W9-BZO-757

Date	Event	Date	Event
1917	Yerkes (1876–1956), with colleagues, published the Army Alpha and Army Beta tests, which were group-administered intelligence tests used for the assessment of military recruits in the United States.	1939	Wechsler (1896–1981) published the Wechsler-Bellevue Intelligence Scale; revisions were issued in 1955, 1981, and 1997 under the titles Wechsler Adult Intelligence Scale, Wechsler Adult Intelligence Scale–Revised, and Wechsler Adult Intelligence Scale–Third Edition.
1918	Otis (1886–1964) published the Absolute Point Scale, a group intelligence test.	1940	P. Cattell (1893–1989) published the Cattell Infant Intelligence Scale.
1919	Monroe (1863–1939) and Buckingham (1876–1962) published the Illinois General Intelligence Scale.	1949	Wechsler Intelligence Scale for Children was published; a revision was issued in 1974 under the title Wechsler Intelligence Scale for Children–Revised and in 1991 under the title Wechsler Intelligence Scale for Children–Third Edition.
1923	Kelly (1884–1961), Ruch (1903–1982), and Terman (1877–1956) published the Stanford Achievement Test.		
	Kohs (1890–1984) published the Kohs Block Design Test, a test of nonverbal reasoning.	1959	Guilford (1897–1988) proposed a Structure of Intellect model of intelligence based on factor analytic methods.
1924	Porteus (1883–1972) published the Porteus Maze Test.	1961	Kirk (1904–1996) and J. J. McCarthy (1927–) published the Illinois Test of Psycholinguistic Ability.
1926	Goodenough (1886–1959) published the Draw-A-Man Test.		
1928	Arthur (1883–1967) published the Point Scale of Performance Tests.	1963	R. B. Cattell (1905–1998) proposed a theory of fluid and crystallized intelligence.
1931	Stutsman (1894–1980) published the Merrill-Palmer Scale of Mental Tests.	1969	Bayley (1899–1994) published the Bayley Scales of Infant Development; a revision was published in 1993.
1933	Thurstone (1887–1955) proposed a multiple factor analytic approach to the study of human abilities.	1972	D. McCarthy (1906–1974) published McCarthy Scales of Children's Abilities.
	Tiegs (1891–1970) and Clark (1895–1964) published the Progressive Achievement Tests, later renamed the California Achievement Tests.	1975	U.S. Public Law 94-142 passed, proclaiming the right to equal education for all handicapped children.
1936	Lindquist (1901–1978), with colleagues, published the Iowa Every-Pupil Tests of Basic Skills, later named the Iowa Tests of Basic Skills.	1979	Judge Peckham in California ruled in *Larry P. v. Riles* that intelligence tests used for the assessment of African American children for classes for the educable mentally retarded are culturally biased.
	Piaget (1896–1980) published *Origins of Intelligence.*		
	Doll (1889–1968) published the Vineland Social Maturity Scale; a revision by Sparrow (1933–), Balla (1939–1982), and Cicchetti (1937–) was published in 1985 under the title Vineland Adaptive Behavior Scales.	1980	Judge Grady in Illinois ruled in *Parents in Action on Special Education v. Joseph P. Hannon* that intelligence tests are not racially or culturally biased and do not discriminate against African American children.
1938	Bender (1897–1987) published the Bender Visual Motor Gestalt Test.	1986	R. L. Thorndike (1910–1990), Hagen (1915–), and Sattler (1931–) published the Stanford-Binet Intelligence Scale: Fourth Edition, in which a point-scale format replaced the age-scale format of the Stanford-Binet Intelligence Scale: Form L-M.
	Buros (1905–1978) published the first *Mental Measurements Yearbook.*		
	Gessell (1880–1961) published the Gessell Maturity Scale.		

Assessment of Children
Cognitive Applications
Fourth Edition

Jerome M. Sattler
San Diego State University

Jerome M. Sattler, Publisher, Inc.
San Diego

Copyright © 2001 by Jerome M. Sattler, Publisher, Inc.
P.O. Box 3557, La Mesa, California 91944-3557
www.sattlerpublisher.com

All rights reserved. No part of the material protected by this copyright notice may be reproduced or utilized
in any form or by any means, electronic or mechanical, including photocopying, recording, or by any
information storage and retrieval system, without written permission from the copyright owner.

Editorial Services: Sally Lifland and Denise Throckmorton, Lifland et al., Bookmakers
Interior Design: Jerome M. Sattler and Sally Lifland
Cover Design: Jennifer Mathews and Jerome M. Sattler
Proofreaders: Gail Magin, Madge Schworer, and David N. Sattler
Indexers: Jeanne Yost and Susan Patt
Production Coordinators: Sally Lifland and Jerome M. Sattler
Compositor: Omegatype Typography, Inc., Champaign, Illinois
Cover Printer: Phoenix Color
Printer and Binder: Maple-Vail Book Manufacturing Group

This text was set in Times Roman and Helvetica, printed on Highland Plus, Smyth sewn, with Type 2 mylar
lamination and photoembossed cover stock.

Cover: Wassily Kandinsky, *Spitzen im Bogen,* 1927

Library of Congress Catalog Card Number: 00–192723

ISBN 0-9618209-7-7

16 15 14 13 12 11 10 9 8 7 6 5 4 3 2   12 11 10 09 08 07 06 05 04 03 02 01

Printed in the United States of America

To my family
Bonnie Jeanne, Heidi Beth, David Nathan, Deborah Elaine,
Keith Richard, Walter Edwin, Nicole Marie, and Justin Lewis

and

To my mentors
Alfred Binet, David Wechsler, John Chotlos,
Fritz Heider, and William A. Hillix

BRIEF CONTENTS

CONTENTS

SECTION VI. ACHIEVEMENT AND LANGUAGE ABILITIES

Chapter 17. Assessment of Academic Achievement   576

Chapter 18. Assessment of Receptive and Expressive Language   610

SECTION VII. CULTURALLY AND LINGUISTICALLY DIVERSE CHILDREN

Chapter 19. Assessment of Culturally and Linguistically Diverse Children: Background Considerations and Dynamics   635

Chapter 20. Assessment of Culturally and Linguistically Diverse Children: Research Findings and Recommendations   657

LIST OF TABLES

LIST OF FIGURES

LIST OF EXHIBITS

PREFACE

Writing a book is an adventure; to begin with it is a toy and an amusement, then it becomes a master, and then it becomes a tyrant; and the last phase is just as you are about to be reconciled to your servitude–you kill the monster and fling him ... to the public.

—Sir Winston Churchill

The Fourth Edition of *Assessment of Children: Cognitive Applications* has evolved over 40 years. In 1959, I thought of writing a cognitive assessment text that would help students become competent in clinical and psychoeducational assessment and report writing. It took about 14 years for the thought to lead to publication, in 1973. My orientation today is the same as it was when I started: Clinical and psychoeducational assessment must rest on a foundation of sound theory, administration, interpretation, and intervention. A focus on research underpins all of the material in this text, because only research can provide the knowledge we need to evaluate and interpret our assessment instruments.

So as to keep the text a manageable size, the Fourth Edition is published as two independent texts: *Assessment of Children: Cognitive Applications, Fourth Edition* and *Assessment of Children: Behavior and Clinical Applications, Fourth Edition.*

Assessment of Children: Cognitive Applications, Fourth Edition, like the former editions, is designed not only as a teaching text but also as a reference source for students and professionals. It is a major revision. Every chapter has been rewritten to make the text more comprehensive, relevant, readable, up-to-date, and informative. Extensive art work has been added. The text contains new material on ethical guidelines related to assessment, laws pertaining to children with disabilities, the Differential Ability Scales, brief intelligence tests, achievement tests, language tests, and background considerations relevant to the evaluation of culturally and linguistically diverse children. The text has expanded coverage of the Wechsler Intelligence Scale for Children–Third Edition, the Wechsler Adult Intelligence Scale–Third Edition, the Wechsler Preschool and Primary Scales of Intelligence–Revised, the Stanford-Binet Intelligence Scale: Fourth Edition, report writing, general testing techniques, administrative techniques, psychometric considerations, assessment theory, and the assessment process.

The companion volume covers assessment procedures that complement those in *Assessment of Children: Cognitive Applications, Fourth Edition.* These include interviews, behavioral observations, personality tests and checklists, and adaptive behavior scales. *Assessment of Children: Behavioral and Clinical Applications, Fourth Edition* also covers the clinical application of assessment procedures to children with mental retardation, children who are gifted, children with learning disabilities, children with attention-deficit/hyperactivity disorder, children with an autistic disorder, children with sensory disabilities, and children with brain injury.

Assessment of Children: Cognitive Applications, Fourth Edition contains several useful learning aids. These include

- List of major headings and goals and objectives at the beginning of each chapter
- A "Thinking Through the Issues" section; a summary of each major topic area; a list of key terms, concepts, and names, each linked to the page on which it appears; and a series of study questions at the end of each chapter
- Detailed guidelines for administering the major tests covered in the text
- Exercises on report writing
- Detailed analyses of two model psychological reports
- Report writing principles
- Guidelines for evaluating test administration techniques and reports

The text also includes an extensive collection of cartoons touching on assessment, psychology, and education. The cartoons provide humor and relief and serve as a teaching and learning tool.

The assessment process does not begin and end with administering and interpreting tests. Effective assessors need to know not only about assessment instruments but also about (a) children who are normal, as well as those with special needs, (b) the ethical and legal guidelines of the profession, (c) the institutions in which they work, (d) how to communicate both orally and in writing with examinees, their parents, their teachers, and other interested parties, (e) how culture and ethnicity relate to the children assessed, and (f) how to help children.

The field of assessment is not free of controversy. Some question the entire assessment enterprise, claiming that assessment is not related to how children learn and that assessment fails to provide intervention guidelines. Therefore, these critics maintain that current assessment practices should be abandoned. Certainly current assessment practices do not provide all that we might want or need, but assessments are useful, providing information helpful to children, their parents, their teachers, and other interested parties. When you have completed your study of *Assessment of Children: Cognitive Applications, Fourth Edition*, you will be in a better position to understand the controversies surrounding assessment and to form your own opinion about the merits of assessment.

As we enter the 21st century, we must be mindful of the prominent place that litigation occupies in American society. Assessment results, and the decisions reached on the basis of assessment results, may be questioned by others who seek legal recourse to change a diagnosis or recommendation. Therefore, I strongly urge you to assume that everything you do has potential legal consequences. The best strategy is to be prepared. You can do this by (a) following standard procedures scrupulously, (b) maintaining accurate and complete records, and (c) keeping up with the research and clinical literature in your field.

Underlying all assessments are a respect for children and their families and a desire to help children. A thorough assessment should allow us to learn something about the child that we could not learn from simply talking to others about the child, observing the child, or reviewing the child's records. Assessment makes a difference in the lives of children and their families, as well as in the lives of the professionals, including educators, who work with the children and their families.

Early in my career as a psychologist, I learned that clinicians must have a "tolerance for ambiguity." We need that tolerance today just as we did in the 20th century. Much remains to be learned about the nature of intelligence, how best to nurture it, and how best to assess it.

Note to Instructors: An *Instructor's Manual,* written by James O. Rust and Jerome M. Sattler, accompanies *Assessment of Children: Cognitive Applications, Fourth Edition.* The manual contains multiple-choice questions useful for objective examinations.

ACKNOWLEDGMENTS

Two broken down old men sat on a park bench. One said, "I'm here because I never took advice from anybody."

"Shake," said the other man. "I'm here because I took everybody's advice."

—Bill Adler

I wish to acknowledge the contributions of numerous individuals who have written original material for the book or who have assisted in updating various parts of the book:

Dr. Ron Dumont, Fairleigh Dickenson University, who wrote original material on the Differential Ability Scales (Chapter 15)

Dr. Denise Hildebrand, who assisted me in updating the WPPSI–R chapter (Chapter 11) and the Stanford-Binet: IV chapter (Chapter 14) and who wrote original material on the Cognitive Assessment System (Chapter 16)

Dr. Guy M. McBride, Burke County Public Schools, who is co-author of the sections in Chapter 3 on the IDEA

Dr. Rhia Roberts, Dr. Nancy Mather, and Dr. Elizabeth A. Allen, who wrote original material on the Illinois Test of Psycholinguistic Abilities–Third Edition (Chapter 18)

Dr. Joseph Ryan, Central Missouri State University, who is co-author of the two chapters on the WAIS–III (Chapters 12 and 13)

Dr. Donald H. Saklofske, University of Saskatchewan, Canada, who is co-author of the three WISC–III chapters (Chapters 8, 9, and 10)

Dr. Agnes Shine, who wrote original material on the Bayley Scales of Infant Development (Chapter 16)

Dr. Ranae Stetson, Texas Christian University, and Dr. Elton Stetson, Texas A&M–Commerce, who wrote original material for the achievement test chapter (Chapter 17) and the language test chapter (Chapter 18)

Dr. John O. Willis, Rivier College, who wrote original material on the Differential Ability Scales (Chapter 15) and the Test of Written Language–Third Edition (Chapter 18)

I also have been fortunate in receiving the wisdom, guidance, and suggestions of several individuals who willingly gave of their time and energy to read almost all of the manuscript. I wish to express my thanks and appreciation to

Dr. Vincent C. Alfonso, Fordham University
Dr. Ron Dumont, Fairleigh Dickenson University
Dr. William A. Hillix, San Diego State University
Dr. Nancy Mather, University of Arizona
Anne Owen, MA, University of Kansas
Dr. Anthony W. Paolitto, James Madison University
Bonnie J. Sattler, MA, Kaiser Permanente, San Diego
Dr. Lisa Weyandt, Central Washington University
Darlene Wheeler, MA, Riverside Public Schools
Dr. John O. Willis, Rivier College

I also have been fortunate in having the following individuals read one or more chapters of the manuscript. Their excellent feedback was extremely helpful in making the manuscript more scholarly and accurate.

Dr. Achilles N. Bardos, University of Northern Colorado
Dr. Carol Bartz, North Inland Special Education Region, San Diego County
Deborah R. G. Cesario, Attorney, Lozano Smith
Dr. James Deni, Appalachian State University
Dr. Colin D. Elliott, University of California, Santa Barbara
Linda Halperin, Ed. S., Seton Hall University
Dr. Keith Hattrup, San Diego State University
Joel Hastings, MA, Burke County Public Schools
Dr. Larry Hilgert, Valdosta State University
Dr. Sara E. Lynch, East County Special Education Region, San Diego County
Dr. Vanessa Malcarne, San Diego State University
Dr. Susan Maller, Purdue University
Dr. Georg Matt, San Diego State University
Dr. Thomas Massarelli, Seton Hall University
Dr. Guy M. McBride, Burke County Public Schools
Dr. Mary Ann Roberts, University of Iowa
Dr. David N. Sattler, Western Washington University
Dr. Donald H. Saklofske, University of Saskatchewan, Canada
Dr. David Tulsky, The Psychological Corporation
Dr. Larry Weiss, The Psychological Corporation
Peter Wright, Attorney
Dr. Jian Jun Zhu, The Psychological Corporation

A number of students at San Diego State University and Western Washington University read and commented on the manuscript, checked references, proofread the page proofs, and helped in other invaluable ways. Thanks go to

Stefanie Blue	Tina Ann Mathews
Granville Bowman	Pilar Moreno
Victoria Cogar	Verónica Morillón
Leslie Croot	Adria Sandroni
Anna Dotran	Samantha Julie Scott
Gary Drake	Tami Lee Terrones
Jennifer S. Kamenides	Sara Louise Tragesser
Korrie Kashuba	Wakana Tsuru
Jill Kattelman	Kenton Whalen
Christopher Lewis	

My able assistant, Kadir Samuel, helped me in numerous ways in getting the manuscript and book into production. Kadir, thanks for being so special. Your dependability and dedication to getting this book published are much appreciated. I also wish to thank Kartika Y. Widjaja for her assistance.

Brenda Pinedo and Sharon Drum, at Jerome M. Sattler, Publisher, Inc., have been exceptional staff members. Thanks, Brenda and Sharon, for keeping the company office going and helping with the various details involved in getting this book into production.

I would like to thank the staff at the San Diego State Library for their assistance in obtaining books and reprints of articles. James F. Edwards, Steve Isachsen, and Rob Drake, from Instructional Technology Services, and Adam D. Royce, James B. Varnel, and Steve Bednarik, at San Diego State University, were invaluable in helping me with the computer. And Michael Irwin, from the Test Office at San Diego State University, was of great assistance in writing the computer programs necessary to generate several tables. Thank you all for your knowledge and expertise. It is comforting to know that you are available when I get into trouble with the computer, which seems to be a weekly occurrence. Lori Palmer, from the Instructional Technology Service at San Diego State University, and J. Mathews, graphic artist, composed the figures that are in the book. Thank you both.

I also wish to thank the able secretarial staff of the Psychology Department at San Diego State University for relaying messages, notifying me of faxes, and helping me in innumerable other ways. Thank you, Darlene Pickrel, Linda Corio, and Marty Malano.

I want to give a special thanks to Herman Zielinski for his wonderful sense of humor and for his willingness to share his cartoons with the readers of this text.

I also want to acknowledge Roy A. Wallace, West Coast representative from Maple-Vail Book Manufacturing Group. Roy, thank you for your help in getting this book printed. It has always been a pleasure working with you.

My family has been supportive throughout this 8-year project. Thank you, Bonnie, Heidi, David, Deborah, Keith, and Walter, for your encouragement and support.

I also wish to thank my friends and neighbors—Victor Menache, John Tisdale, Shirely Tisdale, Robert Piserchio, and Connie Piserchio—for their support and friendship.

I have been fortunate in having a superb copyediting and production staff help get this book ready for publication. The folks at Lifland et al., Bookmakers are craftpersons and, as the title of their firm indicates, truly "bookmakers." Thank you, Sally Lifland, Denise Throckmorton, and Gail Magin, for your patience and tolerance and for working with me during a 9-month period to make the manuscript clear and readable, grammatically correct, organized, coherent, as free from error as possible, and a work that we can be proud of.

I also want to thank Yoram Mizrahi and the staff at Omega-type for putting my galleys into pages with exceptional expertise. Thank you, Yoram, for doing such an excellent job.

Finally, I wish to acknowledge the role that San Diego State University has played in my life. For almost 36 years, this great university has given me the support and academic freedom needed to pursue my interests in teaching, research, writing, and consultation. Thank you, San Diego State University, for all that you have given me. I hope that in my small way I have returned something to my students and to the university community at large.

ABOUT THE AUTHOR

I grew up in the East Bronx of New York City during the 1930s and 1940s. Both of my parents came to the United States from villages in Poland in the early 1920s. I began my study of psychology at the City College of New York, obtaining my BA in 1952. I received my master's degree in 1953 and my Ph.D. in 1959 from the University of Kansas (KU). While at KU, I was introduced to gestalt and existential psychology and participated in the Veterans Administration clinical psychology training program. My mentors at KU, Fritz Heider and John Chotlos, were extraordinarily gifted and creative psychologists and teachers. In 1954, I was drafted into the U.S. Army and worked as a psychologist in an outpatient mental health clinic.

After graduation, I taught and worked in a child guidance clinic at Fort Hays Kansas State College. In 1961, I accepted a position at the University of North Dakota. In 1965, I joined the staff at San Diego State University (SDSU), where I taught for 29 years. I retired from SDSU in 1994. I am now a Professor Emeritus and Adjunct Professor at SDSU. Also, I am a Diplomate in Clinical Psychology and a Fellow of the American Psychological Association. In 1998, I received the Senior Scientist Award from the Division of School Psychology (Division 16) of the American Psychological Association. Finally, I am the author of *Clinical and Forensic Interviewing of Children and Families: Guidelines for the Mental Health, Education, Pediatric, and Child Maltreatment Fields* and one of the co-authors of the *Stanford-Binet Intelligence Scale: Fourth Edition.*

I had three excellent international experiences. The first was as a Fulbright lecturer at the University of Kebangsaan in Kuala Lumpur, Malaysia, in 1972. The second was as an exchange professor at Katholieke Universiteit in Nijmegen, The Netherlands, in 1983. And the third was as an exchange professor at University College Cork, in Cork, Ireland, in 1989.

When I am not working on a book, I enjoy walking, listening to jazz, watching movies, ballroom dancing, reading, and spending time with my family, including my two grandchildren.

I feel fortunate in having chosen a career that has allowed me the freedom and opportunity to write, teach, conduct research, travel, study, and interact with remarkable students and colleagues. Little did I realize when I started out 40 years ago that *Assessment of Children* would consume a good part of my professional and personal life. And little did I realize that the book would go through four editions, train over 200,000 students and professionals since its initial publication in 1973, be referred to as "the bible" of assessment, be translated into Spanish three times, and be rated by my fellow psychologists as one of the 50 great books in psychology. I am honored, gratified, and humbled by the recognition that *Assessment of Children* has received over the past 28 years.

1

CHALLENGES IN ASSESSING CHILDREN: THE PROCESS

Tests not accompanied by detailed data on their construction, validation, uses, and limitations should be suspect.

—Oscar K. Buros

Purposes of Assessment

Four Pillars of Assessment

Guidelines for Assessment

Objectives of This Text

Steps in the Assessment Process

Thinking Through the Issues

Summary

Goals and Objectives

This chapter is designed to enable you to do the following:

- Identify the purposes of assessment

- Delineate principles guiding the use of tests

- Describe the skills needed to become a competent clinical assessor

- Describe the basic techniques used in the assessment process

- List the steps in the assessment process

Exhibit 1-1
Psychological Reports Do Count: The Case of *Daniel Hoffman v. the Board of Education* of the City of New York

Introduction

The case of *Daniel Hoffman v. the Board of Education of the City of New York* is instructive because it illustrates the important role that testing and psychological reports can play in people's lives. In this case, the psychological report contained a recommendation that was ignored by the school administrators. Years later, when the case was tried, the failure to follow the recommendations became a key issue.

Basis of Litigation

Daniel Hoffman, a 26-year-old man, brought suit against the New York City Board of Education in 1978 to recover damages for injuries resulting from his placement in classes for the mentally retarded. The complaint alleged that (a) the Board was negligent in its original testing procedures and placement of Mr. Hoffman, causing or permitting him to be placed in an educational environment for mentally retarded children and consequently depriving him of adequate speech therapy, which would have improved his only real disability, a speech impediment, and (b) the Board was negligent in failing or refusing to follow adequate procedures for the recommended retesting of Mr. Hoffman's intelligence.

Board of Education's Position

The Board of Education took the position that Mr. Hoffman's IQ of 74, obtained on the Stanford-Binet Intelligence Scale when he was 5 years, 9 months old, indicated that his placement in a class for the mentally retarded was appropriate. They contended that the test was proper, that it was administered by a competent and experienced psychologist, and that it was the unanimous professional judgment of Mr. Hoffman's teachers, based on their evaluation and his performance on standardized achievement tests, that a retest was not warranted. The Board made clear that at the time Mr. Hoffman was in school, its policy was to retest only when retesting was recommended by teachers or requested by parents.

The psychological report, in which the psychologist had recommended that Mr. Hoffman be placed in a class for the mentally retarded, was one of the key documents upon which the entire case rested. Mr. Hoffman entered special education classes and remained in them throughout his school years. However, the key sentence in the 1957 report was as follows: *"Also, his intelligence should be reevaluated within a two-year period so that a more accurate estimation of his abilities can be made"* (italics added).

The Board of Education argued that the psychologist did not literally mean "retesting" because he did not use this word in the report. Although a minority of the court concurred with this interpretation, the majority supported Mr. Hoffman's position that reevaluation meant only one thing—administration of another intelligence test.

Removal from Training Program

In a curious twist of fate, testing, which resulted in the assignment of Mr. Hoffman to special education, also played an important role in removing him from a special workshop program during his late

teenage years. Mr. Hoffman had made poor progress during his school years, and there had been no significant change in his severe speech defect. At the age of 17, he entered a sheltered workshop for retarded youths. After a few months in the program, he was given the Wechsler Adult Intelligence Scale and obtained a Verbal Scale IQ of 85, a Performance Scale IQ of 107, and a Full Scale IQ of 94. His overall functioning was in the Normal range. On the basis of these findings, Mr. Hoffman was not permitted to remain at the Occupational Training Center. On learning of this decision, he became depressed, often staying in his room at home with the door closed.

Mr. Hoffman then received assistance from the Division of Vocational Rehabilitation. At the age of 21, he was trained to be a messenger, but he did not like this work. At the time of the trial, he had obtained no further training or education, had not made any advancement in his vocational life, and had not improved his social life.

Inadequate Assessment Procedures

During the trial it was shown that the psychologist who tested Mr. Hoffman in kindergarten had failed (a) to interview Mrs. Hoffman, (b) to obtain a social history, and (c) to discuss the results of the evaluation with her. If a history had been obtained, the psychologist would have learned that Mr. Hoffman had been tested 10 months previously at the National Hospital for Speech Disorders and had obtained an IQ of 90 on the Merrill-Palmer Scale of Mental Tests.

Verdict and Appeals

The case was initially tried before a jury, which returned a verdict in favor of Mr. Hoffman, awarding him damages of $750,000. This decision was appealed to the Appellate Division of the New York State Supreme Court, which affirmed the jury verdict on November 6, 1978, but lowered damages to $500,000. The New York State Appeals Court overturned the Appellate Court's decision on December 17, 1979, finding that the court system was not the proper arena for testing the validity of educational decisions or for second-guessing such decisions.

THE IMPORTANCE OF THE CASE FOR THE PRACTICE OF SCHOOL AND CLINICAL PSYCHOLOGY

The case of *Daniel Hoffman v. the Board of Education of the City of New York* is one of the first cases in which the courts carefully scrutinized psychological reports and the process of special education placement. The case touches on several important issues involved in the psychoeducational assessment process. Let us consider some of these issues.

1. *Psychological reports do count.* Psychological reports are key documents used by mental health professionals, teachers, administrators, physicians, courts, parents, and children.

2. *Words can be misinterpreted.* A pivotal point in the case was the meaning of the words "reevaluate" and "retest." Some participants in the case, as well as some court judges, assigned

(Continued)

Exhibit 1-1 *(Continued)*

these words different meanings. Therefore, careful attention must be given to the wording of reports. Reports must be written clearly, with findings and recommendations stated as precisely as possible.

3. *IQs change.* Children's IQs do not remain static. Although there is a certain stability after children reach 6 years of age, their IQs do change.

4. *Different tests may provide different IQs.* The three IQs obtained by Mr. Hoffman at 5, 6, and 18 years of age may reflect differences in the content and standardization of the three tests, rather than genuine changes in cognitive performance.

5. *Decisions must be based on more than one assessment approach.* A battery of psychological tests and procedures, along with interviews with parents and teachers and reports from teachers, should be used in the assessment process. All available information should be reviewed before recommendations are made.

6. *The instruments used must be appropriate.* A child who has a speech or language disability may need to be assessed with performance tests in addition to—or in place of—verbal tests.

7. *Previous findings must be reviewed.* Before the formal assessment is carried out, the assessor must determine whether the child has been previously evaluated and, if so, review all relevant assessment findings.

Although many issues were involved in the case of *Daniel Hoffman,* the preceding points are particularly germane to the practice of school and clinical psychology. They illustrate that a psychological evaluation, including the formulation of recommendations, requires a high level of competence. The case also demonstrates that it is incumbent on administrators to carry out the psychologist's recommendations.

Note. The citations for this case are 410 N.Y.S.2d 99 and 400 N.E.2d 317-49 N.Y.2d 121.

You are about to begin a study of assessment procedures that affect children, their families, schools, and society. The assessment procedures covered in this text have their roots in century-old traditions of psychological, clinical, and educational measurement. Psychologists are continuously refining assessment tools, and this text will help you become aware of these refinements.

Those of you who are beginning your study of assessment are likely to be overwhelmed at first by the many details you will encounter in learning how to administer psychological and psychoeducational tests and other assessment procedures and record, score, interpret, and report the results. Your instructor may ask you to review psychometric theory (which refers to the measurement of psychological variables) and to study theoretical views and models that attempt to explain intelligence and other abilities and skills. Some of you also may be exposed to computer-oriented procedures designed for administering tests, conducting interviews, interpreting assessment data, and writing reports. And, of course, all of you will write and develop psychological reports, with or without the aid of computers. This text provides you with tools that will make each of these tasks a little easier. The success of this text will be determined by the competencies that you develop in meeting these challenges.

PURPOSES OF ASSESSMENT

Assessment is a way of gaining some understanding of the child in order to make informed decisions. The purposes of assessment include screening, problem solving, diagnosis, coun-

seling and rehabilitation, and progress evaluation. In some cases, one evaluation may serve several of these purposes.

- A *screening assessment* is a relatively brief evaluation given to identify children who (a) are eligible for certain programs, (b) have a disorder or disability in need of remediation or rehabilitation, or (c) may need a more comprehensive assessment. Screening may involve, for example, evaluating the readiness of children to enter kindergarten programs or programs for the gifted and talented. Decisions based on a screening assessment should not be permanent and should be reversed or further explored if necessary.

- A *focused, or problem-solving, assessment* is a detailed evaluation of a specific area of functioning. The assessment may address a diagnostic question (e.g., Does the child have attention deficit/hyperactivity disorder?) or a skill question (e.g., Does the child exhibit a verbal memory deficit?). The examiner also may include at his or her discretion or clinical judgment additional areas to examine, such as reading ability. With increased time and financial pressures in private medical facilities, schools, health maintenance organizations, and other settings, the focused, or problem-solving, assessment is being used more frequently as an alternative to the longer and more expensive diagnostic assessment.

- A *diagnostic assessment* is a detailed evaluation of a child's strengths and weaknesses in several areas, such as cognitive, academic, language, and social functioning. It involves a range of purposes, including diagnosis (determining the classification that best reflects the child's level and type of functioning), assisting in the determination of mental illness or educational disabilities, and making suggestions for placement and intervention.

- A *counseling and rehabilitation assessment* is similar to a classification/placement assessment except that emphasis is placed on the child's abilities to adjust to and successfully fulfill daily responsibilities. Possible responses to treatment and potential for recovery also are considered.
- A *progress evaluation assessment* focuses on the day-to-day, week-to-week, month-to-month, or year-to-year progress of the child. It is used to evaluate changes in the child's development and skills and to evaluate the effectiveness of intervention procedures.

Questions that should be considered in an assessment include the following:

1. What are the child's age, sex, and grade level (if relevant)?
2. What are the child's and family's ethnicity, culture, and socioeconomic status?
3. Who is the referral source?
4. What is the reason for the referral?
5. What behaviors are of concern to the child's parents, teachers, and significant others?
6. Are there any associated problems or disabilities? If so, what is the nature of the problem or disability—its frequency, duration, and intensity—and what are the antecedents and consequences of the problem or coexisting medical problems (e.g., seizures) of the disability? How severe is the child's problem or disability (e.g., mild, moderate, or severe)? How did the problem or disability come about (e.g., congenital or acquired; if acquired, age at which acquired)? How has the problem affected the child's cognitive ability, language, motor skills, self-concept, interpersonal relationships, and related areas?
7. What stresses are present in the child's life?
8. What roles do the family, school, and community have in affecting the child's performance?
9. What supports does the child have from the family, school, and community?
10. How do the child, family, and teachers perceive and deal with the problem?
11. What is the level of the child's intelligence, including his or her level of verbal and nonverbal ability as well as any other areas of cognitive functioning?
12. How is the child performing academically?
13. What are the main features of the child's temperament, personality, and interpersonal skills?
14. What are the child's strengths and limitations?
15. In what ways have the child's problems affected ordinary activities?
16. What compensatory strategies has the child developed to help him or her cope with difficulties?
17. What expectations do the child, family, and school have for changes in the child's behavior?
18. What interventions are most feasible, including the most appropriate educational program and setting for the child?
19. What realistic goals can be set for the child?
20. What is the prognosis (likely outcome)?
21. (For reevaluations) Has there been any change in the child's functioning and, if so, in what areas have there been changes?

Let's consider some similarities and differences between psychological assessment and psychological testing. Both involve identifying critical questions and areas of concern, planning data collection, and collecting data as needed. They differ in the following ways: *Psychological testing* involves administering tests; the focus is on collecting data. *Psychological assessment* is more encompassing and involves several clinical tools, such as formal and informal tests, observations, and interviews; the focus is not only on collecting data, but also on using clinical skills to interpret the data and synthesize the results. Testing produces findings; assessment gives meaning to the findings within the context of the examinee's life. What children and parents tell you may depend on their (a) personal agenda, (b) need to please you, (c) attitude toward mental illness, (d) attitude toward use of medications, and (e) related issues.

FOUR PILLARS OF ASSESSMENT

The four pillars of assessment—norm-referenced tests, interviews, observations, and informal assessment procedures—can be referred to in the broadest sense as "tests" (see Figure 1-1). More accurately, however, the word *test* applies to any standard procedure used for measuring a sample of behavior. "Standard procedure" refers to the use of the same (a) *item content* (selected to represent the domain of interest), (b) *administration procedure* (directions, wording of items, probing questions, recording of responses, and time limits, where applicable, that are strictly specified and detailed), and (c) *scoring criteria* (objective guidelines that are provided for evaluating responses). Test authors design standard procedures to reduce the effect of personal idiosyncrasies and biases of examiners and to reduce extraneous sources of influence that may affect the examinee's performance.

A useful description of what constitutes a *standardized test* follows (Green, 1981):

A standardized test is a task or set of tasks given under standard conditions and designed to assess some aspect of a person's knowledge, skill, behavior, or personality. A test provides a scale of measurement for consistent individual differences regarding some psychological concept and serves to compare people according to that concept. Tests can be thought of as yardsticks, but they are less efficient and reliable than yardsticks, just as the concept of verbal reasoning ability is more complex and less well understood than the concept of length. A test yields one or more objectively obtained quantitative scores, so that, as nearly as possible, each person is

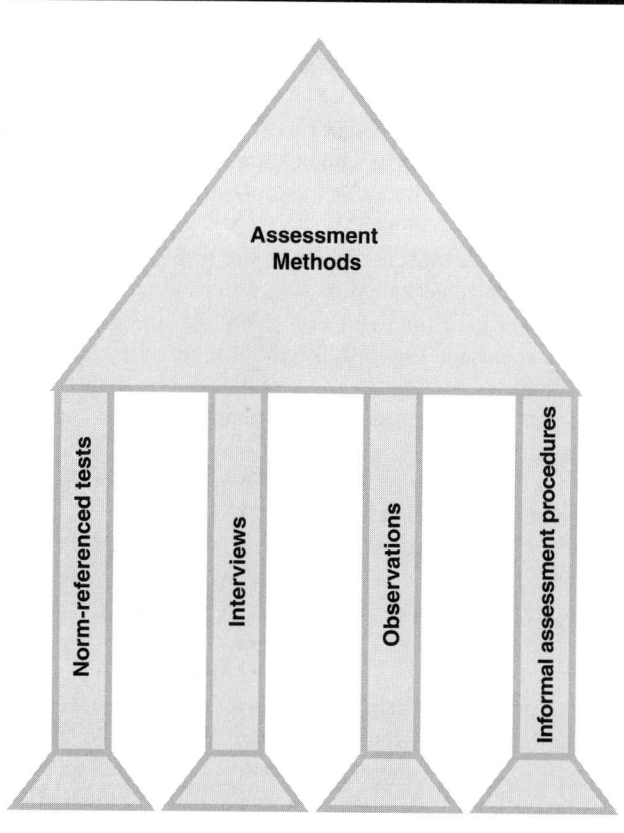

Figure 1-1. Four pillars of assessment.

assessed in the same way. The intent is to provide a fair and equitable comparison among test takers. (p. 1001, with changes in notation)

Norm-Referenced Tests

We have based this text on the premise that norm-referenced tests are indispensable for clinical and psychoeducational assessment. Norm-referenced tests are standardized on a clearly defined group, termed the *norm group,* and scaled so that each score reflects a rank within the norm group (see Chapter 4 for a discussion of psychometric issues). Psychologists have developed norm-referenced tests to assess, for example, intelligence, reading, mathematics, writing, visual-motor skills, gross- and fine-motor skills, and adaptive behavior. Although we are fortunate in having a choice of well-standardized and psychometrically sound tests with which to evaluate children, some tests do not meet acceptable psychometric standards. When you have completed your study of this text, you will be in a better position to evaluate the merits of norm-referenced tests.

Norm-referenced tests provide some degree of quantification of the child's psychological functioning. Quantification (i.e., assigning numbers to responses) serves many purposes, including (a) describing the child's present functioning in

reference to his or her peer group; (b) sorting out the nature of specific cognitive, motor, and behavioral deficits and strengths; and (c) providing a baseline to assist in measuring progress during *and* after treatment or intervention. Norm-referenced tests also are economical and efficient and permit a sampling of behavior within a few hours.

Norm-referenced tests also provide an index for evaluating changes in many different aspects of the child's physical and social world, including developmental changes, the changing nature of the child's cognitive and neurological condition, and the effects of behavioral interventions and other forms of remediation. For example, periodic reevaluations of fine-motor control and integration, reaction time, attention and concentration, cognitive flexibility, and short-term memory may be particularly valuable in evaluating the effects of a medication regimen, particularly when the medications may have toxic side effects.

Interviews

You will gain assessment information by interviewing the child, parents, teachers, and other individuals familiar with the child. (Note that we will be using the term *parents* to refer to the child's parents or to other caregivers, such as foster parents, grandparents, or other relatives who are raising the child.) It is pointless to examine only the child without also interviewing the individuals who play an important role in the child's life.

Unstructured or semi-structured interviews are more informal than formal tests. They give interviewees an opportunity to convey information in their own words—an opportunity that they may not have during the administration of standardized tests. *Unstructured interviews* are usually open-ended, without a set agenda. *Semi-structured interviews* provide a list of questions, but the focus of the interview can be changed as needed. *Structured interviews* provide a rigid, but comprehensive, list of questions usually designed to arrive at a diagnosis.

An unstructured or semi-structured interview with the child, depending on his or her age, is useful, for example, in understanding how the child views the referral, what the child's concerns are about being evaluated, and how the child views his or her family, teachers, and peer group. An unstructured or semi-structured interview with the parent is crucial for obtaining information about the child's family situation, the parent's view of the child's problem, the parent's knowledge about the child's problem or disability (if relevant), parenting styles and discipline techniques, environmental factors that may be contributing to the child's problems (such as marital discord or financial strain), resources available to the family, factors that may interfere with treatment or recovery, the child's prenatal and postnatal development, and the child's medical, social, and academic history. An unstructured or semi-structured interview with the teacher can provide information about the chronicity of the child's symptoms, situations when symptoms are present or absent, specific behaviors that interfere with the child's functioning, factors that may exacerbate the child's behavior, the child's academic strengths and weaknesses, the child's social skills, the child's peer relationships, and the child's school attendance record. Chapters 1, 2, and 3 in *Assessment of Children: Behavioral and Clinical Applications* discuss interviewing techniques (also see Sattler, 1998, for extensive information on clinical and forensic interviewing of children and families).

Observations

You will obtain valuable information by observing the child during the formal assessment, as well as in his or her natural surroundings (e.g., classroom, playground, or home). Direct observation of the child's behavior will allow you to focus on specific target behaviors, determining the frequency, duration, and rate of the target behaviors and comparing the behavior of the referred child to that of a non-referred child in the same setting. Observations in natural surroundings also may help you learn about (a) how the child functions in situations requiring planning, decision making, memory, attention, and related functions; (b) how the child reacts to social stressors (e.g., disagreements with others) and environmental stresses (e.g., noise, high temperature, or poor air quality); and (c) changes in the child's behavior during the day.

Observations will enable you to identify factors that may be contributing to and sustaining the problem behavior, and consequently can be useful in developing interventions. Observations across multiple settings or caregivers and at different times of the day may be beneficial in developing targeted treatment plans. Behavioral observations will give you a better picture of the child and the settings in which he or she functions, and will help you formulate remedial and treatment recommendations. Three chapters present useful information on observations: Chapters 4 and 5 in *Assessment of Children: Behavioral and Clinical Applications* explain how to conduct different types of structured observations and how to record and evaluate the data obtained from the observations and Chapter 7 in this text presents useful guidelines for conducting observations during testing.

Informal Assessment Procedures

You may need to supplement standardized norm-referenced tests with informal and other assessment procedures such as the following:

- Criterion-referenced tests are designed to determine whether individuals have reached some pre-established level or standard of performance, usually in some academic subject area or skill area. Districtwide and teacher-made criterion-referenced tests will give you information about the child's competencies in mastering the classroom curriculum.

- Written language samples, including essays, term papers, and answers to test questions, obtained under various conditions, will help you evaluate the breadth of the child's writing skills.
- Informal tests or procedures, such as phonics tests or rate of reading (words per minute) from classroom curricula, will help you evaluate factors that may contribute to the child's reading skills.
- Prior and current school records will give you a picture of the child's achievement record, behavior, and attendance in school over time and may allow you to compare the child's present test results with former test results (if available).
- Personal documents, such as diaries, poems, stories, drawings, and musical compositions, may help you learn about the child's thoughts and perceptions at the time the documents were written.
- Self-monitoring records that the child keeps of his or her specific actions, thoughts, or feelings or the events preceding or following a behavior can be useful for understanding the child (see Chapter 5 in *Assessment of Children: Behavioral and Clinical Applications*).
- Role playing can help you see how the child behaves in a contrived (or simulated) situation. For example, if you want to see how the child feels about having to speak in front of the classroom, you can create a situation by assuming the role of the teacher and asking the child to play himself or herself.

A vast realm of informal and other assessment procedures have been developed for different purposes. In addition to using published procedures, you will have opportunities to develop your own informal assessment procedures. However, any assessment procedure that has unknown or questionable technical adequacy (e.g., unknown reliability and validity) must be used cautiously. Informal assessments are particularly helpful when developing interventions. This text describes several informal and other assessment procedures that merit use in evaluations. There is, however, no chapter devoted exclusively to informal tests and procedures.

Comment on the Four Pillars of Assessment

The four pillars of assessment—norm-referenced tests, interviews, observations, and informal assessment procedures—complement one another and form a firm foundation for making decisions about children. You must first interpret each procedure in its own right and then weave information from the various sources together so that the final tapestry is integrated, understandable, meaningful, and consistent. You should resolve major discrepancies in your findings before you make diagnostic decisions or recommendations. For example, if the intelligence test results indicate that the child is currently functioning in the mentally retarded range and the interview findings and adaptive behavior results suggest a level of functioning that is below average but not in the mentally retarded range, do not make a diagnosis of mental retardation; instead, report your findings and discuss the implications of your findings. As another example, before you recommend that a child who is gifted receive special class placement, consider the feelings and wishes of the child, parents, and teacher. Does the child want to leave his or her present classroom? Is he or she working close to capacity? Will the new setting be more stimulating or create undue anxiety? Special class placement decisions always call for an understanding of the present setting, the alternative setting, and how changes in the settings may affect the child, his or her family, and the teachers involved.

When you perform a clinical or psychoeducational assessment of a child, select strategies with developmental processes in mind (i.e., consider what is normal for the child's age and gender). *Never evaluate a child without considering formal or informal developmental norms.* Standardized tests usually provide such norms, but you should base informal assessment procedures on a developmental perspective as well.

Several guidelines are available that will give you approximate norms for many different behaviors. If you use assessment techniques that do not have well-established national norms, obtain local norms (e.g., norms developed for one specific school or community) or develop informal norms to help you evaluate the child's performance more accurately. Chapter 4 in this text describes statistical procedures that will aid you in this effort.

A *multimethod assessment approach* is advocated in this text. It consists of the following elements (see Figure 1-2): (a) obtaining information from several sources and reviewing the child's record and previous evaluations; (b) using several assessment methods, including norm-referenced tests, interviews, observations, and informal assessment procedures, as needed; and (c) assessing several areas, as needed (e.g., intelligence, memory, achievement, visual, auditory, oral language, adaptive behavior, and social-emotional-personality). A well-rounded assessment will provide information about the child's medical, developmental, academic, familial, and social history, as well as about the child's present cognitive,

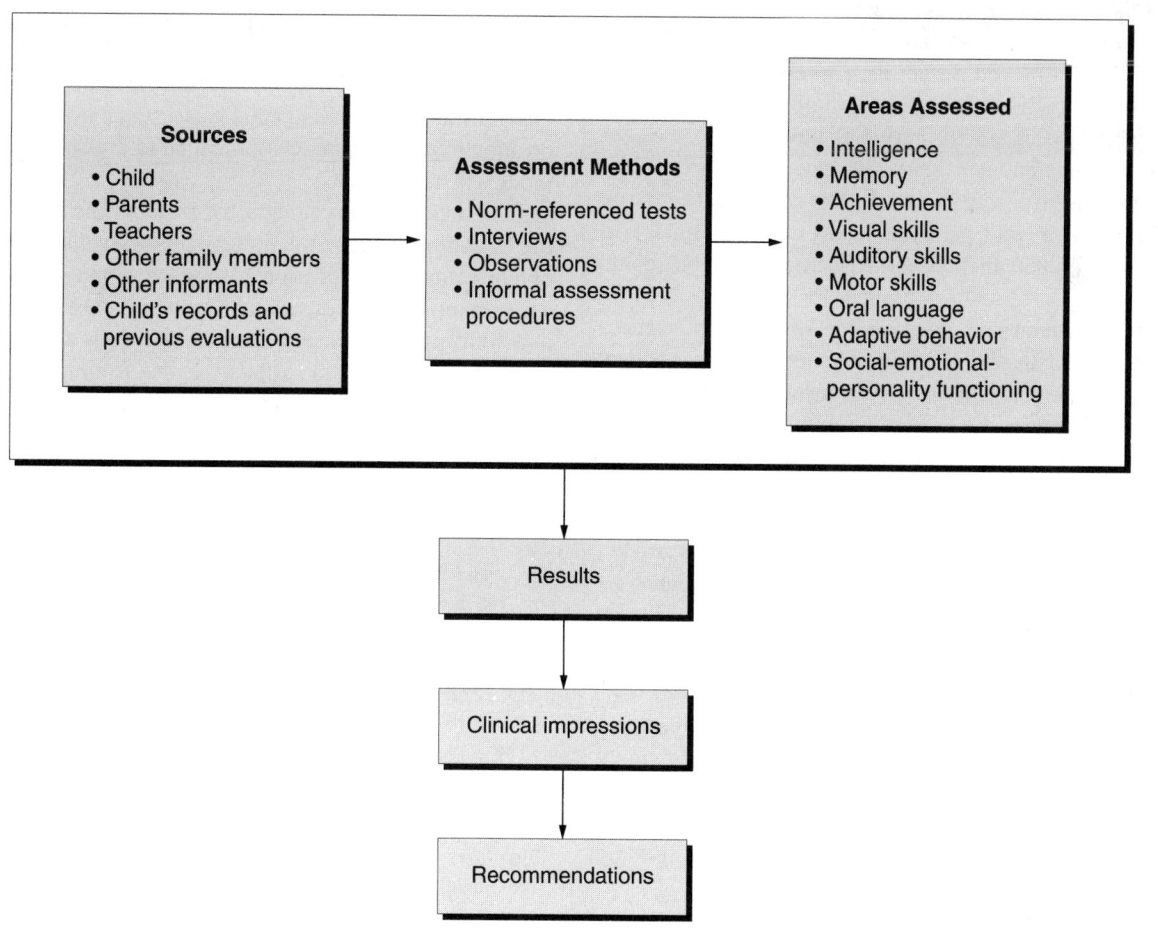

Figure 1-2. Multimethod assessment approach.

academic, social, behavioral, and interpersonal functioning. Thus, you should use a multidimensional assessment battery to do the following:

- Determine the child's strengths and weaknesses and understand the nature, presence, and degree of any disabling conditions
- Cross-validate impressions provided by multiple informants
- Determine the conditions that inhibit or support the acquisition of appropriate skills
- Provide baseline information prior to the implementation of an intervention program
- Develop useful instructional programs and guide individuals in selecting appropriate educational and vocational programs
- Monitor cognitive, academic, or social changes in the child
- Measure the impact of the instructional programs

Consider carefully what assessment procedures will be most effective and efficient and whether additional assessment procedures will contribute to the evaluation. For example, federal and state laws require that children who receive special education services be reevaluated every 3 years to determine whether they continue to qualify for services. If you evaluate a child as part of this process and he or she is doing fine behaviorally and socially, you do not need to conduct an in-depth personality assessment. In fact, according to the Individuals with Disabilities Education Act (Public Law 105-17), the educational reevaluation team decides what areas or types of assessment are needed (see Chapter 3). The nature of the referral question, together with personnel and time constraints, will help you determine which assessment procedures you should use.

Other assessment procedures also may be useful, particularly in evaluating the child's reaction to interventions, but they are not within the scope of this text. They include psychophysiological measures, such as recordings of blood pressure, heart rate, respiratory rate, muscle electrodermal activity, electrical response of the skin, and height and weight.

An effective clinician has the abilities to (a) choose and evaluate assessment approaches, (b) administer and score assessment instruments, (c) interpret and report assessment results, and (d) engage in professionally responsible assessment. To become competent in each of these areas, you must gain knowledge about the following:

- Formal and informal assessment approaches and the types of information obtainable from different assessment approaches
- Statistical properties of assessment instruments, how to interpret test scores, and how to explain commonly reported scores
- How to administer and score assessment instruments
- How to evaluate the appropriateness of the norm group when interpreting the test scores of an individual or group

- How to use multiple sources of assessment information for decision making while recognizing the limitations of using a single score in making decisions
- The rationale underlying the use of qualifying scores for placement
- The consequences of assessment-related decisions and how to avoid decisions that might have unintended negative consequences
- Personality, temperament, and psychopathology
- The meaning of test bias and how to avoid using tests in a biased manner
- How to communicate assessment results to others
- The code of ethics of your profession
- Relevant federal and state laws governing assessment practices

This text presents information in each of these areas to help you become a competent clinician.

Assessment results reflect the child's performance *at a particular time and place.* Learning *why* the child performed as he or she did requires a careful study of the entire clinical history and assessment results. The assessment results usually will not tell you what the child might be able to do under a different set of testing conditions. If you want to know what the child is capable of doing under altered testing conditions, you can use testing-of-limits procedures (see Chapter 7).

Assessments should not end with the report. Make every attempt to be available to work with the child, parents, and referral source on an as-needed basis. You may be in the best position to monitor the recommended interventions and then modify them as needed.

It is important that you recognize both the strengths and the limitations of assessment techniques. Although you will obtain valuable information from both formal and informal assessment techniques, neither provides perfectly reliable and valid information nor samples the complete domain of the child's repertoire of skills, thoughts, feelings, and behavior. In addition, assessment techniques vary in their degree of precision. Measurement error, for example, may be associated with the tests, the setting in which you conduct the evaluation, and the child (e.g., the child's motivation, willingness to guess, or level of alertness). Measurement error may also vary among different parts of the same test and among different age groups. The less objective the assessment technique (e.g., role playing), the more care you will need to exercise in using it and in interpreting the examinee's responses. Consequently, it is best to view assessment results as *approximations* of the domains that they address.

You also must consider the context in which the child functions in evaluating the assessment results and in formulating interventions. To be effective, the intervention plan must have *ecological validity.* This means that you must consider how the child's environment—including immediate family, extended family, subculture, neighborhood, school, and even the larger community—affects the child. The environmental contingencies a child faces play a crucial role in affecting his or her behavior, not only during the testing situation but also outside the testing situation. If you focus exclusively on test results and fail to consider the child's environment, the proposed interventions may fail.

Therefore, a skilled assessor evaluates what effects seem to have been caused by an impoverished environment and tries to separate these effects from other factors such as genetic disposition or family interactions. Let's look at a concrete example of how one environmental condition—poverty—may affect children's development. Poverty is associated with poor nutrition, poor health care, poor self-esteem, and poor educational and vocational opportunities (Ramey & Ramey, 1990). Poverty may have devastating effects on children, including (a) delays in their development (involving delays in language, reasoning ability, and the quality of their social interactions with peers and teachers); (b) lowered aspirations (often accompanied by hostility toward mainstream society, which they see as excluding them from equal opportunities); (c) apathy; and (d) school failure or withdrawal. Children who live in poverty have increased health risks. These risks include having low birth weight, a sexually transmitted disease or AIDS, a high blood lead level, increased physical injuries, growth retardation, anemia, asthma, dental problems, and problems secondary to lack of vaccinations (Tarnowski & Rohrbeck, 1992). To counteract such trends, our society needs to ensure that all children are raised in an environment that will foster their growth and development. Unless this happens, interventions will likely be less effective if the children being assessed come from an environment characterized by poverty. When you work with children who are at the poverty level, you may need to refer their parents to appropriate community agencies for help.

GUIDELINES FOR ASSESSMENT

When you evaluate a child, never focus exclusively on the child's test scores or numbers; instead, interpret the scores by asking yourself what they suggest about the child's competencies. Each child has a range of competencies and limitations that you can evaluate by both quantitative and qualitative means. Note that your aim is to assess both limitations *and* competencies; the focus should not be only on problems.

The following guidelines form an important foundation for the clinical and psychoeducational use of tests and for the assessment process.

ASSESSMENT GUIDELINES

1. Assessment techniques should be used for the benefit of the child.
2. Assessment is a systematic process of arriving at an understanding of a child.
3. Tests should be administered under standard conditions (e.g., using the exact wording in the test manuals and following administration instructions and time limits precisely).
4. Tests should be scored according to well-defined rules.
5. Test scores may be adversely affected by numerous factors in the child, such as poor comprehension of English; temporary states of fatigue, anxiety, or stress; uncooperative behavior and limited motivation; disturbances in temperament or personality; or physical illnesses or disorders.
6. Evidence should demonstrate that tests have adequate reliability and validity (see Chapter 4).
7. Useful assessment strategies include comparing the child's performance with that of other children (i.e., normative comparisons) and evaluating the child's unique profile of scores (i.e., examining individual patterns, which is referred to as the *idiographic approach*).
8. Assessment interpretations are developed by use of inductive methods (i.e., gathering information about the child and then drawing conclusions) as well as deductive methods (i.e., proposing a hypothesis about the child's behavior and then collecting information that relates to it).
9. Assessment conclusions and recommendations should be based on all sources of information obtained about the child and not on any single piece of information.
10. Tests are samples of behavior.
11. Tests do not directly reveal traits or capacities, but they allow you to make inferences about these areas.
12. Tests measure the child's performance based on answers to a set of test items administered at a particular time and place. Tests that measure either general cognitive abilities or specific skills are sometimes referred to as "achievement tests," "ability tests," "aptitude tests," or "readiness tests." These designations reflect the different emphases of item content in the tests (e.g., content focusing on reading a passage vs. general reasoning problems). However, the four types of tests should all be considered measures of achievement.
13. Test results should be interpreted in relation to other behavioral data and to case history information (including the child's cultural background and primary language) and never in isolation.
14. Tests may need to be readministered after a child has been in a specific program for a period of time (e.g., after 1 year).
15. Tests intended to measure the same area may yield different scores (e.g., two different achievement tests administered to a child may give scores that differ).

Tests and other assessment procedures are powerful tools, but their effectiveness will depend on your knowledge and skill. When wisely and cautiously used, assessment procedures can assist you in helping children, parents, teachers, and other professionals obtain valuable insights. When used inappropriately, they can mislead those who must make important life decisions, thus causing harm and grief. The case of *Daniel*

Hoffman in Exhibit 1-1 shows how assessment results affect many people and directly affect the lives of children and their parents. As a result of clinical and psychoeducational evaluations, actions are taken and critical decisions are made. You must be careful about the words you choose when you write reports and communicate with the children, their families, and other professionals. Your work represents a major professional contribution to the lives of children and adolescents, to their families, to their schools, and to society.

OBJECTIVES OF THIS TEXT

This text should help you make (a) sensible evaluations of psychological tests and other assessment procedures and (b) effective decisions about children who are referred to you for evaluation. *Effective decision making is the hallmark of clinical and psychoeducational assessment.* Reaching these goals will help you become a skilled clinician. The term *clinician* is used in this text to refer to individuals who have been trained in any number of different professional areas such as clinical psychology, school psychology, counseling psychology, educational psychology, special education, social work, speech therapy, psychiatry, and medicine. To become a skilled clinician, you will need to develop a number of technical and clinical skills. You should also have a background in testing and measurement, statistics, child development, personality theory, and child psychopathology. Knowledge in each of these areas will help you administer and interpret tests, arrive at conclusions, and formulate interventions and recommendations. If you are evaluating children with severe sensory or motor disabilities (e.g., deafness, blindness, or cerebral palsy), you may need to work collaboratively with teachers or other experts knowledgeable about these disabilities. A study of remedial and educational techniques used to treat and educate special-abilities children will help those of you who plan to work in school settings.

The technical and clinical skills needed to be a competent clinical assessor include the abilities to do the following:

1. Establish and maintain rapport with children
2. Use effective listening and interviewing techniques appropriate for interviewing parents, children, and teachers
3. Evaluate the psychometric properties of tests
4. Select an appropriate assessment battery
5. Administer and score tests and other assessment tools by following standardized procedures
6. Observe and evaluate behavior
7. Perform informal assessments
8. Interpret assessment results
9. Use assessment findings to develop effective interventions
10. Communicate assessment findings effectively both orally and in writing
11. Adhere to ethical standards
12. Read and interpret research in clinical and psychoeducational assessment
13. Keep up with federal and state laws and regulations concerning the assessment and placement of children with special needs

In using this text, consider the following cautions. First, this text is not a substitute for test manuals or for texts on child development or child psychopathology; it supplements material contained in test manuals and summarizes major findings in the areas of child development and psychopathology. Second, this text cannot substitute for clinically supervised experiences. Each student should receive supervision in all phases of assessment, including test selection, administration, scoring, and interpretation; report writing; and communication of results and recommendations. Ideally, every student should examine children who have mental retardation, learning disabilities, or developmental delays, as well as normal and gifted children, in order to develop skills with different populations. Third, although this text covers the major psychological instruments used in the individual assessment of children, it does not cover every psychological assessment instrument currently published or even a fraction of the thousands of informal assessment procedures used by clinicians and researchers. However, the principles you will learn in this text will enable you to evaluate many kinds of assessment tools with a more discerning eye.

It is important for you to keep abreast of current research concerning assessment and intervention throughout your training and career. You will want to pay close attention to research on the reliability and validity of the tests, interview

"It's about Benny, doctor. He's just come from school with an IQ of 104! Should I put him right to bed?"

Copyright © 1955, Cowles Magazines, Inc.

procedures, observational techniques, behavioral checklists, and other assessment techniques that you use. Research findings will provide you with a base from which you can evaluate your assessment techniques and recommendations. You also may want to conduct research on intelligence testing, tests of special abilities, interviewing, observation, and other assessment procedures. Although much of the material in this text is relevant to this task, you still need to be acquainted with current research findings to carry out meaningful research.

You will find some information in this text about federal regulations, such as the Individuals with Disabilities Education Act (see Chapter 3). In order to work with special needs children, however, you will have to become thoroughly knowledgeable about state and federal regulations concerning assessment procedures, particularly if the assessment involves identification for placement in educational programs. Especially important are topics related to nonbiased assessment, classification of disabling conditions, eligibility criteria for many special programs, individualized educational programs, rights of parents, and confidentiality and safekeeping of records.

STEPS IN THE ASSESSMENT PROCESS

You can think of the assessment process as comprising the 11 steps discussed below (see Figure 1-3). These steps represent a multistage assessment process involving planning, collecting data, evaluating results and formulating hypotheses, developing recommendations, communicating results and recommendations, conducting reevaluations, and following up on the child's performance as needed.

Step 1: Review Referral Information

When you receive a referral, read it carefully and, if necessary, consult with the referral source to clarify any ambiguous or vague information. For example, if a teacher asks you to find out why a child is having difficulty in class, you will want to know what kind of difficulty the teacher is referring to, in order to keep from going off in a misleading direction. You will want to know what the referral source expects you to accomplish, and you will want to identify the areas that the referral source is most concerned about. If you can't identify these areas, you will have difficulty in formulating an appropriate assessment strategy. If you understand the referral question and the expectations that the referral source has about what you can and cannot accomplish, then you will begin the assessment on a firm footing.

You want to establish a good working relationship with the referral source. This will facilitate reviewing the available information, as well as determining what further information you need and what decisions and options are available. Com-

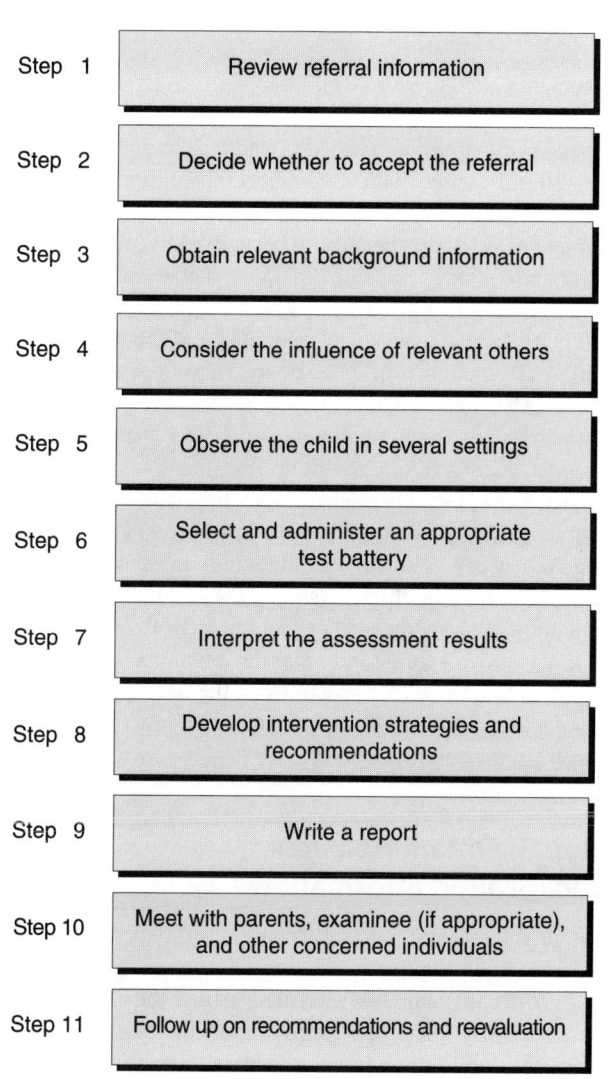

Figure 1-3. Steps in the assessment process.

munication and decision making will be easier if you and the referral source share a common vocabulary and agree about the referral questions. However, you may need to clarify the issues involved in a particular case with the referral source and reconceptualize or redefine the referral question.

Discuss the reasons for individual assessment with the referral source, and spell out any potential benefits and limitations. Some school districts have pre-referral committees, established to work with teachers who have concerns about students' academic or behavioral performance. Pre-referral committees may recommend possible interventions. They may also reduce the number of children unnecessarily referred for individual assessment, making it easier to provide prompt and intensive services to those most in need of individual assessment.

Step 2: Decide Whether to Accept the Referral

You do not need to give all children who are referred to you a complete battery of tests. Ask yourself questions such as these: Is formal testing needed? Can I answer the concerns of the referral source with assessment procedures other than formal testing? Are there other professionals who are more competent to handle the referral because of its highly specialized nature? For example, a child who has recently sustained a head injury would be best served by neuropsychological and neurological assessments. Similarly, if the referral indicates (or if you discover in the course of your evaluation) that the child has had a sudden change in personality or cognitive behavior, certain physical complaints (e.g., nausea, dizziness, headache, vomiting, undue sleeplessness, difficulty in arousal from sleep, listlessness, easy fatiguability, blurred or double vision, motor weakness or clumsiness, loss or reduction in sensory acuities), or alterations in sensations (e.g., pain, numbness, tingling, ringing in the ears), you should immediately ask for a medical consultation (Boll, 1987). Generally, if you can't figure out what the examinee's problem is, refer the examinee to a specialist in the appropriate area. If you decide to conduct the evaluation, obtain written permission from the parents to do so.

Step 3: Obtain Relevant Background Information

Obtain information relevant to the child's medical, social, psychological, linguistic, educational, and physical development. You can obtain this information from the child, the parents, teachers, and others familiar with the child's problem; from the child's cumulative school records (including records from previous schools); from previous psychological evaluations (if performed); from medical reports; and from reports from other agencies (if applicable). Have the parents complete the Background Questionnaire (see *Assessment of Children: Behavioral and Clinical Applications*) and have the teacher complete the School Referral Questionnaire (see *Assessment of Children: Behavioral and Clinical Applications*). Note whether there have been any risk factors or predisposing factors for psychological or psychoeducational problems during pregnancy and delivery, early childhood, or later developmental periods and whether there is a family history of any disorders related to the referral question. In school settings, you will want to note information about what the child has or has not learned and what corrective instructional actions have been taken by the school staff (such as the remedial approaches used, changes in curricula, and changes in instructional approach). Also obtain samples of the child's classroom work (e.g., essays, writing samples, drawings, constructions). If you plan to contact other sources to obtain information about the child, be sure to have the parents sign a release-of-information consent form. If the child was recently hospitalized, ask the hospital staff about their opinion of the child's readiness to return to school and about any factors that might interfere with the child's schooling.

Step 4: Consider the Influence of Relevant Others

To evaluate the child's problems fully, it is critical that you interview the parents, the teachers, and other relevant adults and siblings. Determine each parent's preferred language and use an interpreter as needed (see Chapter 19 for information about using an interpreter). Carefully explain to the parents the policies of the clinic, the school, or your own practice; the limits of confidentiality; the fees; the time constraints; and what you think you can accomplish. Give them the opportunity to ask questions, and answer their questions as simply, clearly, and directly as possible. If you interview the parents and teachers, find out about how they view the problem, what they have done to alleviate the problem, and their role in maintaining the problem (see Chapter 2 in *Assessment of Children: Behavioral and Clinical Applications*). Because different adults see the child in different settings and play different roles with the child, do not be surprised to find disagreements in the reports adults give about the same child. When the assessment findings do not agree with the parents' or teachers' accounts of what the child can do, investigate the reasons for the disagreement. Do not assume that conflicting reports are wrong; rather, consider them to be reports based on different samples of behavior. Ideally you should observe how the behaviors of parents, teachers, and siblings affect the child.

Step 5: Observe the Child in Several Settings

As you administer tests, you also need to observe the child's behavior. Knowing *how* the child performs on a test—information that supplements the more objective test information—will help you individualize the clinical evaluation. Careful observation also may help you, for example, to develop hypotheses about the child's coping behaviors and to learn about the child's flexibility and willingness to communicate clearly with others. You will want to observe the child in other settings as well.

Home and classroom visits provide added benefits, including the opportunity to establish rapport with the child, the parents, and teachers and to observe the physical characteristics of the child's environments, such as the layout and structure of the home and the classroom. Developing a collaborative relationship with the child's parents and teachers will be important during both assessment and intervention phases. Avoid interfering with regular home or classroom routines, and remind the teacher that you don't want the specific child to know that you are there to observe him or her.

Ask teachers or parents to follow their usual routine when you are present. As a result of your visit to the classroom, you should be able to answer questions such as these: How would you describe the classroom environment? Is the curriculum appropriate for the child and is it being implemented effectively? What instructional strategies and rewards are being used? Although you should make every effort to reduce the parents' or teachers' anxiety about your visit, parents and teachers must understand that their behavior may be part of the problem and that changes in their behavior may be part of the solution. The behaviors of the child and parents or the child and teachers are usually so intertwined that it is almost impossible to examine one without the other. Chapter 4 in *Assessment of Children: Behavioral and Clinical Applications* describes procedures for observing the home and classroom in more detail.

Step 6: Select and Administer an Appropriate Test Battery

An effective assessment strategy requires that you develop a plan and choose tests and other assessment procedures to meet your goal. Table 1-1 presents guidelines for evaluating tests and other assessment procedures; Figure 1-4 shows components of tests or subtests. Carefully study the information contained in each test manual, including evidence on the reliability and validity of the test and the normative data. For information on a vast number of tests, consult the latest edition of the *Mental Measurements Yearbook*. Consult *Standards for Educational and Psychological Testing* (AERA, APA, & NCME, 1999) for information about technical and professional standards for test construction and use. Journals that publish test reviews and research on assessment include *Psychological Assessment, Journal of Psychoeducational Assessment, Psychology in the Schools, School Psychology Review, Journal of Clinical Psychology, Journal of School Psychology, Educational and Psychological Measurement, Intelligence, Applied Psychology Measurement,* and *Journal of Educational Psychology.*

Colleagues working in your school or agency also can be a helpful source of information. List-serve groups on the Internet—such as the one sponsored by the National Association of School Psychologists (NASP)—are another source for information about tests, other assessment procedures, and public laws governing special education. In the NASP list-serve group, individual school psychologists share information and ask questions about issues that arise in their work. Finally, Table F-7 in Appendix F presents Web sites that are valuable for the fields of school psychology and clinical psychology.

Selecting group or individual tests. In deciding whether to use group or individually administered tests, consider the nature of the referral question and whether the referral question can be answered without administering a battery

---

Table 1-1
Guidelines for Evaluating a Test

Information about the Test

1. What is the name of the test?
2. Who are its authors?
3. Who published it?
4. When was it published?
5. Is there an alternative form available?
6. How much does it cost (including the cost of the test, answer sheets, scoring services, etc.)?
7. How long does it take to administer?
8. Is there a test manual?
9. How recently was the test revised?
10. What is the purpose of the test?
11. What are the qualifications needed to administer and interpret the test?
12. What was the standardization group?
13. How representative was the standardization group?
14. What is the reliability of the test?
15. What reliability measures are provided?
16. How valid is the test for its stated purposes?
17. What validity measures are provided?
18. If a factor analysis has been performed, what were the results?
19. How clear are the directions for administration and scoring?
20. Are the scoring procedures clear?
21. Are the scales used for reporting scores clearly and carefully described?
22. Are norms reported in an appropriate form, usually standard scores or percentile ranks?
23. Are the populations to which the norms refer clearly defined and described?
24. If more than one form is available, are there tables showing equivalent scores on the different forms?
25. Is computer scoring available?

Examinee Considerations

26. What prerequisite skills are needed by the examinee to complete the test?
27. In what languages or modes of communication can the test be administered?
28. Is the vocabulary level of the test's directions appropriate for the examinee?
29. How are the test items presented?
30. How are the test items responded to?
31. What stated and unstated adaptations can be made in presentation and response modes?
32. How much is the test affected by gender and ethnic bias?
33. Will the test materials be interesting to the examinee?
34. Is the test suitable for individual or group administration?

---

of individual tests. How important is it that tests be administered individually? Would group tests be as effective as individual tests in answering the referral question? Are there any motivational, personality, linguistic, or physically disabling factors that may impair the examinee's performance on

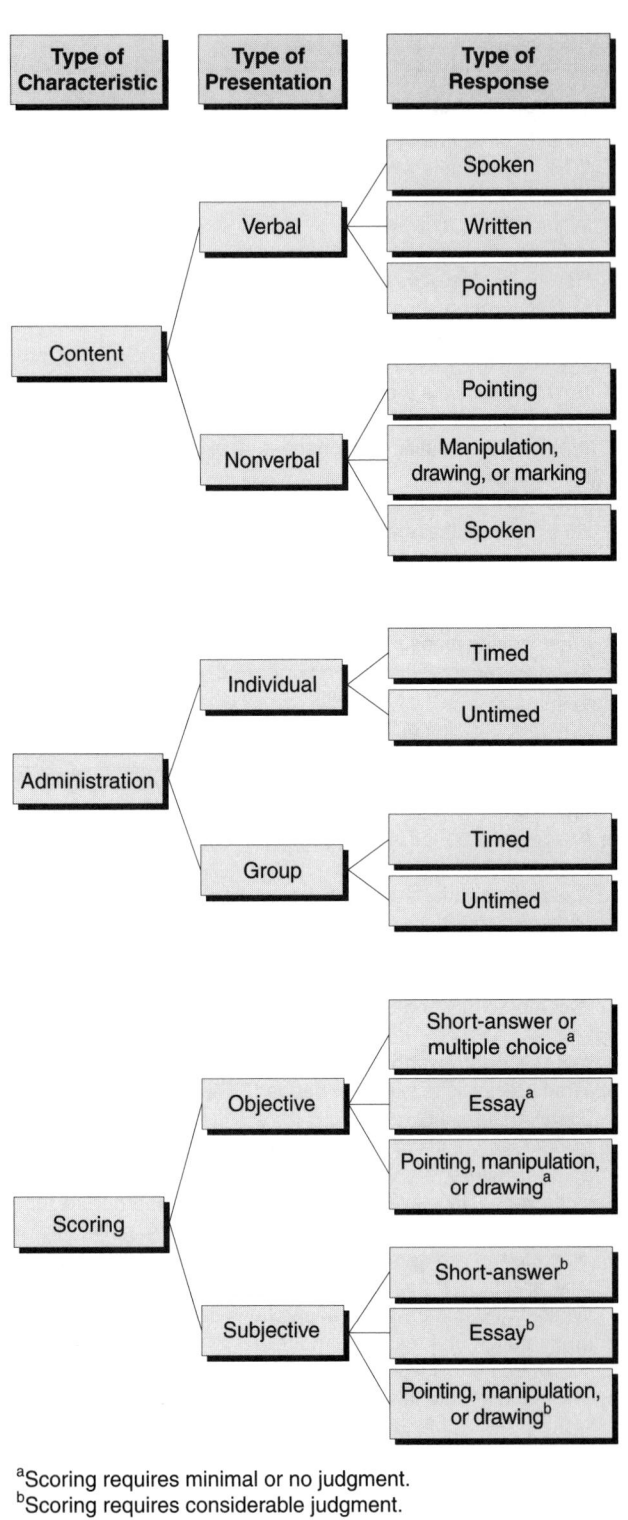

aScoring requires minimal or no judgment.
bScoring requires considerable judgment.

Figure 1-4. Components of tests or subtests. Note that some tests have subtests that are timed and others that are untimed. Also, some group tests are sometimes administered individually.

Copyright © 1997, John P. Wood. Reprinted with permission.

group tests? When there is reason to question the validity of the results of group tests or when you need to observe the examinee's performance, you should administer individual tests.

Group tests are less frequently used in the assessment of special children for four reasons (Newcomer & Bryant, 1993). First, group tests usually require some degree of reading proficiency, and many children with special needs have reading difficulties. Individually administered tests, in contrast, usually rely on examiners to read the test directions and interact verbally with examinees. (Obviously, individually administered tests designed to measure reading ability will require examinees to read.)

Second, because examinees taking group tests typically fill in bubbles, circle letters, or underline answers instead of giving their answers orally, it is difficult to determine whether they know the answers or are merely guessing. Students with visual perceptual problems or attention problems may have difficulty using answer sheets. They may, for example, follow instructions to skip too-difficult items but forget to also skip the corresponding item on the answer sheet. Also, group-administered tests do not allow you to observe how the examinee goes about solving problems.

Third, group tests tend to use recognition rather than recall, requiring examinees to select one answer from among the several that are given. Although some individually administered tests require the examinee to select an answer from four choices (e.g., Peabody Picture Vocabulary Test–III, Peabody Individual Achievement Test–Revised Normative

Update, and Comprehensive Test of Nonverbal Intelligence), examinees most often answer questions directly rather than choosing the correct answer.

Fourth, examinees taking group tests can get lost, bored, fatigued, or indifferent without examiners' ever knowing that these behaviors or feelings are present or having a chance to intervene. With individual tests, examiners can monitor these factors and take steps to reduce their influence by providing encouragement, bringing examinees back to focus, taking short breaks, or maintaining momentum and motivation.

Individually administered tests are more expensive in both cost and time than group-administered tests, but they are essential as supplements to—or sometimes replacements for—group-administered tests. Individually administered tests also are useful because they provide a second opinion when results of group-administered tests may be in question, and they are usually mandated when children are evaluated for special education services.

Selecting the test battery. Select the test battery on the basis of the information you have about the child and the available tests. Consider, for example, the referral question and the child's age, physical capabilities, language proficiency, and prior test results. Also consider teacher, parental, and medical reports. With respect to the available tests, consider their age-appropriateness and the recency of the norms, as well as reliability and validity, objectivity, ease of administration, and time requirements. Recognize that no one test can give you all the information you need to perform a comprehensive evaluation of the child. An objective measure of intelligence, for example, provides little or no information about the child's word recognition and reading comprehension abilities; competencies in arithmetical operations and spelling; behavior outside of the test situation; self-concept; attitudes toward peers, siblings, and parents; temperament and personality; adaptive behavior; or interpersonal skills. To conduct a thorough evaluation, you will need to supplement a measure of intellectual ability with other assessment measures. Nonetheless, a measure of intellectual ability may be needed to address issues of remediation (e.g., Does the child have a specific learning disability in reading?) or general developmental concerns. Your personal preferences, based on your experience and evaluations, also will guide you in selecting the most appropriate tests.

You should address (or at least consider) the following factors in a complete individual appraisal of a child (Keogh, Major-Kingsley, Omori-Gordon, & Reid, 1982):

- Age (years, months)
- Gender
- Residence location (rural, small town, suburban, urban)
- Grade level (preschool or specific grade in elementary school, high school, college)
- Ethnicity (how examinee identifies himself or herself, such as African American, Asian American, Euro American, Hispanic American, Native American, mixed ancestry, other)
- Family history (birth order, number of siblings, pertinent family health history, resources for change)
- Socioeconomic status, or SES (upper class, upper-middle class, middle class, lower-middle class, lower class)
- Language (if bilingual or non-English, specify languages, language competence in each language, and language spoken at home if different from that at school)
- Educational history (age-appropriate grade placement, retained in grade, changed schools often, spent most of educational career in special classes)
- Physical and health status (sensory deficits, physical disabilities, neurological impairment, chronic illness, medications, compensatory behavior, and other relevant aspects)
- Intellectual ability (repertoire of skills, knowledge, learning style)
- Oral language (receptive and expressive)
- Achievement (reading, including decoding, phonemic awareness, reading comprehension, and reading fluency; mathematics, including math computations and math applications; and written language, including spelling, writing mechanics, and written expression)
- Activity level (kind and amount of movement displayed during a specific period in a specific context)
- Attention (ability to filter out extraneous stimuli and focus selectively on a task over a period of time)

SCHOOLIES © 1998 by John P. Wood

I marked them all "True." I just can't believe that you'd ever lie to us.

Copyright © 1998, John P. Wood. Reprinted with permission.

- Adaptive skills (self-help skills and ability to move about in the environment)
- Work and study skills (study habits, including length of time spent studying, frequency of studying, when and where studying takes place; note-taking strategies; study strategies such as writing and answering study questions; text-reading strategies; use of supplementary materials; use of computer software; and use of the World Wide Web and on-line encyclopedias)
- Auditory perception (ability to identify, discriminate, interpret, and organize elements of acoustical stimuli)
- Fine-motor coordination (ability to integrate small muscles, usually in conjunction with visual perception)
- Gross-motor activity (degree of coordination and ability to organize movements of the large muscle groups)
- Memory (ability to store and retrieve information, regardless of mode of input)
- Visual perception (ability to identify, discriminate, interpret, and organize physical elements of visual stimuli)
- Personal and emotional functioning (ability to relate to others, to express and modulate emotions, and to show a range of emotions)

Administering the test battery.   When you administer a test battery, you need to know how to present the test materials, how to interact with examinees, how to score responses, and how to complete the record booklets (or test protocols or test forms). To score responses accurately, you need to (a) understand the scoring principles and scoring criteria discussed in the test manuals and (b) guard against allowing "halo" effects (i.e., when a judgment about one characteristic of a person is influenced by another characteristic or general impression of that person) that might bias your scoring. You also may want to learn about how the child functions with additional cues, a process referred to as testing-of-limits (see Chapter 7). The material in this text will help you in each of these areas and complements the material contained in test manuals.

Step 7: Interpret the Assessment Results

After you have administered and scored the tests and have gathered the background, interview, and observational information, you will interpret the findings. Interpretations should never rely solely on test scores. Your judgments, for example, of the child's speech, voice quality, language, motor skills, physical appearance, posture, gesture, and affect are as important as the interviews, responses to questionnaires and behavior checklists, case history, and other kinds of observations. Interpreting the findings is one of the most challenging of all assessment activities, as it will draw on your knowledge of children, test theory, developmental psychology, personality theory, and psychopathology. The interpretive process involves (a) integrating the assessment data, (b) mak-

ing judgments about the meaning of the data, and (c) exploring the implications of the data regarding diagnosis, placement, and intervention.

As you integrate and interpret the assessment data, you will want to consider questions such as the following:

- Are the test scores from similar measures congruent or incongruent? For example, if you administered two different arithmetic tests, are the percentile ranks similar? How might you account for any discrepancies between the two measures? For example, were there differences in the standardization groups, differences in item types, or differences in the times at which the two tests were administered to the child?
- Are the test results congruent with the other pieces of information about the examinee, such as his or her educational level, academic grades, teacher and parent reports, or occupational level (in the case of adolescents and adults)? What patterns are present in the assessment results?
- Are there any discrepancies in the information you obtained from the child, parents, teachers, and other sources? If so, what might account for the discrepancies? Is it possible that, rather than being discrepancies, the differences simply reflect behaviors of the child in different settings or contexts?
- Do the current findings appear to be reliable and valid? For example, did the examinee have motivational difficulties or difficulties understanding the English language? Were there problems with the administrative test procedures? Did any other factors affect the reliability and validity of the assessment results?
- Do the assessment results suggest implications for remediation and intervention?

All of the information you gather should be understood in relation to the child as a whole. Because the information will come from many different sources, it may not be easy to integrate. But integration is essential, particularly in sorting out findings and in establishing trends. Many chapters in this text will assist you with interpreting assessment results. As you interpret the findings, evaluate the extent to which biological and environmental factors may have contributed to the problem and the relative importance of each. Additionally, you want to determine the child's strengths and weaknesses and the adaptive resources the child and his or her family have available to cope with the problem and make changes that will contribute to remediating the problem.

In making interpretations, you will also formulate hypotheses and seek independently verifiable confirming evidence. You should either regard as tentative or drop any hypotheses supported by only one piece of minor evidence. You should retain hypotheses supported by more than one piece of evidence—especially if the supporting data come from more than one source (e.g., test results *and* observations). Also, seek evidence that may disconfirm each hypothesis. When you complete this process, advance the supported hypotheses. Keep in mind that these are still hypotheses—that is, tentative and unproven explanations of a complex set of data—but they are explanations that you can offer with some degree of confidence. Use your judgment in deciding whether a response reflects the examinee's habitual style or is a temporary and transient expression. For example, is the impulsiveness demonstrated by the child related to the test question, to the psychological evaluation, to temporary conditions, or to a habitual style? Although you must be careful not to overinterpret every minuscule aspect of the examinee's performance, there are occasions when hypotheses developed from unique responses may prove to be valuable. For example, if a child ends a sentence completion item with a statement that he or she was sexually molested, you will want to follow up this response.

Recognize that test scores do not tell us about the home and school environment, the quality of the instruction that the child has received in school, the quality of the child's textbooks, peer pressures, the SES of the family, and other factors that may influence the child's test performance. You will need to obtain information about these factors from caregivers and teachers and consider their effect on the child's performance.

As a beginning examiner, you are not expected to have the well-developed clinical skills and insights to make skilled interpretations. Developing these skills takes time. With experience, you will learn how to integrate knowledge obtained from various sources—including class lectures, textbooks, test manuals, practicum, and internship—and will begin to feel more comfortable making interpretations.

Step 8: Develop Intervention Strategies and Recommendations

In addition to interpreting the assessment findings, you may need to formulate interventions and recommendations; in school settings you may also need to determine eligibility for a special education program and work with an educational team to formulate an individualized education program (IEP; see Chapter 3). To formulate interventions and recommendations, you will need to rely on the same body of information you used to interpret the findings, as well as on data from other sources. These include information obtained from the fields of clinical psychology, assessment theory, developmental psychology, educational psychology, psychopathology, and psychoeducational interventions. This text provides general information on how to formulate recommendations. However, it is not designed to cover remediation or intervention procedures in depth. You will obtain this knowledge from other texts and sources that cover behavioral interventions, educational interventions, psychotherapy, counseling techniques, and rehabilitation counseling, as well as from supervision and clinical experience.

Traditional forms of psychometric assessment usually do not provide information about the conditions that will best facilitate the child's ability to learn—for example, how the type of material, rate and modality of presentation, cues, and reinforcements differentially affect learning. Information about these and related factors could help us design more effective intervention programs which might improve the cognitive ability and skills of children. An integration of experimental and clinical/psychoeducational approaches, which has been in the making for many years, has yet to occur. Until this union occurs, we must use the procedures available (inferences from performance on standard tests, informal tests, and specialized procedures, and inferences from observations) to determine the conditions that will best facilitate the child's ability to learn and succeed in the classroom. For example, what you did to help the child function more effectively during the assessment may suggest recommendations. *Currently, developing interventions is as much an art as it is a science.*

The assessment report should not merely enumerate the examinee's deficits, or areas of failure, and which behaviors should be targeted for change; it also should specify abilities that he or she might be able to use to master tasks. By identifying compensatory abilities, you establish a basis for developing intervention strategies. Consider, for example, how the examinee's deficits can be circumvented, which sensory processing modalities are most intact, and the specific needs and capacities of the examinee. Examinees with language processing deficits, for example, may respond better to programs that employ visual materials, whereas those with visual-perceptual processing deficits may learn more quickly with concrete and specific verbally mediated materials. In the case of highly distractible examinees, short intervention sessions conducted in a minimally distracting environment might be appropriate.

You also should consider factors in the school that may interfere with the child's ability to learn and profit from schooling. Consider, for example, whether modifications are needed in the courses the child is taking, the teaching methods used in the classroom, the scheduling of courses, and the physical layout of the building. Also consider whether the child needs any type of assistance, can tolerate a full day or only a half day, needs special equipment to help with communications, or needs to be reassigned to another teacher or a new school. Evaluate how flexible, accepting of children with special needs, and patient the child's present teacher is, and whether she or he has a positive and supportive attitude and is willing to take suggestions and work with other professionals.

Schools may offer some of the following services for students with disabilities (Sink & Tracy, 1988): speech and language training; remedial classes in basic academic subjects; adaptive physical education; computer-assisted instruction; tutoring for mainstream classes; social skills retraining; mobility and transportation assistance; academic, vocational, and personal counseling; and career development and employment assistance. You will need to consider which of these or other resources are available in the particular school district.

Diagnosing educational disabilities is a complex and difficult task. It is often even more difficult to specify with certainty the procedures needed to ameliorate an examinee's problems, to create appropriate conditions for learning, and to foster psychological development, social adjustment, and successful participation in the community. Concern with intervention should not tempt us to go beyond the limits of our present knowledge. We can, however, use the knowledge and experience we have gained to suggest treatment interventions and corresponding methods of evaluating progress, apply these interventions in a careful and thoughtful manner, and then examine the data and test our hypotheses to see whether the treatment produced the desired effect.

In spite of the problems associated with developing interventions in school settings, you should work with the examinee's teachers to establish a set of instructional objectives that the teachers can use. Objectives for teachers can include determining the tasks that they will use, arranging a hierarchy of instructional objectives, eliminating behaviors incompatible with effective instruction, and teaching the tasks most needed by the child. You also will need to consider the child's and family's resources (such as family support and financial resources) and the role of the parents in developing, implementing, and evaluating the intervention strategies.

Step 9: Write a Report

Your findings and recommendations can help the children you evaluate as well as their parents, teachers, and other interested parties, but the value of your contribution will depend on your ability to communicate these findings and recommendations. Recognize that many different people may read your report, including parents, teachers, counselors, psychiatrists, probation officers, pediatricians, neurologists, social workers, attorneys, and, depending on his or her age, the examinee.

You need to write the report as clearly as possible shortly after you complete the evaluation. Include in the report your findings, interpretations, and recommendations. One of the best ways to learn how to write a report is to study reports written by competent clinicians. Throughout this text you will find reports that illustrate clear writing, skillful analysis, and good clinical judgment. Use these reports only as general guides; ideally, you should develop your own style and approach to report writing. Because the psychological report is a crucial part of the assessment process, it deserves your care and attention. A study of the material in Chapter 21 will help you master some fundamentals of report writing.

Step 10: Meet with Parents, the Examinee (if appropriate), and Other Concerned Individuals

After you have written the report, you may want to discuss the results with the child, the child's parents, and the referral source. You may also be called on to present your results at a staff conference or even in a court of law. All face-to-face contacts will require you to be skillful in explaining your findings and recommendations. If children or parents are at the conference, you will need to help them understand the findings, encourage their participation, and reduce any anxiety or defensiveness. By becoming familiar with the content of this text, you will be better able to present and support your findings. Chapter 3 in *Assessment of Children: Behavioral and Clinical Applications* provides some guidelines for conferring with parents.

Step 11: Follow Up on Recommendations and Reevaluation

Effective delivery of services requires close monitoring of recommendations, interventions, and changes in the child's development. Both short- and long-term follow-ups are important components of the assessment process. Short-term follow-ups (within 2 to 6 weeks) are needed to identify interventions that prove to be ineffective, either because of changes in the situation or because the interventions were inadequate from the beginning. You also may discover other issues requiring additional assessment after you review the initial response to the intervention.

Long-term follow-ups are important because examinees change as a result of development, life experiences, and treat-

From *Mainstreaming Series: Individualized Educational Programming (IEP),* Copyright © 1977 by Judy A. Schrag, Thomas N. Fairchild, and Bart L. Miller, published by Teaching Resources Corporation, Hingham, Massachusetts. Reprinted with permission. All rights reserved.

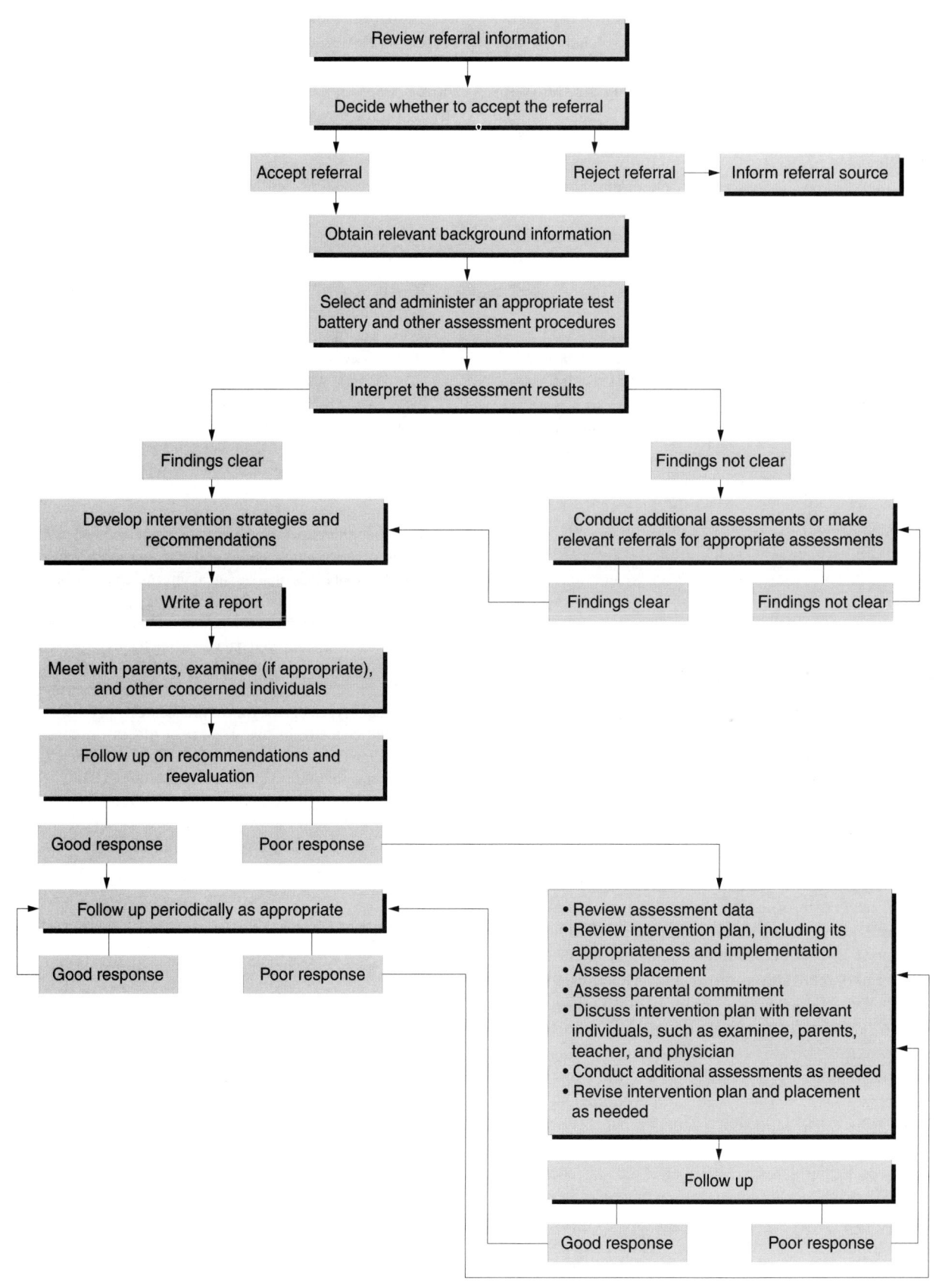

Figure 1-5. Flowchart of a decision-making model for clinical and psychoeducational assessment.

ment; consequently, you should not consider an assessment to be an end point. For example, an evaluation conducted when the child is 2 years old may have little meaning a year later, except as a basis for comparison. Reevaluation is an important means of monitoring and documenting the child's response to an intervention, the stability of symptoms, the progression of a disease process, or the course and rate of recovery. Repeated assessment is especially important when a medical intervention procedure (e.g., chemotherapy or brain surgery) or a behavioral intervention procedure (e.g., a cognitive rehabilitation program) is used. Repeated assessment is also required when you place children in special education programs or when preschool children have developmental disabilities. If the child has an IEP, you will want to determine whether the goals and objectives of the plan are being met and how best to change the plan if change is needed.

The assessment recommendations are not the final solution to the child's difficulties. Recommendations are starting points for the clinician and for those responsible for implementing the interventions. Assessment should be an ongoing process, with modifications made to the intervention plans as the child's needs change or when the plans are ineffective. Effective consultation requires monitoring the child's progress with both short-term and long-term follow-up contacts as needed.

Comment on Steps
in the Assessment Process

Formulating an assessment plan begins with selecting an appropriate battery of tests, deciding on whom to interview, deciding on what types of observations are needed, and modifying the original plan as additional questions develop from the assessment findings. Sometimes you will want to (a) change or add tests or other assessment procedures as a result of the information you obtain early in the assessment process or (b) schedule further assessments in order to gain additional needed information. Here is an example of how you might modify your original plan: Your original plan does not call for an in-depth developmental history interview with the mother to obtain further information. However, the interview with the child reveals a period of hospitalization last summer. Consequently, you decide that you need to interview the mother to obtain further information. Finally, as you review your findings, you may decide that the child needs a specialized assessment, such as a neuropsychological evaluation or a speech and language evaluation. In this case, you would refer the child to an appropriate specialist.

The steps in the assessment process are not necessarily fixed in the order presented here. For example, sometimes you might formulate hypotheses after you review the referral and background information. These hypotheses will guide you in your selection of assessment tools. As you conduct the examination and review the results, your initial hypotheses will be modified and new ones proposed.

You also can think of the steps in the assessment process as a model for making decisions about the child. Figure 1-5 presents a flowchart depicting a decision-making model for clinical and psychoeducational assessment. In addition to the 11 steps in the assessment process, Figure 1-5 offers strategies for how to proceed when the assessment findings are not clear or when the examinee does not benefit from the intervention.

THINKING THROUGH THE ISSUES

1. Most of you will be able to master the skills needed to evaluate, select, and administer assessment instruments and to record, score, and interpret test responses. However, there is more to clinical assessment than simply mastering techniques. You will have to work with many different types of children and families. Why have you embarked upon the study of assessment of children? What experiences have you had that have influenced your decision? What do you hope to gain upon completing this course of study? What skills do you now have and what kinds of experiences do you think you will need to become an effective clinical assessor?

2. The four pillars of assessment—norm-referenced tests, interviews, observations, and informal assessment procedures—provide different kinds of assessment information. In what ways do the various assessment procedures overlap? Why would it be useful to integrate the information from the four different methods—that is, what do you gain by using the four methods rather than using one or two methods only? What kinds of problems do you foresee in integrating the information obtained from the four major types of assessment procedures?

3. You can conceive of the assessment process as consisting of several interrelated steps. What problems can occur at each step that might interfere with your ability to complete the assessment? What might you do to prevent such problems? If problems occur, what can you do to recover and continue the assessment? What negative effects might result?

SUMMARY

Purposes of Assessment

1. Assessment is a process of gaining some understanding of the child in order to make informed decisions.

2. A screening assessment is a relatively brief evaluation given to identify children who (a) are eligible for certain programs, (b) have a disorder or disability in need of remediation or rehabilitation, or (c) may need a more comprehensive assessment.

3. A focused, or problem-solving, assessment is a detailed evaluation of a specific area of functioning.

4. A diagnostic assessment is a detailed evaluation of the child's strengths and weaknesses in several areas, such as cognitive, academic, language, and social functioning.

5. A counseling and rehabilitation assessment is similar to a classification/placement assessment except that emphasis is placed on the child's abilities to adjust to and successfully fulfill daily responsibilities.

6. A progress evaluation assessment focuses on the day-to-day, week-to-week, month-to-month, or year-to-year progress of the child.

7. Psychological testing involves administering tests; the focus is on collecting data.

8. Psychological assessment is more encompassing and involves several clinical tools, such as formal and informal tests, observations, and interviews; the focus is not only on collecting data, but also on using clinical skills to interpret the data and synthesize the results.

Four Pillars of Assessment

9. The word *test* can apply to any standard procedure used for measuring a sample of behavior.

10. "Standard procedure" refers to the use of the same item content, administration procedure, and scoring criteria.

11. A standardized test is a task or set of tasks given under standard conditions and designed to assess some aspect of a person's knowledge, skill, behavior, or personality.

12. Norm-referenced tests are standardized on a clearly defined group, termed the *norm group,* and scaled so that each score reflects a rank within the norm group.

13. Norm-referenced tests provide some degree of quantification of the child's psychological functioning.

14. Norm-referenced tests also provide an index for evaluating changes in many different aspects of the child's physical and social world.

15. You will gain assessment information by interviewing the child, parents, teachers, and other individuals familiar with the child.

16. Unstructured interviews are usually open-ended, without a set agenda.

17. Semi-structured interviews provide a list of questions, but the focus of the interview can be changed as needed.

18. Structured interviews provide a rigid, but comprehensive, list of questions usually designed to arrive at a diagnosis.

19. You will obtain valuable information by observing the child during the formal assessment, as well as in his or her natural surroundings.

20. Observations will enable you to identify factors that may be contributing to and sustaining the problem behavior, and consequently can be useful in developing interventions.

21. You may need to supplement standardized norm-referenced tests with informal and other assessment procedures.

22. The four pillars of assessment complement one another and form a firm foundation for making decisions about children.

23. You must first interpret each procedure in its own right and then weave information from the various sources together so that the final tapestry is integrated, understandable, meaningful, and consistent.

24. Never evaluate a child without considering formal or informal developmental norms.

25. A multimethod assessment approach is advocated in this text. It consists of obtaining information from several sources and reviewing the child's record and previous evaluations, using several assessment techniques, and assessing several areas.

26. Consider carefully what assessment procedures will be most effective and efficient and whether additional assessment procedures will contribute to the evaluation.

27. Learning *why* the child performed as he or she did requires a careful study of the entire clinical history and assessment results.

28. Assessments should not end with the report.

29. It is important that you recognize both the strengths and the limitations of assessment techniques.

30. To be effective, the intervention plan must have ecological validity.

Guidelines for Assessment

31. Your aim is to assess both the limitations and the competencies of the child; the focus should not be only on problems.

32. Tests and other assessment procedures are powerful tools, but their effectiveness will depend on your knowledge and skill.

33. Effective decision making is the hallmark of clinical and psychoeducational assessment.

34. This text is not a substitute for test manuals or for texts on child development or child psychopathology.

35. This text cannot substitute for clinically supervised experiences.

36. It is important for you to keep abreast of current research concerning assessment and intervention throughout your training and career.

37. In order to work with special needs children, you will have to become thoroughly knowledgeable about state and federal regulations concerning assessment procedures, particularly if the assessment involves identification for placement in educational programs.

Steps in the Assessment Process

38. The steps in the assessment process are reviewing referral information; deciding whether to accept the referral; obtaining relevant background information; considering the influence of relevant others; observing the child in several settings; selecting and administering an appropriate test battery; interpreting the assessment results; developing intervention strategies and recommendations; writing a report; meeting with parents, the examinee, and other concerned individuals; and following up on recommendations and reevaluation.

KEY TERMS, CONCEPTS, AND NAMES

Daniel Hoffman v. the Board of Education of the City of New York (p. 2)
Screening assessment (p. 3)
Focused, or problem-solving, assessment (p. 3)
Diagnostic assessment (p. 3)
Counseling and rehabilitation assessment (p. 4)
Progress evaluation assessment (p. 4)
Psychological testing (p. 4)
Psychological assessment (p. 4)
Standardized test (p. 4)
Norm-referenced tests (p. 5)
Interviews (p. 5)
Norm group (p. 5)
Unstructured interviews (p. 5)
Semi-structured interviews (p. 5)
Structured interviews (p. 5)
Observations (p. 6)
Informal assessment procedures (p. 6)
Multimethod assessment approach (p. 7)
Ecological validity (p. 8)

STUDY QUESTIONS

1. What relevance does the case of *Daniel Hoffman* have to the practice of school and clinical psychology?

2. Discuss the purposes of assessment. Include in your discussion how psychological assessment differs from psychological testing.

3. What are the four pillars of assessment, and how do they complement one another?

4. What are some important guidelines for assessment?

5. What technical and clinical skills do you need to become a competent clinical assessor?

6. Describe the main steps in the assessment process.

2

CHALLENGES IN ASSESSING CHILDREN: THE CONTEXT

It is probably unwise to spend much time in attempts to separate off sharply certain qualities of man, such as his intelligence, from such emotional and vocational qualities as his interest in mental activity, carefulness, determination to respond effectively, persistence in his efforts to do so; or from his amount of knowledge; or from his moral or aesthetic tastes.

—Edward L. Thorndike

Classification and Labeling

The Need to Consider Ethnic and Cultural Diversity

Controversy Regarding the Use of Standardized Tests

Useful Theoretical Perspectives for Assessment

Factors That Affect Test Scores

Accounting for Poor Performance

Use of Computers in the Assessment Process

Concluding Comment on Challenges in Assessing Children

Thinking Through the Issues

Summary

Goals and Objectives

This chapter is designed to enable you to do the following:

- Explain the purposes of classification and labeling
- Describe the controversies surrounding the use of standardized tests
- Compare the developmental perspective, normative-developmental perspective, and cognitive-behavioral perspective
- Describe the process of integrating assessment data
- Delineate the role of computers in the assessment process

This chapter provides additional background material for carrying out a clinical assessment. It focuses on such issues as classification and labeling, the need to consider ethnic and cultural diversity, controversy regarding the use of tests, theoretical perspectives useful for assessment, factors to consider in interpreting assessment data, and the use of computers in the assessment process. The material in this chapter, combined with the material in Chapter 1, will give you an appreciation of issues involved in clinical and psychoeducational assessments.

CLASSIFICATION AND LABELING

A comprehensive assessment process involves (a) gathering information, (b) formulating hypotheses about a problem, (c) gaining insights about the individual, (d) arriving at a formal diagnosis, and (e) constructing an intervention plan (Achenbach & Edelbrock, 1989). A formal diagnosis is usually based on a classification system created by a professional organization, such as the one designed by the American Psychiatric Association and found in its *Diagnostic and Statistical Manual of Mental Disorders* (*DSM-IV;* American Psychiatric Association, 1994). A diagnosis is made by evaluating all of the information accumulated about the individual and seeing whether there is a pattern of problems that matches a category present in the classification system.

Table 2-1 shows the major disorders that are usually first diagnosed in infancy, childhood, and adolescence, according to *DSM-IV.* There are several other disorders whose essential features are considered to be the same in children and adults; therefore, no special categories are provided for children. Examples are depression, gender identity disorder, substance-related disorders, mood disorders, and schizophrenia.

Classification systems have two major features (Zigler, 1982): First, they provide rules for placing an individual into a specific class; these rules establish the system's reliability (see Chapter 4). Second, they provide information about the correlates of class membership—that is, what we know about all individuals given a certain class designation. The strength of these class correlates establishes the system's validity (see Chapter 4).

Making a formal diagnosis is a complex task. Any system used to classify individuals, such as the *DSM-IV,* must be based on ordered and group distinctions so that the classifications in the system reflect intrinsic distinctions among individuals assigned to different classifications (Achenbach & Edelbrock, 1989). For example, the characteristics associated with an attention-deficit/hyperactivity disorder should differ in important ways from those associated with a conduct disorder. Group distinctions, called taxonomic distinctions, allow us "to link cases that share useful similarities and to distinguish between cases that differ in important ways. Although diagnostic terms often convey an aura of clinical authority, they can be no more valid than their taxonomic underpinnings" (Achenbach & Edelbrock, 1989, p. 55). Ongoing research is needed to see whether the empirical underpinnings and clinical relevance of *DSM-IV* are fully supported.

Some clinicians object to diagnosis and classification, maintaining that labels (a) have a medical, disease-oriented connotation, (b) provide no explanation of the child's difficulties, (c) tell us nothing about the steps necessary for remediation, (d) lead to self-fulfilling prophecies, (e) are used to excuse the child's behavior, and (f) lead to a preoccupation with finding the correct label rather than focusing on treatment. These objections are all legitimate when classification is misused. Classification, when properly used, can lead to suggestions for remediation and to searches for the sources of the child's difficulties. Further, diagnosis and classification lend organization to the complex and heterogeneous area of exceptionality and aid in the study of etiology, development of hypotheses about the individual child's needs, development of programs, evaluation of the outcomes of intervention programs, communication with professionals, problem solving, obtaining services, and obtaining needed funding. Diagnostic labels are useful in record keeping, statistical reporting, and the administration of treatment programs and research. Diagnostic labels also help to point out areas in which study is needed, and they serve as a rallying point for groups of parents who have children with a specific disability.

Labeling also may have beneficial consequences such as increasing altruism and understanding on the part of those who must deal with deviant behavior. For example, the label "mental retardation" may elicit more protective, altruistic responses from people than does the label "normal." For some parents, labels provide closure and a sense of relief that their child's problem is understood. Without labels, parents and others may develop unrealistically high expectations, which in turn can lead to failure, frustration, and low self-esteem on the part of the child. Labels also afford legal protections to the individual. Schools, for example, must offer services to children who have certain disabilities. When students leave secondary school, accurate labels also ensure protections in vocational and postsecondary settings.

Thus, despite the very real dangers of their misuses, the potential advantages of diagnosis and classification justify their use. The clinician should not, however, treat the diagnosis or classification as an end in itself. The unique characteristics and needs of the individual child must always remain the center of attention, and remediation of problems must be the goal of the assessment process.

Self-Fulfilling Prophecy—How Accurate?

It has been alleged that placing a label such as "mentally retarded" on a child initiates a *self-fulfilling prophecy.* In other words, individuals will lower their expectations of labeled

Disorder	Description
Mental Retardation	Significantly subaverage intellectual functioning (an IQ of approximately 70 or below) with onset before age 18 years and concurrent deficits or impairments in adaptive functioning
Learning Disorders	Academic functioning substantially below that expected, given the child's chronological age, measured intelligence, and age-appropriate education
Reading Disorder	Reading achievement substantially below that expected
Mathematics Disorder	Mathematical ability substantially below that expected
Disorder of Written Expression	Writing skills substantially below those expected
Developmental Coordination Disorder	Performance of daily activities that require motor coordination substantially below that expected, given the child's chronological age and measured intelligence
Communication Disorders	Difficulties in speech or language, including expressive language disorder, mixed receptive-expressive language disorder, phonological disorder, and stuttering
Autistic Disorder	Markedly abnormal or impaired development in social interaction and communication and markedly restricted repertoire of activities and interests
Attention-Deficit/Hyperactivity Disorder	Persistent pattern of inattention and/or hyperactivity-impulsivity that is more frequent and severe than is typically observed in children at a comparable level of development
Conduct Disorder	Repetitive and persistent pattern of behavior in which the basic rights of others or major age-appropriate societal norms or rules are violated
Oppositional Defiant Disorder	Recurrent pattern of negativistic, defiant, disobedient, and hostile behavior toward authority figures that occurs more frequently than is typically observed in children of comparable age and developmental level and that leads to significant impairment in social, academic, or occupational functioning
Feeding and Eating Disorders of Infancy or Early Childhood	Persistent feeding and eating disturbances
Pica	Persistent eating of nonnutritive substances, including the eating of paint, plaster, string, hair, or cloth by younger children and the eating of animal droppings, sand, insects, leaves, and pebbles by older children
Rumination Disorder	Repeated regurgitation and rechewing of food that develops in an infant or child after a period of normal functioning
Feeding Disorder of Infancy or Early Childhood	Persistent failure to eat adequately, as reflected in significant failure to gain weight or significant weight loss, absent any gastrointestinal or other general medical condition severe enough to account for the feeding disturbance
TIC Disorders	
Tourette's Disorder	Multiple motor or vocal tics (sudden, rapid, recurrent, nonrhythmic, stereotyped motor movements or vocalizations)
Chronic Motor or Vocal Tic Disorder	Either motor tics *or* vocal tics, but *not both*
Transient Tic Disorder	Single or multiple motor tics and/or vocal tics
Elimination Disorders	
Encopresis	Involuntary or intentional expulsion of feces into inappropriate places
Enuresis	Repeated voiding of urine during the day or at night into bed or clothes, which most often is involuntary but occasionally may be intentional
Other Disorders	
Separation Anxiety Disorder	Excessive anxiety (beyond that which is expected for the child's developmental level) concerning separation from the home or from those to whom the child is attached
Selective Mutism	Persistent failure to speak in specific social situations (e.g., at school, with playmates) where speaking is expected, despite speaking in other situations
Reactive Attachment Disorder	Markedly disturbed and developmentally inappropriate social relatedness in most contexts that begins before age 5 years and is associated with grossly pathological care
Stereotypic Movement Disorder	Motor behavior that is repetitive, often seemingly driven, and nonfunctional

Source: Adapted from *DSM-IV* (American Psychiatric Association, 1994).

children to such an extent that children are not encouraged to reach their potentials. Although negative stereotypes are often associated with behavioral deviancy labels (e.g., conduct disorder) and with labels indicating low levels of intellectual functioning (e.g., mental retardation), research indicates that, in classrooms, children's *actual* classroom performances are a much more potent force in influencing teachers' expectancies than are labels assigned to the children (Brophy & Good, 1970; Dusek & O'Connell, 1973; Good & Brophy, 1972; Yoshida & Meyers, 1975). This is so because observation of a child's classroom behavior over weeks and months plays the pivotal role in the formation of the teacher's expectancies. When a teacher learns that a new student in the class has been diagnosed as having a learning disability, the teacher is likely to form provisional expectations generated by the label. The teacher will modify these expectations, however, if the child performs at grade level; the teacher will temper the initial impression with observations of the child's classroom performance. Thus, although labels may initiate expectations, they often hold little power once the observer obtains *direct* information about the child's functioning.

The benefits of a diagnostic label in the above example should also be considered. A child who, unknown to the teacher, learns at a significantly slower rate than classmates may be assigned work that is too difficult and may respond to such assignments with maladaptive behaviors (e.g., disrupting the class, noncompliance). Had the teacher been made aware of the diagnostic label of mental retardation, expectations for classroom assignments could have been modified accordingly and the development of the child's maladaptive behaviors avoided.

Arbitrariness of Classification Systems

Classifications such as *moderate mental retardation* (intelligence quotient [IQ] of 40 to 54) and *mild mental retardation* (IQ of 55 to 69) are arbitrary cutoffs on a continuum of intelligence test scores. A child with an IQ of 54 has obtained a score nearly identical to that of a child with an IQ of 55, but their classifications differ. Similarly, a child with an IQ of 68 is like a child with an IQ of 70; yet, if other conditions such as deficits in adaptive behavior are present as well, we may label only the former child as mentally retarded. In developing your assessment findings and recommendations, be guided by the child's *performance* and not by a classification system of arbitrary cutoff scores on an intelligence test. However, you should adhere to a classification system's specific cutoff points and labels when reporting test results, reporting exactly where the child fits with respect to these cutoffs. Similarly, if you are using the *DSM-IV* criteria to make a diagnosis, you must adhere to the criteria set forth in its classification system to make a meaningful *DSM-IV* diagnosis.

Comment on Classification and Labeling

The use of labels and classifications should not cloud our ability to recognize and respect children's resiliency. Even when we arrive at an accurate label to characterize children's problems or disabilities, we still know relatively little about the following areas: (a) how children process, store, and retrieve information; (b) how differing environments affect learning; and (c) how intellectual growth is best nurtured. We should not expect children who receive the same label to perform in the same ways. Children classified as mentally retarded, for example, differ among themselves in their abilities, learning styles, and temperaments. They may surprise you with their intelligence and humanity if you view them without preconceptions. Although labels are important in the diagnostic process and in communicating with professionals, parents, and teachers, you must not allow labels to regiment and restrict the ways you observe and work with children.

Copyright © 1983, Downstown. Reprinted with permission of Universal Press Syndicate.

Finally, we must not allow the advantages of labeling to make us complacent about the potentially negative effects of labeling. Labels do set up expectancies, and such expectancies may influence our behavior, especially when we have *limited contact* with the referred child. In some situations, it is conceivable that the expectations generated by labels could be so powerful as to lead to severe restrictions of the child's opportunities. Little is known about the frequency of such occurrences, but even the thought of such a possibility is a potent reminder of the importance of maintaining a balanced perspective when employing diagnostic labels. Furthermore, we must be careful not to succumb to the temptation to lie in order to obtain services for students.

THE NEED TO CONSIDER ETHNIC AND CULTURAL DIVERSITY

However much we subscribe to the philosophy that well-normed standardized tests provide the most reliable and valid means of assessment, we also must recognize the cultural diversity of children. Because the children you evaluate will represent different ethnic and cultural backgrounds, you must consider their backgrounds in selecting tests and interpreting findings. Ethnic groups have unique mores and customs, languages, and family and social interaction patterns. Differences among African Americans, Euro Americans, Hispanic Americans, Native Americans, and Asian Americans, for example, may be related to the importance placed on certain types of knowledge in their culture and to their temperaments and patterns of familial and social interactions. And within each ethnic group, there are subgroups with different mores and customs, language dialects, and perhaps even family and social interaction patterns. You must consider factors related to ethnicity in interpreting test results and in working with children and their families.

Horowitz and O'Brien (1989) explain the implications of a multicultural society for our work as clinicians:

We are a nation of diversity. Though the "melting pot" that would diminish diversity was a metaphor applied to the United States for many years, it has become increasingly apparent that this metaphor does not fit reality. The diversity of the United States, deriving from the presence of strong and different cultures—cultures that shape and form the children they nurture—is unlikely to disappear in the next 100 years. Culture should be viewed as the overriding organizer of environmental stimulation for the child.... We must strive to understand the strengths of the different cultures that are the source of these pervasive influences or we will not succeed in educating all children to their maximum capabilities....

The cultural backgrounds and heritages of all individuals are reflected in values, in patterns of behavior, in the character of emotional responses, in world views, in historical and ahistorical perspectives, and in compatibility with the institutions of the general society. Understanding, respecting, and working in constructive ways with individuals from the diverse cultures that define the United States go beyond the notions of poverty, disadvantage, or even tolerance; a real attempt to understand and appreciate diversity must inform the design of both research and social policy. (p. 445)

Chapters 19 and 20 discuss ethnic groups in more detail.

CONTROVERSY REGARDING THE USE OF STANDARDIZED TESTS

The past several decades have seen numerous attacks on the use of standardized ability and achievement tests and tests of personality. Ethnic minority groups (and other groups as well) claim that educators and psychologists use standardized tests to allocate limited educational resources and to penalize children whose family, socioeconomic status, and cultural experiences are different from those of Euro American middle-class children. The very foundations of assessment practices have been questioned, including the tools that are used and the situations in which assessments are conducted. Some critics maintain that intelligence tests and achievement tests are culturally biased and thus harmful to African American children and children of other ethnic groups. Others believe that some of the activities of school psychologists and clinical child psychologists are not in the best interests of children. These activities include labeling children, testing children without fully informing the parents or children of the possible consequences of the testing, moving children from regular classrooms to potentially damaging special classes, and fostering mechanistic procedures for making decisions. Courts (e.g., Judge Peckham in *Larry P. v. Wilson Riles*) have issued decisions limiting the freedom of psychologists to use and select tests for evaluation and placement decisions. Other critics contend that standardized, norm-referenced tests are imperfect in what they measure, foster limited conceptualizations of human ability, and have little or no utility in the classroom.

Certainly the critics of testing are correct in some cases; for example, no advocate of testing would deny that tests are imperfect measures or that they can be interpreted (or misinterpreted) in such a way that they limit conceptions of human ability. Nevertheless, test advocates believe that standardized tests, if they are administered and interpreted carefully and ethically, have valid uses. Their use may increase accountability—without testing, for example, how can we know whether our educational system is working? Standardized tests provide at least a rough indication of change in ability; they may, in fact, be the best indicators of change we have. They are our best yardstick for evaluating a student's ability in specific subject areas as well as in overall intellectual ability. They are usually more reliable and valid—and less biased—than teacher-made tests. They allow teachers (and the community at large) to see how students in one school compare with students in other schools across town or across the nation. They help school districts identify curriculum strengths and weaknesses and develop programs to address those weaknesses. They serve to motivate parents and teachers to seek help for students whose test performance is poor. Similarly, they may serve to motivate students who perform poorly on tests (although, unfortunately, poor test results may be more likely to discourage than to motivate students). They encourage teachers to provide extra help to students who score well on the tests and yet perform poorly in school. And they provide a profile of abilities useful in vocational planning and counseling.

As a result of testing, children gain access to special programs that can help them become more effective learners. Testing used in this way also enables us to make the most efficient use of limited resources, identifying and providing help to those students who are most in need of assistance. Tests establish a standard for evaluating the extent to which children of all ethnic groups have learned the basic cognitive and academic skills necessary for survival in our culture.

Few critics have proposed reasonable alternatives to present assessment methods. In fact, alternative procedures for estimating children's ability or personality have limitations equal to, if not greater than, those associated with standardized tests. Most people, including teachers, are not trained to judge objectively and accurately children's intellectual ability, achievements, perceptual-motor ability, personality, or type and degree of psychopathology. Eliminating tests would add more subjectivity and bias to the assessment process. If alternative assessment procedures replace standardized tests, the alternative procedures should be technically adequate and information should be provided about with which populations the alternative procedures work best (Bracken, 1994).

The criticisms of testing have resulted in improved practice. Test publishers now select normative groups that are representative of the population and take steps to ensure that test items are as free from cultural bias as possible. Examiners need to consider cultural differences when they administer and interpret tests. Tests must be administered in the child's preferred language. And the norms must be based on tests standardized in the language in which the tests are administered. (However, if the test is a nonverbal one and the *only* change is the language in which the directions are given, then the norms based on directions in English may be appropriate.) Schools and clinicians are required to keep accurate records authorizing evaluations and must allow parents to see their children's records. In these and other ways assessment practices have become more accountable.

We are accountable, as clinicians-in-training and as professionals, to the children we serve, to their parents, to the schools, and to the larger community. We cannot ignore the many valid criticisms of tests and test practices simply because we do not like to hear them. However, we need to be prepared to respond to and defend against unwarranted attacks in both the scientific community and popular media. We must continue to develop procedures and instruments that will better serve our nation's children. We must adhere scrupulously to the procedures now available to protect our clients, and we need to continue to conduct research to better

understand our assessment practices. Although none of us likes having our shortcomings pointed out, especially in public, we must listen to our critics and follow the best scientific and clinical practices possible. These practices need to be based not only on empirical observations, but also on a sound theoretical foundation.

USEFUL THEORETICAL PERSPECTIVES FOR ASSESSMENT

Three perspectives are useful in guiding the assessment process: the developmental perspective, the normative-developmental perspective, and the cognitive-behavioral perspective. This text attempts to integrate the three perspectives. Let us briefly examine each of them.

Developmental Perspective

A *developmental perspective* proposes that the interplay between genetic disposition and environmental influences follows a definite, nonrandom form and direction. This interplay assures that development proceeds toward specific goals: learning to walk and talk, developing complex coordinated movements, gradually developing more complex thinking skills, and reaching sexual maturity. However, there are intraindividual (i.e., within the individual) and interindividual (i.e., between individuals) differences in the rate and timing of development. Thus, both within the individual and across individuals, different areas of development—such as physical, cognitive, social, language, and speech—develop at different rates. Newly developed skills bring challenges to children, especially at critical points in development such as puberty. Exhibit 2-1 looks at the process of language acquisition from a developmental perspective.

The developmental perspective also emphasizes that biological, psychological, and social factors constantly interact to shape and modify children's development. The environments that play a role in children's development—including family, peer, school, and work environments—are interdependent. Children "evoke differential reactions from the environment as a result of their physical and behavioral characteristics, and environments contribute to individual development through the feedback they provide" (Compas, Hinden, & Gerhardt, 1995, p. 270). Maladaptive behaviors may be manifest, at least in part, when there is a mismatch between children's needs and the opportunities afforded them by their environments. This may happen, for example, when the expectations or demands of the environments either exceed the children's capacities or conflict with the children's abilities.

Another important principle of the developmental perspective is that growth is both qualitative and quantitative. For example, as development proceeds, organizational and adaptational changes emerge. At first, children's thoughts are

---

Exhibit 2-1
Language Acquisition from a Developmental Perspective

Three general stages demarcate the changes in development that children go through in acquiring verbal language: a prelinguistic communication stage, a stage of lexical expansion, and a stage of grammatical expansion.

1. *Prelinguistic communication stage.* In this stage, which covers the period from birth to approximately 12 months of age, language foundations are being prepared, although language as is used by adults is not present. A rudimentary system of movements and vocalizations enables the infant to communicate basic biological and social needs. Additionally, infants are able to perceive certain aspects of human communication and recognize voices. At about 8 months of age, the infant engages in more persistent communicative signaling. Gestures, facial expressions, and vocalizations begin to interact in a complex manner, eventually followed by the emergence of first words early in the second year of life.

2. *Lexical expansion stage.* In this stage, which covers the period of approximately 12 to 24 months, the child increases semantic (meaning) knowledge and phonological (sound organization and production ability) knowledge. The child acquires semantic knowledge, in part, by

assigning more features to the lexical representation of the verbal concept. These "features" are presented as the child's representation of encoded perceptual information. An example...involves the word *doggie*. Initially, this label may apply to any four-legged animal. As additional features are acquired—e.g., hoofs, horns, says moo—the child begins to subdivide the larger category or concept into units more closely aligned with adult representation. Acquisition of semantic knowledge then is a function of the child's analyzing the environment and applying increasingly complex feature contrasts to a general set of verbal labels. (Crary et al., 1988, p. 252)

The child acquires phonological knowledge by learning contrasts between various sounds of language on the basis of differences in meaning that result from using different sounds. During this stage of language development, the child's task is to extract and analyze meaningful perceptions from the environment, and subsequently to attach linguistic significance to these perceptions in terms of semantic and phonological features. A sudden growth in vocabulary, rapid phonological expansion, and the emergence of multiword utterances characterize the final period of the lexical expansion stage.

3. *Grammatical expansion stage.* In this stage, which runs from approximately 2 to 4 years of age and beyond, dramatic growth occurs in all aspects of grammar. Phonological productions become increasingly complex, and spoken utterances increase in length and syntactic complexity. By the age of 6 years, the child's basic phonological system approximates that of adults.

It is at the end of the prelinguistic communication stage that adults begin to recognize the productions of children as meaningful words. Some of the words used by children during the early lexical expansion stage do not have the same meaning for adults as they do for children. Children, like adults, use words to refer to objects or events occurring in the environment, but the referents for children's words may be idiosyncratic. Finally, there is considerable variability in the rate and style of language development among children. For example, some children tend to be more verbal, providing a greater number of multiword utterances at an early age, whereas other children use gestures in conjunction with single words to communicate their message. These variations in language development may be related to the style of language learning employed by children at a later stage of development, but no firm evidence exists at the present time to support this hypothesis.

Source: Adapted from Crary, Voeller, and Haak (1988).

---

dominated by what they see and touch. By approximately 2 years of age, they begin to develop expressive language recognizable to familiar adults and to recall some prior actions and responses; thinking tends to be egocentric. By about age 7, thought processes become more systematic and skills needed to solve concrete problems develop. By age 11 or so, most children think abstractly and make logical deductions without the necessity of direct experience. A developmental perspective focuses on individual changes that occur during the developmental process.

Normative-Developmental Perspective

A *normative-developmental perspective* evaluates and attempts to account for changes in children's cognitions, affect, and behavior in relation to a reference group, usually composed of children of the same age and gender as the referred child (Edelbrock, 1984). *Cognitions* refer to mental processes, including perception, memory, and reasoning, by which children acquire knowledge, make plans, and solve problems. *Affect* refers to the experience of emotion or feeling. The normative-developmental perspective considers (a) demographic variables, such as the child's age, grade, gender, ethnicity, and socioeconomic status (SES); (b) developmental variables, such as language, motor, social, and self-help skills; and (c) the influence of prior development on current and future development.

Normative data are useful in various ways (Edelbrock, 1984). First, normative data provide information about how a particular child's development compares with that of average

Baby Blues   by Rick Kirkman and Jerry Scott

Copyright © 1994, Rick Kirkman and Jerry Scott. Reprinted with permission of King Features Syndicate.

children. Norms allow you to establish reasonable treatment goals and evaluate the clinical significance of changes resulting from interventions. Second, normative data guide you in selecting appropriate target areas and behaviors that need change—for example, deciding that a child is not growing as expected or is not developing age-appropriate skills. Third, normative data allow you to compare information acquired from different sources. Comparing information from parents and teachers, for example, will help you learn about the consistency of children's behavior in different settings. Fourth, normative data may help you to identify behaviors with unusually low or high rates (i.e., behaviors that occur more or less often than expected), transient behaviors (e.g., anxiety associated with enrolling at school), behaviors that are rela-

tively normal for a particular age group (e.g., fear of strangers in very young children), and situational variables that may place the child at risk for developing problem behaviors (e.g., adverse home environments or classrooms). Finally, normative data assist in research investigations by allowing investigators to form relatively homogeneous groups and to compare participant samples across studies.

Cognitive-Behavioral Perspective

A *cognitive-behavioral perspective* focuses on the importance of (a) cognitions as major determinants of emotion and behavior, including the child's thoughts and ways of processing information; (b) the role that cognitions such as values,

Calvin and Hobbes   by Bill Watterson

Copyright © 1993, Bill Watterson. Reprinted with permission of Universal Press Syndicate.

beliefs, self-statements (including perceived self-confidence or self-efficacy based on prior experiences), problem-solving strategies, expectancies, images, and goals play in the development of maladaptive behavior (e.g., withdrawal or task avoidance can result when a child believes that she or he has little self-worth); and (c) the individual and environmental influences that may shape and control the child's and family's thoughts, feelings, and behavior (e.g., sounds from spinning objects—that is, auditory stimuli—reinforce the child to continue the stereotyped activity, or social responses from others, such as verbal comments, elicited by a child's aggressive behavior, increase that behavior).

The cognitive-behavioral perspective emphasizes the importance of empirical validation throughout the assessment and treatment processes. Quantitative measures such as frequency counts, measures of duration, measures of intensity, and times of occurrence are used to document the relevant behavior of the child. In addition, self-monitoring assessment can provide data about thoughts, feelings, and behavior (see Chapter 5 in *Assessment of Children: Behavioral and Clinical Applications*). Self-monitoring assessment also provides the child with a sense that the child is an active participant in the assessment and intervention.

The cognitive aspect of a cognitive-behavioral perspective acknowledges that cognitions, although private, mediate learning and behavior. Cognitions and behavior also are functionally related: change in one can cause changes in the other. The primary concerns are with how behavior varies as a function of changes in a child's cognitions and environment and how cognitions, behavior, and the environment can be modified to produce the desired outcome. Cognitive and affective factors influence how the child responds to problems and to the interventions.

The behavioral aspect of a cognitive-behavioral perspective proposes that environmental contingencies, such as setting factors (e.g., heat, light, noise, crowding conditions, and condition of buildings), natural reinforcers, and distractors, also mediate behavior and learning. Thus, for example, acting out can result when environmental stimuli become associated with aversive experiences. Particular attention is given to the antecedents and consequences of a specific behavior—the events that precede and follow it. The belief underlying this approach, termed *behavioral analysis* or *functional analysis*, can be simply represented as follows: antecedents → behavior → consequences. Behavior analysis (or functional analysis) looks at behavior without resort to indirect measures. *Assessment of Children: Behavioral and Clinical Applications* discusses functional behavior assessment as used in the schools.

The cognitive-behavioral assessment process can become a valuable educational tool (Turk & Kerns, 1985). First, asking a child about the factors that exacerbate or reduce a problem behavior implicitly suggests that the problem behavior is subject to various controlling forces. Second, asking a child to monitor his or her thoughts and feelings related to the problem behavior or to describe the circumstances surrounding the problem behavior may help the child identify environmental events that instigate the problem behavior. Third, asking the child to monitor others' responses to the problem behavior highlights the importance of others' roles in relationship to the problem behavior. Thus, by means of the assessment process, the child is helped to understand that the problem behavior is not inexplicable and uncontrollable.

Integration of the Three Perspectives

The propositions that follow, which are based on developmental, normative-developmental, and cognitive-behavioral perspectives, serve as an important foundation for the assessment of children (Bretherton, 1993; Campbell, 1989; Edelbrock, 1984; Luiselli, 1989; Masten & Braswell, 1991; Millon, 1987; Turk & Kerns, 1985).

PROPOSITIONS RELATED TO NORMAL FUNCTIONING IN CHILDREN

1. Children are rapidly changing and evolving individuals, showing changes that are both quantitative and qualitative.
2. Children possess relatively enduring biological dispositions that give a consistent coloration and direction to their experiences.
3. Children's temperaments, early experiences, learning histories, and cultural backgrounds simultaneously interact to affect the development and nature of their emerging psychological structures, abilities, and functions.
4. Children develop relatively stable behaviors, cognitions, and affects that stem partially from generalized learning and from similarities that exist among related situations.
5. Children's cognitions can be major determinants of emotion and behavior.
6. Children gradually replace reflexive, sensory-bound, and concrete behavior with more conceptual, symbolic, and cognitively mediated behavior.
7. Children may develop abilities that are not fully expressed in their behavior at a particular stage of development but that may be expressed at a later stage of development.
8. Children's physical maturation plays an especially important role in influencing their behavior during infancy and childhood.
9. Children's chronological age and developmental status (i.e., the level at which they are functioning) will affect their behavior.
10. Children's motives and emotions become more refined, advanced, and controlled over the course of their development.
11. Children engage in behaviors and seek situations that are rewarding.
12. Children's behavior that is appropriate at one age may be inappropriate at another age.
13. Children's sense of self and capacity for interpersonal relationships develop, in large part, from the parent-child relationship.

14. Children's behavior can be influenced by physiological and neuromuscular factors.
15. Children can be stimulated by sensory events, such as pleasant sounds or sights, that encourage them to continue a behavior in which they are engaged.
16. Children's development can be better understood by reference to normative data.

PROPOSITIONS RELATED TO DEVIANT FUNCTIONING IN CHILDREN

17. Children's problems are influenced by complex interactions of biological, psychological, and environmental factors.
18. Children's maladaptive behavior may be related to their cognitions (e.g., emotional problems may be caused by distortions or deficiencies in thinking).
19. Children's problems that have the most serious long-term consequences occur early, express themselves in several forms, are pervasive across settings, and persist throughout the children's development.
20. Children with similar psychological disorders may have different behavioral symptoms, and children with different psychological disorders may have similar behavioral symptoms.
21. Children's referrals for assessment and treatment are influenced by their parents' perceptions and interpretations of behavior and by their parents' psychological and emotional states.
22. Children may have transient problems (such as fears and worries, nightmares, bedwetting, and tantrums) characteristic of a particular developmental period; these problems, if atypical of the child's developmental period, may serve as a warning signal for the development of more serious problems and, therefore, must be handled skillfully.
23. Children may have developmental problems that reflect (a) an exaggeration or distortion of age-appropriate behaviors (e.g., attachment problems in infancy), (b) difficult transitions from one developmental period to the next (e.g., noncompliance in toddlers and preschoolers), or (c) age-related but maladaptive reactions to environmental, particularly familial, stress (e.g., school difficulties among older children associated with moving or with a parent's loss of a job).
24. Children's environments during their formative years are usually highly structured (except possibly in highly dysfunctional families) and closely monitored by parents and other caregivers. Children's interactions with others in their environments contribute to shaping their behavior, and children, in turn, also help shape their environments.
25. Children's families function on a continuum from highly functional to highly dysfunctional.
26. Children's families that function well overall may continue to function adequately during stressful periods. For example, the families may cope with the stress, protect

"She double-clicked her first icon!"

Copyright © 1996, Ted Goff. Reprinted with permission.

their members, adjust to role changes within the family, and continue to carry out their functions. Supportive intervention may still be beneficial for these families.

27. Children's families that function poorly may make their members more susceptible to stress. For example, a family may induce maladaptive behavior or illness in its members, be unable to protect its members from maladaptive reactions, and induce in its members persistent problems that are likely to require treatment.
28. Children whose parents experience distorted thought processes will likely have difficulty communicating with their parents. Similarly, parents who have distorted thought processes will likely have difficulty communicating with their children. In such situations, children's abilities to adapt flexibly and appropriately to new situations will be restricted.
29. Children must receive interventions appropriate to their developmental level.

FACTORS THAT AFFECT TEST SCORES

Figure 2-1 shows a useful model that helps us recognize the factors that may influence test scores. First there are innate and background factors and then intervening variables, which include the child's personality, the assessment situation, test demands, and random variation. Although the relative importance of each of these factors will vary with the examinee, you must always consider them when you evaluate the examinee's test scores.

The influence of innate factors on intelligence test scores has been a matter of concern since the inception of the testing movement. Although we still have no definitive information about the precise contribution of heredity, heredity does make

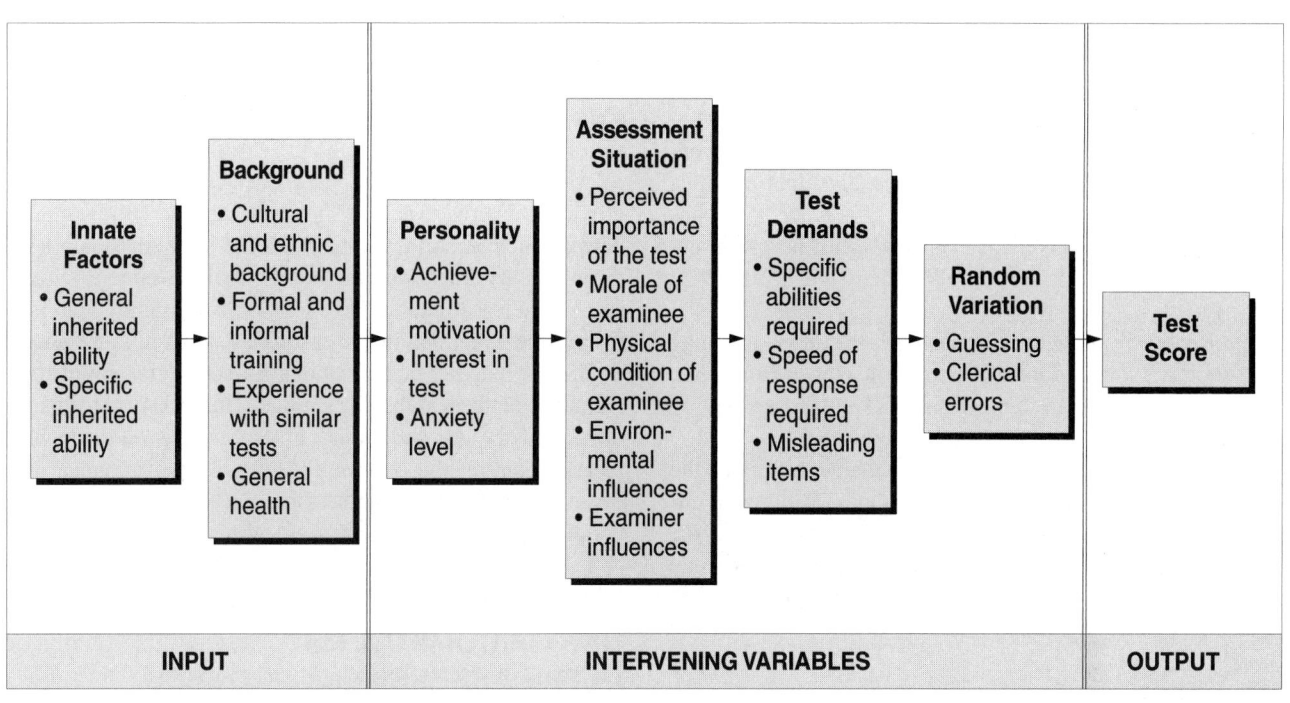

Figure 2-1. Variables that affect a test score. Reprinted and adapted by permission of the publisher from D. A. Goslin, *The Search for Ability: Standardized Testing in Social Perspective,* p. 130. Copyright 1963, Russell Sage Foundation.

a significant contribution to intellectual functioning (see Chapter 6), and perhaps to personality and temperament as well. We do not know, however, the specific extent to which genetic factors can be altered by environmental conditions.

Here are some examples of how the examinee's background and personality, the situation, the test demands, and random variation may affect test scores.

1. *Demand characteristics.* An examinee may think that the situation requires a certain type of response in order to obtain a desired outcome—for example, an examinee may believe that he or she must say that an instruction is understood in order to avoid embarrassing himself or herself and therefore fail to ask for a needed clarification.

2. *Response bias.* An examinee's response to one item may influence how she or he responds to the next item—for example, after saying yes to several items in a row, the examinee may say yes to the next item when the response otherwise would have been no.

3. *Characteristics of the population being assessed.* The type of psychological or physical problems the examinee has may affect how she or he responds to items—for example, an examinee who has a pervasive developmental disorder may give unusual responses, or an examinee with visual defects may have difficulty seeing pictures.

4. *Social desirability.* An examinee may have a tendency to present herself or himself or someone else in a

favorable light—for example, an examinee may say that she studies hard when she does not or agree with everything the examiner says because she believes that it is impolite to disagree with an authority figure.

5. *Misperception of items.* An examinee's replies may be affected by memory difficulties, misperception of questions, or attending to irrelevant parts of a question—for example, an examinee who does not hear the instruction to work "as quickly as possible" may work too slowly and consequently lose points on a test.

6. *Instruction format.* The format or wording of oral or written instructions may affect the examinee's replies—for example, an examinee's reading difficulties may affect his ability to answer printed questions unrelated to the evaluation of reading proficiency.

7. *Response format.* The type of response required—such as oral or written one-word answers, answers requiring a complete thought, true/false answers, pointing responses—may affect the examinee's replies—for example, an examinee may be more anxious when questions require a full thought in response, or an examinee with motor impairment of the upper extremities may not be able to write answers that she could express orally.

8. *Setting variables.* The location of the evaluation (school, home, clinic, jail, hospital), the time of day when the test is administered, seating arrangements, and other related factors may affect the examinee's responses—for example,

an examinee may be more anxious when tested in an aversive environment such as a juvenile detention setting than when tested at school.

9. *Previous testing experiences.* An examinee's responses may be affected by previous testing experiences— for example, an examinee who has taken the test in the recent past may remember some of the items and thus obtain a falsely elevated score. Usually, practice effects are not a concern if at least 9 months elapse before the test is readministered (see Chapter 4 for further discussion of practice effects).

10. *Reactive effects.* An examinee's response pattern may be altered by the assessment procedure itself—for example, an examinee may begin to view his problems differently by the time you reach the tenth interview question.

11. *Examiner-examinee variables.* Characteristics of the particular examiner and examinee, such as age, culture, gender, and appearance, may affect the examinee's *and* the examiner's performance—for example, an examinee may view an examiner who is 25 years old as being less competent than a middle-aged examiner.

ACCOUNTING FOR POOR PERFORMANCE

When examinees perform poorly on tests, you will want to try to explain their poor performance. This is a difficult task, however, because poor performance may occur for several reasons (see Figure 2-2). Both individual and environmental factors play a role in poor performance. Let's see how this is so. Take the case of a child who fails to stack blocks when you ask him or her to do so. Possible causes of the child's poor performance include limited hearing, vision, English proficiency, comprehension, spatial reasoning, and visual-motor ability; temporary inefficiencies; situational stress; negativistic behavior; peer-group pressure to fail; and neurological impairment. Similarly, when an examinee fails a test that requires repeating digits, the failure may be caused by difficulty in sequencing; limited short-term memory; lack of attention, motivation, auditory acuity, understanding of task demands, effort, or strategy usage; or peer-group pressure to do poorly. You will need to analyze the child's entire performance carefully and integrate information from other assessment sources to arrive at a plausible explanation of his or her poor performance. In addition, you may need to administer specialized tests that can help to pinpoint specific areas of difficulty.

Because assessment information is usually obtained during a single time period, an examinee's performance may not reflect how she or he would perform if she or he were more comfortable, stimulated or inspired, healthier, or less upset by family anxieties. *Tests provide information about how the examinee performs at a specific time under specific conditions.* For example, a child's overall IQ may not reveal how the child's abilities are changing over time. Some children

who appear to be slow learners at the time you assess them, may be storing information that they will not reveal until later. Children also may have skills that are not adequately measured by standardized tests. You should always look for signs of creativity or special talents not directly addressed by the objective test scores.

Also recognize that the test scores obtained on individually administered tests may not represent the child's typical performance. A child who works at his or her optimum level during the examination may not work at the same level outside of the test situation. On the other hand, a child who fails to take the examination seriously may perform more poorly on the test than in other situations. Of course, the child's performance on the test may be similar to his or her performance outside of the test situation. Although it may be difficult to clearly interpret the *reasons* for a child's performance, you do know that the child can perform in a certain way under the conditions in which the tests were administered.

USE OF COMPUTERS IN THE ASSESSMENT PROCESS

Computers can facilitate the administration and scoring of verbal tests and interviews, the recording and analysis of data involved in the observation of behavior, the preparation of reports, and the transmission of data (Goldstein, 1987). Computers present test items in the same manner to each examinee, allowing for a high level of standardization. Computers are not influenced by halo effects. They provide consistent conditions from day to day in the administration of tests, thereby helping to eliminate the risk of bias that may be present when examiners administer tests, conduct interviews, or observe examinees.

In the area of interviewing, for example, computer interviews consistently present questions according to predetermined rules, thereby standardizing the interview and eliminating individual biases and memory difficulties that human interviewers may have (Farrell, 1991). In addition, examinees may be less embarrassed to reveal personal material to a computer.

In the area of observation of behavior, computer-assisted data collection has several advantages, including the following (Bloom, Hursh, Wienke, & Wolf, 1992): "the ability to (a) collect data on several behaviors at once, (b) store an entire day of data and get a quick report at the end of the day, (c) identify the frequency, duration and sequence of behaviors to gain a precise picture of student performance across time, and (d) save time by eliminating the need for making recording sheets, tallying recorded data, etc." (p. 174). In addition, "computer systems that record the onset and offset times of behaviors are also more faithful to the 'stream' of behavior than manual or mechanical systems that involve simple frequency counts or that impose arbitrary time intervals on the data" (Farrell, 1991, p. 164).

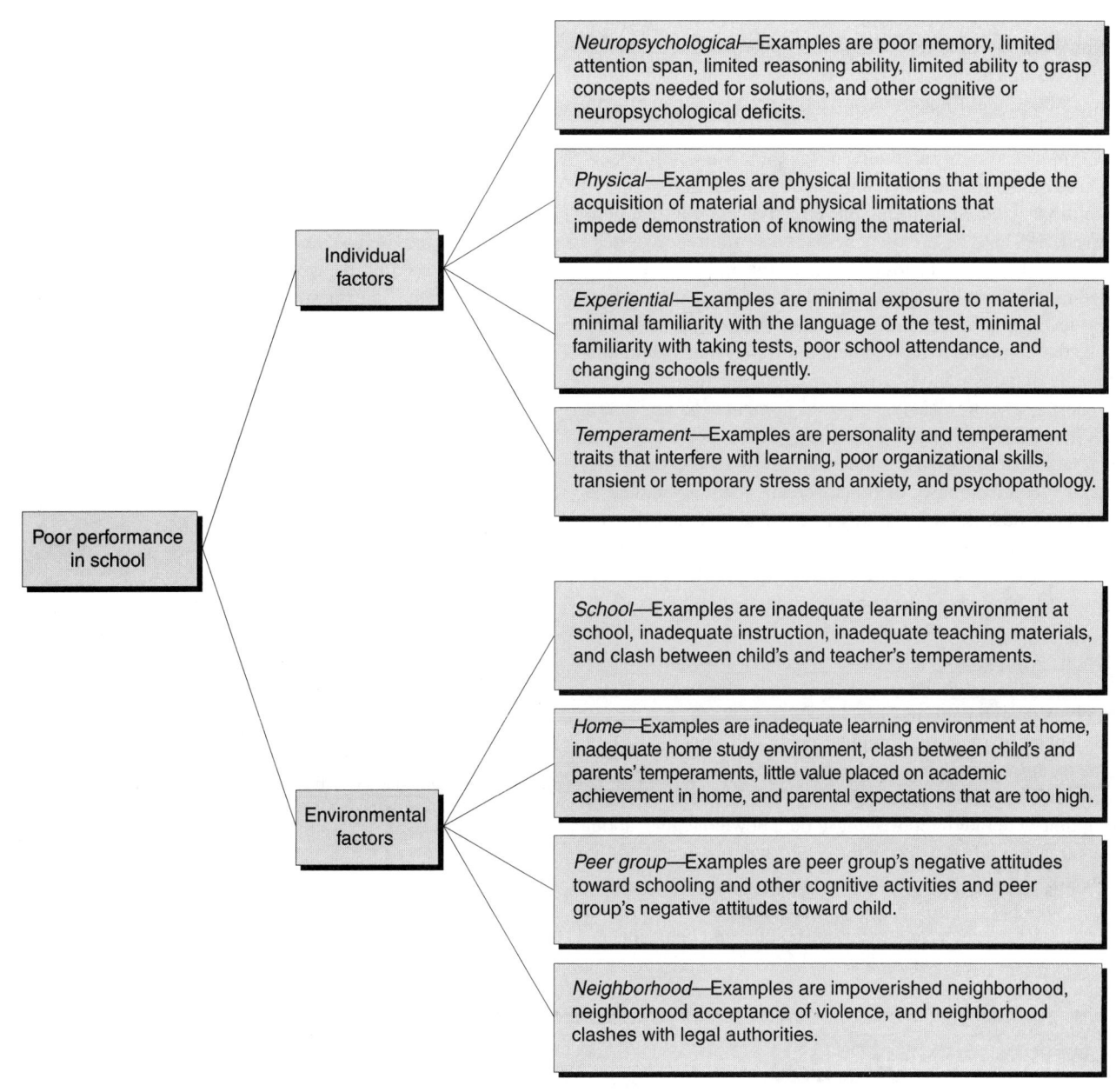

Figure 2-2. Major factors that should be considered in accounting for poor performance in school.

In the area of intellectual assessment, computers are used to compute scores and create reports. Computers can (a) convert raw scores to standard scores; (b) evaluate which scores in a profile are statistically significantly different; (c) present percentile ranks, grade and age equivalents for scores, and confidence intervals; and (d) perform other statistical calculations as needed (Honaker & Fowler, 1990). A definite advantage of computer programs is that they reliably convert accurately entered raw scores to standard scores and provide reliable statistical analyses. These statistical analyses serve as the basis for reports generated by computer programs.

Computer-generated reports provide information about levels of intellectual functioning, as well as about intellectual strengths and weaknesses, based on the examinee's scores.

The advantages of using computers for assessment purposes hold only if the computer program is not flawed. Software programs can be corrupted. Therefore, it behooves psychologists to carefully check all computer-generated reports to make sure that what the reports say seems logical. A report is not logical if it concludes that the examinee has above-average ability overall, after listing all the subtest scores as below average.

An important advantage of computers is that they can be used for research purposes because they can store, retrieve, and analyze vast amounts of data. Computers can record psychophysiological measures such as reaction time, movement time, latency, and finger pressure more precisely than human examiners can.

Computer systems are being developed to assist in selecting assessment instruments, making diagnoses, designing interventions, and monitoring the effectiveness of treatment (Farrell, 1991). These expert systems use inference or reasoning to draw conclusions based on the information provided to the computer. For example, if data from a structured interview, a physical examination, and observations were entered, the computer would generate a report that included a probable diagnosis and treatment recommendation.

There are some disadvantages to computer-administered tests. For example, computer-administered tests are effective only with examinees who understand how to use the computer keyboard, mouse, or touch screen. If the examinee is left unattended, there is no way to evaluate whether the examinee understands each question. It is unlikely that young children or examinees who are severely psychologically disturbed will be able to take computer-administered tests without assistance. In addition, it is difficult at present for computers to administer tests that require manipulation of three-dimensional materials, such as tests that involve making block design patterns or using peg boards.

A major danger of computer-generated reports is that some examiners may not be able to interpret the results accurately and explain them to others. Professionals who use computer-generated reports must be knowledgeable about how all of the information in the report was obtained and the basis for the interpretations. To be optimally useful, computer-generated reports need to include data obtained from the case history, interview, prior test results, and behavior ob-

servations, along with test data. Another danger is that untrained individuals may have access to the computer and generate reports without understanding the implications of the reports' findings and conclusions. We recommend that you not use "canned" computerized reports. Instead, select a report-writing program that will allow you to insert, omit, and clarify information with ease, using the clinical judgments and insights you obtained from a study of the child's entire results and record.

We need research to determine the validity of interpretive reports generated by computer programs (Honaker & Fowler, 1990). Here are some questions that need to be considered: Do computerized psychological reports assist the decision-making process of the clinician? Do they add useful information beyond the profile of scores? Do they produce interpretations that may be harmful to the child?

Concerns that computers may replace clinicians have been addressed (Honaker & Fowler, 1990):

There is a growing consensus that computer-assisted testing and interpretation can be a time- and cost-effective aid in psychological assessment, but few believe today that the computer will supplant the clinician.... "There must be a clinician between the computer and the client." Computers can produce psychological reports, but a psychological assessment requires the integration of test material with a whole range of other data including history, interviews, and behavioral observations. Even the very best psychological reports, whether they are written by a clinician or generated by a computer, are of little value without a competent clinician who can put the results into the context of the [client's] life. A report from a well-designed interpretation system that is based on a valid test can provide a useful source of hypotheses for the clinician, but it is the task of the clinician to examine those hypotheses in light of the clinical history and behavioral observations. Computer technology can assist clinicians by providing useful, cost-effective ways to give the public better and more efficient services. (p. 540)

Copyright © 1996, John P. Wood. Reprinted with permission.

New challenges await professionals who use computers in their clinical work. Computer-generated reports and assessment procedures raise many new legal, ethical, clinical, professional, and philosophical issues. For example, it is imperative that computer records, like all other assessment records, be kept confidential. To do so, we must consider who has access to the equipment, where the disks are stored, and whether reports will be sent by e-mail to other parties. If the examinee is adversely affected by the suggestions offered in an invalid computerized report, who is responsible for any harm caused—the clinician, the software manufacturer, or both? Our guidelines are still evolving along with the technology.

CONCLUDING COMMENT ON CHALLENGES IN ASSESSING CHILDREN

You should carry out the assessment of intelligence and special abilities with sensitivity and concern for the child and the child's family. As you perform an assessment, consider the child's expectancies regarding the assessment, how your appearance (such as clothing, grooming, and ethnicity) and other personal attributes may affect the way the child and the child's parents view you, and how your expectations, biases, and cultural values might affect the assessment. Be ready to consider new findings that emerge during the assessment and modify your assessment plan. Also, recognize that the assessment process can be time-consuming and that there may not be sufficient time available to conduct as comprehensive an assessment as you would like for each child you evaluate.

Assessment is a means to an end, not an end in itself. Assessments are conducted to obtain information needed to make decisions that will benefit the child. We recommend that you carry out assessments only when there is a problem to be addressed, a question to be answered about the child's functioning, or a decision to be reached about the child's educational placement. Collecting assessment information with little regard for how the information may be used is improper and unprofessional. Each evaluation must be conducted with full recognition of how it might affect the child, his or her family, and those who will use the findings. Good assessment practice requires that you be clear about the purposes of the assessment and the adequacy of the instruments or procedures used in the assessment.

A clinical or psychoeducational evaluation is unique in that a highly able and skilled professional devotes his or her exclusive attention to one child for a period ranging from at least 1 to several hours and perhaps across several sessions. This may never have happened before in the child's life, and it may never happen again. It is a relationship based on trust and collaborative problem solving. An implied contract exists between the examinee and examiner: The examinee will do his or her best to answer the questions posed by the examiner, and the examiner, in turn, will use the best procedures available for the assessment and follow the ethical guidelines of his or her profession.

This text focuses on how assessment information can be used to make informed decisions about children. To be effective as a clinician, you must be willing to (a) entertain alternative hypotheses, (b) revise your initial impressions of the examinee, and (c) reduce your reliance on memory by keeping good records and reviewing them periodically, as needed. Although assessment information is critical for making decisions, the assessment information takes on meaning only when it is integrated by the clinician. It is the clinician who is at the center of the assessment process and who is ultimately responsible for integrating assessment information and formulating decisions about the child.

The typical clinical assessment is not completely ecologically valid because it minimizes demands faced by children in their natural environments and is structured to help examinees compensate for or mask functional impairments. The assessment setting does this by providing (a) a quiet and structured environment to reduce attention and concentration difficulties; (b) frequent breaks and rest periods to lessen problems with endurance, perseverance, and fatigue; (c) clear and repetitive instructions to deal with difficulties in task orientation, orientation to new tasks, and memory; and (d) active cues, prompts, and encouragement to deal with difficulties in motivation, initiation, and response inhibition (Sbordone, 1988). In addition, current formal tests do not replicate the demands of a normal school setting, such as the need to integrate or retain data over time or to apply information or skills to new contexts (Ylvisaker, 1986).

Limitations can be overcome, in part, by observing how the children you are assessing function in their natural environment. For example, note how they perform daily activities (e.g., feeding, dressing, grooming, personal hygiene, toileting, communicating, interacting with others, playing), use language, use motor skills, cope with different environments, accomplish new learning, and use strategies in different settings. If you are able to observe children functioning in different environments—including home, school, playground, and examination room—you will obtain a more complete picture of their adaptive and coping abilities, including how they process information, how they behave, and how they handle distractions, information overload, competition, failure, negative feedback for making errors or for misbehaving, and other stressors (Marquardt, Stoll, & Sussman, 1988). These observations also may give you clues about children's level of orientation, anxiety, confusion, distractibility, impulsivity, initiative, inhibition, concreteness, flexibility, organization, judgment, and similar behaviors. When it is not possible to observe the child in the natural environment, a detailed history obtained from parents, teachers, and others or adaptive behavior scales completed by the parents (see Chapter 2 in *Assessment of Children: Behavioral and Clinical Applications*) may provide ecologically valid information. Although naturalistic assessment possesses greater ecological validity, standardized assessment provides a comparative framework by which to gauge the child's behavior. Ideally, both naturalistic and standardized assessment data would be obtained in a comprehensive evaluation of a child.

The assessment field will become more viable and productive if it can move beyond a primarily diagnostic role. Diagnosis and classification—which includes providing a unique profile of the child's abilities, temperament, and personality—must be linked with effective interventions that will promote and enhance the child's learning, help the child cope with her or his problems, and, where needed, promote the child's recovery of function. Although the task of establishing clinically valid linkages between assessment and intervention methodologies is formidable, it is a worthy goal.

Assigning a diagnostic label, such as attention-deficit/ hyperactivity disorder (ADHD), is only part of the assessment process. You will still need to determine children's instructional needs, regardless of diagnosis. In the area of reading, this would entail determining not only their reading levels, but also their strengths and weaknesses associated with reading, the type of reading instruction they are currently receiving, and what adjustments are needed in their instruction.

The assessment procedures covered in this text are typically used for the evaluation of one child, rather than a group, and serve to identify the nature and severity of the child's dysfunctional behavior, as well as his or her strengths, assets, and adaptive capabilities. Remember that, to fully understand a child's behavior, you must consider the broader social context in which the child and his or her family function. As you read about assessment procedures in this text and elsewhere, keep in mind the different purposes that they best serve.

This text provides guidelines designed to promote the usefulness and fairness of assessment and intervention procedures. We believe that clinical and psychoeducational assessment represents one of the most effective ways of promoting the mental health and educational success of children from all ethnic, cultural, and socioeconomic backgrounds. Each child represents a separate challenge for you, the examiner; this book aims to increase your ability to rise effectively to the challenge.

This text is dedicated to the principle that tests of intelligence and special abilities, interviews, observations, informal tests, and other assessment procedures provide the cornerstones for the consultation process. These cornerstones help us to identify the observable manifestations of childhood disorders and, when linked with our knowledge of child development and psychopathology, form the foundation for assessment decisions. Objective measurements (a) help us make independent judgments about a child's level of functioning, (b) are useful in determining the extent of psychopathology, and (c) are helpful in communicating with other professionals. Knowledge gained about the behavioral correlates of psychological and physical illness is an important contribution to the study of children. Ideally, each clinical and psychoeducational assessment should be a learning opportunity for both the clinician and the child. Knowledgeable and responsible use of intelligence and special ability tests, as well as other assessment procedures, will be of value to the child, to those responsible for his or her care and education, and, ultimately, to society as a whole.

THINKING THROUGH THE ISSUES

1. What types of information will you need to help you arrive at a diagnostic impression? And what will it take to make you confident of your diagnostic impression, once it is reached?
2. What would the science of psychology be without classification and labels?
3. Do you think there ever will be a time when tests are not under attack? Explain your answer.
4. How does theory enrich the assessment process?
5. Consider the role you think computers should play in psychological assessment, the reasons for your position, and the arguments against your position.

SUMMARY

Classification and Labeling

1. A comprehensive assessment process involves (a) gathering information, (b) formulating hypotheses about a problem, (c) gaining insights about the individual, (d) arriving at a formal diagnosis, and (e) constructing an intervention plan.
2. Some clinicians object to diagnosis and classification, maintaining that labels have negative consequences.
3. Classification, when properly used, has several positive consequences.
4. Labeling may have beneficial consequences such as increasing altruism and understanding on the part of those who must deal with deviant behavior.
5. Although negative stereotypes are often associated with behavioral deviancy labels and with labels indicating low levels of intellectual functioning, research indicates that, in classrooms, children's actual classroom performances are a much more potent force in influencing teachers' expectancies than are labels assigned to the children.
6. Classifications such as moderate mental retardation and mild mental retardation are arbitrary cutoffs on a continuum of intelligence test scores.
7. Although labels are important in the diagnostic process and in communicating with professionals, parents, and teachers, you must not allow labels to regiment and restrict the ways you observe and work with children.

The Need to Consider Ethnic and Cultural Diversity

8. You must consider children's backgrounds in selecting tests and interpreting findings and in working with their families.
9. Ethnic groups have unique mores and customs, languages, and family and social interaction patterns.

Controversy Regarding the Use of Standardized Tests

10. Some critics maintain that intelligence tests and achievement tests are culturally biased and thus harmful to African American children and children of other ethnic groups.
11. Test advocates believe that standardized tests, if they are administered and interpreted carefully and ethically, have valid uses.
12. Few critics have proposed reasonable alternatives to present assessment methods.
13. The criticisms of testing have resulted in improved practice.

Copyright © 1996, John P. Wood. Reprinted with permission.

Useful Theoretical Perspectives for Assessment

14. Three perspectives are useful in guiding the assessment process: the developmental perspective, the normative-developmental perspective, and the cognitive-behavioral perspective.
15. A developmental perspective proposes that the interplay between genetic disposition and environmental influences follows a definite, nonrandom form and direction.
16. A normative-developmental perspective evaluates and attempts to account for changes in children's cognitions, affect, and behavior in relation to a reference group, usually composed of children of the same age and gender as the referred child.
17. A cognitive-behavioral perspective focuses on the importance of (a) cognitions as major determinants of emotion and behavior, including the child's thoughts and ways of processing information; (b) the role that cognitions such as values, beliefs, self-statements, problem-solving strategies, expectancies, images, and goals play in the development of maladaptive behavior; and (c) the individual and environmental influences that may shape and control the child's and family's thoughts, feelings, and behavior.

Factors That Affect Test Scores

18. Many factors interact to affect test scores. In addition to innate and background factors, there are intervening variables, which include the child's personality, the assessment situation, test demands, and random variation.

Accounting for Poor Performance

19. You will need to analyze the child's entire performance carefully and integrate information from other assessment sources to arrive at a plausible explanation of his or her poor performance.
20. You may need to administer specialized tests that can help to pinpoint specific areas of difficulty.
21. Tests provide information about how the examinee performs at a specific time under specific conditions.

Use of Computers in the Assessment Process

22. Computers can facilitate the administration and scoring of verbal tests and interviews, the recording and analysis of data involved in the observation of behavior, the preparation of reports, and the transmission of data.
23. Use of computers in the assessment process has both advantages and disadvantages.
24. New challenges await professionals who use computers in their clinical work.

Concluding Comment on Challenges in Assessing Children

25. Assessment is a means to an end, not an end in itself.
26. A clinical or psychoeducational evaluation is unique in that a highly able and skilled professional devotes his or her exclusive attention to one child for a period ranging from at least 1 to several hours and perhaps across several sessions.
27. To be effective as a clinician, you must be willing to (a) entertain alternative hypotheses, (b) revise your initial impressions of the examinee, and (c) reduce your reliance on memory by keeping good records and reviewing them periodically, as needed.
28. The typical clinical assessment is not completely ecologically valid because it minimizes demands faced by children in their natural environments and is structured to help examinees compensate for or mask functional impairments.
29. The assessment field will become more viable and productive if it can move beyond a primarily diagnostic role.
30. Tests of intelligence and special abilities, interviews, observations, informal tests, and other assessment procedures provide the cornerstones for the consultation process.
31. Knowledgeable and responsible use of intelligence and special ability tests, as well as other assessment procedures, will be of value to the child, to those responsible for his or her care and education, and, ultimately, to society as a whole.

KEY TERMS, CONCEPTS, AND NAMES

Classification and labeling (p. 24)
Self-fulfilling prophecy (p. 24)
Arbitrariness of classification systems (p. 26)
Ethnic and cultural diversity (p. 27)
Controversy regarding the use of standardized tests (p. 27)
Developmental perspective (p. 28)
Normative-developmental perspective (p. 29)
Cognitions (p. 29)
Affect (p. 29)
Cognitive-behavioral perspective (p. 30)
Propositions related to normal functioning in children (p. 31)
Propositions related to deviant functioning in children (p. 32)
Factors that affect test scores (p. 32)
Demand characteristics (p. 33)
Response bias (p. 33)
Social desirability (p. 33)
Setting variables (p. 33)
Reactive effects (p. 34)
Accounting for poor performance (p. 34)
Computers in the assessment process (p. 34)

STUDY QUESTIONS

1. Discuss classification and labeling. Include in your discussion the advantages and disadvantages of each.
2. Why is it important to consider how ethnic and cultural patterns may affect the assessment process?
3. Why has testing come under attack, and how has testing been defended?
4. Compare and contrast developmental, normative-developmental, and cognitive-behavioral perspectives.
5. Describe at least seven propositions, based on the developmental, normative-developmental, and cognitive-behavioral perspectives, related to normal and deviant functioning in children.
6. Discuss the major factors that may affect test scores. Include in your discussion the role of intervening variables.
7. How would you go about accounting for why examinees do poorly on tests?
8. Discuss some of the advantages and disadvantages of using computers in the assessment process.
9. Discuss some of the challenges involved in assessing children.

3

ETHICAL, LEGAL, AND PROFESSIONAL APPLICATIONS OF ASSESSMENT PRACTICES

It is easy for critics to produce logical arguments against testing children. Mislabeling, of course, can deny a child educational opportunities and damage the self-image of the child. Yet most such arguments remain at the abstract level. The exceptions are a few well-publicized cases. What we do not hear about are the thousands of cases in which well-trained professional psychologists, working with caring teachers and loving parents, quietly identify the sources of children's frustrations and place them in an environment in which growth and success, not frustration, become the norm. We also do not hear about the other thousands of cases in which children remain frustrated because well-meaning teachers and parents fail or refuse to have a child tested because they "don't believe in testing." It is the psychological equivalent of refusing to take a child to a doctor because you "don't believe in doctors." Psychologists, like physicians, sometimes make mistakes; but it is a much bigger mistake to regard errors as the norm, and behave as though Binet, Simon, Terman, and Wechsler and all the other great names in the assessment field had never been born, and as though psychologists had no expertise to offer in this field.

—William A. Hillix

Goals and Objectives

This chapter is designed to enable you to do the following:

- Become acquainted with ethical standards related to assessment

- Understand the components of the Individuals with Disabilities Education Act (IDEA), Section 504, the Americans with Disabilities Act (ADA), and the Family Educational Rights and Privacy Act of 1974, as these laws pertain to assessment

- Discuss the outcomes of major lawsuits involving assessment procedures and interpretations of the IDEA

- Know the laws regarding confidentiality and privileged communication

- Understand when you need to report child maltreatment

- Recognize the challenges of being an expert witness

- Understand forensic assessments

Ethical Responsibilities of Psychologists

Overview of Four Federal Laws Regarding Children
  with Disabilities

Individuals with Disabilities Education Act (IDEA)

Section 504 of the Rehabilitation Act of 1973

Americans with Disabilities Act (ADA)

Comment on the IDEA '97, Section 504, and the ADA

Confidentiality of Assessment Findings and Records

The Challenges of Being an Expert Witness

Forensic Assessment

Thinking Through the Issues

Summary

Please note that the information contained in this chapter is not intended to constitute legal advice or to substitute for obtaining legal advice from your agency's or school's attorney or from your own attorney. Furthermore, the information may not reflect current legal developments.

ETHICAL RESPONSIBILITIES OF PSYCHOLOGISTS

The Ethical Standards of the American Psychological Association (APA; 1994a) serve as guidelines for the work of psychologists and provide general guidance for all assessment specialists. You must carefully study the standards in order to understand the responsibilities associated with your work as an assessment specialist. Recognize that an action may be legal but unethical. For example, it is legal but unethical to date a client. Similarly, it is legal to conduct a mental status evaluation of a parent involved in a child custody dispute at the request of the court, but the evaluation would be unethical if you were seeing the parent in therapy.

The following ethical guidelines set out minimum requirements for psychologists who perform psychological assessments (adapted from the American Psychological Association, 1994a). Although these guidelines were written by and for psychologists, they also apply to other assessment professionals.

APA ETHICAL GUIDELINES

1. *Training.* The psychologist who works with children and their families has sufficient education, training, and expertise in child and family development, child psychopathology, and adult psychopathology to conduct assessments. Those working in a specialty area such as neuropsychology, behavioral medicine, custody proceedings, or child maltreatment have additional training in that area. The psychologist also keeps abreast of the latest developments in the field.

2. *Consultation.* The psychologist consults with other professionals when in doubt about assessment findings.

3. *Knowledge of federal and state law.* The psychologist is knowledgeable about the relevant federal and state laws concerning assessment, such as laws governing children with disabilities, child maltreatment, family violence, and custody evaluations.

4. *Awareness of personal and societal biases and non-discriminatory practice.* The psychologist is aware of any personal biases regarding age, sex, race, ethnicity, national origin, religion, sexual orientation, disability, language, culture, and socioeconomic status that may interfere with an objective evaluation and subsequent recommendations. The psychologist recognizes and strives to overcome any such biases or withdraws from the evaluation if the biases cannot be overcome.

5. *Avoidance of multiple relationships.* The psychologist avoids potential conflicts of interest. For example, a psychologist who is functioning as a therapist does not take on additional roles with the client—such as evaluating the client in a child custody dispute, a child maltreatment case, or any other situation related to a legal matter—if the assessment would affect the ongoing relationship the psychologist has with the client.

6. *Informed consent.* The psychologist obtains informed consent from parents (or caregivers) to conduct the assessment with the child.

7. *Confidentiality and disclosure of information.* The psychologist must protect the confidentiality of the information obtained during the evaluation. The only exceptions are when the client (or guardian) gives consent to release the information, when the psychologist is working with other professionals within an agency, or when failure to release information would violate the law.

8. *Multiple methods of data gathering.* The psychologist uses several sources to gather information about the examinee, including psychological tests, interviews, observations, previous psychological and psychiatric reports, and records from schools, hospitals, and other agencies. No decision should be made using a single data source.

9. *Interpretation of data.* The psychologist interprets data cautiously and appropriately, considers alternative interpretations, and avoids overinterpreting data.

10. *Explanation of assessment findings.* The psychologist explains the results of the assessment and the recommendations in a clear and understandable manner to the parents, the referral source, and, where appropriate, the child.

11. *Records and data.* The psychologist maintains raw data, written records, and copies of all audiotapes, videotapes, and computer disks. Clients have the right of access to their test results and are provided with a copy of the psychological report when requested. Security of tests, test results, test reports, and computer disks is maintained.

12. *Reliability and validity.* The psychologist clearly states in the report any doubts concerning the reliability or validity of the test results.

13. *Understanding the power of recommendations.* The psychologist recognizes that the recommendations may alter the lives of others and is aware of his or her social responsibilities.

14. *Recognition of competencies.* The psychologist recognizes his or her own competencies and the limitations of assessment and intervention techniques.

15. *Public statements.* The psychologist makes accurate public statements about diagnostic and assessment services.

16. *Explaining financial costs.* The psychologist makes sure that the client clearly understands the financial costs connected with the assessment before the assessment begins.

17. *Research.* The psychologist, when conducting research on assessment, considers the dignity and welfare of the participants in the research project.

Obviously, some of the above recommendations do not apply to young children; all of the recommendations apply to adolescents, however. Psychologists who do not follow these guidelines may be sued for wrongful use or misuse of assessment instruments, wrongful use of derived data, misinterpretation of assessment data, invasion of privacy, and violation of confidentiality. To reduce professional liability, fully inform the client about (a) the purpose of the evaluation, (b) the results of the evaluation (including findings and recommendations), (c) the potential uses of the results, and (d) the individuals who may have access to the report. You should follow standard practice in administering tests and make specific and detailed notes about the interview, observation, and all other relevant assessment procedures.

The American Psychological Association (1990) has also provided guidelines for working with ethnically, linguistically, and culturally diverse populations. The main points of the guidelines follow.

APA GUIDELINES FOR WORKING WITH ETHNICALLY, LINGUISTICALLY, AND CULTURALLY DIVERSE POPULATIONS

1. Psychologists educate their clients about the processes of psychological intervention, such as goals and expectations; the scope and legal limits of confidentiality; and the psychologist's theoretical orientation.
   a. Whenever possible, psychologists provide information in writing along with oral explanations.
   b. Whenever possible, the written information is provided in the language understandable to the client.
2. Psychologists are cognizant of relevant research and practice issues as related to the population being served.
   a. Psychologists acknowledge that ethnicity and culture affect behavior and take those factors into account when working with various ethnic/racial groups.
   b. Psychologists seek out educational and training experiences to enhance their ability to address the needs of various populations more appropriately and effectively. These experiences include cultural, social, psychological, political, economic, and historical material specific to the particular ethnic group being served.
   c. Psychologists recognize the limits of their competence and expertise. Psychologists who do not possess knowledge and training about an ethnic group seek consultation with, and/or make referrals to, appropriate experts.
   d. Psychologists consider the validity of a given instrument or procedure and interpret resulting data while keeping in mind the cultural and linguistic characteristics of the person being assessed. Psychologists are aware of the instrument's reference population and possible limitations of such instruments with other populations.
3. Psychologists recognize ethnicity and culture as significant parameters in understanding psychological processes.

   a. Psychologists, regardless of ethnic/racial background, are aware of how their own cultural background/experiences, attitudes, values, and biases influence psychological processes. They make efforts to correct any prejudices and biases.
   b. Psychologists' practice incorporates an understanding of the client's ethnic and cultural background. This includes the client's familiarity and comfort with the majority culture, as well as ways in which the client's culture may add to or improve various aspects of the majority culture and/or of society at large.
   c. Psychologists help clients increase their awareness of their own cultural values and norms, and they facilitate discovery of ways clients can apply this awareness to their own lives and to society at large.
   d. Psychologists seek to help clients determine whether a problem stems from racism or bias in others so that the client does not inappropriately personalize problems.
   e. Psychologists consider not only diagnostic issues, but also the cultural beliefs and values of the client and his or her community in providing intervention.
4. Psychologists respect the roles of family members and community structures, hierarchies, values, and beliefs within the client's culture.
   a. Psychologists identify resources in the family and the larger community.
   b. Clarification of the role of the psychologist and the expectations of the client precede intervention. Psychologists seek to ensure that both the psychologist and the client have a clear understanding of what services and roles are reasonable.
5. Psychologists respect clients' religious and/or spiritual beliefs and values, including attributions and taboos, since they affect world view, psychosocial functioning, and expressions of distress.
   a. Part of the psychologist's role when working in minority communities is to become familiar with indigenous beliefs and practices and to respect them.
   b. Effective psychological intervention may be aided by consultation with spiritual practitioners relevant to the client's cultural and belief systems.
6. Psychologists interact in the language requested by the client or, if this is not feasible, make an appropriate referral.
   a. Problems arise when the psychologist does not understand the language of the client. In such a case, the psychologist refers the client to a mental health professional who knows the client's language. If this is not possible, the psychologist offers the client a translator with cultural knowledge and an appropriate professional background. When no translator is available, a trained paraprofessional from the client's culture is used as a translator/culture broker.
   b. If translation is necessary, the psychologist does *not* retain the services of a translator who may have a dual role with the client and could thus jeopardize the validity of evaluation or the effectiveness of intervention.

c. Psychologists interpret and relate test data in terms understandable and relevant to the needs of those assessed.

7. Psychologists consider the impact of adverse social, environmental, and political factors in assessing problems and designing interventions.
   a. The types of intervention strategies to be used match the client's level of need.
   b. Psychologists work within the cultural setting to improve the welfare of all persons concerned.

8. Psychologists work to eliminate biases, prejudices, and discriminatory practices.
   a. Psychologists acknowledge relevant discriminatory practices at the social and community level that may be affecting the psychological welfare of the population being served.
   b. Psychologists are cognizant of sociopolitical contexts in conducting evaluations and providing interventions; they develop sensitivity to issues of oppression, sexism, elitism, and racism.

9. Psychologists working with culturally diverse populations should document culturally and sociopolitically relevant factors in the records:
   a. Number of generations in the country
   b. Number of years in the country
   c. Fluency in English
   d. Extent of family support (or disintegration of family)
   e. Community resources
   f. Level of education
   g. Change in social status as a result of coming to this country (for immigrant or refugee)
   h. Intimate relationships with people of different backgrounds
   i. Level of stress related to acculturation

Finally, the American Psychological Association (1998) also has provided guidelines for conducting evaluations in child protection matters. The guidelines that follow supplement the APA ethical guidelines presented earlier.

APA GUIDELINES FOR CONDUCTING EVALUATIONS IN CHILD PROTECTION MATTERS

I. *Orienting Guidelines*
   1. The primary purpose of the evaluation is to provide relevant, professionally sound results or opinions in matters where a child's health and welfare may have been or may in the future be harmed.
   2. In child protection cases, the child's interest and well-being are paramount.
   3. The evaluation addresses the particular psychological and developmental needs of the child and parent(s) that are relevant to child protection issues such as physical abuse, sexual abuse, neglect, and serious emotional harm.

II. *General Guidelines: Preparing for a Child Protection Evaluation*
   4. The role of the psychologist conducting evaluations is that of professional expert who strives to maintain an unbiased, objective stance.
   5. The serious consequences of psychological assessment in child protection matters place a heavy burden on psychologists.
   6. Psychologists gain specialized competence.
   7. Psychologists are aware of personal and societal biases and engage in nondiscriminatory practice.
   8. Psychologists avoid multiple relationships.

III. *Procedural Guidelines: Conducting a Psychological Evaluation in Child Protection Matters*
   9. The scope of the evaluation is determined by the psychologist and is guided by the nature of the referral question.
   10. Psychologists performing psychological evaluations in child protection matters obtain appropriate informed consent from all adult participants and, as appropriate, inform the child participant. Psychologists need to be particularly sensitive to informed consent issues.
   11. Psychologists inform participants about the disclosure of information and the limits of confidentiality.
   12. Psychologists use multiple methods of data gathering.
   13. Psychologists neither overinterpret nor inappropriately interpret clinical or assessment data.
   14. The psychologist conducting a psychological evaluation in a child protection matter provides an opinion regarding the psychological functioning of an individual only after conducting an evaluation of the individual adequate to support the opinion or conclusion.
   15. Recommendations, if offered, are based on whether the child's health and welfare have been or may be seriously harmed.
   16. Psychologists clarify financial arrangements.
   17. Psychologists maintain appropriate records.

The National Association of School Psychologists (NASP; 1994, adapted from p. 1 of insert) advocates the following assessment practices.

NASP ASSESSMENT GUIDELINES

NASP endorses assessment practices that are tailored to the needs of the individual student in the context of a comprehensive service delivery system that facilitates educational progress for all children.

Evidence from practice and research indicates the following:

- Specialized training and skills in areas of psychological and educational assessment are needed by those engaged in such practices.

- Assessment and intervention should be designed to produce positive outcomes for the child.
- Multidisciplinary team assessment must include multiple sources of information, multiple procedures, and multiple settings in order to yield a comprehensive understanding of a child's abilities.
- Assessment and intervention must be multidimensional and based on the needs of the child.
- Family systems and home environments substantially influence the development of all children and should be addressed in assessment.
- Parent-professional and, where appropriate, child-professional collaboration is crucial to decision making, as well as to the identification of childrens' and families' needs.
- Longitudinal assessment is needed to evaluate and document progress or response to interventions.
- Assessment information should guide intervention strategies.

Therefore, the National Association of School Psychologists endorses assessment practices that have the following characteristics:

- Relevant to the referral question
- Based on the characteristics of children and related environments
- Comprehensive in addressing the educational, cognitive, and mental health needs of the child
- Linked to efforts to resolve the problem through prevention and/or early intervention
- Directly linked to relevant intervention designs for the child
- Not limited to any single methodology or theoretical framework
- Nondiscriminatory in terms of ethnicity, gender, native language, family, or socioeconomic status
- Technically adequate and used for the purposes for which they were developed and/or validated

OVERVIEW OF FOUR FEDERAL LAWS REGARDING CHILDREN WITH DISABILITIES

by Jerome M. Sattler and Guy McBride

In addition to understanding the ethical principles that guide your practice as a psychologist, you need to be aware of four federal laws that apply to the practice of assessment: the Individuals with Disabilities Education Act (IDEA; also referred to as IDEA '97), Section 504 of the Rehabilitation Act of 1973 (Section 504), the Americans with Disabilities Act (ADA), and the Family Educational Rights and Privacy Act (FERPA). We will devote most of our attention to the IDEA '97 because it provides the most extensive guidelines for assessment of children with disabilities.

To read the literature about special education law, you need to know several terms and acronyms (see Table 3-1) and understand which agencies are responsible for implementing the various laws. The U.S. Department of Education (DOE) is responsible for enforcing the laws passed by Congress dealing with civil rights (Section 504 and the ADA) as applied to the public schools, as well as those dealing with educational rights (IDEA '97 and FERPA). Within the Department of Education, various agencies are assigned specific responsibilities for ensuring compliance by the states and by local school systems, and these are usually referred to as *local educational agencies* (LEAs).

The Office for Special Education and Rehabilitative Services (OSERS) in the DOE is responsible for enforcing the IDEA '97 and wrote the federal regulations issued in May 1999 to clarify the IDEA '97. These federal regulations have the force of law, whereas policy letters issued by OSERS do not. However, policy letters may later be incorporated into the regulations.

Within OSERS is the Office for Special Education Programs (OSEP). This office has specific administrative, monitoring, and state-support responsibilities for special education. If OSERS finds that a state is not in compliance with the IDEA '97, federal special education funding can be withheld from a state or school until compliance is assured. States and schools have the right to appeal the withholding of funds to federal courts. OSERS has a basic mandate: to affirm the

SCHOOLIES © 1998 by John P. Wood

Nice going, Mom. You took me to the dentist for new fillings and now I can't get through the metal detector at school.

Copyright © 1998 by John P. Wood. Reprinted with permission.

Table 3-1
Terms Associated with Federal Laws Related to Children with Disabilities

Americans with Disabilities Act (ADA). A law that makes it illegal to discriminate against any individual based on his or her disability. It provides similar rights to school children as does Section 504 of the Vocational Rehabilitation Act. Both laws are enforced by the Office for Civil Rights.

Assistive technology (AT). Any item or piece of equipment, whether acquired commercially off the shelf, modified, or customized, used to increase, maintain, or improve the functional capabilities of a child with a disability. Examples of AT devices are word prediction software, adapted keyboards, voice recognition and synthesis software, head pointers, enlarged print, Braille printers, hearing aids, and communication boards. (Sec. 300.5)

Assistive technology service. Any service that directly assists a student with a disability in the selection, acquisition, or use of an assistive technology device. (Sec. 300.6)

Behavioral intervention plan (BIP). A plan that is created for a student whose behavior impedes his or her learning or the learning of others and that details, as needed, positive behavioral interventions, strategies, supports, and other relevant interventions. (Sec. 300.346)

BIA. Bureau of Indian Affairs.

CFR. Code of Federal Regulations.

DOE. United States Department of Education.

Due process. The steps and rules established to ensure fairness in providing educational opportunities to all children.

ED. United States Department of Education.

Education Department General Administrative Regulations (EDGAR). Federal regulations pertaining to all students in schools receiving federal funds, including special education students. (Sec. 300.30)

Education for the Handicapped Act (EHA). An act originally passed in 1975, amended in 1990 and renamed the Individuals with Disabilities Education Act (IDEA) and amended again in 1997 (IDEA '97).

Educational service agency (ESA). A regional public multi-service agency authorized by state law to develop, manage, and provide services or programs to Local Education Agencies or similar public institutions or agencies having administrative control and direction over a public elementary or secondary school. (Sec. 300.10)

EPSDT. Early periodic screening, diagnosis, and treatment.

ESEA. Elementary and Secondary Education Act of 1965.

Extended school year (ESY). The time outside the regular school year, usually during the summer vacation. Each public agency shall ensure that educational and educationally related extended school year services are available as necessary to provide a FAPE for children with a disability. (Sec. 300.309)

Family Policy Compliance Office (FPCO). A separate office under the U.S. Department of Education that is responsible for enforcing the Family Educational Rights and Privacy Act.

FEOG. Full educational opportunity goal.

FERPA. Family Educational Rights and Privacy Act (also known as the Buckley Amendment).

Free appropriate public education (FAPE). Special education and related services provided without charge (at public expense) under public supervision and direction. (Sec. 300.13)

Functional behavioral assessment (FBA). An assessment that considers situational, environmental, and behavioral factors related to a child's problems. An FBA is needed when the behavior of a student with a disability (a) places the student or others at risk of injury, (b) results in the destruction or loss of property, or (c) diminishes the self-concept of the student. If an FBA has not been completed, it is required after a change of placement resulting from a disciplinary removal. The assessment includes the development of a comprehensive treatment plan that may become part of the IEP.

GEPA. General Education Provisions Act.

Independent Educational Evaluation (IEE). An educational evaluation obtained independently by parents. If the evaluation meets state requirements, the IEP team is obligated to consider it but not necessarily to accept its findings and recommendations. (Sec. 300.502)

Individualized Education Program (IEP). A written statement that describes the special education and related services (such as transition services, specific accommodations, and special modifications) needed for a student with a disability. The IEP is developed, reviewed, and revised in meetings by the IEP team. (Sec. 300.340)

Individualized Education Program team (IEP team). A group of individuals, which includes the student's parents, responsible for developing, reviewing, or revising an IEP for a child with a disability. (Sec. 300.16)

Individualized Family Service Plan (IFSP). A plan developed for infants or toddlers with a disability. For children transitioning from an infant-toddler program to a preschool program, an IFSP may be used in place of an IEP if all the components required of the IEP are present, if the IFSP continues to be appropriate, and if the parents agree to its use. (Sec. 300.342)

Individuals with Disabilities Education Act (IDEA). The federal law designed (a) to ensure that all children with disabilities have available to them a free appropriate public education that emphasizes special education and related services designed to meet their unique needs and prepare them for employment and independent living; (b) to ensure that the rights of children with disabilities and their parents are protected; (c) to assist states, localities, educational service agencies, and federal agencies in providing for the education of all children with disabilities; and (d) to assess and ensure the effectiveness of efforts to educate children with disabilities. (Sec. 300.1)

Individuals with Disabilities Education Law Reporter (IDELR). A commonly cited legal reference that contains the full text of major federal statutes and regulations, IDEA policy rulings, Section 504 policy rulings, federal and state court decisions, and state educational agency appeals decisions.

Least restrictive environment (LRE). For students with disabilities, the environment that allows them to be educated to the maximum extent appropriate with students who are nondisabled. Students with disabilities, including students in public or private institutions or other care facilities, are to be placed in special classes or separate schools or to be removed from the regular educational environment only if the nature or severity of the disability is such that they cannot be educated in regular classes, even with the use of supplementary aids and services. (Sec. 300.550)

(Continued)

Table 3-1 (*Continued*)

LEP. Limited English proficiency.

Local Educational Agency (LEA). A public Board of Education or other public authority legally constituted within a state either for administrative control or direction of, or to perform a service function for, public elementary or secondary schools. The jurisdiction may be a city, county, township, school district, or other political subdivision of a state or a combination of school districts or counties recognized in a state as an administrative agency for its public elementary or secondary schools. (Secs. 300.18; 300.10)

Native language. The language or mode of communication normally used by an individual. In the case of a child, it may be the language normally used by the parents of the child or the language used by the child in the home or learning environment. For an individual with deafness, blindness, or no written language, it could be sign language, Braille, or oral communication. (Sec. 300.19)

Nonacademic services and activities. Services and activities that afford children with disabilities an opportunity to participate in school activities. These services and activities may include counseling, athletics, transportation, health services, recreational activities, special interest groups or clubs sponsored by the public agency, referrals to agencies that provide assistance to individuals with disabilities, employment of students, and assistance in making outside employment available. (Sec. 300.306)

NPRM. Notice of proposed rulemaking.

Office for Civil Rights (OCR). An agency of the U.S. Department of Education responsible for enforcing Section 504 and the ADA in the public schools.

Office of Special Education and Rehabilitative Services (OSERS). An agency of the U.S. Department of Education responsible for enforcing the IDEA '97 in the public schools.

Office of Special Education Programs (OSEP). An agency of the U.S. Department of Education charged with monitoring state compliance with the IDEA '97.

OHI. Other health impairment.

OMB. Office of Management and Budget.

Related services. Transportation and such developmental, corrective, and other supportive services as are required to assist a child with a disability to benefit from special education. (Sec. 300.24)

SEA. State Education Agency.

Section 504 of the Vocational Rehabilitation Act of 1973. A federal law that makes it illegal for any agency to discriminate against an otherwise qualified individual solely because of a disability.

Services Plan. A plan developed for private school children designated by the LEA as entitled to receive services. (Sec. 300.455)

Severe discrepancy. A number arrived at by comparing scores on a test of intellectual ability with scores on tests that measure achievement in one or more of the following areas: oral expression, listening comprehension, written expression, basic reading skill, reading comprehension, mathematics calculation, or mathematics reasoning. (Sec. 300.541)

SPED (Special Education). Informal abbreviation often used in discussions of special education, especially on the Internet.

SPEDLAW (Special Education Law). Informal abbreviation often used in discussions of special education law, especially on the Internet.

Student with a disability. A student who has mental retardation, a hearing impairment (including deafness), a speech or language impairment, a visual impairment (including blindness), serious emotional disturbance, an orthopedic impairment, autism, traumatic brain injury, another health impairment, a specific learning disability, deaf-blindness, multiple disabilities, or developmental delay (for children aged 3 through 5 to 9 years) and who, by reason thereof, needs special education and related services. (Secs. 300.7; 300.313)

Supplementary aids and services. Supports that are provided in regular education classes or other education-related settings to enable children with disabilities to be educated with nondisabled children to the maximum extent appropriate. (Sec. 300.28)

Transition services. A coordinated set of activities for a student with a disability that promotes movement from school to post-school activities, including postsecondary education, vocational training, employment, continuing and adult education, adult services, independent living, or community participation. Transition services are based on the individual student's needs. They take into account the student's preferences and interests and include instruction, related services, community experiences, the development of employment and other post-school adult living objectives, and, if appropriate, acquisition of daily living skills and a functional vocational evaluation. (Sec. 300.29)

Note. Section numbers refer to the IDEA '97.

rights of children who are disabled and needing special education services to receive a *free appropriate public education (FAPE)* in the least restrictive environment (LRE).

Section 504 and the ADA apply to all children with disabilities, including those eligible under the IDEA '97. However, students who qualify for services under Section 504 do not necessarily qualify for services under the IDEA '97. The requirements of Section 504 and the ADA are virtually identical with respect to school systems. These two laws are en-

forced by the Office for Civil Rights (OCR), which is part of the DOE. The requirements of the IDEA '97 are more elaborate than those of Section 504 or the ADA. The requirements of both Section 504 and the ADA will be met if the requirements for services under the IDEA '97 are met.

The Family Educational Rights and Privacy Act (FERPA) applies to all students, including those who are disabled. The Family Policy Compliance Office in the Office of Management in the DOE administers FERPA. This act forms the foundation for the confidentiality rights of children with disabilities and is enforceable through the federal court system. Furthermore, if a school does not comply with FERPA, funding for appropriate federal programs can be terminated. Confidentiality is discussed later in this chapter.

INDIVIDUALS WITH DISABILITIES EDUCATION ACT (IDEA)

by Jerome M. Sattler and Guy McBride

In 1975, Congress passed Public Law 94-142, the Education for All Handicapped Children Act. Congress designed the law to assure the right to a FAPE for all children with disabilities. Before the law was passed, "more than half of the children with disabilities in the United States did not receive appropriate educational services, and a million children with disabilities were excluded entirely from the public school system" (Federal Register, March 12, 1999, p. 12414). The law incorporated many of the ethical principles discussed earlier in this chapter.

In 1990, Congress updated Public Law 94-142 and changed its name to the Individuals with Disabilities Education Act (IDEA; Public Law 101-476). In 1997, the IDEA was reauthorized and amended (Public Law 105-17; referred to as IDEA '97). In March 1999, regulations implementing the IDEA '97 were issued. Several principles form the foundation of the IDEA '97:

1. Children with disabilities must receive a FAPE that provides special education and related services, including nonacademic and extracurricular services and activities, designed to meet their unique needs and prepare them for employment and independent living. (Sec. 300.1)
2. Each child being considered for special education and related services must receive a full, individualized, and appropriate evaluation. The evaluation must identify all of the child's special education needs, even if these needs are not commonly related to the child's disability. (Sec. 300.352)
3. Children with disabilities who are eligible for special education and related services must have an Individualized Education Program (IEP). (Secs. 300.341-300.350)
4. Children with disabilities should be educated with children who are not disabled in the LRE. (Sec. 300.550)
5. Children with disabilities and their parents must be given the opportunity to participate in meetings where decisions will be made regarding the identification, evaluation, or placement of the children or regarding the provision of a FAPE to the children. (Sec. 300.501)
6. All procedural safeguards must be followed. A copy of the procedural safeguards must be provided to parents. (Secs. 300.500; 300.504)
7. Schools are responsible for finding, identifying, and evaluating children, including private school students (such as students in religious schools), with disabilities

who are in need of special education and related services. (Secs. 300.125; 300.451)
8. School districts are obliged to offer some services to children with disabilities enrolled at private schools after the children have been properly identified (Sec. 300.450). These services can be offered even when there is no dispute over the appropriateness of public school programs. However, "no private school child with a disability has an individual right to receive some or all of the special education and related services that the child would receive if enrolled in a public school" (Sec. 300.454).
9. Special education and related services may be provided to parentally placed private school children with disabilities on the premises of private schools, including religious schools, in a manner that does not violate the establishment clause of the first amendment to the U.S. Constitution and is consistent with applicable state constitutions and laws. (Sec. 300.456)
10. The amount spent on services offered to children with disabilities at private schools must be a proportional amount of the federal funds allocated for all disabled children in the school district (Sec. 300.453).
11. Children with disabilities enrolled at private schools who are designated to receive services from the LEA are entitled to a services plan comparable to an IEP (Sec. 300.452). A representative from the private school should participate, if possible, at each services plan meeting.
12. Children with disabilities must be provided services to the extent necessary to enable them to progress appropriately in the general curriculum and advance appropriately toward achieving the goals set out in their IEP. (Secs. 300.121; 300.347)
13. Informed written consent of parents must be obtained before conducting any evaluation and before special education and related services are initially implemented for a child with a disability. (Sec. 300.505)
14. Parents of children with disabilities must be given feedback through such means as periodic report cards on the children's progress with the same frequency as parents of children who are not disabled. (Sec. 300.347(a)(7)(ii))
15. States, localities, educational service agencies, and federal agencies are required to implement services to provide for the education of all children with disabilities. (Sec. 300.1)

Some of the key provisions of the IDEA '97 are as follows.

1. It establishes safeguards for the identification, evaluation, and placement of children with disabilities. (Sec. 300.503)
2. It requires that states take steps to ensure children with disabilities equitable access to their programs and remove barriers that prevent such access. (Appendix B)
3. It requires the IEP team to consider whether a child with disabilities requires assistive technology devices and ser-

vices in order to receive a FAPE. (Secs. 300.5; 300.6; 300.8)

4. It requires that a full continuum of alternative placements be considered for children with disabilities (regular classrooms, special education classrooms, nonpublic schools, home instruction, instruction in hospitals). (Sec. 300.130)

5. It requires the development of an IEP for children between 3 and 21 years or an Individualized Family Service Plan (IFSP) for children between birth and 2 years 11 months. (Sec. 300.132)

6. It requires that parents be fully informed of all information relevant to their children in their native language or other mode of communication. This includes providing notice of the IEP meeting to the parents in their native language or other primary mode of communication and arranging for an interpreter at the meeting, as needed. (Secs. 300.500; 300.503)

7. It gives parents the right to have access to their child's records and to actively participate in each IEP meeting. (Sec. 300.562)

8. It gives parents the right to an independent evaluation of their children at public expense if they disagree with the evaluation conducted by the school. However, if the public school initiates a hearing and the hearing officer determines that the school's evaluation was appropriate, the parent has a right to an independent assessment, but not at public expense. (Sec. 300.502)

9. It requires that schools consider an evaluation obtained by parents at their own expense if the evaluation meets agency criteria. (Sec. 300.502)

10. It requires that a group of qualified professionals and the parents decide on the child's eligibility for special education and related services. (Sec. 300.534)

11. It requires that information about children be kept confidential in accordance with FERPA requirements. However, it requires that a child's IEP be accessible to regular education teachers, special education teachers, related service providers, and any other service provider who is responsible for its implementation. It also states that each teacher and service provider shall be informed of his or her specific responsibilities related to the implementation of a child's IEP and the specific accommodations, modifications, and supports that must be provided for the child in accordance with the IEP. (Secs. 300.571; 300.342)

12. It requires that schools provide services, modifications, or accommodations that children with disabilities need in order to receive a FAPE. (Sec. 300.346)

13. It requires that children with disabilities be disciplined only for the same reasons or length of time as children without disabilities. (Sec. 300.520)

14. It provides procedures for parents and schools to resolve disputes (through mediation and impartial due process hearings) relating to the identification, evaluation, and educational placement of a child with a disability or the provision of a FAPE for the child. (Secs. 300.503-300.513)

15. It requires that during the due process hearing or judicial proceeding, unless the parties agree otherwise, the child involved in the dispute shall remain in his or her current educational placement. This is commonly referred to as "stay put." (Sec. 300.514)

Additional rights and privileges (e.g., extension of eligibility rights) may be granted by a state, but a state cannot reduce the protections provided by the IDEA '97. You should become familiar with the procedures and regulations mandated for use in the schools in your state.

Least Restrictive Environment (LRE)

Earlier in this chapter you read about the IDEA mandate requiring, to the maximum extent appropriate, that all children with disabilities be placed in the LRE. The LRE mandate means that children with disabilities are to be educated with children who are not disabled when appropriate, not to the "maximum extent possible." This is also referred to as "mainstreaming." The determination of the LRE for each child with a disability is made by the IEP team based on the child's individual needs.

The IEP team is composed of the following individuals: (a) the parents, (b) at least one general education teacher of the child if the child is or may be participating in general education, (c) at least one special education teacher of the child (or special education provider), (d) a representative of the school who is qualified to provide specialized instruction or supervise special education teachers and is knowledgeable about the general curriculum and available resources, (e) an individual who can interpret the instructional implications, (f) other individuals who have knowledge or special expertise about the child (invited by the parent or the agency), and (g) the child, when appropriate. The determination of the knowledge or special expertise of any individual shall be made by the party who invited the individual to be a member of the IEP team.

Students should not be removed from age-appropriate regular education classrooms solely because of needed modifications to the general curriculum. In fact, there is a statutory presumption in the IDEA '97 that children with disabilities will be educated in the regular education classroom if, with appropriate services, the child can receive a FAPE. Services should be provided at the child's home school or in a school as near to his or her home school as possible.

Some special educators and parents advocate full inclusion as the LRE for children with disabilities. In its pure form, *full inclusion* requires that all services for the child be provided within the general education classroom. Some courts are particularly sympathetic to this philosophy when the needs of young children who are mentally retarded are being considered (e.g., *Sacramento City School District v. Rachel H.,* 1994). Although the terms *mainstreaming* and *full*

SCHOOLIES © 1999 by John P. Wood

Copyright © 1999 by John P. Wood. Reprinted with permission.

Federal regulations issued in May 1999 require that school systems maintain a full continuum of alternative placements to meet the needs of children with disabilities for special education and related services. The following range of services (from least to most restrictive), though not defined in the law, suggests options that states might adopt: (a) individual special education services in the general education classroom, (b) direct instruction in a resource room, (c) self-contained instruction in a special education classroom with integration as appropriate, (d) separate public day school for students with disabilities, (e) separate private day school for students with disabilities, (f) public or private residential facility, (g) homebound instruction, and (h) instruction in a hospital or institution.

The regulations require the IEP team to consider whether the child can be educated in the LRE with the use of appropriate supplementary aids and services. If the IEP team determines that a less restrictive setting is not appropriate, even with supplementary aids and services, the team can then consider a more restrictive placement along the continuum that is appropriate to the child's individual needs. Further, a student need not fail in the regular classroom before another placement can be considered. Conversely, the IDEA does not require that a student demonstrate achievement at a specific performance level as a prerequisite for placement in a regular classroom.

inclusion do not have legal meaning, they reflect the legislative mandate requiring educators to place children with disabilities in the LRE to the maximum extent appropriate. Although educational philosophies regarding inclusion may differ, the IDEA '97 requires that every public school system maintain a full continuum of services for its children.

The rationale for full inclusion is that it (a) increases academic achievement, (b) provides social benefits such as self-esteem, social skills, and parental involvement, (c) prepares students with disabilities for careers and living in society, and (d) reduces stigma. The arguments against full inclusion are that it (a) places an inappropriate burden on general education teachers who are not trained to work with students with disabilities, (b) requires an excessive amount of teacher time and energy, (c) isolates students with disabilities and increases stigma, (d) denies students with disabilities special services, and (e) diminishes the intensity of the services provided. Thus, full inclusion for children with disabilities is controversial (Gottlieb, Alter, & Gottlieb, 1991; Hornby, 1992; Salend, 1990). The Circuit Court of Appeals for the Fourth District ruled that the social needs of the child assume a subordinate role to the educational needs of the child in formulating an appropriate educational program (*Hartmann v. Loudoun County Board of Education,* 1997).

In determining the LRE for a child with a disability, the IEP team must carefully consider all options. The team must determine the services needed to provide a FAPE in a setting that is as close to the general education program as feasible. The IEP must be reviewed at least annually.

Testing and Evaluation Procedures

Let's now examine some of the provisions of the IDEA '97 as they pertain to the evaluation of children. The evaluations shall be administered by trained and knowledgeable personnel. The testing and evaluation procedures must meet the following standards (guidelines adapted from the Federal Register, March 12, 1999, Sec. 300.532, p. 12455 and Sec. 300.520, p. 12453).

1. *Assessment procedures must be nondiscriminatory.*

2. *Assessment procedures must be administered in the child's native language or other mode of communication, unless it is clearly not feasible to do so.* Native language refers to the language normally used by the child in the home or learning environment. For a child who is deaf or blind or for a child who has no written language, native language refers to the mode of communication that is normally used by the child, such as sign language, Braille, or oral communication.

3. *Assessment instruments used with a child with limited English proficiency must measure the extent to which the child has a disability and needs special education, not the child's English language skills.*

4. *A variety of assessment tools and strategies must be used to evaluate the child.*

5. *Standardized tests must be validated for the specific purpose for which they are used.*

6. *Standardized tests must be administered by trained and knowledgeable personnel in accordance with the instructions provided by the test producer.*

7. The report must include information about instances when standard test administration procedures are not followed.

8. The instruments and other evaluation procedures should assess specific areas of educational need, not only general intelligence.

9. The test results obtained with children who have impaired sensory, manual, or speaking skills should accurately reflect their academic or cognitive abilities, not their impaired sensory or communication skills.

10. No single procedure is used as the sole criterion to determine whether a child has a disability or to determine an appropriate educational program.

11. All areas related to the suspected disability should be assessed, including, if appropriate, health, vision, hearing, social and emotional status, general intelligence, academic performance, communicative status, and motor abilities.

12. The evaluation must be sufficiently comprehensive to identify all of the child's special education and related services needs, not just those associated with his or her disability classification. "Related services means transportation and such developmental, corrective, and other supportive services as are required to assist a child with a disability to benefit from special education, and includes speech-language pathology and audiology services, psychological services, physical and occupational therapy, recreation, including therapeutic recreation, early identification and assessment of disabilities in children, counseling services, including rehabilitation counseling, orientation and mobility services, and medical services for diagnostic or evaluation purposes. The term also includes school health services, social work services in schools, and parent counseling and training" (Sec. 300.24, pp. 12423–12424, March 12, 1999).

13. Only technically sound instruments shall be used to assess cognitive, behavioral, physical, and developmental factors.

14. The assessment tools and strategies used must provide information that will help in determining the educational needs of the child.

15. When a child with disabilities has been removed from his or her current educational placement for more than 10 school days or when the behavior of a child with disabilities interferes with the education of himself or herself or that of others, a functional behavioral assessment shall be conducted and a behavioral intervention plan shall be developed and implemented. A functional behavioral assessment would consider situational, environmental, and behavioral factors related to the child's problems and may require the parent's consent if the team decides that special assessment procedures are needed. However, if the functional behavioral assessment is based only on a review of existing data, parental permission is not required. (See *Assessment of Children: Behavioral and Clinical Applications* for more information about functional behavioral assessments.) *Assessment of Children: Behavioral and Clinical Applications* describes the additional standards specified in the law for the evaluation of children with specific learning disabilities.

The main purposes of an initial evaluation or reevaluation under the IDEA are to provide the IEP team with the data it needs to determine (a) whether a child has a disability (as defined below, under "Determination of Disability") and is eligible for special education and related services and (b) the child's unique strengths and needs. Remember, the IEP team must include an individual who can interpret the instructional implications and evaluation results. The IDEA '97 requires the school district to complete an evaluation within a reasonable time after receipt of a referral, but an IEP must be developed within 30 days of the eligibility decision.

The IEP is developed by the IEP team. In developing the IEP, the IEP team will want to answer several questions:

1. What is the child's level of performance in reading? in mathematics? in spelling? in written language? in cognitive functioning? in other areas?
2. What are the child's unique educational and psychological needs?

If the child has a disability and needs special education, the IEP team will also consider the following questions:

1. What areas need remediation?
2. What goals are appropriate?
3. What special education and related services are needed to enable the child to meet the goals formulated in the IEP and to participate in the general education curriculum?
4. What will be the LRE?

Procedural Safeguards and Parent Involvement

Procedural safeguards were included in the IDEA '97 in order to ensure that (a) the rights of children with disabilities and their parents are protected, (b) children with disabilities and their parents are provided with the information they need to make informed decisions about the children's educational opportunities, and (c) procedures and mechanisms are in place to resolve disagreements between the parents and the school district. The term *parent* refers to a natural or adoptive parent of a child, a guardian, a person acting in the place of a parent (such as a grandparent or stepparent with whom the child lives or a person who is legally responsible for the child's welfare), a surrogate parent who has been appointed by a public agency, or a qualified foster parent (unless prohibited by state law). (A qualified foster parent is one who has an ongoing parental relationship, is willing to make educational decisions, and has no conflict of interest.)

Here are useful practices to ensure that procedural safeguards are followed:

1. Give the parents prior written notice of the evaluation in easy-to-understand wording and in the primary language used in the home.

2. Invite the parents, as appropriate, to attend a meeting with staff personnel before the formal assessment is begun to assist in determining the scope of the assessment that is needed, based on a review of existing data. This is a good time to answer any questions the parents have. What you explained should be summarized and logged in your records.

3. Inform the parents at the meeting (or, if the parents are unable to appear, notify them in writing or through documented telephone calls or by a home visit or video conferencing) about (a) the nature of the problem; (b) the purpose of the assessment; (c) all instruments, records, and information-gathering procedures that will be used; (d) possible uses of information gathered; and (e) due process, procedural safeguards, confidentiality, and parent access to records. Due process rights must be provided to the parents whether or not they attend a meeting.

4. Provide written information about the following procedural safeguards upon the initial referral for evaluation. Parents have the following rights:

   • To obtain an evaluation from outside of the school system
   • To have the local education agency inform them in writing about their child's evaluation
   • To have the local education agency obtain their consent for the evaluation in writing
   • To inspect and review any education records relating to their child that the school collects, maintains, and uses
   • To inspect and review all education records with respect to the identification, evaluation, and educational placement of the child
   • To have school personnel explain and interpret the child's records
   • To have copies of their child's evaluation report and other relevant records and reports if they cannot see the records in person
   • To have their representative inspect and review their child's records
   • To present complaints
   • To be informed of the child's placement, pending the outcome of any due process proceeding
   • To receive a description of the procedures used for students placed in an interim alternative educational setting
   • To receive an explanation of the procedures they must follow if they want their child to go to a private school at public expense
   • To use mediation procedures in cases of disagreement with the placement of their child
   • To have a due process hearing if mediation is not successful
   • To appeal to a state level (if applicable)
   • To engage in a civil action if they are not satisfied that the child's placement and services are providing a FAPE

   • To receive payment of attorneys' fees in certain cases
   • To receive information about how to file a complaint with the state education department

If there is reason to believe that the parents are illiterate, convene a meeting to discuss their rights in a language they understand. If schools fail to give parents information about their rights and responsibilities in a language that the parents can understand and if the parents request reimbursement for private school tuition, the parents may be reimbursed even if they did not follow the prior notice requirements of the IDEA '97.

5. Before conducting an initial evaluation, obtain from the parents at the meeting (or in some other manner if you do not hold a meeting) the following: (a) written consent for you to perform the assessment (the consent form can also serve as documentation that the parents received their due process rights if a statement to that effect is included in the consent form); (b) written consent for you to obtain and share information with other sources, as appropriate; (c) information on languages used in the home; (d) parental perceptions of the child's problem, adaptive behavior, and temperament and personality; and (e) information about the child's medical history, the home environment, and any other related issues (see *Assessment of Children: Behavioral and Clinical Applications*).

Parents have the right to refuse permission for the school to conduct an evaluation. When this happens, the local education agency may use mediation or invoke due process procedures, state laws permitting. The IDEA '97 specifies that parental consent is not required to review existing data as part of an evaluation or a reevaluation or to administer a test or another assessment procedure that is administered to all children, unless consent is required of parents of all children.

For initial evaluations, the parents' written consent is required. For reevaluations, the parents' permission is not required if they failed to respond to request(s) for reevaluation or to attend a reevaluation IEP team meeting. The local education agency also needs to demonstrate that it has taken reasonable measures to obtain their consent.

If the parents refuse to consent to additional testing for a child's reevaluation, schools have several options in those states that allow schools to ask for a due process hearing. First, the school can ask a group of professionals (which may be the IEP team) to review existing data to see whether there is sufficient information to make a determination of eligibility and needs. Second, the school may ask for mediation. Third, the school may ask a hearing officer to order the evaluation. In no case can the school dismiss the child from the program simply because the parent refuses consent.

In those states that do not permit schools to take parents to a due process hearing when the parents refuse consent for a reevaluation, the IEP team may still review the data or go to mediation. If, however, the IEP team finds that it has insuffi-

SCHOOLIES © 1999 by John P. Wood

Your parents demanded that the board pressure the superintendent to compel the principal to order me to tell you to try a little harder.

Copyright © 1999 by John P. Wood. Reprinted with permission.

cient data and cannot gain voluntary parental compliance, it may have to dismiss the child from the program.

If parents disagree with any aspect of the evaluation process or recommended interventions, they are entitled to seek resolution of their grievances through (from least to most formal) (a) nonbinding mediation, (b) appeal to the state department of education, (c) hearings/arbitration, and (d) formal legal proceedings at the court level. To participate adequately in these hearings, you will need to learn how to testify as an expert witness (discussed later in this chapter). The IDEA '97 specifically prohibits schools from using mediation to delay parents in exercising their legal rights before a hearing officer. Courts have held, however, that parents must exhaust administrative remedies (due process hearings and appeals) before coming to state or federal court (e.g., *Jackson v. New Hyde Park Memorial High School,* 1999).

Statewide Assessments

The IDEA '97 requires that state- or districtwide group tests administered to children without disabilities also be administered to children with disabilities. The IEP should provide guidance on the accommodations needed for the student to take the group-administered tests or any alternative assessments. If the IEP team determines that a child cannot participate in group testing, it must explain why and it must use an alternative assessment based on state-approved guidelines.

Following are examples of what can be done to accommodate students with disabilities on group-administered tests:

- *Flexible scheduling*—extending time to complete the test, allowing breaks as needed, administering the test over two or more sessions, and administering the test over two or more days
- *Flexible setting*—administering the test individually or in small groups, providing special lighting, and providing special acoustics during testing
- *Revised test format*—using Braille editions or large-print editions, increasing the space between test items, reducing the number of test items per page, and increasing the size of answer bubbles on the answer sheet
- *Revised test directions*—simplifying language in the directions, providing additional examples, providing cues (e.g., arrows) on answer forms, and highlighting verbs in instructions
- *Use of aids for test items*—allowing use of a visual magnification device, auditory amplification device, auditory tape of test items, and masks to maintain place
- *Use of aids for test responses*—allowing use of a tape recorder, typewriter, word processor, pointer, communication boards, and adaptive writing instruments
- *Use of an aide to help students*—having an aide read directions, repeat oral comprehension items, read or sign test items, provide cues to maintain on-task behavior, and record answers given by the student

For children unable to participate in a state- or district-wide assessment program, states must provide alternative assessments. These may include (a) observation of the child's learning environment (sometimes called ecological assessment), (b) use of curriculum-based measurement, and (c) analysis of the student's work products (sometimes referred to as authentic assessment or portfolio assessment). The IDEA '97 requires that state educational agencies develop guidelines for alternative assessments and provide reports to the public about the number of children with disabilities (but not their names) participating in regular assessments and alternative assessments.

If an IEP team recommends exemption from state- or districtwide testing, the parent must be informed as to why the assessment was inappropriate and how the child will be assessed. Exemption from statewide assessments may result in a child's being denied the right to receive a diploma because he or she failed to demonstrate competency. Parents should also be informed of the long-term implications of an exemption decision.

Determination of Disability

After the evaluation is completed, the IEP team determines whether the student has one of 14 defined disabilities (see Table 3-2). Disabilities include "mental retardation, a hearing impairment including deafness, a speech or language impairment, a visual impairment including blindness, serious emotional disturbance (hereafter referred to as emotional

Table 3-2
Fourteen Disability Categories in the IDEA '97

1. *Autism.* A developmental disability, generally evident before age 3, that significantly affects verbal and nonverbal communication and social interaction and that adversely affects a child's educational performance. Symptoms may range from mild to severe. Other characteristics often associated with autism are engagement in repetitive activities and stereotyped movements, resistance to environmental change or change in daily routines, and unusual responses to sensory experiences. The term does not apply if a child's educational performance is adversely affected primarily because the child has an emotional disturbance.

2. *Deaf-blindness.* Concomitant hearing and visual impairments, the combination of which causes such severe communication and other developmental and educational needs that a child who is deaf and blind cannot be accommodated in special education programs solely for children with deafness or children with blindness.

3. *Deafness.* A hearing impairment that is so severe that the child is impaired in processing linguistic information through hearing, with or without amplification, and that adversely affects a child's educational performance.

4. *Emotional disturbance.* A condition in which one or more of the following characteristics is exhibited over a long period of time and to a marked degree, which adversely affects a child's educational performance: (a) an inability to learn that cannot be explained by intellectual, sensory, or health factors; (b) an inability to build or maintain satisfactory interpersonal relationships with peers and teachers; (c) inappropriate types of behavior or feelings under normal circumstances; (d) a general pervasive mood of unhappiness or depression; and (e) a tendency to develop physical symptoms or fears associated with personal or school problems. The term includes schizophrenia, but does not apply to children who are socially maladjusted unless it is determined that they have an emotional disturbance.

5. *Hearing impairment.* An impairment in hearing, whether permanent or fluctuating, that adversely affects a child's educational performance but does not meet the definition of deafness in this section.

6. *Mental retardation.* Significantly subaverage general intellectual functioning, existing concurrently with deficits in adaptive behavior and manifested during the developmental period, that adversely affects a child's educational performance.

7. *Multiple disabilities.* Concomitant impairments (such as mental retardation-blindness, mental retardation-orthopedic impairment, etc.) that, in combination, cause such severe educational needs that the child cannot be accommodated in special education programs solely for one of the impairments. The term does not include deaf-blindness.

8. *Orthopedic impairment.* A severe orthopedic impairment that adversely affects a child's educational performance. The term includes impairments caused by congenital anomaly (e.g., clubfoot, absence of some limb, etc.), impairments caused by disease (e.g., poliomyelitis, bone tuberculosis, etc.), and impairments from other causes (e.g., cerebral palsy, amputations, and fractures or burns that cause contractures).

9. *Other health impairment.* Limited strength, vitality, or alertness, including a heightened alertness to environmental stimuli, that results in limited alertness with respect to the educational environment and that adversely affects a child's educational performance. It may be due to a chronic or acute health problem—such as asthma, attention deficit disorder or attention- deficit/hyperactivity disorder, diabetes, epilepsy, a heart condition, hemophilia, lead poisoning, leukemia, nephritis, rheumatic fever, or sickle cell anemia.

10. *Specific learning disability.* A disorder in one or more of the basic psychological processes involved in understanding or in using language, spoken or written, that may manifest itself in an imperfect ability to listen, think, speak, read, write, spell, or do mathematical calculations. It may include perceptual disabilities, brain injury, minimal brain dysfunction, dyslexia, and developmental aphasia. It does not include learning problems that are primarily the result of visual, hearing, or motor disabilities; of mental retardation; of emotional disturbance; or of environmental, cultural, or economic disadvantage.

11. *Speech or language impairment.* A communication disorder, such as dysfluency (stuttering), impaired articulation, a language impairment, or a voice impairment, that adversely affects a child's educational performance.

12. *Traumatic brain injury.* An acquired injury to the brain caused by an external physical force, resulting in total or partial functional disability or psychosocial impairment or both, that adversely affects a child's educational performance. The term applies to open or closed head injuries resulting in impairments in one or more areas such as cognition; language; memory; attention; reasoning; abstract thinking; judgment; problem-solving; sensory, perceptual, and motor abilities; psychosocial behavior; physical functions; information processing; and speech. The term does not apply to brain injuries that are congenital or degenerative or were induced by birth trauma.

13. *Visual impairment.* An impairment in vision that, even with correction, adversely affects a child's educational performance. The term includes both partial sight and blindness.

14. *Developmental delays.* Delays in physical development, cognitive development, communication development, social or emotional development, and/or adaptive development experienced by children between 3 and 9 years of age who, by reason thereof, need special education and related services.

Note. These definitions have been adapted from the Federal Register, March 12, 1999, pp. 12421–12422.

disturbance), an orthopedic impairment, autism, traumatic brain injury, an other health impairment, a specific learning disability, deaf-blindness, or multiple disabilities" (Sec. 300.7). In addition, children between 3 and 9 years of age may receive services if they are experiencing developmental delays in physical, cognitive, communication, social, emotional, or adaptive development when state and local educational agencies determine that the "developmental delay" is a disability.

To find a child eligible for services under the IDEA '97, the IEP team must find not only that the child has one of the

SCHOOLIES © 2000 by John P. Wood

WHO WANTS TO BE A GRADUATE

X = 3?

Final answer?

A MORE POPULAR APPROACH TO STATE TESTING.

Copyright © 2000 by John P. Wood. Reprinted with permission.

and toddlers served under Part C of the IDEA in 1997 was 193,376.

Table 3-3 also shows that there was an increase in every disability category covered under the IDEA (except deaf-blindness, which showed about a 2% decrease) in the period from 1988 (or 1992) to 1998. The increase was over 20% in 8 of the 12 disability categories. The largest increases were in other health impairments (279.87%), traumatic brain injury (200.86%), and autism (172.86%). Improvements in identifying children with attention-deficit/hyperactivity disorder might account for the increased number of children in the other health impairments category. The increases in traumatic brain injury and autism also might be associated with improvements in identification or with a genuine increase in the occurrence of these disabilities.

A gender breakdown is available for 1994 for the following three disability categories for elementary and secondary-age students (U.S. Department of Education, 1994):

- Specific learning disability—69% males, 31% females
- Mental retardation—59% males, 41% females
- Emotional disturbance—79% males, 21% females

Overall, more than two-thirds of all students receiving special education are male (U.S. Department of Education,

14 defined disabilities but also that the disability adversely affects the child's educational performance. The definitions shown in Table 3-2 are used in most states, but states may use different labels and their own criteria for the determination of disabilities, as long as the criteria are consistent with the federal law.

In deciding whether a child is disabled for purposes of qualifying for special education and related services, the IEP team needs to consider all relevant information and ensure that all of the information is well documented. A child may not be eligible if the determining factor is lack of instruction in reading or math or limited English proficiency and the child does not meet the eligibility requirements described above. Once the IEP team determines that a child has a disability, the team has to determine whether the child requires special education and related services to meet her or his needs. If so, the IEP team must develop an IEP.

Table 3-3 shows the number of children with psychological and physical disorders, from ages 6 through 21, who received services in schools in the United States during the 1997–98 academic year under the IDEA. The largest group of children receiving services was those with specific learning disabilities (51.48%), followed by children with speech and language impairments (19.95%), mental retardation (11.28%), and emotional disturbances (8.51%). These four categories contained 91.22% of all children receiving services. The remaining 8.78% of the children had multiple disabilities, hearing impairments, orthopedic impairments, other health impairments, visual impairments, autism, deaf-blindness, or traumatic brain injury. The number of infants

Table 3-3
Number of Children Ages 6 to 21 Served Under the Individuals with Disabilities Education Act (IDEA) in 1997–98, by Disability and Percentage Change from 1988–89 to 1997–98

Disability	Number	Percent	Percent change
Specific learning disabilities	2,748,497	51.48	38.13
Speech or language impairments	1,065,074	19.95	10.54
Mental retardation	602,111	11.28	4.64
Emotional disturbances	454,363	8.51	21.97
Multiple disabilities	106,758	2.00	26.93
Hearing impairments	69,537	1.30	21.98
Orthopedic impairments	67,422	1.26	43.03
Other health impairments	190,935	3.58	279.87
Visual impairments	26,015	0.49	16.07
Autism[a]	42,487	0.80	172.86
Deaf-blindness	1,454	0.03	–2.07
Traumatic brain injury[a]	11,895	0.22	200.86
All disabilities	5,338,483	100.90	29.42

[a]The percentage changes for autism and traumatic brain injury reflect changes since 1992–93.
Source: Adapted from U.S. Department of Education (1999), pp. A-2, A-3, A-4, and II-39.

1998). The disproportion, while difficult to account for, may be related to (a) physiological or maturational differences between males and females, (b) differences in the behavior of males and females, and (c) the methods used to identify students, which may be somewhat biased against males.

The school placements of children covered by the IDEA for the 1996–97 school year were as follows (U.S. Department of Education, 1999, adapted from p. A-51).

- 45.75% were in a *regular class.* This placement includes students who receive most of their education program in a regular classroom and receive special education and related services either outside the regular classroom for less than 21% of the school day or within the regular classroom.
- 28.47% were in a *resource room.* This placement includes students who receive special education and related services outside the regular classroom for at least 21% but not more than 60% of the school day. It may include students placed in resource rooms, with part-time instruction in a regular class.
- 21.43% were in a *separate class.* This placement includes students who receive special education and related services outside the regular classroom for more than 60% of the school day. Students may be placed in self-contained special classrooms, with part-time instruction in regular classes, or placed in self-contained classrooms full-time on a regular school campus.
- 3.10% were in a *separate school.* This placement includes students who receive special education and related services in separate day schools for students with disabilities for more than 50% of the school day.
- 0.70% were in a *residential facility.* This placement includes students who receive special education and related services in a public or private residential facility, at public expense, for more than 50% of the school day.
- 0.54% were *homebound* or in a *hospital environment.* This placement includes students who receive special education and related services in a home-based or hospital program.

Individualized Education Program (IEP)

The IEP is an important document because it spells out the needs of the child with a disability and how the educational agency will satisfy these needs. It is also important because it is the first document that the parents' attorney will review, and its contents are the most likely to be challenged in a due process hearing or court of law. Table F-2 in Appendix F shows an example of an IEP form.

The IDEA '97 provides detailed and specific guidelines about how an IEP should be developed, reviewed, and altered as necessary. An IEP should provide a statement of the services the child needs to progress in meeting annual goals, to advance in the general curriculum, and to participate in extracurricular activities and other nonacademic activities. It is a team effort, bringing together the skills and resources of the educational staff and parents. Each word in the term *Individualized Education Program* has a particular meaning: *individualized* means that the program is focused on the unique needs of a specific child; *education* means that the program is directed toward learning activities; and *program* refers to specific and clearly formulated annual goals and objectives and the means of reaching those goals and objectives.

The IEP meeting, in part, serves as a communication vehicle between the parents and school personnel. The meeting enables the two parties to jointly decide the child's needs, what services will be provided to meet those needs, and what the anticipated outcomes may be. Furthermore, it allows for resolution of any differences between the parents and school personnel concerning the special educational needs of the child with a disability.

The IEP team needs to keep in mind this axiom: "The IEP determines placement." The components of the IEP described below are not discrete elements; rather, they reflect a process to be completed in logical order. An IEP team leader who opens a team meeting by recommending a placement *prior* to a consideration of the child's strengths, needs, and goals and objectives may be guilty of a serious procedural violation.

The basic components of an IEP are as follows:

1. A description of the child's present levels of educational performance and his or her individual, unique needs. The IEP team considers data collected from all sources and determines how the child's disability may affect his or her performance within the general education curriculum.
2. Concrete, realistic, and measurable goals specifying what the child should achieve within a 1-year period. Examples of annual goals include (a) the student will demonstrate mastery of third-grade reading with 90% accuracy as measured by third-grade reading tests; (b) the student will spell at a level that is 90% of that expected for her age group; (c) the student will write a five-sentence paragraph with appropriate punctuation and grammar with 90% accuracy; and (d) the student will control aggressive behavior toward other students by walking away from potential confrontations 100% of the time and practicing suitable replacement behaviors, such as running around the track, hitting a punching bag, or writing about angry feelings in a journal.

    In arriving at instructional goals and objectives, the IEP team considers (a) program content, (b) the conditions under which the learning takes place, and (c) the level of performance, as well as the child's (d) learning style (or preferred learning modalities), (e) rate of learning, and (f) need for structure. The written goals and objectives should provide for accountability, motivate children, facilitate teacher-parent communication, and focus attention on learning activities.

3. Short-term benchmarks, or instructional objectives, that are observable and measurable and correspond to manageable units of instruction. These objectives are similar to annual goals, but they focus on specific functions that the child can achieve in a short time in order to attain the annual goal. Examples of instructional objectives include (a) the student will write 20 letters with fewer than 2 illegible letters by Nov. 1, 2001; (b) the student will read fourth-grade material at 40 to 60 words per minute with fewer than 5 errors by Dec. 1, 2001; (c) the student will button and unbutton his coat within 2 minutes without making any errors by Jan. 15, 2001; and (d) the student will raise her hand and be recognized by the teacher before contributing opinions and answers in 9 out of 10 instances by March 15, 2001.

4. A description of the special education and related services as well as the supplementary aids needed by the child. All special services required to meet the unique needs of the child should be specified.

5. A description of any individual modifications that need to be made in the administration of state- and district-wide assessment programs of student achievement and how the child will be assessed if the state- and district-wide programs are determined to be inappropriate.

6. The date on which special services will begin, the location of the services, the anticipated length of time for which services will be given, and the number of minutes per day, week, month, or year that the services will be provided. The IEP must be developed before special education and related services are provided to the child. Before special education services can be provided, the parents must give their consent to the placement in writing.

7. A statement of needed transition services for the child when age 14 is reached (or younger, if a younger age is determined to be appropriate by the IEP team). The focus should be on the child's course of study, such as participation in advanced placement courses or a vocational education program.

8. A statement of needed transition services for the child when age 16 is reached (or younger, if a younger age is determined to be appropriate by the IEP team), as well as a statement of interagency responsibilities or any linkages needed among agencies. The focus might be on one or more of the following: instruction, related services, community experiences, employment, post-school adult living objectives, daily living skills, and a functional vocational evaluation. The student has a right to participate in writing this part of the IEP, and the student's needs, preferences, and interests must be considered. Table F-3 in Appendix F shows a form useful in designing an individual transition plan.

9. A statement that the student was notified of his or her rights at least 1 year before the student reached the age of majority under state law. These rights pertain to special education services such as available programs, changes in programs, and assessments, as well as any other rights previously accorded to the parent, including the right to inspect educational records.

10. Justification for the child's placement. The IEP must be designed, to the maximum extent appropriate, to instruct a child in the LRE. The IEP should include a statement about the modifications needed for the child to be successful in a general education curriculum. If the child cannot be educated within the general education environment, the IEP must provide justification for placement in a more restrictive setting.

11. A description of the objective criteria and evaluation procedures, as well as relevant schedules, for determining whether the child is achieving the goals and objectives. Reports must be made to parents at least as often as they are made to parents of children who are not disabled.

12. A statement of how the child's parents will be regularly informed of their child's progress toward the goals and objectives and the extent to which the progress is sufficient to enable the child to meet the goals.

13. Strategies, such as positive behavioral supports and interventions, in the case of children whose behavior impedes their learning or that of others.

14. Consideration of the language needs of the child, particularly as those needs relate to the child's IEP, for a child who has limited English proficiency.

15. Provision for instruction in Braille for a child who is blind or visually impaired, unless the IEP team determines that instruction in Braille is not appropriate.

16. Consideration of the communication abilities of the child. For example, in the case of a child who is hearing impaired, the assessment focuses on the child's (a) communication needs, (b) preferred mode of communication, (c) linguistic needs, (d) hearing loss and potential for using residual hearing, (e) academic levels, and (f) social, emotional, and cultural needs, including opportunities for peer interactions and communication.

17. A statement of the child's needs for assistive technology.

Each local educational agency shall take steps to ensure that at least one of the child's parents has an opportunity to be present and participate at each IEP meeting. Specifically, the local educational agency shall notify the parents of the purpose, time, and location of the meeting early enough to ensure that they can attend or reschedule. Additionally, the parents must be informed that they may invite someone who has knowledge or special expertise regarding their child, and they must be informed about who will be attending the IEP meeting.

The meeting must be scheduled at a mutually convenient time and place. If the student is 14 years old (or younger, if appropriate), the local educational agency shall invite the student. If the public agency is unable to convince the parents that they should attend the IEP meeting, the meeting may be

"Oscar, I do not consider 'beating some sense into their stubborn little heads' an acceptable behavioral objective."

Courtesy of *Phi Delta Kappan* and the artist, Bardulf Ueland.

conducted without a parent in attendance. However, the public agency must document its attempts to arrange the IEP meeting. This includes keeping detailed records of telephone calls, written correspondence, and visits to the home and businesses. And the school district must provide a copy of the IEP to the parents.

Because they feel uncomfortable at the meeting, some parents may prefer to receive information passively, rather than contribute actively. By encouraging parents to share their perceptions about their child's needs (and their own needs related to helping the child excel in school), you may enable them to take a more active role in the meeting.

The IDEA '97 discourages parents and schools from bringing an attorney to an IEP meeting. If parents do bring an attorney to the IEP meeting, they will not be reimbursed for attorneys' fees incurred during the meeting unless the meeting was ordered by a hearing officer or court or allowed by the state.

An IEP meeting is not a democratic process; decisions are reached not by majority rule, but by consensus. The IEP team members (public agency personnel and parents) are equal participants in the IEP process. If the parties reach consensus, the IEP goes into effect. If not, and if the parents had previously given written consent for their child to be placed in special education, the public agency has the legal obligation to formulate and implement an IEP. The parents may file for a due process hearing to resolve any disagreements.

Discipline Procedures

The IDEA '97 regulations dealing with suspensions and expulsions are complex. Schools must maintain a record of the total consecutive and cumulative days that a child has been suspended. If a child has been suspended for 10 school days or fewer in a school year, the child may be disciplined in the same manner as a child without a disability.

If a child with a disability is removed for disciplinary reasons from her or his current educational placement for more than 10 consecutive school days (or for a series of shorter suspensions that cumulatively total more than 10 school days), resulting in a change in placement in a school year, the school district must ensure that the following steps are taken (see Figure 3-1):

1. An IEP team meeting must be convened, and the parents must be notified of the change in the child's placement resulting from a code of conduct violation that applies to all children. A change in placement would occur if (a) the school suspended a child for more than 10 consecutive school days or (b) the IEP team determined that a series of short-term suspensions totaling more than 10 school days constituted a pattern because they cumulated to more than 10 school days in a school year and because factors such as the length of each removal, the total amount of time the child was removed, and the proximity of the removals to one another had imposed an unreasonable limitation on the child's right to a FAPE.

2. Either before or not later than 10 business days after first removing the student for more than 10 school days, if the school district has not previously conducted a functional behavioral assessment, the team must convene an IEP meeting to develop a functional behavioral assessment plan. As soon as practicable after developing a functional behavioral assessment plan and conducting the assessment, the public agency shall convene another IEP meeting to develop a behavioral intervention plan for the child. If the child has a behavioral intervention plan, the IEP team shall review it and modify it as necessary not later than 10 business days after removing the student for more than 10 school days. These meetings may be combined.

3. A hearing officer may order a change in the child's placement to an appropriate interim alternative educational setting for not more than 45 days if the child's behavior is likely to result in injury to the child or to others. If ordered by a hearing officer, the IEP team will determine the most appropriate setting. A public agency may convene the IEP team and unilaterally change a child's placement for not more than 45 days if the child was in possession of a weapon in school or at a school function or knowingly possessed or used illegal drugs or sold or solicited the sale of a controlled substance while at school or a school function. If the parents appeal the permanent placement recommended by the IEP team, at the end of the 45 days the school must (a) return the child to the original placement,

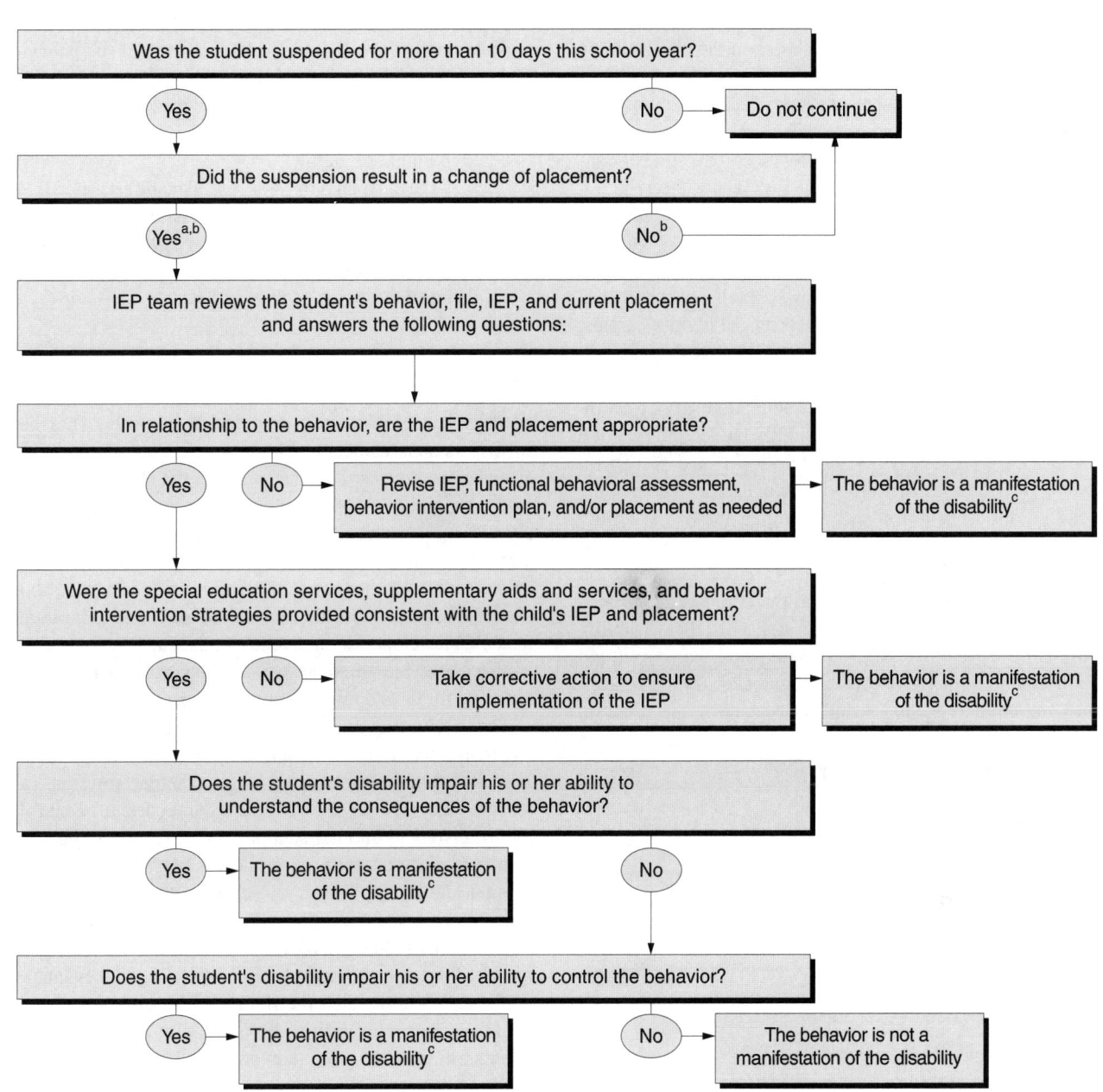

a The IEP team must conduct a manifestation determination hearing to determine whether there is a relationship between the student's disability and the behavior subject to the disciplinary action. This hearing must take place no later than 10 school days after the date of a decision resulting in a disciplinary change of placement (a removal of more than 10 consecutive days or short-term suspensions of more than 10 days total that constitute a pattern).

b If the student had a previous behavior intervention plan (BIP), it must be reviewed, whether or not there was a change of placement. If a functional behavioral assessment (FBA) was not previously completed within 10 business days after the 11th cumulative day of suspension, the IEP team must develop an assessment plan to complete an FBA and a BIP. A school administrator and the student's special education teacher must determine and provide the services needed for the student to progress in the general curriculum and to meet the IEP goals.

c The student cannot be removed for another day if that removal would result in a change of placement (other than a 45-day interim placement for bringing drugs or weapons to school), unless the school and the parents otherwise agree. A free appropriate public education (FAPE) must be provided in the least restrictive environment (LRE).

Figure 3-1. Procedural requirements for the disciplinary suspension of students served under the IDEA '97. Flow chart developed with the assistance of Guy McBride.

(b) obtain a 45-day extension from a hearing officer, or (c) obtain an injunction from a court barring the child from his or her original school based on the child's being a danger to himself or herself or to others.

4. The IEP team shall meet not later than 10 school days after the date a decision is made to change a student's placement for more than 10 school days for a code of conduct violation. The IEP team shall consider the relationship between the child's disability and the behavior subject to disciplinary action (referred to as a *manifestation determination review*). The IEP team does this by reviewing evaluation and diagnostic results, observational information, information supplied by the child's parents, and the child's IEP and placement. The IEP team will need to determine whether the IEP and placement were appropriate and whether special education services, supplementary aids and services, and behavior intervention strategies consistent with the child's IEP and placement were provided. The team will then decide whether the child's disability did or did not impair his or her ability (a) to understand the impact and consequences of the aberrant behavior and (b) to control the aberrant behavior.

5. If the IEP team concludes that (a) the IEP was inappropriate or implemented inappropriately, (b) the disability impaired the child's ability to understand the impact and consequences of the aberrant behavior, or (c) the disability impaired the child's ability to control the aberrant behavior, then the aberrant behavior is considered to be a manifestation of the disability. If the IEP team arrives at

any of these conclusions, the team must take immediate steps to remediate the deficiencies in the child's IEP or placement. If the IEP team determines that the behavior was *not* a manifestation of the disability, then the child is subject to the same disciplinary procedures that a child without disabilities receives, with certain exceptions noted in number 6 below.

6. Even if the misbehavior was not a manifestation of the child's disability, the child with a disability does not lose the right to a FAPE under the IDEA '97 during a long-term suspension or expulsion or when placed in an alternative interim setting.

Reviews and Reevaluations

Reviews and reevaluations serve several purposes. They help to (a) evaluate whether the child continues to be eligible for special education services (i.e., whether the child continues to have a disability); (b) evaluate the child's progress; (c) identify any difficulties with the IEP and determine the reasons for such difficulties; (d) identify new areas for instruction; (e) determine whether any further information is needed about the child's present levels of performance and educational needs; (f) develop new intervention plans to meet new needs that have been identified; and (g) provide feedback to those responsible for developing and implementing the plan.

The child's IEP should be reviewed periodically—but not less than once a year—to determine whether the goals and objectives are being achieved and whether revisions are needed. A review of the IEP may be needed (a) when the child transfers to another school district, (b) when there is a change in placement, or (c) on the anniversary of the child's original placement. The school also must reevaluate a child with a disability if conditions warrant it or if the child's parent or teacher requests a reevaluation, but at least once every 3 years. Table F-4 in Appendix F shows a triennial evaluation worksheet. Additionally, the IDEA '97 requires that parents of children with disabilities be notified at least as often as parents of children who are nondisabled (through report cards or other means) about how the children are progressing in meeting their annual goals and objectives.

Here are some typical questions that might be addressed on a reevaluation.

- Are the goals and objectives of the IEP being achieved? For example, has the student's reading (or mathematics, written expression, etc.) level improved?
- What progress is the student making toward achieving the objectives of the regular curriculum?
- If improvement has occurred, what has been most helpful?
- If improvement has not occurred, what factors might account for the lack of improvement (e.g., ineffective instruction, sporadic provision of services, student not attending school regularly, student not doing homework)?
- Is the student still eligible for special education services? If so, what is her or his disability?

SCHOOLIES © 1999 by John P. Wood

Here's your new student and a stack of blank incident report forms.

Copyright © 1999 by John P. Wood. Reprinted with permission.

- Are the previously identified problem areas (e.g., phonological awareness, verbal memory, executive functions) still weaknesses?
- Are any new problems apparent? If so, what are they?
- How does the student's identified condition (e.g., ADHD, autistic disorder, learning disability, mental retardation) affect her or his education (e.g., academic performance, classroom behavior, and completion of homework)?
- Would changes in instructional strategies, educational placement, services provided, or home-school instruction be of benefit?
- Would the use of assistive technology (e.g., word processor, calculator, text reading program) help the student's learning and academic performance?
- How much would additional accommodations or modifications (e.g., extended testing time, use of large print materials) help the student demonstrate academic proficiency?
- If accommodations or modifications have been used, which ones are no longer appropriate?
- What strategies are appropriate to assist the student in transitioning from special education to regular education?
- Should the student have an alternative plan developed if she or he is no longer eligible for special education?
- What accommodations or modifications are reasonable to implement in the general education setting to help the student be successful if she or he is no longer in special education? How should progress in regular education be monitored?

The assessment principles that apply to the initial evaluation also apply to the reevaluation. To conduct the reevaluation, you will need to (a) review existing evaluation data, including results from teacher-made and statewide tests, (b) obtain information about the child's functioning from the teacher and parents, (c) observe the student in various settings, and (d) determine what additional data are needed—such as data obtained from rating scales, medical evaluations, and informal procedures. Formal psychological testing may not be needed for reevaluations if there is sufficient information to make the appropriate decisions and recommendations without the additional testing. Formal psychological testing, however, remains a useful part of a reevaluation when handicapping conditions, beyond or other than those previously identified, are suspected; when the student's level of functioning has changed notably; when there are gaps in the previous assessment; or when the student's parent or guardian requests the administration of formal tests. The parents are not required to justify their request. If the parents wanted their child to be tested for some other reason (e.g., aptitude for a certain trade), the school could deny the request and the parents would have the option of requesting a due process hearing. Documentation of progress by use of standardized tests may also be warranted when an exit from special education is being considered. Generally, if the IEP team agrees that the present placement is appropriate, extensive evaluation is likely not needed.

Parents are an integral part of the reevaluation process. The IDEA '97 requires that local education agencies (a) notify parents of their right to request standardized instruments or other assessments at the time of reevaluation, (b) notify parents that their child needs to be reevaluated, (c) describe the procedures that will be used in the reevaluation, and (d) obtain written parental consent for additional assessments. However, consent for the additional assessments is not required if the local education agency takes reasonable steps to obtain parental consent and the parents fail to respond to the request.

The IDEA Part C: Infants and Toddlers with Disabilities

Public Law 99-457, passed in 1986, amended Public Law 94-142 to (a) authorize an early intervention program for infants and toddlers who have a disability and for their families and (b) extend all the rights and protections of Public Law 94-142 to children with disabilities from ages 3 through 5 years. The IDEA '97 reauthorized the law, which is now referred to as Part C: Infants and Toddlers with Disabilities. At a state's discretion, infants and children from birth to age 2 years also can receive services if they are raised in an adverse environment (such as in a family in which there is child abuse or neglect) or if they are at risk of having substantial developmental delays if early intervention services are not provided.

Once a child is identified, an Individualized Family Service Plan (IFSP) is developed with parental consent. The IFSP includes a statement of (a) the child's present levels of development, (b) the family's strengths and weaknesses, (c) major outcomes that can be expected, (d) specific services to be provided, (e) the place where intervention services will be provided, (f) the dates of initiation and the duration of these services, (g) the name of the child's service coordinator, and (h) steps to be taken to support the transition of the toddler to preschool or to appropriate service providers. Like an IEP, an IFSP should be reviewed at least once a year and revised as needed.

Court Interpretations of the IDEA

The IDEA, which is a complex and intricate law covering a myriad of issues pertaining to the education of children with disabilities, has been the subject of much litigation since its inception. Its sheer volume—and the hundreds of issues it addresses—leaves the IDEA open to different interpretations. Courts become involved in interpreting and implementing the provisions of the IDEA because the IDEA permits a party adversely affected by an administrative decision to obtain a judicial review. The IDEA gives courts broad discretion to grant appropriate relief to the party who prevails at a hearing. This section provides information about how U.S. Circuit Courts of Appeals and the U.S. Supreme Court have interpreted the

IDEA, based on cases heard in the 1990s and a seminal case heard in the 1982. Although you may not be able to prevent litigation, the information contained in this section should help to prepare you for any litigation that does occur.

Evolving case law is expanding understanding of the requirements of the IDEA. For example, the IDEA has always said that children are entitled to nonmedical-related services if they are needed to receive a FAPE. However, the courts disagreed as to just how "medical service" was to be defined. But in 1999 the U.S. Supreme Court, in *Cedar Rapids Community School District v. Garret F.,* said that if a service was needed to provide a FAPE and it did not have to be provided by a doctor, then the child was entitled to the service no matter what the cost.

No case is a "sure" win, either for the parents or for public entities. The prudent practitioner remembers that the old maxim "There are two sides to every argument" has particular significance within the context of litigation. There are several reasons why the outcome of any litigation is uncertain. Statutes and case decisions are interpreted differently by different judges, attorneys, and educators in different parts of the country. One Circuit Court of Appeals may issue a ruling that is in direct conflict with a ruling from another Circuit Court of Appeals. One judge will hold that a ruling stands for a certain legal principle and another judge will hold the opposite; that is the nature of law. Even within the same Circuit Court of Appeals, two seemingly similar cases may have different outcomes. One case is decided based on a child's educational progress, and the other case is decided based on the procedures followed by the school district in providing services to the child. Still, an understanding of the rulings of the two highest level courts in the nation may reduce the need for litigation associated with the IDEA.

Decisions from a U.S. District Court are appealed to a U.S. Circuit Court of Appeals; rulings from a U.S. Circuit Court of Appeals are appealed to the U.S. Supreme Court. The U.S. Supreme Court usually hears cases only when there is either a split ruling between two or more circuit courts or a compelling public policy question at issue. Rulings from the U.S. Supreme Court and the U.S. Circuit Court of Appeals for your state are binding on lower courts of your state. Rulings from other courts, including other U.S. Circuit Courts of Appeals, may influence courts in your jurisdiction, but they do not carry the same weight as the rulings of your own U.S. Circuit Court of Appeals.

If you are seeking legal authority or justification for a position, read the full text of the cases you are interested in, do a complete search of relevant cases, and remember that different courts may have issued contrary rulings. Cases are available on the Internet (e.g., LEXIS database at www.lexis-nexis.com or FindLaw at www.findlaw.com) and in publications found in law school libraries, such as the *Individuals with Disabilities Education Law Reporter* (IDELR) and *West's Federal Reporter* (3rd edition or later). The following subsections discuss some important issues dealt with in various IDEA cases.

Critical issues for the courts. When federal courts hear cases challenging decisions made under the IDEA, their focus is on whether the school district complied with the regulations set forth in the IDEA. Courts will attempt to determine whether the child has received (a) a FAPE; (b) services tailored to meet his or her unique needs and reasonably calculated to enable the child to receive educational benefits (courts will determine this in part by evaluating the IEP and how it has been implemented and by reviewing the child's attendance record, grades, personal conduct, and academic achievement); and (c) an education in a setting with his or her nondisabled peers to the maximum extent appropriate (*Burlington v. Massachusetts Department of Education,* 1996; *Poolaw v. Bishop,* 1995; *Stockton v. Barbour County Board of Education,* 1997; *Walczak v. Florida Union Free School District,* 1998).

Protection under the IDEA would be unwarranted if a student had not received a disability diagnosis and an IEP had not been developed. Allowing a student the safeguards and benefits of the IDEA before she or he is diagnosed as being disabled not only would be premature but also would take resources away from students who have been diagnosed as disabled (*Doe v. Board of Education of the Elyria City Schools,* 1998). Similarly, a gifted child with a learning disability who is performing *adequately* in school and whose curriculum has been modified to help her or him function better in the classroom may not qualify for services under the IDEA, even though she or he is not achieving up to her or his potential (*Norton v. Orinda Union School District,* 1999).

Educational benefit. The standard for measuring educational benefit under the IDEA is not merely whether the placement is reasonably calculated to provide the child with educational benefits but, rather, whether the child makes progress toward the goals set forth in the IEP (*County of San Diego v. California Special Education Hearing Office,* 1996). Acquisition of reading, writing, spelling, and arithmetic skills and improvement in test scores are other measures of educational benefit. The IDEA does not specify any level of educational benefit that must be provided through an IEP, but the services must be appropriate for each child with a disability. However, the educational placement does not have to be the best possible one, or one that maximizes the potential of the child, or one designed to have the child achieve outstanding results in school (*Board of Education v. Rowley,* 1982; *Board of Education of Montgomery County v. Brett Y.,* 1998; *Cronkite v. Long Beach Unified School District,* 1999; *E. S. v. Independent School District, No. 196,* 1998; *Walczak v. Florida Union Free School District,* 1998; *Yankton School District v. Schramm,* 1996).

Whether a child with a disability is making progress in school (or, more technically, receiving a FAPE) depends on how the courts interpret the entire record (*Fort Zumwalt School District v. Clynes,* 1997). When the courts rule that the school district is not providing an appropriate education, the courts can require the school to pay for alternative services, which could include placement in a residential facility (*Mrs. B. v. Milford Board of Education,* 1997; *Ojai Unified School District v. Jackson,* 1993).

Role of administrative law judge (or hearing officer). An administrative law judge's decision is given considerable weight by courts when the decision shows careful, impartial consideration of all the evidence and demonstrates sensitivity to the complexities of the issues presented (*County of San Diego v. California Special Education Hearing Office,* 1996). The responsibility for determining whether a challenged IEP will provide a child with an appropriate education initially rests with administrative hearing and review officers, whose rulings are subject to independent judicial review (*Walczak v. Florida Union Free School District,* 1998). "The IDEA does not grant federal courts a license to substitute their own notions of a sound educational policy for those of the local school authorities, or to disregard the findings developed in state administrative proceedings" (*Hartmann v. Loudoun County Board of Education,* 1997). Furthermore, when a case is appealed, the party challenging the state administrative hearing officer's decision has the burden of proof (*E.S. v. Independent School District, No. 196,* 1998). Although courts are required to give due weight to the results of administrative hearings, courts also are required to make an independent decision based on a preponderance of evidence available to them in the proceedings (*Stockton v. Barbour County Board of Education,* 1997).

Evaluation procedures. It is the school district's duty to ensure that evaluations are conducted by a multidisciplinary team that includes at least one teacher or other specialist with knowledge of the child's suspected disability (*Seattle School District v. B.S.,* 1996). The IDEA grants schools the right to conduct their own 3-year evaluation of a student in special education. Schools are not compelled to rely on an independent evaluation obtained by the parents (*Andress v. Cleveland Independent School District,* 1995; *Johnson v. Duneland School Corporation,* 1996). Furthermore, the Fourth Circuit Court of Appeals said that psychological evaluations provide important information in formulating an IEP (*Board of Education of Montgomery County v. Brett Y.,* 1998). (Note that public entities are required to consider parent-initiated evaluations if the evaluations meet agency criteria.)

Individualized education program (IEP). Courts will consider several areas in evaluating whether an IEP is reasonably calculated to provide meaningful educational benefits. For example, they will consider whether the program is (a) individualized, based on the student's assessment and performance; (b) administered in the LRE; (c) provided in a coordinated manner; and (d) demonstrated to produce positive academic and nonacademic benefits (*Cypress-Fairbanks Independent School District v. Michael F.,* 1997). Schools do not violate the IDEA when they rely on information obtained by other schools to develop their own IEPs, as long as the information is relevant (*Poolaw v. Bishop,* 1995).

School districts bear the burden of proving compliance with the IDEA in an administrative hearing, including proving the appropriateness of the evaluation and the subsequent IEP. School districts, however, are not required to prove the *inappropriateness* of any competing plans advocated by parents (*Carlisle Area School v. Scott P.,* 1995; *Seattle School District No. 1 v. B.S.,* 1996). In addition, as long as the student is benefiting from his or her education, it is up to the school district, and not up to the parents, to determine the appropriate interventions (*E.S. v. Independent School District No. 196,* 1998). Parents "are not entitled to dictate educational methodology or to compel a school district to supply a specific program to their disabled child" (*Tucker v. Calloway County Board of Education,* 1998).

In evaluating the adequacy of an IEP, the courts will examine the facts available at the time the IEP was written, and not facts pertinent at a later date. However, the implementation of the IEP is a continuing activity and must be evaluated as such. A school district cannot "ignore the fact that an IEP is clearly failing, nor can it continue to implement year after year, without change, an IEP which fails to confer educational benefits on the student" (*O'Toole v. Olathe District Schools Unified School District No. 233,* 1997).

An IEP will satisfy the requirements of the IDEA only if it is likely to produce progress, not regression or trivial educational advancement (*M.C. and G.C. v. Central Regional School District,* 1996). The IEP must offer a meaningful basis for measuring a student's progress (*Cleveland Heights v. Boss,* 1998) and contain strategies that attempt to reduce the incidence of serious problem behavior that impairs a student's educational progress (*M.C. and G.C. v. Central Regional School District,* 1996). As long as the IEP is reasonably developed to enable a child to receive educational benefits, there is no denial of a FAPE (*Board of Education of Montgomery County v. Brett Y.,* 1998; *Board of Education v. Rowley,* 1982). If a child's intervention requires consistent implementation, both inside and outside the classroom, the IEP must include provisions for parent training; if not, the school district can be held liable for compensatory services because of an improper IEP (*M.C. and G.C. v. Central Regional School District,* 1996).

Least restrictive environment (LRE). The IDEA requires that a child with a disability be placed in a general education classroom if she or he can receive an appropriate education with the help of supplementary aids and support services. These services include "resource rooms, itinerant instruction, … speech and language therapy, special education training for the regular teacher, behavior modification programs, or any other available aids or services appropriate to the child's particular disabilities. The school must also make efforts to modify the regular education program to accommodate a disabled child …. Thus, even if a child with disabilities cannot be educated satisfactorily in a regular education classroom, the child must still be included in school programs with nondisabled children wherever possible" (*Oberti v. Board of Education of the Borough of Clementon School District,* 1993).

When a child presents a clear and present danger to others, a school may petition a hearing officer to order the child's removal from the school. Consistent with previous case law, the IDEA '97 requires the hearing officer to determine whether the school made reasonable efforts to minimize the risk of harm in the child's current placement. If the school did not have an appropriate behavioral plan or if the plan was not properly administered, the courts may rule in favor of the parents and child—even if the school's documentation of dangerous behavior is extensive (*Oberti v. Board of Education of the Borough of Clementon School District,* 1993).

The IDEA requires that a child's placement have some educational benefit and be delivered in the LRE—the IDEA does not, however, require schools to provide an optimal education (*Carlisle Area School v. Scott P.,* 1995). Ideally, courts will consider several issues in interpreting the LRE provision of the IDEA. These include (a) the extent to which the school district has made a reasonable effort to accommodate the child in a general education classroom; (b) the educational benefits available to the child in a general education classroom as compared with the benefits provided in a special education class; (c) the nonacademic benefits of interaction with children who are not disabled; (d) the possible negative effects on the other students and teacher of including the child in a general education classroom; and (e) the cost of mainstreaming the child in a general education classroom (*Oberti v. Board of Education of the Borough of Clementon School District,* 1993; *Sacramento City School District v. Rachel H.,* 1994). Furthermore, "the school bears the burden of proving compliance with the mainstreaming requirement of IDEA, regardless of which party (the child and parents or the school) brought the claim under IDEA before the district court" (*Oberti v. Board of Education of the Borough of Clementon School District,* 1993).

School districts need to consider the relative costs of various alternative placements. If these estimated costs are inflated, schools can lose credibility in the court's eyes (*Sacramento City School District v. Rachel H.,* 1994). The norm in American public education is for children to be educated in day programs if they reside at home and receive the support of their families. A residential program is more restrictive than a local extended day program (*Walczak v. Florida Union Free School District,* 1998).

Courts also have recognized that mainstreaming is not always possible: "The IDEA's broad mandate to provide handicapped children with a FAPE designed to meet the unique needs of each handicapped child is fairly imprecise in its mechanics. This vagueness reflects Congress' clear intent to leave educational policy-making to state and local education officials.... School officials therefore retain maximum flexibility to tailor education programs as closely as possible to the needs of each handicapped child .... In some cases, such as where the child's handicap is particularly severe, it will be impossible to provide any meaningful education to the student in a mainstream environment" (*Poolaw v. Bishop,* 1995). "Mainstreaming is not appropriate when the nature or severity of the disability is such that education in general education classes with use of supplementary aids and services cannot be achieved satisfactorily" (*Hartmann v. Loudoun County Board of Education,* 1997). The social benefits of mainstreaming are subordinate to the requirement that children with a disability receive educational benefit (*Hartmann v. Loudoun County Board of Education,* 1997).

Private school placement.   Parents who send their child to a private school or treatment center *without* the consent of the state or local school authorities—before, during, or after a review hearing to address their request for a change in placement—do so at their own financial risk. Schools must have the opportunity to evaluate the child and to develop an IEP before the parents remove the child from the public schools. School districts do not have to pay for the cost of education, including special education and related services, for a child with a disability at a private school (a) if the school district made a FAPE available to the child in a timely manner and (b) if the parents elected to place the child in a private school or facility *without* approval of the school district (*Burlington v. Massachusetts Department of Education,* 1996; *Foley v. Special School District of St. Louis County,* 1998; *Heather S. v. State of Wisconsin,* 1997; *K.R. v. Anderson Community School Corporation,* 1997; *Kathleen H., Larry H., and Daniel H. v. Massachusetts Department of Education,* 1998; *Russman v. Board of Education of the Enlarged City School District of the City of Watervliet,* 1998; *Thomas R. W. v. Massachusetts Department of Education,* 1997; *Tucker v. Calloway County Board of Education,* 1998). However, reimbursement after a unilateral placement is possible when the school district has engaged in a serious procedural failure, such as failing to locate children with disabilities who are in need of services (*Doe v. Metropolitan Nashville Public Schools,* 1998).

Courts will consider that placement of a child in a residential treatment facility is appropriate when (a) the placement is supportive of the child's education, (b) a child's medical, social, or emotional problems that require residential placement are intertwined with educational problems, and (c) the placement is primarily to help the child benefit from special education (*County of San Diego v. California Special Education Hearing Office,* 1996; *Schoenfeld v. Parkway School District,* 1998; *Stockton v. Barbour County Board of Education,* 1997; *Walczak v. Florida Union Free School District,* 1998). But courts will not award reimbursement costs for a residential placement simply because the placement would enable the child to reach his or her full potential (also see "Educational benefit" above; *Walczak v. Florida Union Free School District,* 1998).

Special services provided in public schools. The IDEA does not require schools to provide medical services, but it does require schools to provide related services that will enable students to attend school if these services do not have to be provided by a licensed physician. The cost to the school system is not a factor if the services are needed for the child to receive a FAPE (*Cedar Rapids Community School District v. Garret F.,* 1999; *Morton Community Unit School District v. J.M.,* 1998).

A special service requested by parents, such as transportation from a private school to a public school for speech therapy, need not be granted by the school district if the service is not related to the child's disability. However, other considerations also should be taken into account in evaluating transportation needs, such as (a) the child's age, (b) the distance the child must travel, (c) the nature of the area through which the child must pass, (d) the child's access to private assistance in making the trip, and (e) the availability of other forms of public assistance in route, such as crossing guards or public transit (*Donald B. v. Board of School Commissioners of Mobile County,* 1997). The "related services" provision of the IDEA refers to services that may be required to help a child with a disability benefit from special education.

Stay-put provision. The IDEA requires that school districts permit children to remain in their current educational placement during any administrative hearings, as well as during any additional proceedings, unless the parents and the school district otherwise agree, until a decision has been reached about the child's placement. The stay-put provision has two purposes. First, it gives parents the choice of keeping their child in her or his existing program until their dispute with the school district is resolved. Second, it prevents schools from having unilateral authority to exclude disabled students from school.

The stay-put provision applies to students currently enrolled in special education—it does not automatically apply to every student who files an application for special education. If this were permitted, then "an avenue will be open for disruptive, non-disabled students to forestall any attempts at routine discipline by simply requesting a disability evaluation and demanding to 'stay put'" (*Rodiriecus v. Waukegan School District,* 1996). However, there may be circumstances in which a child with a disability who has not yet been identified by the school district or who has been misidentified will be permitted to stay in her or his present class until the dispute has been resolved. Courts will examine psychological reports and teacher evaluations to assist them in deciding how to rule and whether to grant preliminary injunctions.

Overall, in order for the courts to invoke the stay-put provision, "the student must be or reasonably should have been determined to be eligible through the administrative procedures of the IDEA" (Office for Special Education Programs Memorandum No. 95-16, cited in *Rodiriecus v. Waukegan*

School District, 1996). Therefore, "before a court invokes the IDEA placement protection provision, petitioners must reasonably demonstrate that the school officials knew of, or should have known of, a student's genuine disability" (*Rodiriecus v. Waukegan School District,* 1996). However, parents (a) may unilaterally withdraw their child from a public school placement, (b) are not bound by the "stay-put" requirement, and (c) do not need to request a due process hearing prior to withdrawing their child from school (*Burlington v. Massachusetts Department of Education,* 1996).

Special services provided in religious schools. The IDEA creates a neutral government program that dispenses aid to individual children with disabilities, not to schools. Therefore, if a child with a disability chooses to enroll in a sectarian school, the Establishment Clause of the Constitution does not prevent the school district from furnishing the child with special services to facilitate the child's education, such as a sign language interpreter or physical and occupational therapy (*Zobrest v. Catalina Foothills School District,* 1993; *Peck v. Lansing School District,* 1998). Direct grants of government aid to sectarian schools, however, are not covered by the IDEA (*Zobrest v. Catalina Foothills School District,* 1993).

Compensatory education. In order for a student to receive compensatory education beyond his or her 21st year, the school district must flagrantly fail to comply with the requirements of the IDEA—that is, the school district must have engaged in a pattern of gross and prolonged deprivation of the student's right to a FAPE (e.g., waiting 30 months or longer to locate an appropriate placement for a child, unduly delaying a hearing, failing to place a child in a facility that can provide an appropriate education; *Carlisle Area School v. Scott P.,* 1995).

Disabilities covered under the IDEA. The IDEA does not require a school district to fund the cost of special education for medical, social, or emotional problems that are not directly related to a child's learning problems (*Board of Education of Montgomery County v. Brett Y.,* 1998). For example, a child who fails to attend school because of defiance toward his or her parents is behaving in a way that is likely unrelated to a learning problem. Once a student's misbehavior has been found to be unrelated to his or her disability, there is no justification for treating him or her differently from a child who is not disabled.

The IDEA requires states to provide children with a disability the right (i.e., access) to a FAPE. However, the provisions of the IDEA were not designed to shield special education students from the normal consequences of their actions if their actions have nothing to do with their disabilities (*Doe v. Board of Education of Oak Park,* 1997).

In order to implement eligibility criteria, the courts will review the child's record and come to some decision about the appropriate diagnosis. For example, schools might maintain that "conduct disorder" is the proper diagnosis, whereas parents might maintain that "serious emotional disturbance" is the proper diagnosis (*Muller v. Committee on Special Education of the East Islip Union Free School District,* 1998; *Springer v. Fairfax County School Board,* 1998). Children with a conduct disorder only or those who are socially maladjusted only may not be eligible to receive services under the IDEA, whereas those who are emotionally disturbed are eligible for services. However, children who have a conduct disorder (or who are socially maladjusted) and who also are emotionally disturbed would be eligible for services if otherwise qualified.

Notification of parental rights.   Courts will look closely at the record submitted by the schools to see whether the parents were informed of their rights under the IDEA, including their right to a due process hearing (*Thompson v. Board of the Special School District No. 1,* 1998).

Individual rights to sue.   Parents have the right to sue a state in order to receive services mandated by the IDEA (*Marie O., Gabriel C., and Kyle G. v. Edgar and Spagnolo,* 1997).

Representation in court.   The IDEA grants parents ample procedural rights to ensure their active involvement in all stages of the development and implementation of their child's IEP, even through administrative hearings. However, non-attorneys, including a non-attorney parent, do not have the right to represent another person (or their child) in federal court (*Collinsgru v. Palmyra Board of Education,* 1998; *Shevtsov v. Los Angeles Unified School District,* 1998; *Wenger v. Canastota Central School District,* 1998). Under the Federal Rules of Civil Procedure, some courts have appointed counsel to represent a child if the court believes that the child's position merits consideration in court (*Wenger v. Canastota Central School District,* 1998).

Reimbursement.   Once a court holds that (a) the provisions of the IDEA have been violated, (b) exhaustive administrative remedies were tried before the child was placed in another school, and (c) the original school has been notified, the court can grant appropriate relief, including payment for tuition at a private school and attorneys' fees. For example, when (a) the IEP has been shown to be inappropriate, (b) parents have followed the procedures outlined in the IDEA '97, and (c) private placement has been found to be appropriate, then the courts may order a school system to reimburse the parents for their expenses associated with the private placement (*Hines v. Tullahoma City School System,* 1998; *Kari H. v. Franklin Special School District,* 1997; *Ridgewood Board of Education v. N.E.,* 1999). Reimbursement to the parents can be made retroactively (*Burlington v. Massachusetts Department of Education,* 1996).

The major problem faced by litigants on both sides of these expensive disputes is that the IDEA does not define what standards should be applied to determine whether a child's IEP is appropriate. In *Florence County School District Four v. Carter* (1993), for example, the Fourth Circuit Court of Appeals considered that an IEP with a goal of 4 months' progress in a year's time for a bright child with a learning disability only guaranteed that she would fall further and further behind. The circuit court affirmed the district court's conclusion that the IEP, therefore, failed to provide Shannon Carter with a FAPE—that is, with "more than trivial or minimal progress." Data submitted by the parents showing that the child had made a year's progress in a year's time in a private school was accepted as evidence to support the parents' claim that the private school setting provided the proper educational setting. The court awarded the parents retroactive private school tuition and legal fees.

In *Houston Independent School District (HISD) v. Bobby, Joyce, and Caius R.* (2000), the Fifth Circuit Court of Appeals denied tuition reimbursement. In this case, the child had made at least a year's progress in reading, math, and written language during the last full year at a public school. The Fifth Circuit Court of Appeals provided the following guidelines for evaluating an educational program for a child with a disability: (a) the program is individualized and based on the student's assessment and performance, (b) the program is administered in the LRE, (c) the services are provided in a coordinated and collaborative manner by the key "stakeholders," and (d) positive academic and nonacademic benefits for the child are demonstrated. The court also pointed out that parents needed to show more than minor failures on the part of the school in implementing their child's IEP for the court to rule that their child failed to receive educational benefit from the IEP.

There is nothing in the IDEA that limits the federal district court's authority to award reimbursement costs against the state educational agency, the local educational agency, or both. Either or both agencies may be held liable for failing to provide a child with a FAPE. Furthermore, if the parent is the prevailing party, the State Department of Education or school district must pay any properly documented expenses incurred during the period in which the child remains in her or his present educational setting, even if the expenses are unreasonable or excessive (*St. Tammany Parish School Board v. State of Louisiana,* 1998).

When the parents unilaterally and inappropriately place a child in a facility, however, the parents may not receive reimbursement for the period during which the child remained in this educational setting (Federal Regulations, Sec. 300.403; *Tucker v. Calloway County Board of Education,* 1998). If the parents were to receive reimbursement in this situation, "any parent could take his or her chances on an initial unilateral placement, banking on the likelihood that appeals would be drawn out for several months and probably over the course of one or two school years, and thereby artificially force the school district to pay for at least the later years of a placement which it had not approved" (*Tucker v. Calloway County Board of Education,* 1998).

In order to determine who is the prevailing party, courts must use judgment in deciding *what* was achieved by the party starting the lawsuit (i.e., the litigant) and *how* it was achieved. In general, the prevailing party must succeed on some significant issue in the litigation that relates to the benefit the party sought in bringing the lawsuit. The outcome does not have to be "identical to the relief demanded in the complaint, provided the relief obtained is of the same general type.... The most critical factor is the degree of success obtained" (*G.M. v. New Britain Board of Education,* 1999). Courts may rule that the prevailing party is not entitled to recover the full amount of legal fees when the party does not prevail on all issues (*Jason W. v. Houston Independent School District,* 1998).

Courts should consider several factors in arriving at an appropriate and reasonable level of reimbursement for attorneys' fees (*Florence County School District Four v. Carter,* 1993; *Thompson v. Board of the Special School District No. 1,* 1998). These factors include "(1) the time and labor required for litigation; (2) the novelty and difficulty of the questions presented; (3) the skill required to perform the legal services properly; (4) the preclusion of other employment by the attorney due to acceptance of the case; (5) the customary fee; (6) whether the fee is fixed or contingent; (7) time limitations imposed by the client or the circumstances; (8) the amount of time involved and the result obtained; (9) the experience, reputation, and ability of the attorneys; (10) the 'undesirability' of the case; (11) the nature and length of the professional relationship with the client; and (12) awards in similar cases" (*Jason D. W. v. Houston Independent School District,* 1998).

Even though a school district changes its procedures as a result of a hearing or trial, the courts may rule that attorneys are not entitled to fees if the same remedy could have been obtained without resort to administrative or legal process (*Soroko v. Arlington County Public Schools,* 1997). The Fourth Circuit Court of Appeals' reasoning in *Soroko* was as follows: "Allowing an award of attorneys' fees under these circumstances would encourage potential litigants and their attorneys to pursue legal claims prior to attempting a simpler resolution and would discourage schools from taking any action whatsoever once an administrative proceeding or lawsuit was underway for fear that any action on their part would give rise to a claim by a plaintiff that he [or she] prevailed and was entitled to attorneys' fees."

A parent who is an attorney and acts as counsel for his or her child in proceedings under the IDEA is not entitled to attorneys' fees because the parent generally is not capable of exercising independent judgment (*Doe v. Board of Education of Baltimore County,* 1998). Allowing an attorney–parent to recover attorneys' fees for representing his or her own child in proceedings under the IDEA would not ensure that a child

would benefit from the best legal services that could be obtained from an independent third party.

An attorney who is licensed to practice before the federal bar but not licensed to practice before a particular state bar may not be entitled to receive attorneys' fees from a school district, even though she or he wins the case under the IDEA at a state administrative hearing (*Z.A. & Bobby A. v. San Bruno Park School District,* 1999). The laws of each state should be reviewed regarding this issue. A parent or guardian who is *not* the prevailing party in a federal lawsuit involving the IDEA is not entitled to reimbursement for attorneys' fees (*Lambeau v. Arlington County School Board,* 1997; *Soroko v. Arlington County Public Schools,* 1997; *Warner v. Independent School District No. 625,* 1998).

The time period during which the prevailing party in a lawsuit can file for award of attorneys' fees under the IDEA is governed by the state statute of limitations; it is, for example, 4 years in Florida (*Zipperer v. The School Board of Seminole County, Florida,* 1997), 3 years in California (California Education Code, Sec. 56505j), and 2 years in New Jersey (*Ridgewood Board of Education v. N.E.,* 1999). In some locations courts may limit the time to a matter of 2 to 3 weeks (Peter W. D. Wright, Esq., personal communication, August 1999).

The IDEA does not provide for compensatory or punitive damages stemming from educational malpractice. Some

THE I.E.P. TEAM WAS SOMEWHAT SURPRISED WHEN ALBERT BROUGHT THE FAMILY'S ATTORNEY

Courtesy of Herman Zielinski.

courts and attorneys have noted that malpractice is a breach of a standard of care, and there are no clear standards of practice in education that can be breached (Peter W. D. Wright, Esq., personal communication, August 1999). The Ninth and Fourth Circuit Courts of Appeals ruled that it would be inconsistent with the structure of the IDEA to award damages for pain and suffering, damages for emotional distress, or other consequential damages (*Sellers v. School Board of the City of Manassas, Virginia,* 1998; *Shevtsov v. Los Angeles Unified School District,* 1998). However, the Third Circuit Court of Appeals noted that "we do not preclude the awarding of monetary damages…" when there is a violation of the IDEA (*W.B. v. Matula,* 1995).

Parents cannot seek reimbursement under Section 504 or the Americans with Disabilities Act (see below) for improper education of their child until they have exhausted their administrative remedies under the IDEA (*Babicz v. The School Board of Broward County,* 1998).

SECTION 504 OF THE REHABILITATION ACT OF 1973

Section 504 of the Rehabilitation Act of 1973 (Public Law 93-112) was designed to protect individuals with disabilities from discrimination in any setting receiving funds from the federal government. This act, as well as the ADA, mandates that reasonable accommodations be made for children (and adults) with disabilities so that they will have access to needed services. Examples of needed services in school settings are access to classrooms, buses, and other means of transportation and the opportunity to participate in extracurricular activities.

Section 504 offers protections to children who are or were disabled so that they are not discriminated against. For example, a school could not deny enrollment to a student simply because he had once been hospitalized for emotional problems, nor could a school discriminate against a child by designating HIV-positive status as a disability. However, if there is no current disability, the school would not be liable for any additional services to either of these children. Only if a child currently has a disability and needs additional services in order to receive a FAPE (to progress in the curriculum and to enjoy the same opportunities all other children possess to participate in extracurricular activities) would a school be liable. All children covered under the IDEA '97 are also covered under Section 504.

Following are some of the similarities between Section 504 and the IDEA '97:

- They both embrace the concept that a child with a disability is entitled to equal opportunities to engage in nonacademic as well as academic activities.
- They both allow children to be disciplined for up to 10 days in the same manner as other children.
- They both prohibit discriminatory treatment.

- They both require that a school system provide a FAPE for every child with a disability.
- They both describe a FAPE as consisting of education in general education classes, education in regular classes with the use of supplementary services, or special education and related services in separate classrooms for all or portions of the school day.
- They both follow the principle that special education could include specially designed instruction in classrooms, at home, or in private or public institutions, and may be accompanied by such related services as speech therapy, occupational and physical therapy, and psychological counseling and medical diagnostic services necessary to the child's education.

Here are some of the differences between the two laws:

- The IDEA '97 does not provide services for a child who has a temporary disability (e.g., a broken arm), whereas under Section 504 the child could be eligible for temporary modifications or accommodations.
- The IDEA '97 provides some funding for services to children with disabilities, whereas Section 504 does not.
- The IDEA '97 imposes more formal and intricate procedural requirements than Section 504 does. Section 504 does not require a written plan or a written consent from the parent, although most schools draw up a written agreement (which may be called a "504 Plan") to document that they have met their obligations.
- The IDEA '97 provides for services only if the services are needed to help a child meet the goals of the IEP and make progress in the general curriculum. Section 504 provides for services even if the services are only to help a child without a need for special educational services progress in the general curriculum. For example, a child in a wheelchair might need special transportation to get to and from school but no special educational services. This child would be eligible under Section 504 but not under the IDEA '97.
- The IDEA '97 requires a detailed reevaluation plan only if there is a change of placement that might result in the child's losing all services (except, of course, if the child is too old for any benefits or graduates with a regular diploma), whereas Section 504 requires a reevaluation before changing the placement of a child with a disability (although it does not define a reevaluation). Conducting a manifestation determination review before suspending the child for more than 10 days would meet the requirements of Section 504.
- The IDEA '97 stipulates that the school is liable for providing the student with a FAPE even if the child's behavior was not a manifestation of the child's disability, whereas under Section 504 the school would have no liability for services.

Two cases that went before a federal appeals court under Section 504 are those of Kelly DeBord (*DeBord v. Board of Education of the Ferguson-Florissant School District,* 1997) and Jacob Todd (*Todd v. Elkins School District,* 1998). Kelly DeBord was prescribed a dosage of Ritalin that exceeded the recommended dosage in the *Physician's Desk Reference* (PDR). The school nurse refused to administer the prescribed dosage because the school had a policy of following the recommendations contained in the PDR. The school offered several accommodations to allow Kelly's parents to administer the drug, but the parents sought relief from the courts. The appeals court ruled that the school has the right to establish guidelines for the administration of drugs. Schools that have objective standards for implementing services do not have to modify those standards if they believe that there is potential liability in following the modified procedure. Courts look favorably on standards applied equally to all students.

Jacob Todd was a fourth-grade special education student with muscular dystrophy. While he was being pushed in a wheelchair to the playground by a fellow student, he fell from the wheelchair and—because he was unbuckled—sustained a broken leg. Jacob's IEP did not provide for an adult aide, although one was available to assist him if needed; instead, the school district had Jacob's peers transport him to recess at times in order to minimize his isolation and to encourage relationships with other students. Jacob's parents asked for damages, claiming that school officials had violated Jacob's rights under Section 504. The parents claimed that the school was indifferent to and had intentionally disregarded their son's safety and had denied him the right to participate in various programs. An appeals court affirmed the district court's ruling that the school district did *not* discriminate against Jacob. The school district's policy did not markedly depart from accepted professional judgment, practice, or standards. Furthermore, the school district did not show bad faith or gross misjudgment.

AMERICANS WITH DISABILITIES ACT (ADA)

The Americans with Disabilities Act (ADA) of 1990 (Public Law 101-336) provides protection from discrimination for individuals with disabilities in all settings, regardless of whether federal funds are involved. The U.S. Supreme Court interpreted the ADA in three rulings handed down in 1999. In each case, by a 7-to-2 vote, the Supreme Court ruled that people with physical impairments who can function normally when they wear their glasses or take their medicine generally cannot be considered disabled and therefore do not come under the protection of the ADA (*Albertsons v. Kirkingburg,* 1999; *Murphy v. UPS,* 1999; *Sutton v. United Airlines,* 1999). The justices said that the law was not designed to protect individuals with treatable impairments such as poor eyesight, hypertension, or diabetes.

COMMENT ON THE IDEA '97, SECTION 504, AND THE ADA

Interpretations of the IDEA '97, Section 504, and the ADA involve complex judgments on the part of (a) educators and professionals working in schools, (b) administrative hearing officers at both the local and state levels, (c) judges from U.S. District Courts, (d) judges from U.S. Circuit Courts of Appeals, and (e) justices from the U.S. Supreme Court. It is admirable that our nation wants to provide a FAPE to all children. But what is not admirable is the amount of litigation associated with the IDEA. *Educational methodology decisions are best left to experts—namely, educators—and not judges or attorneys.* Members of the legal profession are not acquainted with curriculum standards, teaching methods, children with disabilities, or educational interventions. They have not taught in the classroom or worked with children with special needs, their parents, or administrators. For these and other reasons, members of the legal profession must listen to teachers and understand that teachers are in the best position to judge how children should be taught and what is needed in the classroom. Of course it is important that schools understand and follow the laws related to education.

The courts have stated that educational methodology decisions are best left to educators (*Logue v. Unified School District,* 1998). However, when school districts fail to use appropriate educational practices and children fail to learn, they leave the door open for courts to dictate educational practice. Schools have a good chance that courts will rule in their favor if they (a) show that the child progressed in their program; (b) have expert witnesses testify in support of their program; (c) used methods that are current and accepted in the field; and (d) supply evidence that they have provided both teacher and parent training, where needed.

It is critical that schools keep accurate records of all meetings, as well as copies of consent forms, IEPs, and anything else related to a child's assessment and intervention plans. Courts may scrutinize the child's entire school record. They will look carefully at the IEP to determine whether the provisions listed in the plan were carried out and whether the goals and objectives relate to the child's disability. Failure to develop and include appropriate plans can be just as damaging as failure to carry out the plans properly. The IDEA '97, and the rules and regulations interpreting it, apply only to events that took place *after* the regulations were published—the regulations do not apply retroactively (*O'Toole v. Olathe District Schools Unified School District No. 233,* 1997).

Congress included procedural safeguards in the IDEA in an attempt to promote fair classification. School placement decisions are important to students and families, and they should not be undertaken lightly or arbitrarily. Congress held that schools are accountable for the accuracy of their classifications and for the appropriateness of their programs. School personnel are obliged to specify the basis upon which they classify children and must demonstrate that programs are likely to benefit the child.

Courts need to consider that the diagnostic process involves both art and science—that is, both subjective and objective processes. For example, in *Muller v. Committee on Special Education of the East Islip Union Free School District* (1998), the school psychologist employed by the school district arrived at a "conduct disorder" diagnosis, whereas the psychologist working for a private residential facility arrived at a diagnosis of "seriously emotionally disturbed." As noted earlier, the former diagnosis meant that the child was not eligible for special education services, whereas the latter diagnosis meant that the child might be eligible for these services. If the child was deemed eligible for services, the private residential facility could receive payment from the school district. On what basis can the court determine which diagnosis is correct? In cases where a school's evaluation is in dispute, we believe that the procedure that is fair to all parties is for the school to have the child tested by a neutral third party with expertise in the area of disability and no vested interests. Following this procedure might prevent litigation. If both sides approve the evaluator, one significant area of contention is bypassed. For example, a child might be tested at a local college or university training center. In high-stakes litigation (which includes most litigation), schools should consider bringing in outside experts.

The IDEA '97 extends protection to children who are suspended from school if the school knew or should have known that the child had a disability. A school would be deemed to know about the child's possible disability if (a) a parent had ever written a letter to a teacher or other school official indicating that his or her child might have a disability or (b) the behavior of the child was such that it should have indicated to a reasonable teacher or school official that the child might have a disability. The IDEA '97 does provide, however, that protections under the IDEA would not apply if the school system (a) evaluated the child previously and found the child ineligible or (b) informed the parents of their rights and that an evaluation was not needed and the parents did not appeal.

Parents and children should never be coerced or intimidated into accepting the school's placement decision and the IEP. The IEP team must take care to express decisions about eligibility, placement, program goals, and the review process in clear, understandable, and jargon-free language. Even so, some parents will have difficulty comprehending their child's IEP and education program. Schools should do their best to help these parents gain the necessary understanding.

Schools must listen to parents and be flexible in their approaches to formulating IEPs. Parents are less likely to hire an attorney when they understand how the school arrived at the recommendations and when they believe that their concerns are being addressed. For example, it may be prudent for a school to grant the wish of parents who want their child to attend general education classes for 80% of the day rather than 50% of the day, as preferred by the school. What evidence is there that the child's education will be more significantly enhanced by a 50/50 split than by an 80/20 split? If

there is such evidence, then it behooves the school to present it to the parents in a comprehensible way. Following the letter of the law may not be enough to avoid litigation. Rather, there must be an effort by schools to work cooperatively with parents, to ensure that the parents' position is given credence, and to recognize that the education of children with disabilities sometimes involves trial and error. Having the parents "on board" is the best and safest way to proceed.

Both schools and parents need to realize that interpretation of the IDEA by the courts is controversial. In addition, interpretation of the IDEA and Section 504, as well as the role of the ADA in special education disputes, is still evolving and changing. There is no simple way to predict how the courts will rule. In some cases the federal courts will uphold the administrative hearing officers, whereas in similar cases they will not. Parents electing to pursue their cases under the IDEA '97 through state court systems may obtain rulings that differ from those in cases decided by federal courts. The U.S. Circuit Courts of Appeals may affirm or reverse the rulings of the U.S. District Courts, and the U.S. Supreme Court may affirm or reverse the rulings of the U.S. Circuit Courts of Appeals. The unpredictable nature of court rulings should make both parents and schools want to avoid litigation. Even in situations where the law might not require a school system to provide services, spending a little extra money to benefit a child may prove to be a wiser decision than giving money to attorneys just to prove a point. And once litigation begins, there is no certainty that the school will receive a favorable decision.

Case law is evolving on the issue of awarding compensatory or punitive damages under the IDEA '97, Section 504, and the ADA. Some court decisions suggest that compensatory or punitive damages can be awarded when the schools have shown bad faith, gross professional misjudgment, or intentional discrimination (*Hoekstra v. Independent School District,* 1996; *Sellers v. Manassas,* 1998). Until or unless the U.S. Supreme Court rules on this issue, liability may depend on where the litigation occurs. This is just one of many unsettled issues illustrating the need for professionals to remain current on case law in the field.

An ambiguous component of the IDEA '97 is its call for racially or culturally nondiscriminatory assessment procedures. It does not clearly define what such procedures might be; in fact, the law does not specify *any* acceptable or unacceptable assessment procedures. However, when the IDEA discusses mental retardation, it uses the terminology "significantly subaverage general intellectual functioning." The term "significantly subaverage" likely means two or more standard deviations below the mean of a standardized test of intelligence. This and other statements suggest that the IDEA recognizes the importance of standardized tests in the assessment process.

Another shortcoming of the IDEA is the lack of guidance concerning ways of determining the child's native language. When a child speaks more than one language, how do we determine the child's "native language"?

It is to be hoped that in the future the courts will recognize their limitations and defer to the judgment of specialists in education when it comes to educational matters. Until that happens, all professionals who work in (or with) schools with children who may have disabilities need to be aware of how the IDEA is interpreted by the courts, how to follow the provisions of the IDEA as carefully as possible, and how to take precautions to avoid costly litigation.

Overall, the IDEA '97, Section 504, and the ADA represent an attempt by the federal government to assure that children with disabilities (a) receive a meaningful, free, and appropriate public education; (b) are afforded equal opportunities and access to services and programs that are the same as or similar to the programs available to students who do not have disabilities; (c) are provided with a meaningful plan to aid in a smooth transition from public school to adulthood; and (d) enter an adulthood free of discriminatory practices by employers and free of physical and structural environmental barriers. The ultimate measure of the usefulness of these laws is the quality of the education received by each child (and adult) with a disability, how the education is used to benefit the child and society, and how society integrates individuals with disabilities into the mainstream of daily living. For further information about the law and special education, see Jacob-Timm and Hartshorne (1998), Turnbull (1993), and Yell (1998).

CONFIDENTIALITY OF ASSESSMENT FINDINGS AND RECORDS

Confidentiality and privileged communication play an important role in assessment. The best sources of information about confidentiality are the ethical principles of your profession and appropriate state and federal laws. Note the subtle distinction between confidentiality and privileged communication in the following descriptions.

- *Confidentiality* is an ethical practice, the obligation never to reveal information obtained in an assessment (or through any professional relationship) without specific consent from the client. It protects the client from unauthorized disclosures of information given in confidence to a clinician.
- *Privileged communication* is a legal right granted by state and federal laws. It protects clients from having their disclosures to certain professionals—such as psychologists, marriage and family counselors, social workers, attorneys, clergy, and physicians, including psychiatrists—revealed during legal proceedings without their informed consent. (Check your state law to learn whether your profession is bound by privileged communication.)

It is important to understand that minors are generally entitled to the same confidential relationship as adults. Federal regulations define a minor as "a person who has not attained the age of majority specified in the applicable state law, or if no age of majority is specified in the applicable state law, the age of eighteen years" (42 C.F.R., Part 2, 1993).

Exceptions to Confidentiality and Privileged Communication

Confidential and privileged communications may need to be suspended in some cases (Federal law, 42 C.F.R, Part 2, 1993). Three exceptions to confidentiality and privileged communication are as follows:

1. *When there is a reasonable suspicion of child maltreatment* (i.e., child abuse or neglect), you are legally obliged to report it to the authorities.
2. *When the examinee poses a physical threat to another person,* you must warn the prospective victim.
3. *When the examinee is a minor and poses a threat to himself or herself* (e.g., any situation that places the minor in danger of death, where the delay of medical treatment would pose a health risk to the minor, or where treatment is needed to decrease physical pain), you are required to notify those responsible for the child.

These three exceptions involve the principle that *when there is a clear and imminent danger to another individual, to society, or to the child directly, confidentiality must be breached.* However, you will need to use considerable judgment in deciding when confidentiality should be breached. First, what behaviors or conditions are grounds for "reasonable suspicion" that the child has been maltreated? (See below.) Second, what behaviors indicate that the child poses a "physical threat to another person"? And third, what behaviors indicate that the child poses a "threat to herself"?

Strict confidentiality cannot be maintained within schools, clinics, hospitals, prisons, and other agencies because agency personnel involved in the case usually have access to the child's records. You must explain this to the examinee. Review your state law for guidance about confidentiality and privileged communications and the exceptions to breaking confidentiality.

Reporting Child Maltreatment

Because reporting child maltreatment requires a breach of confidentiality, it is important to know under what circumstances child maltreatment should be reported to the authorities. (For further information about theories of child maltreatment, assessment of child maltreatment, and intervention in cases of child maltreatment, see Sattler, 1998.)

Responsibility of professionals to report child maltreatment. With the encouragement of the Federal Child Abuse Prevention and Treatment Act, passed by Congress in 1974 and amended and renewed several times, all 50 states in the United States have passed laws about who should report child maltreatment. State laws generally require that individuals working with children—such as child caregivers, teachers, physicians, psychologists, psychiatrists, social workers, marriage and family therapists, counselors, and clergy (in some states)—report child maltreatment when there is reasonable suspicion. These individuals are sometimes referred to as mandated reporters. Regulatory statutes use the term *reasonable suspicion* to mean that a person should consider the possibility of child maltreatment if there are facts that could cause a reasonable person in a similar position to come to the same conclusion. It means "reasonable cause to believe" or "reasonable cause to know or suspect." In addition, members of the public can voluntarily (unless state law says that every adult must report a reasonable suspicion of child maltreatment) notify Child Protective Services or law enforcement if they suspect that child maltreatment has occurred or is occurring. In most, if not all, states, an individual making a report of child maltreatment in good faith is given immunity.

Visible indications of possible child physical abuse include bruises, broken bones, dislocations, burns with unusual patterns, scalded feet or hands, discolored skin, welts, human bites, and injuries to the eyes, ears, nose, or mouth. Signs of possible neglect include a child who appears hungry, is unwashed, has unkempt hair, is improperly dressed for the weather, or shows signs of malnutrition. The key is to be especially alert to injuries that are unexplained, that do not make sense, or that cannot be associated with normal accidents or illnesses or natural disasters.

Role of reporting party. The role of the reporting party is not to determine or to prove that maltreatment did in fact occur but, rather, to report a reasonable suspicion of maltreatment. By talking with the individual who discloses the possible maltreatment, the reporting party should be able to determine whether there is sufficient reason to make a report. It is then the responsibility of trained investigators to prove the maltreatment.

Here are some pointers to follow when a child discloses that she or he has been maltreated (Connaway, 1996; Poole & Lamb, 1997). You are encouraged to share these pointers with other psychologists and other mandated reporters such as teachers, nurses, school counselors, and health care providers.

1. Pay close attention to your body language. You want to convey interest in what the child says, but not shock, horror, or indifference.
2. You may be the only person this child feels comfortable confiding in, so don't discourage the child from talking to you or give the impression that you are not available to listen.
3. If a child makes a disclosure, don't try to obtain all the details.
4. Listen attentively and then ask the child if he or she wants to say anything else. Follow up and clarify what the child tells you when appropriate.
5. Do not ask the child to demonstrate an event that requires the child to remove her or his clothes.
6. Do not tell the child that you think he or she was or wasn't abused. Your role is to listen carefully, not to make inferences or decisions about whether the maltreatment occurred.
7. Do not give selective reinforcements to things that the child says, such as "good girl" or "Yes, that's what I want to know."
8. Do not use any words that suggest fantasy or a play mode, such as *pretend* or *imagine* or *make believe*.
9. If you have a reasonable suspicion that the child was maltreated, notify the appropriate authorities of what you learned immediately after the interview.
10. Write down the exact words used by the child in the disclosure; the date, time, and place of the disclosure; and any other relevant information about the child's behavior and the situation in which the disclosure was made.

Discussing Confidentiality with Children and Parents

Children and parents must be informed about confidentiality and its limits. Psychologists may be reluctant to discuss confidentiality with examinees because they believe that it might hamper rapport. In addition, some agencies do not have clearcut policies about discussing confidentiality with children and parents. Still, it is important to explain confidentiality to both children and their parents. Discussing confidentiality is an ethical and legal obligation and is evidence that you have followed proper procedures if you are sued. We suggest that when discussing confidentiality you follow your agency's policy, which should be based on (a) your state laws, (b) the ethical principles of your profession, (c) the child's age, (d) the child's level of comprehension, (e) the parents' level of comprehension, and (f) relevant clinical observations. However, you may need to work toward changing your agency's policy if the agency is not following proper procedures.

Some suggestions about how you might handle the issue of confidentiality during an examination follow. These suggestions should not be carried out unless they have been approved by your supervisor or agency and are consistent with your state's regulations and laws. Raising the issue of confidentiality may protect you and the agency you work for and may even help build rapport (examinees might regard you as honest and open when you do so).

1. *Present statements about confidentiality on a consent form.* It's good practice to inform the parents (and older children) about confidentiality and its limits in writing. Then they can read and sign the form before the evaluation begins. This form must follow your state laws and any agency policy that is more specific than the state laws. The statement about the limits of confidentiality might read as follows (with additions as needed): "I understand that if the examiner has reason to believe that a client (a) is being physically, emotionally, or sexually abused or neglected; (b) intends to hurt someone else; or (c) intends to hurt himself or herself, the proper authorities must be notified."

2. *Discuss the issue of confidentiality directly with the child.* To children older than 5 years who have an appropriate level of understanding, you might say, "I want you to know that there are some things you might tell me that I must share with your parents or other people. This could happen if you tell me that someone has hurt you, if you plan to hurt someone else, or if you plan to hurt yourself in some way. Do you understand?… I also may share other things with your parents, because it is important that they know how you are feeling because they want to help you. Do you have any questions?"

3. *Discuss the issue of confidentiality with parents who have control of the information about their minor children.* In this situation you might say, "I will not release information you have shared with me unless I have your consent or am compelled to do so by the courts. However, I'm legally obligated to report to the proper authorities if I learn that your child has been physically, emotionally, or sexually abused or neglected; if you plan to hurt someone; or if your child plans to hurt someone. I also will try to get you help if you are planning to hurt yourself or your child. Do you have any questions?"

4. *Discuss confidentiality when the issue of maltreatment, self-harm, or harming others is raised.* If the child or parent says that abuse or neglect occurred or talks about suicidal ideations or harming others, you might say, "Remember what we discussed about sharing what you say when we first started talking? After hearing what you just told me, I must tell [law enforcement, Child Protective Services, and so forth]." Then explain why you are going to do so.

Confidentiality of School and Other Institutional Records

The Family Educational Rights and Privacy Act (FERPA; Public Law 93-830) was first enacted in 1974 by Congress and has been amended several times. The law is designed to protect the privacy of children's educational records (i.e., all records, files, and documents and any material in the records related to their parents). FERPA gives parents the right to (a) inspect and review their children's education records, (b) request that the records be amended if mistakes have been made, and (c) partially control disclosures of the information contained in the records. When a student turns 18 or enters college, the rights transfer from the parents to the student. School personnel can disclose information from the records without prior consent only under certain conditions specified in the law. The information, for example, can be shared with school officials and teachers and other recognized authorities or agencies. One agency that can receive confidential information is the Department of Social Services, when failure to divulge the information could put the child in danger. When information is disclosed, schools need to document the disclosures, with certain exceptions as specified in the law. The exceptions include the following: when the disclosure is

Don't go! I'm sure Billy's page 3 of the Behavior Management Plan within his third Comprehensive Individual Assessment's Individual Education Plan is here somewhere.

Courtesy of Daniel Miller.

made (a) to the parent or eligible student, (b) to a school official within the school system, (c) to a party with written consent from the parent or eligible student, (d) to an official party seeking information, or (e) to a party directed by a federal grand jury or other law enforcement subpoena to receive the records. Electronic data stored on floppy disks, hard disks, CD-ROM disks, or any other means of storage must be guarded as carefully as traditional paper files (i.e., locked in a secure file cabinet).

THE CHALLENGES OF BEING AN EXPERT WITNESS

A psychologist may be called on to testify in court or at special hearings conducted in schools or agencies. For example, a psychologist may be asked to give her or his opinion about the examinee's (a) need for special programs, (b) mental status, (c) adaptive skills, and/or (d) general adjustment. Testifying as an expert witness can be a difficult experience, especially in court or courtlike settings. Court procedures are radically different from those followed in mental health settings, medical settings, and schools. A witness in court may be expected to respond to many questions with a simple one-word answer. "Isn't it true that…?" is a form that questions often take, and little opportunity is afforded to qualify responses. The courtroom is a place where issues are framed in black-and-white terms; it is not a place where complex philosophical or educational issues are either debated or resolved.

Differences Between the Scientific Method and the Adversarial System

Psychologists are trained as scientists and professionals, but they are not trained in the art of litigation. They recognize that behavior is not a matter of absolutes; rather, there are many plausible explanations that can be offered to account for behavior. Further, they are trained to participate in a dialog with colleagues and clients, in a search for the best possible explanation for behavior. When psychologists become involved in the legal system, they may be unprepared for what they will encounter (Newman, 1991):

The adversarial system used to litigate cases differs from the scientific method. It seeks to answer moral and legal questions in an absolute ("yes" or "no") fashion. The trier of fact, either the judge or jury, must consider both sides to every argument. Each side is presented in its most positive light, and then the two sides are weighed against each other. No matter how convincing each side may be, only one side can prevail. In the adversarial system there is little room for qualifiers or contingencies. The defendant, for example, is either guilty or not guilty, competent or incompetent, morally responsible or irresponsible, negligent or not liable. The trier of fact can—and actually must—consider all relevant factors and circumstances. The ultimate answer, however, to any question must be an unequivocal "yes" or "no." (pp. 242–243, with changes in notation)

The goal of the mental health system is to promote mental health, while the goal of the legal system is to promote justice. These goals can clash when the two systems come into contact. Yet the two systems hold similar values, particularly in rejecting deceit and exploitive use of power; both emphasize fairness, honesty, and competence in expert testimony, recognize limitations in current scientific knowledge, and stress the advancement of human welfare (Melton, 1994).

Attorney Peter W. D. Wright (personal communication, August 1999) observed that, ironically, psychology is usually more relevant than law to the outcome of litigation. The outcome of any litigation is based primarily on perception, empathy, projection, and similar psychological principles. Thus, the selective perception of facts and testimony and the judge or jury's identification with one party or the other may play a greater role in the decision than the actual facts and law.

Testifying as an Expert Witness

Time of discovery. During the information-gathering period before trial—a period known as the *time of discovery*—you may be asked to give a deposition. A *deposition* refers to the questioning of a witness who is under oath by an opposing attorney. The responses are written down or recorded for use in court at a later date. At the deposition, the opposing attorney will want to learn about your involvement in the case, your findings, how you arrived at your conclusions and recommendations, and related matters. The attorney is likely to refer to your report and other related materials. Questions at the deposition tend to be phrased in an open-ended manner, which invites you to expand on your responses, whereas cross-examination questions at trial tend to be closed-ended and require brief, specific answers (Pope, Butcher, & Seelen, 1993).

The purpose of the deposition is for the opposing attorney to find out information that will assist his or her client. You need to answer truthfully, but you usually will be advised by your attorney to give minimal answers—that is, to offer no information whatsoever beyond that needed to truthfully answer the questions asked. (You will want to use the same strategy when you testify in court.) Depositions, in some sense, serve as fishing expeditions, designed to help the opposing attorney learn what can be used later in the case. The answers that you give during a deposition and in court should be made equally carefully. Remember that your answers at the deposition are given under oath and can be used later to impeach you if they differ from those given in testimony at trial.

The direct examination. When you are sworn in as an expert witness in court (or at an administrative hearing) and answer the questions posed to you by your attorney, you are under direct examination. (Your attorney is usually the one who asked you to perform the evaluation or who is representing the agency for whom you conducted the evaluation.) You will be asked to present your findings, recommendations, and opinions. It is the attorney's responsibility to ask the questions skillfully so that you can present your findings in a clear, logical, and understandable manner. To do this, the attorney must know a great deal about the case.

When you testify as an expert witness, expect to answer questions similar to those asked at the deposition, including questions about (a) your professional background, credentials, and experience (see Table 3-4), (b) the amount of contact you have had with the examinee, (c) the history of the examinee's difficulties, and (d) the procedures you used to evaluate the examinee and to draw conclusions and arrive at the recommendations. Many of these questions about the examinee can be answered by referring to your report. You will want to carefully review your report, recommendations, and deposition transcript prior to testifying.

An expert witness can and should rely on notes or other materials for information that cannot be readily recalled. This process, called *refreshing recollection,* is an acceptable and accurate means of providing information to the court. However, you don't want to read from your notes; use them only to verify facts or other information. It is important that you inform your or the agency's attorney that you plan to bring notes or other materials to court to assist you with your testimony. Also discuss with the attorney whether these documents may be detrimental to the case if and when they are inspected by the opposing attorney. Keys to being an expert witness are to adhere closely to your findings, to be familiar with current research findings in your field, and to make interpretations cautiously.

Your role as an expert witness is to provide information to the court so that the court can reach an appropriate decision. In your testimony, present your findings, the implications of the findings, and your conclusions. A logical, carefully reasoned

Table 3-4
Examples of Questions Asked of an Expert Witness

Background

1. Please state your name.
2. What is your present occupation?
3. For those unfamiliar with the term psychologist, please explain to us what a psychologist is.
4. How does a psychologist differ from other professionals, such as psychiatrists or social workers?
5. By whom and where are you employed?
6. How long have you been so employed?
7. Do you have a particular specialty in your work?
8. What services are provided at your organization?
9. What are your specific duties?
10. Describe your prior work history.
11. What education have you had to allow you to do this work? Tell me about your undergraduate degree and institution, graduate degree and institution, and specialized training in the field while you were in school.
12. (If pertinent to testimony) Did you have to write a thesis or research paper to obtain your graduate degree?
13. What is a thesis?
14. What was the topic of your thesis?
15. How many hours of research were involved?
16. Was your thesis published?
17. (If yes) Where was it published?
18. Have you had any other specialized training in your field, such as on-the-job training and seminars and continuing education?
19. (If yes) Tell me about this specialized training.

Publications and Professional Experience

20. In the state where you reside, what are the licensing procedures for psychologists?
21. Are you licensed in your state?
22. (If no) Why are you not licensed?
23. Have you published any books or articles that deal with your work?
24. (If yes) Please describe each publication, including title, topic, publisher, length, and approximate amount of time spent on the publication.
25. Are you presently on the teaching staff of any college or university?
26. (If yes) What classes do you teach?… How long have you been teaching?… Do you have other teaching experience?
27. Have you presented any papers on the subject of _____ to professional symposiums?
28. (If yes) When?… Where?… What specific subjects?
29. Are you a member of any professional organizations?
30. (If yes) What organizations?… Have you ever served as an officer or in any special capacity for that organization?… (If yes) In what capacity did you serve?
31. Have you received any honors or awards for your work in the field of _____ ?
32. (If yes) Tell me about them.
33. Have you appeared on local or national television concerning your work in this area?
34. (If yes) Tell me about your appearance.
35. Have there been newspaper or magazine articles written concerning your efforts in the field of _____ ?
36. (If yes) Tell me about these articles.

37. Have you received any national recognition for your work?
38. (If yes) Tell me about that.

Experience as an Expert Witness

39. Have you previously testified as an expert in the superior courts of this state regarding (reason for lawsuit or prosecution)?
40. (If yes) Tell me about that.
41. Have you testified as an expert in the courts of any other states?
42. (If yes) Which states?
43. How many times have you testified as an expert on the topic of (reason for lawsuit or prosecution)?

Familiarity with Subject Matter

44. Are you familiar with recent literature/articles/research in the area of (reason for lawsuit or prosecution)?
45. Do you subscribe to any professional journals that deal with (reason for lawsuit or prosecution)?
46. (If yes) What journals?
47. Do you routinely keep up with the literature in this field?
48. What is the present state of knowledge in your profession on the characteristics of the (child with attention deficit/hyperactivity disorder, child with a brain injury, child with a learning disability, etc.)?
49. Can you give any examples? [Produce a comprehensive bibliography that can be used in court.]
50. Do you devote all of your professional time to this field, or do you do work in other areas?
51. (If other areas) Tell me about these other areas.
52. Please explain how you came to be involved in your area of expertise.
53. Can you estimate the number of children you have talked to who have been (type of child cited)?
54. What services do you offer these children?

Research on Subject Matter

55. Have you participated in any research regarding these children?
(If yes, go to question 56; if no, go to question 76.)
56. In what way did you participate?
57. Was anyone else involved in this research?… (If yes) Who?
58. What was the goal of your study?
59. How many children were involved in the study?
60. Did you use accepted scientific methodology in conducting your research?
61. Did you follow approved and established statistical methods in compiling your data?
62. Please explain those methods.
63. What verification procedures were followed to ensure the authenticity of your data?
64. Have other similar studies been conducted?
65. Can you give us some examples?
66. Have you compared the information you gathered with information obtained from the work of other experts in your field?
(If yes, go to question 67; if no, go to question 69.)
67. How do they compare?

(Continued)

Table 3-4 (*Continued*)

68. Is their information consistent with yours?
69. What use is made of this information within your profession?
70. Have these characteristics gained general acceptance in your profession?
71. How can you know that to be true?
72. Are these characteristics and responses relied on by members of your profession in forming opinions or in making inferences regarding the diagnosis and treatment of these children?
73. Are they helpful to you in other ways?
74. In your experience, is the information revealed by your studies and those of other researchers in your field known to the average person?
75. On what do you base that opinion?

Compliance with Subpoena

76. Have you complied fully with each and every element of the subpoena to produce material?
77. Are there any items that you did not make available to me?
78. Were any of these documents altered in any way?
79. Were any of them recopied, erased, written over, enhanced, edited, or added to in any way since the time each was originally created?
80. Are the photocopies you gave me true and exact replicas of the original documents without any revision?
81. Have any documents falling within the scope of the subpoena or otherwise relevant to the case been lost, stolen, misplaced, destroyed, or thrown away?
82. Are any documents you made, collected, handled, or received that are within the scope of this subpoena or otherwise relevant to the case absent from the documents made available to me?

Evaluation of Child

83. How many times do you normally like to see a child during an evaluation?
84. Did you have an opportunity to interview/evaluate (child's name)?
85. Who contacted you to evaluate (child's name)?
86. Before meeting with (child's name), what did you do to familiarize yourself with the case?
87. Before meeting with (child's name), did you talk with anyone? (If yes, go to question 88; if no, go to question 90.)
88. With whom?
89. What type of information did you hope to obtain from (person met with)?
90. Did you look at any reports in this case before meeting with (child's name)? (If yes, go to question 91; if no, go to question 94.)
91. From whom did you get the reports?
92. How did you use the information that you obtained from (persons or reports)?
93. How much weight did you attribute to information learned from sources other than the child?
94. Is meeting with an adult before talking to the child an accepted practice within your profession?
95. How long were your meetings with (child's name)?
96. Were your interviews an acceptable length of time, considering the child's age and level of development?

97. How many times did you meet with (child's name)?
98. How much time would you estimate that you spent with (child's name) in total?
99. How much time would you estimate that you have spent on this case?
100. Where did your meetings with (child's name) take place?
101. When evaluating a child for (reason for referral), what procedures do you typically use for your evaluation?
102. Tell me about the procedures you use, such as their reliability, validity, norm group, and any other relevant information about them.
103. Why do you use these procedures?
104. Do you typically follow the same protocol?
105. Are the procedures you have just described an accepted means of assessment in your profession? (If yes, go to question 106; if no, go to question 108.)
106. Which procedures are not accepted?
107. Why aren't they accepted?
108. How many children have you evaluated using this protocol?
109. Do you regularly keep records of what was found during your evaluation? (If yes, go to question 110; if no, go to question 112.)
110. Please describe what is kept in these records.
111. When are these records completed?
112. Is there anything you can do or attempt to do to ensure that what a child is telling you is not something that was related to the child by a third person?
113. (If yes) Tell me about that.
114. Please describe how (child's name) appeared during your evaluations and how (he, she) acted during the interview.
115. During the course of your evaluation, did (child's name) express any reluctance to talk about anything? (If yes, go to question 116; if no, go to question 118.)
116. What was the child reluctant to talk about?
117. How did you respond to the child's reluctance?
118. Did you arrive at a diagnosis? (Go to either question 119 or question 120.)
119. (If yes) What was it?... How confident are you of your diagnosis?
120. (If no) Why didn't you arrive at a diagnosis?
121. Would other evaluators arrive at the same (diagnosis, conclusions/recommendations)?
122. (If no) Why not?
123. Do you have any doubts about the reliability or validity of the assessment findings?
124. (If yes) Tell me about your doubts.
125. What recommendations did you make?
126. What was the basis for your recommendations?
127. Is there anything else you want to tell us about your findings?
128. (If yes) Go ahead.
129. After meeting with (child's name), did you offer (him, her) any further services?
130. (If yes) What services did you offer the child?
131. Did you offer or suggest any referral services to (child's name)?
132. (If yes) What referral services did you recommend to the child and family?

Source: Questions 1–73 from *Investigation and Prosecution of Child Abuse* (2nd ed., pp. 353–395), by the American Prosecutors Research Institute of the National Center for the Prosecution of Child Abuse. Copyright 1993 by the American Prosecutors Research Institute. Adapted and reprinted with permission. Questions 76–82 adapted from Pope, Butcher, and Seelen (1993). Questions 81–115 and 127–130 adapted and reprinted with permission from *Using Expert Witnesses in Child Abuse and Neglect Cases* (pp. 28–29), by M. Zehnder, St. Paul: Minnesota County Attorneys Association. Copyright 1994 by the Minnesota County Attorneys Association.

presentation will help the court reach a proper decision. As an expert witness, you may be asked to predict whether the defendant will engage in dangerous behavior in the future. This is an area fraught with difficulty. You must be aware of the current research literature before giving an opinion. Long-term predictions of violence by expert witnesses have low accuracy (Poythress, 1992). In some cases, you may be asked to explain to the court the impact of the trauma or illness on the victim and what future treatment the victim may need. Your role as an expert witness may be critical in deciding the outcome of the case, including a determination of the amount of damages awarded the client.

The cross-examination. The opposing attorney will cross-examine you in court. The cross-examination follows the direct examination. Be prepared for the opposing attorney to scrutinize your credentials, your report, and your recommendations, as well as your expertise and credibility. The opposing attorney may ask you about the following:

* *Your education,* especially if you do not have a doctoral degree: "Isn't it true that a Ph.D. is the accepted degree for the practice of psychology?"
* *Your experience:* "You're not a medical doctor, are you? Then, how can you tell us about the effects of brain damage?"
* *The amount of time that you spent with the examinee:* "Do you mean that you spent only two hours testing the child?"
* *Your ability to make recommendations:* "Do you think that you know the child well enough to make a recommendation based on a two-hour evaluation?"
* *The type of recommendations that you made:* "How can you be sure that the child should be placed with the mother (or has been abused, or needs a classroom for children with learning disabilities rather than a special tutor)?"
* *Your publications,* if you have published a book or an article: "Isn't it true that on page 17 you wrote that children are not reliable informants?"
* *Your assessment techniques:* "Isn't it true that intelligence tests are culturally biased?"

The opposing attorney may attempt to discredit you by trying to show that your assessment procedures were faulty, that you are a "hired gun," that you have a questionable character, that your current testimony conflicts with testimony you gave in prior trials, that your publications are inconsistent, or that you lack knowledge about the subject matter (Schultz, 1990). In addition, the opposing attorney may do anything within the legal limits of courtroom procedure to impugn your testimony. Because court hearings are based on the adversarial process, there are few absolute truths; the verdict or decision often depends on which party presents a more convincing case.

Suggestions for Testifying as an Expert Witness

The following suggestions should help you prepare to testify as an expert witness (American Prosecutors Research Institute of the National Center for the Prosecution of Child Abuse, *Investigation and Prosecution of Child Abuse,* 2nd ed., pages 387–389, copyright 1993 by the American Prosecutors Research Institute, adapted and reprinted with permission).

PREPARATION

1. Be prepared. Always know the pertinent facts of the case better than anyone else in the courtroom. Determine the key legal issues. Also be up to date on the empirical findings in the area. Don't merely rely on in-depth knowledge of a single case.
2. Request a pre-trial conference with the attorney who is calling you as a witness to learn what information is expected from you and to provide education to the attorney about the subject matter of your testimony. In addition, review other cases in which you have given similar testimony, and discuss potential cross-examination questions and answers.
3. Avoid using professional jargon. Review your testimony with the attorney who is calling you as a witness, and identify any difficult words. When preparing your testimony, use a thesaurus to find simple and clear alternative words that the judge and jury will understand.
4. Provide the attorney who is calling you as a witness with a list of qualification and foundation questions—that is, questions the attorney can ask to establish your credentials. Also, provide the attorney with an up-to-date resume of your professional credentials and educational background.
5. Wear professional and conservative clothing.
6. Maintain a ready file of literature, including monographs, articles, and books, about the specialty area in which you will be offering expert testimony. Make these available to the attorney calling you so that he or she will be more educated on your subject. Also, be sure that the attorney is aware of anything you have written about the subject of your testimony.
7. If you are deposed by the opposing counsel, avoid holding the deposition in your office. By meeting in your personal office, you give the attorney a chance to look around at the various reference books and texts on your shelves. The attorney could then challenge you in court with one of your own reference books. A conference room or an attorney's office is a more neutral place for your meeting.
8. Avoid sitting for a deposition with opposing counsel until you are fully prepared, know the facts of your case, have spoken to the attorney who is calling you as a witness, and have reviewed the relevant references in the professional literature. The attorney who is calling you as a witness will usually be present during your deposition.

9. Segregate your personal notes and work products from the case file. Do not show them to the opposing counsel without either the permission of the attorney who is calling you as a witness or a court order.

10. At a deposition, have a "game plan." One plan is to impress the attorney questioning you with *all* the facts that support your position to encourage settlement of the case. If you expect the case to go to trial, then another plan is to answer the questions honestly but narrowly. Always discuss the "game plan" with the attorney who is calling you as a witness.

11. Always tell the truth, and strive to be fair and objective.

12. If you anticipate that the opposing attorney will also be calling an expert witness, suggest to the attorney who is calling you as a witness that you spend time preparing him or her to deal with the other expert witness. You can even sometimes sit with the attorney in court and suggest areas of cross-examination on the spot.

COURTROOM BEHAVIOR

13. Remember, when you are approaching the courthouse or are inside it, anyone you pass may be a judge, juror, hostile witness, or opposing attorney. Always conduct yourself accordingly. This also means that you do not discuss the case in any public place, including hallways, over lunch at a nearby restaurant, or in the restroom. Do not chat informally with the opposing attorney or any other person on his or her staff.

14. When you enter the courtroom, do not do anything that will draw attention to your behavior. Before sitting down in the witness stand, make brief eye contact with the judge and jury. Adjust the chair and microphone so you don't have to lean forward to answer questions.

15. Before answering each question, control the situation by consciously pausing. This allows the judge and jury to mentally shift from hearing the attorney's question to listening to your answer. For example:

   Q: State your name and occupation.
   [Three-count pause]
   A: My name is _____. I am a psychologist for the _____.

   Q: How long have you been employed?
   [Three-count pause]
   A: I have been working there for _____ years.

16. Answer each question with a declarative statement rather than a word or phrase. The opposing attorney may want the judge and jury to hear only his or her question. By using the three-count pause, the declarative sentence, and looking directly at the jury, you will take psychological control away from the attorney.

17. When answering questions, don't guess. If you don't know, say you don't know, but don't let the cross-examiner get you in the trap of answering question after question with "I don't know."

18. Understand the question before you attempt to give an answer. If necessary, ask that it be repeated. You can't possibly give a truthful and accurate answer unless you understand the question.

19. Listen carefully to each question. Keep a sharp lookout for questions with a double meaning and questions that assume you have testified to a fact when you have not done so.

20. Answer the question asked and then stop, especially on cross-examination. Don't volunteer information not called for by the question you are asked.

21. Your choice of words is important. Develop your ability to use words that not only depict what happened but also convey the impression you intend. Here are some examples of positive "soft" words, followed by negative "hard" words in parentheses: *mother* (woman, respondent, abuser), *father* (subject, suspect, defendant), *child* (juvenile, youth), *cut* (laceration, open wound), *molest* (rape, sexually assault), and *bruise* (contusion). Note how the hard and soft words leave different impressions.

22. Speak loudly enough so that everyone can hear you, yet softly enough so that you can raise your voice to emphasize a point. This is especially important if the proceedings are being audiotaped or videotaped.

23. Avoid distracting behaviors such as eating mints, chewing gum, dangling noisy bracelets, or fumbling through a file.

24. Give an audible answer that the court reporter can hear. Don't nod your head; say yes or no instead. The court reporter is recording everything you say.

25. Don't look at the attorney who called you as a witness or at the judge for help when you are on the witness stand. You are responsible for your testimony.

26. Beware of questions involving distances and time. If you make an estimate, make sure that everyone understands that you are estimating. Think clearly about distances and intervals of time. Be sure your estimates are reasonable.

27. Don't be afraid to look the jurors in the eye. Jurors are naturally sympathetic to witnesses and want to hear what they have to say. Look at them most of the time and speak to them as frankly and openly as you would to a friend or neighbor.

28. Don't argue with the attorney cross-examining you. The attorney has every right to question you. The attorney who called you should object if the other attorney asks an inappropriate question. Don't answer a question with a question unless the question you are asked is not clear.

29. Don't lose your temper, no matter how hard you are pressed. If you lose your temper, you have played right into the hands of the cross-examiner.

30. Be courteous. Courtesy is one of the best ways to make a good impression on the judge and jury. Address the judge as "Your Honor."

31. If asked whether you have talked to the attorney who is calling you as a witness or to an investigator, admit it

freely. If you are being paid a fee, admit without hesitation that you are receiving compensation.

32. Avoid joking, wisecracks, and condescending comments or inflections. A trial is a serious matter.

EXPERT TESTIMONY

33. Most people learn visually. Use blackboards, diagrams, charts, etc., liberally. While standing at the blackboard or easel, turn around and talk to the judge and jury. Inevitably, witnesses not following this instruction get into an inaudible conversation with the blackboard.

34. Draw in proportion. Before drawing anything—think! Don't start with the cliché "Well, I am not much of an artist." Draw in proportion, and never refer to "here" and "there." If you use vague terms, a court that is reviewing the proceedings (e.g., an appeals court) will not understand what you mean. Describe what you draw verbally, and number each relevant representation.

35. Never read from notes unless absolutely necessary. If you must, announce the fact that you are doing so and state your reason—that is, refreshing memory, need for specificity, etc. Be aware that the attorney cross-examining you will likely have a right to see the notes and perhaps all of the documents that you took to the stand. That is why it is important that you tell your or the agency's attorney that you plan to bring these materials to court.

36. An opposing attorney may cross-examine you using articles, books, other people's opinions, or things you have said. You may be confronted with something that appears contradictory in an effort to show that your opinion is inconsistent with these other sources. Ask to see the book or article to which the opposing attorney refers. Read it, and compare what you read with what the attorney has said. Often, you will find that something has been taken out of context or misinterpreted by the attorney. You can then demonstrate not only that you are correct, but that the article or book agrees with your statement.

CONCLUSION

37. When you finish testifying, nod to the judge and jury and say "thank you."

38. After each appearance as an expert witness, check with the attorney or others for a critique of your performance. Use the critique to improve the way you testify in the future. If there are transcripts, obtain a copy of your testimony and critique it yourself.

Effectiveness of Testimony

Your effectiveness as an expert witness will be judged on the following issues (Myers, 1993):

- Did you consider all relevant facts?
- How much confidence can be placed in the accuracy of the facts underlying your opinion?

- Did you show an adequate understanding of the pertinent clinical and scientific principles involved in the case? Did you use methods of assessment and analysis recognized as appropriate by professionals in your field?
- Were the inferences you drew logical?
- Were your assumptions reasonable?
- Were you reasonably objective?

Your testimony will be judged on whether it was "logical, consistent, explainable, objective, and defensible" (Myers, 1993, p. 179). See Brodsky (1991) for more information about testifying in court as an expert witness.

FORENSIC ASSESSMENT

Both clinical and forensic assessments involve obtaining a case history, evaluating the mental status of the examinee, and giving a battery of psychological tests. However, a clinical assessment frequently includes the development of an intervention plan to help the child and family, whereas a *forensic assessment* provides the referral source with an objective opinion about the examinee (e.g., the specific cause of any abnormal test findings or statement of prognosis, the amount and types of future psychological services needed), regardless of whether it helps the child and her or his family. Forensic assessments can nonetheless be therapeutic for children and their families, especially in cases of maltreatment in which painful secrets are revealed and safety plans are initiated. In addition to evaluating a child's emotional status and perceptual, sensory, intellectual, motor, and cognitive skills, the forensic evaluation should assess daily living skills such as academic, communication, social, and vocational skills (Kreutzer, Harris-Marwitz, & Myers, 1990). Generally, clinicians serve as advocates for their clients, whereas forensic evaluators serve as fact finders.

Purposes of Forensic Assessments

The following are some of the purposes of forensic assessments.

- In legal cases involving personal injury, the aim is to arrive at a judgment about how a specific event—such as an accident, exposure to a chemical or toxic substance, malfunctioning equipment, medical negligence, or situational stress—may have contributed to any psychological or medical problems of the examinee.
- In child custody evaluations, the aim is to help the court learn about the strengths and weaknesses of each parent and about the factors that will promote the best interests of the child.
- In civil litigation for psychiatric hospitalization, the aim is to help decide whether the examinee's commitment should be voluntary or involuntary (i.e., at the parents' request in the case of a child).

- In child maltreatment evaluations, the aim is to evaluate the child's functioning and to recommend interventions. In addition, those who work in Child Protective Services or law enforcement will evaluate whether the child was maltreated, whether the child's report and the reports of others of the maltreatment are credible, whether the child is at risk for further maltreatment, and what steps should be taken to protect the child.

The courts might ask forensic clinicians to answer questions such as the following (Koocher & Keith-Spiegel, 1990): Was the child abused sexually? Which parent should be given custody of the child? Was the adolescent competent to waive his or her *Miranda* rights (the rights of a person accused of a crime to have counsel and not to incriminate himself or herself) when he or she was arrested?

Clinical assessments with children usually are conducted at the request of parents, schools, or health care providers. Forensic assessments, in contrast, are requested by attorneys, courts, or insurance companies, but they may also be requested by parents or by adolescents directly; in cases of child maltreatment, forensic assessments are usually required by law.

Questions Asked in a Personal Injury Case

When the forensic assessment relates to a personal injury case in which a child is involved, the referral source will usually request answers to the following questions:

1. Does the examinee have psychological problems? If so, what types of problems are present and how severe are the problems?
2. Did the examinee have any psychological problems before the event? If so, what were they?
3. Did the event exacerbate the examinee's psychological problems? If so, what proportion of the examinee's psychological problems might be associated with the event?
4. Are the problems the examinee is reportedly having commonly observed following similar types of events?
5. Are there other factors not related to the event that contribute to the examinee's psychological problems? If so, what are these factors?
6. Is the examinee reporting the problems accurately? If not, what is interfering with the accuracy of the reports?
7. Are the examinee's parents reporting the problems accurately? If not, what might be the reasons for the inaccuracies?
8. Is the examinee exaggerating the problems? If so, what might be the reasons for the exaggerations?
9. Are the parents exaggerating the examinee's problems? If so, what might be the reasons for the exaggerations?
10. To what extent will the examinee recover from the event? How much confidence do you have in your estimate of recoverability?

11. What type of treatment does the examinee need?
12. For what length of time will the examinee need treatment?
13. Will the examinee need reevaluations in the future? If so, how often will they be needed?

Explaining a Forensic Assessment

The forensic clinician will usually inform the examinee about the nature and purpose of the assessment, including how the assessment will be conducted and what the examinee's role will be. Here is an example of what might be said to an adolescent and her or his family regarding a personal injury case:

"I am Dr. (Mr., Ms.) _____. I have been retained by _____ to evaluate you in connection with your recent automobile accident.

"I will ask you questions about your past and current life and about the accident. I want to learn about you, your interests, how you think and feel about things in general, and about other things as well." [In some cases, the clinician might add, "I also may recommend that you complete some psychological tests."]

"You may not want to answer some of my questions, and that is your right. However, if you don't want to answer some questions, I will advise the attorneys about which questions you did not answer. OK?

"You can telephone your attorney at any time during the evaluation, and I'll arrange for you to make your call in private if you want to.

"Please remember that the results of my evaluation will be given to your attorney [or other referring party] and will also be read by the other party in the dispute. You should also keep in mind that I may be asked to testify in court about the things we talk about or do today. This means that the results of my evaluation are not private or confidential."

You would, of course, have to modify these statements for a younger child.

Use of the Results of a Forensic Assessment

The results of the forensic assessment will be used in litigation (a legal proceeding, which can take place in or out of court) either to support or to refute a particular claim. A forensic clinician must know how to conduct a clinical assessment, must know the specific legal issues relevant to the referral, and must be familiar with formal court procedures. Because the results of a forensic assessment will probably be cited in a legal proceeding, it is critical that you make thorough, well-documented case notes. (Of course, this advice holds for clinical assessments as well, because they too may be used in legal proceedings.) Be sure you carefully clarify the purpose of the assessment (e.g., an investigation or a mediation) with the attorney or other referral source and obtain all of the examinee's relevant records (Koocher & Keith-Spiegel, 1990). Also consider any potential conflicts of interest, and apprise the referral source of your areas of competence.

Rendering an Opinion

Because forensic clinicians must evaluate their findings in relation to the questions that are posed by the attorneys, they may render an opinion, such as the following: "There is a reasonable certainty that the accident contributed to the examinee's psychological problems" or "In my opinion, his memory problems were present before the injury and no additional memory problems developed after the injury." *Opinions should be supported by or based on the data obtained in the evaluation.* Because the forensic assessment is part of an adversarial system, the forensic clinician will usually be cross-examined by the opposing attorney. Forensic clinicians must be prepared to defend their opinions, to maintain clear and complete records, and to justify their procedures and conclusions. (See Adams and Rankin, 1996, for more information about conducting forensic psychological evaluations.)

Precariousness of Dual Roles

Mental health professionals who become involved in cases of child maltreatment are in a precarious role when they both investigate the allegation of maltreatment and treat either the child victim or the perpetrator (Melton, 1994). Melton advocates that mental health professionals focus on clinical evaluation (for the purpose of treatment planning, not legal investigation) and treatment. Furthermore, Melton believes that "mental health professionals should not offer an opinion about whether a particular child was abused or whether he or she told the truth, and courts should not admit such an opinion...[because] such opinions are inherently misleading and prejudicial, and...they should be excluded from evidence" (pp. 111–112). These opinions, Melton argues, involve common sense inferences—not specialized knowledge—and are within the province of the judge and the jury. However, mental health professionals do make a unique contribution in cases of child maltreatment by conducting diagnostic evaluations and recommending interventions. The legal system will therefore need to define the role of mental health professionals in cases of child maltreatment.

We hope our colleagues will step forward as ethical professionals, as thoughtful experts, and as wise advocates in cases in which their knowledge and expertise can legitimately inform decision makers and advance the well-being of children.

—Gerald P. Koocher and Patricia C. Keith-Spiegel

THINKING THROUGH THE ISSUES

1. Why is it important to have a code of ethical behavior for assessment-related clinical activities?
2. In what ways has the IDEA affected the practice of psychological assessment in the schools and in the community?
3. Has the IDEA improved assessment procedures? What is the basis for your answer?
4. In what ways may the IDEA have adversely affected the practice of school psychology?
5. How would you decide whether to recommend that a child with a disability be placed in a general education classroom?
6. What specific advice would you give to a parent of a child with disabilities about placing the child in a general education classroom?
7. How can psychological reports assist teachers in developing better IEPs?
8. Should issues involving assessment and special education practices be resolved in the courts? If yes, why? If no, why not, and where should they be resolved?
9. How do you think you would react if you were a parent and were told that your child had a disability?
10. How would you react if you learned that an examinee was being maltreated?
11. What information would you want to have before you reported suspected child maltreatment?
12. Given your personal history and training, what concerns you the most about your possible performance as an expert witness? In what areas do you think you would do well? How could you prepare yourself for this experience?

SUMMARY

Ethical Responsibilities of Psychologists

1. The Ethical Standards of the American Psychological Association serve as guidelines for your work as a psychologist.
2. The standards emphasize that psychologists need to have sufficient training in their specialty area, to consult with other professionals when in doubt about assessment findings, to know federal and state laws concerning assessment, to be aware of personal and societal biases and nondiscriminatory practices, to avoid multiple relationships, to obtain informed consent from parents to conduct the assessment with the child, to protect the confidentiality of the assessment information, to use multiple methods of data gathering, to interpret the data cautiously and appropriately, to explain assessment findings clearly, to maintain assessment data, to state the reliability and validity of the assessment results in the report, to understand the power of recommendations, to recognize their own competencies, to make accurate public statements, to explain financial costs to the client, and to conduct research in a manner that considers the dignity and welfare of the client.
3. It is also important to follow the American Psychological Association guidelines for work with ethnically, linguistically, and culturally diverse populations. These guidelines stress the importance of understanding the client's ethnic and cultural background in administering and interpreting assessment instruments.

4. Following the guidelines of the National Association of School Psychologists is important for psychologists who work in the schools.

Overview of Four Federal Laws Regarding Children with Disabilities

5. In addition to understanding the ethical principles that guide your practice as a psychologist, you need to be aware of four federal laws critical to the practice of assessment: the Individuals with Disabilities Education Act (IDEA; also referred to as IDEA '97), Section 504 of the Rehabilitation Act of 1973 (Section 504), the Americans with Disabilities Act (ADA), and the Family Educational Rights to Privacy Act (FERPA).

Individuals with Disabilities Education Act (IDEA)

6. In 1975, Congress passed Public Law 94-142, the Education for all Handicapped Children Act.
7. Congress designed the law to assure the right to a free appropriate public education (FAPE) for all children with disabilities.
8. In 1990, Congress updated Public Law 94-142 and changed its name to the Individuals with Disabilities Education Act (IDEA; Public Law 101-476).
9. In 1997, the IDEA was reauthorized and amended (Public Law 105-17; referred to as IDEA '97).
10. In March 1999, regulations implementing the IDEA '97 were issued.
11. The principles and key provisions that form the foundation of the IDEA '97 are summarized in items 12 to 22 below.
12. Children with disabilities must receive a FAPE that provides special education and related services, including nonacademic and extracurricular services and activities, designed to meet their unique needs and prepare them for employment and independent living.
13. Each child being considered for special education and related services must receive a full, individualized, and appropriate evaluation. The evaluation must identify all of the child's special education needs, even if these needs are not commonly related to the child's disability.
14. Children with disabilities who are eligible for special education and related services must have an Individualized Education Program (IEP).
15. Children with disabilities should be educated with children who are not disabled in the LRE.
16. Children with disabilities and their parents must be given the opportunity to participate in meetings where decisions will be made regarding the identification, evaluation, or placement of the children or regarding the provision of a FAPE to the children.
17. All procedural safeguards must be followed. A copy of the procedural safeguards must be provided to parents.
18. Schools are responsible for finding, identifying, and evaluating children, including private school students, with disabilities who are in need of special education and related services.
19. Children with disabilities must be provided services to the extent necessary to enable them to progress appropriately in the general curriculum and advance appropriately toward achieving the goals set out in their IEP.
20. Informed written consent of parents must be obtained before conducting any evaluation and before special education and

related services are initially implemented for a child with a disability.
21. Parents of children with disabilities must be given feedback through such means as periodic report cards on the children's progress with the same frequency as parents of children who are not disabled.
22. States, localities, educational service agencies, and federal agencies are required to implement services to provide for the education of all children with disabilities.
23. The IDEA '97 establishes safeguards for the identification, evaluation, and placement of children with disabilities.
24. The IDEA '97 requires that states take steps to ensure children with disabilities equitable access to their programs and remove barriers that prevent such access.
25. The IDEA '97 requires the IEP team to consider whether a child with disabilities requires assistive technology devices and services in order to receive a FAPE.
26. The IDEA '97 requires that a full continuum of alternative placements be considered for children with disabilities (regular classrooms, special education classrooms, nonpublic schools, home instruction, instruction in hospitals).
27. The IDEA '97 requires the development of an IEP for children between 3 and 21 years or an Individualized Family Service Plan (IFSP) for children between birth and 2 years 11 months.
28. The IDEA '97 requires that parents be fully informed of all information relevant to their children in their native language or other mode of communication. This includes providing notice of the IEP meeting to the parents in their native language or other primary mode of communication and arranging for an interpreter at the meeting, as needed.
29. The IDEA '97 gives parents the right to have access to their child's records and to actively participate in each IEP meeting.
30. The IDEA '97 gives parents the right to an independent evaluation of their children at public expense if they disagree with the evaluation conducted by the school. However, if the public school initiates a hearing and the hearing officer determines that the school's evaluation was appropriate, the parent has a right to an independent assessment but not at public expense.
31. The IDEA '97 requires that schools consider an evaluation obtained by parents at their own expense if the evaluation meets agency criteria.
32. The IDEA '97 requires that a group of qualified professionals and the parents decide on the child's eligibility for special education and related services.
33. The IDEA '97 requires that information about children be kept confidential in accordance with FERPA requirements. However, it requires that a child's IEP be accessible to regular education teachers, special education teachers, related service providers, and any other service provider who is responsible for its implementation. The IDEA '97 also states that each teacher and service provider shall be informed of his or her specific responsibilities related to the implementation of a child's IEP and the specific accommodations, modifications, and supports that must be provided for the child in accordance with the IEP.
34. The IDEA '97 requires that schools provide services, modifications, or accommodations that children with disabilities need in order to receive a FAPE.
35. The IDEA '97 requires that children with disabilities be disciplined only for the same reasons or length of time as children without disabilities.

36. The IDEA '97 provides procedures for parents and schools to resolve disputes (through mediation and impartial due process hearings) relating to the identification, evaluation, educational placement of a child with a disability or the provision of a FAPE for the child.

37. The IDEA '97 requires that during the due process hearing or judicial proceeding, unless the parties agree otherwise, the child involved in the dispute shall remain in his or her current educational placement. This is commonly referred to as "stay put."

38. The LRE of the IDEA also is referred to as "mainstreaming."

39. The IEP team is composed of the following individuals: (a) the parents, (b) at least one general education teacher of the child if the child is or may be participating in general education, (c) at least one special education teacher of the child (or special education provider), (d) a representative of the school who is qualified to provide specialized instruction or supervise special education teachers and is knowledgeable about the general curriculum and available resources, (e) an individual who can interpret the instructional implications, (f) other individuals who have knowledge or special expertise about the child (invited by the parent or the agency), and (g) the child, when appropriate.

40. The team must determine services needed to provide a FAPE in a setting that is as close to the general education program as feasible.

41. The IEP must be reviewed at least annually.

42. Federal regulations issued in May 1999 require that school systems maintain a full continuum of alternative placements to meet the needs of children with disabilities for special education and related services.

43. The regulations require the IEP team to consider whether the child can be educated in the LRE with the use of appropriate supplementary aids and services.

44. Assessment procedures must be nondiscriminatory.

45. Assessment procedures must be administered in the child's native language or other mode of communication, unless it is clearly not feasible to do so.

46. Assessment instruments used with a child with limited English proficiency must measure the extent to which the child has a disability and needs special education, not the child's English language skills.

47. A variety of assessment tools and strategies must be used to evaluate the child.

48. Standardized tests must be validated for the specific purpose for which they are used.

49. Standardized tests must be administered by trained and knowledgeable personnel in accordance with the instructions provided by the test producer.

50. The report must include information about instances when standard test administration procedures are not followed.

51. The instruments and other evaluation procedures should assess specific areas of educational need, not only general intelligence.

52. The test results obtained with children who have impaired sensory, manual, or speaking skills should accurately reflect their academic or cognitive abilities, not their impaired sensory or communication skills.

53. No single procedure is used as the sole criterion to determine whether a child has a disability or to determine an appropriate educational program.

54. All areas related to the suspected disability should be assessed, including, if appropriate, health, vision, hearing, social and emotional status, general intelligence, academic performance, communicative status, and motor abilities.

55. The evaluation must be sufficiently comprehensive to identify all of the child's special education and related services needs, not just those associated with his or her disability classification.

56. Only technically sound instruments shall be used to assess cognitive, behavioral, physical, and developmental factors.

57. The assessment tools and strategies used must provide information that will help in determining the educational needs of the child.

58. When a child with disabilities has been removed from his or her current educational placement for more than 10 school days or when the behavior of a child with disabilities interferes with the education of himself or herself or that of others, a functional behavioral assessment shall be conducted and a behavioral intervention plan shall be developed and implemented.

59. The main purposes of an initial evaluation or reevaluation under the IDEA are to provide the IEP team with the data it needs to determine (a) whether a child has a disability and is eligible for special education and related services and (b) the child's unique strengths and needs.

60. Procedural safeguards must be followed in implementing the provisions of the IDEA.

61. If parents disagree with any aspect of the evaluation process or recommended interventions, they are entitled to seek a resolution of their grievances through (from least to most formal) (a) nonbinding mediation, (b) appeal to the state department of education, (c) hearings/arbitration, and (d) formal legal proceedings at the court level.

62. The IDEA '97 requires that state- or districtwide group tests administered to children without disabilities also be administered to children with disabilities.

63. For children unable to participate in a state- or districtwide assessment program, states must provide alternative assessments. After the evaluation is completed, the IEP team determines whether the student has one of 14 defined disabilities.

64. The 14 disabilities are autism, deaf-blindness, deafness, emotional disturbance, hearing impairment, mental retardation, multiple disabilities, orthopedic impairment, other health impairment, specific learning disability, speech or language impairment, traumatic brain injury, visual impairment, and developmental delays.

65. The largest group of children receiving services in 1997–98 was those with specific learning disabilities (51.48%), followed by children with speech and language impairments (19.95%), mental retardation (11.28%), and emotional disturbances (8.51%). These four categories contained 91.22% of all children receiving services. The remaining 8.78% of the children had multiple disabilities, hearing impairments, orthopedic impairments, other health impairments, visual impairments, autism, deaf-blindness, or traumatic brain injury.

66. The school placements of children covered by the IDEA for the 1996–97 school year were as follows: 45.75% were in a regular class, 28.47% were in a resource room, 26.43% were in a separate class, 3.10% were in a separate school, 0.70% were in a residential facility, and 0.54% were homebound or in a hospital environment.

67. The IEP is an important document because it spells out the needs of the child with a disability and how the educational agency will satisfy these needs.

68. An IEP should provide a statement of the services the child needs in order to progress in meeting annual goals, to advance in the general curriculum, and to participate in extracurricular activities and other nonacademic activities.

69. The IDEA '97 regulations dealing with suspensions and expulsions are complex.

70. The child's IEP should be reviewed periodically—but not less than once a year—to determine whether the goals and objectives are being achieved and whether revisions are needed.

71. Parents are an integral part of the reevaluation process.

72. Public Law 99-457, passed in 1986, amended Public Law 94-142 to (a) authorize an early intervention program for infants and toddlers who have a disability and for their families and (b) extend all the rights and protections of Public Law 94-142 to children with disabilities from ages 3 through 5 years. Once a child is identified, an Individualized Family Service Plan (IFSP) is developed with parental consent.

73. The IDEA has been the subject of much litigation since its inception. Its sheer volume—and the hundreds of issues it addresses—leaves the IDEA open to different interpretations.

Section 504 of the Rehabilitation Act of 1973

74. Section 504 of the Rehabilitation Act of 1973 (Public Law 93-112) was designed to protect individuals with disabilities from discrimination in any setting receiving funds from the federal government.

Americans with Disabilities Act (ADA)

75. The Americans with Disabilities Act (ADA) of 1990 (Public Law 101-336) provides protection from discrimination for individuals with disabilities in all settings, regardless of whether federal funds are involved.

Comment on the IDEA '97, Section 504, and the ADA

76. Interpretations of the IDEA '97, Section 504, and the ADA involve complex judgments on the part of (a) educators and professionals working in schools, (b) administrative hearing officers at both the local and state levels, (c) judges from U.S. District Courts, (d) judges from U.S. Circuit Courts of Appeals, and (e) justices from the U.S. Supreme Court.

77. Educational methodology decisions are best left to experts—namely, educators—and not judges or attorneys.

78. Parents and children should never be coerced or intimidated into accepting the school's placement decision and the IEP.

79. Schools must listen to parents and be flexible in their approaches to formulating IEPs.

80. Both schools and parents need to realize that interpretation of the IDEA by the courts is controversial.

Confidentiality of Assessment Findings and Records

81. Confidentiality is an ethical practice, the obligation never to reveal information obtained in an assessment (or through any professional relationship) without specific consent from the client. It protects the client from unauthorized disclosures of information given in confidence to a clinician.

82. Privileged communication is a legal right granted by state and federal laws. It protects clients from having their disclosures to certain professionals—such as psychologists, marriage and family counselors, social workers, attorneys, clergy, and physicians, including psychiatrists—revealed during legal proceedings without their informed consent. (Check your state law to learn whether your profession is bound by privileged communication.)

83. Three exceptions to confidentiality and privileged communication are as follows: (a) When there is a reasonable suspicion of child maltreatment (i.e., child abuse or neglect), (b) when the examinee poses a physical threat to another person, and (c) when the examinee is a minor and poses a threat to himself or herself (e.g., any situation that places the minor in danger of death, where the delay of medical treatment would pose a health risk to the minor, or where treatment is needed to decrease physical pain).

84. State laws generally require that individuals working with children—such as child caregivers, teachers, physicians, psychologists, psychiatrists, social workers, marriage and family therapists, counselors, and clergy (in some states)—report child maltreatment when there is reasonable suspicion that maltreatment has occurred.

85. Regulatory statutes use the term *reasonable suspicion* to mean that a person should consider the possibility of child maltreatment based on facts that could cause a reasonable person in a similar position to come to the same conclusion.

86. The role of the reporting party is not to determine or to prove that maltreatment did in fact occur but, rather, to report a reasonable suspicion of maltreatment.

87. Children and parents must be informed about confidentiality and its limits.

88. The Family Educational Rights and Privacy Act (FERPA; Public Law 93-830) is designed to protect the privacy of children's educational records (i.e., all records, files, and documents and any material in the records related to their parents).

89. FERPA gives parents the right to (a) inspect and review their children's education records, (b) request that the records be amended if mistakes have been made, and (c) partially control disclosures of the information contained in the records.

The Challenges of Being an Expert Witness

90. A psychologist may be called on to testify in court or at special hearings conducted in schools or agencies.

91. Testifying as an expert witness can be a difficult experience, especially in court or courtlike settings, because the adversarial system used to litigate cases differs from the scientific method.

92. During the information-gathering period before trial—a period known as the time of discovery—you may be asked to give a deposition.

93. When you are sworn in as an expert witness in court (or at an administrative hearing) and answer the questions posed to you by your attorney, you are under direct examination.

94. An expert witness can and should rely on notes or other materials for information that cannot be readily recalled.

95. Your role as an expert witness is to provide information to the court so that the court can reach an appropriate decision.

96. Be prepared for the opposing attorney to scrutinize your credentials, your report, and your recommendations, as well as your expertise and credibility.

97. There are many things that you can and should do to prepare to testify as an expert witness.
98. Your testimony will be judged on whether it was logical, consistent, explainable, objective, and defensible.

Forensic Assessment

99. Both clinical and forensic assessments involve obtaining a case history, evaluating the mental status of the examinee, and giving a battery of psychological tests. However, a clinical assessment frequently includes the development of an intervention plan to help the child and family, whereas a forensic assessment provides the referral source with an objective opinion about the examinee.
100. The results of the forensic assessment will be used in litigation (a legal proceeding, which can take place in or out of court) either to support or to refute a particular claim.
101. Mental health professionals who become involved in cases of child maltreatment are in a precarious role when they both investigate the allegation of maltreatment and treat either the child victim or the perpetrator.

KEY TERMS, CONCEPTS, AND NAMES

Ethical responsibilities of psychologists (p. 42)
APA ethical guidelines (p. 42)
Informed consent (p. 42)
APA guidelines for working with ethnically, linguistically, and culturally diverse populations (p. 43)
APA guidelines for conducting evaluations in child protection matters (p. 44)
NASP assessment guidelines (p. 44)
Local educational agencies (LEAs) (p. 45)
Office for Special Education and Rehabilitative Services (OSERS) (p. 45)
Office for Special Education Programs (OSEP) (p. 45)
Free appropriate public education (FAPE) (p. 47)
Public Law 94-142 (p. 48)
Individuals with Disabilities Education Act (IDEA) (p. 48)
Public Law 101-476 (p. 48)
Public Law 105-17 (p. 48)
IDEA '97 (p. 48)
Least restrictive environment (LRE) (p. 49)
Full inclusion (p. 49)
Testing and evaluation procedures (p. 50)
Procedural safeguards and parent involvement (p. 51)
Statewide assessments (p. 53)
Determination of disability (p. 53)
Eligibility for special education (p. 55)
Individualized Education Program (IEP) (p. 56)
Discipline procedures (p. 58)
Manifest determination review (p. 60)
Reviews and reevaluations (p. 60)

The IDEA Part C: Infants and Toddlers with Disabilities (p. 61)
Court interpretations of the IDEA (p. 61)
Cedar Rapids Community School District v. Garret F. (p. 62)
Section 504 of the Rehabilitation Act of 1973 (p. 68)
Americans with Disabilities Act (ADA) (p. 69)
Confidentiality (p. 71)
Privileged communication (p. 71)
Reporting child maltreatment (p. 71)
Discussing confidentiality with children and parents (p. 72)
Family Educational Rights and Privacy Act (FERPA) (p. 73)
The challenges of being an expert witness (p. 73)
Adversarial system (p. 73)
Testifying as an expert witness (p. 74)
Time of discovery (p. 74)
Deposition (p. 74)
The direct examination (p. 74)
Refreshing recollection (p. 74)
The cross-examination (p. 77)
Suggestions for testifying as an expert witness (p. 77)
Effectiveness of testimony (p. 79)
Forensic assessment (p. 79)
Purposes of forensic assessments (p. 79)
Questions asked in a personal injury case (p. 80)
Explaining a forensic assessment (p. 80)
Use of the results of a forensic assessment (p. 80)
Rendering an opinion (p. 81)
Precariousness of dual roles (p. 81)

STUDY QUESTIONS

1. Discuss the ethical standards related to assessment.
2. Discuss the IDEA as it relates to assessment. Include in your discussion (a) testing and evaluation procedures, (b) IEPs, (c) parents' rights, and (d) the least restrictive environment (LRE).
3. Discuss court cases concerning interpretation of the IDEA.
4. Discuss Section 504 of the Rehabilitation Act of 1973 and the Americans with Disabilities Act.
5. Discuss the confidentiality of assessment findings and records and privileged communication. Include in your discussion the Family Educational Rights and Privacy Act of 1974.
6. Discuss the issues involved in reporting child maltreatment.
7. Discuss the challenges of testifying as an expert witness.
8. What are some of the issues involved in reporting suspected cases of child maltreatment?
9. Discuss the types of questions that may be asked during a cross-examination.
10. What is involved in a forensic assessment? Include in your discussion (a) the purposes of forensic assessments, (b) questions asked in a personal injury case, (c) explaining a forensic assessment, (d) use of the results of a forensic assessment, (e) rendering an opinion, and (f) the precariousness of dual roles.

4

USEFUL STATISTICAL AND MEASUREMENT CONCEPTS

We conquer the facts of nature when we observe and experiment upon them. When we measure them we have made them our servants. A little statistical insight trains them for invaluable work.

—Edward L. Thorndike

Goals and Objectives

This chapter is designed to enable you to do the following:

- Recognize the primary scales of measurement

- Understand the main measures of central tendency and measures of dispersion

- Explain the value of the normal curve and how you can use it to generate standard scores

- Discuss the role of correlation and regression in evaluating test scores

- Understand the importance of reliability and validity in evaluating tests

- Describe methods for obtaining confidence intervals

- Explain the role of factor analysis in evaluating tests

A knowledge of statistical and measurement concepts will enhance your understanding of tests, test manuals, and research articles and will enable you to evaluate the psychometric properties of intelligence tests, special ability tests, and interview and observational data more effectively. *Psychometrics* refers to the quantitative assessment of an individual's psychological traits or attributes. This chapter reviews basic statistical and measurement concepts; for more information, refer to statistics and measurement texts.

THE WHY OF PSYCHOLOGICAL MEASUREMENT AND STATISTICS

Measurement in psychology is different from physical measurement. In our everyday experience, the numbers we assign to the physical properties of objects, such as height, weight, and length, reflect some property of the object that we can perceive directly. Psychological measurement can never be as precise as physical measurement because it measures intangibles. Still, psychological measurement conveys meaningful and important information about people. Psychological measurement is designed to measure attributes of the person, such as intelligence, motor skills, reading ability, adaptive behavior, and extroversion-introversion. Psychological measurement produces a test score, or rating, that is said to reflect the attribute. Measurement in psychology is designed to measure not the entire person, but only specific attributes of the person. Attributes selected for measurement are often related to cognitive ability, achievement skills, personality, temperament, attitudes, interests, and vocational preferences.

Statistical procedures reduce large amounts of data to manageable and understandable forms for use in the study of populations and samples, in decision making, and in making reliable inferences from observational data. Statistics help us to communicate information about test scores, and they assist us in drawing conclusions about those scores. Without statistics it would be impossible to evaluate chance variations in the scores we obtain. Only by using statistics can we tell whether (a) a child's scores on a test administered at two different times differ significantly, (b) a child's scores on two different tests differ significantly, or (c) the scores of two different children on the same test differ significantly.

Remember that test scores are imperfect measures; statistics can help us determine the amount of error present in test scores. A conclusion based on statistical analysis of test scores is limited, however. It tells us nothing about how the scores were obtained, what the test scores mean, or how they should be interpreted. And test scores also do not tell us whether the examinee performed at his or her best level or whether the testing conditions were favorable. Other kinds of information will shed light on these areas.

Measurement enables us to compare and contrast many of the phenomena that we find in the world. Individual difference is what psychology is all about. People differ: Some are energetic, others lethargic; some are extroverted, others introverted; some are well adjusted, others maladjusted; some are good readers, others poor readers. Measurement helps us describe and measure this variability. And through the application of psychological theories, we will gain some understanding of why people differ on various traits and characteristics.

Measurement is a process of assigning numerals to objects or events according to certain rules. In physical measurement, the use of a ruler or a scale implies that we are following rules to measure the length or weight of an object. In psychological measurement, the use of a 5-point rating scale (e.g., 1 = very uncooperative, 5 = very cooperative) to rate a child's level of cooperativeness, after observing the child on a playground for 10 minutes, implies that we also are following a measurement rule to measure behavior. Obviously, physical measurement is more precise than psychological measurement, but both techniques qualify as measurement procedures. Thus, the measurement process, whether physical or psychological, consists of (a) defining a dimension (e.g., height) or behavior (e.g., cooperativeness) to be measured, (b) determining the measurement operations, (c) specifying the rules of measurement, and (d) using a scale of units to express the measurement.

In most cases of physical measurement, an instrument like a ruler, a scale, or an electronic calculator is used to obtain a number. In many cases of psychological measurement, a formal test plays a role similar to that of the physical instrument. At other times, however, the human observer makes a direct judgment. Even in the case of physical measurement, a human observer—for example, a witness describing a suspect—often must estimate a variable like height without the help of an instrument.

DESCRIPTIVE STATISTICS

Descriptive statistics summarize data obtained about a sample of individuals. Descriptive statistics include measurements on a scale, measures of central tendency, measures of dispersion, properties of the normal curve, and correlations. Table 4-1 shows symbols commonly used in statistics and psychometrics. These symbols are a shorthand method of describing important characteristics of a test formula or norm group. This list is for reference, not for memorization. As you gain more experience in the field, the symbols will become familiar to you.

Scales of Measurement

Data can be ordered by various methods. In most cases, we use one of four types of scales: nominal, ordinal, interval, or ratio. A scale is a system for assigning values or scores to some measurable trait or characteristic. We can then subject the values to various mathematical procedures to determine

Table 4-1
Common Statistical and Psychometric Symbols and Abbreviations

Symbol	Definition	Symbol	Definition
a	Intercept constant in a regression equation	SE_E, SE_{est}	Standard error of estimate
b	Slope constant in a regression equation	SEM, SE_m,	Standard error of measurement
c	Any unspecified constant	SE_{meas}, S_m,	
CA	Chronological age	s_m, s_{meas},	
cf	Cumulative frequency	or s_{err}	
DQ	Developmental quotient	t	t test
f	Frequency	T	T score; standard score with a mean of 50 and standard deviation of 10
F	Test statistic in analysis of variance and covariance	x	Deviation score $X - \overline{X}$; indicates how far the score falls above or below the mean of the group
IQ	Intelligence quotient		
M	Mean (see also $\overline{X}$)	X	Raw score
MA	Mental age	$\overline{X}$	Mean
Md or Mdn	Median	Y	A second raw score
n	Number of cases in a subsample	z	z score; standard score with a mean of 0 and standard deviation of 1
N	Number of cases in a sample		
p	Probability or proportion	σ	Standard deviation of a population
P	Percentile	σ^2	Variance of a population
Q	Semi-interquartile range; half the difference between Q_3 and Q_1	Σ	"Sum of"; ΣX means to add up all the Xs (scores)
Q_1	First quartile score (25th percentile score)	ΣX	Sum of Xs
Q_3	Third quartile score (75th percentile score)	ΣX^2	Sum of squared Xs (square first, then add)
r	Pearson correlation coefficient	$(\Sigma X)^2$	Squared sum of Xs (add first, then square the total)
r^2	Coefficient of determination; the proportion of variance in Y attributable to X	ΣXY	Sum of cross products of X and Y (multiply each $X \times Y$, then add)
r_{pb}	Point biserial correlation coefficient	ϕ	Phi coefficient; a correlation coefficient for a 2×2 contingency table
r_s or ρ	Spearman rank-difference correlation coefficient (also referred to as rho)	χ^2	Chi square
r_{xx}	Reliability coefficient	$<$	Less than
r_{xy}	Validity coefficient (x represents the test score and y the criterion score)	$>$	Greater than
		$\geq$	Greater than or equal to
R	Coefficient of multiple correlation	$\leq$	Less than or equal to
$rel.\,f$	Relative frequency	$\pm$	Plus or minus
S, s, or SD	Standard deviation of the sample	$\sqrt{}$	Square root
S^2	Variance of the sample	$\neq$	Not equal to

relationships between the traits or characteristics of interest and other measured behaviors. These scales range from lower-ordered ones (nominal, ordinal) to higher-ordered ones (interval, ratio). The higher-ordered scales possess all the properties of lowered-ordered scales but have additional properties of their own.

Nominal scales. The lowest level of measurement is a *nominal measurement scale. Nominal* means "name." A

nominal scale consists of a set of nonordered categories, with one name for each item being scaled. The numbers, letters, or names usually represent mutually exclusive categories but cannot be arranged in any meaningful order. The categories are merely labels. An example of nominal scaling is the assignment of numbers to baseball players (the numbers do not reflect the players' abilities) or the designation of examinees as male or female. Although nominal scales are of limited usefulness because they allow only for classification, they are still valuable. Some variables, such as sex, ethnicity, and geographic area, can only be described by nominal scales.

Ordinal scales.   The next level of measurement is an *ordinal measurement scale*. Like a nominal scale, it classifies items, but it has the property of order (or magnitude) as well. The variable being measured is ranked, or ordered, according to the amount of some characteristic or dimension, without regard for differences in the distance between scores. An example of ordinal scaling is the ranking of persons from highest to lowest based on class standing. An ordinal scale tells us who is first, second, and third; it does not tell us, for example, whether the distance between the first- and second-ranked scores is the same as the distance between the second- and third-ranked scores. The difference between the first- and second-ranked grade point averages could be .10 (e.g., 3.30 versus 3.20), but the difference between the second- and third-ranked grade point averages could be .80 (e.g., 3.20 versus 2.40). Another type of ordinal scale is a rating scale, such as

No anxiety	Mild anxiety	Moderate anxiety	Severe anxiety	Extreme anxiety
1	2	3	4	5

Interval scales.   The third level of measurement is an *interval measurement scale*. It classifies like a nominal scale and orders like an ordinal scale, but it adds an arbitrary zero point and equal units. Examples of interval scales are the Celsius scale, which measures temperature, and the Wechsler Intelligence Scale for Children–III (WISC–III), which measures intelligence and reports test scores (or standard scores). On the WISC–III, an increase of 10 IQ points from 100 to 110 reflects the same amount of change as an increase from 120 to 130. However, it makes no sense to say that a child with an IQ of 150 is twice as intelligent as a child with an IQ of 75, because interval scales lack a true zero point and because an IQ of zero has no meaning. Similarly, it makes no sense to say that a temperature reading of 0° reflects a complete lack of temperature, although you can say that the difference between 10°C and 20°C is the same as the difference between 60°C and 70°C.

Ratio scales.   The highest level of measurement is a *ratio measurement scale*. It has a true zero point, equal intervals between adjacent units, and equality of ratios, in addition to order and classification. Because there is a meaningful zero point, a true ratio exists between measurements made on a ratio scale. Weight is one example of a characteristic measured on a ratio scale; an individual who weighs 150 pounds is twice as heavy as one who weighs 75 pounds. Reaction time, like weight, has a true zero point, and a reaction time of 2,000 milliseconds is exactly twice as long as one of 1,000 milliseconds. Because most psychological characteristics do not permit the measurement of an absolute zero point (such

as zero intelligence), we rarely find ratio scales in psychology. Often we must be content with interval scales or the weaker ordinal and nominal scales.

Measures of Central Tendency

The three most commonly used *measures of central tendency* are the mean, the median, and the mode. These measures are used to describe the typical or center scores of a set of scores.

Mean.   The *mean* (M or $\bar{X}$) is the arithmetic average of all the scores in a set of scores. To compute the mean, divide the sum of all the scores by the total number of scores in the set (N). The formula is

$$M = \frac{\Sigma X}{N}$$

where M = mean of the scores
Σ = sum of scores
N = number of scores

Example: The mean for the four scores 2, 4, 6, and 8 is

$$M = \frac{2+4+6+8}{4} = \frac{20}{4} = 5$$

The mean is responsive to the exact position of each score in a distribution, including extreme scores. Consequently, extreme scores in a data set can affect the mean such that it becomes a poor measure of central tendency. For example, the mean of the four scores 2, 4, 6, and 32 is 11. Overall, however, the mean is the preferred measure of central tendency. It is appropriate for both interval and ratio scale data.

Median.   The *median* (*Mdn*) is the middle point in a set of scores arranged in order of magnitude: 50% of the scores lie at or above the median, and 50% of the scores lie at or below the median. If there is an even number of scores, the median is the number halfway between the two middlemost scores and therefore is not any of the actual scores. If there is an odd number of scores, the median is simply the middlemost score.

To compute the median, arrange the scores in order of magnitude from highest to lowest. Then count up (or down) through half the scores. Table 4-2 illustrates the procedure for both an even number and an odd number of scores in a distribution. In the first column there are eight scores. To obtain the median, count up four scores from the bottom and then determine the number that lies halfway between the fourth and fifth scores (the two middlemost scores). In the second column there are seven scores. To obtain the median, count up four scores from the bottom; the median is the fourth score. The median divides a distribution into two equal halves; the number of scores above the median is the same as the number below.

Table 4-2
Calculation of the Median

X (even number of scores)	X (odd number of scores)
130	130
128	128
125	125
124 ← 123.5 median	124 ← 124 median
123	123
120	120
110	110
108	

When distributions are "skewed" (i.e., the bulk of the scores are at either the high end or the low end of the set), the median is a better measure of central tendency than the mean. The median is not affected disproportionately by outliers—scores that deviate extremely from the other scores in the set. The median is an appropriate measure of central tendency for ordinal, interval, or ratio scale data.

Mode. The *mode* is the score in a set of scores that occurs more frequently than any other. In some sets two scores occur more often than any other score but with the same frequency as each other; in such cases we say that the distribution is bimodal—there are two modes in the set. When more than two scores occur more frequently than any other score and with the same frequency as each other, the distribution is said to be multimodal—there are multiple modes in the set.

The mode is greatly affected by chance and has little or no mathematical usefulness. However, it does tell us what score is most likely to occur and is therefore useful in analyzing qualitative data (e.g., What was the most frequently occur-

ring classification in the group?). It is the only appropriate measure of central tendency for nominal scale data.

Measures of Dispersion

Dispersion refers to the variability of scores in a set of scores. The range is the simplest measure of the dispersion of a group of scores. More frequently used measures of dispersion are the variance and standard deviation.

Range. The *range* (*R*) is the distance between the highest and lowest scores in a set. We compute the range by subtracting the lowest score in the set from the highest score. The formula is

$$R = H - L$$

where R = range
H = highest score
L = lowest score

Example: The range for the distribution 50, 80, 97, and 99 is

$$R = 99 - 50 = 49$$

The range is easily calculated; however, it is not a sensitive measure of dispersion because it is determined by the locations of only two scores. The range tells us nothing about the distribution of scores located between the high and low scores, and a single score can grossly change the result. Still, the range provides some information that can be useful in understanding a set of scores.

Variance. *Variance* (S^2) is a statistical measure of the amount of spread in a set of scores: the greater the spread, the greater the variance. Unlike the range, the variance takes into account every score in the group. When two different sets of scores have the same mean but different variances, it means that one set has a larger spread of scores than the other. The variance is obtained by comparing every score in a distribution to the mean of the distribution. The variance is the average squared deviation of scores from the mean. To compute

MOMMA by Mell Lazarus. Courtesy of Mell Lazarus and Field Newspaper Syndicate.

the deviation of an individual score, subtract the mean from each score. Scores that have values greater than the mean will yield positive values, whereas scores that have values less than the mean will yield negative values. Because the deviations will be squared in computing the variance, the negative values will become positive. The variance for a sample is computed in the following way:

$$S^2 = \frac{\Sigma(X - \bar{X})^2}{N - 1}$$

where
S^2 = variance of the scores
Σ = sum
X = raw score
$\bar{X}$ = mean
N = number of scores

Example: The variance for the four scores 2, 4, 6, and 8 is

$$S^2 = \frac{(2 - 5)^2 + (4 - 5)^2 + (6 - 5)^2 + (8 - 5)^2}{3}$$

$$= \frac{9 + 1 + 1 + 9}{3} = \frac{20}{3} = 6.67$$

Standard deviation. The *standard deviation* (*SD*) is the square root of the variance, representing the average of the squared deviations from the mean. It is sometimes represented by the lowercase Greek letter σ (sigma), and it is an important and commonly used measure of the extent to which scores deviate from the mean. The standard deviation is often used in the field of testing and measurement. It also is used in calculating the Deviation IQ, which is discussed later in this chapter. The standard deviation is obtained by taking the square root of the variance. The formula for calculating the standard deviation of a sample is

$$SD = \sqrt{\frac{\Sigma(X - \bar{X})^2}{N - 1}}$$

Example: The standard deviation for the four scores 2, 4, 6, and 8 in the example above is

$$SD = \sqrt{\frac{(2 - 5)^2 + (4 - 5)^2 + (6 - 5)^2 + (8 - 5)^2}{N - 1}}$$

$$= \sqrt{\frac{9 + 1 + 1 + 9}{3}} = \sqrt{\frac{20}{3}} = \sqrt{6.67} = 2.582$$

The variance and the standard deviation are both useful as measures of dispersion and in the calculation of *z* scores, which are discussed later in the chapter.

Normal Curve

The *normal* (or bell-shaped) *curve* (see Figure 4-1) is a common type of distribution. Many psychological traits are dis-

tributed roughly along a normal curve. An important feature of the normal curve is that it enables us to calculate exactly how many cases fall between any two points under the curve. Small deviations do not appreciably affect the conclusions reached by assuming a perfect normal distribution, which is fortunate, for real data are never perfectly normal.

Figure 4-1 shows the precise relationship between the standard deviation and the proportion of cases under a normal curve. It also shows the percentages of cases that fall within one, two, and three standard deviations above and below the mean. Approximately 68% of the cases fall within +1 *SD* and –1 *SD* of the mean (34% of the cases are between the mean and 1 *SD* above the mean, and 34% of the cases are between the mean and 1 *SD* below the mean). As we move away from the mean, the number of cases diminishes. The areas between +1 *SD* and +2 *SD* and between –1 *SD* and –2 *SD* each represent approximately 14% of the cases. Between +2 *SD* and +3 *SD* and between –2 *SD* and –3 *SD* from the mean, there are even fewer cases—each area represents approximately 2% of the distribution. We will return to the normal curve when we consider standard scores.

Correlations

Correlations tell us about the degree of association or co-relationship between two variables, including the strength and direction of their relationship. We determine the strength of the relationship by the absolute magnitude of the *correlation coefficient;* the maximum value is +1.00 or –1.00. The sign of the coefficient reflects the direction of the relationship. A positive correlation (+) indicates that higher scores on one variable are associated with higher scores on the second variable (e.g., more hours spent studying with a higher GPA). It also indicates that lower scores on one variable are associated with lower scores on the second variable (e.g, fewer hours spent studying with a lower GPA). Conversely, a negative correlation (–) signifies an inverse relationship—that is, high scores on one variable are associated with low scores on the other variable (e.g., a large number of days absent with a low GPA). Thus, correlation coefficients range in value from –1 to +1.

Correlations are used in prediction. The higher the correlation between two variables, the more accurately we can predict the value of one variable when we know the value of the other variable. A correlation of –1.00 or +1.00 means that we can perfectly predict a person's score on one variable if we know the person's score on another variable. In contrast, a correlation of .00 indicates that we can't predict scores on one variable from our knowledge of scores on the other variable (e.g., weight and GPA).

It is important to distinguish between the strength of the correlation and the direction of the correlation. A correlation above .50, either positive or negative, indicates a moderate to strong relationship between the two variables. When we consider the *strength* of the relationship, it doesn't matter

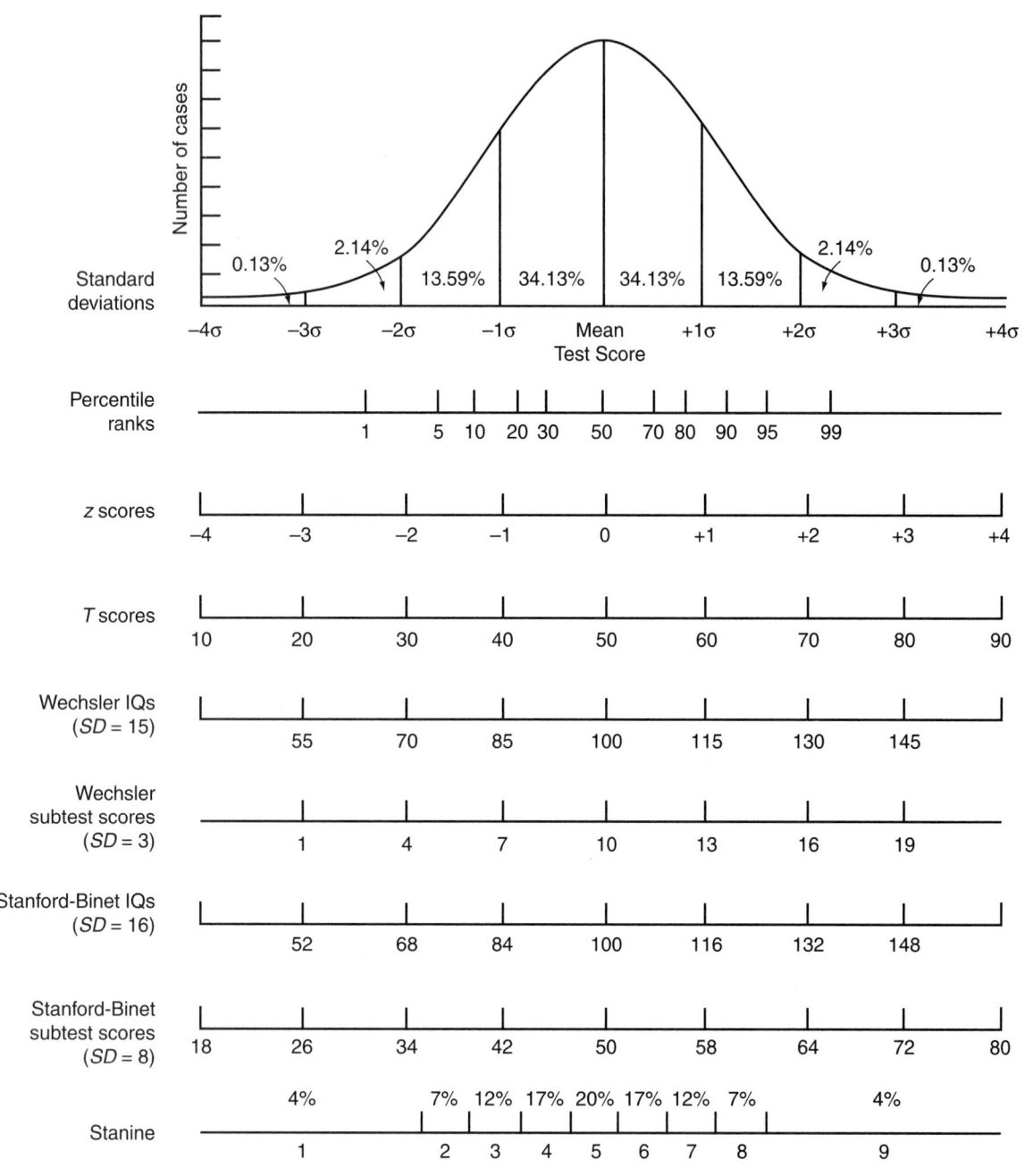

Figure 4-1. Relationship of the normal curve to various types of standard scores.

whether the correlation is positive or negative (e.g., whether r = +.50 or r = −.50). However, we also need to know the *direction* of the relationship between the scores—that is, whether it is positive or negative.

Variables can be related nonlinearly. If a curvilinear relationship exists between two variables, the correlation coefficient will underestimate the true degree of association. *Curvilinear* implies that the relationship can be portrayed better by a curve than by a straight line. An example of a cur-

vilinear relationship is the one between age and coordination. Children younger than 10 years of age and adults older than 60 years of age have poorer coordination than individuals between 10 and 60 years of age.

Figure 4-2 shows scatterplots for eight different relationships. A scatterplot presents a visual picture of the relationship between two variables, X and Y. Each point in the scatterplot represents a pair of scores for one examinee—a score on the X variable and a score on the Y variable. Plot A

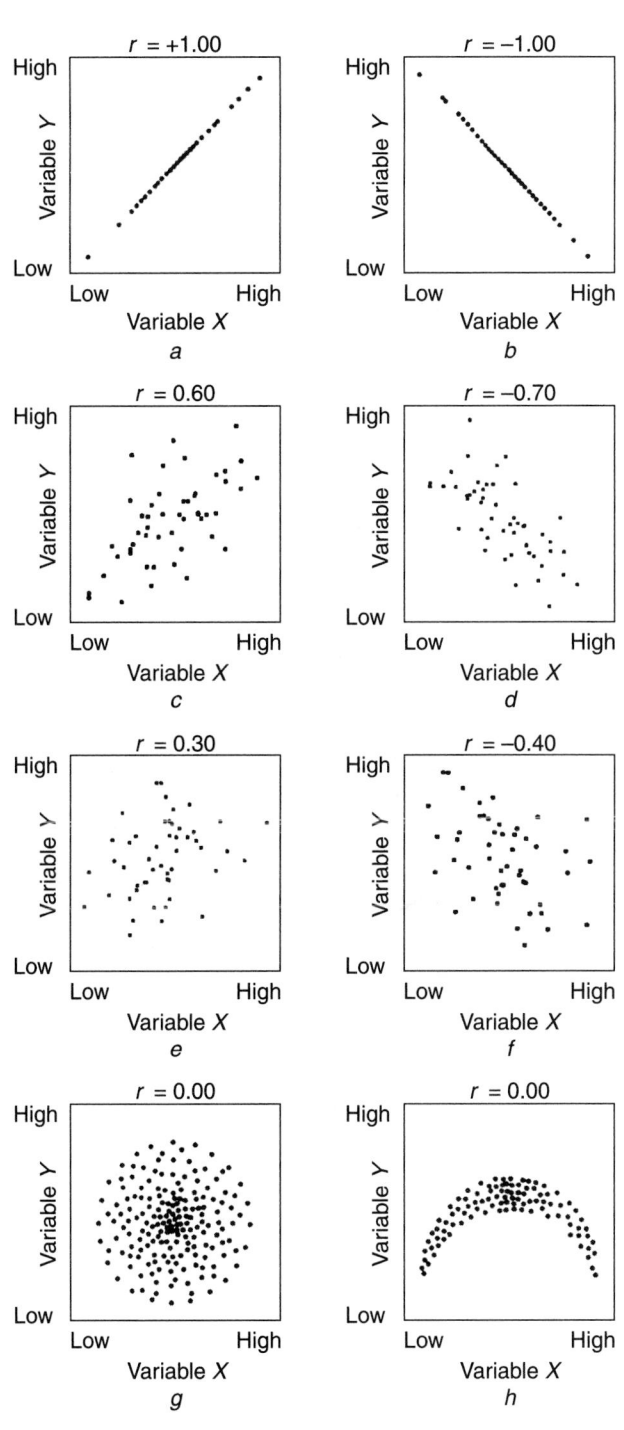

Figure 4-2. Scatter diagrams illustrating various degrees of relationship.

Y) to the lower right (high *X*, low *Y*). Plots C through F show varying degrees of relationship between *X* and *Y*. Plot G shows no relationship between *X* and *Y* (*r* = 0.00). And Plot H shows a curvilinear relationship between *X* and *Y;* the dots fall along a curved line.

The most common correlation coefficient is the *Pearson correlation coefficient,* symbolized by *r.* Several assumptions must be met to use Pearson's *r:* (a) the two variables are continuous and normally distributed, (b) a linear relationship exists between these variables, and (c) the predictor variable predicts as well at the high-score ranges as at the low-score ranges. When there is a restriction of range (i.e., the scores are homogeneous), the resulting correlation is lowered.

When the assumptions of Pearson's *r* cannot be met, the Spearman r_s (rank-difference) method can be used (see Table 4-3). This method uses ranks of the scores instead of the scores themselves. A rank is a number given to a score that represents its order in a distribution. For example, in a set of 10 scores, the highest score receives a rank of 1, the fifth score from the top receives a rank of 5, and the lowest score receives a rank of 10.

Correlations should *not* be used to infer cause and effect. Research indicates, for example, that there is a large positive correlation between reading speed and IQ. This means that people who read quickly tend to obtain higher scores on intelligence tests than do people who read slowly. We cannot infer, however, that reading speed *causes* high intelligence or that people will obtain higher intelligence test scores if they increase their reading speed. It may be that the ability to read quickly and the ability to obtain high scores on intelligence tests are both associated with other factors, such as verbal ability, time spent reading, alertness, or quick reaction time. Table 4-3 shows formulas for computing several correlation coefficients.

When we want to know how much variance in one variable is explained by another variable, we must square the correlation coefficient. For example, if we want to know how much variance in school grades we can account for by knowing students' scores on an intelligence test, we first compute a correlation coefficient. Let's say we find that *r* = .60. Squaring *r* (.60) gives .36, or 36%. Consequently, we can say that knowing their intelligence test scores allows us to account for 36% of the variance in students' school grades. This value may not seem large, but given that other factors—such as the number of children in the classroom and the child's personality—account for significantly less variance, IQ tests are currently the best predictor of overall school/academic performance. However, reading tests, for example, are usually more highly related to children's reading ability than are intelligence tests. Similarly, mathematics tests are usually more highly related to children's mathematics ability than are intelligence tests.

The value r^2 is known as the *coefficient of determination.* Just as in interpreting a correlation coefficient, knowing the coefficient of determination does not establish a cause and effect relationship between the two variables.

shows a perfect positive linear relationship between *X* and *Y* (*r* = 1.00); the dots fall into a straight line from the lower left (low *X*, low *Y*) to the upper right (high *X*, high *Y*). Plot B shows a perfect negative linear relationship (*r* = −1.00); the dots fall into a straight line from the upper left (low *X*, high

Table 4-3
A Variety of Correlation Coefficients

Name	Description of variables	Formula
Pearson product-moment correlation coefficient (r)	Both variables continuous (on interval or ratio scale)	$$r = \frac{N\,\Sigma XY - (\Sigma X)(\Sigma Y)}{\sqrt{[N\,\Sigma X^2 - (\Sigma X)^2][N\,\Sigma Y^2 - (\Sigma Y)^2]}}$$ where r = correlation coefficient N = number of paired scores ΣXY = sum of the product of the paired X and Y scores ΣX = sum of the X scores ΣY = sum of the Y scores ΣX^2 = sum of the squared X scores $(\Sigma X)^2$ = square of the sum of the X scores ΣY^2 = sum of the squared Y scores $(\Sigma Y)^2$ = square of the sum of the Y scores
Spearman rank-difference correlation coefficient (Spearman r, r_s, or ρ)	Both variables on an ordinal scale (rank-ordered)	$$r_s = 1 - \frac{6\Sigma D^2}{N(N^2 - 1)}$$ where D = difference between ranks for each person N = number of paired scores
Point biserial correlation coefficient (r_{pb})	One variable continuous (on interval or ratio scale), the other genuinely dichotomous (usually on nominal scale)	Formula for r can be used (see above). The dichotomous variable can be coded 0 or 1. For example, if sex is the dichotomous variable, 0 can be used for females and 1 for males (0 = females, 1 = males), or vice versa.
Phi (ϕ) coefficient	Both variables dichotomous (on nominal scales)	1. $$\phi = \frac{BD - AD}{\sqrt{(A + B)(C + D)(A + C)(B + D)}}$$ where A, B, C, and D are the four cell frequencies 2. $$\phi = \sqrt{\frac{\chi^2}{N}}$$ where χ^2 = chi square N = total number of observations

Regression Equation

You can use the correlation coefficient, together with other information, to construct a linear equation for predicting the score on one variable when you know the score on another variable. (A linear equation is one in which the relationship between the variables can be represented on a graph by a straight line.) This equation, called the *regression equation*, has the following form:

$$Y_{\text{pred}} = bX + a$$

where Y_{pred} = predicted score on Y
   b = slope of the regression line

X = known score on X
a = Y intercept of the regression line

The slope of the regression line is defined as

$$b = r\frac{SD_Y}{SD_X}$$

where r = correlation between the X and Y scores
   SD_Y = standard deviation of the Y scores
   SD_X = standard deviation of the X scores

The formula for calculating b directly from raw data is

$$b = \frac{N \, \Sigma XY - (\Sigma X)(\Sigma Y)}{N \, \Sigma X^2 - (\Sigma X)^2}$$

The intercept a, or regression constant, is then determined as follows:

$$a = \overline{Y} - b\overline{X}$$

where
$\overline{Y}$ = mean of the Y scores
b = slope of the regression line
$\overline{X}$ = mean of the X scores

Example: To find the regression equation for the following pairs of scores (X, Y), we first calculate X^2, Y^2, and XY.

X	Y	X^2	Y^2	XY
7	9	49	81	63
2	3	4	9	6
6	4	36	16	24
6	5	36	25	30
3	1	9	1	3
$\Sigma = 24$	22	134	132	126

$$\overline{X} = 4.8 \quad \overline{Y} = 4.4$$

The slope is then given by

$$b = \frac{5(126) - 24(22)}{5(134) - (24)^2} = \frac{630 - 528}{670 - 576} = \frac{102}{94} = 1.09$$

and the regression constant by

$$a = 4.40 - 1.09(4.80) = 4.40 - 5.23 = -.83$$

These data can now be substituted into the regression equation:

$$Y_{\text{pred}} = 1.09X - .83$$

The correlation coefficient for these data is

$$r = \frac{5(126) - 24(22)}{\sqrt{[5(134) - (24)^2][5(132) - (22)^2]}}$$

$$= \frac{102}{\sqrt{94(176)}} = \frac{105}{\sqrt{16,544}} = \frac{102}{128.62} = .79$$

Standard Error of Estimate

A measure of the accuracy of the predicted Y scores is the *standard error of estimate:*

$$SE_{\text{est}} = SD_Y\sqrt{1 - r_{XY}^2}$$

where
SD_Y = standard deviation of the Y scores
r_{XY}^2 = square of the correlation between the X and Y scores

The standard error of estimate is the standard deviation, a measure of the amount by which the observed or obtained

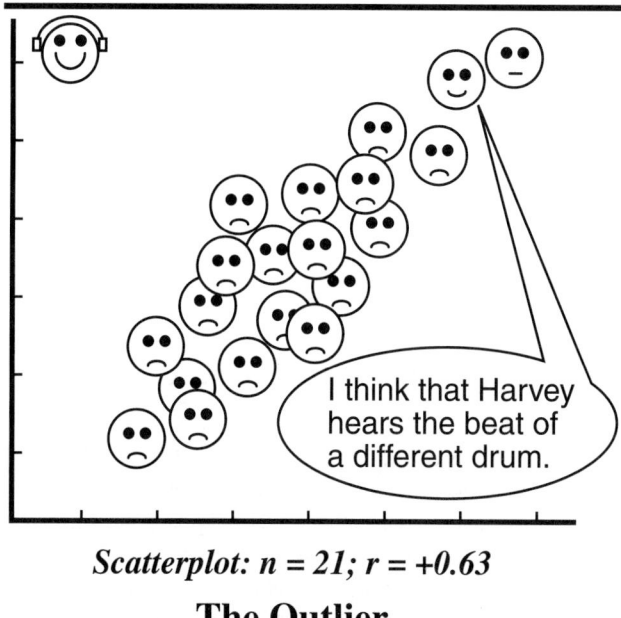

Scatterplot: n = 21; r = +0.63

The Outlier

Courtesy of David Likely.

scores in the sample differ from the predicted scores. The higher the correlation between X and Y, the smaller the standard error of estimate and hence the greater the average accuracy of the predictions. A +1.00 correlation coefficient means that you can make perfect predictions of Y if you know X; a .00 correlation means that knowledge of X does not improve your prediction of Y.

Example: The standard error of estimate for a test with a standard deviation of 15 and a .60 correlation between X and Y is

$$SE_{\text{est}} = 15\sqrt{1 - .60^2}$$

$$= 15\sqrt{1 - .36}$$

$$= 15(.80) = 12$$

Thus, we can say that the predicted score (Y) will be within ±12 at the 68% confidence level.

MULTIPLE CORRELATION

Multiple correlation is a statistical technique for determining the relationship between one variable and several other variables. The coefficient of multiple correlation is represented as R. When we use several variables for a prediction, the prediction is likely to be more accurate and powerful than if we base the prediction on a single variable only. A principal drawback to using multiple correlation, however, is that large samples are usually required when several variables are used in an analysis. Usually, over 100 subjects or at least 20 subjects per variable—for example, 200 subjects if 10 variables are being studied—are needed to arrive at a stable prediction equation. A good example of the use of multiple correlation is in the prediction of college performance. High school grades, intelligence test scores, and educational attainment of parents are measures that correlate positively with performance in college. By using these measures in a multiple correlation, we can predict academic performance in college with more accuracy than by using any of these measures alone.

NORM-REFERENCED MEASUREMENT

In *norm-referenced measurement,* we compare an examinee's performance with the performance of a specific group of subjects. A norm provides an indication of the average, or typical, performance of a specified group and the spread of scores above and below the average. Norms are needed because the number of correct responses in itself is not very meaningful. For example, knowing that a child obtained a score of 20 or correctly answered 70% of the items on a test is of little use unless we also know how other children performed on the same test; we need a relevant normative population. We could compare the child's score with those of a representative population of children in the United States, or those of the children in the child's school, or those of a special population. We can make such a comparison by converting the child's raw score into some relative measure, called a derived score. A *derived score* indicates the child's standing relative to the norm group, and it allows us to compare the child's performance on one test with her or his performance on other tests.

Evaluating the Norm Group

Before we discuss derived scores, let's consider some factors important in the evaluation of a normative group. These include (a) the representativeness of the norm group, (b) the number of cases in the norm group, and (c) the relevance of the norm group.

Representativeness. The representativeness of the norm group refers to how characteristic the group is of a particular population. The norm group should match as closely as possible the major demographic characteristics of the population as a whole. For psychological and psychoeducational assessment, the most salient of these characteristics are age, grade level, gender, geographic region, ethnicity, and SES. We also need to know when the norms were established to determine whether the norms are current and useful.

Size. The number of subjects in the norm group should be large enough to assure that the test scores are stable and that the subgroups in the population are adequately represented.

Usually, the larger the number of subjects in the norm group, the more stable the norms. If we are going to use the test for several age groups, then the sample should contain at least 100 subjects for each age group represented in the norm group.

Relevance. To interpret an examinee's score properly, we need a representative norm group against which to evaluate his or her scores. For some purposes, national norms may be the most relevant (e.g., when we want to find out how an examinee ranks within a national population), whereas for other purposes, local norms may be preferred (e.g., when we want to find out how an examinee ranks within a local population). The examiner interpreting the test should have the skill and insight needed to select the proper norm group for each examinee being evaluated. If the norm group is different from the one customarily used by most examiners, the report should clearly state which norm group was used.

TYPES OF DERIVED SCORES

The major types of derived scores used in norm-referenced measurement are standard scores, percentile ranks, stanines, normal-curve equivalents, age-equivalent scores, grade-

"I could have done better, but I didn't want to depart too far from the accepted norm."

Courtesy of Germaine Vanselow, Cartoonist, Bill Vanselow.

equivalent scores, and ratio IQs. As the following discussion indicates, the various derived scores differ in their usefulness.

Standard Scores

Standard scores are raw scores that have been transformed to have a designated mean and standard deviation. They express how far an examinee's score lies from the mean of the distribution in terms of the standard deviation.

A *z score* is one type of standard score. It has a mean of 0 and a standard deviation of 1. Therefore, most *z* scores lie between –3.0 and +3.0. A *z* score of –2.5 indicates that the raw score fell below the mean score of the group by two and one-half standard deviations. Frequently, we transform *z* scores into other standard scores to eliminate the + and – signs. For example, a *T score* is a standard score based on a distribution with a mean of 50 and a standard deviation of 10. The *Deviation IQ* is another standard score; it has a mean of 100 and a

standard deviation of 15 or 16, depending on the test used. All of the Wechsler scales (WISC–III, WPPSI–R, and WAIS–III) provide Deviation IQs with a mean of 100 and a standard deviation of 15. The Stanford-Binet Intelligence Scale: Fourth Edition provides Deviation IQs with a mean of 100 and a standard deviation of 16.

Table 4-4 shows formulas for computing various standard scores. A general formula for converting standard scores from one system to another is

$$\text{New standard score} = \left(\frac{X_{\text{old}} - M_{\text{old}}}{SD_{\text{old}}}\right)SD_{\text{new}} + M_{\text{new}}$$

where

X_{old} = score on old system

M_{old} = mean of old system

SD_{old} = standard deviation of old system

SD_{new} = standard deviation of new system

M_{new} = mean of new system

Table 4-4
Formulas for Computing Various Standard Scores

Score	*Example*
z score $$z = \frac{X - \overline{X}}{S}$$ where z = *z* score corresponding to the individual raw score X X = individual raw score $\overline{X}$ = mean of sample S = standard deviation of sample	The *z* score for an individual with a raw score of 50 in a group having a mean of 30 and standard deviation of 10 is calculated as follows: $$z = \frac{50 - 30}{10} = 2.00$$ Thus, the *z* score for this individual is 2.00.
T score $T = 10(z) + 50$ where T = *T* score corresponding to the individual raw score X 10 = standard deviation of the *T* distribution z = *z* score corresponding to the individual raw score X 50 = mean of the *T* distribution	The *T* score for an individual with a *z* score of 2 is calculated as follows: $$T = 10(2) + 50 = 70$$ Thus, the *T* score for this individual is 70.
Deviation IQ $\text{D IQ} = 15(z) + 100$ where D IQ = Deviation IQ corresponding to the individual raw score X 15 = standard deviation of the Deviation IQ distribution z = *z* score corresponding to the individual raw score X 100 = mean of the Deviation IQ distribution	The Deviation IQ for an individual with a *z* score of 2 is calculated as follows: $$\text{D IQ} = 15(2) + 100 = 130$$ Thus, the D IQ for this individual is 130.

Example: A standard score of 60 in a *T* distribution ($M = 50$, $SD = 10$) is converted to a Deviation IQ ($M = 100$, $SD = 15$) as follows:

$$\text{Deviation IQ} = \left(\frac{60 - 50}{10}\right)15 + 100$$

$$= \left(\frac{10}{10}\right)15 + 100 = (1)15 + 100 = 115$$

Percentile Ranks

Percentile ranks are derived scores that permit us to determine an individual's position relative to the standardization sample (or any other specified sample). A percentile rank is a point in a distribution at or below which the scores of a given percentage of individuals fall. If 63% of the scores fall at or below a given score, then that score is at the 63rd percentile rank. *Quartiles* are percentile ranks that divide a distribution into four equal parts, with each part containing 25% of the norm group. Deciles, a less common percentile rank, divide a distribution into 10 bands, each of which contains 10% of the norm group. Exhibit 4-1 shows some procedures for calculating percentile ranks.

Interpretation of percentile ranks is simple and straightforward. For example, a child who obtains a percentile rank of 35 on an intelligence test has scored the same as or better than 35% of the children in the norm sample. However, the psychometric properties of percentile ranks limit their usefulness in data analysis. The primary difficulty is that we can't assume that the units along the percentile distribution are equal. Raw score differences between percentile ranks are smaller near the mean than at the extremes of the distribution. Therefore, percentile ranks cannot be added, subtracted, multiplied, or divided. In order to use them in statistical tests, we must normalize percentile ranks by converting them to another scale.

Normal-Curve Equivalents

Normal-curve equivalents (NCEs) are standard scores with a mean of 50 and a standard deviation of 21.06. NCEs divide the normal curve into 100 equal units (see Table BC-1 on the back endsheets of the book). Unlike percentile ranks, which cannot be used for statistical analyses, NCEs can be used for such purposes because they can legitimately be added, subtracted, multiplied, and divided.

Stanines

Stanines (a contraction of "standard nine") provide a single-digit scoring system with a mean of 5 and a standard deviation of 2. The scores are expressed as whole numbers from 1 to 9. When we convert scores to stanines, the shape of the original distribution changes into a normal curve. The percentages of scores at each stanine are 4, 7, 12, 17, 20, 17, 12, 7, and 4, respectively (refer back to Figure 4-1). Stanines have drawbacks, though, such as loss of information associated with large categories and categories that are not equal intervals. The main advantage of stanines is that they produce single-digit scores.

SCHOOLIES © 1999 by John P. Wood

Sorry—I'm not allowed to talk to anyone outside of my percentile.

Copyright © 1999 by John P. Wood. Reprinted with permission.

Age-Equivalent Scores and Grade-Equivalent Scores

We obtain *age-equivalent scores* and *grade-equivalent scores* by determining the average score obtained on a test by different groups of children who vary in age or grade placement. For example, if the average score of 10-year-old children on a test is 15 items correct out of 25, then any child obtaining a score of 15 receives an age-equivalent score of 10-0 (10 years 0 months). We find an age-equivalent score by computing the mean raw score on a test for a group of children of a specific age.

Similarly, we find a grade-equivalent score by computing the mean raw score on a test obtained by children in a specific grade. If the mean score of seventh graders on an arithmetic test is 30, then we say that a child obtaining a score of 30 has arithmetical knowledge at the seventh-grade level (or a grade-equivalent score that equals the seventh-grade level). We express grade-equivalent scores in tenths of a grade (e.g., 5.5 refers to average performance of children at the middle of the fifth grade). This is in contrast to age-equivalent scores, which are expressed in years and months. A grade-equivalent score, therefore, refers to the level of test performance of an

Exhibit 4-1
Calculating Percentile Ranks

The following formula is used to determine the percentile rank for a score in a distribution:

$$\text{Percentile rank} = \frac{\left(\frac{X - \text{lrl}}{i}\right)\text{fw} + \Sigma\text{fb}}{N} \times 100$$

where X = raw score
  lrl = lower real limit of the target interval or score
  i = width of the target interval or score
  fw = frequency within the target interval or score
  Σfb = sum of frequencies (number of scores occurring) below the target interval or score
  N = total number of scores

To compute the lower real limit of a whole number, simply subtract .5 from the number; to get the upper real limit, add .5 to the number. The width of the target interval or score (i) is obtained by subtracting the lower real limit from the upper real limit.

Example 1
Let's compute the percentile rank for a score of 110 in the following distribution:

	X	f
	120	5
	119	10
Target interval for a score of 110 →	110	20
	100	40
	90	10
	80	5
		$N = 90$

where lrl = 109.5
  i = 1
  fw = 20
  Σfb = 55
  N = 90

Substituting these values into the percentile rank formula yields the following:

$$\text{Percentile rank} = \frac{\left(\frac{X - \text{lrl}}{i}\right)\text{fw} + \Sigma\text{fb}}{N} \times 100$$

$$= \frac{\left(\frac{110 - 109.5}{1}\right)20 + 55}{90} \times 100$$

$$= \frac{\left(\frac{.5}{1}\right)20 + 55}{90} \times 100$$

$$= \frac{(.5)20 + 55}{90} \times 100$$

$$= \frac{10 + 55}{90} \times 100$$

$$= \frac{65}{90} \times 100$$

$$= .72 \times 100$$

Percentile rank is 72nd percentile, or 72. Thus, a score of 110 exceeds 72% of the scores in the distribution.

The formula given here for calculating percentile ranks can be used with both grouped (organized into classes of more than one value) and ungrouped (organized into classes of single values) data. When the distribution is ungrouped and all the intervals are 1, a simplified version of the formula can be used:

$$\text{Percentile rank} = \left(\frac{.5\text{fw} + \Sigma\text{fb}}{N}\right) \times 100$$

Example 2
Let's compute the percentile rank for a score of 4 in the following distribution:

	X	f
	5	3
Target interval for a score of 4 →	4	5
	3	4
	2	3
	1	2
		$N = 17$

where fw = 5
  Σfb = 9
  N = 17

Substituting these values into the percentile rank formula for ungrouped data with intervals of 1 yields

$$\text{Percentile rank} = \left(\frac{.5\text{fw} + \Sigma\text{fb}}{N}\right) \times 100$$

$$= \left(\frac{.5\text{fw} + \Sigma\text{fb}}{N}\right) \times 100$$

$$= \frac{.5(5) + 9}{17} \times 100$$

$$= \frac{2.5 + 9}{17} \times 100$$

$$= \frac{11.5}{17} \times 100$$

$$= .68 \times 100$$

Percentile rank is 68th percentile, or 68. Thus, a score of 4 exceeds 68% of the scores in the distribution.

average student at that grade level. It does *not* mean that the student is performing at a level consistent with curricular expectations for that grade level at his or her particular school. Note that a dash is used for age equivalents (e.g., 10-0) and a decimal for grade equivalents (e.g., 5.5).

Other terms for age-equivalent scores.   Other terms for age-equivalent scores are *mental age* (MA) and *test age.* Mental age, however, may not always refer to a specific group of children with a known level of mental ability. For example, on the 1972 norms for the Stanford-Binet: Form L-M, mental age scores do not refer to scores associated with children of a certain age; they simply represent a number of points obtained by the child on the test. Chapter 6 discusses the interpretation of MAs. The WISC–III, Wechsler Preschool and Primary Scale of Intelligence–Revised (WPPSI–R), and Stanford-Binet Intelligence Scale: Fourth Edition manuals present test ages for raw scores on each of their subtests.

Interpretation of age-equivalent and grade-equivalent scores.   Age-equivalent and grade-equivalent scores require careful interpretation because, for the following reasons, they can be misleading (Bennett, 1982; Berk, 1981, 1984; Thorndike & Hagen, 1977):

1. Within an age-equivalent or grade-equivalent distribution of scores, the scores may not represent equal units. For example, the difference between second grade– and third grade–equivalent scores may not be the same as the difference between eleventh grade– and twelfth grade–equivalent scores.
2. Because many grade equivalents are obtained by interpolation (estimating a value between two given values or points) and extrapolation (extending norms to scores not actually obtained in the standardization sample), no children may have actually obtained the scores.
3. Grade equivalents encourage comparison with inappropriate groups. For example, we should not say that a second grader who obtains a grade equivalent of 4.1 in arithmetic is functioning like a fourth grader at the beginning of the school year; the fourth grade is the wrong comparison group. The second-grade student shares with the average fourth grader the number of items right on the test—not other attributes associated with fourth-grade mathematical skills. We should think of the grade equivalent of 4.1 in reference only to the child's second-grade comparison group.
4. Identical grade-equivalent scores on different tests may mean different things. For example, grade-equivalent scores of 4.6 on two tests of mathematics may mean that the examinee has mastered different mathematical content on the two tests.
5. Grade equivalents assume that growth is constant throughout the school year, an assumption that may not be warranted.
6. At junior and senior high school levels, age equivalents and grade equivalents may have little meaning for school subjects not taught at those levels or for skills that reach their peak at an earlier age.
7. Grade equivalents exaggerate small differences in performance; a score slightly below the median may result in a grade level equivalent one or two years lower.
8. Grade equivalents vary from test to test, from subtest to subtest within the same test, and from percentile to percentile, thereby complicating any type of comparison.
9. Grade-equivalent scores depend on promotion practices in different schools and on the particular curriculum being used in different grades and in different schools.
10. Age-equivalent and grade-equivalent scores tend to be based on ordinal scales that cannot support the computation of important statistical measures, such as the standard error of measurement.

We have seen that age-equivalent and grade-equivalent scores are psychometrically impure; however, they still may be useful on some occasions (Hoover, 1984). Age-equivalent and grade-equivalent scores place performance in a developmental context, provide information that parents and the public can easily understand, and reduce misinterpretations. (Percentile ranks, for example, are often misinterpreted as indicating the percentage of questions that the child answered correctly.) Instead of abandoning age-equivalent and grade-equivalent scores, psychometricians should construct better tests that use these scores and educate people in their use (Hoover, 1984).

Ratio Intelligence Quotients

In order to interpret age-equivalent or grade-equivalent scores, we must know the child's chronological age (CA). Knowing the child's MA and CA allows us to make a judgment about the child's relative performance. For example, a child with a CA of 10-0 and an MA of 12-0 has performed at an above-average level, whereas a child with a CA of 10-0 and an MA of 8-0 has performed at a below-average level.

When IQs were first introduced, they were defined as ratios of mental age to chronological age, multiplied by 100 to eliminate the decimal: $IQ = MA/CA \times 100$. Substituting an MA of 12 and a CA of 10 into the formula yields a *ratio IQ* of 120 ($IQ = 12/10 \times 100 = 120$). Unfortunately, because the standard deviation of the ratio IQ distribution does not remain constant with age, IQs for different ages are not comparable—the same IQ has different meanings at different ages. The use of the Deviation IQ, which is a standard score (see the section on standard scores in this chapter), effectively avoids this problem. We do not recommend the use of ratio IQs, except when you want to make a crude approximation of the child's level of ability and standard scores are not available. This may happen, for example, when the individual being assessed is chronologically too old for a test or chronologically too young for a test.

Relationships Among Derived Scores

All derived scores are obtained from raw scores. Different derived scores are merely different expressions of an examinee's performance. We can convert one type of derived score to another type. The most frequently used conversion in the area of intelligence testing is from standard scores (e.g., scaled scores or Deviation IQs) to percentile ranks. Although standard scores are the preferred derived scores, percentile ranks—and, on occasion, age equivalents—also are useful. The latter two scores may be helpful in describing the child's performance to parents or teachers.

Do not use the abbreviation "%" or "%tile" for "percentile rank" because these abbreviations may lead to confusion of percentile rank with percent correct. Instead, we recommend that you spell out the words *percentile rank.*

Figure 4-1 shows the relationships among various derived scores. If a test has a mean Deviation IQ of 100, a standard deviation of 15, and scores that are normally distributed, we can precisely determine the percentile rank associated with each IQ. Let's see how we can compute percentile rank associated with Wechsler IQs at several standard deviation points.

An IQ of 100 represents the 50th percentile rank, because an IQ of 100 is the median (as well as the mean) of the distribution. In this example, an IQ of 115 represents the point that is +1 *SD* away from the mean. We obtain the percentile rank associated with this IQ—the 84th percentile—by adding 50% to 34%. The 50% represents the proportion of the population below the mean of 100, and the 34% represents the proportion of the population between the mean and +1 *SD* away from the mean. The key is to recognize that an IQ of 115 is +1 *SD* above the mean because 15 is the standard deviation of the distribution.

Using the same rationale, we can compute the percentile rank associated with an IQ of 130. An IQ of 130 is +2 *SD* away from the mean. We know that the area below the mean represents 50% of the population, the area from the mean to +1 *SD* represents approximately 34% of the population, and the area from +1 *SD* to +2 *SD* represents approximately 14% of the population (see Figure 4-1). To arrive at the percentile rank for an IQ of 130, we add the percentages: 50 + 34 + 14 = 98th percentile rank.

Now try to figure out for yourself the percentile rank associated with an IQ of 85. You subtract 34 from 50, because an IQ of 85 corresponds to the point that is –1 *SD* away from the mean. The answer you should obtain is the 16th percentile rank. The percentile rank associated with an IQ of 70 is the 2nd percentile rank (50 – 34 – 14 = 2).

The above examples hold only for tests with *M* = 100 and *SD* = 15 (e.g., WISC–III, WPPSI–R, and WAIS–III). For tests that have *M* = 100 and *SD* = 16, such as the Stanford-Binet Intelligence Scale: Fourth Edition, the percentile ranks associated with the IQs are slightly different except at the mean. The IQ of 100 is still at the 50th percentile rank, but an IQ of 116 (not 115) is at the 84th percentile rank because the *SD* of the test is 16.

Let's look at two more examples. Because an IQ of 116 is at the 84th percentile rank on the Stanford-Binet Intelligence Scale: Fourth Edition but at the 86th percentile rank on the WISC–III, the IQs on the two scales are not directly comparable. Similarly, an IQ of 70 is at the 3rd percentile rank on the Stanford-Binet Intelligence Scale: Fourth Edition but at the 2nd percentile rank on the WISC–III. Although a 1-percentile difference may not appear to be major, it can loom as an important factor when placement decisions are being made, especially if the 1-percentile difference places the child in a different classification (e.g., from the Borderline level to the Mental Retardation level). A glance at Table BC-1 on the inside back cover will show you the percentile ranks associated with the Deviation IQs found on the Stanford-Binet Intelligence Scale: Fourth Edition, Wechsler tests, and other tests.

STATISTICAL SIGNIFICANCE

When we want to know whether the difference between two or more scores can be attributed to chance or to some systematic (and perhaps hypothesized) cause, we need to run a test of *statistical significance.* "Significance" in statistics refers to whether the results differ from what would be expected on the basis of chance alone. Statisticians have agreed that it is reasonable to accept results as statistically significant if the results would occur by chance 5% or less of the time. Thus, the lower the probability that the results would occur by chance, the greater the probability that the results are real. The least significant acceptable probability level is .05 (5 times in 100); greater significance is indicated by lower probabilities, such as .01 (1 time in 100) or .001 (1 time in 1,000). Tests of significance can be used to evaluate differences between two or more means, differences between a score and the mean of the scale, and whether correlations differ from zero (or chance). The expression $p < .05$ means that the results have a probability level of less than .05 (or 5 times in 100) of occurring by chance, whereas the expression $p > .05$ means that the results have a probability level of greater than .05 (or more than 5 times in 100) of occurring by chance.

Tests of significance, although highly useful, don't tell us the complete story. When we test to see whether two or more means are significantly different, we also need to consider the values of the means, the degree to which they differ, and the direction of the difference. For example, the mean difference between two groups may be statistically significant and yet have no practical significance. Thus, if one group has a mean of 100 and the other has a mean of 101, the significance test may yield a p value less than .05, but the difference of only 1 point may have little practical usefulness. When we test to see whether a correlation coefficient differs significantly from chance, we also need to know how powerful the coefficient is (or how powerful its strength of association is). When the sample size is large enough, the correlation coefficient may be statistically significant and yet reflect only a weak association between the two variables. Thus, a Pearson correlation coefficient of .20 is significant when the sample size is 100, but the level of variance explained is low ($.20^2 = 4\%$).

RELIABILITY

A psychological or psychoeducational measure must be reliable if it is to be useful. *Reliability* refers to the consistency of measurements. Consistency has several meanings, including that the measure is (a) consistent within itself (internal reliability), (b) consistent over time (test-retest reliability), (c) consistent with an alternate form of the measure (alternate form reliability), and (d) consistent when used by another rater or observer (interrater or interobserver reliability). We can quantify the various forms of reliability, as we will show below.

Test results need to be reliable—that is, dependable, reproducible, and stable. Reliability is expressed with a reliability coefficient or with the standard error of measurement, which is derived from the reliability coefficient. We should not trust the results from a test if its reliability coefficient is low. We particularly need high reliabilities, usually .80 or higher, for tests used in individual assessment.

The Theory of Reliability of Measurement

When we administer the same test to an examinee on several occasions, the examinee will likely earn different scores. Sometimes the score changes in a systematic way (regular increase or decrease in scores), and sometimes the score changes in a random or unsystematic way. A test is considered unreliable if scores are subject to random, unsystematic fluctuations; obviously a test is not dependable if it randomly yields different scores when readministered. Reliability of measurement refers to the extent to which random or unsystematic variation affects the measurement of a trait, characteristic, or quality.

According to classical psychometric theory, the test score is composed of two components: *true score* and *error score.* The concept of "true score" refers to the measurement process, not to the underlying content category. Thus, the true score represents a combination of all the factors that lead to consistency in measurement of a characteristic. The examinee's true score is a hypothetical construct; we cannot observe it. However, we can hypothesize that if we repeatedly gave the examinee the test, a distribution of scores around the true score would result. The mean of this distribution, which is assumed to be normal, would approximate the true score. The theory assumes that (a) the examinee possesses stable traits, (b) errors are random, and (c) the obtained test score results from the addition of true and error scores. The reliability coefficient, then, represents a ratio of the true score variance to the observed score variance.

Reliability Coefficients

The *reliability coefficient* expresses the degree of consistency in the measurement of test scores. The symbol used to denote a reliability coefficient is the letter r with two identical subscripts (e.g., r_{xx} or r_{tt}). Reliability coefficients range from 1.00 (indicating perfect reliability) to .00 (indicating the absence of reliability). As noted earlier, types of reliability coefficients include test-retest reliability, alternate form reliability, internal consistency reliability, and interrater reliability. We use the Pearson product-moment correlation formula (see Table 4-3) to compute test-retest and alternate form reliability coefficients, specialized formulas to compute internal consistency reliability coefficients, and several different methods to compute interrater reliability. Table 4-5 shows some procedures for determining reliability. Psychologists prefer reliabilities above .80 for clinical and psychoeducational tasks, and reliabilities at or above .90 for decision-making tasks. Subtests with reliabilities between .70 and .79 are relatively reliable; between .60 and .69, marginally reliable; and below .60, unreliable.

Test-retest reliability. *Test-retest reliability* is an index of stability, a measure of how consistent scores are over time. The usual procedure for obtaining a test-retest reliability coefficient is to administer the same test to the same group on two different occasions, usually within a short period of time (e.g., 2 weeks to a month). The obtained correlation, sometimes called the *coefficient of stability,* represents the extent to which the test is consistent over time.

The test-retest correlation is affected by factors associated with the specific administrations of the test and with what the examinees have remembered or learned in the interim. Thus, any variables that affect the examinees' performance on one occasion but not on the other will affect the coefficient of stability. Typical influencing variables include differences in administration (different examiners, different rooms, different times of the day) or differences in the examinees (fatigue, moodiness, motivation). Errors due to poorly constructed test items are not germane to test-retest reliability because the same test items are usually administered on both occasions. Generally, the shorter the retest interval, the higher the reliability coefficient, because within a shorter span of time there are fewer reasons for examinees' scores to change. With individual intelligence tests, test-retest reliabilities are higher when the retest interval is less than 10 months and when the examinees are older than 15 years (Schuerger & Witt, 1989).

The test-retest reliability coefficient may not be an appropriate measure to use for behavioral checklists and scales, observational procedures, and related forms of measurement. For example, a low test-retest reliability coefficient indicates that the instrument is providing readings that differ on the two times that the measurement was conducted. However, this should not automatically mean that the instrument is faulty—that is, that there is measurement error. It may be that

Table 4-5
Some Procedures Used to Determine Reliability

Procedure	Description
Spearman-Brown correction formula $$r_{nn} = \frac{kr_{tt}}{1 + (k-1)r_{tt}}$$ where r_{nn} = estimated reliability coefficient k = number of items on the revised version divided by number of items on the original version of the test r_{tt} = reliability coefficient before correction	An *internal consistency reliability* formula used to evaluate the effect that lengthening or shortening a test will have on the reliability coefficient. The formula increases the reliability estimate when the test is lengthened.
Cronbach's coefficient alpha (α) formula $$r_{tt} = \left(\frac{n}{n-1}\right)\left(\frac{S_t^2 - \Sigma(S_i^2)}{S_t^2}\right)$$ where r_{tt} = coefficient alpha reliability estimate n = number of items on the test S_t^2 = variance of the total scores on the test $\Sigma(S_i^2)$ = sum of the variances of individual item scores	An *internal consistency reliability* formula used when a test has no right or wrong answers. This formula provides a general reliability estimate that simultaneously considers all of the ways of splitting items. It is an efficient method of measuring internal consistency. Coefficient alpha essentially indicates the average intercorrelation between test items and any set of items drawn from the same domain.
Kuder-Richardson formula 20 (KR_{20}) $$r_{tt} = \left(\frac{n}{n-1}\right)\left(\frac{S_t^2 - \Sigma pq}{S_t^2}\right)$$ where r_{tt} = reliability estimate n = number of items on the test S_t^2 = variance of the total scores on the test Σpq = sum of the product of p and q for each item p = proportion of people getting an item correct q = proportion of people getting an item incorrect	An *internal consistency reliability* formula used for calculating the reliability of a test in which the items are scored 1 or 0 (or right or wrong). It provides a general method that simultaneously considers all of the ways of splitting items. It is a special form of coefficient alpha for use with dichotomous items.
Product-moment correlation coefficient formula See Table 4-3 for formula.	A formula used to estimate *test-retest reliability* or *equivalent form* or *parallel form reliability*.

the behaviors being measured have changed. Consequently, you should carefully consider whether low test-retest reliabilities are associated with poorly designed instruments or with actual changes in the child's behavior, attitudes, temperament, or other characteristics being measured.

Alternate form reliability. We measure *alternate form reliability,* also called *equivalent* or *parallel form reliability,* by administering two equivalent tests to the same group of examinees. If the two forms of the test are equivalent, they should have the same means and variances and their reliability coefficient should be high (i.e., .80 or higher). If there were no error in measurement, examinees should earn the same score on both forms of the test. Additionally, to be truly parallel, each equivalent item on the two forms should have

the same response split (number of individuals answering each item right or wrong) and the same correlations with other scores on the criterion measures. This level of similarity is difficult, if not impossible, to achieve.

To determine alternate form reliability, we give two forms of the same test to a large sample. We give half of the sample form A followed by form B, and we give the other half of the sample form B followed by form A. Scores from the two forms are then correlated, yielding a reliability coefficient that we call a *coefficient of equivalence.* Alternate form reliability coefficients are subject to some of the same influences as test-retest reliability coefficients, such as decreased reliability as we lengthen the interval between the tests. Because we do not test examinees twice with the same items, however, there is less chance than there is with the test-retest method that memory or specific item content will affect the scores. Alternate forms usually are easier to construct for tests that measure intellectual ability or specific academic abilities than for those that measure personality, temperament, or motivation, as these latter constructs usually are more difficult to define.

Internal consistency reliability. We base *internal consistency reliability* on the scores individuals obtain during one test administration. We obtain one type of internal consistency coefficient by dividing the test into two equivalent halves (*split-half reliability*). This division creates two alternate forms of the test. The most common way of dividing the test is to assign odd-numbered items to one form and even-numbered items to the other. This procedure assumes that all items measure the same trait or construct. We usually use the Spearman-Brown correction formula to estimate reliability by the split-half method. The formula corrects for test length because each half is, of course, only half as long as the whole test, and—all things being equal—longer tests are more reliable than shorter ones (see Table 4-5).

Another type of internal consistency reliability coefficient uses intercorrelations among comparable parts of the same test. Special formulas—such as Cronbach's formula for coefficient alpha and the Kuder-Richardson formula 20—measure the uniformity, or homogeneity, of items throughout the test (see Table 4-5). *Cronbach's coefficient alpha,* a general reliability coefficient that can be used for different scoring systems, is based on the variance of the test scores and on the variance of the item scores. The *Kuder-Richardson formula 20 coefficient,* a special case of coefficient alpha, is useful for tests scored as pass/fail or right/wrong. We obtain the coefficient by calculating the proportion of people who pass and fail each item and the variance of the test scores. Both coefficients represent the mean of all possible split-half coefficients that could be obtained by various test splittings. Higher estimates of reliability are associated with more homogeneous items.

Internal consistency reliability estimates are not appropriate for timed tests, and they do not take into account changes over time. Generally, the size of the internal consistency coefficient increases with greater test length.

Interrater Reliability

When an assessment requires the examiner to be a rater of a child's behavior, we need another type of reliability procedure called *interrater reliability, examiner reliability,* or *scorer reliability.* Interrater reliability refers to the degree to which the ratings are free from error variance associated with either the rater or the examiner. We assess interrater reliability by having two (or more) raters independently rate examinees' behaviors.

We can use several indices of agreement to evaluate interrater reliability, including percentage agreement, kappa, the product-moment correlation coefficient, and the intraclass

correlation coefficient. Chapter 5 in *Assessment of Children: Behavioral and Clinical Applications* describes these procedures. The most common measure of interrater reliability is percentage agreement. This statistic tells us the number of raters who gave the same rating to the behavior or criterion being judged (e.g., 80% gave a rating of 5). Percentage agreement is not strictly a reliability coefficient because it provides no information about the measurement procedure itself. Furthermore, percentage agreement does not take into account that chance alone would lead to some agreements. However, percentage agreement does tell us the extent to which two or more raters arrived at the same score or rating. In this sense, percentage agreement contributes to our understanding of the objectivity of the scoring, a factor in reliability.

Factors Affecting Reliability

The following factors affect the reliability of a test:

1. *Test length.* The more items there are on a test, the greater the reliability is likely to be.

2. *Homogeneity of items.* The more homogeneous the items on a test are, the greater the reliability is likely to be.

3. *Test-retest interval.* The smaller the interval between administration of two tests, the smaller the chance of change and hence the higher the reliability is likely to be.

4. *Variability of scores.* The greater the variance of scores on a test, the higher the reliability estimate is likely to be. Small changes in performance have a greater impact on the reliability of a test when the range, or spread, of scores is narrow than when it is wide. Therefore, on a given test, homogeneous samples (those with a small variance) will probably yield lower reliability estimates than heterogeneous samples (those with a large variance).

5. *Guessing.* The less guessing that occurs on a test (i.e., the less often examinees respond to items randomly), the higher the reliability is likely to be. Even guessing that results in correct answers introduces error into the score.

6. *Variation within the test situation.* The fewer variations there are in the test situation, the higher the reliability is likely to be. Examinee factors, such as misunderstanding instructions, illness, and daydreaming, and examiner factors, such as misreading instructions and making scoring errors, introduce an indeterminate amount of error into the testing procedure.

7. *Sample size.* Although not directly related to reliability, the sampling error associated with the reliability coefficient will be smaller when the sample size is larger. This is seen when you consider the sampling error of *r:*

$$Sr_{xx} = \frac{1 - r_{xx}^2}{\sqrt{n-1}}$$

A reliability estimate of .80 based on a sample size of 26 yields an estimated standard error of .07, whereas one based on a sample of 201 yields an estimated standard error of .03, a value less than half as large. Larger samples thus provide a more dependable estimate of reliability. Reliability coefficients are more meaningful when the sample represents a large group, as well as when the examinees assessed closely resemble the sample on which the reliability coefficient was based.

Reliability of an Individual Examinee's Assessment Data

A test that is reliable for one group may not be reliable for every subgroup of the population or for every individual examinee. The reliability of a score obtained on an individually administered test may be affected by idiosyncratic examinee and examiner factors. Unreliable results may be obtained, for example, if examinees are uncooperative or anxious or have difficulty following the instructions or if examiners are incompetent. Examinees tested under these and other circumstances may perform differently when tested on another occasion by the same or another examiner; the initial results may thus be unreliable. Of course, we should never use a test that has inadequate reliability to make decisions about an examinee.

Four major factors contribute to the variability of test scores and of the information obtained from the interview and observation: characteristics of the examinee, characteristics of the test items or interview questions, situational conditions, and characteristics of the examiner. Let's examine each of these factors in more detail.

Examinee characteristics. Several examinee characteristics contribute to variability of test scores. They include the examinee's (a) overall level of ability, (b) test-taking skills, (c) ability to comprehend instructions, (d) mastery of specific test content, (e) health, (f) fatigue, (g) motivation, (h) affect, (i) comprehension of the task requirements, (j) techniques for solving particular test items, (k) level of practice with particular items, (l) anticipation of different types of items, (m) fluctuations in attention or memory, (n) willingness to guess, and (o) response to distractions.

A reliable and valid assessment is possible only if the examinee is willing and able to give you accurate information. Consequently, when you evaluate the examinee's responses, particularly during the interview, you will need to consider the examinee's age, intellectual ability, cognitive development, emotional and social development, receptive and expressive language competence, self-awareness, degree of psychological disturbance, and culture and ethnicity, as well as the reason for which the evaluation is being conducted.

Some potential sources of error associated with examinees are their attitudes; understanding of questions; memory; interpretation of events; language; affect; personal likes, dislikes, and values; and behavior. Let's examine these potential sources of error in more detail.

1. *Errors associated with examinees' attitudes.* Examinees who are angry or uncooperative or who want to give socially desirable answers may not give useful information. The validity of the information also will be compromised if examinees are under stress, are resistant, lack trust, feel pressured to give certain responses, or fear reprisal or punishment if they are truthful. Examinees may also intentionally try to distort their behavior in order to convince you that they have some type of disturbance. If you suspect that there is deliberate distortion, look for incongruities in the examinee's behavior and evaluate whether the examinee might have a motive for deception (e.g., desire to obtain a large monetary award or a special school program); consider both the examinee's cognitive level *and* the examinee's moral level of development in assessing the possible deception. Examinees who come voluntarily for help are likely to give more accurate information than are those who are coerced to come (Bellack & Hersen, 1980).

One of the worst things that can happen to a child during the assessment is to be confronted with an "obvious lie" that is actually the truth. Children may occasionally tell you things that seem utterly outrageous and impossible, but later turn out to be true. Therefore, be cautious about confronting a child with what appears to be an untruth, unless you have convincing evidence.

2. *Errors associated with examinees' understanding of the test directions and interview questions.* When an examinee fails to understand the test directions or interview questions and yet does not ask you to rephrase the questions or does not say, "I don't understand," he or she usually will give misleading information. Such misunderstandings are likely to occur when examinees have hearing difficulties that have not been corrected, have cognitive limitations, have language comprehension difficulties, or are embarrassed to tell you that they do not understand the questions.

3. *Errors associated with examinees' memory.* Examinees may have difficulty recalling information in the interview, including important developmental milestones, and may have memory lapses. Sometimes, rather than saying they don't know, they may guess or make up information on tests, as well as during the interview.

4. *Errors associated with examinees' interpretation of events.* Examinees may distort what happened to them or to others. People tend to interpret their own behavior in a manner consistent with the image they have of themselves. Examinees also may exaggerate or minimize the significance of events.

5. *Errors associated with examinees' language.* Examinees may have difficulty finding the correct words to describe their thoughts and feelings or previous events. They may misuse words and thereby unintentionally give wrong information.

6. *Errors associated with examinees' affect.* The fears and anxieties that some examinees have may impede their ability to give accurate replies. For example, withdrawal, overtalkativeness, giggling, and loss of voice are possible

manifestations of anxiety or of coping and defensive behaviors; these reactions, if present, will likely contribute to the unreliability of the assessment.

7. *Errors associated with examinees' personal likes, dislikes, and values.* Examinees may fail to cooperate simply because you belong to an ethnic, economic, age, or gender group that differs from theirs. Thus, for example, examinees may like you because you both have the same skin color or are of the same gender. Or, they may dislike you because you are too young or dressed in a way that they don't like. Reactions to the examiner that are not objective are called *reactive effects.*

8. *Errors associated with examinees' behavior.* Examinees may behave in the assessment—or when they are observed in the playroom or at home—in a way that differs from their usual behavior. For example, they may be more cooperative, use more polished language, or treat people with more respect than they usually do. Examinees may also be too distraught or preoccupied to talk coherently. These types of behavior or change, which are associated with the knowledge of being evaluated, are another kind of reactive effect.

Test items.   The characteristics of test items (or interview questions) that contribute to variability of test scores include (a) a chance element that determines whether the examinees do or do not know a particular fact or word, (b) test items that measure different variables, (c) unequal familiarity with the item types among the examinees, (d) different interpretations of the wording of items among the examinees, and (e) scoring guidelines that do not acknowledge correct but unusual responses.

Situational conditions.   The assessment situation itself may be a source of unreliability, in which case we say that *situational bias* exists. Situational factors that contribute to variability of test scores and interview responses include external conditions such as heat, light, ventilation, and noise; delays in starting the assessment; the location of the assessment; the time of the assessment; the chance assignment of an examinee to an examiner; and temporary fluctuations in the behavior of the examiner and examinee. Thus, evaluating a child before nap time or when the child is sleepy or hungry may lead to an unreliable evaluation, as may evaluating a child after you have had a sleepless night.

Examiner characteristics.   Examiner characteristics that may potentially contribute to unreliability include errors associated with techniques and style; personal needs; personal likes, dislikes, and values; understanding of the examinee; attention to the physical environment; selective perceptions and expectancies; ethnicity; test administration; scoring techniques; recording techniques; interpretations; and theoretical position. Let's first examine each of these sources and then look at ways to reduce potential examiner bias and errors.

1. *Errors associated with the examiner's techniques and style.* You can influence the examinee's responses by the way in which you word a question, your choice of follow-up responses, the tone of your voice, your facial expressions (particularly those following responses from the examinee), your posture, and other verbal and nonverbal behaviors (see Chapter 1 in *Assessment of Children: Behavioral and Clinical Applications* on interviewing techniques). Errors may occur for the following reasons:

- You fail to establish rapport.
- You use ambiguous or vague questions.
- You ask more than one question at a time.
- You use complex and abstract words.
- You use biased wording.
- You time questions poorly.
- You ask many "why" questions and put the examinee on the defensive.
- You ask many leading questions.
- You are insensitive to the examinee's mood.
- You fail to monitor your verbal and nonverbal behavior.
- You fail to gather enough information to reach valid conclusions.

Examiner bias occurs when your actions either directly or indirectly induce the examinee to respond in a way that he or she did not intend or to distort his or her communications to please you. Sometimes you may not even realize that you are influencing the examinee's responses (Kleinmuntz, 1967). Asking "Shall we move on?" or glancing at your watch can effectively limit further discussion. A loaded statement such as "I take it that you are happy to accept your new class schedule" may leave the examinee with little choice but to agree. Similarly, the examinee is not likely to contest a statement that begins with "A good kid like you would think...."

2. *Errors associated with the examiner's personal needs.* Your personal needs may affect the way you conduct the assessment and the topics you approach and avoid. If you are anxious about sexual orientation, for example, you may fail to probe this area or you may avoid it altogether. Similarly, if you have strong feelings about certain issues such as abortion or religion, you may have difficulty discussing these topics. In a similar vein, excessive questions about a topic are improper when the questions further your needs rather than the needs of the examinee or the goals of the assessment. For example, excessive probing of the examinee's sexual behavior, when there are no indications of any problems in this area, may be a reflection of the needs of the examiner rather than a reflection of good assessment techniques. Finally, you may want the examinee to obtain high scores because you value high scores.

3. *Errors associated with the examiner's personal likes, dislikes, and values.* Your personal likes, dislikes, and values may influence how you relate to the examinee. For example, if you like examinees who are attractive, or those who dress well, or those from a specific age group, or those who have a rich voice, or those who belong to a specific ethnic group,

you may conduct assessments with these examinees differently than you do assessments with examinees who lack these characteristics. You may unknowingly signal your pleasure or displeasure to examinees you are attracted to or not attracted to, respectively. Diagnostic impressions also may be tainted in these cases.

You may be susceptible to the examinee's nonverbal behavior. For example, examinees who make eye contact, smile, have an attentive posture, or show interest in you may encourage you to probe topics and ask follow-up questions. In contrast, you may be disinclined to probe and ask follow-up questions when examinees fail to make eye contact, frown, have an inattentive posture, or fail to show interest in you.

Another type of error occurs when you compare your values with those of the examinee and find the examinee's values lacking (e.g., you are against spanking, but the parent is in favor of it). Your goal as an examiner is to understand the examinee's values, not to measure him or her against your personal standards. The way you perceive similarities and differences between you and the examinee also may affect how you conduct the evaluation.

You may be attracted to the odors of some examinees and repelled by those of others. Nevertheless, you must not let your attitude toward an examinee's body odor, perfume, or after-shave lotion influence either the length or the direction of the evaluation. Awareness of odors is subtle and often preconscious. By recognizing your preferences for odors, you will be in a better position to guard against allowing these preferences to bias the assessment. As stated above, reactions that are not objective are reactive effects. Errors will occur if you fail to recognize your biases and attend to them.

4. *Errors associated with the examiner's understanding of the examinee.* You are likely to make errors when you fail to consider the examinee's age, cognitive level, or culture or when you misunderstand what the examinee says. These errors may occur, for example, when you have difficulty understanding the examinee's speech or language, are preoccupied with other thoughts, are distracted by noise (such as a loud school bell or airplane passing overhead), or have hearing difficulties that have not been corrected.

5. *Errors associated with the examiner's failure to attend to the physical environment.* If you do not prepare the assessment room properly—that is, minimize distractions, keep the room temperature comfortable, assure adequate lighting, disconnect or turn off a regular phone or cell phone, and have comfortable seats, for example—the assessment may suffer.

6. *Errors associated with the examiner's selective perceptions and expectancies.* Bias occurs when you have selective perceptions and expectancies that diminish your ability to listen to the examinee or lead you to make judgments based on limited information. Following are three examples: First, you may miss important communications if you have preconceived notions about the examinee and allow these preconceptions to influence what you attend to and what

areas you probe. Second, you may distort information if you listen only to things that you believe are important or that confirm your expectancies. Third, you may interpret marginal behavior as the full expression of the behavior. For instance, you may interpret marginally aggressive behavior as aggressive behavior because the referral indicated that the child has a history of aggressive behavior.

7. *Errors associated with the examiner in cross-ethnic, cross-cultural, or cross-class situations.* Bias can occur when you distort replies or make inaccurate inferences simply because of racial or class differences (also see Chapter 2). For example, it would be wrong to infer that an Asian American or Native American examinee was evasive because she or he won't look you in the eye; for these examinees, such behavior is a sign of respect.

8. *Errors associated with the examiner's test administration.* Carelessness in the wording of instructions and questions, the presentation of test materials, and/or the timing of questions will invalidate the test scores.

9. *Errors associated with the examiner's scoring.* Some examiners have liberal scoring standards, whereas others have conservative scoring standards. If you fail to adhere to the scoring guidelines, you will generate unreliable test scores.

10. *Errors associated with the examiner's recording of data.* You may make recording errors simply because of careless notations or because you omitted, added, or subtly changed details. Or you may make recording errors because of your preconceived ideas—you hear what you want to hear or what you expect to hear. These errors can occur when you are making notes either during the evaluation proper or after the evaluation is completed.

11. *Errors associated with the examiner's interpretation of observations and information.* If you make inferences beyond your observations or beyond the information you obtain, you lose objectivity. For example, the speech of an examinee may be characterized as "deliberate" by one examiner, as "slow and dull" by another examiner, and as "depressed and despondent" by still another examiner. To be objective, your notes should accurately reflect the examinee's behavior—for example, that the examinee "spoke slowly" or "paused several seconds before responding." Use adjectives that best describe the behavior of the examinee. *Don't draw inferences unless you have sufficient information.* Interpretation errors are more likely to occur when the behavior of the examinee is ambiguous.

When you are unable to form judgments about the examinee's behavior, you may opt for the middle ground. That is, you may take a neutral position—for example, "the examinee's behavior was neither aggressive nor passive." This statement is fine if your observation was accurate. However, if it was not and you failed to observe some important behavior, you may fail to probe valuable leads.

12. *Errors associated with the examiner's theoretical position.* These errors come about when you interpret all behavior from a preconceived position. Not all of the child's

behaviors are likely to be related to an unresolved Oedipus complex, being an oldest child, having been adopted, or having an inappropriate reinforcement history.

Ways to Reduce Examiner Bias and Errors in the Assessment

Here are some strategies for improving the reliability and validity of the assessment:

1. *Become an expert in administering tests, conducting interviews, and performing observations.* The more proficient you become in administering, scoring, and interpreting tests and in conducting interviews and observations, the more attention you will be able to devote to the examinee. As an expert, you will likely be more objective in the assessment and less susceptible to bias. And plan to remain an expert by frequently reviewing your techniques for administering and scoring tests, for conducting interviews, and for observing examinees. Finally, follow standard procedures in administering tests.

2. *Develop self-awareness.* Become aware of personal needs that may adversely affect how you conduct the assessment, and find ways to suppress them. Recognize your attitudes, values, and objectives and how they relate to examinees from different ethnic, cultural, or socioeconomic groups. Develop an awareness of your nonverbal and verbal behavior. Be aware not only of the communications of the examinee and your reactions to them but also of your communications and how the examinee may perceive them. Minimize selective perceptions, theoretical preconceptions, and expectancies that may distract you from eliciting information and from making appropriate decisions. You want to develop a neutral stance toward all examinees, even though you may be distracted by their personal appearance, deformities, body piercings, and so forth.

3. *Relate to the examinee.* Listen carefully to the examinee. Give your undivided interest and attention to the examinee. Show your acceptance of the examinee. Maintain an attitude of professional interest and concern. When examinees are fearful and anxious, try even harder to establish rapport. For example, make frequent supportive comments to show them that you understand their fears and anxieties and can accept them. When examinees are fearful and anxious or hostile and resentful, listen carefully to them and take the pressure off by interjecting light conversation. If you continue to detect anxiety or defensiveness, stay relaxed and try to get them to relax by making small talk before broaching or returning to anxiety-laden topics. When examinees will not cooperate simply because of who you are, you can do nothing to change your status. You can, however, show them that you can be trusted and want to help them.

4. *Gather additional information.* When you have doubts about the reliability of the test results and other information you obtain, use more than one test to measure the same ability, ask questions in different ways or at different times, or ask both the examinee and someone else about the same areas. You can evaluate the validity of the information you obtain by checking against tests scores obtained from the school, school grades, baby books, medical records, and other formal and informal records, where applicable.

5. *Attend to recordings.* Shortly after the evaluation is over, check your scoring on all the tests that you administered and the accuracy of your notes. If you do not take notes, record (by writing or tape recorder) the information you obtained and your impressions soon after the assessment. *Remember that you should record verbatim actual responses to test questions.*

6. *Develop hypotheses.* Study all sources of information about the examinee. Cross-validate inferences and predictions. Closely review the data before you make inferences. Recognize the limitations of your theoretical approach. Be open to alternative explanations.

You must strive to overcome any conditions that will impede your effectiveness as an examiner. In case of substantial doubts about your findings, arrange to have the examinee eval-

Copyright © 1987, Bill Hoest. Reprinted with permission of King Features Syndicate, Inc. World rights reserved.

uated by another examiner, and then compare the results of the two evaluations. Your goal is to be vigilant and objective, yet always caring.

Now let's turn to a statistical procedure that lets us determine how much an examinee's score would vary if he or she were repeatedly tested.

Standard Error of Measurement

Because measurement error is usually associated with a test score, there is almost always some uncertainty about an examinee's true score. The *standard error of measurement* (SEM), or standard error of a score, is an estimate of the amount of error associated with an examinee's obtained score. It is directly related to the reliability of a test: the lower the reliability, the higher the standard error of measurement, and conversely, the higher the reliability, the lower the standard error of measurement. Large standard errors of measurement reflect less precise measurements and require larger confidence intervals for the obtained score (see the following subsection). Of course, the size of the SEM is also related to the standard deviation of the metric (i.e., the measurement scale)—the larger the standard deviation of the metric, the larger the SEM. Thus, for example, the SEM will be larger when the total score has a mean of 100 and standard deviation of 16 than when the total score has a mean of 50 and a standard deviation of 8.

The standard error of measurement is the standard deviation of the distribution of error scores. We can compute it from the reliability coefficient of the test by multiplying the standard deviation (SD) of the test by the square root of 1 minus the reliability coefficient (r_{xx}) of the test:

$$\text{SEM} = SD\sqrt{1 - r_{xx}}$$

This equation indicates that as the reliability of a test increases, the standard error of measurement decreases. With a reliability coefficient of 1.00, the standard error of measurement would be zero. With a reliability coefficient of .00, the standard error of measurement would be equal to the standard deviation of the scores in the sample.

Confidence Intervals for Obtained Scores

When we report a score for a psychological test, such as an intelligence test, we also should report how certain we are that an interval around the examinee's obtained score contains his or her true score. We usually do this by reporting a *confidence interval*—that is, a band or range of scores around the obtained score that likely includes the examinee's true score.

The confidence interval may be large or small, depending on the degree of certainty we desire. Traditionally, we select points that represent the 68%, 95%, or 99% level of confidence, although we also can use the 85% or 90% level. We

can think of a 95% confidence interval as the range in which we will find an examinee's true score 95% of the time. The statistical chances are only 5 in 100 that an examinee's true score lies outside this confidence interval. It is not possible, however, to construct a confidence interval within which an examinee's true score is certain to lie unless the entire distribution of scores is included.

Although you can usually use confidence intervals for several scores obtained by an examinee on a test (such as subtest scaled scores), we recommend that you use them primarily for the overall score, such as the WISC–III Full Scale IQ, because it is this score that you usually use to make diagnostic and classification decisions. *Individuals who use the test findings need to know that the IQ and other major scores used to make decisions about the child are not perfectly accurate because they inherently contain measurement error.* Consequently, you should report confidence intervals associated with the IQ and other similar overall scores.

There are two methods for obtaining confidence intervals. One is based on the child's obtained score and the conventional standard error of measurement. The other is based on the estimated true score (discussed shortly) and the standard error of measurement associated with the estimated true score (also called the *standard error of estimation*). The following guidelines will help you to select which type of confidence interval to use. Note that in all of the examples in this section, the confidence intervals have been rounded up to the next whole number.

Confidence interval for obtained score without reference to the estimated true score.   When you base the confidence interval solely on the examinee's obtained score, without reference to her or his estimated true score, use the standard error of measurement for obtained scores.

Confidence interval formula for conventional standard error of measurement.   We obtain the confidence interval by using the following formula:

$$\text{Confidence interval} = \text{obtained score} \pm z(\text{SEM})$$

The formula shows that two values are needed in addition to the child's test score: the z score associated with the confidence level chosen and the standard error of measurement. You can obtain the z score from a normal distribution table, which you can find in most statistics textbooks. We used a normal distribution table to obtain the following values for the five most common levels of confidence:

$$68\% \text{ level, } z = 1.00$$
$$85\% \text{ level, } z = 1.44$$
$$90\% \text{ level, } z = 1.65$$
$$95\% \text{ level, } z = 1.96$$
$$99\% \text{ level, } z = 2.58$$

You will usually find the SEM in the manual that accompanies a test, or you can compute it using the formula given previously. You compute the upper limit of the confidence interval by adding the product $(z)(\text{SEM})$ to a child's score, and the lower limit by subtracting the product from a child's score (thus the plus/minus symbol ± in the equation).

Constructing the confidence interval using the conventional standard error of measurement. Here is an example of how to construct a confidence interval, given a standard error of measurement of 3 and an IQ of 100. First we need to select a confidence level. Let's say that we select the 95% level. The z score associated with the 95% level, as we have seen, is 1.96. To obtain the confidence interval, we multiply this value by the standard error of measurement, 3, and add a ± sign to the result to represent the upper and lower limits of the interval. Thus, the confidence interval is 100 ± 6. The value 6 is then added to and subtracted from the obtained score to determine the specific band, or interval, associated with the obtained score. The upper limit of the interval is given by

$$\text{Confidence interval (upper limit)} = 100 + 1.96(3)$$
$$= 100 + 6 = 106$$

and the lower limit of the interval is given by

$$\text{Confidence interval (lower limit)} = 100 - 1.96(3)$$
$$= 100 - 6 = 94$$

Because the z score we used was associated with the 95% level, we can say that the chances that the child's true score is between 94 and 106 are about 95 out of 100.

For an IQ of 100 (with SEM = 3), the interval would be 100 ± 3 (97 to 103) at the 68% confidence level, 100 ± 4 (96 to 104) at the 85% confidence level, 100 ± 5 (95 to 105) at the 90% confidence level, and 100 ± 8 (92 to 108) at the 99% confidence level. The last band indicates that the chances that the child's true score is between 92 and 108 are about 99 out of 100. Notice that we must increase the band width to increase our level of confidence (or degree of certainty).

As another example, let's construct several confidence intervals for a child who obtains an IQ of 80 on a test for which the SEM = 5. We would complete the equation for the 90% level of confidence in the following way:

$$\text{Confidence interval} = \text{score} \pm z(\text{SEM})$$
$$= 80 \pm 1.65(5)$$
$$= 80 \pm 8 = 72 \text{ to } 88$$

For the 99% level of confidence, the equation would be as follows:

$$\text{Confidence interval} = 80 \pm 2.58(5)$$
$$= 80 \pm 13 = 67 \text{ to } 93$$

Rationale for using the conventional standard error of measurement to construct confidence intervals. Glutting, McDermott, and Stanley (1987) pointed out that if you want to answer the question "What is the best measure of an examinee's *current* functioning in the performance area assessed by a specific test?" (p. 613), then the proper score to interpret is the obtained score, without recourse to the estimated true score. Their reasoning follows:

The obtained score is the proper score to interpret...because the question pertains exclusively to a single examinee on a given test at a particular point in time. Moreover, long-standing conventions in clinical practice, contemporary social policy, and law require that psychologists use obtained scores for diagnostic and classificatory decisions....

In instances where a single examinee is tested alone, and not as a member of an explicit group, the expected error of measurement (in the statistical sense) is zero because the examinee's score is the mean of the group ($N = 1$) and the obtained score "regresses" toward this mean because of error of measurement. For the lone-tested individual, confidence limits must be constructed around the obtained score by using the standard error of measurement procedure.... The standard error of measurement is a *personal* statistic that, theoretically, is computable for a single examinee and independent of a test's reliability and mean. It yields confidence limits that are applicable when the psychologist does not know to which specific subgroup of the general population the examinee belongs. In diagnostic classification, because one cannot presume to know beforehand the resultant assignment of an examinee to a specific clinical or exceptional subgroup, psychologists are compelled to use scores and confidence limits that are personally focused. (pp. 612–613)

Appendixes A, B, C, and E show the confidence intervals for the WISC–III (Table A-1), WPPSI–R (Table B-1), WAIS–III (Table C-1), and Stanford-Binet Intelligence Scale: Fourth Edition (Table E-1) based on the obtained score and the conventional standard error of measurement—that is, without recourse to the estimated true score or the standard error of estimation. Use of an examinee's specific age group in these tables allows you to obtain the most accurate confidence interval.

Confidence limits for obtained scores with reference to the estimated true score. Glutting et al. (1987) also pointed out that if you are interested in answering the question "What is the best *long-run* (stable) measure of an examinee's functioning in the performance area assessed by a specific test *relative to other examinees in a particular reference group*?" (p. 612), then the proper score to interpret is the estimated true score. They go on to note that

the "reference group" could include all examinees in the standardization sample for the test, or some independent clinical subgroup of those examinees (i.e., the gifted or mentally retarded), or examinees comprising subsets similar to the examinee in age, sex, score level, and other relevant characteristics. In this situation, the estimated true score is the appropriate score for interpretation, as it considers the mean and reliability for the specific reference group in question and corrects for mean regression on that basis. (p. 613, with changes in notation)

Because the WISC–III is widely used, it will be used in this section to illustrate how confidence limits are obtained with reference to the estimated true score. Table D-2 in Appendix D shows the confidence intervals, by age, for the WISC–III Full Scale IQ, Verbal Scale IQ, and Performance Scale IQ based on the estimated true score and the appropriate standard error of measurement. You simply apply the confidence intervals in Table D-2, as noted below, to the obtained score, just as you do those in Table A-1. You also can use Table D-2 for the WPPSI–R and WAIS–III and for any test with $M = 100$ and $SD = 15$ that has a reliability coefficient of .85 to .98.

Confidence interval formula using the estimated true score. The formula used to obtain the estimated true score is

$$T = r_{xx}X + (1 - r_{xx})\overline{X}$$

where T = estimated true score
r_{xx} = reliability of the test
X = obtained score
$\overline{X}$ = mean of the test

For a test with a mean of 100, the formula simplifies to the following:

$$T = 100 + r_{xx}(X - 100)$$

The formula used to obtain the standard error of estimation (SE_E) is as follows:

$$SE_E = r_{xx}\text{SEM}$$

where SE_E = standard error of estimation (or standard error of measurement of the true score)
r_{xx} = reliability of the test
SEM = standard error of measurement of the test

Thus, the estimated true score for an obtained WISC–III Full Scale IQ of 60 (where $r_{xx} = .96$) would be

$$
\begin{aligned}
T &= .96(60) + .04(100) \\
&= 57.60 + 4 = 62
\end{aligned}
$$

And the standard error of estimation would be

$$SE_E = .96(3.20) = 3.07$$

(Note that the WISC–III manual reports an SEM = 3.20 for the Full Scale IQ, not an SEM = 3.00.)

Using confidence intervals with reference to the estimated true score. Because the confidence intervals are centered around the estimated true score, the intervals become asymmetrical when applied to the obtained score. The asymmetry is greatest for values farthest from the mean, because regression to the mean is greater at the extremes of the distribution than at the center of the distribution. In fact, for scores at or near the mean, there is no asymmetry at all—the confidence intervals are equal around the mean. For example, as Table 4-6 shows, at the 68% confidence level for the WISC–III Verbal Scale at age 10 (Section K) the confidence level of an IQ of 40 is 40 + 0 to 40 + 6 (40 to 46), whereas for an IQ of 91 at this same age the confidence level is 91 – 3 to 91 + 4 (88 to 95). The procedure used to obtain the confidence intervals in Table D-2 in Appendix D is the same as that used by The Psychological Corporation in the construction of the confidence intervals in the WISC–III manual.

To use Table D-2 in Appendix D, follow this procedure. First, use the list at the beginning of the table to find which section of the table represents the examinee's age, the appropriate test (WISC–III, WPPSI–R, or WAIS–III), and the appropriate scale (i.e., Full Scale, Verbal Scale, or Performance Scale). Then select one confidence level from the columns labeled 68%, 85%, 90%, 95%, and 99%. The values in the table under the appropriate confidence level will allow you to calculate the lower (L) and upper (U) limits of the confidence interval for the obtained IQ. If the value is *positive* (when no sign precedes the value, the + sign is understood), *add* the absolute value to the obtained IQ. If the value is *negative* (a – sign precedes the absolute value), *subtract* the absolute value from the obtained IQ. Usually, you will find the lower limit by subtracting an absolute value from the obtained IQ, and you will find the upper limit by adding an absolute value to the obtained IQ.

The following example shows how a confidence interval is calculated. To calculate the confidence interval for a 6-year-old child who obtains a WISC–III Full Scale IQ of 46, see Table D-2, Section K, in Appendix D. Section K shows that the values at the 68% confidence level for the lower and upper limits of the confidence interval are 0 and 6, respectively. (Table 4-6 shows Section K.) Because both values are positive, you can obtain the lower and upper limits of the confidence interval by adding the absolute values to the obtained IQ. The resulting confidence interval is 46 to 52 (lower limit is 46 + 0 = 46; upper limit is 46 + 6 = 52).

Note that, although you calculate them for the estimated true score, the values for the confidence intervals are applied to the obtained score. Also note that you do not provide the estimated true score in the report. It is used only to generate the confidence interval.

Table D-2 in Appendix D is based on the examinee's age and not on average values for the total sample; this is in contrast to the WISC–III manual, where the confidence intervals are based on the total sample. *Use of the child's specific age group allows you to obtain the most accurate confidence interval.*

Comment on confidence intervals. In clinical and psychoeducational assessments, questions usually center on how the examinee is functioning at the time of the referral. Therefore, we recommend that you use the confidence interval based on the child's obtained score, without recourse to the child's estimated true score. If you follow this recommendation, use the confidence intervals for the obtained score

Table 4-6
Part of Table D-2 in Appendix D Showing Confidence Intervals Based on the Estimated True Score for Wechsler Scales

K. WISC–III—Verbal Scale—Ages 10, 11, 12, 14, 16, and Average; WISC–III—Full Scale—Ages 6, 9, 11, 13, and 14; WPPSI–R—Performance Scale—Age 5; WPPSI–R—Verbal Scale—Average; WPPSI–R—Full Scale—Ages 5½, 6, and 6½; WAIS–III—Performance Scale—Age 25–29, 55–64, and 70–74 (r_{xx} = .95)

68%			85%			90%			95%			99%		
IQ	*L*	*U*	*IQ*	*L*	*U*	*IQ*	*L*	*U*	*IQ*	*L*	*U*	*IQ*	*L*	*U*
40–46	0	6	40–41	−2	8	40–44	−2	8	40–45	−3	9	40–45	−5	11
47–53	−1	6	42–58	−2	7	45–55	−3	8	46–54	−4	9	46–54	−6	11
54–66	−1	5	59–61	−3	7	56–64	−3	7	55–65	−4	8	55–65	−6	10
67–73	−2	5	62–78	−3	6	65–75	−4	7	66–74	−5	8	66–74	−7	10
74–86	−2	4	79–81	−4	6	76–84	−4	6	75–85	−5	7	75–85	−7	9
87–93	−3	4	82–98	−4	5	85–95	−5	6	86–94	−6	7	86–94	−8	9
94–106	−3	3	99–101	−5	5	96–104	−5	5	95–105	−6	6	95–105	−8	8
107–113	−4	3	102–118	−5	4	105–115	−6	5	106–114	−7	6	106–114	−9	8
114–126	−4	2	119–121	−6	4	116–124	−6	4	115–125	−7	5	115–125	−9	7
127–133	−5	2	122–138	−6	3	125–135	−7	4	126–134	−8	5	126–134	−10	7
134–146	−5	1	139–141	−7	3	136–144	−7	3	135–145	−8	4	135–145	−10	6
147–153	−6	1	142–158	−7	2	145–155	−8	3	146–154	−9	4	146–154	−11	6
154–160	−6	0	159–160	−8	2	156–160	−8	2	155–160	−9	3	155–160	−11	5

and the conventional standard error of measurement—Table A-1 in Appendix A; the WISC–III manual does *not* provide a similar table. However, when you want to know how the child might perform over a longer period in relation to a specific reference group, use the confidence interval based on the estimated true score—Table D-2 in Appendix D. Again, the confidence intervals shown in Table D-2 are more appropriate than those shown in the WISC–III manual because they are based on the examinee's specific age and not on the total sample.

Confidence Intervals for Predicted Scores

Earlier in the chapter we discussed regression equations and the standard error of estimate associated with the predicted score. The standard error of estimate allows us to establish a confidence interval around a predicted score. This confidence interval is obtained in the following way:

$$\text{Confidence interval} = Y_{\text{pred}} \pm z(SE_{\text{est}})$$

The confidence interval for predicted scores is similar to the confidence interval for obtained test scores. If we use a *z* score of 1, then the standard error of estimate tells us that we can expect the predicted score to fall within the range bounded by the standard error of estimate about 68% of the time. If we want to have more confidence in the prediction,

we can use a *z* score associated with, for example, the 95% confidence level (*z* = 1.96) or the 99% confidence level (*z* = 2.58). However, with higher levels of confidence, we must expand the band (or range) around the predicted score.

The following three examples illustrate how we can establish several confidence intervals. In each case, let's assume that $SE_{\text{est}} = 5$ and $Y_{\text{pred}} = 15$.

- For the 68% level of confidence, the confidence interval is 15 ± 1.00(5). Thus, the confidence interval associated with the predicted score of 15 is 10.00 to 20.00 (there is a 68% chance that *Y* falls within this range).
- For the 95% level of confidence, the confidence interval is 15 ± 1.96(5). Thus, the confidence interval associated with the predicted score of 15 is 5.20 to 24.80 (there is a 95% chance that *Y* falls within this range).
- For the 99% level of confidence, the confidence interval is 15 ± 2.58(5). Thus, the confidence interval associated with the predicted score of 15 is 2.10 to 27.90 (there is a 99% chance that *Y* falls within this range).

Repeated Evaluations

When the retest interval is short, it may be difficult to interpret the results of repeated evaluations because of *practice effects* or other retest factors. Let's see why this is so, using intelligence tests as the model.

1. *Practice effects cannot be easily differentiated from changes associated with clinical improvement.* Practice effects refer to changes in performance (usually gains) that result from prior exposure to a task. A higher retest score may be the result of an intervention or of learning, or it might simply be related to prior exposure to the task. For example, are the higher intelligence test scores obtained by a child with a brain injury on retesting related to practice effects or to the child's improved cognitive functioning? We can attempt to answer this question by seeing how the child performs on other tasks. When the change on the retest is greater than one standard error of measurement, we can be more confident that the score reflects a reliable change. Of course, additional factors—such as motivation, concentration, time of day, and so forth—also may influence the child's retest performance.

2. *Practice effects may not occur to the same extent in all populations.* Practice effects that are typically seen among examinees with average ability may not occur among mentally retarded examinees, gifted examinees, or examinees with known cerebral dysfunction. Practice effects may differ as a function of the examinee's age or other variables.

3. *Practice effects vary for different types of tasks.* Nonverbal tasks (such as those found on the Wechsler Performance Scale) usually show more practice effects than verbal tasks (such as those found on the Wechsler Verbal Scale; see Chapters 8 through 12 for a discussion of the Wechsler tests). Even tasks within the same performance area (or within the same verbal area) may show different practice effects. Practice effects may be minimal on finger-tapping and strength-of-grip tests (see *Assessment of Children: Behavioral and Clinical Applications* for a description of tests that measure these functions).

4. *Practice effects may be affected by the length of time that elapsed between administration of the tests.* Shorter testretest intervals produce greater practice effects than do longer intervals.

5. *Test-retest results may vary as a function of scores on the first test.* Children with low initial scores tend to score somewhat higher on retest, and children with high initial scores tend to score somewhat lower on retest. This phenomenon is called regression to the mean, and it reflects the tendency for a retest score to be closer to the mean than the initial test score because of random factors that vary between the initial test and retest performances.

6. *Differences in results may be difficult to interpret when the initial test and the retest are different.* If you measure intelligence by test A on the first occasion and by test B on the second, changes in IQ may be produced by differences between the two tests and not changes in the examinee. An understanding of the properties of different tests, including how they are related to each other, is critical in evaluating retest changes.

7. *Differences in results may depend on the item content covered throughout the test.* A test that covers a wide age range may tap different abilities at different ages, even though the test is said to measure only one ability or skill. For example, an intelligence test that covers ages 2 years through 18 years may measure different components of intelligence at 2 years than at 15 years. In such cases, it will be difficult to compare test results at these two ages and know precisely what any changes in test scores mean.

When examinees are expected to show gains on retest and do not, they may have a subtle learning deficit. This can happen, for example, when examinees are brain injured or when they are being reevaluated after brain surgery or chemotherapy.

For the results of repeated evaluations to be maximally useful, we would need data on the differential effects of practice in relation to such factors as item content, age, gender, ability level, and illness (type, location, and chronicity). A database that provided normative retest changes on various tests with specific normal and clinical populations would be extremely helpful in evaluating practice effects. Any clinical significance attributed to changes in test scores should be corroborated by other assessment and clinical data; validity data would be particularly important in this regard. Until such data become available for each test that you use, be careful in interpreting retest findings.

ITEM RESPONSE THEORY

Traditionally, test developers look at certain values for each item on a test to see whether the item is performing properly. One value is *item difficulty:* the percentage of examinees who answer an item correctly. It ranges from 0.0 for an item with maximum difficulty (everyone in the sample answers incorrectly) to +1.0 for an item with no difficulty (everyone in the sample answers correctly). A second value is *item discrimination:* how an item discriminates between examinees who do well on the test as a whole and those who do poorly. It ranges from –1.0 to +1.0. A +.8 value for an item reflects excellent discrimination, whereas values from –.2 to +.2 indicate poor discrimination. A –.9 value reflects a reverse discriminator—examinees who performed poorly on the test answered the item correctly more often than examinees who did well on the test. This may occur when the item is keyed incorrectly, when there is more than one correct answer (as in a multiple-choice test), or when the item is ambiguous.

Another approach, called *item response theory* (IRT) or *latent trait model* (LTM), is also used to analyze individual items. Item response theory provides useful information about the relationships between the attribute being measured and the test responses through the use of three parameters: item discrimination, item difficulty, and a "guessing" parameter that reflects the probability that a correct response will occur by chance. A test developer places this information in mathematical equations to guide in the construction of a test. The mathematical equations can also be illustrated graphically in an item characteristic curve. An *item characteristic curve* (ICC) is the line that results when we graph the

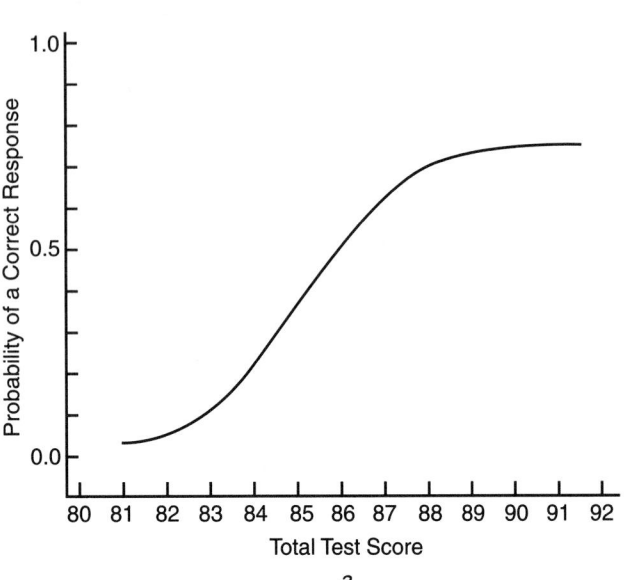

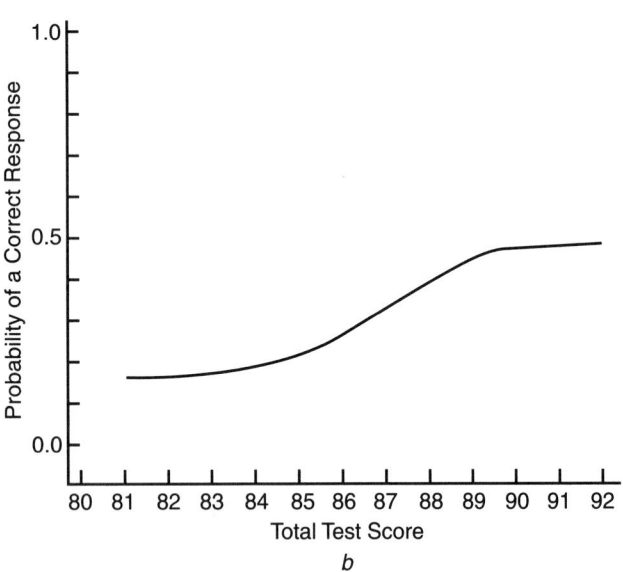

Figure 4-3. Two item characteristic curves.

relationship between the probability of passing an item and the examinee's position on the construct being measured.

Figure 4-3 shows item characteristic curves for two items on an intelligence test. Curve A reflects a good item: Examinees with high intelligence test scores are more likely to pass the item than are those with low intelligence test scores. Curve B reflects a difficult item that has little discriminating power: Examinees with low intelligence test scores are almost as likely to pass the item as those with high intelligence test scores. The slope of the curve tells you how effective the item is. A positive slope (i.e., one that rises from the lower left to the upper right) means that the item is a good discriminator, whereas a flat slope means that the item is a poor discriminator.

Here is another example of how an item characteristic curve is used (Allen & Yen, 1979):

Item characteristic curves can be useful in identifying items that perform differently for different groups of examinees. For example, a test developer may be concerned that some reading-comprehension items dealing with farms may measure different processes for rural children and urban children. To examine this question, the test developer would administer the test to both groups of children and determine the item characteristic curve for each item in each group. If an item is measuring the same thing in both groups, the item characteristic curves for that item should look the same in both groups. If the item is measuring different things in the two groups, the item characteristic curves can appear different. Items whose item characteristic curves are substantially affected by the group membership of the examinees can be revised or deleted from the test. (pp. 129–130, with changes in notation)

Item response theory also is useful in adaptive testing (Anastasi, 1989).

One of the most important applications of item response theory is to be found in computer-administered adaptive testing, also described as individualized, tailored, and response-contingent testing. This procedure adjusts item coverage to the responses actually given by each examinee. As the individual responds to each item, the computer chooses the next item on the basis of the individual's response history up to that point. Essentially each person takes a test that is tailor-made to fit his or her performance. The test stops when enough information is available to reach a preestablished reliability; this is equivalent to reducing the error of measurement to an acceptable level. The person's test score is based not on the number of items passed, but on the predetermined score of each of the items passed, as determined by its difficulty level, discriminative value, and susceptibility to guessing. The item "score" represents the best estimate of the ability level at which the likelihood of passing the item is 50-50. Adaptive testing is thus made possible by the use of item response theory in developing the item pool. (p. 479, with changes in notation)

DIFFERENTIAL ITEM FUNCTIONING

Differential item functioning (DIF) is a procedure designed to tell us whether test items function differently in different groups (Zumbo, 1999). The procedure is based on the principle that if different groups of examinees have the same level of proficiency, then they should perform similarly on individual test items regardless of their group membership. Differential item functioning occurs when examinees from different groups show differing probabilities of success on the item after the groups have been matched on the underlying ability (i.e., overall score on the test) that the item is intended to measure.

Differential item functioning can occur in a uniform or non-uniform manner. It is uniform if the difference in the probability of success is consistent across all levels of ability (e.g., the item favors all females regardless of ability). It is non-uniform if the difference in the probability of success between the groups is not constant across ability levels—that is, there is an interaction effect (e.g., the item favors females of low ability and males of high ability). The procedure is useful for detecting item bias, but the assumptions of the procedure (for instance, that the test item measures a single trait, that the overall test is fair, and that the abilities measured by the test are equivalently distributed across all groups) may be questionable in certain instances. Finally, removing items judged as biased may not result in a fairer test (Camilli, 1993).

VALIDITY

The *validity* of a test refers to the extent to which a test measures what it is supposed to measure, and therefore the appropriateness with which we can make inferences based on the test results. We can use test results for many purposes, including educational placements, program training, job qualification, and diagnosis. Unless the test is valid for the particular purpose we are using it for, though, we cannot use the results with confidence. Because we use tests for many different purposes, there is no single type of validity appropriate for all testing purposes.

The process of test validation revolves around two issues: (a) what a test measures and (b) how well it measures it. In the following subsections, we will consider procedures that reflect different strategies for analyzing validity. Recognize that no test is valid for all purposes or valid in the abstract; tests are valid only for a specific purpose. Furthermore, validity is not a matter of all or nothing, but a matter of degree. When you evaluate a test, you should consider the various lines of evidence used to support the validity of the test, as discussed below. You want to select tests that are valid for your purposes. For example, if you want to select the best applicants for a position, you should consider the criterion-related validity of the test. However, if you want to measure achievement, you should focus on the content validity of the test. Studies of the validity of a test should continue long after the publication of the test. The test publisher is responsible for furnishing evidence that the test is valid for specific purposes, and the examiner is responsible for the valid use of test results. Let us now consider the three principal varieties of validity: content validity, criterion-related validity, and construct validity.

Content Validity

Content validity refers to whether the items on a test represent the domain that the test is supposed to measure. In evaluating content validity, we must consider the appropriateness of the type of items, the completeness of the item sample, and the way in which the items assess the content of the domain involved. Issues relevant to these considerations include the following: (a) Does the test measure the domain of interest? (b) Are the test questions appropriate? (c) Does the test contain enough information to cover appropriately what it is supposed to measure? (d) What is the level of mastery at

which the content is being assessed? If we can answer these four questions satisfactorily, the test has good content validity. For example, a mathematics test designed for children between 6 and 17 years would have good content validity if the test systematically sampled the material found in several mathematics books used in grades 1 through 12.

We can build content validity into a test by including only items that measure the trait or behavior of interest. Content validity does not require that we measure all possible elements of a content area, but rather that those measured represent the area. Part of the validation process for any educational or psychological test is to determine the representativeness of the test. Do not confuse content validity with face validity. *Face validity* refers to what the test appears to measure, not what it actually does measure. Face validity is important because if the test does not appear to measure what it is supposed to measure, examinees may become skeptical and not perform adequately. Although face validity is, in itself, a desirable feature of a test, it is not always necessary. In some personality tests, items that do not have face validity are included in order to detect malingering.

Criterion-Related Validity

Criterion-related validity refers to the relationship between test scores and some type of criterion or outcome, such as ratings, classifications, or other test scores. The criterion, like the test, must possess adequate psychometric properties: It should be readily measurable, free from bias, and relevant to the purposes of the test. The test and criterion should have a complementary relationship; otherwise we could not use the criterion to determine whether the test measures the trait or characteristic it was designed to measure. There are two types of criterion-related validity: concurrent (or diagnostic) and predictive (or prognostic).

Concurrent validity. *Concurrent validity* refers to whether test scores are related to some currently available criterion measure. Let's suppose we have a test designed to place children in a special math class. If we find that the test scores correlate with the teachers' assessment of the children's knowledge of math or with classroom performance in math, we can say that the test has concurrent validity. Because the test scores correlate with teacher ratings, we can use the test to replace teacher ratings if we want an estimate of the children's math ability.

Predictive validity. *Predictive validity* refers to the correlation between test scores and future performance on a relevant criterion. The predictive validity coefficient answers the following question: Is the score obtained on the test an accurate predictor of future performance on the criterion? An example of predictive validity is the accuracy with which a reading readiness test administered at the beginning of the first grade predicts reading performance at the end of the first grade. Predictive validity is important in many psychoeducational contexts.

We determine predictive validity by giving a test to a group that has yet to perform on the criterion of interest. Then we subsequently measure the group's performance on the criterion. The correspondence between the two scores provides a measure of the predictive validity of the test. If the test possesses high predictive validity, persons scoring high on the test will perform well on the criterion measure. Likewise, those scoring low on the test will perform poorly on the criterion. If the predictive validity of a test is low, there will be an erratic and unpredictable relationship between the test scores and subsequent performance on the criterion.

Comment on criterion-related validity.   Both concurrent and predictive validity involve establishing a relationship between a test and a criterion measure. When the criterion measure is available immediately, we are evaluating evidence of concurrent validity; when the criterion measure is available in the future, we are evaluating evidence of predictive validity. More importantly, the choice of concurrent or predictive validity evidence depends on the objectives of measurement. If we want to know how a child functions now (Can Jill read at her current grade level now?), we need evidence of concurrent validity. If we want to know how she will function in the future (Is it likely that Jill will be able to read at the third-grade level next year?), we need evidence of predictive validity.

Construct Validity

Construct validity refers to the extent to which a test measures a psychological construct (i.e., an inferred entity) or trait. Two components of construct validity are convergent validity and discriminant validity. *Convergent validity* refers to how well performances on different measures of the same domain in different formats (e.g., teacher and parent forms or multiple-choice test and essay test formats) correlate positively. *Discriminant validity,* sometimes called *divergent validity,* is the opposite of convergent validity. Different constructs are chosen to measure different characteristics; therefore, tests designed to measure unrelated constructs should not correlate. You should consider both convergent validity and discriminant validity when you assess a test's construct validity.

Examples of constructs include intelligence, self-esteem, concept formation, speed of information processing, nonverbal reasoning, and mechanical aptitude. We can use several procedures to determine how the items in a test relate to the theoretical constructs that the test purports to measure. They include specifying the meaning of the construct, distinguishing the construct from other constructs, and specifying how measures of the construct relate to other variables. We obtain evidence for construct validity when

- we find a relationship between the test items and a theory related to how the items were selected. For example, we can

say that a test of intelligence has construct validity if children who obtain high scores on the test also have better recall, understanding of concepts, imagination, grades in school, teacher ratings of scholarship, and parental ratings of intelligence than those who have low scores on the test.

- we conduct a factor analysis and find that the test measures the constructs underlying the test. For example, if we correlate the test with other similar measures and conduct a factor analysis, the results will provide information about which tests share common variance or communality (described below), and thus measure the same construct. A factor analysis of the WISC–III indicates that the subtests in the test share common variance and that the test has a meaningful verbal component and a meaningful performance component, thereby supporting the use of separate verbal and performance scores (see Chapter 8).

- we find that scores on a test relate more closely to those on other tests measuring the same construct (referred to as convergent validation) than to those on tests that are supposed to measure different constructs (referred to as discriminant validation). Thus, when a test of reading correlates more highly with other tests of reading than it does with tests of mathematics, we can say that the reading test has convergent and discriminant validity.

- we find that the test scores correlate with related measures. For example, suppose we give a test of leadership quality to a sample of college students, place them in small groups of six students, and give each group a task to perform. We then have raters who are unfamiliar with the students' test scores rate each student on his or her leadership qualities. A positive correlation between the test and the ratings provides evidence that the test has construct validity.

Other ways to demonstrate construct validity include designing experimental studies to evaluate the construct and showing developmental changes in the test scores.

Predictive Utility

A concept related to predictive validity is predictive utility. *Predictive utility* refers to the extent to which a test agrees with a criterion measure in classifying individuals as to their membership in a category. For example, suppose a preschool inventory administered to a group of children at 5 years of age classifies 10% of the children as "at risk" for learning difficulties. Three years later, at the end of the third grade, we give the children an achievement test. Children falling below the 15th percentile rank on the test are classified as having learning difficulties. We refer to the battery at the end of the third grade as the criterion measure. We need to know the predictive utility of the preschool inventory if we want to know how well it predicts which children will have learning difficulties in the future. Validity coefficients are not adequate for this purpose; instead, we use various agreement indices, as noted below.

We evaluate predictive utility by determining the percentage of correct classifications the test (or battery of tests) makes—that is, how accurately the test assigns individuals to specific groups or categories based on cut-off scores. We can do this by determining the extent to which the test and the independent criterion measure make the same classifications. We can depict the results in a 2 × 2 matrix, as shown in Figure 4-4. In Figure 4-4 the test criterion or classification criterion is whether children were "at risk." The "at risk" designation could be for learning difficulties, pervasive developmental disorder, conduct disorder, or any other category. We usually base the outcome criterion (or criterion measure) on the individual's performance, on diagnoses given by mental health professionals, or on ratings given by teachers.

The four cells in the matrix represent the following types of agreement (alternative terminology for the type of agreement is shown in parentheses):

(*a*) *Valid positive* (*hit*). The test assigned the child to the at-risk classification (referred to as the positive classification), which was confirmed by the criterion measure. *Positive* here means that the child is classified as being at risk for having problems or a poor outcome. (In medical terminology, *positive* means having a disease or illness.)

(*b*) *False positive* (*false alarm*). The test assigned the child to the at-risk classification, which was not confirmed by the criterion measure.

(*c*) *False negative* (*miss*). The test assigned the child to the no-risk classification (referred to as the negative classifica-

tion), which was not confirmed by the criterion measure. *Negative* here means that the child is classified as not being at risk for having problems or a poor outcome. (In medical terminology, negative means not having a disease or illness.)

(*d*) *Valid negative* (*correct rejection*). The test assigned the child to the no-risk classification, which was confirmed by the criterion measure.

We measure the effectiveness of a test in predicting a criterion by adding the frequencies in (*a*) and (*d*) and dividing by the total frequency:

$$\text{Effectiveness} = \frac{a + d}{a + b + c + d}$$

Thus, if the four cells had the frequencies $a = 45$, $b = 15$, $c = 5$, and $d = 35$, the effectiveness of the test would be

$$\text{Effectiveness} = \frac{45 + 35}{100} = .80, \text{ or } 80\% \text{ accurate}$$

For early screening instruments, in particular, it would be valuable to have information about validity and predictive utility.

Treatment Validity or Clinical Utility

Another aspect of validity is *treatment validity,* or *clinical utility.* A test is said to have treatment validity, or clinical

		Outcome criterion		
		Poor outcome	Good outcome	Total
Test criterion	At risk	Valid positive (hit) (*a*)	False positive (false alarm) (*b*)	*a + b*
	Not at risk	False negative (miss) (*c*)	Valid negative (correct rejection) (*d*)	*c + d*
	Total	*a + c*	*b + d*	*a + b + c + d*

Figure 4-4. Model for assessing the predictive utility of a test. The *valid positive rate* is $a/(a + c)$; it is also referred to as the true positive rate, hit rate, or index of sensitivity, and reflects the probability that people who had a poor outcome will be correctly identified by the test criterion. The *false positive rate* is $b/(b + d)$; it is also referred to as the false alarm rate, and reflects the probability that people who had a good outcome will be incorrectly identified by the test criterion. The *false negative rate* is $c/(a + c)$; it is also referred to as the miss rate or under-referral rate, and reflects the probability that people who had a poor outcome will be incorrectly identified by the test criterion. The *valid negative rate* is $d/(b + d)$; it is also referred to as the true negative rate, the correct rejection rate, or index of specificity, and reflects the probability that people who had a good outcome will be correctly identified by the test criterion. The *efficiency rate* is $a/(a + b)$; it reflects the probability that people identified by the test criterion as being at risk will have a poor outcome. The *overall accuracy rate* is $(a + d)/(a + b + c + d)$; it is also referred to as the overall hit rate or overall correct classification, and reflects the probability that people identified by the test criterion as being either at risk or not at risk will have the predicted outcome.

utility, if knowledge of the test results leads to constructive changes in the examinee's life. For example, suppose the results of a spatial test indicate that the examinee has excellent ability for constructing objects. The test is said to have treatment validity, or clinical utility, if the results motivate the examinee to pursue a course of study in a field related to his or her special ability.

Factors Affecting Validity

Because validity coefficients are a type of correlation coefficient, they are affected by such factors as (a) the range of attributes being measured (narrowing the range of either the test or the criterion measure will reduce the size of the validity coefficient, referred to as restriction of range) and (b) the length of the interval between the administration of the two measures (longer intervals will tend to lower the size of the validity coefficient). The concurrent validity and predictive validity of the IQ (and other test scores) are also affected by examinee-related factors and by criterion-related factors.

　1. *Examinee-related factors.* These factors include the examinees' test-taking skills, anxiety, degree of rapport with the examiner, motivation, speed, understanding of test instructions, physical handicaps, language skills, educational opportunities, and familiarity with the test material. Deficiencies in any of these factors will decrease validity. Thus, for example, test results are not valid when examinees are uncooperative or highly distractible, when they fail to understand the test instructions or the wording of the test questions, when they have physical handicaps that interfere with their ability to take the tests (and no adjustments have been made by the examiner), or when they have limited comprehension of English.

　2. *Criterion-related factors.* Let's look at achievement test scores, a commonly used criterion for evaluating the validity of intelligence tests, as an example of how deficiencies in the criterion might affect validity. Achievement test scores may be affected (a) by the quality of teaching, the quality of textbooks, and the quality of the curriculum and (b) by the examinees' levels of ability, motivation, effort, classroom behavior, study skills, relationships with teachers and peers, and home environment (e.g., parent encouragement, study facilities, and resources in the home such as a computer and access to the World Wide Web). Thus, for example, the criterion will be affected by poor quality of teaching and textbooks, an inadequate curriculum, and a student's poor study skills and inadequate home environment. An unreliable or deficient criterion will decrease validity.

If the criterion measure shows no variability (e.g., teachers rated all students as "moderately active"), then the validity of the test (e.g., one designed to measure hyperactivity) will be zero. We cannot say that the test shows differences in classroom behavior when no differences exist according to the teachers. It is a case of trying to predict the unpredictable or of trying to find differences where none exist.

Alternatively, if we obtain the criterion measure on a sample that is more heterogeneous than the group for which the test is intended, validity estimates will be spuriously (falsely) high. For example, suppose we try to validate a test of artistic ability, which is designed to screen children nominated by their teachers as showing artistic talent, on a random sample of school children. The random sample will be more heterogeneous than the group for whom the test was originally intended (children nominated as having artistic talent). The resulting validity coefficient is likely to be spuriously high—it will show that the test has good discrimination (i.e., differentiating children who have artistic ability from those who do not). We can determine the relative amount of overestimation by comparing the validity coefficient obtained from using the random sample with the one obtained by using a sample of children nominated for their artistic talent.

The criterion measure also should be free of contamination; raters should not know how each child performed on the initial test. The ratings (criterion measure) should represent an independent assessment of each child in the study.

Predictive validity can be affected by intervening events and contingencies. You therefore need to consider everything you know about the examinee in evaluating predictive validity. For example, do emotionally disturbed examinees have an acute or chronic condition? If they have an acute state of disturbance, their intellectual efficiency or efficiency on an achievement test is likely to be hampered, resulting in nonrepresentative test results. If a later therapeutic intervention—such as drugs, psychotherapy, foster-home placement, or environmental manipulation—promptly improves the examinee's performance, we must question the validity or representativeness of the initial test results. However, if examinees have a chronic condition, such as irreversible brain damage or chronic schizophrenia, their test results may *not* be invalid, because in these cases their level of ability may not change. If the examinees' performance on the test reflects how they would likely perform during the next several weeks after the assessment, you can consider the evaluation to be valid. As Deutsch, Fishman, Kogan, North, and Whiteman (1964) stated:

If the time interval between the test administration and the criterial assessment is lengthy, a host of situational, motivational, and maturational changes may occur in the interim. An illness, an inspiring teacher, a shift in aspiration level or in direction of interest, remedial training, an economic misfortune, an emotional crisis, a growth spurt or retrogression in the abilities sampled by the test—any of these changes intervening between the testing and the point or points of criterion assessment may decrease the predictive power of the test. (pp. 136–137)

If you have reason to question the validity of your test results, state your reservations in the psychological report. If you seriously question the validity of the findings, consider destroying the test protocol or marking the word "invalid" over the face sheet. When an examinee deviates from some earlier level of functioning, it may not invalidate the results, however, because his or her current level of functioning may be different from the earlier level. In some cases, you may need to estimate the earlier level of functioning based on prior test results, school grades, or parental reports. This is sometimes required in cases of brain injury, for example. In such cases, we refer to the earlier level of functioning as the premorbid level—that is, the level at which the examinee was functioning prior to the onset of the brain injury.

META-ANALYSIS

A single study seldom provides definitive answers to research questions. Instead, progress in science is achieved through the accumulation of findings from numerous studies on a particular issue. Traditionally, researchers relied on narrative literature reviews (i.e., reviewing the research literature by inspecting the findings and arriving at generalizations) to fulfill this function. However, these reviews often suffered from methodological flaws: Narrative reviews of the same body of research sometimes led to different conclusions because of subjective judgments, preferences, and reviewer bias.

Meta-analysis is an alternative to the narrative literature review and avoids many of its flaws. Meta-analysis makes explicit use of rigorous research techniques (including quantitative methods) to sum up a body of separate but similar studies for the purpose of integrating the findings. Researchers have successfully applied meta-analysis within the social, behavioral, and biomedical sciences.

Meta-analysis is particularly useful in validity generalization studies. Researchers examine, when possible, an entire population of studies that present evidence on the validity of a particular test instrument. The empirical findings from these validity studies (e.g., validity coefficients and scores showing between-group differences) are converted to a common metric and then evaluated for consistency (i.e., generalizability or robustness) across different populations, test conditions, criterion measures, and the like. Findings from meta-analyses highlight trends evident in the data and allow researchers and practitioners to obtain valuable information about the validity of the test under study.

Although meta-analysis has many potential benefits and is widely used to synthesize research findings, its conclusions may be compromised by shortcomings of the studies reviewed and of the meta-analytic methods. Matt and Cook (1994) provide a careful examination of factors that may decrease the validity of meta-analysis and offer methods for handling these difficulties. For further information about meta-analysis, see Cooper (1989), Hunter and Schmidt (1990), Light and Pillemer (1984), Rosenthal (1984), and Wolf (1986).

FACTOR ANALYSIS

Factor analysis is a mathematical procedure used to analyze the intercorrelations of a group of tests (or other variables) that have been administered to many individuals. Factor analysis is based on the assumption that we can account for the intercorrelations with some underlying set of (unobservable) factors that are fewer than the tests (or variables) themselves. In the field of intelligence, we might use factor analysis, for example, to determine the number of different mental abilities that account for the pattern of intercorrelations among subtests in an intelligence test.

The findings from factor analysis tell us the extent to which varying numbers of factors account for the correlations among tests. We define a factor as that which a cluster of interrelated tests have in common. We can think of factors as reflecting the underlying processes that have created the correlations among variables. Factors, like the test scores from which they are derived, only describe the relationships observed in the data. There is no implication that the observed scores are somehow caused by the factors or vice versa. As Anastasi (1992) observed, "[Factors] do not represent underlying causal entities" (p. 614).

Factor analysis also tells us the extent to which each test loads on, or is correlated with, the factors. *Factor loadings* are simply correlations between factors and tests. The loadings indicate the weight of each factor in determining performance on each test. (Notice that the word *test* also can refer to a subtest or other parts of a test that have separate scores.) An *exploratory factor analysis* is used to determine the number and kinds of factors contained in a set of variables. It is designed to maximize the variance accounted for in the data set. A *confirmatory factor analysis* can be used to test a theory about the nature of the processes underlying the tests—that is, how well a hypothesized set of factors fits the data.

Procedures Used in Factor Analysis

Most factor analysis programs work by extracting first the factor that accounts for the largest proportion of variance, then the factor that accounts for the next largest proportion, and so on. Usually, the first unrotated factor is a *general factor* on which most variables have high loadings. We find a general factor when all subtests have a considerable amount of overlap, such as in an intelligence test. In an intelligence test, the first general factor is considered to reflect general intelligence, called *g*. In other cases, such as in a multidimensional test of personality, there may be two or three important factors but no single factor on which all variables load.

Rather than attempting to interpret the original factors, however, researchers usually rotate the matrix of factor loadings to make the factor structure clearer. The rotation rearranges the factors so that, ideally, for every factor there are some tests with high loadings on the factor and other tests with low loadings on the factor. The order in which the factors were originally extracted is not always preserved in the rotation; in particular, researchers usually cannot discern the first unrotated factor. We call the factors resulting from the rotation *group factors*. It is up to the researcher or test developer to name or interpret each factor by looking at the content of the tests that have high loadings on the factor.

After all of the common factor variance is extracted and the rotation completed, there still may be a significant amount of variance that has not been analyzed. We call this variance that is present in one test but not in the other tests under study *specific factor variance, specific variance,* or *specificity.*

Components of Variance

In a factor analysis, we can divide the variance associated with a test or subtest into three categories: communality, specificity, and error variance. Let's now look at these three categories.

1. *Communality.* Communality refers to that part of the total variance that we can attribute to common factors (those that appear in more than one test). The formula for obtaining communality is as follows:

$$h_t^2 = a_{t1}^2 + a_{t2}^2 + \cdots + a_{tm}^2$$

where h_t^2 = communality of test t
$a_{t1}^2, \ldots, a_{tm}^2$ = loading of test t on factor 1, …, factor m

For the WISC–III data in Table 4-8 in the next part of the chapter, the communality estimate for the Similarities subtest is

$$h_t^2 = .72^2 + .29^2 + .21^2 + .11^2 = .66$$

2. *Specificity.* Specificity refers to that part of the total variance that is due to factors specific to the particular test, not to measurement error or common factors. We obtain the proportion of specific variance in the following way:

$$s_t^2 = r_{tt} - h_t^2$$

where s_t^2 = variance specific to test t
r_{tt} = reliability of test t
h_t^2 = communality of test t

The proportion of specific variance for the WISC–III Similarities subtest (see Table 4-8 in the next part of the chapter) is

$$s_t^2 = .81 - .66 = .15$$

3. *Error variance.* Error variance refers to that part of the total variance that remains when we subtract the reliability of the test from the total variance. We obtain it by using the following formula:

$$e_t^2 = 1 - r_{tt}$$

where e_t^2 = error variance of test t
r_{tt} = reliability of test t

Error variance for the Similarities subtest is

$$e_t^2 = 1 - .81 = .19$$

Table 4-7
Average Intercorrelations for Four WISC–III Subtests

Subtest	S	V	PA	BD
S	—	.69	.39	.49
V	.69	—	.40	.46
PA	.39	.40	—	.37
BD	.49	.46	.37	—

Note. Abbreviations: S = Similarities, V = Vocabulary, PA = Picture Arrangement, BD = Block Design.
Source: Adapted from Wechsler (1991, p. 281).

When *specific* variance exceeds *error* variance, we can conclude that the subtest has some specificity. In the example above, this was not the case; therefore, we conclude that Similarities does not have adequate specificity.

Illustration of Factor Analysis

Let's examine how we might apply factor analysis to the WISC–III. Table 4-7 shows a partial set of WISC–III subtest intercorrelations (for 4 of the 13 WISC–III subtests). These correlations are based on the entire standardization group (N = 2,200). A factor analysis of the complete WISC–III intercorrelation table would help us determine, for example, whether the WISC–III measures a single general ability or two or more specific abilities.

If the WISC–III measures general intellectual ability, children with an abundance of this ability should perform well on all of the subtests, and those with a small amount of this ability should do poorly. Applied to the intercorrelations in Table 4-7, this means that children who do well on Similarities should also do well on the other three subtests, whereas those who do poorly on Similarities should also do poorly on the other three subtests. If children's scores on the four subtests are highly correlated, we can reasonably conclude that the subtests have something in common.

Subtests correlate with other each other to different degrees. When specific abilities are more salient than general or group abilities, the correlations among subtests should be lower or variable. Since the correlations in Table 4-7 are high, we might conclude that there is a general ability factor in these four subtests of the WISC–III. Something more than a general factor may be present when the correlations are not consistently high—some abilities are important for some subtests but not for others.

The factor analytic findings for the entire WISC–III are shown in Chapter 8. They indicate that both a general factor and group factors are present in the test. Additionally, several subtests have adequate subtest specificity. Table 4-8 shows the median general factor and group factor loadings, reliability, communality, specificity, and error variance for the Similarities, Vocabulary, Block Design, and Picture Arrangement subtests. We consider loadings above .70 on the general factor to be substantial, as are loadings above .30 or .40 on the group factors. The loadings indicate that Similarities, Vocabulary, and Block Design are good measures of the general factor, and that Picture Arrangement is a fair measure of the general factor. Additionally, Similarities and Vocabulary load highly on the Verbal Comprehension group factor, Block Design loads highly on the Perceptual Organization group factor and moderately on the Verbal Comprehension factor, and Picture Arrangement loads moderately on both the Perceptual Organization and Verbal Comprehension factors. None of these four subtests loads highly on either the Freedom from Distractibility group factor or the Processing Speed group factor. Of the four subtests, only the Picture Arrangement and Block Design subtests have adequate specificity, because on these two subtests specific variance (specificity) exceeds error variance.

Other Uses of Factor Analysis

We use factor analysis to determine the homogeneity of a test and to develop better tests. Homogeneity is the extent to which the items of a test measure the same quality or attribute. In investigations of homogeneity, the input data are the scores of each individual on each item of the test. We compute intercorrelations of the items (not people) and then subject them to a factor analytic procedure. We also can apply factor analysis to data other than test scores. For example, we can apply it to ratings of personality traits or behaviors of people, thus grouping the variables measured by the rating scales according to their similarities. In addition, we can study the underlying constructs associated with a test or group of tests, which is a way of summarizing and putting many measures into some ordered perspective. For instance, we can consider the WISC–III verbal group factor as the construct underlying the subtests in that cluster.

Comment on Factor Analysis

Factor analysis is a complex statistical method. The same set of data can yield different results depending on the factor analytic method used, the number of factors retained, and the rotations of the factors. In addition, the naming of factors is rather arbitrary. For example, one test developer may label a factor as "Verbal Comprehension," whereas another may identify it as "Receptive Oral Language." Thus, although factor analysis is a useful procedure, we must carefully interpret the results obtained from it.

OTHER USEFUL PSYCHOMETRIC CONCEPTS

Occasionally, you will find that two or more tests that are believed to measure the same ability give different results. Discrepancies may occur, for example, because of examinee characteristics, testing conditions, examiner characteristics, or psychometric properties of the tests. Chapter 7 discusses the first three areas in more detail. Now we will discuss discrepancies associated with the psychometric properties of tests (L. Atkinson, January 1993, personal communication; Bracken, 1987, 1988):

1. *Floor effects.* The lower limits of scores on tests may differ. The test floor is the lowest possible score obtainable on an assessment instrument. You need to consider the test floor because it indicates how well the instrument can discriminate among examinees in the lower ranges of functioning; it tells you which populations can and cannot validly be tested with the instrument. Floor effects thus refer to the number of easy items available at the lowest level of the test to distinguish among children whose ability is below average.

Let's illustrate how floor effects operate on the WISC–III. The lowest Full Scale IQ obtainable on the WISC–III is 40 (see WISC–III manual, Table A.4, p. 253). This indicates

Table 4-8
General Factor Loadings, Group Factor Loadings, Reliability, Communality, Specific Variance, and Error Variance for Four WISC–III Subtests

WISC–III subtests	General factor	Group factors				Reliability (r_{tt})	Communality (h_t^2)	Specificity (s_t^2)	Error (e_t^2)
		Factor A, Verbal Comprehension	Factor B, Perceptual Organization	Factor C, Freedom From Distractability	Factor D, Processing Speed				
S	.78	.72	.29	.21	.11	.81	.66	.15	.19
V	.79	.79	.23	.16	.17	.87	.73	.12	.13
PA	.60	.34	.38	.02	.28	.76	.24	.45	.24
BD	.74	.30	.67	.26	.19	.87	.64	.19	.13

Note. Abbreviations: S = Similarities, V = Vocabulary, PA = Picture Arrangement, BD = Block Design.

that the WISC–III does not offer valid IQs for children functioning more than four standard deviations below the mean of the test (which is 100). A special case of the test floor is the subtest floor, which reflects the lowest obtainable score on a subtest. Knowledge of subtest floors is important for profile analysis (i.e., when you compare scores among subtests). For example, subtest floors for the 13 WISC–III subtests for the age group 6 years, 0 months to 6 years, 3 months vary between standard scores of 1 and 4 (see WISC–III manual Table A.1, p. 217). Therefore, when you examine a WISC–III profile of a child who is functioning at the lower levels of the test, her or his performance may simply reflect the scores available on the subtests and not the child's true abilities. If you are concerned when you are assessing a child that the WISC–III subtest floors may not be adequate, consider using an alternative instrument.

2. *Ceiling effects.* The upper limits of scores on tests may differ. Analogous to the test floor, the test ceiling is the highest score obtainable on an instrument. You need to consider the test ceiling because it indicates how well the instrument will discriminate among examinees in the upper ranges of functioning and which populations can and cannot validly be tested with the instrument. Ceiling effects thus refer to the number of difficult items available at the highest level of the test to distinguish among children whose ability is above average.

Let's now look at ceiling effects on the WISC–III. The test ceiling of the WISC–III Full Scale IQ is 160 (see WISC–III manual, Table A.4, p. 254). This indicates that the WISC–III does not offer valid IQs for individuals functioning more than four standard deviations above the mean. As with subtest floors, knowledge of subtest ceilings is important for profile analysis. Subtest ceilings on the WISC–III vary from 17 to 19. Therefore, when you examine a WISC–III profile of a child who is functioning at the upper limits of the test, his or her performance may simply reflect the scores available on the subtests and not the child's true abilities. Again, if you are concerned about the WISC–III subtest ceilings in a particular assessment, consider using an alternative instrument.

3. *Item gradients.* Item gradients may differ on various tests. Item gradients refer to the ratio of item raw scores to standard scores, or the number of raw score points required to earn 1 standard score point. In other words, item gradients help us see "how rapidly standard scores increase as a function of a child's success or failure on a single test item" (Bracken, 1987, p. 322). Item gradients tell us how steeply items are arranged within a test. Tests that have steep gradients (the difficulty level of items changes rapidly, which means that a change of a single raw score point produces a large change in the standard score) are less sensitive to small or moderate differences in ability or skill development than are tests with gradual gradients. This means that tests with steep gradients are less effective in assessing a child's abilities or skills than tests with more gradual gradients (Bracken, 1987).

Now let's look at both the WISC–III and the WPPSI–R to see how item gradients operate. We will use the Information

subtest to illustrate how item gradients operate on these two Wechsler tests. Table 4-9 shows the scaled score equivalents of raw scores for the WPPSI–R and WISC–III Information subtest for standard scores of 1 to 6 (obtained from the WPPSI–R manual, Table 25, p. 182 and the WISC–III manual, Table A.1, p. 217). For the WISC–III, an examinee between the ages of 6 years 0 months (6-0) and 6 years 3 months (6-3) with one correct answer obtains a scaled score of 4, and an examinee with three correct answers obtains a scaled score of 6. Three correct answers (i.e., 3 raw score points), therefore, place the examinee's performance at two standard deviations above the bottom on this section of the WISC–III Information subtest (the *SD* for the Wechsler subtests is 3 scaled scores). This means that the Information subtest has a steep gradient and will not discriminate well among children who are functioning at the low end of the subtest.

By comparison, on the WPPSI–R Information subtest, an examinee between 6–0 and 6–3 years must earn 14 raw score points to obtain a scaled score of 4 and 17 raw score points to earn a scaled score of 6. The ratio of raw scores to scaled scores is greater for the WPPSI–R (17:6) than for the WISC–III (3:6) for this age group and at this level of functioning (i.e., at the lowest 2 *SD*s of the subtest). Therefore, other factors being equal (e.g., subtest reliability, subtest floor), the WPPSI–R Information subtest would be more useful in discriminating among 6-year-old children whose general fund of information is poor. This is because at this age range and ability level, the WPPSI–R Information subtest has a relatively gradual gradient; that is, it samples the information domain more broadly than does the WISC–III Information subtest. The general rule is that the greater the ratio of raw scores to standard scores, the more discriminating the test or subtest.

4. *Norm table layout differences.* Norm tables may have different age-span layouts. For example, age-span layouts may be in 1-month, 3-month, or 4-month intervals; these differences may lead to divergent scores for the same ages.

5. *Age-equivalent or grade-equivalent differences.* Age-equivalent or grade-equivalent scores on the tests may not

Table 4-9
Scaled Score Equivalents of Raw Scores on the WISC–III and WPPSI–R Information Subtest

WPPSI–R raw score	WISC–III raw score	Scaled score
0–9	—	1
10–11	0	2
12–13	—	3
14–15	1	4
16	2	5
17	3	6

Source: Courtesy L. Atkinson, personal communication, January 1993.

coincide, even though the standard scores are similar on the two tests.

6. *Reliability differences.* Tests with low reliability will produce less stable scores than tests with high reliability.

7. *Different procedures used to assess skill areas.* Even though both tests have the same label for a skill area (e.g., "reading"), they may be measuring different skills: One test may be measuring word recognition, whereas the other test may be measuring comprehension.

8. *Different test content.* Both tests may be measuring the same skill area but contain different content. For example, although both tests may be measuring arithmetic, they may sample different arithmetical principles or concepts.

9. *Differences in publication dates.* Tests published in different years may yield scores that differ because of changes in the norm groups.

10. *Sampling differences.* Tests normed on different samples may yield scores that differ because the samples are not comparable. For example, one sample might contain more educated people than another, which would tend to make the average score higher.

You must, therefore, study the psychometric properties of each test instrument you consider using. You also must pay attention to psychometric properties when you compare the results from two or more tests.

COMMENT ON USEFUL STATISTICAL AND MEASUREMENT CONCEPTS

Despite all attempts to develop reliable and valid tests, you must recognize the following:

- No test is completely reliable (i.e., without some error).
- Validity does not exist in the abstract but must be anchored to specific purposes for which the test is given.
- Every examinee's behavior fluctuates from time to time and from situation to situation.
- Any test contains only a sample of all possible questions related to the domain of interest.
- Tests purporting to measure the same construct may give different results for a particular examinee.
- A test measures a sample of behavior or a construct at one point in time.
- A one-day difference in the day in which a test is administered may yield dramatic differences in scores if the norms change radically with slight changes in age.
- The examinee might have performed differently with a different examiner.
- Test scores will likely change to some degree during an examinee's development.

The above propositions are only a sample of the many critical issues essential for an understanding of statistical and measurement concepts. The concepts in this chapter should help you in your study of psychological and psychoeduca-

tional tests. You are encouraged to read additional test and measurement texts.

Exercise 4-1. Reviewing a Test

Select a test that is covered in this text. Read the test manual carefully. Before you read any reviews of the test, evaluate the test using the following 23 points. Then compare your review with one in this text, the *Mental Measurements Yearbook,* or another source.

1. Title
2. Author(s)
3. Publisher
4. Purpose of test
5. Ages (or grade levels)
6. Date of publication and dates of norming
7. Cost, including replacement costs for protocols and other consumables
8. Equipment needed for administration and scoring
9. Time required for administration and scoring
10. Number of forms
11. Basis for item selection
12. Types of items
13. Type of scoring
14. Evidence of validity
15. Evidence of reliability
16. Norms
17. Interpretation guidelines
18. Desirable features
19. Undesirable features
20. Quality of manual
21. Availability of computer scoring
22. General evaluation
23. References

THINKING THROUGH THE ISSUES

1. Even though you will seldom compute standard deviations and carry out significance tests when you administer and score tests, you will often use standard scores and other statistical concepts to interpret test results. In what ways will a knowledge of statistics and psychometric concepts be useful to you as a clinician?

2. Before you use a test, how important is it that you become familiar with its reliability, validity, and standardization?

3. Under what circumstances would you use tests that do not have adequate reliability or validity?

4. How can you evaluate the reliability and validity of informal test procedures, such as interviews or tests that do not have norms?

SUMMARY

1. A knowledge of statistical and measurement concepts will enhance your understanding of tests, test manuals, and research articles and will enable you to evaluate the psychometric properties

of intelligence tests, special ability tests, and interview and observational data more effectively.

2. *Psychometrics* refers to the quantitative assessment of an individual's psychological traits or attributes.

The Why of Psychological Measurement and Statistics

3. Psychological measurement is designed to measure attributes of the person, such as intelligence, motor skills, reading ability, adaptive behavior, and extroversion-introversion.

4. Psychological measurement produces a test score, or rating, that is said to reflect the attribute.

5. Statistics help us to communicate information about test scores, and they assist us in drawing conclusions about those scores.

6. Without statistics it would be impossible to evaluate chance variations in the scores we obtain.

7. Test scores are imperfect measures; statistics can help us determine the amount of error present in test scores.

8. Measurement is a process of assigning numerals to objects or events according to certain rules.

9. The measurement process, whether physical or psychological, consists of (a) defining a dimension or behavior to be measured, (b) determining the measurement operations, (c) specifying the rules of measurement, and (d) using a scale of units to express the measurement.

Descriptive Statistics

10. Descriptive statistics summarize data obtained from one or more individuals.

11. Descriptive statistics include measurements on a scale, measures of central tendency, measures of dispersion, properties of the normal curve, and correlations.

12. Data can be ordered by various methods. In most cases, we use one of four types of scales: nominal, ordinal, interval, or ratio.

13. A nominal scale consists of a set of nonordered categories, with one name for each item being scaled.

14. Like a nominal scale, an ordinal measurement scale classifies items, but it has the property of order as well. The variable being measured is ranked, or ordered, according to the amount of some characteristic or dimension, without regard for differences in the distance between scores.

15. An interval measurement scale classifies like a nominal scale and orders like an ordinal scale, but it adds an arbitrary zero point and equal units.

16. A ratio scale has a true zero point, equal intervals between adjacent units, and equality of ratios, in addition to order and classification.

17. The three most commonly used measures of central tendency are the mean, the median, and the mode.

18. The mean is the arithmetic average of all the scores in a set of scores.

19. The median is the middle point in a set of scores arranged in order of magnitude.

20. The mode is the score in a set of scores that occurs more frequently than any other.

21. Dispersion refers to the variability of scores in a set of scores.

22. The range represents the distance between the highest and lowest scores in a set.

23. Variance (S^2) is a statistical measure of the amount of spread in a set of scores: the greater the spread, the greater the variance.

24. The standard deviation (*SD*) is the square root of the variance, representing the average of the squared deviations from the mean.

25. The normal (or bell-shaped) curve is a common type of distribution. The distributions of many psychological traits are roughly normal.

26. Correlations tell us about the degree of association or co-relationship between two variables, including the strength and direction of their relationship.

27. We determine the strength of the relationship by the absolute magnitude of the correlation coefficient; the maximum value is +1.00 or −1.00.

28. If a curvilinear relationship exists between two variables, the correlation coefficient will underestimate the true degree of association.

29. The most common correlation coefficient is the Pearson correlation coefficient, symbolized by *r*.

30. When the assumptions of Pearson's *r* cannot be met, the Spearman r_s (rank-difference) method can be used.

31. Correlations should not be used to infer cause and effect.

32. The square of the correlation coefficient represents the proportion of variance in one variable that is accounted for by the other variable.

33. You can use the correlation coefficient, together with other information, to construct a linear equation for predicting the score on one variable when you know the score on another variable. This equation is called the regression equation.

34. A measure of the accuracy of the predicted *Y* scores in a regression equation is the standard error of estimate.

Multiple Correlation

35. Multiple correlation is a statistical technique for determining the relationship between one variable and several other variables.

36. The coefficient of multiple correlation is represented as *R*.

Norm-Referenced Measurement

37. In norm-referenced measurement, we compare an examinee's performance with the performance of a specific group of subjects.

38. A norm provides an indication of the average, or typical, performance of a specified group and the spread of scores above and below the average.

39. The representativeness of the norm group refers to how characteristic the group is of a particular population.

40. The number of subjects in the norm group should be large enough to assure that the test scores are stable and that the subgroups in the population are adequately represented.

41. To interpret an examinee's score properly, we need a representative norm group against which to evaluate his or her scores.

Types of Derived Scores

42. Standard scores are raw scores that have been transformed to have a designated mean and standard deviation.

43. Percentile ranks are derived scores that permit us to determine an individual's position relative to the standardization sample (or any other specified sample).

44. Normal-curve equivalents (NCEs) are standard scores with a mean of 100 and a standard deviation of 21.06.

45. Stanines (a contraction of "standard nine") provide a single-digit scoring system with a mean of 5 and a standard deviation of 2.
46. Age-equivalent scores and grade-equivalent scores are obtained by determining the average score obtained on a test by different groups of children who vary in age or grade placement.
47. Other terms for age-equivalent scores are mental age (MA) and test age.
48. Although age-equivalent and grade-equivalent scores can be misleading and are psychometrically impure, they still may be useful on some occasions.
49. When IQs were first introduced, they were defined as ratios of mental age to chronological age, multiplied by 100 to eliminate the decimal: $IQ = MA/CA \times 100$.
50. The different derived scores are merely different expressions of an examinee's performance.

Statistical Significance

51. When we want to know whether the difference between two or more scores can be attributed to chance or to some systematic (and perhaps hypothesized) cause, we need to run a test of statistical significance.
52. "Significance" in statistics refers to whether the results differ from what would be expected on the basis of chance alone.
53. Statisticians have agreed that a reasonable level of statistical significance is one in which the observed results (or more extreme results) would happen 5% of the time or less by chance alone.

Reliability

54. Reliability refers to the consistency of measurements. Test results need to be reliable—that is, dependable, reproducible, and stable.
55. Reliability is expressed with a reliability coefficient or with the standard error of measurement, which is derived from the reliability coefficient.
56. Reliability of measurement refers to the extent to which random or unsystematic variation affects the measurement of a trait, characteristic, or quality.
57. The reliability coefficient represents a ratio of the true score variance to the observed score variance.
58. The reliability coefficient expresses the degree of consistency in the measurement of test scores.
59. The symbol used to denote a reliability coefficient is the letter r with two identical subscripts.
60. Test-retest reliability is an index of stability, a measure of how consistent scores are over time.
61. The test-retest correlation is affected by factors associated with the specific administrations of the test and with what the examinees have remembered or learned in the interim.
62. The test-retest reliability coefficient may not be an appropriate measure to use for behavioral checklists and scales, observational procedures, and related forms of measurement.
63. We measure alternate form reliability, also called equivalent or parallel form reliability, by administering two equivalent tests to the same group of examinees.
64. We base internal consistency reliability on the scores individuals obtain during one test administration.
65. Internal consistency reliability estimates are not appropriate for timed tests, and they do not take into account changes over time.

66. Interrater reliability refers to the degree to which the ratings are free from error variance associated with either the rater or the examiner.
67. Several factors (including test length, homogeneity of items, test-retest interval, variability of scores, guessing, variation within the test situations, and sample size) affect reliability.
68. Strategies for improving the reliability and validity of the assessment include (a) becoming an expert in administering tests, conducting interviews, and performing observations; (b) developing self-awareness; (c) relating to the examinee; and (d) gathering additional information; attending to recordings; and developing hypotheses.
69. The standard error of measurement (SEM), or standard error of a score, is an estimate of the amount of error associated with an examinee's obtained score. It is directly related to the reliability of a test: the lower the reliability, the higher the standard error of measurement, and conversely, the higher the reliability, the lower the standard error of measurement.
70. We usually report a confidence interval for a score—that is, a band or range of scores around the obtained score that likely includes the examinee's true score—to express our degree of certainty in the score.
71. There are two methods for obtaining confidence intervals. One is based on the child's obtained score and the conventional standard error of measurement. The other is based on the estimated true score and the standard error of measurement associated with the estimated true score.
72. We recommend that the obtained score and the conventional standard error of measurement be used to construct confidence intervals for scores that measure the examinee's current functioning.
73. It may be difficult to interpret the results of repeated evaluations when the retest interval is short.
74. Practice or retest effects (a) cannot be easily differentiated from changes associated with clinical improvement; (b) may not occur to the same extent in all populations; (c) vary for different types of tasks; (d) may be affected by the length of time that elapsed between administration of the tests; (e) may vary as a function of scores on the first test; (f) may be difficult to interpret when the initial test and the retest are different; and may depend on the item content covered throughout the test.

Item Response Theory

75. Item response theory provides useful information about the relationships between the attribute being measured and the test responses through the use of three parameters: item discrimination, item difficulty, and a "guessing" parameter that corresponds to the probability that a correct response will occur by chance.

Differential Item Functioning

76. Differential item functioning (DIF) is a procedure designed to tell us whether test items function differently in different groups.

Validity

77. The validity of a test refers to the extent to which a test measures what it is supposed to measure, and therefore the appropriateness with which we can make inferences based on the test results.

78. Content validity refers to whether the items on a test represent the domain that the test is supposed to measure.
79. Face validity refers to what the test appears to measure, not what it actually does measure.
80. Criterion-related validity refers to the relationship between test scores and some type of criterion or outcome, such as ratings, classifications, or other test scores.
81. Concurrent validity refers to whether test scores are related to some currently available criterion measure.
82. Predictive validity refers to the correlation between test scores and future performance on a relevant criterion.
83. Construct validity refers to the extent to which a test measures a psychological construct (i.e., an inferred entity) or trait.
84. Convergent validity refers to how well performances on different measures of the same domain in different formats correlate positively.
85. Discriminant validity, sometimes called divergent validity, is the opposite of convergent validity. Different constructs are chosen to measure different characteristics; therefore, tests designed to measure unrelated constructs should not correlate.
86. Predictive utility refers to the extent to which a test agrees with a criterion measure in classifying individuals as to their membership in a category.
87. A test is said to have treatment validity, or clinical utility, if knowledge of the test results leads to constructive changes in the examinee's life.
88. Because validity coefficients are a type of correlation coefficient, they are affected by such factors as the range of attributes being measured and the length of the interval between the administration of the two measures.
89. Reliability is a necessary but not sufficient condition for validity.

Meta-Analysis

90. Meta-analysis makes explicit use of rigorous research techniques (including quantitative methods) to sum up a body of separate but similar studies for the purpose of integrating the findings.

Factor Analysis

91. Factor analysis is a mathematical procedure used to analyze the intercorrelations of a group of tests (or other variables) that have been administered to many individuals.
92. The findings from factor analysis tell us the extent to which varying numbers of factors account for the correlations among tests.
93. An exploratory factor analysis is used to determine the number and kinds of factors contained in a set of variables. It is designed to maximize the variance accounted for in the data set.
94. A confirmatory factor analysis can be used to test a theory about the nature of the processes underlying the tests—that is, how well a hypothesized set of factors fits the data.
95. In a factor analysis, we can divide the variance associated with a test or subtest into three categories: communality, specificity, and error variance.

Other Useful Psychometric Concepts

96. Results from two or more similar tests may differ for a variety of reasons, including the following: floor effects, ceiling effects, item gradients, norm table layout differences, age- or grade-equivalent differences, reliability differences, different procedures used to assess skill areas, different test content, differences in publications dates, and sampling differences.

KEY TERMS, CONCEPTS, AND NAMES

Psychometrics (p. 87)
Descriptive statistics (p. 87)
Nominal measurement scale (p. 88)
Ordinal measurement scale (p. 89)
Interval measurement scale (p. 89)
Ratio measurement scale (p. 89)
Measures of central tendency (p. 89)
Mean (p. 89)
Median (p. 89)
Mode (p. 90)
Measures of dispersion (p. 90)
Range (p. 90)
Variance (p. 90)
Standard deviation (p. 91)
Normal curve (p. 91)
Correlations (p. 91)
Correlation coefficient (p. 91)
Pearson correlation coefficient (r) (p. 93)
Coefficient of determination (p. 93)
Regression equation (p. 94)
Standard error of estimate (p. 95)
Multiple correlation (R) (p. 95)
Norm-referenced measurement (p. 96)
Derived scores (p. 96)
Standard scores (p. 97)
z score (p. 97)
T score (p. 97)
Deviation IQ (p. 97)
Percentile ranks (p. 98)
Quartiles (p. 98)
Normal-curve equivalents (p. 98)
Stanines (p. 98)
Age-equivalent scores (p. 98)
Grade-equivalent scores (p. 98)
Mental age (p. 100)
Test age (p. 100)
Ratio intelligence quotient (p. 100)
Statistical significance (p. 101)
Reliability (p. 102)
True score (p. 102)
Error score (p. 102)
Reliability coefficient (p. 102)
Test-retest reliability (p. 102)
Coefficient of stability (p. 102)
Alternate form reliability (p. 103)
Equivalent form reliability (p. 103)
Parallel form reliability (p. 103)
Coefficient of equivalence (p. 103)
Internal consistency reliability (p. 104)
Split-half reliability (p. 104)
Cronbach's coefficient alpha (p. 104)
Kuder-Richardson formula 20 coefficient (p. 104)

STUDY QUESTIONS

1. Discuss why psychological measurement and statistics are useful.
2. Compare and contrast nominal, ordinal, interval, and ratio scales.
3. Discuss the three measures of central tendency.
4. Discuss measures of dispersion.
5. Discuss the normal curve.
6. Discuss correlations.
7. Discuss the regression equation.
8. What is the standard error of estimate?
9. Briefly discuss multiple correlation.
10. What are some important features of norm-referenced testing?
11. Describe and evaluate the following derived scores: standard scores, percentile ranks, normal-curve equivalents, stanines, age- and grade-equivalent scores, and ratio intelligence quotients.
12. Discuss the concept of statistical significance.
13. Discuss the concept of reliability. Include in your discussion (a) the theory of reliability of measurement, (b) reliability coefficients, (c) test-retest reliability, (d) alternate form reliability, (e) internal consistency reliability, (f) interrater reliability, (g) factors affecting reliability, (h) reliability of an individual examinee's assessment data, and (i) ways to reduce examiner bias and errors in the assessment.
14. What is the standard error of measurement?
15. Discuss confidence intervals. Include in your discussion why confidence intervals are important and the difference between confidence intervals based on the obtained score and intervals based on the estimated true score.
16. Discuss the problems associated with repeated evaluations or practice effects.
17. Discuss item response theory.
18. Discuss differential item functioning.
19. Discuss the concept of validity. Include in your discussion various types of validity, predictive utility, and the factors affecting validity.
20. Discuss meta-analysis.
21. Discuss factor analysis.
22. Discuss why two or more similar tests may differ in the scores they provide.

5

HISTORICAL SURVEY
AND THEORIES OF INTELLIGENCE

Philosophy of science without history is empty; history of science without philosophy is blind.

—Immanuel Kant

Goals and Objectives

This chapter is designed to enable you to do the following:

- Identify the 19th- and 20th-century investigators who shaped our theories of intelligence

- Provide and discuss definitions of intelligence

- Describe factor analytic approaches to the study of intelligence

- Discuss information-processing approaches to intelligence

- Examine other approaches to the study of intelligence

- Discuss the form intelligence tests may take in the future

This chapter provides a brief history of developments in the field of intelligence testing. It describes the contributions of pioneer and contemporary theorists and test developers, and it summarizes several major definitions of intelligence. Let's begin our historical survey with 19th-century developments.

NINETEENTH-CENTURY AND EARLY TWENTIETH-CENTURY DEVELOPMENTS

In 1838, Jean Esquirol (1772–1840) was one of the first scientists to make a clear distinction between mental incapacity and mental illness. He made a distinction between "idiots," who never developed their intellectual capacities, and "mentally-deranged persons," who lost abilities they once possessed. Esquirol tried to develop methods for differentiating between the two groups, focusing first on physical measurements and then on speech patterns. His descriptions of the verbal characteristics associated with various levels of "idiocy" can be regarded as the first crude mental test.

In the latter part of the 19th century, psychology emerged as a separate discipline. The psychophysical methods developed by Ernst H. Weber (1795–1878) and Gustav T. Fechner (1801–1887) and the statistical studies of mental processes initiated by Sir Francis Galton (see below) formed the background for much of the work that would take place in the 20th century. (See the inside front cover of this textbook for a listing of historical landmarks in cognitive and educational assessment.)

Developments in England

Galton's contribution. Sir Francis Galton (1822–1911) is regarded as the father of the testing movement. He developed the statistical concepts of regression to the mean and correlation, a contribution that permitted the psychometric field to develop and flourish. These statistical concepts allowed for the study of intelligence over time, as well as for the study of the relationships between the intelligence test scores of parents and their children.

In 1869, Galton published *Hereditary Genius,* in which he offered a statistical explanation for inherited mental characteristics and estimated the number of "geniuses" that could be expected in a particular sample of people. In his 1883 publication *Inquiries into Human Faculty,* which was a collection of 40 articles written between 1869 and 1883, Galton presented his views on human faculties and considered the problems involved in measuring mental characteristics. In 1884, he set up a psychometric laboratory at the International Health Exhibition, which he later reestablished at University College, London. The laboratory was open to the public (see Figure 5-1), and for a small fee measures of physical and mental capacities were provided. Galton assumed that, because our knowledge of the environment reaches us through the senses, people with the highest intelligence also should have the best sensory discrimination abilities. The sensory discrimination assumption led him to develop tests of sensory discrimination and motor coordination to study mental

ANTHROPOMETRIC
LABORATORY

For the measurement in various ways of Human Form and Faculty.

Entered from the Science Collection of the S. Kensington Museum.

This laboratory is established by Mr. Francis Galton for the following purposes:—

1. For the use of those who desire to be accurately measured in many ways, either to obtain timely warning of remediable faults in development, or to learn their powers.

2. For keeping a methodical register of the principal measurements of each person, of which he may at any future time obtain a copy under reasonable restrictions. His initials and date of birth will be entered in the register, but not his name. The names are indexed in a separate book.

3. For supplying information on the methods, practice, and uses of human measurement.

4. For anthropometric experiment and research, and for obtaining data for statistical discussion.

Charges for making the principal measurements:
THREEPENCE each, to those who are already on the Register. FOURPENCE each, to those who are not:— one page of the Register will thenceforward be assigned to them, and a few extra measurements will be made, chiefly for future identification.

The Superintendent is charged with the control of the laboratory and with determining in each case, which, if any, of the extra measurements may be made, and under what conditions.

Figure 5-1. An announcement for Galton's Laboratory.
Reproduced by permission of the Photo Science Museum, London, England.

functioning. These tests generally proved to be invalid, however, and therefore limited his work on the measurement of intelligence. (See Johnson, McClearn, Yuen, Nagoshi, Ahern, and Cole, 1985, for an analysis of 6,500 individual records obtained from Galton's laboratory.)

Pearson's contribution. Karl Pearson (1857–1936), Galton's close friend and biographer, was a professor of applied mathematics and mechanics at University College, London. Pearson was active in the fields of eugenics, anthropology, and psychology. Furthering Galton's work, Pearson developed the product-moment correlation formula for linear correlation, the multiple correlation coefficient, the partial correlation coefficient, the phi coefficient, and the chi-square test for determining how well a set of empirical observations conforms to an expected distribution (goodness of fit).

Developments in the United States

James McKeen Cattell's contribution. James McKeen Cattell (1860–1944) studied with Wilhelm Wundt at Leipzig, where Wundt founded the first psychological laboratory in

1879. Wundt believed that the aim of psychology was to analyze the content of consciousness: Psychology should focus on the study of immediate experience, principally by self-observation or introspection. Cattell, however, left Wundt to serve as an assistant in Galton's anthropometric laboratory and was influenced by Galton's theories. Instead of following Wundt's introspective approach to psychology, Cattell, like Galton, focused on the study of individual differences in behavior. Upon his return to the United States, Cattell established a psychological laboratory at the University of Pennsylvania. In 1890, he published an article in the journal *Mind* in which he first used the term "mental test." He described 50 different measures that primarily assessed sensory and motor abilities; they differed little from those designed by Galton. In 1891, Cattell moved to Columbia University to continue his work on measurement.

Cattell stressed that psychology must rest on a foundation of measurement and experimentation. Foreseeing the practical application of tests as tools for diagnostic evaluations and for the selection of individuals for training, he compiled a battery of tests for evaluating a variety of skills and capacities. Some tests he included were Dynamometer Pressure, Rate of Movement (speed with which an individual moved a specified distance), Sensation-Areas (two-point discrimination), Least Noticeable Difference in Weight, Reaction-Time for Sound, Time for Naming Colors, Bisection of a 50-cm Line, Judgment of Ten Seconds' Time, and Number of Letters Remembered on Once Hearing. Although the battery was not predictive of cognitive development or educational achievement, Cattell's contributions were valuable to the field of psychology. He moved the assessment of mental ability out of the field of abstract philosophy and demonstrated that mental ability could be studied experimentally and practically.

Other developments in the United States. Psychological tests made a public debut in the United States at the 1893 Chicago World's Fair, where Hugo Munsterberg (1863–1916) and Joseph Jastrow (1863–1944) collaborated on a demonstration testing laboratory. Munsterberg came from Germany to the United States to take over William James's laboratory at Harvard. In Germany, Munsterberg had developed perceptual, memory, reading, and information tests for children. For a small fee, visitors to the exhibit could take tests of "mental anthropometry" and learn how their performance compared to that of others.

In the early 1890s, Franz Boas (1858–1942) at Clark University and J. Gilbert at Yale University studied how children responded to various tests. Boas studied the validity of simple sensorimotor tests by using teachers' estimates of children's "intellectual acuteness" as a criterion. Gilbert, also studying simple sensorimotor tests, found only two tests—rate of tapping and judgment of distances—that could distinguish "bright" from "dull" children.

Clark Wissler (1870–1947; 1901) investigated the validity of several tests that he thought were related to cognitive processes. Most of his tests also measured simple sensory func-

tions. Using the correlational methods of Galton and Pearson, he found low relationships among the test scores of simple sensory functions themselves and between the test scores of simple sensory functions and school grades in a sample of college-age individuals. Stella Sharp (1898) also reported that tests similar to those used by Binet and Henri (see "Developments in France") were providing unreliable results. Sharp, however, studied only seven graduate students; the weak correlations were not surprising for this small, homogeneous sample. Unfortunately, as a result of their serious methodological shortcomings, the studies by Wissler and Sharp led investigators to believe that mental measurement was not a fruitful field to study.

Developments in Germany

In Germany at the turn of the century, four individuals contributed to the field of assessment. Emil Kraepelin (1855–1926), a psychiatrist and one of Wundt's first pupils, introduced complex tests for measuring mental functioning, including tests of perception, memory, motor functions, and attention in adults. Kraepelin worked in the field of psychopathology and based many of his tests on abilities necessary for daily functioning. Kraepelin recognized the importance of repeated examinations in order to reduce chance variation.

Herman Ebbinghaus (1850–1909) worked on tests of memory, computation, and sentence completion. One procedure he developed was a predecessor of the group-administered intelligence test. It was a timed completion task containing passages with missing words. The examinee's task was to fill in as many blanks in the passage as possible within a 5-minute period. Ebbinghaus developed his tests in response to requests from teachers in Breslau, Germany, for help in evaluating the academic aptitude of the city's school children.

Carl Wernicke (1848–1905), well known in Poland and Germany for his investigations of brain localization, developed a set of questions designed to detect mental retardation. The questions—such as "What is the difference between a ladder and a staircase?"—emphasized conceptual thinking. In 1908, Theodor Ziehen (1862–1950) published a test battery that contained questions requiring generalizations, such as "What have an eagle, a duck, a goose, and a stork in common?" In Wernicke's and Ziehen's work we see the beginning of the trend away from sensorimotor functions and toward the kinds of cognitive functions emphasized in modern intelligence tests.

Developments in France

In France at the end of the 19th century, Alfred Binet (1857–1911), Victor Henri (1872–1940), and Theodore Simon (1873–1961) developed methods for the study of mental functions. They believed that the key to measuring intelligence was to focus on higher mental processes instead of simple sensory functions. Their work culminated in the development of the

Exhibit 5-1
Description of the 1905 Binet-Simon Scale

1. Visual coordination. The degree of coordination of movement of the head and eyes is noted as a lighted match is passed slowly before the subject's eyes.
2. Grasping provoked tactually. A small wooden cube is placed in contact with the palm or back of the child's hand. He or she must grasp it and carry it to his or her mouth, and coordinated grasping and other movements are noted.
3. Grasping provoked visually. Same as 2, except that the object is placed within the child's reach, but not in contact with him or her. The examiner, to catch the child's attention, encourages him or her orally and with appropriate gestures to take the object.
4. Awareness of food. A small bit of chocolate and a piece of wood of similar dimensions are successively shown to the child, and signs of recognition of the food and attempts to take it are noted carefully.
5. Seeking food when a slight difficulty is interposed. A small piece of the chocolate used in the previous test is wrapped in a piece of paper and given to the subject. Observations are made of the child's manner of getting the food and separating it from the paper.
6. The execution of simple orders and the imitation of gestures. The orders are mostly such as might be understood from the accompanying gestures alone.
   (This is the limit for idiots as experimentally determined.)
7. Verbal knowledge of objects. The child must touch his or her head, nose, ear, etc., and also hand the examiner on command a particular one of three well-known objects: cup, key, string.
8. Knowledge of objects in a picture as shown by finding them and pointing them out when they are called by name.
9. Naming objects designated in a picture.
   (This is the upper limit for 3-year-old normal children. The three preceding tests are not in order of increasing difficulty, for whoever passes 7 usually passes 8 and 9 also.)
10. Immediate comparison of two lines for discrimination as to length.
11. Reproduction of series of three digits immediately after oral presentation.
12. Discriminating between two weights: (a) 3 and 12 grams, (b) 6 and 15 grams, and (c) 3 and 15 grams.
13. Suggestibility. (a) Modification of 7: an object not among the three present is asked for. (b) Modification of 8: "Where [in the picture] is the patapoum? the nitchevo?" (These words have no meaning.) (c) Modification of 10: the two lines to be compared are of equal length.
    (Test 13 is admitted to be a test not of intelligence but of "force of judgment" and "resistance of character.")
14. Definitions of familiar objects—house, horse, fork, mamma.
    (This is the limit for 5-year-old normal children, except that they fail on Test 13.)
15. Repetition of sentences of 15 words each, immediately after hearing them spoken by the examiner.
    (This is the limit for imbeciles.)
16. Providing differences between various pairs of familiar objects recalled in memory: (a) paper and cardboard, (b) a fly and a butterfly, and (c) wood and glass.
    (Test 16 alone effectively separated normal children of 5 and 7 years.)
17. Immediate memory of pictures of familiar objects. Thirteen pictures pasted on two pieces of cardboard are presented simultaneously. The child looks at them for 30 seconds and then gives the names of those recalled.
18. Drawing from memory two different designs shown simultaneously for 10 seconds.
19. Repetition of series of digits after oral presentation. Three series of three digits each, three of four each, three of five, etc., are presented until not one of the three series in a group is repeated correctly. The number of digits in the longest series that the child repeats is his or her score.
20. Providing from memory the resemblance among familiar objects: (a) a wild poppy (red) and blood, (b) an ant, a fly, a butterfly, and a flea, and (c) a newspaper, a label, and a picture.
21. Rapid discrimination of lines. A line of 30 cm is compared successively with 15 lines varying from 35 to 31 cm. A more difficult set of comparisons is then made of a line of 100 mm with 12 lines varying from 103 to 101 mm.
22. Arranging in order five weights—15, 12, 9, 6, and 3 grams—of equal size.
23. Identification of the missing weight from the series in Test 22 from which one weight has been removed. The remaining weights are not presented in the right order. This test is given only when Test 22 is passed.
    (This is given as the most probable limit for morons.)
24. Finding words to rhyme with a given word after the process has been illustrated.
25. Supplying missing words at the end of simple sentences, one for each sentence. This is the Ebbinghaus completion method simplified.
26. Construction of a sentence to embody three given words: Paris, gutter, fortune.
27. Replying to 25 questions of graded difficulty, such as "What is the thing to do when you are sleepy?" "Why is it better to continue with perseverance what one has started than to abandon it and start something else?"
    (Test 27 alone reveals the moron.)
28. Providing the time that it would be if the large and the small hands of the clock were interchanged at 4 minutes to 3 and at 20 minutes after 6. A much more difficult test is given to those who succeed in the inversion—namely, explaining the impossibility of the precise transposition indicated.
29. Drawing what a quarto-folded paper with a piece cut out of the once-folded edge would look like if unfolded.
30. Explaining distinctions between abstract terms, such as liking and respecting a person, being sad and being bored.

1905 Binet-Simon Scale (see Exhibit 5-1). Part of the impetus for the development of the 1905 scale was the French government's request that Binet and Simon find a way to identify school-aged children who had mental retardation. The scale contained many of the items that the investigators had previously developed and written about. We can consider the 1905 scale as the first practical intelligence test, for the 30 items were ranked by level of difficulty and were accompanied by relatively precise instructions for administration.

Unlike previous attempts at developing intelligence tests, the 1905 scale reflected an acknowledgment of age-based cognitive development. It objectively diagnosed degrees of mental retardation and became the prototype for subsequent scales for the assessment of mental ability. Binet and Simon revised their scale in 1908 and again in 1911. Items were added and the range was extended. The goal was to develop a scale that would precisely determine whether a child was performing at the average level of children of the same age.

Comments on Nineteenth-Century Theorists

Developments in the field of intelligence testing proceeded differently in England, the United States, Germany, and France. The English were concerned with statistical analyses; the Americans focused on the implementation of Binet's ideas for developing a scale and statistical methods for examining test data; the Germans emphasized the study of psychopathology and more complex mental functions; and the French focused on clinical experimentation. The early test constructors also had varied reasons for developing tests. Galton and Pearson devised tests to aid in the study of heredity; James McKeen Cattell was interested in the study of individual differences in behavior; and Binet was interested primarily in determining levels of intellectual functioning. For additional information about the intelligence-testing movement, see Boring (1950), Linden and Linden (1968), Peterson (1925), Sokal (1987), and Tuddenham (1962).

The "laboratory" period in mental measurement was from 1880 to 1905, during which time psychologists formulated general psychological principles and studied individual differences. The search for a means to measure intelligence focused on sensation, attention, perception, association, and memory tasks. The work of Binet, Ebbinghaus, and others had a unifying thread—the application of methods used in experimental psychological laboratories to solve practical problems presented by educators from their communities. The interplay of these forces gave birth to the field of applied psychology and ushered in a new era in psychometrics.

TWENTIETH-CENTURY DEVELOPMENTS

Goddard's Contribution

After the introduction of the Binet-Simon Scales, the testing movement flourished in the United States. Henry H. Goddard (1866–1957; 1908), the director of the Psychological Laboratory at the Vineland Training School, introduced the 1905 scale in the United States in 1908, and two years later, the 1908 scale (Goddard, 1910). He adapted the 1908 scale by making minor revisions and standardizing it on 2,000 American children. For many years, it was the most commonly used version of the Binet-Simon Scale in the United States. Psychologists restricted the early use of the scale almost entirely to the evaluation of individuals with mental retardation.

Goddard's view of intelligence was different from that of Binet, who conceptualized it as a shifting complex of interrelated functions. Instead, Goddard believed that intelligence consisted of a single underlying function. "Further, he believed that this unitary function was largely determined by heredity, a view much at variance with Binet's optimistic proposals for mental [ability]" (Tuddenham, 1962, p. 490).

Terman's Contribution

Lewis M. Terman (1877–1956; 1911), at Stanford University, observed that the 1908 scale had great practical and theoreti-

Figure 5-2. Alfred Binet.

Figure 5-3. Lewis M. Terman. Courtesy of Stanford University.

cal value and suggested several supplemental tests. He became interested in the intellectual assessment of school children and, after studying Goddard's work, collaborated with H. G. Childs in publishing a provisional revision of the Binet-Simon Scale in 1912 (Terman & Childs, 1912). In 1916, he published a modified, extended, and standardized form of this revision called the Stanford Revision and Extension of the Binet-Simon Scale. Although the 1916 Stanford-Binet incorporated the ideas of Binet and Simon, Terman deserves credit for his thorough and accurate implementation of the method suggested by Binet and his colleagues. The standardization of the 1916 scale was a major contribution to the field of mental measurement.

Terman adopted Louis William Stern's (1871–1938) concept of *mental quotient,* which is found by dividing mental age by chronological age, for use in the 1916 Stanford-Binet. Stern originally introduced the concept at the German Congress of Psychology in Berlin in 1912. He also described the concept in his book *The Psychological Methods of Testing Intelligence* (1914). Stern's rationale for the development of the mental quotient was, in part, as follows:

It is perfectly clear how valuable the measurement of mental retardation is, particularly in the investigation of abnormal children. It has, however, been shown recently that the simple computation of the absolute difference between the two ages is not entirely adequate for this purpose, because this difference does not mean the same thing at different ages.... Only when children of approximately equal age-levels are under investigation can this value suffice: for all other cases the introduction of the mental quotient will be recommended.... This value expresses not the difference, but the ratio of mental to chronological age and is thus partially independent of the absolute magnitude of chronological age. The formula is, then: mental quotient = mental age ÷ chronological age. (pp. 41–42)

Terman and his associates renamed this ratio the *intelligence quotient (IQ)* when they produced the 1916 version of the Binet-Simon Scale. It was renamed the Stanford-Binet after Stanford University, where Terman was a professor, and Alfred Binet. Although the IQ has become an extremely useful means for classifying persons, Wolf (1969) noted that it is questionable whether Binet "would have accepted even Terman's elaborate standardization as a valid basis for calculating IQ's" (p. 236).

Yerkes' Contribution

Soon after Goddard introduced the Binet scales in the United States, discontent with the age-scale format of the test began to surface. The leading spokesperson against the age-scale format was Robert M. Yerkes (1876–1956), who, with Bridges and Hardwick, published the Point Scale in 1915. Yerkes (1917) believed that the age-scale format was radically different from the point-scale format, both in how the tests are standardized and scored and how items are selected.

In an *age-scale format,* such as the 1916 Stanford-Binet Scale, items are standardized on a group of children at several age levels. Those items passed by a majority of children at a particular age are assigned to that level. For example, an item passed by the majority of 7-year-olds would be assigned to the 7-year age level. Partial credit in months is given for each item passed beyond the basal level. The child's mental age is the basal age plus the credit in months that he or she earned on the remainder of the items. In a *point-scale format,* points are assigned based on the correctness and quality of the child's responses, as well as (in some cases) the speed of the responses. The raw scores for the items are then converted into standard scores, which in turn are converted into an overall score.

The age-scale and point-scale formats also differ in how items are selected. In age scales, items are selected on the assumption that important forms of behavior appear at various points in development, while in point scales, items are selected to measure specific functions. The Terman Revision of the Stanford-Binet (as well as two later revisions) was an age scale; it contained a heterogenous collection of items, with different items at different age groups. Point scales—particularly the Wechsler series, discussed later in the chapter—theoretically have the same types of items at every age.

Revisions of the Stanford-Binet

Lewis Terman and Maud Merrill (1888–1978) revised the 1916 Stanford-Binet in 1937 and 1960. In 1972, new norms were published using Deviation Quotients for the first time in the scale, instead of the ratio IQ. In 1986, Robert Thorndike, Elizabeth Hagen, and Jerome M. Sattler published a point-scale version of the test—the Stanford-Binet Intelligence Scale: Fourth Edition (see Chapter 14).

Figure 5-4. David Wechsler. Courtesy of The Psychological Corporation.

Wechsler's Search for Subtests

Like Yerkes, David Wechsler (1896–1981) was interested in developing a point scale. After studying the standardized tests available during the 1930s, he selected 11 different subtests to form a scale. He called it the Wechsler-Bellevue Intelligence Scale, Form I. This scale was the forerunner of the Wechsler Intelligence Scale for Children–Third Edition (WISC–III), Wechsler Preschool and Primary Scale of Intelligence–Revised (WPPSI–R), and Wechsler Adult Intelligence Scale–Third Edition (WAIS–III).

Sources of the subtests in the first Wechsler scale included the Army Alpha (for the Information and Comprehension subtests), the 1916 Stanford-Binet (for the Comprehension, Arithmetic, Digit Span, Similarities, and Vocabulary subtests), the Healy Picture Completion Tests and other tests containing picture completion items (for the Picture Completion subtest), the Army Group Examinations (for the Picture Arrangement subtest), the Kohs Block Design Test (for the Block Design subtest), and the Army Beta (for the Digit Symbol and Coding subtests). Wechsler designed original material for all of the subtests, although in some cases items differed only slightly from those appearing in the other intelligence tests.

Wechsler's search for subtests was guided by a focus on the global nature of intelligence—he considered intelligence to be a part of the larger construct of personality. He hoped that his scales would aid in psychiatric diagnosis. The Wechsler scales were designed to consider factors contributing to the effective intelligence of the individual; Wechsler made no attempt to design a series of subtests to measure "primary abilities" (the basic units that make up general ability or intelligence—see Thurstone later in this chapter) or to order the subtests into a hierarchy of relative importance. The overall IQ obtained from the Wechsler scale represented an index of general mental ability.

Comments on Early Twentieth-Century Developments

Introduction of the Binet-Simon Scale stimulated the development of clinical psychology in the United States and elsewhere. Jenkins and Paterson (1961) noted that "probably no psychological innovation has had more impact on the societies of the Western world than the development of the Binet-Simon scales" (p. 81). Tuddenham (1962) expressed a similar opinion:

The success of the Stanford-Binet was a triumph of pragmatism, but its importance must not be underestimated, for it demonstrated the feasibility of mental measurement and led to the development of other tests for many special purposes. Equally important, it led to a public acceptance of testing which had important consequences for education and industry, for the military, and for society generally. (p. 494)

Practical demands and interest in the concept of IQ pushed the development of the testing movement despite a lack of support from any particular school or system. Although there were several researchers and test developers in the field of test construction during the first years of the 20th century, Binet and Simon were the first to have their scale recognized as a practical means of measuring mental ability. Success came to Binet and Simon when they measured intelligence in general terms, abandoning the attempt to analyze intelligence into its component parts. In addition, the scale helped "school systems identify students who were likely to learn less rapidly than most of their peers and who, therefore, were candidates for special education" (Siegler, 1992, p. 185). With the introduction of the Binet-Simon Scale, intelligence testing became a popular assessment technique throughout the United States. The 1986 revision of the Stanford-Binet represents the latest step in the evolution of Binet's original idea.

Psychologists continue to develop tests to measure cognitive ability. Testing has become a common practice in schools, clinics, industry, and the military, influencing public policy, business, and scientific psychology. The testing movement, although subject to criticism, continues to thrive in the United States and in many other parts of the world.

We now examine how several theorists define intelligence and how the method of factor analysis, specifically, contributes to our understanding of intelligence. Factor analysts have played a powerful role in shaping 20th-century developments in the field of assessment.

DEFINITIONS OF INTELLIGENCE

Two symposia addressing definitions of intelligence were conducted in 1921 (*Journal of Educational Psychology, 12,* 1921) and in 1986 (Sternberg & Detterman, 1986). There were 13 psychologists at the first symposium and 24 at the second. Table 5-1 presents the major concepts used by the contributors at both symposia to define intelligence.

Across the two symposia, there were commonalities in the definitions of intelligence provided by the presenters (Sternberg & Berg, 1986). Prominent in the definitions were at-

Table 5-1
Terms Used to Define Intelligence in Two Symposia

Terms	1921 (percent)	1986 (percent)
Higher-level components, which include abstract reasoning, representation, problem solving, and decision making	57	50
Adaptation needed to meet the demands of the environment effectively	29	13
Ability to learn	29	17
Physiological mechanisms	29	8
Elementary processes, such as perception, sensation, and attention	21	21
Overt behavioral manifestations represented by effective or successful responses	21	21
Speed of mental processing	14	13
g	14	17
Restricted to academic/cognitive abilities	14	8
Metacognition (knowledge about cognition)	7	17
Executive processes	7	25
Interaction of processes and knowledge	0	17
Knowledge	7	21
Discrete set of abilities, such as spatial, verbal, and auditory	7	17
That which is valued by culture	0	29

Source: Adapted from Sternberg and Berg (1986).

tributes such as *adaptation to the environment, basic mental processes,* and *higher-order thinking* (e.g., *reasoning, problem solving,* and *decision making*). The major areas of difference were the increased emphasis placed by 1986 symposium participants on (a) metacognition and executive processes (see the discussion of information-processing approaches later in the chapter), (b) knowledge and the interaction between knowledge and mental processes, and (c) context, particularly the value culture places on intelligence.

Terman (1921), one of the psychologists at the 1921 symposium, defined intelligence as the ability to carry on "abstract thinking." He was well aware of the danger of placing too much emphasis on the results of one particular test:

We must guard against defining intelligence solely in terms of ability to pass the tests of a given intelligence scale. It should go without saying that no existing scale is capable of adequately measuring the ability to deal with all possible kinds of material on all intelligence levels. (p. 131)

Terman's comments are still valid and appropriate today. Exhibit 5-2 provides other definitions of intelligence.

Binet (Binet & Simon, 1905) regarded intelligence as a collection of faculties: judgment, practical sense, initiative, and the ability to adapt to circumstances. He based his selection of tests, however, on an empirical criterion—namely, whether the tests differentiated older from younger children. Whether the tests were actually measuring intelligence, however, was based only on Binet's opinion (i.e., "face value").

For Wechsler (1958), intelligence is composed of qualitatively different abilities (see Exhibit 5-2). He argued, however, that intelligence is not the mere sum of abilities, because intelligent behavior is also affected by the way the abilities are combined and by motivation. Wechsler took a pragmatic view of intelligence, stating that intelligence can be recognized by what it enables us to do. From Wechsler's perspective, the measurement of various aspects of intellectual ability is possible; however, intelligence test scores do not fully capture intelligence. Although his theory was partially empirically based, he did not supply empirical referents for terms—such as "aggregate," "global," "purposefully," and "rationally"—that he used in his definition of intelligence.

Clearly, there are many ways to define intelligence. The confusion concerning different definitions and methods of measuring intelligence is linked to the fact that intelligence is an attribute, not an entity, and that it reflects the summation of the learning experiences of the individual (Wesman, 1968). Tests of intelligence, tests of achievement, tests of abilities, and tests of aptitude measure similar abilities that reflect the level of achievement of individuals; their names merely reflect the aspect selected for study or investigation. In summary, *all ability tests measure what the individual has learned.* Definitions of intelligence emphasize the ability to adjust or adapt to the environment, the ability to learn, or the ability to perform abstract thinking (e.g., to use symbols and concepts).

Exhibit 5-2
Some Definitions of Intelligence

Anastasi (1986)	"Intelligence is not an entity within the organism but a quality of behavior. Intelligent behavior is essentially adaptive, insofar as it represents effective ways of meeting the demands of a changing environment. Such behavior varies with the species and with the context in which the individual lives" (pp. 19–20).		*genuine problems or difficulties* that he or she encounters, and, when appropriate, to create an effective product—and must also entail the potential *for finding or creating problems*—thereby laying the groundwork for the acquisition of new knowledge" (pp. 60–61).
Binet (in Terman, 1916)	"The tendency to take and maintain a definite direction; the capacity to make adaptations for the purpose of attaining a desired end; and the power of autocriticism" (p. 45).	Humphreys (1979)	"… the resultant of the processes of acquiring, storing in memory, retrieving, combining, comparing, and using in new contexts information and conceptual skills; it is an abstraction" (p. 115).
Binet & Simon (1916)	"… judgment, otherwise called good sense, practical sense, initiative, the faculty of adapting one's self to circumstances. To judge well, to comprehend well, to reason well, these are the essential activities of intelligence" (pp. 42–43).	Hunt (1985)	Intelligence is a collective term that refers to the possession of useful knowledge and special information-processing capabilities.
Carroll (1997b)	"… IQ represents the degree to which, and the rate at which, people are able to learn, and retain in long-term memory, the knowledge and skills that can be learned from the environment (that is, what is taught in the home and in school, as well as things learned from everyday experience)" (p. 44).	Pellegrino (1986)	"Intelligence is implicitly determined by the interaction of organisms' cognitive machinery and their sociocultural environment. … [There is] the need to consider cultural values and context in any understanding of intelligence" (p. 113).
Das (1973)	"… the ability to plan and structure one's behavior with an end in view" (p. 27).	Sattler (this text)	"Intelligent behavior reflects the survival skills of the species, beyond those associated with basic physiological processes."
Detterman (1986)	"Intelligence can best be defined as a finite set of independent abilities operating as a complex system" (p. 57).	Snow (1986)	Intelligence is part of the internal environment that shows through at the interface between person and external environment as a function of cognitive task demands.
Estes (1986)	"… intelligence … is a multifaceted aspect of the processes that enable animate or inanimate systems to accomplish tasks that involve information processing, problem solving, and creativity" (p. 66).	Spearman (1923)	"… everything intellectual can be reduced to some special case of educing either relations or correlates" (p. 300).
Freeman (1955)	"… *adjustment or adaptation of the individual to his* [or her] *total environment,* or to limited aspects of it. … the capacity to reorganize one's behavior patterns so as to act more effectively and more appropriately in novel situations. … the *ability to learn.* … the extent to which [a person] is educable. … the *ability to carry on abstract thinking.* … the effective use of concepts and symbols in dealing with … a problem to be solved" (pp. 149, 150).	Sternberg (1986)	"… *mental activity involved in purposive adaptation to, shaping of, and selection of real-world environments relevant to one's life*" (p. 33).
		Stoddard (1943)	"… the ability to undertake activities that are characterized by (1) difficulty, (2) complexity, (3) abstractness, (4) economy, (5) adaptiveness to a goal, (6) social value, and (7) the emergence of originals, and to maintain such activities under conditions that demand a concentration of energy and a resistance to emotional forces" (p. 4).
Gardner (1983)	"… a human intellectual competence must entail a set of skills of problem solving—enabling the individual *to resolve*	Wechsler (1958)	"The aggregate or global capacity of the individual to act purposefully, to think rationally and to deal effectively with his [or her] environment" (p. 7).

Common to many definitions of intelligence are the following six major interdependent aspects of intelligence (Snow, 1986):

1. *Knowledge-based thinking* involves "the incorporation of concisely organized prior knowledge into purposive thinking" (p. 133).
2. *Apprehension* includes the idea that persons "not only feel, strive, and know, but also know that they feel, strive, and know, and can anticipate further feeling, striving, and knowing; they monitor and reflect upon their own experiences, knowledge, and mental functioning in past, present, and future tenses" (p. 134).
3. *Adaptive purposeful striving* "includes the notion that one can adopt or shift strategies in performance to use what strengths one has in order to compensate for one's weaknesses" (p. 134).
4. *Fluid-analytic reasoning* refers to "agile, analytic reasoning of the sort that enables significant features and dimensions of problems, circumstances, and goals to be decontextualized, abstracted, and interrelated rationally" (p. 134).
5. *Mental playfulness* involves tolerance for ambiguity and pursuit of novelty (the ability to create interesting problems to solve and interesting goals toward which to strive) and the ability to explore alternative ideas, strategies, and purposes.
6. *Idiosyncratic learning* refers to adaptive learning, reassembly, and strategy shifting within the same test or task.

"After 20 years of schooling, your aptitude test shows that you're skilled at just one thing—taking tests."

Courtesy of H. L. Schwadron.

When 1,020 experts in the fields of psychology, education, sociology, and genetics were asked to rate 13 behavioral descriptions of important elements of intelligence, their ratings showed a high degree of consensus about what constitutes intelligence (Snyderman & Rothman, 1987). Following are the highlights of the results (behavioral descriptive phrase and percentage of respondents who rated it as important):

1. Abstract thinking or reasoning (99.3%)
2. Problem-solving ability (97.7%)
3. Capacity to acquire knowledge (96.0%)
4. Memory (80.5%)
5. Adaptation to one's environment (77.2%)
6. Mental speed (71.7%)
7. Linguistic competence (71.0%)
8. Mathematical competence (67.9%)
9. General knowledge (62.4%)
10. Creativity (59.6%)
11. Sensory acuity (24.4%)
12. Goal-directedness (24.0%)
13. Achievement motivation (18.9%)

The respondents also indicated that they believe intelligence tests adequately measure most of these important elements of intelligence.

INTRODUCTION TO FACTOR ANALYTIC THEORIES OF INTELLIGENCE

The factor analytic theorists fall into two camps: those who espouse a general-factor (*g*) theory of intelligence and those who favor a multiple-factor theory. Galton first proposed that individuals possess both a general intellectual ability, which is present in the whole range of their mental abilities, and some special aptitudes. In contrast, Thorndike, Kelley, and Thurstone asserted that intelligence is composed of many independent faculties, such as mathematical, mechanical, and verbal faculties. Spearman introduced statistical techniques, such as factor analysis, that allowed for the testing of these rival theories.

Although factor analysts disagree about how intelligence is organized—whether intelligence is a general unitary function or a composite of several independent abilities—many accept the theory of general intelligence, while still maintaining that intelligent behavior is multidimensional. Part of the difficulty with factor analytic approaches to the study of intelligence is that the outcomes of factor analysis vary depending on the nature of the data, the type of statistical procedure used, and the proclivities of the investigator who chooses the labels to designate the factors. *We should view factor labels as descriptive categories and not as accurate reflections of underlying entities.* Although factor analysts have made significant contributions to the field of intelligence, there are limitations associated with their statistical methods, just as there are limitations associated with the methods of other theorists.

SPEARMAN'S TWO-FACTOR THEORY OF INTELLIGENCE

Charles E. Spearman (1863–1945) was one of the early proponents of a factor analytic approach to intelligence. Spearman (1927) proposed a two-factor theory of intelligence to account for the patterns of correlations observed among group tests of intelligence. His theory stated that a general factor (g) plus one or more specific factors (s) per test account for performance on intelligence tests (see Figure 5-5). Spearman thought of the g *factor* as general mental energy, with complicated mental activities containing the greatest amount of g. The g factor is involved in deductive operations linked with the skill, speed, intensity, and extent of intellectual output. The cognitive activities associated with g are, in part, the ability to determine the relationship between two or more ideas and the ability to find a second idea associated with a previously stated one.

According to Spearman, the g factor is an index of general mental ability or intelligence, and it represents the "inventive," as contrasted with the "reproductive," aspect of mental ability (Jensen, 1979). Tests with high g loadings require conscious and complex mental effort, such as that needed for reasoning, comprehension, and hypothesis-testing tests (e.g., matrix relations, generalizations, verbal analogies, arithmetic problems, paragraph comprehension, and perceptual analogies). In contrast, tests with low g loadings are less complex, emphasizing recognition, recall, speed, visual-motor abilities, and motor abilities (e.g., maze speed, crossing out numbers, counting groups of dots, simple addition, and tapping speed).

Jensen (1993) also observed that several lines of evidence indicate the following with respect to g:

Individual differences with respect to diverse tests of mental abilities that range in complexity from simple reaction time to abstract reasoning are all positively correlated in the population. The g factor is common to every type of cognitive performance, whatever other ability factors may be involved (e.g., verbal, spatial, numerical, musical, etc.), and is the crucial factor in most tests' practical validity. The correlation of g with many other variables indicates

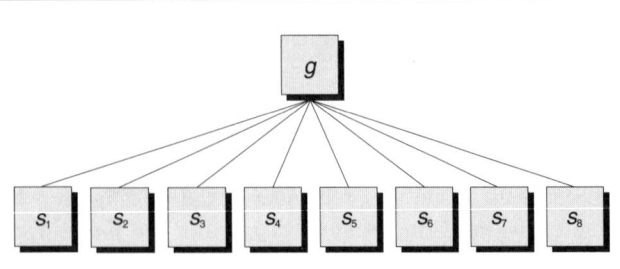

Figure 5-5. Spearman's two-factor theory of intelligence. *g* refers to the general factor, or general ability, and *s* to specific factors.

that, as a product of evolution, g is profoundly enmeshed with many organismic variables. A theory based on empirical evidence links g to neural processes involved in the speed and efficiency of information processing. (p. 127, with changes in notation)

Although evidence strongly supports the idea that g is important in human ability and is an excellent predictor of occupational success in many different fields (Olea & Ree, 1994), this does not mean that g is an entity. We can accept the evidence for Spearman's g without accepting Spearman's explanation of g as "mental energy, or any other explanation that suggests a unitary something underlying the behavioral phenomena" (Humphreys, Parsons, & Park, 1979, p. 75). For more information about g, see Jensen (1998).

THORNDIKE'S MULTIFACTOR THEORY OF INTELLIGENCE

Edward L. Thorndike's (1874–1949) multifactor theory of intelligence postulates that intelligence is the product of many interconnected but distinct intellectual abilities. Certain mental activities have elements in common and combine to form clusters. Three such clusters have been identified: social intelligence (dealing with people), concrete intelligence (dealing with things), and abstract intelligence (dealing with verbal and mathematical symbols) (Thorndike, 1927). Thorndike's conceptions were based on a theoretical perspective, not on statistical methods.

THURSTONE'S MULTIDIMENSIONAL THEORY OF INTELLIGENCE

The view of human intelligence the most divergent from Spearman's is that of Louis L. Thurstone (1887–1955). Thurstone (1938) maintained that we cannot regard intelligence as a unitary trait. According to Thurstone, human intelligence possesses a certain systematic organization, with a structure that we can infer from a statistical analysis of the patterns of intercorrelations found in a group of tests. Using a method of factor analysis suitable for analyzing factors simultaneously (centroid method), he identified the following factors as the primary mental abilities: verbal, perceptual speed, inductive reasoning, number, rote memory, deductive reasoning, word fluency, and space or visualization. Thurstone believed that we can divide intelligence into these multiple factors, each of which has equal weight. He went on to develop the Primary Mental Abilities Tests to measure these factors. Although Thurstone's multidimensional theory at first eliminated g as a significant component of mental functioning, subsequent research showed that the primary factors correlated moderately among themselves, leading Thurstone to postulate the existence of a second-order factor that may be related to g.

GUILFORD'S STRUCTURE OF INTELLECT THEORY

The most prominent multifactor theorist in the United States is J. P. Guilford (1967). He developed the three-dimensional *Structure of Intellect model* as a means for organizing intellectual factors. One dimension represents the operations involved in processing information, a second dimension represents contents, and a third dimension represents products. Thus, we can understand intellectual activities in terms of the mental operation performed, the content on which the mental operation is performed, and the resulting product. The model posits 120 possible factors: five different *operations* (cognition, memory, divergent production, convergent production, and evaluation), four types of *content* (figural, symbolic, semantic, and behavioral), and six *products* (units, classes, relations, systems, transformations, and implications) ($5 \times 4 \times 6 = 120$; see Figure 5-6). A combination of one element from each of the three dimensions yields a factor, such as Cognition of Semantic Units. Cognition refers to the operations dimension, semantic to the content dimension, and units to the product dimension. In this example, the factor refers to knowing what a word means and explaining it.

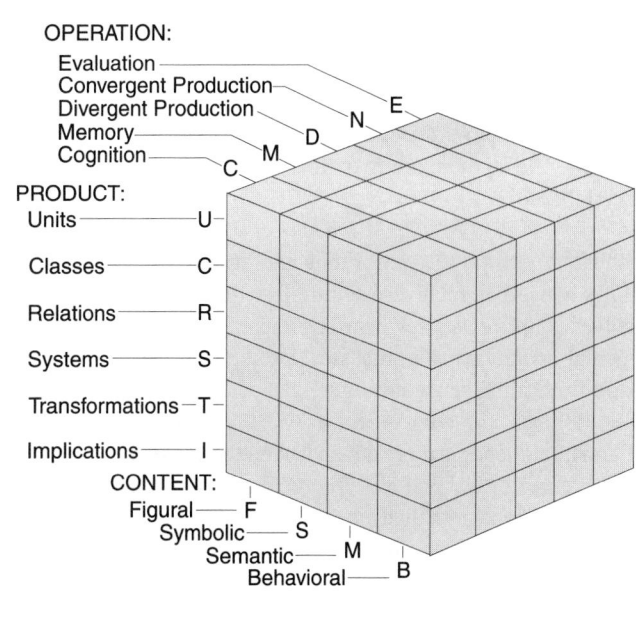

Figure 5-6. Guilford's Structure of Intellect model.

VERNON'S HIERARCHICAL THEORY OF INTELLIGENCE

In Philip E. Vernon's (1950) hierarchical theory of intelligence (see Figure 5-7), *g*, or general ability, is at the highest level. The two major group factors at the next level are verbal-educational and spatial-mechanical. At lower levels are subdivisions of these group factors (or minor group factors). Included in the verbal-educational factor are creative abilities, verbal fluency, and numerical factors. Included in the

spatial-mechanical factor are spatial, psychomotor, and mechanical information factors. Specialized factors unique to certain tests emerge at the next level. Factors low in the hierarchy refer to narrow ranges of behavior, while those high in the hierarchy refer to a wide variety of behaviors. Vernon (1965) believed that we must consider a general group factor (*g*) in any attempt to understand or measure intelligence. This belief has substantial support across numerous studies, as indicated by positive intercorrelations among cognitive tests administered to representative populations.

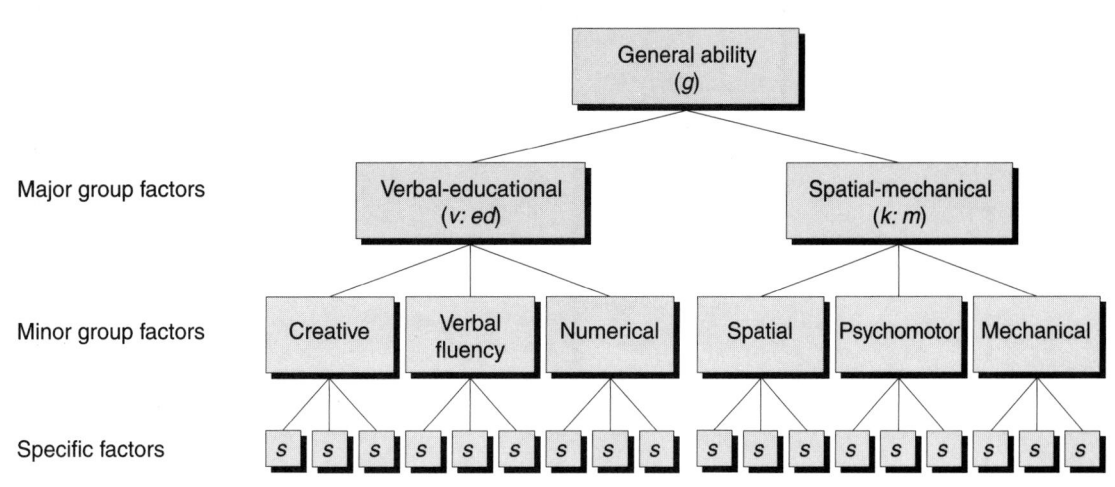

Figure 5-7. Vernon's hierarchical model of intelligence.

CATTELL AND HORN'S FLUID AND CRYSTALLIZED THEORY OF INTELLIGENCE

According to Raymond B. Cattell and John Horn (Cattell, 1963; Horn, 1967, 1968, 1978a, 1978b, 1985, 1998; Horn & Cattell, 1967), there are two types of intelligence—fluid and crystallized.

1. *Fluid intelligence.* Fluid intelligence refers to essentially nonverbal, relatively culture-free mental efficiency. It involves adaptive and new learning capabilities and is related to mental operations and processes. Examples of tasks that measure fluid intelligence are figure classifications, figural analyses, number and letter series, matrices, and paired associates. Fluid intelligence is more dependent on the physiological structures (e.g., cortical and lower cortical regions) that support intellectual behavior than is crystallized intelligence. Fluid intelligence increases until some time during adolescence,

when it plateaus; it then begins to decline because of the gradual degeneration of physiological structures. Fluid intelligence is more sensitive to the effects of brain injury than is crystallized intelligence. Fast processing speed and a large working memory appear to be related to fluid intelligence. As children mature, "age-related changes in processing speed lead to changes in working memory that, in turn, lead to changes in performance on tests of fluid intelligence" (Fry & Hale, 1996, p. 237).

2. *Crystallized intelligence.* Crystallized intelligence refers to acquired skills and knowledge that are developmentally dependent on exposure to culture. It involves overlearned and well-established cognitive functions and is related to mental products and achievements. Examples of tasks that measure crystallized intelligence are vocabulary, general information, abstract word analogies, and mechanics of language. Crystallized intelligence is highly influenced by formal and informal educational factors throughout the life span, and it thus increases at least through middle adulthood. Fluid intelligence is the basis for the development of crystallized intelligence.

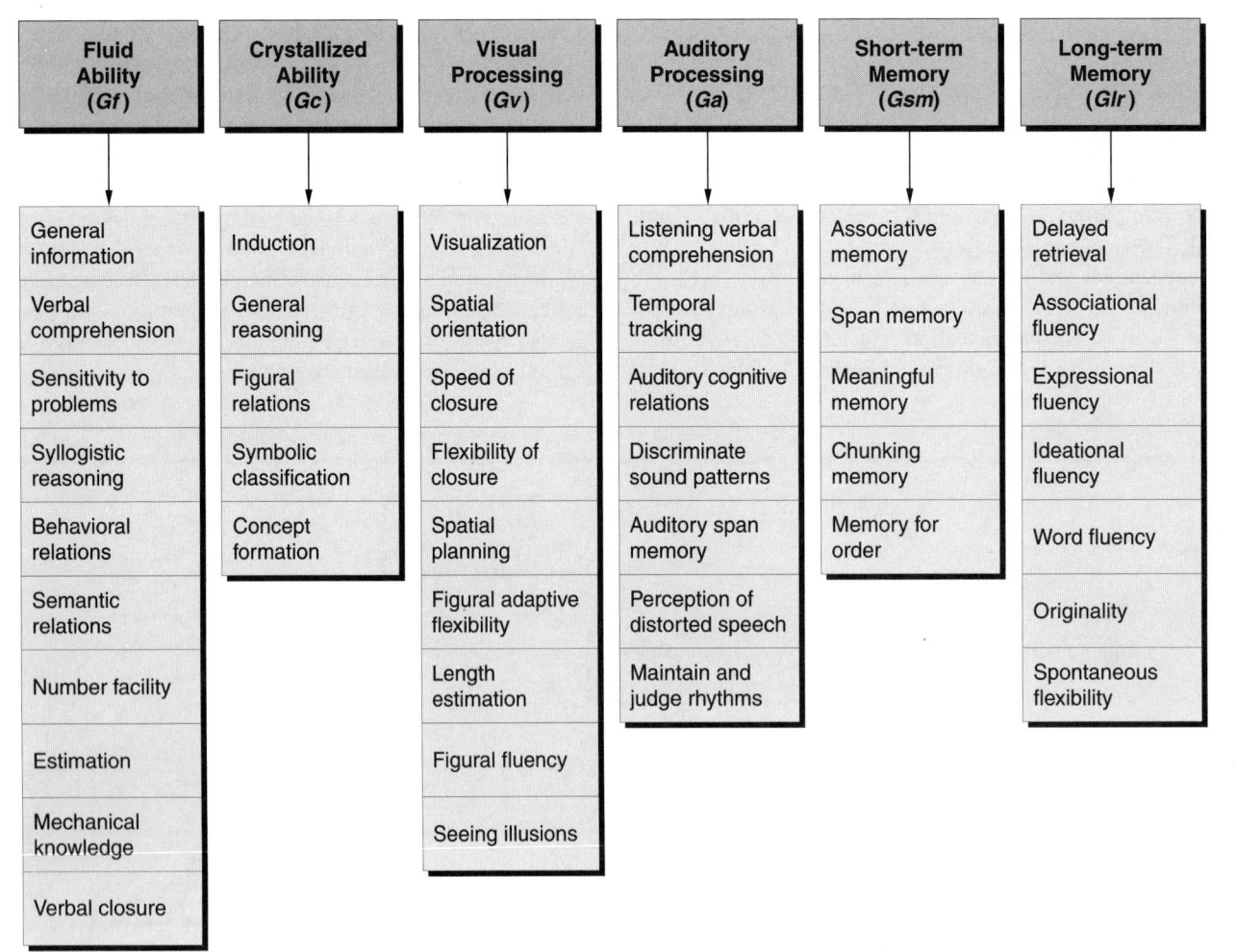

Figure 5-8. Horn's model of intelligence. Adapted from Horn (1998).

Some tasks, such as arithmetic reasoning, inductive verbal reasoning, and syllogistic reasoning, load equally on fluid and crystallized intelligence. The Stanford-Binet: Fourth Edition, WISC–III, WPPSI–R, WAIS–III, Differential Ability Scale, and Cognitive Assessment System contain measures of both fluid and crystallized intelligence. Tasks that measure fluid intelligence (e.g., WAIS–III Matrix Reasoning) may require more concentration and problem solving than do tasks that measure crystallized intelligence (e.g., WISC–III Vocabulary and Information), which tap retrieval and application of general knowledge abilities. The proportion of tasks that measure fluid intelligence (Gf), crystallized intelligence (Gc), and other types of intelligence vary on different intelligence tests (Horn, 1998).

Horn (1985) argued against the concept of general intelligence, maintaining that research does not support a unitary theory. Instead, he asserted that intellectual ability is composed of several distinct functions that probably have genetic underpinnings and that take different courses of development over the life span. For example, fluid ability and visual thinking decline with age, whereas crystallized ability and long-term acquisition and retrieval show no such decline.

Horn (1998) modified the theory by proposing 55 primary abilities replicated in factor analytic studies and 9 second-stratum abilities (see Figure 5-8). Definitions of the second-stratum abilities follow (adapted from Horn, 1987, p. 220; 1998, p. 62):

1. *Fluid ability:* A broad pattern of reasoning, seriation, sorting, and classifying.
2. *Crystallized ability:* A broad pattern of the achievements and knowledge that are emphasized in acculturation.
3. *Visual processing:* A facility for visualizing and mentally manipulating figures and responding appropriately to spatial forms.
4. *Auditory processing:* A pattern of skills involved in listening and responding appropriately to auditory information.
5. *Short-term memory:* A broad pattern of immediate awareness, alertness, and retrieval of material recently acquired.
6. *Long-term memory:* A facility in retrieving information stored in "long-term memory."
7. *Processing speed:* An ability to rapidly scan and react to simple tasks.
8. *Decision speed:* An ability to provide answers quickly to tasks of slight or moderate difficulty.
9. *Quantitative knowledge:* An ability to understand and apply mathematical concepts.

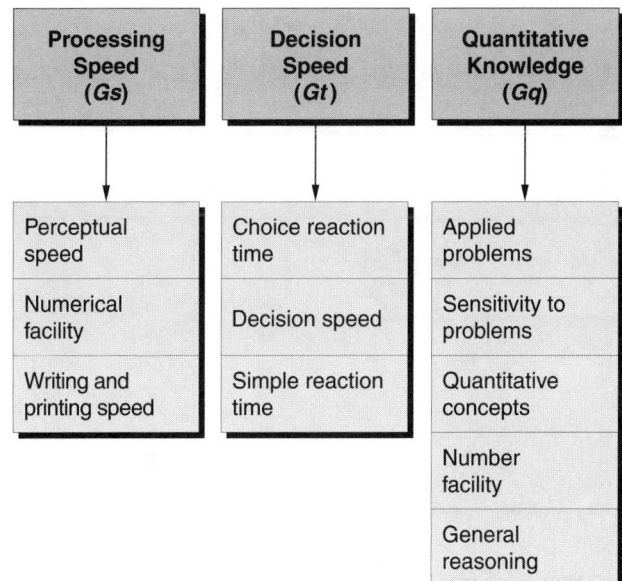

CARROLL'S THREE-STRATUM FACTOR ANALYTIC THEORY OF COGNITIVE ABILITIES

John B. Carroll (1997c) proposed a three-stratum factor analytic theory of cognitive abilities (see Figure 5-9). The theory, which was based on a review of 465 research studies, postulates that there are many distinct individual differences in cognitive ability and that the relationships among these individual differences can be classified into three strata, or levels. "All of the abilities covered by the theory are assumed to be 'cognitive' in the sense that cognitive processes are critical to the successful understanding and performance of tasks requiring these abilities, most particularly in the *processing of mental information.* In many cases, they go far beyond the kinds of intelligences measured in typical batteries of intelligence tests" (Carroll, 1997c, p. 126).

Here is an outline of the three levels of Carroll's theory:

1. *Narrow (Stratum I).* The first level consists of 65 narrow abilities comprising levels of mastery in various cognitive areas (e.g., general sequential reasoning, reading comprehension, memory span, visualization, speech sound discrimination, originality/creativity, numerical facility, and simple reaction time).

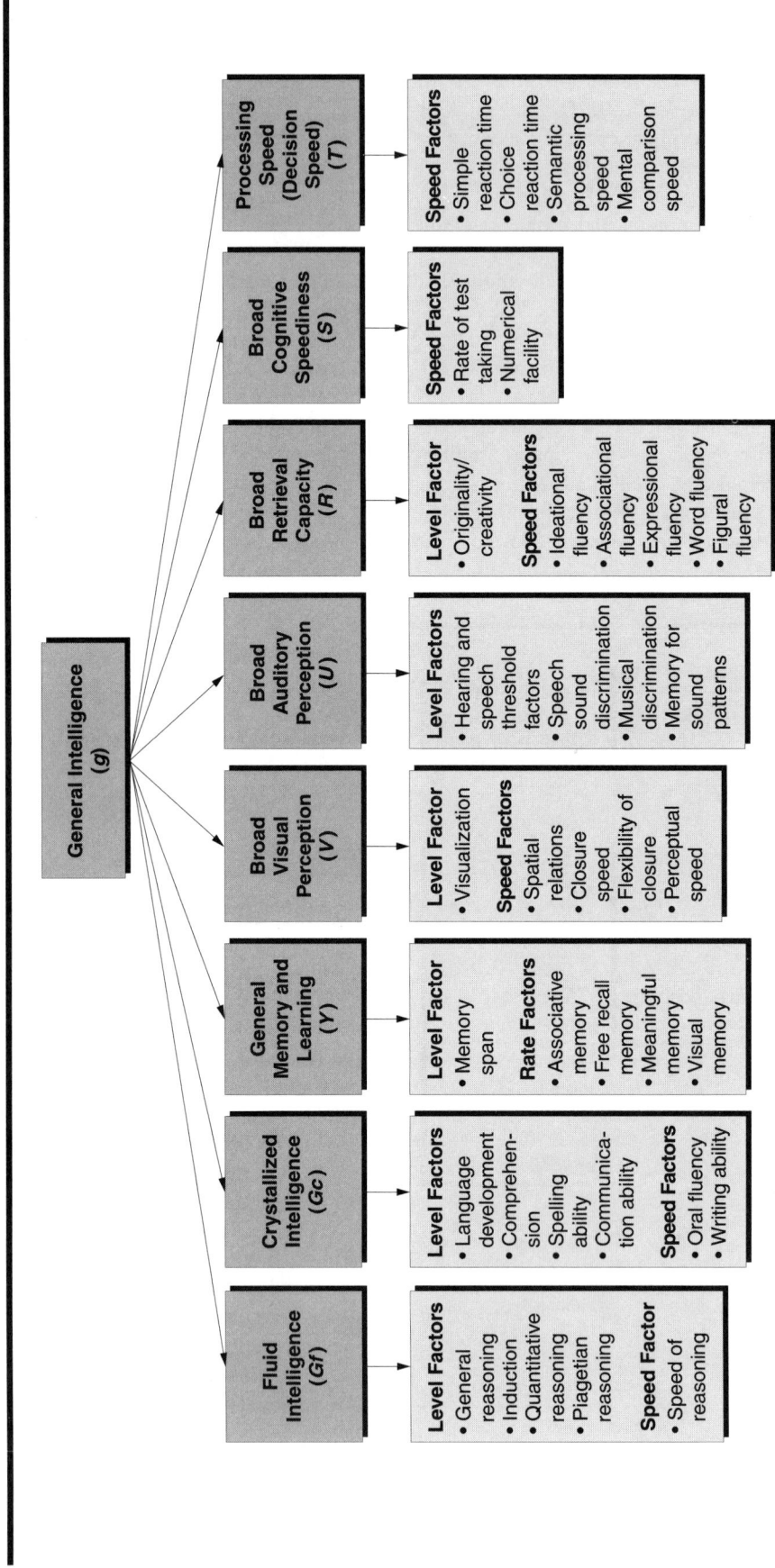

Figure 5-9. The Carroll structure of mental abilities. Adapted from Carroll (1993a).

142

2. *Broad (Stratum II).* The second level is composed of eight broad factors: fluid intelligence, crystallized intelligence, general memory and learning, broad visual perception, broad auditory perception, broad retrieval capacity, broad cognitive speediness, and processing speed (decision speed).

3. *General (Stratum III).* The third level is composed of a general factor, or *g*.

Carroll's (1997c) theory constitutes "a provisional statement about the enumeration, identification, and structuring of the total range of cognitive ability discovered thus far" (p. 124). Carroll's theory was expected to replace, expand, or supplement previous theories of the structure of cognitive abilities, such as Thurstone's theory of primary mental abilities, Guilford's structure-of-intellect theory, Cattell-Horn's Gf-Gc theory, or Wechsler's theory of verbal and performance components of intelligence. A hierarchical confirmatory factor analysis provides support for the three-stratum theory (Bickley, Keith, & Wolfle, 1995). For further information about Carroll's theory, see his book *Human Cognitive Abilities* (1993).

CAMPIONE, BROWN, AND BORKOWSKI'S INFORMATION-PROCESSING THEORY OF INTELLIGENCE

Information-processing conceptions of intelligence focus on the ways individuals mentally represent and process informa-

tion. Information-processing models of cognitive activities categorize mental processes by the different operations performed during various tasks. In these models, human cognition is conceived of as occurring in a series of discrete stages, with information received being operated on at one stage and then passed on as input to the next stage for further processing. Mental processes, then, are composed of specific covert cognitive behaviors "which transform and manipulate information between the time it enters as a stimulus and the time a response to it is selected" (Torgesen, 1979, p. 516).

According to Swanson (1985),

The information processing framework assumes that a number of component operations or processing stages occur between a stimulus and a response. It is assumed that all behavior of a human information processing system is the result of combinations of these various processing stages. Typically, two theoretical components are postulated in information processing analysis: a structural component, which defines the constraints of a particular processing stage (e.g., sensory storage, short-term memory, long-term memory), and a functional component, which describes the operations of the various stages. Of particular interest in the area of intelligence are functional components or strategies that must be performed if a task is to be successfully completed. (pp. 226–227)

Joseph Campione and Ann Brown (1978) used an information-processing framework to develop a general theory of intelligence, which was expanded by John Borkowski (1985). Their theory postulates that intelligence has two basic components:

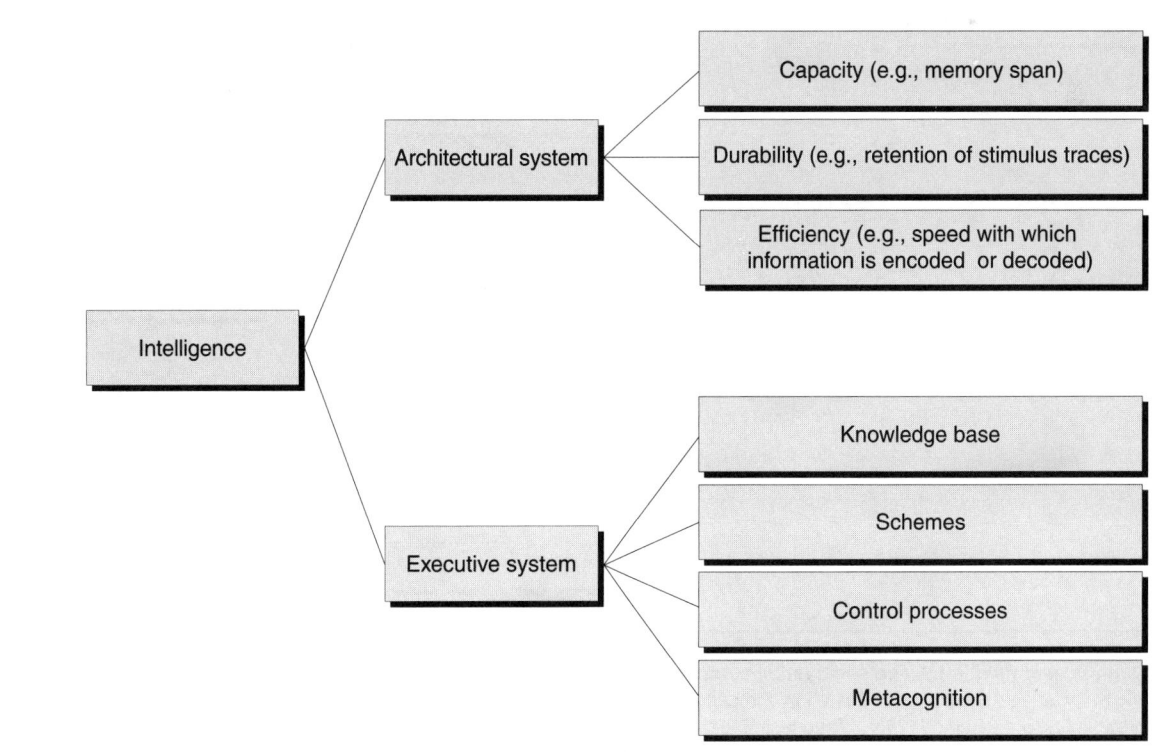

Figure 5-10. Campione, Brown, and Borkowski's model of intelligence.

an architectural system, which represents a structural component, and an executive system, which represents a control component (see Figure 5-10). Exhibit 5-3 describes the theory in more detail.

Figure 5-11 shows how cognitive, motivational, and self-system components interact to facilitate metacognitive processes. The following are examples of some of these interactions (Borkowski & Burke, 1996, adapted from pp. 238–240).

1. A child is taught to use a learning strategy and, with repetition, comes to learn about the attributes of that strategy. The attributes of this *specific strategy knowledge* include the effectiveness of the strategy, the range of its appropriate applications, and the proper use of the strategy with a variety of tasks.

2. A child learns other strategies and repeats them in multiple contexts. The child comes to understand when, where, and how to employ each strategy. In this way, specific strategy knowledge is enlarged and enriched.

3. A child gradually develops the capacity to select strategies appropriate for some tasks (but not others) and to adjust the strategies accordingly by monitoring performance, especially when essential strategy components have not been adequately learned in the past.

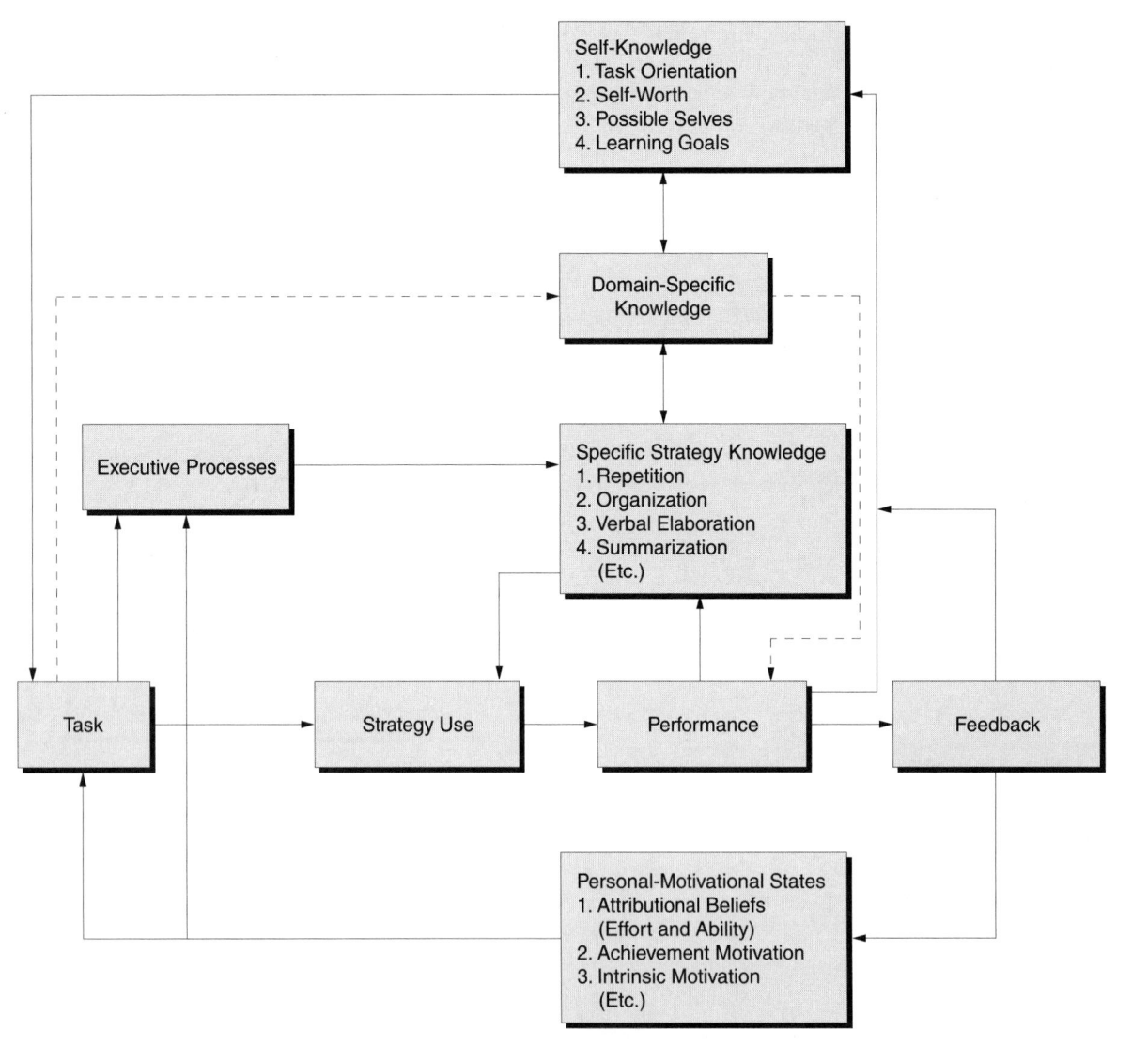

Figure 5-11. Cognitive, motivational, and self-system components of metacognition: The complete model. Note that the model has a Domain-Specific Knowledge "bypass," as indicated by the dashed lines. Reprinted and adapted, with permission of the publisher and author, from J. G. Borkowski and J. E. Burke (1996), "Theories, Models, and Measurement of Executive Functioning: An Information Processing Perspective," in Lyon, G. R., & Krasnegor, N. A. (Eds.). (1996). *Attention, memory and executive function* (p. 240). Baltimore: Paul H. Brookes Publishing Company.

Exhibit 5-3
Components of an Information-Processing Theory

The Architectural System

The architectural system refers to biologically/genetically based properties necessary for processing information, such as memory span, retention of stimulus traces, and efficiency (or speed of encoding and decoding information). These properties are closely linked to the perceptual skills of individuals and reflect sensory activity and nervous system integrity. They are relatively impervious to improvement by the environment and are essential to basic cognitive operations, such as perception and short-term memory. Thus, the architectural system corresponds to the major stores, or the system's hardware.

Properties of structures in the architectural system include *capacity,* or the amount of space available in the units (e.g., number of slots in short-term memory and amount of filing space in long-term memory); *durability,* or the rate at which information is lost; and *efficiency of operation,* or the temporal characteristics associated with selection and storage of information (e.g., speed of encoding, rate of memory search, rapidity with which attention is altered, and duration of alertness). The architectural system registers and responds to sensory input.

The Executive System

The executive system refers to environmentally learned components that guide problem solving, including (a) a *knowledge base* (retrieval of knowledge from long-term memory), (b) *schemes* (such as those found in Piagetian theory), (c) *control processes* (e.g., rehearsal strategies), and (d) *metacognition* (introspective knowledge). The four components can be viewed as complementary, overlapping, hypothetical constructs. Although they are assumed to be independent, future research may find that they are actually interdependent.

The components of the executive system are skills that emerge from experience and from instruction in complex problem-solving tasks. These executive function skills enable the individual to engage in creative, adaptive learning by initiating and regulating retrieval of knowledge from long-term memory, modifying the knowledge base, and mediating problem solving. They allow the individual to rise above rote, nonstrategic learning. These skills appear to be products of enriched learning experiences and hence are highly modifiable. From a developmental standpoint, the study of executive function processes might include (a) self-control and search tasks for *toddlers*; (b) problem-solving tasks that require simple planning and rulelike behavior for *preschoolers and young children*; and (c) tasks that require complex planning, self-monitoring, and maintenance of multiple pieces of information in working memory for *older school-age children and adults* (Welsh & Pennington, 1988).

Knowledge Base

Knowledge plays a central role in intelligent behavior because "knowledge informs perceptions, provides a home for new memories amidst the storage of old ones, and informs cognitive routines and strategies in the face of complex problems" (Borkowski, 1985, p. 112).

Schemes

In the Piagetian perspective, schemes refer to abstract cognitive structures by which individuals assimilate or accommodate new information. Schemes (or rules of thinking) are the active and constructive aspects of human intelligence. In Piagetian theory, the major stages of cognitive development—sensorimotor, preoperational, concrete operational, and formal operational (see Table 5-2, ahead)—represent groups of schemes. Passage from one stage to another occurs when there is a major change in the scheme. Piaget's theory is discussed later in the chapter.

Control Processes

Control processes refer to the rules and strategies that aid in memorizing, understanding, problem solving, and other cognitive activities. Strategic behaviors—such as self-checking, rehearsal, and other self-instructional procedures—can be taught to promote greater strategy generalization. Children who possess sophisticated cognitive strategies and skilled routines are likely to become efficient, effective problem solvers who can create strategies to meet new cognitive challenges.

Metacognition

Metacognition refers to thoughts about thoughts or awareness of one's own thought processes and strategies of thought. Two aspects of metacognition are declarative knowledge ("knowing that") and procedural knowledge ("knowing how"). Declarative knowledge refers to one's knowledge and awareness of factors that impede or facilitate cognition. Procedural knowledge refers to knowledge of the procedures that one employs to regulate cognitive activities.

Metacognition helps to inform and regulate cognitive routines and strategies. The integration of metacognitive knowledge with strategic behaviors results in more effective problem solving. The metacognitive components involved in intelligence include (a) recognizing the existence of a problem, (b) defining the nature of the problem, (c) choosing steps to solve the problem, (d) representing information about the problem, (e) allocating resources, (f) monitoring solutions, and (g) evaluating solutions. Metacognition aids in planning, self-monitoring, and ingenuity, and it may lead to strategy selection, self-reflection, and even the generation of new strategies.

Examples of metacognition include (a) knowing that a strategy which worked for one task might need to be slightly modified for a new task, (b) knowing that some strategies will work for several tasks, (c) knowing how to retrieve information from memory, (d) knowing whether there is sufficient information to accomplish a goal, (e) knowing whether a problem solution was performed correctly, and (f) knowing how to deal with uncertainty when one encounters a logical dilemma. Puzzlement is an experiential aspect of metacognition and may be "both a source of new metacognitive knowledge and a cue for utilizing stored knowledge about appropriate strategies to confront the problem at hand" (Borkowski,1985, p. 135).

Source: Adapted from Borkowski (1985).

4. As strategic and executive processes become refined, the child gradually recognizes the general utility and importance of being strategic and forms beliefs about self-efficacy. Children learn to attribute successful (and unsuccessful) learning outcomes to effort expended in strategy deployment (rather than to luck) and to understand that mental competencies can be enhanced through self-directed actions. After many cognitive acts, the child is provided with or infers feedback about the successfulness of performance and its specific cause(s) (e.g., "Because I prepared well for the test, I received a good grade"). This feedback is essential for shaping personal-motivational states.

5. A child accumulates general knowledge about the world, as well as domain-specific knowledge (e.g., mathematics), as he or she develops.

6. A child imagines what her or his future career might be or what she or he will become in the future. This brings forth "hoped-for" and "feared" possible selves. These images provide the impetus for achieving important short-term and long-term goals, such as becoming a competent student in order to eventually become a successful lawyer (or teacher or electrician).

STERNBERG'S TRIARCHIC THEORY OF INTELLIGENCE

Robert J. Sternberg (1986) divides human intelligence into three dimensions: componential, experiential, and contextual.

Componential Dimension

The componential dimension relates intelligence to the internal mental mechanisms of the individual, and Sternberg refers to these mental mechanisms as "information-processing components." A component is "a mental process that may translate a sensory input into a mental representation, transform one mental representation into another, or translate a mental representation into a motor output" (Sternberg, 1986, p. 24). There are three basic types of components: metacomponents, performance components, and knowledge acquisition components.

1. *Metacomponents.* These are higher-order processes used in planning, monitoring, and evaluating the performance of a task. Metacomponents tell other components what to do and when to do it.

2. *Performance components.* These are strategies used in the execution of a task.

3. *Knowledge acquisition components.* These are processes used in learning new things. The three knowledge acquisition components are (a) selective encoding, (b) selective combinations, and (c) selective comparison. Selective encoding is a process of separating relevant from irrelevant information in problem-solving situations. Selective combination is a process of forming a new and integrated "knowledge structure" from relevant encoded information. Selective comparison is also a process involving the comparison of the new knowledge structure with previously encoded information.

Experiential Dimension

The experiential dimension of Sternberg's theory relates intelligence to both the external and the internal worlds of the individual, and it specifies the point at which intelligence is most critically involved in an individual's ability to cope with tasks or situations. Intelligence deals with novelty *and* with the automatization of mental processes. As experience with a task or situation increases, the need to deal with novelty decreases and automatic processes or routines take over. Thus, Sternberg believes that it is difficult—if not impossible—to compare levels of intelligence fairly across sociocultural groups. Even if a test requires members of different groups to exercise the same performance components, because of differences in previous environmental experiences the test is unlikely to be equivalent for the groups in terms of novelty and the degree to which the groups have automatized the performance.

Contextual Dimension

The contextual dimension relates intelligence to the external world of the individual. It emphasizes adaptation to, selection of, and shaping of the environment. Environmentally adaptive requirements can differ widely from one culture to another and thus can be evaluated only in context. When attempts to adapt to a given environment fail and it is not practical or possible to select a new environment, environmental shaping may be the best tactic to employ—the individual must attempt to change the environment.

DAS, NAGLIERI, AND KIRBY'S PLANNING-ATTENTION-SIMULTANEOUS-SUCCESSIVE PROCESSING (PASS) MODEL OF INTELLIGENCE

J. P. Das, Jack Naglieri, and John R. Kirby have proposed a planning, attention, simultaneous, and successive processing model to categorize cognitive ability (Das, Naglieri, & Kirby, 1994). The model, based in part on Aleksandr Luria's (1966a, 1966b) work in neuropsychology, postulates that four cognitive processes are involved in intellectual functioning. *Planning processes* involve cognitive control, knowledge, intentionality, and self-regulation. *Attentional processes* allow for focused cognitive activity. *Simultaneous processing*

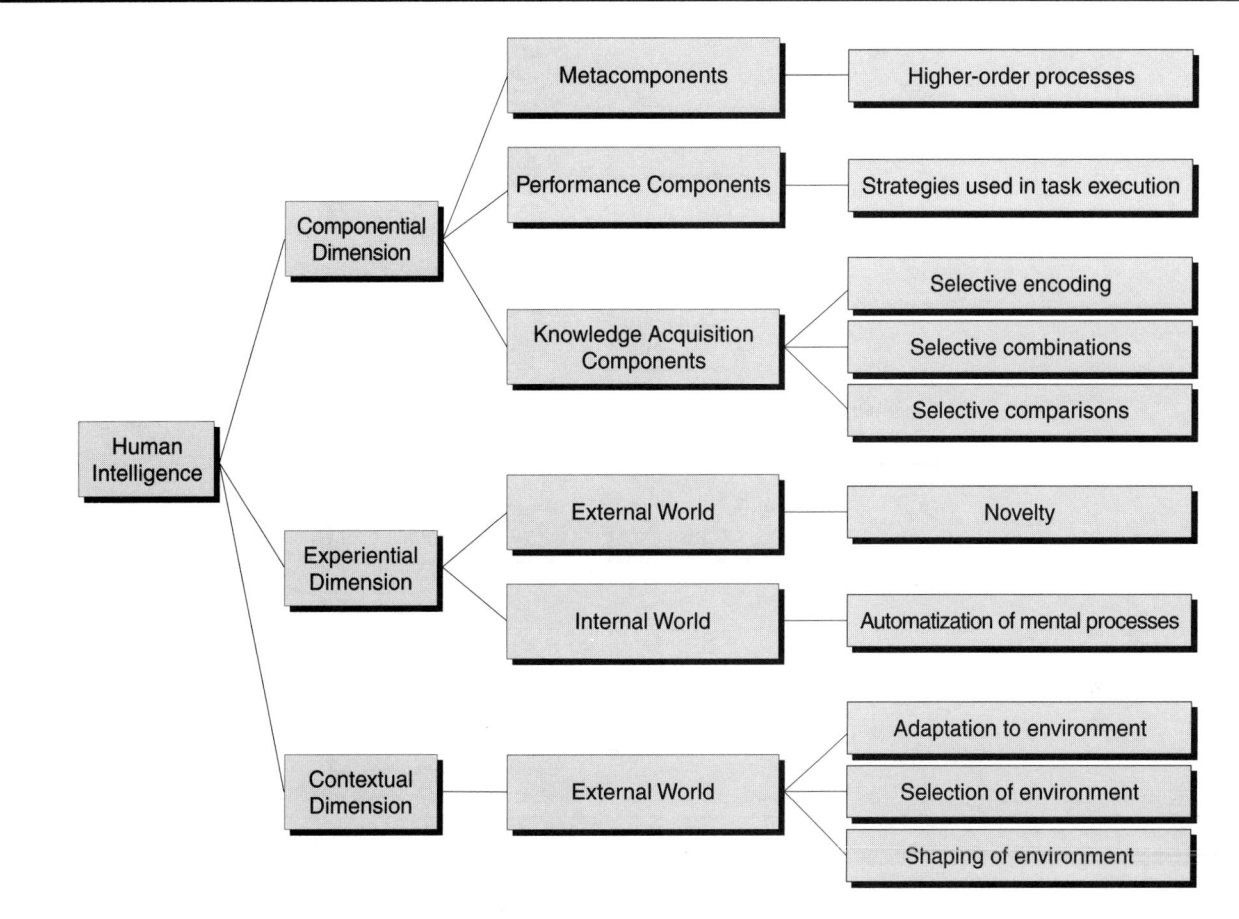

Figure 5-12. Sternberg's triarchic theory of intelligence.

involves perception of stimuli as a whole or the understanding of grammatical statements requiring integration of words into a meaningful idea. *Successive processing* involves operating on stimuli arranged in sequence in order to make a decision; processing occurs in a sequence-dependent, temporally based series. The four processes operate together when a person is working on intellectual tasks, although some processes play a stronger role than others, depending on the task. The Cognitive Assessment System (CAS) was designed according to the PASS theory (see Chapter 16).

GARDNER'S MULTIPLE INTELLIGENCE THEORY

Howard Gardner (Gardner, 1983; Gardner, 1998; Gardner, Kornhaber, & Wake, 1996) posits several relatively autonomous intellectual competencies, or multiple intelligences (see Exhibit 5-2 for Gardner's definition of intelligence). He has identified eight competencies and two tentative compe-

tencies, but allows that more may be discovered. The competencies are as follows:

1. *Linguistic intelligence* (e.g., capacities involved in the use of language for communication)
2. *Musical intelligence* (e.g., rhythmic and pitch abilities involved in composing, singing, and playing music)
3. *Logical-mathematical intelligence* (e.g., logical thinking, numerical ability)
4. *Spatial intelligence* (e.g., perceiving the visual world, transposing and modifying one's initial perceptions, recreating aspects of one's visual experience)
5. *Bodily-kinesthetic intelligence* (e.g., dancing, acting, athletics)
6. *Intrapersonal intelligence* (e.g., knowledge of self, including the ability to identify one's feelings, intentions, and motivations)
7. *Interpersonal intelligence* (e.g., ability to discern other individuals' feelings, beliefs, and intentions)
8. *Naturalist intelligence* (e.g., ability to discern patterns in nature)

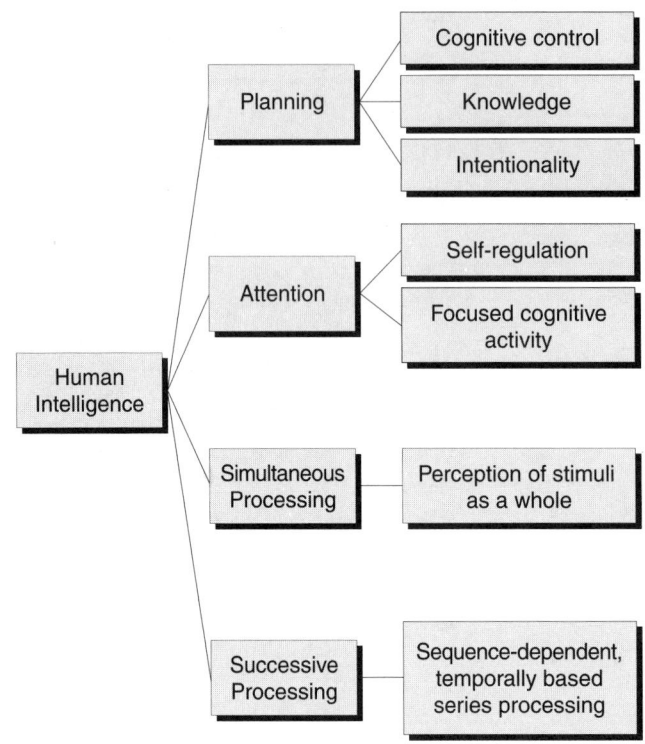

Figure 5-13. Das, Naglieri, and Kirby's planning-attention-simultaneous-successive processing (PASS) model of intelligence.

9. *Spiritual intelligence* (tentative; e.g., concern with cosmic or existential issues and recognition of the spiritual as an ultimate state of being)

10. *Existential intelligence* (tentative; e.g., concern with ultimate issues)

The competencies can be viewed as building blocks out of which thought and action develop. The components constitute the basis of human symbol-using capacities, and they interact to produce a diverse mixture of human talents that we can employ to achieve societal ends. Clearly, combinations of several intelligences are usually involved in behavior.

Gardner proposes that the multiple intelligence theory be used as a basis for assessing children; the resulting multiple intelligence profile might be useful for guidance and education. Gardner believes that we can assess children's intellectual competencies through planned observations. For example, we can teach infants patterns and then test the infants to see whether they remember the patterns. We can give preschool children blocks, puzzles, games, and other tasks. Their block constructions may provide information about spatial and kinesthetic intelligence, their ability to relate a set of stories may reveal information about linguistic capacities, and their ability to operate a simple machine may give information about kinesthetic and logical-mathematical skills. "The future musician may be marked by perfect pitch; the child gifted in personal matters, by his [or her] intuitions about the motives of others; the budding scientist, by his [or her] ability to pose provocative questions and then follow them up with appropriate ones" (Gardner, 1983, p. 386).

Gardner suggests that different assessment strategies are required for evaluating children of different ages. Testing for spatial ability, for example, might include hiding an object from a 1-year-old, giving a jigsaw puzzle to a 6-year-old, and giving a Rubik's cube to a preadolescent. Developing a reasonably accurate picture of a child's abilities may require 5 to 10 hours of observation of regular classroom activities over the course of a month. Table 16-1 in Chapter 16 shows a checklist for evaluating children's multiple intelligences. Gardner has not, however, developed a standardized test to measure these different types of intelligence.

STERNBERG'S SUCCESSFUL INTELLIGENCE THEORY

Sternberg (1996) offered another theory of intelligence, referred to as *successful intelligence,* that focuses on "the ability to adapt to, shape, and select environments to accomplish one's goals and those of one's society and culture" (Sternberg & Kaufman, 1998, p. 494). His successful intelligence theory complements his triarchic theory presented earlier in the chapter. Individuals with successful intelligence are able

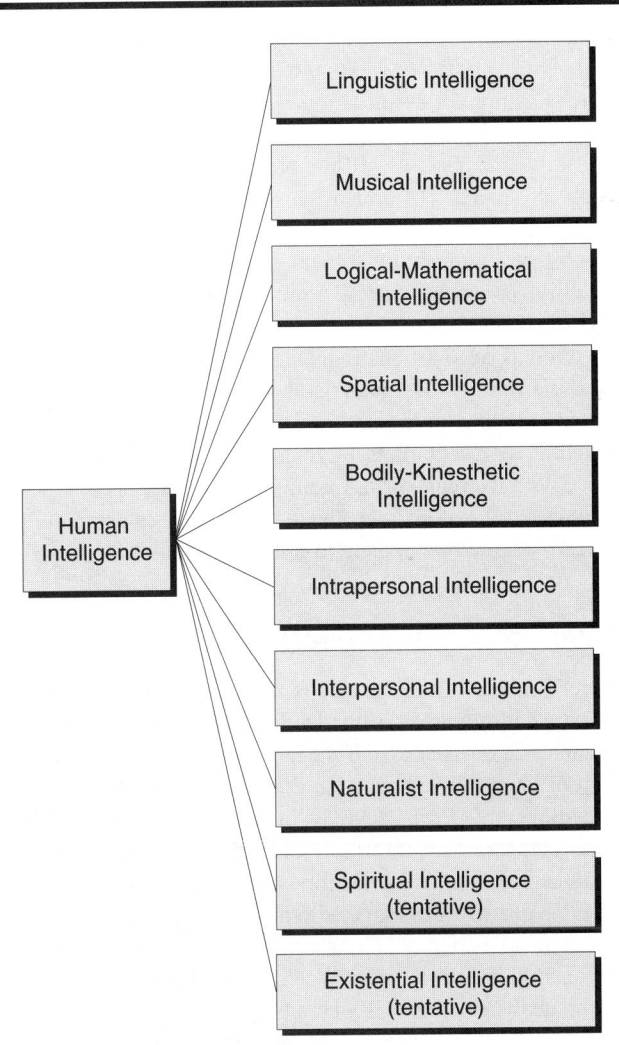

Figure 5-14. Gardner's multiple intelligence theory.

to discern their strengths and weaknesses and then determine ways to use their strengths and minimize their weaknesses.

The three broad areas associated with successful intelligence are analytical, creative, and practical abilities.

1. *Analytic abilities.* Analytic abilities are useful in analyzing and evaluating one's life options. They include "identifying the existence of a problem, defining the nature of the problem, setting up a strategy for solving the problem, and monitoring one's solution" (Sternberg & Kaufman, 1998, p. 494).

2. *Creative abilities.* Creative abilities help to generate problem-solving options, to promote one's ideas that may not be popular, and to convince others of the value of the ideas.

3. *Practical abilities.* Practical abilities are those applied to real-world problems in order "to implement options and to make them work.... A key aspect of practical intelligence is the acquisition and use of tacit knowledge, which is knowledge of what one needs to know to succeed in a given environment that is not explicitly taught and that usually is not verbalized" (Sternberg & Kaufman, 1998, p. 494).

Underlying the theory of successful intelligence is the premise that schools—by focusing too narrowly on analytical and memory abilities and failing to promote creative and practical abilities—do not use children's multiple abilities. The theory emphasizes the importance of other aspects of intelligence and their usefulness in our society. These aspects are not typically measured well by standardized intelligence tests.

CECI'S BIO-ECOLOGICAL THEORY OF INTELLIGENCE

The bio-ecological theory of intelligence attempts to explain the development of intelligent behavior using four perspectives

© 1999 Thaves / Reprinted with permission. Newspaper dist. by NEA, Inc.

Copyright © 1999 Thaves/ Reprinted with permission.

(Ceci, Rosenblum, de Bruyn, & Lee, 1997). First, intelligence is composed of multiple cognitive abilities rather than of one pervasive general factor. Second, although genes play an important role in the development of intelligence by setting the upper and lower limits of development, it is the interplay of genetic-environmental interactions at various points in development that produces changes in intelligence. Third, cognitive processes depend on the context in which cognition takes place. This context includes the motivational properties of environmental features and the individual's mental representation of the task (such as how the problem is represented in memory). Fourth, noncognitive intrinsic abilities, including temperament (e.g., restless, impulsive), physical traits (e.g., skin color, facial features), and motivation (e.g., seeking rewards, lack of interest in seeking rewards), are highly important in the development of intelligence. All four perspectives must be considered in understanding the development of intelligence.

PIAGET'S DEVELOPMENTAL THEORY OF INTELLIGENCE

Jean Piaget (1896–1980) perceived intelligence as a form of biological adaptation to one's environment. The individual is constantly interacting with the environment, trying to maintain a balance between personal needs and environmental demands. Cognition extends the scope of biological adaptation by allowing the individual to move from the immediate action level to a symbolic level through the process of internalization.

Cognitive processes emerge through a developmental progression that is neither a direct function of biological development nor a direct function of learning; rather, the emergence represents a reorganization of psychological structures resulting from organismic-environmental interactions. Social development, play, and art, for example, have large cognitive-structural components. These views led Piaget to disregard the dichotomy between maturation and learning and that between cognitive and social-emotional components of development.

According to Piaget, two inherent tendencies govern interactions with the environment: organization and adaptation. *Organization* is the tendency to combine two or more separate schemes into one higher-order, integrated scheme. *Schemes* are individual structures that produce changes in cognitive development—such as those involved in grasping an object or comprehending the concept of time (i.e., they are a kind of mini-system forming a framework into which incoming sensory data can fit).

Adaptation contains two complementary processes: assimilation and accommodation. *Assimilation* is a process of taking in information and experiences and fitting them into the schemes or concepts that one has already mastered. *Accommodation,* in turn, is a process whereby existing cognitive structures and behaviors are modified to consider new information and experiences. Both assimilation and accommodation occur simultaneously whenever we adapt to environmental events, but the particular balance between the two is likely to vary from situation to situation.

An example of assimilation is make-believe play with an object. Initially, the child ignores special features of the object and responds to it as if it were something else. The child displays accommodation when he or she learns a new scheme by imitating someone else's behavior. For example, if you give a young child a hair brush and he or she shakes it, the child is assimilating. If you demonstrate how to brush your hair with the hair brush and the child does what you do, the child is accommodating. Assimilative processes permit intelligence to go beyond a passive coping with reality, while accommodative processes prevent intelligence from constructing representations of reality that have no correspondence with the real world. Intelligence represents the rational processes—the processes that show the greatest independence from internal and environmental regulation.

Developmental Aspects

Piaget's model of intelligence is a hierarchical one, in which cognitive development is divided into four major periods, each characterized by stages and substages. Each stage represents a form of cognitive organization that is more complex than the preceding one. Each stage is invariant and universal. The stages, representing a form of biological adaptation, emerge from the individual's interaction with the environment.

Table 5-2 outlines Piaget's four periods of cognitive development. As development proceeds, different types of organization and adaptation occur. At first, children's perceptions dominate their thoughts. By about 2 years of age, the child has begun to develop language and memory for actions and prior responses, although the child's thinking is still egocentric. By about 7 years of age, the child's thought processes have become more systematic and concrete problem-solving skills have begun to develop. By 11 to 12 years, the child can think abstractly, construct theories, and make logical deductions without the need for direct experience. Piaget's developmental model assumes that mental organization operates as a totality, includes rules of transformation, is self-regulating, changes with development to give rise to new higher levels of organization, and differs at each level in the complexity of the rules of transformation and self-regulation (Elkind, 1981).

Piagetian vs. Psychometric Approaches

The goals of Piagetian assessment are to disclose the nature of mental organization at successive age levels and to provide information about stages of cognitive development. Although the Piagetian and psychometric approaches to intelligence differ in perspective, they are similar in several ways and complement each other (see Table 5-3). For example, the psychometric evaluation of intelligence is valuable in documenting the degree of delay of children with disabilities, pre-

Table 5-2
Outline of Piaget's Periods of Cognitive Development

Periods/Stages	Approximate ages	Characteristic behaviors
I. Sensorimotor period	Birth to 2 years	Child passes through six stages, beginning with the exercise of simple reflexes and ending with the first signs of internal, or symbolic, representations of actions.
1. Exercising reflexes	Birth to 1 month	Simple reflex activity is exhibited; sensorimotor schemes are exercised.
2. Primary circular reactions	1 to 4 months	Activities involve only the infant's own body and are endlessly repeated. First adaptations are acquired, such as integration and coordination of activities (e.g., finger sucking or watching one's hands).
3. Secondary circular reactions	4 to 8 months	Procedures are developed to make interesting sights persist; reactions also involve events or objects in the external world (e.g., shaking a rattle to hear the noise).
4. Coordination of secondary schemes	8 to 12 months	Two or more previously acquired schemes are combined to obtain a goal; acts become clearly intentional (e.g., reaching behind a cushion for a ball).
5. Tertiary circular reactions	12 to 18 months	Trial-and-error behavior and goal-seeking activity are designed to produce novel results; movements are purposely varied and the results observed (e.g., pulling a pillow nearer in order to get a toy resting on it).
6. Intention of new means through mental combination	18 to 24 months	Mental combinations appear; representational thought begins (e.g., using a stick to reach a desired object).
II. Preoperational period	2 to 7 years	Child acquires language and symbolic functions (e.g., ability to search for hidden objects, perform delayed imitation, engage in symbolic play, and use language).
III. Concrete operations period	7 to 11 years	Child develops conservation skills; mental operations are applied to real (concrete) objects or events.
IV. Formal operations period	11 years and upward	Child can think abstractly, formulate hypotheses, use deductive reasoning, and check solutions.

dicting school success, and assessing brain injury and psychopathology, whereas the Piagetian approach is valuable in diagnosing learning difficulties and designing educational interventions.

There is presently no comprehensive battery of Piagetian tests of intelligence, although some success has been achieved with the development of sensorimotor scales (Uzgiris & Hunt, 1975). Studies have found positive correlations between Piagetian measures and psychometric scales of intelligence in infant, preschool, and school-age populations (Bat-Haee, Mehyrar, & Sabharwal, 1972; Dodwell, 1961; Dudek, Lester, Goldberg, & Dyer, 1969; Elkind, 1961; Goldschmid, 1967; Gottfried & Brody, 1975; Humphreys & Parsons, 1979; Kaufman, 1972b; Keasey & Charles, 1967; Keating, 1975; Lester, Muir, & Dudek, 1970; Orpet, Yoshida, & Meyers, 1976; Rogers, 1977; Wasik & Wasik, 1976). In particular, Piagetian measures—such as the ability to use formal operations, to understand the principle of conservation, and to use sensorimotor operations—relate to psychometric measures of intelligence, although Piagetian tasks have unique elements

not present in psychometric measures of intelligence. The significant correlations between Piagetian tests and psychometric tests indicate that children who achieve high scores on psychometric tests of intelligence are not merely "good test-takers"; they have advanced levels of cognitive development in several areas.

COMMENT ON MODERN VIEWS OF INTELLIGENCE

An integrated theory of intelligence would encompass the interdependency of biological, cognitive, motivational, and behavioral factors (Sternberg, 1986). All of these factors influence performance on intelligence tests.

1. *Biological factors.* The biological basis for intelligence, which is partly dependent on genetic factors, includes structural aspects of the brain and physiological processes involved in brain development and brain functioning.

Table 5-3
Comparison of Piagetian and Psychometric Approaches to Intelligence

	Differences	
Similarities	Piagetian	Psychometric
1. Both accept genetic determinants of intelligence.	1. Assumes that there are factors that give development a definite nonrandom direction	1. Assumes that tested intelligence is randomly distributed in a given population, with the distribution following the normal curve
2. Both accept maturational determination of intelligence.	2. Is concerned with intraindividual changes occurring in the course of development	2. Is concerned with interindividual differences
3. Both use nonexperimental methodology.		
4. Both attempt to measure intellectual functions that the child is expected to have developed by a certain age.	3. Views mental growth as the formation of new mental structures and the emergence of new mental abilities; assumes that mental growth is qualitative and presupposes significant differences in the thinking of younger versus older children	3. Views the course of mental growth as a curve, from which the amount of intelligence at some criterion age can be predicted on the basis of intelligence at any preceding age
5. Both conceive of intelligence as being essentially rational.		
6. Both assume that maturation of intellectual process is complete during late adolescence.		
7. Both are capable of predicting intellectual behavior outside the test situation.	4. Assumes that genetic and environmental factors interact in a functional and dynamic manner with respect to their regulatory control over mental activity	4. Assumes that genetic and environmental contributions to intelligence can be measured

Note. Similarity items 5, 6, and 7 obtained from Dudek, Lester, Goldberg, and Dyer (1969); the remainder of the table adapted from Elkind (1974).

2. *Cognitive factors.* Cognitive factors involved in intelligence center on two kinds of cognition: metacognition (knowledge about and control of one's cognition) and ordinary cognition (what is known and controlled by metacognition). For example, metacognition as knowledge involves awareness of what one does and does not know. Metacognition as a control process involves strategies for solving a problem. Ordinary cognition encompasses the cognitive steps actually used by the individual to solve the problem.

3. *Motivational factors.* Motivational factors involved in intelligence include the magnitude, direction, and disposition of the individual's motivation. For example, the level of interest an individual has in learning and the specific area of interest affect what the individual will learn.

4. *Behavioral factors.* Behavioral factors involved in intelligence emphasize what the individual does rather than what she or he thinks. Domains of behavioral interest include the academic domain (behavior exhibited in such subjects as language, mathematics, science, social science, and arts), social domain (behavior exhibited in interaction with other people), and practical domain (behavior exhibited in activities of daily living).

Current hierarchical theories of intelligence lie somewhere between Spearman's and Thurstone's views. They stress a general factor (*g*) at the top of the hierarchy, several broad classes of abilities in the middle, and primary factors at the bottom. Intelligence is multifaceted and hierarchically organized, with a general factor entering into many cognitive tasks

and narrow group factors and specialized abilities forming the core of abilities. The IQ should be viewed as a somewhat arbitrary summary index of many abilities. Because the various intelligence tests sample different combinations of abilities, an individual's IQ is likely to vary—sometimes dramatically—from one test to another, depending on the abilities included in the different tests. The hierarchical model, although it may not fit the complexities of the interrelationships of human ability perfectly, is a useful approximation (Deary & Stough, 1996; Humphreys et al., 1979).

The Campione-Brown-Borkowski formulation is an exciting theory of intelligence for those engaged in intellectual assessment. The theory places various cognitive assessment tasks in a broad-based model. It emphasizes that (a) intelligent behavior represents a dynamic interaction of structural and control components, (b) child-rearing practices and quality of education are important determinants of functional components (i.e., executive system abilities), (c) environmental enrichments are important for all children who have the requisite ability structure (i.e., in the architectural system), and (d) intelligent behavior is dependent on biologically/genetically based components, as well as on culturally based educational-environmental enrichments. The Campione-Brown-Borkowski theory, with other information-processing approaches, provides valuable guidelines for developing psychometric tests, intervention strategies, and remediation programs.

Psychologists have criticized Guilford's model for several reasons. First, it fails to reproduce the essentially hierarchical nature of intelligence test data, with minor factors, major factors, and a general factor (Eysenck, 1967). One outstanding and consistent finding is that various intelligence tests measure a basic commonality, as evidenced by the positive correlations among relevant tests and between different factors. This finding suggests a central factor in intellectual activity, which Guilford fails to mention in his model. Second, many of the three-way combinations in the model are logical indications of ways to construct tests, but they are not indications of distinct human abilities. Third, results from factor analytic studies do not provide convincing support for Guilford's model (Horn & Knapp, 1973). In fact, some factor analytic results provide as much support for randomly determined theories as they do for the Structure of Intellect theory.

Sternberg's triarchic theory is important because it combines internal aspects of intelligence (such as problem solving and reasoning) with external aspects of intelligence (such as experience and practice). However, more information is needed about how the three subtheories relate to one another. Additionally, the theory mixes personality characteristics (confidence, sociability) with intelligence and consequently clouds the theory of intelligence (Eysenck, M., 1994). Furthermore, the theory is limited because "components are positively correlated and do not, in general, exhibit sufficient generality to provide a basis for understanding individual differences in intelligence" (Brody, 1992, p. 125).

Sternberg's theory of successful intelligence is important because it points out that there are many real-life intelligent decisions that are not adequately measured by current standardized tests. The theory also points out the value of considering intelligent behavior in a wider context. Unfortunately, a reliable and valid measure of successful intelligence does not yet exist.

Although Gardner's theory is provocative, it is by no means novel. His linguistic intelligence corresponds closely to crystallized intelligence, and his logic-mathematical ability is similar to Cattell and Horn's fluid intelligence (Bouchard, 1984). Additionally, other theorists have recognized a spatial or visualization factor and an auditory organization factor (which subsumes musical ability).

There are several further difficulties with the theory of multiple intelligences (Bouchard, 1984; Carroll, 1997c; Eysenck, 1994; Sternberg, 1985, 1991). First, many would argue that bodily-kinesthetic skill, musical ability, and personal intelligence do not belong in the lists of intelligences, as the latter is more appropriately assigned to the realm of personality and the former are poorly correlated with effective functioning. Second, a plethora of evidence indicates that the eight competencies, or intelligences, are not independent; that is, a modest correlation exists among most cognitive abilities. For example, logical-mathematical and spatial abilities correlate highly; individuals who score highly on some measures of intelligence also score highly on other measures of intelligence. Third, the components of each type of intelligence are not clear. Fourth, rather than the term "multiple intelligences," *multiple talents* or *multiple abilities* might be more appropriate terminology. Finally, the current

instruments used to assess multiple intelligence do not have acceptable psychometric properties. "It is very difficult, if not impossible, to quantify performance on them; assessments take place over extremely long periods of time, and it is questionable whether anything approaching objective scoring is even possible.... Those who are advocating this type of approach need to demonstrate the psychometric soundness of their instruments" (Sternberg, 1991, p. 266)

Let's now look at some other issues related to test construction and the nature of intelligence. When we evaluate factors, we must recognize that it is extremely difficult, if not impossible, to devise tests for *pure* factors or pure measures of ability (Horn, 1987). Take, for example, a test designed to measure constructional ability (e.g., reproducing patterns with blocks). To measure this ability, examiners must give examinees instructions about what they should do. Because the ability to understand instructions differs among examinees, a test designed to measure constructional ability to some extent involves verbal comprehension as well. In addition, verbal facility (e.g., verbalizing what movements are necessary to place the blocks in the correct alignment) may also help some examinees solve the constructional task. Thus, in this example, it is difficult to separate constructional ability from verbal ability—the two may not be independent.

Even tests designed to measure more narrow abilities, such as memory span, may involve broader abilities related to short-term acquisition and retrieval functions. For example, recency effects (i.e., material presented near the end of a fairly long series tends to be recalled better than material presented early or in the middle of the series) or primacy effects (i.e., material presented early in a series is more likely to be recalled than material presented in the middle of the series) may be involved (Horn, 1987). Thus, as Horn (1987) points out, "a test designed to measure at one level of breadth always measures, to some extent, narrower and broader abilities, and a test designed to measure one kind of capacity—a cognitive operation, say—always measures, to some extent, other capacities. Abilities are not different in the same sense that marbles and apples are different. The distinctions among abilities are shades of gray" (p. 208).

Horn's (1998) observations about the nature of intelligence are also important. He noted that the results from many studies indicate that humans express distinctly different patterns of achievements that reflect different aspects of intelligence. Different intelligences emerge from different combinations of genetic and environmental (e.g., schooling) determinants. Environmental experiences vary among "individuals in intensity, length, and quality. The different intelligences that emerge thus reflect a variety of neurological, experiential, developmental, genetic, and life achievement influences" (Horn, 1998, p. 76).

Contemporary views of intelligence emphasize both biological and developmental influences. Genetically determined cognitive ability is always viewed as being modified by experience. Measures of intelligence sample only a limited spectrum of intellectual ability, and the responses provided by

Exhibit 5-4
Intelligence Tests in the Future: What Form Will They Take and What Purposes Will They Serve?

John Horn

Realistic appraisal, based on historical analysis, suggests that the tests used to measure intellectual abilities in applied settings in the future will be very similar to the tests used in the latter part of the 20th century. However, if the technology of measurement for applied purposes follows advancements in scientific understanding of human intelligence, then we can expect that intelligence tests of the future will have the following characteristics:

1. Be structured to provide for measurements of many separate abilities, ranging from elementary processes to broad but distinct dimensions of intelligence
2. Involve, perhaps, abilities to comprehend and assimilate information that comes to one via the continuous flow of TV-like presentations
3. Contain subtests designed to indicate features of temporal integration of information, auditory organization, and elementary cognitive processing of information
4. Derive more from the study of adulthood development than from the study of childhood development

The mainstreams of cognitive psychology will be diverted more and more into the study of intelligence and thus will influence the shape of practical tests. Tests will be used less and less to measure global intelligence just for the sake of measuring it or to make objectionable distinctions; more testing will be done to help identify particular ability strengths and weaknesses. Theories about intelligence will improve, and more test construction will be based on sound theory.

Lauren B. Resnick

What is the likelihood that IQ tests as we currently know them will still be in use in the schools in the near future? What new kinds of tests of aptitude and intelligence can we reasonably look for? IQ tests or some similar kinds of assessment instrument are likely to be functionally necessary in the schools as long as the present form of special education for the children with disabilities remains with us—or until we are prepared to spend substantially more public resources on education for all children than we are now doing. Further, I have suggested that there is a very real possibility of a revival of interest in IQ tests in the educational mainstream as a protective response by school people threatened with legal responsibility for ensuring that all children, even the very hard-to-teach, learn. I believe these two areas—special education and the school's legal responsibility—are the things to watch in the future for new developments in global IQ measurement.

What new kinds of tests can we expect? I have suggested the possibility of a serious shift in the science, and therefore the technology, of intelligence testing. Aptitude tests useful for monitoring instruction and adapting it to individual differences are essentially nonexistent today. Current work on the cognitive analysis of intelligence and aptitude tests may be able to provide the basis for much more systematic and refined matching of instructional treatments to aptitudes. We can particularly look forward to this development as work on the cognitive components of intelligence shifts attention from performance on the tests themselves to the learning processes that underlie both skillful test performance and skillful performance in school subject matters.

Ann L. Brown and Lucia A. French

We would like to see an extension of the predictive power of intelligence tests so that we are able to (a) predict school failure prior to its occurrence and (b) predict potential adult competence by a consideration of performance on tests of everyday reasoning. To achieve these ends, we will need to invest considerable energy in ethnographic surveys and experimental testing programs directed at improving our scanty knowledge in two main areas. First we need sensitive indices of early cognitive incompetence that are related to subsequent academic intelligence. Secondly we need theories and measures of functional literacy, minimal competence, and mundane cognition, so that we can begin to predict life adaptation as well as academic success. We would also like to see an increased emphasis on the diagnosis and remediation of cognitive deficits, of both the academic and the everyday variety.

William W. Turnbull

My view is that we are likely to see evolutionary rather than quantum changes in intelligence tests, at least as they are used in academic settings. We are likely to see tests that provide separate scores on a variety of abilities. They are likely to be standard scores. The ratio defining the IQ may by then have been abandoned everywhere and the term IQ may have disappeared into psychological and educational history.

Norman Frederiksen

Realistic simulations of real-life problem situations might be used to supplement the usual psychological tests and thus to contribute to the database needed to develop a broader conception of intelligence. It is possible to develop scoring systems that describe intelligent behavior in ways that go far beyond the number-right score, that make possible the measurement of qualitative variables, such as problem-solving strategies and styles, and that may even provide information about some of the information-processing components of intelligent behavior. Many of the scores based on simulations are reliable, their interrelationships are consistent across different groups of subjects, and some of them predict real-life criteria that are not well predicted by conventional tests. Our glimpse of a broader picture of human intelligence suggests that the structure of intellect of the future will include a much broader spectrum of intelligent behaviors. Furthermore, it will not be a static model but will be one that recognizes the interactions involving test formats, subject characteristics, and the settings in which the problems are encountered. The structure of intelligence is not necessarily a fixed structure but one that may vary as the subjects learn and as the circumstances are altered.

(Continued)

Exhibit 5-4 *(Continued)*

Earl Hunt and James Pellegrino

Microcomputers can serve as automated testing stations for use in psychometric assessment. There are economic advantages in conducting aptitude and intelligence testing with such stations. Is it possible to improve the quality of cognitive assessment by extending the range of cognitive abilities to be assessed? Two types of extension are considered: modifying and expanding testing procedures for psychological functions that are components of conventional tests, and the extension of testing to psychological functions not generally assessed by conventional intelligence or aptitude tests. Computerized presentations will make relatively little difference in our ways of testing verbal comprehension. Computer-controlled testing could well extend the ways in which we evaluate spatial-visual reasoning and memory. The impact of testing on the evaluation of reasoning is unclear. Computer-controlled item presentation makes it possible to conceive of tests of learning and attention, neither of which is evaluated in most psychometric programs today.

Robert J. Sternberg

New tests of intelligence, in comparison to previous ones, will (a) be more heavily based on psychological theories (e.g., basing items on theories of information processing), (b) have more breadth (i.e., measuring a broader set of abilities), (c) measure the processes underlying intelligence (e.g., distinguishing between reasoning and perceptual processing), (d) measure the practical side of intelligence (i.e, measuring what happens in everyday life), (e) measure the ability to cope with novelty (i.e., coping with the unfamiliar and strange), (f) measure synthetic and insightful thinking (i.e., creating new products that show examinees' ability to think synthetically and even creatively), (g) merge testing and learning functions (e.g., merging measuring what has been learned with a program of instruction for teaching intellectual skills), (h) measure learning styles (e.g., finding out how individuals solve problems, such as by verbal or spatial means), (i) measure learning potential (e.g., measuring the child's ability to profit from instruction), (j) use computerized adaptive testing (e.g., having the computer present items at an appropriate level of difficulty given the examinee's past performance), and (k) use dynamic computerized testing (e.g., having the computer respond differently as a function of the answer given by the examinee). Also, in the future, the longevity of tests will be reduced more frequently and replaced with better measures of intelligence.

Rich E. Snow

We need to study and measure mental playfulness and idiosyncracy. We also need to study and measure conative [refers to volition or striving] and affective aspects of cognitive performance because there is growing reason to expect subtle intersections between individual differences in motivation, volition, anxiety, and so forth, and individual differences in intellectual performance.

Source: Brown and French (1979, adapted from p. 270); Frederiksen (1986, adapted from p. 451); Horn (1979, adapted from p. 239); Hunt and Pellegrino (1985, p. 207); Resnick (1979, adapted from p. 252); Sternberg (1986); Snow (1986, adopted from pp. 137–138), Turnbull (1979, adapted from p. 281). Citations from 1979 originally appeared in *Intelligence*, 1979, *3* (3).

individuals on intelligence tests are related to their unique learning histories. Contemporary views suggest that intelligence is a more global concept than was previously imagined. For possible ideas of what form intelligence tests will take in the future, see Exhibit 5-4. Whatever perspective you adopt toward conceptions of intelligence, recognize that the unique learning histories of individuals influence the ways in which they manifest their intelligence.

THINKING THROUGH THE ISSUES

1. Review the 1905 Binet-Simon Scale in Exhibit 5-1 to gain an appreciation of the variety of items it contained. What items in this scale are the forerunners of assessment procedures currently in use?

2. Psychologists are continually developing and modifying theories of intelligence. How can a study of historical developments in the field of intelligence aid you as a clinician?

3. Do you think the IQ concept will survive in the 21st century? If so, in what form?

4. How do you think lay people conceptualize intelligence differently from professionals in the field?

5. With which model or models of intelligence do you agree, and why?

6. How could the many definitions of intelligence be unified into a single theory? Would this be useful? Why or why not?

7. Which theoretical perspective do you believe most adequately explains your style of thinking? Least adequately? Explain.

8. Gardner and others believe that observations of children's behavior can provide more useful indices of children's cognitive ability than the current standardized tests of intellectual ability. Do you agree or disagree? Explain.

9. Observe a child for 15 minutes. To what extent can you evaluate the child's level of vocabulary, reasoning, social comprehension, short- and long-term memory, spatial ability, and other forms of problem-solving ability? How reliable and valid do you believe your observations are? What are some difficulties in conducting observations designed to obtain information about cognitive ability? What can you do to reduce such difficulties?

Intelligence testing in the 21st century.

Courtesy of Hugh Mahon and Jerome M. Sattler.

SUMMARY

Nineteenth-Century and Early Twentieth-Century Developments

1. Esquirol's descriptions of the verbal characteristics associated with various levels of "idiocy" can be regarded as the first crude mental test.

2. In the latter part of the 19th century, the psychophysical methods developed by Weber and Fechner and the statistical studies of mental processes initiated by Galton formed the background for much of the work that would take place in the 20th century.

3. Galton is regarded as the father of the testing movement.

4. Pearson developed the product-moment correlation formula for linear correlation, the multiple correlation coefficient, the partial correlation coefficient, the phi coefficient, and the chi-square test for determining how well a set of empirical observations conforms to an expected distribution (goodness of fit).

5. Cattell established a psychological laboratory at the University of Pennsylvania. In 1890, he published an article in the journal *Mind* in which he first used the term "mental test."

6. Psychological tests made a public debut in the United States at the 1893 Chicago World's Fair, where Munsterberg and Jastrow collaborated on a demonstration testing laboratory.

7. As a result of serious methodological shortcomings in studies by Wissler and Sharp at the end of the 19th century, investigators were led to believe that mental measurement was not a fruitful field to study.

8. In Germany at the turn of the century, Kraepelin, Ebbinghaus, Wernicke, and Ziehen made contributions to the field of testing.

9. In France at the end of the 19th century, Binet, Henri, and Simon developed methods for the study of mental functions. They believed that the key to measuring intelligence was to focus on higher mental processes instead of simple sensory functions.

10. The work of Binet, Ebbinghaus, and others had a unifying thread—the application of methods used in experimental psychological laboratories to solve practical problems presented by educators from their communities. The interplay of these forces gave birth to the field of applied psychology and ushered in a new era in psychometrics.

Twentieth-Century Developments

11. Goddard adapted the 1908 Binet-Simon Scale by making minor revisions and standardizing it on 2,000 American children.

12. In 1916, Terman published a modified, extended, and standardized form of the Binet-Simon Scale called the Stanford Revision and Extension of the Binet-Simon Scale.

13. Terman adopted Stern's concept of mental quotient and named it the intelligence quotient (IQ).

14. Believing that a point-scale arrangement has better psychometric properties than an age-scale format, Yerkes developed one of the first point scales in the 20th century.

Copyright © 1992 United Feature Syndicate, Inc.

15. Terman and Merrill revised the 1916 Stanford-Binet in 1937 and again in 1960.
16. Wechsler systematized and organized a series of subtests into a standardized point scale, guided by a conception of intelligence that emphasized its global nature.
17. The success of the Binet-Simon Scales and their derivatives launched the 20th-century testing movement in the United States and many other countries.

Definitions of Intelligence

18. Prominent in the definitions of intelligence are attributes such as adaptation to the environment, basic mental processes, and higher-order thinking (e.g., reasoning, problem solving, and decision making).
19. All ability tests measure what the individual has learned.
20. Definitions of intelligence emphasize the ability to adjust or adapt to the environment, the ability to learn, or the ability to perform abstract thinking.
21. Common to many definitions of intelligence are six major interdependent aspects of intelligence: knowledge-based thinking, apprehension, adaptive purposeful striving, fluid-analytic reasoning, mental playfulness, and idiosyncratic learning.
22. Experts in the fields of psychology, education, sociology, and genetics generally agree that the following terms refer to important elements of intelligence: abstract thinking or reasoning, the capacity to acquire knowledge, problem-solving ability, adaptation to one's environment, creativity, general knowledge, linguistic competence, mathematical competence, memory, and mental speed.

Introduction to Factor Analytic Theories of Intelligence

23. Some factor analytic theorists (e.g., Spearman and Vernon) proposed a general theory of intelligence, whereas others (e.g., Thorndike, Kelley, and Thurstone) viewed intelligence as composed of many independent faculties. Many theorists now accept the theory that general intelligence coexists with separate independent abilities.

Spearman's Two-Factor Theory of Intelligence

24. Spearman proposed a two-factor theory of intelligence, emphasizing a general factor (*g*) and one or more specific factors (*s*).

Thorndike's Multifactor Theory of Intelligence

25. Thorndike described three kinds of intelligence—social, concrete, and abstract.

Thurstone's Multidimensional Theory of Intelligence

26. Thurstone described eight primary mental factors (verbal, perceptual speed, inductive reasoning, number, rote memory, deductive reasoning, word fluency, and space or visualization). In his later work he postulated a second-order factor that may be similar to *g*.

Guilford's Structure of Intellect Theory

27. Guilford maintained that we must consider three classes of variables in any account of intellectual abilities: the activities or operations performed (operations), the material or content on which the operations are performed (content), and the product that is the result of the operations (products).

Vernon's Hierarchical Theory of Intelligence

28. Vernon's hierarchical approach to intelligence emphasized the *g* factor, followed by verbal-educational and spatial-mechanical group factors, which can be broken down further into minor group factors.

Cattell and Horn's Fluid and Crystallized Theory of Intelligence

29. Cattell and Horn proposed that there are two types of intelligence—fluid and crystallized. Fluid intelligence refers to essentially nonverbal, relatively culture-free mental efficiency. It involves adaptive and new learning capabilities and is related to mental operations and processes. Crystallized intelligence refers to acquired skills and knowledge that are developmentally dependent on exposure to culture. It involves overlearned and well-established cognitive functions and is related to mental products and achievements.
30. Horn's modification of the theory now includes nine second-stratum abilities, two of which are fluid ability and crystallized ability; the remaining seven abilities are visual processing, auditory processing, short-term memory, long-term memory, processing speed, decision speed, and quantitative knowledge.

Carroll's Three-Stratum Factor Analytic Theory of Cognitive Abilities

31. Carroll proposed a three-stratum factor analytic theory of cognitive abilities. The first level consists of 65 narrow abilities comprising levels of mastery in various cognitive areas. The second level is composed of eight broad factors: fluid intelligence, crystallized intelligence, general memory and learning, broad visual perception, broad auditory perception, broad retrieval capacity, broad cognitive speediness, and processing speed. The third level is composed of a general factor, or *g*.

Campione, Brown, and Borkowski's Information-Processing Theory of Intelligence

32. The Campione, Brown, and Borkowski information-processing theory of intelligence has two major components. One is the architectural system (the structural component), whose structures differ in such characteristics as capacity, durability, and efficiency of operation. The other is the executive system (functional component), which contains such components as a knowledge base, schemes, control processes, and metacognition. It stresses the dynamic interplay of structural and functional components.

Sternberg's Triarchic Theory of Intelligence

33. Sternberg's triarchic theory of intelligence consists of the componential dimension, which relates to internal world of the individual; the experiential dimension, which relates to both the external and the internal worlds of the individual; and the contextual dimension, which relates to the external world of the

individual. We must consider all three parts in the study of intelligence.

Das, Naglieri, and Kirby's Planning-Attention-Simultaneous-Successive Processing (PASS) Model of Intelligence

34. Das, Naglieri, and Kirby have proposed a planning, attention, simultaneous, and successive processing model to categorize cognitive ability.

Gardner's Multiple Intelligence Theory

35. Gardner posits the existence of at least eight relatively autonomous intellectual competencies: linguistic intelligence, musical intelligence, logical-mathematical intelligence, spatial intelligence, bodily-kinesthetic intelligence, intrapersonal intelligence, interpersonal intelligence, and naturalistic intelligence. Unfortunately, Gardner has not proposed a reliable and valid way to measure these competencies throughout the developmental period.

Sternberg's Successful Intelligence Theory

36. Sternberg offered another theory of intelligence, referred to as successful intelligence, that complements his triarchic theory. It has three components: analytic, creative, and practical abilities.

Ceci's Bio-Ecological Theory of Intelligence

37. Ceci's theory of intelligence contains the following four perspectives: (a) intelligence is composed of multiple cognitive abilities, (b) it is the interplay of genetic-environmental interactions at various points in development that produces changes in intelligence, (c) cognitive processes depend on the context in which cognition takes place, and (d) noncognitive intrinsic abilities are highly important in the development of intelligence.

Piaget's Developmental Theory of Intelligence

38. Piaget's model of intelligence is a hierarchical one, in which cognitive development is divided into four major periods: sensorimotor, preoperational, concrete operations, and formal operations.
39. Piagetian and psychometric approaches to intellectual assessment complement each other. Both approaches accept genetic and maturational determinants and emphasize the rational nature of intelligence. The Piagetian approach emphasizes developmental changes and the emergence of new mental structures, whereas the psychometric approach emphasizes the normal distribution of intelligence and interindividual differences.

Comment on Modern Views of Intelligence

40. An integrated theory of intelligence would encompass the interdependency of biological, cognitive, motivational, and behavioral factors.
41. Current hierarchical theories of intelligence stress a general factor (*g*) at the top of the hierarchy, several broad classes of abilities in the middle, and primary factors at the bottom.
42. When we evaluate factors, we must recognize that it is extremely difficult, if not impossible, to devise tests for *pure* factors or pure measures of ability.

43. Contemporary views of intelligence emphasize both biological and developmental influences. Genetically determined cognitive ability is always viewed as being modified by experience.
44. Measures of intelligence sample only a limited spectrum of intellectual ability, and the responses provided by individuals on intelligence tests are related to their unique learning histories.

KEY TERMS, CONCEPTS, AND NAMES

Crystallized intelligence (p. 140)
Carroll (p. 141)
Three-stratum factor analytic theory of cognitive abilities (p. 141)
Information-processing theory of intelligence (p. 143)
Campione (p. 143)
Brown (p. 143)
Borkowski (p. 143)
Architectural system (p. 145)
Capacity (p. 145)
Durability (p. 145)
Efficiency of operation (p. 145)
Executive system (p. 145)
Knowledge base (p. 145)
Schemes (p. 145)
Control processes (p. 145)
Metacognition (p. 145)
Sternberg (p. 146)
Triarchic theory of intelligence (p. 146)
Componential dimension (p. 146)
Metacomponents (p. 146)
Performance components (p. 146)
Knowledge acquisition components (p. 146)
Experiential dimension (p. 146)
Contextual dimension (p. 146)
Das (p. 146)
Naglieri (p. 146)
Kirby (p. 146)
PASS model of intelligence (p. 146)
Planning processes (p. 146)
Attentional processes (p. 146)
Simultaneous processing (p. 146)
Successive processing (p. 147)
Gardner (p. 147)
Multiple intelligence theory (p. 147)
Successful intelligence theory (p. 148)
Analytic abilities (p. 149)
Creative abilities (p. 149)
Practical abilities (p. 149)
Ceci (p. 149)
Bio-ecological theory of intelligence (p. 149)
Piaget (p. 150)
Developmental theory of intelligence (p. 150)

Organization (Piaget) (p. 150)
Schemes (Piaget) (p. 150)
Adaptation (Piaget) (p. 150)
Assimilation (Piaget) (p. 150)
Accommodation (Piaget) (p. 150)
Sensorimotor period (p. 151)
Primary circular reactions (p. 151)
Secondary circular reactions (p. 151)
Tertiary circular reactions (p. 151)
Preoperational period (p. 151)
Concrete operations period (p. 151)
Formal operations period (p. 151)

STUDY QUESTIONS

1. Compare and contrast work on intellectual assessment in the United States, Germany, France, and England during the 19th century and the early years of the 20th century.
2. Discuss Terman's contribution to the field of intelligence testing.
3. Discuss the contributions of Yerkes and Wechsler to the testing movement.
4. What effect did the Binet-Simon Scales have in the United States during the early 20th century?
5. Provide several definitions of intelligence. What commonalities and differences exist?
6. Compare and contrast the work of the following factor analytic theorists: Spearman, Thorndike, Thurstone, Guilford, Vernon, Cattell and Horn, and Carroll.
7. Discuss information-processing approaches to intelligence.
8. Discuss Sternberg's triarchic theory of intelligence.
9. Discuss Das, Naglieri, and Kirby's PASS theory of intelligence.
10. Discuss Gardner's multiple intelligence theory.
11. Discuss Ceci's bio-ecological theory of intelligence.
12. Discuss Sternberg's successful intelligence theory.
13. Discuss Piaget's developmental theory of intelligence.
14. What are some similarities and differences between Piagetian and psychometric approaches to intelligence?
15. What form will intelligence tests take in the future?

6

ISSUES RELATED TO THE MEASUREMENT AND CHANGE OF INTELLIGENCE

It is in connection with intelligence and the tests which measure it that some of the most violent polemics in psychology and in all the behavioral sciences have raged. These polemics have concerned the nature of man's intellectual capacities, how they should be measured, how mutable they are, and what the implication of the decisions on these issues should be for educating and improving the race.

—J. McVicker Hunt

Goals and Objectives

This chapter is designed to enable you to do the following:

- Describe the contribution of hereditary and environmental factors in intellectual functioning

- Discuss personality, social, and gender influences on intelligence

- Discuss the stability and change of intelligence

- Discuss the relationship between intellectual development and assessment

- Compare curriculum-based measurement and norm-referenced measurement

- Define MA (mental age) and discuss its limitations and usefulness

- Understand the relationship of reaction time to intelligence

- Discuss biological correlates of intelligence

- Describe the values and limitations of intelligence testing

The assessment of intelligence requires the ability to administer, score, and interpret tests; knowledge of variables associated with the measurement and change of intelligence; and knowledge of the social and political implications of the use of intelligence tests. An understanding of the issues discussed in this chapter will help you become a more effective clinician.

Wilson (1978b) succinctly described the importance of intelligence for the individual:

Among the capabilities of human beings, none is as distinctive nor as central to his or her adaptive potential as intelligence. It is tied to the recently evolved regions of the brain, particularly the association areas of the neocortex. It furnishes an enormous integrative capability by which the experiences of the past can be brought to bear adaptively on the problems of the present and the anticipations of the future. As a species characteristic, it progresses from the rudimentary sensorimotor coordinations of infancy to the abstract reasoning of the adult, and the transformation is so drastic that the line of continuity is inferential rather than direct. It is perhaps the most widely studied capability of man, and in recent years, by far the most controversial. (p. 940, with changes in notation)

Verbal ability, an important component of intelligence, is likely a complex collection of factors, dependent on such psychological processes as "access to lexical memory, the ability to manipulate information in working memory, rapid consolidation of information into long-term memory, the possession of knowledge about how to process discourse in general, and the possession of knowledge about the topic of the discourse being comprehended" (Hunt, E., 1987, p. 388). Some of these factors, Hunt suggests, are closely linked to underlying brain processes, such as efficiency of consolidation of information into long-term memory, whereas other factors are associated with exposure to learned material, such as possession of specific knowledge (e.g., names of the presidents of the United States).

RELATIONSHIP BETWEEN HUMAN INTELLIGENCE AND THE BRAIN

Intellectual activity appears to involve several regions of the brain, particularly when complex tasks are performed (Haier, 1990). In addition, different cognitive strategies may be primarily dependent on separate areas of the brain (e.g., frontal, temporal, parietal, or occipital) and on different combinations of areas (e.g., frontal plus temporal, frontal plus parietal, frontal plus occipital, or temporal plus parietal). With the advent of brain imaging technologies such as positron emission tomography (PET), we may be closer to answering questions about brain/intelligence relationships. Questions that are important to address include the following (Haier, 1990, adapted from p. 371):

1. What are the neural foundations of higher cognitive properties of the human cerebral cortex?
2. What essential properties of the brain give rise to conscious awareness?

3. Why is thinking easy for normal people and difficult for individuals with schizophrenia?
4. Given the degree of similarity between the human brain and those of other species, what makes humans unique?

Detterman (1994) also observed that there is a relationship between human intelligence and the brain and noted the value of measuring intelligence as well. He pointed out the following:

The average brain weighs approximately 3 to 4 pounds. It is composed of at least 100 billion neurons and many more supporting cells. Each neuron is composed of an axon and multiple dendrites. Neurons and supporting cells generate the neural transmitters and inhibitors that allow nerve cells to communicate with each other. The neural environment is further complicated by the effects of hormones and other agents produced in the brain and elsewhere. Over half of our 10,000 genes are thought to regulate nervous system development and functioning.

Now consider intelligence. There is no doubt that there is measurable variability in human intellectual ability. Research demonstrates that intelligence tests are highly reliable. If two versions of the same test are given within a short span of time (e.g., 2 months), the correlation between the test scores will be impressively high. Intelligence tests predict important things like number of years of schooling completed, school performance, and the scores on other tests of intelligence and achievement. The reasons for these correlations may be debatable, but the empirical fact of the correlations is indisputable. IQ tests correlate with other measures of mental functioning more highly than any other kind of psychological test correlates with other measures of its own kind. Even more impressive is the correlation of IQ tests with validity measures (e.g., around .50). Validity measures for IQ tests, as a group, are higher than for any other kind of psychological test. For example, personality tests don't correlate nearly as highly with appropriate personality validity indices as IQ tests correlate with appropriate intellectual validity indices. There is little doubt that it is possible to obtain both reliable and valid measures of intelligence. The important question is, what factors correlate with the development of intelligence? In other words, what roles do nature and nurture play in the expression of intelligence? (p. 35, with additions and changes in notation).

GENETIC PROGRAMMING, MATURATIONAL STATUS, AND ENVIRONMENTAL INFLUENCE

Genetic programming, maturational status, and environmental influence interact to affect the course of mental development (Wilson, 1978b). The genetic influence for many behaviors reflects a high degree of preorganization and priming laid down in the brain structure by evolution. Gene actions are likely to be associated with the growth patterns of various human behaviors, precocity, and deficits in developmental status. Distinctive cycles of gene action operate in conjunction with the maturational state of the child. A prominent feature of the epigenetic process (a process of continuous feedback and modulation that directs development toward specific targets, or end states) is individual differences in the rate of development and in the timing of particular phases. Thus, intellectual growth for any given child reflects the interaction of many complex factors (see Figure 6-1).

During the first 2 years of life, changes in maturational status affect mental development. In the first stages of infancy, primitive sensorimotor functions are the major components of mental development. Between ages 18 and 24 months, a significant transition occurs during which the child's symbolic functions are enhanced (also see the discussion of Piaget in Chapter 5). It is in this period that the child becomes able to draw on internalized memories of experience as an aid in comprehending present experiences.

Wilson (1978b) described the interaction of the genetic influences, maturational status, and the environment between ages 18 and 24 months in the following way:

… cognitive functions turn more toward the symbolizing and synthesizing functions that figure so prominently in the growth of intelligence.… The efficiency and scope of these symbolizing functions become a predictable attribute of each individual's mental status, and the variations in efficiency become translated into the normal distribution of intelligence. Such variations must ultimately have their roots in epigenetic processes that determine the integrative power of the brain. Within the normal range of environments, these processes unfold in accordance with the intrinsic scheduling of the genetic program, and it is at this level that the synchronies in mental development may be found. (p. 947)

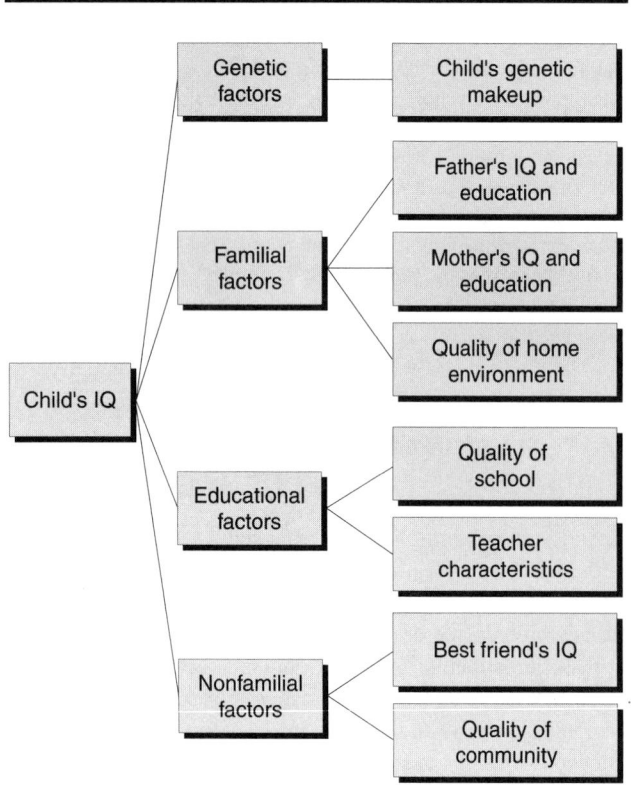

Figure 6-1. Some genetic and environmental factors that may influence a child's IQ. Adapted from Coon, Carey, and Fulker (1992).

INTELLECTUAL FUNCTIONING: HEREDITARY INFLUENCES

An estimate of the *heritability of a trait* describes the proportion of the variation of a trait in a given population that is attributable to genetic differences in that population. The degree of heritability ranges from 0% to 100%. A value of .50 for the heritability of IQ in a given population means that 50% of the observed variation in IQs in that population is attributable to genetic differences among the members of the population and 50% of the observed variation is attributable to other sources. A heritability estimate refers only to *population* variance in a trait; it is not applicable to an individual.

Children do not inherit an IQ. They inherit a collection of genes, called a *genotype,* that is related to intelligence. The expression of the genotype, called the *phenotype* (the observable performance of individuals), results from the interaction of the genotype with environmental experiences.

Genes set the upper and lower limits of the phenotype, but the environment determines where in this range intellectual functioning will fall. The current nature-nurture controversy is reducible to the single issue of how wide the range of reaction is. Those who favor environmental explanations argue for a wide reaction range of 50, 70, or even 100 IQ points. Those who emphasize genetic determinants assert that the reaction range within which environmental variables operate is more narrow, generally around 25 points. (Zigler & Farber, 1985, p. 400, with changes in notation)

Genotype exerts a significant influence on cognitive patterning and development. Genes, for example, program (a) the physiological mechanisms that control intellectual growth, (b) how stimuli are responded to, and (c) predispositions to learn certain things easily. Thus, for example, some children are better with verbal material and other children are better with spatial material. In addition, "The same genotype can manifest itself in different ways at different ages and the ultimate expression of the genotype may depend upon complex factors…" (Hay, 1999, p. 80). This means, for example, that young children with good spatial ability may excell at block building and when they reach adulthood they may excell at designing buildings.

A *polygenic model* is useful for understanding the heritability of intelligence. This model assumes that intelligence is a result of the combined action and influence of many genes rather than of a single gene. Techniques of biometrical genetics clearly indicate that intelligence is under polygenic inheritance (Hay, 1999).

Heritability estimates for human intelligence are obtained by examining the correlations between groups of individuals of different degrees of kinship, such as monozygotic twins (twins developing from a single egg, or identical twins) and dizygotic twins (twins developing from two eggs, or fraternal twins). Figures on heritability must remain *estimates* because we cannot perform experimental manipulations of human matings. The best estimate is that genetic variation appears to account for at least 50% of the individual differences in intelligence test scores, with the remainder attributed to environmental (or nongenetic) forces (Plomin & DeFries, 1980; Rodgers, Rowe, & May, 1994; Scarr, 1991). Examples of nongenetic influences are psychosocial factors (e.g., parenting styles), prenatal and postnatal biological factors (e.g., nutrition and illness), and nontransmissable DNA event factors (e.g., somatic mutations of DNA that occur in cells outside the gonads; Plomin & Petrill, 1997). Because 50% of the variation in general intellectual ability is *not* related to genetic influences, some degree of external or environmental control over the development of intelligence is possible.

There is considerable evidence that both general intelligence and specific intellectual abilities—such as verbal, spatial, numerical, and perceptual abilities—are under genetic influence (Loehlin, Horn, & Willerman, 1994). This means that genetically related family members show higher correlations in intelligence and in specific abilities than do genetically unrelated individuals who share the same family environments (see Table 6-1). In other words, the more similar people are genetically, the more highly related are their IQs. Table 6-1 also indicates that (a) the IQs of genetically related individuals reared apart are similar even though they do not share the same family environment, (b) the IQs of family members living together are more similar than those of adoptive family members who are not genetically related, and (c) the IQs of identical twins (monozygotic twins) are more similar than those of fraternal twins (dizygotic twins), whether the twins are reared together or apart (Plomin & Petrill, 1997).

Other research suggests that shared family environments appear to have a decreasing influence on intellectual functioning as children grow older (Loehlin, Horn, & Willerman,

Separated at birth, the Mallifert twins meet accidentally

© 2000 from cartoonbank.com. All Rights Reserved.

1989). In addition, "the genetic influence on intelligence becomes increasingly important throughout the life span… [with heritability increasing] from about 40% in childhood to about 60% in early adulthood to about 80% later in life" (Plomin & Petrill, 1997, p. 60). There is also ample evidence

Table 6-1
Summary of Family, Twin, and Adoption Studies Showing the Relationship Between IQs of Persons with Different Degrees of Relationship

Relationship	Degree of genetic relatedness	Degree of shared family environment	Correlation of IQs	Number of pairs
Identical twins reared together	100%	100%	.86	4,672
Identical twins reared apart	100%	0%	.76	158
Fraternal twins reared together	50%	100%	.55	8,600
Fraternal twins reared apart	50%	0%	.35	112
Biological siblings reared together	50%	100%	.47	26,473
Biological siblings reared apart	50%	0%	.24	203
Unrelated children reared together	0%	100%	.30	714
Parent and offspring living together	50%	100%	.42	—[a]
Parent and offspring living apart	50%	0%	.24	—[a]
Parent and adoptive child living together	0%	100%	.30	—[a]

[a]Not specified in Plomin and Petrill (1997).
Source: Adapted from Bouchard and McGue (1981), Scarr (1997a), and Plomin and Petrill (1997).

that during development (a) monozygotic twins come to be more similar than dizygotic twins from infancy on, (b) biological siblings appear more similar than adopted siblings, especially by the end of adolescence, (c) similarities between fraternal twins decline from infancy to adolescence, and (d) similarities between adopted siblings decline from infancy to adolescence (Scarr, 1991).

INTELLECTUAL FUNCTIONING: ENVIRONMENTAL INFLUENCES

What are the environmental variables that may play a role in the development of intelligence? In Figure 6-1, you saw some general ones. Now let's look at specific environmental factors that are likely to enhance the development of intelligence (Spitz, 1996, adapted from pp. 176–177):

- Access to stimulating or enriching experiences
- Adult-assisted consolidation and extension of new skills
- Adult-assisted exploration
- Adult-assisted teaching of basic skills
- Positive reinforcement by adults
- Caregivers who help the child learn problem-solving skills
- Cultural beliefs that foster learning, problem solving, and acquisition of knowledge
- Access to sources of knowledge
- Open exploration
- Good medical care
- Accomplished mentors
- Good nutrition
- Parental involvement in the child's learning and education
- Parents who believe in the importance of stimulation and learning
- Parents with a good education
- A high level of caregiving
- A high level of social support
- Minimal noise level
- Minimal environmental crowding
- Rich, responsive language environment
- Secure attachment to a caregiver
- Good social and physical settings
- Good school attendance
- Schools that foster achievement expectancy
- Stable neighborhoods

These variables are unlikely to work in isolation; they interact (or covary) with genetic and other environmental variables. Let's now consider some of these variables and related issues in more detail.

Perinatal and Early Developmental Influences on Intelligence

Considerable research has stemmed from interest in the effects of perinatal factors on intellectual functioning in children. *Perinatal factors* include prenatal variables (e.g., abnormal fetus, prenatal stress or injury); general birth process variables (e.g., abnormal delivery, instrument delivery, delivery difficulties); and neonatal variables (e.g., brain damage, hemorrhage, other physical malfunctions in the neonate). Related, too, are factors affecting the mother during pregnancy, including illness, weight gain, blood pressure, smoking, drugs, alcohol, anxiety, pelvic abnormalities, and complications from previous pregnancies.

The weight of an infant at birth is an important variable that reflects intrauterine growth. Difficulties occurring during intrauterine life can lead to a reduction in potential for intellectual and physical development. Low birth weight (a weight of less than 2,500 grams, or 5.50 lb) and very low birth weight (defined as a weight of less than 1,500 grams, or 3.30 lb) may be associated with intrauterine difficulties and represent an increased risk factor. Maternal factors associated with low or very low birth weight include low socioeconomic status (SES), extremes of maternal age, short stature, cigarette smoking, the presence of certain pathologic states (e.g., hypertension, renal disease, uncontrolled diabetes), and low maternal weight gain during pregnancy.

Advances in medical care have dramatically improved the survival rate of very low birth weight children. At school age, the intelligence test scores and achievement test scores of very low birth weight children tend to be lower than those of normal birth weight children (Hack, Breslau, Aram, Weissman, Klein, & Borawski-Clark, 1992; Klein, Hack, & Breslau, 1989). Very low birth weight children also tend to have more difficulties in visuomotor and fine-motor functions, expressive language, and memory and exhibit more hyperactive behavior than normal birth weight children. Although the precise reasons are not clear, the biological factors that place these children at risk include a wide range of prenatal conditions, birth complications, and neonatal diseases. In addition, because very low birth weight children frequently come from lower socioeconomic status homes, lower social status appears to be an additional risk factor.

Research suggests that the effects of perinatal stress on intellectual functioning are small. Early biological insult may affect subsequent intellectual functioning, but present instruments are not sufficiently sensitive to detect measurable differences in intelligence between normal children and those who experienced perinatal stress.

Nutrition and Intelligence

Vulnerability to malnutrition is greatest during the 40 weeks of gestation and the first few years after birth, the most critical periods in the growth of brain tissue. Nutritional stress can lead to learning difficulties by affecting the central nervous system (Lozoff, 1989). Malnutrition may prevent the expression of the full genetic potential for mental development and interfere with concentration, motivation, social interaction, and time required for learning. Nutritional inadequacy also increases the risk of infection and interferes with immune mechanisms.

Inadequate amounts of vitamins and minerals may lead to lower intellectual functioning in children (Eysenck & Schoenthaler, 1997). Supplementing children's diets with vitamins and minerals has been found to raise children's nonverbal IQs by an average of about 9 points, but does not affect verbal IQs. The positive effects of vitamin and mineral supplementation appear to be greatest for young children who have dietary deficiencies, with little effect beyond the teenage years. In technologically advanced countries, however, nutritional variables do not appear to be substantially related to intelligence (Brody, 1992).

Family Background, Home Environmental Variables, and Intelligence

Many studies have demonstrated that psychosocial factors in the home play an important role in the development of children's intelligence (Hanson, 1975; Marjoribanks, 1972; McCall, Appelbaum, & Hogarty, 1973; Mercy & Steelman, 1982; Sameroff, Seifer, Baldwin, & Baldwin, 1993; Wilson, 1983; Wolf, 1966). These factors include (a) the intellectual environment of the home (such as the quality of language models available, opportunities for enlarging vocabulary, feedback about appropriate language usage, and opportunities for language practice), (b) stimulation in the home (such as pressures for achievement, activity, intellectuality, and independence), (c) type of punishment regime (such as very severe or very mild), and (d) the presence of family risk factors (such as parental unemployment, limited maternal education, authoritarian parental attitudes, rigid maternal behavior, father's absence from home, and large family size). The results of these studies indicate that family background and home environmental variables are significantly correlated with children's IQ, with many of the correlations being above $r = .50$.

The correlation between a family's socioeconomic status and children's intelligence test scores is on average about .33 (Bouchard & Segal, 1985). In the WISC–III standardization sample, mean parental education was the most powerful predictor of IQs (Vanderploeg, Schinka, Baum, Tremont, & Mittenberg, 1998). Pointing out that variables such as the parents' level of education tap parental heredity, not just environmental factors, Bouchard and Segal hypothesized that two-thirds to three-fourths of the average IQ differences between children in the various social classes are genetic in origin. Home environmental factors, however, may not be independent of family background characteristics. Measures of pressure for achievement, motivation, and language development and provisions for general learning, for example, may serve as surrogate measures of parental IQ and education. In addition, home environment measures may be related to the genetic makeup of parents.

Overall, research on the relationship between the home environment and intelligence test scores suggests that the home environment has an important influence on the early intellectual development of children but plays only a minor role in the intellectual development of postadolescents (Brody, 1992). Thus, family environmental influences "may fade and be of diminishing importance for mature intellectual development" (Brody, 1992, p. 173).

Poverty and Intelligence

Research indicates that persistent poverty has more detrimental effects on children's intelligence test scores and school achievement than does transitory poverty (McLoyd, 1998). Reasons for diminished cognitive functioning in poor children include high rates of perinatal complications, reduced access to health-promoting resources, increased exposure to lead, and inadequate home-based cognitive stimulation. "These factors, along with lower teacher expectancies and poorer academic-readiness skills, also appear to contribute to lower levels of school achievement among poor children" (McLoyd, 1998, p. 185). Some research indicates that 5-year-olds in chronic poverty obtain IQs that are about 9 points lower than those of nonpoor children (Duncan, Brooks-Gunn, & Klebanov, 1994).

Family Configuration and Intelligence

Zajonc (1976) proposed a *confluence model* to account for the effect of family configuration on intellectual development. The model relates intellectual development to several family configuration variables, including birth order, family size, and sibling birth intervals. The model postulates that the intellectual environment to which the child is exposed mediates cognitive development. Specifically, it proposes that family size is negatively correlated with IQ, and that later-born children in large families frequently obtain lower intelligence test scores than earlier-born children. Zajonc hypothesized that a large family provides a less stimulating intellectual environment than does a small family. However, the model explains only a very small amount of the total variance in IQ. One of the difficulties in interpreting research on birth order is that larger families tend to come from lower socioeconomic classes and it may be difficult to control for the effects of socioeconomic status (Bouchard & Segal, 1985).

Malleability and Change in Intelligence

Schooling and intelligence. Inequality of schooling plays a minor role in individual differences in IQ. Research suggests that between 2% and 10% of the variance in cognitive functioning may be associated with school quality (Bouchard & Segal, 1985). The high correlation between years of schooling completed and IQ (r = .69) may indicate that bright individuals continue in school; it may also mean that schooling increases IQ. Few studies have addressed these issues. The evidence suggests, however, that each extra year of education adds about 1 point to the expected adult IQ of the individual.

Preschool enrichment programs are designed to modify the course of early development so that the child with social disadvantages will be better prepared for public school. A meta-analysis of 72 studies involving Head Start programs indicated that, at the conclusion of the program, children in the program had higher IQs than children who were not in the program, as well as gains on readiness and achievement measures (U.S. Department of Health and Human Services, 1985). However, 2 years after the program's conclusion, there were no educationally meaningful differences between children who had attended Head Start and those who had not. Parents of Head Start children saw the program as benefiting the children as well as themselves, and many parents participated in the program. Children whose parents were highly involved in the program tended to perform better on cognitive tests than children whose parents were less involved. With respect to child-rearing practices and attitudes toward the value of education, few, if any, meaningful differences were noted between parents whose children were enrolled in Head Start and those whose children were not. Other research on preschool intervention suggests "that preschool interventions cannot eliminate differences in academic and intellectual performance associated with variations of parental and demographic characteristics of children" (Brody, 1997, p. 326).

Although the long-term influences of preschool programs on intellectual functioning do not appear to be large, preschool enrichment programs may change achievement orientation, school competence, educational attainment, and career accomplishments. In addition, small overall differences may reflect large differences for given individual children—some children are significantly influenced by such programs. Unfortunately, because the data regarding the effectiveness of preschool enrichment programs are subject to several different interpretations, firm conclusions cannot be drawn about the impact of the programs on children's later intellectual development. Research on attempts to increase general intelligence in school-age populations suggests that changes in IQ are relatively small—generally about 7.5 points or less (Brody, 1992). Furthermore, "there is no evidence that general intelligence can be substantially changed as a result of experimental interventions" (Brody, 1992, p. 186).

We also need to consider, however, that the results of efforts to improve human intelligence and thinking may not be measured by traditional intelligence tests. There is ample research to suggest that some aspects of intelligent behavior can be taught, at least to a limited extent (Perkins & Grotzer, 1997). Effective interventions help individuals (a) reorganize how they approach cognitive tasks and (b) make more effective use of their abilities. What is needed is more research to determine the best methods for enhancing intelligence, and

the extent to which these methods can enhance intellectual functioning.

Malleability of intelligence judged from adoption studies. Adoption studies provide a useful way of studying the malleability of intelligence—the capacity for change. Although the variables used in adoption studies are difficult to control (e.g., who is put up for adoption, who is adopted, and who is studied), reasonable estimates of the malleability of intelligence suggest that the adoptive environment can produce about a 10- to 12-point IQ gain (for children adopted into favorable environments) or loss (for children adopted into unfavorable environments; Locurto, 1990). Locurto concluded that "*there appear to be limits in the extent to which even the most substantial environmental changes can affect IQ*" (p. 290). Overall, the biological background of adopted children is clearly more important in determining the IQs of older children than the characteristics of the adoptive families (Brody, 1992).

Generational increases in intelligence. In several economically advanced nations, the intelligence of the population has increased by approximately 15 points between 1940 and 1990, or by about 3 IQ points per decade (Lynn, 1987, 1990). Lynn proposes that environmental improvements account in part for the rise in intelligence test scores. These improvements include better nutrition and health, smaller families, provision of more nursery education, and greater availability of cognitively stimulating toys, board games, computer games, books, radio, and television. Lynn (1990) suggests that "nutrition is a more important determinant of intelligence than is generally supposed" (p. 282). Increases in intelligence parallel increases in height and weight. Improvements in nutrition have led to increases in brain size and probably to improvements in the brain's neurological development and functional efficiency.

Flynn (1987), however, argues that the apparent increases in intelligence represent only the populations' improved ability to take intelligence tests. Emanuelsson and Svensson (1990) suggest that improved educational opportunities may partly account for the increase in IQs. What is not in dispute is the rise in intelligence tests scores over the period. And, according to Brody (1992), the changes in secular intelligence reported by Lynn remain mysterious: Although "nutrition and educational changes may be responsible, we have no explanation for these changes that is not speculative" (p. 196). Therefore, we need further research to determine the most reasonable explanation to account for the rise in IQs.

COMMENT ON HEREDITARY AND ENVIRONMENTAL INFLUENCES ON INTELLECTUAL FUNCTIONING

Although heredity sets limits on a child's potential, it is the environment that permits that potential to be actualized. Heredity does not set the final limits on human intelligence because intelligence is always expressed in an environment that either promotes or restricts intellectual development. Consequently, researchers should try to determine which environmental factors—such as nutrition, educational systems, home environments, and personal experiences—nurture or impede intellectual development. We should then develop strategies that will best enhance children's cognitive functioning. Environmental interventions that produce significant changes in intelligence, however, are likely to be complex, time consuming, and costly.

Although intelligence is malleable to some extent, it is difficult to change (Brody, 1997). Furthermore, "individual differences in IQ influence the individual's encounters with the environment and help to shape and define that environment.... Intelligence is not defined solely by the social world we encounter—it defines the intellectual world we create for ourselves" (p. 328). Overall "there is little evidence that any single source of environmental influence is highly correlated with IQ. Variables as diverse as exposure to lead in air and water supplies, quality and quantity of schooling, and birth order may each exert a small but discernible influence on intelligence. It may be difficult to increase scores on intelligence tests because the environmental influences on tests are diverse" (Brody, 1992, p. 214).

Intelligence develops within a cultural context, and cultures differ in how they value mental abilities (Hunt, 1997). For example, the inability to read is a substantial problem for individuals in our culture but not for those in a nonliterate society. Intelligent behavior depends partly on acquired knowledge. Acquired knowledge is influenced by the way a culture stores and transmits knowledge and how individuals in that culture extract information from their environment.

Hunt (1997) also pointed out that

Genetics counts.... Twin, kinship, and adoption studies have more than proven the point that genetic variance in intelligence is substantial. It is not clear why we need to tie down the numbers to the second or third decimal point.

What we do need to do is to go beyond statistics to investigate the mechanisms of genetic action, including the interaction between genetic predisposition and the environment. No one inherits a genetic compulsion to watch television or innate knowledge of the answers to intelligence-test questions. We inherit blueprints for constructing proteins; all else follows from interactions! What we need to do is to understand the causal pathways, at both the molecular genetics and the psychological-social ends of the continuum between genes and behavior. (p. 549)

There is some evidence that the genetic effect on intelligence test scores is larger in more stimulating environments (such as are found in middle and upper social classes) and smaller in less stimulating environments (such as are found in the working class; Fischbein, 1980). Fischbein hypothesized that, although it seems paradoxical, "equality of opportunity, with optimal stimulation for everyone, might lead to a greater proportion of genetic variance in intelligence test score differences" (p. 61). And Brody (1997) noted, "As

Western societies become more egalitarian in providing greater opportunity for individuals to be exposed to adequate schooling, individual differences in the ability to profit from those exposures will increasingly determine the intellectual accomplishments of individuals" (p. 328).

A heritability index of .50 for intellectual ability does not mean that genetic and nongenetic factors make an equal contribution to the intellectual ability of every child at every intelligence level (McCall, 1994). Very poor environments, for example, may exert a disproportionately depressing effect on a child's genetic potential for intellectual ability. Also, home environments likely change over the course of a child's development and are not the same for all children in the family. Each child in the family likely experiences a unique combination of particular environments throughout his or her development.

An individual's score on an intelligence test does not permit us to make inferences about either genetic influences (the biological substrate) or environmental influences (the psychosocial substrate; Humphreys, 1971). The independent contributions of these two components are impossible to assess in the individual case. Intelligence tests measure acquired behavior and yield an estimate of a child's current level of performance (or observed behavior). It is impossible to make inferences from this level of behavior to another level, termed "innate potential." *We cannot observe potential—all we can observe is actual behavior.* Furthermore, performance on any test reflects the complex and pervasive cumulative effects of education and upbringing. One cannot abstract an index or estimate of innate potential from the child's interactions with the environment or from something measurable in the child's behavior. In the assessment situation, the focus is on what the child can or cannot do—not on the child's innate potential.

That there are genetic and environmental substrates for intelligence does not mean that a child's intelligence is fixed and unchangeable (Humphreys & Davey, 1988).

In fact, the genetic and environmental substrates for intelligence provide for change, not for stability. It is widely assumed that the genetic substrate is polygenic. The many genes involved do not express themselves simultaneously at the moment of conception to produce a unitary entity. Instead, it is probable that the multiple genes express themselves at different times during development, and do so independently. The environmental substrate is also a complex of many determinants that impinge on the organism at various times during development. There is little basis in either substrate for the conception of intelligence as a stable entity. (pp. 191–192, with changes in notation)

INTELLECTUAL FUNCTIONING: PERSONALITY AND GENDER INFLUENCES

Research suggests that there are developmental trends in the personality patterns of children and adults who show increases in IQ (McCall, Appelbaum, & Hogarty, 1973).

Gains in IQ are associated with independence and competitiveness during the preschool years; with independence, scholastic competitiveness, self-initiation, and problem-solving approaches during the elementary school years; and with interpersonal distance, coldness, and introversion during adulthood. "These shifts may reflect the changing sources of educational experiences and motivation for intellectual achievement beginning with the family, then the competition with peers at school, and finally the self-education and intrinsic motivations that characterize maturity" (McCall et al., 1973, p. 71).

Research on gender differences in cognitive ability points to the following conclusions (Hyde & McKinley, 1997):

1. *Verbal ability.* Gender differences in general verbal ability are essentially nonexistent. However, gender differences may exist within particular verbal abilities; for example, males have more reading and stuttering difficulties than females.

2. *Mathematical ability.* Gender differences in mathematical ability are essentially nonexistent. Developmentally, girls tend to be somewhat better than boys at computations in both elementary school and middle school, but not in high school. At any age, there is no gender difference in the understanding of mathematical concepts. "Finally, in terms of problem solving, there is no gender difference in elementary school or middle school, but there is a small-to-moderate difference favoring boys in high school and men during the college years" (p. 35).

3. *Spatial ability.* Gender differences exist in two of three types of spatial ability. Males have better spatial perception ability than females (e.g., sensing positions of horizontality or verticality) and better mental rotation ability (e.g., rotating mentally a three-dimensional object depicted in two dimensions). However, males and females have similar spatial visualization ability (e.g., locating a simple figure within a complex one).

4. *Variability in performance.* The genders differ in variability of performance. Males show more variable performance than females on some tests of general knowledge, quantitative ability, spatial ability, and spelling, but not on other types of cognitive tests.

5. *Temporal changes.* Gender differences in cognitive ability decreased between 1960 and 1990. Although the reasons for the decline are not clear, possible reasons include methodological artifacts and socialization practices.

STABILITY AND CHANGE OF INTELLIGENCE

The stability of IQs through childhood and adolescence depends on measurement factors, genetic factors, and environmental factors. We will now consider how each of these factors relates to *IQ constancy*—the extent to which IQs remain consistent from one age to another. Constancy refers to the amount of change found in test scores when the test is repeated after an interval, such as 6 months or more.

Measurement Factors and Their Effect on IQ Constancy

The measurement factors that affect a child's initial test scores also affect subsequent test scores. These factors include the following:

- Types of test items
- Placement of test items
- Time interval between the original test and the retest
- The way the tests are administered and scored
- Situational factors (e.g., rapport, fatigue, physical well-being, attitude, motivation, attention span, frustration tolerance, self-confidence, level of aspiration, anxiety, and reaction to failure)
- Test-taking experience (e.g., differential exposure to practice and coaching)

Additionally, when you use a different test for the retest, any changes in scores may simply be due to differences between the tests. The tendency of extreme scores to regress toward the mean also affects the stability of test scores (see Chapter 4).

Test-retest correlations tend to be lower with increasing time intervals between measurements. Thus, test-retest correlations obtained after a 3-year interval tend to be lower than those obtained after a 2-month interval. Correlations between childhood IQs and adulthood IQs show more stability as children develop (Plomin, DeFries, & Fulker, 1988). For example, correlations between children's IQs and their adult IQs are about .25 if the first test is taken at 1 year of age, .40 if at 2 years of age, and about .60 if at 3 years of age.

Gains on retest are likely to be larger on performance items than on verbal items because examinees can develop a set of problem-solving strategies that they can apply to the same or similar problems. A child may solve puzzles and block designs, for example, more easily on a repeated administration because he or she is familiar with the materials and can use problem-solving strategies that proved successful previously. Another factor that may contribute to changes in test scores is speed of responding. Many tests are timed, and bonus points are awarded for giving correct answers quickly, which probably increases practice effects.

Genetic Factors and Their Effect on IQ Constancy

Changes in IQ may be related to genetically based developmental trends. Some children have a continuous growth pattern, others have spurts and pauses, and still others have a discontinuous curve.

Environmental Factors and Their Effect on IQ Constancy

Environmental factors contribute to fluctuations in intelligence in two ways. First, physical and emotional factors (e.g., physical illness, emotional trauma, or separation from parents), often transitory in nature, may affect a child's test performance. Second, changes in cognitive stimulation or motivation may alter the child's level of performance.

Prediction of Intelligence from Infant Tests

Tests designed for infants assess sensorimotor functions primarily and do not appear to be measuring the same factors that are measured by tests given to preschool and older children. As the content of tests changes with age, shifting from perceptual-motor to more cognitively oriented functions, the tests become better predictors of intelligence (Humphreys & Davey, 1988). Thus, infant tests cover a period in which important qualitative changes occur in children's development. One difficulty in obtaining reliable scores from infants is their proneness to developmental spurts and lags.

Humphreys and Davey (1988) analyzed the intercorrelations from the Louisville Twin Project (Wilson, 1983), which were based on developmental test scores (Bayley Scales of Infant Development) and intelligence test scores (Stanford-Binet Intelligence Scale: Form L-M, McCarthy Scales of Children's Abilities, and the Wechsler Intelligence Scale for Children–Revised) obtained from twins from 3 months of age to 15 years of age. The investigators drew the following conclusions from their analyses:

1. Changes in intelligence appear to be smooth and continuous, beginning at 12 months of age.
2. Even though intelligence shows a degree of stability during the school years, on a long-term basis a great deal of change is possible in a child's intelligence test scores.
3. For tests given between 12 months and 9 years of age, developmental measures and intelligence tests appear to be measuring a general intelligence factor. (Data about trends in ages after 9 years were not available, but it is likely that the same trends hold at later years.)
4. Change in intellectual development is more rapid during the preschool years than during the school years. This may be due to the rapid increase of the preschool child's repertoire of knowledge and new additions to the repertoire that may not be correlated with the previous knowledge base. These factors can lead to increased performance on intelligence test measures.

To say that scores on infant and toddler developmental tests bear no relationship to intelligence test scores obtained in childhood is an overstatement. Although for normal children correlations are low and not adequate for clinical application, they do attain statistical significance at certain ages, especially after the age of 18 months (see Table 6-2).

Table 6-2
Median Correlations Across Studies Between Infant Test Scores and Childhood IQ

Age at childhood test (years)	Age at infant test (months)				Overall
	1 to 6	7 to 12	13 to 18	19 to 30	
8 to 18	.06	.25	.32	.49	.28
5 to 7	.09	.20	.34	.39	.25
3 to 4	.21	.32	.50	.59	.40
	.12	.26	.39	.49	

Note. Decimal entries indicate median correlation. Marginal values indicate the average of the median r's presented in that row/column. Median r's were based on 3 to 34 different r's and were obtained from 3 to 12 studies.
Source: Adapted from McCall (1979).

Wilson (1978a) conducted a longitudinal study of children tested at 3, 6, 9, 12, 18, and 24 months with the Bayley Scales and at 3 years with the Stanford-Binet: Form L-M. The results indicated that the correlations increased in size as the children became older (see Table 6-3). The highest correlations were between 24 and 36 months of age ($r = .73$). The pattern of correlations, Wilson explained, was coherent and orderly. Additionally, the substantial gain in predictive power at 18 months suggested "an emerging dimension of cognitive functioning that becomes more fully operative with age, but that is only modestly related to earlier functions" (Wilson,

Table 6-3
Intercorrelations Between Mental Development Scores at Ages 3 Months to 36 Months

Months	Months						
	3	6	9	12	18	24	36
3		.57	.44	.44	.37	.22	.20
6			.58	.53	.42	.25	.26
9				.57	.43	.30	.34
12					.55	.43	.38
18						.61	.57
24							.73

Note. N is between 177 and 335 for each correlation.
Source: Reprinted, with a change in notation, from R. S. Wilson, "Sensorimotor and Cognitive Development," in F. D. Minifie and L. L. Lloyd (Eds.), *Communicative and Cognitive Abilities—Early Behavioral Assessment* (Baltimore, MD: University Park Press, 1978), p. 138. Copyright 1978 by University Park Press.

1978a, p. 138). In addition, a study of 152 children in the Rochester Longitudinal Study found that Verbal Scale IQs on the WPPSI at age 4 years were highly similar ($r = .72$) with those obtained by the children on the WISC–R at 13 years (Sameroff, Seifer, Baldwin, & Baldwin, 1993).

Predictive power of infant tests for children with developmental disabilities. Infant Developmental Quotients that fall in the average or superior range have less predictive power than do those at very low levels. Willerman and Fiedler (1977), for example, found that infant developmental scores did not predict the unusual intellectual achievements of a group of gifted children tested at 4 and 7 years of age. The picture changes dramatically, though, for infants who have been identified as having a developmental disability. For such children, correlations between infant test scores and childhood IQs are much higher, ranging in some studies from $r = .50$ to .97 (Broman & Nichols, 1975; Brooks-Gunn & Lewis, 1983; Fishler, Graliker, & Koch, 1965; Fishman & Palkes, 1974; Illingworth & Birch, 1959; Keogh & Kopp, 1978; Knobloch & Pasamanick, 1960; VanderVeer & Schweid, 1974; Werner, Honzik, & Smith, 1968). For example, infants with serious developmental handicaps (such as Down syndrome or a major congenital malformation) who have below-average scores on infant tests during their first 20 months of life are likely to obtain low IQs at later periods of development. A majority (73%) of infants who were moderately to profoundly retarded, as assessed by the Bayley Scales, were still classified as severely retarded 1 to 3 years after the initial assessment (Brooks-Gunn & Lewis, 1983). Infants who score in mentally retarded ranges on developmental scales during their first year of life have a high probability of obtaining scores in the mentally retarded range during their school years. Infants with very low Developmental Quotients (e.g., 25 or lower) are likely to remain severely incapacitated.

The above findings are based on groups. *In assessing individuals, it is imperative that you never make a diagnosis of mental retardation based on a single test score in infancy (or at any age).* Despite the high correlations for infants who initially score in the developmentally disabled range, infants who are slow at an early age may gain rapidly at subsequent ages. Consequently, before making a diagnosis you should always retest a child who was identified as having a disability as an infant. It is also prudent to be conservative in making predictions from very high scores.

Relationship of Visual Novelty Preference During Infancy to Later Intelligence

A moderate relationship (*Mdn r* = .45) exists between measures of information processing in infancy—namely, visual recognition memory—and measures of intellectual ability in childhood, at least up to the age of 12 years (Fagan 1984a, 1984b; Fagan & Singer, 1983; McCall, 1994; McCall & Mash, 1995; Rose & Feldman, 1995; Rose, Feldman, Wallace, & Cohen, 1991). In recognition memory tasks given to infants, the infants must recognize the recurrence of a specific pattern. During the initial presentation of the stimulus, infants likely form a mental representation of the stimulus. When subsequent stimuli are shown to infants, the stimuli are judged in terms of their similarity to the mental representation. Infants with higher novelty scores—that is, those who spend more time looking at a novel stimulus—tend to have higher IQs in later childhood than those who spend less time looking. However, measures of infant recognition memory are not necessarily stable, with an estimated reliability of about .40 (Brody, 1992).

The visual novelty performance tasks require several types of information processes—including encoding, cortical representation, discrimination of features, and judgments of similarity—that are important in recognizing class or category membership. Performance on these tasks appears to represent a type of information processing—"that is, the ability to encode the familiar stimulus, remember it, compare a presented stimulus with the remembered engram, recognize the familiar stimulus when it is represented, discriminate a new stimulus from the familiar or engram, and encode the new stimulus into memory" (McCall & Carriger, 1993, pp. 76–77).

McCall (1994) hypothesized that the ability of infants to inhibit attention to, or disengage from, less salient stimuli might be crucial to the prediction of later IQ. Furthermore, the concept of inhibition also appears to play a role in the cognitive development of children, as well as of adults. Mature intelligence involves the ability to inhibit attending to information that is irrelevant to the solution of a problem. Processing speed (such as speed of encoding) may also be included in both infant measures of development and measures of intelligence at later ages (Rose & Feldman, 1995). This line of research then suggests "that some of the basic mechanisms subserving general intellectual ability have their origin in infant capabilities" (Rose et al., 1991, p. 804). It also suggests that one reason for the relatively weak predictive power of infant intelligence measures may be that we are not measuring the intellectual skills in infants that best predict later intellectual development.

IQs as Predictors of Adult Educational and Occupational Success

Research has also focused on the relationship between childhood IQs and later occupational success. McCall (1977), for example, reported that IQs obtained for a sample of children between 3 and 18 years of age were significant predictors of educational and occupational status at 26 years of age and older. The correlations between IQ and attained educational and occupational success rose until 7 to 8 years of age and remained stable thereafter at about $r = .50$. IQs obtained from children as young as 5 years correlated moderately with adult IQs ($r = .50$ and higher). Research with adults indicates that intelligence test scores are a reasonably good predictor of job performance in many different occupations, with an estimated $r = .53$ based on 400 studies (Hunter & Hunter, 1984). A review of military databases totaling 82,000 trainees found an average correlation of $r = .63$ between intellectual ability and job training performance (Hunter, 1986).

Comment on Stability and Change of Intelligence

The constancy of the IQ is influenced by the age of the child at initial testing and by the length of the interval between the test and the retest. *The older the child is when first tested and the shorter the interval is between tests, the greater the constancy of the IQ.* Infant scales have limited predictive power, except for children who have been identified as having a disability, because the items the scales contain are primarily of a perceptual-motor nature. Preschool intelligence tests have more content reflecting cognitive ability and therefore have greater predictive value. Intelligence test scores of school-aged children show even more stable correlations with scores obtained after 5 years of age and those obtained in adulthood. Generally, IQs obtained *before* 5 years of age have to be interpreted cautiously. When a child is 5 years old or older, however, his or her IQ tends to remain relatively stable, although individual fluctuations may be great. Additionally, children with high IQs tend to show more change than do children with low IQs (McCall et al., 1973).

Although their test scores may fluctuate, most children tend to retain a similar position relative to their age group. The IQ of any given child may change by as much as 20 points, but for most children measured intelligence remains relatively stable after 5 years of age (Zigler, Balla, & Hodapp, 1984). *Despite high test-retest correlations, we must conduct frequent and periodic testing if we are going to use test scores for guidance or placement decisions.* There is sufficient variability in individual growth patterns to warrant evaluation any time you need to make decisions about a child.

IQs tend to remain relatively constant because of (a) the invariance of genetic factors, (b) the relative stability of the environment for any particular individual, (c) developmental irreversibility (current developmental status exerts a strong influence on future development), and (d) the overlap of abilities measured by intelligence tests at different ages (Ausubel, Novak, & Hanesian, 1978). Any long-term predictions must take into account that unassessed traits or unpredictable future circumstances may radically alter the course of an individual's intellectual development. *You must use ex-* *treme caution in predicting a child's future level of intellectual functioning.*

RELATIONSHIP BETWEEN INTELLECTUAL DEVELOPMENT AND ASSESSMENT

The following propositions, based on research, are useful in understanding the relationship between intellectual development and assessment (Brody, 1992; Horn, 1998; Scarr, 1991, 1997b; Siegler & Richards, 1982; Sternberg, 1990).

1. *Various forces play different roles at different points in children's intellectual development.* During early development, infants are passive and biology plays a major role in determining their behavior. However, infants also engage in behaviors that elicit feedback from others. Infants, as well as older children, have different behavioral characteristics that will evoke different sets of responses from others during their development. All individuals selectively attend to and learn from their environment, with selections that are partially genetically based.

2. *As young children develop, (a) parental influence wanes, (b) contacts with others assume greater importance, (c) they have a greater voice in selecting their own experiences, (d) their behavior continues to elicit feedback from others, and (e) the environment influences them differently.*

3. *There is increasing differentiation of abilities with age—that is, the number of abilities and factors influencing behavior increases with age.* Thus, "abstract or symbol intelligence changes in its organization as age increases from a fairly unified and general ability to a loosely organized group of abilities or factors" (Garrett, 1946, p. 373).

4. *The way in which genetic and environmental influences combine to affect intelligence changes over an individual's life.* In other words, IQ is not a measure of the same construct at all points in a person's life.

5. *The structure of intelligence remains stable across development, but the content that fills in this structure changes.* Thus, there may be a single general type of intelligence at preschool ages and during adolescence, but this intelligence may be perceptual-motor in nature at the early level and involve abstract reasoning at the older level.

6. *The amount of information acquired during development increases with age—that is, the absolute level of intelligence increases during development.* This type of intelligence increases fairly rapidly until early adolescence, increases less rapidly from early to middle adolescence, and then levels off during middle to late adolescence. In adulthood, fluid intelligence (also referred to as fluid reasoning or *Gf*), short-term memory (*Gsm*), and processing speed (*Gs*) decline with age, whereas crystallized intelligence (also referred to as acculturation knowledge or *Gc*) and long-term storage and retrieval (*Glr*) may show little decline with age or even increase with

age. Age-related declines may be associated with physiological changes in the brain, including a loss of brain tissue. Thus, although some abilities deteriorate with advancing age, there is learning and consolidation of other abilities.

7. *Overall, development is determined by interactions between environmental stimuli and children's inherent predispositions.* Children determine their own experiences by both selecting and eliciting reactions from environmental stimuli, but children "vary in their susceptibility to environmental events and contingencies" (Scarr, 1991, p. 70). In addition, the intellectual skills that children develop depend on their cultural experiences.

8. *When children have equal opportunities to learn, individual differences in learning are likely to be associated with individual genetic variation.*

9. *When children do not have equal opportunities to learn, individual differences in learning are likely to be associated with differences in opportunities to learn.*

10. *Reliable quantitative measurements of children's general intelligence can be obtained from at least 4 or 5 years onward.* For children of these ages, measures of general intelligence possess considerable stability over a period of several years. The stability of IQ increases with age and decreases with the length of the interval between the tests.

11. *Quantitative measurements of intelligence accurately predict children's future performance in school.* Again, predictive accuracy increases with age and decreases with the length of the interval between the initial test and the eventual outcome measure.

12. *Children's use of logical reasoning skills is influenced by factors other than understanding of the logic itself.* These factors include memory, linguistic understanding, and ability to select the appropriate representation for the problem.

MENTAL AGE

We can think of *mental age* as a developmental measure that indicates the child's level of cognitive functioning. We can also conceive of it as a level of achievement, which may indicate a child's readiness to learn, and a level of cerebral development (Jensen, 1979).

MA Defined

Mental age (MA) divided by chronological age (CA) and multiplied by 100 produces the ratio IQ, used on the 1916 and 1937 versions of the Stanford-Binet Intelligence Scale and on other tests as well. The MA provides an age-equivalent for the child's raw score, whereas the IQ indicates a child's performance relative to children who are at his or her own chronological age. We can define MA as the degree of general mental ability possessed by the average child of a chronological age corresponding to the MA score. For example, we can view a child who receives an MA score of 6 as having general mental ability of an average 6-year-old child.

Limitations of MA Scores

Chapter 4 discussed the limitations of MA scores and test-age equivalent scores from a statistical viewpoint; this section discusses other considerations. First, differences between MA units are not the same throughout the developmental period because mental growth does not follow a linear function. For example, the difference between MAs of 2 and 3 is much greater than the difference between MAs of 10 and 11. By about 5 years of age, the rate of mental growth begins to decrease, and by about 13 years of age, mental age has little meaning because mental growth is close to its limits at this age.

Second, the same MA may mean different things for different children. Children with the same MA may have different skills, different interests, different experiences, different academic successes and failures, and different rates of progress in school. Here are some examples of the many ways of obtaining the same MA (John Willis, personal communication, January 2000). One child might pass almost all the items up to the MA level and fail almost all the items above it. Another child might have widely scattered passes and failures well below and above the MA level. A third child might have a distinct pattern of strengths and weaknesses around the overall MA level. These factors should always be considered when we use MAs or test-age equivalents.

Comment on MA Scores

The MA, or age-equivalent, score obtained on an intelligence test provides useful information about the child's repertoire of knowledge. It reflects a more absolute level of performance than does the IQ, as it is the test-score equivalent of the 50th percentile rank in a given norm group. In contrast, the standard score on an intelligence test (or Deviation IQ, Composite Score, or IQ) provides no information about the size of the individual's repertoire of skills and knowledge. Unlike many other psychologists, Humphreys (1985) believes that we should retain the MA concept because it provides some understanding, although coarse, of the individual's absolute level of performance. Use of MA scores also makes public understanding of test results more concrete. Humphreys' position has merit.

DISTINCTION BETWEEN INTELLIGENCE TESTS AND ACHIEVEMENT TESTS

Both intelligence tests and achievement tests sample aptitude, learning, and achievement to some degree, and both sample responses in the child's repertoire at the time of assessment. The two types of tests differ on several dimensions, however (Humphreys, 1971). Intelligence tests are broader in scope than achievement tests and sample from a wider range of experiences. Because intelligence tests assess learning that occurs in a wide variety of settings, they are more valid estimators of future performance than are achievement tests. Achievement tests, such as reading and mathematics tests, are heavily dependent on formal learning acquired in school or at home. They appear to be more culture-bound and to sample more specific skills than intelligence tests. Intelligence tests stress the ability to apply information in new and different ways, whereas achievement tests stress mastery of factual information. In summary, intelligence tests measure less formal achievements than do achievement tests, which measure acquired information.

CURRICULUM-BASED MEASUREMENT VS. NORM-REFERENCED MEASUREMENT

As you learned in Chapter 4, *norm-referenced measurement* is used to evaluate a student's performance in relation to the performance of others on the same measure. In other words, we compare a student's performance with that of a normative group. We use *curriculum-based measurement,* on the other hand, to identify a student's status with respect to an established standard of performance—that is, to measure levels of mastery. In curriculum-based measurement, we compare a student's performance to some predetermined criterion, rather than to the performance of other students. In curriculum-based measurement, standardized samples of student performance on curricular materials are obtained (Deno & Fuchs, 1987).

Curriculum-based measurement provides information relevant to instructional decisions, such as whether a child is ready to go to the next level of instruction, whether there are certain subskills that require more attention than others, and which curriculum materials might best help the child master the necessary skills. For example, a series of tests can be developed with four levels of reading mastery:

I. Ability to read beginning-level basal readers and most of the curriculum materials found in grades one and two.
II. Ability to read all levels of basal readers and most of the curriculum materials found in elementary school.
III. Ability to read most newspapers and most of the curriculum materials found in high school.
IV. Ability to read college-level material.

Examples of questions that may be addressed in curriculum-based measurement include the following (Marston, 1989):

1. How many words did the student read correctly from a grade-level word list in 1 minute?
2. How many words did the student write during a 3-minute interval, given a topic sentence?
3. How many words did the student spell correctly from a grade-level word list, given words dictated every 7 seconds?
4. How many problems did the student solve correctly from a list of grade-level computational problems?

The following statements could be derived from curriculum-based measurement:

- "Jim can read 90% of the material at Level II of the reading mastery program."
- "Luis can spell 80% of the words in the unit word list."
- "Judith can subtract three-place numbers without error."

These statements refer to performance on a given criterion, without reference to the level of performance of other members of the group. A mastery level of performance is established as part of the instructional objective, and the child's test performance is described relative to this level (e.g., mastery at the 90% level).

In curriculum-based assessment, examiners may have the opportunity to observe how the student goes about solving the problem. However, observation is not possible when the student does not reveal how he or she solved the problem.

Comparison of Curriculum-Based Measurement and Norm-Referenced Measurement

Curriculum-based measurement differs from norm-referenced measurement primarily in the scale used for measurement. In norm-referenced measurement, the middle of the scale is usually anchored to an average level of performance for a particular norm group, with the units of the scale being a function of the distribution of scores above and below the average level. In curriculum-based measurement, "the scale is usually anchored at the extremities—a score at the top of the scale indicating complete or perfect mastery of some defined abilities, or at the bottom indicating complete absence of those abilities. The scale units consist of subdivisions of this total scale range" (Ebel, 1971, p. 282).

Advantages and Disadvantages of Curriculum-Based Measurement

Curriculum-based measurement has several advantages (Deno & Fuchs, 1987). It improves the match between testing and teaching, it enables direct appraisal of the extent to which a student is performing successfully in the curriculum, it helps to determine the effectiveness of instructional interventions, and it enables communication between regular and special education teachers and between teachers and parents.

Curriculum-based measurement also has several limitations, especially when it is used to emphasize facts rather than structures of understanding. In some cases, rote learning may replace understanding. Additionally, curriculum-based measurement

has the appeal of novelty and innovation. It may seem to offer more meaningful measures of achievement, as well as escape from some of the problems inherent in norm-referenced measurements. But it creates special problems. First, there is the problem of selecting and later defending a unique set of ideas and abilities that each student will be expected to learn. Second, there is the problem of rational definition of a particular level of test performance that will indicate attainment of each objective. Third, there is the problem of repeated testing of those who do not reach the criterion initially, plus the problem of creating multiple parallel test forms for use in the repeated testing. Finally, there is the problem of reporting only two levels of an achievement that exists at many different levels, and of treating an achievement ever so slightly above the criterion as completely satisfactory, while an achievement ever so slightly below is treated as completely unsatisfactory. (Ebel, 1975, p. 85, with changes in notation)

Other disadvantages include the lack of national norms and the small sample sizes for local norms.

Comment on Curriculum-Based Measurement

Curriculum-based measurement tests focus primarily on lower-order skills that can easily be sequenced, such as math calculation, spelling, and decoding (Nancy Mather, personal communication, January 2000). These types of tests are not as easily developed for academic areas requiring higher levels of cognition, such as reading comprehension or math problem solving. They are also more useful in the elementary grades, where more emphasis is placed on tasks involving rote processes.

Curriculum-based measurement may diminish the feeling of competition among children because the children are competing with themselves in striving to advance their own skills, regardless of where they stand in relation to other children. But curriculum-based measurement cannot eliminate competition among children because those performing at lower levels are likely to feel inferior to those at more advanced levels. Substituting "level of ability" for "percentile rank" may be simply a cosmetic change. It is doubtful that replacing norm-referenced tests with curriculum-based tests would eliminate offensive comparisons among children.

Norm-referenced measurement and curriculum-based measurement have different roles in the assessment process, and both contribute to our understanding of a child's abilities. We should view them as complementary methods of evaluation. Curriculum-based measurement procedures are useful for assessing specific skill areas in order to evaluate behavior relative to behavioral objectives and individual teaching programs, whereas norm-referenced measurement procedures are especially useful in measuring individual differences among children in order to determine levels of relative proficiency. For more information about curriculum-based measurement, see Shinn (1989, 1998).

REACTION TIME AND INTELLIGENCE

As noted in Chapter 5, early attempts by Galton and Cattell to use reaction time as a measure of intelligence were unsuccessful. In the 1980s, there was a revival of interest in reaction time as a measure of intelligence. Current interest is focused on studying the speed of information processing through several procedures (Vernon, 1983). These include the following:

1. *Speed of encoding, or inspection time (IT)*. The individual must decide, in a visual inspection-time task, which of two vertical lines, exposed for an extremely short period of time, is longer; in an auditory inspection-time task, which of two tones, exposed for an extremely short period of time, is higher.

2. *Efficiency of short-term memory scanning*. The individual must decide whether a digit in a string of digits is novel or one that has been presented previously.

3. *Speed of information retrieval from long-term memory*. The individual must decide whether two words are the same or different.

4. *Simple and choice reaction time*. The individual must press a button when a light of a particular color or another stimulus appears.

Dependent measures include (a) reaction time, measured as the interval between stimulus onset and the lifting of the finger from the rest button; (b) movement time, measured as the time required to move the finger from the rest button to the response button; and (c) inspection time, measured as the shortest exposure duration necessary to make accurate discriminations between two simple stimuli.

Research indicates that reaction time (or the speed of information processing) and short-term memory are related to intelligence (Miller & Vernon, 1992). Individuals with fast reaction times (i.e., ability to identify stimuli presented for extremely short times) and good short-term memory tend to perform better on intelligence tests than those with slow reaction times and poor short-term memory. The best estimate of the correlation of reaction time with IQ is about −.30 (Miller & Vernon, 1992); the negative correlation reflects the fact that higher IQs are associated with shorter (faster) reaction times. When more than one measure of reaction time is used, the correlation between reaction time and IQ may increase, and more complex reaction-time measures have higher correlations with IQs than do less complex reaction-time measures. The relationship between inspection time (IT) and IQ is stronger with the Performance IQ than with the Verbal IQ (Nettelbeck, 1987). This suggests that perceptual sampling, as measured by IT, is more closely related to cognitive tasks involving visual organization and integration. IT has moderate to high reliability, about .70. We still do not know whether measures of choice reaction time reflect a single process or a number of complex processes.

With children ages 4 to 6 years old, reaction time and intelligence are poorly related (Miller & Vernon, 1996). However, for children 8 to 11 years old, a moderate relationship has been reported between inspection time and intelligence ($r = -.38$; Hutton, Wilding, & Hudson, 1997). More research is needed on the relationship between reaction time and intelligence with young children and children in the middle years.

The responses in a choice reaction-time task appear to be simple—namely, lifting a finger from a rest button and then pressing a button or a screen. However, choice reaction-time measures are not simple, nor do they appear to be pure measures of a unitary process (Detterman, 1987). Unlike Jensen and Vernon (1986), who maintain that choice reaction time is a simple task, Detterman argues that choice reaction time represents a complex set of processes, only some of which are related to intelligence. These processes may include individuals' understanding of instructions, familiarity with the equipment, motivation, sensory acuity, speed-accuracy tradeoff, attention, memory, search strategy, response selection (touching a screen or touching a keyboard), response execution, and use of feedback (e.g., how individuals monitor their responses).

Correlations between IT and IQ cannot be easily interpreted (Nettelbeck, 1987). It is still not clear whether IT reflects perceptual speed, general intelligence, neural efficiency, or the ability to maintain concentration. Also unclear is to what extent IT is influenced by personality differences and individual differences in sensitivity, concentration, level of noise within the perceptual system, and adaptation effects, variables that may be beyond voluntary control. Cognitive strategies that can be under voluntary control also may influence IT.

In summary, we still do not understand the reasons for the relationships between choice reaction-time measures and measures of intelligence or whether any basic cognitive processes are being assessed accurately by reaction-time measures (Stankov & Roberts, 1997). The size of the correlations may be related to a number of factors, including practice, strategies, response bias, visual angle effects, stimulus-response compatibility, sequential dependency, temporal uncertainty, and size and intensity of the stimulus. Similarly, there is much to learn about the reasons for the correlations between inspection time and intelligence. Problems involve the adequacy of the procedures used to present the stimuli, practice effects, accuracy of measurement, and related factors. On the basis of the available evidence, we should not make premature judgments about the nature of intelligence and elementary perceptual processing: "In the search for understanding the mechanisms underlying the various strata of intelligence it must be acknowledged that many different processes (whose number is currently undetermined) probably contribute to each factor of 'intelligence'...it is improbable that any one facet of human cognitive abilities should be considered dominant in determining 'intelligence'" (Stankov & Roberts, 1997, p. 81).

BIOLOGICAL CORRELATES OF INTELLIGENCE

Event-Related Brain Potential and Intelligence

Since the beginning of electroencephalography, researchers have explored whether a relationship exists between brain-wave patterns and intelligence. Event-related brain potentials (ERPs) provide a measure of neural efficiency or spread of neural information processing. The procedure consists of measuring the electrical activity of the brain by placing electrodes on the scalp. When a stimulus is shown to an individual, his or her brain's response to the stimulus can be measured by voltage changes recorded by an amplifier known as an electroencephalograph. The result is an electroencephalogram (EEG).

The two main sensory modalities that researchers have investigated are visual and auditory, with most research concentrating on the visual modality. When researchers derive the event-related brain potential from the visual modality, it is called the *visual evoked response* or *VER*. Researchers obtain VER latencies by placing electrodes over the occipital lobes of the individual's cortex, presenting flashes of light to the individual's eyes, and then finding the latency of the response from the brain-wave recordings. The evoked response is obtained by computer analysis of repeated responses to the flashes of light. The VER is a useful measure of brain activity arising from sensory stimulation.

Research on the relationship between ERPs and intelligence is inconclusive (Vernon, 1997). The results depend on the type of stimulus and the component of electrical activity measured (such as the latency, the amplitude, or the length of the contour perimeter of the wave form). Researchers who found a significant relationship between IQ and ERP latencies observed that higher IQs were associated with shorter (faster) latencies. It is unlikely, however, that a single measure of brain electrical activity will soon replace conventional intelligence tests (Deary & Caryl, 1993).

Cerebral Glucose Metabolism and Intelligence

Current technology such as positron emission tomography (PET) enables researchers to study cerebral action. For example, the rate at which glucose is metabolized by the brain and indices of blood flow can be used to infer brain activity. Research indicates that, on various cognitive tasks, individuals who have high IQs show more brain activity and less consumption of energy than individuals who have low IQs (Vernon, 1997). These results suggest that individuals who have high IQs have "greater 'brainpower' at their disposal but use their brainpower more efficiently when called upon to do so" (Vernon, 1997, adapted from p. 247). Many questions remain, of course, and this technology and research is still in its infancy.

Nerve Conduction Velocity and Intelligence

Another way of looking at the biological correlates of intelligence is to study nerve conduction velocity, which "refers to the speed with which electrical impulses are transmitted along nerve fibers and synapses" (Vernon, 1997, p. 247). Research in this area is inconclusive, with studies reporting both significant and nonsignificant findings (Vernon, 1997).

Comment on Biological Correlates of Intelligence

Sternberg (1991) cautioned that the significant relationships reported between biological measures and intelligence may be an artifact of the methods used to obtain measures of brain functioning (Sternberg, 1991): "I believe that the biological approach is interesting and has great potential. But we need to refrain from making speculative claims, whether from wave forms or even from choice reaction-time experiments, that are linked to neuronal conduction accuracy or speed in ways that are totally speculative" (p. 265). Obviously, we need more research on the biological correlates of intelligence.

THE TESTING OF INTELLIGENCE: PROS AND CONS

Intelligence testing has generated much controversy in recent years. Some psychologists maintain that the development of intelligence tests is one of the most significant contributions of the field of psychology; other psychologists believe that intelligence tests have many serious shortcomings. Figure 6-2 summarizes the major assets and limitations of intelligence tests,

and Table 6-4 presents misconceptions about intelligence tests and intelligence testing.

Intelligence tests have been criticized because the IQ does not relate closely to several measures of everyday functioning. But can we expect any one measure to correlate highly with behaviors that are multidetermined? Individuals with the same IQ vary widely in their social competence, as well as in the expression of their talents (Zigler & Farber, 1985). These divergences result from personality and motivational factors that arise from each individual's unique socialization history. For example, the child with mental retardation who is restricted and catered to may never develop independence, whereas the child who is gifted and "whose talents are unappreciated or viewed as troublesome may bow to pressures to conform and become an…underachiever" (Zigler & Farber, 1985, p. 398). Because of the many determinants of behavior, the IQ should not be expected to be an infallible indicator of everyday functioning.

Intelligence is a broad concept that reflects an individual's information-processing capacities and possession of useful knowledge. Intelligence tests measure only a part of a domain that reflects intelligent behavior. For example, intelligence tests often fail to measure (a) the child's ability to carry out tasks that require complex planning and integration

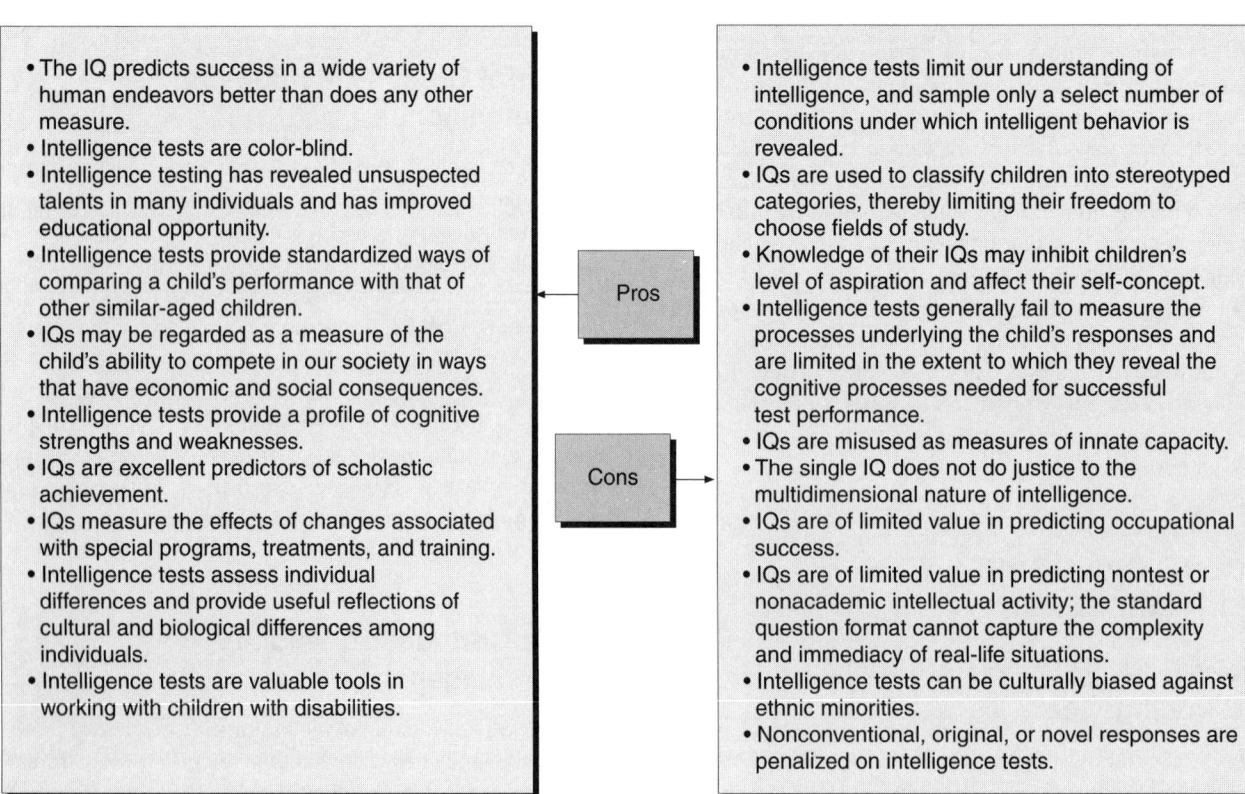

- The IQ predicts success in a wide variety of human endeavors better than does any other measure.
- Intelligence tests are color-blind.
- Intelligence testing has revealed unsuspected talents in many individuals and has improved educational opportunity.
- Intelligence tests provide standardized ways of comparing a child's performance with that of other similar-aged children.
- IQs may be regarded as a measure of the child's ability to compete in our society in ways that have economic and social consequences.
- Intelligence tests provide a profile of cognitive strengths and weaknesses.
- IQs are excellent predictors of scholastic achievement.
- IQs measure the effects of changes associated with special programs, treatments, and training.
- Intelligence tests assess individual differences and provide useful reflections of cultural and biological differences among individuals.
- Intelligence tests are valuable tools in working with children with disabilities.

Pros

Cons

- Intelligence tests limit our understanding of intelligence, and sample only a select number of conditions under which intelligent behavior is revealed.
- IQs are used to classify children into stereotyped categories, thereby limiting their freedom to choose fields of study.
- Knowledge of their IQs may inhibit children's level of aspiration and affect their self-concept.
- Intelligence tests generally fail to measure the processes underlying the child's responses and are limited in the extent to which they reveal the cognitive processes needed for successful test performance.
- IQs are misused as measures of innate capacity.
- The single IQ does not do justice to the multidimensional nature of intelligence.
- IQs are of limited value in predicting occupational success.
- IQs are of limited value in predicting nontest or nonacademic intellectual activity; the standard question format cannot capture the complexity and immediacy of real-life situations.
- Intelligence tests can be culturally biased against ethnic minorities.
- Nonconventional, original, or novel responses are penalized on intelligence tests.

Figure 6-2. Intelligence testing: Pros and cons.

Table 6-4
Some Misconceptions About Intelligence Tests and Testing

Misconception	Comment
Intelligence tests measure innate intelligence.	IQs always are based on the individual's interactions with the environment; they never measure innate intelligence exclusively.
IQs are fixed and immutable and never change.	IQs change in the course of development, especially from birth through 5 years of age. Even after 5 years of age, significant changes in intelligence can occur.
Intelligence tests provide perfectly reliable scores.	No intelligence test has perfect reliability. Test scores are only estimates of a person's ability. Every test score should be reported as a statement of probability (or odds): "There is a 90% chance that the child's IQ falls between ___ and ___."
Intelligence tests measure all we need to know about a person's intelligence.	No single intelligence test measures the entire spectrum of abilities related to intellectual behavior. Some tests measure verbal and nonverbal abilities, but do not adequately measure other areas, such as mechanical skills, creativity, and social intelligence. Other tests measure only verbal and nonverbal abilities. Any test only *samples* the individual's repertoire of skills.
All intelligence tests measure the same thing.	Although tests of intelligence often correlate highly, different intelligence tests measure different abilities. Therefore, we should not expect scores on an intelligence test that measures only one factor to be similar to those on an intelligence test that measures a multiplicity of factors.
IQs obtained from different tests are interchangeable.	Although there is some overlap among intelligence tests, IQs may not be interchangeable—especially when the standard deviations of the tests are different.
A battery of tests can tell us everything that we need to know to make judgments about a person's competence.	No battery of tests can give us a complete picture of any person's abilities.

of multiple pieces of information and (b) the ability to make decisions with changing circumstances. Test scores provide a statistical indication of the extent to which a person has acquired information and thinks abstractly, but test scores should *not* be directly equated with intelligence. Test scores are a useful index of ability, but they may reflect test-taking sophistication, personality, and attitudinal characteristics as well.

Intelligence and the Social Order

We cannot divorce intelligence tests, as presently constituted, from the social order of our society, which values excellence in judgment, reasoning, and comprehension over other kinds of excellence. Because IQ tests measure potential for success in school, intelligence tests are value-laden. They reflect such socially valued factors as schooling, verbal abilities, and abstraction and concept formation skills. These are important skills in industrialized societies, but, of course, they are not the only important skills. Psychologists are continually trying to develop methods to measure and reinforce intellectual abilities and skills (e.g., creativity) other than those currently associated with intelligence tests (also see Gardner's approach in Chapter 5). We need such efforts because our current tests tap only part of the spectrum of human abilities.

Still, intelligence tests generally do a good job in predicting success in school, are extremely useful in neuropsychological assessment, and measure important abilities and skills valued in many cultures.

The real importance of the IQ is that it has something of a threshold character—below some very low point on the IQ distribution, people do not function well in society, nor can any of their latent talents be manifested. "There seems to be no other human defect ... as severely limiting as a very low intelligence. Deafness, blindness, physical deformity, paralysis—all are not incompatible with achievement, athletic enjoyment, and self-realization. Very low intelligence, on the other hand, seems a different order of misfortune ..." (Jensen, 1974, p. 434).

A central criticism, perhaps at the heart of many other criticisms, is that psychologists and educators use intelligence tests to allocate the limited resources of our society. Intelligence test results are used to provide rewards or privileges, such as special classes for the gifted, admission to college or advanced study, and employment. Those who do not qualify for these resources may misdirect their anger at the tests, because they see the tests as denying them opportunity for success. For reasons that are still unclear, the IQ has come to be associated not only with an individual's ability to perform certain tasks, but also with his or her essential worth: "To have a low IQ is seen as the equivalent of having low caste" (Hudson, 1972, p. 15). We must squelch this overvaluation surrounding the IQ; it has no constructive place in our society.

Limitations Associated with the Assessment Setting

Because the intelligence test is administered in a controlled, standardized setting and usually in an examiner's office, there is little or no opportunity for the examinee to reformulate the problem, develop an original solution, delay the response, use library resources, seek advice, or settle for a less than optimal solution (Frederiksen, 1986). Additionally, "The cognitive processes that are involved in taking a test may depend not only on the format of the test and thus the mode of responding to a problem but also on such personal characteristics as the level of expertise of the [child] in the area of the problems posed and on the nature of the setting and situation in which the problems are presented" (Frederiksen, 1986, p. 451). Finally, unlike problems in natural situations, items on intelligence tests involve only one or a few variables at a time and are highly structured and organized by the test authors. Consequently, intelligence test items fail to mirror the complexities of real-life challenges. Future work in assessment needs to address these important issues.

Value of Intelligence Testing

Intelligence testing is part of a relatively young and developing science of human abilities. Although there are weaknesses in the technology of the science of human abilities, there is a solid scientific basis for the practice of mental-ability testing (Carroll & Horn, 1981). Furthermore, the differential psychology of cognitive abilities can do much to improve the human condition. The robustness of current research on cognitive development augurs well for the future of intelligence testing.

The IQs obtained from standardized intelligence tests can be extremely helpful in work with children who do or do not have disabilities. As the best available long-range predictor of outcome and adjustment, the IQ provides teachers, parents, and psychologists with some idea about the child's capabilities. Furthermore, because intelligence tests provide some measure of the child's developmental limitations and impairments, teachers, parents, and psychologists are able to devise an individualized curriculum that falls within the range of the child's level of development and developmental expectations.

Humphreys (1985) provides a useful summary of many of the issues addressed in this chapter:

There appears to be continuity in the development of intelligence from 12 months to 17 years. This development is along a single dimension on which children change both absolutely and relatively to each other during this time frame. This hypothesis accounts for the intercorrelations of test scores during the many occasions for which data are available.... Change proceeds smoothly and, apparently, inexorably. One must use different content to measure intelligence at 12 months and at 17 years, but it is not necessary to invoke the difference in content to explain the low correlation between intelligence test scores during this interval of time. The rate of relative change is most rapid early in development, but has become relatively level by the time of school entrance. The rate stabilizes, but change continues.

The construct of general intelligence that emerges *requires* one to infer a multiplicity of causes of individual differences. One subset of these causes is certainly the many genes involved [in intellectual functioning]. There is widespread agreement that the inheritance of intelligence is polygenic. Although these genes are largely fixed at the time of conception, there is no reason to consider their resultant an entity. To the extent that there are genetic determinants of instability, individual genes in the complex may be "coming on line" at different times during development. It also is clear that there are environmental determinants of the intellectual repertoire, and there are both genetic and environmental determinants of the many structures within the central nervous system. Both sets of determinants affect how those structures are used in the acquisition of the behaviors sampled by standard intelligence tests. (pp. 222–223)

Humphreys (1986) also notes that the construct of general intelligence, as we measure it, is a mathematical construct. "Even a high heritability coefficient, or correlations with reaction time, brain waves, and physique, cannot establish intelligence as a fixed capacity or any other kind of entity. The construct is behavioral and has associated functional correlates..." (p. 433).

DuBois (1972) concluded from his study of the testing movement that "whether measurement leads to an increase in educational opportunity depends on administrators of education programs as well as on the psychometricians who devise the tests. In the [20th century] the applications of psychological and educational measurements have increased enormously through the joint efforts of both administrators and test technicians. By and large these applications have improved educational opportunity" (p. 55).

Perhaps the increases in IQ that have been observed across generations will one day start to manifest themselves in people's behavior. To date [1998], signs that increases in IQ are reflected in more intelligent everyday behavior have been conspicuous by their absence.

—Robert J. Sternberg and James C. Kaufman

THINKING THROUGH THE ISSUES

1. Some writers maintain that genetics plays no role in the development of intelligence. What is your opinion, and what is it based on?
2. Is it possible to separate the effects of genetics and environment on the development of intelligence? What is the basis for your answer?

3. In your opinion, what can be done in the home to stimulate intellectual growth and development?
4. What type of study would you propose to investigate the role of familial factors in intellectual development?
5. What experiences contributed most to the development of your intelligence during your childhood and adolescence?
6. What experiences diminished your intellectual growth?
7. How is an older child's level of cognitive ability different from a younger child's? Is it simply a quantitative difference?
8. What is your position on the pros and cons associated with intelligence testing? Should intelligence tests, as we now know them, continue to be used? If so, why? If not, what techniques can we use to assess cognitive abilities in a relatively quick, efficient, reliable, and valid manner?

SUMMARY

1. Among the capabilities of human beings, none is as distinctive or as central to their adaptive potential as intelligence.

Relationship Between Human Intelligence and the Brain

2. Intellectual activity appears to involve several regions of the brain, particularly when complex tasks are performed.

Genetic Programming, Maturational Status, and Environmental Influence

3. Genetic programming, maturational status, and environmental influence interact to affect the course of mental development.
4. During the first 2 years of life, changes in maturational status affect mental development.

—Pity the test doesn't measure all her skills..........

From *OF CHILDREN*, *3rd edition*, by G. R. LeFrancois © 1980. Reprinted with permission of Wadsworth, a division of Thomson Learning. Fax 800 730-2215.

Intellectual Functioning: Hereditary Influences

5. An estimate of the heritability of a trait describes the proportion of the variation of a trait in a given population attributable to genetic differences in that population.
6. Children do not inherit an IQ. They inherit a collection of genes, called a genotype, that is related to intelligence. The expression of the genotype, called the phenotype (the observable performance of individuals), results from the interaction of the genotype with environmental experiences.
7. The best estimate is that genetic variation appears to account for at least 50% of individual differences in intelligence test scores, with the remainder attributed to environmental (or nongenetic) forces.
8. There is considerable evidence that both general intelligence and specific intellectual abilities—such as verbal, spatial, numerical, and perceptual abilities—are under genetic influence.
9. There is also ample evidence that during development (a) monozygotic twins come to be more similar than dizygotic twins from infancy on, (b) biological siblings appear more similar than adopted siblings, especially by the end of adolescence, (c) similarities between fraternal twins decline from infancy to adolescence, and (d) similarities between adopted siblings decline from infancy to adolescence.

Intellectual Functioning: Environmental Influences

10. Several environmental factors are likely to enhance the development of intelligence, including stimulating and enriching experiences, good medical care and nutrition, parental involvement in the child's learning, a rich language environment, and a good physical environment.
11. At school age, the intelligence test scores and achievement test scores of very low birth weight children tend to be lower than those of normal birth weight children.
12. Research suggests that the effects of perinatal stress on intellectual functioning are small.
13. Vulnerability to malnutrition is greatest during the 40 weeks of gestation and the first few years after birth, the most critical periods in the growth of brain tissue.
14. Malnutrition may prevent the expression of the full genetic potential for mental development and interfere with concentration, motivation, social interaction, and time required for learning.
15. The positive effects of vitamin and mineral supplementation appear to be greatest for young children who have dietary deficiencies, with little effect beyond the teenage years.
16. The correlation between a family's socioeconomic status and children's intelligence test scores is on average about .33.
17. Overall, research on the relationship between the home environment and intelligence test scores suggests that the home environment has an important influence on the early intellectual development of children but plays only a minor role in the intellectual development of postadolescents.
18. Research indicates that persistent poverty has more detrimental effects on children's intelligence test scores and school achievement than does transitory poverty.
19. The confluence model explains a very small amount of the total variance in IQ.
20. Inequality of schooling plays a minor role in individual differences in IQ.

21. A meta-analysis of 72 studies involving Head Start programs indicated that, at the conclusion of the program, children in the program had higher IQs than children who were not in the program, as well as gains on readiness and achievement measures.

22. Although the long-term influences of preschool programs on intellectual functioning do not appear to be large, preschool enrichment programs may change achievement orientation, school competence, educational attainment, and career accomplishments.

23. Research on attempts to increase general intelligence in school-age populations suggests that changes in IQ are relatively small—generally about 7.5 points or less.

24. The adoptive environment can produce about a 10- to 12-point IQ gain (for children adopted into favorable environments) or loss (for children adopted into unfavorable environments).

25. In several economically advanced nations, the intelligence of the population has increased by approximately 15 points between 1940 and 1990, or by about 3 IQ points per decade.

26. Lynn proposes that environmental improvements account in part for the rise in intelligence test scores.

27. Flynn argues that the apparent increases in intelligence represent only the populations' improved ability to take intelligence tests.

Comment on Hereditary and Environmental Influences on Intellectual Functioning

28. Although heredity sets limits on a child's potential, it is the environment that permits that potential to be actualized.

29. Although intelligence is malleable, it is also resistant to change.

30. Intelligence develops within a cultural context, and cultures differ in how they value mental abilities.

31. An individual's score on an intelligence test does not permit us to make inferences about either genetic influences (the biological substrate) or environmental influences (the psychosocial substrate).

Intellectual Functioning: Personality and Gender Influences

32. Research suggests that there are developmental trends in the personality patterns of children and adults who show increases in IQ. Gains in IQ are associated with independence and competitiveness during the preschool years; with independence, scholastic competitiveness, self-initiation, and problem-solving approaches during the elementary school years; and with interpersonal distance, coldness, and introversion during adulthood.

33. Research on gender differences in cognitive ability indicates that gender differences in general verbal ability and mathematical ability are essentially nonexistent; males have better spatial perception ability and better mental rotation ability than females, whereas there are no gender differences in spatial visualization ability; males show more variable performance on some tests of cognitive ability; and gender differences have become smaller between 1960 and 1990.

Stability and Change of Intelligence

34. The stability of IQs obtained across childhood and adolescence is a function of measurement factors, genetic factors, and environmental factors.

35. The measurement factors that affect a child's initial test performance also affect subsequent test performance.

36. Test-retest correlations tend to be lower with increasing time intervals between measurements.

37. Gains on retest are likely to be larger on performance items than on verbal items because examinees can develop a set of problem-solving strategies that they can apply to the same or similar problems.

38. Changes in IQ may be related to genetically based developmental trends. Some children have a continuous growth pattern, others have spurts and pauses, and still others have a discontinuous curve.

39. Environmental factors contribute to fluctuations in intelligence in two ways. First, physical and emotional factors (e.g., physical illness, emotional trauma, or separation from parents), often transitory in nature, may affect a child's test performance. Second, changes in cognitive stimulation or motivation may alter the child's level of performance.

40. Tests designed for infants assess sensorimotor functions primarily and do not appear to be measuring the same factors that are measured by tests given to preschool and older children.

41. As the content of tests changes with age, shifting from perceptual-motor to more cognitively oriented functions, the tests become better predictors of intelligence.

42. Although for normal children correlations between infant tests and later intelligence tests are low and not adequate for clinical application, they do attain statistical significance at certain ages, especially after the age of 18 months.

43. Infant Developmental Quotients that fall in the average or superior range have more limited predictive power than do those at very low levels.

44. In an individual assessment, it is imperative that you never make a diagnosis of mental retardation based on a single test score in infancy (or at any age).

45. A moderate relationship (*Mdn r* = .45) exists between measures of information processing in infancy—namely, visual recognition memory—and measures of intellectual ability in childhood.

46. The ability of infants to inhibit attention to, or disengage from, less salient stimuli might be crucial to the prediction of later IQ.

47. Research has shown that IQs obtained at the age of 5 years correlate moderately with adult IQs (*r* = .50 and higher).

48. Research with adults indicates that intelligence test scores are a reasonably good predictor of job performance in many different occupations, with an estimated *r* = .53 based on 400 studies.

49. The older the child is when first tested and the shorter the interval between tests, the greater the constancy of the IQ.

50. The IQ of any given child may change by as much as 20 points, but for most children measured intelligence remains relatively stable after 5 years of age.

51. Despite high test-retest correlations, we must conduct frequent and periodic testing if we are going to use test scores for guidance or placement decisions.

Relationship Between Intellectual Development and Assessment

52. Research on the relationship between intellectual development and assessment indicates the following. Various forces play different roles at different points in children's intellectual development. Environmental influences take on a greater role as chil-

dren develop. There is increasing differentiation of abilities with age. The way in which genetic and environmental influences combine to affect intelligence changes over an individual's life. The structure of intelligence remains stable across development, but the content that fills in this structure changes. The amount of information acquired during development increases with age. Overall, development is determined by interactions between environmental stimuli and children's inherent predispositions. When children have equal opportunities to learn, individual differences in learning are likely to be associated with individual genetic variation. When children do not have equal opportunities to learn, individual differences in learning are likely to be associated with differences in opportunities to learn. Reliable quantitative measurements of children's general intelligence can be obtained from at least 4 or 5 years onward. Quantitative measurements of intelligence accurately predict children's future performance in school. Children's use of logical reasoning skills is influenced by factors other than understanding of the logic itself.

Mental Age

53. We can define MA as the degree of general mental ability possessed by the average child of a chronological age corresponding to the MA score.
54. MA scores are limited in that differences between MA units are not the same throughout the developmental period because mental growth does not follow a linear function. Furthermore, the same MA may mean different things for different children. Children with the same MA may have different skills, different interests, different experiences, different academic successes and failures, and different rates of progress in school.
55. The MA score, or age-equivalent score, obtained on an intelligence test provides useful information about the child's repertoire of knowledge. It reflects a more absolute level of performance than does the IQ, as it is the test-score equivalent of the 50th percentile rank in a given norm group.

Distinction Between Intelligence Tests and Achievement Tests

56. Both intelligence tests and achievement tests sample aptitude, learning, and achievement to some degree, and both sample responses in the child's repertoire at the time of assessment. But intelligence tests measure less formal achievements than do achievement tests, which measure acquired information.

Curriculum-Based Measurement vs. Norm-Referenced Measurement

57. Curriculum-based measurement is used to identify a student's status with respect to an established standard of performance—that is, to measure levels of mastery.
58. Curriculum-based measurement improves the match between testing and teaching, enables direct appraisal of the extent to which a student is performing successfully in the curriculum, helps to determine the effectiveness of instructional interventions, and enables communication between regular and special education teachers and between teachers and parents.
59. Curriculum-based measurement is limited when it is used to emphasize facts rather than structures of understanding, when

rote learning is emphasized rather than understanding, and when national norms are not available.

Reaction Time and Intelligence

60. Research indicates that reaction time (or the speed of information processing) and short-term memory are related to intelligence; the correlation is in the range of −.30.
61. We still do not understand the reasons for the relationships between choice reaction-time measures and measures of intelligence or whether any basic cognitive processes are being assessed accurately by reaction-time measures.

Biological Correlates of Intelligence

62. Research on the relationship between ERPs and intelligence is inconclusive.
63. Research indicates that, on various cognitive tasks, individuals who have high IQs show more brain activity and less consumption of energy than individuals who have low IQs.
64. Research in the areas of nerve conduction velocity and intelligence is inconclusive.

The Testing of Intelligence: Pros and Cons

65. Intelligence testing has generated much controversy in recent years.
66. Some psychologists maintain that the development of intelligence tests is one of the most significant contributions of the field of psychology; other psychologists believe that intelligence tests have many serious shortcomings.
67. Intelligence is a broad concept that reflects an individual's information-processing capacities and possession of useful knowledge.
68. Intelligence tests measure only a part of a domain that reflects intelligent behavior.
69. Test scores are a useful index of ability, but they may reflect test-taking sophistication, personality, and attitudinal characteristics as well.
70. We cannot divorce intelligence tests, as presently constituted, from the social order of our society, which values excellence in judgment, reasoning, and comprehension over other kinds of excellence.
71. The real importance of the IQ is that it has something of a threshold character—below some very low point on the IQ distribution, people do not function well in society, nor can any of their latent talents be manifested.
72. A central criticism, perhaps at the heart of many other criticisms, is that psychologists and educators use intelligence tests to allocate the limited resources of our society.
73. Because the intelligence test is administered in a controlled, standardized setting and usually in an examiner's office, there is little or no opportunity for the examinee to reformulate the problem, develop an original solution, delay the response, use library resources, seek advice, or settle for a less than optimal solution.
74. Intelligence testing is part of a relatively young and developing science of human abilities.
75. Although there are weaknesses in the technology of the science of human abilities, there is a solid scientific basis for the practice of mental-ability testing.

76. As the best available long-range predictor of outcome and adjustment, the IQ provides teachers, parents, and psychologists with some idea about the child's capabilities.

77. Overall, the testing movement has improved educational opportunity in the 20th century.

KEY TERMS, CONCEPTS, AND NAMES

Genetic programming (p. 161)
Maturational status (p. 162)
Heritability of a trait (p. 162)
Genotype (p. 162)
Phenotype (p. 162)
Polygenic model (p. 162)
Environmental influences (p. 164)
Perinatal factors (p. 164)
Nutrition and intelligence (p. 164)
Family background, home environmental variables, and intelligence (p. 165)
Family configuration and intelligence (p. 165)
Confluence model (p. 165)
Malleability and change in intelligence (p. 165)
Generational increases in intelligence (p. 166)
Gender differences in cognitive ability (p. 168)
Stability and change of intelligence (p. 168)
IQ constancy (p. 168)
Prediction of intelligence from infant tests (p. 169)
Visual novelty preference during infancy and later intelligence (p. 170)
IQs as predictors of adult educational and occupational success (p. 170)
Relationship between intellectual development and assessment (p. 171)
Mental age (p. 172)
Distinction between intelligence tests and achievement tests (p. 172)
Norm-referenced measurement (p. 173)
Curriculum-based measurement (p. 173)
Reaction time and intelligence (p. 174)
Inspection time and intelligence (p. 174)
Event-related brain potential and intelligence (p. 175)
Visual evoked response (VER) (p. 175)
Cerebral glucose metabolism and intelligence (p. 175)
Nerve conduction velocity and intelligence (p. 175)
Pros and cons of intelligence testing (p. 176)
Intelligence and the social order (p. 176)
Limitations associated with the assessment setting (p. 178)
Value of intelligence testing (p. 178)

STUDY QUESTIONS

1. Discuss the interaction of genetic programming, maturational status, and environmental influence as it affects intellectual functioning.
2. Discuss hereditary influences on intellectual functioning.
3. Discuss environmental influences on intellectual functioning. Include in your discussion such areas as (a) perinatal and early developmental influences on intelligence, (b) nutrition and intelligence, (c) influence of family background and home environment on intelligence, (d) family configuration and intelligence, (e) malleability and change in intelligence, and (f) generational increases in intelligence.
4. Compare and contrast hereditary and environmental influences on intellectual functioning.
5. Discuss personality and gender influences on intellectual functioning.
6. Discuss factors that are related to the stability of and changes in intelligence.
7. Discuss the relationship of visual novelty preference during infancy to later intelligence.
8. Discuss IQs as predictors of adult educational and occupational success.
9. Discuss the relationship between intellectual development and assessment.
10. Discuss the concept of mental age.
11. Identify and explain several differences between intelligence and achievement tests.
12. Compare and contrast curriculum-based measurement and norm-referenced measurement.
13. What is known about reaction time and intelligence?
14. Discuss the biological correlates of intelligence. Include in your discussion (a) event-related brain potential, (b) cerebral glucose metabolism, and (c) nerve conduction velocity and intelligence.
15. Discuss the pros and cons of intelligence testing. Include in your discussion (a) intelligence and the social order, (b) limitations of the assessment setting, and (c) the value and limitations of intelligence testing.

7

ADMINISTERING TESTS TO CHILDREN

Tests can enrich the teacher's insight or the therapist's understanding only when the details are looked at in relation to the child's experience in the test situation—what he was coping with and how.

—Lois B. Murphy

Goals and Objectives

This chapter is designed to enable you to do the following:

- Describe examiner characteristics associated with efficient testing skills

- Learn how to establish rapport with children

- Observe children in a test situation

- Learn how to administer tests skillfully

- Understand how to motivate children

- Recognize problems associated with administering tests

This chapter will help you learn how to administer tests to children. Other chapters in the text will describe how to administer tests to children with specific types of special needs. Administering tests to children requires skill and patience. You need to obtain their confidence and cooperation; otherwise the results may not accurately reflect their abilities. You also want to provide a setting that allows children to demonstrate the best of their capabilities.

EXAMINER CHARACTERISTICS

Before we discuss issues related to administering tests to children, let's look at your role as the examiner, together with relevant research findings on how examiners administer and score tests. An appreciation of the examiner's role will provide an important foundation for your training as a clinician.

Examiner Skills

To be able to work successfully with children, you need to have tact, diplomacy, ingenuity, patience, understanding, warmth, and respect. A competent examiner is flexible, vigilant, and self-aware and genuinely enjoys working with children. A sense of humor and the ability to work under less than favorable conditions also help. For example, a preschool child who is uncooperative, pushes away test materials, and remains silent will test the skills of even the most competent examiner. Recognize that subjective factors, such as your personal style, the child's physical and mental health, the setting, interruptions during testing, your level of preparation, the child's language facility, and the child's and your ethnicity and social class, invariably affect the testing situation. Still, your task is to adhere to standardized procedures and obtain cooperation from even the most intractable child.

Flexibility. When you evaluate children, you must be prepared to adjust your testing techniques, even as you adhere to standardized procedures. For example, you may need to take rest breaks, allow additional time for the child to explore and become familiar with the surroundings, or arrange for more than one testing session. If you do take a break, do so after a test or between the subtests of a test. You may need to employ considerable effort to establish and maintain rapport. The adjustments you make should help reduce the child's fatigue and alleviate his or her anxiety.

When a child has a known weakness, such as a physical disability or a language impairment, begin with tests in the battery that do not accentuate that weakness. Selecting appropriate tests will facilitate rapport and lead to more reliable and valid test results. Generally, it is better to select an appropriate test than to alter an inappropriate one. And, you do not want to use the same test battery for all children. For example, the Stanford-Binet: Fourth Edition Pattern Analysis subtest, which does not use time bonuses, is more appropriate than the WISC–III Block Design subtest for an examinee

with a mild motor or visual disability. Similarly, for a young child with some reasonably strong and some weak abilities, the Stanford-Binet: Fourth Edition, with its wider age range, might be more useful than the relatively narrow WISC–III. For an examinee who cannot speak clearly or use a pencil well, the Peabody Picture Vocabulary Test–III (which uses a multiple-choice format) and the Peabody Individual Achievement Test-R NU reading comprehension, math, and spelling subtests (which also use a multiple-choice format) would be better selections than other standardized achievement tests that require more writing or verbal responses.

If you cannot successfully test a child, the child's parents may be able to provide information about the child's language ability, motor ability, social skills, self-sufficiency, mental development, and overall development. A semistructured interview with the parents would be helpful on such occasions (see *Assessment of Children: Behavioral and Clinical Applications*). So, too, would the Vineland Adaptive Behavior Scales (see *Assessment of Children: Behavioral and Clinical Applications*), which is a standardized interview for quantifying the parents' observations and information about their child.

Vigilance. Administering tests should not become so automatic that you forget the child, the setting, and the reason for the evaluation. What should become routine is your handling of the test procedures. What should *never* become routine is how you attend to the child. You will always need to be vigilant, attending to details like making certain that the child has the necessary physical abilities to proceed with the test, noting whether the child has any sensory impairments that may affect performance, observing whether the child is making his or her best effort, determining when to offer encouragement and praise, and deciding when to take breaks. Whenever a child's interest in the task wanes, you will need to offer encouragement and support. Addressing problem behaviors may be taxing. For example, how do you decide whether a particular behavior reflects helplessness or manipulation? And, once you decide, what actions should you take? Although such questions are difficult to answer, with experience you will gain a sense of how to deal with these and similarly challenging issues.

Self-awareness. Strive to understand your temperament and your attitudes toward children in general and, in particular, toward children with special needs and children from cultural and linguistic backgrounds that differ from your own. Not all of you will be (or should be expected to be) equally effective in working with children of all ages, with all types of children with special needs, and with all ethnic and cultural groups. If you are having difficulty establishing rapport with certain children, try to determine why. *Whenever you recognize that you are not fully capable of establishing rapport with a child, you should disqualify yourself from evaluating the child and ask a colleague to conduct the assessment.* It is only through encounters with many types of

Table 7-1
Illustrations of Positive and Negative Examiner Nonverbal Behaviors

Positive or appropriate nonverbal behavior	Negative or inappropriate nonverbal behavior
Facial expressions	
Warm, inviting smile	Cold, frowning, frozen, rigid, or "poker-faced" expression
Good eye contact (be aware, though, that some cultures find this particular behavior offensive)	Avoidance of or poor eye contact: eyes downcast, peering, staring, darting around the room, fixating
Eyes at same level as interviewee's eyes	Eyes at level higher or lower than interviewee's eyes
Appropriately varied and animated facial expressions	Lifting eyebrow critically, nodding head excessively, yawning
Mouth relaxed; occasional smiles	Inappropriate slight smile, pursing or biting lips
Body posture	
Body posture oriented to encourage interpersonal interaction	Body posture oriented to discourage interpersonal interaction
Leaning slightly toward the interviewee	Laid-back, or "propped-up cadaver" look, feet on the desk
Facing the interviewee squarely	Not facing the interviewee squarely, giving the cold shoulder
Relaxed active movement, conveying interest in the interviewee	Rigid posture, communicating cold, impersonal attitude
Settling back in chair, indicating willingness to listen	Sitting on the edge of chair as if ready to jump to feet
Sitting with arms and legs uncrossed, communicating openness	Sitting with arms and legs crossed, communicating closedness
Establishing optimal comfort zone between interviewer and interviewee (3–4 feet in the United States, although there are cultural differences about the preferred space)	Leaving too much or too little distance between interviewer and interviewee (comfort zone for culture violated)
Vocal behaviors	
Warm, interested, natural voice	Cold, impersonal, mumbling, monotonic voice; lacking interest in the interviewee; halting speech
Appropriate volume and pitch	Voice too loud or too quiet
Appropriate rate of speech	Speech too fast, too abrupt, too terse, too animated, or too slow
Fluency in language use	Stammering, halting or hesitant speech
Responsive noises ("umm hmm," "ah ha," etc.)	Clearing throat repeatedly, nervous laughter
Silence suggesting that the interviewee has time to think or elaborate	Silence that causes undue anxiety or suggests that the interviewee should change his or her response
Interrupting when appropriate to clarify, summarize, or reflect meanings	Interrupting frequently and inappropriately
Gestures, mannerisms, and motor behavior	
Outstretched arm or welcoming wave (culture dependent)	Cold, impersonal greeting; brusque seating gesture
Firm handshake	Limp or crushing handshake
Cessation of activity when interviewee enters	Continuing to look at papers on desk or to write when interviewee enters
Closing door to indicate privacy	Allowing door to be open (unfortunately, concern for the examiner's protection may dictate leaving the door ajar)
Unplugging phone	Not unplugging phone, answering telephone
Engaging in no distracting gestures	Looking repeatedly at watch, smoking cigarettes, chewing gum, playing or fidgeting with objects, fumbling with stopwatch, cracking knuckles, clicking ballpoint pen, running hands through hair, rubbing or scratching body, yawning, constantly shifting body position, swinging legs, crossing and uncrossing legs or arms, nodding head continuously, twitching nervously, tapping pen or pencil
Taking minimal notes and continuing to look at interviewee	Taking excessive notes and seldom looking at interviewee

Note. Positive and negative nonverbal behaviors do not apply to all cultural groups.
Source: Adapted from Zima (1983).

children and openness to self-evaluation and evaluation by others that you will learn the limits of your abilities. You should continually seek such knowledge by monitoring your behaviors and reactions and requesting feedback from colleagues.

Becoming self-aware also means listening to yourself. Become attuned to your thoughts, feelings, and actions, and learn how to deal with them appropriately during the evaluation. At times you will need to suppress your reactions so that you can remain objective. You are strongly encouraged to videotape several evaluations and study the videotapes to see how your needs, values, and standards emerged during the evaluations and how they affected your testing techniques and the hypotheses you formed about the examinees. Having an experienced colleague or supervisor view the tapes and provide feedback is also beneficial. Remember that you will need to obtain parental permission to videotape a test session with a child.

Supervision from an experienced psychologist during training should provide you with the feedback and guidance you need to deal with difficult situations involving children with special needs and their parents. In school settings, supervisors can alert you to policy and procedural safeguards associated with special education laws (see Chapter 3). What you learn in the classroom and from books can never prepare you for every eventuality that you will find in your work.

You want to make sure that, if you use glasses or hearing aids, you wear them to conduct the evaluation. You also should attend to your personal needs, such as food, drink, and use of the restroom, before the evaluation begins.

To help develop your assessment skills, you might ask yourself the following questions about your role as an examiner:

- Do you recognize how your standards affect the judgments you make? For example, do you think that it is acceptable for an adolescent to be lazy because you were lazy as a 12-year-old? If so, do you say to yourself, "Why can't these parents be like my parents and leave her alone?"
- Can you determine the basis for your hypotheses? For example, if you hypothesize that an adolescent is hiding some facts about an issue, is your hypothesis based on what he said, the way he looked when he said it, the way he reacted to your questions, or a combination of these factors?
- Are you aware of the style or tone of your communications? For instance, if you are speaking more rapidly with one examinee than with others, why are you doing so? Or if you are speaking in a condescending manner to an examinee, why are you doing so?
- Are you aware of personal biases, such as a sensitivity to certain words or concepts, that may distract you from listening in an unbiased manner? For example, do you flinch when you hear the terms *homosexual, gay,* and *lesbian*? Do you panic when you hear the word *abuse* because you were once abused? What can you do about these reactions so that they do not interfere with your ability to listen effectively?

Self-awareness also includes knowledge of your body language, including your facial expressions and gestures; the way you sit, hold your head, and direct your eyes; the small vocal sounds you make; and other nonverbal mannerisms. Watch out for frowning, puckering your lips, biting your fingernails, cracking your knuckles, tapping a foot or finger, twisting your hair or a paper clip, rocking, scratching, or shaking your head. When they are anxious or uncomfortable,

examiners often do these things and are not aware of doing them. *Your body language conveys meaning to the examinee.* Monitor it and use it to promote a positive testing relationship (see Table 7-1). A well-timed smile or nod of the head conveys to the examinee your interest and attention. You usually want to avoid body language that sends negative messages. For example, frowning or shaking your head may discourage the examinee from talking further or from working on a puzzle or other test materials. Also avoid distracting mannerisms such as humming a song, as they may cause the examinee to lose track of what he or she wants to say or interfere with the examinee's concentration. Because idiosyncratic mannerisms may distract examinees and usually serve no purpose during the evaluation, work hard to eliminate them or at least reduce the frequency of their occurrence.

Eye contact.   Eye contact is important. It helps examinees gauge the extent of your interest. You want to maintain eye contact with examinees but not stare or gaze intently at them. You also do not want to bury your head in the test manual and fail to look at the examinee. By occasionally looking away and then resuming your eye contact, you give examinees some breathing room, especially when they are having trouble responding to a question.

Appearance.   Dress appropriately and maintain acceptable grooming. You do not want to be too formal or too casual or present an unkempt appearance. Any of these may create psychological distance or discomfort and interfere with the examinee's performance.

Examiner Expectancy Effects

Your test administration should not be influenced by your personal impressions of the examinee, a reaction (as you learned in Chapter 1) called the *halo effect.* A halo effect occurs when you overrate the responses of a child whom you perceive as extremely capable or underrate the responses of a child whom you perceive as less capable. You may base these impressions, for example, on teacher reports, the child's appearance or behaviors, the quality of early responses, or previous experience with the child. In the testing of a child with special needs, you do not want to be overly liberal in scoring simply because the child tried hard to answer the questions. Alfred Binet and David Wechsler carefully sought to diminish halo effects with their standardization procedures, but examiners, too, must take precautions to avoid giving more credit or less credit than the child deserves.

There is room for subjectivity because many items on individual intelligence tests call for open-ended responses rather than fixed responses (such as those on a multiple-choice test). Open-ended responses are more susceptible to the halo effect because they may be ambiguous or may not be included in the scoring guide of the test. Only a limited number of scoring examples are included in most test scoring guides.

SCHOOLIES © 1997 by John P. Wood

SLOW STUDENTS CROSSING

Boy, we bomb one state test and we're labelled for life.

Copyright © 1997 by John P. Wood.

Social-psychological research indicates that, in experiments, the experimenter's hypotheses or expectancies may exert some subtle influence over how participants perform by affecting how the experimenter behaves with these individuals. For example, early data returns in an experiment may lead the experimenter to develop expectancies that subtly affect the experimenter's attitudes in later interactions with those who are participating in the study (Rosenthal, 1966). Administering an individual intelligence test is in some ways similar to conducting an experiment. Background information on the examinee may lead the examiner to formulate a hypothesis, although vague, regarding the examinee's level of intelligence; this hypothesis may affect the examiner-examinee relationship. Similarly, examiners obtain information about an examinee's ability as the test proceeds, and this information is likely to give rise to expectancies about the examinee's ability. You must not allow the halo effect to influence your judgment about how to administer and score tests. (See Sattler, 1992, pages 113–114, for a list of studies evaluating expectancy effects for responses given to intelligence tests.)

The elimination of halo effects in administering, scoring, and evaluating intelligence and other ability tests is a difficult goal. It is probably impossible to eliminate your positive or negative reactions to a child completely; however, it *is* possible and necessary to reduce the influence of these reactions on your test administration and scoring. Be sure that, when interacting with examinees you believe are capable, you do not smile more frequently, sustain eye contact longer, offer more support, act friendlier, give more praise, repeat ques-

tions more frequently, create a warmer atmosphere, or score responses more leniently. Similarly, do not give cues that signal disinterest or disdain to examinees you believe are less capable on certain tasks. You must become aware of your reactions to each child and be especially alert to possible halo effects in your test administration and scoring of responses.

A special type of expectancy effect may occur when an examinee appears to be approaching a basal level or ceiling level on a test. This is a level at which the test will be continued if a certain number of items are passed or discontinued if a certain number of items are failed, respectively. You may subconsciously assist the examinee or score too leniently when the examinee has almost established a basal, and you may do the opposite as the examinee attempts the last few items for a long-awaited ceiling on a grueling test. It is essential to continue testing and scoring as thoughtfully and accurately as possible, even in these circumstances.

Variability Among Examiners

Research on expectancy effects and on examiner differences (see Sattler, 1992, pages 113–115, for a review) indicates that not all examiners score the same intelligence test responses in the same way. Also, examiners sometimes allow their or the examinee's sex, race, or ethnicity to affect the score they obtain for the examinee. Chapter 20 reviews studies on the examiner's race and ethnicity as variables in testing children.

Research on the role of the examiner confirms clinical impressions that the evaluation setting has elements of subjectivity. You must try to reduce any sources of subjectivity related to how you administer and score tests. If you do not, the validity of the child's score may be in question. You should become aware of your scoring habits when faced with vague or ambiguous responses: Are you lenient or rigorous in your judgments? Always try to be fair, consistent, and accurate in your application of the scoring criteria. For assistance in obtaining information about your administrative techniques, see Table 7-2. During the early phases of your career, answer the questions in Table 7-2 after every assessment you complete. An observer (such as a course instructor, course assistant, or fellow student) can use the list to evaluate your performance, too. An understanding of child psychology, child exceptionality, test manuals, and the material in this book, coupled with a willingness to evaluate and reflect on your testing skills, will enable you to achieve a high level of competence in evaluating children.

Research Findings on the Examiner-Examinee Relationship

When children are acquainted (or familiar) with the examiner, does their performance on individual ability and achievement tests improve? Fuchs and Fuchs (1986) decided to find out by examining the results of 22 studies. These studies involved 1,489 children who took tests measuring intelligence, speech/

Table 7-2
Checklist for General Test Administration Practices

GENERAL TEST ADMINISTRATION PRACTICES CHECKLIST

Examiner: _____   Date: _____

Examinee: _____   Age: _____

Observer: _____   Test administered: _____

Scale: 1 = Very Poor   2 = Poor   3 = Satisfactory   4 = Good   5 = Excellent

Circle One

1 2 3 4 5   1. Established rapport before beginning the test

1 2 3 4 5   2. Prepared the child for the examination

1 2 3 4 5   3. Arranged the test environment to minimize distractions

1 2 3 4 5   4. Avoided distracting mannerisms

1 2 3 4 5   5. Showed interest in the child

1 2 3 4 5   6. Gave the child ample encouragement and support

1 2 3 4 5   7. Wore appropriate, nondistracting attire

1 2 3 4 5   8. Spoke at an appropriate volume for the setting

1 2 3 4 5   9. Appeared open and accepting of the child's feelings

1 2 3 4 5   10. Seemed at ease with the child

1 2 3 4 5   11. Maintained frequent eye contact with the child

1 2 3 4 5   12. Had the necessary materials present and organized

1 2 3 4 5   13. Arranged the materials conveniently

1 2 3 4 5   14. Placed the manual so that the child could not read it

1 2 3 4 5   15. Arranged the materials so that the child could not review test items other than the one(s) in use

1 2 3 4 5   16. Manipulated the materials with ease and confidence

1 2 3 4 5   17. Read all directions verbatim

1 2 3 4 5   18. Used accurate timing procedures

1 2 3 4 5   19. Used unobtrusive timing procedures

1 2 3 4 5   20. Recorded responses in the record booklet

1 2 3 4 5   21. Paced the examination to suit the child's needs and temperament

Circle One

1 2 3 4 5   22. Explained test procedures adequately

1 2 3 4 5   23. Used developmentally appropriate vocabulary

1 2 3 4 5   24. Showed awareness of signs of fatigue

1 2 3 4 5   25. Handled fatigue appropriately

1 2 3 4 5   26. Showed awareness of emotional upsets

1 2 3 4 5   27. Handled emotional upsets appropriately

1 2 3 4 5   28. Took needed breaks

1 2 3 4 5   29. Handled the child's attempts to manipulate the situation

1 2 3 4 5   30. Gave appropriate explanations or clarifications

1 2 3 4 5   31. Made inquiries in a nonthreatening manner

1 2 3 4 5   32. Used additional questions to clarify, not to improve, the child's answers

1 2 3 4 5   33. Praised the child appropriately (e.g., did not praise correct answers, praised *effort*)

1 2 3 4 5   34. Handled disruptions adequately

1 2 3 4 5   35. Responded honestly and positively to the child's questions in ways consistent with the test instructions

1 2 3 4 5   36. Used open-ended questions when appropriate, not closed ones

1 2 3 4 5   37. Introduced the test and explained what the examiner and child would be doing together

1 2 3 4 5   38. Adhered to standardized procedures

1 2 3 4 5   39. Appeared professional—neither too stiff or robotic nor too casual

1 2 3 4 5   40. Ended the session appropriately

Copyright © 1997 by John P. Wood.

language proficiency, educational achievement, and similar areas. The results indicated that examiner familiarity raised the children's test performance, on the average, by about 4.2 scaled-score points. The increase in points was greater (on the average, about 7.6 scaled-score points) when the children were of low SES, when they were tested on comparatively difficult tests, and when they knew the examiner for a relatively long time. Fuchs and Fuchs (1989) also reported that in 14 of the studies in which African American, Hispanic American, and Euro American children served as subjects, the ethnic minority children scored about 11 points higher with a familiar examiner than with an unfamiliar examiner. Euro American children, in contrast, performed similarly with familiar and unfamiliar examiners. This research did not examine the race or ethnicity of the examiners. The results, however, must be interpreted with caution because the increase in scores may be associated in part with how the examiners scored the responses, rather than solely with changes in the examinees' performance (Fuchs & Fuchs, 1986).

The results of this study do suggest that situational factors may affect the performance of children of low SES and of ethnic minorities to a greater extent than they do the performance of children of high SES and of Euro American ethnic backgrounds. We need more research to determine the effects of examiner variables and situational factors on children's test performances. Let's now consider some ideas that can help prepare you for the first meeting.

PREPARING FOR THE FIRST MEETING

In preparing for the first meeting, you should study the referral question and review available background material. If the parents have completed the Background Questionnaire (see *Assessment of Children: Behavioral and Clinical Applications*), review it. Also review teacher reports, medical reports, police reports, and prior evaluations of the child and the parents, if available. If the referral information leads you to select tests you do not often use, review the test manuals and materials carefully. If your knowledge of the presenting problem is rusty, review relevant literature. If the referral question is beyond your competence, refer the case to someone else. Before scheduling the evaluation, you may wish to recommend that the child have an up-to-date medical examination. Pay particular attention to information about any health-related difficulties that might interfere with the child's evaluation. Finally, make sure that the examination room is ready.

As noted in Chapter 1, in school settings there may be a pre-referral team meeting to decide whether an assessment is needed and, if so, how it should proceed. Participants at the meeting may include a guidance counselor, classroom teacher, school nurse, school administrator, psychologist, and parent. If the team decides that an assessment is warranted, the parent will be asked to sign the necessary documents to start the evaluation process. If the team decides that an assessment is not warranted, it may consider other alternatives for providing the child with services (see Chapter 3).

ESTABLISHING RAPPORT

The process of establishing rapport begins when the parent conveys to the child that the child will be meeting with a psychologist. You want to allay parental anxieties about the evaluation when you arrange the appointment for the child.

Explain what you will be doing with the child, such as looking at how the child understands words and pictures, determining which types of activities are easy for the child and which are more difficult, and finding out how the child expresses ideas and interests. Assure the parent that most children find the activities pleasant and that you are looking forward to meeting the child. Instruct the parent to refrain from telling the child that the child will be playing games with you. If the parent says this, the child may ask you after a few minutes, "So when do we play the games?" You want the parent to have an understanding of what you are going to do because it is the parent who will initially prepare the child for the evaluation.

When you will be conducting the evaluation at the child's school, it will be helpful to share with the child's teacher the same information that you gave to the parent. Eliciting cooperation from the teacher also may help in developing rapport with the child.

When a parent is with the child, first introduce yourself to the parent, and then introduce yourself to the child using the child's first name. You might say to an older child, "Hello Duane. I'm Dr. _____, a psychologist who works here. We're going to be working together for a while with words and pictures while your mother [father] waits out here for us." This simple introduction serves several functions. First, it emphasizes, through use of the examiner's formal title, that the relationship is a professional one. Second, it makes clear that you and the child will be engaging in some activity. Finally, it tells the child where the parent will be during the meeting, thus helping to alleviate anxiety that the child may have about separation. You should keep your introductory comments to a minimum.

With young children, consider avoiding use of the title "doctor" because young children may become anxious when they hear the word. For example, children who have had extensive medical care may associate the word "doctor" with getting injections.

If the child is young, you might bring a toy and at first try to keep the parent seated so that you can kneel at the child's level. Initially, give most of your attention to the parent and let the child look you over. Gradually make friends with the child as he or she becomes used to your presence. When the child seems comfortable, invite the child and, depending on the child's age, the parent into your room. But do not abruptly remove the child from an interesting activity. With young children, you might begin simply by saying "We're going to do some things together," or "We're going to work on some fun things together," or "Time to do some things now; I'll show you where they are."

A brief and frank account of the purpose of the evaluation may be helpful with older children. You might say,

We will be doing some things together, and most children enjoy doing them. Some things that we'll be doing will be easy and some will be hard. That's because some things are for children younger than you and some things are for children older than you. So don't worry if you can't get all the answers right. I don't expect you to know all the answers, but I want you to do your very best.

For evaluating school children, here is another possible introduction (John Willis, personal communication, October 1999):

My job is helping teachers learn how to teach students better. What I do in this school is work with one student at a time so that I can help the teacher do a better job of teaching that student. Your teacher(s) and parent(s) wanted me to do that with you. You know that everybody has his or her own best ways of learning, and that some people are better at certain things and some people are better at others. My job is to find out what you are best at and what things are hardest for you. I need to know what you've already learned and what you have not learned yet. I hope to find out what are the best ways for you to learn, so I can tell your teachers to do more of those things. Before we are done, I will also be asking you for your opinions about the best ways for you to learn and about what you like and don't like.

To do all this, I need to ask you to do all kinds of different things. Some of them will be much too easy, so please don't be offended when I ask you something from _____ grade. Some of them will be much too hard because they are for students in [middle school/high school/college]. You won't know all of them because you haven't been to [middle school/high school/college] yet. It may worry you because I cannot tell you if you are right or wrong on the things we do, but I will go over the results with you later.

Tailor your remarks to the needs of the child. Be confident and encouraging, making it clear that you want the child to do her or his best. Convey your sincere interest in seeing the child succeed. Reassure the child of your unconditional acceptance and support, even when she or he fails items. Although your first comments are important in establishing rapport, *efforts to build and maintain rapport should continue throughout the evaluation.*

Make the tasks as pleasant as you can, even though some of them will be difficult for the child to perform. Learning to encourage effort, as opposed to rewarding responses, takes practice. Always check the test manuals to learn what prompts and words of encouragement are suggested by the test developers.

Do not allow other children to be in the room. Having another child in the room can be disruptive, and the feelings of the child who is not getting your attention can be hurt. Avoid these problems by requesting, at the time you make the appointment, that the parent arrange for someone to take care of any siblings. Occasionally, a child will ask about your previous evaluation with a sibling or schoolmate. Be very clear that you are not allowed to discuss evaluations except with parents, teachers, and other official people.

Allaying Apprehensions of Younger Children

Sometimes young children will scream and cry in the waiting room. In such cases, pause a few minutes before you enter the waiting area to see if the child's distress is brief and if the parents can calm the child (Kanfer, Eyberg, & Krahn, 1992). If the child continues to cry, try to distract the child by offering him or her a toy and engaging briefly in play.

Separation from the parent may be an issue particularly with children who are under the age of 6 years or who are agitated; sometimes older children will not want to separate from their parents. To ease the separation, first spend some time talking with the parent in the child's presence, and then point out where the parent will be waiting. Offer your hand to the child and say, "Come with me to the office." Or you could ask, "Would you like to leave your dolly [toy] here with your mother, or would you like to bring it with you?" (Kanfer et al., 1992, p. 56). The question gives the child some choice and control and thus may help reduce anxiety. You can coax a hesitant child by showing the child a toy and encouraging him or her to go into your office to play with it. If these strategies fail, you can ask the parent to come into your office with the child. As the child relaxes, you can ask the parent to leave, reassuring the parent that the child will be safe.

If the child insists that the parent stay in the room, place the parent behind the child, out of the child's line of vision. You don't want the parent to give the child cues or interfere with the evaluation in any way. Tell the parent not to give any form of verbal encouragement (or nonverbal encouragement either) to the child. If a parent holds a small child on her or his lap, make sure that the chair is low enough so that together their knees fit underneath the table. *However, if the parent is suspected of having abused or neglected the child or if the evaluation is part of a custody dispute, do not evaluate the child in the presence of a parent.* (See Sattler, 1998, for further information about child maltreatment interviewing and child custody evaluations.)

It is permissible to allow the parent (who has no allegation of child maltreatment pending against him or her) to sit in an observation room with a one-way mirror. Viewing the testing may help the parent understand the test results better.

Allaying Apprehensions of Older Children

When you first meet older children, they may be apprehensive. Possible concerns center on such issues as medical treatment ("Will I get needles?"), removal from home ("Am I going to be 'put away'?"), competency ("Will I have my head examined? How?"), self-concept ("Will they find that I'm crazy or 'dumb'?"), "something extra" ("Is this going to go on my report card?" or "Is this going to count in my grades?"), and being singled out ("Why am I the only one in the family to come?" or "How come the other kids at school don't come?" or "What will I tell my friends about why I had to leave class today?"). To allay their apprehensions and reduce their anxiety, you will need to deal with these and other concerns.

To the older child, you want to convey through questions and comments that you will treat her or him professionally, with decency, safety, and respect. Be honest with the child, tailoring your comments to her or his age and level of understanding. For example, at the beginning of the evaluation, you will want to inform the child about the reason for the evaluation by saying something like "Your parents are concerned about your school work being difficult for you, and I'm here to find out how we can help you." You can also say, "Your parents are concerned that you're not doing as well as you're capable of doing, and I'm here to find out how we can help you."

Older children may be curious about what you are going to do with the information you obtain: how much of the information you are going to share with parents, guardians, school, or court (see Chapter 3) and what will happen to them after you complete the evaluation. What you say about these matters will depend on the referral question, what you learn during the evaluation, your school or agency policy, your state law, or some combination of these factors. Even if children are not curious about these matters, share with them the steps in the evaluation procedure and, if feasible, tell them that you will meet with them to discuss the results and recommendations. Anything you can do to calm them will be helpful. You might say, "After we finish today, I'll review the results and then I'll ask you and your parents to meet with me so that we can plan what to do next."

Children (and adults) may wonder about you. They may wonder about who you are, your competency (especially if you are a psychologist-in-training), what you know about them, whose side you are on, and how your actions will affect what eventually happens to them. Be prepared to address these and other concerns. Children may not express their thoughts and feelings directly, so observe them carefully. It may help to let children know that you recognize their apprehensions: "Tracey, I know how difficult it is for many young people to come to a new place and talk with new people."

It also is helpful to learn what the child thinks is the reason for the evaluation. You might ask, "Did your parents talk to you about coming to see me?" or "What kind of place did you think this would be?" Correct any misconceptions. If you think it will reduce the child's anxiety, explain that you do not give shots and that after the session is over he or she can go home or back to class.

Examinees who are students may need to know how long the assessment will take and what they will be missing in class. If a child is anxious about missing a special event—such as a school play, an exam, or a class he or she particularly enjoys—because of the evaluation, reassure the student that you will stop in time. It may be necessary to alter your schedule so that the student does not miss a crucial class or test, but your flexibility will be rewarded by greatly enhanced rapport.

You also may need to make arrangements with the student's teachers so that the student is not penalized for missing class. Some teachers may not be flexible and will treat the evaluation session as an unexcused absence if you do not intervene. Unless the student is reassured about such issues, test validity may be impaired. It is a good idea to talk to the student's teachers 2 or 3 days in advance to find a good time to schedule the evaluation.

Despite your efforts, a few children may not want to speak with you or take any tests. They may be wary of strangers, uncertain as to why you want to evaluate them, resentful of having been coerced to come to the evaluation, reluctant to confide anything that may get back to their parents, or fearful of talking about painful or frightening experiences (Kessler, 1988). If children won't talk openly with you, see whether they are willing to answer test questions or play a game. Asking a reluctant child to draw may serve as an ice-breaker. Empathize with the fears and resentments of wary children, and offer them support and reassurance. In some cases, however, there may be nothing that you can do to allay apprehensions. This is especially likely when the child is actively psychotic, is extremely hyperactive, has an extreme anxiety disorder, or is markedly deficient in attention and motivation. Older children who have undergone recent testing in other situations (such as by court-appointed referral) also may be resistant to testing, despite your assurances that the tests are different and serve a clearly different purpose.

When you encounter children who are unusually tense, who resist responding to the test questions, who are unable to concentrate, who in other ways fail to give forth their best effort, or who simply will not or cannot cooperate, be prepared to stop the evaluation and reschedule it. If you have prepared properly and done your best to establish rapport, there is no reason to take a rejection personally. Even the most empathic and experienced examiners are sometimes unable to carry out an evaluation.

Helping Children Feel at Ease

Helping children maintain a sense of self-esteem and self-acceptance is essential to bringing about a successful relationship. Encourage children to respond to each question and to take a chance even when they are reluctant. By giving encouragement, you may both reduce their anxiety and help to sustain their interest level. When children become fatigued, take a short break. If they are still fatigued after the break, discontinue testing. If you sense that children are frustrated, you might say something like "That was a bit difficult, but no one is expected to get them all right. Now let's try another one." By letting children know that you recognize that the questions are becoming more difficult and by verbally acknowledging their reactions, you will help children maintain their self-esteem. Because the directions in the test manuals cannot cover every contingency, be prepared to use tact and common sense when difficulties arise.

In most cases, after a short introduction, you can begin with the test materials as a way of continuing to establish rapport. Children like to do things, and they will usually find responding to questions or solving puzzlelike tasks engaging and challenging. Encourage children to do their best. Accompany your supportive comments with appropriate facial expressions and modulations of your voice. More than almost any other procedure, early experiences of success in answering test questions will help children relax quickly. If there are practice items, be sure to give them.

You must be willing, however, to listen to and be attentive to children's needs, rather than adhering mechanically to your agenda. Teglasi and Freeman (1983) cite an example of a case in which a male examiner put his needs before those of the child. The examiner interacted the "obligatory" few minutes with an 11-year-old girl. The girl felt comfortable enough to bring up a concern that was directly germane to the referral problem. She described the difficulties she was having finding a quiet place to study in her home. Instead of listening to and responding to her legitimate concerns, the examiner's response was "Well, we've spent enough time talking; shall we get started with the test?"

Rapport may be affected in several ways, some obvious and others not. For example, do *not* say "Good answer" or "That's right" or "You're doing great" every time the child responds. In most tests, it is not part of the standard administrative procedure to inform the examinee about whether a response is correct or incorrect. Also, if you use excessive praise early in the test, you face a dilemma when the test questions become more difficult and failures are more common. You must then either abandon your previous approach, with the obvious implication that praise is no longer deserved, or continue to use praise when the child is probably aware that her or his performance is inadequate. The latter may cause the child to distrust you and hence interfere with your relationship and, ultimately, the child's performance. Consequently, give brief, natural, and casual praise for the child's *effort*—"You're trying hard and that's good"—rather than for the *results* of her or his effort. Do not get into the habit of responding differently to correct and incorrect responses, such as saying "Good" to correct answers and "Okay" to incorrect answers or saying "Un-huh" with a rising inflection to correct responses and "Un'huh" with a falling inflection to incorrect responses. Finally, adopt a uniform method of recording all responses because if you do not do so, you may provide cues to the examinee. For example, if you write out only incorrect responses or those that need to be checked and simply record a score for correct responses, the examinee may recognize how he or she is performing (e.g., "She only writes down the ones I'm unsure of or the ones that I must be getting wrong").

Also, give the child a choice only when you intend to leave the decision up to him or her. Do *not* ask, "Do you want to come into my room now?" unless you are prepared to accept no as an answer. You don't want to say "Do you want to get started?" and then, after the child says no, say, "Well, we're going to get started" (Teglasi & Freeman, 1983). Similarly, if the child asks "When can I take a break?" do not say, "Any time you want" when you don't mean it (e.g., the child responds with "Now" and you then say, "Well, let's finish this first").

Do not do or say anything that may diminish the child's self-respect. Avoid attempting to motivate the child by making comparisons between the child and another child or by encouraging competition. Try to maintain the child's cooperation at all times. Remember that you need to *earn* the child's attention and cooperation.

In summary, you don't want to introduce extraneous material that may increase the child's anxiety, perplex the child, or reduce the child's motivation, as was done in the following incident (Teglasi & Freeman, 1983). The examiner said to the examinee, "These are getting hard. They are so hard that even I don't know some of the answers. Do you sometimes wonder if your teachers know the answers to tests that they give you? So you're not really expected to know all of them … now even I don't know the answers to some of these. I look them up in a book." The child simply looked perplexed after listening to all this.

After you complete the evaluation, praise the child for her or his effort, *if* the praise was deserved. Say, for example, "Thank you for trying your best" or "I appreciated your effort" or "Thanks for coming today and being so cooperative." You don't have to give the child a reward, but sometimes providing a pencil, eraser, or sticker can be a nice gesture. Do not give the child a cola drink or food unless you have the parent's permission.

Maintaining Limits on Permissible Behavior

Your attempts to maintain control of the testing situation may not always be successful. Some children, for example, may try to gain control by requesting water frequently or by being

SCHOOLIES © 2000 by John P. Wood

Oooh, that's a tragic miss there.

It must have been a mis-read, Alan.

Yep, not much of a chance for him now…

TELEVISED HIGH STAKES TESTING

Copyright © 2000 by John P. Wood.

uncooperative. Your patience may be tried. You do not want to be rigid and unyielding. Instead, be flexible and do what is necessary to get the child to participate in the assessment. You can gather hints about how to proceed from the child's verbal statements, nonverbal behavior, age, and background.

Be sure that the child understands the limits of behavior, and let there be no doubt as to who is in charge. If control becomes an issue, stop the testing until you settle the matter. You may need to take a break, play a game, retreat to easier items, or use some other tactic, but do not allow things to get out of hand. Do not permit the relationship to degenerate into a power struggle. Sometimes you cannot avoid a modest degree of unpleasantness, especially with unhappy, rebellious children, but establish as much rapport as you can and elicit the child's best effort.

Individual Variability Among Examinees and in the Examiner-Examinee Relationship

Each encounter with a child will have its own dynamics. Procedures that are effective with one child may not work with another. Thus, each test administration is subtly different. Even though you should follow the test procedures precisely, your interactions will (and should) differ with every child. Following are some examples of how evaluations vary. Note that the differences are not violations of standard procedures, unless otherwise noted in a test manual.

1. Because some children respond slowly and others quickly, evaluations will take varying amounts of time.
2. The number of follow-up questions you ask will depend on a child's initial responses to the questions. (If you prudently query a response and later discover that your probe was not permitted by the test manual, you can neatly cross out the question and the examinee's answer, not counting the answer in the scoring but preserving it for analysis.)
3. On tests where two trials are allowed, some children may need both trials, while others will need only one.
4. Some children need few, if any, breaks during the evaluation, while others need many.
5. Changes in how you feel (e.g., your mental or physical health) may affect how you administer the test that day.
6. Your attitude toward the examinee may affect how you establish rapport and administer the tests, as was noted earlier in the chapter.

These sources of examinee and examiner variability *usually* will not diminish the overall reliability or validity of the test results. They contributed to the standard error of measurement of the test score during standardization. To ensure good test administration, however, you need to be aware of how you and the examinee are feeling on the day you are testing, how you are responding to the examinee, and how the examinee is responding to you and to the test situation, and then make the appropriate adjustments.

© 2000 from cartoonbank.com. All Rights Reserved.

OBSERVING EXAMINEES

Your observations of examinees will depend on their age and the setting in which you conduct the evaluation. It will be helpful to observe examinees' personal appearance, nonverbal behavior, and verbal behavior, both in the test situation and in interactions with others, especially parents, teachers, siblings, and peers. Observations conducted during the administration of psychological tests are especially valuable because they are made under relatively standard conditions and allow for comparisons among different examinees. As examinees are working, observe them inconspicuously. Do not stare or do or say anything that might distract, embarrass, or irritate them. Be discreet when you are recording observations and scoring responses.

Whenever you observe a behavior that deviates from normal—such as perseveration (persistent repetition of the same thought or response) or echolalia (inappropriate repetition of speech previously uttered by another speaker)—note where and when the behavior occurs and what happens afterwards. For example, does the behavior occur on all tests, some tests only, or certain items only? Does it happen at the beginning of the session, during the middle, or at end, when the examinee may be fatigued or frustrated? Can the examinee recover on his or her own or is assistance needed from you? How does the examinee react to his or her behavior (e.g., concerned or indifferent)? Overall, what purpose might the behavior serve, if any?

You also need to be aware of how the examinee responds to extraneous stimuli. For example, what is the examinee's response to the following distractions: voices, music, or noises outside the testing room; pictures in the room; sounds in the room, such as that of a fan, a computer, or a clock; or any interruptions?

Also observe the examinee's manner of responding to questions. Table 7-3 provides a detailed list of questions to help you

do this. It contains questions about the examinee's attitude, attention, affect, language, visual skills, visual-motor skills, motor skills, and behavior. And Table 7-4 will assist you in recognizing indicators of psychological problems associated with the child's behavior. Don't feel overwhelmed by the list of behavioral indicators—you are not required to observe all of them. The purpose of the list is to show possibilities.

You also need to observe how the child performs on various types of test items and materials. The following questions will help you in carrying out these observations (Nancy Marron, personal communication, October 1999).

- How well does the child recognize errors and then proceed to make changes to help solve the problems?
- Does the child continue to repeat the same mistakes over and over, especially on items requiring assembly?
- Does the child appear to know what he or she does and does not know?
- Does the child learn anything from successful completion of early test items?
- Does the child take apart puzzles or block designs that are correct?
- Does the child use both hands, one hand, or the right hand for the right side of the design and the left hand for the left

NON SEQUITUR by WILEY

NON SEQUITUR © Wiley Miller. Dist. by UNIVERSAL PRESS SYNDICATE. Reprinted with permission. All rights reserved.

Table 7-3
Questions to Consider About the Child's Behaviors During the Assessment

Attitude

Attitude Toward the Examiner
1. How does the child relate to you (e.g., shy, frightened, bold, aggressive, friendly, respectful, cooperative, negativistic, or overly eager to please)?
2. Does the child's attitude toward you change over the course of the examination? If so, in what way and when does the change occur?
3. Does the child try to induce you to give answers to questions? If so, in what way?
4. Does the child maintain reasonable eye contact with you?
5. Does the child watch you closely to discover whether his or her responses are correct?
6. Does the child do things that might distract you? If so, what things does the child do?
7. Does the child refrain from interrupting you?

Attitude Toward the Test Situation
1. What is the child's attitude toward himself or herself (e.g., poised, confident, self-derogatory, boastful, or objective)?
2. What is the child's attitude toward taking the tests (e.g., relaxed, tense, irritable, withdrawn, expansive, eager, reluctant, or interested)?
3. Does the child's interest vary during the examination? If so, in what way?
4. Is the child aware of time limits on timed tasks? If so, how does this awareness affect his or her performance?
5. Does the child appear to be making his or her best effort?
6. How does the child react to probing questions (e.g., reconsiders the answer, defends the first answer, quickly says "I don't know," or becomes silent)?
7. Do any of the test items produce in the child reactions such as anxiety, stammering, blushing, or a change in mood or behavior? If so, what type of item?
8. Is the child easily frustrated? If so, how is this frustration expressed and on what tasks?
9. Does the child block on some items ("I know, but I just can't think") or wait a long time before answering? If blocking or waiting occurs, is it on easy items, difficult items, or all items?
10. Does the child need to be urged to respond? If so, does the urging lead to a response?
11. What degree of assistance does the child need to assure an adequate response to the task (e.g., modeling, verbal prompts, physical prompts, or physical guidance)?

Attention

Overall Attention
1. How well does the child attend to the test?
2. Does the child respond consistently to his or her name?
3. Is the child easily distracted? If so, what kind of stimuli seems to distract the child most easily (e.g., visual or auditory)?
4. For what length of time can the child participate in an activity?
5. How difficult is it to regain the child's attention when it is lost?

Following Directions
1. Does the child wait until the directions have been given before he or she begins a task?
2. What is the child's level of comprehension of the instructions and test questions?

3. Does the child show confusion? If so, how is the confusion expressed (e.g., asks for clarification or repetition when he or she is unsure of the instructions or messages or looks perplexed)?
4. Is it necessary to repeat instructions or questions, or does the child say "What?" frequently? If so, what does the need for repetition suggest (e.g., a hearing problem, limited understanding of English, attention difficulties, poor comprehension, or an effort on the child's part to obtain more time to think about the question)?
5. Is there any other evidence of a possible hearing problem (e.g., asks you to speak louder or repeat instructions, watches your mouth intently, or cannot understand what you are saying when his or her back is turned to you)?

Affect
1. What is the quality of the child's affect (e.g., happy, sad, elated, angry, agitated, anxious, fearful, flat, labile)?
2. Is the child's affect appropriate to the situation and task demands?
3. Does the child show incongruity of affect between verbal and nonverbal behaviors (e.g., frowning while discussing how happy he or she feels)?
4. Is there any suggestion of a possible affective disturbance? If so, what are the signs?

Language
Speech, Expressive Language, and Receptive Language
1. What is the quality of the child's speech (e.g., rapid, slow, high-pitched, unusually loud or soft, characterized by appropriate or inappropriate rhythm, or difficult to understand)?
2. Does the child converse spontaneously or only in response to questions?
3. How much effort does the child need to produce speech? (Note any visible struggles, facial grimaces, body posturing, deep breathing, or hand gestures.)
4. What is the child's typical phrase length (e.g., single words, short phrases, or complete sentences)?
5. If the child makes speech errors, to what can the errors be attributed (e.g., problems with remembering what you asked, expressive language, receptive language, fluency, organization, pronunciation, or sentence structure)?
6. Does the child have difficulty with word retrieval ("I know what that is but forgot what it's called")? If so, what is the difficulty?
7. Does the child seem to understand what you are saying? If not, what is the difficulty?
8. Is there any suggestion of a possible thought disorder? If so, what are the signs?

Gestures and Nonverbal Behavior
1. Does the child understand gestures?
2. Does the child use nonverbal behaviors appropriately when speaking? If not, what behaviors are inappropriate?

Content of Communications
1. How accurately does the child express himself or herself?
2. Do the child's responses reflect personal concerns or egocentrism? If so, what are the responses?
3. Does the child avoid certain topics? If so, which topics?

(Continued)

Table 7-3 (Continued)

4. How competent is the child in the use of words and grammar?
5. Does the child's language contain objects, actions, and events in a variety of relationships?
6. Does the child use words for social communication?
7. Does the child verbalize several possibilities and perspectives?
8. What is the quality of the child's responses (e.g., brief answers or detailed, thoughtful answers)?
9. Can the child assume the role or viewpoint of another?
10. Does the child take turns appropriately in conversations?

Visual, Visual-Motor, and Motor Skills

1. Are there any signs that the child has a visual problem (e.g., holds some of the test materials close to his or her eyes or seems to be straining to see the test stimuli)? If so, what are the signs?
2. How well does the child perform motor tasks (e.g., walking, jumping, kicking, or throwing a ball, using scissors, turning pages, holding a pencil, drawing, and using pegs)?
3. What is the tempo of the child's body movements (e.g., normal, slow, fast, impulsive, or hesitant)?
4. Are the child's motor movements appropriate for his or her age and situation?
5. Does the child show signs of motor difficulties (e.g., rhythmic shaking of extremities, excessive wriggling and squirming, marked overactivity or underactivity relative to the situation, tics, or stereotyped movements)? If so, what are the signs?
6. Does the child have any motor or sensory impairments that would obviously affect his or her test performance? If so, what are the impairments?
7. How does the child perform visual-motor tasks (e.g., proceeds systematically, proceeds in a trial-and-error manner, uses the same hand for all tasks, or uses different hands for different tasks)?

Behavior

Work Habits

1. What is the child's work tempo (e.g., fast, slow, or moderate)?
2. How does the child approach tasks (e.g., responds impulsively, acts thoughtfully, gives up easily, insists on continuing to work

on difficult items, thinks aloud, revises answers frequently, or only gives final answer)?
3. If there is a delay in responding, what might it be due to?
4. Does the child write out answers on the table with a finger, continually ask you for clarification, or use other means to solve the problems?
5. How readily does the child become fatigued?

Problem Behavior

1. Does the child exhibit any inappropriate or unacceptable behaviors? If so, what are the behaviors?
2. Does the child seem to have blank periods or moments (when he or she suddenly stops speaking for a few seconds or longer or stops working on a test)?

Reaction to Failure

1. How does the child react to difficult items (e.g., retreats, becomes aggressive, works harder, tries to cheat, becomes evasive, or openly admits failure)?
2. How does the child react to failure (e.g., apologizes, rationalizes, broods, accepts failure calmly, or becomes angry or humiliated)?

Reinforcers

1. How responsive is the child to verbal and physical reinforcers (e.g., reacts to praise gracefully or awkwardly or is motivated by praise to work harder)?
2. What schedule of reinforcement is needed to sustain effort?
3. For a child with a severe disability, is food needed to teach a new behavior or skill, or will nonedible reinforcers do?
4. If there is problem behavior, what consequences are most effective in reducing the problem behavior?

Note. This table should be used in conjunction with Table 7-4, which shows indicators of possible psychological problems observed in the evaluation.
Source: Adapted from Finkle, Hanson, and Hostetler (1983); Hartley (1990); O'Neil (1984); Silver and Hagin (1990); Zimmerman and Woo-Sam (1985).

side of the design when working with items requiring assembly?

- Does the child show anxiety when he or she detects that speed is important?
- Are high scores on verbal questions the result of brief, succinct answers or the result of rambling responses that finally include sufficient information to yield a high score?
- What is the pattern of the child's successes and failures (e.g., mostly successes and then failures; a repeated pattern of success followed by failure, such as one success and three failures followed by another success and then three failures)?

- Does the child respond too quickly, before you have even completed the question?
- Does the child ask repeatedly when the test will be over?
- How does the child react to probing questions and follow-up questions (cooperatively, defensively, inflexibly)?
- Does the child accept or refuse an offered break in testing?

Skill in observing behavior requires training and practice; it does not occur automatically when you find yourself in a situation where you have to observe a child. You must be alert, perceptive, and attentive to the child's behavior. Make notes as you observe the child rather than relying on your

Table 7-4
Indications in the Evaluation Suggesting Possible Psychological Difficulties

Relation to Examiner

1. *Clinging*—Clings to examiner, seeks physical contact, demands constant attention and direction
2. *Confused*—Is bewildered, perplexed, or puzzled
3. *Negative*—Opposes and resists examiner's initiative; makes guarded, evasive replies or is deliberately silent; is manipulative or defiant; refuses to cooperate
4. *Overcompliant*—Goes along with examiner passively; fails to assert self reasonably
5. *Withdrawn*—Seems preoccupied, avoids eye contact with examiner, acts aloof or distant, responds mechanically, exhibits no sustained emotional relatedness

Motor Behavior

6. *Body asymmetries*—Has facial asymmetry such as drooping of one side of the face or weakness in one arm only; has other body asymmetries
7. *Extremely limited use of gestures*—Fails to use gestures as would normally be expected, given his or her cultural background
8. *Extremely relaxed posture forms*—Slouches or acts inappropriately relaxed
9. *Hyperactive/impulsive*—Has difficulty staying seated; gets up frequently; moves fast; exhibits vigorous, impulsive bursts of locomotion
10. *Involuntary body movements*—Displays at-rest tremors (tremors that appear when the examinee is still), choreiform movements (jerky, involuntary movements or spasms of short duration), tics (e.g., tic-like movements, usually of eyes, lips, or cheeks), dyskinesias (defects in voluntary movement), dystonias (disordered muscle tone and posture), or intention tremors (tremors that appear when the examinee is to perform an action)
11. *Motor difficulties*—Displays akathesia (motor restlessness shown by pacing or continual movements), akinesia (lowered level of muscle activity), athetoid movements (slow, recurring, writhing movements of arms and legs), or deviant locomotion (walks on toes, whirls on own longitudinal axis, or runs in small circles)
12. *Motor retardation*—Sits unusually still; is sluggish; has slow, feeble, or labored movements; walks slowly; evidences delays in performing movements
13. *Muscle tone difficulties*—Displays atonia (no muscle tone), flaccidity (slumps, lets arms dangle limply, has slack facial muscles), or hypotonia (low muscle tone)
14. *Nervous habits*—Taps; "drums" with hands or feet; grinds teeth; sucks tongue; bites lips, nails, hands, or cuticles; sucks body parts (fingers, hair, etc.); picks skin, scabs, or nose; twists hair
15. *Odd mannerisms, including peculiar rhythmic or stereotypic movements*—Exhibits odd, stylized movements, postures, or actions (e.g., maintains uncomfortable or inappropriate postures of trunk or extremities; flaps or oscillates hands; wiggles fingers or positions them bizarrely); grimaces (i.e., makes bizarre facial movements); engages in complex motor rituals, usually idiosyncratic; performs compulsive rituals (such as touching and counting things or folding arms in order to avoid germs, dirt, etc.); darts and lunges peculiarly; sits in one peculiar position for a long time; rocks; sways; bangs head; rolls; engages in repetitive jumping; rubs head round and round with hand; nods head constantly

16. *Poor gross motor coordination*—Is awkward, stiff, or clumsy; stumbles
17. *Restlessness*—Is fidgety or restless, paces up and down, makes frequent unnecessary movements
18. *Squirming*—Wriggles, squirms, moves or shifts restlessly in chair
19. *Tense musculature*—Holds body taut or strained, keeps body rigid, clenches jaws, grips arms of chair, hands tremble

Affect

20. *Angry affect*—Is angry, hostile, antagonistic, touchy, or violent; erupts easily; throws things or threatens to
21. *Anxious affect*—Is fearful, apprehensive, overconcerned, tense, or worried; speaks in a frightened tone of voice; has tremor; has sweaty palms
22. *Blunted affect*—Has restricted range and intensity of emotional expression, has expressionless face and voice, lacks emotional response to distressing topics
23. *Depressed affect*—Is sad, has mournful look, breaks into tears, speaks in a monotone, frequently sighs deeply, voice chokes on distressing topic
24. *Gross excitement*—Throws things, runs, jumps around, waves arms wildly, shouts, screams
25. *Hypomanic affect*—Smiles unduly; is inappropriately euphoric and elated
26. *Incongruous affect*—Expresses affect not in keeping with the verbal content or context of the material (e.g., changes in affect are precipitated by minimal or no external stimulus)
27. *Irritable affect*—Screams, cries, is agitated or excited
28. *Labile affect*—Has sudden mood changes
29. *Perplexed affect*—Looks puzzled, cannot explain or understand experiences
30. *Silly affect*—Engages in excessive clowning; is giddy, playfully silly, or facetious; makes silly jokes and flippant remarks
31. *Suspicious affect*—Is wary, guarded, or distrustful of the examiner (e.g., constantly questions the intentions or goodwill of examiner)

Vocal Production

32. *Abnormal prosody (dysprosody)*—Uses questionlike "melody" (rising inflection) for statements; chants; uses sing-song melody; has hollow-sounding or scanning speech; has monotonic speech; exhibits other manneristic changes in pitch, intonation, stress, phrasing, and rhythm
33. *Articulation difficulties (dysarthria)*—Has speech characterized by additions (adding a sound or sounds to a word, as in *piln* for *pin*), substitutions (substituting a sound or sounds for those in a word, as in *zat* for *rat*), omissions (omitting a sound or sounds from a word, as in *ight* for *fight*), or distortions (distorting the sound or sounds in a word)
34. *Fluency difficulties*—Engages in repetitious or prolonged speech (e.g., repeats sounds, syllables, or words, as in *he-he-he-he-he goes,* or prolongs sounds in a word, as in *bbbbbbbed*)

(Continued)

Table 7-4 *(Continued)*

35. *No speech or delayed speech*—Has no speech or a delay of more than 1 year in the appearance of individual speech sounds

36. *Pressured speech*—Has speech that is abundant, accelerated, loud, or difficult to interrupt

37. *Slow speech*—Leaves long pauses before answering and long pauses between words

38. *Underproductive speech*—Fails to answer questions, gives monosyllabic answers, has to be pressured for an answer, does not elaborate

39. *Loud voice*—Is boisterous, shouts, sings loudly, shrieks, squeals

40. *Low voice*—Has a weak, soft, whispering, monotonous, or almost inaudible voice

Language and Thought

41. *Agrammatism*—Has difficulty ordering words grammatically, omitting key syntactical words (e.g., "woman ran street" for "woman ran into the street")

42. *Anomia*—Has difficulty finding the right word (e.g., "He, uh, just hurried along" for "He ran"; "the thing you put in your mouth" for "the spoon")

43. *Blocking*—Shows interruption of a train of speech before a thought or idea has been completed

44. *Circumstantiality*—Has a pattern of speech that is indirect, reaching its goal idea belatedly; has speech filled with tedious details and parenthetical remarks

45. *Clanging*—Uses sound patterns rather than meaningful words, which results in impaired intelligibility of speech and redundancy of words

46. *Derailment*—Goes off course in speech so that there are vague connections between the ideas or no apparent connections at all

47. *Distractible speech*—Stops repeatedly in the middle of a sentence or idea and changes the subject in response to a nearby stimulus, such as an object on a desk or the examiner's clothing or appearance

48. *Echolalia*—Echoes words or phrases used by the examiner, either immediately or after a delay

49. *Illogicality*—Has speech characterized by illogical conclusions

50. *Incoherence*—Has speech that is essentially incomprehensible at times

51. *Loss of goal*—Fails to follow a chain of thought through to its natural conclusion (e.g., begins with a particular subject and then wanders away from it, never to return to it)

52. *Neologisms*—Uses new or unconventional words or phrases whose derivation cannot be understood. Neologisms can be created through (a) structural changes, where syllables are scrambled (*helicopter* is produced as *copiheter*); (b) semantic changes, where a word that has similar connotative meanings is used (*pull-ons* for *boots*); and (c) phonological changes, where sounds are exchanged (*brod* for *bread*)

53. *Paragrammatism*—Uses verbs, clauses, or prepositional phrases incorrectly

54. *Paraphasia*—Substitutes incorrect words for other words (e.g., *cow* instead of *spoon*; "The flower is *on* the garden" instead of "The flower is *in* the garden")

55. *Perseveration*—Persistently repeats words, ideas, or subjects that may at first be meaningful, but whose continuation is inappropriate

56. *Phonemic paraphasia*—Mispronounces words by making sounds or syllables that are out of sequence (e.g., *amihal* for *animal*)

57. *Poverty of amount of speech*—Restricts the amount of spontaneous speech (e.g., gives brief, concrete, and unelaborated replies to questions and rarely provides unprompted additional information)

58. *Poverty of content of speech*—Restricts the information conveyed by speech (e.g., gives replies that are long enough, but convey little information; tends to use language that is vague, overabstract or overconcrete, repetitive, and stereotyped)

59. *Self-reference*—Refers the subject under discussion back to himself or herself, even when someone else is talking

60. *Stilted speech*—Speaks in an excessively stilted or formal manner (e.g., tends toward rather quaint and outdated speech or speech that appears pompous, distant, or overpolite)

61. *Syntactic errors*—Orders words in an unconventional way (e.g., "My house, well, I live in, well, my house, uh, I live in" for "I live in my house")

62. *Tangentiality*—Replies to questions or statements in an oblique, tangential, or even irrelevant way (e.g., when asked to pick up the blue notebook, picks up the blue car and says "Car")

63. *Telegraphic speech*—Omits connectives, prepositions, modifiers, and refinements of language in speech

64. *Topical or referential identification problems*—Has difficulty selecting the appropriate referent when speaking (e.g., when asked "Did you put the book on my desk?" responds "My desk is clean")

65. *Word approximations*—Uses old words in a new and unconventional way or develops new words by using conventional rules of word formation

Attention

66. *Aberrant attentional behaviors*—Is clearly preoccupied with listening to self-induced, nonvocal sounds such as scratching or tapping; is visually preoccupied with hand or finger movements; bangs, rubs, or flicks; covers ears or eyes

67. *Aberrant, eccentric, or odd behavior with objects*—Engages in peculiar or inappropriate behavior with objects (e.g., passively lets objects fall on and off hand; flicks at objects; feels, strokes, rubs, or scratches objects; is preoccupied with trivial specks, breaks, points, and the like in objects; uses objects in a bizarre, idiosyncratic manner; spins objects; remains preoccupied with the same object or activity; uses objects ritualistically; ignores objects; holds an object in an undifferentiated fashion with no visual attention on it; mouths or sucks objects; taps; stares at objects or at nothing in particular; engages in repetitive banging)

68. *Blank spells*—Has abrupt interruptions of attention that last a few seconds or longer

69. *Disorganized behavior*—Engages in inconsistent behavior that changes abruptly; exhibits fragmented behavior, without coherent goal direction

70. *Self-mutilation*—Bites, scratches, or hits self; bangs head

Source: Adapted, in part, from Fish (1985).

memory, and be aware of your relationship with, and reactions to, the child. Have a pad of paper handy on which to write your comments about the child's behavior or record any statements that you believe are essential to understanding the child. Observing behavior carefully will help you make appropriate inferences from your observations.

Observing Personal Appearance

Make note of the examinee's height, weight, clothing, hairstyle, grooming, and general appearance. For example, notice whether the examinee's dress is clean, neat, disheveled, dowdy, dirty, atypical, or appropriate; whether the examinee has body odors; and whether there are signs of malnutrition (e.g., the examinee is underweight, is small in stature, appears lethargic, has a limited attention span, or has eyes that lack luster). In observing an older examinee, note whether his or her breath smells ordinary or from alcohol or another substance and whether there are abrasions or needle marks on the forearms or inside the elbows.

These observations may give you clues about the examinee's physical and neurological development and conditions that the examinee may suffer from, such as bulimia (an eating disorder characterized by repeated episodes of binge eating followed by inappropriate compensatory behaviors such as self-induced vomiting), anorexia (an eating disorder characterized by a refusal to maintain a minimally normal body weight, leading to a body weight of less than 85% of that expected), substance abuse, medical illness, physical abuse, or neglect. Your impressions will guide you in conducting the evaluation, in formulating hypotheses, and in determining possible areas to probe in the evaluation. For example, if an examinee reeks of alcohol but denies drinking, consider probing the inconsistency further. The examinee's physical appearance may give you clues about the examinee's attitude toward himself or herself and the group the examinee belongs to or admires. The way children dress also may be a reflection of their parents' or their peers' values. Keep in mind that you should not continue the evaluation if an adolescent is inebriated because you will not obtain a picture of how he or she functions under normal circumstances.

Observing Nonverbal Behavior

Be aware of the examinee's nonverbal behavior, or body language (see Tables 7-3 and 7-5). Body language may tell you about the examinee's (a) moods, (b) openness for communication or distance from you, (c) amount and range of expressive gestures, and (d) idiosyncratic or symptomatic patterns of body movements (Atakan & Cooper, 1989). Here are things to look for in the examinee's body language:

- *Facial expressions*—alert, angry, anxious, bland, calm, distressed, grimacing, habitually perplexed, sad, scowling, seductive, sleepy, smiling, staring into space, tics, vacant stare

Table 7-5
Examples of the Meanings of Nonverbal Behaviors

Nonverbal behavior	Possible meaning
Direct eye contact	Readiness for interpersonal communication, attentiveness, staring, an effort to be invasive, defiance
Staring at or fixating on a person or object	Confrontational defiance, preoccupation, possible rigidness or anxiety
Tight lips (pursed together)	Stress, determination, anger, hostility, anxiety
Shaking head from left to right	Disagreement, disapproval, disbelief, uncertainty
Slouching in chair, turned away from examiner	Sadness, discouragement, resistance to discussion, disengagement, boredom
Trembling, fidgety hands	Anxiety, anger, fear of self-disclosure, fear of failure (test anxiety)
Foot-tapping	Impatience, anxiety, excessive energy, boredom
Whispering	Difficulty in revealing material, hoarse throat, shyness, uncertainty
Silence	Reluctance to talk, preoccupation, shyness, fear, waiting, thinking
Clammy hands, shallow breathing, pupil dilation, paleness, blushing, rashes on neck	Fearfulness, arousal—positive (excitement, interest) or negative (anxiety, embarrassment), drug intoxication

Note. These meanings do not hold for all cultural groups. Also note that some nonverbal behaviors may suggest more than one thing and that the same behavior can have a positive or negative meaning.
Source: Adapted from Cormier and Cormier (1979).

- *Posture*—crossing and recrossing legs, legs and arms drawn close to trunk, legs and arms outstretched, recumbent, relaxed, rigid, slouched, stooped, tense
- *Gestures, mannerisms, and motor behavior*—abnormal staring, agitation, biting lips, clumsiness, finger pointing, clenching fists, flapping hands, hyperactivity, hypoactivity, inappropriate posturing, repetitive movements, rituals, rocking, rolling eyes to ceiling, self-stimulation, stereotypic movements, tremors, twitches, winking or eye blinking
- *Vocal behaviors*—saying "ah-uh," barking, clacking, coughing, saying "eeee," grunting, gurgling, hawking, hissing, saying repetitive or meaningless words or phrases, screeching, sniffling, spitting, sucking, saying "uh-uh," whistling

- *Senses*—looking closely at things, straining to see, straining to hear, sniffing or tasting test materials, holding test materials close to the eyes and rotating the materials as if microscopically examining them
- *Attention*—ability to attend to visual stimuli, scan or follow your movement, respond to sounds, follow your simple requests; extent to which the examinee is attentive or distractible or has variable attention

Observing Verbal Behavior

As you converse with the examinee, note voice and speech qualities, clarity of expression, fluency, grammar, cohesiveness of communications, comprehension, length and frequency of pauses, ability to converse, and ability to maintain a train of thought. Language usage is a guide to the examinee's personality and thought processes, as are the tempo, quality, and content of the examinee's verbal responses (see Table 7-3). Pay careful attention to the examinee's language, and consider what is normal for his or her age. For children who have mastered speech, look for possible language processing difficulties, particularly in spontaneous language samples. Language distortions may be related to psychological disorders, or to health-related disorders such as brain damage or drug intoxication (see Table 7-4).

If you observe voice or speech deviations, consider why they occurred and whether you need to recommend a speech, medical, or neuropsychological evaluation. Deviations such as omitting sounds (e.g., saying "ing" for "thing"), substituting sounds (e.g., saying "den" for "then"), or distorting sounds (e.g., saying "lan" for "pan") suggest an articulation disorder. Other deviations, such as saying "dad" for "pad" or "run" for "bun," suggest difficulty in distinguishing sounds. In still other cases, voice or speech deviations may suggest anxiety, inattention, auditory sensory difficulties, an underlying language disorder, or brain injury.

The following are indicators of possible language problems in examinees of various ages:

1. For an 18-month-old, absence of any attempt to say meaningful words
2. For a 24-month-old, failure to use phrases communicatively, unintelligible speech, and inappropriate use of language
3. For a 3- to 5-year-old, lack of speech, unintelligible speech, and failure to speak in sentences
4. For a 5- to 6-year-old, substituting easy sounds for difficult ones, consistently dropping word endings, faulty sentence structure, noticeable nonfluency, and abnormal rhythm, rate, and inflection of speech
5. For a 7-year-old, distorting, omitting, or substituting sounds and abnormal rhythm, rate, and inflection of sounds

Observing Attention, Mood, Affect, and Attitude

Your observation of the examinee's nonverbal and verbal behavior will provide you with information about her or his (a) ability to attend to testing materials, (b) mood and affect, (c) orientation (i.e., to person, place, and time), and (d) attitude toward the test situation and toward you. The questions in Table 7-3 will help in the evaluation of these areas, and the indicators in Table 7-4 will help you recognize disturbances in mood and affect.

Observing Vision

If you see any of the following signs in a child who has *not* been previously referred for possible visual difficulties, recommend to the parents and child that the child have a vision examination:

- Rubs eyes excessively
- Shuts or covers one eye, tilts head, or thrusts head forward
- Has difficulty reading or doing close visual work
- Blinks excessively or is irritable when doing close visual work
- Tires easily after visual work
- Moves head excessively when reading
- Holds books too close to or too far from eyes

Bent Offerings   by Don Addis

YOU **SAY** YOU'RE OKAY, BUT YOUR BODY LANGUAGE SAYS DIFFERENT!

© 1991 Creators Syndicate, Inc.

7-20

By permission of Don Addis and Creators Syndicate.

The Far Side   by Gary Larson

happy   depressed

angry   pensive

excited   suicidal

How to recognize the moods of an Irish setter

THE FAR SIDE © 1992 FAR WORKS, INC. Used by permission. All rights reserved.

- Is inconsistent in reading print at different distances (e.g., is able to read a book but not material written on the blackboard)
- Is unable to see distant objects clearly
- Squints or frowns when using eyes
- Loses place while reading, skips words or lines of print
- Has poor sitting posture while reading (e.g., places face close to book)
- Walks overcautiously or runs into objects not directly in line of vision
- Has difficulty judging distances
- Has crossed eyes
- Has red-rimmed, encrusted, or swollen eyelids
- Has inflamed or watery eyes
- Has recurring sties
- Reports that eyes itch, burn, or feel scratchy
- Reports that he or she cannot see well
- Complains of dizziness, headaches, or nausea following close visual work
- Reports blurred or double vision
- Reports spots before eyes
- Reports that lights bother him or her when reading
- Reports that eyes are tired after reading

- Attends to the left side of space and neglects the right (or vice versa)

If a child does not show or report these signs, do not assume that the child's vision is adequate. A child may have visual defects—such as slight astigmatism or a binocular visual defect that can impede reading—without having observable symptoms. Whenever you uncover signs of a possible visual problem, refer the child to an optometrist or ophthalmologist. The test results may be invalid if the child's performance was adversely affected by problems with vision.

Observing Hearing

If a child has *not* been previously referred for possible hearing difficulties and you detect any behavior that suggests a hearing deficit, refer the child to an audiologist or a physician. General signs of hearing difficulty include the following:

- Lack of normal response to sound
- Lack of interest in general conversation
- Inattentiveness
- Difficulty following oral directions
- Failure to respond when spoken to
- Frequent requests to have the speaker repeat what was said
- Mistakes in carrying out spoken instructions
- Intent observation of the speaker's lips (lipreading, speechreading) rather than looking at the speaker's eyes in face-to-face encounters
- Leaning forward to hear the speaker
- Habitually turning one ear toward the speaker
- Cupping hand behind ear
- Unusual voice quality (e.g., monotonous or high pitched)
- Abnormally loud or soft speech
- Faulty pronunciation
- Poor articulation
- Frequent earaches or discharges from ears

Specific language problems that may indicate hearing difficulties include the following:

- Difficulty discriminating consonant sounds (e.g, the child hears *bet* for *bed, tab* for *tap*)
- Difficulty discriminating and learning short vowel sounds
- Difficulty sounding out a word, sound by sound (e.g., the child has difficulty saying *k-a-t* for *cat*)
- Difficulty relating printed letters such as *f, pl,* and *ide* to their sounds
- Difficulty separating sounds that make up blends (e.g., the child has difficulty determining that *fl* has the sounds /f/ … /l/)
- Better spelling and reading of sight words (using the whole-word or look-say method of reading) than of phonetic words (a phoneme represents the smallest unit of speech)

Children with an undiagnosed hearing deficit may perform poorly on tests because they fail to hear the instructions and questions, not because of cognitive or other ability limitations. Children may have a temporary hearing loss due to allergies, sinus infections, colds, or other intermittent ear, nose, and throat problems. In cases where a significant hearing problem is documented or suspected, ask the child to repeat a few complex sentences before you administer a test (e.g., "Jill opened the door when she heard someone knock"). If the child repeats the sentences correctly, you can be reasonably confident that the child's hearing proficiency is sufficient for you to administer most tests. Conversely, if the child fails to repeat the sentences correctly, you might want to recommend that the child receive a hearing evaluation before you administer the battery of tests. If the child usually wears a hearing aid, be sure that the child wears it during the evaluation and verifies for you that it is functioning properly. In the public school system, the child should—at a minimum—have been screened for hearing problems prior to referral for a psychoeducational evaluation.

Observing Visual-Motor and Motor Behavior

The questions in Table 7-3 will help you assess the child's visual-motor and motor behavior during the evaluation. In addition, Table 7-4 lists indicators of disturbances in motor behavior.

Be sure to note how the child walks (e.g., whether his or her feet tend to drop and point toward the ground or remain relatively parallel to the ground, as is normal; whether the child walks with the torso pitched forward from the waist; whether the child's gait is smooth, hesitant, uncoordinated, or spastic; whether the child walks in a straight line or at an angle; whether the child bumps into furniture; and whether the child demonstrates asymmetrical arm movements). Also observe how the child performs simple motor tasks (e.g., how the child jumps, kicks or throws a ball, uses scissors, turns pages, holds a pencil, uses pegs, and so forth). Evaluate the child's performance according to what is expected for his or her age. When it is age appropriate, ask the child to write his or her name on the test protocol. This will give you information about the child's preferred hand for writing, pencil grip, ability to form letters, and preferred writing style (i.e., print or cursive).

Observing Waiting Room Behavior

Observations begin when you first see the child in the waiting room. If a parent is with the child, note how the parent and child interact. Even a brief period of observation—say, 30 seconds—can provide useful information about the child, the parent, and the parent-child interaction.

During your initial observations of interactions of the parent, child, and sibling (if present), be guided by the following questions:

Parent (or other caregiver)

1. What is the parent doing? For example, if the parent is talking to the child, what is the nature of the conversation? Does the parent talk quietly and calmly; yell at, scold, or reprimand the child; or converse in some other manner?
2. Does the parent sit close to or at a distance from the child?
3. Does the parent maintain eye contact with the child?
4. What are the parent's facial expressions?
5. How does the parent respond to the child's requests? Does the parent help or ignore the child?
6. Does the parent look relaxed or tense? If the parent looks tense, does he or she cry or sob, pound fists, drum fingers, chew fingers, tap feet, or verbally express anger or dismay?
7. How does the parent react to the child (e.g., with acceptance, reassurance, or rejection) if the child is distressed?
8. Does the parent seem preoccupied?
9. Is the parent caring and affectionate?

Child

10. What is the child doing? If the child is playing or doing homework, what is the child playing or what kind of homework is the child doing?
11. Does the child talk to the parent? If so, what do they talk about?
12. Does the child cling to the parent?
13. What are the child's facial expressions?
14. How does the child respond to the parent's requests? Does the child comply with or refuse to comply with the requests?
15. Does the child seek help from the parent? If so, what kind of help does the child seek?
16. Does the child look relaxed or tense? If the child looks tense, does he or she cry, run around, pace, flail arms, kick, verbalize fear or distress, or withdraw by remaining silent and immobile?
17. How does the child separate from the parent?

Sibling (Answer only if one or more siblings are present.)

18. How do the sibling's appearance and behavior differ from those of the referred child?
19. Does the parent treat the sibling differently from the referred child? If so, how?
20. How does the referred child interact with his or her sibling (e.g., avoidance, parallel play, cooperative play, overt hostility)?

If the child came alone, note whether the child was on time and whether the child was able to find the office by herself or himself. Also note how she or he came to your office (such as by public transportation, on foot, by bicycle, or by car). Was it age appropriate for the child to come alone and in that manner?

Observing Children in Their Natural Environments

When you observe children with special needs in natural settings, note how they perform daily activities, use language, use motor skills, cope with different environments, accomplish new learning, and use cognitive strategies in different settings. By observing how children function in different environments, you will gain a better picture of their adaptive and coping abilities, including how they behave, process information, and cope with distractions and information overload, as well as how they deal with successes, failures, and competition (Marquardt, Stoll, & Sussman, 1988). These observations may also give you clues about such characteristics as their level of orientation, anxiety, confusion, distractibility, impulsivity, initiative, inhibition, concreteness, flexibility, organization, and judgment. In addition, a detailed history obtained from parents, teachers, and others may provide information that enhances the results of the observation.

Behavior and Attitude Checklist

You can use the Behavior and Attitude Checklist, shown in Table 7-6, to record a child's reactions in the testing situation. The checklist is a guide for summarizing a child's behavior; it does not cover all contingencies that may arise during the evaluation. You may find it helpful in formulating descriptions of some children but not others.

GATSB: Guide to the Assessment of Test Session Behavior for the WISC–III and WIAT

The GATSB is a 29-item behavior-rating instrument that uses a three-point scale ("usually applies," "somewhat applies," and "doesn't apply") to rate the examinee's behavior during the administration of the WISC–III and the Wechsler Individual Achievement Test (WIAT; Glutting & Oakland, 1993). The items are grouped into three factors: Avoidance (which accounts for 49% of the variance), Uncooperative Mood (which accounts for 11% of the variance), and Inattentiveness (which accounts for 8% of the variance). Reliability is acceptable, with an average internal consistency reliability of .92 for the Total Score and reliabilities of between .84 and .88 for the three factors. Construct and criterion validity are acceptable. Factor analyses support the use of the three fac-

School psychologist on the way to work

Courtesy of Daniel Miller.

tors. Research indicates that children who show compliant behaviors, as measured by the GATSB (e.g., attentiveness and cooperativeness), during the administration of the WISC–III obtain Full Scale IQs that are about 7 to 10 points higher than those of children who show noncompliant behaviors (Glutting, Youngstrom, Oakland, & Watkins, 1996).

GENERAL SUGGESTIONS FOR ADMINISTERING TESTS

When you begin to administer tests, you are likely to be anxious. You must professionally juggle the many required tasks: establishing rapport, administering items, keeping the materials ready, responding appropriately to the child, precisely recording the child's responses, observing the child's behavior, and scoring the child's responses. In time, many of these procedures will become routine for you, but even the most experienced examiners should review their test procedures periodically. Periodic reviews are needed because even experienced examiners may be deviating from the standardized procedures without realizing it—perhaps by inserting their own words in the directions, taking liberties in reading the questions and in asking follow-up questions and probes, failing to record all responses, failing to probe ambiguous responses, or questioning responses unnecessarily.

Test manuals usually present valuable suggestions for administering tests. Study these suggestions carefully. The following tips for administering tests supplement or reemphasize points often found in test manuals. *When tests have specific guidelines that differ from those presented below, always follow the guidelines shown in the test manuals.* Some of the material in this section was adapted from Robinson and Harris (1980).

Table 7-6
Behavior and Attitude Checklist

BEHAVIOR AND ATTITUDE CHECKLIST

Child's name: _____   Examiner: _____

Age: _____   Date of report: _____

Test(s) administered: _____   Date of examination: _____

Instructions: Place an X on the appropriate line for each scale.

I. Attitude toward examiner:
1. cooperative   ____ : ____ : ____ : ____ : ____   uncooperative
2. friendly   ____ : ____ : ____ : ____ : ____   hostile

II. Attitude toward test situation:
3. relaxed   ____ : ____ : ____ : ____ : ____   tense
4. does not give up easily   ____ : ____ : ____ : ____ : ____   gives up easily
5. tries best   ____ : ____ : ____ : ____ : ____   does not try best
6. benefits from feedback   ____ : ____ : ____ : ____ : ____   doesn't benefit from feedback
7. interested in materials   ____ : ____ : ____ : ____ : ____   not interested in materials

III. Attitude toward self:
8. confident   ____ : ____ : ____ : ____ : ____   not confident
9. proud   ____ : ____ : ____ : ____ : ____   self-derogatory

IV. Work habits:
10. fast   ____ : ____ : ____ : ____ : ____   slow
11. answers carefully   ____ : ____ : ____ : ____ : ____   answers impulsively
12. thinks silently   ____ : ____ : ____ : ____ : ____   thinks aloud
13. careful   ____ : ____ : ____ : ____ : ____   careless
14. attentive   ____ : ____ : ____ : ____ : ____   inattentive
15. flexible   ____ : ____ : ____ : ____ : ____   inflexible
16. organized   ____ : ____ : ____ : ____ : ____   disorganized
17. efficient problem-solving style   ____ : ____ : ____ : ____ : ____   inefficient problem-solving style

V. Behavior:
18. at ease   ____ : ____ : ____ : ____ : ____   hyperactive
19. normal   ____ : ____ : ____ : ____ : ____   bizarre or unusual
20. remains in seat   ____ : ____ : ____ : ____ : ____   out of seat
21. regulates behavior   ____ : ____ : ____ : ____ : ____   fails to regulate behavior

VI. Reaction to failure:
22. aware of failure   ____ : ____ : ____ : ____ : ____   unaware of failure
23. works harder after failure   ____ : ____ : ____ : ____ : ____   gives up easily after failure
24. calm after failure   ____ : ____ : ____ : ____ : ____   agitated after failure

VII. Reaction to praise:
25. accepts praise gracefully   ____ : ____ : ____ : ____ : ____   accepts praise awkwardly
26. works harder after praise   ____ : ____ : ____ : ____ : ____   retreats after praise

VIII. Expressive language:
27. expresses self easily   ____ : ____ : ____ : ____ : ____   expresses self with difficulty
28. good articulation   ____ : ____ : ____ : ____ : ____   poor articulation
29. direct responses   ____ : ____ : ____ : ____ : ____   vague responses
30. converses spontaneously   ____ : ____ : ____ : ____ : ____   speaks only when spoken to
31. reality-oriented language   ____ : ____ : ____ : ____ : ____   bizarre language

IX. Receptive language:
32. good understanding   ____ : ____ : ____ : ____ : ____   poor understanding
33. repetition not needed   ____ : ____ : ____ : ____ : ____   repetition needed
34. clarification not needed   ____ : ____ : ____ : ____ : ____   clarification needed

X. Visual-motor skills:
35. fast reaction time   ____ : ____ : ____ : ____ : ____   slow reaction time
36. careful and planned   ____ : ____ : ____ : ____ : ____   trial-and-error
37. skillful movements   ____ : ____ : ____ : ____ : ____   awkward movements

XI. Graphomotor skills:
38. legible handwriting   ____ : ____ : ____ : ____ : ____   illegible handwriting
39. appropriate pencil grasp   ____ : ____ : ____ : ____ : ____   awkward pencil grasp
40. smooth line quality   ____ : ____ : ____ : ____ : ____   tremulous line quality

XII. Gross motor skills:
41. good motor coordination   ____ : ____ : ____ : ____ : ____   defective motor coordination

XIII. Overall test results:
42. reliable   ____ : ____ : ____ : ____ : ____   unreliable
43. valid   ____ : ____ : ____ : ____ : ____   invalid

In general, you should know your task well enough that the test administration flows automatically, leaving you free to observe the child's behavior. You do not want to have to stop to read a paragraph in the manual about how to give the test, because if you do you may lose control of the situation; instead of waiting for you, the child may get up, start to play games, or tell you that he or she wants to go home. In addition, you should know your instructions well and know how to find materials quickly. You should become so familiar with the test materials that you can introduce and remove them without breaking the interaction and flow between you and the child. We recommend that you always look at the test manual when you give the test instructions and ask the test questions. The way to gain proficiency in administering tests is to practice, practice, and practice.

It is advisable to complete the administration of any single test in one test session or, at most, two test sessions separated by no more than one day. If, instead, you administer parts of the same test over a week or two or even more, you run the risk that the child will be placed in a different norm age group (e.g., 7-0-0 instead of 6-11-25).

Let's now look at some suggestions on arranging the physical environment, arranging the test materials, giving instructions and asking questions, timing items, encouraging replies, clarifying responses, recording responses, and scoring responses.

ARRANGING THE PHYSICAL ENVIRONMENT

1. *Administer the test in a room with minimal distractions.* You and the test materials should be the most important stimuli in the room. Ideally, your office or evaluation room should be free of distraction and located in a quiet setting (or at least have good sound insulation). Although at times you may have to settle for conditions that fall short of the ideal, you must *never* test when the conditions would adversely affect the child's performance. You may need to work hard to establish rapport with administrators and secretaries and help them understand the need for appropriate testing conditions.

2. *Control your materials.* Do not permit the child to play with the test manual or materials or to hold pencils, pens, or toys, except when they are needed for a test. Unless the test manual specifically prohibits it, you may, however, permit the child to turn pages in test booklets that contain items (e.g., the pictures in the Wechsler Picture Completion subtest). This allows the child to proceed at his or her own pace and encourages rapport. You do not have to do this routinely, though.

With infants up to 6 months your materials can be in sight, but with older children the only materials visible or accessible should be those needed for the task at hand. Your test box should be on a low chair beside you, placed such that, when the box is open, the back of the box lid faces the child. Stay between the box and the child, keeping the box out of the child's reach. Position the test manual in such a way that the child does not see any of the answers in it. Check to see that the testing box contains all necessary materials *before* you begin testing.

3. *Make sure the child is comfortable.* For example, the chair and table should be supportive and at appropriate heights, the lighting should be sufficient, and the ventilation adequate. If the child's feet do not touch the floor, arrange a solid box or block for them. A high chair or booster seat is optimal for young children who are able to sit upright on their own (usually by about 6 months of age); they are accustomed to it, it is comfortable, and it provides foot support.

ARRANGING THE TEST MATERIALS

1. *Administer items from the child's left to right in the order given in the test manual.* Even arrange demonstration items in this way. This rule of thumb simply brings some uniformity to the test administration.

2. *Place stimulus materials in front of the child one at a time so that the child can see the blocks, cards, or other materials clearly.* Some beginning examiners inadvertently cover materials as they place them on the table. Unless the test manual instructs otherwise, the child needs to be able to see your full movements as you arrange materials in demonstration items.

3. *Complete one row at a time in constructing sample block designs, starting each row at the child's left and working to the right.* This procedure helps to assure that you administer the sample items in the same way to each child. Be sure that the child can easily reach the blocks or other stimulus materials.

4. *Recognize that you have the option of holding or not holding the test booklet, unless the test manual gives specific instructions on what to do.* For example, you can leave the booklet flat on the table and turn the pages (or cards) over for each succeeding item, but be sure that the child cannot read the manual. It is a good idea to place the manual on a bookstand.

5. *To avoid needless distractions, keep the testing table clear of all extraneous materials.* Return all materials to the test box immediately after you use them.

GIVING INSTRUCTIONS AND ASKING QUESTIONS

1. *Adhere to test instructions exactly if you want to use the test norms.* You should (a) use the exact wording in reading the instructions and test questions, (b) maintain accurate timing, (c) present the materials as indicated in the test manual, (d) use the exact wording in the test manual for probing questions, and (e) follow the scoring instructions precisely. This means, for example, that you must not ad lib, add extraneous words, leave out any words from the instructions or the test questions, or change any test directions because you think that the child could perform better on a particular task with altered directions. Like an actor, practice reading your "lines" until you can deliver them verbatim, but with a natural tone and rhythm.

2. *Consider the child's age and ability level as you engage the child in conversation and give the test instructions, and modify your tempo accordingly.* You want to strive for a natural quality in your voice and behavior. This is especially important on memory tests, where it is necessary to speak in a clear and even-toned fashion.

3. *Avoid unusual facial expressions or modulations in your voice that may give the child cues about her or his performance.*

4. *Do not tell the child whether her or his responses are correct.* If the child asks, you can say that it is against the rules to tell the answers but you can answer general questions when you have finished. In addition, you do not want to give the child any clues about what you expect.

5. *Repeat the instructions for the first trial of a test on successive trials or items if you believe that it would be helpful, unless the test manual notes otherwise.* However, you usually should not explain any of the words used in the directions or in the test questions. Be sure to follow the instructions in the test manuals.

6. *Do not repeat items designed to measure memory.*

7. *Do not spell out words unless the test manual permits this.*

8. *Phrase requests as mild commands (such as "Tell me another reason …") unless prohibited from doing so by the test manual.* This is preferable to asking the child whether she or he knows the answer. "Can you tell me …?" and "Do you know …?" often result in a simple "No," whereas a mild command may encourage the child to try to answer the question.

9. *Recognize that a child's responses may provide valuable clues about her or his developmental level, language usage, range of opportunities and experiences, and other relevant areas.* Therefore, it is good practice to inquire into any unusual responses at any time during an evaluation.

10. *Be especially sensitive to cultural patterns as they may relate to the child's responses.* Specifically, you need to determine whether the child truly does not know how to define a word, give a similarity, or come up with an appropriate answer (depending on the test) or whether the child is merely giving a response based on cultural experiences that differ from those of the mainstream culture. Therefore, query responses that suggest regionalisms or slang or that may have cultural bearings. For example, you can say, "Give me another meaning for …" or "Give me another answer to the question …."

11. *Do not routinely inquire after every response, even though inquiry might give you insight into what the child is thinking, or ask any leading questions during the administration of a test.*

12. *Talk to the child, if you want to, before or after you administer nonverbal tests that can be administered without—or with minimal—verbal instructions* (e.g., Leiter International Performance Scale-Revised, the pantomime version of the Comprehensive Test of Nonverbal Intelligence, or the Universal Nonverbal Intelligence Test; see Chapter 16). Typ-ically, the nonverbal instructions apply to the test administration procedure and test content, not to the interactions between you and the child. Study each test manual carefully to learn the requirements for administering the test (John Willis, personal communication, October 1999).

TIMING ITEMS

1. *Do not tell the child how much time is allotted on tests that have time limits unless the test manual says otherwise.* If the child asks, you might tell the child to give an answer as soon as he or she knows it. Begin timing as soon as you show the item to the child.

2. *Note whether the child takes an excessive amount of time to give answers or to begin working with the blocks, pictures, or other test materials.* This will give you information about the child's response style. If the child "dawdles" at the beginning of a timed test, signaling that he or she is unaware that the test is timed, remind the child to work as quickly as he or she can, as permitted by the test manual.

3. *Once the test has begun, do not stop timing a test (or subtest) that requires timing unless permitted to do so by the manual.*

4. *Do not give the child formal credit for any correct responses given after the time limit unless permitted to do so by the manual.*

5. *Always record the child's response and the amount of time the child took to respond.*

6. *Use your judgment about how much additional time the child needs to complete a task so that you do not abruptly halt the test administration.*

ENCOURAGING REPLIES

1. *Seldom accept the first "I don't know" response that the child gives.* Instead, ask the child to try to answer, unless the question appears to be too difficult for her or him. You can say something like "Try to give an answer" or "Try to answer it in some way, if you can."

2. *Encourage a child who is hesitant to respond or guess* (e.g., say, "Just try it" or "I think you can do it"). Hesitancy might be indicated by frequent "I don't know" responses, shoulder shrugs, or "No" responses, especially to questions that you might expect the child to answer correctly. However, do not press the child to give an answer.

3. *Do not cue the child to indicate approval or disapproval of her or his verbal responses or nonverbal performance, except when indicated in the test manual.*

CLARIFYING RESPONSES

1. *Ask the child to repeat a response if you are uncertain about what the child said.* To reduce the need for repetition, pay close attention to everything the child says. The purpose of questioning is to clarify ambiguous responses.

2. *Do not probe obviously incorrect responses.*

3. *When a response contains one part that is correct and one that is incorrect, ask the child for his or her preference and score the response accordingly.*

4. *Avoid giving the child the impression that you are discontinuing a test because of repeated failure.*

5. *Repeat the entire question (if it is allowed) when a child asks to have part of a question repeated.*

6. *Always remember to consult the test manual for guidelines on how to probe, and follow those guidelines when specified.*

7. *Note how the child responds to your queries.* For example, some children are encouraged by follow-up questions, while others resent such questioning.

RECORDING RESPONSES

1. *Pace the evaluation so that you can comfortably and accurately record the child's responses.* For example, if the child is reading words quickly and you can't easily record his or her incorrect responses, you might say, "I'd like you to wait for a little while in between words" or "Say the next word when I say it's okay."

2. *Develop efficient ways to record responses.* Practice writing quickly and learn as many useful abbreviations as possible. Learn how to finish writing the answer to one question while beginning to ask the next. Learn how to write without looking at the paper.

The following abbreviations will prove useful in recording responses (Wechsler, 1991):

- "P" for Pass
- "F" for Fail
- "Q" for Query
- "DK" for Don't Know
- "NR" for No Response
- "Inc." for Incomplete
- "R" for Rotation or for Reversals or transpositions, as in digit- and sentence-repetition tests
- "T" for exceeding Time limit
- "OTP" for Over Time Pass, when an examinee passes the item after the time limit has expired
- "REP" for Repeating an item at the examinee's request
- "PO" for Pointing to a correct response instead of giving the response orally
- "PF" for Pointing to an incorrect response instead of giving the response orally

You can also use abbreviations for phrases that the examinee tends to repeat. For example, if an examinee says "I have no clue" frequently, spell this phrase out the first time and then use an abbreviation such as "IHNC."

3. *Record the child's answers in the spaces provided in the record booklets.* Be as accurate as possible in recording the child's responses, and don't change or embellish the child's words. Incorrect recording of the child's responses may affect the scoring of the responses after you complete the test. Exercise judgment in recording parts of the response

that have limited relevance to the test question. In the margin of the record booklet, note behaviors of interest and other observations, hypotheses, and relevant information. Record the child's responses in a way that does not interfere with your ongoing relationship.

As noted above, in some cases you may want to record the time it takes the child to respond to a question or prompt. A helpful method is to use a dot (.) to represent one second of elapsed time. For example, the notation "....... 5 Q ...." means that the child hesitated for 7 seconds before giving the answer "5" and, when queried, took another 9 seconds to give a response to the query.

4. *For items that require the arrangement of stimulus materials, be sure to record the child's arrangement as soon as the child completes the item.*

SCORING RESPONSES

1. *Usually score the child's responses immediately after they are given.* Shield from the child, as unobtrusively as possible, the scores you place in the record booklet. Position the record booklet so that the child does not see answers to questions or get feedback on prior or current responses. You might want to place the record booklet on a clipboard and hold it at an angle from the child.

2. *Study the scoring criteria for each test so that you know which are correct, questionable, and incorrect answers.* Try to discern the type of response called for by an item and the type of scoring for each response. For example, some types of responses to the same question may receive a higher score than others; on the WISC–III, conceptual or abstract responses receive 2 points and concrete or functional responses receive 1 point. The scoring sections of test manuals usually provide guidelines to help you arrive at the proper score. When the test manual does not provide guidelines, study the sample responses in the test manual to determine the type of response that should receive credit. Try to determine the rationale for assigning different point values to apparently similar responses in the manual. If you can understand the reasoning, you will be able to score other responses more accurately. A careful study of the scoring sections of test manuals will be a good investment of time, will help you decrease mistakes, and will help you become a proficient examiner.

On the WISC–III, WPPSI–R, WAIS–III, Stanford-Binet: Fourth Edition, and other tests that employ entry and discontinuance points (i.e., specific items where you begin a subtest and where you stop giving a subtest), you must score the responses *immediately* at these points so that you can follow the correct procedures. As you are administering a test, place a question mark to the left of the number of any item that was difficult to score. Give special attention to these items when you recheck your scoring. *Always carefully recheck your scoring after the evaluation.*

3. *Recognize that the scoring examples shown in test manuals are guides.* They do not cover all possible correct or incorrect answers, except when the test manual so specifies.

A few tests, such as some of the language tests published by Pro-Ed, give credit only for responses listed in the manual, even though other responses are correct according to standard dictionaries. Be sure to re-read the test manual, and be certain of the scoring rules for the test you are using.

4. *In general, on intelligence test or achievement test items that require an oral response, give credit for correct responses that the child gives in any form of communication, unless explicitly forbidden to do so by the test manual.* Alternative forms of communication include writing, typing on a computer or typewriter, sign language, Braille, fingerspelling, and teletouch. If the child has not given a correct response, it is never appropriate to give credit for an item simply because you *think* the child knows the answer.

5. *If the child gives several responses to an item, ask the child which response she or he wants to give, unless prohibited from doing so by the test manual.*

6. *Give the child credit if she or he answers verbal questions correctly at any time during the test, unless prohibited from doing so by the test manual.* This guideline does *not* apply to immediate memory questions, however.

Departures from Standard Procedures

We have seen that, to use the test norms with confidence, you must administer the test following standard procedures. This means, for example, that you must use the exact words of the questions, the specific test materials, and the specified time limits. We do not know how small deviations in test procedures affect scores. Each test has a standard error reflecting deviations caused by the nuances in the examiner-examinee relationship, the conditions of the evaluation, the time of day, and other similar factors. We hope that when small changes occur in rapport or in other aspects of the test situation, the resulting score will remain within the range of the standard error, but we never know this with certainty. Examples of other possible minor modifications in test administration include using Braille, large print format, signing, or auditory amplification with children who have visual or auditory difficulties and who know how to use the communication method. Any modifications that are used to administer a test should be noted on the test record form.

Whether norms are violated when test procedures are modified depends on the extent of the modifications. As noted, minor modifications may not invalidate the use of test norms. However, serious modifications—such as rephrasing questions when the child does not understand them, repeating memory items because the child was not paying attention, giving a few more seconds on a timed test, or using a multiple-choice procedure for items that call for definitions—are likely to invalidate the test results.

Modifications may have other unintended consequences (Erin & Koenig, 1997). First, modifications may affect the skill that the test was intended to measure. For example, a phonics test that requires the examinee to look at three pictures and determine which one starts with a given consonant blend, such as *st,* would not be measuring the intended skill if the examiner described the pictures to a blind child or if Braille words were substituted for the picture. Second, eliminating items from a test usually reduces both the reliability of the test and the content breadth of the test. For example, eliminating half of the verbal items on a decoding test for a child with a hearing impairment would decrease the reliability of the test and provide less information about the child's decoding skills. Finally, information from modified tests can be misinterpreted because there usually is no precise way to evaluate the information.

Although your goal is to follow standard procedures whenever possible, you may need to make occasional exceptions to obtain some estimate of the child's ability without regard to norms. For example, if the child is depressed, you may want to extend the time limits on the test. When you must use modifications, report the resulting scores as "estimates" based on departures from standard procedures, and interpret them cautiously in light of the departures. The estimated scores are likely to be less precise, and predictions about future levels of functioning cruder than would otherwise be the case. A plus in using adapted test procedures is that they may provide information about what the children can or cannot do, and they may suggest ways to facilitate the children's interactions with the environment. Always include a statement in the report (and a footnote in any table of test scores that you develop) explaining how and why you deviated from standard instructions and cautioning the reader about how the deviations may affect the test scores and any interpretations attached to the scores.

The following case illustrates the value of using test modifications with a child with a severe disability.

Tommy was 8 years old and had a severe disability (athetoid-type cerebral palsy, characterized by slow, recurring, writhing movements of the arms and legs and the presence of facial grimaces). He had no oral speech and communicated only by painstakingly pointing out numbers that corresponded to words or phrases taped to the tray of his wheelchair. Tommy appeared to the examiner to be alert, curious, and eager to participate in the assessment. The examiner attempted to administer the Pictorial Test of Intelligence, a test that requires the child to point to one of four pictures that corresponds to the correct answer to a verbal question. However, Tommy was unable to make the movements necessary to differentiate between the pictures, even though they were printed on a large card. As a modification of the standard procedure, the examiner read each test item and then pointed in turn to each of the four pictures. When the examiner pointed to the choice Tommy wished to make, the child wiggled in his wheelchair. Because of the problem of interpreting Tommy's movements, many of the items had to be administered several times. After an hour and a half of this exhausting procedure, both examiner and child finished the test with a sense of real accomplishment. Tommy, a boy who had been suspected of having mental retardation, had earned a standard score of 120.

In this case, the modifications deviated from the standard procedures used to administer the test, but they did not alter the structure of the test procedures or give undue clues to the examinee. The score should be reported, with a note that it was obtained under modified administrative procedures and should be interpreted with caution.

Incentives and their effects. The systematic use of incentives during the administration of a test is a departure from standard procedures. Researchers have extensively studied the effects of incentives such as praise, candy, and money—called *social* or *token reinforcement*—on children's test performance. Analysis of the results of 34 studies (Sattler, 1992, page 110), with normal children and children with disabilities of various ethnic groups, presented a mixed picture: 41% of the studies indicated that incentives or feedback did not affect test scores, while 59% of the studies indicated that the effects on test scores were variable, sometimes raising tests scores and sometimes lowering test scores.

The differences between studies finding significant effects and those finding nonsignificant effects are difficult to discern. In some studies, token reinforcement increased scores on the Wechsler Verbal Scale but not on the Performance Scale. There is no readily available explanation to account for such differential effects. One could hypothesize that incentives are more effective in situations calling for speed and quick reaction time; yet some findings indicate the opposite effect. Social and token reinforcers in these studies do not appear to be related to the children's ethnicity or SES.

The research findings suggest that many children view the standard test situation as inherently rewarding—that is, the children do not need any special reinforcers. Children may enjoy the special attention from and acceptance by an adult examiner. The standard testing condition in those experiments that reported nonsignificant findings was apparently one in which the children were motivated to perform at their maximum level; they did not need additional social or token reinforcement or feedback to perform more effectively. However, in those experiments that reported significant findings, reinforcers sometimes increased and sometimes decreased the children's motivation and performance.

The research on incentives and their effects on intelligence test scores is hampered by the lack of information about the validity of the scores obtained under the incentive conditions. It may be that the most valid scores are those obtained under conditions similar to those found in the child's environment. If teachers and parents do not use incentives in teaching children, the scores obtained using reinforcement procedures may be less valid than those obtained under standard conditions. Scores obtained through the use of specific reinforcements may be more valid in environments that use reinforcements. These hypotheses need exploration and testing. At present there is little evidence that scores obtained using tangible or social reinforcement provide better estimates of children's abilities than those obtained under standard administrative conditions. And it is important to remember that most tests are not standardized with the use of reinforcers. Therefore, incentives should not be routinely used. If they are

used in exceptional circumstances, such as with an extremely uncooperative child, their use should be noted in the psychological report.

Testing-of-limits. Generally, the only modifications you should make to standard administrative procedures are those discussed in the test manuals (e.g., changing the order of tests if necessary or eliminating spoiled tests) or those necessary to test children who have disabilities that interfere with using standard procedures. However, there may be times when you want to go beyond the standard test procedures—referred to, as noted in Chapter 1, as *testing-of-limits*—to gain additional information about the child's abilities. Testing-of-limits refers to giving the child a series of help steps (or more time or additional cues) to determine whether he or she can solve the problems with the additional help. The information gleaned from testing-of-limits can be useful, especially in clinical or psychoeducational settings. Testing-of-limits will give you information about the child's ability to learn and the type and amount of assistance needed to raise the child's level of performance. Testing-of-limits is also referred to as interactive assessment, dynamic assessment, mediated learning, instruction-oriented method, and graduated prompts method. *When you score the test and report the results obtained under standard procedures, you do not give credit for any items that the child passed during testing-of-limits.*

Use testing-of-limits only after you have administered the entire test using standard procedures. Otherwise, the additional cues you use in testing-of-limits may help the child on the remaining items of a test. Such increases in scores, for example, have been reported for the Block Design and Picture Arrangement subtests of the WISC and Wechsler-Bellevue Intelligence Scale (Sattler, 1969). Following are some examples of modifications that may be used in testing-of-limits.

Providing additional cues. To determine how much help the child needs to solve a problem, give the child a series of cues. First, readminister failed items, telling the child that there is another solution or arrangement and asking her or him to try to find it. Or, you might reproduce the child's construction (e.g., a block design pattern or picture arrangement layout exactly as the child arranged it), tell the child that there is an error, and ask her or him to find it and correct it. If this procedure does not lead to a correct solution, you can show the child the first step in solving the problem. For example, you can place the upper left-hand corner block in its correct position or arrange the first picture of an item in the Picture Arrangement subtest. Then provide additional cues as needed, such as arranging a second block in its correct position or placing a second card in the right order.

Some examinees who fail items on the Block Design subtest or Pattern Analysis subtest—especially nine-block items—are able to succeed if they assemble the blocks inside the square box rather than on the table. You can also try demonstrating one item and seeing whether the examinee can then solve additional ones. Some examinees benefit from verbal explanations of puzzles and other nonlanguage tests. You can try gradually escalating from a single simple hint to a complete discussion of strategy. Progress slowly so that you can determine both the kind and the amount of help the examinee needs.

If you want to find out whether the child can benefit from cues that you give after he or she fails to read a word (or words) correctly, you can use the following procedure. First, evaluate the errors that were made. Then determine what cues might be useful. For example, if the child misreads the word *slam,* making an error on the *sl* consonant blend, write the last phonemes *am,* show the letters to the child, and ask the child to read them. If the child makes a mistake, read the letters correctly. Then write the letters *sl,* show them to the child, and ask the child if he or she knows any words beginning with *sl.* Give the child some examples if he or she fails to give any. Then show the word *slam* again and ask the child to read it.

Another way to see what help the child needs to read a word is to cover the word with a business card and then reveal the word one phoneme or syllable at a time, beginning at the end. After each successive revelation, have the child pronounce the letters as a whole—for instance, *-am, -lam, slam.*

Another approach is to provide additional structure. For instance, if the child becomes disoriented when asked to throw a ball, you might put a line on the floor to better orient the child.

In general, you might show the child the first step in reaching the correct solution (as above) or tell the child which part of the original response was incorrect and then ask the child to try the problem again. Overall, you can break down and simplify the tasks until it becomes clear to you what the child can and cannot do with help, how much help is needed, and under what conditions the child can succeed.

The above procedures will help you to determine the extent to which the child can benefit from additional cues. The more cues the child needs before she or he achieves success, the greater the child's possible degree of learning disorder or cognitive deficit. Be sure to explain your technique and findings in the report.

Changing the stimulus modality. You may want to explore whether the manner in which you administered the questions—the stimulus modality—influenced the child's performance. For example, if the child fails problems in oral form, can he or she solve them in written form? Or, if the child fails math word problems, can he or she solve the problems if they are rewritten in the form of math number problems?

It is handy to make and keep printed copies of the oral math questions on the WISC–III and WAIS–III Arithmetic subtests and other similar subtests. One set would be the problems copied from the manual and another would be the same problems presented as paper-and-pencil computation pages. See whether a child who failed an item orally can do it

when given a printed copy of the words and scratch paper. If not, see whether the child knows how to perform the arithmetic steps involved in the problem. You do not want to make assumptions about mental arithmetic ability, attention, concentration, and working memory when the real problem is that the child has not yet learned the necessary arithmetic skills.

Changing the response modality. You may want to see whether the child can succeed if you allow her or him to respond in another manner. For example, if the child fails a free-recall procedure, can she or he succeed with a multiple-choice procedure? (If you use a multiple-choice procedure, be sure to randomly vary the position of the correct answer on successive items.) Or, if the child fails to respond correctly when not allowed to use pencil and paper or a calculator, can she or he solve the problems *with* these aids?

Establishing methods used by the child. A child may use one of several ways to solve a problem. On Digit Span memory tests, for example, the child can solve the task by grouping the digits in sets of two, three, or more digits (4-1-2-5 as 41, 25), by recalling them as a number (4-1-3 as four hundred and thirteen), or by recalling them as distinct digits in sequence (4-1-3 as 4-1-3). The method used by the child may indicate the type of memory strategies used by the child. To learn how the child went about solving a problem, simply ask what method he or she used: "How did you go about solving the problem?" You might add, if needed, "I would like to hear you think aloud, OK?" Some children will be able to verbalize their method, but others will not, even though they answered correctly.

Eliminating time limits. When a child did not complete an item or a subtest (e.g., a Wechsler Block Design subtest item or the Wechsler Coding subtest) because he or she reached the time limit and you had to stop the test, you can readminister the item or subtest (after the evaluation) without time limits, deleting references to speed or time limits in the directions. This procedure will help you determine whether the child can eventually solve the problem, and the results can have implications for classroom interventions.

If speed is a problem for the child, you might not want to use tests that include time bonuses in the scoring. For example, for a slow-working child, the Stanford-Binet: Fourth Edition Pattern Analysis subtest or the Differential Ability Scale Pattern Construction Alternative Procedure subtest would be preferable to the WISC–III Block Design subtest. The WAIS–III includes an optional procedure for the Digit Symbol-Coding subtest in which the examinee simply copies symbols as quickly as possible. This procedure allows you to see how much of the examinee's success or difficulty on the actual subtest was attributable to graphomotor speed.

Asking probing questions. Occasionally examinees will give responses or make constructions (with blocks, picture arrangement cards, or other materials) that are vague or idiosyncratic. If you want to, you can go back to these items, repeating the item and response and then saying "Tell me more about what you mean" or reconstructing the design and then saying "Tell me about what you assembled; explain it to me." You also can say, "Tell me about how you arranged the cards." Such probing questions may give you insight into how examinees approached the tasks, as well as into their cognitive processes. You may learn, for example, whether the examinee recognizes incongruities in the final product, corrects errors, or tries to make sense of an incorrect design or seemingly random arrangement of the cards. If you want to understand how the examinee went about trying to solve the problem, you can say, "Tell me what you are thinking about as you try to solve the problem" or "Tell me why you think your answer [or what you did] is correct." Leading questions, which are generally prohibited by the test manuals, may help you better determine whether the examinee knows the information or is capable of solving the problem.

With preschool children, however, probing questions may not elicit what you want to know. For example, the question "Why did you choose that picture?"—intended to elicit information about task characteristics—may bring a response related to the child's motivation ("I'm smart," "I was tired," or "I didn't try hard"). Of course, motivation-related responses might be useful, depending on your goals.

Increasing motivation. You may want to give the child additional incentives after the standardized administration has been completed to see whether incentives increase her or his performance. You can use additional praise or a tangible reward. If the child improves as a result of your asking her or him to try harder, you might conclude that lack of motivation influenced her or his initial performance. This information may be useful in designing an intervention.

Comment on testing-of-limits. As a result of the help provided during testing-of-limits, the child may pass particular items or subtests. During the test proper, too, the child may solve a problem after the time limit. In such cases, you can note in your report that the child benefited from additional help or time and the implications of the child's successes, but, as noted earlier, do not change the child's test scores. You should, of course, give the child credit for any work completed within the allotted time limit, following the procedures described in the test manual.

If examinees succeed as a result of testing-of-limits, you may be able to separate failures associated with response slowing, inertia, or interference from failures associated with actual loss or inability to perform the task. The aim of all testing-of-limits is to better understand the examinee's cognitive ability: Do the additional cues or added time enable the child to succeed?

The information you obtain from testing-of-limits—such as whether the child benefited from verbal cues, demonstrations, concrete examples, elimination of time limits, or some combination of these—also may help you plan interventions. The techniques that help the child in the evaluation may be models for methods that would allow the child to learn more effectively in school and may, therefore, provide some of your most useful recommendations. Keep this idea in mind, too, as you assess and review the effectiveness of the behavioral interventions you used to help the child concentrate, stay on task, and make his or her best effort. Assessment results need to be applied to interventions useful in schools, and other places as well, whenever possible.

One of the major problems associated with testing-of-limits is that *it may invalidate future assessments.* Giving cues, extra time, and additional practice, for example, will likely help some children solve the tasks. If the child is retested, higher scores on retest may reflect practice effects rather than changes in ability (also see Chapter 4 on repeated evaluations and practice effects). Therefore, carefully consider the benefits and costs of testing-of-limits. If you will need to retest the child with the same test soon (e.g., within 12 to 24 months), then you should not use testing-of-limits. How the examinee does on the retest may give you more useful information than testing-of-limits. This may be especially true in cases of traumatic brain injury, where the examinee is slowly regaining functions and you plan to test repeatedly. Also, if the examinee will be referred to another agency for further evaluation, you may not want to test limits. However, if your goal is either to evaluate the limits of the child's abilities on the test or to determine the child's problem-solving approaches and there is no reason to plan on a retest within the next 12 to 24 months, you may want to consider testing-of-limits.

Talking to Parents of Infants and Toddlers

You may find it difficult to handle both a parent and a young child in your office or testing room. During the formal assessment, give most of your attention to the young child. But you also want to talk with a parent about her or his child. The parent may feel restrained when talking in the child's presence, especially if the parent is sad or angry; these are feelings that an infant or toddler may pick up on. In such cases, and with older children, you will need to schedule a separate appointment to interview the parent about her or his concerns, information you need, or issues you want to discuss, such as discipline techniques (see Chapter 2 in *Assessment of Children: Behavioral and Clinical Applications* for more information about interviewing parents).

Be aware of the feelings of the parents. Parents have limited experience with testing; they may be uninformed about the meaning of test results, biased by reading in the media about the role of testing, anxious about their child's behavior, and defensive about their child's need for testing. By honestly reassuring parents, avoiding technical language or psychological jargon, and addressing their concerns whenever possible, you can help to alleviate their anxiety. We must constantly guard against using jargon and technical concepts

Courtesy of Herman Zielinski.

in our discussions with parents and teachers because, even though we take these concepts for granted, they are not familiar to most parents (and teachers).

Remember that you are the parents' ally in providing the best possible care for the child. (Obviously, in cases of alleged child maltreatment, this statement may not apply; see Sattler, 1998.) Resist the temptation to assign blame, remembering that any behavior you see in the child (and in the child-parent interaction) is a product of a long series of complex interactions. Remain friendly, helpful, warm, objective, and credible. Most parents respond positively to kind words about their caretaking and teaching, as well as their patience and effort. Show them that you recognize their affection, their commitment, and the problems with which they are coping. These recommendations are especially important for dealing with anxious or defensive parents. Parents and caregivers will need to respect and value your views if they are to accept the results of your evaluation and carry out your suggested interventions.

ADMINISTERING TESTS TO CHILDREN WITH SPECIAL NEEDS

Suggestions for administering tests to children with special needs—whether because of age, language differences, or cultural patterns—are made in several chapters of the text. Special skills are required to test children who have emotional disturbance, behavior disorders, autism, attention deficit/hyperactivity disorder, brain injury, or physical impairments; these children will often challenge the resources of even the most competent and experienced examiners.

When you examine children with special needs, ask them if they need help and allow them to accept or refuse your help. Do not provide assistance without first asking. You can say, "Do you need help?" or "How should I help you?" Be patient, listen, and let them speak for themselves. You may repeat what they said to confirm that you understand them, but do not second guess them or assume that you know what they are trying to express.

Speak directly to the child with special needs, as you would to any other child. Do not direct your conversation to a parent, attendant, assistant, or nearby companion as if the child were not present. Children with special needs are children first. They should be treated with the same courtesy and respect that you would accord any other children.

Give children with special needs time to acclimate to the surroundings. Position them in their preferred way. Be sure that they have access to the adaptive equipment that they normally use, such as glasses or a hearing aid. If at all possible, evaluate them in a setting that is familiar to them. For example, a blind child may demonstrate more skilled behaviors in a familiar, rather than an unfamiliar, environment. Although you should try to complete the assessment in one session, sometimes you will need to see an infant, a young child, or a child with special needs on more than one occasion to complete the evaluation.

Following are some suggestions to help you administer tests to children with behavioral difficulties (Herschell, Greco, Filcheck, & McNeil, in press; Schwean & Saklofske, 1998). Remember that it is important to fit the strategy to the individual child with whom you are working. What works well with one child may not work with another. You need to be observant and sometimes even creative in figuring out what will work with a child who is difficult to manage.

1. *Know the test procedures so completely that you can give the child your full attention.*

2. *Sit next to the child rather than across the desk, if necessary.* If the child's attention wanders, gently say the child's name and ask him or her to listen to you.

3. *Establish some simple rules to assist in behavioral management.* For example, before the formal testing you might say, "For the rest of our time together today, there are only two rules. One is to sit in this chair, and the other is to follow directions. I'll give the directions slowly so that you can understand them. OK? Good; then let's get started."

4. *Direct the child in how to sit appropriately, when necessary.* For example, you might say, "There is a special way to sit so that I know you're ready for what we're about to do. This is how it looks. [Model good sitting posture and ask the child to try it.] That's great. You sit nice and straight right here at the table, really quiet without moving, and then I know you're ready to go on. Thank you."

5. *Use something appealing to the child as an incentive for cooperative behavior.* For example, show the child some stickers and have the child point to ones that she or he particularly likes. Then say, "I'm glad you like that one. I'll give it to you just as soon as we finish this part of our work." The stickers themselves sometimes work as reinforcers in that children may work hard simply to fill a page with stickers.

6. *Acknowledge the child's efforts and make other pleasant remarks as the child listens, sits in the chair, waits until instructions are completed before beginning a task, uses a moderate volume in speaking, follows directions, or otherwise behaves appropriately.*

7. *Use directive statements that emphasize desired behaviors.* For example, say: (a) "Greg, please hand me the blocks" rather than "I need those blocks back"; (b) "Greg, please show me how a big boy walks quietly" rather than "Greg, please stop running"; (c) "Greg, show me how still and tall you can sit" rather than "Greg, stop squirming, fussing, and looking around the room."

8. *Ignore or redirect behaviors such as whining, yelling, and complaining.* For example, if the child whines and says "This is too hard. I hate this," you might say, "I really appreciate that you're working so hard. I know some of these problems are tough. We'll take a break as soon as we've finished a little bit more. OK, all ready?"

9. *Use "when-then," "if-then," "either-or," and two-choice statements to aid in behavioral management.* For example, you might say, "When you've finished looking at that picture, then we can start on this page"; "As soon as you're in your chair, I'll show you some interesting pictures"; "If you sit straight, then we can move on"; "Either I'll put the puzzle in the box or you may do it"; or "Would you rather draw first or write some sentences first?"

10. *Verbally cue the child that you are ready to start a test by saying "Ready?" or something similar.*

11. *Make eye contact with the child before presenting the directions for an item.*

12. *Be sensitive to the child's needs.* Take short breaks, as needed, after the child has completed a task, rather than immediately after the child misbehaves. Provide breaks when the child looks extremely tired, bored, or uncomfortable or under any other circumstance that might impair the test results. Remember that young children and children for whom the testing situation is difficult need short testing sessions. A few short sessions are often preferable to one long session.

13. *Remove all distractions from the testing room.*

14. *Keep any test materials not in use out of the child's reach.*

15. *Speak slowly and emphasize key words to help the child better comprehend the instructions and items.*

16. *Learn what activities the child will engage in before coming to see you and what activities are planned for the time the child will be away from his or her class.* If possible, take these activities into account when you schedule the assessment. This is especially important if you think that the prior activities will interfere with the assessment or that missing an activity will cause resentment.

17. *Encourage the child to slow down.* For example, say, "Take your time and think it through" if she or he answers questions too quickly or acts carelessly.

18. *Acknowledge the child's frustration.* Say, as appropriate, "These are getting difficult, but try them anyway" (or something similar). If applicable, you can repeat the information with which you introduced the evaluation: "Remember what I said earlier: Some of these will be much too hard because they are for students in [middle school/high school/college]. You won't know all of them because you haven't been to [middle school/high school/college] yet."

Many of the techniques you use to test children who do not have disabilities can be used with children with special needs, but their application may seem demanding to the special needs children. Children who do not have disabilities typically do not require as much encouragement since they are accustomed to answering test questions. Children with special needs, in contrast, may feel at a disadvantage in the test situation. Those who have physical limitations may appear clumsy and awkward, and they may feel self-conscious. They must cope not only with specific deficits associated with their disability (such as inadequate sight or hearing) but perhaps also with the anxiety and uncertainty of their parents. Anxiety associated with repeated medical examinations, peer difficulties, and related factors also may have influenced their affective development and, indirectly, their cognitive development. Their reactions to the test situation may depend largely on how they perceive themselves outside the test situation. They may be aware of their disabilities and reluctant to expose their disabilities in the evaluation. You will need to be patient and supportive to establish rapport and elicit their optimal performance.

Administering tests to children with special needs poses various challenges.

1. You may develop false impressions of their intellectual ability if they have communication difficulties, such as speech or hearing deficiencies.
2. You may have to take many breaks if they are unaccustomed to doing concentrated work for long periods and fatigue easily.
3. You may have trouble deciding whether their attention difficulties, when present, are associated with physical deficiencies, with medication (if used), or with cognitive or neurological deficiencies.
4. You may have difficulty in establishing rapport with children who have heightened dependency.
5. You may have to deal with their heightened anxiety on timed tests.
6. You need to be sure that they understand the test directions fully throughout the testing process.

Children with special needs may be suspicious of easy items that appear to underestimate their ability (Ursula

Willis, personal communication, October 1999). They may react by taking the test less seriously and consequently may fail items that they could have passed. Be careful to explain to children both before the test proper and occasionally during the test itself that the test was designed to have very easy items and very difficult items for all children.

Preschool children in special education programs are usually accustomed to a great deal of direction and feedback from teachers. This is especially true of children with an autistic disorder or a pervasive developmental disorder. The children may become puzzled when you do not give them similar amounts of guidance and reinforcement. They may take a lack of reinforcement as an indication that they are making errors. In such situations, considerable ingenuity will be required on your part to remain within the test administration rules without discouraging the child (John Willis, personal communication, October 1999).

To make valid inferences about a child's ability based on his or her test performance, you must be confident that the child understands the test instructions. Scores should not reflect a child's failure to understand the task requirements. If the child's receptive or expressive disability is so severe that you cannot be sure whether he or she understands the test directions, you have several options. One is to continue to administer the test and then evaluate whether the child seems to understand the task. Another is to discontinue the test. A third is to develop practice items (if the test does not have practice items) or to use additional practice items (if the test has practice items) to make certain that the child understands the task. You can do this by (a) borrowing items from earlier versions of the test or from similar tests or (b) making up items. Although the latter procedures violate the test standardization and must be discussed in the report, these adaptations may be preferable to spoiling the test by beginning it before the child understands the task.

In evaluating the cognitive abilities of children with special needs, do not confuse sensory deficits—for example, visual, auditory, kinesthetic, or tactile deficits—with cognitive deficits. A child may have one or more sensory or motor difficulties and yet have adequate cognitive abilities. If you use timed tests, supplement them with tests that are not timed but that still adequately assess the child's skill repertoire. If children show undue stress when they work under time pressure, consider discontinuing the timed test or giving the test but not timing it or scoring it. *When assessing their cognitive abilities, you must not penalize special needs children because of their sensory or motor deficits.* Select tests that allow them to respond at their optimal level. For example, select tests without time limits, or at least avoid tests that give bonus points for fast work. Tests of cognitive ability should assess their cognitive abilities and not the extent of their physical abilities.

During parent interviews, ask the parents about signs, signals, or gestures that the children understand or use. Also ask the parents, teachers, and aides about when the children are most alert during the day. Through observation and informal testing, determine the degree to which the children are physically able to respond to the tests. This involves informally evaluating their (a) basic abilities, including vision, hearing, speech, sitting balance, and arm-hand use (e.g., voluntary movement to activate a switch, to press a key on a keyboard, or to use another device); (b) reading and writing skills (for school-age children); and (c) ability to communicate, including the ability to indicate yes or no by either verbal or nonverbal means. You can informally evaluate them by observing, if appropriate, how they perform such tasks as describing a picture, putting a puzzle together, reading and then writing a short sentence, and responding to simple questions. During these activities, note how they respond to your questions, perform motor tasks, and succeed on the tasks.

After you have become familiar with their problems and the limitations associated with their disabilities, select tests that are appropriate for their functional abilities. Depending on the child, you may have to omit tests or items that require physical or sensory abilities. For example, you may have to eliminate items that require deftness in object manipulation or drawing when you test children with disabilities of the upper extremities.

Some children with special needs are accustomed to receiving tangible reinforcers as motivators (e.g., candy, stickers, bubblegum, raisins, Cheerios). In such cases, be sure you have parental permission to use these primary reinforcers. One of the best motivators, in addition to positive reinforcement, is to arrange the activities so that the child intermittently experiences successes. You can do this by administering a test that you believe the child will succeed on after administering some tests that were difficult for the child. You also can take a break after three or four subtests and then go to an activity that you know the child enjoys or is competent at (based on parent or teacher reports), such as drawing airplanes or building with Legos. This additional activity does not have to be related to the test proper or to the referral. And the activity itself can be structured as a subtest: "Now I want you to draw me a picture of an airplane" or "You see these Legos. They are not all alike. I want you to build something with them."

Let the parent know, if he or she is present, that you do not expect the child to pass all of the test items; acknowledge from the beginning that some items are simply too difficult. Never tell a parent that a child has "failed" an item.

Some children with severe disabilities have paraprofessionals (i.e., aides or assistants) who work closely with them during much or all of the day. Possibly, the child will need to have the paraprofessional or parent present during the examination. In such cases, it is helpful to explain to the parent or paraprofessional before the evaluation that you are using tests with rigid rules for asking questions and giving help, so you will be behaving differently from how teachers behave. The reason for these rigid rules is to have standardized test results that can be compared over time with confidence. The rules ensure that every examiner administers the test in precisely the same way, even if some procedures do not seem reasonable. With children who have severe communication problems, you may need to explain to the parents or paraprofessionals that you might occasionally ask for assistance and that you will tell them exactly what you need within the rules for the test.

A FINAL THOUGHT—THROUGH A CHILD'S EYES

As repeatedly observed in this chapter, examinees play an active role in how you administer tests. They will react to you, as you react to them. Sometimes you may actually receive feedback from the children you test. Exhibit 7-1 presents a tongue-in-cheek example of such feedback.

Exhibit 7-1
" . . . On the Other Foot"

My name is Timmy Jones and I am in the third grade. I am as smart as anyone in the Elm Street School, including grown-ups. I even learned their language. Take that woman who tested me last week. Here's the report I have written about her.

Psychological Report

Name: Audrey O'Neill
Age: Uncertain
Profession: School Psychologist

Observation of behavior: Mrs. O'Neill is below average height and weight. It was a cold, wet day and she was limping slightly. Her grooming leaves something to be desired. Her clothing was dark and several years behind the style, "comfortable" shoes evidenced lack of concern with the impression made on others, long straight hair would be more appropriate on a younger person, and her fingernails were dirty—she looks as if she spends her spare time refinishing furniture. The bag she carried her test equipment in has seen better days. The whole impression she gave was one of mild involutional depression.

Mrs. O'Neill actually lost her way to the supply closet where she had set up makeshift quarters, even though she has been using it all semester. This was my first time and I found it right away. Attempts to establish rapport were clumsy, and interview techniques emphasized the negative. Of course I don't beat up on my little brother. And what did she mean by asking if everyone in my family has the same last name? She was distracted by the sound of the band practicing in the next room and preoccupied by the three phone calls that interrupted the testing session.

Test performance: Mrs. O'Neill made three errors administering the Stanford-Binet: Fourth Edition. All the better examiners use the WISC–III anyway. During a 90-minute testing session she managed to misplace her reading glasses once, her glass case twice, and her pen three times. Her handwriting is almost completely illegible, and she dropped three of the blocks. She transposed numbers twice, once administering digits forward and once transcribing a phone message. She definitely became nervous when I went into my hyperactive act, and has a hard time tolerating drumming fingers, tapping feet, etc.

Strengths and weaknesses: She is high in long-term memory and informational background. She remembered my sister and brother, and asked about my grandmother's health. She is low in short-term memory, concentration, and auditory skills (such as auditory reception and discrimination, and auditory figure-ground). She is also low in sequencing, both auditory and visual. She had problems with fine-motor skills and spatial orientations. Her motor coordination is gross.

Social relationships: Both child and peer relationships are in need of improvement. The children who greeted her in the hall are all either failing in school, from broken homes, or from the socioeconomic level that my parents do not allow me to associate with. Nor does she handle peer relationships well. It took us 12 minutes and 48 seconds by the new stopwatch I got for my birthday to get from one end of the hall to the supply closet because every grown-up we passed had to stop and tell her something. No wonder she is not more task-oriented.

Summary: Mrs. O'Neill is of approximately average native endowment for her cultural group membership. However, she is not functioning well because of (a) mild depression and (b) learning disabilities, which are developmental and therefore at her age will get worse. Peer relationships distract her from her work.

Recommendations:

1. Mrs. O'Neill could probably continue to perform her duties adequately in a simpler and more protected setting. Perhaps she could be transferred to the Gilmanton Corners Village School.
2. A program for identifying the gifted would improve her child contacts and broaden her perspective.
3. She should stop eating lunch alone while working on records. Not only did she get three mayonnaise stains on my cumulative folder, but she is heading for a good case of professional burn-out.

Timothy Jones
Grade 3
The Elm Street School

Source: Reprinted, with changes in notation, with permission of the publisher and author from Audrey Myerson O'Neill, "…On the Other Foot," *Journal of School Psychology*, 1981, *19*, pp. 71–72. Copyright 1981, Pergamon Journals, Ltd.

THINKING THROUGH THE ISSUES

1. How does the process of establishing rapport with children differ with the age of the child (infancy through 18 years)? With what age groups do you believe you have the most strengths in establishing rapport? Why? What can you do to improve your skills in establishing rapport with other age groups? How do you think children view you?
2. How can you eliminate or diminish the impact of halo effects in your test administration, in the impressions you develop of the child, and in your report?
3. Because no two test administrations are alike, what do we mean when we report that test results were obtained under standard administration procedures?

SUMMARY

Examiner Characteristics

1. To be able to work successfully with children, you need to have tact, diplomacy, ingenuity, patience, understanding, warmth, and respect.
2. A competent examiner is flexible, vigilant, and self-aware and genuinely enjoys working with children.
3. When you evaluate children, you must be prepared to adjust your testing techniques, even as you adhere to standardized procedures.
4. If you cannot successfully test a child, the child's parents may be able to provide information about the child's language ability, motor ability, social skills, self-sufficiency, mental development, and overall development.
5. Administering tests should not become so automatic that you forget the child, the setting, and the reason for the evaluation. What should become routine is your handling of the test procedures.
6. Strive to understand your temperament and your attitudes toward children in general and, in particular, toward children with special needs and children from cultural and linguistical backgrounds that differ from your own.
7. Whenever you recognize that you are not fully capable of establishing rapport with a child, you should disqualify yourself from evaluating the child and ask a colleague to conduct the assessment.
8. Self-awareness includes knowledge of your body language, including your facial expressions and gestures; the way you sit, hold your head, and direct your eyes; the small vocal sounds you make; and other nonverbal mannerisms.
9. Your test administration should not be influenced by your personal impressions of the examinee, a reaction called the halo effect.
10. Research on the role of the examiner confirms clinical impressions that the evaluation setting has elements of subjectivity.
11. You must try to reduce any sources of subjectivity related to how you administer and score tests.
12. Research indicates that examiner familiarity raised children's test performance on individual ability and achievement tests, on the average, by about 4.2 scaled-score points.

Preparing for the First Meeting

13. In preparing for the first meeting, you should study the referral question and review available background material.

Establishing Rapport

14. The process of establishing rapport begins when the parent conveys to the child that the child will be meeting with a psychologist.
15. If the child is young, you might bring a toy and at first try to keep the parent seated so that you can kneel at the child's level.
16. A brief and frank account of the purpose of the evaluation may be helpful with older children.
17. Tailor your remarks to the needs of the child.
18. Although your first comments are important in establishing rapport, efforts to build and maintain rapport should continue throughout the evaluation.
19. Make the tasks as pleasant as you can, even though some of them will be difficult for the child to perform.
20. If the parent is suspected of having abused or neglected the child or if the evaluation is part of a custody dispute, do not evaluate the child in the presence of a parent.
21. To allay the apprehensions of the older child, you want to convey through questions and comments that you will treat him or her professionally, with decency, safety, and respect.
22. Helping children maintain a sense of self-esteem and self-acceptance is essential to bringing about a successful relationship.
23. In most cases, after a short introduction, you can begin with the test materials as a way of continuing to establish rapport.
24. You must be willing to listen to and be attentive to the children's needs, rather than adhering to your agenda.
25. Give the child a choice only when you intend to leave the decision up to him or her.
26. Each encounter with a child will have its own dynamics, and procedures that are effective with one child may not work with another.

Observing Examinees

27. It will be helpful to observe examinees' personal appearance, nonverbal behavior, and verbal behavior, both in the test situation and in interactions with others, especially parents, teachers, siblings, and peers.
28. Observations conducted during the administration of psychological tests are especially valuable because they are made under relatively standard conditions and allow for comparisons among different examinees.
29. Whenever you observe a behavior that deviates from normal, note where and when the behavior occurs and what happens afterwards.
30. Be aware of how the examinee responds to extraneous stimuli.
31. Skill in observing behavior requires training and practice; it does not occur automatically when you find yourself in a situation where you have to observe a child.
32. You must be alert, perceptive, and attentive to the child's behavior.
33. Make note of the examinee's height, weight, clothing, hairstyle, grooming, and general appearance.
34. Your observations may give you clues about the examinee's physical and neurological development and conditions that the examinee may suffer from.
35. Be aware of the examinee's nonverbal behavior, or body language.
36. Body language may tell you about the examinee's (a) moods, (b) openness for communication or distance from you, (c) amount and range of expressive gestures, and (d) idiosyncratic or symptomatic patterns of body movements.

Courtesy of Herman Zielinski.

37. Note the examinee's voice and speech qualities, clarity of expression, fluency, grammar, cohesiveness of communications, comprehension, length and frequency of pauses, ability to converse, and ability to maintain a train of thought.

38. Language usage is a guide to the examinee's personality and thought processes, as are the tempo, quality, and content of the examinee's verbal responses.

39. Your observation of the examinee's nonverbal and verbal behavior will provide you with information about her or his (a) ability to attend to testing materials, (b) mood and affect, (c) orientation (i.e., to person, place, and time), and (d) attitude toward the test situation and toward you.

40. Look for signs of visual, auditory, speech, or visual-motor and motor difficulties.

41. Observations begin when you first see the child in the waiting room.

42. When you observe children with special needs in natural settings, note how they perform daily activities, use language, use motor skills, cope with different environments, accomplish new learning, and use cognitive strategies in different settings.

43. The GATSB is a 29-item behavior-rating instrument that uses a three-point scale to rate the examinee's behavior during the administration of the WISC–III and the Wechsler Individual Achievement Test.

General Suggestions for Administering Tests

44. In general, you should know your task well enough that the test administration flows automatically, leaving you free to observe the child's behavior.
45. It is advisable to complete the administration of any single test in one test session or, at most, two test sessions separated by no more than one day.
46. Administer the test in a room with minimal distractions.
47. Control your materials.
48. Make sure the child is comfortable.
49. Administer items from the child's left to right in the order given in the test manual.
50. Place stimulus materials in front of the child one at a time so that the child can see the blocks, cards, or other materials clearly.
51. Complete one row at a time in constructing sample block designs, starting each row at the child's left and working to the right.
52. Recognize that you have the option of holding or not holding the test booklet, unless the test manual gives specific instructions on what to do.
53. To avoid needless distractions, keep the testing table clear of all extraneous materials.
54. Adhere to test instructions exactly if you want to use the test norms.
55. Consider the child's age and ability level as you engage the child in conversation and give the test instructions, and modify your tempo accordingly.
56. Avoid unusual facial expressions or modulations in your voice that may give the child cues about her or his performance.
57. Do not tell the child whether her or his responses are correct.
58. Repeat the instructions for the first trial of a test on successive trials or items if you believe that it would be helpful, unless the test manual notes otherwise.
59. Do not repeat items designed to measure memory.
60. Phrase requests as mild commands (such as "Tell me another reason…") unless prohibited from doing so by the test manual.
61. Do not tell the child how much time is allotted on tests that have time limits unless the test manual says otherwise.
62. Note whether the child takes an excessive amount of time to give answers or to begin working with the blocks, pictures, or other test materials.
63. Seldom accept the first "I don't know" response that the child gives.
64. Ask the child to repeat a response if you are uncertain about what the child said.
65. Do not probe obviously incorrect responses.
66. When a response contains one part that is correct and one that is incorrect, ask the child for his or her preference and score the response accordingly.
67. Avoid giving the child the impression that you are discontinuing a test because of repeated failure.
68. Repeat the entire question (if it is allowed) when a child asks to have part of a question repeated.

69. Always remember to consult the test manual for guidelines on how to probe, and follow those guidelines when specified.
70. Pace the evaluation so that you can comfortably and accurately record the child's responses.
71. Develop efficient ways to record responses.
72. Record the child's answers in the spaces provided in the record booklets.
73. Usually score the child's responses immediately after they are given.
74. Study the scoring criteria for each test so that you know which are correct, questionable, and incorrect answers.
75. Recognize that the scoring examples shown in test manuals are guides.
76. In general, give credit for correct responses that the child gives in any form of communication, including writing, typing on a computer or typewriter, sign language, Braille, fingerspelling, or teletouch, unless explicitly forbidden to do so by the test manual.
77. Any modifications that are used to administer a test should be noted on the test record form.
78. Research on the effects of incentives on test performance gives a mixed picture, with some studies showing no effect and others showing minimal or some effect.
79. Testing-of-limits is a procedure used to gain additional information about the child's abilities.
80. Testing-of-limits is also referred to as interactive assessment, dynamic assessment, mediated learning, instruction-oriented method, and graduated prompts method.
81. When you score the test and report the results obtained under standard procedures, you do not give credit to any items that the child passed during testing-of-limits.
82. Use testing-of-limits only after you have administered the entire test using standard procedures.
83. One of the major problems associated with testing-of-limits is that it may invalidate future assessments. Therefore, carefully consider the benefits and costs of testing-of-limits.

Administering Tests to Children with Special Needs

84. Special skills are required to test children who have emotional disturbance, behavior disorders, autism, attention-deficit/hyperactivity disorder, brain injury, or physical impairments; these children will often challenge the resources of even the most competent and experienced examiners.
85. Speak directly to children with special needs, as you would to any other child.
86. Give children with special needs time to acclimate to the surroundings.
87. Remember that it is important to fit the strategy to the individual child with whom you are working. What works well with one child may not work with another.
88. Many of the techniques you use to test children who do not have disabilities can be used with children with special needs, but their application may seem demanding to the special needs children.
89. To make valid inferences about a child's ability based on his or her test performance, you must be confident that the child understands the test instructions.
90. In evaluating the cognitive abilities of children with special needs, do not confuse sensory deficits—for example, visual, auditory, kinesthetic, or tactile deficits—with cognitive deficits.

91. During parent interviews, ask the parents about signs, signals, or gestures that the children understand or use.
92. Ask the parents, teachers, and aides about when the children are most alert during the day.
93. After you have become familiar with their problems and the limitations associated with their disabilities, select tests that are appropriate for their functional abilities.
94. Some children with special needs are accustomed to receiving tangible reinforcers as motivators (e.g., candy, stickers, bubble-gum, raisins, Cheerios). In such cases, be sure you have parental permission to use these primary reinforcers.

KEY TERMS, CONCEPTS, AND NAMES

Examiner characteristics (p. 184)
Examiner expectancy effects (p. 186)
Halo effect (p. 186)
Establishing rapport (p. 189)
Observing examinees (p. 194)
GATSB (p. 203)
Departures from standard procedures (p. 208)
Incentives (p. 209)
Social or token reinforcement (p. 209)
Testing-of-limits (p. 209)
Administering tests to children with special needs (p. 212)

STUDY QUESTIONS

1. What are some of the skills of effective examiners?
2. Discuss examiner expectancy effects, variability among examiners, and the examiner-examinee relationship. Cite relevant research in your discussion.
3. Explain how an examiner should initiate the process of establishing rapport with children. Cite research studies in your discussion.
4. Discuss the process of establishing rapport with both young children and school-aged children.
5. What should examiners observe when they administer tests?
6. What are some general suggestions for administering tests?
7. Discuss the problems associated with departures from standard procedure. When would you depart from standard procedure and why?
8. Discuss research findings on the use of incentives and feedback.
9. Discuss testing-of-limits.
10. What are some important issues in administering tests to children with special needs?

8

WECHSLER INTELLIGENCE SCALE FOR CHILDREN–III (WISC–III): DESCRIPTION

by Jerome M. Sattler and Donald H. Saklofske

Mind is the great lever of all things; human thought is the process by which human ends are ultimately answered.
—Daniel Webster

Goals and Objectives

This chapter is designed to enable you to do the following:

- Evaluate the psychometric properties of the WISC–III
- Administer the WISC–III in a competent and professional way
- Evaluate short forms of the WISC–III
- Compare the WISC–III with other Wechsler tests
- Evaluate the assets and limitations of the WISC–III

The Wechsler Intelligence Scale for Children–Third Edition (WISC–III) is the latest version of the Wechsler scales for children 6 through 16 years old (Wechsler, 1991; see Figure 8-1). Wechsler is cited as the author of the WISC–III, even though he died in 1982; the staff of The Psychological Corporation authored the revision. The WISC–III was published in 1991, 17 years after the previous edition, called the WISC–R (Wechsler, 1974). The primary reasons for revising the test were to (a) update the norms, (b) strengthen its psychometric properties, (c) revise and add items and subtests, and (d) give the test a more contemporary look. Wechsler (1949) developed his first children's intelligence test, the WISC, as a downward extension of the adult intelligence test, the Wechsler-Bellevue Intelligence Scale (Wechsler, 1939).

The WISC–III contains 13 subtests that make up a Verbal Scale and a Performance Scale. The five subtests in the Verbal Scale are Information, Similarities, Arithmetic, Vocabulary, and Comprehension. The five subtests in the Performance Scale are Picture Completion, Coding, Picture Arrangement, Block Design, and Object Assembly. The three remaining subtests—Digit Span in the Verbal Scale and Symbol Search and Mazes in the Performance Scale—are designated as supplementary subtests but, nevertheless, measure important dimensions of cognitive ability. Exhibit 8-1 shows items similar to those on the WISC–III. The WISC–III retains about 73% of the WISC–R items (not including the Coding subtest), either in the original or in a slightly modified form. Symbol Search is the only subtest new to the WISC–III.

STANDARDIZATION OF THE WISC–III

The WISC–III was standardized on 2,200 children who were selected to be representative of children in the United States. The demographic characteristics used to obtain a stratified sample were age, race/ethnicity, geographic region, and parental education (used as a measure of socioeconomic status). There were 11 age groups—ranging from 6 through 16 years—in the standardization group, with 100 boys and 100

Figure 8-1. Wechsler Intelligence Scale for Children–III. Courtesy of The Psychological Corporation.

Exhibit 8-1
WISC–III–Like Items

Information (30 questions)
How many legs do you have?
What must you do to make water freeze?
Who discovered the North Pole?
What is the capital of France?

Similarities (19 questions)
In what way are a pencil and a crayon alike?
In what way are tea and coffee alike?
In what way are an inch and a mile alike?
In what way are binoculars and microscope alike?

Arithmetic (24 questions)
If I have one piece of candy and get another one, how many
   pieces will I have?
At 12 cents each, how much will 4 bars of soap cost?
If a suit sells for ½ of the regular price, what is the cost of a $120
   suit?

Vocabulary (30 words)
What is a ball?
What does *running* mean?
What is a poem?
What does *obstreperous* mean?

Comprehension (18 questions)
Why do we wear shoes?
What is the thing to do if you see someone dropping his package?
In what two ways is a lamp better than a candle?
In the United States, why are we tried by a jury of our peers?

Digit Span (15 items; 8 in Digits Forward, 7 in Digits Backward)
The task is to repeat digits presented by the examiner in a forward direction in one part (2 to 9 digits in length; example: 1-8)
and in a backward direction in the other part (2 to 8 digits in
length; example: 6-4-9).

Picture Completion (30 items)
The task is to identify the essential missing part of the picture,
such as (a) a car without a wheel, (b) a dog without a leg, and
(c) a buggy without a wheel (see below).

Coding (59 items in Coding A and 119 items in Coding B)
The task is to copy symbols from a key (see below).

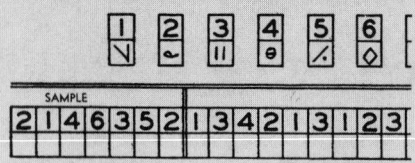

Picture Arrangement (14 items)
The task is to arrange a series of pictures into a meaningful
sequence (see below).

Block Design (12 items)
The task is to reproduce stimulus designs using four or nine
blocks (see below).

Object Assembly (5 items)
The task is to arrange pieces into a meaningful object (see
below).

Symbol Search (45 items in Part A and 45 items in Part B)
The task is to decide whether a stimulus figure (a symbol)
appears in an array (see below).

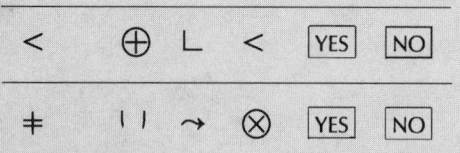

Mazes (10 items)
The task is to complete a series of mazes (see below).

Note. The questions resemble those that appear on the WISC–III but are not actually from the test, except for the sample items shown for
Symbol Search and Mazes. Chapter 9 describes each subtest in more detail. Pictures courtesy of The Psychological Corporation.

girls in each age group. As for race/ethnic membership, children were from the following groups: Euro American, African American, Hispanic American, or Other (composed of Native American, Eskimo, Aleut, Asian American, and Pacific Islander categories). The four geographical regions sampled were Northeast, North Central, South, and West. Within each age group, children were selected so that they matched as closely as possible the proportions found in the 1988 U.S. Census data with regard to race/ethnicity, geographic region, and parental education.

Table 8-1 shows the educational status and geographic location by race/ethnic group of the standardization sample. Parents in the Euro American and Other classifications had the most education—51.5% of the Euro American group and 57.2% of the Other group had some college education, while 27.9% of the African American group and 19.9% of the Hispanic American group had some college education. The majority of the Euro American and African American samples came from the North Central and South regions, while the majority of the Hispanic American and Other samples came from the South and West. The race/ethnic proportions in the sample were 70.1% Euro American, 15.4% African American, 11.0% Hispanic American, and 3.5% Other.

Tables 2.2 through 2.5 in the WISC–III manual indicate that parent education level was stratified within race, race was stratified within geographic region, and these variables match the 1988 U.S. Census data with remarkable accuracy.

The WISC–III sampling procedure is notably superior to that used on the WISC–R, which stratified race by Euro American versus NonEuro American categories only. In addition, actual cases were used, without weighting for any demographic variable, to obtain the normative data for the WISC–III. The sampling methodology was excellent.

DEVIATION IQS, SCALED SCORES, AND TEST-AGE EQUIVALENTS

The WISC–III, like the WPPSI–R and WAIS–III, uses the Deviation IQ ($M = 100$, $SD = 15$) for the Verbal Scale, Performance Scale, and Full Scale IQs and scaled scores ($M = 10$, $SD = 3$) for the 13 individual subtests. An IQ is computed by comparing the examinee's sum of scaled scores with the scores earned by a representative sample of his or her age group. After each subtest is scored, raw points are summed and converted to scaled scores within the examinee's own age group through use of Table A.1 in the WISC–III manual (pages 217–249). Age groups are in 4-month intervals for children between 6-0-0 (years, months, days) and 16-11-30.

In the WISC–III manual, the table used to obtain IQs (Table A.4, pages 253–254) is based on the 10 standard subtests. The three supplementary subtests—Digit Symbol, Symbol Search, and Mazes—are not used in the calculation of IQs

Table 8-1
Demographic Characteristics of WISC–III Standardization Sample: Education and Geographic Region by Ethnic Group

Demographic variable	Ethnic group (percent)			
	Euro American	African American	Hispanic American	Other[a]
Amount of education				
Eight years or less	1.6	7.1	30.0	5.7
Some high school	8.6	22.7	23.6	8.6
High school graduate	38.4	42.2	26.4	28.6
Some college	29.4	18.8	14.5	22.9
College graduate	22.1	9.1	5.4	34.3
Total	100.1	99.9	99.9	100.1
Geographic region				
Northeast	20.5	12.3	9.1	17.1
North Central	31.2	20.8	6.4	14.3
South	30.0	60.4	43.6	20.0
West	18.3	6.5	40.9	48.6
Total	100.0	100.0	100.0	100.0

Note. Race/ethnic distribution in total group was as follows: Euro American = 70.1%, African American = 15.4%, Hispanic American = 11.0%, Other = 3.5%.
[a]*Other* represents the following groups: Native American, Eskimo, Aleut, Asian American, and Pacific Islander.
Source: Adapted from Wechsler (1991).

unless a standard subtest is either spoiled or not given. When a supplementary subtest is substituted for a standard subtest, the reliability and validity of the IQs are unknown because the supplementary subtests were not used in generating the IQ tables. In fact, there is no information in the WISC–III manual about the reliability and validity of the test when supplementary subtests are used to compute the IQ. One statement in the manual (page 5), however, indicates that when a supplementary subtest was substituted for a standard subtest, mean changes ranging from .1 to .3 point occurred. Nevertheless, be cautious when using supplementary subtests to compute an IQ.

The WISC–III manual provides guidelines for use of the three supplementary subtests. These instructions, in part, indicate that Digit Span may substitute for any Verbal Scale subtest, Mazes may substitute for any Performance Scale subtest, and Symbol Search may substitute for Coding *only*. Unfortunately, the WISC–III manual fails to discuss how these recommendations were determined or to cite findings to support its recommendations. According to a spokesperson for The Psychological Corporation (personal communication, Aurelio Prifitera, January 1992), the last guideline was designed to prevent the Performance Scale IQ from being too heavily weighted with subtests that have relatively low *g* loadings.

Prorating Procedure

The WISC–III manual provides Table A.8 (page 258) for prorating sums of scaled scores when only four Verbal Scale subtests and four Performance Scale subtests are administered. Tellegen and Briggs (1967) provided another procedure (see Exhibit 8-4 in this chapter) for computing IQs obtained on an abbreviated version of any Wechsler test (also referred to as a short form). Their procedure considers the intercorrelations between the specific subtests administered; prorating does not take the intercorrelations into account. Later in the chapter we discuss how you can obtain estimated IQs for several short-form combinations using the Tellegen and Briggs procedure. We need research to determine which procedure—prorating or the Tellegen and Briggs procedure—produces more valid IQs.

Test-Age Equivalents

When David Wechsler first developed the WISC, he believed that the mental-age concept was potentially misleading and therefore decided not to use it in calculating IQs. (See Chapter 4 for a discussion of the mental-age concept.) Wechsler rejected the notion that mental age represents an absolute level of mental capacity or that the same mental age in different children represents identical intelligence levels. Soon after the initial publication of the WISC, however, he recognized that mental-age equivalents or test-age equivalents (the average age associated with a score on a subtest)

could be useful. Therefore, in later publications of the WISC, WISC–R, and WISC–III, the test manuals provided test-age equivalents (see Table A.9, page 259, in the WISC–III manual). Test-age equivalents are essentially mental-age (MA) scores.

Test ages are obtained directly from the raw scores on each subtest. Because a scaled score of 10 represents the mean, the test-age equivalents of the raw scores reflect the average score for each specific age group. An *average* test-age equivalent is obtained by summing the individual subtest test ages and dividing the sum by the number of subtests. To obtain a *median* test age, you should rank order test ages from high to low and locate the middle-most test age. The median is more appropriate than the mean because test ages are not equal-unit scores (see Chapter 4).

The WISC–III test-age equivalent scores can be compared with mental-age or test-age scores from other tests. By so doing, parents, teachers, and others may better understand the child's level of intellectual functioning. Research with the WISC–R suggests that test ages have adequate validity, based on high correlations with the Stanford-Binet: Form L-M mental age ($r = .88$; Sutton, Koller, & Christian, 1982) and the Peabody Individual Achievement Test ($r = .82$; Huberty & Koller, 1984). We need similar studies with the WISC–III.

RELIABILITY OF THE WISC–III

The WISC–III has outstanding reliability. For example, the Full Scale, Verbal Scale, and Performance Scale have internal consistency reliability coefficients of .89 or above over the entire age range covered in the standardization group. Average internal consistency reliability coefficients, based on the 11 age groups, are .96 for the Full Scale IQ, .95 for the Verbal Scale IQ, and .91 for the Performance Scale IQ (see Table 8-2). The internal consistency reliability coefficients for ages 6 to 16 years range from .94 to .97 for the Full Scale IQ, .92 to .96 for the Verbal Scale IQ, and .89 to .94 for the Performance Scale IQ. The lowest internal consistency reliability coefficient ($r = .89$) is at 14 years for the Performance Scale IQ, but this coefficient is close to .90.

Subtest Reliabilities

The internal consistency reliabilities for the subtests are lower than those for the Verbal Scale, Performance Scale, and Full Scale (see Table 8-2). This would be expected because there are fewer items in the subtests than in the scales. The average internal consistency reliabilities range from a low of .69 for Object Assembly to a high of .87 for Vocabulary and Block Design. For the 11 age groups, median subtest internal consistency reliabilities range from a low of .76 at 13 years to a high of .83 at 8 years (see Table 8-3). Internal consistency reliabilities across the ages are generally similar.

Table 8-2
Average Internal Consistency Reliability Coefficients, Test-Retest Reliability Coefficients, and Standard Errors of Measurement for WISC–III Subtests and Scales

Subtest or scale	Average internal consistency reliability r_{xx}	Average test-retest reliability r_{tt}	Average SEM
Information	.84	.85	1.23
Similarities	.81	.81	1.30
Arithmetic	.78	.74	1.41
Vocabulary	.87	.89	1.08
Comprehension	.77	.73	1.45
Digit Span	.85	.73	1.17
Picture Completion	.77	.81	1.44
Coding	.79	.77	1.42
Picture Arrangement	.76	.64	1.48
Block Design	.87	.77	1.11
Object Assembly	.69	.66	1.67
Symbol Search	.76	.74	1.48
Mazes	.70	.57	1.64
Verbal Scale IQ	.95	.94	3.53
Performance Scale IQ	.91	.87	4.54
Full Scale IQ	.96	.94	3.20

Note. Reliabilities for 11 of the 13 subtests (except Coding and Symbol Search) are split-half correlations. For Coding and Symbol Search, the reliability coefficients are test-retest coefficients obtained on a sample of about 60 children in six different age groups (retest interval not given in WISC–III manual). Verbal Scale, Performance Scale, and Full Scale reliability coefficients are based on a formula for computing the reliability of a composite group of tests. Digit Span, Mazes, and Symbol Search were not included in the calculation of the reliability coefficients for the Verbal Scale IQ, Performance Scale IQ, and Full Scale IQ.
Source: Adapted from Wechsler (1991).

Standard Errors of Measurement

The average standard errors of measurement (SEMs) in IQ points are 3.20 for the Full Scale, 3.53 for the Verbal Scale, and 4.54 for the Performance Scale (see Table 8-2). As with all Wechsler scales, you can place more confidence in IQs based on the Full Scale than in those based on either the Verbal or the Performance Scale. In addition, you can place more confidence in IQs obtained from the Verbal Scale than in those obtained from the Performance Scale.

The SEMs for the subtests in scaled-score points range from 1.08 to 1.45 for the Verbal Scale subtests and from 1.11 to 1.67 for the Performance Scale subtests. Within the Verbal

Table 8-3
Range and Median Internal Consistency Reliabilities of WISC–III Subtests in 11 Age Groups

Age (in years)	Range of r_{xx}	Median r_{xx}
6	.69–.82	.79
7	.65–.84	.77
8	.65–.88	.83
9	.66–.85	.80
10	.69–.89	.79
11	.65–.88	.79
12	.66–.89	.81
13	.70–.90	.76
14	.60–.91	.77
15	.61–.92	.82
16	.67–.90	.82
Average	.69–.87	.78

Source: Adapted from Wechsler (1991).

Scale, Vocabulary has the smallest average SEM (1.08) and Comprehension has the largest average SEM (1.45). Within the Performance Scale, Block Design has the smallest average SEM (1.11) and Object Assembly has the largest average SEM (1.67). Chapter 4 discusses the SEM.

Test-Retest Reliability

In the standardization sample, the stability of the WISC–III was assessed by having 353 children from age groups 6, 7, 10, 11, 14, and 15 years retested after an interval of 12 to 63 days (*Mdn* = 23 days; Wechsler, 1991). For statistical analyses, the six age groups were then combined into three age groups (6–7 years, 10–11 years, and 14–15 years). In the three age groups, the stability coefficients were, respectively, .92, .95, and .94 for the Full Scale IQ; .90, .94, and .94 for the Verbal Scale IQ; and .86, .88, and .87 for the Performance Scale IQ. These test-retest reliability coefficients indicate that the WISC–III provides stable IQs for the Full Scale and Verbal Scale, but less stable IQs for the Performance Scale because of practice effects (see Chapter 4).

The stability coefficients for the subtests ranged from a low of .54 for Mazes at 14–15 years to a high of .93 for Vocabulary at 14–15 years. Average test-retest reliabilities for the subtests ranged from .57 for Mazes to .89 for Vocabulary (see Table 8-2). As expected, average internal consistency reliabilities are somewhat higher than average test-retest reliabilities (*Mdn* r_{xx} = .78 versus *Mdn* r_{tt} = .74).

Several studies report test-retest correlations for various groups of children with special needs. As Table 8-4 shows,

Table 8-4
Long-Term Stability of the WISC–III

Sample	N	Test-retest interval	M change			r			Reference
			Verbal Scale	Performance Scale	Full Scale	Verbal Scale	Performance Scale	Full Scale	
ADHD	37	30 mo	1.55	4.81	2.93	.86	.74	.84	Schwean & Saklofske (1998)
Sp Ed	667	34 mo	−.64	−.27	−.51	.87	.87	.91	Canivez & Watkins (1998)
LD	50	36 mo	.70	.20	.13	.76	.71	.82	Stavrou & Flanagan (1996)
LD	60	36 mo	−4.30	−2.80	−3.70	.79	.70	.78	Zhu, Woodell, & Kreiman (1997)
LD	80	36 mo	−1.40	−2.10	−2.00	.84	.87	.88	Finkelson & Stavrou (1999)
MR	70	36 mo	−3.14	−.56	−1.66	.91	.81	.92	Bolen (1998)
LD	54	36 mo	−3.54	.14	−2.06	.83	.78	.87	Smith, Smith, Bramlett, & Hicks (1999)

Note. ADHD = attention-deficit/hyperactivity disorder, Sp Ed = special education, LD = learning disability, MR = mental retardation.

the test-retest correlations for periods about 30 to 36 months ranged from .76 to .91 for the Verbal Scale (*Mdn r* = .84), from .70 to .87 for the Performance Scale (*Mdn r* = .78), and from .78 to .92 for the Full Scale (*Mdn r* = .87). These findings, along with those reported in the WISC–III manual, support the stability of WISC–III scores over both shorter and longer periods with both "typical" children and children with special needs.

Canivez and Watkins (1999) reported stability coefficients for various demographic groups for a sample of 642 students who were evaluated twice for special education eligibility over a mean test-retest interval of 2.83 years. The results, which are shown in Table 8-5, indicate that long-term stability coefficients for the Verbal Scale, Performance Scale, and Full Scale are similar across gender, ethnicity, and age. In all cases, the Full Scale IQ had the highest stability coefficients of the three scales.

Changes in IQs. Table 8-6 shows the mean test-retest IQs and standard deviations for the Verbal Scale, Performance Scale, and Full Scale for the three combined age groups reported in the WISC–III manual. On average, from the first to the second testing, the Full Scale IQ increased by 7.0 to 8.4 points, the Verbal Scale IQ increased by 1.7 to 3.3 points, and the Performance Scale IQ increased by 11.5 to 13.5 points. These statistically significant increases, which likely result from practice effects, are 4 to 6 times greater for the Performance Scale than for the Verbal Scale.

When the WISC–III is administered a second time, children are likely to have greater gains on the Performance subtests than on the Verbal Scale subtests. This may occur because they are able to recall (a) the types of items they encountered the first time and (b) the strategies they used to solve the problems (Kaufman, 1990a). During the first administration, children

may perceive the Performance Scale subtests as more novel than the Verbal Scale subtests. On retest, the Performance Scale items may become less novel and perhaps more of a test of long-term memory and ability to apply previous learning sets than a test of adaptability and flexibility.

Table 8-5
WISC–III Stability Coefficients for Various Demographic Groups Studied by Canivez and Watkins (1999)

Demographic group	Verbal Scale	Performance Scale	Full Scale
Female	.88	.86	.92
Male	.85	.87	.91
Euro American	.86	.86	.91
African American	.83	.87	.89
Hispanic American	.86	.76	.87
Age 6 years at first testing	.80	.87	.89
Age 7 years at first testing	.86	.81	.89
Age 8 years at first testing	.85	.82	.87
Age 9 years at first testing	.88	.91	.94
Age 10 years at first testing	.82	.86	.90
Age 11 years at first testing	.89	.89	.94
Age 12 years at first testing	.87	.89	.92
Age 13 years at first testing	.93	.87	.95

Note. The sample contained 642 students who were evaluated twice for special education eligibility over a mean test-retest interval of 2.83 years.

Table 8-6
Test-Retest WISC–III IQs for Three Age Groups

Age (in years)	Scale	First testing		Second testing		
		Mean IQ	SD	Mean IQ	SD	Change
6–7	Verbal	100.8	12.7	102.5	12.3	+ 1.7*
(N = 111)	Performance	102.7	14.8	114.2	17.6	+11.5**
	Full	101.6	13.0	108.6	14.3	+ 7.0**
10–11	Verbal	100.3	13.7	102.2	13.8	+ 1.9**
(N = 119)	Performance	99.0	13.1	112.0	15.2	+13.0**
	Full	99.6	13.1	107.3	14.4	+ 7.7**
14–15	Verbal	99.4	13.8	102.7	14.5	+ 3.3**
(N = 123)	Performance	99.6	15.3	112.1	16.7	+12.5
	Full	99.2	14.5	107.6	15.5	+ 8.4**

Note. Test-retest intervals ranged from 12 to 63 days, with a median retest interval of 23 days. Table 8-7 shows the *t*-test formula used to evaluate the mean changes.
 *p < .01
**p < .001
Source: Reprinted, with a change in notation, from *WISC–III Manual* (pages 170–172). *Wechsler Intelligence Scale for Children: Third Edition.* Copyright © 1991 by The Psychological Corporation, a Harcourt Assessment Company. Reproduced by permission. All rights reserved. "Wechsler Intelligence Scale for Children" and "WISC–III" are trademarks of The Psychological Corporation registered in the United States of America and/or other jurisdictions.

Large retest gains on the Performance Scale are a major concern in interpreting the results when the WISC–III is readministered after a period of only 2 to 9 weeks. For periods longer than 9 weeks, gains on retest are likely to be lower because practice effects tend to diminish over time. The average gains for the short period were over ⅔ of a standard deviation on the Performance Scale and about ½ of a standard deviation on the Full Scale. The gain on the retest, however, may have nothing to do with increased ability per se; it may simply reflect exposure to the test materials or practice effects.

Other research shown in Table 8-4 indicates that for students in special education (which includes the categories special education, ADHD, LD, and MR), mean changes over a 3-year period in Verbal Scale, Performance Scale, and Full Scale IQs are less than 5 points.

Carefully consider whether you want to use the WISC–III for repeated evaluations, especially if you plan to use the results obtained on the retest for placement, eligibility, or diagnostic decisions. If the time between tests is relatively short (e.g., less than 9 months), consider using another individually administered well-standardized test of cognitive ability, such as the Stanford-Binet Intelligence Scale-IV, for the reexamination.

Changes in subtest scaled scores. Table 8-7 shows the changes in subtest scaled scores from the first to the second administration for the three combined age groups in the standardization sample. The largest gains were for Picture Arrangement (increases of 2.7 to 3.3 scaled-score points), and the smallest gains were for Vocabulary (increases of 0 to .2 scaled-score point) and Comprehension (increases of 0 to .5 scaled-score point). Tests of significance that we conducted for this chapter indicated that the changes in subtest scaled scores were significantly greater than chance in 34 of the 39 *t* tests. It is difficult to know why Picture Arrangement subtest scaled scores showed gains of almost 1 standard deviation on retest, especially since its internal consistency reliability coefficient is at the median reliability of the Performance Scale subtests. Perhaps, aided by the color of the pictures, the children retained a clear memory of the story elements of the pictures. On the retest, they then may have solved the arrangements more quickly and accurately and thus gained bonus points.

Confidence Intervals

This text presents two types of confidence intervals. The first type, in Table A-1 in Appendix A, is based on the obtained score and the SEM. The second type, in Table D-2 in Appendix D, uses the estimated true score and the standard error of estimation (SE_E). The rationale behind each method is discussed in Chapter 4. Both tables show confidence intervals for the 68, 85, 90, 95, and 99% levels for the Verbal Scale, Performance Scale, and Full Scale, and both provide confidence

Table 8-7
Test-Retest Gains on WISC–III Subtests for Three Age Groups

Subtest	Age (in years)		
	6–7 (N = 111)	10–11 (N = 119)	14–15 (N = 123)
Information	.4*	.3*	.7***
Similarities	.5**	.7***	1.2***
Arithmetic	.1	.4*	.4*
Vocabulary	0.0	.2	.2*
Comprehension	.5*	0.0	.3
Digit Span	.6**	.7***	.9***
Picture Completion	1.2***	2.0***	2.1***
Coding	1.8***	2.2***	1.9***
Picture Arrangement	3.3***	2.9***	2.7***
Block Design	.9***	1.2***	1.0***
Object Assembly	1.5***	1.5***	1.7***
Symbol Search	1.8***	1.4***	1.4***
Mazes	1.1***	1.0***	1.0***

Note. Test-retest intervals range from 12 to 63 days, with a median retest interval of 23 days. The *t* test used to evaluate the mean changes on each subtest employed a repeated-measures formula:

$$t = \frac{M_1 - M_2}{\sqrt{\left(\frac{SD_1}{\sqrt{N_1}}\right)^2 + \left(\frac{SD_2}{\sqrt{N_2}}\right)^2 - 2r_{12}\left(\frac{SD_1}{\sqrt{N_1}}\right)\left(\frac{SD_2}{\sqrt{N_2}}\right)}}$$

*p < .05
**p < .01
***p < .001
Source: Means and standard deviations obtained from Wechsler (1991), pages 170–172.

intervals for each age level of the test, as well as for the average of the age levels. *Use the child's specific age group—not the average of the 11 age groups—to obtain the most accurate confidence interval.*

The confidence intervals, based on the conventional SEM, for the three scales have the following range: at the 95% level of confidence, from ±6 to ±8 for the Verbal Scale, from ±7 to ±10 for the Performance Scale, and from ±5 to ±7 for the Full Scale. The range is greatest for the Performance Scale because this scale is less reliable than either the Verbal Scale or the Full Scale. Similar relationships hold for the other levels of confidence. As noted in Chapter 4, we recommend that you use the confidence intervals based on the conventional SEM.

VALIDITY OF THE WISC–III

Criterion Validity

Several studies have investigated the criterion validity of the WISC–III by correlating the test with the WISC–R, WPPSI–R, WAIS–III, Stanford-Binet: Fourth Edition, other intelligence tests, and measures of achievement and school grades. Table 8-8 shows the mean correlations between the WISC–III Full Scale and other intelligence tests, achievement tests, and school grades. Although Table 8-8 is not exhaustive, the representative studies listed show that the WISC–III has satisfactory criterion validity. Mean correlations between the WISC–III Full Scale and other measures are as follows (Zimmerman & Woo-Sam, 1997): (a) *r* = .72 with other intelligence tests, (b) *r* = .71 with the Peabody Picture Vocabulary Test, (c) *r* = .54 with measures of reading achievement, and (d) *r* = .64 with measures of arithmetic achievement.

WISC–III and WISC–R. Approximately 73% of the items on the WISC–R are also found on the WISC–III. It seems plausible, therefore, that the research concerning the validity of the WISC–R generally applies to the WISC–III. Studies related to the validity of the WISC–R indicate that it had adequate construct, concurrent, and predictive validity for many types of children, with and without disabilities, in the age range covered by the test (see Sattler, 1992 for a review).

In the two concurrent validity studies reported in the WISC–III manual, the correlations between the WISC–III and WISC–R were .86 and .90 Verbal Scale, .73 and .81 for the Performance Scale, and .86 and .89 for the Full Scale. Mean IQs were *lower* on the WISC–III than on the WISC–R by about 5 to 6 points.

There have been at least 33 predictive validity studies that have compared the WISC–III and the WISC–R. Most studies have been based on results from reevaluations of special education students carried out about 2 to 3 years after the initial evaluation with the WISC–R. Twenty-two studies were reviewed by Weiss (1995), and we have reviewed an additional 11 studies (Ackerman, Weir, Holloway, & Dykman, 1995; Bolen, Aichinger, Hall, & Webster, 1995; Gaskill & Brantley, 1996; Gunter, Sapp, & Green, 1995; Lyon, 1995; Sabatino, Spangler, & Vance, 1995; Sapp, Abbott, Hinckley, & Rowell, 1997; Slate, 1995b; Slate & Jones, 1995; Slate & Saarino, 1995; Vance, Maddux, Fuller, & Awadh, 1996). In all but two of these 33 studies, WISC–III IQs were *lower* than those of the WISC–R. The median changes were as follows (WISC–III—WISC–R):

Mdn Verbal Scale IQ change = –5.40
(range of +1.50 to –14.57)

Mdn Performance Scale IQ change = –6.06
(range of +4.56 to –13.09)

Mdn Full Scale IQ change = –5.97
(range of +3.19 to –18.09)

Because the WISC–III generally yields lower IQs than the WISC–R, decrements of about 6 IQ points between the two

Table 8-8
Summary of WISC–III Criterion Validity Studies

Criterion	Verbal Scale	Performance Scale	Full Scale	Criterion	Verbal Scale	Performance Scale	Full Scale
CLEF				Visual Motor Integration	.50	.57	.37
Expressive	.67	.40	.60	WISC–R	.77	.72	.79
Receptive	.47	.18	.35	WAIS–R			
DAS	.75	.75	.85	Verbal	.85	—	—
DTLA–3	.66	.54	.70	Performance	—	.74	—
Group-administered achievement tests				Full Scale	—	—	.88
Total	.74	.57	.74	WAIS–III			
Reading	.70	.43	.66	Verbal	.94	—	—
Mathematics	.63	.58	.68	Performance	—	.86	—
Written Language	.56	.46	.57	Full Scale	—	—	.93
Halstead-Reitan Neuropsychological Battery				WIAT			
Tactual PerformanceTest—Total time	−.39	−.64	−.58	Total Composite	.64	.50	.60
Tactual PerformanceTest—Memory	.19	.45	.37	Reading Composite	.50	.42	.65
Finger Tapping	−.40	−.37	−.45	Math Composite	.69	.70	.73
K-ABC	.55	.66	.70	Language Composite	.48	.15	.57
KAIT	—	—	.88	Writing Composite	.58	.45	.56
K-BIT	.79	.60	.80	Woodcock-Johnson--R			
K-TEA				Broad Math	.54	.36	.47
Math	.57	.42	.65	Broad Reading	.47	.13	.37
Reading	.60	.19	.53	Broad Written Language	—	—	.47
Matrix Analogies Short Form	—	—	.67	WPPSI–R	.85	.73	.85
Otis-Lennon School Ability Test	.64	.65	.56	WRAML			
Peabody Picture Vocabulary Test–Revised	.67	.43	.61	Visual	.41	.46	.50
Stanford-Binet: IV	.69	.56	.74	Learning	.26	.24	.27
School grades				General Memory	.52	.43	.53
GPA	.42	.39	.47	Verbal	.60	.36	.54
Mathematics	.35	.35	.41	WRAT–3			
English	.36	.31	.40	Arithmetic	.72	.60	.74
Reading	.44	.39	.48	Spelling	.58	.55	.63
Spelling	.28	.32	.36	Reading	.65	.55	.65
TONI–2	—	.67	—	WRAT–R			
TOVA	.006	.119	.134	Arithmetic	.41	.34	.32
				Spelling	.13	.12	.15
				Reading	.25	.27	.30

Source: This table is based on the following studies: Ackerman and Dykman (1995); Beal (1995); Canivez (1995); Canivez (1996); Carvajal, Hayes, Miller, Holly, Wiebe, and Weaver (1993); Carvajal, Hayes, Lackey, Rathke, Wiebe, and Weaver (1993); Chae (1999); Doll and Boren (1993); Donders (1995); Dumont, Cruse, Price, and Whelley (1996); Graf and Hinton (1997); Hishinuma and Yamakawa (1993); Hodapp and Hass (1997); Konold, Maller, and Glutting (1998); Lavin (1996a, b, c); Law and Faison (1996); Levinson and Folino (1994); Lukens and Hurrell (1996); Mackinson, Leigh, and Anthony (1997); Mealer, Morgan, and Luscomb (1996); Phelps, Leguori, Nisewaner, and Parker (1993); Phelps (1996); Prewett (1995); Quereshi and Seitz (1994); Rust and Lindstrom (1996); Rust and Yates (1997); Saklofske, Schwean, Yackulic, and Quinn (1994); Saklofske, Schwean, and O'Donnell (1996); Schultz (1997); Slate, Jones, Graham, and Bower (1992); Slate, Jones, Graham, and Bower (1994); Slate (1995); Smith, Smith, and Smithson (1995); Thompson, Browne, Schmidt, and Boer (1997); Thompson and Sota (1998); Vance and Fuller (1995); Ward, Garcia, Trebon, Ward, and Erwin (1995); Wechsler (1991); Weiss and Prifitera (1995); Wodrich and Kush (1998).

tests do not reflect meaningful changes in a child's ability. Interpret such changes simply as scores on two similar tests that have different norms. Nevertheless, large differences between scores on the WISC–III and the WISC–R may reflect meaningful changes in the child's ability. You need to take these differences into account when you evaluate children first tested on the WISC–R and retested with the WISC–III.

WISC–III and WPPSI–R. Because the WISC–III and WPPSI–R overlap at ages 6 to 7–3 years, one must know the relationship between the two tests for this age group. A sample of 188 normal 6-year-old children was administered the WISC–III and WPPSI–R in counterbalanced order within a 12- to 62-day period (*Mdn* = 21 days; Wechsler, 1991). The correlations between the tests were .85 for the Verbal Scale, .73 for the Performance Scale, and .85 for the Full Scale. These correlations should be high because the two tests have as many as 35 items in common.

For the Verbal Scale, Performance Scale, and Full Scale, mean IQs were *higher* on the WISC–III than on the WPPSI–R. The average difference was 4.0 points on the Full Scale, 1.9 points on the Verbal Scale, and 5.9 points on the Performance Scale.

WISC–III and WAIS–III. Because the WISC–III and WAIS–III overlap at ages 16 to 17 years, it is important to have information about the relationship between the two tests for this age group. The WISC–III and WAIS–III were administered in counterbalanced order to a sample of 184 16-year-olds (Wechsler, 1997). The interval between the two test administrations ranged from 2 to 12 weeks (*Mdn* = 4.6 weeks). The correlations were .88 for the Verbal Scale, .78 for the Performance Scale, and .88 for the Full Scale.

For the 11 subtests that the WISC–III and WAIS–III have in common, correlations ranged from a low of .31 for Picture Arrangement to a high of .83 for Vocabulary (*Mdn r* = .73). Subtests on the Verbal Scale have higher correlations (range of .60 to .83, *Mdn r* = .74) than do those on the Performance Scale (range of .31 to .80, *Mdn r* = .64).

For the Verbal Scale, Performance Scale, and Full Scale, mean IQs were slightly higher on the WAIS–III than on the WISC–III. The average difference was 0.5 point on the Verbal Scale (103.5 vs. 103.0), 0.4 point on the Performance Scale (104.9 vs. 104.5), and 0.7 point on the Full Scale (104.6 vs. 103.9). These results suggest that the two scales yield comparable IQs. However, these findings are based on a relatively small sample with predominantly average ability and should not be generalized to individuals at the extremes of the intelligence distribution.

Research is needed on the comparability of the WISC–III and WAIS–III in clinical populations, in gifted populations, and in mentally retarded populations. In addition, because the results reported previously were based on a counterbalanced design (i.e., giving the WAIS–III followed by the WISC–III to half the sample and the WISC–III followed by the WAIS–III to the other half of the sample), the scores on the second test administered are affected by practice effects. To examine further the comparability of the WAIS–III and WISC–III, results from independent administrations of the two tests to random samples and results from different groups of exceptional adolescents are needed.

Comment on the criterion validity of the WISC–III. The validity studies cited in the WISC–III manual and the research literature support the criterion validity of the WISC–III. However, you should not consider the WISC–III and WPPSI–R or the WISC–III and WAIS–III to be parallel forms in the overlapping age groups. The WISC–III yields *higher* mean Full Scale IQs than the WPPSI–R by about 4 points, and slightly *lower* mean Full Scale IQs than the WAIS–III. The various Wechsler tests also provide somewhat different Verbal Scale IQs and Performance Scale IQs.

If you administer one Wechsler test after another Wechsler test, small changes on the second test could be related to intervening events in the child's life or, more likely, practice effects, errors of measurement, or different norm groups. For example, 2 years separate the standardization of the WISC–III and the WPPSI–R, and 6 years separate the standardization of the WISC–III and the WAIS–III. We do not know why the WISC–III yields higher mean IQs than the WPPSI–R and slightly lower mean IQs than the WAIS–III; we need continued research on the relationship between the WISC–III and other measures of ability and achievement.

Construct Validity

There is strong evidence that the WISC–III yields both a measure of general intelligence and specific factors, as noted in studies reported in the WISC–III manual and in the research literature. However, there is a difference of opinion about how many specific factors the test yields (e.g., three or four specific factors). Later in the chapter we consider the results of several factor analytic studies of the WISC–III.

INTERCORRELATIONS BETWEEN SUBTESTS AND SCALES

Inspection of the intercorrelations between WISC–III subtests and scales (see Table C.12, page 281, in the WISC–III manual) indicates that, in the total group, correlations between the 13 subtests range from a low of .14 to a high of .70 (*Mdn r* = .355). The highest intercorrelations are between Vocabulary and Information (.70), Vocabulary and Similarities (.69), Similarities and Information (.66), Comprehension and Vocabulary (.64), Comprehension and Similarities (.59), and Arithmetic and Information (.57). The lowest intercorrelations are between Mazes and Digit Span (.14), Mazes and Coding (.15), Mazes and Vocabulary (.17), Mazes and Comprehension (.17), Mazes and Similarities (.18), Mazes and Information (.18), and Coding and Picture Completion (.18).

MR. WOODHEAD © 1998 by John P. Wood

Panel 1: I'm a great student. I have a perfect 4.0 grade-point average.

Panel 2: Wow! 4.0!! You must learn a lot!

Panel 3: Who said anything about learning?

Copyright © 1998 by John P. Wood.

In the total group, the Verbal Scale subtests correlate more highly with each other (*Mdn r* = .55) than do the Performance Scale subtests (*Mdn r* = .33). Average correlations between each of the Verbal Scale subtests and the Verbal Scale range from .42 to .78 (*Mdn r* = .72); those between the Performance Scale subtests and the Performance Scale range from .32 to .65 (*Mdn r* = .45). Thus, the Verbal Scale subtests have more in common with each other than do the Performance Scale subtests (see Table 8-9).

Average correlations between each of the 13 individual subtests and the Full Scale range from .31 to .74 (*Mdn r* = .58). Vocabulary has the highest correlation with the Full Scale (.74), followed by Information (.72), Similarities (.72), Block Design (.66), Arithmetic (.65), Comprehension (.64), Picture Completion (.58), Object Assembly (.58), Symbol Search (.56), Picture Arrangement (.52), Digit Span (.43), Coding (.33), and Mazes (.31). Thus, five of the standard Verbal Scale subtests, plus Block Design, correlate more highly with the Full Scale than do the other subtests (see Table 8-9). Vocabulary has the highest correlation with the Verbal Scale (.78), and Block Design has the highest correlation with the Performance Scale (.65). These findings support the use of the WISC–III as a measure of general mental ability. Although the subtests vary in their correlations with the Full Scale IQ and in their respective reliabilities, the estimation of general intellectual functioning, as measured by the Full Scale IQ, appears justified.

WISC–III AND PARENT EDUCATION

Table 8-10 shows the relationship between WISC–III IQs and level of parent education (Granier & O'Donnell, 1991). The sample consisted of 1,194 children, ages 6 through 16 years, who were included in the WISC–III standardization group.

Children whose parents had a college education had higher mean IQs (*M* IQ = 106.01) than children whose parents had a ninth-grade education or less (*M* IQ = 86.38)—a difference of about 20 points. If we consider parent education and socioeconomic status as interchangeable variables, then these results are similar to those reported for the WISC–R (Kaufman & Doppelt, 1976; also reproduced in Sattler, 1992).

Table 8-9
Average Correlations Between WISC–III Subtests and Scales

Subtest	Verbal Scale	Performance Scale	Full Scale
Information	.75	.55	.72
Similarities	.75	.55	.72
Arithmetic	.62	.54	.65
Vocabulary	.78	.56	.74
Comprehension	.67	.49	.64
Digit Span	.42	.35	.43
Picture Completion	.52	.54	.58
Coding	.29	.32	.33
Picture Arrangement	.45	.49	.52
Block Design	.57	.65	.66
Object Assembly	.48	.60	.58
Symbol Search	.44	.58	.56
Mazes	.23	.35	.31

Source: Adapted from Wechsler (1991), Table C.12 (page 281).

Table 8-10
Relationship Between Parent Education Level and WISC–III IQs

Parent education level	Verbal Scale IQ	Performance Scale IQ	Full Scale IQ
Less than 9th grade	85.60	89.80	86.38
9th through 11th grade	91.63	94.04	92.10
High school diploma	97.82	98.33	97.72
Some college	100.84	100.92	100.82
College graduate	106.03	105.17	106.01

Source: Reprinted with permission of the authors, M. Granier and L. O'Donnell (1991), *Children's WISC–III scores: Impact of parent education and home environment.* Copyright 1991 by The Psychological Corporation.

WISC–III AND ETHNIC STATUS

Table 8-11 shows the relationship between WISC–III IQs and ethnic status in a sample of children from the standardization sample (Prifitera et al., 1998). Mean IQs of Euro American children were about 15 points higher than those of African American children and about 9 points higher than those of Hispanic American children. Euro American children had Verbal Scale IQs and Performance Scale IQs that were essentially similar to each other, as did African American children, whereas Hispanic American children had somewhat higher Performance Scale IQs than Verbal Scale IQs. When we examine Verbal Scale/Performance Scale differences in African American and Hispanic American samples, we find that a majority of African American children had higher Verbal Scale IQs than Performance Scale IQs (57.1% vs. 40.5%), whereas a majority of Hispanic American children had higher Performance Scale IQs than Verbal

Scale IQs (69.0% vs. 26.4%). The results for the Hispanic American children likely are related to their Spanish-language background.

FACTOR ANALYSIS OF THE WISC–III

The WISC–III manual presents a maximum-likelihood factor analysis of the standardization sample based on four age clusters (6–7, 8–10, 11–13, and 14–16 years), but not for the 11 separate age groups. The results indicate that a four-factor model best describes the WISC–III (see Figure 8-2). These factors (which are called indexes in the WISC–III manual) are labeled as follows:

- Verbal Comprehension Index (Information, Similarities, Vocabulary, Comprehension)
- Perceptual Organization Index (Picture Completion, Picture Arrangement, Block Design, Object Assembly)
- Freedom from Distractibility Index (Arithmetic, Digit Span)
- Processing Speed Index (Coding, Symbol Search)

The term *Verbal Comprehension Index* describes a hypothesized verbal-related ability underlying the index for both item content (verbal) and mental processes (comprehension). Verbal Comprehension measures verbal knowledge and understanding obtained through both informal and formal education, and it reflects the application of verbal skills to new situations. This factor appears to measure a variable common to most of the Verbal Scale subtests. For the total sample, Vocabulary, Information, Similarities, and Comprehension have the highest loadings on the Verbal Comprehension Index, followed by Arithmetic, which has a moderate loading. Three Performance Scale subtests—Picture Completion, Picture Arrangement, and Block Design—also have small loadings on the Verbal Comprehension Index.

How can we account for the loadings that these three Performance Scale subtests have on Verbal Comprehension? First, verbal mediation may in part be involved in successful performance on Picture Completion and Picture Arrangement, and even on Block Design (e.g., "I need two divided sides to make each triangle here"). Second, the high *g* loadings associated with Block Design (see below) may explain its correlation with Verbal Comprehension. And third, these three Performance Scale subtests, together with the Verbal Scale subtests, may be highly related to a more general cognitive factor.

The term *Perceptual Organization Index* describes a hypothesized performance-related ability underlying the index for both item content (perceptual) and mental processes (organization). Perceptual Organization measures the ability to interpret and organize visually perceived material within a time limit. This index appears to measure a variable common to several of the Performance Scale subtests. For the total sample, Block Design and Object Assembly have high loadings on the Perceptual Organization Index, followed by Picture Comple-

Table 8-11
Relationship Between Ethnic Group Membership and WISC–III IQs

Ethnicity	N	M Verbal Scale IQ	M Performance Scale IQ	M Full Scale IQ
Euro American	1543[a]	103.6	102.9	103.5
African American	338	90.8	88.5	88.6
Hispanic American	242	92.1	97.7	94.1

[a]Personal communication, L. Weiss, June 1999.
Source: Adapted from Prifitera, Weiss, and Saklofske (1998).

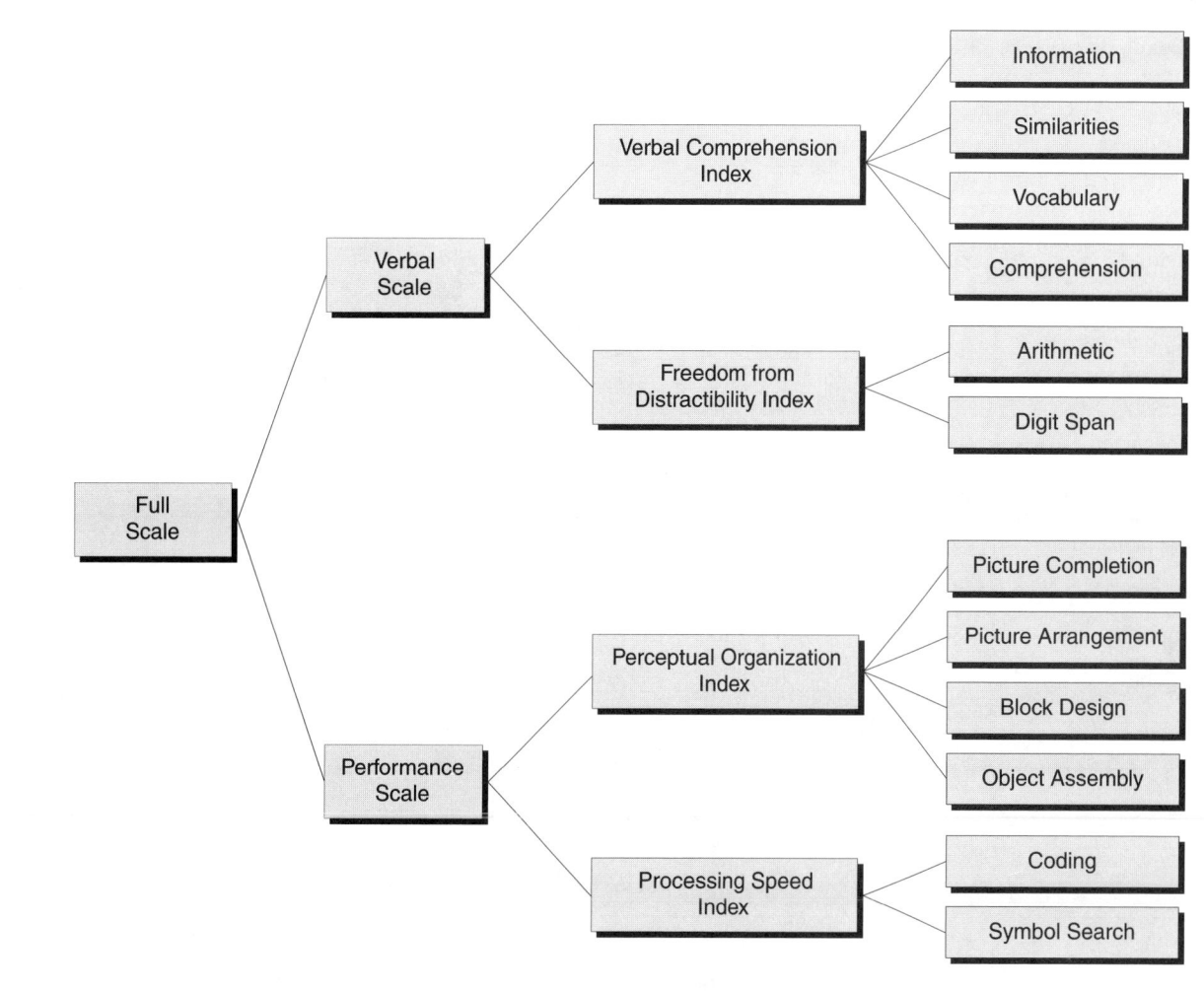

Figure 8-2. Structure of the WISC–III.

tion, which has a moderate loading, and Picture Arrangement, Mazes, and Symbol Search, which have small loadings.

The term *Freedom from Distractibility Index* describes a hypothesized memory-related ability underlying the index for both item content (verbal) and mental processes (memory). Freedom from Distractibility measures the ability to sustain attention, concentrate, and exert mental control. Several other labels have been proposed for this factor, including (a) Working Memory (Prifitera et al., 1998) or Working Memory Efficiency (Kranzler, 1997), (b) Quantitative Reasoning (Carroll, 1997a; Keith & Witta, 1997), (c) Sequencing (Little, 1992), and (d) Memory (Little, 1992). According to Little (1992), inferences about distractibility should be made from behavioral observations, not from scores on an intelligence test. For the total sample, Arithmetic and Digit Span have moderate loadings on the Freedom from Distractibility Index.

The term *Processing Speed Index* describes a hypothesized processing speed ability underlying the index for both item content (perceptual) and mental process (speed). Processing Speed measures the ability to process visually per-

ceived nonverbal information quickly, with concentration and rapid eye-hand coordination being important components. For the total sample, Symbol Search and Coding have high loadings on the Processing Speed Index.

The factor analytic results give empirical support to interpretation of the Verbal Scale IQ and Performance Scale IQ as separately functioning entities in the WISC–III. *The factor structure of the WISC–III into verbal and nonverbal components closely agrees with the actual organization of the subtests.*

The four-factor model has also received support from other studies (Blaha & Wallbrown, 1996; Donders & Warschausky, 1997; Grice, Krohn, & Logerquist, 1999; Hishinuma & Yamakawa, 1993; Keith & Witta, 1997; Konold, 1999; Konold, Kush, & Canivez, 1997; Maller & Ferron, 1997; Roid, Prifitera, & Weiss, 1993; Roid & Worrall, 1997; Tupa, Wright, & Fristad, 1997). Some studies and reviewers, however, do not support the four-factor model. Carroll (1993b), for example, reported that the factorial structure of the WISC–III is unclear, particularly with respect to the Freedom from Distractibility

Table 8-12
Factor Loadings of WISC–III Subtests for 11 Age Groups Following Principal Factor Analysis

Subtest	Age (in years)											
	6	7	8	9	10	11	12	13	14	15	16	Av.[a]
Factor A—Verbal Comprehension												
Information	68	71	75	60	72	68	76	79	71	76	80	72
Similarities	74	64	75	69	79	70	73	70	73	71	76	72
Arithmetic	58	39	56	30	65	43	53	48	54	41	59	47
Vocabulary	65	76	72	78	85	79	80	81	82	74	81	79
Comprehension	56	71	66	62	70	64	71	66	71	54	69	66
Digit Span	51	27	43	18	40	24	18	29	25	27	28	26
Picture Completion	36	21	36	39	45	38	35	30	41	47	31	37
Coding	01	07	12	12	18	12	13	14	15	14	07	11
Picture Arrangement	36	32	28	25	32	30	29	26	31	46	34	34
Block Design	44	17	30	26	29	20	31	34	31	27	42	30
Object Assembly	28	24	25	31	26	25	22	21	09	29	30	25
Symbol Search	32	23	29	14	22	19	17	06	24	24	19	20
Mazes	17	02	17	02	06	00	06	13	–05	09	–02	07
Factor B—Perceptual Organization												
Information	20	24	33	27	23	28	33	24	39	25	22	29
Similarities	21	24	35	30	19	30	29	22	20	27	33	29
Arithmetic	24	13	41	28	22	23	10	27	24	23	16	30
Vocabulary	35	20	36	16	15	22	17	28	19	19	22	23
Comprehension	13	09	21	20	20	16	26	14	11	29	17	19
Digit Span	18	20	21	07	17	09	11	–05	04	20	11	16
Picture Completion	45	55	56	50	42	58	62	60	49	58	56	55
Coding	10	15	14	11	12	09	10	04	10	14	03	14
Picture Arrangement	23	24	23	32	32	40	42	37	53	47	25	38
Block Design	57	64	64	65	78	64	67	44	56	57	62	67
Object Assembly	64	64	70	61	70	60	66	40	68	55	59	66
Symbol Search	25	21	32	26	26	30	27	32	28	31	31	32
Mazes	30	26	32	30	51	17	40	51	14	36	31	36

(Continued)

Table 8-12 *(Continued)*											

	Age *(in years)*										
Subtest	6	7	8	9	10	11	12	13	14	15	16	Av.[a]

Factor C—Freedom from Distractibility

Subtest	6	7	8	9	10	11	12	13	14	15	16	Av.
Information	16	33	09	42	−15	24	21	15	13	32	10	23
Similarities	18	30	22	36	05	33	20	27	18	26	06	21
Arithmetic	36	51	−07	54	08	67	51	27	54	62	40	48
Vocabulary	06	11	25	31	−19	18	23	09	20	28	07	16
Comprehension	18	04	16	05	13	18	13	08	12	32	−01	12
Digit Span	13	36	−30	42	18	49	39	22	47	46	22	41
Picture Completion	25	09	07	17	−17	13	05	28	20	21	22	09
Coding	10	03	09	16	−00	15	12	05	06	15	06	10
Picture Arrangement	53	31	53	06	08	−11	11	10	00	02	30	02
Block Design	23	37	21	28	03	29	45	59	40	48	17	26
Object Assembly	23	19	01	21	−12	14	38	45	10	32	25	12
Symbol Search	22	44	10	25	−02	09	18	11	12	19	13	17
Mazes	45	33	11	00	10	09	01	05	21	23	51	08

Factor D—Processing Speed

Subtest	6	7	8	9	10	11	12	13	14	15	16	Av.
Information	10	06	23	19	17	08	08	07	09	13	10	11
Similarities	02	17	11	07	16	08	16	12	18	12	10	11
Arithmetic	17	28	36	26	15	18	17	31	10	20	37	21
Vocabulary	09	20	17	14	26	16	16	16	09	38	14	17
Comprehension	13	10	21	21	22	19	24	28	18	36	20	21
Digit Span	13	09	29	16	25	21	17	44	12	17	34	19
Picture Completion	24	22	09	17	17	10	08	03	07	10	04	10
Coding	61	56	71	72	68	63	64	72	62	73	70	63
Picture Arrangement	25	43	20	37	37	20	27	26	15	26	28	28
Block Design	17	18	25	13	17	26	17	33	25	30	31	19
Object Assembly	21	18	21	08	13	18	16	19	28	28	21	16
Symbol Search	60	47	66	70	66	64	64	61	64	60	76	63
Mazes	22	02	20	13	17	18	11	05	25	25	12	15

Note. Decimal points omitted.
[a]Av. = average of 11 age groups.

and Processing Speed Indexes. Little (1992) did not support for the four-factor model presented in the WISC–III manual. He noted that the Verbal Comprehension and Perceptual Organization Indexes account for approximately 45% of the variance, whereas the Freedom from Distractibility and Processing Speed Indexes account for only 2–3% and 4–5% of the variance, respectively.

Kamphaus, Benson, Hutchinson, and Platt (1994) concluded from their research that the Freedom from Distractibility and Processing Speed Indexes are much weaker than either the Verbal Comprehension or the Perceptual Organization Index. Parker and Atkinson (1994) reported, based on the standardization data, that the Arithmetic subtest contributed substantially to the Freedom from Distractibility Index, whereas Digit Span made almost no contribution to this index. Similarly, they noted that the Processing Speed Index is defined more by Coding than by Symbol Search. Kush (1996) found no evidence for the Freedom from Distractibility Index in his study.

We conducted a principal factor analysis using the standardization data. The results indicated that a four-factor model holds overall (see Table 8-12). However, there is little support for the Freedom from Distractibility Index at ages 6, 8, 10, 13, and 16 years, because at these ages either Arithmetic or Digit Span has a loading of less than .30 on this index. Although questions have been raised about the appropriateness of the four-factor model, we will still offer information in this text about the model because the model may be helpful in interpreting the WISC–III. However, interpretations of the Freedom from Distractibility Index and Processing Speed Index must be made with caution.

Factor Analytic Findings Related to Age

The factor analytic findings show a diverse pattern with age (see Table 8-13). It is difficult to explain why the pattern of correlations is not consistent at all ages. The pattern of factor loadings may be a function either of measurement error or of the fact that all subtests are related to g to some extent, in which case it would not reflect underlying developmental trends. Following is a brief summary of the age-related findings for each index.

1. *Verbal Comprehension Index*. Vocabulary, Information, Comprehension, Similarities, and Arithmetic load on the Verbal Comprehension Index above .30 at every age level. Three of the Performance Scale subtests—Picture Completion, Block Design, and Picture Arrangement—load above .30 on this index at several age levels.

2. *Perceptual Organization Index*. Object Assembly, Block Design, and Picture Completion load on the Perceptual Organization Index above .30 at every age level. Also, Picture Arrangement loads on this index above .30 at ages 9, 10, 11, 12, 13, and 14; and Symbol Search loads above .30 at ages 8, 11, 13, 15, and 16. Only a few of the Verbal Scale

subtests load on the Perceptual Organization Index over the 11 age levels.

3. *Freedom from Distractibility Index*. Digit Span loads on the Freedom from Distractibility Index at ages 7, 8, 9, 11, 12, 14, and 15; and Arithmetic loads on this index at ages 6, 7, 8, 9, 11, 12, 14, 15, and 16. Other subtests also load on the Freedom from Distractibility Index at various ages.

4. *Processing Speed Index*. Coding and Symbol Search load on the Processing Speed Index above .30 at every age level. In addition, other subtests load above .30 on this index at more than one age: Picture Arrangement at ages 7, 9, and 10; Arithmetic at ages 7, 13, and 16; and Block Design at ages 13, 15, and 16.

WISC–III Manual Cautions for Index Score Interpretations

A curious statement is found on page 20 of the WISC–III manual concerning the Processing Speed and Freedom from Distractibility Index scores. The statement (italicized below) was made in the context of a study of 38 gifted children who were administered the WISC–III. The children obtained higher scores on the Verbal Comprehension, Perceptual Organization, and Freedom from Distractibility Indexes than on the Processing Speed Index ($Ms = 126.9, 125.8, 123.0,$ and 110.2, respectively). The Psychological Corporation interpreted these findings to mean that the Freedom from Distractibility and Processing Speed Indexes are not as highly related to general intellectual ability as the Verbal Comprehension and Perceptual Organization Indexes. *"Scores on these indexes can be expected to vary independently of FSIQ [Full Scale IQ] scores* [italics added]. This finding emphasizes the reason that the index scores are not referred to as IQ scores" (Wechsler, 1991, p. 210).

The statement that "Scores on these scales can be expected to vary independently of FSIQ scores" is misleading. First, the WISC–III manual did not present any data to support this assertion, except for index means. In fact, the Freedom from Distractibility Index mean was almost as high as the Verbal Comprehension Index mean and the Perceptual Organization Index mean. Second, the subtests that make up the third and fourth indexes correlate significantly with the Full Scale (Symbol Search $r = .56, p < .001$; Coding $r = .33, p < .001$; Arithmetic $r = .65, p < .001$; Digit Span $r = .43, p < .001$; all correlations based on the total group). In some cases, these subtests have as high or higher a correlation with the Full Scale as do other subtests. For example, the correlations of Picture Completion and Picture Arrangement with the Full Scale are .58 and .52, respectively. Furthermore, Arithmetic, Digit Span, and Symbol Search are either good or fair measures of g. We believe that it is misleading to say that Processing Speed and Freedom from Distractibility scores "vary independently of FSIQ scores."

According to a spokesperson for The Psychological Corporation (personal communication, Aurelio Prifitera, November 1991), they included this statement in the WISC–III

Table 8-13
Summary of Major Trends of Principal Factor Analysis on WISC–III, by Age Level and for the Average of the Total Sample

Age (in years)	Subtests with loadings of .30 or higher on Verbal Comprehension	Subtests with loadings of .30 or higher on Perceptual Organization	Subtests with loadings of .30 or higher on Freedom from Distractibility	Subtests with loadings of .30 or higher on Processing Speed
6	V, I, C, S, A, DS, BD, PC, PA, SS	OA, BD, PC, V, MA	PA, MA, A	CD, SS
7	V, I, C, S, A, PA	BD, OA, PC	A, SS, BD, DS, MA, I, S	CD, SS, PA
8	V, I, C, S, A, DS, PC, BD	OA, BD, PC, V, S, I, SS, MA	A, SS, BD, DS, I, MA, S	CD, SS, A
9	V, S, C, I, PC, OA, A	BD, OA, PC, PA, MA, S	A, DS, I, S, V	CD, SS, PA
10	V, I, C, S, A, DS, PC, PA	BD, OA, MA, PC, PA	None	CD, SS, PA
11	V, S, I, C, A, PC, PA	BD, OA, PC, PA, SS, S	A, DS, S	SS, CD
12	V, I, S, C, A, PC	BD, OA, PC, PA, MA	A, BD, DS	CD, SS
13	V, I, S, C, A, PC	PC, MA, BD, OA, PA, SS	BD, OA	CD, SS, DS, BD, A
14	V, S, I, C, A, PC, PA, BD	OA, BD, PA, PC, I	A, DS, BD	SS, CD
15	I, V, S, C, PC, PA, A	PC, BD, OA, MA, SS	A, BD, DS, I, C, OA	CD, SS, V, C, BD
16	V, I, S, C, A, BD, PA, PC	BD, OA, PC, S, SS, MA	MA, A, PA	SS, CD, A, DS, BD
Av.	V, I, S, C, A, PC, PA	BD, OA, PC, PA, MA, SS, A	A, DS	CD, SS

Note. Abbreviations: I = Information, S = Similarities, A = Arithmetic, V = Vocabulary, C = Comprehension, DS = Digit Span, PC = Picture Completion, CD = Coding, PA = Picture Arrangement, BD = Block Design, OA = Object Assembly, SS = Symbol Search, MA = Mazes, Av. = average of 11 age groups.
There were four factors at each age level, except at age 10 years where there were three factors.

manual to emphasize that examiners should never use the Freedom from Distractibility or Processing Speed Index score as an independent estimate of a child's Full Scale IQ. We agree fully with this recommendation. In the nine years since publication of the WISC–III, no published studies that we are aware of have shown that the Processing Speed and Freedom from Distractibility Indexes vary independently of the Full Scale. However, these two indexes do account for less variance than the Verbal Comprehension and Perceptual Organization Indexes (Keith, 1997).

WISC–III Subtests as Measures of *g*

Examination of the loadings on the first unrotated factor in a principal-components analysis that we conducted for this chapter allows one to determine the extent to which the WISC–III subtests measure general intelligence, or *g*. Overall, the WISC–III is a fair measure of *g*, with 43% of its variance attributed to *g*.

The WISC–III subtests form three clusters with respect to the measurement of *g* (also see Table 8-14):

- Vocabulary, Information, Similarities, Block Design, Arithmetic, and Comprehension are *good* measures of *g*.
- Object Assembly, Picture Completion, Symbol Search, Picture Arrangement, and Digit Span are *fair* measures of *g*.
- Coding and Mazes are *poor* measures of *g*.

The subtests in the Verbal Scale have higher *g* loadings than those in the Performance Scale (52%, on the average, for the Verbal Scale subtests; 36%, on the average, for the Performance Scale subtests). Highest loadings are for Vocabulary, Information, and Similarities in the Verbal Scale and Block Design, Object Assembly, and Picture Completion in the Performance Scale. Any one of the five standard Verbal Scale subtests serves as a good measure of *g*, but only Block Design in the Performance Scale serves as a good measure of *g*.

Subtest Specificity

Subtest specificity refers to the proportion of a subtest's variance that is both reliable (i.e., not due to error of measurement) and distinctive to the subtest (see Chapter 4 for further information about subtest specificity). Although the individual subtests on the WISC–III overlap in their measurement properties (i.e., the majority of the reliable variance for most subtests is common factor variance), many possess sufficient specificity at some ages to justify interpretation of specific subtest functions.

Throughout the age range covered by the WISC–III, Digit Span, Picture Arrangement, and Block Design have ample specificity (see Table 8-15). In addition, Picture Completion, Coding, and Mazes have ample specificity at 10 of the 11 age levels. Each of the seven remaining subtests shows a unique

Table 8-14
WISC–III Subtests as Measures of *g*

Good measure of *g*			Fair measure of *g*			Poor measure of *g*		
Subtest	Average loading of *g*	Proportion of variance attributed to *g* (%)	Subtest	Average loading of *g*	Proportion of variance attributed to *g* (%)	Subtest	Average loading of *g*	Proportion of variance attributed to *g* (%)
Vocabulary	.79	62	Object Assembly	.66	44	Coding	.44	20
Information	.78	61	Picture Completion	.66	44	Mazes	.37	13
Similarities	.78	60	Symbol Search	.62	38			
Block Design	.74	56	Picture Arrangement	.60	36			
Arithmetic	.74	54	Digit Span	.51	26			
Comprehension	.70	50						

Table 8-15
Amount of Specificity in WISC–III Subtests for 11 Ages and Average

Subtest	Ages with ample specificity	Ages with adequate specificity	Ages with inadequate specificity
Information	11, Av.	8–10, 12–16	6, 7
Similarities	6, 14	11, 12, 15, 16, Av.	7–10, 13
Arithmetic	6, 7, 10, 13, 15, Av.	16	8, 9, 11, 12, 14
Vocabulary	6, 11	7, 8, 12–16, Av.	9, 10
Comprehension	6, 8–11, Av.	12	7, 13–16
Digit Span	6–16, Av.	—	—
Picture Completion	6–11, 13–16, Av.	—	12
Coding	6, 7, 9–16, Av.	—	8
Picture Arrangement	6–16, Av.	—	—
Block Design	6–16, Av.	—	—
Object Assembly	9, 13, 15	6	7, 8, 10–12, 14, 16, Av.
Symbol Search	7, 10–16, Av.	—	6, 8, 9
Mazes	6–14, 16, Av.	—	15

Note. Av. = average of the 11 age groups. Kaufman's (1975) rule of thumb was used to classify the amount of specificity in each subtest. Subtests with ample specificity have specific variance that (a) reflects 25% or more of the subtest's total variance (100%) and (b) exceeds the subtest's error variance. Subtests with adequate specificity have specific variance that (a) reflects between 15% and 24% of the subtest's total variance and (b) exceeds the subtest's error variance. Subtests with inadequate specificity have specific variance that either (a) is less than 15% of the subtest's total variance or (b) is equal to or less than the subtest's error variance.

Specific variance is obtained by subtracting the squared multiple correlation (from the maximum-likelihood factor analysis with varimax rotation) from the subtest's reliability (r_{xx} – SMC) (A. Silverstein, personal communication, October 1991). Error variance is obtained by subtracting the subtest's reliability from 1.00 ($1 - r_{xx}$).

pattern of specificity—that is, the ages at which each has ample, adequate, or inadequate specificity differ. Similarities, Arithmetic, Comprehension, and Object Assembly have inadequate specificity for at least five ages.

Subtests with inadequate specificity should *not* be interpreted as measuring specific functions. These subtests, how-

ever, can be interpreted as (a) good, fair, or poor measures of *g* (see Table 8-14) and (b) representing a specific index (i.e., Verbal Comprehension, Perceptual Organization, Freedom from Distractibility, or Processing Speed; see Table 8-13), where appropriate. Once you have determined which subtest scaled scores are significantly different from the mean of their scale and, in some cases, from one another and have analyzed performance on all relevant subtests, you may be able to draw meaningful conclusions about an examinee's cognitive strengths or weakness. We call this process profile analysis. (See Chapter 10 for a discussion of profile analysis.) Thus, low scores on Coding and Symbol Search and average or high scores on the other subtests suggest that the child has difficulty in processing information rapidly. However, a high score on Coding and a low score on Symbol Search do not suggest general difficulty in processing information rapidly because the scores are not in the same direction.

Index Scores

To obtain index Deviation Quotients, use the following tables in the WISC–III manual:

- Table A.5 (page 255) for Verbal Comprehension (Information, Similarities, Vocabulary, and Comprehension)
- Table A.6 (page 256) for Perceptual Organization (Picture Completion, Block Design, Object Assembly, and Picture Arrangement)
- Table A.7 (page 257) for Freedom from Distractibility (Arithmetic and Digit Span)
- Table A.7 (page 257) for Processing Speed (Coding and Symbol Search)

If you want to obtain a purer measure of the Perceptual Organization Index (as discussed above under Factor Analysis of the WISC–III), use the scaled scores from Picture Completion, Block Design, and Object Assembly and Table A-23 in Appendix A to obtain an estimated Deviation Quotient.

RANGE OF SUBTEST SCALED SCORES

The WISC–III provides a range of scaled scores from 1 to 19. However, this range is not possible for all subtests at all ages of the test, particularly at 6 years and at 11 through 16 years. The WISC–III is so constructed that children receive credit even when they fail all items. For example, at 6 years they receive 2 scaled-score points credit and at 7 through 16 years 1 scaled-score point credit on Information, Similarities, Picture Arrangement, and Block Design even when they fail all items on these subtests.

After the age of 11 years, the ceiling level (i.e., the highest scaled score that can be obtained on a subtest) drops for one or more subtests; however, the drop is no more than 2 scaled-score points. Table 8-16 shows the maximum scaled scores for each subtest by age. The failure to have the same maximum scaled score at the upper limits (i.e., a scaled score of 19) throughout the test primarily affects how the profiles of bright children aged 14 years and older are interpreted. (When Mazes is included, we have particular difficulty in interpreting the profiles of bright children ages 11 through 16 years.)

Table 8-16
Maximum WISC–III Subtest Scaled Scores by Age

Subtest	Maximum scaled score	Age (in years)
Information	19	6 to 14
	18	15
	17	16
Similarities	19	6 to 16
Arithmetic	19	6 to 15
	18	16
Vocabulary	19	6 to 16
Comprehension	19	6 to 15
	18	16
Digit Span	19	6 to 16
Picture Completion	19	6 to 13
	18	14 to 15
	17	16
Coding	19	6 to 16
Picture Arrangement	19	6 to 16
Block Design	19	6 to 15
	18	16
Object Assembly	19	6 to 15
	18	16
Symbol Search	19	6 to 15
	18	16
Mazes	19	6 to 10
	18	11 to 12
	17	13 to 16

You can appropriately apply profile analysis techniques at all ages for only Similarities, Vocabulary, Digit Span, Coding, and Picture Arrangement. For older gifted children, you can apply profile analysis uniformly only when all scaled scores are 17 or below. Applying profile analysis uniformly to all subtests could be misleading with older gifted children because they cannot obtain the same number of scaled-score points on all subtests. However, the failure to have the same scaled-score range at all age levels and for all subtests is usually only a minor difficulty because all subtests provide scores for at least a range of 1 to 17.

RANGE OF FULL SCALE IQS

The range of WISC–III Full Scale IQs is 40 to 160. This range is insufficient for children who are extremely low or extremely high functioning and is not available at all ages of the test. For example, the highest possible IQ that adolescents aged 16–8 years can obtain is 154; the lowest possible

IQ that children 6–0 years old can obtain is 46. In addition, every child receives at least 10 scaled-score points for giving *no* correct answers to any subtest. In fact, a 6-year-old who failed every item would receive 14 scaled-score points.

The Psychological Corporation recognizes that awarding scaled-score points for no successes might be a problem. It therefore recommends that examiners compute IQs on each scale only when the child obtains raw scores greater than 0 on at least three subtests on each scale. Similarly, it recommends that examiners compute a Full Scale IQ only when the child obtains raw scores greater than 0 on three Verbal Scale *and* three Performance Scale subtests. This is a rule of thumb, rather than an empirically based recommendation, but it does have merit. However, we need research to determine whether this rule of thumb or other procedures are valid for computing IQs. The WISC–III manual provides no validity data to support this recommendation.

If we follow The Psychological Corporation's recommended procedure, what is the lowest possible IQ that a 6-year-old child can receive? If the child obtained raw scores of 1 on Information, Similarities, Comprehension, Picture Completion, Picture Arrangement, and Block Design and a raw score of 0 on each of the remaining four subtests, the resulting IQs would be as follows: Verbal Scale IQ = 58 (13 scaled-score points), Performance Scale IQ = 55 (13 scaled-score points), and Full Scale IQ = 53 (26 scaled-score points). Six 1-point successes thus yield an IQ of 53. Therefore, the WISC–III may not provide accurate IQs for young children who are functioning at two or more standard deviations below the mean of the scale. In other words, the WISC–III does not appear to sample a sufficient range of cognitive abilities for low-functioning children. Also, you will not derive much useful clinical data from a test on which the child responds correctly to only six items. If a child fails all or most of the items on the WISC–III, administer another intelligence test designed for children who are low functioning.

ADMINISTERING THE WISC–III

The procedures discussed in Chapter 7 for administering psychological tests will help you administer the WISC–III. However, you must also master the specific standardized procedures needed to administer the test, discussed in the WISC–III manual. Be careful not to confuse administration procedures for the WPPSI–R or WAIS–III with those for the WISC–III, because some subtests with the same name have different instructions and time limits. The guidelines in Chapter 9, which supplement those in the WISC–III manual, will help you administer the WISC–III. The suggestions in Exhibit 8-2 and the checklist in Exhibit 8-3 also should help you learn how to administer the WISC–III. In addition, Table A-15 in Appendix A presents special procedures for administering the WISC–III Performance subtests to children who

are hearing impaired. By mastering the administrative procedures early in your testing career, you will be better able to focus on the equally important tasks of learning how to observe the child and how to interpret the test results. Figure 8-3 shows the cover page of the WISC–III Record Form.

Subtest Sequence

Administer the subtests in the order specified in the manual unless you have a compelling reason to use another order. For example, a compelling reason might be giving a child who is extremely bored or frustrated a different subtest or a subtest of his or her choice for motivation. Another reason might be giving a child with a sensory handicap selected subtests. However, using the standard sequence of administration provides you with a baseline for evaluating children whom you will test in the future; it is also an order comparable to that used by other examiners. Following the specified order in the WISC–III manual, which alternates nonverbal and verbal subtests, may also help to maintain the child's interest in the tasks.

The test begins with the Picture Completion subtest. The rationale for giving this subtest first is that "Picture Completion provides an engaging, nonthreatening task" (Wechsler, 1991, p. 14). This statement, however, may not hold for all children. For example, for a child who has difficulty with perceptual discrimination, Picture Completion may be neither engaging nor nonthreatening. Similarly, a child with test anxiety may feel anxious at the beginning of the test, regardless of the subtest you administer first. You must therefore carefully attend to the child's behavior, especially at the beginning of the test. Do not assume that the order of the subtests will automatically reduce a child's anxiety level or help a child feel relaxed. Research is needed to learn how the order of administering the subtests affects children's anxiety level and performance in general.

Scoring WISC–III Responses

You may find it difficult to score ambiguous responses on the Similarities, Vocabulary, and Comprehension subtests. Carefully studying the scoring criteria, scoring guidelines, and scoring examples in the WISC–III manual will help you to score responses. Then, recognize that, although the WISC–III manual provides detailed scoring guidelines for each subtest, the sample responses in the manual simply cannot cover all possible responses that children will give. For this reason, you will have to use judgment in scoring responses. It will be helpful to study similar examples with different scores in the WISC–III manual. Once you figure out why apparently similar responses are given different scores, you will have insight into the reasoning behind the scoring guidelines.

Exhibit 8-2
Supplementary Instructions for Administering the WISC–III

Preparing to Administer the WISC–III

1. Study the instructions in the WISC–III manual, and practice administering the test before you give it to a child to fulfill a class assignment. It is a good idea to take the test yourself before you study it thoroughly.

2. Organize your test materials before the child comes into the room. Make sure that all test materials—including stimulus booklets, blocks, cards, puzzle pieces, Record Form, stopwatch, and pencils—are in the kit. Arrange the Picture Arrangement cards in numerical sequence. Have extra blank paper on which to take notes if needed.

3. Keep materials, other than those needed for the test, off the table (e.g., soda cans, pocketbook, keys).

4. Complete the top of the Record Form (examinee's name, sex, school, grade, examiner, and handedness).

5. Enter the date tested and date of birth, calculate the chronological age (CA), and put it in the box provided. Months are considered to have 30 days for testing purposes. Check the chronological age by adding the chronological age to the date of birth to obtain the date of testing.

Administering the WISC–III Subtests

6. Administer the subtests in the order presented in the manual, except in rare circumstances. Do not change the wording on any subtest. Read the directions exactly as shown in the manual. Do not ad lib.

7. Start with the appropriate item on each subtest and follow discontinuance criteria. You must be thoroughly familiar with the scoring criteria *before* you give the test.

8. Write down verbatim all of the child's responses that are pertinent to the test, testing situation, and referral question or that are otherwise helpful in understanding the child. Write clearly, and do not use unusual abbreviations. Record time accurately in the spaces provided on the Record Form. Use a stopwatch (or a wristwatch with a digital timer) to administer the timed WISC–III subtests.

9. Clearly and accurately complete the Record Form (see Figure 8-3), and *record all responses relevant to the test and testing situation verbatim*. This will (a) give you an opportunity to review your scoring after the test has been administered, (b) provide a record for qualitative analysis, (c) provide a document in cases of litigation, and (d) keep the child from discovering that your writing signals an error and your not writing indicates that the response was correct.

10. Question all ambiguous or unscorable responses, writing "(Q)" after each questionable response. Question all responses followed by a "(Q)" in the WISC–III manual.

11. Introduce the test by saying something like "We will be doing a lot of different things today. Some will be easy and some will be hard. I'd like you to do the best you can. OK?" Make eye contact with the child from time to time, and use the child's first name when possible. Watch for signs that the child needs a break (for example, a stretch, a drink, or a trip to the bathroom). Between subtests say something like "Now we'll do something different." At the end of the test, thank the child for coming and for being cooperative (if appropriate).

12. The following procedure will be helpful if your scoring template does not have a number at the end of each row. To facilitate the scoring of the Coding subtest, write the cumulative total number of symbols up to and including that row at the end of each row of the Coding scoring template. For the Coding A template, the numbers that should be written at the ends of rows 1 through 8, respectively, are 3, 11, 19, 27, 35, 43, 51, and 59. For the Coding B template, the cumulative totals are 14, 35, 56, 77, 98, and 119; these numbers should be written at the ends of rows 1 through 6. After you write the numbers, laminate the template to prolong its life (Danielson, 1991).

13. On subtests that grant bonus points for speed, make sure that the score you circle on the Record Form corresponds to the time taken by the child to complete the item. In no case give bonus points for 0-point answers.

Scoring and Calculating the IQ

14. Recognize that although the Verbal subtests are generally easier to administer than the Performance subtests, they are more difficult to score.

15. Carefully score each protocol and recheck your scoring. If you failed to question a response when you should have and the response is obviously not a 0 response, give the child the most appropriate score based on the child's actual response.

16. If a subtest was spoiled, write "spoiled" by the subtest total score and on the front cover of the Record Form next to the name of the subtest. If the subtest was not administered, write "NA" in the margin of the Record Form next to the subtest name and on the front of the Record Form.

17. Add the raw scores for each subtest carefully. Make sure that you give credit for items not administered below the starting-point items. Be sure to add the points associated with the circled numbers on the Record Form for all subtests that have bonus points.

18. Transfer subtest scores to the front of the Record Form under Raw Scores. After transferring all raw scores to the front page of the Record Form, check that the raw scores on the front page match those noted inside the Record Form for each subtest.

(Continued)

Exhibit 8-2 *(Continued)*

19. Transform raw scores into scaled scores by using Table A.1 on pages 217 to 249 of the WISC–III manual. Be sure to use the page of Table A.1 that is appropriate for the child's age and the correct row and column for each transformation. For example, to convert a raw score on Picture Completion (the first subtest administered) to a scaled score, you must use the column in the lower half of Table A.1 ("Performance Subtests") that shows the raw scores for the Picture Completion subtest and their corresponding scaled scores.

20. In converting raw scores to scaled scores, be aware that the order of subtests on the front of the Record Form is different from the order of subtests in Table A.1 (pages 217–249) in the WISC–III manual. The order of subtests on the Record Form is the order in which you administer the subtests, whereas the order of subtests in Table A.1 is how they are arranged in each scale—the six Verbal subtests in the upper half of the table and the seven Performance subtests in the lower half of the table.

21. Add the scaled scores for the five standard Verbal subtests to compute the sum of the scaled scores. Do not use Digit Span to compute the Verbal score unless you have substituted it for another Verbal subtest. Add the scaled scores for the five standard Performance subtests. Do not include Symbol Search or Mazes to compute the Performance score unless you have substituted Symbol Search for Coding or Mazes for another Performance subtest. You can include both Mazes and Symbol Search to compute the Performance score if you have substituted Symbol Search for Coding and Mazes for some other Performance subtest. Sum the Verbal and the Performance subtest scaled scores to obtain the sum for the Full Scale. Double check all of your additions.

22. Convert the sums of scaled scores for the Verbal, Performance, and Full Scales by using the appropriate conversion tables in Appendix A (pages 251 to 254) in the WISC–III manual. Use Table A.2 for the Verbal Scale, Table A.3 for the Performance Scale, and Table A.4 for the Full Scale. Be sure to use the correct table for the appropriate scale. Record the IQs on the front of the Record Form.

23. Recheck all of your work. If the IQ was obtained by use of a short form, write "SF" beside the appropriate IQ. If IQs were prorated, write "PRO" beside each appropriate IQ.

24. If fewer than five subtests were administered in the Verbal section or fewer than five subtests in the Performance section, use the Tellegen and Briggs short-form procedure described on page 256 of this text to compute the IQ. This procedure is the most reliable one for prorating IQs. You can also consult Tables A-22 to A-26 in Appendix A. These tables provide estimated Full Scale Deviation Quotients for several combinations of short forms based on the Tellegen and Briggs procedure.

25. Make a profile of the examinee's scaled scores on the front of the Record Form by plotting the scores on the graph provided.

26. Look up the confidence intervals for the Full Scale IQ, Verbal Scale IQ, and Performance Scale IQ in Table A-1 or D-2 in Appendixes A and D of this text. Use Table A-1 unless you are making a long-term prediction; in that case, use Table D-2. All confidence intervals in Tables A-1 and D-2 are based on the examinee's exact age group, as well as on the total sample. Normally, the confidence intervals are not used with the Verbal and Performance IQs, unless one of these is the only IQ reported. Write the confidence intervals on the front cover of the Record Form in the space provided.

27. Look up the percentile rank and classification for each of the IQs in Tables BC-1 and BC-2 on the inside back cover of this text. You can also use Tables A.2, A.3, and A.4 (pages 251–254) in the WISC–III manual for the percentile ranks and Table 2.8 (page 32 in the WISC–III manual) for classifications.

28. If you want to obtain test-age equivalents, use Table A.9 on page 259 of the WISC–III manual. They can be placed (in parentheses) in the right margin of the box that contains the scaled scores. For test-age equivalents *above* those in the table, use the highest test-age equivalent and a plus sign. For test-age equivalents *below* those in the table, use the lowest test-age equivalent and a minus sign.

29. If you want to, you can enter the four index scores on the front cover of the Record Form. The Deviation Quotients associated with the index scores can be obtained from Tables A.5, A.6, and A.7 in the WISC–III manual, pages 255 to 257.

30. Be sure to check the scores you enter into any computer program you use to assist you in writing a report.

Summary

31. In summary, read the directions verbatim, pronounce words clearly, query at the appropriate times, start with the appropriate item, discontinue at the proper place, place items properly before the child, use correct timing, and follow the specific guidelines in the manual for administering the test.

Exhibit 8-3
Administrative Checklist for the WISC–III

ADMINISTRATIVE CHECKLIST FOR THE WISC–III

Name of examiner: _____   Date: _____

Name of examinee: _____   Name of observer: _____

(Note: *If an item is not applicable, mark NA to the left of the number.*)

Picture Completion	Circle One	
1. Reads directions verbatim	Yes	No
2. Reads directions clearly	Yes	No
3. Pronounces words in queries clearly	Yes	No
4. Begins with appropriate item	Yes	No
5. Places booklet flat on table, close to child	Yes	No
6. Begins timing after last word of instructions	Yes	No
7. Gives a maximum of 20 seconds on each item	Yes	No
8. Gives correct answers for sample item and items 1 and 2 if child fails these items	Yes	No
9. Does not give correct answers for items 3–30	Yes	No
10. Prompts with "Yes, but what's missing?" no more than one time	Yes	No
11. Prompts with "A part is missing in the picture. What is it that is missing?" no more than one time	Yes	No
12. Prompts with "Yes, but what is the most important part that is missing?" no more than one time	Yes	No
13. Inquires correctly on items 6, 13, 21, 23, 26, and 28 when certain responses are given	Yes	No
14. Gives credit for correct responses made after the prompt	Yes	No
15. Administers items in reverse order, when the first or second item administered is failed, to children ages 8 to 16 until they pass two consecutive items	Yes	No
16. Gives credit for items not administered when those items precede two consecutive successes	Yes	No
17. Gives credit for a correct oral or pointing response	Yes	No
18. Gives 1 point credit for each correct response	Yes	No
19. Gives no credit for correct responses given after time limit	Yes	No
20. Records 0 or 1 point for each item	Yes	No
21. Discontinues subtest after five consecutive failures	Yes	No
22. Adds points correctly	Yes	No

Comments: _____

_____

Information	Circle One	
1. Reads directions verbatim	Yes	No
2. Reads directions clearly	Yes	No
3. Reads items verbatim and clearly	Yes	No

Information	Circle One	
4. Starts with appropriate item	Yes	No
5. Gives sufficient time for child to respond to each question	Yes	No
6. Gives correct answer for item 1 if child fails item	Yes	No
7. Does not give correct answers for items 2–30	Yes	No
8. Says "Explain what you mean" or "Tell me more about it" for responses that are not clear	Yes	No
9. Gives prompts when the child's response suggests that the child has misheard or misunderstood the exact meaning of the question	Yes	No
10. Repeats question if child says he (she) does not understand it	Yes	No
11. Inquires correctly on items 4, 8, 16, 18, 19, 21, 24, 26, 28, 29, and 30 when certain responses are given	Yes	No
12. Gives credit for correct responses made after the prompt (or inquiry)	Yes	No
13. Administers items in reverse order, when the first or second item administered is failed, to children ages 8 to 16 until they pass two consecutive items	Yes	No
14. Does not ask leading questions or spell words	Yes	No
15. Gives credit for items not administered when those items precede two consecutive successes	Yes	No
16. Gives 1 point credit for each correct response	Yes	No
17. Records 0 or 1 point for each item	Yes	No
18. Discontinues subtest after five consecutive failures	Yes	No
19. Records responses	Yes	No
20. Adds points correctly	Yes	No

Comments: _____

_____

Coding	Circle One	
1. Reads directions verbatim	Yes	No
2. Reads directions clearly	Yes	No
3. Correctly selects either Coding A or B	Yes	No
4. Provides two no. 2 graphite pencils without erasers	Yes	No
5. Removes Coding Response Sheet from the Record Form	Yes	No

(Continued)

Exhibit 8-3 *(Continued)*

Coding　　　　　　　　　　　**Circle One**

6. Provides a smooth work surface — Yes No
7. Provides extra Coding Response Sheet for left-handed children — Yes No
8. Points to the key while reading the first part of the instructions — Yes No
9. Points to the proper forms (e.g., star, ball, triangle, circle, box with two lines) while reading instructions — Yes No
10. Follows directions in the manual for pointing to sample items while reading directions — Yes No
11. Praises child's success on each sample item by saying "yes" or "right" — Yes No
12. Corrects child's mistakes on sample items — Yes No
13. Does not begin subtest until child clearly understands the task — Yes No
14. Gives proper instructions after child completes the sample items and understands the task — Yes No
15. Provides proper caution the first time child omits item or does only one type: "Do them in order. Don't skip any." Then points to the next item and says "Do this one next." — Yes No
16. Provides caution about omitting or skipping item only one time — Yes No
17. Reminds child to continue until told to stop (when needed) — Yes No
18. Does not time the sample items — Yes No
19. Begins timing immediately after completing instructions — Yes No
20. Allows 120 seconds unless child is finished sooner — Yes No
21. Records time accurately — Yes No
22. Uses scoring stencil to score subtest — Yes No
23. Places a mark through each incorrect box — Yes No
24. Adds number of correct boxes or subtracts number of incorrect boxes from number attempted — Yes No
25. Gives time-bonus credits appropriately on Coding A — Yes No
26. Gives no time-bonus credits on Coding B — Yes No
27. Records correct number of items — Yes No

Comments: _____

Similarities

1. Reads directions verbatim — Yes No
2. Reads directions clearly — Yes No
3. Reads items verbatim and clearly — Yes No
4. Begins with sample item and then item 1, regardless of child's age — Yes No
5. Allows sufficient time for child to respond to each question — Yes No

Similarities　　　　　　　　**Circle One**

6. Gives correct answers for items 1 and 2 if child fails these items — Yes No
7. Does not give correct answers for items 3–19 — Yes No
8. Gives an example of a 2-point response if a 1-point response is given on item 6 or item 7 — Yes No
9. Queries every response followed in the WISC–III manual by a "(Q)", even if it is a 0-point response — Yes No
10. Queries vague responses — Yes No
11. Prompts with "Explain what you mean" or "Tell me more about it" and no other statement to query a response — Yes No
12. Does not query a clearcut response — Yes No
13. Asks "Now which one is it?" each time a child's response contains both a correct and an incorrect answer — Yes No
14. Gives 1 point credit for each correct response to items 1–5 — Yes No
15. Gives 1 or 2 points credit for each correct response to items 6–19 — Yes No
16. Records 0, 1, or 2 points as appropriate — Yes No
17. Discontinues after four consecutive failures — Yes No
18. Records responses — Yes No
19. Adds points correctly — Yes No

Comments: _____

Picture Arrangement

1. Reads directions verbatim — Yes No
2. Reads directions clearly — Yes No
3. Gives sample item to all children and then item 1 to children ages 6 to 8 or item 3 to children ages 9 to 16 — Yes No
4. Has cards arranged in numerical sequence and places all cards in correct numerical order from child's left to child's right — Yes No
5. Rearranges sample item in correct order by moving cards one at a time to a new row and then points to each card as story is told — Yes No
6. Allows child 10 seconds to look at correct arrangement on sample item — Yes No
7. Begins timing after last word of instructions — Yes No
8. Records time in the Record Form — Yes No
9. Stops timing when child is obviously finished with each arrangement — Yes No
10. Gives a second trial on items 1 and 2 when child fails first trial — Yes No
11. Does not give a second trial on items 1 and 2 when child passes first trial — Yes No
12. Does not give a second trial on items 4–14 — Yes No
13. Uses correct time limits — Yes No

(Continued)

Exhibit 8-3 *(Continued)*

Picture Arrangement	Circle One	
14. Gives 2 points credit for each correct response to items 1 and 2 given on first trial or 1 point credit for each correct response given on second trial	Yes	No
15. Administers items 1 and 2 in that sequence if children between ages 9 and 16 fail item 3	Yes	No
16. Allows child to continue working on arrangement after time limit has expired when child is nearing completion of task	Yes	No
17. Records exact amount of time taken to solve each item	Yes	No
18. Records child's exact arrangement (in letters) in Record Form	Yes	No
19. Gives correct number of points credit, including time-bonus credit, for items 3–14	Yes	No
20. Gives no time-bonus credit to WODAHS arrangement for item 14	Yes	No
21. Discontinues after three consecutive failures	Yes	No
22. Adds points correctly	Yes	No

Comments: _____

_____

Arithmetic	Circle One	
1. Reads items verbatim	Yes	No
2. Reads items clearly	Yes	No
3. Starts with appropriate item	Yes	No
4. Places booklet properly in front of child for items 1–5 and for items 19–24	Yes	No
5. Uses correct timing	Yes	No
6. Gives correct answers for items 1 and 2 if child fails them	Yes	No
7. Does not give correct answers for items 3–24	Yes	No
8. Explains the concept of "cover up" on item 3 without using card for demonstration if child does not understand it	Yes	No
9. Does not allow child to use pencil and paper	Yes	No
10. Allows child to use a finger to "write" on the table	Yes	No
11. Administers items in reverse order, when the first or second item administered is failed, to children ages 7 to 16 until they pass two consecutive items	Yes	No
12. Reads items 19–24 aloud to children who have visual problems or reading difficulties	Yes	No
13. Records exact amount of time taken to solve each problem	Yes	No
14. Begins timing immediately after each problem has been read	Yes	No
15. Repeats a problem only once	Yes	No
16. Records time from the end of the first reading of problem to when the response is made, even when problem is read again	Yes	No

Arithmetic	Circle One	
17. Asks child to select one of two responses when it is not clear which response is the final choice by saying "You said _____ and you said _____. Which one do you mean?"	Yes	No
18. Gives no credit for correct responses given after time limit	Yes	No
19. Gives 1 point credit for each correct response on items 1–18	Yes	No
20. Gives 2 points credit for each correct response given within 1 to 10 seconds on items 19–24	Yes	No
21. Gives credit for correct numerical quantity even when unit is not given	Yes	No
22. Gives credit when child spontaneously corrects an incorrect response within time limit	Yes	No
23. Records 0, 1, or 2 points as appropriate	Yes	No
24. Discontinues after three consecutive failures	Yes	No
25. Records responses	Yes	No
26. Adds points correctly	Yes	No

Comments: _____

_____

Block Design	Circle One	
1. Reads items verbatim	Yes	No
2. Reads items clearly	Yes	No
3. Turns blocks slowly to show different sides as instructions are read	Yes	No
4. Starts with appropriate item	Yes	No
5. Places blocks and cards properly	Yes	No
6. Constructs model or places Stimulus Booklet approximately 7 inches from child's edge of the table	Yes	No
7. Places model or Stimulus Booklet somewhat to the left of the child's midline for right-handed children and somewhat to the right of midline for left-handed children	Yes	No
8. Constructs designs 1 and 2 properly	Yes	No
9. Presents pictures in the Stimulus Book with the unbound edge toward child	Yes	No
10. Lays out blocks so that different colored surfaces face up on different blocks	Yes	No
11. Lays out blocks so that only one block has a red-and-white side facing up for the two- and four-block designs and only two blocks have a red-and-white side facing up for the nine-block designs	Yes	No
12. Scrambles blocks between designs	Yes	No
13. Begins timing after the last word of instructions	Yes	No
14. Records time in the Record Form	Yes	No
15. Uses correct time limits	Yes	No
16. Stops timing when child is obviously finished with design (except for items 1–3)	Yes	No

(Continued)

Exhibit 8-3 *(Continued)*

Block Design	Circle One	
17. Allows child to continue working on design after time limit when child has nearly completed task	Yes	No
18. Gives a second trial on items 1–3 when child fails first trial	Yes	No
19. Does not give a second trial on items 4–9	Yes	No
20. Uses the correct number of blocks for each item	Yes	No
21. Says "But, you see, the blocks go this way" and corrects child's design the first time child rotates a design	Yes	No
22. Gives instructions about need to correct a rotated design only once during the test	Yes	No
23. Uses the appropriate instructions for item 3 depending on whether the child started the subtest with item 1 or 3	Yes	No
24. Gives 2 points each when child gets items 1–3 correct on the first trial	Yes	No
25. Gives 1 point each when child gets items 1–3 correct on the second trial	Yes	No
26. Gives correct number of points, including time-bonus credits, for items 4–12	Yes	No
27. Gives no credit for correct responses given after time limit	Yes	No
28. Circles on the Record Form a Y (Yes) or N (No) for each item	Yes	No
29. Stops child on items 1–3 when time limit has expired on first trial and gives second trial	Yes	No
30. Records exact amount of time taken to solve each item	Yes	No
31. Administers items 1 and 2 in normal sequence to children ages 8 to 16 when trial 1 of item 3 is failed followed by either a pass or fail on trial 2	Yes	No
32. Begins the directions for item 1 by assembling the model when child fails the second trial of item 3	Yes	No
33. Records 0–7 points as appropriate	Yes	No
34. Discontinues after two consecutive failures	Yes	No
35. Adds points correctly	Yes	No

Comments: _____

_____

Vocabulary	Circle One	
1. Reads directions verbatim	Yes	No
2. Reads directions clearly	Yes	No
3. Pronounces words clearly	Yes	No
4. Starts with appropriate item	Yes	No
5. Gives sufficient time for child to respond to each word	Yes	No

Vocabulary	Circle One	
6. Queries every response followed in the WISC–III manual by a "(Q)," even if it is a 0-point response	Yes	No
7. Queries vague responses	Yes	No
8. Does not query a clearcut response	Yes	No
9. Gives the 2-point answer for item 1 if child gives a 0- or 1-point response	Yes	No
10. Does not give correct answers for items 2–30 if child misses items	Yes	No
11. Does not give credit for a pointing response	Yes	No
12. Prompts "Listen carefully" for misheard words	Yes	No
13. Does not spell any words	Yes	No
14. Gives credit for items not administered when those items precede perfect (2-point) scores on the first two items administered to children ages 9 to 16	Yes	No
15. Administers items in reverse order, when child fails or gives a 1-point response to first or second item administered, to children ages 9 to 16 until they obtain perfect (2-point) scores on two consecutive items	Yes	No
16. Inquires about vague responses, regionalisms, or slang responses	Yes	No
17. Gives 1 or 2 points credit for each correct response	Yes	No
18. Records 0, 1, or 2 points as appropriate	Yes	No
19. Discontinues after four consecutive failures	Yes	No
20. Records responses	Yes	No
21. Adds points correctly	Yes	No

Comments: _____

_____

Object Assembly	Circle One	
1. Reads directions verbatim	Yes	No
2. Reads directions clearly	Yes	No
3. Starts with sample item	Yes	No
4. Administers all items	Yes	No
5. Uses shield correctly	Yes	No
6. Presents puzzles with pieces arranged properly	Yes	No
7. Begins timing immediately after last word of instructions	Yes	No
8. Stops timing when child is obviously finished	Yes	No
9. Records time accurately	Yes	No
10. Records number of junctures correctly completed within time limit	Yes	No
11. Gives no credit for correct responses given after time limit	Yes	No
12. Gives 10-second exposure after assembling sample item (apple)	Yes	No
13. Demonstrates correct arrangement on item 1 (girl) if child's assembly is incomplete	Yes	No

(Continued)

Exhibit 8-3 *(Continued)*

Object Assembly	**Circle One**	
14. Does not demonstrate correct arrangement on items 2–5 even if child's arrangements are incomplete	Yes	No
15. Does not give name of object for items 3–5	Yes	No
16. Records 0–10 points as appropriate	Yes	No
17. Gives proper time-bonus credit	Yes	No
18. Adds points correctly	Yes	No

Comments: _____

_____

Comprehension

1. Reads items verbatim	Yes	No
2. Reads items clearly	Yes	No
3. Begins with item 1 for all children	Yes	No
4. Repeats question if child has difficulty remembering it or has not responded after 10–15 seconds	Yes	No
5. Encourages a hesitant child to speak	Yes	No
6. Queries every response followed in the WISC–III manual by a "(Q)," even if it is a 0-point response	Yes	No
7. Queries vague responses	Yes	No
8. Does not query a clearcut response, especially one that is not followed in the WISC–III manual by a "(Q)"	Yes	No
9. Gives a few 2-point answers for item 1 if child gives a 0- or 1-point response	Yes	No
10. Does not give correct answers for items 2–18 if child fails or does not give a 2-point response	Yes	No
11. Prompts for second response on items 2, 6, 7, 11, 12, 15, 17, and 18 only when first response is right	Yes	No
12. Prompts for a second response only once per designated item	Yes	No
13. Records 0, 1, or 2 points as appropriate	Yes	No
14. Discontinues after three consecutive failures	Yes	No
15. Records responses	Yes	No
16. Adds points correctly	Yes	No

Comments: _____

_____

Symbol Search

1. Reads directions verbatim	Yes	No
2. Reads directions clearly	Yes	No
3. Correctly selects either Part A or Part B	Yes	No
4. Provides two no. 2 graphite pencils without erasers	Yes	No
5. Proceeds with test items only when child understands the task	Yes	No
6. Points from child's left to right when giving instructions for sample item	Yes	No

Symbol Search — **Circle One**

7. Offers praise such as "Yes" or "Right" when child marks correct answers for the two practice items	Yes	No
8. Gives correct instructions when child fails practice items	Yes	No
9. Opens booklet to page 2 after child completes practice items	Yes	No
10. Points to correct part of booklet as instructions are read for subtest items	Yes	No
11. Turns page briefly to show child third page of items	Yes	No
12. Begins timing after completing instructions	Yes	No
13. Reminds child, if needed, to go in order and to continue task until told to stop	Yes	No
14. Discontinues after 120 seconds	Yes	No
15. Places a mark through each incorrect item	Yes	No
16. Records numbers of correct and incorrect items properly	Yes	No
17. Obtains score by subtracting number of incorrect from number of correct items attempted	Yes	No

Comments: _____

_____

Digit Span

1. Begins with item 1	Yes	No
2. Reads directions verbatim	Yes	No
3. Reads directions clearly	Yes	No
4. Administers both trials of each item	Yes	No
5. Pronounces digits singly and distinctly, at the rate of one digit per second and without chunking digits	Yes	No
6. Drops voice inflection slightly on last digit	Yes	No
7. Pauses after each sequence to allow child to respond	Yes	No
8. Gives sample item for Digits Backward	Yes	No
9. Gives the correct answer for sample item on Digits Backward if child fails item	Yes	No
10. Gives both trials of each item on Digits Forward and on Digits Backward	Yes	No
11. Discontinues Digits Forward after failure on both trials of any item and then gives Digits Backward	Yes	No
12. Discontinues Digits Backward after failure on both trails of any item	Yes	No
13. Gives 1 point for each trial passed	Yes	No
14. Records successes and failures in Record Form	Yes	No
15. Records responses	Yes	No
16. Adds points correctly	Yes	No

Comments: _____

_____

(Continued)

Exhibit 8-3 *(Continued)*

Mazes	Circle One	
1. Reads directions verbatim	Yes	No
2. Reads directions clearly	Yes	No
3. Begins with appropriate item	Yes	No
4. Provides two no. 2 graphite pencils without erasers	Yes	No
5. Exposes sheet properly (with arrow pointed toward examiner)	Yes	No
6. Folds Mazes Response Booklet so that only one page is exposed	Yes	No
7. Provides a smooth work surface	Yes	No
8. Demonstrates the correct solution if child fails Maze 1	Yes	No
9. Demonstrates the correct solution if child fails Maze 2	Yes	No
10. Gives credit for all preceding items if child aged 8 to 16 obtains a perfect score on Maze 4	Yes	No
11. Administers Mazes 1–3 in normal sequence if child aged 8 to 16 obtains no more than partial credit on Maze 4	Yes	No
12. Demonstrates sample maze and administers Mazes 1–3 in normal sequence if child aged 8 to 16 fails Maze 4	Yes	No
13. Begins timing after last word of instructions	Yes	No
14. Records number of errors in the appropriate column on Report Form	Yes	No
15. Uses "pencil point on paper" caution appropriately	Yes	No
16. Uses "begins outside center of box" caution appropriately	Yes	No
17. Uses "begins at the exit" caution appropriately	Yes	No
18. Uses "don't stop" caution appropriately	Yes	No
19. Uses "not allowed to start over" caution appropriately	Yes	No
20. Uses "does not completely clear the exit" caution appropriately	Yes	No
21. Does examiner portion of sample appropriately	Yes	No
22. Points to boy or girl figure in each maze as instructions are read	Yes	No
23. Uses correct timing for each maze	Yes	No
24. Records time accurately	Yes	No
25. Discontinues after two consecutive failures	Yes	No
26. Adds points correctly	Yes	No

Comments: _____

_____

Other Aspects of Test Administration

	Circle One	
1. Establishes rapport	Yes	No
2. Is well organized	Yes	No

Other Aspects of Test Administration	Circle One	
3. Has all needed materials in kit	Yes	No
4. Has extra paper and pencils	Yes	No
5. Makes smooth transition from subtest to subtest	Yes	No
6. Provides support between subtests as needed	Yes	No
7. Focuses child's attention on tasks	Yes	No
8. Handles behavior problems appropriately	Yes	No
9. Makes the test experience positive	Yes	No

Comments: _____

_____

Front Page of Record Form

	Circle One	
1. Transfers raw scores for each subtest to front page of Record Form correctly	Yes	No
2. Converts raw scores to scaled scores for each subtest correctly	Yes	No
3. Adds scaled scores for Verbal Scale correctly	Yes	No
4. Adds scaled scores for Performance Scale correctly	Yes	No
5. Adds scaled scores for Full Scale correctly	Yes	No
6. Converts sum of scaled scores in Verbal Scale to IQ correctly	Yes	No
7. Converts sum of scaled scores in Performance Scale to IQ correctly	Yes	No
8. Converts sum of scaled scores in Full Scale to IQ correctly	Yes	No
9. Completes profile of subtest scores correctly	Yes	No
10. Completes identifying information section on front of Record Form correctly; assumes that all months have 30 days for purposes of calculating the chronological age; does not round up age (e.g., does not round 8 years-2 months-28 days to 8 years, 3 months); calculates chronological age accurately	Yes	No
11. Writes child's name, date, and examiner's name on Coding sheet and on Symbol Search and Mazes forms, if subtests are given	Yes	No

Overall Assessment of Test Administration

Circle One: Excellent   Good   Average   Poor   Failing

Overall strengths: _____

Overall weaknesses: _____

Other comments: _____

Wechsler Intelligence Scale
for Children – Third Edition

Name_____ Sex _____

School_____ Grade _____

Examiner_____ Handedness _____

Subtests	Raw Scores	Scaled Scores					
Picture Completion							
Information							
Coding							
Similarities							
Picture Arrangement							
Arithmetic							
Block Design							
Vocabulary							
Object Assembly							
Comprehension							
(Symbol Search)		( )					
(Digit Span)	( )						
(Mazes)		( )					
Sum of Scaled Scores		Verbal	Perfor.	VC	PO	FD	PS

Full Scale Score   OPTIONAL

	Year	Month	Day
Date Tested			
Date of Birth			
Age			

	Score	IQ/ Index	%ile	— % Confidence Interval
Verbal				–
Performance				–
Full Scale				–
VC				–
PO				–
FD				–
PS				–

Subtest Scores

	Verbal						Performance						
	Inf	Sim	Ari	Voc	Com	DS	PC	Cd	PA	BD	OA	SS	Mz

IQ Scores

VIQ	PIQ	FSIQ

Index Scores (Optional)

VCI	POI	FDI	PSI

Copyright © 1991, 1986, 1974, 1971 by The Psychological Corporation
Standardization edition copyright © 1989 by The Psychological Corporation
Copyright 1949 by The Psychological Corporation
Copyright renewed 1976 by The Psychological Corporation
All rights reserved. Printed in the United States of America.

THE PSYCHOLOGICAL CORPORATION®
HARCOURT BRACE JOVANOVICH, INC.

2 3 4 5 6 7 8 9 10 11 12 A B C D E

Ψ®

09–980004

Figure 8-3. Cover page of WISC–III Record Form. *Wechsler Intelligence Scale for Children: Third Edition.* Copyright © 1991 by The Psychological Corporation, a Harcourt Assessment Company. Reproduced by permission. All rights reserved. "Wechsler Intelligence Scale for Children" and "WISC–III" are trademarks of The Psychological Corporation registered in the United States of America and/or other jurisdictions.

249

Some examiners are more lenient than others in giving credit, and at times even the same examiners may not consistently follow their own (relative) standards. For example, they may be strict on some occasions and lenient on others. Studies have reported dramatic differences in the scoring standards of examiners. For example, in one study, 99 school psychologists gave IQs ranging from 63 to 117 to the *same* WISC protocol (Massey, 1964)! In other studies with graduate-student examiners (Miller et al., 1970) and with members of the American Psychological Association (Miller & Chansky, 1972), examiners differed by as many as 17 points in scoring the same WISC protocol.

Starting-Point Scoring Rule

Occasionally, you may have doubts about whether the child passed items at the starting point (the starting-point items are those that the child must pass before you continue with the subtest). When this happens, you will need to administer previous items in the subtest. The WISC–III manual does not provide guidance on how to score items that the examinee fails *below* the starting point. The WISC–R manual, however, did provide such guidance: *If subsequent scoring of the items indicates that the early items were administered unnecessarily, give the child full credit for these items even if only partial or no credit was earned* (adapted from Wechsler, 1974, p. 59). We recommend that you follow the same procedure on the WISC–III. (Lawrence Weiss, Project Director for the WISC–III from The Psychological Corporation, supports this recommendation; personal communication, October 1991.) In other words, if the child failed (or received only partial credit for) one or more items *below* the starting point but further checking indicates that, in fact, the child correctly answered the items at the starting point, give *full credit* for those items that precede the starting-point items. This rule usually applies to children aged 7 years and older because they may have starting points above the first item on certain subtests.

Here is an example of how to use the starting-point scoring rule. You administer items 5 and 6 on the Information subtest to an 8-year-old child and are uncertain of how to score the responses. You then administer items 4 and 3, which the child clearly fails, and then items 2 and 1, which the child clearly passes. You follow this procedure because the directions for the subtest state that the child must pass two consecutive items before you administer the rest of the subtest. Because the child passed items 1 and 2, you continue giving the subtest with item 7. After the examination, you decide that the child did indeed pass items 5 and 6. The starting-point scoring rule requires that the child receive full credit for items 3 and 4, even though the two items were failed, because these two items are *below* the starting-point items 5 and 6, which the child passed.

The starting-point scoring rule favors the child by ensuring that you do not penalize him or her for failing items that, as it turned out, you did not have to administer. The starting-point scoring rule is an attempt to maintain standardized scoring procedures.

Discontinuance-Point Scoring Rule

The discontinuance-point scoring rule applies to situations in which you have doubts about whether the child failed the items at the discontinuance point and you then administer additional items in the subtest (see page 43 of the WISC–III manual). (The discontinuance-point items are those that the child must fail before you discontinue the subtest.) The discontinuance-point scoring rule is as follows: *If subsequent scoring of the items indicates that the additional items were administered unnecessarily, do not give the child credit for items that were passed after the discontinuance point.*

Here is an example of how to use the discontinuance-point scoring rule. You administer the first 15 words of the Vocabulary subtest and are uncertain of how to score the child's responses to words 11 through 14. You then administer additional words. The child knows words 15 and 16 but not words 17 to 21. You therefore discontinue the subtest after word 21. After the test is over, you check your scoring and decide that the child's answers on words 11 to 14 were wrong. The discontinuance-point scoring rule requires that you *not* give the child credit for words 15 and 16, even though the child's definitions were correct, because these words occur after you should have discontinued the subtest.

In contrast with the starting-point scoring rule, the discontinuance-point scoring rule does not favor the child. This scoring rule prevents the child from receiving credit for items that, as it turned out, you did not have to administer. This rule is another attempt to maintain standardized scoring procedures.

Repetition of Items

When a child says "I don't know," you must decide whether the response means that he or she (a) does not know the answer, (b) is not confident of the answer and is unwilling to take a risk, (c) is being uncooperative and does not want to answer the question, or (d) has been inattentive and therefore does not know what the question is. If you decide that motivation is an issue, encourage the child to attempt an answer by repeating the question or by asking it again at some later point, especially if the child says "I don't know" to an easy question. Better yet, the first time a child says "I don't know," say something like "I want you to try your hardest on each question. Try your best to answer each question. If you are not sure, go ahead and take your best guess." You can also say, "It's OK to answer even if you are not sure." Give the child credit if the question is answered correctly. Exception: never repeat items on Digit Span.

Use of Probing Questions and Queries

Use probing questions when responses are ambiguous, vague, or incomplete or when probing is indicated by a "(Q)" following a response in the WISC–III manual. The "(Q)" means that you need to query the response because it is vague. In order to receive the appropriate credit, the examinee must give the response shown after the "(Q)" or a similar response. Therefore, the entire response—the initial answer plus the response to the query—is used in determining the appropriate credit.

In addition to the responses shown in the WISC–III manual, you will also need to query some responses that are not provided in the manual. For example, you can acknowledge negativistic or mistrustful responses and then ask for clarification. If a child says "Freedom of speech is relative, so at times it is improper when it incites people," you could say, "Well, try to give some answers that other people think are reasonable." You will have to be alert to recognize responses requiring this kind of probing. You also will need to probe verbal responses that are incomplete, indefinite, or vague. Ask additional questions (i.e., use queries or probing questions) when you are unsure of how to score a response; however, do not ask additional questions to elicit a higher quality response from the child unless the WISC–III manual so indicates.

Spoiled Responses

An explicit scoring rule on the WISC–III is that you give a score of 0 to a spoiled response (see pages 50–51 in the WISC–III manual). A spoiled response is one that initially was partially correct, but was spoiled by the child's incorrect elaboration on the initial response. For example, if a child says that *clock* means "Goes ticktock" and then says, in response to your query, "It's the engine on a motorcycle," the response is spoiled. The child's elaboration reveals her or his misconception about the meaning of the word *clock,* and hence the response receives a score of 0.

If the child adds additional irrelevant information that is not contrary to fact, then a correct initial response is not spoiled. For example, if a child defines *donkey* as "An animal," the response is still scored 2 points if he or she then adds, "Eeyore is a donkey. My aunt has donkeys on her farm. Some donkeys are grey. I like donkeys. Another word for donkey is a swear word, but I can't say it."

Modifying Standard Procedures

Research with the WISC–R indicates that children are likely to obtain higher scores on some subtests when they are encouraged to talk about their problem-solving procedures, think about their answers before responding, explain their picture arrangements, or solve problems after receiving a series of cues (Herrell & Golland, 1969; Post, 1970; Sattler, 1969; Schwebel & Bernstein, 1970). We would expect similar results on the WISC–III. If you use such modifications, employ them only *after* the standard administration and completion of the entire test. Such modifications may be helpful in assessing the child's ability to benefit from learning strategies or cues, but they may invalidate the test results if you use the modifications during the standard administration.

Potential Administrative Problems on Arithmetic and Picture Arrangement

Although unlikely, there can be subtle administrative problems on the Arithmetic and Picture Arrangement subtests. For example, on Arithmetic, you ask children to read problems 19 through 24. Because you begin timing when children finish reading each of these problems, slow readers have more time to solve the problems than fast readers. Some children may also intentionally slow their reading to solve the problems before timing begins. The effect, if any, that reading speed has on the speed of solving the problems is unknown. Because children receive bonus points for speed on items 19 through 24, differences in reading speed and in problem-solving strategies may affect their scores.

Another potential problem with Arithmetic is that some children may feel anxious when they read the problems aloud. We do not know how anxiety affects the ability to solve problems. In addition, for children with a reading disability, their struggle to read the items may interfere with their ability to comprehend the material. And finally, there seems to be a subtle difference in administration when the examiner reads items 19 through 24 aloud to children who cannot read and when children read the problems aloud by themselves. When the examiner reads the problems, memory plays an important role because the children do not look at the questions; examiners also likely differ in their reading speed and enunciation. When the children read the problems, memory plays a minor role because they look at the problems while they work on them.

On Picture Arrangement, not all children receive the same type of help. Let's consider how this might happen. All children start with the sample item and are told the story elements of the arrangement. Young children (6 to 8 years) are then administered items 1 and 2 and again told the story elements of the arrangements. In contrast, older children (9 to 16 years) are not given any story elements when they begin item 3. We do not know whether hearing the story elements on the first two items helps children solve later items.

Problems in Administering the WISC–III

The following are common problems encountered by beginning examiners when they administer the WISC–III and other intelligence tests (as applicable).

Problems Related to Establishing Rapport

1. Failing to establish rapport
2. Interrogating the examinee while trying to establish rapport
3. Failing to be sensitive to the examinee's need for a break
4. Rushing the examinee
5. Showing impatience or frustration

Problems Related to Speech

6. Reading questions too quickly or too slowly
7. Making enunciation errors

Problems Related to Layout of Test Materials

8. Failing to position record booklet so that the examinee cannot observe recorded responses
9. Leaving unessential materials on the table

Problems Related to Test Administration

10. Failing to record all responses in their entirety and verbatim
11. Burying the head in the manual, with little eye contact and attention to the examinee
12. Providing hints not shown in the manual, such as defining or explaining words
13. Providing nonverbal cues
14. Calculating chronological age incorrectly
15. Failing to adhere to guidelines for giving help or prompting
16. Failing to adhere to guidelines for giving second trials
17. Failing to adhere to standardized instructions
18. Ignoring proper time limits
19. Failing to begin timing immediately after reading problems requiring timing
20. Failing to stop timing when the examinee obviously has finished
21. Failing to question ambiguous or vague responses and responses similar to those with a "(Q)" in the WISC–III manual
22. Questioning unnecessarily
23. Failing to credit responses
24. Failing to follow the starting rule
25. Failing to follow the discontinuance rule
26. Testing-of-limits after an item or subtest has been administered instead of after the entire test has been administered
27. Repeating questions or items when the manual says not to do so
28. Allowing paper and pencil when the instructions forbid this practice

Problems Related to Scoring

29. Incorrectly transferring raw scores to the front of the protocol
30. Incorrectly converting raw scores to scaled scores

31. Incorrectly converting scaled scores to IQs
32. Prorating incorrectly
33. Giving time-bonus credits incorrectly
34. Using inappropriate norms
35. Failing to give a score of 0 to an incorrect response
36. Failing to use the scoring guidelines appropriately
37. Adding raw scores incorrectly
38. Adding scaled scores incorrectly
39. Failing to give credit for items not administered below the starting point
40. Giving credit for items passed above the discontinuance point
41. Failing to give credit for items missed below the starting point
42. Failing to score a subtest
43. Computing an IQ by including a supplementary subtest, in addition to the five standard subtests in either the Verbal Scale or the Performance Scale or both scales

Several studies have documented that examiners make errors in administering and scoring the WISC–III and other Wechsler tests (Klassen & Kishor, 1996; Levenson, Golden-Scaduto, Aiosa-Karpas, & Ward, 1988; Slate & Hunnicutt, 1988; Slate, Jones, Coulter, & Covert, 1992; Wagoner, 1988). For example, Klassen and Kishor (1996) reported clerical errors in 42% of the WISC–III protocols administered by seven master's level psychologists (range of 75 to 105 protocols per examiner). Only one of the seven examiners had no errors. The most common errors were in (a) the addition of raw scores (79%), (b) the transformation of raw scores to scaled scores (9%), (c) the addition of scaled scores (9%), and (d) the transformation of scaled scores to IQs (2%). A similar rate of errors was reported for the WISC–R. Wagoner (1988) found that examiners made an average of 8.4 errors per protocol, which resulted in errors in 34% of the Full Scale IQs.

Another study found that 15 graduate students, who administered 60 tests, committed a total of 468 errors, with 7.8 errors per protocol (range of 1 to 37 errors; Alfonso, Johnson, Patinella, & Rader, 1998). Most of the errors were failures to (a) query, (b) record responses verbatim, (c) report Full Scale IQs correctly, (d) report Verbal Scale IQs correctly, and (e) add individual subtest scores correctly.

Examiners may commit scoring errors for a variety of reasons, including the following (Slate & Hunnicutt, 1988):

- They received poor training in test administration.
- They encountered ambiguous scoring criteria in the test manual.
- They were careless.
- They had a poor relationship with the examinee.
- They were suffering from personal stress or fatigue.
- They became bored with administering the test.

To avoid scoring and administration errors, carefully review how you administer and score each subtest. Assign tentative scores as you administer the test, and always rescore each item after the entire test is completed. If you are unsure of how to score a response while testing and the item is involved in establishing a starting point (also referred to as a basal level) or discontinuance point (also referred to as a ceiling level), always err on the side of safety: *It is better to administer an item that may be critical to a starting point or discontinuance point than to invalidate the subtest!*

Although administration, scoring, and clerical errors will decrease with practice and effective feedback, we recommend that you make a mental checklist of your findings, such as the following:

- "How is it possible that this 8-year-old child has a scaled score of only 5 on Object Assembly when each puzzle was successfully completed in the required time?"
- "With no Verbal Scale subtest scaled scores exceeding 9, how is it possible to have a Verbal Scale IQ of 109 unless I added incorrectly, misread the table, or added in the optional subtests to increase the Verbal score?"
- "Was it possible that I made scoring errors on this protocol because I was tired today? If so, I need to go back and recheck all of the calculations."

If possible, make a videotape of your test administration, review it yourself, and then have a fellow student review it carefully to critique your performance. Another option is to have an observer view your test administration from behind a two-way mirror. Be alert to possible sources of error—both covert and overt—in your test administration, and take appropriate steps to prevent these errors from occurring. Also check the Record Form to be sure that you have completed it accurately. And, again, have a fellow student review the Record Form and give you feedback. In many training programs, your instructor or teaching assistant will give you feedback about your testing techniques by reviewing a videotape of your test administration or by observing your test administration. The keys to proper test administration are to

follow standard test procedures and to be an objective, but sensitive and supportive, examiner.

Examples follow of cases in which examiners were *not* sensitive to the child's needs or influenced the child's performance inappropriately (from Teglasi & Freeman, 1983, adapted from pp. 232–234, 239).

Example 1: Failure to recognize nonverbal cues. Before administering the test, the examiner discussed with the child issues connected with the child's stealing. Later, when questioned on the Comprehension subtest about finding someone's wallet, the child looked distressed, but the examiner did not recognize the distress. *Comment:* Be sensitive to nonverbal and verbal cues. An alert examiner would have said something like "Now, this question has nothing to do with our previous discussion. This is one of the questions I ask everyone." Or the examiner could have waited to discuss the potentially emotionally arousing "stealing" issue until *after* the child completed the test. Always consider how any discussion may affect rapport.

Example 2: Failure to recognize and stifle incongruent comments. The examiner wanted to say something supportive to the examinee after the Digit Span subtest, on which the examinee had obtained a low score. The examiner said, "Are you aware that you have a very good memory?" The child said, "No, I have a lousy one. I forget things all the time." *Comment:* Be sure that any reinforcing comments you make are congruent with the examinee's performance and are given at appropriate times. Also, praise the examinee's efforts, not his or her performance.

Example 3: Failure to follow standard procedures. The examiner watched a 10-year-old assemble the horse on the Object Assembly subtest, leaving one piece out. When the child said "Finished," the examiner pointed to the extra piece. The child quickly corrected the error and was given full credit. *Comment:* Do not give nonverbal cues, such as the one in this

Courtesy of David Wilcox.

example. Such cues are not part of the standard procedure, and their use may invalidate the test results.

Example 4: Failure to be neutral. Only when the child's arrangement on the Picture Arrangement subtest was correct did the examiner ask, "Finished?" If the child was still checking an incorrect sequence, the examiner was silent. The child soon caught on. *Comment:* Do not give verbal cues that may alert examinees to how well they are doing.

Example 5: Failure to follow directions. The examiner, noting that an examinee had misplaced only one block in a complicated design on the Block Design subtest, said, "Be sure to check your answer." *Comment:* Do not ad lib directions, especially when your comments may help the examinee obtain higher scores. Follow the directions in the WISC–III manual as closely as possible.

SHORT FORMS OF THE WISC–III

Short forms of the WISC–III (and other Wechsler scales) may be used for following reasons (Silverstein, 1990c):

- Screening purposes, when the short form may be followed by administration of the rest of the test
- Research purposes, to obtain an estimate of the intellectual level of an examinee
- A quick check on an examinee's intellectual status, when the obtained IQ is peripheral to the referral question

Ideally, selection of a short form should be based on (a) acceptable reliability and validity, (b) the ability of the short form to answer the referral question and provide clinically useful information, (c) the examinee's physical capabilities, and (d) the amount of time available for administering the test.

In research studies, short-form IQs often are evaluated by correlating them with Full Scale IQs, by examining mean differences between the two IQs, and by comparing the intelligence classifications provided by the two IQs. These three criteria, however, may not be useful for the following reasons. First, it is virtually certain that there will be high correlations between short-form and Full Scale IQs (Silverstein, 1990c). Second, with sufficiently large samples, a significant difference between short-form IQs and Full Scale IQs is likely to occur, thereby reducing the importance of this analysis. Third, it is likely that the short-form IQs and Full Scale IQs will yield different classifications. Goh (1978), for example, found that short-form WISC–R IQs misclassified 45% of a group of 142 children. Because of such findings, be sure to use other considerations to determine the appropriateness of a short form, such as (a) the reliability and validity of the short form, (b) examinee characteristics, and (c) time constraints. Also recognize that the use of a short form greatly magnifies any administrative errors or the effect of selecting an inappropriate subtest for a particular child. *If you need a classification for a clinical or psychoeducational purpose or need information for programming decisions, do* not *use a short form.*

Selecting the Short Form

Table A-16 in Appendix A lists the 10 most valid short-form combinations of two, three, four, and five WISC–III subtests, plus short forms for rapid screening and for examinees with a hearing impairment. The reliability and validity coefficients shown in Table A-16 were calculated using the standardization data and the Tellegen and Briggs (1967) procedure, which takes into account the reliabilities of the subtests used in the short form. Exhibit 8-4 shows the formulas used to compute the reliability and validity of the short-form combinations.

An inspection of the coefficients in Table A-16 indicates that the 10 best four- and five-subtest short-form combinations have validity coefficients of .90 or higher. The best three-subtest short-form combinations have validity coefficients of .87 to .89, while the best two-subtest short-form combinations have validity coefficients of .81 to .86. Overall, for the combinations shown in Table A-16, the more subtests used in the short form, the higher the validity and reliability of the estimated IQ.

Because the reliabilities and validities of the various short forms are high, clinical considerations also should guide you in selecting the short form. For example, if you want to use a four-subtest short form, consider selecting a combination of two Verbal Scale and two Performance Scale subtests to obtain some representation of both verbal and performance skills in the short form.

An examinee's physical capabilities also may guide you in selecting a short form. Examinees with marked visual impairment or severe motor dysfunction of the upper extremities will have difficulty with Performance Scale tasks. In such cases, the Verbal Scale (or subtests that form the Verbal Comprehension Index) serves as a useful short form. For examinees who are hearing impaired, the Performance Scale (or subtests that form the Perceptual Organization Index) alone is a useful short form. Administer these short forms by using the child's preferred mode of communication and, if possible, supplement your evaluation by using other tests designed to accommodate the special physical abilities of the child (see Chapter 16). The WISC–III short forms shown in Table 8-17 have been studied in various populations or proposed for various groups.

Converting Short-Form Scores into Deviation Quotients

After you administer the short form, you will need to convert the scaled scores to a Full Scale IQ estimate. Simple proration and regression procedures are not applicable in this case because they do not deal adequately with the problem of subtest reliability (Tellegen & Briggs, 1967). The more accept-

Table 8-17
WISC–III Short Forms That Have Been Studied or Proposed for Various Populations

Number of subtests	Subtests in short form	Population
2	Vocabulary and Block Design[a]	Clinical populations
	Information and Picture Completion[b]	Gifted
4	Similarities, Arithmetic, Picture Completion, and Block Design[c]	Clinical populations
5	Picture Completion, Information, Coding, Block Design, and Vocabulary[d]	Learning disabilities or gifted
6	Vocabulary, Similarities, Picture Completion, Block Design, Arithmetic, and Coding[e]	Clinical populations
	Similarities, Vocabulary, Picture Completion, Block Design, Arithmetic, and Digit Span[f]	Clinical populations
8	Information, Similarities, Vocabulary, Comprehension, Picture Completion, Picture Arrangement, Block Design, and Object Assembly[g]	All children
	Similarities, Vocabulary, Picture Completion, Block Design, Arithmetic, Digit Span, Coding, and Symbol Search[h]	Traumatic brain injury

[a]Campbell, 1998; Herrera-Graf, Dipert, and Hinton, 1996.
[b]Linville, Rust, and Kim, 1999.
[c]Kaufman, Kaufman, Balgopal, and McLean, 1996.
[d]Beal, Dumont, Branche, and Cruse, 1996; Dumont and Faro, 1993; Mark, Beal, and Dumont, 1998.
[e]Campbell, 1998.
[f]Donders, 1997.
[g]Prifitera et al., 1998.
[h]Donders and Warschausky, 1997.

able procedure is to transform the short-form scores into the familiar Wechsler-type Deviation Quotient, which has a mean of 100 and a standard deviation of 15. Exhibit 8-4 shows the procedure for converting the short-form scores into a Deviation Quotient. This procedure holds for all Wechsler tests. Although this approach does not eliminate the many problems associated with short forms, it is statistically appropriate for computing Full Scale IQs.

We used the Tellegen and Briggs (1967) procedure to obtain estimated WISC–III Deviation Quotients for the 10 best short-form dyads, triads, tetrads, and pentads (see Tables A-22, A-23, A-24, and A-25 in Appendix A, respectively). The notes in Tables A-22, A-23, A-24, and A-25 also describe other short-form

combinations, some of which are useful for screening hearing-impaired children. Table A-26 in Appendix A provides Deviation IQs for combinations of six, seven, and eight subtests, along with the reliability and validity for each combination.

Reduced-Item Short-Form Procedures

In the Yudin WISC–III short-form procedure (originally proposed by Yudin in 1966), every other item is administered on most subtests. Hobby (1980) described a short-form procedure (also applicable to the WISC–III) in which only odd items are administered on most subtests. It is similar to the Yudin procedure, but has more specific basal and ceiling procedures and correction factors. Research indicates that the Yudin procedure results in a moderate loss of validity and reliability, less reliable profile data, and IQs that differ from those obtained on the Full Scale (studies cited in Sattler, 1992).

Reduced-item short-form procedures also may be inappropriate to use as screening devices. It is difficult to imagine a situation in which administration of a reduced-item short form would be followed by administration of the remaining items in the original scale. However, a short form that uses all of the items in selected subtests can be useful as a screening instrument and, if necessary, be followed by other subtests.

Reduced-item short forms represent a *radical* departure from the standard administration. Because half of the items are excluded, the difficulty of the items increases more rapidly, while the opportunity for practice decreases equally rapidly (personal communication, Leslie Atkinson, January 1992). Research has usually involved administering the entire scale and generating validity coefficients only for the relevant half. This procedure is different from simply administering half of the items. For these reasons we recommend that reduced-item short forms *not* be used, and we therefore will not describe how to administer reduced-item short forms in this text.

Two Two-Subtest Short-Form Combinations

A two-subtest combination that is popular as a short-form screening instrument is Vocabulary plus Block Design. These two subtests have excellent reliability, correlate highly with the Full Scale over a wide age range, and are good measures of *g*. If this combination is chosen, Table A-22 in Appendix A can be used to convert the sum of scaled scores directly into an estimated Full Scale IQ. The composite has satisfactory reliability and validity ($r_{xx} = .91$ and $r = .86$).

Another useful two-subtest short form is Information plus Block Design. These two subtests also have moderate correlations with the Full Scale, have consistently high reliabilities, and are good measures of *g*. If this combination is chosen, Table A-22 in Appendix A can be used to convert the

Exhibit 8-4
Obtaining Deviation Quotients, Plus Reliability and Validity Coefficients, for Wechsler Short Forms

Computing the Deviation Quotient of the Short Form

The following formula is used to compute the Deviation Quotient for a short form:

$$\text{Deviation Quotient} = \left(\frac{15}{S_c}\right)(X_c - M_c) + 100$$

where
$S_c = S_s\sqrt{n + 2\Sigma r_{jk}}$ (standard deviation of composite score)
X_c = composite score (sum of subtest scaled scores in the short form)
M_c = normative mean, which is equal to $10n$
S_s = subtest standard deviation, which is equal to 3
n = number of component subtests
Σr_{jk} = sum of the correlations between component subtests

This equation considers the number of subtests in the short form, the correlations between the subtests, and the total scaled-score points obtained on the short form.

A more straightforward computational formula for obtaining the Deviation Quotient is as follows:

$$\text{Deviation Quotient} = (\text{composite score} \times a) + b$$

where
$a = \dfrac{15}{S_c}$

$b = \dfrac{100 - n(150)}{S_c}$

Table D-6 in Appendix D can be used in obtaining the appropriate a and b constants. In using Table D-6, first select the heading corresponding to the number of subtests in the short form. The first column under each heading is Σr_{jk}. This term represents the sum of the correlations between the subtests making up the composite score. To obtain Σr_{jk}, use the WISC–III correlation table for the group closest in age to the examinee (Tables C.1–C.12 on pages 270–281 of the WISC–III manual). With two subtests in the short form, only one correlation is needed. With three subtests in the short form, three correlations are summed (1 with 2, 1 with 3, and 2 with 3). With four subtests in the short form, six correlations are summed (1 with 2, 1 with 3, 1 with 4, 2 with 3, 2 with 4, and 3 with 4). With five subtests in the short form, 10 correlations are summed (1 with 2, 1 with 3, 1 with 4, 1 with 5, 2 with 3, 2 with 4, 2 with 5, 3 with 4, 3 with 5, and 4 with 5). After Σr_{jk} is calculated, the values for the two constants are obtained under the appropriate heading.

The procedure used to obtain the Deviation Quotient can be summarized as follows:

1. Sum the scaled scores of the subtests in the short form to obtain the composite score.
2. Sum the correlations between the subtests to obtain Σr_{jk}.
3. Find the appropriate a and b constants in Table D-6 in Appendix D after Σr_{jk} has been calculated.

4. Compute the Deviation Quotient by using the composite score and the a and b constants.

Example: A three-subtest short form composed of the Arithmetic, Vocabulary, and Block Design subtests is administered to a 6-year-old child. The child obtains scaled scores of 7, 12, and 13 on the three subtests. The four steps are as follows:

1. The three scaled scores are summed to yield a composite score of 32.
2. The correlations between the three subtests are obtained from Table C.1 (page 270) of the WISC–III manual (Arithmetic and Vocabulary, .50; Arithmetic and Block Design, .51; Vocabulary and Block Design, .53). These are summed to yield 1.54 (Σr_{jk}).
3. The appropriate row in Table D-6 in Appendix D is the third one under the heading "3 Subtests." The values for the constants a and b are 2.0 and 40, respectively.
4. The formula

$$\text{Deviation Quotient} = (\text{composite score} \times a) + b$$

is used to obtain a Deviation Quotient of 104:

$$104 = (32 \times 2.0) + 40$$

Computing the Reliability Coefficient of the Short Form

The following formula is used to obtain the reliability of the short form:

$$r_{ss} = \frac{\Sigma r_{ii} + 2\Sigma r_{ij}}{k + \Sigma 2r_{ij}}$$

where
r_{ss} = reliability of the short form
r_{ii} = reliability of subtest i
r_{ij} = correlation between any subtests i and j
k = number of component subtests

Example: The reliability of the two-subtest combination of Vocabulary and Block Design is calculated in the following way, given r_{ii} (Vocabulary) = .87, r_{ii} (Block Design) = .87, and r_{ij} (Vocabulary and Block Design) = .46:

$$r_{ss} = \frac{1.74 + .92}{2 + .92} = \frac{2.66}{2.92} = .91$$

Computing the Validity Coefficient of the Short Form

The following formula is used to obtain the validity of the short form:

$$r'_{pw} = \frac{\Sigma\Sigma r_{jl}}{\sqrt{k + 2\Sigma r_{ij}}\sqrt{t + 2\Sigma r_{lm}}}$$

where
r'_{pw} = modified coefficient of correlation between the composite part and the composite whole

(Continued)

Exhibit 8-4 *(Continued)*

r_{jl} = correlation between any subtest j included in the part and any subtest l included in the whole, where any included correlation between a subtest and itself is represented by its reliability coefficient

r_{ij} = correlation between subtests i and j

r_{lm} = correlation between subtests l and m

k = number of component subtests

t = number of subtests included in the whole

To obtain $\Sigma\Sigma r_{jl}$, total the following three sums: (a) the sum of the reliabilities of the component subtests, (b) twice the sum of the intercorrelations among the component subtests

$(2\Sigma r_{ij})$, and (c) the sum of the intercorrelations between any component subtest and any noncomponent subtest.

Example: The validity of the two-subtest combination of Vocabulary and Block Design is calculated in the following way, given r_{ii} (Vocabulary) = .87, r_{ii} (Block Design) = .87, and r_{ij} (Vocabulary and Block Design) = .46. In this example, all 13 WISC–III subtests are used; in other cases, only the 10 standard subtests may be used.

$$r'_{pw} = \frac{1.74 + .92 + 9.74}{\sqrt{2 + 2(.46)}\sqrt{13 + 2(28.91)}}$$

$$= \frac{12.40}{(1.71)(8.42)} = \frac{12.40}{14.40} = .86$$

Source: Adapted from Tellegen and Briggs (1967).

---

sum of scaled scores directly into an estimated Full Scale IQ. The composite has satisfactory reliability and validity (r_{xx} = .90 and r = .85).

Two Four-Subtest Short-Form Combinations

Two excellent four-subtest short forms are (a) Information, Vocabulary, Block Design, and Symbol Search and (b) Arithmetic, Vocabulary, Block Design, and Symbol Search. Both of these combinations contain two Verbal Scale subtests and two Performance Scale subtests. The composites for both forms have satisfactory reliability and validity (r_{xx} = .93 and r = .91; r_{xx} = .92 and r = .90, respectively). These short forms take longer to administer than the two-subtest short forms described above, but they can provide more clinical and diagnostic information (e.g., additional information about concentration and attention). You can use Table A-24 in Appendix A to convert the sum of scaled scores on these two four-subtest short forms directly into an estimated Deviation Quotient. You also can use these short forms to obtain estimated Deviation IQs for the Verbal Scale (e.g., Information and Vocabulary) and Performance Scale (e.g., Block Design and Symbol Search) (see Table A-22 in Appendix A).

One Six-Subtest Short-Form Combination

A six-subtest short-form combination that consists of Information, Similarities, Vocabulary, Picture Completion, Block Design, and Object Assembly is useful to obtain the Verbal Comprehension Index score (Information, Similarities, and Vocabulary), the Perceptual Organization Index score (Picture Completion, Block Design, and Object Assembly), and

an estimated Deviation Quotient for the entire scale. The composite has satisfactory reliability and validity (r_{xx} = .95 and r = .91). You can use Table A-26 in Appendix A to convert the sums of scaled scores on these six subtests into an estimated Deviation Quotient. Table A-23 in Appendix A provides the estimated Deviation Quotients for the Verbal Comprehension Index score and the Perceptual Organization Index score.

One Seven-Subtest Short-Form Combination

A useful seven-subtest short-form combination is Information, Similarities, Vocabulary, Comprehension, Picture Completion, Block Design, and Object Assembly. The composite has satisfactory reliability and validity (r_{xx} = .95 and r = .91). Table A-26 in Appendix A can be used to convert the sums of the scaled scores on these seven subtests into an estimated Full Scale IQ. To obtain an estimated Deviation IQ for the Verbal Scale and the Performance Scale, consult Table A-24 in Appendix A for the Verbal Scale (four subtests) and Table A-23 in Appendix A for the Performance Scale (three subtests).

Two Eight-Subtest Short-Form Combinations

One useful eight-subtest short-form combination is Information, Similarities, Vocabulary, Comprehension, Picture Completion, Picture Arrangement, Block Design, and Object Assembly. The composite has satisfactory reliability and validity (r_{xx} = .95 and r = .92). Table A-26 in Appendix A can be used to convert the sum of the scaled scores on these eight subtests into an estimated Full Scale IQ. To obtain an estimated Deviation IQ for the Verbal Scale and the Performance Scale, consult Table A-24 in Appendix A for both the Verbal Scale (four subtests) and the Performance Scale (four subtests). Prifitera et al. (1998) refer to this short form as the "General Ability Index."

Another useful eight-subtest short-form combination is Information, Arithmetic, Vocabulary, Digit Span, Coding, Block Design, Object Assembly, and Symbol Search. This composite has satisfactory reliability and validity (r_{xx} = .95 and r = .93). Table A-26 in Appendix A can be used to convert the sum of the scaled scores on these eight subtests into an estimated Full Scale IQ. To obtain an estimated Deviation IQ for the Verbal Scale and the Performance Scale, consult Table A-24 in Appendix A. To obtain an estimated Deviation Quotient for both the Freedom from Distractibility Index and the Processing Speed Index, see Table A-22 in Appendix A.

Short Forms for Quick Administration and Scoring

If you want to give a short form that can be administered quickly and scored relatively easily, consider the following combinations (reliabilities shown in parentheses): two subtests—Information and Picture Completion (r_{tt} =.88; r = .79); three subtests—Information, Arithmetic, and Picture Completion (r_{xx} = .90; r = .85); and four subtests—Information, Arithmetic, Picture Completion, and Coding (r_{xx} = .90; r = .88). These short forms, although they do not fall into the 10-best-combinations category, are effective as screening tools and have in their favor, as noted earlier, quick administration with a minimum of scoring problems. You can use Tables A-22, A-23, and A-24 in Appendix A, respectively, to convert the sum of scaled scores on these combinations directly to an estimated Deviation Quotient. The footnotes at the bottoms of these tables indicate which columns to use to obtain estimated Deviation Quotients for these short-form combinations.

A word of caution is in order, however: Even though the Information and Picture Completion short form takes less time to administer and is easier to score than Vocabulary and Block Design, you do not gain any information about how the child copes with a less structured task (Vocabulary) or uses problem-solving strategies (Block Design) when you use this short form. For the extra time involved, you will obtain more valuable clinical information by using Vocabulary and Block Design in a two-subtest short form (or in a longer short-form combination). We recommend that you consider using Vocabulary and Block Design in a short form if you need to administer one.

Short-Form Subtest Scatter

Tables A-17 to A-21 in Appendix A show whether the observed scatter (the highest scaled score minus the lowest scaled score) on all the short forms in Table A-16 in Appen-

dix A (a) represents a reliable scaled-score range and (b) is unusual. Table A-16 indicates that in the two-subtest short form composed of Vocabulary and Block Design, a range of 4 points between the two scores represents a reliable scaled-score range (i.e., a range of 4 or greater represents nonchance difference at the .05 level). A range of 6 (or more) occurs in less than 10% of the population and should be considered unusual. Less credence can be placed in the estimated short-form IQ when the scatter is larger than expected.

Comment on Short Forms of the WISC–III (and Short Forms of Other Tests as Well)

Short forms save time and are useful screening devices, but they have certain disadvantages.

1. IQs are less stable with short forms than with the full battery of subtests.
2. Information is lost about cognitive strengths and weaknesses, as well as about the pattern of variability among subtest scaled scores.
3. The opportunity to observe the examinee's problem-solving methods over a range of situations is lost.
4. Information about nonverbal ability is lost when you administer short forms composed of Verbal Scale subtests only, and information about verbal ability is lost when you administer short forms composed of Performance Scale subtests only.
5. The internal consistency reliability of the IQ is reduced when short forms are used.

If you are thinking about using a short form, weigh the time saved against the validity lost. In addition, consider what kind of decision you will make based on the short-form scores. The most efficient testing strategy for a particular situation will depend, in part, on the goal of the evaluation—whether it is for a general assessment of intelligence, classification, selection, or screening.

Even when you administer all of the subtests, the IQ you obtain on any intelligence test is merely an *estimate* of the cognitive abilities possessed by a child. When you use only a few subtests, the estimate may be far less adequate than that provided by the Full Scale. Educational and clinical situations call for more, rather than less, extensive cognitive evaluation. Consequently, administer the Full Scale to increase the diagnostic information you can obtain and to reduce placement errors, unless there is some compelling reason to administer a short form. Compelling reasons might be situations in which (a) the examinee is ready to quit testing, (b) the physical capabilities of the examinee make some subtests inappropriate, or (c) in-depth testing is not needed for a reevaluation and no change of placement or eligibility for a special education program is being contemplated. *We do not recommend short forms for placement, educational, or clinical decision-making purposes.*

The Psychological Corporation (1999) publishes an abbreviated Wechsler test, called the Wechsler Abbreviated Scale of Intelligence (WASI), that covers ages 6 years to 89 years. It contains four subtests—Vocabulary, Similarities, Block Design, and Matrix Reasoning—and is described more fully in Chapter 16. This test also may be used for screening purposes.

CHOOSING BETWEEN THE WISC–III AND THE WPPSI–R AND BETWEEN THE WISC–III AND THE WAIS–III

The WISC–III overlaps with the WPPSI–R for ages 6–0–0 to 7–3–15 and with the WAIS–III for ages 16–0–0 to 16–11–30. The overlap in ages between the WISC–III and the WPPSI–R and between the WISC–III and the WAIS–III is especially helpful in retest situations. For example, a child first administered the WISC–III at age 6 years can be retested with the WPPSI–R at any time during the next 15 months. Similarly, a 16-year-old who initially was given the WAIS–III can be retested with the WISC–III up until his or her 17th birthday. However, because the WISC–III and the WPPSI–R share many items, the two tests are not truly independent instruments.

In the overlapping age ranges, Atkinson (personal communications, January 1992 and April 1998) compared the WISC–III with the WPPSI–R and the WISC–III with the WAIS–III on several criteria, including mean subtest reliability, Full Scale reliability, mean subtest floor (mean number of correct items needed to obtain a scaled score of 1), mean subtest ceiling (mean number of correct items needed to obtain the highest scaled score), item gradients (number of correct items needed to go from the floor to the mean and from the mean to the ceiling, the relationship of raw-score points to scaled-score points), Full Scale floor, and Full Scale ceiling. Let us now discuss Atkinson's recommendations.

WISC–III vs. WPPSI–R

The child's age and ability level should be taken into account in choosing between the WISC–III and the WPPSI–R.

a. *For ages 6–0 to 6–11,* the WISC–III and WPPSI–R are comparable in all respects except for measures of item gradients. Item gradient statistics suggest the following:
  • The WPPSI–R is a better choice for children with below-average ability.
  • The WISC–III is a better choice for children with above-average ability.
  • Either test is adequate for children with average ability.

b. *For ages 7–0 to 7–3,* the WISC–III has superior subtest reliabilities, higher subtest ceilings, and better item gradients both above and below the mean. In other respects, the two tests are comparable. Therefore,

• The WISC–III is a better choice for all children at ages 7–0 to 7–3.

The following example illustrates how you can obtain a more thorough sampling on the WPPSI–R than on the WISC–III for a 6-year-old child with below-average ability. To obtain a scaled score of 5 on Information, a 6-year-old child needs a raw score of 16 on the WPPSI–R but a raw score of only 2 on the WISC–III.

Atkinson's recommendations differ somewhat from those presented in the WISC–III manual. The WISC–III manual (page 8) recommends that for all overlapping ages you use the WISC–III for children with average or above-average ability and the WPPSI–R for children with below-average ability. We suggest that you follow Atkinson's recommendations.

WISC–III vs. WAIS–III

Atkinson makes the following recommendations:

• The WISC–III is a better choice for adolescents with below-average ability.
• Either test is adequate for adolescents with average ability.
• The WAIS–III is a better choice for adolescents with above-average ability.

The following example illustrates how you can obtain a more thorough sampling on the WISC–III than on the WAIS–III for an adolescent aged 16–8 with below-average ability. On Information, to obtain a scaled score of 5, the adolescent needs a raw score of 14 on the WISC–III but a raw score of only 5 on the WAIS–III.

Comment on Choosing Between the WISC–III and the WPPSI–R or Between the WISC–III and the WAIS–III

Atkinson's recommendations are based on internal psychometric data. However, we still need to address the issue of validity. In addition, the WAIS–III has some additional advantages when compared with the WISC–III, such as (a) two new subtests (Matrix Reasoning and Letter-Number Sequencing) and (b) newer norms. In the final analysis, the choice of a test in the overlapping ages should depend on the validity of the inferences you can make from the scores. To this end, we need additional validity studies that compare the WISC–III with the WPPSI–R and the WISC–III with the WAIS–III in their overlapping age ranges, using samples of both normal and exceptional children.

ADMINISTERING THE WECHSLER TESTS TO CHILDREN WITH DISABILITIES

You will need to evaluate the sensorimotor abilities of children with disabilities before you administer a Wechsler test (or any test). If you find that the child has a visual, hearing, or motor problem that may interfere with his or her ability to take one or more subtests, do not administer those subtests. Table 8-18 shows the physical abilities needed to take a Wechsler test. Obviously, if you give the directions aloud, the child must be able to hear what you say. On most of the Performance subtests, the child must be able to see the items and use his or her hands to solve the problems.

If you want to administer a Wechsler test to a child with a physical disability, you will need to administer the subtests without providing cues to the child. If your modifications go beyond simply permitting the child to respond in her or his

preferred mode of communication or using alternative procedures to present the items, the results may be invalid.

Verbal Scale Subtests

You can administer all of the Verbal Scale subtests aloud to a child whose hearing is intact. If the child cannot hear but can read, you can type the Information, Comprehension, Similarities, and Vocabulary questions on cards and show the cards to the child, one at a time. However, visually presenting the Arithmetic and Digit Span items poses more difficulties because time limits are involved in the Arithmetic subtest and because visual presentation of the items is quite different from oral presentation, especially with Digit Span. In addition, the child needs to be able to read for this mode of presentation. Therefore, you may have to omit Digit Span when you test children with a hearing impairment. If you do so, make a note of the omission in your report. If the child cannot respond by speaking, you can accept written replies (or those typed on a typewriter or computer) to any of the Verbal Scale subtests.

Performance Scale Subtests

Adaptations of the Performance Scale subtests center on the child's method of responding. You can give the Picture Completion subtest to a child who has adequate vision and who can describe the missing part either orally or in writing (or typed on a typewriter or computer) or by pointing to it. It is sometimes helpful to provide the examinee with a small, pointed stick that is soft and dull enough not to mar the pictures. You cannot easily adapt Block Design, Object Assembly, Coding, Digit Symbol (WAIS–III), Mazes, Animal Pegs (WPPSI–R), or Geometric Design (WPPSI–R) for a child whose arm-hand use is severely impaired. However, you can adapt the Picture Arrangement subtest for a child who has an arm-hand impairment. On this subtest, ask the child to tell you the order that he or she wants. The child can do this, for example, orally or by writing or typing. You can adapt Symbol Search by pointing to each item and having the child say, type, or indicate by head movements whether the symbol is or is not in the array. Table A-15 in Appendix A provides detailed instructions for administering the WISC–III Performance Scale subtests to a child who is hearing impaired.

Table 8-18
Physical Abilities Necessary and Adaptable for Subtests on the Wechsler Scales

Subtest	Physical ability			
	Vision	Hearing	Oral speech	Arm-hand use
Information	S	A	A	W
Comprehension	S	A	A	W
Arithmetic	S	A	A	W
Similarities	S	A	A	W
Vocabulary	S	A	A	W
Digit Span	N	R	A	W
Picture Completion	R	A	O	P or W
Coding, Digit Sym[a]	R	A	N	R
Picture Arrangement	R	A	O	A
Block Design	R	A	N	R
Object Assembly	R	A	N	R
Symbol Search	R	A	O	P or W
Mazes	R	A	N	R
Sentences	S	A	A	W
Animal Pegs	R	A	O	A
Geometric Design	R	A	N	R

Note. The codes are as follows:

A—This ability is required for standard administration, but the subtest is adaptable.

N—This ability is not required.

O—Examinees who are able to speak can say their answers.

P—Examinees who are able to point can point to their answers.

R—This ability is required. Adaptation is not feasible if this function is absent or more than mildly impaired.

S—Examinees who are able to read can be shown the questions. If the examinee cannot read, hearing is necessary. If neither the ability to read nor the ability to hear is present, the subtest should not be administered.

W—Examinees who are able to write can write their answers.

[a]Digit Sym = Digit Symbol—Coding.

Advantages of Two Separate Scales

The division of the Wechsler subtests into a Verbal Scale and a Performance Scale is helpful in testing children with disabilities. You can administer the Verbal Scale to a child with a visual impairment or to a child with severe motor disabilities. And you can administer the Performance Scale to a child with a hearing impairment or to a child who has little or no speech. If you also administer the Verbal Scale to a child with a hearing impairment, you can compare the child's performance on the Verbal Scale and the Performance Scale to evaluate the child's verbal deficit. *In such cases, however, do not include the Verbal Scale in the computation of the IQ; use only the Performance Scale as the best estimate of the child's intellectual ability.*

Unknown Effects of Modifications

Without empirical findings, there is no way to know how the suggested modifications affect the reliability and validity of the scores. Yet, when you cannot follow standard procedures because disabilities prevent the child from comprehending the instructions or manipulating the materials, you will need to use modifications if you want to administer the test. *When you use modifications, consider the resulting score as only an approximation of the score that the child might obtain under standardized procedures.* You should describe any modifications of test procedures in the psychological or psychoeducational report.

ASSETS OF THE WISC–III

The WISC–III is a well-standardized test, with excellent reliability and adequate concurrent and construct validity. The 13 subtests are divided into a Verbal Scale section and a Performance Scale section. A valuable feature of the test is that all children take a comparable battery of subtests. The following are specific assets of the WISC–III:

1. *Excellent standardization.* The standardization procedures were excellent, sampling four geographical regions, both sexes, the major ethnic groups (Euro American, African American, Hispanic American, and Other), and the entire socioeconomic status range. The standardization group well represents the nation as a whole for the age groups covered by the test.

2. *Excellent overall psychometric properties.* The WISC–III has excellent reliability for the IQs generated by the Verbal Scale, Performance Scale, and Full Scale. Studies suggest that the WISC–III has adequate validity.

3. *Useful diagnostic information.* The WISC–III provides diagnostic information useful for the assessment of cognitive abilities of elementary- and high-school-age children who are functioning within four standard deviations from the mean (± 4 *SD*). It also provides data likely to be helpful in planning special school programs, perhaps tapping important developmental or maturational factors needed for school success, especially in the lower grades. The Verbal Scale IQ, Performance Scale IQ, and index scores are helpful in clinical and psychoeducational work and aid in the assessment of brain-behavior relationships.

4. *Good administration procedures.* The procedures described in the WISC–III manual for administering the test are excellent. The examiner actively probes the child's

responses to evaluate the breadth of the child's knowledge and to determine whether the child really knows the answer. On items that require two reasons for maximum credit, the examiner asks the child for another reason when only one reason is given. These procedures ensure that the test does not penalize the child for failing to understand the demands of the questions. The emphasis on probing questions and queries is extremely desirable.

5. *Good manual and interesting test materials.* The WISC–III manual is easy to use; it provides clear directions and tables. Examiners are aided by instructions printed in a color that differs from that of other text material. The test materials also are interesting to children.

6. *Helpful scoring criteria.* The scoring criteria generally are helpful. The Similarities and Vocabulary scoring guidelines, for example, detail the rationale for 2-, 1-, and 0-point scores. Several examples demonstrate the application of the scoring principles. The scoring guidelines present several examples, and those that must be queried are indicated by a "(Q)."

7. *Usefulness for children with disabilities.* You can administer the Verbal Scale alone to children who have visual or motor impairments and the Performance Scale alone to children who are hearing impaired.

8. *Extensive research and clinical literature base.* There is a vast amount of research and case material concerning the WISC–III (and prior editions of the test) that is useful in interpreting the test.

LIMITATIONS OF THE WISC–III

Although the WISC–III is overall an excellent instrument, some problems do exist.

1. *Limited floor and ceiling.* The test is not applicable for extremely low or extremely high functioning children.

2. *Low reliability of individual subtests.* Reliability coefficients for the individual subtests are lower than .80 at most ages, and when the reliabilities are lower than .80 the scores may not be dependable. In addition, during the standardization of the scale The Psychological Corporation did not obtain test-retest scores for the Coding and Symbol Search subtests for each age level of the test; therefore, we do not know the accuracy of the reliability estimates (these are based on adjacent ages) for the ages at which the two subtests were not readministered.

3. *Nonuniformity of subtest scaled scores.* Because the range of scaled scores on all subtests is less than 19 at some of the older ages, there may be some minor problems in profile analysis at the upper extremes of scores. All subtests, however, do have a range of at least 1 to 17 for all ages.

4. *Difficulty in interpreting norms when a supplementary subtest is substituted for a regular subtest.* With the norms based on only the 10 standard subtests, there is no way of knowing precisely what the scores mean when one of the

supplementary subtests (Digit Span, Mazes, or Symbol Search) is substituted for a regular subtest. Make a substitution of this kind, therefore, only in unusual circumstances, and label the results "tentative" when you report the scores.

5. *Possible difficulties in scoring responses.* Work with the WISC–R suggests that Similarities, Vocabulary, and Comprehension may be difficult to score. The WISC–III manual cites a study in which there was high agreement among examiners in the scores they gave to these subtests (and to the Mazes subtest as well). These results are encouraging, but additional studies are needed. We recommend that you consult colleagues if you are uncertain about scoring responses.

6. *Large practice effects on the Performance Scale.* The large practice effects on the Performance Scale, close to one standard deviation, suggest that the WISC–III may give misleading scores in retest situations. This is especially true when the retest interval is less than 9 weeks. The implication is that the WISC–III may not be useful for gauging change and progress in children retested within a short time. (See Chapter 4 for further information about practice effects or repeated evaluations.) Think carefully about whether you want to use the WISC–III for a retest when you have previously given the test, and consider what the retest results may mean if you readminister the test.

7. *Lack of independence of some items in the WISC–III and WPPSI–R.* At least 23 items overlap on the WISC–III and WPPSI–R, primarily on the Information, Vocabulary, Picture Completion, and Mazes subtests. This overlap is unfortunate for at least two reasons. First, it means that the WISC–III and WPPSI–R are not independent parallel forms at the overlapping age levels (6–0 to 7–3 years). Second, it means that children tested with the WPPSI–R and then with the WISC–III (or vice versa) may have an advantage on the second test because of practice effects. There should be no overlapping items on the WISC–III and WPPSI–R.

8. *Problems for children who do not place a premium on speed.* Because several of the subtests reward speed (all Performance Scale subtests and also the Arithmetic subtest), the test may penalize children who are from ethnic groups that do not place a premium on speed (see Chapter 19) or who work in a slow, deliberate, or thoughtful manner.

9. *Poor quality of some test materials.* The templates on the Coding and Symbol Search subtests are poorly constructed and may rip (Danielson, 1991). In addition, the puzzle pieces used in the Object Assembly subtest are of light construction and have a tendency to be jarred apart as the examinee adds additional pieces to each puzzle. The pieces on the horse puzzle are gray on both sides; this can cause confusion and increase assembly time for children who inadvertently turn over one of the pieces.

CONCLUDING COMMENT ON THE WISC–III

The WISC–III has been well received by those who use tests to evaluate children's and adolescents' intellectual ability. It has excellent standardization, reliability, and concurrent and construct validity, and useful administrative and scoring guidelines are provided. The manual is outstanding, and much thought and preparation have gone into the revision. The WISC–III will likely serve as a valuable instrument in the assessment of children's intelligence for many years to come.

THINKING THROUGH THE ISSUES

1. Although the concept behind the Wechsler tests was by no means unique when Wechsler developed the tests, the tests did make a substantial impact on the assessment field. Why do you think the Wechsler tests were so successful as clinical assessment instruments?

2. The Wechsler tests do not provide interchangeable scores. What problems do you foresee in using different Wechsler tests with children in the overlapping ages when two Wechsler tests are appropriate?

3. When would you use the WISC–III index scores?

4. How would you explain why the WISC–III Verbal Scale subtests are better measures of *g* than the Performance Scale subtests are?

5. What can you do to develop proper WISC–III administrative techniques?

AND ANOTHER THING... SOMETIMES I THINK YOU LOVE THIS WISC MORE THAN YOU LOVE ME!

THAT'S ABSURD!.... I RESPECT IT... I VALUE IT... I TRUST IT...BUT LOVE IT?.... NO. ABSOLUTELY NOT!

HERM

IT WAS JUST A TYPICAL MARITAL SPAT IN THE LIFE OF A TYPICAL SCHOOL PSYCHOLOGIST

Courtesy of Herman Zielinski.

6. When do you think WISC–III short forms would be appropriate to use?

7. How might the limitations of the WISC–III affect its clinical usefulness?

Question: What letter comes after T?
Answer: Well, that's easy—V.

SUMMARY

1. The WISC–III was published in 1991, 17 years after the previous edition, called the WISC–R.

2. The WISC–III contains 13 subtests that make up a Verbal Scale and a Performance Scale.

3. The five subtests in the Verbal Scale are Information, Similarities, Arithmetic, Vocabulary, and Comprehension.

4. The five subtests in the Performance Scale are Picture Completion, Coding, Picture Arrangement, Block Design, and Object Assembly.

5. The three remaining subtests—Digit Span in the Verbal Scale and Symbol Search and Mazes in the Performance Scale—are designated as supplementary subtests.

Standardization of the WISC–III

6. The WISC–III was standardized on 2,200 children who were selected to be representative of children in the United States.

Deviation IQs, Scaled Scores, and Test-Age Equivalents

7. The WISC–III, like the WPPSI–R and WAIS–III, uses the Deviation IQ ($M = 100$, $SD = 15$) for the Verbal, Performance, and Full Scale IQs and scaled scores ($M = 10$, $SD = 3$) for the 13 individual subtests.

8. Because a scaled score of 10 represents the mean, the test-age equivalents of the raw scores reflect the average score for each specific age group.

9. The WISC–III test-age equivalent scores can be compared with mental-age or test-age scores from other tests.

Reliability of the WISC–III

10. The WISC–III has outstanding reliability. For example, the Full Scale, Verbal Scale, and Performance Scale have internal consistency reliability coefficients of .89 or above over the entire age range covered in the standardization group.

11. Average internal consistency reliability coefficients, based on the 11 age groups, are .96 for the Full Scale IQ, .95 for the Verbal Scale IQ, and .91 for the Performance Scale IQ.

12. The internal consistency reliabilities for the subtests are lower than those for the Verbal Scale, Performance Scale, and Full Scale.

13. The average standard errors of measurement (SEMs) in IQ points are 3.20 for the Full Scale, 3.53 for the Verbal Scale, and 4.54 for the Performance Scale.

14. Test-retest reliability coefficients indicate that the WISC–III provides stable IQs for the Full Scale and Verbal Scale, but less

stable IQs for the Performance Scale because of practice effects.

15. The stability coefficients for the subtests ranged from a low of .54 for Mazes at 14–15 years to a high of .93 for Vocabulary at 14–15 years.

16. On average, from the first to the second testing, the Full Scale IQ increased by 7.0 to 8.4 points, the Verbal Scale IQ increased by 1.7 to 3.3 points, and the Performance Scale IQ increased by 11.5 to 13.5 points.

17. Large retest gains on the Performance Scale are a major concern in interpreting the results when the WISC–III is readministered after a period of only 2 to 9 weeks. For periods longer than 9 weeks, gains on retest are likely to be lower because practice effects tend to diminish over time.

18. Use the child's specific age group—not the average of the 11 age groups—to obtain the most accurate confidence interval.

Validity of the WISC–III

19. Mean correlations between the WISC–III Full Scale and other measures are $r = .72$ with other intelligence tests, $r = .71$ with the Peabody Picture Vocabulary Test, $r = .54$ with measures of reading achievement, and $r = .64$ with measures of arithmetic achievement.

20. Studies indicate that the WISC–III generally yields IQs that are about 6 IQ points lower than those of the WISC–R.

21. WISC–III IQs are about 4.0 points higher than WPPSI–R IQs.

22. Research suggests that the WISC–III and WAIS–III yield comparable IQs, although scores on the WISC–III tend to be slightly lower.

23. You should not consider the WISC–III and WPPSI–R or the WISC–III and WAIS–III to be parallel forms in the overlapping age groups.

24. There is strong evidence that the WISC–III yields both a measure of general intelligence and specific factors, as noted in studies reported in the WISC–III manual and in the research literature. However, there is a difference of opinion about how many specific factors the test yields (e.g., three or four specific factors).

Intercorrelations Between Subtests and Scales

25. Intercorrelations between WISC–III subtests and scales indicate that, in the total group, correlations between the 13 subtests range from a low of .14 (Mazes and Digit Span) to a high of .70 (Vocabulary and Information; $Mdn\ r = .355$).

26. In the total group, the Verbal Scale subtests correlate more highly with each other ($Mdn\ r = .55$) than do the Performance Scale subtests ($Mdn\ r = .33$).

WISC–III and Parent Education

27. Children whose parents had a college education had higher mean WISC–III IQs (M IQ = 106.01) than children whose parents had a ninth-grade education or less (M IQ = 86.38)—a difference of about 20 points.

WISC–III and Ethnic Status

28. Mean IQs of Euro American children on the WISC–III were about 15 points higher than those of African American children

and about 9 points higher than those of Hispanic American children.

Factor Analysis of the WISC–III

29. The results of a factor analysis indicate that a four-factor model best describes the WISC–III: Verbal Comprehension (Information, Similarities, Vocabulary, Comprehension), Perceptual Organization (Picture Completion, Picture Arrangement, Block Design, Object Assembly), Freedom from Distractibility (Arithmetic, Digit Span), and Processing Speed (Coding, Symbol Search).

30. The WISC–III subtests form three clusters with respect to the measurement of *g*: Vocabulary, Information, Similarities, Block Design, Arithmetic, and Comprehension are *good* measures of *g*; Object Assembly, Picture Completion, Symbol Search, Picture Arrangement, and Digit Span are *fair* measures of *g*; Coding and Mazes are *poor* measures of *g*.

Range of Subtest Scale Scores

31. The WISC–III provides a range of scaled scores from 1 to 19. However, this range is not possible for all subtests at all ages of the test, particularly at 6 years and at 11 through 16 years.

Range of Full Scale IQs

32. The range of WISC–III Full Scale IQs is 40 to 160. This range is insufficient for children who are extremely low or extremely high functioning and is not available at all ages of the test.

Administering the WISC–III

33. Common problems encountered by beginning examiners when they administer the WISC–III and other intelligence tests (as applicable) include problems related to establishing rapport, speech, layout of test materials, test administration, and scoring.

34. To ensure that scoring is standardized at the starting and discontinuance points, credit any items failed below the starting-point items when the child passes the starting-point items, and do not credit any items passed above the discontinuance-point items when the child fails the discontinuance-point items.

35. The WISC–III requires the use of many probing questions and queries. Spoiled responses are scored 0.

36. Certain modifications in test procedures have been found to increase children's scores on the WISC–R. Similar modifications probably will affect WISC–III scores. Use such modifications only *after* the standard administration.

Short Forms of the WISC–III

37. Short forms of the WISC–III (and other Wechsler scales) may be used for (a) screening purposes, when the short form may be followed by administration of the rest of the test; (b) research purposes, to obtain an estimate of the intellectual level of an examinee; or (c) a quick check on an examinee's intellectual status, when the obtained IQ is peripheral to the referral question.

38. In comparison with the Full Scale IQ, short-form IQs may be less stable, impede profile analysis, and result in misclassifications. Do not use short forms for any placement, educational, or clinical decision-making purpose.

Choosing Between the WISC–III and the WPPSI–R and Between the WISC–III and the WAIS–III

39. For ages 6–0 to 6–11, the WPPSI–R is a better choice than the WISC–III for children with below-average ability, the WISC–III is a better choice than the WPPSI–R for children with above-average ability, and either test is adequate for children with average ability. For ages 7–0 to 7–3, the WISC–III is a better choice for all children than the WPPSI–R.

40. The WISC–III is a better choice than the WAIS–III for adolescents with below-average ability, either test is adequate for adolescents with average ability, and the WAIS–III is a better choice than the WISC–III for adolescents with above-average ability.

Administering the Wechsler Tests to Children with Disabilities

41. You will need to evaluate the sensorimotor abilities of children with disabilities before you administer a Wechsler test (or any test). If you find that the child has a visual, hearing, or motor problem that may interfere with his or her ability to take one or more subtests, do not administer those subtests.

42. If you want to administer a Wechsler test to a child with a physical disability, you will need to administer the subtests without providing cues to the child. If your modifications go beyond simply permitting the child to respond in her or his preferred mode of communication or using alternative procedures to present the items, the results may be invalid.

Assets of the WISC–III

43. The strengths of the WISC–III include excellent standardization, useful diagnostic information, good administration procedures, good manual and interesting test materials, helpful scoring criteria, usefulness for children with disabilities, and extensive research and clinical literature base.

Limitations of the WISC–III

44. The limitations of the WISC–III include limited floor and ceiling, low reliability of individual subtests, nonuniformity of subtest scaled scores, difficulty in interpreting norms when a supplementary subtest is substituted for a regular subtest, possible difficulties in scoring responses, large practice effects on the Performance Scale, lack of independence of some items in the WISC–III and WPPSI–R, problems for children who do not place a premium on speed, and poor quality of some test materials.

Concluding Comment on the WISC–III

45. The WISC–III will likely serve as a valuable instrument in the assessment of children's intelligence for many years to come.

KEY TERMS, CONCEPTS, AND NAMES

WISC–III (p. 221)
WISC–III Verbal Scale (p. 221)
WISC–III Performance Scale (p. 221)

STUDY QUESTIONS

1. Discuss the WISC–III. Include in your discussion the following issues: standardization, Deviation IQs, test-age equivalents, reliability, and validity.
2. Explain two procedures for developing confidence intervals.
3. Describe and interpret the intercorrelations between WISC–III subtests and scales.
4. Describe and interpret WISC–III factor analytic findings.
5. Discuss administrative considerations when using the WISC–III.
6. Discuss WISC–III short forms, including their values and limitations.
7. For overlapping ages, explain how you would go about choosing between the WISC–III and the WPPSI–R and between the WISC–III and the WAIS–III.
8. Identify the most important factors to consider in administering the WISC–III (and other Wechsler tests) to children with disabilities.
9. Discuss the strengths and limitations of the WISC–III.
10. Identify common administrative and scoring errors on the WISC–III, and describe what measures you could take to minimize and avoid these mistakes.

9

WISC–III SUBTESTS

by Jerome M. Sattler and Donald H. Saklofske

Wit is brushwood, judgment is timber. The first makes the brightest flame, but the other gives the most lasting heat.
—Hebrew proverb

The knowledge of words is the gate to scholarship.
—Woodrow Wilson

The true art of memory is the art of attention.
—Samuel Johnson

Goals and Objectives

This chapter is designed to enable you to do the following:

- Critically evaluate the 13 WISC–III subtests
- Describe the rationales, factor analytic findings, reliability and correlational highlights, and administrative and interpretive considerations for the 13 WISC–III subtests

Information

Similarities

Arithmetic

Vocabulary

Comprehension

Digit Span

Picture Completion

Coding

Picture Arrangement

Block Design

Object Assembly

Symbol Search

Mazes

Thinking Through the Issues

Summary

This chapter provides information that will help you administer, score, and interpret the 13 WISC–III subtests. Included in the chapter are the rationale, factor analytic findings, reliability and correlational highlights, administrative suggestions, and interpretive suggestions for each subtest. The factor analytic findings discussed in this chapter are based on the factor analysis and principal-components analysis that we conducted on the WISC–III standardization data, obtained from the WISC–III manual and presented in Chapter 8. Similarly, the reliability and correlational findings reported in this chapter are based on the WISC–III standardization data presented in the WISC–III manual. Although the research literature concerning the psychometric properties and clinical interpretation of the WISC–III continues to grow, the standardization data are the most comprehensive, complete, and representative available to date. Reliabilities for the Coding and Symbol Search subtests are test-retest correlations, and those for the remaining 11 subtests are split-half correlations corrected by the Spearman-Brown formula (see Chapter 4). You need to review Chapter 7 before you administer the WISC–III.

Table D-3 in Appendix D summarizes (a) the abilities purportedly measured by each WISC–III subtest, (b) background factors influencing performance, (c) implications of high and low subtest scaled scores, and (d) instructional implications. Table D-3 deserves careful study and is a useful reference for report writing. Recognize that the standard administration of all subtests on the WISC–III Verbal Scale and Performance Scale requires the child to hear, pay attention, listen, understand directions, and retain the directions while solving problems. In addition, all Performance Scale subtests require the child to have adequate vision, and some Performance Scale subtests also require the child to have adequate motor skills. Some items on the Arithmetic subtest also require adequate vision.

Many of the WISC–III subtests have enough subtest specificity at most ages (see Table 8-15 in Chapter 8) to provide reliable estimates of specific abilities, or at least to permit development of hypotheses about the underlying cognitive functions that the subtests may measure. The subtests that have sufficient specificity at most ages are Information, Similarities, Vocabulary, Digit Span, Picture Completion, Picture Arrangement, Block Design, Symbol Search, and Mazes. Arithmetic, Comprehension, and Coding have ample or adequate specificity at some ages only. Speed plays an important role in awarding points on some of the Performance Scale subtests. For example, on the Picture Arrangement, Block Design, and Object Assembly subtests, children who are 12 years of age or older need to receive time-bonus credits to obtain a scaled score of 10 or higher (Dumont & Faro, 1993).

The best estimates of abilities are provided by the Full Scale, followed by the Verbal Scale and the Performance Scale, indexes, other combinations of subtests, and, finally, individual subtests. For example, the Full Scale IQ, derived from 10 subtests, provides the best estimate of general ability. The Verbal Scale IQ, derived from a combination of five Verbal Scale subtests, yields more accurate information about a child's verbal skills than does a single Verbal Scale subtest, such as Vocabulary. Similarly, the Performance Scale IQ, derived from a combination of five Performance Scale subtests, yields more accurate information about a child's nonverbal skills than does a single Performance Scale subtest, such as Picture Completion. Arithmetic and Digit Span together provide more information about working memory than does either subtest alone. Finally, Coding and Symbol Search together provide more information about immediate short-term memory and encoding ability than does either subtest alone.

As you read about each subtest, you will find questions to guide you in your test administration. Answering these questions will help you evaluate and interpret the child's performance. In addition to the child's scores, always consider the quality of the child's responses and the pattern of his or her successes and failures. Recording the child's responses verbatim, along with pertinent behavioral observations, will help you evaluate the test results, especially when you review the test protocol later. An accurate record is also important if you need to testify at an administrative hearing or in court or if other professionals need to review the record.

In administering the subtests, use the exact wording of the questions or items and never add explanations or give synonyms. The same guideline holds for the directions that introduce each subtest. Restrict your deviations to those listed in the manual, except when common sense dictates that you say something that is needed (e.g., "Tell me when you're finished"). The aim is to administer the test in a standardized manner. Never include in the calculation of an IQ a subtest that was spoiled (e.g., through improper timing or mistakes in administration).

Scoring responses to some of the Wechsler subtests—such as Vocabulary, Comprehension, and Similarities—can be challenging. Although the WISC–III manual provides adequate guidelines, the guidelines cannot cover every contingency. Therefore, you will sometimes have to use judgment in scoring responses, especially borderline ones. Always query unclear or borderline responses unless the manual says otherwise. Score the best response when a child gives multiple acceptable responses for an item. Also, if a child gives both a correct and an incorrect response for an item, ask, "Now, which one is it?" and then base your score on the answer. Do the best job possible with the scoring guidelines given in the manual. However, whenever you have any doubt about the scoring of a response, you are encouraged to consult a colleague.

This chapter also discusses testing-of-limits. As noted in Chapter 7, *always conduct testing-of-limits after you administer the entire test following standard procedures.* Testing-of-limits is useful for (a) following up leads about the child's functioning obtained during the standard administration, (b) testing clinical hypotheses, and (c) evaluating whether additional cues or extra time helps the child solve problems. As noted in Chapter 7, *testing-of-limits may invalidate repeated evaluations and should be used cautiously.* A useful complement to the WISC–III is the WISC–III PI (Kaplan, Fein, Kramer, Delis, & Morris, 1999; see Chapter 16 for a review), which is a standardized instrument for conducting testing-of-limits procedures (e.g., to determine whether a low score on Vocabulary is due to low ability, expressive language difficulties, or word retrieval difficulties).

This text, unlike the WISC–III manual, uses the term *mental retardation* instead of the term *intellectual deficiency* to describe children who may be significantly below average in their intellectual ability. *Mental retardation* is the term used in *DSM-IV* and by the American Association on Mental Retardation. Consequently, we believe that *mental retardation* is the preferred term for describing children who are functioning two or more standard deviations below the mean.

Let us now turn to a discussion of each of the 13 WISC–III subtests. Note that we recommend that, from an examinee who cannot speak, you accept written or typed answers or signed answers (assuming you know American Sign Language or use an interpreter).

Question: Before we start, what is your name and address?
Answer: TMcGuire@AOL.com
Question: What is your date of birth?
Answer: July fifteenth.
Question (follow up): What year?
Answer: Every year.
Question: And how tall are you?
Answer: A little bit higher than the bathroom sink.

INFORMATION

The Information subtest requires the child to answer questions dealing with various types of content, including quantitative content (items 2, 3, 6, 10, 11, and 29), calendar information (items 4, 7, 8, 9, and 15), science (items 5, 12, 17, 19, 24, 26, 27, and 30), geography (items 14, 16, 18, 21, and 25), and history (items 13, 20, 22, 23, and 28; Kaplan et al., 1999). The subtest contains 30 questions. Children can usually answer the questions with a brief statement. They need only show that they know facts; they need not find relationships between these facts.

Rationale

The amount of knowledge a child has acquired may depend on his or her (a) natural endowment, (b) education (both formal and informal), and (c) cultural opportunities, experiences, and interests. The subtest samples the knowledge that average children with average opportunities should have acquired through typical home and school experiences (in the American culture). The child's responses and comments provide clues about her or his range of information, alertness to the environment, social or cultural background, and attitudes

toward school and school-like tasks (e.g., the child may say, "Those questions are hard, just like my teacher asks").

High scores may not necessarily indicate cognitive competence; children may have acquired isolated facts but may not know how to use the facts appropriately or effectively. In addition, intellectual drive may contribute to higher scores. Successful performance on the Information subtest requires memory for habitual, overlearned material (i.e., information that the child has likely been exposed to repeatedly), especially in older children. Thus, Information provides clues about the child's ability to store and retrieve acquired knowledge.

Factor Analytic Findings

The Information subtest is the second-best measure of *g* in the WISC–III (61% of its variance can be attributed to *g*), and it contributes substantially to the Verbal Comprehension Index (average loading = .72). Specificity is either ample or adequate at ages 8 through 16 years and is inadequate at ages 6 and 7 years.

Reliability and Correlational Highlights

Information is a reliable subtest (r_{xx} = .84), with reliability coefficients above .70 at all of the 11 age groups (range of .73 to .88). It correlates better with Vocabulary (r = .70) and Similarities (r = .66) than with any of the other subtests. It has a moderately high correlation with the Full Scale (r = .72) and the Verbal Scale (r = .75) and a moderate correlation with the Performance Scale (r = .55).

Administrative Suggestions

Here are some administrative suggestions for the Information subtest.

Background Considerations
- The Information subtest is untimed, is easy to administer, and has simple and direct questions.
- Give the prompts noted in the WISC–III manual for specific items, and inquire about responses that are not clear. For example, on item 8, if the child first says "5," ask, "How many counting the weekend?" If the child then says "2," ask, "How many altogether, all week?"
- Do not spell, define, or explain any words for the child even though the WISC–III manual does not specifically say that you should not do so.
- You can repeat a question when the child's response suggests that the question was misunderstood.
- Record answers verbatim.

Starting Considerations
- All children 6 to 7 years old (and older children suspected of mental retardation) begin with item 1, children 8 to 10 years old begin with item 5, children 11 to 13 years old

begin with item 8, and children 14 to 16 years old begin with item 11.

- If a child 8 to 16 years old earns a score of 0 on either of the first two items you administer, give the preceding items in *reverse order* until two consecutive items are passed.

Scoring Considerations

- Scoring is straightforward: A correct response receives 1 point and an incorrect response, 0.
- Give credit for any response that is of the same caliber as those listed in the Acceptable Responses section of the WISC–III manual.
- If a child 8 to 16 years old earns 2 points on the first two items administered, give full credit for all preceding items.
- When you administer the items in reverse order, give credit for any items not administered that precede two consecutive successes.
- Ask the child to choose the best answer if two or more answers to a question are given, and score that answer.

Discontinuance Considerations

- The subtest is discontinued after five consecutive failures.

Interpretive Suggestions

Note the quality of the child's answers, style of responding, and pattern of successes and failures.

- Is the child thinking through the questions, responding impulsively, or simply guessing?
- Does the child appear confident or hesitant when responding?
- Does the child give peculiar responses? If so, in what way? What does your inquiry reveal?
- Does the child frequently say, "I know this answer, but I can't think of it" or "I don't know"?
- Are the child's answers imprecise and roundabout? Difficulty in giving precise answers, such as saying "When it is hot" for *summer* or "When it is cold" for *winter,* may suggest word-retrieval difficulties.
- Are the child's answers close to the correct answer or completely off base?
- Are the child's answers wordy? Overly long responses or responses filled with extraneous information may suggest an obsessive-compulsive orientation—a child with this orientation sometimes feels compelled to prove how much he or she knows. Alternatively, excessive responses may simply reflect the child's desire to impress you. Consider the child's entire test performance, plus other relevant information, when you interpret such behavior.
- Does the child seem to be inhibited in making responses? Inability to recall an answer may suggest that the question is associated with conflict-laden material. For example, a child may not be able to recall the number of legs on a dog

because of an earlier traumatic experience with dogs. If possible, follow up your hypotheses during an interview with the child (see Chapter 2 in *Assessment of Children: Behavioral and Clinical Applications*).

- What is the pattern of the child's successes and failures? Failures on easy items coupled with successes on more difficult ones may suggest poor motivation, anxiety, temporary inefficiency, boredom, or an inconsistent environment. Alternatively, this pattern may indicate a problem with retrieval of information from long-term memory. When you suspect such a problem, analyze the content of the failed items, as noted above. Content analysis may provide clues about the child's interests, areas about which you might want to inquire after you complete the WISC–III, or areas that need remediation.

Low scores on the Information subtest may indicate a poor range of factual knowledge and information, poor memory, hostility to a pre-school or school-type task, a tendency to give up easily, or low achievement orientation. Low scores also may occur because the child has a foreign language background.

If you think the child may have word-retrieval problems, you can use a multiple-choice testing-of-limits procedure (Holmes, 1988). This procedure may help you differentiate deficits associated with word-retrieval difficulties from those associated with lack of knowledge. After you complete the *entire test,* go back to the item (or items) that the child had difficulty with and give the child three answers to choose from. For example, for item 13 you might ask, "Was he a king or an explorer or a writer?" Be sure to randomly vary the position of the correct answer in the series (i.e., put the correct answer sometimes as the first choice, sometimes as the second, and sometimes as the third). If the child answers the multiple-choice questions correctly, you may infer that

HOW WOULD YOU SCORE THIS?

Courtesy of R. Gould and Jerome M. Sattler.

the child has a word-retrieval difficulty and not a lack of knowledge. However, do not use scores from the multiple-choice procedure to calculate an IQ.

The range of scaled scores from 1 to 19 at ages 6–0 to 13–11 years aids in profile analysis for children in this age range. However, profile analysis is slightly more restricted at ages 14–0 to 15–11 years and ages 16–0 to 16–11 years, where the scaled scores range from 1 to 18 and 1 to 17, respectively.

Question: What are the four seasons?
Answer: Baseball, football, basketball, and hockey.
Question: What are four other seasons?
Answer: Mustard, ketchup, salt, and pepper.

SIMILARITIES

The Similarities subtest requires the child to answer questions about how objects or concepts are alike. The subtest contains 19 pairs of words; the child must state the similarity between the two items in each pair.

Rationale

On the Similarities subtest, the child, in addition to perceiving the common elements of the paired terms, must bring the common elements together into a concept to answer the questions. Thus, the subtest appears to measure verbal concept formation—the ability to place objects and events together into a meaningful group. To do this, the child may need to organize, abstract, and find relationships that are not at first obvious. Although concept formation can be a voluntary, effortful process, it also can reflect well-automatized verbal conventions. Performance on the subtest may be related to cultural opportunities and interest patterns. Memory may also be involved. Success initially depends on the child's ability to comprehend the meaning of the task.

Factor Analytic Findings

Similarities is the third-best measure of *g* in the WISC–III (60% of its variance can be attributed to *g*), and it contributes substantially to the Verbal Comprehension Index (average loading = .72). Specificity is either ample or adequate at ages 6, 11, 12, 14, 15, and 16 years and inadequate at ages 7 through 10 and 13 years.

Reliability and Correlational Highlights

Similarities is a reliable subtest (r_{xx} = .81), with reliability coefficients above .70 at all of the 11 age groups (range of .77 to .84). It correlates better with Vocabulary ($r = .69$) and In-

formation ($r = .66$) than with any of the other subtests. It has a moderately high correlation with the Full Scale ($r = .72$) and the Verbal Scale ($r = .75$) and a moderate correlation with the Performance Scale ($r = .55$).

Administrative Suggestions

Here are some administrative suggestions for the Similarities subtest.

Background Considerations
- The subtest is not timed.
- Note whether the child understands the task.
- Tell the child the 2-point answer if the child gives a 1-point answer to item 6 or 7; do this to help the child give 2-point responses on later items.
- Query unclear or ambiguous responses, as well as those listed in the sample responses in the WISC–III manual that are marked "(Q)."

Starting Considerations
- All children begin with the sample item and then are administered item 1.
- Give the child the correct answer on items 1 and 2 if either of these items is failed.

Scoring Considerations
- Score the best response when a child gives multiple acceptable responses for an item.
- The scoring examples are not an exhaustive list of responses.
- Items 1 to 5 are scored as 1 or 0. These items are generally easy to score.
- Items 6 to 19 are scored as 2, 1, or 0. A conceptual response, such as a general classification, receives a score of 2; a more concrete response, such as a specific property of the item, receives a score of 1; and an incorrect response receives a score of 0. Items 6 to 19 may be difficult to score.
- A careful study of the sample responses in the scoring guide in the WISC–III manual will help you become more proficient in scoring Similarities responses.
- Study—and master—the general scoring principles, which clarify the rationales for 2, 1, and 0 scores (see page 84 in the WISC–III manual).

Discontinuance Considerations
- The subtest is discontinued after four consecutive failures.

As noted, careful study of the sample responses in the scoring guide will help you determine which responses you need to query and which responses should receive 2, 1, and 0 scores. Research on the prior edition of the test indicated that ambiguous Similarities responses are difficult to score (Sattler, Andres, Squire, Wisely, & Maloy, 1978). Scoring difficulties may arise from the inadequate number of examples in the WISC–III manual and from the difficulty of establishing precise criteria that apply to all responses, including ambiguous and idiosyncratic ones.

Interpretive Suggestions

Observing the child's typical level of conceptualization will help you understand the style of her or his thinking. Are the child's answers on a concrete, a functional, or an abstract level? Concrete answers typically refer to qualities of the objects (or stimuli) that can be seen or touched (apple-banana: "Both have a skin"). Functional answers typically concern a function or use of the objects (apple-banana: "You eat them"). Finally, abstract answers typically refer to a more universal property or to a common classification of the objects (apple-banana: "Both are fruits").

You can tell, in part, whether the child's response style is concrete, functional, or abstract by the numbers of 0-, 1-, and 2-point responses. Zero or 1-point responses suggest a more concrete and functional conceptualization style, while 2-point responses suggest a more abstract conceptualization style. However, a 2-point response does not necessarily reflect abstract thinking ability and may simply be an overlearned response. For example, there may be a difference between the 2-point response "Both fruits" for apple-banana and the 2-point response "Artistic expressions" for painting-statue. Although it receives 2 points, the former may be an overlearned response, whereas the latter may reflect a more abstract level of conceptual ability.

Furthermore, if the child earns 1 point on several items, the child may have a good breadth of knowledge but not depth. If the child generally earns 2 points for each correct response but responds correctly to only a few items, the child may have a good depth of knowledge but less breadth.

Also note whether the child gives *overinclusive responses.* These are responses that are so general that several objects are included in the concept. For example, the reply "Both contain molecules" to a question asking for the similarity between an apple and a banana is overinclusive because it does not delimit the particular characteristics of these two objects. Overinclusive responses may be a subtle indication of unusual thinking.

Observe how the child handles any frustration induced by the subtest questions. For example, when the child has difficulty answering the questions, does the child become negativistic and uncooperative, or does he or she continue to try to answer the questions? A child who responds with "They are not alike" may be displaying negativism, avoidance of the task demands, suspiciousness, a coping mechanism, or a lack of knowledge. To determine which of these may account for the child's response, compare the child's style of responding to the Similarities questions with his or her style of responding to questions on other subtests and during the interview.

Low scores on the Similarities subtest may indicate poor conceptual thinking, difficulty in seeing relationships, difficulty in selecting and verbalizing appropriate relationships between two objects or concepts, an overly concrete mode of thinking, rigidity of thought processes, or negativism.

If you think the child may have word-retrieval problems, you can use a multiple-choice testing-of-limits procedure, similar to the one discussed for the Information subtest, after you complete the *entire test.*

The range of scaled scores from 1 to 19 at all ages aids in profile analysis.

Question: In what way are an orange and a pear alike?
Answer: Both give me hives.

ARITHMETIC

The Arithmetic subtest requires the child to answer simple to complex problems involving arithmetical concepts and numerical reasoning. The subtest contains 24 problems, with 5 presented on picture cards, 13 presented orally, and 6 presented in written form. Many of the arithmetic problems are

Reprinted with special permission of King Features Syndicate.

similar to those commonly encountered by children in school, although the child is not permitted to use paper and pencil to solve the problems. Individual items may be repeated, but timing continues during the repetition of any item.

The problems on the Arithmetic subtest require various skills. Problems 1 and 2 require direct counting of discrete objects. Problems 3, 4, and 5 require subtraction, using objects as the stimuli. Problems 6 and 17 require simple division. Problems 7 to 14 and problem 16 require simple addition or subtraction. Problem 15 involves multiplication (or addition). Problems 18 to 24 require the use of automated number facts and subtle mathematical reasoning operations, such as identifying relevant relationships at a glance, understanding task requirements, and understanding probability.

Rationale

The problems on the Arithmetic subtest require the child to follow verbal directions, concentrate on selected parts of questions, hold information in working memory, and use numerical operations. Depending on the problem, the child may need knowledge of addition, subtraction, multiplication, or division operations. The emphasis of the problems is not on mathematical knowledge per se, but on mental computation and concentration. Concentration is especially important for the more complex problems.

The Arithmetic subtest measures numerical reasoning—the ability to solve arithmetical problems. It requires the use of noncognitive functions (concentration and attention) in conjunction with cognitive functions (knowledge of numerical operations). Success on this subtest is influenced by education, interests, fluctuations of attention, and transient emotional reactions such as anxiety. Like the Vocabulary and Information subtests, Arithmetic involves memory and prior learning; however, it also requires concentration and the active application of select skills to unique situations.

Information-processing strategies, as well as mathematical skills, may underlie performance on the Arithmetic subtest (Stewart & Moely, 1983). These strategies may include (a) rehearsal (e.g., to remember the information presented in the task) and (b) recognition of an appropriate response (e.g., to continue using a correct strategy or change an incorrect strategy). Mathematical skills include the ability to comprehend and integrate verbal information presented in a mathematical context, together with numerical ability (i.e., the ability to perform the necessary calculations).

Factor Analytic Findings

The Arithmetic subtest is a good measure of g (54% of its variance can be attributed to g), and it contributes moderately to the Freedom from Distractibility Index (average loading = .48) and minimally to the Perceptual Organization Index (average loading = .30). Specificity is either ample or adequate at ages 6, 7, 10, 13, 15, and 16 years and inadequate at 8, 9, 11, 12, and 14 years.

Reliability and Correlational Highlights

Arithmetic is a relatively reliable subtest (r_{xx} = .78), with reliability coefficients above .70 at all of the 11 age groups (range of .71 to .82). It correlates better with Information (r = .57) and Similarities (r = .55) than with any of the other subtests. It has a moderately high correlation with the Full Scale (r = .65) and the Verbal Scale (r = .62) and a moderate correlation with the Performance Scale (r = .54).

Administrative Suggestions

Here are some administrative suggestions for the Arithmetic subtest.

Background Considerations
- Reassure a child who is anxious about his or her arithmetical skills.
- All items are timed, with items 1 to 17 having a 30-second time limit; item 18, a 45-second time limit; and items 19 to 24, a 75-second time limit.
- Do not permit the child to use pencil and paper to solve the problems.
- Allow the child to write with his or her fingers if he or she wants to.
- Begin timing as soon as you finish reading the problem.
- Repeat an item only once, and continue timing as you repeat the item.
- When two responses are given, ask the child which one is right.
- Give the child additional time to complete a problem if the child seems to be on the verge of solving it when the time limit is reached. This will give you information about the child's ability to solve the problem. Record the response and the amount of time the child took to respond. Although you do not give formal credit for correct responses given after the time limit, you can include information about the child's ability to solve such problems in the report.
- The first five and the last six Arithmetic items are in the Stimulus Booklet, which also contains the Picture Completion and Block Design stimuli. Items 6 to 18, which are in the WISC–III manual, are read aloud to the child.

Starting Considerations
- Children 6 years old (and older children suspected of mental retardation) begin with item 1, children 7 to 8 years old begin with item 6, children 9 to 12 years old begin with item 12, and children 13 to 16 years old begin with item 14.

- If a child 8 to 16 years old earns a score of 0 on either of the first two items you administer, give the preceding items in *reverse order* until two consecutive items are passed.

Scoring Considerations
- All items are scored 1 or 0, with 1 additional time-bonus point on items 19 to 24.
- When you administer the items in reverse order, give credit for any items not administered that precede two consecutive successes.

Discontinuance Considerations
- The subtest is discontinued after three consecutive failures.

Interpretive Suggestions

Observe the child's reactions to the items.

- Is the child anxious (e.g., exhibits panic behaviors when you suggest doing math problems)?
- If the child is anxious, how does the child deal with this anxiety (e.g., calms down, remains anxious, gives up easily, becomes angry, makes excuses, tries to leave the situation)?
- What approach does the child use to solve problems (e.g., counts on fingers, draws with a finger on the table, imagines the numbers in her or his head)?
- Does the child show temporary inefficiencies such as anxiety, blocking, or transient concentration difficulties?
- Does the child recognize when a mistake has been made?
- Does the child attempt to correct perceived errors?
- Does the child ask you to repeat questions?
- If the answer is incorrect, does the child show an understanding of the process required (e.g., understands that the problem requires addition or multiplication)?
- Are the child's responses given hurriedly, without sufficient thought?

Try to determine the reasons for the child's failures. Possible reasons are poor knowledge of arithmetical operations, inadequate conceptualization of the problem, anxiety, poor concentration, misunderstanding of the problem, and carelessness.

Low scores on the Arithmetic subtest may indicate inadequate ability in mental arithmetic, poor concentration, distractibility, anxiety (e.g., over a school-like task or because of worry over personal problems), blocking toward mathematical tasks, or poor school achievement (perhaps associated with rebellion against authority or with cultural background).

After you complete the standard administration of the *entire* WISC–III, you might want to further explore the reasons for the child's failures by going back to the questions. You might say, for example, "Let's try this one again. Tell me how you solved the problem." If necessary, you can ask the child to think aloud to see how the child tried to solve the problem.

Allowing the child to use paper and pencil is another testing-of-limits procedure that may help you find out whether the child has poor arithmetical knowledge or atten-

tion and concentration difficulties. If the child can solve the problems with paper and pencil, the failure is not associated with lack of arithmetical knowledge; rather, the errors may relate to attention or concentration difficulties that inhibit mental computation. Use of paper and pencil reduces the load on the child's working memory (Kaplan et al., 1999). If the child fails the items in both situations, the failures more likely reflect difficulties with arithmetical knowledge, although attention and concentration difficulties may also be interfering with the child's ability to solve written arithmetic problems. Inspect the written work to see whether the child misaligns numbers, sequences computational steps incorrectly, performs calculations carelessly, or has poor mastery of basic arithmetical operations. A tendency to misalign numbers may indicate spatial difficulties.

If you think the child may have word-retrieval problems, you can use a multiple-choice testing-of-limits procedure similar to the one discussed for the Information subtest. Finally, in some cases you can allow the child to use a calculator, to see whether this helps him or her solve the problems.

The information you obtain from testing-of-limits may help you to differentiate between failures caused by temporary inefficiency and those caused by limited knowledge. Successful delayed performance, for example, may indicate temporary inefficiency or a slow, painstaking approach to problem solving. Of course, do not give the child credit for answering any items correctly during testing-of-limits. (Refer to Chapter 7 for more information about testing-of-limits.)

The range of scaled scores from 1 to 19 at ages 6–0 to 15–11 years aids in profile analysis. However, from 16–0 to 16–11 years, profile analysis is based on scaled scores that range from only 1 to 18.

Question: If I cut a pear in thirds, how many pieces will I have?
Answer: One.
Question (testing-of-limits): Are you sure I'll have only one piece?
Answer: Yes, and I'll have the other two pieces.

VOCABULARY

The Vocabulary subtest requires the child to listen as you read words aloud and then to define the words. This subtest contains 30 words arranged in order of increasing difficulty. The child is asked to explain the meaning of each word (e.g., "What is a …?" or "What does … mean?").

Rationale

The Vocabulary subtest, a test of word knowledge, assesses several cognitive factors—such as the child's learning ability, fund of information, richness of ideas, memory, concept formation, and language development—that may be closely related to her or his educational experiences and environment. Because the number of words known by a child correlates with her or his ability to learn and to accumulate information, the subtest provides an excellent estimate of intellectual ability. Performance on the subtest is stable over time and relatively resistant to neurological deficit and psychological disturbance. Scores on Vocabulary therefore provide a useful index of the child's general mental ability.

Factor Analytic Findings

The Vocabulary subtest is the best measure of g in the WISC–III (62% of its variance can be attributed to g), and it contributes substantially to the Verbal Comprehension Index (average loading = .79). Specificity is either ample or adequate at ages 6 through 8 and 11 through 16 years and inadequate at ages 9 and 10 years.

Reliability and Correlational Highlights

Vocabulary ties with Block Design as one of the two most reliable subtests (r_{xx} = .87) in the WISC–III. The reliability coefficients for Vocabulary are above .70 in all of the 11 age groups (range of .79 to .91). It correlates better with Information (r = .70), Similarities (r = .69), and Comprehension (r = .64) than with any of the other subtests. It has a moderately high correlation with the Full Scale (r = .74) and the Verbal Scale (r = .78) and a moderate correlation with the Performance Scale (r = .56).

Administrative Suggestions

Here are some administrative suggestions for the Vocabulary subtest.

Background Considerations
- The subtest is not timed.
- Pronounce each word clearly and correctly. You must be especially careful about how you pronounce the words, because you are not allowed to show the words to the child or to spell them.
- Have the child repeat the word to you when you suspect that the child has not heard a word correctly. If the child heard the word incorrectly, say, "Listen carefully. What does…mean?"
- Tell young children (or older children who may have mental retardation) the 2-point answer when they give a 0- or 1-point response to the first word of the Vocabulary subtest. Use this procedure, designed to encourage 2-point responses, only on the first item.
- The scoring guidelines following each item in the WISC–III manual list many responses that you should query, shown by a "(Q)." Study these guidelines carefully so that you can recognize responses that you need to query.

- Carefully record the child's definitions, and be sure to write down all of the child's answers, whether they are correct or incorrect.
- The nature of the child's response should determine whether you query it during the standard administration. For example, if the child's answer clearly defines a homonym, repeat the question by saying "What else does…mean?" However, if the child's response is peculiar (e.g., possibly indicative of a thought disorder), delay querying until you have finished the entire test. Then during testing-of-limits, you might say, "To the word…you said…. Tell me more about your answer."

Starting Considerations
- Children 6 to 8 years old (and older children suspected of mental retardation) begin with item 1, children 9 to 10 years old begin with item 3, children 11 to 13 years old begin with item 5, and children 14 to 16 years old begin with item 7.
- If a child 9 to 16 years old earns a score of 0 or 1 on either of the first two items you administer, give the preceding items in *reverse order* until the child has two consecutive perfect scores (2 points).

Scoring Considerations
- All items are scored 2, 1, or 0.
- If the child earns 2-point scores on both of the first two items administered, assign full credit for all preceding items (i.e., items 1 and 2 for children 9 to 10 years, items 1 to 4 for children 11 to 13 years, and items 1 to 6 for children 14 to 16 years).
- When you administer the items in reverse order, give credit for any items not administered that precede two consecutive successes.
- Award 2 points for good synonyms, major uses, or general classifications.
- Award 1 point for vague responses, less pertinent synonyms, or minor uses.
- Do not consider the child's elegance of expression in scoring the response.
- Give credit for all meanings recognized by standard dictionaries.
- Give 0 points for obviously wrong answers, for regionalisms or slang not found in dictionaries, and for pointing responses only.
- Vocabulary is one of the more difficult subtests to score, and sometimes it may be difficult to apply the scoring criteria given in the WISC–III manual.
- Inquiring about borderline responses and carefully studying the scoring guidelines will help you resolve some scoring problems that arise as you give the subtest.
- When you have any doubt about the acceptability of a response, ask the child for another meaning of the word.

Discontinuance Considerations
- The subtest is discontinued after four consecutive failures (scores of 0).

Interpretive Suggestions

The following guidelines are useful for observing and evaluating Vocabulary responses (Taylor, 1961).

- Is the child definitely familiar with the word or only vaguely familiar with it?
- What is the quality of the child's definitions (e.g., precise and brief, indirect and vague, or verbose and lengthy)?
- Are the child's responses objective, or do they relate to personal experiences?
- Does the child confuse the word with another one that sounds like it?
- If the child does not know the meaning of a word, does he or she guess?
- Does the child readily say, "I don't know" and shake off further inquiries, or does the child pause, ponder, or think aloud about the item?
- Does the child show signs of a possible hearing difficulty?
- Does the child appear to hear the words correctly or hear them with some distortion?
- Does the child easily express what he or she means, or does the child struggle?
- Does the child have mechanical difficulties with pronouncing words properly?
- Does the child seem uncertain about how best to express what he or she thinks?
- Does the child use gestures to illustrate his or her responses or even depend on them exclusively?

- Are the child's responses synonyms for the stimulus word (e.g., thief: "A burglar"), or do they describe an action (e.g., thief: "Takes stuff")?
- Does the child describe a particular feature of the object (e.g., donkey: "It has four legs") or try to fit it into some category (e.g., donkey: "A living creature that is kept in a barn")?
- Are there any emotional overtones or references to personal experiences in the child's responses (e.g., alphabet: "I hate to write")?
- Does seeing the printed word during testing-of-limits help the child define the word?

The child's responses to the Vocabulary subtest may reveal something about her or his language skills, background, cultural milieu, social development, life experiences, responses to frustration, and thought processes. Try to determine the basis for incorrect responses, and distinguish among guesses, clang associations (i.e., responses that appear to be based on the sound of the stimulus word rather than on its meaning), idiosyncratic associations, and bizarre associations. Whenever a child gives peculiar responses, mispronounces words, or has peculiar inflections, inquire further. Occasionally, you can identify language disturbances in the word definitions of children with a pervasive developmental disorder.

Low scores on the Vocabulary subtest may indicate poor word knowledge, poor verbal comprehension, poor verbal skills and language development, limited educational background, difficulty in verbalization, or a home environment in which verbalization was not encouraged. Low scores, however, may also occur with children who speak English as a second language.

If you think the child may have word-retrieval problems, at the end of *entire test* you can use a multiple-choice testing-of-limits procedure, similar to the one discussed for the Information subtest.

The range of scaled scores from 1 to 19 at all ages aids in profile analysis.

Question: What does imitate mean?
Answer: What does imitate mean?

COMPREHENSION

The Comprehension subtest requires the child to explain situations, actions, or activities that relate to events familiar to most children. The questions cover several content areas, including knowledge of one's body, interpersonal relations, and social mores. The subtest contains 18 questions.

Rationale

On the Comprehension subtest, the child must understand given situations and provide answers to specific problems.

Courtesy of Herman Zielinski.

Success depends on the child's possession of practical information, plus an ability to draw on previous experiences. Responses may reflect the child's knowledge of conventional standards of behavior, extensiveness of cultural opportunities, and level of development of conscience or moral sense. Success suggests that the child has common sense, social judgment, and a grasp of social conventionality. These characteristics imply an ability to use facts in a pertinent, meaningful, and emotionally appropriate manner. Success is also based on the child's ability to verbalize acceptable actions.

Factor Analytic Findings

The Comprehension subtest is a good measure of g (50% of its variance can be attributed to g), and it contributes substantially to the Verbal Comprehension Index (average loading = .66). Specificity is adequate at ages 6 and 8 through 12 years and inadequate at ages 7 and 13 through 16 years.

Reliability and Correlational Highlights

Comprehension is a relatively reliable subtest (r_{xx} = .77), with reliability coefficients above .70 at all ages. It correlates better with Vocabulary (r = .64), Similarities (r = .59), and Information (r = .56) than with any of the other subtests. It has a moderately high correlation with the Full Scale (r = .64) and the Verbal Scale (r = .67) and a moderately low correlation with the Performance Scale (r = .49).

Administrative Suggestions

Here are some administrative suggestions for the Comprehension subtest.

Background Considerations
- The subtest is not timed.
- Tell the child the correct 2-point response on the first item if the child gives a 1- or 0-point response. This procedure is designed to encourage the child to give 2-point responses, but it is used on the first item only.
- Study carefully the examples following each item in the WISC–III manual so that you will know which types of responses, labeled "(Q)," need further inquiry. The examples indicate that you should query many 0- and 1-point responses.
- Queries allow you an opportunity to evaluate more thoroughly the extent of the child's knowledge. However, do not query obviously less complete 1-point responses in an attempt to improve the child's score on other items for which a complete one-idea answer receives 2 points.
- On the eight items (2, 6, 7, 11, 12, 15, 17, and 18) that require two ideas for full credit (2 points), ask the child for a second idea when he or she gives only one correct idea. Do this so that you do not penalize the child automatically for not giving two ideas. However, you can ask

for a second idea only one time for each of these eight items. Do not ask for a second idea if the first response is incorrect. In scoring these eight items, note that the two responses must reflect two of the general-concept categories listed in the WISC–III manual.
- Ask the child to explain any unusual responses.
- Record the child's responses verbatim during the initial presentation of the items and during the inquiry phase so that you have a complete record with which to evaluate the responses.
- If the child does not give an answer after 10 to 15 seconds, it is a good idea to repeat the question.
- The instructions in the WISC–III manual are explicit about the help you can give the child. You can encourage the child if hesitancy is shown, ask the child to further explain unclear or ambiguous answers, ask the child for a second response on items requiring two responses if the child's first response is correct, and give the child the correct answer if the first item is failed. No other help, such as defining or spelling words, can be given.
- The Record Form has an asterisk next to those items that require you to ask for a second response.

Starting Considerations
- All children begin with item 1.

Scoring Considerations
- Study the scoring guidelines carefully, because the Comprehension subtest is difficult to score; children may give responses that differ from those provided in the WISC–III manual.
- All items are scored 2, 1, or 0. The most complete or best response receives a score of 2; a less adequate response, 1; and an incorrect response, 0.
- Score the response given to your query rather than the initial response if, in response to your query, the child alters her or his response.

Discontinuance Considerations
- The subtest is discontinued after three consecutive failures.

Interpretive Suggestions

Responses to the Comprehension questions may provide information about the child's personality style, ethical values, and social and cultural background. Unlike the Information questions, which usually elicit precise answers, the Comprehension questions may elicit more complex and idiosyncratic replies. Because the questions involve judgment of social situations, answers may reflect the child's social attitudes. Some responses may reveal understanding *and* acceptance of social mores, whereas others may reveal understanding *but not* acceptance of social mores. A child may know the right answers but not practice them. In fact, one study reported that scores on Comprehension are not related to clinicians' ratings of children's social competence (Lipsetz, Dworkin, & Erlenmeyer-Kimling, 1993). Some children may maintain that they do not have to abide by social conventions, believing that such matters do not pertain to them personally.

A child's replies may reveal initiative, self-reliance, independence, self-confidence, helplessness, indecisiveness, inflexibility, manipulative tendencies, naive perceptions of problems, cooperative solutions, hostility, aggression, or other traits. For example, a child with a dependent personality style might describe seeking help from his or her mother (or others) when faced with a problem situation.

The following are possible interpretations of Comprehension subtest responses that may reveal characteristics of the child's social judgment.

Question 1: "What is the thing to do when you cut your finger?"

Answer: "You should be more careful and not cut your finger" (a possible indication of a moralistic response; Taylor, 1961).

Answer: "Fingers can fall off or be cut off and maybe they could be sewed on" (a possible indication of preoccupation with aggression and retribution; Brooks, 1979).

Question 2: "What are you supposed to do if you find someone's wallet or purse in a store?" (All examples for this question are from Zimmerman & Woo-Sam, 1985.)

Answer: "Give it back, say you didn't take it" (a possible indication of guilt).

Answer: "Give it to your mother" (a possible indication of passivity).

Answer: "Take the money" (a possible indication of sociopathy or subculture values).

Answer: "Don't do nothing" (a possible indication of difficulty in coping).

Answer: "I never stole anything" (a possible indication of denial).

Question 3: "What is the thing to do if a boy (girl) much smaller than yourself starts to fight with you?" (Most examples are from Taylor, 1961).

Answer: "He should not hit you" (a possible indication of a moralistic response).

Answer: "I should not fight" (a possible indication of a defensive response).

Answer: "I would tell my mother" (a possible indication of dependency).

Answer: "I would beat them up real good" (a possible indication of aggressive behavior).

Answer: "I would run and hide" (a possible indication of a fearful response from a child who may have been bullied).

Note how the child responds to the questions (Taylor, 1961):

- Do the child's failures indicate misunderstanding of the meaning of a word or the implications of a particular phrase?
- Does the child provide a complete answer or just part of one?
- Does the child respond to the entire question or only to a part of it?
- Does the child seem to be objective, seeing various possibilities and choosing the best possible response?
- Is the child indecisive, unable to give firm answers?
- Are the child's responses too quick, indicating failure to consider the questions in their entirety?
- Does the child recognize when her or his answers are sufficient or insufficient?
- How does the child respond when you ask her or him for another good answer (e.g., becomes impatient, flustered, challenged by the request)?

Because Comprehension requires considerable verbal expression, the subtest may be sensitive to mild language impairments and to disordered thought processes. Be alert to language deficits (such as word-retrieval difficulties), circumstantial or tangential speech, or other expressive difficulties.

Low scores on the Comprehension subtest may indicate poor social judgment, failure to take personal responsibility (e.g., overdependency, immaturity, limited involvement with others), overly concrete thinking, difficulty in expressing ideas verbally, a creative individual looking for unusual solutions, or negativism. One study (Beebe, Pfiffner, & McBurnett, 2000) indicates that Comprehension scores are significantly related to mothers' reports of conduct problems ($r = -.31$), leadership skills ($r = .27$), and popularity ($r = .20$) and to teachers' reports of conduct problems ($r = -.28$), adaptability ($r = .33$), social skills ($r = .33$), leadership skills ($r = .45$), and popularity ($r = .25$). The sample for this study comprised 142 children with attention-deficit/hyperactivity disorder and 30 children without problems, aged 6 to 11 years.

If you think the child may have word-retrieval problems, you can use a multiple-choice testing-of-limits procedure similar to the method discussed for the Information subtest. You also can conduct an extensive inquiry about any responses as part of testing-of-limits after you complete the *entire test*.

The range of scaled scores from 1 to 19 at ages 6–0 to 15–11 years aids in profile analysis. At 16–0 to 16–11 years, however, profile analysis is somewhat hindered because the scaled scores range only from 1 to 18.

Question: What would you do if you were lost in the woods? Answer: I'd use my cell phone, pager, or global positioning satellite device.

DIGIT SPAN

The Digit Span subtest, a supplementary subtest, requires the child to repeat a series of digits that you read aloud. The subtest has two parts: Digits Forward, which contains series ranging in length from two to nine digits, and Digits Backward, which contains series ranging in length from two to eight digits. There are two series of digits for each sequence length.

Although Digit Span is a supplementary subtest, administering it may give you useful diagnostic information. Considering the small investment of time and energy required to give it, we recommend that you administer Digit Span routinely.

Rationale

Digit Span is primarily a measure of the child's short-term sequential auditory memory and attention. In addition, the task assesses a child's ability to retain several elements that have no logical relationship to one another. Because a child must recall auditory information and repeat the information aloud in proper sequence, the task also requires sequencing skills. However, a child's performance on the Digit Span subtest may be negatively affected by anxiety.

Digits Forward primarily involves rote learning and memory, whereas Digits Backward requires transformation of the stimulus input prior to responding. On Digits Backward, not only must the child hold the mental image of the numerical sequence longer (usually) than on Digits Forward; the child also must mentally manipulate the sequence before restating it. High scores on Digits Backward may indicate flexibility, good tolerance for stress, and excellent concentration. Digits Backward requires more complex cognitive processing than does Digits Forward and has higher loadings on g than does Digits Forward (Jensen & Osborne, 1979).

Because of differences between the two tasks, it is useful to consider Digits Forward and Digits Backward separately. Digits Forward appears to involve primarily sequential processing and short-term memory, while Digits Backward appears to involve both planning ability and sequential processing (and may provide some insight into working memory). Additionally, Digits Backward may involve the abilities to (a) form mental images and (b) scan an internal visual display formed from an auditory stimulus. However, more research is needed to explore the role of visualization on the Digits Backward portion of the subtest.

Factor Analytic Findings

The Digit Span subtest is a fair measure of g (26% of its variance can be attributed to g), and it contributes moderately to the Freedom from Distractibility Index (average loading = .41). Specificity is ample at all ages.

Reliability and Correlational Highlights

Digit Span is a reliable subtest (r_{xx} = .85), with reliability coefficients above .70 at all ages (range of .79 to .91). It correlates better with Arithmetic (r = .43) than with any of the other subtests. It has a moderately low correlation with the Full Scale (r = .43), the Verbal Scale (r = .42), and the Performance Scale (r = .35).

Administrative Suggestions

Here are some administrative suggestions for the Digit Span subtest.

Background Considerations
- The child should not be able to see the digits in the WISC–III manual or on the Record Form before or during the administration of the Digit Span subtest.
- The subtest is not timed.
- Read the digits clearly at one per second, and *drop* your inflection on the last digit in the series. Then pause to allow the child to respond. Practice reading speed with a stopwatch.
- Do not break the digits into groups by unintentionally spacing them as you read them. If you do so, you may provide the child with a mnemonic device—chunking—that helps him or her recall the digits better.
- It is permissible to make eye contact with the child during the administration of Digit Span if you want, because eye contact does not affect the examinee's performance (Goldfarb, Plante, Brentar, & DiGregorio, 1995; Plante, Plante, Rahm, Brentar, & Couchman, 1997).
- Never repeat any of the digits on either trial of a series during the subtest proper.
- Always administer both trials of each series.
- After you complete Digits Forward, give the sample Digits Backward item and then the rest of Digits Backward. Give Digits Backward even if the child fails both trials of item 1 on Digits Forward.
- On Digits Backward, if the child passes the sample two-digit series (on either the first or the second trial), go to the two-digit series in the subtest proper. If the child fails the sample series, read the specific directions in the WISC–III manual that explain how the child should repeat the series.
- One procedure for recording the number of digits correctly recalled in each series is to place on the Record Form either a mark designating a correct answer above each digit correctly recalled or a mark designating an incorrect answer on each digit missed.
- An even better procedure is to record the exact sequence given by the child in the available space.
- Do not use Digit Span to compute an IQ when you administer the five standard Verbal Scale subtests.
- Request an audiological examination whenever you have any doubt about a child's hearing. Because this subtest contains no contextual cues (i.e., you only present several random series of digits), children with a hearing impairment are especially prone to failure or poor performance.

Starting Considerations
- All children begin with the first trial of Digits Forward.

Scoring Considerations
- Score all items 2 (passed both trials), 1 (passed one trial), or 0 (failed both trials) on both Digits Forward and Digits Backward.
- Give a child credit for each trial that is passed.

Discontinuance Considerations
- The subtest is discontinued after the child fails both trials on any one item in each part.

Interpretive Suggestions

A good record can greatly help you evaluate and interpret a child's performance. A child who consistently misses the last digit in the first series and then successfully completes the second series differs from one who fails to recall any of the digits in the first series but successfully completes the second. Similarly, the short-term memory of a child who responds to the sequence 3-4-1-7 with "3-1-4-7" is better than that of the child who says "9-8-5-6." The scoring system described in the WISC–III manual does not distinguish between these or other failure patterns.

Observe whether the child's failures involve leaving out one or more digits, transposing digits, interjecting incorrect digits, producing more digits than were given, giving a series of digits in numerical order (e.g., 6-7-8-9), or recalling only the first and last digits. The child who recalls the correct digits but in an incorrect sequence is more likely to have a deficit in immediate auditory sequential memory than in immediate auditory memory. Contrariwise, the child who fails to recall the correct digits may have a deficit in immediate auditory memory. The child who fails the first trial but passes the second trial may be displaying a learning-to-learn pattern or a need to practice a bit to achieve success.

Consider the following questions:

- Is the child's performance effortless, or does the child seem to concentrate hard?
- Does the child view the task as interesting, boring, or difficult?
- Is the child aware of her or his errors, or does the child think that her or his answers are always correct?
- Does the child understand the difference between Digits Backward and Digits Forward?
- Are the errors the child makes on Digits Backward similar to or different from those made on Digits Forward?
- How does the child react as the Digits Backward series proceeds (e.g., becomes stimulated and encouraged or tense, anxious, and frustrated)?
- Does the child perform better on Digits Forward than on Digits Backward? (If so, the more complex operations required on Digits Backward may induce anxiety in the child.)

- Does the child make more errors on Digits Forward than on Digits Backward? (This may mean that the child views Digits Backward as more of a challenge and therefore mobilizes more of her or his resources, such as giving added concentration and attention.)
- What strategy does the child use to recall the digits (e.g., simply repeating what is heard, rehearsing the numbers before repeating them back to you, visualizing the numbers in her or his head, using a finger to write the digits, chunking the digits, or repeating back the numbers after an extended period of time)?
- What types of errors does the child make (e.g., an omission error by leaving one digit out of the correct sequence, an addition error by adding one or more digits to the correct sequence, a perseveration error by repeating one or more digits, a sequential error by giving the correct digits but in the wrong sequence, or a sequence reversal error by giving the correct digits but with two or more reversed; Kaplan et al., 1999)?

Some grouping techniques introduce meaning into the task so that separate digits become numbers grouped into hundreds, tens, or other units (e.g., 3-1-7 becomes three hundred seventeen). If the child uses grouping, the function underlying the task may be changed from one of attention to one of concentration.

The WISC–III manual does not provide separate scaled scores for Digits Forward and Digits Backward. There are,

Courtesy of Herman Zielinski.

however, two useful tables in the WISC–III manual that show how the standardization group performed on Digits Forward and on Digits Backward. Table B.6 (page 267 of the WISC–III manual) shows the longest Digits Forward span and the longest Digits Backward span recalled by the children. The median Digits Forward span was 5 at ages 6 to 8 years, 6 at ages 9 to 14 years, and 7 at ages 15 and 16 years. The median Digits Backward span was 3 at ages 6 to 8 years, 4 at ages 9 to 13 years, and 5 at ages 14 to 16 years. Across all age groups, children had a median Digits Forward span of 6 (range of 5 to 7) and a median Digits Backward span of 4 (range of 3 to 5; see Table 9-1). These results indicate that children usually produce longer spans on Digits Forward than on Digits Backward by about two digits.

Table B.7 (page 268 of the WISC–III manual) shows the extent to which children recalled more digits forward than backward and vice versa. In all age groups and in the total sample, children recalled more digits forward than backward (*Mdn* difference = 2 at 10 of the 11 age groups and in the total sample, except at age 15, where *Mdn* difference = 1). Thus, you can consider as noteworthy raw-score differences of 3 points (or more) between Digits Forward and Digits Backward. The percentage of children in the standardization group who recalled more digits backward than forward was 3.8% in the total group, with a range from .5% at 8 years to 10.5% at 15 years (see Table 9-2). Table 9-2 indicates that a larger percentage of older children than younger children recalled more digits backward than forward.

Table 9-2
Percentage of Children in WISC–III Standardization Group Who Recalled More Digits Backward than Digits Forward, by Age

Age	Percent
6	1.0
7	1.0
8	.5
9	1.5
10	2.5
11	2.5
12	4.0
13	4.0
14	6.0
15	10.5
16	9.0
All ages	3.8

Note. There were 200 children at each age level.
Source: Adapted from Wechsler (1991), Table B.7 (page 268).

Low scores on the Digit Span subtest may indicate anxiety, inattention, distractibility, a possible learning deficit, difficulty in auditory sequential processing, poor short-term auditory memory, boredom, difficulty in shifting, impaired hearing, or negativism.

Testing-of-limits after the *entire test* is over may give you some understanding of the child's Digit Span performance. You might ask the child how he or she went about remembering the numbers. You also can determine whether the child does better if he or she writes down the numbers and whether the child can recall letters better than numbers.

The range of scaled scores from 1 to 19 at all ages aids in profile analysis.

Question: We want to see if you're eligible for our memory training class. Repeat the following: 6 Z 4 J 5 Y 9 A 1 P 7 W 3 D 8 G 2 S 9 T 4 K.
Answer: Huh?
Reply: You're eligible.

PICTURE COMPLETION

The Picture Completion subtest requires the child to identify the single most important missing detail in 30 drawings of common objects, animals, and people—such as a box, a cat, and a face. The child's task is to name or point to the essential missing portion of the incomplete picture within the 20-second time limit.

Table 9-1
Median Number of Digits Recalled on WISC–III Digits Forward and Digits Backward, by Age

Age	Median Forward	Median Backward
6	5	3
7	5	3
8	5	3
9	6	4
10	6	4
11	6	4
12	6	4
13	6	4
14	6	5
15	7	5
16	7	5
All ages	6	4

Note. There were 200 children at each age level.
Source: Adapted from Wechsler (1991), Table B.6 (page 267).

Rationale

On the Picture Completion subtest, the child must recognize the object depicted, appreciate its incompleteness, and determine the missing part. It is a test of visual discrimination—the ability to differentiate between essential and nonessential details. Picture Completion requires concentration, reasoning (or visual alertness), visual organization, and long-term visual memory (as the items require a child to have stored and retrieve information about the complete figure).

Picture Completion also may measure perceptual and conceptual abilities involved in visual recognition and identification of familiar objects. Perception, cognition, judgment, and delay of impulse all may influence performance. The time limit on the subtest places additional demands on the child. The richness of the child's life experiences also may affect her or his performance on the subtest.

Factor Analytic Findings

The Picture Completion subtest is a fair measure of g (44% of its variance can be attributed to g), and it contributes moderately to the Perceptual Organization Index (average loading = .55) and minimally to the Verbal Comprehension Index (average loading = .37). Specificity is either ample or adequate at ages 6 through 11 and 13 through 16 years and inadequate at age 12 years.

Reliability and Correlational Highlights

Picture Completion is a relatively reliable subtest (r_{xx} = .77), with reliability coefficients above .70 at all age groups (range of .72 to .84). It correlates better with Block Design (r = .52), Object Assembly (r = .49), and Information (r = .47) than with any of the other subtests. It has a moderate correlation with the Full Scale (r = .58), the Performance Scale (r = .54), and the Verbal Scale (r = .52).

Administrative Suggestions

Here are some administrative suggestions for the Picture Completion subtest.

Background Considerations
- The Picture Completion subtest is easy to administer. Leave the booklet flat on the table and turn over the cards one at a time to show consecutive pictures.
- Allow the child to turn the pages in the test booklet if the child wants to and you are sure that you can set the pace.
- Have the child point to where the part is missing on the picture if the child has severe speech difficulties.
- The WISC–III manual provides no guidance about the placement of the stopwatch. We recommend that the child see the stopwatch so that she or he understands that the subtest is timed. However, do not tell the child that you are timing him or her.
- The WISC–III manual indicates that, if necessary, you may give each of three guiding statements *once* to help the child understand the subtest requirements: (a) If the child names the object pictured, ask the child what is missing in the picture. (b) If the child names a part that is off the card, ask the child what part *in* the picture is missing. (c) If the child mentions a nonessential missing part, ask the child for the most important missing part.
- In response to inexact or made-up words that are ambiguous, say, "Show me where."
- Record each incorrect response verbatim.
- Record the time the child takes to respond.
- Ask the child to point to the missing part on the card if ambiguous responses are given on items 6, 13, 21, 23, and 28.
- In other cases as well, whenever there is any doubt about the child's verbal or pointing response, ask for clarification.
- On item 29, give credit to "rib" or "spoke" (personal communication, spokesperson Lawrence Weiss, for The Psychological Corporation, September 1991).
- Although the letters are missing on the buttons of the telephone (item 23), a spokesperson for The Psychological Corporation advised that you not give credit to a response mentioning this omission because it is an unessential missing part (personal communication, Lawrence Weiss, January 1992). If this is the first unessential missing part mentioned by the child, say, "Yes, but what is the most important part that is missing?"

Starting Considerations
- All children begin with the same sample item. Then children 6 to 7 years old (and older children suspected of mental retardation) are administered item 1; children 8 to 9 years old, item 5; children 10 to 13 years old, item 7; and children 14 to 16 years old, item 11.
- If a child 8 to 16 years old earns a score of 0 on either of the first two items you administer, give the preceding items in *reverse order* until two consecutive items are passed.

Scoring Considerations
- All items are scored 1 or 0 (pass-fail).
- If a child 8 to 16 years old obtains a perfect score on the first two items that you administer, give the child full credit for all of the preceding items.
- When you administer the items in reverse order, give credit for any items not administered that precede two consecutive successes.
- Give credit for any reasonable response; the response does not have to be the exact name of the missing part.
- An item is failed if a child points to the correct place but gives a wrong verbal response.

Discontinuance Considerations
- The subtest is discontinued after five consecutive failures.

Interpretive Suggestions

As you administer the subtest, consider the following:

- Does the child understand the task?
- Does the child respond with a word, with a description of the missing detail, or by pointing?
- Does the child mainly give verbal responses or pointing responses?
- Does the child respond impulsively, saying anything that comes to mind, or does the child search for the right answer?
- Does the child find fault with himself or herself or with the picture after failing an item?
- Does the child benefit from any guiding statements given, such as "Yes, but what is the *most important part* that is missing?"
- What is the child's rate of response (e.g., quick and impulsive or slow and deliberate)?
- Is the child fearful of making an error, hesitant, or suspicious?
- Is the child aware of being timed? If so, does the timing make the child anxious or prompt the child to change the pace of responding?
- Does the child frequently use nondescriptive speech, such as "It's that thing there"?
- Does the child give roundabout definitions of words (sometimes called circumlocutions)? Circumlocutions may suggest word-retrieval difficulties.
- Does the child have trouble producing the right word (sometimes referred to as dysnomia)? Dysnomia may suggest word-retrieval difficulties.
- Does the child repeatedly say that nothing is missing? Such a response may reflect negativism.
- Does the child hold the booklet close to his or her face or put his or her face close to the booklet? Such a habit may suggest visual difficulties.

If the child's performance leaves any doubt about her or his visual skills, request a visual examination.

Observe whether perseveration occurs. A child displays perseveration, for example, by saying "ear" for each picture portraying an animal (pictures 1, 3, and 5). "Ear" is the correct answer for picture 1, but not for the subsequent pictures depicting animals.

The Picture Completion items can be classified as pattern-symmetry items (1, 2, 3, 4, 5, 9, 10, 12, 13, 14, 15, 25, 26, 27, and 30) or knowledge-based items (6, 7, 8, 11, 16, 17, 18, 19, 20, 21, 22, 23, 24, 28, and 29; Kaplan et al., 1999). Studying the child's error pattern will give you information about where the errors occurred. Pattern-symmetry failures may reflect visual-spatial problems, whereas failures on knowledge-based items may reflect limited exposure to the environment.

Comparing a child's Picture Completion score with those on Block Design and Object Assembly may help you distinguish between visuospatial difficulties and visual-motor diffi-

culties. Picture Completion is the only task on the WISC–III Performance Scale that does not require a motor component.

The child who usually responds in less than 5 seconds may be more impulsive, more confident, and, if correct, more skilled than the child who takes more time. The child who responds correctly *after* the time limit (for which no credit is received) may be more skilled than the child who fails the item even with additional time. Because the pass-fail scoring does not make provisions for such qualitative factors, carefully evaluate individual variations in each case and discuss these qualitative factors in the written report. Delayed correct responses may suggest temporary inefficiency, insecurity, depression, or simply a slow and diligent approach, whereas extremely quick but incorrect responses may reflect impulsivity.

Low scores on the Picture Completion subtest may indicate anxiety affecting concentration and attention, preoccupation with irrelevant details, or negativism ("Nothing is missing").

After you administer the subtest, you can inquire about the child's perceptions of the task: "How did you go about coming up with the answer?" or "How did you decide when to give an answer?" Inquire about any noteworthy or unclear answers. The child's behavior during this subtest may provide insight into how she or he reacts to time pressure. As a testing-of-limits procedure, you can ask the child to look again at the pictures that were missed. You might say, "Look at this picture again. Before, you said that … was missing. That's not the part that's missing. Look for something else." In some cases, you may ask the child to describe or name the picture, especially when many items are missed. The factor analytic results suggest that verbal reasoning may help children detect the missing part of the pictures.

The range of scaled scores from 1 to 19 at ages 6–0 to 13–11 years aids in profile analysis. However, profile analysis is limited at ages 14–0 to 15–11 years and 16–0 to 16–11 years, where the scaled scores range from 1 to 18 and 1 to 17, respectively.

Question: What are 12, 14, and 16?
Answer: That's easy; MTV, Fox, and Cartoon Network.

CODING

The Coding subtest requires that the child copy symbols paired with other symbols. The subtest consists of two separate and distinct parts. Each part uses a key. In Coding A, the key consists of five shapes—a star, a circle, a triangle, a cross, and a square. Within each shape, there is a special mark (a vertical line, two horizontal lines, a horizontal line, a circle, and two vertical lines, respectively). The child must place within each test shape (which is empty) the mark that is within the key shape. There are 5 practice shapes, followed by 59 shapes in the subtest proper.

In Coding B, the key consists of boxes containing one of the numbers 1 to 9 in the upper part and a symbol in the lower part. Each number is paired with a different symbol. The test stimuli are boxes whose upper part contains a number and lower part is empty. The child must write in the empty box the symbol that is paired with the number in the key. There are 7 practice boxes, followed by 119 boxes in the subtest proper.

Rationale

Coding assesses the child's ability to learn an unfamiliar task. The subtest involves speed and accuracy of visual-motor coordination, speed of mental operation (processing speed), attentional skills, visual acuity, visual scanning and tracking (repeated visual scanning between the code key and answer spaces), short-term memory for new learning (paired-associate learning of an unfamiliar code), cognitive flexibility (in shifting rapidly from one pair to another), handwriting speed, and, possibly, motivation. Success depends not only on comprehension of the task but also on fine-motor skills. The subtest is sensitive to visuoperceptual difficulties.

Coding B also may involve a verbal-encoding process if the child attaches verbal descriptions to the symbols. For example, a child may label the + symbol as a "plus sign" or "cross" and the V symbol as the letter "V." A child may improve his or her performance when using verbal labels to code the symbols. Consequently, Coding B can be described as measuring the ability to learn combinations of symbols and shapes and the ability to make associations quickly and accurately. Coding A also can involve a verbal-encoding process, but to a lesser degree. Coding A and Coding B thus may involve separate information-processing modes. "The speed and accuracy with which the child performs the task are a measure of the child's intellectual ability. At each step in the task the [child] must inspect the next digit, go to the proper location in the table, code the information distinguishing the symbol found, and carry this information in short-term memory long enough to reproduce the symbol in the proper answer box" (Estes, 1974, p. 745). Thus, you can conceptualize Coding as an information-processing task involving the discrimination and memory of visual pattern symbols.

Factor Analytic Findings

The Coding subtest is a poor measure of g (20% of its variance can be attributed to g—range of 10 to 30% in the 11 age groups), and it contributes substantially to the Processing Speed Index (average loading = .63). Specificity is ample at ages 6, 7, and 9 through 16 years and inadequate at age 8 years.

Reliability and Correlational Highlights

Coding is a relatively reliable subtest (r_{xx} = .79), with reliability coefficients above .70 at ages 6, 7, 10, 11, 14, and 15

(range of .70 to .90). Unfortunately, there are no reliability coefficients provided in the WISC–III manual for ages 8, 9, 12, 13, and 16 because children were not retested at these ages. It correlates better with Symbol Search (r = .53) than with any of the other subtests and has a moderately low correlation with the Full Scale (r = .33) and the Performance Scale (r = .32) and a low correlation with the Verbal Scale (r = .29).

Administrative Suggestions

Here are some administrative suggestions for the Coding subtest.

Background Considerations
- Because Coding may penalize a child with visual defects or with specific motor disabilities, do not give the subtest to a child with either of these disabilities. If you give it to a child with either of these disabilities, do not include it in the final calculation of the IQ.
- Coding may also penalize a left-handed child, if the way the child writes causes the child to cover the key immediately above the line of writing. If this is the case, the child will have to lift her or his hand repeatedly during the task to view the key. If the child is left-handed, the WISC–III manual suggests that you place an extra Coding Response Sheet to the right of the child's sheet and have the child work with the separate key during both the practice items and the subtest proper.
- Each part of the subtests has a time limit of 120 seconds; however, practice items are not timed.
- Observe how the child proceeds with the task. Note any differences in the quality of the symbols drawn early and late in the task. If the child stops working after the first line, say, "Continue on the next line." Count these instructions as part of the 120-second time limit.
- If the child skips around, filling in symbols for like shapes or like numbers first, instruct the child to proceed in order: "Do them in order. Don't skip any." Count these instructions as part of the 120-second time limit.

Starting Considerations
- Children under 8 years of age are administered Coding A, whereas children 8 years of age and older are administered Coding B.
- The Coding subtest items are located in the Record Form.
- Tear the page out of the Record Form to administer this subtest.
- Administer the subtest on a smooth drawing surface.
- Be sure to record the child's name, the date, and your name at the top of the Coding Response Sheet.
- You and the child should each use a no. 2 graphite pencil without an eraser.
- Correct the child's mistakes immediately when you administer the practice items.
- Do not begin the subtest until the child clearly understands the task.

Scoring Considerations

- On Coding A, allot 1 point for each correct item, and give up to 6 additional time-bonus points for a perfect score.
- On Coding B, give 1 point for each correct item, but *do not* give any time-bonus points.
- Do not include the responses to the practice items in scoring either Coding A or Coding B.
- Do not penalize the child for imperfectly drawn symbols as long as the symbols can be clearly identified as the keyed symbols.
- Give credit for symbols that are spontaneously corrected within the time limit.
- Use the template to score the child's responses.
- If your scoring template does not have a number above each box, write the numbers in. After you write in the numbers, laminate the template to prolong its life (Danielson, 1991).
- If you want to record the pace at which the child completes the Coding items, first arrange the seating so that you can observe the child's performance (R. Dumont and J. Willis, personal communication, March 2000). Second, have your own copy of the Coding sheet, and number every box on the sheet. Third, position the sheet so that it is upside down, to facilitate transcription. Finally, at the end of the 30-, 60-, and 90-second intervals, record on your numbered Coding sheet the symbol that the child has reached. Write these numbers down on the WISC–III protocol next to the Coding raw score entry (e.g., 12/10/11/14). The WISC–III PI presents norms for this procedure (Kaplan et al., 1999).

Discontinuance Considerations

- Coding A and Coding B are each discontinued after 120 seconds, unless the child has finished before that time.

Interpretive Suggestions

Following are some useful questions to guide your observation:

- Does the child understand the task?
- Does the child understand and proceed correctly after you give an explanation?
- Does the child use one hand to hold the paper in place and the other hand to draw the symbols?
- Is the child impulsive?
- Is the child meticulous?
- Does the child seem overly anxious?
- Does the child display tremor?
- Does the child's speed increase or decrease as the subtest proceeds?
- Are the child's symbol marks well executed, barely recognizable, or incorrect?
- Do the child's symbol marks show any distortions, such as reversals? If so, do the distortions appear only once, occasionally, or each time the child draws the symbol mark? How many different symbols are distorted?

- Does the child draw the same symbol repeatedly even though the numbers change (perseveration)?
- Is the child penalized for lack of speed, inaccuracy, or both?
- Are the child's failures due to inadequate form perception or to poor attention?
- Does the child check each symbol with the sample, or does the child seem to remember the symbols (e.g., not look up at the code at the top of the page)?
- Does the child recheck every symbol before moving on to the next one?
- Does the child pick out one number only and skip the others?
- Is the child's work smooth and orderly, or does the child seem confused at times and have difficulty finding his or her place?
- Is the child aware of any errors?
- Do the child's errors occur in some regular manner?
- How does the child react to errors?
- Is the child persistent?
- Does the child need urging to continue the task?
- Does the child appear bored with the task?
- Does the child hold the pencil in an appropriate way (e.g., pencil grip appropriate or pencil grip too tight, hand steady or hand shaking)?
- Does the child try to use an eraser from another pencil or another source? If so, does the child seem to realize that an eraser is not supposed to be used?
- Does the child stop in the middle of the task, stretch, sigh, look around, and talk?

Answers to the above questions will provide information about the child's attention span, method of working, and other behaviors. If the child makes many errors, consider whether the errors might be due to impulsivity, poor self-monitoring and poor self-correction, or visual-motor difficulties (Kaplan et al. 1999). An increase in speed, coupled with correct copying of symbols, suggests that the child is adjusting well to the task. A decrease in speed, coupled with incorrect copying of symbols, suggests that the child may be showing fatigue. And a decrease in speed, coupled with correct copying of symbols, suggests that the child may be bored, distracted, or fatigued. Some research suggests that motor speed, but not incidental learning, is related to Coding scores (Kelly & Britton, 1996).

In the standardization group, there was a consistent decrease from the first 30-second interval to the second 30-second interval by about 3 Coding items and a less consistent decrease from the second interval to the third interval (Kaplan et al., 1999). Children referred for learning problems have a similar rate of decrease (about 2 to 3 Coding items) after the first 30-second interval (Dumont, Farr, Willis, & Whelley, 1998). Thus, a slight decrease in the number of Coding items successfully completed after the first 30-second interval is the norm, rather than the exception.

Coding is particularly useful for evaluating a child's attention when you suspect attentional difficulties, such as in cases of attention-deficit/hyperactivity disorder, anxiety, or a traumatic brain injury. If other tests indicate that the child has adequate response speed and visual acuity, then poor scores on Coding are likely to be associated with attentional deficits and not visuoperceptual difficulties per se. A slow and deliberate approach may suggest depressive features.

Distortion of forms may mean that the child has difficulties with perceptual functioning. Ask the child about any symbol that was written peculiarly to find out whether it has some symbolic meaning to the child. Perseveration may suggest neurological difficulties that should be investigated further. Boredom might be present with a bright child who is not challenged by the task.

Low scores on the Coding subtest may indicate visual-motor coordination difficulties, distractibility, anxiety, visual defects, poor pencil control, poor motivation, excessive concern for detail in reproducing symbols (perfectionism), lethargy or boredom, or impulsivity.

After the *entire test* is over, you can go back to the Coding subtest and ask the child about how the symbol-number combinations were remembered. This testing-of-limits procedure may give you insight about the strategies the child used on the task. You also may want to go over each symbol that was copied wrong and ask the child to tell you whether it looks like the symbol in the key.

The range of scaled scores from 1 to 19 at all ages aids in profile analysis.

Question: What is celebrated on Thanksgiving Day?
Answer: My cousin's birthday.

PICTURE ARRANGEMENT

The Picture Arrangement subtest requires the child to place a series of pictures in logical order. The subtest contains 14 series, or items, similar to short comic strips. Your task is to first place individual cards with pictures in front of the child in a specified disarranged order and then ask the child to rearrange the pictures in the "right" order to tell a story that makes sense. The number of pictures per set ranges from three to six. The only motor action required of the child is to change the position of the pictures.

Rationale

The Picture Arrangement subtest measures the child's ability to comprehend and evaluate a situation. To accomplish the task, the child must grasp the general idea of a story. Although some children take a trial-and-error approach to the subtest, success usually depends on an appraisal of the total situation depicted in the pictures.

Picture Arrangement is considered to be a measure of nonverbal reasoning that involves planning ability, anticipa-

tion, visual organization, and temporal sequencing. The subtest measures the ability to anticipate the consequences of initial acts or situations, as well as the ability to interpret social situations. Some children may generate covert, analytical, verbal descriptions of alternative story sequences to guide them in arranging the stimulus cards. In such cases, the subtest may measure verbal sequencing processes as well. The capacity to anticipate, judge, and understand the possible antecedents and consequences of events is important in lending meaningful continuity to everyday experiences.

Factor Analytic Findings

The Picture Arrangement subtest is a fair measure of g (36% of its variance can be attributed to g), and it contributes minimally to the Perceptual Organization Index (average loading = .38) and to the Verbal Comprehension Index (average loading = .34). Specificity is ample at all ages.

Reliability and Correlational Highlights

Picture Arrangement is a relatively reliable subtest (r_{xx} = .76), with reliability coefficients of .70 or above at all of the age groups (range of .70 to .84). It correlates better with Block Design (r = .41), Information (r = .40), Vocabulary (r = .40), and Similarities (r = .39) than with any of the other subtests. It has a moderate correlation with the Full Scale (r = .52) and a moderately low correlation with the Performance Scale (r = .49) and the Verbal Scale (r = .45).

Administrative Suggestions

Here are some administrative suggestions for the Picture Arrangement subtest.

Background Considerations
- Administer one set of cards at a time to the child.
- Place the Picture Arrangement cards at least 3 or 4 inches away from the edge of the table. Arrange them from the child's left to right, in the order specified in the WISC–III manual.
- For the sample item, the cards are laid out *before* you give the instructions, while for the regular items, the cards are laid out *after* you give the instructions.
- When you present the sample item and demonstration (trial 2 of items 1 and 2), move each card down to a new row rather than shifting the cards within their original row.
- Give two trials for items 1 and 2.
- Coach the child (as indicated in the WISC–III manual) if either item 1 or item 2 is failed.
- Each item is timed, with 45 seconds allowed for items 1 to 11 and 60 seconds allowed for items 12 to 14.
- If the child does not tell you when he or she is finished, ask promptly. Stop timing when the child is obviously finished, though, even if the child does not tell you.

- When the child places the cards from his or her right to left, ask the child to tell you where the story begins.
- Record the child's Picture Arrangement sequence as soon as you pick up the cards.
- The instructions emphasize that the child should work as quickly as possible.
- When the child is perfectionistic in arranging the cards, tell the child that the cards do not have to be perfectly straight (or aligned).

Starting Considerations
- All children begin with the sample item. Then children 6 to 8 years old (and older children suspected of mental retardation) are administered item 1, and children 9 to 16 years, item 3.
- If a child 9 to 16 years old fails item 3, administer items 1 and 2 in normal sequence.
- As you present the demonstration items to the child (i.e., the sample item and trial 2 of items 1 and 2), be sure not to accidentally cover the pictures with your hand—the child must be able to see all the pictures and follow your movements when you rearrange the pictures.

Scoring Considerations
- Items 1 and 2 are scored as 2, 1, or 0. Items 3 to 14 are scored as 5, 4, 3, 2, or 0, with 2 points for the correct arrangement and up to 3 additional time-bonus points.
- Give 1 point for an alternative arrangement on item 14, but do not give time-bonus points for the alternative arrangement.
- If you begin the subtest with item 3 and item 3 is passed, give the child credit for items 1 and 2.

Discontinuance Considerations
- The subtest is discontinued after three consecutive failures.

Interpretive Suggestions

The Picture Arrangement subtest gives you the opportunity to observe how the child approaches a performance task involving planning ability.

- Does the child look at all of the cards first before starting to arrange them?
- Does the child examine the cards, come to some decision, and then reassess his or her decision while arranging the cards?
- Does the child proceed quickly, without stopping to reconsider decisions?
- Does the child arrange the cards in one order and then rearrange them several times?
- Does the child pick up the cards and attempt to look at the back of them for any cues?

- Are the child's failures due to lack of understanding of the task, such as leaving the pictures in their original order?
- Are low scores the result of not being able to place the pictures in the proper sequence, an impulsive and careless style of responding, or a slow and perfectionistic style of responding?
- What type of errors does the child make? For instance, are cards placed in a perfunctory or random manner, or is one card always moved to the same position?
- Is the child persistent, discouraged, impulsive, or rigid?
- What types of trial-and-error patterns does the child use?
- How does the child's approach to the Picture Arrangement items compare with his or her approach to the Block Design and Object Assembly items?
- Does the child consistently employ the same patterns when searching for solutions? If not, what are the different patterns employed, and what might account for when and where they are used?
- How do task content, fatigue, and mood changes influence the child's approach to the items?
- Does the child talk aloud while solving the problems? If so, do the child's verbalizations give you any insight about how the child perceives the task?
- Does coaching help the child grasp the point of the arrangement, story, or task requirements if you coach the child on trial 2 of items 1 and 2?
- Does the child offer to put the cards back in the box after the task is over?
- Does the child ask about his or her performance (e.g., "Did I get that right?")?

The child's performance on the Picture Arrangement subtest may give you information about her or his reasoning. Failures may be due to difficulties in logical reasoning. However, faulty solutions may also result from overlooking details (e.g., on the CASH item, the child may fail to use the time on the clock as a clue to the correct arrangement). One study indicates that scores on Picture Arrangement are not related to clinicians' ratings of children's social competence (Lipsetz et al., 1993). However, another study indicates that Picture Arrangement scores are significantly related to teachers' reports of conduct problems ($r = -.27$), social skills ($r = .30$), and leadership ($r = .31$; Beebe et al., 2000).

Children older than 8 years may be displaying reasoning difficulties when they regularly make young, immature arrangements. Children with mental retardation, children with brain injuries, and children with behavior disorders may show reasoning difficulties on Picture Arrangement. Although children with mild behavior disorders usually produce logical stories, they may rush through the task or reveal their anxieties and preoccupations by unusual arrangements, such as neglecting details for the sake of a particular theme.

Low scores on the Picture Arrangement subtest may indicate difficulty with visual organization and sequential processing, difficulty in anticipating events and their consequences, inattentiveness, anxiety, failure to use cues, difficulty working under time pressure, impulsivity, or poor visual acuity and discrimination.

After the *entire test* is over, you can conduct one of the following useful testing-of-limits procedures.

1. *Give additional time.* One at a time, lay out the arrangements that the child had partially completed correctly and give the child additional time to complete them.

2. *Give cues on failed items.* Place the first card before the child and say, "Here is the first picture. What goes next?" If one card does not help the child, place the second correct card next to the first one and say, "What picture goes next?" In some cases you may need to arrange even more than one or two cards to help the child. The child who solves the problems with cues may have more ability than the child who fails in spite of receiving cues. Introduce such graded help only after you have completed the entire test because such help during the test can raise Picture Arrangement scores (Sattler, 1969).

3. *Use a multiple-choice procedure.* One at a time, present three arrangements—one correct and two incorrect. Ask the child to indicate which one makes the most sense.

4. *Ask for a different sequence.* Ask the child to arrange the stories, one at a time, in a sequence different from the incorrect arrangements.

5. *Ask the child to tell you about his or her arrangements and make up a story.* One way to do this is to ask the child to explain or describe one or more arrangements. Select items that you think may help you understand the child's thought patterns better. You may want to focus on items that the child failed. However, you can also select items that the child passed; even correct arrangements do not necessarily mean that the child interpreted the series correctly. Because the last two items tried are likely to be the most complex for the child, you might select them if you have no other specific choices.

Arrange the cards for each item separately, in the order given by the child. Then say, "Tell what is happening in the pictures" or "Make up a story" or "Tell me what the pictures show." Although Picture Arrangement is not standardized as a projective technique, the child may project feelings, affect, and experiences in the process of telling stories.

A second version of this procedure involves randomly placing the DOG sequence of cards before the child and then asking the child to make up a story about *one* of the cards. After the child has completed the story and you have removed the cards, arrange the WALK sequence of cards randomly and ask the child to tell a story about one of those cards. You can follow this procedure for any other items that you administered during the test proper.

Consider the following in evaluating the stories:

- Are the child's stories logical, fanciful, confused, or bizarre?

- Are the child's stories creative or conventional?
- Does the child reveal any themes in the stories, such as self-oriented, socially oriented, or repetitive themes?
- Are the child's incorrect arrangements a consequence of incorrect perceptions of details in the pictures or of failure to consider some details?
- Does the child consider all the relationships in the pictures?
- Are the child's sequences correct, although the point of the story is missed?
- Are the child's sequences incorrect, although the point of the story is grasped?

The range of scaled scores from 1 to 19 at all ages aids in profile analysis.

Question: What is the capital of Greece?
Answer: G.

BLOCK DESIGN

The Block Design subtest requires the child to reproduce designs, using three-dimensional blocks that have a red surface, a white surface, and a surface cut diagonally into half red and half white. The subtest contains 12 items. The child uses blocks to assemble a design identical to a model constructed by the examiner (items 1 and 2) or to a two-dimensional, red-and-white picture (items 3 to 12). The items are arranged in order of increasing difficulty.

Rationale

On the Block Design subtest, the child must perceive and analyze forms by breaking down a whole (the design) into its parts and then assembling the components into the identical design. This process is called analysis and synthesis. To succeed, the child must use visual organization and visual-motor coordination. Success also involves the application of logic and reasoning to spatial relationship problems. Consequently, you can consider Block Design to be a nonverbal concept-formation task requiring perceptual organization, spatial visualization, and abstract conceptualization. You also can view it as a constructional task involving spatial relations and figure-ground separation.

Different strategies can be used to assemble the blocks (Rozencwajg, 1991). One is a *global strategy* in which the child assembles blocks in a stepwise trial-and-error procedure; with this strategy, the child does not analyze the components of the model. A second is an *analytical strategy* in which the child forms a representation of the model and then decomposes the design into blocks. Once the blocks have been identified, the child selects and orients them before placing them in the design.

A child's performance on Block Design may be affected by rate of motor activity and vision. However, do not interpret inadequate performance as *direct* evidence of inadequate visual form and pattern perception, because the ability to discriminate block designs (i.e., to perceive the designs accurately at a recognition level) may be intact even when the ability to reproduce the designs is impaired. The child's performance on Picture Completion may help you evaluate her or his performance on Block Design.

Factor Analytic Findings

The Block Design subtest is the best measure of *g* among the Performance Scale subtests. It is the fourth-best measure of *g* in the WISC–III (56% of its variance can be attributed to *g*), and it contributes substantially to the Perceptual Organization Index (average loading = .67) and minimally to the Verbal Comprehension Index (average loading = .30). Specificity is ample at all ages.

Reliability and Correlational Highlights

Block Design is a reliable subtest (r_{xx} = .87), with reliability coefficients above .70 at all of the age groups (range of .77 to .92). It correlates better with Object Assembly (r = .61), Picture Completion (r = .52), and Arithmetic (r = .52) than with any of the other subtests. It has a moderately high correlation with the Full Scale (r = .66) and the Performance Scale (r = .65) and a moderate correlation with the Verbal Scale (r = .57). It correlates better with the Verbal Scale than do any of the other subtests on the Performance Scale.

Administrative Suggestions

Here are some administrative suggestions for the Block Design subtest.

Background Considerations
- The area on your desk that you use to administer Block Design should be clear of other blocks and materials.
- Construct the design for item 1 by laying out the two blocks from the child's left to right.
- Construct the design for item 2 by completing, from the child's left to right, the first row (i.e., the top row of the design from the child's perspective) and then the second row.
- Scramble the blocks before you administer each new design, and place before the child the exact number of blocks needed for each item.
- Two blocks are used for item 1, four blocks for items 2 to 9, and nine blocks for items 10 to 12.
- A variety of block surfaces should face up (i.e., only one block with a red-and-white side facing up for the two- and four-block designs, and only two blocks with a red-and-white side facing up for the nine-block designs).

- Show the child the correct orientation only after the first time the child rotates a design.
- Ask the child to tell you when items 1, 2, 3, 10, 11, and 12 are completed if you have any doubt about when he or she is finished. In such cases, say, "Tell me when you have finished." Give this instruction routinely on items 4 to 9, as indicated in the WISC–III manual, and repeat it on the other items as needed.
- Record the exact amount of time it takes the child to construct each design, and record whether the child successfully constructs the design.
- All items are timed, with item 1 having a maximum of 30 seconds; items 2 to 5, 45 seconds; items 6 to 9, 75 seconds; and items 10 to 12, 120 seconds.

Starting Considerations
- Children 6 to 7 years old (and older children suspected of mental retardation) begin with item 1, and children 8 to 16 years old, item 3.
- When you demonstrate the sample items, put them together slowly. Be careful not to cover the blocks with your hand; the child needs to see what you are doing. Make the designs so that they are in the appropriate direction for the child. This means that you will be making the designs upside down. Don't make a design right side up and then turn the whole thing around to face the child.
- If a child 8 to 16 years old fails item 3, administer items 1 and 2 in normal sequence.

Scoring Considerations
- Items 1 to 3 are scored 2 (correct on trial 1), 1 (correct on trial 2), or 0 (failed on trial 1 and trial 2).
- Items 4 to 12 are given 4 points for correct completion and up to 3 additional time-bonus points.
- Give a score of 0 to designs that are rotated more than 30°.
- Give the child credit for items 1 and 2 if you begin the subtest with item 3 and the child passes item 3 on the first trial.

Discontinuance Considerations
- The subtest is discontinued after two consecutive failures.

Interpretive Suggestions

Block Design is an excellent subtest for observing the child's problem-solving approach and fine-motor skills. Consider the following issues:

- Is the child hasty and impulsive or deliberate and careful?
- Does the child slowly and methodically check each block with the design or rarely check her or his work?
- Does the child give up easily or become frustrated when faced with possible failure, or does the child persist and keep on working even after the time limit is reached?

- Does the child use only one approach, or does the child alter her or his approach as the need arises?
- Does the child use a slow approach or a rapid trial-and-error approach?
- Is the child excessively concerned with lining up the blocks precisely?
- Does the child study the designs first before attempting to construct them?
- Does the child appear to have a plan when assembling the blocks?
- Does the child construct the design in units of blocks, or does the child work in a piecemeal fashion?
- Does the child understand the principle of using individual blocks to construct the designs?
- Does the child try to place the blocks on the picture of the design?
- Does the child express concerns about differences between blocks?
- Does the child interpret white portions of the design card as open spaces in the assembled designs?
- Does the child use a solid red or solid white block surface for a red-and-white surface?
- Does the child say that her or his designs are correct when, in fact, they are not?
- Are the child's designs correct but rotated?
- Does the child rotate single blocks?
- Can the child rotate a row of blocks at the bottom when the blocks are in the wrong direction, or does she or he start the entire design over again?
- Does the child show any indications of fine-motor difficulties such as tremor or clumsiness?
- Does the child offer to put the blocks back in the box after the task is over?

Excessive fumbling or failure to check the pattern may indicate anxiety. Visuoperceptual difficulties may be indicated if the child moves or twists around to improve his or her perspective on the design or if the child leaves space between the blocks in the assembled design. Try to differentiate between excessive cautiousness as a personality style and excessive slowness as a possible indication of depression or boredom. Children who continually recheck their work with the model may be revealing insecurities or obsessive tendencies.

Conduct testing-of-limits after you have administered the *entire test,* because if you don't, you will violate standard procedures and the cues you give may lead to higher scores (Sattler, 1969). One useful testing-of-limits procedure is to select an item that the child has incorrectly constructed, assemble the incorrect reproduction, and ask the child if the reproduction is the same as or different from the original design. If the child recognizes that his or her design is incorrect and can tell you the specific errors (e.g., "A red-and-white block goes here, not a white block"), the child may have a visual-motor execution problem rather than a visual-motor recognition problem.

Another testing-of-limits procedure involves showing the child the Block Design card (or assembled design) for a design that the child failed. As you give the directions, place one row or block in its correct position. Say, "Let's try some of these again. I'm going to put together some of the blocks. I'll make the top row [or arrange the first block]. Now you go ahead and finish it. Make one like this. Tell me when you have finished." If the child still fails, arrange additional blocks. Record the amount of help the child needs to reproduce the design accurately. A child who needs many cues to reproduce the designs may have weaker spatial reasoning ability than a child who needs only a few cues. In some cases, the additional cues may not help the child reproduce the designs.

Other testing-of-limits procedures are also possible. One is to show the child three different arrangements, only one of which is correct. Then ask the child to point to the arrangement that is the same as the one on the card. Be sure to vary the placement of the correct design. Another procedure is to ask the child to tell you how he or she goes about making the block design pattern.

The range of scaled scores from 1 to 19 at ages 6–0 to 15–11 years aids in profile analysis. However, at 16–0 to 16–11 years, profile analysis is somewhat hindered because scaled scores range only from 1 to 18.

Question: In what direction does the sun rise?
Answer: Near Kansas City.

OBJECT ASSEMBLY

The Object Assembly subtest requires a child to put jigsaw puzzle pieces together to form common objects: a girl (seven pieces), a car (seven pieces), a horse (six pieces), a ball (six pieces), and a face (nine pieces). There is one sample item: an apple (four pieces).

Rationale

The Object Assembly subtest is mainly a test of the child's skill at synthesis—putting things together to form familiar objects. It requires visual-motor coordination, with motor activity guided by visual perception and sensorimotor feedback. Object Assembly also is a test of visual organizational ability, for the child needs visual organization to produce an object out of parts that may not be immediately recognizable. To solve the jigsaw puzzles, the child must be able to grasp an entire pattern by anticipating the relationships among its individual parts. The tasks require some constructive ability, as well as perceptual skill—the child must recognize individual parts and place them correctly in the incomplete figure.

The child's performance also may be related to her or his rate and precision of motor activity; persistence, especially when much trial and error is required; and long-term visual memory (having stored information about the object to be formed).

Factor Analytic Findings

The Object Assembly subtest is a fair measure of g (44% of its variance can be attributed to g), and it contributes substantially to the Perceptual Organization Index (average loading = .66). Specificity is either ample or adequate at ages 6, 9, 13, and 15 years and inadequate at ages 7, 8, 10, 11, 12, 14, and 16 years.

Reliability and Correlational Highlights

Object Assembly is a marginally reliable subtest (r_{xx} = .69), with reliability coefficients above .70 at ages 6, 9, 13, 15, and 16 years and between .60 and .69 at ages 7, 8, 10, 11, 12, and 14 years (range of .60 to .76). It correlates better with Block Design (r = .61) than with any of the other subtests. It has a moderate correlation with the Full Scale (r = .58), a moderately high correlation with the Performance Scale (r = .60), and a moderately low correlation with the Verbal Scale (r = .48).

Administrative Suggestions

Here are some administrative suggestions for the Object Assembly subtest.

Background Considerations
- All children are administered every item, beginning with the sample item and continuing with items 1 to 5.
- Place all the pieces right side up in the disarranged pattern specified in the diagram on the Object Assembly Layout Shield. Arrange the pieces close to the child so that he or she does not waste time reaching for them.
- All items are timed. The first item has a maximum of 120 seconds; the next two items, 150 seconds each; and the last two items, 180 seconds each.
- As soon as you complete the directions for each item, begin timing.
- Observe time limits carefully on each item. Record the elapsed time precisely, because the child receives additional points for quick execution on all items.
- Be sure that the child does not see the pages of the WISC–III manual that contain pictures of the correctly assembled objects.
- Use the Object Assembly Layout Shield not only to set up the individual puzzle parts but also to shield the WISC–III manual.

- If the child turns over any piece, promptly and unobtrusively turn it right side up.
- As in other subtests, you may have to ask the child to tell you when he or she is finished by saying "Tell me when you have finished." You may need to give this instruction on items 2 to 5 even though the directions in the WISC–III manual do not say you should do so.
- Record the number of junctures completed within the time limit.

Starting Considerations
- Tell the child the name of the object that you are constructing only on the first two Object Assembly items.

Scoring Considerations
- The girl (item 1), car (item 2), and horse (item 3) have a maximum score of 8 (6 points plus 2 time-bonus points for perfect assembly), whereas the ball (item 4) and face (item 5) items have a maximum score of 10 (7 points plus 3 time-bonus points for perfect assembly).
- Give points for partially correct assemblies on all items.
- When you give partial scores, count the number of junctures completed when the time limit has been reached.

Discontinuance Considerations
- The subtest is discontinued after the fifth puzzle is administered.

Because all items are given to all children, young school-aged children may experience some frustration on Object Assembly. Future research should investigate the potential effects a discontinuance criterion would have on Object Assembly. For example, would it reduce young children's anxiety level without affecting the reliability and validity of the subtest?

Interpretive Suggestions

Object Assembly is an especially good subtest for observing the child's thinking style and work habits. Some children envision the complete object almost from the start and either recognize or have an imperfect understanding of the relations of the individual parts to the whole. Other children merely try to fit the pieces together by trial-and-error methods. Still others have initial failure, followed by trial and error, and then sudden insight and recognition of the object.

Observe the child's performance, including responses to errors and the handling of frustration.

- Does the child (a) demand to know what the object is before constructing it, (b) insist that pieces are missing, or (c) say that the object doesn't make sense?
- Does the child recognize what the object is before putting the pieces together?
- Does the child know the name of the object but still have difficulty assembling it? For example, does the child say,

"It's a soccer ball," but continue to attempt to assemble a nonrounded shape?

- Does the child peek over the shield when you are putting out the pieces?
- If low scores are earned, are they due to, for example, temporary inefficiency (such as reversal of two parts) or spending a long time lining up each piece precisely, which results in loss of time-bonus credits?
- What is the child's problem-solving approach to the task (e.g., trial and error, a systematic and apparently planned process, random placement of pieces)?
- What is the tempo of the child's performance (e.g., slow, deliberate, fast, impulsive)?
- Does the child spend a long time with one piece, trying to position it in an incorrect location? (If so, this behavior may indicate anxiety or rigidity.)
- Which hand does the child prefer to use to assemble the puzzles?
- What is the quality of the child's motor coordination (e.g., smooth, jerky, uncoordinated, suggesting tremor)?
- Does the child offer to put the pieces back in the box after the task is completed?

Low scores on the Object Assembly subtest may indicate visual-motor difficulties, visuoperceptual problems, poor planning ability, difficulty in perceiving a whole, minimal experience with construction tasks, limited interest in assembly tasks, limited persistence, difficulty working under time pressure, or impulsivity.

After you administer the subtest, ask the child about any constructions that may be peculiar or unusual (such as pieces placed on top of each other). You can use testing-of-limits procedures similar to those described for the Picture Arrangement and Block Design subtests after you have administered the *entire test*. For example, you can introduce a series of graduated cues, such as placing one or more pieces in the correct location. Note the amount of help the child needs to complete the task successfully. The child who needs only a few cues to complete the object may have better underlying perceptual organization skills, not evident during the standard administration of the subtest, than the child who needs many cues.

Another testing-of-limits approach is to ask the child to visualize the object in her or his mind before you lay out the puzzle pieces. For example, say, "Think of how a horse looks" and then give the child the horse item. See if this instruction helps the child assemble the puzzle. An additional procedure is to show the child a picture of the completed object and see whether the child is able to put the pieces together correctly with the aid of a picture. Still another procedure is to ask the child to tell you how each object was put together.

The range of scaled scores from 1 to 19 at ages 6-0 to 15-11 years aids in profile analysis. However, at ages 16-0 to 16-11 years, profile analysis is somewhat hindered because scaled scores range only from 1 to 18.

Question: Count as high as you can.
Answer: One, two, three, four, five, six, seven, eight, nine, pause, fast forward, rewind, play, and record.

SYMBOL SEARCH

The Symbol Search subtest, a supplementary subtest, requires the child to look at a symbol and then decide whether the symbol is present in an array of symbols. The target symbols in both parts, A and B, of the subtest usually are nonsense shapes and designs, as are the symbols in the arrays.

Do not use Symbol Search to compute the IQ when you give the five standard Performance Scale subtests. Kaufman (1994) recommends that Symbol Search replace Coding in the calculation of the Performance Scale IQ and Full Scale IQ because it correlates more highly with the Performance Scale IQ than Coding and also has higher loadings on the Perceptual Organization Index. Tables A-13 and A-14 in Appendix A present the Performance Scale IQs and Full Scale IQs that result from this substitution. However, we recommend that you not substitute Symbol Search for Coding until research indicates that the substitution provides more valid IQs than those provided by using the procedure described in the WISC–III manual. Interestingly, Glutting, Youngstrom, Ward, Ward, and Hale (1997) recommend that Symbol Search and Mazes be omitted from the battery altogether unless future research documents their utility.

Rationale

On the Symbol Search subtest, the child looks at a stimulus figure (target stimulus), scans an array, and decides whether the stimulus figure appears in the array. The task involves perceptual discrimination, speed and accuracy, attention and concentration, short-term memory, and cognitive flexibility (in shifting rapidly from one array to the next). Visual-motor coordination plays a role, although a minor one, because the only motor movement is that of drawing a slash. Part B is more complex than Part A because there are two target stimulus figures instead of one and five symbols in the test array instead of three.

Most of the symbols used in the Symbol Search subtest are difficult to encode verbally. However, the child may verbally encode some symbols if verbal descriptions can be attached to them. These include, for example, ± (plus or minus), L (L shape), > (greater than sign), ∩ (inverted U), and ⊢ (a T on its side). Research is needed to learn whether children verbally encode these or other symbols and whether the encoding helps their performance.

As in the Coding subtest, the speed and accuracy with which the child performs the task are a measure of the child's intellectual ability. For each item, the child must inspect the target stimulus, go to the array, look at the array items and determine whether the target stimulus is present, and then mark the appropriate box (YES or NO) once a decision is made. Thus, you can conceptualize Symbol Search as a task involving visual discrimination and visuoperceptual scanning.

Factor Analytic Findings

The Symbol Search subtest is a fair measure of g (38% of its variance can be attributed to g), and it contributes substantially to the Processing Speed Index (average loading = .63) and minimally to the Perceptual Organization Index (average loading = .32). Specificity is ample at ages 7 and 10 through 16 years and inadequate at ages 6, 8, and 9 years.

Reliability and Correlational Highlights

Symbol Search is a relatively reliable subtest ($r_{xx} = .76$), with reliability coefficients above .70 at five of the six age groups studied (7, 10, 11, 14, and 15). The one exception is at age 6, where the reliability coefficient is .69 (range of .69 to .82). As with Coding, no reliability coefficients are given for ages 8, 9, 12, 13, and 16 years in the WISC–III manual because no children were retested at these ages. Symbol Search correlates better with Coding ($r = .53$) than with any of the other subtests. It has a moderate correlation with the Full Scale ($r = .56$) and the Performance Scale ($r = .58$) and a moderately low correlation with the Verbal Scale ($r = .44$).

Administrative Suggestions

Here are some administrative suggestions for the Symbol Search subtest.

Background Considerations
- Both Part A and Part B contain two demonstration (sample) items and two practice items. Both parts have 45 items in addition to the two sample and two practice items. Some symbols in Part A and Part B are the same.
- In Part A, there is one target symbol and there are three symbols in the test array. The child must draw a slash (/) through the box labeled YES if the target symbol is also in the array. If the target symbol is not in the test array, the child must draw a slash (/) through the box labeled NO.
- In Part B, there are two target symbols and there are five symbols in the test array. The child must draw a slash (/) through the box labeled YES if *either* of the target symbols is also in the test array. If neither of the target sym-

bols is in the test array, the child must draw a slash (/) through the box labeled NO.
- Each part of the subtest has a time limit of 120 seconds; however, the sample and practice items are not timed.
- Use only the sample items to explain the task further.
- When you administer the practice items, praise the child for getting the items correct. Correct immediately any mistakes the child makes on the practice items, and give the child help if the task is not understood.
- Observe the child's work methods. If the child stops working after the first line, say, "Continue on the next line."
- Tell the child who fails to turn the page to "Go to the next page."
- Remind the child to do the lines in order if any lines are skipped. Count these instructions as part of the 2-minute time limit.
- Children with visual impairments or specific motor disabilities may be penalized on Symbol Search. Therefore, do not give the subtest to a child with either of these impairments. If you do give the subtest to a child with a motor impairment because of clinical interest, do not include the subtest in computing IQs, even when it replaces a standard Performance Scale subtest.

Starting Considerations
- The Symbol Search subtest is in a separate booklet (WISC–III Symbol Search Response Booklet).
- Symbol Search Part A is administered to children 6 to 7 years old, whereas Symbol Search Part B is administered to children 8 to 16 years old.
- Write the child's name, the date, and your name in the space provided on the Symbol Search Response Booklet, and note the child's handedness.
- Administer the subtest on a smooth drawing surface.
- Do not go to the practice items until the child demonstrates understanding of the task.
- The child needs to have a clear view of the three sample items.
- Both you and the child should use a no. 2 graphite pencil without an eraser.
- Do not begin the subtest until the child understands the task.

Scoring Considerations
- Only score items that the child attempts within the allotted 120 seconds (personal communication, Lawrence Weiss, spokesperson for The Psychological Corporation, January 1992).
- Align the scoring template properly when you score the subtest.
- The score on each part is arrived at by subtracting the number of incorrect responses from the number of correct responses. In scoring the subtest, do not include either skipped items or items that the child did not reach.

- Do not give any credit for the sample or practice items.
- There are no time-bonus credits on either Part A or Part B.

Discontinuance Considerations
- The subtest is discontinued after 120 seconds unless the child completes the items before the time expires.

Interpretive Suggestions

Following are useful questions to guide your observation:

- Does the child use one hand to hold the paper in place and the other hand to draw the symbols?
- Is the child impulsive?
- Is the child meticulous?
- Does the child seem overly anxious?
- Does the child display tremor?
- Does the child's speed increase or decrease as the subtest proceeds?
- Are the child's slash marks (/) well executed, or are they barely recognizable?
- Does the child draw the slash mark slowly or quickly?
- Does the child work slowly and therefore lose points?
- Does the child make many errors? If so, is the child aware of them? If the child is aware of the errors, how does he or she react to the errors?
- Do the child's errors occur in some regular manner?
- Does the child fail to understand the task once the task is started?
- Does the child respond more slowly to NO items?
- Is the child penalized for lack of speed, for inaccuracy, or for both?
- Does the child recheck every item before moving on to the next one?
- Does the child frequently look back and forth between the target symbols and the search group?
- Is the child's work smooth and orderly, or does the child seem confused at times and have difficulty finding his or her place?
- Is the child persistent?
- Does the child need repeated urging to continue the task?
- Is the child bored with the task?
- Does the child hold the pencil in an appropriate way?
- Does the child try to use an eraser from another pencil or another source? If so, does the child seem to realize that an eraser is not supposed to be used?
- Does the child stop in the middle of the task, stretch, sigh, look around, and talk?

Answers to these questions may give you information about the child's attention, persistence, impulsive tendencies, compulsive tendencies, and depressive tendencies. An increase in speed, coupled with correct marks, suggests that the child is adjusting well to the task. A decrease in speed, coupled with incorrect marks, suggests that the child may be showing fatigue. It may be of interest to compare children who obtain the same score in different ways. For example, suppose two children get a score of 10, but one child has 10 correct responses and zero errors and the other child has 20 correct responses and 10 errors. These two children display different styles of working. The first child is a slow, careful, and meticulous worker, but may be unwilling (or unable) to work quickly, whereas the second child is a faster worker, but is rather careless and impulsive.

Children may be penalized on the Symbol Search subtest if they (a) are unable to make quick decisions, (b) respond slowly and carefully, (c) are compulsive and constantly check the stimulus figure(s) against those in the array, or (d) are impulsive and fail to check the array figures against the stimulus figure(s).

With children who make many errors, you may want to go over each item on which an error occurred, after the *entire test* is completed. You can point to an item on which an error occurred and say, "Tell me about your answer" or "Tell me about why you marked NO [or YES]." Another testing-of-limits procedure is to provide highly distractible children with a ruler or paper guide to see whether one of these aids improves their performance.

Compare the child's response style on Symbol Search with that on other subtests. If there are differences, what might account for them? Consider, for example, the nature of the subtests, the child's motivation, the child's scores on all of the subtests, and the order in which the subtests were administered (i.e., at the beginning, middle, or end of the examination).

The range of scaled scores from 1 to 19 at ages 6–0 to 15–11 years aids in profile analysis. However, at ages 16–0 to 16–11 years, profile analysis is somewhat limited because scaled scores range only from 1 to 18.

Question: Say the alphabet.
Answer: A, B, C, D, E, F, G, H, I, J, K, L, M, N, O, P, Q, R, S, T, U, V, WWW DOT, X, Y, Z.

MAZES

The Mazes subtest, a supplementary subtest, requires the child to solve paper-and-pencil mazes that differ in level of complexity. Mazes consists of one sample problem and 10 problems in the subtest proper. Ask the child to draw a line from the center of each maze to the outside without crossing any of the lines that indicate walls. Although Mazes need not be administered routinely, administering it to children who are either language impaired or from a different culture, in particular, may give you useful information. If you do administer Mazes, though, do not use it to compute the IQ when you also give the five standard Performance Scale subtests.

Rationale

To complete the Mazes subtest successfully, the child must (a) attend to the directions, which cover locating a route from the entrance to the exit, avoiding blind alleys, crossing no lines, and holding the pencil on the paper, and (b) execute the task, which involves remembering and following the directions, using visual-motor coordination, and resisting the disruptive effect of an implied need for speed. The Mazes subtest appears to measure the child's planning ability and perceptual-organizational ability—that is, the ability to plan and follow a visual pattern. To succeed, a child must have visual-motor control, combined with speed and accuracy.

Factor Analytic Findings

The Mazes subtest is the poorest measure of g in the test (13% of its variance can be attributed to g), and it contributes minimally to the Perceptual Organization Index (average loading = .36). Specificity is ample at ages 6 through 14 and 16 years and inadequate at age 15 years.

Reliability and Correlational Highlights

Mazes is a relatively reliable subtest (r_{xx} = .70), with reliability coefficients above .70 at ages 6, 7, 8, 10, 13, and 14 years and between .61 and .68 at ages 9, 11, 12, 15, and 16 years (range of .61 to .80). It correlates better with Block Design (r = .31) than with any of the other subtests. It has a low correlation with the Full Scale (r = .31), the Performance Scale (r = .35), and the Verbal Scale (r = .23).

Administrative Suggestions

Here are some administrative suggestions for the Mazes subtest.

Background Considerations
- All items are timed.
- The first four mazes have a maximum of 30 seconds each; the fifth maze, 45 seconds; the sixth maze, 60 seconds; the seventh and eighth mazes, 120 seconds; and the ninth and tenth mazes, 150 seconds.
- Give the child the cues described in the WISC–III manual when certain errors are made. The first time these errors occur, tell the child that an error was made and give the child the appropriate cue. The cues are designed to help the child, especially if the child does not understand what to do.
- In the first printing of the WISC–III manual, there is an incorrect direction on page 157 for Maze 3. The sentence says, "If the child completes the maze within the time limit with no more than one error, proceed to Maze 4." *Disregard this direction because it conflicts with the dis-*

continuance rule. The discontinuance rule states that you should discontinue Mazes after two consecutive failures. Therefore, administer Maze 4 when the child passes Maze 1 and Maze 2, regardless of the number of errors made on Maze 3.

Starting Considerations
- The Mazes subtest is contained in a separate booklet (WISC–III Mazes Response Booklet).
- Administer the subtest on a smooth drawing surface.
- Use a no. 2 graphite pencil without an eraser to demonstrate the sample item, and give a no. 2 pencil without an eraser to the child.
- Write the child's name, the date, and your name in the space provided on the Mazes Response Booklet.
- Children 6 to 7 years old (and older children suspected of mental retardation) begin with the sample maze followed by item 1, whereas children 8 to 16 years old begin with item 4.
- If a child 8 to 16 years old earns 2 points on Maze 4, give her or him full credit for all preceding mazes.
- If a child 8 to 16 years old earns 1 point (partial credit) on Maze 4, administer Mazes 1 to 3 in normal sequence.
- If a child 8 to 16 years old earns 0 points on Maze 4, give the sample maze and then administer items 1 to 3 in normal sequence.

Scoring Considerations
- The number of errors the child makes determines the child's score.
- Scores for the mazes range from 0 to 5 points each, with Mazes 1 to 6 having a maximum score of 2; Maze 7, a maximum score of 3; Mazes 8 and 9, a maximum score of 4; and Maze 10, a maximum score of 5.
- The table in the WISC–III manual on page 159 shows how to score the child's performance.
- Carefully study the sample responses that illustrate the scoring criteria (see pages 160–164 in the WISC–III manual).

Discontinuance Considerations
- The subtest is discontinued after two consecutive failures.

Interpretive Suggestions

Consider the following questions as you observe the child's performance.

- Does the child understand the task?
- Does the child study the mazes extensively and appear to plan a route before proceeding?
- Does the child show signs of tremor, difficulty in controlling the pencil, or difficulty in drawing uniform lines?
- Does the child solve the mazes correctly after the time limit has expired?
- Does the child cross lines? If so, is this tendency related to poor visual-motor coordination or to impulsivity?

Frank and Ernest

THE MAZE IS NO PROBLEM, I'M JUST WATCHING MY DAIRY INTAKE.

© 1998 Thaves / Reprinted with permission. Newspaper dist. by NEA, Inc.

Copyright © 1998 by Thaves.

- Does the child appear to improve her or his performance from one maze to the next?
- If an error is made, is the child aware of the error?
- Does the child say anything that suggests anxiety (e.g., "The little boy is trapped in the center of the maze")?
- Does the child say that similar mazes are done at home?
- Does the child ask for feedback concerning her or his performance?

These observations (and the child's overall success rate) will provide information about the child's motor planning, speed, execution, impulsivity, and sustained attention. Errors on Mazes may be indicative of impulsivity (overshooting alleys and exits); loss of control or poor coordination (walls cut through); or excessive caution, perfectionism, or depression (correct completion *after* time limits).

Low scores on the Mazes subtest may indicate poor visual-motor organization, inefficient planning ability, difficulty in delaying action, impulsivity, inability to sustain attention, or boredom.

As a testing-of-limits procedure, you can ask the child to tell you his or her strategy for solving the task.

The range of scaled scores from 1 to 19 at ages 6–0 to 10–11 years aids in profile analysis. However, profile analysis is somewhat hindered at 11–0 to 12–11 years and 13–0 to 16–11 years, where the scaled scores range from 1 to 18 and 1 to 17, respectively.

Question: What do you call a baby goat?
Answer: Matilda would be a nice name.

THINKING THROUGH THE ISSUES

1. In what ways do the WISC–III subtests share common properties, and in what ways do they differ?

2. What other subtests would you like to see incorporated in the WISC–III? Why?
3. If you were evaluating a child with language impairments, which subtests would you administer if you were trying to minimize the impact of the impairments on performance? Why?
4. If you were evaluating a child with motor impairments, which subtests would you administer? Why?
5. If you were evaluating a child with both language and motor impairments, which subtests would you administer? Which ones might be least useful? Why?

SUMMARY

1. The standard administration of all subtests on the WISC–III Verbal Scale and Performance Scale requires the child to hear, pay attention, listen, understand directions, and retain the directions while solving problems.
2. All Performance Scale subtests require the child to have adequate vision, and some Performance Scale subtests also require the child to have adequate motor skills.
3. The best estimates of abilities are provided by the Full Scale IQ, followed by the Verbal Scale and the Performance Scale, indexes, other combinations of subtests, and, finally, individual subtests.
4. Recording the child's responses verbatim, along with pertinent behavioral observations, will help you evaluate the test results, especially when you review the test protocol later.
5. Always conduct testing-of-limits after you administer the *entire test* following standard procedures.

Information

6. Information measures the child's available information acquired as a result of natural endowment, education, and cultural opportunities, experiences, and interests. Memory is an important aspect of performance on the subtest. The subtest is the second-best measure of *g* in the WISC–III and contributes to the Verbal Comprehension Index. Subtest specificity is

ample or adequate at most ages. Information is a reliable subtest (r_{xx} = .84). It is easy to administer and score.

Similarities

7. Similarities measures verbal concept formation. The subtest is the third-best measure of g and contributes to the Verbal Comprehension Index. Subtest specificity is ample or adequate at 6 of the 11 ages. Similarities is a reliable subtest (r_{xx} = .81). It is easy to administer, but it can be difficult to score.

Arithmetic

8. Arithmetic measures numerical reasoning ability. The subtest is a good measure of g and contributes to the Freedom from Distractibility Index and to the Perceptual Organization Index. Subtest specificity is ample or adequate at 6 of the 11 ages. Arithmetic is a reasonably reliable subtest (r_{xx} = .78). It is easy to administer and score.

Vocabulary

9. Vocabulary measures learning ability, fund of information, richness of ideas, memory, concept formation, and language development. The subtest is an excellent measure of g and contributes to the Verbal Comprehension Index. Subtest specificity is adequate at 9 of the 11 ages. Vocabulary is a reliable subtest (r_{xx} = .87). It is relatively easy to administer, but it can be difficult to score.

Comprehension

10. Comprehension measures social judgment: the ability to use facts in a pertinent, meaningful, and emotionally appropriate manner. The subtest is a good measure of g and contributes to the Verbal Comprehension Index. Subtest specificity is adequate at 6 of the 11 ages. Comprehension is a relatively reliable subtest (r_{xx} = .77). It is easy to administer, but it can be difficult to score.

Digit Span

11. Digit Span is a supplementary subtest that measures short-term sequential auditory memory and attention. The subtest is a fair measure of g and contributes to the Freedom from Distractibility Index. Subtest specificity is ample at all ages. Digit Span is a reliable subtest (r_{xx} = .85). It is easy to administer and score. Administer it routinely, even though you do not use it to compute the IQ when you also administer the five standard Verbal subtests.

Picture Completion

12. Picture Completion measures the ability to differentiate between essential and nonessential details. It requires concentration, reasoning, visual organization, and long-term visual memory. The subtest is a fair measure of g and contributes to the Perceptual Organization Index and to the Verbal Comprehension Index. Subtest specificity is ample or adequate at 10 of the 11 ages. Picture Completion is a reasonably reliable subtest (r_{xx} = .77). It is easy to administer and relatively easy to score.

Coding

13. Coding measures visual-motor coordination, speed of mental operation, attentional skills, visual acuity, visual scanning and tracking, short-term memory, and cognitive flexibility. The subtest is a poor measure of g and contributes to the Processing Speed Index. Subtest specificity is adequate at 10 of the 11 ages. Coding is a relatively reliable subtest (r_{xx} = .79). It is easy to administer and score.

Picture Arrangement

14. Picture Arrangement measures nonverbal reasoning ability. It may be viewed as a measure of planning ability—that is, the ability to comprehend and evaluate a total situation. The subtest is a fair measure of g and contributes to the Perceptual Organization Index and to the Verbal Comprehension Index. Subtest specificity is ample at all ages. Picture Arrangement is a relatively reliable subtest (r_{xx} = .76). It is easy to administer and score.

Block Design

15. Block Design measures nonverbal concept formation and requires perceptual organization, spatial visualization, and abstract conceptualization. The subtest is the best measure of g among the Performance Scale subtests and contributes to the Perceptual Organization Index and to the Verbal Comprehension Index. Subtest specificity is ample at all ages. Block Design is a reliable subtest (r_{xx} = .87). Block Design can be difficult to administer, but it is easy to score.

Object Assembly

16. Object Assembly measures visual organizational ability. The subtest is a fair measure of g and contributes to the Perceptual Organization Index. Specificity is ample or adequate at 4 of the 11 ages. Object Assembly is a marginally reliable subtest (r_{xx} = .69). It can be difficult to administer, but it is relatively easy to score.

Symbol Search

17. Symbol Search is a supplementary subtest that measures perceptual discrimination, speed and accuracy, attention and concentration, short-term memory, and cognitive flexibility. The subtest is a fair measure of g and contributes to the Processing Speed Index and to the Perceptual Organization Index. Subtest specificity is ample at 8 of the 11 ages. Symbol Search is a relatively reliable subtest (r_{xx} = .76). It is easy to administer and score.

Mazes

18. Mazes is a supplementary subtest that measures planning ability and perceptual-organizational ability. The subtest is the poorest measure of g in the test and contributes to the Perceptual Organization Index. Subtest specificity is ample at 10 of the 11 ages. Mazes is a relatively reliable subtest (r_{xx} = .70). It is easy to administer, but it can be difficult to score.

KEY TERMS, CONCEPTS, AND NAMES

WISC–III Information (p. 268)
WISC–III Similarities (p. 270)
WISC–III Arithmetic (p. 271)
WISC–III Vocabulary (p. 273)
WISC–III Comprehension (p. 275)
WISC–III Digit Span (p. 277)
WISC–III Picture Completion (p. 280)
WISC–III Coding (p. 282)
WISC–III Picture Arrangement (p. 285)
WISC–III Block Design (p. 287)
WISC–III Object Assembly (p. 289)
WISC–III Symbol Search (p. 291)
WISC–III Mazes (p. 293)

STUDY QUESTION

Discuss the rationale, factor analytic findings, reliability and correlational highlights, and administrative and interpretive considerations for each of the WISC–III subtests: Information, Similarities, Arithmetic, Vocabulary, Comprehension, Digit Span, Picture Completion, Coding, Picture Arrangement, Block Design, Object Assembly, Symbol Search, and Mazes.

10

INTERPRETING THE WISC–III

by Jerome M. Sattler and Donald H. Saklofske

The gifts of nature are infinite in their variety, and mind differs from mind almost as much as body from body.
—Quintilian

Goals and Objectives

This chapter is designed to enable you to do the following:

- Describe profile analysis for the WISC–III and other Wechsler batteries

- Analyze and evaluate WISC–III scores from multiple perspectives

- Develop hypotheses for WISC–III patterns and responses

- Report WISC–III findings to parents and others

This chapter will help you interpret the WISC–III. It covers (a) profile analysis, (b) how to determine whether differences between the Verbal Scale IQ and the Performance Scale IQ are significant, (c) how to determine whether differences among subtest scaled scores are significant, (d) how to obtain base rates of differences between various scores that occurred in the standardization group, (e) how to develop hypotheses about a child's WISC–III scores, and (f) how to interpret a child's WISC–III result. Because the WISC–III and other Wechsler scales have Deviation IQs with a mean of 100 and standard deviation of 15 and subtests have a mean of 10 and standard deviation of 3, you can statistically evaluate profiles across the scales, across the indexes, and across the subtests.

After you statistically evaluate any Verbal Scale-Performance Scale discrepancy, index score discrepancies, and subtest discrepancies and the profile of subtest scaled scores, you will need to interpret the findings. This chapter, along with the information presented in Chapters 8 and 9, will help you accomplish this goal. In addition, a knowledge of theories of intelligence and intellectual functioning (see Chapters 5 and 6), normal child development, child psychopathology and exceptional children (see *Assessment of Children: Behavioral and Clinical Applications*), and clinical decision making will help you make more valid interpretations.

PROFILE ANALYSIS

Profile analysis (sometimes referred to as scatter analysis) is a procedure for analyzing an examinee's pattern of scaled scores and IQs. Some profiles show extreme variability (e.g., subtest scaled scores from 1 to 19); others, moderate variability (e.g., subtest scaled scores from 5 to 15); and still others, minimal variability (e.g., subtest scaled scores from 8 to 12). You can examine the pattern of subtest scaled scores within the Verbal Scale, within the Performance Scale, and within the entire scale. You can also examine the relationship (a) between the Verbal Scale IQ and Performance Scale IQ, (b) among the four index scores, and (c) between or among the subtest scaled scores.

In the early days of the Wechsler and Wechsler-type scales, psychologists hoped that profile analysis would increase diagnostic precision. There were attempts not only to examine the pattern of subtest and IQ scores but also to discern new patterns or combinations (e.g., Bannatyne, 1974). Unfortunately, these efforts have not yielded the clinical results hoped for. *Profile analysis with the WISC–III, WPPSI–R, and WAIS–III cannot be used for classification purposes or to arrive at a diagnostic label.* Profile analysis is problematic because the Wechsler subtests are not as reliable as the IQs from the three scales and because the subtests do not measure unique cognitive processes. Still, profile analysis can provide information about a child's cognitive strengths and weaknesses and can help in developing hypotheses about the child's cognitive functioning.

Aim of Profile Analysis

Although the WISC–III Full Scale IQ is an invaluable measure of general intellectual ability, the IQ by itself (which represents an average of all the scores) tells us little about the underlying scores upon which it is based. For example, a Full Scale IQ of 100 may reflect subtest scaled scores that range (a) between 8 and 12, (b) between 5 and 15, or (c) between 1 and 19. Therefore, profile analysis aims to describe the child's unique ability pattern and, in so doing, go beyond the information contained within the Full Scale IQ. Knowledge of ability patterns can help in formulating interventions.

The following are some examples of various types of profiles.

1. A flat profile with all scores much above average (e.g., from 14 to 16) suggests that the child is gifted intellectually and may profit from instruction that capitalizes on his or her exceptional intellectual skills.
2. A flat profile with scores all much below average (e.g., from 2 to 4) suggests that the child has limited intellectual ability and needs specialized instruction.
3. A profile with peaks and valleys (e.g., from 3 to 16) suggests special strengths and weaknesses and may provide hypotheses about the child's cognitive style and suggest possible interventions.
4. A profile of subtest scaled scores within normal limits (e.g., 8 to 12) suggests average ability and does not indicate any exceptionality.

The goal of profile analysis is to generate hypotheses about the child's abilities. The hypotheses generated need to be checked against other information about the examinee. When the hypotheses appear to be reasonable, they can be used to (a) clarify the functional nature of a child's learning problems, (b) arrive at treatment recommendations, (c) develop educational programs, and (d) recommend a vocational placement.

Intersubtest variability may result, for example, from temporary inefficiencies, poor motivation, vision or hearing problems, poor concentration, rebelliousness, special aptitudes or weaknesses, learning disabilities, or uneven or disturbed school or home experiences. You will need to determine which, if any, of these interpretations is appropriate. In each case, you will have to seek the best explanation of the child's profile, using information obtained from the test and other relevant sources. Even variability that is outside of "normal limits" may not indicate the presence of psychopathology or exceptionality; rather, variability may simply portray the child's cognitive style.

You can analyze profiles from two frames of reference. One compares the examinee's scores to those the norm group—an *interindividual comparison*. The other method compares the examinee's scores to her or his own unique profile—an *intraindividual comparison*. In either case, you will use scaled scores based on the norm group.

All strengths or weaknesses are relative to some standard or frame of reference, either the performance of the child's age peers or the child's own pattern of abilities. In your written and oral report, clearly indicate which standard you are using when you discuss the examinee's abilities.

Interindividual Comparison

The simplest way to approach a subtest profile analysis is to evaluate the scores in reference to the norm group. A mean of 10 (coupled with a standard deviation of 3) serves as the reference point for the norm group.

You may want to use the three-category approach shown in Table 10-1 to describe Wechsler subtest scaled scores. Use the absolute value of the scaled scores to guide your analysis: (a) scaled scores of 13 to 19 always indicate a strength (one to three standard deviations above the mean); (b) scaled scores of 8 to 12 always indicate average ability (within one standard deviation from the mean); and (c) scaled scores of 1 to 7 always indicate a weakness (one to three standard deviations below the mean).

After you describe the subtest scaled scores and the abilities they are associated with, you might also note the percentile ranks associated with the subtest scaled scores. Percentile ranks provide a more precise description of the child's level of functioning (see Table D-1 in Appendix D), and you are encouraged to include percentile ranks in your reports.

Here are some illustrations of how to describe scaled scores:

- "She has strengths in abstract reasoning (91st percentile) and vocabulary knowledge (84th percentile)."
- "His weaknesses are in spatial visualization organization (5th percentile) and sustained attention for auditory information (9th percentile)."
- "She has average ability in all of the verbal comprehension subtests; all scores were between the 25th and 75th percentiles."
- "His abilities in … are above average (in the 84th to 98th percentiles)."
- "Within the verbal domain, her skills range from below average (16th percentile) to average (63rd percentile). Her range of knowledge, concept formation, … are all average, while her short-term memory is below average."

Table 10-1
A Three-Category Approach to Classifying Wechsler Scaled Scores

Scaled score	Description	Percentile rank
1 to 7	Weakness or below average	1st to 16th
8 to 12	Average	25th to 75th
13 to 19	Strength or above average	84th to 99th

You also can use a finer gradation—five categories instead of three categories—to describe the subtest scaled scores. Table 10-2 shows the five categories.

Whether you use the three- or the five-category system to describe subtest scaled scores is a matter of your or your instructor's preference. You may prefer one system for some reports and the other system for others. Overall, the five-category system is generally preferable to the three-category system because it allows for greater detail in describing scores, especially scores at the low and high ends. As you study the qualitative descriptions of the subtest scaled scores, notice that if all scores are 8 or above, the child has no weaknesses relative to his or her age peers. If all scores are 7 or below, the child has no strengths relative to his or her age peers. *Remember, however, that the child may have cognitive strengths or weaknesses in areas not measured by the test.*

Intraindividual Comparison

When you evaluate a child's unique pattern of scaled scores, you are making an intraindividual comparison, or using an *ipsative approach*. The focus is on describing areas in which the examinee's abilities are better developed or more poorly developed. As noted above, you still use the absolute values of the scaled scores to make an intraindividual comparison (i.e., scaled scores of 13 to 19 are always strengths; scaled scores of 8 to 12 are always average; and scaled scores of 1 to 7 are always weaknesses).

Avoid reporting that scaled scores of 8 or higher reflect a weakness or that scaled scores of 7 or lower reflect a strength. For example, if, of the 10 subtest scaled scores in a profile, nine are 18 or 19 and one is 13, 13 still represents a strength (it is at the 84th percentile rank) even though it is the lowest score in the profile. You do not want to imply that a scaled

Table 10-2
A Five-Category Approach to Classifying Wechsler Scaled Scores

Scaled score	Description	Percentile rank
1 to 4	Exceptional weakness or very poorly developed or far below average	1st to 2nd
5 to 7	Weakness or poorly developed or below average	5th to 11th
8 to 12	Average	25th to 75th
13 to 15	Strength or well developed or above average	84th to 95th
16 to 19	Exceptional strength or very well developed or superior	98th to 99th

score of 13 indicates limited ability or a weakness or deficit. It is the absolute score (in this case, a scaled score of 13), not a comparison with any other score, that reflects the examinee's level of ability. In interpreting this profile, you can report that, although a scaled score of 13 indicates a strength in the ability measured, the ability is not as well developed as are the examinee's other abilities.

Following are some key phrases to use in an intraindividual comparison:

- Relative to his (her) own level of ability
- Within his (her) overall average (above-average or below-average) level of functioning
- Reflects a better developed ability
- Relatively more developed
- Relative strength
- Strength
- Reflects a less developed ability
- Relatively less developed
- Relative weakness
- Weakness

Here are some examples of how these phrases can be used in various profiles:

- This statement was based on Wechsler Verbal Scale scaled scores of 3 to 7: "Relative to her own level of verbal ability, her social comprehension is her best developed ability, but still at a below-average level (16th percentile)." "Relative to her own level of verbal ability" is the key phrase, reflecting a comparison based on the examinee's individual profile. Note, however, that the absolute values of the scaled scores are still used for an intraindividual profile analysis. Her scaled score of 7 does not indicate a strength, even though it is the highest score in the profile. Also note that the phrase "but still at a below-average level" helps the reader understand that, although social comprehension is the examinee's best ability, it is still below average.
- This statement was based on Wechsler scaled scores of 7 to 15 over the 10 standard subtests and a Full Scale IQ of 113: "Within her overall above-average level of functioning, her command of word knowledge is a considerable strength (95th percentile)." "Within her overall above-average level of functioning" is the key phrase, preparing the reader for some comment related to the child's individual profile.
- In a profile with nine Wechsler subtest scaled scores below 4 and one subtest scaled score of 9, you could report that the scaled score of 9, at the 37th percentile, reflects a "better developed ability relative to the child's other abilities." (In this example, 9 of the 10 scores reflect weaknesses relative to the child's age group.)
- In a profile with nine Wechsler subtest scaled scores above 16 and one subtest scaled score of 10, you could report that the score of 10, at the 50th percentile, reflects a "less well developed, albeit average, ability relative to the child's other abilities." (In this example, one score is average and the rest are above average relative to the child's age group.)

Establishing Significant Differences

To be able to say that one score is meaningfully (i.e., statistically significantly) higher than another score, you must first determine that the difference between the two scores does not represent chance variation—you cannot simply look at two scores and say that one is meaningfully (or statistically significantly) higher or lower than the other. Recall from earlier chapters that two numerically different scores may not reflect a meaningful difference, because they are based on tests (or subtests) that are not perfectly reliable. A statistically significant difference indicates a high probability that skill levels measured by the two scores you are comparing are different. In other words, the difference is greater than that which might be expected to occur simply by chance.

One approach to profile analysis is to determine whether certain scores differ significantly from each other; we call this the *significant difference approach*. For example, you might want to compare the Verbal Scale IQ and Performance Scale IQ, the index scores, or certain subtest scaled scores. To make these comparisons, you will need to answer questions like the following:

- Do the IQs on the Verbal Scale and Performance Scale differ significantly from each other?
- Do the index scores (of interest) differ significantly from one another?
- Do the subtest scaled scores (of interest) differ significantly from the means of their respective scales?
- Do the subtest scaled scores (of interest) differ from one another?

You have the option of making none, some, or all of these comparisons. However, if you decide to compare two scores or a score with a mean, you must find out whether they differ significantly from each other. Information presented later in this section will help you make these comparisons.

Base Rates

A second approach to profile analysis is to determine the frequency with which the differences between scores in the child's profile occurred in the standardization sample; we call this the *base rate approach* or *probability-of-occurrence approach*. Tables discussed later in the chapter will help you obtain base rates of Verbal Scale–Performance Scale differences, differences between subtests, and amount of scatter in profiles. Let's now look at how to conduct a profile analysis.

Primary Methods of Profile Analysis

The methods most commonly used for profile analysis are the following:

Method 1.   Compare the examinee's Verbal Scale IQ and Performance Scale IQ.

Method 2.   Compare each Verbal Scale subtest scaled score with the examinee's mean Verbal Scale scaled score.

Method 3.   Compare each Performance Scale subtest scaled score with the examinee's mean Performance Scale scaled score.

Method 4.   Compare each subtest scaled score with the examinee's mean subtest scaled score based on all subtests administered.

Method 5.   Compare sets of the examinee's individual subtest scaled scores.

Method 6.   Compare the examinee's Verbal Comprehension, Perceptual Organization, Freedom from Distractibility, and Processing Speed Index scores.

Method 7.   Compare the examinee's subtest scaled scores in each index with the respective mean index score.

Method 8.   Compare the examinee's range of subtest scaled scores with that found in the standardization sample.

Method 9.   Compare the examinee's intrasubtest scatter with that found in the standardization sample.

Notice that the first and sixth methods involve comparing IQs and indexes, respectively, whereas the other methods involve comparing scaled scores. Methods 2–3 and Method 4 are alternative approaches to profile analysis. You would use Methods 2 and 3 together or Method 4 alone, not Methods 2, 3, *and* 4. Ordinarily, you would decide between Methods 2–3 and Method 4 on the basis of the difference between the Verbal Scale IQ and the Performance Scale IQ. If the difference is significant or unusual, use Methods 2 and 3. Thus, if the difference between an examinee's Verbal Scale IQ and Performance Scale IQ is significant or unusual, first compare each Verbal Scale subtest to the mean Verbal Scale scaled score and then compare each Performance Scale subtest to the mean Performance Scale scaled score. Method 4 (comparing each subtest score to the overall mean scaled score) might be preferred if the difference between the examinee's Verbal Scale and Performance Scale IQs was neither significant nor unusual. Now let us examine each of these methods in more detail.

Method 1: Compare Verbal Scale and Performance Scale IQs.   Table A-2 in Appendix A provides the critical values for comparing the Verbal Scale IQ and Performance Scale IQ for the 11 WISC–III age groups. These values range from 10 to 13 at the .05 level and from 13 to 17 at the .01 level. You should not use an average critical value based on the entire standardization group, because this value may be misleading in some cases. Rather, use the values for a specific age group to evaluate differences between an examinee's Verbal Scale IQ and Performance Scale IQ. Exhibit 10-1 describes the procedure that was used to obtain the crit-

---

Exhibit 10-1
Procedure Used to Determine Whether Two Scores in a Profile Are Significantly Different

In order to establish whether differences between scores in a profile are reliable, it is necessary to apply statistical procedures to the profile. As always, we cannot be 100% certain that the difference between any two subtest scores is reliable. A confidence level must therefore be selected, such as a 95% level of certainty that the differences are significant. In order to determine whether the difference between two scales or subtests or tests is reliable, the following formula can be used:

$$\text{Difference Score} = z\sqrt{\text{SEM}_A^2 + \text{SEM}_B^2}$$

The Difference Score refers to the magnitude of the difference between scales or subtests A and B. The z refers to the normal curve value associated with the desired confidence level. If we select the 95% level, the associated z value is 1.96. The terms under the square root sign refer to the SEM (standard error of measurement) associated with each scale or subtest or test. Many test manuals provide these SEMs.

The following example illustrates how to determine whether there is a significant difference between two scaled scores. Let

us say that we are interested in determining the value needed to represent a significant difference between the WISC–III Verbal and Performance Scales for children in the standardization group. The average SEMs associated with these two scales are 3.60 and 4.66, respectively, as indicated in the WISC–III manual. We know from a normal curve table that at the 95% confidence level the z value is 1.96. Substituting these values into the formula yields the following:

$$\text{Difference Score} = 1.96\sqrt{3.60^2 + 4.66^2} = 12$$

Differences between these two scales that are at or above this value are significant at the 95% level of confidence. A larger difference (15) is needed for the 99% confidence level. These values appear in the small rectangle of Table A-2 in Appendix A. All values in Tables A-2, B-2, and C-2 in Appendixes A, B, and C were obtained by following the above procedure. For the 99% confidence level, the z value of 2.58 is used in the equation.

ical values shown in Table A-2 in Appendix A. You can use this procedure to determine the needed critical values for any comparison involving two scales, two indexes, or two subtests. The values in Table A-2 are similar to the ones in Table B.1 in the WISC–III manual; however, they differ in two ways. First, the values in Table A-2 are in whole numbers instead of decimals. Second, the values are shown for the .05 and .01 significance levels instead of the .15 and .05 significance levels.

Table A-3 in Appendix A shows the probabilities associated with various differences between the WISC–III Verbal Scale IQ and Performance Scale IQ. This table provides an estimate of the probability of obtaining a given or greater discrepancy by chance. It shows probabilities from .001 (1 in 1,000) to .50 (50 in 100, or 1 out of 2). Thus, at age 6 years, there is a 1 in 1,000 chance that a difference of 19.74 points between the Verbal Scale IQ and Performance Scale IQ will be found. On the other hand, at this same age, there is a 50% chance that a difference of 4.02 points will be found between the Verbal Scale IQ and Performance Scale IQ.

Table B.2 (p. 262) in the WISC–III manual shows the cumulative percentages in the standardization sample that obtained various Verbal Scale IQ–Performance Scale IQ differences in *both directions*. The mean Verbal Scale–Performance Scale difference in both directions was 10.0, and the median difference in both directions was 8.0. Approximately 25% of the sample had a Verbal Scale-Performance Scale difference in one or the other direction of 14 points or higher, and approximately 83% of the sample had a Verbal Scale–Performance Scale difference in one or the other direction of 3 points or higher.

The cumulative percentages shown in Table B.2 of the WISC–III manual are absolute values (i.e., they represent bidirectional differences, combining both Verbal Scale > Performance Scale and Performance Scale > Verbal Scale values). Unfortunately, there is no statement in the WISC–III manual that the cumulative frequencies in Table B.2 are absolute values. In addition, Table B.2 does not provide the frequencies with which differences between the Verbal Scale IQ and Performance Scale IQ occurred in the standardization sample in either direction alone. Without this information, the actual occurrence in the standardization sample of Verbal Scale > Performance Scale and Performance Scale > Verbal Scale values cannot be known. An examinee can have a Verbal Scale–Performance Scale discrepancy in one direction only.

After the publication of the WISC–III, the actual frequencies with which differences between the Verbal Scale IQ and Performance Scale IQ (and between the index scores) occurred in the standardization sample in either direction alone were provided by The Psychological Corporation (personal communication, Larry Weiss, spokesperson for The Psychological Corporation, July 2000). Tables A-4 and A-5 in Appendix A show these frequencies. Table A-4 shows, for example, that a Verbal Scale > Performance Scale discrepancy of 15 points was obtained by 11.8% of the standardization sample, whereas Table A-5 shows that a Performance

Scale > Verbal Scale discrepancy of 15 points was obtained by 14.3% of the standardization sample.

If you do not use Tables A-4 and A-5 in Appendix A, *you must divide the frequencies in Table B.2 by 2 to obtain the base rate in one direction.* Since dividing by 2 gives only approximate frequencies, we recommend that you use the actual frequencies, now that they are available.

Method 2: Compare each Verbal Scale subtest scaled score with the mean Verbal Scale scaled score. Table A-6 in Appendix A provides critical values for comparing each of the Verbal Scale subtests with the mean of the standard five Verbal Scale subtests or the mean of the six Verbal Scale subtests for each of the 11 WISC–III age groups. For example, typical critical values for 6-year-old children on the five standard Verbal Scale subtests range from 3.01 to 3.51 at the .05 level and from 3.60 to 4.20 at the .01 level. Table B.3 (pages 263–264) in the WISC–III manual gives values for the .15 and .05 significance levels. The values in Table A-6 are overly liberal (i.e., they often lead to significant differences that may not be true differences) when more than one comparison is made.

Table B.3 in the WISC–III manual also gives the cumulative frequencies with which various differences occurred in the standardization sample between an examinee's scaled score on each subtest and his or her average WISC–III Verbal Scale scaled score. The table shows, for example, that a difference of 3.40 points between the scaled score on Information and the mean Verbal Scale score (derived from the scores on the five standard subtests) was obtained by 5% of the standardization sample. This table should be used only for differences that have first been shown to be reliable (see the .05 significance level column in Table B.3 in the WISC–III manual or in Table A-6 in Appendix A). Differences of 3.40 to 4.20 points between each subtest scaled score and the mean Verbal Scale score were obtained by 5% of the standardization sample.

Method 3: Compare each Performance Scale subtest scaled score with the mean Performance Scale scaled score. Table A-6 in Appendix A provides critical values for comparing each of the Performance Scale subtests with the mean of the standard five Performance Scale subtests or the mean of the six Performance Scale subtests for each of the 11 WISC–III age groups. For example, typical critical values for 6-year-old children for the five standard Performance Scale subtests range from 3.03 to 3.62 at the .05 level and from 3.62 to 4.34 at the .01 level. Table B.3 (pages 263–264) in the WISC–III manual gives values for the .15 and .05 significance levels. The values in Table A-6 are overly liberal (i.e., they often lead to significant differences that may not be true differences) when more than one comparison is made.

Table B.3 in the WISC–III manual also gives the cumulative frequencies with which various differences occurred in the standardization sample between an examinee's scaled score on each subtest and her or his average WISC–III Performance Scale scaled score. The table shows, for example, that a difference of 4.40 points between the scaled score on Picture Completion and the mean Performance Scale score (derived from the scores on the five standard subtests) was obtained by 5% of the standardization sample. This table should be used only for differences that have first been shown to be reliable (see the .05 significance level column in Table B.3 in the WISC–III manual or in Table A-6 in Appendix A). Differences of 4.20 to 5.40 points between each subtest scaled score and the mean Performance Scale score were obtained by 5% of the standardization sample.

Method 4: Compare each subtest scaled score with the mean subtest scaled score.
Table A-6 in Appendix A provides critical values for each of the 11 age groups in the WISC–III for 10, 11, 12, and 13 subtests. For example, typical critical values for 6-year-old children for the 10 standard subtests range from 3.43 to 4.25 at the .05 level and from 4.02 to 4.97 at the .01 level. This approach to profile analysis is less often used than Methods 2 and 3. The values in Table A-6 are overly liberal (i.e., they often lead to significant differences that may not be true differences) when more than one comparison is made.

Method 5: Compare sets of individual subtest scaled scores.
Table A-2 in Appendix A provides critical values for comparing sets of subtest scaled scores for each of the 11 age groups of the WISC–III. They range from 3 to 5 at the .05 level and from 4 to 7 at the .01 level. The values in Table A-2 for subtest comparisons are overly liberal (i.e., they often lead to significant differences that may not be true differences) when more than one comparison is made. They are most accurate when you plan to make specific comparisons before you administer the test; for example, you plan to compare Comprehension with Information or Block Design with Object Assembly. Table A-2 is similar to Table B.4 in the WISC–III manual. It differs in two ways. First, Table A-2 provides values in whole numbers instead of decimals. Second, it provides values for the .05 and .01 significant levels instead of the .15 and .05 significance levels.

Table A-11 in Appendix A gives the base rates for differences between sets of subtest scaled scores that occurred in 1%, 5%, and 15% of the standardization group. Differences between sets of subtest scaled scores that occurred in 15% or less of the standardization group can be considered somewhat rare or unusual differences. The table shows, for example, that when Information is subtracted from Similarities, a difference of 7 points occurred in 1% of the standardization group, 5 points in 5% of the standardization group, and 4 points in 15% of the standardization group.

Before making multiple comparisons, determine the difference between the highest and lowest subtest scaled scores. If this difference is 6 scaled-score points or more, a significant difference at the .05 level is indicated. Differences of 6 scaled-score points or more between subtests can then be interpreted. If the difference between the highest and lowest

subtest scaled scores is less than 6 scaled-score points, multiple comparisons should not be made between individual subtest scaled scores. (The Note to Table A-2 in Appendix A shows the formula that was used to compute the significant difference. The formula considers the average standard error of measurement for each of the 13 subtests and the studentized range statistic.)

Method 6: Compare the Verbal Comprehension, Perceptual Organization, Freedom from Distractibility, and Processing Speed Index scores.
Table A-2 in Appendix A presents the differences between sets of Verbal Comprehension, Perceptual Organization, Freedom from Distractibility, and Processing Speed Deviation IQs needed to reach the .05 and .01 significance levels. Table A-9 in Appendix A shows the probabilities associated with various differences between WISC–III index scores. The method used to interpret differences between index scores is similar to the one used to interpret differences between Verbal Scale IQs and Performance Scale IQs (see Method 1 above).

Table B.2 (page 262) in the WISC–III manual also shows the cumulative percentages in the standardization sample that obtained various index score differences in both directions. As with the Verbal Scale–Performance Scale differences, the cumulative percentages shown in Table B.2 are absolute values (i.e., they represent bi-directional differences). The actual frequencies with which differences between the index scores occurred in the standardization sample in either direction alone are shown in Tables A-4 and A-5 in Appendix A (personal communication, Larry Weiss, spokesperson for The Psychological Corporation, July 2000). Table A-4 shows, for example, that a Verbal Comprehension > Perceptual Organization discrepancy of 20 points was obtained by 6.6% of the standardization sample, whereas Table A-5 shows that a Perceptual Organization > Verbal Comprehension discrepancy of 20 points was obtained by 7.0% of the standardization sample. Use Tables A-4 and A-5 in Appendix A to obtain the base rates for differences between index scores, not Table B.2 in the WISC–III manual.

Be sure to compare an index score with another index score and not with the Verbal Scale or the Performance Scale IQ. This is important because one or more subtests in the index are also in the Verbal Scale or Performance Scale. For example, if you compared the Processing Speed Index with the Performance Scale, you would be including overlapping subtests in the comparison.

Method 7: Compare subtest scaled scores in each index with the respective mean index score.
Table A-8 in Appendix A provides the critical values for comparing WISC–III subtest scaled scores in each index with the respective index mean. Critical values for the subtests in the Verbal Comprehension Index range from 2.48 to 2.99 at the .05 level and from 3.00 to 3.62 at the .01 level. For the Perceptual Organization Index, they range from 2.60 to 3.12 at the .05 level and from 3.19 to 3.82 at the .01 level. For the Freedom from Distractibility Index, the value is 2.06 at the

.05 level and 2.59 at the .01 level. For the Processing Speed Index, the critical value is 2.30 at the .05 level and 2.88 at the .01 level. The procedure used for this method is similar to that described above for Methods 2 and 3. Table A-8 is similar to Table B.3 in the WISC–III manual. Again, the differences in the two tables lie in the significance levels shown (.05 and .01 instead of .15 and .05) and the use of whole numbers instead of decimals.

Method 8: Compare the range of subtest scaled scores with that found in the standardization sample.

Let's look at two ways to evaluate intersubtest scatter by using data from the standardization sample.

1. *Overall scaled-score range.* One method is to compare the examinee's scaled-score range to the range found in the standardization sample. The subtest scaled-score range provides information about the variability (or scatter) in an examinee's WISC–III profile. The overall scaled-score range indicates the distance between the two most extreme scaled scores. It is obtained by subtracting the lowest scaled score from the highest scaled score. For example, in a profile where the highest scaled score is 15 and the lowest scaled score is 3, the range is 12, since $15 - 3 = 12$. If the highest score in the profile is 10 and the lowest score is 5, the range is 5, since $10 - 5 = 5$.

In the standardization sample, the median scaled-score range was 7 points for the 10 standard subtests on the Full Scale, 4 points for the five standard subtests on the Verbal Scale, and 6 points for the five standard subtests on the Performance Scale (see Table B.5, page 266, in the WISC–III manual). The scaled-score range is based on only two scores and therefore fails to take into account the variability among all 10 (or 11, 12, or 13) subtest scaled scores. The range index is still useful, however, because it provides base rate information about what occurred in the standardization sample. It also is a relatively simple measure of variability that can be compared with more complex indices of variability, such as the standard deviation of the 10 subtests and the number of subtests on which scaled scores deviate significantly from the overall mean scaled score.

2. *Scaled-score range based on specific subtest scaled scores.* A second method is to compare the range between the absolute highest and lowest subtest scaled scores with that found in the standardization sample. This method focuses on such questions as the following: Given that the highest scaled score is 17, what would be an unusual range of scatter? To answer this and similar questions, see Table A-10 in Appendix A. This table shows the base rate scatter in the standardization sample based on the highest scaled score in a profile minus the lowest scaled score for scaled scores ranging from 6 to 17+. The table gives the value representing 15% or less of the cases when the lowest scaled score is subtracted from the highest scaled score in the WISC–III standardization group. For example, for the five Verbal Scale subtests, a scatter of 9 points occurred in 15% or less of the standardization group when the highest scaled score was 17 or higher (the

lowest scaled score needed to produce this amount of scatter was 8). The table also shows that as the highest scaled score decreases, the range of scatter is reduced (e.g., for the five Verbal Scale subtests, 9 points was the range of scatter when the highest scaled score was 17+, and 6 points was the range of scatter when the highest scaled score was 8).

Method 9: Compare the intrasubtest scatter with that found in the standardization sample.

We can evaluate intrasubtest scatter by looking at the frequency with which scores on consecutive items on a subtest differ. Following are examples of how this form of intrasubtest scatter is computed follow: A score of 1 followed by a score of 0, or a score of 0 followed by a score of 1, equals 1 scatter point; a score 2 followed by a score of 0, or the reverse, equals 2 scatter points. Intrasubtest scatter was not found to be significantly different among children born prematurely, children with speech and language difficulties, children with learning disabilities, children with other health-related impairments, and children in the standardization sample (Dumont & Willis, 1995). These results suggest that intrasubtest scatter should not be used as a diagnostic indicator of disability, at least for the groups studied in this investigation. We also need studies of intrasubtest scatter in other clinical groups, such as children with traumatic brain injury.

Looking at intrasubtest scatter, however, might have some clinical value when the amount of intrasubtest scatter is unusual. The data in Table 10-3 are helpful in making this

Table 10-3
Intrasubtest Scatter in the WISC–III Standardization Group for Eight WISC–III Subtests

Subtest	M intrasubtest scatter	Unusual intrasubtest scatter[a]
Information	4.4	7
Similarities	7.3	12
Arithmetic	3.2	6
Vocabulary	8.5	14
Comprehension	7.4	11
Picture Completion	6.1	9
Picture Arrangement	14.6	25
Block Design	9.4	17

[a]Intrasubtest scatter that represents less than 10% of the standardization group.
Note. The numbers in the table are raw-score points. Following is an example of how to read the table: On Information, the mean amount of intrasubtest scatter was 4.4 raw-score points; the amount of intrasubtest scatter was 7 raw-score points in less than 10% of the standardization group. Note that for Picture Arrangement, the tabulation of intrasubtest scatter begins with item 3 (WALK), whereas for Block Design, the tabulation of intrasubtest scatter begins with item 4.
Source: Adapted from Dumont and Willis (1995).

determination. For the eight WISC–III subtests for which computing intrasubtest scatter makes sense (Information, Similarities, Arithmetic, Vocabulary, Comprehension, Picture Completion, Picture Arrangement, and Block Design), the table presents (a) the mean intrasubtest scatter found in the standardization sample and (b) the amount of intrasubtest scatter found in the scores of less than 10% of the children in the standardization sample.

Statistically Reliable vs. Empirically Observed IQ Differences

We have seen that there are two types of complementary measures that can assist in profile analysis—statistically reliable differences and empirically observed base rates. Table A-2 in Appendix A presents the differences required between the Verbal Scale and Performance Scale IQs and between index scores for statistical significance. Tables A-4 and A-5 in Appendix A give the actual (i.e., empirically observed) base rates of the frequencies of differences between the IQs and between the index scores for the standardization sample.

Whether an occurrence is "unusual" depends on how one defines the term. A difference that occurs in 15% or 20% of the population may be considered unusual by some, whereas others may consider a difference unusual only if it occurs in no more than 5% or 10% of the population. We believe that all statistically significant differences between scores, regardless of whether they are unusual, deserve consideration in evaluating an examinee's profile of abilities. However, we also believe that you can be more confident about the hypotheses you form when the difference is significant *and* unusual. We suggest that, in order to be considered unusual, the difference (range or other phenomenon) should occur in 10% to 15% or less (in one direction) of the standardization sample.

Let's look at two examples. First, a 6-year-old examinee has a Verbal Scale–Performance Scale IQ difference of 12 points, which is statistically significant at the .05 level. This means that the Verbal Scale–Performance Scale IQ difference is reliable and unlikely to be the result of measurement error (i.e., chance). Differences that are greater than chance may reflect differential functioning in the abilities measured by the Verbal Scale and Performance Scale and by the index scores. From Table B.2 we find that a difference of 12 points or more in one direction between the Verbal Scale IQ and Performance Scale IQ occurred in approximately 17.9% (35.8% in Table B.2, divided by 2) of the standardization sample. This 12-point difference, therefore, is statistically significant but not very unusual. Whether the 12-point difference is clinically meaningful is an empirical question.

Second, a 6-year-old examinee obtains a Verbal Scale–Performance Scale IQ difference of 20 points, which is significant at the .01 level. From Table B.2 we find that a difference of 20 points or more in one direction between the Verbal Scale IQ and Performance Scale IQ occurred in ap-

proximately 6.1% (12.3% in Table B.2, divided by 2) of the standardization sample. This 20-point difference, therefore, is not only statistically significant but also unusual.

Clinical acumen, the examinee's medical history, behavioral observations, and the results of other tests that the examinee has taken will help you interpret differences between the Verbal Scale IQ and Performance Scale IQ and differences between the index scores. Recognize that several variables—such as the examinee's cultural and linguistic background and educational level—may influence the magnitude and direction of the Verbal Scale IQ–Performance Scale IQ discrepancy. For example, examinees who are in honors programs in school or in advanced placement classes may have significantly higher Verbal Scale IQs than Performance Scale IQs, and examinees with non-English linguistic backgrounds and those from some specific ethnic groups (e.g., Native Americans) may have significantly lower Verbal Scale IQs than Performance Scale IQs (see Chapter 20). Therefore, differences between the Verbal Scale IQs and Performance Scale IQs of examinees from non-English linguistic backgrounds are probably related to their language background and should be interpreted accordingly.

Procedure to Follow in Determining Whether Subtest Scaled Scores Are Significantly Different from the Mean

The following procedure will help you determine whether a subtest scaled score is significantly different from the mean of its respective scale (based on 5, 6, or 7 subtests) or the mean based on 10, 11, 12, or 13 subtests.

Step 1.   Write the names of the subtests and their respective scaled scores on a sheet of paper.

Step 2.   Sum the five (or six) Verbal Scale subtest scaled scores.

Step 3.   Compute the mean of the Verbal Scale subtests by dividing the sum of the Verbal Scale subtest scaled scores by 5 (or 6).

Step 4.   Calculate the deviation from the mean for each Verbal Scale subtest by subtracting each Verbal Scale subtest scaled score from the Verbal Scale mean. Enter these deviations, with the appropriate sign (+ or −), opposite the scaled scores.

Step 5.   Sum the five (or six or seven) Performance Scale subtest scaled scores.

Step 6.   Compute the mean of the Performance Scale subtests by dividing the sum of the Performance Scale subtest scaled scores by 5 (or 6 or 7).

Step 7.   Calculate the deviation from the mean for each Performance Scale subtest by subtracting each Performance Scale subtest scaled score from the Performance Scale mean. Enter these deviations, with the appropriate sign (+ or −), opposite the scaled scores.

Step 8. Compute the mean of the overall subtests by dividing the sum by 10 (or 11, 12, or 13).

Step 9. Calculate the deviation from the overall mean for each subtest scaled score by subtracting each scaled score from the overall mean. Enter these deviations, with the appropriate sign (+ or –), opposite the scaled scores.

Step 10. Determine whether the deviations from the Verbal Scale and Performance Scale means are significant by using Table A-6 in Appendix A. The values in Table A-6 reflect significant differences at the .05 and .01 levels of probability. Be sure to use the appropriate column in Table A-6 to obtain the significant deviations. For example, use column 2 when you administer the five standard Verbal Scale subtests, and use column 3 when you administer Digit Span as a sixth Verbal Scale subtest. Similarly, use column 2 when you administer the five standard Performance Scale subtests, and use column 3 when you administer Symbol Search as a sixth Performance Scale subtest.

Step 11. Place an asterisk next to each subtest deviation that is significantly above or below the mean.

Step 12. After the asterisk, write an *S* to indicate a strength or a *W* to indicate a weakness.

Table 10-4 illustrates the above steps and shows how to determine whether the subtest scaled scores differ significantly from the mean of (a) the Verbal Scale scaled scores, (b) the Performance Scale scaled scores, and (c) all the scaled scores for a 6-year-old child. In the example shown in Table 10-4, none of the Verbal Scale subtest scaled scores differed significantly from the Verbal Scale mean. The Coding subtest scaled score was significantly lower than the Performance Scale mean. The Information and Digit Span scaled scores were significantly lower than the overall mean, while the Picture Completion, Block Design, and Object Assembly scaled scores were significantly higher. (In determining whether a scaled score is significantly different from the mean, disregard the plus or minus sign in Table 10-4.) You may now infer that the difference between the Coding subtest scaled score and the child's mean Performance Scale scaled score is not a chance difference. The results suggest that the abilities reflected by the Picture Completion, Block Design, and Object Assembly subtest scaled scores are strengths and the abilities reflected by the Information and Digit Span subtest scaled scores are weaknesses.

The critical values used in the preparation of Table 10-4 are based on the assumption that the scores on all subtests in a scale are to be compared with the mean score for that scale. Therefore, use only one significance level (either .05 or .01)

Table 10-4
An Example of Profile Analysis on the WISC–III: Comparing Each Subtest Score to Various Mean Scaled Scores

		Deviation from		
Subtest	*Scaled score*	*Verbal average*	*Performance average*	*Overall average*
Information	4	–2.2	—	–4.3* *W*
Similarities	7	+.8	—	–1.3
Arithmetic	6	–.2	—	–2.3
Vocabulary	8	+1.8	—	–.3
Comprehension	7	+.8	—	–1.3
Digit Span	5	–1.2	—	–3.3* *W*
Picture Completion	13	—	+2.2	+4.7* *S*
Coding	6	—	–4.8* *W*	–2.3
Picture Arrangement	9	—	–1.8	+.7
Block Design	12	—	+1.2	+3.7* *S*
Object Assembly	14	—	+3.2	+5.7* *S*
Mazes	—	—	—	—
Symbol Search	—	—	—	—

M Verbal scaled score: 37 ÷ 6 = 6.2
M Performance scaled score: 54 ÷ 5 = 10.8
M overall scaled score: 91 ÷ 11 = 8.3

Note. S = strength, W = weakness. See Table A-6 in Appendix A to obtain deviations that are significant.
*Significant at the .05 level.

to determine the critical values. *Do not mix levels of significance for this type of comparison.*

Comment on Verbal Scale–Performance Scale Difference Approaches

As noted earlier, when evaluating a Verbal Scale–Performance Scale difference, you should determine whether the difference is likely to have occurred by chance—we call this the *reliability-of-difference approach*. Differences that are not significant do not warrant your attention, because they are likely to have occurred by chance. Verbal Scale–Performance Scale differences may be significant, yet occur with some frequency in the population. Thus, the discrepancy may be reliable but not unusual. Whether a significant difference has practical significance is open to question. Although a statistically significant difference may have less diagnostic relevance when it occurs in a large proportion of the standardization sample (this is where the base rate information about Verbal Scale–Performance Scale differences helps in interpretation), the difference still tells you something about the child's abilities. Therefore, given a significant difference only, you can still formulate hypotheses about the child's cognitive strengths and weaknesses.

The standard error of measurement of each scale is used in the reliability-of-difference approach, and the correlation between the two scales is used in the probability-of-occurrence approach. Both approaches assist in clinical judgment; however, neither should be used in a mechanical fashion or as a replacement for clinical judgment.

Comment on Profile Analysis

When a difference between subtests or a difference between the Verbal Scale and Performance Scale is statistically significant, it is large enough that it cannot be attributed to chance (i.e., measurement error). The WISC–III manual recommends that you use the .15 level of significance as the minimum level for determining whether there are significant differences between subtest scaled scores and between the Verbal Scale and Performance Scale IQs. In contrast, we recommend that you use the .05 level of significance as the minimum level, to reduce the chances of making a Type I error. By using the more stringent confidence level (.05 instead of .15), you will accept fewer differences between scores as true differences when they are in fact *not* true differences.

Do not use scores on individual subtests to attempt precise descriptions of specific cognitive skills; rather, use them to generate hypotheses about the child's abilities. You can derive more reliable estimates of specific abilities from the Verbal Scale IQ (verbal or verbal comprehension abilities) and the Performance Scale IQ (performance, perceptual organization, or nonverbal abilities) than from individual subtest scaled scores. The index scores also provide more reliable information about abilities than do individual subtest scaled

scores. In fact, of the 133 separate reliability coefficients for the 13 subtests at the 11 age groups of the test, fewer than half (65) are .80 or above. Of these, only seven are .90 or above: Vocabulary at ages 14 and 15, Digit Span at age 15, and Block Design at ages 13, 14, 15, and 16. *The remaining 68 reliability coefficients are below .80 and are not sufficiently reliable for decision-making or classification purposes* (see Table 5.1 on page 166 of the WISC–III manual). However, reliability coefficients of .70 or above on subtests are useful for generating hypotheses.

The difference between an examinee's subtest scaled score and the mean scaled score is a statistically more accurate measure than the difference between pairs of subtest scaled scores. Use of the mean scaled score has the additional advantage of reducing the accumulation of errors associated with multiple comparisons.

What might account for a certain profile of scores? To attempt to answer this question, you must consider both stable factors (also referred to as trait characteristics or long-term factors) and transient conditions (also referred to as state characteristics or short-term factors). Stable factors include the child's cognitive skill development, age, sex, cultural group, socioeconomic status, education, special training, social and physical environment, family background, ethnicity, temperament, personality, and psychopathology. Transient conditions include the health status of the child (e.g., short-term illnesses), the amount of sleep the child had the previous night, the degree of tension in the home, any acute trauma that the child has faced (with possible post-traumatic stress disorder reactions), test anxiety, and adverse (or expected) drug reactions. Variability of subtest scores may even be simply a reflection of the unreliability of the subtest scaled scores, factors associated with examiner characteristics, or factors associated with the assessment situation.

Profile analysis is a useful tool for evaluating intraindividual variability in various ability and achievement areas. Variability of scores, however, may only represent uneven skill development. This variability is not a sufficient basis for making decisions about psychopathology or causes of and cures for uneven development. Again, you should view profile analysis as a clinical tool to be used *together with* other assessment strategies in developing hypotheses about the examinee's ability. Glutting, McDermott, and Konold (1997) described nine core WISC–III profiles and a method for determining whether a child's profile differs from the core profile associated with the child's Full Scale IQ. A related analysis of profile types is provided by Konold, Glutting, McDermott, Kush, and Watkins (1999).

A SUCCESSIVE-LEVEL APPROACH TO TEST INTERPRETATION

The following six-level approach to test interpretation can help you better understand an examinee's performance on a Wechsler test (see Figure 10-1).

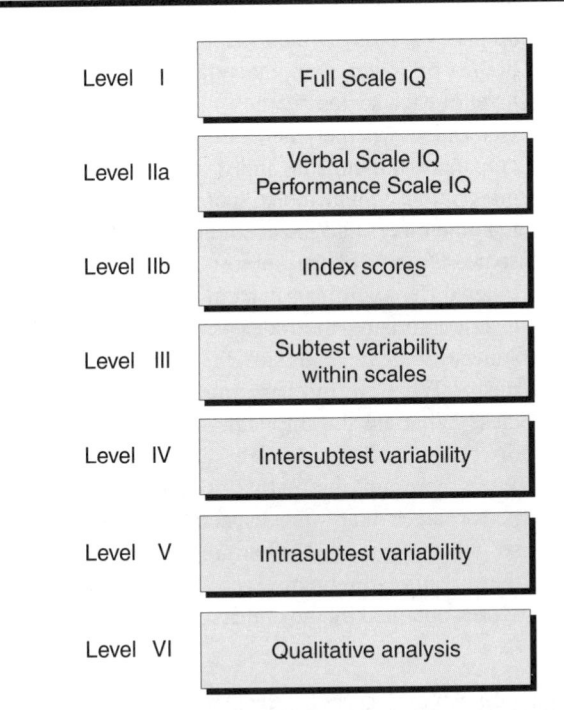

Level I	Full Scale IQ
Level IIa	Verbal Scale IQ Performance Scale IQ
Level IIb	Index scores
Level III	Subtest variability within scales
Level IV	Intersubtest variability
Level V	Intrasubtest variability
Level VI	Qualitative analysis

Figure 10-1. A successive-level approach to Wechsler test interpretation.

Level I: Full Scale IQ. The first level focuses on the Full Scale IQ. In most cases, the Full Scale IQ is the most reliable and valid estimate of the child's intellectual ability provided by the test. It is the primary numerical and quantitative index, providing information about the child's relative standing in the general population (as represented by the standardization group). The Full Scale IQ is a global estimate of the child's level of cognitive ability; it assesses both crystallized and fluid intelligence. The Full Scale IQ is usually used to obtain the descriptive classification of the child's IQ level (e.g., Very Superior, Superior, High Average, Average, Low Average, Borderline, and Mentally Deficient; see Table BC-2 on the inside back cover). Converting the Full Scale IQ to a percentile rank (see Table BC-1 on the inside back cover) will help you interpret this score for individuals who are not familiar with standard scores.

The Full Scale IQ is also "the most parsimonious and powerful predictor of academic achievement obtainable from the WISC–III" (Glutting et al., 1997, p. 300). We therefore recommend, as does Slate (1994), that the Full Scale IQ be used in a regression formula to determine whether a severe discrepancy exists between ability and achievement in establishing a diagnosis of learning disability (see *Assessment of Children: Behavioral and Clinical Applications*), unless there is a compelling reason to use either the Verbal Scale IQ or the Performance Scale IQ (e.g., if the examinee has a sensory deficit—such as a visual, auditory, or motor deficit—

that interferes with her or his ability to take selected subtests).

Level IIa: Verbal Scale IQ and Performance Scale IQ. The second level focuses on the Verbal Scale IQ and Performance Scale IQ and the extent to which there is a significant difference between the two. The Verbal Scale IQ provides information about verbal comprehension skills, while the Performance Scale IQ covers perceptual organization skills. You can use Table BC-1 to obtain the percentile ranks associated with these two IQs.

Level IIb: Index scores. An alternative second-level procedure is to focus on the four index scores (Verbal Comprehension, Perceptual Organization, Freedom from Distractibility, and Processing Speed) and the extent to which there are significant differences among them. You can use Table BC-1 to obtain the percentile ranks associated with the index scores and Table A-1 in Appendix A to obtain confidence intervals.

Level III: Subtest variability within scales. The third level focuses on (a) deviations of the verbal subtest scaled scores from the mean of the Verbal Scale and (b) deviations of the performance subtest scaled scores from the mean of the Performance Scale. You can develop hypotheses about strengths and weaknesses from these analyses.

Level IV: Intersubtest variability. The fourth level focuses on comparisons between sets of subtest scaled scores or among clusters of subtest scaled scores. Although these comparisons are open to the errors associated with multiple comparisons, they are valuable for generating hypotheses about the examinee's intellectual abilities.

Level V: Intrasubtest variability. The fifth level focuses on the pattern of raw scores within each subtest. Within a subtest, the items are arranged in order of difficulty, which will help you to evaluate the pattern of successes and failures. Here are two examples:

- A child who passes the first item, fails the next four, passes the next one, fails the next four, and overall passes a total of four items shows a different pattern from a child who passes the first four items and fails the remainder, although both children receive 4 raw-score points. The child with the markedly uneven pattern may have cognitive or attentional inefficiencies that need to be explored further.

- A pattern of missing easy items and succeeding on more difficult items may occur among bright children who are bored by the easy items and thus give careless or even nonsense replies, only to become challenged by more difficult items that allow them to demonstrate their skills. It is sometimes evident, for example, on the Digit Span subtest, where a child may be observed to perform better on the more demanding backwards task. This pattern also may suggest inconsistent attention or effort resulting from anxiety or other factors.

Level VI: Qualitative analysis. The sixth level focuses on specific item failures and the content of the responses, or what we call "qualitative analysis." Inspecting responses to specific items can aid you in understanding the child's knowledge of specific information, such as knowledge of the concept *half* on the Arithmetic subtest. You also may use a child's unique or idiosyncratic responses to formulate hypotheses that might explain scaled scores that deviate from the means of their respective scales.

Give careful attention to unique or highly personal responses. For example, a child with paranoid tendencies may give querulous, distrustful, or legalistic responses (e.g., "I'm being tricked," "Why are you writing everything down?" "Are you going to use my answers against me?"), whereas a child who is depressed may give slow, hesitant, and blocked responses, interspersed with self-deprecatory remarks (e.g., "I'm worthless," "These things are tiring," "I've never been good at this," "Sure takes a lot of energy to do this puzzle"). Also evaluate nonverbal responses (e.g., grimaces, laughter, crying, tone of voice, motor movements) that accompany the verbal responses.

STEPS IN ANALYZING A WECHSLER PROTOCOL

Use the following steps in analyzing a Wechsler protocol.

Step 1. Evaluate the reliability of the test scores.

Step 2. Evaluate the validity of the test scores.

Step 3. Examine the Full Scale IQ and its percentile rank, and evaluate the implications of this score.

Step 4. Examine the Verbal Scale IQ and its percentile rank, and evaluate the implications of this score.

Step 5. Examine the Performance Scale IQ and its percentile rank, and evaluate the implications of this score.

Step 6. Determine whether there is a significant discrepancy between individual the Verbal Scale and Performance Scale IQs. If there is a significant discrepancy, which IQ is higher? What is the base rate for the discrepancy? What are the implications of the discrepancy?

Step 7. Determine whether there are significant discrepancies between individual subtest scaled scores and the means of their respective scaled scores. If there is a significant discrepancy, is the subtest scaled score lower or higher than the mean? What is the base rate for the discrepancy? What are the implications of the discrepancy? Note the absolute level of each subtest scaled score that differs significantly from its respective mean score.

Step 8. Determine whether there are subtest scaled scores that differ significantly from each other. If so,

which ones? What are the implications of each discrepancy? Note which subtest scaled score is higher or lower than the other and the absolute level of each scaled score.

Step 9. Determine whether there are any significant discrepancies among the index scores. If so, which ones? Note which index score is higher or lower than the others and the absolute level of each index score. Do any of the subtest scaled scores on an index differ significantly from the mean of the subtests comprising the index score? If so, are these subtest scaled scores lower or higher than the mean? What are the base rates for the discrepancies? What are the implications of any significant discrepancies?

Step 10. Were there any qualitative features of the child's performance that were especially noteworthy? Is so, what were they? What are the implications of these features by themselves and in relation to the scores obtained by the child?

COMPARISONS BETWEEN THE VERBAL SCALE AND PERFORMANCE SCALE

When you develop hypotheses about a child's performance on the Verbal Scale and Performance Scale, the hypotheses should be based primarily on the individual subtests that make up the respective scales. However, some general observations about the two scales still can be made.

Interpretation of the Verbal Scale and Performance Scale

The Verbal Scale draws on the child's accumulated experience. The items on the scale usually require the child to respond verbally with what is likely learned information. The questions (input) are presented orally, and the child gives responses (output) orally. You can consider the Verbal Scale as an index of verbal ability and verbal comprehension and a reflection of crystallized intelligence.

The Performance Scale is more dependent than the Verbal Scale on the child's immediate problem-solving ability. The items on the scale usually require the child to apply previously acquired skills to a novel set of demands. The stimuli (input) are nonverbal (aside from the directions), and most are presented visually. The child's solutions (output) require motor responses and, to a lesser extent, verbal responses. You can consider the Performance Scale as an index of nonverbal ability and perceptual organization and a reflection of fluid intelligence.

Items on the Verbal Scale and Performance Scale can be solved by the use of verbal strategies, nonverbal strategies, or a combination of the two. For example, the Verbal Scale subtests Arithmetic and Digit Span can be solved by verbal processing as well as by nonverbal processing, including visualization strategies. On Performance Scale subtests such as Coding, Picture Completion, Picture Arrangement, and Symbol Search, either nonverbal or verbal strategies can be used (e.g., language activity in the form of overt verbal responses or mediating symbolic activity).

Let's examine more closely the subtests on the Performance Scale to understand the possible influence of verbal abilities on a child's performance:

- Coding B depends on the ability to learn associations between digits and symbols, and these associations can be encoded verbally.
- Picture Completion depends on a knowledge of "the way the world is," and this knowledge may be imparted by verbal means.
- Picture Arrangement depends on the ability to properly sequence the pictures, an ability that may involve verbal processing (as well as visual processing).
- Symbol Search depends on the ability to scan symbols rapidly, an ability facilitated by attaching verbal descriptions to symbols.
- Block Design and Object Assembly depend on the ability to visualize configurations in space and therefore may not depend on verbal processing.
- Mazes depends on the ability to follow a visual pattern and therefore may not depend on verbal processing.

Overall, there may be no *pure* tests of nonverbal ability on the WISC–III or other Wechsler tests.

Table D-4 in Appendix D presents a summary of the interpretive rationales, possible implications of high and low scores, and instructional implications for the Verbal Scale, Performance Scale, and Full Scale. Again, note that these descriptions are to guide your interpretations.

Formulating Hypotheses About Verbal Scale–Performance Scale Discrepancies

A significant difference between the Verbal Scale and Performance Scale may indicate the following:

- Interest patterns
- Cognitive style
- Deficiencies or strengths in processing information
- Deficiencies or strengths in modes of expression
- Deficiencies or strengths in the ability to work under time pressure (such as the time constraints on the Performance Scale)
- Sensory deficiencies
- Brain injury
- Psychopathology
- Behavioral problems, such as limited motivation or rebelliousness
- A home or school environment in which language or materials differ from those commonly used in our culture

You will need to evaluate the child's entire performance, clinical history, and background information to arrive at the most reasonable hypothesis to account for a significant difference between scores on the Verbal Scale and Performance Scale. Always formulate hypotheses about a Verbal Scale–Performance Scale difference in relationship to the child's *absolute* Verbal Scale IQ, Performance Scale IQ, and Full Scale IQ, and only when the difference is significant. This means, for example, that you would not say that a child with a Verbal Scale IQ of 150 and a Performance Scale IQ of 125 had a performance deficit, even though the Performance Scale IQ is significantly lower than the Verbal Scale IQ. In this case, both abilities are well developed, with verbal skills even better developed than performance skills. Similarly, you should view a child with a Verbal Scale IQ of 68 and a Performance Scale IQ of 50 as having deficits in both verbal and nonverbal areas, even though the Verbal Scale IQ is significantly higher than the Performance Scale IQ. As stated previously, the Verbal Scale IQ of 68 may be a relative strength for this child, but it is not an absolute one.

A Verbal Scale–Performance Scale discrepancy may be used to generate hypotheses about an examinee's cognitive functioning, but should not be used to diagnose or classify an individual or to conclude that a disability is present. A Verbal Scale–Performance Scale discrepancy should never be used as the sole criterion for making a diagnosis of learning disability, brain injury, or mental retardation. Here are some examples of hypotheses to consider when Verbal Scale > Performance Scale and when Performance Scale > Verbal Scale.

ILLUSTRATIVE HYPOTHESES FOR VERBAL SCALE > PERFORMANCE SCALE

1. Verbal skills are better developed than performance skills.
2. Verbal processing is better developed than visuospatial processing.
3. Auditory-vocal processing skills are better developed than visual-motor discrimination skills.
4. Knowledge acquired through accumulated experience is better developed than immediate problem-solving ability.
5. Ability to retrieve verbal information from long-term memory is better developed than immediate problem-solving ability.
6. The examinee may have difficulties with practical tasks.
7. Performance deficits may exist.
8. Limitations may be present in visual-motor integration.
9. The examinee may have difficulties in performing speeded or timed tasks or may have a deliberate response style.

ILLUSTRATIVE HYPOTHESES FOR PERFORMANCE SCALE > VERBAL SCALE

1. Performance skills are better developed than verbal skills.
2. Visuospatial processing is better developed than verbal processing.
3. Visual-motor discrimination skills are better developed than auditory-vocal processing skills.

4. Immediate problem-solving ability is better developed than knowledge acquired as a result of accumulated experience.

5. Immediate problem-solving ability is better developed than ability to retrieve verbal information from long-term memory.

6. The examinee may have difficulties with verbal tasks.

7. Language deficits or cultural differences may exist.

8. Limitations may be present in auditory conceptual skills and auditory processing skills.

9. The examinee may have difficulties in working effectively without time pressure or may have a nondeliberate response style.

COMPARISONS BETWEEN INDEX SCORES

Formulate hypotheses about index scores only when they are significantly different from each other (see Table A-2 in Appendix A). Tables A-4 and A-5 in Appendix A show the frequencies with which given discrepancies between the WISC–III index scores occur in the standardization sample. You can find a summary of interpretive rationales for Wechsler index scores in Table D-4 in Appendix D. In all cases, to determine the best explanation of an examinee's index score, carefully analyze his or her entire performance on the test, other test scores, and case history information. Caruso and Cliff (1999) provide procedures for obtaining more reliable index scores.

Interpretations of the Verbal Comprehension Index (Information, Similarities, Vocabulary, and Comprehension) and the Perceptual Organization Index (Picture Completion, Block Design, and Object Assembly) are similar to those of the Verbal Scale and Performance Scale, respectively. The Verbal Comprehension Index provides a purer measure of verbal comprehension than does the Verbal Scale IQ, just as the Perceptual Organization Index provides a purer measure of perceptual organization than does the Performance Scale IQ. When the scaled scores on the subtests that comprise the Verbal Comprehension Index or the Perceptual Organization Index are in a similar direction (e.g., all above average or all below average), you are on firm ground in interpreting the index. However, when the scaled scores on the subtests that comprise an index differ in direction (e.g., some above average and some below average), the index should not be interpreted.

The Freedom from Distractibility Index (Digit Span and Arithmetic) appears to be a measure of working memory or short-term acquisition and retrieval. A child's performance may be related to (a) cognitive variables, such as sequencing, short-term memory, working memory, numerical skills, and auditory processing skills, and (b) behavioral variables, such as anxiety and distractibility. The name Freedom from Distractibility is somewhat misleading because this index should never be unequivocally interpreted as a measure of distractibility. Although distractibility can certainly result in lower scores on this index, it can also impair performance on other subtests. And other factors may lead to lower scores on this

index. When the Arithmetic and Digit Span subtest scaled scores are both high or low, you can have more confidence in interpreting the Freedom from Distractibility Index than when the scaled scores on the two subtests are not consistent.

The Processing Speed Index (Coding and Symbol Search) appears to measure immediate short-term memory, ability to sustain attention, encoding ability, perceptual discrimination ability, fine motor skills, and cognitive flexibility. When the Coding and Symbol Search scaled scores are both high or low, you can have more confidence in interpreting the Processing Speed Index than when the scaled scores on the two subtests are inconsistent.

COMPARISONS BETWEEN SUBTESTS

If you find significant differences between subtest scaled scores (see Table A-2 in Appendix A), you will need to interpret the findings. Several parts of this text will help you do so. First, Table 10-5 shows suggested abilities and factors associated with the 13 WISC–III subtests (as well as with additional WAIS–III subtests). Second, much of the material in this and the preceding two chapters is relevant to interpreting subtest scaled scores. Third, the suggestions that follow are also useful. *Any hypotheses about subtest scaled scores should be developed through the study of the child's entire test performance and clinical history.*

The following list illustrates ways of comparing Wechsler subtests. Note that the list does not include all possible comparisons, nor does it reflect all possible interpretations. However, these examples should help you develop interpretations for other subtest comparisons as well. Treat all hypotheses developed from subtest comparisons as tentative, not definitive. In Appendix D, see Table D-3 for a summary of interpretive rationales for the WISC–III subtests and Table D-5 for suggested remediation activities for combinations of subtests. Develop your hypotheses based on both significant differences between subtest scaled scores and the absolute values of the subtest scaled scores. Thus, *scaled scores of 10 or higher should never be described as reflecting absolute weaknesses, and scaled scores of 9 or lower should never be described as reflecting absolute strengths.* Also, see Table D-1 in Appendix D for percentile ranks and qualitative descriptions associated with subtest scaled scores.

COMPARISONS OF VERBAL SCALE SUBTESTS

1. *Information (I) and Comprehension (C).* This comparison relates the amount of information retained (Information) to the ability to use information (Comprehension). Information requires factual knowledge, while Comprehension requires both factual knowledge and judgment.

- I > C: High Information and low Comprehension may suggest adequate general knowledge but difficulty in synthesizing and using information to solve problems involving the social world.

Table 10-5
Suggested Abilities or Factors Associated with WISC–III and WAIS–III Subtests

Information (I)	Similarities (S)	Arithmetic (A)	Vocabulary (V)	Comprehension (C)	Digit Span (DS)	Letter–Number Seq. (LN)	Picture Completion (PC)	Picture Arrangement (PA)	Block Design (BD)	Object Assembly (OA)	Coding (CD)	Mazes (MA)	Symbol Search (SS)	Matrix Reasoning (MR)	M Suggested abilities or factors
	S		V												___ Abstract thinking
		A			DS	LN					CD		SS	MR	___ Attention
		A			DS	LN									___ Auditory memory
	S														___ Categorical thinking
				C				PA							___ Common-sense reasoning
		A			DS	LN	PC					MA	SS	MR	___ Concentration
I	S		V	C											___ Crystallized ability
I			V	C				PA							___ Cultural opportunities at home
I	S		V												___ Extent of outside reading
		A			DS						CD				___ Facility with numbers
									BD	OA		MA	SS		___ Fine motor coordination
		A			DS		PC	PA	BD	OA	CD		SS	MR	___ Fluid ability
		A			DS	LN					CD		SS		___ Freedom from distractibility
I			V												___ Fund of information
I	S	A	V	C			PC								___ Long-term memory
		A													___ Mathematics knowledge
							PC	PA	BD	OA		MA		MR	___ Nonverbal reasoning
		A			DS	LN					CD				___ Numerical ability
									BD		CD	MA	SS	MR	___ Perception of abstract stimuli
							PC	PA		OA					___ Perception of meaningful stimuli
							PC	PA	BD	OA		MA	SS	MR	___ Perceptual organization
								PA				MA			___ Perceptual planning ability
									BD		CD				___ Perceptual reproduction
								PA	BD	OA					___ Perceptual synthesis
								PA				MA			___ Planning ability
											CD		SS		___ Processing speed
									BD	OA	CD		SS		___ Psychomotor speed
I			V												___ Richness of early environment
I		A	V												___ School learning
					DS	LN		PA			CD				___ Sequencing
		A			DS	LN					CD		SS		___ Short-term memory
				C				PA							___ Social judgment
							PC		BD	OA		MA		MR	___ Spatial perception
						LN			BD	OA	CD	MA	SS	MR	___ Sustained energy or persistence
I	S		V	C											___ Verbal comprehension
	S		V												___ Verbal concept formation
	S		V	C											___ Verbal expression
	S	A		C											___ Verbal reasoning
							PC				CD		SS		___ Visual memory
									BD	OA	CD	MA	SS		___ Visual-motor coordination
							PC	PA							___ Visual organization
							PC	PA	BD	OA	CD	MA	SS	MR	___ Visual processing
		A			DS						CD				___ Working memory

Note. M = mean of the subtest scaled scores for the ability or factor.

313

- I < C: Low Information and high Comprehension may suggest limited factual knowledge but good ability to use this limited knowledge to make appropriate judgments.

2. *Information (I) and Similarities (S).* This comparison relates the amount of information retained (Information) to the ability to engage in conceptual thinking (Similarities).

- I > S: High Information and low Similarities may suggest adequate general knowledge but difficulty in using factual knowledge conceptually.
- I < S: Low Information and high Similarities may suggest that conceptual reasoning is better developed than grasp of general knowledge or that exposure to general knowledge is deficient.

3. *Comprehension (C) and Arithmetic (A).* The Comprehension and Arithmetic subtests both require reasoning ability—for instance, the ability to analyze a given set of material and recognize the elements needed for the solution of the specified problem.

- C > A: High Comprehension and low Arithmetic may suggest that reasoning ability is adequate in social situations but not in situations involving numbers.
- C < A: Low Comprehension and high Arithmetic may suggest that reasoning ability is better in mathematical tasks than in social settings.

4. *Digit Span (DS) and Arithmetic (A).* The Digit Span and Arithmetic subtests both require facility with numbers and ability in immediate recall. Comparing the two subtests may provide an index of the relative balance between short-term attention (Digit Span) and long-term concentration (Arithmetic) or between short-term memory and long-term memory.

- DS > A: High Digit Span and low Arithmetic may suggest that attention is better developed than concentration or that short-term memory is better developed than long-term memory.
- DS < A: Low Digit Span and high Arithmetic may suggest that concentration is better developed than attention or that long-term memory is better developed than short-term memory.

5. *Similarities (S) and Comprehension (C).* Similarities and Comprehension both involve conceptualizing skills. Similarities usually requires a single-word response, while Comprehension requires an extended response that interrelates a set of ideas (referred to as propositional thinking).

- S > C: High Similarities and low Comprehension may suggest good abstract thinking but difficulty in applying conceptualizing ability to solve problems in the social world. This pattern also may suggest a verbal-expressive deficit involving propositional thinking.

- S < C: Low Similarities and high Comprehension may suggest a deficit in verbal concept formation in comparison with real-world conceptualizing ability.

6. *Similarities (S) and Arithmetic (A).* Similarities and Arithmetic both require conceptual thinking, one dealing with verbal material and the other with numerical symbols.

- S > A: High Similarities and low Arithmetic may suggest that conceptual thinking is better developed with verbal material than with numerical symbols.
- S < A: Low Similarities and high Arithmetic may suggest that conceptual thinking is better developed with numerical symbols than with verbal material.

7. *Similarities (S) and Vocabulary (V).* Both Similarities and Vocabulary measure level of abstract thinking and ability to form concepts, but Similarities is a better measure of these abilities.

- S > V: High Similarities and low Vocabulary may suggest good ability to think abstractly but limited ability to understand or express the meaning of individual words.
- S < V: Low Similarities and high Vocabulary may suggest difficulty in forming abstract concepts but good ability to understand or express the meaning of individual words.

8. *Digits Forward (DS-F) and Digits Backward (DS-B).* Both components of Digit Span—Digits Forward and Digits

Courtesy of Herman Zielinski.

Backward—involve short-term memory and attention. Digits Backward, however, involves more complex attentional processes and requires working memory.

- DS-F > DS-B: High Digits Forward and low Digits Backward (differences of 3 or more raw-score points) may indicate that the child did not put forth the extra effort needed to master the more difficult task of recalling digits backward in sequence. Alternatively, it may indicate good auditory sequential memory but poor working memory (or poor short-term visual memory based on auditory information, a tentative hypothesis).

- DS-F < DS-B: Low Digits Forward and high Digits Backward may indicate that the child views Digits Backward as a challenge rather than as a task involving mere repetition of numbers. Alternatively, it may indicate poor auditory sequential memory but good working memory (or good short-term visual memory based on auditory information, a tentative hypothesis).

9. *Similarities (S) and Digit Span (DS).* Similarities and Digit Span have little overlap in their measurement properties, although both are included in the Verbal Scale.

- S > DS: High Similarities and low Digit Span may reflect good conceptualizing ability coupled with poor rote auditory memory for digits.

- S < DS: Low Similarities and high Digit Span may suggest poor conceptualizing ability coupled with good rote auditory memory for digits.

COMPARISONS OF VERBAL SCALE AND PERFORMANCE SCALE SUBTESTS

1. *Similarities (S) and Block Design (BD).* Similarities and Block Design both reflect abstract reasoning ability. They require the abstraction of relations among stimulus items.

- S > BD: High Similarities and low Block Design may suggest that abstract reasoning ability is better with verbal stimuli than with nonverbal stimuli.

- S < BD: Low Similarities and high Block Design may suggest that abstract reasoning ability is better with nonverbal stimuli than with verbal stimuli.

2. *Picture Arrangement (PA) and Comprehension (C).* Picture Arrangement and Comprehension both contain stimuli concerned with social interaction. The comparison relates knowledge of social conventions (Comprehension) to the capacity to anticipate and plan in a social context (Picture Arrangement).

- PA > C: High Picture Arrangement and low Comprehension may suggest sensitivity to interpersonal nuance, but a disregard for social conventions. It also may reflect appropriate judgments but poor expressive language. Or it may suggest better ability to use visual cues than verbal cues in social situations.

- PA < C: Low Picture Arrangement and high Comprehension may suggest an understanding of social situations in the abstract, but difficulty in deciding what the situations mean or what actions to take once involved in the situations. It also may suggest better ability to use verbal cues than visual cues in social situations.

3. *Picture Completion (PC) and Arithmetic (A).* Picture Completion and Arithmetic both involve concentration. However, on Picture Completion concentration is on an externalized form—a visual stimulus—while on Arithmetic concentration is on an internalized stimulus—a memory trace.

- PC > A: High Picture Completion and low Arithmetic may suggest good attention to visual detail, but not to an auditory stimulus.

- PC < A: Low Picture Completion and high Arithmetic may suggest adequate concentration on an auditory stimulus, but inattention to visual detail.

COMPARISONS OF PERFORMANCE SCALE SUBTESTS

1. *Picture Completion (PC) and Picture Arrangement (PA).* This comparison provides an estimate of attention to detail (Picture Completion) versus organization of detail (Picture Arrangement). Both Picture Completion and Picture Arrangement involve perception of details, but Picture Arrangement also requires logical ordering of details, or sequencing.

- PC > PA: High Picture Completion and low Picture Arrangement may suggest that perception of details is better developed for nonsequencing tasks than for tasks requiring sequencing and organization.

- PC < PA: Low Picture Completion and high Picture Arrangement may suggest that perception of details is less well developed for nonsequencing tasks than for tasks requiring sequencing and organization.

2. *Picture Completion (PC) and Block Design (BD).* This comparison relates visuoperception (Picture Completion) to visual-motor-spatial coordination (Block Design).

- PC > BD: High Picture Completion and low Block Design may suggest adequate nonspatial visuoperceptual ability but inadequate visuospatial ability.

- PC < BD: Low Picture Completion and high Block Design may suggest inadequate nonspatial visuoperceptual ability but adequate visuospatial ability.

3. *Object Assembly (OA) and Picture Arrangement (PA).* This comparison relates inductive reasoning (working from parts to a whole; Object Assembly) to sequencing (Picture Arrangement). Both tasks require synthesis into a whole without a model, but Picture Arrangement also involves sequencing.

- OA > PA: High Object Assembly and low Picture Arrangement may suggest that visual inductive reasoning skills are better developed than visual sequencing skills.
- OA < PA: Low Object Assembly and high Picture Arrangement may suggest that visual inductive reasoning skills are less well developed than visual sequencing skills.

4. *Coding (CD) and Symbol Search (SS).* This comparison relates two subtests with abstract perceptual stimuli that tap into perceptual discrimination, speed and accuracy, and attention and concentration. However, Symbol Search requires more cognitive flexibility than does Coding, and Coding requires better perceptual-motor integration than does Symbol Search. In comparison to Coding, Symbol Search appears to involve (a) scanning a smaller visual field, as the stimulus array is smaller; (b) a briefer duration of visual working memory, as there is less information needed to make a decision; (c) a simpler decision-making process, as there are two choices instead of 10; (d) a simpler motor response, such as drawing a straight line rather than making more complex figures; (e) less verbal recoding (for instance, it doesn't require recognizing that "a cross goes with the 2"); and (f) fewer distractions, since the examinee proceeds down the page in one direction instead of proceeding left-to-right to complete each row (John MacDonald, personal communication, June 1999).

What is missing in the picture?

Copyright © 1977 American Publishing Corporation and adapted.

- CD > SS: High Coding and low Symbol Search may suggest better performance on a visual-motor task when the stimuli do not require constant shifting between symbols.
- CD < SS: Low Coding and high Symbol Search may suggest better performance on a visual-motor task that requires constant shifting between symbols than on one where the symbols are fixed. It may also suggest poor perceptual-motor integration when a task requires more than drawing a straight line.

COMPARISONS OF THREE OR MORE SUBTESTS

1. *Block Design (BD), Object Assembly (OA), and Mazes (MA).* The Block Design, Object Assembly, and Mazes subtests require visual-motor coordination and planning; they involve motor activity guided by perceptual organization. The role of visual organization differs in the three subtests. On Block Design, the child uses visual organization in a process of analysis (recognizing how the pattern can be broken down) and synthesis (recognizing how to build the pattern out of the blocks). On Object Assembly, the child uses visual organization to arrange parts into a meaningful pattern. The child may develop a mental concept of the whole from the parts because there is no visual representation of the whole, whereas on Block Design a drawing of the whole design is provided for the child. On Mazes, the child may use visual organization in planning and foresight. Thus, the term *visual organization* refers to a different function on each of these three subtests.

- BD > MA: High Block Design and low Mazes may suggest that visual organization skills involving analysis and synthesis are better developed than those involving planning and foresight. It may also suggest poor visual-motor control in that blocks are easier to manipulate than a pencil.
- BD < MA: Low Block Design and high Mazes may suggest that visual organization skills involving analysis and synthesis are less well developed than those involving planning and foresight.
- OA > BD: High Object Assembly and low Block Design may suggest that nonverbal inductive reasoning skills (working from parts to a whole) are better developed than nonverbal deductive reasoning skills (working from a whole to parts). Additionally, it may suggest difficulty in interpreting figure-ground relationships.
- OA < BD: Low Object Assembly and high Block Design may suggest that nonverbal inductive reasoning skills are less well developed than nonverbal deductive reasoning skills or that a deficit exists in the ideation required to form a visual representation of the objects.

2. *Vocabulary (V), Information (I), and Comprehension (C).* All three subtests involve verbal processing, but in different contexts.

- V, I > C: High Vocabulary and Information coupled with low Comprehension may suggest an inability to use verbal ability and general knowledge fully in life situations and may therefore indicate impaired judgment.

- V, I < C: Low Vocabulary and Information coupled with high Comprehension may suggest limited concept formation, except when conceptualizing ability is applied to solving problems in the social world.

- V, C > I: High Vocabulary and Comprehension coupled with low Information may suggest good concept formation and ability to solve problems in the social world, but limited general knowledge.

- V, C < I: Low Vocabulary and Comprehension coupled with high Information may suggest that the child's store of general information is not backed up by an in-depth vocabulary or an ability to solve problems in the social world.

3. *Information (I), Arithmetic (A), and Comprehension (C) versus Similarities (S), Vocabulary (V), and Digit Span (DS).* This comparison contrasts subtests that have relatively long verbal questions (Information, Arithmetic, Comprehension) with those that have relatively short verbal questions (Similarities, Vocabulary, Digit Span).

- I, A, C > S, V, DS: High Information, Arithmetic, and Comprehension coupled with low Similarities, Vocabulary, and Digit Span may suggest better performance when verbal stimuli are long than when they are short. The child may put forth more effort to attend to verbal material that is of a relatively long duration. The pattern also may reflect an ability to benefit from the contextual cues contained in the longer questions.

- I, A, C < S, V, DS: Low Information, Arithmetic, and Comprehension coupled with high Similarities, Vocabulary, and Digit Span may suggest better performance when verbal stimuli are short than when they are long. The child may put forth more effort to attend to verbal material that is of a relatively short duration. This pattern also may suggest a receptive language impairment associated with deriving meaning from spoken language.

4. *Similarities (S), Vocabulary (V), and Comprehension (C) versus Information (I), Arithmetic (A), and Digit Span (DS).* This comparison contrasts subtests that require a fair amount of verbal expression (Similarities, Vocabulary, Comprehension) with those that require relatively little verbal expression (Information, Arithmetic, Digit Span).

- S, V, C > I, A, DS: High Similarities, Vocabulary, and Comprehension coupled with low Information, Arithmetic, and Digit Span may suggest better performance when tasks require a fair amount of verbal expression than when they require relatively little verbal expression. One possibility is that the child is challenged by tasks that primarily require verbal expression.

- S, V, C < I, A, DS: Low Similarities, Vocabulary, and Comprehension coupled with high Information, Arithmetic, and Digit Span may suggest better performance

when tasks require relatively little verbal expression than when they require a fair amount of verbal expression. One possibility is that the child puts forth effort only when tasks require minimal verbal expression. Additionally, this pattern may be associated with communication problems or shyness associated with speaking in relatively lengthy sentences.

5. *Picture Completion (PC), Picture Arrangement (PA), and Object Assembly (OA) versus Block Design (BD), Coding (CD), and Symbol Search (SS).* This comparison contrasts subtests that contain relatively meaningful perceptual stimuli (Picture Completion, Picture Arrangement, Object Assembly) with those that have relatively abstract perceptual stimuli (Block Design, Coding, Symbol Search).

- PC, PA, OA > BD, CD, SS: High Picture Completion, Picture Arrangement, and Object Assembly coupled with low Block Design, Coding, and Symbol Search may suggest better performance when visual stimuli are meaningful than when they are abstract or nonmeaningful.

- PC, PA, OA < BD, CD, SS: Low Picture Completion, Picture Arrangement, and Object Assembly coupled with high Block Design, Coding, and Symbol Search may suggest better performance when visual stimuli are abstract than when they are concrete.

6. *Picture Completion (PC) and Picture Arrangement (PA) versus Block Design (BD), Object Assembly (OA), and Mazes (MA).* Five of the seven Performance Scale subtests involve perceptual organization (the exceptions are Coding

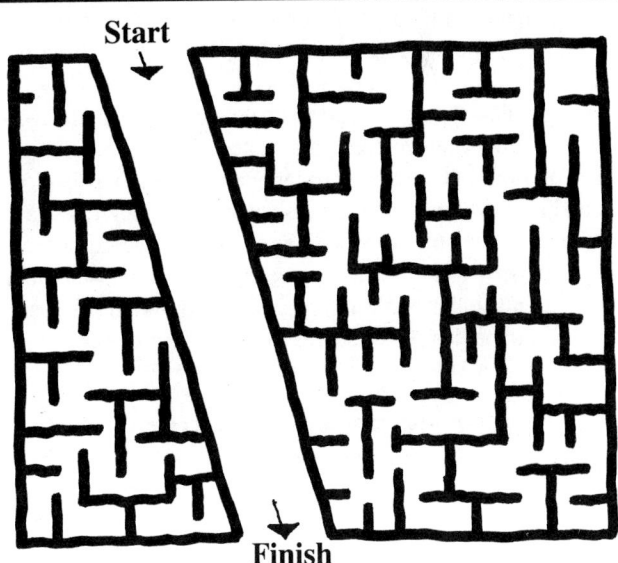

Start

Finish

See if you can find your way through this perplexing maze

Copyright © 1977 American Publishing Corporation and adapted.

and Symbol Search). All of the Performance Scale subtests involve speed. This comparison of five of the Performance Scale subtests distinguishes the two subtests that involve primarily perceptual organization (Picture Completion and Picture Arrangement) from the three that involve both perceptual organization and visual-motor coordination (Block Design, Object Assembly, and Mazes).

- PC, PA > BD, OA, MA: High Picture Completion and Picture Arrangement coupled with low Block Design, Object Assembly, and Mazes may suggest better performance when tasks require only perceptual organization than when they require both perceptual organization and visual-motor coordination.
- PC, PA < BD, OA, MA: Low Picture Completion and Picture Arrangement coupled with high Block Design, Object Assembly, and Mazes may suggest better performance when tasks require both perceptual organization and visual-motor coordination than when they require only perceptual organization.

ESTIMATED PERCENTILE RANKS AND TEST-AGE EQUIVALENTS FOR RAW SCORES

When you are preparing to explain test results to teachers, parents, physicians, attorneys, or other people involved in the assessment, it is helpful to convert subtest scaled scores to percentile ranks and to convert raw scores to test-age equivalents. Table D-1 in Appendix D gives the estimated percentile ranks and qualitative descriptions for each WISC–III (and WPPSI–R and WAIS–III) subtest scaled score. You should never estimate an IQ based on only one subtest scaled score.

Table 21 (page 259) in the WISC–III manual gives the test-age equivalents for raw scores on each subtest. The test-age equivalents provide approximate developmental levels for the child's achievement on a subtest. For example, a raw score of 7 on Information is roughly equivalent to a developmental age level of 6–6 years. As noted in Chapter 4, test-age equivalents have many drawbacks; therefore, we do not recommend their routine use. The exception is for discussions with parents and other similar parties who may more easily understand these types of scores than standard scores.

SUGGESTIONS FOR REPORTING SCALES AND SUBTESTS

Following are summaries of some essential features of the three WISC–III scales and 13 subtests. You can use this material to discuss results with parents and the referral source, as well as in the writing of your report.

Full Scale

Usually, the Full Scale IQ is the best measure of cognitive ability. It measures general intelligence, scholastic aptitude, and readiness to master a school curriculum. The child's Full Scale IQ is affected by motivation, interests, cultural opportunities, natural endowment, neurological integrity, attention span, ability to process verbal information (particularly on the verbal subtests), ability to process visual information, and psychomotor ability (particularly on the performance subtests).

Verbal Scale

The Verbal Scale IQ is a measure of verbal comprehension. This includes the application of verbal skills and information to the solution of new problems, the ability to process verbal information, and the ability to think with words. The Verbal Scale provides information about language processing, reasoning, attention, verbal learning, and memory. The child's Verbal Scale IQ may be affected by his or her motivation, interests, cultural opportunities, natural endowment, attention span, and ability to process verbal information.

Performance Scale

The Performance Scale IQ is a measure of perceptual organization. This includes the ability to think in visual images and to manipulate these images with fluency and relative speed, to reason without the use of words (in some cases), and to interpret visual material quickly. The Performance Scale provides information about visual processing, planning and organizational ability, attention, nonverbal learning, and memory. The child's Performance Scale IQ may be affected by her or his motivation, interests, cultural opportunities, natural endowment, attention span, ability to process visual information, and psychomotor ability.

Information

The Information subtest provides a measure of how much general factual knowledge the child has acquired from his or her environment. The child is asked to answer a series of questions that cover a range of material on several subjects. The subtest provides valuable information about the child's range of factual knowledge and long-term memory. Performance may be influenced by cultural opportunities, outside interests, richness of early environment, reading, and school learning.

Similarities

The Similarities subtest provides a measure of the child's ability to select and verbalize appropriate relationships between two objects or concepts. The child is asked to state how two things are alike. A response indicating an abstract classification receives more credit than a response indicating a concrete classification. The subtest provides valuable information about the child's verbal concept formation and long-term memory. Performance may be influenced by cultural opportunities, interests, reading habits, and school learning.

Arithmetic

The Arithmetic subtest provides a measure of the child's facility in mental arithmetic. The child is asked to solve several different types of arithmetic problems involving addition, subtraction, multiplication, division, and problem solving. The subtest provides valuable information about the child's numerical reasoning ability, concentration, attention, short-term memory, and long-term memory. Performance may be influenced by the child's attitude toward school and level of anxiety.

Vocabulary

The Vocabulary subtest provides a measure of the child's word knowledge. The child is asked to define individual words of increasing difficulty. The subtest provides valuable information about the child's verbal skills, language development, and long-term memory. Performance may be influenced by cultural opportunities, education, reading habits, and familiarity with English.

Comprehension

The Comprehension subtest provides a measure of the child's social judgment and common sense. The child is asked to answer questions dealing with various problem situations that, in part, involve interpersonal relations and social mores. The subtest provides valuable information about the child's knowledge of conventional standards of behavior. Performance may be influenced by cultural opportunities, ability to evaluate and draw from experiences, and moral sense.

Digit Span

The Digit Span subtest provides a measure of the child's short-term memory. In this two-part subtest, the child is asked to repeat series of digits given orally by the examiner. Each series in the first part is to be repeated as given by the examiner, and each series in the second part is to be repeated in reverse order. The subtest provides valuable information about the child's rote memory, attention, and concentration. Performance may be influenced by level of anxiety.

Picture Completion

The Picture Completion subtest provides a measure of the child's ability to differentiate essential from nonessential details. The child is shown pictures of objects from everyday life and is asked to indicate the single most important part missing from each picture. The subtest provides valuable information about the child's ability to concentrate on visually perceived material and alertness to details. Performance may be influenced by cultural experiences and alertness to the visual aspects of the environment.

Coding

The Coding subtest provides a measure of the child's ability to learn a code rapidly. The child is shown a key in which several symbols are matched with other symbols. Then the child is shown one symbol and is asked to put the matching symbol in the blank space. The subtest provides valuable information about speed and accuracy of eye-hand coordination, short-term visual memory, and attentional skills. Performance may be influenced by rate of motor activity and by motivation.

Picture Arrangement

The Picture Arrangement subtest provides a measure of the child's ability to comprehend and evaluate social situations. The child is presented with pictures in a mixed-up order and is asked to rearrange them in a logical sequence. The pictures are similar to those seen in short comic strips. The subtest provides valuable information about the child's ability to attend to details, alertness, planning ability, and visual sequencing. Performance may be influenced by cultural opportunities.

Block Design

The Block Design subtest provides a measure of the child's spatial visualization and nonverbal reasoning ability. The child is asked to use blocks to assemble a design identical to one made by the examiner or one pictured on a card. The subtest provides valuable information about the child's ability to analyze and synthesize visuospatial material and the child's visual-motor coordination. Performance may be influenced by rate of motor activity.

Object Assembly

The Object Assembly subtest provides a measure of the child's ability to synthesize concrete parts into a meaningful whole and the child's visual-motor coordination. The child is asked to assemble jigsaw puzzle pieces correctly to form common objects. The subtest provides valuable information about the child's ability to visualize a whole from its parts, organizational ability, sense of spatial relations, and visual-motor coordination. Performance is influenced by rate of motor activity, persistence, and experience with part-whole relationships.

Symbol Search

The Symbol Search subtest provides a measure of the child's visual discrimination and visuoperceptual scanning ability. After looking at the target symbol (or two target symbols in the second part of the subtest), the child looks at another group of symbols and indicates whether the target symbol (or at least one of the two target symbols) is in the group of symbols. The subtest provides valuable information about the child's perceptual discrimination, speed and accuracy, attention and concentration, and short-term memory. Performance may be influenced by rate of motor activity and motivation and perhaps by cognitive flexibility. Cognitive flexibility refers to an ability to shift between the target symbols and the other groups of symbols as they change for each item.

Mazes

The Mazes subtest provides a measure of the child's planning ability and perceptual organizational ability involved in following a visual pattern. The child is shown a maze and is asked to draw a continuous line that shows a way out of the maze without running into a blocked passage. The mazes are of increasing difficulty. The subtest provides valuable information about planning ability, foresight, visual-motor control, and attention and concentration. Performance may be influenced by visual-motor organization ability and ability to delay actions—that is, to not act impulsively.

COMMENT ON INTERPRETING
THE WISC–III

In interpreting the WISC–III (as well as any other test), it is critical that you consider all sources of information, including the child's educational history, previous assessment results, other current assessment results, developmental history, cultural and linguistic background, family environment, health history, and temporary situational factors. If the Full Scale IQ does not appear to be a valid estimate of the child's ability, consider the Verbal Scale IQ or the Performance Scale IQ as a possible substitute. In this case, also consider following up with another intelligence test.

You should never delete subtests in computing the Full Scale IQ (or in computing the Verbal Scale IQ or Performance Scale IQ) simply because an examinee scored poorly on the subtests. There is no justification for this practice. In contrast, you should always delete subtests in computing the Full Scale IQ (or in computing the Verbal Scale IQ or Performance Scale IQ) when the subtests are spoiled during their administration, when the child has a physical disability that invalidates the use of the subtests, or when there is a priori evidence that certain subtests (or scales) should not be administered or used to compute an IQ (e.g., it is known that the Verbal Scale subtests should not be used to compute an IQ for children with a severe hearing impairment or for Native American children, and that the Performance Scale subtests should not be used to compute an IQ for children with a severe visual impairment).

In interpreting the child's performance on the WISC–III (and on other tests as well), you should also consider several factors that have been discussed in this and other chapters of the book:

1. The child's level of performance, such as whether the child's scaled scores reflect strengths, weaknesses, or average ability
2. The quality of the child's performance, such as the child's language, affect, attention, and approach to the tasks (e.g., systematic or unsystematic), as well as how the child related to the examiner
3. The problem-solving strategies used by the child, such as the child's verbalizations to herself or himself and whether the child checked solutions, repeated key elements of problems, recognized when solutions were correct or incorrect, found alternative ways of solving problems, and formulated plans to solve problems

Throughout this process you should focus on typical behaviors as well as on those that might reflect psychopathology.

Sometimes examinees have difficulty completing tasks. For example, tasks requiring speed and quick execution, such as Coding or Symbol Search, may be taxing for depressed children. Although depressed children's performance on these tasks may not reflect their level of cognitive ability, the tasks are still valuable because they provide information not readily obtained from interviews or observations conducted in natural settings. Coding, for example, can give you clues about the child's ability to follow a complex set of instructions, visual scanning processes, and learning ability. Symbol Search gives you clues about visual scanning and the ability to shift rapidly. You may not want to report a score for these subtests for children who are depressed, but you can use the results to develop hypotheses to guide your clinical judgments.

An illustration follows of how quantitative and qualitative information can be woven into a report and how a child's profile can be discussed in a report. The report, only parts of which are shown below, was based on the administration of the WISC–III to an adolescent female named Helen, aged 16 years 11 months. Her scores were as follows:

Information 12	Picture Completion 9
Similarities 12	Coding 11
Arithmetic 8	Picture Arrangement 5
Vocabulary 10	Block Design 9
Comprehension 9	Object Assembly 9
Digit Span 6	

Verbal Scale IQ   101
Performance Scale IQ   91
Full Scale IQ   94

Helen's short-term auditory sequential memory is relatively less well developed than her overall verbal skills. The subtest measuring short-term auditory sequential memory involves repeating a sequence of digits from immediate memory. Her weakness in short-term auditory sequential memory may be due to temporary inefficiency caused by anxiety or inattention. However, it is important to note that neither anxiety nor inattention appeared to affect her performance on other subtests adversely. Therefore, it is more likely that her weakness in short-term auditory sequential memory for digit sequences indicates difficulty forming in memory an adequate mental image of the correct digit sequence. Helen was often able to recall the correct digits but in the wrong sequence, indicating a weakness in auditory sequential memory specifically rather than in general auditory memory per se.

Helen's visual sequencing ability is relatively less well developed than her other nonverbal skills. Helen's average attention to visual detail, coupled with her below-average visual sequencing ability, indicates that although her perception of visual details is adequate, her ability to organize and sequence these details is poor. Moreover, it is important to note that both Helen's verbal and her nonverbal weaknesses lie in her sequencing ability in different domains—auditory sequencing and visual sequencing. This may indicate an inefficiency in her general sequential processing abilities, although further testing would be needed to substantiate this hypothesis. It is unclear how Helen's weakness in auditory and visual sequencing has affected her academic performance at school; this needs to be investigated. However, her overall average verbal and nonverbal skills indicate that she has the ability to perform adequately in school.

When a significant Verbal Scale–Performance Scale split occurs, the Full Scale IQ may be a misrepresentation of the individual's functioning level. In this situation, the Full Scale IQ may represent a forced average of rather disparate primary skills. What meaning, for example, can we attach to an IQ of 100 that results from a Verbal Scale IQ of 130 and a Performance Scale IQ of 70? Although the IQ of 100 may be the best overall estimate of the child's cognitive level, the child is not likely to be average either in situations calling for verbal reasoning or in those requiring nonverbal reasoning. Unfortunately, there is little research that can help us understand how examinees with large Verbal Scale–Performance Scale discrepancies function outside the test situation.

To a lesser extent, a similar problem exists in interpreting the Verbal Scale IQ and Performance Scale IQ when there is an exceptionally large amount of variability among the subtests within each scale. Consider a child who obtains a score of 10 on each subtest and comes out with a Full Scale IQ of 100. Then consider another child who obtains a score of 1 on five verbal subtests and a score of 19 on five performance subtests, again with a resulting Full Scale IQ of 100. What is the meaning of the 100 IQ in each case? Obviously, these two children differ in their pattern of ability. Should a Full Scale IQ be reported in the second case? If not, how do we handle situations requiring the reporting of one number (e.g., in the determination of mental retardation or when a discrepancy formula is involved)? And when is the variability of scores sufficient that we should not report the Full Scale IQ or use it in eligibility decisions? There are no simple answers to these difficult questions. Answers to these and similar questions await further research.

The score that a child obtains on each WISC–III scale and subtest is multidetermined. This means that any one scale or subtest likely measures many different abilities. Consequently, a high score or a low score does not indicate which particular functions are well developed or not well developed. This information will come only from a sifting of all WISC–III scores, scores obtained on other tests, qualitative information, testing-of-limits, and the child's clinical history.

As noted in Chapter 8, the WISC–III may not be the instrument of choice for evaluating the cognitive abilities of children who function at either an extremely low or an extremely high level. In both cases, there may be too few items on the test—that is, not enough easy items for low-functioning children and not enough challenging ones for high-functioning children. Profile analysis also is hindered because the highest scaled scores are not available on each subtest throughout all of the age ranges covered by the test.

Interpreting the WISC–III is a challenging activity. The WISC–III gives an estimate of the child's level of intellectual functioning. We need to emphasize the word *estimate*. The WISC–III provides useful, but limited, information about the range, depth, and real-world applications of a child's intellectual ability.

The WISC–III (and other Wechsler tests) should not be used to evaluate personality and temperament, to diagnose psychopathology, or to determine brain lateralization. Instead, the WISC–III should be used to learn about the child's intellectual ability and to generate hypotheses to account for the child's functioning on the test. There is a world of difference between reporting that the child performed in an impulsive manner and reporting that the WISC–III test results indicate that the child has ADHD. Once we go beyond the confines of the IQs provided by the Full Scale, Verbal Scale, and Performance Scale, the ground becomes loose and wobbly. Interpretations become more impressionistic and less reliable and valid. When on this ground, step carefully, continually getting your bearings from research findings, other sources of information, and clinical experience.

Chapters in *Assessment of Children: Behavioral and Clinical Applications* discuss whether there are WISC–III patterns that can distinguish clinical groups of children (e.g., those with learning disabilities or those with ADHD) from normal children. In terms of profile analysis, we know of no WISC–III patterns that can reliably distinguish clinical groups from normal groups.

PSYCHOLOGICAL EVALUATION

The psychological evaluation in Exhibit 10-2 illustrates how the WISC–III can contribute to the assessment of a youngster with emotional difficulties. For illustrative purposes the report focuses on only the WISC–III. We would, of course, use several assessment procedures for a thorough assessment.

Exhibit 10-2
Analysis of and Line-by-Line Notations on a Psychological Evaluation of an Emotionally
Disturbed 7-Year-Old Examined with the WISC–III

INTRODUCTORY REMARKS

On the following pages is a case study of an emotionally disturbed child. Jim, a 7-year-old boy referred for evaluation because of antisocial behavior, was administered the WISC–III. His Full Scale IQ of 113 is classified in the High Average range of intelligence. There was a significant 15-point difference between his Verbal Scale IQ (119) and Performance Scale IQ (104). Most subtest scores were above average, with the exception of those on two performance subtests (Object Assembly and Coding). These results suggest that his nonverbal skills may be more variable than his verbal skills. Note that several of his answers were related to his antisocial behavior pattern. This case illustrates that emotional disturbance may not necessarily affect cognitive functioning.

ANALYSIS OF THE REPORT

Identifying Data
The report begins with the traditional identification data. In an actual report, the child's last name would be included.

Test Administered
This part of the report cites the test name (or names) and test scores. It is optional, because the name of the test and major WISC–III scores (Verbal, Performance, and Full Scale IQs) can be included in the body of the report. Often the subtest scores are not included in the report.

Reason for Referral
This section, which usually begins the narrative portion of the report, explains the reason for the evaluation. It documents what the psychologist sees as the purpose for the evaluation and helps to develop the focus of the recommendations. It also may contain information about the child that is related to the referral question.

Background Information
This section describes portions of Jim's background that might be pertinent to the issues under consideration. The first paragraph sets the stage for a historical understanding of the problem and provides information as to possible resources available within the family for remediation. The second paragraph cites in more detail the behaviors that led to Jim's referral. The third paragraph focuses on school behavior and recent changes in problem behaviors.

Behavioral Observations
This section describes Jim's behavior during the examination, with particular emphasis on his approach to the test and behavior reflective of his unique style.

Assessment Results and Clinical Impressions
This section begins with a description of Jim's overall test performance. Normative data and confidence levels are then reported. The confidence bands for IQs are found in Table A-1 in Appendix A. The percentile ranks for IQs are found in Table BC-1 on the inside back cover of this text.

The second paragraph discusses the discrepancy between his Verbal and Performance Scale IQs. Table A-2 in Appendix A gives values that indicate significant differences between scaled scores and between individual subtest scores. Table A-6 in Appendix A gives values that indicate significant differences between individual subtest scores and their respective mean scaled scores.

The third paragraph describes Jim's strengths and weaknesses based on his subtest scores. Jim's numerical reasoning, range of knowledge, and language usage are well developed, as suggested by his scores on Arithmetic, Information, and Vocabulary, respectively. Less adequate are his visual-motor coordination and psychomotor speed, as indicated by his scores on Object Assembly and Coding. (Table D-3 in Appendix D provides a summary interpretation of skills associated with the individual WISC–III subtests.)

The fourth paragraph describes some idiosyncratic responses that may reflect Jim's behavior problem, and the last paragraph provides a brief summary of Jim's overall level of functioning.

Recommendations
Recommendations are made before the final summary. Note that because the evaluation did not include personality tests, the recommendations call for further testing and evaluation.

Summary
The final section of the report summarizes the major findings and recommendations.

(Continued)

Exhibit 10-2 *(Continued)*

THE REPORT WITH LINE-BY-LINE NOTATIONS

Name: Jim
Date of birth: July 17, 1993
Chronological age: 7-4

Date of examination: November 20, 2000
Date of report: November 21, 2000
Grade: Second

Tests Administered
Wechsler Intelligence Scale for Children–III

VERBAL SCALE		PERFORMANCE SCALE	
Information	14	Picture Completion	12
Similarities	12	Coding	6
Arithmetic	15	Picture Arrangement	13
Vocabulary	13	Block Design	14
Comprehension	12	Object Assembly	8

Verbal Scale IQ = 119
Performance Scale = 104
Full Scale IQ = 113 ± 7 at the 95% confidence level

Reason for Referral

1	Jim, a 7-year, 4-month-old boy, was referred to the clinic by	1–2 who was referred and who made the referral
2	his aunt for evaluation because of involuntary defecation,	2–3 specific behavior leading to referral
3	fecal smearing, enuresis, and stealing.	

Background Information

4	According to Jim's aunt, Jim was born out of wedlock and	4–7 early infancy and family background
5	never knew his natural father. He was separated from his	
6	mother at 6 months of age, when she developed leukemia	
7	from which she died a year later. Since that time, Jim has	
8	lived with a paternal aunt and her three children, who range	8–10 family constellation
9	in age from 8 to 18 years. The aunt has been divorced twice.	
10	Jim calls his aunt "mother" and thought of her first husband	10–11 attachment to parental figures
11	as his father. This man, who had been in the family as long	
12	as Jim, has not been involved with the family since he	12–14 time of early separation from parental figure
13	divorced the aunt. Jim was 2½ years old at the time of the	
14	divorce. His aunt described having made incomplete and	14–16 past parental behaviors that may relate to Jim's
15	ineffective attempts at toilet training during this period of	current problems
16	turmoil. Last year Jim's aunt remarried. During the 6 months	16 recent family changes
17	that the marriage lasted, Jim formed no attachment to his	17–18 Jim's relationship to new family member
18	second step-uncle.	
19	Jim's aunt reported that he has bowel movements in the	19–22 encopresis
20	bathtub; he smears feces on the walls or leaves them in	
21	trash cans around the house. He also soils himself	
22	frequently. He wanders around the house at night, and	22–24 "wandering" behavior
23	sometimes vanishes for hours while in the park or on his way	
24	home from school. His aunt stated that he stole a stopwatch	24–27 stealing behavior
25	from the principal's office, and food and money from other	
26	places. Apparently, he makes an effort to be discovered	
27	when he steals.	
28	Jim is an excellent student, although he is difficult to	28–29 level of academic achievement and deviant class-
29	handle because of his opposition and defiance. His	room behavior
30	behavior in the past three months has been changing.	29–33 recent changes in behavior
31	There has been a decrease in encopresis and fecal	
32	smearing, and an increase in stealing and aggressive	
33	behavior.	

(Continued)

Exhibit 10-2 *(Continued)*

Behavioral Observations

34	Jim is a small, thinly built, energetic child. He was
35	cooperative and friendly during the evaluation. His test
36	behavior was characterized by competitiveness, tenacity,
37	and anxiety. He seemed to want to answer all of the
38	questions correctly and was reluctant to give up on any
39	question. On the Information subtest, he responded to
40	"What are the four seasons of the year?" with "Spring" and
41	"Fall," but could not remember the other seasons. He had
42	to be encouraged to go on to the next question, and three
43	times later he spontaneously returned to the season
44	question, adding "Winter" and "Summer." Jim seemed to
45	need continual assurance from the examiner that he was
46	answering the items correctly. He often asked, "Have I
47	gotten them all right?"

34	appearance
35	overall response to being tested
35–39	response to test materials
39–44	example of response to a test question
44–46	style of relating to examiner
46–47	example of test behavior

Assessment Results and Clinical Impressions

48	With a chronological age of 7-4, Jim achieved a Verbal
49	Scale IQ of 119, a Performance Scale IQ of 104, and a Full
50	Scale IQ of 113 ± 7 on the WISC–III. His overall
51	performance is classified in the High Average range and is
52	equal to or higher than that of 80% of the children his age
53	(81st percentile). The chances that the range of scores from
54	106 to 120 includes his true IQ are about 95 out of 100.
55	The present measure of his level of intellectual functioning
56	appears to be valid.
57	Although there was a 15-point difference between the
58	Verbal and Performance Scales, this difference was
59	associated primarily with his low scores on two
60	Performance Scale subtests. Whereas his verbal skills are
61	uniformly well developed, his performance skills show more
62	variability, with some abilities well developed and others
63	less well developed. Overall (with the exception of two of
64	the Performance subtest scores), Jim consistently
65	demonstrated above-average skills as assessed by the
66	WISC–III.
67	Within the verbal area, his numerical reasoning ability,
68	range of knowledge, and language usage are excellent.
69	Social comprehension and concept formation abilities are
70	also strong. Within the performance area, his analytic and
71	synthetic ability, planning and anticipation ability, and ability
72	to differentiate essential from nonessential details are all
73	well developed. Less adequate are skills associated with
74	visual-motor coordination and with psychomotor speed. It is
75	difficult to account for his lower scores in these two areas in
76	light of his overall above-average ability. Perhaps the
77	scores reflect temporary inefficiency due to fatigue, or
78	perhaps they simply indicate that his abilities in these areas
79	are not as well developed.
80	The test results suggest that Jim's behavioral
81	problems, for the most part, have not interfered with his
82	intellectual functioning. His psychomotor speed and
83	visual-motor coordination are less adequately developed
84	than his other abilities, but his overall functioning is better
85	than average. There were suggestions of preoccupation with
86	stealing, but it is difficult to determine the extent of this
87	preoccupation.

48	chronological age
48–49	Verbal Scale IQ and Performance Scale IQ
49–50	Full Scale IQ and confidence band
51	normative classification based on Full Scale IQ
52–54	percentile rank and confidence range of IQ
55–56	validity of test result
57–58	discrepancy between IQs
58–60	variability noted in Performance area
60–61	description of verbal skills
61–63	description of nonverbal skills
63–66	summary of performance on WISC–III
67–70	verbal skill strengths
70–73	nonverbal skill strengths
73–74	nonverbal skill weaknesses
74–76	relation of weaknesses to overall ability
76–79	possible reasons for low scores
80–82	effect of behavior problems on cognitive functioning
82–84	psychomotor weaknesses
84–85	level of overall functioning
85–86	relation of specific responses to behavior problems
86–87	limits of interpretation

(Continued)

Exhibit 10-2 *(Continued)*

Recommendations

88 On the basis of the present limited evaluation, it is
89 recommended that a personality evaluation be conducted.
90 Furthermore, the seriousness of his behavioral disturbance
91 suggests that therapy should be initiated for both Jim and his
92 aunt. Every attempt should be made to obtain further
93 information about his home environment and to determine
94 which factors in the home may be reinforcing his deviant
95 behavior pattern. His aunt should be actively engaged in the
96 development of a treatment program.

88   limitations of current testing
89   recommendation for personality testing
90–92   therapeutic interventions

92–95   needed additional information about home
        environment

95–96   suggested intervention

Summary

97   Jim, with a chronological age of 7-4, achieved an IQ of 113 ±
98   7 on the WISC–III. This IQ is at the 81st percentile and in the
99   High Average range. The chances that the range of scores
100 from 106 to 120 includes his true IQ are about 95 out of 100.
101 The test results appear to give a valid indication of his
102 present level of intellectual functioning. Jim's verbal skills
103 were uniformly well developed, but there was some
104 variability in his performance skills. The findings suggest
105 that his behavioral problems are not significantly interfering
106 with his cognitive skills. A personality evaluation was
107 recommended, along with a treatment program that would
108 involve Jim and his aunt.

97   chronological age
97–98   IQ and name of test
98–99   percentile rank and normative classification of IQ
99–100   confidence limits associated with IQ
101–102   validity of test results
102–103   verbal skills
103–104   variability of nonverbal skills
104–106   possible effects of behavior problems
          on intellectual functioning
106–108   recommendations

109 (Signature)
110 Jo Lynn Mack, M.A.

TEST YOUR SKILL

Exhibit 10-3 presents five sets of exercises designed to sharpen your skill in interpreting the WISC–III (and WPPSI–R and WAIS–III). Each excerpt in Exhibit 10-3 illustrates one or more inadequacies of description or interpretation. Find the mistakes in the sentences. After you have completed your analysis, compare your evaluations with those shown in the Comment section of each exercise set.

THINKING THROUGH THE ISSUES

1. In interpreting the WISC–III, you can use various procedures. How does profile analysis help in evaluating a child's WISC–III performance? What problems are associated with profile analysis?
2. The successive-level approach to test interpretation is based on a hierarchical model. What is the logic underlying the hierarchy?
3. The Verbal Scale IQ and Performance Scale IQ are important features of the WISC–III. How might a child function with a Verbal Scale IQ of 120 and a Performance Scale IQ of 80? How might another child function with a Verbal Scale IQ of 80 and a Performance Scale IQ of 120?

Find the elephant

Copyright © 1977 American Publishing Corporation and adapted.

Exhibit 10-3
Test-Your-Skill Exercises for the WISC–III

Directions: Read each item to determine where it is inadequate. Then compare your evaluations with those in the Comment section that follows each part.

Part 1. Unnecessary Technical Information

1. A difference of 4 points between her Information and Comprehension scores is significant at the 5% level.
2. Mark did not score zero on any Comprehension items. He had 12 2-point responses and 5 1-point responses.
3. On the Comprehension subtest, Bill scored 18; 10 is average and 19 is the ceiling.
4. On Block Design, she failed items 3, 4, and 5.
5. Bill scored 5 points on the Similarities subtest.
6. He missed the Picture Arrangement item about rain.
7. The Digit Span is an optional subtest and was not used in computing the IQ.
8. On the WISC–III, the majority of her scores hovered around a scaled score of 12.
9. A total scaled score of 52 yielded a Performance IQ score of 102.
10. On the Information subtest, she earned a scaled score of 13, which is 1 standard deviation above the mean of 10.
11. Bannatyne's recategorization system reveals particular strength in the Visuo-Spatial area (prorated IQ = 127).
12. Frank appears to be weak in the areas dealing with Freedom from Distractibility.
13. A review of Glenda's Verbal scores indicates significance at the .05 level in her Vocabulary and Comprehension tests.
14. Her score on Coding was 4 points lower than her score on Block Design and 5 points lower than her score on Object Assembly.
15. A mean scaled score of 9 was obtained on the 10 subtests.
16. Intersubtest scatter was minimal.

Comment on Part 1

1. This information is too technical to present in a report. Furthermore, the sentence does not give the direction of the difference. The primary focus should be on differences between each subtest and the mean of the Verbal or Performance Scale. The intersubtest comparisons of interest should be made only after comparisons with the mean of each scale have been made. Also, it is not necessary to present significance levels.
2. Stress what the child *did* do, not what he or she did not do.
3. It is not necessary to report this technical information. *Suggestion:* "Bill's social reasoning and verbal comprehension are well developed."
4. Delete this sentence from the report unless there is some significance to the pattern of missed items. If there is, discuss the significance of the pattern.
5. Reference to "5 points" is potentially misleading. The reader does not know whether the 5 points refers to a raw score or a standard score. This sentence should be rewritten to convey the child's knowledge of what is required on the Similar-

ities subtest. *Suggestion:* If his score is below average (scaled score of 7 or below) and significantly below his Verbal Scale mean, you could say, "Bill's conceptual thinking ability is less well developed (at the 16th percentile) than are his other verbal skills."
6. Unless it makes an important point, do not include such information.
7. This sentence provides unnecessary technical information and should be deleted.
8. It is preferable to discuss percentile ranks rather than scaled scores, because they are more easily understood by parents and teachers.
9. It is not necessary to report the total scaled score.
10. Standard deviation is a technical concept and should not be used in the report. The scaled scores should be interpreted rather than cited. *Suggestion:* "His range of knowledge is above average."
11. Most readers will not understand the reference to Bannatyne's recategorization system. Also, citing a prorated IQ of 127 may cause confusion. The reader does not know how this IQ compares with the Full Scale IQ. Delete this sentence, substituting a more useful interpretation of the test scores.
12. "Freedom from Distractibility" is a technical term that may not be understood by most readers of the report. *Suggestion:* "Frank had difficulties with short-term memory."
13. This is a poorly written sentence that fails to communicate useful information. It does not tell whether the abilities measured by these subtests are well or poorly developed. Also, it is not necessary to present the significance level. *Suggestion:* Assuming that her Comprehension score was significantly higher than her Vocabulary score, you could say, "In the verbal area, Glenda's social reasoning ability is better developed than her word knowledge."
14. This sentence fails to present useful information. The reader does not know whether these scores reflect strengths or weaknesses. *Suggestion:* "Her sequencing and visual memory abilities are weaker than her spatial and perceptual organization abilities."
15. It is not necessary to report the mean score.
16. This sentence will have little meaning to the average reader. *Suggestion:* If all scores on the Verbal Scale subtests are between 9 and 11, you could say, "On verbal tasks, his performance was consistently within the Average range."

Part 2. Poor Writing

1. His score on the WISC–III was equivalent to an IQ of approximately 98.
2. Within the Verbal Scale, her abilities ranged from average to very superior when compared to those of other children in her chronological age group.
3. Average abilities were indicated in Pat's attention and concentration and how well they are used in conjunction with

(Continued)

Exhibit 10-3 *(Continued)*

solving basic arithmetic problems, and in her auditory vocal sequencing memory.

4. The examination of the results displayed a significant amount of point discrepancy between the Verbal and Performance IQ scores of 37 points.
5. The Verbal scores were close-knit in the solidly average range from 9 through 11.
6. In the area of math, the regular classroom teacher might make use of concrete situations to add meaning and to reinforce the total experiential background.
7. All of Mary's scores were respectable and adequate, with the exception of Digit Span where she received a 7.
8. Bill has better mental than nonverbal abilities.
9. Statistical factors and the tenor of his test performance indicate an excellent chance (95%) that his test performance would fall consistently (other things being equal) within the range of 117 to 129.
10. Jim's high scores on the Performance Scale suggest that he has well-developed abilities in the conception of his environment.
11. *The following description was written about a 6-year-old's performance on the Block Design subtest:* She gave up easily even after putting the blocks into the design but not recognizing it as it was supposed to be, thus dismantling the design she made.
12. *The following sentence was written for Verbal subtest scores between 9 and 11:* Her verbal subtest scores appear to be within the average range.
13. The accuracy of his intrasubtest scores were intermittent on many of his subtests. He missed items in such proportions that he was able to complete all of the subtests.
14. His other outstanding score that was indicated was his performance in the Picture Completion subtest.
15. In reviewing her Performance Scale subtest scores, there appears to be a significance at the .05 level between her Object Assembly and Block Design.
16. The Verbal test profile showed a peek for the Comprehension subtest.
17. She showed a retarded score on the ability to see spatial relationships.

Comment on Part 2

1. The IQ achieved by a child is a specific number. You do not have to write "approximately 98." The notion of "approximately" is handled by the confidence interval or precision range. *Suggestion:* "He obtained a Full Scale IQ of 98 ± 6 on the WISC–III. This score is in the Average classification."
2. It is redundant to write "when compared to those of other children of her chronological age group." Including this phrase every time a child's ability is discussed would unnecessarily lengthen the report. The phrase should be deleted.

3. This sentence is poorly constructed and redundant in places. *Suggestion:* "She has average short-term memory ability and mathematical skills."
4. This sentence is awkward. *Suggestion:* One way of expressing the difference between the two scales is as follows: "The fact that the Performance Scale was 37 points higher than the Verbal Scale indicates that visual nonverbal skills are better developed than auditory processing skills." Other possible interpretations are discussed in Chapter 9.
5. This sentence is too colloquial. *Suggestion:* "All of his Verbal Scale scores were in the Average range."
6. The recommendations should be clearer. *Suggestion:* "To increase his mathematics skills, John's regular classroom teacher might make math more meaningful by incorporating it into daily activities. For example, he could be shown how to use mathematics to buy groceries and to make a budget."
7. The term "respectable" is not appropriate for describing a test score. It implies that some scores are "not respectable." Also, the reference to a score of 7, without some explanation, is not informative to the reader. *Suggestion:* "All of Mary's abilities appear to be developed at an average level, with the exception of short-term memory for digits, which is relatively weak."
8. The WISC–III Verbal Scale and Performance Scale both measure "mental" abilities. The writer may have meant to write "verbal" instead of "mental."
9. The term "statistical factors" is too general, and the phrase "tenor of his performance" is vague. *Suggestion:* "Joe obtained an IQ of 123 ± 6. The chances that the range of scores from 117 to 129 includes his true IQ are about 95 out of 100."
10. "Conception of his environment" is a vague phrase. *Suggestion:* "Jim's nonverbal abilities are well developed."
11. The point of this sentence is not clear. Why is there a "thus"? Did the child dismantle the design before allowing the examiner to record her performance? *Suggestion:* "She behaved impulsively when reproducing block designs, dismantling the designs, whether correct or not, as soon as they were completed."
12. This sentence is too tentative, because the scores are in the Average range. *Suggestion:* "Her verbal subtest scores are in the Average range."
13. The wording of these two sentences is awkward and is likely to confuse most readers. Also, the first sentence is grammatically incorrect because the subject of the sentence ("accuracy") takes a singular verb ("was"). *Suggestion:* "On many subtests he failed easy items but passed more difficult ones."
14. This sentence is awkwardly written. *Suggestion:* "He showed outstanding ability in a task requiring alertness to details."
15. This sentence is poorly constructed. Also, it is not necessary to state probability levels in the report. *Suggestion:* Assuming that the score on Block Design was significantly higher than the score on Object Assembly, the sentence

(Continued)

Exhibit 10-3 *(Continued)*

---

could read, "On performance tasks, her deductive reasoning ability is stronger than her inductive reasoning ability."

16. The correct word is "peak," not "peek." Furthermore, this information, by itself, is not informative. Was the Comprehension score above average, average, or below average? Was it significantly different from the other scores? *Suggestion:* Assuming that the Comprehension score of 10 was significantly above the mean of the Verbal subtests, the sentence could read, "The area in which she showed the strongest verbal ability is social reasoning and judgment (at the 50th percentile)."

17. The score itself is not retarded, although it may reflect a weakness or poorly developed skill in a specific area. *Suggestion:* If the score on Object Assembly is low, it is preferable to say, "Her spatial visualization skills are not well developed, as indicated by her weak performance in completing puzzle items."

Part 3. Technical Errors

1. A lower score on Information (scaled score 9) shows poor range of knowledge.

2. Average to above-average scores were obtained by George in the sequencing area, with a prorated IQ of 103 in the Sequencing I area and a prorated IQ of 120 in the Sequencing II area.

3. Henry scored in the average intellectual range on the WISC–III, with a mental age of 7-2 and a chronological age of 7-6.

4. Five of the 12 WISC–III subtests were 2 standard deviations from the mean, indicating that her performance was in the very superior range.

5. The 10-point difference between Brandon's Verbal and Performance Scale IQs approaches significance at the 5 percent level, suggesting that his verbal skill development is somewhat ahead of his nonverbal development.

6. Her Full Scale IQ of 109 ± 6 just barely reaches the Above Average classification.

7. The range of scores from 6 to 16 indicates good performance.

8. Her scores ranged from a classification of Very Superior to Borderline Mentally Deficient.

9. The Picture Completion score was significantly lower than the Picture Arrangement score. Because these two subtests are somewhat similar in the testing of detail, reasoning ability, and perceptual organization, the Picture Completion subtest may have been spoiled.

10. Bill's IQ of 114 ± 7 classifies him in a range from average, high average, to superior intellectual functioning.

11. *On the basis of a range of scores from 12 to 19 (Verbal Scale IQ = 142, Performance Scale IQ = 131, Full Scale IQ = 140), the following statement was made:* His subtest scores show great variability, indicating he has definite strengths and weaknesses.

12. Bill achieved a Verbal Scale score of 65, a Performance Scale score of 61, and a Full Scale IQ of 118.

13. Her scaled score of 3 on Information places her in the Mentally Retarded range.

14. *The following statement was made on the basis of a Verbal Scale IQ of 107 and a Performance Scale IQ of 111:* Her Performance Scale IQ is higher than her Verbal Scale IQ.

Comment on Part 3

1. Scaled scores of 9 or higher on any of the Wechsler subtests do not indicate "poor" ability. A scaled score of 9 is only one-third of a standard deviation below the mean scaled score of 10; it is within the Average range.

2. The reference to Sequencing I and Sequencing II areas is vague. Reporting IQs for these areas is confusing.

3. The WISC–III does not use mental ages, but it provides test-age equivalents for the 13 subtests. These test ages should be used cautiously. Mental ages usually are not given in a report.

4. This statement is not accurate because it focuses on some of the subtests, rather than on the Full Scale, to characterize the child's overall level of ability. The child would not have superior ability if the remaining subtest scaled scores were below 6. Furthermore, "standard deviations" is a technical term and should not be included in the report.

5. It is not necessary to put in the report the technical information contained in this sentence ("approaches significance at the 5% level"). Because the 10-point difference is not significant, it is not appropriate to infer that verbal development is better than nonverbal development. This inference should be made only when there is a significant discrepancy between the Verbal and Performance Scale IQs.

6. A Full Scale IQ of 109 receives an Average classification, not an Above Average classification. *Suggestion:* "Her Full Scale IQ of 109 ± 6 is classified in the Average range." If there is reason to suspect a higher level of functioning than the test scores indicate, discuss your concerns.

7. This range from 6 (9th percentile) to 16 (98th percentile) indicates both strengths and weaknesses. Do not say that this range indicates good performance only.

8. It is preferable to report percentiles for individual subtests. Classification labels should be used for the Full Scale and occasionally, if desired, for the Verbal and Performance Scales. *Suggestion:* "Her scores on the WISC–III ranged from the 5th to the 91st percentile."

9. It is not appropriate to conclude that a subtest may be "spoiled" or invalid because the score is lower than the score on another subtest. A subtest is spoiled when it is improperly administered or when the child does not attend to the task, not when a child's score on it is low. Focus on the implications of the findings (strengths and weaknesses) rather than on the procedures used to arrive at the implications. Any interpretations of the discrepancy between the two subtest scores should relate to characteristics of the child. For example, "Although Tom's visual perception and attention to detail skills are strong, his application of these skills to social situations is less well developed."

(Continued)

Exhibit 10-3 *(Continued)*

10. Although a precision range is attached to the IQ (in this case, ± 9), cite only one classification for the obtained IQ. In this case, an IQ of 114 falls into the High Average classification. Presenting more than one classification is confusing.

11. There are no weaknesses in this profile. The sentence might be rephrased to reflect relative strengths. *Suggestion:* "All of his scores were above average. However, there were areas that reflect special strengths relative to his own level of functioning." This statement should be followed with a discussion of the child's relative strengths.

12. This sentence mixes up scaled scores and IQs. Report IQs for the three scales, not total scaled scores. For example, "Bill achieved a Verbal Scale IQ of 118, a Performance Scale IQ of 115, and a Full Scale IQ of 118." Then add a precision range.

13. Classifications should be used primarily for the Full Scale IQ. On some occasions, classifications can also be used for the Verbal and Performance Scale IQs, but they should never be used for subtest scores. *Suggestion:* A phrase such as "considerably below average" or "represents a weakness" can be used to describe a scaled score of 3. Or you might say, "Her knowledge of factual information is limited and at the 1st percentile rank."

14. Although this statement is literally correct, it should be deleted because the 4-point difference is not statistically significant. *Suggestion:* "Her verbal and nonverbal skills are not significantly different from each other, being at the 68th and 77th percentiles, respectively."

Part 4. Inaccurate or Incomplete Interpretations

1. His low Information score reflects potential repressive mechanisms at work.

2. In response to the question "In what way are anger and joy alike?" she said, "telling about something that you do." Clinical interpretation of this statement suggests that it is probably an emotional indication of aggression.

3. Two subtests deviate significantly from his average Verbal subtest score: Vocabulary (high) and Arithmetic (low).

4. A high Picture Completion subtest score and a low Coding subtest score may predict difficulty in reading.

5. Bill's Full Scale IQ was achieved with a 15-point difference between his Verbal Scale and Performance Scale scores, in favor of the latter. This difference suggests an action-oriented person.

6. A high score on Coding reflects a high and sustained energy level.

7. Discrepancies between this WISC–III administration and the one given three years ago may be due to Henry's variable attention and memory span or possibly examiner differences.

8. The 13-point difference between Helen's Verbal Scale and Performance Scale scores indicates that her Verbal Scale subtest scores are significantly higher than her Performance Scale subtest scores.

9. Lack of social judgment and immature responses were noted on the Comprehension subtest (scaled score 7).

10. Bill scored high on Object Assembly because he was persistent in his attempt to assemble the objects.

11. The 15-point discrepancy between Mary's Verbal Scale IQ and Performance Scale IQ indicates that she has a learning disability.

12. The consistency of his scores probably indicates that John is functioning at his capacity.

13. His lowest score was on the Picture Completion subtest, where he received a scaled score of 12.

14. A weakness in another modality—i.e., hearing—was evident in the Digit Span subtest score.

15. Her high Verbal subtest scores indicate that she is able to express herself with little difficulty.

16. Based on his scores, he would be considered a slow learner or a low average student.

17. *The following statement was based on a Similarities scaled score of 15 and a Digit Span scaled score of 10:* She has good conceptualizing ability and poor rote memory for digits.

18. The 40-point difference between Greg's Verbal Scale IQ and Performance IQ can probably be accounted for by the fact that at age 6, Greg has not yet developed the visual-motor skills he needs to do his best on the nonverbal part of the WISC–III.

19. Comprehension requires social adaptation, practical judgment, and self-direction.

20. The intrasubtest scatter may indicate a lack of persistence.

21. *The following sentences were based on scaled scores of 13 or higher, with the exception of a 10 on Block Design:* His weaknesses seemed to be in visual-motor coordination and spatial orientation. His lowest and only average score was on the Block Design subtest.

22. Another relatively low score occurred in the Performance Scale, indicating attentional skill weakness.

23. Her verbal skills appear significantly better developed than her performance skills, suggesting that her ability to respond automatically with what is already known may be more developed than her ability to use past experiences and previously acquired skills to solve new problems.

24. He scored relatively high on Digit Span and Coding.

25. The fact that her Similarities score was lower than her Comprehension score implies some difficulty involving fear and emotional excesses.

26. *The following interpretation was based on scaled scores of 8 on Picture Completion, 7 on Picture Arrangement, 10 on Block Design, 7 on Object Assembly, and 9 on Coding:* On two tests, Picture Arrangement and Object Assembly, she scored in the low average range. Because these tests measure skills similar to those measured by tests on which she scored higher, it appears probable that she did not apply the same effort on these tests or that there is some other intervening factor such as poor visual acuity.

27. *The following statement was based on a Verbal Scale IQ of 129, a Performance Scale IQ of 100, and a Full Scale IQ of*

(Continued)

Exhibit 10-3 *(Continued)*

117: Monica's verbal skills appear to be somewhat more developed than her performance skills.

28. A review of her Verbal tests does not appear to indicate any areas of significance.

29. A third factor on the test generally denotes poor attention, poor concentration, and poor ability to screen out extraneous influences.

30. In the area of acquired knowledge, which assesses life experiences, social-educational exposure, and learning, he obtained an average score.

31. *The following sentence was based on a Verbal Scale IQ of 98, a Performance Scale IQ of 131, and a Full Scale IQ of 114:* The discrepancy between her verbal and performance scores is significant and may suggest that she is compensating for her lack of verbal abilities with her superior performance abilities to achieve good grades in school.

32. *The following statement was based on a Verbal Scale IQ of 95, a Performance Scale IQ of 131, and a Full Scale IQ of 113:* An examination of the overall results of this WISC–III session indicates that Frank is very strong in areas where using one's hands is important.

33. His low functioning on Coding may relate to his apparently weak background in school-related tasks.

34. On the Coding subtest the child is asked to attach a meaningless symbol to a number.

35. Because she tried hard, she passed many items.

Comment on Part 4

1. This hypothesis should be supported by more information before it is offered in the report. A low Information score may result from several factors, such as limited schooling, few interests, and inadequate stimulation.

2. There is no basis for making this interpretation. Nothing in the response appears to warrant an interpretation of aggression.

3. This type of sentence does not describe the child's strengths and weaknesses. *Suggestion:* "Although her verbal ability is average, her verbal comprehension is a strength (84th percentile rank), whereas her ability to perform mental arithmetic is a weakness (9th percentile rank)."

4. Reading involves many different skills, and only a reliable and valid reading test should be used to evaluate reading proficiency. It should not be evaluated by an intelligence test. Intelligence tests can assist in assessing some cognitive skills of children; however, no single test can be used to evaluate every type of cognitive and perceptual-motor skill. In interpreting subtest scores, discuss only the abilities that are associated with the subtests.

5. It is interesting to attempt to use patterns of intelligence-test scores for developing hypotheses about personality style. Verbal-Performance discrepancies alone, however, should not be used to substantiate such hypotheses. Discrepancy scores should be used in conjunction with other test scores and analysis of behavior to develop hypotheses.

6. There is little research to support this interpretation. Remember, you have only a sample of the child's performance in a limited, controlled, and formal encounter. You do not know whether the level of energy displayed during the test can be sustained outside of the examination setting.

7. There are many possible reasons why changes may occur in the test scores; it is potentially misleading to offer only two of these reasons. Differences in test scores may be associated with, for example, maturational changes, growth spurts, changes in item content, motivation, situational variables, or environmental changes. Unless you know which reasons are most probable, it is better not to speculate.

8. Although this statement is literally correct, it fails to inform the reader of the possible implications of this profile. *Suggestion:* "Helen's verbal comprehension skills are better developed than her perceptual organization skills."

9. "Lack of" is a strong statement. A scaled score of 8 is at the 25th percentile rank. It is incorrect to interpret a scaled score of 7 as indicating a "lack of social judgment." *Suggestion*: If Comprehension was the child's relatively weakest area and if the responses were immature, a better way to state these findings would be to say, "Amy's social judgment is relatively weak (at the 25th percentile), as indicated by her immature responses to questions relating to social situations."

10. Many children are persistent and still fail items. There is more involved in success on the Object Assembly items than mere persistence. Persistence may help a child in solving various tasks, but unless it is coupled with adequate cognitive ability, the child's performance is not likely to be successful. *Suggestion*: "In completing puzzle items, Bill was persistent and worked quickly and accurately. His high score in this area reflects his strong abilities in understanding spatial relationships and in perceptual organization."

11. Intelligence test scores in and of themselves should never be used as a basis for establishing the presence of a learning disability. Many factors, especially a discrepancy between estimates of intelligence and achievement, usually must be taken into account in arriving at a classification of learning disability. *Suggestion*: "The 15-point discrepancy between Mary's Verbal and Performance Scale IQs indicates that her verbal abilities are better developed than her nonverbal abilities."

12. This interpretation is problematic. A child may have consistently low or consistently high scores for various reasons. Some depressed children have uniformly low test scores; some gifted children have uniformly high test scores. In the latter case, the test may not have an adequate ceiling. Test results provide information about current functioning, not capacity. It is better not to use the term "capacity" in a report. This sentence should be deleted.

13. A score of 12 is above average. To say that it is his lowest score, although correct, is potentially misleading. Do not cite a scaled score without explaining what the score means. *Suggestion*: "His alertness to details is above average, but it is not as well developed as are his other abilities."

(Continued)

Exhibit 10-3 *(Continued)*

14. Hearing ability is required by all of the subtests unless sign language or pantomime instructions are used. Digit Span appears to measure attention span and other abilities; it is not primarily a measure of hearing. *Suggestion:* "Jim's auditory attention span and short-term memory for digits are weak."

15. There is no one-to-one relationship between verbal knowledge, as revealed by high Verbal subtest scores, and expressive skills. There are many intelligent individuals who have expressive difficulties (in writing or in speech). This statement should be supported by observation of the examinee's behavior.

16. The WISC–III provides information about cognitive functioning; it does not provide direct information about school performance. It is risky to apply labels such as "slow learner" or "low average student" based solely on the WISC–III (or on any other intelligence test). *Suggestion:* "His scores on the WISC–III indicate that he is functioning in the Low Average range."

17. A scaled score of 10 is in the Average range and should not be considered "poor." The sentence should be rewritten. *Suggestion:* "She has excellent concept formation skills and average rote memory ability."

18. The explanation offered for the child's Verbal Scale–Performance Scale discrepancy is probably incorrect. The items on the WISC–III Performance Scale call for cognitive skills primarily. Although visual-motor skills are necessary for some items, they are not the major determinant of success on the Performance items. Indeed, if the writer's reasoning were correct, there would be no way for children who were maturationally average to obtain superior nonverbal scores. Additionally, scaled scores are normed in reference to children of the same age as the child being tested; therefore lower scores indicate abilities that are less well developed than those of other children of the same age.

19. Comprehension, like all of the other WISC–III subtests, is a test of cognition. Practical judgment is probably measured by the subtest. There is no way to evaluate the extent to which the subtest taps social adaptation or self-direction, however. Also, the concept of self-direction is vague.

20. Intrasubtest variability indicates an uneven pattern of performance. It is a great leap, and likely an improper one, to infer "lack of persistence" solely on the basis of intrasubtest variability. Furthermore, "intrasubtest scatter" is a technical concept that is better left out of the report. *Suggestion:* "There were many failures on easy items and successes on more difficult ones." Then offer an interpretation of this pattern.

21. These "weaknesses" are relative and should be labeled as such. A second problem is that the connection between these two sentences is ambiguous; the two sentences should be tied together with a transitional phrase. *Suggestion:* "Unlike his overall level of performance, which is above average, Bill's visual-motor coordination and spatial orientation are average."

22. The Performance Scale measures more than attentional skill. If the writer is referring to one particular Performance Scale subtest, this subtest should be specifically mentioned.

23. This interpretation is misleading. Verbal subtests do not simply require automatic responding; they also require judgment, problem solving, conceptualization, and attention.

24. Mentioning subtest names is not informative. It is better to discuss the abilities tapped by the subtests than to simply name the subtests. *Suggestion:* "His strongest abilities in relation to his other skills are in short-term auditory memory and processing and short-term visual memory."

25. This interpretation has little, if any, basis from either a clinical or a research perspective. It should be deleted from the report.

26. This interpretation includes a number of inaccuracies. First, because most of the subtest scores are not significantly different from one another, it is preferable not to imply that there are meaningful differences in the pattern of subtest scores, with the exception of Block Design, which is higher than Picture Arrangement and Object Assembly. Second, because each WISC–III Performance subtest requires somewhat different cognitive skills, it is stretching the point to say that similar skills are measured by all of the Performance Scale subtests. Third, the hypothesis that the child may not have applied the same effort to all of the subtests should be based on observational data, not on subtest scores alone. Fourth, it is highly unlikely that visual acuity problems are responsible for this pattern of scores. *Suggestion:* "Her nonverbal skills, such as visual perception, spatial orientation, nonverbal reasoning, attention to detail, and visualizing a whole from its parts, range from the 16th to 50th percentile."

27. This sentence, although literally correct, does not give sufficient emphasis to the 29-point Verbal-Performance discrepancy. *Suggestion:* "Monica's verbal skills (97th percentile) are significantly better developed than her performance skills (50th percentile)." Then describe her strengths and relatively less well developed abilities.

28. This sentence fails to present the child's level of performance. Also, the term "significance," as used here, is vague. The sentence should be deleted and a discussion of the child's test performance substituted.

29. The writer is referring to the Freedom from Distractibility factor. This factor—like all factors, scales, and subtests—measures both strengths and weaknesses. The sentence reads as if the factor only measured weaknesses. Also, this sentence should convey how the child performed on this factor. *Suggestion:* "John has poor attention and concentration and has difficulty in screening out distracting influences."

30. All areas of an intelligence test are related to some degree to the individual's life experiences, social-educational exposure, and learning. It is inaccurate and misleading to single out one area. Furthermore, most readers are unfamiliar with a reference to the "area of acquired knowledge." The writer should describe the skills tapped by these subtests.

(Continued)

Exhibit 10-3 *(Continued)*

Suggestion: "Jim is average in his range of information, arithmetical ability, and word knowledge."

31. This interpretation is problematic. This child does not "lack" verbal abilities. Her scores suggest that some abilities are better developed than others. Her good performance in school should not be attributed to compensation for average verbal skills. The logic of this inference is not clear. *Suggestion:* "Her performance abilities are significantly better developed than her verbal abilities." This statement can then be followed with an analysis of the specific pattern of scores.

32. The Performance Scale does not measure fine or gross motor skills, as is implied in this statement. Rather, it measures cognitive skills and visual-motor coordination and integration. It is the integration of cognitive and motor skills that is required for success on many Performance Scale items. *Suggestion:* "Frank's excellent nonverbal cognitive skills (98th percentile rank) are considerably better developed than are his verbal cognitive skills (39th percentile rank)."

33. Low functioning on the Coding subtest may be associated with several factors. The basis for the interpretation should be described in the report. Also, the interpretation fails to discuss the underlying abilities measured by the Coding subtest.

34. This is not a clear description of the task. Coding requires the child to use a key or to learn a key. The symbols may be meaningful to some children. The statement, as written, makes it sound as if the child were required to do something actively—attach a symbol to a number—when in fact the symbol-number association (or combination) is given in the subtest. A better way to describe Coding A would be to say, "The Coding task is a psychomotor task that requires the child to rapidly copy simple figures associated with different shapes." A preferred way to describe Coding B would be to say, "The Coding task is a psychomotor task that requires the child to rapidly copy symbols associated with numbers."

35. "Trying hard" does not seem to be sufficient for obtaining success on the subtests. Some children may try hard and still not succeed. In describing this child's efforts, focus on the behavior without referring to test scores. *Suggestion:* "She appeared hard-working while taking the test."

Part 5. Inappropriate Recommendations

1. The significant difference between his Verbal Scale IQ and Performance Scale IQ indicates a need for further investigation into his intellectual ability.

2. Because of the extreme scatter in her nonverbal abilities, Julie should be examined by a neurologist and given appropriate medical tests to confirm or eliminate the possibility of neurological impairment.

Comment on Part 5

1. If this recommendation were made each time there was a significant difference between a child's verbal and performance skills, thousands of hours of needless testing would take place. A significant difference simply means that the difference between the scores is not a chance difference. It does not mean that there is a problem. Some individuals have a varied pattern of skills; this pattern does not necessarily call for further investigation, unless other factors are present. The recommendation should tell the reader why further investigation is needed—what might be learned in further investigation that could be helpful to the child.

2. There are two problems with this sentence. First, using the term "scatter" without explanation may mislead readers. It is preferable to use the word "variability." Second, the sentence raises the question of the reason for a referral to a neurologist. It is inappropriate to recommend a neurological evaluation simply on the basis of variability of scores. A neurological examination is a costly procedure. There should be some pathognomonic signs (refers to a group of symptoms that are diagnostic "trademarks" of a particular disease or disorder) of brain damage (see *Assessment of Children: Behavioral and Clinical Applications*) in the test findings, observations, or case history before this recommendation is made.

4. If you had the opportunity, what would you do to improve the WISC–III?

5. Suppose a parent asked you to respond to the question "What is my child's potential?" based on results from the WISC–III. How would you answer?

SUMMARY

Profile Analysis

1. Profile analysis (sometimes referred to as scatter analysis) is a procedure for analyzing an examinee's pattern of scaled scores and IQs.

2. Profile analysis with the WISC–III, WPPSI–R, and WAIS–III cannot be used for classification purposes or to arrive at a diagnostic label.

3. You can analyze profiles from two frames of reference. One compares the examinee's scores to those of the norm group—an interindividual comparison. The other method compares the examinee's scores to her or his own unique profile—an intraindividual comparison. In either case, you will use scaled scores based on the norm group.

4. Scaled scores of 13 to 19 always indicate a strength; scaled scores of 8 to 12 always indicate average ability; scaled scores of 1 to 7 always indicate a weakness.

5. When you evaluate a child's unique pattern of scaled scores, you are making an intraindividual comparison, or using an ipsative

approach. The focus is on describing areas in which the examinee's abilities are better developed or more poorly developed.

6. To be able to say that one score is meaningfully (i.e., statistically significantly) higher than another score, you must first determine that the difference between the two scores does not represent chance variation—you cannot simply look at two scores and say that one is meaningfully (or statistically significantly) higher or lower than the other.

7. One approach to profile analysis is to determine whether certain scores differ significantly from each other; we call this the significant difference approach.

8. A second approach to profile analysis is to determine the frequency with which the differences between scores in the child's profile occurred in the standardization sample; we call this the base rate approach or probability-of-occurrence approach.

9. The primary methods of profile analysis begin with evaluating Verbal Scale IQ–Performance Scale IQ differences and end with evaluating intrasubtest scatter.

10. Both statistically reliable differences and empirically observed base rates can assist in profile analysis.

11. All statistically significant differences between scores, regardless of whether they are unusual, deserve consideration in evaluating an examinee's profile of abilities. However, you can be more confident about the hypotheses you form when the difference is significant *and* unusual.

12. In order to be considered unusual, the difference (range or other phenomenon) should occur in 10% to 15% or less (in one direction) of the standardization sample.

13. Neither the reliability-of-difference approach nor the probability-of-occurrence approach should be used in a mechanical fashion or as a replacement for clinical judgment.

14. We recommend that you use the .05 level of significance as the minimum level when you evaluate differences between two scores, to reduce the chances of making a Type I error.

15. You can derive more reliable estimates of specific abilities from the Verbal Scale IQ and the Performance Scale IQ than from individual subtest scaled scores.

A Successive-Level Approach to Test Interpretation

16. A successive-level approach to test interpretation is helpful in understanding the examinee's performance. The six levels of the approach are (a) Full Scale IQ, (b) Verbal Scale IQ and Performance Scale IQ or Index scores, (c) subtest variability within scales, (d) intersubtest variability, (e) intrasubtest variability, and (f) qualitative analysis.

Steps in Analyzing a Wechsler Protocol

17. Following a series of 10 steps will help you evaluate a child's performance on a Wechsler test. The steps focus on evaluating the reliability and validity of the test scores, evaluating the actual scores obtained by the child, determining whether there are significant discrepancies between the scores, and evaluating qualitative features of the child's performance.

Comparisons Between the Verbal Scale and Performance Scale

18. The Verbal Scale draws on the child's accumulated experience, whereas the Performance Scale is more dependent on the child's immediate problem-solving ability. Both scales may involve verbal and nonverbal strategies in the solution of problems.

19. A significant difference between the Verbal Scale and Performance Scale may indicate interest patterns, cognitive style, deficiencies or strengths in processing information, deficiencies or strengths in modes of expression, deficiencies or strengths in the ability to work under time pressure, sensory deficiencies, brain injury, psychopathology, behavioral problems, or a home or school environment in which language or materials differ from those commonly used in our culture.

20. A higher Verbal Scale IQ than Performance Scale IQ may indicate that verbal processing skills are better developed than visuospatial processing skills. A higher Performance Scale IQ than Verbal Scale IQ may indicate that visuospatial processing skills are better developed than verbal processing skills.

Comparisons Between Index Scores

21. The Verbal Comprehension Index provides a purer measure of verbal comprehension than does the Verbal Scale IQ, just as the Perceptual Organization Index provides a purer measure of perceptual organization than does the Performance Scale IQ.

22. The Freedom from Distractibility Index appears to be a measure of working memory or short-term acquisition and retrieval.

23. The Processing Speed Index appears to measure immediate short-term memory, ability to sustain attention, encoding ability, perceptual discrimination ability, fine motor skills, and cognitive flexibility.

Comparisons Between Subtests

24. Any hypotheses about subtest scaled scores should be developed through the study of the child's entire test performance and clinical history.

25. Scaled scores of 10 or higher should never be described as reflecting absolute weaknesses, and scaled scores of 9 or lower should never be described as reflecting absolute strengths.

Estimated Percentile Ranks and Test-Age Equivalents

26. When you are preparing to explain test results to teachers, parents, physicians, attorneys, or other people involved in the assessment, it is helpful to convert subtest scaled scores to percentile ranks and to convert raw scores to test-age equivalents.

Suggestions for Reporting Scales and Subtests

27. Present the essential features of the WISC–III scales and subtests when you discuss results with parents and the referral source.

Comment on Interpreting the WISC–III

28. In interpreting the WISC–III (as well as any other test), it is critical that you consider all sources of information, including the child's educational history, previous assessment results, other current assessment results, developmental history, cultural and linguistic background, family environment, health history, and temporary situational factors.

29. You should never delete subtests in computing the Full Scale IQ (or in computing the Verbal Scale IQ or Performance Scale IQ) simply because an examinee scored poorly on the subtests.

30. When a significant Verbal Scale–Performance Scale split occurs, the Full Scale IQ may be a misrepresentation of the individual's functioning level. In this situation, the Full Scale IQ may represent a forced average of rather disparate primary skills.

31. To a lesser extent, a similar problem exists in interpreting the Verbal Scale IQ and Performance Scale IQ when there is an exceptionally large amount of variability among the subtests within each scale.

32. The score that a child obtains on each WISC–III scale and subtest is multidetermined.

33. The WISC–III provides useful, but limited, information about the range, depth, and real-world applications of a child's intellectual ability.

34. The WISC–III (and other Wechsler tests) should not be used to evaluate personality and temperament, to diagnose psychopathology, or to determine brain lateralization. Instead, the WISC–III should be used to learn about the child's intellectual ability and to generate hypotheses to account for the child's functioning on the test.

KEY TERMS, CONCEPTS, AND NAMES

Profile analysis (p. 299)
Interindividual comparison (p. 300)
Intraindividual comparison (p. 300)
Ipsative approach (p. 300)
Significant difference approach (p. 301)
Base rate approach (p. 301)
Probability-of-occurrence approach (p. 301)
Primary methods of profile analysis (p. 302)
Statistically reliable IQ differences (p. 306)
Empirically observed IQ differences (p. 306)
Reliability-of-difference approach (p. 308)
Successive-level approach to test interpretation (p. 308)
Steps in analyzing a Wechsler protocol (p. 310)

STUDY QUESTIONS

1. Discuss the intent of profile analysis, methods of profile analysis, and approaches to profile analysis on the WISC–III.

2. Describe the successive-level approach to interpreting the WISC–III.

3. Discuss how to interpret differences between the WISC–III Verbal Scale and Performance Scale and between index scores.

4. Discuss how to interpret differences between WISC–III subtests. Cite at least seven subtest comparisons in your presentation.

5. What are some general considerations in interpreting the WISC–III?

11

WECHSLER PRESCHOOL AND PRIMARY SCALE OF INTELLIGENCE–REVISED (WPPSI–R)

Written with assistance from Denise Hildebrand

From the child of five to myself is but a step. But from the new-born baby to the child of five is an appalling distance.
—Leo Tolstoy

Goals and Objectives

This chapter is designed to enable you to do the following:

• Evaluate the psychometric properties of the WPPSI–R

• Describe the rationale, factor analytic findings, reliability and correlational highlights, and administrative and interpretive considerations for the 12 WPPSI–R subtests

• Describe profile analysis for the WPPSI–R

• Analyze and evaluate WPPSI–R scores from multiple perspectives

• Evaluate and describe the assets and limitations of the WPPSI–R

The Wechsler Preschool and Primary Scale of Intelligence–Revised (WPPSI–R; Wechsler, 1989) is designed to assess the cognitive ability of young children. This chapter should be read in conjunction with Chapters 8, 9, and 10, concerning the WISC–III. Because the WISC–III and the WPPSI–R are similar, you can apply many of the psychometric, clinical, and psychoeducational approaches used with the WISC–III to the WPPSI–R. However, because the WPPSI–R has not been as widely used or researched as the WISC–III, you need to be more cautious in interpreting the WPPSI–R.

The WPPSI–R (see Figure 11-1) is appropriate for use with children from 3 years 0 months to 7 years 3 months of age. Unfortunately, the WPPSI–R is not completely distinct from the WISC–III; some items overlap with those on four WISC–III subtests (Picture Completion, Mazes, Vocabulary, and Information). This overlap limits the retesting of children with a different Wechsler test.

The WPPSI–R contains 12 subtests (see Exhibit 11-1), grouped into a Performance Scale and a Verbal Scale. The five standard subtests within the Performance Scale are Object Assembly, Geometric Design, Block Design, Mazes, and Picture Completion. The five standard subtests within the Verbal Scale are Information, Comprehension, Arithmetic, Vocabulary, and Similarities. The two optional subtests are Animal Pegs in the Performance Scale and Sentences in the Verbal Scale. Nine of the 12 subtests are similar to those in the WISC–III (Object Assembly, Block Design, Mazes, Picture Completion, Information, Comprehension, Arithmetic, Vocabulary, and Similarities), and three are unique to the WPPSI–R (Sentences, Animal Pegs, and Geometric Design). Essentially, the WPPSI–R is a downward extension of the WISC–III, except at 6 to 7¼ years, where the two tests overlap.

STANDARDIZATION

The WPPSI–R was standardized on 1,700 children: 100 boys and 100 girls in each of eight age groups from 3 to 7 years, and one group of 50 boys and 50 girls from 7 years 0 months to 7 years 3 months of age. The 1986 U.S. Census data were used to select representative children for the normative sample. Euro American children and non-Euro American children were included in the sample, based on the ratios found in the census for four geographical regions in the United States (Northeast, North Central, South, and West).

Figure 11-1. Wechsler Preschool and Primary Scale of Intelligence–Revised. From the Wechsler Preschool and Primary Scale of Intelligence–Revised. Copyright © 1989 by The Psychological Corporation. Reproduced by permission. All rights reserved.

Exhibit 11-1
WPPSI–R-Like Items

Object Assembly (6 items)
There are two types of tasks: (a) placing pieces into a form board and (b) assembling jigsaw puzzles. An example of an Object Assembly item is shown below.

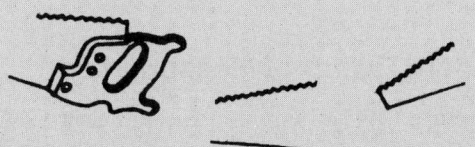

Geometric Design (16 items)
The task for the first seven items is to select the matching design from four choices. The task for the last nine items is to copy a geometric design shown on a printed card. The designs include a circle, square, triangle, and diamond.

Block Design (14 designs)
The task is to reproduce designs using three or four blocks.

Mazes (11 mazes)
The task is to find paths through a series of mazes.

Picture Completion (28 items)
The task is to identify the essential missing part of the picture:

A picture of a doll without a leg
A picture of a rabbit without an ear
A picture of a car without a wheel

Animal Pegs
The task is to place appropriate colored pegs into the corresponding holes on a board. The colored pegs are matched with four different animals. The Animal Pegs task is shown in the photograph of the WPPSI–R (see Figure 11-1).

Information (27 items)

Point to the picture that shows the one you cut with.
How many legs does a cat have?
In what kind of store do we buy meat?
How many pennies make a dime?

Comprehension (15 items)

Why do you need to take a bath?
Why do we have farms?
What makes a sailboat move?

Arithmetic (23 items)

A card showing squares of different sizes is placed in front of the child. The examiner says, "Here are some squares. Which one is the biggest? Point to it."
Bill had 1 penny and his mother gave him 1 more. How many pennies does he now have?
Judy had 4 books. She lost 1. How many books does she have left?
Jimmy had 7 bananas and he bought 8 more. How many bananas does he have altogether?

Vocabulary (25 items)

The examiner shows the child a picture of a dog and says, "What is this?"
What is a boot?
What does "nice" mean?
What does "annoy" mean?

Similarities (20 items)

The examiner shows the child a picture of objects that go together and says, "Look at these pictures. They're all alike— they all go together. Now look at these pictures. Which one is like these?"
You can read a book and you can also read a _____.
In what way are a quarter and a dollar alike?
In what way are a cow and a pig alike?

Sentences (12 items)
The task is to repeat sentences given orally by the examiner:

Birds fly.
Ted eats apples in the morning.
The children like to visit the city every Saturday during the summer.

DEVIATION IQS, SCALED SCORES, AND TEST-AGE EQUIVALENTS

Deviation IQs and Scaled Scores

The WPPSI–R, like the WISC–III and the WAIS–III, uses Deviation IQs ($M = 100$, $SD = 15$) for the Verbal Scale IQ, Performance Scale IQ, and Full Scale IQ, and scaled scores ($M = 10$, $SD = 3$) for the subtests. An IQ is computed by comparing the child's scores with the scores earned by a repre-

sentative sample of his or her own age group. After each subtest is scored, raw-score totals are converted to scaled scores within the child's own age group through use of Table 25 in the WPPSI–R manual (pages 170–186). Age groups are divided into 16 three-month intervals from 2-11-16 (years, months, days) to 6-11-15, and 1 four-month interval from 6-11-16 to 7-3-15.

IQs are based on the 10 standard subtests (see Table 27, pages 188–189 in the WPPSI–R manual). The two optional subtests are not used in computing IQs unless a standard subtest is spoiled or omitted. When a subtest must be excluded on the Performance Scale, substitute Animal Pegs, and when a subtest must be excluded on the Verbal Scale, substitute Sentences. When an optional subtest is substituted for a standard subtest, the exact reliability and validity of the IQs are not known because the optional subtests were not used in the original construction of the tables used to generate IQs.

Prorating Procedure

When fewer than 10 subtests are administered, you can compute IQs either by prorating or by using a short-form procedure designed to estimate the Performance Scale IQ, Verbal Scale IQ, and Full Scale IQ. Table 26 on page 187 of the WPPSI–R manual is used to prorate sums of the scaled scores when you administer four of the subtests in each scale. To compute IQs when fewer than 10 subtests are administered, you also can use the Tellegen and Briggs (1967) procedure described later in this chapter. Unlike prorating, their procedure considers the intercorrelations between the specific subtests administered.

Test-Age Equivalents

Table 28 (page 190) of the WPPSI–R manual shows test-age equivalents. The test ages were determined by obtaining the raw score corresponding to a scaled score of 10 at each age level. Because a scaled score of 10 represents the mean, the test-age equivalents of the raw scores shown in Table 28 reflect the average score for each particular age group. Review the discussion in Chapter 4 of the assets and limitations of test-age equivalents before you use this statistic.

RELIABILITY

The WPPSI–R Performance Scale IQ, Verbal Scale IQ, and Full Scale IQ have excellent reliability at eight of the nine age groups covered by the test. From ages 3 to 6½ years, the reliabilities for all three IQs range from .90 to .97; this range is excellent. At age 7 years, however, the reliability coefficients for the Performance Scale IQ and Verbal Scale IQ (r_{xx} = .85 and .86, respectively) are less satisfactory than that for the Full Scale IQ (r_{xx} = .90). The lower reliability coefficients at the 7-year level are probably related to ceiling effects. (Ceiling effects exist when a test has too few items at the upper levels to reliably measure the abilities of high-functioning children.) Across the nine age groups, the average internal consistency reliabilities are .92 for the Performance Scale IQ, .95 for the Verbal Scale IQ, and .96 for the Full Scale IQ (see Table 11-1).

Subtest Reliabilities

The internal consistency reliabilities for the subtests are lower than those for the three scales, as would be expected (see Table 11-1). The average internal consistency subtest reliabilities range from a low of r_{xx} = .63 for Object Assembly to a high of r_{xx} = .86 for Similarities. For the nine age groups, median subtest reliabilities are highest for ages 3, 3½, 4, 4½, and 5 years (*Mdn r_{xx}* ranges from .830 to .870), followed by age 6 years (*Mdn r_{xx}* = .780), age 5½ years (*Mdn r_{xx}* = .775), age 6½ years (*Mdn r_{xx}* = .745), and, at the lowest level, age 7 years (*Mdn r_{xx}* = .660). The lowest subtest reliabilities are found at age 7 years (see Table 11-2).

Standard Errors of Measurement

The average standard errors of measurement (SEM) in IQ points are 3.00 for the Full Scale, 4.24 for the Performance Scale, and 3.35 for the Verbal Scale (see Table 11-1). As with all Wechsler tests, more confidence can be placed in IQs based on the Full Scale than in IQs based on either the Performance Scale or the Verbal Scale alone. The average SEMs for the subtests in scaled-score points range from 1.16 to 1.82 for the Performance Scale subtests and from 1.12 to 1.34 for the Verbal Scale subtests. Within the Performance Scale,

Table 11-1
Average Reliability Coefficients and Standard Errors of Measurement for WPPSI–R Subtests and Scales

Subtest or scale	Average internal consistency reliability r_{xx}	Average test-retest reliability r_{tt}	Average SEM
Object Assembly	.63	.59	1.82
Geometric Design	.79	.67	1.37
Block Design	.85	.80	1.16
Mazes	.77	.52	1.44
Picture Completion	.85	.82	1.16
Animal Pegs	.66	.66	1.75
Information	.84	.81	1.20
Comprehension	.83	.78	1.24
Arithmetic	.80	.71	1.34
Vocabulary	.84	.75	1.20
Similarities	.86	.70	1.12
Sentences	.82	.79	1.27
Performance IQ	.92	.88	4.24
Verbal IQ	.95	.90	3.35
Full Scale IQ	.96	.91	3.00

Note. Reliability coefficients for all subtests except Animal Pegs are split-half coefficients corrected by the Spearman-Brown formula. For Animal Pegs, the reliability coefficient is a test-retest coefficient.
Source: Adapted from Wechsler (1989).

Table 11-2
Range and Median: WPPSI–R Subtest Reliabilities

Age	Range	Median
3 years	.63–.90	.850
3½ years	.63–.89	.845
4 years	.66–.89	.870
4½ years	.56–.93	.840
5 years	.59–.86	.830
5½ years	.57–.86	.775
6 years	.66–.86	.780
6½ years	.66–.83	.745
7 years	.54–.86	.660
Average	.63–.86	.825

Table 11-3
Test-Retest WPPSI–R IQs

Scale	First testing		Second testing		Change[a]
	Mean IQ	SD	Mean IQ	SD	
Performance IQ	101.8	14.4	108.1	16.6	+6.3
Verbal IQ	101.4	14.7	104.2	16.3	+2.8
Full Scale IQ	101.7	14.4	106.8	16.6	+5.1

[a]All mean change scores are significant at $p < .001$.
Source: Adapted from Wechsler (1989).

Block Design and Picture Completion have the smallest SEMs (1.16 for both). Within the Verbal Scale, Similarities, Information, and Vocabulary have the smallest SEMs (1.12, 1.20, and 1.20, respectively).

Test-Retest Reliability

In the standardization sample, the stability of the WPPSI–R was assessed by retesting 175 children from two age groups (3–0 to 4–11 and 5–0 to 7–3) after an interval of 3 to 7 weeks ($M = 4$ weeks; Wechsler, 1989). The stability coefficients for the combined groups were r_{tt} = .87, .89, and .91 for the Performance Scale, Verbal Scale, and Full Scale, respectively. These results indicate that the WPPSI–R provides stable IQs for the Full Scale, but slightly less stable IQs for the Performance Scale and Verbal Scale. The stability coefficients for the subtests ranged from a low of r_{tt} = .52 for Mazes to a high of r_{tt} = .82 for Picture Completion (see Table 11-1). As expected, the internal consistency reliabilities are somewhat higher than the test-retest reliabilities (*Mdn* r_{xx} = .82 versus *Mdn* r_{tt} = .73).

Changes in IQs. Table 11-3 shows the mean test-retest IQs and standard deviations for the Performance Scale, Verbal Scale, and Full Scale for the one combined retested group. From the first to the second testing, the Full Scale IQ increased by 5.1 points, the Performance Scale IQ increased by 6.3 points, and the Verbal Scale IQ increased by 2.8 points. These statistically significant increases, which likely resulted from practice effects, are more than two times greater for the Performance Scale than for the Verbal Scale. Studies are needed to evaluate the stability of the WPPSI–R with other samples of children and over the longer periods of time, such as 3 years, that often elapse between cognitive assessments under the IDEA (see Chapter 3). The greater gains

on the Performance Scale than on the Verbal Scale may be associated with examinees' ability to better recall the types of items on the Performance Scale and the strategies previously worked out to solve them (Kaufman, 1990). Small retest gains on the Performance Scale, consequently, probably do not reflect true gains in intelligence.

Changes in subtest scaled scores. From the first to the second testing, the changes in subtest scaled scores, which again were probably related to practice effects, were as follows: Object Assembly, +1.2; Geometric Design, 0; Block Design, +1.3; Mazes, +1.0; Picture Completion, +.9; Animal Pegs, +.7; Information, +.4; Comprehension, +.4; Arithmetic, +.4; Vocabulary, –.2; Similarities, +.9; and Sentences, +.4. The changes in subtest scores, which ranged from –.2 (Vocabulary) to +1.3 (Block Design), were significant for 10 of the 12 subtests. The two exceptions were Geometric Design, where there was no change, and Vocabulary, where the change was minimal. Generally, subtests on the Performance Scale showed greater practice effects (*M* change = .85) than did those on the Verbal Scale (*M* change = .45).

Confidence Intervals

Table B-1 in Appendix B shows the confidence intervals for the 68, 85, 90, 95, and 99% levels for the WPPSI–R Performance Scale IQ, Verbal Scale IQ, and Full Scale IQ, by age level, based on the conventional SEM (see Chapter 4). These confidence intervals are generally similar throughout the nine WPPSI–R age groups. For the Full Scale IQ, they range between 6 and 8 points at the 95% confidence level. The confidence intervals are narrower for the Full Scale IQ and Verbal Scale IQ than for the Performance Scale IQ, and narrower at ages 3 to 5 years than at ages 5½ to 7 years. You should use the child's specific age group to obtain the most accurate confidence interval. For further discussion of confidence intervals and how to report them, see Chapter 4. If you want to use the confidence interval based on the standard error of estimation (see Chapter 4 for a discussion of how and when to use this confidence interval), see Table D-2 in Appendix D.

VALIDITY

Let's now turn to evaluating the concurrent validity and construct validity of the WPPSI–R.

Concurrent Validity

Table 11-4 summarizes WPPSI–R concurrent validity studies. These studies indicate that the WPPSI–R has excellent concurrent validity, as indicated by strong correlations with several different intelligence and achievement tests. The median correlation between the WPPSI–R and various intelligence tests is .74, while the median correlation between the WPPSI–R and various achievement tests is .62.

Construct Validity

Several factor analytic studies (Gyurke, Stone, & Beyer, 1990; LoBello & Gulgoz, 1991; Wechsler, 1989) support the construct validity of the WPPSI–R. These studies support a two-factor structure corresponding to the Verbal Scale and Performance Scale of the test. The WPPSI–R also provides a fair measure of general intelligence (g).

Comment on the Validity of the WPPSI–R

Studies indicate that the WPPSI–R has adequate concurrent and construct validity, with some exceptions. Because the WPPSI–R has an inadequate floor for children in the lowest age ranges, there are not enough easy items to provide accurate diagnostic information for children with severe mental retardation (Flanagan & Alfonso, 1995). Similarly, the limited ceiling makes it difficult to assess high-functioning children.

The WPPSI–R and the WISC–III should *not* be considered parallel forms. The WISC–III manual (Wechsler, 1991) suggests that when children are tested with both the WPPSI–R and the WISC–III, WISC–III scores will probably exceed WPPSI–R scores by 2 points on the Verbal Scale IQ, 6 points on the Performance Scale IQ, and 4 points on the Full Scale IQ. This generalization may not hold for children at the lower levels or upper levels of the IQ distribution. The increase in WISC–III scores may be associated with the two different sets of norms or with ceiling effects on the WPPSI–R. Because the WISC–III is designed for older children, it has a higher ceiling for 6- and 7-year-olds; therefore, children of these ages can obtain higher scores on the WISC–III than on the WPPSI–R (Wechsler, 1991). Consequently, higher WISC–III scores for children tested earlier on the WPPSI–R may have nothing to do with intervening events that affected a child's cognitive ability, but may simply reflect a different set of norms based on different standardization samples or a different set of items. The probability that the change in Full

Table 11-4
WPPSI–R Criterion Validity Studies

Criterion	Verbal Scale	Performance Scale	Full Scale
	Median correlation		
WPPSI	.86	.74	.83
WISC–R	.69	.73	.81
WISC–III	.85	.73	.85
Stanford-Binet: IV	.56	.71	.74
McCarthy Scales	.63	.58	.68
CMMS	.18	.49	.37
K-BIT	.75	.44	.63
Draw-A-Person	—	—	.30
K-ABC	.42	.41	.49
Stanford-Binet: L-M	.85	.75	.82
Woodcock-Johnson	.76	.36	.66
PPVT–R	.33	.30	.36
BBCS	.63	.43	.70
SON–R	.49	.82	.80
Achievement tests			
Listening	.72	.29	.65
Reading	.51	.27	.85
Mathematics	.62	.35	.60
Word analysis	.44	.16	.38

Note. Abbreviations: WPPSI = Wechsler Preschool and Primary Scale of Intelligence; WISC–R = Wechsler Intelligence Scale for Children–Revised; WISC–III = Wechsler Intelligence Scale for Children–Third Edition; CMMS = Columbia Mental Maturity Scale; PPVT–R = Peabody Picture Vocabulary Test–Revised; BBCS = Bracken Basic Concept Scale; SON–R= Snijders-Omen Nonverbal Intelligence Test–Revised.

Source: Carvajal, Parks, Bays, Logan, Lujano, Page, and Weaver (1991); Carvajal, Parks, Logan, and Page (1992); Carvajal, Parks, Parks, Logan, and Page (1993); Faust and Hollingsworth (1991); Gerken and Hodapp (1992); Harrington, Kimberly, and Dai (1992); Kaplan, Fox, and Paxton (1991); Karr, Carvajal, Elser, Bays, Logan, and Page (1993); Lassiter and Bardos (1995); Laughlin (1995); McCrowell and Nagle (1994); Milrod and Rescorla (1991); Moore, O'Keefe, and Lawhon (1998); Quereshi and Seitz (1994); Schneider and Gervais (1991); Tellegen (1997); Wechsler (1991).

Scale IQ is genuine, however, increases with the size of the difference above 4 points.

Similarly, a child first tested with the WISC–III (e.g., at the age of 6 years) and then retested with the WPPSI–R (e.g., at the age of 7 years) may show a decrease of about 4 IQ points on the retest. Again, decreases of up to 4 IQ points may be solely a function of the different norms, not a reflection of decrements in the child's intellectual ability. Decreases beyond 4 points, however, may suggest decrements in ability.

Studies suggest that the WPPSI–R yields IQs similar to those of the Stanford-Binet: IV and McCarthy Scales of Children's Abilities for children in the normal range of functioning. However, the WPPSI–R IQs are not comparable to those of the K-ABC or the Woodcock-Johnson Tests of Cognitive Ability. Scores on the K-ABC were generally about 6 points higher than those on the WPPSI–R, while scores on the Woodcock-Johnson were generally about 4.5 points lower than those on the WPPSI–R. WPPSI–R test-age equivalents have been found to be similar to those on the WISC–III for 23 overlapping items (Sattler & Atkinson, 1993).

INTERCORRELATIONS BETWEEN SUBTESTS AND SCALES

Intercorrelations between subtests and scales reflect the degree of relationship between various sections of the WPPSI–R. Average intercorrelations between the 12 subtests range from a low of $r = .24$ (Mazes and Sentences) to a high of $r = .66$ (Information and Comprehension). The median intercorrelation is $r = .41$. The highest intercorrelations are between Information and Comprehension ($r = .66$), Information and Vocabulary ($r = .60$), Comprehension and Vocabulary ($r = .60$), Information and Arithmetic ($r = .59$), Information and Similarities ($r = .57$), and Information and Sentences ($r = .55$). The lowest intercorrelations are between Mazes and Sentences ($r = .24$), Object Assembly and Sentences ($r = .25$), Geometric Design and Vocabulary ($r = .26$), Object Assembly and Comprehension ($r = .26$), Mazes and Comprehension ($r = .26$), Mazes and Vocabulary ($r = .26$), and Animal Pegs and Vocabulary ($r = .26$). Note that the Verbal Scale subtests have higher intercorrelations than the Performance Scale subtests and that the lowest correlations are between subtests in different scales (e.g., Mazes and Sentences or Object Assembly and Sentences).

FACTOR ANALYSIS

For this text, we conducted a principal-components analysis with varimax rotation using the WPPSI–R standardization data. Two principal factors were found at all age levels except for age 7 years, where a three-factor solution also was appropriate. In the three-factor solution, Mazes and Animal Pegs were the only subtests that had loadings above .40 on the third factor. The two-factor solution best explains the WPPSI–R throughout all of its age levels; this finding agrees with factor analytic studies cited earlier. The six subtests in the Verbal Scale best represent the Verbal factor (or Verbal Comprehension) at all ages: Comprehension, Information, Vocabulary, Sentences, Similarities, and Arithmetic. Five of the six subtests in the Performance Scale best represent the Performance factor (or Perceptual Organization) at most ages: Block Design, Geometric Design, Object Assembly,

Mazes, and Animal Pegs, but not Picture Completion (see Figure 11-2 and Table 11-5).

Picture Completion does not consistently load on the Performance factor at all ages. It has higher loadings on the Verbal factor than on the Performance factor at age 3 years, and it has satisfactory loadings on both the Verbal and the Performance factor at ages 3½, 4, 4½, 6½, and 7 years. It clearly loads on the Performance factor only at ages 5, 5½, and 6 years. For all ages combined, Picture Completion has a substantial loading on both the Verbal and the Performance factor, but higher loadings on the Performance factor. At 3 years, you can obtain a purer measure of the Performance factor by using only Object Assembly, Geometric Design, Block Design, and Mazes (adding Animal Pegs if you like).

WPPSI–R Subtests as Measures of *g*

Examination of the loadings on the first unrotated factor in the principal-component analysis allows one to determine the extent to which the WPPSI–R subtests measure *g*. Overall, the WPPSI–R is a fair measure of *g*, with 45% of its variance attributed to *g*. We find higher *g* loadings at ages 3 to 5 years (average loadings range from 45% to 50%) than at ages 5 to 7 years (average loadings range from 34% to 44%), with age 7 years having the lowest *g* loadings (average loading is 34%).

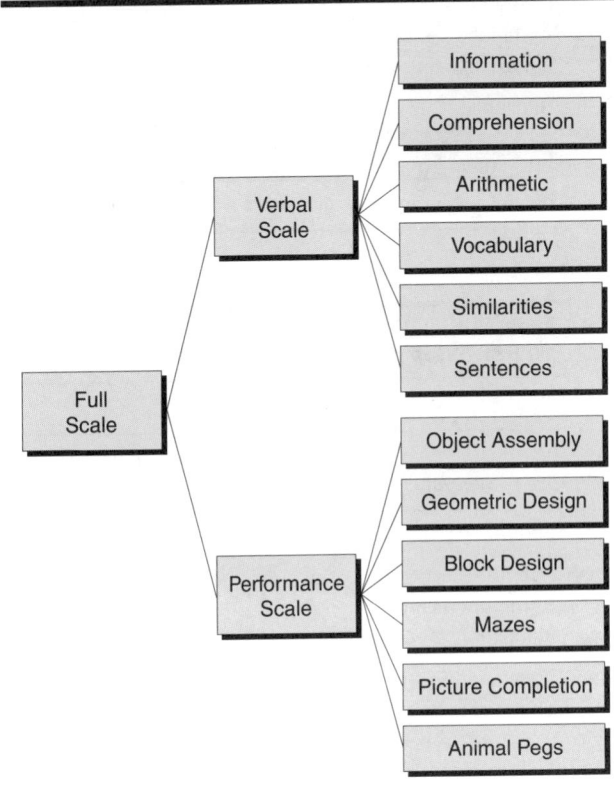

Figure 11-2. Structure of the WPPSI–R.

Table 11-5
Factor Loadings of WPPSI–R Subtests (Varimax Rotation)

Subtest	Age group									
	3	3½	4	4½	5	5½	6	6½	7	Av.
Factor A—Verbal										
Object Assembly	21	15	08	12	23	13	06	30	02	14
Geometric Design	38	29	22	19	−03	17	20	16	09	18
Block Design	12	22	34	26	45	23	18	39	15	26
Mazes	25	15	26	23	13	−04	24	06	13	15
Picture Completion	63	55	49	53	32	22	22	41	41	41
Animal Pegs	18	19	30	28	41	26	15	24	24	24
Information	83	79	81	77	80	73	78	79	70	78
Comprehension	80	87	85	84	80	77	79	75	75	81
Arithmetic	59	69	70	63	62	52	64	65	66	62
Vocabulary	79	79	77	83	81	79	78	82	70	79
Similarities	73	72	78	74	72	75	68	71	65	72
Sentences	72	77	71	76	73	75	76	61	73	74
Factor B—Performance										
Object Assembly	70	68	75	76	64	66	76	68	77	72
Geometric Design	69	75	75	77	80	67	65	72	55	72
Block Design	69	77	74	76	65	80	78	72	78	75
Mazes	69	69	63	63	79	73	69	75	50	69
Picture Completion	37	53	55	56	65	62	66	55	44	57
Animal Pegs	52	58	64	65	38	50	48	31	36	52
Information	32	33	34	37	25	22	28	26	30	31
Comprehension	21	20	19	21	07	10	04	13	08	16
Arithmetic	43	39	38	44	50	54	40	36	30	44
Vocabulary	13	13	18	16	08	17	21	18	26	17
Similarities	25	30	24	28	29	20	30	25	−05	26
Sentences	22	13	27	19	22	13	13	29	16	19

Note. Av. = Average. Decimal points omitted. Factors based on principal-components analysis.

Table 11-6
WPPSI–R Subtests as Measures of *g*

Good measure of *g*			Fair measure of *g*		
Subtest	Average loading of *g*	Proportion of variance attributed to *g* (%)	Subtest	Average loading of *g*	Proportion of variance attributed to *g* (%)
Information	.79	63	Picture Completion	.69	47
Arithmetic	.76	57	Block Design	.68	47
Comprehension	.72	52	Sentences	.68	46
Similarities	.72	51	Geometric Design	.61	37
Vocabulary	.71	51	Object Assembly	.57	33
			Mazes	.56	32
			Animal Pegs	.52	27

Note. Criteria used to classify subtests are as follows: good—50% or more of variance attributed to *g*; fair—26–49% of variance attributed to *g*; poor—0–25% of variance attributed to *g*.

The WPPSI–R subtests form two clusters with respect to the measurement of *g:* (a) Information, Arithmetic, Comprehension, Similarities, and Vocabulary are good measures of *g;* and (b) Picture Completion, Block Design, Sentences, Geometric Design, Object Assembly, Mazes, and Animal Pegs are fair measures of *g* (see Table 11-6). The subtests in the Verbal Scale have higher *g* loadings than do those in the Performance Scale. In the Verbal Scale, Information has the highest loading, while in the Performance Scale, Picture Completion and Block Design have the highest loadings. Any of the five standard Verbal Scale subtests can be used as a good measure of *g*. Although no Performance Scale subtest is a good measure of *g*, Picture Completion and Block Design are fair to good measures of *g* at each of the nine age levels.

At each age level, most Verbal Scale subtests have higher *g* loadings than do the Performance Scale subtests. The consistency of this finding is striking. There are only two age levels at which any Verbal Scale subtest contributes less than 40% to the measurement of *g:* at age 6 years, Comprehension (38%), and at age 7 years, Similarities (26%). Block Design is a fair to good measure of *g* at each of the nine age levels. Picture Completion is a fair to good measure of *g* at every age level.

WPPSI–R Subtest Specificity

Subtest specificity refers to the proportion of a subtest's variance that is both reliable (i.e., not due to errors of measure-

ment) and distinctive to the subtest (see Chapter 4 for further information about subtest specificity). Although the individual subtests on the WPPSI–R overlap in their measurement properties (i.e., the majority of reliable variance for most subtests is common factor variance), most possess sufficient specificity at some age levels to justify interpretation of specific subtest functions (see Table 11-7).

Throughout the age range covered by the WPPSI–R, Picture Completion is the only subtest that has ample specificity, and Object Assembly is the only subtest that has inadequate specificity. Each of the 10 other subtests shows a unique pattern of specificity—that is, each subtest's specificity differs for different ages. More subtests have inadequate specificity at ages 4, 5½, 6½, and 7 years than at the other ages.

Subtests with inadequate specificity should *not* be interpreted as measuring specific functions. Subtests that fall within the adequate specificity category should be cautiously interpreted. Subtests with inadequate specificity, however, can be interpreted as measuring *g* (see Table 11-6), if appropriate, and one of the principal factors (Verbal or Performance), as appropriate (see Table 11-5).

Factor Analysis of the WPPSI–R Compared to the WISC–III

The factor structure of the WPPSI–R is generally similar to that of the WISC–III, particularly in terms of the Verbal

---

Table 11-7
WPPSI–R Subtest Specificity

Subtest	Ages with ample specificity	Ages with adequate specificity	Ages with inadequate specificity
Object Assembly	—	—	3–7, Av.
Geometric Design	6, 7	3–3½, 4½, Av.	4, 5–5½, 6½
Block Design	3	3½–5, 6, 7, Av.	5½, 6½
Mazes	3–4½, 6, 7, Av.	—	5–5½, 6½
Picture Completion	3–7, Av.	—	—
Animal Pegs	3, 5, 6–7, Av.	—	3½–4½, 5½
Information	—	3½, 4½	3, 4, 5–7, Av.
Comprehension	—	3, 5–5½	3½–4½, 6–7, Av.
Arithmetic	3, 5½, 6½	3½, 4½, 6, Av.	4, 5, 7
Vocabulary	4	3, 5–5½, Av.	3½, 4½, 6–7
Similarities	3–3½, 4½–6, Av.	4	6½–7
Sentences	3–4	4½–5, Av.	5½–7

Note. Av. = average of the nine age groups. Kaufman's (1975) rule of thumb was used to classify the amount of specificity in each subtest. Subtests with *ample specificity* have specific variance that (a) reflects 25% or more of the subtest's total variance *and* (b) exceeds the subtest's error variance. Subtests with *adequate specificity* have specific variance that (a) reflects 15–24% of the subtest's total variance *and* (b) exceeds the subtest's error variance. Subtests with *inadequate specificity* have specific variance that is either (a) less than 15% of the subtest's total variance *or* (b) equal to or less than the subtest's error variance.

Comprehension and Perceptual Organization factors. The primary difference between the WPPSI–R and WISC–III factor structures is that two additional WISC–III factors have sometimes been identified; these factors have been labeled Freedom from Distractibility and Processing Speed. The differences in the factor structures of the two tests may be due to the fact that the two tests contain somewhat different subtests. Developmental changes in cognitive structure might also account for the different factor structures.

RANGE OF FULL SCALE IQS AND OF SUBTEST SCALED SCORES

Knowledge of the range of IQs available at each age level of the test will help you to (a) evaluate children at the extreme ranges of intelligence, (b) monitor children's performance over time, and (c) conduct a profile analysis. Let's now look at the range of IQs and the range of subtest scaled scores on the WPPSI–R and then examine guidelines for evaluating IQs and subtest scaled scores at the extremes of the WPPSI–R IQ range.

IQ Ranges

The WPPSI–R Full Scale IQs range from 41 to 160 (see Table 26 of the WPPSI–R manual). The WPPSI–R manual recommends that IQs be computed only when the child has a minimum of 1 raw-score point on three Performance Scale subtests and 1 raw-score point on three Verbal Scale subtests. When this rule is followed, it is not until 5¾ years that a child can obtain a Full Scale IQ as low as 41 (six raw-score points of 1 and four raw-score points of 0). With this rule, the lowest Full Scale IQ possible at 3 years is 65, barely two standard deviations below the mean (see Table 11-8). (The lower limits of the ranges shown in Table 11-8 may vary depending on the combination of subtests for which the child earns raw-score points.) The lowest possible Performance Scale IQ at 3 years is 66, and the lowest possible Verbal Scale IQ is 71 (three raw-score points of 1 and two raw-score points of 0 on each scale). Even without this rule, a 3-year-old scoring zero on all subtests would be given a Full Scale IQ of 62. Because the lower limit of IQs provided by the WPPSI–R is not consistent throughout the scale, it will be difficult to use the WPPSI–R to monitor changes in the performance of a child who functions more than two standard deviations below the mean (see the example that follows).

IQs at the lower limits. The following example illustrates the IQs a 3-year-old child obtains with raw-score points of 1 on the Object Assembly, Geometric Design, Block Design, Information, Arithmetic, and Vocabulary subtests and raw-score points of 0 on the four remaining subtests. Six 1-point raw scores give the child a Performance Scale IQ of 66 (22 scaled-score points), a Verbal Scale IQ of

Table 11-8
WPPSI–R Performance Scale, Verbal Scale, and Full Scale IQ Ranges

Age	Performance Scale	Verbal Scale	Full Scale
3 years	66–160	71–160	65–160
3¼ years	62–160	67–160	61–160
3½ years	61–160	66–160	59–160
3¾ years	56–160	63–160	56–160
4 years	52–160	58–160	51–160
4¼ years	49–160	54–160	47–160
4½ years	48–160	54–160	46–160
4¾ years	47–160	53–160	45–160
5 years	47–160	48–160	43–160
5¼ years	45–160	48–160	42–160
5½ years	45–160	47–160	42–160
5¾ years	45–160	46–160	41–160
6 years	45–160	46–160	41–160
6¼ years	45–160	46–160	41–160
6½ years	45–156	46–157	41–160
6¾ years	45–156	46–152	41–160
7 years	45–156	46–152	41–160

Note. Age 7 represents a 4-month interval. Ranges were obtained by using data from Table 25, "Scaled Score Equivalents of Raw Scores," and Table 27, "IQ Equivalents of Sums of Scaled Scores," in the WPPSI–R manual. Ranges were based on the 10 standard subtests using the suggested criterion in the WPPSI–R manual that examinees must have three raw scores of at least 1 on the Performance Scale and three raw scores of at least 1 on the Verbal Scale in order for an IQ to be computed. The lower limits of the IQ range represent the lowest IQs that can be obtained. Other combinations of successes and failures will produce slightly higher IQs at the lower limits of the range.

71 (26 scaled-score points), and a Full Scale IQ of 65 (48 scaled-score points). This example demonstrates that the WPPSI–R may not provide precise IQs for a child who is functioning two or more standard deviations below the mean of the test. Research is needed to determine the validity of the WPPSI–R for mildly and moderately mentally retarded children. If a child fails all or most of the items on the WPPSI–R, administer a test that provides a more precise estimate of the child's ability.

Another example illustrates how the restricted range of IQs at the earliest year levels of the test may seriously affect the interpretation of a child's performance. On the first administration, a 3-year-old boy obtains a Full Scale IQ of 65; when retested at 5¼ years, he obtains a Full Scale IQ of 41. The 24-point drop between the first and second examinations may be purely an artifact of the IQs available at each age level of the test. As previously noted, at the earliest year levels of the test, the floor is much higher than at the later year levels–that is, the test norms do not provide the lowest possible IQs at the youngest ages for which the test was intended. Thus, when examinations are given 2 (or more) years apart to a low-functioning child, it is not possible to determine whether there has been a serious decrement in functioning. In the preceding example, you should assume there was no decrement in the child's mental ability during the interval between the two examinations. The lower score on the second test administration is most likely merely a reflection of how the test was constructed.

IQs at the upper limits.   In contrast with the restricted and variable range of IQs available at the lower limits of the WPPSI–R, a Full Scale IQ of 160—the upper limit of the WPPSI–R IQ range—can be obtained at every age level. The uniform ceiling is an advantage when you reexamine a child who is functioning three or four standard deviations above the mean. Although the ceiling level on the Full Scale is uniform throughout the WPPSI–R, the ceiling levels on the Performance Scale and Verbal Scale are less uniform (see Table

11-8). The highest Performance Scale IQ available at ages 6½ to 7 years is 156, while the highest Verbal Scale IQ available at age 6½ years is 157 and at ages 6¾ and 7 years is 152. However, these restricted ranges at the upper ages are a minor problem.

Subtest Scaled-Score Ranges

The major problem with the WPPSI–R scaled-score ranges is at the first-year level of the test, where points are given even when all items are failed. For example, at age 3 years, children receive 5 or 6 scaled-score points on Geometric Design, Mazes, Picture Completion, Information, Comprehension, Similarities, and Sentences even when they fail every item (see Table 11-9). Object Assembly is the only subtest on which a child can obtain a scaled score as low as 1 at age 3 years. This problem is related to the limited floor that was previously discussed. For example, 3-year-old children receive up to 43 scaled-score points even when they fail every item on the 10 standard subtests; the corresponding IQ is 62. Also, for one or more of the subtests at each of the 17 age groups, it is not

Table 11-9
WPPSI–R Subtest Scaled-Score Ranges

Age (in years)	Subtest											
	OA	GD	BD	MA	PC	AP	I	C	A	V	S	Se
3	1–19	5–19	4–19	5–19	5–19	2–19	5–19	6–19	3–19	3–19	6–19	5–19
3¼	1–19	4–19	4–19	4–19	4–19	1–19	4–19	6–19	3–19	2–19	5–19	4–19
3½	1–19	4–19	4–19	3–19	4–19	1–19	4–19	5–19	3–19	2–19	5–19	3–19
3¾	1–19	3–19	3–19	2–19	3–19	1–19	3–19	5–19	2–19	2–19	4–19	3–19
4	1–19	2–19	3–19	1–19	2–19	1–19	2–19	4–19	1–19	2–19	3–19	3–19
4¼	1–19	1–19	3–19	1–19	1–19	1–19	2–19	3–19	1–19	1–19	3–19	2–19
4½	1–19	1–19	3–19	1–19	1–19	1–19	2–19	3–19	1–19	1–19	3–19	2–19
4¾	1–19	1–18	2–19	1–19	1–19	1–19	1–19	3–19	1–19	1–19	2–19	2–19
5	1–19	1–18	1–19	1–19	1–19	1–19	1–19	2–19	1–19	1–19	2–19	1–19
5¼	1–19	1–17	1–19	1–19	1–19	1–19	1–19	2–19	1–19	1–19	2–19	1–19
5½	1–18	1–17	1–19	1–19	1–19	1–19	1–19	2–18	1–19	1–19	1–19	1–19
5¾	1–18	1–17	1–19	1–19	1–19	1–19	1–19	1–18	1–19	1–19	1–19	1–19
6	1–17	1–17	1–19	1–19	1–19	1–19	1–19	1–18	1–19	1–19	1–19	1–19
6¼	1–17	1–17	1–19	1–19	1–19	1–19	1–19	1–18	1–18	1–19	1–18	1–19
6½	1–16	1–16	1–18	1–18	1–19	1–19	1–18	1–17	1–17	1–19	1–18	1–19
6¾	1–16	1–16	1–18	1–18	1–18	1–19	1–17	1–17	1–16	1–19	1–17	1–19
7	1–16	1–16	1–18	1–18	1–18	1–19	1–17	1–17	1–16	1–19	1–17	1–17

Note. Abbreviations: OA = Object Assembly, GD = Geometric Design, BD = Block Design, MA = Mazes, PC = Picture Completion, AP = Animal Pegs, I = Information, C = Comprehension, A = Arithmetic, V = Vocabulary, S = Similarities, Se = Sentences. Age 7 represents a 4-month interval. Ranges are based on Table 25, "Scaled Score Equivalents of Raw Scores," in the WPPSI–R manual.

possible to obtain a range of scaled scores from 1 to 19 (see Table 25 in the WPPSI–R manual, pages 170–176).

The WPPSI–R manual, as noted before, advises that IQs not be computed (as we did in the previous example) unless the child obtains at least one success on each of three Verbal Scale and three Performance Scale subtests. However, because the WPPSI–R manual provides no documentation to support this recommendation, consider it as tentative. For example, we don't know whether IQs based on five, four, or even fewer subtests that have raw scores of 1 are reliable and valid. In addition, it is unclear whether the IQs obtained using the recommendation given in the WPPSI–R manual are reliable and valid.

There is a minor problem at the upper limits of the last two years of the test. At age 7 years, for example, a child can obtain 19 scaled-score points on only two subtests—Animal Pegs and Vocabulary. In addition, at age 7 years there is a low ceiling (scaled score of 16) on three subtests—Object Assembly, Geometric Design, and Arithmetic. Finally, on some subtests a child reaches the ceiling level of 19 scaled-score points midway through the age range (e.g., at age 4½ years for Geometric Design and at age 5¼ years for Object Assembly and Comprehension), after which the maximum number of scaled-score points available is reduced.

The failure to have a uniform scaled-score range throughout all age levels of the test means that profile analysis cannot be performed routinely, particularly at the lower and upper limits of the scaled-score range. For example, research with a sample of 52 gifted 3- to 5-year-old children showed that the ceiling level of the WPPSI–R was limited for high-functioning children (Kaplan, 1992). Therefore, in interpreting children's profiles, consider the available range of scaled scores for that child's specific age. Also recognize that, because the maximum scaled score obtainable is not the same for all subtests, Verbal Scale-Performance Scale comparisons and subtest comparisons may not be appropriate for high-functioning children.

NORMATIVE CHANGES ON ANIMAL PEGS

Because Animal Pegs has exactly the same number of items, scoring procedure, and time limits in the WPPSI and in the WPPSI–R, we can examine how the norms have changed over the 22-year period between publication of the two versions of the test. At ages 4 to 6½ years, where the two forms overlap, children usually must earn more raw-score points on the WPPSI–R than on the WPPSI to obtain the same scaled score. The changes range from –1 to +17 raw-score points (*Mdn* change = +4 raw-score points).

Changes Related to Age and Ability Level

The normative changes on the Animal Pegs subtest tend to be related to both the child's age and the child's ability level.

Table 11-10
Median Changes on WPPSI–R Animal Pegs Subtest

Scaled-score range	Ages		
	4–4½	4¾–5¾	6–6½
1–9	1	8	6
11–19	8	3	1

Children usually most affected by the changes are (a) those between 4 and 4½ years with above-average ability (e.g., with scaled scores above 10) and (b) those between 4¾ and 6½ years with below-average ability (e.g., with scaled scores below 10). These groups usually need to be more proficient (in speed, accuracy, or both) to maintain the same relative position on the WPPSI–R that they had on the WPPSI. In contrast, changes for 4-year-olds with below-average ability and 5- to 6½-year-olds with above-average ability are slight (see Table 11-10). Overall, changes are greatest at age 4 years (*Mdn* change = 7 raw-score points) and smallest at age 6½ years (*Mdn* change = 1 raw-score point; see Table 11-11).

Table 11-11 shows the additional raw-score points that a child needs for seven representative scaled scores at ages 4, 5¼, and 6½ years. A 4-year-old child needs, for example, 13 more raw-score points on the WPPSI–R than on the WPPSI to earn a scaled score of 19. Translated into time require-

Table 11-11
Raw Score Changes on WPPSI–R Animal Pegs Subtest

Scaled score	Age group			
	4	5¼	6½	*Mdn*[a]
1	0	0	0	0
4	1	7	17	7
7	2	13	1	9
10	7	7	1	7
13	11	3	0	3
16	9	3	0	3
19	13	5	2	5
Mdn[b]	7	4	1	4

Note. Based on Table 25 in the WPPSI–R manual and Table 21 in the WPPSI manual. The raw scores shown in the table are at the lower limits of the range of raw scores for each scaled score. Animal Pegs is called Animal House on the WPPSI.
[a]Over 11 age intervals from 4 though 6½ years.
[b]Over the range of scaled scores from 1 through 19.

ments, this means that to earn the highest scaled score, a 4-year-old with a perfect performance must work 1 minute *faster* on the WPPSI–R than on the WPPSI (30" on the WPPSI–R and 1'30" on the WPPSI). Another way to understand the changes on Animal Pegs is to note that a 4-year-old with a raw score of 52 earns a scaled score of 19 on the WPPSI and a scaled score of 15 on the WPPSI–R. For a 6½-year-old child, a raw score of 15 earns a scaled score of 4 on the WPPSI and a scaled score of 1 on the WPPSI–R. These are some of the dramatic normative changes reflected on the Animal Pegs subtest.

Accounting for Normative Changes on Animal Pegs

What accounts for the normative changes on Animal Pegs? The WPPSI norms indicate that school-age children with above-average ability were already near or at the ceiling level; therefore, few changes could be expected in their performance. School-age children with below-average ability were not at the ceiling level; therefore, they had room for improvement and, in fact, did become more proficient. Perhaps during the years between the initial standardization and the revision, young children have had better nutrition or increased exposure to manipulative experiences at preschool or at home. The normative changes may also be due to unknown differences between the WPPSI–R and WPPSI standardization groups. Overall, the data indicate that children must be more proficient on the WPPSI–R than on the WPPSI Animal Pegs subtest to maintain the same relative scaled-score position.

ADMINISTERING THE WPPSI–R

The general administrative suggestions described for the WISC–III (see Chapter 8) are also appropriate for the WPPSI–R. The two tests have common problems in administration and scoring. Because many subtest names are the same in both scales, you must be careful not to substitute WISC–III directions for WPPSI–R directions or vice versa.

The suggestions in Exhibit 11-2, which supplement those given in other parts of this chapter, and the checklist in Exhibit 11-3 will help you administer the WPPSI–R. You can review the checklist before you administer the test, complete it as you review a videotape of your test administration, or have another student or colleague complete it while observing you administer the test (in person or on videotape). The checklist also can be used by a course instructor, teaching assistant, or colleague to evaluate your test administration. Of course, you should always follow and read from the manual when administering the WPPSI–R (and other tests as well).

Because many important instructions are buried in dense text, in learning how to administer the WPPSI–R you should study and highlight details of when to demonstrate correct verbal or nonverbal responses, when to correct the examinee,

and when to give second trials. If you do not administer the WPPSI–R routinely (and especially if you use the WISC–III often), you will need to review these details before administering the WPPSI–R. Young children will be more sensitive than older children and adolescents to delays during testing.

Physical Abilities Required for the WPPSI–R

The physical abilities children need to take the WPPSI–R are similar to those required to take the WISC–III (see Table 8-18 in Chapter 8). Examinees must have adequate visual-motor skills to manipulate the Performance Scale materials. Alternative ways of administering the WPPSI–R are few, because young children who cannot speak usually will not be able to write their answers and those who cannot hear usually will not be able to read the questions. Still, some of the suggestions for administering the WISC–III to children with physical impairments are applicable to the WPPSI–R (see Chapter 8).

Testing-of-Limits on the WPPSI–R

The general testing-of-limits suggestions presented in Chapter 8 are also useful with the WPPSI–R.

Short Forms of the WPPSI–R

Short forms of the WPPSI–R have the same advantages and disadvantages as those of the WISC–III (see Chapter 8). It is of crucial importance that you never use short forms for classification or selection purposes. Short forms can be used for screening or research studies, however. The information in Table B-8 in Appendix B can help you in the selection of a short form. This table, based on the average of the total standardization group, shows the best WPPSI–R short forms for combinations of two, three, four, and five subtests. Because the short forms of a given length in Table B-8 are mutually interchangeable, you can use clinical or other considerations to select the short form. Tables B-14, B-15, and B-16 in Appendix B give the estimated WPPSI–R Full Scale IQ equivalents for various short-form dyads, triads, and tetrads, respectively.

An inspection of the coefficients in Table B-8 indicates that the four- and five-subtest short-form combinations all have reliability coefficients of .93 or higher and validity coefficients of .91 or higher. These are higher than the coefficients for the shorter combinations. Consequently, if time permits, give a four- or five-subtest combination rather than a two- or three-subtest combination. If you need an estimate of separate verbal and performance abilities, do not include Picture Completion in the short form because it does not load on the Performance factor at all ages. If, however, your goal is simply to administer a general cognitive screening measure, you can use Picture Completion because it is a good measure

---

Exhibit 11-2
Administering the WPPSI–R

1. Complete the top of the record form.
2. Using date of testing and date of birth, calculate the chronological age (CA) and put it in the box provided. On the WPPSI–R, CA must be stated in years, months, and days.
3. Administer the subtests in the order presented in the manual, except in rare circumstances. Do not change the wording on any subtest. Read the directions exactly as shown in the manual. Do not ad lib or provide hints that are not in the manual.
4. Start with the appropriate item on each subtest, and follow the discontinuance criteria. You must know the correct scoring criteria *before* you give the test.
5. Write all responses completely and legibly. Do not use unusual abbreviations. Record time accurately.
6. Question all ambiguous or unscorable responses, writing (Q) after each questioned response.
7. Be patient when working with children in the WPPSI–R age group. Several breaks may be needed during the evaluation.
8. On Comprehension, if a child gives only one reason in response to Question 11, request a second reason.
9. Carefully score each protocol, recheck the scoring, and transfer subtest scores to the Raw Score column on the front of the record form. If you have failed to question a response when you should have and the response is obviously not a 0 response, give the child the most appropriate score.
10. If a subtest was spoiled, write *spoiled* by the subtest total score and on the front of the record form where the raw and scaled scores appear. If for some reason a subtest was not administered, write *NA* in the margin on the record form next to the subtest name and on the front of the record form.
11. Transform raw scores into scaled scores by using Table 25 on pages 170–186 of the WPPSI–R manual. Be sure to use the page of the table that is appropriate for the child's age and the correct row and column for each transformation.
12. Base the Performance Score on the total of the scaled scores on the five standard Performance Scale subtests. Base the Verbal Score on the total of the scaled scores on the five standard Verbal Scale subtests. Do not use Animal

Pegs to compute the Performance Score unless you substitute it for another Performance subtest. Similarly, do not use Sentences to compute the Verbal Score unless you substitute it for another Verbal subtest. Add the Performance Score and the Verbal Score together to obtain the Full Scale Score.
13. If fewer than five subtests were administered in the Performance section or fewer than five subtests in the Verbal section, use the Tellegen and Briggs short-form procedure described in Chapter 8 of this text to compute the IQ.
14. Obtain the IQs from Table 27 in the WPPSI–R manual. Be sure to use the correct section of the table for each of the three IQs—page 188 for the Performance and Verbal IQs and page 189 for the Full Scale IQ. Record the IQs. Next, recheck all of your work. If the IQ was obtained by use of a short form, write *SF* beside the appropriate IQ.
15. Determine the confidence intervals for the Full Scale IQ, Performance Scale IQ, and Verbal Scale IQ, using Table B-1 in Appendix B. Normally, the confidence intervals are not used with the Performance Scale or Verbal Scale IQs unless these are the only IQs reported.
16. Determine the percentile rank and classification for each of the IQs, using Tables BC-1 and BC-2 on the inside back cover of this text.
17. If desired, use the material on page 190 (Table 28) of the WPPSI–R manual to obtain test-age equivalents. They can be placed (in parentheses) in the right-hand margin on the cover page of the record form next to the scaled score. For test-age equivalents above those in the table, use the highest test-age equivalent and a plus sign. For test-age equivalents below those in the table, use the lowest test-age equivalent and a minus sign.
18. In summary, be sure to read directions verbatim, pronounce words clearly, query at the appropriate times, start with the appropriate item, discontinue at the proper place, place items properly before the child, use correct timing, refrain from repeating questions except where the manual permits it, and follow the specific guidelines in the manual for administering the test.

Source: Adapted and revised from material written by M. L. Lewis for the WPPSI. Courtesy of M. L. Lewis.

---

of cognitive functioning. As noted in Chapter 8, we do not recommend the use of reduced-item short forms, such as proposed by Yudin (1966).

Tables B-9 to B-14 in Appendix B show whether the observed scatter (the highest scaled score minus the lowest scaled score) on all the short forms in Table B-8 in the Appendix is (a) significant and (b) within the expected range. Table B-9 indicates that in the two-subtest short form composed of Block Design and Comprehension, a range of 4 points between the two scores indicates a nonchance difference at the .05 level. A range of 6 points occurs in less than

10% of the population and should be considered unusual. Less credence can be placed in the estimated short-form IQ when the scatter is larger than expected.

Choosing Between the WPPSI–R and the WISC–III

The WPPSI–R overlaps with the WISC–III for ages 6-0-0 to 7-3-15 years. Consequently, you must decide which form to use when you test children of these ages. Atkinson (personal

Exhibit 11-3
Administrative Checklist for the WPPSI–R

ADMINISTRATIVE CHECKLIST FOR THE WPPSI–R

Name of examiner: _____   Name of examinee: _____

Date: _____   Name of observer: _____

(Note: *If an item is not applicable, mark NA next to the number.*)

Object Assembly	Circle One	
1. Reads directions verbatim	Yes	No
2. Reads directions clearly	Yes	No
3. Administers all items	Yes	No
4. Uses shield correctly	Yes	No
5. Presents puzzles with pieces arranged properly	Yes	No
6. Records time accurately	Yes	No
7. Gives appropriate prompt once only if child dawdles on items 1 and 2	Yes	No
8. Demonstrates correct arrangement if child fails item 1	Yes	No
9. Does not demonstrate correct arrangement if child fails items 2–6	Yes	No
10. Does not give prompts on items 3–6	Yes	No
11. Discontinues appropriately	Yes	No

Comments: _____

_____

Information	Circle One	
1. Reads items verbatim	Yes	No
2. Reads items clearly	Yes	No
3. Queries at appropriate times	Yes	No
4. Demonstrates correct answer if child fails item 1	Yes	No
5. Does not demonstrate correct answer if child fails items 2–27	Yes	No
6. Records responses	Yes	No
7. Discontinues appropriately	Yes	No

Comments: _____

_____

Geometric Design	Circle One	
1. Reads directions verbatim	Yes	No
2. Reads directions clearly	Yes	No
3. Uses prompts appropriately for items 1–7	Yes	No
4. Gives correct answer if child fails item 1	Yes	No

Geometric Design	Circle One	
5. Does not give correct answer if child fails items 2–16	Yes	No
6. Uses black-lead primary pencils with erasers	Yes	No
7. Uses sheet of cardboard or other firm, smooth surface for items 8–16 if table top is not smooth	Yes	No
8. Folds sheets correctly on items 8–16	Yes	No
9. Queries appropriately	Yes	No
10. Discontinues appropriately	Yes	No

Comments: _____

_____

Comprehension	Circle One	
1. Reads items verbatim	Yes	No
2. Reads items clearly	Yes	No
3. Queries at appropriate times	Yes	No
4. Asks for a second response if child gives only one answer on item 11	Yes	No
5. Gives correct answer if child gives 0- or 1-point responses on items 1 and 2	Yes	No
6. Does not give correct answer if child fails or does not give 2-point responses on items 3–15	Yes	No
7. Records responses	Yes	No
8. Discontinues appropriately	Yes	No

Comments: _____

_____

Block Design	Circle One	
1. Reads directions verbatim	Yes	No
2. Reads directions clearly	Yes	No
3. Begins with appropriate item	Yes	No
4. Places blocks and cards properly	Yes	No
5. Provides demonstration and an explanation on first trial when administering items 1–3 and item 6	Yes	No

(Continued)

Exhibit 11-3 *(Continued)*

Block Design — Circle One

6. Provides demonstration without explanation on first trial when administering items 4, 5, and 7–14 — Yes No
7. Provides demonstration and an explanation on second trial when administering items 6, 8, and 10–14 — Yes No
8. Provides demonstration without explanation on second trial when administering items 1–5, 7, and 9 — Yes No
9. Discontinues appropriately — Yes No

Comments: _____

Arithmetic

1. Reads items verbatim — Yes No
2. Reads items clearly — Yes No
3. Starts with appropriate item — Yes No
4. Uses correct timing — Yes No
5. On items 1–11, proceeds to next item if child shows no sign of responding after 10 or 15 seconds — Yes No
6. Asks for clarification when two responses are given — Yes No
7. Gives credit when child answers correctly only by holding up fingers — Yes No
8. Gives no credit when child holds up correct number of fingers but gives incorrect verbal responses — Yes No
9. Probes on item 11 if child leaves incorrect number of blocks — Yes No
10. Probes on item 14 if child says "one" — Yes No
11. Gives credit for items 1–7 if child passes items 8 and 9 — Yes No
12. Places items properly — Yes No
13. Records responses — Yes No
14. Discontinues appropriately — Yes No

Comments: _____

Mazes

1. Reads directions verbatim — Yes No
2. Reads directions clearly — Yes No
3. Uses red-lead pencil — Yes No

Mazes — Circle One

4. Gives child black-lead primary pencils without erasers — Yes No
5. Begins with appropriate item — Yes No
6. Exposes sheet properly — Yes No
7. Gives correct demonstration — Yes No
8. Provides "cautions" correctly — Yes No
9. Uses correct timing — Yes No
10. Gives credit for Mazes 3B and 4B if Mazes 3A and 4A have been passed — Yes No
11. Discontinues appropriately — Yes No

Comments: _____

Vocabulary

1. Reads directions verbatim — Yes No
2. Reads directions clearly — Yes No
3. Pronounces words clearly — Yes No
4. Queries at appropriate times — Yes No
5. Gives correct answer if child misses item 1 — Yes No
6. Does not give correct answer if child misses items 2–25 — Yes No
7. Records responses — Yes No
8. Discontinues appropriately — Yes No

Comments: _____

Picture Completion

1. Reads directions verbatim — Yes No
2. Reads directions clearly — Yes No
3. Reads words clearly — Yes No
4. Begins with appropriate item — Yes No
5. Places booklet properly — Yes No
6. Gives child at least 15 seconds to respond to items 1 and 2 — Yes No
7. Gives child at least 30 seconds to respond to items 2–28 — Yes No
8. Gives correct answer if child gives incorrect answers on items 1–4 — Yes No
9. Gives the prompt "Yes, but what is missing?" no more than twice for items 4–28 — Yes No

(Continued)

Exhibit 11-3 *(Continued)*

Picture Completion	Circle One	
10. Gives the prompt "A part is missing in the picture. What is it that is missing?" no more than twice for items 4–28	Yes	No
11. Inquires correctly on items 16, 17, 22, and 28 when specified responses are given	Yes	No
12. Discontinues appropriately	Yes	No

Comments: _____

_____

Similarities

	Circle One	
1. Reads directions verbatim	Yes	No
2. Reads directions clearly	Yes	No
3. Reads items verbatim and clearly	Yes	No
4. Queries at appropriate times	Yes	No
5. Gives correct answer if child gives incorrect answers on items 1, 7, 13, and 14	Yes	No
6. Does not give correct answer if child gives incorrect answers on items 2–6, 8–12, and 15–20	Yes	No
7. Gives an example of a 2-point response if child gives a 1-point response on item 13	Yes	No
8. Queries appropriately	Yes	No
9. Records responses	Yes	No
10. Discontinues appropriately	Yes	No

Comments: _____

_____

Animal Pegs

	Circle One	
1. Reads directions verbatim	Yes	No
2. Reads directions clearly	Yes	No
3. Demonstrates tasks clearly	Yes	No
4. Uses correct timing	Yes	No
5. Gives correct prompt or caution when child hesitates after completing first row	Yes	No
6. Gives correct prompt or caution when child loses the sense of the task	Yes	No
7. Gives correct prompt or caution no more than twice when child selects pegs of one color and completes that color before starting another	Yes	No

Animal Pegs

	Circle One	
8. Gives correct prompt or caution when child removes pegs after completing one row and starts over again	Yes	No

Comments: _____

_____

Sentences

	Circle One	
1. Reads directions verbatim	Yes	No
2. Reads directions clearly	Yes	No
3. Reads sentences verbatim	Yes	No
4. Reads sentences slowly, distinctly, and with natural intonation	Yes	No
5. Reads sentences at rate of about 2 syllables per second	Yes	No
6. Starts with correct item	Yes	No
7. Gives correct answer if child fails items 1, 2, and 6	Yes	No
8. Does not give correct answer if child fails items 3–5 and 7–12	Yes	No
9. Records responses	Yes	No
10. Discontinues appropriately	Yes	No

Comments: _____

_____

Overall Evaluation of Test Administration

Circle One: Excellent Good Average Poor Very Poor

Overall strengths: _____

_____

_____

Overall weaknesses: _____

_____

_____

Other comments: _____

_____

_____

_____

communication, January 1992) suggests that the WPPSI–R is a better choice for children with below-average ability, the WISC–III is a better choice for children with above-average ability, and either test is adequate for children with average ability. (Chapter 8 discusses the reasons for his recommendations.) However, research is still needed to determine which test provides the most reliable and valid scores at different ages and ability levels.

INTRODUCTION TO THE WPPSI–R SUBTESTS

The following sections look at the 12 WPPSI–R subtests. For each subtest, a brief description is presented, followed by a discussion of the rationale, factor analytic findings, reliability and correlational highlights, and administrative and interpretive considerations. The factor analytic findings discussed in this chapter are based on the principal-components analysis with varimax rotation, described earlier in the chapter, that we conducted on the WPPSI–R standardization data obtained from the WPPSI–R manual. Similarly, the reliability and correlational findings reported in this chapter are based on the WPPSI–R standardization data presented in the WPPSI–R manual.

Table D-3 in Appendix D summarizes (a) the abilities purportedly measured by each WPPSI–R subtest, (b) background factors influencing performance, (c) implications of high and low subtest scaled scores, and (d) instructional implications. Table D-3 deserves careful study and is a useful reference for report writing.

Recognize that the standard administration of all subtests on both the Verbal Scale and the Performance Scale requires the child to hear, pay attention, listen, understand directions, and retain the directions while solving problems. In addition, all Performance Scale subtests require the child to have adequate vision, and some Performance Scale subtests also require the child to have adequate motor skills.

The best estimates of abilities are provided by the Full Scale IQ, followed by the Verbal Scale and Performance Scale IQs, combinations of subtests, and, finally, individual subtests. For example, the Verbal Scale IQ, derived from a combination of five Verbal Scale subtests, yields more accurate information about an examinee's verbal skills than does a single Verbal Scale subtest, such as Vocabulary. Similarly, the Performance Scale IQ, derived from a combination of five Performance Scale subtests, yields more accurate information about an examinee's nonverbal skills than does a single Performance Scale subtest, such as Picture Completion.

As you read about each subtest, you will find questions to guide you in your test administration. Answering these questions will help you evaluate and interpret the child's performance. In addition to the child's scores, always consider the quality of the child's responses and the pattern of her or his successes and failures. Recording the examinee's responses carefully, along with pertinent behavioral observations, will also help you evaluate the test results, especially when you review the test protocol later. An accurate record is also important if you need to testify at an administrative hearing or in court or if other professionals need to review your findings.

In administering the subtests, use the exact wording of the questions or items; never add explanations or give synonyms. The same guideline holds for the directions that introduce each subtest. Deviate from the instructions listed in the manual only when common sense dictates that you say something that is needed (e.g., "Tell me when you're through"). The aim is to administer the test in a standardized manner. In calculating an IQ, never include a subtest that was spoiled (e.g., through improper timing or mistakes in administration). You need to review Chapter 7 before you administer the WPPSI–R.

Scoring responses to some of the Wechsler subtests—such as Vocabulary, Comprehension, and Similarities—can be challenging. Although the WPPSI–R manual provides adequate guidelines, the guidelines cannot cover every contingency. Therefore, you sometimes will have to use judgment in scoring responses, especially borderline ones. Always query unclear or borderline responses unless the manual says otherwise. Do the best job possible with the scoring guidelines given in the manual. However, when you have any doubt about the scoring of a response, you are encouraged to consult a colleague.

As noted in Chapter 7, *if you want to conduct testing-of-limits, always do so after you administer the entire test following standard procedures.* Testing-of-limits is useful for (a) following up leads about the child's functioning obtained during the standard administration, (b) testing clinical hypotheses, and (c) evaluating whether additional cues or extra time will help the child solve problems. As noted in Chapter 7, *testing-of-limits may invalidate repeated evaluations and should be used cautiously.*

This text, unlike the WPPSI–R manual, uses the term "mental retardation" instead of the term "intellectually deficient" to describe examinees who may be significantly below average in their intellectual ability. "Mental retardation" is the term used in *DSM-IV* and by the American Association on Mental Retardation. Consequently, we believe that "mental retardation" is the preferred term for describing examinees who are functioning two or more standard deviations below the mean.

Let's now turn to a discussion of each of the 12 WPPSI–R subtests.

OBJECT ASSEMBLY

Object Assembly requires the child to put three rectangular pieces into their appropriate recesses in a frame or to put jigsaw pieces together to form common objects: a flower (four pieces), a car (three pieces), a teddy bear (four pieces), a face (five pieces), and a dog (four pieces).

Rationale

The rationale presented for WISC–III Object Assembly also applies to WPPSI–R Object Assembly (see Chapter 9). However, there are some subtle differences in the items on the two tests. One difference is that the first WPPSI–R Object Assembly item is a form-board item and does not require the child to make a meaningful picture; there are no form-board items on the WISC–III. A second difference is that the WISC–III items have more pieces than do the WPPSI–R items. A third difference is that one WISC–III item has a longer time limit (180 seconds) than any WPPSI–R items.

Factor Analytic Findings

Object Assembly is a fair measure of g (33% of its variance may be attributed to g), and it contributes substantially to the Performance factor (*Mdn* loading = .70). Specificity is inadequate at all ages.

Reliability and Correlational Highlights

Object Assembly is a marginally reliable subtest (r_{xx} = .63), with reliability coefficients below .70 at seven of the nine age groups. Two exceptions are at ages 4 years and 6 years, where the reliability coefficients are both .70. It correlates better with Block Design (r = .52) than with any of the other subtests. It has a moderate correlation with the Full Scale (r = .50) and the Performance Scale (r = .56) and a moderately low correlation with the Verbal Scale (r = .37).

Administrative Suggestions

Here are some administrative suggestions for the Object Assembly subtest.

Background Considerations

- Place all the pieces right side up in the disarranged pattern specified in the diagram on the Object Assembly Layout Shield. Place the pieces close to the child so that the child does not waste time reaching for them.
- All items are timed. Items 1 to 4 have a maximum of 120 seconds, and items 5 and 6 have a maximum of 150 seconds.
- As soon as you complete the directions for each item, begin timing.
- Observe time limits carefully on each item and record the elapsed time precisely, because the child receives additional points for quick execution of items 3 to 6.
- Be sure that the child does not see the pages of the WPPSI–R manual containing pictures of the correctly assembled objects.
- Use the Object Assembly Layout Shield not only to set up the individual puzzle parts but also to shield the WPPSI–R manual.

- If the child turns over any piece, promptly and unobtrusively turn it right side up.
- As in other subtests, you may have to ask the child to tell you when he or she is finished by saying "Tell me when you are through." You may need to give this instruction on items 4 to 6, even though the directions in the WPPSI–R manual do not say you should do so.
- On items 1 and 2, if the child does not appear to understand the need to work quickly (e.g., dawdles or seems to be playing with pieces), say, "Now hurry!" You can give this instruction once during item 1 and once during item 2, but not on any other items.
- Record the number of pieces (referred to as "cuts" in the manual) completed within the time limit.
- Stop timing when the child finishes. If you are not certain whether the child is finished, ask him or her.
- If the child is still working on a puzzle and the time limit has been reached, it is permissible to allow the child to continue. However, you must record the child's arrangement at the expiration of the time limit.

Starting Considerations

- There is no sample item, but the first item is demonstrated before the child attempts it.
- All children begin with the first item.

Scoring Considerations

- The maximum score for the rectangles (item 1) is 3 points on each trial; for the flowers, it is 4 points; for the car, it is 5 points (2 points plus 3 time-bonus points); for the teddy bear (item 4), it is 6 points (3 points plus 3 time-bonus points for perfect assembly); for the face (item 5), it is 8 points (5 points plus 3 time-bonus points for perfect assembly); and for the dog (item 6), it is 6 points (3 points plus 3 time-bonus points).
- Give credit for any correctly joined parts in an incomplete assembly at the expiration of the time limit.
- There are special scoring rules for item 1. When trial 2 is administered because the child did not obtain a perfect score on trial 1, do not give any credit for trial 2 even if it is completed correctly. Trial 2 is administered only to help the child understand the task requirements.

Discontinuance Considerations

- The subtest is discontinued after 0 points are earned on three consecutive items.

Interpretive Suggestions

The interpretive suggestions for the WISC–III Object Assembly are relevant for the WPPSI–R Object Assembly. When you perform a profile analysis, take into account that the full range of scaled scores from 1 to 19 is available only at ages 3 to 5¼ years (see Table 11-9).

AFTER HIS THIRD STOPWATCH TURNS UP
MISSING, THEODORE DECIDES TO TAKE
DRASTIC MEASURES.

Courtesy of Herman Zielinski.

GEOMETRIC DESIGN

Geometric Design has two parts. In the first part, the child makes visual discriminations; in the second part, the child copies designs with a pencil. The subtest contains 16 items. Items 1 to 7 require visual recognition and discrimination, and items 8 to 16 require visual-motor coordination.

Rationale

The first part of Geometric Design (items 1 to 7) involves perceptual recognition and discrimination ability. The child must match a target figure with one of the four figures below it. Because attention is also probably involved, an impulsive child who makes quick, careless choices may perform poorly, especially if the child fails to scan all four options.

The second part of the subtest (items 8 to 16) involves perceptual and visual-motor ability, visual construction, and eye-hand coordination. Previous experience with paper and pencil can help the child succeed on this part of the subtest. Adequate reproduction of the designs requires fine motor development, perceptual discrimination ability, and ability to integrate perceptual and motor processes. The child must shift attention between the stimulus and the reproduction and must monitor her or his performance.

The extent to which perceptual recognition and discrimination abilities are forerunners of visual-motor skills is not known. Perhaps there are two (or more) distinct processes

measured by the two different parts of Geometric Design; research investigating this hypothesis is needed.

Factor Analytic Findings

Geometric Design is a fair measure of g (37% of its variance may be attributed to g), and it contributes substantially to the Performance factor (*Mdn* loading = .72). Specificity is ample or adequate at ages 3, 3½, 4½, 6, and 7 years and inadequate at ages 4, 5, 5½, and 6½ years.

Reliability and Correlational Highlights

Geometric Design is a relatively reliable subtest (r_{xx} = .79), with reliability coefficients above .70 at eight of the nine age groups. The one exception is at age 7 years, where the reliability coefficient is .68. It correlates better with Block Design (r = .49) than with any of the other subtests. It has a moderate correlation with the Full Scale (r = .54) and the Performance Scale (r = .58) and a moderately low correlation with the Verbal Scale (r = .41).

Administrative Suggestions

Here are some administrative suggestions for the Geometric Design subtest.

Background Considerations

- Although there are no time limits, remove each item after about 30 seconds if the child is unable to cope with the task or is unable to produce a recognizable copy.
- If the child seems hesitant on Part 1, you may give the prompt "Show me which one."
- If the child seems reluctant to try Part 2, encourage the child by saying "Do the best you can."
- On item 12, which contains two designs, ask, "Are you finished?" if the child draws only one of the designs.
- Record on the Record Form the child's response to item 17.

Starting Considerations

- The child should have a smooth drawing surface for Part 2, the drawing part.
- All children begin with item 1.

Scoring Considerations

- Items 1 to 7 are scored 0 or 1 point; items 8 to 16 are scored 0, 3, 4, 6, 8, or 12 points.
- The WPPSI–R manual presents detailed guidelines for scoring items 8 to 16, which will require careful study.
- If the child makes two attempts at drawing a design, only score the second attempt.
- Although previous research indicated that the WPPSI Geometric Design was difficult to score (e.g., Morsbach, McGoldrick, & Younger, 1978; Sattler, 1976), research

described in the WPPSI–R manual suggests that the new scoring rules have improved scoring accuracy. Other research, however, indicates that Geometric Design is still difficult to score (Whitten, Slate, Jones, & Shine, 1994). The major scoring difficulty is that as many as 12 different criteria must be evaluated on a single design in arriving at a score.

Discontinuance Considerations

- The subtest is discontinued after three consecutive failures on Part 1 and after two consecutive failures on Part 2. Administer Part 2 even when Part 1 has been discontinued.

Interpretive Suggestions

Consider the following questions:

- How does the child hold the pencil?
- In which hand does the child hold the pencil?
- Does the child use one hand to hold the paper in place and the other hand to draw the designs?
- Does the child understand the task?
- Are the child's drawings done with extreme care and deliberation or impulsively?
- Does the child display tremor?
- Are the child's drawings excessively dark, excessively light, or just about right?
- Does the child seem overly anxious?
- Does the child trace the design with a finger before drawing it?
- Does the child count the loops or sides of figures before drawing a design?
- Are the designs drawn haphazardly?
- Does the child glance at the design briefly and then draw it from memory?
- Does the child rotate the design card or paper (or both)?
- Does the child make frequent erasures? If so, on what figures or parts of figures (e.g., curves, angulations, overlapping parts, or open figures)?
- Does the child's speed increase or decrease as the subtest proceeds?
- What part of a design does the child draw first?
- In what direction does the child move in copying the designs? For example, does the child draw the designs from top down, bottom up, inside out, or outside in?
- Does the child change direction of movement from design to design?
- Does the child use sketching?
- Does the child show unusual blocking on any design?
- Does the child start over making the designs? If so, how many times does this happen?
- How much space does the child use to draw the design? For example, is the drawing approximately the same size as the original or greatly reduced or expanded?
- How accurate are the child's drawings? For example, are the designs well executed or barely recognizable?

- If the child makes errors, what kind are they? For example, are the errors associated with straightness of lines; orientation of lines; gaps in lines; gaps at intersections, closure points, or corners; overshoots; curved or wavy lines; vertical lines; circles; triangles; oval figures; square figures; or relationships between figures? Does the child recognize any errors? Does the child express dissatisfaction over poorly executed drawings?
- Is the child persistent?
- Is the child bored with the task?
- Does the child talk to himself or herself as the subtest proceeds?
- How does the child's behavior on Part 1 compare with his or her behavior on Part 2? For example, is the child equally at ease on both parts, or is the child more anxious on one part than on the other? What other differences in behavior are present, if any?
- What comments does the child make about the designs?
- Does the child show signs of fatigue?
- Does the child need encouragement to complete the drawings?
- Does the child spend approximately the same amount of time on each design?
- How long did the child need to complete the task?
- Was the amount of time taken by the child excessively long or unusually short?
- Does the child express satisfaction with the end product?

You do not need the special copyrighted blank paper from the test publisher to administer Geometric Design. You can fold an ordinary sheet of paper in half, writing on each half of the paper the number of the design and "top" and "bottom" (relative to the child's frame of reference). Keep the paper folded for the second design so that there is no possible distraction from the first drawing.

Low scores on the Geometric Design subtest may indicate poor perceptual-motor ability, deficient eye-hand coordination, or developmental immaturity. Even some high-functioning young children may have difficulty obtaining high scores, because the motor ability needed for successful performance (the ability to grasp a pencil appropriately, make contact with paper, and draw appropriate lines) is associated with maturational processes that may be independent of the development of cognitive processes.

When you do a profile analysis, take into account that the full range of scaled scores from 1 to 19 is available only at ages 4¼ to 4½ years (see Table 11-9).

BLOCK DESIGN

Block Design requires the child to reproduce 14 designs using flat one- or two-colored tiles. The child follows a model, sometimes assembled out of sight, to construct the first seven items and follows pictures of designs to construct the last seven items.

Rationale

The rationale described for WISC–III Block Design also applies to WPPSI–R Block Design (see Chapter 9).

Factor Analytic Findings

Block Design is a fair measure of g (47% of its variance may be attributed to g), and it contributes substantially to the Performance factor (*Mdn* loading = .76). Specificity is ample or adequate at ages 3, 3½, 4, 4½, 5, 6, and 7 years and inadequate at ages 5½ and 6½ years.

Reliability and Correlational Highlights

Block Design is a reliable subtest (r_{xx} = .85), with reliability coefficients above .70 at all of the age groups. It correlates better with Picture Completion ($r = .46$), Arithmetic ($r = .46$), and Mazes ($r = .45$) than with any of the other subtests. It has a moderate correlation with the Full Scale ($r = .62$) and the Performance Scale ($r = .64$) and a moderately low correlation with the Verbal Scale ($r = .48$).

Administrative Suggestions

Here are some administrative suggestions for the Block Design subtest.

Background Considerations

- Study the directions carefully *before* you give the subtest, because the complicated directions for demonstrations and second trials are too long to read or even review while testing. This is especially important if you do not give the subtest frequently.
- The area on your desk that you use to administer Block Design should be clear of all other blocks and materials.
- The child needs to be seated parallel to the edge of the table.
- For Designs 1 to 5, you use six blocks that are solid red on one side and solid white on the other; for Designs 6 to 14, you use eight blocks that are solid red on one side and half red and half white on the other side.
- For Designs 1 to 8, the child works directly from block models that you construct; for Designs 9 to 14, the child works from pictures of block designs.
- For Designs 1 to 8, construct the designs behind the Layout Shield, which is positioned about 8 to 10 inches from the child. After you set up the block pattern, remove the shield.
- When you set up a design, the top edge of the design should face the child and the lower edge should face you.
- After you set up a design, move the block model to a position approximately 7 inches from the child's edge of the table.
- The placement of the model is "a little to the left of a line perpendicular to the child's body if the child is right-

handed and to the child's right if the child is left-handed" (Wechsler, 1989, p. 54).
- When you present the pictures of block patterns for Designs 9 to 14, the unbound edge of the Stimulus Booklet should be toward the child.
- All items are timed. The time limits are 30 seconds for Designs 1 to 6, 45 seconds for Design 7, and 75 seconds for Designs 8 to 14.
- Begin timing after you give the last word of the directions.
- Stop timing when the child is obviously finished, even if the child does not tell you that a design is finished.
- There are two trials for every design. If the child passes trial 1 of a design, go to the next design. On Designs 1 to 7 and Design 9, if the child fails trial 1, demonstrate the correct solution and then go to trial 2. On Design 8 and Designs 10 to 14, there are no demonstrations; if the child fails trial 1, go to trial 2.
- Ask, "Is that right?" if the child leaves a definite gap in the design but positions the block correctly.
- Only correct the first two rotations that occur.

Starting Considerations

- Children younger than 6 years begin with item 1, while children 6 years and older begin with item 6.
- If a child aged 6 years or older passes Design 6 on the first trial, go to Design 7 and give the child full credit for Designs 1 to 5.
- If a child aged 6 years or older fails the first trial of Design 6, administer the second trial. Then administer the preceding items in *reverse order* until two consecutive items are passed on the first trial; at that point, go to Design 7.

Scoring Considerations

- An item is failed only when the child fails both trials.
- When you administer items in reverse order, give credit for any items not administered that precede two consecutive successes.
- On items 1 through 7, 2 points are given for successful performance on trial 1, 1 point for successful performance on trial 2, and 0 points for failure on both trials. On items 8 to 14, the child receives 3 points for correct completion and 4 additional time-bonus points.
- On the WPPSI–R, unlike the WISC–III, rotations are corrected twice, but not penalized unless they are complete reversals.

Discontinuance Considerations

- The subtest is discontinued after three consecutive failures.

Interpretive Suggestions

The interpretive suggestions for the WISC–III Block Design subtest are relevant for the WPPSI–R Block Design subtest (see Chapter 9). When you perform a profile analysis, take into account that the full range of scaled scores from 1 to 19 is available only at ages 5 to 6¼ years (see Table 11-9).

MAZES

Mazes requires the child to solve paper-and-pencil mazes that differ in level of complexity. Seven of the 11 mazes are similar to those on the WISC–III. Mazes 1 to 4 are horizontal mazes, and Mazes 5 to 11 are box mazes. Mazes is a standard subtest in the WPPSI–R, whereas in the WISC–III it is an optional subtest.

Rationale

The rationale presented for WISC–III Mazes also applies to WPPSI–R Mazes (see Chapter 9).

Factor Analytic Findings

Mazes is a fair measure of g (32% of its variance may be attributed to g), and it contributes substantially to the Performance factor (*Mdn* loading = .69). Specificity is ample at ages 3, 3½, 4, 4½, 6, and 7 years and inadequate at ages 5, 5½, and 6½ years.

Reliability and Correlational Highlights

Mazes is a relatively reliable subtest (r_{xx} = .77), with reliability coefficients above .70 at eight of the nine age groups. The one exception is at age 7 years, where the reliability coefficient is .65. It correlates better with Block Design (r = .45) and Geometric Design (r = .43) than with any of the other subtests. It has a moderate correlation with the Full Scale (r = .50) and the Performance Scale (r = .54) and a moderately low correlation with the Verbal Scale (r = .38).

Administrative Suggestions

Here are some administrative suggestions for the Mazes subtest.

Background Considerations

- The Mazes subtest is contained in a separate booklet.
- Present each maze separately.
- Expose only one page of the booklet at a time.
- A small E, which appears on the page, will help you orient the page.
- Administer the subtest on a smooth drawing surface.
- Use a no. 2 red-lead pencil to demonstrate the sample item, and give a no. 2 black-lead pencil without an eraser to the child.
- Write the child's name, the date, and your name in the space provided on the Mazes Booklet.
- You may need to use several cautions, specified on page 69 of the manual, on the first maze that you administer.

- In some cases, you may need to give cautions to the child on later mazes, in addition to those given on the first maze.
- You can hold the child's pencil on the first item if you see the child having trouble.
- Time each maze.
- Give Mazes 1 to 7 a maximum of 45 seconds; Maze 8, 60 seconds; Maze 9, 75 seconds; and Mazes 10 and 11, 135 seconds.
- Allow the child to finish each maze (especially if the child wants to or is about to complete it), regardless of the errors the child made, because interruptions may generate anxiety and confusion and leave the child with a sense of failure.

Starting Considerations

- Children below the age of 5 years begin with Maze 1A, and those 5 years of age and older begin with Maze 3A.
- If a child aged 5 years or older passes Mazes 3A and 3B, give him or her full credit for the first two mazes and proceed to Maze 4.
- If a child aged 5 years or older does not pass Mazes 3A and 3B, administer the first two mazes before administering Maze 4, unless the discontinuance criterion has been met. In this case, you must use the directions for children aged 3 to 4 years.

Scoring Considerations

- Scoring Mazes requires considerable judgment. You must become familiar with special terms, such as "blind alley," "clear crossing of a wall," "overshoot," "false exit," and "false start," which designate specific features of the mazes or of the child's performance. Likewise, you must point out these features to the child in the sample item.
- Consider items 1 to 4 failed only when the child fails both trials.
- Some examiners make a considerable number of scoring errors on Mazes (Whitten et al., 1994). The major error is the failure to add points for Maze 3B and Maze 4B when the child makes no errors on Maze 3A and Maze 4A.

Discontinuance Considerations

- The subtest is discontinued after two consecutive failures.

Interpretive Suggestions

The interpretive suggestions for WISC–III Mazes are relevant for WPPSI–R Mazes (see Chapter 9). Be sure to study the child's failures. Notice, for example, whether there is a pattern to the failures and whether there are signs of tremor or other visual-motor difficulties. Evaluating the child's failures on Mazes may help you form hypotheses about the child's performance. Let's look at the examples in Figure 11-3. In Example 1, the girl did not complete the maze, but made no errors as far as her performance went. In Example 2, the boy entered a blind alley, thereby making an error. In the first

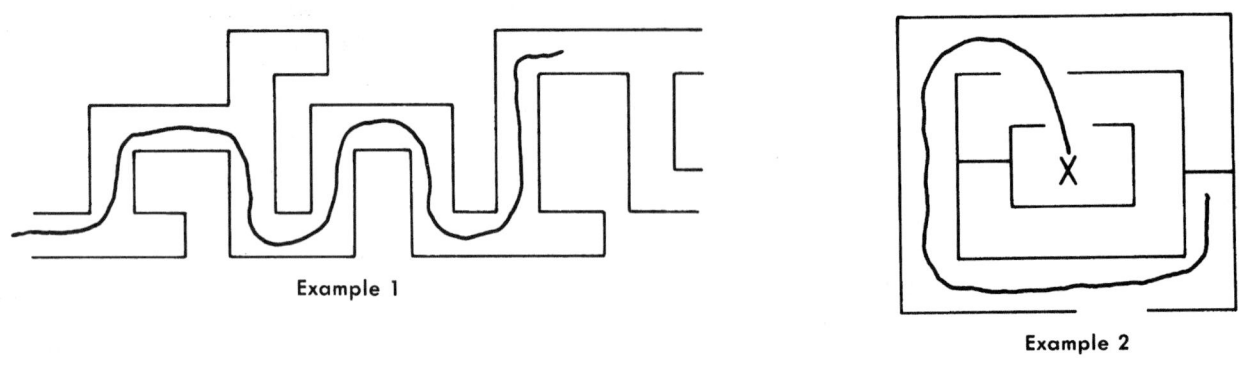

Example 1

Example 2

Figure 11-3. Two examples of failures on the Mazes subtest. From the Wechsler Preschool and Primary Scale of Intelligence–Revised. Copyright © 1989 by The Psychological Corporation. Reproduced by permission. All rights reserved.

case you should wonder why the girl stopped short before reaching the goal. Perhaps she has limited perseverance, perhaps she takes things for granted and assumes that others will understand her, or perhaps she is easily distracted. The second performance may be that of an impulsive child who works well until he is about to complete a task and then is unable to do so correctly. These hypotheses are tentative, subject to modification after study of the child's performance on the entire subtest, other subtests on the test, and other data such as background information.

When the entire test is finished, you might want to return to Mazes to inquire into the child's performance on any mazes of interest. For example, you could ask, "Why did you go that way?"

When you perform a profile analysis, take into account that the full range of scaled scores from 1 to 19 is available only at ages 4 to 6¼ years (see Table 11-9).

IT'S FOR YOU

Courtesy of David Wilcox.

PICTURE COMPLETION

Picture Completion requires the child to identify the single most important missing element in each of 28 drawings of common objects, such as a doll, car, and jacket. Unfortunately, 10 of the 28 items are also on the WISC–III. The child's task is to name or point to the essential missing portion of the incomplete picture.

Rationale

The rationale described for WISC–III Picture Completion also applies to WPPSI–R Picture Completion (see Chapter 9).

Factor Analytic Findings

Picture Completion is a fair measure of g (47% of its variance may be attributed to g), and it contributes moderately to the Performance factor (*Mdn* loading = .55) and the Verbal factor (*Mdn* loading = .41). Specificity is ample at all ages.

Reliability and Correlational Highlights

Picture Completion is a reliable subtest (r_{xx} = .85), with reliability coefficients above .70 at all of the age groups. It correlates better with Information (r = .47), Block Design (r = .46), and Arithmetic (r = .45) than with any of the other subtests. It has a moderate correlation with the Full Scale (r = .61), the Performance Scale (r = .54), and the Verbal Scale (r = .54).

Administrative Suggestions

Here are some administrative suggestions for the Picture Completion subtest.

Background Considerations

- Picture Completion is easy to administer. Simply leave the booklet flat on the table and turn over the cards to show each consecutive picture.
- Show the pictures one at a time.
- Allow the child to turn the pages in the test booklet if the child wants to and you are sure that you can set the pace.
- Although there are no exact time limits, allow items 1 and 2 a minimum of 15 seconds, and items 3 to 28 a minimum of 30 seconds. This procedure differs from that for the WISC–III, where there is a maximum time limit of 20 seconds.
- Record the amount of time taken by the child to make each response.
- You can give several different prompts on the first three items when the meaning of the child's response is ambiguous, when the child gives the name of the picture, or when the child mentions a part that is off the picture.
- You can give some prompts only twice on items 4 to 28 ("Yes, but what is missing?" and "A part is missing in the picture. What is it that is missing?").
- There are also prompts you must give on items 1 to 4 if the child does not respond by the end of the minimum exposure time.
- There are specific prompts for items 16, 17, 22, and 28.

Starting Considerations

- Children younger than 5 years of age begin with the sample item, and those 5 years of age and older begin with item 3.
- If a child aged 5 years or older fails item 3, administer the sample item and then item 4.

Scoring Considerations

- When a child aged 5 years or older passes item 3, give credit for the first two items.
- A verbal response is not needed for credit.
- A verbal response that is a synonym for the correct answer receives credit.
- A correct pointing response accompanied by an incorrect verbal response is scored as a failure.

Discontinuance Considerations

- The subtest is discontinued after five consecutive failures.

Interpretive Suggestions

The interpretive suggestions for the WISC–III Picture Completion subtest are relevant for the WPPSI–R Picture Completion subtest (see Chapter 9). On the WPPSI–R Picture Completion subtest, however, a child may have difficulty in identifying the missing part of some pictures (e.g., the face item and the suit jacket item) because the manner in which the pictures are drawn may be confusing. The factor analytic results suggest that verbal reasoning may help the child to detect the missing part of the pictures.

When you perform a profile analysis, take into account that the full range of scaled scores from 1 to 19 is available only at ages 4¼ to 6½ years (see Table 11-9).

ANIMAL PEGS

Animal Pegs, which is a substitute for WISC–III Coding and is known as Animal House on the WPPSI, requires the child to place colored pegs in holes on a board according to a key at the top of the board. It is a timed subtest (maximum time of 5 minutes) that places a premium on speed. A perfect score obtained in 9 seconds or less is awarded 70 raw-score points, and one obtained in 5 minutes is awarded 12 raw-score points.

Rationale

Animal Pegs requires the child to associate signs with symbols. Memory, attention span, goal awareness, concentration, finger and manual dexterity, and learning ability may all be involved in the child's performance. Research with WPPSI Animal House indicates that it correlated significantly with a measure of learning ($r = .71$) and a measure of motor skill ($r = -.69$) in a sample of 36 children 5 to 6 years old (Sherman, Chinsky, & Maffeo, 1974). The latter correlation was negative because motor skill was measured via reaction time, with lower reaction times indicating better motor skill. The combination of learning and motor skill scores led to a better prediction of Animal House scores than did the learning scores by themselves. Thus, Animal Pegs likely involves both motor and learning abilities.

Factor Analytic Findings

Animal Pegs is a fair measure of g (27% of its variance may be attributed to g), and it contributes moderately to the Performance factor (*Mdn* loading = .50). Specificity is ample at ages 3, 5, 6, 6½, and 7 years and inadequate at ages 3½, 4, 4½, and 5½ years.

Reliability and Correlational Highlights

Animal Pegs is marginally reliable (test-retest $r_{xx} = .66$). However, this reliability coefficient is only an estimate of the reliability of the subtest, because the WPPSI–R manual reports only one test-retest reliability coefficient based on a combined sample of 175 children in two age groups (36 to 59 months and 60 to 87 months). (All tables in this text use a reliability coefficient of .66 for Animal Pegs.) The subtest correlates better with Block Design ($r = .37$) than with any of the other subtests. It has a moderately low correlation with the Full Scale ($r = .45$), the Performance Scale ($r = .43$), and the Verbal Scale ($r = .37$).

Administrative Suggestions

Here are some administrative suggestions for the Animal Pegs subtest.

Background Considerations

- Note whether the child is right-handed or left-handed before administering Animal Pegs. Knowing this will help you decide where to place the box of pegs before the child.
- Encourage the child to use her or his preferred hand.
- If the child stops working after the first row, tell the child to "Go on to the next line." Count these instructions as part of the 5-minute time limit.
- If the child skips around, filling in peg symbols for the same animal first, tell the child to proceed in order: "Do them one right after the other. Don't skip any." You can give this instruction only twice.
- If the child does not understand the need to work quickly, say, "Now hurry!" Again, you can give this instruction only twice.
- Animal Pegs is an optional subtest, so you do not have to administer it. If you have time, though, you should administer the subtest because it provides useful information about important developmental skills.

Starting Considerations

- All children begin the same way.

Scoring Considerations

- The raw score is based on time and the number of errors plus omissions (see pages 168-169 in the WPPSI–R manual).
- If you administer Animal Pegs as the sixth Performance Scale subtest, do not use it to compute the IQ.

Discontinuance Considerations

- The subtest is discontinued after 5 minutes or when the child has finished—whichever comes first.

Interpretive Suggestions

Consider the following questions:

- How does the child proceed with the task?
- Does the child use one hand or both hands to place the pegs?
- If the child uses one hand, which hand is it?
- What is the quality of the child's finger and manual dexterity?
- Is the child impulsive or meticulous?
- Does the child seem overly anxious?
- Does the child display tremor?
- Does the child's speed increase or decrease as the subtest proceeds?
- Is the child penalized for lack of speed, for inaccuracy, or for both?
- Does the child understand the task?
- Does the child take out the pegs after completing a row?

"I feel pretty silly putting pegs in holes when I have a personal computer at home."

Copyright © 1988 by Wm. Hoest Enterprises, Inc. Reprinted with permission.

- Does the child understand and proceed correctly after being given an explanation?
- Does the child check each item with the key row, or does the child seem to remember the color pairings (e.g., not look up at the key at the top of the page)?
- Does the child recheck every peg before moving on to the next one?
- Does the child work smoothly and in an orderly fashion, or does the child seem confused at times and have difficulty finding his or her place?
- Does the child put in pegs under one type of animal rather than working across a row?
- Is the child aware of any errors?
- Do the child's errors occur in some regular manner?
- How does the child react to making errors?
- Is the child persistent?
- Does the child need repeated urging to continue the task?
- Is the child bored with the task?
- Does the child hold the pegs in an appropriate way?
- Does the child stop in the middle of the task, stretch, sigh, look around, and talk?

Answers to the above questions will provide information about the child's attention span, method of working, and other behaviors. An increase in speed, coupled with correct performance, suggests that the child is adjusting well to the task. A decrease in speed, coupled with incorrect performance, suggests that the child may be showing fatigue. Carefully follow the scoring procedures provided on page 103 of the WPPSI–R manual.

Low scores on the Animal Pegs subtest may indicate visual-motor coordination difficulties, distractibility, visual defects, poor short-term visual memory, or lethargy.

When you perform a profile analysis, take into account that the full range of scaled scores from 1 to 19 is available at nearly all ages of the test—from 3¼ to 7 years (see Table 11-9).

INFORMATION

Information has 27 questions that sample a broad range of knowledge about factual material. Unfortunately, three of the questions are exactly the same as in the WISC–III, and one is essentially the same. Most items require the child to provide a simply stated fact or facts.

Rationale

The rationale presented for WISC–III Information also applies to WPPSI–R Information (see Chapter 9). The WPPSI–R questions, however, appear to assess that part of the child's knowledge of the environment that the child gains from the home environment rather than from formal education.

Factor Analytic Findings

Information is the best measure of g in the test (63% of its variance may be attributed to g), and it contributes substantially to the Verbal factor (*Mdn* loading = .79). Specificity is adequate at ages 3½ and 4½ years and inadequate at ages 3, 4, 5½, 6, 6½, and 7 years.

Reliability and Correlational Highlights

Information is a reliable subtest (r_{xx} = .84), with reliability coefficients above .70 at eight of the nine age groups. The one exception is at age 7 years, where the reliability coefficient is .62. It correlates better with Comprehension ($r = .66$) than with any of the other subtests. It has a moderately high correlation with the Full Scale ($r = .71$) and the Verbal Scale ($r = .75$) and a moderate correlation with the Performance Scale ($r = .52$).

Administrative Suggestions

Here are some administrative suggestions for the Information subtest.

Background Considerations

- The Information subtest is untimed, is easy to administer, and has simple and direct questions.
- Items 1 to 6 use pictures as stimuli and require either a pointing or a verbal response.
- For items 1 to 6, place the unbound edge of the Stimulus Booklet toward the child.
- Read items 7 to 27 aloud; all but one of these items require a verbal response from the child.

- Query any responses that are incomplete or unclear ("Tell me more about it"), but never ask leading questions or make leading comments ("This animal lives on a farm; does that help?").

Starting Considerations

- All children begin with item 1.
- If the child fails item 1, give him or her the correct answer.

Scoring Considerations

- Each item is scored 1 or 0 (pass-fail).
- On the first six items, which are picture items, give a score of 0 if the child points to the correct picture but gives an incorrect verbal response.
- The sample answers to question 12 in the WPPSI–R manual do not mention grooming products that come in plastic bottles, such as shampoo or liquid soap. Because the term "etc." appears in the scoring criteria, we can assume that credit should be given for responses that mention any substances that come in plastic bottles.
- The suggested answers for question 13 do not mention that acceptable answers should include the names of any mammals because all mammals produce milk when feeding their newly born offspring. Therefore, give credit for any mammal that the child names.
- The scoring criteria for question 14 do not include "planet," yet a planet shines in the sky at night. Give credit for "planet," "comet," and other astronomical terms.
- To receive credit, the child is required to give two correct answers on item 16 and three correct answers on item 17.
- On item 17, an answer referring to the animal kingdom can include birds, fish, insects, worms, and other non-mammalian species.

Discontinuance Considerations

- The subtest is discontinued after five consecutive failures.

Interpretive Suggestions

The interpretive suggestions for the WISC–III Information subtest are relevant for the WPPSI–R Information subtest (see Chapter 9). When you perform a profile analysis, take into account that the full range of scaled scores from 1 to 19 is available only at ages 4¾ to 6¼ years (see Table 11-9).

COMPREHENSION

The Comprehension subtest contains 15 questions that require the child to explain actions or activities related to familiar events. None of the items overlap with those in the WISC–III. Content areas of the items include health and hygiene, environmental concerns, interpersonal relations, and societal conventions.

Rationale

The rationale presented for WISC–III Comprehension also generally applies to WPPSI–R Comprehension (see Chapter 9). Linguistic skill and logical reasoning, however, may play a more important role in WPPSI–R Comprehension than in the WISC–III version.

Factor Analytic Findings

Comprehension is a good measure of g (52% of its variance may be attributed to g), and it contributes substantially to the Verbal factor (*Mdn* loading = .80). Specificity is adequate at ages 3, 5, and 5½ years and inadequate at ages 3½, 4, 4½, 6, 6½, and 7 years.

Reliability and Correlational Highlights

Comprehension is a reliable subtest (r_{xx} = .83), with reliability coefficients above .70 at eight of the nine age groups. The one exception is at age 7 years, where the reliability coefficient is .59. It correlates better with Information (r = .66) and Vocabulary (r = .60) than with any of the other subtests. It has a moderate correlation with the Full Scale (r = .61), a moderately high correlation with the Verbal Scale (r = .70), and a moderately low correlation with the Performance Scale (r = .41).

Administrative Suggestions

Here are some administrative suggestions for the Comprehension subtest.

Background Considerations

- The subtest is not timed.
- You can repeat a question as needed, but do not alter the wording in any way.
- If the child does not answer within 10 or 15 seconds, you should repeat the question.
- Query any response followed by a "(Q)."
- On items 1 and 2, if the child fails, give her or him the correct answer.
- Ask for a second reason on item 11 if the child gives only one reason.
- Ask the child to explain any unusual responses.
- Record the child's responses verbatim during the initial presentation of the items and during the inquiry phase so that you have a complete record with which to evaluate the responses.

Starting Considerations

- All children begin with item 1.

Scoring Considerations

- All items are scored 2, 1, or 0, depending on the conceptual level of the response.

- Judgment is occasionally needed to score Comprehension responses. Consider the content of the response and the quality of the child's verbalizations in scoring the responses.

Discontinuance Considerations

- The subtest is discontinued after four consecutive failures.

Interpretive Suggestions

The interpretive suggestions for the WISC–III Comprehension subtest are relevant for the WPPSI–R Comprehension subtest (see Chapter 9). When you perform a profile analysis, take into account that the full range of scaled scores from 1 to 19 is not available at any of the age levels in the test (see Table 11-9).

ARITHMETIC

Arithmetic contains 23 items, two of which are also on the WISC–III. Arithmetic requires the child to demonstrate his or her understanding of concepts that may be precursors to numerical reasoning and to show his or her knowledge of numerical concepts. The problems on Arithmetic reflect various skills. Problems 1 to 7 entail perceptual judgments involving biggest, tallest, longest, more, most, shortest, and same. Problems 8 to 10 require direct counting of concrete quantities. Problem 11 involves complex counting. Problems 12 to 23 are arithmetic reasoning tasks presented aloud by the examiner. Most problems involve simple addition or subtraction.

Rationale

The rationale presented for WISC–III Arithmetic also generally applies to WPPSI–R Arithmetic (see Chapter 9), although the skills required for WPPSI–R Arithmetic are likely to be less dependent on the child's formal education. The first seven WPPSI–R questions, which require the child to make comparisons and perceptual discriminations, appear to measure nonverbal reasoning ability and verbal concepts; these seven problems use quantitative concepts and language without involving the explicit use of numbers.

Factor Analytic Findings

Arithmetic is a good measure of g (57% of its variance may be attributed to g), and it contributes substantially to the Verbal factor (*Mdn* loading = .64) and moderately to the Performance factor (*Mdn* loading = .40). Perhaps it loads on the Performance factor because the items employing pictures of sets of objects may be visually analyzed and then verbally compared. For children who have not memorized sums and differences (i.e., number facts), the verbally framed problems may require mental visualization or finger counting. Of course, other factors may be involved as well, and research is needed to help us understand the strategies that children might develop to solve problems on the Arithmetic subtest. Specificity is ample or adequate at ages 3, 3½, 4½, 5½, 6, and 6½ years and inadequate at ages 4, 5, and 7 years.

Reliability and Correlational Highlights

Arithmetic is a reliable subtest (r_{xx} = .80), with reliability coefficients above .70 at eight of the nine age groups. The one exception is at age 7, where the reliability coefficient is .66. It correlates better with Information (r = .59) than with any of the other subtests. It has a moderate correlation with the Full Scale (r = .67), the Verbal Scale (r = .63), and the Performance Scale (r = .55).

Administrative Suggestions

Here are some administrative suggestions for the Arithmetic subtest.

Background Considerations

- Reassure a child who is anxious about his or her arithmetical skills.
- The first 7 items are presented in the form of pictures, the next 3 in the form of blocks, and the last 13 in the form of oral questions.
- Pointing responses are required on the first 7 items and oral responses (holding up the correct number of fingers also is credited) on the last 16 items.
- The first 11 problems have no time limit, while the last 12 items have a 30-second time limit.
- Do not permit the child to use pencil and paper to solve the problems.
- Allow the child to write with a finger if he or she wants to.
- Record the time taken by the child to solve each problem.
- Pay careful attention to the special contingent instructions in the WPPSI–R manual for item 14.
- Encourage the child to verbalize his or her responses to the verbal items.

Starting Considerations

- Children under 6 years of age begin with item 1, and children aged 6 and older begin with item 8.
- Give the child who is 6 years or older credit for items 1 to 7 when items 8 and 9 (the entry point items) are passed.
- When a child who is 6 years or older fails item 8 or 9, administer items 10 and 11 and then items 1 to 7 before administering item 12, unless the discontinuance criterion has been met.

Scoring Considerations

- All items are scored 1 or 0 (pass-fail).
- When a child spontaneously changes his or her answer, score the second response, provided it is given within the time limit on a timed item.

- Holding up the correct number of fingers but giving an incorrect verbal response is scored as a failure. However, holding up the correct number of fingers without giving a verbal response is scored as a pass.

Discontinuance Considerations

- The subtest is discontinued after five consecutive failures.

Interpretive Suggestions

The interpretive suggestions presented for the WISC–III Arithmetic subtest are relevant for the WPPSI–R Arithmetic subtest (see Chapter 9). When you perform a profile analysis, take into account that the full range of scores from 1 to 19 is available only at ages 4 to 6 years (see Table 11-9).

VOCABULARY

Vocabulary contains 25 words, six of which also appear on the WISC–III subtest. Vocabulary requires the child to identify pictured stimuli and to define words. For items 1 to 3, the child must give the correct name of a pictured object; for items 4 to 25, the child must explain aloud the meaning of each word.

Rationale

The rationale presented for WISC–III Vocabulary also generally applies to WPPSI–R Vocabulary (see Chapter 9). Formal education, however, is less likely to be an influence in vocabulary development for preschool children than for older children. Experiences at home and in the community are likely to be the major contributing factors in the vocabulary development of preschool children.

Factor Analytic Findings

Vocabulary is a good measure of *g* (51% of its variance may be attributed to *g*), and it contributes substantially to the Verbal factor (*Mdn* loading = .79). Specificity is ample or adequate at ages 3, 4, 5, and 5½ years and inadequate at ages 3½, 4½, 6, 6½, and 7 years.

Reliability and Correlational Highlights

Vocabulary is a reliable subtest (r_{xx} = .84), with reliability coefficients above .70 at all age groups. It correlates better with Information (r = .60) and Comprehension (r = .60) than with any of the other subtests. It has a moderate correlation with the Full Scale (r = .61) and the Verbal Scale (r = .68) and a moderately low correlation with the Performance Scale (r = .42).

Administrative Suggestions

Here are some administrative suggestions for the Vocabulary subtest.

Background Considerations

- The subtest is not timed.
- There are two parts to the Vocabulary subtest. Part 1 (items 1 to 3) has picture items, and Part 2 (items 4 to 25) has verbal items.
- For items 4 to 25, be especially careful about how you pronounce each word, because the child must hear the word in order to define it—you cannot spell the word for the child.
- When you suspect that the child has not heard a word correctly, have the child repeat the word to you. If the child heard the word incorrectly, say, "What is a _____?" or "What does _____ mean?"
- All ambiguous responses must be queried.
- All sample responses in the manual followed by a "(Q)," as well as any similar responses, must be queried.
- Ask the child for another meaning if the response is a regionalism, slang word, or colloquialism.
- Give the child the correct answer to the first item if the child fails it, but do not give the correct answer to any other item.
- Carefully record the child's definitions, and write down all of the child's answers, whether they are correct or incorrect.
- A procedure used on Arithmetic contaminates the second Vocabulary item, because the second Vocabulary picture is exactly the same as the picture used on the second Arithmetic item. On Arithmetic, which is administered before Vocabulary, the child is told the name of the picture. Consequently, success on the second Vocabulary item may be a function of the child's short-term memory rather than of her or his vocabulary ability. However, you still must give credit to a correct response.

Starting Considerations

- All children begin the subtest with the first word. This procedure differs from the one used for the WISC–III, where the beginning word depends on the child's age.

Scoring Considerations

- Do not give credit for responses based on homonyms. When the definition of a homonym is given, always ask the child, "What else does _____ mean?"
- Items 1 to 3 are scored 1 or 0 (pass-fail), and items 4 to 25 are scored 2, 1, or 0.
- Give credit for all meanings recognized by standard dictionaries.
- Award 2 points for a good synonym, major use, general classification, definitive primary feature, less definitive primary feature, or example of an action or causal relation

(for verbs). Award 1 point for a vague response, less pertinent synonym, minor use, nondefinitive attribute, nonelaborated example, correct definition of a related form of the word, or demonstration of the word.
- Scoring requires considerable judgment, particularly because the WPPSI–R manual provides too few sample responses. Examiners have been found to make numerous scoring errors on this subtest (Whitten et al., 1994).

Discontinuance Considerations

- The subtest is discontinued after five consecutive failures, starting with item 4.

Interpretive Suggestions

The administrative suggestions presented for the WISC–III Vocabulary subtest are relevant for the WPPSI–R Arithmetic subtest (see Chapter 9). When you perform a profile analysis, take into account that the full range of scaled scores from 1 to 19 is available from ages 4¼ to 7 years (see Table 11-9).

SIMILARITIES

The Similarities subtest contains 20 questions, one of which is on the WISC–III. The child explains how objects or concepts are alike and is asked to give verbal analogies. Responses may involve perceptual reasoning and verbal reasoning on the early items and verbal reasoning or conceptual thinking on the later items.

Items 1 to 6 require the child to point to the object that is similar to the target object in the pictured array. Items 7 to 12 require a response to a simple analogy that is read aloud by the examiner. Items 13 to 20, which are similar to those on the WISC–III, require a conceptual reasoning response.

Rationale

The rationale described for WISC–III Similarities generally applies to WPPSI–R Similarities for items 13 to 20 (see Chapter 9). Items 1 to 6 appear to measure reasoning based on classification involving perceptual elements. Items 7 to 12 primarily involve simple analogic reasoning, but they may be solved by other means as well.

Because over half of the items are either perceptual reasoning or simple analogic thinking items, the subtest may be measuring logical thinking (or even vocabulary development in some cases), rather than verbal concept formation, especially at the earlier levels of the subtest. In fact, on items 7 to 12, a child may not need to attend to the first half of the statement to get the item correct. For example, a child need only attend to the second half of item 8 ("…you also ride in a _____") to get the right answer. Thus, we do not know whether the simple analogy items measure the beginning stages of conceptual reasoning ability or vocabulary ability or verbal reasoning skills or some combination of these abilities.

Factor Analytic Findings

Similarities is a good measure of *g* (51% of its variance may be attributed to *g*), and it contributes substantially to the Verbal factor (*Mdn* loading = .72). Specificity is ample or adequate at ages 3, 3½, 4, 4½, 5, 5½, and 6 years and inadequate at ages 6½ and 7 years.

Reliability and Correlational Highlights

Similarities is a reliable subtest (r_{xx} = .86), with reliability coefficients above .70 at eight of the nine age groups. The one exception is at age 7 years, where the reliability coefficient is .54. It correlates better with Information (*r* = .57) than with any of the other subtests. It has a moderate correlation with the Full Scale (*r* = .62) and the Verbal Scale (*r* = .65) and a moderately low correlation with the Performance Scale (*r* = .45).

Administrative Suggestions

Here are some administrative suggestions for the Similarities subtest.

Background Considerations

- The subtest is not timed.
- There are three different parts to the subtest: Part 1 contains picture items (items 1 to 6), Part 2 contains sentence completion items (items 7 to 12), and Part 3 contains verbal analogy items (items 13 to 20).
- Items 1 to 6 are in a separate booklet, while items 7 to 20 are in the manual.
- In Part 1, the child has to point to the correct answer. In Part 2, the child has to give a word to complete a sentence. In Part 3, the child has to say how two concepts are similar.
- Always query unclear or ambiguous responses.
- Always query responses that are followed by a "(Q)" in the manual.
- Provide demonstrations if the child fails the first one or two items in Parts 1 and 2 or if the child gives a 0- or 1-point answer in Part 3.

Starting Considerations

- All children begin with item 1.

Scoring Considerations

- The scoring procedures on the WPPSI–R differ from those on the WISC–III.
- Items 1 to 12 are scored 1 or 0 (pass-fail).
- On items 13 to 20, a conceptual response, such as a general classification, receives a score of 2; a more concrete response, such as a specific property of the item, receives a score of 1; and an incorrect response receives a score of 0.

- Scoring should be relatively easy on items 1 to 12, but is more difficult on items 13 to 20, where more judgment is required. Carefully study the scoring guidelines in the WPPSI–R manual for items 13 to 20. Less-than-full-credit responses to items 13 and 14 must be corrected by the examiner. You should write a D (demonstrated) on the record form when you correct the examinee.

Discontinuance Considerations

- The subtest is discontinued after three consecutive failures on items 1 to 6 and after five consecutive failures on items 7 to 20.

Interpretive Suggestions

The administrative suggestions presented for the WISC–III Similarities subtest are relevant for the WPPSI–R Similarities subtest (see Chapter 9). When you perform a profile analysis, take into account that the full range of scaled scores from 1 to 19 is available only at ages 5½ to 6 years (see Table 11-9).

SENTENCES

Sentences, an optional subtest, contains 12 sentences, ranging in length from 2 to 18 words. The child repeats verbatim sentences that you read aloud. When Sentences is administered as a sixth Verbal Scale subtest, it is not counted in calculating the IQ.

Rationale

Sentences measures short-term auditory memory, which involves attention, concentration, auditory perception, listening comprehension, immediate recall, auditory processing, and the ability to verbalize what is recalled. However, the subtest may measure different processes, depending on the child's age. For children 5 years and older, Sentences may primarily measure short-term memory ability; for children younger than 5 years, it may measure verbal knowledge and comprehension as well as (or more than) short-term memory.

Factor Analytic Findings

Sentences is a fair measure of *g* (46% of its variance may be attributed to *g*), and it contributes substantially to the Verbal factor (*Mdn* loading = .72). Specificity is ample or adequate at ages 3, 3½, 4, 4½, and 5 years and inadequate at ages 5½, 6, 6½, and 7 years.

Reliability and Correlational Highlights

Sentences is a reliable subtest (r_{xx} = .82), with reliability coefficients above .70 at all age groups. It correlates better with

Information (*r* = .55) than with any of the other subtests. It has a moderate correlation with the Full Scale (*r* = .59) and the Verbal Scale (*r* = .65) and a moderately low correlation with the Performance Scale (*r* = .41).

Administrative Suggestions

Here are some administrative suggestions for the Sentences subtest.

Background Considerations

- Read the sentences slowly and distinctly, with a natural intonation. Use a reading rate of about two syllables per second.
- If the child does not understand the requirements of the task, give him or her demonstrations and second tries.

Starting Considerations

- Children aged 3 to 4 years start with sentence 1, whereas those aged 5 years and older start with sentence 6.
- If a child aged 5 years or older does not earn a perfect score on Sentence 6, give the preceding items in *reverse order* until two consecutive items are passed.

Scoring Considerations

- When you score the responses, ignore faulty pronunciation.
- Articulation errors are acceptable if the errors are not idea errors.
- Scoring responses on Sentences requires careful attention to the types of errors made by the child. Typical errors include omissions, transpositions, additions, and substitutions of words.
- If a child aged 5 years or older earns a perfect score on Sentence 6, give him or her full credit for Sentences 1 to 5.
- When you administer the items in reverse order, give credit for any items not administered that precede two consecutive successes.
- Items receive 0 to 5 points, depending on the length of the sentence and the number of errors the child makes.

Discontinuance Considerations

- The subtest is discontinued after three consecutive failures.

Interpretive Suggestions

Consider the following questions:

- Is the child's performance effortless, or does the child seem to concentrate highly?
- Does the child view the task as interesting, boring, or difficult?
- Is the child aware of her or his errors, or does the child think that her or his answers are always correct?
- What strategy does the child use to recall the sentences (e.g., simply repeating what is heard, rehearsing the sentences before repeating them back to you, visualizing the sentences in her or his head, using a finger to write the words, or repeating back the sentences after an extended period of time)?
- What types of errors does the child make (e.g., omission—leaving one word out of the correct sequence; addition—adding one or more words to the correct sequence; perseveration—repeating one or more words; sequential error—giving the correct words but in the wrong sequence; sequence reversal—giving the correct words but reversing two or more of them; adding idiosyncratic or peculiar words; or adding the same incorrect words to several sentences (e.g., "my dog")?
- Does the child make errors primarily at the beginning, middle, or end of sentences?
- Does the child miss sentences partially or completely?
- Are any tangential thoughts added to the sentences? If so, what are they?

Evaluating the quality of the child's responses may help you learn about particular features of the child's short-term auditory memory ability. For example, missing a few words suggests minor inefficiencies, while missing all or most of the words suggests more serious short-term auditory memory, language, or hearing problems.

Low scores on the Sentences subtest may indicate anxiety, inattention, distractibility, difficulty in auditory sequential processing, poor short-term auditory memory, or negativism.

When you perform a profile analysis, take into account that the full range of scaled scores from 1 to 19 is available only at ages 5 to 6¾ years (see Table 11-9).

INTERPRETING THE WPPSI–R

Most of the material in Chapter 9 on the WISC–III also pertains to the WPPSI–R. The methods of interpretation—such as the successive-level approach, profile analysis, Performance Scale–Verbal Scale comparisons, and subtest comparisons—are essentially the same for both the WISC–III and the WPPSI–R. Table D-3 in Appendix D can help you to interpret the WPPSI–R subtests, as well as to write reports. It summarizes the abilities considered to be measured by the subtests found in all the Wechsler tests, and it deserves careful study. Table D-4 in Appendix D provides a summary of the interpretive rationales for the Full Scale, Verbal Scale, and Performance Scale of the Wechsler tests. Table D-5 in Appendix D presents suggested remediation activities for combinations of Wechsler subtests.

Table BC-2 on the inside back cover shows the classifications associated with WPPSI–R IQs. Table BC-1 on the inside back cover gives the percentile ranks for the WPPSI–R Full Scale IQ, Performance Scale IQ, and Verbal Scale IQ. Table D-1 in Appendix D presents the percentile ranks associated with subtest scaled scores.

Use subtest scaled scores for generating hypotheses about the child's abilities, but not for determining specific cognitive skills with precision. You can derive the most reliable estimates of specific abilities from the Performance Scale IQ (performance or perceptual organization abilities) and the Verbal Scale IQ (verbal or verbal comprehension abilities), not from individual subtest scaled scores. In fact, of the 108 separate reliability coefficients for the 12 subtests at the nine age groups of the test, only 60 are at .80 or above, and of these, only 3 are at .90 or above—Information at ages 3 and 4½ years and Picture Completion at age 4½ years. The remaining 48 reliability coefficients are below .80 and are not sufficiently reliable for decision-making or classification purposes (see Table 9 on page 128 of the WPPSI–R manual). Many of the 12 subtests have inadequate specificity at several of the nine age levels. Of the 108 specificity loadings, 49 (45%) show inadequate specificity and can be interpreted only as part of their IQ scale or factor, not separately.

Because the WPPSI–R and WISC–III have nine subtest types in common, most of the information in this text on the WISC–III is pertinent to the WPPSI–R. We encourage you to review Chapter 9, which discusses the WISC–III subtests.

Because profile analysis on the WPPSI–R is similar to that on the WISC–III, review the material in Chapter 10 that describes WISC–III profile analysis before you undertake a WPPSI–R profile analysis. Although we know much less about profile analysis on the WPPSI–R than on other Wechsler tests, the procedures can still be useful in generating hypotheses about a child's strengths and weaknesses.

The following six methods of profile analysis on the WPPSI–R are essentially the same as those described for the WISC–III (see Chapter 10). One difference, however, is that you must use the tables in Appendix B appropriate for the WPPSI–R. Another difference is that we do not use Index scores in profile analysis on the WPPSI–R because the Performance Scale and Verbal Scale adequately describe the organization of the test.

Method 1: Compare Performance Scale IQ with Verbal Scale IQ.

Table B-2 in Appendix B provides critical values for comparing the Performance Scale IQ and the Verbal Scale IQ for the nine age groups of the WPPSI–R. The critical values for each age, as shown in Table B-2, are as follows (.05/.01 significance level):

- 10/13 at ages 3 to 4½ years
- 11/14 at age 5 years
- 12/15 at age 5½ years
- 11/14 at age 6 years
- 12/16 at age 6½ years
- 16/21 at age 7 years

These values indicate that an average critical value based on the entire group would be misleading in some cases. Therefore, use the values for the child's specific age group to evaluate differences between the child's Performance Scale IQ and Verbal Scale IQ. Table B-3 in Appendix B shows the probabilities associated with various differences between the Performance Scale and Verbal Scale.

Table B-4 in Appendix B presents the percentage of children in the standardization group who obtained a given discrepancy between the Verbal Scale and Performance Scale. This table shows, for example, that between 25% and 50% of the population in each WPPSI–R age group had a 10-point difference (in either direction) between the two IQs.

Table B-5 in Appendix B shows the frequency of Verbal Scale IQ–Performance Scale IQ discrepancies at various IQ levels in the standardization group. The mean Verbal Scale IQ–Performance Scale IQ discrepancy was 10.81 points. Children with IQs below 79 had the smallest mean Verbal Scale–Performance Scale discrepancy ($M = 8.92$), while children with IQs from 110 to 119 had the largest Verbal Scale–Performance Scale discrepancy ($M = 11.89$).

Method 2: Compare each Performance Scale subtest scaled score with the mean Performance Scale subtest scaled score.

Table B-6 in Appendix B provides the critical values for comparing each Performance subtest scaled score with the mean Performance subtest scaled score for each of the nine age groups of the WPPSI–R. Typical values for 3-year-old children on the five standard Performance Scale subtests, for example, range from 2.65 to 3.96 at the .05 level and from 3.16 to 4.72 at the .01 level. The values in Table B-6 are overly liberal (i.e., they often lead to significant differences that may not be true differences) when more than one comparison is made.

Table 14 (page 136) in the WPPSI–R manual presents the frequencies with which various differences between a child's score on each subtest and his or her average WPPSI–R Performance Scale score occurred in the standardization sample. Use this table only for differences that have been found to be reliable.

Method 3: Compare each Verbal Scale subtest scaled score with the mean Verbal Scale subtest scaled score.

Table B-6 in Appendix B provides the critical values for comparing each Verbal subtest scaled score with the mean Verbal subtest scaled score for each of the nine age groups of the WPPSI–R. Typical values for 3-year-old children on the five standard Verbal Scale subtests, for example, range from 2.30 to 3.10 at the .05 level and from 2.75 to 3.70 at the .01 level. These values are lower than those on the Performance Scale. The values in Table B-6 are overly liberal (i.e., they often lead to significant differences that may not be true differences) when more than one comparison is made.

Table 14 (page 136) in the WPPSI–R manual presents the frequencies with which various differences between a child's score on each subtest and her or his average WPPSI–R Verbal Scale score occurred in the standardization sample. Use this table only for differences that have been found to be reliable.

Method 4: Compare each subtest scaled score with the mean subtest scaled score.   Table B-6 in Appendix B provides the critical values for comparing each subtest scaled score with the mean subtest scaled score for each of the nine age groups of the WPPSI–R for 10, 11, and 12 subtests. For a 3-year-old, for example, they range from 2.62 to 4.72 at the .05 level and from 3.05 to 5.49 at the .01 level for the 10 standard subtests. The values in Table B-6 are overly liberal (i.e., they often lead to significant differences that may not be true differences) when more than one comparison is made.

Table 14 (page 136) in the WPPSI–R manual presents the frequencies with which various differences between a child's score on each subtest and his or her average WPPSI–R score occurred in the standardization sample. Use this table only for differences that you have found to be reliable.

Method 5: Compare sets of subtest scaled scores.   Table B-2 in Appendix B provides the critical values for comparing sets of subtest scaled scores for each of the nine age groups of the WPPSI–R. They range from 3 to 6 at the .05 level and from 4 to 7 at the .01 level. The values in Table B-2 for subtest comparisons are overly liberal (i.e., they lead to some significant differences that may not actually be true differences) when more than one comparison is made. They are most accurate when a priori planned comparisons are made, such as Comprehension versus Information or Block Design versus Object Assembly. Chapter 10 provides additional information on making comparisons between subtests.

Before you make multiple comparisons, determine the difference between the highest and lowest subtest scaled scores. A difference of 6 scaled-score points or more is significant at the .05 level, so you can interpret differences between subtests that are 6 or more scaled-score points apart. If the difference between the highest and lowest subtest scaled scores is less than 6 scaled-score points, do not make multiple comparisons between individual subtest scaled scores. (The Note to Table B-2 in Appendix B shows the formula used to compute the significant difference. The formula considers the average SEM for each of the 12 subtests and the studentized range statistic.)

Method 6: Compare the examinee's intersubtest scatter with that found in the standardization sample.   Table B-7 in Appendix B provides the range of subtest scaled scores within the Verbal Scale, Performance

Scale, and Full Scale at five IQ levels ($\leq$79, 80–89, 90–109, 110–119, 120+) in the standardization sample. The mean scaled-score range was 7 points for the 10 standard subtests on the Full Scale, 5 points for the five standard subtests on Verbal Scale, and 6 points for the five standard subtests on the Performance Scale. The scaled-score ranges were generally similar in the six IQ groups. (See Chapter 4 for further discussion about the use of the range statistic.)

ASSETS OF THE WPPSI–R

The WPPSI–R is a well-standardized test, with good reliability and validity. The 12 subtests are divided into a Performance Scale section and a Verbal Scale section, and the test provides a Performance Scale IQ, Verbal Scale IQ, and Full Scale IQ. These breakdowns are helpful in clinical and psychoeducational evaluations. Parts of the test can be administered to children limited by sensory impairments (e.g., the Verbal Scale to children with a severe visual impairment and the Performance Scale to children with a severe hearing impairment). Specific assets of the WPPSI–R include the following.

1. *Excellent standardization.* The standardization procedures were excellent, sampling four geographical regions, both sexes, Euro American children and non-Euro American children, and the entire socioeconomic status range. The standardization group well represents the nation as a whole in 1986 for the age groups covered by the test.

2. *Excellent overall psychometric properties.* The WPPSI–R has excellent reliability for the Performance Scale IQ, Verbal Scale IQ, and Full Scale IQ, with a minor exception at 7 years, where the Performance Scale IQ and Verbal Scale IQ have reliabilities below .90. The WPPSI–R has adequate concurrent and construct validity.

3. *Useful diagnostic information.* The WPPSI–R provides diagnostic information useful for the assessment of cognitive abilities of preschool- and early-elementary-school-age children who are functioning within two standard deviations from the mean. In addition, the test is useful for mildly mentally retarded children who are between 4 and 7 years old and for moderately mentally retarded children who are between 5 and 7 years old. It also furnishes data likely to be helpful in planning special school programs, perhaps tapping important developmental or maturational factors needed for school success in the lower grades.

4. *Good administrative procedures.* The procedures described in the WPPSI–R manual are excellent. The examiner actively queries responses to evaluate the breadth of the examinee's knowledge and to determine whether the child truly knows the answers. The emphasis on probing questions can lead to valuable information.

5. *Good manual.* The WPPSI–R manual is easy to use; it provides clear directions and tables. Examiners are aided by instructions printed in a color contrasting with that of the

other text material. The manual provides helpful abbreviations for recording the examinee's responses.

6. *High interest level.* Most young children enjoy taking the test; the mixture of performance and verbal items, as well as the varied test materials, helps to maintain their interest. The conversational give-and-take of the verbal tasks and the variety of performance tasks allow you to interact with children and make useful observations.

LIMITATIONS OF THE WPPSI–R

Although the WPPSI–R is an excellent instrument overall, some problems exist.

1. *Low reliability of individual subtests.* Reliability coefficients for the individual subtests are lower than .80 at some ages. In these cases, the subtest scaled scores may not be dependable. In addition, there are no test-retest scores for the Animal Pegs subtest at each age level of the test; this reflects poor test construction. Because the WPPSI–R manual presents only one test-retest reliability coefficient for Animal Pegs, the same reliability coefficient had to be used to generate the SEMs and other statistical information for each age level of the test; the accuracy of these estimates is unknown.

2. *Limited floor.* The WPPSI–R has an inadequate floor—that is, it does not clearly differentiate among children who perform at the lower end of the test. IQs range from 41 to 160, but the lower limit of this range is reached only at 5¼ years.

3. *Nonuniformity of subtest scaled scores.* Because the range of scaled scores on all subtests is not uniform, there are problems in profile analysis, particularly at the lower and upper limits of the scaled-score range.

4. *Long administration time.* Administration may take too long for some children, although fatigue should not often be a problem for older children. We know little about how 3- to 4-year-olds maintain attention on the test. With younger children or children with a disability, two test sessions may be needed. However, because this procedure differs from that used when the test was standardized, we have no way of determining whether the break between testing sessions affects a child's scores. Empirical data are needed to clarify the effect of two test sessions on children's test scores.

5. *Possible difficulties in scoring responses.* Some responses to Geometric Design, Vocabulary, Similarities, and Comprehension may be difficult to score. We recommend that you consult with colleagues when you have difficulty scoring responses.

6. *Problems for some linguistically and culturally diverse children and children who do not place a premium on speed.* The long administration time, demands for concentration and attention, and need to clarify answers may make some children uncomfortable, particularly linguistically and culturally diverse children who are unaccustomed to pro-

longed or intense periods of problem-solving activity. In addition, the test may penalize children who (a) are from a cultural group that does not place a premium on speed (see Chapter 19) or (b) prefer to work in a slow, deliberate, and thoughtful manner.

7. *Overlap with the WISC–III.* The WPPSI–R and the WISC–III have at least 23 overlapping items, primarily on Picture Completion, Mazes, Vocabulary, and Information. This overlap is unfortunate for at least two reasons. First, it means that the WPPSI–R and the WISC–III are not independent, parallel forms at the overlapping age levels (6 to 7¼ years). Second, it means that children tested with the WPPSI–R and then with the WISC–III (or vice versa) have an advantage on the second test because of practice effects. We recommend that, on the next revision of the WPPSI–R, items overlapping with the WISC–III be eliminated.

CONCLUDING COMMENT

Overall, the WPPSI–R represents a major contribution to the field of intelligence testing of young children. It serves as an important instrument for this purpose.

PSYCHOLOGICAL EVALUATION

The psychological evaluation in Exhibit 11-4 illustrates how the WPPSI–R was used to evaluate a child who was developmentally delayed. The report summarizes information obtained from parents and from a kindergarten teacher and cites both qualitative and quantitative information obtained during the assessment. The examiner uses profile analysis to develop some assessment information and bases recommendations on the test results and background information.

TEST YOUR SKILL

The WISC–III Test Your Skill Exercises in Chapter 10 also pertain to the WPPSI–R. If you have not reviewed these exercises recently, we encourage you to do so now. In addition, three exercises that pertain only to the WPPSI–R follow. Each exercise contains a description or interpretation of WPPSI–R subtest results. Analyze the mistakes made in the exercises, and then compare your answers with those given in the Comments section.

1. Tom's excellent performance on Block Design and Geometric Design suggests that he has good ability in analyzing school situations and has high moral judgment.

2. The Geometric Design subtest presented problems for her and she fell in the slow learning category.

3. The following interpretation was given to these WPPSI–R Performance Scale scores—Object Assembly, 12; Picture Completion, 15; Mazes, 13; Geometric Design, 14; and

Exhibit 11-4
Psychological Evaluation: A Child with Developmental Immaturity Evaluated by the WPPSI–R

Name: Amanda
Date of birth: November 25, 1994
Chronological age: 5-6

Date of examination: June 12, 2000
Date of report: June 15, 2000
Grade: Kindergarten

Test Administered
Wechsler Preschool and Primary Scale of Intelligence–Revised Edition (WPPSI–R):

VERBAL SCALE		PERFORMANCE SCALE	
Information	8	Animal Pegs	5
Vocabulary	13	Picture Completion	6
Arithmetic	10	Mazes	8
Similarities	7	Geometric Design	7
Comprehension	9	Object Assembly	9

Verbal Scale IQ = 95
Performance Scale IQ = 80
Full Scale IQ = 87 ± 6 at the 95% confidence level

Reason for Referral
Amanda's parents requested the evaluation because they were concerned about her rate of mental development. Her parents described her as being a slow learner and as having a short attention span. Amanda's developmental landmarks were all reached slightly later than is average. For example, she began walking at 16 months and did not begin speaking until 28 months. The results of a neurological examination were negative. Her parents consider her to be a well-adjusted child who is generally happy at home and with other children. There is one other sibling in the family, a 10-year-old boy, who the parents believe is gifted.

Amanda's kindergarten teacher described her as being a willing worker when supervised by an adult. When she is on her own, however, her attention often wanders aimlessly. In class, her retention appears to be limited; she is distracted by anything that crosses her vision and by extraneous sounds. She tends to perceive situations as parts, not wholes, and because she fixes her attention on small details she fails to understand many situations. In class she speaks slowly and uses phrases that are more characteristic of a 3-year-old than a 5-year-old.

General Observations
Amanda is of average height and weight for her age. Although an articulation problem was evident, her speech was understandable. She was unable to pronounce "sh" sounds and mixed up sounds—for example, saying "amimal" for "animal." She exhibited some awkwardness in motor coordination. Her walking gait was uneven, and she had some difficulty in turning the pages of a test booklet. At times she was restless during the testing. For example, she squirmed in her chair and played with her hair and the buttons on her clothing. For the most part, she was cooperative and attempted to answer the questions and do the tasks asked of her.

Test Results
The WPPSI–R results were as follows: Verbal Scale IQ of 95 (37th percentile), Performance Scale IQ of 80 (9th percentile), and Full Scale IQ of 87 ± 6. The chances that her true score is between 81 and 93 are about 95 out of 100. Her overall performance is classified in the Low Normal range and is ranked at the 20th percentile. Given the good rapport between Amanda and the examiner and her ability to follow directions, the present results are valid.

Amanda's performance skills are not as well developed as are her verbal skills. The 15-point difference between her scores on the verbal and performance parts of the scale suggests that visual-motor ability, perceptual ability, ability to attend to perceptual details, and persistence are at a level of development that is below normal. In contrast, not only do her verbal skills show more variability than do her performance skills, but also the overall level of verbal development is within the Average range. A noticeable strength was her word knowledge. She was able to define words at a level that was higher than the norm for her age peers and above the average of her verbal scaled scores. For example, she gave satisfactory definitions to such common vocabulary words as "fur," "join," and "diamond." These results are consistent with Amanda's teacher's report that she has good vocabulary. Her arithmetic skills appear to be at an average level.

Amanda's answers were usually short, precise, and direct. Her failures were manifested by incorrect answers and by her saying "No" when she did not know the correct answer. She seemed to experience more difficulty on the Similarities subtest, which measures logical thinking, than on most other verbal subtests. Instead of giving analogies, she frequently repeated part of the question in her answer or gave associations. For example, to the question "You ride in a train and you also ride in a _____ ," she said "Choo-choo." Her difficulty in grasping con-

(Continued)

Exhibit 11-4 *(Continued)*

cepts suggests some immaturity in reasoning. Initially, she refused to complete the Animal Pegs subtest, but with encouragement and support finally proceeded with the task. Her refusal to do this task, too, suggests immaturity.

Recommendations
The results of the intellectual evaluation suggest that Amanda has better developed verbal than nonverbal cognitive abilities. She will need encouragement and attention, however, because she may tend to remove herself from difficult situations by inattention or by simply refusing to try. Her parents should be helped to accept her present level of development and not place unrealistic demands on her. Special programs to improve Amanda's muscle coordination and speech are recommended.

Summary
In summary, on the WPPSI–R, Amanda, with a chronological age of 5-6, obtained a Full Scale IQ of 87 ± 6, which is in the

Low Average classification and at the 20th percentile rank. The chances that the range of scores from 81 to 93 includes her true IQ are about 95 out of 100. The results appear to be a valid estimate of her present level of intellectual functioning. Case history material suggests a pattern of developmental immaturity for Amanda. She has better verbal skills than performance skills. Visual-motor coordination and other perceptual skills are less well developed than her vocabulary ability. Amanda's responses were immature, as was her behavior. Amanda will need support and encouragement. Her parents should be helped to accept her at her present level of functioning. Special programs were recommended to improve her muscle coordination and speech.

(Examiner's signature)

_____

Examiner

Block Design, 12: While her two lowest scores on the Performance Scale were above average, they may suggest some visual acuity problems.

Comments

1. These interpretations are totally inaccurate. Block Design and Geometric Design do not assess moral judgment or ability to analyze school situations. *Suggestion:* "Tom has above-average visual perception, nonverbal reasoning, and fine motor abilities."
2. A label (such as "slow learner") should never be applied to a child based on one subtest score. *Suggestion:* "Her perceptual-motor skills were weak."
3. None of these subtest scores are significantly different from the mean of the Performance Scale ($M = 13.2$); therefore, this interpretation is erroneous. Furthermore, even if Block Design and Animal House scores were significantly lower than the mean Performance Scale score, it is unlikely that "visual acuity problems" would be the reason for the low scores. Visual acuity is also required for the other Performance Scale subtests on which the child performed adequately. Finally, all Performance Scale subtest scores are above average, thereby lessening the possibility that the child has visual acuity problems.

THINKING THROUGH THE ISSUES

1. Consider the WPPSI–R in relation to the WISC–III. How does the WPPSI–R differ from the WISC–III?
2. Do the limitations of the WPPSI–R affect its clinical usefulness? Explain your position.

3. What other kinds of subtests would you like to see incorporated in the WPPSI–R? Why?
4. If you were going to evaluate a 6-year-old child and decided to use a Wechsler test, would you choose the WPPSI–R or the WISC–III? Why?
5. If you were evaluating a preschooler with a language impairment, what parts of the WPPSI–R would be most useful in estimating the child's cognitive ability? What might the child's scores on the Verbal Scale subtests indicate?

SUMMARY

1. The Wechsler Preschool and Primary Scale of Intelligence–Revised (WPPSI–R) is designed to assess the cognitive ability of young children.
2. The age range for which the WPPSI–R is appropriate is 3 years 0 months to 7 years 3 months.
3. The WPPSI–R is not completely distinct from the WISC–III; some items overlap with those on the WISC–III.
4. The WPPSI–R contains 12 subtests, grouped into a Performance Scale and a Verbal Scale.
5. The five standard subtests within the Performance Scale are Object Assembly, Geometric Design, Block Design, Mazes, and Picture Completion.
6. The five standard subtests within the Verbal Scale are Information, Comprehension, Arithmetic, Vocabulary, and Similarities.
7. The two optional subtests are Animal Pegs in the Performance Scale and Sentences in the Verbal Scale.

Standardization

8. The WPPSI–R was standardized on 1,700 children: 100 boys and 100 girls in each of eight age groups from 3 to 7 years, and one group of 50 boys and 50 girls from 7 years 0 months to 7 years 3 months.

Deviation IQS, Scaled Scores, and Test-Age Equivalents

9. The WPPSI–R, like the WISC–III and the WAIS-III, uses Deviation IQs ($M = 100$, $SD = 15$) for the Verbal Scale IQ, Performance Scale IQ, and Full Scale IQ, and scaled scores ($M = 10$, $SD = 3$) for the subtests.

Reliability

10. The WPPSI–R Performance Scale IQ, Verbal Scale IQ, and Full Scale IQ have excellent reliability at eight of the nine age groups covered by the test.
11. From ages 3 to 6½ years, the reliabilities for all three IQs range from .90 to .97; this range is excellent. At age 7 years, however, the reliability coefficients for the Performance Scale IQ and Verbal Scale IQ ($r_{xx} = .85$ and $.86$, respectively) are less satisfactory than that for the Full Scale IQ ($r_{xx} = .90$).
12. The average internal consistency subtest reliabilities range from a low of $r_{xx} = .63$ for Object Assembly to a high of $r_{xx} = .86$ for Similarities.
13. The average standard errors of measurement (SEM) in IQ points are 3.00 for the Full Scale, 4.24 for the Performance Scale, and 3.35 for the Verbal Scale.
14. Test-retest changes are greater on the Performance Scale than on the Verbal Scale by about 3.5 points.
15. Test-retest change scores on the subtests ranged from $-.2$ (Vocabulary) to $+1.3$ (Block Design).
16. Confidence intervals are available for the WPPSI–R at five levels of confidence by age.

Validity

17. The WPPSI–R has excellent concurrent validity, as indicated by strong correlations with several different intelligence and achievement tests.
18. The median correlation between the WPPSI–R and various intelligence tests is .74, while the median correlation between the WPPSI–R and various achievement tests is .62.
19. Studies support a two-factor structure for the WPPSI–R corresponding to the Verbal Scale and Performance Scale of the test.
20. The WPPSI–R provides a fair measure of general intelligence (*g*).
21. The WPPSI–R and the WISC–III should not be considered parallel forms.

Intercorrelations Between Subtests and Scales

22. Average intercorrelations between the 12 subtests range from a low of $r = .24$ (Mazes and Sentences) to a high of $r = .66$ (Information and Comprehension).

Factor Analysis

23. The WPPSI–R subtests form two clusters with respect to the measurement of *g:* (a) Information, Arithmetic, Comprehension, Similarities, and Vocabulary are good measures of *g;* and (b) Picture Completion, Block Design, Sentences, Geometric Design, Object Assembly, Mazes, and Animal Pegs are fair measures of *g*.
24. The Verbal Scale subtests have higher *g* loadings than do the Performance Scale subtests.

25. Throughout the age range covered by the WPPSI–R, Picture Completion is the only subtest that has ample specificity, and Object Assembly is the only subtest that has inadequate specificity.
26. Each of the 10 other subtests shows a unique pattern of specificity—that is, each has ample, adequate, or inadequate specificity at different ages.
27. The factor structure of the WPPSI–R is generally similar to that of the WISC–III, particularly in terms of the Verbal Comprehension and Perceptual Organization factors.
28. The primary difference between the WPPSI–R and WISC–III factor structures is that two additional WISC–III factors have sometimes been found; these factors have been labeled Freedom from Distractibility and Processing Speed.

Range of Full Scale IQs and of Subtest Scaled Scores

29. The WPPSI–R Full Scale IQs range from 41 to 160.
30. The WPPSI–R may not provide precise IQs for a child who is functioning two or more standard deviations below the mean of the test.
31. The WPPSI–R provides a uniform ceiling level for the Full Scale throughout all the ages of the test, but not for the Verbal Scale and Performance Scale.
32. The failure to have a uniform scaled-score range throughout all age levels of the test means that profile analysis cannot be performed routinely, particularly at the lower and upper limits of the scaled-score range.

Normative Changes on Animal Pegs

33. Generally, a child must be more proficient on the WPPSI–R Animal Pegs subtest than on the WPPSI to maintain the same relative position on the subtest.

Administering the WPPSI–R

34. The administrative considerations that apply to the WISC–III generally apply to the WPPSI–R. Because the WPPSI–R is used with a younger age group than the WISC–III is, there are some problems in adapting the subtests to alternative sensory modalities for children with sensory or motor handicaps.
35. Short forms of the WPPSI–R have the same advantages and disadvantages as those of the WISC–III.
36. Research is needed to determine whether the WPPSI–R or the WISC–III is more valid at the overlapping ages of 6 to 7¼ years.

Object Assembly

37. Object Assembly is a fair measure of *g* and contributes to the Performance factor. Subtest specificity is inadequate at every age, and reliability is marginal ($r_{xx} = .63$). Administrative procedures differ somewhat from those for the WISC–III version.

Geometric Design

38. Geometric Design measures perceptual recognition and discrimination in younger children and perceptual and visual-motor ability, visual construction, and eye-hand coordination in older children. It is a fair measure of *g* and contributes to the Performance factor. Subtest specificity is ample or adequate at

five of the nine age groups, and reliability is relatively good (r_{xx} = .79). The subtest is difficult to score.

Block Design

39. Block Design is a fair measure of g and contributes to the Performance factor. Subtest specificity is ample or adequate at seven of the nine age groups, and reliability is good (r_{xx} = .85). The subtest requires skill to administer.

Mazes

40. Mazes is a fair measure of g and contributes to the Performance factor. Subtest specificity is ample at six of the nine age groups, and reliability is relatively good (r_{xx} = .77). Scoring requires considerable judgment. Administrative procedures differ from those used on the WISC–III version.

Picture Completion

41. Picture Completion is a fair measure of g and contributes to both the Performance and the Verbal factor. Subtest specificity is ample at all ages, and reliability is good (r_{xx} = .85). Administration is relatively easy.

Animal Pegs

42. Animal Pegs is an optional subtest on the WPPSI–R. The subtest measures memory, attention span, goal awareness, concentration, finger and manual dexterity, and learning ability. It is a fair measure of g and contributes to the Performance factor. Subtest specificity is ample at five of the nine age groups, and reliability is marginal (r_{xx} = .66). Administration is relatively easy.

Information

43. Information is the best measure of g in the test and contributes to the Verbal factor. Subtest specificity is adequate at only two of the nine age groups, and reliability is good (r_{xx} = .84). Judgment is needed in scoring responses.

Comprehension

44. Comprehension is a good measure of g and contributes to the Verbal factor. Subtest specificity is adequate at only three of the nine age groups, and reliability is good (r_{xx} = .83). Judgment is needed to score responses.

Arithmetic

45. Arithmetic is a good measure of g and contributes to both the Verbal and the Performance factor. Subtest specificity is ample or adequate at six of the nine age groups, and reliability is good (r_{xx} = .83). Scoring is easy.

Vocabulary

46. Vocabulary is a good measure of g and contributes to the Verbal factor. Subtest specificity is ample or adequate at four of the nine age groups, and reliability is good (r_{xx} = .84). Judgment is needed to score responses.

Similarities

47. Similarities is a good measure of g and contributes to the Verbal factor. Subtest specificity is ample or adequate at seven of the nine age groups, and reliability is good (r_{xx} = .86). Judgment is needed to score the last eight items.

Sentences

48. Sentences is an optional subtest on the WPPSI–R. It measures short-term auditory memory, involving immediate recall and attention. The subtest is a fair measure of g and contributes to the Verbal factor. Subtest specificity is ample or adequate at five of the nine age groups, and reliability is good (r_{xx} = .82). Scoring requires considerable skill.

Interpreting the WPPSI–R

49. Although the considerations that apply to profile analysis on the WISC–III apply to profile analysis on the WPPSI–R, you need to take more care in using profile analysis on the WPPSI–R because we know less about the scale.

Assets of the WPPSI–R

50. Assets of the WPPSI–R include its excellent standardization, excellent overall psychometric properties, useful diagnostic information, good administrative procedures, good manual, and high interest level.

Limitations of the WPPSI–R

51. Limitations of the WPPSI–R include the low reliability of its individual subtests, its limited floor, nonuniformity of its subtest scaled scores, its long administration time, possible difficulties in scoring responses, problems for some linguistically and culturally diverse children and children who do not place a premium on speed, and its overlap with the WISC–III.

Concluding Comment

52. Overall, the WPPSI–R represents a major contribution to the field of intelligence testing of young children. It serves as an important instrument for this purpose.

KEY TERMS, CONCEPTS, AND NAMES

STUDY QUESTIONS

1. Describe the purpose of the WPPSI–R, and then discuss its standardization, reliability, and validity.
2. Describe WPPSI–R factor analytic findings.
3. Discuss general administrative considerations for the WPPSI–R.
4. Discuss the strengths and limitations of WPPSI–R short forms.
5. Discuss the rationale, factor analytic findings, reliability and correlational highlights, and administrative and interpretive considerations for each of the following WPPSI–R Performance Scale subtests: Object Assembly, Geometric Design, Block Design, Mazes, Picture Completion, and Animal Pegs.
6. Discuss the rationale, factor analytic findings, reliability and correlational highlights, and administrative and interpretive considerations for each of the following WPPSI–R Verbal Scale subtests: Information, Comprehension, Arithmetic, Vocabulary, Similarities, and Sentences.
7. Briefly describe profile analysis on the WPPSI–R.
8. Discuss the strengths and limitations of the WPPSI–R.

12

WECHSLER ADULT INTELLIGENCE SCALE–III (WAIS–III): DESCRIPTION

by Jerome M. Sattler and Joseph J. Ryan

We should take care not to make the intellect our god; it has, of course, powerful muscles, but no personality.

—Albert Einstein

Standardization

Deviation IQs and Scaled Scores

Reliability

Validity

Intercorrelations Between Subtests and Scales

Factor Analysis

Range of Subtest Scaled Scores

Range of Full Scale IQs

Comparison of the WAIS–III and WAIS–R

Administering the WAIS–III

Short Forms of the WAIS–III

Choosing Between the WAIS–III and the WISC–III

Thinking Through the Issues

Summary

Goals and Objectives

This chapter is designed to enable you to do the following:

- Evaluate the psychometric properties of the WAIS–III
- Learn how to administer the WAIS–III
- Select useful WAIS–III short forms
- Choose between the WAIS–III and the WISC–III in the overlapping ages

The Wechsler Adult Intelligence Scale–III (WAIS–III; Wechsler, 1997) is the latest edition of an intelligence test introduced in 1939. In its original version, it was called the Wechsler-Bellevue Intelligence Scale, Form I (Wechsler, 1939), after David Wechsler and Bellevue Hospital in New York City, where Wechsler served as chief psychologist. Other editions included the Wechsler-Bellevue Intelligence Scale, Form II, published in 1946; the WAIS, published in 1955; and the WAIS–R, published in 1981. The Wechsler Intelligence Scale for Children–III (WISC–III) and the Wechsler Preschool and Primary Scale of Intelligence–Revised (WPPSI–R) also are derivatives of the 1939 adult scale.

The WAIS–III contains 14 subtests grouped into a Verbal Scale and a Performance Scale (Figure 12-1). The six standard subtests within the Verbal Scale are Vocabulary, Similarities, Arithmetic, Digit Span, Information, and Comprehension. The five standard subtests within the Performance Scale are Picture Completion, Digit Symbol—Coding, Block Design, Matrix Reasoning, and Picture Arrangement. The three remaining subtests are Letter–Number Sequencing in the Verbal Scale and Symbol Search and Object Assembly in the Performance Scale. Letter–Number Sequencing and Symbol Search are designated as supplementary subtests because they contribute only to index scores, which are essentially factor scores and will be discussed later in the chapter. Object Assembly is designated as an optional subtest because, although it is not included in any index score, it does provide useful clinical information about perceptual organization.

Although numerous modifications have been made in the third edition, the basic structure remains similar to that of the WAIS–R. More than 68% (113) of the 165 WAIS–R items (excluding Digit Symbol—Coding) are retained in the WAIS–III, in either the original or modified form. One of the primary differences between the WAIS–R and the WAIS–III

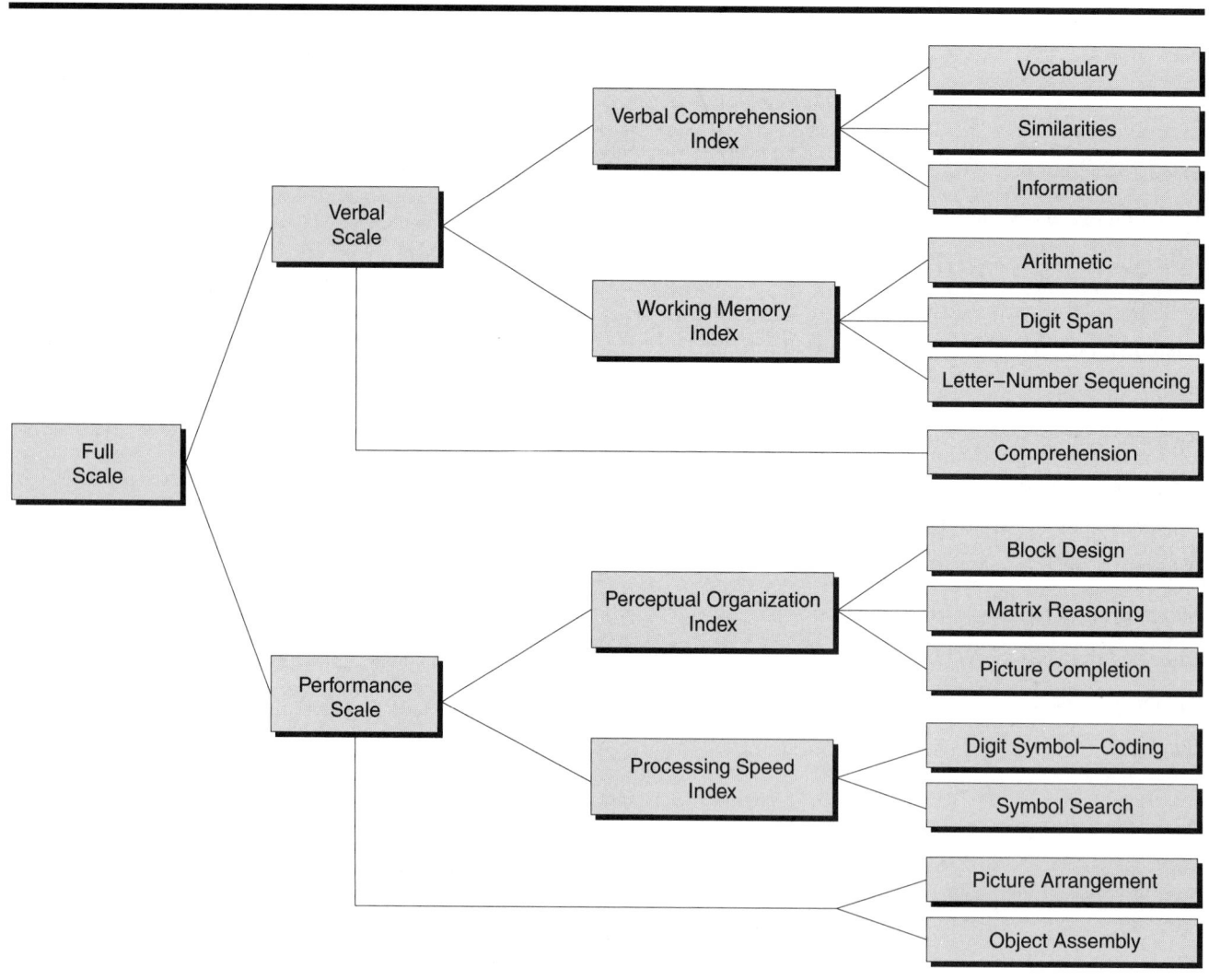

Figure 12-1. Structure of the WAIS–III.

is that the latest revision covers a broader age range: The age range of 16 years 0 months to 74 years 11 months for the WAIS–R has been extended to an age range of 16 years 0 months to 89 years 11 months for the WAIS–III.

STANDARDIZATION

The WAIS–III was standardized on 2,450 individuals selected to be representative of the late-adolescent and adult population in the United States during the early to mid 1990s. The demographic characteristics used to obtain a stratified sample were age, sex, race/ethnicity, educational level, and geographic region.

In the standardization sample, there were 13 age groups: 16–17, 18–19, 20–24, 25–29, 30–34, 35–44, 45–54, 55–64, 65–69, 70–74, 75–79, 80–84, and 85–89 years. In each age group between 16 and 64 years, there were 100 males and 100 females. In the age groups from 65 to 89 years, there were more women than men, in proportions consistent with the U.S. Census data (i.e., 65–69 years: 90 males and 110 females; 70–74 years: 88 males and 112 females; 75–79 years: 83 males and 117 females; 80–84 years: 54 males and 96 females; 85–89 years: 32 males and 68 females).

With respect to race/ethnicity, individuals were classified as Euro American ($N = 1,925$), African American ($N = 279$), Hispanic American ($N = 181$), or other ($N = 65$).

The five educational categories ranged from less than or equal to 8 years of education to greater than or equal to 16 years of education. For individuals in the age range 16 to 19 years, parental education, rather than the individual's educational level, was used to stratify the samples.

The four geographic regions sampled were Northeast, North Central, South, and West. Table 12-1 shows the educational status and geographic location by race/ethnicity of the standardization sample.

A comparison of the percentage of persons in each of 10 occupational categories in the standardization sample and in the corresponding United States noninstitutionalized civilian population shows mild discrepancies between the sample and the population (Tulsky, Zhu, & Prifitera, 1999). For example, 3.2% of those in the standardization sample were managers, while 6.9% of those in the U.S. population were so classified; 8.6% of those in the standardization sample were administrative support and clerical specialists, while 16.7% of the population was in this category. These discrepancies should not detract from the representativeness of the standardization sample, however. The WAIS–III was co-normed with the Wechsler Memory Scale–III (WSM–III; Wechsler, 1997), using a sample of individuals 16 to 89 years old ($N = 1,250$). In addition, a sample of individuals 16 to 19 years old ($N = 142$) was given both the WAIS–III and the Wechsler Individual Achievement Test (WIAT; Wechsler, 1991). This sample was referred to as a "linking sample" in the *WAIS–III—WMS–III Technical Manual*. The co-norming of the WAIS–III and WMS–III will enable you to evaluate an examinee's memory

Table 12-1
Demographic Characteristics of WAIS–III Standardization Sample: Education and Geographic Region by Race/Ethnic Group

Demographic variable	Race/ethnic group (percent)			
	Euro American	African American	Hispanic American	Other
Amount of education				
≤ 8 years	9.8	13.3	29.8	6.2
9–11 years	10.3	17.2	18.2	13.8
12 years	36.1	34.4	25.4	24.6
13–15 years	23.8	23.3	19.3	32.3
≥ 16 years	19.9	11.8	7.2	23.1
Total	99.9	100.0	99.9	100.0
Geographic region				
Northeast	19.2	16.5	7.7	16.9
North Central	26.4	30.8	7.7	24.5
South	32.4	37.3	66.9	35.4
West	21.9	15.4	17.7	23.1
Total	99.9	100.0	100.0	100.1

Note. Race/ethnic distribution in total group was as follows: Euro American, 78.6%; African American, 11.4%; Hispanic American, 7.4%; Other, 2.6%.
Source: Adapted from The Psychological Corporation (1997).

functions in relation to his or her level of intellectual functioning. Similarly, linking the WAIS–III and WIAT will help you evaluate an examinee's achievement level in relation to his or her level of intellectual functioning.

DEVIATION IQS AND SCALED SCORES

The WAIS–III, like the WISC–III and WPPSI–R, uses the Deviation IQ ($M = 100$, $SD = 15$) for the Verbal Scale, Performance Scale, and Full Scale IQs, and standard scores ($M = 10$, $SD = 3$) for the 14 individual subtests. An IQ is computed by comparing the examinee's scores with the scores earned by a representative sample of his or her age group. After each subtest is scored, raw point totals are converted to scaled scores within the examinee's own age group through use of Table A.1 in the *WAIS–III Administration and Scoring Manual* (Wechsler, 1997; pp. 181–194). Age groups are 2-year intervals for individuals 16 to 19 years, 5-year intervals for individuals in the age ranges 20 to 34 years and 65 to 89 years, and 10-year intervals for persons between 35 and 64 years old. In the *WAIS–III Administration and Scoring Manual*, the table used to obtain IQs (Table A.3, pages 195–198) is based on the 11 standard subtests.

The two supplementary subtests, Letter–Number Sequencing and Symbol Search, are not used in the calculation of IQs unless the former replaces Digit Span and the latter replaces Digit Symbol—Coding. The optional subtest, Object Assembly, is not used in the calculation of IQs unless it is substituted for a Performance Scale subtest. Little is known about the exact reliability and validity of the IQs when a supplementary or optional subtest is substituted for a standard subtest, because only the standard subtests were used in the construction of the tables used to generate IQs. Moreover, the Letter–Number Sequencing subtest was not administered to the entire standardization sample—only to the 1,250 individuals who also completed the WMS–III. According to the *WAIS–III Administration and Scoring Manual* (page 54), a series of statistical analyses using the normative sample demonstrated that Matrix Reasoning may be replaced by Object Assembly in the determination of the Performance Scale IQs and Full Scale IQs without affecting scores, but no statistical data were provided to support this statement. Because Object Assembly has a lower reliability than Matrix Reasoning ($r_{xx} = .70$ vs. $r_{xx} = .90$), the reliabilities of the Performance Scale IQ and Full Scale IQ are likely to be lower when Object Assembly is substituted for Matrix Reasoning.

Research based on the standardization sample indicates that using Matrix Reasoning instead of Object Assembly yields a slightly higher reliability for the Performance Scale IQ (Tulsky et al., 1999). When the Performance Scale IQ is based on Picture Completion, Block Design, Picture Arrangement, Digit Symbol—Coding, and Object Assembly, the reliability is .93. When Matrix Reasoning replaces Object Assembly, the reliability is .94.

The two WAIS–III manuals (*WAIS–III Administration and Scoring Manual* and *WAIS–III—WMS–III Technical Manual*) provide guidelines for use of the supplementary and optional subtests. These instructions, in part, indicate that Letter–Number Sequencing may substitute only for Digit Span in determining the Verbal Scale IQ, and Symbol Search may replace only Digit Symbol—Coding in calculating the Performance Scale IQ. These substitutions are permitted only when one or both of the designated subtests have been spoiled. The optional subtest, Object Assembly, may be substituted for any spoiled Performance Scale subtest when the examinee is in the age range 16 to 74 years. Unfortunately, the two WAIS–III manuals fail to discuss how these recommendations were reached. Practitioners need to know if there is any research to support these recommendations. We believe that it is reasonable to substitute any subtests as needed because all of the subtests have adequate reliability. In addition, it is likely that the IQs computed with Letter–Number Sequencing, Symbol Search, and Object Assembly will be reliable and valid. However, research studies are needed to determine what actual effects subtest substitutions have on the obtained IQs.

Scaled Scores

The *WAIS–III Administration and Scoring Manual* provides two tables for determining subtest scaled scores. The principal one is Table A.1, on page 181. This table is used in converting raw scores to scaled scores relative to the examinee's own age group. The second one is Table A.2, on page 194, which provides supplemental norms. This table is based on a census-matched reference group of persons ranging in age from 20 to 34 years ($N = 600$). *The subtest scaled scores in Table A.2 are not age-corrected and should never be used for the computation of IQs or index scores.* The scores in Table A.2, however, can be used when you want to compare an older examinee's scaled scores with those of a young-adult group.

Prorating Procedure

Use Table A.10 on page 203 of the *WAIS–III Administration and Scoring Manual* to prorate sums of scaled scores when you administer only five Verbal Scale subtests and four Performance Scale subtests. Tellegen and Briggs (1967) provide another procedure (see Chapter 8) for computing IQs obtained on an abbreviated version of the test (also referred to as a short form). Their procedure considers the intercorrelations between the specific subtests administered; prorating does not take the intercorrelations into account. Later in this chapter we discuss how you can obtain estimated IQs for several short-form subtest combinations using the Tellegen and Briggs procedure. We need research to determine which procedure—prorating or the Tellegen and Briggs procedure—produces more valid IQs.

RELIABILITY

The WAIS–III has excellent reliability. The three scales have internal consistency reliability coefficients of .93 or above over the entire age range covered in the standardization sample. Average internal consistency reliability coefficients, based on the 13 age groups, are .98 for the Full Scale IQ, .97 for the Verbal Scale IQ, and .94 for the Performance Scale IQ (see Table 12-2). The reliability coefficients for ages 16 to 89 years range from .97 to .98 for the Full Scale IQ, .96 to .98 for the Verbal Scale IQ, and .93 to .96 for the Performance Scale IQ. Similar findings have been reported for Euro American males and African American males with substance abuse disorders (Ryan, Arb, Paul, & Kreiner, 2000).

Subtest Reliabilities

The internal consistency reliabilities for the subtests are lower than those for the three scales, as would be expected. The average internal consistency reliabilities range from a low of .70 for Object Assembly to a high of .93 for Vocabulary (see Table 12-2). For the 13 age groups, median subtest

Table 12-2
Reliability Coefficients and Standard Errors of Measurement for WAIS–III Subtests, Scales, and Index Scores

Subtest, scale, or index	Average internal consistency reliability (r_{xx})	Average test-retest reliability (r_{tt})	Average SEM
Vocabulary	.93	.88	.79
Similarities	.86	.83	1.12
Arithmetic	.88	.84	1.05
Digit Span	.90	.73	.94
Information	.91	.94	.91
Comprehension	.84	.79	1.21
Letter–Number Sequencing	.82	.71	1.30
Picture Completion	.83	.82	1.25
Digit Symbol—Coding	.84	.91	1.19
Block Design	.86	.77	1.14
Matrix Reasoning	.90	.76	.97
Picture Arrangement	.74	.68	1.53
Symbol Search	.77	.80	1.43
Object Assembly	.70	.68	1.66
Verbal Scale IQ	.97	.95	2.55
Performance Scale IQ	.94	.93	3.67
Full Scale IQ	.98	.96	2.30
Verbal Comprehension	.96	.95	3.01
Perceptual Organization	.93	.90	3.95
Working Memory	.94	.90	3.84
Processing Speed	.88	.92	5.13

Note. Reliabilities for Digit Symbol—Coding and Symbol Search are test-retest stability coefficients. Reliabilities for the other 12 of the 14 subtests are split-half correlations.
Source: Technical Manual of the Wechsler Adult Intelligence Scale: Third Edition/Wechsler Memory Scale: Third Edition. Copyright © 1997 by The Psychological Corporation. Reproduced by permission. All rights reserved. "Wechsler Adult Intelligence Scale," "Wechsler Memory Scale," and "WMS" are registered trademarks of The Psychological Corporation.

reliabilities range from .83 to .87 (see Table 12-3). Thus, there are no distinct differences in subtest internal consistency reliabilities as a function of age. Similarly high reliabilities have been reported for several clinical samples, including patients with substance abuse disorders, Alzheimer's disease, Hun-

tington's disease, Parkinson's disease, traumatic brain injury, epilepsy, schizophrenia, alcohol abuse, mental retardation, attention-deficit/hyperactivity disorder, learning disabilities, and hearing impairments (Ryan et al., 2000; Zhu, Tulsky, & Rolfhus, 1999).

The highest reliabilities are found among the six standard Verbal Scale subtests (average reliabilities range from .84 to .93). Vocabulary ($r_{xx} = .93$) is the most reliable Verbal Scale subtest. Average reliabilities among the five standard Performance Scale subtests range from .74 to .90. Matrix Reasoning is the most reliable Performance Scale subtest ($r_{xx} = .90$). Reliability coefficients for 10 of the 11 standard subtests and for Letter–Number Sequencing and Object Assembly are split-half correlations corrected by the Spearman-Brown formula (see Chapter 4). For Digit Symbol—Coding and Symbol Search, the reliability estimates are test-retest stability coefficients, because the items comprising these subtests do not lend themselves to the split-half calculation procedure.

Standard Errors of Measurement

The average standard errors of measurement (SEMs) in IQ points are 2.30 for the Full Scale, 2.55 for the Verbal Scale, and 3.67 for the Performance Scale (see Table 12-2). Thus, as with all Wechsler scales, you can place more confidence in IQs based on the Full Scale than in those based on either the Verbal Scale or the Performance Scale. In addition, you can

Table 12-3
Range and Median Internal Consistency Reliabilities of WAIS–III Subtests for 13 Age Groups

Age group	Range r_{xx}	Median r_{xx}
16–17	.70–.90	.83
18–19	.70–.93	.87
20–24	.70–.94	.84
25–29	.71–.92	.86
30–34	.66–.94	.86
35–44	.71–.93	.86
45–54	.75–.92	.86
55–64	.72–.94	.88
65–69	.77–.95	.87
70–74	.68–.93	.87
75–79	.59–.93	.84
80–84	.64–.94	.87
85–89	.50–.93	.83
Average	.70–.93	.85

Source: Adapted from The Psychological Corporation (1997).

place more confidence in IQs obtained from the Verbal Scale than in those obtained from the Performance Scale.

Across the 13 age groups, the standard errors of measurement for the subtests in scaled-score points range from .67 (at 65–69 years) to 1.50 (at 35–44 years and 75–79 years) for the Verbal Scale subtests and from .73 (at 65–69 years) to 2.12 (at 85–89 years) for the Performance Scale subtests. Within the Verbal Scale, Vocabulary has the smallest average SEM (.79) and Letter–Number Sequencing has the largest average SEM (1.30). Among the six standard Verbal Scale subtests, Comprehension has the largest SEM (1.21). Within the Performance Scale, Matrix Reasoning has the smallest average SEM (.97) and Object Assembly has the largest average SEM (1.66).

Among the five standard Performance Scale subtests, Picture Arrangement has the largest average SEM (1.53).

Test-Retest Stability

In the standardization sample, the stability of the WAIS–III was assessed by having 394 individuals from the 13 age groups (approximately 30 individuals from each age group) retested after an interval ranging from 14 to 84 days ($M = 34.6$ days; Wechsler, 1997). Individuals were then combined into four age groups (16–29 years, 30–54 years, 55–74 years, and 75–89 years) for statistical analyses. The uncorrected stability coefficients were, respectively, .91, .96, .96, and .96

Table 12-4
Test-Retest Stability Coefficients of the WAIS–III for Four Age Groups

Subtest, scale, or index	Age group (in years)				
	16–29	30–54	55–74	75–89	Av.[a]
Vocabulary	.85	.93	.92	.85	.91
Similarities	.73	.85	.84	.82	.83
Arithmetic	.80	.87	.86	.83	.86
Digit Span	.75	.79	.85	.69	.83
Information	.92	.93	.93	.94	.94
Comprehension	.67	.80	.83	.75	.81
Letter–Number Sequencing	.48	.74	.77	.71	.75
Picture Completion	.66	.79	.82	.82	.79
Digit Symbol—Coding	.80	.84	.85	.91	.86
Block Design	.77	.86	.77	.76	.82
Matrix Reasoning	.70	.69	.78	.72	.77
Picture Arrangement	.60	.70	.62	.71	.69
Symbol Search	.69	.80	.77	.80	.79
Object Assembly	.64	.78	.76	.65	.76
Verbal Scale IQ	.91	.95	.97	.94	.96
Performance Scale IQ	.83	.88	.91	.93	.91
Full Scale IQ	.91	.96	.96	.96	.96
Verbal Comprehension	.89	.95	.96	.93	.95
Perceptual Organization	.79	.86	.89	.89	.88
Working Memory	.82	.90	.90	.85	.89
Processing Speed	.83	.87	.89	.92	.89

[a] Av. = Average

Source: Technical Manual of the Wechsler Adult Intelligence Scale: Third Edition/Wechsler Memory Scale: Third Edition. Copyright © 1997 by The Psychological Corporation. Reproduced by permission. All rights reserved. "Wechsler Adult Intelligence Scale," "Wechsler Memory Scale," and "WMS" are registered trademarks of The Psychological Corporation.

for the Full Scale IQ; .91, .95, .97, and .94 for the Verbal Scale IQ; and .83, .88, .91, and .93 for the Performance Scale IQ. Thus, the WAIS–III provides stable IQs for the Full Scale, Verbal Scale, and Performance Scale (see Table 12-4).

The stability coefficients for the subtests ranged from a low of .48 for Letter–Number Sequencing at 16–29 years to a high of .94 for Information at 75–89 years (see Table 12-4). Average test-retest reliabilities for the subtests ranged from .69 for Picture Arrangement to .94 for Information (see Table 12-4). Average internal consistency reliabilities are somewhat higher than average test-retest reliabilities ($M\ r_{xx}$ = .84 versus $M\ r_{xx}$ = .78).

Two reasons help to explain why the test-retest stability of the Performance Scale is lower than the test-retest stability of the Verbal Scale. First, Performance Scale subtests are more vulnerable than Verbal Scale subtests to practice effects. Second, retest reliability is limited by internal reliability. Because the Performance Scale subtests have lower internal reliability than the Verbal Scale subtests, we would expect lower retest reliability for the Performance Scale subtests.

Changes in IQs. Table 12-5 shows the mean test-retest IQs and standard deviations for the Verbal Scale, Performance Scale, and Full Scale for the four age groups. On average, from the first to the second testing, the Full Scale IQ increased by 3.2 to 5.7 points, the Verbal Scale IQ increased by 2.0 to 3.2 points, and the Performance Scale IQ increased by 3.7 to 8.3 points. As mentioned above, these statistically significant increases, which likely result from practice effects, are greater for the Performance Scale than for the Verbal Scale. In addition, as Table 12-5 indicates, there is a trend for retest IQ gains on the Full Scale and Performance Scale to diminish with age. Studies with the WAIS–R also show that retest gains decreased with age (Ryan, Paolo, & Brungardt, 1992; Wechsler, 1981). Perhaps the smaller practice effects with age indicate an age-related drop in incidental learning, a component of fluid intelligence.

Studies are needed to evaluate the stability of the WAIS–III with other samples, including adolescents and adults, and over longer periods of time. Such research would be helpful in determining how IQs on the WAIS–III change over time in different populations and in different age groups. Although, in general, stability coefficients are high for the WAIS–III, there is no way of knowing the precise stability of scores for any individual examinee. This is true for all tests—it is not unique to the WAIS–III.

Changes in subtest scaled scores. Table 12-6 shows the changes in subtest scaled scores from the first to the second administration. The largest changes were for Picture Completion (increases of .9 to 2.4 scaled-score points), and the smallest changes were for Matrix Reasoning (decrease of .1 to an increase of .3). The retest changes were significantly greater than chance in 36 of the 56 t tests that we conducted. It is difficult to know why the Picture Completion subtest showed the largest retest gains.

Table 12-5
Test-Retest WAIS–III IQs for Four Age Groups

Age group	Scale	First testing Mean IQ	SD	Second testing Mean IQ	SD	Change
16–29 (N = 100)	VS	101.4	11.9	104.6	12.6	+3.2*
	PS	101.6	12.2	109.8	12.7	+8.2*
	FS	101.7	11.7	107.4	12.4	+5.7*
30–54 (N = 100)	VS	99.3	14.4	101.3	14.9	+2.0*
	PS	99.9	13.8	108.2	16.6	+8.3*
	FS	99.6	14.3	104.7	15.7	+5.1*
55–74 (N = 100)	VS	99.0	14.1	101.1	14.2	+2.1*
	PS	99.1	14.2	104.8	15.7	+5.7*
	FS	99.0	14.3	102.9	15.0	+3.9*
75–89 (N = 100)	VS	98.9	13.0	101.3	14.7	+2.4*
	PS	99.4	15.2	103.1	18.7	+3.7*
	FS	99.0	14.1	102.2	16.3	+3.2*

*$p < .001$.

Note. Abbreviations: VS = Verbal Scale; PS = Performance Scale; FS = Full Scale.

Source: Technical Manual of the Wechsler Adult Intelligence Scale: Third Edition/Wechsler Memory Scale: Third Edition. Copyright © 1997 by The Psychological Corporation. Reproduced by permission. All rights reserved. "Wechsler Adult Intelligence Scale," "Wechsler Memory Scale," and "WMS" are registered trademarks of The Psychological Corporation.

Knowing the relationship between subtest gain scores and the internal consistency reliabilities of the subtests is helpful in evaluating the gain scores. Calculation of the Spearman rank-order correlations between the magnitude of gain from the initial test to retest and the reliability of the subtests yielded correlations of –.56, –.63, –.52, and –.57 in the age groups 16–29, 30–54, 55–74, and 75–89 years, respectively. These coefficients are significant at $p < .05$ using a one-tailed test, suggesting that practice effects are likely to be smaller for the most reliable subtests.

Changes in index scores. Table 12-6 shows the changes in index scores from the first to the second administration. The largest changes were for Perceptual Organization (increases of 2.7 to 7.4 points), and the smallest changes were for Working Memory (increases of 1.3 to 3.1 points). Although the oldest age group (75–89 years) had smaller gains on retest than the other age groups on Perceptual Organization, Working Memory, and Processing Speed, it had the

Table 12-6
Test-Retest Gains or Losses on the WAIS–III for Four Age Groups

Subtest or index	Age group			
	16–29	*30–54*	*55–74*	*75–89*
Vocabulary	0.2	0.1	0.2	0.4*
Similarities	0.6**	0.3	0.4*	0.7***
Arithmetic	0.6***	0.3	0.3	0.5**
Digit Span	0.5*	0.4*	0.4**	–0.1
Information	0.6***	0.6***	0.5***	0.6***
Comprehension	0.4*	0.1	0.1	0.3
Letter–Number Sequencing	0.1	0.7**	0.3	0.5
Picture Completion	2.3***	2.4***	1.6***	0.9***
Digit Symbol—Coding	1.2***	1.1***	0.8***	0.6***
Block Design	1.0***	0.7***	0.2	0.3
Matrix Reasoning	0.1	0.3	0.2	–0.1
Picture Arrangement	1.2***	1.2***	1.2**	0.7**
Symbol Search	1.0***	0.5**	0.5*	–0.2
Object Assembly	2.3***	1.6***	1.0***	0.9**
Verbal Comprehension	2.5***	2.1***	1.9***	3.2***
Perceptual Organization	7.3***	7.4***	4.0***	2.7**
Working Memory	2.9**	3.1***	2.2***	1.3
Processing Speed	6.0***	4.6***	3.8***	1.3

*p < .05.
**p < .01.
***p < .001.

Source: Adapted from The Psychological Corporation (1997).

largest gain of the four age groups on Verbal Comprehension. In summary, all groups showed significant gains on retest, with the exception of the 75–89-year age group on Working Memory and Processing Speed, where the increases were not statistically significant.

Confidence Intervals

This text presents tables for two types of confidence intervals. The first is Table C-1 in Appendix C, which is based on the obtained score and the standard error of measurement (SEM). The second is Table D-2 in Appendix D, which uses the estimated true score and the standard error of estimation (SE_E). The *WAIS–III Administration and Scoring Manual* (Tables A.3–A.9), in contrast, provides confidence intervals based on the estimated true score only and for the total group only. The

procedures discussed in Chapter 4 concerning proper use of the SEM and the SE_E apply to the WAIS–III and to all tests. We recommend that you use Table C-1 in Appendix C (based on the obtained score and the SEM) to obtain the confidence intervals for individual test administrations.

Table C-1 in Appendix C shows the 68, 85, 90, 95, and 99% confidence intervals based on the obtained score and the SEM for the 13 age groups and the total standardization sample. In contrast, Table D-2 in Appendix D shows the 68, 85, 90, 95, and 99% confidence intervals based on the estimated true score and the SE_E. If you need to use Table D-2 in Appendix D for any purpose, you will need to know the reliability coefficient for each WAIS–III scale in each age group. The first part of Table D-2 in Appendix D shows the specific part of the table that you should use for each age and scale. The confidence intervals in this text are more appropriate than the ones in the *WAIS–III Administration and Scoring Manual* because they are based on the examinee's specific age.

VALIDITY

Because the WAIS–III is a recently published test, relatively little is known about its validity. Approximately 70% of the items on the WAIS–III are from the WAIS–R—only about 30% are new. It seems plausible, therefore, that research concerning the validity of the WAIS–R applies to the WAIS–III. Studies related to the validity of the WAIS–R indicate that the WAIS–R had adequate concurrent and construct validity for many different types of normal and clinical samples in the age range 16 to 74 years (Sattler, 1992). In addition, the *WAIS–III—WMS–III Technical Manual* (The Psychological Corporation, 1997) presents studies that focus on the content, concurrent, and construct validity of the WAIS–III. These studies are summarized below.

Content Validity

The degree to which test items are representative of the defined construct or domain under study provides evidence of content validity. Expert professional judgment plays an integral part in determining content validity. Three primary steps were taken to ensure adequate content validity of the WAIS–III: (a) comprehensive literature reviews were completed to identify problematic items within the WAIS–R; (b) items from the WAIS–R, along with suggested new items provided by psychologists, were scrutinized by consultants for content coverage and relevance, as well as for possible revision or deletion; and (c) surveys and focus groups composed of clinical practitioners and assessment professionals were used to further evaluate item content, usefulness, and relevance. Finally, an advisory panel of psychologists and researchers reviewed and critiqued the results of steps a, b, and c. The panel also made recommendations concerning the development of new subtests, improvement of existing subtests, development of summary scores, and selection of individual test items (The Psychological Corporation, 1997).

Concurrent Validity

The degree to which a test is related to an established criterion measure, when both instruments are administered at approximately the same time, reflects concurrent validity. The *WAIS–III—WMS–III Technical Manual* reports the findings of a series of studies in which the WAIS–III was given along with the WAIS–R, WISC–III, Stanford-Binet: Fourth Edition, Standard Progressive Matrices, and measures of memory and academic achievement. Let's review these findings.

WAIS–III and WAIS–R. A sample of 192 persons between 16 and 74 years of age was administered the WAIS–III and WAIS–R in counterbalanced order (i.e., one group was given first one test and then the other test; the two tests were then given in reverse order to the second group), within a 2- to 12-week period (The Psychological Corporation, 1997). The median retest interval was 4.7 weeks. The group was predominantly Caucasian (79.2% Euro American, 11.5% African American, 6.8% Hispanic American, 2.5% other) and composed of approximately equal numbers of men and women (48.4% males, 51.6% females). The correlations between the tests were .94 for the Verbal Scale, .86 for the Performance Scale, and .93 for the Full Scale. For the 11 subtests that appear in both versions of the test, correlations ranged from a low of .50 for Picture Completion to a high of .90 for Vocabulary (*Mdn r* = .77). Subtests on the Verbal Scale had higher correlations (range of .76 to .90, *Mdn r* = .81) than did those on the Performance Scale (range of .50 to .77, *Mdn r* = .69). The high correlations are not surprising, because most items are the same in both tests. What is less clear is why the correlations were relatively low for some of the Performance Scale subtests, particularly Picture Completion.

The low correlation on Picture Completion may have resulted from the fact that Picture Completion was the subtest most substantially modified in the revision. Only 40% of the WAIS–R Picture Completion items were retained in the WAIS–III, and all items on the WAIS–III Picture Completion subtest were enlarged and colored.

For the Verbal Scale, Performance Scale, and Full Scale, mean IQs were *lower* on the WAIS–III than on the WAIS–R. The average difference was 1.2 points on the Verbal Scale (102.2 vs. 103.4), 4.8 points on the Performance Scale (103.5 vs. 108.3), and 2.9 points on the Full Scale (102.9 vs. 105.8). These results are consistent with previous findings that individuals tend to score lower on new tests than on older ones (Flynn, 1984, 1987, 1998).

The relationship between the WAIS–R and the WAIS–III needs further investigation. For example, because the individuals used to compare the WAIS–R and the WAIS–III were all younger than 75 years old and generally of average ability, we have no way of knowing whether the two tests produce comparable IQs at other ages and ability levels. Until additional research becomes available, you need to be cautious when interpreting results for individuals tested with the WAIS–R and then with the WAIS–III. However, preliminary research suggests that individuals with average ability who are between 16 and 74 years of age will likely obtain somewhat lower scores on the WAIS–III than on the WAIS–R.

When a counterbalanced design is used to evaluate changes from one Wechsler test to another, the scores on the second test are confounded by practice effects—that is, by prior exposure to the first test. This is even more of a factor when there are overlapping items on the two tests. Thus, the results for the second test are not clean; only the results for the first test are uncontaminated. In order to ascertain whether scores on two tests differ, we need to have data from independent test administrations. In the study reported in the *WAIS–III WMS–III Technical Manual* in which the WAIS–III and the WAIS–R were counterbalanced, the independent test data would be data from the first administration of each test only. Unfortunately, these data were not provided by the test publisher. Practice effects have probably made the means in the tables a bit high.

WAIS–III and WISC–III. Because the WAIS–III and WISC–III overlap at ages 16 to 17 years, we need information about the relationship between the two tests for this age group. The WAIS–III and WISC–III were administered in counterbalanced order to a sample of 184 16-year-olds (The Psychological Corporation, 1997). The interval between the two administrations ranged from 2 to 12 weeks (*Mdn* = 4.6 weeks). The correlations were .88 for the Verbal Scale, .78 for the Performance Scale, and .88 for the Full Scale.

For the 11 subtests that the WAIS–III and WISC–III have in common, correlations ranged from a low of .31 for Picture Arrangement to a high of .83 for Vocabulary (*Mdn r* = .73). Subtests on the Verbal Scale have higher correlations (range of .60 to .83, *Mdn r* = .74) than do those on the Performance Scale (range of .31 to .80, *Mdn r* = .64).

For the Verbal Scale, Performance Scale, and Full Scale, mean IQs were slightly higher on the WAIS–III than on the WISC–III. The average difference was 0.5 point on the Verbal Scale (103.5 vs. 103.0), 0.4 point on the Performance Scale (104.9 vs. 104.5), and 0.7 point on the Full Scale (104.6 vs. 103.9). These results suggest that the two scales yield comparable IQs. However, these findings are based on a relatively small sample with predominantly average ability and should not be generalized to individuals at the relative extremes of the intelligence distribution.

Research is needed on the comparability of the WAIS–III and WISC–III in groups composed of individuals who have clinical problems, who are gifted, or who have mental retardation. In addition, because the results reported previously were based on a counterbalanced design, the scores on the second test administered are affected by practice effects. To examine further the comparability of the WAIS–III and WISC–III, we need results from independent administrations of the two tests to random samples and results from different groups of exceptional adolescents.

WAIS–III and Stanford-Binet: IV. Twenty-six normal individuals (*M* age = 28.5) were administered both the WAIS–III and the Stanford-Binet: IV (Thorndike, Hagen, &

Sattler, 1986b) within an unspecified time frame. The mean scores were highly similar. On the Stanford-Binet: IV, the mean composite score was 114.8 (*SD* = 12.1), and on the WAIS–III, the mean Full Scale IQ was 113.3 (*SD* = 12.2). Correlations between the Stanford-Binet and WAIS–III were .78 for the Verbal Scale IQ, .89 for the Performance Scale IQ, and .88 for the Full Scale IQ.

Other concurrent validity studies. Table 12-7 summarizes the results of studies, primarily reported in the *WAIS–III—WMS–III Technical Manual*, in which the WAIS–III was correlated with other tests of cognitive ability, achievement, and memory. The table also includes the relationship between years of education and IQs for a sample of participants in the WAIS–III standardization group who were 25 years old or older (Tulsky & Ledbetter, 2000). Based on the magnitude and pattern of correlations across the different measures, it appears that the WAIS–III has satisfactory concurrent validity. For the most part, the WAIS–III Full Scale correlates more highly with other tests of intelligence (*Mdn r* = .88) than it does with tests of academic achievement (*Mdn r* = .72) and memory (Mdn r = .60) and with years of education (*Mdn* = .55). However, we need additional studies using different populations and different ability, achievement, and memory tests.

The relationship between the WAIS–III and the Wechsler Abbreviated Scale of Intelligence (WASI; The Psychological Corporation, 1999) was reported in the WASI manual (see Chapter 16 for a description of the WASI). A sample of 248 persons between 16 and 89 years of age was administered the two tests within a 2- to 12-week period (*M* retest interval was 4 weeks). Correlations were .82 for the Verbal Scale, .84 for the Performance Scale, and .92 for the Full Scale. For the four subtests that appear in both tests, correlations were .88 for Vocabulary, .76 for Similarities, .83 for Block Design, and .66 for Matrix Reasoning (*Mdn r* = .79). Mean IQs were highly similar on the two tests.

Construct Validity

One method of assessing construct validity is factor analysis. Factor analysis can be used to determine the structure and components of intelligence as measured by a given test. Our principal-axis factor analysis of the WAIS–III standardization sample indicates that all 14 subtests measure general intelligence (*g*) with a moderate or high degree of success. Our results provide support for interpretation of the Verbal Scale IQ and Performance Scale IQ as separate entities and the Full Scale IQ as a global measure of intelligence. For the majority of the age groups, support for the four index scores also was found (see the section on factor analysis later in this chapter).

The pattern of intercorrelations discussed below provides evidence of convergent and discriminant validity, which are forms of construct validity. Convergent validity is demonstrated when tasks that theoretically tap similar functions correlate more highly with each other than with tasks that

Table 12-7
Summary of WAIS–III Criterion-Related Validity Studies

Criterion	WAIS–III		
	VS IQ	*PS IQ*	*FS IQ*
Wechsler Adult Intelligence Scale–Revised	.94	.86	.93
Wechsler Intelligence Scale for Children–III	.88	.78	.88
Stanford-Binet: IV	.78	.89	.88
Standard Progressive Matrices	.49	.79	.64
Wechsler Individual Achievement Test			
Reading Composite	.79	.61	.76
Math Composite	.81	.69	.81
Language Composite	.70	.53	.68
Writing Composite	.69	.55	.68
Wechsler Memory Scale–III			
Immediate Memory Composite	.53	.54	.57
General Memory Composite	.56	.56	.60
Working Memory Composite	.62	.65	.68
Wechsler Abbreviated Scale of Intelligence	.88	.84	.92
Years of education	.55	.46	.55

Note. Abbreviations: VS = Verbal Scale, PS = Performance Scale, FS = Full Scale.

Source: Adapted from The Psychological Corporation (1997, 1999) and from Tulsky and Ledbetter (2000).

theoretically measure different functions. Discriminant validity is demonstrated when tasks that purport to measure different functions yield relatively low or nonsignificant correlations. The pattern of intercorrelations reveals that tasks measuring similar functions (e.g., Vocabulary and Similarities) correlate more highly with each other than do tasks measuring different functions (e.g., Digit Span and Block Design).

INTERCORRELATIONS BETWEEN SUBTESTS AND SCALES

Inspection of the intercorrelations between WAIS–III subtests and scales (see Table 4.12, page 98, in the *WAIS–III WMS–III Technical Manual*) indicates that, in the total group, correlations between the 14 subtests range from a low of .26 to a high of .77 (*Mdn r* = .48). The highest subtest intercorrelations are between Vocabulary and Information (.77), Vocabulary and Similarities (.76), Vocabulary and Comprehension (.75), Information and Similarities (.70), Information and Comprehension (.70), Comprehension and Similarities (.70), and Digit Symbol—Coding and Symbol Search (.65). The lowest subtest intercorrelations are between Object Assembly and Digit Span (.26), Object Assembly and Letter–Number Sequencing (.29), Picture Completion and Digit Span (.30), Object Assembly and Digit Symbol—Coding (.33), Digit Span and Picture Arrangement (.33), Digit Symbol—Coding and Digit Span (.36), and Digit Span and Block Design (.36).

In the total group, the Verbal Scale subtests correlate more highly with each other (*Mdn r* = .57) than do the Performance Scale subtests (*Mdn r* = .49). Average correlations between the Verbal Scale subtests and the Verbal Scale range from .51 to .83 (*Mdn r* = .76); those between the Performance Scale subtests and the Performance Scale range from .50 to .69 (*Mdn r* = .64). Thus, the Verbal Scale subtests have more in common with each other than do the Performance Scale subtests (see Table 12-8).

Average correlations between the 14 individual subtests and the Full Scale range from .52 to .80 (*Mdn r* = .66). Vocabulary has the highest correlation with the Full Scale (.80), followed by Information (.76) and Similarities (.76), Comprehension (.75), Arithmetic (.72), Matrix Reasoning (.69), Symbol Search (.66) and Block Design (.66), Letter–Number Sequencing (.64), Picture Arrangement (.63), Picture Completion (.60), Object Assembly (.59), Digit Symbol—Coding (.53), and Digit Span (.52). Thus, five of the six standard Verbal Scale subtests and one standard Performance Scale subtest (Matrix Reasoning) correlate more highly with the Full Scale than do the other subtests (see Table 12-8). Vocabulary has the highest correlation with the Verbal Scale (.83), and Symbol Search has the highest correlation with the Performance Scale (.69). Overall, the Verbal Scale subtests have higher correlations with the Full Scale (*Mdn r* = .75) than do the Performance Scale subtests (*Mdn r* = .63).

FACTOR ANALYSIS

Factor Analyses Reported in the *WAIS–III—WMS–III Technical Manual*

The *WAIS–III—WMS–III Technical Manual* reports a series of exploratory factor analyses (principal-axis method) of the standardization sample. The 2,450 adolescent and adult individuals were clustered into five age groups (16–19, 20–34, 35–54, 55–74, and 75–89 years), and their scores on 13 of the 14 subtests were analyzed (the Object Assembly subtest was excluded). The results indicated that, for the most part, a four-factor model best describes the WAIS–III. These factors are labeled Verbal Comprehension, Perceptual Organization, Working Memory, and Processing Speed. The factor names are attempts at labeling the postulated unitary ability that accounts for the interrelated performance on the subtests of each factor.

The term *Verbal Comprehension* reflects a hypothesized verbal-related ability reflected in item content (verbal) and mental processes (comprehension). Acquired verbal-related knowledge and verbal reasoning are likely measured by this factor. This factor is correlated most closely with scores on the Vocabulary, Information, Comprehension, and Similarities subtests.

The term *Perceptual Organization* describes a hypothesized performance-related ability reflected in item content (perceptual) and mental processes (organization). Nonverbal reasoning, attentiveness to detail, and visual-motor integration are likely measured by this factor. This factor is correlated most closely with scores on the Block Design, Matrix Reasoning, Picture Completion, and Picture Arrangement subtests for three of the four age groups. However, a well-defined Perceptual Organization factor does not emerge for persons in the age range 75–89 years (see Table 4.16, page 108, in the *WAIS–III—WMS–III Technical Manual*).

The term *Working Memory* reflects a hypothesized memory-related ability that requires the holding of information "online" so that manipulations or calculations can be

Table 12-8
Average Correlations Between WAIS–III Subtests and Verbal, Performance, and Full Scales

Subtest	Verbal Scale	Performance Scale	Full Scale
Vocabulary	.83	.65	.80
Similarities	.77	.65	.76
Arithmetic	.70	.63	.72
Digit Span	.51	.47	.52
Information	.79	.63	.76
Comprehension	.76	.62	.75
Letter–Number Seq.	.62	.57	.64
Picture Completion	.53	.60	.60
Digit Symbol—Coding	.49	.50	.53
Block Design	.59	.66	.66
Matrix Reasoning	.64	.65	.69
Picture Arrangement	.59	.60	.63
Symbol Search	.57	.69	.66
Object Assembly	.50	.64	.59

Source: Technical Manual of the Wechsler Adult Intelligence Scale: Third Edition/Wechsler Memory Scale: Third Edition. Copyright © 1997 by The Psychological Corporation. Reproduced by permission. All rights reserved. "Wechsler Adult Intelligence Scale," "Wechsler Memory Scale," and "WMS" are registered trademarks of The Psychological Corporation.

Table 12-9
Factor Loadings of WAIS–III Subtests for 13 Age Groups and the Average of All Age Groups Following Principal Factor Analysis (Four-Factor Solution, Oblimin Rotation)

Subtest	16–17	18–19	20–24	25–29	30–34	35–44	45–54	55–64	65–69	70–74	75–79	80–84	85–89	Av.[a]
						Age group								
Factor A—Verbal Comprehension														
Vocabulary	87	87	86	95	85	92	81	89	85	77	90	91	77	91
Similarities	63	69	83	83	80	74	67	78	69	79	71	79	59	77
Arithmetic	34	31	28	49	32	15	38	20	33	20	40	58	13	27
Digit Span	–03	–03	05	27	–07	03	11	10	–01	15	29	15	19	01
Information	76	87	84	85	83	76	72	77	86	63	85	92	76	84
Comprehension	79	78	82	82	78	86	84	66	90	69	82	78	80	81
Letter–Number Seq.	05	00	00	19	02	08	–08	10	27	–10	19	12	02	03
Picture Completion	09	05	04	08	10	17	16	17	42	17	12	05	45	12
Digit Symbol—Cod.	12	07	02	–02	11	02	–02	–02	03	05	04	04	02	03
Block Design	07	06	–02	–02	07	–08	07	–09	07	–02	–01	22	03	–03
Matrix Reasoning	25	10	11	12	26	11	34	25	17	01	06	41	–01	11
Picture Arrangement	30	38	29	35	43	39	20	49	20	29	21	35	44	31
Symbol Search	–08	00	–01	01	–08	05	05	06	01	10	–13	–06	00	–01
Object Assembly	03	09	08	–03	–01	04	05	14	02	02	02	04	25	03
Factor B—Perceptual Organization														
Vocabulary	–04	–07	–01	–10	00	–06	04	–16	–09	–02	–07	–08	07	–08
Similarities	11	18	–01	03	09	–01	23	11	09	13	14	–02	24	08
Arithmetic	04	19	31	18	–03	25	17	17	23	07	01	–03	25	13
Digit Span	17	13	–02	08	–04	–08	–05	07	07	–05	–04	–15	08	–01
Information	02	–07	–03	–03	–04	02	17	00	–08	08	02	01	–07	–03
Comprehension	00	12	07	08	03	06	–14	10	16	05	14	14	08	06
Letter–Number Seq.	–12	–12	05	32	13	09	10	–09	–18	08	14	16	–08	01
Picture Completion	44	26	45	62	57	47	41	47	37	41	56	73	04	48
Digit Symbol—Cod.	–10	–09	08	–10	–08	04	00	–02	05	00	–01	08	17	–04
Block Design	67	79	74	73	54	79	67	65	68	65	66	42	62	70
Matrix Reasoning	45	25	54	53	18	59	45	45	52	45	42	29	62	49
Picture Arrangement	31	07	36	32	49	26	55	33	32	54	32	29	08	35
Symbol Search	23	19	34	16	27	12	12	18	24	08	14	21	26	15
Object Assembly	74	61	79	81	78	74	76	68	60	77	75	65	54	74

(Continued)

Table 12-9 (*Continued*)

Subtest	16–17	18–19	20–24	25–29	30–34	35–44	45–54	55–64	65–69	70–74	75–79	80–84	85–89	Av.[a]
							Age group							

Factor C—Working Memory

Subtest	16–17	18–19	20–24	25–29	30–34	35–44	45–54	55–64	65–69	70–74	75–79	80–84	85–89	Av.[a]
Vocabulary	–07	02	09	10	08	–06	05	05	04	16	–06	04	13	02
Similarities	02	04	01	07	00	13	07	00	07	–14	–01	08	–01	–02
Arithmetic	39	29	40	13	56	53	21	56	45	62	40	25	50	50
Digit Span	60	62	75	38	77	62	69	58	71	50	25	62	55	67
Information	02	01	05	06	04	18	09	14	14	24	06	–11	10	06
Comprehension	07	–07	–09	–07	00	–08	01	18	–08	09	01	–04	11	00
Letter–Number Seq.	86	92	79	37	67	72	73	61	40	63	06	73	71	61
Picture Completion	09	14	11	–07	17	–09	06	05	–12	–06	–15	25	–11	–02
Digit Symbol—Cod.	06	04	04	01	02	06	05	01	04	02	–10	64	29	04
Block Design	26	08	19	22	15	12	09	25	14	11	16	11	09	18
Matrix Reasoning	18	51	21	23	46	24	02	24	30	47	29	12	14	33
Picture Arrangement	–03	38	–06	–04	–06	20	–13	–07	03	05	03	18	00	01
Symbol Search	06	01	02	–03	07	08	04	06	12	09	12	72	14	06
Object Assembly	–17	–02	–10	–06	00	–12	09	–13	–03	–05	–08	–08	–31	–10

Factor D—Processing Speed

Subtest	16–17	18–19	20–24	25–29	30–34	35–44	45–54	55–64	65–69	70–74	75–79	80–84	85–89	Av.[a]
Vocabulary	13	10	–01	00	03	14	01	13	15	06	08	08	–06	06
Similarities	01	–01	04	01	–01	04	–08	00	12	11	14	10	09	03
Arithmetic	18	18	00	16	09	03	13	01	02	05	11	02	06	00
Digit Span	09	08	12	16	05	16	–03	03	05	01	37	–11	–08	05
Information	06	03	01	–03	07	–08	–09	–01	–04	01	–01	–10	20	–02
Comprehension	–08	02	01	01	07	00	17	–01	–08	11	–13	–08	–17	–03
Letter–Number Seq.	04	05	00	12	02	02	13	24	35	26	44	–28	17	16
Picture Completion	16	19	17	02	–03	18	17	15	19	30	15	–20	41	19
Digit Symbol—Cod.	70	76	75	85	64	67	79	82	74	66	80	25	57	73
Block Design	–04	–02	–01	01	18	07	09	06	09	16	06	38	17	02
Matrix Reasoning	–02	02	06	08	–06	–01	10	05	00	02	05	18	05	–05
Picture Arrangement	00	–10	10	14	01	–09	14	06	30	–07	20	04	37	09
Symbol Search	74	72	61	78	62	62	72	65	61	63	76	19	63	70
Object Assembly	14	13	00	02	07	08	01	13	26	05	–02	10	–01	06

Note. Decimal points omitted.
[a]Av. = Average of 13 age groups.

performed (analogous to a mental scratch pad). Short-term memory is likely measured by this factor. This factor is correlated most closely with scores on the Arithmetic, Digit Span, and Letter–Number Sequencing subtests.

The term *Processing Speed* reflects a hypothesized performance-related ability involving perceptual processing and speed as reflected in both mental and psychomotor performance. Quickness in processing visual information is likely measured by this factor. This factor is correlated most closely with scores on the Digit Symbol—Coding and Symbol Search subtests for four of the age groups. However, in the age group 75–89 years, the factor is more complex, with substantial loadings on Block Design, Picture Completion, and Picture Arrangement (see Table 4.21, page 109, in the *WAIS–III—WMS–III Technical Manual*).

Exploratory factor analyses were conducted separately for Euro American ($N = 1,925$), African American, ($N = 279$), and Hispanic American ($N = 181$) groups in the standardization sample (Tulsky et al., 1999). The four-factor model was judged appropriate for each ethnic group, except for minor variations in factor pattern loadings. In the African American sample, the factor loading on Arithmetic was split between the Verbal Comprehension and Working Memory factors. In the Hispanic American sample, Picture Arrangement was split between the Verbal Comprehension and Perceptual Organization factors and the Arithmetic subtest did not contribute meaningfully to the Working Memory factor.

Factor Analysis Conducted by Ryan and Sattler

To further clarify the underlying structure of the WAIS–III, we conducted a principal-axis factor analysis (extraction limited to two iterations) followed by oblimin rotation (a type of orthogonal rotation that has the goal of obtaining a simple structure while allowing the factors to be correlated with each other) on the total sample and on each of the 13 age groups. All 14 subtests were included in the analyses, and a four-factor solution was specified. As you can see in Table 12-9, a four-factor solution characterizes the WAIS–III, but the subtests that load on each factor vary somewhat with age. For example, for the Verbal Comprehension factor, Vocabulary, Similarities, Information, and Comprehension are present at every age group and in the total group. However, three Performance Scale subtests—Picture Arrangement, Matrix Reasoning, and Picture Completion—also correlate at .30 or above with the Verbal Comprehension factor at one or more ages. Picture Arrangement, in particular, correlates at .30 or above with Verbal Comprehension at eight age groups and in the total group. Arithmetic also correlates at .30 or above with the Verbal Comprehension factor at eight age groups.

Picture Completion, Block Design, Matrix Reasoning, Picture Arrangement, and Object Assembly load on the Perceptual Organization factor (.30 or above) at 9 to 13 age

groups and in the total group. Only one Verbal Scale subtest—Letter–Number Sequencing—loads on the Perceptual Organization factor (.30 or above), and it does so at only one age group (25–29 years).

Arithmetic, Digit Span, and Letter–Number Sequencing load on the Working Memory factor (.30 or above) at 9 to 12 age groups and in the total group. Three Performance Scale subtests—Matrix Reasoning, Picture Arrangement, and Object Assembly—also load on the Working Memory factor at one or more age groups (and in the total group in the case of Matrix Reasoning).

Digit Symbol—Coding and Symbol Search load on the Processing Speed factor (.30 or above) at 12 age groups and in the total group. Other subtests that load on the factor (.30 or above) at one or more age groups include Letter–Number Sequencing, Picture Completion, Digit Span, and Block Design.

There is no easy explanation for this pattern of subtest loadings. Perhaps a Performance Scale subtest like Picture Arrangement also has a strong verbal processing component. In addition, why some subtests have meaningful loadings on a factor at some ages and not at others cannot be readily explained. Differences may be due to sampling differences or measurement error or some unknown factor related to developmental trends. Table 12-10 summarizes the major trends in the factor analysis by age level.

Later in this chapter you will read about index scores based on the factor analysis conducted by The Psychological Corporation. Overall, our factor analysis supports the work of The Psychological Corporation, albeit with some discrepancies. Similarly, a factor analysis of the WAIS–III in a clinical sample of 152 patients with a variety of psychiatric or neurological disorders generally supported a four-factor model (Ryan & Lopez, 1999), although the Arithmetic subtest could not be uniquely assigned to any factor.

WAIS–III Subtests as Measures of *g*

Examination of the loadings on the first unrotated factor in the principal-axis factor analysis allows one to determine the extent to which the WAIS–III subtests measure general intelligence, or *g*. Overall, the WAIS–III is a fair measure of general intelligence, with 50% of its variance attributed to *g*.

The WAIS–III subtests form two clusters with respect to the measurement of *g*: (a) Vocabulary, Similarities, Information, Comprehension, Arithmetic, Block Design, and Matrix Reasoning are good measures of *g*, and (b) Symbol Search, Picture Arrangement, Letter–Number Sequencing, Picture Completion, Object Assembly, Digit Symbol—Coding, and Digit Span are fair measures of *g* (see Table 12-11). The subtests in the Verbal Scale have higher *g* loadings (55%, on the average) than those in the Performance Scale (44%, on the average). Highest loadings are for Vocabulary, Similarities, and Information in the Verbal Scale and for Block Design, Matrix Reasoning, and Symbol Search in the Performance Scale.

Table 12-10
Summary of Principal Factor Analysis on WAIS–III by Age Group and for the Average of the Total Sample

Age group	Number of factors	Subtests with loadings of .30 or higher on Verbal Comprehension	Subtests with loadings of .30 or higher on Perceptual Organization	Subtests with loadings of .30 or higher on Working Memory	Subtests with loadings of .30 or higher on Processing Speed
16–17	4	V, S, A, I, C, PA	PC, BD, MR, PA, OA	A, DS, LN	CD, SS
18–19	4	V, S, A, I, C, PA	BD, OA	DS, LN, MR, PA	CD, SS
20–24	4	V, S, I, C	PC, BD, MR, PA, SS, OA	A, DS, LN	CD, SS
25–29	3	V, S, A, I, C, PA	LN, PC, BD, MR, PA, OA	DS	CD, SS
30–34	4	V, S, A, I, C, PA	PC, BD, PA, OA	A, DS, LN, MR	CD, SS
35–44	4	V, S, I, C, PA	PC, BD, MR, OA	A, DS, LN	CD, SS
45–54	4	V, S, A, C, MR	PC, BD, MR, PA, OA	DS, LN	CD, SS
55–64	4	V, S, I, C, PA	PC, BD, MR, PA, OA	A, DS, LN	CD, SS
65–69	4	V, S, A, I, C, PC	PC, BD, MR, PA, OA	A, DS, LN, MR	LN, CD, SS
70–74	4	V, S, I, C	PC, BD, MR, PA, OA	A, DS, LN, MR	PC, CD, SS
75–79	3	V, S, A, I, C	PC, BD, MR, PA, OA	A	DS, LN, CD, SS
80–84	3	V, S, A, I, C, MR, PA	PC, BD, OA	DS, LN	BD
85–89	4	V, S, I, C, PC, PA	BD, MR, OA	A, DS, LN, OA	PC, CD, SS
Av.	4	V, S, I, C, PA	PC, BD, MR, PA, OA	A, DS, LN, MR	CD, SS

Note. Abbreviations: V = Vocabulary, S = Similarities, A = Arithmetic, C = Comprehension, DS = Digit Span, I = Information, LN = Letter–Number Sequencing, PC = Picture Completion, CD = Digit Symbol—Coding, BD = Block Design, MR = Matrix Reasoning, PA = Picture Arrangement, SS = Symbol Search, Av. = Average.

Table 12-11
WAIS–III Subtests as Measures of *g*

Subtest	Good measure of g		Subtest	Fair measure of g	
	Average loading of g	Proportion of variance attributed to g (%)		Average loading of g	Proportion of variance attributed to g (%)
Vocabulary	.83	69	Symbol Search	.70	49
Similarities	.79	62	Picture Arrangement	.66	44
Information	.79	62	Letter–Number Seq.	.65	42
Comprehension	.77	59	Picture Completion	.64	41
Arithmetic	.75	56	Object Assembly	.62	38
Block Design	.72	52	Digit Symbol—Coding	.59	35
Matrix Reasoning	.72	52	Digit Span	.57	32

Subtest Specificity

Subtest specificity refers to the proportion of a subtest's variance that is both reliable (i.e., not due to errors of measurement) and distinctive to the subtest (see Chapter 4 for further information about subtest specificity). Although individual subtests on the WAIS–III overlap in their measurement properties (i.e., the majority of the reliable variance for most subtests is common factor variance), many possess sufficient specificity at some ages to justify interpretation of specific subtest functions (see Table 12-12).

Throughout the age range covered by the WAIS–III, Arithmetic, Digit Span, Information, Digit Symbol—Coding, Block Design, and Matrix Reasoning have ample or adequate

Table 12-12
Amount of Specificity in WAIS–III Subtests for 13 Age Groups and the Average of All Age Groups

Subtest	Age groups with ample specificity	Age groups with adequate specificity	Age groups with inadequate specificity
Vocabulary	85–89	16–24 30–64 70–84, Av.	25–29 65–69
Similarities	16–17 85–89	18–19 25–29 35–64 80–84, Av.	20–24 30–34 65–69 70–79
Arithmetic	16–17 35–64 70–89, Av.[a]	18–19 20–34 65–69	—
Digit Span	16–89, Av.	—	—
Information	16–17	18–89, Av.	—
Comprehension	16–17	18–24 30–34 70–74 80–84, Av.	25–29 35–69 75–79 85–89
Letter–Number Sequencing	30–34 45–54 70–74 85–89 Av.	18–19	16–17 20–29 35–44 55–69 75–84
Picture Completion	16–79 85–89, Av.	—	80–84
Digit Symbol—Coding	16–89, Av.	—	—
Block Design	16–17 20–44 55–64 75–89, Av.	18–19 45–54 65–74	—
Matrix Reasoning	16–89 Av.	—	—
Picture Arrangement	16–17 25–29 35–44 65–69 85–89	70–74	18–19 20–24 30–34 45–64 75–84, Av.
Symbol Search	30–44	45–54 Av.	16–29 55–89
Object Assembly	—	45–54	16–44 55–89, Av.

[a] Av. = Average.

specificity. In addition, the Picture Completion subtest has ample specificity at 12 of the 13 age groups. Each of the seven remaining subtests shows a unique pattern of specificity—that is, the ages at which each has ample, adequate, or inadequate specificity differ. Vocabulary, Similarities, Comprehension, Letter–Number Sequencing, Picture Arrangement, Symbol Search, and Object Assembly have inadequate specificity at some ages.

Subtests with inadequate specificity should *not* be interpreted as measuring specific functions. These subtests, however, can be interpreted as (a) good or fair measures of *g* (see Table 12-12) and (b) representing a specific factor (i.e., Verbal Comprehension, Perceptual Organization, Working Memory, or Processing Speed; see Table 12-10), where appropriate. The application of profile analysis also may help with the interpretation of individual subtests. (See Chapter 10 for a discussion of profile analysis.) Once you have determined which subtest scaled scores are significantly different from the mean of their scale and, in some cases, from one another, you may be able to draw meaningful conclusions about an examinee's cognitive strengths or weaknesses. Thus, low scores on Digit Symbol—Coding and Symbol Search and average or high scores on the other subtests may indicate difficulty in processing information rapidly. However, a high score on Digit Symbol—Coding coupled with a low score on Symbol Search does not suggest general difficulty in processing information rapidly, because the picture is mixed.

Index Scores

The *WAIS–III Administration and Scoring Manual* and the *WAIS–III—WMS–III Technical Manual* indicate that the following combinations of subtests are the most robust for the determination of index scores (*index scores* is another term for *factor scores*):

- *Verbal Comprehension Index*: Sum of scaled scores on Vocabulary, Similarities, and Information
- *Perceptual Organization Index*: Sum of scaled scores on Picture Completion, Block Design, and Matrix Reasoning
- *Working Memory Index*: Sum of scaled scores on Arithmetic, Digit Span, and Letter–Number Sequencing
- *Processing Speed Index*: Sum of scaled scores on Digit Symbol—Coding and Symbol Search

These sums can be converted to index scores ($M = 100$, $SD = 15$; consult Tables A.6, A.7, A.8, and A.9, pages 199–202 in the *WAIS–III Administration and Scoring Manual*). If there are large discrepancies among the subtests within a factor, the index score may not provide useful information on that factor. In such cases, be extremely cautious in using the index score. The decision to interpret an individual's WAIS–III subtest scaled scores according to this four-factor model should be based in part on the individual's specific subtest profile. For example, it would be misleading to compute a

Processing Speed Index score for scaled scores of 5 and 13 on Symbol Search and Digit Symbol—Coding, respectively, because the two scores are too dissimilar. The average score would tell us little about this factor. However, it would be appropriate to compute a Processing Speed Index score for scaled scores of 12 and 13 on the two subtests, as these scores are highly similar.

The specific referral questions, time constraints, and the reason for testing should help you decide whether to administer (a) the standard 11 subtests or (b) the standard 11 subtests plus the two supplementary subtests to obtain IQs and also index scores. You can obtain index scores that are more reliable than those reported in the test manual by consulting Caruso and Cliff (1999).

In analyzing a WAIS–III protocol, use all available information about the examinee, including the referral question, the medical history, your observations of the examinee during the examination, and other test data. Of course, you will need to understand how to interpret the test. Use the index scores only for evaluating the examinee's strengths and weaknesses and for generating hypotheses about the examinee's abilities; do not use the index scores for obtaining the Full Scale IQ. When you refer to index scores in a report, it is preferable to use percentile ranks to describe the examinee's performance, but the Deviation IQs associated with the index scores also can be reported.

You should generally use the index scores only at ages where the subtests have ample loadings (.30 or above) on the factor; be cautious in using the index scores at other ages. The following list shows the ages at which it is appropriate to interpret index scores:

- Verbal Comprehension Index score: All ages
- Perceptual Organization Index score: Ages 16–17, 20–29, 35–79 years
- Working Memory Index score: Ages 16–17, 20–24, 30–44, 55–74, 85–89 years
- Processing Speed Index score: Ages 16–79, 85–89 years

Table 12-13
Maximum WAIS–III Subtest Scaled Scores by Age Group

Subtest	Maximum scaled score	Age group
Vocabulary	19	16–34, 70–89
	18	35–69
Similarities	19	16–24, 65–89
	18	25–29, 55–64
	17	30–34
Arithmetic	19	16–17, 70–89
	18	18–24, 55–69
	17	25–54
Digit Span	19	16–89
Information	19	16–24, 70–89
	18	25–69
Comprehension	19	16–89
Letter–Number Seq.	19	16–89
Picture Completion	19	75–89
	18	16–74
Digit Symbol—Coding	19	16–89
Block Design	19	16–89
Matrix Reasoning	19	45–89
	18	20–44
	17	16–19
Picture Arrangement	19	16–19, 55–89
	18	35–54
	17	20–34
Symbol Search	19	16–89
Object Assembly	19	16–89

RANGE OF SUBTEST SCALED SCORES

The WAIS–III provides a range of scaled scores from 1 to 19. The test is constructed so that, even if they fail every item on every subtest, examinees are awarded at least 1 scaled-score point. On two subtests (Picture Arrangement and Object Assembly), examinees are awarded 2 or more scaled-score points, depending on their age, even if they fail all items. For example, on Picture Arrangement, examinees are awarded 2 points at ages 55–64 years, 3 points at ages 65–74 years, 4 points at ages 75–84 years, and 5 points at ages 85–89 years when they fail all items. On Object Assembly, examinees between 70 and 89 years of age are given 2 scaled-score points when they fail all items. Thus, the range of subtest scaled scores from 1 to 19 does not apply to all subtests at all ages.

Table 12-13 shows the maximum possible scaled score for each subtest by age group. The fact that the test does not have the same maximum scaled score throughout primarily affects interpretation of the profiles of gifted examinees. For example, for a 16-year-old, it will be difficult to compare Matrix Reasoning with Symbol Search because the highest possible scaled score is 17 on Matrix Reasoning but 19 on Symbol Search.

You can apply profile analysis techniques appropriately at all ages for seven subtests only—Digit Span, Comprehension, Letter–Number Sequencing, Digit Symbol—Coding, Block Design, Symbol Search, and Object Assembly. Applying profile analysis uniformly to all subtests would be misleading, as examinees cannot obtain the same number of scaled-score points on all subtests. However, the failure to have the same scaled-score range at all age groups and for all subtests is usually only a minor difficulty because most subtests have a scaled-score range of at least 1 to 17.

RANGE OF FULL SCALE IQS

The range of WAIS–III Full Scale IQs for all age groups is 45 to 155. This range is insufficient for examinees with moderate to severe mental retardation and for extremely gifted individuals. The WAIS–III is designed so that every examinee receives at least 11 scaled-score points for giving *no* correct answers to any subtest. Because this is potentially problematic, the *WAIS–III Administration and Scoring Manual* recommends that you compute a Verbal Scale IQ only when the examinee obtains raw scores greater than 0 on at least three Verbal Scale subtests. Likewise, the manual indicates that you should compute a Performance Scale IQ only when the examinee earns raw scores greater than 0 on at least three Performance Scale subtests. Finally, the manual says that you should compute a Full Scale IQ only when the examinee obtains raw scores greater than 0 on three Verbal Scale *and* three Performance Scale subtests. This is a rule of thumb, not an empirically based recommendation (because the two WAIS–III manuals provide no validity data), but it is useful. We need validity data to show whether this procedure or other procedures for computing IQs are valid when examinees obtain many zero raw scores.

If we follow the above recommendation, what is the lowest possible IQ that an individual can receive? If an examinee who is 27 years old obtains raw scores of 1 on the Similarities, Digit Span, Comprehension, Picture Completion, Matrix Reasoning, and Block Design subtests and raw scores of 0 on the remaining five subtests, the resulting IQs will be as follows: Verbal Scale IQ = 48 (6 scaled-score points), Performance Scale IQ = 47 (5 scaled-score points), and Full Scale IQ = 45 (11 scaled-score points). Six 1-point successes thus yield an IQ of 45.

In the case of an examinee who is 80 years old or older, the lowest Full Scale IQ that can be obtained is 48, not 45, when the examinee obtains raw scores of 1 on the Similarities, Digit Span, Comprehension, Picture Completion, Matrix Reasoning, and Picture Arrangement subtests and raw scores of 0 on the remaining five subtests. The resulting IQs will be as follows: Verbal Scale IQ = 51 (9 scaled-score points), Performance Scale IQ = 54 (12 scaled-score points), and Full Scale IQ = 48 (21 scaled-score points).

The preceding examples indicate that the WAIS–III may not provide precise IQs for individuals who are functioning at two or more standard deviations below the mean of the test, because the test does not sample a sufficient range of cognitive abilities for very low-functioning individuals. If an examinee fails most of the items on the WAIS–III, consider administering another intelligence test that may give you a more accurate estimate of her or his level of cognitive ability.

COMPARISON OF THE WAIS–III AND WAIS–R

Although similar to its predecessor, the WAIS–III differs from the WAIS–R in some important ways.

1. As previously noted, the revision contains three new subtests. Matrix Reasoning replaces Object Assembly as a standard subtest of the Performance Scale; the latter is now an optional subtest. Letter–Number Sequencing and Symbol Search are new supplementary subtests.

2. The Digit Symbol—Coding subtest includes two new supplementary procedures: Digit Symbol—Incidental Learning and Digit Symbol—Copy. On the WAIS–R, this subtest involved only copying symbols; there was no recall procedure.

3. Full-color illustrations are used in the WAIS–III.

4. The age range of the WAIS–III now extends to 89 years; in the WAIS–R, the oldest age was 74 years.

5. The WAIS–III contains four factors—Verbal Comprehension, Perceptual Organization, Working Memory, and Processing Speed—whereas the WAIS–R contained only the first two of these factors plus an additional factor called Freedom from Distractibility.

6. Scoring guidelines and administrative procedures for most of the subtests have been modified. For example, changes have been made in the order in which subtests are administered, the order of items, starting points, discontinuance criteria, and allotment of bonus points.

7. When examinees earn raw scores of 0 on all 11 WAIS–III subtests, the Full Scale IQ score extends to 45 at all 13 age groups in the standardization sample. In the WAIS–R, a Full Scale IQ of 45 could be obtained only at ages 18–19 years, 20–24 years, and 25–34 years.

8. The revision deemphasizes speed of performance within the Performance Scale by removing Object Assembly from the calculation of the Performance Scale IQ and decreasing the number of items with time-bonus points in the remaining subtests. However, unlike the WAIS–R, the WAIS–III has a supplementary subtest (Symbol Search) that measures primarily processing speed.

9. The revision places increased emphasis on measuring fluid intelligence and working memory.

10. The number of items has been increased on Picture Completion, Vocabulary, Digit Symbol—Coding, Similarities, Block Design, Arithmetic, Digit Span, Picture Arrangement, Comprehension, and Object Assembly and decreased on Information.

Table 12-14 highlights the changes in the WAIS–III.

ADMINISTERING THE WAIS–III

The procedures discussed in Chapter 7 for administering psychological tests will help you administer the WAIS–III. However, you must also master the special procedures developed for the WAIS–III, whether or not you are familiar with any other test. Be careful not to confuse administration procedures for the WISC–III or WAIS–R with those for the WAIS–III; some subtests with the same name have different standardized instructions and time limits. The general problems in administering the WISC–III, discussed in Chapter 8, also apply to the WAIS–III. Following are some potential problems.

Table 12-14
Highlights of Changes in WAIS–III

Area or subtest	Changes from WAIS–R
Age range	Extended 15 years to cover the age range from 16-0 to 89-11.
Standardization	1995 census data were used, and the sample was increased from 1,880 to 2,450 participants.
Stratification variables	Generally similar, but the number of age groups was increased from 9 to 13 and residence and occupational variables were dropped.
Number of subtests	14 instead of 11, with Matrix Reasoning, Number–Letter Sequencing, and Symbol Search added.
Supplementary procedures	Two new supplementary procedures were added: Digit Symbol—Incidental Learning and Digit Symbol—Symbol Copy.
Reliability	Reliability coefficients generally higher than those for the WAIS–R.
Validity	Validity coefficients generally similar to those for the WAIS–R.
Scoring examples	Somewhat expanded and placed with the subtest proper instead of in the back of the manual.
General administrative changes	Order of administering subtests was changed, item order was changed on some subtests, starting points were changed on some subtests, samples were added on some subtests, discontinuance criteria were changed on some subtests, bonus-point allotment was changed on some subtests, and easier items were added to most subtests.
Computation of IQ	No change, but the WAIS–III manual stipulates that three Verbal and three Performance subtests must have raw scores greater than 0.
Intelligence classification and range	Uses "Extremely Low" instead of "Mentally Retarded" to classify IQs below 70.
Record Form	Last four pages of the Record Form are a profile page, score conversion page, discrepancy analysis page, and demographics page. Allows for the determination of subtest strengths and weaknesses and confidence limits. More space is provided to write responses for Information, Comprehension, Vocabulary, and Similarities. Starting points, discontinuance rules, time limits, and prompts to help facilitate administration are included. A separate booklet contains Symbol Search, Digit Symbol—Incidental Learning, and Digit Symbol—Copy. For Digit Symbol—Coding, the space between the key and stimulus items was increased to reduce the possibility that left-handed individuals will cover the key as they work. Increased space is provided for recording behavioral observations. Unlike the WAIS–R, the WAIS–III does not ask for examinee's occupation, ethnicity, handedness, or place of examination.
Types of scores	Provides IQs ($M = 100$, $SD = 15$) for Verbal, Performance, and Full Scales; index scores ($M = 100$, $SD = 15$) for four factors; percentile ranks for IQs and index scores; subtest scaled scores; discrepancy scores for IQs and index scores; and deviation scores for the 14 subtests. WAIS–R provided IQs for Verbal, Performance, and Full Scales, along with scaled scores and age-corrected scores for the 11 subtests.
Confidence intervals	Confidence intervals in the *WAIS–III Administration and Scoring Manual* are based on the estimated true score method; no confidence intervals are given in the WAIS–R manual.
Factor structure	The manual proposes a model with four factors (Verbal Comprehension, Perceptual Organization, Working Memory, and Processing Speed) that differ from the three factors found on the WAIS–R.
g loading	About the same.
Art work	Color is used instead of black and white for Picture Completion and Matrix Reasoning subtests; some visual stimuli have been enlarged; art work has a more contemporary appearance.
Test-retest changes	Retest changes are generally comparable.
Ceiling to floor level of IQ	The range of IQs is 45 to 155 for all age groups; on the WAIS–R, it was from 45 to 150, but not for all age groups.
Subtests for which scaled scores of 1 to 19 are available	More subtests have a range of 1 to 19 scaled-score points.

(Continued)

Table 12-14 *(Continued)*	
Area or subtest	*Changes from WAIS–R*
Picture Completion	Contains 25 instead of 20 items, with 10 modified and 15 new items. All pictures are enlarged and in color. Five reversal items to lower the floor of the subtest are included. Querying guidelines have been clarified and expanded.
Vocabulary	Contains 33 instead of 35 items, with 25 retained and 8 new items. Administration has been changed so that words are presented orally and also displayed in a stimulus book. A reverse sequence procedure is used if an examinee does not obtain perfect scores on the first two items given. The discontinuance rule has been changed from five to six consecutive failures. Additional scoring examples are provided.
Digit Symbol—Coding	Contains one additional row. Symbols have been slightly enlarged, and the name of the subtest has changed. The time limit has been changed from 90 seconds to 120 seconds.
Similarities	Contains 19 instead of 14 items, with 11 retained and 8 new items. The first five items (reversal items) are given only to examinees who fail to obtain perfect scores on items 6 and 7. Additional sample scoring items are provided.
Block Design	Contains 14 instead of 9 items, with 9 retained and 5 new items (4 easy, 1 difficult). Easy items are administered in reverse order to obtain a basal if an examinee fails or obtains only 1 point on items 5 and 6. Changes have been made in bonus-point allotment; designs have been enlarged.
Arithmetic	Contains 20 instead of 14 items, with all WAIS–R items retained (some with wording changes) and 6 items added. Four easy items are administered in reverse order to examinees who obtain a score of 0 on item 5 or 6. Bonus points are given for speed on items 19 and 20 only.
Matrix Reasoning	New 26-item untimed subtest replaces Object Assembly in computation of the Performance IQ. Each item consists of a matrix from which a section is missing and five response choices.
Digit Span	Contains 15 instead of 14 sets of digits, with one 2-digit set added to Digits Forward. Supplementary norms are provided for Digits Forward, Digits Backward, and Digits Forward minus Digits Backward for each age group in the standardization sample.
Information	Contains 28 instead of 29 items, with 19 retained and 9 new items (2 easy, 7 hard). A procedure for administering items in reverse sequence has been added for examinees who miss item 5 or 6. The discontinuance rule has been changed from five to six consecutive scores of 0. Additional sample scoring items have been included.
Picture Arrangement	Contains 11 instead of 10 items, with 5 modified and 6 new items (2 easy, 4 hard). Five items have 1-point scores for plausible alternative arrangements; the WAIS–R had four such items. Stimuli have been enlarged and printed on card stock.
Comprehension	Contains 18 instead of 16 items, with 12 retained and 6 new items (2 easy, 4 hard). The subtest begins with item 4; if the examinee does not obtain perfect scores on items 4 and 5, items 1–3 are given in reverse order to meet the basal requirement. More sample scoring items are provided.
Symbol Search	New supplementary subtest containing 60 items. It may be substituted for Digit Symbol—Coding in IQ computation if that subtest has been spoiled.
Letter–Number Sequencing	New supplementary subtest containing 7 sets of number-letter combinations. It may be substituted for Digit Span in IQ computation if that subtest has been spoiled.
Object Assembly	Optional subtest may be substituted for any Performance subtest for individuals 16–74 years old. Contains 5 instead of 4 items, with 3 retained and 2 new items. The layout shield is now freestanding.

Problems Related to Establishing Rapport

1. Failing to establish rapport
2. Interrogating the examinee while trying to establish rapport
3. Failing to be sensitive to the examinee's need for a break
4. Rushing the examinee
5. Showing impatience or frustration

Problems Related to Speech

6. Reading questions too quickly or too slowly
7. Making enunciation errors

Problems Related to Layout of Test Materials.

8. Failing to position the record booklet so that the examinee cannot observe recorded responses
9. Leaving unessential materials on the table

Problems Related to Test Administration

10. Failing to record all responses verbatim
11. Burying the head in the manual, with little eye contact and attention to the examinee
12. Providing hints not shown in the manual, such as defining or explaining words
13. Providing nonverbal cues
14. Calculating chronological age incorrectly
15. Failing to adhere to guidelines for giving help or prompting
16. Failing to adhere to guidelines for giving second trials
17. Failing to adhere to standardized instructions
18. Ignoring proper time limits
19. Failing to begin timing immediately after reading problems requiring timing
20. Failing to stop timing when the examinee obviously has finished
21. Failing to question ambiguous or vague responses and responses similar to those with a "(Q)" in the WAIS–III manual
22. Questioning unnecessarily
23. Failing to credit responses
24. Failing to follow the starting rule
25. Failing to follow the discontinuance rule
26. Testing-of-limits after an item or subtest has been administered instead of after the entire test has been administered
27. Repeating questions or items when the manual says not to do so
28. Allowing paper and pencil when the instructions forbid this practice

Problems Related to Scoring

29. Incorrectly transferring raw scores to the front of the protocol
30. Incorrectly converting raw scores to scaled scores
31. Incorrectly converting scaled scores to IQs
32. Prorating incorrectly
33. Giving time-bonus credits incorrectly
34. Using inappropriate norms
35. Failing to give a score of 0 to an incorrect response
36. Failing to use the scoring guidelines appropriately
37. Adding raw scores incorrectly
38. Adding scaled scores incorrectly
39. Failing to give credit for items not administered below the starting point
40. Giving credit for items passed above the discontinuance point
41. Failing to give credit for items missed below the starting point
42. Failing to score a subtest
43. Including a supplementary subtest, in addition to the six standard subtests in the Verbal Scale and five standard subtests in the Performance Scale, in computing an IQ
44. Using both Digit Symbol—Coding and Symbol Search to compute an IQ
45. Substituting Letter–Number Sequencing for a subtest other than Digit Span in computing an IQ
46. Substituting Symbol Search for a subtest other than Digit Symbol—Coding in computing an IQ

Study the instructions in the *WAIS–III Administration and Scoring Manual* and become thoroughly familiar with the test materials before you give the test. Although the Verbal Scale subtests are generally easier to administer than the Performance Scale subtests, they are more difficult to score. You should use a stopwatch when you administer the timed WAIS–III subtests. Assign tentative scores as you administer the test, and then rescore each item after you finish administering the test. If you are unsure how to score a response during the test proper and the item is needed to establish a starting point (also referred to as a basal level) or discontinuance point (also referred to as a ceiling level), always err on the side of administering additional items, even though these items may not be critical to establishing the starting or discontinuance point. Administering additional items will ensure that you do not invalidate the test by failing to establish a basal level or ceiling level.

The Record Form should be clearly and accurately completed—*record all responses relevant to the test and testing situation verbatim.* You need to check all calculations carefully, including the conversion of raw scores to scaled scores and scaled scores to IQs and index scores. In converting raw scores to scaled scores, be aware that the order of subtests on the Score Conversion Page (page 12 of the Record Form) is *not* the same as the order of subtests in Table A.1 (pages 181–194) in the *WAIS–III Administration and Scoring Manual.* On the Score Conversion Page, the subtests appear in the order in which they are administered; in Table A.1, the subtests are ordered by scale—the seven Verbal Scale subtests in the upper half of the table and the seven Performance Scale subtests in the lower half. Be sure to use the appropriate column in Table A.1 for converting raw scores to scaled scores. For example, to convert a raw score on Picture Completion (the first subtest administered) to a scaled score, you must use the column in the lower half of Table A.1 (Performance Scale Subtests) that shows raw scores for the Picture Completion subtest and its corresponding scaled scores. The suggestions in Exhibit 12-1 and the checklist in Exhibit 12-2 also will help you learn how to administer the WAIS–III.

Physical Abilities Required for the WAIS–III

Examinees need to have adequate hearing and language functioning in order to be administered the Verbal Scale subtests, and adequate vision and visual-motor ability in order to be administered the Performance Scale subtests. The suggestions

Exhibit 12-1
Supplementary Instructions for Administering the WAIS–III

1. Study and practice administering the test repeatedly before you give it to an examinee to fulfill a class assignment.
2. Organize your test materials before the examinee comes into the room. Make sure that all test materials—including stimulus booklets, blocks, cards, puzzle pieces, Record Form, Response Booklet, stopwatch, and pencils—are in the kit. Arrange the Picture Arrangement cards in numerical sequence. Have extra blank paper on which to make notes if needed.
3. Complete the top of page 1 of the Record Form (examinee's name, examiner's name, examinee's age, and date of testing) and the top of page 14 (Demographics Page) of the Record Form (date tested, examinee's date of birth, age, name, ID, sex, address, highest level of education, and examiner's name). It also is a good idea to add the examinee's occupation. If you have this information available, it saves time to enter it in advance.
4. Calculate the chronological age (CA)—months are considered to have 30 days for testing purposes—and put it in the box provided on the Demographics Page (page 14 of the Record Form). Also, note that days of age are *not* rounded up to the nearest month. Thus, the age 19 years 11 months and 29 days is 19 years 11 months, not 20 years 0 months.
5. Before beginning the first subtest, introduce the scale using the explanation on page 63 of the *WAIS–III Administration and Scoring Manual.* Use your judgment in deciding whether the examinee needs further explanation of the reason for the examination. However, try not to use the word *intelligence,* because telling the examinee that he or she is about to take an intelligence test may cause unnecessary anxiety and negatively affect performance.
6. Administer the subtests in the order presented in the *WAIS–III Administration and Scoring Manual,* except in rare circumstances. Do not change the wording of the directions or the wording of questions on any subtest. Read the directions and items verbatim from the *WAIS–III Administration and Scoring Manual.* This means that you do *not* omit words, introduce new words, or ad lib.
7. Start with the appropriate item on each subtest, and follow all basal and discontinuance criteria. You must be knowledgeable about the scoring criteria before you administer the test.
8. Record verbatim all of the examinee's responses that are pertinent to the test, testing situation, or referral question or that are otherwise helpful in understanding the examinee. Write clearly, and do not use unusual abbreviations. Record the time accurately in the spaces provided in the Record Form.
9. Question all ambiguous, incomplete, or unscorable responses, using the directions or instructions suggested in the *WAIS–III Administration and Scoring Manual* for questioning. Write "(Q)" after each questioned response. Question all responses followed by a "(Q)" in the *WAIS–III Administration and Scoring Manual.*
10. When an examinee says "I don't know" to an item but then passes more difficult items on the same subtest, readminister the earlier item after the examinee has reached the ceiling level if you believe that he or she may know the answer to that item.
11. If an examinee says "I can't do it" or stops working on an item before the time limit has expired, gently urge her or him to proceed by saying "Just try once more; see if you can do it" or "Try it just a little longer."
12. Carefully score each protocol, recheck scoring, and transfer subtest scores to the Score Conversion Page (page 12 of the Record Form) under the column labeled Raw Score.
13. If a subtest was spoiled, write "spoiled" by the subtest total score and on the Score Conversion Page where you entered the raw scores and scaled scores. If you did not administer a subtest, write "NA" in the margin of the Record Form and on the Score Conversion Page.
14. Transform raw scores into scaled scores through use of Table A.1 (pages 181–194) in the *WAIS–III Administration and Scoring Manual.* Be sure to use the page of Table A.1 that is appropriate for the examinee's age and the correct row and column for each transformation. If you also use the scaled scores based on the reference group of persons aged 20–34 years old (page 194 of the manual), be sure they are entered in the appropriate column on the Score Conversion Page. *Never use the reference group scaled scores to compute IQs or index scores.*
15. Add the scaled scores for the six standard Verbal Scale subtests to compute the sum of the scaled scores. Do not use Letter–Number Sequencing to compute the Verbal Scale score unless you have substituted it for Digit Span. Add the scaled scores for the five standard Performance Scale subtests. Do not include Symbol Search or Object Assembly unless you have substituted Symbol Search for Digit Symbol—Coding or Object Assembly for another Performance subtest. Sum the Verbal and the Performance Scale subtest scaled scores to obtain the sum for the Full Scale. Recheck your addition on all subtests and scales.
16. Administer the Letter–Number Sequencing and Symbol Search subtests if you want to obtain index scores. Do not use these two subtests in computing IQs when you administer the six standard Verbal Scale and five standard Performance Scale subtests.
17. Substitute the Letter–Number Sequencing subtest in computing the Verbal Scale and Full Scale IQs if the Digit Span subtest was spoiled or if you did not administer it. Similarly, substitute Symbol Search in computing the Performance Scale and Full Scale IQs if the Digit Symbol—Coding subtest was spoiled or if you did not administer it. Substitute the Object Assembly subtest in computing the Performance Scale and Full Scale IQs if any of the standard Performance Scale subtests were not administered.
18. Obtain the IQs from Tables A.3 through A.5 (pages 195–198) of the *WAIS–III Administration and Scoring Manual.*

(Continued)

Exhibit 12-1 *(Continued)*

There are tables for the Verbal Scale (A.3), the Performance Scale (A.4), and the Full Scale (A.5). Obtain the index scores from Tables A.6 through A.9 (pages 199–202). Be sure to use the correct table for each of the three IQs and each of the four index scores. Record the IQs and index scores on the Profile Page of the Record Form (page 11). Next, recheck all of your work. If any IQs were obtained by use of a short form, write "SF" beside the appropriate IQs. If any IQs were prorated, write "PRO" beside the appropriate IQs. If fewer than five subtests were administered in the Verbal Scale or fewer than four subtests were administered in the Performance Scale, use the Tellegen and Briggs short-form procedure, described in Chapter 8, to compute the IQ. You also can consult Tables C-21 through C-25 in Appendix C in this text. These tables provide estimated Full Scale Deviation Quotients for several short forms based on the Tellegen and Briggs procedure.

19. If you would like, plot the IQ scores, index scores, and subtest scores on the graph provided on the Profile Page of the Record Form .

20. Obtain a percentile for each IQ and index score from Tables A.3 through A.9 in the *WAIS–III Administration and Scoring Manual.*

21. Obtain a confidence interval for each IQ and index score from Table C-1 in Appendix C of this text.

22. Complete the appropriate part of the Score Conversion Page (page 12) of the Record Form to determine the examinee's strengths and weaknesses for the individual subtests. Enter the scaled scores in the appropriate spaces for the subtests you administered, and follow the instructions given on pages 60 and 61 in the *WAIS–III Administration and Scoring Manual.*

23. Complete the Discrepancy Analysis Page (page 13) of the Record Form to compute the discrepancy between the Verbal and Performance Scale IQs and the differences between all combinations of the index scores. Evaluate the statistical significance of each difference, and note the frequency with which each difference was found in the standardization sample. Also note the difference between the longest Digits Forward and the longest Digits Backward on Digit Span. Follow the instructions for analyzing score discrepancies provided on pages 61 to 62 of the *WAIS–III Administration and Scoring Manual* for Table B.1 and in this text. Use Tables C-4 and C-5 in Appendix C to obtain the appropriate base rate that you need to complete the last column of the Discrepancy Analysis Page, which is labeled "Frequency of difference in standardization sample."

24. In summary, read the directions verbatim, enunciate clearly and pronounce words correctly, query at the appropriate times, start with the appropriate item, obtain a basal where needed, discontinue at the appropriate location, use correct timing, arrange items properly before the examinee, and follow the specific administration guidelines in the *WAIS–III Administration and Scoring Manual.*

presented in Chapter 8 for administering the WISC–III to examinees with disabilities should be studied carefully.

Auditory functions. Examinees with an undiagnosed hearing deficit may obtain low scores not because of cognitive limitations, but because they fail to understand the instructions and questions. Sometimes examinees may have a temporary hearing loss due to an allergy, sinus infection, cold, or other intermittent ear, nose, and throat problem. You will need to consider the following questions in evaluating the examinee's auditory ability:

• How well does the examinee understand conversation when the speaker is outside of the examinee's field of vision?

• Does the examinee watch the speaker's mouth intently during conversation?

• Is there evidence that the examinee has an auditory discrimination deficit (e.g., mistakes *winter* for *winner*)?

• Does the examinee frequently need to have instructions repeated?

• When the volume of speech is increased, does the examinee's comprehension of spoken language improve?

In cases where a significant hearing problem is documented or suspected, ask the examinee to repeat a few complex sentences before you administer the test (e.g., "The lawyer's closing argument convinced him"). If the examinee repeats the sentences correctly, you can be reasonably confident that hearing proficiency is sufficient for you to administer the WAIS–III. Conversely, if the examinee fails to repeat the sentences correctly, recommend a hearing evaluation and postpone administering the test until you obtain the results of the hearing evaluation. If the examinee usually wears a hearing aid, be sure that it is worn during the examination and verify that it is in good operating order.

Language functions. Note any language difficulties that the examinee may have. Always consider the examinee's age and ethnicity and what is normal language for her or his age group. For adolescents and adults, normal speech is fluent (i.e., produced with little or no effort, about 100 to 125 words per minute, with phrases of five or more words strung together between pauses; Albert, Goodglass, Helm, Rubens, & Alexander, 1981) and is free of articulation difficulties, gross grammatical errors, and word substitutions. In contrast, abnormal speech may be nonfluent (i.e., slow, laboriously

Exhibit 12-2
Administrative Checklist for the WAIS–III

ADMINISTRATIVE CHECKLIST FOR THE WAIS–III

Name of examiner: _____   Name of examinee: _____

Date: _____   Name of observer: _____

(Note: *If an item is not applicable, mark NA next to the number.*)

Picture Completion	Circle One	
1. Reads directions verbatim	Yes	No
2. Reads directions clearly	Yes	No
3. Pronounces words in queries clearly	Yes	No
4. Places booklet flat on table, close to examinee	Yes	No
5. Begins with item 6	Yes	No
6. Begins timing after last word of instructions	Yes	No
7. Allows a maximum of 20 seconds on each item	Yes	No
8. Gives the prompt "Yes, but what's missing?" only once	Yes	No
9. Gives the prompt "Something is missing in the picture. What is it that is missing?" only once	Yes	No
10. Gives the prompt "Yes, but what is the most important part that is missing?" only once	Yes	No
11. If the examinee fails item 6, responds by saying "You see the doorknob is missing"	Yes	No
12. If the examinee fails item 7, responds by saying "You see the nose piece is missing"	Yes	No
13. Administers items in reverse order when examinee scores 0 on item 6 or 7	Yes	No
14. Attempts to establish a basal level	Yes	No
15. Inquires correctly on items 8, 10, and 19	Yes	No
16. Allows credit for items not administered when those items precede two consecutive successes	Yes	No
17. Allows credit for a correct spoken or pointing response	Yes	No
18. Allows 1 point credit for each correct response	Yes	No
19. Allows no credit for correct responses given after time limit	Yes	No
20. Records 0 to 1 point for each item	Yes	No
21. Discontinues subtest after five consecutive failures	Yes	No
22. Adds points correctly	Yes	No

Comments: _____

_____

Vocabulary	Circle One	
1. Reads directions verbatim	Yes	No
2. Reads directions clearly	Yes	No
3. Pronounces words clearly	Yes	No
4. Begins with item 4	Yes	No
5. Places booklet flat on table, close to examinee	Yes	No
6. Allows sufficient time for examinee to respond to each word	Yes	No
7. Queries every response followed in the WAIS–III manual by "(Q)," even if it is a 0-point response	Yes	No
8. Queries vague responses	Yes	No
9. Does not query a clearcut response, especially one that is not followed by a "(Q)" in the WAIS–III manual	Yes	No
10. Administers items in reverse order when examinee fails or gives a 1-point response to item 4 or 5	Yes	No
11. Attempts to establish a basal level	Yes	No
12. Inquires about vague responses, regionalisms, or slang responses	Yes	No
13. Limits inquiries to "Tell me more about it" or "Explain what you mean"	Yes	No
14. Allows 1 or 2 points credit for each correct response	Yes	No
15. Records 0, 1, or 2 points as appropriate	Yes	No
16. Discontinues after six consecutive failures	Yes	No
17. Records responses	Yes	No
18. Add points correctly	Yes	No

Comments: _____

_____

Digit Symbol—Coding

	Circle One	
1. Reads directions verbatim	Yes	No
2. Reads directions clearly	Yes	No
3. Provides two no. 2 graphite pencils without erasers	Yes	No
4. Provides a smooth work surface	Yes	No

(Continued)

Exhibit 12-2 *(Continued)*

Digital Symbol—Coding	Circle One	
5. Points to the key while reading the first part of the instructions	Yes	No
6. Points to the proper boxes, numbers, and symbols while reading the instructions	Yes	No
7. Follows directions in the manual for pointing to sample items while reading directions	Yes	No
8. Does not time sample items	Yes	No
9. Gives proper instructions after examinee completes the sample items and clearly understands the task	Yes	No
10. Praises examinee's success on each sample item by saying "yes" or "right"	Yes	No
11. Corrects examinee's mistakes on sample items	Yes	No
12. Explains use of key again if examinee fails the sample items	Yes	No
13. Does not begin subtest until examinee clearly understands the task	Yes	No
14. Provides proper caution the first time examinee omits an item or does only one type: "Do them in order. Don't skip any." Then points to the next item and says "Do this one next."	Yes	No
15. Reminds the examinee to continue until told to stop (when needed)	Yes	No
16. Begins timing immediately after completing instructions	Yes	No
17. Allows 120 seconds	Yes	No
18. Records time accurately	Yes	No
19. Uses scoring template to score subtest	Yes	No
20. Does not give credit for sample items, incorrectly drawn items, or items completed out of sequence	Yes	No
21. Records correct number of items	Yes	No
22. If Digit Symbol—Incidental Learning is administered and examinee fails to complete four rows within 120 seconds, marks examinee's progress at 120 seconds and allows additional time for examinee to work to the end of the fourth row	Yes	No
23. Reads directions verbatim on Digit Symbol—Incidental Learning Pairing	Yes	No
24. Has examinee write answers in Response Booklet	Yes	No
25. Uses cardboard or opaque paper to cover pairing items	Yes	No

Digital Symbol–Coding	Circle One	
26. Presents Digit Symbol—Incidental Learning Free Recall task by pointing to the blank area at the bottom of the page	Yes	No
27. Uses scoring template to score Digit Symbol—Incidental Learning Pairing	Yes	No
28. Records correct number of responses for Digit Symbol—Incidental Learning Pairing	Yes	No
29. Records correct number of responses for Digit Symbol—Incidental Learning Free Recall	Yes	No
30. Administers the Digit Symbol—Copy task after examinee completes the last subtest	Yes	No

Comments: _____

_____

Similarities

	Circle One	
1. Reads directions verbatim	Yes	No
2. Reads directions clearly	Yes	No
3. Reads items verbatim and clearly	Yes	No
4. Begins with item 6	Yes	No
5. Allows sufficient time for examinee to answer each question	Yes	No
6. Gives example of 2-point response if examinee gives 1-point response to item 6	Yes	No
7. Says "They are both musical instruments" if examinee gives a 0-point response to item 6	Yes	No
8. Administers items 1–5 in reverse order if examinee fails or obtains a score of 1 on item 6 or 7	Yes	No
9. Attempts to establish a basal level	Yes	No
10. Queries every response followed in the WAIS–III manual by a "(Q)," even if it is a 0-point response	Yes	No
11. Queries vague responses	Yes	No
12. Says "What do you mean?" or "Tell me more about it" if examinee's response is unclear	Yes	No
13. Does not query a clearcut response	Yes	No
14. Asks "Now which one is it?" each time an examinee's response contains both a correct and an incorrect answer	Yes	No
15. Assigns 1 point credit for each correct response to items 1–5	Yes	No
16. Assigns 1 or 2 points credit for each correct response to items 6–19	Yes	No
17. Records 0, 1, or 2 points as appropriate	Yes	No
18. Discontinues after four consecutive failures	Yes	No
19. Records responses	Yes	No

(Continued)

Exhibit 12-2 *(Continued)*

Similarities	Circle One	
20. Assigns credit for items not administered when those items precede perfect scores on two consecutive items	Yes	No
21. Adds points correctly	Yes	No

Comments: _____

_____

Block Design

	Circle One	
1. Reads directions verbatim	Yes	No
2. Reads directions clearly	Yes	No
3. Turns blocks slowly to show different sides as instructions are read	Yes	No
4. Begins with item 5	Yes	No
5. Places blocks and cards properly	Yes	No
6. Constructs model or places Stimulus Booklet approximately 7 inches from the edge of the table closest to examinee	Yes	No
7. Places model or Stimulus Booklet a little to the left of examinee's midline for right-handed examinees and a little to the right of midline for left-handed examinees	Yes	No
8. Constructs designs 5 and 6 properly	Yes	No
9. Administers items in reverse order if examinee fails or obtains 1 point on item 5 or 6	Yes	No
10. Attempts to establish a basal level	Yes	No
11. Assigns credit for items not administered when those items precede perfect scores (2 points) on two consecutive items	Yes	No
12. Presents pictures in the Stimulus Book with the unbound edge toward the examinee	Yes	No
13. Arranges blocks so that only one block has the red-and-white side facing up for the four-block designs and only three blocks have the red-and-white side facing up for the nine-block designs	Yes	No
14. Scrambles blocks between designs	Yes	No
15. Begins timing after the last word of instructions	Yes	No
16. Records time in the Record Form	Yes	No
17. Uses correct time limits	Yes	No
18. Stops timing when examinee is obviously finished with the design	Yes	No
19. Allows examinee to continue working on design after time limit when examinee is nearing completion of task	Yes	No

Block Design

	Circle One	
20. Gives a second trial on items 1–6 when examinee fails first trial	Yes	No
21. Does not give a second trial on items 7–14	Yes	No
22. Uses the correct number of blocks for each item	Yes	No
23. Says "But, you see, the blocks go this way" and corrects examinee's design the first time examinee rotates a design	Yes	No
24. Gives instructions about need to correct a rotated design only once during the test	Yes	No
25. Assigns 2 points when examinee gets items 5 and 6 correct on the first trial	Yes	No
26. Assigns 1 point when examinee gets items 5 and 6 correct on the second trial	Yes	No
27. Assigns correct number of points, including time-bonus credits, for items 7–14	Yes	No
28. Assigns no credit for correct responses given after time limit	Yes	No
29. Circles, on the Record Form, a Y (Yes) or N (No) for each item	Yes	No
30. Stops examinee on items 1–6 when time limit has expired on the first trial and gives second trial	Yes	No
31. Records exact amount of time taken to solve each item	Yes	No
32. Discontinues subtest after three consecutive failures	Yes	No
33. Adds points correctly	Yes	No

Comments: _____

_____

Arithmetic

	Circle One	
1. Reads directions verbatim	Yes	No
2. Reads directions clearly	Yes	No
3. Begins with item 5	Yes	No
4. Uses correct timing	Yes	No
5. Administers items in reverse order when item 5 or 6 is failed	Yes	No
6. Attempts to establish a basal level	Yes	No
7. Forbids examinee to use pencil and paper	Yes	No
8. Allows examinee to use a finger to "write" on the table	Yes	No
9. Records exact amount of time required to solve each problem	Yes	No

(Continued)

Exhibit 12-2 *(Continued)*

Arithmetic	Circle One
10. Begins timing immediately after each problem has been read	Yes No
11. Repeats a problem only once	Yes No
12. Records time from the end of the first reading of problem to when the response is made, even when problem is read again	Yes No
13. Assigns no credit for correct responses given after time limit	Yes No
14. Assigns 1 point credit for each correct response on items 1–18	Yes No
15. Assigns 2 points credit for each correct response given within 1 to 10 seconds on items 19–20	Yes No
16. Assigns credit for correct numerical quantity even when unit is not given	Yes No
17. Gives credit when examinee spontaneously corrects an incorrect response within time limit	Yes No
18. Records 0, 1, or 2 points as appropriate	Yes No
19. Discontinues after four consecutive failures	Yes No
20. Record responses	Yes No
21. Adds points correctly	Yes No

Comments: _____

_____

Matrix Reasoning	Circle One
1. Reads directions verbatim	Yes No
2. Reads directions clearly	Yes No
3. Begins with sample items A, B, and C	Yes No
4. Places booklet flat on the table, close to examinee	Yes No
5. Presents pictures in the booklet with unbound edge toward examinee	Yes No
6. Demonstrates the correct way to solve the problem if any sample item is failed	Yes No
7. Proceeds to item 4 regardless of examinee's performance on sample items	Yes No
8. Assigns full credit for items 1, 2, and 3 if examinee earns perfect scores (1 point) on both items 4 and 5	Yes No
9. Administers items 1, 2, and 3 in reverse sequence when examinee fails item 4 or 5	Yes No
10. Attempts to establish a basal level	Yes No
11. Circles examinee's numerical responses on Record Form	Yes No

Matrix Reasoning	Circle One
12. Discontinues subtest after four consecutive scores of 0 or four scores of 0 on five consecutive items	Yes No
13. Adds points correctly	Yes No

Comments: _____

_____

Digit Span	Circle One
1. Reads directions verbatim	Yes No
2. Reads directions clearly	Yes No
3. Begins with item 1	Yes No
4. Administers both trials of each item	Yes No
5. Pronounces digits singly and distinctly, at the rate of one digit per second and without chunking digits	Yes No
6. Drops voice inflection slightly on last digit	Yes No
7. Pauses after each sequence to allow examinee to respond	Yes No
8. Administers Digits Backward even if examinee obtains a score of 0 on Digits Forward	Yes No
9. Gives sample item for Digits Backward	Yes No
10. Gives examinee the correct answer to sample item if examinee fails the item on Digits Backward	Yes No
11. Gives both trials of each item on Digits Forward and on Digits Backward	Yes No
12. Discontinues Digits Forward after failure on both trials of any item	Yes No
13. Discontinues Digits Backward after failure on both trials of any item	Yes No
14. Assigns 1 point for each trial passed	Yes No
15. Records responses	Yes No
16. Adds points correctly	Yes No

Comments: _____

_____

Information	Circle One
1. Reads directions verbatim	Yes No
2. Reads directions clearly	Yes No
3. Reads items verbatim and clearly	Yes No
4. Begins with item 5	Yes No
5. Gives sufficient time for examinee to respond to each question	Yes No

(Continued)

Exhibit 12-2 *(Continued)*

Information	Circle One	
6. Administers items 1, 2, 3, and 4 in reverse sequence when examinee fails item 5 or 6	Yes	No
7. Attempts to establish a basal level	Yes	No
8. Says "Yes, but what direction is that?" if examinee points in response to item 6	Yes	No
9. Asks "What scale?" if examinee fails to indicate which temperature scale in response to item 21	Yes	No
10. Says "Explain what you mean" or "Tell me more about it" for responses that are not clear	Yes	No
11. Repeats the question when examinee's response suggests that examinee misheard or misunderstood the exact meaning of the question	Yes	No
12. Assigns credit for correct responses made after the inquiry	Yes	No
13. Avoids asking leading questions or spelling words	Yes	No
14. Assigns credit for items not administered when those items precede two consecutive successes	Yes	No
15. Assigns 1 point credit for each correct response	Yes	No
16. Records 0 or 1 point for each item	Yes	No
17. Discontinues after six consecutive failures	Yes	No
18. Records responses	Yes	No
19. Adds points correctly	Yes	No

Comments: _____

_____

Picture Arrangement

	Circle One	
1. Reads directions verbatim	Yes	No
2. Reads directions clearly	Yes	No
3. Begins with item 1 in all cases	Yes	No
4. Has cards prearranged in numerical sequence and places all cards in correct numerical order from examinee's left to examinee's right	Yes	No
5. Proceeds to trial 2 if examinee fails trial 1 of an item	Yes	No
6. Rearranges cards in trial 1 in correct order by moving cards one at a time to a new row and then points to each card as story is told	Yes	No
7. Rearranges cards in trial 1 in original numerical order and says "Now, you put them in the right order"	Yes	No
8. Begins timing after last word of instructions	Yes	No

Picture Arrangement	Circle One	
9. Records exact amount of time taken to complete each item or trial	Yes	No
10. Records, in the Response Order column of the Record Form, the exact order in which examinee arranges the cards	Yes	No
11. Stops timing when examinee is obviously finished or when the time limit has expired on each item	Yes	No
12. Does not give a second trial on items 2–11	Yes	No
13. Uses correct time limits	Yes	No
14. Assigns 2 points credit for a correct response given to item 1, trial 1	Yes	No
15. Assigns 1 point credit for a correct response given to item 1, trial 2	Yes	No
16. Allows examinee to continue working on arrangement after time limit has expired when examinee is nearing completion of task	Yes	No
17. Gives correct number of credit points on each item	Yes	No
18. Discontinues after four consecutive failures	Yes	No
19. Adds points correctly	Yes	No

Comments: _____

_____

Comprehension

	Circle One	
1. Reads directions verbatim	Yes	No
2. Reads directions clearly	Yes	No
3. Begins with item 4	Yes	No
4. Gives full credit for items 1–3 if examinee earns full credit (2 points) on items 4 and 5	Yes	No
5. Administers items 1–3 in reverse sequence if examinee obtains a score of 0 or 1 on item 4 or 5	Yes	No
6. Attempts to establish a basal level	Yes	No
7. Repeats question if examinee requests or if examinee has not responded after 10–15 seconds	Yes	No
8. Encourages hesitant examinee to speak, saying "Yes" or "Go ahead"	Yes	No
9. Queries every response followed in the WAIS–III manual by a "(Q)," even if it is a 0-point response	Yes	No
10. Queries vague or ambiguous responses, saying "Explain what you mean" or "Tell me more about it"	Yes	No
11. Does not query a clearcut response	Yes	No

(Continued)

Exhibit 12-2 *(Continued)*

Comprehension	Circle One
12. Prompts for second response on items 5, 6, 7, 10, and 13 only when first response is correct	Yes No
13. Prompts for a second response only once per designated item	Yes No
14. Records 0, 1, or 2 points as appropriate	Yes No
15. Discontinues after four consecutive failures	Yes No
16. Records responses	Yes No
17. Adds points correctly	Yes No

Comments: _____

Symbol Search

	Circle One
1. Reads directions verbatim	Yes No
2. Reads directions clearly	Yes No
3. Provides two no. 2 graphite pencils without erasers	Yes No
4. Points from examinee's left to right when giving instructions for sample item 1	Yes No
5. Gives proper instructions for sample items 2 and 3	Yes No
6. Offers praise such as "Good" or "Right" when examinee marks correct answers for the three practice items	Yes No
7. Gives correct instructions when examinee fails practice items	Yes No
8. Proceeds with test items only when examinee understands the task	Yes No
9. Opens the Response Booklet to expose the first two pages of the subtest after examinee completes the practice items	Yes No
10. Points to correct part of booklet as instructions are read for subtest items	Yes No
11. Turns page briefly to show examinee third and fourth pages of items	Yes No
12. Begins timing after completing instructions	Yes No
13. Reminds examinee, if needed, to go in order and to continue the task until told to stop	Yes No
14. Discontinues after 120 seconds	Yes No
15. Uses Symbol Search template to score responses	Yes No
16. Records numbers of correct and incorrect items accurately	Yes No
17. Obtains score by subtracting number of incorrect from number of correct items attempted	Yes No

Symbol Search

Comments: _____

Letter–Number Sequencing

	Circle One
1. Reads directions verbatim	Yes No
2. Reads directions clearly	Yes No
3. Administers all five practice items	Yes No
4. Corrects examinee if she or he makes an error on any practice item and repeats instructions as necessary	Yes No
5. Proceeds with the subtest even if examinee fails all practice items	Yes No
6. Administers item 1 after practice items	Yes No
7. Pronounces digits and letters singly and distinctly, at the rate of one number or letter per second (without chunking)	Yes No
8. Records responses	Yes No
9. Gives all three trials of each item	Yes No
10. Pauses after each sequence to allow examinee to respond	Yes No
11. Assigns 1 point for each trial passed	Yes No
12. Gives credit when the letters are recalled in sequence before the numbers, as long as the numbers and the letters are recalled in sequence	Yes No
13. Discontinues after all three trials of an item are failed	Yes No
14. Adds points correctly	Yes No

Comments: _____

Object Assembly

	Circle One
1. Reads directions verbatim	Yes No
2. Reads directions clearly	Yes No
3. Begins with item 1	Yes No
4. Uses shield correctly	Yes No
5. Presents puzzles with pieces arranged properly	Yes No
6. Demonstrates correct arrangement on item 1 (man) if examinee's assembly is incorrect	Yes No
7. Does not demonstrate correct arrangement on items 2–5, even if examinee's arrangements are incomplete or incorrect	Yes No
8. Administers all items	Yes No

(Continued)

Exhibit 12-2 *(Continued)*

Object Assembly	Circle One	
9. Begins timing immediately after last word of instructions	Yes	No
10. Stops timing when examinee is obviously finished	Yes	No
11. Allows examinee to continue working on a puzzle after time limit when examinee is nearing completion	Yes	No
12. If examinee turns over a piece, promptly and unobtrusively turns it right side up	Yes	No
13. Records time accurately	Yes	No
14. Records number of junctures correctly completed within time limit	Yes	No
15. Assigns no credit for correct responses given after time limit	Yes	No
16. Records points appropriately and accurately	Yes	No
17. Assigns proper time-bonus credit	Yes	No
18. Adds points correctly	Yes	No

Comments: _____

_____

Digit Symbol—Copy

	Circle One	
1. Reads directions verbatim	Yes	No
2. Reads directions clearly	Yes	No
3. Provides two no. 2 graphite pencils without erasers	Yes	No
4. Provides a smooth work surface	Yes	No
5. Demonstrates by copying the first three symbols into the empty boxes	Yes	No
6. Corrects examinee's mistakes on sample items	Yes	No
7. Avoids timing sample items	Yes	No
8. Begins timing immediately after completing instructions	Yes	No
9. Records time accurately	Yes	No
10. Discontinues after 90 seconds	Yes	No
11. Records correct number of items	Yes	No
12. Uses scoring template to score subtest	Yes	No
13. Avoids giving credit for sample items, incorrectly drawn items, or items completed out of sequence	Yes	No

Comments: _____

_____

Other Aspects of Test Administration	Circle One	
1. Establishes rapport before testing	Yes	No
2. Encourages effort and offers appropriate feedback	Yes	No
3. Is well organized	Yes	No
4. Has needed material in kit	Yes	No
5. Has extra paper and pencils	Yes	No
6. Adheres to standardized instructions	Yes	No
7. Is fluid with the administration of the test	Yes	No
8. Has test materials and protocol out of examinee's view	Yes	No
9. Makes smooth transition from subtest to subtest	Yes	No
10. Provides support between subtests as needed	Yes	No
11. Focuses examinee's attention on tasks	Yes	No
12. Takes breaks when appropriate (needed)	Yes	No
13. Handles minor levels of anxiety and other behavior problems appropriately	Yes	No
14. Makes the test experience positive	Yes	No

Comments: _____

_____

Score Conversion Page of Record Form

	Circle One	
1. Transfers raw scores for each subtest to Score Conversion Page correctly	Yes	No
2. Converts raw scores to scaled scores for each subtest correctly	Yes	No
3. Adds scaled scores for Verbal Scale accurately	Yes	No
4. Adds scaled scores for Performance Scale accurately	Yes	No
5. Adds scaled scores for Full Scale accurately	Yes	No
6. Adds scaled scores for Verbal Comprehension Index accurately	Yes	No
7. Adds scaled scores for Perceptual Organization Index accurately	Yes	No
8. Adds scaled scores for Working Memory Index accurately	Yes	No
9. Adds scaled scores for Processing Speed Index accurately	Yes	No
10. Determines subtest strengths and weaknesses correctly	Yes	No
11. Completes Optional Procedures box for Digit Symbol—Incidental Learning and Digit Symbol —Copy correctly	Yes	No

Comments: _____

_____

(Continued)

Exhibit 12-2 *(Continued)*

Profile Page | Circle One

1. Transfers sums of scaled scores for IQs and indexes to Profile Page correctly — Yes No
2. Converts sum of scaled scores in Verbal Scale to IQ correctly — Yes No
3. Converts sum of scaled scores in Performance Scale to IQ correctly — Yes No
4. Converts sum of scaled scores in Full Scale to IQ correctly — Yes No
5. Converts sum of scaled scores in Verbal Comprehension Index to Deviation IQ correctly — Yes No
6. Converts sum of scaled scores in Perceptual Organization Index to Deviation IQ correctly — Yes No
7. Converts sum of scaled scores in Working Memory Index to Deviation IQ correctly — Yes No
8. Converts sum of scaled scores in Processing Speed Index to Deviation IQ correctly — Yes No
9. Enters percentiles and confidence intervals for IQs and Indexes correctly — Yes No
10. Completes profile of subtest scores correctly — Yes No
11. Completes profile of IQ scores correctly — Yes No
12. Completes profile of index scores correctly — Yes No

Comments: _____

Discrepancy Analysis Page

1. Enters IQs and index scores correctly — Yes No
2. Calculates difference scores correctly — Yes No
3. Enters selected significance level — Yes No
4. Enters frequency of difference in standardization sample data for each discrepancy comparison correctly, dividing each tabled frequency in half — Yes No
5. Enters longest Digits Forward span correctly — Yes No
6. Enters longest Digits Backward span correctly — Yes No
7. Calculates difference between Digits Forward and Digits Backward correctly — Yes No

Comments: _____

Demographics Page

1. Completes identifying information section correctly: assumes that all months have 30 days for purposes of calculating the chronological age; does not round up age (for example,

Demographics Page | Circle One

64 years 4 months 28 days is rounded to 64 years 4 months) — Yes No
2. Completes behavioral observation section and records the examinee's race and occupation under the "Other Notes." If the examinee is retired, records the preretirement occupation — Yes No
3. Writes examinee's name, the date, and the examiner's name on Symbol Search Response Booklet, if subtest is given. Circles whether the examinee is right- or left-handed — Yes No

Comments: _____

Overall Evaluation of Test Administration

Circle One: Excellent Good Average Poor Failing

Qualitative feedback: _____

Overall strengths: _____

Areas needing improvement: _____

Other comments: _____

produced, with shortened phrase length) and contain word substitutions (e.g., the examinee says *writer* instead of *pencil*) and grammatical errors. Informal procedures that can help you gauge the examinee's language ability include asking the examinee to

- perform simple actions (e.g., "Place the book on the table"),
- answer simple factual questions (e.g., "Is a hammer good for painting a house?"), or
- name simple objects (e.g., pencil, watch, finger) that you show him or her.

If the tasks you give to the examinee (following verbal commands, answering simple questions of fact, or naming common objects) are age-appropriate, difficulty in performing any of them suggests impaired language comprehension or naming difficulties. Such failures are sometimes noted in examinees who have aphasia (see *Assessment of Children: Behavioral and Clinical Applications*).

It will be difficult to obtain valid scores on the Verbal Scale subtests when examinees have either significant language comprehension deficits or significant language expressive difficulties, such as dysnomia (i.e., naming difficulties) or other language production difficulties. However, examinees with a language impairment should be able to take the Performance Scale subtests if they understand the instructions. You may communicate instructions nonverbally, through gesture or by performing simple actions that the examinee imitates. Table A-15 in Appendix A provides some guidelines for nonverbally administering the Performance Scale subtests. For example, to administer the Block Design subtest to an examinee with impaired language comprehension, begin with item 5. Place four blocks in front of the examinee, and turn each block to show the different sides while pointing in a manner that focuses the examinee's attention on the different colors. Next, arrange the blocks into design 5 and give the examinee four additional blocks. Then, point to the examinee, point to the blocks, and point to the completed model. If the examinee fails an item or does not respond, assemble the examinee's blocks to match the design and then point first to the examinee's blocks and then to the model. Then, scramble the examinee's blocks, point to the examinee, point to the scrambled blocks, and point to the model.

Visual functions.   You will need to determine whether the examinee has adequate visual ability to be administered the nonverbal subtests. In all cases, review the referral material, health history, and recent medical findings. Before formal testing, you can screen for visual acuity by having the examinee read a brief paragraph (if the examinee should be able to read) or describe pictures (if the examinee is a poor reader). It is always good practice to ask the examinee whether she or he wears glasses or is color blind before you begin testing. It also is good practice to ask the examinee whether she or he can see the designs and numbers clearly

when you introduce the Digit Symbol—Coding and Symbol Search subtests during the standard administration.

In addition to visual acuity problems, be alert for deficits in primary visual perception or visual scanning, especially if the examinee has a history of stroke or degenerative brain disease. For example, completely misidentifying the Picture Completion items may suggest visual agnosia, whereas consistent failure to use all of the Picture Arrangement cards may reflect inattention to one side of space. When an examinee has a visual perceptual problem, the standard WAIS–III administration procedures may not be appropriate.

Kaplan, Fein, Morris, and Delis (1991) provide useful strategies for administering WAIS–III subtests to individuals with visual perceptual or visual scanning difficulties. For example, when you administer Picture Completion to an examinee with impaired visual acuity, you might place a sheet magnifier directly over the individual items as you present them. Or, when you administer Picture Arrangement to an examinee with left-sided visual neglect, you can place the cards vertically in the examinee's intact visual field and instruct the examinee to arrange the cards from top to bottom. Although these changes modify the standard procedure and may make use of the norms questionable, they appear to be relatively minor modifications. Still, it would be helpful to have research about the effects of these modifications on WAIS–III scores.

Obviously, it is inappropriate to administer the WAIS–III Performance Scale to examinees with uncorrected visual impairments. However, you can administer the Verbal Scale subtests to estimate their language-based cognitive functioning. The only necessary modification of standard instructions is on the Comprehension subtest. To avoid confusion, instruct examinees (where needed) to answer items 4 and 12 as if they were fully sighted (Shindell, 1989).

Motor functions.   Some types of motor problems may affect examinees' performance on the WAIS–III. These include (a) motor slowing, (b) arthritis in the fingers and hands, (c) dystonic disorders (involuntary, abnormal postures or spasms of the muscles of the head, neck, trunk, or extremities that are painful and interfere with the examinee's ability to engage in voluntary movements), (d) postural tremors (tremors that occur when muscles are activated and the limbs are maintained in certain positions, such as when the arms are held outstretched; the tremors are absent when the limbs are relaxed), (e) intention tremors (tremors that interfere with voluntary movements; the tremors are absent when the examinee is inactive, but when she or he attempts to perform exacting, precise movements, the affected limb begins to oscillate, making the movement difficult or impossible to execute), and (f) medication-induced motor impairment. Motor problems may be present in hemiplegia and progressive movement disorders such as Parkinson's disease.

In most cases, you can evaluate the verbal-comprehension cognitive ability of examinees with severe motor difficulties by administering the WAIS–III Verbal Scale subtests. Hemiplegic individuals who have an intact dominant upper extremity can be evaluated with both Verbal Scale and Performance Scale subtests. For those who have an intact nondominant hand only, omit the Digit Symbol—Coding and Symbol Search subtests, but attempt to administer the remaining Performance Scale subtests.

Subtest Sequence

Administer the subtests in the order specified in the manual unless you have a compelling reason to use another order. For instance, in the case of an examinee who is extremely bored or frustrated, you could give a different subtest or a subtest of the examinee's choice to spark motivation. Or, only selected subtests might be given to an examinee with a sensory handicap, as noted above. Other compelling reasons for adjusting the order of administration would be to accommodate examinees who fatigue easily (e.g., those who are physically ill or elderly) or display marked anxiety about the testing situation. Examinees who fatigue easily may be given subtests such as Digit Span, Arithmetic, Digit Symbol—Coding, or Symbol Search early in the session, when their energy level and attention-concentration skills may be at a peak. Anxious examinees may be started with subtests that are relatively nonthreatening and do not have strict time limits (e.g., Information, Comprehension, or Vocabulary). However, examinees with test anxiety are likely to feel anxious when they begin the test, regardless of which subtest is given first.

Using the standard sequence of administration provides you with a baseline for evaluating examinees whom you will test in the future; it also ensures that the order you use is comparable to that used by other examiners. Following the order specified in the WAIS–III manual, which alternates nonverbal and verbal subtests, also may help to maintain the examinee's interest in the tasks.

If you elect to administer 13 subtests, simply omit Object Assembly. If you give the 11 standard subtests and omit Letter–Number Sequencing, Symbol Search, and Object Assembly, follow the order presented in Table 3.2 on page 37 in the *WAIS–III Administration and Scoring Manual*.

The *WAIS–III Administration and Scoring Manual* states that "Picture Completion was moved to the initial position in the sequence because it provides a colorful, nonverbal introduction to the scale, which should help the examinee 'warm up' to the testing situation" (p. 36). However, for examinees who have difficulty with perceptual discrimination or who respond slowly, Picture Completion may actually induce frustration and reduce motivation to continue with the test. Therefore, carefully attend to the examinee's behavior, especially at the beginning of the test session. Do not assume that the order of the WAIS–III subtests will automatically reduce every examinee's anxiety level. We need research to learn about how the order in which the subtests are administered affects examinees' anxiety level and test performance.

Some examinees—such as those who are depressed and work slowly or those with a neurological disorder or psychiatric disorder—may not be able to complete the test in a single session. In such cases, schedule breaks to coincide with the end of a subtest so that testing can easily be resumed at a later time. In the rare instance when a subtest must be interrupted prior to completion, resume administration of the subtest where you stopped, except on Similarities, Block Design, Matrix Reasoning, and Picture Arrangement. On these subtests, the easy items provide some examinees with the practice they need to succeed at more difficult items. Therefore, if you must interrupt one of these subtests, readminister the first few items at the next session so that the examinee can establish a mental set that may help her or him succeed on the harder items. Naturally, changes in standard administration procedures may affect the validity of the test, but minor changes do not appear to be critical.

Starting Rules

Six of the 14 subtests begin with the first item (Digit Span, Letter–Number Sequencing, Digit Symbol—Coding, Picture Arrangement, Symbol Search, and Object Assembly). Of the remaining eight subtests, three begin with the fourth item (Vocabulary, Comprehension, and Matrix Reasoning), three begin with the fifth item (Information, Arithmetic, and Block Design), and two begin with the sixth item (Picture Completion and Similarities). If the examinee obtains maximum scores on the first two subtest items administered, which are designated as basal items, assign him or her credit for the items that precede the basal items, even though these items were not given. If the examinee does not obtain maximum credit on *both* of the basal items, administer the preceding items in reverse sequence until the maximum score is obtained on two consecutive items. If the examinee obtained maximum credit on the starting item, count it as a success in the reverse sequence.

Occasionally, you may have doubts about whether the examinee passed both basal items. When this happens, you will need to administer earlier items in the subtest. The *WAIS–III Administration and Scoring Manual* does not provide guidance on how to credit items that the examinee fails *below* the starting point. We recommend the following starting-point scoring rule: *If subsequent scoring of the items indicates that the early items were administered unnecessarily, give the examinee full credit for these items even if the examinee earned only partial or no credit.* In other words, if the examinee failed (or received only partial credit for) one or more items below the starting point but further checking indicates that, in fact, the examinee correctly answered the items at the starting point, give full credit for those items that precede the basal items. This starting-point scoring rule favors the examinee by ensuring that the examinee is not penalized for failing items that should not have been administered in the first place. The starting-point scoring rule also helps to maintain standardized scoring procedures.

Discontinuance Rules

Of the 14 subtests in the test, 11 have discontinuance rules—they are discontinued after a specified number of consecutive items are failed. The three subtests without discontinuance rules are Object Assembly, Digit Symbol—Coding, and Symbol Search. On the 11 subtests with discontinuance rules, you will need to administer additional items until you are certain the discontinuance criterion has been met. If you administer additional items in a subtest because you are not sure whether the items at the discontinuance point were failed, use the following discontinuance-point scoring rule to determine how to credit the additional items (Wechsler, 1997): *If subsequent scoring of the items indicates that the additional items were administered unnecessarily, do not give the examinee credit for items passed after the discontinuance point.* This scoring rule prevents the examinee from receiving credit for items that did not need to be administered. This rule constitutes an attempt to maintain standardized scoring procedures.

Repetition of Items

Use judgment in deciding when to repeat questions. However, you *cannot* repeat the Digit Span or Letter–Number Sequencing items.

Use of Probing Questions and Queries

Use probing questions when responses are ambiguous, vague, or incomplete or when querying is indicated by a "(Q)" in the scoring section of the *WAIS–III Administration and Scoring Manual*. When a response is followed by a "(Q)," the examinee must give the response shown after the "(Q)" in order to get the appropriate credit. Thus, the entire response—the initial answer plus the response to the query—is used in determining the appropriate credit.

Spoiled Responses

An explicit scoring rule on the WAIS–III is that you give a score of 0 to a spoiled response (see pages 48–49 in the *WAIS–III Administration and Scoring Manual*). A spoiled response is one that initially was partially correct, but was spoiled by the examinee's incorrect elaboration on the initial response. For example, let's suppose an examinee defines *summer* as "One of the seasons." This is a 1-point answer. In response to a query, however, the examinee replies, "The cold time of year." This elaboration reveals the examinee's misconception about the meaning of *summer*, and the response receives a score of 0.

Modifying Standard Procedures

Use modifications in test administration designed for testing-of-limits (see Chapter 7) only *after* the entire WAIS–III has been administered according to standard procedures. Modifications may be helpful in clinical assessment, but they may invalidate the scores if they are used during the standard administration. Also recognize that testing-of-limits procedures may invalidate the WAIS–III for future assessments. In cases where the WAIS–III will need to be readministered in order to monitor the examinee's progress (e.g., the examinee is in a treatment or rehabilitation program that requires periodic monitoring), do not use testing-of-limits.

How to Proceed When a Basal Level Is Not Established

The *WAIS–III Administration and Scoring Manual* (first printing) does not provide directions for continuing or discontinuing a subtest when a basal level is not established. The subtests that require a basal level—that is, perfect scores on two consecutive items—are Picture Completion, Vocabulary, Similarities, Block Design, Arithmetic, Matrix Reasoning, Information, and Comprehension. There are many possible cases in which a basal level will not be established. The following three examples illustrate failure to establish a basal level (i.e., 2-point responses on two consecutive items)

Courtesy of Herman Zielinski.

on the Vocabulary subtest: (a) An examinee earns 1 point on item 5, 2 points on item 4, 0 points on item 3, 2 points on item 2, and 1 point on item 1. (b) Another examinee earns 1 point on item 5, 1 point on item 4, 1 point on item 3, 0 points on item 2, and 2 points on item 1. (c) A third examinee earns 1 point on each of the first five items.

In any situation in which a basal level is not established, we recommend that the discontinuance procedure be followed for the subtest. (David Tulsky, spokesperson for The Psychological Corporation, fully supports this recommendation; personal communication, May 1998.) This recommendation means that it is not necessary to establish a basal level in order to continue with a subtest. The basal criterion, however, is important for deciding whether to administer the items in a subtest in reverse order. Maintaining standard procedures is critical if all examinees are to be given the same opportunities to demonstrate their competencies. Further, when all examiners follow the same test procedures, users of the test can have more confidence in the results obtained by different examiners.

SHORT FORMS OF THE WAIS–III

It takes approximately 75 minutes (range of 60 to 90 minutes) to administer the 11 standard WAIS–III subtests (Wechsler, 1997). This time estimate is based on normal individuals in the standardization sample and may not generalize to clinical populations. In fact, among patients at a medical center, administration time for the 11 standard WAIS–III subtests was an average of 91 minutes (range of 54 to 136 minutes; Ryan, Lopez, & Werth, 1998).

When time is at a premium, you can use a short form of the WAIS–III as a screening device (when administration of the short form may be followed by administration of the remaining subtests), for research purposes (to describe the intellectual level of a group), or for a quick check on an individual's intellectual status (and only when the IQ is peripheral to the referral question; Silverstein, 1990b). Ideally, you should select a short form based on such criteria as acceptable reliability and validity, the ability of the short form to answer the referral question and provide clinically useful information, the examinee's physical capabilities, and the amount of time available for test administration. Short forms of the WAIS–III have the same advantages and disadvantages as short forms of the WISC–III. Chapter 8 discusses the use of short forms; review this material as needed. Let's now consider different WAIS–III short forms.

Selecting the Short Form

Table C-15 in Appendix C lists the 10 best short-form combinations of two, three, four, and five WAIS–III subtests. It also gives short forms designed to optimize time and scoring and

those designed for use with hard-of-hearing individuals. The reliability and validity coefficients shown in Table C-15 were calculated using the standardization data and the Tellegen and Briggs (1967) procedure, which takes into account the reliabilities of the subtests used in the short form. Exhibit 8-4 in Chapter 8 shows the formulas used to compute the reliability and validity of the short-form combinations.

An inspection of the coefficients in Table C-15 indicates that the 10 best two-, three-, four-, and five-subtest short-form combinations all have reliability coefficients of .90 or above. In fact, all four- and five-subtest combinations have reliability coefficients of .94 or above. Overall, for the combinations shown in Table C-15, the more subtests used in the short form, the higher the reliability of the estimated IQ.

You also need to consider the validity of the short-form combinations. The validity coefficients are .90 or above for all four- and five-subtest short forms shown in Table C-15. For the three-subtest short-form combinations, 8 out of the 10 best combinations have validity coefficients of .90, and the other two are .899. Finally, the validity coefficients for the 10 best two-subtest short-form combinations range from .853 to .881. The best two-, three-, four-, and five-subtest short-form combinations, based on validity and reliability, are as follows:

- Vocabulary and Matrix Reasoning
- Vocabulary, Information, and Block Design
- Vocabulary, Information, Block Design, and Matrix Reasoning
- Vocabulary, Arithmetic, Information, Picture Completion, and Matrix Reasoning

All of the subtests in the best two-, three-, and four-subtest combinations are excellent measures of *g*.

You also want to consider the short-form combinations that you can use for a rapid screening, taking into account the purpose of the screening and the physical capacities of the examinee. We recommend the following short-form combinations for rapid screening (with substitutions as needed):

- Information and Matrix Reasoning (good measures of *g*)
- Arithmetic, Information, and Matrix Reasoning (good measures of *g*)
- Arithmetic, Information, Picture Completion, and Matrix Reasoning (either good or fair measures of *g*)
- Arithmetic, Information, Picture Completion, Digit Symbol—Coding, and Matrix Reasoning (either good or fair measures of *g*)

Because many of the short forms of the WAIS–III have high reliability and validity, clinical considerations should guide you in selecting a short form. For instance, if you want to use a four-subtest short form, consider selecting a combination of two Verbal Scale and two Performance Scale subtests to obtain some representation of both verbal and performance skills in your screening.

Sometimes you may want to use a short form to screen for some specific type of problem, such as a memory problem

(Arithmetic, Digit Span, and Letter–Number Sequencing) or a visual-motor speed problem (Digit Symbol—Coding and Symbol Search). In these cases, you should not use the estimated Deviation IQ obtained on the specialized short form as a measure of intelligence, because the specialized short form may lead to an underestimate of the examinee's IQ if you have prior evidence that the examinee has a possible weakness in the areas measured by the specific subtests. Instead, we recommend that you administer a short form that does not include the subtests in question to derive an estimated IQ. The procedures we recommend allow you to screen for level of intelligence, screen for a particular problem, and screen for problems associated with the difference between two short-form measures (e.g., two verbal measures vs. two performance measures).

An examinee's physical capabilities may guide you in selecting a short form. As stated above, examinees with marked visual impairment or severe motor dysfunction of the upper extremities will have difficulty with the Performance Scale subtests. In these cases, the Verbal Scale (or subtests that form the Verbal Comprehension Index score) serves as a useful short form. For hearing-impaired examinees, the Performance Scale (or subtests that form the Perceptual Organization Index score) is a useful short form. Administer these short forms by using the examinee's preferred mode of communication and, if possible, supplement your evaluation by using other tests designed to accommodate the special physical abilities of the examinee.

After the short form has been given, you will need to convert the scaled scores to an estimated Deviation IQ. Tables C-21 through C-25 in Appendix C provide the estimated Deviation IQs for short-form combinations of two, three, four, five, six, and seven subtests that (a) have the best validity, (b) can be administered and scored rapidly, (c) can be given to hard-of-hearing individuals, and (d) can be used to obtain index scores. If the short form you select is not in one of these tables, follow the procedures outlined in Exhibit 8-4 in Chapter 8 to convert the composite scores to Deviation Quotients. Use Table D-6 in Appendix D to obtain the appropriate a and b constants. To obtain r_{jk} use the section of Table A.1 (pages 218–230 in the *WAIS–III WMS–III Technical Manual*) that corresponds to the examinee's age group.

The estimated Deviation Quotients shown in Appendix C for the short forms that comprise the four index scores differ somewhat from those shown in the *WAIS–III Administration and Scoring Manual*. The Psychological Corporation constructed its norms by using a z score conversion of the scaled scores, transforming the scores to a distribution with $M = 100$ and $SD = 15$, and then smoothing out irregularities in the distribution (personal communication, David Tulsky of The Psychological Corporation, May 1998). The Tellegen and Briggs (1967) procedure uses a linear transformation of the scaled scores without smoothing. Research with a clinical sample of 74 individuals indicated that the two methods produced mean Deviation Quotients that were essentially identical (Sattler & Ryan, 1998). In addition, the two methods

produced index scores that were within 1 point of each other in 95% or more of the cases. Finally, correlations between the index scores generated by the two methods ranged from .965 to .999. We recommend that you use The Psychological Corporation's values on pages 199 to 202 of the manual. However, if you wish to compare the four index short forms with other short forms proposed in this text, then the Deviation IQs shown in Appendix C are appropriate.

Tables C-16 to C-20 in Appendix C show whether the observed scatter (the highest scaled score minus the lowest scaled score) on all the short forms in Table C-15 in the Appendix is (a) significant and (b) within the expected range. Table C-16, for example, indicates that in the short form composed of Information and Digit Symbol—Coding, a range of 3 points between the two scores represents a nonchance difference at the .05 level. A range of 6 points occurs in less than 10% of the population and should be considered unusual. Less credence can be placed in the estimated short-form IQ when the scatter is larger than expected.

Satz-Mogel Abbreviated Procedure

The Yudin short-form procedure, which reduces the number of items within subtests, is known as the Satz-Mogel short form when applied to the WAIS–III (Ryan, Lopez, & Werth, 1999; Satz & Mogel, 1962). Research with the WAIS–R and WAIS–III indicates that this procedure provides IQs with high validity coefficients (Ryan et al., 1999; Silverstein, 1982). However, poor correlations have been reported between estimated subtest scaled scores and actually obtained scores (Evans, 1985). Estimated scaled scores have been found to exceed the range of ±2 scaled-score points from actually obtained scores in over 25% of the 81 cases studied (Evans, 1985). Additionally, when the Satz-Mogel procedure is used, some or all of the subtest scaled scores show relatively poor reliability and stability (Paolo & Ryan, 1993; Silverstein, 1990a; 1990b), rendering the data unsuitable for profile analysis (Mattis, Hannay & Meyers, 1992). Because of these and other limitations discussed in Chapter 8, we do not recommend the use of reduced-item short forms.

Two Two-Subtest Short-Form Combinations

A two-subtest combination that is popular as a short-form screening instrument is Vocabulary plus Block Design. These two subtests have moderate correlations with the Full Scale, have consistently high reliabilities, and are good measures of g. Administration time for this short form in a clinical sample averaged 26 minutes (range of 16 to 40 minutes; Ryan et al., 1998). If this combination is chosen, Table C-21 in Appendix C can be used to convert the sum of scaled scores directly into an estimated Full Scale IQ. The reliability of the composite is high ($r_{xx} = .93$ for the average of the 13 age groups in the standardization sample).

Another useful two-subtest short form is Vocabulary plus Matrix Reasoning. These two subtests also have moderate correlations with the Full Scale, have consistently high reliabilities, and are good measures of *g*. Administration time for this short form in a clinical sample averaged 22 minutes (range of 9 to 39 minutes; Ryan et al., 1998). If this combination is chosen, Table C-21 in Appendix C can be used to convert the sum of scaled scores directly into an estimated Full Scale IQ. The reliability of the composite is high (r_{xx} = .94 for the average of the 13 age groups in the standardization sample).

Two Four-Subtest Short-Form Combinations

Two excellent four-subtest short forms are (a) Information, Arithmetic, Picture Completion, and Block Design and (b) Information, Arithmetic, Picture Completion, and Matrix Reasoning. Both of these combinations contain two Verbal Scale subtests and two Performance Scale subtests. They both have high reliability (r_{xx} = .95 for the average of the 13 age groups in the standardization sample). Although these short forms take longer to administer than the two-subtest short forms mentioned above, they provide more clinical and diagnostic information (e.g., additional information about concentration and attention). You can use Table C-23 in Appendix C to convert the sum of scaled scores on these two four-subtest short forms directly into an estimated Deviation Quotient. You also can use these short forms to obtain estimated Deviation IQs for the Verbal Scale (Information and Arithmetic) and Performance Scale (e.g., Picture Completion and Block Design; see Table C-21 in Appendix C). The Information, Arithmetic, Picture Completion, and Matrix Reasoning combination requires less time to administer than the Information, Arithmetic, Picture Completion, and Block Design combination. In a clinical sample, average administration times were 26 minutes (range of 10 to 58 minutes) and 31 minutes (range of 12 to 55 minutes), respectively, for these two short forms (Ryan et al., 1998). Table C-23 shows other excellent four-subtest short-form combinations.

One Six-Subtest Short-Form Combination

A six-subtest short-form combination that consists of Vocabulary, Similarities, Information, Picture Completion, Block Design, and Matrix Reasoning is useful to obtain the Verbal Comprehension Index score (Vocabulary, Similarities, and Information), the Perceptual Organization Index score (Picture Completion, Block Design, and Matrix Reasoning), and an estimated Deviation Quotient for the entire scale. In a clinical sample, average administration time was 53 minutes (range of 21 to 100 minutes; Ryan et al., 1998). You can use Table C-25 in Appendix C to convert the sum of scaled scores on these six subtests into an estimated Deviation IQ. Table C-22 in Appendix C provides the Deviation IQs for the Verbal Comprehension Index score and the Perceptual Organization Index score.

Two Seven-Subtest Short-Form Combinations

One potentially useful seven-subtest short-form combination is Information, Arithmetic, Digit Span, Similarities, Picture Completion, Block Design, and Digit Symbol—Coding (Ward, 1990). Research with the WAIS–III indicates that this short form reduces administration time by more than 50% (Ryan et al., 1998); provides estimates of the Verbal Scale IQ, Performance Scale IQ, and Full Scale IQ; and possesses excellent reliability (Ryan & Ward, 1999). This seven-subtest short form has a reliability coefficient of .96 for the average of the 13 age groups in the standardization sample. In a clinical sample, average administration time was 46 minutes (range of 29 to 68 minutes; Ryan et al., 1998). Additionally, this short form has performed well both as a screening instrument and as a substitute for the standard WAIS–III in normal and clinical samples (Axelrod, Ryan, & Ward, 2001; Pilgrim, Meyers, Bayless, & Whetstone, 1999; Ryan & Ward, 1999). Table C-25 in Appendix C can be used to convert the sum of the scaled scores on these seven subtests into an estimated Full Scale IQ. To obtain an estimated Deviation IQ for the Verbal Scale and Performance Scale, consult Appendix C Table C-23 for the Verbal Scale (four subtests) and Table C-22 for the Performance Scale (three subtests).

Another potentially useful seven-subtest short-form combination is Information, Arithmetic, Digit Span, Similarities, Picture Completion, Matrix Reasoning, and Digit Symbol—Coding (Ryan, 1999; Ryan, Ament, & Axelrod, 2000; Ryan & Ward, 1999). This combination has a reliability coefficient of .97 for the average of the 13 age groups in the standardization sample. In a clinical sample, average administration time was 41 minutes (range of 25 to 67 minutes; Ryan et al., 1998). Table C-25 in Appendix C can be used to convert the sum of the scaled scores on these seven subtests into an estimated Full Scale IQ. To obtain an estimated Deviation IQ for the Verbal Scale and Performance Scale, consult Appendix C Table C-23 for the Verbal Scale (four subtests) and Table C-22 for the Performance Scale (three subtests).

CHOOSING BETWEEN THE WAIS–III AND THE WISC–III

The WAIS–III overlaps with the WISC–III for ages 16-0-0 to 16-11-30. The overlap in ages between the WAIS–III and the WISC–III is especially helpful in retest situations. For example, an adolescent first administered the WAIS–III at 16 years of age can be retested with the WISC–III at any time during the next 11 months. In the overlapping ranges, Atkinson (personal communication, April 1998) compared the WAIS–III and the WISC–III on several criteria, including mean subtest reliability, Full Scale reliability, mean subtest floor, mean subtest ceiling, item gradients (number of correct items needed to go from the floor to the mean and from the mean to the ceiling and the relationship of raw-score points to scaled-score points), Full Scale floor, and Full Scale ceiling. He makes the following recommendations:

- The WISC–III is a better choice for adolescents with below-average ability.
- Either test is adequate for adolescents with average ability.
- The WAIS–III is a better choice for adolescents with above-average ability.

The following example illustrates how you can obtain a more thorough sampling on the WISC–III than on the WAIS–III for a 16-year, 8-month-old adolescent with below-average ability. To obtain a scaled score of 5 on Information, the adolescent needs a raw score of 14 on the WISC–III but a raw score of only 5 on the WAIS–III.

The previous recommendations are based on internal psychometric data. The issue of validity still needs to be addressed. In the final analysis, the choice of a test in the overlapping ages should be based on the validity of the inferences that you can make from the scores on it. To this end, validity studies that compare the WAIS–III with the WISC–III in their overlapping age ranges, using samples of both normal and exceptional adolescents, would be helpful.

THINKING THROUGH THE ISSUES

1. In what situations would it be appropriate to administer the WAIS–III? In what situations would it be inappropriate to administer the WAIS–III?
2. How well do the items on the WAIS–III relate to everyday cognitive functions?
3. Under what circumstances would you administer an abbreviated form of the WAIS–III? How might you decide which subtests to administer?
4. Do you think that the type of medication an examinee is taking can influence his or her WAIS–III performance? If so, what types of medications might you be concerned about?
5. If an examinee did not sleep well the night before a WAIS–III examination, might this have an impact on her or his performance? What are some of the signs of excessive fatigue? What subtests might be affected adversely by excessive fatigue?
6. What are some clinical situations in which repeat testing with the WAIS–III would be an appropriate recommendation?
7. How can you relate theories of intelligence to the composition of the WAIS–III?

SUMMARY

1. The Psychological Corporation published the WAIS–III in 1997, 16 years after the former edition, the WAIS–R. The WAIS–III is similar to its predecessor, with more than 68% of the items retained, as well as the original Digit Symbol subtest, which was slightly modified. Matrix Reasoning, a standard sub-

test, and Letter–Number Sequencing and Symbol Search, two supplementary subtests, are new. The WAIS–III is applicable to adolescents and adults from 16-0-0 to 89-11–30 years of age.

Standardization

2. Standardization of the test was excellent and included Euro American, African American, Hispanic American, and other ethnic groups.
3. The WAIS–III is co-normed with the Wechsler Memory Scale–III and linked with the Wechsler Individual Achievement Test.

Deviation IQs and Scaled Scores

4. The WAIS–III provides Deviation IQs for the Verbal Scale, Performance Scale, and Full Scale ($M = 100$, $SD = 15$) and standard scores for the 14 subtests ($M = 10$, $SD = 3$).

Reliability

5. The internal consistency reliabilities of the Verbal Scale, Performance Scale, and Full Scale are excellent (average r_{xx} of .97, .94, and .98, respectively). Average subtest internal consistency reliabilities range from .70 to .93, and average test-retest reliabilities range from .76 to .94. Reliabilities for the Verbal Scale, Performance Scale, and Full Scale are higher than those for the individual subtests.
6. Vocabulary is the most reliable Verbal Scale subtest, and Matrix Reasoning is the most reliable Performance Scale subtest.
7. Average standard errors of measurement are 2.55 for the Verbal Scale, 3.67 for the Performance Scale, and 2.30 for the Full Scale. The most confidence can be placed in the Full Scale, followed by the Verbal Scale and then the Performance Scale.
8. On average, test-retest reliability was lowest for Picture Arrangement ($r_{tt} = .69$) and highest for Information ($r_{tt} = .94$).
9. Increases in IQ produced by practice effects (after approximately a 1-month interval) averaged from 3.2 to 5.7 points on the Full Scale, 2.0 to 3.2 points on the Verbal Scale, and 3.7 to 8.3 points on the Performance Scale.

Validity

10. Studies reported in the *WAIS–III WMS–III Technical Manual* and other sources suggest that the WAIS–III has acceptable concurrent validity. Correlations between the Full Scale IQ and other measures of intelligence, achievement, and memory range from .57 to .93.
11. The *WAIS–III WMS–III Technical Manual* indicates that in the overlapping ages the WAIS–III provides *lower* IQs than does the WAIS–R, by about 3 points, and *higher* IQs than does the WISC–III, by about 1 point.

Intercorrelations Between Subtests and Scales

12. The Verbal Scale subtests correlate more highly with each other (*Mdn r* = .57) than do the Performance Scale subtests (*Mdn r* = .49). Correlations between the Verbal Scale subtests and the Verbal Scale (*Mdn r* = .76) are higher than those between the Performance Scale subtests and the Performance Scale (*Mdn r* = .64). The Verbal Scale subtests also have higher correlations with the Full Scale (*Mdn r* = .75) than do the Performance Scale subtests (*Mdn r* = .63).

Factor Analysis

13. Factor analysis of the WAIS–III standardization data indicated that four factors account for the test's structure at most age groups: Verbal Comprehension, Perceptual Organization, Working Memory, and Processing Speed. The best measures of g are Vocabulary, Similarities, Information, Comprehension, Arithmetic, Block Design, and Matrix Reasoning.

14. Because several WAIS–III subtests have an adequate degree of subtest specificity, interpretation of profiles of subtest scaled scores is on firm ground for these subtests.

15. The index scores are formed by the following combinations of subtests: (a) Vocabulary, Similarities, and Information for Verbal Comprehension; (b) Picture Completion, Block Design, and Matrix Reasoning for Perceptual Organization; (c) Arithmetic, Digit Span, and Letter–Number Sequencing for Working Memory; and (d) Digit Symbol—Coding and Symbol Search for Processing Speed.

Range of Subtest Scaled Scores

16. The subtest scaled-score range is 1 to 19, but not at all age groups. For some age groups and for some subtests, the highest scaled score attainable is 17. For persons in the age groups 80–84 years and 85–89 years, the lowest attainable scaled scores on the Picture Arrangement subtest are 4 and 5, respectively.

Range of Full Scale IQs

17. The range of Full Scale IQs for all age groups is 45 to 155. This range means that the WAIS–III does not adequately assess the cognitive ability of examinees who are either severely retarded or exceptionally gifted.

Comparison of the WAIS–III and WAIS–R

18. The WAIS–III differs from the WAIS–R in several ways. The most noticeable changes are the addition of three new subtests (Letter–Number Sequencing, Matrix Reasoning, and Symbol Search), two new factors (Working Memory and Processing Speed), and full color for many of the pictures. Items have been added or changed on every subtest, and numerous administrative changes have been made.

Administering the WAIS–III

19. Developing proper administrative procedures early in your testing and assessment career is an important step in becoming a competent clinician.

20. Examiners may make administrative errors. These include failing to follow the scoring rules, failing to complete the Record Form properly, failing to adhere to directions, failing to probe ambiguous responses, and failing to follow starting-point and discontinuance procedures.

21. Adequate hearing and language functions are required for the Verbal Scale subtests, and adequate vision and visual-motor ability are needed for the Performance Scale subtests. If you have any doubts about the examinee's auditory functions, language functions, visual functions, or motor functions, use screening procedures to determine whether the examinee has any deficits in that area.

22. You should follow the standard order of administering the subtests in all but the most exceptional circumstances.

23. Some examinees may not be able to complete the full battery of subtests in a single session. In such cases, schedule breaks to coincide with the end of a subtest so that testing can easily be resumed at a later time.

24. To ensure that scoring is standardized at the starting and discontinuance points, credit any items failed below the starting-point items when the examinee passes the starting-point items, and do not credit any items passed above the discontinuance-point items when the examinee fails the discontinuance-point items.

25. The WAIS–III requires the use of many probing questions and queries. Give spoiled responses a score of 0.

26. Because modifications in test procedures may increase the examinee's scores, use modifications only *after* the standard administration.

27. In any situation in which a basal level is not established, follow the discontinuance procedure for the subtest.

Short Forms of the WAIS–III

28. Short forms of the WAIS–III, although practical, have several disadvantages. Short-form IQs may be less stable, impede profile analysis, and result in misclassifications. Do not use short forms for any placement, educational, or clinical decision-making purpose.

29. If you need to use a short form for screening purposes, follow the procedures advocated by Tellegen and Briggs to determine the Deviation IQs.

Choosing Between the WAIS–III and the WISC–III

30. Although you can view the WISC–III and WAIS–III as alternative forms for examinees aged 16-0-0 to 16-11-30 years, we recommend that you give the WISC–III to examinees with below-average ability, either test to examinees with average ability, and the WAIS–III to examinees with above-average ability.

KEY TERMS, CONCEPTS, AND NAMES

Wechsler-Bellevue Intelligence Scale (p. 376)
WAIS–III standardization (p. 377)
WAIS–III Deviation IQ (p. 377)
WAIS–III scaled scores (p. 378)
Prorating procedure (p. 378)
Reliability of the WAIS–III (p. 378)
Subtest reliabilities of the WAIS–III (p. 378)
Standard errors of measurement of the WAIS–III (p. 379)
Stability of the WAIS–III (p. 380)
Changes in WAIS–III IQs (p. 381)
Changes in WAIS–III subtest scaled scores (p. 381)
Confidence intervals for WAIS–III IQs (p. 382)
Content validity of the WAIS–III (p. 382)
Concurrent validity of the WAIS–III (p. 383)
Construct validity of the WAIS–III (p. 384)
WAIS–III subtest intercorrelations (p. 384)
Factor analysis of the WAIS–III (p. 385)
WAIS–III Verbal Comprehension factor (p. 385)
WAIS–III Perceptual Organization factor (p. 385)
WAIS–III Working Memory factor (p. 385)
WAIS–III Processing Speed factor (p. 388)

STUDY QUESTIONS

1. Discuss the following topics with respect to the WAIS–III: standardization, Deviation IQs, scaled scores, reliability, and validity.
2. Describe and interpret WAIS–III factor analytic findings.
3. Discuss important factors involved in administering the WAIS–III.
4. Discuss WAIS–III short forms, including their value and limitations.

13

WAIS–III SUBTESTS AND INTERPRETING THE WAIS–III

by Jerome M. Sattler and Joseph J. Ryan

For it is not intelligence that makes us truly human, but how we use it.

—Bryan Appleyard

Goals and Objectives

This chapter is designed to enable you to do the following:

- Describe the rationale, factor analytic findings, reliability and correlational highlights, and administrative and interpretive considerations for the 14 WAIS–III subtests

- Describe profile analysis for the WAIS–III

- Analyze and evaluate WAIS–III scores from multiple perspectives

- Evaluate and describe the assets and limitations of the WAIS–III

This chapter describes the 14 subtests in the WAIS–III and issues involved in the interpretation of the test. A brief description of each subtest is followed by a discussion of its rationale, factor analytic findings, reliability and correlational highlights, and administrative and interpretive considerations. The factor analytic findings discussed in this chapter are based on the principal-axis factor analysis (described in Chapter 12) that we conducted on the WAIS–III standardization data, obtained from the correlation matrices in the *WAIS–III–WMS–III Technical Manual.* Similarly, the reliability and correlational findings reported in this chapter are based on the WAIS–III standardization data presented in the WAIS–III manual.

Table D-3 in Appendix D summarizes (a) the abilities purportedly measured by each WAIS–III subtest, (b) background factors influencing performance, (c) implications of high and low subtest scaled scores, and (d) instructional implications. Table D-3 deserves careful study and is a useful reference for report writing. Table 10-5 in Chapter 10 also highlights suggested abilities or factors measured by the WAIS–III subtests.

Recognize that the standard administration of all subtests on the WAIS–III Verbal Scale and Performance Scale requires the examinee to hear, pay attention, listen, understand directions, and retain the directions while solving problems. In addition, all Performance Scale subtests require the examinee to have adequate vision, and some Performance Scale subtests also require the examinee to have adequate motor skills.

The best estimates of abilities are provided by the Full Scale, followed by the Verbal Scale and the Performance Scale, indexes, other combinations of subtests, and, finally, individual subtests. For example, the Full Scale IQ, derived from 11 subtests, provides the best estimate of general ability. The Verbal Scale IQ, derived from a combination of six Verbal Scale subtests, yields more accurate information about an examinee's verbal skills than does a single Verbal Scale subtest, such as Vocabulary. Similarly, the Performance Scale IQ, derived from a combination of five Performance Scale subtests, yields more accurate information about an examinee's nonverbal skills than does a single Performance Scale subtest, such as Picture Completion. Arithmetic, Digit Span, and Letter–Number Sequencing together provide more information about working memory than does any of the three subtests alone. Finally, Digit Symbol—Coding and Symbol Search together provide more information about processing speed than either subtest alone.

As you read about each subtest, you will find questions to guide you in your test administration. Answering these questions will help you evaluate and interpret the examinee's performance. In addition to the examinee's scores, always consider the quality of the examinee's responses and the pattern of his or her successes and failures. Recording the examinee's responses carefully, along with pertinent behavioral observations, will help you evaluate the test results, especially when you review the test protocol later. An accurate record is also vital if you need to testify at an administrative hearing or in court or if other professionals need to review the record.

In administering the subtests, use the exact wording of the questions or items and never add explanations or give synonyms. The same guideline holds for the directions that introduce each subtest. Restrict your deviations to those listed in the manual, except when common sense dictates that you say something that is needed (e.g., "Tell me when you're finished"). The aim is to administer the test in a standardized manner. Never include in the calculation of an IQ a subtest that was spoiled (e.g., through improper timing or mistakes in administration). Review Chapter 7 before you administer the WAIS–III.

Scoring responses to some of the Wechsler subtests—such as Vocabulary, Comprehension, and Similarities—can be challenging. Although the WAIS–III manual provides adequate guidelines, the guidelines cannot cover every contingency. Therefore, you will sometimes have to use judgment in scoring responses, especially borderline ones. Always query unclear or borderline responses unless the manual says otherwise. Do the best job possible with the scoring guidelines given in the manual. However, whenever you have any doubt about the scoring of a response, consult a colleague.

This chapter also discusses testing-of-limits. As noted in Chapter 7, *always conduct testing-of-limits after you administer the entire test following standard procedures.* Testing-of-limits is useful for (a) following up leads about the examinee's functioning obtained during the standard administration, (b) testing clinical hypotheses, and (c) evaluating whether additional cues or extra time helps the examinee solve problems. As noted in Chapter 7, *testing-of-limits may invalidate repeated evaluations and should be used cautiously.*

This text, unlike the WAIS–III manual, uses the term *mental retardation* instead of the term *extremely low* to describe examinees who may be significantly below average in their intellectual ability. *Mental retardation* is the term used in *DSM-IV* and by the American Association on Mental Retardation. Consequently, we believe that *mental retardation* is the preferred term for describing examinees who are functioning two or more standard deviations below the mean.

Let us now turn to a discussion of each of the 14 WAIS–III subtests. Note that we recommend that, from an examinee who cannot speak, you accept written or typed answers or signed answers (assuming you know American Sign Language or use an interpreter).

VOCABULARY

The Vocabulary subtest contains 33 words arranged in order of increasing difficulty. Each word is presented orally and in print, and the examinee is asked to explain the meaning of each word aloud.

Rationale

The Vocabulary subtest, a test of word knowledge, assesses several cognitive factors—such as the examinee's learning ability, fund of information, richness of ideas, memory, concept formation, and language development—that may be closely related to the examinee's educational experiences and environment. Because the number of words known by an examinee correlates with learning ability and with the ability to learn and to accumulate information, the subtest provides an excellent estimate of intellectual ability. Performance on the subtest is stable over time and relatively resistant to psychological disturbance and to neurological deficit that does not involve significant aphasia or language dysfunction. Scores on Vocabulary therefore provide a useful index of the examinee's general mental ability.

Factor Analytic Findings

The Vocabulary subtest is the best measure of g in the scale (69% of its variance may be attributed to g). This subtest contributes substantially to the Verbal Comprehension Index (average loading = .91). Specificity is either ample or adequate for 11 age groups (16–17 through 20–24, 30–34 through 55–64, 70–74 through 85–89 years); at two age groups (25–29, 65–69 years), it is inadequate.

Reliability and Correlational Highlights

Vocabulary is the most reliable subtest in the scale ($r_{xx} = .93$), with reliability coefficients at or above .90 at all of the 13 age groups (range of .90 to .95). It correlates better with Information ($r = .77$) than with any other subtests. It has a high correlation with the Full Scale ($r = .80$) and the Verbal Scale ($r = .83$) and a moderate correlation with the Performance Scale ($r = .65$).

Administrative Suggestions

Here are some administrative suggestions for the Vocabulary subtest.

Background Considerations

- The subtest is not timed.
- After the first three items are administered, you can pronounce the words rather than giving the instruction "Tell me what ... means."
- Pronounce each word clearly and correctly.
- Have the examinee repeat the word to you when you suspect that the examinee has heard a word correctly. If the examinee heard the word incorrectly, say, "Listen carefully. What does ... mean?"
- The scoring guidelines following each item in the WAIS–III manual list many responses that you should query, shown by a "(Q)." Study these guidelines carefully so that you can recognize responses that you need to query. The

examples indicate that many 0- and 1-point responses should be queried. When a 2-point response is accompanied by a "(Q)," it is the entire response, including the elaboration, that is worth 2 points.

- Carefully record all of the examinee's answers, whether they are correct or incorrect.
- The nature of the examinee's response should determine whether you query it during the standard administration. For example, if the examinee's answer clearly defines a homonym, repeat the question by saying "What else does ... mean?" However, if the examinee's response is peculiar (e.g., possibly indicative of a thought disorder), delay querying until you have completed administering the *entire test.* Then during testing-of-limits, you might say, "To the word ... you said .... Tell me more about your answer."

Starting Considerations

- Place the Stimulus Booklet before the examinee, point to the appropriate word, and say the word.
- All examinees begin with item 4.
- If the examinee earns a score of 0 or 1 on either word 4 or word 5, administer items 1, 2, and 3 in *reverse sequence* until the examinee has two consecutive perfect scores (2 points).
- Unlike on the WISC–III, when the examinee gives a 0- or 1-point definition of the first basal word (i.e., item 4), do not give him or her any help.

Scoring Considerations

- All items are scored 2, 1, or 0.
- If the examinee earns 2-point scores on items 4 and 5, assign full credit for items 1, 2, and 3.
- When you administer the items in reverse order, give credit for any items not administered that precede two consecutive successes.
- Award 2 points for good synonyms, major uses, one or more definitive or primary features of the object, a general classification to which the word belongs, a correct figurative use of the word, several correct descriptive features that cumulate in an adequate response, or an example of an action or causal relation (for verbs).
- Award 1 point for vague responses, less pertinent synonyms, minor uses, an unelaborated example using the word, a concrete unelaborated definition, or a correct definition of a related form of the word.
- Award 0 points for obviously wrong answers, for regionalisms or slang not found in dictionaries, and for a pointing response only.
- Do not consider the examinee's elegance of expression in scoring the response.
- Give credit for all meanings recognized by standard dictionaries.
- Vocabulary is one of the more difficult subtests to score, and it may be difficult to apply the scoring criteria given in the WAIS–III manual.

- Inquiring about borderline responses and carefully studying the scoring guidelines will help you resolve scoring problems that arise as you give the subtest.
- When you have any doubt about the acceptability of a response, ask the examinee for another meaning of the word.

Discontinuance Considerations

- The subtest is discontinued after six consecutive item failures (scores of 0).

Interpretive Suggestions

The following guidelines are useful for observing and evaluating Vocabulary responses (Taylor, 1961).

- Is the examinee definitely familiar with the word or only vaguely familiar with it?
- What is the quality of the examinee's definitions (e.g., precise and brief, indirect and vague, or verbose and lengthy)?
- Are the examinee's responses objective, or do they relate personal experiences?
- Does the examinee confuse the word with another one that sounds like it?
- If the examinee does not know the meaning of a word, does the examinee guess?
- Does the examinee readily say, "I don't know" and shake off further inquiries, or does the examinee pause, ponder, or think aloud about the item?
- Does the examinee show signs of a possible hearing difficulty?
- Does the examinee appear to hear the words correctly or hear them with some distortion?
- Does the examinee express the meaning of the words easily or with difficulty?
- Does the examinee have mechanical difficulties pronouncing words properly?
- Does the examinee seem uncertain about how best to express his or her thoughts?
- Does the examinee use gestures to illustrate his or her responses or even depend on them exclusively?
- Are the examinee's responses synonyms for the stimulus word (e.g., thief: "A burglar"), or do they describe an action (e.g., thief: "Takes stuff")?
- Does the examinee describe a particular feature of the object (e.g., donkey: "It has four legs") or try to fit it into some category (e.g., donkey: "A living creature that is kept in a barn")?
- Are there any emotional overtones or reference to personal experiences in the examinee's responses (e.g., alphabet: "I hate to write")?
- Does the examinee define the words in order or skip around? Does this behavior have any significance (based on the examinee's behavior during the entire test)?

The examinee's responses to the Vocabulary subtest may reveal something about her or his language skills, background, cultural milieu, social development, life experiences, responses to frustration, and thought processes. Try to determine the basis for incorrect responses, and distinguish among guesses, clang associations (i.e., responses that appear to be based on the sound of the stimulus word rather than on its meaning), idiosyncratic associations, and bizarre associations. Whenever an examinee gives peculiar responses, mispronounces words, or has peculiar inflections, inquire further. Occasionally, you can identify language disturbances in the word definitions of examinees with a thought disorder.

Low scores on the Vocabulary subtest may indicate poor word knowledge, poor verbal comprehension, poor verbal skills and language development, limited educational background, difficulty in verbalization, or a home environment in which verbalization was not encouraged. Low scores, however, may also occur with examinees who speak English as a second language.

If you think the examinee may have word-retrieval problems, at the end of the *entire test* you can use a multiple-choice testing-of-limits procedure, similar to the one discussed for the Information subtest.

The range of scaled scores from 1 to 19 at ages 16–34 and 70–89 aids in profile analysis. However, profile analysis is slightly more restricted at ages 35–69, where the scaled scores range from 1 to 18.

Copyright © 1998 by John P. Wood.

SIMILARITIES

The Similarities subtest contains 19 pairs of words; the examinee is asked to explain the similarity between the two words in each pair.

Rationale

On the Similarities subtest, the examinee, in addition to perceiving the common elements of the paired terms, must bring the common elements together into a concept to answer the questions. Thus, the subtest appears to measure verbal concept formation—the ability to place objects and events together into a meaningful group. To do this, the examinee may need to organize, abstract, and find relationships that are not at first obvious. Although concept formation can be a voluntary, effortful process, it also can reflect well-automatized verbal conventions. Performance on the subtest may be related to cultural opportunities and interest patterns. Memory may also be involved. Success initially depends on the examinee's ability to comprehend the meaning of the task.

Factor Analytic Findings

Similarities is tied with Information as the second-best measure of g in the scale (62% of its variance may be attributed to g). This subtest contributes substantially to the Verbal Comprehension Index (average loading = .77). Specificity is either ample or adequate for eight age groups (16–17, 18–19, 25–29, 35–44 through 55–64, 80–84 through 85–89 years); at five age groups (20–24, 30–34, 65–69 through 75–79 years), it is inadequate.

Reliability and Correlational Highlights

Similarities is a reliable subtest (r_{xx} = .86), with reliability coefficients at or above .81 at all of the 13 age groups (range of .81 to .89). It correlates better with Vocabulary (r = .76), Information (r = .70), and Comprehension (r = .70) than with any of the other subtests. It has a moderately high correlation with the Full Scale (r = .76) and the Verbal Scale (r = .77) and a moderate correlation with the Performance Scale (r = .65).

Administrative Suggestions

Here are some administrative suggestions for the Similarities subtest.

Background Considerations

- Note whether the examinee understands the task.
- The subtest is not timed.
- Query unclear or ambiguous responses, as well as those listed in the sample responses in the manual that are marked "(Q)."

Starting Considerations

- All examinees begin with item 6.
- On item 6, if the examinee gives a 1-point response, give an example of a 2-point response. If the examinee does not know the answer to item 6, give the 2-point answer.
- If the examinee receives a score of 0 or 1 on either item 6 or item 7, administer items 1 to 5 in *reverse* order until the examinee has two consecutive perfect scores (1 point each).

Scoring Considerations

- If the examinee obtains 2-point scores on both items 6 and 7, assign full credit for items 1 to 5 (5 points).
- When you administer the items in reverse order, give credit for any items not administered that precede two consecutive successes.
- Score the best response when an examinee gives multiple acceptable responses for an item.
- Items 1 to 5 are scored as 1 or 0. These items are generally easy to score.
- Items 6 to 19 are scored as 2, 1, or 0. A conceptual response, such as a general classification, receives a score of 2; a more concrete response, such as a specific property of the item, receives a score of 1; and an incorrect response receives a score of 0. These items may be difficult to score.
- A careful study of the sample responses in the scoring guide in the WAIS–III manual will help you become more proficient in scoring Similarities responses.
- Study—and master—the general scoring principles, which clarify the rationales for 2, 1, and 0 scores (see page 112 in the WAIS–III manual).

Discontinuance Considerations

- The subtest is discontinued after four consecutive failures.

Interpretive Suggestions

Observing the examinee's typical level of conceptualization will help you understand the style of her or his thinking. Are the examinee's answers on a concrete, a functional, or an abstract level? Concrete answers typically refer to qualities of the objects (or stimuli) that can be seen or touched (apple-banana: "Both have a skin"). Functional answers typically concern a function or use of the objects (apple-banana: "You eat them"). Finally, abstract answers typically refer to a more universal property or to a common classification of the objects (apple-banana: "Both are fruits").

You can tell, in part, whether the examinee's response style is concrete, functional, or abstract by the numbers of 0-, 1-, and 2-point responses. Zero or 1-point responses suggest a more concrete and functional conceptualization style, while 2-point responses suggest a more abstract conceptualization style. However, a 2-point response does not necessarily reflect abstract thinking ability and may simply be an overlearned response. For example, there may be a difference between the 2-point response "Both fruits" for apple-banana and the 2-point response "Artistic expressions" for painting-statue. Although it receives 2 points, the former may be an overlearned response, whereas the latter may reflect a more abstract level of conceptual ability.

Furthermore, if the examinee earns 1 point on several items, the examinee may have a good breadth of knowledge but not depth. If the examinee generally earns 2 points for each correct response but responds correctly to only a few items, the examinee may have a good depth of knowledge but less breadth.

Also note whether the examinee gives *overinclusive responses*. These are responses that are so general that several objects are included in the concept. For example, the reply "Both contain molecules" to a question asking for the similarity between an apple and a banana is overinclusive because it does not delimit the particular characteristics of these two objects. Overinclusive responses indicate unusual thinking.

Observe how the examinee handles any frustration induced by the subtest questions. For example, when the examinee has difficulty answering the questions, does the examinee become negativistic and uncooperative, or does she or he continue to try to answer the questions? An examinee who responds with "They are not alike" may be displaying negativism, avoidance of the task demands, suspiciousness, a coping mechanism, or a lack of knowledge. To determine which of these may account for the examinee's response, compare the examinee's style of responding to the Similarities questions with her or his style of responding to questions on other subtests and during the interview.

Low scores on the Similarities subtest may indicate poor conceptual thinking, difficulty in seeing relationships, difficulty in selecting and verbalizing appropriate relationships between two objects or concepts, an overly concrete mode of thinking, rigidity of thought processes, or negativism.

If you think the examinee may have word-retrieval problems, you can use a multiple-choice testing-of-limits procedure, similar to the one discussed for the Information subtest, after you complete the *entire test*.

The range of scaled scores from 1 to 19 at ages 16–24 and 65–89 aids in profile analysis for examinees in these age ranges. However, profile analysis is slightly more restricted at ages 25–64, where the scaled scores range from 1 to 18.

ARITHMETIC

The Arithmetic subtest contains 20 items; 17 are given orally, and the other three use blocks along with oral directions.

Rationale

The problems on the Arithmetic subtest require the examinee to follow verbal directions, concentrate on selected parts of questions, hold information in working memory, and use numerical operations. Depending on the problem, the examinee may need knowledge of addition, subtraction, multiplication, or division operations. The emphasis of the problems is not on mathematical knowledge per se, but on mental computation and concentration. Concentration is especially important for the more complex problems.

The Arithmetic subtest measures numerical reasoning— the ability to solve arithmetical problems. It requires the use of noncognitive functions (concentration and attention) in conjunction with cognitive functions (knowledge of numerical operations). Success on this subtest is influenced by education, interests, fluctuations of attention, and transient emotional reactions such as anxiety. Like the Vocabulary and Information subtests, Arithmetic involves memory and prior learning; however, it also requires concentration and the active application of select skills to unique situations.

Information-processing strategies, as well as mathematical skills, may underlie performance on the Arithmetic subtest (Stewart & Moely, 1983). These strategies may include (a) rehearsal (e.g., to remember the information presented in the task) and (b) recognition of an appropriate response (e.g., to continue using a correct strategy or change an incorrect strategy). Mathematical skills include the ability to comprehend and integrate verbal information presented in a mathematical context, together with numerical ability (i.e., the ability to perform the necessary calculations).

Factor Analytic Findings

Arithmetic is a good measure of *g* (56% of its variance may be attributed to *g*). This subtest contributes moderately to the Working Memory Index (average loading = .50). Subtest specificity is either ample or adequate for all age groups.

Reliability and Correlational Highlights

Arithmetic is a reliable subtest (r_{xx} = .88), with reliability coefficients at or above .77 at all of the 13 age groups (range of .77 to .91). It correlates better with Information (r = .63) and Vocabulary (r = .60) than with any of the other subtests. It has a moderately high correlation with the Full Scale (r = .72) and the Verbal Scale (r = .70) and a moderate correlation with the Performance Scale (r = .63).

Administrative Suggestions

Here are some administrative suggestions for the Arithmetic subtest.

Background Considerations

• Reassure an examinee who is anxious about his or her arithmetical skills.
• All problems are timed, with items 1 to 6 having a time limit of 15 seconds; items 7 to 11, 30 seconds; items 12 to 19, 60 seconds; and item 20, 120 seconds.

- Do not permit the examinee to use pencil and paper to solve the problems, but allow the examinee to write with his or her fingers if he or she wants to. However, do not allow the examinee to wet his or her finger because writing with a damp finger may leave almost as clear a mark as writing with a pencil.
- Begin timing as soon as you finish reading the problem.
- Repeat an item only once, and continue timing as you repeat the item.
- When two responses are given, ask the examinee which one is right.
- Give the examinee additional time to complete a problem if he or she seems to be on the verge of solving it when the time limit is reached. This will give you information about the examinee's ability to solve the problem. Record the response and the amount of time the examinee took to respond. Although you do not give formal credit for correct responses given after the time limit, you can include information about the examinee's ability to solve such problems in the report.
- All items are administered verbally. This is unlike the WISC–III, where a booklet is used to present some of the items to the examinee.

Starting Considerations

- All examinees begin with item 5.
- If the examinee fails either item 5 or item 6, administer items 1 to 4 in *reverse sequence* until the examinee obtains credit on two consecutive items.

Scoring Considerations

- All items are scored 1 or 0 (pass-fail), with 1 additional time-bonus point possible on items 19 and 20.
- If the examinee gives correct responses (1-point answers) to both items 5 and 6, give the examinee full credit for items 1 to 4.
- When you administer the items in reverse order, give credit for any items not administered that precede two consecutive successes.

Discontinuance Considerations

- The subtest is discontinued after four consecutive failures.

Interpretive Suggestions

Observe the examinee's reactions to the items.

- Is the examinee anxious (e.g., exhibits panic behaviors when you suggest doing math problems)?
- If the examinee is anxious, how does the examinee deal with this anxiety (e.g., calms down, remains anxious, gives up easily, becomes angry, makes excuses, tries to leave the situation)?
- What approach does the examinee use to solve problems (e.g., counts on fingers, draws with a finger on the table, imagines the numbers in her or his head)?

- Does the examinee show temporary inefficiencies such as anxiety, blocking, or transient concentration difficulties?
- Does the examinee recognize when a mistake has been made?
- Does the examinee attempt to correct perceived errors?
- Does the examinee ask you to repeat questions?
- If the answer is incorrect, does the examinee show an understanding of the process required (e.g., understands that the problem requires addition or multiplication)?
- Are the examinee's responses given hurriedly, without sufficient thought?

Try to determine the reasons for the examinee's failures. Possible reasons are poor knowledge of arithmetical operations, inadequate conceptualization of the problem, anxiety, poor concentration, forgetfulness (e.g., not recalling the first part of the question, especially on items 12 and 19), misunderstanding of the problem, impulsivity, and carelessness.

Low scores on the Arithmetic subtest may indicate inadequate ability in mental arithmetic, poor concentration, distractibility, anxiety (e.g., over a school-like task or because of worry over personal problems), blocking toward mathematical tasks, or poor school achievement (perhaps associated with rebellion against authority or with cultural background).

After you complete the standard administration of the *entire test,* you might want to further explore the reasons for the examinee's failures by going back to the questions. You might say, for example, "Let's try this one again. Tell me how you solved the problem." If necessary, you can ask the examinee to think aloud. This will help you determine how the examinee went about solving the problem.

Allowing the examinee to use paper and pencil is another testing-of-limits procedure that may help you find out whether the examinee has poor arithmetical knowledge or attention and concentration difficulties. If the examinee can solve the problems with pencil and paper, the failure is not associated with lack of arithmetical knowledge; rather, the errors may relate to attention, concentration, or memory difficulties that inhibit mental computation. Use of paper and pencil reduces the load on the examinee's working memory (Kaplan et al., 1999). If the examinee fails the items in both situations, the failures more likely reflect difficulties with arithmetical knowledge, although attention and concentration difficulties may also be interfering with the examinee's ability to solve written arithmetic problems. Inspect the written work to see whether the examinee misaligns numbers, sequences computational steps incorrectly, performs calculations carelessly, or has poor mastery of basic arithmetical operations. A tendency to misalign numbers may indicate spatial difficulties.

If you think the examinee may have word-retrieval problems, you can use a multiple-choice testing-of-limits procedure similar to the one discussed for the Information subtest. Finally, in some cases you can allow the examinee to use a calculator, to see whether this helps him or her solve the problems.

The information you obtain from testing-of-limits may help you to differentiate between failures due to temporary inefficiency and those due to limited knowledge. Successful delayed performance, for example, may indicate temporary inefficiency or a slow, painstaking approach to problem solving. Of course, do not give the examinee credit for answering any items correctly during testing-of-limits. (Refer to Chapter 7 for more information about testing-of-limits.)

The range of scaled scores from 1 to 19 at ages 70–89 years aids in profile analysis. However, from 18 to 34 years and from 55 to 69 years, profile analysis is based on scaled scores that range from only 1 to 18; and from 25 to 54 years, profile analysis is based on scaled scores that range from only 1 to 17.

DIGIT SPAN

The Digit Span subtest has two parts: Digits Forward, which contains series of numbers ranging in length from two to nine digits, and Digits Backward, which contains series of numbers ranging in length from two to eight digits. The examinee listens to a series of digits given orally by the examiner and then repeats the digits. There are two sets of digits of each length.

Rationale

Digit Span is primarily a measure of the examinee's short-term sequential auditory memory and attention. In addition, the task assesses an examinee's ability to retain several elements that have no logical relationship to one another. Because an examinee must recall auditory information and repeat the information aloud in proper sequence, the task also requires sequencing skills. However, an examinee's performance on the Digit Span subtest may be negatively affected by anxiety.

Digits Forward primarily involves rote learning and memory, whereas Digits Backward requires transformation of the stimulus input prior to responding. On Digits Backward, not only must the examinee hold the mental image of the numerical sequence longer (usually) than on Digits Forward; the examinee also must mentally manipulate the sequence before restating it. High scores on Digits Backward may indicate flexibility, good tolerance for stress, and excellent concentration. Digits Backward requires more complex cognitive processing than does Digits Forward and has higher loadings on *g* than does Digits Forward (Jensen & Osborne, 1979).

Because of differences between the two tasks, it is useful to consider Digits Forward and Digits Backward separately. Digits Forward appears to involve primarily sequential processing and short-term memory, while Digits Backward appears to involve both planning ability and sequential processing (and may provide some insight into working memory). Additionally, Digits Backward may involve the abilities to (a) form mental images and (b) scan an internal visual display formed from an auditory stimulus. However, more research is needed to explore the role of visualization on the Digits Backward portion of the subtest.

Factor Analytic Findings

The Digit Span subtest is a fair measure of *g* (32% of its variance may be attributed to *g*). This subtest contributes substantially to the Working Memory Index (average loading = .67). Specificity is ample for all age groups.

Reliability and Correlational Highlights

Digit Span is a reliable subtest (r_{xx} = .90), with reliability coefficients at or above .84 at all of the 13 age groups (range of .84 to .93). It correlates better with Letter–Number Sequencing (*r* = .57) and Arithmetic (*r* = .52) than with any of the other subtests. It has a moderate correlation with the Full Scale (*r* = .52) and the Verbal Scale (*r* = .51) and a moderately low correlation with the Performance Scale (*r* = .47).

Administrative Suggestions

Here are some administrative suggestions for the Digit Span subtest.

Background Considerations

- The examinee should not be able to see the digits in the WAIS–III manual or on the Record Form before or during the administration of the Digit Span subtest.
- Do not time the subtest.
- Read the digits clearly at one per second, and *drop your inflection* on the last digit in the series. Then pause to allow the examinee to respond. Practice reading speed with a stopwatch.
- Do not break the digits into groups by unintentionally spacing them as you read them. If you do so, you may provide the examinee with a mnemonic device—chunking—that helps him or her recall the digits better.
- Never repeat any of the digits on either trial of a series during the subtest proper.
- Always administer both trials of each series.
- After you complete Digits Forward, give the sample Digits Backward item and then the rest of Digits Backward. Give Digits Backward even if the examinee fails both trials of item 1 on Digits Forward.
- If the examinee fails the first sample item on Digits Backward, give the examine the correct answer and then present the second sample item. If the examinee fails the second sample item, do not give the right answer.
- Request an audiological examination whenever you have any doubt about an examinee's hearing. Because this subtest contains no contextual cues (i.e., you only present several random series of digits), examinees with a hearing impairment are especially prone to failure or poor performance.

- One procedure for recording the number of digits correctly recalled in each series is to place on the Record Form either a mark designating a correct answer above each digit correctly recalled or a mark designating an incorrect answer on each digit missed.
- An even better procedure is to record the exact sequence given by the examinee in the available space.
- On the WAIS–III Digit Span is a regular subtest, whereas on the WISC–III it is a supplementary subtest.

Starting Considerations

- All examinees begin with the first trial of Digits Forward.

Scoring Considerations

- Score all items 2 (passed both trials), 1 (passed one trial), or 0 (failed both trials) on both Digits Forward and Digits Backward.

Discontinuance Considerations

- The subtest is discontinued after the examinee fails both trials on any one item in each part.

Interpretive Suggestions

A good record can greatly help you evaluate and interpret an examinee's performance. An examinee who consistently misses the last digit in the first series and then successfully completes the second series differs from one who fails to recall any of the digits in the first series but successfully completes the second. Similarly, the short-term memory of an examinee who responds to the sequence 3-4-1-7 with "3-1-4-7" is better than that of the examinee who says "9-8-5-6." The scoring system described in the WAIS–III manual does not distinguish between these or other failure patterns.

Observe whether the examinee's failures involve leaving out one or more digits, transposing digits, interjecting incorrect digits, producing more digits than were given, giving a series of digits in numerical order (e.g., 6-7-8-9), or recalling only the first and last digits. The examinee who recalls the correct digits but in an incorrect sequence is more likely to have a deficit in immediate auditory sequential memory than in immediate auditory memory. Alternatively, the examinee who fails to recall the correct digits may have a deficit in immediate auditory memory. The examinee who fails the first trial but passes the second trial may be displaying a learning-to-learn pattern or a need to practice to achieve success.

Consider the following questions:

- Is the examinee's performance effortless, or does the examinee seem to concentrate hard?
- Does the examinee view the task as interesting, boring, or difficult?
- Is the examinee aware of her or his errors, or does the examinee think that her or his answers are always correct?

- Does the examinee understand the difference between Digits Backward and Digits Forward?
- Are the errors made on Digits Backward similar to or different from those made on Digits Forward?
- How does the examinee react as the Digits Backward series proceeds (e.g., becomes stimulated and encouraged or tense, anxious, and frustrated)?
- Does the examinee perform better on Digits Forward than on Digits Backward? (If so, the more complex operations required on Digits Backward may induce anxiety in the examinee.)
- Does the examinee make more errors on Digits Forward than on Digits Backward? (This may mean that the examinee views Digits Backward as more of a challenge and therefore mobilizes more of her or his resources, such as giving added concentration and attention.)
- What strategy does the examinee use to recall the digits (e.g., simply repeating what is heard, rehearsing the numbers before repeating them back to you, visualizing the numbers in her or his head, using a finger to write the digits, chunking the digits, or repeating back the numbers after an extended period of time)?
- What types of errors does the examinee make (e.g., an omission error by leaving one digit out of the correct sequence, an addition error by adding one or more digits to the correct sequence, a perseveration error by repeating one or more digits, a sequential error by giving the correct digits but in the wrong sequence, a sequence reversal error by giving the correct digits but with two or more reversed; Kaplan et al., 1999)?

Some grouping techniques introduce meaning into the task so that separate digits become numbers grouped into hundreds, tens, or other units (e.g., 3-1-7 becomes three hundred seventeen). If the examinee uses grouping, the function underlying the task may be changed from one of attention to one of concentration.

The WAIS–III manual does not provide separate scaled scores for Digits Forward and Digits Backward. There are, however, two useful tables in the WAIS–III manual that show how the standardization group performed on Digits Forward and on Digits Backward. Table B.6 (page 212 of the WAIS–III manual) shows the longest Digits Forward span and the longest Digits Backward span recalled by the examinees. The median Digits Forward span was 7 at ages 16 to 54 years and 6 at ages 55 to 89 years. The median Digits Backward span was 5 at ages 16 to 54 years and 4 at ages 55 to 89 years. Across all age groups, examinees had a median Digits Forward span of 6 (*Mdn* range of 6 to 7) and a median Digits Backward span of 5 (*Mdn* range of 4 to 5; see Table 13-1). These results indicate that examinees usually produce longer spans on Digits Forward than on Digits Backward by about one digit.

Table B.7 (page 213 of the *WAIS–III Administration and Scoring Manual*) shows the extent to which examinees recalled more digits forward than backward and vice versa. In

Table 13-1
Median Number of Digits Recalled on WAIS–III Digits Forward and Digits Backward, by Age Group

Age group	Median	
	Forward	Backward
16–17	7	5
18–19	7	5
20–24	7	5
25–29	7	5
30–34	7	5
35–44	7	5
45–54	6	4
55–64	6	4
65–69	6	4
70–74	6	4
75–79	6	4
80–84	6	4
85–89	6	4
Average	6	5

Source: Adapted from Wechsler (1997), Table B.6 (page 212).

Table 13-2
Percentage of Individuals in Standardization Group Who Recalled More WAIS–III Digits Backward than Digits Forward, by Age Group

Age group	Percent
16–17	4.0
18–19	5.0
20–24	2.0
25–29	5.0
30–34	4.5
35–44	5.0
45–54	1.5
55–64	5.0
65–69	4.0
70–74	3.0
75–79	4.0
80–84	3.3
85–89	2.0
Average	3.8

Source: Adapted from Wechsler (1997), Table B.7 (page 213).

all age groups and in the total sample, examinees recalled more digits forward than backward (*Mdn* difference = 2 at 12 of the 13 age groups and in the total sample; *Mdn* difference = 1 at ages 80–84). Thus, you can consider as noteworthy raw-score differences of 3 points (or more) between Digits Forward and Digits Backward. The percentage of examinees in the standardization group who recalled more digits backward than forward was only 3.8% in the total group (range of 1.5% to 5%; see Table 13-2).

Low scores on the Digit Span subtest may indicate anxiety, inattention, distractibility, a possible learning deficit, difficulty in auditory sequential processing, poor short-term auditory memory, boredom, difficulty in shifting, impaired hearing, or negativism. Repetition of ≤ 4 digits forward and ≤ 3 digits backward by an otherwise alert examinee with adequate hearing may reflect a lack of effort or poor test-taking motivation (Iverson & Franzen, 1994).

Testing-of-limits after the *entire test* is over may give you some understanding of the examinee's Digit Span performance. You might ask the examinee how he or she went about remembering the numbers. You also can determine whether the examinee does better if he or she writes down the numbers and whether the examinee can recall letters better than numbers.

The range of scaled scores from 1 to 19 at all ages aids in profile analysis.

INFORMATION

The Information subtest contains 28 questions that sample a broad range of general knowledge. Items cover content associated with calendar information (items 1, 4, and 7), science (items 3, 5, 14, 21, 22, 25, and 27), geography (items 6, 9, 13, 15, 16, 24, and 26), and history (items 8, 10, 11, 12, 17, 18, 19, 20, 23, and 28). Each item is scored 1 or 0 (pass-fail). The questions can usually be answered with a simply stated fact. The examinee is not required to find relationships between facts in order to receive credit.

Rationale

The amount of knowledge an examinee has acquired may depend on her or his (a) natural endowment, (b) education (both formal and informal), and (c) cultural opportunities, experiences, and interests. The subtest samples the knowledge that average individuals with average opportunities should have acquired through typical home, school, and work experiences. The examinee's responses and comments provide clues about her or his range of information, alertness to the environment, and social or cultural background. For adolescents, responses may reflect attitudes toward school and school-like tasks (e.g., the adolescent may say, "Those questions are hard, just like my teacher asks").

High scores may not necessarily indicate cognitive competence; examinees may have acquired isolated facts but may not know how to use the facts appropriately or effectively. In addition, intellectual drive may contribute to higher scores. Successful performance on the Information subtest requires memory for habitual, overlearned material (i.e., information that the examinee has likely been exposed to repeatedly). Thus, Information provides clues about the examinee's ability to store and retrieve acquired knowledge.

Factor Analytic Findings

Information is tied with Similarities as the second-best measure of *g* in the scale (62% of its variance may be attributed to *g*). This subtest contributes substantially to the Verbal Comprehension Index (average loading = .83). Specificity is ample or adequate for all age groups.

Reliability and Correlational Highlights

Information is a reliable subtest (r_{xx} = .91), with reliability coefficients at or above .89 at all of the 13 age groups (range of .89 to .93). It correlates better with Vocabulary (*r* = .77) than with any of the other subtests. It has a moderately high correlation with the Full Scale (*r* = .76) and the Verbal Scale (*r* = .79) and a moderate correlation with the Performance Scale (*r* = .63).

Administrative Suggestions

Here are some administrative suggestions for the Information subtest.

Background Considerations

- The Information subtest is untimed, is easy to administer, and has simple and direct questions.
- Give the prompts noted in the WAIS–III manual for item 6 ("Yes, but what direction is that?") and item 21 ("What scale?").
- Record answers verbatim.
- Do not spell, define, or explain any words for the examinee even though the WAIS–III manual does not specifically say that you should not do so.
- Inquire about responses that are not clear.
- You can repeat a question when the examinee's response suggests that the question was misunderstood.

Starting Considerations

- All examinees begin with item 5.
- If an examinee earns a score of 0 on either item 5 or item 6, give the preceding items in *reverse order* until the examinee passes two consecutive items.

Scoring Considerations

- Scoring is straightforward: A correct response receives 1 point and an incorrect response, 0.
- Give credit for any response that is of the same caliber as those listed in the Acceptable Responses section of the WAIS–III manual.
- If an examinee obtains 1 point on questions 5 and 6, give full credit for the four preceding items.
- When you administer the items in reverse order, give credit for any items not administered that precede two consecutive successes.
- Ask the examinee to choose the best answer if two or more answers are given to a question, and score that answer.

Discontinuance Considerations

- The subtest is discontinued after six consecutive failures.

Interpretive Suggestions

Note the quality of the examinee's answers, style of responding, and pattern of successes and failures.

- Is the examinee thinking through the questions, responding impulsively, or simply guessing?
- Does the examinee appear confident or hesitant when responding?
- Does the examinee give peculiar responses? If so, in what way? What does your inquiry reveal?
- Does the examinee frequently say, "I know this answer, but I can't think of it" or "I don't know"?
- Are the examinee's answers imprecise and roundabout? Difficulty in giving precise answers, such as saying "When it is hot" for *summer* or "When it is cold" for *winter,* may suggest word-retrieval difficulties.
- Are the examinee's answers close to the correct answer or completely off base?
- Are the examinee's answers wordy? Overly long responses or responses filled with extraneous information may suggest an obsessive-compulsive orientation—an examinee with this orientation sometimes feels compelled to prove how much he or she knows. Alternatively, excessive responses may simply reflect the examinee's desire to impress you. Consider the examinee's entire test performance, plus other relevant information, when you interpret such behavior.
- Does the examinee seem to be inhibited in making responses? Inability to recall an answer may suggest that the question is associated with conflict-laden material. For example, an examinee may not be able to recall the number of legs on a dog because of an earlier traumatic experience with dogs. If possible, follow up your hypotheses during an interview with the examinee (see Chapters 1 and 2 in *Assessment of Children: Behavioral and Clinical Applications*).

• What is the pattern of the examinee's successes and failures? Failures on easy items coupled with successes on more difficult ones may suggest poor motivation, anxiety, temporary inefficiency, boredom, or an inconsistent environment. Alternatively, this pattern may indicate a problem with retrieval of information from long-term memory. When you suspect such a problem, analyze the content of the failed items, as noted above. Content analysis may provide clues about the examinee's interests, areas about which you might want to inquire after you complete the WAIS–III, or areas that need remediation.

Low scores on the Information subtest may indicate a poor range of factual knowledge and information, poor memory, hostility to a school-type task, a tendency to give up easily, and low achievement orientation. Low scores also may be associated with examinees who have a foreign language background.

If you think the examinee may have word-retrieval problems, you can use a multiple-choice testing-of-limits procedure (Holmes, 1988). This procedure may help you differentiate deficits associated with word-retrieval difficulties from those associated with lack of knowledge. After you complete the *entire test,* go back to the item (or items) that the examinee had difficulty with and give the examinee three answers to choose from. For example, for item 3 you might ask, "Is it square, or like a triangle shape, or round?" Be sure to randomly vary the position of the correct answer in the series (i.e., put the correct answer sometimes as the first choice, sometimes as the second, and sometimes as the third). If the examinee answers the multiple-choice questions correctly, you may infer that the problem is word-retrieval difficulty, not a lack of knowledge. Do not use scores from the multiple-choice procedure to calculate an IQ.

The range of scaled scores from 1 to 19 at ages 16–24 and 70–89 years aids in profile analysis for examinees in these age ranges. However, profile analysis is slightly more restricted at ages 25–69, where the scaled scores range from 1 to 18.

COMPREHENSION

The Comprehension subtest contains 18 questions covering a wide range of situations and problems. Questions deal with such issues as government operations and laws, health standards, and social mores.

Rationale

On the Comprehension subtest, the examinee must understand given situations and provide answers to specific problems. Success depends on the examinee's possession of practical information, plus an ability to draw on previous experiences. Responses may reflect the examinee's knowledge of conventional standards of behavior, extensiveness of cultural opportunities, and level of development of conscience or moral sense. Success suggests that the examinee has common sense, social judgment, and a grasp of social conventionality. These characteristics imply an ability to use facts in a pertinent, meaningful, and emotionally appropriate manner. Success is also based on the examinee's ability to verbalize acceptable actions.

Factor Analytic Findings

The Comprehension subtest is a good measure of g (59% of its variance may be attributed to g). This subtest contributes substantially to the Verbal Comprehension Index (average loading = .81). Specificity is ample or adequate for six age groups (16–17 through 20–24, 30–34, 70–74, 80–84 years); at seven age groups (25–29 through 65–69, 75–79, 85–89 years), it is inadequate.

Reliability and Correlational Highlights

Comprehension is a reliable subtest (r_{xx} = .84), with reliability coefficients at or above .79 at all of the 13 age groups (range of .79 to .87). It correlates better with Vocabulary (r = .75), Information (r = .70), and Similarities (r = .70) than with any of the other subtests. It has a moderately high correlation with the Full Scale (r = .75) and the Verbal Scale (r = .76) and a moderate correlation with the Performance Scale (r = .62).

Administrative Suggestions

Here are some administrative suggestions for the Comprehension subtest.

Background Considerations

• The subtest is not timed.
• Study carefully the examples following each item in the WAIS–III manual so you will know which type of responses, labeled "(Q)," need further inquiry. The examples indicate that you should query many 0- and 1-point responses.
• Queries allow you an opportunity to evaluate more thoroughly the extent of the examinee's knowledge. However, do not query obviously incomplete 1-point responses in an attempt to improve the examinee's score on other items for which a complete one-idea answer receives 2 points.
• On the five items (5, 6, 7, 10, and 13) that require two ideas for full credit (2 points), ask the examinee for a second idea when only one correct idea is given. Do this so that you do not penalize the examinee automatically for not giving two reasons. However, you can ask for a second idea only one time for each of these five items. Do not ask for a second idea if the first response is incorrect. In scoring these five items, note that the two responses must re-

flect two of the general-concept categories listed in the WAIS–III manual.

- Ask the examinee to explain any unusual responses.
- If the examinee does not give an answer after 10 to 15 seconds, it is a good idea to repeat the question.
- Record the examinee's responses verbatim during the initial presentation of the items and during the inquiry phase so you have a complete record with which to evaluate the responses.
- The Record Form has an asterisk next to those items that require you to ask for a second response.

Starting Considerations

- All examinees begin with item 4.
- If an examinee earns a score of 0 or 1 on either item 4 or item 5, administer items 1 to 3 in *reverse order* until the examinee passes two consecutive items.

Scoring Considerations

- Study the scoring guidelines carefully, because the Comprehension subtest is difficult to score; examinees may give responses that differ from those provided in the WAIS–III manual.
- Score items 1 to 3 as 1 or 0 and items 4 to 18 as 2, 1, or 0. The most complete or best response receives a score of 2; a less adequate response, 1; and an incorrect response, 0.
- Score the response given to your query rather than the initial response if, in response to your query, the examinee alters her or his response.
- When you administer the items in reverse order, give credit for any items not administered that precede two consecutive successes.

Discontinuance Considerations

- The subtest is discontinued after four consecutive failures (0-point responses).

Interpretive Suggestions

Responses to the Comprehension questions may provide information about the examinee's personality style, ethical values, and social and cultural background. Unlike the Information questions, which usually elicit precise answers, the Comprehension questions may elicit more complex and idiosyncratic replies. Because the questions involve judgment of social situations, answers may reflect the examinee's social attitudes. Some responses may reveal understanding *and* acceptance of social mores, whereas others may reveal understanding *but not* acceptance of social mores. An examinee may know the right answers but not practice them. Some examinees may maintain that they do not have to abide by social conventions, believing that such matters do not pertain to them personally.

An examinee's replies may reveal initiative, self-reliance, independence, self-confidence, helplessness, indecisiveness, inflexibility, manipulative tendencies, naive perceptions of problems, cooperative solutions, hostility, aggression, or other traits. For example, an examinee with a dependent personality style might describe seeking help from others when faced with a problem situation (e.g., on the "forest" item).

Note how the examinee responds to the questions (Taylor, 1961):

- Do the examinee's failures indicate misunderstanding of the meaning of a word or the implications of a particular phrase?
- Does the examinee provide a complete answer or just part of one?
- Does the examinee respond to the entire question or only to a part of it?
- Does the examinee seem to be objective, seeing various possibilities and choosing the best possible response?
- Is the examinee indecisive, unable to give firm answers?
- Are the examinee's responses too quick, indicating failure to consider the questions in their entirety?
- Does the examinee recognize when his or her answers are sufficient or insufficient?
- How does the examinee respond when you ask him or her for another good answer (e.g., becomes impatient, flustered, challenged by the request)?

Because Comprehension requires considerable verbal expression, the subtest may be sensitive to mild language impairments and to disordered thought processes. Be alert to language deficits (such as word-retrieval difficulties), circumstantial or tangential speech, or other expressive difficulties.

Low scores on the Comprehension subtest may indicate poor social judgment, failure to take personal responsibility (e.g., overdependency, immaturity, limited involvement with others), overly concrete thinking, difficulty in expressing ideas verbally, a creative individual looking for unusual solutions, or negativism.

If you think the examinee may have word-retrieval problems, you can use a multiple-choice testing-of-limits procedure similar to the method discussed for the Information subtest. You also can conduct an extensive inquiry about any responses as part of testing-of-limits after you complete the *entire test*.

The range of scaled scores from 1 to 19 at all ages aids in profile analysis.

LETTER–NUMBER SEQUENCING

The Letter–Number Sequencing subtest, a supplementary subtest, contains seven items, each consisting of three trials. Each trial requires the examinee to sequentially order a series of numbers and letters that are orally presented in a specified random order. Although Letter–Number Sequencing is a supplementary subtest, administering it may give you useful diagnostic or clinical information, especially when the examinee may have problems with attention. Also, you need to administer Letter–Number Sequencing to compute the Working Memory Index score.

Rationale

To complete the Letter–Number Sequencing subtest successfully, the examinee must (a) simultaneously track letters and numbers, (b) arrange the numbers in ascending order; (c) arrange the letters in alphabetical order, following the numbers; and (d) perform both mental operations without forgetting any part of the series. The Letter–Number Sequencing subtest involves attention, short-term auditory memory, and information processing. The *WAIS–III—WMS–III Technical Manual* (The Psychological Corporation, 1997) identifies the construct measured by this task as *working memory*—a dynamic short-term memory storage system of limited capacity, used to hold information that is being processed (Baddeley, 1990). Some research suggests that Letter–Number Sequencing measures primarily attention and memory and, to a lesser extent, visuospatial functions and processing speed (Crowe, 2000).

Factor Analytic Findings

The Letter–Number Sequencing subtest is a fair measure of g (42% of its variance may be attributed to g). This subtest contributes substantially to the Working Memory Index (average loading = .61). Specificity is either ample or adequate for five age groups (18–19, 30–34, 45–54, 70–74, 85–89 years); at eight age groups (16–17, 20–24, 25–29, 35–44, 55–64, 65–69, 75–79, 80–84 years), it is inadequate.

Reliability and Correlational Highlights

Letter–Number Sequencing is a reliable subtest (r_{xx} = .82), with reliability coefficients at or above .75 at all of the 13 age groups (range of .75 to .88). It correlates better with Digit Span (r = .57) and Arithmetic (r = .55) than with any of the other subtests. It has a moderate correlation with the Full Scale (r = .64), the Verbal Scale (r = .62), and the Performance Scale (r = .57).

Administrative Suggestions

Here are some administrative suggestions for the Letter–Number Sequencing subtest.

Background Considerations

- The subtest is not timed.
- Read the numbers and letters clearly, at the rate of one per second.
- Practice reading speed with a stopwatch.
- Never repeat any of the numbers or letters on any trial of a series during the subtest proper.
- Always administer all three trials of each series.

- On the Record Form, you can record the letters and numbers correctly recalled in each series either by placing a check mark above each letter or digit correctly recalled or by putting a mark designating an incorrect answer on each letter or number missed. A better procedure, however, is to record the exact response given by the examinee in the available space on the Record Form.
- Because this subtest contains no cues (i.e., you present only a random series of letters and numbers), hard-of-hearing examinees may be especially prone to failure.
- Letter–Number Sequencing is not used in the computation of the IQ when the six standard Verbal Scale subtests are administered.
- Whenever you have any doubt about the examinee's auditory acuity, request an audiological examination.

Starting Considerations

- All examinees begin with the practice items and then are administered item 1.
- If an examinee fails a practice item, correct her or him and repeat the instructions as necessary.
- Even if all the practice items are failed, proceed with item 1.

Scoring Considerations

- Give the examinee credit for each trial passed.
- Give credit for any response that is in the correct sequence, regardless of whether the numbers or the letters are said first (e.g., for item 1, trial 1, give credit for the response "L-2"). (David Tulsky, spokesperson for The Psychological Corporation, supports this procedure; personal communication, May 1998.)

Discontinuance Considerations

- The subtest is discontinued after failure on all three trials of an item.

Interpretive Suggestions

Consider the following questions:

- Is the examinee's performance effortless, or does the examinee have to concentrate?
- Does the examinee view the task as interesting, boring, or difficult?
- Is the examinee aware of his or her errors, or does the examinee think that his or her answers are always correct?
- What strategy does the examinee use to recall the numbers and letters (e.g., simply repeating what is heard, rehearsing the numbers and letters before repeating them back to you, visualizing the numbers and letters in his or her head, using a finger to write the numbers and letters, or repeating back the numbers and letters after an extended period of time)?
- What type of errors does the examinee make (e.g., an omission error by leaving one number or letter out of the correct sequence, an addition error by adding one or more numbers or letters to the correct sequence, a perseveration

error by repeating one or more numbers or letters, a sequential error by giving the correct numbers and letters but in the wrong sequence, a sequence reversal error by giving the correct numbers and letters but reversing two or more numbers and letters, an auditory discrimination error by saying the letter *d* instead of *t*)?

A good record can help you evaluate the examinee's performance. For example, an examinee who consistently fails to recall the last item in a Letter–Number series (for "T-9-A-3," says "3–9–A") is different from an examinee who says an incorrect letter (for "T-9-A-3," says "3-9-A-D"). Failing to recall a letter or number may reflect poor attention-concentration, whereas mistaking T for D may reflect an auditory discrimination problem. Unfortunately, the scoring system does not distinguish among failure patterns. For example, the examinee who places one letter out of sequence in a six-item series obtains the same score as the examinee who misses all six items, even though the second examinee's performance is more inefficient than the first examinee's. Also note whether the examinee misses letters primarily, numbers primarily, or both letters and numbers. Finally, although an examinee receives credit for giving the letters first and then the numbers, such a response demonstrates poor understanding of the directions or inability to follow the directions.

Low scores on the Letter–Number Sequencing subtest may indicate poor short-term auditory memory, anxiety, inattention, distractibility, a possible learning deficit, difficulty in auditory sequencing, auditory processing, impulsivity, or negativism. Low scores on Letter–Number Sequencing, Block Design, and Symbol Search may suggest visuospatial difficulties, as well as processing speed difficulties.

PICTURE COMPLETION

The Picture Completion subtest requires the examinee to identify the single most important missing detail in 25 drawings of common objects, animals, and people—such as a chair, a cow, and a face. The examinee's task is to name or point to the essential missing portion of the incomplete picture within the 20-second time limit.

Rationale

On the Picture Completion subtest, the examinee must recognize the object depicted, appreciate its incompleteness, and determine the missing part. It is a test of visual discrimination—the ability to differentiate between essential and nonessential details. Picture Completion requires concentration, reasoning (or visual alertness), visual organization, and long-term visual memory (as the items require an examinee to have stored and retrieve information about the complete figure).

Picture Completion may also measure perceptual and conceptual abilities involved in visual recognition and identification of familiar objects. Perception, cognition, judgment, and

delay of impulse all may influence performance. The time limit on the subtest places additional demands on the examinee. The richness of the examinee's life experiences may also affect her or his performance on the subtest.

Factor Analytic Findings

The Picture Completion subtest is a fair measure of *g* (41% of its variance may be attributed to *g*). This subtest contributes moderately to the Perceptual Organization Index (average loading = .48). Specificity is ample at 12 of the 13 age groups; for one age group (80–84 years), it is inadequate.

Reliability and Correlational Highlights

Picture Completion is a reliable subtest ($r_{xx} = .83$), with reliability coefficients at or above .76 at all of the 13 age groups (range of .76 to .88). It correlates better with Block Design ($r = .52$) and Object Assembly ($r = .52$) than with any of the other subtests. It has a moderate correlation with the Full Scale ($r = .60$), the Performance Scale ($r = .60$), and the Verbal Scale ($r = .53$).

Administrative Suggestions

Here are some administrative suggestions for the Picture Completion subtest.

Background Considerations

- Picture Completion is easy to administer. Leave the booklet flat on the table and turn over the cards one at a time to show consecutive pictures.
- Allow the examinee to turn the pages in the test booklet if the examinee wants to and you are sure that you can set the pace.
- Have the examinee point to where the part is missing on the picture if the examinee has severe speech difficulties.
- The WAIS–III manual provides no guidance about the placement of the stopwatch. We recommend that the examinee see the stopwatch so that he or she understands that the subtest is timed. However, do not tell the examinee that you are timing the subtest.
- Give the examinee the correct answers for items 6 and 7 if these items are missed.
- The WAIS–III manual indicates that, if necessary, you may give each of three guiding statements *once* to help the examinee understand the subtest requirements: (a) If the examinee names the object pictured, ask the examinee what is missing in the picture. (b) If the examinee names a part that is off the card, ask the examinee what part *in the* picture is missing. (c) If the examinee mentions a nonessential missing part, ask the examinee for the most important missing part.

- In response to inexact or made-up words that are ambiguous, say, "Show me where."
- Record each incorrect response verbatim.
- Record the time the examinee takes to respond.
- Ask the examinee to point to the missing part on the card if ambiguous responses are given on items 8 (pitcher) and 10 (leaf).
- In other cases as well, whenever there is any doubt about the examinee's verbal or pointing response, ask for clarification.

Starting Considerations

- All examinees begin with item 6.
- If an examinee earns a score of 0 on either item 6 or item 7, administer items 1 to 5 in *reverse order* until the examinee passes two consecutive items.

Scoring Considerations

- Score all items 1 or 0 (pass-fail).
- Give the examinee full credit for items 1 to 5 if 1 point is obtained on questions 6 and 7.
- When you administer the items in reverse order, give credit for any items not administered that precede two consecutive successes.
- Give credit for any reasonable response; the response does not have to be the exact name of the missing part.
- An item is failed if the examinee points to the correct place but gives a wrong verbal response.

Discontinuance Considerations

- The subtest is discontinued after five consecutive failures.

Interpretive Suggestions

As you administer the subtest, consider the following:

- Does the examinee understand the task?
- Does the examinee respond with a word, with a description of the missing detail, or by pointing?
- Does the examinee mainly give verbal responses or pointing responses?
- Does the examinee respond impulsively, saying anything that comes to mind, or does the examinee search for the right answer?
- Does the examinee find fault with herself or himself or with the picture after failing an item?
- Does the examinee benefit from any guiding statements given, such as the instruction to name the most important missing part of the picture?
- What is the examinee's rate of response (e.g., quick and impulsive or slow and deliberate)?
- Is the examinee fearful of making an error, hesitant, or suspicious?
- Is the examinee aware of being timed? If so, does the timing make the examinee anxious or prompt the examinee to change the pace of responding?

- Does the examinee frequently use nondescriptive speech, such as "It's that thing there"?
- Does the examinee give roundabout definitions of words (called circumlocutions)? Circumlocutions may suggest word-retrieval difficulties.
- Does the examinee have trouble producing the right word (referred to as dysnomia)? Dysnomia may suggest word-retrieval difficulties.
- Does the examinee repeatedly say that nothing is missing? Such a response may reflect negativism.
- Does the examinee's response pattern suggest perseveration (e.g., says "Tooth" for each picture portraying a person, when "Tooth" is the correct answer for picture 1, but not for the subsequent pictures of humans)?
- Does the examinee hold the booklet close to her or his face or put her or his face close to the booklet? Such a habit may suggest visual difficulties.

In addition, record each incorrect response verbatim, and record the time the examinee takes to respond. If the examinee's performance leaves any doubt about his or her visual skills, request a visual examination.

The Picture Completion items can be classified as pattern-symmetry items (1, 2, 3, 4, 7, 10, 11, 15, 16, 17, 19, 20, 21, 22, and 23) or knowledge-based items (5, 6, 8, 9, 12, 13, 14, 18, 24, and 25). Studying the examinee's error pattern will give you information about where the errors occurred.

Comparing an examinee's Picture Completion score with those on Block Design and Object Assembly may help you distinguish between visuospatial difficulties and visual-motor difficulties. Picture Completion is the only task on the WAIS–III Performance Scale that does not require a motor component.

The examinee who usually responds in less than 5 seconds may be more impulsive, more confident, and, if correct, more skilled than the examinee who takes more time. The examinee who responds correctly *after* the time limit (for which no credit is received) may be more skilled than the examinee who fails the item even with additional time. Because the pass-fail scoring does not make provisions for such qualitative factors, carefully evaluate individual variations in each case and discuss these qualitative factors in the written report. Delayed correct responses may suggest temporary inefficiency, insecurity, depression, or simply a slow and diligent approach, whereas extremely quick but incorrect responses may reflect impulsivity.

Low scores on the Picture Completion subtest may indicate anxiety affecting concentration and attention, preoccupation with irrelevant details, or negativism ("Nothing is missing").

After you administer the subtest, you can inquire about the examinee's perceptions of the task: "How did you go about coming up with the answer?" or "How did you decide when to give an answer?" Inquire about any noteworthy or unclear answers. The examinee's behavior during this subtest may provide insight into how he or she reacts to time pressure. As a testing-of-limits procedure, you can ask the examinee to look again at those pictures that are missed. You might say, "Look at this picture again. Before, you said that … was missing. That's not the part that's missing. Look for something else." In some cases, you may ask the examinee to describe or name the picture, especially when many items are missed. The factor analytic results suggest that verbal reasoning may help examinees detect the missing part of the pictures.

The range of scaled scores from 1 to 19 at ages 75–89 years aids in profile analysis. However, profile analysis is limited at ages 16–74 years, where the scaled scores range from 1 to 18.

DIGIT SYMBOL—CODING

The Digit Symbol—Coding subtest is similar to Coding B on the WISC–III. The subtest requires the examinee to copy symbols that are paired with numbers. The key consists of nine boxes, each of which contains one of the numbers 1 to 9 and a symbol. Each test box contains a number in the upper portion; the lower portion is empty. In the empty space, the examinee must draw the symbol that is paired with the number in the key. There are 7 sample boxes, followed by 133 boxes in the subtest proper.

The Digit Symbol—Coding subtest contains two optional procedures. They are intended to help you determine what skills may be deficient if the examinee performs poorly on the subtest; they are not used to compute IQs. *Digit Symbol—Incidental Learning* is a measure of the examinee's ability to recall (a) the associated number-symbol pairs (this part is called Pairing) and (b) the individual symbols, independent of the numbers (this part is called Free Recall). For you to administer Digit Symbol—Incidental Learning, the examinee has to complete at least four rows of symbols on Digit Symbol—Coding. The examinee may need more than 120 seconds to meet this requirement; symbols completed after the time limit do not count in the Digit Symbol—Coding score. You must note the last item completed at the end of 120 seconds if you give the examinee more than 120 seconds to complete at least four rows of symbols.

The second optional procedure is administered at the end of the WAIS–III and is called *Digit Symbol—Copy*. This task, which is in a separate Response Booklet, requires the examinee to draw, on the blank below the box, the symbol that appears in the box.

Rationale

Digit Symbol—Coding assesses the examinee's ability to learn an unfamiliar task. The subtest involves speed and accuracy of visual-motor coordination, speed of mental operation (processing speed), attentional skills, visual acuity, visual scanning and tracking (repeated visual scanning between the code key and answer spaces), short-term memory for new learning (paired-associate learning of an unfamiliar code), cognitive flexibility (in shifting rapidly from one pair to another), handwriting speed, and, possibly, motivation. Success depends not only on comprehension of the task but also on fine-motor skills. The subtest is sensitive to visuoperceptual difficulties.

Digit Symbol—Coding can be described as measuring the ability to learn combinations of symbols and numbers and the ability to make associations quickly and accurately. The speed and accuracy with which the examinee performs the task are a measure of the examinee's intellectual ability. At each step in the task the examinee must inspect the next digit, go to the proper location in the table, code the information distinguishing the symbol found, and carry this information in short-term memory long enough to reproduce the symbol in the proper answer box (Estes, 1974). Thus, you can conceptualize Digit Symbol—Coding as an information-processing task involving the discrimination and memory of visual pattern symbols.

The optional procedures are intended to help you determine the reason for a deficient performance on Digit Symbol—Coding. Let's look at three examples. First, a low score on Digit Symbol—Coding, a low score on Digit Symbol—Incidental Learning, and an average score on Digit Symbol—Copy suggest that the examinee may have performed poorly on Digit Symbol—Coding because the stimuli were not remembered well. Second, a low score on Digit Symbol—Coding, a low score on Digit Symbol—Copy, and an average score on Digit Symbol—Incidental Learning suggest that the low score on Digit Symbol—Coding may reflect impaired graphomotor speed. Finally, a low score on Digit Symbol—Coding, a low score on Digit Symbol—Incidental Learning, and a low score on Digit Symbol—Copy suggest that the low score on Digit Symbol—Coding may reflect impaired memory as well as impaired graphomotor speed. Of course, other interpretations exist, such as poor concentration, inattention, or limited motivation.

Factor Analytic Findings

Digit Symbol—Coding is a fair measure of g (35% of its variance may be attributed to g). This subtest contributes substantially to the Processing Speed Index (average loading = .73). Specificity is ample for all age groups.

Reliability and Correlational Highlights

Digit Symbol—Coding is a reliable subtest ($r_{xx} = .84$), with reliability coefficients at or above .81 at all of the 13 age groups (range of .81 to .87). It correlates better with Symbol Search ($r = .65$) than with any of the other subtests. It has a moderate correlation with the Full Scale ($r = .53$) and the Performance Scale ($r = .50$) and a moderately low correlation with the Verbal Scale ($r = .49$).

Administrative Suggestions

Here are some administrative suggestions for the Digit Symbol—Coding subtest.

Background Considerations

Digit Symbol—Coding

- Because Digit Symbol—Coding may penalize an examinee with visual defects or with specific motor disabilities, do not give the subtest to an examinee with either of these disabilities. If you give it to an examinee with these disabilities, do not include it in the final calculation.
- The space between the key and the stimulus items is larger than it was on the former edition of the test because left-handed examinees occasionally covered the sample immediately above the line of writing. Unlike the WISC–III manual, the WAIS–III manual does not suggest that you place an extra Digit Symbol—Coding Response Sheet to the right of the examinee's sheet. However, the subtest may still penalize left-handed examinees, if the way they write causes them to cover the sample immediately above the line of writing. In this case, the examinee will have to lift his or her hand repeatedly during the task to view the key. If this happens, place an extra Digit Symbol—Coding Response Sheet to the right of the examinee's sheet.
- Observe how the examinee proceeds with the task. Note any differences in the quality of the symbols drawn early and late in the task. Tell the examinee who stops working after the first line to "Continue on the next line." Count these instructions as part of the 120-second time limit.
- If the examinee skips around, filling in symbols for like shapes or like numbers first, instruct the examinee to proceed in order: "Do them in order. Don't skip any."
- Laminate the template to prolong its life.

Digit Symbol—Incidental Learning and Digit Symbol—Copy

- The Response Booklet used for Symbol Search is also used for Digit Symbol—Incidental Learning and Digit Symbol—Copy.
- Administer Digit Symbol—Incidental Learning after the Digit Symbol—Coding subtest.
- Do not time either the Pairing phase or the Free Recall phase of Digit Symbol—Incidental Learning.
- Observe how the examinee proceeds with the task. Note any differences in the quality of the symbols drawn early and late in the task.
- The WAIS–III manual advises on page 16 that Digit Symbol—Copy be administered at the end of the test.

Starting Considerations

Digit Symbol—Coding

- The Digit Symbol—Coding subtest items are located in the primary test protocol.

- Administer the subtest on a smooth drawing surface.
- You and the examinee should each use a no. 2 graphite pencil without an eraser.
- Correct an examinee's mistakes immediately when you administer the sample items.
- Do not begin the subtest until the examinee clearly understands the task.

Digit Symbol—Incidental Learning and Digit Symbol—Copy

- You and the examinee should each use a no. 2 graphite pencil without an eraser.
- Correct the examinee's mistakes immediately when you administer the sample items of Digit Symbol—Copy.
- When you administer the Free Recall part of Digit Symbol—Incidental Learning, cover the Pairing items with a blank sheet of paper sufficiently opaque that the examinee cannot see through it. Also, be sure that the examinee does not see the Digit Symbol—Copy page.
- Sometimes an examinee will stop after completing the first row of Digit Symbol—Incidental Learning. In such cases, give the Response Booklet back to the examinee, point to the second row, and say, "Please complete the second row as well." (David Tulsky, spokesperson for The Psychological Corporation, advised that the above directions be used in such instances; personal communication, May 1998.)
- The instructions for Digit Symbol—Incidental Learning say to fill in the numbers one after another. However, if the examinee skips around, allow him or her to do so. Do not say anything in addition to the instructions (David Tulsky, spokesperson for The Psychological Corporation, April 2000).
- When you administer Digit Symbol—Copy, fold over the page in the Response Booklet so that the examinee does not see the Digit Symbol—Incidental Learning page.

Scoring Considerations

Digit Symbol—Coding

- One point is allotted for each correct item.
- No time-bonus points are awarded.
- Do not include the responses to the sample items in scoring the subtest.
- Use the template to score the examinee's responses.
- Do not penalize the examinee for an imperfectly drawn symbol as long as the symbol can be clearly identified as the keyed symbol.
- Give credit for symbols that are spontaneously corrected within the time limit.
- Do not give credit for any items completed out of sequence.

Digit Symbol—Incidental Learning

- One point is allotted for each correct Pairing response and 1 point for each correct Free Recall response.

Digit Symbol—Copy

- Give credit for responses that are clearly identifiable, even though imperfect, and any spontaneous corrections.
- Do not give credit for the seven sample items or any items completed out of sequence.
- Note that there is an error in the Response Booklet for Digit Symbol—Copy (page 7). For the first item in the second row (#14), the Response Booklet shows a three-sided U-shaped figure open to the left. However, the Digit Symbol Scoring Template for this item shows a three-sided U-shaped figure open at the top. We recommend that, for this item, you disregard what is shown on the Digit Symbol Scoring Template and give credit for a drawing of a three-sided U-shaped figure open to the left.

Discontinuance Considerations

Digit Symbol—Coding

- The subtest is discontinued after 120 seconds, unless the examinee completes it before that time.

Digit Symbol—Incidental Learning

- The subtest is discontinued when the examinee has completed each part, as there is no time limit.

Digit Symbol—Copy

- The subtest is discontinued after 90 seconds, unless the examinee completes it before that time.

Interpretive Suggestions

Following are some useful questions to guide your observations:

- Does the examinee understand the task?
- Does the examinee understand and proceed correctly after you give an explanation?
- Does the examinee use one hand to hold the paper in place and the other hand to draw the symbols?
- Is the examinee impulsive?
- Is the examinee meticulous?
- Does the examinee seem overly anxious?
- Does the examinee display tremor?
- Does the examinee's speed increase or decrease as the subtest proceeds?
- Are the examinee's symbol marks well executed, barely recognizable, or incorrect?
- Do the examinee's symbol marks show any distortions, such as reversals? If so, do the distortions appear only once, occasionally, or each time the examinee draws the symbol mark? How many different symbols are distorted?
- Does the examinee draw the same symbol repeatedly even though the numbers change (perseveration)?

- Is the examinee penalized for lack of speed, inaccuracy, or both?
- Are the examinee's failures due to inadequate form perception or to poor attention?
- Does the examinee check each symbol with the sample, or does the examinee seem to remember the symbols (e.g., not look up at the code at the top of the page)?
- Does the examinee recheck every symbol before moving on to the next one?
- Does the examinee pick out one number only and skip the others?
- Is the examinee's work smooth and orderly, or does the examinee seem confused at times and have difficulty finding her or his place?
- Is the examinee aware of any errors?
- Do the examinee's errors occur in some regular manner?
- How does the examinee react to errors?
- Is the examinee persistent?
- Does the examinee need urging to continue the task?
- Does the examinee appear bored with the task?
- Does the examinee hold the pencil in an appropriate way (e.g., pencil grip appropriate or pencil grip too tight, hand steady or hand shaking)?
- Does the examinee try to use an eraser from another pencil or another source? If so, does the examinee seem to realize that an eraser is not supposed to be used?
- Does the examinee stop in the middle of the task, stretch, sigh, look around, and talk?
- How are symbols drawn by the examinee on the Pairing and Free Recall parts of Digit Symbol—Incidental Learning? This information should be used in conjunction with results from Digit Symbol—Coding to develop hypotheses about the examinee's performance (e.g., the examinee has difficulty drawing some symbols in all procedures or has more success earlier in the task than later).
- How does the examinee's approach to Digit Symbol—Copy compare with that to Digit Symbol—Coding? Are there any differences in performance (e.g., quality of symbols drawn, level of anxiety, type of pencil grip, number of items completed)?

Answers to the above questions will provide information about the examinee's attention span, method of working, and other behaviors. If the examinee makes many errors, consider whether the errors might be due to impulsivity, poor self-monitoring and poor self-correction, or visual-motor difficulties (Kaplan et al., 1999). An increase in speed, coupled with correct copying of symbols, suggests that the examinee is adjusting well to the task. A decrease in speed, coupled with incorrect copying of symbols, suggests that the examinee may be showing fatigue. And a decrease in speed, coupled with correct copying of symbols, suggests that the examinee may be bored, distracted, or fatigued.

Digit Symbol—Coding is particularly useful for evaluating an examinee's attention when you suspect attentional difficulties, such as in cases of attention-deficit/hyperactivity disorder, anxiety, or a traumatic brain injury. If other tests indicate that the examinee has adequate response speed and visual acuity, then poor scores on Digit Symbol—Coding are likely to be associated with attentional deficits and not visuo-perceptual difficulties per se. A slow and deliberate approach may suggest depressive features.

Distortion of forms may mean that the examinee has difficulties with perceptual functioning. Ask the examinee about any symbol written peculiarly to find out whether it has some symbolic meaning to the examinee. Perseveration may suggest neurological difficulties that should be investigated further. Boredom might be present with a bright examinee who is not challenged by the task.

Low scores on the Digit Symbol—Coding subtest may indicate visual-motor coordination difficulties, distractibility, anxiety, visual defects, poor pencil control, poor motivation, excessive concern for detail in reproducing symbols (perfectionism), lethargy or boredom, or impulsivity.

After the *entire test* is over, you can go back to the Digit Symbol—Coding subtest and ask the examinee about how the symbol-number combinations were remembered. This testing-of-limits procedure may give you insight about the strategies the examinee used on the task. You also may want to go over each symbol that was copied wrong and ask the examinee to tell you whether it looks like the symbol in the key.

The range of scaled scores from 1 to 19 at all ages aids in profile analysis.

TRAVIS CONCLUDES THAT "WHISTLING WHILE YOU WORK" MAY NOT ALWAYS BE A GOOD IDEA, SUCH AS WHEN A CLIENT IS TRYING TO CONCENTRATE ON THE CODING SUBTEST

Courtesy of Herman Zielinski.

BLOCK DESIGN

The Block Design subtest contains 14 items. The examinee is shown a two-dimensional red-and-white picture of an abstract design and then must reproduce the design using three-dimensional red and white plastic blocks. All blocks contain the identical surfaces: two red surfaces, two white surfaces, and two red-and-white surfaces.

Rationale

On the Block Design subtest, the examinee must perceive and analyze forms by breaking down a whole (the design) into its parts and then assembling the components into the identical design. This process is called analysis and synthesis. To succeed, the examinee must use visual organization and visual-motor coordination. Success also involves the application of logic and reasoning to spatial relationship problems. Consequently, you can consider Block Design to be a nonverbal concept formation task requiring perceptual organization, spatial visualization, and abstract conceptualization. You can also view it as a constructional task involving spatial relations and figure-ground separation.

Different strategies can be used to assemble the blocks (Rozencwajg, 1991). One is a *global strategy* in which the examinee assembles blocks in a stepwise trial-and-error procedure; with this strategy, the examinee does not analyze the components of the model. A second is an *analytical strategy* in which the examinee forms a representation of the model and then decomposes the design into blocks. Once the blocks have been identified, the examinee selects and orients them before placing them in the design.

An examinee's performance on Block Design may be affected by rate of motor activity and vision. However, do not interpret inadequate performance as *direct* evidence of inadequate visual form and pattern perception, because the ability to discriminate block designs (i.e., to perceive the designs accurately at a recognition level) may be intact even when the ability to reproduce the designs is impaired. The examinee's performance on Picture Completion may help you evaluate her or his performance on Block Design.

Factor Analytic Findings

The Block Design subtest is tied with Matrix Reasoning as the best measure of *g* among the Performance Scale subtests (52% of its variance may be attributed to *g*). This subtest contributes substantially to the Perceptual Organization Index (average loading = .70). Specificity is either ample or adequate for all age groups.

Reliability and Correlational Highlights

Block Design is a reliable subtest (r_{xx} = .86), with reliability coefficients at or above .76 at all of the 13 age groups (range of .76 to .90). It correlates better with Object Assembly ($r =$ .61) and Matrix Reasoning ($r = $.60) than with any of the other subtests. It has a moderate correlation with the Full Scale ($r = $.66), the Performance Scale ($r = $.66), and the Verbal Scale ($r = $.59).

Administrative Suggestions

Here are some administrative suggestions for the Block Design subtest.

Background Considerations

- The area on your desk that you use to administer Block Design should be clear of other blocks and materials.
- For items 1 to 5, construct a model and ask the examinee to reproduce the model.
- Construct the design for items 1 and 2 by laying out the two blocks from the examinee's left to right.
- Construct the design for items 3 and 5 by completing, from the examinee's left to right, the first row (i.e., the top row of the design from the examinee's perspective) and then the second row.
- If the examinee earns a score of 0 or 1 on either item 5 or item 6, administer items 1, 2, 3, and 4 in *reverse sequence* until the examinee has two consecutive perfect scores.
- A variety of block surfaces should face up (i.e., only one block with a red-and-white side facing up for the four-block designs, and only three blocks with a red-and-white side facing up for the nine-block designs).
- Use two blocks for designs 1 and 2, four blocks for designs 3 to 9, and nine blocks for designs 10 to 14.
- All items are timed. Items 1 to 4 have a maximum of 30 seconds; items 5 to 9, 60 seconds; and items 10 to 14, 120 seconds.
- Scramble the blocks before you administer each new design. Place before the examinee the exact number of blocks needed for each item (4 blocks for items 1 and 2, 8 blocks for items 3 to 5, 4 blocks for items 6 to 9, and 9 blocks for items 10 to 14).
- Items 1 to 6 have two trials; items 7 to 14 have only one trial.
- Do not administer the second trial on items 1 to 6 if the examinee succeeds on the first trial.
- Administer the second trial on items 1 to 6 if the examinee fails trial 1 (i.e., wrong solution or correct solution after the time limit).
- Show the examinee the correct orientation only after the first time a design is rotated by 30° or more.
- For some examinees, you may want to begin Block Design with item 1. In this case, use the introduction to item 5 and adjust the item instructions to accommodate this sequencing.
- Record the exact amount of time it takes the examinee to construct each design, and record whether the examinee successfully constructs the design.

Starting Considerations

- All examinees begin with item 5.
- When you demonstrate the sample items, put them together slowly. Be careful not to cover the blocks with your hand; the examinee needs to see what you are doing. Make the designs so that they are in the appropriate direction for the examinee. This means that you will be making the designs upside down. Don't make a design right side up and then turn the whole arrangement around to face the examinee.
- Place the model approximately 7 inches from the edge of the table closest to the examinee. You want the examinee to look down at the model, not at its sides.
- For right-handed examinees, place the model a little to the left of a line perpendicular to the examinee's body. For left-handed examinees, place the model a little to the right of a line perpendicular to the examinee's body.
- The examinee should be seated facing the edge of the table.
- Place the unbound edge of the Stimulus Booklet or the model perpendicular to the examinee's body.

Scoring Considerations

- If the examinee earns 2-point scores on both items 5 and 6 (i.e., correct performance on the first trial), assign full credit for items 1, 2, 3, and 4.
- When you administer the items in reverse order, give credit for any items not administered that precede two consecutive successes.
- On items 1 to 6, give 2 points for successful completion on the first trial and give 1 point for successful completion on the second trial. On items 7 to 14, give 4 points for a correct completion and give up to 3 additional time-bonus points for quick execution.
- Give a score of 0 to designs that are rotated more than 30°.

Discontinuance Considerations

- The subtest is discontinued after three consecutive failures.

Interpretive Suggestions

Block Design is an excellent subtest for observing the examinee's problem-solving approach and fine-motor skills. Consider the following issues:

- Is the examinee hasty and impulsive (e.g., rarely checks his or her work) or deliberate and careful (e.g., methodically checks each block with the design)?
- Does the examinee give up easily or become frustrated when faced with possible failure, or does the examinee keep on working even after the time limit is reached?
- Does the examinee use only one approach, or does the examinee alter his or her approach as the need arises?
- Does the examinee use a slow approach or a rapid trial-and-error approach?

- Is the examinee excessively concerned with lining up the blocks precisely?
- Does the examinee study the designs first before attempting to construct them?
- Does the examinee appear to have a plan when assembling the blocks?
- Does the examinee construct the design in units of blocks, or does the examinee work in a piecemeal fashion?
- Does the examinee understand the principle of using individual blocks to construct the designs?
- Does the examinee try to place the blocks on the picture of the design?
- Does the examinee express concerns about differences between blocks?
- Does the examinee interpret white portions of the design card as open spaces in the assembled designs?
- Does the examinee use a solid red or solid white block surface for a red-and-white surface?
- Does the examinee say that his or her designs are correct when, in fact, they are not?
- Are the examinee's designs correct but rotated?
- Does the examinee rotate single blocks?
- Can the examinee rotate a row of blocks at the bottom when the blocks are in the wrong direction, or does he or she start the entire design over again?
- Does the examinee show any indications of fine motor difficulties such as tremor or clumsiness?
- Does the examinee offer to put the blocks back in the box after the task is over?

Excessive fumbling or failure to check the pattern may indicate anxiety. Visuoperceptual difficulties may be indicated if the examinee moves or twists around to improve her or his perspective on the design or if the examinee leaves space between the blocks in the assembled design. Try to differentiate between excessive cautiousness as a personality style and excessive slowness as a possible indication of depression or boredom. Examinees who continually recheck their work with the model may be revealing insecurities or obsessive tendencies.

Conduct testing-of-limits after you have administered the *entire test,* because if you don't, you will violate standard procedures and the cues you give may lead to higher scores (Sattler, 1969). One useful testing-of-limits procedure is to select an item that the examinee has incorrectly constructed, assemble the incorrect reproduction, and ask the examinee if the reproduction is the same as or different from the original design. If the examinee recognizes that his or her design is incorrect and can tell you the specific errors (e.g., "A red-and-white block goes here, not a white block"), the examinee may have a visual-motor execution problem rather than a visual-motor recognition problem.

Another testing-of-limits procedure involves showing the examinee the Block Design card (or assembled design) for a design that he or she failed. As you give the directions, place one row or block in its correct position. Say, "Let's try some

of these again. I'm going to put together some of the blocks. I'll make the top row [or arrange the first block]. Now you go ahead and finish it. Make one like this. Tell me when you have finished." If the examinee still fails, arrange additional blocks. Record the amount of help the examinee needs to reproduce the design accurately. An examinee who needs many cues to reproduce the designs may have weaker spatial reasoning ability than an examinee who needs only a few cues. In some cases, the additional cues may not help the examinee reproduce the designs.

Other testing-of-limits procedures are also possible. One is to show the examinee three different arrangements, only one of which is correct. Then ask the examinee to point to the arrangement that is the same as the one on the card. Be sure to vary the placement of the correct design. Another procedure is to ask the examinee to tell you how the block design pattern was made.

The range of scaled scores from 1 to 19 at all ages aids in profile analysis.

You also can use other constructional tasks, such as the Bender-Gestalt or the Greek Cross item from the Reitan-Indiana Aphasia Screening Test (see *Assessment of Children: Behavioral and Clinical Applications*), to investigate a hypothesis of impaired visuospatial manipulation and motor output. For example, discovering that the examinee has difficulty reproducing the Bender-Gestalt designs, recognizes her or his errors, but can't improve the designs on repeated attempts would be consistent with an hypothesis of impaired visual-motor output.

MATRIX REASONING

The Matrix Reasoning subtest is composed of 26 nonverbal reasoning tasks that involve pattern completion, analogy, classification, or serial reasoning. The items consist of individually presented colored matrices, each of which is missing a part. The examinee is directed to look at all aspects of each matrix carefully and select the missing part from an array of five choices at the bottom of the page.

Rationale

The Matrix Reasoning subtest involves perceptual reasoning ability without a speed component. Analogic reasoning, attention to detail, and concentration are required for successful performance; spatial ability may be involved for some examinees. Experience with part-whole relationships may be helpful, as may a willingness to respond when uncertain. Some research suggests that Matrix Reasoning has a strong verbal mediation component and a minor visuoperceptual and visuospatial construction skill component as well (Dugbartey, Sanchez, Rosenbaum, Mahurin, Davis, and Townes, 1999). This study also reported a .75 correlation between Matrix Reasoning and the CTONI, a nonverbal measure of intelligence (see Chapter 16).

Factor Analytic Findings

The Matrix Reasoning subtest is tied with Block Design as the best measure of g in the Performance Scale (52% of its variance may be attributed to g). This subtest contributes moderately to the Perceptual Organization Index (average loading = .49) and to a limited extent to the Working Memory Index (average loading = .33). Specificity is ample for all age groups.

Reliability and Correlational Highlights

Matrix Reasoning is a reliable subtest (r_{xx} = .90), with reliability coefficients at or above .84 at all of the 13 age groups (range of .84 to .94). It correlates better with Block Design (r = .60) and Arithmetic (r = .58) than with any of the other subtests. It has a moderate correlation with the Full Scale (r = .69), the Performance Scale (r = .65), and the Verbal Scale (r = .64).

Administrative Suggestions

Here are some administrative suggestions for the Matrix Reasoning subtest.

Background Considerations

- Matrix Reasoning is relatively easy to administer. Simply leave the stimulus booklet flat on the table and turn the cards over one at a time to show each item.
- The subtest is untimed.
- The examinee may respond orally or by pointing.
- If 30 seconds have elapsed and the examinee still has not answered, encourage him or her to respond. If the examinee fails to respond after an additional 15 to 30 seconds, proceed to the next item (Tulsky et al., 1999).

Starting Considerations

- All examinees begin with the three sample items, A, B, and C. These items are intended to help the examinee understand the subtest instructions.
- Administer the three sample items more than once if needed.
- Give the examinee as much help as he or she needs to understand how the subtest works.
- Proceed to item 4, even if the examinee fails items A, B, and C.
- If the examinee fails either item 4 or item 5, administer matrices 1, 2, and 3 in *reverse sequence* until the examinee passes two consecutive items.

Scoring Considerations

- All responses are scored 1 or 0 (pass-fail).
- If the examinee answers items 4 and 5 correctly, give credit for items 1, 2, and 3.
- When you administer the items in reverse order, give credit for any items not administered that precede two consecutive successes.

Discontinuance Considerations

- The subtest is discontinued after either four consecutive failures or four failures in five consecutive items.

Interpretive Suggestions

Consider the following questions:

- What is the tempo of the examinee's responses (e.g. fast, slow, deliberate, impulsive, careful)?
- Are there any signs of a response set (i.e., examinee points to the same numbered choice for each item)?
- If the examinee takes more than a minute to respond, what might the reasons be for the long response time (e.g., depression, thoughtfulness, inability to make a decision, anxiety, hope that the right answer will somehow come to her or him)?
- How does the examinee's pattern of responding in this subtest compare with her or his responses on other subtests?
- Are there any indications of visual difficulties that might impede the examinee's performance (e.g., visual acuity difficulties, color blindness)?
- Are there any signs of negativism or uncooperative behavior? If so, what are the signs?

After you administer the *entire test,* you can inquire about the examinee's approach to the task in order to gain insight into his or her problem-solving strategies.

Low scores on the Matrix Reasoning subtest may indicate poor perceptual organization, poor reasoning, poor attention to detail, poor concentration, impulsivity, or negativism.

PICTURE ARRANGEMENT

The Picture Arrangement subtest requires the examinee to arrange a series of pictures in a logical sequence. Each of the 11 series of pictures is presented in a specified disarranged order, and the examinee is asked to rearrange the pictures in the "right" order to tell a story. One set of cards is presented at a time. Little motor action is required, as the pictures must simply be shifted to make a meaningful story.

Rationale

The Picture Arrangement subtest measures the examinee's ability to comprehend and evaluate a situation. To accomplish the task, the examinee must grasp the general idea of a story. Although some examinees take a trial-and-error approach to the subtest, success depends on an appraisal of the total situation depicted in the cards.

Picture Arrangement is considered to be a measure of nonverbal reasoning that involves planning ability, anticipation, visual organization, and temporal sequencing. The subtest measures the ability to anticipate the consequences of initial acts or situations, as well as the ability to interpret social situations. Some examinees may generate covert, analytical, verbal descriptions of alternative story sequences to guide them in arranging the stimulus cards. In such cases, the subtest may measure verbal sequencing processes as well. The capacity to anticipate, judge, and understand the possible antecedents and consequences of events is important in lending meaningful continuity to everyday experiences.

Factor Analytic Findings

The Picture Arrangement subtest is a fair measure of g (44% of its variance may be attributed to g). This subtest contributes to a limited extent to the Perceptual Organization Index (average loading = .35) and to the Verbal Comprehension Index (average loading = .31). Specificity is either ample or adequate for six age groups (16–17, 25–29, 35–44, 65–69, 70–74, 85–89 years); at seven age groups (18–19, 20–24, 30–34, 45–54, 55–64, 75–79, 80–84 years), it is inadequate.

Reliability and Correlational Highlights

Picture Arrangement is relatively reliable (r_{xx} = .74), with reliability coefficients at or above .66 at all of the 13 age groups (range of .66 to .81). It correlates better with Information (r = .54) and Vocabulary (r = .53) than with any of the other subtests. It has a moderate correlation with the Full Scale (r = .63), the Performance Scale (r = .60), and the Verbal Scale (r = .59).

Administrative Suggestions

Here are some administrative suggestions for the Picture Arrangement subtest.

Background Considerations

- Administer one set of cards at a time to the examinee.
- Place the Picture Arrangement items at least 3 or 4 inches away from the edge of the table. Arrange them from the examinee's left to right, in the order specified in the WAIS–III manual.
- Each item is timed, with 30 seconds allowed for item 1, 45 seconds for item 2, 60 seconds for items 3 and 4, 90 seconds for items 5 and 6, and 120 seconds for items 7 to 11.
- Record the examinee's Picture Arrangement sequence as soon as you pick up the cards.
- When the examinee places the cards from her or his right to left, ask the examinee to tell you where the story begins.
- If the examinee does not tell you when she or he is finished, ask promptly. Stop timing when the examinee is obviously finished, though, even if the examinee does not tell you.
- When the examinee is perfectionistic in arranging the cards, tell the examinee that the cards do not have to be perfectly straight (or aligned).

Starting Considerations

- All examinees begin with item 1.

Scoring Considerations

- Only the first item has two trials, and it is scored 2 (for correct performance on trial 1), 1 (for correct performance on trial 2), or 0 (failure on both trials).
- Items 2 to 11 are scored either 0 or 2, with the exception of items 5 to 9, where 1 point is given for an acceptable variation of the correct arrangement.
- Unlike on the WISC–III, where bonus points can be earned on items 3 to 14 for speed, there are no bonus points on the WAIS–III Picture Arrangement subtest.

Discontinuance Considerations

- The subtest is discontinued after four consecutive failures.

Interpretive Suggestions

The Picture Arrangement subtest gives you the opportunity to observe how the examinee approaches a performance task involving planning ability.

- Does the examinee look at all of the cards first before starting to arrange them?
- Does the examinee examine the cards, come to some decision, and then reassess his or her decision while arranging the cards?
- Does the examinee proceed quickly, without stopping to reconsider decisions?
- Does the examinee arrange the cards in one order and then rearrange them several times?
- Does the examinee pick up the cards and attempt to look at the back of them for any cues?
- Are the examinee's failures due to lack of understanding of the task, such as leaving the pictures in their original order?
- Are low scores the result of not being able to place the pictures in the proper sequence, an impulsive and careless style of responding, or a slow and perfectionistic style of responding?
- What types of errors does the examinee make? For instance, are cards placed in a perfunctory or random manner, or is one card always moved to the same position?
- Is the examinee persistent, discouraged, impulsive, or rigid?
- What types of trial-and-error patterns does the examinee use?
- How does the examinee's approach to the Picture Arrangement items compare with his or her approach to the Block Design and Object Assembly items?
- Does the examinee consistently employ the same patterns when searching for solutions? If not, what are the different patterns employed, and what might account for when and where they are used?

- How do task content, fatigue, and mood changes influence the examinee's approach to the items?
- Does the examinee talk aloud while solving the problems? If so, do the examinee's verbalizations give you any insight into how the examinee perceives the task?
- Does the examinee offer to put the cards back in the box after the task is over?
- Does the examinee ask about his or her performance (e.g., "Did I get that right?")?

The examinee's performance on the Picture Arrangement subtest may give you information about her or his reasoning. Failures may be due to difficulties in logical reasoning. Examinees with mental retardation, brain injuries, or behavior disorders may show reasoning difficulties on Picture Arrangement. Although examinees with mild behavior disorders usually produce logical stories, they may rush through the task or reveal their anxieties and preoccupations by unusual arrangements, such as neglecting details for the sake of a particular theme.

Low scores on the Picture Arrangement subtest may indicate difficulty with visual organization and sequential processing, difficulty in anticipating events and their consequences, inattentiveness, anxiety, failure to use cues, difficulty working under time pressure, impulsivity, or poor visual acuity and discrimination.

After the *entire test* is over, you can conduct one of the following useful testing-of-limits procedures.

1. *Give additional time.* One at a time, lay out the arrangements that the examinee had partially completed correctly and give the examinee additional time to complete them.

2. *Give cues on failed items.* Place the first card before the examinee and say, "Here's the first picture. What goes next?" If one card does not help the examinee, place the second correct card next to the first one and say, "What picture goes next?" In some cases you may need to arrange even more than one or two cards to help the examinee. The examinee who solves the problems with cues may have more ability than the examinee who fails in spite of receiving cues. Introduce such graded help only after you have completed the *entire test* because such help during the test can raise Picture Arrangement scores (Sattler, 1969).

3. *Use a multiple-choice procedure.* One at a time, present three arrangements—one correct and two incorrect. Ask the examinee to indicate which one makes the most sense.

4. *Ask for a different sequence.* Ask the examinee to arrange the stories, one at a time, in a sequence different from the incorrect arrangements.

5. *Ask the examinee to tell you about his or her arrangements and make up a story.* One way to do this is to ask the examinee to explain or describe one or more arrangements. Select items that you think may help you understand the examinee's thought patterns better. You may want to focus on items that the examinee failed. However, you can also select items that the examinee passed; even correct arrangements do not necessarily mean that the examinee interpreted the series correctly. Because the last two items tried are likely to be the most complex for the examinee, you might select them if you have no other specific choices.

Arrange the cards for each item separately, in the order given by the examinee. Then say, "Tell what is happening in the pictures" or "Make up a story" or "Tell me what the pictures show." Although Picture Arrangement is not standardized as a projective technique, the examinee may project feelings, affect, and experiences in the process of telling stories.

A second version of this procedure involves randomly placing the CAP sequence of cards before the examinee and then asking the examinee to make up a story about one of the cards. After the examinee has completed the story and you have removed the cards, arrange the BAKE sequence of cards randomly and ask the examinee to tell a story about one of those cards. You can follow this procedure for any other items that you administered during the test proper.

Consider the following in evaluating the stories:

- Are the examinee's stories logical, fanciful, confused, or bizarre?
- Are the examinee's stories creative or conventional?
- Does the examinee reveal any themes in the stories, such as self-oriented, socially oriented, or repetitive themes?
- Are the examinee's incorrect arrangements a consequence of incorrect perceptions of details in the pictures or of failure to consider some details?
- Does the examinee consider all the relationships in the pictures?
- Are the examinee's sequences correct, although the point of the story is missed?
- Are the examinee's sequences incorrect, although the point of the story is grasped?

The range of scaled scores from 1 to 19 at ages 16–19 and 55–89 years aids in profile analysis. However, profile analysis is slightly more restricted at ages 35–74, where the scaled scores range from 1 to 18, and at ages 20–34, where the scaled scores range from 1 to 17.

SYMBOL SEARCH

The Symbol Search subtest, a supplementary subtest, requires the examinee to look at two symbols and decide whether either one is present in an array of five symbols. The subtest contains 60 items.

Rationale

On the Symbol Search subtest, the examinee looks at two figures (target stimulus), scans an array of five items, and decides whether either stimulus figure appears in the array. The task involves perceptual discrimination, speed and accuracy, attention and concentration, short-term memory, and cognitive flexibility (in shifting rapidly from one array to the next). Visual-motor coordination plays a role, although a minor one, because the only motor movement is that of drawing a slash.

Most of the symbols used in the Symbol Search subtest are difficult to encode verbally. However, the examinee may verbally encode some symbols if verbal descriptions can be attached to them. These include, for example, ± (plus or minus), ⌐ (L shape), > (greater than sign), ∩ (inverted U), and ⊢ (a T on its side). Research is needed to learn whether examinees verbally encode these or other symbols and whether the encoding helps their performance.

As in the Digit Symbol—Coding subtest, the speed and accuracy with which the examinee performs the task are a measure of the examinee's intellectual ability. For each item, the examinee must inspect the target stimulus, go to the array, look at the array items and determine whether either of the stimulus figures is present, and then mark the appropriate box (YES or NO) once a decision is made. Thus, you can conceptualize Symbol Search as a task involving visual discrimination and visuoperceptual scanning.

Factor Analytic Findings

The Symbol Search subtest is a fair measure of *g* (49% of its variance may be attributed to *g*). This subtest contributes substantially to the Processing Speed Index (average loading = .70). Specificity is either ample or adequate for three age groups (30–34 through 45–54 years); at 10 age groups (16–17 through 25–29, 55–64 through 85–89 years), it is inadequate.

Reliability and Correlational Highlights

Symbol Search is a relatively reliable subtest (r_{xx} = .77), with reliability coefficients at or above .74 at all of the 13 age groups (range of .74 to .82). It correlates better with Digit Symbol—Coding (r = .65) than with any of the other subtests. It has a moderate correlation with the Full Scale (r = .66), the Performance Scale (r = .69), and the Verbal Scale (r = .57).

Administrative Suggestions

Here are some administrative suggestions for the Symbol Search subtest.

Background Considerations

- Each item has two target symbols and five symbols in the test array. The examinee must draw a slash (/) through the box labeled YES if either of the target symbols is also in the test array. If neither of the target symbols is in the test array, the examinee must draw a slash (/) through the box labeled NO.

- The subtest has a time limit of 120 seconds.
- Briefly show the third and fourth pages of the Response Booklet when you give the instructions for item 1, and then fold the booklet so that the examinee sees only the first page of items.
- Observe the examinee's work methods. Remind the examinee to do the items in order if any items are skipped.
- Unlike on the WISC–III, where the Symbol Search subtest consists of two separate parts, Symbol Search on the WAIS–III has only one part.
- Examinees with visual impairments or specific motor disabilities may be penalized on Symbol Search. Therefore, do not give the subtest to an examinee with either of these impairments. If you do give the subtest to an examinee with a motor impairment because of clinical interest, do not include the subtest in computing IQs, even when it replaces a standard Performance Scale subtest.

Starting Considerations

- The Symbol Search subtest is in a separate booklet (WAIS–III Response Booklet).
- Write the examinee's name, the date, and your name in the space provided on the Symbol Search Response Booklet, and note the examinee's handedness.
- Administer the subtest on a smooth drawing surface.
- There are three sample items and three practice items.
- The examinee needs to have a clear view of the three sample items.
- Do not go to the practice items until the examinee appears to understand the task.
- On the practice items, give the examinee help if he or she does not understand the task.
- When you administer the practice items, praise the examinee for doing the items correctly. Correct any mistakes the examinee makes immediately.
- The sample and practice items are not timed.
- Both you and the examinee should use a no. 2 graphite pencil without an eraser.
- Do not begin the subtest until the examinee understands the task.

Scoring Considerations

- Only score items that the examinee attempts within the allotted 120 seconds.
- Align the scoring template properly when you score the subtest.
- The score is arrived at by subtracting the number of incorrect responses from the number of correct responses. In scoring the subtest, do not include either skipped items or items that the examinee did not reach.
- Mark as wrong an item that has both YES and NO marked.
- Do not to give any credit for the sample or practice items.
- There are no time-bonus credits on the subtest.

Discontinuance Considerations

- The subtest is discontinued after 120 seconds unless the examinee completes it before that time.

Interpretive Suggestions

Following are useful questions to guide your observations.

- Does the examinee use one hand to hold the paper in place and the other hand to draw the symbols?
- Is the examinee impulsive?
- Is the examinee meticulous?
- Does the examinee seem overly anxious?
- Does the examinee display tremor?
- Does the examinee's speed increase or decrease as the subtest proceeds?
- Are the examinee's slash marks (/) well executed, or are they barely recognizable?
- Does the examinee draw the slash mark slowly or quickly?
- Does the examinee work slowly and therefore lose points?
- Does the examinee make many errors? If so, is the examinee aware of them? If the examinee is aware of the errors, how does she or he react to the errors?
- Do the examinee's errors occur in some regular manner?
- Does the examinee fail to understand the task once it is begun?
- Does the examinee respond more slowly to NO items?
- Is the examinee penalized for lack of speed, for inaccuracy, or for both?
- Does the examinee recheck every item before moving on to the next one?
- Does the examinee frequently look back and forth between the target symbols and the search group?
- Is the examinee's work smooth and orderly, or does the examinee seem confused at times and have difficulty finding his or her place?
- Is the examinee persistent?
- Is the examinee bored with the task?
- Does the examinee hold the pencil in an appropriate way?
- Does the examinee try to use an eraser from another pencil or another source? If so, does the examinee seem to realize that an eraser is not supposed to be used?
- Does the examinee stop in the middle of the task, stretch, sigh, look around, and talk?

Answers to these questions may give you information about the examinee's attention, persistence, impulsive tendencies, compulsive tendencies, and depressive tendencies. An increase in speed, coupled with correct marks, suggests that the examinee is adjusting well to the task. A decrease in speed, coupled with incorrect marks, suggests that the examinee may be showing fatigue. It may be of interest to compare examinees who obtain the same score in different ways. For example, suppose two examinees get a score of 10, but one examinee has 10 correct responses and zero errors and the other examinee has 20 correct responses and 10 errors. These two examinees likely have different styles of working. The first examinee may be a slow, careful, and meticulous worker, but may be unwilling (or unable) to work quickly, whereas the second examinee may be a quick worker, but rather careless and impulsive.

Examinees may be penalized on the Symbol Search subtest if they (a) are unable to make quick decisions, (b) respond slowly and carefully, (c) are compulsive and constantly check the stimulus figures against those in the array, or (d) are impulsive and fail to check the array figures against the stimulus figures.

With examinees who make many errors, you may want to go over each item on which an error occurred after the *entire test* is completed. You can point to an item on which an error occurred and say, "Tell me about your answer" or "Tell me about why you marked a NO [or YES]." Another testing-of-limits procedure is to provide highly distractible examinees with a ruler or paper guide to see whether one of these aids improves their performance.

Compare the examinee's response style on Symbol Search with that on other subtests. If there are differences, what might account for them? Consider, for example, the nature of the subtests, the examinee's motivation, the examinee's scores on all of the subtests, and the order in which the subtests were administered (i.e., at the beginning, middle, or end of the examination).

The range of scaled scores from 1 to 19 at all ages aids in profile analysis.

OBJECT ASSEMBLY

The Object Assembly subtest, which is an optional subtest, requires the examinee to put jigsaw pieces together to form common objects: a man (six pieces), a profile of a face (seven pieces), an elephant (six pieces), a house (nine pieces), and a butterfly (seven pieces).

Rationale

The Object Assembly subtest is mainly a test of the examinee's skill at synthesis—putting things together to form familiar objects. It requires visual-motor coordination, with motor activity guided by visual perception and sensorimotor feedback. Object Assembly also is a test of visual organizational ability, for the examinee needs visual organization to produce an object out of parts that may not be immediately recognizable. To solve the jigsaw puzzles, the examinee must be able to grasp an entire pattern by anticipating the relationships among its individual parts. The tasks require some constructive ability, as well as perceptual skill—the examinee must recognize individual parts and place them correctly in the incomplete figure. The examinee's performance also may be related to his or her rate and precision of motor activity;

persistence, especially when much trial and error is required; and long-term visual memory (having stored information about the object to be formed).

Factor Analytic Findings

The Object Assembly subtest is a fair measure of g (38% of its variance may be attributed to g). This subtest contributes substantially to the Perceptual Organization Index (average loading = .74). Specificity is adequate for one age group (45–54 years); at the other 12 age groups, it is inadequate.

Reliability and Correlational Highlights

Object Assembly is the least reliable of the WAIS–III subtests (r_{xx} = .70), with reliability coefficients at or above .50 at all of the 13 age groups (range of .50 to .75). It correlates better with Block Design (r = .61) than with any of the other subtests. It has a moderate correlation with the Full Scale (r = .59), the Performance Scale (r = .64), and the Verbal Scale (r = .50).

Administrative Suggestions

Here are some administrative suggestions for the Object Assembly subtest.

Background Considerations

- All examinees are administered all five items.
- Place all the pieces right side up in the disarranged pattern specified in the diagram on the Object Assembly Layout Shield. Arrange the pieces close to the examinee so that she or he does not waste time reaching for them.
- All items are timed. The first two items have a time limit of 120 seconds each, and the last three items, 180 seconds each.
- After you read the instructions for each item, begin timing.
- Observe time limits carefully on each item. Record the elapsed time precisely, because the examinee receives additional points for quick execution on all items.
- Stop timing when the examinee is obviously finished, even if the examinee does not say that she or he is finished. However, if you are not sure that the examinee is finished, say, "Are you finished?" or "Tell me when you have finished."
- Be sure that the examinee does not see the pages of the WAIS–III manual that contain pictures of the correctly assembled objects.
- Use the Object Assembly Layout Shield not only to set up the individual puzzle parts but also to shield the WAIS–III manual.
- If the examinee turns over any piece, promptly and unobtrusively turn it right side up.
- Provide help on item 1 (see Starting Considerations) but not on any other item.

- Do not tell the examinee the name of any of the objects, as you do on the first two WISC–III items. Even if the examinee asks, you cannot tell her or him what the object is.

Starting Considerations

- All examinees begin with item 1.
- If the examinee fails the first item, show her or him how the puzzle is put together. Make sure that the examinee can follow your assembly. Do not give help on any other item.

Scoring Considerations

- The man (item 1) has a maximum score of 8 (5 points plus 3 time-bonus points for perfect assembly), the profile (item 2) has a maximum score of 12 points (9 points plus 3 time-bonus points for perfect assembly), the elephant (item 3) has a maximum score of 11 points (8 points plus 3 time-bonus points for perfect performance), the house (item 4) has a maximum score of 10 points (7 points plus 3 time-bonus points for perfect performance), and the butterfly (item 5) has a maximum score of 11 points (8 points plus 3 time-bonus points for perfect performance).
- Give points for partially correct assemblies on all items.
- When you give partial scores, count the number of junctures completed when the time limit has been reached.

Discontinuance Considerations

- The subtest is discontinued after the last puzzle is administered.

Interpretive Suggestions

Object Assembly is an especially good subtest for observing the examinee's thinking style and work habits. Some examinees envision the complete object almost from the start and either recognize or have an imperfect understanding of the relations of the individual parts to the whole. Other examinees merely try to fit the pieces together by trial-and-error methods. Still others have initial failure, followed by trial and error, and then sudden insight and recognition of the object.

Observe the examinee's performance, including responses to errors and handling of frustration.

- Does the examinee (a) demand to know what the object is before constructing it, (b) insist that pieces are missing, or (c) say that the object doesn't make sense?
- Does the examinee recognize what the object is before putting the pieces together?
- Does the examinee know the name of the object but still have difficulty assembling it? For example, does the examinee say, "It's a face," but continue to have trouble putting it together?
- Does the examinee peek over the shield when you are putting out the pieces?
- If low scores are earned, are they due to, for example, temporary inefficiency (such as reversal of two parts) or

spending a long time lining up each piece precisely, which results in loss of time-bonus credits?

- What is the examinee's problem-solving approach to the task (e.g., trial and error, systematic and apparently planned process, random placement of pieces)?
- What is the tempo of the examinee's performance (e.g., slow, deliberate, fast, impulsive)?
- Does the examinee spend a long time with one piece, trying to position it in an incorrect location? (If so, this behavior may indicate anxiety or rigidity.)
- Which hand does the examinee prefer to use to assemble the puzzles?
- What is the quality of the examinee's motor coordination (e.g., smooth, jerky, uncoordinated, suggesting tremor)?
- Does the examinee offer to put the pieces back in the box after the task is completed?

Low scores on the Object Assembly subtest may indicate visual-motor difficulties, visuoperceptual problems, poor planning ability, difficulty in perceiving a whole, minimal experience with construction tasks, limited interest in assembly tasks, limited persistence, difficulty working under time pressure, or impulsivity.

After you administer the subtest, ask the examinee about any constructions that may be peculiar or unusual (such as pieces placed on top of each other). You can use testing-of-limits procedures similar to those described for the Picture Arrangement and Block Design subtests after you have administered the *entire test*. For example, you can introduce a series of graduated cues, such as placing one or more pieces in the correct location. Note the amount of help the examinee needs to complete the task successfully. The examinee who needs only a few cues to complete the object may have better underlying perceptual organization skills, not evident during the standard administration of the subtest, than the examinee who needs many cues.

Another testing-of-limits approach is to ask the examinee to visualize the object in his or her mind before you lay out the puzzle pieces. For example, say, "Think of how a face looks" and then give the examinee the profile item. See if this instruction helps the examinee assemble the puzzle. An additional procedure is to show the examinee a picture of the completed object and see whether she or he can put the pieces together correctly with the aid of the picture. Still another procedure is to ask the examinee to tell you how each object was put together.

The range of scaled scores from 1 to 19 at all ages aids in profile analysis.

INTERPRETING THE WAIS–III

Almost all of the material in Chapter 10 on interpreting the WISC–III pertains to the WAIS–III. For example, the successive level approach to test interpretation, profile analysis, Verbal Scale–Performance Scale comparisons, factor score (or index score) comparisons, and subtest comparisons are similar for both tests. The estimated percentile ranks for subtest scaled scores are shown in Table D-1 in Appendix D. This table also shows suggested qualitative descriptions associated with scaled scores. Table BC-2 on the inside back cover shows the classifications associated with WAIS–III IQs. (Note, however, that the WAIS–III uses "Extremely Low" in place of "Mentally Retarded" for IQs of 69 and below.) In Appendix D, Table D-3 summarizes the interpretive rationales, background factors, possible implications of high and low scores, and instructional implications for subtests on all of the Wechsler tests. Table D-4 presents information about the three scales and the four index scores, and Table D-5 gives suggested remediation activities for combinations of Wechsler subtests.

Profile Analysis

As noted above, approaches to profile analysis are basically the same on the WAIS–III as on the WISC–III (see Chapter 10). The main difference is that you must use the tables in Appendix C for the WAIS–III. The approach to profile analysis that follows is a combined one: Differences between IQs and scaled scores are evaluated based on statistical significance, as well as on base rates of such differences that occur in the standardization sample.

Method 1: Compare Verbal Scale and Performance Scale IQs. Table C-1 in Appendix C provides critical values for comparing the Verbal Scale IQs and Performance Scale IQs for 16- to 17-year-olds, for 18- to 19-year-olds, and for the average of the standardization sample. For examinees 16 to 17 years old and 18 to 19 years old, a difference of 10 points is required at the .05 level and 13 points at the .01 level. The critical values are 9 at the .05 level and 12 at the .01 level for the average of the standardization group. The values in Table C-1 in Appendix C range from 7 to 10 at the .05 level and from 10 to 13 at the .01 level. Thus, an average critical value based on the entire standardization sample would be misleading in some cases (compare Table C-1 in Appendix C with Table B.1 on page 205 of the *WAIS–III Administration and Scoring Manual*). Therefore, use the values for a specific age group to evaluate differences between an examinee's Verbal Scale IQ *and* Performance Scale IQ. Table C-3 in Appendix C shows the probabilities associated with various differences between the WAIS–III Verbal Scale IQs and Performance Scale IQs.

Table B.2 (pages 206–207) in the *WAIS–III Administration and Scoring Manual* shows the cumulative percentages in the standardization sample that obtained various Verbal Scale IQ–Performance Scale IQ differences in *both directions*. The mean Verbal Scale–Performance Scale difference in both directions was 8.6, and the median difference in both directions was 7.0. Approximately 20% of the sample had a Verbal Scale–Performance Scale difference in one or the other direction of 14 points or higher, and approximately 81% of the sample had a Verbal Scale–Performance Scale difference in one or the other direction of 3 points or higher.

The cumulative percentages shown in Table B.2 of the *WAIS–III Administration and Scoring Manual* are absolute values (i.e., they represent bi-directional differences, combining both Verbal Scale > Performance Scale *and* Performance Scale > Verbal Scale values). Unfortunately, in the first printing of the manual, there is no statement that the cumulative frequencies in Table B.2 are absolute values. In addition, Table B.2 does not provide the frequencies with which differences between the Verbal Scale IQ and Performance Scale IQ occurred in the standardization sample in either direction alone. Without this information, it is difficult to determine the actual occurrence in the standardization sample of each kind of difference between the Verbal Scale IQ and Performance Scale IQ. An examinee can have a Verbal Scale-Performance Scale discrepancy in one direction only.

After the publication of the WAIS–III, the actual frequencies with which differences between the Verbal Scale IQ and Performance Scale IQ (and between the index scores) occurred in the standardization sample in either direction alone were provided by The Psychological Corporation (Tulsky, Rolfhus, & Zhu, 2000). Tables C-4 and C-5 in Appendix C show these frequencies. Use these tables to obtain the base rate frequencies to complete the last column ("Frequency of difference in standardization sample") of the Discrepancy Analysis Page in the WAIS–III Record Form. Table C-4 shows, for example, that a Verbal Scale > Performance Scale discrepancy of 24 points was obtained by 2.1% of the standardization sample, whereas Table C-5 shows that a Performance Scale > Verbal Scale discrepancy of 24 points was obtained by 1.0% of the standardization sample.

If you do not use Tables C-4 and C-5 in Appendix C, *you must divide the frequencies in Table B.2 by 2 to obtain the base rate in one direction.* Since dividing by 2 gives only approximate frequencies, we recommend that you use the actual frequencies, now that they are available.

Our recommended procedure, to use Tables C-4 and C-5 in Appendix C to obtain the base rates for Verbal Scale–Performance Scale differences, differs from the one stated in the *WAIS–III Administration and Scoring Manual.* Page 61 of the manual says

Using Table B.2, find the difference obtained by the examinee in the Amount of Discrepancy column. Then, read across the row to the column corresponding to the relevant discrepancy score (e.g., VIQ–PIQ). Record that value in the appropriate space on the Discrepancy Analysis Page of the Record Form.

As noted above, the values in Table B.2 are absolute values. Therefore, they should not be used to determine the frequency with which any one examinee's Verbal Scale–Performance Scale discrepancy occurred in the standardization sample.

Tables D.1 to D.5 (pages 300–309) in the *WAIS–III WMS–III Technical Manual* present the frequency distributions of

Verbal Scale IQ–Performance Scale IQ differences in both directions at five ability levels; these again are absolute values. These tables indicate that the magnitude of differences in both directions increases as IQ level increases. The mean differences as a function of IQ level were as follows: IQ ≤ 79: 6.1; IQ 80–89: 7.6; IQ 90–109: 8.6; IQ 110–119: 9.6; IQ ≥ 120: 10.3. When we look at specific differences, we find, for example, that a 10-point difference in one or the other direction occurred in 20.6% of individuals with a Full Scale IQ less than or equal to 79, whereas 48.1% of individuals with a Full Scale IQ greater than or equal to 120 had a 10-point difference in one or the other direction. Thus, individuals with lower IQs have a smaller average Verbal Scale–Performance Scale difference than those with higher IQs. If you need to use the values for the examinee's specific ability range in Tables D.1 to D.5 of the *WAIS–III WMS–III Technical Manual* to establish the base rate for differences between the Verbal Scale IQ and Performance Scale IQ, you should *divide the values in these tables by 2 to get an estimate of the base rate of Verbal Scale–Performance Scale differences for one direction only in the standardization group.*

Method 2: Compare each Verbal Scale subtest scaled score with the mean Verbal Scale scaled score. Table C-6 in Appendix C provides critical values for comparing each of the Verbal Scale subtests with the mean of the standard six Verbal Scale subtests or the mean of the standard six subtests plus Letter–Number Sequencing. The critical values range from 2.02 to 2.83 at the .05 level and from 2.41 to 3.36 at the .01 level when the standard six Verbal Scale subtests are administered. The critical values range from 2.09 to 3.15 at the .05 level and from 2.48 to 3.72 at the .01 level when seven subtests are considered. Also provided are the critical values for comparing each Verbal Scale subtest with the mean of six subtests when Letter–Number Sequencing is substituted for Digit Span.

Table B.3 (pages 208–209) in the *WAIS–III Administration and Scoring Manual* gives the cumulative frequencies with which various differences occurred in the standardization sample between an examinee's scaled score on each subtest and her or his average WAIS–III Verbal Scale scaled score. The table shows, for example, that a difference of 2.83 points between the scaled score on Vocabulary and the Verbal Scale average, composed of scores on the six standard subtests, was obtained by 5% of the standardization sample. Use this table only for differences that have first been shown to be reliable (i.e., see the significance level columns in Table B.3 in the *WAIS–III Administration and Scoring Manual* or Table C-6 in Appendix C). Differences of 2.83 to 4.67 points between each subtest scaled score and the average Verbal Scale score were obtained by 5% of the standardization sample.

Table C-7 in Appendix C provides the frequencies with which each Verbal Scale subtest scaled score differs from the mean Verbal Scale scaled score when Letter–Number Sequencing is substituted for Digit Span.

Method 3: Compare each Performance Scale subtest scaled score with the mean Performance Scale scaled score. Table C-6 in Appendix C provides critical values for comparing each of the Performance Scale subtests with the mean of the standard five Performance Scale subtests, the mean of the standard five subtests plus Symbol Search, the mean of the standard five subtests plus Object Assembly, or the mean of the standard five subtests plus both Symbol Search and Object Assembly. The critical values range from 2.40 to 3.37 at the .05 level and from 2.88 to 4.04 at the .01 level when the five standard Performance Scale subtests are administered. The critical values range from 2.50 to 3.57 at the .05 level and from 2.97 to 4.24 at the .01 level when the five standard subtests plus Symbol Search are considered. The critical values range from 2.59 to 4.01 at the .05 level and from 3.07 to 4.75 at the .01 level when all seven Performance Scale subtests are given. Table C-6 also provides the critical values for comparing each Performance Scale subtest with the mean of six subtests when Symbol Search is substituted for Object Assembly.

Table B.3 (pages 208–209) in the *WAIS–III Administration and Scoring Manual* gives the cumulative frequencies with which various differences occurred in the standardization sample between an examinee's scaled score on each subtest and his or her average WAIS–III Performance Scale scaled score. The table shows, for example, that a difference of 3.8 points (or higher) between the scaled score on Picture Completion and the Performance Scale average, composed of scores on the five standard subtests, was obtained by 5% of the standardization sample. Use this table only for differences that have first been shown to be reliable (i.e., see the significance level columns in Table B.3 in the *WAIS–III Administration and Scoring Manual* or Table C-6 in Appendix C). Differences of 3.6 to 4.4 between each subtest scaled score and the average Performance Scale score were obtained by 5% of the standardization sample.

Table C-8 in Appendix C provides the frequencies with which each Performance Scale subtest scaled score differs from the mean Performance Scale scaled score for the five standard Performance Scale subtests plus Symbol Search. And Table C-9 in Appendix C provides the frequencies with which each Performance Scale subtest scaled score differs from the mean Performance Scale scaled score when Symbol Search is substituted for Digit Symbol—Coding.

Method 4: Compare each subtest scaled score with the mean of (a) the standard 11 subtests, (b) the standard 11 subtests plus Letter–Number Sequencing, (c) the standard 11 subtests plus Letter–Number Sequencing and Symbol Search, and (d) all 14 subtests. Table C-6 in Appendix C provides critical values for comparing subtest scaled scores with the mean of the standard 11 subtests. They range from 2.24 to 4.05 at the .05 level and from 2.62 to 4.73 at the .01 level. When Letter–Number Sequencing is added, critical values range from 2.27 to 4.12 at the .05 level and from 2.64 to 4.79 at the .01 level.

When both Letter–Number Sequencing and Symbol Search are added, critical values range from 2.30 to 4.17 at the .05 level and from 2.67 to 4.85 at the .01 level. If all 14 subtests are administered, the critical values range from 2.33 to 4.58 at the .05 level and from 2.69 to 5.29 at the .01 level.

Table B.3 (pages 208–209) in the *WAIS–III Administration and Scoring Manual* gives the cumulative frequencies with which various differences occurred in the standardization sample between an examinee's scaled score on each subtest and her or his average WAIS–III scaled score based on the 11 standard subtests and on the 11 index score subtests. The table shows, for example, that a difference of 3.36 points (or higher) between the scaled score on Vocabulary and the mean scaled score, composed of scores on the 11 standard subtests, was obtained by 5% of the standardization sample. Use this table only for differences that have first been shown to be reliable (i.e., see the significance level columns in Table B.3 in the *WAIS–III Administration and Scoring Manual* or Table C-6 in Appendix C). Differences of 3.36 to 4.82 points between each subtest scaled score and the mean scaled score were obtained by 5% of the standardization sample.

Table C-10 in Appendix C provides the frequencies with which each of the 11 standard subtest scaled scores plus Letter–Number Sequencing differs from the mean scaled score.

Method 5: Compare each subtest scaled score with the mean of (a) the 11 standard subtests, but with Letter–Number Sequencing substituted for Digit Span, and (b) the standard 11 subtests, but with Symbol Search in place of Digit Symbol—Coding. Table C-6 in Appendix C provides critical values for comparing subtest scaled scores with the mean of the 11 subtests when Letter–Number Sequencing is substituted for Digit Span. They range from 2.26 to 4.05 at the .05 level and from 2.64 to 4.74 at the .01 level. When Symbol Search is substituted for Digit Symbol—Coding, critical values range from 2.25 to 4.05 at the .05 level and from 2.63 to 4.73 at the .01 level.

Tables C-11 and C-12 in Appendix C provide the frequencies with which each of the 11 subtest scaled scores in each of the combinations above differs from the respective mean scaled score.

Method 6: Compare pairs of individual subtest scaled scores. Table C-2 in Appendix C provides critical values for comparing pairs of subtest scaled scores. The values range between 3 and 5 scaled-score points at the .05 level and between 4 and 6 scaled-score points at the .01 level. The values in Table C-2 for subtest comparisons are overly liberal (i.e., they indicate significant differences that may not be true differences) when more than one comparison is made. They are most accurate when a priori planned comparisons are made, such as Comprehension versus Picture Arrangement or Digit Span versus Arithmetic. (See Chapter 10 for additional information that can guide interpretations of subtest comparisons.)

Before making *multiple comparisons,* determine the difference between the highest and lowest subtest scaled scores. If this difference is 6 scaled-score points or more, a significant difference at the .05 level is indicated. You can then interpret differences of 6 or more scaled-score points between subtests. If the difference between the highest and lowest subtest scaled scores is less than 6 scaled-score points, do not make multiple comparisons between individual subtest scaled scores. The Note to Table A-2 in Appendix A shows the formula used to compute the significant difference between the highest and lowest subtest scaled scores. The formula considers the average standard error of measurement for each of the 14 subtests and the studentized range statistic.

Method 7: Compare Verbal Comprehension, Perceptual Organization, Working Memory, and Processing Speed Index scores. Table C-2 in Appendix C presents the differences between sets of Verbal Comprehension, Perceptual Organization, Working Memory, and Processing Speed Index scores (in the form of Deviation IQs) needed to reach the .05 and .01 significance levels for ages 16–17 years and 18–19 years and for the average of the standardization sample. Table C-13 in Appendix C shows probabilities associated with various differences between WAIS–III index scores.

Table B.2 (pages 206–207) in the *WAIS–III Administration and Scoring Manual* also shows the cumulative percentages in the standardization group that obtained various index score differences in both directions. As with the Verbal Scale–Performance Scale differences, the cumulative percentages shown in Table B.2 are absolute values (i.e., they represent bi-directional differences). As noted earlier, the actual frequencies with which differences between the index scores occurred in the standardization sample in either direction alone are shown in Tables C-4 and C-5 in Appendix C. Use these tables to obtain the base rate frequencies to complete the last column ("Frequency of difference in standardization sample") of the Discrepancy Analysis Page in the WAIS–III Record Form. Table C-4 shows, for example, that a Verbal Comprehension > Perceptual Organization discrepancy of 20 points was obtained by 5.8% of the standardization sample, whereas Table C-5 shows that a Perceptual Organization > Verbal Comprehension discrepancy of 20 points was obtained by 6.0% of the standardization sample.

Tables D.1 to D.5 (pages 300–309) in the *WAIS–III WMS–III Technical Manual* present the frequency distributions of pairs of index score differences in both directions at five ability levels; these again are absolute values. As with the Verbal Scale IQs and Performance Scale IQs, the differences between pairs of index scores vary in relationship to Full Scale IQ, as well as to the type of comparison under consideration. For example, the mean difference between Working Memory and Processing Speed was 10.3 in either direction for individuals with a Full Scale IQ less than or equal to 79, whereas the mean difference was 13.7 in either direction for individuals with a Full Scale IQ greater than or equal to 120; the

mean difference between Perceptual Organization and Processing Speed was 7.5 in either direction for individuals with a Full Scale IQ less than or equal to 79, whereas the mean difference was 12.4 in either direction for individuals with a Full Scale IQ greater than or equal to 120. If you need to use the values for the examinee's specific ability range in Tables D.1 to D.5 of the *WAIS–III WMS–III Technical Manual* to establish the base rate for differences between the index scores, you should *divide these values by 2 to get an estimate of differences between the index scores for one direction only in the standardization group.*

Method 8: Compare subtest scaled scores in each index with the respective index mean. Table C-6 in Appendix C provides the critical values for comparing WAIS–III subtest scaled scores in the total sample with the respective index mean. Critical values for the Verbal Comprehension Index range from 1.70 to 2.03 at the .05 level and from 2.09 to 2.48 at the .01 level. For the Perceptual Organization Index, they range from 2.05 to 2.32 at the .05 level and from 2.51 to 2.85 at the .01 level. For the Working Memory Index, they range from 2.00 to 2.36 at the .05 level and from 2.46 to 2.89 at the .01 level. For the Processing Speed Index, they are 2.08 at the .05 level and 2.61 at the .01 level.

Table C-14 in Appendix C provides the frequencies with which each subtest scaled score in each index differs from the respective mean index scaled score.

Method 9: Compare the range of subtest scaled scores with that found in the standardization sample. The subtest scaled-score range provides information about the variability (or scatter) in an examinee's WAIS–III profile. The scaled-score range indicates the distance between the two most extreme scaled scores. It is obtained by subtracting the lowest scaled score from the highest scaled score. For example, in a profile where the highest scaled score is 15 and the lowest scaled score is 3, the range is 12, since 15 − 3 = 12.

In the standardization sample, the median scaled-score range was 7 points for the 11 standard subtests on the Full Scale, 5 points for the six standard subtests on Verbal Scale, and 5 points for the five standard subtests on the Performance Scale (see Table B.5, page 211, *WAIS–III Administration and Scoring Manual*). The scaled-score range is based on only two scores and therefore fails to take into account the variability among all 11 (or 12, 13, or 14) subtest scaled scores. The range index is still useful, however, because it provides base rate information about what occurred in the standardization sample. It also is a relatively simple measure of variability that can be compared with more complex indices of variability, such as the standard deviation of the 11 subtests and the number of subtests on which scaled scores deviate significantly from the overall mean scaled score. Research on the WAIS–R standardization sample indicated that the range is as useful a measure of variability as is the standard deviation or the number of tests that differ significantly from the mean (Matarazzo, Daniel, Prifitera, & Herman, 1988). However, we need research to determine whether this finding also applies to the WAIS–III.

Statistically Reliable vs. Empirically Observed IQ Differences

We have seen that there are two types of complementary measures that can assist in profile analysis—statistically reliable differences and empirically observed base rates. Table C-2 in Appendix C presents the differences required between the Verbal Scale and Performance Scale IQs and between index scores for statistical significance. Tables C-4 and C-5 in Appendix C give the actual (i.e., empirically observed) base rates of the frequencies of differences between the IQs and between the index scores for the standardization sample, and Table C-2 in Appendix C gives the statistical significance.

Whether an occurrence is unusual or rare depends on how one defines "unusual." A difference that occurs in 15% or 20% of the population may be considered unusual by some, whereas others may consider a difference unusual only if it occurs in 5% or 10% of the population. We believe that all significant differences, regardless of whether they are unusual, deserve consideration in evaluating an examinee's profile of abilities. However, we also believe that we can be more confident about the hypotheses we form when the difference is *also* unusual or rare. We suggest that, in order to be considered unusual or rare, the difference should occur in 15% or less (in one direction) of the standardization sample.

Let's look at two examples. First, an examinee has a Verbal Scale–Performance Scale IQ difference of 9 points, which is significant at the .05 level. This means that the Verbal Scale–Performance Scale IQ difference is reliable and unlikely to be the result of chance. Differences that are greater than chance may reflect differential functioning in the abilities measured by the Verbal Scale and Performance Scale and index scores. From Table B.2 we find that a difference of 9 points or more in one direction between the Verbal Scale IQ and Performance Scale IQ occurred in approximately 21.3% (42.7% in Table B.2, divided by 2) of the standardization sample. This 9-point difference, therefore, is statistically significant but not necessarily unusual or rare. Whether the 9-point difference is clinically meaningful is an empirical question.

Second, an examinee obtains a Verbal Scale–Performance Scale IQ difference of 26 points, which is significant at the .01 level. From Table B.2 we find that a difference of 26 points or more in one direction between the Verbal Scale IQ and Performance Scale IQ occurred in approximately 1% (2.0% in Table B.2, divided by 2) of the standardization sample. This 26-point difference, therefore, is not only statistically significant but also unusual or rare.

Clinical acumen, the examinee's medical history, behavioral observations, and the results of other tests the examinee has taken will help you interpret differences between Verbal Scale IQs and Performance Scale IQs and differences between index scores. Recognize that several variables—such as the examinee's ethnicity, linguistic background, and educational level—may influence the magnitude and direction of the Verbal Scale IQ–Performance Scale IQ discrepancy. For example, examinees with graduate-level education may have significantly higher Verbal Scale IQs than Performance Scale IQs, and examinees with non-English linguistic backgrounds and those from some ethnic minority groups (e.g., Native Americans) may have lower Verbal Scale IQs than Performance Scale IQs (Kaufman, 1990). Therefore, differences between the Verbal Scale IQs and Performance Scale IQs of examinees from non-English linguistic backgrounds are probably related to their language background and should be interpreted accordingly.

Age and WAIS–III Subtest Performance

The age norms on the WAIS–III allow us to determine how scaled-score points are awarded to individuals in each age group as a function of raw-score points (Ryan, Sattler & Lopez, 2000). Table 13-3 was constructed in the following way: First, for each age group in the reference group (ages 20–34 years), we located the raw score associated with the scaled score of 10. Then, for each raw score obtained from the reference group, we located the scaled score associated with that raw score in each age group. This procedure allowed us to compare all of the age groups on every subtest.

Table 13-3 indicates that there were few differences between older and younger people in verbal ability, but large differences in nonverbal ability. For example, individuals in the 85–89-year age group (and individuals in other older age groups as well) show little, if any, difference from the reference group (ages 20–34 years) on Information, Vocabulary, and Comprehension (0 or 1 scaled-score point); slight differences on Arithmetic, Similarities, and Digit Span (2 or 3 scaled-score points); a moderate difference on Letter–Number Sequencing (5 scaled-score points); and large differences on all of the Performance Scale subtests (6 to 9 scaled-score points).

Within the Performance Scale, measurable differences in ability begin with the 45–54-year age group. Subtests that assess speed of information processing show the greatest difference as one moves from the younger to the older groups. For example, in the reference group (20–34 years), a raw score of 33 on Symbol Search yields a scaled score of 10. However, at ages 85–89 years, the same raw score yields a scaled score of 19. Similarly, in the reference group, a raw score of 76 on Digit Symbol—Coding yields a scaled score of 10. However, at ages 85–89 years, the same raw score yields a scaled score of 18. The 9 and 8 additional scaled-score points awarded at ages 85–89 years change the percentile ranks for raw scores of 33 and 76 from 50th to 99th.

These findings suggest that older adults are not as proficient as younger adults at tasks involving working memory, process-

Table 13-3
Additional Scaled-Score Points Awarded on WAIS–III Subtests, by Age Group, When the Reference Group (Ages 20–34 Years) Receives a Scaled Score of 10

Subtest	Age group												
	16–17	*18–19*	*20–24*	*25–29*	*30–34*	*35–44*	*45–54*	*55–64*	*65–69*	*70–74*	*75–79*	*80–84*	*85–89*
Vocabulary	1	0	0	0	−1	−1	−2	−1	−1	−1	−1	1	1
Similarities	0	0	0	0	−1	−1	−1	0	1	1	1	2	3
Arithmetic	0	0	0	0	−1	−1	−1	−1	0	0	0	1	2
Digit Span	0	0	0	0	0	0	0	1	1	1	2	2	3
Information	0	0	0	0	−1	−1	−2	−1	−1	−1	−1	0	0
Comprehension	1	0	0	0	−1	−1	−2	−1	−1	−1	0	1	1
Letter–Number Sequencing	0	0	0	0	0	0	1	2	2	3	4	4	5
Picture Completion	0	0	0	0	0	0	0	1	1	2	3	4	6
Digit Symbol—Coding	0	−1	−1	0	0	0	1	3	4	5	6	7	8
Block Design	0	0	0	0	0	0	1	2	3	4	5	5	6
Matrix Reasoning	−1	0	0	0	0	0	1	2	3	4	5	5	6
Picture Arrangement	0	0	0	0	0	0	1	2	3	4	5	6	6
Symbol Search	0	−1	0	0	0	0	1	2	3	5	6	8	9
Object Assembly	0	0	0	0	0	0	1	2	3	4	6	6	7

Note. Negative values indicate performance that exceeds that of the reference group of persons 20 to 34 years old. The table indicates that raw scores yielding a scaled score of 10 in the WAIS–III reference group (ages 20–34 years) yield, in most cases, the same or higher scaled scores in the nine age groups over 34 years. The greatest change is at ages 75–89 years. For example, in the reference group, a raw score of 76 on Digit Symbol—Coding yields a scaled score of 10; but at ages 85–89 years, this same raw score yields a scaled score of 18. The 8 additional scaled-score points awarded at ages 85–89 years change the percentile rank for a raw score of 76 from 50 to 99. Symbol Search exhibits the most change of any WAIS–III subtest, showing a steady increment in scaled-score points from age 35 to age 89.

The greatest changes are consistently shown on the Performance Scale subtests. On the Verbal Scale subtests, the increment in scaled-score points is never greater than 5 points, with most changes being either plus or minus 1 or 2 points. Information, Comprehension, and Vocabulary show the least amount of change with advancing age. The one exception on the Verbal Scale subtests is Letter–Number Sequencing. On this subtest, for a performance that is average in the reference group, 5 additional points are awarded at ages 85–89 years and 4 additional points at ages 75–84 years.

The positive values in this table actually reflect less proficient ability. This is more graphically revealed when the raw-score points needed at the various age groups to obtain an average scaled score are examined. For example, as we have seen, on Digit Symbol—Coding a raw score of 76 yields a scaled score of 10 for the reference group. At ages 85 to 89 years, however, a raw score of only 33 is required to obtain a scaled score of 10. Thus, individuals in the oldest age group need 43 fewer raw-score points than do those in the reference group to obtain average status in their age group.

ing speed, perceptual organization, and the capacity to handle mental operations that involve nonverbal abstract reasoning. If we view the performance tasks as measures of fluid intelligence and the verbal tasks as measures of crystallized intelligence, then the WAIS–III age norms indicate that fluid abilities are not as well developed as crystallized abilities in older people. *These differences do not reflect changes in intel-* *ligence with age; rather, they show only how older adults compare with younger adults.* To study changes in intelligence with age, we would need to have longitudinal data to see how 80-year-olds, for example, functioned on these same tasks when they were 20-year-olds. The WAIS–III norms indicate that, in some respects, people of advanced age differ in ability from those who are younger. Longitudinal research on twins indicates that performance on Block Design declines steadily from 60 to 90 years, whereas there is little or no age-related change in performance on Vocabulary (McArdle, Prescott, Hamagami, & Horn, 1998). These findings support the hypothesis that fluid intelligence, but not crystallized intelligence, shows a marked decrement with advancing age.

COMPARISONS BETWEEN WAIS–III SUBTESTS

The following list illustrates how you can compare WAIS–III subtests not covered in Chapter 10. Note that the list does not include all possible comparisons, nor does it reflect all possible interpretations. However, these examples should help you develop interpretations for other subtest comparisons as well. Treat all hypotheses developed from subtest comparisons as tentative, not definitive. In Appendix D, see Table D-3 for a summary of interpretive rationales for the WAIS–III subtests and Table D-5 for suggestive remediation activities for combinations of subtests. Develop your hypotheses based on both significant differences between subtest scaled scores and the absolute values of the subtest scaled scores. Thus, *never describe scaled scores of 10 or higher as reflecting absolute weaknesses, and never describe scaled scores of 9 or lower as reflecting absolute strengths.* Also, see Table D-1 in Appendix D for percentile ranks and qualitative descriptions associated with Wechsler subtest scaled scores.

COMPARISON OF VERBAL SCALE SUBTESTS

1. *Digit Span (DS) and Letter–Number Sequencing (LN).* This comparison relates two subtests that measure short-term auditory memory. In Digit Span the stimuli are numbers only, whereas in Letter–Number Sequencing the stimuli are both numbers and letters and the task involves a greater degree of information processing.

- DS > LN: High Digit Span and low Letter–Number Sequencing may suggest adequate immediate short-term auditory memory when the task requires passive recall without information processing but less adequate short-term memory when the task requires rote memorization, information processing, and the ability to mentally visualize the stimuli.
- DS < LN: Low Digit Span and high Letter–Number Sequencing may suggest inadequate immediate short-term auditory memory when the task requires primarily passive recall but adequate short-term memory when the task is more challenging and requires rote memorization, information processing, and the ability to mentally visualize the stimuli.

COMPARISONS OF PERFORMANCE SCALE SUBTESTS

1. *Matrix Reasoning (MR) and Block Design (BD).* This comparison relates two subtests that measure nonverbal rea-

soning ability. Matrix Reasoning requires analogic perceptual reasoning and has no time limits, whereas Block Design requires analysis and synthesis and has time limits.

- MR > BD: High Matrix Reasoning and low Block Design may suggest adequate analogic perceptual reasoning ability but inadequate perceptual analysis and synthesis skills when working under time pressure.
- MR < BD: Low Matrix Reasoning and high Block Design may suggest inadequate perceptual reasoning ability but adequate spatial visualization ability when working under time pressure.

2. *Matrix Reasoning (MR) and Picture Arrangement (PA).* This comparison relates nonverbal reasoning ability (Matrix Reasoning) to the capacity to anticipate and plan in a social context with time limits (Picture Arrangement).

- MR > PA: High Matrix Reasoning and low Picture Arrangement may suggest adequate analogic perceptual reasoning ability but inadequate ability to anticipate and plan in a social context when working under time pressure.
- MR < PA: Low Matrix Reasoning and high Picture Arrangement may suggest inadequate analogic perceptual reasoning ability but adequate ability to anticipate and plan in a social context when working under time pressure.

3. *Matrix Reasoning (MR) and Picture Completion (PC).* This comparison relates analogic nonverbal reasoning ability (Matrix Reasoning) to attention to detail under time pressure (Picture Completion).

- MR > PC: High Matrix Reasoning and low Picture Completion may suggest adequate analogic perceptual reasoning ability but inadequate ability to attend to details when working under time pressure.
- MR < PC: Low Matrix Reasoning and high Picture Completion may suggest inadequate analogic perceptual reasoning ability but adequate ability to attend to details when working under time pressure.

4. *Matrix Reasoning (MR) and Object Assembly (OA).* This comparison relates analogic nonverbal reasoning ability (Matrix Reasoning) to inductive reasoning (working from parts to a whole), visual-motor coordination, and speed of performance (Object Assembly).

- MR > OA: High Matrix Reasoning and low Object Assembly may suggest adequate analogic perceptual reasoning ability but inadequate inductive reasoning and visual-motor coordination when working under time pressure.
- MR < OA: Low Matrix Reasoning and high Object Assembly may suggest inadequate analogic perceptual reasoning ability but adequate inductive reasoning and visual-motor coordination when working under time pressure.

5. *Matrix Reasoning (MR) and Digit Symbol—Coding (CD).* This comparison relates analogic nonverbal reasoning ability (Matrix Reasoning) to perceptual discrimination abil-

ity, speed and accuracy, and attention (Digit Symbol—Coding).

- MR > CD: High Matrix Reasoning and low Digit Symbol—Coding may suggest adequate analogic perceptual reasoning ability but inadequate perceptual discrimination ability, speed and accuracy, and attention.
- MR < CD: Low Matrix Reasoning and high Digit Symbol—Coding may suggest inadequate analogic perceptual reasoning ability but adequate perceptual discrimination ability, speed and accuracy, and attention.

6. *Matrix Reasoning (MR) and Symbol Search (SS).* This comparison relates analogic nonverbal reasoning ability (Matrix Reasoning) to perceptual discrimination, speed and accuracy, and attention and concentration (Symbol Search).

- MR > SS: High Matrix Reasoning and low Symbol Search may suggest adequate analogic perceptual reasoning ability but inadequate perceptual discrimination ability, speed and accuracy, and attention and concentration.
- MR < SS: Low Matrix Reasoning and high Symbol Search may suggest inadequate analogic perceptual reasoning ability but adequate perceptual discrimination ability, speed and accuracy, and attention and concentration.

COMPARISONS OF VERBAL AND PERFORMANCE SCALE SUBTESTS

1. *Similarities (S) and Matrix Reasoning (MR).* This comparison relates the ability to engage in conceptual thinking (Similarities) to analogic nonverbal reasoning ability (Matrix Reasoning).

- S > MR: High Similarities and low Matrix Reasoning may suggest adequate ability to use factual knowledge conceptually but inadequate analogic nonverbal reasoning ability.
- S < MR: Low Similarities and high Matrix Reasoning may suggest that conceptual reasoning is less well developed than analogic nonverbal reasoning ability.

2. *Comprehension (C) and Matrix Reasoning (MR).* This comparison relates the ability to use information to solve hypothetical everyday problems involving the social world (Comprehension) to analogic nonverbal reasoning ability (Matrix Reasoning).

- C > MR: High Comprehension and low Matrix Reasoning may suggest adequate ability to use information to solve hypothetical everyday problems but inadequate analogic nonverbal reasoning ability.
- C < MR: Low Comprehension and high Matrix Reasoning may suggest that the ability to use information to solve hypothetical everyday problems involving the social world is less well developed than analogic nonverbal reasoning ability.

3. *Vocabulary (V) and Matrix Reasoning (MR).* This comparison relates the ability to understand or express the

meanings of individual words (Vocabulary) to analogic nonverbal reasoning ability (Matrix Reasoning).

- V > MR: High Vocabulary and low Matrix Reasoning may suggest adequate ability to understand or express the meanings of individual words but inadequate analogic nonverbal reasoning ability.
- V < MR: Low Vocabulary and high Matrix Reasoning may suggest inadequate ability to understand or express the meanings of individual words but adequate analogic nonverbal reasoning ability.

COMPARISONS OF THREE OR MORE SUBTESTS

1. *Matrix Reasoning (MR), Block Design (BD), and Picture Completion (PC).* Matrix Reasoning, Block Design, and Picture Completion all require perceptual reasoning, attention to detail, and concentration. In addition, both Matrix Reasoning and Block Design may involve spatial ability.

- MR, BD > PC: High Matrix Reasoning and Block Design and low Picture Completion may suggest that spatial reasoning ability is better developed than nonspatial reasoning ability.
- MR, BD < PC: Low Matrix Reasoning and Block Design and high Picture Completion may suggest that spatial reasoning ability is less well developed than nonspatial reasoning ability.

2. *Matrix Reasoning (MR), Block Design (BD), and Picture Arrangement (PA).* Matrix Reasoning, Block Design, and Picture Arrangement all require perceptual reasoning, attention to detail, and concentration. In addition, both Matrix Reasoning and Block Design may involve spatial ability.

- MR, BD > PA: High Matrix Reasoning and Block Design and low Picture Arrangement may suggest that spatial reasoning ability is better developed than nonspatial reasoning ability applied to social situations.
- MR, BD < PA: Low Matrix Reasoning and Block Design and high Picture Arrangement may suggest that spatial reasoning ability is less well developed than nonspatial reasoning ability applied to social situations.

3. *Matrix Reasoning (MR), Block Design (BD), Vocabulary (V), and Information (I).* Matrix Reasoning and Block Design require perceptual reasoning and fluid intelligence, whereas Vocabulary and Information reflect the extent of previously learned and stored verbal material and crystallized intelligence.

- MR, BD > V, I: High Matrix Reasoning and Block Design and low Vocabulary and Information may suggest that spatial reasoning ability and novel problem-solving capacities are better developed than education-related capacities dependent on well-learned verbal facts and relationships.
- MR, BD < V, I: Low Matrix Reasoning and Block Design and high Vocabulary and Information may suggest that spatial reasoning and novel problem-solving skills are less

well developed than capacities dependent on well-learned facts and relationships.

4. *Digit Span (DS), Letter–Number Sequencing (LN), Digit Symbol—Coding (CD), and Symbol Search (SS).* Digit Span and Letter–Number Sequencing require short-term auditory memory and attention and concentration, whereas Digit Symbol—Coding and Symbol Search require short-term visual memory and attention and concentration.

- DS, LN > CD, SS: High Digit Span and Letter–Number Sequencing and low Digit Symbol—Coding and Symbol Search may suggest that short-term auditory memory is better developed than short-term visual memory.
- DS, LN < CD, SS: Low Digit Span and Letter–Number Sequencing and high Digit Symbol—Coding and Symbol Search may suggest that short-term visual memory is better developed than short-term auditory memory.

ASSETS OF THE WAIS–III

The WAIS–III is a well-standardized test, with excellent reliability and good concurrent and construct validity. The 14 subtests are divided into a Verbal Scale and a Performance Scale, and the test provides a Verbal Scale IQ, Performance Scale IQ, and Full Scale IQ. When the two supplementary subtests are administered in conjunction with the standard 11 subtests, the test also yields four index scores: Verbal Comprehension, Perceptual Organization, Working Memory, and Processing Speed. This procedure is helpful in clinical and psychoeducational work and in the assessment of brain-behavior relationships. A valuable feature of the test is that most examinees take a comparable battery of subtests. Parts of the test can be administered to examinees limited by sensory impairment (for example, the Verbal Scale may be given to blind individuals or to those with motor handicaps, and the Performance Scale may be given to hard-of-hearing individuals). Here are some other assets of the WAIS–III:

1. *Excellent standardization.* The standardization procedures were excellent, sampling four geographical regions; both sexes; White, Black, Hispanic, and other racial/ethnic groups; and the entire socioeconomic status range. The standardization sample well represents the nation as a whole for the age groups covered by the test.

2. *Excellent overall psychometric properties.* The WAIS–III has excellent reliability for the IQs and index scores. The studies in the *WAIS–III—WMS–III Technical Manual* indicate good concurrent and construct validity, although more research is needed to evaluate the different forms of validity of the latest edition of the test; this is especially true of the index scores.

3. *Good administration procedures.* The procedures described in the *WAIS–III Administration and Scoring Manual* are excellent. The examiner actively probes responses to evaluate the breadth of the examinee's knowledge and to determine whether the individual truly knows the answer. On items that require two reasons for maximum credit, examinees are asked for another reason when they give only one reason. These procedures ensure that the test does not penalize examinees for failing to understand the demands of the questions. The emphasis on probing questions and queries is extremely desirable. Also desirable is the inclusion of practice items on some subtests.

4. *Good manual.* The *WAIS–III Administration and Scoring Manual* is easy to use; it provides clear directions and tables. Examiners are aided by instructions printed in a different color from that of other text material. The manual provides helpful abbreviations for recording the examinee's responses, such as P for Pass, F for Fail, Q for Query/Question, DK for Don't Know, NR for No Response, Inc. for Incomplete, PC for Points Correctly, and PX for Points Incorrectly. The *WAIS–III WMS–III Technical Manual* provides extensive information concerning the validity, reliability, and interpretation of the test.

5. *Helpful scoring criteria.* The criteria for scoring replies have been carefully prepared. The Vocabulary and Similarities scoring guidelines, for example, detail the rationale for 2-, 1-, and 0-point scores. Several examples demonstrate application of the scoring principles. Many typical responses are provided and scored, and those deemed to need further inquiry are indicated by a "(Q)." Scoring criteria and sample responses for the Vocabulary, Comprehension, and Similarities subtests are placed with the subtest proper, rather than in appendixes in the back of the manual.

6. *Decreased reliance on timed performance.* Although speed of performance is important on the WAIS–III, the new Matrix Reasoning subtest has no time limits and the Object Assembly subtest, which relies heavily on bonus points for quick completion, is now an optional subtest and is not required for calculation of the IQ or index scores. The number of bonus points possible for quick performance has been reduced on some subtests. The reduced time requirements appear to be an asset in testing elderly examinees.

7. *Co-norming with an individual measure of memory and linking to a measure of academic achievement.* The WAIS–III was co-normed with the Wechsler Memory Scale–III (WMS–III; Wechsler, 1997) for all 13 age groups in the WAIS–III standardization sample. For persons in the age range 16–19 years, the WAIS–III was linked with the Wechsler Individual Achievement Test (WIAT; The Psychological Corporation, 1992). These procedures provide information about what scores to expect on the WMS–III and WIAT when you know the examinee's scores on the WAIS–III, and vice versa.

LIMITATIONS OF THE WAIS–III

Although the WAIS–III is, overall, an excellent instrument, some problems do exist.

1. *Limited floor and ceiling.* The test is not applicable for severely retarded or extremely gifted individuals.

2. *Low reliability of three subtests.* Reliability coefficients for the Picture Arrangement, Symbol Search, and Object Assembly subtests are lower than .80 at most ages.

3. *Nonuniformity of subtest scaled scores.* Because the range of scaled scores is less than 19 on some subtests, there may be minor problems in profile analysis in some age groups at the lower and upper extremes of scores.

4. *Difficulty in interpreting norms when you substitute a supplementary subtest for a regular subtest.* With norms for the three IQs based on 11 standard subtests, there is no way of knowing precisely what scores mean when you substitute one of the supplementary subtests (Letter–Number Sequencing and Symbol Search) or the optional subtest (Object Assembly) for a regular subtest. You should make a substitution of this kind only in unusual circumstances and, when you report the results, label them "tentative."

5. *Possible difficulties in scoring responses.* Work with previous editions of the WAIS suggests that Similarities, Vocabulary, and Comprehension may be difficult to score. The *WAIS–III WMS–III Technical Manual* cites a series of scoring studies in which there was high agreement among examiners in the scores they gave to these subtests (and to the Information subtest as well). These results are encouraging, but researchers need to replicate them.

6. *Poor quality or design of some test materials.* The templates for scoring the Digit Symbol—Coding and Symbol Search subtests are poorly constructed and may tear and disintegrate quickly.

CONCLUDING COMMENT ON THE WAIS–III

Overall, the WAIS–III represents a major contribution to the field of intelligence testing of adolescents and adults. It serves as an important instrument for this purpose.

THINKING THROUGH THE ISSUES

1. Which subtests on the WAIS–III do you like the most, and which ones do you like the least?
2. Do you believe that the WAIS–III is culturally biased? Explain your reasoning.
3. Why do you think some cognitive functions differ between older and younger people?
4. How would the WAIS–III assist in a vocational assessment?
5. How could the results of the WAIS–III be useful in designing rehabilitation programs?
6. How does the WAIS–III differ from the WISC–III? Compared to the WISC–III, what are some unique features of the WAIS–III?
7. Should the WAIS–III be considered a neuropsychological instrument? What is the basis for your answer?
8. Is it possible for an examinee to fake cognitive problems on the WAIS–III? If so, in what assessment situations might faking be a potential problem?
9. Which WAIS–III subtest results might be most distorted by depression and by anxiety?

SUMMARY

Vocabulary

1. Vocabulary measures learning ability, fund of information, richness of ideas, memory, concept formation, and language development. The subtest is an excellent measure of g and contributes to the Verbal Comprehension Index. Subtest specificity is adequate at 11 age groups. Vocabulary is a reliable subtest (r_{xx} = .93). It is relatively easy to administer but can be difficult to score.

Similarities

2. Similarities measures verbal concept formation. The subtest ties with Information as the second-best measure of g and contributes to the Verbal Comprehension Index. Subtest specificity is ample or adequate at 8 age groups. Similarities is a reliable subtest (r_{xx} = .86). It is easy to administer but can be difficult to score.

Arithmetic

3. Arithmetic measures numerical reasoning ability. The subtest is a good measure of g and contributes to the Working Memory Index. Subtest specificity is ample or adequate at all age groups. Arithmetic is a reliable subtest (r_{xx} = .88). It is easy to administer and score.

Digit Span

4. Digit Span measures short-term sequential auditory memory and attention. The subtest is a fair measure of g and contributes to the Working Memory Index. Subtest specificity is ample at all age groups. Digit Span is a reliable subtest (r_{xx} = .90). It is easy to administer and score.

Information

5. Information measures the range of information the examinee has acquired as a result of natural endowment; education; and cultural opportunities, experiences, and interests. Memory is an important aspect of performance on the subtest. The subtest ties with Similarities as the second-best measure of g in the test and contributes to the Verbal Comprehension Index. Subtest specificity is ample or adequate at all age groups. Information is a reliable subtest (r_{xx} = .91). It is easy to administer and score.

Comprehension

6. Comprehension measures social judgment—the ability to use facts in a pertinent, meaningful, and emotionally appropriate manner. The subtest is a good measure of g and contributes to the Verbal Comprehension Index. Subtest specificity is ample or adequate at 6 age groups. Comprehension is a reliable subtest (r_{xx} = .84). It is easy to administer but can be difficult to score.

Letter–Number Sequencing

7. Letter–Number Sequencing is a supplementary subtest that measures attention, short-term auditory memory, and information processing. The subtest is a fair measure of g and contributes to the Working Memory Index. Subtest specificity is ample or adequate at 5 age groups. Comprehension is a reliable subtest (r_{xx} = .82). It is easy to administer and score.

Picture Completion

8. Picture Completion measures the ability to differentiate between essential and nonessential details. It requires concentration, reasoning, visual organization, and long-term visual memory. The subtest is a fair measure of g and contributes to the Perceptual Organization Index and to the Verbal Comprehension Index. Subtest specificity is ample at 12 of the 13 age groups. Picture Completion is a reasonably reliable subtest (r_{xx} = .83). It is easy to administer and relatively easy to score.

Digit Symbol—Coding

9. Digit Symbol—Coding measures visual-motor coordination, speed of mental operation, attentional skills, visual acuity, visual scanning and tracking, short-term memory, and cognitive flexibility. The subtest is a fair measure of g and contributes to the Processing Speed Index. Subtest specificity is ample at all age groups. Digit Symbol—Coding is a reliable subtest (r_{xx} = .84). It is easy to administer and score.

Block Design

10. Block Design measures nonverbal concept formation and requires perceptual organization, spatial visualization, and abstract conceptualization. The subtest ties with Matrix Reasoning as the best measure of g among the Performance Scale subtests and contributes to the Perceptual Organization Index. Subtest specificity is either ample or adequate at all age groups. Block Design is a reliable subtest (r_{xx} = .86). It can be difficult to administer but is easy to score.

Matrix Reasoning

11. Matrix Reasoning measures perceptual reasoning ability without a speed component. Analogic reasoning, attention to detail, and concentration are required for successful performance. The subtest ties with Block Design as the second best measure of g among the Performance Scale subtests and contributes to the Perceptual Organization Index and to a limited extent to the Working Memory Index. Subtest specificity is ample at all age groups. Matrix Reasoning is a reliable subtest (r_{xx} = .90). It is relatively easy to administer and score.

Picture Arrangement

12. Picture Arrangement is a measure of nonverbal reasoning that involves planning ability, anticipation, visual organization, and temporal sequencing. The subtest is a fair measure of g and contributes to the Perceptual Organization Index and to the Verbal Comprehension Index. Subtest specificity is either ample or adequate at six age groups. Picture Arrangement is a relatively reliable subtest (r_{xx} = .74). It is easy to administer and score.

Symbol Search

13. Symbol Search is a supplementary subtest that measures perceptual discrimination, speed and accuracy, attention and concentration, short-term memory, and cognitive flexibility. The subtest is a fair measure of g and contributes to the Processing Speed Index. Subtest specificity is either ample or adequate at three age groups. Symbol Search is a relatively reliable subtest (r_{xx} = .77). It is easy to administer and score.

Object Assembly

14. Object Assembly is an optional subtest that measures synthesis skill and visual organizational ability. The subtest is a fair measure of g and contributes to the Perceptual Organization Index. Specificity is adequate for one age group. Object Assembly is a relatively reliable subtest (r_{xx} = .70). It can be difficult to administer but relatively easy to score.

Interpreting the WAIS–III

15. Interpreting the WAIS–III is similar to interpreting the WISC–III.
16. The WAIS–III norms indicate that there are few differences between older and younger people in verbal ability, but large differences, in favor of younger people, in nonverbal ability.

Comparisons Between WAIS–III Subtests

17. Comparisons between the WAIS–III subtests may prove useful in generating hypotheses about the examinee's performance.

Assets of the WAIS–III

18. The assets of the WAIS–III include its excellent standardization, excellent overall psychometric properties, good administrative procedures, good manual, helpful scoring criteria, decreased reliance on timed performance, and co-norming with the WMS–III.

Limitations of the WAIS–III

19. The limitations of the WAIS–III include limited floor and ceiling, low reliability of three subtests, nonuniformity of subtest scaled scores, difficulty in interpreting norms when you substitute a supplementary subtest for a regular subtest, possible difficulty in scoring responses, and poor quality or design of some test materials.

Concluding Comment

20. Overall, the WAIS–III represents a major contribution to the field of intelligence testing of adolescents and adults. It serves as an important instrument for this purpose.

KEY TERMS, CONCEPTS, AND NAMES

STUDY QUESTIONS

1. Discuss the rationale, factor analytic findings, reliability and correlational highlights, and administrative and interpretive considerations for each of the WAIS–III subtests: Vocabulary, Similarities, Arithmetic, Digit Span, Information, Comprehension, Letter–Number Sequencing, Picture Completion, Digit Symbol—Coding, Block Design, Matrix Reasoning, Picture Arrangement, Symbol Search, and Object Assembly.

2. Discuss the intent of profile analysis, methods of profile analysis, and approaches to profile analysis on the WAIS–III.

3. Discuss the assets and limitations of the WAIS–III.

14

STANFORD-BINET INTELLIGENCE SCALE: FOURTH EDITION

General intelligence is well established as one of the most significant phenotypic human attributes. It is the behavioral attribute that distinguishes us from other species. Human intelligence accounts for our ability to transform our environment, to create culture and to record as well as transmit culture to future generations.

—David Lubinski and Lloyd G. Humphreys

1937 and 1960 Stanford-Binet Intelligence Scales

Introduction to the SB: IV

Standardization

Composite Scores, Standard Age Scores, and Test-Age Equivalents

Reliability

Validity

Correlations Between Subtests and Between Subtests and the Composite Score

SB: IV Composite Scores and Stratification Variables

Factor Analysis

Administering the SB: IV

Vocabulary

Comprehension

Absurdities

Verbal Relations

Pattern Analysis

Copying

Matrices

Paper Folding and Cutting

Quantitative

Number Series

Equation Building

Bead Memory

Memory for Sentences

Memory for Digits

Memory for Objects

Interpreting the SB: IV

A Successive-Level Approach to Test Interpretation

Comparisons Between Factor Scores That Can Guide Interpretations

Comparisons Between Subtests That Can Guide Interpretations

Additional Suggestions for Using and Interpreting the SB: IV

Assets of the SB: IV

Limitations of the SB: IV

Concluding Comment on the SB: IV

Thinking Through the Issues

Summary

Goals and Objectives

This chapter is designed to enable you to do the following:

• Describe the different forms of the Stanford-Binet Intelligence Scale

• Evaluate the psychometric properties of the Stanford-Binet Intelligence Scale: Fourth Edition (SB: IV)

• Describe the rationale, factor analytic findings, reliability, correlational highlights, and administrative and interpretive considerations for the 15 SB: IV subtests

• Describe profile analysis for the SB: IV

• Analyze and evaluate SB: IV scores from a multiple-factor perspective

• Evaluate the assets and limitations of the SB: IV

Figure 14-1. Stanford-Binet Intelligence Scale: Fourth Edition. Courtesy Riverside Publishing Company.

The Stanford-Binet Intelligence Scale: Fourth Edition (SB: IV; Thorndike, Hagen, & Sattler, 1986a) contains 15 subtests and covers an age range of 2 to 23 years (see Figure 14-1 and Exhibit 14-1). The SB: IV uses a point-scale format similar to that of the Wechsler tests. Prior editions of the Stanford-Binet Intelligence Scales, as noted in Chapter 5, used an age-scale format. Table 14-1 summarizes some major characteristics of the earlier versions of the Binet-Simon Scales and the Stanford-Binet Intelligence Scale.

1937 AND 1960 STANFORD-BINET INTELLIGENCE SCALES

1937 Stanford-Binet Scales

In 1937, after 21 years, Terman and Merrill revised the 1916 Stanford-Binet Intelligence Scale. They designed two new forms, Form L and Form M. Reviewers recognized the 1937 revision as a milestone in the progress of individual testing of intelligence. The scale was better standardized than the

former version, two forms were available, and there were more performance items at the earlier levels. New types of items were added at the preschool and adult levels, and more use was made of differential scoring of the same items. Terman and Merrill improved the memory items, wording of questions, year-level assignments, and scoring of the Vocabulary items. They extended the scale downward to year level II, with items appearing at half-year levels between years II and V, and upward to the Superior Adult III level. They also added items for year levels XI and XII.

The scales had excellent reliability (ranging from .98, for examinees with IQs below 70, to .90, for examinees with IQs above 129) and acceptable validity (r of .40 to .50 with school success). Factor analytic studies indicated that most of the items loaded heavily on a common factor, although group factors (e.g., verbal, memory, visualization, spatial, and reasoning) also were reported.

The 1937 scales represented a significant improvement over the 1916 scale. The scales were better statistically and had many clinical applications—the scales were efficient instruments for diagnosing mental retardation and for gaining

Exhibit 14-1
Stanford-Binet Intelligence Scale: Fourth Edition–Like Items

1. Vocabulary (14 pictures, 32 words)
The task on the first 14 items is to name the pictured object. Words 15 through 46 are both given orally and shown to the examinee; the examinee must define these words.

train   dime   taut   cryptography

2. Bead Memory (42 items)
The task is to reproduce bead patterns by finding them in photographs or placing beads on a stick (see Figure 14-1).

3. Quantitative (40 questions)
The task is to solve quantitative problems.

Match

Count the number of blocks in the picture.
What is the smallest whole number that can be divided evenly by 1, 2, and 3?
How many 12-inch-by-12-inch tiles will be needed to cover a floor that is 6 feet by 6 feet?

4. Memory for Sentences (42 items)
The task is to repeat successively longer sentences.

Say: Small cow.
Say: High clouds appeared on the horizon.
Say: The field of science can aid mankind by discovering many useful things.

5. Pattern Analysis (42 items)
For the first six items, the task is to complete a form board (see Figure 14-1). For the remaining items, the task is to reproduce stimulus designs using two, three, four, six, or nine blocks (see Figure 14-1). An example of a Pattern Analysis design is shown below.

6. Comprehension (42 questions)
The task is to point to body parts (at earlier levels) and to answer questions dealing with social comprehension.

Point to the doll's foot (see Figure 14-1).
Why do we have nurses?
What advantages does an airplane have over a car?
Why do we have a Congress?

7. Absurdities (32 items)
The task is to identify the incongruity in pictures, such as those depicting writing with a spoon, riding a bicycle that has one wheel missing, and a map of the United States with Florida on the West coast.

8. Memory for Digits (14 series/12 series)
Digits Forward: The task is to recall series of digits, three to nine digits in lenth, in the order given (Example: 3-9-5).
Digits Reversed: The task is to recall series of digits, two to seven digits in length, in *reverse* order (Example: 5-8-9-4).

9. Copying (28 items)
The task is to reproduce designs with blocks (items 1 to 12) or to copy simple and complex geometric designs—such as lines, rectangles, and partial circles—that are shown on cards.

10. Memory for Objects (14 items)
The task is to recall pictured objects in the exact sequence in which they were presented. The examinee points to the pictured items on a card that contains both the stimulus items and distractor items. For example, the examinee is first shown a picture of a knife and a dog and then shown a card containing pictures of a knife, dog, spoon, cat, and house.

11. Matrices (26 items)
The task is to select the object, design, or letter that best completes the matrix. An example of a Matrices item is shown below.

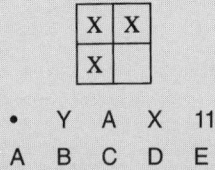

•	Y	A	X	11
A	B	C	D	E

12. Number Series (26 items)
The task is to predict the numbers in a series. To succeed, the examinee must discern the pattern in the series.

5 , 4 , 3, , ___ , ___ ,
4 , 4 , 4 , 4 , ___ , ___ ,
14 , 13 , 12 , 11 , ___ , ___ ,
10 , 2 , 11 , 2 , 12 , ___ , ___ ,

13. Paper Folding and Cutting (18 items)
The task is to select the picture that shows how a folded and cut piece of paper would look unfolded.

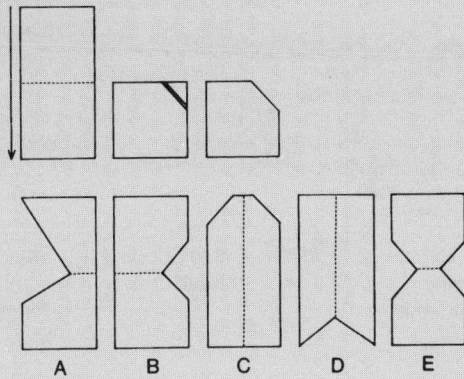

A   B   C   D   E

14. Verbal Relations (18 items)
The task is to indicate how the first three items are alike but different from the fourth.

How are a dog, cow, and pig alike but different from a bird?
How are a car, truck, and motorcycle alike but different from a bicycle?

15. Equation Building (18 items)
The task is to arrange numbers and mathematical signs (+, −, ÷, etc.) into an equation.

4   2   6   +   =
¼   2   7   1   −   ÷   =

Note. These items are similar to those on the Stanford-Binet: IV, but they are not actually from the test.

Table 14-1
Some Characteristics of the Binet-Simon and Stanford-Binet Scales from 1905 to 1972

Scale year	Authors	Number of tests	Year levels covered	Modifications made in revisions	Limitations
1905	Binet and Simon	30	Very low grade idiots to upper elementary grades	—	Poor standardization ($N=50$) Inadequate range Tests did not always discriminate No objective scoring method
1908	Binet and Simon	59	III to XIII	New tests added Some tests eliminated, especially at the idiot level Tests grouped according to age commonly passed Mental-age concept introduced	Inadequate standardization ($N=203$) No credit given for fractions of a year Lower year level tests too easy, higher year level tests too difficult Inadequate scoring and administrative procedures Unequal numbers of tests at different year levels Almost the same limitations as noted for 1905 scale
1911	Binet and Simon	54	III to Adult	New tests added, some eliminated Credit given for fraction of a year Tests shifted More detail added to instructions Adult year level included	Almost the same limitations as noted for 1908 scale; there were no fundamental changes
1916	Terman	90	III to Superior Adult I	New tests added Some tests revised Location changed for some tests Scoring and administrative procedures changed and better organized Alternative tests introduced IQ concept introduced Representative sampling attempted	Poor standardization at the extremes Only one form Inadequate standardization ($N=1,000$ native-born Californian children and 400 adults) Inadequate measure of adult mental capacity Too heavily weighted with verbal and abstract materials Inadequate scoring and administrative procedures at some points Some tests dated by the 1930s Some tests placed at wrong age level Too much credit for rote memory
1937	Terman and Merrill	129	II to Superior Adult III	Standardization improved ($N=3,184$) Two forms (L and M) provided More performance tests included at earlier year levels	Equal variability not present at all ages Sample not fully representative of general population Some tests difficult to score Ceiling too low for above-average adolescents
1960	Terman and Merrill	142	II to Superior Adult III	Best tests from Forms L and M incorporated in one form (L-M) New group of children used to check changes in test difficulty ($N=4,498$) Some tests relocated, dropped, or rescored Deviation IQ used, with $M=100$ and $SD=16$ Age 18 years used as ceiling level, rather than 16 years Scoring principles clarified	Too heavily weighted with verbal materials Originality and creative abilities not measured Inadequate for very superior students Abstract verbal tests appeared at too low a level and rote memory tests appeared at too high a level Restandardization procedures not appropriate
1973	Thorndike	—	—	Restandardized in 1972 ($N=2,100$)	—

insights into a examinee's temperament. The 1937 Stanford-Binet combined facets of a clinical interview with those of an objective assessment.

The 1937 scales, however, had several problems. Verbal items were too highly emphasized, an age-scale format was used instead of a point-scale format, the ceiling was inadequate, some item placements were incorrect, rote memory items were emphasized, administration procedures were faulty in places, statistical data were not complete, only one score was provided, g was inadequately measured, some items were inappropriate for adults, and there were some clinical limitations (e.g., comparing verbal and performance deficits was difficult). Despite these difficulties, the 1937 scales were extremely popular: they yielded acceptable validity coefficients, served as the standard for the development of other tests of cognitive ability, and functioned as important tools in clinical and educational settings.

1960 Stanford-Binet Scale: Form L-M

In 1960, Terman and Merrill revised the 1937 scales, although the 1960 edition was not a genuine revision. Terman and Merrill selected the best items from Form L and Form M of the 1937 scales and combined them into a new form. They did not obtain a new standardization group; instead, to check on changes in item difficulty, they used a sample of 4,498 participants who had taken the scale between 1950 and 1954. New material was not introduced, nor were the essential features of the scale changed. With the 1960 revision, there was only one form. The 1960 Form L-M manual did not present validity data; rather, validity rested on the fact that the same types of items were used as in the 1937 scales.

An important development in Form L-M was the replacement of the 1937 scale's IQ tables, which represented the conventional ratio IQ, with Deviation IQs for ages 2 to 18 years. The Deviation IQ is a normalized standard score with a mean of 100 and a standard deviation of 16. It expresses the deviation of the ratio IQ from the mean ratio IQ at each age level. The Deviation IQ controls for the variability in IQ distributions that was present in the former editions. A specific IQ at different ages in Form L-M indicates close to the same relative ability or standing regardless of the age of the examinee.

Reviewers expressed dissatisfaction with how the Deviation IQs were constructed in the 1960 scale and with the norming sample, however. Additionally, reviewers criticized the 1960 scale for being too heavily weighted with verbal materials, for not measuring creative abilities, and for having some items improperly placed. Nonetheless, the 1960 revision produced acceptable validity coefficients and remained one of the standard instruments for the assessment of children's intelligence until it was revised in the 1980s.

1972 Norms

In 1972, Robert Thorndike, working with The Riverside Publishing Company, published revised norms for the 1960 Form L-M. Except for two minor changes in the test procedures (Thorndike substituted a more attractive female doll card and the word "charcoal" for "coal"), the subtests in the scale and the directions for scoring and administration were the same. The standardization group for the revision consisted of a representative sample of 2,100 participants, with approximately 100 participants at each Stanford-Binet year level. Thorndike used a special procedure, based on test scores from the group-administered Cognitive Abilities Tests, to stratify each age sample so as to ensure proportionate representation of all ability levels. Unlike the 1960 norms, which did not include non-Euro Americans in the standardization group, the 1972 norms contained African Americans and Spanish-surnamed individuals as well as Euro Americans. Participants were excluded from the normative sample, however, if English was not the primary language spoken in the home. The greatest differences in test scores between the 1972 and 1960 norms were found at the preschool level. For a similar performance, the 1972 norms yielded IQs that were about 10 points lower than those given by the 1960 norms. (See Sattler, 1982, for a comprehensive review of administrative and interpretive procedures for the Stanford-Binet: Form L-M.)

INTRODUCTION TO THE SB: IV

Some continuity is maintained between the SB: IV and prior editions. The latest edition has in common with prior editions such item types as vocabulary (both pictures and words), comprehension, picture absurdities, paper folding and cutting, copying, repeating digits, memory for sentences, copying a bead chain from memory, similarities, form-board items, and quantitative items. Within each of these types, items were revised and new items were added. In addition, new types of items were added, including memory for objects, number series, and equation building. Every effort was made to design items with culture-fair content. A panel of ethnic minority reviewers evaluated the items for biased content.

The SB: IV contains 15 subtests, but not all subtests are used at every age level (see Table 14-2). Some subtests are administered at the preschool and elementary school ages only (e.g., Absurdities and Copying), while others are administered at the upper year levels only (e.g., Number Series and Equation Building). Of the 15 subtests, only six appear at every age—Vocabulary, Comprehension, Pattern Analysis, Quantitative, Bead Memory, and Memory for Sentences.

A *three-level hierarchical model* guided the construction of the scale. The model postulates (a) g (a general intelligence factor) at the highest level of interpretation; (b) crystallized, fluid, and short-term memory factors at the second level; and (c) more specific factors—such as verbal reasoning, quantitative reasoning, and abstract visual reasoning—at the third level. The specific factors at the third level, plus short-term memory at the second level, form four area scores in the SB: IV. Within each area, specific subtests are designated (see Table 14-2); however, a factor analysis was not

Table 14-2
Areas, Subtests, and Age Spans for Stanford-Binet: IV

Designated area	Subtest	Age span
Verbal Reasoning	Vocabulary	2 to 23
	Comprehension	2 to 23
	Absurdities	2 to 14
	Verbal Relations	12 to 23
Abstract/Visual Reasoning	Pattern Analysis	2 to 23
	Copying	2 to 13
	Matrices	7 to 23
	Paper Folding and Cutting	12 to 23
Quantitative Reasoning	Quantitative	2 to 23
	Number Series	7 to 23
	Equation Building	12 to 23
Short-Term Memory	Bead Memory	2 to 23
	Memory for Sentences	2 to 23
	Memory for Digits	2 to 23
	Memory for Objects	7 to 23

used for the placement of subtests into areas. The Composite Score reflects the highest level, and it is considered the best estimate of *g* in the scale.

STANDARDIZATION

The SB: IV was standardized on 5,013 individuals in 17 age groups. The sample was selected to be representative of the U.S. population according to the 1980 census data. The demographic characteristics used to obtain a stratified sample were age, gender, race/ethnicity, socioeconomic status, community size, and geographic region. Because the final sample included too many children with high SES backgrounds, a weighting procedure was used to make the sample conform to the census data. The number of individuals ranged from 194 in the 18-0 to 23-11 age group to 460 in the 5-0 to 5-11 group.

COMPOSITE SCORES, STANDARD AGE SCORES, AND TEST-AGE EQUIVALENTS

Raw scores are converted into three types of standard scores: standard age scores (or scaled scores) for the subtests ($M = 50$, $SD = 8$), area scores ($M = 100$, $SD = 16$), and a Composite Score ($M = 100$, $SD = 16$). The Composite Score is similar to the Deviation IQ employed on the Wechsler tests. The Wechsler tests use a standard deviation of 15, however, while the SB: IV uses a standard deviation of 16, consistent with previous editions of the Stanford-Binet. The raw score obtained by the examinee on each subtest is converted into a *standard age score* within the examinee's own age group through tables in the *Guide for Administering and Scoring the Fourth Edition*. The manual divides age groups into 4-

month intervals from 2 to 6 years (the one exception is a 3½-month interval at age 2-0-0 to 2-3-15), 6-month intervals from 6 to 12 years, 1-year intervals from 12 to 18 years, and a 6-year interval from 18 to 23-11 years.

The procedure used in the SB: IV allows you to compute area and Composite Scores when less than the entire battery is administered. You do not need to use proration or special short-form procedures to compute area or Composite Scores. After you obtain the subtest scaled scores, you enter them in a table that provides area standard age scores ($M = 100$, $SD = 16$). The *area score* can be obtained by use of one or more of the subtest scaled scores that make up the area.

The area standard scores then can be converted to a *Composite Score* through use of a table on pages 187 and 188 in the *SB: IV Guide*. This table is divided into two sections; one is for ages 2-0-0 to 9-11-15, and the other is for ages 9-11-16 to 23-11-15. As with the areas scores, you can obtain the Composite Score by use of one, two, three, or four area scores.

As you will read shortly, we advocate that you use factor scores in place of area scores. Consequently, we will highlight the factor scores in this chapter. However, you still must use the area score tables in the *SB: IV Guide* to compute the Composite Score and the factor scores.

The *Stanford-Binet: Fourth Edition Technical Manual* provides a table (Table G.1) of test-age equivalents to facilitate interpretation of a examinee's performance. Chapter 4 of this text discusses the advantages and disadvantages associated with the use of test-age equivalents.

RELIABILITY

The Composite Score of the SB: IV has excellent reliability. The internal consistency reliability coefficients for the Composite Score range from $r_{xx} = .95$ to .99 over the 17 age groups. The median Composite Score reliability is $r_{xx} = .97$. The reliabilities of the factor scores are discussed later in this chapter.

As expected, the reliabilities for the subtests are less satisfactory than those for the Composite Score (see Table 14-3). The median subtest reliabilities range from a low of $r_{xx} = .73$ for Memory for Objects to a high of $r_{xx} = .94$ for Paper Folding and Cutting. Subtest reliabilities differ somewhat according to age group, ranging from a low of $r_{xx} = .66$ for Memory for Objects at age 10 years to a high of $r_{xx} = .96$ for Pattern Analysis at ages 18-23.

Standard Errors of Measurement

The median standard error of measurement (SEM) in standard-score points is 2.8 for the Composite Score (see Table 14-3). Of the subtests, Paper Folding and Cutting and Pattern Analysis have the smallest median SEMs (2.0 and 2.3 scaled-score points, respectively), and Memory for Objects and Memory for Digits have the largest median SEMs (4.2 and 3.3 scaled-score points, respectively).

Table 14-3
Median Reliability Coefficients and Standard Errors of Measurement for Stanford-Binet: IV Subtests, Factor Scores, and Composite Score

Subtest, factor, and Composite Score	Median r_{xx}	Median SEM
Subtest		
Vocabulary	.87	2.9
Comprehension	.89	2.6
Absurdities	.87	2.9
Verbal Relations	.91	2.4
Pattern Analysis	.92	2.3
Copying	.87	2.9
Matrices	.90	2.5
Paper Folding and Cutting	.94	2.0
Quantitative	.88	2.8
Number Series	.90	2.5
Equation Building	.91	2.4
Bead Memory	.87	2.9
Memory for Sentences	.89	2.6
Memory for Digits	.83	3.3
Memory for Objects	.73	4.2
Factor		
Verbal Comprehension	.95	3.6
Nonverbal Reasoning/Visual	.96	3.2
Memory	.91	4.8
Composite		
Composite score	.97	2.8

Source: Adapted, in part, from Thorndike et al. (1986b).

Test-Retest Stability

The stability of the SB: IV was evaluated by retesting two groups (57 children with a mean age of 5-2 and 55 children with a mean age of 8-1) after an interval of 2 to 8 months (Thorndike et al., 1986b). For the 5-year-olds, the stability coefficient was excellent for the Composite Score (r_{xx} = .91). Stability coefficients for the eight subtests ranged from r_{tt} = .56 for Bead Memory to r_{tt} = .78 for Memory for Sentences. For the 8-year-olds, the stability coefficient was again excellent for the Composite Score (r_{xx} = .90). Stability coefficients for the 12 subtests ranged from r_{tt} = .28 for Quantitative to r_{tt} = .86 for Comprehension.

In both groups, children obtained higher scores on the second testing. The mean Composite Score change was 8.2 points for the 5-year-olds and 6.4 points for the 8-year-olds. For the individual subtests in the 5-year-old sample, mean changes ranged from a low of 1.5 scaled-score points on Vocabulary to a high of 4.3 scaled-score points on Copying. For the individual subtests in the 8-year-old sample, mean changes ranged from a low of 1.2 scaled-score points on Memory for Objects to a high of 3.7 scaled-score points on Pattern Analysis. Highly stable Composite Scores were also reported for a sample of 71 African American and Euro American preschool children (r_{xx} = .84; Lamp & Krohn, 1990).

The test-retest reliability coefficients indicate that the Composite Score is substantially more reliable than the individual subtest scores. The average change noted for the Composite Score was about half of a standard deviation. Individual subtests showed considerable fluctuation in scores, suggesting that they may not provide stable measures of ability.

Confidence Intervals

Table E-1 in Appendix E shows the 68, 85, 90, 95, and 99% confidence intervals based on the conventional standard error of measurement (see Chapter 4) for the three factor scores—Verbal Comprehension, Nonverbal Memory/Visualization, and Memory—and for the Composite Score for all age groups in the standardization sample. Table E-1 does not provide confidence intervals for the average of the age groups because the composition of the scale changes at various age levels. Additionally, the confidence intervals change considerably with age. For example, the confidence interval for the Composite Score at the 68% level is 4 for 2-year-olds and 2 for 10-year-olds. Therefore, you need to use confidence intervals for the examinee's specific age group.

VALIDITY

Several studies have investigated the criterion validity of the SB: IV by correlating it with other intelligence tests such as the WISC–III, WISC–R, WPPSI–R, WAIS–R, and Stanford-Binet: Form L-M and with measures of achievement (see Table 14-4). Table 14-4 indicates that the SB: IV has satisfactory criterion validity. For example, with other intelligence tests the SB: IV has correlations that range from .44 to .78. The SB: IV has a median r = .57 with tests of reading achievement, a median r = .64 with tests of mathematics achievement, and a median r = .50 with measures of spelling. However, Composite Scores may not adequately reflect the intelligence level of children functioning in the severely mentally retarded range (Spruill, 1996).

The construct validity of the SB: IV is acceptable. First, raw scores increase as a function of age. Second, factor analyses support several dimensions of the scale, such as adequate to high g loadings of the subtests and specific factors at various age levels of the scale. Third, all of the subtests correlate moderately to highly positively with the Composite Score.

Table 14-4
Criterion Validity Studies for the Stanford-Binet: IV

Criterion	SB: IV Composite	Criterion	SB: IV Composite
Bayley Mental Scale	.55	SRA Educational Ability Scales	.42
Bracken Basic Concept Scale	.75	Test of Cognitive Skills	.51
British Ability Scales	.66	Vineland Adaptive Behavioral Composite	.70
Columbia Mental Maturity Scale	.44	WAIS–R	.68
Goodenough-Harris Drawing Test	.40	WISC–R	.77
K-ABC	.80	WISC–III	.81
K-TEA		Woodcock-Johnson Tests of Achievement–R	
Math	.65	Knowledge	.59
Reading	.65	Language	.48
Spelling	.59	Math	.57
Leiter International Performance Scale	.78	Reading	.57
Matrix Analogies Test	.73	WPPSI–R	.61
McCarthy Scales of Children's Abilities	.77	WRAT–R	
Peabody Individual Achievement Test	.86	Reading	.52
PPVT–R	.58	Arithmetic	.64
Stanford-Binet: Form L-M	.69	Spelling	.42

Source: This table is based on the following studies: Atkinson, Bevc, Dickens, and Blackwell (1992); Blakeslee (1987); Brown and Morgan (1991); Carvajal, Gerber, Hewes, and Weaver (1987); Carvajal, Gerber, and Smith (1987); Carvajal, Hardy, Harmon, Sellers, and Holmes (1987); Carvajal, Hardy, Smith, and Weaver (1988); Carvajal, Karr, Hardy, and Palmer (1988); Carvajal and McKnab (1990); Carvajal, McKnab, Gerber, Hewes, and Smith (1989); Carvajal, McVey, Sellers, Weyand, and McKnab (1987); Carvajal, Parks, Bays, and Logan (1991); Carvajal and Weyand (1986); Greene, Sapp, and Chissom (1990); Hartwig, Sapp, and Clayton (1987); Hayden, Furlong, and Linnemeyer (1988); Hendershott, Searight, Hatfield, and Rogers (1990); Hollinger and Baldwin (1987); Hollinger and Baldwin (1990a, b); Howell and Bracken (1992); Johnson, Howie, Owen, Baldwin, and Luttman (1993); Karr, Carvajal, and Palmer (1992); Knight, Baker, and Minder (1990); Krohn and Lamp (1989); Lewis-O'Donnell (1986); Livesay (1986); Lukens (1988); Lukens (1990); McCall, Yates, Hendricks, Turner, and McNabb (1989); McCallum and Karnes (1987); Phelps (1989); Phelps, Bell, and Scott (1988); Prewett and Farhney (1994); Robinson, Dale, and Landesman (1990); Rothlisberg (1987; 1990); Rothlisberg and McIntosh (1991); Smith, St. Martin, and Lyon (1989); Thorndike, Hagen, and Sattler (1986a).

CORRELATIONS BETWEEN SUBTESTS AND BETWEEN SUBTESTS AND THE COMPOSITE SCORE

Intercorrelations provide information about the relationships of the SB: IV subtests to each other and to the Composite Score. Median correlations between the subtests range from a low of $r = .29$ to a high of $r = .73$ ($Mdn\ r = .47$). The highest median correlations ($r = .60$ and above) are between Vocabulary and Comprehension ($r = .73$), Vocabulary and Verbal Relations ($r = .71$), Quantitative and Number Series ($r = .67$), Matrices and Number Series ($r = .66$), Number Series and Equation Building ($r = .64$), Vocabulary and Memory for Sentences ($r = .64$), Comprehension and Verbal Relation ($r = .63$), Vocabulary and Absurdities ($r = .62$), Quantitative and Equation Building ($r = .61$), Paper Folding and Cutting and Number Series ($r = .61$), and Pattern Analysis and Paper Folding and Cutting ($r = .60$).

The lowest median correlations (less than $r = .40$) are between Memory for Objects and Paper Folding and Cutting ($r = .29$), Memory for Objects and Equation Building ($r = .30$), Memory for Objects and Verbal Relations ($r = .32$), Memory for Objects and Absurdities ($r = .33$), Memory for Digits and Copying ($r = .33$), Memory for Digits and Comprehension ($r = .34$), Memory for Digits and Absurdities ($r = .34$), Memory for Digits and Pattern Analysis ($r = .35$), Memory for Sentences and Paper Folding and Cutting ($r = .35$), Memory for Objects and Pattern Analysis ($r = .36$), Memory for Digits and Verbal Relations ($r = .36$), Memory for Digits and Paper Folding and Cutting ($r = .37$), Memory for Objects and Comprehension ($r = .38$), and Memory for Sentences and Equation Building ($r = .38$).

Median correlations between the subtests and the Composite Score range from $r = .60$ to $r = .82$ ($Mdn = .74$). Quantitative and Number Series have the highest correlation with the Composite Score ($r = .82$ for both), followed by Vocabulary ($r = .81$), Matrices ($r = .78$), and Comprehension and Verbal Relations ($r = .76$ for both). Memory for Objects has the lowest correlation with the Composite Score ($r = .60$), followed by Memory for Digits ($r = .64$), Copying ($r = .66$), Absurdities ($r = .72$), and Bead Memory ($r = .72$). Thus, reasoning and verbal comprehension subtests have the highest correlations with the Composite Score and memory subtests have the lowest correlations.

SB: IV COMPOSITE SCORES AND STRATIFICATION VARIABLES

Table 4.5 in the Technical Manual shows the relationship between Composite Scores and the demographic characteristics of the standardization sample for three age groups: (a) 2 to 6, (b) 7 to 11, and (c) 12 to 18-23. Differences between males' and females' mean Composite Scores were less than 2

Table 14-5
Relationship of Stanford-Binet: IV Composite Scores to Sex, Race, Parental Education, Parental Occupation, and Community Size

Demographic variables		M	SD
Sex	Males	99.1	16.0
	Females	100.4	15.1
Race	Asian American	99.9	15.4
	African American	91.0	13.2
	Hispanic American	94.9	13.4
	Native American	94.7	17.7
	Euro American	103.5	15.8
Parental education	1. Less than high school	94.4	14.8
	2. High school graduate	99.0	14.3
	3. 1 to 3 years college	103.4	15.2
	4. College graduate	110.1	14.4
Parental occupational group	1. Managerial/professional	108.0	15.3
	2. Technical/sales	101.5	14.3
	3. Service occupations	93.5	15.7
	4. Farming/forestry	96.0	16.7
	5. Precision production	96.8	16.6
	6. Operators, fabricators, other	94.0	15.0
Community size	1. 1,000,000 or more	98.6	15.8
	2. 300,000 to 999,999	98.5	17.9
	3. 100,000 to 299,999	100.4	14.4
	4. 25,000 to 99,999	103.0	14.1
	5. 2,500 to 24,999	98.1	16.6
	6. Less than 2,500	101.0	14.8

Note. These are mean Composite Scores based on the median scores of the three age groups listed in Table 4.5 of the *Technical Manual for the Stanford-Binet: Fourth Edition.*
Source: Adapted from Thorndike et al. (1986b).

points. Thus, sex differences are not large enough to assume any practical significance on the scale. Mean Composite Scores of Euro American examinees were about 10 to 17 points higher than those of African American examinees: 14 points at ages 2 to 6 (104.7 vs. 91.0), 10 points at ages 7 to 11 (102.6 vs. 92.7), and 17 points at ages 12 to 18-23 (103.5 vs. 86.1). Euro American examinees also obtained higher scores than other ethnic groups, except at ages 7 to 11, where Asian American examinees obtained a mean Composite Score of 103.6 and Euro American examinees a mean Composite Score of 102.6. This difference, however, is not meaningful. Table 14-5 shows the mean Composite Scores based on the median scores of the three age groups for the demographic characteristics.

Mean Composite Scores show a clear relationship to parental education and parental occupational groups: Composite Scores of children whose parents were college graduates were about 16 points higher, on the average, than those of children whose parents had less than a high school education (110.1 vs. 94.4). Similarly, Composite Scores of children of managerial and professional workers were 14 points higher, on the average, than those of children of operators, fabricators, and others (108.0 vs. 94.0). Community size differences varied depending on the age group in the standardization sample. For example, in the 2 to 6 age group, the range was about 5 points (103.4 vs. 98.1) for cities with 1,000,000 or more versus towns with 2,500 to 24,999. In the 7 to 11 age group, the range was about 12 points (103.0 vs. 91.4) for cities with 25,000 to 99,999 versus cities with 300,000 to 999,999. Finally, in the 12 to 18-23 age group, the range was about 8 points (102.6 vs. 94.4) for cities with 25,000 to 99,999 versus towns with 2,500 to 24,999.

FACTOR ANALYSIS

This section first presents the results of a principal-components analysis with varimax rotation conducted on the standardization sample data by the text author. The principal-components analysis differs from the one presented in the Technical Manual. A principal-components analysis lends itself to the development of factors that may be useful in guiding interpretations needed for clinical and psychoeducational evaluations.

Table 14-6 summarizes the results of the principal-components analysis. At ages 2 to 6, a two-factor solution best characterizes the scale: Verbal Comprehension and Nonverbal Reasoning/Visualization. At ages 7 to 18-23, a three-factor solution is most appropriate: Verbal Comprehension, Nonverbal Reasoning/Visualization, and Memory.

The *Verbal Comprehension factor* score measures verbal knowledge and understanding obtained through formal and informal education, as well the ability to apply verbal skills to new situations. The *Nonverbal Reasoning/Visualization factor* score reflects the ability to interpret and organize visually perceived material, to perform basic arithmetical operations using

Table 14-6
Stanford-Binet Intelligence Scale: Fourth Edition Subtest Loadings on Factor A (Verbal Comprehension), Factor B (Nonverbal Reasoning/Visualization), and Factor C (Memory) for 17 Age Levels Following Varimax Rotation

Subtest	2	3	4	5	6	7	8	9	10	11	12	13	14	15	16	17	18[a]	Mdn.
														Age level				

Factor A—Verbal Comprehension

Subtest	2	3	4	5	6	7	8	9	10	11	12	13	14	15	16	17	18[a]	Mdn.
Vocabulary	75	76	78	73	79	71	77	79	70	81	72	76	79	78	75	78	77	77
Comprehension	66	78	76	82	74	71	79	75	66	68	52	70	68	62	68	46	63	68
Absurdities	53	72	60	59	44	41	50	49	46	51	72	40	49	–	–	–	–	50
Verbal Relations	–	–	–	–	–	–	–	–	–	–	61	53	67	70	75	60	67	67
Pattern Analysis	28	34	29	32	24	17	26	28	18	27	49	27	23	21	26	15	28	27
Copying	13	28	34	28	18	16	27	19	30	29	74	24	–	–	–	–	–	25
Matrices	–	–	–	–	–	10	20	13	18	28	43	37	33	24	38	25	25	25
Paper Folding and Cut.	–	–	–	–	–	–	–	–	–	–	18	22	37	28	31	23	24	24
Quantitative	33	32	42	40	36	40	44	34	41	50	38	52	49	38	56	41	40	41
Number Series	–	–	–	–	–	18	27	23	26	32	33	29	33	25	41	24	28	28
Equation Building	–	–	–	–	–	–	–	–	–	–	01	23	34	38	45	19	22	23
Bead Memory	11	20	36	40	26	31	28	26	31	42	35	40	29	10	29	30	14	29
Memory for Sentences	67	64	56	59	63	60	58	51	64	63	42	69	57	39	51	45	56	58
Memory for Digits	–	–	–	–	–	26	20	21	27	22	17	46	25	15	15	20	32	22
Memory for Objects	–	–	–	–	–	20	16	08	11	28	15	43	17	18	15	25	07	17

Factor B—Nonverbal Reasoning/Visualization

Subtest	2	3	4	5	6	7	8	9	10	11	12	13	14	15	16	17	18[a]	Mdn.
Vocabulary	17	29	36	38	27	35	30	32	45	35	36	33	33	33	37	30	38	33
Comprehension	37	32	34	32	25	29	30	26	45	33	47	29	40	45	39	28	27	32
Absurdities	44	33	42	43	43	48	49	49	69	58	27	45	44	–	–	–	–	44
Verbal Relations	–	–	–	–	–	–	–	–	–	–	03	45	32	30	34	37	45	34
Pattern Analysis	64	66	71	71	70	55	72	69	77	64	39	60	76	61	71	51	32	66
Copying	58	70	62	60	53	48	52	52	49	46	–04	32	–	–	–	–	–	52
Matrices	–	–	–	–	–	23	57	63	57	55	47	65	63	64	60	58	65	60
Paper Folding and Cut.	–	–	–	–	–	–	–	–	–	–	25	67	65	71	63	70	65	65
Quantitative	43	63	68	70	64	48	40	43	54	35	49	59	56	58	54	60	47	54
Number Series	–	–	–	–	–	14	57	59	61	48	68	74	61	73	69	69	70	64
Equation Building	–	–	–	–	–	–	–	–	–	–	51	58	42	60	51	73	72	58
Bead Memory	55	65	63	63	63	56	57	42	48	54	33	51	50	36	51	40	38	51
Memory for Sentences	12	26	37	39	63	20	26	15	16	26	24	19	16	13	20	18	19	20
Memory for Digits	–	–	–	–	–	19	24	20	14	25	33	35	25	24	25	26	28	25
Memory for Objects	–	–	–	–	–	19	37	22	30	36	21	31	32	26	19	16	18	24

(Continued)

Table 14-6 *(Continued)*																		

Subtest	Age level																	Mdn.
	2	3	4	5	6	7	8	9	10	11	12	13	14	15	16	17	18ª	

Factor C—Memory

Subtest	2	3	4	5	6	7	8	9	10	11	12	13	14	15	16	17	18ª	Mdn.
Vocabulary	–	–	–	–	–	22	22	28	29	26	44	24	33	35	32	32	29	29
Comprehension	–	–	–	–	–	26	15	21	21	25	43	20	30	38	21	36	28	26
Absurdities	–	–	–	–	–	25	14	13	04	16	13	42	30	–	–	–	–	15
Verbal Relations	–	–	–	–	–	–	–	–	–	–	12	07	16	17	16	33	15	16
Pattern Analysis	–	–	–	–	–	32	17	22	19	29	14	28	27	27	28	12	29	27
Copying	–	–	–	–	–	26	16	10	22	37	37	82	–	–	–	–	–	26
Matrices	–	–	–	–	–	53	31	37	40	41	29	31	33	37	31	20	25	32
Paper Folding and Cut.	–	–	–	–	–	–	–	–	–	–	15	15	15	14	17	04	17	15
Quantitative	–	–	–	–	–	11	22	29	27	44	40	23	38	49	39	33	40	36
Number Series	–	–	–	–	–	80	28	33	38	52	30	36	43	32	36	42	34	36
Equation Building	–	–	–	–	–	–	–	–	–	–	29	18	29	18	24	27	17	24
Bead Memory	–	–	–	–	–	14	24	37	34	29	45	31	43	43	47	29	49	36
Memory for Sentences	–	–	–	–	–	36	50	61	53	45	67	37	57	65	57	69	64	57
Memory for Digits	–	–	–	–	–	57	81	55	71	71	60	38	64	70	74	64	66	65
Memory for Objects	–	–	–	–	–	42	44	53	58	37	63	30	53	51	54	32	61	52

Note. Abbreviation: Paper Folding and Cut. = Paper Folding and Cutting. Decimal points omitted. Factor loadings are for a two-factor solution at ages 2 to 6 and for a three-factor solution at ages 7 to 18–23.
ª Represents ages 18–23.

visual cues or verbal cues, to visualize patterns, to demonstrate visual-motor skills, and to use reasoning to solve problems. Both reasoning and visualization are key components of this factor. The *Memory factor* measures the ability to attend or concentrate, or short-term memory, but also may involve sequencing skills.

SB: IV Subtests as Measures of *g*

As shown in Table 14-7, all of the SB: IV subtests are either good or moderate measures of *g* (the general intelligence factor). Based on the median of the 17 age levels, the subtests with the highest loadings are Vocabulary (.80), Number Series (.79), Quantitative (.77), Comprehension (.75), Matrices (.74), Absurdities (.72), Memory for Sentences (.71), and Pattern Analysis (.70). The subtests with moderate *g* loadings are Paper Folding and Cutting (.69), Bead Memory (.68), Verbal Relations (.68), Equation Building (.67), Copying (.61), Memory for Digits (.60), and Memory for Objects (.54). The subtests with high *g* loadings include both verbal and nonverbal subtests.

Subtest Specificity

Subtest specificity refers to the proportion of a subtest's variance that is both reliable (i.e., not due to errors of measurement) and distinctive to the subtest. Although individual subtests on the SB: IV overlap in their measurement properties (i.e., the majority of the reliable variance for most subtests is common factor variance), many possess sufficient specificity to justify interpretation of specific subtest functions (e.g., interpreting Verbal Relations as a measure of conceptual thinking; see Table 14-8). Of the 15 subtests in the scale, 11 have ample or adequate specificity at all age levels. These subtests are Absurdities, Verbal Relations, Pattern Analysis, Copying, Matrices, Paper Folding and Cutting, Number Series, Equation Building, Bead Memory, Memory for Sentences, and Memory for Digits. The four subtests with inadequate specificity at one or more ages are Vocabulary, Comprehension, Quantitative, and Memory for Objects.

At ages at which subtests have inadequate specificity, do not interpret the scores as measuring specific functions, and give cautious interpretation to subtests that have adequate specificity. You can interpret these subtests, however, as measuring *g*

Table 14-7
Stanford-Binet: IV Subtests as Measures of *g*

	Good measure of *g*			Fair measure of *g*	
Subtest	Median loading of *g*	Percentage of variance attributable to *g*	Subtest	Median loading of *g*	Percentage of variance attributable to *g*
Vocabulary	.80	64	Paper Folding and Cutting	.69	48
Number Series	.79	62	Bead Memory	.68	46
Quantitative	.77	60	Verbal Relations	.68	46
Comprehension	.75	56	Equation Building	.67	45
Matrices	.74	55	Copying	.61	37
Absurdities	.72	52	Memory for Digits	.60	36
Memory for Sentences	.71	50	Memory for Objects	.54	29
Pattern Analysis	.70	49			

Table 14-8
Amount of Specificity in Stanford-Binet: IV Subtests

Ample specificity		Adequate specificity		Inadequate specificity	
Subtest	Ages	Subtest	Ages	Subtest	Ages
Vocabulary	2 and 15	Vocabulary	10, 12–13, 16–18	Vocabulary	3–9, 11, 14
Comprehension	2, 7, 10–13, 16–18	Comprehension	3–4, 14–15	Comprehension	5–6, 8–9
Absurdities	2–9, 11–14	Absurdities	10	Quantitative	6, 18
Verbal Relations	12–18	Pattern Analysis	14	Memory for Objects	12
Pattern Analysis	2–13, 15–18	Copying	12		
Copying	2–11, 13	Quantitative	14–16		
Matrices	7–18	Number Series	7, 12–13, 16–18		
Paper Folding and Cutting	12–18	Memory for Sentences	18		
Quantitative	2–5, 7–13, 17	Memory for Digits	10		
Number Series	8–11, 14–15				
Equation Building	12–18				
Bead Memory	all ages				
Memory for Sentences	2–17				
Memory for Digits	7–9, 11–18				
Memory for Objects	7–11, 13–18				

Note. Age 18 includes ages 18 through 23. The procedure described by Kaufman (1975) was used to evaluate the specificity of the subtests.

and the appropriate factor (Verbal Comprehension, Nonverbal Reasoning/Visualization, or Memory).

Obtaining Factor Scores

Of the 15 subtests in the battery, the following 12 subtests, based on their factor loadings, are useful in obtaining the three factor scores:

VERBAL COMPREHENSION

- Sum of scaled scores on Vocabulary, Comprehension, Absurdities, and Memory for Sentences at ages 2 to 7
- Sum of scaled scores on Vocabulary, Comprehension, and Absurdities at ages 8 to 14
- Sum of scaled scores on Vocabulary, Comprehension, and Verbal Relations at ages 15 to 18-23

NONVERBAL REASONING/VISUALIZATION

- Sum of scaled scores on Pattern Analysis, Copying, Quantitative, and Bead Memory at ages 2 to 11
- Sum of scaled scores on Pattern Analysis, Matrices, Quantitative, and Bead Memory at ages 12 to 18-23

MEMORY (NOT CALCULATED FOR AGES 2 TO 6)

- Sum of scaled scores on Memory for Digits and Memory for Objects at age 7
- Sum of scaled scores on Memory for Sentences, Memory for Digits, and Memory for Objects at ages 8 to 18-23

In addition to the subtests noted above, other subtests can be used to obtain factor scores. For the Verbal Comprehension factor, you can use Verbal Relations at ages 12 to 14. For the Nonverbal Reasoning/Visualization factor, you can use Matrices and Number Series at ages 9 to 11, Number Series and Equation Building at ages 12 to 18-23, and Paper Folding and Cutting at ages 13 to 18-23. Table 14-9 shows the grouping of the subtests for factor scores at various age levels. Because the subtests in the SB: IV are not continuous throughout the scale and because different subtests are administered at different ages, the factor structure of the scale differs at different ages. Exhibit 14-2 shows a worksheet for computing factor scores, with sample computations, and Exhibit 14-3 presents another form for computing factor scores. The factor scores are highly reliable ($r_{xx} = .91$ to .96, with SEMs of 3.2 to 4.8; see Table 14-3).

Factor analytic studies of the SB: IV report varied findings. Some studies generally replicate the results reported above. For example, Thorndike (1990), using the principal-axis factoring method on the standardization sample, reported two general factors—a verbal and a nonverbal factor—for younger children and three general factors—verbal, abstract/visual, and short-term memory factors for older children. Kline (1989) found strong support for the two-factor and

Table 14-9
Suggested Subtest Combinations for Factor Scores at Various Age Ranges for the Stanford-Binet: IV

Factor score	Age	Subtest combination
Verbal Comprehension	2 through 7	Vocabulary Comprehension Absurdities Memory of Sentences
	8 through 14	Vocabulary Comprehension Absurdities
	15 through 18–23	Vocabulary Comprehension Verbal Relations
Nonverbal Reasoning/ Visualization	2 through 11	Pattern Analysis Copying Quantitative
	12 through 18–23	Pattern Analysis Matrices Quantitative Bead Memory
Memory	2 through 6	None
	7	Memory for Digits Memory for Objects
	8 through 18–23	Memory for Sentences Memory for Digits Memory for Objects

Note. Other subtests may be added or substituted to obtain factor scores. For the Verbal Comprehension factor, Verbal Relations can be used at ages 12, 13, and 14. For the Nonverbal Reasoning/ Visualization factor, (a) Matrices and Number Series can be used at ages 9, 10, and 11; (b) Number Series and Equation Building at ages 12 through 18–23; and (c) Paper Folding and Cutting at ages 13 through 18–23.

three-factor models provided in this chapter. Additional factor analytic studies (e.g., Gridley & McIntosh, 1991; Kaplan & Alfonso, 1997; Kline, 1989; Molfese, Yaple, Helwig, Harris, & Connell, 1992) generally supported a two-factor model (or in some cases a three-factor model) for ages 2 to 6 years. With older children, however, Gridley and McIntosh (1991) identified four factors—Verbal Reasoning, Quantitative Reasoning, Abstract/Visual Reasoning, and Memory. Boyle (1990) also found that the four factors hold up reasonably well, but recommended that Absurdities, Copying, and Memory for Objects be excluded in calculating individual area scores. Keith, Cool, Novak, White, and Pottebaum (1988) support a four-factor model, except at ages 2 to 6,

Exhibit 14-2
Worksheet for Computing Factor Scores for Stanford-Binet: IV

WORKSHEET FOR COMPUTING FACTOR SCORES FOR STANFORD-BINET: IV

Examinee's name: Jim   Examiner's name: Bill Smith
Date: November 1, 1987   Age: 6-11
Date of birth: December 1, 1980   Sex: M

VERBAL COMPREHENSION	STANDARD SCORE
Ages 2 through 7	
SUBTEST	
1 Vocabulary (VR)	40
6 Comprehension (VR)	45
7 Absurdities (VR)	30
4 Memory for Sentences (STM)	43
STEPS	
1. Sum of standard scores on Vocabulary + Comprehension + Absurdities	115
2. Verbal Reasoning (VR) Area SAS (p. 183 of *Guide* for 3 subtests)	73
3. Short-Term Memory (STM) Area SAS (multiply the standard score by 2)	86
4. Sum of (2) + (3)	159
5. **Verbal Comprehension Factor Score** (p. 187 of *Guide* for 2 area scores)	77
Ages 8 through 14	
SUBTEST	
1 Vocabulary (VR)	____
6 Comprehension (VR)	____
7 Absurdities (VR)	____
STEPS	
1. Sum of standard scores on Vocabulary + Comprehension + Absurdities	
2. Verbal Reasoning (VR) Area SAS (p. 183 of *Guide* for 3 subtests)	____
3. **Verbal Comprehension Factor Score** (p. 187 or 188 of *Guide* for 1 area score)	____
Ages 15 through 18–23	
SUBTEST	
1 Vocabulary (VR)	____
6 Comprehension (VR)	____
14 Verbal Relations (VR)	____
STEPS	
1. Sum of standard scores on Vocabulary + Comprehension + Verbal Relations	
2. Verbal Reasoning (VR) Area SAS (p. 183 of *Guide* for 3 subtests)	
3. **Verbal Comprehension Factor Score** (p. 188 of *Guide* for 1 area score)	____

NONVERBAL REASONING/VISUALIZATION	STANDARD SCORE
Ages 2 through 11	
SUBTEST	
5 Pattern Analysis (A/VR)	33
9 Copying (A/VR)	30
3 Quantitative (QR)	33
2 Bead Memory (STM)	35
STEPS	
1. Sum of standard scores on Pattern Analysis + Copying	63
2. Abstract/Visual Reasoning (A/VR) Area SAS (p. 184 of *Guide* for 2 subtests)	57
3. Quantitative Reasoning (QR) Area SAS (multiply the standard score by 2)	66
4. Short-Term Memory (STM) Area SAS (multiply the standard score by 2)	70
5. Sum of (2) + (3) + (4)	193
6. **Nonverbal Reasoning/Visualization Factor Score** (p. 187 or 188 of *Guide* for 3 area scores)	58
Ages 12 through 18–23	
SUBTEST	
5 Pattern Analysis (A/VR)	____
11 Matrices (A/VR)	____
3 Quantitative (QR)	____
2 Bead Memory (STM)	____
STEPS	
1. Sum of standard scores on Pattern Analysis + Matrices	____
2. Abstract/Visual Reasoning (A/VR) Area SAS (p. 184 of *Guide* for subtests)	____
3. Quantitative Reasoning (QR) Area SAS (multiply the standard score by 2)	____
4. Short-Term Memory (STM) Area SAS (multiply the standard score by 2)	____
5. Sum of (2) + (3) + (4)	____
6. **Nonverbal Reasoning/Visualization Factor Score** (p. 188 of *Guide* for 3 area scores)	____

(Continued)

Exhibit 14-2 *(Continued)*

MEMORY	STANDARD SCORE	MEMORY	STANDARD SCORE
Age 7		**Ages 8 through 18–23**	
SUBTEST		SUBTEST	
8 Memory for Digits (STM)	___	4 Memory for Sentences (STM)	___
10 Memory for Objects (STM)	___	8 Memory for Digits (STM)	___
		10 Memory for Objects (STM)	___
STEPS		STEPS	
1. Sum of standard scores on Memory for Digits + Memory for Objects	___	1. Sum of standard scores on Memory for Sentences + Memory for Digits + Memory for Objects	___
2. Short-Term Memory (STM) Area SAS (p. 186 of *Guide* for 2 subtests)	___	2. Short-Term Memory (STM) Area SAS (p. 186 of *Guide* for 3 subtests)	___
3. **Memory Factor Score** (p. 187 of *Guide* for 1 area score)	___	3. **Memory Factor Score** (p. 187 or 188 of *Guide* for 1 area score)	___

where three factors emerged (Memory could not be separated from Reasoning). Ownby and Carmin (1988) support a four-factor model, except at ages 2 and 10, where the four factors did not consistently apply. Reynolds, Kamphaus, and Rosenthal (1988) found little support for a four-factor solution. The results of these studies indicate that a multiple-factor model, rather than a single-factor model, best accounts for the correlations between subtests. However, it is not clear what the precise factor structure of the SB: IV is.

ADMINISTERING THE SB: IV

Items in each SB: IV subtest are arranged in order of increasing difficulty, with two items of approximately equal difficulty at each level. Letters designate levels. You use the levels to determine entry and discontinuance points. Figure 14-2 shows the front page of the record booklet. A guide by Delany and Hopkins (1987) provides useful information for administering the SB: IV.

Adaptive Testing

All examinees are initially given the Vocabulary subtest, called the *routing subtest.* Using the examinee's score on this subtest, with his or her chronological age, you determine the entry level for the other subtests from a routing chart.

The routing subtest and routing chart, however, may not be accurate for mentally retarded children and perhaps other groups. One study (Bissette, 1987) and several field reports have indicated that the entry levels are too high for trainable mentally retarded (TMR) children. In fact, the entry levels suggested in the *SB: IV Guide* tend to be above TMR children's ceiling levels on most subtests. You will have to adjust the entry level to the examinee's probable level of performance.

Basal level and ceiling level. The *basal level* on the SB: IV refers to the two consecutive levels at which the examinee passes all four items, and the *ceiling level* refers to the two consecutive levels at which the examinee fails three of the four items or all four items. The ceiling level is the point at which you discontinue a subtest. When you obtain a double basal level, use the lower basal level to calculate the raw score. When you obtain a double ceiling level, use the higher ceiling level to obtain the raw score. These procedures consider all of the examinee's actual failures and successes. A complete administration of the SB: IV requires you to establish one basal level and one ceiling level. When the examinee does not reach either a basal or a ceiling level, you can report scores but with the notation "Estimate" following the scores.

Chronological age. The examinee's chronological age can be obtained by subtracting her or his date of birth from the date of examination. Record chronological age in years and months, with 16 or more days rounded to the next higher month.

Timing of items. Of the 15 subtests in the SB: IV, only one—Pattern Analysis—is timed. (In several subtests, the presentation of stimulus items is timed.) In the other subtests, you must judge whether sufficient time has elapsed before you go on to the next item.

Scratch paper. The examinee may use scratch paper on the Quantitative, Number Series, and Equation Building subtests. Collect the scratch paper after you administer the subtest.

Exhibit 14-3
Alternative Worksheet for Computing Factor Scores for Stanford-Binet: IV

ALTERNATIVE WORKSHEET FOR COMPUTING FACTOR SCORES FOR STANFORD-BINET: IV

Examinee's name: _____   Date: _____   Age: _____

Examiner's name: _____

Steps:

1. Identify the subtests for the factor for the examinee's age.
2. Enter only those subtest scores in the Score column.
3. Find the total for the subtests in each area.
4. Look up the Area SAS for each total (Thorndike et al., 1986a, pp. 183–186).
5. Find the total of the Area SASs.
6. Look up the Composite SAS for the examinee's age (Thorndike et al., 1986a, p. 187 or 188).
7. Look up and enter percentile ranks for all scores (Thorndike et al., 1986b, p. 129).

Verbal Comprehension (ages 2 to 18–23)

Subtest	Ages	Score	Area SAS	Percentile rank
Verbal Reasoning Subtests				
1. Vocabulary	2–23			
2. Comprehension	2–23			
3. Absurdities	2–14			
4. Verbal Relations	15–23			
Total				
Short-Term Memory Subtests				
1. Memory for Sentences	2–7			
Total				
Sum of Area SASs				
Composite SAS				

Nonverbal Reasoning/Visualization (ages 2 to 18–23)

Subtest	Ages	Score	Area SAS	Percentile rank
Abstract/Visual Reasoning Subtests				
1. Pattern Analysis	2–23			
2. Copying	2–11			
3. Matrices	12–23			
Total				
Quantitative Reasoning Subtests				
1. Quantitative	2–23			
Total				
Short-Term Memory Subtests				
1. Bead Memory	2–23			
Total				
Sum of Area SASs				
Composite SAS				

Memory (ages 7 to 18–23)

Subtest	Ages	Score	Area SAS	Percentile rank
Short-Term Memory Subtests				
1. Memory for Digits	7–23			
2. Memory for Objects	7–23			
3. Memory for Sentences	8–23			
Total				
Sum of Area SASs				
Composite SAS				

Source: Courtesy of John Willis.

9-74539

STANFORD-BINET INTELLIGENCE SCALE

RECORD BOOKLET

Stanford-Binet Intelligence Scale: Fourth Edition

Name ______________________

______________________ Sex ______

Ethnicity NA H B W/NH O/AA PI Other ______

	YEAR	MONTH	DAY
Date of Testing	____	____	____
Birth Date	____	____	____
Age	____	____	____

School ______________________

Grade ______________________

Examiner ______________________

Father's Occupation: ______________________

Mother's Occupation: ______________________

FACTORS AFFECTING TEST PERFORMANCE
Overall Rating of Conditions

Optimal — Good — Average — Detrimental — Seriously detrimental

	RAW SCORE	STANDARD AGE SCORE *
Verbal Reasoning		
1 Vocabulary	____	____
6 Comprehension	____	____
7 Absurdities	____	____
14 Verbal Relations	____	____
Sum of Subtest SAS's		
Verbal Reasoning SAS		
Abstract/Visual Reasoning		
5 Pattern Analysis	____	____
9 Copying	____	____
11 Matrices	____	____
13 Paper Folding & Cutting	____	____
Sum of Subtest SAS's		
Abstract/Visual Reasoning SAS		
Quantitative Reasoning		
3 Quantitative	____	____
12 Number Series	____	____
15 Equation Building	____	____
Sum of Subtest SAS's		
Quantitative Reasoning SAS		
Short-Term Memory		
2 Bead Memory	____	____
4 Memory For Sentences	____	____
8 Memory For Digits	____	____
10 Memory For Objects	____	____
Sum of Subtest SAS's		
Short-Term Memory SAS		
Sum of Area SAS's		____

	COMPOSITE SCORE *
Test Composite	____
Partial Composite	____
Partial Composite based on ______	

	1 2 3 4 5	
Attention		
a) Absorbed by task	|__|__|__|__|__|	Easily distracted
Reactions During Test Performance		
a) Normal activity level	|__|__|__|__|__|	Abnormal activity level
b) Initiates activity	|__|__|__|__|__|	Waits to be told
c) Quick to respond	|__|__|__|__|__|	Urging needed
Emotional Independence		
a) Socially confident	|__|__|__|__|__|	Insecure
b) Realistically self-confident	|__|__|__|__|__|	Distrusts own ability
c) Comfortable in adult company	|__|__|__|__|__|	Ill-at-ease
d) Assured	|__|__|__|__|__|	Anxious
Problem-Solving Behavior		
a) Persistent	|__|__|__|__|__|	Gives up easily
b) Reacts to failure realistically	|__|__|__|__|__|	Reacts to failure unrealistically
c) Eager to continue	|__|__|__|__|__|	Seeks to terminate
d) Challenged by hard tasks	|__|__|__|__|__|	Prefers only easy tasks
Independence of Examiner Support		
a) Needs minimum of commendation	|__|__|__|__|__|	Needs constant praise and encouragement
Expressive Language		
a) Excellent articulation	|__|__|__|__|__|	Very poor articulation
Receptive Language		
a) Excellent sound discrimination	|__|__|__|__|__|	Very poor sound discrimination

Was it difficult to establish rapport with this person?

Easy \|__\|__\|__\|__\|__\| Difficult

***Be sure that all Standard Age Scores (SAS's) are based on the tables in the *Guide* with the number 9-74502 on the cover.**

The Riverside Publishing Company

Robert L. Thorndike
Elizabeth P. Hagen
Jerome M. Sattler

© 1986 The Riverside Publishing Company. All rights reserved.

Figure 14-2. Cover page of Stanford-Binet Intelligence Scale: Fourth Edition record booklet. Reprinted with permission of the Riverside Publishing Company from *Stanford-Binet Intelligence Scale: Fourth Edition*, by R. L. Thorndike, E. P. Hagen, and J. M Sattler. The Riverside Publishing Company, 8420 W. Bryn Mawr Avenue, Chicago, IL 60631. Copyright 1986.

Administrative checklist. The administrative checklist shown in Exhibit 14-4 should help you learn how to administer the SB: IV.

Physical Abilities Necessary for the SB: IV

The examinee must have adequate hearing and speech for the verbal subtests and adequate vision or visual-motor ability for the nonverbal subtests (see Table 14-10). As discussed in Chapter 8, in administering the test to an examinee with a physical disability, you must find ways to give the items without providing cues to the answers. Alternative ways to administer the subtests to children younger than 6 or 7 years are restricted by the limited writing and reading skills of the children. Most of the discussion in Chapter 8 about the adaptive administration of the WISC–III also pertains to the SB: IV.

Short Forms of the SB: IV

The *Guide for Administering and Scoring the Fourth Edition* and the Technical Manual suggest several short forms. Three of the most useful are as follows:

1. *Two-subtest short form.* This short form is composed of Vocabulary and Pattern Analysis. The two subtests are administered at all ages of the test.
2. *Four-subtest short form.* This short form is composed of Vocabulary, Bead Memory, Quantitative, and Pattern Analysis. These four subtests are administered at all ages of the test.
3. *Six-subtest short form.* This short form is composed of Vocabulary, Bead Memory, Quantitative, Memory for Sentences, Pattern Analysis, and Comprehension. These six subtests are administered at all age levels of the test. Additionally, this short form yields estimates of two factor scores: Verbal Comprehension (Vocabulary, Comprehension, and Memory for Sentences) and Nonverbal Reasoning/Visualization (Pattern Analysis, Quantitative, and Bead Memory). When the complete test (15 subtests) is administered, Memory for Sentences is part of the Verbal Comprehension factor at ages 2 to 7 and part of the Memory factor after age 7. But, because Memory for Sentences also has high loadings on the Verbal Comprehension factor, you can use it to obtain a Verbal Comprehension factor score when you administer the six-subtest short form at any age.

Short forms on the SB: IV have the same advantages and disadvantages as they do on the Wechsler tests (see Chapter 8). Use short forms primarily for screening purposes.

Research studies have reported the following results for SB: IV short forms. The four-subtest short form is useful for screening students referred for a learning disability (Lawson & Evans, 1996). It has a high correlation with the Total Composite ($r = .95$) and a relatively short administration time. The six-subtest short form is useful for students who are below average in functioning (i.e., Composite Scores of less

Table 14-10
Physical Abilities Necessary and Adaptable for Stanford-Binet Intelligence Scale: IV

Subtest	Vision	Hearing	Oral speech	Arm-hand use
Vocabulary	Xr	Xa	Xa	Xw
Comprehension	Xr	Xa	Xa	Xw
Absurdities	X	Xa	Xa	Xw
Verbal Relations	Xr	Xa	Xa	Xw
Pattern Analysis	X	Xa	–	X
Copying	X	Xa	–	X
Matrices	X	Xa	Xo	Xa
Paper Folding and Cutting	X	Xa	Xo	Xa
Quantitative	X	Xa	Xa	Xw
Number Series	Xa	Xa	Xa	Xw
Equation Building	Xa	Xa	Xa	Xw
Bead Memory	X	Xa	–	X
Memory for Sentences	–	X	Xa	Xw
Memory for Digits	–	X	Xa	Xw
Memory for Objects	X	Xa	Xa	Xw

Note. The codes are as follows:
X—This ability is required. Adaptation is not feasible if this function is absent or more than mildly impaired.
Xa—This ability is required for standard administrations, but the subtest is adaptable.
Xo—Examinees who are able to speak can say their answers.
Xr—Examinees who are able to read can be shown the questions. If the examinee cannot read, hearing is necessary. If neither the ability to read nor the ability to hear is present, the subtest should not be administered.
Xw—Examinees who are able to write can write their answers.

than 79; Atkinson, 1991) and for those who are developmentally disabled (DeLamatre & Hollinger, 1990).

Two-, four-, and six-subtest short forms used with above-average college students yielded scores that were about 4 to 5 points lower than the Composite Score, thereby underestimating the students' ability levels; correlations between the short form and the standard form ranged from .66 to .76 (Nagle & Bell, 1993).

Both four-subtest and six-subtest short forms were found to be highly correlated ($r = .93$ and .95, respectively) in a sample of 18- and 19-year-olds (Carvajal & Gerber, 1987). Similarly, both four-subtest and six-subtest short forms were found to be highly correlated with the Composite Score ($r = .93$ and .96, respectively) in a group of low-achieving students (Prewett, 1992).

Exhibit 14-4
Administrative Checklist for the Stanford-Binet: IV

ADMINISTRATIVE CHECKLIST FOR THE STANFORD-BINET: IV

Name of examiner: _____   Date: _____

Name of examinee: _____   Name of observer: _____

(Note: *If an item is not applicable, mark NA to the left of the number.*)

Vocabulary	**Circle One**	
1. Starts at appropriate entry level	Yes	No
2. Obtains a basal level (passing all items at two consecutive levels or passing item 1) before continuing	Yes	No
3. Reads directions verbatim	Yes	No
4. Reads directions clearly	Yes	No
5. Pronounces oral vocabulary items (15–46) distinctly and correctly	Yes	No
6. Queries responses when appropriate	Yes	No
7. After about 20 seconds with no response, asks, "Do you want to try this?"	Yes	No
8. Records responses verbatim using appropriate abbreviations	Yes	No
9. Scores items quickly	Yes	No
10. Scores items correctly	Yes	No
11. Obtains a ceiling level (failing 3 of 4 items or all 4 items at two consecutive levels)	Yes	No
12. Administers 4th item at ceiling level	Yes	No
13. Adds points correctly	Yes	No

Comments: _____

Bead Memory	**Circle One**	
1. Starts at appropriate entry level	Yes	No
2. Obtains a basal level (passing all items at two consecutive levels or passing item 1) before continuing	Yes	No
3. Reads directions verbatim	Yes	No
4. Reads directions clearly	Yes	No
5. Uses stimuli	Yes	No
6. Exposes each picture for 4.5 to 5.5 seconds	Yes	No
7. Does not repeat any item	Yes	No
8. Scores items correctly	Yes	No
9. Obtains a ceiling level (failing 3 of 4 items or all 4 items at two consecutive levels)	Yes	No
10. Administers 4th item at ceiling level	Yes	No
11. Adds points correctly	Yes	No

Comments: _____

Quantitative		
1. Starts at appropriate entry level	Yes	No
2. Obtains a basal level (passing all items at two consecutive levels or passing item 1) before continuing	Yes	No

Quantitative	**Circle One**	
3. Reads directions verbatim and clearly	Yes	No
4. Reads items distinctly and correctly	Yes	No
5. Gives credit if proper block face is up, even if it is in a different orientation from the examiner's	Yes	No
6. Provides pencil and scratch paper for Levels L– V	Yes	No
7. Records responses verbatim	Yes	No
8. Scores items correctly	Yes	No
9. Obtains a ceiling level (failing 3 of 4 items or all 4 items at two consecutive levels)	Yes	No
10. Administers 4th item at ceiling level	Yes	No
11. Adds points correctly	Yes	No

Comments: _____

Memory for Sentences		
1. Starts at appropriate entry level	Yes	No
2. Corrects errors on sample items	Yes	No
3. Obtains a basal level (passing all items at two consecutive levels or passing item 1) before continuing	Yes	No
4. Reads directions verbatim and clearly	Yes	No
5. Reads items steadily, distinctly, and correctly, dropping voice at end of each item	Yes	No
6. Does not repeat any item	Yes	No
7. Records responses	Yes	No
8. Scores items correctly (e.g., does not penalize contractions)	Yes	No
9. Obtains a ceiling level (failing 3 of 4 items or all 4 items at two consecutive levels)	Yes	No
10. Administers 4th item at ceiling level	Yes	No
11. Adds points correctly	Yes	No

Comments: _____

Pattern Analysis		
1. Starts at appropriate entry level	Yes	No
2. Obtains a basal level (passing all items at two consecutive levels or passing item 1) before continuing	Yes	No
3. Reads directions verbatim	Yes	No
4. Reads directions clearly	Yes	No
5. Says, "Let's try another one" when appropriate	Yes	No

(Continued)

Exhibit 14-4 *(Continued)*

Pattern Analysis	Circle One	
6. Administers sample items correctly (for entry levels higher than C)	Yes	No
7. Gives appropriate feedback	Yes	No
8. Reads items distinctly and correctly	Yes	No
9. Uses stimuli (e.g., form-board pieces, cubes, box lid) correctly and efficiently	Yes	No
10. Gives exact number of cubes needed to make the pattern for items 11–42	Yes	No
11. Provides corrective feedback on reversals for sample items only	Yes	No
12. Uses stopwatch correctly for items 7–42	Yes	No
13. Uses diagram to record incorrect patterns	Yes	No
14. Scores items correctly, including P, F, RF, and TF	Yes	No
15. Obtains a ceiling level (failing 3 of 4 items or all 4 items at two consecutive levels)	Yes	No
16. Administers 4th item at ceiling level	Yes	No
17. Adds points correctly	Yes	No

Comments: _____

_____

Comprehension	Circle One	
1. Starts at appropriate entry level	Yes	No
2. Obtains a basal level (passing all items at two consecutive levels or passing item 1) before continuing	Yes	No
3. Reads directions verbatim	Yes	No
4. Reads directions clearly	Yes	No
5. Reads items distinctly and correctly	Yes	No
6. Does not explain any words or items	Yes	No
7. Queries responses correctly, including responses expressing attitudes instead of direct answers	Yes	No
8. Reads back examinee's response if asked how many responses have been given and lets examinee decide	Yes	No
9. Asks for second response when appropriate	Yes	No
10. Uses stimuli	Yes	No
11. Scores items correctly	Yes	No
12. Obtains a ceiling level (failing 3 of 4 items or all 4 items at two consecutive levels)	Yes	No
13. Administers 4th item at ceiling level	Yes	No
14. Adds points correctly	Yes	No

Comments: _____

_____

Absurdities	Circle One	
1. Starts at appropriate entry level	Yes	No
2. Obtains a basal level (passing all items at two consecutive levels or passing item 1) before continuing	Yes	No
3. Reads directions verbatim	Yes	No

Absurdities	Circle One	
4. Reads directions clearly	Yes	No
5. Administers sample item for Levels A–B only	Yes	No
6. Gives appropriate feedback	Yes	No
7. Reads items distinctly and correctly	Yes	No
8. Queries correctly	Yes	No
9. Records responses verbatim	Yes	No
10. Scores items correctly	Yes	No
11. Obtains a ceiling level (failing 3 of 4 items or all 4 items at two consecutive levels)	Yes	No
12. Administers 4th item at ceiling level	Yes	No
13. Adds points correctly	Yes	No

Comments: _____

_____

Memory for Digits	Circle One	
1. Starts at appropriate entry level	Yes	No
2. Administers sample item correctly	Yes	No
3. Obtains a basal level (passing all items at two consecutive levels or passing item 1) before continuing	Yes	No
4. Reads directions verbatim	Yes	No
5. Reads directions clearly	Yes	No
6. Administers Digits Forward and Digits Reversed	Yes	No
7. Reads items distinctly and correctly at a rate of one per second, dropping voice at the end of each item	Yes	No
8. Does not repeat any item	Yes	No
9. Records responses verbatim	Yes	No
10. Scores items correctly	Yes	No
11. Obtains a ceiling level (failing 3 of 4 items or all 4 items at two consecutive levels)	Yes	No
12. Administers 4th item at ceiling level	Yes	No
13. Adds points correctly	Yes	No

Comments: _____

_____

Copying	Circle One	
1. Starts at appropriate entry level	Yes	No
2. Collects blocks after each item	Yes	No
3. Gives examinee correct number of blocks	Yes	No
4. Leaves examiner's model standing	Yes	No
5. Obtains a basal level (passing all items at two consecutive levels or passing item 1) before continuing	Yes	No
6. Reads directions verbatim	Yes	No
7. Reads directions clearly	Yes	No
8. Uses stimuli (e.g., blocks, Record Booklet, pencil with eraser) appropriately	Yes	No
9. Writes each item number on Record Booklet	Yes	No
10. Scores items correctly	Yes	No

(Continued)

Exhibit 14-4 *(Continued)*

Copying	Circle One	
11. Obtains a ceiling level (failing 3 of 4 items or all 4 items at two consecutive levels)	Yes	No
12. Administers 4th item at ceiling level	Yes	No
13. Adds points correctly	Yes	No

Comments: _____

_____

Memory for Objects

	Circle One	
1. Starts at appropriate entry level	Yes	No
2. Administers both sample items and gives appropriate feedback	Yes	No
3. Obtains a basal level (passing all items at two consecutive levels or passing item 1) before continuing	Yes	No
4. Reads directions verbatim	Yes	No
5. Reads directions clearly	Yes	No
6. Records responses in order	Yes	No
7. Does not repeat any item	Yes	No
8. Scores items correctly	Yes	No
9. Obtains a ceiling level (failing 3 of 4 items or all 4 items at two consecutive levels)	Yes	No
10. Administers 4th item at ceiling level	Yes	No
11. Adds points correctly	Yes	No

Comments: _____

_____

Matrices

	Circle One	
1. Starts at appropriate entry level	Yes	No
2. Obtains a basal level (passing all items at two consecutive levels or passing item 1) before continuing	Yes	No
3. Reads directions verbatim	Yes	No
4. Reads directions clearly	Yes	No
5. Administers 4 sample items and	Yes	No
gives appropriate feedback	Yes	No
6. Records responses for items 1–22	Yes	No
7. Has examinee record responses in Record Booklet for items 23–26	Yes	No
8. Scores items correctly	Yes	No
9. Obtains a ceiling level (failing 3 of 4 items or all 4 items at two consecutive levels)	Yes	No
10. Administers 4th item at ceiling level	Yes	No
11. Adds points correctly	Yes	No

Comments: _____

_____

Number Series

1. Starts at appropriate entry level	Yes	No
2. Administers both sample items and gives appropriate feedback	Yes	No
3. Obtains a basal level (passing all items at two consecutive levels or passing item 1) before continuing	Yes	No
4. Reads directions verbatim	Yes	No

Number Series

	Circle One	
5. Reads directions clearly	Yes	No
6. Does not read any items to examinee	Yes	No
7. Provides pencil and scratch paper	Yes	No
8. Records responses	Yes	No
9. Gives prompt for next item if time exceeds approximately 2 minutes	Yes	No
10. Scores items correctly	Yes	No
11. Obtains a ceiling level (failing 3 of 4 items or all 4 items at two consecutive levels)	Yes	No
12. Administers 4th item at ceiling level	Yes	No
13. Adds points correctly	Yes	No

Comments: _____

_____

Paper Folding and Cutting

1. Starts at appropriate entry level	Yes	No
2. Obtains a basal level (passing all items at two consecutive levels or passing item 1) before continuing	Yes	No
3. Demonstrates sample items 1 and 2 (and no others) with paper and scissors	Yes	No
4. Reads directions verbatim	Yes	No
5. Reads directions clearly	Yes	No
6. Circles responses	Yes	No
7. Scores items correctly	Yes	No
8. Obtains a ceiling level (failing 3 of 4 items or all 4 items at two consecutive levels)	Yes	No
9. Administers 4th item at ceiling level	Yes	No
10. Adds points correctly	Yes	No

Comments: _____

_____

Verbal Relations

1. Starts at appropriate entry level	Yes	No
2. Obtains a basal level (passing all items at two consecutive levels or passing item 1) before continuing	Yes	No
3. Reads directions verbatim	Yes	No
4. Reads directions clearly	Yes	No
5. Queries responses appropriately	Yes	No
6. Records responses verbatim	Yes	No
7. Scores items correctly	Yes	No
8. Obtains a ceiling level (failing 3 of 4 items or all 4 items at two consecutive levels)	Yes	No
9. Administers 4th item at ceiling level	Yes	No
10. Adds points correctly	Yes	No

Comments: _____

_____

Equation Building

1. Starts at appropriate entry level	Yes	No
2. Administers both sample items and gives appropriate feedback	Yes	No

(Continued)

Exhibit 14-4 *(Continued)*

Equation Building	Circle One	
3. Obtains a basal level (passing all items at two consecutive levels or passing item 1) before continuing	Yes	No
4. Reads directions verbatim	Yes	No
5. Reads directions clearly	Yes	No
6. Provides pencil and scratch paper	Yes	No
7. Records responses verbatim	Yes	No
8. Gives prompt for next item if time exceeds approximately 2 minutes	Yes	No
9. Scores items correctly, including true sentences not listed in the item book	Yes	No
10. Obtains a ceiling level (failing 3 of 4 items or all 4 items at two consecutive levels)	Yes	No
11. Administers 4th item at ceiling level	Yes	No
12. Adds points correctly	Yes	No

Comments: _____

Other Aspects of Test Administration and Scoring

	Circle One	
1. Establishes rapport	Yes	No
2. Introduces test appropriately	Yes	No
3. Is well organized and prepared (e.g., has necessary materials, including paper, pencils, and stopwatch)	Yes	No
4. Has only materials necessary for the current test visible	Yes	No
5. Transitions well from subtest to subtest	Yes	No
6. Scores items at an appropriate pace	Yes	No
7. Attends to examinee appropriately	Yes	No
8. Gives praise appropriately	Yes	No
9. Makes the test a positive experience	Yes	No
10. Records behavioral observations	Yes	No
11. Completes front page of Record Booklet correctly	Yes	No
12. Determines entry level correctly	Yes	No

Other Aspects of Test Administration and Scoring

	Circle One	
13. Adjusts entry levels appropriately	Yes	No
14. Administers subtests in appropriate order	Yes	No
15. Uses Appendix A of Handbook to guide administration	Yes	No
16. Transfers raw scores to front page of Record Booklet correctly	Yes	No
17. Writes "Estimate" after a subtest score in which no basal level or ceiling level was obtained	Yes	No
18. Converts subtest raw scores to scaled scores correctly	Yes	No
19. Calculates standard age scores correctly	Yes	No
20. Calculates factor scores correctly	Yes	No
21. Calculates Composite Score correctly	Yes	No
22. Completes profile correctly	Yes	No
23. Records percentile ranks correctly	Yes	No
24. Records classifications correctly	Yes	No
25. Completes identifying information on Record Booklet correctly	Yes	No
26. Calculates examinee's age correctly	Yes	No
27. Puts examinee's name, date, and examiner's name on all pieces of paper	Yes	No

Comments: _____

Overall Assessment of Test Administration

Circle One: Excellent   Good   Average   Poor   Failing

Overall strengths: _____

Overall weaknesses: _____

Other comments: _____

Source: Courtesy of Christina D. Adams (with adaptions and assistance from John O. Willis).

A five-subtest nonverbal battery consisting of Bead Memory, Pattern Analysis, Copying, Memory for Objects, and Matrices is recommended for screening students with a hearing impairment, with a speech/language impairment, or with limited English language proficiency (Glaub & Kamphaus, 1991). This subtest short form was found to correlate highly ($r = .95$) with the Composite Score.

A seven-subtest short form consisting of Vocabulary, Bead Memory, Quantitative, Pattern Analysis, Comprehension, Matrices, and Number Series was found to be useful for evaluating gifted children ($r = .90$; McCallum & Karnes, 1990).

Content Area Scores

The SB: IV provides four content area scores: Verbal Reasoning, Abstract/Visual Reasoning, Quantitative Reasoning, and Short-Term Memory. Because some factor analyses do not support these four content area scores, they should be used with caution. If you do use them, see Spruill (1988) for confidence intervals. The four content area scores, however, need to be calculated to obtain the Composite Score and to obtain the factor scores. Factor scores are preferred over content area scores for interpretative purposes.

Profile Sheet

After you score the scale and compute the factor scores, plot the examinee's scores on a profile sheet (see Exhibit 14-5). The profile sheet has entries for the Composite Score, factor scores, and subtest scores. It provides a visual picture of the examinee's performance.

Recommended Subtest Battery

Table 14-11 shows the subtest battery that is recommended for each age level of the SB: IV. The 8-subtest and 10-subtest combinations shown in Table 14-11 are based on factor analysis, time considerations, and clinical and psychoeducational usefulness.

- At ages 2 to 6, the recommended 8-subtest battery is Vocabulary, Comprehension, Pattern Analysis, Quantitative, Bead Memory, Memory for Sentences, Absurdities, and Copying.
- At ages 7 to 11, the recommended 10-subtest battery is Vocabulary, Comprehension, Pattern Analysis, Quantitative, Bead Memory, Memory for Sentences, Absurdities, Copying, Memory for Digits, and Memory for Objects.

- At ages 12 to 14, the recommended 10-subtest battery is Vocabulary, Comprehension, Pattern Analysis, Quantitative, Bead Memory, Memory for Sentences, Absurdities, Matrices, Memory for Digits, and Memory for Objects.
- At ages 15 to 18-23, the recommended 10-subtest battery is Vocabulary, Comprehension, Pattern Analysis, Quantitative, Bead Memory, Memory for Sentences, Verbal Relations, Matrices, Memory for Digits, and Memory for Objects.

The use of these combinations will save administration time and will help you to interpret the test results and make placement decisions. You can use the other three subtests—Paper Folding and Cutting, Number Series, and Equation Building—for special diagnostic purposes. Let's now discuss each of the subtests.

VOCABULARY

The Vocabulary subtest contains 46 items divided into a picture vocabulary section (items 1 to 14) and an oral vocabulary section (items 15 to 46). For the picture vocabulary items, the examinee names the picture or gives the most pertinent detail

Table 14-11
Recommended Subtest Battery for Each Age of the Stanford-Binet: IV

	Subtest	2	3	4	5	6	7	8	9	10	11	12	13	14	15	16	17	18[a]
1	Vocabulary	•	•	•	•	•	•	•	•	•	•	•	•	•	•	•	•	•
6	Comprehension	•	•	•	•	•	•	•	•	•	•	•	•	•	•	•	•	•
7	Absurdities	•	•	•	•	•	•	•	•	•	•	•	•	•				
14	Verbal Relations														•	•	•	•
5	Pattern Analysis	•	•	•	•	•	•	•	•	•	•	•	•	•	•	•	•	•
9	Copying	•	•	•	•	•	•	•	•	•	•							
11	Matrices											•	•	•	•	•	•	•
13	Paper Folding and Cutting																	
3	Quantitative	•	•	•	•	•	•	•	•	•	•	•	•	•	•	•	•	•
12	Number Series																	
15	Equation Building																	
2	Bead Memory	•	•	•	•	•	•	•	•	•	•	•	•	•	•	•	•	•
4	Memory for Sentences	•	•	•	•	•	•	•	•	•	•	•	•	•	•	•	•	•
8	Memory for Digits						•	•	•	•	•	•	•	•	•	•	•	•
10	Memory for Objects						•	•	•	•	•	•	•	•	•	•	•	•
	Number of subtests	8	8	8	8	8	10	10	10	10	10	10	10	10	10	10	10	10

[a] Represents ages 18–23.

Exhibit 14-5
Profile Sheet for the Stanford-Binet: IV

Name: _____   Sex: _____   Date of examination: _____

Date of birth: _____   CA: _____   Examiner's name: _____

Percentile rank	Standard score	Summary scores				Standard score	Verbal Comprehension					Nonverbal Reasoning/Visualization								Memory			Percentile rank
		Verbal Comprehension	Nonverbal Reasoning/Visualization	Memory	Composite Score		Vocabulary	Comprehension	Absurdities	Memory for Sentences	Verbal Relations	Pattern Analysis	Copying	Quantitative	Bead Memory	Matrices	Number Series	Equation Building	Paper Folding and Cutting	Memory for Sentences	Memory for Digits	Memory for Objects	
99+	156	•	•	•	•	78	•	•	•	•	•	•	•	•	•	•	•	•	•	•	•	•	99+
99+	152	•	•	•	•	76	•	•	•	•	•	•	•	•	•	•	•	•	•	•	•	•	99+
99+	148					74																	99+
99+	144	•	•	•	•	72	•	•	•	•	•	•	•	•	•	•	•	•	•	•	•	•	99+
99	140	•	•	•	•	70	•	•	•	•	•	•	•	•	•	•	•	•	•	•	•	•	99
99	136	•	•	•	•	68	•	•	•	•	•	•	•	•	•	•	•	•	•	•	•	•	99
98	132					66																	98
96	128	•	•	•	•	64	•	•	•	•	•	•	•	•	•	•	•	•	•	•	•	•	96
93	124	•	•	•	•	62	•	•	•	•	•	•	•	•	•	•	•	•	•	•	•	•	93
89	120	•	•	•	•	60	•	•	•	•	•	•	•	•	•	•	•	•	•	•	•	•	89
84	116					58																	84
77	112	•	•	•	•	56	•	•	•	•	•	•	•	•	•	•	•	•	•	•	•	•	77
69	108	•	•	•	•	54	•	•	•	•	•	•	•	•	•	•	•	•	•	•	•	•	69
60	104	•	•	•	•	52	•	•	•	•	•	•	•	•	•	•	•	•	•	•	•	•	60
50	100					50																	50
40	96	•	•	•	•	48	•	•	•	•	•	•	•	•	•	•	•	•	•	•	•	•	40
31	92	•	•	•	•	46	•	•	•	•	•	•	•	•	•	•	•	•	•	•	•	•	31
23	88	•	•	•	•	44	•	•	•	•	•	•	•	•	•	•	•	•	•	•	•	•	23
16	84					42																	16
12	80	•	•	•	•	40	•	•	•	•	•	•	•	•	•	•	•	•	•	•	•	•	12
7	76	•	•	•	•	38	•	•	•	•	•	•	•	•	•	•	•	•	•	•	•	•	7
4	72	•	•	•	•	36	•	•	•	•	•	•	•	•	•	•	•	•	•	•	•	•	4
2	68					34																	2
1	64	•	•	•	•	32	•	•	•	•	•	•	•	•	•	•	•	•	•	•	•	•	1
1	60	•	•	•	•	30	•	•	•	•	•	•	•	•	•	•	•	•	•	•	•	•	1
1−	56	•	•	•	•	28	•	•	•	•	•	•	•	•	•	•	•	•	•	•	•	•	1−
1−	52					26																	1−
1−	48	•	•	•	•	24	•	•	•	•	•	•	•	•	•	•	•	•	•	•	•	•	1−
1−	44	•	•	•	•	22	•	•	•	•	•	•	•	•	•	•	•	•	•	•	•	•	1−

of the picture. For the oral vocabulary items, the examinee explains orally the meaning of each word. The subtest is administered at all ages, and each item is scored 1 or 0.

Rationale

The rationale presented for the WISC–III Vocabulary subtest generally applies to the SB: IV oral vocabulary section (see Chapter 9). Formal education is less likely to be an influence for picture vocabulary than for oral vocabulary. Experience is likely to be the major contributing factor to the vocabulary development of preschool children.

The purpose of the picture vocabulary section is to determine whether the examinee correctly identifies a picture by any of its appropriate names. Picture vocabulary involves visual perception and retrieval and word recall abilities. In complex pictures, the examinee must appreciate the main element in the picture. Correct association of the word with the object, the ability to vocalize the word, and the ability to comprehend the spoken word are all important. These skills represent emergent aspects of language use. The subtest emphasizes the examinee's ability to comprehend what the spoken word stands for and not the examinee's articulation skills.

Factor Analytic Findings

Vocabulary is a good measure of g (64% of its variance may be attributed to g). This subtest contributes substantially to the Verbal Comprehension factor (Mdn loading = .77). Specificity is ample or adequate at ages 2, 10, 12, 13, and 16-18 years and inadequate at ages 3-9, 11, 14, and 15 years.

Reliability and Correlational Highlights

Vocabulary is a reliable subtest (r = .87). It correlates better with Comprehension (r = .73) than with any of the other subtests. It has a high correlation with the Composite Score (r = .81).

Administrative and Interpretive Considerations

The administrative and interpretive considerations presented for the WISC–III Vocabulary subtest generally apply to the SB: IV Vocabulary subtest (see Chapter 9). On the SB: IV, however, different administrative procedures are used for the picture vocabulary and oral vocabulary sections.

Carefully study "General Guidelines for Scoring the Vocabulary Test" (Appendix A) in the *Stanford-Binet: Fourth Edition Guide* so that you will know which responses need further inquiry. The examples indicate that you should query many responses. Unlike the WISC–III, on which you score vocabulary responses 2, 1, or 0, the SB: IV uses 1 or 0 only.

Here are some questions that will help you evaluate an examinee's performance on the picture vocabulary items (Taylor, 1961, adapted from pp. 308–309):

- Does the examinee find some responses for every picture, or does the examinee say, "I don't know"?
- Does the examinee try to find a new word for each picture, or does the examinee use the same word several times, successively or at intervals?
- Does the examinee seem to grope for the correct word, or does the examinee seem to say the first word that comes to mind?
- Do the examinee's errors show associations easily recognizable as such (e.g., dog for lamb) or meaningful to those around him or her (e.g., "Daddy go" for car)?
- Does the examinee's naming show that pictures are perceived in a global way (e.g., stick for hammer) or with an appreciation for fine details?
- Are the examinee's errors the result of a carryover from a previous picture or from other familiar verbal patterns?
- What is the quality of the examinee's enunciation (e.g., does the examinee miss or drop consonants, saying *boo-* for book or *fla-* for flag)?

When an examinee has poor articulation, check with the parent about nuances in sound productions that may mean different words to the examinee but be only barely perceptible to outsiders. Observe whether gestures accompany or replace verbal responses and whether they are relevant and meaningful or only incidental. If they are the examinee's only form of response, do they indicate that the examinee is familiar with the picture?

The picture vocabulary items can be used for testing-of-limits in the following ways (Taylor, 1961, adapted from pp. 309–310):

1. *Gestures.* To evaluate how the examinee expresses herself or himself without words, show the picture of the scissors (or hammer, bat, or shovel) and say, "Show me what it does" or "Show me what we do with it." For an examinee who does not seem to understand language, demonstrate what you want. Note the following:

- Does the examinee use varied appropriate gestures, or does the examinee use the same gestures with all pictures?
- Are the examinee's means of expression mostly manual, facial, or both?
- Does the examinee use the same gesture for objects that belong to the same category?
- Does the examinee describe animals by their sounds and movements, describe tools by their use, or point to a book in the room to indicate a book?

Observations of an examinee's use of gestures can be of considerable diagnostic significance with respect to development of communication.

2. *Alternative naming.* If the examinee has designated an object either in words or through gestures, you may ask, "What else could it be?" The examinee may find a second response, producing a synonym, a better word, or a better gesture.

3. *Pointing.* The picture material can also be used in a multiple-choice procedure to investigate language comprehension. Here is a suggested procedure: Present four pictures to the examinee and say, "Where is the flower [etc.]?" The examinee can indicate his or her answer by pointing, nodding at the pictures, or some other means. For a severely handicapped examinee who is unable to point accurately or to turn his or her head freely, the pictures should be spread far enough apart to avoid equivocal responses, yet near enough so that they all remain in the examinee's line of vision. Here are some guidelines for observing the examinee's performance during this procedure.

- Does the examinee scan the four pictures for the proper picture or respond haphazardly?
- Does the examinee point to the correct picture only?
- Does the examinee know at least the general area in which the item belongs? For example, does the examinee point to a hammer when asked for a bat?
- Does the examinee seem to see all the pictures correctly, or does the examinee make unexpected errors?
- Are errors possibly attributable to sensory difficulties? For example, if the examinee points to the wrong picture, is it because of poor perception, eyesight, or hearing?

- Does the examinee seem to know the difference between what a hammer looks like and what a bat looks like?
- Does the examinee seem to hear the difference between the words, such as the difference between the words "flag" and "flower"?

Children who are not disabled usually can point to the pictures adequately before—or at least at the same age as—they can find names for them. Often children can point correctly to something long before they are able to name it. Does the examinee have better receptive language ability than expressive language ability? The above procedure is valuable for examinees with language delay or sensory difficulties.

COMPREHENSION

The Comprehension subtest contains 42 items, 6 of which require a pointing response (items 1 to 6) and 36 of which require a verbal response (items 7 to 42). The first six items measure knowledge of body parts; the remaining items cover understanding of basic physiological processes and hygiene, environmental hazards, societal practices, and political and economic activities. The items tap the examinee's comprehension of survival skills, social skills, economic skills, and political skills. The subtest is administered at all ages, and each item is scored 1 or 0.

Rationale

The rationale described for the WISC–III Comprehension subtest generally applies to the SB: IV Comprehension subtest (see Chapter 9). Additionally, the pointing items involve some appreciation of the proper location of body parts. Items at the upper level of the subtest involve comprehension of the political and economic process, particularly the role of government in our society. These upper-level items provide insight into an individual's understanding of how her or his society functions.

Factor Analytic Findings

Comprehension is a good measure of g (56% of its variance may be attributed to g). This subtest contributes substantially to the Verbal Comprehension factor (*Mdn* loading = .68). Specificity is ample or adequate at all ages except ages 5 to 6 and 8 to 9.

Reliability and Correlational Highlights

Comprehension is a reliable subtest ($r = .89$). It correlates better with Vocabulary than with any of the other subtests ($r = .73$). It has a moderately high correlation with the Composite Score ($r = .76$).

Courtesy of Herman Zielinski.

Administrative and Interpretive Considerations

The administrative and interpretive considerations presented for the WISC–III Comprehension subtest generally apply to the SB: IV Comprehension subtest (see Chapter 9). Carefully study "General Guidelines for Scoring the Comprehension Test" (Appendix B) in the *SB: IV Guide* so that you will know which responses need further inquiry. The examples indicate that many responses should be queried. Unlike the WISC–III, on which Comprehension responses are scored 2, 1, or 0, the SB: IV uses only a two-point system—1 or 0.

ABSURDITIES

The Absurdities subtest contains 32 items. Items 1 to 4 are in multiple-choice format and require a pointing response, whereas items 5 to 32 are in an open-ended format and require an oral response. On items 5 to 32, the examinee is asked to state the essential incongruity in the picture. The subtest is administered at ages 2 to 14 years, and each item is scored 1 or 0.

Rationale

Absurdities requires the examinee to recognize what is visually depicted in the stimulus picture, appreciate that there is some incongruity, and determine what that incongruity is. Success depends, in part, on the examinee's perception of detail, alertness, concentration, and social understanding. The task is conceptual and involves some understanding of right and wrong. Performance on the multiple-choice items in part reflects the examinee's ability to delay impulses.

Factor Analytic Findings

Absurdities is a good measure of *g* (52% of its variance may be attributed to *g*). This subtest contributes moderately to the Verbal Comprehension factor (*Mdn* loading = .50) and Nonverbal Reasoning/Visualization factor (*Mdn* loading = .44). Specificity is ample or adequate at all ages.

Reliability and Correlational Highlights

Absurdities is a reliable subtest (*r* = .87). It correlates better with Vocabulary (*r* = .62) and with Comprehension (*r* = .59) than with any of the other subtests. It has a moderately high correlation with the Composite Score (*r* = .72).

Administrative and Interpretive Considerations

Items 1 to 4 are easy to score because they are multiple-choice items. Items 5 to 32, however, may be difficult to score because the examinee may give ambiguous responses.

Courtesy of Herman Zielinski.

The item book lists typical responses needing inquiry. Study this section so that you will know which responses to query and which to score as pass or fail. If an examinee says that nothing is foolish, encourage another response. The factor analytic findings suggest that examinees may use both verbal and nonverbal processes to arrive at an answer.

VERBAL RELATIONS

The Verbal Relations subtest contains 18 items, each consisting of four words. All four words have something in common, but the first three words also share one characteristic that the fourth word does not have. The examinee must state what is true about the first three words that is not true of the fourth word. The subtest is administered at ages 12 to 18–23 years, and each item is scored 1 or 0.

Rationale

Verbal Relations involves perceiving the common elements of three terms, bringing these common elements together in a concept, and contrasting the common elements with a fourth term. Because the fourth term is both similar to and different from the first three terms, the Verbal Relations subtest involves both verbal concept formation and reasoning—the ability to place objects and events together in a meaningful group and then decide how the meaningful group contrasts with a member of another group. Verbal Relations also may involve the ability to view facts from several angles simultaneously and coordinate the multiple relationships involved, the ability to test and discard hypotheses, and flexibility.

Factor Analytic Findings

Verbal Relations is a fair measure of g (46% of its variance may be attributed to g). This subtest contributes substantially to the Verbal Comprehension factor (*Mdn* loading = .67). Specificity is ample for all ages.

Reliability and Correlational Highlights

Verbal Relations is a reliable subtest (r_{xx} = .91). It correlates better with Vocabulary than with any of the other subtests (r = .71). It has a moderately high correlation with the Composite Score (r = .76).

Administrative and Interpretive Considerations

The interpretive suggestions presented for the WISC–III Similarities subtest generally apply to the SB: IV Verbal Relations subtest (see Chapter 9). Verbal Relations, however, requires a different type of conceptualization than does Similarities, and it also requires reasoning ability. Consequently, it is more difficult to determine the precise cause for failure on the Verbal Relations subtest.

Carefully study "General Guidelines for Scoring the Verbal Relations Test" (Appendix E) in the *SB: IV Guide* so that you will know which responses need further inquiry. Unlike the WISC–III, on which Similarities responses are scored 2, 1, or 0, the SB: IV uses only a two-point system—1 or 0.

PATTERN ANALYSIS

The Pattern Analysis subtest contains 42 items. The first six items require the examinee to place pieces in appropriate recesses on the form board; the remaining items use two-dimensional black-and-white pictures of abstract designs. On items 7 to 24, you construct a model; on items 25 to 42, you show pictures of designs. The number of blocks used varies from one block on items 7 to 10 to nine blocks on items 39 to 42.

Items 7 to 42 are timed. Items 7 to 18 and 25 to 30 have a maximum of 30 seconds each; items 19 to 24 and 31 to 36, 45 seconds; items 37 and 38, 60 seconds; and items 39 to 42, 90 seconds. The subtest is administered at all ages, and each item is scored 1 or 0.

Rationale

The rationale described for the WISC–III Block Design subtest generally applies to the Pattern Analysis subtest (see

Chapter 9). The form-board items, however, primarily measure visual-motor ability and recognition and manipulation of forms. Additionally, "the form-board items require accurate spatial skills and a sensitivity to form differences, plus an awareness of the match between block outline and the corresponding hole in the form board. The latter becomes crucial when the form board is reversed" (Wilson, 1978b, p. 947).

Factor Analytic Findings

Pattern Analysis is a good measure of g (49% of its variance may be attributed to g). This subtest contributes substantially to the Nonverbal Reasoning/Visualization factor (*Mdn* loading = .66). Specificity is ample or adequate at all age levels.

Reliability and Correlational Highlights

Pattern Analysis is a reliable subtest (r_{xx} = .92). It correlates better with Paper Folding and Cutting (r = .60) and Matrices and Number Series (r = .55 for both) than with any of the other subtests. It has a moderately high correlation with the Composite Score (r = .74).

Administrative and Interpretive Considerations

The administrative and interpretive considerations presented for the WISC–III Block Design subtest generally apply to the Pattern Analysis subtest (see Chapter 9). Probably the examinee can reproduce the models constructed out of blocks more easily than those shown in pictures. Because this is the only timed subtest in the scale, notice whether timing increases the examinee's anxiety or affects his or her performance in other ways.

COPYING

The Copying subtest contains 28 items divided into two sections. In the first section (items 1 to 12), the examinee constructs a cube tower by following a model that you construct with three or four blocks. In the second section (items 13 to 28), the examinee copies printed line drawings. The drawings range from a straight line to multiple rectangular objects and cubes. The examinee makes the drawings directly in the record booklet. The subtest is administered at ages 2 to 13 years, and each item is scored 1 or 0. There is no time limit.

Rationale

Copying involves visual-motor ability and eye-hand coordination. Previous experience with pencil and paper may help the examinee. Adequate reproduction of the designs requires appropriate fine motor development, perceptual discrimination ability, and ability to integrate perceptual and motor processes. The examinee must shift attention between the stimulus and the reproduction and monitor her or his performance. Constructing a cube tower involves psychomotor dexterity and sustained goal-oriented activity. The examinee must retain the instructions in memory and must organize her or his production "to match the examiner's model, with the necessary intermediate steps of comparison and adjustment" (Wilson, 1978b, p. 947).

Factor Analytic Findings

Copying is a fair measure of g (37% of its variance may be attributed to g). This subtest contributes moderately to the Nonverbal Reasoning/Visualization factor (*Mdn* loading = .52). Specificity is ample or adequate at all ages.

Reliability and Correlational Highlights

Copying is a reliable subtest (r_{xx} = .87). It correlates better with Pattern Analysis than with any of the other subtests (r = .50). It has a moderate correlation with the Composite Score (r = .66).

Administrative and Interpretive Considerations

The Copying subtest is difficult to score, particularly for items 13 to 28 (also see Mason, 1992). Each of these designs has up to 10 special scoring criteria. Study the scoring criteria carefully to become proficient in scoring this subtest (Appendix D in the *SB: IV Guide*).

Useful observational guidelines are as follows:

1. How does the examinee hold the pencil?
2. In which hand does the examinee hold the pencil?
3. Does the examinee use one hand to hold the paper in place and the other hand to draw the designs?
4. Does the examinee understand the task?
5. Are the examinee's drawings done with extreme care and deliberation or impulsively?
6. Does the examinee display tremor?
7. Does the examinee seem overly anxious?
8. Does the examinee trace the design with a finger before drawing it?
9. Does the examinee count the loops or sides of figures before drawing a design?
10. Are the designs drawn haphazardly?
11. Does the examinee glance at the design briefly and then draw from memory?
12. Does the examinee rotate the card or paper (or both)?

13. Does the examinee make frequent erasures? If so, on what parts of figures (e.g., curves, angulations, overlapping parts, or open figures)?
14. Does the examinee's speed increase or decrease as the subtest proceeds?
15. What part of a design does the examinee draw first?
16. In what direction does the examinee work in copying the designs? For example, does the examinee draw the designs from top down or bottom up, or from inside out or outside in? Does the examinee change direction of movement from design to design?
17. Does the examinee use sketching?
18. Does the examinee show unusual blocking on any design?
19. Does the examinee start over when drawing the designs? If so, how many times does this happen?
20. How much space does the examinee use to draw the design (e.g., is the drawing about the same size as the original or greatly reduced or expanded)?
21. How accurate are the examinee's drawings? For example, are the designs well executed or barely recognizable? If the designs show any distortions, what kind are they?
22. Does the examinee spend approximately the same amount of time on each design?
23. Does the examinee recognize his or her errors?
24. How does the examinee react to making errors?
25. Is the examinee persistent?
26. Is the examinee bored with the task?
27. What comments does the examinee make about the designs?
28. Does the examinee express dissatisfaction over poorly executed drawings?
29. Does the examinee show signs of fatigue?
30. Does the examinee need encouragement to complete the drawings?
31. How long did the examinee need to complete the task?
32. Was the amount of time taken by the examinee about average or excessively long or unusually short?
33. Does the examinee express satisfaction with the end product?

MATRICES

The Matrices subtest contains 26 items, each composed of either a four-figure configuration (items 1 to 12) or a nine-figure configuration (items 13 to 26). Items 1 to 12 show pictures of animals, people, or geometric figures; items 13 to 22 show geometric figures only; and items 23 to 26 show letters only. Items 1 to 22 are multiple-choice items, whereas items 23 to 26 require a written response. The examinee selects the best alternative to complete the matrix. In each item, the missing figure has some logical relationship to the other figures in the matrix. The subtest is administered at ages 7 to 18-23 years, and each item is scored 1 or 0.

Rationale

Matrices involves perceptual reasoning ability and requires analogic reasoning, attention to detail, concentration, and possibly spatial ability. Experience with part-whole relationships may be helpful, as may a willingness to respond when uncertain.

Factor Analytic Findings

Matrices is a good measure of g (55% of its variance may be attributed to g). This subtest contributes substantially to the Nonverbal Reasoning/Visualization factor (*Mdn* loading = .60). Specificity is ample at all ages.

Reliability and Correlational Highlights

Matrices is a reliable subtest (r_{xx} = .90). It correlates better with Number Series (r = .66) than with any of the other subtests. It has a moderately high correlation with the Composite Score (r = .78).

Administrative and Interpretive Considerations

Matrices is simple to score because there is only one correct response for each item. The varied item content suggests that the subtest is not a pure measure of nonverbal or figural reasoning. The subtest uses both abstract stimuli and meaningful stimuli, and the last four items use letters. Impulsive examinees may have difficulty with the tasks because of the detailed nature of the stimuli. Table 14-12 shows the possible processes involved in solving the items on the Matrices subtest.

PAPER FOLDING AND CUTTING

The Paper Folding and Cutting subtest contains 18 items. The examinee first looks at a sequence of drawings showing a piece of paper being folded and cut and then selects the diagram that shows how the folded and cut paper would look unfolded. (In the early items you make cuts in a piece of paper, whereas in later items you show pictures that depict where the cuts are made.) Items vary from simple one-fold and one-cut problems to multiple-fold-and-cut snowflake-like designs. The subtest is administered at ages 12 to 18-23 years, and each item is scored 1 or 0.

Rationale

Paper Folding and Cutting involves visualization, spatial ability, the integration of visual and spatial abilities, and at-

tention to visual clues. Successful performance requires visualization of what the folded and cut paper would look like if the paper were unfolded.

Factor Analytic Findings

Paper Folding and Cutting is a fair measure of g (48% of its variance may be attributed to g). This subtest contributes substantially to the Nonverbal Reasoning/Visualization factor (*Mdn* loading = .65). Specificity is ample at all ages.

Reliability and Correlational Highlights

Paper Folding and Cutting is a reliable subtest (r_{xx} = .94). It correlates better with Number Series (r = .61) and Pattern Analysis (r = .60) than with any of the other subtests. It has a moderately high correlation with the Composite Score (r = .74).

Administrative and Interpretive Suggestions

Because all items are in a multiple-choice format, scoring is easy on the Paper Folding and Cutting subtest. Observe how the examinee responds to the items.

- Does the examinee understand the instructions?
- Is the examinee perplexed by the task?
- Does the examinee find the task too abstract?
- Is the examinee challenged by the task?

The subtest may help you identify individuals with excellent visualization skills.

QUANTITATIVE

The Quantitative subtest contains 40 problems that cover a range of quantitative concepts. Early items involve matching and addition primarily; later items involve subtraction, division, multiplication, and algebra. Solutions require an understanding (or use) of ordinality, mathematical language, comparisons, utilization of space, mixing, interest, and logic. The stimulus materials are dice-like blocks for the first 12 items and pictures or word problems for items 13 to 40. Item content varies, including whole numbers, objects, money, fractions, and measurement. Table 14-13 presents the processes, content, and stimulus material for each item on the Quantitative subtest. The subtest is administered at all ages, and each item is scored 1 or 0.

Rationale

The rationale presented for the WISC–III Arithmetic subtest generally applies to the Quantitative subtest of the SB: IV (see Chapter 9). The skills required for the earlier Quantita-

Table 14-12
Processes Involved in Solving Items on the Matrices Subtest of the Stanford-Binet: IV

Item	Processes involved in solving items	Item	Processes involved in solving items
Sample 1	Find a likeness	12	Find a like relationship using shape and number
Sample 2	Find a likeness	13	Find a like relationship using addition and subtraction
Sample 3	Find a likeness or change shape and shading	14	Find a like relationship using addition and subtraction
Sample 4	Change orientation and shading or change orientation	15	Find a like relationship using size, color, and orientation
1	Find a likeness	16	Find a like relationship using the number of elements and reversal of color
2	Find a likeness or a like relationship using physical characteristics	17	Find a like relationship using subtraction and orientation
3	Find a likeness or a like relationship using size and shape	18	Find a like relationship using size, color, and orientation
4	Change size	19	Find a like relationship using addition, subtraction, size, color, and shape
5	Find a like relationship using size and shape	20	Find a like relationship using subtraction
6	Find a like relationship using physical characteristics	21	Find a like relationship using subtraction
7	Find a relationship using addition and orientation	22	Find a like relationship using color and orientation
8	Change size, shape, and shading or change size and shading	23	Find a like relationship using letter sequence, orientation, and number of elements
9	Find a like relationship using size and shape	24	Find a like relationship using letter sequence, orientation, and number of elements
10	Change size and shading or change size, shape, and shading	25	Find a like relationship using letter sequence, orientation, and number of elements
11	Find a like relationship using shape and size	26	Find a like relationship using letter sequence and orientation

Source: Courtesy of Jeannine Feldman.

tive items, however, are less likely to be dependent on formal education than are those required for the WISC–III Arithmetic subtest. Items 1 to 3 and 6 to 8 on the Quantitative subtest require the examinee to make perceptual discriminations, and they appear to measure nonverbal reasoning ability.

Factor Analytic Findings

Quantitative is a good measure of *g* (60% of its variance may be attributed to *g*). This subtest contributes moderately to the Nonverbal Reasoning/Visualization factor (*Mdn* loading = .54) and to the Verbal Comprehension factor (*Mdn* loading = .41). Specificity is ample or adequate at most ages, with the exception of ages 6 and 18–23, where it is inadequate.

Reliability and Correlational Highlights

Quantitative is a reliable subtest (r_{xx} = .88). It correlates better with Number Series (*r* = .67) and Equation Building (*r* = .61) than with any of the other subtests. It has a high correlation with the Composite Score (*r* = .82).

Administrative and Interpretive Considerations

As on the WISC–III Arithmetic subtest, use testing-of-limits procedures to determine the reasons for the examinee's failures. You might say, for example, "Let's try this one again. Tell me how you solved the problem." The examinee may fail the items because of poor knowledge of arithmetical

Table 14-13
Analysis of the Quantitative Subtest on the Stanford-Binet: IV by Process and Content Variables and Stimulus Material

Item	Process	Content	Stimulus material	Item	Process	Content	Stimulus material
1	Matching	Whole nos.	Blocks	21	Comparing	Objects	Picture
2	Matching	Whole nos.	Blocks	22	Mixing	Whole nos./mon.	Word problem
3	Matching	Whole nos.	Blocks	23	Addition	Objects	Picture
4	Counting	Whole nos.	Blocks	24	Comparing	Objects	Picture
5	Counting	Whole nos.	Blocks	25	Division	Whole nos.	Word problem
6	Matching	Whole nos.	Blocks	26	Division	Whole nos./mon.	Word problem
7	Matching	Whole nos.	Blocks	27	Division	Whole nos./mon.	Word problem
8	Matching	Whole nos.	Blocks	28	Utilization of space	Objects	Word problem
9	Addition/counting	Whole nos.	Blocks	29	Converting numbers	Fractions/dec.	Word problem
10	Addition/counting	Whole nos.	Blocks	30	Mixing	Whole nos./mon.	Word problem
11	Addition/counting	Whole nos.	Blocks	31	Multiplication	Whole nos./mon.	Word problem
12	Ordinality/reasoning	Whole nos.	Blocks	32	Applying math logic	Measurement	Word problem
13	Addition/counting	Whole nos.	Picture	33	Applying math logic	Measurement	Word problem
14	Subtraction	Whole nos.	Picture	34	Applying math logic	Measurement	Word problem
15	Applying concepts	Objects	Picture	35	Utilization of space	Measurement	Word problem
16	Measuring	Objects	Picture	36	Applying math logic	Money	Word problem
17	Division	Objects	Picture	37	Applying math logic	Money	Word problem
18	Matching	Objects	Picture	38	Applying math logic	Measurement	Word problem
19	Division	Whole nos.	Word problem	39	Applying math logic	Whole nos.	Word problem
20	Utilization of space	Objects	Picture	40	Applying math logic	Whole nos.	Word problem

Note. Abbreviations: Whole nos. = Whole numbers; Whole nos./mon. = Whole numbers/money; Fractions/dec.= Fractions/decimals.

operations, inadequate conceptualization of the problem, temporary inefficiency or anxiety, poor concentration, carelessness, or some combination of these or other factors.

NUMBER SERIES

The Number Series subtest contains 26 items. The examinee is presented with five to seven numbers arranged in a logical sequence and is asked to give (either orally or in writing) the two numbers that would come next in the series. The subtest is administered at ages 7 to 18-23 years, and each item is scored 1 or 0.

Rationale

Number Series involves using logical reasoning and concentration in working with numbers. The examinee must come to some understanding of the relationship between numbers in a set, or discover the rationale underlying the series, and apply this understanding to arrive at a solution. Correct solutions may involve trial and error, persistence, and/or flexibility.

The subtest measures analogic reasoning with quantitative materials.

Factor Analytic Findings

Number Series is a good measure of g (62% of its variance may be attributed to g). This subtest contributes substantially to the Nonverbal Reasoning/Visualization factor (*Mdn* loading = .64). Specificity is ample at all ages.

Reliability and Correlational Highlights

Number Series is a reliable subtest (r_{xx} = .90). It correlates better with Quantitative (r = .67) and Matrices (r = .66) than with any of the other subtests. It has a high correlation with the Composite Score (r = .82).

Administrative and Interpretive Considerations

Number Series is easy to score. Note how the examinee proceeds to answer the items.

SCHOOLIES

What happened to your tolerance for diverse viewpoints?

Copyright © 1996 by John P. Wood.

- Does the examinee give responses quickly or slowly?
- Does the examinee appear confident or anxious?
- How does the examinee handle failures?
- Does the examinee show flexibility in shifting from ascending to descending series?
- Does the examinee find any series especially difficult, such as those with fractions or those with both numbers and letters?
- How much time does the examinee need to solve the problems?

EQUATION BUILDING

The Equation Building subtest contains 18 items. Each item consists of a series of four to five numbers followed by three to four signs. The examinee must rearrange the numbers and signs to make a true number sentence, or equation. Paper and pencil can be used. The examinee can give responses either orally or in writing. Although there is no time limit, allow at least 2 minutes per item. The subtest is administered at ages 12 to 18-23, and each item is scored 1 or 0.

Rationale

Equation Building involves working with relationships among numbers, which in turn involves logic, flexibility, and trial and error. The examinee's task is to manipulate mathe-

matical signs of operation and numbers to form a valid equation. Consider the subtest as a type of mathematical anagram.

Factor Analytic Findings

Equation Building is a fair measure of g (45% of its variance may be attributed to g). This subtest contributes moderately to the Nonverbal Reasoning/Visualization factor (Mdn loading = .58). Specificity is ample at all ages.

Reliability and Correlational Highlights

Equation Building is a reliable subtest (r_{xx} = .91). It correlates better with Number Series (r = .64) and Quantitative (r = .61) than with any of the other subtests. It has a moderately high correlation with the Composite Score (r = .74).

Administrative and Interpretive Considerations

Equation Building is relatively easy to score. In addition to those in the scoring guide, give credit to the following solutions and other correct solutions that you learn about:

4. $4 - 1 + 2 = 5$
8. $3 \times 6 \div 2 = 3 \times 3$
13. $8 \div 2 \times 1 = 4$
15. $5 + 4 + 1 = 13 - 3$
16. $5 - 6 + 9 = 4 \times 2$
    $9 - 2 \times 4 + 5 = 6$

Observe the examinee's reactions to this subtest.

- How flexible is the examinee?
- Does the examinee enjoy the challenge or find the tasks burdensome?
- Does the examinee work well with fractions?
- Does the examinee know how to use parentheses?
- How does the examinee handle failure?

BEAD MEMORY

The Bead Memory subtest contains 42 items. Beads are of four shapes (round; cylindrical; cone; and flattened round, or saucer-like) and three colors. Items 1 to 10 use photographs of the beads, and items 11 to 42 use a plastic base and stick and real beads. For items 1 to 10, you show the examinee one or two beads for 2 or 3 seconds, and the examinee then must point to the correct bead(s) in the photograph. On these items, the order in which the examinee points to the beads does not matter. For items 11 to 42, you show a photograph of two to eight beads arranged vertically on a stick. After 5 seconds, you remove the photograph and ask the examinee to construct the design. On these items, the examinee must arrange the shapes and colors exactly as they are arranged in the photograph. There is no time limit. The subtest is administered at all ages, and each item is scored 1 or 0.

Rationale

Bead Memory involves short-term memory for visual stimuli, form perception and discrimination, spatial relations, alertness to detail, attention, and concentration. Additionally, for items 11 to 42, which require the examinee to place the beads on the stick, the subtest involves eye-hand coordination.

Factor Analytic Findings

Bead Memory is a fair measure of g (46% of its variance may be attributed to g). This subtest contributes moderately to the Nonverbal Reasoning/Visualization factor (*Mdn* loading = .51) and to a limited extent to the Memory factor (*Mdn* loading = .36). Specificity is ample at all ages.

Reliability and Correlational Highlights

Bead Memory is a reliable subtest (r_{xx} = .87). It correlates better with Number Series (r = .54) and Matrices and Quantitative (r = .52 for both) than with any of the other subtests. It has a moderately high correlation with the Composite Score (r = .72).

Administrative and Interpretive Suggestions

Bead Memory is easy to administer. Note, however, that in order to administer this subtest, you must determine that the examinee can identify at least three of the four shapes. If the examinee cannot, do not administer the subtest.

Observe how the examinee proceeds. Note, for example, the following:

- Does the examinee show tremor? If so, to what extent does it interfere with the task?
- What is the tempo of the examinee's responses?
- Does the examinee verbalize as work progresses?
- Does the examinee find the task enjoyable or burdensome?
- Does the examinee arrange the shapes correctly but choose the wrong color, or vice versa?
- When the examinee fails, how many of the beads are incorrect?
- What might have caused the examinee's failures?
- How many near successes does the examinee have?

MEMORY FOR SENTENCES

The Memory for Sentences subtest contains 42 items. You read each item aloud and ask the examinee to repeat it. The examinee must repeat the sentence exactly to receive credit. The sentences range in complexity and length from simple 2-word phrases to statements of 22 words. The subtest is administered at all ages, and each item is scored 1 or 0.

Rationale

Memory for Sentences measures immediate recall and attention. The subtest involves short-term auditory memory, which includes attention, concentration, listening comprehension, and auditory processing. Because success may depend on verbal facility, failure may not reflect poor memory ability. For children 5 years and older, scores may be related primarily to memory ability, but for younger children, scores may reflect verbal knowledge and comprehension rather than immediate recall ability per se.

Factor Analytic Findings

Memory for Sentences is a good measure of g (50% of its variance may be attributed to g). This subtest contributes moderately to the Verbal Comprehension factor (*Mdn* loading = .58) and to the Memory factor (*Mdn* loading = .57). Specificity is ample or adequate at all ages.

Reliability and Correlational Highlights

Memory for Sentences is a reliable subtest (r_{xx} = .89). It correlates better with Vocabulary (r = .64) and Comprehension (r = .58) than with any of the other subtests. It has a moderately high correlation with the Composite Score (r = .73).

Administrative and Interpretive Considerations

Memory for Sentences is easy to administer. Read the sentences clearly and in a steady voice. Here are some questions for you to consider:

- What kinds of errors did the examinee make—omissions, substitutions, additions, changes in words, or changes in the order of words?
- Did the examinee add any idiosyncratic or peculiar words?
- Did the examinee make errors toward the beginning, middle, or end of sentences?
- Did the examinee completely miss sentences, or were there only a few errors in each sentence?

Missing a few words suggests minor temporary inefficiencies, whereas not recalling any words in the sentences suggests more serious memory problems.

MEMORY FOR DIGITS

The Memory for Digits subtest has two parts: Digits Forward and Digits Reversed. Score and administer each part separately. Each item is presented orally at a rate of one digit per second. Digits Forward has 14 items. It begins with three digits per item and goes up to nine digits per item. Digits Reversed has 12 items. It begins with two digits per item and goes up to seven digits per item. The raw score is equal to the sum of the raw scores on Digits Forward and Digits Reversed. The subtest is administered at ages 7 to 18-23 years, and each item is scored 1 or 0.

Rationale

The rationale presented for the WISC–III Digit Span subtest applies to the SB: IV Memory for Digits subtest (see Chapter 9).

Factor Analytic Findings

Memory for Digits is a fair measure of g (36% of its variance may be attributed to g). This subtest contributes substantially to the Memory factor ($Mdn = .65$). Specificity is ample or adequate at all ages.

Reliability and Correlational Highlights

Memory for Digits is a reliable subtest ($r_{xx} = .83$). It correlates better with Memory for Sentences ($r = .56$) and Number Series ($r = .52$) than with any of the other subtests. It has a moderate correlation with the Composite Score ($r = .64$).

Administrative and Interpretive Considerations

The administrative and interpretive considerations presented for the WISC–III Digit Span subtest also are relevant for the Memory for Digits subtest (see Chapter 9).

MEMORY FOR OBJECTS

The Memory for Objects subtest contains 14 items. Stimulus cards containing a picture of an object are shown to the examinee at a rate of one per second. After the stimulus cards are shown, the examinee is shown a response card containing several objects, including the objects on the stimulus cards. The examinee is asked to point to the stimulus objects. There is no time limit. The response cards contain 5 to 12 pictured objects. To receive credit, the examinee must point to the correct objects in the exact order in which they were presented. The subtest begins with two stimulus objects per item and ends with eight stimulus objects per item. The subtest is administered at ages 7 to 18-23 years, and each item is scored 1 or 0.

Rationale

Memory for Objects measures immediate recall and attention. The subtest involves short-term visual memory, which includes attention, concentration, visual comprehension, and

visual processing. Because performance may depend on recognition of objects, the examinee's success may be enhanced by familiarity with objects or by labeling of objects.

Factor Analytic Findings

Memory for Objects is a fair measure of g (29% of its variance may be attributed to g). This subtest contributes moderately to the Memory factor (Mdn loading = .52). Specificity is ample at all ages, except for age 12 years, where it is inadequate.

Reliability and Correlational Highlights

Memory for Objects is a moderately reliable subtest ($r_{xx} = .73$). It correlates better with Memory for Digits and Bead Memory ($r = .44$ for both) than with any of the other subtests. It has a moderate correlation with the Composite Score ($r = .60$).

Administrative and Interpretive Considerations

Memory for Objects is easy to administer. Look for possible patterns in the errors made by the examinee.

- Did the examinee point to the correct objects but in the wrong order?
- Were the examinee's errors toward the beginning, middle, or end of the series?
- Did the examinee completely miss the order, or were only a few errors made?

The examinee who points to the correct objects but in the wrong order or who misses only one or two objects at the end of a long series may have less serious memory problems than one who makes many errors.

Observe how the examinee approaches the task.

- Does the examinee name the objects as you point to them?
- Is the examinee aware of any errors?
- How does the examinee react to failure?

INTERPRETING THE SB: IV

Much of the material in Chapter 10 on interpreting the WISC–III pertains to the SB: IV. Profile analysis, the successive-level approach to test interpretation, factor-score comparisons, and subtest comparisons are essentially the same for the WISC–III and the SB: IV. Read or review Chapter 10 before you read the rest of this chapter.

The information in Table E-9 in Appendix E can help you to interpret and write reports on the SB: IV. The table summarizes the abilities thought to be measured by each subtest, background factors that may influence subtest performance, implications of high and low scores, and instructional implications. This table deserves careful study.

Table BC-2 on the inside back cover shows the classifications associated with the SB: IV Composite Scores. Table BC-1 on the inside back cover shows the percentile ranks for the Composite Scores and for the factor scores. If you have any questions about the validity of the Composite Score, consider whether the separate factor scores may be more valid. Table E-10 in Appendix E shows the percentile ranks associated with the subtest scores.

Like the Wechsler subtests, the individual SB: IV subtests should not be viewed as a means of determining specific cognitive skills with precision. Rather, subtest scores should be used to generate hypotheses about the examinee's abilities. The most reliable estimates of specific abilities are derived from the Verbal Comprehension factor, Nonverbal Reasoning/Visualization factor, and Memory factor, not from the individual subtest scores. Consider all hypotheses you develop from the SB: IV in relation to all other sources of data.

Profile Analysis

Profile analysis can be used to formulate tentative hypotheses about an examinee's strengths and weaknesses. As noted previously, the approaches to profile analysis for the SB: IV are generally the same as those for the WISC–III (see Chapter 10). The main difference is that you must use different tables in the Appendix.

Method 1: Compare Verbal Comprehension, Nonverbal Reasoning/Visualization, and Memory factor scores. Table E-3 in Appendix E provides the critical values for comparing the Verbal Comprehension, Nonverbal Reasoning/Visualization, and Memory factor scores. These values range from 8 to 15 points. Because the range is large, no single critical value is appropriate for all comparisons. Consequently, use the values shown for each age group. (Table E-6 in Appendix E shows the probabilities associated with various differences between factor scores.)

Table E-7 in Appendix E presents the percentage of individuals in the standardization group who obtained a given discrepancy between the factor scores. The table, for example, shows that between 25% and 50% of the population had a median discrepancy (in either direction) of from 9 to 13 points between Verbal Comprehension and Nonverbal Reasoning/Visualization factor scores.

Method 2: Compare each Verbal Comprehension factor subtest scaled score with the mean Verbal Comprehension factor scaled score. Table E-4 in Appendix E provides the critical values for comparing Verbal Comprehension subtests with the mean of the Verbal Comprehension subtests. These values range from 5.18 to 6.18 at the .05 level and from 6.37 to 7.51 at the .01 level.

Table E-5 in Appendix E gives the frequencies with which various differences between subtest scores and aver-

age SB: IV Verbal Comprehension scores occurred in the standardization sample. The table shows, for example, that 5% of the standardization sample at ages 2 to 7 obtained a difference as large as 7.02 points between the scaled score on Vocabulary and the Verbal Comprehension factor average. Use this table only when differences are statistically significant. Five percent of the standardization sample obtained differences of approximately 5 to 9 points between each subtest score and the respective average Verbal Comprehension factor score.

Method 3: Compare each Nonverbal Reasoning/ Visualization factor subtest scaled score with the mean Nonverbal Reasoning/Visualization factor scaled score. Table E-4 in Appendix E provides the critical values for comparing Nonverbal Reasoning/Visualization subtests with the mean of the Nonverbal Reasoning/Visualization subtests. These values range from 5.22 to 6.15 at the .05 level and from 6.35 to 7.42 at the .01 level.

Table E-5 in Appendix E gives the frequencies with which various differences between subtest scores and average SB: IV Nonverbal Reasoning/Visualization scores occurred in the standardization sample. The table shows, for example, that 5% of the standardization sample at ages 2 to 11 obtained a difference as large as 9.41 points between the scaled score on Pattern Analysis and the Nonverbal Reasoning/Visualization factor average. Use this table only when differences are statistically significant. Five percent of the standardization sample obtained differences of approximately 10 to 12 points between each subtest score and the respective average Nonverbal Reasoning/Visualization factor score.

Method 4. Compare each Memory factor subtest scaled score with the mean Memory factor scaled score. Table E-4 in Appendix E provides the critical values for comparing Memory subtests with the mean of the Memory subtests. These values range from 5.98 to 7.51 at the .05 level and from 7.34 to 9.73 at the .01 level.

Table E-5 in Appendix E gives the frequencies with which various differences between subtest scores and average SB: IV Memory scores occurred in the standardization sample. The table shows, for example, that 5% of the standardization sample at age 7 obtained a difference as large as 8.29 points between the scaled score on Memory for Digits and the Memory factor average. Use this table only when differences are statistically significant. Five percent of the standardization sample obtained differences of approximately 8 to 11 points between each subtest score and the respective average Memory factor score.

Method 5. Compare sets of individual subtest scores. Table E-2 in Appendix E provides the critical values for comparing sets of subtest scaled scores. These values range between 6 and 10 at the .05 level and between 8 and 14 at the .01 level. The values in Table E-2 in Appendix E for

Table 14-14
Subtest Age Ranges in *SD* Units for the Stanford-Binet: IV

Subtest	+4 (82–75)	+3 (74–67)	+2 (66–59)	+1 (58–51)
Vocabulary	2-0-0 to 17-11-15	17-11-16 to 23-11-15	—	—
Comprehension	2-0-0 to 12-11-15	12-11-16 to 15-11-15	15-11-16 to 23-11-15	—
Absurdities	2-0-0 to 9-11-15	9-11-16 to 11-11-15	11-11-16 to 14-11-15	—
Verbal Relations	11-11-16 to 13-11-15	13-11-16 to 17-11-15	17-11-16 to 23-11-15	—
Pattern Analysis	2-0-0 to 8-11-15	8-11-16 to 10-5-15	10-5-16 to 14-11-15	14-11-16 to 23-11-15
Copying	2-0-0 to 7-5-15	7-15-16 to 9-11-15	9-11-16 to 11-11-15	11-11-16 to 13-11-15
Matrices	6-11-16 to 14-11-15	14-11-16 to 23-11-15	—	—
Paper Folding and Cutting	11-11-16 to 13-11-15	13-11-16 to 15-11-15	15-11-16 to 23-11-15	—
Quantitative	2-0-0 to 14-11-15	14-11-16 to 17-11-15	17-11-16 to 23-11-15	—
Number Series	6-11-16 to 12-11-15	12-11-16 to 15-11-15	15-11-16 to 23-11-15	—
Equation Building	9-11-16 to 23-11-15	—	—	—
Bead Memory	2-0-0 to 23-11-15	—	—	—
Memory for Sentences	2-0-2 to 23-11-15	—	—	—
Memory for Digits	6-11-16 to 16-11-15	16-11-16 to 23-11-15	—	—
Memory for Objects	6-11-16 to 10-11-15	10-11-16 to 23-11-15	—	—

Subtest	−1 (50–42)	−2 (41–34)	−3 (33–26)	−4 (25–18)
Vocabulary	2-0-0 to 2-3-15	2-3-16 to 3-3-15	3-3-16 to 5-11-15	5-11-16 to 23-11-15
Comprehension	2-0-0 to 2-3-15	2-3-16 to 3-3-15	3-3-16 to 6-5-15	6-5-16 to 23-11-15
Absurdities	2-0-0 to 2-11-15	2-11-16 to 4-3-15	4-3-16 to 6-5-15	6-5-16 to 14-11-15
Verbal Relations	11-11-16 to 13-11-15	13-11-16 to 23-11-15	—	—
Pattern Analysis	2-0-0 to 2-3-15	2-3-16 to 3-3-15	3-3-16 to 5-3-15	5-3-16 to 23-11-15
Copying	2-0-0 to 2-11-15	2-11-16 to 3-11-15	3-11-16 to 6-5-15	6-5-16 to 13-11-15
Matrices	6-11-16 to 7-11-15	7-11-16 to 10-5-15	10-5-16 to 16-11-15	16-11-16 to 23-11-15
Paper Folding and Cutting	11-11-16 to 15-11-15	15-11-16 to 23-11-15	—	—
Quantitative	2-0-0 to 3-7-15	3-7-16 to 4-11-15	4-11-16 to 6-11-15	6-11-16 to 23-11-15
Number Series	6-11-16 to 8-11-15	8-11-16 to 11-11-15	11-11-16 to 23-11-15	—
Equation Building	11-11-16 to 15-11-15	15-11-16 to 23-11-15	—	—
Bead Memory	2-0-0 to 3-3-15	3-3-16 to 4-3-15	4-3-16 to 6-5-15	6-5-16 to 23-11-15
Memory for Sentences	2-0-0 to 2-11-15	2-11-16 to 3-11-15	3-11-16 to 5-11-15	5-11-16 to 23-11-15
Memory for Digits	—	6-11-16 to 9-5-15	9-5-16 to 17-11-15	17-11-16 to 23-11-15
Memory for Objects	—	6-11-16 to 9-11-15	9-11-16 to 23-11-15	—

subtest comparisons are overly liberal (i.e., they lead to too many significant differences) when you make more than one comparison. They are most accurate when a priori planned comparisons are made (such as Memory for Sentences versus Memory for Digits or Pattern Analysis versus Matrices).

Before you make multiple-subtest comparisons (i.e., when you compare more than one set of subtest scores), determine the difference between the highest and lowest subtest scores. A difference of 13 scaled-score points between the highest and lowest scaled scores is significant at the .05 level. (This critical difference is for the 12 subtests that make up the factor scores; excluded are Paper Folding and Cutting, Number Series, and Equation Building. If you administer all 15 subtests, the critical difference between the highest and lowest subtest scores is 14.) You can then interpret differences of 13 scaled-score points or greater. If the difference between the highest and lowest subtest scaled scores is less than 13 scaled-score points, do not make multiple comparisons between individual subtest scores.

Ranges for Subtests, Short Forms, Factor Scores, and Composite Scores

Table E-8 in Appendix E presents the ranges in standard age scores (or scaled scores) for each subtest, for the three short forms, for the three factors, and for the two Composite Scores in the SB: IV by age level. The discussion that follows summarizes the highlights of Table E-8.

Range of subtests.   There are no subtests in the SB: IV that provide the full range of scores (from −3 *SD*s to +3 *SD*s from the mean or more) over the entire age range covered by the subtest (see Table 14-14). This nonuniformity of scaled scores complicates the use of profile analysis. Some examples are instructive. (a) Although the Vocabulary subtest provides a ±3 *SD* range of scores from ages 3-3-16 to 23-11-15, Bead Memory provides this range only beginning with age 4-3-16. (b) There are no scores on Verbal Relations, Paper Folding and Cutting, or Equation Building that run below −2 *SD*s from the mean. (c) The full ±3 *SD* range of scores is available only for ages 3-3-16 to 10-5-15.

You cannot apply profile analysis to subtest scores without considering the available score ranges. Any statements about the examinee's differential strengths and weaknesses may be inappropriate unless you consider the available subtest ranges. Consequently, refer to Table E-8 in Appendix E when you evaluate each examinee's profile.

Subtests that do not have adequate ceilings for the age ranges they cover (at least +3 *SD*s from the mean) are as follows:

- Comprehension at age 15-11-16 and on
- Absurdities at age 11-11-16 and on
- Verbal Relations at age 17-11-16 and on
- Pattern Analysis at age 10-5-16 and on
- Copying at age 9-11-16 and on
- Paper Folding and Cutting at age 15-11-16 and on
- Quantitative at age 17-11-16 and on
- Number Series at age 15-11-16 and on

Subtests that do not have adequate floors for the age ranges they cover (at least −3 *SD*s from the mean) are as follows:

- Vocabulary at age 3-3-15 and below
- Comprehension at age 3-3-15 and below
- Absurdities at age 4-3-15 and below
- Verbal Relations at all ages
- Pattern Analysis at age 3-3-15 and below
- Copying at age 3-11-15 and below
- Matrices at age 10-5-15 and below
- Paper Folding and Cutting at all ages
- Quantitative at age 4-11-15 and below

Table 14-15
Age Ranges That Span ±2.1 to 3 *SD*s and ±3.1 to 4 *SD*s on the Stanford-Binet: IV for Subtests, Short Forms, Factors, and Composite Scores

Subtest, short form, factor, and Composite Score	±2.1 to 3 SD	±3.1 to 4 SD
Subtest		
V	3-3-16 to 23-11-15	5-11-16 to 17-11-15
C	3-3-16 to 15-11-15	6-5-16 to 12-11-15
A	4-3-16 to 11-11-15	6-5-16 to 9-11-15
VR	—	—
PA	3-3-16 to 10-5-15	5-3-16 to 8-11-15
CP	3-11-16 to 9-11-15	6-5-16 to 7-5-15
M	10-5-16 to 23-11-15	—
PF	—	—
Q	4-11-16 to 17-11-15	6-11-16 to 14-11-15
NS	11-11-16 to 15-11-15	—
EB	—	—
BM	4-3-16 to 23-11-15	6-5-16 to 23-11-15
MS	3-11-16 to 23-11-15	5-11-16 to 23-11-15
MD	9-5-16 to 23-11-15	—
MO	9-11-16 to 23-11-15	—
Short Form		
2-Subtest	3-3-16 to 17-11-15	4-7-16 to 12-11-15
4-Subtest	3-7-16 to 23-11-15	4-11-16 to 16-11-15
6-Subtest	3-3-16 to 23-11-15	4-3-16 to 14-11-15
Factor		
VC	3-3-16 to 23-11-15	4-3-16 to 15-11-15
NR/V	3-7-16 to 23-11-15	4-11-16 to 16-11-15
Mem	7-11-16 to 23-11-15	8-11-16 to 23-11-15
Composite		
Factor battery	3-3-16 to 23-11-15	4-3-16 to 17-11-15
Full battery	3-3-16 to 23-11-15	4-3-16 to 23-11-15

Note. Abbreviations: V = Vocabulary; C = Comprehension; A = Absurdities; VR = Verbal Relations; PA = Pattern Analysis; CP = Copying; M = Matrices; PF = Paper Folding and Cutting; Q = Quantitative; NS = Number Series; EB = Equation Building; BM = Bead Memory; MS = Memory for Sentences; MD = Memory for Digits; MO = Memory for Objects; VC = Verbal Comprehension; NR/V = Nonverbal Reasoning/Visualization; Mem = Memory. Subtest short forms are as follows: 2 subtests: Vocabulary and Pattern Analysis; 4 subtests: Vocabulary, Bead Memory, Quantitative, and Pattern Analysis; 6 subtests: Vocabulary, Bead Memory, Quantitative, Memory for Sentences, Pattern Analysis, and Comprehension. See Table 14-9 for subtests that form the factor scores.

- Number Series at age 11-11-15 and below
- Equation Building at all ages
- Bead Memory at age 4-3-15 and below
- Memory for Sentences at age 3-11-15 and below
- Memory for Digits at age 9-5-15 and below
- Memory for Objects at age 9-11-15 and below

Fortunately, five of the six subtests (Vocabulary, Comprehension, Quantitative, Bead Memory, and Memory for Sentences) that cover all ages provide a range of scores of ±2.1 to 3 SDs for ages 4-11-16 to 15-11-15. Table 14-15 shows the

ages at which each subtest, three short forms, three factor scores, and two Composite Scores (based on factor scores and the full battery) span ±2.1 to 3 and ±3.1 to 4 SDs from the mean.

Range for short forms. The ranges for three useful short forms are as follows (see Tables 14-15 and 14-16):

- The Vocabulary plus Pattern Analysis short form has a range of scores of ±2.1 to 3 SDs from ages 3-3-16 to

Table 14-16
Short Forms, Factors, and Composite Score Ranges on the Stanford-Binet: IV

Short form, factor, and Composite Score	+4 (164–149)	+3 (148–133)	+2 (132–117)	+1 (116–101)
Short Form				
2-Subtest short form	2-0-0 to 12-11-15	12-11-16 to 17-11-15	17-11-16 to 23-11-15	—
4-Subtest short form	2-0-0 to 16-11-15	16-11-16 to 23-11-15	—	—
6-Subtest short form	2-0-0 to 15-11-15	15-11-16 to 23-11-5	—	—
Factor				
Verbal Comprehension factor	2-0-0 to 15-11-15	15-11-16 to 23-11-15	—	—
Nonverbal Reasoning/Visualization factor	2-0-0 to 16-11-15	16-11-16 to 23-11-15	—	—
Memory factor	2-0-0 to 23-11-15	—	—	—
Composite				
Composite Score (factor scores)	2-0-0 to 17-11-15	17-11-16 to 23-11-15	—	—
Composite Score (full battery)	2-0-0 to 23-11-15	—	—	—

Short form, factor, and Composite Score	−1 (100–84)	−2 (83–68)	−3 (67–52)	−4 (51–36)
Short Form				
2-Subtest short form	2-0-0 to 2-3-15	2-3-16 to 3-3-15	3-3-16 to 4-7-15	4-7-16 to 23-11-15
4-Subtest short form	2-0-0 to 2-7-15	2-7-16 to 3-7-15	3-7-16 to 4-11-15	4-11-16 to 23-11-15
6-Subtest short form	2-0-0 to 2-7-15	2-7-16 to 3-3-15	3-3-16 to 4-3-15	4-3-16 to 23-11-15
Factor				
Verbal Comprehension factor	2-0-0 to 2-3-15	2-3-16 to 3-3-15	3-3-16 to 4-3-15	4-3-16 to 23-11-15
Nonverbal Reasoning/Visualization factor	2-0-0 to 2-11-15	2-11-16 to 3-7-15	3-7-16 to 4-11-15	4-11-16 to 23-11-15
Memory factor	—	6-11-16 to 7-11-15	7-11-16 to 8-11-15	8-11-16 to 23-11-15
Composite				
Composite Score (factor scores)	2-0-0 to 2-7-15	2-7-16 to 3-3-15	3-3-16 to 4-3-15	4-3-16 to 23-11-15
Composite Score (full battery)	2-0-0 to 2-7-15	2-7-16 to 3-3-15	3-3-16 to 4-3-15	4-3-16 to 23-11-15

Note. Subtest short forms are as follows: 2 subtests: Vocabulary and Pattern Analysis; 4 subtests: Vocabulary, Bead Memory, Quantitative, and Pattern Analysis; 6 subtests: Vocabulary, Bead Memory, Quantitative, Memory for Sentences, Pattern Analysis, and Comprehension. See Table 14-9 for subtests that form the factor scores.

17-11-15 only. The ±3.1 to 4 *SD* range spans ages 4-7-16 to 12-11-15.

- The Vocabulary, Pattern Analysis, Quantitative, and Bead Memory short form has a range of scores of ±2.1 to 3 *SD*s from ages 3-7-16 to 23-11-15. The ±3.1 to 4 *SD* range spans ages 4-11-16 to 16-11-15.

- The Vocabulary, Comprehension, Pattern Analysis, Quantitative, Bead Memory, and Memory for Sentences short form has a range of scores of ±2.1 to 3 *SD*s from ages 3-3-16 to 23-11-15. The ±3.1 to 4 *SD* range spans ages 4-3-16 to 14-11-15.

Range for factor scores. The ranges for the factor scores are as follows:

- The Verbal Comprehension factor has a range of scores of ±2.1 to 3 *SD*s for ages 3-3-16 to 23-11-15. The ±3.1 to 4 *SD* range spans ages 4-3-16 to 15-11-15.

- The Nonverbal Reasoning/Visualization factor has a range of scores of ±2.1 to 3 *SD*s for ages 3-7-16 to 23-11-15. The ±3.1 to 4 *SD* range spans ages 4-11-16 to 16-11-15.

- The Memory factor has a range of scores of ±2.1 to 3 *SD*s for ages 7-11-16 to 23-11-15. The ±3.1 to 4 *SD* range spans ages 8-11-16 to 23-11-15.

Ranges for Composite Scores. The ranges for the Composite Scores are as follows:

- The Composite Score for the factor score battery has a range of scores of ±2.1 to 3 *SD*s for ages 3-3-16 to 23-11-15. The ±3.1 to 4 *SD* range spans ages 4-3-16 to 17-11-15.

- The Composite Score for the full battery has a range of scores of ±2.1 to 3 *SD*s for ages 3-3-16 to 23-11-15. The ±3.1 to 4 *SD* range spans ages 4-3-16 to 23-11-15.

The ranges for the two Composite Scores on the SB: IV (i.e., the Composite Score for the factor battery and the Composite Score for the full battery) are such that the floor is not sufficient to classify children as mentally retarded until they reach age 3-3-16. In fact, the lowest Composite Score a 2-0-0 can receive on either the factor battery or the full battery is 95. The lowest score drops to 87 at 2-3-16, 80 at 2-7-16, 73 at 2-11-16, and 66 at 3-3-16. Thus, at the 2-year-old level, the SB: IV is suitable for the evaluation of exceptionally gifted children but not for the evaluation of children with mental retardation.

A SUCCESSIVE-LEVEL APPROACH TO TEST INTERPRETATION

The successive-level approach to interpreting the SB: IV is similar to the one described for the Wechsler tests in Chapter 10. Let's look at the approach again, however, because there are some subtle differences.

I. *The Composite Score.* At the first level of interpretation is the Composite Score. It provides a global estimate of the examinee's level of cognitive ability. The examinee's in-

telligence classification is based on the Composite Score (see Table BC-2 on the inside back cover sheets). Converting the Composite Score into a percentile rank (see Table BC-1 on the inside back cover sheets) will help you to interpret this score for persons not familiar with standard scores.

II. *Factor scores.* At the second level of interpretation are the absolute levels of the three factor scores and the extent to which there are differences between them.

III. *Subtest variability within factors.* At the third level of interpretation are the deviations of the subtests from the mean of the Verbal Comprehension factor or Nonverbal Reasoning/Visualization factor or Memory factor. You can develop hypotheses about strengths and weaknesses from these analyses.

IV. *Intersubtest variability.* At the fourth level of interpretation are comparisons between sets of subtests or among clusters of subtests. Although these comparisons are open to the errors associated with multiple comparisons, they are valuable for generating hypotheses. (Table E-10 in Appendix E provides the percentile ranks for subtest scaled scores.)

V. *Intrasubtest variability.* At the fifth level of interpretation are the patterns of performance within each individual subtest. Because the items in each subtest are arranged in order of difficulty, you can evaluate patterns of successes and failures. For example, an examinee who passes the first item, fails the next four, passes the next one, fails the next four, and overall passes a total of four items shows a different pattern from one who passes the first four items and fails the remainder, although both examinees receive the same raw score. The examinee with the markedly uneven pattern may have cognitive or attentional inefficiencies that you should explore further.

VI. *Qualitative analysis.* At the sixth level of interpretation are specific item failures and the content of the responses, or qualitative analysis. Inspecting responses to specific items can aid you in understanding the examinee's knowledge of specific information, such as how to count coins on the Quantitative subtest or the meaning of specific words on the Vocabulary subtest. Always evaluate both the verbal and the nonverbal responses.

COMPARISONS BETWEEN FACTOR SCORES THAT CAN GUIDE INTERPRETATIONS

Your evaluation of the SB: IV factor scores depends primarily on your hypotheses about the individual subtests that make up the respective factor scores. Some general observations can be made about the three factors, however.

Interpretation of Verbal Comprehension, Nonverbal Reasoning/Visualization, and Memory Factors

The Verbal Comprehension factor depends on the examinee's accumulated experience. The items in this factor usually tap into the examinee's repertoire of verbal knowledge. Questions are presented either verbally or visually, and the examinee gives the responses. The Verbal Comprehension factor might be considered an index of verbal ability and crystallized intelligence.

The Nonverbal Reasoning/Visualization factor, in contrast, is more dependent on the examinee's immediate problem-solving ability. The stimuli are nonverbal and are presented visually. Solutions require motor, pointing, or verbal responses. The Nonverbal Reasoning/Visualization factor might be considered an index of nonverbal ability and fluid intelligence.

The Memory factor is dependent on the examinee's ability to sustain attention. Also involved are short-term memory, encoding ability (including sequencing ability), use of rehearsal strategies, ability to shift mental operations rapidly on symbolic material, and ability to self-monitor. These processes are similar to those described for the Freedom from Distractibility factor on the WISC–III (see Chapter 10).

Solving problems that make up the Verbal Comprehension, Nonverbal Reasoning/Visualization, and Memory factors involves both verbal and nonverbal strategies. Within the Verbal Comprehension factor, Absurdities may involve visualization strategies more than the other subtests. Within the Nonverbal Reasoning/Visualization factor, Quantitative and Matrices may involve verbal strategies more than Pattern Analysis, Copying, or Bead Memory. Within the Memory factor, Memory for Sentences may involve verbal processing more than the other subtests.

Formulating Hypotheses About Factor Score Discrepancies

Significant differences in an examinee's factor scores may lead to hypotheses about one or more of the following:

- Interest patterns
- Cognitive style
- Psychopathology
- Deficiencies or strengths in processing information
- Sensory deficiencies
- Motivational changes

You must decide which interpretations apply, based on the examinee's entire performance and clinical history.

Formulate hypotheses about factor scores in relationship to the examinee's absolute Verbal Comprehension, Nonverbal Reasoning/Visualization, and Memory factor scores, and only when the differences are significant. Thus, for example, you would not say that an examinee with a Verbal Comprehension factor score of 140 and a Memory factor score of 120 had a memory deficit. In this case, both verbal comprehension and memory are well developed. Similarly, you should view an examinee with a Nonverbal Reasoning/Visualization factor score of 65 and a Memory score of 50 as having deficits in both nonverbal and memory areas; do not consider the higher Nonverbal Reasoning/Visualization score of 65 as an absolute strength.

ILLUSTRATIVE HYPOTHESES FOR VERBAL COMPREHENSION > NONVERBAL REASONING/VISUALIZATION

1. Verbal skills are better developed than performance skills.
2. Auditory-vocal processing skills are better developed than visual discrimination skills.
3. Knowledge acquired through accumulated experience is better developed than immediate problem-solving ability.
4. Practical tasks are more difficult than nonpractical tasks.
5. Performance deficits may exist, including deficits in copying skills.
6. Limitations in visual-motor integration may be influencing performance.

ILLUSTRATIVE HYPOTHESES FOR VERBAL COMPREHENSION > MEMORY

1. Verbal skills are better developed than short-term memory skills.
2. Long-term memory is better developed than short-term memory.
3. Limitations in attention, possibly due to anxiety and distractibility, may be influencing performance.

ILLUSTRATIVE HYPOTHESES FOR NONVERBAL REASONING/VISUALIZATION > VERBAL COMPREHENSION

1. Performance skills are better developed than verbal skills.
2. Visual-motor discrimination skills are better developed than auditory-vocal processing skills.
3. Immediate problem-solving ability is better developed than knowledge acquired as a result of accumulated experience.
4. Reading skill and performance on academic tasks are not satisfactory.
5. A language deficit may exist.
6. Limitations in auditory conceptual skills and auditory processing skills may be influencing performance.

ILLUSTRATIVE HYPOTHESES FOR NONVERBAL REASONING/VISUALIZATION > MEMORY

1. Nonverbal reasoning skills are better developed than short-term memory skills.
2. Visual-motor discrimination skills are better developed than memory skills.
3. Immediate problem-solving ability is better developed than memory skills.
4. Limitations in attention, possibly due to anxiety and distractibility, may be influencing performance.

ILLUSTRATIVE HYPOTHESES FOR MEMORY > VERBAL COMPREHENSION

1. Short-term memory skills are better developed than verbal skills.
2. Short-term memory is better developed than long-term memory.

3. Encoding ability (such as sequencing ability) is better developed than knowledge acquired as a result of accumulated experience.
4. Reading skill and performance on academic tasks are not satisfactory.
5. A language deficit may exist.

ILLUSTRATIVE HYPOTHESES FOR MEMORY > NONVERBAL REASONING/VISUALIZATION

1. Short-term memory skills are better developed than nonverbal reasoning and visualization skills.
2. Short-term memory skills are better developed than visual-motor discrimination skills.
3. Encoding ability (such as sequencing ability) is better developed than immediate problem-solving ability.
4. Practical tasks are more difficult than nonpractical tasks.
5. Performance deficits may exist, including deficits in copying skills.
6. Limitations in visual-motor integration may be influencing performance.

COMPARISONS BETWEEN SUBTESTS THAT CAN GUIDE INTERPRETATIONS

If you find that the differences between subtest scaled scores are significant (see Table E-2 in Appendix E), you must translate the findings into meaningful descriptions. It is not easy to interpret differences between subtest scores. The material in this chapter will help you in making interpretations. Table 14-17 charts suggested abilities and factors associated with the 15 SB: IV subtests. View the interpretations that follow as hypotheses that may help you understand an examinee's abilities. However, you need to investigate these hypotheses through a study of the examinee's entire test performance and clinical history.

The following list of subtest comparisons does not include all possible comparisons, nor does it reflect all possible interpretations. Based on these examples, however, you should be able to develop other comparisons and formulate other interpretations. Treat all hypotheses as tentative. Never consider interpretations derived from profile analysis as definitive. (See Table E-9 in Appendix E for a summary of interpretive rationales and suggested remediation activities for the SB: IV subtests.) Develop hypotheses based on both significant differences between subtest scores and the absolute values of the subtest scores. Thus, scaled scores of 50 or higher never reflect absolute weaknesses, and scaled scores of 49 or lower never reflect absolute strengths.

COMPARISONS OF VERBAL COMPREHENSION FACTOR SUBTESTS

1. *Vocabulary (V) and Comprehension (C).* Both subtests involve verbal processing, but in different contexts.

• V > C: High Vocabulary and low Comprehension may suggest inability to apply verbal skills and general knowledge fully in life situations and may therefore indicate impaired judgment.
• V < C: Low Vocabulary and high Comprehension may suggest limited concept formation, except when conceptualizing ability is applied to solving problems in the social world.

2. *Vocabulary (V) and Verbal Relations (VR).* Both Vocabulary and Verbal Relations measure level of abstract thinking and ability to form concepts, but Verbal Relations is a better measure of these abilities.

• VR > V: High Verbal Relations and low Vocabulary may suggest good ability to think abstractly but limited ability to understand the meaning of words.
• VR < V: Low Verbal Relations and high Vocabulary may suggest difficulty in forming abstract concepts but good ability to understand the meaning of individual words.

3. *Verbal Relations (VR) and Comprehension (C).* Verbal Relations and Comprehension both involve conceptualizing skills. Verbal Relations usually requires a single-word response, whereas Comprehension requires an extended response that interrelates a set of ideas (i.e., propositional thinking).

• VR > C: High Verbal Relations and low Comprehension may suggest good abstract thinking but difficulty in applying conceptualizing ability to problem solving in the social world. This pattern also may suggest a verbal-expressive deficit involving propositional thinking.
• VR < C: Low Verbal Relations and high Comprehension may suggest a deficit in verbal concept formation relative to real-world conceptualizing ability.

4. *Comprehension (C) and Absurdities (A).* Comprehension and Absurdities both reflect social intelligence. The comparison relates knowledge of social conventions (Comprehension) to the ability to discern incongruities in visually presented material (Absurdities).

• A > C: High Absurdities coupled with low Comprehension may suggest good observational skills but limited understanding of social conventions.
• A < C: Low Absurdities coupled with high Comprehension may suggest an understanding of social conventions but difficulty in using observational skills.

5. *Vocabulary (V) and Memory for Sentences (MS).* Vocabulary and Memory for Sentences both involve verbal processing (particularly from 2 to 7 years). Comparing the two subtests may provide an index of the relative balance between long-term memory (Vocabulary) and short-term memory (Memory for Sentences).

• V > MS: High Vocabulary and low Memory for Sentences may suggest that long-term memory is better developed than short-term memory.

Table 14-17
Suggested Abilities or Factors Associated with the 15 Subtests of the Stanford-Binet: IV

Vocabulary (V)	Comprehension (C)	Absurdities (A)	Verbal Relations (VR)	Pattern Analysis (PA)	Copying (CP)	Matrices (M)	Paper Folding and Cutting (PF)	Quantitative (Q)	Number Series (NS)	Equation Building (EB)	Bead Memory (BM)	Memory for Sentences (MS)	Memory for Digits (MD)	Memory for Objects (MO)	M	Suggested abilities or factors
V			VR												—	Abstract thinking
		A			CP	M	PF	Q	NS	EB	BM	MS	MD	MO	—	Attention
								Q				MS	MD		—	Auditory memory
			VR												—	Categorical thinking
	C														—	Common-sense reasoning
		A			CP	M	PF	Q	NS	EB	BM	MS	MD	MO	—	Concentration
V	C		VR												—	Crystallized ability
V	C	A													—	Cultural opportunities at home
V			VR												—	Extent of outside reading
								Q	NS	EB					—	Facility with numbers
				PA	CP										—	Fine motor coordination
				PA				Q	NS	EB	BM	MS	MD	MO	—	Fluid ability
		A						Q			BM	MS	MD	MO	—	Freedom from distractibility
V															—	Fund of information
V			VR					Q							—	Long-term memory
								Q	NS	EB					—	Mathematics knowledge
				PA		M	PF								—	Nonverbal reasoning
								Q	NS	EB					—	Numerical ability
				PA		M	PF				BM				—	Perception of abstract stimuli
V(P)		A				M								MO	—	Perception of meaningful stimuli
				PA	CP	M	PF				BM				—	Perceptual organization
						M									—	Perceptual planning ability
				PA	CP						BM				—	Perceptual reproduction
				PA			PF								—	Perceptual synthesis
				PA											—	Psychomotor speed
V															—	Richness of early environment
V								Q	NS	EB					—	School learning
									NS		BM	MS	MD	MO	—	Sequencing
								Q		EB	BM	MS	MD	MO	—	Short-term memory
	C														—	Social judgment
				PA	CP		PF				BM				—	Spatial perception
				PA		M	PF			EB					—	Sustained energy on persistence
V	C	A	VR												—	Verbal comprehension
V			VR												—	Verbal concept formation
V	C		VR												—	Verbal expression
	C	A						Q		EB					—	Verbal reasoning
							PF				BM			MO	—	Visual memory
				PA	CP						BM				—	Visual-motor coordination
		A	PA			M	PF				BM				—	Visual processing
								Q	NS	EB	BM	MS	MD	MO	—	Working memory

Note. V(P) = Picture Vocabulary and *M* = mean of the subtest scaled scores or factor.

- V < MS: Low Vocabulary and high Memory for Sentences may suggest that short-term memory is better developed than long-term memory.

6. *Comprehension (C) and Memory for Sentences (MS).* Both Comprehension and Memory for Sentences involve verbal processing (particularly from 2 to 7 years). This comparison provides an estimate of verbal reasoning versus short-term verbal memory.

- C > MS: High Comprehension and low Memory for Sentences may suggest that verbal reasoning is better developed than short-term verbal memory.
- C < MS: Low Comprehension and high Memory for Sentences may suggest that verbal reasoning is not as well developed as short-term verbal memory.

COMPARISONS OF NONVERBAL REASONING/VISUALIZATION FACTOR SUBTESTS

1. *Pattern Analysis (PA) and Copying (CP).* This comparison relates visual-spatial ability to visual-motor ability.

- PA > CP: High Pattern Analysis and low Copying may suggest adequate visual-spatial ability but inadequate visual-motor ability.
- PA < CP: Low Pattern Analysis and high Copying may suggest inadequate visual-spatial ability but adequate visual-motor ability.

2. *Pattern Analysis (PA) and Matrices (M).* Both Pattern Analysis and Matrices involve nonverbal reasoning ability. In Pattern Analysis, however, the reasoning has to do with analysis and synthesis, whereas in Matrices the reasoning is more analogic.

- PA > M: High Pattern Analysis and low Matrices may suggest adequate analysis and synthesis skills but inadequate analogic reasoning skills.
- PA < M: Low Pattern Analysis and high Matrices may suggest inadequate analysis and synthesis skills but adequate analogic reasoning skills.

3. *Pattern Analysis (PA) and Paper Folding and Cutting (PF).* Both Pattern Analysis and Paper Folding and Cutting involve visual-spatial ability, but Paper Folding and Cutting is a purer measure of this ability. In Pattern Analysis the examinee is provided with a concrete representation of the design, whereas in Paper Folding and Cutting the examinee must discern how the design would look when the folded and cut paper was unfolded.

- PA > PF: High Pattern Analysis and low Paper Folding and Cutting may suggest that visual-spatial ability is more adequate when the stimulus is concrete.
- PA < PF: Low Pattern Analysis and high Paper Folding and Cutting may suggest that visual-spatial ability is less adequate when the stimulus is concrete.

4. *Pattern Analysis (PA) and Quantitative (Q).* This comparison relates nonverbal spatial reasoning to numerical reasoning.

- PA > Q: High Pattern Analysis and low Quantitative may suggest adequate nonverbal spatial reasoning ability but inadequate numerical reasoning ability.
- PA < Q: Low Pattern Analysis and high Quantitative may suggest inadequate nonverbal spatial reasoning ability but adequate numerical reasoning ability.

5. *Pattern Analysis (PA) and Bead Memory (BM).* Pattern Analysis and Bead Memory both involve visual discrimination and spatial relations. In Bead Memory, however, these skills are measured in the context of a short-term visual memory task, whereas in Pattern Analysis these skills are measured using stimuli that remain in view during the task. Additionally, Pattern Analysis has a strong reasoning component, whereas Bead Memory does not.

- PA > BM: High Pattern Analysis and low Bead Memory may suggest that visual discrimination and spatial relations skills are adequate when short-term memory is not involved but are inadequate when short-term memory is involved.
- PA < BM: Low Pattern Analysis and high Bead Memory may suggest that visual discrimination and spatial relations skills are adequate when short-term memory is involved but are inadequate when short-term memory is not involved.

6. *Quantitative (Q) and Number Series (NS).* Both Quantitative and Number Series involve numerical reasoning ability, but Number Series is a better measure of this ability.

- Q > NS: High Quantitative and low Number Series may suggest adequate understanding of mathematical concepts but inadequate numerical reasoning ability.
- Q < NS: Low Quantitative and high Number Series may suggest inadequate understanding of mathematical concepts but adequate numerical reasoning ability.

7. *Quantitative (Q) and Equation Building (EB).* Both Quantitative and Equation Building involve numerical reasoning ability, but Equation Building requires more logical reasoning and flexibility in rearranging and manipulating mathematical symbols.

- Q > EB: High Quantitative and low Equation Building may suggest adequate understanding of mathematical concepts but inadequate logical reasoning and flexibility in the use of mathematical symbols.
- Q < EB: Low Quantitative and high Equation Building may suggest inadequate understanding of mathematical concepts but adequate logical reasoning and flexibility in the use of mathematical symbols.

8. *Number Series (NS) and Equation Building (EB).* Both Number Series and Equation Building involve numeri-

cal reasoning. Equation Building, in addition, involves knowledge of conventional arithmetical operations and flexibility in the use of mathematical symbols.

- NS > EB: High Number Series and low Equation Building may suggest adequate numerical and logical reasoning ability but inadequate knowledge of conventional operations and limited flexibility in the use of mathematical symbols.
- NS < EB: Low Number Series and high Equation Building may suggest inadequate numerical and logical reasoning ability but adequate knowledge of conventional operations and flexibility in the use of mathematical symbols.

COMPARISONS OF MEMORY FACTOR SUBTESTS

1. *Memory for Sentences (MS), Memory for Digits (MD), Memory for Objects (MO), and Bead Memory (BM).* The Memory for Sentences, Memory for Digits, Memory for Objects, and Bead Memory subtests all involve short-term memory. Differences exist among the four subtests, however, in the stimuli used to elicit responses (meaningful or nonmeaningful) and the processing modality (auditory or visual; see Figure 14-3). Memory for Sentences involves meaningful stimuli presented in the auditory modality. Memory for Digits involves nonmeaningful stimuli presented in the auditory modality. Memory for Objects involves meaningful stimuli presented in the visual modality. Bead Memory involves nonmeaningful stimuli presented in the visual modality.

The subtests also load on different factors. Bead Memory loads on the Nonverbal Reasoning/Visualization factor, whereas the other three subtests load on the Memory factor. (Memory for Sentences also loads on the Verbal Comprehension factor throughout the scale.) In Bead Memory the stimuli are presented simultaneously (or as a group or as a gestalt), whereas in the other subtests the stimuli are shown sequentially.

- MS > MD: High Memory for Sentences and low Memory for Digits may suggest adequate short-term memory for meaningful material but inadequate short-term memory for nonmeaningful material.
- MS < MD: Low Memory for Sentences and high Memory for Digits may suggest inadequate short-term memory for meaningful material but adequate short-term memory for nonmeaningful material.

- MS > MO: High Memory for Sentences and low Memory for Objects may suggest that, for meaningful stimuli, short-term auditory memory is adequate but short-term visual memory is inadequate.
- MS < MO: Low Memory for Sentences and high Memory for Objects may suggest that, for meaningful stimuli, short-term auditory memory is inadequate but short-term visual memory is adequate.
- MD > BM: High Memory for Digits and low Bead Memory may suggest that, for nonmeaningful material, short-term auditory memory is adequate but short-term visual memory is inadequate.
- MD < BM: Low Memory for Digits and high Bead Memory may suggest that, for nonmeaningful material, short-term auditory memory is inadequate but short-term visual memory is adequate.
- BM > MO: High Bead Memory and low Memory for Objects may suggest that short-term visual memory is adequate for nonmeaningful material but inadequate for meaningful material.
- BM < MO: Low Bead Memory and high Memory for Objects may suggest that short-term visual memory is inadequate for nonmeaningful material but adequate for meaningful material.

2. *Memory for Digits—Digits Forward (MD-F) versus Digits Reversed (MD-R).* The two components of Memory for Digits—Digits Forward and Digits Reversed—both involve attention. Digits Reversed, however, involves more complex attentional processes.

- MD-F > MD-R: High Digits Forward and low Digits Reversed (differences of 3 or more raw-score points) may indicate that the extra effort needed to master the more difficult task of recalling digits in reversed sequence was not put forth. Alternatively, it may indicate good auditory memory but poor short-term visual memory based on auditory information (a tentative hypothesis).
- MD-F < MD-R: Low Digits Forward and high Digits Reversed may indicate that Digits Reversed was seen as a challenge rather than as a task involving mere repetition of numbers.

3. *Memory for Sentences (MS) and Memory for Objects (MO) versus Memory for Digits (MD) and Bead Memory (BM).* This comparison contrasts subtests that measure short-term memory for meaningful material (Memory for Sentences, Memory for Objects) with those that measure short-term memory for nonmeaningful material (Memory for Digits, Bead Memory; see Figure 14-3).

- MS, MO > MD, BM: High Memory for Sentences and Memory for Objects coupled with low Memory for Digits and Bead Memory may suggest better short-term memory

	Meaningful memory	Nonmeaningful memory
Auditory memory	Memory for Sentences	Memory for Digits
Visual memory	Memory for Objects	Bead Memory

Figure 14-3. Classification of four memory subtests on the Stanford-Binet Intelligence Scale: Fourth Edition.

when the material is meaningful than when it is nonmeaningful.

- MS, MO < MD, BM: Low Memory for Sentences and Memory for Objects coupled with high Memory for Digits and Bead Memory may suggest better short-term memory when the material is nonmeaningful than when it is meaningful.

4. *Memory for Sentences (MS) and Memory for Digits (MD) versus Memory for Objects (MO) and Bead Memory (BM).* This comparison contrasts short-term auditory memory with short-term visual memory (see Figure 14-3).

- MS, MD > MO, BM: High Memory for Sentences and Memory for Digits and low Memory for Objects and Bead Memory may suggest better short-term auditory memory than short-term visual memory.
- MS, MD < MO, BM: Low Memory for Sentences and Memory for Digits and high Memory for Objects and Bead Memory may suggest poorer short-term auditory memory than short-term visual memory.

5. *Bead Memory (BM) versus Memory for Sentences (MS), Memory for Digits (MD), and Memory for Objects (MO).* This comparison contrasts a subtest that uses simultaneously presented stimuli with subtests that use sequentially presented stimuli.

- BM > MS, MD, MO: High Bead Memory and low Memory for Sentences, Memory for Digits, and Memory for Objects may suggest better short-term memory with stimuli presented simultaneously than with stimuli presented sequentially.
- BM < MS, MD, MO: Low Bead Memory and high Memory for Sentences, Memory for Digits, and Memory for Objects may suggest poorer short-term memory with stimuli presented simultaneously than with stimuli presented sequentially.

COMPARISONS OF VERBAL COMPREHENSION, NONVERBAL REASONING/VISUALIZATION, AND MEMORY FACTOR SUBTESTS

1. *Verbal Relations (VR) and Pattern Analysis (PA).* Verbal Relations and Pattern Analysis both reflect abstract reasoning ability. They require the abstraction of relations among stimulus items. However, Verbal Relations reflects verbal processing, whereas Pattern Analysis reflects nonverbal processing.

- VR > PA: High Verbal Relations and low Pattern Analysis may suggest that abstract reasoning ability is better with verbal stimuli than with nonverbal stimuli.
- VR < PA: Low Verbal Relations and high Pattern Analysis may suggest that abstract reasoning ability is better with nonverbal stimuli than with verbal stimuli.

2. *Comprehension (C) and Quantitative (Q) versus Vocabulary (V), Verbal Relations (VR), and Memory for Digits (MD).* This comparison contrasts subtests that have relatively long verbal questions (Comprehension and Quantitative) with those that have relatively short verbal questions (Vocabulary, Verbal Relations, Memory for Digits).

- C, Q > V, VR, MD: High Comprehension and Quantitative coupled with low Vocabulary, Verbal Relations, and Memory for Digits may suggest better performance when the verbal stimuli are long than when they are short. The examinee may put forth more effort to attend to verbal material of a relatively long duration. The pattern also may reflect the examinee's ability to benefit from the contextual cues contained in the longer questions.
- C, Q < V, VR, MD: Low Comprehension and Quantitative coupled with high Vocabulary, Verbal Relations, and Memory for Digits may suggest better performance when verbal stimuli are short than when they are long. The examinee may put forth more effort to attend to verbal material of a relatively short duration. This pattern also may suggest an auditory processing deficit associated with deriving meaning from spoken language.

3. *Vocabulary (Oral) (V(O)), Comprehension (C), and Verbal Relations (VR) versus Absurdities (A), Quantitative (Q), and Number Series (NS).* This comparison contrasts subtests that require a fair amount of verbal expression (Vocabulary (Oral), Comprehension, and Verbal Relations) with those that require relatively little verbal expression (Absurdities, Quantitative, and Number Series).

- V(O), C, VR > A, Q, NS: High Vocabulary (Oral), Comprehension, and Verbal Relations coupled with low Absurdities, Quantitative, and Number Series may suggest better performance when the tasks require a moderate amount of verbal expression than when they require relatively little verbal expression. One possibility is that the examinee may put forth extra effort in situations that require verbal expression.
- V(O), C, VR < A, Q, NS: Low Vocabulary (Oral), Comprehension, and Verbal Relations coupled with high Absurdities, Quantitative, and Number Series may suggest better performance when the tasks require relatively little verbal expression than when they require a moderate amount of verbal expression. One possibility is that the examinee may put forth effort only when tasks require minimal verbal effort. Additionally, this pattern may be associated with communication problems or shyness when the examinee must speak in relatively long sentences.

4. *Absurdities (A) versus Pattern Analysis (PA), Matrices (M), and Paper Folding and Cutting (PF).* This comparison contrasts a subtest that contains relatively meaningful perceptual stimuli (Absurdities) with those that have relatively abstract perceptual stimuli (Pattern Analysis, Matrices, and Paper Folding and Cutting). (Matrices contains some meaningful stimuli as well, but primarily at the younger ages.)

- A > PA, M, PF: High Absurdities coupled with low Pattern Analysis, Matrices, and Paper Folding and Cutting may suggest better performance when the visual stimuli are meaningful than when they are abstract or nonmeaningful.
- A < PA, M, PF: Low Absurdities coupled with high Pattern Analysis, Matrices, and Paper Folding and Cutting may suggest better performance when the visual stimuli are abstract than when they are concrete.

5. *Vocabulary (V), Verbal Relations (VR), and Quantitative (Q) versus Bead Memory (BM), Memory for Sentences (MS), Memory for Digits (MD), and Memory for Objects (MO).* This comparison contrasts subtests that involve long-term memory (Vocabulary, Verbal Relations, and Quantitative) with those that involve primarily short-term memory (Bead Memory, Memory for Sentences, Memory for Digits, and Memory for Objects).

- V, VR, Q > BM, MS, MD, MO: High Vocabulary, Verbal Relations, and Quantitative coupled with low Bead Memory, Memory for Sentences, Memory for Digits, and Memory for Objects may suggest better performance on tasks requiring long-term memory than on those requiring short-term memory.
- V, VR, Q < BM, MS, MD, MO: Low Vocabulary, Verbal Relations, and Quantitative coupled with high Bead Memory, Memory for Sentences, Memory for Digits, and Memory for Objects may suggest better performance on tasks requiring short-term memory than on those requiring long-term memory.

6. *Pattern Analysis (PA), Paper Folding and Cutting (PF), and Bead Memory (BM) versus Quantitative (Q) and Matrices (M).* This comparison distinguishes subtests that may tap spatial visualization processes from subtests with perceptual tasks that do not tap these processes.

- PA, PF, BM > Q, M: High Pattern Analysis, Paper Folding and Cutting, and Bead Memory coupled with low Quantitative and Matrices may suggest better performance when perceptual tasks require spatial visualization than when they do not.
- PA, PF, BM < Q, M: Low Pattern Analysis, Paper Folding and Cutting, and Bead Memory coupled with high Quantitative and Matrices may suggest poorer performance when perceptual tasks require spatial visualization than when they do not.

ADDITIONAL SUGGESTIONS FOR USING AND INTERPRETING THE SB: IV

The following are additional suggestions for interpreting the SB: IV. You will usually need other information to confirm any of the following hypotheses.

- Some subtests may be less culturally loaded than others. Candidates include Paper Folding and Cutting, Matrices, Pattern Analysis, Number Series, and Bead Memory.
- Some subtests may be especially sensitive to brain damage that affects conceptual processes or visualization or flexibility in rearranging materials. Possible candidates are Pattern Analysis, Matrices, Paper Folding and Cutting, Verbal Relations, and Equation Building. Other subtests may be sensitive to brain damage that affects short-term memory (Bead Memory, Memory for Sentences, Memory for Digits, Memory for Objects), long-term memory (Vocabulary, Verbal Relations, Quantitative), or judgment and reasoning (Comprehension, Absurdities, Matrices).
- The four memory subtests—Bead Memory, Memory for Sentences, Memory for Digits, and Memory for Objects—may prove to be especially helpful in assessment of learning disabled examinees. These subtests permit comparisons of simultaneous and successive processing, auditory and visual processing, and meaningful and nonmeaningful processing.
- The three numerical ability subtests—Quantitative, Number Series, and Equation Building—provide a powerful measure of quantitative skills. These subtests may be especially useful in counseling students about their mathematical talents.
- Four subtests provide potentially useful information about spatial perception skills—Pattern Analysis, Copying, Paper Folding and Cutting, and Bead Memory. These subtests may prove to be useful in identifying examinees with visual-spatial talents.
- The Nonverbal Reasoning/Visualization factor subtests along with the Memory for Objects subtest may be a useful screening tool for measuring the cognitive skills of hearing-impaired children.
- The Vocabulary, Comprehension, Memory for Sentences, Memory for Digits, Verbal Relations, and Number Series subtests may be a useful screening tool for measuring the cognitive skills of visually impaired children.
- The Pattern Analysis subtest may provide some clues about how the examinee performs under time pressure.

ASSETS OF THE SB: IV

The SB: IV is a well-standardized test, with excellent internal consistency reliability and adequate concurrent validity. Of the 15 subtests in the scale, 12 subtests are recommended for routine use. These 12 subtests form three factors:

- Verbal Comprehension: Vocabulary, Comprehension, Absurdities at ages 2 to 14, Memory for Sentences at ages 2 to 7, and Verbal Relations at ages 15 to 18–23
- Nonverbal Reasoning/Visualization: Pattern Analysis, Copying (at ages 2 to 11), Quantitative, Bead Memory, and Matrices (at ages 12 to 18–23)

• Memory: Memory for Sentences (at ages 8 to 18–23), Memory for Digits, and Memory for Objects

The three remaining subtests—Paper Folding and Cutting, Number Series, and Equation Building—should be considered as supplementary, to be used for special purposes. The division of the scale into two factors at lower age levels (ages 2 to 6) and three factors at elementary and high school years is helpful in clinical and psychoeducational work and aids in the assessment of brain-behavior relationships. Following is a summary of the assets of the SB: IV:

1. *Good validity.* The SB: IV has adequate concurrent validity, demonstrated by acceptable correlations with several ability measures.

2. *High reliabilities.* The internal consistency reliabilities of the Composite Score and factor scores are extremely high (*Mdn r_{xx}* ranges from .91 to .97), with standard errors of measurement of less than 5 points. Because the Technical Manual provides reliability data, standard errors of measurement, and intercorrelations of subtest scores by one-year age intervals, as well as median reliabilities, you can evaluate the scale's properties throughout its entire age range. You can establish confidence intervals for the Composite Score for each of the 17 separate age groups, thereby providing estimates that are specifically applicable to each examinee's chronological age.

3. *Excellent standardization.* The standardization procedures were excellent, with sampling based on geographical region, community size, ethnic group, age, gender, and socioeconomic status. A weighting procedure was used to make the sample conform to the 1980 census data.

4. *Good administration procedures.* The procedures described in the Manual are excellent. The examiner actively probes borderline responses, and for several subtests the Manual provides examples of responses needing probing.

5. *Adequate administrative guidelines and test materials.* The administrative guidelines are adequate, although cumbersome. The use of both letters and numbers for items complicates use of the scale. The test directions, however, are easy to read. The art work and photos are clear, and the materials are well constructed. The easel format for administering the subtests is a decided advantage. The sample items on many subtests help the examinee understand the task requirements. Finally, the minimal time requirements are an advantage for those examinees who do not perform well under time pressure.

6. *Helpful scoring criteria.* The criteria for scoring the responses have been carefully prepared. The Vocabulary, Comprehension, and Verbal Relations scoring guidelines, for example, detail the rationale for 1 and 0 scores. Several examples demonstrate the application of the scoring principles. The Manual provides scores for many typical responses and places those responses needing further inquiry under a query section.

LIMITATIONS OF THE SB: IV

Although the SB: IV is, overall, an excellent instrument, some problems do exist.

1. *Lack of a comparable battery throughout the age ranges covered.* The SB: IV does not provide a comparable battery of subtests at all ages. This means that scores examinees obtain at different ages are based on different combinations of subtests. Only six subtests run throughout the scale (Vocabulary, Comprehension, Pattern Analysis, Quantitative, Bead Memory, and Memory for Sentences). Two subtests begin at the lowest age levels but stop during the adolescent years (Absurdities and Copying). Four subtests begin at age 7 years and run to the upper age level (Matrices, Number Series, Memory for Digits, and Memory for Objects). One subtest begins at age 12 and goes to the upper age level (Equation Building). Only at two ages can an examinee take all 15 subtests (ages 12 and 13). The lack of continuity across ages and within subtests makes it difficult to monitor changes in performance on individual subtests and may make it difficult to perform longitudinal studies.

2. *Variable range of scores.* The SB: IV fails to provide the same range of Composite Scores, factor scores, and subtest scores throughout the scale. For example, at ages 2-0-0 to 12-11-15 the highest Composite Score is 164. The Composite Scores then begin to drop, and at the age of 17-11-16 the highest Composite Score is 149. This means that if every item was answered correctly, the scores of an examinee tested first at age 12 and again at age 17 would differ by 15 points (about 1 standard deviation).

Similarly, examinees cannot obtain a Composite Score as low as 36 at all age levels. For example, the lowest possible scores at the 2-year level are 95 (2-0-0), 87 (2-3-16), 80 (2-7-16), and 73 (2-11-16). Only at age level 3-3-16 can scores more than 2 *SD*s below the mean be obtained. This limited floor means that you cannot establish a diagnosis of mental retardation with the SB: IV for children who are between 2 and 3 years of age.

The nonuniformity of scores also holds for all comparable combinations of subtests, either in factors or otherwise established. Applying profile analysis uniformly to all subtests would be misleading for individual cases because examinees cannot obtain the same number of scaled-score points on all subtests.

3. *Limited support for four area scores.* Factor analysis does not support the four area scores throughout the age levels of the scale. Thus, the routine use of area scores is not recommended. Factor scores are useful in describing the examinee's abilities, however.

4. *Difficulty in scoring responses.* When responses on Verbal Relations, Comprehension, and Vocabulary subtests differ from those in the *SB: IV Guide,* they may be difficult to score. The Copying subtest also is difficult to score.

5. *Difficulty in interpreting norms for subtests that have estimated scaled-score values at some ages.* Figure 2 in the

SB: IV Guide lists nine subtests that have estimated standard score values. For example, the *SB: IV Guide* gives estimated standard score values for ages 15, 16, and 17 years for the Absurdities subtest. Although for these years the raw scores can be converted into standard scores, the *SB: IV Guide* does not provide descriptive statistics for these age levels. Similarly, the *SB: IV Guide* does not give descriptive statistics for any of the ages at which the subtest scores are estimated. Therefore, we recommend that subtests be used only for ages at which the *SB: IV Guide* provides descriptive statistics.

6. *Lack of information about the procedure for establishing cutoff criteria.* Neither the *SB: IV Guide* nor the Technical Manual provides information concerning how the cutoff criteria (the number of items that should be administered before the test is discontinued) were determined (i.e., empirically or intuitively).

7. *Overly long administration time.* Because the SB: IV has only one timed subtest, examinees can take an inordinate amount of time to solve the problems. Even when the examinee does not take too much time to respond, administering the complete battery to an adolescent examinee may take 2 hours or more.

8. *Incorrect entry level points.* The entry level points indicated in the SB: IV may not be appropriate for all examinees. Therefore, you may unnecessarily prolong the test and give examinees items that are too difficult at the beginning of the test.

CONCLUDING COMMENT ON THE SB: IV

The SB: IV is a useful instrument for assessing the cognitive ability of young children, adolescents, and young adults. It has some shortcomings, however. The most serious of these are the lack of a comparable battery throughout the age levels covered by the scale and the nonuniformity of Composite Scores, factor scores, and scaled scores. Consequently, you cannot evaluate profiles and changes in test performance without considering how the scale is constructed. In each case, you must attend to the range of scores provided by the scale for the examinee's specific age. Keep these considerations in mind, especially when you must make critical decisions about the examinee.

THINKING THROUGH THE ISSUES

1. What unique features does the SB: IV have compared to the Wechsler tests?
2. How might the SB: IV assist in the diagnosis of learning disability?
3. When would you want to use the SB: IV instead of one of the Wechsler tests?
4. How would the limitations of the SB: IV affect its clinical usefulness?

SUMMARY

1. The SB: IV represents a significant departure from former editions, although it has some continuity with former editions.

1937 and 1960 Stanford-Binet Intelligence Scales

2. The 1937 and 1960 editions of the Stanford-Binet were generally well received, although there were criticisms associated with their emphasis on verbal material, age-scale format, ceiling procedure, item placements, emphasis on rote memory, administrative procedures, inappropriateness for use with adults, and use in clinical situations. The scales produced acceptable validity coefficients, however, and remained popular until the 1980s.

Introduction to the SB: IV

3. Only 6 of the 15 subtests run consecutively throughout the scale.

Standardization

4. The standardization sample was based on the 1980 U.S. Census data, but weighting procedures were used because the sample contained too many children with high SES backgrounds.

Composite Scores, Standard Age Scores, and Test-Age Equivalents

5. The SB: IV continues to use $M = 100$ and $SD = 16$ for the area scores and the Composite Score. The subtests use $M = 50$ and $SD = 8$.

Reliability

6. Internal consistency reliabilities are excellent for the Composite Score (*Mdn* r_{xx} = .97, *Mdn* SEM = 2.8). Reliabilities for the subtests are less satisfactory (r_{xx} ranges from .73 to .94). Stability coefficients are satisfactory for the Composite Score (r_{tt} ranges from .90 to .91), but not for some of the subtests (r_{tt} ranges from .28 to .86).

Validity

7. Validity studies comparing the SB: IV with other intelligence tests indicate satisfactory criterion validity (range from .44 to .78). SB: IV Composite Scores and IQs on other tests may not be comparable, however, especially in gifted or mentally retarded populations.

Correlations Between Subtests and Between Subtests and the Composite Score

8. Correlations are higher among the verbal subtests and nonverbal subtests than among the memory subtests. The memory subtests have low correlations with most other subtests. The subtests with the highest correlations with the Composite Score are Quantitative, Number Series, Vocabulary, Matrices, Comprehension, and Verbal Relations (all above .75).

SB: IV Composite Scores and Stratification Variables

9. The relationships between SB: IV Composite Scores and demographic characteristics indicate that African American children tend to score 10 to 17 points lower than Euro American children. There is about a 14-point difference between children in the highest and lowest socioeconomic status groups (108 vs. 94). Differences associated with gender were minimal, but some meaningful differences were associated with community size.

Factor Analysis

10. A principal-components analysis of the SB: IV supports two factors at ages 2 to 6—Verbal Comprehension and Nonverbal Reasoning/Visualization—and three factors at ages 7 to 18-23—Verbal Comprehension, Nonverbal Reasoning/Visualization, and Memory. The subtests that make up these factors differ at different ages.
11. All SB: IV subtests are either good or moderate measures of g. Those with the highest g loadings are Vocabulary, Number Series, Quantitative, Comprehension, and Matrices.
12. Of the 15 subtests in the SB: IV, only Vocabulary, Comprehension, Quantitative, and Memory for Objects have inadequate specificity at some ages.
13. Factor scores are the preferred way to identify meaningful psychological dimensions on the SB: IV. The factor scores are highly reliable.

Administering the SB: IV

14. The routing procedure used on the SB: IV may not apply to mentally retarded children. Entry level points for these children may have to be lower than those indicated in the record booklet. The entry level should be adjusted in testing a mentally retarded examinee (and other examinees as well, if necessary).
15. A complete administration of the SB: IV requires establishing a basal level (two consecutive levels at which the examinee passes all four items) and a ceiling level (two consecutive levels at which the examinee fails three or four items).
16. The examinee must have specific physical abilities to take the subtests, but some modifications may be made for physically handicapped children.
17. Short forms can be used for screening purposes.
18. A profile sheet is useful in plotting the examinee's scores. It can be used with the recommended battery for each age group or with the entire battery.
19. Use of the subtest battery recommended for each age level of the SB: IV will save administration time and help with the interpretation of test results and making of placement decisions.

Vocabulary

20. The rationale for the WISC–III Vocabulary subtest generally applies to the oral section of the SB: IV Vocabulary subtest. Formal education is less likely to influence the picture section of the Vocabulary subtest than the oral section. The subtest is a good measure of g and contributes to the Verbal Comprehension factor. It is a reliable subtest ($r_{xx} = .87$). Scoring requires considerable judgment.

Comprehension

21. The rationale for the WISC–III Comprehension subtest generally applies to the SB: IV Comprehension subtest. The subtest is a good measure of g and contributes to the Verbal Comprehension factor. It is a reliable subtest ($r_{xx} = .89$). Scoring requires considerable judgment.

Absurdities

22. Absurdities measures the ability to isolate the incongruities and absurdities in visual material. Success depends on perception of detail, alertness, concentration, and social understanding. The subtest is a good measure of g and contributes to the Verbal Comprehension factor. It is a reliable subtest ($r_{xx} = .87$) and relatively easy to administer.

Verbal Relations

23. Verbal Relations measures verbal concept formation and reasoning ability. It is a fair measure of g and contributes to the Verbal Comprehension factor. It is a reliable subtest ($r_{xx} = .91$) but may be difficult to score.

Pattern Analysis

24. The rationale for the WISC–III Block Design subtest generally applies to most of the items on the SB: IV Pattern Analysis subtest. The form-board items, however, primarily measure visual-motor ability and recognition and manipulation of forms. The subtest is a good measure of g and contributes to the Nonverbal Reasoning/Visualization factor. It is a reliable subtest ($r_{xx} = .92$) and is easy to score.

Copying

25. The Copying subtest measures visual-motor ability and eye-hand coordination. The subtest is a fair measure of g and contributes to the Nonverbal Reasoning/Visualization factor. It is a reliable subtest ($r_{xx} = .87$). The subtest may be the most difficult SB: IV subtest to score.

Matrices

26. Matrices measures analogic reasoning, attention to detail, and concentration. The subtest is a good measure of g and contributes to the Nonverbal Reasoning/Visualization factor. It is a reliable subtest ($r_{xx} = .90$) and is easy to administer.

Paper Folding and Cutting

27. Paper Folding and Cutting measures visualization, spatial ability, the integration of visual and spatial abilities, and attention to visual cues. The subtest is a fair measure of g and contributes to the Nonverbal Reasoning/Visualization factor. It is a reliable subtest ($r_{xx} = .94$) and is easy to score.

Quantitative

28. The rationale presented for the WISC–III Arithmetic subtest generally applies to the Quantitative subtest, although formal education probably has less influence on performance on the early Quantitative items. The subtest is a good measure of g and

contributes to the Nonverbal Reasoning/Visualization factor. It is a reliable subtest (r_{xx} = .88) and is easy to score.

Number Series

29. Number Series measures use of logical reasoning and concentration in working with numbers. The subtest is a good measure of g and contributes to the Nonverbal Reasoning/Visualization factor. It is a reliable subtest (r_{xx} = .90) and is easy to score.

Equation Building

30. Equation Building involves working with relationships among numbers, which in turn involves logic, flexibility, and trial and error. The subtest is a fair measure of g and contributes to the Nonverbal Reasoning/Visualization factor. It is a reliable subtest (r_{xx} = .91) and is relatively easy to score.

Bead Memory

31. Bead Memory measures short-term visual memory and involves form perception and discrimination, spatial relations, and alertness to detail. The subtest is a fair measure of g and contributes to the Nonverbal Reasoning/Visualization factor and, to a limited extent, the Memory factor. It is a reliable subtest (r_{xx} = .87) and is easy to administer.

Memory for Sentences

32. Memory for Sentences involves short-term auditory memory for meaningful material and measures immediate recall and attention. The subtest is a good measure of g and contributes to the Verbal Comprehension factor at ages 2 to 7 and Memory factor at ages 8 to 18-23. The Verbal Comprehension factor is a reliable subtest (r_{xx} = .89) and is easy to administer.

Memory for Digits

33. The rationale for the WISC–III Digit Span subtest applies to the Memory for Digits subtest. The subtest is a fair measure of g and contributes to the Memory factor. It is a reliable subtest (r_{xx} = .83) and is easy to administer.

Memory for Objects

34. Memory for Objects involves short-term visual memory and is therefore a measure of immediate recall and attention. The subtest is a fair measure of g and contributes to the Memory factor. It is a moderately reliable subtest (r_{xx} = .73) and is easy to administer.

Interpreting the SB: IV

35. Although the same considerations that apply to profile analysis on the WISC–III apply to the SB: IV, take more care in using profile analysis with the SB: IV because less is known about it. Table E-9 of Appendix E summarizes the proposed interpretive rationales and possible implications of high and low scores.
36. The nonuniform scaled-score ranges for subtests, short forms, factor scores, and Composite Scores complicate the use of profile analysis on the SB: IV. Perform profile analysis by considering the available score ranges, as shown in Table E-8 in Appendix E.

A Successive-Level Approach to Test Interpretation

37. As with the Wechsler tests, consider using a successive-level approach to test interpretation with the SB: IV.

Comparisons Between Factor Scores That Can Guide Interpretations

38. The Verbal Comprehension factor is dependent on the examinee's accumulated experience. The Nonverbal Reasoning/Visualization factor is dependent on the examinee's immediate problem-solving ability. The Memory factor is dependent on the examinee's ability to sustain attention. All three factors involve verbal and nonverbal strategies in the solution of problems.
39. Interpret significant differences between factor scores by considering the examinee's entire performance and clinical history and always in relationship to the examinee's absolute level of functioning.
40. A Verbal Comprehension factor score higher than both Nonverbal Reasoning/Visualization and Memory factor scores suggests that auditory processing skills may be better developed than visual processing and memory skills. A Nonverbal Reasoning/Visualization factor score higher than Verbal Comprehension and Memory factor scores suggests that nonverbal processing skills may be better developed than verbal and memory processing skills. A Memory factor higher than the Verbal Comprehension and Nonverbal Reasoning/Visualization factor scores suggests that short-term memory skills may be better developed than verbal and nonverbal reasoning skills.

Comparisons Between Subtests That Can Guide Interpretations

41. Treat any hypotheses generated from subtest comparisons as tentative and formulate them in relation to the absolute levels of the examinee's subtest scores.

Additional Suggestions for Using and Interpreting the SB: IV

42. Special combinations of subtests in the SB: IV may prove useful in generating interpretive hypotheses.

Assets of the SB: IV

43. The assets of the SB: IV include its good validity, high reliabilities, excellent standardization, good administration procedures, well-constructed and well-designed materials, and helpful scoring criteria.

Limitations of the SB: IV

44. The limitations of the SB: IV include the lack of a comparable battery throughout the age ranges covered, variable range of scores, limited support for four area scores, difficulty in scoring some subtests, difficulty in interpreting norms for subtests that have estimated scaled scores at some ages, lack of information about the procedure for establishing cutoff criteria, overly long administration time, and incorrect entry level points for some examinees.

Concluding Comment on the SB: IV

45. The SB: IV is a useful instrument for assessing the cognitive ability of young children, adolescents, and young adults. However, profile analysis cannot be performed in a routine manner—the range of scores available for each subtest and age must be considered.

KEY TERMS, CONCEPTS, AND NAMES

Three-level hierarchical model (p. 459)
SB: IV standardization sample (p. 460)
Standard age score (p. 460)
Area score (p. 460)
Composite Score (p. 460)
SB: IV test-age equivalents (p. 460)
Reliability of the SB: IV (p. 460)
Standard errors of measurement of the SB: IV (p. 460)
Stability of the SB: IV (p. 461)
Validity of the SB: IV (p. 461)
SB: IV subtest intercorrelations (p. 462)
Stratification variables on the SB: IV (p. 463)
SB: IV Verbal Comprehension factor (p. 463)
SB: IV Nonverbal Reasoning/Visualization factor (p. 463)
SB: IV Memory factor (p. 465)
SB: IV subtests as measures of g (p. 465)
Subtest specificity on the SB: IV (p. 465)
Factor scores on the SB: IV (p. 467)
Adaptive testing (p. 469)
Routing subtest (p. 469)
Basal level (p. 469)
Ceiling level (p. 469)
Physical abilities necessary for the SB: IV (p. 472)
Short forms of the SB: IV (p. 472)
Profile sheet for the SB: IV (p. 477)
SB: IV Vocabulary (p. 477)
SB: IV Comprehension (p. 480)
SB: IV Absurdities (p. 481)
SB: IV Verbal Relations (p. 481)
SB: IV Pattern Analysis (p. 482)
SB: IV Copying (p. 482)
SB: IV Matrices (p. 483)
SB: IV Paper Folding and Cutting (p. 484)
SB: IV Quantitative (p. 484)
SB: IV Number Series (p. 486)
SB: IV Equation Building (p. 487)
SB: IV Bead Memory (p. 487)
SB: IV Memory for Sentences (p. 488)
SB: IV Memory for Digits (p. 488)
SB: IV Memory for Objects (p. 489)
Profile analysis (p. 490)
Standard age score (or scaled-score) ranges (p. 492)
Successive-level approach to interpreting the SB: IV (p. 494)
Formulating hypotheses about factor score discrepancies on the SB: IV (p. 495)
Comparisons between subtests on the SB: IV (p. 496)

STUDY QUESTIONS

1. Discuss the SB: IV. Include in your discussion the following issues: standardization, Composite Score, test-age equivalents, reliability, and validity.
2. Describe and interpret correlations on the SB: IV (a) between subtests and (b) between subtests and the Composite Score.
3. Describe and interpret the SB: IV Composite Scores with respect to the stratification variables used in the standardization sample.
4. Describe and interpret SB: IV factor analytic findings.
5. Discuss SB: IV administrative considerations.
6. Discuss SB: IV short forms.
7. Discuss the rationale, factor analytic findings, reliability and correlational highlights, and administrative considerations for each of the SB: IV subtests: Vocabulary, Comprehension, Absurdities, Verbal Relations, Pattern Analysis, Copying, Matrices, Paper Folding and Cutting, Quantitative, Number Series, Equation Building, Bead Memory, Memory for Sentences, Memory for Digits, and Memory for Objects.
8. Discuss the intent of profile analysis, methods of profile analysis, and approaches to profile analysis on the SB: IV. Include in your discussion the effect of score ranges on profile analysis.
9. Discuss how to interpret differences between SB: IV factor scores.
10. Discuss how to interpret differences between SB: IV subtests. Cite at least seven subtest comparisons in your presentation.
11. What are some general considerations in interpreting the SB: IV?
12. Discuss the assets and limitations of the SB: IV.

15

DIFFERENTIAL ABILITY SCALES

by Ron Dumont, John Willis, and Jerome M. Sattler

The truth is rarely pure and never simple.

—Oscar Wilde

Goals and Objectives

This chapter is designed to enable you to do the following:

- Evaluate the psychometric properties of the DAS

- Become competent in administering the DAS

- Compare the DAS with other individual ability tests

- Evaluate the assets and limitations of the DAS

The *Differential Ability Scales* (*DAS*; Elliott, 1990a) is an individually administered battery of 17 cognitive subtests and 3 achievement tests for children and adolescents between the ages of 2 years 6 months (2-6 years) and 17 years 11 months (17-11 years). The DAS was designed to measure specific abilities and provide profiles of strengths and weaknesses. The DAS contains a *Preschool Level* battery for ages 2-6 to 5-11 and a *School-Age Level* battery for ages 6-0 to 17-11. The Preschool Level battery is further divided into a lower Preschool Level battery for ages 2-6 to 3-5 and an upper Preschool Level battery for ages 3-6 to 5-11 (see Table 15-1). Exhibit 15-1 shows items similar to those on the DAS.

There are 17 cognitive subtests, designated as *core subtests* (12 subtests) or *diagnostic subtests* (5 subtests; see Table 15-1). The core subtests are used to compute (a) the *General Conceptual Ability* (*GCA*) composite, which is defined as "the general ability of an individual to perform complex mental processing that involves conceptualization and transformation of information" (Elliott, 1990b, page 20), and (b) the *Verbal Ability, Nonverbal Ability, Nonverbal Reasoning Ability,* and *Spatial Ability cluster* scores. The diagnostic subtests are useful in interpreting examinees' strengths and weaknesses, but they are not used to assess complex mental processing.

The DAS does not use the terms "intelligence" and "IQ" because Elliott (1990b) maintains that (a) there are many definitions of intelligence, (b) the terms are subject to widespread misunderstanding, and (c) the GCA score is a purer measure of *g* when compared to the IQs provided by the Wechsler tests and Stanford-Binet: IV. However, as noted in Chapter 5 of this text, there is much consensus among experts about the concept of intelligence.

A *Special Nonverbal Composite* can also be computed at the lower Preschool Level (composed of Block Building and Picture Similarities) and at the School-Age Level (composed of Recall of Designs, Pattern Construction, Matrices, and Sequential and Quantitative Reasoning). The Special Nonverbal Composite is useful for assessing examinees with hearing impairments or with other types of language disabilities. The upper Preschool Level includes a Nonverbal Ability cluster (composed of Picture Similarities, Pattern Construction, and Copying) as part of the standard cognitive battery.

Table 15-1 also shows some other features of the DAS. One is that there are only four subtests that run through both the Preschool Level and the School-Age Level—namely, Pattern Construction, Recall of Digits, Recognition of Pictures, and Recall of Objects. Another feature is that Block Building and Recall of Objects are not administered at all ages within their level. A third feature is that Block Building serves two purposes; it is a core subtest at the lower Preschool Level and a diagnostic subtest at the upper Preschool Level.

The DAS refers to the age ranges covered by the subtests as usual, extended, or out-of-level (see page 4 of the Handbook).

- The *usual age range* refers to the ages at which the subtests are ordinarily administered.
- The *extended age range* refers to the ages at which the subtests also can be administered for diagnostic purposes.

Table 15-1
Structure of the DAS

Subtests	Preschool Level		School-Age Level
	2-6 to 3-5	3-6 to 5-11	6-0 to 17-11
Core Cognitive Subtests			
Block Building	■		
Verbal Comprehension	■	■[a]	
Picture Similarities	■	■[b]	
Naming Vocabulary	■	■[a]	
Pattern Construction		■[b]	■[c]
Copying		■[b]	
Early Number Concepts		■	
Word Definitions			■[a]
Similarities			■[a]
Matrices			■[b]
Seq. & Quantitative Reasoning			■[b]
Recall of Designs			■[c]
Diagnostic Cognitive Subtests			
Recall of Digits	■	■	■
Recognition of Pictures	■	■	■[d]
Block Building		■	
Matching Letter-Like Forms		■[e]	
Recall of Objects		■[f]	■
Speed of Information Processing			■
Achievement Tests			
Basic Number Skills			■
Spelling			■
Word Reading			■

Note. All core subtests form the GCA at their respective year levels.
[a] Part of the Verbal Ability cluster.
[b] Part of the Nonverbal Ability cluster.
[c] Part of the Spatial Ability cluster.
[d] Ages 6-0 to 7-11 only.
[e] Ages 4-6 to 5-11 only.
[f] Ages 4-0 to 5-11 only.
Source: Adapted from Elliott (1990a).

- The *out-of-level age range* refers to the ages at which the subtests can be administered to examinees who function at unusually high or low levels for their age.

This chapter focuses on the usual age ranges covered by the subtests.

Exhibit 15-1
DAS–Like Items

Verbal Comprehension (36 items)
The task is to point to pictures or manipulate objects in response to oral instructions from the examiner.

Show me the dog's collar.
Give me the things that make noise.
Put the ball in the glove.
Give me all the orange rectangles and the green ovals.

Naming Vocabulary (26 items)
The task is to give the name of an object or a picture. For example, the examinee might be shown a picture of a table, a square, or a rocket and asked, "What is this called?"

Word Definitions (42 items)
The task is to define individual words.

Tell me what a pyramid is.
What's an altar?
What does tremor mean?
What's an emblem?

Similarities (34 items)
The task is to state how three things are similar or go together.

What are all these things: hammer, chisel, saw?
How are these things alike: house, tent, igloo?
How do these things go together: love, hate, fear?

Block Building (12 items)
The task is to reproduce two- or three-dimensional block designs using four or eight wooden blocks.

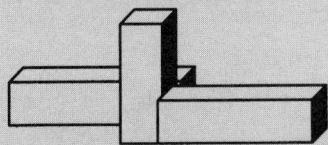

Picture Similarities (32 items)
The task is to place a card with a picture under the one of four displayed pictures that the card shares an element or concept with.

Here is a row of pictures:

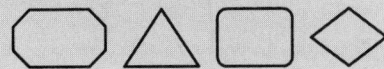

Which picture goes with this one?

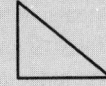

Copying (20 items)

The task is to draw abstract geometric designs such as a square or an inverted U.

Recall of Designs (21 items)
The task is to draw abstract geometric designs from memory after viewing each design for 5 seconds.

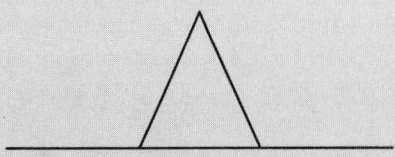

Pattern Construction (26 items)
The task is to construct geometric designs with flat squares or solid cubes.

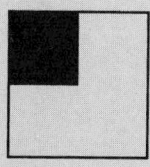

Matrices (33 items)
The task is to select the figure that best completes the matrix.

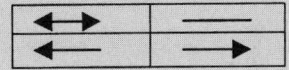

Sequential and Quantitative Reasoning (39 items)
On some items, the task is to provide the missing figure needed to complete a series of abstract figures. On other items, the task is to figure out how the numbers in each of two pairs relate and then apply the rule to another number to complete a third pair.

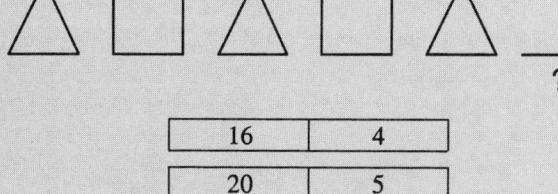

16	4
20	5
4	?

Early Number Concepts (28 items)
The task is to demonstrate knowledge of numerical concepts such as size, number, order, addition, and subtraction.

Here are some big leaves, and here are some small leaves. Here are trees that go with them. Show me all the trees that go with the big leaves.

(Continued)

Exhibit 15-1 *(Continued)*

Point to the number that shows how many circles there are in this picture.

○ ○ ○   1 2 3 4 5

Show me the third box.

☐ ☐ ☐ ☐ ☐

Look at this row of numbers. Which one has been left out?

1 2 3 4 5 7 8 9

Matching Letter-Like Forms (27 items)
The task is to find an identical match to an abstract figure from six choices.

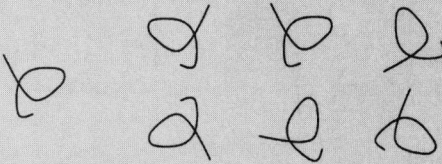

Recall of Digits (36 items)
The task is to correctly recall digits that were presented orally.

Say this after me: 5-8-7-6.

Recognition of Pictures (20 items)
The task is to recognize, in a group of four to seven similar pictures, the one, two, three, or four pictures that had been briefly presented previously.

Look at this picture:

[The picture is exposed for 5 seconds.]

Can you find it here?

Recall of Objects–Immediate (20 items)
The task is to recall as many pictures as possible from memory after viewing pictures on a card for 20 or 60 seconds.

Recall of Objects–Delayed (20 items)
The task is to recall from memory, after approximately a 15- to 20-minute delay, the pictures that were presented in the Recognition of Pictures subtest.

Speed of Information Processing (8 items)
The task is to scan a row of figures or numbers and mark, as quickly as possible, the figure that contains the most parts or the greatest number.

Mark the largest number in each row:

233   262   263   293

812   782   822   832

Basic Number Skills (48 items)
The task is to solve paper-and-pencil math computation problems.

5	31		1/3
+ 2	× 66	3 ÷ 26	+ 1/6

Spelling (70 items)
The task is to write dictated words.

but
milk
preposition
susceptibility

Word Reading (90 items)
The task is to read aloud increasingly difficult words.

on
late
horoscope
virology

The three achievement tests in the DAS—Basic Number Skills, Spelling, and Word Reading—were co-normed with the cognitive battery. The co-norming allows for an ability-achievement discrepancy analysis.

STANDARDIZATION

The DAS was standardized on 3,475 examinees selected to be representative of noninstitutionalized, English-proficient children and adolescents living in the United States during 1987–1989. The sample was stratified on age, sex, ethnicity, parental educational level, educational preschool enrollment, and geographic region. Individuals with mild perceptual, speech, and motor impairments were included in the sample. An additional group of 600 African American and Hispanic American examinees (not included in establishing the norms) was tested during standardization to study item bias and prediction bias and ensure that item-scoring rules were not discriminatory.

Table 15-2 shows the educational status and geographic location by ethnic group of the standardization sample. Indi-

Table 15-2
Demographic Characteristics of DAS Standardization Sample: Education and Geographic Region by Ethnic Group

Demographic variable	Ethnic group (percent)			
	Euro American	African American	Hispanic American	Other
Amount of education				
11 years or less	10.4	29.1	52.8	17.1
High school	38.8	42.4	28.2	25.6
Some college	28.6	19.9	13.6	25.6
College graduate	22.2	9.3	5.5	31.3
Total	100.0	100.6	100.1	99.7
Geographic region				
Northeast	20.5	14.6	14.6	11.4
North Central	30.0	19.2	7.3	22.8
South	31.0	56.9	30.9	19.9
West	18.5	9.3	47.3	48.4
Total	100.0	99.9	100.1	102.5

Note. Ethnic distribution in the total group was as follows: Euro American = 70.3%, African American = 15.2%, Hispanic American = 11.0%, Other = 3.5%.
Source: Adapted from Elliott (1990b).

viduals were classified as Euro American (N = 2,443), African American (N = 525), Hispanic American (N = 382), and Other (N = 125). The sample was 70.3% Euro American, 15.2% African American, 11.0% Hispanic American, and 3.6% Other. The four parental education categories ranged from less than 12 years of education to at least 16 years of education. The four geographic regions sampled were Northeast, North Central, South, and West. Parents in the Euro American and Other classifications had the most education; 50.8% of the Euro American group and 56.9% of the Other group had some college education, while 29.2% of the African American group and 19.1% of the Hispanic American group had some college education. The majority of the Euro American and African American examinees came from the North Central and South regions, while the majority of the Hispanic American and Other examinees came from the South and West. The sample closely matched Bureau of the Census data for 1988.

COMPOSITE SCORES, *T* SCORES, AND TEST-AGE EQUIVALENTS

The DAS uses standard scores (M = 100, SD = 15) for the Verbal Ability cluster, Nonverbal Ability cluster, Nonverbal Reasoning Ability cluster, Spatial Ability cluster, GCA, and three achievement Composite Scores. It uses T scores (M = 50, SD = 10) for the 17 cognitive core and diagnostic subtests. In calculating DAS scores, raw-score points are converted to ability scores, which are based on item response theory (see pages 331–343 of the Handbook for information about ability scores). The ability scores are then converted to T scores within the examinee's own age (see Table 1 on pages 280–373 in the Manual). Age groups are in 2-month intervals for examinees ages 2-6 to 7-11 and in 6-month intervals for examinees 8-0 years and older. Then, the T scores are summed to obtain cluster scores (see Table 2 on page 374 in the Manual), and the cluster scores are summed to obtain the GCA (see Table 3 on page 384 in the Manual).

Table 11 (pages 408–409) in the Manual provides age-equivalent scores for the cognitive subtests and for the achievement tests. No age-equivalent scores are available for the cluster scores or for the GCA. Chapter 4 of this text discusses the advantages and disadvantages of age-equivalent scores.

RELIABILITY

The DAS has excellent reliability (see Tables 15-3 and 15-4). Average internal consistency reliability coefficients for the GCA are .90, .94, and .95 on the lower Preschool Level, upper Preschool Level, and School-Age Level, respectively. For the clusters, average internal consistency reliability coefficients are (a) .88 for the Verbal Ability cluster in the upper

Table 15-3
Average Internal Consistency Reliability Coefficients, Median Test-Retest Reliability Coefficients, and Standard Errors of Measurement for DAS Preschool Level Cognitive Subtests, Clusters, and GCA

Subtest, cluster, and GCA	Average internal consistency r_{xx}	Median test-retest reliability r_{tt}	Average SEM
Verbal Comprehension	.84	.79	3.95
Naming Vocabulary	.78	.85	4.69
Block Building	.77	.67	4.76
Picture Similarities	.76	.60	4.92
Pattern Construction	.88	.67	3.40
Copying	.86	.70	3.79
Early Number Concepts	.86	.75	3.69
Matching Letter-Like Forms	.85	.65	3.73
Recall of Digits	.87	.80	3.54
Recall of Objects	.71	.58	5.33
Recognition of Pictures	.73	.56	5.20
Verbal Ability	.88	.86	5.15
Nonverbal Ability	.89	.83	4.92
GCA (Lower)	.90	.90	4.63
GCA (Upper)	.94	.94	3.51

Note. Reliabilities for 11 subtests (except Recall of Objects) are based on item response theory. For Recall of Objects, the reliability coefficients are coefficient alpha. Verbal, Nonverbal, and GCA reliability coefficients are based on a formula for computing the reliability of a composite group of tests. Diagnostic subtests were not included in calculating the reliability coefficients for the Verbal, Nonverbal, and GCA clusters.
Source: Adapted from Elliott (1990b).

Table 15-4
Average Internal Consistency Reliability Coefficients, MedianTest-Retest Reliability Coefficients, and Standard Errors of Measurement for DAS School-Age Level Cognitive Subtests, Clusters, and GCA

Subtest, cluster, and GCA	Average internal consistency reliability r_{xx}	Median test-retest reliability r_{tt}	Average SEM
Word Definitions	.83	.84	4.09
Similarities	.79	.76	4.65
Matrices	.82	.70	4.28
Seq. & Quan. Reas.	.85	.74	3.87
Recall of Designs	.84	.73	4.01
Pattern Construction	.91	.83	2.93
Recall of Digits	.87	.78	3.66
Recall of Objects	.76	.63	4.94
Speed of Info. Processing	.91	.79	2.98
Verbal Ability	.88	.88	5.13
Nonverbal Reasoning Ability	.90	.82	4.77
Spatial Ability	.92	.85	4.19
GCA	.95	.91	3.25

Note. Reliabilities for seven subtests (except Recall of Objects and Speed of Information Processing) are based on item response theory. For Recall of Objects and Speed of Information Processing, the reliability coefficients are coefficient alpha. Verbal, Nonverbal Reasoning, Spatial, and GCA reliability coefficients are based on a formula for computing the reliability of a composite group of tests. Diagnostic subtests were not included in calculating the reliability coefficients for the Verbal, Nonverbal Reasoning, Spatial, and GCA clusters.
Source: Adapted from Elliott (1990b).

Preschool Level and School-Age Level, (b) .89 and .90 for the Preschool Nonverbal Ability cluster and School-Age Nonverbal Reasoning Ability cluster, and (c) .92 for the Spatial Ability cluster.

The internal consistency reliabilities for the subtests are usually lower than those for the GCA and the four clusters, as would be expected (see Tables 15-3 and 15-4). The average internal consistency subtest reliabilities range from .71 for Recall of Objects to .88 for Pattern Construction at the Preschool Level and .76 for Recall of Objects to .91 for Speed of Information Processing and Pattern Construction at the School-Age Level (see Tables 15-3 and 15-4). Tables 15-5 and 15-6 show the range of median internal consistency reliabilities for the Preschool Level and School-Age Level cognitive subtests.

Standard Errors of Measurement

The average standard errors of measurement (SEM) in standard-score points are shown in Table 15-3 for the Preschool Level and Table 15-4 for the School-Age Level. These tables show that you can place more confidence in scores based on

Table 15-5
Range and Median Internal Consistency Reliabilities of DAS Preschool Level Cognitive Subtests at Six Age Groups

Age (in years)	Range of r_{xx}	Median r_{xx}
2-6	.68–.86	.72
3	.74–.90	.78
3-6	.66–.88	.83
4	.70–.89	.82
4-6	.66–.88	.79
5	.67–.90	.84
Average	.71–.88	.81

Source: Adapted from Elliott (1990b).

Table 15-6
Range and Median Internal Consistency Reliabilities of DAS School-Age Level Cognitive Subtests at 12 Age Groups

Age (in years)	Range of r_{xx}	Median r_{xx}
6	.66–.90	.83
7	.69–.89	.83
8	.71–.90	.84
9	.76–.92	.84
10	.76–.91	.84
11	.78–.92	.83
12	.77–.92	.85
13	.76–.93	.86
14	.77–.92	.85
15	.78–.93	.85
16	.75–.92	.84
17	.73–.94	.83
Average	.70–.91	.83

Source: Adapted from Elliott (1990b).

the GCA than in those based on the Verbal Ability, Nonverbal Ability, or Spatial Ability cluster. In addition, you can place more confidence in scores obtained from the Spatial Ability cluster than in those obtained from the Nonverbal Ability, Nonverbal Reasoning Ability, and Verbal Ability clusters.

Test-Retest Stability

The stability of the DAS was measured by having 393 individuals from four age groups (ages 3-6 to 4-5, 5-0 to 6-3, 5-9

to 6-11, and 12-0 to 13-11) retested after an interval of 2 to 7 weeks (M = 30 days). The median stability coefficients (see Tables 15-3 and 15-4), corrected for restriction of range, are .90 and .95 for the GCA, .86 to .88 for the Verbal Ability cluster, .82 to .83 for the Nonverbal Ability cluster and Nonverbal Reasoning Ability cluster, and .85 for the Spatial Ability cluster. Thus, the DAS provides fairly stable GCA and cluster scores. Stability coefficients for subtests ranged from a low of .38 for Recall of Objects–Delayed at ages 3-6 to 4-5 to a high of .90 for Pattern Construction at ages 12-0 to 13-11 ($M\ r_{tt}$ = .72).

Tables 15-7 and 15-8 show test-retest changes for the subtests, clusters, and GCA at the Preschool Level and the School-Age Level, respectively. On average, from the first to

Table 15-7
Test-Retest Changes on DAS Cognitive Preschool Level Subtests, Clusters, and GCA

Subtest, cluster, and GCA	Ages (in years) (N = 100) 3-6 to 4-5	Ages (in years) (N = 90) 5-0 to 6-3
Verbal Comprehension	2.0**	0.6
Naming Vocabulary	0.6	0.8
Picture Similarities	1.8	4.2***
Pattern Construction	2.3**	2.9***
Copying	0.6	−1.0[a]
Early Number Concepts	0.4	1.3**
Block Building	0.1	—
Matching Letter-Like Forms	2.2[b]	2.5**
Recall of Digits	2.3***	−0.4
Recall of Objects–Immediate	2.6[b]*	5.5[a]***
Recall of Objects–Delayed	−1.2[b]	2.3[a]*
Recognition of Pictures	1.0	1.2
Verbal Ability	2.1**	1.2
Nonverbal Ability	3.3[c]***	4.5[a]***
GCA	3.0[d]***	3.4[a]***

Note. Test-retest intervals ranged from 2 to 6 weeks, with a median retest interval of 30 days.
* p < .05.
** p < .01.
*** p < .001.
[a] N = 88.
[b] N = 44.
[c] N = 99.
[d] N = 97.
Source: Adapted from Elliott (1990b).

Table 15-8
Test-Retest Changes on DAS Cognitive School-Age Level Subtests, Clusters, and GCA

Subtest, cluster, and GCA	Ages (in years) (N = 81) 5-9 to 6-11	Ages (in years) (N =122) 12-0 to 13-11
Word Definitions	1.2	2.3***
Similarities	1.8**	3.8***
Matrices	3.4***	3.7***
Sequential & Quantitative Reas.	3.5***	4.1***
Recall of Designs	0.5	3.9***
Pattern Construction	4.9***	4.9***
Recall of Digits	1.3*	1.9a**
Recall of Objects–Immediate	6.2***	9.0***
Recall of Objects–Delayed	4.3b**	5.5c***
Recognition of Pictures	0.5	1.8
Speed of Information Processing	3.2***	1.9a
Verbal Ability	2.5***	5.1***
Nonverbal Reasoning Ability	5.8***	6.6***
Spatial Ability	4.7***	7.6***
GCA	5.1***	7.8***

Note. Test-retest intervals ranged from 2 to 6 weeks, with a median retest interval of 30 days.
  * $p < .05$.
 ** $p < .01$.
*** $p < .001$.
a $N = 120$.
b $N = 74$.
c $N = 115$.
Source: Adapted from Elliott (1990b).

ognition of Pictures (average increases of .05 to 1.8 points). For the six core subtests, the average gain ranged from 1.2 to 2.3 points for Word Definitions to 4.9 points for Pattern Construction.

Table 15-9
Summary of DAS Preschool Level Criterion Validity Studies

Criterion	Verbal Ability	Nonverbal Ability	GCA
WPPSI–R			
Verbal Scale	.74	.57	.77
Performance Scale	.60	.77	.80
Full Scale	.74	.74	.85
SB: IV			
Verbal Reasoning	.72	.55	.67
Abstract-Visual Reasoning	.54	.64	.64
Quantitative Reasoning	.44	.51	.48
Short-Term Memory	.66	.46	.62
Composite	.74	.69	.77
MSCA			
Verbal	.79	.37	.69
Perceptual Performance	.64	.66	.74
Quantitative	.72	.39	.56
GCI	.84	.55	.79
Memory	.66	.50	.63
WJ–R PSSC	.56	.67	.67
K-ABC			
Sequential Processing	.62	.75	.74
Simultaneous Processing	.50	.45	.49
Mental Processing Composite	.63	.67	.68
PPVT–R			.84
TACL–R			.75
CMMS			.61

Source: Adapted from Elliott (1990b, pp. 218–225). *Differential Ability Scales.* Adapted by permission. Copyright © 1983 by Colin D. Elliott. U.S. adaptation copyright © 1990 by The Psychological Corporation, a Harcourt Assessment Company. Reproduced by permission of the Publisher, The Psychological Corporation. All rights reserved. "Differential Ability Scales" and "DAS" are trademarks of The Psychological Corporation.

the second testing the GCA increased by 3.0 to 7.8 points, the Verbal Ability cluster increased by 1.2 to 5.1 points, the Nonverbal Ability cluster increased by 3.3 to 6.6 points, and the Spatial Ability cluster increased by 4.7 to 7.6 points.

At the Preschool Level, the largest change in subtest *T* scores was for Recall of Objects–Immediate (average increases of 2.6 to 5.5 points), whereas the smallest change was for Copying (average decrease of 1 to an increase of .6 point). Memory likely accounts for the large increase on Recall of Objects–Immediate, whereas copying objects does not appear to benefit from additional memory.

At the School-Age Level, the largest change in *T* scores was for Recall of Objects–Immediate (average increases of 6.2 to 9.0 points), whereas the smallest change was for Rec-

When the DAS is readministered after 2 to 7 weeks, examinees are likely to have greater gains on the subtests in the Nonverbal Ability, Nonverbal Reasoning Ability, and Spatial Ability clusters than on the subtests in the Verbal Ability cluster. This may be because they are able to recall (a) the types of items they were administered the first time and (b) the strategies they used to solve the problems (Kaufman, 1990). During the first administration, examinees may perceive the subtests in the Nonverbal Ability, Nonverbal Reasoning Ability, and Spatial Ability clusters as more novel than those in the Verbal Ability cluster. On retest, these items may become less novel and perhaps more a test of long-term memory and ability to apply previous learning sets than a test of adaptability and flexibility.

Large retest gains on the Nonverbal Ability, Nonverbal Reasoning Ability, and Spatial Ability clusters raise concerns about interpreting retest results after a short period. For periods longer than 7 weeks, gains on retest are likely to be lower because practice effects tend to diminish over time. The gain on the retest may have nothing to do with increased ability per se: it may simply reflect exposure to the test materials or practice effects.

Studies are needed to evaluate the stability of the DAS with other samples, including preschoolers and adolescents, and over longer periods of time. Such research would be helpful in learning about how cognitive abilities change on the DAS over time.

Carefully consider whether you want to use the DAS for repeated evaluations, especially if you plan to use the results obtained on the retest for placement, eligibility, or diagnostic decisions. If the time between testing is relatively short, consider using another individually administered, well-standardized test of cognitive ability for the reexamination.

Confidence Intervals

The DAS Summary Page (see page 537) has space for recording scores as confidence bands rather than as single scores. For the cluster scores, GCA, and Special Nonverbal Composite, the confidence band is provided when you look up the score.

VALIDITY

The studies in Tables 15-9 and 15-10 indicate that the DAS has satisfactory concurrent validity. The GCA correlates highly with other measures of intelligence (M r = .76) as well as with tests of academic achievement (M r = .60). The DAS yields both a measure of general intelligence and specific factors noted by both confirmatory and exploratory factor analysis, as reported in the Handbook. The validity studies in these tables are based on relatively small samples with predominantly average ability; consequently, the results should not be generalized to individuals at the relative extremes of the intelligence distribution or to individuals with disabilities.

Table 15-10
Summary of DAS School-Age Level Criterion Validity Studies

Criterion	Verbal Ability	Nonverbal Reasoning Ability	Spatial Ability	GCA
WISC–R				
Verbal	.84	.72	.41	.82
Performance	.45	.63	.73	.73
Full Scale	.77	.77	.64	.87
WISC–III				
Verbal	.82	.56	.58	.75
Performance	.41	.72	.75	.75
Full Scale	.72	.74	.75	.85
SB: IV				
Composite	.70	.78	.66	.87
K-ABC				
Sequential	.18	.24	.62	.46
Simultaneous	.35	.68	.74	.78
Mental Proc. Composite	.32	.56	.81	.75
WJ–R	.64	.50	.51	.65
PPVT–R	.57	.38	.16	.56
K-ABC				
Achievement	.64	.72	.39	.78
BASIS				
Math	.42	.58	.38	.58
Spelling	.44	.44	.31	.49
Reading	.58	.56	.39	.63
K-TEA				
Math	.55	.59	.41	.69
Spelling	.38	.44	.25	.53
Reading	.56	.43	.32	.57
Group Achievement Tests (grades 1–12)				
Total Math scores	.54	.64	.46	.66
Total Reading scores	.66	.51	.41	.63
Spelling	.54	.42	.16	.44

Source: Adapted from Elliott (1990b, pp. 225–234, 245–249). *Differential Ability Scales.* Adapted by permission. Copyright © 1983 by Colin D. Elliott. U.S. adaptation copyright © 1990 by The Psychological Corporation, a Harcourt Assessment Company. Reproduced by permission of the Publisher, The Psychological Corporation. All rights reserved. "Differential Ability Scales" and "DAS" are trademarks of The Psychological Corporation. Also from Dumont, Cruse, Price, and Whelley (1996) and Dumont, Willis, Farr, McCarthy, and Price (2000).

CORRELATIONS BETWEEN SUBTESTS AND SCALES

Correlations between the 20 subtests range from a low of .07 (Picture Similarities and Recall of Objects–Delayed) to a high of .68 (Recall of Objects–Immediate and Recall of Objects–Delayed). The median correlation between all subtests is .28. The highest correlations are between Verbal Comprehension and Naming Vocabulary (.61 and .64, respectively, at the lower Preschool Level and upper Preschool Level) and Definitions and Similarities (.64 at the School-Age Level). The lowest correlations are between Block Building and Picture Similarities (.28) at the lower Preschool Level, between Naming Vocabulary and Pattern Construction (.28) at the upper Preschool Level, and of Word Definitions and Similarities with Recall of Designs (.38 for both) at the School-Age Level.

Table 15-11 presents average correlations between the Preschool Level cognitive subtests and the clusters and GCA. Early Number Concepts has the highest correlation with the GCA (.82), followed by Verbal Comprehension (.79), Naming Vocabulary (.71), Pattern Construction (.67), Picture Similarities and Copying (.65), Block Building (.58), Matching Letter-Like Forms (.51), Recognition of Pictures (.47), Recall of Digits (.44), and Recall of Objects (.22).

Table 15-12 presents average correlations between the School-Age Level cognitive subtests and the clusters and GCA. Sequential and Quantitative Reasoning has the highest

Table 15-11
Average Correlations Between DAS Preschool Level Cognitive Subtests, Clusters, and GCA

Subtest	Verbal Ability	Nonverbal Ability	GCA
Verbal Comprehension	.90	.51	.79
Naming Vocabulary	.91	.41	.71
Block Building	.37	.60	.58
Picture Similarities	.40	.73	.65
Pattern Construction	.38	.76	.67
Copying	.36	.75	.65
Early Number Concepts	.62	.62	.82
Matching Letter-Like Forms	.34	.52	.51
Recall of Digits	.41	.31	.44
Recall of Objects	.19	.19	.22
Recognition of Pictures	.37	.41	.47

Source: Adapted from Elliott (1990b, p. 199). *Differential Ability Scales.* Adapted by permission. Copyright © 1983 by Colin D. Elliott. U.S. adaptation copyright © 1990 by The Psychological Corporation, a Harcourt Assessment Company. Reproduced by permission of the Publisher, The Psychological Corporation. All rights reserved. "Differential Ability Scales" and "DAS" are trademarks of The Psychological Corporation.

Table 15-12
Average Correlations Between DAS School-Age Level Cognitive Subtests, Clusters, and GCA

Subtest	Verbal Ability	Nonverbal Reasoning Ability	Spatial Ability	GCA
Word Definitions	.90	.53	.45	.74
Similarities	.91	.53	.46	.75
Matrices	.48	.89	.55	.76
Sequential & Quan. Reasoning	.57	.89	.55	.79
Recall of Designs	.42	.49	.88	.71
Pattern Construction	.47	.60	.88	.77
Recall of Digits	.30	.30	.22	.33
Recall of Objects	.27	.25	.26	.31
Speed of Information Proc.	.20	.22	.21	.25

Source: Adapted from Elliott (1990b, p. 200). *Differential Ability Scales.* Adapted by permission. Copyright © 1983 by Colin D. Elliott. U.S. adaptation copyright © 1990 by The Psychological Corporation, a Harcourt Assessment Company. Reproduced by permission of the Publisher, The Psychological Corporation. All rights reserved. "Differential Ability Scales" and "DAS" are trademarks of The Psychological Corporation.

Table 15-13
Relationship Between Parent Education Level and DAS GCA

Parent education level	GCA (lower Preschool Level)	GCA (upper Preschool Level)	GCA (School-Age Level)
Less than high school	89.70	89.44	90.07
High school	99.26	96.73	97.85
Some college	104.24	102.20	101.60
College graduate	105.34	108.49	109.67

Source: Based on the DAS standardization sample. *Differential Ability Scales.* Adapted by permission. Copyright © 1983 by Colin D. Elliott. U.S. adaptation copyright © 1990 by The Psychological Corporation, a Harcourt Assessment Company. Reproduced by permission of the Publisher, The Psychological Corporation. All rights reserved. "Differential Ability Scales" and "DAS" are trademarks of The Psychological Corporation.

correlation with the GCA (.79), followed by Pattern Construction (.77), Matrices (.76), Similarities (.75), Word Definitions (.74), Recall of Designs (.71), Recall of Digits (.33), Recall of Objects (.31), and Speed of Information Processing (.25). Average correlations between subtests and the GCA range from .22 to .82 (*Mdn r = .65*).

GCA AND PARENT EDUCATION

Table 15-13 shows the relationship between GCA and level of parent education in the standardization group. GCA scores increase with the level of education attained by the examinee's parents. For example, school-age examinees of parents with a college education had the highest average GCAs (109.67), while school-age examinees whose parents had a ninth-grade education or less had the lowest average GCA (90.07). If we consider parent education and socioeconomic status as somewhat interchangeable variables, then these re-

sults are similar to those reported for the WISC–III (see Chapter 8).

FACTOR ANALYSIS

The factor analyses reported in the Manual indicate that one factor emerges at ages 2-6 to 3-5, two factors (Verbal and Nonverbal) emerge at ages 3-6 to 5-11, and three factors (Verbal, Nonverbal Reasoning, and Spatial) emerge at ages 6-0 to 17-11. Factor analyses by Keith (1990) and Stone (1992) also support a three-factor structure of the core subtests for school-age examinees.

Cognitive Subtests as Measure of *g*

Table 15-14 presents the average *g* loadings for the cognitive subtests at both the Preschool Level and the School-Age Level. The best measures of *g* are Early Number Concepts,

Table 15-14
DAS Subtests as Measures of *g* at the Preschool and School-Age Levels

	Good measure of *g*			Fair measure of *g*			Poor measure of *g*	
Subtest	Average loading of *g*	Proportion of variance attributed to *g* (%)	Subtest	Average loading of *g*	Proportion of variance attributed to *g* (%)	Subtest	Average loading of *g*	Proportion of variance attributed to *g* (%)
Early Number Concepts[a]	.82	67	Similarities[b]	.69	48	Recognition of Pictures[a]	.49	24
Seq. & Quan. Reasoning[b]	.76	58	Naming Vocabulary[a]	.69	48	Recognition of Pictures[b]	.42	18
Verbal Comprehension[a]	.76	58	Word Definitions[b]	.68	46	Recall of Digits[a]	.47	22
Matrices[b]	.71	50	Pattern Construction[a]	.49	35	Recall of Digits[b]	.36	13
			Pattern Construction[b]	.70	49	Recall of Objects[a]	.26	7
			Recall of Designs[b]	.63	40	Recall of Objects[b]	.35	12
			Copying[a]	.59	35	Speed of Inf. Processing[b]	.28	8
			Matching Let. Forms[a]	.55	30			
			Picture Similarities[a]	.53	28			
			Block Building[a]	.51	26			

[a] Preschool Level.
[b] School-Age Level.
Source: Adapted from Elliott (1990b, p. 202–206). *Differential Ability Scales.* Adapted by permission. Copyright © 1983 by Colin D. Elliott. U.S. adaptation copyright © 1990 by The Psychological Corporation, a Harcourt Assessment Company. Reproduced by permission of the Publisher, The Psychological Corporation. All rights reserved. "Differential Ability Scales" and "DAS" are trademarks of The Psychological Corporation.

**Table 15-15
Age at Which the DAS Cognitive Subtests Provide for the Lowest and Highest T Score**

Subtest	Age of lowest T score (20)	Age of highest T score (80)
Block Building	3-9	3-5
Verbal Comprehension	2-9	5-2
Picture Similarities	3-9	5-11
Naming Vocabulary	3-3	6-8
Early Number Concepts	4-9	5-8
Copying	4-6	7-11
Pattern Construction	4-6	14-11
Word Definitions	7-9	17-11
Similarities	7-6	17-11
Matrices	6-3	13-5
Sequential and Quantitative Reasoning	8-0	13-5
Recall of Designs	6-6	17-11
Matching Letter-Like Forms	5-9	5-2
Recall of Digits	4-0	13-11
Recall of Objects	5-0	17-11
Recognition of Pictures	4-6	7-5
Speed of Information Processing	7-6	17-11

Source: Adapted from pages 280–373 in the *DAS Administration and Scoring Manual* (Elliott, 1990a).

Sequential and Quantitative Reasoning, Verbal Comprehension, and Matrices. The poorest measures of *g* are Speed of Information Processing, Recall of Objects, Recall of Digits, and Recognition of Pictures.

Subtest Specificity for Cognitive Subtests

Although individual cognitive subtests on the DAS overlap in their measurement properties (i.e., the majority of the reliable variance for most cognitive subtests is common factor variance), they possess sufficient specificity to justify the interpretation of specific subtest functions.

RANGE OF SUBTEST SCALED SCORES

The DAS provides a range of *T* scores from 20 to 80, but this range is not available at all ages of the test. Table 15-15 shows the ages at which the lowest and highest *T* scores can

be obtained. None of the 17 cognitive subtests provides a *T* score of 20 at age 2-6, and only 5 of the 17 cognitive subtests provide a *T* score of 80 at age 17-11. For example, although the Sequential and Quantitative Reasoning subtest is designed for ages 6 to 17, it is possible to obtain the full range of *T* scores only between the ages of 8 and 13. The range limitations, however, are usually associated with the youngest and oldest ages at which the subtests are administered.

The failure to have the same range of *T* scores throughout the test may affect profile analysis. On the core subtests at the upper Preschool Level, Verbal Comprehension and Early Number Concepts have limited ceilings (maximum *T* scores are 71 and 75, respectively, at age 5-11, for example), and Early Number Concepts, Copying, Pattern Construction, Recall of Digits, and Recognition of Pictures have limited floors (minimum *T* scores of 30, 31, 30, 25, and 28, respectively, at age 3-6, for example).

On the core subtests of the School-Age Level, Pattern Construction, Matrices, Sequential and Quantitative Reasoning, and Recall of Digits have limited ceiling levels (maximum *T* scores of 75, 75, 70, and 75, respectively, at age 17-11, for example), and Word Definitions, Similarities, Sequential and Quantitative Reasoning, Recall of Designs, and Speed of Information Processing have limited floors (minimum *T* scores of 30, 30, 32, 24, and 32, respectively, at various ages). The range limitations, however, are usually associated with the youngest and oldest ages at which the subtests are administered.

All of the subtests at ages 8 to 17 of the School-Age Level battery, however, have *T* scores as low as 20. Children of low ability between the ages of 6 and 8 can also be assessed with the upper Preschool Level tests whose subtest floors extend down to a *T* score of 20.

RANGE OF GCAs

The GCAs range from 44 to 175. This range is not available at all ages. For example, the highest GCA that examinees age 17-11 can obtain is 156; the lowest GCA that examinees age 2-6 can obtain is 53.

Depending on the examinee's age, if an examinee of low ability has little success at the ages covered by the battery you initially selected, you may be able to administer subtests from a lower level of the test. Conversely, if an examinee has high ability and has few failures at the ages covered by the battery you initially selected, you can administer subtests from a higher level of the test. For example, all subtests at the Preschool Level and School-Age Level have overlapping normative data for children ages 5-0 to 6-11. Consequently, the Preschool Level subtests can be administered to children ages 6-0 to 6-11 for whom the School-Age Level is too high. Similarly, the School-Age subtests can be administered to children ages 5-0 to 5-11 for whom the Preschool Level is too low. In such cases, the examinee's raw scores can be converted to ability scores and then to *T* scores.

If one subtest cannot be administered (or is spoiled), you can obtain a General Conceptual Ability Composite by prorating. However, when more than one subtest is invalid, do not calculate a General Conceptual Ability Composite. For examinees of very low ability, Table 5 (pages 385–389) in the Manual provides norms for obtaining extended GCA scores as low as 25. However, because the extended GCA norms are extrapolated, they have a greater degree of error than do the standard norms and must be used with caution.

OVERVIEW OF ADMINISTRATION PROCEDURES

The DAS uses a form of tailored testing to reduce testing time and examinee frustration. Each subtest has age-related starting points, which are shown on the Record Form with a black triangle (see Figure 15-1) and in the subtest directions. Subtests are administered from the starting-point item to the stopping-point item, called the *decision point*. Decision points are shown on the Record Form with a black diamond (see Figure 15-1) and in the subtest directions. If an examinee has passed at least three items and failed at least three items in a subtest, testing stops at the decision point. If an examinee has not failed at least three items at the first decision point, testing continues until the next decision point. If the examinee has not passed at least three items at the first decision point, items are administered from an earlier starting point and the subtest is continued from this point. The tailored-testing procedure is designed to make testing more efficient for the examiner and less tiring for examinees.

Testing normally stops only at decision points. However, when an examinee fails a series of items before reaching a decision point, an alternative stopping rule may be employed. The alternative stopping rules differ from subtest to subtest and are shown on the Record Form and in the subtest directions. For example, the alternative stopping rule for Sequential and Quantitative Reasoning is five failures in six consecutive items. If an examinee has passed at least three items but then fails five out of six consecutive items before the decision point, this subtest may be discontinued.

The DAS employs unscored sample items (e.g., see items A and B in Figure 15-1) in several subtests to help the examinee understand the task. Teaching items (some scored and some unscored) are also used to provide additional help after examinees fail items (e.g., items 16 and 17 in Figure 15-1). Teaching procedures include repeating and rephrasing the question or instruction, providing clues, demonstrating the correct response, and giving positive feedback.

Let's now turn to a description of each of the DAS subtests. Note that the ages presented for each subtest reflect the usual ages covered by the subtest, not the extended ages. Exhibits 15-2 and 15-3 provide checklists for the Preschool Level and School-Age Level, respectively, to help you learn how to administer the DAS.

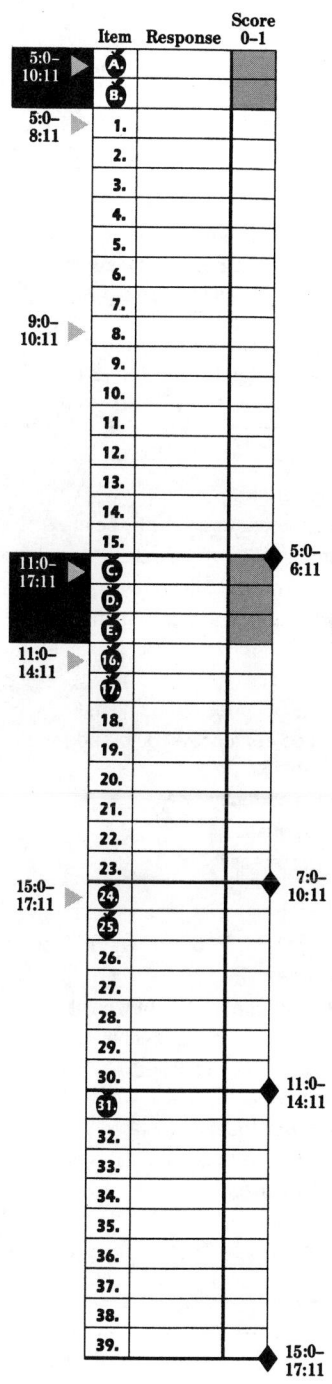

Figure 15-1. Section of DAS Record Form for Sequential and Quantitative Reasoning subtest. From the School-Age Record Form of the Differential Ability Scales. *Differential Ability Scales.* Adapted by permission. Copyright © 1983 by Colin D. Elliott. U.S. adaptation copyright © 1990 by The Psychological Corporation, a Harcourt Assessment Company. Reproduced by permission of the Publisher, The Psychological Corporation. All rights reserved. "Differential Ability Scales" and "DAS" are trademarks of The Psychological Corporation.

Exhibit 15-2
Administrative Checklist for DAS Preschool Level Subtests

ADMINISTRATIVE CHECKLIST FOR THE DAS PRESCHOOL LEVEL SUBTESTS

Name of examiner: _____   Date: _____

Name of examinee: _____   Name of observer: _____

(Note: *If an item is not applicable, mark NA to the left of the number.*)

Block Building — Circle One

1. Builds model in front of examinee — Yes   No
2. Leaves model for examinee, except on item 1 — Yes   No
3. Reads directions verbatim but naturally — Yes   No
4. Corrects and explains rotation errors — Yes   No
5. Gives second try if needed — Yes   No
6. Records responses — Yes   No
7. Adds points correctly — Yes   No

Comments: _____
_____

Verbal Comprehension

1. Begins at appropriate age entry point — Yes   No
2. Repeats items only once if asked — Yes   No
3. Reads directions verbatim but naturally — Yes   No
4. Makes sure examinee is paying attention — Yes   No
5. Holds out hand for instructions that include "Give me..." — Yes   No
6. Lines up toys but does not name them — Yes   No
7. Has examinee demonstrate knowledge of colors and shapes — Yes   No
8. Discontinues correctly — Yes   No
9. Records responses — Yes   No
10. Adds points correctly — Yes   No

Comments: _____
_____

Picture Similarities

1. Begins at appropriate age entry point — Yes   No
2. Reads directions verbatim but naturally — Yes   No
3. Provides teaching on all failed teaching items — Yes   No
4. Always provides teaching on item 3 — Yes   No
5. Clarifies ambiguous placements — Yes   No
6. Discontinues correctly — Yes   No
7. Records responses — Yes   No
8. Adds points correctly — Yes   No

Comments: _____
_____

Naming Vocabulary

1. Begins at appropriate age entry point — Yes   No
2. Provides teaching on all failed teaching items — Yes   No
3. Reads directions verbatim but naturally — Yes   No
4. Questions appropriately — Yes   No
5. Records responses — Yes   No
6. Discontinues correctly — Yes   No
7. Adds points correctly — Yes   No

Comments: _____
_____

Recall of Objects–Immediate — Circle One

1. Allows proper exposure time for each trial — Yes   No
2. Uses correct timing — Yes   No
3. Names each item during directions — Yes   No
4. Reads directions verbatim but naturally — Yes   No
5. Pronounces items clearly — Yes   No
6. Records time — Yes   No
7. Does not tell examinee of delayed-recall trial — Yes   No
8. Records responses — Yes   No
9. Adds points correctly — Yes   No

Comments: _____
_____

Pattern Construction

1. Begins at appropriate age entry point — Yes   No
2. Provides model, picture, and demonstration as appropriate — Yes   No
3. Reads directions verbatim but naturally — Yes   No
4. Corrects rotation errors — Yes   No
5. Begins and stops timing correctly — Yes   No
6. Provides correct teaching on all two-trial items — Yes   No
7. Sketches incorrect items in area provided on protocol — Yes   No
8. Decides between standard and alternative-procedures before ending test — Yes   No
9. Discontinues correctly — Yes   No
10. Records responses — Yes   No
11. Adds points correctly — Yes   No

Comments: _____
_____

Early Number Concepts

1. Begins at appropriate age entry point — Yes   No
2. Provides teaching on all failed teaching items — Yes   No
3. Gives second trial on item 1 if response is less than perfect — Yes   No
4. Reads directions verbatim but naturally — Yes   No
5. Discontinues correctly — Yes   No
6. Records responses — Yes   No
7. Adds points correctly — Yes   No

Comments: _____
_____

Recall of Objects–Delayed

1. Administers subtest after 10- to 30-minute delay — Yes   No
2. Records start time for delayed trial — Yes   No
3. Places picture card face down in front of examinee — Yes   No

(Continued)

Exhibit 15-2 *(Continued)*

Recall of Objects—Delayed	**Circle One**	
4. Reads directions verbatim but naturally	Yes	No
5. Records time	Yes	No
6. Records responses	Yes	No
7. Adds points correctly	Yes	No

Comments: _____

_____

Copying

1. Begins at appropriate age entry point	Yes	No
2. Reads directions verbatim but naturally	Yes	No
3. Labels each sheet of paper	Yes	No
4. Presents paper with longer edge as base	Yes	No
5. Allows examinee to erase	Yes	No
6. Discontinues correctly	Yes	No
7. Allows spontaneous second attempt	Yes	No
8. Adds points correctly	Yes	No

Comments: _____

_____

Matching Letter-Like Forms

1. Administers sample A to all ages	Yes	No
2. Begins at appropriate age entry point	Yes	No
3. Provides teaching on all failed teaching items	Yes	No
4. Reads directions verbatim but naturally	Yes	No
5. Discontinues correctly	Yes	No
6. Records responses	Yes	No
7. Adds points correctly	Yes	No

Comments: _____

_____

Recall of Digits

1. Reads directions verbatim but naturally	Yes	No
2. Pronounces digits clearly	Yes	No
3. Reads digits at proper rate—two digits per second	Yes	No
4. Refrains from repeating number sequence	Yes	No
5. Establishes basal and ceiling correctly	Yes	No
6. Records responses	Yes	No
7. Adds points correctly	Yes	No

Comments: _____

_____

Recognition of Pictures

1. Administers sample A and B to all examinees	Yes	No
2. Provides teaching on all failed teaching items	Yes	No
3. Begins at appropriate age entry point	Yes	No
4. Refrains from naming any items	Yes	No
5. Keeps stopwatch running	Yes	No
6. Exposes pictures for correct amount of time	Yes	No
7. Models behavior by looking at page during exposure	Yes	No

Recognition of Pictures	**Circle One**	
8. Asks appropriate question only once per item	Yes	No
9. Reads directions verbatim but naturally	Yes	No
10. Records responses	Yes	No
11. Adds points correctly	Yes	No

Comments: _____

_____

Other Aspects of Test Administration and Scoring

1. Establishes rapport	Yes	No
2. Introduces test appropriately	Yes	No
3. Is well organized and prepared (e.g., has necessary materials, including paper, pencils, and stopwatch)	Yes	No
4. Has only materials necessary for the current test visible	Yes	No
5. Administers subtests in appropriate order	Yes	No
6. Transitions well from subtest to subtest	Yes	No
7. Scores items at an efficient pace	Yes	No
8. Attends to examinee appropriately	Yes	No
9. Gives praise appropriately	Yes	No
10. Makes the test a positive experience	Yes	No
11. Completes identifying information on back page of Record Form correctly	Yes	No
12. Records behavioral observations on back page of Record Form	Yes	No
13. Calculates examinee's age correctly on back page of Record Form	Yes	No
14. Converts raw scores to ability scores correctly	Yes	No
15. Calculates T scores correctly	Yes	No
16. Calculates cluster scores correctly	Yes	No
17. Calculates GCA correctly	Yes	No
18. Completes profile correctly on Summary Page of Record Form	Yes	No
19. Records scores for diagnostic subtests correctly on Summary Page of Record Form	Yes	No

Comments: _____

_____

Overall Assessment of Test Administration

Circle One: Excellent Good Average Poor Failing

Overall strengths: _____

Overall weaknesses: _____

Other comments: _____

Exhibit 15-3
Administrative Checklist for the DAS School-Age Level Cognitive Subtests and Achievement Tests

ADMINISTRATIVE CHECKLIST FOR DAS SCHOOL-AGE LEVEL COGNITIVE SUBTESTS AND ACHIEVEMENT TESTS

Name of examiner: _____ Date: _____

Name of examinee: _____ Name of observer: _____

(Note: *If an item is not applicable, mark NA to the left of the number.*)

Recall of Designs — Circle One

1. Begins with samples A, B, and C — Yes No
2. Administers samples correctly with feedback — Yes No
3. Begins at appropriate age entry point — Yes No
4. Reads directions verbatim but naturally — Yes No
5. Correctly labels each sheet of paper — Yes No
6. Presents paper with longer edge as base — Yes No
7. Refrains from helping or coaching — Yes No
8. Prevents examinee from comparing drawings to original drawings — Yes No
9. Allows spontaneous second attempt — Yes No
10. Adds points correctly — Yes No

Comments: _____

Word Definitions

1. Begins at appropriate age entry point — Yes No
2. Repeat items if asked or if examinee mishears word — Yes No
3. Reads directions verbatim but naturally — Yes No
4. Pronounces words clearly — Yes No
5. Varies form of question to avoid stilted presentation — Yes No
6. Provides teaching on first two items administered if examinee fails these items — Yes No
7. Queries appropriately — Yes No
8. Discontinues correctly — Yes No
9. Records responses — Yes No
10. Adds points correctly — Yes No

Comments: _____

Recall of Objects–Immediate

1. Allows proper exposure time for each trial — Yes No
2. Names each item during directions — Yes No
3. Names items during the 60 seconds — Yes No
4. Reads directions verbatim but naturally — Yes No
5. Pronounces items clearly — Yes No
6. Records time — Yes No
7. Does not tell examinee of delayed-recall trial — Yes No

Recall of Objects–Immediate — Circle One

8. Records responses — Yes No
9. Adds points correctly — Yes No

Comments: _____

Pattern Construction

1. Begins at appropriate age entry point — Yes No
2. Provides model, picture, and demonstration as appropriate — Yes No
3. Reads directions verbatim but naturally — Yes No
4. Corrects rotation errors — Yes No
5. Times items correctly — Yes No
6. Provides correct teaching on all two-trial items — Yes No
7. Sketches incorrect items in area provided in Record Booklet — Yes No
8. Decides between standard and alternative procedures before ending test — Yes No
9. Discontinues correctly — Yes No
10. Records responses — Yes No
11. Adds points correctly — Yes No

Comments: _____

Matrices

1. Begins with samples A, B, and C — Yes No
2. Provides teaching on failed items as required — Yes No
3. Always provides teaching on sample D — Yes No
4. Begins at appropriate age entry point — Yes No
5. Reads directions verbatim but naturally — Yes No
6. Discourages impulsive responses if necessary — Yes No
7. Discontinues correctly — Yes No
8. Records responses — Yes No
9. Adds points correctly — Yes No

Comments: _____

Recall of Objects–Delayed

1. Administers subtest after 10- to 30-minute delay — Yes No
2. Records start time for delayed trial — Yes No

(Continued)

Exhibit 15-3 *(Continued)*

Recall of Objects–Delayed	Circle One	
3. Places picture card face down in front of examinee	Yes	No
4. Reads directions verbatim but naturally	Yes	No
5. Records time	Yes	No
6. Records responses	Yes	No
7. Adds points correctly	Yes	No

Comments: _____

Similarities		
1. Begins with sample A	Yes	No
2. Acknowledges correct response on sample and teaching items	Yes	No
3. Provides teaching on all failed items as required	Yes	No
4. Begins at appropriate age entry point	Yes	No
5. Repeats items once if asked or if examinee misunderstands instructions	Yes	No
6. Reads directions verbatim but naturally	Yes	No
7. Pronounces words clearly	Yes	No
8. Discontinues correctly	Yes	No
9. Records responses	Yes	No
10. Adds points correctly	Yes	No

Comments: _____

Sequential and Quantitative Reasoning		
1. Begins at appropriate age entry point	Yes	No
2. Begins with correct sample items	Yes	No
3. Acknowledges correct response on sample and teaching items	Yes	No
4. Provides teaching on all failed teaching items	Yes	No
5. Reads directions verbatim but naturally	Yes	No
6. Discontinues correctly	Yes	No
7. Records responses	Yes	No
8. Adds points correctly	Yes	No

Comments: _____

Recall of Digits		
1. Reads directions verbatim but naturally	Yes	No
2. Pronounces digits clearly	Yes	No
3. Reads digits at proper rate—two digits per second	Yes	No
4. Refrains from repeating number sequence	Yes	No
5. Establishes basal and ceiling correctly	Yes	No
6. Records responses	Yes	No
7. Adds points correctly	Yes	No

Comments: _____

Speed of Information Processing	Circle One	
1. Begins at appropriate age entry point	Yes	No
2. Gives correct sample items	Yes	No
3. Provides teaching on all failed items	Yes	No
4. Encourages examinee to work quickly	Yes	No
5. Changes to lower level if necessary	Yes	No
6. Checks accuracy of each trial in an obvious manner	Yes	No
7. Times items correctly	Yes	No
8. Reads directions verbatim but naturally	Yes	No
9. Adds points correctly	Yes	No

Comments: _____

Basic Number Skills		
1. Begins at appropriate age entry point	Yes	No
2. Provides scrap paper	Yes	No
3. Encourages examinee to complete items	Yes	No
4. Reads directions verbatim but naturally	Yes	No
5. Establishes basal and ceiling levels correctly	Yes	No
6. Records responses	Yes	No
7. Adds points correctly	Yes	No

Comments: _____

Spelling		
1. Begins at appropriate age entry point	Yes	No
2. Establishes basal and ceiling levels correctly	Yes	No
3. Encourages examinee to guess if unsure	Yes	No
4. Reads directions verbatim but naturally	Yes	No
5. Presents each item in isolation, in sentence, in isolation	Yes	No
6. Reads items correctly and clearly	Yes	No
7. Repeats items once if necessary	Yes	No
8. Includes name of item where appropriate	Yes	No
9. Records responses	Yes	No
10. Adds points correctly	Yes	No

Comments: _____

Word Reading		
1. Begins at appropriate age entry point	Yes	No
2. Discontinues correctly	Yes	No
3. Does not provide coaching or instructions on items	Yes	No
4. Reads directions verbatim but naturally	Yes	No
5. Records responses	Yes	No
6. Adds points correctly	Yes	No

Comments: _____

(Continued)

Exhibit 15-3 (Continued)

Other Aspects of Test Administration and Scoring	Circle One	
1. Establishes rapport	Yes	No
2. Introduces test appropriately	Yes	No
3. Is well organized and prepared (e.g., has necessary materials, including paper, pencils, and stopwatch)	Yes	No
4. Has only materials necessary for the current test visible	Yes	No
5. Administers subtests in appropriate order	Yes	No
6. Transitions well from subtest to subtest	Yes	No
7. Scores items at an efficient pace	Yes	No
8. Attends to examinee appropriately	Yes	No
9. Gives praise appropriately	Yes	No
10. Makes the test a positive experience	Yes	No
11. Completes identifying information on back page of Record Form correctly	Yes	No
12. Records behavioral observations on back page of Record Form	Yes	No
13. Calculates examinee's age correctly on back page of Record Form	Yes	No
14. Converts raw scores to ability scores correctly	Yes	No
15. Calculates *T* scores correctly	Yes	No

Other Aspects of Test Administration and Scoring	Circle One	
16. Calculates cluster scores correctly	Yes	No
17. Calculates GCA correctly	Yes	No
18. Completes profile correctly on Summary Page of Record Form	Yes	No
19. Records percentile ranks for achievement tests correctly on Summary Page of Record Form	Yes	No

Comments: _____

_____

Overall Assessment of Test Administration

Circle One: Excellent   Good   Average   Poor   Failing

Overall strengths: _____

Overall weaknesses: _____

Other comments: _____

_____

WORD DEFINITIONS

The Word Definitions subtest, which is a core cognitive subtest, requires the examinee to define words that you present orally. The subtest contains 42 words. It is administered at ages 6 to 17. Each item is scored 1 or 0. Word Definitions assesses acquired verbal knowledge, language comprehension, and fluency. The rationale presented for the WISC–III Vocabulary subtest applies to the DAS Word Definitions subtest (see Chapter 9).

Factor Analytic Findings

Word Definitions is a fair measure of *g* (46% of its variance can be attributed to *g*), and it contributes substantially to the Verbal Ability cluster (average loading = .79). Specificity is ample at all ages.

Reliability and Correlational Highlights

Word Definitions is a reliable subtest (r_{xx} = .83), with reliability coefficients above .70 at all ages (range of .75 to .84). It correlates better with Similarities (*r* = .64) than with any of the other subtests. It has a moderately high correlation with the GCA (*r* = .74), a high correlation with the Verbal Ability cluster (*r* = .90), a moderate correlation with the Nonverbal Reasoning Ability cluster (*r* = .53), and a moderately low correlation with the Spatial Ability cluster (*r* = .45).

Administrative Considerations

Examples of correct and incorrect responses are listed in alphabetical order in the Manual to help with scoring. If an examinee has difficulty hearing a word, you may repeat the word, spell the word, or write it out on paper. This procedure differs from that used on the Wechsler tests and Stanford-Binet: IV. Incorrect responses that might be associated with the mishearing of words are marked with an asterisk. This subtest requires you to question a broader range of vague or incomplete responses than are questioned on the WISC–III Vocabulary subtest.

SIMILARITIES

The Similarities subtest, which is a core cognitive subtest, requires the examinee to tell how three words go together, what they all are, or how they are similar. The subtest contains 34 three-word items. It is administered at ages 6 to 17. Five items are scored 2, 1, or 0, and 29 items are scored 1 or 0.

SCHOOLIES D 1999 by John P. Wood

Well, are there any questions from chapter five that your attorney will let you answer?

Copyright © 1999 by John P. Wood.

The subtest assesses acquired verbal knowledge, language comprehension, language fluency, verbal inductive reasoning, vocabulary and verbal development, logical and abstract thinking, and ability to distinguish between essential and superficial features.

Factor Analytic Findings

Similarities is a fair measure of g (48% of its variance can be attributed to g), and it contributes substantially to the Verbal Ability cluster (average loading = .81). Specificity is ample at ages 6 to 15 years and adequate at ages 16 to 17.

Reliability and Correlational Highlights

Similarities is a relatively reliable subtest (r_{xx} = .79), with reliability coefficients above .70 at all ages (range of .73 to .84). It correlates better with Word Definitions (r =.64) than with any of the other subtests. It has a moderate correlation with the GCA (r = .75), a high correlation with the Verbal Ability cluster (r = .91), a moderate correlation with the Nonverbal Reasoning Ability cluster (r = .53), and a moderately low correlation with the Spatial Ability cluster (r = .46).

Administrative Considerations

Scoring examples are listed in the Manual in alphabetical order. You may repeat the words one time only.

The DAS Similarities subtest differs from the Similarities subtest on the Wechsler tests. On the DAS Similarities sub-

test, three target words are used instead of two. Scoring also differs; credit is given on the DAS for a superordinate class response but not for a subordinate response. The DAS Similarities subtest also differs from the Verbal Relations subtest on the Stanford-Binet: IV, which requires an explanation of how three words are alike and different from a fourth.

The DAS requires you to question incorrect responses that show some understanding of the concept. The first two items administered also are teaching items if the examinee gives an incorrect response.

MATRICES

The Matrices subtest, which is a core cognitive subtest, requires the examinee to select the response that best completes a matrix. The subtest contains 33 items. Each matrix problem is a square of four or nine cells, with a blank cell in the lower right-hand corner. The examinee chooses the correct response from four to six alternatives. The subtest is administered at ages 6 to 17. Each item is scored 1 or 0. The subtest assesses nonverbal inductive reasoning ability, ability to formulate and test hypotheses, verbal mediation, and visual perception.

Factor Analytic Finding

Matrices is a good measure of g (50% of its variance can be attributed to g), and it contributes substantially to the Nonverbal Reasoning Ability cluster (average loading = .74). Specificity is ample at all ages.

Reliability and Correlational Highlights

Matrices is a reliable subtest (r_{xx} = .82), with reliability coefficients above .70 at all ages (range of .72 to .87). It correlates better with Sequential and Quantitative Reasoning (r = .58) than with any of the other subtests. It has a moderately high correlation with the GCA (r = .76), a moderately low correlation with the Verbal Ability cluster (r = .48), a high correlation with the Nonverbal Reasoning Ability cluster (r = .89), and a moderate correlation with the Spatial Ability cluster (r = .55).

Administrative Considerations

Correct responses are highlighted in bold blue ink on the Record Form, which must be shielded from the examinee. You need to turn the test booklet sideways for correct presentation.

SEQUENTIAL AND QUANTITATIVE REASONING

The Sequential and Quantitative Reasoning subtest, which is a core cognitive subtest, requires the examinee to solve problems dealing with sequential and quantitative material. The subtest contains 39 items. Items 1 through 15 are presented in a single-use booklet in which the examinee draws the missing figure in the appropriate space. For items 16–39, the examinee responds orally, typically with a single oral response, to problems presented in the booklet. Written answers also are acceptable. The stimuli are two pairs of numbers related by the same arithmetic rule (e.g., the second number is 3 greater than the first number, or the second number is twice as great as the first number less 1). The examinee must derive the rule from the two pairs and apply the rule to another number to create a third pair that follows the same rule. The subtest is administered at ages 6 to 17. Each item is scored 1 or 0.

Sequential and Quantitative Reasoning assesses the ability to perceive relationships, draw conclusions (inductive reasoning), formulate and test hypotheses, use analytic reasoning, and retrieve long-term information. Overall, the subtest measures nonverbal reasoning ability. The early items measure visual perceptual-motor skills, and the later items require arithmetic computation skills.

Factor Analytic Findings

Sequential and Quantitative Reasoning is a good measure of g (58% of its variance can be attributed to g), and it contributes substantially to the Nonverbal Reasoning Ability cluster (average loading = .80). Specificity is ample at all ages.

Reliability and Correlational Highlights

Sequential and Quantitative Reasoning is a reliable subtest (r_{xx} = .85), with reliability coefficients above .75 at all ages (range of .78 to .88). It correlates better with Matrices ($r = .58$) than with any of the other subtests. It has a moderately high correlation with the GCA ($r = .79$), a moderate correlation with the Verbal Ability cluster ($r = .57$), a high correlation with the Nonverbal Reasoning Ability cluster ($r = .89$), and a moderate correlation with the Spatial Ability cluster ($r = .55$).

Administrative Considerations

You can use a separate piece of paper instead of the booklet furnished by the publisher. Pages 244 (items 1–15) and 246 (items 16–39) in the Manual show the correct responses.

RECALL OF DESIGNS

The Recall of Designs subtest, which is a core cognitive subtest, requires the examinee to reproduce pictured designs that are exposed to view for 5 seconds and then removed. The subtest contains 21 items. It is administered at ages 6 to 17. Items 1–16 are scored 2, 1, or 0, whereas items 17–21 are scored 3, 2, 1, or 0.

Recall of Designs assesses the ability to encode and retain visual-spatial information and use motor skills, short-term visual recall, spatial orientation, and drawing skills.

Factor Analytic Findings

Recall of Designs is a fair measure of g (40% of its variance can be attributed to g), and it contributes moderately to the Spatial Ability cluster (average loading = .69). Specificity is ample at all ages.

Reliability and Correlational Highlights

Recall of Designs is a reliable subtest (r_{xx} = .84), with reliability coefficients above .70 at all ages (range of .72 to .87). It correlates better with Pattern Construction ($r = .57$) than with any of the other subtests. It has a moderately high correlation with the GCA ($r = .71$), a moderately low correlation with both the Verbal Ability cluster ($r = .42$) and the Nonverbal Reasoning Ability cluster ($r = .49$), and a high correlation with the Spatial Ability cluster ($r = .88$).

Despite the obvious memory demand, Recall of Designs has relatively low correlations with other DAS subtests requiring memory, as follows: Recognition of Pictures ($r = .35$), Recall of Objects–Immediate ($r = .25$), Recall of Objects–Delayed ($r = .22$), and Recall of Digits ($r = .19$).

Administrative Considerations

For the Recall of Designs subtest, the examinee draws the designs on paper that has been cut into sheets approximately 4 inches high by 5 inches wide. After the examinee completes the subtest, staple or paper-clip these sheets of paper together. Alternatively, you can use an 8½- by 11-inch sheet of paper and fold it into quarters. For each subsequent design, turn the page over to a new folded section. This method allows you to have all of the designs on two pieces of paper.

The examinee is allowed to draw the designs a second time if the second drawing is done spontaneously (i.e., the instructions do not permit you to tell the examinee that a second attempt is possible). Erasing is permitted.

After the examinee completes each drawing, write the item number in the upper right-hand corner of each sheet (or of each quadrant of the folded sheet of paper), and draw an arrow on the sheet indicating the top of the design, especially if the examinee rotates the sheet. Making these notations is important, because scoring is based on correct orientation. Carefully study the scoring procedures in Appendix B (pages 417–431) of the Manual. You will need practice to become proficient in the use of the two transparent scoring templates.

Scoring focuses on the essential features of the designs drawn by the examinee. Added lines are acceptable if they are due to poor coordination or if the examinee indicated that they are not intended to be part of the final design. Small gaps are also acceptable if they appear to be due to crudeness rather than a failure to remember the designs. Decorative additions as well as overworked, feathered, or scribbled lines are generally acceptable. The examinee may use one of the edges of the paper as one line of drawing.

PATTERN CONSTRUCTION

The Pattern Construction subtest, which is a core cognitive subtest, requires the examinee to reproduce 26 designs. The stimulus booklet contains pictures of two-dimensional designs, while the blocks or squares used by examinees are three-dimensional. The examinee must disregard the third dimension when constructing the designs. The subtest assesses visual-spatial ability, perception of spatial orientation, analysis of visual data, and nonverbal reasoning. The rationale presented for the WISC–III Block Design subtest generally applies to the Pattern Construction subtest (see Chapter 9).

Pattern Construction is administered at ages 3 to 17. The subtest is scored in two ways: standard and alternative (unspeeded). Standard scoring considers speed and accuracy, whereas alternative scoring considers accuracy only (within the time limits allotted). Scores range from 0 to 5 points under standard scoring and from 0 to 2 points under alternative scoring.

The alternative scoring is useful when you believe that considering speed of response may invalidate the score (e.g., the examinee has a physical handicap, an attentional problem, or an overly deliberate approach). The two versions of this subtest appear to measure the same construct (Elliott, 1990b).

There is a typographical error on page 221 of some printings of the Manual. The starting-point samples are wrong for two age groups (ages 7 to 12 and 13 to 17). The directions for ages 7 to 12 (page 221) should read "Sample C and Item 8" instead of "Sample B and Item 8," and the directions for ages 13 to 17 should read "Sample D and Item 14" instead of "Sample C and Item 14."

Factor Analytic Findings

At the Preschool Level, Pattern Construction is a fair measure of g across all ages (35% of its variance can be attributed to g), and it contributes substantially to the Nonverbal Ability cluster (loading = .61). Specificity is ample at all ages.

At the School-Age Level, Pattern Construction is also a fair measure of g across all ages (49% of its variance can be attributed to g), and it contributes substantially to the Spatial Ability cluster (loading = .82). Specificity is ample at all ages.

Reliability and Correlational Highlights

At the Preschool Level, Pattern Construction is a highly reliable subtest (r_{xx} = .88), with reliability coefficients above .75 at all ages (range of .80 to .90). It correlates better with Block

Building and Early Number Concepts (r = .48 for both) than with any of the other subtests. It has a moderately high correlation with the GCA (r = .67), a moderately low correlation with the Verbal Ability cluster (r = .38), and a high correlation with the Nonverbal Ability cluster (r = .76).

At the School-Age Level, Pattern Construction is also a highly reliable subtest (r_{xx} = .91), with reliability coefficients above .85 at all ages (range of .87 to .93). It correlates better with Recall of Designs (r = .57) than with any of the other subtests. It has a high correlation with the GCA (r = .77), a moderately low correlation with the Verbal Ability cluster (r = .47), a moderately high correlation with the Nonverbal Reasoning Ability cluster (r = .60), and a high correlation with the Spatial Ability cluster (r = .88).

Administrative Considerations

Examinees who are ages 3 to 6 begin with flat squares that have black sides and yellow sides. Examinees who are ages 7 to 17 begin with three-dimensional blocks that have, in addition to black sides and yellow sides, black-and-yellow sides divided diagonally and black-and-yellow sides divided vertically. Items range from two- to nine-block patterns. Flat squares appear less confusing to young examinees (Elliott, 1990b).

The Record Form has the following helpful notations:

- M (model) refers to cases where the examiner builds the pattern in front of the examinee and then leaves the completed model in place while the examinee builds the design.
- P (picture) refers to cases where the examiner shows the examinee a design from either Booklet 2 (items 1–7) or Booklet 1 (sample C through item 26) and then leaves the picture in full view while the examinee completes the pattern.
- D (demonstrate) refers to cases where the examiner builds the pattern using the examinee's own blocks and then mixes the pattern up and has the examinee try again.

In five specific cases, there are multiple notations—for example, "M, P" on item 1 means that the examiner creates the model *and* shows the picture to the examinee.

Some examinees try to complete the patterns by building their designs directly on top of the model or picture. On early items, this strategy may be helpful. On the later items, however, where the picture is smaller than the blocks, this strategy does not work. Encourage examinees not to make their design directly on the picture if they try to do so on later items.

Rotations of 30° or more receive a score of 0. When rotations occur on any item, point out the rotation to the examinee after it occurs and show the examinee how the pattern should be made.

Timing is important because bonus points are given for quick execution in the standard scoring procedure. Timing begins when the instructions are completed and ends when the design is completed. Stop timing when the examinee indicates by word or gesture that he or she is finished.

Pattern Construction allows for an alternative scoring procedure. If you believe that time limits will invalidate the subtest (e.g., a motor impairment hampers the examinee or the examinee is overly slow or overly thoughtful), use the alternative scoring procedure. The alternative scoring procedure is described on page 221 of the Manual and also on the Record Form. Usually, you will need to administer more items if you use the alternative scoring procedure.

Items 24–26 are administered as part of the alternative scoring procedure only. You do not need to choose between the two types of procedures in advance. However, you must decide which one to use before you complete the subtest.

BLOCK BUILDING

The Block Building subtest, which is both a core and a diagnostic cognitive subtest, requires the examinee to copy two- and three-dimensional models or designs using wooden blocks. The subtest contains 12 items. All examinees start with item 1. Block Building is administered at ages 2-6 to 3-5. Item 1 is scored 2, 1, or 0, while items 2–12 are scored 1 or 0.

Block Building measures visuoperceptual ability, problem-solving ability, hand-eye coordination, and spatial orientation; it also may involve verbal encoding strategies. The subtest is designed to measure, in young examinees, abilities similar to those measured by the Copying subtest.

Factor Analytic Findings

Block Building is a fair measure of g (26% of its variance can be attributed to g). The subtest does not contribute to any cluster. Specificity is ample at all ages.

Reliability and Correlational Highlights

Block Building is a relatively reliable subtest ($r_{xx} = .77$), with reliability coefficients above .65 at all ages (range of .68 to .84). It correlates better with Copying ($r = .51$) than with any of the other subtests. It has a moderate correlation with the GCA ($r = .58$), a moderately low correlation with the Verbal Ability cluster ($r = .37$), and a moderately high correlation with the Nonverbal Ability cluster ($r = .60$).

Administrative Considerations

The Preschool Record Form shows each design and its correct orientation. Rotations of 45° or more receive a score of 0 on items 2–12. You must correct all rotations on each item.

Second attempts are allowed in two instances. One is on item 1, when the examinee builds the tower by placing the

blocks on end (small side down) and fails to complete it. The other is on items 1–7, when the structure topples before 3 seconds. Second attempts are not allowed for rotation errors.

VERBAL COMPREHENSION

The Verbal Comprehension subtest, which is a core cognitive subtest, requires the examinee to show understanding of oral instructions by pointing or by performing the action that you request (e.g., carrying out the request to "Put the cat in the box"). The subtest contains 36 items. Verbal Comprehension assesses understanding of language (including understanding of syntax and prepositional and relational concepts), ability to follow verbal directions, and short-term auditory memory.

Verbal Comprehension is administered at ages 2-6 to 6. Examinees ages 2-6 to 3-11 start with item 1, while examinees ages 4 to 6 start with item 13. All items are scored 1 or 0.

On items 1–6, which use a picture of a Teddy Bear, the task for the examinee is to point to several requested features of the bear. Items 7–18 use a variety of small toys. The task for the examinee is to follow your request (e.g., "Give me the marble") or to demonstrate knowledge of the object(s) (e.g., "Give me all things that make a sound"). Items 19–29 use a set of wooden objects (e.g., trees and houses). The task for the examinee is to demonstrate knowledge of language (e.g., below, far, top). And items 30–36 use colored plastic chips of varying shapes. The task is to demonstrate understanding of complex instructions (e.g., "Put a green square over a black diamond").

Factor Analytic Findings

Verbal Comprehension is a good measure of g (58% of its variance can be attributed to g). The subtest contributes substantially to the Verbal Ability cluster (average loading = .81). Specificity is ample at all ages.

Reliability and Correlational Highlights

Verbal Comprehension is a reliable subtest ($r_{xx} = .84$), with reliability coefficients above .70 at all ages (range of .74 to .86). It correlates better with Naming Vocabulary ($r = .64$) than with any of the other subtests. It has a moderately high correlation with the GCA ($r = .79$), a high correlation with the Verbal Ability cluster ($r = .90$), and a moderate correlation with the Nonverbal Ability cluster ($r = .51$).

Administrative Considerations

Read the items directly from the protocol. You may repeat instructions one time if the examinee has not responded to the item or if the examinee asks for repetition. Say, "Listen carefully" if you need to gain the examinee's attention.

PICTURE SIMILARITIES

The Picture Similarities subtest, which is a core cognitive subtest, requires the examinee to place a picture card below the picture (one of four) that it best goes with. The subtest contains 32 items. Picture Similarities assesses nonverbal reasoning abilities, including the ability to solve nonverbal problems, identify pictures, formulate and test hypotheses about the relationship among different pictures in a set, use verbal mediation, and attach meaning to pictures.

Picture Similarities is administered at ages 2-6 to 6. Examinees ages 2-6 to 4-5 start with item 1, while examinees ages 4-6 to 6 start with item 11. All items are scored 1 or 0.

Factor Analytic Findings

Picture Similarities is a fair measure of g (28% of its variance can be attributed to g), and it contributes moderately to the Nonverbal Ability cluster (average loading = .55). Specificity is ample at all ages.

Reliability and Correlational Highlights

Picture Similarities is a relatively reliable subtest ($r_{xx} = .76$), with reliability coefficients above .30 at all ages (range of .33 to .84). It correlates better with Early Number Concepts ($r = .44$) than with any of the other subtests. It has a moderately high correlation with the GCA ($r = .65$), a moderately low correlation with the Verbal Ability cluster ($r = .40$), and a moderately high correlation with the Nonverbal Ability cluster ($r = .73$).

Administrative Considerations

Give the examinee one card at a time, with the instruction to place the card under the one picture (out of four) that it best goes with. Vertical lines between the pictures in the test book facilitate scoring. If the placement of a card is not clear, ask the child to tell which picture the card should be placed under.

NAMING VOCABULARY

The Naming Vocabulary subtest, which is a core cognitive subtest, requires the examinee to name real objects (items 1 and 2) or pictured objects (items 3–24). The subtest assesses recognition language, expressive language ability, general language development, and word retrieval from long-term memory.

The subtest covers ages 2-6 to 6. Examinees ages 2-6 to 4-5 start with item 1, while examinees ages 4-6 to 6 start with item 8. All items are scored 1 or 0.

Factor Analytic Findings

Naming Vocabulary is a fair measure of g (48% of its variance can be attributed to g), and it contributes moderately to the Verbal Ability cluster (average loading = .71). Specificity is ample at all ages.

Reliability and Correlational Highlights

Naming Vocabulary is a relatively reliable subtest ($r_{xx} = .78$), with reliability coefficients above .60 at all ages (range of .64 to .84). It correlates better with Verbal Comprehension ($r = .64$) than with any of the other subtests. It has a moderately high correlation with the GCA ($r = .71$), a high correlation with the Verbal Ability cluster ($r = .91$), and a moderately low correlation with the Nonverbal Ability cluster ($r = .41$).

Administrative Considerations

Correct answers are shown on the Record Form as well as on pages 83–85 in the Manual.

EARLY NUMBER CONCEPTS

The Early Number Concepts subtest, which is a core cognitive subtest, requires the examinee to demonstrate knowledge of number abilities. The subtest contains 28 items. It measures such number abilities as reciting, counting, matching, comparing, recognizing, and solving number problems.

Early Number Concepts is administered at ages 2-6 to 6. Examinees ages 2-6 to 4-5 begin with item 1 (counting and pointing), and examinees ages 4-6 to 6 begin with item 2. Item 1 is scored 6, 5, 4, 3, 2, 1, or 0, while items 2–28 are scored 1 or 0.

Item 1 (counting and pointing to 10 chips) has a maximum of 6 points (up to 3 points for counting correctly and up to 3 points for pointing correctly). If fewer than 6 points are earned on the first administration of item 1, administer the item again. Give the examinee the higher of the two scores obtained.

Factor Analytic Findings

Early Number Concepts is a good measure of g (67% of its variance can be attributed to g), and it does not contribute to either the Verbal Ability cluster or the Nonverbal Ability cluster. Specificity is ample at all ages.

Reliability and Correlational Highlights

Early Number Concepts is a reliable subtest ($r_{xx} = .86$), with reliability coefficients above .50 at all ages (range of .53 to .88). It correlates better with Verbal Comprehension ($r = .61$)

than with any of the other subtests. It has a high correlation with the GCA ($r = .82$) and moderately high correlations with the Verbal Ability cluster ($r = .62$) and the Nonverbal Ability cluster ($r = .62$).

Administrative Considerations

Be sure to read Appendix A ("Scoring Procedure for Early Number Concepts," pages 415–416) in order to understand the scoring procedure for item 1. Some items require a verbal response, while other items require a pointing response.

COPYING

The Copying subtest, which is a core cognitive subtest, requires the examinee to copy geometric figures. The subtest contains 20 items. It measures fine motor ability and the ability to perceive similarities between figures. Items vary from a simple straight line to complex geometric figures. The subtest is not timed.

Copying is administered at ages 3-6 to 6. Examinees ages 3-6 to 4-11 start with item 1, and examinees ages 5-0 to 5-11 start with item 5. Item 1 is scored 1 or 0; items 2–11, 13, 14, 19, and 20 are scored 2, 1, or 0; and items 12 and 15–18 are scored 3, 2, 1, or 0.

Factor Analytic Findings

Copying is a fair measure of *g* (35% of its variance can be attributed to *g*), and it contributes moderately to the Nonverbal

Copyright © 1999 by John P. Wood.

Ability cluster (average loading = .61). Specificity is ample at all ages.

Reliability and Correlational Highlights

Copying is a reliable subtest ($r_{xx} = .86$), with reliability coefficients above .80 at all ages (range of .82 to .88). It correlates better with Block Building ($r = .51$) than with any of the other subtests. It has a moderately high correlation with the GCA ($r = .65$), a moderately low correlation with the Verbal Ability cluster ($r = .36$), and a moderately high correlation with the Nonverbal Ability cluster ($r = .75$).

Administrative Considerations

Examinees draw their designs on pieces of paper approximately 4 inches high by 5 inches wide. After the subtest is completed, clip or staple together the sheets of paper. An alternative method is to fold an 8½- by 11-inch sheet of paper into quarters and have the examinee draw on a folded part of the page. For each subsequent design, turn the page over to a new section. If you use this procedure, multiple drawings will be on one piece of paper.

The examinee is allowed a second attempt to draw a design. However, allow the second attempt only if the examinee requests it spontaneously. When there are two drawings, score the better of the two attempts.

The scoring of the final design is dependent on correct orientation. Be sure to number each sheet (or quadrant of the 8½- by 11-inch paper) in the upper right-hand corner and draw an arrow indicating the top of the paper after each design is drawn, especially if the examinee rotates the sheet.

Carefully study the scoring procedures in Appendix B (pages 417–431) of the Manual. You will need to use the two transparent scoring templates provided in the kit. Use Set B (not A) to score straightness of lines.

RECALL OF OBJECTS

The Recall of Objects subtest, which is a diagnostic cognitive subtest, requires the examinee to recall objects from memory. It is administered at ages 4 to 17. The examinee is shown a card with pictures of 20 common objects. Three trials are given, with exposure times of 60 seconds, 20 seconds, and 20 seconds, respectively. On the first trial, you say the names of the objects aloud for the examinee. After the card is removed, the examinee is asked to recall as many objects as possible in any order (with a time limit of 60 seconds on trial 1 and 40 seconds on trials 2 and 3).

The Recall of Objects subtest also has a delayed-recall trial. After you complete the three trials, you administer two nonverbal subtests (which together take about 10 to 30 minutes) and then administer the delayed-recall trial (time limit of 60 seconds). Usually, the delayed-recall trial will be about 10 to 15 minutes after the initial subtest. Examinees, however, are not informed that they will be asked to recall the objects again.

The subtest assesses (a) short-term verbal memory, including verbal encoding, rehearsal, and retrieval strategies (e.g., use of a semantic clustering strategy—retrieving all the animals and then all the vehicles—versus use of a serial clustering strategy—retrieving the items in the exact order in which they are presented on the page); (b) short-term visual memory; or (c) a combination of the two.

One point is awarded for each correctly recalled object. If all 20 items are correctly remembered on the first and second trials, the third trial is not administered; however, examinees are credited with 20 points for the third trial.

Factor Analytic Findings

At the Preschool Level, Recall of Objects is a poor measure of g (7% of its variance can be attributed to g). The subtest does not contribute to any cluster. Specificity is ample at all ages.

At the School-Age Level, Recall of Objects is also a poor measure of g (12% of its variance can be attributed to g). The subtest does not contribute to any cluster. Specificity is ample at all ages.

Reliability and Correlational Highlights

At the Preschool Level, Recall of Objects is a relatively reliable subtest ($r_{xx} = .71$), with reliability coefficients above .65 at all ages (range of .66 to .77). It correlates better with Recall of Objects–Delayed ($r = .47$) than with any other subtest. It has low correlations with the GCA ($r = .22$), the Verbal Ability cluster ($r = .19$), and the Nonverbal Ability cluster ($r = .19$).

At the School-Age Level, Recall of Objects is also a relatively reliable subtest ($r_{xx} = .76$), with reliability coefficients above .65 at all ages (range of .67 to .83). It correlates better with Recall of Objects–Delayed ($r = .68$) than with any other subtest. It has a moderately low correlation with the GCA ($r = .31$) and low correlations with the Verbal Ability cluster ($r = .27$), the Nonverbal Reasoning Ability cluster ($r = .25$), and the Spatial Ability cluster ($r = .26$).

Administrative Considerations

If one of the three trials is spoiled or unscorable, estimate the three-trial score by multiplying the sum of the two trials by 1.5 and rounding the result up to a whole number.

On the first trial, the pictures are exposed to the examinee as the directions are given and the pictures are named. On the second and third trials, the directions are given *before* the card is exposed.

The delayed-recall trial should be administered after a delay of at least 10 minutes, but no more than 30 minutes. In the event that these time limits cannot be met, the Manual notes that no tests or tasks should be given whose content could interfere with the content of the delayed-recall trial. Administer the delayed-recall trial in the sequence presented on the Record Form to ensure that the intervening subtests will not be likely to interfere with the recall trial.

Observe how the examinee recalls the objects.

- Does the examinee remember them in the order in which they appear on the card or by categories?
- Does the examinee improve her or his performance on each trial, or does performance worsen?
- Are only some types of items remembered?
- Are items recalled primarily by their position on the card?

Record the examinee's responses as clearly as possible. For example, distinguish clearly between "ball" and "bowl." Give credit for reasonable synonyms such as "rat" for "mouse." However, do not give credit for repeated names or for items repeated with similar names (e.g., "rat" and "mouse"). If an examinee asks if it is all right to repeat words, say it is ok.

The table in the Manual for converting ability scores to T scores has the column for Recall of Digits *after* the column for Recall of Objects. This is opposite to the order in which the subtest scores appear on the Record Form. Consequently, be careful to use the correct column when converting the Recall of Objects ability score to a T score.

The Manual and Record Form give the appropriate time limits for administering the subtest. Allow the examinee to continue recalling items for a reasonable time after the time limits have expired; however, do not give credit for any items recalled after the time limit. Note the last item recalled at the end of the time limit (e.g., place a line under that item), and record the items recalled after the time limit. Examinees who continue to recall items correctly after the time limit may have better memory ability than those who do not recall any additional items.

RECALL OF DIGITS

The Recall of Digits subtest, which is a diagnostic cognitive subtest, requires the examinee to recall a sequence of digits that you read aloud. The subtest contains 36 items. Sequences range from two to nine digits in length. The digit sequences are arranged in eight blocks, with each block containing two to five sequences with the same number of digits. The subtest measures short-term auditory sequential memory. The rationale presented for the WISC–III Digit Span subtest applies to the Recall of Digits subtest (see Chapter 9). The subtest is administered at ages 3 to 17. Each item is scored either 1 or 0, with 1 point awarded only when the examinee recalls all the digits in the item in the correct sequence.

Factor Analytic Findings

At the Preschool Level, Recall of Digits is a poor measure of g (22% of its variance can be attributed to g). The subtest does not contribute to any cluster. Specificity is ample at all ages.

At the School-Age Level, Recall of Digits is also a poor measure of g (13% of its variance can be attributed to g). The subtest does not contribute to any cluster. Specificity is ample at all ages.

Reliability and Correlational Highlights

At the Preschool Level, Recall of Digits is a reliable subtest ($r_{xx} = .87$), with all reliability coefficients above .80 at all ages (range of .85 to .90). It correlates better with Early Number Concepts ($r = .41$) than with any of the other subtests. It has moderately low correlations with the GCA ($r = .44$), the Verbal Ability cluster ($r = .41$), and Nonverbal Ability cluster ($r = .31$).

At the School-Age Level, Recall of Digits is also a reliable subtest ($r_{xx} = .87$), with all reliability coefficients above .80 at all ages (range of .85 to .88). It correlates better with Sequential and Quantitative Reasoning ($r = .29$) than with any of the other subtests. It has moderately low correlations with the GCA ($r = .33$), the Verbal Ability cluster ($r = .30$) and the Nonverbal Reasoning Ability cluster ($r = .30$) and a low correlation with the Spatial Ability cluster ($r = .22$).

Administrative Considerations

The Recall of Digits subtest has basal-level and ceiling-level rules. All examinees start with item 1. If the examinee passes the first item of the first set, proceed to the next set. Continue with the first item of each set until the examinee fails the first item. Then go back to the previous set and administer the remaining items in that set. If the examinee fails more than one item in a set, continue backward until the examinee has no more than one failure in the set. This block becomes the basal level. Test forward until the examinee passes no more than one item in a set. That set becomes the ceiling level. If a basal level is not established (all item sets have more than one error), count all the correct items to obtain the raw score.

The basal-level and ceiling-level rules were established to help you move quickly through the subtest. The rules assume that if the examinee passes the first item of a set, he or she would probably pass the other items in the same set. Once an examinee fails the first item in a set or passes only one item in a set, you move to fill in the prior set.

On this subtest, unlike the other cognitive subtests, credit is given for items not administered below the basal level.

Items are administered at a rate of two digits per second. This procedure differs from that used on the Wechsler tests and on the Stanford-Binet: IV, where digits are read at the rate of one per second. Practice reading digits at the rate of two per second with a metronome or clock.

On the Record Form, you can record whether the items were correct or incorrect or you can record the actual digits recalled by the examinee. The latter procedure is recommended because it will give you information about failures—a generalized memory problem (remembering few numbers but in correct sequence), a sequencing problem (remembering all the correct numbers but in the wrong order), an intrusion problem (intermixing correct and incorrect numbers), or some other type of problem.

Unlike the Wechsler tests and the Stanford-Binet: IV, the DAS has no items that measure the ability to recall digits in reverse.

RECOGNITION OF PICTURES

The Recognition of Pictures subtest, which is a diagnostic cognitive subtest, requires the examinee to find, among a group of pictures, one or more pictures that were previously shown to him or her. The subtest contains 20 items. All of the pictured objects in each item represent a single category (e.g., toys or vehicles). A picture of one to four objects (referred to as target objects) is shown for 5 seconds (items 1–15) or 10 seconds (items 16–20). Then another picture is shown that contains the target objects plus distractor objects. The task is to point to the target objects. Success depends on recall of visual images. The subtest is administered at ages 3 to 7. Each item is scored 1 or 0. Recognition of Pictures measures short-term visual memory.

Factor Analytic Findings

At the Preschool Level, Recognition of Pictures is a poor measure of g (24% of its variance can be attributed to g). The subtest does not contribute to any cluster. Specificity is ample at all ages.

At the School-Age Level, Recognition of Pictures is also a poor measure of g (18% of its variance can be attributed to g). The subtest does not contribute to any cluster. Specificity is ample at all ages.

Reliability and Correlational Highlights

At the Preschool Level, Recognition of Pictures is a relatively reliable subtest ($r_{xx} = .73$), with reliability coefficients above .50 at all ages (range of .54 to .80). It correlates better with Early Number Concepts ($r = .43$) than with any other subtest. It has moderately low correlations with the GCA ($r = .47$), the Verbal Ability cluster ($r = .37$), and the Nonverbal Ability cluster ($r = .41$).

At the School-Age Level, Recognition of Pictures is also a relatively reliable subtest ($r_{xx} = .70$), with reliability coefficients above .65 at the three usual ages covered by the subtest (range of .66 to .74). It correlates better with Recall of Designs ($r = .35$) than with any other subtest. It has a moderately low correlation with the GCA ($r = .38$), a low correlation with the Verbal Ability cluster ($r = .28$), and moderately low correlations with the Nonverbal Reasoning Ability cluster ($r = .33$) and Spatial Ability cluster ($r = .35$).

Administrative Considerations

Time the exposure of the items carefully. If the examinee points to a single target figure when two or more target figures are shown, ask if there are any more target figures. This query may be made only once per item.

Because Recognition of Pictures is usually administered to examinees between the ages of 3 and 8, even though it is normed for all ages of the test (ages 2-6 to 17), only the Preschool Record Form contains the scoring key for the subtest. Therefore, you must use the Preschool Record Form to administer the subtest, regardless of the examinee's age. The key on the Preschool Record Form is presented in two ways: how you see the card and how the examinee sees the card.

SPEED OF INFORMATION PROCESSING

The Speed of Information Processing subtest, which is a diagnostic cognitive subtest, requires the examinee to mark the circle with the most boxes in each row or to mark the highest number in each row. The subtest is administered at ages 6 to 17. Three booklets are used. Booklet A is for ages 6 to 8, Booklet B for ages 9 to 12, and Booklet C for ages 13 to 17. Each booklet contains eight pages—two practice pages and six test pages. Each page contains five to eight rows of figures (i.e., circles containing one to four small squares) or numbers.

The task is a relatively simple one, and almost all examinees should succeed. Each page is scored from 0 to 6 points depending on the speed of completion. The subtest measures mental speed.

Factor Analytic Findings

The Speed of Information Processing subtest is a poor measure of g (8% of its variance can be attributed to g), and it does not contribute to any cluster. Specificity is ample at all ages.

Reliability and Correlational Highlights

Speed of Information Processing is a highly reliable subtest ($r_{xx} = .91$), with reliability coefficients above .86 at all ages (range of .86 to .94). It correlates better with Sequential and Quantitative Reasoning and Pattern Construction ($r = .22$ for both) than with any other subtests. It has low correlations with the GCA ($r = .25$), the Verbal Ability cluster ($r = .20$), the Nonverbal Reasoning cluster ($r = .22$), and the Spatial Ability cluster ($r = .21$).

Administrative Considerations

Examinees who are given Booklet A are asked to complete the entire booklet. However, if examinees who are given Booklet B or Booklet C make two or more errors on two of the first four test pages, give them the booklet that is one level easier (Booklet B for those who started with Booklet C and Booklet A for those who started with Booklet B).

You turn the page of the booklet for the examinee after each page is completed. Timing begins when the examinee makes a mark in the first row and stops when the examinee makes a mark in the last row. Encourage the examinee to work quickly by saying, for example, "Do these as quickly as you can." Provide feedback to the examinee as described on page 257 of the Manual. The Manual advises that you disregard the results when an examinee makes numerous errors, because the subtest is probably not tapping what it is intended to measure.

MATCHING LETTER-LIKE FORMS

The Matching Letter-Like Forms subtest, which is a diagnostic cognitive subtest, requires the examinee to look at a figure on one page and identify, by pointing, that same figure on another page that contains six identical figures, five of which have been rotated to varying degrees. The examinee must select the one figure whose orientation is identical to the target figure's. The subtest contains 27 items.

Matching Letter-Like Forms is administered at ages 4 to 5. Each item is scored 1 or 0. The subtest measures visual discrimination and spatial orientation.

Factor Analytic Findings

Matching Letter-Like Forms is a fair measure of g (30% of its variance can be attributed to g), and it does not contribute to any cluster. Specificity is ample at all ages.

Reliability and Correlational Highlights

Matching Letter-Like Forms is a reliable subtest ($r_{xx} = .85$), with reliability coefficients above .45 at all ages (range of .49 to .87). It correlates better with Pattern Construction ($r = .45$) than with any other subtest. It has a moderate correlation with the GCA ($r = .51$), a moderately low correlation with the Verbal Ability cluster ($r = .34$), and a moderate correlation with the Nonverbal Ability cluster ($r = .52$).

Administrative Considerations

Correct responses are highlighted in bold green ink on the Record Form. Be sure to record the examinee's actual responses so that you can analyze errors.

BASIC NUMBER SKILLS

The Basic Number Skills test, which is an achievement test, requires the examinee to solve computational problems that are presented in a workbook. The test contains 48 items, grouped into six sets of eight items arranged approximately in order of increasing difficulty. The items cover recognition of printed numbers; the four basic arithmetic operations (adding, subtracting, multiplying, and dividing); and calculations using whole numbers, decimal fractions, common fractions, and percentages. The test is administered at ages 6 to 17. Basic Number Skills measures concepts and skills that underlie competence in arithmetical reasoning and calculations.

Reliability and Correlational Highlights

Basic Number Skills is a highly reliable test ($r_{xx} = .87$), with reliability coefficients above .80 at all ages (range of .82 to .90). It correlates better with Sequential and Quantitative Reasoning ($r = .57$) than with any other subtest. It has a moderately high correlation with the GCA ($r = .60$), a moderately low correlation with the Verbal Ability cluster ($r = .48$), a moderate correlation with the Nonverbal Reasoning Ability cluster ($r = .59$), and a moderately low correlation with the Spatial Ability cluster ($r = .45$).

Administrative Considerations

Basic Number Skills uses a basal-level and ceiling-level format. The basal level is no more than three failures within one eight-item block. The ceiling level is no more than three passes within one eight-item block. The Basic Number Skills test does not assess the ability to perform mathematics applications. Therefore, you will need to use another math test to evaluate this ability (see Chapter 18).

SPELLING

The Spelling test, which is an achievement test, requires the examinee to write words from dictation. The test contains 70 items, divided into 10 sets of seven items each. It is administered at ages 6 to 17. The test measures spelling proficiency.

Copyright © 1998 by John P. Wood.

Reliability and Correlation Highlights

Spelling is a highly reliable test ($r_{xx} = .92$), with reliability coefficients above .89 at all ages (range of .90 to .94). It correlates better with Word Definitions and with Sequential and Quantitative Reasoning ($r = .49$ for both) than with any other subtest. It has a moderate correlation with the GCA ($r = .52$), moderately low correlations with the Verbal Ability cluster and the Nonverbal Reasoning Ability cluster ($r = .49$ for both), and a low correlation with the Spatial Ability cluster ($r = .34$).

Administrative Considerations

Study the basal-level and ceiling-level procedures for the Spelling test carefully (pages 267–268 of the Manual). The Record Form provides spaces for marking spelling errors (see pages 273–275 of the Manual).

WORD READING

The Word Reading test, which is an achievement test, requires the examinee to read aloud a series of single words of increasing difficulty. The test is administered at ages 6 to 17. Word Reading contains 90 words, separated into nine sets of 10 words each. The test measures word reading.

Reliability and Correlational Highlights

Word Reading is a highly reliable test ($r_{xx} = .92$), with reliability coefficients above .65 at all ages (range of .68 to .95). It correlates better with Word Definitions ($r = .57$) than with any other subtest. It has a moderately high correlation with the GCA ($r = .60$), moderate correlations with the Verbal Ability cluster ($r = .59$) and the Nonverbal Reasoning Ability cluster ($r = .52$), and a moderately low correlation with the Spatial Ability cluster ($r = .40$).

Administrative Considerations

Begin the test at the starting point for the examinee's age, as indicated on the Record Form. If the examinee has at least three passes on any items, discontinue the test when there are eight failures within a block of 10 words. If the examinee has fewer than three passes on any items, drop back to an earlier starting point and continue testing. Record the examinee's attempts phonetically for later analysis. The Manual (page 278) provides guidelines to help you categorize the examinee's reading errors. Word Reading, as its name implies, measures only one aspect of reading—word recognition. To assess reading vocabulary, reading comprehension, reading fluency, or other reading skills, you will need to administer another reading test (see Chapter 18 of this text).

INTERPRETING THE DAS

Much of the material in Chapter 10 on interpreting the WISC–III pertains to the DAS. Profile analysis, the successive-level approach to test interpretation, cluster score comparisons, and subtest comparisons are conceptually the same for the WISC–III and the DAS, although the procedures differ. Read or review Chapter 10 before you read the rest of this chapter.

Chapters 2, 4, and 5 of the DAS Handbook provide useful information for interpreting the DAS. The Manual and Table 5.1 (page 89) in the Handbook show the descriptive classifications for the GCA, cluster scores, and subtest scores. Table BC-1 on the inside back cover of this text shows the percentile ranks for the GCA (column with $M = 100$, $SD = 15$), and Table F-8 in Appendix F shows the percentile rank for the T scores ($M = 50$, $SD = 10$).

Do not view the individual subtests as a means of determining specific cognitive skills with precision. You derive the most reliable estimates of specific abilities from the Verbal Ability, Nonverbal Ability, Nonverbal Reasoning Ability, and Spatial Ability clusters and the GCA, not from the individual subtest scores. Instead, use subtest scores to generate hypotheses about an examinee's abilities. Consider all hypotheses you develop from the DAS in relation to all other sources of data about the examinee.

The lower Preschool Level and School-Age Level offer a Special Nonverbal Composite (Block Building and Picture Similarities at the lower Preschool Level and Recall of Designs, Pattern Construction, Matrices, and Sequential and Quantitative Reasoning at the School-Age Level). The upper Preschool Level has a Nonverbal Ability cluster (Picture Similarities, Pattern Construction, and Copying) that can be interpreted as a Special Nonverbal Composite.

Profile Analysis

Profile analysis can be used to formulate tentative hypotheses about an examinee's strengths and weaknesses. As noted above, the approaches to profile analysis for the DAS are conceptually similar to those for the WISC–III (see Chapter 10). However, there are unique procedures that you need to follow on the DAS.

Step 1: Evaluate the GCA and cluster scores.

The GCA is the most reliable and valid score in the DAS. It is an excellent measure of general cognitive ability, as well as the best predictor of overall academic achievement (Youngstrom, Kogos, & Glutting, 1999). However, the Special Nonverbal Composite may be a more accurate measure of cognitive ability when examinees have a hearing impairment, a language impairment, or other disabilities that might invalidate their overall performance.

You should find first the confidence band and the percentile rank for the examinee's GCA score (see pages 379–383 in the Manual) and then the classification (see page 54 in the Manual). Next, examine the differences between the cluster scores. The Summary page of the Record Form (see Figure 15-2) shows the *average* differences between cluster scores needed for statistical significance at the .05 level (see Chapter 4 of this text for a discussion of significance levels). For example, at the School-Age Level, a difference of 16 or more points between two cluster scores (e.g., between Verbal Ability and Spatial Ability or between Verbal Ability and Nonverbal Reasoning Ability) would be statistically significant at the .05 level.

The numbers printed below the boxes for the cluster scores show the *average* difference between each cluster score and the GCA needed for statistical significance at the .05 level. Again, for the School-Age Level, a difference of 9 or more points between a cluster score and the GCA would be significant at the .05 level. Tables B.1 and B.4 (pages 290, 292, 293) of the Handbook provide the differences required for statistical significance at the .15, .05, and .01 levels at each age level.

The Handbook states that if the cluster scores contributing to the GCA are significantly diverse, you should conclude "that the GCA alone provides an incomplete description of the child's cognitive abilities as measured by the subtests" (p. 88). However, no external validity studies are presented to support this statement. Consequently, until such evidence is presented, you should view this recommendation as tentative.

Similarly, the Handbook states that "Significant differences between the subtest scores within each cluster constrain the interpretation of that cluster score: The cluster score provides an incomplete or misleading description of the child's ability" (p. 88). Again, no external validity studies are presented to support this statement. This recommendation, like the one made for the GCA, should be viewed as tentative until external validity studies are available.

When you discuss individual cluster scores that are significantly different from each other or from the GCA, you should also consider how frequently such differences occurred in the DAS standardization sample (see Tables B.2 and B.3 of the Handbook). Differences that are statistically significant (unlikely to occur by pure chance) are not necessarily unusual. For example, Table B.2 of the Handbook shows that a 16-point difference between cluster scores, which is significant at the .05 level, was found in approximately 25% of the standardization sample.

Step 2: Evaluate within-cluster differences. The second step is to consider the variability within each cluster. The DAS Record Form (see Figure 15-2) also shows the *average* differences required between the subtests that compose each cluster score for statistical significance at the .05 level. These numbers are printed just below the adjacent boxes for

the subtest scores in each cluster. For example, a difference of 12 or more points between Word Definitions and Similarities on the School-Age Level would be statistically significant at the .05 level. Tables B.1 and B.4 (pages 290, 292, 293) of the Handbook provide the differences required for statistical significance at the .15, .05, and .01 levels at each age level. Chapter 5 of the Handbook suggests that if the subtests within a cluster score are significantly different from each other, the cluster score is not a complete summary of the examinee's ability in that area. Again, no evidence is presented to support this recommendation.

Step 3: Evaluate differences between subtests and the mean core *T* score. Table 3 in the Manual (pages 379–381) provides mean *T* scores based on the sum of the examinee's *T* scores for the core subtests. You should compare each of the examinee's core and diagnostic subtest scores with the mean core *T* score. The difference between the subtest *T* score and the mean core *T* score required for statistical significance at the .05 level is printed directly below the box for the subtest score on the Record Form (see Figure 15-2). If a subtest *T* score differs from the examinee's mean core *T* score by the amount shown on the Record Form (or more), you should interpret that subtest as a strength or a weakness. Differences required at other significance levels (.15 and .01) are shown in Table B.5 (page 294) of the Handbook.

The frequencies of various differences between subtest *T* scores and the mean core *T* score are shown in Tables B.6, B.7, and B.8 (pages 295–297) of the Handbook. Again, when evaluating a difference between scores, you should consider not only the statistical significance of the difference (likelihood of a difference that large or larger occurring by pure chance) but also how common differences that large or larger may be in the test's standardization sample (frequency of occurrence, or base rate).

Step 4: Compare each subtest *T* score with the other subtest *T* scores. Table B.9 (pages 298–299) of the Handbook shows the differences required between all pairs of cognitive subtests for statistical significance at the .15 and .05 levels. Because these values are not adjusted for multiple comparisons, they are overly liberal and would lead to too many significant differences if you made more than one comparison. They are most accurate when a priori planned comparisons are made to test a hypothesis you have developed (such as Recall of Objects versus Recall of Digits or Pattern Construction versus Matrices). These types of comparisons are not routinely recommended by Elliott.

Step 5: Qualitative analysis. This level of interpretation focuses on specific item failures and the content of the responses, or qualitative analysis. Inspecting responses to specific items can aid in evaluating the examinee's knowledge of specific information, such as how to read numerals on the

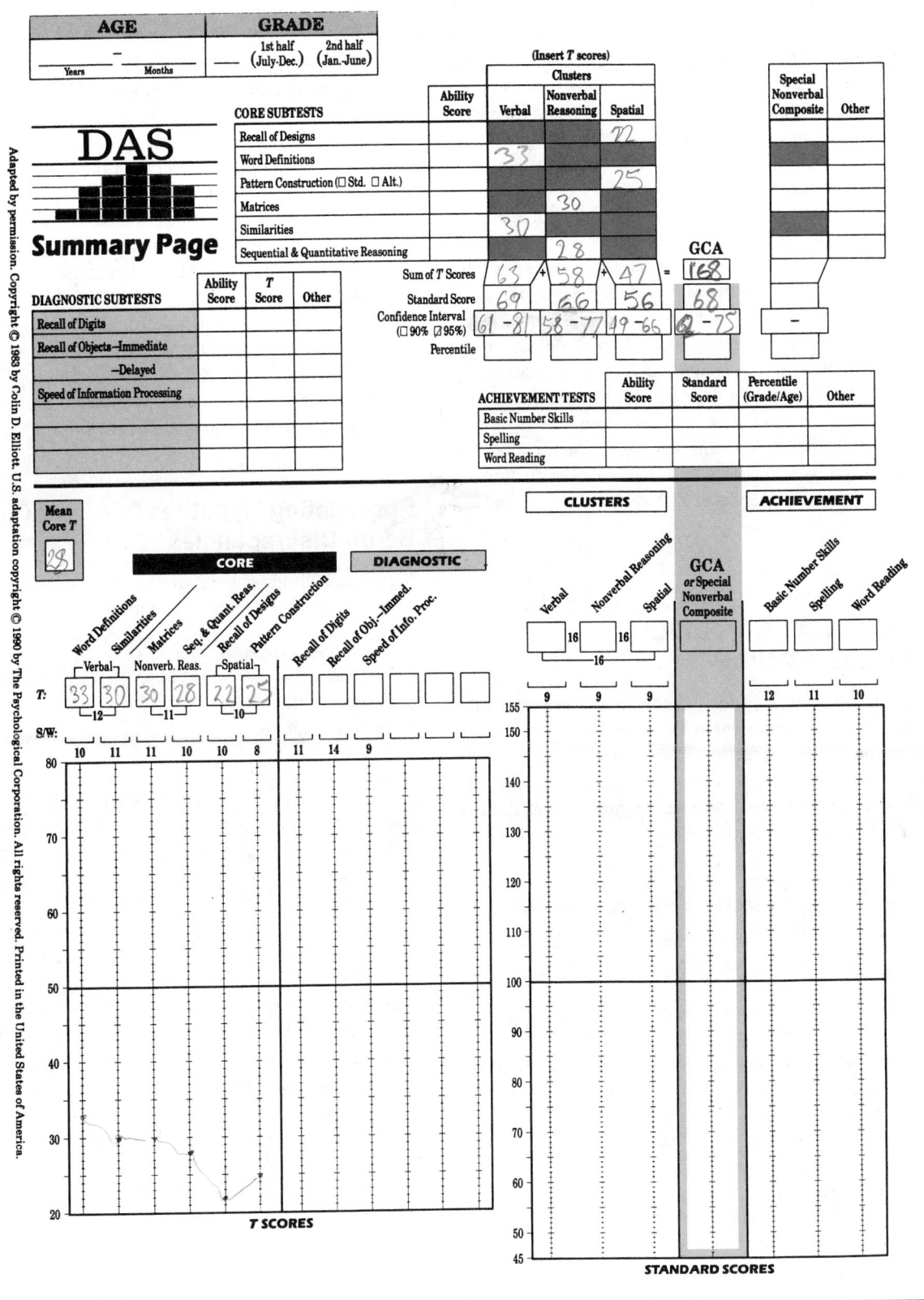

Figure 15-2. Summary Page of DAS School-Age Record Form. From the School-Age Record Form of the Differential Ability Scales. *Differential Ability Scales.* Adapted by permission. Copyright © 1983 by Colin D. Elliott. U.S. adaptation copyright © 1990 by The Psychological Corporation, a Harcourt Assessment Company. Reproduced by permission of the Publisher, The Psychological Corporation. All rights reserved. "Differential Ability Scales" and "DAS" are trademarks of The Psychological Corporation.

Early Number Concepts subtest or the meaning of specific words on the Word Definitions subtest. Always evaluate the examinee's verbal and nonverbal responses. When interpreting verbal and nonverbal responses to individual items, remember that these responses are one-time events that may not be typical of the examinee's usual behavior. Consistent patterns of responses to items may be more meaningful than a response to a single item. For example, again on Early Number Concepts, you might see that an examinee counts well orally on most items that call for that skill but consistently has difficulty reading and interpreting printed numbers. Similarly, on Word Definitions, an examinee might do well whenever she or he is able to think of a synonym for a word but consistently have difficulty explaining a definition when a synonym does not come readily to mind. Another examinee might do well on most Pattern Construction items that are symmetrical but become confused by items on which the two sides or top and bottom are not mirror images of each other.

COMPARISONS BETWEEN CLUSTER SCORES THAT CAN GUIDE INTERPRETATIONS

The evaluation of the cluster scores depends in part on the hypotheses you generate about the individual subtests that make up the respective factor scores, especially as there are only two subtests in each School-Age Level cluster. Some general observations can, however, be made about the two upper Preschool and three School-Age Level clusters.

Interpretation of Verbal Ability, Nonverbal Reasoning Ability, Spatial Ability, and Preschool Nonverbal Ability Clusters

The Verbal Ability cluster is based on accumulated experience. The items in this cluster usually assess the examinee's repertoire of verbal knowledge and concepts. Questions are presented either verbally or visually, and the examinee gives the responses orally or, on the Preschool Verbal Comprehension subtest, through actions. The Verbal Ability cluster might be considered an index of verbal reasoning and crystallized intelligence.

The Nonverbal Reasoning Ability cluster, in contrast, is more dependent on immediate problem-solving, or inductive fluid reasoning, ability. The stimuli are nonverbal (visual matrices and printed symbols or numbers) and are presented visually. Solutions require motor, pointing, or verbal responses. The Nonverbal Reasoning Ability cluster might be considered an index of nonverbal ability and fluid intelligence (Keith, 1990).

The Spatial Ability cluster is dependent on visual and spatial perception, mental imagery, ability to mentally manipulate visual images, and, to a minor extent, visual-motor coordination. One of the Spatial Ability subtests, Recall of

Designs, requires the examinee to draw designs from memory after the model has been removed. However, the correlations of Recall of Designs with other subtests involving memory (Recall of Objects, Recognition of Pictures, and Recall of Digits) are much lower than the correlation with Pattern Construction (Handbook, pages 314–326).

The upper Preschool Nonverbal Ability cluster appears to be based on a mixture of spatial ability (Pattern Construction and Copying subtests) and fluid reasoning ability (Picture Similarities).

Solving problems that make up the Verbal Ability, Nonverbal Reasoning Ability, Spatial Ability, and Preschool Nonverbal Ability clusters involves both verbal and nonverbal strategies. An examinee may reveal a preference for either verbal or nonverbal strategies for solving the problems.

Formulating Hypotheses About Cluster Score Discrepancies

Significant differences in an examinee's cluster scores may lead to hypotheses about one or more of the following:

- Cognitive style
- Deficiencies or strengths in processing information
- Sensory deficiencies
- Interest patterns
- Psychopathology
- Motivational changes

You must decide which interpretations apply, based on the examinee's entire performance and clinical history.

Formulate hypotheses about cluster scores in relationship to the examinee's absolute Verbal Ability, Spatial Ability, Nonverbal Reasoning Ability, or Preschool Nonverbal Ability cluster score, and only when the differences are significant. Thus, for example, you would not say that an examinee with a Verbal Ability cluster score of 140 and a Nonverbal Reasoning Ability cluster score of 120 had a deficit in fluid reasoning. In this case, both verbal comprehension and nonverbal reasoning are well developed. Similarly, you should view an examinee with a Nonverbal Reasoning Ability cluster score of 65 and a Spatial Ability cluster of 50 as having deficits in both nonverbal reasoning and spatial areas; do not consider the higher Nonverbal Reasoning Ability score of 65 as an absolute strength.

ILLUSTRATIVE HYPOTHESES FOR VERBAL ABILITY > NONVERBAL REASONING ABILITY

1. Verbal skills may be better developed than nonverbal reasoning skills.
2. Auditory-vocal processing skills may be better developed than visual skills.
3. Knowledge acquired through accumulated experience is better developed than immediate problem-solving ability.
4. Limitations in visual-perceptual abilities may be influencing performance.

ILLUSTRATIVE HYPOTHESES FOR
VERBAL ABILITY > SPATIAL ABILITY

1. Verbal skills may be better developed than spatial skills.
2. Auditory-vocal processing skills may be better developed than visual discrimination skills.
3. Knowledge acquired through accumulated experience is better developed than immediate problem-solving ability.
4. Practical tasks may be more difficult than nonpractical tasks.
5. Limitations in visual-motor integration may be influencing performance.

ILLUSTRATIVE HYPOTHESES FOR
NONVERBAL REASONING ABILITY > VERBAL ABILITY

1. Nonverbal reasoning skills may be better developed than verbal skills.
2. Visual skills may be better developed than auditory-vocal processing skills.
3. Immediate problem-solving ability is better developed than knowledge acquired as a result of accumulated experience.
4. A language deficit may exist.
5. Limitations in auditory conceptual skills and auditory processing skills may be influencing performance.

ILLUSTRATIVE HYPOTHESES FOR
SPATIAL REASONING > VERBAL ABILITY

1. Performance skills may be better developed than verbal skills.
2. Visual-motor skills may be better developed than auditory-vocal processing skills.
3. Immediate problem-solving ability may be better developed than knowledge acquired as a result of accumulated experience.
4. A language deficit may exist.
5. Limitations in auditory conceptual skills and auditory processing skills may be influencing performance.

ILLUSTRATIVE HYPOTHESES FOR
NONVERBAL REASONING ABILITY > SPATIAL ABILITY

Nonverbal reasoning skills may be better developed than spatial skills.

ILLUSTRATIVE HYPOTHESES FOR
SPATIAL ABILITY > NONVERBAL REASONING ABILITY

Spatial skills may be better developed than nonverbal reasoning skills.

ILLUSTRATIVE HYPOTHESES FOR
VERBAL ABILITY > PRESCHOOL NONVERBAL ABILITY

1. Verbal skills may be better developed than nonverbal reasoning skills.
2. Verbal skills may be better developed than spatial skills.
3. Auditory-vocal processing skills may be better developed than visual skills.

4. Knowledge acquired through accumulated experience is better developed than immediate problem-solving ability.
5. Limitations in visual-motor integration may be influencing performance.

ILLUSTRATIVE HYPOTHESES FOR
PRESCHOOL NONVERBAL ABILITY > VERBAL ABILITY

1. Performance skills may be better developed than verbal skills.
2. Visual-motor skills may be better developed than auditory-vocal processing skills.
3. Nonverbal reasoning skills may be better developed than verbal skills.
4. Immediate problem-solving ability may be better developed than knowledge acquired as a result of accumulated experience.
5. A language deficit may exist.
6. Limitations in auditory conceptual skills and auditory processing skills may be influencing performance.

COMPARISONS BETWEEN SUBTESTS THAT CAN GUIDE INTERPRETATIONS

If you find that the differences between subtest T scores are significant (see Table B.9, pages 298–299 in the Handbook), you must translate the findings into meaningful descriptions. It is not easy to interpret differences between subtest scores, and you must be cautious, as the subtests are less reliable than the cluster scores and GCA. The material in this chapter will help you in making interpretations.

View the interpretations that follow as hypotheses that may help you understand an examinee's abilities. However, you need to investigate these hypotheses through a study of the examinee's entire test performance and clinical history.

The following list of subtest comparisons does not include all possible comparisons, nor does it reflect all possible interpretations. Based on these examples, however, you should be able to develop other comparisons and formulate other interpretations. Treat all hypotheses as tentative. Never consider interpretations derived from profile analysis as definitive. Develop hypotheses based on both significant differences between subtest scores and the absolute values of the subtest scores. Thus, T scores of 50 or higher never reflect absolute weaknesses, and T scores of 49 or lower never reflect absolute strengths. You must be certain that your hypotheses do not contradict one another and do not contradict established facts. For example, do not report in one place that the examinee may have a weakness in spatial abilities and in another place that the examinee may have a strength in spatial abilities.

COMPARISON OF VERBAL ABILITY CLUSTER SUBTESTS

Word Definitions (WD) and Similarities (S). Both subtests involve verbal processing, but in different contexts. Word Definitions typically requires the use of more expressive skills than does Similarities. Both measure aspects of abstract thinking and ability to form concepts, but Similarities is a better measure of these abilities.

- WD > S: High Word Definitions and low Similarities may suggest difficulty in forming abstract concepts but good ability to understand the meaning of individual words.
- WD < S: Low Word Definitions and high Similarities may suggest good ability to think abstractly but limited ability to understand and express the meaning of individual words.

COMPARISON OF SPATIAL ABILITY SUBTESTS

Pattern Construction (PC) and Recall of Designs (RD). This comparison relates visual-spatial ability to visual-motor ability with a memory component.

- PC > RD: High Pattern Construction and low Recall of Designs may suggest adequate visual-spatial ability but inadequate visual-motor memory ability.
- PC < RD: Low Pattern Construction and high Recall of Designs may suggest inadequate visual-spatial ability but adequate visual-motor memory ability.

COMPARISON OF NONVERBAL REASONING ABILITY CLUSTER SUBTESTS

Matrices (MS) and Sequential and Quantitative Reasoning (SQR). The Matrices and Sequential and Quantitative Reasoning subtests both involve fluid reasoning abilities, but Sequential and Quantitative Reasoning requires knowledge of and facility with formal arithmetic operations (for items 16–39) and step-by-step sequential reasoning. Matrices requires visual perceptual abilities, including the ability to evaluate the pattern as a whole.

- MS > SQR: High Matrices and low Sequential and Quantitative Reasoning may suggest good visual perceptual abilities but inadequate knowledge of formal arithmetic operations.
- MS < SQR: Low Matrices and high Sequential and Quantitative Reasoning may suggest good knowledge of formal arithmetic operations but inadequate visual perceptual abilities.

COMPARISON OF MEMORY SUBTESTS

The Recognition of Pictures (RP), Recall of Digits (RDig), and Recall of Objects (RO) subtests all involve short-term memory. Differences exist among the subtests, however, in the stimuli used to elicit responses—that is, whether the stimuli are meaningful or nonmeaningful and whether the items are presented orally or visually. On Recognition of Pictures, the stimuli are meaningful and presented visually, and a pointing response is required. On Recall of Digits, the stimuli are nonmeaningful and presented orally, and an oral response is required. On Recall of Objects, the stimuli are meaningful and presented visually, and a verbal response is required.

1. *Recall of Objects (RO) versus Recall of Digits (RDig).* This comparison contrasts subtests that measure short-term memory for meaningful versus nonmeaningful material and for visual versus auditory material.

- RO > RDig: High Recall of Objects and low Recall of Digits may suggest better short-term memory for meaningful visually presented material than for nonmeaningful orally presented material.
- RO < RDig: High Recall of Digits and low Recall of Objects may suggest better short-term memory for nonmeaningful orally presented material than for meaningful visually presented material.

2. *Recognition of Pictures (RP) versus Recall of Digits (RDig).* This comparison contrasts subtests that measure short-term memory for meaningful versus nonmeaningful material as well as short-term memory for visual versus auditory material.

- RP > RDig: High Recognition of Pictures and low Recall of Digits may suggest better short-term memory for meaningful visually presented material than for nonmeaningful orally presented material.
- RP < RDig: High Recall of Digits and low Recall of Objects may suggest better short-term memory for nonmeaningful orally presented material than for meaningful visually presented material.

3. *Recall of Objects–Immediate (ROi) versus Recall of Objects–Delayed (ROd).* Recall of Objects–Immediate and Recall of Objects–Delayed both measure short-term memory. However, the delayed portion requires incidental learning—holding in memory information that was not directly asked for.

- ROi > ROd: High Recall of Objects–Immediate and low Recall of Object–Delayed may suggest better immediate short-term memory than delayed short-term memory.
- ROi < ROd: High Recall of Objects–Delayed and low Recall of Object–Immediate may suggest better delayed short-term memory than immediate short-term memory.

ASSETS OF THE DAS

The DAS is a well-standardized test, with excellent internal consistency reliability and adequate concurrent validity. Following is a summary of the assets of the DAS:

1. *Good validity.* The DAS has adequate concurrent validity, demonstrated by acceptable correlations with several ability measures, and good construct validity.

2. *High reliabilities.* The internal consistency reliabilities of the GCA and cluster scores are high. Average inter-

nal consistency reliability coefficients for the GCA are .90, .94, and .95 (lower Preschool, upper Preschool, and School-Age, respectively), and averages for the clusters are .88 for both the Verbal Ability clusters (upper Preschool and School-Age), .89 and .90 for the Preschool Nonverbal Ability cluster and School-Age Nonverbal Reasoning Ability cluster, respectively, and .92 for the Spatial Ability cluster.

Because the Manual and Handbook provide reliability data, standard errors of measurement, and intercorrelations of subtest scores by one-year or half-year age intervals, you can evaluate the scale's properties throughout its entire age range. You can establish confidence intervals for all the scores at each of the age groups, thereby providing estimates that are specifically applicable to each examinee's chronological age.

3. *Excellent standardization.* The standardization procedures were excellent, with sampling based on geographical region, community size, ethnic group, age, gender, and socioeconomic status. An additional group of ethnic minority examinees was used to ensure that the items were nondiscriminatory.

4. *Good administration procedures.* The procedures described in the Manual are good. The examiner actively probes borderline responses, and for several subtests the Manual provides examples of responses needing probing. You also have flexibility in selecting subtests to administer. Discontinuance procedures may reduce examinees' sense of failure and frustration.

5. *Good administrative guidelines and test materials.* The administrative guidelines are thorough, although complex (see limitations below). The directions are easy to read. The artwork is clear, and the materials are well constructed. The sample and teaching items on several subtests help the examinee understand the task requirements.

6. *Helpful scoring criteria.* The criteria for scoring the responses have been carefully prepared. The Word Definitions and Similarities scoring guidelines, for example, detail the rationale for 1 and 0 scores. The Manual provides scores for many typical responses and identifies those responses needing further inquiry.

7. *GCA based on high g loadings.* The GCA score is based on only those subtests with the highest g loadings—the core subtests.

8. *Special Nonverbal Composite.* Provision of a Special Nonverbal Composite is useful for examinees with a hearing impairment or language disability.

9. *Efficiency.* The core subtests can be administered relatively quickly.

10. *Good Handbook.* The Handbook presents a thorough treatment of development, standardization, psychometric properties, factor analyses, and interpretation of the scales and subtests.

11. *Co-norming with achievement tests.* The co-norming facilitates some types of ability-achievement discrepancy analysis.

LIMITATIONS OF THE DAS

Although the DAS is, overall, an excellent instrument, some problems do exist.

1. *Lack of a comparable battery throughout the age ranges covered.* The GCAs obtained at the Preschool and School-Age Levels are based on different combinations of subtests. No subtest runs throughout the battery in the usual age range covered by the test.

2. *Variable range of scores.* The DAS fails to provide the same range of GCA scores, cluster scores, and subtest scores throughout the test. For example, the highest GCA that adolescents age 17-11 can obtain is 156; the lowest GCA that examinees age 2-6 can obtain is 53. Applying profile analysis uniformly to all subtests would be misleading for individual cases because at certain ages examinees cannot obtain the same number of *T*-score points on all subtests.

3. *Difficulty in scoring responses.* Although the Manual provides clear explanations and scoring examples, considerable judgment must be exercised in scoring responses on Word Definitions, Similarities, Recall of Designs, and Copying.

4. *Only two subtests per cluster at the School-Age Level.* The limited number of subtests in the Verbal Ability, Nonverbal Reasoning Ability, and Spatial Ability clusters means that if scores on the two component subtests in a cluster differ significantly, the cluster does not adequately summarize (according to the Manual) the examinee's pattern of abilities.

5. *Limited assessment of verbal expression, especially at the Preschool Level.* The Verbal Comprehension subtest does not require the examinee to speak at all. Naming Vocabulary requires only one-word responses. There is no Preschool subtest that requires expressive language from the examinee. Even at the School-Age Level, there is no subtest comparable to the Comprehension subtests of the Stanford-Binet: IV or Wechsler tests. An examinee could respond to almost all of the DAS Vocabulary and Similarities items with one- or two-word answers.

6. *Complexity of the organization of the test and administration and scoring guidelines.* The structure of the DAS, the diversity of abilities assessed, the several levels of the test, and the test's flexibility in administration make learning the test challenging.

CONCLUDING COMMENT ON THE DAS

The DAS is a useful instrument for assessing the cognitive ability of young children and adolescents. The test covers a wide age range, the materials are child friendly, and administration is time efficient. It is particularly valuable for the assessment of 2- and 3-year-old children. Few other cognitive ability tests are available for the assessment of this age group.

The DAS also some shortcomings, though, as noted above. The most serious of these are the lack of a comparable battery throughout the age levels covered by the scale and the nonuniformity of GCAs, cluster scores, and subtest scores. Consequently, you cannot evaluate profiles and changes in test performance without considering how the scale is constructed. In each case, you must attend to the range of scores provided by the scale for the examinee's specific age. Keep these considerations in mind, especially when you must make critical decisions about the examinee. Overall, the DAS is a valuable contribution to the field of assessment of cognitive ability.

THINKING THROUGH THE ISSUES

1. What unique features does the DAS have compared to the Wechsler tests and the Stanford-Binet: IV?
2. How might the DAS assist in the diagnosis of learning disability?
3. When would you want to use the DAS instead of one of the Wechsler tests or the SB: IV?
4. How would the limitations of the DAS affect its clinical usefulness?

SUMMARY

1. The Differential Ability Scales (DAS) is an individually administered battery of 17 cognitive subtests and 3 achievement tests for children and adolescents between the ages of 2-6 and 17-11.
2. The DAS was designed to measure specific abilities and provide profiles of strengths and weaknesses.
3. The DAS contains a Preschool Level battery for ages 2-6 to 5-11 and a School-Age Level battery for ages 6-0 to 17-11.
4. The Preschool Level battery is further divided into a lower Preschool Level and an upper Preschool Level.
5. The 17 cognitive subtests are grouped into 12 core cognitive subtests and 5 diagnostic subtests.
6. The subtests in the core cognitive area are used to compute the GCA and the Verbal Ability, Nonverbal Ability, Nonverbal Reasoning Ability, and Spatial Ability cluster scores. The cluster scores also are called composite scores.

Standardization

7. The DAS was standardized on 3,475 examinees selected to be representative of noninstitutionalized, English-proficient children and adolescents living in the United States during 1987–1989.

Deviation Composite Scores, *T* Scores, and Test-Age Equivalents

8. The DAS uses standard scores ($M = 100$, $SD = 15$) for the Verbal Ability cluster, Nonverbal Ability cluster, Nonverbal Reasoning Ability cluster, Spatial Ability cluster, GCA, and three achievement Composite Scores. It uses *T* scores ($M = 50$, $SD = 10$) for the 17 cognitive core and diagnostic subtests.

Reliability

9. Average internal consistency reliability coefficients for the GCA are .90, .94, and .95 on the lower Preschool Level, upper Preschool Level, and School-Age Level, respectively.

10. Average internal consistency reliability coefficients for the clusters are (a) .88 for the Verbal Ability cluster in the upper Preschool Level and School-Age Level, (b) .89 and .90 for the Preschool Nonverbal Ability cluster and School-Age Nonverbal Reasoning Ability cluster, and (c) .92 for the Spatial Ability cluster.
11. The average internal consistency subtest reliabilities range from .71 to .91.
12. The average standard errors of measurement (SEM) in standard score points are 3.80 for the GCA, 5.14 for the Verbal Ability cluster, 4.85 for the Nonverbal Ability cluster, 4.77 for the Nonverbal Reasoning cluster, and 4.19 for the Spatial Ability cluster.
13. The test-retest stability coefficients are .89 and .94 for the GCA, .84 to .89 for the Verbal Ability cluster, .79 to .86 for the Nonverbal Ability cluster and Nonverbal Reasoning Ability cluster, and .79 to .90 for the Spatial Ability cluster. Stability coefficients for all subtests ranged from .38 to .90.
14. On average, from the first to the second testing the GCA increased by 3.0 to 7.8 points, the Verbal Ability cluster increased by 1.2 to 5.1 points, the Nonverbal Ability cluster increased by 3.3 to 6.6 points, and the Spatial Ability cluster increased by 4.7 to 7.6 points.
15. At the Preschool Level, the largest test-retest change was for Recall of Objects–Immediate and the smallest change was for Copying.
16. At the School-Age Level, the largest change was for Recall of Objects–Immediate and the smallest was for Recognition of Pictures.
17. For the six core subtests at the School-Age Level, the average gain ranged from 1.2 points to 4.9 points.

Validity

18. The DAS has satisfactory concurrent validity. The GCA correlates highly with other measures of intelligence ($M\ r = .76$) as well as with tests of academic achievement ($M\ r = .60$).

Correlations Between Subtests and Scales

19. Correlations between the 20 subtests range from .07 to .68. The median correlation between all subtests is .28.

GCA and Parent Education

20. Examinees' GCA scores are related to level of parental education.

Factor Analysis

21. Factor analyses indicate that one factor emerges at ages 2-6 to 3-5, two factors at ages 3-6 to 5-11, and three factors at ages 6-0 to 17-11.
22. All subtests possess sufficient specificity to justify the interpretation of specific subtest functions.

Range of Subtest Scaled Scores

23. None of the 17 cognitive subtests provides a *T*-score range of 20 to 80 at all ages.

Range of GCAs

24. The GCAs range from 44 to 175. This range is not available at all ages.

Overview of Administration Procedures

25. The DAS uses a form of tailored testing to reduce testing time.
26. The DAS employs unscored sample items, as well as scored and unscored teaching items.

Word Definitions

27. Word Definitions assesses acquired verbal knowledge, language comprehension, and fluency. It is a fair measure of g and contributes substantially to the Verbal Ability cluster. It is a reliable subtest.

Similarities

28. Similarities assesses acquired verbal knowledge, language comprehension, language fluency, verbal inductive reasoning, vocabulary and verbal development, logical and abstract thinking, and ability to distinguish between essential and superficial features. It is a fair measure of g and contributes substantially to the Verbal Ability cluster. It is a relatively reliable subtest.

Matrices

29. Matrices assesses nonverbal inductive reasoning ability, ability to formulate and test hypotheses, verbal mediation, and visual perception. It is a good measure of g and contributes substantially to the Nonverbal Reasoning Ability cluster. It is a reliable subtest.

Sequential and Quantitative Reasoning

30. Sequential and Quantitative Reasoning assesses the ability to perceive relationships, draw conclusions (inductive reasoning), formulate and test hypotheses, use analytic reasoning, and retrieve long-term information. It is a good measure of g and contributes substantially to the Nonverbal Reasoning Ability cluster. It is a reliable subtest. The early items measure visual perceptual-motor skills, and the later items require arithmetic computation skills.

Recall of Designs

31. Recall of Designs assesses the ability to encode and retain visual-spatial information and use motor skills, short-term visual recall, spatial orientation, and drawing skills. It is a fair measure of g and contributes moderately to the Spatial Ability cluster. It is a reliable subtest. Despite the obvious memory demand, it has relatively low correlations with other DAS subtests requiring memory.

Pattern Construction

32. Pattern Construction assesses visual-spatial ability, perception of spatial orientation, analysis of visual data, and nonverbal reasoning. It is a fair measure of g across all ages and contributes substantially to the Nonverbal Ability cluster at the Preschool Level and to the Spatial Ability cluster at the School-Age Level. It is a highly reliable subtest. It is scored in two ways: standard (considers speed and accuracy) and alternative (considers accuracy only).

Block Building

33. Block Building measures visuoperceptual ability, problem-solving ability, hand-eye coordination, and spatial orientation; it also may involve verbal encoding strategies. It is a fair measure of g and does not contribute to any cluster. It is a relatively reliable subtest.

Verbal Comprehension

34. Verbal Comprehension assesses understanding of language (including understanding of syntax and prepositional and relational concepts), ability to follow verbal directions, and short-term auditory memory. It is a good measure of g and contributes substantially to the Verbal Ability cluster. It is a reliable subtest.

Picture Similarities

35. Picture Similarities assesses nonverbal reasoning abilities including the ability to solve nonverbal problems, identify pictures, formulate and test hypotheses about the relationship among different pictures in a set, use verbal mediation, and attach meaning to pictures. It is a fair measure of g and contributes moderately to the Nonverbal Ability cluster. It is a relatively reliable subtest.

Naming Vocabulary

36. Naming Vocabulary assesses recognition of pictures, expressive language ability, general language development, and word retrieval from long-term memory. It is a fair measure of g and contributes moderately to the Verbal Ability cluster. It is a relatively reliable subtest.

Early Number Concepts

37. Early Number Concepts measures such number abilities as reciting, counting, matching, comparing, recognizing, and solving number problems. It is a good measure of g, but it does not contribute to any cluster. It is a reliable subtest.

Copying

38. Copying measures fine-motor ability and the ability to perceive similarities between figures. Items vary from a simple straight line to complex geometric figures. It is a fair measure of g and contributes moderately to the Nonverbal Ability cluster. It is a reliable subtest.

Recall of Objects

39. Recall of Objects assesses (a) short-term verbal memory, (b) short-term visual memory, or (c) a combination of the two. It has both immediate and delayed-recall trials. It is a poor measure of g and does not contribute to any cluster. It is a relatively reliable subtest.

Recall of Digits

40. Recall of Digits measures short-term auditory sequential memory. It is a poor measure of g and does not contribute to any cluster. It is a reliable subtest.

Recognition of Pictures

41. Recognition of Pictures measures short-term visual memory. It is a poor measure of *g* and does not contribute to any cluster. It is a relatively reliable subtest.

Speed of Information Processing

42. Speed of Information Processing measures mental speed. It is a poor measure of *g* and does not contribute to any cluster. It is a highly reliable subtest.

Matching Letter-Like Forms

43. Matching Letter-Like Forms measures visual discrimination and spatial orientation. It is a fair measure of *g* and does not contribute to any cluster. It is a reliable subtest.

Basic Number Skills

44. Basic Number Skills, an achievement test, measures concepts and skills that underlie competence in arithmetical reasoning and calculations. It is a highly reliable test. Items cover recognition of printed numbers; the four basic arithmetic operations; and calculations using whole numbers, decimal fractions, common fractions, and percentages.

Spelling

45. Spelling, an achievement test, measures spelling proficiency. It is a highly reliable test.

Word Reading

46. Word Reading, an achievement test, measures sight reading. It is a highly reliable test.

Interpreting the DAS

47. Do not view the individual subtests as a means of determining specific cognitive skills with precision.
48. Derive the most reliable estimates of specific abilities from the Verbal Ability, Nonverbal Ability, Nonverbal Reasoning Ability, and Spatial Ability clusters and the GCA.
49. The Special Nonverbal Composite (lower Preschool Level and School-Age Level) and the Nonverbal Ability cluster (upper Preschool Level) can be used to evaluate nonverbal abilities.
50. Profile analysis can be used to formulate tentative hypotheses about an examinee's strengths and weaknesses.
51. Interpretation of the DAS involves a multi-step process for developing and testing hypotheses.
52. Evaluate each aspect of the DAS, including information regarding significant differences between scores as well as the frequencies of any difference.

Comparisons Between Cluster Scores That Can Guide Interpretations

53. The Verbal Ability cluster might be considered an index of verbal reasoning and crystallized intelligence.
54. The Nonverbal Reasoning Ability cluster might be considered an index of nonverbal ability and fluid intelligence.

55. The Spatial Ability cluster might be considered an index of visual, spatial perception, mental imagery, ability to mentally manipulate visual images, and, to a minor extent, visual-motor coordination.
56. The upper Preschool Nonverbal Ability cluster might be considered a mixed index of spatial ability and fluid reasoning ability.
57. Formulate hypotheses about cluster scores in relationship to the examinee's absolute Verbal Ability, Spatial Ability, Nonverbal Reasoning Ability, or Preschool Nonverbal Ability cluster score, and only when the differences are significant.

Comparisons Between Subtests That Can Guide Interpretations

58. Interpret differences between subtest scores cautiously, and only in relation to the examinee's entire performance and clinical history.

Assets of the DAS

59. The DAS is a well-standardized test, with excellent internal consistency reliability and adequate concurrent validity.
60. The administrative guidelines are helpful, and the Handbook is good.

Limitations of the DAS

61. The DAS lacks a comparable battery throughout the ages covered and has a variable range of scores.
62. Other difficulties include difficulty in scoring some subtests, the limited number of subtests in clusters, limited assessment of verbal expression (especially at the Preschool Level), and the complexity of the organization of the test and administration and scoring guidelines.

Concluding Comment on the DAS

63. The DAS is a useful instrument for assessing the cognitive ability of young children and adolescents. Interpretation must take into account the structure of the test and the range of scores available for each subtest and age.

KEY TERMS, CONCEPTS, AND NAMES

STUDY QUESTIONS

1. Discuss the DAS. Include in your discussion its standardization, the GCA, reliability, and validity.
2. Discuss correlations on the DAS, including correlations between subtests, between subtests and the cluster scores, and between subtests and the GCA.
3. Describe DAS cluster scores with respect to the stratification variables used in the standardization sample.
4. Discuss DAS factor analytic findings.
5. Discuss DAS administrative considerations.
6. Discuss the DAS Special Nonverbal Composite.
7. Discuss the rationale, factor analytic findings, reliability and correlational highlights, and administrative considerations for each of the DAS cognitive subtests: Word Definitions, Similarities, Matrices, Sequential and Quantitative Reasoning, Recall of Designs, Pattern Construction, Block Building, Verbal Comprehension, Picture Similarities, Naming Vocabulary, Early Number Concepts, Copying, Recall of Objects, Recall of Digits, Recognition of Pictures, Speed of Information Processing, and Matching Letter-Like Forms.
8. Discuss the DAS Basic Number Skills, Spelling, and Word Reading achievement tests.
9. Discuss the intent of profile analysis, methods of profile analysis, and approaches to profile analysis on the DAS. Include in your discussion the effect of score ranges on profile analysis.
10. Discuss how to interpret differences between DAS cluster scores.
11. Discuss how to interpret differences between DAS subtests. Cite at least five subtest comparisons in your presentation.
12. What are some general considerations in interpreting the DAS?
13. Discuss the assets and limitations of the DAS.

16

ASSESSMENT OF INTELLIGENCE
WITH SPECIALIZED MEASURES

*Many would, in fact, offer the intelligence test
as the major achievement of psychology in guiding
everyday practical affairs.*

—Richard A. Weinberg

Goals and Objectives

This chapter is designed to enable you to do the following:

- Describe several individually administered brief tests of intelligence.

- Compare and contrast brief tests of intelligence.

- Recognize which tests are appropriate for the assessment of children with specific disabilities.

This chapter covers several specialized instruments for the assessment of cognitive ability. Some of the tests are specialized because they are limited to a specific (a) age range, such as infancy or early childhood, or (b) area of cognitive ability, such as nonverbal reasoning or figural reasoning. The chapter also discusses some informal ways to evaluate children's cognitive ability.

The individually administered tests of intelligence surveyed in this chapter can make valuable additions to your fund of assessment techniques; they are especially useful in situations in which it is not feasible or practical to administer the WISC–III, WPPSI–R, WAIS–III, Stanford-Binet Intelligence Scale: IV, or DAS. The tests described in this chapter can be used for screening and follow-up evaluations and for assessing children with or without disabilities. Some tests in this chapter require a pointing response only, and instructions may be pantomimed. You can master some tests in this chapter (e.g., the Slosson Intelligence Test–Revised) relatively quickly and easily, whereas others (e.g., the Bayley Scales of Infant Development–II) require considerable training. In any case, every assessment requires skill in establishing rapport with the examinee, recognizing signs of psychopathology, and interpreting assessment findings.

Critical decisions, such as placement decisions or predictions about future academic or vocational success, normally should not be based solely on any of the tests described in this chapter, because they have limited validity and reliability, have out-of-date norms, measure only some limited domain of ability, or need further research. The WISC–III, WPPSI–R, WAIS–III, Stanford-Binet Intelligence Scale: IV, and DAS are recommended for the assessment of intelligence when a child has the necessary physical capacities to respond to the test questions, when the child is of appropriate age to take the test, when time is not at a premium, and when the IQ is to be used for making critical decisions. When verbal responses cannot be elicited from the child, when sensory or motor handicaps limit the child's performance, or when time is at a premium and only a screening decision is being made, however, specialized intelligence tests, brief intelligence tests, or brief forms of longer intelligence tests can be useful.

The matrix-type tests covered in this chapter (and other chapters as well) can be used for testing-of-limits, if needed. Useful testing-of-limits procedures include (a) asking children to describe their approach or strategy while they are solving the problems; (b) asking children to describe the principles or reasons behind their solutions after they give their answers; (c) giving children feedback on correct performance, incorrect performance, or both and seeing how this feedback affects their performance; and (d) showing children the correct solution when they fail and seeing how this feedback affects their performance.

This chapter (as well as other chapters of the text) covers several individually administered tests of intelligence. McGrew and Flanagan (1998) have proposed that parts of different tests be selected to create a customized assessment, a

Copyright © 1999 by John P. Wood.

technique termed the "cross-battery approach." With this approach, you can obtain more precise information about different areas of cognitive functioning. Glutting, Watkins, and Youngstrom (in press), however, have raised several concerns about the cross-battery approach. Three of these relate to the comparability of scores obtained from different instruments, effects associated with modifying the order of subtests, and sampling and norming issues. Therefore, you should study the work of McGrew and Flanagan and that of Glutting et al. before you use the cross-battery approach.

BAYLEY SCALES OF INFANT DEVELOPMENT–II

by Agnes Shine and Jerome M. Sattler

The Bayley Scales of Infant Development–II (BSID–II; Bayley, 1993) is an individually administered test of infant mental and motor development. It is a revision of the 1969 edition. Changes included extending the age range (1 to 42 months), expanding the content, and deleting uninteresting and difficult-to-administer items. The test takes about 30 minutes to administer to children up to 15 months of age and about 60 minutes to administer to children older than 15 months of age.

The three scales on the BSID–II are as follows:

• The Mental Scale contains 178 items that measure recognition memory, habituation, visual preference, visual acuity skills, problem solving, number concepts, language, and social development.

- The Motor Scale contains 111 items that measure quality of movement, sensory integration, motor planning, fine and gross motor skills, and perceptual-motor integration.
- The Behavior Rating Scale contains 30 items designed to obtain information about how the examiner views the child's behavior (e.g., persistence, affect, cooperation, fine and gross motor movement, and frustration level).

Scores

Raw scores on the Mental Scale and Motor Scale are converted to standard scores ($M = 100$, $SD = 15$); however, the BSID–II does not provide a single composite score. The Behavior Rating Scale uses a Likert-type rating scale (range of 1 to 5 points) and provides percentile ranks for the raw scores.

Standardization

The BSID–II was standardized on a sample of 1,700 children divided into 17 age groups, with 50 males and 50 females in each age group. The sample matched 1988 U.S. Census data with respect to gender, race/ethnicity, geographic region, and parental educational level.

Reliability

Internal consistency reliability coefficients range from .78 to .93 ($Mdn \ r_{xx} = .88$) for the Mental Scale, from .79 to .91 ($Mdn \ r_{xx} = .84$) for the Motor Scale, and from .82 to .92 ($Mdn \ r_{xx} = .88$) for the Behavior Rating Scale. Standard errors of measurement for the Mental Scale and Motor Scale are 5.21 and 6.01, respectively. Stability coefficients, based on a sample of 175 children who were retested after a 1- to 16-day period, are .87 for the Mental Scale and .78 for the Motor Scale. Interrater reliabilities for the Behavior Rating Scale range from .57 to .80. Correlations between the Mental and Motor Scales range from .24 to .72 ($Mdn \ r_{xx} = .44$), with no apparent reason to explain the pattern of correlations.

Validity

The BSID–II Mental Scale has acceptable concurrent validity, as noted by significant correlations with other tests of cognitive abilities. The concurrent validity of the Motor Scale, however, is not as well established. Factor analyses in the Manual generally support the construct validity of the Behavior Rating Scale, although its factor structure may be more complex than is reported in the Manual (Thompson, Wasserman, & Matula, 1996). Mean scores on the BSID–II of several groups of children with developmental disabilities provide support for the discriminant validity of the test. A study of at-risk children reported that the BSID–II has acceptable convergent and divergent validity (Goldstein, Fogle, Wieber, & O'Shea, 1995).

Comment on the BSID–II

The BSID–II is the best available measure for the assessment of infants. The norm group is excellent, and technical properties, overall, are good. For more information about the BSID–II, see Black and Matula (2000).

COGNITIVE ASSESSMENT SYSTEM
by Denise K. Hildebrand and Jerome M. Sattler

The Cognitive Assessment System (CAS; Naglieri & Das, 1997) is an individually administered test of cognitive ability designed for children between the ages of 5 and 17 years. It takes about 1 hour to administer. The test is based on the PASS model, a derivative of Luria's neuropsychologically based model (see Chapter 5). PASS is an acronym for four components—planning, attention, simultaneous processing, and successive processing—hypothesized to represent basic cognitive processing. Although each component has a distinct function, all are related.

- Planning is a mental activity that involves setting goals, selecting strategies for task completion, and monitoring the effectiveness of strategies and of one's own behavior in implementing plans.
- Attention is the process by which an individual focuses on relevant stimuli and ignores irrelevant stimuli over a sustained period of time.
- Simultaneous processing involves viewing information holistically (e.g., spatially).
- Successive processing involves the sequencing of information using temporal order links or chain-like progressions.

The four components are all used in a cognitive act. For example, when you read a textbook, planning processes allow you to scan topic headings to determine the gist of the content, attentional processes assist you in focusing on the text and ignoring extraneous sounds or activities, simultaneous processes help you to integrate words into ideas through text comprehension, and successive processes aid you in understanding sentences based on syntactic relationships. For more information on the CAS, see *CAS Interpretive Handbook* (Naglieri & Das, 1997) and *Essentials of CAS Assessment* (Naglieri, 1999a).

Subtests

The 13 subtests are as follows:

Planning

- The Matching Numbers subtest requires underlining the two numbers in a row that are the same.
- The Planned Codes subtest requires using codes on the top to complete boxes, each of which has a letter and an empty box beneath it.

- The Planned Connections subtest requires connecting numbers or connecting numbers and letters in sequential order.

Attention

- The Expressive Attention subtest requires identifying pictures of animals or words in color on a page that has distracting elements.
- The Number Detection subtest requires identifying numbers on a page that has distracting elements.
- The Receptive Attention subtest requires identifying pictures that have similar lexical elements but differ perceptually.

Simultaneous Processing

- The Nonverbal Matrices subtest requires selecting the item that best completes the matrix.
- The Verbal-Spatial Relations subtest requires matching a verbal description with its pictorial counterpart.
- The Figure Memory subtest requires recognizing a geometric design that is embedded within a larger design.

Successive Processing

- The Word Series subtest requires repeating words read aloud by the examiner.
- The Sentence Repetition subtest requires repeating sentences read aloud by the examiner.
- The Speech Rate subtest requires repeating a three-word series 10 times (for ages 5 to 7).
- The Sentence Questions subtest requires answering questions about sentences read aloud by the examiner (for ages 8 to 17).

The CAS has two batteries, with 8 subtests in the Basic Battery (Matching Numbers, Planned Codes, Expressive Attention, Number Detection, Nonverbal Matrices, Verbal-Spatial Relations, Word Series, and Sentence Repetition) and 13 subtests in the Standard Battery. Each battery provides scores for the Planning, Attention, Simultaneous Processing, and Successive Processing Scales.

Scores

Standard scores are provided for the subtests ($M = 10$, $SD = 3$), four scales ($M = 100$, $SD = 15$), and Full Scale ($M = 100$, $SD = 15$). The subtests are scored in different ways. On Matching Numbers, Planned Codes, and Expressive Attention, the completion time and number of correct items are combined into a ratio score and then summed across items to produce a raw score. On Number Detection and Receptive Attention, an accuracy score, which is the number of correct responses minus the number of incorrect responses (termed *false detections*), is obtained. The ratio score is then the ratio of the accuracy score to the total time for each item. Ratio scores are summed across the items to obtain a raw score for

each of these subtests. The raw score for Speech Rate is based on the total time needed to complete the subtest. Planned Connections, Nonverbal Matrices, Verbal-Spatial Relations, Figure Memory, Word Series, Sentence Questions, and Sentence Repetition are scored 1 (correct) or 0 (incorrect).

Standardization

The CAS was standardized on a stratified random sample representative of the 1990 U.S. Census. A sample of 2,200 children ages 5 to 17 was selected based on age, gender, race, region, community setting, classroom placement, educational classification (e.g., learning disability), and parental educational level.

Reliability

Internal consistency reliabilities range from .75 to .89 (*Mdn* $r_{xx} = .82$) for the subtests, from .88 to .93 (*Mdn* $r_{xx} = .90$) for the scales, and from .95 to .97 (*Mdn* $r_{xx} = .96$) for the Full Scale on the Standard Battery. On the Basic Battery, Full Scale reliabilities range from .85 to .90 (*Mdn* $r_{xx} = .87$). The average standard error of measurement is 5.4 for the Full Scale on the Basic Battery and 3.1 for the Full Scale on the Standard Battery. The average SEMs for the four scales on the Standard Battery range from 4.2 to 6.2 (*Mdn* SEM = 4.3). For the individual subtests, the average SEMs range from 1.0 to 1.5 (*Mdn* SEM = 1.4).

Test-retest reliability was assessed on a sample of 215 children who spanned the entire age range. Test-retest intervals ranged from 9 to 73 days (*Mdn* = 21 days). Median stability coefficients are $r_{xx} = .73$ for the subtests and $r_{xx} = .82$ for the Basic and Standard Batteries. On the Standard Battery, mean retest scores increased by 4 points on the Planning and Successive Scales, 5 points on the Simultaneous Scale, and 6 points on the Attention and Full Scales. On the Basic Battery, mean retest scores increased by 2 points on the Successive Scale, 3 points on the Planning Scale, 4 points on the Simultaneous Scale, and 5 points on the Attention and Full Scales.

Validity

The validity of the CAS was examined using content, construct, and criterion-related approaches. Construct validity was assessed by examining raw-score changes as a function of age, computing correlations between the subtests and scales, and conducting factor analyses. The results indicated appropriate developmental trends. For example, mean scores for Planned Connections, which are based on completion time, decreased with age. Correlations between subtests and scales were generally in keeping with theoretical tenets (e.g., subtests within scales correlated more highly than subtests between scales). However, several subtests also correlated moderately with subtests on other scales. For example, Planned Codes on the Planning Scale is moderately correlated ($r = .43$) with Receptive Attention on the Attention Scale. Confirmatory factor analysis supports the four-factor PASS configuration, but exploratory factor analysis supports only a three-factor solution. Other analyses also indicate that the Planning and Attention Scales are confounded in the PASS model (Carroll, 1993a, 1995).

Correlations between the CAS and WISC–III are .69 in a regular education sample, .66 in a sample of students with mental retardation, and .71 in a sample of children with learning disabilities. Correlations between the CAS and the Woodcock-Johnson–Revised range from .50 to .67 (*Mdn r* = .49) on the Standard Battery and from .44 to .64 (*Mdn r* = .46) on the Basic Battery.

Other results indicated that strategy use increases with age, with older children implementing more effective strategies than younger children. Children who use strategies also obtain higher scores on the Planning subtests than those who do not. The performance of children in special groups (e.g., children with attention-deficit/hyperactivity disorder, mental retardation, reading disabilities, traumatic brain injury, or serious emotional disturbance or children who are gifted) was similar to what would be expected (also see Gutentag, Naglieri, & Yeates, 1998).

Comment on the CAS

As a theoretically based test, the CAS offers an alternative framework for examining and interpreting cognitive ability. For example, an examinee's performance can be evaluated on processing strengths and weaknesses that may be amenable to academic intervention. Several intervention programs have been developed based on the PASS model. For example, the PASS Remedial Program (PREP; Das, Carlson, Davidson, & Longe, 1997) is designed to improve student performance on the PASS processes, particularly simultaneous and successive processes within the reading domain. Students are trained to improve specific simultaneous or successive processing skills and then to generalize these skills to academic tasks (e.g., word identification). Research suggests that students improve on both word identification and word decoding skills after completing the program.

Despite the strong theoretical ties to cognitive processing theory, the CAS presents some interpretive difficulties. The possible confounding of the Planning and Attention components may make interpretation of these component scores somewhat problematic. The four-factor solution reported by Naglieri and Das (1997) has not been replicated by others (Kranzler & Keith, 1999). Given the distinctive nature of the four component processes, Naglieri and Das (1990) argued that the PASS model precludes the formulation of a composite, or Full Scale, score, yet they provide a Full Scale Score on the CAS. Because the CAS is a relatively new measure of cognitive processing, more research is required to evaluate its clinical and diagnostic utility.

COMPREHENSIVE TEST OF NONVERBAL INTELLIGENCE

The Comprehensive Test of Nonverbal Intelligence (CTONI; Hammill, Pearson, & Wiederholt, 1997) is an individually administered test of intelligence that contains six subtests designed to measure problem solving, reasoning, and abstract thinking abilities. The test is designed for individuals between the ages of 6 and 89 years. Each subtest has 25 test items and 3 practice items, instructions can be pantomimed or given orally, and examinees point to the best answer from five options. The test takes about 40 to 60 minutes to administer.

Subtests

The six subtests are as follows:

- The Pictorial Analogies subtest requires determining the relationship between two pictures and then applying this relationship to new pictures.
- The Geometric Analogies subtest requires determining the relationship between geometric patterns and then applying this relationship to new patterns.
- The Pictorial Categories subtest requires determining the relationship between pictured objects.
- The Geometric Categories subtest requires determining the relationship between geometric objects.
- The Pictorial Sequences subtest requires determining the sequential relationship among pictured objects.
- The Geometric Sequences subtest requires determining the sequential relationship among geometric figures.

SCHOOLIES © 1999 by John P. Wood

I don't care much for the ABC's. When do we learn about the ESPN's?

Copyright © 1999 by John P. Wood.

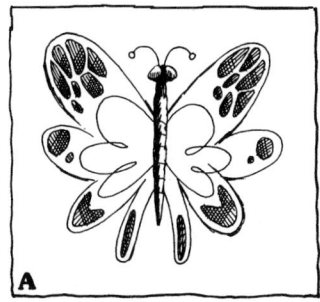 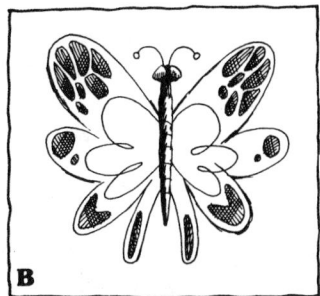 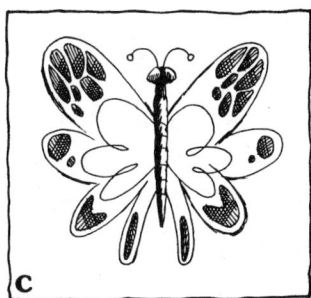 

Which one is different?

Copyright © 1977 American Publishing Corporation and adapted.

The six subtests form three quotients (or composites):

- The Pictorial Nonverbal Intelligence Quotient (PNIQ), which measures problem-solving and reasoning abilities based on familiar pictures, contains the Pictorial Analogies, Pictorial Categories, and Pictorial Sequences subtests.
- The Geometric Nonverbal Intelligence Quotient (GNIQ), which measures problem-solving and reasoning abilities based on abstract figures, contains the Geometric Analogies, Geometric Categories, and Geometric Sequences subtests.
- The Nonverbal Intelligence Quotient (NIQ), which measures nonverbal problem-solving and reasoning abilities, contains all six subtests.

Scores

Raw scores for the three composites are converted into standard scores ($M = 100$, $SD = 15$), which can then be converted into percentiles and age-equivalent scores. Standard scores on the subtests have $M = 10$ and $SD = 3$. Although the Manual shows a range of IQs from 35 to 165, this range is not possible at each age group. In fact, there is no way to compute IQs of 35, 36, and 37, even though they are shown in the Manual. At some ages, the lowest IQs that can be obtained are in the 60s (ages 6 and 7) or 50s (ages 8 and 9). Similarly, at some ages, the highest IQs that can be obtained are in the 130s and 140s (ages 17, 18, and 19 to 69).

Standardization

The standardization sample consisted of 2,901 individuals from 30 states and the District of Columbia, including some students with disabilities enrolled in general education classes. The standardization group was stratified by age, geographic region, gender, race, residence, and ethnicity, following 1990 U.S. Census data.

Reliability

The CTONI has excellent internal consistency reliabilities for the three composites: $r_{xx} = .97$ for the Nonverbal Intelligence Quotient, $r_{xx} = .95$ for the Geometric Nonverbal Intelligence Quotient, and $r_{xx} = .93$ for the Pictorial Nonverbal Intelligence Quotient.

The average SEMs are 2.60 for the Nonverbal Intelligence Quotient, 3.40 for the Geometric Nonverbal Intelligence Quotient, and 4.00 for the Pictorial Nonverbal Intelligence Quotient. Hence, more confidence can be placed in the Nonverbal Intelligence Quotient than in either the Geometric or the Pictorial Nonverbal Intelligence Quotient alone. Internal consistency reliability coefficients for ethnic groups, genders, and students with disabilities ranged from .93 to .98 for the three composites.

The test-retest reliability coefficients reported in the Manual were based on two different administrations 1 month apart. Instructions for the first administration were pantomimed, whereas instructions for the second administration were given orally; this procedure is not customary. The test-retest samples consisted of 33 third-graders and 30 eleventh-graders. The test-retest reliability coefficients in the combined sample were .92 for the Nonverbal Intelligence Quotient, .91 for the Geometric Nonverbal Intelligence Quotient, and .87 for the Pictorial Nonverbal Intelligence Quotient. The test-retest reliability coefficients for the subtests ranged from .80 to .87. The mean score for the three composites changed by less than .5 point on the two administrations (e.g., the Nonverbal Intelligence Quotient was 99.9 on the first administration and 100.3 on the second administration).

Validity

Content validity was established by selecting items that were relevant to the theoretical rationale of the test, showing that the items had satisfactory discrimination and difficulty levels, and showing that differences between gender, ethnic, and learning disabled groups were minimal. Construct validity, as shown by a factor analysis reported in the Manual, indicates that the test comprises one factor that can be labeled *nonverbal intelligence*. Correlations between the subtests and the factor ranged from .50 to .71. Concurrent validity is acceptable, as noted by correlations that range from .70 to .90 between the CTONI and other individually administered tests of intelligence.

Comment on the CTONI

Although the CTONI appears to have adequate reliability and validity, there are some concerns that need to be addressed. First, the pictured objects are drawn relatively small, and in some cases they are poorly drawn. Therefore, younger examinees, in particular, may have difficulty recognizing some pictures. Second, because the test has a limited floor for 6- and 7-year-olds, it cannot distinguish degrees of mental retardation at these age groups. Third, there is no information in the Manual on how gifted children perform on the test. Fourth, the ceiling level fluctuates so that the highest attainable scores range from 139 (ages 30 to 49) to 165 (ages 6 to 12). Fifth, the Manual fails to provide information on how scores from the CTONI compare with scores on other intelligence tests. These limitations indicate that further studies are needed to evaluate the test.

DETROIT TESTS OF LEARNING APTITUDE–4

The Detroit Tests of Learning Aptitude–4 (DTLA–4; Hammill, 1998) is an individually administered test of intelligence designed for children ages 6 to 17 years. The DTLA was originally published in 1935 and was revised in 1985, 1991, and 1998. The fourth edition has new materials, 10 subtests instead of 11 (Picture Fragments was deleted), a new standardization group, colored pictures, and no time limit for the Story Sequences subtest. The test takes about 1 to 2 hours to administer.

Subtests

The 10 subtests are as follows:

Verbal Subtests

- The Word Opposites subtest measures knowledge of antonyms.
- The Sentence Imitation subtest measures meaningful memory for sentences.
- The Story Construction subtest measures story-telling ability.
- The Basic Information subtest measures range of general information.
- The Word Sequences subtest measures attention and short-term memory.

Nonverbal Subtests

- The Design Sequences subtest measures visual discrimination ability and short-term memory for nonmeaningful stimuli.
- The Reversed Letters subtest measures attention, visual sequencing, memory, and fine motor ability.
- The Design Reproduction subtest measures attention, short-term memory, and fine motor ability.
- The Symbolic Relations subtest measures problem-solving and abstract reasoning abilities.
- The Story Sequences subtest measures the ability to organize pictures into a meaningful sequence.

The DTLA–4 provides different types of composites. First, all 10 subtests combine to form the General Mental Ability Composite. Then, there are three domain composites further divided into more specialized composites. However, the three domain composites have the same 10 subtests, regrouped in different ways; consequently, the composites are not independent, but the comparisons within each composite are independent. The domain composites are as follows:

- The Linguistic Domain Composite contains the Verbal Composite and Nonverbal Composite.
- The Attentional Domain Composite contains the Attention-Enhanced Composite and Attention-Reduced Composite.
- The Motoric Domain Composite contains the Motor-Enhanced Composite and Motor-Reduced Composite.

Finally, the 10 subtests are regrouped into composites that follow other theoretical models. Again, these regroupings reflect only reorganization of the 10 subtests.

Scores

The DTLA–4 yields five types of scores: raw scores, subtest standard scores ($M = 10$, $SD = 3$), composite standard scores ($M = 100$, $SD = 15$), percentiles, and age-equivalent scores. The Manual shows a range of IQs from 34 to 164; however, this range is not possible at each age group. In fact, there is no way to compute IQs of 34 and 35 for any age group, even though the Manual shows these IQs (e.g., the lowest IQs available at ages 6-0 to 7-5 range from 42 to 49). Similarly, the upper limit IQ of 164 is not obtainable at all ages (e.g., the highest IQs available at ages 16 to 17 range from 151 to 156).

Standardization

The standardization sample consisted of 1,350 children residing in 37 states. The sample was stratified by age, geographic region, gender, race, rural or urban residence, ethnicity, family income, educational attainment of parents, and disability of the child, following 1996 U.S. Census data.

Reliability

The DTLA–4 has excellent internal consistency reliabilities for the General Mental Ability Quotient (r_{xx} = .96) and the composite scores (r_{xx} ranges from .90 to .97). The average standard error of measurement is 3.00 for the General Mental Ability Quotient. For the three composites, the SEMs range from 3.00 to 4.00. The test-retest reliability coefficient of the General Mental Ability Quotient in a sample of 98 students in third to twelfth grades, tested 1 week apart, is .97, with a mean change of 3 points. The stability coefficients are .96 for the Verbal Quotient and .92 for the Nonverbal Quotient and range from .71 to .96 (*Mdn* r_{xx} = .84) for the subtests.

Validity

Content validity was established by selecting items that were relevant to the theoretical rationale of the test, by showing that the items had satisfactory discrimination and difficulty levels, and by showing that there were minimal differences between gender and ethnic groups.

Construct validity, as shown by a factor analysis, indicates that the DTLA–4 contains two factors—Verbal Ability and Nonverbal Ability. Correlations between the five verbal subtests and the Verbal Ability factor range from .51 to .87. Correlations between the five nonverbal subtests and the Nonverbal Ability factor range from .51 to .70.

The Manual does not report any criterion-related validity studies for the DTLA–4. The Manual does report satisfactory criterion-related validity studies for the DTLA–3, but the two editions of the test differ somewhat.

A concurrent validity study with a sample of 264 students indicates satisfactory correlations between the DTLA–4 General Mental Ability Quotient and the Hammill Multiability Achievement Test (*r* from .37 to .65). Another study showed satisfactory correlations between the DTLA–4 General Mental Ability Quotient and the Comprehensive Scales of Student Abilities for a sample of 77 students (*r* from .52 to .69).

Comment on the DTLA–4

The DTLA–4 has excellent reliability. Although further information is needed about its validity, information on the DTLA–3 suggests that the DTLA–4 likely will have satisfactory validity. Factor analysis supports a Verbal factor and a Nonverbal factor. It would be useful to have information about how children who are gifted and children with mental retardation perform on the test. The Story Sequence subtest demands more of examinees than similar picture arrangement tests because examinees do not manipulate the pictures. Research also is needed on the reliability of examiners'

Copyright © 1999 by John P. Wood.

scores because considerable judgment is needed to score some subtests. Overall, the DTLA–4 appears to be a useful measure of general intelligence.

INFANT PSYCHOLOGICAL DEVELOPMENT SCALE

The Infant Psychological Development Scale (Uzgiris & Hunt, 1975) measures intellectual processes associated with natural stages of development for infants and young children between the ages of 2 weeks and 2 years. It is an informal test that contains eight subscales developed on the basis of Piagetian theory, each measuring the development of a specific ability. The subscales consist of a number of separate ordinal steps, with each step delineating a stage in the development of the ability. The subscales are as follows:

1. Object Permanence (15 steps)
2. Use of Objects as Means (9 steps)
3. Learning and Foresight (5 steps)
4. Development of Schemata (11 steps)
5. Development of an Understanding of Causality (10 steps)
6. Conception of Objects in Space (11 steps)
7. Vocal Imitation (8 steps)
8. Gestural Imitation (5 steps)

Wachs (1975) reported that scores on most subscales of the Infant Psychological Development Scale were significantly related to later performance on the Stanford-Binet:

SCHOOLIES

I was not horsing around. I was developing my kinesthetic intelligence.

Copyright © 1997 by John P. Wood.

Form L-M only if infants were 18 months of age or older at the time of testing. The one exception was Object Permanence. Scores on this subscale obtained at 12, 15, 18, 21, and 24 months were significantly related to later Stanford-Binet performance. This subscale also showed the most consistently significant pattern of relationships across all five age levels. The development of object permanence (which involves understanding what happens to an object or person when out of sight) early in life may play an important role in cognitive development. This finding was essentially supported in a study of children with severe and profound retardation (Kahn, 1983). Object Permanence and Vocal Imitation were found to be the best predictors of language development in the sample.

The Infant Psychological Development Scale can be used to design developmentally sequenced curriculum programs. A manual by Dunst (1980) provides information on clinical and educational uses of the scale and ways to estimate a developmental age. Evidence of the concurrent validity of the developmental ages was obtained by administering the Bayley Scales of Infant Development to a group of infants with disabilities (Heffernan & Black, 1984).

INFORMAL ASSESSMENT OF MULTIPLE INTELLIGENCES

In Chapter 5, you read about Gardner's multiple intelligence theory. You can use the informal checklist shown in Table 16-1

to obtain information from teachers or parents about seven of Gardner's skill or talent areas. With adaptations, the checklist can also be given to children. It should be used in conjunction with other sources of assessment information.

KAUFMAN ADOLESCENT AND ADULT INTELLIGENCE TEST

The Kaufman Adolescent and Adult Intelligence Test (KAIT; Kaufman & Kaufman, 1993) is an individually administered test of intelligence designed for individuals ages 11 to 85+ years. The KAIT assesses crystallized and fluid abilities; it includes a mental status examination and delayed recall subtests. The core subtests in the KAIT take about 1 hour to administer, and the additional subtests take about another 30 minutes.

Subtests

The 11 subtests are as follows:

Crystallized Scale

Core Battery

- The Definitions subtest measures word knowledge and verbal concept formation.
- The Auditory Comprehension subtest measures understanding and comprehension of oral information.
- The Double Meanings subtest measures the ability to find a word, given two clues for each of two distinct meanings.

Extended Battery

- The Famous Faces subtest measures the fund of acquired information.

Fluid Scale

Core Battery

- The Rebus Learning subtest measures the ability to learn and apply new information.
- The Logical Steps subtest measures logical reasoning and application of logical relationships to solve problems.
- The Mystery Codes subtest measures the ability to detect logical relationships and apply them to novel problems.

Extended Battery

- The Memory for Block Designs subtest measures the ability to construct geometric designs from memory.

Delayed Recall Scale

Extended Battery

- The Rebus Delayed Recall subtest measures memory for previously learned visual information.

Table 16-1
Checklist for Assessing Students' Multiple Intelligences

CHECKLIST FOR ASSESSING STUDENTS' MULTIPLE INTELLIGENCES

Name of student: _____   Date: _____

Name of rater: _____   Teacher's name: _____

Directions: Check each item that applies.

Linguistic Intelligence

____ Writes better than average for age

____ Spins tall tales or tells jokes and stories

____ Has a good memory for names, places, dates, or trivia

____ Enjoys word games

____ Enjoys reading books

____ Spells words accurately (or, if in preschool, does developmental spelling that is advanced for age)

____ Appreciates nonsense rhymes, puns, tongue twisters, etc.

____ Enjoys listening to the spoken word (stories, commentary on radio, talking books, etc.)

____ Has a good vocabulary for age

____ Communicates to others in a highly verbal way

Other linguistic strengths: _____

_____

Logical-Mathematical Intelligence

____ Asks a lot of questions about how things work

____ Computes arithmetic problems in his or her head quickly (or, if in preschool, math concepts are advanced for age)

____ Enjoys math class (or, if in preschool, enjoys counting and doing other things with numbers)

____ Finds math computer games interesting (or, if no exposure to computers, enjoys other math or counting games)

____ Enjoys playing chess, checkers, or other strategy games (or, if in preschool, enjoys board games requiring counting squares)

____ Enjoys working on logic puzzles or brainteasers (or, if in preschool, enjoys hearing logical nonsense such as in *Alice's Adventures in Wonderland*)

____ Enjoys putting things in categories or hierarchies

____ Likes to experiment in a way that shows higher order cognitive thinking processes

____ Thinks on a more abstract or conceptual level than peers

____ Has a good sense of cause-effect for age

Other logical-mathematical strengths: _____

_____

Spatial Intelligence

____ Reports clear visual images

____ Reads maps, charts, and diagrams more easily than text (or, if in preschool, enjoys looking at more than text)

____ Daydreams more than peers

____ Enjoys art activities

____ Draws figures that are advanced for age

____ Likes to view movies, slides, or other visual presentations

____ Enjoys doing puzzles, mazes, "Where's Waldo?" or similar visual activities

____ Builds interesting three-dimensional constructions for age (e.g., LEGO buildings)

____ Gets more out of pictures than words while reading

____ Doodles on workbooks, worksheets, or other materials

Other spatial strengths: _____

_____

Bodily-Kinesthetic Intelligence

____ Excels in one or more sports (or, if in preschool, shows physical prowess advanced for age)

____ Moves, twitches, taps, or fidgets while seated for a long time in one spot

____ Cleverly mimics other people's gestures or mannerisms

____ Loves to take things apart and put them back together again

____ Puts her or his hands all over something she or he has just seen

____ Enjoys running, jumping, wrestling, or similar activities (or, if older, shows these interests in a more "restrained" way—e.g., punching a friend, running to class, jumping over a chair)

____ Shows skill in a craft (e.g., woodworking, sewing, mechanics) or good fine motor coordination in other ways

____ Has a dramatic way of expressing herself or himself

____ Reports different physical sensations while thinking or working

____ Enjoys working with clay or other tactile experiences (e.g., fingerpainting)

Other bodily-kinesthetic strengths: _____

_____

Musical Intelligence

____ Tells you when music sounds off-key or disturbing in some other way

____ Remembers melodies of songs

____ Has a good singing voice

____ Plays a musical instrument or sings in a choir or other group (or, if in preschool, enjoys playing percussion instruments and/or singing in a group)

(Continued)

Table 16-1 (Continued)

Musical Intelligence (Continued)

____ Has a rhythmic way of speaking and/or moving

____ Unconsciously hums to himself or herself

____ Taps rhythmically on the table or desk as he or she works

____ Is sensitive to environmental noises (e.g., rain on the roof)

____ Responds favorably when a piece of music is put on

____ Sings songs that he or she has learned outside of the classroom

Other musical strengths: _____

_____

Interpersonal Intelligence

____ Enjoys socializing with peers

____ Seems to be a natural leader

____ Gives advice to friends who have problems

____ Seems to be street-smart

____ Belongs to clubs, committees, or other organizations (or, if in preschool, seems to be part of a regular social group)

____ Enjoys informally teaching other kids

____ Likes to play games with other kids

____ Has two or more close friends

____ Has a good sense of empathy or concern for others

____ Others seek out his or her company

Other interpersonal strengths: _____

_____

Intrapersonal Intelligence

____ Displays a sense of independence or a strong will

____ Has a realistic sense of her or his strengths and weaknesses

____ Does well when left alone to play or study

____ Marches to the beat of a different drummer in her or his style of living and learning

____ Has an interest or hobby that she or he doesn't talk much about

____ Has a good sense of self-direction

____ Prefers working alone to working with others

____ Accurately expresses how she or he is feeling

____ Is able to learn from her or his failures and successes in life

____ Has high self-esteem

Other intrapersonal strengths: _____

_____

Source: Reprinted, with changes in notation, with permission of the publisher from T. Armstrong, *Multiple Intelligences in the Classroom,* copyright 1994 by Association for Supervision and Curriculum Development, pp. 29–31.

- The Auditory Delayed Recall subtest measures memory for previously learned auditory information.

Mental Status

- The Mental Status subtest measures orientation and attention. It is not part of any battery.

Scores

Raw scores are converted to scaled scores for the subtests ($M = 10$, $SD = 3$) and to standard scores for the Fluid and Crystallized Scales and the Composite Intelligence Scale ($M = 100$, $SD = 15$). Percentile ranks are also provided. For the Mental Status subtest, qualitative descriptors are provided. A computerized scoring and report-writing program is available.

Standardization

The KAIT was standardized on a representative sample of 2,000 individuals, based on 1990 U.S. Census data. The norm sample was matched on such characteristics as gender, examinee or parental education, ethnicity, and geographic re-

gion, although participants from the West were somewhat overrepresented and those from the Northeast were somewhat underrepresented.

Reliability

Internal consistency reliabilities range from .71 to .93 (*Mdn* $r_{xx} = .89$) for 10 subtests and from .95 to .97 for the Fluid and Crystallized Scales and the Composite Intelligence Scale. Stability coefficients for a sample of 153 individuals who were retested after 6 to 99 days ($M = 31$ days) range from .87 to .94 (*Mdn* $r_{tt} = .94$) for the Fluid and Crystallized Scales and the Composite Intelligence Scale and from .63 to .95 (*Mdn* $r_{tt} = .78$) for the subtests. The Mental Status Exam yielded acceptable reliabilities.

Validity

The KAIT has adequate construct validity and concurrent validity. Factor analyses indicate that the test provides a Crystallized factor and a Fluid factor. Correlations with other tests of intelligence are in the .55 to .85 range.

Comment on the KAIT

The KAIT is a useful test of cognitive ability for adolescents and adults. It has an adequate norm group, and administration and scoring are easy. However, more studies are needed to evaluate its use with individuals functioning at the lower levels of intelligence.

KAUFMAN ASSESSMENT BATTERY FOR CHILDREN

The Kaufman Assessment Battery for Children (K-ABC; Kaufman & Kaufman, 1983) is an individually administered test of intelligence and achievement designed for children ages 2-6 to 12-5. The K-ABC has four scales: Sequential Processing, Simultaneous Processing, Achievement, and Nonverbal. The test takes about 45 minutes to administer to preschool children and about 75 minutes to administer to those of school age.

Subtests

The 15 subtests are as follows:

Sequential Processing Scale

- The Hand Movements subtest requires reproducing sequences of raps on a table, using the fist, palm, or side of the hand.
- The Number Recall subtest requires repeating a series of numbers.
- The Word Order subtest requires touching or pointing to a series of silhouettes of objects in the order in which they are named by the examiner. Some items also include an interference task.

Simultaneous Processing Scale

- The Magic Window subtest requires identifying a picture that is passed slowly behind a window so that only part of the picture is visible at any one time.
- The Face Recognition subtest requires selecting, from a group of photographs, the photograph of a face previously seen.
- The Gestalt Closure subtest requires identifying an object or scene in a partially completed drawing (ink blot).
- The Triangles subtest requires reproducing a design by using several identical rubber triangles.
- The Matrix Analogies subtest requires selecting the picture or design that best completes a visual analogy.
- The Spatial Memory subtest requires recalling the location of pictures randomly arranged on a page.
- The Photo Series subtest requires arranging a series of photographs in a meaningful order.
- The Faces and Places subtest requires naming fictional characters, famous persons, and well-known places.

Achievement Scales

- The Arithmetic subtest requires identifying numbers, counting, computing, and demonstrating other mathematical skills.
- The Riddles subtest requires naming a concrete or abstract verbal concept after having been given several of its characteristics.
- The Reading/Decoding subtest requires identifying letters and reading and pronouncing words.
- The Reading/Understanding subtest requires reading sentences silently and then acting out the commands given in the sentences.

Not all subtests are administered at every age. Only three subtests run throughout the ages covered by the test: Hand Movements, Gestalt Closure, and Faces and Places. Thus, composite scores are derived from different combinations of subtests, depending on the child's age. Of the 15 subtests in the K-ABC, no more than 13 are administered to any one child.

The scales are designed to measure the following processes:

- The Sequential Processing Scale measures the ability to solve problems that require the arrangement of stimuli in sequential or serial order.
- The Simultaneous Processing Scale measures the ability to solve spatial, analogic, or organizational problems that require the processing of many stimuli at once.
- The Achievement Scale measures factual knowledge.
- The Nonverbal Scale, composed of those subtests from the Sequential and Simultaneous Processing Scales that do not require words (Hand Movements, Face Recognition, Triangles, Matrix Analogies, Spatial Memory, and Photo Series), measures nonverbal reasoning ability; these subtests can be administered through gestures and require movement responses.

The Sequential and Simultaneous Processing Scales are hypothesized to reflect the child's style of problem solving and information processing. Scores from these two scales are combined to form the Mental Processing Composite, which serves as the measure of intelligence on the K-ABC. The Sequential and Simultaneous Processing Scales were designed to reduce the effects of verbal processing and gender and ethnic bias. In contrast, the Achievement Scale is more heavily loaded with verbal stimuli. The subtests on the Achievement Scale were kept separate from those on the Sequential and Simultaneous Processing Scales in an effort to distinguish between knowledge acquired by exposure to environmental stimulation or educational opportunities and knowledge that results from an integration of sequential and simultaneous processing.

Scores

Raw scores for the subtests are converted into scaled scores ($M = 10$, $SD = 3$); those on the scales are converted into standard scores ($M = 100$, $SD = 15$). An index of mental ability, called the Mental Processing Composite, is derived only from scores on the Simultaneous and Sequential Processing Scales. The Mental Processing Composite is more heavily weighted with Simultaneous Processing subtests than with Sequential Processing subtests. Chatman, Reynolds, and Willson (1984) provide tables that show levels of interscale and subtest variability and frequencies of significant interscale and intrascale differences on the K-ABC.

Standardization

The standardization of the K-ABC was designed to match 1980 U.S. Census data. Stratification variables included age, sex, geographic region, socioeconomic status (parental education), race or ethnicity, and community size. However, the match was not entirely successful, as Hispanic Americans were underrepresented by 24% and African Americans with limited education were underrepresented by 10%. A total of 2,000 children between the ages of 2-6 and 12-5 were tested, with 200 to 300 children, equally divided by sex, at each of nine age levels.

Reliability

Internal consistency reliabilities for the Mental Processing Composite and the Achievement Scale are excellent for preschool children ($r_{xx} = .91$ and $.93$, respectively) and for school-age children ($r_{xx} = .94$ and $.97$). Average internal consistency reliabilities for the other three scales are satisfactory, ranging from .86 to .93. The Mental Processing Composite has an average standard error of measurement of 4.6 points for preschool children and 3.5 points for school-age children. The highest average correlation is between the Simultaneous and Achievement Scales for school-age children ($r = .66$), whereas the lowest average correlation is between the Sequential and Simultaneous Processing Scales for preschool children ($r = .41$).

Stability of the K-ABC, measured over a retest interval of 2 to 4 weeks for three samples of children (N of 70 to 92), is adequate, with median coefficients of .88 for the Mental Processing Composite and .95 for the Achievement Scale. Median gains in scores were 4.9 points for the Mental Processing Composite and 2.0 points for the Achievement Scale.

Validity

Evidence of construct validity is presented in the form of increases in subtest raw scores with age. According to the Manual, factor analysis supports the organization of the K-ABC into three scales. However, Strommen's (1988) factor analysis did not support the three factors. He concluded that caution is needed in interpreting the K-ABC in the manner proposed by the test authors.

Copyright © 1999 by John P. Wood.

Evidence of concurrent validity is presented in the form of correlations of the K-ABC with various individual and group tests of intelligence and achievement. Median correlations between the Mental Processing Composite and other intelligence tests range from .50 to .70. Correlations of the K-ABC with various achievement tests administered 6 to 12 months after the K-ABC indicate adequate predictive validity. Median correlations with the total score on the achievement tests were .56 for the Mental Processing Composite and .80 for the Achievement Composite.

Comment on the K-ABC

There are some practical and theoretical issues that need to be considered in using the K-ABC. The norms are over 18 years old and are likely out of date. The use of the term "mental processing" for some subtests and "achievement" for other subtests is misleading because both types of subtests measure mental processing. The heavy reliance on short-term memory and attention tasks reduces the test's effectiveness in evaluating children with attention and short-term memory difficulties. The terms "simultaneous processing" and "sequential processing" are ambiguous (Keith, 1985). The limited range of standard scores at some ages makes it difficult to evaluate children with mental retardation or children who are gifted. Finally, instructional strategies based on K-ABC profiles are questionable (Ayres & Cooley, 1986; Fisher, Jenkins, Bancroft, & Kraft, 1988; Goetz & Hall, 1984). The K-ABC may prove to be useful in certain situations, particularly when information is needed about nonverbal cognitive abilities. However, the K-ABC should not be used as the primary instrument for identifying the intellectual abilities of children.

KAUFMAN BRIEF INTELLIGENCE TEST

The Kaufman Brief Intelligence Test (K-BIT; Kaufman & Kaufman, 1990) is an individually administered test of intelligence designed to measure verbal and nonverbal abilities in a quick, efficient manner. It contains two subtests—Vocabulary and Matrices—that cover ages 6 to 90 years, and it takes approximately 15 to 30 minutes to administer.

Subtests

The two subtests are as follows:

- The Vocabulary subtest requires naming pictured objects and giving the word that best completes the partially spelled word.
- The Matrices subtest requires choosing, from a multiple-choice array, the figure that best shows a relationship with the stimulus figure.

Scores

Raw scores are converted into standard scores ($M = 100$, $SD = 15$) for both the subtests and the IQ Composite. In addition, percentile ranks, normal curve equivalents, and stanines are provided.

Standardization

The standardization sample consisted of 2,022 individuals stratified by geographic region, socioeconomic status, and race or ethnicity, following 1990 U.S. Census data.

Reliability

Internal consistency reliability coefficients range from .88 to .98 ($M\ r_{xx} = .94$) on the IQ Composite, from .89 to .98 ($M\ r_{xx} = .93$) on the Vocabulary subtest, and from .74 to .95 ($M\ r_{xx} = .88$) on the Matrices subtest. Internal consistency reliabilities are somewhat higher for adults ($r_{xx} = .94$ to .97) than for children ($r_{xx} = .85$ to .92).

On the IQ Composite, the mean standard error of measurement is 4.2 points for children ages 4 to 19 and 2.7 points for adults ages 20 to 90 (M SEM = 3.9). On the Vocabulary subtest, it is 4.5 points for children ages 4 to 19 and 2.7 points for adults ages 20 to 90 (M SEM = 4.1). On the Matrices subtest, it is 5.8 points for children ages 4 to 19 and 3.8 points for adults ages 20 to 90 (M SEM = 5.4). Correlations between the Vocabulary and Matrices subtests range from .38 to .75 ($M\ r = .59$).

Test-retest reliability coefficients are based on a sample of 232 individuals ages 5 to 89, retested after 12 to 145 days ($M = 21$ days). The sample was divided into four age groups—5 to 12 years, 13 to 19 years, 20 to 54 years, and 55 to 89 years. Test-retest reliability coefficients for the total sample range from .92 to .95 on the IQ Composite, from .86 to .97 on the Vocabulary subtest, and from .80 to .92 on the Matrices subtest. Mean score changes for the IQ Composite, Vocabulary subtest, and Matrices subtest ranged from 1.7 to 4.1 points.

Validity

Construct validity was established by showing that raw scores increase with age, selecting items that theoretically relate to intellectual functioning, and showing satisfactory item discrimination and difficulty levels. Criterion-related validity is satisfactory, as noted by correlations ranging from .23 to .80 with several measures of intelligence and from .14 to .86 with several measures of achievement.

Comment on the K-BIT

The K-BIT has satisfactory reliability and validity. The test appears to be useful as a screening measure of verbal and nonverbal abilities. However, the test should not be substituted for a comprehensive measure of intellectual abilities.

LEITER INTERNATIONAL PERFORMANCE SCALE–REVISED

The Leiter International Performance Scale–Revised (Leiter–R; Roid & Miller, 1997) is an individually administered nonverbal test of intelligence designed for children and adolescents between the ages of 2 and 20 years. The Leiter–R contains two batteries—Visualization and Reasoning, Attention and Memory—with 10 different subtests in each battery. The test is administered largely through pantomimed instructions and takes about 90 minutes to administer. Not all subtests are administered at every age.

The Leiter–R is an updated version of its predecessor in design and presentation. The test was designed following factor analytic models of intelligence proposed by Carroll (see Chapter 5 in this text) and by Gustafson (see Sattler, 1992). The test uses colorful chips, cards, pictures, and stimulus easels. Four rating scales are also provided to assess children's psychosocial behaviors; these scales are not covered in this review.

Subtests

The 20 subtests are as follows:

Visualization and Reasoning Battery

- The Figure Ground subtest requires identifying a stimulus figure embedded within a complex background.

- The Design Analogies subtest requires completing abstract analogies presented in matrix form.
- The Form Completion subtest requires assembly of fragmented puzzle pieces to form a whole.
- The Matching subtest requires matching a visual stimulus with an identical design.
- The Sequential Order subtest requires completing pictorial and figural sequences.
- The Repeated Patterns subtest requires completing a pictorial or figural pattern.
- The Picture Context subtest requires identifying a missing part of a picture.
- The Classification subtest requires organizing or classifying materials according to their salient characteristics.
- The Paper Folding subtest requires identifying, as fast as possible, what a paper figure would look like if it were folded.
- The Figure Rotation subtest, appropriate at ages 11 to 20, requires identifying rotated two- or three-dimensional objects.

Attention and Memory Battery

- The Associated Pairs subtest requires selecting the correct member of a pair of objects after the complete pair is briefly shown.
- The Immediate Recognition subtest, appropriate at ages 4 to 10, requires remembering objects that were shown briefly.
- The Forward Memory subtest requires recall of a sequence of objects.
- The Attention Sustained subtest requires identifying a target stimuli embedded within a picture.
- The Reverse Memory subtest requires pointing, in reverse order, to the stimuli pointed to by the examiner.
- The Visual Coding subtest requires identifying, from a key, the appropriate stimulus to complete a pair.
- The Spatial Memory subtest requires recalling the layout of pictured objects after a 10-second exposure.
- The Delayed Pairs subtest requires recalling objects presented on the Associated Pairs subtest about 30 minutes after it has been administered.
- The Delayed Recognition subtest requires recalling objects presented on the Immediate Recognition subtest about 30 minutes after it has been administered.
- The Attention Divided subtest requires attending to stimuli while performing a competing task.

The Visualization and Reasoning Battery assesses fluid reasoning and visual-spatial abilities, while the Attention and Memory Battery assesses attention, memory, and learning processes. The two batteries have the following composites:

Visualization and Reasoning Battery

- Brief IQ Screener (ages 2 to 20)
- Full Scale IQ (ages 2 to 20)
- Fluid Reasoning (ages 2 to 20)

- Fundamental Visualization (ages 2 to 5)
- Spatial Visualization (ages 11 to 20)

Attention and Memory Battery

- Memory Screener (ages 2 to 20)
- Associative Memory (ages 6 to 20)
- Memory Span (ages 6 to 20)
- Attention (ages 6 to 20)
- Memory Process (ages 6 to 20)
- Recognition Memory (ages 4 to 10)

Scores

Each battery provides composite standard scores ($M = 100$, $SD = 15$), subtest scaled scores ($M = 10$, $SD = 3$), percentile ranks, normal curve equivalents, age equivalents, and growth scores.

Standardization

The Visualization and Reasoning Battery of the Leiter–R was standardized on 1,719 children, adolescents, and young adults, while the Attention and Memory Battery was standardized on 763 children, adolescents, and young adults. There were between 41 and 100 individuals per age level for the Visualization and Reasoning Battery and between 42 and 86 individuals per age level for the Attention and Memory Battery. The normative sample was stratified on the basis of gender, race, socioeconomic status, community size, and geographic region, according to 1993 U.S. Census data.

Reliability

Average internal consistency reliabilities range from .75 to .90 ($Mdn\ r_{xx} = .82$) for the Visualization and Reasoning Battery subtests and from .67 to .87 for the Attention and Memory Battery subtests ($Mdn\ r_{xx} = .82$). Composite reliabilities range from .88 to .93 ($Mdn\ r_{xx} = .89$) for the Visualization and Reasoning Battery and from .75 to .93 ($Mdn\ r_{xx} = .86$) for the Attention and Memory Battery. The SEM is 4.24 for the Full Scale IQ on the Visualization and Reasoning Battery. SEMs range from 4.74 to 6.71 for the Attention and Memory Composites.

Test-retest reliability for the Visualization and Reasoning Battery was studied in a sample of 163 children and adolescents, ages 2 to 20 (Mdn age = 8-11), who were tested after intervals of 10 to 25 days ($M = 14$ days; personal communication, David Madsen, January 2000). The stability coefficients range from .61 to .90 ($Mdn\ r_{tt} = .80$) for the subtests and from .83 to .96 ($Mdn\ r_{tt} = .91$) for the composites. The increase in the Full Scale IQ from the first to the second administration was 4.0 points at ages 2 to 5, 6.7 points at ages 6 to 10, and 6.0 points at ages 11 to 20.

The stability of the Attention and Memory Battery was examined in a sample of 45 children and adolescents ages 6 to 17 years (Mdn age = 10-11). Stability coefficients range from .61 to .85 (Mdn r_{tt} = .74) for the composites and from .55 to .85 (Mdn r_{tt} = .61) for the subtests. Changes in composite scores ranged from 3.8 on Memory Span to 7.9 on Recognition and Attention. Changes in subtest scores were less than 2 points.

Validity

Concurrent validity is acceptable, as noted by a .86 correlation between the Leiter–R and the WISC–III in a sample of 126 children ages 6 to 16. Correlations between the Leiter–R and several individual and group achievement tests range from .26 to .82. Factor analyses suggest that the Leiter–R measures the following factors:

- Fluid Reasoning, Broad Visualization, Attention, and Memory at ages 4 to 5
- Nonverbal Reasoning, Visuospatial, Attention, Recognition, and Associated Span at ages 6 to 10
- Nonverbal Reasoning, Visuospatial, Attention, Associative, and Span Working Memory at ages 11 to 20

The *g* loadings of the subtests range from .26 to .66 (*Mdn g* loading = .59) at ages 2 to 5, from .26 to .65 at ages 6 to 10 (*Mdn g* loading = .46), and from .24 to .70 (*Mdn g* loading = .56) at ages 11 to 20.

Copyright © 1996 by John P. Wood.

Comment on the Leiter–R

The Leiter–R provides an acceptable measure of nonverbal intelligence for children, adolescents, and young adults between 2 and 20 years. The normative sample matches the U.S. population fairly well on important stratifying variables at the total sample level. Internal consistency reliabilities are acceptable, but changes in composite scores on retest tend to be somewhat large. Factor analyses generally support the theoretical underpinnings of the test. The test is particularly useful for examinees who have little or no useful speech or who have limited motor coordination.

PIAGETIAN TESTS

Piagetian theory provides insight into a child's thinking processes. Representative informal Piagetian tests, with approximate age norms, are shown in Exhibit 16-1 for ages 5 to 11 years. The tests cover the understanding of conservation, logical operations, and seriation. Many other Piagetian tests are available; these were selected because they require few special materials and can be administered quickly and easily.

RAVEN'S PROGRESSIVE MATRICES

Raven's Progressive Matrices (Raven, Court, & Raven, 1986; Raven, Raven, & Court, 1998a, b, c), originally introduced in 1938, is a nonverbal test of reasoning ability based on figural stimuli. It can be administered individually or to a group. The test measures the ability to form comparisons, to reason by analogy, and to organize spatial perceptions into systematically related wholes. Raven's Progressive Matrices comes in the following forms:

- The Coloured Progressive Matrices is a 36-item test applicable at ages 5 to 11. Colors are used in this form to attract and hold the attention of the children.
- The Standard Progressive Matrices is a 60-item test applicable at ages 6 to 17, although it also can be administered to adults. It contains five sets of 12 items.
- The Advanced Progressive Matrices is a 48-item test applicable to older adolescents and adults, particularly individuals with more than average intellectual ability. There are 12 problems in Set I and 36 problems in Set II.
- Parallel forms of the Coloured Progressive Matrices (Raven et al., 1998b) and the Standard Progressive Matrices (Raven et al., 1998c) were published in 1998, along with an expanded version of the Standard Progressive Matrices (Raven et al., 1998c) and norms for the Advanced Progressive Matrices (Raven et al., 1998a).

In each form, the examinee is presented with a matrix-like arrangement of figural symbols and must complete the

Exhibit 16-1
Examples of Piagetian Tasks

Conservation of Number

This conservation task measures the child's understanding that variations in the configuration of a row of objects do not affect the number of objects.

Materials: 20 checkers

Procedure: Present two rows of 10 checkers in one-to-one correspondence. Say: "Do the two rows contain the same numbers of checkers?" If the child says "No," help him or her to understand that both rows have the same number of checkers. Then spread apart the row closer to the child. Say: "Do the rows have the same number, or does one row have more? How do you know?"

Age: 5 to 6 years

Conservation of Continuous Quantity: Solids

This conservation task measures the child's understanding that changes in the shape of a solid do not change the quantity of that solid.

Materials: Two balls of clay, identical in size, shape, and weight

Procedure: Show the two balls of clay to the child. Say: "Do the two balls have the same amount of clay?" If the child says "No" or if there is any doubt about the child's understanding, encourage the child to make them the same. Then say, "Suppose I roll one of the balls into a hot dog. Will there be as much clay in the hot dog as in the ball? Will they both have the same amount of clay?" After the child answers, roll one of the balls into a sausage shape. Say: "Is there as much clay in the hot dog as in the ball? Do they both have the same amount of clay?" After the child responds, say: "Why did you say that?"

Age: 6 years

Conservation of Length

This conservation task measures the child's understanding that the comparative length of objects is unaffected by their relative positions.

Materials: Two unsharpened pencils, identical in length and color

Procedure: Place the two pencils in a horizontal position, one directly beneath the other, about 1 inch apart. Say: "Are the two pencils the same length?" After the child agrees that the two pencils are the same length, take the pencil closest to the child and turn it 45 degrees. Say: "Are the two pencils still the same length? Why?"

Age: 6 years

Conservation of Weight

This conservation task measures the child's understanding that changes in the shape of an object do not cause changes in its weight.

Materials: Two balls of clay, identical in size, shape, and weight

Procedure: Give the two balls of clay to the child. Say: "Do the two balls weigh the same?" If the child says "No" or if there is any doubt, encourage the child to make them the same. Then say: "Suppose I roll one of the balls into a hot dog. Will the hot dog weigh the same as the ball?" After the child answers, roll one of the balls into a sausage shape. Say: "Do they both weigh the same?" After the child responds, say: "Why is that?"

Age: 6 years

Seriation: Size

This test of seriation measures the child's understanding that objects can be put in order according to their size.

Materials: 12 sticks, 10 of which range in length from 9 to 16.2 cm, each being .8 cm longer than the preceding one; one of which is midway between sticks 3 and 4 in length; and one of which is midway between sticks 7 and 8 in length

Procedure: Place the first 10 sticks before the child in random order, but all in the vertical direction. Say: "Look at these sticks carefully. I want you to put them in order. Put them in order so that the very smallest comes first, and then the next smallest, and then the next smallest, all the way to the biggest. Go ahead."

After the child finishes arranging the set of sticks, give him or her the additional stick that goes between the 7th and 8th sticks. Say: "Here's an extra stick. You put it in the right place where it belongs."

After the child inserts the stick, remove it, give the child the second stick, and say: "Here's another stick. Put this stick in the right place where it belongs."

Age: 7 years

Conservation of Continuous Quantity: Liquids

This conservation test measures the child's understanding that variations in the shape of a container of liquid do not affect the quantity of that liquid.

Materials: Two identical large glasses that contain equal quantities of water and three identical small glasses that are empty

Procedure: With the child watching, pour water from one large glass into the three small glasses. Say: "Now I have this one to drink [point to the large glass with water] and you have all three glasses of water to drink. Will you have more to drink, or will I have more to drink? How do you know?"

Age: 8 years

Additive Classification: Visual

This test of logical operations measures the child's ability to group objects according to a common attribute.

Materials: Two large red squares, two small red squares, two large blue squares, two small blue squares, two large red cir-

(Continued)

Exhibit 16-1 *(Continued)*

cles, two small red circles, two large blue circles, two small blue circles, two white sheets of paper

Procedure: Place the 16 squares and circles in random order before the child. Say: "Tell me what you see." After the child finishes the description, say: "See these two sheets of paper [point to the sheets of paper]? I want you to put some of the blocks on one sheet and the others on the other sheet. Put those together on each sheet that you think belong together." After the blocks have been placed on the two sheets, remove the blocks and scramble them. Say: "Now put them together on each sheet another way." Repeat this procedure one additional time.

Age: 9 years for three classifications

Class Inclusion

This test of logical operations measures the child's understanding of the relationship among a group of objects.

Materials: Four white squares, two blue squares, three blue circles

Procedure: Show the child the objects and say:

1. "Are all the blue ones circles? Why?"
2. "Are all the squares white? Why?"
3. "Are there more circles or more blue things? Why?"
4. "Are there more blue things than there are squares, or the same number, or fewer? Why?"

Age: 10 years for questions 1 and 2; after 10 years for questions 3 and 4

matrix by selecting the appropriate missing symbol from a group of symbols (see Figure 16-1). In the easier sets, a design is shown, with a piece appearing to have been cut out. In other sets, individual pieces are arranged in either a 2 × 2 or a 3 × 3 matrix. One piece or design is left out of the matrix, and the examinee must select, from a group of six to eight choices, the one that best completes the matrix. Each form takes between 15 and 30 minutes to administer. A short form of Raven's Advanced Progressive Matrices may be a reasonable alternative to the full test as a quick screening measure for identifying students who are gifted (Ablard & Mills, 1996).

Subtests

There are no subtests on Raven's Progressive Matrices.

Scores

Raw scores are converted into percentile ranks.

Standardization

Numerous normative studies have been done since Raven's Progressive Matrices was originally published. The most recent compendiums of North American normative studies were published in 1986 (Raven & Summers, 1986) and 1998 (Raven et al., 1998a, 1998b, and 1998c). Included in these compendiums are norms for the Coloured Progressive Matrices, Standard Progressive Matrices, and Advanced Progressive Matrices.

The U.S. norms are based on weighting separate samples of children in various areas of the United States. No attempt was made to use a stratified random sampling procedure.

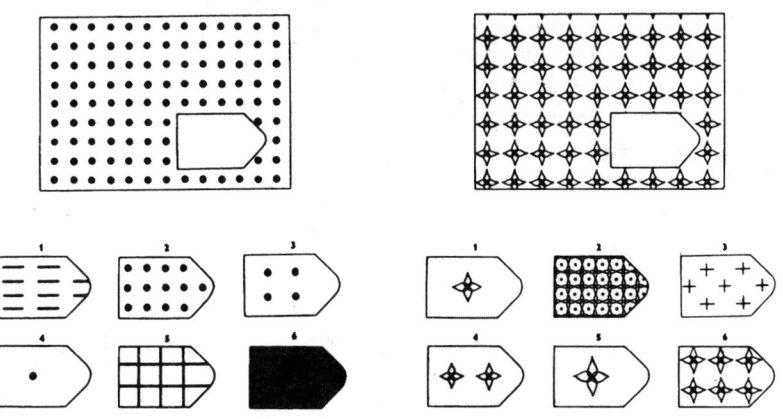

Figure 16-1. Sample Progressive Matrices items. Reprinted by permission of J. C. Raven, Ltd.

Because of the large samples employed in various school districts, however, the norms are probably representative of the school-age population. Tables F-5 and F-6 in Appendix F present the 1986 norms for the Coloured Progressive Matrices and the Standard Progressive Matrices. There was no standardization group for the parallel forms published in 1998.

Reliability

Split-half reliabilities range from .65 to .94 for the Coloured Progressive Matrices (Raven et al., 1986). For the Standard Progressive Matrices, a split-half reliability coefficient of .86 is the best estimate (Raven, Court, & Raven, 1983). Test-retest reliabilities are adequate for each form, ranging from .71 to .93. The lowest reliabilities are for young children (Raven, 1938, 1960, 1965; Raven et al., 1986).

Validity

The three forms have adequate concurrent validity, as established by correlations with intelligence tests and achievement tests (Raven et al., 1986; Raven & Summers, 1986). Concurrent validity coefficients between Raven's Progressive Matrices and other intelligence tests are in the .50s to .80s; concurrent validity coefficients with achievement tests are in the .30s to .60s.

The structure of Raven's Progressive Matrices is not clear. Some research suggests that the test contains primarily a *g* factor (Inductive or Reasoning), whereas others indicate that it contains two, three, or more factors (Burke, 1958; Carlson & Jensen, 1980; Corman & Budoff, 1974; Dillon, Pohlmann, & Lohman, 1981; Keir, 1949; MacArthur, 1960; MacArthur & Elley, 1963; Rimoldi, 1948; Schmidtke & Schaller, 1980; Wiedl & Carlson, 1976).

A single dimension (*g*) is inadequate to account for performance on the Coloured Progressive Matrices. The three factors for the Coloured Progressive Matrices have been labeled I—Closure and Abstract Reasoning by Analogy (items A7, A9, A10, Ab2, B2, B3, Ab4, Ab5, Ab7, Ab8, B4, B6); II—Pattern Completion through Identity and Closure (items B8, B9, B10, B11, B12); and III—Simple Pattern Completion (items A2, A3, A4, A5, B1; Carlson & Jensen, 1980). However, a one-factor solution best accounts for performance on the Advanced Progressive Matrices (Alderton & Larson, 1990; Arthur & Woehr, 1993).

Comment on Raven's Progressive Matrices

Raven's Progressive Matrices is a useful measure of nonverbal reasoning ability. The norms gathered from various groups are helpful, but all three versions of the test need to be normed on a representative sample of the U.S. population.

The ease of administration (instructions can be pantomimed) and the limited sensory demands make the test a useful supplementary screening device for children and adults with severe language, auditory, or physical disabilities. In addition, it is useful in testing children who do not speak English or who have limited command of English, as it is a culturally reduced test. Because the test provides a measure of intelligence based on figural reasoning only, it likely will not provide a valid estimate of cognitive ability for examinees who are not capable of doing figural-reasoning tasks. Supplementing Raven's Progressive Matrices with a vocabulary test may be valuable when you need to screen children.

SLOSSON INTELLIGENCE TEST–PRIMARY

The Slosson Intelligence Test–Primary (SIT–P; Erford, Vitali, & Slosson, 1999) is a screening test of intelligence designed for children between the ages of 2 and 7 years. The Verbal Scale contains 121 items that measure concept formation, vocabulary, general information, quantitative skills, sentence memory, digit span, and social comprehension. The Nonverbal Scale contains 90 items that measure constructional ability, perceptual-motor speed, and gross and fine motor coordination. Several verbal items were adapted from the Slosson Intelligence Test–Revised. The test takes about 15 to 30 minutes to administer.

Subtests

There are no subtests on the SIT–P.

Scores

All items are scored 1 (correct) or 0 (incorrect). The SIT–P provides standard scores ($M = 100$, $SD = 15$) for the Verbal Scale, Nonverbal Scale, and Total Scale; percentile ranks; and age equivalents. Age-equivalent scores are presented for ages 1-0 to 11-3, although no children in the norm group were below age 2-0 or above age 7-11.

Standardization

The SIT–P was standardized in 1995 and 1996 on a sample of 834 children living in Virginia and Maryland. The number of children in the six age groups (ages 2 to 7) ranged from 45 to 137. Although the authors state that the sample was similar to the U.S. population ages 2 to 7 in terms of race, sex, and community size and slightly higher in socioeconomic level, this claim does not appear fully warranted. For example, Hispanic American children were underrepresented (7% in the standardization sample vs. 11% in the population), while

Euro American children were overrepresented (77.4% in the standardization sample vs. 71% in the population).

Reliability

Internal consistency reliabilities range from .81 to .97 (M r_{xx} = .98) for the Total Scale, from .79 to .97 (M r_{xx} = .95) for the Verbal Scale, and from .72 to .93 (M r_{xx} = .97) for the Nonverbal Scale. Test-retest reliabilities are not reported in the Manual.

Validity

Correlations between the SIT–P Total Scale and the Stanford-Binet: IV Composite and WISC–III Full Scale IQ are .65 (N = 834) and .74 (N = 164), respectively. Correlations between the SIT–P Total Scale and the SIT–R, PPVT–R, and Expressive One Word Picture Vocabulary Test–Revised are .69 (N = 298), .54 (N = 172), and .46 (N = 172), respectively. Means and standard deviations are not reported for any of the tests used in the concurrent validity studies.

Comment on the SIT–P

The SIT–P might serve as a useful screening test of intelligence for young children if further studies support its stability and validity. We especially need information about how mean scores on the SIT–P compare with those on other standardized tests and whether there is factor analytic support for the two scales. The norm group is also less than desirable. Furthermore, it is a questionable practice to report age equivalents that go beyond the age groups in the standardization sample. Finally, studies are needed to investigate interexaminer scoring reliability.

SLOSSON INTELLIGENCE TEST–REVISED

The Slosson Intelligence Test–Revised (SIT–R; Slosson, 1996, 1998) is a screening test of verbal intelligence designed for individuals ages 4 to 18+ years. The SIT was originally published in 1963 and was renormed in 1981. The SIT–R was normed in 1991 and renormed in 1998.

The SIT–R consists of 187 items that measure vocabulary, general information, concept formation, comprehension, quantitative ability, and auditory memory. All questions are presented verbally and require spoken responses. None of the questions are timed, and the test takes between 10 and 30 minutes to administer. Scoring is fairly objective.

Subtests

There are no subtests on the SIT–R.

Scores

All items are scored 1 (correct) or 0 (incorrect). The SIT–R provides standard scores (M = 100, SD = 16) for the Total Standard Score, percentile ranks, and age equivalents. Age-equivalent scores are presented for ages 2.3 to 3.8, although no children in the norm group were below age 4.

Standardization

The SIT–R was standardized on a sample of 1,854 individuals in the United States. The sample was designed to match the U.S. population in terms of age, ethnicity, educational level, occupation, and region, based on the 1990 *World Almanac*. However, there are considerable disparities between the standardization group and the population. For example, the professional occupational group was overrepresented (27% in the standardization sample vs. 23% in the population), whereas the production, craft, and repair occupational group was underrepresented (8% in the standardization sample vs. 13% in the population). African American children were underrepresented (12% in the standardization sample vs. 14% in the population), while Euro Americans were overrepresented (83% in the standardization sample vs. 74% in the population). In addition, no information is presented about other individual ethnic groups such as Hispanic American or Asian American; instead, these groups are included in the "Other" category. Finally, there were considerable disparities in city size between the standardization group and the population. For example, cities with populations of 1 million or more were underrepresented (1% in the standardization group vs. 9% in the population), while cities of 10,000 to 24,999 were overrepresented (18% in the standardization group vs. 5% in the population).

Reliability

Internal consistency reliabilities range from .88 to .97 (*Mdn* r_{xx} = .95), and standard errors of measurement range from 2.88 to 5.50 (*Mdn* SEM = 3.72). The test-retest reliability with a sample of 41 individuals (ages not given) over a 1-week period is .96, but no test-retest means are reported.

Validity

In 1998, calibrated norm tables were published using an anchoring procedure that gave certain weights to the 1991 SIT–R norms; however, the test was not restandardized. The Manual reports correlations of (a) .83 between the WISC–III Full Scale IQ and the SIT–R Total Standard Score in a sample of 191 individuals (ages not reported) and (b) .65 between the Stanford-Binet: IV and the SIT–R Total Score in a sample of 293 individuals (ages not reported). Mean differences between the SIT–R and the WISC–III and Stanford-Binet: IV

SCH[...]

It s[...]
the[...]

2 [...]
3 [...]
4 [...]

Academic Documents

Copyright © 1999 by John P. Wood.

were about 2 points or less. No studies with children with disabilities are reported.

Comment on the SIT–R

The Slosson Intelligence Test–Revised might have some merit as a screening device if further studies support its stability and validity. Advantages include short administration time and the relative ease with which it can be used by personnel who have minimal training in the administration of individual intelligence tests. However, it is a questionable practice to report age equivalents that go beyond the age groups in the standardization sample. The SIT–R should not be used as a substitute for the Stanford-Binet: IV, WISC–III, WPPSI–R, or DAS, especially in assessing children with disabilities.

TEST OF NONVERBAL INTELLIGENCE–3

The Test of Nonverbal Intelligence–3 (TONI–3; Brown, Sherbenou, & Johnsen, 1997) was originally published in 1982 and was revised in 1990 and again in 1997. The TONI–3 is designed to measure problem-solving and abstract reasoning abilities. The TONI–3 has 10 fewer items than the previous edition, more psychometric information about the adult sample, and a new standardization group.

The TONI–3 consists of Forms A and B, each comprising 5 training items and 45 abstract/figural problem-solving items arranged in increasing order of difficulty. Items are in a

...tiple-choice format, with either four or six options. Ex-...nees answer by pointing to the best option. Instructions ...antomimed. The TONI–3 covers ages 6 to 89 years and ... about 15 minutes to administer.

...tests

...are no subtests on the TONI–3.

...es

...res are converted into standard scores ($M = 100$, $SD =$ ... centile ranks, and age-equivalent scores. The Manual snows a range of IQs from 60 to 150. However, this range is not possible at 17 of the 23 age groups (e.g., the range of IQs at ages 6-0 to 6-5 is 70 to 150).

Standardization

The standardization sample consisted of 3,451 individuals residing in 28 states. Children in the normative sample were from general education classes containing children with and without disabilities. The standardization group was stratified by age, geographic region, gender, race, and ethnicity, following 1990 U.S. Census data.

Reliability

Internal consistency reliabilities are excellent and range from .89 to .97 ($M\ r_{xx} = .93$). Alternate-form reliabilities range from .74 to .95 ($M\ r_{xx} = .84$). Several alternate-form reliability coefficients are below .80 at eight age groups (ages 7, 8, 10, 14, 15, 17, 18, and 50–59). These alternate-form reliabilities are below preferred levels. The average standard errors of measurement are 4.00 for both Form A and Form B (range of 3.00 to 5.00 points).

Test-retest reliabilities on both forms over a 1-week period ranged from .89 to .94 for three age groups—ages 13, 15, and 19–40. Because the Manual did not provide means and standard deviations for the first and second tests, we cannot determine the magnitude of change between the two administrations.

Validity

Content validity was established by selecting items that were relevant to the theoretical rationale of the test, showing that the items had satisfactory discrimination and difficulty levels, and showing that there were minimal differences between gender, ethnic, gifted, and learning disabled groups. Correlations between the TONI–3 and other individual tests of intelligence range from .51 to .76. Construct validity is satisfactory, as noted by an increase in raw scores with age, a strong general factor obtained by factor analysis, and satisfactory correlations between each item and the total score.

Although the TONI–3 can differentiate individuals with mental retardation from those without mental retardation, it is limited in its ability to identify gifted individuals. This is indicated by a $M = 111$ on Form A and a $M = 109$ on Form B for 134 children who were gifted (ages not indicated).

Comment on TONI–3

The TONI–3 is useful as a screening measure of nonverbal reasoning ability for children and adults. However, we do not recommend that the TONI–3 be used in place of the Wechsler tests, the Stanford-Binet Intelligence Scale: Fourth Edition, or the DAS, because it measures intelligence based on figural reasoning only. Like Raven's Progressive Matrices and other figural reasoning tests, the TONI–3 may not be a valid measure of intelligence for examinees whose figural reasoning ability is limited. Limitations of the TONI–3 include the less-than-satisfactory alternate-form reliabilities, the inability to distinguish degrees of mental retardation at all ages, and the possibility that the test does not adequately measure the abilities of gifted examinees. We also need information about how scores on the TONI–3 compare with those on other individual tests of intelligence, because the Manual did not report means and standard deviations for the concurrent validity studies. Using the TONI–3 in conjunction with a verbal test may be a better screening procedure than using the test alone.

UNIVERSAL NONVERBAL INTELLIGENCE TEST

The Universal Nonverbal Intelligence Test (UNIT; Bracken & McCallum, 1998) is an individually administered nonverbal test of intelligence designed for children between the ages of 5 and 17 years. Eight standardized language-free gestures (head nodding, head shaking, open-hand shrugging, palm rolling, pointing, hand waving, stop, and thumbs up) are used to administer the test. A video is available to assist in learning how to administer the test. The Manual includes a chapter dedicated to fairness in testing and addresses the topic through a wide variety of subjective and objective analyses.

Subtests

The six subtests are as follows:

- The Symbolic Memory subtest measures sequential short-term visual memory.
- The Cube Design subtest measures visual-spatial reasoning.
- The Spatial Memory subtest measures short-term memory for abstract material.

- The Analogic Reasoning subtest measures symbolic reasoning.
- The Object Memory subtest measures short-term recognition memory and recall of symbolic material.
- The Mazes subtest measures reasoning and planning abilities.

The six subtests combine to form the following five scales and three batteries:

Scales

- The Memory Scale consists of Symbolic Memory, Object Memory, and Spatial Memory.
- The Reasoning Scale consists of Analogic Reasoning, Cube Design, and Mazes.
- The Symbolic Scale consists of Symbolic Memory, Object Memory, and Analytic Reasoning.
- The Nonsymbolic Scale consists of Spatial Memory, Cube Design, and Mazes.
- The Full Scale consists of all six subtests.

Batteries

- The Abbreviated Battery consists of Symbolic Memory and Cube Design and takes about 15 minutes to administer.
- The Standard Battery consists of Symbolic Memory, Cube Design, Spatial Memory, and Analogic Reasoning and takes about 30 minutes to administer.
- The Extended Battery consists of the six subtests and takes about 45 minutes to administer.

Scores

The UNIT provides standard scores ($M = 100$, $SD = 15$) for the IQs, scaled scores ($M = 10$, $SD = 3$) for the subtests, percentile ranks, and test-age equivalents.

Standardization

The standardization group contained 2,100 children and adolescents, ages 5 to 17 (175 examinees at each age level). An additional 1,765 children were used in reliability, validity, and test-fairness studies. The norming sample was representative of the 1995 U.S. Census with respect to sex, race, Hispanic origin, region of the country, classroom placement, special education services, and parental educational attainment.

Reliability

Average internal consistency reliabilities for the Abbreviated, Standard, and Extended Battery Full Scale IQs are .91, .93, and .93, respectively, with corresponding SEMs of 4.50, 3.99, and 4.10. Average internal consistency coefficients for the four individual scales range from .87 to .91. Average internal consistency reliabilities for the subtests range from .64

to .91 (Mdn r_{xx} = .80). Internal consistency reliabilities are also reported for the clinical/exceptional group, African Americans, and Hispanic Americans. These coefficients are consistently high.

Test-retest reliability was studied in a sample of 197 children ages 5 to 17 over an interval of approximately 3 weeks (M = 20.3 days). Average subtest stability coefficients are from .57 to .83 (Mdn r_{tt} = .65) for the subtests; from .75 to .79 (M r_{tt} = .77) for the Memory, Reasoning, Symbolic, and Nonsymbolic Scales in the Extended Battery; and from .79 to .84 (Mdn r_{tt} = .81) for the Full Scale IQ in the three batteries.

Gains in scores due to practice effects vary somewhat across the age span. Increases are about 3 to 5 points at ages 5 to 7 and ages 11 to 13, but up to 14 to 15 points at ages 8 to 10. It is not clear why this age level experienced greater retest gains. The Manual also presents useful information about subtest floors, ceilings, and item gradients.

Validity

Concurrent validity is acceptable, with correlations ranging from .54 to .82 between the UNIT and other individual tests of intelligence. Factor analyses provide support for two factors—Reasoning and Memory—and for a strong g factor.

Comment on the UNIT

The UNIT is an acceptable measure of nonverbal cognitive ability for children between the ages of 5 and 17. It is well standardized and can be administered in a nonverbal fashion. More research is needed, though, to see how the test compares with other measures of intelligence.

WECHSLER ABBREVIATED SCALE OF INTELLIGENCE

The Wechsler Abbreviated Scale of Intelligence (WASI; The Psychological Corporation, 1999) is a brief individually administered test of intelligence designed for individuals from age 6 to 89 years. It contains four subtests—Vocabulary, Block Design, Similarities, and Matrix Reasoning. The first three are similar to subtests of the same name on the WISC–III and WAIS–III; the fourth is similar to the Matrix Reasoning subtest on the WAIS–III. The WASI takes about 30 minutes to administer. A two-subtest short form—Vocabulary and Matrix Reasoning—takes about 15 minutes to administer.

Subtests

The four subtests are as follows:

- The Vocabulary subtest measures expressive vocabulary, verbal knowledge, and fund of information. Items 1 to 4 require naming pictures, and items 5 to 42 require oral definitions of individual words.

- The Block Design subtest measures perceptual organization. All 13 items require assembling two-dimensional block patterns within a time limit.
- The Similarities subtest measures verbal concept formation and abstract verbal reasoning ability. Items 1 to 4 are multiple-choice pictorial items and require a pointing response; items 5 to 26 are presented orally and require an oral response.
- The Matrix Reasoning subtest measures nonverbal reasoning ability. In all 35 items, the task is to point to the one appropriate design out of five that best completes the matrix.

Standardization

The WASI was standardized on a stratified national sample on the basis of gender, race/ethnicity, educational level, and geographical region, according to 1997 U.S. Census figures. The sample contained 2,245 individuals (1,100 children ages 6 to 16 and 1,145 adults ages 17 to 89), with approximately 100 individuals in each of 23 age groups.

Scores

The WASI yields subtest T scores (M = 50, SD = 10) and IQs (M = 100, SD = 15) for the Verbal Scale IQ (Vocabulary and Similarities), the Performance Scale IQ (Block Design and Matrix Reasoning), and the two Full Scale IQs, one based on the four subtests and one on the Vocabulary and Matrix Reasoning combination. Age-equivalent scores and percentile ranks are also provided, as well as a table for estimating ranges on the WISC–III and WAIS–III from the WASI.

T scores range from 20 to 80, although this range is not available at every age. For example, the lowest T scores at age 6 are 34 for Matrix Reasoning, 32 for Block Design, 30 for Similarities, and 20 for Vocabulary. And the highest T scores at age 15-8 are 67 for Matrix Reasoning, 69 for Block Design, and 77 for Similarities and Vocabulary. The IQ range for the four-subtest combination is from 50 to 160, although this range is not available at every age. For example, the lowest IQ for children age 6 who fail every item on all four subtests is 68. The highest IQ for children age 15-8 who pass every item is 147.

Reliability

In the children's sample, internal consistency reliabilities are excellent for the four-subtest IQ combination (range of .95 to .97, M r_{xx} = .96). In fact, internal consistency reliabilities for all four IQs are .92 or higher. In the adult sample, internal consistency reliabilities are also high for the four-subtest IQ combination (range of .96 to .98, M r_{xx} = .98), as well as for the other IQs (.92 or higher). The SEM for the four-subtest combination is 3.85 in the children's sample and 2.97 in the adult sample.

In the children's sample, internal consistency reliabilities for the subtests are satisfactory for Vocabulary (range of .86 to .93, $M\ r_{xx} = .89$), Similarities (range of .81 to .91, $M\ r_{xx} = .87$), Block Design (range of .84 to .93, $M\ r_{xx} = .90$), and Matrix Reasoning (range of .86 to .96, $M\ r_{xx} = .92$). In the adult sample, internal consistency reliabilities for the subtests are satisfactory for Vocabulary (range of .91 to .98, $M\ r_{xx} = .94$), Similarities (range of .84 to .96, $M\ r_{xx} = .92$), Block Design (range of .90 to .94, $M\ r_{xx} = .90$), and Matrix Reasoning (range of .88 to .96, $M\ r_{xx} = .96$).

Stability coefficients for the four-subtest combination were excellent in a sample of 116 children ages 6 to 16 ($r_{tt} = .93$) and in a sample of 106 adults ages 17 to 89 ($r_{tt} = .92$) who were retested 2 to 12 weeks after the initial test. Stability coefficients for the four IQs range from .85 to .93 in the children's sample and from .87 to .92 in the adult sample. Stability coefficients for the subtests range from .76 to .84 in the children's sample and from .81 to .90 in the adult sample. On retest, IQs based on the four-subtest combination increased by about 5 points in the children's sample and by about 2.5 points in the adult sample.

Validity

Concurrent validity studies indicate that the WASI has high correlations with various measures of intelligence, ability, and achievement. For example, in a sample of 176 children, there was a correlation of .87 between the four-subtest WASI combination and WISC–III Full Scale IQs, with a .2 difference between the IQs ($M = 105.2$ vs. $M = 105.4$). In a sample of 248 adults, the correlation was .92 between the four-subtest WASI Full Scale IQ and the WAIS–III, with a .4 difference between the two IQs ($M = 104.0$ vs. $M = 103.6$). The WASI has adequate construct validity, as noted by moderate subtest intercorrelations and by the results of factor analyses that provide support for two factors on the WASI. Studies of several samples of children with exceptionalities also are reported in the Manual, providing support for the clinical utility of the WASI.

The Manual provides two additional useful tables. Table B.3 shows the differences between WASI Verbal and Performance IQs needed at the .15 and .05 significance levels by age group and for the total children's sample (a difference of 11 points is required at the .05 level) and the total adult sample (a difference of 9 points is required at the .05 level). Table B.4 shows the percentage of examinees whose Verbal IQ and Performance IQ differed by the given amount.

Comment on the WASI

The WASI is a useful screening test for obtaining estimates of overall intelligence for children and adults. It follows the organization and format of the other Wechsler tests, except that it uses T scores instead of scaled scores. The psychometric properties of the WASI are excellent. However, the WASI should not be used as a replacement for either the WISC–III or the WAIS–III.

WECHSLER INTELLIGENCE SCALE FOR CHILDREN–III AS A PROCESS INSTRUMENT

The Wechsler Intelligence Scale for Children–III as a Process Instrument (WISC–III PI; Kaplan, Fein, Kramer, Delis, & Morris, 1999) is an individually administered assessment procedure that complements the WISC–III. Because several cognitive processes may be involved in the solution of each WISC–III subtest, further assessment is usually needed to determine which process is deficient when examinees perform poorly. The WISC–III PI is designed to provide information about the possible reasons examinees do poorly on the WISC–III.

Although the primary purpose of the WISC–III PI is to investigate poor performance on the WISC–III, it can also be used for testing-of-limits (see Chapter 7 in this text) and to obtain additional information about an examinee's cognitive strengths and weaknesses. The entire WISC–III PI need not be administered; administer only those portions needed to help clarify an examinee's performance on the WISC–III.

Let's look at two examples of how the WISC–III PI may be useful. First, the WISC–III PI can help you evaluate whether failures are associated with expressive difficulties or with receptive difficulties. Second, by comparing scores from the WISC–III and WISC–III PI Coding subtests, you can evaluate rate of performance over time (30-second intervals), errors made, incidental learning, and the role of graphomotor speed.

The WISC–III PI contains 19 subtests; 13 are variants of WISC–III subtests, and 6 are standard WISC–III subtests that have additional scoring procedures.

Subtests

The 13 new subtests are as follows:

- The Information Multiple Choice subtest is a multiple-choice version of the WISC–III Information subtest.
- The Coding–Incidental Learning Recall subtest has three parts. Paired Associate Symbol Recall requires remembering symbols associated with specific digits. Free Recall Task requires remembering as many symbols as possible, without associating them with any digits. Paired Associate Digit Recall requires remembering digits associated with specific symbols.
- The Coding–Symbol Copy subtest requires copying a symbol into a box beneath it.
- The Arithmetic Addendum subtest requires solving, with the aid of pencil and paper, problems that were failed on the WISC–III.

- The Written Arithmetic subtest requires solving WISC–III Arithmetic items presented in a paper-and-pencil format.
- The Block Design PI subtest has two parts. Part A (Unstructured) is similar to the WISC–III Block Design subtest but includes six new designs. The examinee determines the number of blocks needed to construct each design. Part B (Structured) requires assembling Block Designs that were failed on Part A with the help of a transparent grid overlay placed over the stimulus designs.
- The Block Design Multiple Choice subtest is a multiple-choice, motor-free variation of the WISC–III Block Design subtest.
- The Vocabulary Multiple Choice subtest is a multiple-choice version of the WISC–III Vocabulary subtest.
- The Picture Vocabulary subtest is a receptive-language multiple-choice version of the WISC–III Vocabulary subtest.
- The Letter Span subtest requires repeating letters in the sequence given by the examiner, with the first trial consisting of nonrhyming letters and the second trial consisting of rhyming letters.
- The Spatial Span subtest has two parts. The forward part requires reproducing a sequence of cubes tapped by the examiner. The backward part requires reproducing, in reverse order, a sequence of cubes tapped by the examiner.
- The Elithorn Mazes subtest requires drawing a path from the bottom of each maze, through a specified number of dots, to an exit at the top of the maze.
- The Sentence Arrangement subtest requires rearranging cards with words on them so that the words make a reasonable sentence.

The six WISC–III subtests that have additional scoring procedures are Picture Completion, Information, Arithmetic, Block Design, Vocabulary, and Digit Span.

Scores

Subtest raw scores are converted into scaled scores ($M = 10$, $SD = 3$), but there are no overall or partial composite scores. Qualitative observations and supplemental scores are available for 16 subtests. Here are some examples.

- On Picture Completion, you record whether responses were verbal, nonverbal, or both.
- On Information, Arithmetic, Vocabulary, and Digit Span, you record correct responses and whether the examinee asked for repetition or gave no response.
- On Coding–Symbol Copy, you record the number of correct symbols completed during four 30-second intervals and the total number of errors.
- On Block Design, you record breaks in configurations, use of extra blocks, a partial score for each design, and correct scores.
- On Letter Span, you obtain scores for nonrhyming and rhyming trials.
- On Spatial Span, you obtain scores for forward and backward spans.

- On Elithorn Mazes, you obtain scores for motor planning, motor imprecision errors, rule violation, and latency, as well as a total raw score without bonus points.
- On Sentence Arrangement, you obtain a total raw score without bonus points.

Standardization

The standardization sample consisted of 825 children, with 275 of the total representing children with special needs (i.e., children with attention-deficit/hyperactivity disorder, learning disorders, language impairment, mental retardation, or closed head injury). Demographic characteristics of the standardization sample were stratified by age, geographic region, gender, race, ethnicity, and parental educational level, following 1995 U.S. Census data.

Reliability

Internal consistency reliabilities for the 19 subtests range from .35 to .95 ($M\ r_{xx} = .80$). At 4 of the 11 age groups (ages 6, 7, 13, 16), more than half of the internal consistency reliability coefficients were below .80. Overall, of the 199 internal consistency reliabilities, 92 (or 46%) were below .80. The highest internal consistency reliabilities are for Vocabulary Multiple Choice, Block Design PI, and WISC–III Block Design Supplemental Score. The lowest internal consistency reliabilities are for Elithorn Mazes and Sentence Arrangement.

The average SEMs range from .65 on Vocabulary Multiple Choice and WISC–III Block Design Partial Score to 2.41 on Block Design Multiple Choice Total Score.

The test-retest reliability coefficients were based on a sample of 180 children, divided into three age groups, tested on two separate occasions ranging from 2 to 5 weeks apart ($M = 23$ days). Stability coefficients (for the 15 subtests studied) range from .41 to .88. Only two of the subtests produced a change in mean score of more than 4.0 points—Block Design PI Part A and Block Design PI Part B.

The effect of administering the WISC–III PI during the standard administration of the WISC–III was also studied for the Information, Arithmetic, Block Design, and Vocabulary WISC–III subtests. The sample consisted of 39 children who were tested on two occasions, ranging from 11 to 45 days apart ($M = 24.3$ days). Test-retest reliability coefficients for the three WISC–III subtests range from .61 to .88, with mean score changes of 1.07 on Information, 1.10 on Arithmetic, 1.65 on Block Design, and 1.37 on Vocabulary. This study suggests that administering WISC–III PI subtests during the standard administration of the WISC–III has some effect on test-retest scores.

Validity

Because much of the WISC–III PI is an extension or revision of the WISC–III, content validity is established based on previous studies of the WISC–III and the WAIS–R NI (Kaplan, Fein, Morris, & Delis, 1991). An item analysis was performed to correct and reevaluate the psychometric properties obtained during research trials and standardization studies.

The Manual reports several criterion-related validity studies for the standardization sample, as well as for several clinical groups. The pattern of correlations between the WISC–III PI and other measures of ability and achievement indicates that the WISC–III PI has satisfactory concurrent validity. For example, the pattern of correlations with the WISC–III indicates that subtests with similar content have a moderate to high degree of correlation (r ranges from .41 to .88 for the WISC–III PI and six similar WISC–III subtests), whereas subtests with differing content have lower correlations.

Comment on the WISC–III PI

The WISC–III PI is a unique instrument for obtaining qualitative information about examinees' cognitive abilities. It supplements the WISC–III by providing several additional pieces of information that increase understanding of failures on several WISC–III subtests. However, the WISC–III PI is not an independent instrument for assessing overall cognitive ability, nor does it provide an in-depth evaluation of neuropsychological functioning. Instead, it provides qualitative information to assist in understanding cognitive, perceptual, and motor processing. Some of the subtests on the WISC–III PI are to be administered immediately after the corresponding WISC–III subtests. This procedure can affect examinees' performances on the remaining WISC–III subtests. Therefore, more research is needed to determine how the inclusion of WISC–III PI subtests affects examinees' performance on the standard WISC–III subtests. In addition, we need research to evaluate how the administration of the WISC–III PI affects retest scores on the WISC–III.

WIDE RANGE INTELLIGENCE TEST

The Wide Range Intelligence Test (WRIT; Glutting, Adams, & Sheslow, 2000) is a brief individually administered test of intelligence designed for individuals ages 4 to 85 years. A hierarchical model of intelligence forms the theoretical basis for the test. At the first level is the General IQ. At the second level are verbal (or crystallized) intelligence and visual (or fluid) intelligence. At the third level are the component subtests that make up verbal intelligence and visual intelligence. The test takes about 30 minutes to administer.

Subtests

The four subtests are as follows:

Verbal Intelligence

- The Verbal Analogies subtest measures conceptual ability.
- The Vocabulary subtest measures vocabulary knowledge.

Visual Intelligence

- The Matrices subtest measures nonverbal reasoning ability.
- The Diamonds subtest measures visual-spatial ability.

Scores

The WRIT yields standard scores for the three IQs and the subtests ($M = 100$, $SD = 15$), percentile ranks, and age-equivalent scores.

Standardization

The WRIT was standardized on a stratified sample representative of 1997 U.S. Census data. A sample of 2,285 individuals ages 4 to 85 was selected based on age, gender, ethnicity, regional residence, and parents' level of educational achievement (for school-aged children) or adult's level of educational achievement.

Reliability

Mean internal consistency reliabilities are .95 for the General IQ, .94 for the Verbal IQ, .92 for the Visual IQ, .84 for Verbal Analogies, .91 for Vocabulary, .90 for Matrices, and .93 for Diamonds. Mean SEMs are 4.7 for the General IQ, 5.1 for the Verbal IQ, and 5.9 for the Visual IQ.

The stability of the WRIT was studied in a sample of 100 individuals from the standardization group who were retested after a 6- to 115-day period (M interval = 30.5 days). Mean stability coefficients were .91 for the General IQ, .90 for the Verbal IQ, .83 for the Visual IQ, .90 for Verbal Analogies, .83 for Vocabulary, .70 for Matrices, and .69 for Diamonds. Mean gains from the first to the second test were about 5.7 points for the General IQ, 4.5 points for the Verbal IQ, and 6.6 points for the Visual IQ.

Validity

Construct validity was supported by various factor analyses indicating that either a one-factor or a two-factor solution—Verbal and Visual—is appropriate for the WRIT. Correlations between the WRIT and the WISC–III in a sample of 100 children ages 6 to 16 were high: .90 between the General IQ and the Full Scale IQ, .85 between the Verbal IQ and the Verbal Scale IQ, and .78 between the Visual IQ and the Performance Scale IQ. The General IQ was .6 point higher than the Full Scale IQ. Correlations between the WRIT and the WAIS–III in a sample of 100 adults ages 16 to 79 also were high: .91 between the General IQ and the Full Scale IQ, .90 between the Verbal IQ and the Verbal Scale IQ, and .85 between the Visual IQ and the Performance Scale IQ. The General IQ was .5 point lower than the Full Scale IQ. Median correlations between the WRIT General IQ and the WRAT–3 in four samples of children and adults were .53 with Reading, .46 with Math, and .48 with Spelling.

Comment on the WRIT

The WRIT is a well-standardized brief intelligence test that covers a wide age range. It has excellent psychometric properties. Helpful tables in the Manual relate the WRIT to the WRAT–3 in terms of prevalence of discrepancies. More research is needed to investigate how the WRIT compares with other brief intelligence tests.

WOODCOCK-JOHNSON III® TESTS OF COGNITIVE ABILITIES

(The review of the Woodcock-Johnson III is based on prepublication materials received from the Riverside Publishing Company. Any changes made in these materials after this text went to press are not reflected here.)

The Woodcock-Johnson III® Tests of Cognitive Abilities (WJ III COG; Woodcock, McGrew, & Mather, 2001) is an individually administered battery of tests of cognitive abilities designed for ages 2 to 90+ years. However, not all the tests are administered at the youngest age levels. Although many features of the revised edition (Woodcock & Johnson, 1989) are retained in the WJ III COG, several new tests and clusters have been added. The WJ III COG has 10 tests in the Standard Battery and 10 additional ones, for a total of 20, in the Extended Battery. All of the WJ III COG tests are contained in two easel books.

Cattell, Horn, and Carroll's theories of the structure of intelligence (see Chapter 5 in this text) provide the theoretical basis for the WJ III COG. The tests are divided into seven clusters, derived from this model: Comprehension-Knowledge, Long-Term Retrieval, Visual-Spatial Thinking, Auditory Processing, Fluid Reasoning, Processing Speed, and Short-Term Memory. The WJ III COG also contains a Brief Intellectual Ability measure composed of Verbal Comprehension, Concept Formation, and Visual Matching. The test takes about 40 minutes to 2 hours to administer.

Tests

The 20 tests are as follows:

Standard Battery

- The Verbal Comprehension test measures word knowledge.
- The Visual-Auditory Learning test measures meaningful memory.
- The Spatial Relations test measures visual-spatial ability.
- The Sound Blending test measures the ability to synthesize sounds.
- The Concept Formation test measures inductive and fluid reasoning.
- The Visual Matching test measures visual perceptual speed.
- The Numbers Reversed test measures short-term auditory memory.

- The Incomplete Words test measures auditory analysis and auditory closure.
- The Auditory Working Memory test measures short-term auditory memory span.
- The Visual-Auditory Learning-Delayed test measures delayed recall.

Extended Battery

- The General Information test measures acquired knowledge.
- The Retrieval Fluency test measures ideational fluency.
- The Picture Recognition test measures visual recognition memory.
- The Auditory Attention test measures auditory discrimination.
- The Analysis-Synthesis test measures general sequential reasoning.
- The Decision Speed test measures reasoning speed.
- The Memory for Words test measures short-term auditory memory.
- The Rapid Picture Naming test measures cognitive fluency.
- The Planning test measures sequential reasoning.
- The Pair Cancellation test measures sustained attention and concentration.

Scores

The WJ III COG provides standard scores ($M = 100$, $SD = 15$), percentile ranks, age- and grade-equivalent scores, instructional ranges, discrepancy scores, and a Relative Proficiency Index (RPI). The standard scores range from 1 to 200 at every age level of the battery (range obtained from Kevin McGrew, personal communication, September 2000). The RPI, which is a criterion-referenced measure, provides information about the relative ease or difficulty with which the examinee is likely to perform similar grade-level or age-level tasks. For example, an RPI of 5/90 means that when the examinee's average peers perform at a 90% level of success, this examinee is predicted to perform at a 5% level of success. Each test in the Test Record contains age-equivalent and grade-equivalent estimates of the values reported by the computer program. On 4 of the 20 tests—Verbal Comprehension, General Information, Retrieval Fluency, and Rapid Picture Naming—the Manual indicates that credit should be awarded for correct responses given either in English or in another language.

The WJ III COG can be scored only by a computer. A software package comes with each test kit. The computer program also provides confidence bands for the standard scores and percentile ranks. The tests are grouped into 23 overlapping clusters, including the seven clusters derived from the Cattell, Carroll, and Horn theories of intelligence. The overall score on the WJ III COG is called the *General Intellectual Ability* (GIA). In both the Standard and the Extended Battery, it is a differentially *g*-weighted score, not a simple summation of the test scores that make up the GIA. This means that at each age level of the WJ III COG, the tests that make up the GIA have different weights. For example, although there are seven tests that form the GIA in the Standard Battery, Verbal Comprehension contributes 20% of the GIA at ages 3 to 16; 19% at age 2 and ages 17 to 19; 18% at ages 20 to 29; and 17% at ages 30 to 80+. In the Standard Battery at every age, Verbal Comprehension is weighted the highest (or is tied with another test for the highest weight) in computing the GIA. It is usually followed by Concept Formation or Visual-Auditory Learning. The weights are derived from the first principal component in a principal-components analysis and are shown in Appendix C of the Technical Manual. The software program also provides several types of discrepancy analyses, including those between the WJ III COG and the WJ III Tests of Achievement.

Standardization

The WJ III COG, together with the WJ III Test of Achievement (see Chapter 17 in this text), was standardized on a sample of 8,818 individuals selected as representative of the population, based on U.S. Census projections for the year 2000. There were 1,143 preschool children, 4,784 school-aged children and adolescents, 1,165 college and university students, and 1,843 adults. Stratification variables included census region, community size, sex, race, Hispanic origin, type of school, type of college/university, education of adults, and—for the adult sample only—occupational status and occupation of those in the labor force. A weighting procedure was applied to the sample to obtain a distribution that was proportional to the community and individual sampling variables of the U.S. Census projections.

Reliability

The WJ III COG has excellent internal consistency reliability. Median internal consistency reliability coefficients for the GIA-Standard and GIA-Extended are .97 and .98, respectively. Median internal consistency reliability coefficients for the seven clusters associated with the Cattell, Horn, and Carroll model range from .81 to .95. Finally, median internal consistency reliability coefficients for the 20 WJ III COG tests range from .76 to .97 (Mdn r_{xx} = .87). The median SEMs in standard-score points are 2.60 for the GIA-Standard and 2.12 for the GIA-Extended. For the Cattell, Horn, and Carroll clusters, the SEMs range from 3.35 to 6.54.

The stability of the WJ III COG was measured in one study of 1,196 individuals who were in four age groups (ages 2 to 7, 8 to 18, 19 to 44, and 45 to 95) at the time of the initial testing. The sample was retested at various intervals. The stability coefficients for a test-retest interval of less than 1 year range from .71 to .92 for the six subtests shown in the Manual.

Validity

Evidence for construct validity of the WJ III COG comes from several sources. First, several factor analyses support

Copyright © 1999 by John P. Wood.

the Cattell, Horn, and Carroll model. Second, correlations between related clusters are higher than correlations between unrelated clusters. Third, developmental growth curves and content validity analysis support the WJ III COG factors. Concurrent validity is satisfactory, as indicated by acceptable correlations between the GIA and other measures of intelligence (Mdn r = .67; range of .62 to .76).

Comment on the WJ III COG

The WJ III COG is useful for assessing the cognitive ability of children and adults. It covers a wide age range and uses sophisticated computer scoring procedures to calculate scores and discrepancies. However, in using the WJ III COG, it would be important to know the following: (a) what algorithms are used by the computer software program to score the test (as suggested by the AERA, APA, and NCME in their *Standards for Educational and Psychological Testing,* 1999), because there is no way of hand scoring the test to check whether the scores generated by the computer program are accurate in every case; (b) how scores on the WJ III COG compare with those on other tests, especially with children who have disabilities; (c) how stable WJ III COG scores are; (d) whether the range of scores from 1 to 200 is based on actual scores or extrapolated scores at every age level, because this range is greater than 6 standard deviations from the mean; (e) how much difficulty examiners will have in scoring responses given in a language other than English; (f) how to interpret estimated age equivalents on Auditory Working Memory, Auditory Attention, and Planning that are lower than the lowest ages listed in the standardization sample; (g) what the norm group is for the Visual-Auditory Learning-Delayed subtest (i.e., the number of individuals by age group and time period—from 30 minutes to 8 days); (h) what the relationship is between raw scores and standard scores; (i) what factor analyses will tell us about the tests at ages 2 to 5; and (j) how the discrepancy analysis based on WJ III COG scores and WJ III ACH scores compares with discrepancy analyses provided by other tests.

THINKING THROUGH THE ISSUES

1. How are the tests covered in this chapter different from more omnibus tests like the WISC–III and the Stanford-Binet: IV?
2. When would you use a brief test of intelligence?
3. Should the results obtained from brief measures of intelligence be used for decision-making purposes?
4. What are some of the principal differences between standardized tests and informal tests?
5. When would you use an informal measure of intelligence?

SUMMARY

1. The individually administered tests of intelligence surveyed in this chapter can make valuable additions to your fund of assessment techniques; they are especially useful in situations in which it is not feasible or practical to administer the WISC–III, WPPSI–R, WAIS–III, Stanford-Binet Intelligence Scale: IV, or DAS.

Bayley Scales of Infant Development–II

2. The BSID-II is an individually administered test of infant mental and motor development. It is designed for children between the ages of 1 and 42 months and takes about 30 to 60 minutes to administer. Overall, the test has good reliability and validity.

Cognitive Assessment System

3. The CAS is an individually administered test of cognitive ability that focuses on planning, attention, simultaneous processing, and successive processing—the PASS model. It is designed for children between the ages of 5 and 17 and takes about 1 hour to administer. The test has adequate reliability and validity.

Comprehensive Test of Nonverbal Intelligence

4. The CTONI is an individually administered test of intelligence that measures problem-solving, reasoning, and abstract-thinking abilities. It is designed for individuals between the ages of 6 and 89 and takes about 40 to 60 minutes to administer. The test appears to have adequate reliability and validity.

Detroit Tests of Learning Aptitude–4

5. The DTLA–4 is an individually administered test of intelligence designed for children between the ages of 6 and 17. It takes about 1 to 2 hours to administer. The test has excellent reliability, but further information is needed about its validity.

Infant Psychological Development Scale

6. The Infant Psychological Development Scale is an informal test of intellectual processes associated with natural stages of development. It is designed for infants and young children between the ages of 2 weeks and 2 years. The scale can be used to design developmentally sequenced curriculum programs.

Informal Assessment of Multiple Intelligences

7. Teachers or parents can be given an informal checklist on which to rate children in seven of the skill or talent areas postulated by Gardner.

Kaufman Adolescent and Adult Intelligence Test

8. The KAIT is an individually administered test of intelligence that assesses crystallized and fluid abilities. It is designed for individuals between the ages of 11 and 85+ and takes about 1 hour to administer. The test has adequate reliability and validity.

Kaufman Assessment Battery for Children

9. The K–ABC is an individually administered test of intelligence and achievement designed for children ages 2-6 to 12-5. It takes about 45 to 75 minutes to administer. The test has excellent reliability, but there are questions concerning its validity.

Kaufman Brief Intelligence Test

10. The K–BIT is a brief individually administered test of intelligence designed to measure verbal and nonverbal abilities of individuals between the ages of 6 and 90. It takes approximately 15 to 30 minutes to administer. The test has satisfactory reliability and validity.

Leiter International Performance Scale–Revised

11. The Leiter–R is an individually administered nonverbal test of intelligence designed for children and adolescents between the ages of 2 and 20. It takes about 90 minutes to administer. The test has acceptable reliability and validity.

Piagetian Tests

12. Three types of informal Piagetian tests—covering understanding of conservation, logical operations, and seriation—can be administered quickly and easily with few special materials. The tests are designed for children between the ages of 5 and 11.

Raven's Progressive Matrices

13. Raven's Progressive Matrices is a nonverbal test of reasoning ability based on figural stimuli. The test is designed for individuals ages 5 to adult and takes about 15 to 30 minutes to administer. The test has adequate reliability and validity, but needs to be standardized on a representative sample of the population.

Slosson Intelligence Test–Primary

14. The SIT–P is a screening test of intelligence. The test is designed for children between the ages of 2 and 7 and takes about 15 to 30 minutes to administer. More information is needed about the reliability and validity of the test.

Slosson Intelligence Test–Revised

15. The SIT–R is a test of verbal intelligence designed for children and adolescents between the ages of 4 and 18+. It takes about 15 to 30 minutes to administer. More information is needed about the reliability and validity of the test.

Test of Nonverbal Intelligence–3

16. The TONI–3 is test of problem-solving and abstract reasoning abilities. The test is designed for individuals between the ages of 6 and 89 and takes about 15 minutes to administer. The test generally has acceptable reliability and validity, but not for all groups of children who are exceptional.

Universal Nonverbal Intelligence Test

17. The UNIT is an individually administered nonverbal test of intelligence designed for children between the ages of 5 and 17. It takes about 15 to 45 minutes to administer. The test has acceptable reliability and validity.

Wechsler Abbreviated Scale of Intelligence

18. The WASI is a brief individually administered test of intelligence that follows the organization and format of the other Wechsler tests. It is designed for individuals between the ages of 6 and 89 and takes about 30 minutes to administer. The test has excellent reliability and validity.

Wechsler Intelligence Scale for Children–III as a Process Instrument

19. The WISC–III PI is an individually administered assessment procedure that complements the WISC–III. The test is designed to provide information about which process is deficient when examinees perform poorly on the WISC–III. The WISC–III PI has limited reliability but acceptable validity.

Wide Range Intelligence Test

20. The WRIT is an brief individually administered test of intelligence. It is designed for individuals between the ages of 4 and 85 and takes about 30 minutes to administer. The test has excellent reliability and validity.

Woodcock-Johnson III Tests of Cognitive Abilities

21. The WJ III COG is an individually administered battery of tests of cognitive ability. The battery is designed for individuals between the ages of 2 and 90+ and takes from 40 minutes to 2 hours to administer. More information is needed about the test's reliability and validity.

KEY TERMS, CONCEPTS, AND NAMES

STUDY QUESTIONS

1. Discuss the strengths and weaknesses of each of the following intelligence tests, including in your discussion a description of the test, subtests in the test, scores, standardization, reliability, validity, and overall evaluation:

   Bayley Scales of Infant Development–II
   Cognitive Assessment System
   Comprehensive Test of Nonverbal Intelligence
   Detroit Tests of Learning Aptitude–4
   Kaufman Adolescent and Adult Intelligence Test
   Kaufman Assessment Battery for Children
   Kaufman Brief Intelligence Test
   Leiter International Performance Scale–Revised
   Raven's Progressive Matrices
   Slosson Intelligence Test–Primary
   Slosson Intelligence Test–Revised
   Test of Nonverbal Intelligence–3
   Universal Nonverbal Intelligence Test
   Wechsler Abbreviated Scale of Intelligence
   Wechsler Intelligence Scale for Children–III
      as a Process Instrument
   Wide Range Intelligence Test
   Woodcock-Johnson III Tests of Cognitive Abilities

2. Compare and contrast the following intelligence tests: Comprehensive Test of Nonverbal Intelligence, Kaufman Brief Intelligence Test, Wechsler Abbreviated Scale of Intelligence, and Wide Range Intelligence Test.

3. Imagine you were going to create a new brief intelligence test. Given the knowledge you have acquired from this chapter, what type of information would you include in the test and why?

17

ASSESSMENT OF ACADEMIC ACHIEVEMENT

by Ranae Stetson, Elton G. Stetson, and Jerome M. Sattler

Have you ever considered what the mere ability to read means? That it is the key which admits us to the whole world of thought and fancy and imagination? To the company of saint and sage, of the wisest and wittiest at their wisest and wittiest moment? That it enables us to see with the keenest eyes, hear with the finest ears, and listen to the sweetest voices of all time?

—James Russell Lowell

Goals and Objectives

This chapter is designed to enable you to do the following:

* Differentiate among single-subject tests, multiple-subject tests, screening tests, and comprehensive tests and classify achievement measures appropriately

* Describe, evaluate, compare, and contrast individually administered tests of academic achievement

Academic achievement refers to the skills children learn through direct intervention or instruction. Achievement tests, in turn, are designed to assess the skills and abilities acquired from this process. The achievement tests covered in this chapter are individually administered tests designed to assess abilities and skills in specific subject areas, such as reading, mathematics, spelling, writing, and vocabulary, and content knowledge in science and social studies.

TYPES OF ACHIEVEMENT TESTS

There are two types of achievement tests: screening tests and comprehensive tests. Within each type, there are single-subject tests and multiple-subject tests. *Screening tests* are brief tests containing one subtest for each subject area covered, while *comprehensive tests* contain more than one subtest per subject area and cover the subject areas in depth. Let's now look at these types of tests in more detail.

Screening Tests vs. Comprehensive Tests

Screening tests are usually simpler to administer and score than are comprehensive tests. They are useful in determining whether comprehensive tests should be administered. Two examples of screening tests are the Wide Range Achievement Test–3 (WRAT–3; Wilkinson, 1993) and the Wechsler Individual Achievement Test–Screener (WIAT–Screener; The Psychological Corporation, 1992). Both of these tests contain one reading subtest, one math subtest, and one spelling subtest. Although using screening tests can save time, results may be misleading, as they sometimes overestimate or underestimate a child's skills and they do not measure other important achievement areas. To use a screening test effectively, you must be familiar with the skills within a subject area that you need to assess and make sure that the screening test actually measures those skills.

To be classified as a comprehensive achievement test, a test should (a) assess three or more subject areas typically taught in schools, (b) include at least two different subtests for each subject area, and (c) assess both lower and higher levels of cognitive skills within each subject area. An example of a comprehensive test is the Wechsler Individual Achievement Test–Comprehensive Test (The Psychological Corporation, 1992), which includes two subtests each in reading, mathematics, language, and writing. An elaborate multiple-subject test is the Woodcock-Johnson III Tests of Achievement (Woodcock, McGrew, & Mather, 2001), which contains 23 different achievement tests (see Chapter 16 for a review of this test).

Figure 17-1 shows five important skills in each of the three subjects—reading, mathematics, and writing—most often evaluated in a psychoeducational assessment. The skills within a subject are listed hierarchically according to level of cognition.

Notice in Figure 17-1 that letter identification, numeration and rational numbers, and letter formation are at the lower levels of cognition, whereas passage comprehension, problem solving, and constructing paragraphs are at the highest level of cognition. The lower the level assessed, the less reliably one can predict performance on higher level skills. The higher the level assessed, the more reliable the results. Examinees who perform adequately on tests at higher levels of cognition usually will perform well on tests of lower level cognition, while the reverse is not always true. For example, an examinee may perform well on a letter recognition test or on a numeration test and still do poorly on a passage comprehension test or on a math problem-solving test. Because screening tests are usually constructed with only one subtest for each subject area, you must be familiar with the level of cognition that each subtest targets. Unfortunately, many screening tests assess lower rather than higher levels of cognitive skills, and thus their ability to predict overall achievement is reduced. The preferred comprehensive test batteries are those that (a) include subtests at both lower and higher levels of cognitive skills, (b) provide a reliable overall composite of achievement, and (c) supply useful information concerning specific skill areas in need of attention. A test that does not evaluate a particular achievement domain comprehensively should be supplemented with another test or procedure that assesses the domain of interest, to provide a more complete picture of the child's academic abilities. For example, if you are trying to get information on ability to write a meaningful paragraph, a spelling-from-dictation test should be supplemented with a test that requires composing sentences or short stories. That way, you will be in a stronger position to evaluate the child's abilities in the grammar and mechanics of writing.

Single-Subject Tests vs. Multiple-Subject Tests

Single-subject tests typically include several subtests designed to assess different skill areas within one subject. One example of a single-subject test is the Woodcock Reading Mastery Tests–Revised (Woodcock, 1998), which includes six subtests designed to measure various aspects of reading, such as visual-auditory learning, letter identification, word identification, word attack or decoding skills, word comprehension, and passage comprehension. Another example of a single-subject test is the KeyMath–Revised (Connolly, 1997), which includes 13 mathematics subtests divided into basic concepts, operations, and applications categories.

In single-subject tests, subtests are typically arranged from easier to more difficult. For example, in the Woodcock Reading Mastery Tests–Revised, the Visual-Auditory Learning subtest is given before the more difficult Passage Comprehension subtest, and in the KeyMath–Revised, the subtests covering basic concepts such as addition, subtraction, and

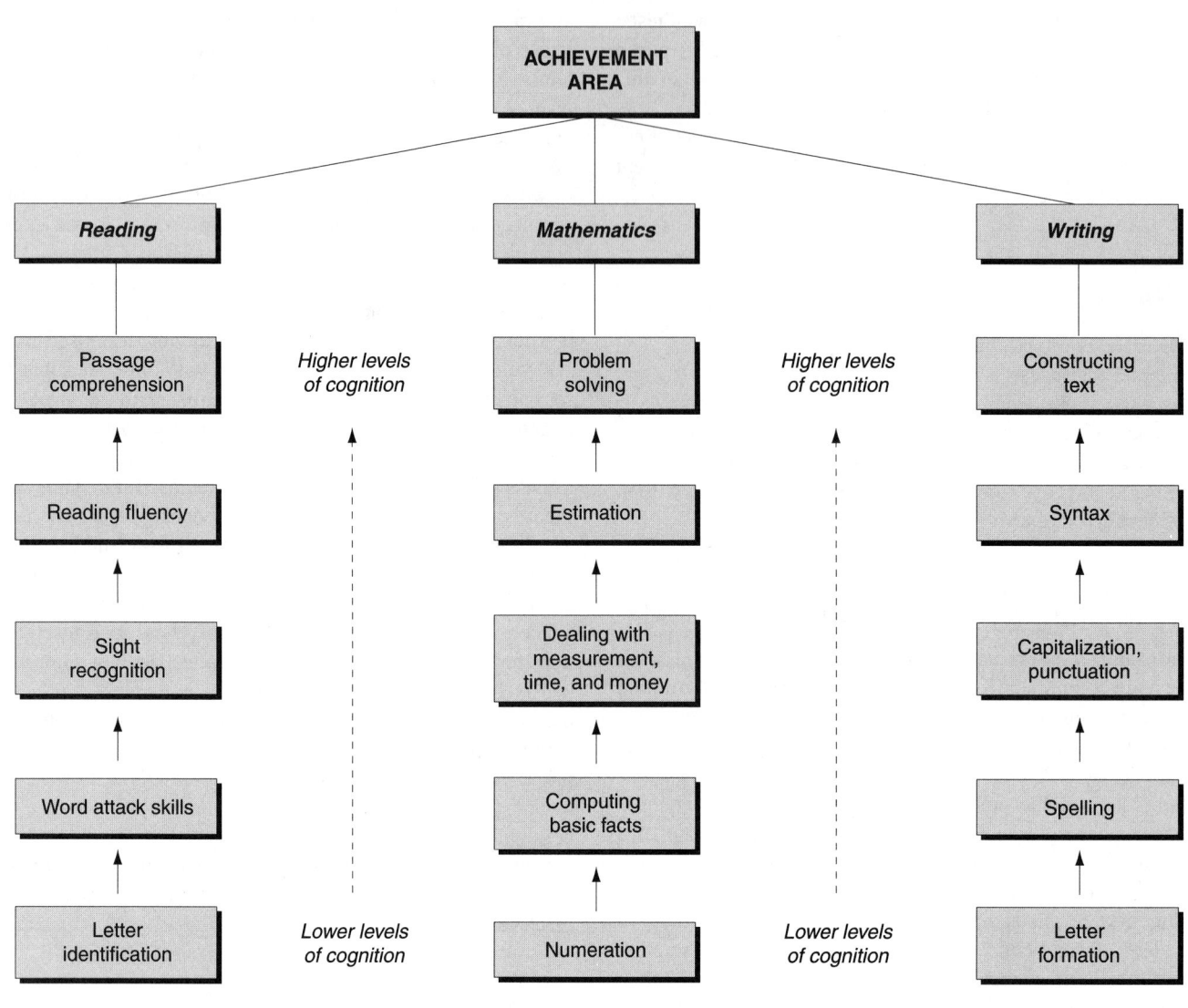

Figure 17-1. Primary skills in reading, mathematics, and writing arranged from highest to lowest level of cognition.

multiplication are given before those covering applications such as measurement, estimating, and problem solving.

Multiple-subject tests are used more often by school psychologists and educators than single-subject tests because they provide information on at least three basic school subjects (e.g., reading, mathematics, and writing). Generally, we recommend that you begin with a multiple-subject test and then use single-subject tests, as needed, to obtain information about the examinee's strengths and weaknesses in specific areas of achievement. However, if the referral question is domain-specific, such as a problem with mathematics, we recommend that you give an in-depth single-subject test.

Seasonal Norms

You should carefully examine the norms tables for tests that have seasonal norms, (e.g., norms for summer, fall, winter, and spring). In some cases, a 1-day difference in when the test is administered may yield a dramatic difference in scores. For example, on the KeyMath–Revised (Connolly, 1988), a fourth-grade examinee who earns 110 raw-score points on January 31 receives a standard score of 100. If the same examinee were tested on February 1, the score would be 86 because of a change in the norms associated with the raw scores. Similar effects are found on other tests with seasonal norms.

HAMMILL MULTIABILITY ACHIEVEMENT TEST

The Hammill Multiability Achievement Test (HAMAT; Hammill, Hresko, Ammer, Cronin, & Quinby, 1998) is a multiple-subject screening test designed for children between the ages of 7 and 17 years. It has two forms (A and B), takes 30 to 60 minutes to administer, and yields four subtest scores (Reading, Writing, Arithmetic, and Facts) and one Composite Quotient (General Achievement). The results help identify areas of difficulty for an examinee who may require a more comprehensive evaluation.

Subtests

The four subtests are as follows:

- The Reading subtest measures reading comprehension and word knowledge, using a modified *cloze procedure.* The cloze procedure requires the examinee to supply key words that have been deleted from a text. Each sentence in the subtest has a word missing. The examinee's task is to select the one word needed to complete each sentence correctly.
- The Writing subtest measures knowledge of spelling and punctuation/capitalization rules. Children are instructed to write from dictation sentences that are sequenced according to grade level. For a child to receive credit for an item, each word must be spelled correctly and the appropriate punctuation marks must be used.

Copyright © 1997 by John P. Wood.

- The Arithmetic subtest measures knowledge of basic number facts and the ability to solve addition, subtraction, multiplication, and division problems. The problems range from simple addition of two single-digit numbers to division of four-digit numbers by three-digit numbers.
- The Facts subtest measures knowledge of basic facts taught in schools in such areas as science, social studies, health, and language arts. The questions relate to factual information, such as days of the week, number of continents, largest ocean, longest river, tallest mountain, and what happens to water when it boils.

Scores

Scoring is 1 (correct) or 0 (incorrect). Raw scores are converted to percentiles, standard scores ($M = 100$, $SD = 15$), and age and grade equivalents. A Composite score called the General Achievement Quotient ($M = 100$, $SD = 15$), which represents the examinee's overall global achievement, is also available. It is calculated by pooling the quotients of the four subtests.

Standardization

The HAMAT was standardized on 1,672 children in grades 1 through 12 who were residing in five states located in the four major geographic regions in the United States. The sample matched the percentages reported in the 1996 U.S. Census data for geographical region, sex, race, residence, ethnicity, family income, educational attainment of parents, and disability. Children in the standardization group attended general classes, and children with disabilities enrolled in these classes were included in the normative sample.

Reliability

Internal consistency reliabilities across both forms range from .74 to .97 ($Mdn\ r_{xx} = .93$) for the subtests and from .93 to .97 ($Mdn\ r_{xx} = .95$) for the Composite score. Alternate-form reliabilities range from .72 to .96 ($Mdn\ r_{tt} = .89$) for the subtests. Alternate-form reliabilities for the Composite score were not provided. Test-retest reliability coefficients for a group of 67 elementary and high school students who took the two forms of the test, 2 weeks apart, ranged from .75 to .97 ($Mdn\ r_{tt} = .81$) for the subtests and from .82 to .97 ($Mdn\ r = .945$) for the Composite score. Interscorer reliabilities range from .94 to .99 ($Mdn\ r_{xx} = .97$) for the subtests and from .97 to .98 ($Mdn\ r = .975$) for the Composite score.

Validity

The content of the HAMAT is highly related to school curricula. Two criterion validity studies are reported in the manual. In one study, 77 children took the HAMAT and the

Comprehensive Scales of Student Abilities, which is a rating scale that provides teacher judgments of academic skills and school-related behaviors. All but one of the 14 correlations between the subtest and Composite scores on the two tests reached or exceeded .60. In the other study, 80 children ranging in age from 8 to 17 years took the HAMAT and the Metropolitan Achievement Test-Seventh Edition. Overall, correlations ranged from .42 to .82 (*Mdn r* = .70) and from .76 to .82 (*Mdn r* = .80) on tests of similar content.

Comment on the HAMAT

Although the Arithmetic subtest is limited to computation, which is a lower level cognitive skill, the other subtests assess higher level skills. The Facts subtest measures knowledge in science and social studies, which most screening tests do not include. The test is easy to administer. The front page of the protocol contains space for summary information, such as all scores, a line graph to connect quotients, standard scores of other tests if available, and comments. The test has acceptable reliability and validity, although additional validity studies are needed. Because this is a screening test, low scores on tests should be followed up with more comprehensive testing. Overall, this is a well-constructed achievement screening test focusing primarily on higher level academic skills.

WECHSLER INDIVIDUAL ACHIEVEMENT TEST–SCREENER

The Wechsler Individual Achievement Test–Screener (WIAT–Screener; The Psychological Corporation, 1992) is an individually administered multiple-subject screening test designed to assess achievement in reading, mathematics, and spelling. It covers ages 5 to 19 years. The test requires about 30 to 60 minutes to administer. The WIAT–Screener includes three subtests: Basic Reading, Mathematics Reasoning, and Spelling. These subtests are the first three subtests of the Wechsler Individual Achievement Test–Comprehensive Test. Scores obtained on the WIAT–Screener can be used to determine whether additional subtests on the Wechsler Individual Achievement Test–Comprehensive Test need to be administered.

Subtests

The three subtests are as follows:

- The Basic Reading subtest assesses lower level cognitive reading skills. It includes items requiring (a) matching a word pronounced by the examiner with another word that begins or ends with the same sound and (b) pronouncing individual words in isolation.
- The Mathematics Reasoning subtest assesses the ability to reason mathematically. Items range from counting objects to solving complex sentence problems requiring knowledge of geometry, measurement, and statistics. Examinees can answer orally or by pointing.
- The Spelling subtest requires writing letters and words dictated by the examiner.

Scores

Scoring is 1 (correct) or 0 (incorrect). Raw scores are converted to standard scores (*M* = 100, *SD* = 15) for both the subtests and the Composite, percentile ranks, stanines, and normal curve equivalents. Age- and grade-based standard scores are available for fall, winter, and spring administrations.

Calvin and Hobbes   by Bill Watterson

CALVIN AND HOBBES © 1990 Watterson. Reprinted with permission of UNIVERSAL PRESS SYNDICATE. All rights reserved.

SCHOOLIES © 1998 by John P. Wood

I don't know the answer, but I'm fascinated by the possibilities.

$\frac{1}{+1}$

Copyright © 1998 by John P. Wood.

Standardization

The standardization sample consisted of 4,252 children in 13 age groups who were enrolled in kindergarten through grade 12. Stratified random sampling was used, following the 1988 U.S. census data. Variables included age, grade, sex, race/ethnicity, geographic region, and parents' educational level.

Reliability

Internal consistency reliabilities range from .74 to .95 ($Mdn\ r_{xx}$ = .91) for the subtests and from .91 to .97 ($Mdn\ r_{xx}$ = .96) for the Composite score. Test-retest reliabilities range from .84 to .95 ($Mdn\ r_{tt}$ = .94) for the subtests and from .93 to .97 ($Mdn\ r_{tt}$ = .95) for the Composite score.

Validity

Content validity was established using both expert judgments and item analysis. Correlations between the WIAT–Screener subtests range from .48 to .89 ($Mdn\ r$ = .67). Correlations between the WIAT–Screener subtests and the Wechsler Intelligence Scale for Children–III Full Scale IQs range from .39 to .84 ($Mdn\ r$ = .60). Criterion validity was assessed by correlating the WIAT–Screener with the Basic Achievement Skills Individual Screener, Kaufman Test of Educational Achievement, Wide Range Achievement Test–Revised, Woodcock-Johnson Psycho-Educational Battery–Revised Tests of

Achievement, and Differential Ability Scales. Correlations between WIAT–Screener subtests and similar subtests on the other tests range from .67 to .88 ($Mdn\ r$ = .83).

Comment on the WIAT–Screener

The WIAT–Screener is easy to administer and score. The Mathematics Reasoning subtest is the most thorough of the three subtests because it targets both lower and higher level cognitive skills in mathematics, including problems involving computation, money, time, geometry, and dealing with extraneous variables. The Reading and Spelling subtests, however, target lower level cognitive skills, like the Reading and Spelling subtests on the Wide Range Achievement Test–3. The Spelling subtest includes 11 potential homonyms in a list of 40 words, such as "eight" (vs. *ate*) or "weak" (vs. *week*; Martelle & Smith, 1994). Spelling these words correctly requires that children also understand the meaning of the word. Overall, the test is well constructed and appears to be a useful screening measure of children's achievement in the three areas.

KAUFMAN TEST OF EDUCATIONAL ACHIEVEMENT–BRIEF FORM

The Kaufman Test of Educational Achievement–Brief Form (K-TEA Brief Form; Kaufman & Kaufman, 1985, 1998) is an individually administered multiple-subject screening test designed to assess school achievement in reading, mathematics, and spelling. The K-TEA Brief Form is designed for children between the ages of 6 and 18 years. The K-TEA Brief Form has a different set of items from those on the Kaufman Test of Educational Achievement–Comprehensive Form. The test takes about 10 to 35 minutes to administer. The K-TEA Brief Form can be used to determine whether additional testing is needed on the K-TEA Comprehensive Form or another comprehensive achievement test.

Subtests

The three subtests are as follows:

- The Mathematics subtest contains two parts. The first part requires paper-and-pencil computation of addition, subtraction, multiplication, and division problems. The second part contains word problems, which are read by the examiner while the examinee looks at a picture related to the problem. Problems can be solved with or without the use of paper and pencil.
- The Reading subtest contains two parts. The first part requires the examinee to name letters and then pronounce a graded list of words. The second part assesses reading comprehension by having the examinee read written commands and act them out.

PEANUTS reprinted by permission of United Feature Syndicate, Inc.

• The Spelling subtest contains 40 words arranged in order of increasing difficulty. The examiner reads a word aloud, reads a sentence containing the word, and then pronounces the word again; the examinee then spells out each word in the test booklet.

Scores

Scoring is 1 (correct) or 0 (incorrect). Raw scores are converted to standard scores ($M = 100$, $SD = 15$) for the subtests and for the Composite. Confidence intervals are provided for the scores, as are percentile ranks, stanines, normal curve equivalents, and grade-equivalent scores.

Standardization

The K-TEA Brief Form was renormed in 1995 and 1996 as part of a coordinated norming program that included the KeyMath–Revised, Kaufman Test of Educational Achievement, Peabody Individual Achievement Test–Revised, and Woodcock Reading Mastery Tests–Revised. The sample included 3,184 K-through-12 students and 245 young adults between the ages of 18 and 22 who resided in 40 states. The sample was representative of 1994 U.S. census data with respect to gender, race/ethnicity, geographic region, parental education, and educational placement. Only some of the sample was administered the complete K-TEA Brief Form.

Reliability

Internal consistency reliability coefficients range from .79 to .97 (*Mdn* r_{xx} = .87) for the subtests and from .91 to .98 (*Mdn* r_{xx} = .94) for the Composite score. Test-retest reliability coefficients on 153 individuals who took the test 6 days apart range from .84 to .90 (*Mdn* r_{tt} = .85) for the subtests and from .92 to .94 (*Mdn* r_{tt} = .93) for the Composite score. Test-retest reliabilities for a sample of 52 children with learning disabilities

who were administered the test over a 3-year period range from .69 for the Math subtest to .88 for the Spelling subtest (*Mdn* r_{tt} = .85; Hewett & Bolen, 1996). Standard errors of measurement are generally in the 4- to 6-point range for the subtests and in the 3- to 4-point range for the Composite score. Intercorrelations among the three subtests range from .55 to .65 (*Mdn r* = .63).

Validity

Content validity was established with the help of curriculum experts and by drawing items from grade-appropriate textbooks. Construct validity is supported by a steady increase in mean raw scores with age. Concurrent validity was assessed by correlating the K-TEA Brief Form with the Wide Range Achievement Test, Peabody Individual Achievement Test, Kaufman Assessment Battery for Children, and Peabody Picture Vocabulary Test–Revised. Correlations between subtests assessing similar content range from .42 to .95 (*Mdn r* = .70). In a criterion-related validity study, the K-TEA Brief Form and the Stanford Binet Intelligence Scale: Fourth Edition were administered to 75 inner-city, low-income, low-achieving students who were referred for evaluation (Prewett & McCaffery, 1993). Correlations between the subtests on the K-TEA Brief Form and the Stanford-Binet Composite score range from .48 on Spelling to .66 on Math (*Mdn r* = 56).

Comment on the K-TEA Brief Form

The K-TEA Brief Form has acceptable psychometric properties to serve as an initial screening test of achievement in mathematics, reading, and spelling. The Spelling subtest is limited to word dictation, which is a lower level cognitive skill. However, the Reading subtest includes a large number of passage comprehension items, and the Mathematics subtest includes numerous word problems; both of these are at higher levels of cognition. The mixture of lower and higher level skills in a single subtest can mask strengths and weaknesses. For example, an examinee with strong decoding skills and weak comprehension skills may receive the same score as an examinee with weak decoding skills and strong comprehension skills or the same score as an examinee with moderate weaknesses in decoding and comprehension skills.

WIDE RANGE ACHIEVEMENT TEST–3

The Wide Range Achievement Test–3 (WRAT–3; Wilkinson, 1993) is a multiple-subject screening test designed to assess the basic skills of reading, arithmetic, and spelling. There are two alternative test forms, Blue and Tan. The WRAT–3 covers an age range from 5 to 75 years and takes about 15 to 30 minutes to administer. The Reading subtest is administered individually, but the Arithmetic and Spelling subtests may be administered either individually or in groups of up to five individuals.

Subtests

The three subtests are as follows:

* The Reading subtest includes 15 letters and 42 individual words.
* The Spelling subtest requires writing one's name, 13 individual letters, and up to 40 individual words of increasing difficulty.
* The Arithmetic subtest contains two parts. Part I requires counting, reading number symbols, and solving simple arithmetic problems presented orally. Part II requires solving, within 15 minutes, up to 40 arithmetic problems presented in a booklet. Items range from adding two single-digit numbers to converting decimals to fractions and reducing algebraic fractions to the lowest common factors.

Scores

Scoring is 1 (correct) or 0 (incorrect). Raw scores are converted to standard scores ($M = 100$, $SD = 15$), grade equivalents, percentile ranks, and normal curve equivalents.

Standardization

The WRAT–3 was standardized on 4,433 children and adults during 1992 and 1993. A nationally stratified sample was selected, based on 1990 U.S. Census data, and matched for age, region, sex, ethnicity, and socioeconomic level. Each age group included from 183 to 200 individuals. All individuals took both forms of the WRAT–3 in a prearranged randomized order. The Reading subtest was administered individually, whereas the Arithmetic and Spelling subtests were administered either individually or in small groups of three to five individuals.

Reliability

Internal consistency reliabilities range from .69 to .95 (*Mdn* r_{xx} = .90) for the subtests, while alternative-form reliabilities range from .82 to .99 (*Mdn* r_{xx} = .92). In a test-retest reliability study involving 142 children between the ages of 6 and 16 who took the same form an average of 37 days apart, test-retest reliabilities ranged from .91 to .98 (*Mdn* r_{tt} = .95). Standard errors of measurement range between 4.5 and 5.9 points for the subtests.

Validity

The manual provides little information about how the items were selected. Many of the items date back to a 1936 edition. Construct validity is evident in that there is a positive correlation

Frank and Ernest

© 1999 Thaves / Reprinted with permission. Newspaper dist. by NEA, Inc.

Copyright © 1999, Thaves. Reprinted with permission of Tom Thaves.

between scores on the subtests and the ages of the individuals. Each subtest shows an increase in mean scores across age groups up to the 45-to-54 group, where the scores begin to fall slightly. Subtest intercorrelations range from .58 to .91 (*Mdn r* = .70). These intercorrelations suggest moderate to high positive relationships among the three subtests.

Concurrent validity studies between the WRAT–3 and three group-administered achievement tests are reported in the manual (California Test of Basic Skills–4th Edition, *N* = 46, ages 8 to 16; California Achievement Test-Form E, *N* = 49, ages 8 to 16; and Stanford Achievement Test, *N* = 31, ages 9 to 15). Correlations range from .41 to .87 (*Mdn r* = .77) for the three subtests. In a group of 100 children between the ages of 6 and 16 who took the WRAT–3 and the Wechsler Intelligence Scale for Children-III, correlations range from .65 to .73 (*Mdn r* = .70) with the Verbal Scale, from .51 to .68 (*Mdn r* = .56) with the Performance Scale, and from .64 to .74 (*Mdn r* = .68) with the Full Scale.

Comment on the WRAT–3

The WRAT–3 is an acceptable screening measure of lower level cognitive skills, one aspect of achievement. The current alternative forms are improvements over past forms of the test. *In administering the test, note that if you use the combined form and give two pretests, you should enter only the higher of the two pretest scores.* If a pretest was not administered, use a score of 15. To obtain an in-depth analysis of an examinee's skills, however, you *must* administer a more comprehensive achievement test. The WRAT–3 contains no measures of essential skills such as reading comprehension, written expression, and math applications.

WOODCOCK-MCGREW-WERDER MINI-BATTERY OF ACHIEVEMENT

The Woodcock-McGrew-Werder Mini-Battery of Achievement (MBA; Woodcock, McGrew, & Werder, 1994) is a multiple-subject screening test of reading, mathematics, writing, and knowledge of science, social studies, and humanities. The test is designed for children and adults between ages 4 and 90+ years and takes about 30 minutes to administer.

Each subtest consists of one or more sections designed to yield a broad measure of achievement. The Reading, Mathematics, and Writing subtest scores are combined to produce a Composite score called the Basic Skills Cluster score. The test is easy to administer.

Subtests

The four subtests are as follows:

• The Reading subtest assesses (a) letter identification and reading of words in isolation, (b) vocabulary and use of

antonyms, and (c) comprehension of missing words in sentences and short passages.

• The Writing subtest has (a) a dictation section that measures knowledge of letters, spelling, punctuation, capitalization, and word usage and (b) a proofreading section that measures knowledge of punctuation, capitalization, word usage, and spelling.

• The Mathematics subtest measures (a) skills in performing mathematical operations involving addition, subtraction, multiplication, geometry, trigonometry, logarithms, and calculus and (b) skills in solving practical mathematical problems, as well as knowledge of mathematical concepts and mathematical vocabulary.

• The Factual Knowledge subtest assesses knowledge of general information in social studies, science, and the humanities. Beginning items are presented in picture form; later items are presented orally by the examiner.

Scores

Scoring is 1 (correct) or 0 (incorrect). Raw scores are converted to standard scores (*M* = 100, *SD* = 15), percentile ranks, and age- and grade-equivalent scores. Raw scores from the Reading, Writing, and Mathematics subtests are combined to form the Basic Skills Composite score. The MBA is the only test reviewed in this chapter that cannot be scored by hand—it *must* be scored by a computer program. The computer program produces a one-page interpretive report that includes age equivalents, grade equivalents, percentile ranks, and standard scores for each of the four subtests as well as for the Basic Skills Composite score. Included in the computer-generated report are a narrative description of what each subtest measures and statements that compare the examinee's performance with that of her or his peer group.

Standardization

All items on the MBA and norms were drawn from the Woodcock-Johnson–Revised Tests of Achievement (Woodcock & Johnson, 1989). The standardization sample included 6,026 individuals (ages 4 to 95) from over 100 geographically diverse communities throughout the United States. They were tested in 1986, 1987, and 1988. Individuals were selected based on region of the country, community size, sex, race, and—for adults—occupational status and occupation.

Reliability

Internal consistency reliabilities range from .70 to .98 (*Mdn r_{xx}* = .93) for the subtests and from .90 to .98 (*Mdn r_{xx}* = .93) for the Basic Skills Composite score. Test-retest reliabilities for sixth graders (*N* = 52), college students (*N* = 53), and adults (*N* = 56) range from .85 to .97 (*Mdn r_{tt}* = .89) for the subtests and from .94 to .97 (*Mdn r_{tt}* = .96) for the Basic Skills Composite score.

Validity

The content of the MBA, which is typically found in school curricula, was reviewed by experts to eliminate ethnic, regional, and gender bias. Concurrent validity is acceptable, as demonstrated by high correlations between the MBA Composite score and Composite scores from other achievement batteries (Woodcock-Johnson–Revised Tests of Achievement, *r* = .82; Kaufman Test of Educational Achievement–Brief Form, *r* = .86; Peabody Individual Achievement Test–Revised, *r* = .87; Wide Range Achievement Test–Revised, *r* = .77). Subtest intercorrelations range from .42 to .88 (*Mdn r* = .71).

Comment on the MBA

The MBA is a well-designed screening test that is easy to administer. Although there is only one subtest for each subject area, the items span several cognitive levels. The standardization procedures are generally good, and the test has acceptable reliability and validity. The test has several limitations, though. First, there is some question about whether all the individuals in the norming sample took the MBA in its final form (Willis, Dumont, & Cruse, 1997). Second, hand scoring is not available, which is a disadvantage if you do not want to use a computer. Further, lack of hand scoring prevents you from checking the accuracy of the computer disk, which may become degraded. Third, the size of the print on the letter recognition portion of the Reading subtest may be too small for some young children. Finally, as on the K-TEA Brief Form, the mixture of lower and higher level items (e.g., reading decoding and reading comprehension) in a single subtest can lead to misinterpretations. Despite these limitations, the MBA appears to provide a short but adequate assessment of overall achievement (Michael, 1998; Sanford, 1998).

WOODCOCK-JOHNSON III® TESTS OF ACHIEVEMENT

(The review of the Woodcock-Johnson III ACH is based on prepublication materials received from the Riverside Publishing Company. Any changes made in these materials after this text went to press are not reflected here.)

The Woodcock-Johnson III® Tests of Achievement (WJ III ACH; Woodcock, McGrew, & Mather, 2001) is an individually administered battery of achievement tests for ages 2 to 90+ years. However, not all of the tests are administered at the youngest age levels. Although many features of the revised edition (Woodcock & Johnson, 1989) are retained in the WJ III ACH, several new tests and clusters have been added. The WJ III ACH has 22 tests, with 12 in the Standard Battery and 10 additional ones in the Extended Battery. The WJ III ACH tests are contained in two easel books.

Tests

The 22 tests are as follows:

Standard Battery

- The Letter-Word Identification test measures reading decoding.
- The Reading Fluency test measures reading speed.
- The Story Recall test measures receptive and expressive language.
- The Understanding Directions test measures language development and listening ability.
- The Calculation test measures the ability to perform mathematical calculations.
- The Math Fluency test measures the ability to work quickly with mathematics facts.
- The Spelling test measures spelling ability.
- The Writing Fluency test measures writing ability.
- The Passage Comprehension test measures reading comprehension.
- The Applied Problems test measures ability to solve practical mathematical problems.
- The Writing Samples test measures quality of written expression or writing ability.
- The Story Recall–Delayed test measures delayed memory.

Extended Battery

- The Word Attack test measures phonological and orthographic coding ability.
- The Picture Vocabulary test measures word knowledge.
- The Oral Comprehension test measures receptive language development.
- The Editing test measures spelling and proofreading ability.
- The Reading Vocabulary test measures vocabulary knowledge.
- The Quantitative Concepts test measures quantitative reasoning and math knowledge.
- The Academic Knowledge test measures extent of knowledge in several academic subjects.
- The Spelling of Sounds test measures phonological and orthographic coding ability.
- The Sound Awareness test measures phonological ability.
- The Punctuation and Capitalization test measures knowledge and application of punctuation and capitalization rules.

Standardization

The WJ III ACH, together with the cognitive battery (WJ III COG), was standardized on a sample of 8,818 individuals selected as representative of the population based on U.S. census projections for the year 2000. There were 1,143 preschool children, 4,784 school-aged children and adolescents, 1,165 college and university students, and 1,843 adults. Stratification variables included census region, community size, sex, race,

Hispanic origin, type of school, type of college/university, education of adults, and—for the adult sample only—occupational status and occupation of those in the labor force. A weighting procedure was applied to the sample to obtain a distribution that was proportional to the community and individual sampling variables of the U.S. census projections for 2000.

Scores

The WJ III ACH provides standard scores ($M = 100$, $SD = 15$), percentile ranks, age- and grade-equivalent scores, instructional ranges, discrepancy scores, and a Relative Proficiency Index (RPI). The standard scores range from 1 to 200 at every age level of the battery (range obtained from Kevin McGrew, personal communication, September 2000). The RPI, which is a criterion-referenced measure, provides information about the relative ease or difficulty with which the examinee will be likely to perform similar grade-level or age-level tasks. For example, an RPI of 5/90 means that when the examinee's average peers perform at a 90% level of success, this examinee is predicted to perform at a 5% level of success. Each test in the Test Record contains age-equivalent and grade-equivalent estimates of the values reported by the computer program.

The WJ III ACH can be scored only by a computer. A software package comes with each test kit. The computer program also provides confidence bands for the standard scores and percentile ranks. Tests are grouped into 19 different overlapping clusters, such as Broad Reading, Oral Language-Standard, Broad Math, Broad Written Language, and Academic Knowledge. The overall cluster, called Total Achievement, is derived from nine tests. The software program provides several types of discrepancy analyses, including those between the WJ III ACH and the WJ III COG.

Reliability

The WJ III ACH has excellent internal consistency reliability. The median internal consistency reliability coefficient for Total Achievement is .98. Median internal consistency reliability coefficients for various clusters range from .85 to .96. Finally, median internal consistency reliability coefficients for the 22 tests range from .76 to .97 ($Mdn\ r_{xx} = .88$). The median SEM is 2.12 for Total Achievement, and SEMs range from 3.00 to 5.81 for the clusters. Interrater reliabilities for tests on which examiners use a range of scores to score the responses (i.e., Writing Samples and Writing Fluency) range from .93 to .99.

The stability of the WJ III ACH was measured in two studies. In one study, 1,196 individuals who were in four age groups (ages 2 to 7, 8 to 18, 19 to 44, and 45 to 95) at the time of the initial testing were retested at various intervals. Stability coefficients, presented for only 4 of the 22 tests and no clusters, range from .85 to .96 for the sample retested within 1 year.

In the second study, 457 children and adolescents who were in four age groups (ages 4 to 7, 8 to 10, 11 to 13, and 14 to 17) at the time of the initial testing were retested. The median stability test-retest reliabilities, which were presented for 17 tests and 12 clusters, range from .69 to .96 ($Mdn\ r_{tt} = .89$) for tests and from .93 to .99 ($Mdn\ r_{tt} = .96$) for clusters.

The Technical Manual presents selected alternate-form correlations, standard errors, item difficulties, and response ogives as evidence for alternate-form equivalence, but it does not present alternate-form reliabilities, except for the Passage Comprehension test.

Validity

The WJ III ACH was compared with the K-TEA and the WIAT in a sample of 52 randomly selected students in grades 1 to 8. The correlation between the WJ III Total Achievement and the K-TEA Battery Composite was .79. The correlation between the WJ III Total Achievement and the WIAT Total Achievement was .65.

Appendix E in the WJ III Technical Manual shows correlations between the cluster scores on the WJ III ACH and WJ III COG. Let's look at the relationship between the WJ III ACH Total Achievement and the WJ III COG GIA-Standard and between the WJ III ACH Broad Reading and the WJ III COG GIA-Standard. Total Achievement is a comprehensive measure of overall achievement, Broad Reading is a comprehensive measure of overall reading achievement, and GIA-Standard is a comprehensive measure of overall cognitive ability.

- Correlations between Total Achievement and GIA-Standard are as follows: .72 at ages 6 to 8, .75 at ages 9 to 13, .81 at ages 14 to 19, .83 at ages 20 to 39, and .88 at ages 40+.
- Correlations between Broad Reading and GIA-Standard as follows: .68 at ages 6 to 8, .66 at ages 9 to 13, .74 at ages 14 to 19, .76 at ages 20 to 39, and .84 at ages 40+.

The correlations generally show an increase with age.

Comment on the WJ III ACH

The WJ III ACH is useful for assessing achievement in children and adults. It covers a wide age range and uses computer scoring procedures to calculate scores and discrepancies. However, in using the WJ III ACH, it would be important to know the following: (a) the algorithms used by the computer software program to score the test (as suggested by the AERA, APA, and NCME in their *Standards for Educational and Psychological Testing,* 1999), because there is no way of hand scoring the test to check whether the scores generated by the computer program are accurate in every case; (b) how scores on the WJ III ACH compare with those on other tests, especially with children who have disabilities; (c) how stable WJ III ACH scores are; (d) the alternate-form reliabilities, as

6-21
©1989 Bil Keone, Inc.
Dist. by Cowles Synd, Inc.

"That's printing and this is cursive writing. In cursive all the letters hold hands."

Reprinted with special permission of King Features Syndicate.

well as the alternate-form means and standard deviations; (e) whether the range of scores from 1 to 200 is based on actual scores or extrapolated scores in every age group, because this range is greater than 6 standard deviations from the mean; (f) how to interpret estimated age equivalents on Math Fluency, Writing Fluency, and Punctuation and Capitalization that are lower than the lowest ages listed in the standardization sample; (g) the relationship between raw scores and standard scores; (h) what factor analyses will tell us about the tests at ages 2 to 5; and (i) how the discrepancy analysis based on WJ III ACH scores and WJ III COG scores compares with discrepancy analyses provided by other tests.

KAUFMAN TEST OF EDUCATIONAL ACHIEVEMENT–COMPREHENSIVE FORM

The Kaufman Test of Educational Achievement–Comprehensive Form (K-TEA; Kaufman & Kaufman, 1985, 1998) is an untimed, individually administered multiple-subject comprehensive test designed to assess achievement in reading, mathematics, and spelling. As noted earlier, the K-TEA and the K-TEA Brief Form contain completely different items.

The K-TEA is designed for children and young adults between the ages of 6 and 22 years. It includes five subtests—

Reading Decoding, Reading Comprehension, Mathematics Applications, Mathematics Computation, and Spelling—and takes about 45 to 70 minutes to administer. An Error Analysis form, which helps to identify possible needed remediations, can be used in the development of an Individualized Education Program (IEP).

Subtests

The five subtests are as follows:

- The Reading Decoding subtest consists of five individual letters and 55 words arranged in order of increasing difficulty.
- The Reading Comprehension subtest measures literal and inferential comprehension of paragraphs of varying lengths. The examinee reads the material aloud or silently, then reads one or two questions below each passage, and responds orally.
- The Mathematics Applications subtest assesses arithmetic concepts, particularly as they relate to real-life situations. Questions are presented orally as the examinee looks at drawings or printed copies of the questions. Paper and pencil may be used if needed, except on two estimation items.
- The Mathematics Computation subtest contains 60 problems covering the four basic arithmetical operations and more complex computations.
- The Spelling subtest assesses written (or oral) spelling.

Scores

Scoring is 1 (correct) or 0 (incorrect). Raw scores are converted to percentiles and standard scores ($M = 100$, $SD = 15$) based on age. Fall and spring grade norms are provided for grades 1 to 12. Also available are grade equivalents, age equivalents, normal curve equivalents, and stanines. In addition to subtest scores, there are three Composite scores (see Table 17-1). Because the Spelling subtest is the only measure of writing skills, there is no Composite score for writing or written language. The Spelling subtest is included in the Total Test Composite, however.

Table 17-1
Composites on the K-TEA Comprehensive Form

Composite	Subtest
Reading	Reading Decoding Reading Comprehension
Mathematics	Mathematics Applications Mathematics Computation
Total Test	Combined scores from the five subtests (with Spelling)

Reprinted with special permission of King Features Syndicate.

Standardization

Standardized in 1985, the K-TEA was renormed in 1995 and 1996 as part of a coordinated norming program that included the KeyMath–Revised, Kaufman Test of Educational Achievement–Brief Edition, Peabody Individual Achievement Test–Revised, and Woodcock Reading Mastery Tests–Revised. The sample included 3,184 K-through-12 students and 245 young adults between the ages of 18 and 22 who resided in 40 states. The sample was representative of 1994 U.S. census data with respect to gender, race/ethnicity, geographic region, parental education, and educational placement. Only some of the sample was administered the complete K-TEA Comprehensive Form.

Reliability

The manual does not report information on the reliability of the 1997 norms. For the 1985 norms, internal consistency reliability coefficients range from .83 to .97 ($Mdn\ r_{xx} = .93$) for the subtests and from .93 to .99 ($Mdn\ r_{xx} = .97$) for the Composite scores. Test-retest reliability coefficients on a sample of 172 individuals (test-retest interval was 35 days) range from .83 to .96 ($Mdn\ r_{tt} = .92$) for the subtests and from .93 to .97 ($Mdn\ r_{tt} = .96$) for the three Composite scores. Another test-retest reliability study (not reported in the manual), involving 60 elementary-grade children, found test-retest reliability coefficients of .90 or higher for the subtests and Composite scores (Shull-Senn, Weatherly, Morgan, & Bradley-Johnson, 1995). Mean standard errors of measurement range from 3.2 to 4.3 points for subtests and from 2.0 to 4.2 points for Composite scores. Correlations between the subtests and Composite scores range from .50 to .95 ($Mdn\ r = .68$). When subtests of similar content were compared, intercorrelations were higher, ranging from .74 to .95 ($Mdn\ r = .93$).

Validity

Content validity was established with the help of educational and testing consultants and by drawing items from grade-appropriate textbooks. Construct validity was established by showing mean increases in raw scores by grade and satisfactory correlations between the subtests and Composite scores ($r = .72$ to .96, $Mdn\ r = .85$).

Concurrent validity is satisfactory, as noted by correlations between Composite scores on the K-TEA and subtests of similar content on the Wide Range Achievement Test and Peabody Individual Achievement Test ($r = .49$ to .90; $Mdn\ r = .82$). Validity coefficients between the K-TEA Composite scores and ability tests such as the Peabody Picture Vocabulary Test–Revised and the Mental Processing Composite of the K-ABC range from .41 to .70 ($Mdn\ r = .63$). When Lavin (1996b) examined the scores of 72 children with behavior disorders who took the K-TEA and the Wechsler Intelligence Scale for Children–Third Edition, correlations ranged from .38 on Spelling to .67 on Math Applications ($Mdn\ r = .53$).

Comment on the K-TEA

The K-TEA is a well-normed, standardized individual test of educational achievement and has good reliability and validity. It is easy to administer. The Error Analysis procedure is a useful tool for understanding the examinee's performance on each subtest. The test, however, does not measure listening comprehension, oral expression, or written expression.

PEABODY INDIVIDUAL ACHIEVEMENT TEST–REVISED

The Peabody Individual Achievement Test–Revised (PIAT–R; Markwardt, 1989, 1997) is a multiple-subject comprehensive test designed to assess achievement in reading, mathematics, writing, and general knowledge. It is designed for children and young adults between the ages of 5 and 22 years and takes about 1 hour to administer. The six PIAT–R subtests are General Information, Reading Recognition, Reading Comprehension, Mathematics, Spelling, and Written Expression. The Written Expression subtest is the only timed subtest. Various combinations of subtests form the Total Reading Composite, the Total Language Composite, and the Total Test Composite (see Table 17-2). A unique feature of the test is that examinees can respond to various subtests orally, with gestures, or in writing.

Subtests

The six subtests are as follows:

- The General Information subtest consists of oral questions related to science, social studies, and fine arts, as well as factual knowledge.
- The Reading Recognition subtest measures the ability to recognize sounds associated with letters and the ability to read words orally.
- The Reading Comprehension subtest measures the ability to comprehend sentences. After the examinee reads a sentence, the page is turned and the examinee points to the one of four pictures that best represents the meaning of the sentence. The examinee is not allowed to look back.
- The Mathematics subtest, presented in a multiple-choice format, measures knowledge and application of mathematical concepts and facts. Items are read aloud by the examiner, and the examinee selects the best response by pointing or responding orally.
- The Spelling subtest requires (a) recognizing letters from their names or sounds and (b) spelling words correctly. The examiner says a word, and the examinee chooses the correct spelling either by responding orally or by pointing.
- The Written Expression subtest assesses (a) prewriting skills such as copying and writing letters, words, and sentences from dictation and (b) the ability to write a story (about a picture).

Table 17-2
Composites on the PIAT–R

Composite	Subtest
Total Reading	Reading Recognition
	Reading Comprehension
Total Language	Spelling
	Written Expression
Total Test	General Information
	Reading Recognition
	Reading Comprehension
	Math
	Spelling

Scores

On all subtests except Written Expression, scoring is 1 (correct) or 0 (incorrect), and raw scores are converted to grade- and age-equivalent scores, standard scores ($M = 100$, $SD = 15$), percentile ranks, normal curve equivalents, and stanines. On the Written Expression subtest, a general achievement score is calculated and grade-based stanines (based on clearly defined scoring categories) and a developmental scaled score are provided. An optional computer program can convert raw scores into derived scores and provide subtest comparisons, confidence intervals, and a narrative report.

Standardization

The PIAT–R was standardized in 1995 and 1996 as part of a coordinated norming program that included the KeyMath–Revised, Kaufman Test of Educational Achievement–Brief Edition, Kaufman Test of Educational Achievement–Comprehensive Edition, and Woodcock Reading Mastery Tests–Revised. The sample included 3,184 K-through-12 students and 245 young adults between the ages of 18 and 22 who resided in 40 states. The sample was representative of 1994 U.S. census data with respect to gender, race/ethnicity, geographic region, parental education, and educational placement. Only some of the sample was administered the complete PIAT–R. The number of children ranged from 204 to 295 in each grade level.

Reliability

Internal consistency reliabilities range from .87 to .98 (Mdn $r_{xx} = .95$) for five of the six subtests (the Written Expression subtest excluded). For the Written Expression subtest, they range from .60 to .91 (Mdn $r_{xx} = .79$), and for the Composite, they range from .95 to .99 (Mdn $r_{xx} = .98$).

Test-retest reliabilities over 2- to 4-week intervals were reported for a sample of 280 examinees. For five of the six subtests (excluding the Written Expression subtest), they range from .65 to .98 (Mdn $r_{tt} = .91$). Reliabilities for Composite scores range from .87 to .99 (Mdn $r_{tt} = .96$). For the Written Expression subtest, test-retest reliability was .56 for 45 first-graders over a 2- to 4-week interval. Interscorer reliability coefficients for the Written Expression Subtest were .58 for one part and .67 for the other part.

Validity

The validity of the PIAT–R is acceptable. The median correlations between the PIAT–R and the Kaufman Test of Educational Achievement were .75 for the Mathematics subtest, .78 for the Spelling subtest, .82 for the Reading subtest, and .86 for the Total Test. For 1,527 children, the median correlation between the PIAT–R Total Test Composite and the Peabody Picture Vocabulary Test was .72.

Comment on the PIAT–R

The PIAT–R is an extensive revision of the original PIAT, first published in 1970. It has acceptable reliability and validity. The updating of the test content, the addition of the Written Expression subtest, and the inclusion of the 1997 norms make the test more useful. Because several of the PIAT–R subtests do not require expressive language, the test can be useful for examinees with adequate receptive language but poor expressive language. The multiple-choice format of the Reading Comprehension, Mathematics, and Spelling subtests is particularly valuable for examinees who cannot talk at all.

Some potential difficulties with the test are as follows. First, the Reading Comprehension subtest may be as much a measure of memory as of reading comprehension. Second, the Mathematics subtest, although it covers a broad array of mathematics skills, does not include any paper-and-pencil computations. Third, the format of the Spelling subtest, which requires the examinee to point to the correct spelling from four possibilities, may not provide an adequate indication of spelling ability (Fitzsimmons & Loomer, 1978; Stetson, 1989a, b). Fourth, the internal consistency reliabilities, test-retest reliabilities, and interscorer reliabilities for the Written Expression subtest are low. Overall, however, the PIAT–R is an acceptable comprehensive test of academic achievement in areas other than written expression.

Copyright © 1999 by John P. Wood.

WECHSLER INDIVIDUAL ACHIEVEMENT TEST

The Wechsler Individual Achievement Test (WIAT; The Psychological Corporation, 1992) is an individually administered multiple-subject comprehensive test covering reading, mathematics, language skills, and writing. It is designed for children and young adults between the ages of 5 and 19 years and takes about 30 to 60 minutes to administer. The eight subtests are Basic Reading, Mathematics Reasoning, Spelling, Reading Comprehension, Numerical Operations, Listening Comprehension, Oral Expression, and Written Expression. The first three subtests form the WIAT–Screener, which was described earlier in this chapter.

Subtests

The eight subtests are as follows:

- The Basic Reading subtest assesses lower level reading skills, ranging from matching words that begin or end with the same sound to pronouncing individual words presented in isolation.
- The Reading Comprehension subtest contains passages of increasing length and difficulty, read silently or aloud by the examinee, followed by an oral question for each passage.
- The Mathematics Reasoning subtest, presented orally with pictures or printed copies of the items, assesses

mathematics abilities such as counting, reading number symbols, and solving simple arithmetic sentence problems. The Numerical Operations subtest assesses skills ranging from writing numerals to solving computation problems involving mixed fractions, negative two-digit integers, and linear equations.

- The Listening Comprehension subtest assesses a range of abilities, from vocabulary knowledge (identifying one of four pictures corresponding to an orally presented word) to comprehension (looking at a picture while a passage is read orally and answering one or two orally presented comprehension questions about the passage).
- The Oral Expression subtest uses large color pictures to assess an examinee's ability to express words, describe scenes, give directions for getting from one place to another, and explain steps in completing tasks such as changing a light bulb in a lamp. Items begin with simple instructions, such as "Look at this picture and tell me a word that means a place where automobiles are parked," and progress to more advanced instructions, such as "Look at this picture of the zoo and tell me everything you can about the picture."
- The Spelling subtest requires writing individual letters from dictation and spelling words of increasing difficulty.
- The Written Expression subtest requires writing a letter to a friend. The letter is then evaluated for ideas and development, organization, unity and coherence, vocabulary, sentence structure and variety, grammar and usage, and capitalization and punctuation.

Scores

Scoring is 1 (correct) or 0 (incorrect) on seven of the eight subtests; on the Written Expression subtest, scoring is either 1 to 6 points (for holistic scoring) or 6 to 24 points (for analytic scoring). Some subjectivity is also involved in scoring on Comprehension, Listening Comprehension, and Written Expression. Raw scores are converted to standard scores ($M = 100$, $SD = 15$), age and grade equivalents, percentile ranks, stanines, and normal curve equivalents. Age-based standard scores and grade-based standard scores are available for fall, winter, and spring. The WIAT subtests form six Composite scores: Reading Composite, Mathematics Composite, Language Composite, Writing Composite, Screener Composite, and Total Composite. Table 17-3 summarizes the subtests that make up each Composite.

Standardization

The standardization sample consisted of 4,252 students in 13 age groups, ranging in age from 5 to 19. The sample was stratified for age, grade, gender, race/ethnicity, geographic region, and parents' education level, based on 1988 U.S. census data. Students, including children in special education, were drawn from public and private schools in 32 states. To link the WIAT with a Wechsler intelligence test, a subset of 1,284 students were also given the Wechsler intelligence test appropriate for their age.

Reliability

Split-half internal consistency reliabilities range from .69 to .95 ($Mdn\ r_{xx} = .88$) for the subtests and from .83 to .98 ($Mdn\ r_{xx} = .93$) for the Composite scores. Standard errors of measurement at the 90% level of confidence range from 10 to 12 points for subtests and from 4 to 6 points for Composite scores. Test-retest reliability coefficients for 367 students in grades 1, 3, 5, 8, and 10 who took the WIAT on two occasions, with a median 17-day retest interval, range from .61 to .96 ($Mdn\ r_{tt} = .85$) for the subtests and from .65 to .97 ($Mdn\ r_{tt} = .93$) for the Composite scores.

Two interscorer reliability studies were conducted for the four subtests that require some subjectivity in scoring. In one study, the interscorer reliability coefficients for the Reading Comprehension and Listening Comprehension subtests ranged from .89 to .99 ($Mdn\ r = .98$). In the other study, the average interscorer reliability coefficient was .93 for the Oral Expression subtest, .89 for one part of the Written Expression subtest, and .79 for another section of the Written Expression subtest.

Validity

Experts in reading, math, speech, and other areas reviewed items in order to establish content validity. Intercorrelations range from .14 to .89 ($Mdn\ r = .52$) for subtests and from .26 to .96 ($Mdn\ r = .81$) for Composite scores. Correlations between WIAT scores and Full Scale IQs on the Wechsler tests range from .30 to .84 ($Mdn\ r = .58$). The highest correlations occurred between the Reading Comprehension subtest and the Full Scale and between the Mathematics Reasoning subtest and the Full Scale. Criterion validity is satisfactory, as noted by adequate to high correlations ($r = .68$ to .88; $Mdn\ r = .81$) between the WIAT and the Basic Achievement Skills Individual Screener, Kaufman Test of Educational Achievement, Wide Range Achievement Test–Revised, and Woodcock-Johnson Psycho-Educational Battery–Revised Tests of Achievement.

Comment on the WIAT

The WIAT has acceptable reliability and validity, but it has some limitations. First, although the scoring criteria are clear and the need for subjectivity has been minimized, four of the subtests require some subjective judgment in scoring. Second, the Basic Reading subtest does not assess phonics or other word-attack skills, areas that are important to reading ability (Ferrara, 1998). Third, the Oral Expression subtest calls for some fairly complex descriptions (however, they are liberally scored). Fourth, the test does not have a sufficient floor for young examinees or a sufficient ceiling for older examinees. Overall, the scores provided for high-scoring older children are not satisfactory.

The WIAT has added value because it contains three subtests (the two language subtests and the Written Expression subtest) that are not usually included in achievement tests. A useful aspect of the test is the ability to compare an examinee's reading comprehension and listening comprehension

Table 17-3
Composites on the WIAT

Composite	Subtest
Reading	Basic Reading
	Reading Comprehension
Mathematics	Mathematics Reasoning
	Numerical Operations
Language	Listening Comprehension
	Oral Expression
Writing	Spelling
	Written Expression
Screener	Basic Reading
	Mathematics Reasoning
	Spelling
Total Composite	Combined scores from the eight subtests

Copyright © 1991 by Lew Little Enterprises, Inc. Reprinted with permission.

with a set of norms based on the same sample. In addition, the link between the WIAT and various Wechsler intelligence tests is an advantage in comparing achievement scores with intelligence test scores. Also useful are tables that show the percentage of examinees who obtained various differences between WIAT and Wechsler scores (referred to as base rates). For those using the WISC–III and WIAT in combination, a computer program is available to assist in writing individualized, comprehensive reports. In addition, an intervention guide is available that provides help in formulating an Individualized Education Program.

DIAGNOSTIC ACHIEVEMENT BATTERY– SECOND EDITION

The Diagnostic Achievement Battery–Second Edition (DAB–2; Newcomer, 1990) is an individually administered multiple-subject comprehensive test consisting of 12 subtests that assess listening, speaking, reading, writing, and mathematics skills. It is untimed, requires about 1 to 2 hours to administer, and is designed for children between the ages of 6 and 14 years.

Subtests

The 12 subtests are as follows:

- The Story Comprehension subtest assesses comprehension of stories read aloud by the examiner.
- The Characteristics subtest assesses the ability to listen to a statement read aloud by the examiner and tell whether the statement is true or false.
- The Synonyms subtest assesses the ability to provide a synonym for each given word.
- The Grammatic Completion subtest assesses knowledge of plurals, possessives, and verb tenses, as well as comparative and superlative adjectives.

- The Alphabet/Word Knowledge subtest assesses letter and word discrimination, letter naming, and pronunciation of words in isolation.
- The Reading Comprehension subtest assesses comprehension of stories read silently.
- The Capitalization subtest assesses the ability to read sentences without any capital letters and then rewrite them using proper capitalization.
- The Punctuation subtest assesses the ability to read sentences without any punctuation and then rewrite them using proper punctuation.
- The Spelling subtest assesses written spelling of individual words that are dictated.
- The Writing Composition subtest assesses the ability to write a story based on three stimulus pictures.
- The Mathematics Reasoning subtest assesses the ability to solve mathematical problems without pencil and paper.
- The Mathematics Calculation subtest assesses, by means of pencil and paper, knowledge of basic calculations, decimals, fractions, and algebraic concepts.

Scores

Scoring is 1 (correct) or 0 (incorrect) except on the Writing Composition subtest, where scores range from 0 to 40. Raw scores are converted to percentiles, standard scores ($M = 10$, $SD = 3$), and grade equivalents. Subtests are combined to form eight Composite Quotients ($M = 100$, $SD = 15$; see Table 17-4). A computer program that scores the test and provides an interpretive report is available.

Standardization

The standardization group consisted of 2,623 students between the ages of 5 and 14 living in 40 states. The number of cases per age group ranged from 86 to 395. The norming

Table 17-4
Composites on the Diagnostic Achievement Battery–Second Edition

Composite	Subtest
Listening	Story Comprehension Characteristics
Speaking	Synonyms Grammatic Completion
Reading	Alphabet/Word Knowledge Reading Comprehension
Writing	Capitalization Punctuation Spelling Writing Composition
Mathematics	Mathematics Reasoning Mathematics Calculation
Spoken Language	Story Comprehension Characteristics Synonyms Grammatic Completion
Written Language	Alphabet/Word Knowledge Reading Comprehension Capitalization Punctuation Spelling Writing Composition
Total Achievement	Combined scores from the 12 core subtests

sample represents children tested in 1982–83, combined with those tested in 1989–90. However, the exact number of students who took the DAB–2 items is unknown. The sample is representative of the nation, according to 1985 U.S. Census data, with regard to age, gender, residence, race, ethnicity, occupation of the parents, and urban/rural geographic region.

Reliability

Internal consistency reliabilities range from .70 to .98 (*Mdn r_{xx}* = .91) for all subtests except Written Composition and from .83 to .99 (*Mdn r_{xx}* = .95) for the Composite score. No internal consistency reliabilities were provided for the Written Composition subtest. Test-retest reliabilities are included for 52 students in grades 1 through 7 who took the Capitalization, Punctuation, and Writing Composition subtests within a 1-week interval, and they range from .83 to .94 (*Mdn r_{tt}* = .87).

Validity

Expert opinion and item analysis data were used to establish the content validity of the DAB–2. Mean scores on the subtests increase proportionately from younger to older ages. In addition, correlations between age/grade and subtest scores range from .49 to .86 (*Mdn r* = .77). Correlations among 94 subtest and Composite scores range from .14 to .90 (*Mdn r* = .45). Concurrent validity was assessed by correlating the DAB–2 subtests with comparable subtests on the Durrell Analysis of Reading Difficulty, KeyMath Diagnostic Arithmetic Test, Test of Language Development–Intermediate, Test of Language Development–Primary, Test of Written Language, Wide Range Achievement Test, and Woodcock Reading Mastery Tests. Correlations with these tests range from .41 to .81 (*Mdn r* = .55).

Comment on the DAB–2

The DAB–2 is a potentially useful test for the assessment of academic ability. It assesses listening and speaking skills that are usually not covered on similar tests. However, there is some question about the representativeness of the standardization sample because the sample was tested during two time periods separated by at least 7 years. Further, some items were subtly changed between the first and second editions. Because the sample tested in 1982–83 did not receive the exact same items as are on the DAB–2, the norms may be inappropriate. Also, the manual does not report any interscorer reliability studies for the Writing Composition subtest. You will need to use the DAB–2 with caution.

DIAGNOSTIC ACHIEVEMENT TEST FOR ADOLESCENTS–SECOND EDITION

The Diagnostic Achievement Test for Adolescents–Second Edition (DATA–2; Newcomer & Bryant, 1993) is an untimed, individually administered multiple-subject comprehensive test for adolescents between the ages of 12 and 18. The 13 subtests (10 core and 3 optional subtests) cover the majority of academic subjects taught in middle and secondary schools. The DATA–2 takes 1 to 2 hours to administer.

Subtests

The 13 subtests are as follows:

Vocabulary and Grammar Subtests

- The Receptive Vocabulary subtest assesses knowledge of synonyms and antonyms.
- The Receptive Grammar subtest assesses the ability to recognize grammatically correct sentences.
- The Expressive Grammar subtest assesses the ability to repeat sentences verbatim.

PEANUTS reprinted by permission of United Feature Syndicate, Inc.

- The Expressive Vocabulary subtest assesses the ability to use a stimulus word correctly in a sentence.

Reading and Writing Subtests

- The Word Identification subtest assesses the ability to read words.
- The Reading Comprehension subtest assesses silent reading ability.
- The Spelling subtest requires spelling words that are dictated.
- The Writing Composition subtest assesses the ability to write a short story.

Mathematics Subtests

- The Math Calculation subtest assesses the ability to solve problems in general mathematics, algebra, and geometry.
- The Math Problem Solving subtest assesses competence in solving math story problems.

Optional Subtests

- The Science Knowledge subtest assesses knowledge of earth science, biology, and chemistry.
- The Social Studies Knowledge subtest assesses knowledge of economics, geography, world history, and civics.
- The Reference Skills subtest assesses the ability to use guide words at the top of dictionary-like pages.

Scores

Scoring is 1 (correct) or 0 (incorrect) except on the Writing Composition subtest, where scoring is based on the number of words containing seven or more letters and on story thematic content. Raw scores are converted to percentile ranks, subtest standard scores ($M = 10$, $SD = 3$), and Composite standard scores ($M = 100$, $SD = 15$). Table 17-5 shows how the Composite scores are generated. A computer program is available to assist with scoring and interpretation of results (Hresko & Schlieve, 1993).

Standardization

The DATA–2 was standardized on 2,085 students from age 12 to 18 years in 19 states, using data collected in two time periods, 1985–86 and 1990–91. Data from the later period were also used to co-norm the DATA–2 and the Scholastic Aptitude Scale, to allow for aptitude-achievement discrepancy analyses. The combined sample population was repre-

Table 17-5
Composites on the DATA–2

Composite	Subtest
Listening	Receptive Vocabulary Receptive Grammar
Speaking	Expressive Grammar Expressive Vocabulary
Reading	Word Identification Reading Comprehension
Writing	Spelling Writing Composition
Mathematics	Math Calculation Math Problem Solving
Achievement Screener	Word Identification Math Calculation Spelling
Total Achievement	Combined scores from the 10 core subtests

sentative of the nation as a whole with regard to age, gender, residence (urban, rural), race, ethnicity, and geographic region, based on the 1990 U.S. census.

Reliability

Internal consistency reliabilities range from .76 to .98 (*Mdn* r_{xx} = .95) for the subtests and from .89 to .99 (*Mdn* r_{xx} = .97) for the Total Achievement Composite score.

Validity

Construct validity was demonstrated by showing that (a) raw scores increase with age and item difficulty and (b) correlations between subtests and Composite scores were satisfactory (range from .13 to .73; *Mdn r* = .45). The concurrent validity of the original DATA was determined by comparing it with several achievement measures, including the Stanford Diagnostic Reading Test, Stanford Diagnostic Mathematics Test, Iowa Test of Basic Skills, and Iowa Test of Educational Development. Correlations between 358 subtest and Composite scores ranged from .14 to .85 (*Mdn r* = .54), and 325 correlations met or exceeded .35. To determine the concurrent validity of the DATA–2, the test was administered to 30 students who were also administered the Wide Range Achievement Test. The correlations ranged from .35 to .90 (*Mdn r* = .64).

Copyright © 1998 by John P. Wood.

Comment on the DATA–2

The DATA–2 may be an acceptable multiple-subject comprehensive measure for secondary students with academic problems. It is easy to administer and score, and it is useful for conducting aptitude-achievement discrepancy analysis when used in conjunction with the Scholastic Aptitude Scale (DeMauro, 1998). However, the test has some shortcomings. There are no reliability data for the Writing Composition subtest, the items may be dated, and the norms from two time periods are co-mingled (Andrews, 1998). You will need to use the test with caution.

WOODCOCK READING MASTERY TESTS–REVISED

The Woodcock Reading Mastery Tests–Revised (WRMT–R; Woodcock, 1987, 1998) is an individually administered single-subject comprehensive test battery of reading skills for children and adults from age 5 to 75+ years. The content of the 1998 publication is the same as in the 1987 version except that there are new 1998 norms based on a sample of more than 3,000 individuals. The test has two alternate forms (G and H), and each has the same four subtests. In addition, Form G has two additional subtests and a supplementary subtest. The test takes about 40 to 45 minutes to administer.

Subtests

The four subtests in both forms are as follows:

- The Word Identification subtest requires pronunciation of isolated words.
- The Word Attack subtest requires pronunciation of either nonsense words (letter combinations that are not actual words) or words with very low frequency of occurrence in English.
- The Word Comprehension subtest requires knowledge of antonyms, synonyms, and analogies.
- The Passage Comprehension subtest requires the ability to identify a key word missing from a short passage (usually two to three sentences in length).

The two additional subtests in Form G are as follows:

- The Visual-Auditory Learning subtest is a controlled learning task that measures the ability to form associations between visual stimuli and oral responses.
- The Letter Identification subtest measures the ability to identify letters presented in uppercase or lowercase forms.

Scores

Scoring is 1 (correct) or 0 (incorrect) except on the Visual-Auditory Learning subtest, where the score reflects the total number of errors. Raw scores are converted W scores, which range from 340 to 606 points, grade- and age-equivalent scores, relative performance indices, instructional ranges, percentile ranks, standard scores ($M = 100$ and $SD = 15$), T scores, stanines, and normal curve equivalents. The Instructional Range (IR) score acts as a guide to the level of instruction perceived as most appropriate for the examinee. Five cluster scores are also provided. Table 17-6 shows the subtests that constitute each cluster.

Standardization

The norms for the 1998 edition were based on a representative sample of 3,184 K-to-12 students and 245 young adults between the ages of 18 and 22. The sample was tested in 1995 and 1996 at 129 sites in 40 states on several test batteries, including the WRMT–R. A stratified multi-stage sampling procedure was used to ensure selection of a nationally representative sample at each age level, based on the 1994 U.S. census data. Of the total sample, approximately one-fifth were randomly assigned to take the WRMT–R. Therefore, 721 persons took the entire WRMT–R as a primary battery. The majority of those not taking the WRMT–R as a primary battery took one or more subtests of the WRMT–R. The numbers of individuals used to norm the subtests were as follows: 2,662 for the Word Identification subtest, 2,151 for the Reading Comprehension subtest, 1,309 for the Visual-Auditory Learning subtest, and 751 for the Word Attack subtest.

Reliability

Internal consistency reliabilities across both forms range from .34 to .99 ($Mdn\ r_{xx} = .94$) for subtests and from .54 to .99 ($Mdn\ r_{xx} = .97$) for clusters. Standard errors of measurement were calculated using W scores; they range from 2 to 7 points ($Mdn = 4$) on subtests and from 1 to 5 ($Mdn = 3$) on cluster scores.

Validity

Content validity was established by outside experts, including experienced teachers and curriculum specialists, who studied the item pool and made recommendations about which items to retain. Concurrent validity is satisfactory, as noted by acceptable correlations for subtests ($r = .25$ to $.90$; $Mdn\ r = .62$) and for total test comparisons ($r = .79$ to $.91$; $Mdn\ r = .85$) between the WRMT–R and the reading subtests of the Woodcock-Johnson Psycho-Educational Battery–Revised Tests of Achievement.

Comment on the WRMT–R

The WRMT–R has been widely used to measure the reading skills of children and adults. The improvements to the 1987/1998 edition include the addition of two readiness tests to Form G, expansion of the Word Comprehension subtest, extension of assessment of an examinee's vocabulary to four content areas, inclusion of a new Short Scale Total Reading score to shorten test administration when necessary, and extension of the test to college and adult groups. Overall, the WRMT-R has adequate reliability and validity and is a satisfactory diagnostic test of reading ability.

WOODCOCK DIAGNOSTIC READING BATTERY

The Woodcock Diagnostic Reading Battery (WDRB; Woodcock, 1997) is an individually administered single-subject comprehensive test of reading ability, covering basic reading skills, reading comprehension, phonological awareness, oral language comprehension, and reading aptitude. The test covers ages 4 to 95 years. It contains 10 tests, each measuring a different aspect of reading achievement, and usually can be completed within 60 minutes. The WDRB comprises subtests selected from several parts of the Woodcock-Johnson Psycho-Educational Battery–Revised Tests of Achievement.

Tests

The ten tests are as follows:

- The Letter-Word Identification test measures symbolic learning through recognizing pictures, identifying letters, and pronouncing words.
- The Word Attack test measures phonic and structural analysis skills through the pronunciation of nonsense words.

Table 17-6
Clusters on the WRMT–R

Cluster	Subtest
Readiness Cluster	Visual-Auditory Learning Letter Identification
Basic Skills Cluster	Word Identification Word Attack
Reading Comprehension Cluster	Word Comprehension Passage Comprehension
Total Reading—Full Scale	Word Identification Word Attack Word Comprehension Passage Comprehension
Total Reading—Short Scale	Word Identification Passage Comprehension

Copyright © 1996 by John P. Wood.

- The Reading Vocabulary test measures understanding of words by requiring the examinee to read words aloud and then identify either a synonym or antonym, as specified.
- The Passage Comprehension test requires reading a sentence or short paragraph and then supplying the missing word (modified cloze technique).
- The Incomplete Word test uses an auditory cloze procedure to measure phonological ability.
- The Sound Blending test measures the ability to synthesize dictated phonemes into whole words.
- The Oral Vocabulary test assesses knowledge of word meanings.
- The Listening Comprehension test uses an oral cloze procedure to measure the ability to comprehend a passage, requiring the examinee to supply the missing final word.
- The Memory for Sentences test measures the ability to remember and repeat phrases and sentences presented orally.
- The Visual Matching test measures matching speed, giving the examinee 3 minutes to locate two identical numbers in each row of six numbers.

The tests combine to form seven clusters (see Table 17-7).

Scores

Scoring is 1 (correct) or 0 (incorrect) except on the Memory for Sentences test, where perfect responses for items 6 to 32 receive 2 points and responses with one error receive 1 point. Raw scores are converted to age- and grade-equivalent scores, relative mastery indices, standard scores ($M = 100$, $SD = 15$), normal curve equivalents, percentile ranks, and instructional and developmental range scores. Scoring can be done by hand or by computer.

Standardization

Standardization data were collected from 6,026 individuals between 1986 and 1988. The sample ranged in age from 4 and 90+ years and closely matched the 1980 U.S. Census on

Table 17-7
Clusters on the WDRB

Cluster	Subtest
Total Reading	Letter-Word Identification Word Attack Reading Vocabulary Passage Comprehension
Broad Reading	Letter-Word Identification Passage Comprehension
Basic Reading Skills	Letter-Word Identification Word Attack
Reading Comprehension	Reading Vocabulary Passage Comprehension
Phonological Awareness	Incomplete Words Sound Blending
Oral Comprehension	Oral Vocabulary Listening Comprehension
Reading Aptitude	Sound Blending Oral Vocabulary Memory for Sentences Visual Matching

such variables as region of the country, community size, gender, and race. For the 916 adults enrolled in colleges or universities and the 1,493 adults not enrolled in any secondary school or college, additional matching variables included education level, occupation status (employed or not employed), type of occupation (white- or blue-collar), and funding level of colleges and universities.

Reliability

Internal consistency reliabilities range from .60 to .98 (*Mdn* r_{xx} = .89) for tests and from .67 to .99 (*Mdn* r_{xx} = .95) for clusters. Test-retest reliabilities for 504 students who retook the WDRB at intervals from 1 to 17 months after the first testing range from .77 to .95 (*Mdn* r_{tt} = .89) for tests and from .87 to .95 (*Mdn* r_{tt} = .95) for clusters (McGrew, Werder, & Woodcock, 1991).

Validity

Items were selected using item validity studies and expert opinions. For four age groups (ages 5, 9, 18, and 50–59), intercorrelations range from .14 to .92 (*Mdn r* = .51) for tests and from .35 to .99 (*Mdn r* = .78) for clusters. Concurrent validity is acceptable, as demonstrated by adequate correlations (*r* = –.02 to .92; *Mdn r* = .63) between the WDRB and other achievement tests, including the Peabody Individual Achievement Test, Basic Achievement Skills Individual Screener, Kaufman Test of Educational Achievement, and Wide Range Achievement Test–Revised.

Comment on the WDRB

The WDRB is an acceptable measure of reading. It is well standardized and covers a wide age range. A particularly valuable feature is the provision of norms for oral comprehension and reading comprehension. A computer program is available for scoring the test.

TEST OF EARLY READING ABILITY–SECOND EDITION

The Test of Early Reading Ability–Second Edition (TERA–2; Reid, Hresko, & Hammill, 1989) is an individually administered single-subject screening test of reading ability designed for children between the ages of 3 and 9 years. The test requires 15 to 30 minutes to administer, and two alternate forms (A and B) are available.

Subtests

Although there are no subtests, the 46 items are grouped into three areas: (a) meaning of print, (b) knowledge of the alphabet, and (c) knowledge of the conventions of print.

- Items in the meaning-of-print area range from naming pictures to identifying syntactically and semantically correct sentences.
- Items in the knowledge-of-the-alphabet area range from identifying letters to indicating the missing word in a poem.
- Items in the conventions-of-print area range from naming letters and numerals to explaining the meaning of homonyms.

Scores

Scoring is 1 (correct) or 0 (incorrect). A computer scoring program is available. Raw scores are converted into percentile ranks, normal curve equivalents, and Reading Quotients (*M* = 100, *SD* = 15).

Standardization

The TERA–2 was standardized on a sample of 1,454 children residing in 15 states. The sample was representative of the U.S. population, as reported in the 1985 census, relative to gender, urban/rural residence, race, geographic region, ethnicity, and age.

Reliability

Internal consistency reliabilities across both forms range from .78 to .98 (*Mdn* r_{xx} = .92) for knowledge areas. The alternate-form reliability coefficient for 49 students between ages 7 and 9 who took both forms within a 2-week interval is .79.

Validity

Content validity was established using experts in the areas of reading, language, and early childhood education. Construct validity was demonstrated by showing that raw scores (a) increase with age and (b) correlate with age (*r* = .74 for both forms). The test discriminated between a sample of children with learning disabilities and a sample of children without learning disabilities. Criterion-related validity was satisfactory, as seen by correlations ranging from .34 to .61 (a median cannot be computed, given the limited information in the manual) between the TERA–2 and Basic School Skills Inventory–Diagnostic and between the TERA–2 and the Paragraph Reading subtest of the Test of Reading Comprehension.

Comment on the TERA–2

The TERA–2 has acceptable reliability; however, the validity studies are limited. It is a useful tool for assessing pre-reading and early reading skills. The availability of two forms is an advantage. Until additional validity studies are conducted, though, further testing of an examinee's reading skills may be needed.

TEST OF READING COMPREHENSION–THIRD EDITION

The Test of Reading Comprehension–Third Edition (TORC–3; Brown, Hammill & Wiederholt, 1995) is single-subject reading test designed for children ages 7 to 17 years. It can be administered individually or in small groups. The test requires 30 to 90 minutes to complete.

Subtests

The four subtests in the General Reading Comprehension Core are as follows:

- The General Vocabulary subtest measures the ability to identify multiple vocabulary words that relate to the same concept.
- The Syntactic Similarities subtest assesses understanding of meaningfully similar, but syntactically different, sentence structures.
- The Paragraph Reading subtest requires reading and understanding of short passages.
- The Sentence Sequencing subtest measures the ability to integrate sentences into meaningful paragraphs.

The five additional diagnostic subtests are as follows:

- The Mathematics subtest measures understanding of words in mathematics.
- The Vocabulary subtest measures understanding of general vocabulary words.
- The Social Studies subtest measures understanding of words in social science.
- The Science Vocabulary subtest measures understanding of words in science.
- The Reading the Directions of Schoolwork subtest is designed for younger children and children with reading difficulties. It measures understanding of written directions commonly found in textbooks.

Scores

Scoring is 1 (correct) or 0 (incorrect). Raw scores for subtests are converted to grade- and age-equivalent scores, percentiles, and standard scores ($M = 10$, $SD = 3$). The General Reading Comprehension Core subtests are combined to form a Reading Comprehension Quotient ($M = 100$, $SD = 15$).

Standardization

The TORC–3 was standardized on a sample of 1,962 students residing in 19 states. The norm group was representative of the U.S. population, as reported in the 1990 census, relative to sex, urban/rural residence, race, geographic region, ethnicity, disability status, and age. Students with disabilities enrolled in general education classes were included in the normative sample.

Reliability

Internal consistency reliabilities range from .83 to .98 ($Mdn\ r_{xx} = .94$) for the subtests and from .96 to .98 ($Mdn\ r_{xx} = .97$) for the Reading Comprehension Quotient. Test-retest reliabilities for 37 students aged 15 to 17 years, who took the test twice within a 2-month interval, range from .79 to .88 ($Mdn\ r_{tt} = .85$).

Validity

Items are the same as those in the original 1978 version and represent content taught in schools at that time. Raw scores increase generally with age from 7 to 12 years, but show little change for children between ages 13 and 17. The correlations between age and subtest scores for children ages 7 to 12 range from .46 to .68 ($Mdn\ r = .57$). The correlations between age and subtest scores for 13- to 17-year-olds range from .01 to .12 ($Mdn\ r = .07$).

Subtest intercorrelations range from .24 to .61 ($Mdn\ r = .45$). Criterion-related validity studies, primarily with former editions of the test, indicate that correlations between the TORC–3 and tests assessing similar content range from .22 to .89 ($Mdn\ r = .59$). Correlations between the TORC–3 and intelligence tests range from .42 to .99 ($Mdn\ r = .62$).

Comment on the TORC–3

The TORC–3 is a comprehensive diagnostic reading test that assesses several reading skills. An advantage of the test is that it can be administered to individuals or groups; however, the authors do not discuss whether students in the norm group were given the test individually or in groups. In spite of the fact that items in the 3rd edition are the same as those in the original 1978 version, new norms were established for the 3rd edition using data collected in 1993–94. The TORC–3 does *not* appear to have acceptable validity as a test of reading comprehension for 13- to 17-year-olds, although more research is needed to evaluate the validity of the test for these ages. The TORC–3 does appear to be a valid measure of reading comprehension for 7- to 12-year-olds. However, the discontinuance procedure may be premature—and thereby not allow for an adequate sampling of reading skills—as examinees have been found to answer questions correctly at levels above the discontinuance level (personal communication, John O. Willis, June 2000).

GRAY ORAL READING TEST–DIAGNOSTIC

The Gray Oral Reading Test–Diagnostic (GORT–D; Bryant & Wiederholt, 1991) is a single-subject comprehensive reading test for children ages 5 to 12 years. There are two alternate forms (A and B), each containing seven subtests. The test takes 50 to 90 minutes to administer.

Subtests

The seven subtests are as follows:

Meaning Cue Subtests

- The Paragraph Reading subtest requires reading passages aloud and responding to comprehension questions.
- The Word Identification subtest measures word recognition and vocabulary.

Function Cue Subtests

- The Morphemic Analysis subtest measures knowledge of inflectional endings, contractions, and compound words.
- The Contextual Analysis subtest measures the use of function cues as they appear in context.
- The Word Ordering subtest measures the ability to arrange words presented in random order into a grammatically correct sentence.

Graphic/Phonemic Cue Subtests

- The Decoding subtest measures the ability to recognize letter sounds and letter blends.
- The Word Attack subtest measures the ability to recognize small words within larger words.

Scores

In the Paragraph Reading subtest, the nine passages are scored from 0 (lowest) to 5 (highest) on three skills: reading rate, reading accuracy, and comprehension. The Total Score for each paragraph is the sum of rate, accuracy, and comprehension scores (maximum score = 15). A Total Paragraph Reading score is then calculated by adding together the Total Scores for all paragraphs. The Total Paragraph Reading score can be converted to percentile ranks, standard scores ($M =$ 10, $SD = 3$), and grade-equivalent scores. For the six remaining subtests, items are scored 1 (correct) or 0 (incorrect). Raw scores can be converted into percentile ranks, standard scores ($M = 10$, $SD = 3$), and grade-equivalent scores. Various subtests are combined to form four Composite scores ($M =$ 100, $SD = 15$). Table 17-8 shows the subtests associated with each of the Composites.

Standardization

The standardization group consisted of 831 students in 13 states who took the test between 1988 and 1990. The sample was representative of the national population, based on 1985 U.S. census data, with regard to gender, residence, race, ethnicity, and geographic area.

Table 17-8
Composites on the GORT–D

Composite	Subtest
Meaning Cue	Paragraph Reading Word Identification
Function Cue	Morphemic Analysis Contextual Analysis Word Ordering
Graphic/Phonemic Analysis	Decoding Word Attack
Total Reading	Combined scores from the seven subtests

Reliability

Internal consistency reliabilities across both forms range from .73 to .98 (*Mdn* $r_{xx} = .93$) for the subtests and from .93 to .99 (*Mdn* $r_{xx} = .97$) for the Composite scores. Alternate-form reliabilities for 200 students who took the two forms 1 week apart range from .67 to .90 (*Mdn* $r_{tt} = .76$) for the subtests and from .72 to .89 (*Mdn* $r_{tt} = .86$) for the Composite scores.

Validity

Items were selected using curriculum materials and expert opinion. Construct validity is supported by increases in raw scores with age. Except on the Paragraph Reading subtest, raw scores tend to reach a ceiling after age 9, lending support to the argument that most decoding skills are learned by age 9, absent reading disabilities or other problems. Correlations among subtests range from .49 to .87 (*Mdn r* = .71) for Form A and from .51 to .86 (*Mdn r* = .66) for Form B. Correlations among the Composites range from .67 to .91 (*Mdn r* = .76) for Form A and from .65 to .89 (*Mdn r* = .76) for Form B.

Criterion-related validity was assessed by correlating the GORT–D with other achievement tests, including the GORT–3, Screening Children for Related Early Educational Needs, and Diagnostic Achievement Battery–Second Edition reading subtests. Correlations among the subtests range from .26 to .83 (*Mdn r* = .56), and correlations among Composite scores range from .26 to .85 (*Mdn r* = .71).

Comment on the GORT–D

The GORT–D is a useful test that assesses reading comprehension and gives insight into specific reading difficulties. However, the standardization group is somewhat small. In addition, more information is needed about the test's reliability and validity.

GRAY ORAL READING TEST– THIRD EDITION

The Gray Oral Reading Test–Third Edition (GORT–3; Wiederholt & Bryant, 1992) is an individually administered single-subject screening test for measuring reading ability. It has two forms (A and B), is appropriate for ages 7 to 18, and takes 15 to 30 minutes to administer. The GORT–3 has 13 separate reading passages of increasing difficulty. Examinees read each passage aloud and then answer five multiple-choice comprehension questions. The test is designed to estimate the highest grade level at which an examinee can achieve 70% to 90% reading accuracy.

Subtests

There are no subtests in the GORT–3.

Scores

Performance on each of the 13 reading passages is evaluated in three specific skill areas, yielding four scores: Rate, Accuracy, Passage Reading (combined Rate and Accuracy), and Comprehension. The raw scores for Rate, Accuracy, and Comprehension are based on a 6-point scale (0 to 5). The score for Passage Reading, based on a 10-point scale, is determined by combining the raw scores for Rate and Accuracy. The less time the examinee requires to read the passage, the more Rate points he or she earns. The fewer mistakes the examinee makes in reading the words, the more Accuracy points she or he earns. One Comprehension point is awarded for each of the five multiple-choice questions answered correctly. Raw scores for Rate, Accuracy, and Passage Reading are converted to standard scores ($M = 10$, $SD = 3$), percentiles, and grade equivalents. The Oral Reading Quotient ($M = 100$, $SD = 15$) is calculated by combining Passage and Comprehension standard scores.

Standardization

The standardization sample consisted of 1,259 students who took the 1986 version of the test and 226 students who took the 3rd edition in 1990. The content of the passages and questions is identical on both versions. The students ranged in age from 7 to 18 years. The sample was representative of the national population, according to the 1990 U.S. census, with respect to gender, area of residence, race, geographic area, and ethnic background.

Reliability

Internal consistency reliabilities across both forms range from .79 to .96 (*Mdn* r_{xx} = .90) and from .95 to .98 (*Mdn* r_{xx} = .96) for the Oral Reading Quotient. Alternate-form reliabilities, based on 100 protocols randomly selected from the 1990 standardization sample (no information is given about retest interval), range from .62 to .82 (*Mdn* r_{tt} = .80). The *SEM* is 1 point for skill areas and 3 points for the Oral Reading Quotient.

Validity

The content validity of the GORT–3 appears satisfactory. Because the test was designed to assess general reading comprehension, content that would require knowledge of specific academic subjects, such as math, science, and social studies, was avoided. Construct validity is supported by high correlations between age and raw scores for Form A (r = .71 to .82; *Mdn r* = .82) and for Form B (r = .75 to .84; *Mdn r* = .84). Raw scores on all subtests increased with age. Two studies reported in the manual indicate that students classified as reading or learning disabled had significantly lower scores than students in the norm group.

Criterion-related validity was examined in studies involving the Iowa Test of Educational Development, California Achievement Test, Gray Oral Reading Test–Diagnostic, Screening Children for Related Early Educational Needs, and Diagnostic Achievement Battery–Second Edition. In all, 180 different correlations were computed; they range from .22 to .89 (*Mdn r* = .57). Correlations between the GORT–3 and the Short Form Test of Academic Aptitude and Scholastic Aptitude Test range from .26 to .85 (*Mdn r* = .50) for Form A and from .21 to .81 (*Mdn r* = .58) for Form B.

Copyright © 1998 by John P. Wood.

Comment on the GORT–3

The GORT–3 provides useful information about reading rate, reading accuracy, passage reading, and reading comprehension. One problem with the test is that the discontinuance procedure may lead to premature termination of testing, and thereby not allow for an adequate sampling of reading skills. A better discontinuance procedure might be two consecutive failed passages, rather than one. Other difficulties include the failure to provide grade norms, the absence of measures of silent reading, and strict scoring rules (personal communication, John O. Willis, June 2000). Nevertheless, the GORT–3 provides a normed measure of reading fluency, an essential reading skill that is not measured by many other reading tests.

CLASSROOM READING INVENTORY– EIGHTH EDITION

The Classroom Reading Inventory–Eighth Edition (CRI–8; Silvaroli, 1997) is an individually administered single-subject informal reading inventory designed to assess general reading skills in children between the ages of 5 and 18 and in adults. It takes 15 to 20 minutes to administer. The CRI–8 is useful for ascertaining instructional reading levels, identifying reading problems that may need more formal testing, and developing appropriate remedial instruction. The standard test contains a Subskills Format, for evaluating the ability to decode words in and out of context and answer comprehension questions, and a Reader Response Format, for evaluating literacy skills. A separate Customized Format is also available to evaluate reading subskills appropriate for high school and adult-education students. All three formats include a pretest (Form A) and a posttest (Form B).

The examinee begins the Subskills Format by reading aloud from graded word lists until he or she misses five or more words on a list. The basal level for passage reading is the highest level at which the examinee scores 100% on the word list. The examinee reads each story in the pretest passages aloud, while the examiner records all reading miscues on the record sheet. After each passage, the examinee answers five comprehension questions. Comprehension questions are of three types: (a) factual (e.g., "What was the name of the horse in the story?"), (b) vocabulary (e.g., "What does the word 'grind' mean?"), and (c) inferential (e.g., "Why is skydiving like being in a dream?"). Performance on each passage is then converted to a percentage score and rating (i.e., independent, instructional, or frustration level) for both reading recognition and comprehension. The posttest contains a second set of passages that can be used either at a later date (to assess growth) or immediately (to assess silent reading comprehension).

The Reader Response Format begins similarly in that the basal level for the reading passages is determined by having the examinee read from a graded word list. However, instead of reading the passages and answering five comprehension questions, the examinee first looks at the picture and/or title accompanying each story and then predicts what the story will be about. Each passage is then read aloud, while the examiner records reading miscues. Once the story has been read, the examiner asks questions intended to elicit a retelling of the story by the examinee, with an emphasis on characters, problems, and outcomes or solutions. The examiner probes for responses from the student, as needed, and evaluates the responses.

Subtests

There are no subtests in the CRI–8.

Scores

The Subskills Format provides scores in three areas: graded word lists, word recognition, and comprehension. The Graded Word List score is based on the examinee's pronunciation of the words in the lists. Each paragraph included in the Graded Passages score is scored separately for word recognition and comprehension. Guidelines are provided in the manual for scoring recognition errors as *significant* or *insignificant,* based on whether the error tends to influence comprehension. Scoring is correct (1), incorrect (0), or partially correct (½).

The Reader Response Format provides four scores: Predicting, Characters, Problem, and Outcome. A 3-point scale is used to score the responses: 1 = low (poor response), 2 = average (adequate response), and 3 = high (excellent response).

Overall, scoring helps to identify four different levels of reading recognition and comprehension ability: (a) *independent level,* the highest reading level at which the examinee can read comfortably without assistance; (b) *instructional level,* the highest reading level at which the examinee can read text with a teacher's guidance at a 95% accuracy level in word recognition and at a 75% or better accuracy level in comprehension; (c) *frustration level,* the level at which the examinee's understanding of what is read is below 90% accuracy and the examinee would likely be frustrated; and (d) *listening or capacity level,* the highest level at which the examinee can comprehend at least 75% of material read aloud by the teacher.

Standardization, Reliability, and Validity

Curiously, the manual provides no data about the standardization sample, reliability, or validity of the CRI–8.

Comment on the CRI–8

The Classroom Reading Inventory–Eighth Edition is an informal assessment measure and does not provide reliability, validity, and normative information. Therefore, unfortunately, the psychometric properties of the test cannot be evaluated. In addition, there is no information about interexaminer reliability. The test includes no information about silent reading, which is a serious deficiency. Although the CRI–8 appears to provide useful information for determining an examinee's reading level, it should not be used for placement decisions. It shares with other informal reading inventories the problem that the grade-level designations for the reading passages are of unknown accuracy. Depending on the reading series used in a particular school, scores from such reading inventories might be misleading (personal communication, John O. Willis, June 2000).

KEYMATH–REVISED: A DIAGNOSTIC INVENTORY OF ESSENTIAL MATHEMATICS

KeyMath–Revised (KeyMath–R; Connolly, 1988, 1997) is an individually administered single-subject comprehensive test of mathematical concepts and skills. It is designed for examinees between the ages of 5 and 22 years. The test is untimed, and administration requires 35 to 45 minutes for primary-grade students and 40 to 50 minutes for older students. The 1997 edition has new norms, but the items are the same as those in the previous edition. There are two alternate forms of the test, A and B.

Subtests

The 13 subtests are as follows:

Basic Concepts Subtests (represent foundational knowledge)

- The Numeration subtest measures knowledge of numbers 0 through 999.
- The Rational Numbers subtest measures knowledge of fractions, decimals, and percentiles.
- The Geometry subtest measures knowledge of spatial and attribute relations, two- and three-dimensional shapes, and coordinate and transformational geometry.

Operations Subtests (represent necessary computational skills)

- The Addition subtest measures the abilities to add objects in sets, to add two- and three-digit numbers with and without regrouping, to use addition with money, and to add fractions with like and unlike denominators.
- The Subtraction subtest measures the ability to subtract objects in sets.
- The Multiplication subtest measures the ability to multiply objects in sets.
- The Division subtest measures the ability to divide objects in sets.
- The Mental Computation subtest measures the ability to work with chains, whole numbers, and rational numbers.

Applications Subtests (represent the use of knowledge and computational skills and assess the highest levels of performance in the test)

- The Measurement subtest measures the ability to make comparisons using nonstandard and standard units (length, area, weight, and capacity).
- The Time and Money subtest measures understanding of the passage of time, the use of clocks, monetary amounts to 1 dollar and 100 dollars, and business transactions.
- The Estimation subtest measures the ability to use whole and rational numbers, measurement units, and computation skills.
- The Interpreting Data subtest measures the ability to use charts, tables, graphs, and probability statistics.
- The Problem Solving subtest measures the ability to solve and understand routine and non-routine problems.

Scores

Scoring is 1 (correct) or 0 (incorrect). Raw scores are converted into scaled scores ($M = 10$, $SD = 3$). Area scores and the Total Test Score are converted into standard scores ($M = 100$, $SD = 15$). Percentile ranks, stanines, and normal curve equivalents also are provided. An optional computer program converts raw scores into standard scores and provides a report.

Standardization

KeyMath–Revised was standardized in 1985 and 1986 on a sample of 1,798. It was renormed in 1995 and 1996 as part of a coordinated norming program that included the KeyMath–Revised, Kaufman Test of Educational Achievement, Peabody Individual Achievement Test–Revised, and Woodcock Reading Mastery Tests–Revised. The sample included 3,184 K-through-12 students and 245 young adults between the ages of 18 and 22 who resided in 40 states. The sample was representative of 1994 U.S. census data with respect to gender, race/ethnicity, geographic region, parental education, and educational placement. Approximately one-fifth ($N = 650$) of the overall sample took the KeyMath–Revised as a primary battery. All reliability and validity analyses are based on the original KeyMath–Revised norms.

Reliability

Split-half internal consistency reliabilities for the subtests range from .11 to .93 ($Mdn\ r_{xx} = .81$) for the fall testing group and from .07 to .94 ($Mdn\ r_{xx} = .85$) for the spring testing group. For the three Area scores and the Total Test score, internal consistency reliabilities range from .66 to .98 ($Mdn\ r_{xx} = .94$) for the fall testing group and from .73 to .99 ($Mdn\ r_{xx} = .96$) for the spring testing group. The median standard errors of measurement for both fall and spring testing groups range from 0.7 to 2.0 (Mdn SEM = 1.1) for subtest scores and from

1.5 to 7.7 (*Mdn* SEM = 2.5) for Area scores. Alternate-form reliabilities (retest interval of 2 to 4 weeks) for 356 students range from .53 to .80 (*Mdn* r_{tt} = .73) for the subtests and from .81 to .92 (*Mdn* r_{tt} = .85) for the Area scores.

Validity

Validity is satisfactory, as demonstrated by relatively high correlations between subtests and Area scores for 488 students (*r* = .53 to .90; *Mdn r* = .80). Criterion validity is satisfactory, as noted by acceptable correlations between the KeyMath–Revised and similar subtest and Area (Composite) scores on (a) the Comprehensive Test of Basic Skills (*Mdn r* = .46 for subtests; *Mdn r* = .62 for Composite scores) and (b) the Iowa Test of Basic Skills (*Mdn r* = .57 for subtests; *Mdn r* = .68 for Composite scores) in a sample of 121 students in grades 1 through 8.

Comment on KeyMath–Revised

KeyMath–Revised provides a comprehensive assessment of mathematical ability, with acceptable reliability and validity. The broad range and diversity of item content and the absence of reading and writing requirements make the Key-

NON SEQUITUR © Wiley Miller. Dist. by UNIVERSAL PRESS SYNDICATE. Reprinted with permission. All rights reserved.

Math–Revised attractive for use with exceptional examinees. The manual contains useful information that can guide teachers and clinicians in designing individualized remediation of arithmetic deficiencies. Each test item has a performance objective that pinpoints specific skills that may need improvement. A separate manual, the *KeyMath Teach and Practice,* provides remediation strategies for use in classrooms and in writing Individualized Education Programs.

TEST OF MATHEMATICAL ABILITIES– SECOND EDITION

The Test of Mathematical Abilities–Second Edition (TOMA–2; Brown, Cronin, & McEntire, 1994) is a single-subject comprehensive mathematics test that can be administered either individually or in groups. The TOMA–2 includes measures of (a) attitudes toward mathematics, (b) understanding of mathematics vocabulary, and (c) familiarity with general mathematical information found in everyday life. The test contains four core subtests—Vocabulary, Computation, General Information, and Story Problems—and one supplemental subtest—Attitude Toward Math. The four core subtests combine to form a Math Quotient. None of the subtests is timed, and administration takes 60 to 120 minutes, depending on the examinee's age and mathematical competencies. The TOMA–2 is appropriate for use with children and young adults ages 8 to 18 years.

Subtests

The four core subtests are as follows:

- The Vocabulary subtest measures understanding of math vocabulary words ranging from simple terms, such as *dozen* and *calendar,* to advanced terms, such as *binomial* and *irrational number.*
- The Computation subtest measures the ability to solve arithmetic problems ranging from adding one-digit numbers to writing in scientific notation. The subtest items sample basic operations, as well as fractions, decimals, money, percentages, and other types of complex mathematical problems.
- The General Information subtest measures knowledge of math used in everyday situations, such as "How many pennies are in a dime?" and "Why can a canceled check be your receipt?"
- The Story Problems subtest measures understanding of mathematical concepts in a meaningful context.

There is one supplementary subtest:

- The Attitude Toward Math subtest assesses attitude toward math. The examinee is asked to agree or disagree with statements such as "Someone who likes math is usually weird" and "My friends like math more than I do." This subtest may be helpful in determining whether an examinee's attitude toward mathematics is affecting her or his achievement in the area or, perhaps, vice versa.

Scores

Scoring is 1 (correct) or 0 (incorrect) on the core subtests and from 1 (No, definitely) to 4 (Yes, definitely) on the Attitude Toward Math subtest. Raw scores for subtests and the Math Quotient are converted to standard scores ($M = 10$ and $SD = 3$, $M = 100$ and $SD = 15$, respectively), percentiles, age equivalents, and grade equivalents.

Standardization

The TOMA–2 was standardized on 2,082 students (336 took the test in 1983, and 1,746 took the test in 1990, 1991, and 1992) between the ages of 8 and 18. They resided in 26 states, representing the four major census districts of the United States. The norm group matched the U.S. population, based on the 1990 census, with regard to gender, race, ethnicity, geographic region, and disability status.

Reliability

Internal consistency reliabilities range from .73 to .96 ($Mdn\ r_{xx} = .93$) for the subtests and from .94 to .98 ($Mdn\ r_{xx} = .97$) for the Math Quotient. The average SEM for the five subtests ranges from 0.7 to 1.2. The SEM for the Math Quotient ranges from 2.1 (for students ages 15 to 18) to 3.7 (for students ages 8 to 8-11). Test-retest reliabilities for a group of 198 elementary and high school students who took the test about 2 weeks apart range from .66 for the Vocabulary subtest to .87 for the Story Problems subtest ($Mdn\ r_{tt} = .81$). Test-retest reliabilities for the Math Quotient range from .91 to .93 ($Mdn\ r_{tt} = .92$).

Validity

According to the authors, the content of the TOMA–2 is closely related to the math content taught in schools. Criterion validity is satisfactory, as demonstrated by adequate correlations (range of .27 to .81; $Mdn\ r = .45$) between the TOMA and the KeyMath Diagnostic Arithmetic Test, the Math subtest from the Peabody Individual Achievement Test, and the Math subtest from the Wide Range Achievement Test for a sample of 38 students with learning disabilities. Satisfactory correlations (from .38 to .72; $Mdn\ r = .67$) were also reported between the TOMA–2 and the SRA Achievement Series in a sample of 290 students.

Comment on the TOMA–2

One advantage of the TOMA–2 is that it can be used as either an individually administered test or a group-administered test. Subtests on mathematical vocabulary, general information, and attitude toward math provide information that is not usually supplied by tests. However, mixing norm samples obtained as far apart as 1983 and 1990–92 is questionable. Another concern is that the manual fails to describe whether the test was administered to the standardization group individually or in groups. These concerns limit the use of the TOMA–2.

TEST OF EARLY MATHEMATICS ABILITY– SECOND EDITION

The Test of Early Mathematics Ability–Second Edition (TEMA–2; Ginsburg & Baroody, 1990) is an individually administered single-subject screening test of mathematics for examinees between the ages of 3 and 8 years. It is untimed, but takes 5 to 15 minutes to administer.

Copyright © 1997 by John P. Wood.

Subtests

There are no subtests; however, the 65 test items can be categorized into informal and formal mathematics items.

- Informal mathematics items assess knowledge of (a) relative magnitude (i.e., larger, smaller, and equal to), (b) simple counting in sequence, counting by twos, threes, and fours, and counting backward, and (c) verbal addition and subtraction.
- Formal mathematics items assess knowledge of (a) reading and writing one-, two-, and three-digit numbers, (b) verbal addition and subtraction, (c) paper-and-pencil addition and subtraction of up to three digits, and (d) concepts such as place value, borrowing, and aligning of numerals in addition or subtraction problems.

Scores

Scoring is 1 (correct) or 0 (incorrect). Raw scores are converted to a Math Quotient ($M = 100$, $SD = 15$), percentile rank, and age- and grade-equivalent scores.

Standardization

The standardization group consisted of 426 children tested in 1982 and 470 additional children tested in 1989, for a total of 896 children. Children in the standardization group ranged in age from 3 to 8 years and resided in 27 states. The norm group was representative of the population, based on 1985 U.S. Census data, with respect to gender, residence, race, ethnicity, and geographical area. There were from 75 to 209 children in each age group.

Reliability

Internal consistency reliabilities range from .92 to .96 ($Mdn\ r_{xx}$ = .94), with standard errors of measurement ranging from 3 to 4 points. No test-retest reliabilities are reported in the manual.

Validity

Content validity was established by selecting items from published works that focus on mathematical knowledge. Construct validity is satisfactory, as demonstrated by a .83 correlation between age and raw score. No studies of concurrent validity are reported in the manual. However, one study with the original version of the test reported a correlation of .49 for 6-year-olds and .59 for 8-year-olds between the TEMA and the Math Calculation subtest of the Diagnostic Achievement Battery–Second Edition. Another study reported correlations of .66 and .79 for normal children and children with learning disabilities, respectively, between the TEMA and the Slosson Intelligence Test (2nd ed.).

Courtesy of Gail Machlis.

Comment on the TEMA–2

The TEMA–2 must be used with caution because of its poor standardization and failure to provide sufficient information about reliability and validity.

THINKING THROUGH THE ISSUES

1. In what ways are achievement tests similar to and different from tests of intelligence?
2. What role might achievement tests have in a psychological assessment?
3. How might the examinee's ethnic background affect her or his performance on achievement tests?
4. Are achievement tests more culturally loaded than tests of intelligence?

SUMMARY

1. Academic achievement refers to the skills children learn through direct intervention or instruction. Achievement tests are designed to assess, for example, skills in reading, mathematics, spelling, writing, and vocabulary and content knowledge in science and social studies.

Types of Achievement Tests

2. The tests described in this chapter are useful for the assessment of academic achievement. Achievement tests can be classified

as screening tests or comprehensive tests. They can be further designated as single-subject tests (e.g., reading or mathematics only) or multiple-subject tests (e.g., reading, mathematics, and spelling).

3. Screening tests typically include one subtest each in reading, mathematics, and spelling. Most screening tests assess only lower levels of achievement skills. They are usually easier to administer and score than comprehensive tests, but they do not supply in-depth information about the examinee's academic strengths and weaknesses and they may yield misleading impressions because of the skills that are not measured by the test.

4. Comprehensive tests usually assess three or more subject areas, include at least two subtests for each subject area, and assess skills requiring both lower and higher levels of achievement.

Hammill Multiability Achievement Test

5. The HAMAT is a multiple-subject screening test that measures skills in reading, writing, and arithmetic and knowledge of general facts about science, social studies, health, and language arts. It is designed for examinees between the ages of 7 and 17. It has two forms, A and B, and takes about 30 to 60 minutes to administer. The test has adequate reliability and validity.

Wechsler Individual Achievement Test–Screener

6. The WIAT–Screener is a multiple-subject screening test that measures achievement in reading, mathematics, and spelling. It is designed for examinees between the ages of 5 and 19 and takes about 30 to 60 minutes to administer. The test has adequate reliability and validity.

Kaufman Test of Educational Achievement–Brief Form

7. The K-TEA Brief Form is a multiple-subject screening test that measures achievement in reading, mathematics, and spelling. It is designed for examinees between the ages of 6 and 18 and takes about 10 to 35 minutes to administer. The test has adequate reliability and validity.

Wide Range Achievement Test–3

8. The WRAT–3 is a multiple-subject screening test that assesses the basic skills of reading, arithmetic, and spelling. It is designed for children and adults between the ages of 5 and 75 and takes about 15 to 30 minutes to administer. The test has adequate reliability and validity.

Woodcock-McGrew-Werder Mini-Battery of Achievement

9. The MBA is multiple-subject screening test of reading, mathematics, writing, and factual knowledge of science, social studies, and humanities. It is designed for children and adults from 4 to 90+ years and takes about 30 minutes to administer. Scoring can be done only by a computer. The test has adequate reliability and validity.

Woodcock-Johnson III Tests of Achievement

10. The WJ III ACH is a multiple-subject comprehensive assessment of academic achievement. It is designed for children and

adults between the ages of 2 and 90+. The test has good reliability and validity, although more information is needed about its psychometric properties.

Kaufman Test of Educational Achievement–Comprehensive Form

11. The K-TEA is a multiple-subject comprehensive assessment of academic achievement in reading decoding, reading comprehension, mathematics applications, mathematics computation, and spelling. It is designed for children and young adults between the ages of 6 and 22 and takes about 10 to 35 minutes to administer. The test has good reliability and validity.

Peabody Individual Achievement Test–Revised

12. The PIAT–R is a comprehensive multiple-subject test battery designed to assess achievement in reading, mathematics, and writing; general knowledge about science, social studies, and fine arts; and encyclopedic knowledge. It is designed for children and young adults between the ages of 5 and 22 and takes about 1 hour to administer. The multiple-choice format in three of the subtests is useful for examinees who cannot give their responses verbally. The test has adequate reliability and validity.

Wechsler Individual Achievement Test

13. The WIAT is a multiple-subject comprehensive test that has eight subtests covering four areas: reading, mathematics, language skills (including oral expression), and writing. It is designed for children and young adults between the ages of 5 and 19 and takes about 30 to 60 minutes to administer. The test has adequate reliability and validity.

Diagnostic Achievement Battery–Second Edition

14. The DAB–2 is a multiple-subject comprehensive test consisting of 12 subtests that assess listening, speaking, reading, writing, and mathematics skills. It is designed for examinees between the ages of 6 and 14 and takes about 1 to 2 hours to administer. The test has adequate reliability and validity, but the representativeness of the sample is questionable.

Diagnostic Achievement Test for Adolescents–Second Edition

15. The DATA–2 is a multiple-subject comprehensive test consisting of 13 subtests that assess reading, mathematics, writing, spelling, listening, and oral expression, as well as science, social studies, and reference skills. It is designed to assess the academic skills of adolescents between the ages of 12 and 18 and takes about 1 to 2 hours to administer. The test has adequate reliability and validity, but there is some question about the standardization data because norms from two time periods are comingled.

Woodcock Reading Mastery Test–Revised

16. The WRMT–R is a single-subject comprehensive test that measures reading ability. It is designed for children and adults from age 5 to 75+ years and takes about 40 to 45 minutes to administer. The test has adequate reliability and validity.

Woodcock Diagnostic Reading Battery

17. The WDRB is a comprehensive single-subject test with 10 subtests that measure basic reading skills, reading comprehension, phonological awareness, oral language comprehension, and reading aptitude. It is designed for children and adults between the ages of 4 and 95 and takes about 60 minutes to administer. The test has adequate reliability and validity.

Test of Early Reading Ability–Second Edition

18. The TERA–2 is a single-subject comprehensive reading test that measures several reading skills. It is designed for children between the ages of 3 and 9 and takes about 15 to 30 minutes to administer. The test has adequate reliability, but validity studies are limited.

Test of Reading Comprehension–Third Edition

19. The TORC–3 is a single-subject comprehensive test with eight subtests that measure general vocabulary, syntactic similarities, paragraph reading, and sentence sequencing, as well as mathematics vocabulary, social studies vocabulary, science vocabulary, and reading directions for schoolwork. It is designed for children between the ages of 7 and 17 and takes about 30 to 90 minutes to administer. The test has adequate reliability and validity, except that it does not appear to have acceptable validity as a test of reading comprehension for 13- to 17-year-olds.

Gray Oral Reading Test–Diagnostic

20. The GORT–D is a single-subject comprehensive measure of reading. The seven subtests measure paragraph reading, word identification, morphemic analysis, contextual analysis, word ordering, decoding, and word attack. It is designed for children between the ages of 5 and 12 and takes about 50 to 90 minutes to administer. More information is needed about the test's reliability and validity.

Gray Oral Reading Test–Third Edition

21. The GORT–3 is a single-subject screening test consisting of 13 reading passages of increasing difficulty. It is designed for children between the ages of 7 and 18 and takes about 15 to 30 minutes to administer. The test has adequate reliability and validity.

Classroom Reading Inventory–Eighth Edition

22. The CRI is a single-subject informal reading test. It is designed for children between the ages of 5 and 18 and for adults, and it takes about 15 to 20 minutes to administer. No standardization, validity, or reliability data are available. The test should not be used for classification purposes.

KeyMath–Revised: A Diagnostic Inventory of Essential Mathematics

23. The KeyMath–Revised is a single-subject comprehensive assessment of mathematical concepts and skills. It is designed for children and young adults between the ages of 5 and 22 and takes about 35 to 50 minutes to administer. The test has acceptable reliability and validity.

Test of Mathematical Abilities–Second Edition

24. The TOMA–2 is a single-subject comprehensive mathematics achievement test that measures attitudes toward mathematics, understanding of mathematics vocabulary, and familiarity with general mathematical information found in everyday life. It is designed for children and young adults between the ages of 8 and 18 and takes about 60 to 120 minutes to administer. Although the test has adequate reliability and validity, the mixing of norm samples is of concern.

Test of Early Mathematics Ability–Second Edition

25. The TEMA–2 is a single-subject screening test of mathematical ability. It is designed for children between the ages of 3 and 8 and takes about 5 to 15 minutes to administer. The manual does not provide sufficient information about the test's reliability and validity.

KEY TERMS, CONCEPTS, AND NAMES

Screening tests (p. 577)
Comprehensive tests (p. 577)
Lower cognitive skills (p. 577)
Higher cognitive skills (p. 577)
Single-subject tests (p. 577)
Multiple-subject tests (p. 578)
Hammill Multiability Achievement Test (p. 579)
Cloze procedure (p. 579)
Wechsler Individual Achievement Test–Screener (p. 580)
Kaufman Test of Educational Achievement–Brief Form (p. 581)
Wide Range Achievement Test–3 (p. 583)
Woodcock-McGrew-Werder Mini-Battery
    of Achievement (p. 584)
Woodcock-Johnson III Tests of Achievement (p. 585)
Kaufman Test of Educational Achievement–
    Comprehensive Form (p. 587)
Peabody Individual Achievement Test–Revised (p. 588)
Wechsler Individual Achievement Test (p. 590)
Diagnostic Achievement Battery–Second Edition (p. 592)
Diagnostic Achievement Test for Adolescents–
    Second Edition (p. 593)
Woodcock Reading Mastery Tests–Revised (p. 595)
Woodcock Diagnostic Reading Battery (p. 596)
Test of Early Reading Ability–Second Edition (p. 598)
Test of Reading Comprehension–Third Edition (p. 599)
Gray Oral Reading Test–Diagnostic (p. 599)
Gray Oral Reading Test–Third Edition (p. 601)
Classroom Reading Inventory–Eighth Edition (p. 602)
KeyMath–Revised: A Diagnostic Inventory of Essential
    Mathematics (p. 603)
Test of Mathematical Abilities–Second Edition (p. 604)
Test of Early Mathematics Ability–Second Edition (p. 605)

STUDY QUESTIONS

1. Discuss the strengths and weaknesses of each of the following achievement tests, including a description of the test, subtests in

the test, scores, standardization, reliability, validity, and overall evaluation:

Hammill Multiability Achievement Test

Wechsler Individual Achievement Test–Screener

Kaufman Test of Educational Achievement–Brief Form

Wide Range Achievement Test–3

Woodcock-McGrew-Werder Mini-Battery of Achievement

Woodcock-Johnson III Tests of Achievement

Kaufman Test of Educational Achievement– Comprehensive Form

Peabody Individual Achievement Test–Revised

Wechsler Individual Achievement Test

Diagnostic Achievement Battery–Second Edition

Diagnostic Achievement Test for Adolescents– Second Edition

Woodcock Reading Mastery Tests–Revised

Woodcock Diagnostic Reading Battery

Test of Early Reading Ability–Second Edition

Test of Reading Comprehension–Third Edition

Gray Oral Reading Test–Diagnostic

Gray Oral Reading Test–Third Edition

Classroom Reading Inventory–Eighth Edition

KeyMath–Revised: A Diagnostic Inventory of Essential Mathematics

Test of Mathematical Abilities–Second Edition

Test of Early Mathematics Ability–Second Edition

2. Compare and contrast screening tests and comprehensive tests. Include in your discussion differences between the two types of tests, the advantages and disadvantages of each, the characteristics of tests that justify their classification as either a screening or a comprehensive test, and how screening and comprehensive tests can be used in designing test batteries.

3. Summarize the advantages and disadvantages of single-subject and multiple-subject achievement tests.

4. Compare and contrast the following five multiple-subject screening tests: Hammill Multiability Achievement Test, Wechsler Individual Achievement Test–Screener, Kaufman Test of Educational Achievement–Brief Form, Wide Range Achievement Test–3, and Woodcock-McGrew-Werder Mini-Battery of Achievement.

5. Compare and contrast the Gray Oral Reading Test–Third Edition, Gray Oral Reading Test–Diagnostic, Woodcock Reading Mastery Tests–Revised, and Woodcock Diagnostic Reading Battery.

6. Select two contrasting comprehensive multiple-subject tests and discuss their similarities and differences. Be sure to note the strengths and limitations of each.

7. Imagine you were going to create a new achievement test. Given the knowledge you have acquired from this chapter, what type of information would you include in the test and why?

18

ASSESSMENT OF RECEPTIVE AND EXPRESSIVE LANGUAGE

by Ranae Stetson, Elton G. Stetson, and Jerome M. Sattler

After all, when you come right down to it, how many people speak the same language, even when they speak the same language?

—Russell Hoban

Goals and Objectives

This chapter is designed to enable you to do the following:

- Describe several of the major individually administered tests of receptive and expressive language

- Compare and contrast individually administered tests of receptive and expressive language

- Recognize which tests are appropriate for the assessment of expressive language

- Recognize which tests are appropriate for the assessment of receptive language

This chapter describes individually administered standardized tests of receptive and expressive language. Language tests are useful because problems with receptive and expressive language may be related to the cognitive and academic difficulties that some students have. Language has five basic components (Gleason, 1997; Lahey, 1988; Nelson, 1993; Owens, 1995):

1. *Semantics*: the meaning of words, phrases, and sentences
2. *Syntax*: the order, or arrangement, of words in sentences that make sense
3. *Morphology*: the meaning of the smaller units within words, such as roots, prefixes, and suffixes
4. *Phonology*: the rules for the formation of speech sounds within words
5. *Pragmatics*: the functional use of language to communicate messages, needs, desires, and meanings to another person

RECEPTIVE AND EXPRESSIVE LANGUAGE

The terms *receptive* and *expressive* language are used to describe how individuals either receive or produce messages (Reed, 1994). *Receptive language* refers to the ability to understand messages through either listening or reading. It includes skills such as meaningful listening, comprehension of speech, and reading comprehension. *Expressive language* refers to the ability to produce or generate meaningful messages through either speech or writing (Hegde, 1995). Standardized tests of language skills may focus only on receptive language, only on expressive language, or on both receptive and expressive language.

Interrelationship of Receptive and Expressive Language

Listening, speaking, reading, and writing are the four basic language processes (see Figure 18-1). Although each process can be assessed separately, language processes do not begin at the same time, develop at the same rate, or develop to the same extent.

Listening (receptive) and *speaking* (expressive) are the first processes to develop, and until about age 8, they remain the most competent of the four language processes. From birth to about age 5, listening and speaking are the primary means of communicating. Children are born with the ability to acquire language, but they are not genetically programmed to speak any particular language. The home environment is the most important influence on how quickly and extensively listening and speaking skills develop. Language role models in the home, such as parents and siblings, determine, in part, the form of the child's vocabulary, syntax, and grammar. Speaking vocabulary is a subset of listening vocabulary.

Children usually do not use in their speech vocabulary that they have not understood during listening.

Development of Reading and Writing

Given the extensive listening and speaking processes already acquired by the normal child when he or she enters the primary grades, development of the *reading* (receptive) and *writing* (expressive) processes becomes the primary goal of instruction in grades 1 through 3. The extent to which a child develops reading and writing skills in school will depend, in part, on what abilities the child brings to school. During the primary grades and much of the elementary years, reading and writing naturally lag behind listening and speaking, for two reasons. First, listening and speaking have a 5- to 6-year head start, given that reading and writing are not usually introduced formally until the child enters school. Second, while listening and speaking evolve and develop quite naturally from birth with little or no formal instruction, effective reading and writing depend both on well-developed listening and speaking and on formal instruction in the complexities of decoding print and translating thought into writing.

Reading is a subset of listening, and writing is a subset of speaking. For example, a passage that a child can learn to read and understand is one that the child would understand easily if it were read aloud by an adult reader. This is important, because when children are not able to understand what they read, a strategy often used is to read the passage aloud to them. Similarly, a composition, once written, usually can be read and understood by the writer, even if it is not understood by those who listen.

Assessment Considerations

When you evaluate a language test, consider whether the test taps into lower level skills, higher level skills, or both lower level and higher level skills. For example, a spelling test that requires the spelling of individual words will reveal less about an examinee's general writing ability than a test that requires the writing of a short composition. Evaluating a composition provides information about several skills, including spelling, depth and use of vocabulary, syntactic and semantic correctness of sentence structure, quality of content, and the ability to organize writing in an appropriate sequence (main points, supporting statements, summary, and conclusions).

You also need to know the methods a test uses to assess receptive language skills such as listening. A test may ask the examinee to point to the one picture among several that represents a word or sentence read aloud by the examiner. Or, the test may require the examiner to read a short passage to the examinee and then ask several questions designed to determine the examinee's ability to understand what was read, make reasonable predictions of what might happen next,

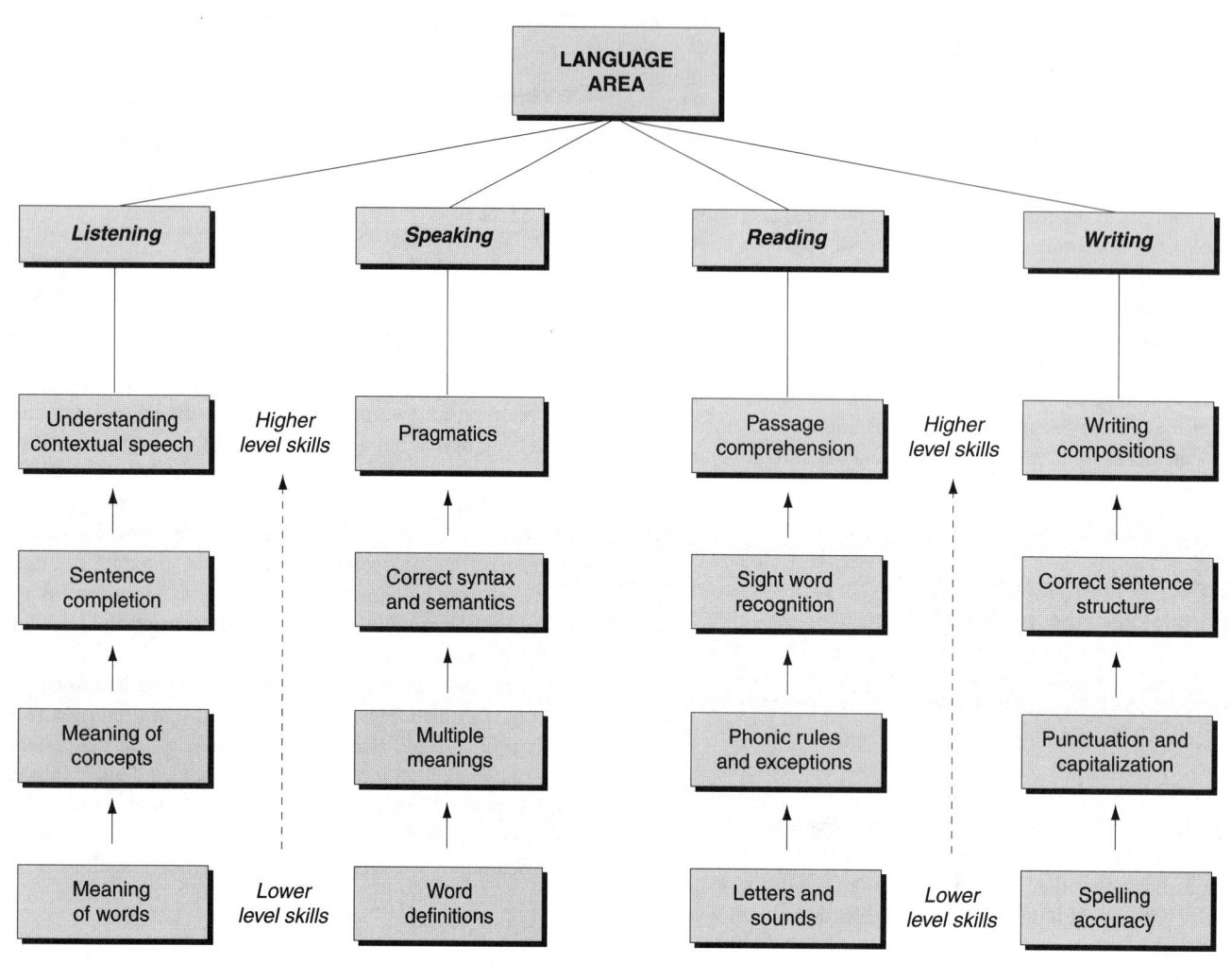

Figure 18-1. Primary skills in listening, speaking, reading, and writing arranged from highest to lowest level of functioning.

recall factual information from the passage, or draw inferences from the information provided.

The tests reviewed in this chapter represent tests of (a) receptive language, (b) expressive language, and (c) both receptive and expressive language. When expressive language skills are found to be deficient, it is important to evaluate receptive language.

Language tests have been criticized for being heavily culturally loaded. This criticism is, of course, accurate, but inescapable, because language tests assess mastery of both a particular language and the culture in which the language is used. As with all assessments, you must carefully consider the examinee's background in evaluating the assessment results.

This chapter does not review the Woodcock Language Proficiency Battery–Revised (WLPB–R; Woodcock, 1991), which is a subset of the tests included in the Woodcock-Johnson Psycho-Educational Battery–Revised, because the latter test, in its revised form (now called the Woodcock-Johnson III), is discussed in Chapter 17 of this text.

BOEHM TEST OF BASIC CONCEPTS–REVISED

The Boehm Test of Basic Concepts–Revised (BTBC–R; Boehm, 1986b) is a pictorial multiple-choice test designed to measure knowledge of concepts thought to be necessary for understanding verbal instructions and for academic achievement in the first few years of school. It covers ages 5 to 7 years. The test can be individually or group administered in either English or Spanish. The BTBC–R has two alternate forms (C and D). The test takes about 30 minutes to administer. An optional test, Applications, contains 26 items designed to assess the ability to attend to, remember, and coordinate two or more concepts and make higher order relational decisions. Applications takes about 10 minutes to administer.

Subtests

There are no subtests. However, the BTBC–R assesses three types of concepts: space, quantity, and time.

Scores

Scoring is 1 (correct) or 0 (incorrect). Derived scores include percentile ranks and normal curve equivalents for the English version. The manual allows you to compare the examinee's performance on individual items with that of the norm sample.

Standardization

The two forms of the test were administered to kindergarten, first-grade, and second-grade children at the beginning and end of the school year. For Form C, 5,577 children took the test at the beginning of the school year, and 5,326 children took it at the end of the school year. For Form D, 4,683 children took the test at the beginning of the school year, and 4,604 children took it at the end of the school year. For the Applications test, 6,923 children took the test at the beginning of the school year, and 6,232 children took it at the end of the school year. Students were selected from 19 cities across the Northeast, Midwest, Southwest, and West. The sample was weighted to match national school enrollment data published in 1978 and 1981 with respect to district size and region.

Reliability

Internal consistency split-half reliability coefficients range from .55 to .85 (Mdn r_{xx} = .77) for Form C, from .57 to .87 (Mdn r_{xx} = .77) for Form D, and from .72 to .82 (Mdn r_{xx} = .76) for the Applications test. Mean standard errors of measurement range from 1.1 to 2.5 (Mdn SEM = 1.5) for Forms C and D and from 1.5 to 1.8 (Mdn SEM = 1.7) for the Applications test. Test-retest reliabilities for 954 examinees who took the same test twice with a 1-week interval ranged from .75 to .88 (Mdn r_{tt} = .76) for Form C, .55 to .85 (Mdn r_{tt} = .79) for Form D, and .69 to .72 (Mdn r_{tt} = .71) for the Applications test. Alternate-form reliability for 625 examinees who took both Form C and Form D range from .65 to .82 (Mdn r_{tt} = .77).

Validity

Items were selected to reflect concepts related to understanding directions and other oral communications and under-

standing reading and mathematics. The 17 concurrent validity studies that compared the BTCB–R with such tests as the Comprehensive Test of Basic Skills, California Achievement Test, Iowa Test of Basic Skills, and HBJ Bookmark Reading Program reported validity coefficients ranging from .24 to .64 (Mdn r = .44).

Comment on the BTBC–R

The BTBC–R provides useful information about children's knowledge of basic concepts. The test has acceptable validity and minimally adequate reliability. The test needs to be renormed, especially if test scores are to be used to compare children's performance with that on other measures. Testing materials also need to be updated.

BOEHM TEST OF BASIC CONCEPTS–PRESCHOOL VERSION

The Boehm Test of Basic Concepts–Preschool Version (BTBC–PV; Boehm, 1986a) is a downward extension of the Boehm–R, designed for children ages 3 to 5 years. It takes about 15 minutes to administer. There are 52 test items that assess knowledge of 26 relational concepts considered necessary for achievement in the beginning years of school (e.g., size—tallest, direction—up, position in space—under, quantity—many, and time—after). The BTBC–PV is a pictorial multiple-choice test in which the child listens to a statement read aloud by the examiner and then points to one of three black-and-white drawings that best represents the correct response. Drawings are on an easel placed in front of the child.

Standardization

The test was standardized on 433 children from the four major regions of the United States. Sample characteristics closely matched the 1980 U.S. Census data. Parents' educational level was used to determine socioeconomic status.

Scores

Scoring is 1 (correct) or 0 (incorrect). Raw scores are converted to percentile ranks and T scores (M = 50, SD = 10). Norms are provided for five age groups: ages 3, 3½, 4, 4½, and 5.

Reliability

Split-half reliabilities range from .80 to .87 (Mdn r_{xx} = .86), and coefficient alphas range from .85 to .91 (Mdn r_{xx} = .87). Standard errors of measurement for the Total score range from 4.6 to 7.0 (Mdn SEM = 5.2).

Validity

Concurrent validity was studied first in a group of 29 preschool children (*M* age = 3-10) who took the BTBC–PV and Form L of the Peabody Picture Vocabulary Test–Revised (PPVT–R). The correlation between the two tests was .63. It was then studied in a group of children with language delays (*M* age = 4-4); the correlation between the BTBC–PV and Form M of the PPVT–R was .57.

Comment on the BTBC–PV

The BTBC–PV appears to be a useful downward extension of the BTBC–R, but more information is needed to evaluate its validity.

BRACKEN BASIC CONCEPT SCALE–REVISED

The Bracken Basic Concept Scale–Revised (BBCS–R; Bracken, 1998) is an individually administered test designed to assess knowledge of basic concepts in children between the ages of 2-6 and 7-11. The 11 subtests in the BBCS–R are designed to assess colors, letters, numbers and counting, sizes, comparisons, shapes, direction and position, self-social awareness, texture and material, quantity, and time and sequence.

All items are presented orally by the examiner, with the aid of a full-color easel. The child points to the appropriate response picture in a multiple-choice format. The test takes about 30 minutes to administer. Concept development is related to intellectual development and academic achievement and, therefore, is an important consideration in preschool assessment.

The BBCS–R is also available in Spanish. However, *the Spanish version can be used only as a criterion-referenced measure,* because the sample size of Spanish-speaking children (*N* = 193) was too small to derive norms.

Subtests

The 11 subtests are as follows:

- The Colors subtest measures the ability to identify primary colors and other basic color terms.
- The Letters subtest measures the ability to identify capital and lower-case letters.
- The Numbers and Counting subtest measures the ability to assign a number value to a set of objects and the ability to recognize single- and double-digit numbers.
- The Sizes subtest measures understanding of concepts of size.
- The Comparisons subtest measures the ability to match or differentiate objects based on one or more of their salient characteristics such as similarity or equality.
- The Shapes subtest measures the ability to identify linear, two-dimensional, and three-dimensional concepts.
- The Directions and Position subtest measures knowledge of terms related to direction.
- The Self-Social Awareness subtest measures knowledge of emotional values, kinship, and personal-social categories.
- The Texture and Materials subtest measures the ability to apply concepts that describe salient characteristics or attributes of an object.
- The Quantity subtest measures understanding of concepts of dimension and quantity.
- The Time and Sequence subtest measures understanding of events that occur along a temporal or sequential continuum and the speed or order of occurrence of those events.

Scores

Scoring is 1 (correct) or 0 (incorrect). There are no derived scores for the first six subtests, as these subtests are combined to form the School Readiness Composite. Derived scores for the School Readiness Composite and the total test Composite include scaled scores (*M* = 100, *SD* = 15), percentile ranks, confidence intervals, and concept-age equivalent scores. Derived scores for the last five subtests include scaled scores (*M* = 10, *SD* = 3), percentile ranks, confidence intervals, and concept-age equivalent scores.

Standardization

The BBCS–R was standardized in 1997. The sample contained 1,100 children between the ages of 2-6 and 8-0. Each age group between 2-6 and 5-11 spanned 2 months, and each included 50 children. Each age group between ages 6-0 and 8-11 spanned 6 months, and each included 100 children. The sample was representative of the U.S. population, based on the 1995 U.S. Census, and was stratified by age, gender, race/ethnicity, region, and parental education level.

Reliability

Internal consistency reliabilities range from .78 to .98 (*Mdn r_{xx}* = .94) for the subtests and from .96 to .99 (*Mdn r_{xx}* = .98) for the total test. Standard errors of measurement range from 0.4 to 1.4 (*Mdn* SEM = .75) for the subtests and from 1.6 to 2.8 (*Mdn* SEM = 1.85) for the total test. Test-retest reliability for 114 children who took the BBCS–R twice, with a 7- to 14-day interval, was .85 for the School Readiness Composite and .92 for the total test. Test-retest reliabilities for the last five subtests range from .73 to .79 (*Mdn r_{tt}* = .77).

Validity

Content for the test items was taken from commonly used tests of academic, language, and cognitive abilities, as well as from early-childhood language arts worksheets, workbooks, texts, and other curricular materials. Correlations between the subtests and the total test ranged from .68 to .92 (*Mdn r* = .86). Concurrent validity was assessed by correlating the total test Composite of the BBCS–R with other receptive language measures, such as the previous version of the test, Peabody Picture Vocabulary Test–III, Preschool Language Scale–Third Edition, Boehm Test of Basic Concepts–Revised, and Boehm Test of Basic Concepts–Preschool Version. Correlations for the total test Composite range from .79 to .90 (*Mdn r* = .84). Correlations between the BBCS–R total test score and the Wechsler Preschool and Primary Scale of Intelligence–Revised Verbal, Performance, and Full Scale IQ scores and the Differential Ability Scale Verbal, Nonverbal, and General Conceptual Ability scores range from .72 to .88 (*Mdn r* = .81).

Comment on the BBCS–R

The BBCS–R is an easy-to-administer test designed to assess basic concepts. It is available in both English and Spanish versions. Psychometric properties are good. Although subtest scores are useful, the School Readiness Composite and total test Composite are the most reliable. The current edition features new norms; updated, full-color pictures with better balance of gender and race; inclusion of the Sizes subtest in the School Readiness Composite; new items in all subtests to extend the age coverage; and a simpler procedure for obtaining basal levels. Panter (1997) observed that the BBCS–R is one of the best overall predictors of kindergarten children's academic growth.

PEABODY PICTURE VOCABULARY TEST–III

The Peabody Picture Vocabulary Test–III (PPVT–III; Dunn & Dunn, 1997) is an individually administered screening test of single-word listening comprehension for standard English. It is designed for individuals between 2-6 and 90+ years of age. There are two alternate forms, IIIA and IIIB. The test is not timed and takes about 10 minutes to administer. It is administered using an easel that holds the test items. Each test item consists of four black-and-white illustrations. The examinee selects the one picture that best represents the meaning of a stimulus word presented orally by the examiner.

In the PPVT–III, 54% of the words are from the former edition, and 46% are new words. The artwork used in the test items is balanced with respect to gender and race representation.

Scores

Scoring is 1 (correct) or 0 (incorrect). Raw scores can be converted to standard scores (*M* = 100, *SD* = 15), percentile ranks, stanines, normal curve equivalents, and age-equivalent scores.

Standardization

The PPVT–III was standardized nationally on a stratified sample of 2,725 examinees aged 2½ to 90+ years (2,000 children and adolescents and 725 persons over age 19), tested at 240 sites. All examinees took both forms, as well as the Expressive Vocabulary Test. Stratification variables included parents' education level (socioeconomic status), race/ethnicity, geographic region, and individuals receiving various special education services in approximately the same proportions as in the U.S. school population.

Reliability

The split-half internal consistency reliabilities for the 25 age groups range from .89 to .97 (*Mdn r_{xx}* = .94) for Form IIIA and from .86 to .96 (*Mdn r_{xx}* = .94) for Form IIIB. Mean standard errors of measurement range from 3.0 to 5.2 points (*Mdn* SEM = 3.7). Alternate-form reliability correlations range from .88 to .96 (*Mdn r_{tt}* = .94). Test-retest reliabilities for 226 randomly selected individuals in four age groups who took the test twice, with intervals of from 8 to 203 days (*M* = 42 days), range from .85 to .90 (*Mdn r_{tt}* = .89) for Form IIIA and from .87 to .91 (*Mdn r_{tt}* = .88) for Form IIIB.

Validity

Content validity was established by drawing items from a pool of standard English words that could be depicted by an illustration and selecting items representative of 20 common content areas such as animals, body parts, and actions. Construct validity was established by showing a steady increase in mean raw scores through the age group 51–60, with greater increases in the early years and more gradual changes in the later years.

Concurrent validity is satisfactory, as noted by acceptable correlations between the PPVT–III and Oral and Written Language Scales (for Form IIIA, *r* = .52 to .76, *Mdn r* = .73; for Form IIIB, *r* = .48 to .71, *Mdn r* = .68). Correlations between the PPVT–III and tests of cognitive abilities (Wechsler Intelligence Scale for Children–Third Edition, Kaufman Adolescent and Adult Intelligence Test, and Kaufman Brief Intelligence Test, 1990) range from .43 to .74 (*Mdn r* = .85).

Comment on the PPVT–III

The PPVT–III serves as a measure of receptive vocabulary. The test is easy to administer and score, has two forms, and has updated illustrations with good gender and ethnic balance. The test has excellent reliability and validity, although additional studies on the validity of the latest edition are needed. Because the PPVT–III measures only one facet of a child's ability repertoire, it is most appropriately used as a screening component in a more comprehensive assessment. Because all individuals in the standardization sample took both forms of the PPVT–III and the EVT, you can more easily make comparisons between the PPVT–III and the EVT.

TEST OF AUDITORY COMPREHENSION OF LANGUAGE–THIRD EDITION

The Test of Auditory Comprehension of Language–Third Edition (TACL–3; Carrow-Woolfolk, 1999a) is an individually administered test of auditory comprehension of receptive language. The test has three subtests designed to assess oral vocabulary, grammatical morphemes, and syntax and sentence structure. The TACL–3 can be administered to children between the ages of 3-0 and 9-11 and requires about 20 to 30 minutes to administer. The third edition represents a major revision and improvement over previous editions. Improvements include new norms, a 20% increase in test items, new stimulus materials, and more user-friendly directions and record booklet. All test materials are in an easel booklet that contains full-color drawings of the stimulus items.

Subtests

The three subtests are as follows:

- The Vocabulary subtest measures understanding of the literal and most common meanings of words in word classes such as nouns, verbs, adjectives, and adverbs.
- The Grammatical Morphemes subtest assesses knowledge of grammatical morphemes (such as prepositions), noun number and case, verb number and tense, noun-verb agreement, derivational suffixes, and pronouns.
- The Elaborated Phrases and Sentences subtest assess the ability to understand syntactically based word relations, elaborated phrase and sentence construction, and conjoined sentences.

Scores

Scoring is 1 (correct) or 0 (incorrect). Derived scores for each subtest include standard scores ($M = 10$, $SD = 3$), percentile ranks, and age-equivalent scores. The three subtests combine to create a Composite Quotient ($M = 100$, $SD = 15$).

Standardization

The standardization sample included 1,102 children aged 3-0 to 9-11 who resided in 24 states. Each age group comprised 127 to 192 children. The demographic characteristics of the sample matched those of the 1997 U.S. Census, as well as projected 2000 demographics.

Reliability

Internal consistency reliabilities across the seven age groups range from .84 to .95 (*Mdn* r_{xx} = .94) for the subtests and

from .95 to .97 (*Mdn* r_{xx} = .97) for the Composite score. Standard errors of measurement across the scale are 1.0 for the subtests and 3.0 for the Composite score. Test-retest reliability coefficients for 29 children who took the TACL–3 twice within a 2-week interval ranged from .86 to .96 (*Mdn* r_{tt} = .88) for the subtests; the test-retest coefficient for the Composite score was .97.

Validity

Content validity is good, based on theoretical and logical assumptions that the assessment of receptive language should involve three components: vocabulary, grammar, and sentence structure. Construct validity was demonstrated by showing increasing scores with age, differential difficulty levels of subtests, and discrimination among clinical groups. Subtest intercorrelations range from .57 to .65 (*Mdn* r = .58). A concurrent validity study was carried out on 23 examinees who took the TACL–3 and the Comprehensive Receptive and Expressive Vocabulary Test. Correlations ranged from .53 to .85 (*Mdn* r = .65) for the subtests and from .65 to .88 (*Mdn* r = .79) for the Composite.

Comment on the TACL–3

The TACL–3 is a well-standardized test of receptive language. It is an improvement over previous editions. However, additional validity studies are needed.

EXPRESSIVE VOCABULARY TEST

The Expressive Vocabulary Test (EVT; Williams, 1997) is an individually administered norm-referenced test of expressive vocabulary and word retrieval for children and adults from 2½ through 90 years. The EVT contains 190 items, requires one-word answers, is untimed, and takes about 10 to 25 minutes to administer.

All items except one use colored pictures as stimuli. The first 38 items require the examinee to name pictures or tell the color or number of items in the picture. The remaining 152 items require the examinee to give synonyms.

The EVT was co-normed with the PPVT–III. Since the PPVT–III measures receptive vocabulary, administering both tests provides information about receptive and expressive vocabulary.

Scores

Scoring is 1 (correct) or 0 (incorrect). Raw scores are converted to standard scores ($M = 100$, $SD = 15$), percentile ranks, normal curve equivalents ($M = 50$, $SD = 21.06$), stanines, and test-age equivalent scores.

Standardization

The EVT was standardized in 1995 and 1996 on a representative sample of 2,725 examinees between the ages of 2½ and 90 years. The sample matched the 1994 U.S. Census data with regard to age, gender, race/ethnicity, geographic region, and socioeconomic status. Children receiving special education services were represented in the norm sample in approximately the same proportions as in the U.S. school population.

Reliability

Internal consistency reliability coefficients range from .70 to .94 (Mdn r_{xx} = .83). Standard errors of measurement range from 2.6 to 6.2 (Mdn SEM = 4.6) in standard-score points. Test-retest reliability for a group of 226 randomly selected individuals in four age groups who took the test twice with a mean interval of 42 days ranged from .75 to .91 (Mdn r_{tt} = .79).

Validity

Items were selected based on frequency and common usage. Construct validity was established by showing mean and standard deviation increases in raw scores with age. Concurrent validity is satisfactory, as noted by acceptable correlations for 25 age groups between the EVT and the Peabody Picture Vocabulary Test–III (correlations range from .62 to .88, Mdn r = .79, with Form IIIA and from .61 to .88, Mdn r = .77, with Form IIIB). Correlations between the EVT and the Listening Comprehension and Oral Expression subtests of the Oral and Written Language Scales range from .23 to .81 (Mdn r = .54). Correlations between the EVT and the WISC–III, Kaufman Adolescent and Adult Intelligence Test, and Kaufman Brief Intelligence Test range from .62 to .79 (Mdn r = .73).

Comment on the EVT

The EVT has good reliability and validity, although additional studies on validity need to be conducted. Although the EVT is probably a good screening instrument for evaluating language ability, it should not be used as the sole measure for identifying a language delay or impairment. Co-norming of the EVT and the PPVT–III is a decided advantage—it allows comparison of expressive and receptive vocabulary ability with two tests normed on the same examinees.

TEST OF EARLY WRITTEN LANGUAGE–SECOND EDITION

The Test of Early Written Language–Second Edition (TEWL–2; Hresko, Herron, & Peak, 1996) contains two subtests that assess written language abilities of children ages 3-0 to 10-11. There are two equivalent forms (Form A and Form B). The TEWL–2 extends the range of the Test of Written Language–Third Edition to younger children, and it takes about 50 minutes to administer.

Subtests

The two subtests are as follows:

- The Basic Writing subtest measures understanding of basic writing, including directionality, punctuation, capitalization, proofing, spelling, sentence combining, syntatic maturity, conceptual vocabulary, and understanding of common activities.
- The Contextual Writing subtest measures the ability to construct a story from a picture. The story is then evaluated in areas such as format, cohesion, thematic maturity, ideation, and structure.

Scores

Scoring is 1 (correct) or 0 (incorrect) for the Basic Writing subtest. For the Contextual Writing subtest, scoring is on a scale of 0 (poor) to 3 (good) for each of 14 target writing abilities. Derived scores include age-equivalent scores, normal curve equivalents, percentile ranks, and quotients (M = 100, SD = 15). If both subtests are given, the two quotients are summed into a Global Writing Quotient (M = 100, SD = 15).

Standardization

The norm group consisted of 1,479 children from 33 states who were between the ages of 3 and 10. Data were collected between 1993 and 1995. Each age group comprised a minimum of 100 children. The sample was representative of the 1990 U.S. Census with regard to gender, urban/rural residence, race, geographic region, ethnicity, age, and disability status.

Reliability

Internal consistency reliabilities for subtests range from .90 to .99 (Mdn r_{xx} = .94) for both Form A and Form B. For the Composite score, they range from .95 to .97 (Mdn r_{xx} = .96) for Form A and from .96 to .97 (Mdn r_{xx} = .97) for Form B. Standard errors of measurement for the combined forms range from 1.5 to 4.7 (Mdn SEM = 3.7) for the subtests and from 2.6 to 3.4 (Mdn SEM = 3.0) for Composites. Test-retest reliabilities for 171 children between the ages of 4 and 9 who took the same form within a 14- to 21-day interval range from .82 to .92 (Mdn r_{tt} = .88) for the subtests and from .91 to .94 (Mdn r_{tt} = .93) for the Composite score. Alternate-form reliabilities range from .83 to .91 (Mdn r_{tt} = .87) for the subtests and from .91 to .93 (Mdn r_{tt} = .93) for the Composite score. Interscorer reliabilities for the Contextual Writing subtest range from .92 to .99 (*Mdn r* = .95).

Validity

Content validity was established by having items selected by subject matter experts and by a change in raw scores with age. Concurrent validity is satisfactory, as noted by correlations of from .24 to .77 (*Mdn r* = .48) between the Basic Writing subtest and comparable measures of writing. Similarly, correlations between the Contextual Writing subtest and comparable measures range from .29 to .90 (*Mdn r* = .47). Finally, correlations between the two subtests and various tests of cognitive abilities range from .22 to .73 (*Mdn r* = .43).

Comment on the TEWL–2

The psychometric properties of the TEWL–2 are moderate to strong. The second edition has several improvements over the first edition. These include two equivalent forms, an increase in the number of test items, and coverage of a wider age range.

TEST OF WRITTEN LANGUAGE– THIRD EDITION

The Test of Written Language–Third Edition (TOWL–3; Hammill & Larsen, 1996) is a test of expressive language for children ages 7-6 to 17-11. It contains eight subtests that measure writing vocabulary, spelling, style, sentence construction, sentence combining, use of language, use of writing conventions, and story construction. It can be administered to either groups or individuals. With the exception of Story Construction, the subtests have no time limits; Story Construction has a 15-minute time limit. The test takes about 90 minutes to administer. Two alternate equivalent forms (A and B) are available.

Testing begins with the examinee writing a story based on a picture. The first five subtests are then administered. The last three subtests are based on an analysis of the story written at the beginning of testing.

The TOWL–3 is similar in format to the TOWL–2 and uses the same stimulus pictures, but some of the subtests have been shortened and simplified.

Subtests

The eight subtests are as follows:

- The Vocabulary subtest measures the ability to use a stimulus word in a written sentence.
- The Spelling subtest measures spelling accuracy in sentences written from dictation.

- The Style subtest measures skills in punctuation and capitalization and in using sentence fragments.
- The Logical Sentences subtest measures editing skills.
- The Sentence Combining subtest measures the ability to rewrite two or more short sentences into a single grammatically correct sentence.
- The Contextual Conventions subtest measures capitalization, punctuation, spelling, and paragraph indents.
- The Contextual Language subtest measures the quality of vocabulary, sentence construction, and grammar.
- The Story Construction subtest measures the quality of the plot, prose, sequence, and character development of the examinee's story and its interest to the reader.

Scores

The first five subtests are scored 1 (correct) or 0 (incorrect). The last three subtests are scored on a scale that ranges from 0 (no response or lowest quantity or quality of response) to 3 (highest quantity or quality of response) for each scoring category. For the first five subtests, testing begins with the first item and is discontinued after three consecutive incorrect items. There are no discontinuance procedures for the last three subtests. Derived scores include percentile ranks and standard scores (*M* = 10, *SD* = 3) for the subtests. Three Composite scores are formed by combining various subtest scores: Contrived Writing Composite (the first five subtests), Spontaneous Writing Composite (the last three subtests), and Overall Writing Composite (all subtests). Composites yield standard scores (*M* = 100, *SD* = 15).

Standardization

The TOWL–3 was normed in 1995 on a sample of 2,217 examinees in grades 2 to 12, residing in 25 states. Examinees with disabilities who were enrolled in general classes were included in the sample. The sample matched 1990 U.S. Census data with regard to gender, urban/rural residence, race, ethnicity, geographic area, educational attainment of the parents, and disabling condition.

Reliability

Internal consistency reliabilities for the subtests range from .60 to .92 (*Mdn* r_{xx} = .84) for Form A and from .60 to .94 (*Mdn* r_{xx} = .84) for Form B. Reliabilities for Composite scores are the same on both forms and range from .89 to .97 (*Mdn* r_{xx} = .95). The standard error of measurement for all subtests is 1.0 standard-score point. For the Composite scores, the SEM is 3.0 standard-score points for both Contrived Writing and Overall Writing and 5.0 standard-score points for Spontaneous Writing. Alternate-form reliabilities range from .60 to .94 (*Mdn* r_{tt} = .84) for the subtests and from .76 to .96 (*Mdn* r_{tt} = .89) for the Composite scores. Interscorer reliabilities for two individuals who each scored 38 protocols ranged from .83 to .97 (*Mdn r* = .94) for the first five subtests, from .80 to .92 (*Mdn r* = .88) for the last three subtests, and from .90 to .97 (*Mdn r* = .97) for the Composite scores.

Validity

The content of the TOWL–3 is related to that of other tests assessing similar skills. Test items demonstrate acceptable levels of difficulty. Mean scores for the subtests tend to increase gradually between ages 7 and 13 years. Between ages 14 and 17, mean scores change little. Subtest intercorrelations range from .33 to .75 (*Mdn r* = .56). Concurrent validity is satisfactory, as noted by acceptable correlations between the TOWL–3 subtests and the Writing subtest of the Comprehensive Scales of Student Abilities (CSSA) for 76 elementary students. Correlations range from .34 to .69 (*Mdn r* = .46) for Form A and from .34 to .67 (*Mdn r* = .52) for Form B. Correlations between the TOWL–3 Composites and the Writing subtest of the CSSA range from .46 to .55 (*Mdn r* = .49) for Form A and from .50 to .59 (*Mdn r* = .59) for Form B. Correlations between the TOWL–3 (combined forms) and the Reading, Math, and General Facts subtests of the CSSA for the same population of 76 examinees range from .34 to .69 (*Mdn r* = .50) for the subtests and from .52 to .70 (*Mdn r* = .61) for the Composite. Correlations between the three Composites of the TOWL–3 and the three Composites of the Comprehensive Test of Nonverbal Intelligence range from .31 to .60 (*Mdn r* = .54) for Form A and from .30 to .57 (*Mdn r* = .43) for Form B.

Comment on the TOWL–3

The TOWL–3 has moderate to good psychometric properties, although more validity studies are needed. The test is useful in evaluating important components of writing. An attractive feature is its use as a group-administered test. Administering and scoring the test is relatively straightforward except for scoring the Style and Logical Sentences subtests, where directions are ambiguous. A computer scoring system that generates a report is available.

TEST OF WRITTEN SPELLING– FOURTH EDITION

The Test of Written Spelling–Fourth Edition (TWS–4; Larsen, Hammill, & Moats, 1999) is a norm-referenced test of written spelling designed for students in grades 1 through 12. The TWS–4 can be either individually administered or group administered and requires about 20 minutes to complete. The TWS–4 has two equivalent forms (A and B), and each form contains 50 words arranged in order of relative difficulty, from easy to hard. The examinee writes words dictated by the examiner. The format closely duplicates that of classroom spelling tests.

Scores

Scoring is 1 (correct) or 0 (incorrect). The test is discontinued after five consecutive misspelled words. Derived scores include standard scores (*M* = 100, *SD* = 15), percentile ranks, spelling ages, and grade-equivalent scores.

Copyright © 1997 by John P. Wood.

Standardization

The standardization group for the TWS–4 was the same as for the TWS–3. For the TWS–3, the standardization group contained 4,097 students from the 1986 norming of the TWS–2 and 855 new cases tested in 1993, for a total of 4,952. No new cases were added to norm the TWS–4. The characteristics of the normative sample matched the 1997 U.S. Census data with regard to gender, urban and rural residence, race, geographic area, and ethnicity. With the exception of the 18-year-old group ($N = 85$), all age groups had from 147 to 593 individuals.

Reliability

Internal consistency reliabilities range from .87 to .96 ($Mdn\ r_{xx}$ = .95) for Form A and from .89 to .97 ($Mdn\ r_{xx}$ = .94) for Form B. Standard errors of measurement for both forms range from 3.0 to 5.0 points (Mdn SEM = 4.0). Alternate-form reliabilities, based on the entire sample, range from .86 to .98 ($Mdn\ r_{tt}$ = .97). Test-retest reliabilities for 41 first-, third-, and sixth-grade students who took the same form twice within a 2-week interval range from .94 to .96 ($Mdn\ r_{tt}$ = .95) for Form A and from .95 to .97 ($Mdn\ r_{tt}$ = .96) for Form B. Interscorer reliability for two individuals who each scored 108 protocols independently was .99 for both forms.

Validity

Content validity is acceptable, based on the selection of words from basal series used in schools and from a core vocabulary list. Construct validity is supported by increases in difficulty level with age. Concurrent validity was studied in a sample of 50 fourth- and fifth-graders who took the TWS–4, Metropolitan Achievement Test, Norm-Referenced Assessment Program for Texas, and Texas Assessment of Academic Skills. Correlations between spelling tests ranged from .59 to .86 ($Mdn\ r$ = .73). Correlations between the TWS–4 and other areas such as reading, mathematics, writing, and language ranged from .28 to .74 ($Mdn\ r$ = .58) for Form A and from .24 to .75 ($Mdn\ r$ = .56) for Form B. Correlations between the TWS–4 and the Otis-Lennon School Ability Index for the same 50 students were .56 for both forms.

Comment on the TWS–4

The TWS–4 is an easy-to-administer written spelling test of 50 words that can be administered to individuals or to a whole class. The test requires examinees to write words, which is preferred over a multiple-choice format. The 1999 version is an improved version. It contains 50 rather than 100 words and has two alternate forms. The standardization sample is less than ideal because individuals were tested at different times. Reliability is acceptable, but more validity research is needed. Overall, the TWS–4 may be an acceptable instrument for assessing written spelling among students from age

Copyright © 1999 by John P. Wood.

6 to 18, but the procedure for obtaining the norm group is questionable.

COMPREHENSIVE RECEPTIVE AND EXPRESSIVE VOCABULARY TEST

The Comprehensive Receptive and Expressive Vocabulary Test (CREVT; Wallace & Hammill, 1994) is an individually administered test designed to assess both receptive and expressive oral vocabulary. It has two equivalent forms, A and B, each of which has two subtests. The CREVT is suitable for examinees ages 4-0 to 17-11 and requires about 20 to 30 minutes to administer. An easel containing full-color photographs is used to administer the Expressive Vocabulary subtest.

Subtests

The two subtests are as follows:

- The Receptive Vocabulary subtest measures vocabulary knowledge.
- The Expressive Vocabulary subtest measures the ability to verbally define words read aloud by the examiner.

Scores

Scoring is 1 (correct) or 0 (incorrect). Derived scores for the subtests and for the General Vocabulary Composite include standard scores ($M = 100$, $SD = 15$), percentile ranks, and age-equivalent scores.

Standardization

The norming sample consisted of 1,920 participants in 33 states who ranged in age from 4-0 to 17-11 and attended regular classes. The sample size of the age groups ranged from 60 to 252. Characteristics of the normative sample with regard to sex, residence, race, ethnicity, geographic area, and disability condition reflected those reported in the 1990 U.S. Census. Specific dates during which the test was administered to the norm group were not reported.

Reliability

Internal consistency reliabilities for the subtests range from .84 to .97 (*Mdn* r_{xx} = .90) for Form A and from .85 to .98 (*Mdn* r_{xx} = .92) for Form B. For the General Vocabulary Composite, the reliabilities range from .90 to .98 (*Mdn* r_{xx} = .95) for Form A and from .92 to .98 (*Mdn* r_{xx} = .95) for Form B. Standard errors of measurement range from 2.1 to 6.0 (*Mdn* SEM = 4.7) for the subtests and from 2.1 to 4.7 (*Mdn* SEM = 3.6) for the Composite. Alternate-form reliabilities range from .74 to .97 (*Mdn* r_{tt} = .91). Test-retest reliabilities for 27 kindergarten children who took the same form twice within a 2-month interval ranged from .79 to .87 (*Mdn* r_{tt} = .84). Among 28 twelfth-graders who took the same form twice within 2 weeks, the range was from .79 to .94 (*Mdn* r_{tt} = .87). Reliabilities were not calculated for the Composite score. Interscorer reliabilities for 42 test records were .99 for both forms of the Receptive Vocabulary subtest, Expressive Vocabulary subtest, and General Vocabulary Composite.

Validity

Content validity of the CREVT is acceptable, as items were selected from several sources that present vocabulary lists. Item difficulty is reflected by generally increasing mean scores at each age level through age 13, but little change afterwards. Correlations between subtests and forms range from .74 to .77 (*Mdn* r = .77). Concurrent validity is acceptable, as noted by correlations of .64 to .97 (*Mdn* r = .83) between the CREVT and other language tests.

Comment on the CREVT

The CREVT is an easy-to-administer test of receptive and expressive vocabulary for children ages 4 to 17 years. The availability of equivalent forms and the short time required to administer the test are positive factors. The test also can be administered via a computer. Additional validity studies are needed, especially with students without disabilities. A valuable feature of the test is that it offers measures of both receptive and expressive vocabulary normed on the same sample.

ORAL AND WRITTEN LANGUAGE SCALES

The Oral and Written Language Scales (OWLS; Carrow-Woolfolk, 1995) is an individually administered test of receptive and expressive language. It has three subtests. The Listening Comprehension and Oral Expression subtests cover ages 3 to 21; the Written Expression subtest covers ages 5 to 21. Testing time is about 5 to 15 minutes for Listening Comprehension, 10 to 25 minutes for Oral Expression, and 10 to 40 minutes for Written Expression.

The test stimuli for the Listening Comprehension and Oral Expression subtests are black-and-white pencil drawings presented on easels. For the Written Expression subtest, the examinee writes his or her responses in a test booklet.

Subtests

The three subtests are as follows:

- The Listening Comprehension subtest measures the abilities needed to understand spoken language, including vocabulary knowledge, grammar skills, and higher order thinking skills.
- The Oral Expression subtest measures the ability to understand and use spoken language.
- The Written Expression subtest measures the ability to apply writing conventions.

Scores

Scoring is 1 (correct) or 0 (incorrect) on the Listening Comprehension and Oral Expression subtests. On the Written Expression subtest, each item is scored 0 to 10 points. The score is determined by comparing the examinee's responses with examples in the manual.

Standard scores ($M = 100$, $SD = 15$), percentile ranks, normal curve equivalents, stanines, and test-age equivalent scores are provided for the subtests and for two Composites—the Oral Composite, which is a combination of the Listening and Oral Expression subtests, and the Language Composite, which is a combination of all three subtests. A computer program is available that provides a score profile, suggested exercises by grade range, a score narrative, and item responses. Supplementary scoring forms are included that allow for detailed item analysis on each of the three scales.

Standardization

The OWLS was normed on a sample of 1,795 children and young adults tested at 74 sites nationwide. The sample was stratified to match the 1991 U.S. Census on gender, race/ethnicity, region, and mother's education level. Children with disabilities also were included in the sample.

Reliability

Internal consistency reliabilities range from .75 to .89 ($Mdn\ r_{xx}$ = .82) for the Listening Comprehension scale, from .76 to .91 ($Mdn\ r_{xx}$ = .87) for the Oral Expression scale, and from .77 to .94 ($Mdn\ r_{xx}$ = .87) for the Written Expression scale. Internal consistency reliabilities for the Oral Composite range from .86 to .94 ($Mdn\ r_{xx}$ = .91). For the Language Composite, internal consistency reliabilities range from .90 to .95 ($Mdn\ r_{xx}$ = .93). Standard errors of measurement range from 5.0 to 7.5 (Mdn SEM = 6.4) for the Listening Comprehension scale, from 4.5 to 7.3 (Mdn SEM = 5.4) for the Oral Expression scale, and from 3.7 to 7.2 (Mdn SEM = 5.4) for the Written Expression scale. Test-retest reliabilities for 137 randomly selected individuals (mean test-retest interval of 8 weeks) range from .58 to .74 ($Mdn\ r_{tt}$ = .70) for Listening Comprehension, from .65 to .80 ($Mdn\ r_{tt}$ = .79) for Oral Expression, and from .76 to .85 ($Mdn\ r_{tt}$ = .76) for the Oral Composite. Test-retest reliabilities in a sample of 84 individuals (mean test-retest interval of 8 weeks) range from .66 to .83 ($Mdn\ r_{tt}$ = .75) for Written Expression and from .81 to .83 for Language Composite ($Mdn\ r_{tt}$ = .82). Interscorer reliabilities on all subtests and Composites range from .90 to .99 ($Mdn\ r$ = .95).

Validity

The content of the OWLS is highly related to content found in classrooms. Construct validity was established by showing steady increases in mean raw scores for the three subtests across the 13 age groups in the sample. Correlations between Listening Comprehension, Oral Expression, and the Oral Composite range from .30 to .79 ($Mdn\ r$ = .64). Concurrent validity between the OWLS Oral Composite and other tests of receptive and expressive language range from .35 to .84 ($Mdn\ r$ = .66). Correlations between the OWLS Oral Composite and tests of academic achievement range from .44 to .89 ($Mdn\ r$ = .75). Correlations between the OWLS Listening Comprehension and Oral Expression and tests of intelligence range from .41 to .74 ($Mdn\ r$ = .58).

Comment on the OWLS

The Oral and Written Language Scales is an acceptable measure of receptive and expressive language. The test has good reliability and validity. Overall, this is an easy-to-use and well-constructed test that can assist in determining delays or disorders in language. It can also be used to compare achievement scores in reading and other academic areas with listening comprehension, oral expression, and written expression scores.

The manuals are clear, explicit, and helpful, and the supplementary item-analysis forms are valuable for interpretation. The multiple-choice pictorial format of the OWLS Listening Comprehension Scale is useful for assessing language skills in children who cannot speak. The use of multiple direct and indirect items, rather than a single writing sample, on the Written Expression scale is helpful for students who write only a few words. The manuals also present useful information on significant differences among the three scales as well as base rates of differences.

TEST OF EARLY LANGUAGE DEVELOPMENT–THIRD EDITION

The Test of Early Language Development–Third Edition (TELD–3; Hresko, Reid, Hammill, 1999) is an individually

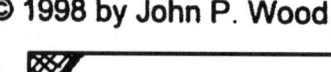

Copyright © 1998 by John P. Wood.

administered test of oral language designed for children between the ages of 2-0 and 7-11. It has two equivalent forms (Form A and B), each of which contains two subtests. The test is untimed and requires about 15 to 40 minutes to administer.

Subtests

The two subtests are as follows:

- The Receptive Language subtest measures understanding of spoken language.
- The Expressive Language subtest measures semantic and syntactic use of oral language.

Scores

Scoring is 1 (correct) or 0 (incorrect). Derived scores for the subtests and the Spoken Language Quotient are standard scores ($M = 100$, $SD = 15$), age-equivalent scores, and percentile ranks.

Standardization

The TELD–3 was normed on a sample of 2,217 children residing in 35 states. Data were collected in two time periods: from 1,309 examinees who took the TELD–2 in 1990–91 and from 908 additional examinees tested in 1996–97. The sample population is representative of the nation, based on the 1997 U.S. Census, with regard to geographical area, gender, race, ethnicity, family income, educational attainment of parents, and disabilities. The age groups consisted of 226 to 494 children.

Reliability

Internal consistency reliabilities for the subtests range from .80 to .95 (Mdn r_{xx} = .92) for Form A and from .81 to .95 (Mdn r_{xx} = .93) for Form B. Reliabilities for the Spoken Language Quotient are the same for both forms and range from .89 to .97 (Mdn r_{xx} = .95). Internal consistency reliabilities for the subtests and the Language Quotient range from .82 to .97 (Mdn r_{xx} = .96). Standard errors of measurement range from 3.0 to 7.0 (Mdn SEM = 4.0) for the subtests and from 3.0 to 5.0 (Mdn SEM = 3.0) for the Spoken Language Composite. Alternate-form reliabilities range from .79 to .94 (Mdn r_{tt} = .83) for Receptive Language and from .80 to .91 (Mdn r_{tt} = .89) for Expressive Language. Test-retest reliabilities for 116 examinees who took the same form with a 2-week interval ranged from .80 to .94 (Mdn r_{tt} = .89) for Form A and from .83 to .98 (Mdn r_{tt} = .92) for Form B.

Validity

Content validity and construct validity of the TELD–3 appear to be satisfactory. Mean scores increase gradually and steadily with each succeeding age group for both subtests and both forms, reflecting item difficulty. Concurrent validity studies have compared performance on the TELD–3 and several other tests designed to measure similar skills: Communication Abilities Diagnostic Test, Clinical Evaluation of Language Fundamentals–Preschool, Expressive One Word Picture Vocabulary Test, Test of Early Language Development–2, Test of Language Development: Primary–3, Peabody Picture Vocabulary Test–Revised, Preschool Language Scale–3, and Receptive One Word Picture Vocabulary Test. Correlations range from .30 to .87 (Mdn r = .56) for the subtests and from .38 to .92 (Mdn r = .64) for the Spoken Language Quotient. Correlations with intelligence tests range from .41 to .76 (Mdn r = .58).

Comment on the TELD–3

The TELD–3 is useful for assessing young children's receptive and expressive language ability. Psychometric properties of the test are moderate to good, but the mixture of norms raises some serious concerns.

TEST OF ADOLESCENT AND ADULT LANGUAGE–THIRD EDITION

The Test of Adolescent and Adult Language–Third Edition (TOAL–3; Hammill, Brown, Larsen, & Wiederholt, 1994) is designed to assess language functioning in adolescents and young adults between the ages of 12-0 and 24-11. The TOAL–3 has eight subtests that assess listening vocabulary and grammar, speaking vocabulary and grammar, reading vocabulary and grammar, and writing vocabulary and grammar. Six of the eight subtests can be group administered. The TOAL–3 requires about 2 hours to administer.

Subtests

The eight subtests are as follows:

- The Listening Vocabulary subtest measures the ability to understand the meaning of individually spoken words.
- The Listening Grammar subtest measures the understanding that spoken sentences using different grammatical or syntactical structures can have similar meanings.
- The Speaking Vocabulary subtest measures the ability to use individual words properly in spoken sentences.
- The Speaking Grammar subtest measures short-term memory for sentences.
- The Reading Vocabulary subtest measures concept formation.
- The Reading Grammar subtest measures the understanding that written sentences using different grammatical or syntactical structures can have similar meanings.
- The Writing Vocabulary subtest measures the ability to use individual words properly in written sentences.

- The Writing Grammar subtest measures the ability to write grammatically and syntactically acceptable sentences.

Scores

Scoring is 1 (correct) or 0 (incorrect). Derived scores for subtests include standard scores ($M = 10$, $SD = 3$) and Composite Quotients ($M = 100$, $SD = 15$). Various subtests combine to form 11 Composite Quotients ($M = 100$, $SD = 15$; see Table 18-1). The General Language Quotient is the best estimate of overall language ability. Grade- and age-equivalent scores are not provided for subtests or for the Composite Quotients.

Standardization

The TOAL–3 was normed on 3,056 individuals ranging in age from 12 to 24 years who took the test between 1980 and 1993. Between ages 12 and 18, groups included from 136 to 536 individuals. For ages 19 through 24, there were from 60 to 82 individuals per group. Characteristics of the sample with regard to gender, residence, race, ethnicity, geographic area, and postsecondary educational status closely matched the 1990 U.S. Census.

Reliability

Internal consistency reliabilities range from .80 to .98 ($Mdn\ r_{xx}$ = .91) for the subtests and from .89 to .98 ($Mdn\ r_{xx}$ = .95) for the Composites. The standard errors of measurement are 1.0 for all subtests and from 2.0 to 5.0 (Mdn SEM = 3.0) for Composite scores. Test-retest reliability was assessed in two studies; one involved 52 11- to 14-year-olds who took the TOAL twice within a 2-week interval, and the other involved 59 college participants ages 18 to 24 who also took the TOAL–3 twice within a 2-week interval. Test-retest reliabilities range from .78 to .90 ($Mdn\ r_{tt}$ = .81) for the subtests and from .82 to .98 ($Mdn\ r_{tt}$ = .92) for the Composite scores. Mean interscorer reliabilities among six raters who scored 15 protocols for the three most subjective subtests were .87 for Writing/Vocabulary, .96 for Speaking/Vocabulary, and .98 for Writing/Grammar.

Validity

Content validity is acceptable, as the content of the items shows a considerable relationship with other tests of language. Item discrimination indices are good. Correlations among subtests range from .11 to .66 ($Mdn\ r$ = .48). Concurrent validity studies involving the TOAL–3 are not reported. However, given the similar nature of the current and past versions, it is likely that current validity indices for this edition are generally similar to those of the former edition.

Table 18-1
Composites on the TOAL–3

Composite	Subtest
Listening	Listening/Vocabulary
	Listening/Grammar
Speaking	Speaking/Vocabulary
	Speaking/Grammar
Reading	Reading/Vocabulary
	Reading/Grammar
Writing	Writing/Vocabulary
	Writing/Grammar
Spoken Language	Listening/Vocabulary
	Listening/Grammar
	Speaking/Vocabulary
	Speaking/Grammar
Written Language	Reading/Vocabulary
	Reading/Grammar
	Writing/Vocabulary
	Writing/Grammar
Vocabulary	Listening/Vocabulary
	Speaking/Vocabulary
	Reading/Vocabulary
	Writing/Vocabulary
Grammar	Listening/Grammar
	Speaking/Grammar
	Reading/Grammar
	Writing/Grammar
Receptive Language	Listening/Vocabulary
	Listening/Grammar
	Reading/Vocabulary
	Reading/Grammar
Expressive Language	Speaking/Vocabulary
	Speaking/Grammar
	Writing/Vocabulary
	Writing/Grammar
General Language	All eight subtests

Comment on the TOAL–3

The TOAL–3 is one of a few tests available that assess all four basic components of oral language: listening, speaking, reading, and writing. Being available for group administration and assessing a wide range of language skills are features that make the TOAL–3 attractive. A computerized scoring and reporting system is available. The test has some limitations, though. Test administration can take almost 2 hours, and moving back and forth between the Test Booklet and Answer Booklet can be cumbersome. The norms for the current version were collected over a 13-year period, between 1980 and 1993, making the norm group difficult to interpret. The difference in mean raw scores on subtests between 12- and 24-year-olds is quite small, and the correlations between age and subtest scores are low, particularly for the 17- to 24-year-old groups. Therefore, it may be difficult to differentiate among age groups for older students. Finally, the manual fails to report validity studies for the current version.

TEST OF LANGUAGE DEVELOPMENT– PRIMARY: THIRD EDITION

The Test of Language Development–Primary: Third Edition (TOLD–P: 3; Newcomer & Hammill, 1997) is an individually administered test of receptive and expressive oral language development designed for children between the ages of 4-0 and 8-11. The six core subtests take 30 to 60 minutes to administer, and the three supplementary subtests take about 30 minutes to administer.

Subtests

The nine subtests are as follows:

Core Subtests

- The Picture Vocabulary subtest measures vocabulary knowledge.
- The Relational Vocabulary subtest measures the ability to understand and orally express the relationship between two words.
- The Oral Vocabulary subtest measures the ability to define words.
- The Grammatic Understanding subtest measures the ability to comprehend the meaning of sentences.
- The Sentence Imitation subtest measures the ability to repeat sentences.
- The Grammatic Completion subtest measures the ability to recognize, understand, and use common English morphological forms.

Supplementary Subtests

- The Word Discrimination subtest measures the ability to recognize differences in speech sounds.
- The Phonemic Analysis subtest measures the ability to segment words into smaller phonemic units.
- The Word Articulation subtest measures the ability to utter important speech sounds.

Scores

Scoring is 1 (correct) or 0 (incorrect). Derived scores include age-equivalent scores, percentile ranks, and standard scores

Copyright © 1999 by John P. Wood.

($M = 10$, $SD = 3$). Six Composite Quotients ($M = 100$, $SD = 15$) are also available (see Table 18-2): Listening, Organizing, Speaking, Semantics, Syntax, and Spoken Language.

Standardization

The standardization sample, tested in 1996, contained 1,000 children between 4 and 8 years of age, residing in 28 states. Each age group had from 107 to 258 individuals. The sample matched the 1990 U.S. Census data with regard to geographic region, gender, race, residence, ethnicity, family income, educational attainment of parents, and disabling condition.

Reliability

Internal consistency reliabilities range from .75 to .94 (Mdn r_{xx} = .88) for the subtests and from .89 to .96 (Mdn r_{xx} = .92) for the Composite scores. Standard errors of measurement range from .6 to 1.5 (Mdn SEM = 1.0) for the subtests and from 3.0 to 5.0 (Mdn SEM = 4.2) for the Composite scores. Test-retest reliabilities for 33 children in kindergarten through second grade who took the test twice within a 4-month interval range from .77 to .90 (Mdn r_{tt} = .84) for the subtests and from .82 to .92 (Mdn r_{tt} = .89) for the Composite scores. Interscorer reliability for two individuals who each independently scored 50 randomly selected test records was .99 on all subtests and Composite scores.

Table 18-2
Composites on the TOLD–P: 3

Composite	Subtest
Spoken Language Quotient (SLQ)	Picture Vocabulary Relational Vocabulary Oral Vocabulary Grammatic Understanding Sentence Imitation Grammatic Completion
Listening Quotient (LiQ)	Picture Vocabulary Grammatic Understanding
Organizing Quotient (OrQ)	Relational Vocabulary Sentence Imitation
Speaking Quotient (SpQ)	Oral Vocabulary Grammatic Completion
Semantics Quotient (SeQ)	Picture Vocabulary Relational Vocabulary Oral Vocabulary
Syntax Quotient (SyQ)	Grammatic Understanding Sentence Imitation Grammatic Completion

Validity

Content validity for the TOLD–P: 3 was established by using item analysis, opinions of experts, and differential item functioning to show the absence of bias in the test items. Mean scores across all subtests increase gradually with each age group, and the correlations between age and subtest scores range from .32 to .62 (*Mdn r* = .55). Correlations between subtests range from .37 to .59 (*Mdn r* = .46) for the six core subtests and from .11 to .42 (*Mdn r* = .17) for the three supplemental subtests. One concurrent validity study showed satisfactory correlations between the TOLD–P: 3 and the Bankson Language Test–Second Edition (*r* = .52 to .97; *Mdn r* = .81).

Comment on the TOLD–P: 3

The TOLD–P: 3 is designed to assess young children's receptive and expressive spoken language competence with respect to semantics, syntax, and phonology. It has acceptable psychometric properties. The addition of two new subtests to assess phonological awareness is a benefit. All pictures have been redrawn to present a more contemporary and appealing

look to children. Each test item was reevaluated using classical item analysis and the newer differential item functioning analysis (to locate and eliminate biased items). Optional software packages for scoring and reporting are available for computer use. Additional validity studies are needed.

TEST OF LANGUAGE DEVELOPMENT–INTERMEDIATE: THIRD EDITION

The Test of Language Development–Intermediate: Third Edition (TOLD–I: 3; Newcomer & Hammill, 1997) is an individually administered test of receptive and expressive language designed for children ages 8-0 to 12-11. The test, which contains six subtests, requires about 30 to 60 minutes to administer. In all subtests except one, the examiner reads the stimulus items and the examinee responds orally. The only exception is the Picture Vocabulary subtest, where the stimuli consist of pictures.

Subtests

The six subtests are as follows:

- The Sentence Combining subtest measures the ability to form a complex sentence from two or more simple sentences.
- The Picture Vocabulary subtest measures vocabulary knowledge.
- The Word Ordering subtest measures the ability to speak in a syntactically correct manner.
- The Generals subtest measures concept formation.
- The Grammatic Comprehension subtest measures the ability to recognize incorrect grammar in spoken sentences.
- The Malapropisms subtest measures the ability to use semantics.

Scores

Scoring is 1 (correct) or 0 (incorrect). Derived scores for the subtests include age-equivalent scores, percentile ranks, and standard scores (*M* = 10, *SD* = 3). There are also five Composite Quotients (*M* = 100, *SD* = 15): Syntax, Semantics, Listening, Speaking, and Spoken Language (see Table 18-3).

Standardization

The standardization group contained 779 children, from age 8 to 12, who lived in 23 states. There were 104 to 201 children in each age group. Tested in 1996, the sample matched the 1990 U.S. Census with regard to geographic region, gender, race, residence, ethnicity, family income, educational attainment of parents, and disabling conditions.

Table 18-3
Composites on the TOLD–I: 3

Composite	Subtest
Spoken Language	Sentence Combining
	Picture Vocabulary
	Word Ordering
	Generals
	Grammatic Comprehension
	Malapropisms
Syntax	Sentence Combining
	Word Ordering
	Grammatic Comprehension
Semantics	Picture Vocabulary
	Generals
	Malapropisms
Listening	Picture Vocabulary
	Malapropisms
	Grammatic Comprehension
Speaking	Sentence Combining
	Word Ordering
	Generals

Reliability

Internal consistency reliabilities range from .80 to .97 ($Mdn\ r_{xx}$ = .88) for the subtests and from .92 to .96 ($Mdn\ r_{xx}$ = .94) for the Composite scores. Standard errors of measurement are 1.0 for the subtests, 3.0 for the Spoken Language and Listening Composites, and 4.0 for the Speaking, Semantics, and Syntax Composites. Test-retest correlations for a sample of 55 fourth-, fifth-, and sixth-graders who took the test twice within a 1-week interval range from .83 to .94 ($Mdn\ r_{tt}$ = .91) for the subtests and from .94 to .96 ($Mdn\ r_{tt}$ = .94) for the Composite scores. Interscorer reliabilities of two staff members who scored 50 test records randomly selected from the sample ranged from .94 to .97 ($Mdn\ r$ = .96).

Validity

Content validity was established using test item and testing format analysis, opinions of experts, item validity, and differential functioning analysis (to show the absence of bias in the test items). Mean scores across all subtests increase gradually with each age group, and the correlations between age and subtest scores range from .32 to .47 ($Mdn\ r$ = .43). Correlations between the subtests range from .38 to .63 ($Mdn\ r$ = .54). One concurrent validity study reported correlations ranging from .74 to .88 ($Mdn\ r$ = .83) for the Composite

scores between the TOLD–I: 3 and the Test of Adolescent and Adult Language–Third Edition.

Comment on the TOLD–I: 3

The TOLD–I: 3, designed for children between the ages of 8-0 and 12-11, measures receptive and expressive language. It has good psychometric properties. The new features are the updated norms, the downward extension of the age range, and the addition of the Picture Vocabulary subtest. A software package for scoring and reporting is available.

COMPREHENSIVE ASSESSMENT OF SPOKEN LANGUAGE

by John O. Willis and Jerome M. Sattler

The Comprehensive Assessment of Spoken Language (CASL; Carrow-Woolfolk, 1999a) is an individually administered test of language proficiency designed for children and young adults between 3 and 21 years of age. The 15 tests are grouped into four language structure categories—Lexical/Semantic, Syntactic, Supralinguistic, and Pragmatic. The tests in each category are further divided into core and supplementary tests. Table 18-4 shows the categories to which the tests belong and the ages at which the tests are administered. The core tests take about 23 minutes to administer at ages 3 and 4, about 40 minutes at ages 5 and 6, about 50 to 60 minutes at ages 7 to 10, and about 45 minutes at ages 11 to 21. The test stimuli are contained in three easel booklets.

Tests

The 15 tests are as follows.

Lexical/Semantic Category

- The Comprehension of Basic Concepts test measures understanding of words representing basic precepts and concepts, based on identifying pictures.
- The Antonyms test measures understanding of antonyms.
- The Synonyms test measures understanding of synonyms.
- The Sentence Completion test measures word retrieval skill—the ability to complete a sentence with a meaningful word.
- The Idiomatic Language test measures knowledge of idioms of the English language.

Syntactic Category

- The Syntax Construction test measures understanding of syntactic rules, based on the ability to generate sentences.
- The Paragraph Comprehension of Syntax test measures understanding of syntax, based on the ability to understand orally presented paragraphs.

Table 18-4
CASL Tests by Language Structure Category and Ages at Which the Tests Are Core or Supplementary

Test and language processing category	Core age range	Supplementary age range
Lexical/Semantic Category		
Basic Concepts— Auditory Comprehension	3 to 4	5 to 6
Antonyms— Expression, Retrieval	5 to 12	13 to 21
Synonyms— Auditory Comprehension	13 to 21	7 to 12
Sentence Completion— Expression with Comprehension, Retrieval	—	3 to 21
Idiomatic Language— Expression	—	11 to 21
Syntactic Category		
Syntax Construction— Expression	3 to 10	11 to 21
Paragraph Comprehension— Auditory Comprehension	5 to 10	3 to 4 11 to 12
Grammatical Morphemes— Expression	11 to 12	7 to 10 13 to 21
Sentence Comprehension— Auditory Comprehension	11 to 12	13 to 21
Grammaticality Judgment— Expression	13 to 21	7 to 12
Supralinguistic Category		
Nonliteral Language— Comprehension with Expression, World Knowledge	7 to 21	—
Meaning from Context— Comprehension with Expression	13 to 21	11 to 12
Inference— World Knowledge	—	7 to 17
Ambiguous Sentences— Comprehension with Expression	—	11 to 21
Pragmatic Category		
Pragmatic Judgment— Expression with Comprehension, World Knowledge	3 to 21	—

Source: Adapted from Carrow-Woolfolk (1999a).

- The Grammatical Morphemes test measures the ability to complete analogies that require knowledge of grammatical word forms.
- The Sentence Comprehension test measures the ability to comprehend the meaning of an orally presented sentence from its syntactic-structure organization.
- The Grammaticality Judgment test measures understanding of grammar.

Supralinguistic Category

- The Nonliteral Language test measures understanding of figurative speech, indirect requests, and sarcasm.
- The Meaning from Context test assesses the ability to comprehend inferentially words that do not require the use of factual knowledge beyond what is given in the dictated sentence. The examinee must explain the meaning of a specific difficult word in the sentence.
- The Inference test measures the ability to integrate, through inference, appropriate world knowledge with information provided in messages spoken by the examiner. The examiner reads a brief "episode" or "schema" and asks the examinee to answer a question that requires both understanding of the sentence(s) and application of background knowledge.
- The Ambiguous Sentences test measures understanding of ambiguous wording.

Pragmatic Category

- The Pragmatic Judgment subtest measures understanding of the use of appropriate language.

Scores

Scoring usually is 1 (correct) or 0 (incorrect). Two items in Syntax Construction and most items in Grammaticality Judgment are scored 2, 1, or 0, and four items in Pragmatic Judgment are scored 3, 2, 1, or 0. Derived scores include the Core Composite score ($M = 100$, $SD = 15$); Category Index scores for the Lexical/Semantic, Syntactic, Supralinguistic, Receptive, and Expressive categories ($M = 100$, $SD = 15$); and, for the individual tests, standard scores ($M = 100$, $SD = 15$), percentile ranks, normal curve equivalents, stanines, and age-equivalent scores.

Standardization

The standardization sample contained 1,700 children and young adults between the ages of 3 and 21 who were tested in 1996 and 1997. The sample was stratified to match the 1994 U.S. Census data with regard to sex, race or ethnic group, geographic region, and mother's educational level. Children with disabilities also were included in the sample.

Reliability

Internal consistency reliabilities range from .64 to .94 (Mdn r_{xx} = .86) for the tests and from .85 to .96 (Mdn r_{xx} = .94) for the Composite and Category Index scores. Standard errors of measurement are 3.6 to 9.0 (Mdn SEM = 5.5) for the tests and 2.8 to 5.8 (Mdn SEM = 3.6) for the Composite and Category Index scores. Test-retest reliabilities for 41 children ages 5 to 6, 38 children ages 8 to 10, and 69 children ages 14 to 16 who took the test twice within 7 to 109 days (Mdn = 42 days) range from .65 to .95 (Mdn r_{tt} = .85) for the tests and from .88 to .96 (Mdn r_{tt} = .93) for the Composite and Category Index scores.

Validity

Content validity was established by using items that pertain to both theoretical and practical language usage and by showing that mean raw scores increase with age. Construct validity is supported by factor analysis showing that the test has one factor at ages 3 to 6 and three factors at ages 7 to 21. The Receptive and Expressive Index scores are used only at ages 7 to 10, the only ages at which they were identified by factor analysis. Correlations among the 15 tests range from .30 to .79 (Mdn r = .61). Concurrent validity is satisfactory, as noted by acceptable correlations of the CASL Core Composite with other language tests (r = .72 to .80, Mdn r = .74) and with a test of cognitive ability (r = .81). Clinical validity studies indicate that children with disabilities obtain lower scores on the CASL than matched control groups.

Copyright © 1998 by John. P. Wood.

Comment on the CASL

The CASL is designed to assess the oral language skills of children and adolescents. It has good psychometric properties. The extensive manual describes in detail the underlying theory, the interpretation of each of the 15 tests, and the interpretation of qualitative information gathered during testing. The wide sampling of oral language skills, open-ended responses on several tests, and clearly defined rules for prompting marginal responses make the CASL particularly useful.

ILLINOIS TEST OF PSYCHOLINGUISTIC ABILITIES–THIRD EDITION

by Rhia Roberts, Nancy Mather, Elizabeth A. Allen, and Jerome M. Sattler

The Illinois Test of Psycholinguistic Abilities–Third Edition (ITPA–3; Hammill, Mather, & Roberts, 2001) is an individually administered test of language ability. The ITPA–3 is based on Osgood's (1957) psycholinguistic model and on Kirk, McCarthy, and Kirk's (1968) interpretation of that model. The test contains 12 subtests, six of which form the Spoken Language Composite and six of which form the Written Language Composite. All 12 subtests form the General Language Composite. The subtests are also regrouped into eight other Composites. The subtests in the Spoken Language Composite are designed for ages 5 to 12 years, whereas the subtests in the Written Language Composite are designed for ages 6-6 to 12-11 years (Donald Hammill, personal communication, October 2000). The latest revision of the ITPA contains new subtests, new Composites, a new standardization group, and a response booklet in which examinees write their answers. The test takes about 1 hour to administer.

Subtests

The 12 subtests are as follows:

Spoken Language Composite

- The Spoken Analogies subtest measures the ability to complete a phrase by identifying the relationships among the words.
- The Spoken Vocabulary subtest measures the ability to identify spoken words when provided with attributes of the words.
- The Morphological Closure subtest measures the ability to complete a partially formed sentence by supplying a final word that is correct grammatically.
- The Syntactic Sentences subtest measures the ability to repeat semantically nonsensical but syntactically correct sentences.

- The Sound Deletion subtest measures the ability to segment spoken words into smaller phonemic units by remembering and uttering the component of a word that remains after a portion is removed from the original stimulus word.
- The Rhyming Sequences subtest measures the ability to apprehend and then repeat a series of rhyming words.

Written Language Composite

- The Sentence Sequencing subtest measures the ability to understand the meaning of written sentences and the relationships among them.
- The Written Vocabulary subtest measures the ability to relate adjectives with appropriate nouns to create meaningful phrases in writing.
- The Sight Decoding subtest measures the ability to pronounce words that contain an irregular element, silent letter(s), or uncommon or low-frequency spelling pattern.
- The Sound Decoding subtest measures the ability to pronounce pseudowords that are phonically regular.
- The Sight Spelling subtest measures the ability to spell the irregular component of words.
- The Sound Spelling subtest measures the ability to spell phonically regular pseudowords.

Scores

Scoring is 1 (correct) or 0 (incorrect). Derived scores are provided for the subtests ($M = 10$, $SD = 3$) and Composites ($M = 100$, $SD = 15$), along with percentile ranks and age-equivalent scores. Subtest scaled scores range from 1 to 20, and General Language Composite standard scores range from 61 to 140, depending on the child's age. However, these ranges are not available at every age. For example, at age 5-0, children earn 35 scaled-score points even when they fail every item on the six Spoken Language subtests. At age 7-0, children earn 29 scaled-score points even when they fail every item on the six Written Language subtests. The highest possible scores that a 12-year-old can obtain are 129 on the Spoken Language Composite, 118 on the Written Language Composite, and 124 on the General Language Composite. There are also some steep changes in age-equivalent scores on several subtests. For example, on the Sound Deletion subtest, a raw score of 16 yields an age-equivalent score of 9-6, while a raw score of 17 yields an age-equivalent score of 11-0. Thus, 1 additional raw-score point changes the age-equivalent score by 1½ years.

Standardization

The ITPA–3 was standardized in 1999–2000 on a sample of 1,522 children in 27 states. The sample is representative of the estimated school-age population for the year 2000 with regard to geographic region, gender, race, rural or urban residence, ethnicity, family income, educational attainment of parents, and children's disabilities.

Reliability

Average internal consistency reliabilities range from .79 to .94 (*Mdn* r_{xx} = .92) for the subtests and from .88 to .99 (*Mdn* r_{xx} = .96) for the Composites. The standard errors of measurement for the Composites range from 2.0 to 5.0 points. Interscorer reliability ranges from .95 to .99 for the subtests (*Mdn* r_{xx} = .98) and from .96 to .99 for the Composites (*Mdn* r_{xx} = .99).

Validity

The content of the ITPA–3 is acceptable, as noted by the consistency of the test's structure with current knowledge about language processing and with Osgood's (1957) psycholinguistic model, acceptable item discrimination and difficulty levels, increases of subtest scores with age, and minimal item bias with respect to gender and ethnicity. Criterion-related validity is good, as noted by acceptable correlations with other language tests (median correlations range from .63 to .81). Construct validity is acceptable, as noted by significant correlations between subtests and by the results of a factor analysis that supports a general language factor, a written language factor, and a spoken language factor.

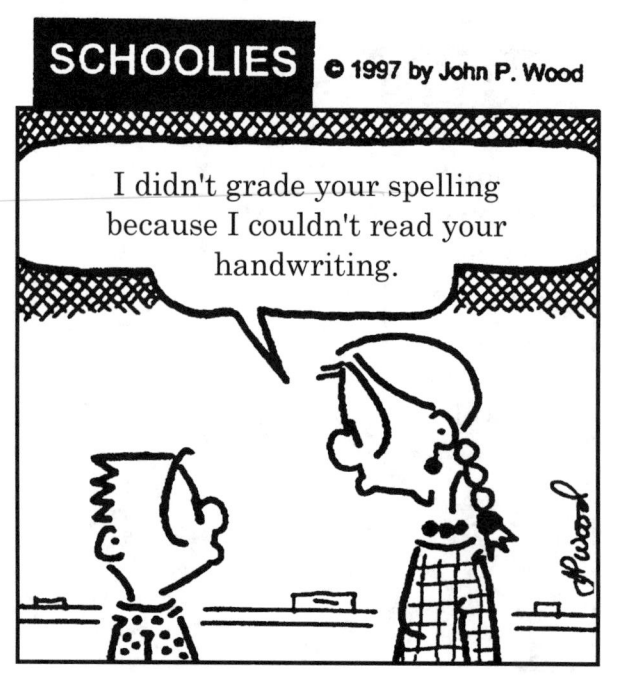

Copyright © 1997 by John P. Wood.

Comment on the ITPA–3

The ITPA–3 is an acceptable measure of oral and written language ability. Useful information is obtained by comparing different composites, such as Spoken Language vs. Written Language. A unique feature in the ITPA–3 is the ability to compare nonword reading and spelling to exception (or irregular) word reading and spelling. In interpreting the ITPA–3, you need to consider the composite score ranges (i.e., the floors and ceilings of the available standard scores) at each age level. In addition, because the range of standard scores changes with age, you must consider the available range when you do repeated evaluations. Because the age-equivalent scores show steep gradients on several subtests, be cautious in interpreting these scores (see Chapter 4 in this text for further discussion of age-equivalent scores). More information is needed about the validity of the test with children with disabilities.

WOODCOCK-MUÑOZ LANGUAGE SURVEYS

The Woodcock-Muñoz Language Survey–English (WMLS–E) and the Woodcock-Muñoz Language Survey–Spanish (WMLS–S; Woodcock & Muñoz-Sandoval, 1993) are individually administered measures of cognitive-academic language proficiency for individuals from age 4 to adulthood. The WMLS–E provides a sampling of competence in oral language, reading, and writing; it is designed as a screening instrument for program placement for students who have English as a second language. The English and Spanish versions each have four tests that assess different aspects of language proficiency. It takes about 15 to 20 minutes to administer.

Tests

The four tests are as follows:

- The Picture Vocabulary test measures vocabulary ability.
- The Verbal Analogies test measures the ability to comprehend and verbally complete a logical word relationship.
- The Letter-Word Identification test measures the ability to recognize letters, letter sounds, and individual words presented in isolation.
- The Dictation test measures prewriting and writing skills.

Scores

Scoring is 1 (correct) or 0 (incorrect). Derived scores include age- and grade-equivalent scores, a Relative Proficiency Index (RPI), W scores, and standard scores ($M = 100$, $SD = 15$). The Relative Proficiency Index, reported as a fraction, compares the examinee's proficiency level (the numerator) to the average proficiency of the comparison group (the denominator). A score of 56/90, for example, means that the examinee is expected to show 56% proficiency on oral language tasks on which others of the same age show 90% proficiency.

Three clusters are also provided ($M = 100$, $SD = 15$): Oral Language, Reading-Writing, and Broad English Ability (see Table 18-5). A unique feature of the cluster scores is the use of the Cognitive-Academic Language Proficiency (CALP) rating, which has a range of 1 (lowest rating) to 5 (highest rating). A Level 1 rating means the examinee has a negligible English (or Spanish) CALP when compared with others of the same age or grade. A Level 5 rating means the examinee has an advanced English (or Spanish) CALP when compared with others of the same age or grade.

Standardization

The standardization sample for the English version of the Woodcock-Muñoz Language Survey included 6,359 individuals between the ages of 2 and 90 from 100 geographically diverse U.S. communities. Data were collected between 1986 and 1988. The sample was stratified to match the U.S. Census data with regard to community and participant variables, including region, community size, gender, race, funding of college/university, and type of college/university, as well as education, occupational status, and income of adults. Norms for the Spanish version are equated to the English norms.

Reliability

Split-half internal consistency reliabilities range from .77 to .98 (*Mdn* r_{xx} = .91) for the tests and from .82 to .99 (*Mdn* r_{xx} = .95) for the clusters. Standard errors of measurement using W scores range from 3.7 to 12.7 (*Mdn* SEM = 5.7) for the tests and from 2.3 to 7.2 (*Mdn* SEM = 4.0) for the clusters. No test-retest studies were reported in the manual.

Validity

Items were selected using item validity studies, as well as expert opinion. Correlations range from .21 to .82 (*Mdn* r = .57)

Table 18-5
Clusters on the WMLS–E

Cluster	Test
Oral Language	Picture Vocabulary Verbal Analogies
Reading-Writing	Letter-Word Identification Dictation
Broad English Ability	All subtests

between tests and from .42 to .97 (*Mdn r* = .91) between clusters. In one study, children from preschool through grade 11 were given the WMLS–E along with various achievement and ability tests. Correlations with achievement tests range from .23 to .71 (*Mdn r* = .56), while correlations with ability tests range from .12 to .89 (*Mdn r* = .54).

Another study looked at the WMLS–E cluster scores and comparable test and cluster scores on the Woodcock Language Proficiency Battery for seven age groups (ages 6 to 79). Correlations range from .87 to .95 (*Mdn r* = .93) for the Oral Language cluster, from .87 to .97 (*Mdn r* = .92) for the Reading-Writing cluster, and from .96 to .99 (*Mdn r* = .97) for the Broad English Ability cluster. In a third study, in which 56 tenth- and eleventh-graders took the WMLS–E and several achievement tests, correlations between tests and Composites were found to range from .14 to .78 (*Mdn r* = .48).

Comment on the WMLS

The WMLS–E and the WMLS–S are useful screening instruments for assessing proficiency in oral language, reading, and writing among both English and Spanish speakers. Their psychometric properties are good. The tests are easy to administer, and directions are simple and clear. In addition, a computer scoring and report-writing program is available. However, scoring can be somewhat complex and time consuming if all the scores are used.

THINKING THROUGH THE ISSUES

1. In what ways are language tests similar to and different from achievement tests?
2. What role might language tests have in a psychological assessment?
3. How might the examinee's ethnic background affect her or his performance on language tests?
4. Are language tests more culturally loaded than achievement tests and tests of cognitive abilities?

SUMMARY

Receptive and Expressive Language

1. Language has five basic components: semantics, syntax, morphology, phonology, and pragmatics.
2. Receptive language involves the ability to understand communications by listening or reading.
3. Expressive language involves the ability to produce or generate meaningful messages through speech or writing.
4. Listening and speaking are the first language processes to develop and remain the most competent through the upper elementary school years. The home environment is the most important influence on the development of listening and speaking.
5. Development of the reading and writing processes, the primary goal of instruction in grades 1 through 3, depends on the depth and breadth of the listening and speaking abilities developed in the preschool years.
6. When expressive language skills are found to be deficient, receptive language should also be evaluated.

Boehm Test of Basic Concepts–Revised

7. The BTBC–R is a pictorial multiple-choice test designed to measure knowledge of concepts thought to be necessary for understanding verbal instructions and for academic achievement in the first few years of school. The test is designed for children in kindergarten through second grade and can be administered in either English or Spanish. The BTBC–R has two alternate forms (C and D), and can be individually or group administered. Administration time is about 30 minutes. The BTBC–R has acceptable validity but weak reliability.

Boehm Test of Basic Concepts–Preschool Version

8. The BTBC–PV is an individually administered test of basic concepts designed for children ages 3 to 5 years. It is a downward extension of the Boehm–R and takes about 15 minutes to administer. The test has acceptable reliability and validity.

Bracken Basic Concept Scale–Revised

9. The BBCS–R is an individually administered test designed to assess 11 basic concepts. Children need only point to the appropriate picture or pictures in a multiple-choice format. The test is designed for children between the ages of 2-6 and 7-11 and takes about 30 minutes to administer. The BBCS–R is also available in a Spanish edition. The test has good reliability and validity.

Peabody Picture Vocabulary Test–III

10. The PPVT–III measures listening comprehension. It is an individually administered screening test for individuals ages 2-6 to 90+ years. Testing time is about 10 minutes. Previous versions of the test have excellent reliability and validity, but additional validity studies need to be conducted on the current edition.

Test of Auditory Comprehension of Language–Third Edition

11. The TACL–3 is an individually administered test designed to assess three specific receptive language skills: oral vocabulary, grammatical morphemes, and syntax and sentence structure. It can be administered to children between the ages of 3-0 and 9-11 and requires about 20 to 30 minutes to administer. The test has good reliability and acceptable validity.

Expressive Vocabulary Test

12. The EVT is an individually administered test of expressive vocabulary and word retrieval for children and adults ages 2½ to 90. It takes about 10 to 25 minutes to administer. The test has good reliability and validity, although additional validity studies need to be conducted.

Test of Early Written Language–Second Edition

13. The TEWL–2 is designed to assess written language abilities for children ages 3-0 to 10-11. There are two subtests, Basic

Writing and Contextual Writing, and two equivalent forms. Administration time is about 50 minutes. The test has good reliability and validity.

Test of Written Language–Third Edition

14. The TOWL–3 is a test of expressive language that measures writing competence in eight skill areas: writing vocabulary, spelling, style, sentence construction, sentence combining, use of language, use of writing conventions, and story construction. It covers ages 7-6 to 17-11 and can be individually or group administered. It takes about 90 minutes to administer. Two equivalent forms are available. The TOWL–3 has acceptable reliability and validity.

Test of Written Spelling–Fourth Edition

15. The TWS–4 is a test of written spelling designed for examinees in grades 1 through 12. It takes about 20 minutes to administer and can be given individually or group administered. It has two equivalent forms. The test has acceptable reliability, but more validity research is needed.

Comprehensive Receptive and Expressive Vocabulary Test

16. The CREVT is an individually administered test designed to assess both receptive and expressive oral vocabulary. It is suitable for use with children and adolescents ages 4-0 to 17-11. It has two forms and requires 20 to 30 minutes to administer. Reliability and content validity data are acceptable.

The Oral and Written Language Scales

17. The OWLS is an individually administered assessment of receptive and expressive language consisting of three subtests: Listening Comprehension, Oral Expression, and Written Expression. The test was designed for individuals ages 3 to 21 (ages 5 to 21 for Written Expression). The test takes about 5 to 40 minutes per subtest to administer. The test has good reliability and validity.

Test of Early Language Development–Third Edition

18. The TELD–3 is an individually administered test of oral language for children between the ages of 2-0 and 7-11. The test has two equivalent forms and requires about 15 to 40 minutes to administer. The test has good reliability and validity.

The Test of Adolescent and Adult Language–Third Edition

19. The TOAL–3 is designed to assess listening vocabulary and grammar, speaking vocabulary and grammar, reading vocabulary and grammar, and writing vocabulary and grammar. It is designed for individuals between the ages of 12-0 and 24-11. It takes about 2 hours to administer. A computerized scoring and reporting system is available. The test has good reliability and validity.

Test of Language Development–Primary: Third Edition

20. The TOLD–P: 3 is an individually administered test of receptive and expressive oral language development for children ages 4-0 to 8-11. Six core subtests and three supplemental subtests assess the ability to understand and use spoken words in meaningful ways, aspects of grammar usage, and the ability to say words correctly and to distinguish between words that sound similar. The six core subtests take 30 to 60 minutes to administer; the three supplemental tests require about 30 minutes to administer. The TOLD–P: 3 has acceptable reliability and validity.

Test of Language Development–Intermediate: Third Edition

21. The TOLD–I: 3 is an individually administered test of receptive and expressive language. The six subtests involve knowledge of sentence construction, picture vocabulary, word ordering, abstract relationships, grammatical comprehension, and malapropisms. It is designed for children ages 8-0 to 12-11 and requires about 30 to 60 minutes to administer. A computer scoring and reporting package is available. The TOLD–I: 3 has good reliability and validity.

Comprehensive Assessment of Spoken Language

22. The CASL is an individually administered test of language proficiency for children and young adults between the ages of 3 and 21. It takes about 23 to 60 minutes to administer, depending on the examinee's age. The 15 tests are grouped into four language structure categories—Lexical/Semantic, Syntactic, Supralinguistic, and Pragmatic. The test has good reliability and validity for the Composite scores.

Illinois Test of Psycholinguistic Abilities–Third Edition

23. The ITPA–3 is an individually administered of language ability designed for children ages 5 to 12 years. It contains 12 subtests and 11 Composites. The test takes about 1 hour to administer. The ITPA–3 has acceptable reliability and validity.

Woodcock-Muñoz Language Surveys

24. The WMLS–E (English) and the WMLS–S (Spanish) are individually administered screening assessments that measure competence in oral language, reading, and writing. The tests are appropriate for use with individuals from age 4 to adult. The WMLS-E and WMLS-S each contain four tests. Each version takes about 15 to 20 minutes to administer. Reliability and validity are good.

KEY TERMS, CONCEPTS, AND NAMES

Semantics (p. 611)
Syntax (p. 611)
Morphology (p. 611)
Phonology (p. 611)
Pragmatics (p. 611)
Receptive language (p. 611)
Expressive language (p. 611)
Language development (p. 611)
Listening process (p. 611)
Speaking process (p. 611)
Reading process (p. 611)
Writing process (p. 611)
Receptive language tests (p. 612)

Boehm Test of Basic Concepts–Revised (p. 612)
Boehm Test of Basic Concepts–Preschool Version (p. 613)
Bracken Basic Concept Scale–Revised (p. 614)
Peabody Picture Vocabulary Test–III (p. 615)
Test of Auditory Comprehension of Language–
    Third Edition (p. 616)
Expressive Vocabulary Test (p. 616)
Test of Early Written Language–Second Edition (p. 617)
Test of Written Language–Third Edition (p. 618)
Test of Written Spelling–Fourth Edition (p. 619)
Comprehensive Receptive and Expressive Vocabulary Test (p. 620)
Oral and Written Language Scales (p. 621)
Test of Early Language Development–Third Edition (p. 622)
Test of Adolescent and Adult Language–Third Edition (p. 623)
Test of Language Development–Primary: Third Edition (p. 625)
Test of Language Development–Intermediate:
    Third Edition (p. 626)
Comprehensive Assessment of Spoken Language (p. 627)
Illinois Test of Psycholinguistic Abilities–Third Edition (p. 629)
Woodcock-Muñoz Language Survey–English
    and Spanish forms (p. 631)

STUDY QUESTIONS

1. Discuss the five basic language components.
2. Discuss the four processes that comprise receptive and expressive language.
3. Discuss the similarities and differences in language development among the following groups: (a) children from birth to grade 3, (b) individuals from their middle and secondary school years to adulthood, and (c) children with learning disabilities.

4. Discuss each of the following tests. Include in your discussion a description of the test, scores, standardization, reliability, and validity, and provide an overall evaluation of the test:

    Boehm Test of Basic Concepts–Revised
    Boehm Test of Basic Concepts–Preschool Version
    Bracken Basic Concept Scale–Revised
    Peabody Picture Vocabulary Test–III
    Test of Auditory Comprehension of Language–Third Edition
    Expressive Vocabulary Test
    Test of Early Written Language–Second Edition
    Test of Written Language–Third Edition
    Test of Written Spelling–Fourth Edition
    Comprehensive Receptive and Expressive Vocabulary Test
    Oral and Written Language Scales
    Test of Early Language Development–Third Edition
    Test of Adolescent and Adult Language–Third Edition
    Test of Language Development–Primary: Third Edition
    Test of Language Development–Intermediate: Third Edition
    Comprehensive Assessment of Spoken Language
    Illinois Test of Psycholinguistic Abilities–Third Edition
    Woodcock-Muñoz Language Surveys

5. Discuss (a) two different tests that assess language skills primarily at the lower levels of development, (b) two different tests that assess language skills primarily at the higher levels of development, and (c) two different tests that assess language skills at both lower and higher levels of development.

19

ASSESSMENT OF CULTURALLY AND LINGUISTICALLY DIVERSE CHILDREN: BACKGROUND CONSIDERATIONS AND DYNAMICS

"First of all," he said, "if you can learn a simple trick, Scout, you'll get along a lot better with all kinds of folks. You never really understand a person until you consider things from his point of view—"

"Sir?"

"—until you climb into his skin and walk around in it."

—Harper Lee

Goals and Objectives

This chapter will enable you to do the following:

- Discuss the concepts of culture, value orientations, and acculturation

- Describe cross-ethnic and cross-cultural assessment

- Understand issues involved with language translations

Background Considerations

Dynamics of Cross-Ethnic and Cross-Cultural Assessment

Assessment of Bilingual Examinees

Interpreters

Test Translations

Thinking Through the Issues

Summary

This and the following chapter emphasize the need to consider cultural variables when you assess culturally and linguistically diverse children. By considering cultural variables, you will be in a better position to establish rapport, administer tests, obtain valid information, arrive at an accurate diagnosis, and formulate meaningful intervention plans. It will not always be easy to evaluate the role that cultural variables play in assessment because members of culturally and linguistically diverse groups differ in how firmly they adhere to their group's cultural traditions and practices. Great diversity exists within any group, especially between recent immigrants and those who have had more opportunity to become acculturated into their new society. Even among those who are acculturated, differences exist in patterns of acculturation. Members of culturally and linguistically diverse groups do not need to reject their cultural heritage to adapt to a new culture; they can choose to value their old traditions and practices while also valuing those of the new culture. *Our society must recognize and preserve cultural diversity and promote culturally sensitive and culturally relevant clinical services.*

In this book, we have been using the terms *Euro American* (to refer to White Americans, Anglo Americans, or Caucasians), *African American* (to refer to Black Americans), *Hispanic American* (to refer to Latinos, Mexican-Americans, and other groups from Latin America), *Asian American* (to refer to Chinese, Japanese, South Sea Islanders, Filipinos, and other Asian groups), and *Native American* (to refer to American Indians and Alaskan Native Americans). The use of these terms does away with color designations and emphasizes the national origin of each group.

We recognize, however, that these terms may not adequately describe children of multicultural heritage. When asked to choose an ethnicity in order to complete school forms, children of multicultural heritage are faced with the dilemma of having to select one ethnicity from among those in their background. Obviously, school forms, and other forms as well, should have a multiethnic category or even several multiethnic categories if information about ethnicity is required.

Within any cultural group, there are differences in values, motivation, social organization, ways of speaking and thinking, and life styles that vary with education, income, class status, geographic origin, assimilation patterns, religious background, and age. Broad generalizations about cultural practices do not do justice to regional, generational, socioeconomic, and idiosyncratic variations. However, knowledge of a child's and family's (a) cultural mores and customs, (b) possible migration experiences, and (c) level of acculturation will help you conduct a more effective assessment. The generalizations in this chapter about culturally and linguistically diverse groups and the majority group must remain generalizations; do not apply them indiscriminately to each child and family. For example, although Euro Americans may be more individualistic than Hispanic Americans, you

"cannot predict with any certainty the level of individualism of a particular person" (Okazaki & Sue, 1995, p. 368). Broad prescriptions, based on generalizations that do not take into account individual variability, are likely to be not only ineffective but also resented by the culturally and linguistically diverse child and his or her family. Use what you know about culturally and linguistically diverse groups and the majority group as background for the assessment, but treat each child as an individual and each family as unique.

The concept of culture is closely intertwined with the concepts of race, ethnicity, and social class. Here are some definitions of these terms (Betancourt & López, 1993, pp. 630–632, with changes in notation):

Culture is the human-made part of the environment, consisting of highly variable systems of meaning that are learned and shared by a people or an identifiable segment of a population. Culture represents designs and ways of life normally transmitted from one generation to another.

Race refers to the physical characteristics, such as skin color, facial features, and hair type, common to a population.

Ethnicity refers to the characterization of a group by its common nationality, culture, or language.

Social class refers to group designations within a society, usually based on occupation, education, or both.

The issues involved in the assessment of culturally and linguistically diverse children are complex because they are woven into the fabric of society. Assessment results have an impact on children's self-esteem and influence their chances of having a successful life. If tests are detrimental to culturally and linguistically diverse children, society must change or eliminate them. If tests are beneficial to culturally and linguistically diverse children, their elimination would be a disservice to countless children. Whenever you use tests, you must ensure that the results are employed for the benefit of the child. This chapter demonstrates how you can accomplish this goal.

BACKGROUND CONSIDERATIONS

The U.S. Bureau of the Census estimates that there were 70.4 million children under age 18 living in the United States as of June 1, 2000. The ethnic affiliation of the children was as follows: Euro American, 64%; African American, 15%; Hispanic American, 16%; Asian American, 4%; and Native American, less than 1%. The Hispanic American children traced their origins to Mexico, Puerto Rico, Cuba, El Salvador, Colombia, Guatemala, Nicaragua, Ecuador, Peru, Honduras, and other Central and South American countries. The Asian American groups included Chinese, Filipino, Japanese, Asian Indian, Korean, Vietnamese, Laotian, Cambodian, Thai, and Hmong.

The U.S. Bureau of the Census projected that Hispanic Americans and Asian Americans will account for more than half the growth in the U.S. population every year for the next half-century and beyond. As a result, the ethnic portrait of America will change dramatically: The population of Euro Americans (non-Hispanic), which as of June 1, 2000 was about 71% of all Americans, will shrink to a bare majority (52.8%) by the year 2050. Because the Hispanic American population is young (mean age is 29 years, the lowest of any ethnic group) and has a high fertility rate, it will likely become the nation's largest minority group by 2005.

It is estimated that by 2050, Hispanic Americans will form 24.3% of the population, up from the current 11.8%, and Asian Americans will make up 9.3%, an increase from the current 3.8%. The African American population will remain relatively constant, rising to about 14.7% from the current 12.2%. The Native American population will stay about the same, showing a small rise from 0.7% to 1.1%. The population as a whole, it is estimated, will rise from 274 million in 2000 to 403 million in 2050.

Problems Faced by Culturally and Linguistically Diverse Groups

In the United States, culturally and linguistically diverse groups may face (a) racism and discrimination, (b) poverty, (c) conflicts associated with acculturation and assimilation, especially when children begin to identify more closely with the majority culture and reject their ethnic culture, (d) problems in dealing with medical, educational, social, and law enforcement organizations, and (e) problems in using standard English. These underlying problems may affect the assessment. In addition, children from culturally and linguistically diverse groups who have a disability can be considered to be minorities within minorities.

Prejudice. A common thread in the experience of culturally and linguistically diverse groups in our society is confronting prejudice. Prejudice is an insidious force that culturally and linguistically diverse groups face at all socioeconomic levels. Prejudice can lead to segregation in housing, inequality before the law, discrimination in employment, and other kinds of social and political discrimination. The experience of prejudice may make culturally and linguistically diverse examinees wary of help offered by the majority group.

Poverty. When we look at the *poverty rate* for families in 1998, we find that Euro American families had the lowest poverty rate (6.1%), followed by Asian Americans (11%), Hispanic Americans (22.7%), and African Americans (23.4%). Over 20% of African American and Hispanic American families were below the poverty level. Information about Native American families is less recent. In 1990, their

poverty rate was 27.2%. In 1998, families were considered to be at the poverty level if they had an income of $16,600 or less.

In 1998, 18.3% of all children were living at or below the poverty level. The breakdown for the ethnic groups was as follows: 10.0% for Euro American non-Hispanic children, 17.5% for Asian American children, 33.6% for Hispanic American children, and 36.4% for African American children. Over 33% of African American and Hispanic American children were living at or below the poverty level.

Poverty can raise children's and parents' stress levels and place them at increased risk for health problems such as obesity, suicide, and alcoholism. Poverty affects maternal health as well as the child's own health and social functioning, both of which may be related to school failure. Poverty also may affect rate of learning, which in turn influences intelligence and academic success. Among the conditions assaulting the central nervous systems of inner-city children are perinatal disease (connected with or occurring during the birth process), malnutrition, infection, anemia, and lead poisoning.

Poverty, as such, is neither a necessary nor a sufficient condition to produce intellectual deficits, especially if nutrition and the home environment are adequate. It is only when these and related factors are inadequate that there are likely to be learning deficits. Imagine, for example, what effect poor nutrition and health care, substandard housing, low family income, prevalent family disorganization, anarchic discipline, diminished personal worth, low expectations, frustrated aspirations, exposure to physical violence in the streets, and other environmental handicaps may have on the development of a child's intellectual skills.

Schooling. When we look at data for 1998 on the *years of school completed* by persons 25 years of age and older, we find that Asian Americans as a group had the highest percentage of individuals with four years of high school or more (84.9%), followed by Euro Americans (83.7%), African Americans (76.0%), and Hispanic Americans (66.5%); for Native Americans in 1990, the figure is 65.6%.

Terminology

In this book, we use the terms *culturally and linguistically diverse group* and *minority group* interchangeably to refer to "a group subordinated in terms of power and privilege to the majority group" (Kumabe, Nishida, & Hepworth, 1985, p. 9). Culturally and linguistically diverse groups are usually referred to in terms of race, ethnicity, nationality, religion, or sex. Although we use the terms *Euro Americans* and *majority group* interchangeably, Euro Americans may not be the majority group in specific geographical areas. We use the term *ethnic group* to refer to the culture of minority groups, the majority group, or both groups.

Civil rights today is, as it has always been in human history, a struggle for the human conscience, and ...we all have a stake in that struggle.... Let history record that we in our time faced our challenges remembering who we are and believing finally in that old adage that we are more than our brother's keeper; that is, on this earth, we are his savior and he is ours.

—Deval Patrick

Culture and Value Orientations

Ethnic groups differ in their value orientations about human nature, the relationship between person and nature, time, activity level, and social relations. Following are some value orientations associated with each area (Kluckhohn, 1958; Spiegel, 1982).

- *Human nature—evil orientation* (people are born with evil inclinations that must be controlled) versus *good orientation* (people are born good) versus *mixed orientation* (people are born with both evil and good inclinations)
- *Relationship between person and nature—subjugation orientation* (people are subjected to natural forces and cannot control them) versus *mastery orientation* (people can gain mastery over nature) versus *harmony orientation* (people can achieve a partnership with nature)
- *Time—past orientation* (traditions, ancestors, and the wisdom of the elderly are valued) versus *present orientation* (life is lived in the here and now) versus *future orientation* (life is planned for tomorrow with an emphasis on newness and youth)
- *Activity level—being orientation* (emphasizes cooperation, seeking harmony with nature, concern with what the

person is, and spontaneous self-expression) versus *doing orientation* (emphasizes achievement, competitiveness, upward mobility in jobs, and controlling feelings) versus *being-in-becoming orientation* (emphasizes what the person is and developing aspects of the self in an integrated manner)
- *Social relations—lineal orientation* (emphasizes clearly established lines of authority) versus *collateral orientation* (emphasizes collective decision making) versus *individual orientation* (emphasizes individuality and autonomy over group goals)

Table 19-1 shows how Euro Americans, African Americans, Hispanic Americans, Asian Americans, and Native Americans may be characterized with respect to the five value orientations discussed above, as well as others. These value orientations should be viewed as rough guides for understanding the five ethnic groups. Not only are the value orientations undergoing change, but there are wide variations within each ethnic group. Furthermore, as noted previously, we cannot know for certain whether any one individual has the same value orientation as his or her cultural group.

It also is useful to consider *cultural styles* in working with ethnic groups. Cultural styles can be placed on a continuum from traditional to modern (Ramirez, 1991). In general, *traditional life styles* emphasize the following:

- A strict distinction between gender roles
- Strong ties to family and community
- The past and present over the future
- The wisdom that comes with increasing age
- Cooperation
- Traditional ceremonies
- Norms, conventions, and respect for authority
- Spirituality and religion in life events

Table 19-1
Value Orientations of Five Ethnic Groups

Area	Euro American	African American	Hispanic American	Asian American	Native American
Human nature	Mixed	Mixed	Good	Good	Good
Person and nature	Mastery	Subjugation	Subjugation	Harmony	Harmony
Time	Future	Present	Past–present	Past–present	Present
Activity level	Doing	Being	Being-in-becoming	Being-in-becoming	Being-in-becoming
Social relations	Individual	Collateral	Collateral	Lineal	Collateral
Handling time	Time is not flexible	Time is defined by rhythm of social relationships	Time is relaxed	Time is a reflection of the eternal	Time is flexible
Aging	Respect youth	Respect elders	Respect elders	Respect elders	Respect elders
Belief system	Rational/empirical belief orientation	Rational/spiritual belief orientation	Spiritual/magic belief orientation	Rational/spiritual belief orientation	Spiritual/magic belief orientation
Group relations	Competition	Cooperation	Cooperation	Cooperation	Cooperation

Modern life styles, in contrast, emphasize

- Flexible boundaries between gender roles
- Individual identities
- The future more than the past or present
- The vitality of youth
- Competition
- What is new and innovative rather than what is traditional
- The right to question norms, conventions, and authority
- Science and secularism in life events

Acculturation

Acculturation is the process of cultural change that occurs in individuals when two cultures meet; it leads the individuals to adopt elements of another culture, such as values and social behaviors. The process of acculturation may involve several phases:

Phase 1: Traditionalism. Individuals maintain and practice mainly the traditions of their culture of origin.

Phase 2: Transitional period. Individuals partake of both the old and the new culture but question basic traditional values and also those of the new culture.

Phase 3: Marginality. Individuals develop anxiety as they try, unsuccessfully, to meet the demands of both the old and the new culture. In the process, they may become isolated from the culture of origin and from the new culture.

Phase 4: Assimilation. Individuals embrace traditions of the new culture and reject practices and customs of their old culture.

Phase 5: Biculturalism. Individuals integrate practices of both the old and the new culture by selectively adapting new customs and maintaining former ones, without losing a sense of identity.

Factors affecting acculturation.   The extent to which individuals maintain or depart from their traditional cultural practices or allow prior cultural practices to coexist with new ones depends on several variables (Kumabe et al., 1985).

1. *History of migration experience.* The nature of the migration experience may influence individuals' self-concepts and how they acculturate to the United States. Consider whether culturally and linguistically diverse groups view themselves as forced to come against their will (e.g., African Americans who were forced to come to the United States as slaves), conquered (e.g., Native Americans or Hispanic Americans), displaced (e.g., Vietnamese), oppressed (e.g., Cubans who were oppressed in Cuba), or voluntary immigrants (e.g., individuals who migrated for professional or personal reasons).

2. *Temporal and geographic distance from the country of origin and its indigenous culture.* Individuals' degree of acculturation may be influenced by their length of residence in the United States, the extent to which they maintain ties with the indigenous culture, and how often they return to their native land. Stronger acculturation to the majority culture is more likely if residence has been long, ties with the indigenous culture are minimal, and returns to the native land are limited.

3. *Place of residence and socioeconomic status in the homeland.* Individuals' acculturation may be influenced by where they lived in the homeland (e.g., in an urban or a rural area) and their status in the homeland (e.g., their economic, occupational, and educational strata). Individuals with rural backgrounds and low socioeconomic status may have more difficulty adjusting to U.S. culture than those who have urban backgrounds and high socioeconomic status (e.g., rural Cambodians versus urban Vietnamese).

4. *Type of neighborhood in the United States.* Individuals who live in a neighborhood with others of the same ethnicity and who have primary ties with their own group are more likely to keep their indigenous traditions than those who live in an integrated neighborhood and frequently interact with other culturally and linguistically diverse groups as well as the majority group.

5. *Ties with immediate and extended family.* Individuals may have difficulty becoming acculturated when they have close ties to their immediate and extended families.

6. *Role of the family's power and authority.* Individuals will have difficulty deviating from family norms when their families insist that they maintain indigenous traditions.

7. *Language and customs.* Individuals may have difficulty acculturating when they primarily speak the language of their homeland, celebrate the holidays of their homeland, and follow the traditions and customs found there. In addition, acculturation may be difficult when individuals have had limited exposure to Western culture in their homeland.

Tables 19-2 and 19-3 provide questions that will help you determine children's and parents' degree of acculturation, including language preference.

Stresses associated with acculturation.   Many aspects of the acculturation process are likely to bring about stress for children and their families (Zambrana & Silva-Palacios, 1989):

- Leaving relatives and friends behind when moving from their homeland to the United States
- Being exposed to customs and mores that differ from those they are accustomed to
- Having difficulty understanding English
- Being taunted because of their ethnic origin
- Being ridiculed because of the way they dress or speak English
- Feeling lonely because they have few friends from their culturally and linguistically diverse group
- Speaking in one language and having their friends answer in another

---

Table 19-2
Interview Questions for Determining an Adolescent's Degree of Acculturation

1. What language do you usually use when you talk with your mother?
2. What language do you usually use when you talk with your father?
3. (If applicable) What language do you usually use when you talk with your sisters and brothers?
4. (If applicable) What language do you usually use when you talk with your grandmother and grandfather?
5. What language do you usually use when you talk with your friends?
6. What language do you usually use when you talk in school?
7. In what language are the television programs you usually watch?
8. In what language are the radio programs you usually listen to?
9. In which language do you usually think?
10. What language do you use for reading?
11. What language do you use for writing?
12. What cultural or ethnic groups live in your neighborhood?
13. What is the cultural or ethnic background of your close friends?
14. What type of foods do you eat at home?
15. What is the ethnic background of your father?
16. What is the ethnic background of your mother?
17. What ethnic or cultural holidays and traditions do you celebrate?
18. What culture do you feel the most proud of?

Table 19-3
Interview Questions for Determining a Parent's Degree of Acculturation

1. What language do you usually use when you talk with your husband (wife)?
2. What language do you usually use when you talk with your child?
3. (If applicable) What language do you usually use when you talk with your brothers and sisters?
4. What language do you usually use when you talk with your friends?
5. What language do you usually use when you shop at the grocery store?
6. In what language are the television programs you usually watch?
7. In what language are the radio programs you usually listen to?
8. In which language do you usually think?
9. What language do you use for reading?
10. What language do you use for writing?
11. What language did you use as a child?
12. What cultural or ethnic groups live in your neighborhood?
13. What is the cultural or ethnic background of your close friends?
14. What type of foods do you eat?
15. What ethnic or cultural holidays and traditions do you celebrate?
16. What culture do you feel the most proud of?

- Feeling pressured to speak only the ethnic language at home
- Being teased at home about not knowing how to speak their ethnic language
- Feeling pressured to speak only English at home
- Having to act as mediators, negotiators, or translators for members of the family who do not speak English

In working with children and families who are in the process of acculturation, consider what phase they may be in. Then, evaluate how they are dealing with the separation from their country of origin, their attitudes toward life in the United States, and their hopes and aspirations, conflicts, and adjustment patterns.

Ethnic Identity and Identification

Ethnic identity refers to "one's sense of belonging to an ethnic group and the part of one's thinking, perceptions, feelings, and behavior that is due to ethnic group membership" (Rotheram & Phinney, 1986, p. 13). Culturally and linguistically diverse youth may have difficulty in developing a clear identity if they must choose between the values of the larger society and those of their own group (Spencer & Markstrom-Adams, 1990). For example, do they choose competition or cooperation? Do they value the family over the individual? Do they celebrate the holidays of their group and miss school, or do they attend school and anger their family?

Stereotypes of children's culturally and linguistically diverse group may also impede their identity formation (Spencer & Markstrom-Adams, 1990). If the majority group, for example, views their culturally and linguistically diverse group negatively (say, as powerless and primitive), how are they to perceive themselves? In addition to hindering identification with the majority group, stereotypes may create anxieties and doubts about their own group. Children may internalize negative portrayals by the majority culture, which, in turn, may lead to low self-esteem and behavioral problems.

Identity formation is impeded when the family fails to discuss ethnic or racial issues with children (Spencer & Markstrom-Adams, 1990). This is likely to happen when the parents are uncomfortable with issues related to race or ethnicity.

Examinees from the same ethnic background have different levels of identification with their ethnic group, reflected, in part, by how they wish to be described. For example, some prefer to be identified as African American rather than Black American, others prefer Latino or Chicano over Hispanic, and still others prefer no specific ethnic identification other than American.

Ethnic identification becomes particularly complex when individuals have a biracial or multicultural heritage (Herring, 1992). One issue is the transmission of a cultural heritage and an ethnic identity from the parents to their children. Parents may emphasize their children's membership in one or another group, or they may simply consider them members of the human race and not focus on race or color. A second issue is how the larger community treats biracial or multicultural children and their families—with acceptance or discrimination, for example. A third issue is how biracial or multicultural children integrate their racial or cultural identifications.

I have a dream that my four little children will one day live in a nation where they will not be judged by the color of their skin but by the content of their character.

—Martin Luther King, Jr.

Health Care Practices

Depending on their degree of acculturation, members of culturally and linguistically diverse groups in the United States may use both traditional and Western methods of healing. Those who use traditional healing methods may be reluctant to reveal their practices to Western health professionals for fear of being misunderstood or deprecated (Kumabe et al., 1985). You will need to gain the family members' trust to learn about their attitudes toward health and illness and about their health and medical care practices. A key question is *What does the family believe causes illness or disease?* (Kumabe et al., 1985). For example, does the family view illness and disease as punishment from God for unacceptable behavior, as an invasion of the body by evil spirits, as a test of their religious faith or courage, or as a challenge to be overcome? Does the family have any folk beliefs or practices that conflict with the tenets of Western medicine? Or, does the family accept illness as part of the life process, seek medical care, and follow medical prescriptions? The family's interpretation of why the child has an illness, disease, or problem will have a direct bearing on what is considered an appropriate intervention (Coll & Meyer, 1993).

Culturally and Linguistically Diverse Groups' Use of Mental Health and Medical Services

Culturally and linguistically diverse groups' use of mental health and medical services may be affected by the following issues, several of which apply to most people:

1. What are the group's cultural values? For example, does the group prefer to solve or treat its problems within the family or extended family?
2. What is the group's attitude toward mental health and illness, physical health and illness, psychological treatment, and medical treatment? For example, does the group accept the need for treatment of medical illnesses but not of psychological illnesses? Does the group view mental illness as carrying a stigma? Do members of the group fear being ostracized if other members find out they are receiving treatment for mental health problems?

3. What is the availability of medical and mental health services? For example, do members of the group face a long waiting list to obtain required services? Can they afford the cost of treatment?
4. How accessible are medical and mental health services? For example, where are the facilities, and what transportation services are available?
5. Who is providing the services? For example, are the practitioners professionals, paraprofessionals, or recent graduates? Will the group accept help from practitioners who are members of another ethnic group or who are males or who are females or who are young?
6. How culturally relevant are the treatment programs? For example, are the treatment programs willing to recognize and use practices that are indigenous to the group's culture?

Factors that may make it difficult for members of culturally and linguistically diverse groups to use the mainstream health care system include the following (Kumabe et al., 1985):

- Perceptions of health and illness that differ from those of the majority culture
- Unfamiliarity with the clinic or hospital setting
- Fear of Western medical practices
- Distrust of Western health care providers because of the prejudice they have experienced
- Fear of being turned in to authorities and deported, if they are illegal immigrants

Some members of culturally and linguistically diverse groups will seek treatment from the mainstream health care system *only* when they have exhausted their own traditional remedies. At times of stress, it can be comforting to turn to familiar cultural and religious roots.

Some culturally and linguistically diverse families (and majority families as well) may wonder whether an examiner who is a female or young or not a "doctor" or who is from another ethnic group possesses sufficient skill and training to help them. If you have any of these characteristics, you may have to demonstrate to or convince the family that you are a competent professional (or professional-in-training).

If the family subscribes to mainstream medical and psychological practices *and* to traditional methods, *consider encouraging them to seek help from both services*. A combined treatment approach may be the most beneficial for these families (Kumabe et al., 1985).

Culture and Communication Styles

Let's now consider how verbal and nonverbal communication styles may lead to difficulties in cross-cultural assessments.

Verbal communication difficulties. You may encounter communication barriers when you work with culturally and linguistically diverse examinees (Kumabe et al., 1985). Culturally and linguistically diverse examinees, as well as examinees who are from the majority group, may be mystified by medical or psychological terminology. They may be reticent about discussing a personal or family problem with an outsider because it "may be perceived as a reflection of personal inadequacy and as a stigma upon the entire family" (Kumabe et al., 1985, p. 130). This is especially true for some Asian American groups. Consequently, be sensitive to any subtle cues that examinees or their parents give you regarding their willingness to talk about personal issues. If you fail to recognize their preferences and mistakenly urge them to be open and direct, they may resent your suggestion and become silent.

Communication difficulties arise when culturally and linguistically diverse examinees view examiners as authority figures. In the presence of authority figures, they may become passive and inhibited in their communications and reluctant to ask questions or express disagreement (Kumabe et al., 1985).

Culturally and linguistically diverse examinees may respond at their own pace to your interview or test questions (Tharp, 1989). Some Native American children, for example, prefer to wait before responding to questions. If they feel hurried, they may resent your intrusion. Do not perceive their hesitation as refusal to talk to you or as resistance. Rather, respect their need for silence between your question and their answer. In contrast, some Native Hawaiians may interrupt your questions or comments because they want to show their involvement; in such cases, don't interpret their interruptions as a sign of rudeness.

Another source of problems is examiners' misinterpretation of examinees' communications. The following exaggerated fictional excerpt illustrates the danger of making interpretations and diagnoses when you are not familiar with the examinee's jargon.

IE: I was at home and this cat I know came in and asked to borrow some ends from me so he could buy some tickets to the show. (IR notes, "Delusions that cats can talk and that ends can be used as money.")

IE: Then, I was shooting the breeze with my chick and the pigs came along and took us to jail. (IR notes, "Fantasies of using a baby chicken to shoot breezes and delusional thinking that pigs can take people to jail.")

IE: I didn't have on my best rags, and they wouldn't let me use a wire to call. (IR notes, "Claims to wear rags of various quality and believes wires can be used to make phone calls. Definite signs of delusions.")

IE: Before the pigs came, I smoked some horse while my chick got high on snow. (IR notes, "Bizarre ideation in thinking that he could smoke a horse and misperceptions that people can use snow to change their mood. Continues to make references to pigs and chicks in his fantasies. Signs of distorted thinking and confusion.")

(*Diagnosis:* Paranoid schizophrenia with delusional material, distorted thinking, and confusion. Psychological treatment needed. Prognosis is guarded.)

Here is the translation in standard English of what the examinee was saying:

I was at home and a guy I know asked to borrow some money to buy tickets to the show. Then, I was talking to my girlfriend and the police came along and took us to jail. I didn't have on my best clothes, and they wouldn't let me use a phone to call. Before the police came, I smoked some heroin while my girlfriend got high on cocaine.

Examiners and examinees may give symptoms different interpretations, depending on their group membership. For example, behavior viewed as hypersensitive or paranoid by a middle-class Euro American examiner may be viewed as reality-oriented coping by a non–Euro American examiner or examinee.

Language may pose a problem in interviewing a family, particularly when the family members have different levels of proficiency in their native language and in English. If the parents prefer to speak Spanish and the child prefers to speak English, for example, you may have difficulty knowing which language to use and whether to use an interpreter. When the child's command of English is better than that of the parents, the child may take advantage of the parents' limited language skills to control the flow of information to the parents. In such situations, the child becomes powerful, thus reversing the usual parent-child relationship. Later in the chapter, we discuss working with an interpreter.

Language considerations for African Americans.   Some African American children and their parents speak a variant of English that linguists call *Black English, nonstandard Black English, Black dialect,* or *Ebonics.* (The term *Ebonics* is a combination of "ebony" and "phonics.") Black English tends to be used by urban African Americans and by African Americans who remain isolated racially and economically in poor African American communities (Lynch & Hanson, 1992). It is primarily used in informal settings, such as at home and among friends, rather than in business or professional settings.

Black English shares many language features with standard English, but it has several distinguishing pronunciational and grammatical features (see Table 19-4). Features include use of "be" to denote an ongoing action ("he be going to school"), dropping of linking verbs ("you smart"), shortened plurals ("thirty cent"), dropping of some final consonants ("las" instead of "last" or "mas" instead of "mask"), and substitution for some pronouns ("that's the person got all the money"). Other markers include substitution of /ks/ for /sk/ in the final position, as in "ax" for "ask," and substitution of the base form for the past, present, or future verb form, as in "he goes" for "he went," "he is going," or "he will go." Black English is a fully formed linguistic system with its own rules of grammar and pronunciation; it has a rich repertoire of forms and usages.

Black English has contributed to American society in many ways (Emmons, 1996):

Table 19-4
Some Differences Between Black English and Standard English

Black English		Standard English	
Usage	Example	Usage	Example
1. Uses *got*	The girls got a cat.	1. Uses *have*	The girls have a cat.
2. Omits *is* and *are*	The cat in the wagon.	2. Uses *is* and *are*	The cat is in the wagon.
3. Omits the third-person singular ending *-s* from some verbs	The man ask the boy what to wear.	3. Uses the *-s* ending on verbs	The man asks the boy what to wear.
4. Omits the *-ed* ending from verbs	The dog get chase by the cat.	4. Uses the *-ed* ending on verbs	The dog was chased by the cat.
5. Uses *do*	The girl do pull the wagon to the boat.	5. Uses *does*	The girl does pull the wagon to the boat.
6. Uses *be* in place of *am, is,* and *are*	The big ball be rolling down the hill.	6. Uses *am, is,* and *are* in place of *be*	The big ball is rolling down the hill.
7. Uses *he be, we be,* and *they be*	They be going home.	7. Uses *he is, we are,* and *they are*	They are going home.
8. Pronounces *th* at beginning of a word as *d*	Des boys kick de ball.	8. Pronounces *th* at the beginning of a word as *th*	These boys kick the ball.
9. Pronounces *th* at end of word as *f*	In the baf, he washed his mouf and played wif a toy.	9. Pronounces *th* at the end of a word as *th*	In the bath, he washed his mouth and played with a toy.
10. Drops the final *r* and *g* from words	My fatha and motha were talkin and laughin.	10. Pronounces the final *r* and *g* in words	My father and mother were talking and laughing.

It has enriched the fabric of American English. Black English is in jazz. Among the hundreds of the jazz world's words that have filtered into the American lexicon are "hip," "cool," "gig," "jiving around," "get high" and "gimme five." Black English is in blues and soul, giving America expressive, often sensual, words and phrases like "hot," "baby," "mojo," "fine," "mess with," "thang" (as doin' my), "take it easy," "slick," "rip-off," "cool out," and "bad." Black English is in Negro spirituals ("Dat Ole Man River," "Ah Got Shoes"). It is in gospel ("Ain't No Devil in Hell Gonna Walk on the Jesus in Me") and through these mediums of expression has found home in the vernacular of the black church. (p. B9)

Black English has its roots in the oral traditions of the African ancestors of African Americans. "Black English evolved from West African languages and slave traders who used a form of pidgin English to communicate with African slaves who were allowed neither to speak their tribal languages nor to learn English in a classroom" (*Los Angeles Times,* 1996, p. M4, with changes in notation). In many African groups, history and traditions were transmitted orally, and the elder who kept this information was a revered member of the community. African American culture maintains the tradition of orality. To *rap, sound,* or *run it down* is a prized oral skill. Sources of prestige among inner-city African American youth include skill in using language in ritual insults, verbal routines, singing, jokes, and storytelling. Oral

skills are esteemed not just at the street level, but at every level of African American culture.

In school, teachers may tell African American children that their dialect is "wrong" and that standard English dialect is "right." By extension, African American children may feel that they are inadequate and inferior to other children who speak standard English. These feelings may extend to the psychological evaluation and may lead to reticence and even withdrawal. Regardless of your ethnicity, there may not be much you can do to alleviate such feelings immediately, but children may begin to talk to you if you are supportive and encouraging. African American children who speak both Black English and standard English have a highly developed skill. *Do not view Black English as inferior to standard English.*

Schools have often failed to appreciate that African American children have spoken and written language skills that are extremely useful, such as "keen listening and observational skills, quick recognition of nuanced roles, rapid-fire dialogue, hard-driving argumentation, succinct recapitulation of an event, striking metaphors, and comparative analyses based on unexpected analogies" (Heath, 1989, p. 370). Schools usually make little effort to help African American children use these skills in the classroom.

Some African Americans continue to use Black English because of habit, ease of usage, peer pressure, and group identification and because it provides a sense of protection, belonging, and solidarity. The social distance between African Americans and Euro Americans contributes to the maintenance of African English. Encouraging African American children to speak in their natural language may enable them to speak more freely about themselves and, thus, may give you a better sample of their language skills. Recognize, however, that some African American children and adults are comfortable using either Black English or standard English, depending on the situation. And use of standard English by African Americans may be important for their social and economic mobility. You must attend carefully to the communications of examinees who speak Black English if you are not familiar with the language.

If, as our folk theories maintain, schools are in the business of improving benefits for society, they have much to learn from the oral and literate traditions of African American family and community life.

—Shirley Brice Heath

Language considerations for Hispanic Americans. Linguistically, Hispanic American children and their families are a heterogeneous group, with wide variations in their degree of mastery of English and Spanish. Some Hispanic American children are equally fluent in both languages, whereas others have difficulty in both languages. When Hispanic American children speak Spanish as their primary language, the Euro American examiner may have difficulty talking with them without an interpreter. Speech patterns of bilingual Hispanic American children can be an intricate mixture of English and Spanish. The complexity of using both languages in the home makes it difficult for some Hispanic American children to become proficient in either language.

Spanish-speaking children may encounter four types of difficulties when they speak their own language.

1. *Borrowing from English.* Because their Spanish vocabulary may be limited, they may borrow from their English vocabulary to complete expressions begun in Spanish. For example, they may say "Yo estaba leyendo cuando it started to rain" (I was reading when it started to rain).

2. *Anglicizing words.* They may "anglicize certain words or…borrow English words to develop specific linguistic patterns (e.g., *'Está reinando'* for 'It's raining' [instead of *'Está lloviendo'*], calling a grocery store a *'groceria'* [instead of *'una tienda de abarrotes'*], or using *'carpeta'* for 'rug' [instead of *'alfombra'*])" (Marin & Marin, 1991, p. 86). English words given Spanish pronunciations and endings are called pochismos. Examples of pochismos include the word *huachar* (from the English verb "to watch"), used instead of the correct Spanish verb *mirar,* and the word *chuzar* (from the English verb "to choose"), used instead of the correct Spanish word *escoger.*

3. *Pronunciation problems.* They may have difficulties in pronunciation and enunciation in both Spanish and English.

4. *Word order problems.* They may maintain Spanish word order while speaking English.

Language considerations for Asian Americans. When Euro American clinicians evaluate Asian Americans, misunderstandings may arise because of the ways Asian Americans use language or pronounce English words. For example, some Asian Americans tend to avoid using the word *no* because they consider it rude to do so. "The word 'yes' can mean 'no' or 'perhaps.' A direct 'no' is avoided because it may cause the same individual to lose face. Hesitance, ambiguity, subtlety, and implicity are dominant in Chinese speech" (Giger & Davidhizar, 1991, p. 361).

Asian languages also are context bound:

Most of the meaningful information is either in the physical context or internalized in the person who receives the information, while relatively little is contained in the verbally transmitted part of the message…. The speaker or sender's true intent is thus often camouflaged in the context of the situation…. Nonverbal communication thus conveys significantly more information in high-context Asian cultures, wherein silence is particularly valued. (Lynch & Hanson, 1992, pp. 232, 233)

Language considerations for Native Americans. There is no universal, traditional Native American language (Everett et al., 1983). Each tribe is likely to have its own language, and within a tribe different dialects may exist. Like other culturally and linguistically diverse groups, Native Americans differ in their command of the English language: "As with any bilingual group, these abilities range from a very articulate command of English to…a limited receptive vocabulary and little or no expressive vocabulary" (Everett et al., 1983, p. 592).

If you speak only English, you may experience difficulties in communicating with Native American children and their parents who speak a native language primarily or who have limited knowledge of English. In addition, you will need to consider that Native Americans are more likely than Euro Americans to be hesitant to speak, to speak softly, to give short responses that lack important details, to fear making a mistake, to be nonassertive, and to be reluctant to offer self-disclosures.

[American] Indians are sort of an invisible people. There are a lot of [American] Indians in this country, and people have no idea of what to expect from us.

—Sheila Tousey

Nonverbal communication difficulties. Nonverbal communications are another potential source of communication difficulties in cross-cultural assessments. Areas of difficulty may include perception and use of personal and interpersonal space (proxemics); body movements (such as facial expressions, posture, and gestures), characteristics of movement, and eye contact (kinesics); and vocal cues used in talking (paralanguage). Misunderstandings of nonverbal communication contribute to sustaining stereotypic interpersonal judgments. Examples of difficulties in nonverbal communication follow.

Proxemics. Hispanic Americans and African Americans tend to stand closer to the person they are talking with than do Euro Americans. When assessing members of these culturally and linguistically diverse groups, Euro American examiners may back away from the examinee. Such behavior may be misinterpreted as aloof, cold, or haughty; as expressing a desire not to communicate; or as a sign of superiority. Euro American examiners, in turn, may mistakenly view the ethnic examinee's behavior as inappropriately intimate or as a sign of pushiness or aggressiveness (Sue, 1990).

Some culturally and linguistically diverse groups will be sensitive to the spatial arrangements in the examination. "Chinese people feel more comfortable in a side-by-side or right-angle arrangement and may feel uncomfortable when placed in a face-to-face situation. Euro Americans prefer to sit face-to-face or at right angles to each other" (Giger & Davidhizar, 1991, p. 363, with changes in notation).

Kinesics. Cultures may interpret the same gestures in different ways. For example, some cultures interpret the thumbs-up gesture as obscene, and to people from Southeast Asia the American bye-bye gesture means "come here." Cultural upbringing also shapes how people move their bodies. For example, people from Northern Europe tend to hold their torsos rigidly, whereas those from the Caribbean tend to move their bodies more fluidly (Dresser, 1996).

Euro Americans usually view smiling as an indication of positive affect. However, to Asian Americans, smiling may suggest weakness. They consider restraint of feeling to be a sign of maturity and wisdom. Thus, Euro American examiners may assume that Asian American examinees are out of touch with their feelings when, in reality, they are following cultural patterns. Many Native Americans and Japanese avoid eye contact as a sign of respect or deference. In such cases, it is wrong to assume that avoidance of eye contact indicates "inattentiveness, rudeness, aggressiveness, shyness, or low intelligence" (Sue, 1990, p. 426).

African Americans tend to make greater eye contact when speaking than when listening. The reverse is true of Euro Americans, who tend to make more eye contact when listening than when speaking. For African Americans, attentiveness is signaled by mere physical proximity. When African American listeners do not look at the speaker, it is wrong to interpret their behavior as sullen, resistant, or uncooperative. And when Euro American listeners look at the speaker, it is wrong to interpret their behavior as undue scrutiny of the speaker (Sue, 1990).

Japanese people tend to present a blank, nearly motionless facial expression that reveals little of their inner feelings to the Western observer. Westerners, in contrast, tend to keep their forehead and eyebrows constantly in motion as they speak. Thus, "simply because of the greater stillness of the Japanese face there tends to be a large amount of Japanese-Western miscommunication: The Japanese are regarded as noncomprehending or even antagonistic" (Morsbach, 1988, p. 206).

Paralanguage. Silence, for Asian Americans, is traditionally a sign of respect for elders. When an Asian American speaker becomes silent, it may not be a cue for the listener to begin talking. "Rather, it may indicate a desire to continue speaking after making a particular point. At other times, silence may be a sign of politeness and respect, rather than a lack of desire to continue speaking" (Sue, 1990, p. 426). Native Americans may remain silent in some situations as an act of patience and respect. Thus, when assessing members of culturally and linguistically diverse groups, do not interpret reticence to speak out as a sign of ignorance or lack of motivation. Sometimes, if you break the silence, you may discourage further elaboration.

Asian Americans, Native Americans, and some Hispanic Americans value indirectness in communications. Use of euphemisms and ambiguity serves as a way of not embarrassing or hurting the feelings of the other person. Native Americans perceive the asking of direct questions (as occurs when you are taking a social history) as rude or incompetent or an invasion of individual privacy. They prefer that the examiner share personal information about himself or herself (self-disclosure) or deduce the problem by instinct. In contrast, Euro Americans accept direct interrogation and an impersonal examiner style (Everett, Proctor, & Cartmell, 1983).

Comment on Background Considerations

When you evaluate children and parents who are members of culturally and linguistically diverse groups, be prepared to consider issues related to ethnic and racial identity, acculturation, language, changing family patterns, sex roles, religious and traditional beliefs, customs for dealing with crisis and change, racism, poverty, social class, health care practices, and the interactions among these factors. Children and parents who maintain strong ties to their culture, particularly recent refugees or immigrants, may be influenced by indigenous cultural beliefs and practices that affect the symptoms they develop, how they understand the symptoms, their coping mechanisms, their help-seeking behavior, their use of services, and their satisfaction with services and clinical outcomes (Chung & Lin, 1994). Knowledge that you gain about these and related issues will help you conduct the assessment, formulate a diagnosis, and develop an intervention plan.

You will likely have the difficult task of evaluating whether behaviors that suggest personality or temperament problems in the majority group reflect similar problems in minority groups. For example, when culturally and linguistically diverse examinees remain silent, speak softly, or avoid extended eye contact, are they revealing shyness, weakness, or reluctance to speak or are they exhibiting politeness and respect? Does expressing emotions in an indirect, understated way with little emotion suggest denial, lack of affect, lack of awareness of one's feelings, deceptiveness, or resistance, or do such expressions suggest a wish to sustain interpersonal harmony (Uba, 1994)? The failure to understand cultural practices can lead to incorrect diagnoses and ineffective interventions.

DYNAMICS OF CROSS-ETHNIC AND CROSS-CULTURAL ASSESSMENT

In cross-ethnic and cross-cultural assessments, your effectiveness will suffer if you display a patronizing attitude, fail to recognize the value of examinees' traditional customs and mores, or are obsessed with the examinees' culture (LaFromboise, Trimble, & Mohatt, 1990). You will be considered patronizing if you expect the worst from examinees or lower your expectations of them. Examinees who are from culturally and linguistically different groups may be especially attentive to any indications of prejudice, superiority, disapproval, or rejection. Trust will be difficult to establish if examinees fear that you are trying to influence their value structure, thereby separating them from their own group and traditions. These individuals want help with their problems, not help in changing cultures. Alienation is the likely result when you focus too much on their customs, mores, and traditions.

Majority Examiner with Minority Examinee

Difficulties in the relationship between a majority examiner and a minority examinee stem from several sources. Because of racial antagonism, minority examinees may find it difficult to react to majority examiners as individuals, and vice versa. Minority examinees may view majority examiners with suspicion and distrust, as part of the hostile majority world. And, because examiners who are from majority groups have been encouraged through education and training to view prejudice as unacceptable, they may deny or suppress negative reactions toward examinees who are from minority groups. When majority examiners begin to feel confused or guilty about their own racial and class identity and allow these feelings to intrude on the relationship or on decisions that need to be made, difficulties are likely to arise. For example, majority examiners may miss subtle cues given by minority examinees, may be too accepting of behaviors, may give credit to borderline or vague responses, or may fail to probe sensitive topics.

Misinterpretations of intercultural communication will occur when minority examinees view majority examiners as immature, rude, and lacking in finesse because they want to get to the point quickly. Similarly, majority examiners should not view minority examinees as evasive and afraid to confront their problems because they communicate indirectly.

Majority examiners must recognize that minority examinees will be judging their behavior. If majority examiners speak bluntly and directly, some minority examinees (such as Asian Americans) may view this behavior as socially disruptive, embarrassing, or even hurtful (Uba, 1994). Minority examinees will also be frustrated when the social cues they give are not picked up by majority examiners.

Minority Examiner with Majority Examinee

Examiners who are from a minority group may experience difficulties in their relationships with examinees who are from the majority group because of the sociocultural aspects of minority-majority interpersonal relations. Conflicts may arise if majority examinees avoid the race issue, deprecate the examiner, have special admiration for the examiner, or view the examiner as all-forgiving or uncritical. Examiners who are from a minority group, on the other hand, may be unsympathetic or punitive because of hostility toward the majority group, or they may overcompensate by being too permissive (denying their hostility toward majority examinees, overidentifying with the majority group, or being overly liberal in scoring the responses of majority examinees). Any of these dynamics can affect the examination process.

Minority Examiner with Minority Examinee of the Same Group

Examiners who are from the same minority group as examinees may be in the best position to obtain reliable and valid information. However, if these examiners also are from the middle class, they may have some difficulties with same-minority examinees who are from the lower class. Difficulties arise in such cases when examiners (a) cannot accept examinees because of their class, (b) become defensive, (c) overidentify with examinees, or (d) view work with minority examinees as lower in status and priority than work with majority examinees. Similarly, difficulties arise when minority examinees perceive these examiners as (a) collaborators with the majority community, (b) objects of jealousy because of their success in the majority community, (c) less competent than majority examiners, or (d) too removed from their problems.

If minority examiners believe that minority examinees' problems primarily stem from sociopolitical or economic factors, they may dismiss the examinees' psychological problems and instead deliver lectures about social-class oppression (Hunt, P. L., 1987). This is unprofessional and unacceptable. Examiners who are members of a minority group walk a fine line between overidentification and objectivity when evaluating minority examinees of the same ethnic background.

Minority Examiner with Minority Examinee of a Different Group

Examiners who are from a minority group may experience difficulties in their relationships with examinees who are from a different minority group. There may be problems associated with racial antagonism, depending on how the groups have been getting along in society at large. Examinees may be envious of these examiners, believing, for example, that they have been given special treatment because of their group membership. The examiners might have similar feelings about the examinees. However, because the examiners and examinees are likely to have had similar experiences with racism and discrimination, minority examiners may have increased empathy for examinees from any minority group.

No oppressive White person can hurt me as much as a Black sister, for no oppressive White person knows so well where to hurt me. Turn this around and it is a Black sister's love and support that can allow me to soar because her power and strength is a reflection of my own strength and power.
—Anonymous (cited by J. van Heeswyk and J. Hibbert)

Possible Distortions in Cross-Ethnic and Cross-Cultural Assessments

Preoccupation with and heightened sensitivity to ethnic differences may lead to distortions, guardedness, and evasiveness on the part of examinees and to guardedness, failure to probe, defensiveness, and feelings of intimidation on the part of examiners. Because responses given by both examinees and examiners require subtle forms of cognitive activity—such as summarizing one's opinion to oneself, estimating the listener's probable reaction, and then deciding whether to convey the opinion accurately to the listener—there is always the potential for both examinees and examiners to distort opinions, attitudes, and even facts. Do some examinees replace genuine feelings with a facade of submissiveness, pleasure, impassivity, or humility? Can examiners be genuine and avoid patronizing? Is any form of social distance between examiners and examinees likely to create difficulties with rapport and communication? These and similar questions are a matter of special concern in cross-ethnic, cross-cultural, and cross-class assessments.

Comment on Cross-Ethnic and Cross-Cultural Assessment

Examiners are not immune to racism and to harboring stereotypes. *It is your responsibility to ensure that any such views you have do not adversely affect the assessment.* Your stereotypes might change, and you must monitor them constantly lest they interfere with your ability to conduct a meaningful assessment.

Despite generalizations made about ethnic relations and about the examiner-examinee relationship in particular, each assessment involves two unique individuals. It is their specific attitudes, values, experiences, and behavior that will determine whether racism and bias enter the assessment. Even examiners and examinees from the same minority group or from the same majority group may be mismatched if they have different values. And, conversely, examiners and examinees from different minority groups or from a minority group and the majority group can work cooperatively when they have similar values and speak the same language. Usually, examiners will be effective when they are tolerant and accepting of examinees, despite value differences. Your goal is to establish a professional relationship—characterized by trust and acceptance—with people of all ethnic groups. If you cannot establish such a relationship, refer the examinee to another psychologist.

Frank and Ernest

Copyright © 1991 by Thaves / Reprinted with permission.

Human beings are more alike than unalike, and what is true anywhere is true everywhere, yet I encourage travel to as many destinations as possible.... Perhaps travel cannot prevent bigotry, but by demonstrating that all peoples laugh, cry, eat, worry, and die, it can introduce the idea that if we try to understand each other, we may even become friends.

—Maya Angelou

ASSESSMENT OF BILINGUAL EXAMINEES

Bilingualism refers to the ability to use two languages. It generally involves the learning of a second language after the primary one, although it may involve the learning of two languages simultaneously. Research indicates that children who are fluently bilingual have advantages over their monolingual peers on both verbal and nonverbal tasks (Bialystok, 1992; Diaz & Klinger, 1991). They have better developed selective attention skills and language processing skills, such as more sensitivity to language structure and syntax and greater flexibility in language usage.

The advantages of bilingualism, however, depend in part on whether (a) children are adding the second language to a well-developed first language and (b) whether the second language is gradually replacing the first language. Hispanic American children, for example, usually learn English as a second language and then use this second language in their school work; they continue, however, to use Spanish at home and in the community, in speaking but seldom in reading. Because of this form of bilingualism, some Hispanic American children fail to develop a sufficient mastery of either language, and learning is more difficult under such conditions.

You can use several informal methods to determine the language preference of a child who speaks more than one language. First, ask the child in which language he or she prefers to be tested. Second, observe which language the child uses in the classroom and at home. Third, ask the teacher and parent to describe the child's language preference, using questions such as those shown in Table 19-5. Finally, ask the teacher to complete the rating scale shown in Table 19-6.

Several formal measures are available to assess bilingual verbal ability; unfortunately, none of those mentioned below has obtained a nationally representative sample of individuals with proficiency in each language of the test. One of the most recent tests is the Bilingual Verbal Ability Tests (BVAT; Muñoz-Sandoval, Cummins, Alvarado, & Ruef, 1998). This individually administered test is composed of three subtests drawn from the Woodcock-Johnson–Revised (1989) Tests of Cognitive Ability—namely, Picture Vocabulary, Oral Vocabulary, and Verbal Analogies. The English version of the test was translated into 15 languages: Arabic, Chinese (simplified and traditional), French, German, Haitain-Creole, Hindi,

Table 19-5
Interview Questions for Teacher and Parent to Determine Child's Language Preference

Questions for Teacher

1. What language does _____ use in the classroom?
2. In what language can _____ read?
3. In what language does _____ speak with his (her) classmates?
4. In what language does _____ write?
5. Overall, how competent is _____ in English?
6. Overall, how competent is _____ in _____ (language)?

Questions for Parent

1. In what language do you speak with _____ ?
2. In what language does your husband (wife) speak with _____ ?
3. In what language do you speak with your husband (wife)?
4. In what language does _____ speak with you?
5. In what language does _____ speak with his (her) father (mother)?
6. (If applicable) In what language does _____ speak with his (her) sisters and brothers?
7. What language does _____ prefer to speak at school?
8. In what language are the television programs _____ watches?
9. In what language do you read stories to _____ ?
10. In what language does _____ prefer to be tested?

Italian, Japanese, Korean, Polish, Portuguese, Russian, Spanish, Turkish, and Vietnamese. Each item is first administered in English. Failed items are then readministered in the examinee's other language. The overall score consists of the number of items answered correctly in either language. Raw scores are converted to standard scores, age- and grade-equivalent scores, percentile ranks, a relative proficiency index, and instructional zones (negligible, very limited, limited, fluent, advanced).

There are several technical problems with the test. First, the test was not standardized in each language. Second, data are not presented about the difficulty level of each translated item in each language. Third, each language version does not include all of the items that are in the English version. Fourth, concurrent validity studies are not presented in each language. Although psychometrically imperfect, the BVAT does provide information that can be helpful in classifying an examinee's proficiency in more than one language. It is particularly useful because it includes languages besides Spanish.

Other individually administered tests that can be used to assess language proficiency in English and in Spanish include the following:

• The Language Assessment Scales–Oral (LAS–O; Duncan & DeAvila, 1990), a paper-and-pencil multiple-choice

Table 19-6
SOLOM Teacher Observation Checklist

STUDENT ORAL LANGUAGE OBSERVATION MATRIX

Student's name: _____   Date: _____

Grade: _____   Teacher's name: _____

Class: _____   Language observed: _____

Directions:
Based on your observation of the student, put an "X" across the category that best describes the student's abilities.

Note. The SOLOM should be administered only by persons who themselves score at level 4 or above in all categories in the language being assessed.

	1	2	3	4	5
A. Comprehension	Does not understand even simple conversation.	Has great difficulty following what is said. Can comprehend only social conversation spoken slowly and with frequent repetitions.	Understands most of what is said at slower-than-normal speed with repetitions.	Understands nearly everything at normal speed, although occasional repetition may be necessary.	Understands everyday conversation and normal classroom discussions.
B. Fluency	Speech is so halting and fragmentary that conversation is impossible.	Usually hesitant and often silent because of language limitations.	Speech in everyday conversation and classroom discussions is frequently disrupted by a search for the correct expression.	Speech in everyday conversation and classroom discussions is generally fluent with occasional lapses while searching for the correct expression.	Speech in everyday conversation and classroom discussions is fluent and effortless and approximates that of a native speaker.
C. Vocabulary	Vocabulary limitations are so extreme that conversation is impossible.	Misuses words, has limited vocabulary, and has difficulty with comprehension.	Frequently uses wrong words. Conversation is somewhat limited because of inadequate vocabulary.	Occasionally uses inappropriate terms or must rephrase ideas because of language inadequacies.	Extent of vocabulary and usage of idiomatic words approximate those of a native speaker.
D. Pronunciation	Pronunciation problems are so severe that speech is unintelligible.	Hard to understand because of pronunciation problems. Must frequently repeat himself or herself in order to be understood.	Pronunciation problems necessitate concentration on the part of the listener and occasionally lead to misunderstanding.	Always intelligible, although the listener is conscious of an accent and occasional inappropriate intonation patterns.	Pronunciation and intonation approximate those of a native speaker.
E. Grammar	Errors in grammar and word order are so severe that speech is unintelligible.	Makes so many grammar and word errors that comprehension is difficult. Must often rephrase or restrict himself or herself to basic speech patterns.	Makes frequent errors of grammar and word order that occasionally obscure meaning.	Occasionally makes grammatical or word order errors, but these do not obscure meaning.	Grammar and word order approximate those of a native speaker.

Note. A total score of about 20 can be considered proficient.
Source: Adapted from SOLOM Teacher Observation, developed by San Jose Area Bilingual Consortium.

oral response test with four levels: preschool age, elementary school age, secondary school age, and adult ages.

- The Language Assessment Scales–Reading and Writing (LAS–R/W; Duncan & DeAvila, 1994) a paper-and-pencil multiple-choice and essay test with three levels (grade 2 through high school)
- The Woodcock-Muñoz Language Survey (Woodcock & Muñoz-Sandoval, 1993), which is reviewed in Chapter 18

After making an informal and formal assessment of language proficiency, classify the child's degree of language proficiency. A useful 5-point classification scale follows:

1. Monolingual speaker of a language other than English (speaks the other language exclusively).
2. Predominantly speaks a language other than English (speaks mostly the other language, but also speaks some English).
3. Bilingual (speaks the other language and English with equal ease).
4. Predominantly speaks English (speaks mostly English, but also speaks some in the other language).
5. Monolingual speaker of English (speaks English exclusively).

INTERPRETERS

When you evaluate an examinee or interview a parent who speaks a language you do not speak, you must employ the services of an interpreter. Language usage can vary depending on such factors as country of origin, ethnicity, economic status, and geographical area. Before you engage an interpreter, ask the child about his or her language preference (see Table 19-2). Also, ask the parents and, if possible, the child's teacher the questions shown in Table 19-5. *Recognize that, no matter how carefully the interpreter makes the translation, the examination is likely to be ineffective if you and the interpreter are not familiar with the examinee's culture, values, and ideology.*

If you employ an interpreter, ask the interpreter to inform the child and parents about her or his role, that she or he is acting as your agent, and that she or he will keep all information confidential. Also have the interpreter tell them that you want to get accurate information, to explain the services clearly, and to make them comfortable in the evaluation. Employing an interpreter will increase the time needed to complete the evaluation; you must schedule accordingly and should consider having more than one session.

Even if the family members speak English as a second language, offer them the services of an interpreter because they may have minimal proficiency in English. Sometimes examinees switch languages during the evaluation in a process called code switching. For example, examinees may change from their primary language to English to discuss topics that would be upsetting if discussed in their primary language.

You should be sure to obtain permission from the child and the parents to use an interpreter. Also, *when you write your report or make notes in the examinee's folder or chart, always note that you used an interpreter.* This is especially important if you quote the examinee.

Difficulties Involving an Interpreter

Although it may not be intentional, interpreters may delete information or make other changes and embellishments in the translations that distort what you and the examinee say. These distortions may lead to inaccurate information. Also, interpreters who are unfamiliar with testing and standardized directions may unintentionally cue the answer when they translate directions or may relay responses from the child inaccurately. You will have no way of knowing whether the interpreter performed exactly the way you intended him or her to perform. Finally, the use of an interpreter may result in loss of rapport between you and the child.

The following are examples of difficulties that can arise when you employ an interpreter:

1. *Failure to reveal symptoms.* Interpreters may not reveal symptoms they believe portray the child or parent in an unfavorable light. Taboo topics for Asian American interpreters, for example, may include sexual matters, financial information, suicidal thoughts, and homicidal thoughts. An interpreter hearing information about these topics may omit details, substitute details, reformulate details, or change the focus of the communication. For example, the interpreter may try to make sense out of disorganized statements made by the examinee and thus prevent you from getting a clear idea of the examinee's mental state.

2. *Mistrust of interpreter.* Some children and parents may be uncomfortable because of the interpreter's age, sex, level of education, relationship to them, or mere presence. They may also distrust the interpreter, fear being judged by the interpreter, fear being misinterpreted, or fear loss of confidentiality.

3. *Preaching to examinees.* Some interpreters, if they believe that the child has strayed from their culture, may preach to the child and parents about the need to follow traditions.

4. *Lack of equivalent concepts.* Some concepts either have no equivalent in other languages or are difficult to translate. Thus, the meaning of important phrases may be lost in translation.

5. *Dialectical and regional differences.* Translations are usually made into a standard language, as translators necessarily have only a limited ability to provide for the many variations that depend on the speaker's country of origin. For example, *toston* means a half-dollar to a Mexican American child but a squashed section of a fried banana to a Puerto Rican child or Cuban child, and the word for kite is *papagayo* in Venezuela, *cometa* in Spain, and *papalote* in Cuba. Some words differ in meaning not only across coun-

tries but within a country as well. For example, the word *guila* means sunny in Sonora, Mexico, but in Mexico City it means prostitute.

6. *Mixture of two languages.* The language familiar to children from culturally and ethnically diverse groups may be a combination of two languages. For Spanish-speaking children, this combination may be Pocho, pidgin, Spanglish, or Tex-Mex. In such cases, a monolingual translation may be inappropriate. Some examples of words that combine English and Spanish are *raite* (ride), *raiteros* (drivers), *lonche* (lunch), *dompe* (dump), *yonke* (junk), *dame un quebrazo* (give me a break), and *los baggies* (baggy jeans).

7. *Changes in difficulty level.* The level of difficulty of words may change because of translation. For example, *animal domestico,* the Spanish equivalent of the common English word *pet,* is an uncommon phrase in Spanish.

8. *Alteration of meaning.* Translation can alter the meaning of words. For example, seemingly harmless English words may translate into Spanish profanity. *Huevo* is the literal translation of the word *eggs,* but the Spanish term *huevón* has more earthy connotations. The context determines the meaning of the word.

9. *Causing offense with colloquial words.* Interpreters may use colloquial words for more formal words and, in the process, inadvertently offend some examinees. For example, use of the Spanish words *pata* for foot and *espinizo* for back, which are more appropriate for animals than for humans, may offend examinees who prefer the more formal words *pie* and *espalda,* respectively.

Suggestions for Working with an Interpreter

Here are some suggestions for working with an interpreter:

1. *Selecting an interpreter.* Select an interpreter who is thoroughly familiar with the examinee's language and, if possible, with the linguistic variations or dialect used by the child's ethnic group. As noted earlier, select an interpreter who also is knowledgeable about the child's culture.

2. *Briefing the interpreter.* Brief the interpreter thoroughly on issues that may affect his or her role. For example, *before* you begin the assessment, discuss with the interpreter (a) the goals of the evaluation, (b) areas you want to cover, (c) the need to address sensitive topics, (d) the level of competence the interpreter has in both languages, (e) the attitude of the interpreter toward the examinee and possible problem areas, (f) the need to translate your questions and comments and those of the examinee word for word, and (g) the need to maintain confidentiality. This means that the interpreter should not add words, delete words, or interpret what the examinee says. Also inform the interpreter not to repeat questions unless requested to do so.

Stress the importance of establishing rapport, maintaining neutrality, not reacting judgmentally to what the examinee says or to what you say, transmitting all the information be-

tween the parties, and preserving the confidentiality of the proceedings. You may need to deal with the feelings and reactions of some interpreters, especially when you discuss extremely sensitive issues such as child maltreatment or rape. Also, the gender of the interpreter may be an issue if there are cultural taboos against males and females discussing certain topics. This is an issue that should be discussed before the assessment.

If the interpreter is translating test questions, stress the importance of (a) following standard procedures (e.g., not prompting or commenting on responses and stating questions exactly), (b) avoiding nonverbal gestures that signal whether the examinee's responses were correct or incorrect, and (c) recording precisely the examinee's responses. A brief explanation of the reasons for following standardized test procedures will help the interpreter better understand his or her role.

3. *Discussing technical terms.* Discuss beforehand any technical terms and concepts that may pose a problem for translation. Ideally, the interpreter should be familiar with terms related to psychological disorders and medical disorders. Encourage the interpreter to conduct a sentence-by-sentence interpretation to ensure that each translated phrase is equivalent to the phrase in the original language, to refrain from giving explanations that you did not ask him or her to provide, and to mirror your affective tone as closely as possible. Use clear, standard, formal English and avoid technical terms and colloquialisms if possible. Even if the interpreter knows the correct translation of your technical term or jargon (e.g., *esquizofrenia* for *schizophrenia*), the examinee may not know that word. Slang words, in particular, are difficult to translate accurately.

4. *Practicing with the interpreter.* Practice with the interpreter *before* the assessment to help the interpreter develop good translating skills.

5. *Selecting a nonfamily member as the interpreter.* Choose an interpreter who is not a family member, a family friend, or someone the family knows, because of possible sensitive subject matter or conflicts of interest.

6. *Involving the interpreter as an assistant.* Engage the interpreter as an assistant, not as a co-examiner. Unless the interpreter is a qualified mental health professional and you give her or him permission to do so, the interpreter should not formulate her or his own questions. If the interpreter does formulate questions, distinguish between her or his questions and yours.

7. *Positioning of self and interpreter.* Face the examinee when you talk to him or her. Position the interpreter at your side, and speak as though the examinee can understand you.

8. *Talking to the interpreter.* Avoid talking to the interpreter about the family in the presence of family members.

9. *Encouraging attention to details.* Encourage the interpreter to tell you about the paralinguistic aspects of the examinee's speech—such as cries, laughter, sighs, stuttering, and melodic voice changes—and where these occurred. After the session, ask the interpreter to describe the quality of

the examinee's vocabulary and language, especially in comparison with that of other children the same age. Although the interpreter's description will not be that of a professional, it may nonetheless be useful.

10. *Speaking and word usage.* Speak in a normal tone of voice; use facial expressions that are not forced or faked; use short, simple sentences; and avoid idioms, colloquialisms, and jargon. Ask the interpreter to alert you to specific translated words that might be too difficult for the examinee to understand. You then can rephrase as needed.

11. *Observing the examinee.* Be attentive to the examinee's reactions, gestures, and facial expressions. If the examinee looks confused or puzzled, try to determine at what point the translation may have gone wrong or whether other factors have interfered with the communication. Do not interrupt the interpreter.

12. *Summarizing and confirming.* Summarize what you have learned at appropriate points, and ask the examinee to confirm your understanding.

13. *Allowing extra time.* As noted previously, allow extra time when you schedule the session, because working with an interpreter will extend the time required to conduct the evaluation.

14. *Reviewing the interpreter's performance.* After you complete the assessment, meet with the interpreter to discuss problems that he or she encountered and to review his or her performance. Include in your report the name and qualifications of the interpreter and any reservations about the reliability and validity of the information you obtained.

15. *Using the interpreter in future sessions.* Use the same interpreter in any future sessions with the examinee and in the post-assessment evaluation, assuming that the interpreter performed adequately.

After you complete the assessment, evaluate the adequacy and the quality of the information. Does the information make sense? Do you believe you have obtained all of the relevant information you need? Are you puzzled by any details? Do you think the interpreter omitted some information? Do you believe the interpreter did her or his job well?

In the post-assessment evaluation, also evaluate the family's understanding of the results and the planned intervention program. Do they seem puzzled? If so, why? Ask them to repeat the major findings and recommendations.

TEST TRANSLATIONS

In an attempt to make intelligence tests (and other tests as well) more appropriate for non-English-speaking children, test items or directions are sometimes translated into their native language. Test translations have the same inherent difficulties as the use of interpreters. These include lack of equivalent concepts in the two languages, minimal or no provision for dialectical or regional variations, and possible changes in the level of difficulty and meaning of translated words.

Studies designed to investigate the effect of Spanish translations of intelligence tests and vocabulary tests reveal no consistent trend. Scores on the Spanish test version may be higher than, similar to, or lower than those on the English version (Bergan & Parra, 1979; Chandler & Plakos, 1969; Chavez, 1982; Eklund & Scott, 1965; Galvan, 1967; Holland, 1960; Keston & Jimenez, 1954; Levandowski, 1975; Myers & Goldstein, 1979; Palmer & Gaffney, 1972; Sattler & Altes, 1984; Sattler, Avila, Houston, & Toney, 1980; Swanson & DeBlassie, 1971; Thomas, 1977). Heavily weighted language-based tests do not appear to provide the most effective way to evaluate Hispanic American children's cognitive skills. Hispanic American children reared in a bilingual environment may not have any "native" language. Although Hispanic American children often learn Spanish in their early years of life, English becomes, in many cases, the predominant mode of communication in their school years.

It is a risky procedure to simply translate a test and still use the English-language norms. Ideally, any translated test should be standardized in the new language on a representative group of individuals. Even then, you must be cautious in using a test normed in, for example, Puerto Rico with a child from, say, Mexico.

THINKING THROUGH THE ISSUES

1. With what ethnic or cultural group do you identify?
2. What are your ethnic group's attitudes toward children with behavioral problems, physical disabilities, or medical illnesses?
3. What are your ethnic group's attitudes toward homelessness, divorce, welfare, and other social issues?
4. How does your ethnic or cultural identity relate to your self-view and self-esteem?
5. How do you feel about members of other ethnic or cultural groups?
6. If you were aware of having your personal biases toward a specific minority group, how would you try to conduct an unbiased assessment?
7. How might your cultural practices and traditions interfere with your ability to understand and relate to examinees from other cultural and ethnic backgrounds?
8. What personal qualities do you have that would be helpful in assessment of culturally and linguistically diverse groups? What personal qualities do you have that would be detrimental?
9. Do you believe that, to be an effective examiner, you must be of the same ethnic group as the examinee? If so, what would you do if you were scheduled to evaluate someone of a different ethnic group?
10. If you were scheduled to be evaluated for your personal problems by someone of an ethnic group different from your own, how would you feel? Would you take any actions to arrange for another professional? If so, why?
11. Do you believe that many problems faced by culturally and linguistically diverse examinees are a direct result of an oppressive society? If so, then what role do you think mental health practitioners have in working with culturally and linguistically diverse groups?

12. Have you ever experienced prejudice? If so, what form of prejudice did you experience, and how did you feel during the experience and afterwards?

13. Do the ethnic groups covered in the chapter retain some unique cultural styles, or have they been largely assimilated?

14. What are some benefits and losses associated with assimilation?

15. What aspects of African American, Hispanic American, Native American, and Asian American cultures do you value the most?

16. How might your development have been different if you had been raised in a culture other than your own?

17. How will it be helpful to you as a clinical assessor to know about the culture of ethnic groups?

18. Can prejudiced examiners be effective clinical assessors? If you do not believe so, then what should be done when an examiner harbors prejudice against an examinee's ethnic group? What ethical guidelines can assist you in answering this question?

19. What experiences have you had with different cultures that have influenced your attitudes and behavior toward children and adults of these groups?

20. What were your reactions to the content of this chapter? For example, was any material disturbing or anxiety provoking? Did any of the material stimulate you to want to learn more about a particular ethnic group or groups?

SUMMARY

1. By considering cultural variables, you will be in a better position to establish rapport, administer tests, obtain valid information, arrive at an accurate diagnosis, and formulate meaningful intervention plans.

2. Our society must recognize and preserve cultural diversity and promote culturally sensitive and culturally relevant clinical services.

3. Broad generalizations about cultural practices do not do justice to regional, generational, socioeconomic, and idiosyncratic variations.

4. Culture is the human-made part of the environment, consisting of highly variable systems of meaning that are learned and shared by a people or an identifiable segment of a population. Culture represents designs and ways of life normally transmitted from one generation to another.

5. Race refers to the physical characteristics, such as skin color, facial features, and hair type, common to a population.

6. Ethnicity refers to the characterization of a group by its common nationality, culture, or language.

7. Social class refers to group designations within a society, usually based on occupation, education, or both.

Background Considerations

8. The U.S. Bureau of the Census estimates that there were 70.4 million children under age 18 living in the United States as of June 1, 2000.

9. The ethnic affiliation of the children was as follows: Euro American, 64%; African American, 15%; Hispanic American, 16%; Asian American, 4%; and Native Americans, less than 1%.

10. It is estimated that by 2050, Hispanic Americans will form 24.3% of the population, up from the current 11.8%, and Asian Americans will make up 9.3%, an increase from the current 3.8%.

11. In the United States, culturally and linguistically diverse groups may face (a) racism and discrimination, (b) poverty, (c) conflicts associated with acculturation and assimilation, especially when children begin to identify more closely with the majority culture and reject their ethnic culture, (d) problems in dealing with medical, educational, social, and law enforcement organizations, and (e) problems in using standard English.

12. In 1998, Euro American families had the lowest poverty rate (6.1%), followed by Asian Americans (11%), Hispanic Americans (22.7%), and African Americans (23.4%).

13. In 1998, 18.3% of all children were living at or below the poverty level. The breakdown for the ethnic groups was as follows: 10.0% for Euro American non-Hispanic children, 17.5% for Asian American children, 33.6% for Hispanic American children, and 36.4% for African American children.

14. In 1998, Asian Americans as a group had the highest percentage of individuals with at least four years of high school or more (84.9%), followed by Euro Americans (83.7%), African Americans (76.0%), and Hispanic Americans (66.5%); for Native Americans in 1990, the figure is 65.6%.

15. Three orientations that can characterize a group's attitude toward human nature are evil orientation, good orientation, and mixed orientation.

16. Three orientations that can characterize a group's attitude toward the relationship between person and nature are subjugation orientation, mastery orientation, and harmony orientation.

17. Three orientations that can characterize a group's attitude toward time are past orientation, present orientation, and future orientation.

18. Three orientations that can characterize a group's attitude toward activity level are being orientation, doing orientation, and being-in-becoming orientation.

19. Three orientations that can characterize a group's attitude toward social relations are lineal orientation, collateral orientation, and individual orientation.

20. Acculturation is the process of cultural change that occurs in individuals when two cultures meet; it leads the individuals to adopt elements of another culture, such as values and social behaviors.

21. The process of acculturation may involve several phases. Individuals may adhere to the traditions of their culture (traditionalism), partake of both the old and the new culture (transitional period), try unsuccessfully to meet the demands of both the old and the new culture (marginality), embrace traditions of the new culture and reject practices of the old culture (assimilation), and integrate practices of both the old and the new culture (biculturalism).

22. Factors affecting acculturation include the history of the person's migration experience, temporal and geographic distance from the country of origin and its indigenous culture, place of residence and socioeconomic status in the homeland, type of neighborhood in the United States, ties with immediate and extended family, role of the family's power and authority, and language and customs.

23. Children (and their families) may face several stresses in dealing with acculturation.

24. Ethnic identity refers to one's sense of belonging to an ethnic group and the part of one's thinking, perceptions, feelings, and behavior that is due to ethnic group membership.

25. Stereotypes of children's culturally and linguistically diverse group may impede their identity formation.

26. Ethnic identification becomes particularly complex when individuals have a biracial heritage.

27. Depending on their degree of acculturation, members of minority groups in the United States may use both traditional and Western methods of healing.

28. The examiner should inquire about what the family believes causes illness or disease.

29. Culturally and linguistically diverse groups' use of mental health and medical services may be affected by the group's cultural values; the group's attitude toward mental health and illness, physical health and illness, psychological treatment, and medical treatment; the availability of medical and mental health services; how accessible the services are to the group; who provides the services; and how culturally relevant the treatment programs are.

30. Factors that may make it difficult for members of culturally and linguistically diverse groups to use the mainstream health care system include perceptions of health and illness that differ from those of the majority culture, unfamiliarity with the clinic or hospital setting, fear of Western medical practices, distrust of Western health care providers because of the prejudice they have experienced, and fear of being turned in to authorities and deported, if they are illegal immigrants.

31. If the family subscribes to mainstream medical and psychological practices *and* to traditional methods, consider encouraging them to seek help from both services. A combined treatment approach may be the most beneficial for these families.

32. You may encounter communication barriers when you work with culturally and linguistically diverse clients.

33. Examiners may misinterpret examinees' communications.

34. Examiners and examinees may give symptoms different interpretations, depending on their group membership.

35. Some African American children and their parents speak a variant of English that linguists call Black English, nonstandard Black English, Black dialect, or Ebonics. (The term *Ebonics* is a combination of "ebony" and "phonics.")

36. Black English shares many language features with standard English, but it has several distinguishing pronunciational and grammatical features.

37. Black English has its roots in the oral traditions of the African ancestors of African Americans.

38. Black English should not be viewed as inferior to standard English.

39. Linguistically, Hispanic American children and their families are a heterogeneous group, with wide variations in their degree of mastery of English and Spanish.

40. Spanish-speaking children may encounter difficulties when they speak their own language because they borrow from English, anglicize words, or have pronunciation and word order problems.

41. When Euro American clinicians evaluate Asian Americans, misunderstandings may arise because of the ways Asian Americans use language or pronounce English words.

42. There is no universal, traditional Native American language. Each tribe is likely to have its own language, and within a tribe different dialects may exist.

43. Native Americans differ in their command of the English language.

44. Nonverbal communications are a potential source of communication difficulties in cross-cultural assessments.

45. Proxemics refers to the perception and use of personal and interpersonal space.

46. Kinesics refers to body movements (such as facial expressions, posture, and gestures), characteristics of movement, and eye contact.

47. Paralanguage refers to the vocal cues used in talking.

48. When you interview children and parents who are members of minority groups, be prepared to consider issues related to ethnic and racial identity, acculturation, language, changing family patterns, sex roles, religious and traditional beliefs, customs for dealing with crisis and change, racism, poverty, social class, health care practices, and the interactions among these factors.

49. Examiners have the difficult task of evaluating whether behaviors that suggest personality or temperament problems in the majority group reflect similar problems in minority groups.

Dynamics of Cross-Ethnic and Cross-Cultural Interviewing

50. In cross-ethnic and cross-cultural assessments, effectiveness will suffer if examiners display a patronizing attitude, fail to recognize the value of examinees' traditional customs and mores, or are obsessed with the examinees' culture.

51. Misinterpretations of intercultural communication will occur when minority examinees view majority examiners as immature, rude, and lacking in finesse because they want to get to the point quickly. Similarly, majority examiners should not view minority examinees as evasive and afraid to confront their problems because they communicate indirectly.

52. Conflicts may arise if majority examinees, when they are interviewed by minority examiners, avoid the race issue, deprecate the examiner, have special admiration for the examiner, or view the examiner as all-forgiving or uncritical. Minority examiners, on the other hand, may be unsympathetic or punitive because of hostility toward the majority group, or they may overcompensate by being too permissive (denying their hostility toward majority examinees or overidentifying with them).

53. Examiners who are from the same minority group as examinees may be in the best position to obtain reliable and valid information. Minority examiners walk a fine line between overidentification and objectivity when interviewing minority examinees of the same ethnic background.

54. Examiners who are from a minority group may experience some difficulties in their relationships with examinees who are from a different minority group because of problems associated with racial antagonism, depending on how the groups have been getting along in society at large.

55. Preoccupation with and heightened sensitivity to ethnic differences may lead to distortions, guardedness, and evasiveness on the part of examinees and to guardedness, failure to probe, defensiveness, and feelings of intimidation on the part of examiners.

56. It is your responsibility to ensure that any stereotypical views you have do not adversely affect the assessment.

57. Examiners will usually be effective when they are tolerant and accepting of examinees, despite value differences. Your goal is to establish a professional relationship, characterized by trust and acceptance.

Assessment of Bilingual Examinees

58. Bilingualism refers to the ability to use two languages.
59. Research indicates that children who are fluently bilingual have advantages over their monolingual peers on both verbal and nonverbal tasks.

Interpreters

60. Before you use an interpreter, learn about the child's language preference.
61. Recognize that, no matter how carefully the interpreter makes the translation, the evaluation is likely to be ineffective if you and the interpreter are not familiar with the examinee's culture, values, and ideology.
62. When you write your report or make notes in the examinee's folder or chart, always note that you used an interpreter. This is especially important if you quote the examinee.
63. There are several potential difficulties in working with interpreters. Interpreters may not reveal symptoms they believe portray the child or parent in an unfavorable light. Some examinees may be uncomfortable with having an interpreter. Some interpreters will preach to examinees instead of being neutral. Some concepts are difficult to translate. Translations sometimes are made with limited provision for dialectical or regional variations. The language familiar to minority children may be a combination of two languages. The level of difficulty of words may change because of translation. Translations can alter the meaning of words. Interpreters may use colloquial words for more formal words and, in the process, inadvertently offend some examinees.
64. Select an interpreter who is thoroughly familiar with the examinee's language and, if possible, with the linguistic variations or dialect used by the child's cultural and linguistic group. Brief the interpreter thoroughly on issues that may affect his or her role. Discuss beforehand any technical terms and concepts that may pose a problem for translation. Practice with the interpreter *before* the interview to help the interpreter develop good translation skills. Because of possible sensitive subject matter or conflicts of interest, choose an interpreter who is not a family member, a family friend, or someone the family knows. Involve the interpreter as an assistant, not as a co-examiner. Face the examinee when you talk to him or her. Avoid talking to the interpreter about the family in the presence of family members. Encourage the interpreter to tell you about the paralinguistic aspects of the examinee's speech. Ask the interpreter to alert you to specific translated words that might be too difficult for the examinee to understand. Summarize what you have learned at appropriate points, and ask the examinee to confirm your understanding. After you complete the interview, meet with the interpreter to discuss problems that he or she encountered and to review his or her performance. Use the same interpreter in any future sessions with the examinee and in the post-assessment evaluation, assuming that the interpreter performed adequately.

Test Translations

65. Test translations have the same inherent difficulties as the use of interpreters. These include lack of equivalent concepts in the two languages, minimal or no provision for dialectical or regional variations, and possible changes in the difficulty and meaning of translated words.
66. Heavily weighted language-based tests do not appear to provide the most effective way to evaluate Hispanic American children's cognitive skills.
67. It is a risky procedure to simply translate a test and still use the English-language norms.
68. Ideally, any translated test should be standardized in the new language on a representative group of individuals.

KEY TERMS, CONCEPTS, AND NAMES

Culture (p. 636)
Race (p. 636)
Ethnicity (p. 636)
Social class (p. 636)
Projections of the U.S. Census Bureau (p. 637)
Poverty rate (p. 637)
Years of school completed (p. 637)
Culturally and linguistically diverse group; minority group (p. 637)
Euro Americans; majority group (p. 637)
Ethnic group (p. 637)
Culture and value orientations (p. 638)
Human nature (p. 638)
Evil orientation (p. 638)
Good orientation (p. 638)
Mixed orientation (p. 638)
Relationship between person and nature (p. 638)
Subjugation orientation (p. 638)
Mastery orientation (p. 638)
Harmony orientation (p. 638)
Time (p. 638)
Past orientation (p. 638)
Present orientation (p. 638)
Future orientation (p. 638)
Activity level (p. 638)
Being orientation (p. 638)
Doing orientation (p. 638)
Being-in-becoming orientation (p. 638)
Social relations (p. 638)
Lineal orientation (p. 638)
Collateral orientation (p. 638)
Individual orientation (p. 638)
Cultural styles (p. 638)
Traditional life styles (p. 638)
Modern life styles (p. 639)
Acculturation (p. 639)
Traditionalism (p. 639)
Transitional period (p. 639)
Marginality (p. 639)
Assimilation (p. 639)
Biculturalism (p. 639)
Ethnic identity (p. 640)
Health care practices (p. 641)
Use of mental health and medical services (p. 641)
Verbal communication difficulties (p. 641)
Black English (p. 642)
Nonverbal communication difficulties (p. 644)

Proxemics (p. 645)

Kinesics (p. 645)

Paralanguage (p. 645)

Dynamics of cross-ethnic and cross-cultural assessment (p. 646)

Bilingualism (p. 648)

Interpreters (p. 650)

Test translations (p. 652)

STUDY QUESTIONS

1. Discuss why it is important to consider cultural variables when you evaluate children and families.

2. How do the concepts of culture, race, ethnicity, and social class differ?

3. What is the ethnic distribution of culturally and linguistically diverse groups in the United States, as discussed in the text?

4. Describe some of the problems faced by culturally and linguistically diverse groups in the United States.

5. What are some key value orientations of culturally and linguistically diverse groups?

6. Discuss acculturation. In your discussion, examine factors affecting acculturation, strategies for dealing with acculturation, and stresses associated with acculturation.

7. Discuss ethnic identity and identification.

8. Discuss some of the factors that may affect culturally and linguistically diverse groups' use of mental and medical health care services.

9. Discuss culture and communication styles. Include in your discussion both verbal and nonverbal communication difficulties. Touch on issues related to proxemics, kinesics, and paralanguage.

10. Discuss cross-ethnic and cross-cultural assessment. Include in your discussion issues related to the following relationships: majority examiner–minority examinee, minority examiner–majority examinee, minority examiner–minority examinee of same group, and minority examiner–minority examinee of different group.

11. Discuss issues involved in working with an interpreter. Include in your discussion difficulties associated with working with an interpreter and suggestions for handling these difficulties.

20

ASSESSMENT OF CULTURALLY AND LINGUISTICALLY DIVERSE CHILDREN: RESEARCH FINDINGS AND RECOMMENDATIONS

In the history of human thinking, the most fruitful developments frequently occur at those points where different lines of thought meet. These lines may have their roots in different cultures, in different times, in different religious traditions. If these are allowed to meet ... a new and interesting way of being will emerge.

—Werner Heisenberg

Arguments Against the Use of Intelligence Tests in Assessing Culturally and Linguistically Diverse Children

Arguments for the Use of Intelligence Tests in Assessing Culturally and Linguistically Diverse Children

Court Cases Involving Assessment Techniques

Intelligence and Racial Differences

Development of Culture-Fair Tests for Assessing Culturally and Linguistically Diverse Children

Evaluating Ethnic and Cultural Factors

Recommendations for the Assessment of Culturally and Linguistically Diverse Children and Their Families

Comment on the Assessment of Culturally and Linguistically Diverse Children

Thinking Through the Issues

Summary

Goals and Objectives

This chapter will enable you to do the following:

- Understand the arguments for and against the use of intelligence tests in assessing culturally and linguistically diverse children

- Describe several factors that may affect how culturally and linguistically diverse children perform in the test situation

- Understand important guidelines for working with culturally and linguistically diverse children

This chapter continues the discussion of assessing culturally and linguistically diverse children. It highlights research over the past 40 years and provides guidelines that you should try to incorporate into your assessment practice. The assessment of culturally and linguistically diverse children is fraught with controversy and often elicits strong emotions. Although we recognize that not everyone will agree with the positions that are offered here, we have tried in this and the preceding chapter to be fair, objective, and impartial.

ARGUMENTS AGAINST THE USE OF INTELLIGENCE TESTS IN ASSESSING CULTURALLY AND LINGUISTICALLY DIVERSE CHILDREN

Several claims have been made about the inappropriateness of using tests—in particular, intelligence tests—with culturally and linguistically diverse children. In fact, Valdé and Figueroa (1994) recommended that "Standardized tests should not be used in any aspect of a decision-making process with bilingual populations. There is no way of minimizing the potential harm to this population resulting from seemingly 'objective' and 'scientific' psychometric tests. All such testing should be discontinued" (p. 203).

We will first consider the major arguments against the use of intelligence tests and then turn to arguments in favor of using them.

1. Intelligence Tests Have a Cultural Bias

The allegation has been made that standard intelligence tests have a strong Euro American, Anglo-Saxon, middle-class bias. In examining test bias, we must first consider the meaning of a test score. Is a test score an indication of past achievement, of aptitude for future achievement, or neither? Arguments concerning test bias rest on which of these interpretations psychologists consider correct. There is an important distinction—and one that psychologists often make—between achievement tests (past learning) and aptitude tests (future learning). This distinction, however, has never been clearly resolved for intelligence tests.

We advocate that intelligence tests and other special ability tests be used as measures of achievement, not as pure measures of aptitude or capacity. Intelligence test scores, representing the interplay of biological factors and environmental factors, reflect past learnings. If culturally and linguistically diverse children obtain low scores, it means that educational systems need to be improved, not that standardized tests should be abandoned.

Measures of test bias.   We now consider statistical criteria used to measure test bias (Flaugher, 1978).

Mean differences.   One position is that a test is biased when it yields lower scores for one group than for another.

This criterion is not acceptable, however, because mean differences are not a legitimate standard for identifying test bias. Because of educational, economic, political, and social disparities among groups in our nation, it would be surprising if there were not mean differences between groups on intelligence and achievement tests. Drasgow (1987) noted that

Measurement bias should not be investigated using the proportion-correct statistic because it confounds bias with between-group differences in the attribute being measured by the test. Between-group differences are expected whenever "environments" of groups differ, and it is clear that environments differ for men, women, Euro Americans, African Americans, and Hispanic Americans. (p. 28, with changes in notation)

Single-group or differential validity.   Another measure of bias is whether a test is an equally good predictor for two (or more) minority groups. There are at least two ways to determine whether this form of test bias is present. One is the *single-group validity approach*. With this approach, a test is said to be biased when a validity coefficient is significantly different from zero for one ethnic group but not for another. The other is the *differential validity approach*. With this approach, a test is considered to be biased when there is a significant difference between two validity coefficients. *The majority of research with culturally and linguistically diverse groups in the United States indicates that these forms of test bias are not commonly present.* That is, psychologists infrequently find either single-group validity bias or differential validity bias. Although there are instances in which single-group or differential validity has been found, "the fact that they are so elusive, difficult to detect, and debatable is good evidence that they are not very potent phenomena relative to all other possible sources of problems in the interaction of minorities and testing" (Flaugher, 1978, p. 674).

Several studies have examined the validity of intelligence or vocabulary tests for culturally and linguistically diverse children. Studies with the WISC–III, WISC–R, Stanford-Binet: Form L-M, PPVT, and Raven's Progressive Matrices indicate that the regression lines for African American children, Euro American children, and Hispanic American children are similar when Wide Range Achievement Test scores and other achievement indices are used as criteria (Bossard, Reynolds, & Gutkin, 1980; Dean, 1979a, 1979b; Hall, Huppertz, & Levi, 1977; Poteat, Wuensch, & Gregg, 1988; Reschly & Sabers, 1979; Reynolds & Gutkin, 1980; Reynolds & Hartlage, 1979). In addition, studies have shown that the concurrent validity of the WISC–III, WISC–R, WISC, and Stanford-Binet: Form L-M with such criteria as the California Achievement Test, Wide Range Achievement Test, Metropolitan Achievement Tests, California Test of Mental Maturity, Stanford Achievement Test, and teacher ratings is excellent for African American, Euro American, Mexican American, and Native American children, with median validity coefficients in the .50s (see Table 20-1). *These findings support the conclusion that intelligence tests generally are equally good predictors for African American, Hispanic American, and Euro American children.*

Table 20-1
Concurrent Validity: Median Correlations Between Intelligence Tests and Achievement Tests for Euro American, African American, and Hispanic American Children

	Achievement area			
	Reading		Arithmetic	
Ethnic group	Number of studies	Mdn r	Number of studies	Mdn r
Euro American	14	.65	12	.59
African American	15	.62	11	.58
Hispanic American	9	.55	9	.57

Note. These median correlations are based on the following studies: Bossard, Reynolds, and Gutkin (1980); Dean (1977a, 1979b); Henderson, Butler, and Goffeney (1969); Henderson, Fay, Lindemann, and Clarkson (1973); Kennedy, Van de Riet, and White (1963); Komm (1978); Oakland (1980, 1983); Oakland and Feigenbaum (1979); Reschly and Reschly (1979); Reynolds and Gutkin (1980); Reynolds and Nigl (1981); Sewell (1979); Sewell and Severson (1974); Svanum and Bringle (1982); Weaver (1968); Weiss, Prifitera, and Roid (1993).

Let's examine more closely one of the studies presented in Table 20-1 (Weiss, Prifitera, & Roid, 1993) because it is especially noteworthy in having an extensive sample ($N = 700$) that was representative of the U.S. population (75% Euro American, 15% African American, and 11% Hispanic American). The WISC–III Full Scale IQ was found to correlate significantly with reading, writing, and math scores obtained on group-administered achievement tests and with math, reading, and English school grades in all three groups. Correlations between the WISC–III Full Scale IQ and group achievement tests ranged from .47 to .67 in the Euro American group, from .50 to .71 in the African American group, and from .47 to .57 in the Hispanic American group. Correlations between the Full Scale IQ and school grades were lower than those for achievement test scores (range of .36 to .46 in the Euro American group, .29 to .53 in the African American group, and .17 to .24 in the Hispanic American group). In supporting the absence of bias, the results are consistent with previous research correlating intelligence test scores with achievement test scores.

In instances where children's language backgrounds differ from that of the standardization group used to develop norms for the test, the test results are likely to be invalid. For example, Native American children may obtain WISC–R Performance Scale IQs that are as much as 25 to 30 points higher than their Verbal Scale IQs (McShane & Plas, 1984; Teeter et al., 1982). Similarly, their Peabody Picture Vocabulary Test scores may be much below scores obtained on performance tests (Naglieri & Yazzie, 1983). Thus, it is important to examine carefully the IQs generated by different

tests. *Verbal tests should never be used alone to estimate children's levels of cognitive ability when English is not their primary language.* And measures of vocabulary, like the Peabody Picture Vocabulary Test–III, Expressive Vocabulary Test, and Comprehensive Receptive and Expressive Vocabulary Test, should *never* be used to estimate the intelligence level of children whose language background considerably differs from the norm group.

One cannot for long have one's feet placed in two canoes.
—Iroquois saying

Differential construct validity. Another method of evaluating the possible bias of intelligence tests is to study whether they measure similar abilities in various culturally and linguistically diverse groups. Studies examining the factor structure of the WISC–III, WISC–R, WISC, WPPSI, DAS, and McCarthy Scales of Children's Abilities for African American, Hispanic American, and Euro American children indicate that these groups have comparable factor structures (Dean, 1980; Greenberg, Stewart, & Hansche, 1986; Gutkin & Reynolds, 1981; Guy, 1977; Jensen & Reynolds, 1982; Johnston & Bolen, 1984; Kaufman & DiCuio, 1975; Kaufman & Hollenbeck, 1974; Keith, Quirk, Schartzer, & Elliott, 1999; Kush & Watkins, 1997; Lawlis, Stedman, & Cortner, 1980; Miele, 1979; Reschly, 1978; Rousey, 1990; Semler & Iscoe, 1966; Silverstein, 1973; Taylor & Ziegler, 1987; Vance, Huelsman, & Wherry, 1976; Vance & Wallbrown, 1978). *These findings suggest that (a) intelligence tests measure the same abilities in Euro American, African American, and Hispanic American children and (b) the Verbal-Performance distinction in some of these tests is appropriate for the three ethnic groups.*

Content bias. Evaluation of content bias focuses on whether the content of particular test items is unfair to some groups of the population. Inspection of standardized intelligence tests across numerous studies has revealed few, if any, items that appear to be biased systematically in favor of one group over another. A useful empirical approach for investigating content bias is to examine item performance statistics group by group to determine the difficulty level of each item. "If a particular item is extraordinarily difficult for culturally and linguistically diverse group members relative to the difficulty of other items in the same test, then that item is a good candidate for suspicion of this kind of bias" (Flaugher, 1978, p. 675, with changes in notation). Studies cited by Flaugher suggest that the elimination of such items from standardized tests makes little if any difference in test scores. In addition, Sandoval and Miille (1980) reported that neither African American, Hispanic American, nor Euro American judges were able to determine accurately which WISC–R items were more difficult for culturally and linguistically diverse students. The ethnic background of the judges made no difference in accuracy of item selection.

Several types of internal psychometric criteria for studying content bias also are available. They include examining differences between groups in (a) the rank order of the percent passing each item, (b) the percent passing adjacent items in the test, (c) the number of persons passing each item when both groups are equated for total score, and (d) the types of item content that discriminate most and least between the two groups (Jensen, 1974a). *Applications of these criteria to the intelligence test and ability test performances of African American and Euro American children and adults have produced no evidence that differences between African Americans and Euro Americans are related to cultural bias* (Jensen, 1974a; Meyer & Goldstein, 1971; Miele, 1979; Nichols, 1971; Olivier & Barclay, 1967; Sandoval, 1979; Sandoval, Zimmerman, & Woo-Sam, 1983). Tests in these investigations included the Stanford-Binet: Form L-M, WISC–R, PPVT, and Raven's Progressive Matrices.

Here is an example of how Miele (1979) applied an internal psychometric criterion to an item on the WISC. He reported that the WISC Comprehension item 4, "What should you do if a child smaller than you begins to fight with you?"—which was singled out by Robert Williams in the CBS documentary "The IQ Myth" as a blatant manifestation of cultural bias—proved to be easier for African American children than for Euro American children. It was the 42nd easiest item for 111 African American children (*M* age = 6-1) and the 47th easiest item for 163 Euro American children (*M* age = 6-2).

Two federal judges—Judge Robert Peckham (in *Larry P. v. Riles*) and Judge John Grady (in *Parents in Action on Special Education v. Joseph P. Hannon*)—also evaluated individual intelligence test items for biased content. (These cases are discussed later in the chapter.) Based solely on looking at the content of the items, both judges believed that some items on the WISC, WISC–R, and Stanford-Binet: Form L-M were culturally biased.

Let's now examine two investigations that sought to determine the accuracy of these judges' opinions about item bias. First, Koh, Abbatiello, and McLoughlin (1984) set out to see whether the seven items singled out by Judge Grady were in fact culturally biased. They studied the test protocols of 180 African American children and 180 Euro American children attending schools in Chicago. The average age of the children was 11½ years. They found that the two ethnic groups did not differ significantly on any item. The notorious "fight" item discussed above was passed by 73% of the African American children and by 71% of the Euro American children.

Second, Sattler (1991) studied the responses of 242 African American children and 242 Euro American children in the fourth, fifth, and sixth grades to the 11 WISC and WISC–R Information and Comprehension subtest items cited by Judge Grady and Judge Peckham as being culturally biased. In addition, Sattler included 14 buffer items (i.e., items that were adjacent in difficulty to the 11 target items) from the same two subtests. The results indicated that 12 of the 25 items were significantly more difficult for the African American

children than for the Euro American children. Of these 12 items, 6 had been singled out by the judges. That is, five of the items said by one or more of the judges to be biased were *not* more difficult for the African American children than for the Euro American children, while six items that were not singled out by the judges were found to be more difficult for the African American children than for the Euro American children. The accuracy of the judges was at a chance level. The results of these two studies indicate that an armchair inspection of test items cannot reveal which items are more difficult for one ethnic group than for another one.

Factors affecting the validity of test results.   We have seen that validity studies can provide evidence about whether a test is or is not biased against a group. But equally important is how psychologists and educators *use* the test results. A test may be valid for a particular purpose but still result in biased decisions if the test results are improperly used or misinterpreted or if the test is poorly administered (e.g., if standard administrative procedures are violated).

Uniqueness of the African American experience.   One of the main thrusts of the cultural-bias argument has been that intelligence tests are not relevant to the experiences of culturally and linguistically diverse children. Williams (1970) maintained that African American children, for example, develop unique verbal skills that are neither measured by conventional tests nor accepted by the middle class–oriented classroom. There has been little, if any, research to support this contention. Furthermore, items on intelligence tests represent important aspects of competence in the common culture; they do not reflect purely middle-class values. For a democratic society to endure, these common cultural forms and practices need to be maintained and extended to the culture as a whole— *"cultural apartheid ought not to be encouraged in this society"* (Ebel, 1975, p. 86, italics added).

Ebel (1975) also noted:

The bias which accounts for poor test performance by some culturally and linguistically diverse persons is not in the tests so much as it is in the culture, and thus is another problem altogether. So long as the tests under scrutiny truly measure the skills necessary to success in the prevailing culture, culturally and linguistically diverse interests are not well served by blaming "test bias" for poor performance.

The tests we use in education ought to be as free of bias as we can make them. But the extent and seriousness of bias in our current educational tests can be, and probably have been, exaggerated. The "well-known" bias of tests against culturally and linguistically diverse group members seems to be more fanciful than factual. (p. 87, with changes in notation)

The argument that intelligence tests are not valid because culturally and linguistically diverse children have not had the same experiences as Euro American middle-class children becomes difficult to accept when we consider that a population quite far removed from Euro American middle-class America actually performs better on nonverbal tests than do

American children themselves. The mean scores of children in Japan on many of the Wechsler Performance Scale subtests are higher than those of the American standardization samples (Lynn, 1977). Lynn believes that these findings indicate that tests such as the Wechsler Performance Scale may be much fairer culturally than many critics have been willing to admit.

Humphreys (1973) also believes that the cultural differences between African Americans and Euro Americans may not be as great as some propose. Although there are obvious environmental differences between the two groups, these differences are not so profound as to require different principles in the explanation of African American and Euro American behavior. "The two groups use a highly similar (if not identical) language, attend similar schools, are exposed to similar curricula, listen to the same radio programs, look at the same commodities, etc. Cultural differences are a question of degree, not of kind" (p. 3).

Selection model. The selection bias of a test refers to whether the test has a differential effect on the number of examinees from various groups who enter certain programs (such as special classes, colleges, or vocational training programs) or are selected for certain jobs. There is little agreement about the best statistical procedure to use to reduce selection bias. Should we use the same cutoff scores for all groups, or should we give some groups extra points? All selection procedures are tied to ethical and social values. Universal acceptance of one set of values will be difficult to achieve.

Validity criteria. A test can only be valid for particular criteria. Criteria vary in such characteristics as importance, reliability, and innovativeness. If we use the wrong criterion to establish validity, the test scores may in fact be biased. For example, a test composed only of verbal items may be valid

for selecting people good at speaking or writing about music, but it may not be valid for selecting individuals who prove talented in producing music. Although the criterion problem is difficult, we should examine thoroughly the criteria used to validate tests.

Atmosphere. If examinees feel out of place or unwelcome when taking a test, they will not give their best performance. If the test situation inhibits examinees' real capacities, the test scores are biased. This type of bias appears to play only a limited role, if any, in most individual assessments, however, because most examiners are careful to obtain the examinee's best performance.

Overinterpretation. When test users generalize from a limited domain of measurement to a broad range of ability, we have legitimate grounds for raising the issue of bias in the results. For example, it is a great leap to say that a child "lacks practical judgment" simply because he or she was unable to answer correctly a few problems on a test.

2. National Norms Are Inappropriate for Culturally and Linguistically Diverse Groups

The argument that national norms based primarily on Euro American, middle-class, Anglo-Saxon samples are inappropriate for culturally and linguistically diverse children has led some writers (e.g., Mercer, 1976) to advocate establishing pluralistic norms. Pluralistic norms are norms derived for individual groups, such as Euro Americans, African Americans, Hispanic Americans, Asian Americans, and Native Americans. Those who favor pluralistic norms believe that it is useful to know how a child's performance compares to that of others in his or her own ethnic group. Pluralistic norms are potentially dangerous, however, because they (a) provide a basis for invidious comparisons among different ethnic groups, (b) may lower expectations of culturally and linguistically diverse children and reduce their level of aspiration to succeed, (c) may have little relevance outside of the child's specific geographic area, and (d) furnish no information about the complex reasons why some ethnic groups tend to score lower than others on intelligence tests (DeAvila & Havassy, 1974). The renorming of tests to provide pluralistic norms is inappropriate because it does not involve test modifications, nor does it consider whether we should use the test at all with culturally and linguistically diverse children (Bernal, 1972). And the use of pluralistic norms gives rise to new questions—what norms should we use for a child who has a Mexican father and a Hungarian mother?

Some charge that norms for the major individual intelligence tests are based entirely on the performance of middle-class Euro Americans. This simply is not true. The Stanford-Binet: Fourth Edition, WISC–III, WPPSI–R, WAIS–III, and DAS, for example, have all used excellent sampling procedures

From M. L. Arkava and M. Snow, *Psychological Tests and Social Work Practice*, 1978, p. 39. Courtesy of Charles C Thomas, Publisher, Springfield, Illinois.

to obtain representative samples. Culturally and linguistically diverse groups are represented in each of these norm groups in proportion to their representation in the general population.

National norms reflect the performance of the population as a whole. Because they describe the typical performance of our nation's children, they are important as a frame of reference and as a guidepost for decision making. This is not to say that we should not use other norms, however. We can interpret test results from several frames of reference. But test users and consumers of test information should clearly recognize which norms were used and why they were selected.

3. Culturally and Linguistically Diverse Groups Are Handicapped in Test-Taking Skills

Another argument says that culturally and linguistically diverse children are handicapped in taking tests because of deficiencies in motivation, test practice, and reading; failure to appreciate the achievement aspects of the test situation; and limited exposure to the culture. Thus, they may be deficient in the ability to employ test-taking skills, choose proper problem-solving strategies, and balance speed and power. They may also exhibit test anxiety. Western culture emphasizes achievement and problem solving, and by the time children begin school, they are usually ready to accept intellectual challenge. Some culturally and linguistically diverse children may fail to comprehend or accept the achievement aspects of the test situation, however. They may view the assessment as an enjoyable child-adult encounter, rather than as an opportunity to achieve; or, if they recognize the problem-solving aspects of the situation, they may ignore them. For example, Native American children may not work quickly on timed tests because of a desire not to compete with others.

Although culturally and linguistically diverse children may have adequate information processing capacities, such as the storage and retrieval system they need to answer questions correctly, they may fail in practice because they have not been *exposed* to the material (Zigler & Butterfield, 1968). For example, they may respond incorrectly to the question "What is a gown?" because they have never heard the word *gown*. Motivational factors may also affect the performance of some culturally and linguistically diverse children; they may know what a gown is, but respond with "I don't know" to terminate as quickly as possible the unpleasantness of interacting with a strange and demanding adult. Additionally, they may be more wary of adults, more motivated to secure adults' attention and praise, less motivated to be correct for the sake of correctness alone, or more willing to settle for lower levels of achievement success. *Therefore, the low intelligence test scores of some children may be a consequence of limited exposure to test content or motivational factors.*

There is some evidence that some minority children have limited test-taking skills. But this is true of some majority children as well. We do not know how pervasive this limita-

tion is among minority children or to what degree it lowers their performance on tests. Further research is needed in this area. However, we do know that there is little evidence that African American children learn in ways that are fundamentally different from the ways Euro American children learn (Frisby, 1993).

4. Euro American Examiners Depress the Scores of Minority Children

A fourth argument postulates that rapport and communication problems exist between Euro American examiners and minority children. These problems are said to interfere with the ability of minority children to respond to the test items.

With African American children. The anxiety, insecurity, latent prejudice, and other reactions to contemporary African American-Euro American relations experienced by Euro American clinicians in their work with African American children may be transmitted to the children in several ways. Examiners may exhibit paternalism, overidentification, overconcern, excessive sympathy, indulgence, reactive fear, or inhibition. African American children, in turn, may exhibit fear and suspicion, verbal constriction, strained and unnatural reactions, or a facade of stupidity to avoid appearing "uppity." Some may deliberately score low to avoid personal threat; others may view the test as a means for Euro Americans, not African Americans, to get ahead in society. Although many of these behaviors, patterns, and perceptions are likely to exist and are important phenomena in their own right, there is no way of knowing to what extent they affect African American children's test scores (Sattler, 1970, 1973).

Some psychologists believe that Euro American examiners impair the intelligence test performance of African American children. A careful study of the research literature refutes the myth of racial examiner effects, however. In 25 of the 29 published studies dealing with racial examiner effects on individual intelligence tests or other cognitive measures, the investigators found no significant relationship between the race of the examiner and the examinees' scores (Sattler & Gwynne, 1982). *It is apparent from this body of research that in the overwhelming majority of cases Euro American examiners have not impaired the intelligence test performance of African American children.*

This finding is more impressive when we consider the wide range of tests, grade levels, geographic areas, and dates of administration encompassed by these studies. The tests included the WISC, WAIS, WPPSI, Stanford-Binet: Form L-M, PPVT, Draw-A-Man, Iowa Test of Preschool Development, and several other tests of cognitive ability. The grade levels of the children in these studies ranged from preschool through grade 12. The geographic locations, though largely urban, included Eastern, Midwestern, Southern, and Western cities. The years of publication ranged from 1964 to 1977.

As noted previously, communication difficulties may be present when examinees from culturally and linguistically diverse groups are evaluated. Because misunderstandings may result in mistrust and sustain stereotypic judgments, examiners must try to reduce the likelihood of any misunderstandings. Differences in dialect may be one source of difficulty. Some argue that African American children do not clearly understand Euro American examiners, and this causes their scores to be lower than those they obtain when tested by African American examiners. Scientific studies, however, have not supported this position. Quay (1972, 1974), for example, reported that African American children scored no higher on the Stanford-Binet: Form L-M when an African American examiner administered it in Black dialect than when an examiner administered it in standard English. There is increasing evidence that African American children are bidialectical: They have the ability to comprehend Black dialect and standard English equally well (Genshaft & Hirt, 1974; Hall, Turner, & Russell, 1973; Harver, 1977; Levy & Cook, 1973).

Although research indicates that the ethnicity of the examiner does not usually affect African American children's performance on intelligence tests, examiners should not be indifferent to the examinee's ethnicity. Examiners must be alert to any nuances in the test situation suggesting that their ethnicity is adversely affecting the child. Testing children from different cultures is a demanding task. At times it may be difficult to understand their responses, and you must make every effort to enlist their best efforts.

With Hispanic American children. Stereotypes held by the Euro American examiner about the Hispanic American examinee or by the Hispanic American examinee about the Euro American examiner may interfere with rapport. The two groups are often keenly aware of the differences that divide them, and feelings of resentment—stemming from a mutual lack of understanding—may be present on both sides. Euro Americans generally do not know much about the customs and values of Hispanic Americans, nor are they knowledgeable about the conditions that exist in the *barrio* (section of town in which some Hispanic Americans live). The Hispanic American examinee's language may serve as a cue for group identification, and, like skin color, it may influence the examiner-examinee relationship. Examiners must become aware of and try to overcome any stereotypes that they may have. If they cannot, they should refer the examinee to another psychologist.

The assertion that Euro American examiners are not as effective as Hispanic American examiners in testing Hispanic American children has not received empirical support. For example, Gerken (1978) reported that neither the examiners' ethnicity (Hispanic American or Euro American) nor their language facility (bilingual or monolingual) significantly affected the IQs obtained by Hispanic American kindergarten children on the WPPSI or the Leiter International Performance Scale. Morales and George (1976) found that bilin-

gual Hispanic American first-, second-, and third-graders obtained higher WISC–R Performance IQs when tested by monolingual non-Hispanic American examiners than when tested by bilingual Hispanic American examiners who gave the test directions in both English and Spanish. The children tested by non-Hispanic American examiners also obtained significantly higher scores on the ITPA Grammatical Closure subtest, but not on the Screening Test of Spanish Grammar. These two studies, although limited, suggest that Euro American examiners do not impair the test performance of Hispanic American elementary school children.

Although the studies by Gerken (1978) and Morales and George (1976) provide no support for the assertion that Euro American examiners are less effective than Hispanic American examiners, examiners of both ethnic groups must be aware of stereotyped attitudes toward Hispanic American children that may interfere with their clinical judgments. For example, a study of teachers' attitudes toward Hispanic American third- and fourth-graders who spoke minimally accented, moderately accented, or highly accented English showed that the most favorable ratings were given to the minimally accented speakers and the least favorable ratings to the highly accented speakers (Carter, 1977). Although Hispanic American teachers had more favorable attitudes than Euro American teachers, both groups had more unfavorable attitudes toward the highly accented speakers. These results suggest that examiners may hold stereotypes about children who have accented speech. If you hold such stereotypes, you must not allow them to affect your test interpretations and recommendations or to impair your relationship with Hispanic American children.

5. Test Results Lead to Inadequate and Inferior Education

The argument that test results lead to an inferior education is based on several premises. One is that African American children who are placed in special classes would achieve at a higher level if they were not removed from the regular class. These special classes are said to have an inadequate curriculum and provide an inferior education, and tests are held accountable because they provide a justification for placing children in special classes. This argument was used in the *Larry P. v. Riles* (1979) case. A second premise is that test results produce negative expectancies in teachers. When teachers learn that African American children have low scores, they begin to treat them as if they will perform at a below-average level, which in turn, causes the children to perform poorly, creating a self-fulfilling prophecy.

The role of individual assessments. Although test results may be one link in the educational chain that leads teachers and school administrators to assign children to special classes or programs, teachers usually refer children for individual assessment only after they have performed poorly in school. Most African American children, and most other school children, are never seen for a comprehensive individual psychoeducational assessment. Thus, seldom can we link the school performance of culturally and linguistically diverse children simply to the results of individual psychoeducational assessments.

Expectancy effects. The study of *self-fulfilling prophecy* in the classroom is complex, as it involves teachers' communication of expectations to students, teachers' beliefs about the curriculum, the effectiveness of instruction, student motivation, the quality of the teacher-student relationship, and teacher and student individual difference variables (Brophy, 1983). However, as noted in Chapter 2 of this text, the claim that initial negative expectancies on the part of teachers produce a self-fulfilling prophecy has little scientific merit. In addition to the research cited in Chapter 2, a meta-analysis of 47 teacher-expectation studies found that teacher expectations had no appreciable effect on students' IQs (Smith, 1980).

Are special education classes needed? We also must carefully examine the premise that special education classes for children with mental retardation do not provide the kinds of intervention programs needed by culturally and linguistically diverse children who are functioning in the mentally retarded range. Do low-functioning culturally and linguistically diverse children need special programs emphasizing enrichment and verbal stimulation? Do they benefit from the usual type of program designed for children with mental retardation? Unfortunately, definitive answers to these questions are not available. We need to learn a great deal about the differential effectiveness of special programs—such as resource rooms, tutoring, nongraded classes, and learning centers—and traditional programs designed for low-functioning children.

ARGUMENTS FOR THE USE OF INTELLIGENCE TESTS IN ASSESSING CULTURALLY AND LINGUISTICALLY DIVERSE CHILDREN

The previous discussion suggests that the arguments for the cultural bias of intelligence tests have little, if any, merit. Let us now examine the arguments for the use of intelligence and ability tests with culturally and linguistically diverse children.

1. Intelligence Tests Are Useful in Evaluating Present and Future Functioning

Intelligence test scores of culturally and linguistically diverse children are useful indices of their current cognitive ability. The evidence cited previously indicates that intelligence tests have little or no cultural bias. They generally have the same properties for minority children as they do for majority chil-

dren. Tests can provide valuable information about minority children's cognitive strengths and weaknesses and can help to evaluate change and progress. For example, in cases of brain injury, intelligence and special ability tests help to document the extent of injury (see *Assessment of Children: Behavioral and Clinical Applications*); a comparison of present test results with past results provides a measure of changes as a result of the damage. In cases of psychopathology, tests serve similar purposes.

Doing away with tests would deprive clinicians and educators of vital information needed to assist children. A report sponsored by the American Psychological Association's Board of Scientific Affairs (Cleary, Humphreys, Kendrick, & Wesman, 1975) stressed the importance of evaluation in education: *"Diagnosis, prognosis, prescription, and measurement of outcomes are as important in education as in medicine"* (p. 18, italics added). Standardized intelligence tests provide good indices of future levels of academic success and performance as defined by the majority culture.

2. Tests Are Useful in Obtaining Special Programs

Tests can be useful in obtaining special enrichment programs and services for children. Abandoning formal assessment procedures may deprive minority children with a disability of the opportunity to obtain appropriate attention and services to which they are legally entitled. The problem of poor achievement of African American inner-city children is real; tests have not caused the problem. Tests have been helpful in documenting the severity of the educational deficits. As Green (1978) noted, "The tests are not bigoted villains but color-blind measuring instruments that have demonstrated a social problem to be solved" (p. 669).

3. Tests Are Useful in Evaluating Programs

Tests evaluate the outcomes of school and special programs. They can be used to determine whether children have learned to read or to perform arithmetical operations. Thus, tests provide objective evidence of the effectiveness of school programs. *"As such, far from being a part of the problem, tests are an absolutely essential part of the solution"* (Flaugher, 1974, p. 14, italics added). Those calling for the elimination of testing altogether would, in fact, allow us to release the educational system from any accountability.

4. Tests Are Useful in Revealing Inequalities

By revealing the inequalities in the opportunities available to various groups, tests may provide the stimulus for special intervention to facilitate the maximum development of each child's potentialities. Perhaps some individuals in education should be less concerned with evaluating the unbiased predictive validity of tests and more concerned with facilitating equal opportunity.

5. Tests Are Useful in Providing an Objective Standard

Tests serve as a corrective device by providing information that we cannot obtain easily or reliably by other means. They give students an alternative way of demonstrating academic ability. Tests also provide a measure that is comparable across schools and across time. Test scores do not depend on the predilections of teachers at a specific school or on a student's interpersonal relationship with teachers. Consequently, tests have helped to prevent educational misplacement of children.

Culturally and linguistically diverse groups should favor the use of ability tests; these tests constitute a universal and objective—rather than prejudicial—standard of competence and potential. Other selection methods may decrease the opportunities of culturally and linguistically diverse children. Jensen (1975) observed that "objective means of revealing talents stand to benefit talented members of disadvantaged groups the most, since in their cultural circumstances certain talents are more apt to go unrecognized and underdeveloped" (p. 67). Educational tests encourage and reward individual efforts to learn. If we abandoned tests, programs would be difficult to evaluate and educators might base educational decisions more on the child's ancestry and influence and less on the child's aptitude and merit. Educators might also make curriculum decisions based less on evidence and more on prejudice and caprice.

COURT CASES INVOLVING ASSESSMENT TECHNIQUES

Beginning in the 1970s, courts have heard a number of cases concerning the overrepresentation of minority children in special classes, primarily those for children with mental retardation. Associated with this issue are the related matters of the assessment techniques used to certify placement in special education programs and the value and role of special education. It has been argued that (a) minority children are overrepresented in classes for the educable mentally retarded, (b) special education represents a dead end and provides substandard educational programs, (c) intelligence tests are culturally biased, (d) students with limited facility in English have been inappropriately administered tests requiring extensive facility in English, and (e) a full range of assessment techniques is not being used in arriving at placement decisions. Implied in these arguments is the contention that the children were denied equal protection under the Fourteenth Amendment of the Constitution. In many of the cases that have come before the judiciary, both parties have signed consent agreements, which have attempted to rectify

procedures that were unfair to ethnic minorities. In addition, provisions of the Individuals with Disabilities Education Act have sought to protect the rights of minority children (see Chapter 3 of this book). Let's look at some of these cases.

Larry P. v. Riles

In *Larry P. v. Riles* (495 F. supp. 926, N.D. CA. 1979; 793 F. 2d 969, 9th Cir. 1984) a federal court found the California State Department of Education to be in violation of Title VI of the Civil Rights Act of 1964, the Rehabilitation Act of 1973, and PL 94-142. In October 1979, Judge Robert Peckham ruled that standardized intelligence tests "are racially and culturally biased, have a discriminatory impact against black children, and have not been validated for the purpose of essentially permanent placements of black children into educationally dead-end, isolated, and stigmatizing classes for the so-called educable mentally retarded."

In January 1984, the Ninth Circuit Court of Appeals upheld, by a 2-1 margin, Judge Peckham's ruling in *Larry P. v. Riles*. Judge William B. Enright, the dissenter, noted that proper placement in an EMR (educable mentally retarded) class is a benefit, not a stigmatic dead-end assignment; that before the tests in question can be labeled as discriminatory, there must be evidence that intelligence tests resulted in improper placement in the EMR program, and no such evidence was presented; that the widely recognized IQ tests employed by the defendants have long been hailed for their ability to correct the exact abuse complained of in this case—misevaluation and misplacement; and that educators have long recognized that subjective evaluation, uncorroborated by objective criteria, carries enormous potential for abuse and misplacement based on the personal or cultural values of the evaluator. Judge Enright also noted that the court's decision was striking down the only objective criterion for placement.

In June 1986, the U.S. Circuit Court of Appeals issued an amended decision that reaffirmed the district court's finding of violation of federal statutory law, but reversed the finding of violations of the equal protection clause of the Fourteenth Amendment of the Constitution. In September 1986, the California State Department of Education issued a directive to implement the federal court's decision. The directive stated that individually administered intelligence tests were not to be used for the assessment of any African American child referred for special education services.

In September of 1992, the same court reversed its 1986 amended decision in *Crawford et al. v. Honig et al.* (No. C-89-0014 RFP). The court ruled that parents of African American children have the same rights as all other parents to obtain intelligence tests for the assessment of their children who are in special education or who are being considered for special education services. The only exception is children who are being considered for or in programs for the educable mentally retarded; this ban was in force as of September 2000.

Parents in Action on Special Education v. Joseph P. Hannon

In *Parents in Action on Special Education v. Joseph P. Hannon* (No. 74 C 3586, N.D. Ill. 1980), a federal court ruled that intelligence tests are not culturally biased against African American children. This court stipulated that, when used with other criteria in the assessment process, intelligence tests comply with federal guidelines concerning the use of nondiscriminatory procedures. Judge John Grady noted: "There is no evidence in this record that such misassessments as do occur are the result of racial bias in test items or in any aspect of the assessment process currently in use in the Chicago public school system." He found that the Chicago public school system was complying with federal guidelines.

Georgia Conferences of NAACP v. Georgia

In *Georgia Conferences of NAACP v. State of Georgia* (Eleventh Circuit of Appeals, No. 84-8771, October 29, 1985) and *Marshall v. Georgia* (U.S. District Court for the Southern District of Georgia, CV 482-233, June 28, 1984; amended August 24, 1984), the NAACP alleged that the State of Georgia discriminated against African American children by using evaluation procedures that resulted in their overrepresentation in classes for the educable mentally retarded. Their complaints paralleled those in the *Larry P. v. Riles* case. Both the trial court and the Eleventh Circuit Court of Appeals rejected the claims of the NAACP. The courts noted that there was no evidence of differential treatment of African American and Euro American students. Overrepresentation of African American children in classes for the mentally retarded by itself was not sufficient to prove discrimination.

Mattie T. v. Holladay

In *Mattie T. v. Holladay* (No. DC-75-31-S, 1979), a U.S. district court in Mississippi approved a consent decree stipulating that (a) classification and placement procedures for special education must be evaluated by outside experts, (b) a remedy must be devised to solve the problem of large numbers of African American children in classes for the mentally retarded, and (c) all misclassified children are to be identified and given compensatory education through tutoring or vocational training, even beyond the age of 21.

Diana v. State Board of Education

In *Diana v. State Board of Education* (C-70 37 RFT, N.D. Cal. 1970) a federal court in California invalidated testing procedures that were used to evaluate Mexican American children for placement in special education classes. The school system agreed that linguistically different children would be tested both in their primary language and in English, that primarily nonverbal tests would be used for the assessment of these children's cognitive skills, and that an interpreter would be used if a bilingual examiner was not available.

Comment on Cases Involving Culturally and Linguistically Diverse Children

In the above cases, plaintiffs sometimes characterized individual intelligence tests, a key diagnostic tool in the placement process, as culturally biased and therefore inappropriate for the assessment of African American children. Courts in California agreed with this characterization, whereas courts in Illinois and Georgia did not. Obviously, we will need further judicial rulings to resolve the thorny issues involved in the placement of minority children in special education classes. As some jurists noted in *Daniel Hoffman v. The Board of Education of the City of New York* (see Chapter 1 of this text), the courts may not be the best place to resolve complex issues concerning the fairness of tests and appropriateness of educational procedures.

INTELLIGENCE AND RACIAL DIFFERENCES

During the first year or two of life, African American and Euro American children show few differences in intellectual functioning. At 3 or 4 years of age, however, race and social class differences arise that remain stable during the school years. These findings suggest that "the schools can mostly be exonerated from the charges of creating the African American-Euro American difference in average IQ-test performance or of increasing it during the period of school attendance" (Loehlin, Lindzey, & Spuhler, 1975, pp. 156–157, with changes in notation). The lower scores of African American children may be associated with the increased g loading (see Chapter 5 of this text) of intelligence test items between the ages of 2 and 5 or with certain environmental differences in the African American home or community (Jensen, 1975). The fact that scores of children from culturally and linguistically diverse groups and those of children from Euro American groups continue to differ during the school years, however, may be associated with the quality of schooling. According to Ceci (1991), good schools promote attitudes that may help children take tests, such as the need to attend to questions, monitor responses, sit still, gain rapport, and try to do their best. Memory, reasoning, and deductive reasoning, for example, are all promoted in good schools and are measured by intelligence tests. And the quality of schools in areas where minority children live is often lower than the quality of schools in neighborhoods where Euro American children live.

The present consensus is that we cannot draw valid inferences about genetic differences among races as long as there are relevant systematic differences between races in their cultural patterns and in their psychological environment.

These differences influence the development of cognitive skills in complex ways, and no one has succeeded in either estimating or eliminating their effects. Centuries of discrimination have made meaningless direct comparisons of the mental ability of African Americans and Euro Americans.

In his review of African American and Euro American differences in intelligence, Brody (1992) came to the following conclusions:

After a century of research and speculation about African American–Euro American differences in intelligence it is, I think, fair to say that we know relatively little about the reasons for the difference. We do know that the differences in intelligence test performance are not attributable in any obvious way to bias in the tests and that the differences in test scores reflect differences, not in particular bits of cultural knowledge, but in more general and abstract abilities. And, we know that the differences are related to criteria such as the acquisition of knowledge that are valued by many if not all individuals in both the African American and the Euro American communities of the United States. The reasons for the differences are probably to be found in the distinctive cultural experiences encountered by African American individuals in the United States. (p. 309, with changes in notation)

DEVELOPMENT OF CULTURE-FAIR TESTS FOR ASSESSING CULTURALLY AND LINGUISTICALLY DIVERSE CHILDREN

Attempts to develop tests that are culture fair have not been successful. Williams (1972), for example, developed a 100-item multiple-choice test termed the Black Intelligence Test of Cultural Homogeneity (BITCH), based on items drawn from the African American culture. It is a culture-specific test measuring special information about the inner city. Items deal with African American slang, which is itself not uniform throughout the country. Two examples are

Boot: (a) cotton farmer, (b) African American, (c) Indian, (d) Vietnamese citizen

and

Clean: (a) just out of the bathtub, (b) very well dressed, (c) very religious, and (d) has a great deal

(Answer is b for both items.) Several studies reported that the BITCH has questionable validity (Andre, 1976; Komm, 1978; Long & Anthony, 1974). The test measures knowledge of African American slang, not problem-solving or reasoning abilities. At present, the BITCH does not appear to be useful in the assessment of the cognitive ability of African American children.

Every test is culturally loaded to some extent. Thus, we should distinguish between a test that is culturally loaded and one that is culturally biased (Jensen, 1974a). Although intelligence tests are not culturally biased according to most definitions of test bias, tests do vary in their degree of cultural loading. Every test falls somewhere on a continuum from low

to high cultural loading. For example, picture vocabulary tests, such as the PPVT–III, and portions of the Verbal Scales of the Wechsler tests are *highly culturally loaded* because they use pictorial stimuli that call for specific information associated with a given culture, such as familiarity with the language of the culture and objects representative of the linguistic terms. On the other hand, matrix tests (such as Raven's Progressive Matrices), digit span memory tests, and maze tests are *culturally reduced tests,* because they are less dependent on exposure to specific language symbols. Even these types of tests have some degree of cultural loading, however—they are neither culture fair nor culture free. Table 8.2 (pages 306–309) in Flanagan, McGrew, and Ortiz (2000) classifies the degree of cultural loading (i.e., low, moderate, or high) of subtests of several cognitive ability and special-purpose tests.

Probably no test can be created that eliminates the influence of learning and cultural experiences. The test content and materials, the language in which the questions are phrased, the test directions, the categories for classifying the responses, the scoring criteria, and the validity criteria are all culture bound. In fact, all human experience is affected by the culture, from prenatal development on. As Scarr (1978) observed, "Intelligence tests are not tests of intelligence in some abstract, culture-free way. They are measures of the ability to function intellectually by virtue of knowledge and skills in the culture of which they are a sample" (adapted from p. 339).

EVALUATING ETHNIC AND CULTURAL FACTORS

Your assessment of a culturally and linguistically diverse child who is referred for evaluation of a problem should consider several factors about the child and his or her family. These factors include (a) their degree of acculturation, (b) their cultural and religious beliefs about illness, (c) the family structure and intrafamily relationships, (d) the attitudes of family members toward the child's illness or disability, (e) their attitudes toward medical and mental health professionals and treatment, and (f) their ability to communicate. Questions to consider about each of these factors follow (Bloch, 1983; Kumabe, Nishida, & Hepworth, 1985). (Note that many of these questions are also useful in evaluating any children and families whose practices depart significantly from those of the majority group.)

Acculturation

1. What is the family's cultural group?
2. What is the family's national origin?
3. What is the family's native language?
4. How much English is spoken at home?
5. (If applicable) How long has the family been in the United States?

6. (If applicable) Why did the family come to the United States?

7. To what degree is the family acculturated to American culture?

8. How strongly does each member of the family follow traditional cultural practices?

(Questions 9 through 16 are primarily for recent immigrants.)

9. How did the family get to the United States?

10. How far is the home country from the United States?

11. How often do family members visit their home country?

12. Where did the family live in the home country?

13. What was the socioeconomic status of the family in the home country?

14. Where does the family live in the United States? For example, does the family live in a culturally homogeneous community or in a heterogeneous setting, and does the family live in a safe community?

15. What is the socioeconomic status of the family in the United States?

16. Has there been any role change for the parents since coming to the United States? For example, is the father who formerly was a physician now working as a gardener?

Cultural and Religious Beliefs About Illness

17. What role do cultural or religious factors have in guiding the family's beliefs about the child's illness or disability? For example, does religion play a part in how the family defines the illness or disability, responds to the illness or disability, and accepts the illness or disability? For example, do they see intervention as thwarting God's will or as playing the role of God?

18. What does the family believe caused the child's illness? For example, do family members view the illness or disability as stemming from natural causes, environmental causes, or supernatural causes? Do they view the illness or disability as a punishment for some unnamed wrong? Do they view the illness or disability as divine punishment for sin?

19. How does the family view the role of fate in the child's illness and treatment?

20. Does the family follow traditional health healing practices, and if so, which ones? For example, does the family believe in the power of shamans or healers, the potency of culturally prescribed rituals, the power of religious or other ethnic leaders, or the power of family members with authority?

Family Structure and Intrafamily Relationships

21. What is the family structure (for example, matriarchal or patriarchal)?

22. What are the culturally prescribed rules governing family transactions?

23. What family roles are the members expected to fulfill?

24. What is the family's attitude about sex roles?

25. What is the family's work ethic?

26. How does the family express emotions?

27. How does the family express religious beliefs?

28. What influence does the extended family have on the family? For example, how important are members of the extended family? Do you need to include members of the extended family in designing the interventions? Do you need to conduct a home visit to become acquainted with the members of the extended family and members of the community? Does the family have multiple caregivers and authority figures who need to be included in the intervention plan?

29. What are the family's attitudes and beliefs about sexual matters, exposure of body parts, surgery, use of prescription drugs, discussions of death, and discussions of fears?

30. What customs or beliefs does the family have about child rearing, including ideas about acceptable and unacceptable child behaviors, disciplining and rewarding children, differential expectations for girls and boys, adolescent independence, and appropriate ways for children to show courtesy and respect for adults? What is the family's attitude toward education and careers?

31. What customs or beliefs influence the way the family takes care of infants, including feeding, skin care, hair care, and other areas of personal hygiene?

32. How authoritarian are the parents and other adult authority figures?

33. Who takes care of the children?

Attitudes of Family Members Toward the Illness or Disability

34. What is the attitude of family members toward the child's illness or disability?

35. How does the family treat the child with a problem, illness, or disability? For example, do family members encourage the child to become independent and self-sufficient, or do they foster dependency and isolation?

36. Do they keep the child at home and not allow him or her to go to school? Do they allow the child to go to school but not to play with friends?

37. What role does the family play when and if the child is hospitalized?

38. What role does the family play in following the treatment regimen?

39. What changes have taken place in family roles and functioning because of the child's illness or problem?

Attitudes Toward Medical and Mental Health Professionals and Treatment

40. From whom has the family sought help for the child's illness?

41. Does the family rely on cultural healers, and if so, in what way and for what problems or illnesses?

42. What is the family's attitude toward medical and mental health professionals and toward treatment? For example, do family members believe that they can do little about

their problems? Do they have an attitude of resignation and acceptance, believing that fate has decreed that misfortunes are a part of life? When do they seek treatment? For example, do they delay treatment until the illness has become severe? Do they seek traditional healers before contacting mainstream practitioners? Do they view mental illness as a sign of weakness of character? Do they view treatment as disgraceful, carrying with it shame and a loss of pride?

43. How open is the family in its communication with medical and mental health professionals?
44. Does the family distrust medical and mental health professionals who are from other ethnic groups?
45. Is the family too compliant and dependent on medical and mental health professionals?
46. What are the family's views about the need for treatment for male and female members? For example, do male members have more difficulty than female members in accepting a disability (because they consider it a weakness)? Will male members stop treatment when they have some symptom relief because they view longer term treatment as socially unacceptable? Do male and female members of the family view the disability in the same way?

Ability to Communicate

47. What is the family's proficiency in English?
48. Do family members have adequate receptive ability but inadequate expressive ability, or vice versa?
49. What is the chance that family members will be misunderstood?
50. If an interpreter was employed, how did the interview proceed?

RECOMMENDATIONS FOR THE ASSESSMENT OF CULTURALLY AND LINGUISTICALLY DIVERSE CHILDREN AND THEIR FAMILIES

When working with culturally and linguistically diverse children and their families, show them that you are sensitive to and respect their culture's perspective and value systems and that you are trying to help them. Convey to them an acceptance of their culture. Allow the parents and child to consult other family or community members if they ask to do so.

With culturally and linguistically diverse children and their parents, you may need to spend more time establishing rapport than you would with children and parents from the majority culture, as minority examinees may feel less trusting and particularly vulnerable. Take time to understand the fears, hopes, and aspirations of minority examinees, especially those who are refugees or immigrants. The process of acculturation often carries with it stresses caused by a loss of autonomy and feelings of shame and doubt.

The following guidelines will help you conduct more effective evaluations with minority children and their families. (Also see the Guidelines from the American Psychological Association for working with minority clients, in Chapter 3 of this text.)

LEARN ABOUT THE EXAMINEE'S CULTURE

1. Learn about the child's, family's, and community's cultural values, attitudes, and world view. For example, learn about the family's structure and roles, including distribution of power and authority; marriage customs; mutual obligations; and how the family handles shame. You can learn about the family's structure by reviewing information about the family's size and composition, ages of members, and living arrangements; education and employment of family members; and frequency and nature of contact with family members who are living outside the home. Consider whether the family's cultural practices are related to any of the child's symptoms.
2. Learn about the child's and family's ethnic identification. For example, do they consider themselves African American, Black American, or American? Hispanic American, Latino, Mexican American, or American?
3. Learn about the family's specific cultural patterns related to child rearing—for example, the family's attitudes concerning dating among adolescents, age of independence from the family, and the importance of education for males and females.
4. Consider the family's socioeconomic status and how it may affect the family's values, attitudes, and world view.
5. Learn how the family's community is organized, supported, and developed, including the role of the family in the community, the place of traditional healers, and the role of community leaders.
6. Learn how the sociopolitical system in the United States influences the way the family's minority group is treated.
7. Recognize your ignorance about details of the family's culture, and do not be afraid to let the child and family know that you are *not* aware of some aspects of their value system, world view, and life style. Not only will you learn, but they will appreciate your interest and honesty.
8. Recognize that if you are not a member of the minority group, you may be viewed as "the stranger."

LEARN ABOUT THE EXAMINEE'S LANGUAGE

1. Determine the child's and family's preferred language before you begin the evaluation.
2. Ideally, learn the language spoken by the child and family.
3. Do not assume that, because the child and family speak some English, they can fully understand you.
4. Do not assume that, just because you have some speaking knowledge of the family's language, you can ask meaningful questions in that language or fully understand the family's communications.

5. Employ an interpreter, if needed, and recognize the limitations inherent in doing so.

ESTABLISH RAPPORT

1. Make every effort to encourage the child's and family's motivation and interest.
2. Take time to enlist the child's and family's cooperation.
3. Be diplomatic and tactful. Avoid confrontation, arguments, and kidding, because the child and family may see such actions as disrespectful, rude, or offensive.
4. If taking notes during the evaluation will offend the child or family, write your notes after the evaluation is over. You might also consider using a tape recorder to record your notes.

IDENTIFY STEREOTYPES

1. Recognize any stereotypes and prejudices that you have about the family's ethnic group.
2. Take precautions to ensure that your stereotypes and prejudices do not interfere with your work. If you cannot do so, arrange for another psychologist to evaluate the child.
3. Do not assume that the family follows the minority group's traditional health healing practices or uses traditional healers. Some minority families will be offended if you assume that they believe in traditional healers. Ask them about these matters as needed.

PROMOTE CLEAR COMMUNICATION

1. Speak clearly, and avoid idioms, slang expressions, and statements with implied or double meanings.
2. Ask the parents and the child whom they want at the evaluation. Some families prefer to invite extended family members, whereas others do not.
3. Address all family members present at the evaluation, not just the child and parents.
4. Call children by their proper names. Hispanic Americans, for example, often have two last names, one from each parent. Do not use nicknames unless invited to do so.
5. Monitor your verbal and nonverbal behavior to eliminate words, expressions, and actions that may offend the child and family. Monitoring your nonverbal behavior will not be easy. You must learn whether your behavior changes with members of different minority groups. For example, if you are a majority examiner and work with both minority and majority examinees, do you place yourself farther away from examinees who are from minority groups than from examinees who are from majority groups, spend less time with them, or make more speech errors with them? If so, you may be revealing signs of anxiety or avoidance behavior. Videotape your evaluations and study them carefully for subtle signs of altered communications with different minority groups. Of course, you must first obtain permission to videotape the evaluation session. Then, you should

erase the tapes after you have studied them. In exceptional cases where you plan to use the tapes for research purposes, protect them by storing them in a locked cabinet.
6. Evaluate whether ethnic group differences between you and the child and family may be hampering the evaluation; if so, try to rectify the problems.
7. Be flexible, and use innovative assessment strategies tailored to the needs of the child's ethnic group.

IDENTIFY FAMILY NEEDS

1. Determine the material resources and physical health of the child and family. For example, do they have adequate food, water, clothing, bedding, shelter, and sanitation and proper immunizations? What unmet needs do the child and family have that could affect the assessment and treatment?
2. Determine the psychological and social needs of the child and family. For example, does the child have adequate time for play? What is the child's level of self-esteem? Has the child established friendships? Does the family have adequate leisure time? Are family members able to practice their religious beliefs? Does the child have adequate schooling? Does the home offer a place to study free from distractions? Are the parents able to supervise the child? Is the child forced to assume adult responsibilities prematurely? Is the child exposed to violence on the streets?

IDENTIFY FAMILY ATTITUDES TOWARD HEALTH AND ILLNESS

1. Learn about the child's and family's traditional concepts of illness and healing, traditional rituals, and religious beliefs, and how they differ from those of the majority culture. For example, healing practices that produce bruises on a child may not indicate child abuse, and the shaving of one's head and eyebrows, performed as a sacrifice to wronged ancestors, may not be a sign of mental illness.
2. Learn what the child's and family's expectations are of medical or psychological treatment. For example, when they take medicine, do they expect immediate relief, and if they do not get immediate relief, will they discontinue taking the medicine? Do they believe that only a pill will make them well?
3. Learn what prescribed drugs, over-the-counter drugs, traditional remedies, and illicit drugs the child is taking.

RECOGNIZE THE EXTENT OF THE FAMILY'S ACCULTURATION

1. Recognize that acculturation will take different forms among different ethnic groups. Learn about the extent to which the child and the parents are acculturated.
2. Expect to find differences among children and families from the same minority group in values and level of acculturation and in the problems they face.
3. Learn about the stresses associated with acculturation, particularly for refugee and immigrant groups. Do they feel depressed, angry, or guilty about those left behind in their home country? Do they have any symptoms associ-

ated with posttraumatic stress disorder? If you hold the evaluation after a period of adjustment in the United States, do they complain that nobody cares about them, express fear of failure or feelings of isolation, or have delayed grief reactions? Do they have conflicts in transition periods, such as when the children enter adolescence? Do other refugee or immigrant families reject them when they try to identify with the new culture? How great are the cultural differences between the United States and the home country? Is there intergenerational conflict between the child and parents because the child is acculturating faster than the adults? Does the child feel alienated— rejected both by his or her culture of origin and by the American culture? Is the child accepted by one culture but not the other? Or is he or she accepted by both cultures? Does the family need help in interpreting the laws and regulations of the United States?

4. Obtain information about how the child and family were functioning *before* leaving their home country. For example, children and families who had serious problems before their migration may find their unresolved problems exacerbated in the United States.

ACCEPT THE EXAMINEE'S PERSPECTIVES

1. Show a willingness to (a) accept cultural perspectives other than your own, (b) see the strengths and values of the coping mechanisms of ethnic groups other than your own, and (c) appreciate and respect the viewpoint of each ethnic group with which you work. For example, recognize how your own culture—its values, customs, mores, traditions, and standards—differs from other cultures. Be tolerant of family norms that may have developed in response to stress and prejudice. Include extended family members in the intervention if they are highly involved with the child and family. Also consider contacting traditional healers and practitioners as needed, and work with the established power structures within the child's and family's community.

2. Do not violate the child's and family's culture and traditional beliefs during the evaluation or in formulating intervention plans.

3. Build on the child's and family's strengths, use the family's natural support systems, and help the child remain in his or her natural community in the least restrictive environment.

4. Fully support the premise that society must give each child in the nation an equal opportunity to achieve to the limits of his or her capacity.

5. Recognize that members of minority groups (and members of the majority group as well) often face major social issues. Major social issues include changes in women's roles, changes in the concept of the family, substandard schools, unequal pay scales, dilapidated housing, high dropout rates from school, a shortage of mental

health services in the community, prejudice and discrimination, inaccessibility of mental health services, and irrelevance of treatments.

6. Recognize that families at a low socioeconomic level can provide a healthy, strong, and nurturing environment for their children; *do not equate low socioeconomic status with dysfunction.*

7. Recognize how the sociopolitical system in the United States treats minority groups and how institutional barriers affect minority groups' use of mental health and medical facilities.

8. Consider each child and family as unique, but use what you know about the child's and family's ethnic background to guide you in the evaluation and in formulating intervention plans.

9. Do not use your knowledge of the family's ethnic background to make sweeping stereotypic generalizations or to probe into cultural practices not relevant to the assessment and interventions.

10. Learn about stresses experienced by immigrant children and their families before they came to the United States. For example, have traumatic experiences affected the child's development and the child's and family's perceptions of the world and view of the future?

11. Avoid attributing all the child's and family's problems solely to their minority group status.

12. Have the case reassigned if you find yourself unable to be objective or unwilling to learn about the family's culture.

DEVELOP EFFECTIVE CONSULTATION SKILLS

1. Recognize the limits of your competencies and expertise in working not only with minority groups but with all children and their families.

2. View all examinees as being capable of learning, and hold high expectations for them.

3. Work with school personnel and students in schools to help them understand that all children and their families must be treated as equals, without regard to ethnicity, gender, religion, or disabling condition.

4. Work toward eliminating bias, prejudices, and discrimination in our society.

The above suggestions will help you become a culturally skilled examiner and establish trust with the child and parents. Trust, in turn, will improve the quality of communications. For trust to develop, children and parents must perceive that you have expert knowledge and good intentions and that they can rely on you. *Unless mutual trust develops, the evaluation is doomed to failure.*

You can become more credible in the eyes of minority families by conducting several informal evaluations initially and, in some cases, by visiting the child's home. Be sure to obtain the permission of the parents *before* you visit their home, however. Some minority families are distrustful of a stranger coming to their home, especially if the person is employed by a city, county, state, or federal agency. Minority parents may need time to accept the need for evaluation and treatment. Explain program objectives so that the parents—and the child, where applicable—understand them fully. Repeatedly stress that the welfare of the child is important. Give the parents as much support as they need. Resolve value conflicts to their satisfaction. If the child has a disability, help the parents accept the child's disability and be realistic about it. To orient the examinee's family to the program, recruit parents from the same ethnic group who have children in special programs.

Honesty and reliability can be effective in changing negative opinions about mental health and medical services and about practitioners. By being patient, understanding, competent, and tolerant, you can probably mitigate any hostile feelings that the parents have and help them see that the child's welfare is the concern of all involved.

Improved intercultural communication will ultimately depend on changes in the sociopolitical system. Until our society eliminates racism and discrimination, there will always be vestiges of suspicion and mistrust between people of different ethnicities. As an examiner, you can improve race relations. You can strive to eliminate social inequalities and prejudice from our society by (a) helping children develop pride in their native language and culture, (b) improving families' attitudes toward learning, and (c) helping society and the educational system be more responsive to the attitudes, perceptions, and behaviors of different ethnic groups. These and similar actions will improve the quality of life of the children and families with whom you work.

COMMENT ON THE ASSESSMENT OF CULTURALLY AND LINGUISTICALLY DIVERSE CHILDREN

There are many challenges in assessing children from culturally and linguistically diverse groups. We know that these children have been exposed to environments different from those experienced by majority children, but we are not sure what these differences may mean with respect to test administration and interpretation.

Standardized intelligence tests deal with only a certain part of the broad spectrum of abilities labeled "intelligence"; they measure primarily problem-solving and abstract abilities. Other indices of intelligent behavior need to be considered (see Chapter 5 of this text). Minority children must be given the full benefit of a battery of assessment techniques. Evaluation should tap all available sources of information. Intelligence tests, as imperfect as they undoubtedly are, are a first step toward better understanding and measurement of important aspects of human nature.

Assuming that there is a need to evaluate culturally and linguistically diverse children, which test or tests can be

used? As you read previously in this chapter, some writers want to ban all standardized tests. Although educators and psychologists must be responsive to the needs of children from minority groups, they should not abandon the use of standardized tests in clinical and psychoeducational assessments. The shortcomings of using standardized tests with minority children have been discussed in this chapter, and recommendations have been presented that may pave the way for more appropriate uses of tests.

Calls to ban use of all standardized tests with culturally and linguistically diverse children do not have merit. We believe that standardized tests should continue to be used, but only with recognition of their shortcomings and difficulties when applied to the evaluation of children from minority groups. Standardized tests should be used if they have the potential to contribute to the development of the child. Obviously, standardized tests should never be used when they would physically or emotionally harm any child.

The argument that we cannot accurately measure cognitive ability because individuals have differing linguistic backgrounds is simply false. One could say that each of the 274,000,000 citizens of the United States has experienced a unique and distinct language environment during his or her development. Obviously, it is a matter of degree. We all have communication difficulties, but we do communicate, and often at a high level of understanding. The data are overwhelming and convincing that we can measure, with a moderate degree of success, the cognitive ability of most individuals in our nation, using appropriate standardized tests.

Standardized tests are valuable assessment tools that can counteract the bias and discrimination inherent in subjective evaluations of competence. To deny minority children objective measurement is a disservice to them, to their families, and to society. To call for a ban on standardized tests without providing viable objective and scientific alternatives is simply not acceptable. *The key to evaluating standardized tests is to determine whether they are valid for the purposes for which they are used.* The data are clear: For the most part, standardized tests are valid for use with minority children in conjuction with such criteria as academic performance and school grades. Performance on standardized tests also relates to performance in real-world occupations. It is a myth to say that standardized cognitive ability tests are only valid in school settings (see Chapter 6 in this text).

For additional reading about intelligence, social policy, and changes in intelligence see the following:

- "Intelligence and Social Policy," a special issue of *Intelligence* (1997, *24,* Number 1) that discusses the role of differences in intelligence among groups and how these differences relate to social policy
- Herrnstein and Murray's (1994) *The Bell Curve: Intelligence and Class Structure in American Life*
- Jacoby and Glauberman's (1995) *The Bell Curve Debate: History, Documents, Opinions*

- Neisser's (1998) *The Rising Curve: Long-Term Gains in IQ and Related Measures*

As Cole (1981) noted, "The concern with test bias has arisen out of a broad social concern with equitable treatment of special groups in this society" (p. 1074). In her review of test bias research, Cole offered the following conclusions:

First, we have learned that there is not large-scale, consistent bias against minority groups in the technical validity sense in the major, widely used and widely studied tests. Second, we have learned that the lack of such bias means neither that the use made of the tests is necessarily socially good nor that improvements in the tests cannot be made. Third, we have learned that there are still many subtle aspects of the testing situation that we do not adequately understand and that are promising areas for future research to increase that understanding. However, these areas are not likely to yield results with a direct impact on sociopolitical policy decisions. Finally, and actually foremost, we have learned that whether or not tests are biased, their role is only a small part of the complex social policy issues facing the legislatures, the courts, and the citizenry at large. To pretend that these broader issues are essentially issues of test bias is to be deceived. These policy issues require decisions about values that must be made whether or not tests are involved. (p. 1075)

We must be sure not to lose sight of the importance of our nation's children and of finding ways to help them reach their potentialities. The elimination of intelligence and special ability tests from the schools of our nation will not contribute to this goal. Decisions made about the use of tests should be based on methodologically sound investigations. The evidence from many divergent studies indicates that individual intelligence tests are not culturally biased. They provide a profile of abilities that can be valid for African American, Hispanic American, Asian American, Native American, and other minority children, as well as for Euro American children. This conclusion holds only if standardized tests are administered and interpreted appropriately, taking into account the examinee's cultural and linguistic background and using only tests or portions of tests that are valid.

A culture must be created that allows us to see that one person's gain means the advancement of us all. Over the last 15 years [1980–1995], the concept of the common good has been tragically corrupted. Children grow up in homes where individualism is preeminent and human solidarity is unknown. God has created us to be one family. We can never eradicate racism that corrodes the soul of the nation unless we affirm our membership in that one human family, brothers and sisters, all sacred. I believe this is the central issue of our time. Our lives and destinies are wrapped up together.

The Greeks have a saying that there is no justice in Athens until the uninjured are as indignant as the injured parties. Religious leaders, civil rights leaders, politicians, academics, educators, lawyers, doctors, writers, editors must be committed to creating this culture of the common good.

What an incredible gift to families raising children in these troubled days if we could create a moral vision for America where the affluent are tied to the poor, the secure ones are bound together with the homeless and the well-being of my children and grandchildren is dependent on the health of all children. If a nation could not survive half-slave and half-free, no nation will be blessed if it is half-rich and half-impoverished.

There is something decadent about a city or a nation that denies this human solidarity. There is something corrupting about the assumption that a few have the right to good health, dignified jobs, fine education and decent housing—while others live in misery. It is my deepest conviction that any hope of racial healing is found in this renewed commitment to the common good and creating a culture in which this texture is unmistakably clear.

—George Regas

THINKING THROUGH THE ISSUES

1. Psychologists have not resolved issues surrounding the cultural bias of intelligence tests. What is your position on the controversy? How does the common use or understanding of the term *bias* differ from the technical meanings associated with the term?
2. Why do you think research findings strongly suggest that racial examiner effects do not markedly affect African American and Hispanic American children's intelligence test performance?
3. Children from some minority groups often perform at levels below their Euro American peers, whereas others perform above their Euro American peers on intelligence tests. What might account for these findings? And what might be implications of the findings?
4. Why has the movement to develop culture-fair tests resulted in failure?
5. What procedures do you advocate for the clinical and psychoeducational assessment of culturally and linguistically diverse children?
6. What were your reactions to the content of this chapter? For example, was any material disturbing or anxiety provoking?

SUMMARY

Arguments Against the Use of Intelligence Tests in Assessing Culturally and Linguistically Diverse Children

1. Arguments against the use of intelligence tests in the assessment of culturally and linguistically diverse children include the following: (a) intelligence tests have a cultural bias, (b) national norms are inappropriate for culturally and linguistically diverse groups, (c) culturally and linguistically diverse groups are handicapped in test-taking skills, (d) Euro American examiners depress the scores of minority children, and (e) test results lead to inadequate and inferior education.
2. The overwhelming body of research does not provide support for any of these allegations.

Arguments for the Use of Intelligence Tests in Assessing Culturally and Linguistically Diverse Children

3. Arguments for the use of intelligence tests in the assessment of culturally and linguistically diverse children include the following: They are useful in (a) evaluating present and future functioning, (b) obtaining special programs, (c) evaluating programs, (d) revealing inequalities, and (e) providing an objective standard.

Court Cases Involving Assessment Techniques

4. Beginning in the 1970s, courts have heard a number of cases concerning the overrepresentation of minority children in special classes, primarily those for children with mental retardation.
5. It has been argued that (a) minority children are overrepresented in classes for the educable mentally retarded, (b) special education represents a dead end and provides substandard educational programs, (c) intelligence tests are culturally biased, (d) students with limited facility in English have been inappropriately administered tests requiring extensive facility in English, and (e) a full range of assessment techniques is not being used in arriving at placement decisions.
6. In *Larry P. v. Riles*, a federal court ruled that intelligence were racially and culturally biased.
7. In *Parents in Action on Special Education v. Joseph P. Hannon,* a federal court ruled that intelligence tests were not culturally biased.
8. In *Georgia Conferences of NAACP v. Georgia,* a federal court ruled that there was no evidence of differential treatment of African American and Euro American children in the procedures used to place children in classes for the educable mentally retarded.
9. In *Mattie T. v. Holladay,* a U.S. district court approved a consent decree stipulating that the state of Mississippi reevaluate its procedures used to classify children for classes for the mentally retardated.
10. In *Diana v. State Board of Education,* a federal court invalidated testing procedures used to evaluate Mexican American children for placement in special classes.

Intelligence and Racial Differences

11. The present consensus is that we cannot draw valid inferences about genetic differences among races as long as there are relevant systematic differences between races in their cultural patterns and in their psychological environment.

Development of Culture-Fair Tests for Assessing Culturally and Linguistically Diverse Children

12. Attempts to develop tests that are culture fair have not been successful.
13. Every test is culturally loaded to some extent.
14. Probably no test can be created that eliminates the influence of learning and cultural experiences.

Evaluating Ethnic and Cultural Factors

15. Your assessment of a culturally and linguistically diverse child and his or her family should consider the following factors: (a) their degree of acculturation, (b) their cultural and religious beliefs about illness (c) the family structure and intrafamily relationships, (d) the attitudes of family members toward the child's illness or disability, (e) their attitudes toward medical and mental health professionals and treatment, and (f) their ability to communicate.

Recommendations for the Assessment of Culturally and Linguistically Diverse Children and Their Families

16. When working with culturally and linguistically diverse children and their families, show them that you are sensitive to and respect their culture's perspective and value systems and that you are trying to help them. Convey to them an acceptance of their culture. Allow the parents and child to consult other family or community members if they ask to do so.
17. To become a culturally skilled examiner, learn about the examinee's culture and language, establish rapport, identify any stereotypes you have and take precautions to ensure that they do

---

For Better or For Worse®   by Lynn Johnston

© Lynn Johnston Productions Inc./Dist. by United Feature Syndicate, Inc.

not interfere with the assessment, promote clear communication, identify family needs, identify family attitudes toward health and illness, recognize the extent of the family's acculturation, accept the examinee's perspectives, and develop effective consultation skills.

Comment on the Assessment of Culturally and Linguistically Diverse Children

18. There are many challenges in assessing children from culturally and linguistically diverse groups.
19. We know that culturally and linguistically diverse children have been exposed to environments different from those experienced by majority children, but we are not sure what these differences may mean with respect to test administration and interpretation.
20. Culturally and linguistically diverse children must be given the full benefit of a battery of assessment techniques.
21. Calls to ban use of all standardized tests with culturally and linguistically diverse children do not have merit.
22. Standardized tests are valuable assessment tools that can counteract the bias and discrimination inherent in subjective evaluations of competence.
23. To deny culturally and linguistically diverse children objective measurement is a disservice to them, to their families, and to society.
24. The key to evaluating standardized tests is to determine whether they are valid for the purposes for which they are used.
25. The evidence from many divergent studies indicates that individual intelligence tests are not culturally biased. They provide a profile of abilities that can be valid for African American, Hispanic American, Asian American, Native American, and other culturally and linguistically diverse children, as well as for Euro American children. This conclusion holds only if standardized tests are administered and interpreted appropriately, taking into account the examinee's cultural and linguistic background and using only tests or portions of tests that are valid.

KEY TERMS, CONCEPTS, AND NAMES

STUDY QUESTIONS

1. Critically evaluate the arguments and evidence concerning the use of intelligence tests in assessing culturally and linguistically diverse children.
2. Discuss how response styles affect test scores.
3. Discuss the controversy over intelligence and racial differences.
4. Discuss the use of culture-fair tests in the assessment of culturally and linguistically diverse children.
5. What recommendations would you give for evaluating children who come from culturally and linguistically diverse groups?

21

PRINCIPLES OF REPORT WRITING

A naturalist's life would be a happy one if he had only to observe and never to write.

—Charles Darwin

Introduction to Psychological Report Writing

Sections of a Psychological Report

Overview of Report Writing

Organize Your Findings

Include Relevant Material

Make Interpretations Carefully

Make Generalizations

Convey the Degree of Certainty

Enhance Readability

Focus on the IQ

Interpret Scores

Obtain IQ Classifications

Use Percentile Ranks

Provide Clear Descriptions

Develop Inferences from Test Scores

Describe Profiles Clearly

Make Recommendations Carefully

Use Caution in Extrapolating or Interpolating Scores

Make Diagnoses Cautiously

Communicate Clearly

Describe Any Statistical Concepts

Avoid Bias

Write Concisely

Attend to Grammar and Style

Improve Your Writing Style

Concluding Comment on Report Writing

Test Your Skill

Thinking Through the Issues

Summary

Goals and Objectives

This chapter is designed to enable you to do the following:

- Understand the purposes of a psychological or psychoeducational report

- Understand the sections of a psychological or psychoeducational report

- Develop appropriate skills for communicating your findings and recommendations in the report

- Write a psychological or psychoeducational report

This chapter covers the writing of a psychological report. In school and other settings as well, the report may be referred to as a "psychoeducational report" because the focus is on problems that children have in school. In this chapter we will use "report" or "psychological report" to refer to both psychological reports and psychoeducational reports. First the qualities of a good report are discussed, and then each section of the report is described. Next, we offer 22 principles to serve as guidelines for report writing. After completing this chapter, you should understand the fundamentals of psychological report writing. The final test of your skills, however, will be writing a good report yourself.

Psychological reports may be based on test findings; interviews with the child, his or her parents, and teachers; systematic behavioral observations; and other relevant information gleaned from school records, prior psychological reports, and medical, psychiatric, and other sources. If you are in training at a university or a member of a multidisciplinary team, your report may be based on only one test, one interview, or one systematic behavioral observation. However, when children are referred for a comprehensive evaluation, the report should be based on multiple assessment procedures.

INTRODUCTION TO PSYCHOLOGICAL REPORT WRITING

A psychological evaluation is complete only after the obtained information has been organized, synthesized, and integrated. The traditional medium for presenting assessment information is a report, although you may use other formal and informal means of presentation (e.g., special recording forms or oral communications). The completion of a report is an integral part of the clinical or psychoeducational assessment process. The report should convey clearly and concisely the information obtained, the findings, clinical impressions (where applicable), and specific recommendations. A report may influence a child and family for years to come; its drafting deserves extreme care and consideration (see, for example, the case of *Daniel Hoffman* in Chapter 1). Report writing is one of the defining activities of clinicians.

Qualities of a Good Report

Your report should be well organized and solidly grounded. A good report does not merely present facts. It integrates the testing results, behavioral observations, information gained from interviews, and relevant case history material (which includes current and prior social, educational, psychological, psychiatric, and medical findings and recommendations and prereferral information). The report presents what you have learned about the examinee in a way that shows respect for her or his individuality. This respect for individuality should permeate the entire assessment process; you should view the examinee as an individual in the context of her or his life and not simply as a stimulus for gathering data.

Purposes of the Report

The following are some purposes of a psychological report:

1. To provide accurate assessment-related information (e.g., developmental, medical, and educational history, as well as current interpersonal skills, intellectual and cognitive abilities, motor skills, and personality) to the referral source and other concerned parties
2. To serve as a source of clinical hypotheses, appropriate interventions, and information for program evaluation and research
3. To furnish meaningful baseline information for evaluating (a) the examinee's progress after the interventions have been implemented or (b) changes that occur as a result of time alone
4. To serve as a legal document

Formulating the Report

In formulating and constructing your report, first consider who will be the primary audiences for the report. The target audience may be parents, a general education teacher, special education personnel, a health care provider, an attorney, a judge, or a colleague. In all cases, you want to ensure that the report can be understood by nonprofessionals. Second, consider the circumstances under which the assessment took place, the number of opportunities for observation and interaction, and the behavioral basis for the judgments you make about the examinee. Third, include examples, as appropriate, to illustrate or document selected statements you make in the report. Fourth, make your recommendations with an appreciation of the needs and values of the examinee, his or her family and extended family, the family's resources, the examinee's ethnic and cultural group, the school, and society. Throughout the process, consider how your values affect the way you conduct the assessment, arrive at conclusions and recommendations, and emphasize certain details in the report.

Subjective Elements in the Report

Although you should strive for objectivity and accuracy in writing the report, remember that no report can be completely objective. Every report has elements of subjectivity because the information may be open to different interpretations. Recognize that you introduce subjectivity with each word you use to describe the examinee, each behavior you highlight or ignore, each element of the history you cite, and the sequence you follow in presenting the information. You have already learned that the evaluation procedure also contains many elements of subjectivity.

Promptness in Writing the Report

Write the report as soon as possible after you complete the assessment. You want to record all important details (and not forget any). The referral source needs a prompt reply. Unfortunately, in some settings, there is often a delay between the time someone makes a referral and the initiation of the assessment. You, as the examiner, should not introduce further delay by putting off writing the report.

Contents of the Report

The psychological report should adequately describe the assessment findings, including information about the examinee's history, current problems, assets, and limitations; it should also include behavioral observations and test interpretations. The assessment instruments used should be noted. The value of the psychological report lies in the degree to which it addresses the referral question.

Each report should be an independent document—that is, its content should be comprehensive enough to stand alone. The reader should not need to refer to other materials for illustration or clarification. However, it is perfectly acceptable to refer the reader to past reports for purposes of comparison with the present findings. Test protocols, data sheets, and other assessment information should be filed in the child's private evaluation folder and not attached to the report or placed in the child's cumulative folder.

SECTIONS OF A PSYCHOLOGICAL REPORT

A typical psychological report will have the following sections:

1. Identifying Information
2. Assessment Instruments
3. Reason for Referral
4. Background Information
5. Observations During the Assessment
6. Assessment Results and Clinical Impressions
7. Recommendations
8. Summary
9. Signature

1. Identifying Information

The first part of the report presents relevant identifying information. Include the examinee's name, date of birth, sex, age, and grade in school (if applicable); date(s) of the assessment; date of the report; and the examiner's name. You also may want to state the name of the child's teacher (if applicable) and the names of the child's parents. Also include the name of the organization (e.g., school, clinic, agency, private prac-

tice, or university) sponsoring the assessment (including address, telephone number, and, if available, fax number) and the e-mail address, telephone extension or voice-mail box, or other contact information for the examiner.

Determining the child's chronological age requires attention, beyond just correctly subtracting the child's birthday from the date of testing. Correct computation is worthless if the child's date of birth is wrong. Young children make mistakes, and file folders may have the wrong information. It is a good practice to confirm the child's birthday with a parent.

2. Assessment Instruments

List both formal and informal assessment instruments and techniques that you used to conduct the evaluation. For example, include the names of standardized tests and informal tests and the names of any other techniques that you used, such as the interview and systematic behavioral observation. Spell out all test names completely, followed by their acronym in parentheses.

Some examiners find it helpful to have on hand a hard copy or computer file of brief descriptions of all the tests they use. It is then easy to attach an appendix to the report by (a) photocopying the descriptions of the tests that were used or (b) copying onto a new computer file only the tests used in the evaluation (or deleting from a copy of the original file the tests that were not used). Such appendixes provide useful information to lay readers without cluttering the text of the report.

Summer Vacation!
...but I have a few
more reports to do.

Courtesy of Daniel Miller.

3. Reason for Referral

Citing the reason for referral helps document why the psychological evaluation was conducted. Consider including the following information: (a) name, position, and affiliation (if applicable) of the referral source; (b) why the referral source asked for the assessment; (c) specific questions the referral source has about the examinee; (d) a brief summary of the specific behaviors or symptoms displayed by the examinee that led to the referral; and (e) possible ways the assessment may be used (e.g., to plan remedial measures, treatment, or educational programs).

Here are two examples of a Reason for Referral section.

The Planning and Placement Team of Central Elementary School referred Mikey for an assessment to gain a better understanding of his cognitive and behavioral strengths and weaknesses. This request was prompted by Mikey's distractible behavior, poor work completion, inadequate peer relations, and attention-seeking behaviors in his third-grade class.

In January 1999, Carl had a shunt implanted for increased intracranial pressure and the resection of a glioma. He has just completed a course of radiation therapy, and neuropsychological testing was requested by his physician to assess cognitive changes associated with his treatment and condition.

4. Background Information

In the Background Information section, you may include material obtained from interviews with the parents, teacher(s), and child; from the examinee's educational file; and from previous psychological, psychiatric, and medical accounts. Always acknowledge the sources of the information, and report the dates on which the accounts were written. As noted in Chapter 3, you must have a signed release of information form (usually signed by a parent) to obtain previous psychological or medical reports or similar information from other agencies. You may want to include in this section demographic information, information about the current problems, historical information (including the child's developmental history), information about the family, and information about the parents (see Table 21-1).

As you review the material you obtained from the interviews with the child, parents, teachers, and other informants, estimate the accuracy of the information that they gave you. For example, were they cooperative, confused, or hostile? Was there anything in these interviews suggesting that an interviewee was slanting or distorting information, hiding information, or deliberately giving you misleading information? Were there any gaps in the information? These and similar questions should guide your evaluation of the material that you obtained.

You also will want to compare the information you obtained from different interviewees. What were the similarities and differences in the information obtained from the child, the parents, and the teacher about the child's problems and concerns? How did each interviewee describe the child's behavior? What trends were evident in the developmental history, observational findings, parental reports, teacher reports, medical reports, psychological and psychiatric reports, and police reports (if applicable), and how consistent were the trends?

Don't be surprised to find differences in the information given to you by children, parents, and teachers. For example, they may agree about external symptoms but not about internal ones. If there are differences between the accounts of the parents and child, parents and teacher, or two parents, what might account for the differences? Here are some questions for you to consider:

1. Do the parents and teacher differ in their ability to observe, evaluate, and judge the behavior of the child?
2. Could the variance be associated with different standards for judging deviant behavior or different tolerances for behavioral problems? For example, what the parents consider hyperactive, the teacher may consider normal, or vice versa.
3. Could differences in how the parents and teacher view the child's behavior be due to situational factors? For example, if parents report *fewer* problems than does the teacher, the child may be overindulged at home but treated normally at school. If parents report *more* problems than does the teacher, the child may be experiencing a stressful environment at home (e.g., unsympathetic parents, poor structure and discipline, conflicts with siblings) but a normal environment at school (e.g., even-handed discipline, consistency, clear and reasonable expectations).

Thus, discrepancies between interviewees may suggest that the behaviors of concern are not pervasive or generalizable— the child may actually behave differently at home than at school (Clarizio, 1994). In addition, normal home environments make different demands on students than do normal school environments. Consider all the information you have before arriving at an explanation for any discrepancies between informants.

When information is available from several sources, you will need to organize and interpret it to arrive at a systematic understanding of the child. You will need to consider the child as a whole, given his or her family, culture, and environment. Although the information may not always be clear, you still must sort out the findings and establish trends. Rather than ignoring discrepant information, try to account for it.

Following is a sample Background Information section. The examinee was admitted to a psychiatric hospital on an emergency basis because of bizarre, unpredictable, and out-of-control behavior. His mother reported that he had been talking to himself and may have been having delusions and hallucinations.

Henry, a 12-year, 9-month-old adolescent, is the youngest of five children. He lives with his mother, who has been married three

---

Table 21-1
Types of Background Information That Can Be Included in the Psychological Report

Demographic Information

1. Child's age (repeated from the Identifying Information section)

2. Child's grade in school (if applicable, repeated from the Identifying Information section)

Information About Current Problem

3. Description of the child's current problems and symptoms, if any (including precipitating factors; the frequency, duration, intensity, pervasiveness, and etiology of the problems and symptoms; and how the child is coping with the problems)

Historical Information

4. Child's educational history (including prior school grades, attendance record, previous and current special education services, teacher's perception of the problem, and teacher's observations of the child's behavior and attitudes and the child's relationships with peers and with teachers)

5. Child's present level of academic functioning

6. Child's prior psychological test results (including major findings, diagnostic impressions, recommendations, and follow-up contacts)

7. Child's response to previous interventions, if any were attempted (including what progress has been made, which interventions have been effective, and which Individualized Education Program goals have been attained)

8. Child's significant health history (including types of illnesses and injuries, treatments, and extent of recovery)

9. Child's developmental history (including events in the child's life that may have a bearing on her or his psychological or educational problems, such as the mother's pregnancy, when the child reached developmental milestones, or any traumatic events)

10. Child's physical development (including a description of the child's fine- and gross-motor movements, height and weight, sleep patterns, eating patterns, vision, and audition)

11. Child's social interactions and peer relationships (including degree of emotional maturity and ability to cooperate with peers, parents, siblings, and teachers; to play fair and understand rules; to develop a conscience; to play constructively; and to play alone)

Information About Family

12. Child's current family situation (including family makeup, socioeconomic status, marital status of parents, parents' perceptions of the problem, parents' occupations, parents' education, parents' child-rearing practices, parents' level of involvement with the child, any signs of child maltreatment, how the parents' perception of the problem agrees with those of the child and teacher, description of how the child's problem has affected the family)

13. Nature of the child's home, school, and neighborhood

Information About Parents

14. Parents' ability to give useful information (including the quality of the information they gave, their degree of openness or guardedness, the consistency of the information, and whether they agreed with each other)

15. Parents' attitudes toward the child, the child's school, the child's teachers, the child's friends, the other children in their family, and the neighborhood where they live

16. Parents' involvement with the child (including the amount of time they spend with the child; the activities that they participate in with the child; and their ability to respond to the child's needs, support the child, supervise the child, and discipline the child)

17. Parents' coping ability (including their ability to cope with the child's problem and with the needs of the other siblings)

18. Parents' suggestions for solving the child's problem

---

times. All of the background information was obtained from Henry's mother. Henry last saw his father when he was 5 months old and just beginning to crawl. He first walked alone at 15 months and achieved bowel control at 2 years of age. However, he never achieved bladder control, and he remains enuretic at night.

He attended a Head Start program at the age of 4 and was referred to a child guidance clinic by his Head Start teacher because of behavioral problems. He received a diagnosis of attention-deficit/hyperactivity disorder at that time from his health care provider. When Henry was 5 years old, his maternal grandmother died of a stroke, and Henry became extremely depressed. His mother noted

that shortly afterward Henry told her that he knew in advance that his grandmother was going to die; he claimed that he knew what was going to happen in the future.

At 6 years of age, Henry attempted suicide by throwing himself in front of a car after his mother was hospitalized for hypertension; however, he was not seriously injured. Henry told his mother that he believed that she was going to die and he wanted to die, too. This incident resulted in Henry's referral to Blank County Mental Health Clinic, where he was treated for the suicide attempt and for hyperactivity and enuresis. At the clinic, he started taking medications for his depression and attention-deficit/hyperactivity disorder.

When Henry was 9 years old, his youngest sister, who was then 16 years old, attempted suicide by a drug overdose. Henry was depressed for several months. At the age of 10 years, he was expelled from school for alleged sexually inappropriate behavior, including touching other children's genitalia. He was subsequently transferred to another school, where he currently attends special education classes. He was classified by school personnel as having a behavior disorder. Academically, his grades were average in reading and spelling to below average in mathematics and writing.

The relationship between Henry and his mother has always been close, although recently he has become "difficult to get along with." His mother described Henry as a social isolate—having no friends and preferring to spend his time alone or only with her. No serious medical problems were reported.

5. Observations During the Assessment

One of the challenges in writing a report is to communicate what you have observed during the assessment. A good report carefully describes the examinee's behavior during the evaluation and any observations that you made in the examinee's classroom, home, or hospital setting. Your observations help the reader understand what you consider to be important features of the examinee's behavior. They also lend some objectivity to the report by providing information about what the examinee did that led you to form specific impressions. Finally, information obtained from behavioral observations may be used in the development of intervention plans.

In writing about your observations, recognize the differences between statements that *describe* behavior and those that *interpret* behavior. (See Chapter 7 in this text for guidelines on observing test behavior, and see Chapter 4 in *Assessment of Children: Behavioral and Clinical Applications* for guidelines on observing behavior in natural settings.) A statement that the child was tapping his or her feet during the evaluation is one that describes the child's behavior. A statement that the child was anxious is one that interprets the child's behavior. Both descriptive and interpretive statements are valuable to include in a report. Sometimes it is useful to include a descriptive statement followed by a statement interpreting the behavior or vice versa.

The child's behavior during the evaluation may differ from her or his behavior in other settings. Consequently, you must be careful in generalizing from the child's behavior in the assessment setting. However, the behaviors that you observe during the evaluation are in the child's repertoire.

In describing the child's behavior, focus on the presence of a behavior rather than on its absence. You can cite an almost infinite number of adjectives that did *not* characterize the child's behavior, but such descriptions are relatively useless. Instead, emphasize how the child actually performed. For example, instead of saying "The child was not hyperactive," say, "The child was quiet and calm" or "The child remained still." Similarly, focus on what the behavior suggests rather than on what it doesn't suggest. For example, instead of saying "Her

agility while running suggests no obvious delays in gross-motor development," say, "Her agility while running suggests at least average gross-motor development." An exception is when the referral source asks you to comment on a specific problem or symptom. In such cases, include a statement about the specific problem or symptom, even if it did not occur. Another exception is a comment on a behavior that normally would be expected to occur but is absent.

In the Behavioral Observations section of the report, you can comment on the examinee's physical appearance, reactions to being evaluated, reactions to you, general behavior, activity level, language style, general response style, mood, response to inquiries, response to encouragement, attitude toward self, motor skills, and unusual habits, mannerisms, or verbalizations. You also can include your reaction to the examinee. Four examples of excerpts from a Behavioral Observations section follow.

William is a 5-year, 2-month-old child with blond hair and brown eyes. He was friendly and animated and appeared eager to talk. He was curious about the toys in the room, and he examined each cabinet. During the evaluation, he often squirmed in his seat, exhausting nearly every position possible while remaining on his chair. Despite his frequent squirming, William maintained a high degree of interest throughout the evaluation. He was attentive and followed the questions well, and he established excellent rapport with the examiner.

Regina is a 16½-year-old adolescent whose cosmetics and hairstyle make her look older than she is. She appeared anxious and somewhat sad throughout the evaluation. Her wide-eyed look and clenched hands underscored her anxiety and tension and suggested fearfulness. Although Regina seemed able to relax after talking with the examiner, she was extremely tense when some topics were discussed. In discussing her school performance, for example, she made many self-deprecating remarks, such as "I can't do well in most subjects" and "I'm terrible at that subject." She also responded repeatedly with "I don't know" rather than attempting to answer difficult or personal questions. Despite Regina's anxiety, she occasionally smiled and laughed appropriately.

Karl is a bright-eyed, amiable, 6-year, 3-month-old child of above-average height. He was eager to begin the evaluation and immediately took a seat when I asked him to do so. Initially, he chatted easily with me. However, when I gave him an opportunity to play with the toys in the room, he seemed unsure of himself. He wandered from activity to activity, never staying with any one toy or game. He seemed to be unable to focus his attention. His initial attitude of confidence and self-composure seemed to deteriorate, and he began to whisper his answers. It appeared that he was afraid to respond in the event that I might disapprove of his answers. He was concerned about and sensitive to my opinion of his responses and frequently asked, "Was that OK?" or "Is that right?" Karl appeared disappointed when he could not talk about some things that I asked him to discuss. Even when I gently encouraged him to tell exactly what he meant, he continued to use the same words or added, "I don't know." Karl appeared to relax somewhat as the evaluation progressed. When he realized that I was not critical of responses, he gave his answers in a normal voice and became more assertive. Karl was given a short break because of his restlessness, after which he seemed considerably more relaxed and comfortable.

Frank, a 17-year, 4-month-old adolescent, avoided eye contact with me and, at times, seemed to have difficulty finding the right words to express himself. He showed some signs of anxiety, such as heavy breathing, sniffling a great deal, mumbling, and making short, quick movements with his hands and head. He seemed to answer some questions impulsively, but he would also occasionally say quietly, "No, wait" and then give another answer.

6. Assessment Results and Clinical Impressions

The Assessment Results and Clinical Impressions section consolidates the assessment information you have obtained and provides a comprehensive picture of the assessment findings. Topics covered include assessment findings, precision range of the major score, reliability and validity of the test results, and clinical and diagnostic impressions.

Table 21-2 summarizes typical questions, primarily for school-aged children, that you will want to consider in interpreting the assessment findings. The questions cover such areas as background information, health and developmental history, educational history and current classroom performance, family history, perceptual-motor ability, speech and language ability, attention and information-processing ability, cognitive ability, memory ability, learning ability, affect, motivation, social comprehension, and interpersonal relations; interventions are also covered. Additional questions that are relevant for children with specific types of disabilities are found in *Assessment of Children: Behavioral and Clinical Applications.*

Reliability and validity. Do not report assessment findings unless, in your opinion, they are a valid indication of the child's ability or behavior. If you have any concerns that an assessment finding may not be reliable or valid, clearly state your concerns and the reasons for them at the beginning of the Assessment Results and Clinical Impressions portion of the report.

Of course, you also need to evaluate the reliability and validity of each assessment instrument before you use it by reading the relevant test manuals and other published literature. Do not use tests with poor psychometric properties to make decisions about examinees. After you administer the test, evaluate the reliability and validity of the test results, looking for any factors that might make the test results questionable. As you may recall from Chapter 4, several factors affect reliability, including test length, guessing, and variations in the test instructions or test setting. Test-related or situation-related factors that temporarily impair a child's performance (e.g., loud noises in the environment or medication that causes a child to be drowsy) also affect validity. Because reliability affects validity, you should not consider an unreliable performance to be valid.

In reporting assessment results that you believe are valid (in which case they must be reliable), you might say, "The results of the present testing appear to be valid because Richard's mo-

tivation and attention were good throughout testing." An appropriate way to report results that have questionable validity might be "The intelligence test findings may not be valid and may underestimate Rebecca's abilities because she was ill on the day of the testing" or "Darleen often appeared confused and unwilling to discuss many facets of her life. Consequently, it is doubtful that the limited information she provided about herself was either reliable or valid."

Guidelines for reporting test results. Do not simply report test scores; you also need to integrate and interpret them. Important areas to include in the Assessment Results and Clinical Impressions section are the following:

- Factors that may have affected the assessment results
- Names of the tests you administered
- Test scores, including IQs and other standard scores and major scale scores, such as Verbal and Performance IQs of the Wechsler scales and reading, mathematics, and spelling scores of the achievement tests administered
- Classification of IQ
- Percentile ranks of the major test scores
- Description of the child's strengths and weaknesses, as reflected by the subtest scores and significant differences between the subtest scores and total test score
- Comparison of verbal and nonverbal skills
- Illustrative responses
- Signs suggestive of psychopathology
- Signs suggestive of exceptionality, such as creativity, giftedness, or learning disability
- Interrelationships among test findings
- Interrelationships among all sources of assessment information
- Implications of assessment findings
- Diagnostic impressions

Whenever possible, provide several sources of information to substantiate your interpretations.

Consider what data you should include in or append to the report (Freides, 1993; Matarazzo, 1995). Some clinicians are reluctant to include test data in the report because readers may misunderstand or misinterpret the information. Other clinicians argue that test data should be included in or appended to the report so that qualified readers can evaluate the basis for the examiner's conclusions. You will need to be guided by your agency's policy on this matter. If test data are not included in the report, the data must remain readily available to future examiners with proper release forms or for litigation purposes.

Confidence intervals. Whenever you report an IQ or a similar overall standard score, accompany it with a confidence interval. The confidence interval is a function of both the standard error of measurement and the confidence level: the greater the confidence level (e.g., 99% > 95% > 90% > 85% > 68%) or the lower the reliability of the test (r_{xx} = .80 < r_{xx} = .85 < r_{xx} = .90), the wider the confidence interval. The Appen-

Table 21-2
Questions to Consider After Evaluating a School-Aged Child with Special Needs

Background Information

1. What are the sex, age, ethnicity, and appearance of the child? Appearance includes height, weight, posture, facial expression, eye contact, and personal cleanliness of skin, hair, nails, and teeth.
2. What language does the child speak at home, in school, and in the neighborhood?
3. What are the child's presenting problems, including their frequency, intensity, and duration?
4. Is the child abusing legal substances (e.g., cough syrup, inhalants) or using alcohol or illegal drugs? If so, what is the child taking, how does the child obtain the drugs or alcohol, and for what length of time has the child used these substances?
5. How do the parents, teachers, peers, and others interact with the child?
6. What changes have the parents, teachers, peers, and others made to adjust to the child's problems?
7. What information have the parents been given by teachers, psychologists, or physicians about the child's problems?
8. How do the child and parents view the referral?
9. What are the child's, parents', and teachers' concerns?
10. Do the child and parents believe that the child has problems? If so, how do they describe the child's problems?
11. How well do the child's description of the problems, the parents' description of the problems, and the teacher's description of the problems agree?
12. If there are disagreements among individuals interviewed, in what areas are they?
13. Where does the child display his or her problems (such as at home, at school, at other places)?
14. How old was the child when the parents became aware of the child's problems?
15. How do the parents, child, and teacher handle the child's problems?
16. What do the parents believe might contribute to the child's problems—biological predispositions, deficiencies or delays in basic skill areas, personality and temperament, familial influences, environmental influences, or a combination of any of these factors?

Health and Developmental History

17. What is the child's health history?
18. Are there any indications of visual or auditory difficulties?
19. If the child has visual or auditory difficulties, have glasses or hearing aids been prescribed? If so, does the child have these aids and wear them?
20. Does the child take any medicine that might affect school performance? If so, what is the medicine, and what are the major side effects?
21. Were there any significant events in the child's prenatal, perinatal, or postnatal development that may be related to the current problems? If so, what were these events?

22. Were there any significant medical problems or indications of psychological problems during the child's development? If so, what were they, and did the child receive any significant treatments for them? If so, what treatments did the child receive, and how successful were they?
23. Did the child reach developmental milestones at the expected ages? If not, what milestones were delayed, and when did the child reach these milestones?
24. When did the child's problems emerge?
25. How did the mother's pregnancy progress?
26. During pregnancy, did the mother have any exposure to drugs or any unusual event? If so, what happened?
27. Did the child have hypoxia, neonatal jaundice, head trauma, meningitis, epilepsy, or other illnesses or conditions at birth or shortly thereafter? If so, what condition did the child have, what treatment did the child receive, and what was the outcome of treatment? Were there any residual symptoms? What was the Apgar score?
28. What was the child's temperament as an infant?

Educational History and Current Classroom Performance

29. What school does the child attend?
30. What is the child's grade in school?
31. How long has the child been going to his or her present school?
32. Has the child attended other schools in the past? If so, what schools did the child attend, what were the years of attendance, and what were the reasons for changes from one school to another?
33. What is the child's current school attendance record?
34. If the child has poor attendance, what are the reasons for the poor attendance?
35. What was the child's past school attendance record?
36. If the child had poor attendance, what were the reasons for the poor attendance?
37. Has the child ever been suspended or expelled from school? If so, when did this take place and for what reason?
38. In the past, in what type of classroom settings was the child enrolled?
39. In what type of classroom setting is the child presently enrolled (e.g., resource, multi-level, or self-contained)?
40. How many students are in the classroom?
41. How many teachers and teacher aides are in the classroom?
42. How many classrooms does the child attend?
43. Is the child grouped in a homogeneous setting for various academic subjects? If so, describe (a) the basis for the grouping (e.g., age, cognitive ability, level of academic achievement, optimal learning environment), (b) the level of the child's placement for each academic subject, (c) whether the child has been moved from one group to another, and, if so, (d) the nature of the move (e.g., to a less demanding group or to a more demanding group) and in what subject area(s).

(Continued)

Table 21-2 *(Continued)*

44. How do the parents describe the child's teachers and schooling?

45. Has the child repeated any grades? If so, what grades and what were the reasons for the retention?

46. What specific examples does the teacher give of the child's attention to tasks, impulse control in various situations, and activity level?

47. Does the child's behavior change as a function of the academic subject, teacher, class size, time of day, or other factors? If so, describe the type of change and the basis for it.

48. How well does the child respect the classroom rules?

49. What is the quality of the assignments completed by the child in the classroom and at home?

50. If the child was given psychological or academic tests, what were the results of the evaluation?

51. What is the child's current level of academic functioning (including letter grades and test scores), social functioning in the classroom, and general classroom behavior?

52. What letter grades is the child receiving in each subject area?

53. Has the child shown changes in grade patterns over the course of the academic year? If so, what were the changes (e.g., high in some subjects and low in others; high scores during the beginning of the school year and lower scores as the year progressed; lower or higher scores when there were shifts from rote learning to more conceptual learning)?

54. What standard does the teacher use for grading (e.g., individual effort and improvement, comparison with classmates)?

55. What evaluation techniques does the teacher use as the basis for the grades (e.g., test scores, short quizzes, homework assignments, class participation)?

56. If tests and quizzes are used, what type are they (e.g., multiple choice, true/false, essay, oral response)?

57. Does the child have more difficulty with some evaluation techniques than with others? If so, with which evaluation techniques does the child have most difficulty? Least difficulty?

58. Does the teacher make any special accommodations for the child in the evaluation process? If so, what accommodations does the teacher make (e.g., allowing extra time to complete the test or assignment, substituting oral presentations for essay tests)?

59. Does the child seem to be satisfied with his or her grades?

60. If the child has a reading problem, how does the teacher describe the problem? For example, does the child have difficulty reading new words or nonsense syllables (phonological problem), have difficulty in comprehension, show reluctance in trying to read different words, have a tendency to lose his or her place while reading, read quickly without close inspection, have a tendency to repeat words, hold a book close to his or her face, become bored or

distracted while reading, become easily tired or fatigued, become restless and fidget, follow word by word with a finger, or use an aid (such as a ruler) to underline what is being read?

61. If the child has a writing problem, how does the teacher describe the problem? For example, does the child have problems in capitalization, punctuation, and syntax; write in an incomprehensible manner with poor sentence structure or poor word choice; fail to use notes; fail to outline; fail to use a dictionary or other resources; or fail to rewrite or revise?

62. If the child has a spelling problem, how does the teacher describe the problem? For example, does the child reverse, add, omit, or substitute letters? Does the child sequence sounds incorrectly?

63. If the child has a mathematics problem, how does the teacher describe the problem? For example, does the child have problems with addition, subtraction, multiplication, or division or with more advanced mathematical operations?

64. What teaching methods, materials, and strategies does the teacher use in the various subject areas?

65. How much time does the child spend on homework each night?

66. Approximately how much time should the child spend on his or her homework each night, according to the teacher?

67. What are the child's work habits, rate of learning, learning style, and ability to adapt to new situations?

68. Does the child have any work habits that interfere with his or her school work (e.g., works too quickly or too slowly, has difficulty doing independent work, has difficulty organizing materials needed for the assignment or for homework, has difficulty finding materials in his or her notebook or folder, is easily distracted, fails to record assignments correctly, fails to budget the appropriate amount of time for assignments, has difficulty working neatly, fails to remember or refuses to turn in homework for class)?

Family History

69. What is the composition of the child's family?

70. What is the quality of the relationship between the parents and the child (e.g., parents are uninvolved, cold, overly harsh and controlling, too lax, unable to establish reasonable expectations and limits, too attentive to the child's inappropriate behavior, unable to communicate clearly with the child, inconsistent in handling discipline, or unable to handle the child's misbehavior within an appropriate time)?

71. What is the quality of the relationships between the parents and the child's siblings and among the children in the family?

72. What is the socioeconomic status of the family?

73. Is there a history of child maltreatment, substance abuse, spousal abuse, medical disorders, psychiatric disorders, or learning disorders among the family members? If so, what were the problems or disorders, and which family members had them? Have they received treatment, and if so, what was the outcome of the treatment?

(Continued)

Table 21-2 *(Continued)*

74. Are there any factors in the home that might affect the child's ability to study and learn? If so, what are the factors (e.g., limited language proficiency, lack of privacy for studying, limited economic resources, limited food supplies, physical or mental health problems, family stress), and how do they impede the child's learning and school performance?

75. Does the teacher have an opinion of the family? If so, what is his or her opinion? Consider carefully whether you want to include this information in the report.

Perceptual-Motor Ability

76. What is the quality of the child's fine- and gross-motor coordination? This includes the child's ability to walk, run, and play ball; the child's dominant hand; and the child's ability to have adequate control, balance, strength, and endurance to perform daily living tasks—such as dressing, feeding, toileting, grooming, writing (including use of a pencil and crayon), drawing, using a computer, and other personal activities.

77. What is the quality of the child's perceptual processes? This includes the child's ability to focus appropriately on selected objects, visually track objects or people, and identify and discriminate among objects and features of objects.

Speech and Language Ability

78. What is the quality of the child's speech? This includes speed and quantity, voice quality, prosody, articulation, and speech disturbances.

79. What is the quality of the child's receptive language? This includes the child's understanding of what is spoken to him or her and how the child's comprehension is affected by the length or complexity of the communications, the rate of verbal output, the amount of information communicated, environmental factors, and other conversational demands.

80. What is the quality of the child's expressive language? This includes the quality and amount of the child's automatic language, spontaneous language, and responsive language and the child's ability to use language to express ideas and feelings.

Attention

81. What is the quality of the child's ability to attend to tasks? This includes whether the child can maintain attention long enough to accomplish age-appropriate tasks by focusing on the relevant aspects of a situation and screening out irrelevant visual or auditory background details.

Cognitive Ability

82. What is the quality of the child's cognitive ability? This includes the child's general level of cognitive functioning and problem-solving skills; orientation; judgment; level of abstraction; ability to generate ideas, goals, and alternative strategies; and fund of general knowledge.

Memory Ability

83. What is the quality of the child's memory? This includes the child's immediate memory (e.g., of your name, oral instructions, or a new telephone number) and ability to recall events relative to the recent past (e.g., what he or she did yesterday) and remote past (e.g., what happened 6 months ago and 1 or more years ago).

Learning Ability

84. What is the quality of the child's learning ability? This includes the child's ability to learn new procedures and information.

85. Can the child attend to the essential components of a task long enough to learn it?

86. Does the child benefit from both intrinsic and extrinsic rewards?

87. What materials are of interest to the child and facilitate the child's learning (e.g., color, shape, or size of materials)?

88. What are the optimal rate and duration of presentation of material to the child?

89. Which of the child's modalities best facilitates learning (visual, auditory, tactile, or a combination)?

90. What contents or topics are most meaningful to the child?

91. What procedures best facilitate the child's learning (e.g., reauditorization, stimulation, modeling, analysis of errors)?

92. Which type of cue is most effective in helping the child (verbal, visual, gestural, or a combination)?

93. If verbal cues help, which type are they (e.g., first phoneme of a word, written presentation, first letter of a word, synonyms, opposites, rhymes, use of error responses)?

94. Can the child learn to produce his or her own cues?

95. Is the child's learning affected by *schedule of reinforcement* (continuous, intermittent, immediate, delayed), *type of reinforcement* (verbal, gestural or token, positive or negative), or *dispenser of reinforcement* (self, teacher, clinician, parent)?

96. How do practice and rehearsal affect the child's learning?

97. Is the child's learning random or consistent?

98. Does the child use strategies to help him or her learn? If so, what strategies does the child use?

99. How rapidly does the child learn?

100. If the child can't learn specific behaviors, are there alternative behaviors that he or she can learn?

101. Can the child learn new material, retain it, integrate the knowledge, and apply it to new situations?

102. What are the sources of the difficulty the child has in mastering the material (e.g., difficulty level of materials; meaningfulness of materials; ineffectiveness of cues, instructions, or examples; child's own deficits)?

Affect

103. What is the quality of the child's affect? This includes the child's general affect, range of affect, appropriateness of affect, and emotional lability.

Motivation

104. What is the quality of the child's motivation? This includes the child's motivation to learn, initiative, and interests, activities, and hobbies.

(Continued)

Table 21-2 *(Continued)*

Social Comprehension and Interpersonal Relations Skills

105. What is the overall quality of the child's social comprehension? This includes the child's understanding of socially acceptable responses in various social situations and understanding of the reasons and motivations for social behavior.

Previous Testing

106. Has the child been previously tested? If so, what were the results, and how do the present results compare with past results?

Interventions

107. Has the child received special education services in the past? If so, what services has the child received, what was the Individualized Educational Plan, and were the goals of the plan met?

108. If the child has academic difficulties, has the teacher used interventions to remediate those difficulties? If so, what interventions have been most and least successful, and what are the child's and parents' thoughts about the interventions?

109. What family supports are available, and which ones are missing?

110. How able is the family to provide for the child's needs?

111. Is the child receiving treatment for his or her problems? If so, what is the treatment, and how is the child responding to the treatment?

112. If the child is not receiving treatment, what interventions are needed?

113. What interventions, including services, would the child, parents, and teacher like to receive?

114. What services are available in the community?

115. Are child, parents, and teacher willing to cooperate with intervention efforts?

provide confidence intervals for several intelligence tests. Psychologists usually use a confidence level of 95%.

Suppose that Joe, a 6-year-old child, obtained a Full Scale IQ of 100 on the WISC–III, and you wish to use the 95% level of confidence. Table A-1 in Appendix A shows that for this confidence level and age, the appropriate confidence interval is 7. The recommended way of reporting the IQ using this confidence interval is as follows:

Joe obtained an IQ of 100 ± 7 on the Wechsler Intelligence Scale for Children–III. The chances that his true score is between 93 and 107 are about 95 out of 100.

If you select another confidence level, the range and probability statement will change. For example, the recommended ways of expressing the 68 and 99% levels for Joe are as follows:

Joe obtained an IQ of 100 ± 3 on the Wechsler Intelligence Scale for Children–III. The chances that his true score is between 97 and 103 are about 68 out of 100.

Joe obtained an IQ of 100 ± 9 on the Wechsler Intelligence Scale for Children–III. The chances that his true score is between 91 and 109 are about 99 out of 100.

As the confidence level in the preceding examples increased from 68 out of 100 to 99 out of 100, the confidence interval went from ±3 to ±9. As the confidence level decreases—say, goes from the 99% level to the 68% level—the width of the range for the obtained IQ also decreases. Thus, the more confident you want to be about the child's obtained score, the wider the interval surrounding the score (that is, the confidence interval) must be.

Clinical and diagnostic impressions. When you develop hypotheses about the examinee's performance, consider the examinee's test scores; patterns of test performance; the relationship among test scores; observations about the examinee's verbal and nonverbal behavior during the evaluation; information obtained from systematic behavioral observations; information obtained from interviews with the examinee, the examinee's parents, and the examinee's teachers; prior assessment findings; developmental history; family history; and other relevant case history information. You are on firmer ground for making interpretations when you have consistent findings from several sources. *Use extreme caution in making any interpretations or diagnostic formulations when you have inconsistent assessment information.* Inconsistent assessment information gives rise to questions that you might want to explore further. In any case, never make interpretive or diagnostic statements when there are major discrepancies in the findings or information that you have obtained.

Organizing the assessment results and clinical impressions section. You may choose to organize the assessment results on a *test-by-test basis* (e.g., WISC–III, WIAT, BASC), a *domain-by-domain basis* (e.g., intelligence, achievement, socioemotional), or a *combined test-by-test and domain-by-domain basis*. In deciding how to organize a report, think about the nature of the referral question and which approach you believe will provide the most clarity for the reader. A typical report based on the more common test-by-test organization includes a separate paragraph describing the results of each test or procedure—intelligence test results, visual-motor test results, achievement test results, personality test results, adaptive behavior inventory results, systematic behavior observation results, and so on. A summary paragraph at the end of the section then integrates the main findings.

A typical report based on domain-by-domain organization includes a separate paragraph for each domain of interest— such as intelligence, achievement, and adaptive behavior. Each paragraph reports results from the different assessment procedures relevant to the child's functioning in that domain. For example, a paragraph on achievement skills would include data from the achievement tests, intelligence test subtests related to achievement skills, informal observation of achievement skills, and teacher and parental reports related to achievement skills.

A variant of the domain-by-domain organization is to organize the findings into areas of specific ability, such as comprehension, reasoning, memory, motor ability, spatial ability, and perceptual ability. In each area you might discuss verbal and nonverbal components (where appropriate), expressive and receptive functions, and indices of psychopathology.

As a beginning examiner, you might find the test-by-test organization style easier to use than the domain-by-domain style. If you choose the test-by-test organization style, you should still comment on the relationships among related data—for example, the fact that a child exhibited strong mathematics skills on an achievement test but weak mathematics skills on the Stanford-Binet Intelligence Scale: Fourth Edition or on the subtests of the Differential Aptitude Test that require mathematical reasoning. Whichever style you choose, organize and synthesize all of the assessment findings and present them clearly.

7. Recommendations

Recommendations are an important part of a psychological report. As with the Assessment Results and Clinical Impressions section, base your recommendations on all the information available to you, including the case history, the child's overall level of performance, and the child's strengths and weaknesses. Recommendations may focus on interventions, class placement, treatment, or rehabilitation. The intent is not to look for a "cure" or a "label," but to offer a flexible approach for interventions and appropriate placements. Recommendations should take into consideration the resources of the family and school. If you believe that further assessment is needed before you make a diagnosis or advocate interventions, you may recommend, for example, a neuropsychological evaluation, a medical evaluation, a speech and language evaluation, or a psychiatric evaluation. With sufficient information, you will be in a better position to recommend appropriate interventions. When you make suggestions that involve others (e.g., teachers and parents), it is important that you collaborate with them rather than tell them what to do.

Develop reasonable recommendations. Recommendations should describe realistic and practical intervention goals and treatment strategies. Questions to consider in developing the recommendations include the following:

1. How representative are the present test results?
2. Can the present test results be generalized?
3. Were *all* relevant factors considered in arriving at the recommendations, including test results, observations, parental reports, teacher reports, examinee's self-report, medical evaluations, school grades, prior history, previous psychological test results, and response to prior interventions (if applicable)?
4. What is the examinee's eligibility for special programs?
5. What type of intervention program does the examinee need (behavioral, academic, counseling, or a combination of these)?
6. What are the goals of the intervention program?
7. How can the examinee's strengths be used in an intervention program?
8. How might family members become involved in the treatment plan?
9. Can the recommendations be implemented, given the resources of the family, community, and school?
10. Who can carry out the recommendations?
11. Are the recommendations written clearly and understandably?
12. Are the recommendations sufficiently detailed that they can be easily followed but sufficiently broad to allow for flexibility in implementation?
13. Is there a need for further evaluation? If so, what is needed?
14. Are follow-up evaluations necessary? If so, when and by whom?

You should list the specific recommendations in order of priority. The highest priority recommendations usually address the referral question. However, if you find more pressing problems and have recommendations to alleviate these problems, emphasize them in this section of the report first, and address the referral concerns later. A useful strategy is to begin the recommendation with the basis for your suggestion: "Because of Sarah's below-average reading comprehension skills, it is recommended that ...." "Because Arthur has difficulty memorizing new data, I suggest that ...." "Because of Amy's limited phonological awareness, she might ...."

Involve children, parents, and teachers in the recommendations. Two important aims in making recommendations (and carrying out the assessment as a whole) are to find ways to help the examinee help himself or herself and to involve parents and teachers directly in any therapeutic and educational efforts. The emphasis, however, is on the examinee, on his or her situation, and on identifying avenues for growth and enrichment. Your suggestions for change should be practical, concrete, individualized, and based on sound psychological and educational practice.

If you recommend a specific intervention program by name, be sure to clarify whether the program is an *example* of an appropriate type of intervention or a specific recommendation. Persons reading the report, especially parents, are likely to interpret your recommendations literally. Diagnoses and recommendations for special education, even if done outside the school, are subject to the team processes covered under the Individuals with Disabilities Education Act (see Chapter 3).

Use caution in making long-range predictions. Making predictions about future levels of functioning is difficult and risky. You don't want to lull the reader of the report into thinking that a course of development is fixed. Although you should indicate the examinee's present level of functioning and make suggestions about what can be expected of her or him, any statements dealing with the examinee's performance in the distant future should be made cautiously.

Write the recommendations so that the reader can clearly recognize your degree of confidence in any prediction. Cite test or behavioral data, when needed, to help the reader better understand the recommendations. Your recommendations should individualize the report, highlighting the major findings and their implications for intervention. Table 21-4, presented later in the chapter, provides examples of intervention strategies used in schools.

8. Summary

The Summary section reviews and integrates the information in the prior sections of the report. Ideally, the report itself should be a summary—that is, precise and concise. When you write the Summary section, limit yourself to one or two short paragraphs. Consider including in the summary one key idea (or more as needed) from each part of the report. *Do not include new material in the summary.* The summary might contain a reiteration of the reason for referral, pertinent background information, behavioral observations, assessment results, reliability and validity of the assessment results, classification of scores, examinee's strengths and weakness, examinee's verbal and nonverbal abilities, interrelationship among test scores, special features of the examinee's performance, clinical impressions, and recommendations. You may want to include a single statement in the Summary section that reflects the major recommendation: "The reported findings indicate that Sarah may qualify for special education services under the learning disability _____ (state code)." The psychological evaluations in Exhibits 21-1 and 21-2 (presented later in the chapter) include examples of a summary.

Some people read only the Summary section or rely on it heavily. This is unfortunate, for the body of the report often contains valuable information. Because a Summary section may give readers the idea that they can ignore the body of the report, some examiners choose not to include one. If you do include a Summary section, it may be prudent to refer explicitly to the body of the report at least once within it. We recommend that, for training purposes, you always include a Summary section.

9. Signature

Your name, professional title, and degree should appear at the end of the report, with your signature placed above your printed name. The professional title you use should be in compliance with your state laws. For example, in some states the title "psychologist" should be used only by those who are licensed psychologists. And the title "school psychologist" should be used by psychologists employed by schools. Get into the habit of signing your reports while in training, because an unsigned report in the field may not be considered a legal document. If you are in training, your supervisor will also sign your reports. In some fields (e.g., education), where a multidisciplinary team of examiners is involved in an assessment, the name and title of each member of the team, as well as the name and title of the person who synthesized or compiled the report, needs to be included. The team report also could be signed by each examiner, although in some cases the signature of the compiler may suffice.

Comment on Sections of a Psychological Report

The preceding discussion on organizing a report is a good guide; however, there is no one, unalterable way to organize a report. The way you organize a report depends on your preference, which is governed in part by who will make use of the report. The organization of the report should be logical

FROM THE WALL STREET JOURNAL–PERMISSION, CARTOON FEATURES SYNDICATE.

and convey as clearly as possible the reason for referral, assessment findings and instruments used, other relevant information, interpretations, and recommendations. Sometimes you may want to place the Recommendations section after the Summary section rather than before it. The summary would then focus on the assessment findings—not on the recommendations.

Sometimes one has to say difficult things, but one ought to say them as simply as one knows how.

—G. H. Hardy

OVERVIEW OF REPORT WRITING

This part of the chapter offers 22 principles designed to help you write reports. The principles cover how to organize, interpret, and present the assessment findings. Principles 1 through 6 deal with strategies for including information in the report, Principles 7 through 16 relate to presentation of psychological information, and Principles 17 through 22 concern writing style. Exercises are included to help you evaluate your understanding of the principles. The principles are designed for writing reports containing information from intelligence tests and other objective tests because the focus of this text is on these types of tests. However, the principles are applicable to writing reports based on information from many different clinical sources.

The 22 principles of report writing are as follows.

Strategies for Including Information in the Report

Principle 1. Use a consistent strategy to organize assessment findings; detect common themes that run through and across the assessment findings, integrate the main findings, and adopt a theoretical focus.

Principle 2. Include only relevant material in the report; delete potentially damaging material not germane to the evaluation.

Principle 3. Be extremely cautious in making interpretations based on a limited sample of behavior.

Principle 4. Use all relevant sources of information about the examinee in generating hypotheses, formulating interpretations, and arriving at recommendations.

Principle 5. Be definitive in your writing when the findings are clear; be cautious in your writing when the findings are not clear.

Principle 6. Cite specific behaviors and sources and directly quote the examinee to enhance the report's readability.

Presentation of Psychological Information

Principle 7. Consider the overall IQ, in most cases, to be the best estimate of the child's present level of intellectual functioning.

Principle 8. Interpret the meaning and implications of a child's scores, rather than simply citing test names and scores.

Principle 9. Obtain the classification of IQs and other test scores from the numerical ranges given in the test manuals.

Principle 10. Use percentile ranks whenever possible to describe a child's scores.

Principle 11. Provide clear descriptions of abilities measured by the subtests when appropriate.

Principle 12. Relate inferences based on subtest scores or IQs to the cognitive processes measured by the subtests and scales.

Principle 13. Describe the profile of scores clearly and unambiguously.

Principle 14. Make recommendations carefully, using all available sources of information.

Principle 15. Use scores obtained by extrapolation or interpolation with caution.

Principle 16. Refrain from making diagnoses of psychopathology or educational diagnoses based solely on test scores; consider all sources of information.

Writing Style

Principle 17. Communicate clearly, and do not include unnecessary technical material in the report.

Principle 18. Describe and use statistical concepts appropriately; make sure that you check all calculations carefully and that you accurately report the reliability and validity of the test results.

Principle 19. Eliminate biased terms from the report.

Principle 20. Write a report that is concise but adequate.

Principle 21. Attend carefully to grammar and writing style.

Principle 22. Develop strategies to improve your writing, such as using an outline, revising your first draft, and proofreading your final report.

Now let's look at each principle in greater detail.

ORGANIZE YOUR FINDINGS

Principle 1. Use a consistent strategy to organize assessment findings; detect common themes that run through and across the assessment findings, integrate the main findings, and adopt a theoretical focus.

Although there is no one best method for integrating the assessment findings, using a consistent strategy and keeping clear goals in mind will help. Ideally, the goal of the psychological assessment is to obtain a comprehensive view of the child and his or her life situation while at the same time responding to the referral question. Often, however, the assessment has the narrower focus of addressing a circumscribed referral question.

Before you write the report, look over all of the information you obtained. Consider the following questions:

1. What are the reasons for the referral?
2. What are the backgrounds of the persons for whom the report will be written?
3. What are the major findings you want to report?
4. How do the present results compare with previous ones?
5. What are the major themes you want to develop?
6. How have the findings answered the referral question?
7. What questions remain unanswered?
8. What are the major recommendations you want to present?

As a beginning student—or even as a practitioner—you may have difficulty making sense of the assessment results, especially when they are from several sources. Some findings may be clear, others murky. You may have obtained conflicting results from different tests purporting to measure the same ability or received conflicting information from the child, teacher, and parents. Discuss discrepant findings in the report and provide explanations, when possible. If you cannot explain the findings, report that there is no apparent explanation for the discrepant findings. Caution the reader about the results where appropriate.

Once you have a general understanding of the assessment findings, you are ready to undertake the following three-step process for organizing and interpreting the findings.

Step 1. Detect common themes.   The first step is to detect the common themes and trends that appear in your results. Look over the test results, case history (including developmental history, prior test results, and medical reports), interviews, observations, and any other information you have. Examine the consistencies in the findings; patterns of errors and successes on various tests; major discrepancies among scores; observations of learning style; information obtained from the parents, child, and teachers; and responses to the testing-of-limits (explained in Chapter 7). Gather the information you have about the child's intellectual, social, emotional, and perceptual-motor development from all sources.

The following questions may help you detect common themes.

1. What are the consistent findings and patterns among the test data?
2. What are the divergent findings?
3. Which divergent findings are major and which are minor?
4. What do the themes suggest to you about the examinee's present problems, strengths, weaknesses, coping mechanisms, and possibilities for remediation or change?
5. How do family members, other children, and other adults contribute to the child's difficulties (e.g., anxiety attacks occur only when the examinee's father is present)?

6. What are some important environmental contingencies (e.g., the child has trouble eating in the cafeteria but not at home)?

Step 2. Integrate main findings.   The second step is to consider all the information you have—even information that seems contradictory—as you develop your clinical impressions and recommendations. Recognize that people rarely show the same behavior in every situation. Suppose, for example, that the examinee has memory difficulty with verbal material but not with nonverbal material. Note this variability and take it into account in evaluating the child's memory ability. Variability also may be associated with situational factors, such as fatigue, anxiety, or lack of interest.

Earlier in this chapter we discussed several formats for organizing the Assessment Results and Clinical Impressions section of a report. These included a test-by-test format, a domain-by-domain format, and a combination of the two formats. Regardless of the format you choose, bring together findings that relate to common themes. For example, if a diagnosis of learning disability appears probable, discuss the findings that support this clinical impression. Or if the findings suggest the presence of neurological dysfunction, describe the pertinent facts that led you to this clinical impression. Show how the child's abilities are interrelated by using expressions signaling comparison and contrast, such as *however, but, on the one hand, on the other hand,* or *in comparison with.* When contrasting results, use comparative terms such as *higher, lower, stronger,* or *weaker.*

Be aware of two potential sources of error in integrating findings. One is forming hypotheses prematurely, which may lead you to ignore information that conflicts with your initial conceptualization and to seek data to confirm your premature hypothesis. The second is overgeneralizing based on limited findings. You should not draw conclusions about a child's everyday school behavior from a limited observation period or generalize from the child's behavior in the evaluation to how the child may behave in other settings.

Step 3. Adopt a theoretical perspective.   The third step is to integrate the material using a specific theoretical perspective or an eclectic theoretical perspective. The perspective you adopt may vary from case to case, depending on the context of the particular case, the referral question, and other relevant factors. The major theoretical perspectives related to the assessment focus of this text are developmental, normative-developmental, cognitive-behavioral, and eclectic (see Chapter 2). For example, a cognitive-behavioral perspective may focus on the environmental contingencies related to the problem behavior; the child's and parents' views of themselves, others, and the environment; the child's and parents' attitudes and beliefs; and the historical antecedent events that may be related to the problem behavior. If possible, use a theoretical perspective that not only sheds light on the examinee's behavior but also offers some strategies for remediation and treatment. Often it may be useful to take an eclectic perspective—that is, to interpret findings from more than one theoretical perspective.

INCLUDE RELEVANT MATERIAL

Principle 2. Include only relevant material in the report; delete potentially damaging material not germane to the evaluation.

When you are deciding what material to include in the report, consider the accuracy, relevance, and fairness of the material and how the material augments the reader's knowledge of the examinee. No matter how interesting or factual the information is, information that does not contribute to an understanding of the examinee and the referral question is irrelevant and should be left out. Weigh the value of each statement, particularly how the information will contribute to an understanding of the examinee. If you leave a sentence with highly sensitive information in the report, make its relevance clear and present supporting data. Consider the effect your report will have on various readers, including the child's parents.

Also discuss how much weight you gave to various factors in arriving at your clinical impressions, conclusions, and recommendations. This will help the reader understand your reasoning. In general, include in the report a mix of general implications, specific behavioral illustrations, and some testing details to help the reader understand how you arrived at your clinical impressions.

What information does the reader really need? The reader wants information about the referral question, the findings, your interpretation of the findings, and possible interventions. In most cases, do not include tangential information. For example, information about the father's or mother's sex life usually would be tangential in a report about a child referred for learning problems. In exceptional cases, however, where such information has a direct bearing on the problem, think carefully about the most professional way to phrase the information so that it does not appear to be simply a bit of titillating gossip. When is it worthwhile to note in a report whether the examinee is right handed or left handed or whether the examinee is well groomed? A discussion of the examinee's handedness is worthwhile if there is a question of mixed dominance, and a discussion of the examinee's grooming is useful if it helps the reader understand the examinee's self-concept, attitudes, or familial environment (e.g., parental care and guidance). In other cases, neither handedness nor grooming may be important.

The following are examples of irrelevant or potentially damaging statements:

1. "James told the examiner that his father frequently invited different women over to the house." This information is unlikely to add to an understanding of the child or the test results, and it is potentially damaging to the child and his father. *Suggestion:* Delete it, or, if you are convinced that this statement is relevant, replace it with a statement that may give some insight about the child's feelings—for example, "James expressed resentment about frequent female visitors to his house."

2. "Tara is in excellent health but has food allergies. Some researchers have posited an association between learning disabilities and allergies." The last sentence is controversial. *Suggestion:* Delete the last sentence; however, you can recommend that Tara be referred to a health care provider if she is not already under treatment.

3. "Joe appeared disheveled and dirty at times because his family is on welfare." Don't assume a strong relationship between grooming and limited income. This statement is prejudicial toward people who receive welfare aid. *Suggestion:* The problem here could be corrected by making separate statements—not in the same sentence—about Joe's appearance and his family's income, without assuming a relationship between the two.

4. "Jeffrey's mother has been seen leaving the house at odd hours." This statement may be irrelevant to the case. *Suggestion:* If this statement is relevant, say why it is relevant, explain the word *odd,* cite the source, use the qualifier *reportedly,* or convey the information orally to the referral source; otherwise, delete it.

5. "Mark did not score zero on any Comprehension items." Stress what the child did do, not what the child did not do. This statement serves no useful purpose in a report. *Suggestion:* Delete this sentence from the report.

6. "On Block Design, she failed items 4 and 5." This statement provides little useful information. In addition, the reader does not know what these failures mean. *Suggestion:* Delete this sentence from the report unless there is some special significance to the pattern of missed items. If there is, discuss the significance of the pattern.

7. "Helen scored 5 points on the Digit Span subtest." The reference to 5 points is not useful because the reader does not know what the score means. The 5 points could refer to a raw score or a scaled score. In either case, the reader is at a loss to know how to interpret this score unless she or he knows the test. *Suggestion:* This sentence should be rewritten to convey Helen's relative standing on the Digit Span subtest and explain what the Digit Span subtest measures. For example, if her score is below average (scaled score of 7) and below her Verbal Scale mean, you could write, "Helen's short-term memory ability is less well developed (at the 16th percentile) than are her other verbal skills."

Focusing on the presence of a behavior rather than on its absence will promote clarity in the report. There are many adjectives that do not characterize the examinee's behavior (e.g., not sad, not anxious, not impulsive), but such citations are not illuminating. Instead, emphasize how the examinee did behave (was happy, seemed relaxed, responded carefully). Occasionally, the referral source may ask you to comment on a specific problem or symptom. In such cases, include a statement about the problem or symptom, even if it did not occur.

Exercise 21-1. Evaluating Statements That Are Irrelevant

Read the statements, evaluate them, and then compare your evaluations with those in the Comment section.

1. "Eileen did much better than expected in her communications with me, given the fact that she lives in an impoverished neighborhood."
2. "At one time, she wanted to use my pencil to write out a response, but I explained to her that she should try to talk about herself."

Comment

1. The assumptions here reveal the writer's prejudices. First, the writer labeled the neighborhood "impoverished." A more effective way of presenting information about the child's living conditions would be to describe what was observed in the neighborhood rather than simply labeling it. Second, the writer has made the assumption that poor living conditions lead to poor communications skills, which is a biased assumption. Thus, the writer made a value-laden judgment that the child did much better than expected without presenting a reasonable explanation for this interpretation.
2. Unless this statement illustrates a point, why include it? The statement may distract the reader. In addition, the examiner's refusal to allow the examinee to write out a response may have been an unwise assessment decision because the examinee may have wanted to divulge sensitive material that she was unwilling to say aloud. Examiners should try to be flexible in the ways they allow examinees to express themselves.

MAKE INTERPRETATIONS CAREFULLY

Principle 3. Be extremely cautious in making interpretations based on a limited sample of behavior.

Observations conducted during a short period usually yield a small sample of behavior. Consequently, be careful about the generalizations and inferences you make. Make inferences about underlying traits or processes only with extreme caution, if at all. For example, "Johnny refused to be interviewed and ran away from the office in tears" is better than "Johnny is a negative child who shows hostility toward those who

wish to help him." If the latter statement was based only on the observation that the child ran away from the office in tears, it would be unacceptable because it was an undue generalization. If, however, you can demonstrate that you have enough information to support an interpretation, make it. Also avoid the temptation to assume that a behavior demonstrated in one setting will occur in another setting. For example, do not assume that an examinee who is impulsive in the classroom also is impulsive at home.

The following are examples of statements that make incorrect inferences:

1. "From the start, Derek tended either to repeat questions to himself or to ask the examiner to repeat the questions for him. This appeared to be Derek's attempt to structure or clarify the questions for himself." This behavior *could* reflect the child's attempt to structure the question, but it is not clear how repeating the question helped him to structure it. It also could be a means of controlling the situation, or it could suggest inattention. In addition, the behavior may reflect a delay tactic, a need for additional support, or a coping pattern associated with a hearing deficit. Consider everything you know about the child to arrive at the best interpretation (*if* you need to make one). *Suggestion:* Leave out the last sentence ("This appeared to be …") unless you have other supporting information.
2. "As the examination progressed, he tended to sit with his arms folded or to pick at and scratch his arm when responding to questions. Although, at first, these behaviors made John seem less interested, it appears that he was compensating for his low self-confidence." This interpretation seems to have little merit. In what way do folding arms and scratching arms reflect compensation for low self-confidence? Could these actions simply be a habit or a response to frustration or a reaction to mosquito bites? *Suggestion:* Keep the first sentence and eliminate the second one. Then, describe comments the child made about himself, if any, and note how cooperative he was.
3. "Harry's statements about his inadequacies resulted in an increase in feelings of inferiority and self-deprecating behavior, as shown by an increase in nervous laughter and by impulsive answers." This inference is conjectural. It implies a cause-and-effect relationship between verbal expressions and behavior. There is no way of knowing what the examinee's statements resulted in. *Suggestion:* Limit the statements to a description of his verbalizations and behavior: "When he was asked about his school work, Harry answered impulsively, laughed, and made self-deprecatory remarks." You also could include a comment that he made: "He said, 'I'm a lousy student.'"
4. "Perhaps she played independently because other children could not or did not want to keep up with her." This inference may or may not be correct. To make this statement, you must have supporting information about the other children's behavior and thoughts. *Suggestion:* Omit the

sentence unless information is available about the behavior and thoughts of the other children.

5. This statement was made about a young woman who was observed in a rehabilitation program for developmentally delayed individuals: "Her performance on the assembly line may be somewhat slower than what might be expected of a worker with average intellectual ability." This statement is fine if you know the performance rate of individuals with average intellectual ability. If you do not have this information, leave the statement out. Without the relevant information, it is prejudicial and based on stereotyped notions. You should make statements that compare the examinee with a relevant norm group only when you have information about that group.

Exercise 21-2. Evaluating Statements That Contain Incorrect Inferences

Read the statements, evaluate them, and then compare your evaluations with those in the Comment section.

1. "The child is small for his age and may feel a need to achieve."
2. "Her physical appearance suggested no behavioral problems."
3. "Since there is no evidence of Oedipal conflict in Gunnar's behavior, he must have completely repressed it."
4. "Her rigid approach to the Block Design task may indicate covert feelings of inadequacy."
5. "Her average visual-motor coordination is an indication of field dependence and left-hemisphere processing."
6. "Bill is considered a troublemaker, and this may be due to good social judgment and grasp of social conventionality."
7. "Her IQ of 134 predicts excellent success in school."
8. "On the basis of his IQ of 107, there would be no mismatch between his level of intelligence and the kind of instruction he would receive in the general education classroom."
9. "It must be noted, however, that because Steve is a minority student, the low score of 68 on this intelligence test cannot be used as a valid input toward a nonbiased assessment of this youngster."

Comment

1. Without additional information, these two thoughts are unrelated. *Suggestion:* If the only information available to you about the child's achievement needs is that he is small, do not make this inference.
2. Rarely will a child's physical appearance suggest a behavioral problem. Additionally, this is an example of stating information in the negative. *Suggestion:* This sentence should be omitted.

3. The interpretation has little merit. *Suggestion:* Avoid making such speculative interpretations, especially when they are based on the absence of evidence.
4. It is precarious to interpret a rigid approach to solving a cognitive task, in this case Block Design, as a possible indication of feelings of inadequacy. *Suggestion:* Obtain additional information from other sources before making this type of interpretation.
5. There is no evidence in the literature to back up these two interpretations. *Suggestion:* This statement should be omitted.
6. "Troublemaker" implies a value judgment. *Suggestion:* Whenever you use such a label, cite the basis for using the label. Also, it is far from reasonable to assume that good social judgment and grasp of social conventionality might cause a child to become a "troublemaker."
7. This is an interesting statement. The examiner goes out on a limb, making a statement about future performance on the basis of the IQ alone. The IQ should be used primarily to evaluate current abilities and performance, not to predict future performance. There are many factors (e.g., intelligence, motivation, study habits, and home environment) that affect school performance, and intelligence is only one of them. *Suggestion:* You might state, "Her IQ of 134 indicates that she possesses the cognitive ability to excel in school."
8. This statement may or may not be true. Children with learning disabilities or with emotional, physical, or sensory disabilities may have average (or above-average) scores on an intelligence test. The general education classroom may or may not be suitable for these children. It is improper to conclude, solely on the basis of the IQ, that a general education classroom is the appropriate learning environment. *Suggestion:* Consider the child's performance on several types of tests, classroom behavior, academic performance, and case history before deciding on a classroom placement recommendation.
9. This conclusion may be inaccurate. The minority status of the examinee is not a sufficient basis for concluding that the test results are biased. After all, you should not have administered a test that you know is biased. *Suggestion:* Consider all relevant information in arriving at a decision about the validity of the test results, such as whether the child could understand English (assuming the assessment was conducted in English) or comes from a background similar to that of the children in the standardization group. There are many reasons why an individual assessment might not be considered valid. Maybe the child was sick that day, or there was a tornado drill during the middle of the assessment, or something happened at home that disturbed the child. But minority status *alone* should not invalidate the test results if you have used an appropriately normed test (which, by the way, you are ethically bound to do).

MAKE GENERALIZATIONS

Principle 4. Use all relevant sources of information about the examinee in generating hypotheses, formulating interpretations, and arriving at recommendations.

Conclusions and generalizations should follow logically from the information in the report. Support your conclusions with reliable and sufficient data, and avoid undue generalizations. You can base your inferences and conclusions on several factors, including the assessment results, quality of the interaction between you and the examinee, behavioral observations, case history, medical history, and previous assessment results. Consider all relevant sources of information, and make generalizations only when you have a clear, consistent pattern of behavior. Describe cause-and-effect relationships only when the assessment information is substantial and clear.

Consider the following questions:

1. Are there consistent trends in the information you obtained?
2. Does the child's behavior in the examination correspond with her or his behavior in the classroom and at home?
3. Do the findings point to a clear diagnostic impression?
4. What interventions are likely to be both effective and feasible, given the assessment findings, available facilities and personnel, and family resources?

After you answer these questions, formulate hypotheses and organize the confirming evidence. Entertain alternative hypotheses and revise them as needed. Drop hypotheses supported by only one piece of minor evidence or regard them as tentative. Retain for further consideration hypotheses supported by more than one piece of evidence—especially if the supporting data come from several sources (e.g., from the child, parents, and teacher). Also, carefully review any evidence that may disconfirm hypotheses. Advance only those hypotheses that receive support. Although these hypotheses represent tentative explanations of a complex situation, they may help you in working with the referral source, the child, and the parents and in formulating treatment recommendations.

You can view statements in reports as reflecting one of three levels of clinical inference:

First level. Take the assessment information at face value and keep interpretations to a minimum. *Example:* "Bill obtained an Intelligence Quotient of 109 ± 7 on the WISC–III. The chances that his true score is between 102 and 116 are about 95 out of 100. His IQ is in the Average range and is equal to or higher than that of 73% of children his age (73rd percentile)."

Second level. Present the assessment findings, draw generalizations, and present hypotheses about the causes of the behavior. *Example:* "Sylvia's parents and teacher report that she has mood changes and difficulty getting along with others. Several changes in her mood were observed during the evaluation. Her mood changes suggest that Sylvia may have difficulty controlling her emotions, which may, in part, contribute to her interpersonal difficulties."

Third level. Make the most inclusive interpretations, including explanatory speculations about the examinee's behavior; this level involves clinical hunches, insights, and intuitions (see Figure 21-1). *Example:* "A pervasive pattern of neglect during his formative years, coupled with feelings of self-doubt, suggests a negative self-concept. A negative self-concept may, in part, contribute to his poor school performance."

You may use all three levels of clinical inference in the report. However, as you move up the inferential chain, care-

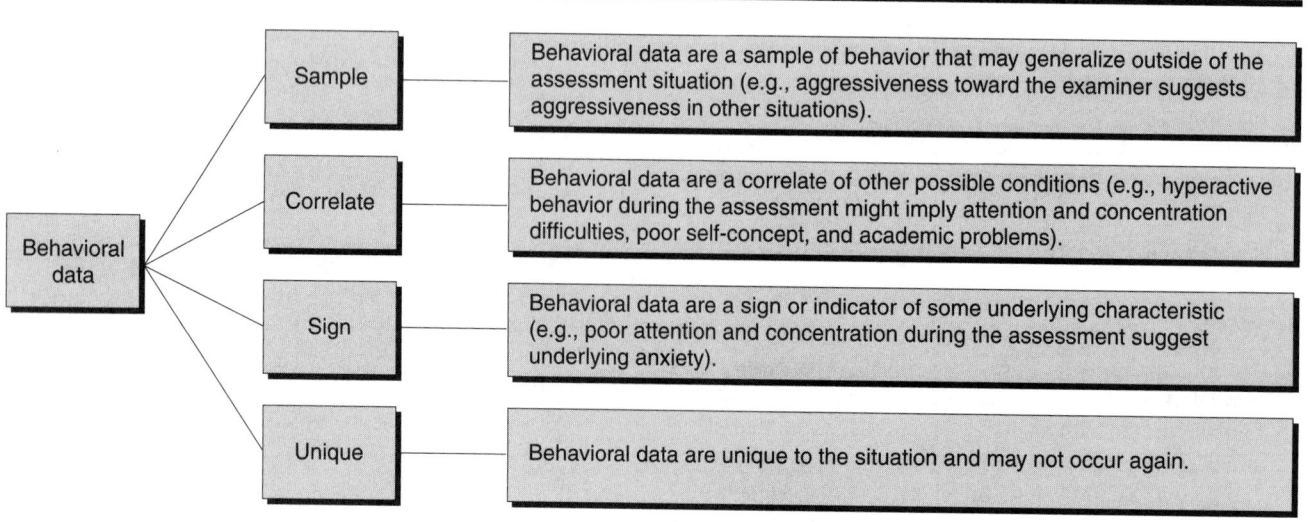

Figure 21-1. Interpreting behavioral data.

fully weigh the assessment information before you decide to offer broad explanatory speculations. If you offer any speculations, label them as such in the report.

When you make a generalization, cite supporting data, particularly if the generalization has important consequences for the child. For example, you might support a statement that Johnny needs special education by stating "Johnny's academic achievement is significantly below that of his age peers, as demonstrated by his performance on the reading and mathematics sections of the Wide Range Achievement Test–3. His intellectual skills, as estimated by the WISC–III, are in the Average range."

The following are examples of statements that convey inappropriate generalizations.

1. "Nancy was weak in numerical reasoning, as evidenced by her missing an easy item on the Arithmetic subtest." Reference to missing one item is not sufficient justification for concluding that a child is weak in numerical reasoning. It is hazardous to generalize from only one failure or one success. *Suggestion:* Use the child's scaled score on the subtest to discuss his or her ability.

2. "On the basis of his Full Scale IQ of 107, it is predicted that Mark will do at least average work in school and that he will excel in athletics." This sentence contains two inappropriate generalizations. First, the 107 IQ indicates that Mark is capable of performing at a average level in school; it does not mean that he will perform at that level. Second, a statement about athletics cannot be made on the basis of a child's performance on an intelligence test.

3. "Charles demonstrated a good attention span, which indicates that he is free from anxiety." Satisfactory performance on the Digit Span or Sentences subtests, for example, does not indicate that the child is free from anxiety. *Suggestion:* The most that can be said is that anxiety did not appear to affect the child's performance in a particular area.

4. This interpretation was based on a WISC–III Verbal IQ of 98 and a Performance IQ of 105: "Her anxious laughter and quick replies of 'I don't know' seem to suggest that overall Mary was less comfortable with verbal tasks than with nonverbal tasks. Whether it is a deficiency of skills in verbal interactions that causes the anxiousness and subsequent poor performance or whether it is the anxiousness that causes a subsequent deficiency in verbal skills is unknown." It is helpful to tie together observations and subtest scores. However, the second sentence is misleading because the examinee does not have a deficiency in verbal skills–she obtained an average score. The statement about causality is unnecessary because it is almost impossible to know what is cause and what is effect simply on the basis of performance on an intelligence test. In addition, the expression "verbal interaction" is ambiguous. *Suggestion:* Leave the second sentence out of the report.

5. "His average score in Arithmetic suggests that he has no difficulties in mathematics." This generalization is too broad. *Suggestion:* "His numerical reasoning ability is average. These results are consistent with his performance in the classroom...."

Exercise 21-3. Evaluating Statements That Contain Inappropriate Generalizations

Read the statements, evaluate them, and then compare your evaluations with those in the Comment section.

1. "Her WISC–III performance suggests that Helena likes and does well in spelling."
2. This statement was based on a WISC–III Similarities scaled score of 6: "She has difficulties in forming verbal concepts that pertain to creativity."

Comment

1. There is little, if any, information obtained from the WISC–III that would support this statement. Also, the word *performance* is ambiguous in discussions of Wechsler scores. The reader does not know whether "Her WISC–III performance" refers to her overall score, her behavior, or her WISC–III Performance Scale IQ only.
2. There is no way of knowing to what extent Similarities involves creativity. There may be some relationship, but research does not support this interpretation. *Suggestion:* "She has difficulties in explaining how two different things (e.g., rabbit and horse) or concepts (e.g., hope and fear) could be alike." If possible, support this statement with additional information obtained, for example, from the interview with the teacher.

CONVEY THE DEGREE OF CERTAINTY

Principle 5. Be definitive in your writing when the findings are clear; be cautious in your writing when the findings are not clear.

Phrases and words such as *probably, it appears, perhaps,* and *it seems* are often used in reports when the writer is not completely sure about his or her conclusions, inferences, or predictions. When the assessment findings are definitive, however, present them confidently. For example, you might write: "The child's current intellectual abilities are classified in the Superior range. The chances that his true score is between 130 and 144 are about 95 in 100." When you do use qualifiers, do not use them redundantly, as in the following sentence: "It *appears* as though he *may* have a *possible tendency* toward *sometimes* saying the wrong thing."

The degree of certainty you convey in your statements should relate to the adequacy of your information. The more current, reliable, complete, and valid the information, the greater your certainty should be. The degree of certainty also should relate to the type of assessment information you are considering. Observed assessment information (such as what you saw an examinee doing) has a greater degree of certainty than prognostic statements (such as what the examinee may do under other conditions or in the future). For example, you can be certain that an examinee was well groomed, spoke clearly, or obtained an IQ of 110. You can only be reasonably certain that an examinee can engage in most sports appropriate for her or his age or that the range from 101 to 115 represents the examinee's IQ. You are even less certain that an examinee will improve her or his performance if transferred to another teacher.

Be definitive when the test findings are clear. For example, when the difference between the WISC–III Verbal and Performance IQs is significant (or when any two subtest scores differ significantly), you can report that one skill, as measured by the scale or subtest, is better developed than the other. There is no need to hedge with such terms as *appears to be* or *may be better than* in these cases. Similarly, when the Verbal Scale is 25 points higher than the Performance Scale, you need a term stronger than *somewhat better,* such as *considerably higher* or *much better developed.* A difference of 25 points indicates that the Verbal and Performance Scale IQs are significantly different.

Do not undermine your message by making excuses either for the test or for the child's test performance. Report, without apology, the results of the evaluation in as objective a manner as possible. The following are examples of apologetic statements.

1. "Nora gave the impression of enjoying herself, and at the same time was willing to try to meet the challenge of the seemingly never-ending questions of the examiner." To whom did the questions seem never-ending? Do not apologize for the examination techniques; apologetic statements tend to belittle your professional status indirectly and may diminish the value of the report.

2. "The examiner is sorry that Edward achieved an IQ of only 85." The words *sorry* and *only* reflect the examiner's personal feelings. If other information led you to expect that the child would perform at a higher level of functioning, note the expectation and the basis for it. Include in the report any doubts about the representativeness of the results. The use of the word *only* leaves the reader wondering why it was included. Your personal values should not be imposed or projected onto either the child or the reader.

Now let's look at examples of overly cautious statements.

1. "The Intelligence Quotient of 120 ± 7 on the WISC–III would seem to indicate a High Average to Superior range of functioning." An IQ of 120 is in the Superior classification, according to the WISC–III Manual. There is no need to hedge. A better statement would be "Mary obtained an Intelligence Quotient of 120 ± 7 on the WISC–III, which is in the Superior range of functioning" or "The Intelligence Quotient of 120 ± 7 indicates that Mary's intellectual abilities are in the Superior range as assessed by the WISC–III."

2. "Jim obtained an IQ on the Stanford-Binet Intelligence Scale: Fourth Edition of approximately 86." The IQ obtained on one evaluation is an estimate of the examinee's intelligence test score and, as stressed in this text, should be accompanied by a confidence interval (i.e., a range of scores). Therefore, the word *approximately* should be eliminated, and a confidence interval should be used instead. For example, "Jim obtained an IQ on the Stanford-Binet Intelligence Scale: Fourth Edition of 86 ± 5.

And here is an example of an overly confident statement that is also probably incorrect.

Calvin and Hobbes   by Bill Watterson

CALVIN AND HOBBES © 1992 Watterson. Reprinted with permission of UNIVERSAL PRESS SYNDICATE. All rights reserved.

1. This statement was based on an IQ of 135 and a reading achievement score of 113: "There is no doubt that the difference between his intelligence test score and achievement test score reflects a learning disability." This assessment may have little basis in fact because the child's performance on the reading test is at the 81st percentile rank, which is above average. There is no reason to expect a perfect relationship between scores on intelligence tests and scores on achievement tests. In fact, correlations between achievement test scores and intelligence test scores are usually in the range of .40 to .60 (see, for example, Table 8-8 in Chapter 8). Also, in comparing two tests you need to make a correction for statistical regression of scores (see Chapter 4) before you conclude that there is a significant discrepancy between the tests.

ENHANCE READABILITY

Principle 6. Cite specific behaviors and sources and directly quote the examinee to enhance the report's readability.

When you describe the examinee's behavior, draw inferences, or make conclusions, add carefully selected examples of the examinee's behavior to illustrate your points. For example, if you say that the examinee gave overly detailed replies, provide an example. Give sources for any information you did not obtain personally. Statements such as "his mother reported," "according to his classroom teacher," "according to the report prepared by the school psychologist," or "according to the police report" provide documentation for the source of your information.

Examples are a particularly valuable way to clarify technical terms. For instance, the statement that the child has poor sequential planning ability may not mean much to a reader. However, if you follow it with the comment that the child is "unable to recall more than two digits in the proper sequence or place four pictures in their proper sequence," the reader will have a better idea of what you mean.

The following are examples of undocumented statements:

1. "Billy has uncontrolled temper tantrums." The source of the statement should be cited. *Suggestion:* "According to Billy's classroom teacher, he cries and stomps his feet when she denies him a privilege. All methods tried by the teacher to prevent these tantrums have proved unsuccessful."
2. "The father has a drug-dependency problem." Either a source should be cited for this statement or the statement should be eliminated. Be careful about accepting such information from sources other than persons likely to have firsthand knowledge of the situation. *Suggestion:* "During an interview with the examiner, Arnold's father stated that he is dependent on heroin."

FOCUS ON THE IQ

Principle 7. Consider the overall IQ, in most cases, to be the best estimate of the child's present level of intellectual functioning.

When the goal of the evaluation is to estimate the child's present level of intelligence, give primary emphasis to the child's general level of intellectual functioning, with the overall IQ serving as the anchor point. For example, the report should convey that a child with an IQ of 130 is superior intellectually, and that a child with an IQ of 70 is limited intellectually. Children with IQs between 90 and 109 should be presented as having average ability.

When you discuss the child's intellectual strengths or weaknesses, keep in mind his or her overall IQ. Also consider the child's overall IQ when you evaluate his or her behavior and performance on achievement tests, visual-motor perception tests, adaptive behavior tests, and so on. On the Wechsler scales, for example, the Full Scale IQ is usually the best estimate of intelligence because it is based on the child's entire test performance. Of lesser importance are the Verbal and Performance IQs, followed in importance by the individual subtest scaled scores. In a few instances (such as with culturally and linguistically diverse examinees or with children with disabilities), a verbal or performance score may be the most representative index of overall cognitive ability.

INTERPRET SCORES

Principle 8. Interpret the meaning and implications of a child's scores, rather than simply citing test names and scores.

The preferred way to report test results is to use *child-oriented statements* (or child-focused statements); these statements focus on the child's performance based on her or his test scores. For example, "John's vocabulary ability is average" is a more child-oriented statement than "John correctly defined 12 vocabulary words, which resulted in a scaled score of 8," which is a *test-oriented statement* (or score-focused statement). Test-oriented reports tend to lose sight of the child and the reason for referral and thus may mean less to parents, court personnel, and other readers. The data you report should clearly and accurately describe the child's performance.

When you report test scores, always add information about the abilities reflected by the scores, unless the meaning of the test scores is clear. You don't want merely to list the scores; instead, you want to help the reader understand what the scores mean. Be sure that your interpretations are well grounded in common clinical usage, research findings, or test rationales. Clearly label any speculations.

Describe the functions you believe may underlie the child's performance on the test. If you do not, readers may assume that the test measures only whatever abilities the name suggests.

When scores differ on two tests that purport to measure the same ability, do not say that the child has an ability that is both "strong" and "weak." Instead, discuss the implications of and possible reasons for the variable pattern. You don't want to present contradictory information without an explanation. When tests that should give similar scores do not, consider giving additional tests to evaluate the child's ability.

Be sure to describe the implications of a child's test performance. Follow the statement "There was a noteworthy difference between Bill's ability to do arithmetical problems and recall numbers" with an explanation of why the difference was noteworthy.

Avoid interpreting intelligence test scores as indicating strengths or weaknesses in specific academic areas such as reading or spelling. To assess these and similar skill areas, use specific achievement tests or curriculum-based measures.

An intelligence test provides an estimate of the child's current level of cognitive ability in the areas measured by that test; it does not assess a child's abilities in all intellectual domains. Consequently, if you make statements about the child's capacity for learning and future performance, do so cautiously, after carefully considering all sources of assessment information.

OBTAIN IQ CLASSIFICATIONS

Principle 9. Obtain the classification of IQs and other test scores from the numerical ranges given in the test manuals.

Tests usually provide some system by which to classify scores. Follow the specified classification system strictly, labeling scores according to what is recommended in the test manual. If you believe that a classification does not accurately reflect the examinee's status, state your concern in the report when you discuss the reliability and validity of the findings.

The Wechsler scales use seven different classifications to describe IQ ranges (see Table BC-2 on the inside back cover). Use these classifications carefully. The classification Average, for example, designates IQs from 90 through 109. Be sure that you do not say that an IQ of 110, which is in the Above Average classification, falls within the Average range.

Use only the overall IQ or Full Scale IQ (except in special cases) to determine a classification, regardless of the range of IQs established by the confidence range. For example, don't say that a child's current level of intellectual functioning, based on an IQ of 123 ± 9, falls into the High Average, Superior, and Very Superior ranges; instead, say that it falls into the Superior range. (Note that this wording emphasizes that the IQ represents the child's *current ability level,* a level that may or may not change.)

USE PERCENTILE RANKS

Principle 10. Use percentile ranks whenever possible to describe a child's scores.

Percentile ranks provide a way of communicating technical findings to readers of the report. Readers may understand percentile ranks more easily than standard scores. You can easily convert Deviation IQs and other types of composite standard scores to percentile ranks (see, for example, Table BC-1 on the inside back cover). However, when two tests use different standard-score systems, the same standard scores will represent different percentile ranks, except at the mean and extremes of the distribution. For example, on the WISC–III ($SD = 15$) a Full Scale IQ of 115 corresponds to the 84th percentile rank, whereas on the Stanford-Binet: Fourth Edition ($SD = 16$) a composite score of 115 corresponds to the 83rd percentile rank. You also can convert scaled subtest scores on the Wechsler tests (and on other tests) to percentile ranks (see Table D-1 in Appendix D).

You can use age-equivalent scores to supplement percentile ranks, or you can use them alone if you cannot convert the scores to percentile ranks (e.g., see Table A.9 in the WISC–III Manual). As we mentioned previously, age- and grade-equivalent scores are not based on equal interval scales and can be misleading (see Chapter 4). On ability and achievement tests, interpret standard scores that fall below the 25th percentile or above the 75th percentile as indicating weaknesses or strengths, respectively, relative to the child's age peers.

In conferences with parents or others, help them understand the difference between percentile ranks and percentage correct. A child's standard score at the 84th percentile rank does not mean that the child correctly answered 84% of the problems; rather, it means that 84% of the norm group scored below that child's standard score. Do not use "%" or "%ile" for percentile ranks; these abbreviations encourage confusion between percentile ranks and percent correct.

You will need to consult the test manual of each test that you use to obtain descriptive information about the test scores and about how the test scores should be used to make classification decisions.

PROVIDE CLEAR DESCRIPTIONS

Principle 11. Provide clear descriptions of abilities measured by the subtests when appropriate.

As noted in Chapter 10, you can interpret subtest scores using either an interindividual (or normative) comparison or an intraindividual comparison. Be sure that it is clear in your report which comparison you are discussing.

There are several ways to describe or interpret the abilities measured by the Wechsler subtests (see Chapter 10 in this text). Table D-3 in Appendix D summarizes these abilities. You will have to decide which description best characterizes the child's performance. Whichever one (or ones) you choose, describe the child's ability clearly. The factor analytic findings also can guide your interpretations. For example, although the WISC–III subtests are grouped into Verbal and Performance Scales, factor analytic findings suggest that Coding and Symbol Search are best interpreted as measuring sustained attention and the ability to process nonmeaningful information rapidly. This would seem to be a more appropriate interpretation than referring to Coding and Symbol Search simply as measures of performance ability.

When you describe the functions measured by a subtest, try to be as specific as possible. For example, if you are writing about Digit Span, identify the type of short-term memory being evaluated (auditory) and the type of content (nonmeaningful). Furthermore, recognize that every subtest provides only a *sampling* of abilities. Subtests such as Arithmetic, for example, do not measure the entire range of mathematical ability. In fact, the Arithmetic subtest may not reliably and systematically measure skills involving addition, subtraction, multiplication, and division. To measure these skills, select a test that is specifically designed to do so, such as the Key Math Diagnostic Arithmetic Test–Revised Normative Update (see Chapter 18). You also may supplement standardized tests with curriculum-based techniques.

Be careful when you discuss abilities, such as verbal comprehension, that apply to more than one subtest. For example, if a child has a Wechsler scaled score of 13 on Vocabulary, also consider the child's scores on the other subtests that measure verbal comprehension (Information, Comprehension, Similarities) before you say that the child has a strength in verbal comprehension. For example, if this child obtained a scaled score of 7 on Information, do not say that verbal comprehension is a strength. Instead use a phrase that refers to Vocabulary but not Information. The same guideline holds for the subtests that measure perceptual organization (Picture Completion, Picture Arrangement, Block Design, Object Assembly) and for those that measure the ability to sustain attention (Coding, Symbol Search).

The following are examples of statements that fail to describe WISC–III subtests or profiles clearly.

1. This statement was based on a Picture Completion scaled score of 7: "She displayed a weakness in her ability to perceive significant features." The phrase "to perceive significant features" is vague. *Suggestion:* "She displayed a weakness in her ability to perceive missing details of pictures."

2. This statement was based on a Picture Arrangement scaled score of 9: "She was average in her ability to anticipate and sequence cause-and-effect social interactions." The phrase "ability to anticipate and sequence cause-and-effect social interactions" is difficult to follow. *Suggestion:* "She exhibited an average (37th percentile) ability to anticipate in a meaningful way what results might be expected from various acts of social behavior."

Table 21-3
WISC–III Profiles Cited in Examples in Guidelines

Subtest	Profile						
	1	2	3	4	5	6	7
Information	—	9	—	8	15	6	7
Similarities	—	10	—	4	14	5	12
Arithmetic	—	14	—	7	13	3	12
Vocabulary	—	9	—	9	14	6	9
Comprehension	—	10	—	8	13	7	10
Digit Span	—	12	—	7	9	8	12
Picture Completion	8	12	16	6	16	5	10
Coding	9	15	13	9	13	10	14
Picture Arrangement	7	13	14	11	14	5	7
Block Design	9	9	12	6	12	5	14
Object Assembly	13	8	13	7	13	4	10
Symbol Search	—	—	—	—	—	—	—
Mazes	—	—	16	—	16	—	—
Verbal Scale IQ	—	102	—	84	123	74	100
Performance Scale IQ	—	110	—	86	125	74	107
Full Scale IQ	—	106	—	84	126	72	104

3. This statement was based on a Digit Span scaled score of 10: "Short-term memory is adequate." Although this description is satisfactory, it could be more precise. *Suggestion:* "Short-term auditory memory for nonmeaningful material is average (50th percentile)."

4. This statement was based on Profile 1 in Table 21-3: "Henry showed a strength on a test of perceptual organization." The statement as such is accurate for the Object Assembly subtest, but it fails to consider that Picture Completion and Block Design also measure perceptual organization. Scores on Picture Completion and Block Design were average. *Suggestion:* "Henry showed a strength in his ability to synthesize concrete parts into meaningful wholes."

Exercise 21-4. Evaluating Statements That Fail to Describe WISC–III Subtests or Profiles Clearly

---

Read the statements, evaluate them, and then compare your evaluations with those in the Comment section.

1. The child obtained a Digit Span score of 15, which was the highest score in the profile: "His highest scaled score was on Digit Span, which is a verbal task."
2. "Jill has ability in the area of perceptual-motor organization, but is less able in numerical reasoning."

Comment

1. Although this statement is technically accurate, you can improve it in two ways. First, instead of listing the name of the subtest, describe what the subtest measures. Second, use a qualitative description for a scaled score of 15. *Suggestion:* "His short-term memory is well developed (95th percentile), as noted by his ability to recall orally presented digits in the order given and in reverse order."
2. This sentence doesn't inform the reader about the child's level of performance. The terms *has ability* and *less able* are vague. *Suggestion:* "Jill's strength is in the area of perceptual-motor organization (84th percentile). Her numerical reasoning skills are within the average range (50th percentile)."

The difference between the right word and the almost right word is the difference between lightning and a lightning bug.
—Mark Twain

DEVELOP INFERENCES FROM TEST SCORES

Principle 12. Relate inferences based on subtest scores or IQs to the cognitive processes measured by the subtests and scales.

Although you should make every effort to discuss the implications of the child's test performance, stay close to the cognitive operations measured by the subtests or scales. You will be in a better position to make generalizations about the

child's abilities if you have information about the child's achievements in school, case history information, behavioral observations, and other assessment information.

Make Generalizations About Intelligence with Caution

Use caution in making generalizations about how examinees will perform in school, on a job, or in other settings based solely or primarily on the results of an intelligence test. Although scores on intelligence tests correlate significantly with school grades, the correlations are moderate, tending to run in the .30s and .40s (see Chapter 8). These correlations mean that intelligence test scores account for only 10–20% of the variance in school grades. Many factors affect school performance besides intelligence, such as learning disabilities, the child's motivation, the child's home environment, and the school curriculum and atmosphere.

Make Generalizations About Other Abilities with Caution

Also make other types of generalizations with caution. For example, the statement "His strengths in immediate auditory memory, numerical reasoning, and visual-motor spatial integration will help him in his understanding of historic events and their link with today's society" may or may not be accurate. Because there is limited, if any, indication in the research literature of a relationship between these skills and the understanding of historic events, it is better not to make this inference.

Exercise Care in Discussing Test Results That Differ from Expectations

How should you discuss test results that differ from what you expected? For example, if an examinee obtains an IQ of 150,

DRABBLE reprinted by permission of UFS, Inc.

but is making grades of C, D, and F in school, do you report that the intelligence test scores are invalid? Or is it better to report that the examinee's poor school performance is probably associated with factors not related to his or her cognitive ability? Conversely, if an examinee with an IQ of 80 achieves a B or A average in school, do you report that the IQ is inconsistent with the examinee's school grades? Grading practices are highly variable, and grades also depend on course content, subject matter, instructor preference, student effort, and class attendance. Unless you have information about each of these factors, be careful about the inferences you make about the relationship between test scores and school grades. When you discuss the examinee's occupational goals or academic performance or potential, consider—in addition to the examinee's IQ—her or his motivation, temperament, interpersonal skills, and other characteristics related to successful occupational or academic performance.

Exercise Care in Discussing Cause-Effect Relationships

Be careful when you discuss cause-and-effect relationships. For example, did the examinee do well in an area because he or she likes the area, or does the examinee like the area because he or she does well in it? In some cases, examinees may like an area that they do not do well in or they may dislike an area that they do well in. Also, to what extent does the examinee's level of performance relate to his or her home environment? Research suggests that there is a relationship between what the parents emphasize in the home and their children's cognitive development, but the relationship is not strong (see Chapter 6). Therefore, a statement such as "His high nonverbal skills are related to the emphasis on sports in his family" may or may not be accurate. In addition, the motor skills involved in sports are different from those involved in individually administered tests of intelligence.

The following are examples of statements that fail to interpret WISC–III subtests or IQs clearly.

1. "Dean performed in the low average range. His cognitive deficits during this examination are inconsistent with his reported B average in school." The words *deficit* and *inconsistent* may not be appropriate. *Suggestion:* Leave out *deficit* and *inconsistent*, but comment on the examinee's test performance and report that the examinee has above-average academic school performance.

2. "She demonstrated below-average performance in visual discrimination tasks and nonverbal reasoning tasks. Despite these skills, she exhibited average performance in analyzing and synthesizing nonverbal information." Why are the words "despite these skills" used to begin the second sentence? Does the writer mean to say, "In contrast with these below-average skills, her skills …"? The writer seems to imply that visual discrimination skills and nonverbal reasoning skills also may be involved in analyzing and synthesizing nonverbal information. This implication may be appropriate, but the writer has not adequately developed it.

3. These interpretations were based on Profile 2 in Table 21-3 (page 699) for a 16-year, 0-month-old female: "Helen demonstrated abilities overall in the Average range, with strengths in nonverbal social intelligence, numerical reasoning, and symbol association skills. Her performance indicates that she may have trouble with her studies at school." The second sentence does not follow from the first one. Why should average overall ability and skills in specific areas lead to the statement that the examinee will have trouble in school? It is risky to make such predictions based on a profile of subtest scores that has no absolute weakness and is in the Average range for the Verbal, Performance, and Full Scales.

4. "The low concentration and attention scores may indicate that Jane's inability to ignore distractions (e.g., nervousness, examiner's note taking, etc.) is indicative of a tendency to give up when items get more difficult (e.g., saying 'I don't know' quickly before thinking about an appropriate response to a test item)." This is a confusing sentence. It is not clear how nervousness is related to an inability to ignore distractions. Saying "I don't know" quickly may have been realistic. If not, what factors suggested to the examiner that the examinee could solve the problems?

5. "Low scores on Information and Arithmetic may indicate weakness in the ability to assimilate given material and then provide a solution for the designated problem." This description attempts to combine functions that we think are involved in the Information and Arithmetic subtests. However, it is not clear how a low score on Information or Arithmetic (or on both) suggests a "weakness in the ability to assimilate given material and then provide a solution for the designated problem." *Suggestion:* "Her range of factual information and ability in mental arithmetic are below average." Support this statement with additional test data, when possible.

Exercise 21-5. Evaluating Statements That Fail to Interpret WISC–III Subtests or IQs Clearly

---

Read the statements, evaluate them, and then compare your evaluations with those in the Comment section.

1. "Her low score on the Arithmetic subtest may be due to her dislike of and disinterest in school mathematics classes."

2. This statement was based on an Information scaled score of 13 and a Comprehension scaled score of 16 for a 13-year-old girl: "Virginia achieved a lower score in her range of knowledge than in her ability to use social judgment, which suggests limited factual knowledge."

Comment

1. Cause-and-effect relationships are difficult to tease out without more information. Perhaps she dislikes mathematics because she is not good at it. *Suggestion:* Leave the sentence out unless you have information to support the hypothesis.

2. This statement is misleading. A standard score of 13 indicates above-average ability. The fact that one subtest score is lower than another does not mean that the lower score reflects limited ability. In this case, Information is not significantly lower than Comprehension (see Table A-2 in Appendix A). *Suggestion:* "Virginia's range of knowledge and ability to use social judgment are above average."

DESCRIBE PROFILES CLEARLY

Principle 13. Describe the profile of scores clearly and unambiguously.

Consider all of the information you have obtained when describing the test profile. Carefully choose the words you use to describe the child's performance. Subtests and scales overlap in their measurement properties; consequently, be careful not to make contradictory statements. Chapter 10 presents terms for describing subtest scores on the WISC–III; these designations apply for all the Wechsler tests and for any test with a mean of 10 and a standard deviation of 3. Follow the guidelines that may be presented in test manuals for interpreting profiles.

Report Significant Differences

Before you state that two abilities are different (or higher/lower or better/more poorly developed), be sure that the scores representing these abilities are significantly different (usually, at the .05 level or below). For example, you do not want to write, "She may favor verbal expressive tasks that allow her to work at her own pace over more structured time-dependent tasks" when the examinee has a Verbal IQ of 106, a Performance IQ of 96, and a Full Scale IQ of 101. Because the Verbal and Performance IQs are about the same, there is little justification for making this inference. Likewise, you do not want to say, "His verbal skills are slightly more well developed than his nonverbal skills" for a Verbal IQ of 86 and a Performance IQ of 82. When two (or more) scores are not significantly different, do not say that one score is slightly better (or poorer) than the other one; rather, point out that the scores reflect similarly developed abilities.

When the Verbal IQ is significantly higher than the Performance IQ, however, you can describe the difference with confidence. For example, for a Verbal IQ of 116 and a Performance IQ of 94, you can say, "Her verbal comprehension skills (84th percentile) are better developed than her perceptual organizational skills (34th percentile)" rather than "Her verbal comprehension skills may be better developed ...."

Emphasize the Direction of Differences

When you report the examinee's scores, compare the examinee's subtest scores, or compare the examinee's Verbal and Performance IQs, always give the level at which the scores fall and the direction of the differences between the scores (or IQs). The statement "She demonstrated a significant difference between Block Design and Object Assembly" is not informative because it gives neither the level of the scores (e.g., average, above average, or below average) nor the direction of the difference (which score was higher or lower than the other).

How to Compare Scores on Different Intelligence Tests

Most intelligence tests, academic achievement tests, and special ability tests yield standard scores. In order to determine whether scores from two tests differ significantly for an individual, the standard scores must be on a common metric—that is, a scale with the same mean and standard deviation. If the scales are different, you must transform them. You can use the z score transformation, described in Table 4-4 in Chapter 4, to do this. After you have transformed the scores, you can use the procedure described in Exhibit 10-1 in Chapter 10 to determine whether the two scores differ significantly.

How to Compare Verbal and Performance IQs

Tables A-2, B-2, and C-2 in Appendixes A, B, and C present the values that reflect significant differences between IQs on the WISC–III, WPPSI–R, and WAIS–III, respectively. Before you say that the Verbal IQ is higher or lower than the Performance IQ (that it reflects a more well developed or less well developed ability), the difference between the two IQs must be statistically significant.

Even when you find a significant difference between the Verbal and Performance Scales, do not routinely recommend further investigation. Significant differences may simply reflect the child's unique cognitive style. Consider all sources of information before you recommend further investigation.

How to Interpret Variability

Interpret the implications of variability of cognitive ability scores with extreme caution, making use of all available sources of information. Variability in scores may reflect the child's cognitive style, or it may be related to other factors such as motivation, bilingualism, ethnic background, psychopathology, temporary inefficiency, or cognitive disturbance. For example, brain damage or depression may lower all scores uniformly or only selected scores. In any event, do not assume that variability in cognitive ability scores always reveals something diagnostically important about the child's functioning, indicates lack of persistence, or suggests better potential. Look for the appropriate explanation for variability by reviewing the entire test performance, behavioral observations, and background information. On instruments that measure special abilities, adaptive behavior, temperament, personality, or other characteristics, use the guidelines in the manuals to interpret variability.

The following are examples of statements that fail to interpret WISC–III profile differences clearly.

1. These statements were based on Profile 4 in Table 21-3 (page 699) for a 15-year-old male: "James's verbal and nonverbal skills are similarly developed and range from average to well below average. His vocabulary ability is better developed than his social comprehension." Because the Vocabulary scaled score is not significantly higher than the Comprehension scaled score (9 vs. 8), this statement is misleading. *Suggestion:* Note that his vocabulary ability and social comprehension are at the 37th and 25th percentile ranks, respectively.

2. "Her average nonverbal and verbal skills varied in a range from average to above-average ability, with particular strengths and weaknesses in certain tasks." This is a confusing sentence. If all scores are average or above average, there are no absolute weaknesses in the profile; the term *weaknesses* refers to skills that are below average (e.g., scaled scores of 7 or lower). *Suggestion:* End the sentence at the comma, eliminating the last part, or use other ways to describe the pattern of scores.

3. This statement was based on a Picture Completion score of 7 and a Block Design score of 12: "There is a marked difference between her visual perception and her visual-motor-spatial coordination." The statement does not give the direction of the difference and is misleading because Block Design also involves visual perception. *Suggestion:* "Her attention to visual details is below average, whereas her spatial visualization ability is average."

4. "Within Becky's scores, a marked difference in ability was found between her Very Superior ability in abstract and concrete reasoning and her Low Average ability in spatial visualization." This is a confusing sentence. Part of the problem is that the writer immediately follows the opening phrase, "within Becky's scores," with a statement about ability levels. *Suggestion:* "Her abstract reasoning ability is excellent, whereas her spatial visualization skills are less well developed but still within the lower limits of the average range." The qualitative descriptions "very superior" and "low average," if used, should begin with lowercase letters. Capitalize qualitative descriptions only when you refer to the classifications associated with the Full Scale, Verbal Scale, or Performance Scale IQs.

5. These statements were based on Profile 5 in Table 21-3 (page 699): "Jamie has one relative weakness in short-term memory. Within her other verbal scores, short-term memory is significantly less developed than her other scores. Her attention is less developed than her concentration. If, in class, Jamie's teacher asked her for some information just presented in class, Jamie probably would have been concentrating, but her average development in attention and short-term memory might cause her to forget the material." This is a confusing paragraph. A scaled score of 9 is average, not weak. In addition, this child has excellent attention skills as reflected by her performance on several subtests, except for Digit Span. What she shows is less developed ability in nonmeaningful immediate auditory memory. It is inappropriate to speculate that this examinee would forget material presented in class. In fact, with her outstanding ability, her recall ability in class may be excellent. Do not stress any score in isolation from the total picture. Finally, "her average development in attention and short-term memory might cause her to forget the material" implies a cause-and-effect relationship that would be difficult to establish and may be erroneous.

Exercise 21-6. Evaluating Statements That Fail to Interpret WISC–III Profile Differences Clearly

Read the statements, evaluate them, and then compare your evaluations to those in the Comment section.

1. This statement was written about Performance subtest scores ranging from 6 to 13: "In nonverbal areas Harry displayed uniformly developed skills."
2. "There is a 9-point difference between his Verbal and Performance IQs, which suggests that his nonverbal abilities are better developed than his verbal abilities."

Comment

1. The statement is incorrect because this range of 7 scaled-score points (from below average to above average) indicates strengths as well as weaknesses. In addition, the term "uniformly developed" is not clear because it fails to describe the level at which the examinee is functioning.
2. A 9-point difference is not statistically significant, and thus the interpretation is incorrect. (See Table A-2 in Appendix A for required differences between WISC–III Verbal and Performance IQs at the .05 and .01 levels.)

Don't write merely to be understood. Write so that you cannot possibly be misunderstood.

—Robert Louis Stevenson

MAKE RECOMMENDATIONS CAREFULLY

Principle 14. Make recommendations carefully, using all available sources of information.

Recommendations are a valuable part of the report. Develop one or more recommendations that you believe may be appropriate and feasible. You want to be on firm ground when you make recommendations. In other words, your recommendations should be based on assessment information, not on hunches or speculation. Be careful not to make any potentially misleading statements. Table 21-4 provides examples of intervention strategies used in schools for children with special needs.

Here is an example of recommendations made on the basis of a 16-year-old female's WISC–III results (Profile 6 in Table 21-3; see page 699).

Frieda may have difficulty processing auditory or visual information presented in the classroom. Presenting material to her in a simplified manner may enable her to better process, retain, and understand concepts. She also might benefit from lessons designed to help her understand logical and sequential cause-and-effect relationships. Frieda's overall scores suggest that she can learn; however, the learning environment should be concrete and repetitive, with many examples provided.

The following are examples of statements that fail to make appropriate recommendations based on the WISC–III.

1. This statement was made on the basis of a Verbal IQ of 108, Performance IQ of 102, and Full Scale IQ of 104: "Victor shows sufficient aptitude to attain advanced degrees, and I recommend that he be considered for a gifted program." This statement is misleading. First, an IQ of 104 may not be sufficient to allow a child to go on to graduate school. We would hesitate to go out on a limb to make such a prediction. Second, it is doubtful that a school would allow a child with an IQ of 104 to enter a gifted program unless the child had special strengths in some academic areas or had special talents that would qualify her or him for the program.
2. This statement was based on an adolescent's WISC–III Verbal IQ of 102, Performance IQ of 96, and Full Scale IQ of 101: "Her overall average ability suggests that she should not be encouraged to pursue a college degree." The recommendation is inappropriate, because students with average ability can complete college successfully. Making predictions about future career success for individuals with average or above-average ability, based solely on the results of an individual intelligence test, is inappropriate and is discouraged.

Exercise 21-7. Evaluating Statements That Fail to Make Appropriate Recommendations Based on the WISC–III

Read the statements, evaluate them, and then compare your evaluations with those in the Comment section.

1. "I believe that Florence's nervous behavior exhibited during the Verbal scale test administration was too profound to discount. It is recommended that this correlation be-

tween nervousness and verbal performance be considered before any definitive assessment is made."
2. "Rachel wants to major in international business. It is recommended that she go into this area. Her strength in social judgment should be useful in international business because of the different cultures and protocols a person must use."

Comment

1. The examiner is concerned about the examinee's level of anxiety, but the recommendation is vague. What does the examiner mean by "before any definitive assessment is made"? Why use the term *correlation?* Why is her "nervous behavior … too profound to discount"? The recommendation should emphasize that the severity of the examinee's anxiety needs to be further investigated. Did her level of anxiety affect the reliability of the test results? In addition, there are some minor stylistic problems. "Scale" should be capitalized, and "test" is superfluous after "scale."
2. This hypothesis is inappropriate. A high score on the Comprehension subtest suggests good social reasoning, but the reasoning measured by the subtest is highly culture bound. The social reasoning skills measured by the subtest, therefore, may not generalize to an understanding of different cultures. Also, it is completely inappropriate to recommend a college major, career, occupation, and so forth for a child based on a subtest score.

USE CAUTION IN EXTRAPOLATING OR INTERPOLATING SCORES

Principle 15. Use scores obtained by extrapolation or interpolation with caution.

You diminish the validity of test scores when you obtain them by extrapolation or interpolation. *Extrapolation* refers to the extension of norms to scores not actually obtained in the standardization sample. *Interpolation* refers to estimating standard scores for raw scores that are not listed in the conversion table in the manual. If a score is extremely high or extremely low, you can report the score as falling above or below the highest or lowest score given in the norms (e.g., "above an IQ of 154" or "below an IQ of 55"). Or you can report the extrapolated score and follow it with the term *estimated*. Similarly, if you report an interpolated score, follow it with the term *estimated*.

MAKE DIAGNOSES CAUTIOUSLY

Principle 16. Refrain from making diagnoses of psychopathology or educational diagnoses based solely on test scores; consider all sources of information.

Base a diagnosis—or hypotheses about possible psychopathology or educational deficiencies—on all relevant sources

Table 21-4
Examples of Intervention Strategies Used in Schools

Environmental Strategies

1. Provide a structured learning environment.
2. Adjust class schedules.
3. Use classroom aides and note takers.
4. Modify non-academic times such as lunch break, recess, and physical education.
5. Change student seating.
6. Use a study carrel.
7. Alter location of personal or classroom supplies for easier access or to minimize distraction.
8. Arrange for regular classes with enrollments much smaller than usual.

Organizational Strategies

1. Modify test delivery.
2. Use tape recorders, computer-aided instruction, and other audiovisual equipment.
3. Select modified textbooks or workbooks.
4. Tailor homework assignments and ensure that required assignments are written down. Provide deadlines for substeps in long-term assignments.
5. Use one-on-one tutorials.
6. Provide peer tutoring.
7. Set time expectations for assignments.
8. Provide cues, such as faces indicating beginning and ending times.
9. Provide tests in segments so that student hands in one segment before receiving the next.
10. Highlight main ideas and supporting details in books.

Behavioral Strategies

1. Use behavioral management techniques.
2. Use behavioral/academic contracts.
3. Use positive reinforcements (rewards).
4. Use negative consequences (punishments).
5. Confer with student's parents (and student, as appropriate).
6. Confer with student's teachers.
7. Establish a home/school communication system for behavior monitoring.
8. Post rules and consequences for classroom behavior.
9. Offer social reinforcers for appropriate behavior.
10. Put student on daily/weekly progress report.
11. Implement self-recording of behaviors.
12. Work with student to devise and implement a new habit to solve a recurring problem.

Presentation Strategies

1. Tape lessons so that the student can listen to them again.
2. Provide mimeographed material for extra practice (e.g., outlines, study guides).

3. Require fewer drill and practice activities.
4. Give both oral and visual instructions for assignments, and check student's recording of them.
5. Vary the method of lesson presentation (e.g., lecture, small groups, large groups, audiovisuals, peer tutors or cross-age tutors, demonstrations, experiments, simulations, games, and one-on-one instruction with adult).
6. Provide for oral testing.
7. Ask student to repeat directions/assignments to show understanding.
8. Arrange for a mentor to work with student in the student's interest area or area of greatest strength.

Methodology Strategies

1. Repeat and simplify instructions about in-class and homework assignments.
2. Supplement verbal instructions with visual instructions.
3. Change instructional pace.
4. Change instructional methods.
5. Move about the room; sometimes stand directly behind inattentive students.
6. Vary speaking tone, volume, and tempo.
7. Make frequent use of maps, globes, charts, timelines, diagrams, illustrations, and demonstrations.
8. Relate unfamiliar or abstract material to concepts familiar to the student.

Curriculum Strategies

1. Change instructional materials.
2. Use supplementary materials.
3. Assess whether student has the necessary prerequisite skills. Determine whether materials are appropriate to the student's current interest and functioning levels.
4. Implement study skill strategies (survey, read, recite, review). Introduce definition of new terms/vocabulary and review to check for understanding.
5. Limit amount of material presented on a single paper.
6. Provide a sample or practice test.
7. Be aware of student's preferred learning style and provide appropriate instruction/materials.

Study Skill Strategies

1. Instruct student to read and survey the material first.
2. Instruct student to develop questions about the material.
3. Instruct student to learn the pertinent facts about the material.
4. Instruct student to recite the pertinent facts learned about the material.
5. Instruct student to review everything he or she learned about the material.

Source: Adapted from *Opportunities for Success* (1996), published by the Colorado Department of Education.

of information about a child and his or her environment. Always use test results in conjunction with interviews, observations, background data, behavior scale profiles, and other sources of information.

The following are examples of statements that are faulty diagnostically.

1. "The low Performance IQ and the high Verbal IQ indicate brain damage." This statement is inappropriate because you must *never* consider a discrepancy between the Verbal and Performance IQs by itself as an indication of brain damage. First, this discrepancy is only one of many possible indicators of brain dysfunction; some individuals with brain damage have a high Performance IQ and a low Verbal IQ. More important, discrepancies between Verbal and Performance IQs may have nothing to do with brain damage; normal children also have this pattern. The discrepancy may simply represent this individual's cognitive style.

2. "His low scores on Arithmetic, Coding, and Digit Span indicate that he has a learning disability and poor reading ability." This statement is unwarranted because you should never use scores on a Wechsler test (or any other individual intelligence test), by themselves, to establish a diagnosis of educational disability. To make a diagnosis of learning disability or reading disability, you need scores on an intelligence test, an achievement test, and other tests as well.

Exercise 21-8. Evaluating Statements That Are Faulty

Read the statements, evaluate them, and then compare your evaluations with those in the Comment section.

1. "Bill achieved an IQ of 112 ± 3. He has just begun kindergarten and needs to develop listening skills and an approach to solving problems."
2. "Her WISC–III IQ of 60 ± 5 indicates that she has mental retardation."

Comment

1. It is difficult to imagine how this child could have achieved an IQ of 112 without having developed some listening and problem-solving skills. The examiner failed to use a transition to indicate that the two sentences were unrelated. If other information leads you to conclude that a child, for example, is more impulsive than the average child of her or his age, clearly indicate this in the report. Always consider what the appropriate normative behavior is for the child's developmental stage.
2. This statement is incorrect because we cannot make a diagnosis of mental retardation based on the IQ alone; we must evaluate adaptive behavior, together with level of intelligence (see *Assessment of Children: Behavioral and Clinical Applications*).

COMMUNICATE CLEARLY

Principle 17. Communicate clearly, and do not include unnecessary technical material in the report.

Good writing is essential if you want your report to be useful. Present your ideas in a logical and orderly sequence, with smooth transitions between topics. You will impede communication if the report contains sentences with unfamiliar or highly technical words, excessive wording, test scores without interpretation, or irrelevant material. Use words that have a low probability of being misinterpreted, that are nontechnical, and that convey your findings as clearly as possible. *Avoid psychological jargon.*

You want the reader to comprehend your report with a minimum of effort. Check carefully that you have written an understandable report, and revise any potentially confusing sentences. You will enhance communication if you write concisely, follow rules of grammar and punctuation, use a consistent style, make clear transitions between different ideas or topics, and give examples of the examinee's performance. Technical and professional writing should leave little room for misinterpretation. Because your report will likely be read by a variety of people who have different levels of psychological knowledge, write it in a way that will be clear to all readers.

Use Clear and Accurate Statements

Make your statements as direct and concrete as possible; avoid vague and abstract ideas and terms that may be difficult to follow. For example, the statement that an examinee's "enthusiasm was slightly off track" is vague, and the statement that an examinee "cultivated a recalcitrant pose" forces the reader to struggle to understand the meaning. If you use a word with multiple meanings, be sure that the meaning is clear from the context in which you use the word. For example, when you use the word *performance,* be sure that the reader knows whether you are referring to the child's behavior during the evaluation, to how the child did on a test, or to the WISC–III, WPPSI–R, or WAIS–III Performance Scale.

As noted in Principle 3, behavioral descriptions usually are preferable to interpretive statements. Describe the examinee's behavior accurately. Choose the term that best says what you want to say. For example, was the examinee *anxious, eager, uninterested,* or *depressed?* Did the examinee *walk, stomp, prance, saunter,* or *race* around the room? Do not say that an examinee *lacks* an ability when what you mean is that the examinee's ability is *weak.* Use *limited, restricted, weak,* or *less well developed* rather than *lack of,* unless *lack of* is literally correct. Also, avoid terms that have medical connotations (such as *diminished* or *depressed*) when you mean *low.*

The word *only,* as in "Sheila raised her hand only twice," may be misleading. If this behavior was the norm, the reader might be incorrectly led to believe that Sheila did not raise her hand as frequently as the other students. Use of the word *just* has similar problems. The words *very* and *quite* add little meaning to a sentence and are best left out.

Be careful with words that have special connotations, such as *intelligent, bright, average,* and *psychopathic.* Use these words only when you have objective information to support their use. Use the word *thinks* or *believes* when you refer to a person's thoughts and the word *feels* when you refer to a person's feelings or emotions.

In professional writing, it is better to be precise when you discuss numbers. For example, the statement "Most children were age three" is vague. *Three* could refer to months or years or even days. Although the context of the report will likely clear up the meaning, it is better to be precise. For example, add *years* if that is what you mean.

Be as specific as possible in your descriptions. For example, instead of saying "There was a small group of children," note the exact size of the group. More detail would enhance the following description: "Joseph is a somewhat apprehensive child, with brown eyes and brown hair." Although the term "apprehensive child" may be accurate, it would be helpful to cite the behaviors that led to this description. Don't use *tends to* or *has a tendency to* to describe a behavior when you have observed the specific behavior. For example, instead of saying "Tommy tends to hit other children," describe what you observed: "Tommy hit his younger brother three times during my visit to his home."

The following section from a "politically correct" report was constructed to humorously illustrate how jargon (or catch words) can reduce the clarity of a report and the reader's understanding of issues. In your reports, you should use conventional terms that are accepted by your profession—not those that are simply "PC."

A POLITICALLY CORRECT REPORT

John is a *cerebrally challenged* child (slow learner) who is *uniquely coordinated* (clumsy) in his movements. In school, he *achieved deficiencies* (failed) in several subjects because of *differently logical* (wrong) answers. He has an *alternative body image* (obese), is *nasally gifted* (large nose), and *vertically challenged* (short). When he sleeps, he is *nasally repetitive* (snores). Occasionally, he *engages in negative attention getting* (misbehaves) and is *temporally challenged* (late) in getting to his classes. His teacher says he is *motivationally deficient* (lazy), and *an expert at incorporating multiple viewpoints* (indecisive). He has been caught committing an *ethically different act* (stealing) and admits to having an *ethical disability* (lying) at times.

Use Transition Words

Transition words help achieve continuity in a report. Transition words may be time links (*then, next, after, while, since*), cause-effect links (*therefore, consequently, as a result*), addition links (*in addition, moreover, furthermore*), or contrast links (*however, but, conversely, nevertheless, although, whereas, similarly*). The *Publication Manual* of the American Psychological Association (1994b) advises that, although the transition word

while is often used in informal writing and conversation to refer to connections other than time (e.g., *while* is used when *whereas* is meant), in scientific and professional writing *while* should be used only to reflect time. Similarly, the *Publication Manual* advises that *since* be used to refer to time and *because* be used when appropriate for transitions. However, O'Conner (1996) notes that there is ample precedent going back 400 to 500 years for using *while* to mean "although" or "whereas" and using *since* to mean "because" or "for the reason that." Obviously, *since* or *while* should not be used when their meaning is not clear and could cause confusion.

Use Standard Terms

You weaken your presentation when you use informal meanings of terms, terms of approximation, stylistic phrases, and colloquial expressions to describe your observations and interpretations. These terms and expressions diminish the professional quality and readability of the report and should not be used unless, of course, you are quoting the examinee.

Avoid the following:

- Informal meanings of terms (*feel* for *believe* or *think*)
- Terms of approximation (*quite a few* or *lots of* rather than a specific number)
- Stylistic phrases (*in terms of*)
- Unnecessary jargon (*structural methodology*)
- Colloquial expressions (*right away* for *now, kids* for *children,* or *lots of* for *many*) and expressions that imply more than you mean (*gang* for *peer group*)
- Offensive terms (*drunk* for *has a drinking problem, retard* for *mentally retarded*)
- Disability-centered language (*learning-disabled child* for *child with a learning disability,* or *brain-injured child* for *child with a brain injury*)

Avoid Technical Terms

To enhance the readability of your report, keep technical descriptions to a minimum. Whenever possible, use common expressions to present the information you have gathered. Technical jargon may confuse the lay reader. It also may communicate meanings different from those you intended to convey. Even professionals do not always agree on the interpretation of psychological terminology.

Be careful when you are using technical terms or concepts to describe the examinee's performance. For instance, do not say, "Mental ability was better than nonverbal ability," because *mental ability* includes both verbal and nonverbal cognitive ability. Likewise, do not say, "There was no significance to be found in the scores," because the term *significance* can be used either in a technical sense (with respect to statistically significant differences between scores) or in defining importance. All scores are significant in the sense of being important, as they tell you something about the child's performance. If you are describing statistical significance, make sure that your description is clear.

You do not need to include general historical or technical information about a test. For example, you do not need to mention that the Stanford-Binet was revised in 1986 or that the WISC–III is a derivative of the adult form of the Wechsler. But a report on the testing of a foreign-born child might note that the Stanford-Binet: Fourth Edition, WISC–III, WPPSI–R, WAIS–III, and DAS were standardized on children in the United States.

The reader does not need to know about the procedures you used to interpret the child's performance or about the specific steps you used to arrive at your interpretations. Don't discuss the statistical methods you used to arrive at your conclusions because you will confuse most readers. Leave references to standard deviations, raw scores, significance levels, scatter, and most other technical concepts out of the report. Focus instead on presenting the findings and their implications.

It is important to identify the scoring system and norms that you used for a particular test, however, especially when you have the choice of using more than one scoring system or set of norms. For example, because there are several scoring systems used with the Bender-Gestalt, such as the Koppitz system and the Hutt system, note in the report which one you used to score the examinee's performance. This is essential for record keeping and will be invaluable in cases of litigation.

It is also important to tell whether test norms are based on the child's age or grade placement. At least one intellectual ability test—the Woodcock-Johnson III—and most achievement tests offer both age and grade norms. If there is much difference between age and grade norms for the examinee, it is usually best to report the results of academic achievement tests using both sets of norms.

The following are examples of unnecessary technical terms and information.

1. "His attention to detail should be strengthened, as indicated by his performance on the Magic Window subtest." A subtest name is likely to have little, if any, meaning to the reader. If you refer to a specific subtest, describe what the subtest measures.
2. "When she reached the ceiling level, she became more restless and serious." The term *ceiling level* may not be understood by the reader. You could say instead, "When the more difficult levels of the test were reached, she ...." If you do use the term *ceiling level,* add "the level at which all or most tests were failed" in parentheses.

Exercise 21-9. Evaluating Statements That Have Unnecessary Technical Terms and Information

---

Read the statements, evaluate them, and then compare your evaluations with those in the Comment section.

1. "The level of agreement for the two observers was > 80%."

2. "His sometimes wandering attention may have contributed to his scatter of subtest scores."

Comment

1. It is preferable to leave technical symbols such as > out of the report, because readers may not be familiar with them. You can, however, describe the symbol in words.
2. "Scatter" is a technical concept and may be misunderstood by lay readers. It is better to use the term *differences* (e.g., "contributed to the marked differences between his subtest scores"). Also, the term *sometimes wandering attention* can be replaced with the word *inattention*.

So far as most of us are concerned there are thousands upon thousands of words that are, with rare exceptions, better left in the dictionary where they won't be misused, waste time, and cause trouble.

—Wendell Johnson

Avoid Confusing and Inappropriate Devices

You may be tempted to inject excitement into your writing by using stylistic techniques appropriate to creative writing— shifts in topic, tense, or mood or surprising or ambiguous statements. These techniques may, however, confuse the reader and should be avoided (American Psychological Association, 1994b). Also, do not use creative embellishments

"It is recommended that hemispheric processing tasks be instituted that take into account the information processing components associated with Processing Speed and Perceptual Organization and disregarding the questionable scatter."

Mrs. Jones
Grade 3

Gee, I'm sure glad that Dr. Wordiness didn't get too technical with that evaluation.

Courtesy of Joanne Davis and Jerome M. Sattler.

or language that attracts undue attention to itself, such as heavy alliteration (repetition of unusual initial consonant sounds in two or more neighboring words or syllables), rhymes, or clichés. If you do, you may distract readers and diminish the focus on your ideas. Use any metaphors with care, and never use mixed metaphors, such as "She tends to go off the deep end and wind up clear out in left field." Simply say, "She is impetuous." Use figurative or colorful expressions (like "dog tired") sparingly; they can make your writing sound labored or unnatural or too casual. When you use synonyms to avoid repetition of terms, choose your words carefully so that you do not unintentionally suggest a different meaning. Pronouns can sometimes be used to reduce repetitions, but you must be certain that the pronoun's antecedent (the word it stands for) is perfectly clear.

Examples of Unclear Statements

The following are examples of statements that can be misinterpreted or are not clear:

1. "His performance is a submaximal representation of his intellectual ability." The word *submaximal* is a poor choice. *Suggestion:* "His scores may underestimate his ability."
2. "He had a tendency to elicit heavy sighs and become visibly frustrated when he was having to discuss his home life." The word *elicit* is used incorrectly. *Suggestion:* Replace *elicit* with *emit* or say, "He sighed heavily and became frustrated when he discussed his home life."
3. "There was no evidence of abnormality in her conversation." The term *abnormality* is likely to be confusing to readers and is potentially misleading. *Suggestion:* "Her conversation was normal."
4. "The seizure impacted his behavior." The seizure is a behavior, so the statement is not clear. Also, the word *impacted* is jargon. *Suggestion:* "He was unable to complete the examination because he had a seizure."
5. "During the examination, Anna engaged in reactive behavior." The term *reactive behavior* is not clear. The sentence forces the reader to guess what the writer means. Instead, describe the child's behavior. *Suggestion:* "During the evaluation, Anna became upset when she discussed her parents' divorce."

Exercise 21-10. Evaluating Statements That May Be Misinterpreted or Are Not Clear

Read the statements, evaluate them, and then compare your evaluations with those in the Comment section.

1. "She also exhibited weaknesses in the Information and Arithmetic standard scores."
2. "Exact verbal interaction was difficult to ascertain."

Comment

1. The emphasis should be on the examinee's abilities, not on scores. Reserve the adjectives *strong* and *weak* or *average* and *normal* for describing abilities. Use the terms *high* and *low* when referring to scores. Also, you usually do not need to discuss in the report the type of scores (standard scores, raw scores, or age scores) used as the basis for your statements. *Suggestion:* "Her general fund of information and arithmetical ability are weaknesses."
2. This is an awkward sentence. *Suggestion:* "The high noise level interfered with my ability to hear what the child was saying."

DESCRIBE ANY STATISTICAL CONCEPTS

Principle 18. Describe and use statistical concepts appropriately; make sure that you check all calculations carefully and that you accurately report the reliability and validity of the test results.

There are preferred ways to describe and use statistical and psychometric concepts such as percentile rank, probability level, range, reliability, and validity. Following are some examples:

- *Percentile rank:* "Her Full Scale IQ is at the 55th percentile rank." (This is preferable to "She is better than 55% of other children.")
- *Probability level:* "The chances that his true score is between 106 and 120 are about 95 out of 100." (This is preferable to "There is a 95–100% probability that his IQ falls between 106 and 120." The use of "100%" is incorrect in the latter statement, as it depicts an improper conceptualization of probability levels.)
- *Range or classification:* "Her overall performance is in the High Average range." (Use the range or classification primarily for the Full Scale IQ and, on occasion, for the Verbal and Performance IQs. Seldom, if ever, use a range or classification for a subtest, as in "Her Vocabulary ability is in the Superior classification.")
- *Reliability and validity:* "The present measure of her level of intellectual functioning appears to be reliable and valid. She was cooperative, motivated, and appeared to do her best." (This is preferable to "On the basis of her consistency, the current results appear to be reliable and valid." An examinee may be consistent, but the scores may still be invalid.)

Underline or italicize statistical terms, leave a space before and after the equal sign, and round off percentage agreement, correlations, and other statistical information to two places beyond the decimal point (e.g., $r = .98$ or $k = .70$).

The following are examples of statements that fail to describe psychometric and statistical concepts appropriately.

1. "The verbal scores may be an underestimation of his true verbal ability because English is his second language.... The test results appear to be reliable and valid." These two sentences are contradictory. If part of the test appears to underestimate an examinee's ability, the test results cannot be valid. Furthermore, the word *true* in the first sentence suggests that the test provides a true measure of an examinee's verbal ability. The WISC–III—or, for that matter, any one test—provides only an estimate of an examinee's ability. The test items sample a range of possible items. No one test samples the entire ability domain.

2. "She enjoyed the performance subtests; hence, the results should be reliable." Enjoyment is not a sufficient reason to conclude that test results are reliable. Additional observations about her test behavior should be included.

Exercise 21-11. Evaluating Statements That Fail to Describe Psychometric and Statistical Concepts Appropriately

---

Read the statements, evaluate them, and then compare your evaluations with those in the Comment section.

1. "Jackie was randomly referred for testing by her teacher."
2. "Statistically speaking, her range of knowledge is poor, as noted by her missing two of the easy items."

Comment

1. It is possible, but highly unlikely, that the teacher randomly referred the child for testing. The statement would be correct if the teacher put the pupils' names in a hat and drew one name randomly or if the teacher used a table of random numbers to select a child for testing. *Suggestion:* "Jackie was referred for the evaluation by her teacher."
2. There are several problems with this sentence. First, poor knowledge is reflected by low scores, not by missing one or two items on a particular subtest. It would be better to describe the child's performance on the subtest as a whole. Second, the phrase *statistically speaking* is a poor choice of words and would be better left out of the sentence. Finally, a statement about the examinee's range of knowledge should be based on all available sources of information, not just two items.

AVOID BIAS

Principle 19. Eliminate biased terms from the report.

Your report should avoid implications of bias. This may be difficult, as biased language is well established in our culture. The use of *man* to denote *humanity* and the use of *he* as a generic pronoun are common examples of gender bias. These terms may convey an implicit message to the reader that women are not included in the reference or that females are unimportant. Where possible, eliminate gender-referenced nouns, pronouns, and adjectives, replacing them with terms that refer to people in general.

Implications of gender bias may also arise from the use of nonparallel terms. *Woman* and *husband* or *man* and *wife,* for example, are not parallel, and using them together may imply differences in the roles of women and men. The terms *husband* and *wife* are parallel, as are *man* and *woman* (American Psychological Association, 1994b). Guard against expressions and clichés that imply unequal roles for men and women.

Refer to members of ethnic groups with nouns and adjectives that are acceptable given the current social trends, the preferences of members of the group being referred to, and the preferences of readers of the report. Consider carefully whether ethnic designations are needed in the report. For example, reporting that a child's teacher is Hispanic American may be important if you are discussing the child's response to the teacher, but not if you are merely citing the teacher as an informant about the child. Generally, the ethnicity of the examinee is useful information to include in the report. If you routinely mention the ethnicity of examinees, mention the ethnicity of the majority group as well as that of minority groups.

Look for signs of stereotyping or prejudice in your writing. For example, do not assume that all welfare clients have limited education or intelligence or that all obese people are unhappy. Do not make inferences about the examinee's family or friends based on knowledge of the examinee's social class or ethnic group. Comparing two ethnic groups may result in irrelevant, negative evaluations of one of the ethnic groups. *Never make evaluative statements about social, ethnic, or gender groups or about members of these groups in a report.*

WRITE CONCISELY

Principle 20. Write a report that is concise but adequate.

The following guidelines will help you write more concise reports.

1. *Avoid wordy sentences.* (a) "Although it cannot be definitely established, it is quite probable that the patient, in all likelihood, is suffering some degree of aphasia" for "The patient is probably aphasic." (b) "The patient was positioned in bed in such a way that he could not move his left leg sideways or bend it at the knee" for "The patient's left leg was immobilized." (c) "His weight is beyond the norms of a typical child" for "He is overweight."
2. *Avoid trite phrases.* (a) "It has come to my attention" for "I learned." (b) "Up to this writing" for "now." (c) "It was observed that he wrote with his left hand" for "He wrote with his left hand." (Item 13 in Table 21-6, on page 726,

lists some wordy expressions and trite phrases and shows their concise equivalents.)

3. *Avoid useless repetitions.* (a) "The twins were exactly identical" for "The twins were identical." (b) "He was small in size" for "He was small." (c) "The family needs to make new changes" for "The family needs to make changes."

4. *Avoid abstract words or phrases.* (a) "She manifested overt aggressive hostility" for "She punched a younger child in the nose." (b) "A minority of the class was misbehaving" for "Five of the 30 children were out of their seats and shouting to one another."

5. *Avoid sentences that are either too long or too short.* The length of sentences is an important factor in readability. Numerous short, choppy sentences can make the text sound disjointed and dull, but long, complicated sentences can render the text difficult to follow. Varying sentence length is a way of maintaining the reader's interest and aiding comprehension. When you need a long sentence to communicate a difficult concept, use simple words and sentence structure.

6. *Avoid long paragraphs.* Restricting the content and length of paragraphs in a report contributes to the report's readability. A paragraph should contain a cohesive and unifying theme and usually should run about four or five sentences. Ordinarily, a paragraph that runs longer than a quarter of a page strains the reader's attention span and impairs the reader's ability to recognize the unifying themes and ideas. If you have written a long paragraph, break it down and reorganize it.

If it is possible to cut a word out, always cut it out.
—George Orwell

ATTEND TO GRAMMAR AND STYLE

Principle 21. Attend carefully to grammar and writing style.

You must follow conventional grammatical rules in writing psychological reports. A good general reference for technical writing is the American Psychological Association's (1994b) *Publication Manual.* For specific questions, consult a dictionary, style manual, or grammar text. Let's now consider some important grammatical, stylistic, and structural aspects of report writing.

1. *Abbreviations.* In general, do not use abbreviations in a report. Terms such as *etc.* can be misleading. Do not use the abbreviation *approx.* for *approximately, TA* for *target adolescent, CC* for *comparison child, E* for *examiner,* or *EE* for *examinee,* or other similar types of abbreviations. If you do need to use abbreviations, anticipate problems the reader might have in understanding them. It is permissible to abbreviate the names of commonly used tests (e.g., *WISC–III* for the Wechsler Intelligence Scale for Children–Third Edition). However, the first time you refer to a test, use its complete name, followed immediately by the accepted abbreviation in parentheses. Similarly, the first time you refer to a university, such as San Diego State University, add its abbreviation (*SDSU*) after its name if you plan to use the abbreviation later in the report. You can use an abbreviation such as *IQ,* however, because it is a familiar term. Always capitalize this term and write it without periods. Avoid acronyms whenever possible.

2. *Capitalization.* Capitalize the first letter of each major word in a test or subtest name, such as Digit Span. Capitalization helps the reader distinguish a particular test or subtest, such as the WISC–III Vocabulary subtest, from the skill that it measures, such as vocabulary. Capitalize the first

Calvin and Hobbes   by Bill Watterson

CALVIN AND HOBBES © 1993 Watterson. Reprinted with permission of UNIVERSAL PRESS SYNDICATE. All rights reserved.

letter of the child's IQ classification, as in Average classification or High Average classification. Do not capitalize terms that refer to abilities, such as language skills or visual-motor abilities, because these terms do not refer to a test. Also, do not capitalize the terms *examiner* and *examinee*.

3. *Hyphens.* The rules for hyphenation are complex. It is helpful to consult a dictionary or other sources, such as *The Chicago Manual of Style* (University of Chicago Press, 1993). A term such as *7-year-old* is usually hyphenated, both as a noun (the 7-year-old) and as a compound adjective (a 7-year-old child). Whatever style you use, be consistent throughout the report.

4. *Punctuation.* Effective punctuation will help clarify your writing and enhance the report's readability. Punctuation cues the reader to the relationship between ideas, as well as to the normal pauses and inflections that help emphasize the main ideas and concepts in the report. The placement of quotation marks sometimes presents a problem. Always place a period or comma before the closing quotation mark. Place a colon, semicolon, or question mark after the closing quotation mark, unless it is part of the quoted material. Again, use a style manual or similar source to check your punctuation.

5. *Tense.* A problem you may encounter with tense is how to determine when to use the past tense and when to use the present tense. In general, refer to the examinee's enduring traits—such as physical characteristics, sex, ethnicity, and intelligence—in the present tense. For example, in the following sentence, the present tense is more appropriate than the past tense: "Leah is a dark-haired, 18-year-old female." However, describe behavior you observed during the evaluation in the past tense, because the child displayed the behavior on a specific past occasion: "John was cooperative during the evaluation" or "Martin held his pen in a firm grip."

In discussing a child's level of intelligence, usually use the present tense: "The child is currently functioning in the Average range of intelligence." If the past tense were used in this sentence, it would sound as if the child were deceased or no longer functioning in the Average range at the time the report was written.

When discussing the testing environment, use the past tense, as in "The classroom was brightly lit and had paintings by many children on the wall." The past tense is more appropriate because the room might not always be brightly lit or have children's paintings on the wall.

6. *Spacing.* When you are planning to send a report to an agency, use single spacing. During your training, however, double space your reports to allow for corrections and the instructor's comments.

The following are examples of statements with stylistic and grammatical difficulties.

1. "His general performance would be described as being within the Average range." The phrase "would be described as" is unnecessary. *Suggestion:* "His general performance is within the Average range."

2. "Phil constantly kept finding things in a drawer of the desk he was being evaluated at to play with throughout the interview, ie. paper clips, rubber bands, pens, etc." This is an awkward sentence, and it contains punctuation mistakes. The abbreviation *i.e.* should have two periods and be followed by a comma. However, *e.g.* (for example) would be a better choice than *i.e.* (that is). In clinical report writing, *etc.* should not be used because the examinee's behaviors should be listed, not left to the reader's imagination. *Suggestion:* "Throughout the evaluation, Phil played with paper clips, rubber bands, and pens that he found in the desk drawer."

3. This statement appeared in a report about an 8-year-old with a Wechsler Verbal Scale IQ of 92, Performance Scale IQ of 112, and Full Scale IQ of 101: "Within a single subtest, his behavior and even speech seemed to deteriorate as the problems got successively more difficult." There are several problems here. First, does the writer mean every subtest, just one subtest, or a few subtests? Second, in what way did the examinee's behavior deteriorate? The word *deteriorate* carries connotations of severe impairment and should be used with caution. Third, to obtain average IQs, the examinee must have been able to perform adequately on several of the subtests. Consequently, whatever deterioration occurred must have been short-lived. *Suggestion:* The writer should give examples of how the child's behavior and speech changed. Also, the writer should avoid using dramatic phrasing in the report, such as "his behavior and even speech," as we discussed earlier. Just saying "his behavior and speech" is sufficient.

4. "She was observed in the outdoor, free play period." Be careful how you modify terms. *Suggestion:* "She was observed outdoors during a free play period."

5. "When approached by a child whom he appeared to dislike, however, Albert threw a ball at the child with one fist." It sounds as if the other child had one fist or Albert threw with one fist, which, of course, is difficult to do. *Suggestion:* "When approached by a child whom he appeared to dislike, Albert threw a ball at him."

Exercise 21-12. Evaluating Statements with Stylistic and Grammatical Difficulties

---

Read the statements, evaluate them, and then compare your evaluations with those in the Comment section.

1. This statement was based on Profile 7 in Table 21-3 (page 699): "Her lack of reflection may prove to be problematic."

2. "The most striking observation was the contrast between his level of interest and motivation during a visual-motor nonverbal task and during a task involving verbal conceptual reasoning. Before answering questions involving arithmetical reasoning, he looked at the examiner in disbelief."

3. "John goes to HMMS."
4. "His mother said, that Fred is lazy."
5. "She scored an IQ score of 111."
6. "Ann has shown scores of average intelligence with a lack of intellectual maturity."
7. "He does not demonstrate good pencil control at the automatic level yet."
8. "Although quite verbal, this 9-year-old girl did not exhibit the egocentric babbling of a less mature child."

Comment

1. This sentence has two problems. First, does the writer really mean *lack of* reflection? If the examinee lacked reflection, how could she perform in the Above-Average range, especially considering that Similarities and other WISC–III subtests may require reflection? Second, the word *problematic* is not clear. The writer likely means that the examinee's impulsiveness might lead to difficulties when she is faced with problem-solving situations.

2. The second sentence doesn't follow from the first. The second sentence should explain the child's different levels of interest and motivation in the two tasks. Instead, it seems to describe a new task. Also, the writer does not tell which task inspired the higher level of interest and motivation.

3. This statement will not be clear to readers who are unfamiliar with the abbreviation. *Suggestion:* "John attends Horace Mann Middle School."

4. There is no need for a comma after the verb, and the placement of the period is incorrect. *Suggestion:* "His mother said that Fred is lazy" or "His mother said, 'Fred is lazy.'"

5. This sentence has two problems. First, referring to IQ as a score is redundant. Second, the source of the IQ should be specified. *Suggestion:* Say, "She obtained a WISC–III IQ of 111 ± 7" and then present other descriptive information as needed, such as the IQ classification and percentile rank.

6. The two ideas in this sentence appear to be in conflict with each other. Although the term *intellectual maturity* is imprecise, average intelligence would seem to be suggestive of intellectual maturity.

7. This statement is confusing because it is not clear to what "automatic level" refers. *A possible restatement:* "John's fine motor control is poorly developed, as can be seen by his inability to write legibly."

8. Observations of behavior should concentrate on what the child did, not on what the child did not do. Why does the writer choose to focus on the "egocentric babbling of a less mature child"? Why does the sentence begin with *Although? Suggestion:* "Jane used mature language in her conversation."

AAAAA—American Association Against Acronym Abuse

IMPROVE YOUR WRITING STYLE

Principle 22. Develop strategies to improve your writing, such as using an outline, revising your first draft, and proofreading your final report.

You should develop writing strategies that suit your needs and style. Here are four effective methods to improve the quality of your writing: (a) use an outline, (b) reread and edit your first draft, (c) use a word processor to write your report, and (d) proofread your report.

Use an Outline

Writing from an outline will help you maintain the logic of the report because you identify the main ideas and subordinate concepts at the outset (American Psychological Association, 1994b). An outline also will help you write more precisely and ensure that you include all pertinent assessment

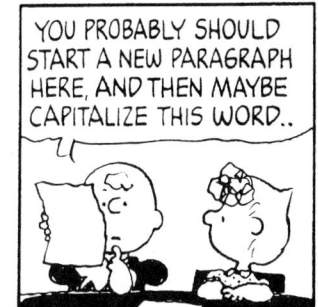

PEANUTS reprinted by permission of United Feature Syndicate, Inc.

information. You can use the outline of the nine sections of a report shown earlier in the chapter as the basis for a more detailed report outline tailored to each case.

Reread and Edit Your First Draft

Check your draft for errors and for vague, ambiguous, or potentially misleading material. Everything in the report should be clear. You want to write a succinct report that deals with relevant issues and avoids undue generalizations and speculations. A guiding theme underlying the 22 principles in this chapter is that reports should be written so that someone who is not in the field of psychology can understand them.

The following checklist may help you assess the quality of your report:

1. Are the identifying data correct? Be sure to check the accuracy of the examinee's name, date of birth, chronological age, and sex; the date of evaluation; your name; and the date of report.
2. Is the referral question stated succinctly?
3. Does the background material contain *relevant* historical information, such as developmental, educational, family, medical, and psychiatric history and prior test results and recommendations?
4. Do the behavioral observations enable the reader to form a clear impression of the examinee and his or her behavior?
5. Are the names of all the assessment procedures noted and spelled correctly in the report?
6. Are the reliability and validity of the assessment findings addressed?
7. Are the test scores, percentile ranks, and other assessment-related data correct?
8. Are the confidence interval and classification of the IQ presented?
9. Is the information obtained from various sources clearly organized, succinct, and integrated, and are the sources of the information noted?
10. Does the report answer the referral question?
11. Are the present results compared with past results (if available) and with the results of other current assessments (if performed, such as a speech and language evaluation), and are any discrepancies noted and discussed?
12. Are themes about the examinee's functioning clearly delineated?
13. Are illustrative examples and descriptions provided?
14. Are any doubts you have about the information, findings, or conclusions stated clearly?
15. Does the report identify questions that remain unanswered or that are answered incompletely?
16. Are the clinical impressions clearly stated?
17. Do the recommendations clearly follow from the findings?
18. Do most or all of the recommendations include the rationale for the recommendation?
19. Are the recommendations clear and practical?
20. Are speculations clearly labeled as such?
21. Is the summary accurate, succinct, self-contained, coherent, and readable?
22. Is the writing style professional and grammatically correct?
23. Is the report free of jargon?
24. Is the report free of biased wording?
25. Is the report free of ambiguities?
26. Is the report straightforward and objective?
27. Does the report focus on the strengths and weaknesses of the examinee, including adaptive capabilities as well as pathology?
28. Is the report of reasonable length? (The length will vary depending on the referral question, the number of tests administered, the number of people interviewed, the number of other procedures that were used, and so forth.)
29. Has the report been run through a spelling and grammar checker?
30. Has the report been proofread carefully?

Use a Computer with a Word-Processing Program to Write the Report

Word-processing programs can help you in writing a report (Matthews, Bowen, & Matthews, 1996). If your computer's word-processing program has a thesaurus, use the thesaurus to make your writing more varied and interesting, but keep your language clear and understandable. The spell-check and grammar-check functions contained in many word-processing programs also are useful, but they can lull you into thinking that a report is in better shape than it really is. In the first-draft stage of development, grammar checkers are most helpful for picking up simple mechanical problems, such as a missing parenthesis or quotation mark, and for picking up writing quirks, such as too many short sentences or overuse of "to be" verbs. However, spell checkers and grammar checkers cannot evaluate the meaningfulness of your writing. You must make those judgments yourself.

When you use a word-processing program, save your work frequently and make a backup copy of the file on a diskette (or other storage device) as a safeguard against inadvertently erasing the file. Remember to update the backup file each time you make revisions. When you are not working on the computer, store the backup disk (or storage device) in a safe place (such as a locked file cabinet). *It is important to treat your computer files and disks (or other storage devices) as carefully as you would treat confidential paper files.*

Some writers prefer to make a printout of the draft and then make changes by hand, which they later enter into the computer. Use the spell-check function as one of the last steps after you have revised and edited the report and have made the necessary changes in the computer.

Table 21-5
Checklist for Accuracy and Completeness of an Intelligence Test Report

CHECKLIST FOR ACCURACY AND COMPLETENESS OF AN INTELLIGENCE TEST REPORT

Examinee's name: _____   Report number: _____

Examiner's name: _____   Date of report: _____

Directions: Use this checklist to evaluate the accuracy and completeness of an intelligence test report. Place a checkmark in the box after you check the item in the report. Write "NA" next to items that are not applicable.

❑ 1. **Report Title**

2. **Identifying Data**
❑   a. Examinee's name
❑   b. Date of birth
❑   c. Age
❑   d. Grade
❑   e. Date of examination
❑   f. Date of report
❑   g. Examiner's name

❑ 3. **Name of Test Administered**

❑ 4. **Reason for Referral**

❑ 5. **Background Information**

6. **Behavioral Observations**
❑   a. Attitude toward examiner
❑   b. Attitude toward test situation
❑   c. Attitude toward self
❑   d. Work habits
❑   e. Reaction to successes
❑   f. Reaction to failures
❑   g. Speech
❑   h. Vocabulary
❑   i. Visual-motor abilities
❑   j. Motor abilities

7. **Test Results and Impressions**
❑   a. Each IQ, area, cluster, scale, or factor score is reported with the appropriate standard score
❑   b. Each IQ, area, cluster, scale, or factor score is based on the correct number of tests or subtests
❑   c. A percentile rank is given for each IQ, area, cluster, scale, or factor score

❑   d. Range designation is given for the Full Scale IQ, composite standard-age score, general conceptual ability score, broad cognitive ability score, or other total score
❑   e. Confidence interval is given for the Full Scale IQ, composite standard-age score, general conceptual ability score, broad cognitive ability score, or other total score
❑   f. Statement describing confidence interval
❑   g. Statement about reliability of test results
❑   h. Statement about validity of test results
❑   i. Statement about a skill described by a percentile rank or qualitative statement (such as strength, weakness, average, above average, or below average)
❑   j. Statements comparing one skill with another skill based on significant differences (and low frequencies [base rates] of differences) between scores on which assessments of skills were based
❑   k. Interpretations based on substantial data
❑   l. Clear recommendations

8. **Summary**
❑   a. Short (about one paragraph)
❑   b. At least one statement (e.g., an idea, thought, or theme) included from each section of the report

9. **Signature**
❑   a. Examiner's name typewritten at end of report
❑   b. Examiner's signature included at end of report

10. **Technical Qualities**
❑   a. Free of spelling errors
❑   b. Free of grammatical errors

Proofread Your Report

As you proofread your report, look for spelling errors, grammatical errors, omitted phrases, and other typing errors. You will need to make fewer major revisions as you gain experience, but you will always need to proofread carefully. You may find it helpful to read your report aloud while proofreading.

Even if you use the spell checker of a word-processing program, do not assume that your word usage is correct—you may have spelled the words correctly, but you may not have used them correctly. Also, you may have used a wrong word form (e.g., *difficulty* for *difficult*) that will elude spell checkers. If you have any questions about word usage, consult a dictionary or grammar text. If you have used a word-

Exhibit 21-1
Psychological Evaluation of a Student with a Reading Problem

PSYCHOLOGICAL EVALUATION

Name of examinee: Bill
Date of birth: April 21, 1992
Chronological age: 7-8
Grade: First

Date of examination: Jan. 15, 1999
Date of report: Jan. 20, 1999
Name of examiner: Phyllis Brown

Test Administered
Wechsler Intelligence Scale for Children–III (WISC–III):

VERBAL SCALE		PERFORMANCE SCALE	
Information	10	Picture Completion	14
Similarities	11	Coding	14
Arithmetic	9	Picture Arrangement	10
Vocabulary	7	Block Design	10
Comprehension	9	Object Assembly	10
Digit Span	7	Mazes	15

Verbal Scale IQ = 95
Performance Scale IQ = 111
Full Scale IQ = 103 ± 7 at the 95% confidence level

Reason for Referral
Bill was administered the WISC–III, with permission of his mother, in order for the examiner to obtain experience in administering and interpreting the WISC–III.

Background Information
Bill, a 7-year, 8-month-old boy, is currently in the first grade. His mother stated that he is experiencing reading difficulties. He reported that his favorite subjects in school are spelling and math and that he likes to "work hard." Outside the school he enjoys building things with Legos.

Behavioral Observations
Bill was pleasant, cooperative, and motivated throughout the testing session. He conversed comfortably with me at the beginning of the session and between subtests. He told me that he was having problems learning to read. During both verbal and nonverbal tasks, he occasionally became fidgety and restless, moving back and forth in the chair, sitting on his knees, and laying his head down on the table. This restless behavior occurred more frequently toward the end of subtests (as the items became more difficult) and as the session progressed. Despite his restlessness, Bill generally remained attentive and on task throughout the session. He was cooperative, put away the puzzle pieces in their boxes, and turned the pages of a subtest booklet when asked to do so. When frustrated, Bill occasionally asked me for help and exclaimed, "That's hard!" or "Can't do this!"

Bill's articulation was often poor, and his speech was occasionally difficult to understand. He often answered in the form of a question, as if unsure of his responses. During the verbal subtests that assessed social comprehension and language devel-

opment, Bill frequently gave long answers or several answers to the same question, some correct and some incorrect.

During two nonverbal subtests, one requiring visual sequencing and another requiring visual-spatial analytic and synthetic abilities, Bill proceeded quickly and systematically when the items were simple. However, as they became more difficult, he proceeded more slowly, often hesitating and moving the cards or blocks to different locations. Bill appeared particularly to enjoy puzzles and tasks involving making designs with blocks, and he said that he was disappointed when these tasks were over. In fact, when the puzzle completion task was over, he was eager to go back and try to complete a puzzle that he could not do earlier.

Assessment Results and Clinical Impressions
With a chronological age of 7-8, Bill achieved a Verbal Scale IQ of 95 (37th percentile), a Performance Scale IQ of 111 (79th percentile), and a Full Scale IQ of 103 ± 7 on the WISC–III. His overall performance is classified in the Average range and is equal to or higher than that of 55% of children his age (55th percentile). The chances that the range of scores from 96 to 110 includes his true IQ are about 95 out of 100. The present measure of his intellectual functioning appears to be reliable and valid because of his cooperativeness and willingness to try.

There is a 16-point difference between Bill's Verbal Scale IQ and Performance Scale IQ, which indicates that his nonverbal skills are better developed than his verbal skills. This difference may reflect a predominantly nonverbal cognitive style or greater interest and motivation during nonverbal than verbal tasks. As previously mentioned, he liked nonverbal tasks involving puzzles and creating designs with blocks. Bill also mentioned that he enjoyed building with Legos, a nonverbal spatially oriented activity.

In the verbal domain, Bill's skills range from below average to average. His range of factual knowledge, logical and abstract reasoning, numerical reasoning, and social comprehension are all average for his age. However, his word knowledge and immediate auditory memory are below average for his age. His word knowledge is less well developed than his overall verbal skills. Within the nonverbal domain, his ability to analyze and synthesize visual-spatial material, his visual sequencing ability, and his ability to synthesize concrete parts into meaningful wholes are average for his age. His ability to differentiate essential from nonessential details, speed and accuracy of eye-hand coordination, and visual-motor control are excellent for his age.

His below-average word knowledge and his excellent psychomotor speed and visual-motor control indicate that Bill performs better on tasks having visual-motor components rather than language components. He performs especially well on tasks requir-

(Continued)

Exhibit 21-1 *(Continued)*

ing visual-motor speed and precision. His excellent ability to differentiate essential from nonessential details, coupled with his poor language development, indicates that his ability to recognize and perceive details of objects visually is better developed than his ability to describe objects verbally.

His overall average verbal skills indicate that he has the ability to perform adequately in school subjects requiring verbal skills, but the reason for his reading difficulties remains unclear. Additional assessment is needed to assess the nature of his reading problems. Furthermore, Bill's nonverbal cognitive skills are well developed for his age, and thus he has the ability to perform well in subjects with nonverbal components.

Recommendations

It is recommended that further evaluation be conducted to assess the nature of his reading difficulties. Bill may also benefit from speech/language therapy and from exercises aimed at enhancing his word knowledge. Therefore, a speech and language evaluation is also recommended. It would be beneficial to capitalize on his affinity for visual-spatial activities by providing him with picture books, objects, puzzles, and other construction activities. During these activities Bill should be encouraged to describe and explain his actions.

Summary

Although Bill, who is 7 years, 8 months old, was occasionally fidgety and restless during the test, he remained attentive, on task, friendly, and cooperative throughout the session. His articulation was somewhat poor, and he occasionally was difficult to understand. He appeared to enjoy particularly tasks involving puzzles and creating designs with blocks. Bill achieved an IQ of 103 ± 7 on the WISC–III. This IQ is at the 55th percentile and in the Average range. The chances that the range of scores from 96 to 110 includes his true IQ are about 95 out of 100. The test results appear to give a reliable and valid estimate of his present level of intellectual functioning. His nonverbal skills are better developed than his verbal skills. Within the verbal domain, most skills are average, except for word knowledge and immediate auditory memory, which are below average for his age. Within the nonverbal domain, he shows strengths in differentiating essential from nonessential details, speed and accuracy of eye-hand coordination, and visual-motor control, and he shows average ability in analyzing and synthesizing visual-spatial material, visual sequencing, and synthesizing concrete parts into meaningful wholes. It is unclear how his reading difficulties are related to his poor language development and vice versa. Further evaluation is needed to assess his reading difficulties. Remedial activities should capitalize on his affinity for visual-spatial materials.

Phyllis Brown, M.A., Certified School Psychologist

---

processing program to write the report, check the final copy to see that it is formatted properly.

SPELLING CHECQUER

Eye halve a spelling chequer
It came with my pea sea
It plainly marques four my revue
Miss steaks eye kin knot sea.
Eye strike a key and type a word
And weight four it two say
Weather eye am wrong oar write
It shows me strait a weigh.

As soon as a mist ache is maid
It nose bee fore two long
And eye can put the error rite
Its rare lea ever wrong.
Eye have run this poem threw it
I am shore your pleased two no
Its letter perfect awl the weigh
My chequer tolled me sew.

—Sauce Unknown

Other Strategies to Improve Your Writing

After you have completed the first draft of your report, use the checklist shown in Table 21-5 to help you evaluate whether you have included all the pertinent details.

Another way you can improve your report-writing skills is by studying reports written by psychologists who write well. A well-written report based on the WISC–III can be found in Exhibit 21-1. It gives a good description of the child's behavior during the evaluation. It discusses the difference between the child's Verbal and Performance IQs and briefly describes each subtest. Finally, it provides recommendations.

Exhibit 21-2 presents a detailed analysis of a psychological report, based on a battery approach, to help you understand the sections of a report. It also may be helpful to review the other reports that are shown throughout this book. The List of Exhibits at the beginning of this text identifies the various places where psychological reports are presented in the text.

The preceding strategies may require you to invest more time in a report than you had anticipated, but these strategies will result in greater accuracy and thoroughness and clearer communication.

Exhibit 21-2
Analysis of and Line-by-Line Commentary on a Psychological Evaluation of a Student with a Learning Problem

INTRODUCTORY REMARKS

Shown on the following pages is a case study of a 9-year-old boy who is experiencing difficulty at home and at school. This case provides a good example of how several sources—including parental interview, test scores, teacher consultation, and behavioral observations—may be used to develop hypotheses about a child's skills and to make recommendations. This well-organized report shows how recommendations can be addressed to the problem areas identified by the test results.

ANALYSIS OF THE REPORT

Identifying Data
Important identifying data about Newt appear at the beginning of the report. In an actual report, Newt's first and last name would be included.

Assessment Instruments
The section on tests administered included in this exhibit (and in other exhibits in this text) provides you with extended original data; such detail is optional in actual reports, where a listing of the test names might be sufficient. You may also cite the child's test scores in the Assessment Results section or provide a table of test scores in an appendix to the report. Although copies of the child's handwriting, spelling, drawings, and other raw data are included in this exhibit for teaching purposes, they may or may not be included in the actual reports.

Reason for Referral
The referral section gives the reason that Newt was referred and who initiated the referral.

Background Information
Background information is necessary because it sets the stage for understanding Newt's life situation and his relationship with others. The two paragraphs in this section deal with relevant educational and family information and medical history.

Behavioral Observations
The report notes the ease with which Newt became comfortable, because level of anxiety can affect test performance. The examiner also describes verbal difficulties observed in informal conversation. Reporting these difficulties may help the reader to isolate possible problem areas, become more alert to the implications of the test results, and consider possible explanations for this behavior. Anecdotal information about Newt's style of problem solving and dealing with frustration tends to complete Newt's profile and leads smoothly into the test data that follow.

Assessment Results and Clinical Impressions
The most notable characteristic of Newt's WISC–III scores is the 24-point discrepancy between his Verbal and Performance Scale IQs. Table A-2 in Appendix A shows that this difference is significant at the .01 level. Thus, the Verbal/Performance difference cannot be attributed to chance. The examiner also determined, from base-rate data in Table A-5 in Appendix A, that this

difference is large enough to be considered an unusual occurrence, occurring in less than 5.2% of the population. The examiner also determined whether the Verbal and Performance subtests differed significantly from their respective means. Each mean was calculated: Verbal Scale subtest $M = 6.2$, Performance Scale subtest $M = 10.2$. The obtained differences between the subtests and their respective scale means were compared with the differences listed in Table A-6 of Appendix A. None of the Verbal subtests were found to differ significantly from the Verbal subtests' mean. However, the score for Coding was significantly lower ($p < .01$) than the mean scaled score for the Performance subtests. The examiner also determined standard scores, confidence levels, and significant interindividual and intraindividual subtest differences before writing the Assessment Results and Clinical Impressions section.

The individual subtest scores suggest that Newt's strengths lie in spatial reasoning ability and perceptual integration. Newt also performed well on tasks requiring holistic, simultaneous processing, while doing less well with tasks that are primarily sequential in nature. Weaknesses were noted in auditory processing skills—that is, short-term auditory memory (low Digit Span score) and psychomotor speed (low Coding score). Verbal subtest scores were consistently below average.

Newt's Draw-A-Person performance was compared with his WISC–III IQ.

Newt's Wechsler Individual Achievement Test scores were then discussed. The examiner pointed out areas of difficulty. Hypotheses about the sources of these difficulties were offered, together with evidence to support the hypotheses.

The Vineland Adaptive Behavior Scales suggested some social immaturity. The examiner suggested that Newt's social immaturity might be related to the limits placed on his freedom of movement and on his responsibilities.

Newt's performance on the Bender-Gestalt was well within normal limits.

Classroom observations, although based on a limited sample of behavior, corroborated the formal assessment results. Newt appears to have difficulty attending to reading assignments.

Recommendations
The Recommendations section lists specific steps for remediation that could be implemented by the family or school staff or by Newt himself. These suggestions include emphasizing language skill development through speech and language therapy, using areas of strength to build skills, and personal counseling for the

(Continued)

Exhibit 21-2 *(Continued)*

family. The first statement is directed to the referral question regarding academic placement. Because placement decisions in a school setting are the responsibility of a multidisciplanary team, the examiner suggests that the assessment findings be considered when eligibility/placement decisions are made. The first three specific recommendations focus on Newt's general needs. The fourth recommendation shows how Newt's strengths could be used in new programs. The fifth recommendation focuses on family involvement. Although the initial referral did not address family stress, information brought up during the assessment

session suggested to the examiner that this area was also important. The last recommendation focuses on Newt's social immaturity.

Summary

The summary provides a concise wrapup of the report and its findings. It introduces no new information, but consolidates the report into a few easily read sentences. It highlights central issues of the report.

THE REPORT WITH LINE-BY-LINE NOTATION

Name: Newt

Date of birth: April 10, 1990

Chronological age: 9-8

Date of examination: December 12, 1999

Date of report: December 15, 1999

Grade: Third

Tests Administered

Wechsler Intelligence Scale for Children–III

VERBAL SCALE		PERFORMANCE SCALE	
Information	4	Picture Completion	13
Similarities	7	Coding	6
Arithmetic	6	Picture Arrangement	9
Vocabulary	8	Block Design	12
Comprehension	7	Object Assembly	13
Digit Span	5	Symbol Search	7

Verbal Scale IQ = 80
Performance Scale IQ = 104
Full Scale IQ = 90 ± 6 at the 95% confidence level

Wechsler Individual Achievement Test

	STANDARD SCORE	PERCENTILE
Basic Reading	67	1
Reading Comprehension	71	3
Listening Comprehension	83	13
Spelling	74	4
Written Expression	76	5
Numerical Operation	88	21
Mathematics Reasoning	94	34

Reading = 64 ± 6 at the 95% confidence level
Mathematics = 90 ± 7 at the 95% confidence level

Writing = 70 ± 8 at the 95% confidence level

Vineland Adaptive Behavior Scales (Survey Form)
Adaptive Behavior Composite = 76 ± 11 at the 95% confidence level, 5th percentile

Naglieri Draw-A-Person
Standard score = 99
Percentile = 47th

Bender-Gestalt
Standard score = 81
Percentile = 10th

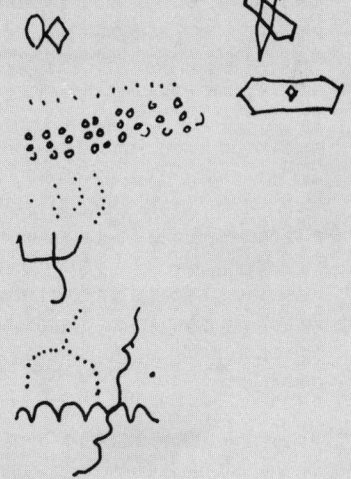

(Continued)

Exhibit 21-2 *(Continued)*

Reason for Referral

1 Newt was referred by his teacher because of learning	1–3 who was referred and reason
2 problems at school, particularly in reading, spelling, and	
3 language arts. His teacher noted that Newt had specific	3–8 teacher's observations
4 problems such as substituting phonetically similar words	
5 when reading aloud (e.g., "chair" for *cheer*, "then" for *when*),	
6 omitting inflectional endings (i.e., *-s*, *-ed*, *-ing*) when reading,	
7 and misspelling words by attempting to spell them	
8 phonetically.	

Background Information

9 Newt, a 9-year, 8-month-old boy, is in the third grade. A	9 current age and grade level
10 recent parental divorce, the death of a grandfather, and the	10–13 current family stress
11 return home of Newt's two older brothers have made for a	
12 tumultuous home setting. Newt's mother seems to be trying	
13 to deal with numerous areas of frustration and tension.	
14 Besides his two older brothers, Newt has a 13-year-old	14–16 family constellation and relationship with siblings
15 sister with whom he is close. Newt appears to be in good	15–16 health history
16 health, and no serious childhood illnesses were reported.	
17 His mother recalled that some of Newt's motor and speech	17–18 developmental history
18 milestones were delayed.	

Behavioral Observations

19 Newt, who arrived with his mother, initially seemed shy with	19 who came to session
20 the examiner. Nevertheless, he willingly came with the	20–22 initial relation with examiner
21 examiner and, except for occasionally laughing anxiously,	
22 seemed relatively at ease. Newt tended to be chatty, with a	22–23 mode of relating during test
23 somewhat disconnected conversational style. Numerous	23–32 language problems and examples
24 sound substitutions and omissions (such as "vorsed" for	
25 *divorced* and "skies" for *disguised*) and syntax errors (often	
26 in tenses as well as subject-verb agreement) were noted in	
27 his spontaneous speech. He also displayed some word	
28 retrieval difficulties, such as labeling dresser knobs as holes;	
29 auditory discrimination difficulties, such as mishearing *cow*	
30 as *car*; and difficulty repeating short sentences (such as	
31 rendering the statement "How many things make a dozen?"	
32 as "How much make a bunch?").	
33 Newt's work style tended to be slow and cautious,	33 general response style
34 and he seemed to want to avoid all errors. Although	34 response to errors
35 generally cooperative, he sometimes wanted to give up	35–37 response to frustration
36 when tasks became difficult, but persisted with mild	
37 verbal encouragement. Overall, his level of activity was	37 activity level
38 age-appropriate, and he reacted appropriately to success	38 response to success and failures
39 and failure.	

Assessment Results and Clinical Impressions

40 On the WISC–III, Newt, with a chronological age of 9-8,	40 WISC–III named, chronological age
41 achieved a Verbal Scale IQ of 80 (9th percentile), a	41 Verbal Scale IQ
42 Performance Scale (nonverbal) IQ of 104 (61st percentile),	42 Performance Scale IQ
43 and a Full Scale IQ of 90 ± 6. The chances his true score is	43–44 Full Scale IQ
44 between 84 and 96 are about 95 out of 100. His overall	44–45 confidence limits
45 performance is classified in the Average range and is equal	45–46 intellectual classification and percentile rank
46 to or higher than that of 25% of children his age. These, as	
47 well as other test results, appear to be reliable and valid.	47 test's reliability and validity

(Continued)

Exhibit 21-2 (Continued)

48 A significant difference of 24 points was noted between 49 Newt's Verbal Scale IQ and Performance Scale IQ. A 50 difference this large occurs in less than 3.1% of the 51 population. Functioning was low average in verbal areas and 52 average in performance areas. Newt has strengths in the 53 areas of spatial reasoning and perceptual integration and 54 weaknesses in the area of processing speed. Further 55 analysis finds that Newt performs well on tasks requiring 56 holistic, simultaneous processing while doing less well with 57 tasks that are primarily sequential in nature.	48–52 Verbal/Performance Scale discrepancy noted and described 52–53 strengths 54 weaknesses 55–56 other strengths 56–57 other weaknesses
58 Qualitatively, many of Newt's verbal responses on the 59 WISC–III were confused and unusual. For example, he 60 named the days of the week when asked for the seasons of 61 the year and responded to the question "How many hours 62 are in a day?" with "28 pounds." In general, his answers 63 tended to be concrete and poorly organized, with a loose, 64 run-on sentence structure.	58–59 qualitative responses on the WISC–III 59–62 conceptual difficulties 62–64 summary of verbal difficulties
65 On the Naglieri Draw-A-Person test, a screening 66 measure of nonverbal ability, Newt scored at the 47th 67 percentile. This result is somewhat higher than the 68 percentile rank associated with his Full Scale WISC–III IQ, 69 but closer to his Performance (nonverbal) IQ.	65–67 Draw-A-Person results 67–69 comparison of Draw-A-Person and WISC–III
70 On the Wechsler Individual Achievement Test, Newt's 71 reading ability (that is, word recognition and passage 72 comprehension) and writing ability (that is, spelling words 73 and writing paragraphs) both rank below the 5th percentile.	70–73 WIAT results
74 Although he knows numerous spelling rules, he has 75 considerable difficulty in employing them appropriately. For 76 example, he spelled the word *play* as *pla*. His reading does 77 not reflect an effective use of phonic skills. For example, he 78 read the word *now* for *know* and said *inside* for *instead*. He	74–78 phonetic difficulties
79 can identify letters reliably. In attempting to read words, he 80 tends to fractionate each phonetic unit and then is often 81 unable to integrate the units effectively. The scores that 82 Newt obtained on his achievement testing, in both the 83 Reading and Writing sections, were well below what we 84 would expect based on his age, grade, and current cognitive 85 ability.	79 ability to identify letters 79–81 reading style 81–85 evaluation of reading and writing scores
86 Newt's arithmetical skills are at the 37th percentile. 87 Although he seems to have mastered simple addition and 88 subtraction skills, including borrowing and carrying, he has 89 difficulty with some age-appropriate arithmetic tasks.	86–89 arithmetic score and discussion of score
90 It is not surprising that this student, who has difficulty in 91 auditory discrimination (for example, saying "masic" for 92 *magic* and "gammel" for *gamble*) and verbal and perceptual 93 sequencing, also has difficulty spelling and reading 94 phonetically. For example, Newt was unable to sequence all	90–94 further comments on Newt's achievement scores
95 the sounds when asked the name of his school. Other 96 common information that he seemed unable to give included 97 his own address, his brother's age, and labels for familial 98 relationships, such as *uncle*.	94–98 examples of information deficits
99 On the Vineland Adaptive Behavior Scales, with Newt's 100 mother as informant, Newt was given an Adaptive Behavior 101 Composite of 76 ± 11, which suggests adaptive functioning	99 Vineland Adaptive Behavior Scales 100 informant described 101–102 scores on Vineland presented and interpreted

(Continued)

Exhibit 21-2 *(Continued)*

102 at the 5th percentile. This indicates that his adaptive level is	
103 moderately low. Newt's freedom and responsibility are	103–107 home environment as it relates to social maturity
104 limited at home, as his mother does not allow him to leave	
105 the yard. His chores at home are few, and his mother still	
106 helps him with many self-care activities, including combing	
107 his hair.	
108 His performance on the Bender-Gestalt suggested no	108–111 Bender-Gestalt results
109 perceptual-motor difficulties (errors = 3, 40th percentile).	
110 His level of perceptual-motor maturation is close to that of	
111 a 7½- to 8-year-old child.	
112 Newt was also observed in his classroom for	112–125 observation in classroom
113 approximately 50 minutes from 9:30 to 10:20 a.m. on	
114 December 8, 1999. The class was engaged in a reading	
115 assignment for the first part of the period and in an	
116 arithmetic assignment for the second part of the period.	
117 During the entire time Newt never raised his hand to answer	
118 a question; several other students did so. He often looked	
119 around the room, stared out the window, and played with his	
120 pencil. Only one other child was similarly distracted. When	
121 asked by his teacher to read, he was unable to sound out	
122 words correctly. However, he did answer a simple arithmetic	
123 problem correctly. His teacher was sensitive to his reading	
124 difficulty and complimented him on his correct arithmetic	
125 response.	

Recommendations

126 Newt may qualify for placement in a program for children	126–133 diagnostic impression
127 with learning disabilities and for a speech/language therapy	
128 program. The scores that Newt obtained on his achievement	
129 testing, in both the Reading and Spelling sections, were well	
130 below what we would expect based on his age, grade, and	
131 current cognitive ability. His school's special education	
132 multidisciplinary team should consider the current	132–136 reference to multidisciplinary team
133 assessment results, along with other information available to	
134 them, when making an eligibility determination. Newt is	
135 experiencing difficulty in school because of language	
136 processing difficulties. The following recommendations are	136–137 recommendations introduced
137 offered:	
138 1. Because of Newt's weakness in language skills, a	138–140 possible goals of program
139 program of education with particular emphasis on	
140 language and language-related skills is recommended.	
141 The program should emphasize oral language, reading,	141–143 additional specifics of language program
142 and writing skills to improve Newt's areas of academic	
143 weakness.	
144 2. Speech and language therapy integrated into the	144–152 speech and language therapy recommended
145 education curriculum would be desirable. It appears that	
146 Newt's weakness in auditory perception might be part of	
147 the basis for his difficulties with oral language, reading,	
148 and writing. If the speech-language pathologist's	
149 assessment supports this assumption, Newt might profit	
150 from intensive work on phonemic awareness skills. The	
151 work on phonemic awareness skills would provide the	
152 underpinning to instruction in reading and writing skills.	
153 3. It would be particularly beneficial for Newt to work on	153–156 phonics recommendation
154 learning to spell the same sounds, syllables, and words	

(Continued)

Exhibit 21-2 *(Continued)*

155 — that he is learning to read. The spelling encoding and 156 — reading decoding would reinforce each other.	
157 — 4. Newt appears to have difficulty with memorization and 158 — retrieval of information. He may need particular help 159 — learning math "facts" and phonic rules. This is an area in 160 — which visual aids might be especially helpful.	157–160 — recommendation for visual aids
161 — 5. Newt's nonverbal spatial strengths should be used in the 162 — remediation program. Teachers can help by making 163 — special, additional efforts to use visual aids as much as	161–163 — how strengths might be used
164 — possible. Charts, diagrams, models, timelines, maps, 165 — globes, illustrations, dioramas, and demonstrations might 166 — prove very helpful to Newt.	164–166 — additional recommendation for visual aids
167 — 6. Newt's mother could use guidance to help sort out and 168 — resolve personal as well as family stress. Some possible	167–168 — goal of involving mother 168–174 — specific issues for mother to resolve
169 — areas on which she might focus would include 170 — encouraging communication among family members, 171 — dealing with hostilities felt toward her husband and older 172 — children, learning how to cope with being a single parent, 173 — and helping her children deal with the issue of the 174 — divorce.	
175 — 7. Newt's mother should be encouraged to help Newt 176 — develop more independent daily living skills. A program 177 — emphasizing social skills should be considered.	175–177 — additional areas for remediation

Summary

178 — Newt, who is 9-8 years old, was referred because of
179 — educational difficulties. His medical history was normal, but
180 — there were some developmental delays. Newt's cooperative
181 — behavior and other factors suggest that the testing results
182 — are reliable and valid. Newt showed unusually diverse
183 — strengths and weaknesses across intellectual areas, with
184 — verbal abilities at a below-average level and performance
185 — abilities at an average level. Overall, Newt obtained a WISC–
186 — III Full Scale IQ of 90 ± 6, which is at the 25th percentile
187 — and in the Average range. He has made little progress in
188 — developing skills in spelling and word recognition. These
189 — deficits are probably manifestations of his language
190 — processing difficulties. Socially, Newt acts like a child
191 — younger than his age. He appears to have a learning
192 — disability and language impairment. Recommendations are
193 — that he be provided with a program focusing on language
194 — and speech therapy. In addition, his family should be advised
195 — to seek counseling to help them resolve their problems in
196 — the home. If there are any questions about this report or
197 — any of these findings, please feel free to contact me at
198 — (201) 123-4567.

178–198 — summary

199 — (Signature of Examiner)
200 — Examiner's name
201 — Examiner's title

199 — signature

Here are some humorous examples of what can happen when writers fail to proofread and correct their work:

- It is important to proofread carfully!
- After a week of therapy, his back was better, and after two weeks it had completely disappeared.
- Why let worry kill you off—let our professional psychologists help!
- At the IEP meeting the student will need a disposition. We will get Ms. Blank to dispose of him.
- The client's past medical history has been remarkably insignificant, with only a 25-pound weight loss in the past four days.
- He has occasional, constant, and infrequent headaches.
- The preschooler has one teenage sibling, but no other abnormalities.
- The adolescent was alert and unresponsive.
- The child was tearful and crying constantly. She also appeared to be depressed.
- The medical history indicates that the X-rated picture of her brain is normal.
- The client has no past history of successful suicides.
- Mr. Jones has been depressed ever since he began seeing me in January 2000.
- The adolescent completed therapy feeling much better except for her original complaints.

Table 21-6 will help you avoid some common pitfalls in report writing; study it carefully. Accompanying each guideline are examples of sentences that fail to meet acceptable standards of communication. Try to figure out the error in the sentence before you read the *Appropriate Statement* column.

Exercise 21-13. Evaluating and Rewriting Sentences

Evaluate the following statements and then rewrite them. Check your evaluations and revisions with those in the Comment section.

1. "This examination with Helen just flew by in terms of time, because the subject answered quickly and without any hitch."
2. "The mother currently shares an apartment with another woman which she doesn't get along with."
3. "He generally answered quickly while malingering over questions about his home."
4. This statement was made about a child with an IQ of 73: "Some consideration of not allowing Tom to do less than his potential should be kept in mind."
5. "Beth's overreaction to criticism very often leads to a type of perseveration that impacts following behaviors until success is again achieved."
6. "Most of our LDs are resourced, but Mark is in a self-contained class because he's both LD and EMH."
7. "His score places him in the 92%ile."

Comment

1. The colloquial expressions "just flew by in terms of time" and "without any hitch" are not appropriate. Also, the term *the subject* is not recommended, even for research reports. *Suggestion:* "Helen was cooperative and well motivated and answered questions quickly."
2. *Which* is not the correct pronoun for "another woman." The proper pronoun would be *whom* (in "with whom"). Also, it is preferable to better identify "the mother" and to leave out the word *currently*. *Suggestion:* "Henry's mother and a woman with whom she doesn't get along share an apartment."
3. *Malingering,* which means pretending to be ill, is used incorrectly in this sentence. *Lingering* was probably intended.
4. This sentence is poorly written. *Suggestion:* "Every effort should be made to encourage Tom to work at a level commensurate with his abilities."
5. The sentence has several problems. First, the word *impacts,* which should not be used at all, is not used properly. Second, the phrase "type of perseveration" is vague. Third, the failure to cite specific behaviors leaves the reader with little concrete information. The writer should describe the child's reaction to criticism and how the child's reaction affected her performance.

CLOSE TO HOME © John McPherson. Reprinted with permission of UNIVERSAL PRESS SYNDICATE. All rights reserved.

Table 21-6
Some Guidelines for Good Report Writing

Guideline	Inappropriate statement	Appropriate statement
1. *Use language that is specific rather than general, definite rather than vague, concrete rather than abstract.*	"The child appeared to be mentally retarded."	"Tom obtained an IQ of 62 ±5 on the Wechsler Intelligence Scale for Children–Third Edition. This level of intelligence falls within the Mentally Retarded range."
2. *Make the verb of a sentence agree with the subject.* Use singular verb forms with singular subjects and plural verb forms with plural subjects.	"All of the students in the class was able to answer the question but Joey." "Lisa's grades are below average but is an accurate reflection of her abilities."	"All of the students in the class except Joey were able to answer the question." "Lisa's grades are below average but appear to be an accurate reflection of her abilities."
3. *Avoid unnecessary shifts in number, tense, subject, voice, or point of view.*	"When he heard about his grade, he complains." "Tom was born in California, but New York was his home in later years."	"When he heard about his grade, he complained." "Tom was born in California but lived in New York in later years."
4. *Avoid sentence fragments.* Fragments often occur when syntax becomes overly complicated.	"Not being sure of himself, several items which should have been easy for him, though he said they were difficult."	"Not being sure of himself, James said that several items were difficult, even though they should have been easy for him."
5. *Avoid redundancies and superfluous material.*	"His confidence was congruent with his abilities, and although he realized he was intelligent, he did not appear to undervalue it or overvalue it but rather seemed to accept it without evaluating it." "He did not appear to be anxious or concerned but was willing to try to succeed within his normal pattern of motivation." "The client complained of numbness and loss of feeling." "The client was excited and agitated." "The client is doing well without problems."	"He displayed a great deal of confidence in his abilities." "His motivation was satisfactory." "The client complained of numbness." "The client was agitated." "The client is doing well."
6. *Make the phrase at the beginning of a sentence refer to the grammatical subject.*	"Administering the Vineland Adaptive Behavior Scales, the mother admitted that enuresis was still a problem." "Analyzing the results of the two tests, the scores indicated below-average functioning." "After climbing the mountain, the view was nice."	"Replying to questions on the Vineland Adaptive Behavior Scales, the mother said that the child was enuretic." "The results of the two tests indicated below-average functioning." "After climbing the mountain, we enjoyed a nice view."
7. *Use verb forms of words rather than noun forms whenever possible.* Using verb forms puts life into reports and helps shorten sentences.	"The principal suggested the implementation of a point system for the improvement of Ricky's playground behavior." "The child is negligent in the details of her work."	"The principal suggested using a point system to improve Ricky's playground behavior." "The child neglects her work."
8. *Do not overuse the passive voice.* Although use of the passive voice is acceptable, its overuse can make a report sound dull. To change a sentence from passive to active voice, make the actor the subject of the sentence.	"Authorization for the absence was given by the teacher." "The previous testing was completed during her former hospitalization."	"The teacher authorized the absence." "Bonnie underwent assessment during her hospital stay earlier this year."

(Continued)

Table 21-6 *(Continued)*

Guideline	Inappropriate statement	Appropriate statement
9. *Provide adequate transitions.* Each sentence in a report should logically follow the previous one. The first sentence in a paragraph should prepare the reader for what follows.	"Richard is above average on memory items. He failed a memory item at an early level of the test."	"Richard's memory ability is above average relative to that of his age peers, even though he failed a memory item at an early level of the test."
10. *Keep related sentence elements together, and keep unrelated elements apart.* Express new thoughts in new sentences.	"Mrs. James has not attended any teacher conferences this year, and she has been married four times."	"Mrs. James has not attended any teacher conferences this year. She has been married four times."
11. *Express coordinate ideas in similar form.* Keep elements that are parallel in thought parallel in form. The content, not the style, should protect the interview report from monotony.	"The patient sat alone at 6 months. At 8 months, crawling began. Walking was noted at 12 months." "The recommendations are to learn a phonics approach and attending an individualized reading class."	"The patient sat alone at 6 months, crawled at 8 months, and walked at 12 months." "The recommendations are to use a phonics approach within an individualized reading class."
12. *Combine or restructure sentences to avoid repeating the same word, phrase, or idea.* Consecutive sentences that have the same subject or describe the same process often require revision.	"Jim's mother said that he had been in an automobile accident last year. His mother also told me that Jim has had memory difficulties since the accident." "Hyperactivity characterized Jim's behavior. He was hyperactive in class and hyperactive on the playground, and he was also hyperactive in the interview."	"Jim's mother said that he has had memory difficulties since his automobile accident last year." "Jim was constantly in motion in the classroom, on the playground, and during the interview."
13. *Omit needless words and phrases. Make every word count.*	"the question as to whether" "whether or not" "he is a man who" "call your attention to the fact that" "due to the fact that" "in order to" "for the purposes of" "in the event that" "in an effort to" "by means of" "in connection with" "for the length of time that" "with the result that" "is supportive of" "to be of great benefit" "in such a state that" "pertains to the problem of" "at this point in time" "am (or are) in agreement with" "insofar as" "with reference to" "many in number" "round in shape" "audible to the ear" "tasted bitter to the tongue" "second time in my life" "quickly with haste"	"whether" "whether" "he" "remind you" or "notify you" "because" "to" "to" or "so that" or "for" "if" "to" "with" "with" "while" "so" "supports" "beneficial" "so" or "such" "concerns" "now" "agree" "so" "regarding" "many" "round" "audible" "tasted bitter" "second time" "quickly"

(Continued)

Table 21-6 (Continued)

Guideline	Inappropriate statement	Appropriate statement
13. (Continued)	"there were several members of the family who said" "they were both alike" "four different teachers said"	"several family members said" "they were alike" "four teachers said"
14. *Avoid misplaced modifiers.* Misplaced modifiers add to confusion and occasionally create unintended humor in a report. Be sure that modifiers qualify the appropriate elements in the sentence. Modifiers should be placed (a) close to the words they modify and (b) away from words that they might mistakenly be taken to modify.	"In response to my instructions, Aaron picked up the ball and walked around the room with his left hand." "Dr. Jones instructed the patient while in the hospital to watch his diet carefully."	"In response to my instructions, Aaron picked up the ball with his left hand and then walked around the room." "While visiting her patient in the hospital, Dr. Jones told him to watch his diet carefully."
15. *Avoid the use of qualifiers.* Words such as *rather, very, little,* and *pretty* are unneeded and are best left out of a report.	"The patient was very attentive." "She was a pretty good student." "a pretty important rule"	"The patient was attentive." "She was a good student" or "She was a mediocre student" or "She had a grade-point average of 3.4." "an important rule"
16. *Use words correctly.* Misused words reflect unfavorably on the writer and discredit the report. Two commonly misused words are *affect* and *effect.*	"The behavior modification approach used by the teacher seems to have had a favorable affect on Edward."	"The behavior modification approach used by the teacher seems to have had a favorable effect on Edward" or "The behavior modification approach used by the teacher seemed to affect Edward favorably."
17. *Avoid fancy words.* The line between fancy words and plain words is sometimes alarmingly fine. The wise writer will avoid an elaborate word when a simple one will suffice. The interview report must not become a two-page exhibition of the writer's professional vocabulary. The best writers use vocabulary true to their own experience.	"The patient exhibited apparent partial paralysis of motor units of the superior sinistral fibers of the genioglossus, resulting in insufficient lingual approximation of the palatoalveolar regions. A condition of insufficient frenulum development was noted, which produced not only sigmatic distortion but also obvious ankyloglossia."	"The patient was tongue-tied."
18. *Do not take shortcuts at the expense of clarity.* Acronyms should be avoided unless they will be understood by all readers. (Even sophisticated readers appreciate having test names written out initially.)	"The PPVT–III, VABS, and WISC–III were administered."	"The following tests were administered: Peabody Picture Vocabulary Test–III (PPVT–III), Vineland Adaptive Behavior Scales (VABS), and Wechsler Intelligence Scale for Children–Third Edition (WISC–III)."
19. *Capitalize proper names of tests.*	"In a previous assessment, he was given the bender and the motor-free test."	"In a previous assessment, he was given the Bender Visual Motor Gestalt Test and the Motor-Free Visual Perception Test."
20. *Put statements in positive form. Make definite assertions. Avoid tame, colorless, hesitating, noncommittal language.* The reader may be dissatisfied with being told only what did not happen; he or she wishes to be told what did happen as well.	"The child did not know his colors." "The child did not have good motor control."	"The child did not name the colors of the red and blue blocks. However, he did separate the blocks by color and matched them to other red and blue objects in the room." "The child stacked two blocks but was unable to stack three blocks."

(Continued)

Table 21-6 *(Continued)*

Guideline	Inappropriate statement	Appropriate statement
21. *Do not affect a breezy manner.* Be professional, avoid pet ideas and phrases, and cultivate a natural rather than a flippant style of writing.	"Would you believe, Ma and Pa had a fuss right in the middle of the interview over when the child began to walk." "Mom said her child was sad."	"The child's parents disagreed as to when the child had first walked." "Mrs. Smith said her child was sad."
22. *Do not overstate.* If you overstate, the reader will be instantly on guard, and everything that precedes your overstatement, as well as everything that follows it, will be suspect in the reader's mind.	"There is no tension in the home." "The client is absolutely brilliant."	"Bill's father reported no tension in the home." "The student scored 141 on the Stanford-Binet Intelligence Scale: Fourth Edition, presented a report card with all As, and was voted 'most intelligent' by the high school faculty."

Source: Adapted from Bates (1985), Gearheart and Willenberg (1980), Kolin and Kolin (1980), and Moore (1969).

6. Many readers will not know what these abbreviations mean. They are best left out; if they are needed, they should be described fully. In addition, it is inappropriate to describe children as "LDs" and "resourced." *Suggestion:* "Mark is in a classroom for children with learning problems."

7. The word *percentile* should be written out.

CONCLUDING COMMENT ON REPORT WRITING

The overall goal of report writing is to use clear and precise language to write a well-integrated and logical report that will be meaningful to the reader and relevant to the child and his or her problems. In formulating the report, consider all sources of information, the possible implications of the information, and the possible interventions. As you work through this material carefully and logically, recognize which statements are based on observations and which are based on inferences. Clearly acknowledge those findings that are substantial and those that are inconclusive. Also acknowledge uncertain or incongruous findings. Don't come to conclusions prematurely. Write a report that informs the reader of your findings and recommendations and responds to the referral question—not a report that becomes an assessment of the reader's ability to understand your language. If the grammar-check function in your word-processing program reports a readability level, try to keep this level at tenth grade or below.

Unfortunately, surveys of teachers and other professional readers indicate that students and clinicians have problems writing effective psychological reports (see Sat-tler, 1992, for references). These problems include omission of supporting data or behavioral referents, poor expression (e.g., use of cliches and jargon, loose use of terms, vagueness), poor organization, inconsistencies, incorrect use of theory, poor differentiation between test data and other data, failure to answer the referral problem, failure to explain the test data, recommendations that are too vague, unrealistic suggestions for the classroom teacher, and either excessive brevity or excessive length and irrelevance. Respondents described good reports as being understandable and enjoyable to read, having excellent interpretations of the test results, explaining the results clearly, explaining how the problem developed, answering specific referral questions, and providing recommendations that could be implemented in the classroom. Good reports also make it clear that the referral source has asked relevant questions that deserve careful answers.

It is helpful to use an evaluative questionnaire, such as the one in Table 21-7, to obtain feedback from teachers and others about the usefulness of your psychological reports. In addition to helping you identify strengths and weaknesses in your written communications, the questionnaire will allow you to learn about the different needs of various referral sources—such as general education classroom teachers, special education teachers, counselors, and speech and language therapists. This information can help you establish realistic expectations on the part of the referral sources about what they can obtain from your report. You will also improve your skills if, some time after the report is written, you evaluate it to determine whether you made helpful recommendations, substantiated your hypotheses, correctly interpreted the data, and included the most important information.

Many tests come with report-writing software. We believe that it is important for you to develop your report-writing

Table 21-7
Evaluation Form for Psychological Reports

We are attempting to determine how well our reports meet the needs of persons who request a psychological assessment for a student. This questionnaire is designed to provide us with information about the extent to which this report provides the information that you requested. Your feedback is important in helping us improve the quality of our service. The first nine items can be answered by checking the appropriate response to each question. The other questions are designed so that you can provide feedback about different aspects of the report.

1. To what extent does this report provide an adequate answer to the referral question(s)?

    _____ adequate   _____ partially adequate   _____ inadequate

2. To what extent does this report provide you with new information or insights about the student?

    _____ very helpful   _____ somewhat helpful   _____ not helpful

3. To what extent does this report confirm the insights that you already had about the student?

    _____ very much   _____ somewhat   _____ none

4. To what extent are the information and insights provided in this report helpful to you in developing new ideas of your own about working with the student?

    _____ very helpful   _____ somewhat helpful   _____ not helpful

5. To what extent does this report provide useful recommendations about instructional strategies that may be appropriate for this student?

    _____ very helpful   _____ somewhat helpful   _____ not helpful   _____ none provided

6. To what extent does this report provide helpful recommendations for dealing with the student's behavior?

    _____ very helpful   _____ somewhat helpful   _____ not helpful   _____ none provided

7. To what extent do the recommendations in this report reflect an understanding of classroom procedures?

    _____ good understanding   _____ some understanding   _____ poor understanding

8. What is your overall evaluation of the usefulness of this report?

    _____ highly useful   _____ somewhat useful   _____ not useful

9. What type of information did you request when you referred this student for a psychological evaluation?

    _____ eligibility for special education services   _____ suggestions for classroom teaching

    _____ information to increase your understanding of the student   _____ other (please specify)_____

10. What, if any, additional information should have been included in this report?

11. What, if any, technical terms were unclear to you?

12. What, if any, information and/or insights from the report are useful in improving your work with this student?

13. What, if any, of the recommendations will you be implementing in your work with this student?

14. What, if any, suggestions can you provide to help the examining psychologist improve the quality of his/her written reports?

15. Please indicate your position and grade level (if appropriate):

    _____ teacher (grade level _____)   _____ administrator/supervisor (level or area _____)

    _____ counselor (level _____)   _____ parent (name_____)

    _____ speech and language clinician (level _____)   _____ other (please specify _____)

    _____ special education teacher (specialty area _____)

Note. Items 4 through 7 pertain to remediation and program development and may not be applicable to reports that deal only with classification and placement decisions.
Source: Reprinted with permission of the publisher and authors from "Evaluating School Psychological Reports, Part I: A Procedure for Systematic Feedback," by R. L. Ownby and F. H. Wallbrown, 1983, *Psychology in the Schools, 20,* p. 44.

Copyright © 1997 by John P. Wood.

skills and learn to write a report independently. However, we suggest that you print out a computer-generated report as a working prototype. Then translate the information in the computer-generated report into your own words, as needed, and form your own hypotheses and interpretations. Every report must be individualized. Remember, *you* are responsible for the content of the report.

The following list summarizes guidelines for writing a clear, succinct, and engaging report:

- Make your presentation straightforward and objective.
- Base your interpretations on the assessment information that you obtained.
- Include the rationale for each recommendation.
- Do not allow personal biases to influence your interpretations or recommendations.
- Do not overinterpret the assessment information.
- Focus on both strengths and weaknesses, adaptive capabilities as well as pathology.
- Admit uncertainty if you are uncertain.
- Be prepared to justify everything you say in the report, because readers may want clarification and because the report may be used in an administrative hearing or in court.
- Avoid writing a report that is so bland it might represent anyone. Instead, try to describe a unique, specific child.
- Make the report tight—strive for clarity and brevity.
- Edit the report carefully to make certain that spelling, grammar, and punctuation are accurate.
- Watch your semantics—avoid overused or nebulous words, colloquial expressions, and stereotyped phrases.
- Avoid using the report as a place to display your learning or to parade a large vocabulary.
- Spell out abbreviated terms the first time you use them (with the abbreviation in parentheses).
- Avoid jargon and arcane terms.
- Refer to parents by name or as "Sam's mother," not "Mom," "Dad," "the mother," or "the father."

Report writing is a process of refining ideas, establishing clarity of expression, and applying expertise to make decisions. The ability to write a clear and meaningful report is an important skill. A good report will contribute to both the assessment and the treatment of the child and her or his family.

TEST YOUR SKILL

The final exercise in this chapter is designed to help you develop the skills needed to write a psychological report based on the WISC–III. There are three parts to the exercise. First, read the WISC–III report in Exhibit 21-3, focusing on the superscript numbers and the words, phrases, or information associated with each superscript number. Your task is to identify the problem, such as an error in punctuation, style, spelling, quantitative information, or interpretation. Second, record your comments on a sheet of paper, using the numbers 1 to 81. Finally, check your comments with those in the Comment section following the report in Exhibit 21-3.

THINKING THROUGH THE ISSUES

1. What should be the function of a psychological report?
2. How might a teacher, a physician, and an attorney differ in the kinds of information they want in a psychological report?
3. Why do you think report writing is so difficult for many students?
4. How would you write a report that is not likely to be misunderstood by the reader?

Exhibit 21-3
Psychological Evaluation Illustrating Several Problems That May Occur in Writing a WISC–III Report

PSYCHOLOGICAL EVALUATION

Name of examinee: Jane Doe

Date of birth: November 12, 1983

Chronological age: 16-8

Grade: High school junior

Date of examination : August, 2000[1]

Date of report: August, 2000[1]

Name of examiner: Alan K. Smith

Test Administered

Wechler Intelligence Scale for Children–III (WISC–III)[2]

VERBAL SCALE		PERFORMANCE SCALE	
Information	7	Picture Completion	9
Similarities	13	Coding	10
Arithmetic	7	Picture Arrangement	10
Vocabulary	11	Block Design	14
Comprehension	11	Object Assembly	13
Digit Span	10		

Verbal Scale IQ = 99

Performance Scale IQ = 108

Full Scale IQ = 104 ± 6 (range of 97 to 110 at the 95% confidence level[3])

Reason for Referral

Jane agreed to act as a subject for a course in psychological assessment at CSU.[4]

Background Information

Jane is a sixteen[5]-year, 9-month[6]-old white female in her junior year at Blank High School. She is enrolled in a precollege curriculum and plans to go to college. She would like to become an Elementary School Teacher.[7] One practice of Janes that was mentioned during the interview was her involvement in a flag corp group.[8] The examiner had previously explained to Jane that she could not be shown her test results.[9] No further background information was obtained.

Behavioral Observations

Jane was[10] a sixteen[5]-year, 9-month[6]-old high school student[11] whose language and behavior appear appropriate to her age and the situation. The most prominent features about Jane were that[12] she was cheerful and cooperative while under observation and insecure during the testing situation.[13] She giggled frequently, especially before answering questions and when she was frustrated.[14] Her answers were often preceded by the word filler "Um", followed by a disclaimer such as "I don't know", "I think", and "I'm no good".[15] These responses suggested some anxiety and nervousness.[16] She seemed more comfortable with the demands of material[17] that required visual attention, physical manipulation, and knowledge organization.[18] Consequently, some variability was apparent during the test.[19]

Her answers were succinct on the initial portions of some subtests and wordy on the latter portions.[20] Her answers were extensive throughout other subtests.[21] She was not consistently methodical in her approach to problem solving[22] and occasionally acted in a haphazard fashion.[23] Her hands are[10] involved in a washing-like motion.[24] Related to the examiner in an approval-seeking manner.[25] She mimicked the examiner exactly during Digits Forward,[26] including timed delay.[27] On a vocabulary test,[28] she unsurely gave[29] multiple responses when a single answer would have sufficed.

Assessment Results and Clinical Impressions

On the WISC–III Jane achieved a Verbal IQ of 99 (47th percentile, which places her in the average range),[30] a Performance IQ of 108 (70th percentile, which places her in the above average range),[30] and a combined full scale[31] IQ of 104 + 6[32] (61st percentile, which places her in the average range[33] of intellectual functioning). The Verbal IQ is near the mean, whereas the Performance IQ is ⅔ standard deviation above the mean.[34] The chances that her true IQ is between 98 and 100[35] are about 95 out of 100. Jane's voluntary participation suggests that the results represent a reliable[36] and valid estimate of her current level of intellectual functioning.

Janes[37] overall functioning is in the average range,[33] although with notable disparity between her verbal and performance[38] IQs.[39] Her nonverbal skills are uniformly well developed,[40] but her verbal skills show considerably more variability.[41] Her verbal skills range from a low average to a superior classification,[42] whereas her nonverbal skills range from an average to superior classification.[42] Her Verbal Scale scores demonstrate accumulated experience[43] and indicate average performance in verbal skills and language development.[44]

On the six verbal subtests, Jane performed at or above the mean of the standardization sample one-half of the time (Similarities, Comprehension[45] and Digit Span).[46] Her performance on the Information and Arithmetic subtests indicated the most notable skill deficits, with performance for each found to be one standard deviation below the mean of the norming sample.[47] Her scaled scores (M = 10, SD = 3)[48] on Arithmetic and Information were significantly lower than her own Verbal Scale mean score ($p < .05$ and $p < .01$, respectively).[49] Information is the second best measure of g among the Verbal Scale subtests.[50] Her performance on Information was anemic[51] and erratic[52] at the Low Average range;[53] she sometimes answered more diffi-

(Continued)

Exhibit 21-3 *(Continued)*

cult items correctly and missed easier ones. On Arithmetic, she responded quickly to items involving simple calculations, but did not take time in responding to more difficult items.[54] Her verbal abilities are extremely diverse and do not fall within the Average range of performance; to characterize her verbal abilities as such would be in error.[55]

Within the non-verbal[56] performance[57] area, her perceptual organizational ability, attention to detail, and visual-motor coordination ability and speed are all well developed.[58] She assembled puzzles quickly, scoring in the 75th percentile.[59] Her analytic and synthetic abilities, nonverbal reasoning ability, and sequencing are superior[60] as assessed by her performance on the Block Design subtest.[61] Block Design is the best measure of general intelligence (*g*) among the Performance Scale subtests.[62]

Her low fund of general information suggests that Jane has not been exposed to the kinds of information that average adolescents acquire through normal home and school experiences.[63] Her low arithmetical reasoning scores suggest that Jane was having difficulty sustaining attention, since this subtest is about halfway to the end of the test.[64] Her good social comprehension scores suggests that her social skills are better developed than her other intellectual skills.[65] Overall, her intellectual level of functioning suggests that she will do well in her

last two years of high school.[66] She appears to be a happy and goal oriented[67] girl,[68] and increased focus can be expected to add definition to her goals with time and increased high school experience.[69]

Summary

Jane, a healthy[70] 16-year, 8-month-old high school student, volunteered to be examined for a demonstration of the WISC–III at a training clinic[71] at CSU.[72] Her test results seem to be reliable and valid.[73] She obtained a WISC–III Full Scale IQ of 104 ± 6, which is in the 51st percentile[74] and in the Average range. She was better overall in performance tasks (70th percentile) than in verbal tasks (47th percentile).[75] She has an uneven pattern of scores, as noted above.[76] She has strengths in three tasks and weakness in two others.[77] She should do well in her last two years of high school, but may not have been exposed to the kinds of information that other adolescents have been exposed to.[78] She appears to know where many of her improficiencies[79] lie and may often simply be fulfilling a "self-fulfilling prophecy."[80]

A.K.S.[81]

COMMENTS ON THE PSYCHOLOGICAL EVALUATION

Note: The numbers below refer to the superscripts in the Psychological Evaluation.

1. The day of the month should be included.
2. *Wechler* is a misspelling—it should be *Wechsler*.
3. The confidence interval is incorrect—it should be 98 to 110.
4. The name of the school should be spelled out completely. It is preferable not to use abbreviations, except for the name of the test. Under "Test Administered," the first use of the abbreviation correctly follows the full name of the test.
5. Age is usually written in Arabic numerals.
6. The correct age is 16-8, not 16-9.
7. The first letter of each word in the phrase "elementary school teacher" should be lowercased.
8. This sentence is awkward and contains punctuation and spelling errors, as well as an inaccuracy. *Janes* should have an apostrophe (*Jane's*) and *corp* should have an *s* (*corps*). The words "during the interview" are not accurate—a formal interview was not conducted, and a test session should not be characterized as an interview. The sentence could be rewritten as follows: "Jane mentioned that she is a member of the flag corps at Blank High School."
9. This sentence provides some information about the testing session, but it does not contribute much to our understanding of the examinee. It would be better to delete it.
10. Use the present tense to describe the examinee's more enduring characteristics ("Jane is a 16-year, 8-month-old")

and the past tense to describe the examinee's behavior, dress, mood, and so forth during the examination ("she *was* cheerful"; "Her hands *were* . . .").
11. This information is in the Background Information section and need not be repeated.
12. The first eight words ("The . . . that") are superfluous and should be deleted.
13. The phrases "while under observation" and "during the testing situation" imply two different periods of the examination. Isn't the examinee under observation throughout the examination? It is not clear when the examinee was cheerful and when she was insecure. Additionally, the words *the* and *situation* can be deleted in the phrase "insecure during the testing situation."
14. It would help if the writer indicated when the examinee giggled—on easy or difficult items, on verbal or nonverbal items.
15. The quotation mark follows the comma or period.
16. *Anxiety and nervousness* is redundant.
17. The words *the demands of* are not needed.
18. A comparative clause beginning with *than* is needed: "She was more comfortable with X than with Y." Additionally, the term *knowledge organization* is vague.
19. This sentence is vague because we do not know to what *variability* refers. Does it refer to behavior, test score, affect, or something else? The variability should be clearly described.

(Continued)

Exhibit 21-3 *(Continued)*

20. The specific subtests or types of subtests should be mentioned.
21. Again, this sentence is vague because we do not know on what subtests (or subtest portions) she gave extensive answers.
22. It would be more helpful if her approach to problem solving were described.
23. *Haphazard* is a strong term and has negative clinical connotations. The examinee's specific behaviors should be mentioned and an appropriate term used to describe these behaviors.
24. This sentence does not provide enough information to the reader, and it almost implies a Lady Macbeth syndrome. When were her hands making a washing-like motion—throughout the test or only on specific items? On what type of items were the hand movements observed?
25. This is not a complete sentence. Complete sentences should always be used in the body of the report. The statement also would benefit from a description of the behaviors associated with her "approval-seeking manner."
26. Most lay readers will not know what *Digits Forward* refers to; instead describe the task.
27. *Timed delay* is vague.
28. The 13 subtests are usually referred to as *subtests*, not tests. The word *test* should be used to describe a complete test, such as the WISC–III or the Leiter International Performance Scale–Revised. The word *Vocabulary* should be capitalized if the term refers to the Vocabulary subtest.
29. "Unsurely gave" is an awkward expression; it should be revised.
30. It is best to use a classification category only for the Full Scale IQ. A report with more than one classification may confuse readers. Also, the classification provided for the Performance IQ is wrong.
31. Both words in the term *Full Scale* should be capitalized.
32. The minus sign (–) is missing in the confidence interval; it should be 104 ± 6.
33. The word *Average* should be capitalized when it designates a range. (For other range designations, such as Above Average or Below Average, capitalize the first letter in each word.)
34. This is technical information and is not needed in the report.
35. The confidence interval is incorrect. It should be 98 to 110.
36. Voluntary participation is not a sufficient reason for concluding that the examinee's performance was reliable. Examinees can volunteer and still not try. The focus should be on the examinee's behavior and not on the reason for the examination, although it may play a role in certain cases.
37. *Janes* should be written with an apostrophe after the *e*: *Jane's.*
38. The words *Verbal* and *Performance* should be capitalized when they refer to IQs or scales.
39. If, as in this case, the difference between the Verbal and Performance Scale IQs is not significant, report that both

areas are developed at a similar level. The wording in this sentence is misleading.
40. Her scaled scores of 9 and 10 indicate average ability; thus, the term *well developed* may be misleading. Additionally, the term *uniformly* is misleading because the scaled scores ranged from 9 to 15 on the Performance Scale.
41. The Verbal Scale scores range from 7 to 13 (6 points), and the Performance Scale scores range from 9 to 14 (5 points). Therefore, it is incorrect to say that the verbal scores "show considerably more variability."
42. Subtest scaled scores should not be referred to as representing ranges or classifications such as high average. Terms such as *strength* (*above average, well developed*) or *weakness* (*below average, poorly developed*) are preferred (see Guideline 2 in this chapter). Additionally, using percentile ranks will help you to discuss subtest scores and the Verbal, Performance, and Full Scale IQs.
43. Both the Verbal Scale and the Performance Scale reflect accumulated experience; this phrase should be therefore either eliminated or revised.
44. It is not clear how language development differs from verbal skills. Isn't language development a part of verbal development?
45. A comma would be helpful after the word *Comprehension.*
46. This statement is not accurate. Her Vocabulary score is also at or above the mean of the standardization group. Additionally, the statement is too technical and should be rewritten.
47. This statement, although literally correct, is awkwardly written and too technical. Many readers would not know what the phrase "one standard deviation below the mean of the norming sample" refers to; it should be deleted.
48. It is not necessary to give the mean and standard deviation of the scaled scores in the narrative of the report.
49. The probability levels should not be included in a report.
50. This information is too technical and should be deleted.
51. *Anemic* is not the correct word in this context.
52. Use *variable* instead of *erratic.*
53. Individual subtest scores should not be classified into formal ranges (see number 42).
54. Instead of saying "but did not take time in responding to more difficult items," the examiner should describe how Jane responded to the more difficult items.
55. The logic of this sentence is unclear. The examinee's Verbal IQ is 99, which is clearly an average score. Consequently, it would be more appropriate to characterize her overall verbal skills as being average.
56. A hyphen is not needed in *nonverbal.*
57. The word *performance* is redundant.
58. The phrases "attention to detail" and "visual-motor coordination ability and speed" likely pertain to the Picture Completion and Coding subtests, respectively. On these two subtests her scores were average: 9 and 10,

(Continued)

Exhibit 21-3 *(Continued)*

respectively. Therefore, the sentence gives misleading information (i.e., "are all well developed").

59. First, this sentence contains an error: the percentile rank should be 84th, not 75th, because the scaled score on Object Assembly is 13. Table D-1 in Appendix D shows the percentile ranks for scaled scores. Second, the sentence can be rephrased to provide more meaningful information. The implications of her performance should be discussed rather than the specific tasks required by the subtest. For example, to describe her performance on Object Assembly you could say, "Her ability to arrange material under time pressure was excellent."

60. Block Design does not measure sequencing ability.

61. The remainder of the sentence ("as assessed by her performance on the Block Design subtest") is not needed.

62. This information is too technical and should be deleted.

63. There usually is no way to corroborate this hypothesis with the limited information obtained during an evaluation. Consequently, this sentence should be deleted.

64. This is a puzzling inference, especially when you consider that some of her best scores were on Object Assembly and Block Design, which were administered during the second half of the test.

65. Comprehension, like all of the other WISC–III subtests, is a measure of cognition. This subtest, therefore, likely measures social judgment and not social skills.

66. A Full Scale IQ of 104 indicates that the examinee probably has the ability to do at least average work in high school. However, because many other factors besides intelligence affect school grades, this statement should be rewritten (e.g., "she possesses the ability to complete high school").

67. Use a hyphen in *goal-oriented* when it modifies a noun (goal-oriented student).

68. *Student* is preferable to *girl*.

69. The last half of this sentence is poorly written; it should be rewritten.

70. Because the term *healthy* was not used in the body of the report, it should not be introduced in the summary. Additionally, unless you have information about the examinee's health, do not make statements about it.

71. The words *training clinic* were not mentioned previously and therefore should not be introduced for the first time in the summary. Furthermore, the examinee was tested as part of a course requirement and not at a training clinic.

72. The summary should be able to stand alone. Thus, it is preferable not to use abbreviations, except for acronyms that are widely known and accepted (e.g., *IQ*).

73. "Seem to be" is a vague phrase. Be more definite when discussing reliability and validity, if at all possible.

74. The correct percentile rank is 61st.

75. Because the Verbal Scale IQ and Performance Scale IQ are not significantly different, this statement is misleading.

76. The summary should repeat the major findings and not refer readers to the body of the report.

77. This sentence is vague.

78. This is a speculative inference and should be deleted.

79. *Improficiencies* is not a word.

80. The concept of a "self-fulfilling prophecy" was not developed in the report proper and is likely to confuse the reader, especially as it comes at the end of the summary.

81. The examiner's full name should be typewritten in this space, followed by his or her degree (e.g., B.A., M.A., Ph.D.) and the word *Examiner*.

5. What type of information might you wish to communicate to the referral source that you would not include in the report? Is it appropriate for such communications to take place?

6. What other report formats, in addition to the one described in the chapter, might be useful for writing reports?

7. When might you use the Evaluation Form for Psychological Reports for your own reports? If you did use it, how could you benefit from the feedback?

8. In addition to this book, what sources can you consult for help in writing better psychological reports?

SUMMARY

1. Psychological reports may be based on test findings; interviews with the child, his or her parents, and teachers; systematic behavioral observations; and other relevant information gleaned from school records, prior psychological reports, and medical, psychiatric, and other sources.

Introduction to Psychological Report Writing

2. A psychological evaluation is complete only after the obtained information has been organized, synthesized, and integrated.

3. The traditional medium for presenting assessment information is a report, although you may use other formal and informal means of presentation.

4. A report may influence a child and family for years to come; its drafting deserves extreme care and consideration.

5. Your report should be well organized and solidly grounded.

6. A good report does not merely present facts. It integrates the testing results, behavioral observations, information gained from interviews, and relevant case history material (which includes current and prior social, educational, psychological, psychiatric, and medical findings and recommendations and prereferral information).

7. The psychological report (a) provides accurate assessment-related information; (b) serves as a source of clinical hypotheses, appropriate interventions, and information for program evaluation and research; (c) furnishes meaningful baseline information

for evaluating the examinee's progress after the interventions have been implemented or changes that occur as a result of time alone, and (d) serves as a legal document.

8. In formulating and constructing your report, consider who will be the primary audiences for the report.

9. Every report has elements of subjectivity because the information may be open to different interpretations.

10. Write the report as soon as possible after you complete the assessment.

11. The psychological report should adequately describe the assessment findings, including information about the examinee's history, current problems, assets, and limitations; it should also include behavioral observations and test interpretations.

12. Each report should be an independent document—that is, its content should be comprehensive enough to stand alone.

Sections of a Psychological Report

13. A typical psychological report includes nine sections: Identifying Information, Assessment Instruments, Reason for Referral, Background Information, Observations During the Assessment, Assessment Results and Clinical Impressions, Recommendations, Summary, and Signature.

14. The Identifying Information section presents relevant identifying information about the examinee and examiner.

15. The Assessment Instruments section lists the formal and informal instruments used to conduct the assessment.

16. The Reason for Referral section summarizes the concerns of the referral source.

17. The Background Information section provides relevant demographic information, information about the current problems, historical information (including the child's developmental history), information about the family, and information about the parents.

18. The Observations During the Assessment section provides a careful description of the child's behavior during the assessment and attempts to capture the child's unique style.

19. The Assessment Results and Clinical Impressions section synthesizes the major findings.

20. The Recommendations section provides realistic and practical intervention goals and treatment strategies.

21. The Summary section reviews and integrates the information in the prior sections of the report.

22. The Signature section of the report contains your name, professional title, and degree.

Overview of Report Writing

23. Twenty-two principles of report writing cover how to organize, interpret, and present the assessment findings.

24. Principle 1. Use a consistent strategy to organize assessment findings; detect common themes that run through and across the assessment findings, integrate the main findings, and use a theoretical focus.

25. Principle 2. Include only relevant material in the report; delete potentially damaging material not germane to the evaluation.

26. Principle 3. Be extremely cautious in making interpretations based on a limited sample of behavior.

27. Principle 4. Use all relevant sources of information about the examinee in generating hypotheses, formulating interpretations, and arriving at recommendations.

BUFORD'S FAMILY HONORS HIS LAST REQUEST THAT HE BE LAID OUT THE WAY MOST OF HIS FRIENDS WOULD REMEMBER HIM

Courtesy of Herman Zielinski.

28. Principle 5. Be definitive in your writing when the findings are clear; be cautious in your writing when the findings are not clear.

29. Principle 6. Cite specific behaviors and sources and directly quote the examinee to enhance the report's readability.

30. Principle 7. Consider the overall IQ, in most cases, to be the best estimate of the child's present level of intellectual functioning.

31. Principle 8. Interpret the meaning and implications of a child's scores, rather than simply citing test names and scores.

32. Principle 9. Obtain the classification of IQs and other test scores from the numerical ranges given in the test manuals.

33. Principle 10. Use percentile ranks whenever possible to describe a child's scores.

34. Principle 11. Provide clear descriptions of abilities measured by the subtests when appropriate.

35. Principle 12. Relate inferences based on subtest scores or IQs to the cognitive processes measured by the subtests and scales.

36. Principle 13. Describe the profile of scores clearly and unambiguously.

37. Principle 14. Make recommendations carefully, using all available sources of information.

38. Principle 15. Use scores obtained by extrapolation or interpolation with caution.

39. Principle 16. Refrain from making diagnoses of psychopathology or educational diagnoses based solely on test scores; consider all sources of information.

40. Principle 17. Communicate clearly, and do not include unnecessary technical material in the report.

41. Principle 18. Describe and use statistical concepts appropriately; make sure that you check all calculations carefully and

that you accurately report the reliability and validity of the test results.

42. Principle 19. Eliminate biased terms from the report.
43. Principle 20. Write a report that is concise but adequate.
44. Principle 21. Attend carefully to grammar and writing style.
45. Principle 22. Develop strategies to improve your writing, such as using an outline, revising your first draft, and proofreading your final report.

Concluding Comment on Report Writing

46. The overall goal of report writing is to use clear and precise language to write a well-integrated and logical report that will be meaningful to the reader and relevant to the child and his or her problems.
47. Report writing is a process of refining ideas, establishing clarity of expression, and applying expertise to make decisions.
48. The ability to write a clear and meaningful report is an important skill.
49. A good report will contribute to both the assessment and the treatment of the child and her or his family.

KEY TERMS, CONCEPTS, AND NAMES

Sections of a psychological report (p. 678)
Confidence interval (p. 682)
Test-by-test basis (p. 686)
Domain-by-domain basis (p. 686)
Principles of report writing (p. 689)
Three levels of clinical inference (p. 694)
Inappropriate generalizations (p. 695)
Child-oriented statements (p. 697)
Test-oriented statement (p. 697)
IQ classifications (p. 698)
Percentile ranks (p. 698)
Extrapolated scores (p. 704)
Interpolated scores (p. 704)
Confusing and inappropriate devices (p. 708)
Bias (p. 710)
Writing strategies (p. 713)

STUDY QUESTIONS

1. What are the purposes of a psychological report?
2. What information is included in each of the following sections of a report: Identifying Information, Assessment Instruments, Reason for Referral, Background Information, Observations During the Assessment, Assessment Results and Clinical Impressions, Recommendations, Summary, and Signature?
3. What strategies can you use to organize assessment findings?
4. What guidelines should you use to decide which material to include in a report?
5. What are some guidelines for making generalizations, interpretations, and diagnoses?
6. What are some important factors to consider in communicating your findings?
7. How can you eliminate biased language from a report?
8. Describe some useful strategies for writing reports.
9. Develop a checklist for evaluating the quality of a psychological report.
10. What are some typical problems that readers encounter in psychological reports?

APPENDIX A

TABLES FOR THE WISC–III

Table A-1
Confidence Intervals for WISC–III Scales and Index Scores Based on Obtained Score Only

Age level	Scale or index	Confidence level				
		68%	85%	90%	95%	99%
6 (6-0-0 through 6-11-30)	Verbal Scale IQ	±4	±6	±7	±8	±10
	Performance Scale IQ	±5	±6	±7	±9	±12
	Full Scale IQ	±3	±5	±6	±7	±9
	Verbal Comprehension	±5	±7	±8	±9	±12
	Perceptual Organization	±5	±7	±8	±9	±12
	Freedom from Distractibility	±6	±8	±9	±11	±14
	Processing Speed	±7	±10	±11	±13	±17
7 (7-0-0 through 7-11-30)	Verbal Scale IQ	±4	±6	±7	±8	±11
	Performance Scale IQ	±5	±7	±8	±9	±12
	Full Scale IQ	±4	±5	±6	±7	±9
	Verbal Comprehension	±5	±7	±8	±9	±12
	Perceptual Organization	±5	±7	±8	±10	±13
	Freedom from Distractibility	±6	±9	±10	±12	±16
	Processing Speed	±7	±10	±12	±14	±18
8 (8-0-0 through 8-11-30)	Verbal Scale IQ	±3	±4	±5	±6	±8
	Performance Scale IQ	±5	±7	±8	±9	±12
	Full Scale IQ	±3	±4	±5	±6	±8
	Verbal Comprehension	±4	±5	±6	±7	±9
	Perceptual Organization	±5	±8	±9	±10	±13
	Freedom from Distractibility	±6	±8	±9	±11	±14
	Processing Speed	±6	±9	±10	±12	±16
9 (9-0-0 through 9-11-30)	Verbal Scale IQ	±4	±6	±7	±8	±10
	Performance Scale IQ	±5	±6	±7	±9	±12
	Full Scale IQ	±3	±5	±6	±7	±9
	Verbal Comprehension	±4	±6	±7	±8	±11
	Perceptual Organization	±5	±7	±8	±10	±13
	Freedom from Distractibility	±7	±9	±11	±13	±16
	Processing Speed	±6	±9	±10	±12	±15
10 (10-0-0 through 10-11-30)	Verbal Scale IQ	±3	±5	±6	±7	±9
	Performance Scale IQ	±5	±6	±7	±9	±12
	Full Scale IQ	±3	±4	±5	±6	±8
	Verbal Comprehension	±4	±6	±7	±8	±10
	Perceptual Organization	±5	±8	±9	±10	±13
	Freedom from Distractibility	±6	±9	±10	±11	±15
	Processing Speed	±6	±9	±10	±12	±16
11 (11-0-0 through 11-11-30)	Verbal Scale IQ	±3	±5	±6	±7	±9
	Performance Scale IQ	±5	±7	±8	±9	±12
	Full Scale IQ	±3	±5	±6	±7	±9
	Verbal Comprehension	±4	±6	±7	±8	±10
	Perceptual Organization	±5	±8	±9	±10	±13
	Freedom from Distractibility	±6	±8	±9	±11	±14
	Processing Speed	±6	±8	±9	±11	±14

(Continued)

Table A-1 (*Continued*)

Age level	Scale or index	Confidence level				
		68%	85%	90%	95%	99%
12 (12-0-0 through 12-11-30)	Verbal Scale IQ	±3	±5	±6	±7	±9
	Performance Scale IQ	±5	±6	±7	±9	±12
	Full Scale IQ	±3	±4	±5	±6	±8
	Verbal Comprehension	±4	±5	±6	±7	±9
	Perceptual Organization	±5	±7	±8	±9	±12
	Freedom from Distractibility	±6	±9	±10	±11	±15
	Processing Speed	±6	±8	±9	±11	±14
13 (13-0-0 through13-11-30)	Verbal Scale IQ	±4	±5	±6	±7	±9
	Performance Scale IQ	±5	±7	±8	±9	±12
	Full Scale IQ	±3	±5	±6	±7	±9
	Verbal Comprehension	±4	±6	±7	±8	±11
	Perceptual Organization	±5	±7	±8	±9	±12
	Freedom from Distractibility	±6	±8	±9	±11	±14
	Processing Speed	±7	±10	±11	±13	±17
14 (14-0-0 through 14-11-30)	Verbal Scale IQ	±3	±5	±6	±7	±9
	Performance Scale IQ	±5	±7	±8	±10	±13
	Full Scale IQ	±3	±5	±6	±7	±9
	Verbal Comprehension	±4	±5	±6	±7	±9
	Perceptual Organization	±5	±8	±9	±10	±13
	Freedom from Distractibility	±6	±9	±10	±11	±15
	Processing Speed	±7	±10	±11	±13	±17
15 (15-0-0 through 15-11-30)	Verbal Scale IQ	±3	±4	±5	±6	±8
	Performance Scale IQ	±4	±5	±6	±7	±9
	Full Scale IQ	±3	±4	±4	±5	±7
	Verbal Comprehension	±4	±5	±6	±7	±9
	Perceptual Organization	±4	±6	±7	±8	±11
	Freedom from Distractibility	±5	±7	±8	±9	±12
	Processing Speed	±5	±7	±8	±9	±12
16 (16-0-0 through 16-11-30)	Verbal Scale IQ	±3	±5	±6	±7	±9
	Performance Scale IQ	±4	±6	±7	±8	±11
	Full Scale IQ	±3	±4	±5	±6	±8
	Verbal Comprehension	±4	±6	±7	±8	±10
	Perceptual Organization	±5	±7	±8	±10	±13
	Freedom from Distractibility	±5	±7	±8	±10	±13
	Processing Speed	±5	±7	±8	±9	±12
Average	Verbal Scale IQ	±4	±5	±6	±7	±9
	Performance Scale IQ	±5	±7	±7	±9	±12
	Full Scale IQ	±3	±5	±5	±6	±8
	Verbal Comprehension	±4	±6	±7	±8	±10
	Perceptual Organization	±5	±7	±8	±10	±13
	Freedom from Distractibility	±6	±8	±9	±11	±15
	Processing Speed	±6	±9	±10	±12	±16

Note. Chapter 4 (pages 109–110) describes the procedure for computing confidence intervals. For the WISC–III Full Scale IQ, the confidence intervals are obtained by the following procedure: The appropriate SEM for the child's age is located in Table 5-2 of the WISC–III Manual. For example, for a 6-year-old child, the SEM = 3.97 for the Verbal Scale IQ. This SEM is multiplied by the respective z value in order to obtain the confidence intervals for the desired level. At the 68% confidence level, the SEM is multiplied by 1 (1 × 3.97 = 4). At the 85% level, the SEM is multiplied by 1.44 (1.44 × 3.97 = 6). At the 90% level, the SEM is multiplied by 1.65 (1.65 × 3.97 = 7). At the 95% level, the SEM is multiplied by 1.96 (1.96 × 3.97 = 8). At the 99% level, the SEM is multiplied by 2.58 (2.58 × 3.97 = 10). Note that the results were rounded to the nearest whole number.

Age level 6 (6-0-0 through 6-11-30)

	I	S	A	V	C	DS	PC	CD	PA	BD	OA	SS
S	4/6	—										
A	4/6	4/5	—									
V	4/6	4/5	4/5	—								
C	5/6	4/6	4/6	4/5	—							
DS	4/6	4/5	4/5	4/5	4/6	—						
PC	5/6	4/5	4/5	4/5	4/6	4/5	—					
CD	5/6	4/6	4/6	4/5	5/6	4/6	4/6	—				
PA	4/6	4/5	4/5	4/5	4/5	4/5	4/5	4/5	—			
BD	4/6	4/5	4/5	4/5	4/5	4/5	4/5	4/5	4/5	—		
OA	5/6	4/6	4/6	4/6	5/6	5/6	5/6	5/6	4/6	4/6	—	
SS	5/6	5/6	5/6	5/6	5/6	5/6	5/6	5/6	5/6	5/6	5/6	—
MA	4/6	4/5	4/5	4/5	4/6	4/5	4/5	4/6	4/5	4/5	5/6	5/6

	VSIQ		VCDQ	FDDQ	PSDQ
PSIQ	12/16	PODQ	13/17	14/19	16/21
		FDDQ	14/19	—	17/22
		PSDQ	16/21	17/22	—

Age level 7 (7-0-0 through 7-11-30)

	I	S	A	V	C	DS	PC	CD	PA	BD	OA	SS
S	4/6	—										
A	5/6	5/6	—									
V	4/6	4/6	4/6	—								
C	5/6	5/6	5/6	5/6	—							
DS	4/5	4/5	4/6	4/5	4/6	—						
PC	4/5	4/5	4/5	4/5	4/6	4/5	—					
CD	5/6	5/6	5/6	5/6	5/6	5/6	4/6	—				
PA	4/5	4/5	4/5	4/5	4/6	4/5	4/5	4/6	—			
BD	4/6	4/6	5/6	4/6	5/6	4/5	4/5	5/6	4/5	—		
OA	5/6	5/6	5/6	5/6	5/7	5/6	5/6	5/7	5/6	5/6	—	
SS	4/6	4/6	5/6	4/6	5/6	4/5	4/5	5/6	4/5	5/6	—	
MA	4/6	4/6	5/6	4/5	5/6	4/5	4/5	5/6	4/5	4/6	5/6	4/6

	VSIQ		VCDQ	FDDQ	PSDQ
PSIQ	13/17	PODQ	13/17	15/20	17/22
		FDDQ	15/20	—	18/24
		PSDQ	16/21	18/24	—

Age level 8 (8-0-0 through 8-11-30)

	I	S	A	V	C	DS	PC	CD	PA	BD	OA	SS
S	4/5	—										
A	4/5	4/5	—									
V	3/4	4/4	4/5	—								
C	4/5	4/5	4/5	3/4	—							
DS	4/5	4/5	4/5	4/4	4/5	—						
PC	4/5	4/5	4/5	4/5	4/5	4/5	—					
CD	4/5	4/5	4/6	4/5	4/5	4/5	4/5	—				
PA	4/5	4/6	5/6	4/5	4/5	4/6	4/6	5/6	—			
BD	4/5	4/5	4/5	4/5	4/5	4/5	4/5	4/5	4/6	—		
OA	5/6	5/6	5/6	4/6	5/6	5/6	5/6	5/6	5/7	5/6	—	
SS	4/5	4/6	5/6	4/5	4/5	4/6	4/6	5/6	5/6	4/6	5/7	—
MA	4/5	4/5	4/6	4/5	4/5	4/5	4/5	4/6	5/6	4/5	5/6	5/6

	VSIQ		VCDQ	FDDQ	PSDQ
PSIQ	11/15	PODQ	12/16	15/19	16/21
		FDDQ	13/17	—	16/21
		PSDQ	14/18	16/21	—

Age level 9 (9-0-0 through 9-11-30)

	I	S	A	V	C	DS	PC	CD	PA	BD	OA	SS
S	4/5	—										
A	4/6	5/6	—									
V	4/5	4/5	4/6	—								
C	4/6	4/6	5/6	4/6	—							
DS	4/5	4/5	4/6	4/5	4/6	—						
PC	4/5	4/5	5/6	4/5	4/6	4/5	—					
CD	4/5	4/5	5/6	4/5	4/6	4/5	4/5	—				
PA	4/6	4/6	5/6	4/6	5/6	4/6	4/6	5/6	—			
BD	4/6	4/5	4/6	4/5	4/5	4/5	4/5	4/5	4/5	—		
OA	4/6	4/6	5/6	4/5	5/6	4/5	4/6	4/6	5/6	4/5	—	
SS	4/6	4/6	5/6	4/6	5/6	4/6	4/6	5/6	5/6	4/5	5/6	—
MA	5/6	5/6	5/7	5/6	5/6	5/6	5/6	5/6	5/7	5/6	5/6	5/7

	VSIQ		VCDQ	FDDQ	PSDQ
PSIQ	12/16	PODQ	13/16	16/21	15/20
		FDDQ	15/19	—	17/22
		PSDQ	14/19	17/22	—

Age level 10 (10-0-0 through 10-11-30)

	I	S	A	V	C	DS	PC	CD	PA	BD	OA	SS
S	4/5	—										
A	4/5	4/5	—									
V	4/5	4/5	4/5	—								
C	4/5	4/5	4/5	4/5	—							
DS	4/5	4/5	4/5	4/4	4/5	—						
PC	4/6	4/6	4/6	4/5	4/6	4/5	—					
CD	4/5	4/5	4/5	4/5	4/5	4/5	4/6	—				
PA	4/6	4/6	4/6	4/5	4/6	4/5	5/6	4/6	—			
BD	4/5	4/5	4/5	3/4	4/5	3/4	4/5	4/5	4/5	—		
OA	5/6	5/6	5/6	4/5	5/6	4/6	5/6	5/6	5/6	4/5	—	
SS	4/6	4/6	5/6	4/5	5/6	4/6	5/6	5/6	5/6	4/5	5/6	—
MA	4/6	4/6	5/6	4/5	5/6	4/6	5/6	5/6	5/6	4/5	5/6	5/6

	VSIQ		VCDQ	FDDQ	PSDQ
PSIQ	11/15	PODQ	12/16	15/19	15/20
		FDDQ	14/18	—	17/22
		PSDQ	14/19	17/22	—

(Continued)

Table A-2 (Continued)

11 (11-0-0 through 11-11-30)

	I	S	A	V	C	DS	PC	CD	PA	BD	OA	SS
S	4/5	—										
A	4/5	4/5	—									
V	3/4	4/5	4/5	—								
C	4/5	4/5	4/6	4/5	—							
DS	4/5	4/5	4/5	4/4	4/5	—						
PC	4/5	4/5	4/6	4/5	4/6	4/5	—					
CD	4/5	4/5	4/5	4/5	4/5	4/5	4/5	—				
PA	4/6	4/6	5/6	4/5	5/6	4/6	5/6	4/6	—			
BD	4/5	4/5	4/5	4/4	4/5	4/5	4/5	4/5	4/6	—		
OA	5/6	5/6	5/6	4/6	5/6	5/6	5/6	5/6	5/7	5/6	—	
SS	4/5	4/5	4/5	4/5	4/6	4/5	4/6	4/5	5/6	4/5	5/6	—
MA	4/6	5/6	5/6	4/6	5/6	4/6	5/6	5/6	5/6	4/6	5/7	5/6

	PSIQ	VSIQ			VCDQ	FDDQ	PSDQ
	PSIQ	12/15		PODQ	13/16	15/19	15/19
				FDDQ	13/17	—	15/20
				PSDQ	13/17	15/20	—

12 (12-0-0 through 12-11-30)

	I	S	A	V	C	DS	PC	CD	PA	BD	OA	SS
S	4/5	—										
A	4/5	4/5	—									
V	3/4	3/4	4/5	—								
C	4/5	4/5	4/6	4/5	—							
DS	4/5	4/5	4/5	3/4	4/5	—						
PC	4/5	4/6	5/6	4/5	4/6	4/5	—					
CD	4/5	4/5	4/6	4/5	4/5	4/5	4/6	—				
PA	4/5	4/5	4/6	4/5	4/5	4/5	5/6	4/5	—			
BD	4/4	4/5	4/5	3/4	4/5	3/4	4/5	4/5	4/5	—		
OA	4/6	4/6	5/6	4/5	5/6	4/6	5/6	5/6	5/6	4/6	—	
SS	4/5	4/5	4/6	4/5	4/5	4/5	5/6	4/5	4/5	4/5	5/6	—
MA	5/6	5/6	5/6	4/5	5/6	4/6	5/7	5/6	5/6	4/6	5/7	5/6

	PSIQ	VSIQ			VCDQ	FDDQ	PSDQ
	PSIQ	11/15		PODQ	11/15	15/19	14/19
				FDDQ	13/17	—	16/21
				PSDQ	13/17	16/21	—

13 (13-0-0 through 13-11-30)

	I	S	A	V	C	DS	PC	CD	PA	BD	OA	SS
S	4/5	—										
A	4/5	4/6	—									
V	3/4	4/5	4/5	—								
C	4/5	5/6	4/6	4/5	—							
DS	4/4	4/5	4/5	3/4	4/5	—						
PC	4/5	5/6	4/6	4/5	5/6	4/5	—					
CD	4/6	5/6	5/6	4/5	5/6	4/5	5/6	—				
PA	4/5	5/6	4/5	4/5	5/6	4/5	5/6	5/6	—			
BD	3/4	4/5	4/5	3/4	4/5	3/4	4/5	4/5	4/5	—		
OA	4/5	5/6	4/6	4/5	5/6	4/5	5/6	5/6	5/6	4/5	—	
SS	4/5	5/6	4/6	4/5	5/6	4/5	5/6	5/6	5/6	4/5	5/6	—
MA	4/6	5/6	5/6	4/5	5/6	4/5	5/6	5/6	5/6	4/5	5/6	5/6

	PSIQ	VSIQ			VCDQ	FDDQ	PSDQ
	PSIQ	12/16		PODQ	12/16	14/18	16/21
				FDDQ	13/17	—	17/22
				PSDQ	15/19	17/22	—

14 (14-0-0 through 14-11-30)

	I	S	A	V	C	DS	PC	CD	PA	BD	OA	SS
S	4/5	—										
A	4/5	4/5	—									
V	3/4	3/4	4/5	—								
C	4/5	4/5	4/6	4/5	—							
DS	4/5	4/5	4/5	3/4	4/5	—						
PC	4/5	4/6	5/6	4/5	5/6	4/6	—					
CD	4/5	4/5	4/6	4/5	5/6	4/6	5/6	—				
PA	4/5	4/5	4/6	4/5	4/6	4/5	5/6	5/6	—			
BD	3/4	3/4	4/5	3/4	4/5	3/4	4/5	4/5	4/5	—		
OA	5/6	5/6	5/7	5/6	5/7	5/6	5/7	5/7	5/7	5/6	—	
SS	4/5	4/5	4/6	4/5	5/6	4/5	5/6	5/6	4/6	4/5	5/7	—
MA	4/5	4/6	5/6	4/5	5/6	4/6	5/6	5/6	5/6	4/5	5/7	5/6

	PSIQ	VSIQ			VCDQ	FDDQ	PSDQ
	PSIQ	12/16		PODQ	12/16	15/20	16/21
				FDDQ	13/17	—	17/22
				PSDQ	15/19	17/22	—

15 (15-0-0 through 15-11-30)

	I	S	A	V	C	DS	PC	CD	PA	BD	OA	SS
S	4/5	—										
A	4/5	4/5	—									
V	3/4	4/5	4/5	—								
C	4/5	4/5	4/5	4/5	—							
DS	3/4	4/5	4/5	3/4	4/5	—						
PC	4/5	4/5	4/5	3/4	4/5	3/4	—					
CD	3/4	4/5	4/5	3/4	4/5	3/4	4/4	—				
PA	4/5	4/6	4/6	4/5	4/6	4/5	4/6	4/5	—			
BD	3/4	3/4	3/4	3/4	4/4	3/4	3/4	3/4	4/5	—		
OA	4/5	4/5	4/5	4/5	4/6	4/5	4/5	4/5	5/6	4/5	—	
SS	4/5	4/5	4/5	3/4	4/5	3/4	4/5	4/4	4/6	3/4	4/5	—
MA	5/6	5/6	5/6	4/6	5/6	4/6	5/6	5/6	5/7	4/6	5/7	5/6

	PSIQ	VSIQ			VCDQ	FDDQ	PSDQ
	PSIQ	10/13		PODQ	12/16	14/18	14/18
				FDDQ	11/15	—	13/17
				PSDQ	11/15	13/17	—

(Continued)

Table A-2 (Continued)

Age level		I	S	A	V	C	DS	PC	CD	PA	BD	OA	SS
16 (16-0-0 through 16-11-30)	S	4/4	—										
	A	4/5	4/5	—									
	V	3/4	3/4	4/5	—								
	C	4/5	4/5	4/6	4/5	—							
	DS	3/4	3/4	4/5	3/4	4/5	—						
	PC	4/5	4/5	4/5	4/5	5/6	4/5	—					
	CD	3/4	3/4	4/4	3/4	4/5	3/4	4/5	—				
	PA	4/5	4/5	4/6	4/5	5/6	4/5	5/6	4/5	—			
	BD	3/4	3/4	4/4	3/4	4/5	3/4	4/5	3/4	4/5	—		
	OA	4/5	4/6	4/6	4/5	5/6	4/5	5/6	4/5	5/6	4/5	—	
	SS	4/5	4/5	4/5	4/5	4/6	4/5	4/5	4/4	4/6	4/4	4/6	—
	MA	4/6	5/6	5/6	4/6	5/6	4/6	5/6	4/5	5/6	4/5	5/6	5/6

Age 16 — IQ box:

	VSIQ
PSIQ	11/14

Age 16 — Deviation Quotient box:

	VCDQ	FDDQ	PSDQ
PODQ	12/16	14/18	13/17
FDDQ	12/16	—	13/17
PSDQ	12/15	13/17	—

Age level		I	S	A	V	C	DS	PC	CD	PA	BD	OA	SS
Average	S	4/5	—										
	A	4/5	4/5	—									
	V	4/5	4/5	4/5	—								
	C	4/5	4/5	4/6	4/5	—							
	DS	4/5	4/5	4/5	4/5	4/5	—						
	PC	4/5	4/5	4/6	4/5	4/6	4/5	—					
	CD	4/5	4/5	4/6	4/5	4/6	4/5	4/6	—				
	PA	4/5	4/5	4/6	4/5	4/6	4/5	4/6	4/6	—			
	BD	4/5	4/5	4/5	3/4	4/5	4/5	4/5	4/5	4/5	—		
	OA	4/6	5/6	5/6	4/6	5/6	4/6	5/6	5/6	5/6	4/6	—	
	SS	4/5	4/5	4/6	4/5	4/6	4/5	4/6	4/6	5/6	4/5	5/6	—
	MA	4/6	5/6	5/6	4/5	5/6	4/6	5/6	5/6	5/6	4/6	5/6	5/6

Average — IQ box:

	VSIQ
PSIQ	12/16

Average — Deviation Quotient box:

	VCDQ	FDDQ	PSDQ
PODQ	12/16	15/19	15/19
FDDQ	13/18	—	16/21
PSDQ	14/18	16/21	—

Note. Abbreviations: I = Information; S = Similarities; A = Arithmetic; V = Vocabulary; C = Comprehension; DS = Digit Span; PC = Picture Completion; CD = Coding; PA = Picture Arrangement; BD = Block Design; OA = Object Assembly; SS = Symbol Search; MA = Mazes; VSIQ = Verbal Scale IQ; PSIQ = Performance Scale IQ; VCDQ = Verbal Comprehension Deviation Quotient; PODQ = Perceptual Organization Deviation Quotient; FDDQ = Freedom from Distractibility Deviation Quotient; PSDQ = Processing Speed Deviation Quotient.

The Index scores are composed of the following subtests: Verbal Comprehension = Information, Similarities, Vocabulary, and Comprehension; Perceptual Organization = Picture Completion, Block Design, and Object Assembly; Freedom from Distractibility = Arithmetic and Digit Span; Processing Speed = Coding and Symbol Search.

Sample reading: At the 6-0-0 level, a difference of 4 points between scaled scores on the Information and Similarities subtests is significant at the 5% level; a difference of 6 points is significant at the 1% level. The first small box shows that a 12-point difference between the Verbal Scale IQ and the Performance Scale IQ is needed for the 5% level, and a 16-point difference is needed for the 1% level. The second small box shows that a difference of 13 points between the Verbal Comprehension Deviation Quotient and the Perceptual Organization Deviation Quotient is needed at the 5% level, and a difference of 17 points is needed at the 1% level.

The values in this table for the subtest comparison are overly liberal when more than one comparison is made for a subtest. They are more accurate when a priori planned comparisons are made, such as Information vs. Comprehension or Digit Span vs. Arithmetic.

All values in this table have been rounded up to the next higher number.

See Chapter 10, Exhibit 10-1 (page 302) for an explanation of the method used to arrive at magnitude of differences.

See Exhibit 8-4 in Chapter 8 (pages 256–257) for the procedure used to obtain the reliability coefficients for the index scores (or short forms).

Silverstein (personal communication, February 1990) suggests that the following formula be used to obtain the value of the significant difference at the .05 level between the highest and lowest subtest scores on the profile that allows for making individual subtest comparisons:

$$D = q \sqrt{\frac{\Sigma \text{SEM}^2}{k}}$$

where D is the significant difference, q is the critical value of the studentized range statistic, SEM is the standard error of measurement of a particular subtest, and k is the number of subtests. For the WISC–III, the q value is 4.68 at the .05 level for 13 and ∞ degrees of freedom and k is 13. The sum of the SEM^2 for the 13 subtests is 1.51 + 1.69 + 1.99 + 1.67 + 2.10 + 1.37 + 2.07 + 2.02 + 2.19 + 1.23 + 2.79 + 2.19 + 2.69 = 25.51 and

$$D = 4.68 \times \sqrt{\frac{25.51}{13}} = 4.68 \times \sqrt{1.96} = 4.68 \times 1.40 = 6.55$$

Thus, a difference of 6 points between the highest and lowest subtest scaled scores represents a significant difference at the .05 level.

Table A-3
Estimates of the Probability of Obtaining Designated Differences Between Individual WISC–III Verbal and Performance IQs by Chance

Probability of obtaining given or greater discrepancy by chance	Age level											
	6	7	8	9	10	11	12	13	14	15	16	Av.[a]
.50	4.02	4.26	3.76	4.02	3.76	3.89	3.76	4.02	4.02	3.18	3.62	3.76
.25	6.90	7.32	6.45	6.90	6.45	6.68	6.45	6.90	6.90	5.45	6.22	6.45
.20	7.68	8.15	7.18	7.68	7.18	7.44	7.18	7.68	7.68	6.07	6.92	7.18
.10	9.90	10.50	9.26	9.90	9.26	9.59	9.26	9.90	9.90	7.83	8.92	9.26
.05	11.76	12.47	11.00	11.76	11.00	11.39	11.00	11.76	11.76	9.30	10.60	11.00
.02	13.98	14.83	13.08	13.98	13.08	13.54	13.08	13.98	13.98	11.05	12.60	13.08
.01	15.48	16.42	14.48	15.48	14.48	14.99	14.48	15.48	15.48	12.24	13.95	14.48
.001	19.74	20.94	18.47	19.74	18.47	19.11	18.47	19.74	19.74	15.61	17.79	18.47

Note. To use Table A-3, find the column appropriate to the examinee's age. Locate the discrepancy that is just *less than* the discrepancy obtained by the examinee. The entry in the first column in that same row gives the probability of obtaining a given or greater discrepancy by chance. For example, the hypothesis that a 6-year-old examinee obtained a Verbal-Performance discrepancy of 17 by chance can be rejected at the .01 level of significance. Table A-3 is two-tailed. See Chapter 10, Exhibit 10-1 (page 302) for an explanation of the method used to arrive at magnitudes of differences.

[a] Av. = Average of 11 age groups.

Table A-4
Frequencies (cumulative percentages) of Differences Between WISC–III Verbal Scale and Performance Scale IQs and Between Index Scores in the Standardization Group When V > P, VC > PO, VC > FD, VC > PS, PO > FD, PO > PS, and FD > PS

Amount of discrepancy	Scales/indexes						
	Verbal > Performance (V > P)	Verbal Comprehension > Perceptual Organization (VC > PO)	Verbal Comprehension > Freedom from Distractibility (VC > FD)	Verbal Comprehension > Processing Speed (VC > PS)	Perceptual Organization > Freedom from Distractibility (PO > FD)	Perceptual Organization > Processing Speed (PO > PS)	Freedom from Distractibility > Processing Speed (FD > PS)
≥40	0.2	0.1	0.1	0.6	0.1	0.2	0.7
39	0.2	0.1	0.2	0.7	0.2	0.3	0.8
38	0.2	0.2	0.2	0.8	0.4	0.4	1.1
37	0.3	0.3	0.2	1.0	0.5	0.6	1.2
36	0.3	0.4	0.3	1.2	0.6	0.6	1.3
35	0.4	0.5	0.4	1.3	0.9	0.8	1.7
34	0.4	0.5	0.5	1.6	1.0	1.0	1.9
33	0.5	0.6	0.6	1.8	1.1	1.1	2.3
32	0.6	0.7	0.7	2.2	1.4	1.3	2.9
31	0.8	0.9	0.8	2.7	1.6	1.7	3.1
30	1.0	1.0	1.2	2.8	1.8	2.1	3.6
29	1.3	1.4	1.5	3.1	2.1	2.4	4.0
28	1.4	1.7	1.6	3.9	2.2	2.8	4.5
27	1.7	2.1	2.2	4.5	2.8	3.5	5.4
26	2.1	2.5	2.6	5.0	3.2	4.0	6.1
25	2.6	3.1	2.8	5.7	3.4	4.6	6.8
24	3.2	3.5	3.4	6.8	4.3	5.6	7.9
23	4.0	4.2	3.8	7.8	4.9	6.5	9.0
22	4.6	5.0	4.5	8.8	5.5	7.2	9.6
21	5.2	5.9	5.3	9.9	6.9	8.2	10.5
20	5.9	6.6	6.1	11.5	8.1	9.4	11.5
19	7.1	7.3	7.2	12.7	8.7	10.9	12.0
18	8.5	8.1	8.5	14.0	10.1	11.9	13.9
17	9.5	9.1	9.3	15.2	11.2	13.2	14.9
16	10.5	11.2	10.3	16.9	12.2	14.7	16.6
15	11.8	12.4	11.8	18.0	13.8	15.8	18.3
14	13.8	14.3	13.4	19.5	14.9	18.3	19.3
13	15.6	16.4	15.4	20.8	17.4	20.3	22.5
12	17.7	18.5	17.4	22.8	19.2	21.7	24.1
11	20.6	20.9	19.0	25.1	21.1	24.9	26.0
10	22.6	23.2	21.4	27.4	23.1	26.3	29.4
9	24.7	25.7	23.9	29.5	25.7	28.1	30.3
8	27.5	27.7	26.0	31.0	27.6	31.0	32.1
7	30.6	30.5	29.1	33.9	30.7	32.7	34.9
6	33.6	33.3	31.6	35.3	34.2	35.1	35.8
5	36.2	36.7	34.6	37.7	36.4	37.7	39.5
4	38.9	39.6	37.5	40.1	40.4	39.7	41.1
3	41.5	42.6	39.8	43.0	43.1	43.3	44.1
2	44.6	45.9	43.3	45.1	45.1	45.3	46.4
1	47.2	49.1	46.9	47.2	48.3	47.6	48.5
0	—	—	—	—	—	—	—
Mdn	8.0	9.0	8.0	11.0	9.0	10.0	11.0

Source: Wechsler Intelligence Scale for Children: Third Edition. Copyright © 1991 by The Psychological Corporation, a Harcourt Assessment Company. Adapted and reproduced by permission. All rights reserved. "Wechsler Intelligence Scale for Children" and "WISC" are trademarks of The Psychological Corporation registered in the United States of America and/or other jurisdictions.

Table A-5
Frequencies (cumulative percentages) of Differences Between WISC–III Verbal Scale and Performance Scale IQs and Between Index Scores in the Standardization Group When P > V, PO > VC, FD > VC, PS > VC, FD > PO, PS > PO, and PS > FD

Amount of discrepancy	Scales/Indexes						
	Performance > Verbal (P > V)	Perceptual Organization > Verbal Comprehension (PO > VC)	Freedom from Distractibility > Verbal Comprehension (FD > VC)	Processing Speed > Verbal Comprehension (PS > VC)	Freedom from Distractibility > Perceptual Organization (FD > PO)	Processing Speed > Perceptual Organization (PS > PO)	Processing Speed > Freedom from Distractibility (PS > FD)
≥40	2.3	0.1	0.1	0.7	0.5	0.8	0.4
39	2.3	0.1	0.1	1.0	0.6	0.9	0.6
38	2.3	0.1	0.1	1.2	0.6	0.9	0.9
37	2.3	0.1	0.3	1.4	0.9	1.1	1.0
36	2.3	0.2	0.4	1.7	1.1	1.3	1.1
35	2.4	0.3	0.6	2.1	1.5	1.7	1.2
34	2.5	0.3	0.9	2.5	1.7	1.9	1.4
33	2.6	0.4	1.1	2.8	2.2	2.1	1.7
32	2.7	0.6	1.1	3.2	2.6	2.5	2.3
31	3.1	0.8	1.3	3.6	2.7	3.0	2.7
30	3.2	1.0	1.5	4.1	3.2	3.3	3.1
29	3.3	1.3	2.0	4.5	3.9	4.1	3.3
28	3.6	1.6	2.4	4.8	4.4	4.4	3.8
27	3.7	1.9	2.9	5.4	5.1	5.0	4.2
26	4.0	2.2	3.5	6.2	5.4	6.0	4.9
25	4.5	2.6	4.0	6.9	6.0	6.5	5.8
24	5.2	3.1	4.6	8.0	6.8	7.4	6.4
23	5.9	3.6	5.1	8.9	7.6	8.3	6.8
22	6.9	4.6	5.9	9.7	8.6	9.0	7.6
21	7.7	6.1	6.7	11.0	9.7	10.1	9.0
20	8.5	7.0	7.9	12.1	10.5	11.2	9.6
19	9.4	7.6	8.6	13.2	11.8	12.2	10.6
18	10.6	8.7	9.9	14.6	13.3	13.3	12.8
17	11.8	10.0	12.1	16.1	14.3	14.9	14.0
16	13.0	11.5	13.4	17.8	16.1	16.1	15.9
15	14.3	13.0	14.9	19.3	18.1	18.1	17.2
14	16.0	14.3	16.8	20.6	19.3	20.1	18.6
13	17.5	16.5	19.5	23.0	21.2	22.1	21.5
12	19.5	18.5	21.1	24.6	23.0	24.3	22.7
11	21.3	20.4	23.5	27.1	25.1	25.9	24.8
10	23.2	22.5	26.4	29.0	27.7	27.9	27.2
9	25.8	25.1	28.9	30.9	29.1	30.1	28.6
8	28.5	27.1	31.3	33.3	31.5	32.2	32.5
7	31.0	29.2	33.5	35.1	35.1	34.5	34.5
6	34.2	32.3	36.0	37.5	36.1	36.2	36.9
5	38.1	35.1	39.0	39.6	39.4	39.6	39.8
4	40.4	38.7	41.4	42.3	43.1	42.8	41.1
3	42.8	42.3	44.1	45.3	44.1	44.7	44.4
2	46.6	45.1	47.6	47.9	47.5	48.0	46.3
1	49.5	48.2	50.7	50.3	49.8	49.6	48.1
0	—	—	—	—	—	—	—
Mdn	9.0	9.0	10.0	11.0	11.0	11.0	10.0

Source: Wechsler Intelligence Scale for Children: Third Edition. Copyright © 1991 by The Psychological Corporation, a Harcourt Assessment Company. Adapted and reproduced by permission. All rights reserved. "Wechsler Intelligence Scale for Children" and "WISC" are trademarks of The Psychological Corporation registered in the United States of America and/or other jurisdictions.

Table A-6
Differences Required for Significance When Each WISC–III Subtest Scaled Score Is Compared to the Mean Subtest Scaled Score for Any Individual Child

Age 6-0-0 through 6-11-30

Subtest	Mean of 4 subtests[a]		Mean of 5 subtests[b]		Mean of 6 subtests[c]		Mean of 6 subtests		Mean of 7 subtests		Mean of 10 subtests	
	.05	.01	.05	.01	.05	.01	.05	.01	.05	.01	.05	.01
Information	3.27	3.96	3.51	4.20	3.64	4.38	—	—	—	—	4.11	4.82
Similarities	2.91	3.52	3.07	3.68	3.16	3.80	—	—	—	—	3.52	4.12
Arithmetic	—	—	3.07	3.68	3.16	3.80	—	—	—	—	3.52	4.12
Vocabulary	2.86	3.46	3.01	3.60	3.09	3.72	—	—	—	—	3.43	4.02
Comprehension	3.19	3.85	3.40	4.07	3.52	4.24	—	—	—	—	3.97	4.65
Digit Span	—	—	—	—	3.28	3.95	—	—	—	—	—	—
Picture Completion	3.04	3.67	3.25	3.90	3.38	4.07	3.35	4.03	3.52	4.18	3.75	4.39
Coding	—	—	3.42	4.09	3.56	4.28	3.53	4.25	3.71	4.40	3.97	4.65
Picture Arrangement	2.85	3.44	3.03	3.62	3.13	3.76	3.10	3.73	3.25	3.85	3.43	4.02
Block Design	2.85	3.44	3.03	3.62	3.13	3.76	3.10	3.73	3.25	3.85	3.43	4.02
Object Assembly	3.35	4.05	3.62	4.34	3.78	4.55	3.76	4.52	3.96	4.69	4.25	4.97
Symbol Search	—	—	—	—	3.89	4.68	—	—	4.07	4.83	—	—
Mazes	—	—	—	—	—	—	3.23	3.88	3.39	4.02	—	—

Subtest	Mean of 11 subtests		Mean of 11 subtests		Mean of 11 subtests		Mean of 12 subtests		Mean of 12 subtests		Mean of 13 subtests	
	.05	.01	.05	.01	.05	.01	.05	.01	.05	.01	.05	.01
Information	4.18	4.89	4.19	4.90	4.18	4.89	4.25	5.11	4.25	5.10	4.43	5.00
Similarities	3.57	4.17	3.58	4.18	3.57	4.17	3.62	4.36	3.62	4.35	3.77	4.25
Arithmetic	3.57	4.17	3.58	4.18	3.57	4.17	3.62	4.36	3.62	4.35	3.77	4.25
Vocabulary	3.48	4.07	3.49	4.08	3.48	4.07	3.54	4.25	3.53	4.24	3.68	4.15
Comprehension	4.04	4.72	4.04	4.73	4.04	4.72	4.10	4.93	4.10	4.93	4.28	4.82
Digit Span	3.73	4.36	—	—	—	—	3.79	4.56	3.78	4.55	3.95	4.45
Picture Completion	3.81	4.45	3.82	4.46	3.81	4.45	3.87	4.65	3.86	4.65	4.03	4.55
Coding	4.04	4.72	4.04	4.73	4.04	4.72	4.10	4.93	4.10	4.93	4.28	4.82
Picture Arrangement	3.48	4.07	3.49	4.08	3.48	4.07	3.54	4.25	3.53	4.24	3.68	4.15
Block Design	3.48	4.07	3.49	4.08	3.48	4.07	3.54	4.25	3.53	4.24	3.68	4.15
Object Assembly	4.32	5.05	4.33	5.06	4.32	5.05	4.39	5.28	4.39	5.28	4.58	5.17
Symbol Search	—	—	4.46	5.22	—	—	4.53	5.45	—	—	4.73	5.33
Mazes	—	—	—	—	3.65	4.27	—	—	3.70	4.45	3.86	4.35

[a]In this column, the entries for Information, Similarities, Vocabulary, and Comprehension are compared to the mean of these four subtests. Similarly, the entries for Picture Completion, Picture Arrangement, Block Design, and Object Assembly are compared to the mean of these four subtests.

[b]In this column, the entries for Information, Similarities, Arithmetic, Vocabulary, and Comprehension are compared to the mean of these five subtests. Similarly, the entries for Picture Completion, Coding, Picture Arrangement, Block Design, and Object Assembly are compared to the mean of these five subtests.

[c]In this column, the entries for Information, Similarities, Arithmetic, Vocabulary, Comprehension, and Digit Span are compared to the mean of these six subtests. Similarly, the entries for Picture Completion, Coding, Picture Arrangement, Block Design, Object Assembly, and Symbol Search are compared to the mean of these six subtests.

(Continued)

Table A-6 (Continued)

Age 7-0-0 through 7-11-30

Subtest	Mean of 4 subtests[a]		Mean of 5 subtests[b]		Mean of 6 subtests[c]		Mean of 6 subtests		Mean of 7 subtests		Mean of 10 subtests	
	.05	.01	.05	.01	.05	.01	.05	.01	.05	.01	.05	.01
Information	3.18	3.84	3.40	4.07	3.50	4.21	—	—	—	—	3.92	4.59
Similarities	3.14	3.79	3.35	4.01	3.44	4.14	—	—	—	—	3.85	4.50
Arithmetic	—	—	3.56	4.26	3.67	4.41	—	—	—	—	4.13	4.84
Vocabulary	3.05	3.68	3.24	3.88	3.32	3.99	—	—	—	—	3.70	4.33
Comprehension	3.35	4.05	3.61	4.32	3.72	4.48	—	—	—	—	4.20	4.92
Digit Span	—	—	—	—	3.19	3.84	—	—	—	—	—	—
Picture Completion	2.77	3.34	2.94	3.52	3.00	3.61	2.99	3.60	3.11	3.68	3.29	3.85
Coding	—	—	3.70	4.43	3.84	4.61	3.83	4.61	4.02	4.77	4.33	5.07
Picture Arrangement	2.77	3.34	2.94	3.52	3.00	3.61	2.99	3.60	3.11	3.68	3.29	3.85
Block Design	3.10	3.75	3.34	4.00	3.44	4.14	3.44	4.14	3.59	4.26	3.85	4.50
Object Assembly	3.61	4.36	3.93	4.71	4.09	4.92	4.09	4.92	4.30	5.10	4.65	5.44
Symbol Search	—	—	—	—	3.50	4.21	—	—	3.66	4.34	—	—
Mazes	—	—	—	—	—	—	3.38	4.06	3.53	4.18	—	—

Subtest	Mean of 11 subtests		Mean of 11 subtests		Mean of 11 subtests		Mean of 12 subtests		Mean of 12 subtests		Mean of 13 subtests	
	.05	.01	.05	.01	.05	.01	.05	.01	.05	.01	.05	.01
Information	3.98	4.65	3.98	4.65	3.98	4.65	4.04	4.85	4.04	4.85	4.21	4.74
Similarities	3.90	4.56	3.91	4.57	3.91	4.57	3.96	4.76	3.96	4.76	4.12	4.65
Arithmetic	4.20	4.91	4.20	4.91	4.20	4.91	4.26	5.12	4.26	5.12	4.44	5.01
Vocabulary	3.75	4.38	3.75	4.39	3.75	4.38	3.80	4.57	3.80	4.57	3.96	4.46
Comprehension	4.27	4.99	4.27	4.99	4.27	4.99	4.33	5.21	4.33	5.21	4.52	5.09
Digit Span	3.59	4.19	—	—	—	—	3.63	4.37	3.63	4.37	3.78	4.26
Picture Completion	3.33	3.89	3.33	3.90	3.33	3.89	3.37	4.05	3.37	4.05	3.50	3.95
Coding	4.40	5.15	4.41	5.15	4.41	5.15	4.47	5.38	4.47	5.38	4.66	5.26
Picture Arrangement	3.33	3.89	3.33	3.90	3.33	3.89	3.37	4.05	3.37	4.05	3.50	3.95
Block Design	3.90	4.56	3.91	4.57	3.91	4.57	3.96	4.76	3.96	4.76	4.12	4.65
Object Assembly	4.73	5.53	4.73	5.53	4.73	5.53	4.81	5.78	4.80	5.78	5.01	5.65
Symbol Search	—	—	3.98	4.65	—	—	4.04	4.85	—	—	4.21	4.74
Mazes	—	—	—	—	3.83	4.48	—	—	3.88	4.66	4.04	4.56

[a]In this column, the entries for Information, Similarities, Vocabulary, and Comprehension are compared to the mean of these four subtests. Similarly, the entries for Picture Completion, Picture Arrangement, Block Design, and Object Assembly are compared to the mean of these four subtests.

[b]In this column, the entries for Information, Similarities, Arithmetic, Vocabulary, and Comprehension are compared to the mean of these five subtests. Similarly, the entries for Picture Completion, Coding, Picture Arrangement, Block Design, and Object Assembly are compared to the mean of these five subtests.

[c]In this column, the entries for Information, Similarities, Arithmetic, Vocabulary, Comprehension, and Digit Span are compared to the mean of these six subtests. Similarly, the entries for Picture Completion, Coding, Picture Arrangement, Block Design, Object Assembly, and Symbol Search are compared to the mean of these six subtests.

(Continued)

Table A-6 (Continued)

Age 8-0-0 through 8-11-30

Subtest	Mean of 4 subtests[a]		Mean of 5 subtests[b]		Mean of 6 subtests[c]		Mean of 6 subtests		Mean of 7 subtests		Mean of 10 subtests	
	.05	.01	.05	.01	.05	.01	.05	.01	.05	.01	.05	.01
Information	2.44	2.94	2.63	3.15	2.71	3.26	—	—	—	—	3.06	3.59
Similarities	2.55	3.08	2.76	3.31	2.86	3.44	—	—	—	—	3.24	3.80
Arithmetic	—	—	3.13	3.75	3.26	3.92	—	—	—	—	3.73	4.37
Vocabulary	2.32	2.80	2.49	2.98	2.55	3.07	—	—	—	—	2.87	3.36
Comprehension	2.49	3.01	2.70	3.23	2.78	3.35	—	—	—	—	3.15	3.69
Digit Span	—	—	—	—	2.86	3.44	—	—	—	—	—	—
Picture Completion	2.97	3.59	3.12	3.74	3.21	3.86	3.20	3.85	3.34	3.96	3.50	4.09
Coding	—	—	3.29	3.94	3.40	4.09	3.39	4.07	3.54	4.20	3.73	4.37
Picture Arrangement	3.37	4.07	3.60	4.31	3.74	4.50	3.73	4.49	3.91	4.64	4.16	4.88
Block Design	2.87	3.47	3.00	3.60	3.08	3.71	3.07	3.69	3.19	3.79	3.33	3.90
Object Assembly	3.65	4.41	3.93	4.71	4.10	4.94	4.10	4.93	4.31	5.11	4.62	5.41
Symbol Search	—	—	—	—	3.74	4.50	—	—	3.91	4.64	—	—
Mazes	—	—	—	—	—	—	3.50	4.22	3.67	4.35	—	—

Subtest	Mean of 11 subtests		Mean of 11 subtests		Mean of 11 subtests		Mean of 12 subtests		Mean of 12 subtests		Mean of 13 subtests	
	.05	.01	.05	.01	.05	.01	.05	.01	.05	.01	.05	.01
Information	3.10	3.62	3.11	3.64	3.11	3.63	3.15	3.78	3.14	3.78	3.28	3.69
Similarities	3.29	3.84	3.30	3.85	3.29	3.85	3.34	4.01	3.33	4.01	3.48	3.92
Arithmetic	3.79	4.43	3.80	4.44	3.80	4.44	3.85	4.63	3.85	4.63	4.02	4.53
Vocabulary	2.90	3.39	2.91	3.41	2.91	3.40	2.94	3.54	2.94	3.54	3.06	3.45
Comprehension	3.19	3.73	3.21	3.75	3.20	3.74	3.24	3.90	3.24	3.90	3.38	3.81
Digit Span	3.29	3.84	—	—	—	—	3.34	4.01	3.33	4.01	3.48	3.92
Picture Completion	3.55	4.15	3.56	4.16	3.55	4.15	3.60	4.33	3.60	4.33	3.76	4.24
Coding	3.79	4.43	3.80	4.44	3.80	4.44	3.85	4.63	3.85	4.63	4.02	4.53
Picture Arrangement	4.23	4.95	4.24	4.96	4.24	4.96	4.31	5.18	4.31	5.18	4.49	5.07
Block Design	3.38	3.95	3.39	3.96	3.38	3.95	3.43	4.12	3.43	4.12	3.57	4.03
Object Assembly	4.70	5.49	4.71	5.50	4.70	5.50	4.78	5.75	4.78	5.75	4.99	5.63
Symbol Search	—	—	4.24	4.96	—	—	4.31	5.18	—	—	4.49	5.07
Mazes	—	—	—	—	3.95	4.62	—	—	4.01	4.82	4.18	4.72

[a] In this column, the entries for Information, Similarities, Vocabulary, and Comprehension are compared to the mean of these four subtests. Similarly, the entries for Picture Completion, Picture Arrangement, Block Design, and Object Assembly are compared to the mean of these four subtests.

[b] In this column, the entries for Information, Similarities, Arithmetic, Vocabulary, and Comprehension are compared to the mean of these five subtests. Similarly, the entries for Picture Completion, Coding, Picture Arrangement, Block Design, and Object Assembly are compared to the mean of these five subtests.

[c] In this column, the entries for Information, Similarities, Arithmetic, Vocabulary, Comprehension, and Digit Span are compared to the mean of these six subtests. Similarly, the entries for Picture Completion, Coding, Picture Arrangement, Block Design, Object Assembly, and Symbol Search are compared to the mean of these six subtests.

(Continued)

Table A-6 (Continued)

Age 9-0-0 through 9-11-30

Subtest	Mean of 4 subtests[a]		Mean of 5 subtests[b]		Mean of 6 subtests[c]		Mean of 6 subtests		Mean of 7 subtests		Mean of 10 subtests	
	.05	.01	.05	.01	.05	.01	.05	.01	.05	.01	.05	.01
Information	2.87	3.47	3.08	3.69	3.16	3.80	—	—	—	—	3.52	4.12
Similarities	2.92	3.53	3.14	3.76	3.22	3.88	—	—	—	—	3.60	4.21
Arithmetic	—	—	3.62	4.34	3.75	4.51	—	—	—	—	4.25	4.98
Vocabulary	2.82	3.41	3.03	3.62	3.09	3.72	—	—	—	—	3.44	4.02
Comprehension	3.20	3.86	3.47	4.15	3.58	4.31	—	—	—	—	4.04	4.74
Digit Span	—	—	—	—	3.09	3.72	—	—	—	—	—	—
Picture Completion	2.95	3.57	3.13	3.75	3.24	3.90	3.26	3.92	3.40	4.04	3.60	4.21
Coding	—	—	3.25	3.89	3.37	4.05	3.38	4.07	3.54	4.20	3.75	4.39
Picture Arrangement	3.31	4.00	3.56	4.27	3.71	4.47	3.73	4.48	3.91	4.64	4.18	4.90
Block Design	2.70	3.27	2.83	3.39	2.91	3.50	2.93	3.52	3.04	3.61	3.18	3.72
Object Assembly	3.18	3.84	3.41	4.08	3.55	4.27	3.56	4.28	3.73	4.42	3.97	4.65
Symbol Search	—	—	—	—	3.71	4.47	—	—	3.91	4.64	—	—
Mazes	—	—	—	—	—	—	4.04	4.86	4.25	5.05	—	—

Subtest	Mean of 11 subtests		Mean of 11 subtests		Mean of 11 subtests		Mean of 12 subtests		Mean of 12 subtests		Mean of 13 subtests	
	.05	.01	.05	.01	.05	.01	.05	.01	.05	.01	.05	.01
Information	3.57	4.17	3.58	4.18	3.58	4.19	3.62	4.35	3.63	4.36	3.78	4.26
Similarities	3.65	4.27	3.66	4.28	3.66	4.28	3.71	4.46	3.71	4.46	3.87	4.36
Arithmetic	4.32	5.05	4.33	5.06	4.33	5.06	4.39	5.28	4.40	5.28	4.59	5.17
Vocabulary	3.48	4.07	3.49	4.08	3.50	4.09	3.54	4.25	3.54	4.26	3.69	4.16
Comprehension	4.11	4.80	4.12	4.81	4.12	4.82	4.18	5.02	4.18	5.02	4.36	4.92
Digit Span	3.48	4.07	—	—	—	—	3.54	4.25	3.54	4.26	3.69	4.16
Picture Completion	3.65	4.27	3.66	4.28	3.66	4.28	3.71	4.46	3.71	4.46	3.87	4.36
Coding	3.81	4.45	3.82	4.46	3.82	4.47	3.87	4.65	3.87	4.66	4.04	4.55
Picture Arrangement	4.25	4.97	4.26	4.98	4.26	4.98	4.32	5.20	4.33	5.20	4.51	5.09
Block Design	3.22	3.76	3.23	3.77	3.23	3.78	3.26	3.92	3.27	3.93	3.40	3.84
Object Assembly	4.04	4.72	4.04	4.73	4.05	4.73	4.10	4.93	4.11	4.94	4.28	4.83
Symbol Search	—	—	4.26	4.98	—	—	4.32	5.20	—	—	4.51	5.09
Mazes	—	—	—	—	4.66	5.45	—	—	4.73	5.69	4.94	5.57

[a]In this column, the entries for Information, Similarities, Vocabulary, and Comprehension are compared to the mean of these four subtests. Similarly, the entries for Picture Completion, Picture Arrangement, Block Design, and Object Assembly are compared to the mean of these four subtests.

[b]In this column, the entries for Information, Similarities, Arithmetic, Vocabulary, and Comprehension are compared to the mean of these five subtests. Similarly, the entries for Picture Completion, Coding, Picture Arrangement, Block Design, and Object Assembly are compared to the mean of these five subtests.

[c]In this column, the entries for Information, Similarities, Arithmetic, Vocabulary, Comprehension, and Digit Span are compared to the mean of these six subtests. Similarly, the entries for Picture Completion, Coding, Picture Arrangement, Block Design, Object Assembly, and Symbol Search are compared to the mean of these six subtests.

(Continued)

Table A-6 (Continued)

Age 10-0-0 through 10-11-30

Subtest	Mean of 4 subtests[a]		Mean of 5 subtests[b]		Mean of 6 subtests[c]		Mean of 6 subtests		Mean of 7 subtests		Mean of 10 subtests	
	.05	.01	.05	.01	.05	.01	.05	.01	.05	.01	.05	.01
Information	2.74	3.31	2.94	3.52	3.03	3.64	—	—	—	—	3.42	4.00
Similarities	2.74	3.31	2.94	3.52	3.03	3.64	—	—	—	—	3.42	4.00
Arithmetic	—	—	3.12	3.73	3.22	3.88	—	—	—	—	3.66	4.29
Vocabulary	2.41	2.91	2.54	3.05	2.59	3.12	—	—	—	—	2.88	3.37
Comprehension	2.89	3.49	3.12	3.73	3.22	3.88	—	—	—	—	3.66	4.29
Digit Span	—	—	—	—	2.89	3.48	—	—	—	—	—	—
Picture Completion	3.26	3.94	3.48	4.17	3.62	4.35	3.62	4.36	3.80	4.50	4.03	4.72
Coding	—	—	3.27	3.92	3.38	4.07	3.39	4.08	3.54	4.20	3.74	4.38
Picture Arrangement	3.26	3.94	3.48	4.17	3.62	4.35	3.62	4.36	3.80	4.50	4.03	4.72
Block Design	2.53	3.06	2.59	3.11	2.64	3.17	2.64	3.18	2.73	3.23	2.78	3.25
Object Assembly	3.47	4.19	3.73	4.47	3.89	4.68	3.89	4.68	4.09	4.85	4.37	5.12
Symbol Search	—	—	—	—	3.73	4.48	—	—	3.92	4.64	—	—
Mazes	—	—	—	—	—	—	3.84	4.62	4.03	4.78	—	—

Subtest	Mean of 11 subtests		Mean of 11 subtests		Mean of 11 subtests		Mean of 12 subtests		Mean of 12 subtests		Mean of 13 subtests	
	.05	.01	.05	.01	.05	.01	.05	.01	.05	.01	.05	.01
Information	3.47	4.05	3.48	4.07	3.48	4.07	3.52	4.23	3.52	4.24	3.67	4.14
Similarities	3.47	4.05	3.48	4.07	3.48	4.07	3.52	4.23	3.52	4.24	3.67	4.14
Arithmetic	3.72	4.34	3.73	4.35	3.73	4.36	3.78	4.54	3.78	4.54	3.94	4.44
Vocabulary	2.91	3.40	2.92	3.41	2.92	3.42	2.95	3.55	2.95	3.55	3.07	3.46
Comprehension	3.72	4.34	3.73	4.35	3.73	4.36	3.78	4.54	3.78	4.54	3.94	4.44
Digit Span	3.29	3.85	—	—	—	—	3.34	4.02	3.34	4.02	3.48	3.93
Picture Completion	4.10	4.79	4.10	4.80	4.11	4.80	4.17	5.01	4.17	5.01	4.35	4.90
Coding	3.79	4.44	3.80	4.45	3.81	4.45	3.86	4.64	3.86	4.64	4.03	4.54
Picture Arrangement	4.10	4.79	4.10	4.80	4.11	4.80	4.17	5.01	4.17	5.01	4.35	4.90
Block Design	2.80	3.28	2.82	3.29	2.82	3.30	2.84	3.42	2.84	3.42	2.96	3.34
Object Assembly	4.44	5.19	4.45	5.20	4.45	5.21	4.52	5.43	4.52	5.44	4.72	5.32
Symbol Search	—	—	4.25	4.96	—	—	4.31	5.18	—	—	4.50	5.08
Mazes	—	—	—	—	4.39	5.13	—	—	4.45	5.35	4.65	5.24

[a]In this column, the entries for Information, Similarities, Vocabulary, and Comprehension are compared to the mean of these four subtests. Similarly, the entries for Picture Completion, Picture Arrangement, Block Design, and Object Assembly are compared to the mean of these four subtests.

[b]In this column, the entries for Information, Similarities, Arithmetic, Vocabulary, and Comprehension are compared to the mean of these five subtests. Similarly, the entries for Picture Completion, Coding, Picture Arrangement, Block Design, and Object Assembly are compared to the mean of these five subtests.

[c]In this column, the entries for Information, Similarities, Arithmetic, Vocabulary, Comprehension, and Digit Span are compared to the mean of these six subtests. Similarly, the entries for Picture Completion, Coding, Picture Arrangement, Block Design, Object Assembly, and Symbol Search are compared to the mean of these six subtests.

(Continued)

Table A-6 *(Continued)*

Age 11-0-0 through 11-11-30

Subtest	Mean of 4 subtests[a]		Mean of 5 subtests[b]		Mean of 6 subtests[c]		Mean of 6 subtests		Mean of 7 subtests		Mean of 10 subtests	
	.05	.01	.05	.01	.05	.01	.05	.01	.05	.01	.05	.01
Information	2.58	3.11	2.75	3.29	2.82	3.39	—	—	—	—	3.17	3.71
Similarities	2.74	3.31	2.94	3.52	3.03	3.64	—	—	—	—	3.43	4.01
Arithmetic	—	—	3.12	3.73	3.22	3.88	—	—	—	—	3.67	4.29
Vocabulary	2.41	2.91	2.54	3.05	2.59	3.12	—	—	—	—	2.89	3.38
Comprehension	3.03	3.66	3.28	3.93	3.41	4.10	—	—	—	—	3.89	4.56
Digit Span	—	—	—	—	2.89	3.48	—	—	—	—	—	—
Picture Completion	3.23	3.90	3.40	4.07	3.50	4.21	3.53	4.24	3.67	4.36	3.89	4.56
Coding	—	—	3.07	3.68	3.13	3.77	3.16	3.80	3.27	3.88	3.43	4.01
Picture Arrangement	3.48	4.21	3.71	4.44	3.84	4.61	3.86	4.64	4.04	4.79	4.31	5.05
Block Design	2.86	3.46	2.95	3.53	3.00	3.61	3.03	3.64	3.13	3.71	3.26	3.81
Object Assembly	3.68	4.44	3.94	4.72	4.09	4.92	4.12	4.95	4.32	5.12	4.63	5.42
Symbol Search	—	—	—	—	3.32	4.00	—	—	3.48	4.13	—	—
Mazes	—	—	—	—	—	—	3.96	4.77	4.15	4.92	—	—

Subtest	Mean of 11 subtests		Mean of 11 subtests		Mean of 11 subtests		Mean of 12 subtests		Mean of 12 subtests		Mean of 13 subtests	
	.05	.01	.05	.01	.05	.01	.05	.01	.05	.01	.05	.01
Information	3.21	3.75	3.21	3.75	3.22	3.77	3.25	3.91	3.26	3.92	3.39	3.82
Similarities	3.47	4.06	3.48	4.07	3.49	4.08	3.52	4.23	3.53	4.24	3.68	4.14
Arithmetic	3.72	4.35	3.73	4.35	3.73	4.37	3.78	4.54	3.78	4.55	3.94	4.44
Vocabulary	2.92	3.41	2.92	3.41	2.93	3.43	2.95	3.55	2.96	3.56	3.07	3.47
Comprehension	3.95	4.62	3.96	4.63	3.97	4.64	4.01	4.83	4.02	4.83	4.19	4.73
Digit Span	3.30	3.86	—	—	—	—	3.34	4.02	3.35	4.03	3.49	3.93
Picture Completion	3.95	4.62	3.96	4.63	3.97	4.64	4.01	4.83	4.02	4.83	4.19	4.73
Coding	3.47	4.06	3.48	4.07	3.49	4.08	3.52	4.23	3.53	4.24	3.68	4.14
Picture Arrangement	4.38	5.12	4.38	5.13	4.39	5.13	4.45	5.35	4.46	5.36	4.65	5.24
Block Design	3.30	3.86	3.30	3.86	3.31	3.87	3.34	4.02	3.35	4.03	3.49	3.93
Object Assembly	4.71	5.50	4.71	5.51	4.72	5.52	4.79	5.75	4.79	5.76	5.00	5.64
Symbol Search	—	—	3.73	4.35	—	—	3.78	4.54	—	—	3.94	4.44
Mazes	—	—	—	—	4.52	5.29	—	—	4.59	5.52	4.79	5.40

[a]In this column, the entries for Information, Similarities, Vocabulary, and Comprehension are compared to the mean of these four subtests. Similarly, the entries for Picture Completion, Picture Arrangement, Block Design, and Object Assembly are compared to the mean of these four subtests.

[b]In this column, the entries for Information, Similarities, Arithmetic, Vocabulary, and Comprehension are compared to the mean of these five subtests. Similarly, the entries for Picture Completion, Coding, Picture Arrangement, Block Design, and Object Assembly are compared to the mean of these five subtests.

[c]In this column, the entries for Information, Similarities, Arithmetic, Vocabulary, Comprehension, and Digit Span are compared to the mean of these six subtests. Similarly, the entries for Picture Completion, Coding, Picture Arrangement, Block Design, Object Assembly, and Symbol Search are compared to the mean of these six subtests.

(Continued)

Table A-6 *(Continued)*

Age 12-0-0 through 12-11-30

Subtest	Mean of 4 subtests[a]		Mean of 5 subtests[b]		Mean of 6 subtests[c]		Mean of 6 subtests		Mean of 7 subtests		Mean of 10 subtests	
	.05	.01	.05	.01	.05	.01	.05	.01	.05	.01	.05	.01
Information	2.52	3.05	2.73	3.27	2.80	3.37	—	—	—	—	3.15	3.69
Similarities	2.58	3.11	2.80	3.35	2.87	3.45	—	—	—	—	3.24	3.80
Arithmetic	—	—	3.38	4.05	3.51	4.22	—	—	—	—	4.02	4.71
Vocabulary	2.29	2.76	2.46	2.94	2.49	3.00	—	—	—	—	2.77	3.24
Comprehension	2.74	3.31	2.99	3.58	3.08	3.70	—	—	—	—	3.50	4.09
Digit Span	—	—	—	—	2.65	3.19	—	—	—	—	—	—
Picture Completion	3.34	4.04	3.57	4.28	3.70	4.45	3.73	4.49	3.90	4.63	4.16	4.87
Coding	—	—	3.03	3.62	3.10	3.73	3.14	3.77	3.25	3.86	3.41	4.00
Picture Arrangement	3.03	3.67	3.20	3.83	3.29	3.96	3.33	4.00	3.46	4.11	3.65	4.28
Block Design	2.64	3.19	2.71	3.25	2.75	3.31	2.79	3.36	2.88	3.41	2.97	3.47
Object Assembly	3.51	4.24	3.77	4.51	3.92	4.71	3.95	4.75	4.14	4.90	4.43	5.18
Symbol Search	—	—	—	—	3.29	3.96	—	—	3.46	4.11	—	—
Mazes	—	—	—	—	—	—	4.05	4.87	4.25	5.04	—	—

Subtest	Mean of 11 subtests		Mean of 11 subtests		Mean of 11 subtests		Mean of 12 subtests		Mean of 12 subtests		Mean of 13 subtests	
	.05	.01	.05	.01	.05	.01	.05	.01	.05	.01	.05	.01
Information	3.19	3.73	3.20	3.74	3.21	3.75	3.24	3.89	3.25	3.90	3.38	3.81
Similarities	3.28	3.84	3.29	3.85	3.30	3.86	3.33	4.00	3.34	4.01	3.48	3.92
Arithmetic	4.09	4.78	4.09	4.79	4.10	4.80	4.15	4.99	4.16	5.00	4.34	4.89
Vocabulary	2.79	3.27	2.80	3.28	2.82	3.29	2.83	3.40	2.84	3.41	2.95	3.33
Comprehension	3.54	4.14	3.55	4.15	3.56	4.16	3.60	4.32	3.61	4.33	3.76	4.24
Digit Span	3.00	3.51	—	—	—	—	3.04	3.65	3.05	3.67	3.17	3.58
Picture Completion	4.23	4.95	4.24	4.95	4.25	4.96	4.30	5.17	4.31	5.18	4.49	5.07
Coding	3.46	4.04	3.47	4.05	3.48	4.06	3.51	4.22	3.52	4.23	3.67	4.13
Picture Arrangement	3.71	4.33	3.71	4.34	3.72	4.35	3.76	4.53	3.77	4.54	3.93	4.43
Block Design	3.00	3.51	3.01	3.51	3.02	3.53	3.04	3.65	3.05	3.67	3.17	3.58
Object Assembly	4.50	5.26	4.51	5.27	4.52	5.28	4.58	5.50	4.59	5.51	4.79	5.40
Symbol Search	—	—	3.71	4.34	—	—	3.76	4.53	—	—	3.93	4.43
Mazes	—	—	—	—	4.65	5.43	—	—	4.72	5.67	4.93	5.55

[a]In this column, the entries for Information, Similarities, Vocabulary, and Comprehension are compared to the mean of these four subtests. Similarly, the entries for Picture Completion, Picture Arrangement, Block Design, and Object Assembly are compared to the mean of these four subtests.

[b]In this column, the entries for Information, Similarities, Arithmetic, Vocabulary, and Comprehension are compared to the mean of these five subtests. Similarly, the entries for Picture Completion, Coding, Picture Arrangement, Block Design, and Object Assembly are compared to the mean of these five subtests.

[c]In this column, the entries for Information, Similarities, Arithmetic, Vocabulary, Comprehension, and Digit Span are compared to the mean of these six subtests. Similarly, the entries for Picture Completion, Coding, Picture Arrangement, Block Design, Object Assembly, and Symbol Search are compared to the mean of these six subtests.

(Continued)

Table A-6 *(Continued)*

Age 13-0-0 through 13-11-30

Subtest	Mean of 4 subtests[a]		Mean of 5 subtests[b]		Mean of 6 subtests[c]		Mean of 6 subtests		Mean of 7 subtests		Mean of 10 subtests	
	.05	.01	.05	.01	.05	.01	.05	.01	.05	.01	.05	.01
Information	2.65	3.20	2.78	3.33	2.83	3.41	—	—	—	—	3.17	3.71
Similarities	3.18	3.84	3.42	4.10	3.54	4.26	—	—	—	—	4.04	4.73
Arithmetic	—	—	3.03	3.63	3.11	3.74	—	—	—	—	3.51	4.11
Vocabulary	2.42	2.93	2.51	3.01	2.53	3.04	—	—	—	—	2.79	3.27
Comprehension	3.22	3.89	3.47	4.16	3.60	4.33	—	—	—	—	4.11	4.81
Digit Span	—	—	—	—	2.68	3.23	—	—	—	—	—	—
Picture Completion	3.31	3.99	3.59	4.30	3.72	4.48	3.73	4.49	3.91	4.64	4.18	4.89
Coding	—	—	3.69	4.41	3.83	4.61	3.84	4.62	4.03	4.78	4.31	5.05
Picture Arrangement	3.13	3.78	3.38	4.05	3.50	4.21	3.51	4.22	3.67	4.35	3.90	4.56
Block Design	2.42	2.93	2.53	3.03	2.55	3.07	2.57	3.09	2.63	3.12	2.69	3.14
Object Assembly	3.18	3.84	3.43	4.11	3.55	4.28	3.57	4.29	3.73	4.42	3.97	4.65
Symbol Search	—	—	—	—	3.55	4.28	—	—	3.73	4.42	—	—
Mazes	—	—	—	—	—	—	3.84	4.62	4.03	4.78	—	—

Subtest	Mean of 11 subtests		Mean of 11 subtests		Mean of 11 subtests		Mean of 12 subtests		Mean of 12 subtests		Mean of 13 subtests	
	.05	.01	.05	.01	.05	.01	.05	.01	.05	.01	.05	.01
Information	3.21	3.75	3.22	3.76	3.22	3.77	3.25	3.91	3.25	3.91	3.39	3.82
Similarities	4.10	4.79	4.11	4.80	4.11	4.81	4.17	5.01	4.17	5.01	4.35	4.90
Arithmetic	3.56	4.16	3.57	4.17	3.57	4.17	3.61	4.34	3.61	4.35	3.77	4.25
Vocabulary	2.81	3.29	2.82	3.30	2.83	3.31	2.85	3.42	2.85	3.43	2.96	3.34
Comprehension	4.17	4.88	4.18	4.89	4.18	4.89	4.24	5.10	4.24	5.10	4.43	4.99
Digit Span	3.01	3.52	—	—	—	—	3.06	3.67	3.06	3.68	3.18	3.59
Picture Completion	4.24	4.96	4.25	4.97	4.25	4.97	4.31	5.18	4.32	5.19	4.50	5.08
Coding	4.38	5.12	4.39	5.13	4.39	5.13	4.45	5.35	4.46	5.36	4.65	5.24
Picture Arrangement	3.95	4.62	3.96	4.63	3.97	4.64	4.02	4.83	4.02	4.83	4.19	4.73
Block Design	2.70	3.16	2.72	3.18	2.72	3.18	2.73	3.29	2.74	3.29	2.85	3.21
Object Assembly	4.03	4.71	4.04	4.72	4.04	4.72	4.09	4.92	4.10	4.92	4.27	4.82
Symbol Search	—	—	4.04	4.72	—	—	4.09	4.92	—	—	4.27	4.82
Mazes	—	—	—	—	4.39	5.13	—	—	4.46	5.36	4.65	5.24

[a]In this column, the entries for Information, Similarities, Vocabulary, and Comprehension are compared to the mean of these four subtests. Similarly, the entries for Picture Completion, Picture Arrangement, Block Design, and Object Assembly are compared to the mean of these four subtests.

[b]In this column, the entries for Information, Similarities, Arithmetic, Vocabulary, and Comprehension are compared to the mean of these five subtests. Similarly, the entries for Picture Completion, Coding, Picture Arrangement, Block Design, and Object Assembly are compared to the mean of these five subtests.

[c]In this column, the entries for Information, Similarities, Arithmetic, Vocabulary, Comprehension, and Digit Span are compared to the mean of these six subtests. Similarly, the entries for Picture Completion, Coding, Picture Arrangement, Block Design, Object Assembly, and Symbol Search are compared to the mean of these six subtests.

(Continued)

Table A-6 (Continued)

Age 14-0-0 through 14-11-30

Subtest	Mean of 4 subtests[a]		Mean of 5 subtests[b]		Mean of 6 subtests[c]		Mean of 6 subtests		Mean of 7 subtests		Mean of 10 subtests	
	.05	.01	.05	.01	.05	.01	.05	.01	.05	.01	.05	.01
Information	2.42	2.92	2.59	3.10	2.65	3.19	—	—	—	—	2.99	3.50
Similarities	2.58	3.12	2.79	3.34	2.87	3.46	—	—	—	—	3.26	3.82
Arithmetic	—	—	3.21	3.84	3.33	4.01	—	—	—	—	3.82	4.47
Vocabulary	2.17	2.62	2.30	2.75	2.32	2.80	—	—	—	—	2.58	3.02
Comprehension	2.99	3.61	3.27	3.91	3.40	4.09	—	—	—	—	3.90	4.56
Digit Span	—	—	—	—	2.87	3.46	—	—	—	—	—	—
Picture Completion	3.38	4.08	3.63	4.35	3.75	4.51	3.76	4.53	3.93	4.67	4.18	4.89
Coding	—	—	3.73	4.47	3.86	4.64	3.87	4.66	4.05	4.80	4.31	5.05
Picture Arrangement	3.11	3.76	3.32	3.98	3.41	4.10	3.42	4.12	3.56	4.22	3.75	4.39
Block Design	2.52	3.04	2.59	3.10	2.59	3.12	2.61	3.14	2.67	3.16	2.69	3.14
Object Assembly	3.84	4.64	4.18	5.01	4.36	5.24	4.37	5.25	4.59	5.44	4.93	5.77
Symbol Search	—	—	—	—	3.59	4.31	—	—	3.75	4.45	—	—
Mazes	—	—	—	—	—	—	3.87	4.66	4.05	4.80	—	—

Subtest	Mean of 11 subtests		Mean of 11 subtests		Mean of 11 subtests		Mean of 12 subtests		Mean of 12 subtests		Mean of 13 subtests	
	.05	.01	.05	.01	.05	.01	.05	.01	.05	.01	.05	.01
Information	3.02	3.53	3.03	3.54	3.03	3.54	3.06	3.68	3.06	3.68	3.18	3.59
Similarities	3.30	3.86	3.31	3.87	3.31	3.87	3.35	4.02	3.35	4.03	3.49	3.93
Arithmetic	3.88	4.53	3.89	4.54	3.89	4.55	3.94	4.74	3.94	4.74	4.11	4.64
Vocabulary	2.59	3.03	2.60	3.05	2.61	3.05	2.62	3.15	2.63	3.16	2.73	3.08
Comprehension	3.95	4.62	3.96	4.63	3.97	4.64	4.02	4.83	4.02	4.83	4.19	4.73
Digit Span	3.30	3.86	—	—	—	—	3.35	4.02	3.35	4.03	3.49	3.93
Picture Completion	4.24	4.96	4.25	4.97	4.25	4.97	4.31	5.19	4.32	5.19	4.50	5.08
Coding	4.38	5.12	4.39	5.13	4.39	5.13	4.46	5.36	4.46	5.36	4.65	5.25
Picture Arrangement	3.80	4.44	3.81	4.45	3.81	4.46	3.86	4.64	3.86	4.65	4.03	4.54
Block Design	2.71	3.16	2.72	3.18	2.72	3.18	2.74	3.29	2.74	3.30	2.85	3.21
Object Assembly	5.01	5.86	5.02	5.87	5.02	5.87	5.10	6.13	5.10	6.14	5.33	6.01
Symbol Search	—	—	4.04	4.72	—	—	4.09	4.92	—	—	4.27	4.82
Mazes	—	—	—	—	4.39	5.13	—	—	4.46	5.36	4.65	5.25

[a]In this column, the entries for Information, Similarities, Vocabulary, and Comprehension are compared to the mean of these four subtests. Similarly, the entries for Picture Completion, Picture Arrangement, Block Design, and Object Assembly are compared to the mean of these four subtests.

[b]In this column, the entries for Information, Similarities, Arithmetic, Vocabulary, and Comprehension are compared to the mean of these five subtests. Similarly, the entries for Picture Completion, Coding, Picture Arrangement, Block Design, and Object Assembly are compared to the mean of these five subtests.

[c]In this column, the entries for Information, Similarities, Arithmetic, Vocabulary, Comprehension, and Digit Span are compared to the mean of these six subtests. Similarly, the entries for Picture Completion, Coding, Picture Arrangement, Block Design, Object Assembly, and Symbol Search are compared to the mean of these six subtests.

(Continued)

Table A-6 *(Continued)*

Age 15-0-0 through 15-11-30

Subtest	Mean of 4 subtests[a]		Mean of 5 subtests[b]		Mean of 6 subtests[c]		Mean of 6 subtests		Mean of 7 subtests		Mean of 10 subtests	
	.05	.01	.05	.01	.05	.01	.05	.01	.05	.01	.05	.01
Information	2.34	2.83	2.49	2.98	2.53	3.04	—	—	—	—	2.83	3.31
Similarities	2.73	3.30	2.95	3.54	3.04	3.66	—	—	—	—	3.46	4.05
Arithmetic	—	—	2.95	3.54	3.04	3.66	—	—	—	—	3.46	4.05
Vocabulary	2.15	2.60	2.26	2.71	2.28	2.74	—	—	—	—	2.51	2.94
Comprehension	2.78	3.36	3.01	3.61	3.11	3.74	—	—	—	—	3.54	4.15
Digit Span	—	—	—	—	2.28	2.74	—	—	—	—	—	—
Picture Completion	2.79	3.37	2.92	3.50	3.02	3.64	3.08	3.71	3.21	3.80	3.38	3.96
Coding	—	—	2.38	2.85	2.42	2.92	2.50	3.00	2.56	3.04	2.62	3.07
Picture Arrangement	3.21	3.88	3.43	4.11	3.58	4.31	3.63	4.37	3.80	4.51	4.07	4.76
Block Design	2.23	2.69	2.23	2.67	2.25	2.71	2.33	2.80	2.37	2.82	2.39	2.80
Object Assembly	3.08	3.71	3.27	3.92	3.41	4.10	3.46	4.16	3.62	4.29	3.85	4.51
Symbol Search	—	—	—	—	3.02	3.64	—	—	3.21	3.80	—	—
Mazes	—	—	—	—	—	—	4.25	5.12	4.48	5.31	—	—

Subtest	Mean of 11 subtests		Mean of 11 subtests		Mean of 11 subtests		Mean of 12 subtests		Mean of 12 subtests		Mean of 13 subtests	
	.05	.01	.05	.01	.05	.01	.05	.01	.05	.01	.05	.01
Information	2.86	3.34	2.87	3.35	2.89	3.38	2.90	3.49	2.92	3.51	3.04	3.42
Similarities	3.51	4.11	3.52	4.11	3.54	4.14	3.57	4.29	3.58	4.31	3.73	4.21
Arithmetic	3.51	4.11	3.52	4.11	3.54	4.14	3.57	4.29	3.58	4.31	3.73	4.21
Vocabulary	2.53	2.96	2.54	2.97	2.56	3.00	2.56	3.08	2.58	3.10	2.68	3.02
Comprehension	3.60	4.20	3.60	4.21	3.62	4.23	3.65	4.39	3.67	4.41	3.82	4.31
Digit Span	2.53	2.96	—	—	—	—	2.56	3.08	2.58	3.10	2.68	3.02
Picture Completion	3.43	4.01	3.43	4.01	3.45	4.04	3.48	4.18	3.50	4.20	3.64	4.11
Coding	2.64	3.09	2.65	3.10	2.68	3.13	2.68	3.22	2.70	3.24	2.80	3.16
Picture Arrangement	4.13	4.83	4.14	4.84	4.16	4.86	4.20	5.05	4.22	5.07	4.40	4.96
Block Design	2.41	2.82	2.42	2.83	2.45	2.86	2.44	2.93	2.46	2.96	2.55	2.88
Object Assembly	3.91	4.57	3.92	4.58	3.93	4.60	3.98	4.78	3.99	4.80	4.16	4.69
Symbol Search	—	—	3.43	4.01	—	—	3.48	4.18	—	—	3.64	4.11
Mazes	—	—	—	—	4.94	5.77	—	—	5.02	6.03	5.24	5.91

[a]In this column, the entries for Information, Similarities, Vocabulary, and Comprehension are compared to the mean of these four subtests. Similarly, the entries for Picture Completion, Picture Arrangement, Block Design, and Object Assembly are compared to the mean of these four subtests.

[b]In this column, the entries for Information, Similarities, Arithmetic, Vocabulary, and Comprehension are compared to the mean of these five subtests. Similarly, the entries for Picture Completion, Coding, Picture Arrangement, Block Design, and Object Assembly are compared to the mean of these five subtests.

[c]In this column, the entries for Information, Similarities, Arithmetic, Vocabulary, Comprehension, and Digit Span are compared to the mean of these six subtests. Similarly, the entries for Picture Completion, Coding, Picture Arrangement, Block Design, Object Assembly, and Symbol Search are compared to the mean of these six subtests.

(Continued)

Table A-6 *(Continued)*

Age 16-0-0 through 16-11-30

Subtest	Mean of 4 subtests[a]		Mean of 5 subtests[b]		Mean of 6 subtests[c]		Mean of 6 subtests		Mean of 7 subtests		Mean of 10 subtests	
	.05	.01	.05	.01	.05	.01	.05	.01	.05	.01	.05	.01
Information	2.39	2.88	2.52	3.01	2.55	3.07	—	—	—	—	2.85	3.34
Similarities	2.61	3.15	2.79	3.34	2.86	3.44	—	—	—	—	3.23	3.78
Arithmetic	—	—	2.91	3.49	3.00	3.60	—	—	—	—	3.40	3.98
Vocabulary	2.33	2.81	2.44	2.93	2.47	2.97	—	—	—	—	2.75	3.22
Comprehension	3.15	3.80	3.42	4.10	3.56	4.28	—	—	—	—	4.08	4.78
Digit Span	—	—	—	—	2.47	2.97	—	—	—	—	—	—
Picture Completion	3.20	3.86	3.38	4.04	3.50	4.21	3.54	4.25	3.69	4.38	3.94	4.61
Coding	—	—	2.45	2.94	2.47	2.97	2.52	3.04	2.58	3.06	2.65	3.10
Picture Arrangement	3.29	3.97	3.48	4.17	3.61	4.35	3.65	4.39	3.82	4.53	4.08	4.78
Block Design	2.45	2.96	2.45	2.94	2.47	2.97	2.52	3.04	2.58	3.06	2.65	3.10
Object Assembly	3.37	4.07	3.58	4.29	3.73	4.48	3.76	4.52	3.94	4.67	4.22	4.94
Symbol Search	—	—	—	—	3.06	3.69	—	—	3.22	3.82	—	—
Mazes	—	—	—	—	—	—	3.97	4.78	4.17	4.94	—	—

Subtest	Mean of 11 subtests		Mean of 11 subtests		Mean of 11 subtests		Mean of 12 subtests		Mean of 12 subtests		Mean of 13 subtests	
	.05	.01	.05	.01	.05	.01	.05	.01	.05	.01	.05	.01
Information	2.88	3.37	2.89	3.38	2.90	3.40	2.92	3.51	2.93	3.52	3.05	3.44
Similarities	3.27	3.82	3.27	3.83	3.29	3.84	3.31	3.98	3.33	4.00	3.46	3.90
Arithmetic	3.44	4.03	3.45	4.03	3.46	4.05	3.50	4.20	3.51	4.22	3.65	4.12
Vocabulary	2.78	3.25	2.78	3.25	2.80	3.27	2.81	3.38	2.82	3.39	2.93	3.31
Comprehension	4.15	4.85	4.15	4.86	4.16	4.87	4.22	5.07	4.23	5.08	4.41	4.97
Digit Span	2.78	3.25	—	—	—	—	2.81	3.38	2.82	3.39	2.93	3.31
Picture Completion	4.00	4.68	4.01	4.69	4.02	4.70	4.07	4.89	4.08	4.90	4.25	4.79
Coding	2.67	3.12	2.68	3.13	2.69	3.15	2.70	3.24	2.71	3.26	2.82	3.18
Picture Arrangement	4.15	4.85	4.15	4.86	4.16	4.87	4.22	5.07	4.23	5.08	4.41	4.97
Block Design	2.67	3.12	2.68	3.13	2.69	3.15	2.70	3.24	2.71	3.26	2.82	3.18
Object Assembly	4.29	5.01	4.29	5.02	4.30	5.03	4.36	5.24	4.37	5.25	4.56	5.14
Symbol Search	—	—	3.45	4.03	—	—	3.50	4.20	—	—	3.65	4.12
Mazes	—	—	—	—	4.57	5.35	—	—	4.64	5.58	4.85	5.46

[a]In this column, the entries for Information, Similarities, Vocabulary, and Comprehension are compared to the mean of these four subtests. Similarly, the entries for Picture Completion, Picture Arrangement, Block Design, and Object Assembly are compared to the mean of these four subtests.

[b]In this column, the entries for Information, Similarities, Arithmetic, Vocabulary, and Comprehension are compared to the mean of these five subtests. Similarly, the entries for Picture Completion, Coding, Picture Arrangement, Block Design, and Object Assembly are compared to the mean of these five subtests.

[c]In this column, the entries for Information, Similarities, Arithmetic, Vocabulary, Comprehension, and Digit Span are compared to the mean of these six subtests. Similarly, the entries for Picture Completion, Coding, Picture Arrangement, Block Design, Object Assembly, and Symbol Search are compared to the mean of these six subtests.

(Continued)

Table A-6 (Continued)

Average

Subtest	Mean of 4 subtests[a]		Mean of 5 subtests[b]		Mean of 6 subtests[c]		Mean of 6 subtests		Mean of 7 subtests		Mean of 10 subtests	
	.05	.01	.05	.01	.05	.01	.05	.01	.05	.01	.05	.01
Information	2.65	3.20	2.82	3.38	2.89	3.48	—	—	—	—	3.25	3.80
Similarities	2.80	3.38	3.01	3.60	3.10	3.73	—	—	—	—	3.50	4.10
Arithmetic	—	—	3.18	3.81	3.29	3.96	—	—	—	—	3.74	4.38
Vocabulary	2.48	3.00	2.63	3.15	2.67	3.22	—	—	—	—	2.97	3.48
Comprehension	2.99	3.62	3.24	3.88	3.35	4.03	—	—	—	—	3.81	4.46
Digit Span	—	—	—	—	2.82	3.40	—	—	—	—	—	—
Picture Completion	3.11	3.76	3.31	3.96	3.42	4.12	3.44	4.14	3.59	4.26	3.81	4.46
Coding	—	—	3.20	3.83	3.30	3.97	3.32	3.99	3.46	4.10	3.66	4.29
Picture Arrangement	3.15	3.81	3.36	4.03	3.48	4.19	3.50	4.21	3.66	4.34	3.89	4.55
Block Design	2.62	3.16	2.71	3.25	2.76	3.32	2.78	3.35	2.87	3.41	2.97	3.48
Object Assembly	3.45	4.17	3.72	4.45	3.87	4.66	3.88	4.67	4.08	4.84	4.37	5.11
Symbol Search	—	—	—	—	3.48	4.19	—	—	3.66	4.34	—	—
Mazes	—	—	—	—	—	—	3.83	4.61	4.02	4.77	—	—

Subtest	Mean of 11 subtests		Mean of 11 subtests		Mean of 11 subtests		Mean of 12 subtests		Mean of 12 subtests		Mean of 13 subtests	
	.05	.01	.05	.01	.05	.01	.05	.01	.05	.01	.05	.01
Information	3.29	3.85	3.30	3.86	3.30	3.86	3.34	4.01	3.34	4.02	3.48	3.92
Similarities	3.55	4.15	3.56	4.16	3.56	4.17	3.60	4.33	3.61	4.34	3.76	4.24
Arithmetic	3.79	4.43	3.80	4.44	3.80	4.45	3.85	4.63	3.86	4.64	4.02	4.53
Vocabulary	3.01	3.51	3.02	3.53	3.02	3.53	3.05	3.66	3.05	3.67	3.18	3.58
Comprehension	3.87	4.52	3.88	4.53	3.88	4.54	3.93	4.73	3.94	4.73	4.10	4.63
Digit Span	3.20	3.74	—	—	—	—	3.24	3.90	3.25	3.91	3.38	3.81
Picture Completion	3.87	4.52	3.88	4.53	3.88	4.54	3.93	4.73	3.94	4.73	4.10	4.63
Coding	3.71	4.34	3.72	4.35	3.73	4.36	3.77	4.53	3.78	4.54	3.94	4.44
Picture Arrangement	3.95	4.61	3.95	4.62	3.96	4.63	4.01	4.82	4.01	4.83	4.19	4.72
Block Design	3.01	3.51	3.02	3.53	3.02	3.53	3.05	3.66	3.05	3.67	3.18	3.58
Object Assembly	4.44	5.19	4.45	5.20	4.45	5.20	4.52	5.43	4.52	5.43	4.72	5.32
Symbol Search	—	—	3.95	4.62	—	—	4.01	4.82	—	—	4.19	4.72
Mazes	—	—	—	—	4.38	5.13	—	—	4.45	5.35	4.65	5.24

[a]In this column, the entries for Information, Similarities, Vocabulary, and Comprehension are compared to the mean of these four subtests. Similarly, the entries for Picture Completion, Picture Arrangement, Block Design, and Object Assembly are compared to the mean of these four subtests.

[b]In this column, the entries for Information, Similarities, Arithmetic, Vocabulary, and Comprehension are compared to the mean of these five subtests. Similarly, the entries for Picture Completion, Coding, Picture Arrangement, Block Design, and Object Assembly are compared to the mean of these five subtests.

[c]In this column, the entries for Information, Similarities, Arithmetic, Vocabulary, Comprehension, and Digit Span are compared to the mean of these six subtests. Similarly, the entries for Picture Completion, Coding, Picture Arrangement, Block Design, Object Assembly, and Symbol Search are compared to the mean of these six subtests.

(Continued)

Table A-6 *(Continued)*

Note. Table A-6 shows the minimum deviations from an individual's average subtest scaled score that are significant at the .05 and .01 levels.

The following formula, obtained from Davis (1959), was used to compute the deviations from average that are significant at the desired significance level: $D = CR \times SEM_{((T/m) - Z_I)}$, where D is the deviation from average, CR is the critical ratio desired, and $SEM_{((T/m) - Z_I)}$ is the standard error of measurement of the difference between an average subtest scaled score and any one of the subtest scaled scores that entered into the average. The standard error of measurement can be obtained from the following formula:

$$SEM_{((T/m) - Z_I)} = \sqrt{\frac{SEM_T^2}{m^2} + \left(\frac{m-2}{m}\right)SEM_{Z_I}^2}$$

where SEM_T^2 is the sum of the squared standard errors of measurement of the m subtests, m is the number of subtests included in the average, T/m is the average of the subtest scaled scores, and $SEM_{Z_I}^2$ is the squared standard error of measurement of any one of the subtest scaled scores. The critical ratio for the .05 level ranges from 2.58 to 2.87, and that for the .01 level from 3.09 to 3.34, depending on the number of subtests. These critical ratios were obtained by use of the Bonferroni inequality, which controls the family-wise error rate at .05 (or .01) by setting the error rate per comparison at .05/m (or .01/m).

The following example illustrates the procedure. We will determine the minimum deviation required for a child's score on the WISC–III Information subtest to be significantly different from his or her average score on the five standard Verbal Scale subtests (Information, Similarities, Arithmetic, Vocabulary, and Comprehension) at the 95% level of confidence. We calculate SEM_T^2 by first squaring the appropriate average standard error of measurement for each of the five subtests and then summing the squares. These standard errors of measurement are in Table 5-2 (page 108) in the WISC–III Manual.

$$SEM_T^2 = (1.56)^2 + (1.31)^2 + (1.31)^2 + (1.27)^2 + (1.50)^2 = 9.73$$

We determine $SEM_{Z_I}^2$ by squaring the average standard error of measurement of the subtest of interest, the Information subtest:

$$SEM_{Z_I}^2 = (1.56)^2 = 2.4336$$

The number of subtests, m, equals 5. Substituting these values into the formula yields the following:

$$SEM_{((T/m) - Z_I)} = \sqrt{\frac{9.73}{(5)^2} + \left(\frac{5-2}{5}\right)2.4336} = 1.359$$

The value, 1.359, is then multiplied by the appropriate z value for the 95% confidence level to obtain the minimum significant deviation (D). Using the Bonferroni correction (.05/5 = .01), we have a z value of 2.58.

$$D = 2.58 \times 1.359 = 3.51$$

Table A-7
Estimates of the Differences Obtained by Various Percentages of the WISC–III Standardization Sample When Each WISC–III Subtest Scaled Score Is Compared to the Mean Scaled Scores for Any Individual Child

Subtest	Verbal average (5 subtests)				Verbal average (6 subtests)			
	10%	5%	2%	1%	10%	5%	2%	1%
Information	2.62	3.12	3.70	4.10	2.80	3.33	3.96	4.39
Similarities	2.62	3.12	3.70	4.10	2.80	3.33	3.96	4.39
Arithmetic	3.23	3.84	4.57	5.06	3.17	3.76	4.47	4.95
Vocabulary	2.48	2.94	3.50	3.87	2.66	3.16	3.75	4.15
Comprehension	3.02	3.59	4.26	4.72	3.17	3.76	4.47	4.95
Digit Span	—	—	—	—	4.08	4.84	5.76	6.37

Subtest	Performance average (5 subtests)				Performance average (6 subtests)				Performance average (6 subtests)			
	10%	5%	2%	1%	10%	5%	2%	1%	10%	5%	2%	1%
Picture Completion	3.42	4.06	4.82	5.34	3.58	4.25	5.06	5.60	3.53	4.19	4.99	5.52
Coding	4.17	4.96	5.89	6.53	4.01	4.76	5.66	6.27	4.24	5.04	5.99	6.63
Picture Arrangement	3.60	4.27	5.08	5.62	3.70	4.39	5.22	5.78	3.70	4.39	5.22	5.78
Block Design	3.04	3.61	4.29	4.75	3.14	3.72	4.43	4.90	3.14	3.72	4.43	4.90
Object Assembly	3.18	3.78	4.50	4.98	3.35	3.98	4.73	5.24	3.28	3.90	4.64	5.13
Symbol Search	—	—	—	—	3.40	4.04	4.80	5.31	—	—	—	—
Mazes	—	—	—	—	—	—	—	—	4.14	4.92	5.85	6.48

Subtest	Full Scale average (10 subtests)				Full Scale average (11 subtests)				Full Scale average (11 subtests)			
	10%	5%	2%	1%	10%	5%	2%	1%	10%	5%	2%	1%
Information	3.10	3.68	4.38	4.85	3.15	3.74	4.45	4.93	3.20	3.80	4.52	5.01
Similarities	3.12	3.70	4.40	4.88	3.17	3.76	4.47	4.95	3.22	3.82	4.52	5.03
Arithmetic	3.42	4.06	4.82	5.34	3.37	4.00	4.75	5.26	3.43	4.08	4.85	5.37
Vocabulary	3.04	3.61	4.29	4.75	3.09	3.67	4.36	4.82	3.14	3.72	4.43	4.90
Comprehension	3.47	4.12	4.89	5.42	3.50	4.16	4.94	5.47	3.51	4.17	4.96	5.50
Digit Span	—	—	—	—	4.22	5.02	5.96	6.60	—	—	—	—
Picture Completion	3.65	4.33	5.15	5.70	3.70	4.39	5.22	5.78	3.70	4.39	5.22	5.78
Coding	4.57	5.43	6.45	7.15	4.54	5.39	6.41	7.10	4.44	5.27	6.27	6.94
Picture Arrangement	3.89	4.63	5.50	6.09	3.94	4.68	5.57	6.17	3.91	4.65	5.52	6.11
Block Design	3.33	3.96	4.71	5.21	3.37	4.00	4.75	5.26	3.33	3.96	4.71	5.21
Object Assembly	3.66	4.35	5.17	5.73	3.71	4.41	5.24	5.81	3.68	4.37	5.20	5.75
Symbol Search	—	—	—	—	—	—	—	—	3.81	4.53	5.38	5.96
Mazes	—	—	—	—	—	—	—	—	—	—	—	—

(Continued)

Table A-7 *(Continued)*

Subtest	Full Scale average (11 subtests)				Full Scale average (12 subtests)				Full Scale average (12 subtests)			
	10%	5%	2%	1%	10%	5%	2%	1%	10%	5%	2%	1%
Information	3.20	3.80	4.52	5.01	3.23	3.84	4.57	5.06	3.23	3.84	4.57	5.06
Similarities	3.22	3.82	4.54	5.03	3.23	3.84	4.57	5.06	3.25	3.86	4.59	5.08
Arithmetic	3.45	4.10	4.87	5.39	3.38	4.02	4.78	5.29	3.42	4.06	4.82	5.34
Vocabulary	3.15	3.74	4.45	4.93	3.17	3.76	4.47	4.95	3.18	3.78	4.50	4.98
Comprehension	3.53	4.19	4.99	5.52	3.55	4.21	5.01	5.55	3.56	4.23	5.03	5.57
Digit Span	—	—	—	—	4.24	5.04	5.99	6.63	4.24	5.04	5.99	6.63
Picture Completion	3.66	4.35	5.17	5.73	3.73	4.43	5.27	5.83	3.71	4.41	5.24	5.80
Coding	4.54	5.39	6.41	7.10	4.42	5.25	6.24	6.91	4.52	5.37	6.38	7.07
Picture Arrangement	3.89	4.63	5.50	6.09	3.94	4.68	5.57	6.17	3.94	4.68	5.57	6.17
Block Design	3.32	3.94	4.68	5.19	3.37	4.00	4.57	5.26	3.37	4.00	4.75	5.26
Object Assembly	3.65	4.33	5.15	5.70	3.71	4.41	5.24	5.80	3.68	4.37	5.20	5.75
Symbol Search	—	—	—	—	3.81	4.53	5.38	5.96	—	—	—	—
Mazes	4.64	5.51	6.55	7.25	—	—	—	—	4.64	5.51	6.55	7.25

Subtest	Full Scale average (13 subtests)			
	10%	5%	2%	1%
Information	3.30	3.92	4.66	5.16
Similarities	3.32	3.94	4.68	5.19
Arithmetic	3.43	4.08	4.85	5.37
Vocabulary	3.25	3.86	4.59	5.08
Comprehension	3.56	4.23	5.03	5.57
Digit Span	4.26	5.06	6.01	6.66
Picture Completion	3.73	4.43	5.27	5.83
Coding	4.41	5.23	6.22	6.89
Picture Arrangement	3.94	4.68	5.57	6.17
Block Design	3.35	3.98	4.73	5.24
Object Assembly	3.70	4.39	5.22	5.78
Symbol Search	3.81	4.53	5.38	5.96
Mazes	4.64	5.51	6.55	7.25

Note. The formula used to obtain the values in this table was obtained from Silverstein (1984):

$$SD_{Da} = 3\sqrt{1 + \overline{G} - 2\overline{T}_a}$$

where SD_{Da} is the standard deviation of the difference for subtest a, 3 is the standard deviation of the scaled scores on each of the subtests, $\overline{G}$ is the mean of all the elements in the matrix (including the diagonal), and $\overline{T}_a$ is the mean of the elements in row or column a of the matrix (again including the diagonal).

Table A-8
Differences Required for Significance When Each WISC–III Subtest Scaled Score Is Compared to the Respective Mean Index Scaled Score for Any Individual Child

Subtest	Mean of Verbal Comprehension subtests		Mean of Perceptual Organization subtests		Mean of Freedom from Distractibility subtests		Mean of Processing Speed subtests	
	.05	.01	.05	.01	.05	.01	.05	.01
Information	2.69	3.26	—	—	—	—	—	—
Similarities	2.79	3.38	—	—	—	—	—	—
Arithmetic	—	—	—	—	2.06	2.58	—	—
Vocabulary	2.48	3.01	—	—	—	—	—	—
Comprehension	3.02	3.65	—	—	—	—	—	—
Digit Span	—	—	—	—	2.06	2.58	—	—
Picture Completion	—	—	2.80	3.43	—	—	—	—
Coding	—	—	—	—	—	—	2.30	2.88
Picture Arrangement	—	—	—	—	—	—	—	—
Block Design	—	—	2.49	3.05	—	—	—	—
Object Assembly	—	—	3.03	3.71	—	—	—	—
Symbol Search	—	—	—	—	—	—	2.30	2.88
Mazes	—	—	—	—	—	—	—	—

Note. Table A-8 shows the minimum deviations from an individual's mean factor scaled score that are significant at the .05 and .01 levels. See the Note in Table A-3 in Appendix A for an explanation of how differences were obtained. The following Bonferroni corrections were used: 2.50 at .05, 3.025 at .01 for Verbal Comprehension; 2.39 at .05, 2.93 at .01 for Perceptual Organization; 2.24 at .05, 2.81 at .01 for Freedom from Distractibility and Processing Speed. The values in this table are based on the total sample.

Table A-9
Estimates of the Probability of Obtaining Designated Differences Between Individual WISC–III Factor Score Deviation Quotients (DQs) by Chance

Probability of obtaining given or greater discrepancy by chance	Verbal Comprehension DQ vs. Perceptual Organization DQ	Verbal Comprehension DQ vs. Processing Speed DQ	Perceptual Organization DQ vs. Processing Speed DQ
.50	4.12	4.88	5.34
.25	7.07	8.38	9.16
.20	7.87	9.33	10.20
.10	10.14	12.02	13.14
.05	12.05	14.28	15.61
.02	14.32	16.98	18.56
.01	15.86	18.80	20.55
.001	20.23	23.97	26.21

Note. The values in Table A-9 are based on the total group. Locate the discrepancy that is just *less than* the discrepancy obtained by the examinee. The entry in the first column in that same row gives the probability of obtaining a given or greater discrepancy by chance. For example, the hypothesis that an examinee obtained a Verbal Comprehension–Perceptual Organization discrepancy of 12 by chance can be rejected at the .10 level of significance. Table A-9 is two-tailed. See Chapter 10, Exhibit 10-1 (page 302) for an explanation of the method used to arrive at the magnitudes of differences.

Table A-10
Lowest Subtest Scaled Score Representing 15% of the Cases or Less in the WISC–III Standardization Group for Various Highest Scaled Scores

Scale	Highest subtest scaled score											
	17+	16	15	14	13	12	11	10	9	8	7	6
Verbal Scale (5 subtests)	8	8	7	6	6	5	4	3	2	2	—	—
Performance Scale (5 subtests)	6	6	5	4	4	3	3	2	1	1	—	—
Full Scale (10 subtests)	5	5	4	3	3	2	2	—	—	—	—	—
Verbal Scale (6 subtests)	7	7	6	5	5	4	4	3	2	2	—	—
Performance Scale (6 subtests)	5	5	4	4	4	3	2	2	1	—	—	—
Full Scale (12 subtests)	5	4	3	2	2	2	2	—	—	—	—	—

Note. The table is read as follows: For five Verbal Scale subtests, when the highest scaled score is 17 (or over), the lowest scaled score representing 15% or less of the WISC–III standardization group is 8. Similarly, for the five Verbal Scale subtests, when the highest scaled score is 8, the lowest scaled score representing 15% or less of the WISC–III standardization group is 2. Occurrence of the scaled scores in this table, as well as all scaled scores below the values in this table, in conjunction with the corresponding highest scaled score can be considered a rare event in the standardization sample. See Schinka et al. (1997) for the percentage of cases in the standardization group for all differences between the lowest and highest scaled scores. In the Schinka et al. publication, the percentage of cases in Table 3 associated with the highest scaled score of 13 and the lowest scaled score of 4 should be 21.1, not 12.1; also, there were no frequencies for the highest scaled score of 6 in Tables 3 and 6 (personal communication, John Schinka, November 1999).

Source: Adapted from Schinka, Vanderploeg, and Curtiss (1997).

Table A-11
Differences Required Between WISC–III Subtests to Be Equal to or Less than 1st, 5th, and 15th Percentile of Scores in the Standardization Sample

Subtest	Percentile	Subtest												
		I	S	A	V	C	DS	PC	CD	PA	BD	OA	SS	MA
I	1st	—	7	8	7	8	9	8	10	9	9	9	9	11
	5th	—	5	6	5	6	7	6	7	7	6	6	7	8
	15th	—	4	4	3	4	5	4	5	4	4	4	5	5
S	1st	7	—	8	7	8	10	9	11	9	9	9	9	11
	5th	5	—	6	5	6	7	6	8	7	7	6	7	8
	15th	4	—	4	3	4	5	4	5	5	4	4	5	5
A	1st	8	8	—	8	8	9	9	10	9	8	9	9	11
	5th	6	6	—	6	6	6	6	7	7	6	7	7	8
	15th	4	4	—	4	4	4	4	5	5	4	5	4	5
V	1st	7	7	8	—	8	10	9	10	9	9	9	10	11
	5th	5	5	6	—	6	7	6	7	7	7	7	7	8
	15th	4	4	4	—	4	5	4	5	5	4	5	5	5
C	1st	8	8	9	8	—	10	9	11	10	10	10	10	11
	5th	6	6	7	5	—	7	7	8	7	7	7	7	8
	15th	4	4	4	4	—	5	5	5	5	5	5	5	5
DS	1st	10	9	8	9	9	—	9	10	10	10	9	9	11
	5th	7	7	6	6	7	—	7	7	8	7	7	7	8
	15th	5	5	4	5	5	—	5	5	5	5	5	5	5
PC	1st	9	9	9	9	9	10	—	11	10	9	9	10	10
	5th	6	6	7	6	7	7	—	8	7	6	6	7	8
	15th	4	4	5	5	5	5	—	5	5	4	4	5	5
CD	1st	10	10	10	10	10	10	10	—	10	11	10	8	11
	5th	8	7	7	7	7	8	8	—	7	7	8	6	8
	15th	5	5	5	5	5	5	5	—	5	5	5	4	6
PA	1st	9	9	9	9	10	10	10	10	—	10	10	10	11
	5th	7	7	7	7	7	7	7	8	—	7	7	7	8
	15th	5	5	5	5	5	5	5	5	—	5	5	5	5
BD	1st	9	9	9	10	9	11	8	10	10	—	8	9	11
	5th	7	7	6	6	7	7	7	8	7	—	6	7	8
	15th	5	5	4	4	5	5	4	5	5	—	4	5	5
OA	1st	9	9	9	9	9	10	8	10	9	8	—	9	10
	5th	7	7	7	7	7	7	7	8	7	6	—	7	8
	15th	5	5	5	5	5	5	4	5	5	4	—	5	5
SS	1st	9	9	9	10	10	10	10	9	9	9	10	—	11
	5th	7	7	7	7	7	8	7	7	7	7	7	—	8
	15th	5	5	5	5	5	5	5	4	5	4	5	—	5
MA	1st	10	10	10	10	10	10	10	10	10	11	10	10	—
	5th	8	8	8	8	8	8	7	8	8	7	7	7	—
	15th	5	5	5	5	5	5	5	5	5	5	5	5	—

Note. Abbreviations: I = Information, S = Similarities, A = Arithmetic, V = Vocabulary, C = Comprehension, DS = Digit Span, PC = Picture Completion, CD = Digit Symbol—Coding, PA = Picture Arrangement, BD = Block Design, OA = Object Assembly, SS = Symbol Search, MA = Mazes.

The table is read as follows: 1% of the WISC–III normative sample had an Information minus Similarities scaled-score difference of 7 or greater. The table provides directional differences. The subtest in the vertical column is always subtracted from the subtest in the horizontal row (e.g., I – S, S – A, A – V, V – C, . . . , MA – SS).

Source: Reprinted and adapted with permission of the publisher and authors from J. A. Schinka, R. D. Vanderploeg, and P. Greblo, "Frequency of WISC–III and WAIS–R Pairwise Subtest Differences," *Psychological Assessment, 10,* pp. 172–173. Copyright 1998 by the American Psychological Association, Inc.

Table A-12
Intrasubtest Scatter in the WISC–III Standardization Group for Eight WISC–III Subtests

Subtest	Intrasubtest scatter representing the mean of the standardization group	Intrasubtest scatter representing less than 10% of the standardization group
Information	4.4	7
Similarities	7.3	12
Arithmetic	3.2	6
Vocabulary	8.5	14
Comprehension	7.4	11
Picture Completion	6.1	9
Picture Arrangement	14.6	25
Block Design	9.4	17

Note. The following is an example of how to read the table: On Information, the mean amount of intrasubtest scatter was 4; the amount of intrasubtest scatter in less than 10% of the standardization group was 7. Note that for Picture Arrangement, the tabulation of intrasubtest scatter begins with item 3 (WALK), whereas for Block Design, the tabulation of intrasubtest scatter begins with item 4. Intrasubtest scatter in this table was obtained by looking at the frequency with which scores on consecutive items on a subtest differ. The following are some examples of how this form of intrasubtest scatter is computed: (a) a score of 1 followed by a score of 0 or a score of 0 followed by a score of 1 equals 1 scatter point, and (b) a score of 2 followed by a score of 0 or the reverse equals 2 scatter points.

Source: Adapted from Dumont and Willis (1995).

Table A-13
Conversion Table for Calculating Performance Scale IQ When Symbol Search Is Substituted for Coding on the WISC–III

Sum of scaled scores	IQ	Sum of scaled scores	IQ	Sum of scaled scores	IQ	Sum of scaled scores	IQ	Sum of scaled scores	IQ
5	44	25	69	45	94	65	119	85	144
6	46	26	71	46	95	66	120	86	145
7	47	27	72	47	97	67	121	87	146
8	48	28	73	48	98	68	123	88	147
9	49	29	74	49	99	69	124	89	149
10	51	30	76	50	100	70	125	90	150
11	52	31	77	51	102	71	126	91	151
12	53	32	78	52	103	72	128	92	152
13	54	33	79	53	104	73	129	93	154
14	56	34	80	54	105	74	130	94	155
15	57	35	82	55	107	75	131	95	156
16	58	36	82	56	108	76	133		
17	59	37	83	57	109	77	134		
18	61	38	84	58	110	78	135		
19	62	39	85	59	112	79	136		
20	63	40	87	60	113	80	138		
21	64	41	89	61	114	81	139		
22	66	42	90	62	115	82	140		
23	67	43	92	63	116	83	141		
24	68	44	93	64	118	84	143		

Source: Adapted with permission of authors and publishers from C. R. Reynolds, S. Sanchez, and V. L. Willson (1996), "Normative Tables for Calculating the WISC–III Performance and Full Scale IQs When Symbol Search Is Substituted for Coding," *Psychological Assessment, 8,* 379. Copyright 1996 by American Psychological Association, Inc.

Table A-14
Conversion Table for Calculating Full Scale IQ When Symbol Search Is Substituted for Coding on the WISC–III

Sum of scaled scores	IQ	Sum of scaled scores	IQ	Sum of scaled scores	IQ	Sum of scaled scores	IQ	Sum of scaled scores	IQ
10	41	50	67	90	94	130	120	170	146
11	42	51	68	91	94	131	121	171	147
12	42	52	69	92	95	132	121	172	148
13	43	53	69	93	96	133	122	173	148
14	44	54	70	94	96	134	123	174	149
15	44	55	71	95	97	135	123	175	150
16	45	56	71	96	98	136	124	176	150
17	46	57	72	97	98	137	125	177	151
18	46	58	73	98	99	138	125	178	152
19	47	59	73	99	100	139	126	179	152
20	48	60	74	100	100	140	127	180	153
21	48	61	75	101	101	141	127	181	153
22	49	62	75	102	102	142	128	182	154
23	50	63	76	103	102	143	129	183	155
24	50	64	77	104	103	144	129	184	155
25	51	65	77	105	104	145	130	185	156
26	52	66	78	106	104	146	130	186	157
27	52	67	79	107	105	147	131	187	157
28	53	68	79	108	105	148	132	188	158
29	54	69	80	109	106	149	132	189	159
30	54	70	81	110	107	150	133	190	159
31	55	71	81	111	107	151	134		
32	56	72	82	112	108	152	134		
33	56	73	82	113	109	153	135		
34	57	74	83	114	109	154	136		
35	58	75	84	115	110	155	136		
36	58	76	84	116	111	156	137		
37	59	77	85	117	111	157	138		
38	59	78	86	118	112	158	138		
39	60	79	86	119	113	159	139		
40	61	80	87	120	113	160	140		
41	61	81	88	121	114	161	140		
42	62	82	88	122	115	162	141		
43	63	83	89	123	115	163	142		
44	63	84	90	124	116	164	142		
45	64	85	90	125	117	165	143		
46	65	86	91	126	117	166	144		
47	65	87	92	127	118	167	144		
48	66	88	92	128	119	168	145		
49	67	89	93	129	119	169	146		

Source: Adapted with permission of authors and publishers from C. R. Reynolds, S. Sanchez, and V. L. Willson (1996), "Normative Tables for Calculating the WISC–III Performance and Full Scale IQs When Symbol Search Is Substituted for Coding," *Psychological Assessment, 8,* 380–381. Copyright 1996 by American Psychological Association, Inc.

Table A-15
Modified Instructions for Administering the WISC–III Performance Scale Subtests to Examinees with Hearing Impairments

PICTURE COMPLETION

Additional Materials
Instruction sheet prepared by the examiner. This sheet should contain the information on pages 60 and 61 of the WISC–III Manual. Only copy the material in color.

Three additional practice items prepared by the examiner. Each practice item consists of a picture with a missing detail on one side of the card and the same picture with the missing detail filled in on the other side of the card. Figure A-A shows the pictures needed for the three practice items. Photocopy these pictures and attach them to the front and back sides of three 3" × 5" cards, as follows:

1. Put the picture of a bird missing a wing on one side of a card and the complete bird on the other side (BIRD).

2. Put the picture of a bow and arrow missing part of the arrow on one side of a card and the complete bow and arrow on the other side (BOW & ARROW).

3. Put the picture of a pair of scissors missing part of the handle on one side of a card and the complete pair of scissors on the other side (SCISSORS).

Procedure
Show the examinee practice item 1 (BIRD). Show the side with the missing detail first and then turn the picture over and show the side with the completed detail. Point to the completed detail. Repeat the procedure with practice item 2 (BOW & ARROW) and practice item 3 (SCISSORS). Present the sample item from the WISC–III Picture Completion booklet. If the examinee can read, show her or him the instruction sheet. Follow the instructions in the WISC–III Manual for the Picture Completion subtest.

CODING

Additional Materials
Instruction sheets prepared by the examiner. One sheet should contain the information for Coding A, which is on pages 71 and 72 of the WISC–III Manual. The other sheet should contain the information for Coding B, which is on pages 72 and 73 of the WISC–III Manual. Only copy the material in color.

Two additional practice Coding forms prepared by the examiner. One is Practice Coding Form A for examinees ages 6 to 7 years. The other is Practice Coding Form B for examinees ages 8 to 16 years. Each form consists of a key and two practice trials. Figures A-B and A-C show the pictures needed for the practice Coding forms. Photocopy these pictures and attach each one to a sheet of paper.

Procedure for Coding A (examinees ages 6–7)
Select Practice Coding Form A. Point to the key (the geometric shape and then the symbol inside the shape). Then go to Trial 1,

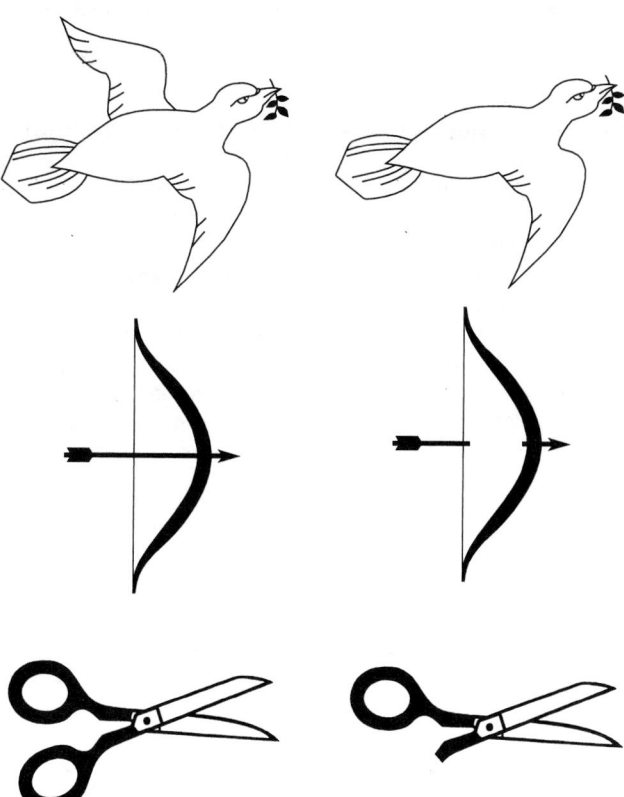

Figure A-A.   Practice items for WISC–III Picture Completion for children who are hearing impaired.

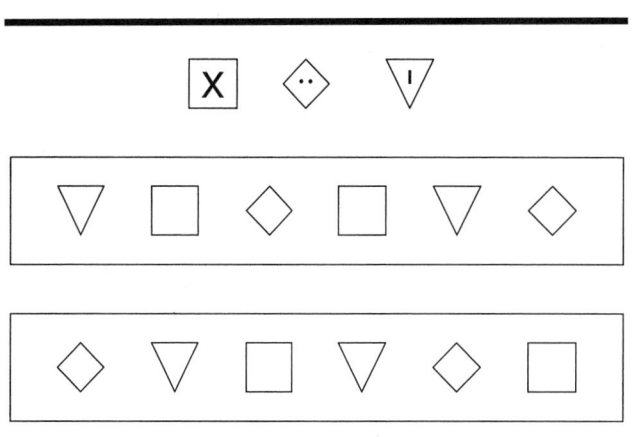

Figure A-B.   Practice items for WISC–III Coding Part A for children who are hearing impaired.

(Continued)

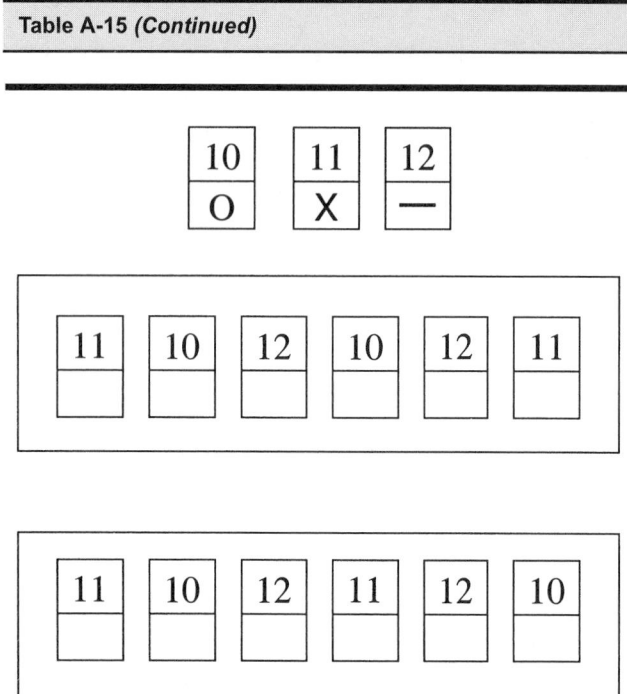

Figure A-C.   Practice items for WISC–III Coding Part B for children who are hearing impaired.

which contains six practice items. Point to the empty geometric shape in the first practice box. Draw the symbol inside the triangle. Follow the same procedure for the second and third geometric shapes. Then point to the examinee and motion for him or her to complete the remaining three shapes. Demonstrate how to complete the first three shapes of Trial 2, following the same procedure as on Trial 1. Have the examinee complete the last three shapes of Trial 2.

If the examinee can read, show him or her the instruction sheet. Take out the Record Booklet and open it to Coding Part A. Point to the examinee, point to the sample box, and motion for the examinee to begin. After the sample items are completed, point to the examinee, point to the first box of the subtest proper, and then with a sweeping motion indicate that the examinee should begin the task. Follow the instructions shown in the WISC–III Manual for the Coding subtest.

Procedure for Coding B (examinees ages 8–16)
Select Practice Coding Form B. Point to the key (the boxes that have a number in the upper half and a symbol in the lower half). Then go to Trial 1, which contains six practice items. Draw the symbol in the first empty box under the number 11. Follow the same procedure for the second and third boxes. Then point to the examinee and motion for her or him to complete the remaining three boxes. Demonstrate how to complete the first three boxes of Trial 2, following the same procedure as on Trial 1. Have the examinee complete the last three boxes of Trial 2.

If the examinee can read, show her or him the instruction sheet. Take out the Record Booklet and open it to Coding Part B. Point to the examinee, point to the sample box, and motion for the examinee to begin. After the sample items are completed, point to the examinee, point to the first box of the subtest proper, and then with a sweeping motion indicate that the examinee should begin the task. Follow the instructions in the WISC–III Manual for the Coding subtest.

PICTURE ARRANGEMENT

Additional Materials
Instruction sheet prepared by the examiner. This sheet should contain the information on pages 86 to 89 of the WISC–III Manual. Only copy the material in color.

Two additional practice items prepared by the examiner. Make each practice item from three white 3" × 5" cards, as follows:

1. Print number 1 on one card, the number 2 on one card, and the number 3 on one card. On the back of each card, print the word *NUMBERS* and the appropriate number.

2. Print the letter A on one card, the letter B on one card, and the letter C on one card. On the back of each card, print the word *LETTERS* and the appropriate letter.

Procedure
For all examinees, present the first practice item (NUMBERS) in the order 2, 3, 1 from the examinee's left to right. Then arrange the cards in correct numerical sequence. Allow the examinee to view the arrangement for 10 seconds. Rearrange the cards in the original order. Motion to the examinee to arrange the cards by pointing to them with a general sweeping motion. If the examinee does not respond or arranges the cards incorrectly, arrange the cards in their correct sequence. Then rearrange the cards in the original administration order and motion to the examinee to arrange the cards. Follow the same procedure for practice item 2 (LETTERS). If the examinee can read, show him or her the instruction sheet. Follow the instructions in the WISC–III Manual for the Picture Arrangement subtest.

BLOCK DESIGN

Additional Materials
Instruction sheet prepared by the examiner. This sheet should contain the information on pages 100 to 104 of the WISC–III Manual. Only copy the material in color.

Procedure
If the examinee can read, show her or him the instruction sheet. For all examinees, motion for the examinee to assemble the design. Point to the examinee, point to the examinee's blocks, and point to the model or the card with the designs. Follow the instructions in the WISC–III Manual for the Block Design subtest.

(Continued)

OBJECT ASSEMBLY

Additional Materials

Instruction sheet prepared by the examiner. This sheet should contain the information on pages 124 to 127 of the WISC–III Manual. Only copy the material in color.

Procedure

If the examinee can read, show him or her the instruction sheet. For all examinees, motion for the examinee to assemble the sample puzzle. Point to the examinee, point to the puzzle pieces, and motion to indicate that the pieces must be put together. Follow the instructions in the WISC–III Manual for the Object Assembly subtest.

SYMBOL SEARCH

Additional Materials

Two instruction sheets prepared by the examiner. One sheet should contain the information for Symbol Search A, which is on pages 145 to 147 of the WISC–III Manual. Only copy the material in color. The other sheet should contain the information for Symbol Search B, which is on pages 147 to 149 of the WISC–III Manual. Only copy the material in color.

Procedure for Symbol Search A (examinees ages 6–7)

The following instructions cover the sample items, practice items, and subtest items.

Sample items. With the Symbol Search Response Booklet before the examinee, move your finger in a sweeping motion, from the examinee's left to right, across the entire row of the first sample item in Part A. Then point to the single target symbol in the first column. Next point to the first symbol in the search group. Then make sure you catch the examinee's eye and shake your head "no" to indicate that the first search symbol does not match the target symbol. You must make sure that the examinee is looking at you each time you shake your head "yes" or "no" or nod your head for any other purpose.

Repeat this procedure two more times. Point to the single target symbol and then to the second search symbol. Shake your head "no." Again point to the single target symbol and then to the third search symbol. This time shake your head "yes" to indicate that the search symbol matches the target symbol. With a no. 2 pencil, mark a slash in the YES box.

For the second sample item in Part A, generally follow the same procedure. However, for this item, shake your head "no" for each search symbol. After the demonstrating the third search symbol, mark a slash in the NO box.

Practice items. Give the examinee a no. 2 pencil. Point to the first row of the practice items and move your finger in a sweeping motion, from the examinee's left to right, along the entire first row. Nod your head to indicate to the examinee to begin. If the examinee places a slash mark in the YES box, nod your head to indicate "good" and go to the second practice item.

If the examinee marks NO on the first practice item, point to the target symbol and then to the second search symbol. Shake

your head to indicate "yes." Then immediately place a slash through the YES box. Do not demonstrate the third symbol.

Point to the second practice item and, by nodding your head, encourage the examinee to do it. If the examinee marks NO, nod your head to indicate "good" and proceed to the regular subtest items (see below). If the examinee marks YES, correct the examinee. Point to the target symbol and each of the three search symbols in turn, shaking your head to indicate "no" each time. Then place a slash through the NO box.

Do not go on to the regular subtest items until the examinee understands the task. You may have to erase your marks and the examinee's marks and ask the examinee to do the sample and/or practice items again.

Subtest items. When the examinee understands the task, open the Symbol Search Booklet to the second page and fold the page over. If the examinee can read, show her or him the first instruction sheet. After the examinee reads the directions, point to the first row to indicate that the examinee should begin the task.

If the examinee cannot read, run your finger down the entire second page. Then turn the booklet to the third page, and again run your finger down the entire page. Then turn to the fourth page, and again run your finger down the entire page. After showing the examinee the three pages of items, turn back to the second page of the booklet. Point to the pencil and then to the first row of the second page, then run your finger down the page, and then nod your head to indicate to the examinee to begin.

If the examinee ceases to work after completing the first row, redirect the examinee's attention to the second row by pointing to the entire second row with a sweeping motion and encourage the examinee to continue. If the examinee stops at the end of the second page, turn the booklet to the third page and encourage the examinee to continue. If the examinee stops at the end of the third page, turn the booklet to the fourth page and encourage the examinee to continue. Allow 120 seconds.

Procedure for Symbol Search B (for examinees ages 8–16)

The instructions cover the sample items, practice items, and subtest items.

Sample items. With the Symbol Search Response Booklet before the examinee, move your finger in a sweeping motion, from the examinee's left to right, across the entire row of the first sample item in Part B. Then point to the two target symbols in the first column. Next point to the first symbol in the search group. Then make sure you catch the examinee's eye and shake your head "yes" to indicate that the first search symbol matches the target symbol. Then with a no. 2 pencil immediately mark a slash in the YES box. You must make sure that the examinee is looking at you each time you shake your head "yes" or "no" or nod your head for any other purpose. Go to the second sample item, without demonstrating the remaining symbols in the first sample item.

For the second sample item in Part B, point to the two target symbols and then to the first search symbol. Shake your head "no" to indicate that the search symbol does not match either of the target symbols. Repeat this procedure four more times. In each case, point to the two target symbols and then to the search

(Continued)

symbol. Shake your head "no" each time. After the last search symbol, make a slash in the NO box.

Practice items. Give the examinee a no. 2 pencil. Point to the first row of the practice items and move your finger in a sweeping motion, from the examinee's left to right, along the entire first row. Nod your head to indicate to the examinee to begin. If the examinee places a slash mark in the YES box, nod your head to indicate "good" and go to the second practice item.

If the examinee marks NO on the first practice item, correct the examinee. Point to the two target symbols and then to the *second* search symbol. Shake your head to indicate "yes." Then immediately place a slash through the YES box. Do not demonstrate the remaining three symbols. Go to the second practice item.

Point to the second practice item and, by nodding your head, encourage the examinee to do it. If the examinee marks NO, nod your head to indicate "good" and proceed to the regular subtest items (see below).

If the examinee marks YES, correct the examinee. Point to the two target symbols and each of the five search symbols in turn, shaking your head to indicate "no" each time. Then place a slash through the NO box.

Do not go on to the regular subtest items until the examinee understands the task. You may have to erase your marks and the examinee's marks and ask the examinee to do the sample and/or practice items again.

Subtest items. When the examinee understands the task, open the Symbol Search Booklet to the sixth page and fold it over. If the examinee can read, show him or her the second instruction sheet. After the examinee reads the directions, point to the first row to indicate that the examinee should begin the task

If the examinee cannot read, run your finger down the entire sixth page. Then turn the booklet to the seventh page, and again run your finger down the entire page. Then turn to the eighth page, and again run your finger down the entire page. After

showing the examinee the three pages of items, turn back to the sixth page of the booklet. Point to the pencil and then to the first row of the sixth page, then run your finger down the page, and then nod your head to indicate to the examinee to begin.

If the examinee ceases to work after completing the first row, redirect the examinee's attention to the second row by pointing to the entire second row with a sweeping motion and encourage the examinee to continue. If the examinee stops at the end of the sixth page, turn the booklet to the seventh page. If the examinee stops at the end of the seventh page, turn the booklet to the eighth page. Allow 120 seconds.

MAZES

Additional Materials

Instruction sheets prepared by the examiner. Only copy the material in color. On one sheet of paper, type the instructions on page 156 of the WISC–III Manual for the sample maze ("See this …me."). On a second sheet of paper, type the instructions on page 156 of the WISC–III Manual for maze 1 ("Now see…Go ahead."). On a third sheet of paper, type the instructions "Now try this one." On the remaining sheets, type the instructions given in the WISC–III Manual for various items.

Procedure

If the examinee can read, show her or him the appropriate instruction sheet. Give the examinee the Response Booklet for the Mazes subtest. Point to the sample item. Point to the figure in the center of the maze and to the opening that leads to the exit. If the examinee can read, show him or her the first instruction sheet. Then, take a pencil and begin to complete the maze. On reaching the opening to the outside of the center, pause and, without lifting your pencil, point to the blind alley. Then point to the correct route and finish your tracing. Give the examinee another copy of the sample maze and motion for the examinee to complete it. Follow the instructions in the WISC–III Manual for the Mazes subtest.

Note. The idea for this table came from the work of Murphy (1957), Neuhaus (1967), Reed (1970), and Sullivan (1978).

Table A-16
Reliability and Validity Coefficients of Proposed WISC–III Short Forms

Dyad				Triad					Tetrad						Pentad					
Short form		r_{tt}	r	Short form			r_{tt}	r	Short form				r_{tt}	r	Short form					r_{tt}	r
V	BD	.911	.862	V	BD	SS	.909	.887	I	V	BD	SS	.931	.910	I	A	V	BD	SS	.940	.918
I	BD	.902	.848	A	V	BD	.921	.884	S	V	BD	SS	.928	.908	S	A	V	BD	SS	.938	.918
S	BD	.893	.842	I	V	BD	.933	.881	A	V	BD	SS	.924	.905	A	V	PC	BD	SS	.931	.917
C	BD	.871	.828	S	V	BD	.928	.878	I	S	BD	SS	.925	.904	I	V	PC	BD	SS	.937	.917
V	SS	.863	.826	I	BD	SS	.905	.877	I	C	BD	SS	.917	.901	I	V	PA	BD	SS	.934	.917
A	V	.886	.825	I	S	BD	.923	.874	I	S	CD	BD	.920	.901	I	V	DS	BD	SS	.938	.917
V	OA	.844	.820	I	C	BD	.912	.874	I	V	CD	BD	.928	.901	S	V	PC	BD	SS	.935	.916
A	BD	.885	.818	S	BD	SS	.900	.873	V	C	BD	SS	.921	.900	I	S	V	BD	SS	.943	.916
I	SS	.852	.817	V	PA	BD	.910	.872	S	V	CD	BD	.924	.900	S	V	PA	BD	SS	.932	.916
S	SS	.841	.814	A	V	OA	.884	.872	A	V	PA	BD	.923	.900	A	V	PA	BD	SS	.929	.915
I	PC[a]	.867	.794	CD	BD	SS[b]	.895	.765	I	A	PC	CD[a]	.900	.881	I	A	DS	PC	CD[a]	.917	.886
A	PC[a]	.838	.797	PC	BD	SS[b]	.893	.830	I	DS	PC	CD[a]	.898	.858	PC	CD	PA	BD	SS[b]	.915	.852
I	CD[a]	.847	.766	PC	PA	BD[b]	.893	.817	A	DS	PC	CD[a]	.892	.838							
I	A[a]	.879	.809	PC	BD	OA[b, d]	.893	.794	PC	PA	BD	SS[b]	.905	.853							
PC	BD[b]	.882	.777	I	A	PC[a]	.896	.852													
BD	SS[b]	.872	.784	I	A	CD[a]	.884	.838													
PA	BD[b]	.869	.777	I	A	DS[a]	.907	.815													
CD	SS[a, c]	.853	.611	A	DS	CD[a]	.881	.756													
				I	DS	CD[a]	.886	.796													
				I	S	V[c]	.932	.829													

Note. Abbreviations: I = Information, V = Vocabulary, BD = Block Design, S = Similarities, DS = Digit Span, A = Arithmetic, PC = Picture Completion, PA = Picture Arrangement, SS = Symbol Search, C = Comprehension, CD = Digit Symbol—Coding.

The first 10 combinations represent the best ones, based on validity. See Exhibit 8-4 (pages 256–257) for formulas used to obtain reliability and validity coefficients.

[a] This combination is useful for a rapid screening.

[b] This combination is useful for examinees who are hearing impaired.

[c] This combination represents the subtests in the Processing Speed Index.

[d] This combination represents the subtests in the Perceptual Organization Index.

Table A-17
Reliable and Unusual Scaled-Score Ranges for WISC–III Selected Two-Subtest Short Forms

Short form		Reliable scaled-score range	Unusual scaled-score range
V	BD	4	6
I	BD	4	6
S	BD	4	5
V	SS	4	6
A	V	4	5
V	OA	4	6
A	BD	4	5
I	SS	4	6
S	SS	4	6
I	PC	4	6
A	PC	4	6
I	CD	4	7
I	A	4	5
PC	BD	4	5
BD	SS	4	6
PA	BD	4	6
CD	SS	5	5

Note. The formula used to obtain the reliable scaled-score range estimate is as follows (Silverstein, 1989):

$$R = q\sqrt{\frac{\Sigma\mathrm{SEM}_i^2}{k}}$$

where

q = critical value of the studentized range for a specified probability level (.05 in this case)

SEM = standard error of measurement of the scores on subtest i

k = number of subtests in the short form

The formula used to obtain the unusual scaled-score range is as follows (Silverstein, 1989):

$$R = q \cdot \sigma\sqrt{1 - \frac{2\Sigma r_{ij}}{k(k-1)}}$$

where

q = critical value of the studentized range for a specified probability level (.10 in this case)

σ = standard deviation of the subtest scores

k = number of subtests in the short form

r_{ij} = correlation between subtests i and j

The table is read as follows: In the two-subtest short form composed of Vocabulary and Block Design, a range of 4 points between the two scores indicates a nonchance difference at the .05 level. A range of 6 occurs in less than 10% of the population and should be considered unusual. Less credence can be placed in the estimated short-form IQ when the scatter is larger than expected.

Table A-18
Reliable and Unusual Scaled-Score Ranges for WISC–III Selected Three-Subtest Short Forms

Short form			Reliable scaled-score range	Unusual scaled-score range
V	BD	SS	4	6
A	V	BD	4	6
I	V	BD	4	5
S	V	BD	4	5
I	BD	SS	4	6
I	S	BD	4	5
I	C	BD	4	6
S	BD	SS	4	6
V	PA	BD	4	6
A	V	OA	5	6
CD	BD	SS	4	6
PC	BD	SS	4	6
PC	PA	BD	4	6
PC	BD	OA	5	6
I	A	PC	4	6
I	A	CD	4	6
I	A	DS	4	6
A	DS	CD	4	7
I	DS	CD	4	7
I	S	V	4	5

Note. See Table A-17 for the formulas.

Table A-19
Reliable and Unusual Scaled-Score Ranges for WISC–III Selected Four-Subtest Short Forms

Short form				Reliable scaled-score range	Unusual scaled-score range
I	V	BD	SS	4	6
S	V	BD	SS	4	6
A	V	BD	SS	4	6
I	S	BD	SS	4	6
I	C	BD	SS	4	6
I	S	CD	BD	4	6
I	V	CD	BD	4	6
V	C	BD	SS	4	6
S	V	CD	BD	4	6
A	V	PA	BD	4	6
I	A	PC	CD	5	7
I	DS	PC	CD	4	7
A	DS	PC	CD	5	7
PC	PA	BD	SS	5	6

Note. See Table A-17 for the formulas.

Table A-20
Reliable and Unusual Scaled-Score Ranges for WISC–III Selected Five-Subtest Short Forms

Short form					Reliable scaled-score range	Unusual scaled-score range
I	A	V	BD	SS	4	6
S	A	V	BD	SS	4	6
A	V	PC	BD	SS	5	6
I	V	PC	BD	SS	4	6
I	V	PA	BD	SS	4	6
I	V	DS	BD	SS	4	7
S	V	PC	BD	SS	4	6
I	S	V	BD	SS	4	6
S	V	PA	BD	SS	5	6
A	V	PA	BD	SS	4	6
I	A	DS	PC	CD	5	7
PC	CD	PA	BD	SS	5	7

Note. See Table A-17 for the formulas.

Table A-21
Reliable and Unusual Scaled-Score Ranges for WISC–III Selected Six-, Seven-, and Eight-Subtest Short Forms

Short form							Reliable scaled-score range	Unusual scaled-score range
I	S	V	PC	CD	OA		5	6
I	S	V	C	PC	BD	OA	5	7
I	S	V	C	PC	PA	BD	OA	5	8
I	A	V	DS	CD	BD	OA	SS	5	8

Note. See Table A-17 for the formulas.

Table A-22
Estimated WISC–III Full Scale Deviation Quotients for Sum of Scaled Scores for 10 Best Short-Form Dyads and Other Combinations

Sum of scaled scores	Combination											
	C2	C3	C4	C5	C6	C7	C8	C9	C10	C11	C12	C13
2	42	45	46	47	47	48	48	48	48	49	49	49
3	45	48	49	50	50	50	51	51	51	51	52	52
4	49	51	52	53	53	53	54	54	54	54	54	55
5	52	54	55	56	56	56	56	57	57	57	57	58
6	55	57	58	59	59	59	59	59	60	60	60	60
7	58	60	61	62	62	62	62	62	63	63	63	63
8	61	63	64	65	65	65	65	65	66	66	66	66
9	65	67	67	68	68	68	68	68	68	69	69	69
10	68	70	70	71	71	71	71	71	71	71	72	72
11	71	73	73	74	74	74	74	74	74	74	74	75
12	74	76	76	77	77	77	77	77	77	77	77	77
13	78	79	79	79	80	80	80	80	80	80	80	80
14	81	82	82	82	82	83	83	83	83	83	83	83
15	84	85	85	85	85	85	85	86	86	86	86	86
16	87	88	88	88	88	88	88	88	89	89	89	89
17	90	91	91	91	91	91	91	91	91	91	91	92
18	94	94	94	94	94	94	94	94	94	94	94	94
19	97	97	97	97	97	97	97	97	97	97	97	97
20	100	100	100	100	100	100	100	100	100	100	100	100
21	103	103	103	103	103	103	103	103	103	103	103	103
22	106	106	106	106	106	106	106	106	106	106	106	106
23	110	109	109	109	109	109	109	109	109	109	109	108
24	113	112	112	112	112	112	112	112	111	111	111	111
25	116	115	115	115	115	115	115	114	114	114	114	114
26	119	118	118	118	118	117	117	117	117	117	117	117
27	122	121	121	121	120	120	120	120	120	120	120	120
28	126	124	124	123	123	123	123	123	123	123	123	123
29	129	127	127	126	126	126	126	126	126	126	126	125
30	132	130	130	129	129	129	129	129	129	129	128	128
31	135	133	133	132	132	132	132	132	132	131	131	131
32	139	137	136	135	135	135	135	135	134	134	134	134
33	142	140	139	138	138	138	138	138	137	137	137	137
34	145	143	142	141	141	141	141	141	140	140	140	140
35	148	146	145	144	144	144	144	143	143	143	143	142
36	151	149	148	147	147	147	146	146	146	146	146	145
37	155	152	151	150	150	150	149	149	149	149	148	148
38	158	155	154	153	153	152	152	152	152	151	151	151

Note. The subtest combinations are as follows:

C2 = I + CD	C4 = C + BD	C5 = BD + SS[b]	C10 = A + BD
C3 = V + SS	V + OA	C6 = V + BD	PC + BD[b]
I + SS	A + PC[a]	C7 = I + PC[a]	C11 = CD + SS[a]
S + SS	PA + BD	C8 = I + BD	C12 = A + V
		C9 = S + BD	C13 = I + A[a]

Abbreviations: V = Vocabulary, S = Similarities, A = Arithmetic, I = Information, C = Comprehension, PC = Picture Completion, CD = Digit Symbol—Coding, BD = Block Design, PA = Picture Arrangement, SS = Symbol Search.

Reliability and validity coefficients associated with each short-form combination are shown in Table A-16. See Exhibit 8-4, pages 256–257, for an explanation of the procedure used to obtain the estimated Deviation Quotients.

[a] This combination is useful for a rapid screening.

[b] This combination is useful for examinees who are hearing impaired.

Table A-23
Estimated WISC–III Full Scale Deviation Quotients for Sum of Scaled Scores for 10 Best Short-Form Triads and Other Combinations

Sum of scaled scores	Combination											
	C2	C3	C4	C5	C6	C7	C8	C9	C10	C11	C12	C13
3	37	39	40	42	43	43	43	43	43	43	44	49
4	39	41	42	45	45	45	45	45	45	45	46	51
5	41	43	45	47	47	47	48	47	47	47	48	53
6	44	46	47	49	49	49	50	49	49	49	50	55
7	46	48	49	51	51	51	52	51	51	51	52	57
8	48	50	51	53	53	53	54	53	53	54	55	59
9	51	52	54	55	55	55	56	55	56	56	57	61
10	53	55	56	57	57	58	58	58	58	58	59	62
11	56	57	58	59	60	60	60	60	60	60	61	64
12	58	59	60	62	62	62	62	62	62	62	63	66
13	60	61	62	64	64	64	64	64	64	64	65	68
14	63	64	65	66	66	66	66	66	66	66	67	70
15	65	66	67	68	68	68	69	68	68	68	69	72
16	67	68	69	70	70	70	71	70	70	70	71	74
17	70	71	71	72	72	72	73	72	72	73	73	76
18	72	73	73	74	74	75	75	75	75	75	75	77
19	74	75	76	77	77	77	77	77	77	77	77	79
20	77	77	78	79	79	79	79	79	79	79	79	81
21	79	80	80	81	81	81	81	81	81	81	81	83
22	81	82	82	83	83	83	83	83	83	83	83	85
23	84	84	85	85	85	85	85	85	85	85	86	87
24	86	86	87	87	87	87	87	87	87	87	88	89
25	88	89	89	89	89	89	90	89	89	89	90	91
26	91	91	91	91	91	92	92	92	92	92	92	92
27	93	93	93	94	94	94	94	94	94	94	94	94
28	95	95	96	96	96	96	96	96	96	96	96	96
29	98	98	98	98	98	98	98	98	98	98	98	98
30	100	100	100	100	100	100	100	100	100	100	100	100
31	102	102	102	102	102	102	102	102	102	102	102	102
32	105	105	104	104	104	104	104	104	104	104	104	104
33	107	107	107	106	106	106	106	106	106	106	106	106
34	109	109	109	109	109	108	108	108	108	108	108	108
35	112	111	111	111	111	111	110	111	111	111	110	109
36	114	114	113	113	113	113	113	113	113	113	112	111
37	116	116	115	115	115	115	115	115	115	115	114	113
38	119	118	118	117	117	117	117	117	117	117	117	115
39	121	120	120	119	119	119	119	119	119	119	119	117
40	123	123	122	121	121	121	121	121	121	121	121	119
41	126	125	124	123	123	123	123	123	123	123	123	121
42	128	127	127	126	126	125	125	125	125	125	125	123
43	130	129	129	128	128	128	127	128	128	127	127	124
44	133	132	131	130	130	130	129	130	130	130	129	126
45	135	134	133	132	132	132	131	132	132	132	131	128
46	137	136	135	134	134	134	134	134	134	134	133	130
47	140	139	138	136	136	136	136	136	136	136	135	132
48	142	141	140	138	138	138	138	138	138	138	137	134
49	144	143	142	141	140	140	140	140	140	140	139	136

(Continued)

Table A-23 *(Continued)*

Sum of scaled scores	Combination											
	C2	*C3*	*C4*	*C5*	*C6*	*C7*	*C8*	*C9*	*C10*	*C11*	*C12*	*C13*
50	147	145	144	143	143	142	142	142	142	142	141	138
51	149	148	146	145	145	145	144	145	144	144	143	139
52	152	150	149	147	147	147	146	147	147	146	145	141
53	154	152	151	149	149	149	148	149	149	149	148	143
54	156	154	153	151	151	151	150	151	151	151	150	145
55	159	157	155	153	153	153	152	153	153	153	152	147
56	161	159	158	155	155	155	155	155	155	155	154	149
57	163	161	160	158	157	157	157	157	157	157	156	151

Note. The subtest combinations are as follows:

C2 = I + DS + CD[a]	C9 = I + BD + SS	C12 = I + A + PC[a]
C3 = A + DS + CD[a]	C10 = S + BD + SS	I + C + BD
C4 = I + A + CD[a]	C11 = PC + PA + BD[b]	A + V + BD
C5 = CD + BD + SS[b]	PC + BD + SS[B]	I + V + BD
C6 = V + BD + SS		PC + BD + OA[b, d]
C7 = V + PA + BD		S + V + BD
C8 = I + A + DS[a]		I + S + BD
A + V + DS		C13 = I + S + V[c]

Abbreviations: V = Vocabulary, S = Similarities, A = Arithmetic, DS = Digit Span, I = Information, C = Comprehension, PC = Picture Completion, CD = Digit Symbol—Coding, BD = Block Design, PA = Picture Arrangement, SS = Symbol Search, OA = Object Assembly.

Reliability and validity coefficients associated with each short-form combination are shown in Table A-16. See Exhibit 8-4, pages 256–257, for an explanation of the procedure used to obtain the estimated Deviation Quotients.

[a] This combination is useful for a rapid screening.

[b] This combination is useful for examinees who are hearing impaired.

[c] This combination represents the subtests in the Verbal Comprehension Index.

[d] This combination represents the subtests in the Perceptual Organization Index.

Table A-24
Estimated WISC–III Full Scale Deviation Quotients for Sum of Scaled Scores for 10 Best Short-Form Tetrads and Other Combinations

Sum of scaled scores	Combination												
	C2	C3	C4	C5	C6	C7	C8	C9	C10	C11	C12	C13	C14
4	34	34	37	39	39	39	40	41	41	41	41	42	42
5	35	36	39	40	41	41	41	42	43	43	43	43	43
6	37	38	41	42	42	43	43	44	44	44	45	45	45
7	39	40	42	44	44	44	45	45	46	46	46	47	47
8	41	42	44	46	46	46	46	47	47	48	48	48	48
9	43	43	46	47	48	48	48	49	49	49	50	50	50
10	45	45	48	49	49	49	50	50	51	51	51	51	52
11	47	47	49	51	51	51	51	52	52	53	53	53	53
12	48	49	51	52	53	53	53	54	54	54	54	55	55
13	50	51	53	54	54	54	55	55	56	56	56	56	56
14	52	53	55	56	56	56	56	57	57	58	58	58	58
15	54	54	56	57	58	58	58	59	59	59	59	60	60
16	56	56	58	59	59	59	60	60	61	61	61	61	61
17	58	58	60	61	61	61	61	62	62	62	63	63	63
18	59	60	62	63	63	63	63	64	64	64	64	64	64
19	61	62	63	64	64	65	65	65	66	66	66	66	66
20	63	63	65	66	66	66	66	67	67	67	67	68	68
21	65	65	67	68	68	68	68	69	69	69	69	69	69
22	67	67	69	69	70	70	70	70	70	71	71	71	71
23	69	69	70	71	71	71	71	72	72	72	72	73	73
24	71	71	72	73	73	73	73	74	74	74	74	74	74
25	72	73	74	74	75	75	75	75	75	75	76	76	76
26	74	74	76	76	76	76	77	77	77	77	77	77	77
27	76	76	77	78	78	78	78	79	79	79	79	79	79
28	78	78	79	80	80	80	80	80	80	80	80	81	81
29	80	80	81	81	81	81	82	82	82	82	82	82	82
30	82	82	83	83	83	83	83	83	84	84	84	84	84
31	83	84	84	85	85	85	85	85	85	85	85	85	85
32	85	85	86	86	86	86	87	87	87	87	87	87	87
33	87	87	88	88	88	88	88	88	89	89	89	89	89
34	89	89	90	90	90	90	90	90	90	90	90	90	90
35	91	91	91	91	92	92	92	92	92	92	92	92	92
36	93	93	93	93	93	93	93	93	93	93	93	94	94
37	94	95	95	95	95	95	95	95	95	95	95	95	95
38	96	96	97	97	97	97	97	97	97	97	97	97	97
39	98	98	98	98	98	98	98	98	98	98	98	98	98
40	100	100	100	100	100	100	100	100	100	100	100	100	100
41	102	102	102	102	102	102	102	102	102	102	102	102	102
42	104	104	103	103	103	103	103	103	103	103	103	103	103
43	106	105	105	105	105	105	105	105	105	105	105	105	105
44	107	107	107	107	107	107	107	107	107	107	107	107	106
45	109	109	109	109	108	108	108	108	108	108	108	108	108
46	111	111	110	110	110	110	110	110	110	110	110	110	110
47	113	113	112	112	112	112	112	112	111	111	111	111	111
48	115	115	114	114	114	114	113	113	113	113	113	113	113
49	117	116	116	115	115	115	115	115	115	115	115	115	115

(Continued)

Table A-24 *(Continued)*

Sum of scaled scores	Combination												
	C2	C3	C4	C5	C6	C7	C8	C9	C10	C11	C12	C13	C14
50	118	118	117	117	117	117	117	117	116	116	116	116	116
51	120	120	119	119	119	119	118	118	118	118	118	118	118
52	122	122	121	120	120	120	120	120	120	120	120	119	119
53	124	124	123	122	122	122	122	121	121	121	121	121	121
54	126	126	124	124	124	124	123	123	123	123	123	123	123
55	128	127	126	126	125	125	125	125	125	125	124	124	124
56	129	129	128	127	127	127	127	126	126	126	126	126	126
57	131	131	130	129	129	129	129	128	128	128	128	127	127
58	133	133	131	131	130	130	130	130	130	129	129	129	129
59	135	135	133	132	132	132	132	131	131	131	131	131	131
60	137	137	135	134	134	134	134	133	133	133	133	132	132
61	139	138	137	136	136	135	135	135	134	134	134	134	134
62	141	140	138	137	137	137	137	136	136	136	136	136	136
63	142	142	140	139	139	139	139	138	138	138	137	137	137
64	144	144	142	141	141	141	140	140	139	139	139	139	139
65	146	146	144	143	142	142	142	141	141	141	141	140	140
66	148	147	145	144	144	144	144	143	143	142	142	142	142
67	150	149	147	146	146	146	145	145	144	144	144	144	144
68	152	151	149	148	147	147	147	146	146	146	146	145	145
69	153	153	151	149	149	149	149	148	148	147	147	147	147
70	155	155	152	151	151	151	150	150	149	149	149	149	148
71	157	157	154	153	152	152	152	151	151	151	150	150	150
72	159	158	156	154	154	154	154	153	153	152	152	152	152
73	161	160	158	156	156	156	155	155	154	154	154	153	153
74	163	162	159	158	158	157	157	156	156	156	155	155	155
75	165	164	161	160	159	159	159	158	157	157	157	157	157
76	166	166	163	161	161	161	160	159	159	159	159	158	158

Note. The subtest combinations are as follows:

C2 = I + DS + PC + CD[a]	C7 = I + V + CD + BD	C12 = A + V + BD + SS
C3 = A + DS + PC + CD[a]	C8 = PC + PA + BD + SS[b]	C13 = I + S + BD + SS
C4 = I + A + PC + CD[a]	C9 = I + C + BD + SS	C14 = S + V + BD + SS
C5 = I + S + CD + BD	C10 = V + C + BD + SS	I + V + BD + SS
C6 = S + V + CD + BD	C11 = A + V + PA + BD	

Abbreviations: V = Vocabulary, S = Similarities, A = Arithmetic, DS = Digit Span, I = Information, C = Comprehension, PC = Picture Completion, CD = Digit Symbol—Coding, BD = Block Design, PA = Picture Arrangement, SS = Symbol Search.

Reliability and validity coefficients associated with each short-form combination are shown in Table A-16. See Exhibit 8-4, pages 256–257, for an explanation of the procedure used to obtain the estimated Deviation Quotients.

[a] This combination is useful for a rapid screening.

[b] This combination is useful for examinees who are hearing impaired.

Sum of scaled scores	Combination										
	C2	C3	C4	C5	C6	C7	C8	C9	C10	C11	C12
5	34	36	38	39	39	39	40	40	41	41	42
6	36	38	39	40	41	41	41	41	42	43	43
7	37	39	41	41	42	42	42	43	44	44	44
8	39	40	42	43	43	43	44	44	45	45	46
9	40	42	43	44	45	45	45	45	46	46	47
10	41	43	45	46	46	46	46	47	48	48	48
11	43	45	46	47	47	47	48	48	49	49	50
12	44	46	48	48	49	49	49	49	50	50	51
13	46	47	49	50	50	50	50	51	52	52	52
14	47	49	50	51	51	51	52	52	53	53	53
15	49	50	52	52	53	53	53	53	54	54	55
16	50	52	53	54	54	54	54	55	56	56	56
17	52	53	55	55	55	55	56	56	57	57	57
18	53	55	56	56	57	57	57	57	58	58	59
19	55	56	57	58	58	58	58	59	59	60	60
20	56	57	59	59	59	60	60	60	61	61	61
21	58	59	60	61	61	61	61	61	62	62	63
22	59	60	61	62	62	62	62	63	63	63	64
23	60	62	63	63	64	64	64	64	65	65	65
24	62	63	64	65	65	65	65	65	66	66	66
25	63	65	66	66	66	66	66	67	67	67	68
26	65	66	67	67	68	68	68	68	69	69	69
27	66	67	68	69	69	69	69	69	70	70	70
28	68	69	70	70	70	70	70	71	71	71	72
29	69	70	71	71	72	72	72	72	73	73	73
30	71	72	72	73	73	73	73	73	74	74	74
31	72	73	74	74	74	74	74	75	75	75	75
32	74	74	75	76	76	76	76	76	76	76	77
33	75	76	77	77	77	77	77	77	78	78	78
34	77	77	78	78	78	78	78	79	79	79	79
35	78	79	79	80	80	80	80	80	80	80	81
36	80	80	81	81	81	81	81	81	82	82	82
37	81	82	82	82	82	82	83	83	83	83	83
38	82	83	83	84	84	84	84	84	84	84	84
39	84	84	85	85	85	85	85	85	86	86	86
40	85	86	86	86	86	87	87	87	87	87	87
41	87	87	88	88	88	88	88	88	88	88	88
42	88	89	89	89	89	89	89	89	90	90	90
43	90	90	90	90	91	91	91	91	91	91	91
44	91	91	92	92	92	92	92	92	92	92	92
45	93	93	93	93	93	93	93	93	93	93	94
46	94	94	94	95	95	95	95	95	95	95	95
47	96	96	96	96	96	96	96	96	96	96	96
48	97	97	97	97	97	97	97	97	97	97	97
49	99	99	99	99	99	99	99	99	99	99	99
50	100	100	100	100	100	100	100	100	100	100	100
51	101	101	101	101	101	101	101	101	101	101	101
52	103	103	103	103	103	103	103	103	103	103	103
53	104	104	104	104	104	104	104	104	104	104	104
54	106	106	106	105	105	105	105	105	105	105	105

(Continued)

Sum of scaled scores	Combination										
	C2	C3	C4	C5	C6	C7	C8	C9	C10	C11	C12
55	107	107	107	107	107	107	107	107	107	107	106
56	109	109	108	108	108	108	108	108	108	108	108
57	110	110	110	110	109	109	109	109	109	109	109
58	112	111	111	111	111	111	111	111	110	110	110
59	113	113	112	112	112	112	112	112	112	112	112
60	115	114	114	114	114	113	113	113	113	113	113
61	116	116	115	115	115	115	115	115	114	114	114
62	118	117	117	116	116	116	116	116	116	116	116
63	119	118	118	118	118	118	117	117	117	117	117
64	120	120	119	119	119	119	119	119	118	118	118
65	122	121	121	120	120	120	120	120	120	120	119
66	123	123	122	122	122	122	122	121	121	121	121
67	125	124	123	123	123	123	123	123	122	122	122
68	126	126	125	124	124	124	124	124	124	124	123
69	128	127	126	126	126	126	126	125	125	125	125
70	129	128	128	127	127	127	127	127	126	126	126
71	131	130	129	129	128	128	128	128	127	127	127
72	132	131	130	130	130	130	130	129	129	129	128
73	134	133	132	131	131	131	131	131	130	130	130
74	135	134	133	133	132	132	132	132	131	131	131
75	137	135	134	134	134	134	134	133	133	133	132
76	138	137	136	135	135	135	135	135	134	134	134
77	140	138	137	137	136	136	136	136	135	135	135
78	141	140	139	138	138	138	138	137	137	137	136
79	142	141	140	139	139	139	139	139	138	138	137
80	144	143	141	141	141	140	140	140	139	139	139
81	145	144	143	142	142	142	142	141	141	140	140
82	147	145	144	144	143	143	143	143	142	142	141
83	148	147	145	145	145	145	144	144	143	143	143
84	150	148	147	146	146	146	146	145	144	144	144
85	151	150	148	148	147	147	147	147	146	146	145
86	153	151	150	149	149	149	148	148	147	147	147
87	154	153	151	150	150	150	150	149	148	148	148
88	156	154	152	152	151	151	151	151	150	150	149
89	157	155	154	153	153	153	152	152	151	151	150
90	159	157	155	154	154	154	154	153	152	152	152
91	160	158	157	156	155	155	155	155	154	153	153
92	161	160	158	157	157	157	156	156	155	155	154
93	163	161	159	159	158	158	158	157	156	156	156
94	164	162	161	160	159	159	159	159	158	157	157

Note. The subtest combinations are as follows:

C2 = I + A + DS + PC + CD[a]   C8 = A + V + PA + BD + SS
C3 = PC + CD + PA + BD + SS[b]   C9 = I + V + PC + BD + SS
C4 = I + V + DS + BD + SS   S + V + PC + BD + SS
C5 = A + V + PA + BD + SS   C10 = S + A + V + BD + SS
C6 = S + V + PA + BD + SS   C11 = I + A + V + BD + SS
C7 = I + V + PA + BD + SS   C12 = I + S + V + BD + SS

Abbreviations: V = Vocabulary, S = Similarities, A = Arithmetic, DS = Digit Span, I = Information, PC = Picture Completion, CD = Digit Symbol—Coding, BD = Block Design, PA = Picture Arrangement, SS = Symbol Search.

Reliability and validity coefficients associated with each short-form combination are shown in Table A-16. See Exhibit 8-4, pages 256–257, for an explanation of the procedure used to obtain the estimated Deviation Quotients.

[a] This combination is useful for a rapid screening.
[b] This combination is useful for examinees who are hearing impaired.

Table A-26
Estimated WISC–III Full Scale Deviation Quotients for Sum of Scaled Scores for One Six-Subtest Short-Form Combination, One Seven-Subtest Short-Form Combination, and Two Eight-Subtest Short-Form Combinations

Sum of scaled scores	Combination				Sum of scaled scores	Combination				Sum of scaled scores	Combination			
	C2	C3	C4	C5		C2	C3	C4	C5		C2	C3	C4	C5
6	42	40	37	32	51	90	82	75	74	96	139	124	114	115
7	43	41	38	33	52	91	83	76	74	97	140	125	114	116
8	44	42	39	34	53	92	84	77	75	98	141	126	115	116
9	45	43	40	35	54	94	85	78	76	99	142	127	116	117
10	46	44	41	36	55	95	86	79	77	100	143	128	117	118
11	47	44	41	37	56	96	87	80	78	101	144	129	118	119
12	48	45	42	38	57	97	88	80	79	102	145	130	119	120
13	49	46	43	39	58	98	89	81	80	103	146	131	120	121
14	50	47	44	40	59	99	90	82	81	104	148	132	120	122
15	51	48	45	41	60	100	91	83	82	105	149	133	121	123
16	52	49	46	42	61	101	92	84	83	106	150	134	122	124
17	54	50	46	43	62	102	92	85	84	107	151	135	123	125
18	55	51	47	43	63	103	93	86	84	108	152	136	124	126
19	56	52	48	44	64	104	94	86	85	109	153	137	125	126
20	57	53	49	45	65	105	95	87	86	110	154	138	125	127
21	58	54	50	46	66	106	96	88	87	111	155	139	126	128
22	59	55	51	47	67	108	97	89	88	112	156	140	127	129
23	60	56	52	48	68	109	98	90	89	113	157	140	128	130
24	61	57	52	49	69	110	99	91	90	114	158	141	129	131
25	62	58	53	50	70	111	100	92	91	115	159	142	130	132
26	63	59	54	51	71	112	101	92	92	116	160	143	131	133
27	64	60	55	52	72	113	102	93	93	117	162	144	131	134
28	65	60	56	53	73	114	103	94	94	118	163	145	132	135
29	67	61	57	53	74	115	104	95	95	119	164	146	133	136
30	68	62	58	54	75	116	105	96	95	120	165	147	134	136
31	69	63	58	55	76	117	106	97	96	121		148	135	137
32	70	64	59	56	77	118	107	97	97	122		149	136	138
33	71	65	60	57	78	119	108	98	98	123		150	137	139
34	72	66	61	58	79	121	108	99	99	124		151	137	140
35	73	67	62	59	80	122	109	100	100	125		152	138	141
36	74	68	63	60	81	123	110	101	101	126		153	139	142
37	75	69	63	61	82	124	111	102	102	127		154	140	143
38	76	70	64	62	83	125	112	103	103	128		155	141	144
39	77	71	65	63	84	126	113	103	104	129		156	142	145
40	78	72	66	64	85	127	114	104	105	130		156	142	146
41	79	73	67	64	86	128	115	105	105	131		157	143	147
42	81	74	68	65	87	129	116	106	106	132		158	144	147
43	82	75	69	66	88	130	117	107	107	133		159	145	148
44	83	76	69	67	89	131	118	108	108	134		160	146	149
45	84	76	70	68	90	132	119	108	109	135		161	147	150
46	85	77	71	69	91	133	120	109	110	136		162	148	151
47	86	78	72	70	92	135	121	110	111	137		163	148	152
48	87	79	73	71	93	136	122	111	112	138		164	149	153
49	88	80	74	72	94	137	123	112	113	139		165	150	154
50	89	81	75	73	95	138	124	113	114	140		166	151	155

(Continued)

Table A-26 *(Continued)*

Sum of scaled scores	Combination				Sum of scaled scores	Combination				Sum of scaled scores	Combination			
	C2	C3	C4	C5		C2	C3	C4	C5		C2	C3	C4	C5
141			152	156	145			155	159	149			159	163
142			153	157	146			156	160	150			159	164
143			154	157	147			157	161	151			160	165
144			154	158	148			158	162	152			161	166

Note. The subtest combinations are as follows:

C2 = I + S + V + PC + BD + OA[a]

C3 = I + S + V + C + PC + BD + OA[b]

C4 = I + S + V + C + PC + PA + BD + OA[c]

C5 = I + A + V + DS + CD + BD + OA + SS[d]

Abbreviations: I = Information, S = Similiarities, A = Arithmetic, V = Vocabulary, C = Comprehension, DS = Digit Span, PC = Picture Completion, CD = Digit Symbol—Coding, BD = Block Design, OA = Object Assembly.

See Exhibit 8-4, pages 256–257, for an explanation of the procedure used to obtain the estimated Deviation Quotients.

[a]The reliability and validity of this combination are r_{xx} = .946 and r = .906, respectively.

[b]The reliability and validity of this combination are r_{xx} = .951 and r = .913, respectively.

[c]The reliability and validity of this combination are r_{xx} = .953 and r = .923, respectively.

[d]The reliability and validity of this combination are r_{xx} = .948 and r = .933, respectively.

APPENDIX B

TABLES FOR THE WPPSI–R

Table B-1
Confidence Intervals for WPPSI–R

Age level	Scale	Confidence level				
		68%	85%	90%	95%	99%
3 (2-11-16 through 3-5-15)	Performance IQ	±4	±6	±7	±8	±10
	Verbal Scale IQ	±3	±5	±5	±6	±8
	Full Scale IQ	±3	±4	±5	±6	±7
3½ (3-5-16 through 3-11-15)	Performance IQ	±4	±6	±7	±8	±10
	Verbal Scale IQ	±3	±5	±5	±6	±8
	Full Scale IQ	±3	±4	±5	±6	±7
4 (3-11-16 through 4-5-15)	Performance IQ	±4	±6	±7	±8	±11
	Verbal Scale IQ	±3	±4	±5	±6	±8
	Full Scale IQ	±3	±4	±5	±6	±7
4½ (4-5-16 through 4-11-15)	Performance IQ	±4	±6	±7	±8	±11
	Verbal Scale IQ	±3	±5	±5	±6	±8
	Full Scale IQ	±3	±4	±5	±6	±8
5 (4-11-16 through 5-5-15)	Performance IQ	±4	±6	±7	±9	±11
	Verbal Scale IQ	±3	±5	±5	±7	±9
	Full Scale IQ	±3	±4	±5	±6	±8
5½ (5-5-16 through 5-11-15)	Performance IQ	±5	±7	±8	±9	±12
	Verbal Scale IQ	±4	±5	±6	±7	±9
	Full Scale IQ	±3	±5	±5	±6	±8
6 (5-11-16 through 6-5-15)	Performance IQ	±4	±6	±7	±9	±11
	Verbal Scale IQ	±4	±6	±6	±7	±10
	Full Scale IQ	±3	±5	±5	±6	±8
6½ (6-5-16 through 6-11-15)	Performance IQ	±5	±7	±8	±9	±12
	Verbal Scale IQ	±4	±6	±7	±8	±10
	Full Scale IQ	±3	±5	±7	±7	±9
7 (6-11-16 through 7-3-15)	Performance IQ	±5	±7	±8	±10	±13
	Verbal Scale IQ	±5	±7	±8	±10	±13
	Full Scale IQ	±4	±6	±6	±8	±10

Note. See the Note in Table A-1 for an explanation of the method used to obtain confidence intervals.

Table B-2
Significant Differences Between Scaled Scores and Between IQs at Each of the Nine Age Levels of the WPPSI–R (.05/.01 significance level)

Age level		OA	GD	BD	MA	PC	AP	I	C	A	V	S
3 (2-11-16 through 3-5-15)	GD	4/6	—									
	BD	4/6	3/4	—								
	MA	4/6	3/4	3/4	—							
	PC	4/5	3/4	3/4	3/4	—						
	AP	5/7	4/5	4/6	4/5	4/5	—					
	I	4/5	3/4	3/4	3/4	3/4	4/5	—				
	C	4/5	3/4	3/4	3/4	3/4	4/5	3/4	—			
	A	5/6	4/5	4/5	4/5	3/4	4/6	3/4	3/5	—		
	V	4/6	3/4	3/4	3/4	3/4	4/5	3/4	3/4	4/5	—	
	S	4/5	3/4	3/4	3/4	3/4	4/5	3/4	3/4	3/5	3/4	—
	SE	4/5	3/4	3/4	3/4	3/4	4/5	3/4	3/4	3/5	3/4	3/4
3½ (3-5-16 through 3-11-15)	GD	4/6	—									
	BD	4/6	3/4	—								
	MA	4/6	3/4	3/5	—							
	PC	4/5	3/4	3/4	3/4	—						
	AP	5/7	4/5	4/5	4/6	4/5	—					
	I	4/5	3/4	3/4	3/4	3/4	4/5	—				
	C	4/5	3/4	3/4	3/4	3/4	4/5	3/4	—			
	A	4/6	3/5	3/5	4/5	3/4	4/6	3/4	3/4	—		
	V	4/6	3/4	3/4	3/5	3/4	4/5	3/4	3/4	3/5	—	
	S	4/5	3/4	3/4	3/4	3/4	4/5	3/4	3/4	3/4	3/4	—
	SE	4/6	3/4	3/4	3/4	3/4	4/5	3/4	3/4	3/5	3/4	3/4
4 (3-11-16 through 4-5-15)	GD	4/5	—									
	BD	4/5	3/4	—								
	MA	4/6	4/5	4/5	—							
	PC	4/5	3/4	3/4	4/5	—						
	AP	5/6	4/6	4/5	5/6	4/5	—					
	I	4/5	3/4	3/4	4/5	3/4	4/5	—				
	C	4/5	3/4	3/4	4/5	3/4	4/5	3/4	—			
	A	4/5	4/5	3/4	4/5	3/4	4/6	3/4	3/4	—		
	V	4/5	3/4	3/4	4/5	3/4	4/5	3/4	3/4	3/4	—	
	S	4/5	3/4	3/4	4/5	3/4	4/5	3/4	3/4	3/4	3/4	—
	SE	4/5	3/4	3/4	4/5	3/4	4/5	3/4	3/4	3/4	3/4	3/4
4½ (4-5-16 through 4-11-15)	GD	5/6	—									
	BD	4/6	3/4	—								
	MA	5/6	4/5	4/5	—							
	PC	4/6	3/4	3/3	3/4	—						
	AP	5/7	4/5	4/5	5/6	4/5	—					
	I	4/6	3/4	3/4	3/5	2/3	4/5	—				
	C	4/6	3/4	3/4	4/5	3/3	4/5	3/4	—			
	A	5/6	3/5	3/4	4/5	3/4	4/6	3/4	3/4	—		
	V	5/6	3/4	3/4	4/5	3/4	4/6	3/4	3/4	4/5	—	
	S	4/6	3/4	3/4	4/5	2/3	4/5	3/4	3/4	3/4	3/4	—
	SE	5/6	3/4	3/4	4/5	3/4	4/6	3/4	3/4	4/5	3/5	3/4
5 (4-11-16 through 5-5-15)	GD	5/6	—									
	BD	4/6	4/5	—								
	MA	5/6	4/5	4/5	—							
	PC	4/6	4/5	3/4	4/5	—						
	AP	5/7	4/6	4/5	4/6	4/5	—					
	I	4/6	4/5	3/4	4/5	3/4	4/5	—				
	C	4/6	4/5	3/4	4/5	3/4	4/5	3/4	—			
	A	5/6	4/5	3/5	4/5	3/5	4/6	4/5	3/5	—		
	V	4/6	4/5	3/4	4/5	3/4	4/5	3/4	3/4	3/5	—	
	S	4/6	4/5	3/4	4/5	3/4	4/5	3/4	3/4	3/5	3/4	—
	SE	5/6	4/5	3/4	4/5	3/4	4/6	3/5	3/4	4/5	3/4	3/4

For age 3: PSIQ — ; VSIQ 10/13
For age 3½: PSIQ — ; VSIQ 10/13
For age 4: PSIQ — ; VSIQ 10/13
For age 4½: PSIQ — ; VSIQ 10/13
For age 5: PSIQ — ; VSIQ 11/14

(Continued)

Table B-2 (Continued)

5½ (5-5-16 through 5-11-15)

Age level		OA	GD	BD	MA	PC	AP	I	C	A	V	S
	GD	5/7	—									
	BD	5/6	4/5	—								
	MA	5/6	4/6	4/6	—							
	PC	5/6	4/5	4/5	4/5	—						
	AP	5/7	5/6	4/6	4/6	4/6	—					
	I	5/6	4/6	4/5	4/5	4/5	5/6	—				
	C	5/6	4/5	4/5	4/5	4/5	4/6	4/6	—			
	A	5/6	4/5	4/5	4/5	4/5	4/6	4/6	4/5	—		
	V	4/6	4/5	3/5	4/5	3/4	4/5	4/5	3/4	3/4	—	
	S	4/6	4/5	3/5	4/5	3/4	4/5	4/5	3/4	3/4	3/4	—
	SE	5/6	4/6	4/6	4/5	4/5	4/6	4/5	4/5	4/5	4/5	4/5

VSIQ / PSIQ box: VSIQ 12/15 · PSIQ 12/15

6 (5-11-16 through 6-5-15)

Age level		OA	GD	BD	MA	PC	AP	I	C	A	V	S
	GD	4/6	—									
	BD	4/5	4/5	—								
	MA	4/6	4/5	4/5	—							
	PC	4/6	4/5	4/5	4/5	—						
	AP	5/6	4/6	4/5	4/6	4/6	—					
	I	4/6	4/5	4/5	4/5	4/5	5/6	—				
	C	4/6	4/5	4/5	4/5	4/5	4/6	4/5	—			
	A	4/5	4/5	4/5	4/5	4/5	4/6	4/5	4/5	—		
	V	4/5	4/5	3/5	4/5	4/5	4/6	4/5	4/5	4/5	—	
	S	4/5	4/5	3/4	3/5	4/5	4/5	4/5	4/5	3/5	3/4	—
	SE	4/6	4/5	4/5	4/5	4/5	4/6	4/5	4/5	4/5	4/5	4/5

VSIQ / PSIQ box: VSIQ 11/14 · PSIQ 11/14

6½ (6-5-16 through 6-11-15)

Age level		OA	GD	BD	MA	PC	AP	I	C	A	V	S
	GD	5/6	—									
	BD	4/6	4/5	—								
	MA	5/6	4/6	4/5	—							
	PC	4/6	4/6	4/5	4/5	—						
	AP	5/6	5/6	4/6	5/6	5/6	—					
	I	4/6	4/5	4/5	4/5	4/5	4/6	—				
	C	5/6	4/6	4/5	4/6	4/6	5/6	4/5	—			
	A	4/6	4/5	4/5	4/5	4/5	4/6	4/5	4/5	—		
	V	4/5	4/5	3/5	4/5	4/5	4/6	4/5	4/5	4/5	—	
	S	4/6	4/6	4/5	4/5	4/5	4/6	4/5	4/6	4/5	4/5	—
	SE	5/6	4/6	4/5	4/6	4/6	5/6	4/5	4/6	4/5	4/5	4/6

VSIQ / PSIQ box: VSIQ 12/16 · PSIQ 12/16

7 (6-11-16 through 7-3-15)

Age level		OA	GD	BD	MA	PC	AP	I	C	A	V	S
	GD	5/7	—									
	BD	5/6	4/5	—								
	MA	5/7	5/6	4/5	—							
	PC	5/7	5/6	4/5	5/6	—						
	AP	5/7	5/6	4/5	5/6	5/6	—					
	I	5/7	5/6	4/6	5/7	5/6	5/7	—				
	C	5/7	5/7	4/6	5/7	5/6	5/7	5/7	—			
	A	5/7	5/6	4/5	5/6	5/6	5/6	5/7	5/7	—		
	V	5/7	4/6	4/5	5/6	4/6	5/6	5/6	5/6	5/6	—	
	S	6/7	5/7	5/6	5/7	5/7	5/7	5/7	5/7	5/7	5/7	—
	SE	5/6	4/6	4/5	5/6	4/6	4/6	5/6	5/6	4/6	4/5	5/6

VSIQ / PSIQ box: VSIQ 16/21 · PSIQ 16/21

(Continued)

Table B-2 (*Continued*)

Note. Abbreviations: OA = Object Assembly, GD = Geometric Design, BD = Block Design, MA = Mazes, PC = Picture Completion, AP = Animal Pegs, I = Information, C = Comprehension, A = Arithmetic, V = Vocabulary, S = Similarities, SE = Sentences.

Sample reading: At age 3 years, a difference of 4 points between scaled scores on the Object Assembly and Geometric Design subtests is significant at the .05 level; a difference of 6 points is significant at the .01 level. The small box shows that at age 3 a 10-point difference between the Performance Scale IQ and Verbal Scale IQ is needed for the .05 level, and a 13-point difference is needed for the .01 level.

The values in this table for the subtest comparisons are overly liberal when more than one comparison is made. They are more accurate when a priori planned comparisons are made, such as Object Assembly vs. Block Design or Information vs. Vocabulary.

See Chapter 10, Exhibit 10-1 (page 302) for an explanation of the method used to arrive at magnitudes of differences.

Silverstein (personal communication, February 1990) suggests that the following formula be used to obtain the value of the significant difference at the .05 level between the highest and lowest subtest scores on the profile that allows for making individual subtest comparisons:

$$D = q\sqrt{\frac{\Sigma \text{SEM}^2}{k}}$$

where D is the significant difference, q is the critical value of the studentized range statistic, SEM is the standard error of measurement of a particular subtest, and k is the number of subtests. For the WPPSI–R, the q value is 4.62 at the .05 level for 12 and ∞ degrees of freedom and k is 12. The sum of the SEM^2 for the 12 subtests is 3.31 + 1.88 + 1.35 + 2.07 + 1.35 + 3.06 + 1.44 + 1.54 + 1.80 + 1.44 + 1.25 + 1.61 = 22.10 and

$$D = 4.62 \times \sqrt{\frac{22.10}{12}} = 4.62 \times \sqrt{1.8417} = 4.62 \times 1.3571 = 6$$

Thus, a difference of 6 points between the highest and lowest subtest scaled scores represents a significant difference at the .05 level.

Table B-3
Estimates of the Probability of Obtaining Designated Differences Between Individual WPPSI–R Performance and Verbal IQs

Probability of obtaining given or greater discrepancy by chance	Age level									
	3	3½	4	4½	5	5½	6	6½	7	Av.[a]
.50	3.43	3.56	3.56	3.56	3.68	4.08	3.82	4.21	3.68	5.49
.25	6.03	6.03	6.03	6.03	6.22	6.90	6.45	7.11	6.22	9.29
.20	6.71	6.71	6.71	6.71	6.92	7.68	7.18	7.92	6.92	10.34
.10	8.65	8.65	8.65	8.65	8.92	9.90	9.26	10.20	8.92	13.33
.05	10.27	10.27	10.27	10.27	10.60	11.76	11.00	12.12	10.60	15.83
.02	12.21	12.21	12.21	12.21	12.60	13.98	13.07	14.41	12.60	18.82
.01	13.52	13.52	13.52	13.52	13.95	15.48	14.48	15.96	13.95	20.84
.001	17.30	17.30	17.30	17.30	17.84	19.80	18.51	20.41	17.84	26.66

Note. To use Table B-3, find the column appropriate to the examinee's age. Locate the discrepancy that is *just less* than the discrepancy obtained by the examinee. The entry in the first column in that same row gives the probability of obtaining the given (or a greater) discrepancy by chance. For example, the hypothesis that a 3-year-old examinee obtained a Performance–Verbal discrepancy of 14 by chance can be rejected at the .01 level of significance. Table B-3 is two-tailed. See Chapter 10, Exhibit 10-1 (page 302) for an explanation of the method used to arrive at magnitudes of differences.

[a] Av. = Average of the nine age groups.

Table B-4
Estimates of the Percentage of Population Obtaining Given Discrepancies Between WPPSI–R Performance and Verbal IQs

Percentage obtaining given or greater discrepancy in either direction	Age level										Percentage obtaining given or greater discrepancy in a specific direction
	3	3½	4	4½	5	5½	6	6½	7	Av.[a]	
50	8.41	8.90	8.78	8.78	9.82	10.45	10.14	9.14	10.76	9.37	25
25	14.01	14.84	14.64	14.64	16.36	17.42	16.90	15.23	17.93	15.62	12.5
20	15.60	16.52	16.29	16.29	18.21	19.39	18.81	16.96	19.95	17.39	10
10	20.11	21.29	21.00	21.00	23.48	25.00	24.25	21.86	25.72	22.41	5
5	23.88	25.29	24.95	24.95	27.89	29.69	28.81	25.97	30.55	26.62	2.5
2	28.39	30.07	29.66	29.66	33.16	35.30	34.24	30.87	36.32	31.65	1
1	31.44	33.29	32.84	32.84	36.71	39.09	37.92	34.18	40.22	35.04	0.5
.1	39.85	42.19	41.62	41.62	46.53	49.54	48.06	43.32	50.97	44.42	.05

Note. To use Table B-4, find the column appropriate to the examinee's age. Locate the discrepancy that is *just less* than the one obtained by the examinee. The first column in that same row gives the percentage of the standardization population obtaining discrepancies as large as or larger than the located discrepancy. For example, for 3-year-old examinees, a Performance–Verbal discrepancy of 15 will be found in between 20% and 25% of the standardization population.

The method used to compute the discrepancy between the Verbal and Performance Scale IQs that reflects the percentage of the population obtaining the discrepancy is as follows:

$$\text{Discrepancy} = \sigma_1 z \sqrt{2 - 2r_{xy}}$$

The first term is the standard deviation of the test, the second is the selected z value, and the last is the correlation between the two scales. For example, for a 3-year-old child the discrepancy between the WPPSI–R Verbal and Performance Scale IQs that represent 5% of the population is

$$15(1.96)\sqrt{2 - 2(.67)} = 23.88$$

[a] Av. = Average of the nine age groups.

Table B-5
Percentage of Cases at or above Each Level of PIQ–VIQ Discrepancy in the WPPSI–R Standardization Sample in Both Directions

PIQ–VIQ discrepancies[a]	Full Scale IQ					
	≤79	80–89	90–109	110–119	120+	All
40	.0%	.4%	.5%	1.0%	1.3%	.6%
39	.0	.4	.6	1.0	1.3	.6
38	.0	.7	1.0	1.4	1.3	.9
37	.0	1.1	1.0	1.4	1.3	1.0
36	.0	1.1	1.3	1.7	1.3	1.2
35	.5	1.1	1.7	1.7	3.2	1.6
34	.0	1.5	1.8	1.7	3.2	1.7
33	.0	1.9	2.5	2.4	3.8	2.3
32	.0	2.2	3.0	3.1	3.8	2.7
31	.0	3.0	3.1	3.4	3.8	2.9
30	.7	3.0	3.7	3.7	4.5	3.4
29	1.4	3.4	4.3	4.7	5.8	4.1
28	1.4	3.7	5.6	5.4	6.4	5.0
27	1.4	3.7	6.2	6.1	8.3	5.6
26	2.8	4.1	6.9	7.5	9.0	6.4
25	2.8	4.1	8.1	8.5	9.0	7.2
24	3.5	5.2	8.8	10.5	12.2	8.4
23	3.5	6.0	10.1	11.5	13.5	9.5
22	4.2	7.5	11.7	12.5	14.7	10.8
21	4.9	9.7	13.9	15.6	15.4	12.9
20	5.6	10.8	15.6	19.7	17.3	14.9
19	7.0	13.8	18.2	20.3	17.9	16.9
18	9.9	16.0	21.5	22.7	20.5	19.8
17	16.2	18.7	23.8	24.7	23.1	22.5
16	18.3	20.9	27.2	26.4	25.0	25.1
15	21.1	23.9	29.4	29.8	31.4	28.1
14	24.6	26.9	32.2	33.6	33.3	31.1
13	28.9	28.4	36.2	39.0	36.5	34.9
12	31.0	31.3	39.2	43.1	39.7	38.0
11	36.6	37.3	43.5	46.4	42.9	42.4
10	41.5	40.7	47.9	52.9	44.9	46.8
9	45.8	46.6	52.8	58.6	52.6	52.2
8	50.7	51.9	56.7	64.7	57.7	56.9
7	54.9	57.1	62.5	69.8	61.5	62.2
6	62.0	63.4	67.3	74.9	67.3	67.6
5	67.6	71.3	72.8	81.4	71.8	73.5
4	73.2	75.7	78.4	85.1	79.5	78.8
3	83.8	82.8	84.6	90.8	87.2	85.6
2	90.8	89.9	91.9	93.9	96.2	91.8
1	95.8	97.8	97.3	98.0	98.1	97.4
0	100.0	100.0	100.0	100.0	100.0	100.0
N	142	268	839	295	156	1700
M	8.92	9.76	10.98	11.89	11.42	10.81
SD	6.61	8.17	8.68	8.67	9.56	8.57
Mdn	8.0	8.0	9.0	10.0	9.0	9.0

[a] For an individual examinee, the entries in this table must be divided by 2 to get an estimate of the percentage of cases at or above a particular PIQ–VIQ discrepancy in *one direction only*.

Source: Adapted with permission of the publisher and authors from J. S. Gyurke, A. Prifitera, and S. A. Sharp, "Frequency of Verbal and Performance IQ Discrepancies on the WPPSI–R at Various Levels of Ability," *Journal of Psychoeducational Assessment*, 1991, *9*, pp. 230–239. Copyright 1991 by The Psychoeducational Corporation.

Table B-6
Differences Required for Significance When Each WPPSI–R Subtest Scaled Score Is Compared to the Mean Scaled Score for Any Individual Child

Age 2-11-16 through 3-5-15

Subtest	Mean of 5 Performance Scale subtests[a]		Mean of 6 Performance Scale subtests		Mean of 5 Verbal Scale subtests[b]		Mean of 6 Verbal Scale subtests	
	.05	.01	.05	.01	.05	.01	.05	.01
Object Assembly	3.96	4.72	4.12	4.92	—	—	—	—
Geometric Design	2.85	3.40	2.93	3.50	—	—	—	—
Block Design	2.91	3.47	3.00	3.58	—	—	—	—
Mazes	2.78	3.32	2.86	3.42	—	—	—	—
Picture Completion	2.65	3.16	2.72	3.24	—	—	—	—
Animal Pegs	—	—	3.97	4.74	—	—	—	—
Information	—	—	—	—	2.30	2.75	2.37	2.82
Comprehension	—	—	—	—	2.45	2.93	2.54	3.02
Arithmetic	—	—	—	—	3.10	3.70	3.26	3.88
Vocabulary	—	—	—	—	2.66	3.18	2.78	3.30
Similarities	—	—	—	—	2.45	2.93	2.54	3.02
Sentences	—	—	—	—	—	—	2.57	3.02

Subtest	Mean of 10 subtests[a, b]		Mean of 11 subtests[b]		Mean of 11 subtests[a]		Mean of 12 subtests	
	.05	.01	.05	.01	.05	.01	.05	.01
Object Assembly	4.72	5.49	5.22	5.60	4.80	5.58	4.90	5.68
Geometric Design	3.21	3.73	3.55	3.80	3.25	3.78	3.32	3.85
Block Design	3.30	3.84	3.65	3.91	3.34	3.89	3.41	3.95
Mazes	3.12	3.63	3.45	3.70	3.16	3.67	3.22	3.74
Picture Completion	2.93	3.41	3.24	3.47	2.97	3.45	3.02	3.51
Animal Pegs	—	—	5.02	5.38	—	—	4.70	5.46
Information	2.62	3.05	2.90	3.11	2.65	3.08	2.70	3.13
Comprehension	2.83	3.30	3.13	3.36	2.87	3.33	2.92	3.39
Arithmetic	3.70	4.31	4.10	4.39	3.76	4.37	3.83	4.45
Vocabulary	3.12	3.63	3.45	3.70	3.16	3.67	3.22	3.74
Similarities	2.83	3.30	3.13	3.36	2.87	3.33	2.92	3.39
Sentences	—	—	—	—	2.87	3.33	2.92	3.39

[a] Animal Pegs excluded.
[b] Sentences excluded.

(Continued)

Table B-6 *(Continued)*

Age 3-5-16 through 3-11-15

Subtest	Mean of 5 Performance Scale subtests[a]		Mean of 6 Performance Scale subtests		Mean of 5 Verbal Scale subtests[b]		Mean of 6 Verbal Scale subtests	
	.05	.01	.05	.01	.05	.01	.05	.01
Object Assembly	3.95	4.72	4.21	5.01	—	—	—	—
Geometric Design	2.71	3.23	2.85	3.39	—	—	—	—
Block Design	2.77	3.31	2.92	3.48	—	—	—	—
Mazes	3.02	3.61	3.20	3.80	—	—	—	—
Picture Completion	2.50	2.99	2.62	3.12	—	—	—	—
Animal Pegs	—	—	4.06	4.83	—	—	—	—
Information	—	—	—	—	2.37	2.83	2.46	2.93
Comprehension	—	—	—	—	2.45	2.92	2.55	3.03
Arithmetic	—	—	—	—	2.98	3.55	3.13	3.73
Vocabulary	—	—	—	—	2.73	3.25	2.86	3.40
Similarities	—	—	—	—	2.37	2.83	2.46	2.93
Sentences	—	—	—	—	—	—	2.71	3.22

Subtest	Mean of 10 subtests[a, b]		Mean of 11 subtests[b]		Mean of 11 subtests[a]		Mean of 12 subtests	
	.05	.01	.05	.01	.05	.01	.05	.01
Object Assembly	4.71	5.48	4.81	5.59	4.80	5.58	4.89	5.68
Geometric Design	3.02	3.52	3.08	3.58	3.07	3.56	3.12	3.62
Block Design	3.12	3.63	3.18	3.69	3.16	3.67	3.22	3.74
Mazes	3.46	4.03	3.53	4.11	3.52	4.09	3.58	4.16
Picture Completion	2.73	3.17	2.78	3.23	2.76	3.21	2.81	3.26
Animal Pegs	—	—	4.63	5.37	—	—	4.70	5.46
Information	2.73	3.17	2.78	3.23	2.76	3.21	2.81	3.26
Comprehension	2.83	3.29	2.89	3.35	2.86	3.33	2.92	3.39
Arithmetic	3.54	4.12	3.62	4.20	3.60	4.18	3.67	4.26
Vocabulary	3.21	3.73	3.27	3.80	3.25	3.78	3.31	3.85
Similarities	2.73	3.17	2.78	3.23	2.76	3.21	2.81	3.26
Sentences	—	—	—	—	3.07	3.56	3.12	3.62

[a] Animal Pegs excluded.
[b] Sentences excluded.

(Continued)

Table B-6 *(Continued)*

Age 3-11-16 through 4-5-15

Subtest	Mean of 5 Performance Scale subtests[a]		Mean of 6 Performance Scale subtests		Mean of 5 Verbal Scale subtests[b]		Mean of 6 Verbal Scale subtests	
	.05	.01	.05	.01	.05	.01	.05	.01
Object Assembly	3.63	4.34	3.86	4.59	—	—	—	—
Geometric Design	3.10	3.70	3.27	3.89	—	—	—	—
Block Design	2.66	3.18	2.79	3.32	—	—	—	—
Mazes	3.38	4.03	3.58	4.26	—	—	—	—
Picture Completion	2.66	3.18	2.79	3.32	—	—	—	—
Animal Pegs	—	—	4.07	4.84	—	—	—	—
Information	—	—	—	—	2.44	2.92	2.54	3.02
Comprehension	—	—	—	—	2.52	3.00	2.62	3.11
Arithmetic	—	—	—	—	2.97	3.55	3.13	3.72
Vocabulary	—	—	—	—	2.52	3.00	2.62	3.11
Similarities	—	—	—	—	2.37	2.83	2.45	2.92
Sentences	—	—	—	—	—	—	2.54	3.02

Subtest	Mean of 10 subtests[a, b]		Mean of 11 subtests[b]		Mean of 11 subtests[a]		Mean of 12 subtests	
	.05	.01	.05	.01	.05	.01	.05	.01
Object Assembly	4.27	4.97	4.36	5.07	4.35	5.05	4.43	5.14
Geometric Design	3.55	4.13	3.62	4.21	3.60	4.18	3.67	4.26
Block Design	2.93	3.41	2.99	3.48	2.97	3.45	3.02	3.51
Mazes	3.93	4.57	4.01	4.66	3.99	4.64	4.07	4.72
Picture Completion	2.93	3.41	2.99	3.48	2.97	3.45	3.02	3.51
Animal Pegs	—	—	4.63	5.38	—	—	4.70	5.46
Information	2.83	3.30	2.89	3.36	2.87	3.33	2.92	3.39
Comprehension	2.93	3.41	2.99	3.48	2.97	3.45	3.02	3.51
Arithmetic	3.55	4.13	3.62	4.21	3.60	4.18	3.67	4.26
Vocabulary	2.93	3.41	2.99	3.48	2.97	3.45	3.02	3.51
Similarities	2.73	3.18	2.79	3.24	2.76	3.21	2.81	3.26
Sentences	—	—	—	—	2.87	3.33	2.92	3.39

[a] Animal Pegs excluded.
[b] Sentences excluded.

(Continued)

Table B-6 *(Continued)*

Age 4-5-16 through 4-11-15

Subtest	Mean of 5 Performance Scale subtests[a]		Mean of 6 Performance Scale subtests		Mean of 5 Verbal Scale subtests[b]		Mean of 6 Verbal Scale subtests	
	.05	.01	.05	.01	.05	.01	.05	.01
Object Assembly	4.28	5.10	4.56	5.42	—	—	—	—
Geometric Design	2.80	3.35	2.94	3.50	—	—	—	—
Block Design	2.60	3.11	2.72	3.24	—	—	—	—
Mazes	3.38	4.04	3.58	4.26	—	—	—	—
Picture Completion	2.23	2.67	2.31	2.74	—	—	—	—
Animal Pegs	—	—	4.07	4.85	—	—	—	—
Information	—	—	—	—	2.29	2.79	2.38	2.83
Comprehension	—	—	—	—	2.44	2.97	2.55	3.04
Arithmetic	—	—	—	—	2.91	3.54	3.07	3.66
Vocabulary	—	—	—	—	2.79	3.39	2.93	3.49
Similarities	—	—	—	—	2.37	2.88	2.47	2.94
Sentences	—	—	—	—	—	—	2.93	3.49

Subtest	Mean of 10 subtests[a, b]		Mean of 11 subtests[b]		Mean of 11 subtests[a]		Mean of 12 subtests	
	.05	.01	.05	.01	.05	.01	.05	.01
Object Assembly	5.12	5.96	5.23	6.08	5.22	6.07	5.32	6.18
Geometric Design	3.12	3.63	3.19	3.70	3.17	3.68	3.23	3.74
Block Design	2.84	3.30	2.89	3.36	2.87	3.34	2.93	3.39
Mazes	3.93	4.57	4.01	4.66	4.00	4.65	4.07	4.73
Picture Completion	2.28	2.65	2.32	2.70	2.30	2.67	2.34	2.71
Animal Pegs	—	—	4.63	5.38	—	—	4.71	5.46
Information	2.63	3.06	2.68	3.11	2.66	3.09	2.71	3.14
Comprehension	2.84	3.30	2.89	3.36	2.87	3.34	2.93	3.39
Arithmetic	3.47	4.04	3.54	4.11	3.52	4.09	3.59	4.16
Vocabulary	3.30	3.84	3.67	3.91	3.35	3.89	3.41	3.96
Similarities	2.73	3.18	2.79	3.24	2.77	3.22	2.82	3.27
Sentences	—	—	—	—	3.35	3.89	3.41	3.96

[a] Animal Pegs excluded.
[b] Sentences excluded.

(Continued)

Table B-6 *(Continued)*

Age 4-11-16 through 5-5-15

Subtest	Mean of 5 Performance Scale subtests[a]		Mean of 6 Performance Scale subtests		Mean of 5 Verbal Scale subtests[b]		Mean of 6 Verbal Scale subtests	
	.05	.01	.05	.01	.05	.01	.05	.01
Object Assembly	4.19	3.36	4.45	5.29	—	—	—	—
Geometric Design	3.38	3.92	3.56	4.23	—	—	—	—
Block Design	2.79	3.21	2.91	3.46	—	—	—	—
Mazes	3.32	3.86	3.50	4.16	—	—	—	—
Picture Completion	2.79	3.21	2.91	3.46	—	—	—	—
Animal Pegs	—	—	4.10	4.88	—	—	—	—
Information	—	—	—	—	2.76	3.30	2.89	3.44
Comprehension	—	—	—	—	2.63	3.14	2.75	3.27
Arithmetic	—	—	—	—	3.01	3.60	3.17	3.77
Vocabulary	—	—	—	—	2.70	3.22	2.82	3.36
Similarities	—	—	—	—	2.63	3.14	2.75	3.27
Sentences	—	—	—	—	—	—	3.04	3.61

Subtest	Mean of 10 subtests[a, b]		Mean of 11 subtests[b]		Mean of 11 subtests[a]		Mean of 12 subtests	
	.05	.01	.05	.01	.05	.01	.05	.01
Object Assembly	4.97	5.78	5.07	5.89	5.06	5.88	5.16	5.98
Geometric Design	3.88	4.51	3.95	4.59	3.94	4.58	4.01	4.66
Block Design	3.06	3.56	3.11	3.62	3.10	3.60	3.15	3.65
Mazes	3.80	4.43	3.88	4.51	3.86	4.49	3.93	4.57
Picture Completion	3.06	3.56	3.11	3.62	3.10	3.60	3.15	3.65
Animal Pegs	—	—	4.64	5.40	—	—	4.72	5.48
Information	3.24	3.77	3.30	3.83	3.28	3.82	3.34	3.88
Comprehension	3.06	3.56	3.11	3.62	3.10	3.60	3.15	3.65
Arithmetic	3.57	4.16	3.64	4.23	3.63	4.21	3.69	4.28
Vocabulary	3.15	3.66	3.21	3.73	3.19	3.71	3.25	3.77
Similarities	3.06	3.56	3.11	3.62	3.10	3.60	3.15	3.65
Sentences	—	—	—	—	3.46	4.02	3.52	4.08

[a] Animal Pegs excluded.
[b] Sentences excluded.

(Continued)

Table B-6 (Continued)

Age 5-5-16 through 5-11-15

Subtest	Mean of 5 Performance Scale subtests[a]		Mean of 6 Performance Scale subtests		Mean of 5 Verbal Scale subtests[b]		Mean of 6 Verbal Scale subtests	
	.05	.01	.05	.01	.05	.01	.05	.01
Object Assembly	4.32	5.16	4.57	5.44	—	—	—	—
Geometric Design	3.69	4.41	3.88	4.61	—	—	—	—
Block Design	3.28	3.92	3.42	4.07	—	—	—	—
Mazes	3.44	4.11	3.60	4.28	—	—	—	—
Picture Completion	3.05	3.64	3.62	3.77	—	—	—	—
Animal Pegs	—	—	4.14	4.92	—	—	—	—
Information	—	—	—	—	3.40	4.06	3.59	4.27
Comprehension	—	—	—	—	3.01	3.59	3.16	3.75
Arithmetic	—	—	—	—	3.01	3.59	3.16	3.75
Vocabulary	—	—	—	—	2.69	3.21	2.81	3.34
Similarities	—	—	—	—	2.69	3.21	2.81	3.34
Sentences	—	—	—	—	—	—	3.47	4.13

Subtest	Mean of 10 subtests[a, b]		Mean of 11 subtests[b]		Mean of 11 subtests[a]		Mean of 12 subtests	
	.05	.01	.05	.01	.05	.01	.05	.01
Object Assembly	5.10	5.94	5.21	6.05	5.20	6.04	5.29	6.14
Geometric Design	4.25	4.95	4.33	5.04	4.33	5.03	4.40	5.11
Block Design	3.68	4.28	3.75	4.35	3.74	4.34	3.80	4.41
Mazes	3.91	4.54	3.98	4.62	3.97	4.61	4.04	4.68
Picture Completion	3.36	3.91	3.41	3.97	3.41	3.96	3.46	4.01
Animal Pegs	—	—	4.66	5.42	—	—	4.74	5.50
Information	4.05	4.71	4.12	4.79	4.12	4.78	4.19	4.86
Comprehension	3.52	4.10	3.58	4.16	3.58	4.15	3.63	4.22
Arithmetic	3.52	4.10	3.58	4.16	3.58	4.15	3.63	4.22
Vocabulary	3.09	3.60	3.14	3.65	3.13	3.64	3.18	3.69
Similarities	3.09	3.60	3.14	3.65	3.13	3.64	3.18	3.69
Sentences	—	—	—	—	3.97	4.61	4.04	4.68

[a] Animal Pegs excluded.
[b] Sentences excluded.

(Continued)

Table B-6 *(Continued)*

Age 5-11-16 through 6-5-15

Subtest	Mean of 5 Performance Scale subtests[a]		Mean of 6 Performance Scale subtests		Mean of 5 Verbal Scale subtests[b]		Mean of 6 Verbal Scale subtests	
	.05	.01	.05	.01	.05	.01	.05	.01
Object Assembly	3.67	4.38	3.89	4.62	—	—	—	—
Geometric Design	3.26	3.89	3.43	4.08	—	—	—	—
Block Design	2.91	3.47	3.04	3.62	—	—	—	—
Mazes	3.20	3.82	3.37	4.01	—	—	—	—
Picture Completion	3.37	4.02	3.55	4.22	—	—	—	—
Animal Pegs	—	—	4.10	4.87	—	—	—	—
Information	—	—	—	—	3.37	4.03	3.55	4.22
Comprehension	—	—	—	—	3.27	3.90	3.43	4.08
Arithmetic	—	—	—	—	3.10	3.70	3.24	3.85
Vocabulary	—	—	—	—	2.98	3.55	3.11	3.70
Similarities	—	—	—	—	2.73	3.25	2.82	3.36
Sentences	—	—	—	—	—	—	3.37	4.00

Subtest	Mean of 10 subtests[a, b]		Mean of 11 subtests[b]		Mean of 11 subtests[a]		Mean of 12 subtests	
	.05	.01	.05	.01	.05	.01	.05	.01
Object Assembly	4.31	5.01	4.39	5.10	4.38	5.10	4.46	5.18
Geometric Design	3.74	4.36	3.81	4.43	3.80	4.42	3.87	4.49
Block Design	3.26	3.79	3.31	3.85	3.30	3.84	3.36	3.89
Mazes	3.67	4.27	3.74	4.34	3.73	4.33	3.79	4.40
Picture Completion	3.89	4.53	3.97	4.61	3.96	4.60	4.03	4.67
Animal Pegs	—	—	4.66	5.41	—	—	4.73	5.49
Information	3.97	4.61	4.04	4.70	4.03	4.69	4.10	4.76
Comprehension	3.82	4.44	3.89	4.52	3.88	4.51	3.95	4.58
Arithmetic	3.59	4.18	3.66	4.25	3.65	4.24	3.71	4.30
Vocabulary	3.43	3.99	3.49	4.05	3.48	4.04	3.54	4.10
Similarities	3.08	3.58	3.13	3.64	3.12	3.62	3.17	3.68
Sentences	—	—	—	—	3.80	4.42	3.87	4.49

[a] Animal Pegs excluded.
[b] Sentences excluded.

(Continued)

Table B-6 *(Continued)*

Age 6-5-16 through 6-11-15

Subtest	Mean of 5 Performance Scale subtests[a]		Mean of 6 Performance Scale subtests		Mean of 5 Verbal Scale subtests[b]		Mean of 6 Verbal Scale subtests	
	.05	.01	.05	.01	.05	.01	.05	.01
Object Assembly	3.87	4.62	4.08	4.85	—	—	—	—
Geometric Design	3.63	4.33	3.82	4.54	—	—	—	—
Block Design	3.10	3.70	3.22	3.83	—	—	—	—
Mazes	3.53	4.21	3.71	4.41	—	—	—	—
Picture Completion	3.48	4.15	3.65	4.34	—	—	—	—
Animal Pegs	—	—	4.13	4.91	—	—	—	—
Information	—	—	—	—	3.06	3.66	3.21	3.81
Comprehension	—	—	—	—	3.55	4.24	3.75	4.46
Arithmetic	—	—	—	—	3.06	3.66	3.21	3.81
Vocabulary	—	—	—	—	2.95	3.52	3.07	3.66
Similarities	—	—	—	—	3.35	3.99	3.52	4.18
Sentences	—	—	—	—	—	—	3.69	4.39

Subtest	Mean of 10 subtests[a, b]		Mean of 11 subtests[b]		Mean of 11 subtests[a]		Mean of 12 subtests	
	.05	.01	.05	.01	.05	.01	.05	.01
Object Assembly	4.52	5.26	4.61	5.35	4.60	5.35	4.68	5.43
Geometric Design	4.20	4.88	4.27	4.96	4.27	4.96	4.34	5.04
Block Design	3.45	4.02	3.51	4.08	3.50	4.07	3.56	4.13
Mazes	4.06	4.72	4.13	4.80	4.13	4.79	4.19	4.87
Picture Completion	3.99	4.64	4.06	4.72	4.05	4.71	4.12	4.78
Animal Pegs	—	—	4.67	5.43	—	—	4.75	5.51
Information	3.53	4.11	3.59	4.18	3.59	4.17	3.64	4.23
Comprehension	4.20	4.88	4.27	4.96	4.27	4.96	4.34	5.04
Arithmetic	3.53	4.11	3.59	4.18	3.59	4.17	3.64	4.23
Vocabulary	3.37	3.92	3.42	3.98	3.42	3.97	3.47	4.03
Similarities	3.92	4.56	3.98	4.63	3.98	4.62	4.04	4.69
Sentences	—	—	—	—	4.20	4.88	4.27	4.95

[a] Animal Pegs excluded.
[b] Sentences excluded.

(Continued)

Table B-6 *(Continued)*

Age 6-11-16 through 7-3-15

Subtest	Mean of 5 Performance Scale subtests[a]		Mean of 6 Performance Scale subtests		Mean of 5 Verbal Scale subtests[b]		Mean of 6 Verbal Scale subtests	
	.05	.01	.05	.01	.05	.01	.05	.01
Object Assembly	4.50	5.37	4.75	5.65	—	—	—	—
Geometric Design	3.90	4.66	4.08	4.86	—	—	—	—
Block Design	2.96	3.53	3.02	3.60	—	—	—	—
Mazes	4.04	4.82	4.23	5.04	—	—	—	—
Picture Completion	3.71	4.43	3.87	4.61	—	—	—	—
Animal Pegs	—	—	4.18	4.98	—	—	—	—
Information	—	—	—	—	4.25	5.08	4.42	5.26
Comprehension	—	—	—	—	4.38	5.23	4.56	5.42
Arithmetic	—	—	—	—	4.08	4.87	4.23	5.03
Vocabulary	—	—	—	—	3.71	4.43	3.81	4.53
Similarities	—	—	—	—	4.58	5.47	4.78	5.69
Sentences	—	—	—	—	—	—	3.70	4.40

Subtest	Mean of 10 subtests[a, b]		Mean of 11 subtests[b]		Mean of 11 subtests[a]		Mean of 12 subtests	
	.05	.01	.05	.01	.05	.01	.05	.01
Object Assembly	5.34	6.22	5.44	6.32	5.43	6.31	5.52	6.40
Geometric Design	4.54	5.28	4.61	5.36	4.60	5.35	4.67	5.42
Block Design	3.22	3.75	3.25	3.78	3.24	3.76	3.27	3.79
Mazes	4.72	5.50	4.80	5.58	4.79	5.57	4.87	5.65
Picture Completion	4.28	4.98	4.34	5.05	4.34	5.04	4.40	5.10
Animal Pegs	—	—	4.74	5.50	—	—	4.80	5.57
Information	4.90	5.70	4.98	5.79	4.98	5.78	5.05	5.86
Comprehension	5.07	5.90	5.16	5.99	5.15	5.99	5.23	6.07
Arithmetic	4.66	5.43	4.74	5.50	4.73	5.50	4.80	5.57
Vocabulary	4.15	4.83	4.21	4.89	4.20	4.88	4.26	4.94
Similarities	5.34	6.22	5.44	6.32	5.43	6.31	5.52	6.40
Sentences	—	—	—	—	4.05	4.71	4.11	4.77

Note. Table B-6 shows the minimum deviations from an individual's average subtest scaled score that are significant at the .05 and .01 levels. See the Note in Table A-6 for an explanation of how the deviations were obtained.

[a] Animal Pegs excluded.

[b] Sentences excluded.

Table B-7
Percentage of Cases at or above Each Level of Scatter in the WPPSI–R Standardization Sample

	Verbal Scale IQ											
	≤79		80–89		90–109		110–119		120+		All	
	Subtests											
Scatter (range)	5	6	5	6	5	6	5	6	5	6	5	6
13	.0	.0	.0	.0	.0	.0	.0	.0	.0	.0	.0	.0
12	.7	.7	.0	.0	.2	.2	.0	.3	.0	.0	.2	.2
11	.7	.7	.4	.4	.6	.7	.3	1.3	.0	1.3	.5	.8
10	1.4	2.1	.8	.8	1.8	2.3	.6	3.6	.6	1.9	1.3	2.3
9	1.4	2.8	2.8	3.2	4.0	5.8	1.9	5.6	2.5	4.5	3.1	5.1
8	2.1	5.7	5.6	7.7	8.3	10.9	6.8	11.5	7.0	13.6	7.0	10.5
7	5.7	12.1	10.5	15.4	16.0	19.7	15.7	21.7	20.0	29.2	14.6	19.8
6	12.8	25.0	20.7	30.8	26.5	34.0	31.8	41.4	36.9	50.6	26.4	35.7
5	32.1	44.3	37.8	49.5	46.0	55.2	53.1	65.3	53.8	70.7	45.6	56.8
4	53.5	62.9	65.0	71.5	68.9	78.6	73.4	84.3	78.5	88.9	68.7	78.3
3	84.9	90.8	82.5	90.2	87.7	92.9	89.8	96.1	92.1	96.0	87.5	93.2
2	95.6	97.9	95.9	98.3	97.8	99.1	97.7	99.4	98.6	100.0	97.4	99.0
1	99.2	99.3	99.6	99.5	100.0	100.0	99.7	100.0	100.0	100.0	99.8	99.9
0	100.0	100.0	100.0	100.0	100.0	100.0	100.0	100.0	100.0	100.0	100.0	100.0
N	140	140	246	246	855	855	305	305	154	154	1700	1700
M	3.91	4.44	4.22	4.68	4.58	5.00	4.71	5.30	4.91	5.57	4.53	5.01
SD	1.68	1.88	1.84	1.85	1.94	1.93	1.81	1.88	1.78	1.79	1.88	1.91
Mdn	4.0	4.0	4.0	4.0	4.0	5.0	5.0	5.0	5.0	6.0	4.0	5.0

	Performance Scale IQ											
	≤79		80–89		90–109		110–119		120+		All	
	Subtests											
Scatter (range)	5	6	5	6	5	6	5	6	5	6	5	6
15	—	.0	—	.0	—	.0	—	.0	—	.0	—	.0
14	.0	.0	.0	.0	.0	.0	.0	.0	.0	1.2	.0	.1
13	.0	.7	.0	.4	.1	.5	.0	.7	.0	1.2	.1	.6
12	.0	2.1	.4	1.2	.8	1.5	.0	1.4	.0	1.8	.5	1.5
11	.0	2.8	1.2	2.7	1.5	2.6	.4	2.5	.6	3.0	1.1	2.6
10	.0	3.5	2.7	5.3	2.5	5.2	1.8	5.7	1.8	7.1	2.2	5.3
9	2.8	7.7	5.3	10.2	7.0	10.8	6.4	12.0	5.3	12.4	6.2	10.8
8	6.3	16.2	10.6	18.9	13.8	20.6	15.5	21.8	10.6	21.8	12.7	20.3
7	17.6	33.1	22.3	32.9	26.0	34.1	27.1	35.5	25.2	36.4	24.9	34.3
6	33.1	50.0	38.9	48.0	42.4	54.1	43.6	54.8	41.6	55.7	41.3	53.1
5	52.1	69.7	59.3	68.8	60.3	72.0	65.0	78.0	60.3	73.8	60.4	72.5
4	71.8	84.5	75.1	83.9	77.3	86.1	82.2	90.3	78.4	87.8	77.6	86.5
3	88.7	96.5	91.7	96.0	91.0	95.8	95.5	98.4	93.6	98.3	92.1	96.6
2	97.2	99.3	98.1	99.8	98.5	99.7	99.4	99.8	99.4	99.5	98.7	99.7
1	100.0	100.0	96.6	100.0	100.0	100.0	100.0	100.0	100.0	100.0	99.9	100.0
0	100.0	100.0	100.0	100.0	100.0	100.0	100.0	100.0	100.0	100.0	100.0	100.0
N	142	142	265	265	837	837	285	285	171	171	1700	1700
M	4.70	5.66	5.05	5.67	5.22	5.82	5.36	6.00	5.16	5.99	5.17	5.83
SD	1.84	2.11	2.03	2.17	2.12	2.15	1.92	2.06	1.92	2.22	2.04	2.14
Mdn	5.0	5.5	5.0	5.0	5.0	6.0	5.0	6.0	5.0	6.0	5.0	6.0

(Continued)

Table B-7 *(Continued)*

Scatter (range)	Full Scale IQ											
	≤79		80–89		90–109		110–119		120+		Overall	
	Subtests											
	10	12	10	12	10	12	10	12	10	12	10	12
16	.0	.0	.0	.0	.0	.0	.0	.0	.0	.0	.0	.0
15	.0	.0	.0	.0	.1	.1	.0	.0	.0	.6	.1	.1
14	.0	.0	.4	.7	.3	.6	.0	.3	.0	1.2	.3	.6
13	.0	.7	.8	1.4	1.1	2.3	.3	1.3	.0	1.8	.8	1.8
12	.0	2.1	2.2	3.3	3.2	4.4	2.0	4.7	1.3	4.4	2.5	4.1
11	.0	2.8	3.8	6.7	6.4	9.2	5.1	9.1	1.9	7.0	4.9	8.0
10	.7	4.9	7.9	13.0	12.5	17.1	9.5	16.9	9.6	16.0	10.1	15.2
9	8.4	16.9	14.2	23.4	22.4	29.4	22.0	30.1	19.9	27.5	19.7	27.3
8	23.2	31.7	30.6	39.4	37.8	46.8	35.9	45.0	37.8	48.7	35.2	44.2
7	41.5	54.2	48.5	58.8	56.8	66.3	62.0	70.8	55.7	68.6	55.1	65.1
6	64.7	76.0	66.4	79.7	75.4	82.9	76.9	86.4	73.0	87.2	73.2	82.8
5	85.8	91.5	87.3	93.5	89.6	95.7	95.2	97.6	91.6	97.5	90.1	95.4
4	92.8	95.7	97.4	99.1	97.9	99.6	99.6	100.0	99.3	99.4	97.9	99.2
3	99.1	100.0	99.6	100.0	99.8	100.0	100.0	100.0	100.0	100.0	99.8	100.0
2	100.0	100.0	100.0	100.0	100.0	100.0	100.0	100.0	100.0	100.0	100.0	100.0
1	100.0	100.0	100.0	100.0	100.0	100.0	100.0	100.0	100.0	100.0	100.0	100.0
0	100.0	100.0	100.0	100.0	100.0	100.0	100.0	100.0	100.0	100.0	100.0	100.0
N	142	142	268	268	839	839	295	295	156	156	1700	1700
M	6.17	6.77	5.59	7.20	7.04	7.54	7.09	7.63	6.90	7.60	6.89	7.44
SD	1.66	1.84	1.98	2.04	2.12	2.10	1.85	1.97	1.85	2.00	2.01	2.05
Mdn	6.0	7.0	6.0	7.0	7.0	7.0	7.0	7.0	7.0	7.0	7.0	7.0

Source: Adapted with permission of the publisher and authors from J. S. Gyurke, A. Prifitera, and S. A. Sharp, "Frequency of Verbal and Performance IQ Discrepancies on the WPPSI–R at Various Levels of Ability," *Journal of Psychoeducational Assessment*, 1991, *9,* pp. 230–239. Copyright 1991 by The Psychoeducational Corporation.

Table B-8
Reliability and Validity Coefficients of Proposed WPPSI–R Short Forms

Dyad				Triad					Tetrad						Pentad						
Short form		r_{tt}	r	Short form			r_{tt}	r	Short form				r_{tt}	r	Short form					r_{tt}	r
BD	I	.890	.859	BD	I	S	.921	.894	BD	PC	I	S	.936	.914	BD	PC	I	A	S	.945	.929
PC	I	.895	.837	BD	I	A	.914	.892	BD	PC	I	SE	.930	.914	BD	PC	I	A	SE	.941	.929
BD	C	.881	.835	BD	PC	I	.919	.888	BD	PC	I	A	.932	.914	BD	PC	I	A	V	.943	.929
I	A	.887	.835	BD	I	V	.918	.887	BD	I	A	S	.934	.913	GD	BD	I	V	S	.940	.928
BD	S	.894	.829	BD	I	SE	.912	.885	BD	PC	I	C	.933	.912	BD	PC	C	A	S	.942	.927
GD	I	.865	.826	BD	A	V	.909	.883	BD	PC	C	A	.927	.911	GD	BD	I	C	S	.939	.927
BD	V	.886	.826	BD	I	C	.918	.882	GD	BD	I	V	.924	.911	BD	PC	I	C	A	.943	.927
BD	A	.880	.824	BD	C	A	.908	.881	BD	PC	I	V	.934	.911	GD	BD	I	A	V	.937	.927
PC	A	.879	.822	BD	PC	C	.912	.881	BD	I	A	V	.932	.910	BD	PC	I	S	SE	.944	.927
I	S	.904	.820	BD	I	A	.915	.881	GD	BD	I	S	.927	.910	GD	BD	PC	I	C	.938	.927

Note. Abbreviations: BD = Block Design, GD = Geometric Design, PC = Picture Completion, I = Information, C = Comprehension, A = Arithmetic, V = Vocabulary, S = Similarities, SE = Sentences.

It is recommended that short-form combinations involving Animal Pegs or Sentences not be used because these two subtests were not used in the construction of the IQ tables. The best two-subtest short-form combination for screening children who are hearing impaired is Block Design and Picture Completion (r_{tt} = .897 and r = .793), followed by Geometric Design and Block Design (r_{tt} = .879 and r = .746). For screening children who are visually impaired, any of the short-form combinations shown in the table involving subtests in the Verbal Scale can be used, such as Information and Arithmetic or Information and Similarities.

Table B-9
Reliable and Unusual Scaled-Score Ranges for WPPSI–R Selected Two-Subtest Short Forms

Short form		Reliable scaled-score range	Unusual scaled-score range
BD	C	4	6
BD	V	4	6
BD	I	4	6
BD	S	4	6
GD	I	4	6
BD	A	4	6
BD	PC	4	6
PC	A	4	6
PC	I	4	6
I	S	4	5
I	A	4	5

Note. See Table A-17 for the formulas.

Table B-10
Reliable and Unusual Scaled-Score Ranges for WPPSI–R Selected Three-Subtest Short Forms

Short form			Reliable scaled-score range	Unusual scaled-score range
BD	PC	C	4	6
BD	C	S	4	6
BD	I	SE	4	6
BD	A	V	4	6
BD	C	A	4	6
BD	PC	I	4	6
BD	I	S	4	6
GD	BD	PC	4	6
BD	I	V	4	6
BD	I	C	4	6
BD	I	A	4	6

Note. See Table A-17 for the formulas.

Table B-11
Reliable and Unusual Scaled-Score Ranges
for WPPSI–R Selected Four-Subtest Short Forms

Short form				Reliable scaled-score range	Unusual scaled-score range
GD	BD	PC	A	5	6
GD	BD	I	V	4	6
GD	BD	I	S	4	6
BD	PC	I	SE	4	6
BD	PC	C	A	4	6
BD	PC	I	S	4	6
BD	PC	I	C	4	6
BD	PC	I	V	4	6
BD	PC	I	A	4	6
BD	I	A	V	5	6
BD	I	A	S	4	6

Note. See Table A-17 for the formulas.

Table B-12
Reliable and Unusual Scaled-Score Ranges
for WPPSI–R Selected Five-Subtest Short Forms

Short form					Reliable scaled-score range	Unusual scaled-score range
GD	BD	MZ	PC	AP	5	7
GD	BD	PC	I	C	4	6
GD	BD	I	V	S	4	6
GD	BD	I	C	S	4	6
GD	BD	I	A	V	4	6
BD	PC	C	A	S	4	6
BD	PC	I	S	SE	4	6
BD	PC	I	A	SE	4	6
BD	PC	I	A	V	4	6
BD	PC	I	A	S	4	6
BD	PC	I	C	A	4	6

Note. See Table A-17 for the formulas.

Table B-13
Reliable and Unusual Scaled-Score Ranges
for WPPSI–R Selected Six-Subtest Short Forms

Short form						Reliable scaled-score range	Unusual scaled-score range
GD	BD	PC	I	C	S	4	7
GD	BD	PC	I	V	S	4	7
GD	BD	PC	I	A	V	4	6

Note. See Table A-17 for the formulas.

Table B-14
Estimated WPPSI–R Full Scale IQ Equivalents for Sum of Scaled Scores for 10 Best Short-Form Dyads

Sum of scaled scores	Combination							
	C2	C3	C4	C5	C6	C7	C8	C9
2	45	45	46	47	47	48	49	50
3	48	48	49	50	50	50	52	52
4	51	51	52	53	53	53	55	55
5	54	55	55	56	56	56	58	58
6	57	58	58	59	59	59	60	61
7	60	61	61	62	62	62	63	64
8	63	64	64	65	65	65	66	66
9	66	67	67	68	68	68	69	69
10	69	70	70	71	71	71	72	72
11	73	73	73	74	74	74	75	75
12	76	76	76	77	77	77	77	78
13	79	79	79	80	79	80	80	80
14	82	82	82	82	82	83	83	83
15	85	85	85	85	85	85	86	86
16	88	88	88	88	88	88	89	89
17	91	91	91	91	91	91	92	92
18	94	94	94	94	94	94	94	94
19	97	97	97	97	97	97	97	97
20	100	100	100	100	100	100	100	100
21	103	103	103	103	103	103	103	103
22	106	106	106	106	106	106	106	106
23	109	109	109	109	109	109	108	108
24	112	112	112	112	112	112	111	111
25	115	115	115	115	115	115	114	114
26	118	118	118	118	118	117	117	117
27	121	121	121	120	121	120	120	120
28	124	124	124	123	123	123	123	122
29	127	127	127	126	126	126	125	125
30	131	130	130	129	129	129	128	128
31	134	133	133	132	132	132	131	131
32	137	136	136	135	135	135	134	134
33	140	139	139	138	138	138	137	136
34	143	142	142	141	141	141	140	139
35	146	145	145	144	144	144	142	142
36	149	149	148	147	147	147	145	145
37	152	152	151	150	150	150	148	148
38	155	155	154	153	153	152	151	150

Note. The subtest combinations are as follows:

C2 = BD + C   C5 = BD + A   C8 = I + S
C3 = BD + V   BD + PC   C9 = I + A
C4 = BD + I   C6 = PC + A
   BD + S   C7 = PC + I
   GD + I

Abbreviations: BD = Block Design, C = Comprehension, A = Arithmetic, PC = Picture Completion, I = Information, S = Similarities, V = Vocabulary, GD = Geometric Design.

Reliability and validity coefficients associated with each short-form combination are shown in Table B-8. See Exhibit 8-4, pages 256–257, for an explanation of the procedure used to obtain the estimated Deviation Quotients.

Table B-15
Estimated WPPSI–R Full Scale IQ Equivalents for Sum of Scaled Scores for 10 Best Short-Form Triads

Sum of scaled scores	Combination								
	C2	C3	C4	C5	C6	C7	C8	C9	C10
3	42	42	43	43	43	44	44	44	45
4	44	44	45	45	46	46	46	46	47
5	46	47	47	48	48	48	48	48	49
6	48	49	49	50	50	50	50	50	51
7	50	51	51	52	52	52	52	52	53
8	52	53	54	54	54	54	54	54	55
9	55	55	56	56	56	56	56	56	57
10	57	57	58	58	58	58	58	59	59
11	59	59	60	60	60	60	60	61	61
12	61	61	62	62	62	62	62	63	63
13	63	64	64	64	64	64	65	65	65
14	65	66	66	66	66	67	67	67	67
15	68	68	68	69	69	69	69	69	69
16	70	70	70	71	71	71	71	71	71
17	72	72	73	73	73	73	73	73	73
18	74	74	75	75	75	75	75	75	75
19	76	76	77	77	77	77	77	77	77
20	78	79	79	79	79	79	79	79	79
21	81	81	81	81	81	81	81	81	82
22	83	83	83	83	83	83	83	83	84
23	85	85	85	85	85	85	85	85	86
24	87	87	87	87	87	87	87	88	88
25	89	89	89	90	90	90	90	90	90
26	91	91	92	92	92	92	92	92	92
27	94	94	94	94	94	94	94	94	94
28	96	96	96	96	96	96	96	96	96
29	98	98	98	98	98	98	98	98	98
30	100	100	100	100	100	100	100	100	100
31	102	102	102	102	102	102	102	102	102
32	104	104	104	104	104	104	104	104	104
33	106	106	106	106	106	106	106	106	106
34	109	109	108	108	108	108	108	108	108
35	111	111	111	110	110	110	110	110	110
36	113	113	113	113	113	113	113	112	112
37	115	115	115	115	115	115	115	115	114
38	117	117	117	117	117	117	117	117	116
39	119	119	119	119	119	119	119	119	118
40	122	121	121	121	121	121	121	121	121
41	124	124	123	123	123	123	123	123	123
42	126	126	125	125	125	125	125	125	125
43	128	128	127	127	127	127	127	127	127
44	130	130	130	129	129	129	129	129	129

(Continued)

Table B-15 *(Continued)*

Sum of scaled scores	Combination								
	C2	C3	C4	C5	C6	C7	C8	C9	C10
45	132	132	132	131	131	131	131	131	131
46	135	134	134	134	134	133	133	133	133
47	137	136	136	136	136	136	135	135	135
48	139	139	138	138	138	138	138	137	137
49	141	141	140	140	140	140	140	139	139
50	143	143	142	142	142	142	142	141	141
51	145	145	144	144	144	144	144	144	143
52	148	147	146	146	146	146	146	146	145
53	150	149	149	148	148	148	148	148	147
54	152	151	151	150	150	150	150	150	149
55	154	153	153	152	152	152	152	152	151
56	156	156	155	155	154	154	154	154	153
57	158	158	157	157	157	156	156	156	155
50	143	143	142	142	142	142	142	141	141
51	145	145	144	144	144	144	144	144	143
52	148	147	146	146	146	146	146	146	145
53	150	149	149	148	148	148	148	148	147
54	152	151	151	150	150	150	150	150	149
55	154	153	153	152	152	152	152	152	151
56	156	156	155	155	154	154	154	154	153
57	158	158	157	157	157	156	156	156	155

Note. The subtest combinations are as follows:

C2 = BD + PC + C   C5 = BD + PC + I   C8 = BD + I + V
C3 = BD + C + S   C6 = BD + I + S   C9 = BD + I + C
C4 = BD + I + SE   C7 = GC + BD + PC   C10 = BD + I + A
    BD + A + V
    BD + C + A

Abbreviations: BD = Block Design, C = Comprehension, A = Arithmetic, PC = Picture Completion, I = Information, S = Similarities, V = Vocabulary, GD = Geometric Design.

Reliability and validity coefficients associated with each short-form combination are shown in Table B-8. See Exhibit 8-4, pages 256–257, for an explanation of the procedure used to obtain the estimated Deviation Quotients.

Table B-16
Estimated WPPSI–R Full Scale IQ Equivalents for Sum of Scaled Scores for 10 Best Short-Form Tetrads

Sum of scaled scores	Combination								
	C2	C3	C4	C5	C6	C7	C8	C9	C10
4	39	40	40	41	41	41	42	43	43
5	41	42	42	42	42	43	44	44	44
6	43	43	44	44	44	45	45	46	46
7	44	45	45	46	46	46	47	47	47
8	46	47	47	47	47	48	49	49	49
9	48	48	49	49	49	50	50	50	51
10	49	50	50	50	51	51	52	52	52
11	51	52	52	52	52	53	53	54	54
12	53	53	53	54	54	54	55	55	55
13	54	55	55	55	56	56	57	57	57
14	56	57	57	57	57	58	58	58	59
15	58	58	58	59	59	59	60	60	60
16	60	60	60	60	60	61	61	62	62
17	61	62	62	62	62	63	63	63	63
18	63	63	63	64	64	64	65	65	65
19	65	65	65	65	65	66	66	66	66
20	66	67	67	67	67	67	68	68	68
21	68	68	68	69	69	69	69	70	70
22	70	70	70	70	70	71	71	71	71
23	71	72	72	72	72	72	73	73	73
24	73	73	73	74	74	74	74	74	74
25	75	75	75	75	75	76	76	76	76
26	76	77	77	77	77	77	78	78	78
27	78	78	78	79	79	79	79	79	79
28	80	80	80	80	80	80	81	81	81
29	81	82	82	82	82	82	82	82	82
30	83	83	83	83	84	84	84	84	84
31	85	85	85	85	85	85	86	86	86
32	87	87	87	87	87	87	87	87	87
33	88	88	88	88	88	89	89	89	89
34	90	90	90	90	90	90	90	90	90
35	92	92	92	92	92	92	92	92	92
36	93	93	93	93	93	93	94	94	94
37	95	95	95	95	95	95	95	95	95
38	97	97	97	97	97	97	97	97	97
39	98	98	98	98	98	98	98	98	98
40	100	100	100	100	100	100	100	100	100
41	102	102	102	102	102	102	102	102	102
42	103	103	103	103	103	103	103	103	103
43	105	105	105	105	105	105	105	105	105
44	107	107	107	107	107	107	106	106	106

(Continued)

Table B-16 *(Continued)*

Sum of scaled scores	Combination								
	C2	C3	C4	C5	C6	C7	C8	C9	C10
45	108	108	108	108	108	108	108	108	108
46	110	110	110	110	110	110	110	110	110
47	112	112	112	112	112	111	111	111	111
48	113	113	113	113	113	113	113	113	113
49	115	115	115	115	115	115	114	114	114
50	117	117	117	117	116	116	116	116	116
51	119	118	118	118	118	118	118	118	118
52	120	120	120	120	120	120	119	119	119
53	122	122	122	121	121	121	121	121	121
54	124	123	123	123	123	123	122	122	122
55	125	125	125	125	125	124	124	124	124
56	127	127	127	126	126	126	126	126	126
57	129	128	128	128	128	128	127	127	127
58	130	130	130	130	130	129	129	129	129
59	132	132	132	131	131	131	131	130	130
60	134	133	133	133	133	133	132	132	132
61	135	135	135	135	135	134	134	134	134
62	137	137	137	136	136	136	135	135	135
63	139	138	138	138	138	137	137	137	137
64	140	140	140	140	140	139	139	138	138
65	142	142	142	141	141	141	140	140	140
66	144	143	143	143	143	142	142	142	141
67	146	145	145	145	144	144	143	143	143
68	147	147	147	146	146	146	145	145	145
69	149	148	148	148	148	147	147	146	146
70	151	150	150	150	149	149	148	148	148
71	152	152	151	151	151	150	150	150	149
72	154	153	153	153	153	152	151	151	151
73	156	155	155	154	154	154	153	153	153
74	157	157	156	156	156	155	155	154	154
75	159	158	158	158	158	157	156	156	156
76	161	160	160	159	159	159	158	157	157

Note. The subtest combinations are as follows:

C2 = GD + BD + PC + AP   C7 = BD + PC + I + S   C8 = BD + PC + I + A
C3 = GD + BD + I + V   BD + PC + I + C   C9 = BD + I + A + V
C4 = GD + BD + I + S   BD + PC + V   C10 = BD + I + A + S
C5 = BD + PC + I + SE
C6 = BD + PC + C + A

Abbreviations: BD = Block Design, C = Comprehension, A = Arithmetic, PC = Picture Completion, I = Information, S = Similarities, V = Vocabulary, GD = Geometric Design, SE = Sentences, AP = Animal Pegs.

Reliability and validity coefficients associated with each short-form combination are shown in Table B-8. See Exhibit 8-4, pages 256–257, for an explanation of the procedure used to obtain the estimated Deviation Quotients.

Table B-17
Estimated WPPSI–R Full Scale IQ Equivalents for Sum of Scaled Scores for 10 Best Short-Form Pentads

Sum of scaled scores	Combination									
	C2	C3	C4	C5	C6	C7	C8	C9	C10	C11
5	37	39	39	39	40	40	40	41	41	41
6	39	40	40	40	41	41	42	42	42	42
7	40	42	42	42	42	42	43	43	43	43
8	41	43	43	43	44	44	44	45	45	45
9	43	44	44	44	45	45	46	46	46	46
10	44	46	46	46	46	46	47	47	47	47
11	46	47	47	47	48	48	48	49	49	49
12	47	48	48	49	49	49	50	50	50	50
13	48	50	50	50	50	50	51	51	51	51
14	50	51	51	51	52	52	52	53	53	53
15	51	52	53	53	53	53	53	54	54	54
16	53	54	54	54	54	54	55	55	55	55
17	54	55	55	55	56	56	56	57	57	57
18	55	56	57	57	57	57	57	58	58	58
19	57	58	58	58	58	58	59	59	59	59
20	58	59	59	59	60	60	60	60	61	61
21	60	61	61	61	61	61	61	62	62	62
22	61	62	62	62	62	63	63	63	63	63
23	62	63	63	63	64	64	64	64	64	65
24	64	65	65	65	65	65	65	66	66	66
25	65	66	66	66	66	67	67	67	67	67
26	67	67	67	68	68	68	68	68	68	68
27	68	69	69	69	69	69	69	70	70	70
28	69	70	70	70	70	71	71	71	71	71
29	71	71	72	72	72	72	72	72	72	72
30	72	73	73	73	73	73	73	74	74	74
31	74	74	74	74	75	75	75	75	75	75
32	75	76	76	76	76	76	76	76	76	76
33	76	77	77	77	77	77	77	78	78	78
34	78	78	78	78	79	79	79	79	79	79
35	79	80	80	80	80	80	80	80	80	80
36	80	81	81	81	81	81	81	82	82	82
37	82	82	82	82	83	83	83	83	83	83
38	83	84	84	84	84	84	84	84	84	84
39	85	85	85	85	85	85	85	86	86	86
40	86	86	86	86	87	87	87	87	87	87
41	87	88	88	88	88	88	88	88	88	88
42	89	89	89	89	89	89	89	89	89	89
43	90	90	91	91	91	91	91	91	91	91
44	92	92	92	92	92	92	92	92	92	92

(Continued)

Table B-17 *(Continued)*

Sum of scaled scores	Combination									
	C2	C3	C4	C5	C6	C7	C8	C9	C10	C11
45	93	93	93	93	93	93	93	93	93	93
46	94	95	95	95	95	95	95	95	95	95
47	96	96	96	96	96	96	96	96	96	96
48	97	97	97	97	97	97	97	97	97	97
49	99	99	99	99	99	99	99	99	99	99
50	100	100	100	100	100	100	100	100	100	100
51	101	101	101	101	101	101	101	101	101	101
52	103	103	103	103	103	103	103	103	103	103
53	104	104	104	104	104	104	104	104	104	104
54	106	105	105	105	105	105	105	105	105	105
55	107	107	107	107	107	107	107	107	107	107
56	108	108	108	108	108	108	108	108	108	108
57	110	110	109	109	109	109	109	109	109	109
58	111	111	111	111	111	111	111	111	111	111
59	113	112	112	112	112	112	112	112	112	112
60	114	114	114	114	113	113	113	113	113	113
61	115	115	115	115	115	115	115	114	114	114
62	117	116	116	116	116	116	116	116	116	116
63	118	118	118	118	117	117	117	117	117	117
64	120	119	119	119	119	119	119	118	118	118
65	121	120	120	120	120	120	120	120	120	120
66	122	122	122	122	121	121	121	121	121	121
67	124	123	123	123	123	123	123	122	122	122
68	125	124	124	124	124	124	124	124	124	124
69	126	126	126	126	125	125	125	125	125	125
70	128	127	127	127	127	127	127	126	126	126
71	129	129	128	128	128	128	128	128	128	128
72	131	130	130	130	130	129	129	129	129	129
73	132	131	131	131	131	131	131	130	130	130
74	133	133	133	132	132	132	132	132	132	132
75	135	134	134	134	134	133	133	133	133	133
76	136	135	135	135	135	135	135	134	134	134
77	138	137	137	137	136	136	136	136	136	135
78	139	138	138	138	138	137	137	137	137	137
79	140	139	139	139	139	139	139	138	138	138
80	142	141	141	141	140	140	140	140	139	139
81	143	142	142	142	142	142	141	141	141	141
82	145	144	143	143	143	143	143	142	142	142
83	146	145	145	145	144	144	144	143	143	143
84	147	146	146	146	146	146	145	145	145	145
85	149	148	147	147	147	147	147	146	146	146
86	150	149	149	149	148	148	148	147	147	147
87	152	150	150	150	150	150	149	149	149	149
88	153	152	152	151	151	151	150	150	150	150
89	154	153	153	153	152	152	152	151	151	151

(Continued)

Table B-17 *(Continued)*

Sum of scaled scores	Combination									
	C2	C3	C4	C5	C6	C7	C8	C9	C10	C11
90	156	154	154	154	154	154	153	153	153	153
91	157	156	156	156	155	155	154	154	154	154
92	159	157	157	157	156	156	156	155	155	155
93	160	158	158	158	158	158	157	157	157	157
94	161	160	160	160	159	159	158	158	158	158

Note. The subtest combinations are as follows:

C2 = GD + BD + MZ + PC + AP
C3 = GD + BD + PC + I + C
C4 = GD + BD + I + V + S
C5 = GD + BD + I + C + S
C6 = GD + BD + I + A + V
      BD + PC + C + A + S

C7 = BD + PC + I + S + SE
C8 = BD + PC + I + A + SE
C9 = BD + PC + I + A + V
C10 = BD + PC + I + A + S
C11 = BD + PC + I + C + A

Abbreviations: BD = Block Design, C = Comprehension, A = Arithmetic, PC = Picture Completion, I = Information, S = Similarities, V = Vocabulary, GD = Geometric Design, SE = Sentences, MZ = Mazes, AP = Animal Pegs.

Reliability and validity coefficients associated with each short-form combination are shown in Table B-8. See Exhibit 8-4, pages 256–257, for an explanation of the procedure used to obtain the estimated Deviation Quotients.

Table B-18
Estimated WPPSI–R Full Scale IQ Equivalents for Sum of Scaled Scores for Three Six-Subtest Short-Form Combinations

Sum of scaled scores	Combination			Sum of scaled scores	Combination			Sum of scaled scores	Combination		
	C2	C3	C4		C2	C3	C4		C2	C3	C4
6	38	38	39	46	84	84	84	86	130	130	130
7	39	39	40	47	85	85	85	87	131	131	131
8	40	40	41	48	86	86	86	88	132	132	132
9	41	41	42	49	87	87	87	89	133	133	133
10	43	43	43	50	89	89	89	90	134	134	134
11	44	44	44	51	90	90	90	91	136	136	135
12	45	45	45	52	91	91	91	92	137	137	136
13	46	46	47	53	92	92	92	93	138	138	138
14	47	47	48	54	93	93	93	94	139	139	139
15	48	48	49	55	94	94	94	95	140	140	140
16	49	50	50	56	95	95	95	96	141	141	141
17	51	51	51	57	97	97	97	97	142	142	142
18	52	52	52	58	98	98	98	98	144	144	143
19	53	53	53	59	99	99	99	99	145	145	144
20	54	54	54	60	100	100	100	100	146	146	146
21	55	55	56	61	101	101	101	101	147	147	147
22	56	56	57	62	102	102	102	102	148	148	148
23	58	58	58	63	103	103	103	103	149	149	149
24	59	59	59	64	105	105	105	104	151	150	150
25	60	60	60	65	106	106	106	105	152	152	151
26	61	61	61	66	107	107	107	106	153	153	152
27	62	62	62	67	108	108	108	107	154	154	153
28	63	63	64	68	109	109	109	108	155	155	155
29	64	64	65	69	110	110	110	109	156	156	156
30	66	66	66	70	111	111	111	110	157	157	157
31	67	67	67	71	113	113	113	111	159	159	158
32	68	68	68	72	114	114	114	112	160	160	159
33	69	69	69	73	115	115	115	113	161	161	160
34	70	70	70	74	116	116	116	114	162	162	161
35	71	71	72	75	117	117	117	115	163	163	163
36	72	72	73	76	118	118	118				
37	74	74	74	77	120	120	119				
38	75	75	75	78	121	121	120				
39	76	76	76	79	122	122	122				
40	77	77	77	80	123	123	123				
41	78	78	78	81	124	124	124				
42	79	79	80	82	125	125	125				
43	80	80	81	83	126	126	126				
44	82	82	82	84	128	128	127				
45	83	83	83	85	129	129	128				

Note. The subtest combinations are as follows:

C2 = GD + BD + PC + I + C + S
C3 = GD + BD + PC + I + V + S
C4 = GD + BD + PC + I + A + V

Abbreviations: BD = Block Design, C = Comprehension, A = Arithmetic, PC = Picture Completion, I = Information, S = Similarities, V = Vocabulary, GD = Geometric Design.

Reliability and validity coefficients associated with each short-form combination are shown in Table B-8. See Exhibit 8-4, pages 256–257, for an explanation of the procedure used to obtain the estimated Deviation Quotients.

APPENDIX C

TABLES FOR WAIS–III

Table C-1
Confidence Intervals for WAIS–III Scales and Index Scores Based on Obtained Score Only

Age group	Scale	Confidence level				
		68%	85%	90%	95%	99%
16–17	Verbal Scale IQ	±3	±5	±5	±6	±8
	Performance Scale IQ	±5	±6	±7	±8	±11
	Full Scale IQ	±3	±4	±5	±6	±7
	Verbal Comprehension	±4	±6	±6	±8	±10
	Perceptual Organization	±5	±6	±7	±8	±11
	Working Memory	±4	±6	±7	±8	±11
	Processing Speed	±6	±8	±10	±11	±15
18–19	Verbal Scale IQ	±3	±4	±5	±5	±7
	Performance Scale IQ	±5	±6	±7	±9	±11
	Full Scale IQ	±3	±4	±4	±5	±7
	Verbal Comprehension	±4	±5	±6	±7	±9
	Perceptual Organization	±5	±7	±8	±9	±12
	Working Memory	±4	±5	±6	±7	±9
	Processing Speed	±6	±8	±10	±11	±15
20–24	Verbal Scale IQ	±3	±4	±5	±6	±7
	Performance Scale IQ	±4	±6	±7	±8	±10
	Full Scale IQ	±3	±4	±4	±5	±7
	Verbal Comprehension	±4	±5	±6	±7	±9
	Perceptual Organization	±4	±6	±7	±8	±10
	Working Memory	±4	±6	±7	±8	±11
	Processing Speed	±6	±9	±10	±11	±15
25–29	Verbal Scale IQ	±3	±4	±5	±5	±7
	Performance Scale IQ	±4	±5	±6	±7	±9
	Full Scale IQ	±3	±4	±4	±5	±6
	Verbal Comprehension	±4	±5	±6	±6	±8
	Perceptual Organization	±4	±5	±6	±7	±9
	Working Memory	±4	±6	±7	±8	±11
	Processing Speed	±6	±8	±9	±11	±15
30–34	Verbal Scale IQ	±3	±4	±5	±5	±7
	Performance Scale IQ	±4	±6	±7	±8	±11
	Full Scale IQ	±3	±4	±4	±5	±6
	Verbal Comprehension	±3	±5	±6	±6	±8
	Perceptual Organization	±5	±6	±6	±7	±9
	Working Memory	±4	±6	±7	±8	±11
	Processing Speed	±5	±8	±9	±11	±15
35–44	Verbal Scale IQ	±3	±4	±5	±5	±7
	Performance Scale IQ	±4	±6	±6	±7	±10
	Full Scale IQ	±3	±4	±4	±5	±6
	Verbal Comprehension	±4	±5	±5	±6	±8
	Perceptual Organization	±4	±6	±7	±8	±10
	Working Memory	±4	±6	±7	±8	±10
	Processing Speed	±5	±8	±9	±10	±13
45–54	Verbal Scale IQ	±3	±4	±5	±5	±7
	Performance Scale IQ	±4	±6	±6	±7	±10
	Full Scale IQ	±3	±4	±4	±5	±6
	Verbal Comprehension	±4	±5	±5	±6	±8
	Perceptual Organization	±4	±6	±7	±8	±11
	Working Memory	±4	±6	±7	±7	±10
	Processing Speed	±5	±8	±9	±10	±13

(Continued)

Table C-1 *(Continued)*

Age group	Scale	Confidence level				
		68%	85%	90%	95%	99%
55–64	Verbal Scale IQ	±3	±4	±4	±5	±7
	Performance Scale IQ	±4	±5	±6	±7	±9
	Full Scale IQ	±3	±3	±4	±5	±6
	Verbal Comprehension	±3	±4	±5	±6	±8
	Perceptual Organization	±4	±5	±6	±7	±9
	Working Memory	±4	±6	±7	±8	±10
	Processing Speed	±5	±7	±8	±10	±13
65–69	Verbal Scale IQ	±3	±4	±4	±5	±6
	Performance Scale IQ	±4	±5	±5	±6	±8
	Full Scale IQ	±2	±3	±4	±4	±5
	Verbal Comprehension	±3	±4	±5	±6	±7
	Perceptual Organization	±4	±5	±6	±7	±9
	Working Memory	±4	±6	±7	±8	±10
	Processing Speed	±5	±7	±8	±10	±13
70–74	Verbal Scale IQ	±3	±4	±5	±5	±7
	Performance Scale IQ	±4	±5	±6	±7	±9
	Full Scale IQ	±3	±4	±4	±5	±6
	Verbal Comprehension	±4	±5	±6	±7	±9
	Perceptual Organization	±4	±6	±7	±8	±10
	Working Memory	±4	±6	±6	±7	±10
	Processing Speed	±5	±8	±9	±10	±13
75–79	Verbal Scale IQ	±3	±4	±5	±6	±7
	Performance Scale IQ	±5	±6	±7	±8	±11
	Full Scale IQ	±3	±4	±5	±5	±7
	Verbal Comprehension	±3	±5	±5	±6	±8
	Perceptual Organization	±5	±7	±8	±9	±12
	Working Memory	±5	±7	±8	±9	±12
	Processing Speed	±6	±8	±9	±10	±14
80–84	Verbal Scale IQ	±3	±4	±5	±5	±7
	Performance Scale IQ	±4	±6	±6	±8	±10
	Full Scale IQ	±3	±4	±4	±5	±6
	Verbal Comprehension	±3	±4	±5	±6	±8
	Perceptual Organization	±5	±6	±7	±9	±11
	Working Memory	±4	±6	±7	±8	±10
	Processing Speed	±6	±8	±9	±10	±14
85–89	Verbal Scale IQ	±4	±5	±6	±6	±8
	Performance Scale IQ	±4	±6	±7	±8	±10
	Full Scale IQ	±3	±4	±5	±6	±7
	Verbal Comprehension	±3	±5	±5	±6	±8
	Perceptual Organization	±5	±7	±8	±10	±13
	Working Memory	±5	±7	±8	±9	±12
	Processing Speed	±6	±8	±9	±10	±13
Average	Verbal Scale IQ	±3	±4	±5	±5	±7
	Performance Scale IQ	±4	±6	±7	±8	±10
	Full Scale IQ	±3	±4	±4	±5	±6
	Verbal Comprehension	±4	±5	±5	±6	±8
	Perceptual Organization	±4	±6	±7	±8	±11
	Working Memory	±4	±6	±7	±8	±10
	Processing Speed	±6	±8	±9	±11	±14

Note. See Table A-1 for an explanation of the method used to obtain confidence intervals. Confidence intervals in Table C-1 were obtained by using the appropriate SEM located in Table 3.4 (page 54) in the *WAIS–III—WMS–III Technical Manual.*

Table C-2
Significant Differences Between WAIS–III Scaled Scores, IQs, and Index Scores at Ages 16 to 17, at Ages 18 to 19, and for the Average of the Thirteen Age Groups (.05/.01 significance levels)

Ages 16–17

	V	S	A	DS	I	C	LN	PC	CD	BD	MR	PA	SS
S	4/5												
A	3/4	4/5											
DS	3/4	4/5	3/4										
I	3/4	4/5	3/4	3/4									
C	3/4	4/5	4/5	3/4	4/5								
LN	4/5	4/6	4/5	4/5	4/5	4/5							
PC	4/5	4/5	4/5	4/5	4/5	4/5	4/5						
CD	4/5	4/5	4/5	4/5	4/5	4/5	4/6	4/5					
BD	3/4	4/5	3/4	3/4	3/4	4/5	4/5	4/5	4/5				
MR	3/4	4/5	3/4	3/4	3/4	4/5	4/5	4/5	4/5	3/4			
PA	4/5	5/6	4/6	4/5	4/5	4/6	5/6	5/6	5/6	4/6	4/6		
SS	4/5	4/6	4/5	4/5	4/5	4/6	5/6	4/6	4/6	4/5	4/5	5/6	
OA	4/5	4/6	4/5	4/5	4/5	4/6	5/6	4/6	4/6	4/5	4/5	5/6	5/6

	VSIQ
PSIQ	10/13

	VCDQ	WMDQ	PSDQ
PODQ	11/14	12/15	14/18
WMDQ	11/14	—	14/18
PSDQ	13/18	14/18	—

Ages 18–19

	V	S	A	DS	I	C	LN	PC	CD	BD	MR	PA	SS
S	3/4												
A	3/4	4/5											
DS	3/4	3/4	3/4										
I	3/4	3/4	3/4	3/4									
C	3/4	4/5	3/4	3/4	3/4								
LN	3/4	4/5	3/4	3/4	3/4	3/4							
PC	4/5	4/5	4/5	4/5	4/5	4/5	4/5						
CD	3/4	4/5	4/5	4/5	4/5	4/5	4/5	4/6					
BD	3/4	4/5	3/4	3/4	3/4	3/4	3/4	4/5	4/5				
MR	3/4	3/4	3/4	3/4	3/4	3/4	3/4	4/5	4/5	3/4			
PA	4/5	4/6	4/5	4/5	4/5	4/6	4/5	5/6	5/6	4/5	4/5		
SS	4/5	4/5	4/5	4/8	4/5	4/5	4/5	5/6	4/6	4/5	4/5	5/6	
OA	4/5	4/6	4/6	4/5	4/5	4/6	4/6	5/6	5/6	4/6	4/5	5/6	5/6

	VSIQ
PSIQ	10/13

	VCDQ	WMDQ	PSDQ
PODQ	11/14	11/15	14/19
WMDQ	9/12	—	13/17
PSDQ	13/17	13/17	—

Average of 13 age groups

	V	S	A	DS	I	C	LN	PC	CD	BD	MR	PA	SS
S	3/4												
A	3/4	3/4											
DS	3/4	3/4	3/4										
I	3/4	3/4	3/4	3/4									
C	3/4	4/5	4/5	3/4	3/4								
LN	3/4	4/5	4/5	4/5	4/5	4/5							
PC	3/4	4/5	4/5	4/5	4/4	4/5	4/5						
CD	3/4	4/5	4/5	3/4	3/4	4/5	4/5	4/5					
BD	3/4	4/5	4/4	3/4	3/4	4/5	4/5	4/5	4/5				
MR	3/4	3/4	3/4	3/4	3/4	4/4	4/5	4/5	3/4	3/4			
PA	4/5	4/5	4/5	4/5	4/5	4/6	4/6	4/6	4/5	4/5	4/5		
SS	4/5	4/5	4/5	4/5	4/5	4/5	4/5	4/5	4/5	4/5	4/5	5/6	
OA	4/5	4/6	4/6	4/5	4/5	5/6	5/6	5/6	4/6	4/6	4/5	5/6	5/6

	VSIQ
PSIQ	9/12

	VCDQ	WMDQ	PSDQ
PODQ	10/13	11/15	13/17
WMDQ	10/13	—	13/17
PSDQ	12/16	13/17	—

Note. Abbreviations: V = Vocabulary, S = Similarities, A = Arithmetic, DS = Digit Span, I = Information, C = Comprehension, LN = Letter–Number Sequencing, PC = Picture Completion, CD = Digit Symbol—Coding, BD = Block Design, MR = Matrix Reasoning, PA = Picture Arrangement, SS = Symbol Search, OA = Object Assembly; VSIQ = Verbal Scale IQ; PSIQ = Performance Scale IQ; VCDQ = Verbal Comprehension Deviation Quotient; PODQ = Perceptual Organization Deviation Quotient; WMDQ = Working Memory Deviation Quotient; PSDQ = Processing Speed Deviation Quotient.

The factor scores are composed of the following subtests: Verbal Comprehension: Vocabulary, Similarities, Information; Perceptual Organization: Picture Completion, Block Design, Matrix Reasoning; Working Memory: Arithmetic, Digit Span, Letter–Number Sequencing; Processing Speed: Digit Symbol—Coding, Symbol Search.

Sample reading: A difference of 4 points between scaled scores on Vocabulary and Similarities is significant at the .05 level; a difference of 5 points is significant at the .01 level. The first small box shows that a 10-point difference between the Verbal Scale IQ and the Performance Scale IQ is needed at the .05 level, and a 13-point difference is needed at the .01 level. The second small box shows that a difference of 11 points is needed between the Verbal Comprehension Deviation Quotient and the Perceptual Organization Deviation Quotient at the .05 level, and a difference of 14 points is needed at the .01 level. The other comparisons between Deviation Quotients are read in a similar manner.

The values in this table for the subtest comparisons are overly liberal when more than one comparison is made for a subtest. They are more accurate when a priori planned comparisons are made, such as Information vs. Comprehension or Digit Span vs. Arithmetic.

All values in this table have been rounded to the next higher number.

See Chapter 10, Exhibit 10-1 (page 302) for an explanation of the method used to arrive at the magnitudes of differences.

See Exhibit 8-4 (pages 256–257) for the procedure used to obtain the reliability coefficients for the index scores (or short forms).

TABLE C-3   **817**

Table C-3
Estimates of Probability of Obtaining Designated Differences Between Individual WAIS–III Verbal and Performance IQs by Chance

Probability of obtaining given or greater discrepancy by chance	Age group													
	16–17	18–19	20–24	25–29	30–34	35–44	45–54	55–64	65–69	70–74	75–79	80–84	85–89	Av.[a]
.50	3.31	3.21	3.10	2.82	3.12	2.89	2.90	2.70	2.48	2.84	3.22	2.96	3.24	2.99
.25	5.69	5.51	5.32	4.85	5.36	4.96	4.97	4.63	4.26	4.88	5.52	5.07	5.57	5.14
.20	6.33	6.13	5.92	5.40	5.97	5.53	5.53	5.15	4.74	5.43	6.14	5.65	6.20	5.72
.10	8.16	7.90	7.63	6.95	7.69	7.12	7.13	6.64	6.11	7.00	7.92	7.28	7.99	7.37
.05	9.70	9.39	9.06	8.26	9.14	8.46	8.47	7.89	7.26	8.32	9.41	8.65	9.49	8.76
.02	11.53	11.16	10.77	9.82	10.86	10.06	10.07	9.38	8.63	9.89	11.18	10.28	11.28	10.41
.01	12.76	12.35	11.93	10.88	12.03	11.14	11.15	10.39	9.56	10.95	12.38	11.38	12.49	11.53
.001	16.28	15.75	15.21	13.87	15.34	14.20	14.22	13.25	12.19	13.96	15.79	14.51	15.93	14.70

Note. To use Table C-3, find the column appropriate to the examinee's age. Locate the discrepancy that is *just less* than the discrepancy obtained by the examinee. The entry in the first column in that same row gives the probability of obtaining the given (or a greater) discrepancy by chance. For example, the probability that a 16-year-old examinee obtained a Verbal-Performance discrepancy of 12 by chance is estimated to be less than 2%. Table C-3 is two-tailed. See Chapter 10, Exhibit 10-1 (page 302) for an explanation of the method used to arrive at magnitudes of differences.

[a]Av. = Average of 13 age groups.

Table C-4
Frequencies (cumulative percentages) of Differences Between WAIS–III Verbal Scale and Performance Scale IQs and Between Index Scores in the Standardization Group When V > P, VC > PO, VC > WM, PO > PS, VC > PS, PO > WM, and WM > PS

Amount of discrepancy	Scales/indexes						
	Verbal > Performance (V > P)	Verbal Comprehension > Perceptual Organization (VC > PO)	Verbal Comprehension > Working Memory (VC > WM)	Perceptual Organization > Processing Speed (PO > PS)	Verbal Comprehension > Processing Speed (VC > PS)	Perceptual Organization > Working Memory (PO > WM)	Working Memory > Processing Speed (WM > PS)
≥40	0.0	0.1	0.4	0.3	0.5	0.1	0.4
39	0.1	0.1	0.4	0.4	0.6	0.2	0.5
38	0.1	0.2	0.4	0.5	0.6	0.2	0.6
37	0.2	0.2	0.4	0.5	0.6	0.2	0.8
36	0.2	0.2	0.4	0.5	0.7	0.3	1.0
35	0.2	0.3	0.4	0.7	0.9	0.3	1.0
34	0.2	0.4	0.6	0.8	1.0	0.4	1.2
33	0.4	0.5	0.6	0.9	1.3	0.7	1.4
32	0.4	0.7	0.7	1.3	1.5	0.9	1.8
31	0.5	1.0	0.8	1.3	1.8	1.1	2.1
30	0.5	1.0	1.0	1.9	2.1	1.4	2.4
29	0.6	1.1	1.2	2.2	2.3	1.5	2.5
28	0.7	1.5	1.8	2.4	2.7	1.9	3.0
27	1.1	1.8	2.2	3.0	3.4	2.2	3.9
26	1.3	2.0	2.4	3.4	4.2	2.7	4.2
25	1.7	2.7	3.1	4.0	4.6	3.2	4.6
24	2.1	3.1	3.3	4.4	5.2	3.8	5.3
23	2.6	4.1	4.2	5.3	6.2	4.2	5.9
22	3.1	4.5	4.8	6.5	7.0	4.6	7.0
21	3.4	5.4	5.6	7.1	8.4	5.7	7.4
20	4.1	5.8	6.2	8.1	9.2	6.0	8.4
19	4.8	7.3	7.4	9.2	10.8	7.8	9.0
18	5.6	8.0	8.6	10.3	11.7	7.8	10.6
17	6.5	9.3	10.3	11.5	13.4	9.2	11.3
16	7.8	10.0	11.7	12.4	14.7	9.7	13.4
15	8.7	11.2	13.7	14.2	16.2	12.4	14.9
14	9.9	12.5	14.6	15.4	17.8	13.4	15.8
13	11.8	14.8	16.6	16.8	19.6	14.2	18.6
12	13.6	16.6	19.0	18.7	21.6	16.2	20.2
11	16.0	18.6	21.1	20.2	23.5	19.4	22.2
10	18.2	21.4	23.4	23.1	26.2	21.4	24.0
9	20.5	23.8	25.1	24.7	27.9	23.8	26.8
8	23.1	26.5	28.3	28.0	30.0	26.6	29.3
7	26.2	29.5	30.2	30.8	32.8	29.8	31.5
6	29.5	32.2	32.9	33.5	35.0	31.7	34.5
5	32.6	35.4	35.8	36.2	38.0	34.7	37.0
4	35.9	38.5	40.3	38.8	40.9	37.8	39.8
3	39.9	41.5	44.9	41.8	43.5	41.8	43.2
2	43.4	46.5	48.2	44.9	46.6	45.0	45.1
1	47.5	49.5	52.2	47.7	49.2	48.5	48.2
0	—	—	—	—	—	—	—
Mdn	7.0	8.0	9.0	8.0	10.0	8.0	9.0

Source: Reprinted and adapted with permission of the authors, The Psychological Corporation, and the publisher of the journal, Zwets and Zeitlinger, from D. S. Tulsky, E. L. Rolfhus, and J. Shu (2000), "Two-Tailed versus One-Tailed Base Rates of Discrepancy Scores in the WAIS–III," *The Clinical Neuropsychologist, 14(3). Wechsler Adult Intelligence Scale: Third Edition.* Copyright © 1997 by The Psychological Corporation, a Harcourt Assessment Company. Reproduced by permission. All rights reserved. "Wechsler Adult Intelligence Scale" and "WAIS" are trademarks of The Psychological Corporation registered in the United States and/or other jurisdictions.

TABLE C-5   **819**

Table C-5
Frequencies (cumulative percentages) of Differences Between WAIS–III Verbal Scale and Performance Scale IQs and Between Index Scores in the Standardization Group When P > V, PO > VC, WM > VC, PS > PO, PS > VC, WM > PO, and PS > WM

Amount of discrepancy	Scales/indexes						
	Performance > Verbal (P > V)	Perceptual Organization > Verbal Comprehension (PO > VC)	Working Memory > Verbal Comprehension (WM > VC)	Processing Speed > Perceptual Organization (PS > PO)	Processing Speed > Verbal Comprehension (PS > VC)	Working Memory > Perceptual Organization (WM > PO)	Processing Speed > Working Memory (PS > WM)
≥40	0.0	0.2	0.1	0.3	0.3	0.2	0.4
39	0.1	0.2	0.1	0.3	0.4	0.2	0.4
38	0.1	0.2	0.1	0.4	0.5	0.2	0.4
37	0.1	0.2	0.5	0.5	0.8	0.6	0.5
36	0.1	0.2	0.5	0.7	1.0	0.7	0.7
35	0.1	0.2	0.5	0.7	1.2	0.7	0.9
34	0.1	0.4	0.5	0.9	1.6	0.7	1.0
33	0.2	0.5	0.6	1.1	1.6	0.9	1.2
32	0.2	0.7	1.0	1.3	1.8	1.0	1.4
31	0.2	0.9	1.2	1.5	2.4	1.2	1.4
30	0.2	1.1	1.3	1.8	2.7	1.4	2.1
29	0.3	1.3	1.4	2.1	3.0	2.0	2.2
28	0.5	1.5	1.4	2.5	3.3	2.7	3.0
27	0.5	2.0	1.6	2.7	3.6	3.0	3.4
26	0.7	2.2	1.9	3.4	4.2	3.1	4.1
25	0.9	2.7	2.2	3.8	4.8	3.8	5.2
24	1.0	2.9	2.8	4.3	5.9	4.3	5.8
23	1.5	3.8	3.1	5.3	6.5	4.7	6.3
22	1.8	4.3	4.0	6.0	7.5	5.2	7.1
21	2.5	5.1	4.6	6.7	8.2	5.8	8.0
20	3.2	6.0	6.0	8.1	9.5	7.0	8.8
19	4.1	6.9	7.0	9.2	10.5	7.7	9.9
18	5.1	8.4	8.0	10.1	11.5	8.4	10.9
17	6.2	9.5	9.5	11.6	13.2	9.6	11.8
16	7.8	10.7	10.8	12.4	14.2	10.9	13.4
15	8.9	11.8	11.8	14.5	16.2	12.0	15.4
14	10.5	13.0	13.5	16.2	17.5	14.2	16.8
13	12.0	15.4	15.0	18.0	19.8	15.4	19.5
12	14.2	16.4	16.6	19.9	21.9	17.9	21.0
11	16.4	19.2	17.8	21.8	23.8	19.5	22.8
10	19.1	20.7	21.4	23.9	26.7	22.7	23.8
9	22.3	23.6	22.6	26.0	28.1	24.1	28.2
8	24.9	26.2	26.6	28.2	30.6	27.3	31.2
7	27.5	28.7	27.3	30.9	32.8	28.5	33.0
6	30.9	31.4	32.2	34.2	35.0	32.4	35.6
5	33.8	33.7	34.1	36.7	38.0	35.0	37.6
4	37.4	37.8	37.4	39.6	39.5	39.5	41.2
3	41.2	39.8	39.2	42.9	42.5	41.8	43.6
2	44.9	43.9	41.4	46.7	46.2	45.9	47.3
1	49.0	45.8	45.4	48.9	48.1	48.6	49.2
0	—	—	—	—	—	—	—
Mdn	7.0	8.0	8.0	9.0	10.0	8.0	9.0

Source: Reprinted and adapted with permission of the authors, The Psychological Corporation, and the publisher of the journal, Zwets and Zeitlinger, from D. S. Tulsky, E. L. Rolfhus, and J. J. Zhu (2000), "Two-Tailed versus One-Tailed Base Rates of Discrepancy Scores in the WAIS–III," *The Clinical Neuropsychologist, 14 (3). Wechsler Adult Intelligence Scale: Third Edition.* Copyright © 1997 by The Psychological Corporation, a Harcourt Assessment Company. Reproduced by permission. All rights reserved. "Wechsler Adult Intelligence Scale" and "WAIS" are trademarks of The Psychological Corporation registered in the United States of America and/or other jurisdictions.

Table C-6
Differences Required for Significance When Each WAIS–III Subtest Scaled Score Is Compared to the Mean Subtest Scaled Score for an Individual Examinee

	Average of all age groups											
	Mean of 2 subtests		Mean of 3 subtests[a]		Mean of 3 subtests		Mean of 5 subtests		Mean of 6 subtests[b]		Mean of 6 subtests	
Subtest	.05	.01	.05	.01	.05	.01	.05	.01	.05	.01	.05	.01
Vocabulary	—	—	1.70	2.09	—	—	—	—	2.02	2.41	—	—
Similarities	—	—	2.03	2.48	—	—	—	—	2.65	3.15	—	—
Arithmetic	—	—	—	—	2.11	2.58	—	—	2.51	2.99	—	—
Digit Span	—	—	—	—	2.00	2.46	—	—	2.30	2.74	—	—
Information	—	—	1.82	2.23	—	—	—	—	2.24	2.67	—	—
Comprehension	—	—	—	—	—	—	—	—	2.83	3.36	—	—
Letter–Number Sequencing	—	—	—	—	2.36	2.89	—	—	—	—	—	—
Picture Completion	—	—	2.32	2.85	—	—	2.87	3.44	3.02	3.59	3.04	3.62
Digit Symbol—Coding	2.08	2.61	—	—	—	—	2.77	3.32	2.91	3.46	2.93	3.48
Block Design	—	—	2.21	2.71	—	—	2.68	3.21	2.81	3.34	2.83	3.37
Matrix Reasoning	—	—	2.05	2.51	—	—	2.40	2.88	2.50	2.97	2.52	3.00
Picture Arrangement	—	—	—	—	—	—	3.37	4.04	3.57	4.24	3.59	4.27
Symbol Search	2.08	2.61	—	—	—	—	—	—	3.37	4.01	—	—
Object Assembly	—	—	—	—	—	—	—	—	—	—	3.85	4.58

	Mean of 7 subtests[c]		Mean of 11 subtests		Mean of 11 subtests		Mean of 11 subtests		Mean of 11 subtests		Mean of 12 subtests	
Subtest	.05	.01	.05	.01	.05	.01	.05	.01	.05	.01	.05	.01
Vocabulary	2.09	2.48	2.24	2.62	2.26	2.64	2.25	2.63	2.26	2.65	2.27	2.64
Similarities	2.76	3.28	3.03	3.54	3.04	3.55	3.04	3.55	3.05	3.56	3.08	3.59
Arithmetic	2.66	3.11	2.86	3.35	2.87	3.36	2.87	3.35	2.88	3.36	2.91	3.38
Digit Span	2.39	2.84	2.60	3.04	—	—	2.61	3.05	—	—	2.64	3.07
Information	2.33	2.72	2.53	2.95	2.54	2.96	2.53	2.96	2.54	2.97	2.56	2.98
Comprehension	2.95	3.50	3.25	3.80	3.26	3.81	3.26	3.81	3.27	3.82	3.31	3.85
Letter–Number Sequencing	3.15	3.72	—	—	3.48	4.07	—	—	3.49	4.08	3.53	4.11
Picture Completion	3.15	3.73	3.25	3.92	3.36	3.93	3.36	3.92	3.36	3.93	3.41	3.96
Digit Symbol—Coding	3.02	3.59	3.20	3.74	3.21	3.75	—	—	—	—	3.26	3.79
Block Design	2.92	3.47	3.08	3.60	3.09	3.61	3.09	3.61	3.10	3.62	3.13	3.64
Matrix Reasoning	2.59	3.07	2.67	3.12	2.68	3.13	2.68	3.13	2.69	3.14	2.71	3.15
Picture Arrangement	3.73	4.43	4.05	4.73	4.05	4.74	4.05	4.73	4.06	4.74	4.12	4.79
Symbol Search	3.52	4.17	—	—	—	—	2.80	4.44	3.81	4.45	—	—
Object Assembly	4.01	4.75	—	—	—	—	—	—	—	—	—	—

(Continued)

TABLE C-6   **821**

Table C-6 *(Continued)*

	Average of all age groups											
	Mean of 12 subtests		Mean of 12 subtests		Mean of 13 subtests		Mean of 13 subtests		Mean of 13 subtests		Mean of 14 subtests	
Subtest	.05	.01	.05	.01	.05	.01	.05	.01	.05	.01	.05	.01
Vocabulary	2.28	2.65	2.29	2.66	2.30	2.67	2.30	2.68	2.31	2.68	2.33	2.69
Similarities	3.08	3.59	3.09	3.60	3.12	3.63	3.12	3.63	3.13	3.64	3.17	3.66
Arithmetic	2.91	3.39	2.92	3.39	2.94	3.42	2.95	3.43	2.95	3.43	2.99	3.45
Digit Span	2.64	3.07	2.65	3.08	2.67	3.10	2.67	3.11	2.68	3.11	2.71	3.13
Information	2.57	2.99	2.57	3.00	2.59	3.01	2.60	3.02	2.60	3.02	2.63	3.04
Comprehension	3.31	3.85	3.32	3.86	3.35	3.89	3.35	3.90	3.36	3.90	3.40	3.93
Letter–Number Sequencing	—	—	—	—	3.58	4.16	3.58	4.17	—	—	3.64	4.20
	Mean of 12 subtests		Mean of 12 subtests		Mean of 13 subtests		Mean of 13 subtests		Mean of 13 subtests		Mean of 14 subtests	
Subtest	.05	.01	.05	.01	.05	.01	.05	.01	.05	.01	.05	.01
Picture Completion	3.41	3.97	3.42	3.98	3.45	4.01	3.46	4.02	3.46	4.02	3.51	4.05
Digit Symbol—Coding	3.26	3.79	3.27	3.80	3.30	3.83	3.30	3.84	3.30	3.84	3.35	3.87
Block Design	3.13	3.65	3.14	3.65	3.17	3.69	3.18	3.69	3.18	3.69	3.22	3.72
Matrix Reasoning	2.71	3.16	2.72	3.17	2.74	3.19	2.75	3.19	2.75	3.20	2.78	3.21
Picture Arrangement	4.12	4.79	4.12	4.80	4.17	4.85	4.18	4.86	4.18	4.86	4.24	4.89
Symbol Search	3.86	4.50	—	—	3.91	4.55	—	—	3.92	4.56	3.98	4.59
Object Assembly	—	—	4.46	5.19	—	—	4.51	5.25	4.52	5.25	4.58	5.29

Note. Table C-6 shows the minimum deviations from an individual's average subtest scaled score that are significant at the .05 and .01 levels. See the note in Table A-6 for an explanation of the method used to obtain the deviations.

[a]In this column, the entries for Vocabulary, Similarities, and Information are compared to the mean of these three subtests. Similarly, the entries for Picture Completion, Block Design, and Matrix Reasoning are compared to the mean of these three subtests.

[b]In this column, the entries for Vocabulary, Similarities, Arithmetic, Digit Span, Information, and Comprehension are compared to the mean of these six subtests. Similarly, the entries for Picture Completion, Digit Symbol—Coding, Block Design, Matrix Reasoning, Picture Arrangement, and Symbol Search are compared to the mean of these six subtests.

[c]In this column, the entries for Vocabulary, Similarities, Arithmetic, Digit Span, Information, Comprehension, and Letter–Number Sequencing are compared to the mean of these seven subtests. Similarly, the entries for Picture Completion, Digit Symbol—Coding, Block Design, Matrix Reasoning, Picture Arrangement, Symbol Search, and Object Assembly are compared to the mean of these seven subtests.

Table C-7
Cumulative Frequencies of Differences from the Mean of Six WAIS–III Verbal Subtests When Letter–Number Sequencing Replaces Digit Span

Subtest	Cumulative percentage				
	25%	10%	5%	2%	1%
Vocabulary	1.60	2.30	2.73	3.25	3.58
Similarities	1.82	2.62	3.11	3.70	4.08
Arithmetic	2.10	3.01	3.57	4.25	4.69
Information	1.73	2.49	2.96	3.51	3.88
Comprehension	1.86	2.66	3.16	3.76	4.15
Letter–Number Seq.	2.53	3.62	4.31	5.12	5.65

Source: Adapted with permission of the publisher from S. G. LoBello, A. P. Thompson, and V. Evani, Supplementary WAIS–III Tables for Determining Subtest Strengths and Weaknesses, *Journal of Psychoeducational Assessment, 16,* Table 3, page 198. Copyright © 1998 by The Psychoeducational Corporation.

Table C-9
Cumulative Frequencies of Differences from the Mean of Five WAIS–III Performance Subtests When Symbol Search Replaces Digit Symbol—Coding

Subtest	Cumulative percentage				
	25%	10%	5%	2%	1%
Picture Completion	2.21	3.17	3.77	4.48	4.94
Block Design	2.03	2.91	3.46	4.11	4.54
Matrix Reasoning	2.12	3.04	3.62	4.30	4.74
Picture Arrangement	2.26	3.25	3.86	4.59	5.06
Symbol Search	2.24	3.22	3.82	4.54	5.01

Source: Adapted with permission of the publisher from S. G. LoBello, A. P. Thompson, and V. Evani, Supplementary WAIS–III Tables for Determining Subtest Strengths and Weaknesses, *Journal of Psychoeducational Assessment, 16,* Table 2, page 198. Copyright © 1998 by The Psychoeducational Corporation.

Table C-8
Cumulative Frequencies of Differences from the Mean of Five WAIS–III Performance Subtests Plus Symbol Search

Subtest	Cumulative percentage				
	25%	10%	5%	2%	1%
Picture Completion	2.30	3.31	3.93	4.67	5.15
Digit Symbol—Coding	2.43	3.49	4.14	4.92	5.43
Block Design	2.14	3.08	3.65	4.34	4.80
Matrix Reasoning	2.23	3.19	3.79	4.51	4.97
Picture Arrangement	2.36	3.39	4.03	4.79	5.28
Symbol Search	2.10	3.01	3.57	4.25	4.69

Source: Adapted with permission of the publisher from S. G. LoBello, A. P. Thompson, and V. Evani, Supplementary WAIS–III Tables for Determining Subtest Strengths and Weaknesses, *Journal of Psychoeducational Assessment, 16,* Table 1, page 198. Copyright © 1998 by The Psychoeducational Corporation.

Table C-10
Cumulative Frequencies of Differences from the Mean of 11 WAIS–III Subtests Plus Letter–Number Sequencing

Subtest	Cumulative percentage				
	25%	10%	5%	2%	1%
Vocabulary	1.64	2.77	3.31	3.93	4.36
Similarities	1.75	2.95	3.53	4.19	4.64
Arithmetic	1.83	3.10	3.70	4.40	4.87
Digit Span	2.29	3.87	4.62	5.50	6.09
Information	1.74	2.95	3.52	4.18	4.63
Comprehension	1.81	3.06	3.66	4.35	4.81
Letter–Numbering Seq.	2.08	3.53	4.21	5.01	5.55
Picture Completion	2.17	3.68	4.39	5.22	5.78
Digit Symbol—Coding	2.32	3.93	4.69	5.58	6.18
Block Design	2.01	3.40	4.07	4.83	5.35
Matrix Reasoning	1.93	3.26	3.89	4.63	5.12
Picture Arrangement	2.10	3.54	4.23	5.03	5.57

Note. The information in this table was obtained by use of Silverstein's (1984) formula, which is shown in the Note to Table A-7 in Appendix A.

TABLE C-12   **823**

Table C-11
Cumulative Frequencies of Differences from the Mean of the Standard 11 WAIS–III Subtests When Letter–Number Sequencing Replaces Digit Span

Subtest	Cumulative percentage				
	25%	10%	5%	2%	1%
Vocabulary	1.61	2.73	3.26	3.87	4.29
Similarities	1.71	2.89	3.45	4.11	4.55
Arithmetic	1.86	3.14	3.75	4.46	4.94
Information	1.70	2.88	3.44	4.09	4.53
Comprehension	1.78	3.00	3.59	4.26	4.72
Letter–Numbering Seq.	2.14	3.63	4.33	5.15	5.70
Picture Completion	2.14	3.63	4.33	5.15	5.70
Digit Symbol—Coding	2.33	3.93	4.70	5.59	6.19
Block Design	1.99	3.36	4.02	4.78	5.29
Matrix Reasoning	1.92	3.24	3.87	4.61	5.10
Picture Arrangement	2.07	3.50	4.18	4.97	5.50

Note. The information in this table was obtained by use of Silverstein's (1984) formula, which is shown in the Note to Table A-7 in Appendix A.

Table C-12
Cumulative Frequencies of Differences from the Mean of the Standard 11 WAIS–III Subtests When Symbol Search Replaces Digit Symbol—Coding

Subtest	Cumulative percentage				
	25%	10%	5%	2%	1%
Vocabulary	1.62	2.74	3.28	3.90	4.32
Similarities	1.71	2.89	3.45	4.10	4.54
Arithmetic	1.84	3.11	3.71	4.41	4.89
Digit Span	2.35	3.97	4.75	5.64	6.25
Information	1.71	2.89	3.45	4.10	4.54
Comprehension	1.77	3.00	3.58	4.26	4.72
Picture Completion	2.15	3.64	4.35	5.17	5.73
Block Design	1.97	3.34	3.99	4.74	5.25
Matrix Reasoning	1.91	3.23	3.86	4.59	5.08
Picture Arrangement	2.07	3.49	4.17	4.96	5.49
Symbol Search	2.08	3.52	4.21	5.01	5.54

Note. The information in this table was obtained by use of Silverstein's (1984) formula, which is shown in the Note to Table A-7 in Appendix A.

Table C-13
Estimates of the Probability of Obtaining Designated Differences Between Individual WAIS–III Index Score Deviation Quotients (DQs) by Chance

Probability of obtaining given or greater discrepancy by chance	Verbal Comprehension DQ vs. Perceptual Organization DQ	Verbal Comprehension DQ vs. Processing Speed DQ	Verbal Comprehension DQ vs. Working Memory DQ	Perceptual Organization DQ vs. Processing Speed DQ	Perceptual Organization DQ vs. Working Memory DQ	Processing Speed DQ vs. Working Memory DQ
.50	3.33	3.99	3.27	4.34	3.69	4.29
.25	5.71	6.84	5.61	7.45	6.34	7.37
.20	6.36	7.61	6.25	8.29	7.05	8.20
.10	8.19	9.81	8.05	10.68	9.09	10.57
.05	9.73	11.66	9.56	12.69	10.80	12.56
.02	11.57	13.86	11.37	15.09	12.84	14.93
.01	12.81	15.35	12.59	16.70	14.21	16.53
.001	16.34	19.57	16.05	21.30	18.12	21.08

Note. The values in Table C-13 are based on the total group. Locate the discrepancy that is *just less* than the discrepancy obtained by the examinee. The entry in the first column in that same row gives the probability of obtaining the given (or a greater) discrepancy by chance. For example, the probability that an examinee obtained a Verbal Comprehension–Perceptual Organization discrepancy of 10 by chance is estimated to be 5%. Table C-13 is two-tailed. See Chapter 10, Exhibit 10-1 (page 302) for an explanation of the method used to arrive at the magnitudes of the differences.

Table C-14
Cumulative Frequencies of Differences from the Mean of WAIS–III Subtests on Verbal Comprehension, Perceptual Organization, Working Memory, and Processing Speed Indices

Subtest	Cumulative percentage				
	25%	10%	5%	2%	1%
Verbal Comprehension					
Vocabulary	1.50	2.15	2.56	3.04	3.36
Information	1.48	2.12	2.51	2.99	3.31
Similarities	1.30	1.87	2.22	2.64	2.92
Perceptual Organization					
Picture Completion	2.06	2.95	3.50	4.17	4.61
Block Design	1.81	2.60	3.09	3.67	4.06
Matrix Reasoning	1.90	2.72	3.23	3.84	4.26
Working Memory					
Arithmetic	1.95	2.79	3.32	3.94	4.37
Digit Span	1.85	2.64	3.14	3.73	4.13
Letter–Number Seq.	1.90	2.73	3.24	3.85	4.27
Processing Speed					
Digit Symbol—Coding	1.44	2.07	2.46	2.92	3.24
Symbol Search	1.44	2.07	2.46	2.92	3.24

Note. The information in this table was obtained by use of Silverstein's (1984) formula, which is shown in the Note to Table A-7 in Appendix A.

TABLE C-15   **825**

Table C-15
Reliability and Validity Coefficients of Proposed WAIS–III Short Forms

Dyad

Short form		r_{tt}	r
V	MR	.945	.881
V	BD	.930	.876
V	A	.941	.875
I	MR[a,b]	.938	.867
I	BD	.922	.865
S	A	.917	.863
S	MR	.922	.861
C	MR	.914	.856
V	I	.955	.853
V	S	.940	.853
I	PC[a]	.911	.836
A	MR[a]	.930	.830
A	PC[a]	.896	.829
I	CD[a]	.909	.824
BD	MR[b]	.925	.790
PC	MR[a,b]	.909	.787
PC	BD[b]	.899	.780
CD	MR[b]	.907	.774
PC	CD[a,b]	.881	.733
DS	LN[c]	.911	.729
CD	SS[d]	.882	.727
I	S	.932	.852
BD	CD	.894	.763
I	A	.936	.850

Triad

Short form			r_{tt}	r
V	I	BD	.954	.906
V	A	PC	.939	.906
V	A	MR	.955	.905
V	A	BD	.947	.905
V	I	MR	.961	.905
V	A	PA	.927	.904
V	S	MR	.954	.902
S	I	MR	.950	.900
V	S	BD	.947	.899
V	C	MR	.950	.899
A	I	MR[a]	.952	.891
A	I	PC[a]	.936	.891
I	PC	MR[a]	.939	.887
I	CD	MR[a]	.938	.886
CD	BD	MR[b]	.931	.834
PC	BD	MR[b]	.934	.832
PC	CD	MR[b]	.922	.830
PC	CD	BD[b]	.917	.810
I	S	DS	.945	.882
V	S	I[e]	.960	.871
A	DS	LN[f]	.936	.820

Tetrad

Short form				r_{tt}	r
V	I	BD	MR	.963	.922
V	A	PC	MR	.955	.921
V	S	A	MR	.962	.920
V	A	BD	PA	.942	.920
V	S	A	BD	.957	.919
V	S	A	PC	.953	.919
V	A	I	BD	.962	.919
V	I	PC	MR	.959	.918
V	DS	I	BD	.950	.918
V	S	A	PA	.946	.912
A	I	PC	MR[a]	.953	.911
DS	I	PC	MR[a]	.950	.905
A	I	CD	MR[a]	.953	.904
A	I	PC	CD[a]	.942	.900
PC	CD	BD	MR[b]	.941	.855
I	A	DS	S	.957	.899
I	S	CD	LN	.941	.918
MR	PC	CD	SS	.933	.865
I	A	PC	BD	.948	.907
S	A	CD	LN	.938	.912

Pentad

Short form					r_{tt}	r
V	A	I	PC	MR	.965	.934
V	S	A	PC	MR	.962	.935
V	A	C	PC	MR	.961	.933
V	S	A	BD	PA	.954	.933
V	DS	I	BD	MR	.967	.933
V	A	I	PC	BD	.962	.932
V	DS	I	PC	MR	.964	.932
V	I	CD	BD	MR	.963	.932
V	A	C	BD	PA	.953	.932
V	A	I	BD	PA	.958	.932
A	I	PC	CD	MR[a]	.955	.921
A	DS	I	PC	MR[a]	.960	.920
DS	I	PC	CD	MR[a]	.953	.915
A	DS	I	PC	CD[a]	.960	.909

Note. Abbreviations: V = Vocabulary, S = Similarities, A = Arithmetic, DS = Digit Span, I = Information, C = Comprehension, LN = Letter–Number Sequencing, PC = Picture Completion, CD = Digit Symbol—Coding, BD = Block Design, MR = Matrix Reasoning, PA = Picture Arrangement, SS = Symbol Search.

The first 10 combinations represent the best ones based on validity. See Exhibit 8-4 (pages 256–257) for formulas used to obtain reliability and validity coefficients.

[a]This combination is useful for a rapid screening.

[b]This combination is useful for examinees who are hearing impaired.

[c]This combination provides an estimate of the Working Memory Index score.

[d]This combination provides an estimate of the Processing Speed Index score.

[e]This combination represents the subtests in the Verbal Comprehension Index.

[f]This combination represents the subtests in the Working Memory Index.

Table C-16
Reliable and Unusual Scaled-Score Ranges for WAIS–III Selected Two-Subtest Short Forms

Short form		Reliable scaled-score range	Unusual scaled-score range
I	CD	3	6
BD	CD	4	6
A	PC	4	6
PC	CD	4	6
CD	MR	4	6
I	PC	4	6
I	BD	3	6
MR	PC	4	6
V	BD	3	5
C	MR	4	5
PC	BD	4	5
I	MR	3	5
S	MR	3	5
V	MR	3	5
S	A	4	5
DS	LN	4	5
A	MR	3	5
V	A	3	5
BD	MR	3	5
I	A	3	5
CD	SS	4	5
I	S	4	4
V	I	3	4
V	S	3	4

Note. See Table A-17 for the formulas.

Table C-17
Reliable and Unusual Scaled-Score Ranges for WAIS–III Selected Three-Subtest Short Forms

Short form			Reliable scaled-score range	Unusual scaled-score range
PC	CD	MR	4	6
I	CD	MR	4	6
PC	CD	BD	4	6
CD	BD	MR	4	6
I	PC	MR	4	6
V	A	PC	4	6
A	I	PC	4	6
I	S	DS	3	6
PC	BD	MR	4	6
V	A	BD	3	5
V	A	PA	4	6
A	DS	LN	4	5
V	A	MR	3	5
A	I	MR	3	5
V	I	BD	3	5
S	I	MR	3	5
V	S	BD	3	5
V	C	MR	3	5
V	I	MR	3	5
V	S	MR	3	5
V	S	I	3	4

Note. See Table A-17 for the formulas.

TABLE C-20   **827**

Table C-18
Reliable and Unusual Scaled-Score Ranges for WAIS–III Selected Four-Subtest Short Forms

Short form				Reliable scaled-score range	Unusual scaled-score range
DS	I	PC	MR	4	6
A	I	PC	CD	4	6
PC	CD	BD	MR	4	6
A	S	CD	LN	4	6
MR	PC	CD	SS	4	6
V	DS	I	BD	3	6
A	I	CD	MR	4	6
I	A	PC	BD	4	6
V	A	PC	MR	4	6
A	I	PC	MR	4	6
V	A	BD	PA	4	6
I	A	DS	S	4	6
V	I	PC	MR	4	6
V	S	A	PC	4	6
V	I	BD	MR	3	6
V	S	A	PA	4	6
V	S	A	BD	4	5
V	A	I	BD	3	5
V	S	A	MR	3	5

Note. See Table A-17 for the formulas.

Table C-19
Reliable and Unusual Scaled-Score Ranges for WAIS–III Selected Five-Subtest Short Forms

Short form					Reliable scaled-score range	Unusual scaled-score range
DS	I	PC	CD	MR	4	7
A	DS	I	PC	CD	4	6
A	I	PC	CD	MR	4	6
A	DS	I	PC	MR	4	6
V	DS	I	PC	MR	4	6
V	I	CD	BD	MR	4	6
V	DS	I	BD	MR	3	6
V	A	C	PC	MR	4	6
V	A	I	PC	BD	4	6
V	A	C	BD	PA	4	6
V	S	A	PC	MR	4	6
V	A	I	PC	MR	4	6
V	S	A	BD	PA	4	6
V	A	I	BD	PA	4	6

Note. See Table A-17 for the formulas.

Table C-20
Reliable and Unusual Scaled-Score Ranges for WAIS–III Selected Six- and Seven-Subtest Short Forms

Short form							Reliable scaled-score range	Unusual scaled-score range
V	S	I	PC	BD	MR		4	6
I	A	DS	S	PC	BD	CD	4	6
I	A	DS	S	PC	MR	CD	4	6

Note. See Table A-17 for the formulas.

Table C-21
Estimated WAIS–III Full Scale Deviation Quotients for Sum of Scaled Scores for 10 Best Short-Form Dyads and Other Combinations

Sum of scaled scores	Combination													
	C2	C3	C4	C5	C6	C7	C8	C9	C10	C11	C12	C13	C14	C15
2	46	47	48	48	48	49	49	49	49	50	50	50	51	52
3	49	50	51	51	51	51	52	52	52	52	53	53	54	55
4	52	53	54	54	54	54	54	55	55	55	56	56	57	57
5	55	56	56	57	57	57	57	58	58	58	58	59	59	60
6	58	59	59	60	60	60	60	60	61	61	61	61	62	63
7	61	62	62	62	63	63	63	63	63	64	64	64	65	65
8	64	65	65	65	66	66	66	66	66	66	67	67	67	68
9	67	68	68	68	68	69	69	69	69	69	70	70	70	71
10	70	71	71	71	71	71	72	72	72	72	72	72	73	73
11	73	74	74	74	74	74	74	75	75	75	75	75	76	76
12	76	77	77	77	77	77	77	77	77	78	78	78	78	79
13	79	80	80	80	80	80	80	80	80	80	81	81	81	81
14	82	82	83	83	83	83	83	83	83	83	83	83	84	84
15	85	85	85	86	86	86	86	86	86	86	86	86	86	87
16	88	88	88	88	89	89	89	89	89	89	89	89	89	89
17	91	91	91	91	91	91	91	92	92	92	92	92	92	92
18	94	94	94	94	94	94	94	94	94	94	94	94	95	95
19	97	97	97	97	97	97	97	97	97	97	97	97	97	97
20	100	100	100	100	100	100	100	100	100	100	100	100	100	100
21	103	103	103	103	103	103	103	103	103	103	103	103	103	103
22	106	106	106	106	106	106	106	106	106	106	106	106	105	105
23	109	109	109	109	109	109	109	108	108	108	108	108	108	108
24	112	112	112	112	111	111	111	111	111	111	111	111	111	111
25	115	115	115	114	114	114	114	114	114	114	114	114	114	113
26	118	118	117	117	117	117	117	117	117	117	117	117	116	116
27	121	120	120	120	120	120	120	120	120	120	119	119	119	119
28	124	123	123	123	123	123	123	123	123	122	122	122	122	121
29	127	126	126	126	126	126	126	125	125	125	125	125	124	124
30	130	129	129	129	129	129	128	128	128	128	128	128	127	127
31	133	132	132	132	132	131	131	131	131	131	130	130	130	129
32	136	135	135	135	134	134	134	134	134	134	133	133	133	132
33	139	138	138	138	137	137	137	137	137	136	136	136	135	135
34	142	141	141	140	140	140	140	140	139	139	139	139	138	137
35	145	144	144	143	143	143	143	142	142	142	142	141	141	140
36	148	147	146	146	146	146	146	145	145	145	144	144	143	143
37	151	150	149	149	149	149	148	148	148	148	147	147	146	145
38	154	153	152	152	152	151	151	151	151	150	150	150	149	148

Note. The subtest combinations are as follows:

C2 = I + CD[a]	C3 = I + PC[a]	C5 = V + BD[c]	C8 = S+ MR[c]	C10 = CD + SS[f]	C13 = CD + SS[f]
BD + CD[b]	C4 = I + BD[c]	C6 = C + MR[c]	V + MR[c]	C11 = I + S[a]	C14 = I + S[a]
A + PC[a]	MR + PC[a,b]	PC + BD[b]	C9 = S + A[c]	V + I[c]	C15 = V + I[c]
PC + CD[a,b]		C7 = I + MR[d]	DS + LN[e]	C12 = I + A	V + S[c]
CD + MR[b]					

Abbreviations: V = Vocabulary, S = Similarities, A = Arithmetic, DS = Digit Span, I = Information, C = Comprehension, LN = Letter–Number Sequencing, PC = Picture Completion, CD = Digit Symbol—Coding, BD = Block Design, MR = Matrix Reasoning, PA = Picture Arrangement, SS = Symbol Search.

Reliability and validity coefficients associated with each short-form combination are shown in Table C-15. See Exhibit 8-4, pages 256–257, for an explanation of the procedure used to obtain the estimated Deviation Quotients.

[a]This combination is useful for a rapid screening.
[b]This combination is useful for examinees who are hearing impaired.
[c]This combination is one of the 10 best dyads.
[d]This combination is useful for a rapid screening and is one of the 10 best dyads.
[e]This combination provides an estimate of the Working Memory factor.
[f]This combination provides an estimate of the Processing Speed factor.

Table C-22

Estimated WAIS–III Full Scale Deviation Quotients for Sum of Scaled Scores for 10 Best Short-Form Triads and Other Combinations

Sum of scaled scores	Combination																
	C2	C3	C4	C5	C6	C7	C8	C9	C10	C11	C12	C13	C14	C15	C16	C17	C18
3	43	43	43	44	45	45	45	46	47	47	47	47	47	48	48	48	51
4	45	45	45	46	47	47	47	48	49	49	49	49	49	49	50	50	52
5	47	47	47	48	49	49	49	50	51	51	51	51	51	51	52	52	54
6	49	49	49	50	51	51	51	52	53	53	53	53	53	53	54	54	56
7	51	51	52	52	53	53	53	54	55	55	55	55	55	55	56	56	58
8	53	54	54	54	55	55	55	56	57	57	57	57	57	57	57	57	60
9	55	56	56	56	57	57	57	58	59	59	59	59	59	59	59	59	62
10	58	58	58	59	59	59	59	60	61	61	61	61	61	61	61	61	63
11	60	60	60	61	61	61	61	62	63	63	63	63	63	63	63	63	65
12	62	62	62	63	63	63	63	64	65	65	65	65	65	65	65	65	67
13	64	64	64	65	65	65	65	66	67	67	67	67	67	67	67	67	69
14	66	66	66	67	67	67	67	68	68	69	69	69	69	69	69	69	71
15	68	68	68	69	69	69	69	70	70	71	71	71	71	71	71	71	73
16	70	70	71	71	71	71	71	72	72	73	73	73	73	73	73	73	74
17	72	73	73	73	73	73	73	74	74	74	75	75	75	75	75	75	76
18	75	75	75	75	75	75	76	76	76	76	76	77	77	77	77	77	78
19	77	77	77	77	77	78	78	78	78	78	78	78	79	79	79	79	80
20	79	79	79	79	79	80	80	80	80	80	80	80	80	81	81	81	82
21	81	81	81	81	82	82	82	82	82	82	82	82	82	83	83	83	84
22	83	83	83	83	84	84	84	84	84	84	84	84	84	84	85	85	85
23	85	85	85	85	86	86	86	86	86	86	86	86	86	86	86	86	87
24	87	87	87	88	88	88	88	88	88	88	88	88	88	88	88	88	89
25	89	89	89	90	90	90	90	90	90	90	90	90	90	90	90	90	91
26	92	92	92	92	92	92	92	92	92	92	92	92	92	92	92	92	93
27	94	94	94	94	94	94	94	94	94	94	94	94	94	94	94	94	95
28	96	96	96	96	96	96	96	96	96	96	96	96	96	96	96	96	96
29	98	98	98	98	98	98	98	98	98	98	98	98	98	98	98	98	98
30	100	100	100	100	100	100	100	100	100	100	100	100	100	100	100	100	100
31	102	102	102	102	102	102	102	102	102	102	102	102	102	102	102	102	102
32	104	104	104	104	104	104	104	104	104	104	104	104	104	104	104	104	104
33	106	106	106	106	106	106	106	106	106	106	106	106	106	106	106	106	105
34	108	108	108	108	108	108	108	108	108	108	108	108	108	108	108	108	107
35	111	111	111	110	110	110	110	110	110	110	110	110	110	110	110	110	109
36	113	113	113	112	112	112	112	112	112	112	112	112	112	112	112	112	111
37	115	115	115	115	114	114	114	114	114	114	114	114	114	114	114	114	113
38	117	117	117	117	116	116	116	116	116	116	116	116	116	116	115	115	115
39	119	119	119	119	118	118	118	118	118	118	118	118	118	118	117	117	116
40	121	121	121	121	121	120	120	120	120	120	120	120	120	119	119	119	118
41	123	123	123	123	123	122	122	122	122	122	122	122	121	121	121	121	120
42	125	125	125	125	125	125	124	124	124	124	124	123	123	123	123	123	122
43	128	127	127	127	127	127	127	126	126	126	125	125	125	125	125	125	124
44	130	130	129	129	129	129	129	128	128	127	127	127	127	127	127	127	126
45	132	132	132	131	131	131	131	130	130	129	129	129	129	129	129	129	127
46	134	134	134	133	133	133	133	132	132	131	131	131	131	131	131	131	129
47	136	136	136	135	135	135	135	134	133	133	133	133	133	133	133	133	131
48	138	138	138	137	137	137	137	136	135	135	135	135	135	135	135	135	133
49	140	140	140	139	139	139	139	138	137	137	137	137	137	137	137	137	135

(Continued)

Table C-22 *(Continued)*

Sum of scaled scores	Combination																
	C2	C3	C4	C5	C6	C7	C8	C9	C10	C11	C12	C13	C14	C15	C16	C17	C18
50	142	142	142	141	141	141	141	140	139	139	139	139	139	139	139	139	137
51	145	144	144	144	143	143	143	142	141	141	141	141	141	141	141	141	138
52	147	146	146	146	145	145	145	144	143	143	143	143	143	143	143	143	140
53	149	149	148	148	147	147	147	146	145	145	145	145	145	145	144	144	142
54	151	151	151	150	149	149	149	148	147	147	147	147	147	147	146	146	144
55	153	153	153	152	151	151	151	150	149	149	149	149	149	149	148	148	146
56	155	155	155	154	153	153	153	152	151	151	151	151	151	151	150	150	148
57	157	157	157	156	155	155	155	154	153	153	153	153	153	152	152	152	149

Note. The subtest combinations are as follows:

C2 = PC + CD + MR[a]	C9 = PC + BD + MR[b]	C14 = V + S + BD[c]
C3 = I + CD + MR[b]	V + A + BD[c]	C15 = V + C + MR[c]
C4 = PC + CD + BD[a]	V + A + PA[c]	C16 = V + I + MR[c]
C5 = CD + BD + MR[a]	A + DS + LN[d]	C17 = V + S + MR[c]
C6 = I + PC + MR[b]	C10 = V + A + MR[c]	C18 = V + S + I[e]
V + A + PC[c]	C11 = A + I + MR[b]	
C7 = A + I + PC[b]	C12 = V + I + BD[c]	
C8 = I + S + DS	C13 = S + I + MR[c]	

Abbreviations: V = Vocabulary, S = Similarities, A = Arithmetic, DS = Digit Span, I = Information, C = Comprehension, LN = Letter–Number Sequencing, PC = Picture Completion, CD = Digit Symbol—Coding, BD = Block Design, MR = Matrix Reasoning, PA = Picture Arrangement, SS = Symbol Search.

Reliability and validity coefficients associated with each short-form combination are shown in Table C-15. See Exhibit 8-4, pages 256–257, for an explanation of the procedure used to obtain the estimated Deviation Quotients.

[a]This combination is useful for a rapid screening.

[b]This combination is useful for examinees who are hearing impaired. It also represents the subtests in the Perceptual Organization Index.

[c]This combination is one of the 10 best short-form triads.

[d]This combination represents the subtests in the Working Memory Index.

[e]This combination represents the subtests in the Verbal Comprehension Index.

TABLE C-23   **831**

Table C-23
Estimated WAIS–III Full Scale Deviation Quotients for Sum of Scaled Scores for 10 Best Short-Form Tetrads and Other Combinations

Sum of scaled scores	Combination															
	C2	C3	C4	C5	C6	C7	C8	C9	C10	C11	C12	C13	C14	C15	C16	C17
4	41	41	42	42	42	43	43	43	44	44	44	44	45	45	46	46
5	42	43	44	44	44	44	45	45	45	45	46	46	46	47	47	48
6	44	44	45	45	46	46	46	47	47	47	47	48	48	48	49	49
7	46	46	47	47	47	48	48	48	48	48	49	49	49	50	50	51
8	47	48	48	49	49	49	50	50	50	50	50	51	51	51	52	52
9	49	49	50	50	50	51	51	51	51	51	52	52	52	53	53	54
10	50	51	52	52	52	52	53	53	53	53	54	54	54	54	55	55
11	52	53	53	53	54	54	54	54	55	55	55	55	55	56	56	57
12	54	54	55	55	55	56	56	56	56	56	57	57	57	57	58	58
13	55	56	56	57	57	57	57	58	58	58	58	58	58	59	59	60
14	57	58	58	58	58	59	59	59	59	59	60	60	60	61	61	61
15	59	59	60	60	60	60	61	61	61	61	61	61	62	62	62	63
16	60	61	61	61	62	62	62	62	62	62	63	63	63	64	64	64
17	62	62	63	63	63	63	64	64	64	64	64	65	65	65	65	66
18	64	64	64	65	65	65	65	65	65	66	66	66	66	67	67	67
19	65	66	66	66	66	67	67	67	67	67	68	68	68	68	68	69
20	67	67	68	68	68	68	68	69	69	69	69	69	69	70	70	70
21	69	69	69	69	70	70	70	70	70	70	71	71	71	71	71	72
22	70	71	71	71	71	71	72	72	72	72	72	72	72	73	73	73
23	72	72	73	73	73	73	73	73	73	73	74	74	74	74	74	75
24	74	74	74	74	74	75	75	75	75	75	75	75	75	76	76	76
25	75	76	76	76	76	76	76	76	76	77	77	77	77	77	77	78
26	77	77	77	78	78	78	78	78	78	78	78	78	78	79	79	79
27	79	79	79	79	79	79	80	80	80	80	80	80	80	80	80	81
28	80	80	81	81	81	81	81	81	81	81	81	81	82	82	82	82
29	82	82	82	82	82	83	83	83	83	83	83	83	83	83	83	84
30	83	84	84	84	84	84	84	84	84	84	85	85	85	85	85	85
31	85	85	85	86	86	86	86	86	86	86	86	86	86	86	86	87
32	87	87	87	87	87	87	87	87	87	87	88	88	88	88	88	88
33	88	89	89	89	89	89	89	89	89	89	89	89	89	89	89	90
34	90	90	90	90	90	90	91	91	91	91	91	91	91	91	91	91
35	92	92	92	92	92	92	92	92	92	92	92	92	92	92	92	93
36	93	93	94	94	94	94	94	94	94	94	94	94	94	94	94	94
37	95	95	95	95	95	95	95	95	95	95	95	95	95	95	95	96
38	97	97	97	97	97	97	97	97	97	97	97·	97	97	97	97	97
39	98	98	98	98	98	98	98	98	98	98	98	98	98	98	98	99
40	100	100	100	100	100	100	100	100	100	100	100	100	100	100	100	100
41	102	102	102	102	102	102	102	102	102	102	102	102	102	102	102	101
42	103	103	103	103	103	103	103	103	103	103	103	103	103	103	103	103
43	105	105	105	105	105	105	105	105	105	105	105	105	105	105	105	104
44	107	107	106	106	106	106	106	106	106	106	106	106	106	106	106	106
45	108	108	108	108	108	108	108	108	108	108	108	108	108	108	108	107
46	110	110	110	110	110	110	109	109	109	109	109	109	109	109	109	109
47	112	111	111	111	111	111	111	111	111	111	111	111	111	111	111	110
48	113	113	113	113	113	113	113	113	113	113	112	112	112	112	112	112
49	115	115	115	114	114	114	114	114	114	114	114	114	114	114	114	113

(Continued)

Table C-23 *(Continued)*

Sum of scaled scores	Combination															
	C2	C3	C4	C5	C6	C7	C8	C9	C10	C11	C12	C13	C14	C15	C16	C17
50	117	116	116	116	116	116	116	116	116	116	115	115	115	115	115	115
51	118	118	118	118	118	117	117	117	117	117	117	117	117	117	117	116
52	120	120	119	119	119	119	119	119	119	119	119	119	118	118	118	118
53	121	121	121	121	121	121	120	120	120	120	120	120	120	120	120	119
54	123	123	123	122	122	122	122	122	122	122	122	122	122	121	123	121
55	125	124	124	124	124	124	124	124	124	123	123	123	123	123	124	122
56	126	126	126	126	126	125	125	125	125	125	125	125	125	124	126	124
57	128	128	127	127	127	127	127	127	127	127	126	126	126	126	127	125
58	130	129	129	129	129	129	128	128	128	128	128	128	128	127	129	127
59	131	131	131	131	130	130	130	130	130	130	129	129	129	129	130	128
60	133	133	132	132	132	132	132	131	131	131	131	131	131	130	132	130
61	135	134	134	134	134	133	133	133	133	133	132	132	132	132	133	131
62	136	136	136	135	135	135	135	135	135	134	134	134	134	133	135	133
63	138	138	137	137	137	137	136	136	136	136	136	135	135	135	136	134
64	140	139	139	139	138	138	138	138	138	138	137	137	137	136	138	136
65	141	141	140	140	140	140	139	139	139	139	139	139	138	138	139	137
66	143	142	142	142	142	141	141	141	141	141	140	140	140	139	141	139
67	145	144	144	143	143	143	143	142	142	142	142	142	142	141	142	140
68	146	146	145	145	145	144	144	144	144	144	143	143	143	143	144	142
69	148	147	147	147	146	146	146	146	145	145	145	145	145	144	145	143
70	150	149	148	148	148	148	147	147	147	147	146	146	146	146	147	145
71	151	151	150	150	150	149	149	149	149	149	148	148	148	147	148	146
72	153	152	152	151	151	151	150	150	150	150	150	149	149	149	150	148
73	154	154	153	153	153	152	152	152	152	152	151	151	151	150	151	149
74	156	156	155	155	154	154	154	153	153	153	153	152	152	152	153	151
75	158	157	156	156	156	156	155	155	155	155	154	154	154	153	154	152
76	159	159	158	158	158	157	157	157	156	156	156	156	155	155	156	154

Note. The subtest combinations are as follows:

C2 = DS + I + PC + MR[a]
C3 = A + I + PC + CD[a]
C4 = PC + CD + BD + MR[b]
C5 = A + S + CD + LN
C6 = MR + PC + CD + SS
C7 = V + DS + I + BD[c]
    A + I + CD + MR[a]

C8 = I + A + PC + BD
C9 = V + A + PC + MR[c]
C10 = V + I + PC + MR[a]
C11 = V + A + BD + PA[c]
C12 = I + A + DS + S
C13 = V + I + PC + MR[c]

C14 = V + S + A + PC[c]
C15 = V + I + BD + MR[c]
    V + S + A + PA[c]
C16 = V + S + A + BD[c]
    V + A + I + BD[c]
C17 = V + S + A + MR[c]

Abbreviations: V = Vocabulary, S = Similarities, A = Arithmetic, DS = Digit Span, I = Information, C = Comprehension, LN = Letter–Number Sequencing, PC = Picture Completion, CD = Digit Symbol—Coding, BD = Block Design, MR = Matrix Reasoning, PA = Picture Arrangement, SS = Symbol Search.

Reliability and validity coefficients associated with each short-form combination are shown in Table C-15. See Exhibit 8-4, pages 256–257, for an explanation of the procedure used to obtain the estimated Deviation Quotients.

[a]This combination is useful for a rapid screening.
[b]This combination is useful for examinees who are hearing impaired.
[c]This combination is one of the 10 best tetrads.

TABLE C-24   **833**

Table C-24
Estimated WAIS–III Full Scale Deviation Quotients for Sum of Scaled Scores for 10 Best Short-Form Pentads and Other Combinations

Sum of scaled scores	Combination										
	C2	C3	C4	C5	C6	C7	C8	C9	C10	C11	C12
5	38	39	41	41	41	42	43	43	43	44	44
6	40	40	42	42	43	43	45	45	45	45	45
7	41	42	43	43	44	45	46	46	46	46	46
8	42	43	45	45	45	46	47	47	47	47	48
9	44	44	46	46	46	47	48	48	48	49	49
10	45	46	47	47	48	49	50	50	50	50	50
11	46	47	49	49	49	50	51	51	51	51	51
12	48	48	50	50	50	51	52	52	52	52	53
13	49	50	51	51	52	52	53	53	54	54	54
14	51	51	52	53	53	54	55	55	55	55	55
15	52	52	54	54	54	55	56	56	56	56	56
16	53	54	55	55	56	56	57	57	57	57	58
17	55	55	56	57	57	58	58	59	59	59	59
18	56	57	58	58	58	59	60	60	60	60	60
19	57	58	59	59	59	60	61	61	61	61	61
20	59	59	60	61	61	61	62	62	62	62	63
21	60	61	62	62	62	63	63	64	64	64	64
22	62	62	63	63	63	64	65	65	65	65	65
23	63	63	64	64	65	65	66	66	66	66	66
24	64	65	66	66	66	67	67	67	67	67	68
25	66	66	67	67	67	68	68	69	69	69	69
26	67	67	68	68	69	69	70	70	70	70	70
27	68	69	70	70	70	70	71	71	71	71	71
28	70	70	71	71	71	72	72	72	72	72	73
29	71	71	72	72	73	73	74	74	74	74	74
30	73	73	74	74	74	74	75	75	75	75	75
31	74	74	75	75	75	76	76	76	76	76	76
32	75	76	76	76	76	77	77	77	77	77	78
33	77	77	78	78	78	78	79	79	79	79	79
34	78	78	79	79	79	79	80	80	80	80	80
35	79	80	80	80	80	81	81	81	81	81	81
36	81	81	82	82	82	82	82	82	82	82	83
37	82	82	83	83	83	83	84	84	84	84	84
38	84	84	84	84	84	85	85	85	85	85	85
39	85	85	85	86	86	86	86	86	86	86	86
40	86	86	87	87	87	87	87	87	87	87	88
41	88	88	88	88	88	88	89	89	89	89	89
42	89	89	89	89	90	90	90	90	90	90	90
43	90	90	91	91	91	91	91	91	91	91	91
44	92	92	92	92	92	92	92	92	92	92	93
45	93	93	93	93	93	94	94	94	94	94	94
46	95	95	95	95	95	95	95	95	95	95	95
47	96	96	96	96	96	96	96	96	96	96	96
48	97	97	97	97	97	97	97	97	97	97	98
49	99	99	99	99	99	99	99	99	99	99	99
50	100	100	100	100	100	100	100	100	100	100	100
51	101	101	101	101	101	101	101	101	101	101	101
52	103	103	103	103	103	103	103	103	103	103	102
53	104	104	104	104	104	104	104	104	104	104	104
54	105	105	105	105	105	105	105	105	105	105	105

(Continued)

Table C-24 *(Continued)*

Sum of scaled scores	Combination										
	C2	C3	C4	C5	C6	C7	C8	C9	C10	C11	C12
55	107	107	107	107	107	106	106	106	106	106	106
56	108	108	108	108	108	108	108	108	108	108	107
57	110	110	109	109	109	109	109	109	109	109	109
58	111	111	111	111	110	110	110	110	110	110	110
59	112	112	112	112	112	112	111	111	111	111	111
60	114	114	113	113	113	113	113	113	113	113	112
61	115	115	115	114	114	114	114	114	114	114	114
62	116	116	116	116	116	115	115	115	115	115	115
63	118	118	117	117	117	117	116	116	116	116	116
64	119	119	118	118	118	118	118	118	118	118	117
65	121	120	120	120	120	119	119	119	119	119	119
66	122	122	121	121	121	121	120	120	120	120	120
67	123	123	122	122	122	122	121	121	121	121	121
68	125	124	124	124	124	123	123	123	123	123	122
69	126	126	125	125	125	124	124	124	124	124	124
70	127	127	126	126	126	126	125	125	125	125	125
71	129	129	128	128	127	127	126	126	126	126	126
72	130	130	129	129	129	128	128	128	128	128	127
73	132	131	130	130	130	130	129	129	129	129	129
74	133	133	132	132	131	131	130	130	130	130	130
75	134	134	133	133	133	132	132	131	131	131	131
76	136	135	134	134	134	133	133	133	133	133	132
77	137	137	136	136	135	135	134	134	134	134	134
78	138	138	137	137	137	136	135	135	135	135	135
79	140	139	138	138	138	137	137	136	136	136	136
80	141	141	140	139	139	139	138	138	138	138	137
81	143	142	141	141	141	140	139	139	139	139	139
82	144	143	142	142	142	141	140	140	140	140	140
83	145	145	144	143	143	142	142	141	141	141	141
84	147	146	145	145	144	144	143	143	143	143	142
85	148	148	146	146	146	145	144	144	144	144	144
86	149	149	148	147	147	146	145	145	145	145	145
87	151	150	149	149	148	148	147	147	146	146	146
88	152	152	150	150	150	149	148	148	148	148	147
89	154	153	151	151	151	150	149	149	149	149	149
90	155	154	153	153	152	151	150	150	150	150	150
91	156	156	154	154	154	153	152	152	152	151	151
92	158	157	155	155	155	154	153	153	153	153	152
93	159	158	157	157	156	155	154	154	154	154	154
94	160	160	158	158	157	157	155	155	155	155	155

Note. The subtest combinations are as follows:

C2 = DS + I + PC + CD + MR[a]   C7 = V + I + CD + BD + MR[b]   C10 = V + S + A + PC + MR[b]
C3 = A + DS + I + PC + CD[a]   V + DS + I + BD + MR[b]   C11 = V + A + I + PC + MR[b]
C4 = A + I + PC + CD + MR[a]   C8 = V + A + C + PC + MR[b]   V + S + A + BD + PA[b]
C5 = A + DS + I + PC + MR[a]   V + A + I + PC + BD[b]   C12 = V + A + I + BD + PA[b]
C6 = V + DS + I + PC + MR[b]   C9 = V + A + C + BD + PA[b]

Abbreviations: V = Vocabulary, S = Similarities, A = Arithmetic, DS = Digit Span, I = Information, C = Comprehension, LN = Letter–Number Sequencing, PC = Picture Completion, CD = Digit Symbol—Coding, BD = Block Design, MR = Matrix Reasoning, PA = Picture Arrangement, SS = Symbol Search.

Reliability and validity coefficients associated with each short-form combination are shown in Table C-15. See Exhibit 8-4, pages 256–257, for an explanation of the procedure used to obtain the estimated Deviation Quotients.

[a]This combination is useful for a rapid screening.

[b]This combination is one of the 10 best pentads.

Table C-25
Estimated WAIS–III Full Scale Deviation Quotients for Sum of Scaled Scores for One Six-Subtest Short-Form Combination and Two Seven-Subtest Short-Form Combinations

Sum of scaled scores	Combination			Sum of scaled scores	Combination			Sum of scaled scores	Combination			Sum of scaled scores	Combination		
	C2	C3	C4		C2	C3	C4		C2	C3	C4		C2	C3	C4
6	43	—	—	41	80	72	72	76	117	106	106	111	154	140	140
7	44	39	39	42	81	73	73	77	118	107	107	112	155	141	141
8	45	40	40	43	82	74	74	78	119	108	108	113	156	142	142
9	46	41	41	44	83	75	75	79	120	109	109	114	157	143	143
10	48	42	42	45	84	76	76	80	121	110	110	115	158	144	144
11	49	42	43	46	85	77	77	81	122	111	111	116		145	145
12	50	43	44	47	86	78	78	82	123	112	112	117		146	146
13	51	44	45	48	87	79	79	83	124	113	113	118		147	147
14	52	45	46	49	88	80	80	84	125	114	114	119		148	148
15	53	46	47	50	90	81	81	85	126	115	115	120		149	149
16	54	47	48	51	91	81	82	86	127	116	116	121		150	149
17	55	48	49	52	92	82	83	87	128	117	116	122		151	150
18	56	49	50	53	93	83	84	88	129	118	117	123		152	151
19	57	50	51	54	94	84	84	89	130	119	118	124		153	152
20	58	51	51	55	95	85	85	90	131	119	119	125		154	153
21	59	52	52	56	96	86	86	91	133	120	120	126		155	154
22	60	53	53	57	97	87	87	92	134	121	121	127		156	155
23	61	54	54	58	98	88	88	93	135	122	122	128		157	156
24	62	55	55	59	99	89	89	94	136	123	123	129		158	157
25	63	56	56	60	100	90	90	95	137	124	124	130		158	158
26	64	57	57	61	101	91	91	96	138	125	125	131		159	159
27	65	58	58	62	102	92	92	97	139	126	126	132		160	160
28	66	59	59	63	103	93	93	98	140	127	127	133		161	161
29	67	60	60	64	104	94	94	99	141	128	128				
30	69	61	61	65	105	95	95	100	142	129	129				
31	70	62	62	66	106	96	96	101	143	130	130				
32	71	63	63	67	107	97	97	102	144	131	131				
33	72	64	64	68	108	98	98	103	145	132	132				
34	73	65	65	69	109	99	99	104	146	133	133				
35	74	66	66	70	110	100	100	105	147	134	134				
36	75	67	67	71	112	101	101	106	148	135	135				
37	76	68	68	72	113	102	102	107	149	136	136				
38	77	69	69	73	114	103	103	108	150	137	137				
39	78	70	70	74	115	104	104	109	151	138	138				
40	79	71	71	75	116	105	105	110	152	139	139				

Note. The subtest combinations are as follows:

C2 = V + S + I + PC + BD + MR[a]
C3 = I + A + DS + S + PC + BD + CD[b]
C4 = I + A + DS + S + PC + MR + CD[c]

Abbreviations: V = Vocabulary, S = Similarities, A = Arithmetic, DS = Digit Span, I = Information, PC = Picture Completion, CD = Digit Symbol—Coding, BD = Block Design, MR = Matrix Reasoning.

Reliability and validity coefficients associated with each short-form combination are shown in Table C-15. See Exhibit 8-4, pages 256–257, for an explanation of the procedure used to obtain the estimated Deviation Quotients.

[a]The reliability and validity of this combination are r_{xx} = .966 and r = .946, respectively.
[b]The reliability and validity of this combination are r_{xx} = .965 and r = .942, respectively.
[c]The reliability and validity of this combination are r_{xx} = .967 and r = .944, respectively.

APPENDIX D

MISCELLANEOUS TABLES FOR THE WECHSLER TESTS

Table D-1
Percentile Ranks and Suggested Qualitative Descriptions for Scaled Scores on the Wechsler Tests

Scaled score	Percentile rank	Qualitative descriptions	
19	99		Exceptional strength or Very well developed or Superior or Excellent
18	99		
17	99		
16	98	Strength or Above average	
15	95		Strength or Well developed or Above average or Good
14	91		
13	84		
12	75	Average	Average
11	63		
10	50		
9	37		
8	25		
7	16		Weakness or Poorly developed or Below average or Poor
6	9	Weakness or Below average	
5	5		
4	2		Exceptional weakness or Very poorly developed or Far below average or Very poor
3	1		
2	1		
1	1		

Table D-2
Confidence Intervals for Wechsler Tests (and Other Tests) Based on Estimated True Score

Use the following chart to locate the section of Table D-2 that shows confidence intervals based on estimated true scores for Wechsler tests (and other tests).

WISC–III

Examinee's age	Verbal Scale	Performance Scale	Full Scale
6 (6-0-0 to 6-11-30)	I	G	K
7 (7-0-0 to 7-11-30)	H	F	J
8 (8-0-0 to 8-11-30)	L	F	L
9 (9-0-0 to 9-11-30)	I	G	K
10 (10-0-0 to 10-11-30)	K	G	L
11 (11-0-0 to 11-11-30)	K	F	K
12 (12-0-0 to 12-11-30)	K	G	L
13 (13-0-0 to 13-11-30)	J	F	K
14 (14-0-0 to 14-11-30)	K	E	K
15 (15-0-0 to 15-11-30)	L	J	M
16 (16-0-0 to 16-11-30)	K	H	L
Average	K	G	L

WPPSI–R

Examinee's age	Verbal Scale	Performance Scale	Full Scale
3 (3-0-0 to 3-5-15)	I	L	M
3½ (3-5-16 to 3-11-15)	I	L	M
4 (3-11-16 to 4-5-15)	I	L	M
4½ (4-5-16 to 4-11-15)	I	L	M
5 (4-11-16 to 5-5-15)	H	K	L
5½ (5-5-16 to 5-11-15)	F	J	K
6 (5-11-16 to 6-5-15)	H	J	K
6½ (6-5-16 to 6-11-15)	F	I	K
7 (6-11-16 to 7-3-15)	A	B	F
Average	K	H	L

WAIS–III

Examinee's age	Verbal Scale	Performance Scale	Full Scale
16–17	L	I	M
18–19	M	I	M
20–24	M	I	N
25–29	M	K	N
30–34	M	I	N
35–44	M	J	N
45–54	M	J	N
55–64	N	K	N
65–69	N	L	N
70–74	M	K	N
75–79	M	I	M
80–84	M	J	N
85–89	L	J	M
Average	M	J	N

(Continued)

Table D-2 *(Continued)*

A. WPPSI–R—Verbal Scale—Age 7 (r_{xx} = .85)

68%			85%			90%			95%			99%		
IQ	L	U	IQ	L	U	IQ	L	U	IQ	L	U	IQ	L	U
40–42	4	14	40–42	2	16	40–42	1	17	40–41	−1	19	40–41	−4	22
43	4	13	43–44	1	16	43–44	0	17	42–45	−1	18	42–45	−4	21
44–49	3	13	45–49	1	15	45–49	0	16	46–47	−2	18	46–48	−5	21
50	3	12	50	0	15	50	−1	16	48–52	−2	17	49–51	−5	20
51–56	2	12	51–55	0	14	51–55	−1	15	53–54	−3	17	52–54	−6	20
57	2	11	56–57	−1	14	56–57	−2	15	55–58	−3	16	55–58	−6	19
58–62	1	11	58–62	−1	13	58–62	−2	14	59–61	−4	16	59–61	−7	19
63	1	10	63–64	−2	13	63–64	−3	14	62–65	−4	15	62–65	−7	18
64–69	0	10	65–69	−2	12	65–69	−3	13	66–67	−5	15	66–68	−8	18
70	0	9	70	−3	12	70	−4	13	68–72	−5	14	69–71	−8	17
71–76	−1	9	71–75	−3	11	71–75	−4	12	73–74	−6	14	72–74	−9	17
77	−1	8	76–77	−4	11	76–77	−5	12	75–78	−6	13	75–78	−9	16
78–82	−2	8	78–82	−4	10	78–82	−5	11	79–81	−7	13	79–81	−10	16
83	−2	7	83–84	−5	10	83–84	−6	11	82–85	−7	12	82–85	−10	15
84–89	−3	7	85–89	−5	9	85–89	−6	10	86–87	−8	12	86–88	−11	15
90	−3	6	90	−6	9	90	−7	10	88–92	−8	11	89–91	−11	14
91–96	−4	6	91–95	−6	8	91–95	−7	9	93–94	−9	11	92–94	−12	14
97	−4	5	96–97	−7	8	96–97	−8	9	95–98	−9	10	95–98	−12	13
98–102	−5	5	98–102	−7	7	98–102	−8	8	99–101	−10	10	99–101	−13	13
103	−5	4	103–104	−8	7	103–104	−9	8	102–105	−10	9	102–105	−13	12
104–109	−6	4	105–109	−8	6	105–109	−9	7	106–107	−11	9	106–108	−14	12
110	−6	3	110	−9	6	110	−10	7	108–112	−11	8	109–111	−14	11
111–116	−7	3	111–115	−9	5	111–115	−10	6	113–114	−12	8	112–114	−15	11
117	−7	2	116–117	−10	5	116–117	−11	6	115–118	−12	7	115–118	−15	10
118–122	−8	2	118–122	−10	4	118–122	−11	5	119–121	−13	7	119–121	−16	10
123	−8	1	123–124	−11	4	123–124	−12	5	122–125	−13	6	122–125	−16	9
124–129	−9	1	125–129	−11	3	125–129	−12	4	126–127	−14	6	126–128	−17	9
130	−9	0	130	−12	3	130	−13	4	128–132	−14	5	129–131	−17	8
131–136	−10	0	131–135	−12	2	131–135	−13	3	133–134	−15	5	132–134	−18	8
137	−10	−1	136–137	−13	2	136–137	−14	3	135–138	−15	4	135–138	−18	7
138–142	−11	−1	138–142	−13	1	138–142	−14	2	139–141	−16	4	139–141	−19	7
143	−11	−2	143–144	−14	1	143–144	−15	2	142–145	−16	3	142–145	−19	6
144–149	−12	−2	145–149	−14	0	145–149	−15	1	146–147	−17	3	146–148	−20	6
150	−12	−3	150	−15	0	150	−16	1	148–152	−17	2	149–151	−20	5
151–156	−13	−3	151–155	−15	−1	151–155	−16	0	153–154	−18	2	152–154	−21	5
157	−13	−4	156–157	−16	−1	156–157	−17	0	155–158	−18	1	155–158	−21	4

(Continued)

Table D-2 *(Continued)*

B. WPPSI–R—Performance Scale—Age 7 (r_{xx} = .86)

68%			85%			90%			95%			99%		
IQ	L	U	IQ	L	U	IQ	L	U	IQ	L	U	IQ	L	U
40	4	13	40–46	1	15	40–46	0	16	40–42	−1	18	40–42	−4	21
41–45	3	13	47–53	0	14	47–53	−1	15	43	−1	17	43	−4	20
46–47	3	12	54–60	−1	13	54–60	−2	14	44–49	−2	17	44–49	−5	20
48–52	2	12	61	−1	12	61–67	−3	13	50	−2	16	50	−5	19
53–54	2	11	62–67	−2	12	68	−3	12	51–56	−3	16	51–56	−6	19
55–59	1	11	68	−2	11	69–74	−4	12	57	−3	15	57	−6	18
60–61	1	10	69–74	−3	11	75	−4	11	58–64	−4	15	58–63	−7	18
62–66	0	10	75	−3	10	76–81	−5	11	65–71	−5	14	64	−7	17
67–69	0	9	76–81	−4	10	82	−5	10	72–78	−6	13	65–71	−8	17
70–73	−1	9	82	−4	9	83–89	−6	10	79–85	−7	12	72–78	−9	16
74–76	−1	8	83–88	−5	9	90–96	−7	9	86–92	−8	11	79–85	−10	15
77–80	−2	8	89	−5	8	97–103	−8	8	93	−8	10	86	−10	14
81–83	−2	7	90–96	−6	8	104–110	−9	7	94–99	−9	10	87–92	−11	14
84–88	−3	7	97–103	−7	7	111–117	−10	6	100	−9	9	93	−11	13
89–90	−3	6	104–110	−8	6	118	−10	5	101–106	−10	9	94–99	−12	13
91–95	−4	6	111	−8	5	119–124	−11	5	107	−10	8	100	−12	12
96–97	−4	5	112–117	−9	5	125	−11	4	108–114	−11	8	101–106	−13	12
98–102	−5	5	118	−9	4	126–131	−12	4	115–121	−12	7	107	−13	11
103–104	−5	4	119–124	−10	4	132	−12	3	122–128	−13	6	108–113	−14	11
105–109	−6	4	125	−10	3	133–139	−13	3	129–135	−14	5	114	−14	10
110–111	−6	3	126–131	−11	3	140–146	−14	2	136–142	−15	4	115–121	−15	10
112–116	−7	3	132	−11	2	147–153	−15	1	143	−15	3	122–128	−16	9
117–119	−7	2	133–138	−12	2	154–160	−16	0	144–149	−16	3	129–135	−17	8
120–123	−8	2	139	−12	1				150	−16	2	136	−17	7
124–156	−8	1	140–146	−13	1				151–156	−17	2	137–142	−18	7
127–130	−9	1	147–153	−14	0				157	−17	1	143	−18	6
131–133	−9	0	154–160	−15	−1				158–160	−18	1	144–149	−19	6
134–138	−10	0										150	−19	5
139–140	−10	−1										151–156	−20	5
141–145	−11	−1										157	−20	4
146–147	−11	−2										158–160	−21	4
148–152	−12	−2												
153–154	−12	−3												
155–159	−13	−3												
160	−13	−4												

(Continued)

Table D-2 *(Continued)*

C. No Wechsler Scale (r_{xx} = .87)

68%			85%			90%			95%			99%		
IQ	*L*	*U*	*IQ*	*L*	*U*	*IQ*	*L*	*U*	*IQ*	*L*	*U*	*IQ*	*L*	*U*
40	3	13	40	1	15	40	0	16	40	−1	17	40–41	−4	20
41–44	3	12	41–44	1	14	41–44	0	15	41–44	−2	17	42–43	−5	20
45–47	2	12	45–48	0	14	45–48	−1	15	45–48	−2	16	44–48	−5	19
48–52	2	11	49–51	0	13	49–51	−1	14	49–51	−3	16	49–51	−6	19
53–55	1	11	52–55	−1	13	52–55	−2	14	52–55	−3	15	52–56	−6	18
56–59	1	10	56–59	−1	12	56–59	−2	13	56–59	−4	15	57–58	−7	18
60–63	0	10	60–63	−2	12	60–63	−3	13	60–63	−4	14	59–64	−7	17
64–67	0	9	64–67	−2	11	64–67	−3	12	64–67	−5	14	65–66	−8	17
68–70	−1	9	68–71	−3	11	68–71	−4	12	68–71	−5	13	67–72	−8	16
71–75	−1	8	72–74	−3	10	72–74	−4	11	72–74	−6	13	73–74	−9	16
76–78	−2	8	75–79	−4	10	75–78	−5	11	75–79	−6	12	75–79	−9	15
79–83	−2	7	80–82	−4	9	79–82	−5	10	80–82	−7	12	80–81	−10	15
84–86	−3	7	83–86	−5	9	83–86	−6	10	83–86	−7	11	82–87	−10	14
87–90	−3	6	87–90	−5	8	87–90	−6	9	87–90	−8	11	88–89	−11	14
91–93	−4	6	91–94	−6	8	91–94	−7	9	91–94	−8	10	90–95	−11	13
94–98	−4	5	95–97	−6	7	95–97	−7	8	95–97	−9	10	96–97	−12	13
99–101	−5	5	98–102	−7	7	98–102	−8	8	98–102	−9	9	98–102	−12	12
102–106	−5	4	103–105	−7	6	103–105	−8	7	103–105	−10	9	103–104	−13	12
107–109	−6	4	106–109	−8	6	106–109	−9	7	106–109	−10	8	105–110	−13	11
110–113	−6	3	110–113	−8	5	110–113	−9	6	110–113	−11	8	111–112	−14	11
114–116	−7	3	114–117	−9	5	114–117	−10	6	114–117	−11	7	113–118	−14	10
117–121	−7	2	118–120	−9	4	118–121	−10	5	118–120	−12	7	119–120	−15	10
122–124	−8	2	121–125	−10	4	122–125	−11	5	121–125	−12	6	121–125	−15	9
125–129	−8	1	126–128	−10	3	126–128	−11	4	126–128	−13	6	126–127	−16	9
130–132	−9	1	129–132	−11	3	129–132	−12	4	129–132	−13	5	128–133	−16	8
133–136	−9	0	133–136	−11	2	133–136	−12	3	133–136	−14	5	134–135	−17	8
137–140	−10	0	137–140	−12	2	137–140	−13	3	137–140	−14	4	136–141	−17	7
141–144	−10	−1	141–144	−12	1	141–144	−13	2	141–144	−15	4	142–143	−18	7
145–147	−11	−1	145–148	−13	1	145–148	−14	2	145–148	−15	3	144–148	−18	6
148–152	−11	−2	149–151	−13	0	149–151	−14	1	149–151	−16	3	149–151	−19	6
153–155	−12	−2	152–155	−14	0	152–155	−15	1	152–155	−16	2	152–156	−19	5
156–159	−12	−3	156–159	−14	−1	156–159	−15	0	156–159	−17	2	157–158	−20	5
160	−13	−3	160	−15	−1	160	−16	0	160	−17	1	159–160	−20	4

(Continued)

Table D-2 *(Continued)*

D. No Wechsler Scale (r_{xx} = .88)

68%			85%			90%			95%			99%		
IQ	L	U	IQ	L	U	IQ	L	U	IQ	L	U	IQ	L	U
40–41	3	12	40	1	14	40–41	0	15	40–45	–2	16	40–44	–5	19
42	2	12	41–42	0	14	42	–1	15	46	–2	15	45–47	–5	18
43–49	2	11	43–49	0	13	43–49	–1	14	47–53	–3	15	48–52	–6	18
50	1	11	50	–1	13	50	–2	14	54	–3	14	53–55	–6	17
51–57	1	10	51–57	–1	12	51–57	–2	13	55–62	–4	14	56–60	–7	17
58	0	10	58–59	–2	12	58	–3	13	63–70	–5	13	61–64	–7	16
59–66	0	9	60–65	–2	11	59–66	–3	12	71	–5	12	65–69	–8	16
67	–1	9	66–67	–3	11	67	–4	12	72–78	–6	12	70–72	–8	15
68–74	–1	8	68–74	–3	10	68–74	–4	11	79	–6	11	73–77	–9	15
75	–2	8	75	–4	10	75	–5	11	80–87	–7	11	78–80	–9	14
76–82	–2	7	76–82	–4	9	76–82	–5	10	88–95	–8	10	81–85	–10	14
83	–3	7	83–84	–5	9	83	–6	10	96	–8	9	86–89	–10	13
84–91	–3	6	85–90	–5	8	84–91	–6	9	97–103	–9	9	90–94	–11	13
92	–4	6	91–92	–6	8	92	–7	9	104	–9	8	95–97	–11	12
93–99	–4	5	93–99	–6	7	93–99	–7	8	105–112	–10	8	98–102	–12	12
100	–5	5	100	–7	7	100	–8	8	113–120	–11	7	103–105	–12	11
101–107	–5	4	101–107	–7	6	101–107	–8	7	121	–11	6	106–110	–13	11
108	–6	4	108–109	–8	6	108	–9	7	122–128	–12	6	111–114	–13	10
109–116	–6	3	110–115	–8	5	109–116	–9	6	129	–12	5	115–119	–14	10
117	–7	3	116–117	–9	5	117	–10	6	130–137	–13	5	120–122	–14	9
118–124	–7	2	118–124	–9	4	118–124	–10	5	138–145	–14	4	123–127	–15	9
125	–8	2	125	–10	4	125	–11	5	146	–14	3	128–130	–15	8
126–132	–8	1	126–132	–10	3	126–132	–11	4	147–153	–15	3	131–135	–16	8
133	–9	1	133–134	–11	3	133	–12	4	154	–15	2	136–139	–16	7
134–141	–9	0	135–140	–11	2	134–141	–12	3	155–160	–16	2	140–144	–17	7
142	–10	0	141–142	–12	2	142	–13	3				145–147	–17	6
143–149	–10	–1	143–149	–12	1	143–149	–13	2				148–152	–18	6
150	–11	–1	150	–13	1	150	–14	2				153–155	–18	5
151–157	–11	–2	151–157	–13	0	151–157	–14	1				156–160	–19	5
158	–12	–2	158–159	–14	0	158	–15	1						
159–160	–12	–3	160	–14	–1	159–160	–15	0						

(Continued)

Table D-2 (Continued)

E. WISC–III—Performance Scale—Age 14 (r_{xx} = .89)

68%			85%			90%			95%			99%		
IQ	L	U	IQ	L	U	IQ	L	U	IQ	L	U	IQ	L	U
40–44	2	11	40–44	0	13	40–43	−1	14	40–43	−2	15	40–44	−5	18
45–46	2	10	45–46	0	12	44–47	−1	13	44–47	−3	15	45–46	−5	17
47–53	1	10	47–53	−1	12	48–52	−2	13	48–52	−3	14	47–53	−6	17
54–55	1	9	54–55	−1	11	53–56	−2	12	53–56	−4	14	54–55	−6	16
56–62	0	9	56–62	−2	11	57–61	−3	12	57–62	−4	13	56–62	−7	16
63–64	0	8	63–64	−2	10	62–65	−3	11	63–65	−5	13	63–64	−7	15
65–72	−1	8	65–71	−3	10	66–70	−4	11	66–71	−5	12	65–72	−8	15
73	−1	7	72–73	−3	9	71–74	−4	10	72–74	−6	12	73	−8	14
74–81	−2	7	74–80	−4	9	75–80	−5	10	75–80	−6	11	74–81	−9	14
82	−2	6	81–82	−4	8	81–83	−5	9	81–83	−7	11	82	−9	13
83–90	−3	6	83–89	−5	8	84–89	−6	9	84–89	−7	10	83–90	−10	13
91	−3	5	90–92	−5	7	90–92	−6	8	90–92	−8	10	91	−10	12
92–99	−4	5	93–98	−6	7	93–98	−7	8	93–98	−8	9	92–99	−11	12
100	−4	4	99–101	−6	6	99–101	−7	7	99–101	−9	9	100	−11	11
101–108	−5	4	102–107	−7	6	102–107	−8	7	102–107	−9	8	101–108	−12	11
109	−5	3	108–110	−7	5	108–110	−8	6	108–110	−10	8	109	−12	10
110–117	−6	3	111–117	−8	5	111–116	−9	6	111–116	−10	7	110–117	−13	10
118	−6	2	118–119	−8	4	117–119	−9	5	117–119	−11	7	118	−13	9
119–126	−7	2	120–126	−9	4	120–125	−10	5	120–125	−11	6	119–126	−14	9
127	−7	1	127–128	−9	3	126–129	−10	4	126–128	−12	6	127	−14	8
128–135	−8	1	129–135	−10	3	130–134	−11	4	129–134	−12	5	128–135	−15	8
136–137	−8	0	136–137	−10	2	135–138	−11	3	135–137	−13	5	136–137	−15	7
138–144	−9	0	138–144	−11	2	139–143	−12	3	138–143	−13	4	138–144	−16	7
145–146	−9	−1	145–146	−11	1	144–147	−12	2	144–147	−14	4	145–146	−16	6
147–153	−10	−1	147–153	−12	1	148–152	−13	2	148–152	−14	3	147–153	−17	6
154–155	−10	−2	154–155	−12	0	153–156	−13	1	153–156	−15	3	154–155	−17	5
156–160	−11	−2	156–160	−13	0	157–160	−14	1	157–160	−15	2	156–160	−18	5

(Continued)

Table D-2 (Continued)

F. WISC–III—Performance Scale—Ages 7, 8, 11, and 13; WPPSI–R—Verbal Scale—Ages 5½ and 6½; WPPSI–R—Full Scale—Age 7 (r_{xx} = .90)

	68%			85%			90%			95%			99%	
IQ	L	U	IQ	L	U	IQ	L	U	IQ	L	U	IQ	L	U
40–42	2	10	40–43	0	12	40–44	−1	13	40–41	−2	14	40–44	−5	17
43–47	1	10	44–46	−1	12	45	−2	13	42–48	−3	14	45	−6	17
48–52	1	9	47–53	−1	11	46–54	−2	12	49–51	−3	13	46–54	−6	16
53–57	0	9	54–56	−2	11	55	−3	12	52–58	−4	13	55	−7	16
58–62	0	8	57–63	−2	10	56–64	−3	11	59–61	−4	12	56–64	−7	15
63–67	−1	8	64–66	−3	10	65	−4	11	62–68	−5	12	65	−8	15
68–72	−1	7	67–73	−3	9	66–74	−4	10	69–71	−5	11	66–74	−8	14
73–77	−2	7	74–76	−4	9	75	−5	10	72–78	−6	11	75	−9	14
78–82	−2	6	77–83	−4	8	76–84	−5	9	79–81	−6	10	76–84	−9	13
83–87	−3	6	84–86	−5	8	85	−6	9	82–88	−7	10	85	−10	13
88–92	−3	5	87–93	−5	7	86–94	−6	8	89–91	−7	9	86–94	−10	12
93–97	−4	5	94–96	−6	7	95	−7	8	92–98	−8	9	95	−11	12
98–102	−4	4	97–103	−6	6	96–104	−7	7	99–101	−8	8	96–104	−11	11
103–107	−5	4	104–106	−7	6	105	−8	7	102–108	−9	8	105	−12	11
108–112	−5	3	107–113	−7	5	106–114	−8	6	109–111	−9	7	106–114	−12	10
113–117	−6	3	114–116	−8	5	115	−9	6	112–118	−10	7	115	−13	10
118–122	−6	2	117–123	−8	4	116–124	−9	5	119–121	−10	6	116–124	−13	9
123–127	−7	2	124–126	−9	4	125	−10	5	122–128	−11	6	125	−14	9
128–132	−7	1	127–133	−9	3	126–134	−10	4	129–131	−11	5	126–134	−14	8
133–137	−8	1	134–136	−10	3	135	−11	4	132–138	−12	5	135	−15	8
138–142	−8	0	137–143	−10	2	136–144	−11	3	139–141	−12	4	136–144	−15	7
143–147	−9	0	144–146	−11	2	145	−12	3	142–148	−13	4	145	−16	7
148–152	−9	−1	147–153	−11	1	146–154	−12	2	149–151	−13	3	146–154	−16	6
153–157	−10	−1	154–156	−12	1	155	−13	2	152–158	−14	3	155	−17	6
158–160	−10	−2	157–160	−12	0	156–160	−13	1	159–160	−14	2	156–160	−17	5

(Continued)

G. WISC–III—Performance Scale—Ages 6, 9, 10, 12, and Average (r_{xx} = .91)

68%			85%			90%			95%			99%		
IQ	L	U	IQ	L	U	IQ	L	U	IQ	L	U	IQ	L	U
40–48	1	9	40	0	11	40–41	−1	12	40–49	−3	13	40–43	−5	16
49–51	0	9	41–48	−1	11	42–47	−2	12	50	−4	13	44–45	−6	16
52–60	0	8	49–51	−1	10	48–52	−2	11	51–60	−4	12	46–54	−6	15
61–62	−1	8	52–59	−2	10	53–58	−3	11	61	−5	12	55–56	−7	15
63–71	−1	7	60–62	−2	9	59–63	−3	10	62–71	−5	11	57–65	−7	14
72–73	−2	7	63–71	−3	9	64–69	−4	10	72	−6	11	66–67	−8	14
74–82	−2	6	72–73	−3	8	70–74	−4	9	73–83	−6	10	68–77	−8	13
83–84	−3	6	74–82	−4	8	75–80	−5	9	84–94	−7	9	78	−9	13
85–93	−3	5	83–84	−4	7	81–86	−5	8	95–105	−8	8	79–88	−9	12
94–95	−4	5	85–93	−5	7	87–91	−6	8	106–116	−9	7	89	−10	12
96–104	−4	4	94–95	−5	6	92–97	−6	7	117–127	−10	6	90–99	−10	11
105–106	−5	4	96–104	−6	6	98–102	−7	7	128	−11	6	100	−11	11
107–115	−5	3	105–106	−6	5	103–108	−7	6	129–138	−11	5	101–110	−11	10
116–117	−6	3	107–115	−7	5	109–113	−8	6	139	−12	5	111	−12	10
118–126	−6	2	116–117	−7	4	114–119	−8	5	140–149	−12	4	112–121	−12	9
127–128	−7	2	118–126	−8	4	120–125	−9	5	150	−13	4	122	−13	9
129–137	−7	1	127–128	−8	3	126–130	−9	4	151–160	−13	3	123–132	−13	8
138–139	−8	1	129–137	−9	3	131–136	−10	4				133–134	−14	8
140–148	−8	0	138–140	−9	2	137–141	−10	3				135–143	−14	7
149–151	−9	0	141–148	−10	2	142–147	−11	3				144–145	−15	7
152–160	−9	−1	149–151	−10	1	148–152	−11	2				146–154	−15	6
			152–159	−11	1	153–158	−12	2				155–156	−16	6
			160	−11	0	159–160	−12	1				157–160	−16	5

H. WISC–III—Verbal Scale—Age 7; WISC–III—Performance Scale—Age 16; WPPSI–R—Verbal Scale—Ages 5 and 6; WPPSI–R—Performance Scale—Average (r_{xx} = .92)

68%			85%			90%			95%			99%		
IQ	L	U	IQ	L	U	IQ	L	U	IQ	L	U	IQ	L	U
40–42	1	9	40–48	−1	10	40–49	−2	11	40–48	−3	12	40–42	−5	15
43–44	1	8	49–51	−2	10	50	−2	10	49–51	−4	12	43–44	−6	15
45–55	0	8	52–60	−2	9	51–61	−3	10	52–60	−4	11	45–55	−6	14
56–57	0	7	61–64	−3	9	62–63	−3	9	61–64	−5	11	56–57	−7	14
58–67	−1	7	65–73	−3	8	64–74	−4	9	65–73	−5	10	58–67	−7	13
68–69	−1	6	74–76	−4	8	75	−4	8	74–76	−6	10	68–69	−8	13
70–80	−2	6	77–85	−4	7	76–86	−5	8	77–85	−6	9	70–80	−8	12
81–82	−2	5	86–89	−5	7	87–88	−5	7	86–89	−7	9	81–82	−9	12
83–92	−3	5	90–98	−5	6	89–99	−6	7	90–98	−7	8	83–92	−9	11
93–94	−3	4	99–101	−6	6	100	−6	6	99–101	−8	8	93–94	−10	11
95–105	−4	4	102–110	−6	5	101–111	−7	6	102–110	−8	7	95–105	−10	10
106–107	−4	3	111–114	−7	5	112–113	−7	5	111–114	−9	7	106–107	−11	10
108–117	−5	3	115–123	−7	4	114–124	−8	5	115–123	−9	6	108–117	−11	9
118–119	−5	2	124–126	−8	4	125	−8	4	124–126	−10	6	118–119	−12	9
120–130	−6	2	127–135	−8	3	126–136	−9	4	127–135	−10	5	120–130	−12	8
131–132	−6	1	136–139	−9	3	137–138	−9	3	136–139	−11	5	131–132	−13	8
133–142	−7	1	140–148	−9	2	139–149	−10	3	140–148	−11	4	133–142	−13	7
143–144	−7	0	149–151	−10	2	150	−10	2	149–151	−12	4	143–144	−14	7
145–155	−8	0	152–160	−10	1	151–160	−11	2	152–160	−12	3	145–155	−14	6
156–157	−8	−1										156–157	−15	6
158–160	−9	−1										158–160	−15	5

845

(Continued)

Table D-2 *(Continued)*

I. WISC–III—Verbal Scale—Ages 6 and 9; WPPSI–R—Verbal Scale—Ages 3, 3½, 4, and 4½; WPPSI–R—Performance Scale—Age 6½; WAIS–III—Performance Scale—Ages 16–17, 18–19, 20–24, 30–34, and 75–79 (r_{xx} = .93)

68%			85%			90%			95%			99%		
IQ	L	U	IQ	L	U	IQ	L	U	IQ	L	U	IQ	L	U
40	1	8	40	−1	10	40–48	−2	10	40–46	−3	11	40–42	−5	14
41–45	0	8	41–45	−1	9	49–51	−3	10	47–53	−4	11	43	−6	14
46–54	0	7	46–54	−2	9	52–63	−3	9	54–60	−4	10	44–56	−6	13
55–59	−1	7	55–59	−2	8	64–65	−4	9	61–67	−5	10	57	−7	13
60–68	−1	6	60–68	−3	8	66–77	−4	8	68–75	−5	9	58–71	−7	12
69–74	−2	6	69–74	−3	7	78–79	−5	8	76–81	−6	9	72–85	−8	11
75–82	−2	5	75–83	−4	7	80–91	−5	7	82–89	−6	8	86	−9	11
83–88	−3	5	84–88	−4	6	92–94	−6	7	90–96	−7	8	87–99	−9	10
89–97	−3	4	89–97	−5	6	95–105	−6	6	97–103	−7	7	100	−10	10
98–102	−4	4	98–102	−5	5	106–108	−7	6	104–110	−8	7	101–113	−10	9
103–111	−4	3	103–111	−6	5	109–120	−7	5	111–118	−8	6	114	−11	9
112–117	−5	3	112–116	−6	4	121–122	−8	5	119–124	−9	6	115–128	−11	8
118–125	−5	2	117–125	−7	4	123–134	−8	4	125–132	−9	5	129–142	−12	7
126–131	−6	2	126–131	−7	3	135–136	−9	4	133–139	−10	5	143	−13	7
132–140	−6	1	132–140	−8	3	137–148	−9	3	140–146	−10	4	144–156	−13	6
141–145	−7	1	141–145	−8	2	149–151	−10	3	147–153	−11	4	157	−14	6
146–154	−7	0	146–154	−9	2	152–160	−10	2	154–160	−11	3	158–160	−14	5
155–159	−8	0	155–159	−9	1									
160	−8	−1	160	−10	1									

J. WISC–III—Verbal Scale—Age 13; WISC–III—Performance Scale—Age 15; WISC–III—Full Scale—Age 7; WPPSI–R—Performance Scale—Ages 5½ and 6; WAIS–III—Performance Scale—Ages 35–44, 45–54, 80–84, 85–89, and Average (r_{xx} = .94)

68%			85%			90%			95%			99%		
IQ	L	U	IQ	L	U	IQ	L	U	IQ	L	U	IQ	L	U
40–49	0	7	40–41	−1	9	40–46	−2	9	40–45	−3	10	40	−5	13
50	0	6	42	−1	8	47–53	−3	9	46–54	−4	10	41–43	−5	12
51–65	−1	6	43–57	−2	8	54–63	−3	8	55–62	−4	9	44–56	−6	12
66–67	−1	5	58	−2	7	64–69	−4	8	63–71	−5	9	57–59	−6	11
68–82	−2	5	59–74	−3	7	70–80	−4	7	72–78	−5	8	60–73	−7	11
83–84	−2	4	75	−3	6	81–86	−5	7	79–87	−6	8	74–76	−7	10
85–99	−3	4	76–91	−4	6	87–96	−5	6	88–95	−6	7	77–90	−8	10
100	−3	3	92	−4	5	97–103	−6	6	96–104	−7	7	91–93	−8	9
101–115	−4	3	93–107	−5	5	104–113	−6	5	105–112	−7	6	94–106	−9	9
116–117	−4	2	108	−5	4	114–119	−7	5	113–121	−8	6	107–109	−9	8
118–132	−5	2	109–124	−6	4	120–130	−7	4	122–128	−8	5	110–123	−10	8
133–134	−5	1	125	−6	3	131–136	−8	4	129–137	−9	5	124–126	−10	7
135–149	−6	1	126–141	−7	3	137–146	−8	3	138–145	−9	4	127–140	−11	7
150	−6	0	142	−7	2	147–153	−9	3	146–154	−10	4	141–143	−11	6
151–160	−7	0	143–157	−8	2	154–160	−9	2	155–160	−10	3	144–156	−12	6
			158	−8	1							157–159	−12	5
			159–160	−9	1							160	−13	5

(Continued)

Table D-2 *(Continued)*

K. WISC–III—Verbal Scale—Ages 10, 11, 12, 14, 16, and Average; WISC–III—Full Scale—Ages 6, 9, 11, 13, and 14; WPPSI–R—Performance Scale—Age 5; WPPSI–R—Verbal Scale—Average; WPPSI–R—Full Scale—Ages 5½, 6, and 6½; WAIS–III—Performance Scale—Age 25–29, 55–64, and 70–74 ($r_{xx} = .95$)

68%			85%			90%			95%			99%		
IQ	L	U	IQ	L	U	IQ	L	U	IQ	L	U	IQ	L	U
40–46	0	6	40–41	–2	8	40–44	–2	8	40–45	–3	9	40–45	–5	11
47–53	–1	6	42–58	–2	7	45–55	–3	8	46–54	–4	9	46–54	–6	11
54–66	–1	5	59–61	–3	7	56–64	–3	7	55–65	–4	8	55–65	–6	10
67–73	–2	5	62–78	–3	6	65–75	–4	7	66–74	–5	8	66–74	–7	10
74–86	–2	4	79–81	–4	6	76–84	–4	6	75–85	–5	7	75–85	–7	9
87–93	–3	4	82–98	–4	5	85–95	–5	6	86–94	–6	7	86–94	–8	9
94–106	–3	3	99–101	–5	5	96–104	–5	5	95–105	–6	6	95–105	–8	8
107–113	–4	3	102–118	–5	4	105–115	–6	5	106–114	–7	6	106–114	–9	8
114–126	–4	2	119–121	–6	4	116–124	–6	4	115–125	–7	5	115–125	–9	7
127–133	–5	2	122–138	–6	3	125–135	–7	4	126–134	–8	5	126–134	–10	7
134–146	–5	1	139–141	–7	3	136–144	–7	3	135–145	–8	4	135–145	–10	6
147–153	–6	1	142–158	–7	2	145–155	–8	3	146–154	–9	4	146–154	–11	6
154–160	–6	0	159–160	–8	2	156–160	–8	2	155–160	–9	3	155–160	–11	5

L. WISC–III—Verbal Scale—Ages 8 and 15; WISC–III—Full Scale—Ages 8, 10, 12, 16, and Average; WPPSI–R—Performance Scale—Ages 3, 3½, 4, and 4½; WPPSI–R—Full Scale—Age 5 and Average; WAIS–III—Verbal Scale—Ages 16–17 and 85–89; WAIS–III—Performance Scale—Ages 65–69 ($r_{xx} = .96$)

68%			85%			90%			95%			99%		
IQ	L	U	IQ	L	U	IQ	L	U	IQ	L	U	IQ	L	U
40	0	5	40–41	–2	7	40–43	–2	7	40–46	–3	8	40–48	–5	10
41–59	–1	5	42–58	–2	6	44–56	–3	7	47–53	–4	8	49–51	–5	9
60–65	–1	4	59–66	–3	6	57–68	–3	6	54–71	–4	7	52–73	–6	9
66–84	–2	4	67–83	–3	5	69–81	–4	6	72–78	–5	7	74–76	–6	8
85–90	–2	3	84–91	–4	5	82–93	–4	5	79–96	–5	6	77–98	–7	8
91–109	–3	3	92–108	–4	4	94–106	–5	5	97–103	–6	6	99–101	–7	7
110–115	–3	2	109–116	–5	4	107–118	–5	4	104–121	–6	5	102–123	–8	7
116–134	–4	2	117–133	–5	3	117–131	–6	4	122–128	–7	5	124–126	–8	6
135–140	–4	1	134–141	–6	3	132–143	–6	3	129–146	–7	4	127–148	–9	6
141–159	–5	1	142–158	–6	2	144–156	–7	3	147–153	–8	4	149–151	–9	5
160	–5	0	159–160	–7	2	157–160	–7	2	154–160	–8	3	152–160	–10	5

(Continued)

Table D-2 *(Continued)*

M. WISC–III—Full Scale—Age 15; WPPSI–R—Full Scale—Ages 3, 3½, 4, and 4½; WAIS–III—Verbal Scale—Ages 18–19, 20–24, 25–29, 30–34, 35–44, 45–54, 70–74, 75–79, 80–84, and Average; WAIS–III—Full Scale—Ages 16–17, 18–19, 75–79, and 85–89 (r_{xx} = .97)

68%			85%			90%			95%			99%		
IQ	L	U	IQ	L	U	IQ	L	U	IQ	L	U	IQ	L	U
40–65	−1	4	40–62	−2	5	40–44	−2	6	40–47	−3	7	40–66	−5	8
66–67	−2	4	63–70	−3	5	45–55	−3	6	48–52	−3	6	67–99	−6	7
68–99	−2	3	71–95	−3	4	56–78	−3	5	53–81	−4	6	100	−7	7
100	−3	3	96–104	−4	4	79–88	−4	5	82–85	−4	5	101–133	−7	6
101–132	−3	2	105–129	−4	3	89–111	−4	4	86–114	−5	5	134–160	−8	5
133–134	−4	2	130–137	−5	3	112–121	−5	4	115–118	−5	4			
135–160	−4	1	138–160	−5	2	122–144	−5	3	119–147	−6	4			
						145–155	−6	3	148–152	−6	3			
						156–160	−6	2	153–160	−7	3			

N. WAIS–III—Verbal Scale—Ages 55–64 and 65–69; WAIS–III— Full Scale—Ages 20–24, 25–29, 30–34, 35–44, 45–54, 55–64, 65–69, 70–74, 80–84, and Average (r_{xx} = .98)

68%			85%			90%			95%			99%		
IQ	L	U	IQ	L	U	IQ	L	U	IQ	L	U	IQ	L	U
40–71	−1	3	40–74	−2	4	40–46	−2	5	40–71	−3	5	40–43	−4	7
72–78	−2	3	75	−2	3	47–53	−2	4	72–78	−4	5	44–56	−4	6
79–121	−2	2	76–124	−3	3	54–96	−3	4	79–121	−4	4	57–93	−5	6
122–128	−3	2	125	−3	2	97–103	−3	3	122–128	−5	4	94–106	−5	5
129–160	−3	1	126–160	−4	2	104–146	−4	3	129–160	−5	3	107–143	−6	5
						147–153	−4	2				144–156	−6	4
						154–160	−5	2				157–160	−7	4

Note. Abbreviations: L = Lower limit of confidence interval, U = Upper limit of confidence interval. The values in the table, when added to the obtained IQ (in the first column), will form the confidence interval. For example, for a 7-year-old, the confidence interval for an obtained IQ of 40 at the 99% confidence level for the WPPSI–R Verbal Scale (see Section A) is 36 to 62 (40 − 4 = 36; 40 + 22 = 62).

The confidence intervals in Table D-2 can be used for any test having the reliability coefficient shown in each section of the table (r_{xx} range of .85 to .98) and a standard score distribution with *M* = 100 and *SD* = 15.

See Chapter 4, pages 110–111, for an explanation of how confidence intervals were computed.

Table D-3
Interpretive Rationales, Implications of High and Low Scores, and Instructional Implications for Wechsler Subtests

Ability[a]	Background factors	Possible implications of high scores	Possible implications of low scores	Instructional implications
Information				
Verbal comprehension Range of factual knowledge Fund of information Long-term memory Acquired knowledge Crystallized ability	Natural endowment Richness of early environment Quality of preschooling or schooling Cultural opportunities Interests and reading patterns	Good range of factual knowledge Good range of information Knowledge of the cultural and educational environment Good memory Enriched background Alertness and interest in the environment Intellectual ambitiousness Intellectual curiosity Urge to collect knowledge	Poor range of factual knowledge Poor range of information Poor memory Hostility to a preschool- or school-type task Tendency to give up easily Foreign background Lack of achievement orientation	Stress factual material by having child read newspaper articles, discuss current events, and do memory exercises Use other enrichment activities, including calendar activities, science and social studies projects, and projects involving animals and their function in society
Similarities				
Verbal comprehension Verbal concept formation Language development Abstract and concrete reasoning abilities Capacity for associative thinking Ability to separate essential from nonessential details Long-term memory Crystallized ability	Education Cultural opportunities Interests and reading patterns Flexibility	Good conceptual thinking Good ability to see relationships Good ability to use logical and abstract thinking Good ability to discriminate fundamental from superficial relationships Good ability to select and verbalize appropriate relationships between two objects or concepts Flexibility of thought processes	Poor conceptual thinking Difficulty in seeing relationships Difficulty in selecting and verbalizing appropriate relationships between two objects or concepts Overly concrete mode of thinking Rigidity of thought processes Negativism	Focus on recognition of differences and likenesses in shapes, textures, and daily surroundings Stress language development, synonyms and antonyms, and exercises involving abstract words, classifications, and generalizations

(Continued)

Table D-3 *(Continued)*

Ability[a]	Background factors	Possible implications of high scores	Possible implications of low scores	Instructional implications
Arithmetic				
Verbal comprehension Numerical reasoning ability Mental computation Quantitative knowledge Application of basic arithmetical processes Concentration Attention Short-term memory Long-term memory Mental alertness Acquired knowledge Fluid ability	Opportunity to acquire fundamental arithmetical processes Quality of preschooling or schooling Ability to attend to stimuli	Facility in mental arithmetic Good ability to apply reasoning skills in the solution of mathematical problems Good ability to apply arithmetical skills in personal and social problem-solving situations Good concentration Good attention Good ability to engage in complex thought patterns, mainly for upper-level items Teacher orientation	Inadequate ability in mental arithmetic Poor concentration Distractibility Anxiety (e.g., over a school-like task or personal problems) Blocking toward mathematical tasks Lack of interest in school achievement (perhaps associated with rebellion against authority or with cultural background)	Develop arithmetical skills Develop concentration skills Use concrete objects to introduce concepts Drill in basic skills Provide interesting "real" problems to solve
Vocabulary				
Verbal comprehension Language development Word knowledge Learning ability Fund of information Richness of ideas Memory Concept formation Long-term memory Verbal fluency Acquired knowledge Crystallized ability	Education Cultural opportunities Interests and reading patterns Richness of early environment Quality of preschooling or schooling	Good word knowledge Good verbal comprehension Good verbal skills and language development Good family or cultural background Good preschooling or schooling Good ability to conceptualize Intellectual striving	Poor word knowledge Poor verbal comprehension Poor verbal skills and language development Limited educational or family background Difficulty with verbalization Foreign language background Lack of encouragement of verbalization in family	Develop working vocabulary Encourage child to discuss experiences, ask questions, and make a dictionary Use other verbal enrichment exercises, including Scrabble, analogy, and other word games

(Continued)

Table D-3 (Continued)

Ability[a]	Background factors	Possible implications of high scores	Possible implications of low scores	Instructional implications
Comprehension				
Verbal comprehension Social judgment Common sense Logical reasoning Application of practical knowledge and judgment in social situations Knowledge of conventional standards of behavior Reasoning Ability to evaluate past experience Moral and ethical judgment Long-term memory Crystallized ability	Cultural opportunities Quality of preschooling or schooling Ability to evaluate and use past experience Development of conscience or moral sense	Good social judgment and common sense Good ability to recognize when practical judgment and common sense are necessary Knowledge of rules of conventional behavior Good ability to organize knowledge Social maturity Ability to verbalize well Wide experience	Poor social judgment Failure to take personal responsibility (e.g., overdependency, immaturity, limited involvement with others) Overly concrete thinking Difficulty in expressing ideas verbally Creativity that leads to looking for unusual solutions Negativism	Help child understand social mores, customs, and societal activities, such as how other children react to things, how the government works, and how banks operate Discuss the actions of others to help children develop an awareness of social relationships and what others expect of them Role-play situations, such as reporting fires, calling police, and calling the plumber
Digit Span				
Verbal comprehension Short-term auditory sequential memory Memory span Rote memory Immediate auditory memory Attention span Concentration Auditory sequential processing Immediate rote recall Fluid ability	Ability to passively receive stimuli Ability to attend to stimuli Auditory acuity and discrimination	Good short-term auditory memory Good rote memory Good immediate recall ability Ability to attend well in a testing situation Good ability to attend to auditory stimuli Cooperation Flexibility in shifting	Anxiety Inattention Distractibility A possible learning deficit Difficulty in auditory sequential processing Negativism Poor short-term auditory memory Boredom Difficulty in shifting	Emphasize listening skills by using sequencing activities, reading a short story and asking the child to recall details, and seeing whether the child can follow directions Use short and simple directions and repeat when necessary Use other memory exercises and memory games
Picture Completion				
Perceptual organization Ability to differentiate essential from nonessential details Identification of familiar objects (visual recognition) Concentration on visually perceived material Alertness to detail Reasoning Visual processing Visual perception (closure) Visual long-term memory Fluid ability	Experiences Alertness to environment Ability to work under time pressure Visual acuity and discrimination Willingness to guess when uncertain	Good perception and concentration Alertness to details Good ability to differentiate between essential and nonessential details Ability to establish a learning set quickly[b]	Anxiety affecting concentration and attention Preoccupation with irrelevant details Negativism ("nothing is missing")	Focus on visual learning techniques stressing individual parts that make up the whole Use perceptual activities that focus on recognizing objects, describing objects, and attention to details (e.g., maps and art work) Improve scanning techniques aimed at identifying missing elements in pictures

(Continued)

Table D-3 *(Continued)*

Ability[a]	Background factors	Possible implications of high scores	Possible implications of low scores	Instructional implications
Coding and Digit Symbol—Coding				
Processing speed Visual-motor coordination or dexterity Speed of mental operation Psychomotor speed Short-term visual memory Visual recall Attention Concentration Symbol-associative skills Visual sequential processing Fluid ability	Rate of motor activity Motivation Visual acuity and discrimination Attention span Ability to work under time pressure	Visual-motor dexterity Good attention and concentration Sustained energy or persistence Ability to learn new material associatively and reproduce it with speed and accuracy Good motivation Desire for achievement Good visual sequential processing	Visual-motor coordination difficulties Distractibility Anxiety Visual defects Poor pencil control Poor motivation Excessive concern for detail in reproducing symbols exactly Lethargy or boredom Impulsivity	Use visual-motor learning exercises, such as developing a code for matching geometric figures and numbers, learning Morse Code, and working on tracing activities
Picture Arrangement				
Perceptual organization Planning ability Interpretation of social situations Nonverbal reasoning ability Attention to details Alertness Visual sequential processing Common sense Anticipation of consequences Fluid ability	Cultural opportunities Ability to work under time pressure Ability to infer cause-and-effect relationships	Planning ability Ability to anticipate in a meaningful way what results might be expected from various acts of behavior Alertness to detail Forethought Sequential thought processes Good ability to synthesize parts into intelligible wholes	Difficulty with visual organization and sequential processing Difficulty in anticipating events and their consequences Inattentiveness Anxiety Failure to use cues Difficulty in working under time pressure Impulsivity Poor visual acuity and discrimination	Focus on cause-and-effect relationships, logical sequential presentations, and part-whole relationships Use story completion exercises Discuss alternative behaviors and endings in stories and events
Block Design				
Perceptual organization Visual-motor coordination Spatial visualization Visual processing Abstract conceptualizing ability Analysis and synthesis Speed of mental processing Fluid ability	Rate of motor activity Color vision Ability to work under time pressure Visual acuity and discrimination Trial-and-error learning	Good visual-motor-spatial integration Good conceptualizing ability Good spatial orientation in conjunction with speed, accuracy, and persistence Good analyzing and synthesizing ability Speed and accuracy in sizing up a problem Good hand-eye coordination Good nonverbal reasoning ability Good trial-and-error methods	Poor visual-motor-spatial integration Visual-perceptual problems Poor spatial orientation Difficulty in working under time pressure Impulsivity Poor ability to size up a problem Poor analyzing and synthesizing ability Poor hand-eye coordination Poor nonverbal reasoning ability	Use puzzles, blocks, spatial-visual tasks, perceptual tasks involving breaking down an object and building it up again, and art work with geometric forms and flannel board Focus on part-whole relationships and working with a model or a key

(Continued)

Table D-3 *(Continued)*

Ability[a]	Background factors	Possible implications of high scores	Possible implications of low scores	Instructional implications
Object Assembly				
Perceptual organization Visual processing Visual-motor coordination Ability to synthesize concrete parts into meaningful wholes Spatial ability Speed of mental processing Fluid ability	Rate of motor activity Familiarity with figures Persistence Experience with part-whole relationships Ability to work toward an unknown goal Ability to work under time pressure Trial-and-error learning	Good visual-motor coordination Good ability to visualize a whole from its parts Ability to perceive a whole, with critical understanding of the relationships of the individual parts Successful trial and error Experience in assembling puzzles Persistence	Visual-motor difficulties Visual-perceptual problems Poor planning ability Difficulty in perceiving a whole Minimal experience with construction tasks Limited interest in assembly tasks Limited persistence Difficulty in working under time pressure Impulsivity	Develop perceptual and psychomotor skills through guided practice in assembling parts into familiar configurations Encourage trial-and-error activities Reinforce persistence Work with puzzles and activities centering on recognition of missing body parts Employ construction, cutting, and pasting activities Focus on interpretation of wholes from minimal cues
Mazes				
Perceptual organization Planning ability Foresight Visual-motor control Eye-hand coordination Attention Concentration Visual processing Spatial scanning	Visual-motor organization Visual acuity and discrimination Ability to delay action	Good perceptual organization Planning efficiency Speed and accuracy Good ability to follow instructions Sustained attention	Poor visual-motor organization Inefficient planning Difficulty in delaying action Impulsivity Inability to sustain attention Boredom	Focus on planning skills, directionality, visual discrimination, and other paper-and-pencil activities emphasizing planning and anticipation Help child evaluate responses prior to emitting them
Symbol Search				
Processing speed Perceptual discrimination Speed of mental operation Psychomotor speed Attention Concentration Short-term visual memory Visual-motor coordination Cognitive flexibility Fluid ability	Rate of motor activity Motivation Ability to work under time pressure Visual acuity and discrimination	Good processing speed Good perceptual discrimination ability Good attention and concentration Sustained energy or persistence Good motivation or desire for achievement Good short-term visual memory	Poor processing speed Poor perceptual discrimination ability Distractibility Visual defects Lethargy or boredom Poor motivation Anxiety Difficulty in working under time pressure Impulsivity Poor short-term visual memory	Use visual-motor scanning exercises, such as looking at two or more objects and deciding if they are the same or different

(Continued)

Table D-3 *(Continued)*

Ability[a]	Background factors	Possible implications of high scores	Possible implications of low scores	Instructional implications
Letter–Number Sequencing				
Working memory Attention Concentration Short-term auditory memory Memory span Information processing Cognitive flexibility Fluid ability	Ability to passively receive stimuli Motivation	Good short-term auditory memory Good working memory Good attention and concentration Persistence	Poor short-term auditory memory Anxiety Inattention Distractibility A possible learning deficit Impulsivity Negativism	Emphasize listening skills by using sequencing activities Use short and simple directions and repeat when necessary Use memory exercises and memory games
Matrix Reasoning				
Perceptual organization Reasoning ability Classification ability Ability to form analogies Attention to detail Concentration Spatial ability Knowledge of part-whole relationships Fluid ability	Persistence Motivation Ability to work toward a goal Ability to use trial and error	Good perceptual organization Good reasoning ability Good attention to detail Persistence Good concentration	Poor perceptual organization Poor reasoning ability Lack of attention to detail Negativism Impulsivity Poor concentration	Use puzzles, blocks, spatial-visual tasks, perceptual tasks involving breaking down an object and building it up again, and art work with geometric forms and flannel board Focus on part-whole relationships
Sentences				
Verbal comprehension Short-term auditory memory Rote memory Immediate auditory memory Attention Concentration Auditory sequential processing Verbal facility Fluid ability	Ability to passively receive stimuli Language development	Good short-term auditory memory Good rote memory Good immediate recall ability Ability to attend well in a testing situation Good ability to attend to auditory stimuli	Anxiety Inattention Distractibility Difficulty with auditory sequential processing Negativism Poor short-term auditory memory	Emphasize listening skills by using sequencing activities, reading a short story and asking the child to recall details, and seeing whether the child can follow directions Use short and simple directions and repeat when necessary Use other memory exercises and memory games
Geometric Design				
Perceptual organization Perceptual-motor ability Visual-motor organization Visualization	Motor ability Finger dexterity	Good perceptual-motor ability Good eye-hand coordination	Poor perceptual-motor ability Deficient eye-hand coordination Developmental immaturity	Use pencil and crayons to develop fine motor skills Use tracing activities with a variety of shapes and designs

(Continued)

Table D-3 *(Continued)*

Ability[a]	Background factors	Possible implications of high scores	Possible implications of low scores	Instructional implications
		Animal Pegs		
Perceptual organization Attention Goal awareness Concentration Finger and manual dexterity Learning ability Short-term visual memory Processing speed Visual sequential processing Fluid ability	Rate of motor activity	Visual-motor dexterity Good concentration Sustained energy or persistence Ability to learn new material associatively and reproduce it with speed and accuracy Good motivation or desire for achievement	Visual-motor coordination difficulties Distractibility Visual defects Poor short-term visual memory Lethargy	Use visual-motor learning exercises, such as sorting coins and putting different-colored objects in bins

Note. Select the appropriate implication(s) based on the entire test protocol and background information.

[a] The first entry under "Ability" is based on factor analytic findings. Other entries are derived from clinical and psychoeducational hypotheses.

[b] Pertains primarily to WPPSI–R.

Source: Adapted, in part, from Blatt and Allison (1968); Freeman (1962); Glasser and Zimmerman (1967); Kaufman (1975); McGrew and Flanagan (1998); Rapaport, Gill, and Schafer (1968); and Searls (1975).

Table D-4
Interpretive Rationales, Implications of High and Low Scores, and Instructional Implications for Wechsler Scales and Index Scores

Ability	Background factors	Possible implications of high scores	Possible implications of low scores	Instructional implications
Full Scale				
General intelligence Scholastic aptitude Academic aptitude Readiness to master a school curriculum	Natural endowment Richness of early environment Extent of schooling Cultural opportunities Interests Rate of motor activity Persistence Visual-motor organization Alertness	Good general intelligence Good scholastic aptitude Readiness to master a school curriculum	Poor general intelligence Poor scholastic aptitude Lack of readiness to master school curriculum	Focus on language development activities Focus on visual learning activities Develop concept formation skills Reinforce persistence
Verbal Scale or Verbal Comprehension Index				
Verbal comprehension Application of verbal skills and information to the solution of new problems Verbal ability Ability to process verbal information Ability to think with words	Natural endowment Richness of early environment Extent of schooling Cultural opportunities Interests	Good verbal comprehension Good scholastic aptitude Knowledge of the cultural milieu Good concept formation Readiness to master school curriculum Achievement orientation	Poor verbal comprehension Poor scholastic aptitude Inadequate understanding of the cultural milieu Poor concept formation Bilingual background Foreign background Lack of readiness to master school curriculum Lack of achievement orientation	Stress language development activities Use verbal enrichment activities Focus on current events Use exercises involving concept formation
Performance Scale or Perceptual Organization Index				
Perceptual organization Ability to think in terms of visual images and manipulate them with fluency, flexibility, and relative speed Ability to interpret or organize visually perceived material within a time limit Nonverbal ability Ability to form relatively abstract concepts and relationships without the use of words	Natural endowment Rate of motor activity Persistence Visual-motor organization Alertness Cultural opportunities Interests	Good perceptual organization Alertness to detail Good nonverbal reasoning ability Persistence Ability to work quickly and efficiently Good spatial ability	Poor perceptual organization Lack of alertness to detail Poor nonverbal reasoning ability Lack of persistence Inability to work quickly and efficiently Poor spatial ability	Focus on visual learning activities Focus on part-whole relationships Use spatial-visual tasks Encourage trial-and-error activities Reinforce persistence Focus on visual planning activities Improve scanning techniques

(Continued)

Table D-4 *(Continued)*

Ability	Background factors	Possible implications of high scores	Possible implications of low scores	Instructional implications
Freedom from Distractibility Index and Working Memory				
Ability to sustain attention Short-term memory Numerical ability Encoding ability Ability to use rehearsal strategies Ability to shift mental operations on symbolic material Ability to self-monitor	Natural endowment Ability to passively receive stimuli	Good ability to sustain attention Good short-term memory Good numerical ability Good encoding ability Good rehearsal strategies Good ability to shift mental operations on symbolic material Good ability to self-monitor	Difficulty in sustaining attention Distractibility Anxiety Short-term retention deficits Encoding difficulties Poor rehearsal strategies Difficulty in rapidly shifting mental operations on symbolic material Inadequate self-monitoring skills	Develop attention skills Develop concentration skills Focus on small, meaningful units of instruction
Processing Speed Index				
Processing speed Perceptual discrimination Speed of mental operation Psychomotor speed Attention Concentration Short-term visual memory Visual-motor coordination Cognitive flexibility Fluid ability	Rate of motor activity Motivation Visual acuity and discrimination Attention span Ability to work under time pressure	Good processing speed Good perceptual discrimination ability Good attention and concentration Sustained energy or persistence Good motivation or desire for achievement Good short-term visual memory	Poor processing speed Poor perceptual discrimination ability Distractibility Visual defects Lethargy or boredom Poor motivation Anxiety Difficulty in working under time pressure Impulsivity Poor short-term visual memory	Develop visual-motor skills Develop concentration skills Focus on learning codes Focus on selecting numbers that match

Table D-5
Suggested Remediation Activities for Combinations of Wechsler Subtests

Subtests	Ability	Activities
Information, Vocabulary, and Comprehension	General knowledge and verbal fluency	(1) Review basic concepts, such as days of the week, months, time, distances, and directions; (2) have children report major current events by referring to pictures and articles from magazines and newspapers; (3) teach similarities and differences in designs, topography, transportation, etc.; (4) have children use dictionary; (5) have children learn new words; (6) have children repeat simple stories; (7) have children explain how story characters are feeling and thinking.
Similarities and Vocabulary	Verbal conceptual	(1) Use show-and-tell games; (2) have children make scrapbooks of classifications such as animals, vehicles, or utensils; (3) have children match abstract concepts; (4) have children find commonality in dissimilar objects; (5) review basic concepts such as days of the week, months, time, directions, and distances.
Digit Span, Arithmetic, Picture Completion, and Picture Arrangement	Attention and concentration	(1) Have children arrange cards in a meaningful sequence; (2) have children learn their telephone number, address, etc.; (3) use spelling word games; (4) use memory games; (5) have children learn days of the week and months of the year; (6) use mathematical word problems; (7) use dot-to-dot exercises; (8) have children describe details in pictures; (9) use tracing activities; (10) use Tinker Toys.
Block Design and Object Assembly	Spatial-visual	(1) Have children identify common objects and discuss details; (2) use guessing games involving description of a person, place, or thing; (3) have children match letters, shapes, numbers, etc.; (4) use jigsaw puzzles; (5) use block-building activities.
Coding, Digit Symbol, Block Design, Object Assembly, Animal Pegs, and Mazes	Visual-motor	(1) Use paper-folding activities; (2) use finger-painting activities; (3) use dot-to-dot exercises; (4) use scissor-cutting exercises; (5) use sky-writing exercises; (6) have children string beads in patterns; (7) use pegboard designs; (8) use puzzles (large jigsaw pieces); (9) have children solve a maze; (10) have children follow a moving object with coordinated eye movements; (11) use tracing exercises (e.g., trace hand, geometric forms, and letters); (12) have children make large circles and lines on the chalkboard; (13) have children copy from patterns; (14) have children draw from memory.

Table D-6
Constants for Converting Wechsler Composite Scores into Deviation Quotients

2 Subtests			3 Subtests			4 Subtests			5 Subtests		
Σr_{jk}	a	b	Σr_{jk}	a	b	Σr_{jk}	a	b	Σr_{jk}	a	b
.78–.92	2.6	48	2.16–2.58	1.8	46	3.95–4.85	1.4	44	6.96–8.83	1.1	45
.66–.77	2.7	46	1.79–2.15	1.9	43	3.21–3.94	1.5	40	5.50–6.95	1.2	40
.54–.65	2.8	44	1.48–1.78	2.0	40	2.60–3.20	1.6	36	4.36–5.49	1.3	35
.44–.53	2.9	42	1.21–1.47	2.1	37	2.09–2.59	1.7	32	3.45–4.35	1.4	30
.35–.43	3.0	40	.97–1.20	2.2	34	1.66–2.08	1.8	28	2.71–3.44	1.5	25
.26–.34	3.1	38	.77–.96	2.3	31	1.29–1.65	1.9	24	2.10–2.70	1.6	20
.19–.25	3.2	36	.59–.76	2.4	28	.98–1.28	2.0	20	1.59–2.09	1.7	15

Source: Reprinted by permission of the publisher and authors from A. Tellegen and P. F. Briggs, "Old Wine in New Skins: Grouping Wechsler Subtests into New Scales," *Journal of Consulting Psychology,* 1967, *31,* p. 504. Copyright 1967 by American Psychological Association.

APPENDIX E

TABLES FOR THE STANFORD-BINET INTELLIGENCE SCALE: FOURTH EDITION

Table E-1
Confidence Intervals for the Stanford-Binet Intelligence Scale: Fourth Edition

Age level	Factor and composite	Confidence level				
		68%	85%	90%	95%	99%
2 (2-0-0 through 2-11-15)	Verbal Comprehension	±4	±6	±6	±8	±10
	Nonverbal Reasoning/Visualization	±6	±8	±9	±11	±14
	Memory	—	—	—	—	—
	Composite	±4	±5	±6	±7	±9
3 (2-11-16 through 3-11-15)	Verbal Comprehension	±4	±6	±6	±7	±9
	Nonverbal Reasoning/Visualization	±4	±6	±6	±8	±10
	Memory	—	—	—	—	—
	Composite	±3	±5	±5	±6	±8
4 (3-11-16 through 4-11-15)	Verbal Comprehension	±4	±5	±6	±7	±9
	Nonverbal Reasoning/Visualization	±4	±5	±6	±7	±9
	Memory	—	—	—	—	—
	Composite	±3	±4	±5	±5	±7
5 (4-11-16 through 5-11-15)	Verbal Comprehension	±4	±5	±6	±7	±9
	Nonverbal Reasoning/Visualization	±3	±5	±5	±6	±8
	Memory	—	—	—	—	—
	Composite	±3	±4	±5	±5	±7
6 (5-11-16 through 6-11-15)	Verbal Comprehension	±5	±7	±7	±9	±12
	Nonverbal Reasoning/Visualization	±4	±6	±6	±8	±10
	Memory	—	—	—	—	—
	Composite	±3	±5	±5	±6	±8
7 (6-11-16 through 7-11-15)	Verbal Comprehension	±5	±7	±7	±9	±12
	Nonverbal Reasoning/Visualization	±4	±6	±7	±8	±11
	Memory	±6	±9	±10	±12	±15
	Composite	±3	±4	±5	±5	±7
8 (7-11-16 through 8-11-15)	Verbal Comprehension	±5	±7	±7	±9	±12
	Nonverbal Reasoning/Visualization	±4	±6	±6	±8	±10
	Memory	±5	±7	±8	±9	±12
	Composite	±3	±4	±5	±5	±7
9 (8-11-16 through 9-11-15)	Verbal Comprehension	±4	±5	±6	±7	±9
	Nonverbal Reasoning/Visualization	±4	±6	±6	±8	±10
	Memory	±5	±8	±9	±10	±14
	Composite	±3	±4	±5	±5	±7
10 (9-11-16 through 10-11-15)	Verbal Comprehension	±4	±5	±6	±7	±9
	Nonverbal Reasoning/Visualization	±3	±5	±5	±6	±8
	Memory	±5	±7	±8	±10	±13
	Composite	±2	±3	±4	±5	±6
11 (10-11-16 through 11-11-15)	Verbal Comprehension	±4	±5	±6	±7	±9
	Nonverbal Reasoning/Visualization	±3	±5	±5	±6	±8
	Memory	±4	±5	±6	±7	±9
	Composite	±2	±3	±4	±5	±6

(Continued)

Age level	Factor and composite	Confidence level				
		68%	85%	90%	95%	99%
12 (11-11-16 through 12-11-15)	Verbal Comprehension	±3	±5	±5	±6	±8
	Nonverbal Reasoning/Visualization	±3	±5	±5	±6	±8
	Memory	±5	±7	±8	±10	±13
	Composite	±2	±3	±4	±5	±6
13 (12-11-16 through 13-11-15)	Verbal Comprehension	±3	±5	±5	±6	±8
	Nonverbal Reasoning/Visualization	±3	±4	±5	±5	±7
	Memory	±5	±7	±7	±9	±12
	Composite	±2	±2	±3	±3	±4
14 (13-11-16 through 14-11-15)	Verbal Comprehension	±3	±5	±5	±6	±8
	Nonverbal Reasoning/Visualization	±3	±5	±5	±6	±8
	Memory	±5	±7	±8	±9	±12
	Composite	±2	±2	±4	±5	±6
15 (14-11-16 through 15-11-15)	Verbal Comprehension	±3	±5	±5	±6	±8
	Nonverbal Reasoning/Visualization	±3	±4	±5	±5	±7
	Memory	±5	±7	±8	±9	±12
	Composite	±2	±2	±4	±5	±6
16 (15-11-16 through 16-11-15)	Verbal Comprehension	±3	±5	±5	±6	±8
	Nonverbal Reasoning/Visualization	±3	±4	±5	±5	±7
	Memory	±5	±7	±8	±9	±12
	Composite	±2	±2	±4	±5	±6
17 (16-11-16 through 17-11-15)	Verbal Comprehension	±3	±4	±5	±5	±7
	Nonverbal Reasoning/Visualization	±3	±4	±5	±5	±7
	Memory	±4	±6	±7	±8	±11
	Composite	±2	±2	±3	±3	±4
18–23 (17-11-16 through 23-11-15)	Verbal Comprehension	±3	±4	±5	±5	±7
	Nonverbal Reasoning/Visualization	±2	±3	±4	±4	±6
	Memory	±4	±6	±6	±8	±10
	Composite	±2	±2	±3	±3	±4

Table E-1 *(Continued)*

Table E-2
Significant Differences Between Stanford-Binet Intelligence Scale: Fourth Edition Subtest Scaled Scores
(.05/.01 significance levels)

Subtest	V	C	A	VR	PA	CP	M	PF	Q	NS	EB	BM	MS	MD
C	8/10													
A	8/11	8/10												
VR	7/10	7/9	6/8											
PA	7/10	7/9	7/10	7/9										
CP	8/11	8/10	8/11	6/8	7/10									
M	8/10	8/10	8/10	7/9	7/9	8/10								
PF	7/9	7/9	7/9	6/8	6/8	7/9	6/8							
Q	8/10	8/10	8/10	7/10	7/9	8/10	7/10	7/9						
NS	8/10	8/10	8/10	7/9	7/9	8/10	7/9	6/8	7/10					
EB	7/8	7/10	7/10	7/9	7/9	6/8	7/9	6/8	7/10	7/9				
BM	8/11	8/11	8/11	7/10	7/10	8/11	8/10	7/9	8/10	8/10	7/10			
MS	8/10	7/9	8/10	7/9	7/9	8/10	7/9	6/8	7/10	7/9	7/9	8/10		
MD	9/11	8/11	8/11	8/11	8/10	9/11	8/11	8/10	8/11	8/11	8/11	9/11	8/11	
MO	10/13	10/13	10/13	9/12	9/12	10/13	10/13	9/12	10/13	10/13	9/12	10/13	10/13	10/14

Note. Abbreviations: V = Vocabulary; C = Comprehension; A = Absurdities; VR = Verbal Relations; PA = Pattern Analysis; CP = Copying; M = Matrices; PF = Paper Folding and Cutting; Q = Quantitative; NS = Number Series; EB = Equation Building; BM = Bead Memory; MS = Memory for Sentences; MD = Memory for Digits; MO = Memory for Objects.

Table E-3
Significant Differences Between Factor Scores on the Stanford-Binet Intelligence Scale: Fourth Edition
(.05/.01 significance levels)

Factor scores	Age																
	2	3	4	5	6	7	8	9	10	11	12	13	14	15	16	17	18–23
VC vs. NRV	13/18	10/14	10/13	9/12	12/15	12/16	12/15	10/14	9/12	9/12	9/12	8/11	9/12	8/11	8/11	8/10	9/12
VC vs. M	—	—	—	—	—	15/19	13/17	13/17	12/16	10/13	12/15	11/14	11/15	11/15	11/15	10/14	9/12
NRV vs. M	—	—	—	—	—	14/19	12/16	13/17	12/15	9/12	12/15	10/14	11/15	11/14	11/14	10/13	11/14

Note. Abbreviations: VC = Verbal Comprehension, NRV = Nonverbal Reasoning/Visualization, M = Memory.
See Table 14-9 (page 467) for subtests comprising each factor.

Table E-4
Differences Required for Significance When Each Stanford-Binet Intelligence Scale: Fourth Edition Subtest Scaled Score Is Compared to the Respective Mean Factor for Any Individual Child

Verbal Comprehension

Subtest	2 through 7		8 through 14		15 through 18–23	
	.05	.01	.05	.01	.05	.01
Vocabulary	6.18	7.51	5.57	6.84	5.57	6.84
Comprehension	5.74	6.99	5.18	6.37	5.18	6.37
Absurdities	6.18	7.51	5.57	6.84	—	—
Memory for Sentences	5.74	6.99	—	—	—	—
Verbal Relations	—	—	—	—	5.26	6.46

Nonverbal Reasoning/Visualization

Subtest	2 through 11		12 through 18–23	
	.05	.01	.05	.01
Pattern Analysis	5.30	6.44	5.22	6.35
Copying	6.15	7.41	—	—
Quantitative	6.02	7.33	5.95	7.24
Bead Memory	6.15	7.14	6.10	7.42
Matrices	—	—	5.50	6.69

Memory

Subtest	7		8 through 18–23	
	.05	.01	.05	.01
Memory for Sentences	—	—	5.98	7.34
Memory for Digits	5.98	7.50	6.60	8.11
Memory for Objects	5.98	7.50	7.51	9.73

Note. See the Note in Table A-6 for an explanation of how differences were obtained.

Table E-5
Estimates of the Differences Obtained by Various Percentages of the Stanford-Binet Intelligence Scale: Fourth Edition Standardization Sample Between a Particular Subtest Score and the Average Subtest Score

Verbal Comprehension Average

Subtest	2 through 7				8 through 14				15 through 18–23			
	10%	5%	2%	1%	10%	5%	2%	1%	10%	5%	2%	1%
Vocabulary	5.90	7.02	8.34	9.24	6.24	7.41	8.81	9.75	4.75	5.64	6.71	7.43
Comprehension	6.47	7.68	9.13	10.11	6.19	7.35	8.74	9.68	5.12	6.08	7.22	8.00
Absurdities	7.92	9.41	11.18	12.38	6.98	8.29	9.86	10.91	—	—	—	—
Verbal Relations	—	—	—	—	—	—	—	—	4.36	5.17	6.15	6.81
Memory for Sentences	7.92	9.41	11.18	12.38	—	—	—	—	—	—	—	—

Nonverbal Reasoning/Visualization Average

Subtest	2 through 11				12 through 18–23			
	10%	5%	2%	1%	10%	5%	2%	1%
Pattern Analysis	7.92	9.41	11.18	12.38	7.80	9.27	11.02	12.20
Copying	8.55	10.15	12.07	13.36	—	—	—	—
Quantitative	8.13	9.66	11.49	12.72	7.59	9.02	10.72	11.87
Bead Memory	8.13	9.66	11.49	12.72	7.80	9.27	11.02	12.20
Matrices	—	—	—	—	7.80	9.27	11.02	12.20

Memory Average

Subtest	2 through 6				7				8 through 18–23			
	10%	5%	2%	1%	10%	5%	2%	1%	10%	5%	2%	1%
Memory for Digits	—	—	—	—	6.98	8.29	9.86	10.91	7.34	8.72	10.37	11.48
Memory for Objects	—	—	—	—	6.98	8.29	9.86	10.91	8.45	10.04	11.93	13.21
Memory for Sentences	—	—	—	—	—	—	—	—	7.52	8.94	10.62	11.76

Note. The following formula was used to compute the estimated differences (Silverstein, 1984):

$$SD_{Da} = 8\sqrt{1 + G - 2T_a}$$

where SD_{Da} is the standard deviation of the difference for subtest a; 8 is the standard deviation of the scaled scores on each of the subtests; G is the mean of all the elements in the matrix (including the diagonal); and T_a is the mean of the elements in row or column a of the matrix (again including the diagonal). This formula is applied to the matrix of subtest intercorrelations, with 1s in the main diagonal. SD_{Da} is multiplied by the respective z value to estimate how large a difference was obtained by 10, 5, 2, or 1% of the standardization sample.

Table E-6
Estimates of the Probability of Obtaining Designated Differences Between Individual Stanford-Binet Intelligence Scale: Fourth Edition Factor Score Deviation Quotients by Chance

Verbal Comprehension vs. Nonverbal Reasoning/Visualization

Probability of obtaining given or greater discrepancy by chance	2	3	4	5	6	7	8	9	10	11	12	13	14	15	16	17	18–23
.50	4.62	3.61	3.44	3.26	4.07	4.22	4.07	3.61	3.26	3.26	3.08	2.88	3.08	2.88	2.88	2.67	3.26
.25	7.81	6.11	5.82	5.52	6.89	7.13	6.89	6.11	5.52	5.52	5.21	4.86	5.21	4.86	4.86	4.51	5.52
.20	8.76	6.85	6.53	6.19	7.73	8.00	7.73	6.85	6.19	6.19	5.84	5.46	5.84	5.46	5.46	5.06	6.19
.10	11.20	8.76	8.35	7.92	9.88	10.23	9.88	8.76	7.92	7.92	7.47	6.98	7.47	6.98	6.98	6.47	7.92
.05	13.31	10.41	9.92	9.41	11.74	12.15	11.74	10.41	9.41	9.41	8.88	8.29	8.88	8.29	8.29	7.68	9.41
.02	15.82	12.37	11.79	11.18	13.96	14.45	13.96	12.37	11.18	11.18	10.55	9.86	10.55	9.86	9.86	9.13	11.18
.01	17.52	13.70	13.05	12.38	15.45	16.00	15.45	13.70	12.38	12.38	11.69	10.91	11.69	10.91	10.91	10.11	12.38
.001	22.41	17.52	16.70	15.84	19.77	20.46	19.77	17.52	15.84	15.84	14.95	13.96	14.95	13.96	13.96	12.94	15.84

Verbal Comprehension vs. Memory

Probability of obtaining given or greater discrepancy by chance	2	3	4	5	6	7	8	9	10	11	12	13	14	15	16	17	18–23
.50	—	—	—	—	—	5.11	4.49	4.35	4.22	3.44	4.07	3.77	3.92	3.92	3.92	3.61	3.26
.25	—	—	—	—	—	8.64	7.59	7.36	7.13	5.82	6.89	6.38	6.64	6.64	6.64	6.11	5.52
.20	—	—	—	—	—	9.69	8.51	8.26	8.00	6.53	7.73	7.16	7.44	7.44	7.44	6.85	6.19
.10	—	—	—	—	—	12.39	10.89	10.56	10.23	8.35	9.88	9.16	9.52	9.52	9.52	8.76	7.92
.05	—	—	—	—	—	14.72	12.94	12.54	12.15	9.92	11.74	10.88	11.31	11.31	11.31	10.41	9.41
.02	—	—	—	—	—	17.50	15.38	14.91	14.45	11.79	13.96	12.93	13.44	13.44	13.44	12.37	11.18
.01	—	—	—	—	—	19.38	17.03	16.50	16.00	13.05	15.45	14.32	14.89	14.89	14.89	13.70	12.38
.001	—	—	—	—	—	24.78	21.78	21.12	20.46	16.70	19.77	18.32	19.04	19.04	19.04	17.52	15.84

Nonverbal Reasoning/Visualization vs. Memory

Probability of obtaining given or greater discrepancy by chance	2	3	4	5	6	7	8	9	10	11	12	13	14	15	16	17	18–23
.50	—	—	—	—	—	4.98	4.22	4.49	4.07	3.26	4.01	3.61	3.92	3.73	3.77	3.44	3.77
.25	—	—	—	—	—	8.43	7.13	7.59	6.89	5.52	6.79	6.11	6.64	6.31	6.37	5.82	6.37
.20	—	—	—	—	—	9.46	8.00	8.51	7.73	6.19	7.61	6.85	7.44	7.08	7.15	6.53	7.15
.10	—	—	—	—	—	12.09	10.23	10.89	9.88	7.92	9.74	8.76	9.52	9.06	9.14	8.35	9.14
.05	—	—	—	—	—	14.37	12.15	12.94	11.74	9.41	11.56	10.41	11.31	10.76	10.86	9.92	10.86
.02	—	—	—	—	—	17.08	14.45	15.38	13.96	11.18	13.75	12.37	13.44	12.79	12.91	11.79	12.91
.01	—	—	—	—	—	18.91	16.00	17.03	15.45	12.38	15.22	13.70	14.89	14.16	14.29	13.05	14.29
.001	—	—	—	—	—	24.19	20.46	21.78	19.77	15.84	19.47	17.52	19.04	18.12	18.28	16.70	18.28

Note. To use Table E-6, find the column appropriate to the examinee's age and locate the discrepancy that is *just less* than the discrepancy obtained by the examinee. The entry in that same row, first column, gives the probability of obtaining a given or greater discrepancy by chance. For example, the hypothesis that a 2-year-old examinee obtained a Verbal-Performance discrepancy of 18 by chance can be rejected at the .01 level of significance. Table E-6 is two-tailed. See Chapter 10, Exhibit 10-1 (page 302) for an explanation of the method used to arrive at magnitudes of difference.

Table E-7
Estimates of the Percentage of Population Obtaining Given Discrepancies Between Stanford-Binet Intelligence Scale: Fourth Edition Factor Scores

Verbal Comprehension vs. Nonverbal Reasoning/Visualization

Percentage obtaining given or greater discrepancy in either direction	2	3	4	5	6	7	8	9	10	11	12	13	14	15	16	17	18–23	Mdn	Percentage obtaining given or greater discrepancy in a specific direction
50	10.66	9.73	8.29	8.14	9.73	9.11	8.70	9.23	7.54	7.69	7.85	7.54	7.38	8.70	7.54	7.85	7.38	8.14	25
25	18.03	16.46	14.02	13.77	16.46	15.40	14.72	15.62	12.75	13.01	13.27	12.75	12.48	14.72	12.75	13.27	12.48	13.77	12.5
20	20.23	18.46	15.73	15.44	18.46	17.27	16.51	17.52	14.31	14.59	14.89	14.31	14.00	16.51	14.31	14.89	14.00	15.44	10
10	25.87	23.61	20.11	19.75	23.61	22.09	21.12	22.41	18.30	18.66	19.04	18.30	17.90	21.12	18.30	19.04	17.90	19.75	5
5	30.73	28.05	23.89	23.46	28.05	26.24	25.09	26.62	21.74	22.17	22.62	21.74	21.27	25.09	21.74	22.62	21.27	23.46	2.5
2	36.53	33.34	28.40	27.89	33.34	31.20	29.82	31.64	25.84	26.35	26.89	25.84	25.28	29.82	25.84	26.89	25.28	27.89	1
1	40.45	36.92	31.45	30.88	36.92	34.55	33.02	35.04	28.61	29.18	29.77	28.61	27.99	33.02	28.61	29.77	27.99	30.88	.5
.1	51.74	47.22	40.23	39.50	47.22	44.19	42.24	44.81	36.60	37.32	38.08	36.60	35.81	42.24	36.60	38.08	35.81	39.50	.05

Verbal Comprehension vs. Memory

Percentage obtaining given or greater discrepancy in either direction	2	3	4	5	6	7	8	9	10	11	12	13	14	15	16	17	18–23	Mdn	Percentage obtaining given or greater discrepancy in a specific direction
50	—	—	—	—	—	10.88	9.73	10.44	9.85	8.70	9.11	8.43	8.70	9.73	10.09	8.00	8.84	9.42	25
25	—	—	—	—	—	18.40	16.46	17.65	16.66	14.72	15.40	14.25	14.72	16.46	17.07	13.52	14.95	15.93	12.5
20	—	—	—	—	—	20.64	18.46	19.80	18.69	16.51	17.27	15.98	16.51	18.46	19.14	15.17	16.77	17.87	10
10	—	—	—	—	—	26.40	23.61	25.33	23.91	21.12	22.09	20.44	21.12	23.61	24.49	19.40	21.45	22.85	5
5	—	—	—	—	—	31.36	28.05	30.09	28.40	25.09	26.24	24.28	25.09	28.05	29.09	23.05	25.48	27.15	2.5
2	—	—	—	—	—	37.28	33.34	35.77	33.76	29.82	31.20	28.87	29.82	33.34	34.58	27.40	30.29	32.27	1
1	—	—	—	—	—	41.28	36.92	39.60	37.78	33.02	34.55	31.97	33.02	36.92	38.29	30.34	33.54	35.74	.5
.1	—	—	—	—	—	52.80	47.22	50.66	47.82	42.24	44.19	40.89	42.24	47.22	48.97	38.81	42.90	45.71	.05

Nonverbal Reasoning vs. Memory

Percentage obtaining given or greater discrepancy in either direction	2	3	4	5	6	7	8	9	10	11	12	13	14	15	16	17	18–23	Mdn	Percentage obtaining given or greater discrepancy in a specific direction
50	—	—	—	—	—	11.41	9.73	10.55	9.67	8.70	8.70	8.43	8.70	9.23	8.97	8.84	8.14	8.91	25
25	—	—	—	—	—	19.30	16.46	17.84	16.86	14.72	14.72	14.25	14.72	15.62	15.17	14.95	13.77	15.06	12.5
20	—	—	—	—	—	21.65	18.46	20.01	18.91	16.51	16.51	15.98	16.51	17.52	17.02	16.77	15.44	16.90	10
10	—	—	—	—	—	27.69	23.61	25.59	24.19	21.12	21.12	20.44	21.12	22.41	21.76	21.45	19.75	21.61	5
5	—	—	—	—	—	32.89	28.05	30.40	28.73	25.09	25.09	24.28	25.09	26.62	25.85	25.48	23.46	25.67	2.5
2	—	—	—	—	—	39.10	33.34	36.14	34.16	29.82	29.82	28.87	29.82	31.64	30.73	30.29	27.89	30.51	1
1	—	—	—	—	—	43.29	36.92	40.01	37.82	33.02	33.02	31.97	33.02	35.04	34.03	33.54	30.88	33.79	.5
.1	—	—	—	—	—	55.37	47.22	51.18	48.38	42.24	42.24	40.89	42.24	44.81	43.53	42.90	39.50	43.22	.05

Note. To use Table E-7, find the column appropriate to the examinee's age and locate the discrepancy obtained by the examinee. The entry in that same row, first column, gives the percentage of the standardization population obtaining discrepancies as large as or larger than the located discrepancy. For example, for a 2-year-old examinee, a Verbal Comprehension–Nonverbal Reasoning/Visualization discrepancy of 30 in either direction on the Stanford-Binet Intelligence Scale: Fourth Edition will be found in between 5 and 10% of the standardization sample. See Table B-4 for an explanation of the method used to arrive at magnitudes of difference.

Table E-8
Ranges of Standard Scores on the Stanford-Binet Intelligence Scale: Fourth Edition for Subtests, Short Forms, Factor Scores, and Composite Scores

Age

Subtests, short forms, factor scores, and composite scores	2-0-0 L	2-0-0 H	2-3-16 L	2-3-16 H	2-7-16 L	2-7-16 H	2-11-16 L	2-11-16 H	3-3-16 L	3-3-16 H	3-7-16 L	3-7-16 H	3-11-16 L	3-11-16 H	4-3-16 L	4-3-16 H	4-7-16 L	4-7-16 H	4-11-16 L	4-11-16 H	5-3-16 L	5-3-16 H	5-7-16 L	5-7-16 H	5-11-16 L	5-11-16 H	6-5-16 L	6-5-16 H	6-11-16 L	6-11-16 H
Vocabulary	42	82	40	82	38	82	35	82	33	82	32	82	30	82	29	82	28	82	28	82	27	82	26	82	25	82	24	82	23	82
Comprehension	40	82	38	82	36	82	34	82	32	82	31	82	30	82	29	82	29	82	28	82	28	82	27	v82	26	82	25	82	24	82
Absurdities	49	82	46	82	43	82	40	82	37	82	36	82	34	82	33	82	32	82	31	82	30	82	29	82	27	82	25	82	22	82
Verbal Relations	—	—	—	—	—	—	—	—	—	—	—	—	—	—	—	—	—	—	—	—	—	—	—	—	—	—	—	—	—	—
Pattern Analysis	44	82	41	82	38	82	36	82	33	82	31	82	30	82	28	82	27	82	26	82	25	82	24	82	23	82	23	82	22	82
Copying	48	82	45	82	42	82	40	82	37	82	35	82	33	82	31	82	30	82	29	82	28	82	27	82	26	82	24	80	23	77
Matrices	—	—	—	—	—	—	—	—	—	—	—	—	—	—	—	—	—	—	—	—	—	—	—	—	—	—	—	—	45	82
Paper Fold. & Cut.	—	—	—	—	—	—	—	—	—	—	—	—	—	—	—	—	—	—	—	—	—	—	—	—	—	—	—	—	—	—
Quantitative	52	82	50	82	47	82	45	82	42	82	40	82	38	82	36	82	34	82	32	82	30	82	29	82	28	82	27	82	25	82
Number Series	—	—	—	—	—	—	—	—	—	—	—	—	—	—	—	—	—	—	—	—	—	—	—	—	—	—	—	—	46	82
Equation Building	—	—	—	—	—	—	—	—	—	—	—	—	—	—	—	—	—	—	—	—	—	—	—	—	—	—	—	—	—	—
Bead Memory	53	82	50	82	46	82	43	82	39	82	36	82	34	82	31	82	30	82	29	82	28	82	27	82	26	82	25	82	24	82
Memory for Sent.	48	82	45	82	42	82	40	82	37	82	34	82	32	82	29	82	28	82	28	82	27	82	26	82	25	82	24	82	23	82
Memory for Digits	—	—	—	—	—	—	—	—	—	—	—	—	—	—	—	—	—	—	—	—	—	—	—	—	—	—	—	—	37	82
Memory for Objects	—	—	—	—	—	—	—	—	—	—	—	—	—	—	—	—	—	—	—	—	—	—	—	—	—	—	—	—	38	82
Two-Sub. S. Form	84	164	79	164	73	164	68	164	62	164	59	164	55	164	52	164	50	164	49	164	46	164	44	164	42	164	41	164	39	164
Four-Sub. S. Form	94	164	89	164	81	164	75	164	68	164	64	164	59	164	55	164	52	164	49	164	46	164	44	164	41	164	40	164	37	164
Six-Sub. S. Form	92	164	86	164	78	164	72	164	65	164	60	164	56	164	51	164	48	164	46	164	43	164	40	164	38	164	36	164	36	164
Verb. Comp.	90	164	83	164	77	164	71	164	65	164	60	164	56	164	51	164	50	164	49	164	47	164	44	164	41	164	39	164	36	164
Nonverb. Reas./Vis.	100	164	94	164	86	164	80	164	72	164	66	164	61	164	56	164	53	164	49	164	46	164	44	164	41	164	39	164	36	164
Memory	—	—	—	—	—	—	—	—	—	—	—	—	—	—	—	—	—	—	—	—	—	—	—	—	—	—	—	—	71	164
Composite—Factor	95	164	87	164	80	164	73	164	66	164	60	164	55	164	50	164	47	164	44	164	41	164	39	164	36	164	36	164	36	164
Composite—Full	95	164	87	164	80	164	73	164	66	164	60	164	55	164	50	164	47	164	44	164	41	164	39	164	36	164	36	164	43	164

(Continued)

Table E-8 (Continued)

Subtests, short forms, factor scores, and composite scores	7-5-16		7-11-16		8-5-16		8-11-16		9-5-16		9-11-16		10-5-16		10-11-16		11-11-16		12-11-16		13-11-16		14-11-16		15-11-16		16-11-16		17-11-16	
	L	H	L	H	L	H	L	H	L	H	L	H	L	H	L	H	L	H	L	H	L	H	L	H	L	H	L	H	L	H
Vocabulary	22	82	21	82	21	82	20	82	20	82	19	82	19	82	18	82	18	82	18	82	18	82	18	82	18	80	18	77	18	72
Comprehension	23	82	22	82	21	82	20	82	19	82	18	82	19	81	18	79	18	75	18	73	18	72	18	69	18	65	18	63	18	60
Absurdities	20	82	18	80	18	79	18	77	18	75	18	74	18	72	18	69	18	66	18	63	18	60	18	58	18	55	18	52	—	—
Verbal Relations	—	—	—	—	—	—	—	—	—	—	—	—	—	—	—	—	45	78	44	76	41	73	39	70	38	68	38	67	38	66
Pattern Analysis	21	81	20	79	19	77	19	74	18	71	18	68	18	66	18	64	18	63	18	61	18	59	18	57	18	57	18	57	18	57
Copying	22	74	22	73	22	71	21	69	21	67	20	64	19	62	18	59	18	57	18	55	—	—	—	—	—	—	—	—	—	—
Matrices	43	82	41	82	39	82	37	82	36	82	34	82	33	82	32	80	30	78	29	76	28	75	27	74	26	73	25	71	24	68
Paper Fold. & Cut.	—	—	—	—	—	—	—	—	—	—	—	—	—	—	—	—	47	78	45	75	43	70	42	67	41	66	40	65	40	65
Quantitative	24	82	22	82	21	82	20	82	20	82	19	82	18	82	18	82	18	78	18	76	18	75	18	74	18	71	18	69	18	66
Number Series	45	82	44	82	42	82	40	82	39	82	37	82	36	81	35	79	33	75	32	70	31	68	31	67	30	66	29	65	28	64
Equation Building	—	—	—	—	—	—	—	—	—	—	—	—	—	—	—	—	47	82	46	82	44	80	43	80	41	78	41	78	39	76
Bead Memory	23	82	22	82	21	82	20	82	19	82	18	82	18	82	18	82	18	82	18	82	18	82	18	82	18	80	18	76	18	76
Memory for Sent.	22	82	21	82	21	82	20	82	20	82	20	82	20	82	18	82	18	82	18	82	18	82	18	82	18	82	18	80	18	76
Memory for Digits	36	82	35	82	34	82	34	82	33	82	32	82	32	82	31	82	30	82	29	80	28	79	27	77	26	75	26	72	25	71
Memory for Objects	38	82	37	82	37	82	35	82	35	82	33	82	33	82	32	74	31	72	30	72	29	71	28	70	28	70	28	69	27	69
Two-Sub. S. Form	36	164	36	164	36	164	36	164	36	159	36	154	36	152	36	150	36	149	36	147	36	144	36	142	36	140	36	137	36	131
Four-Sub. S. Form	36	164	36	164	36	164	36	164	36	164	36	164	36	164	36	162	36	160	36	157	36	156	36	154	36	150	36	145	36	140
Six-Sub. S. Form	36	164	36	164	36	164	36	164	36	164	36	164	36	164	36	162	36	159	36	156	36	154	36	152	36	148	36	145	36	142
Verb. Comp.	36	164	36	164	36	164	36	164	36	164	36	164	36	164	36	161	36	155	36	152	36	149	43	154	42	148	42	143	42	136
Nonverb. Reas./Vis.	36	164	36	164	36	164	36	164	36	164	36	164	36	160	36	164	36	162	36	159	36	157	36	155	36	151	36	145	36	142
Memory	70	164	53	164	52	164	49	164	48	164	46	164	46	164	43	164	41	164	39	164	38	164	36	164	36	164	36	159	36	155
Composite—Factor	36	164	36	164	36	164	36	164	36	164	36	164	36	164	36	164	36	163	36	160	36	157	36	157	36	153	36	150	36	145
Composite—Full	39	164	37	164	36	164	36	164	36	164	36	164	36	164	36	164	38	164	37	163	36	159	38	160	37	157	36	154	36	149

Note. Standard scores for subtests are based on $M = 50$, $SD = 8$. Standard scores for short forms and composites are based on $M = 100$, $SD = 16$.

Short forms are composed of the following subtests:

2-subtest short form: Vocabulary and Pattern Analysis

4-subtest short form: Vocabulary, Pattern Analysis, Quantitative, and Bead Memory

6-subtest short form: Vocabulary, Comprehension, Pattern Analysis, Quantitative, Bead Memory, and Memory for Sentences

Composite—Factor refers to composite based on factor scores; Composite—Full refers to composite based on full battery, using nonextrapolated scores.

See Table 14-9 (page 467) for the subtests that comprise the factor scores.

Table E-9
Interpretive Rationales, Implications of High and Low Scores, and Instructional Implications for Stanford-Binet Intelligence Scale: Fourth Edition Subtests

Ability	Background factors	Possible implications of high scores	Possible implications of low scores	Instructional implications
Vocabulary				
Verbal retrieval Word finding Recall and verbal identification by recognition of familiar objects (Picture Vocabulary) Perceptions (Picture Vocabulary) Verbal comprehension Language development Learning ability Fund of information Richness of ideas Memory Concept formation Long-term memory	Language stimulation Environmental stimulation Alertness to environment Educational experiences Interests	Good word knowledge Good verbal comprehension Good verbal skills and language development Good family or cultural background Good schooling Good ability to conceptualize Intellectual striving	Poor word knowledge Poor verbal comprehension Poor verbal skills and language development Limited educational or family background Difficulty in verbalization Foreign language background Lack of encouragement of verbalization in culture	Develop working vocabulary Encourage child to discuss experiences, ask questions, and make a dictionary Use other verbal enrichment exercises, including Scrabble, analogy, and other word games
Comprehension				
Verbal comprehension Social judgment Common sense Use of practical knowledge and judgment in social situations Knowledge of conventional standards of behavior Ability to evaluate past experience Moral and ethical judgment Reasoning Ability to evaluate situations and give a pertinent response	Extensiveness of cultural opportunities Ability to evaluate and use past experience Development of conscience or moral sense	Good social judgment and common sense Ability to recognize when practical judgment and common sense are necessary Knowledge of rules of conventional behavior Good ability to organize knowledge Social maturity Ability to verbalize well Wide experience	Poor social judgment Failure to take personal responsibility (e.g., overdependency, immaturity, limited involvement with others) Overly concrete thinking Difficulty in expressing ideas verbally Creativity, which leads individual to look for unusual solutions	Help child understand social mores, customs, and societal activities, such as how other children react to things, how the government works, and how banks operate Discuss the actions of others to help children develop awareness of social relationships and what others expect of them Role-play situations, such as reporting fires, calling police, and obtaining help for plumbing problems

(Continued)

Table E-9 (Continued)

Ability	Background factors	Possible implications of high scores	Possible implications of low scores	Instructional implications
Absurdities				
Verbal comprehension Social intelligence Ability to isolate incongruities and absurdities in visual material Attention Concentration	Richness of early environment Interests Cultural opportunities	Good verbal comprehension Good ability to isolate incongruities and absurdities in visual material Good attention Good social intelligence	Poor verbal comprehension Inability to isolate incongruities and absurdities in visual material Distractibility Poor concentration Poor social intelligence	Emphasize how things are organized Focus on visual learning techniques, stressing cause-and-effect relationships
Verbal Relations				
Verbal comprehension Verbal concept formation Conceptual thinking Abstract and concrete reasoning Capacity for associative thinking Ability to separate essential from non-essential details Long-term memory Verbal reasoning Classification Flexible thinking Ability to view facts from various angles at the same time and coordinate the multiple relationships involved Ability to test and discard hypotheses Flexibility and factual knowledge Ability to discriminate on an abstract or ideational level Verbally mediated abstract thinking Receptive and expressive vocabulary General fund of information Verbal retrieval and word finding	Cognitive response style (reflective/ impulsive) Concentration Cognitive flexibility Tolerance for frustration Cultural opportunities Extent of reading Language stimulation Environmental stimulation Educational experiences Interests	Good conceptual thinking Good ability to see relationships Good ability to use logical and abstract thinking Good ability to discriminate fundamental from superficial relationships Good ability to select and verbalize appropriate relationships between two objects or concepts Flexibility of thought processes Good verbal reasoning	Poor conceptual thinking Difficulty in seeing relationships Difficulty in selecting and verbalizing appropriate relationships between two objects or concepts Overly concrete mode of thinking Rigidity of thought processes Negativism Poor verbal reasoning	Focus on recognition of differences and likeness in shapes, textures, and daily surroundings Stress language development, synonyms and antonyms, and exercises involving abstract words, classifications, and generalizations

(Continued)

Table E-9 *(Continued)*				
Ability	*Background factors*	*Possible implications of high scores*	*Possible implications of low scores*	*Instructional implications*
Pattern Analysis				
Nonverbal reasoning Visual-motor coordination Visual-spatial ability Abstract conceptualization Analysis and synthesis Visual discrimination Visual imagery Visual processing Nonverbal conceptualization	Attention Concentration Cognition style Problem-solving strategies Anxiety	Good visual-motor-spatial integration Good conceptualization Good spatial orientation in conjunction with speed, accuracy, and persistence Good analyzing and synthesizing Speed and accuracy in sizing up a problem Good eye-hand coordination Good nonverbal reasoning Good trial-and-error method	Poor visual-motor-spatial integration Visual-perceptual problems Poor spatial orientation	Use puzzles, blocks, spatial-visual tasks, perceptual tasks involving breaking down an object and building it up again, and art work with geometric forms and flannel board Focus on part-whole relationships and working with a model or key
Copying				
Visual-motor ability Eye-hand coordination Fine motor coordination Perceptual discrimination Integration of perceptual and motor processes	Motor ability Experiences	Good visual-motor ability Good eye-hand coordination Good fine motor coordination Good perceptual discrimination Good integration of perceptual and motor processes Good maturation	Poor visual-motor ability Poor eye-hand coordination Poor fine motor coordination Poor perceptual discrimination Poor integration of perceptual and motor processes Maturation delay	Use pencils and crayons to develop fine motor skills Use tracing activities with a variety of shapes and designs
Matrices				
Perceptual reasoning Analogic reasoning Attention to visual detail Concentration Simultaneous processing	Experience with part-whole relationships Willingness to respond when uncertain	Good perceptual ability Good analogic reasoning Good attention to visual detail Good concentration	Poor perceptual ability Difficulty with analogic reasoning Lack of attention to visual detail Poor concentration	Focus on part-whole relationships Develop understanding of sequencing and ordering of events Use patterns to demonstrate how component parts are related

(Continued)

Table E-9 *(Continued)*

Ability	Background factors	Possible implications of high scores	Possible implications of low scores	Instructional implications
Paper Folding and Cutting				
Perceptual organization Visualization Spatial ability Visual-spatial conceptualization Attention to visual cues	Familiarity with figures	Good visualization Good spatial orientation Good conceptualization	Poor visualization Poor spatial orientation Poor conceptualization	Develop visualization skills through use of blocks, geometric figures, and other forms Focus on analyzing how objects are viewed from various perspectives Work with paper cuttings, analyzing how forms look when unfolded
Quantitative				
Numerical reasoning Mental computation Application of basic arithmetical processes Concentration Attention Short-term memory Long-term memory Perception Understanding of mathematical concepts, symbols, and vocabulary Acquired knowledge General fund of information	Educational experiences Environmental stimulation Alertness to environment Interests Opportunities to acquire fundamental arithmetical processes	Facility in mental arithmetic Good ability to apply reasoning skills in the solution of mathematical problems Good ability to apply arithmetical skills in personal and social problem-solving situations Good concentration Good ability to focus attention Ability to engage in complex thought patterns (for upper-level items, particularly) Teacher orientation	Inadequate ability in mental arithmetic Poor concentration Distractibility Anxiety over a school-like task Blocking toward mathematical tasks Poor school achievement (perhaps associated with rebellion against authority or with cultural background) Anxiety (e.g., worry over personal problems)	Develop arithmetical skills Develop concentration skills Use concrete objects to introduce concepts Drill in basic arithmetical skills Develop interesting "real" problems to solve
Number Series				
Numerical reasoning Logical reasoning Concentration	Education Cultural opportunities	Good numerical reasoning Good logical reasoning Good concentration	Poor numerical reasoning Poor logical reasoning Poor concentration	Develop logical reasoning skills

(Continued)

Table E-9 *(Continued)*				
Ability	*Background factors*	*Possible implications of high scores*	*Possible implications of low scores*	*Instructional implications*

Equation Building

Knowledge of numbers Knowledge of conventional arithmetical operations Flexibility in rearranging and manipulating materials Numerical reasoning Logical reasoning Application of basic arithmetical processes Concentration Willingness to engage in trial and error	Education Cultural opportunities	Good knowledge of numbers Good knowledge of conventional arithmetical operations Good ability to rearrange and manipulate arithmetical materials Good numerical reasoning Good logical reasoning Good concentration	Poor knowledge of numbers Poor knowledge of conventional arithmetical operations Poor ability to rearrange and manipulate arithmetical materials Poor numerical reasoning Poor logical reasoning Poor concentration	Develop number skills Help child understand basic arithmetic operations Stress relationships between numbers Use a weighing scale to show how numbers can be equated or balanced

Bead Memory

Short-term visual memory Rote memory Form perception and discrimination Alertness to detail Ability to perceive spatial relations Attention Concentration Simultaneous processing Fluid ability Eye-hand coordination	Ability to receive stimuli passively	Good rote memory Good immediate recall Ability to attend well in a testing situation Good ability to attend to visual stimuli	Anxiety Inattention Distractibility Poor visual memory	Emphasize looking skills by showing pictures and asking child to recall details of pictures Help child learn to discriminate features of objects Ask child to arrange different geometric designs in order and then recall the order Use other memory exercises and games

Memory for Sentences

Freedom from distractibility Short-term memory Rote memory Immediate auditory memory Attention Concentration Auditory sequencing Visualization Perceptual reorganization Fluid ability	Ability to receive stimuli passively	Good rote memory Good immediate recall Ability to attend well in a testing situation Good ability to attend to auditory stimuli Good learning strategies (rehearsal, chunking/grouping)	Anxiety Inattention Distractibility A possible learning deficit Difficulty in auditory sequencing Poor learning strategies (rehearsal, chunking/grouping)	Emphasize listening skills by using sequencing activities, reading a short story and asking child to recall details, and having child follow directions Use short and simple directions and repeat when necessary Use other memory exercises and memory games

(Continued)

Table E-9 *(Continued)*

Ability	Background factors	Possible implications of high scores	Possible implications of low scores	Instructional implications
Memory for Objects				
Short-term visual memory Rote memory Immediate visual memory Alertness to detail Attention Concentration Successive processing	Ability to receive stimuli passively	Good rote memory Good immediate recall Good ability to attend to visual stimuli Ability to attend well in a testing situation	Anxiety Inattention Distractibility A possible learning deficit Difficulty in visual sequencing	Emphasize looking skills by showing pictures and asking child to recall details Help child learn to discriminate features of objects Ask child to arrange pictures in order and then recall order Use other memory exercises and games

Table E-10
Percentile Ranks for Standard Scores on Subtests of the Stanford-Binet Intelligence Scale: Fourth Edition

Standard score	Percentile rank	Standard score	Percentile rank	Standard score	Percentile rank
82	99.99	60	89	38	7
81	99.99	59	87	37	5
80	99.99	58	84	36	4
79	99.98	57	81	35	3
78	99.98	56	77	34	2
77	99.97	55	73	33	2
76	99.94	54	69	32	1
75	99.91	53	64	31	.89
74	99.87	52	60	30	.62
73	99.79	51	55	29	.44
72	99.70	50	50	28	.30
71	99.56	49	45	27	.21
70	99.38	48	40	26	.13
69	99.11	47	36	25	.09
68	99	46	31	24	.06
67	98	45	27	23	.03
66	98	44	23	22	.02
65	97	43	19	21	.02
64	96	42	16	20	.01
63	95	41	13	19	.01
62	93	40	11	18	.01
61	91	39	9		

Note. M = 50, SD = 8.

APPENDIX F

MISCELLANEOUS TABLES

Table F-1
Addresses of Test Publishers

T. M. Achenbach, University Associates in Psychiatry, 1 South
   Prospect Street, Burlington, VT 05401
(802)656-8313
FAX (802)656-2602
http://checklist.uvm.edu

American Association on Mental Retardation, 444 North Capitol
   Street, N.W., Suite 846, Washington, DC 20001-2512
(202)387-1968
(800)424-3688
FAX (202)387-2193
http://www.aamr.org

American Guidance Service, Inc., 4201 Woodland Road,
   Circle Pines, MN 55014-1796
(763)786-4343
(800)328-2560
FAX   (763)786-9077
       (800)471-8457
http://www.agsnet.com

American Orthopsychiatric Association, Inc., 330 Seventh Ave,
   18th floor, New York, NY 10001
(212)564-5930
FAX (212)564-6180
http://www.amerortho.org

Consulting Psychologist Press, Inc., 3803 East Bayshore Road,
   Palo Alto, CA 94303
(415)969-8901
(800)624-1765
FAX (415)969-8608
http://www.ccp-db.com

CTB/McGraw-Hill, 20 Ryan Ranch Road, Monterey, CA 93940
(408)393-0700
(800)538-9547
FAX (800)282-0266
http://www.ctb.com

Denver Developmental Materials, Inc., P.O. Box 20037,
   Denver, CO 80220
(303)355-4729
FAX (303)355-5622

The Devereux Foundation Press, 19 South Waterloo Road,
   Devon, PA 19333
(610)964-3000
(610)964-3090
FAX (610)964-3092
http://www.devereux.org

Modern Curriculum Press, 13900 Prospect Road,
   Cleveland, OH 44316
(201)739-8000
(800)321-3106
FAX (614)771-7360
http://www.pearsonlearning.com/mschool

PRO-ED, 8700 Shoal Creek Boulevard, Austin, TX 78757-6897
(512)451-8246
FAX (800)397-7633
http://www.proedinc.com

The Psychological Corporation, 555 Academic Court,
   San Antonio, TX 78204-2489
(800)228-0752
(210)299-1061
FAX (800)232-1223
http://www.hbtpc.com

Reitan Neuropsychological Laboratory, 2920 South Fourth
   Avenue, Tucson, AZ 85713-4819
(520)882-2022
FAX (520)884-0040

The Riverside Publishing Company, 425 Spring Lake Drive,
   Itasca, IL 60143-9921
(312)714-6194
(800)767-8378
FAX (312)693-2248
http://www.riverpub.com

Slosson Educational Publications, Inc., 140 Pine Street,
   P.O. Box 280, East Aurora, NY 14052
(716)652-0930
(800)828-4800
FAX (716)655-3840
http://www.slosson.com

Stoelting Company, 620 Wheat Lane, Wood Dale, IL 60191
(708)860-9700
FAX (708)860-9775
http://www.stoeltingco.com

Western Psychological Services, 12031 Wilshire Boulevard,
   Los Angeles, CA 90025-1251
(310)478-2061
FAX (310)478-7838
http://www.wpspublish.com

Wide Range, Inc., 15 Ashley Place, Suite 1A, P.O. Box 3410,
   Wilmington, DE 19804-2043
(302)658-4990
(800)221-9728
FAX (302)652-1644
http://www.widerange.com

INDIVIDUALIZED EDUCATION PROGRAM (IEP)

Duration of special education and related services: From ___ / ___ / ___ to ___ / ___ / ___

Student's name: _____   Date of birth: ___ / ___ / ___

School: _____   Grade: _____

I. Area of Eligibility

❏ Autistic   ❏ Mentally disabled   ❏ Specific learning disabled
❏ Behaviorally-emotionally disabled   ❏ EMD ❏ S/PMD ❏ TMD   ❏ Speech-language impaired
❏ Deaf-blind   ❏ Multihandicapped   ❏ Traumatic brain injury
❏ Hearing impaired   ❏ Orthopedically impaired   ❏ Developmentally delayed
                                          ❏ Other health impaired   ❏ Visually impaired

Additional area(s) of need:

_____

_____

II. Consideration of Special Factors

A. Student's overall strengths:

_____

_____

B. Parent's concerns, if any, for enhancing the student's education:

_____

_____

C. Special factors to be considered:

Does the student have behaviors that impede his or her learning or that of others?   ❏ Yes   ❏ No
If yes, describe the behaviors: _____

_____

Does the student have limited English proficiency?   ❏ Yes   ❏ No

If the student is blind or partially sighted, will instruction in or use of Braille be needed?   ❏ Yes   ❏ No
If no, explain: _____

_____

Does the student have any special communication needs?   ❏ Yes   ❏ No
If yes, describe the special communication needs: _____

_____

Does the student require assistive technology devices and/or services?   ❏ Yes   ❏ No
If yes, describe the devices and/or services: _____

_____

D. Other relevant factors for the student:

Does the student require adapted physical education?   ❏ Yes   ❏ No

Is the student's age 14 or older, or will the student turn 14 during the duration of this IEP?   ❏ Yes   ❏ No
If yes, transition services: ❏ Component attached   ❏ Stated in IEP

Has the student been informed of his or her own rights, if age 17 or older?   ❏ Yes   ❏ No

III. Present Level(s) of Educational Performance

Include specific descriptions of strengths and needs that relate to current academic performance, behaviors, and social/emotional development; other relevant information; and how the student's disability affects his or her involvement and progress in the general curriculum.

_____

_____

_____

(Continued)

Table F-2 *(Continued)*

IV. Goals

A. Annual goal:

_____   _____

_____

B. Benchmarks or short-term objectives:

_____

_____

C. How progress toward the annual goal will be measured:

_____

_____

V. Transition

A. By age 14: statement of transition service needs:

This statement should address desired post-school outcome(s) and focus on the student's courses of study that relate to the outcome(s).

_____

_____

B. Standard course of study the student will follow:

Is the student following the district's course of study?   ❑ Yes   ❑ No
If yes, check one of the following:
❑ Career preparation   ❑ College tech preparation   ❑ College preparation   ❑ Occupational preparation

C. By age 16: statement of needed transition services:

Service Areas	Services Needed	Agency Responsible
Instruction		
Related services		
Community experiences		
Employment/adult living skills		
If appropriate, daily living skills and functional vocational education		

Goals and objectives for transition service needs should be written in Section IV.

(Continued)

Table F-2 *(Continued)*

VI. Least Restrictive Environment (Placement)

A. Regular program participation:

Circle the regular class(es) in which the student is enrolled and activities in which the student participates and list the letters for any modifications in the blank provided.

___ Reading	___ Library	___ History	___ Foreign Language	___ Vocational
___ English	___ Music/Art	___ Science	___ Physical Education	___ Recess
___ Spelling	___ Economics	___ Health	___ Chapter I	___ Homeroom
___ Math	___ Social Studies	___ Writing	___ Remediation	___ Extracurricular Activities
___ Language Arts	___ Lunch	___ Assemblies		___ Other

Appropriate supplementary aids, services, modifications, and/or supports for school personnel, if any:

a. grading	f. read loud	l. preferential	q. interpreter/	u. student marks in book
b. modified	g. extended	seating	transliterator	v. technical assistance/
assignments	time	m. video cassette	r. demonstration	inservice
c. alternative	h. portfolio	n. Cranmer-Abacus	teaching	w. multiple test sessions
materials	i. large print	o. dictation to a	s. assistive devices	x. testing in separate
d. graphic	j. audiotapes	scribe	t. computer/	room
organizers	k. Braille/	p. magnification	typewriter/word	y. one test item per page
e. study guide	braillewriter	devices	processor	z. other: _____

Comments (if needed):

_____

For preschool child, describe how the child is involved in a regular program:

_____
_____

B. Anticipated frequency and location of services:

Type of Service	Sessions per Week	or	Month	or	Reporting Period	Amount of Time per Session	Location
Special education	___		___		___	___	_____
	___		___		___	___	_____
	___		___		___	___	_____
Related services	___		___		___	___	_____
❑ None	___		___		___	___	_____
❑ Counseling services	___		___		___	___	_____
❑ Occupational therapy	___		___		___	___	_____
❑ Physical therapy	___		___		___	___	_____
❑ Speech-language	___		___		___	___	_____
❑ Other	___		___		___	___	_____
❑ Transportation	___		___		___	___	_____

C. Continuum of alternative placements:

Check the alternative placements considered by the committee, and circle the decision reached.

School Age
❑ Regular—80% or more of the day with nondisabled peers
❑ Resource—40%–79% of the day with nondisabled peers
❑ Separate—39% or less of the day with nondisabled peers
❑ Public separate school

❑ Private separate school
❑ Public residential
❑ Private residential
❑ Home/hospital

Preschool
❑ Early childhood setting
❑ Part-time early childhood setting/part-time early childhood special education setting
❑ Early childhood special education setting
❑ Separate setting

❑ Residential setting
❑ Home
❑ Itinerant service outside the home
❑ Reverse mainstream setting

D. If the student will be removed for any part of the day (regular class, extracurricular, non-academic activities) from students without disabilities, explain why:

_____
_____
_____

Table F-2 *(Continued)*

VII. Communication with Parents

Explain how and when parents will be informed of the student's progress toward annual goals:

_____

_____

VIII. Testing

State Testing Program: ❑ Regular test administration ❑ Test administration with accommodations
Alternative Assessments: ❑ Computerized adaptive tests ❑ Alternative assessment portfolio

IX. Extended School Year Status

❑ Is not eligible for extended school year
❑ Is eligible for extended school year
❑ Eligibility is under consideration and will be determined by ___ / ___ / ___.

X. IEP Team

The following individuals were present and participated in the development and writing of the IEP.

Signature	Position	Date
	LEA Representative	
	Regular Education Teacher	
	Special Education Teacher	
	Parent	

XI. IEP Team Addendum

The following additional individuals were present and participated in the development and writing of the IEP.

Signature	Position	Date
	LEA Representative	
	Regular Education Teacher	
	Special Education Teacher	
	Parent	

XII. Reevaluation

This IEP was reviewed at reevaluation and was found to be appropriate. An annual review of this IEP will be concluded on or before ___ / ___ / ___.

Signature	Position	Date
	LEA Representative	
	Regular Education Teacher	
	Special Education Teacher	
	Parent	

Source: Adapted and reprinted with permission from *North Carolina State Forms,* Exceptional Children Division, Department of Public Instruction, July 2000.

TRANSITION PLANNING CHECKLIST

Student: _____ School: _____ Anticipated date of graduation: _____

Completed by: _____ Relationship to student: _____ Date: _____

Directions: Check each item that might help the student prepare for adult living after graduation.

Instructional Area

- ❑ Review graduation requirements and progress
- ❑ Enroll in college preparation classes
- ❑ Take PSAT
- ❑ Take SAT/ACT
- ❑ Gather college/university information
- ❑ Gather community college information
- ❑ Determine college entrance requirements
- ❑ Submit college application(s)
- ❑ Enroll in college tech-prep classes
- ❑ Enroll in vocational classes
- ❑ Refer to Vocational Rehabilitation
- ❑ Enroll in JROTC classes
- ❑ Meet with recruiter
- ❑ Take Armed Services Vocational Aptitude Battery
- ❑ Enroll in driver's education class
- ❑ Sign up for driver's training (car)
- ❑ Enroll in functional curriculum
- ❑ Learn banking/money management skills
- ❑ Learn job-seeking/interviewing skills
- ❑ Learn to read bus schedules
- ❑ Participate in social skills class(es)/groups
- ❑ Participate in communication skills class
- ❑ Participate in anger management group
- ❑ Other: _____

Employment and Adult Living Area

- ❑ Do career exploration activities
- ❑ Participate in job shadowing experiences
- ❑ Participate in job sampling experiences
- ❑ Participate in community-based training
- ❑ Participate in an internship
- ❑ Participate in an apprenticeship
- ❑ Secure on-the-job training opportunities
- ❑ Have a vocational assessment done
- ❑ Receive part-time employment assistance
- ❑ Seek competitive employment
- ❑ Submit post-school application(s)
- ❑ Interview (full-time employment)
- ❑ Enroll in a specialized vocational school
- ❑ Enter a work adjustment program
- ❑ Explore supported employment options
- ❑ Explore sheltered workshop options
- ❑ Other: _____
- ❑ Live at home
- ❑ Explore supervised living options
- ❑ Choose appropriate supervised living option
- ❑ Receive referral for residential placement
- ❑ Live independently in house/apartment
- ❑ Identify local housing options and costs
- ❑ Live in a dormitory
- ❑ Other: _____

Community Experience Area

- ❑ Visit community colleges
- ❑ Visit four-year colleges/universities
- ❑ Use public transportation
- ❑ Locate and visit public utility companies
- ❑ Locate and visit health care provider(s)
- ❑ Use public laundromats
- ❑ Participate in shopping experience(s)
- ❑ Go to DMV for driver's test
- ❑ Register for Selective Service
- ❑ Get personal ID card
- ❑ Participate in "Travel Training" experiences
- ❑ Visit banks, libraries, restaurants, etc.
- ❑ Explore community recreation activities
- ❑ Register for community recreation activity(ies)
- ❑ Participate in community support group
- ❑ Explore leisure activities
- ❑ Participate in leisure activity(ies)
- ❑ Explore hobby options
- ❑ Participate in church and/or youth group
- ❑ Other: _____

Daily Living Area

- ❑ Acquire laundry skills
- ❑ Acquire cooking skills
- ❑ Acquire household cleaning skills
- ❑ Acquire ironing skills
- ❑ Acquire household and personal safety skills
- ❑ Acquire personal budgeting skills
- ❑ Acquire bill paying skills
- ❑ Acquire personal hygiene skills
- ❑ Acquire grooming/dressing skills
- ❑ Acquire an understanding of insurances
- ❑ Acquire tax filing skills
- ❑ Understand basics of good citizenship
- ❑ Learn ways to relate to opposite sex
- ❑ Identify transportation options
- ❑ Identify available financial assistance
- ❑ Apply for financial assistance
- ❑ Explore guardianship options
- ❑ Apply for guardianship
- ❑ Explore adult service provider options
- ❑ Identify needed adult services
- ❑ Apply for adult services
- ❑ Identify medical needs
- ❑ Apply for Medicaid, SSI, etc.
- ❑ Apply for food stamps
- ❑ Receive adult case management
- ❑ Other: _____

Note. This checklist should be used in conjunction with the Individualized Education Program form in Table F-2.
Source: Adapted and reprinted with permission of Burke County Public Schools, North Carolina.

Table F-4
Triennial Review Worksheet

TRIENNIAL REVIEW WORKSHEET

Name of student: _____   Date: _____

Grade: _____   Teacher: _____

IEP team members: _____

Review Current IEP and Performance	**Circle One**		
1. Is the student meeting current goals and objectives? If no, describe the student's difficulties _____ _____	Yes	No	N/A
2. Does the student appear to be functioning at the same level that was noted in the IEP? If no, describe the change _____ _____	Yes	No	N/A
3. Are there any related services that need to go through an eligibility process? If yes, describe the services _____ _____	Yes	No	N/A
4. Will the student be making a change to a new school? If yes, describe the change _____ _____	Yes	No	N/A
5. Is the student likely to be promoted? If no, describe the reason _____ _____	Yes	No	N/A
6. Are there any problems with establishing appropriate transition services? If yes, describe the problems _____ _____	Yes	No	N/A
7. Are there any problems with understanding the student's needs? If yes, describe the problems _____ _____	Yes	No	N/A

Review Trends over Last Three Years

8. Have special education services for the student changed during the last three years? If yes, describe the changes _____ _____	Yes	No	N/A
9. Have there been any IEP goals that the student could not meet? If yes, describe the goals _____ _____	Yes	No	N/A
10. Has the student needed extensive modifications to pass courses? If yes, describe which courses and what modifications were made _____ _____	Yes	No	N/A
11. Has the student's overall academic growth been satisfactory? If no, describe the areas that have been unsatisfactory _____ _____	Yes	No	N/A

(Continued)

Table F-4 *(Continued)*			

12. Has the student been committed to schoolwork?   Yes   No   N/A
    If no, describe the reasons for poor commitment _____
    _____

Review the Most Recent Eligibility

13. At the last eligibility meeting, was the nature of the student's disability clear?   Yes   No   N/A
    If no, describe why it was unclear _____
    _____

14. At the last eligibility meeting, was there agreement about eligibility?   Yes   No   N/A
    If no, describe the disagreements _____
    _____

15. Was the eligibility decision based on the student's presumed needs instead of assessment data?   Yes   No   N/A
    If yes, describe the student's presumed needs _____
    _____

Review Assessment Components Used at Last Eligibility Meeting

16. At the last eligibility meeting, were test results supportive of the eligibility decision?   Yes   No   N/A
    If no, describe why the results were not supportive _____
    _____

17. Do the student's previous assessment findings seem accurate compared with current observations?   Yes   No   N/A
    If no, describe the inaccuracies _____
    _____

Miscellaneous

18. Does the student want to continue in special education?   Yes   No   N/A
    If no, describe why not _____
    _____

19. Does the parent want the student to continue in special education?   Yes   No   N/A
    If no, describe why not _____
    _____

20. Has the student expressed a major complaint about any educational issue?   Yes   No   N/A
    If yes, describe the complaint _____
    _____

21. Has the parent expressed a major complaint about any educational issue?   Yes   No   N/A
    If yes, describe the complaint _____
    _____

22. Does the student need to be evaluated in any areas?   Yes   No   N/A
    If yes, tell in what areas and explain the need _____
    _____

Summary of Committee's Recommendations

_____
_____
_____
_____

Source: Adapted and reprinted with permission of Martin Wilson (unpublished manuscript).

Table F-5
Norms for the Coloured Progressive Matrices

Total score	Age (in years)												
	5½ (5.03 to 5.08)	6 (5.09 to 6.02)	6½ (6.03 to 6.08)	7 (6.09 to 7.02)	7½ (7.03 to 7.08)	8 (7.09 to 8.02)	8½ (8.03 to 8.08)	9 (8.09 to 9.02)	9½ (9.03 to 9.08)	10 (9.09 to 10.02)	10½ (10.03 to 10.08)	11 (10.09 to 11.02)	11½ (11.03 to 11.09)
35							99	97	95	95	94	94	88
34						98	97	95	93	93	90	89	75
33					98	96	95	93	90	89	83	77	65
32				99	96	94	93	90	85	78	75	64	57
31				97	94	92	90	85	76	65	66	56	50
30			99	95	92	90	85	76	67	60	57	50	44
29			97	93	90	86	76	67	60	55	50	44	39
28			95	91	87	81	68	60	55	50	44	39	34
27		98	93	90	83	75	63	55	50	45	40	34	29
26		96	92	87	79	69	58	50	45	40	35	30	25
25	98	94	90	84	75	64	54	45	39	35	30	25	21
24	96	92	87	80	70	59	50	39	34	30	25	21	17
23	94	90	84	75	65	54	45	34	30	25	21	17	14
22	93	87	80	70	60	50	41	29	25	21	17	14	12
21	90	83	75	65	55	45	36	25	21	17	14	12	10
20	87	79	70	60	50	41	30	21	17	14	12	10	8
19	83	75	65	55	45	36	24	17	14	12	10	8	6
18	79	70	60	50	41	31	20	14	12	10	8	6	5
17	75	66	55	45	37	25	15	12	10	8	6	5	4
16	70	61	50	39	31	18	12	10	8	6	5	4	2
15	66	56	44	33	24	13	10	8	6	5	4	2	
14	62	50	36	24	16	10	8	6	5	4	2		
13	56	39	25	15	10	7	6	5	4	2			
12	48	26	15	10	7	5	5	4	2				
11	31	17	10	7	5	3	4	2					
10	16	10	7	5	3	1	2						
9	10	6	5	3	1								
8	6	3	3	1									
7	2	1											
6	1												

Note: These are smoothed norms for U.S. children.
Source: Reprinted with permission of the authors and publisher from J. C. Raven and B. Summers, *Manual for Raven's Progressive Matrices and Vocabulary Scales—Research Supplement No. 3*, 1986, p. 36. London: H. K. Lewis & Co.

Table F-6
Norms for the Standard Progressive Matrices

Age (in years)

Total score	6½ (6.03 to 6.08)	7 (6.09 to 7.02)	7½ (7.03 to 7.08)	8 (7.09 to 8.02)	8½ (8.03 to 8.08)	9 (8.09 to 9.02)	9½ (9.03 to 9.08)	10 (9.09 to 10.02)	10½ (10.03 to 10.08)	11 (10.09 to 11.02)	11½ (11.03 to 11.08)	12 (11.09 to 12.02)	12½ (12.03 to 12.08)	13 (12.09 to 13.02)	13½ (13.03 to 13.08)	14 (13.09 to 14.02)	14½ (14.03 to 14.08)	15 (14.09 to 15.02)	15½ (15.03 to 15.08)	16 (15.09 to 16.02)	16½ (16.03 to 16.08)
59																					99
58																				99	98
57																			99	97	95
56															99	99	99	99	97	95	90
55														99	99	98	97	97	94	93	85
54													99	97	97	96	95	95	92	90	80
53												99	97	95	95	94	93	93	90	87	75
52											99	98	96	94	93	92	92	92	86	82	70
51										99	97	96	94	92	92	90	90	90	81	75	65
50									99	98	95	94	92	90	90	86	87	87	75	69	59
49								99	97	96	94	92	90	86	86	81	82	82	68	64	54
48							99	97	96	94	92	90	86	81	81	75	75	74	63	59	50
47							98	96	94	92	90	86	81	75	75	70	68	67	58	54	46
46						99	97	94	92	90	86	81	75	70	70	65	63	62	54	50	43
45						98	96	92	90	86	81	75	70	65	65	61	58	57	50	47	39
44					99	96	94	90	87	81	75	70	65	61	61	57	54	53	46	43	35
43					98	95	92	87	83	75	70	65	61	57	57	53	50	50	42	39	31
42				99	97	94	90	83	79	70	65	61	57	53	53	50	46	46	39	36	25
41				98	95	92	87	79	75	65	61	57	53	50	50	46	42	42	35	31	18
40				97	94	90	83	75	70	61	57	53	50	46	46	42	38	39	31	25	15
39			99	96	92	87	79	70	64	57	53	50	46	43	42	38	34	35	24	18	13
38			98	94	90	83	75	66	59	53	50	46	42	39	38	34	29	31	18	15	11
37			97	92	87	79	70	61	54	50	46	42	38	35	34	30	24	24	15	13	10
36			95	90	83	75	66	57	50	46	42	38	34	31	30	24	19	17	12	12	9
35		97	93	87	79	70	61	53	46	42	37	34	30	24	24	19	16	14	11	10	8
34	99	96	91	84	75	67	57	50	43	39	33	30	25	18	19	16	13	13	10	9	7
33	98	95	89	81	71	63	53	46	40	35	29	25	20	15	15	13	11	11	9	8	6
32	97	94	87	78	68	60	50	43	37	32	25	20	16	12	12	11	10	10	8	7	6
31	96	91	85	75	65	56	46	40	34	28	21	16	14	11	11	10	9	9	7	6	5
30	95	89	82	72	61	53	43	37	31	25	18	14	12	10	9	9	8	8	6	5	4

(Continued)

885

Table F-6 (Continued)

Age (in years)

Total score	6½ (6.03 to 6.08)	7 (6.09 to 7.02)	7½ (7.03 to 7.08)	8 (7.09 to 8.02)	8½ (8.03 to 8.08)	9 (8.09 to 9.02)	9½ (9.03 to 9.08)	10 (9.09 to 10.02)	10½ (10.03 to 10.08)	11 (10.09 to 11.02)	11½ (11.03 to 11.08)	12 (11.09 to 12.02)	12½ (12.03 to 12.08)	13 (12.09 to 13.02)	13½ (13.03 to 13.08)	14 (13.09 to 14.02)	14½ (14.03 to 14.08)	15 (14.09 to 15.02)	15½ (15.03 to 15.08)	16 (15.09 to 16.02)	16½ (16.03 to 16.08)
29	93	87	78	69	58	50	40	34	28	22	15	12	11	9	8	7	6	5	5	4	2
28	91	85	75	65	56	47	37	31	25	19	14	11	10	8	7	6	5	4	4	3	1
27	89	82	71	62	53	44	34	28	22	16	12	10	9	7	6	5	4	3	2	1	
26	87	78	68	59	50	41	31	25	19	14	11	9	8	6	5	4	3	2	1		
25	85	75	65	56	47	38	28	22	17	13	10	8	7	6	4	3	2	1			
24	83	72	62	53	44	35	25	19	15	11	9	7	6	5	3	2	1				
23	81	69	59	50	42	32	22	17	13	10	8	6	6	4	2	1					
22	78	66	56	47	39	29	19	15	11	9	7	6	5	3	1						
21	75	63	53	44	36	25	17	13	10	8	6	5	4	2							
20	72	60	50	41	32	20	15	11	8	7	6	4	3	1							
19	69	57	46	38	29	17	13	10	7	6	5	3	2								
18	66	53	43	34	25	14	11	8	6	5	4	2	1								
17	62	49	39	30	20	11	10	7	5	4	3	1									
16	59	45	35	24	15	10	8	6	4	3	2										
15	55	40	30	18	13	8	7	5	3	2	1										
14	49	33	24	13	10	7	6	4	2	1											
13	39	25	18	10	8	6	5	3	1												
12	26	18	13	8	6	5	4	2													
11	18	13	10	6	5	4	3	1													
10	14	10	7	5	4	3	2														
9	10	7	5	4	3	2	1														
8	7	5	4	3	2	1															
7	5	4	3	2	1																
6	4	3	2	1																	
5	3	2	1																		
4	2	1																			
3	1																				

Note. These are smoothed norms for U.S. children.
Source: Reprinted with permission of the authors and publisher from J. C. Raven and B. Summers, *Manual for Raven's Progressive Matrices and Vocabulary Scales—Research Supplement No. 3*, 1986, p.15. London: H. K. Lewis & Co.

Table F-7
John O. Willis's and David N. Sattler's Recommendations for Web Sites for School Psychology and Clinical Psychology

Web site	Description
General Sources	
http://www.socialpsychology.org/clinical.htm	Clinical psychology resources
http://www.klis.com/chandler	Pediatric psychiatry pamphlets for various disorders
http://www.psywww.com	PsychWeb, psychology resources
http://www.psychref.com	PsychREF, psychology resources
http://www.schoolpsychology.net	School Psychology Resources Online
Assessment	
http://www.brain.com	Brain resources and home IQ test
http://www.unl.edu/Buros	Buros Institute of Mental Measurement
http://www.indiana.edu/~intell/index.html	History and theory of intelligence testing
http://www.nwrel.org/eval/index.html	Northwest Regional Ed. Lab. classroom assessment
http://www.psychassess.bizland.com/main.htm	Psychological Assessment Online
http://www.plattsburgh.edu/psyclink	PsychLink, software and other resources
Psychology	
http://www.apa.org/monitor	American Psychological Association *Monitor*
http://www.mypsychologist.com	Cognitive assessment resources by Jack Naglieri
http://www.dac.neu.edu/cp/consult	Global School Psychology Network
http://home.earthlink.net/~psychron/homepage.htm	Language acquisition resources by Ron Anderson
http://www.brainconnection.com	Information and resources about the brain
http://www.iapsych.com	Institute for Applied Psychometrics
http://www.psyched.net	PsychEd Solutions Network
http://web.univnorthco.edu/pub2/~bardos/apa.html	Psychology instruction links
http://www.hwi.com/tygger/edpsych/default.html	Review of cognitive development theories
http://alpha.fdu.edu/~dumont	School psychology resources by R. Dumont and J. Willis
http://facpub.stjohns.edu/~ortiz/spwww.html	WWW school psychology home page
Psychology and Psychiatry Organizations	
http://www.aacap.org	American Academy of Child and Adolescent Psychiatry
http://www.apa.org	American Psychological Association
http://www.psychologicalscience.org	American Psychological Society
http://www.naspweb.org	National Association of School Psychologists
http://www.indiana.edu/~div16/index.html	School Psychology (APA Division 16)
http://www.apa.org/divisions/div12	Society for Clinical Psychology (APA Division 12)
Learning Disabilities, Nonverbal Learning Disabilities, and Attention-Deficit/Hyperactivity Disorder	
http://www.allkindsofminds.org	All Kinds of Minds learning resources
http://www.eyenet.org	American Academy of Ophthalmology
http://www.asha.org	American Speech-Language-Hearing Association

(Continued)

Table F-7 *(Continued)*	
Web site	*Description*

Learning Disabilities, Nonverbal Learning Disabilities, and Attention-Deficit/Hyperactivity Disorder *(Continued)*

Web site	Description
http://familyvillage.wisc.edu/lib_capd.html	Central Auditory Processing Disorder resources
http://www.chadd.org	Children and Adults with ADHD
http://www.cogcon.com	Cognitive Concepts, Earobics for reading improvement
http://www.interdys.org	International Dyslexia Association
http://www.reading.org/contact	International Reading Association
http://www.ldanatl.org	Learning Disabilities Association of America
http://www.ldonline.org	LDOnLine
http://www.hopkins.k12.mn.us/pages/north/ld_research	Learning disabilities research and resources site
http://www.ldresources.com	Learning disabilities resources
http://www.nationalreadingpanel.org	National Reading Panel
http://www.neuropsychologycentral.com	Neuropsychology Central
http://www.nldontheweb.org	Nonverbal learning disorder resources
http://www.rfbd.org	Recording for the Blind & Dyslexic
http://www.schwablearning.org	Schwab Foundation for Learning
http://www.hood.edu/seri	Special Education Resources on the Internet

Deaf and Hard of Hearing

Web site	Description
http://www.agbell.org	Alexander Graham Bell Association
http://commtechlab.msu.edu/sites/aslweb/browser.htm	American Sign Language dictionary and instruction
http://dww.deafworldweb.org/asl	American Sign Language dictionary
http://www.deafchildren.org	American Society for Deaf Children
http://dww.deafworldweb.org/int/us	Deaf America Web
http://www.educ.kent.edu/deafed	Deaf education resources
http://gri.gallaudet.edu	Gallaudet Research Institute
http://www.nad.org	National Association of the Deaf
http://ctl.augie.edu/perry/ear/heardis.htm	Parent's guide for deaf and hearing impaired instruction
http://www.shhh.org	Self Help for Hard of Hearing People

Blindness and Visual Impairment

Web site	Description
http://www.eyenet.org	American Academy of Ophthalmology
http://www.acb.org	American Council of the Blind
http://www.nfb.org	National Federation of the Blind

Physical Disabilities

Web site	Description
http://www.ussailing.org/swsn/adaptive.htm	Adaptive recreational programs
http://www.charcot-marie-tooth.org	Charcot-Marie-Tooth Association
http://funrsc.fairfield.edu/~jfleitas/contents.html	Children with chronic illnesses resources
http://www.disabilityresource.com	Disability resources
http://www.spinewire.com	Disability resources
http://www.rarediseases.org	National Organization for Rare Disorders
http://www.spinalcord.org	National Spinal Cord Injury Association
http://www.tourette-syndrome.com	National Tourette Syndrome Association
http://www.well.com/user/sssa/sssainfo.htm	Sotos Syndrome Support Association
http://www.tash.org	TASH Disability Advocacy Worldwide
http://www.ucpa.org	United Cerebral Palsy

(Continued)

Table F-7 (Continued)

Web site	Description
Medical Information	

Web site	Description
http://www.healthfinder.gov	Dept. of Health and Human Services health resources
http://www.dbpeds.org	Developmental-Behavioral Pediatrics Online Community
http://www.mayohealth.org	Mayo Clinic medical information
http://www.medscape.com	Medscape medical resources
http://www.merck.com	Merck, link to Merck Manual of Medical Information
http://www.health.org	National Clearinghouse for Drug and Alcohol Information
http://www.nih.gov/health	National Institutes of Health information resources
http://www.nlm.nih.gov	National Library of Medicine
http://www.nlm.nih.gov/medlineplus	NIH Medline Plus health information
http://www.icondata.com/health/pedbase/index.htm	Pediatric medical database
http://www.sfirx.com	Sigler & Flanders, drug reference site
http://www.hon.ch	Health On the Net Foundation

Mental Retardation/Intellectual Challenge

Web site	Description
http://www.aamr.org	American Association on Mental Retardation
http://nads.org	National Association for Down Syndrome
http://www.thenadd.org	NADD, for both mental illness and mental retardation
http://www.psychiatry.com	Psychiatry information and resources
http://www.thearc.org	The Arc, mental retardation and related disabilities

Emotional, Behavioral, Obsessive-Compulsive Disorders

Web site	Description
http://www.counseling.org	American Counseling Association
http://www.counselorlink.com	Counseling links
http://cecp.air.org/fba/default.htm	Functional behavior assessment
http://www.air-dc.org/cecp/guide/default.htm	Guide to safe schools
http://mfba.duq.edu	Multimodal functional behavioral assessment
http://ocfoundation.org	Obsessive-Compulsive Foundation
http://www.pbis.org	Positive Behavioral Interventions & Supports

Autism and Pervasive Developmental Disorders

Web site	Description
http://www.hyperlexia.org	American Hyperlexia Association
http://www.udel.edu/bkirby/asperger	Asperger Syndrome resources
http://www.autismndi.com	Autism Network for Dietary Intervention
http://www.autism-society.org	Autism Society of America
http://www.autism.org	Center for the Study of Autism
http://www.health.state.ny.us/nysdoh/eip/autism/index.htm	Clinical practice guidelines for autism, NY Dept. of Health
http://info.med.yale.edu/chldstdy/autism/index.html	Developmental Disabilities Clinic, Yale Child Study Center
http://www.lovaas.com	Lovaas Institute for Early Intervention, Autism resources
http://www.albany.edu/psy/autism/autism.html	New York Autism Network
http://people.sca.uqam.ca/~sqa/sqa_home_e.html	Quebec Society for Autism and Developmental Disorders
http://www.unc.edu/depts/teacch	Treatment and education of children with autism

(Continued)

Table F-7 *(Continued)*

Web site	Description
Law and Government	
http://www.usdoj.gov/crt/ada/adahom1.htm	Americans with Disabilities Act
http://www.access.gpo.gov/nara/cfr	Code of Federal Regulations
http://ericae.net	Educational Resources Information Center
http://www.ed.gov/pubs/socialpromotion	Ending social promotion, U.S. Dept. of Education
http://ocfo.ed.gov/fedreg/finrule.htm	Federal Register, Final Regulations
http://www.protectionandadvocacy.com/not99nap.htm	IDEA's Parental Notice Requirement
http://www.ideapractices.org	IDEA practices by IDEA Partnerships
http://www.ed.gov/offices/OSERS/IDEA	IDEA '97, U.S. Department of Education
http://www.ed.gov/pubs/offices/OSERS/IDEA/regs.html	IDEA '97 regulations
http://www.dssc.org/frc	Federal Resource Center for Special Education
http://findlaw.com	Legal reference search engine
htt://lrp.com	Legal resources, LRP Publications
http://nces.ed.gov/surveys	National Center for Education Statistics
http://www.nichcy.org	National Information Center for Children with Disabilities
http://www.dhhs.gov/progorg/ocr/ocrhmpg.html	Office for Civil Rights
http://mhnet.org/law/index.html	Psychiatry and law resources
http://www.ldonline.org/ld_indepth/legal_legislative/ edlaw504.html	Section 504, Perry Zirkel commentary
http://www.ed.gov/offices/OCR/placpub.html]	Section 504, OCR information
http://www.ed.gov/offices/OCR/hq5269.html	Section 504, OCR information
http://nces.ed.gov/pubs98/condition98/c9845a01.html	Special education demographic information
http://www.wrightslaw.com/subscribe.htm	Special education law and advocacy resources
http://www.edlaw.net	Special education laws and regulations
http://www.census.gov	U.S. Census Bureau
http://www.ed.gov	U.S. Department of Education
http://www.usdoj.gov	U.S. Department of Justice
Special Education Organizations	
http://www.cec.sped.org	Council for Exceptional Children
http://www.edc.org/collaborative	Urban Special Education Leadership Collaborative

Table F-8
Percentile Ranks for Standard Scores with a Mean of 50 and Standard Deviation of 10 or 15

Standard score	SD 10	SD 15	Standard score	SD 10	SD 15	Standard score	SD 10	SD 15	Standard score	SD 10	SD 15
95	99.99	99.87	72	99	93	49	46	47	26	1	5
94	99.99	99.83	71	98	92	48	42	45	25	1	5
93	99.99	99.79	70	98	91	47	38	42	24	.47	4
92	99.99	99.74	69	97	90	46	34	39	23	.35	4
91	99.99	99.69	68	96	88	45	31	37	22	.26	3
90	99.99	99.62	67	96	87	44	27	34	21	.19	3
89	99.99	99.53	66	95	86	43	24	32	20	.13	2
88	99.99	99	65	93	84	42	21	30	19	.10	2
87	99.99	99	64	92	82	41	18	27	18	.07	2
86	99.98	99	63	90	81	40	16	25	17	.05	1
85	99.98	99	62	88	79	39	14	23	16	.03	1
84	99.97	99	61	86	77	38	12	21	15	.02	1
83	99.95	99	60	84	75	37	10	19	14	.02	1
82	99.93	98	59	82	73	36	8	18	13	.01	1
81	99.90	98	58	79	70	35	7	16	12	.01	1
80	99.87	98	57	76	68	34	5	14	11	—	.47
79	99.81	97	56	73	66	33	4	13	10	—	.38
78	99.74	97	55	69	63	32	4	12	9	—	.31
77	99.65	96	54	66	61	31	3	10	8	—	.26
76	99.53	96	53	62	58	30	2	9	7	—	.21
75	99	95	52	58	55	29	2	8	6	—	.17
74	99	95	51	54	53	28	1	7	5	—	.13
73	99	94	50	50	50	27	1	6			

REFERENCES

Ablard, K. E., & Mills, C. J. (1996). Evaluating abridged versions of the Raven's Advanced Progressive Matrices for identifying students with academic talent. *Journal of Psychoeducational Assessment, 14,* 54–64.

Achenbach, T. M., & Edelbrock, C. S. (1989). Diagnostic, taxonomic, and assessment issues. In T. H. Ollendick & M. Hersen (Eds.), *Handbook of child psychopathology* (pp. 53–73). New York: Plenum.

Ackerman, P. T., & Dykman, R. A. (1995). Reading-disabled students with and without comorbid arithmetic disability. *Developmental Neuropsychology, 11,* 351–371.

Ackerman, P. T., Weir, N. L., Holloway, C. A., & Dykman, R. A. (1995). Adolescents earlier diagnosed as dyslexic show major IQ declines on the WISC–III. *Reading and Writing: An Interdisciplinary Journal, 7,* 163–170.

Adams, R. L., & Rankin, E. J. (1996). A practical guide to forensic neuropsychological evaluations and testimony. In R. L. Adams, O. A. Parsons, J. L. Culbertson, & S. J. Nixon (Eds.), *Neuropsychology for clinical practice: Etiology, assessment, and treatment of common neurological disorders* (pp. 455–487). Washington, DC: American Psychological Association.

AERA, APA, & NCME. (1999). *Standards for educational and psychological testing.* Washington, DC: American Educational Research Association.

Albert, M. L., Goodglass, H., Helm, N. A., Rubens, A. B., & Alexander, M. P. (1981). *Clinical aspects of dysphasia.* New York: Springer-Verlag.

Albertsons v. Kirkingburg, 119 S. Ct. 2162 (1999), LEXIS 4369.

Alderton, D. L., & Larson, G. E. (1990). Dimensionality of Raven's Advanced Progressive Matrices items. *Educational & Psychological Measurement, 50,* 887–900.

Alfonso, V. C., Johnson, A., Patinella, L., & Rader, D. E. (1998). Common WISC–III examiner errors: Evidence from graduate students in training. *Psychology in the Schools, 35,* 119–125.

Allen, M. J., & Yen, W. M. (1979). *Introduction to measurement theory.* Monterey, CA: Brooks/Cole.

American Prosecutors Research Institute. (1993). *Investigation and prosecution of child abuse* (2nd ed.). Alexandria, VA: Author.

American Psychiatric Association. (1994). *Diagnostic and statistical manual of mental disorders* (4th ed.). Washington, DC: Author.

American Psychological Association. (1990). *Guidelines for providers of psychological services to ethnic, linguistic, and culturally diverse populations.* Washington, DC: Author.

American Psychological Association. (1994a). *Guidelines for child custody evaluations in divorce proceedings.* Washington, DC: Author.

American Psychological Association. (1994b). *Publication manual of the American Psychological Association* (4th ed.). Washington, DC: Author.

American Psychological Association. (1998, February). *Guidelines for psychological evaluations in child protection matters.* Washington, DC: Author.

Anastasi, A. (1986). Intelligence as a quality of behavior. In R. J. Sternberg & D. K. Detterman (Eds.), *What is intelligence?* (pp. 19–21). Norwood, NJ: Ablex.

Anastasi, A. (1989). Ability testing in the 1980's and beyond: Some major trends. *Public Personnel Management, 18,* 471–485.

Anastasi, A. (1992). What counselors should know about the use and interpretation of psychological tests. *Journal of Counseling & Development, 70,* 610–615.

Andre, J. (1976). Bicultural socialization and the measurement of intelligence. *Dissertation Abstracts International, 36,* 3675D–3676B. (University Microfilms No. 75–29, 904)

Andress v. Cleveland Independent School District, 64 F.3d 176 (5th Cir. 1995), LEXIS 24373.

Andrews, J. V. (1998). Review of the Diagnostic Achievement Test for Adolescents, Second Edition. In J. C. Impara & B. S. Plake (Eds.), *The thirteenth mental measurements yearbook.* Lincoln: University of Nebraska Press.

Armstrong, T. (1994). *Multiple intelligences in the classroom.* Alexandria, VA: Association for Supervision and Curriculum Development.

Arthur, W., & Woehr, D. J. (1993). A confirmatory factor analytic study examining the dimensionality of the Raven's Advanced Progressive Matrices. *Educational & Psychological Measurement, 53,* 471–478.

Atakan, Z., & Cooper, J. E. (1989). Behavioural Observation Schedule (BOS), PIRS 2nd edition: A revised edition of the PIRS (WHO, Geneva, March 1978). *British Journal of Psychiatry, 155,* 78–80.

Atkinson, L. (1991). Short forms of the Stanford-Binet Intelligence Scale, Fourth Edition, for children with low intelligence. *Journal of School Psychology, 29,* 177–182.

Atkinson, L., Bevc, I., Dickens, S., & Blackwell, J. (1992). Concurrent validities of the Stanford-Binet (Fourth Edition), Leiter, and Vineland with developmentally delayed children. *Journal of School Psychology, 30,* 165–173.

Ausubel, D. P., Novak, J. D., & Hanesian, H. (1978). *Educational psychology: A cognitive view* (2nd ed.). New York: Holt, Rinehart and Winston.

Axelrod, B. N., Ryan, J. J., & Ward, L. C. (2001). Evaluation of the seven-subtest short forms of the Wechsler Adult Intelligence Scale–III in a clinical sample. *Archives of Clinical Neuropsychology, 16,* (page numbers not available).

Ayres, R. R., & Cooley, E. J. (1986). Sequential versus simultaneous processing on the K-ABC: Validity in predicting learning success. *Journal of Psychoeducational Assessment, 4,* 211–220.

Babicz v. The School Board of Broward County, 135 F.3d 1420 (11th Cir. 1998), LEXIS 3120.

Baddeley, A. (1990). *Human memory: Theory and practice.* London: Erlbaum.

Bannatyne, A. (1974). Diagnosis: A note on recategorization of the WISC scaled scores. *Journal of Learning Disabilities, 7,* 272–274.

Bates, J. D. (1985). *Writing with precision* (rev. ed.). Washington, DC: Acropolis Books.

Bat-Haee, M. A., Mehyrar, A. H., & Sabharwal, V. (1972). The correlation between Piaget's conservation of quantity tasks and three measures of intelligence in a select group of children in Iran. *Journal of Psychology, 80,* 197–201.

Bayley, N. (1993). *Bayley Scales of Infant Development* (2nd ed.). San Antonio: The Psychological Corporation.

Beal, A. L. (1995). A comparison of WISC–III and OLSAT–6 for the identification of gifted students. *Canadian Journal of School Psychology, 11,* 120–129.

Beal, A. L., Dumont, R., Branche, A. H., & Cruse, C. L. (1996). Practical implications of differences between the American and Canadian norms for WISC–III and a short form for children with learning disabilities. *Canadian Journal of School Psychology, 12,* 7–14.

Beebe, D. W., Pfiffner, L. J., & McBurnett, K. (2000). Evaluation of the validity of the Wechsler Intelligence Scale for Children–Third Edition Comprehension and Picture Arrangement subtests as measures of social intelligence. *Psychological Assessment, 12,* 97–101.

Bellack, A. S., & Hersen, M. (1980). *Introduction to clinical psychology.* New York: Oxford University Press.

Bennett, R. E. (1982). The use of grade and age equivalent scores in educational assessment. *Diagnostique, 7,* 139–146.

Bergan, J. R., & Parra, E. B. (1979). Variations in IQ testing and instruction and the letter learning and achievement of Anglo and bilingual Mexican-American children. *Journal of Educational Psychology, 71,* 819–826.

Berk, R. A. (1981). What's wrong with using grade-equivalent scores to identify LD children? *Academic Therapy, 17,* 133–140.

Berk, R. A. (1984). *Screening and diagnosis of children with learning disabilities.* Springfield, IL: Charles C Thomas.

Bernal, E. M., Jr. (1972, February). *Assessing assessment instruments: A Chicano perspective.* Paper prepared for the Regional Training Program to Serve the Bilingual/Bicultural Exceptional Child, Montal Educational Associates, Sacramento, CA.

Betancourt, H., & López, S. R. (1993). The study of culture, ethnicity, and race in American psychology. *American Psychologist, 48,* 629–637.

Bialystok, E. (1992). Selective attention in cognitive processing: The bilingual edge. In R. J. Harris (Ed.), *Cognitive processing in bilinguals* (pp. 501–513). Amsterdam, Netherlands: North-Holland.

Bickley, P. G., Keith, T. Z., & Wolfle, L. M. (1995). The three-stratum theory of cognitive abilities: Test of the structure of intelligence across the life span. *Intelligence, 20,* 309–328.

Binet, A., & Simon, T. (1905). Méthodes nouvelles pour le diagnostic du niveau intellectuel des anormaux. *L'Année Psychologique, 11,* 191–244.

Binet, A., & Simon, T. (1916). *The development of intelligence in children* (E. S. Kit, Trans.). Baltimore: Williams & Wilkins.

Bissette, D. C. (1987). *Area score patterning of the Stanford-Binet (4th Edition) with trainable mentally retarded students.* Unpublished manuscript, Biola University at La Mirada, CA.

Black, M. M., & Matula, K. (2000). *Essentials of Bayley Scales of Infant Development–II assessment.* New York: Wiley.

Blaha, J., & Wallbrown, F. H. (1996). Hierarchical factor structure of the Wechsler Intelligence Scale for Children–III. *Psychological Assessment, 8,* 214–218.

Blakeslee, D. E. (1987). *Psychometric properties, subtest patterning and concurrent validity of the Stanford-Binet Intelligence Scale, Fourth Edition with emotionally disturbed children (public school setting).* Unpublished doctoral dissertation, Biola University, La Mirada, CA.

Blatt, S. J., & Allison, J. (1968). The intelligence test in personality assessment. In A. I. Rabin (Ed.), *Projective techniques in personality assessment* (pp. 421–460). New York: Springer.

Bloch, B. (1983). Bloch's assessment guide for ethnic/cultural variations. In M. S. Orque, B. Bloch, & L. S. A. Monrroy (Eds.), *Ethnic nursing care: A multicultural approach* (pp. 49–75). St. Louis: Mosby.

Bloom, L. A., Hursh, D., Wienke, W. D., & Wolf, R. K. (1992). The effects of computer assisted data collection on students' behavior. *Behavioral Assessment, 14,* 173–190.

Board of Education of Montgomery County v. Brett Y, 155 F.3d 557 (4th Cir. 1998), LEXIS 27378.

Board of Education v. Rowley, 458 U.S. 176 (1982), LEXIS 10.

Boehm, A. E. (1986a). *Boehm Test of Basic Concepts–Preschool Version.* San Antonio: The Psychological Corporation.

Boehm, A. E. (1986b). *Boehm Test of Basic Concepts–Revised.* San Antonio: The Psychological Corporation.

Bolen, L. M. (1998). WISC–III score changes for EMH students. *Psychology in the Schools, 35,* 327–332.

Bolen, L. M., Aichinger, K. S., Hall, C. W., & Webster, R. E. (1995). A comparison of the performance of cognitively disabled children on the WISC–R and WISC–III. *Journal of Clinical Psychology, 51,* 89–94.

Boll, T. J. (1987). The role of neuropsychology in the general practice of child and adolescent psychology. *Journal of Child & Adolescent Psychotherapy, 4,* 13–18.

Boring, E. G. (1950). *A history of experimental psychology* (2nd ed.). New York: Appleton-Century-Crofts.

Borkowski, J. G. (1985). Signs of intelligence: Strategy generalization and metacognition. In S. R. Yussen (Ed.), *The growth of reflection in children* (pp. 105–144). Orlando: Academic Press.

Borkowski, J. G., & Burke, J. E. (1996). Theories, models, and measurements of executive functioning: An information processing perpective. In G. R. Lyon & N. A. Krasnegor (Eds.), *Attention, memory and executive function* (pp. 235–261). Baltimore: Paul H. Brookes.

Bossard, M. D., Reynolds, C. R., & Gutkin, T. B. (1980). A regression analysis of test bias on the Stanford-Binet Intelligence Scale. *Journal of Clinical Child Psychology, 9,* 52–54.

Bouchard, T. J., Jr. (1984). [Review of *Frames of the mind: The theory of multiple intelligence*]. *American Journal of Orthopsychiatry, 54,* 506–508.

Bouchard, T. J., Jr., & McGue, M. (1981). Familial studies of intelligence: A review. *Science, 212,* 1055–1058.

Bouchard, T. J., Jr., & Segal, N. L. (1985). Environment and IQ. In B. B. Wolman (Ed.), *Handbook of intelligence: Theories, measurements, and applications* (pp. 391–464). New York: Wiley.

Boyle, G. J. (1990). Stanford-Binet IV Intelligence Scale: Is its structure supported by LISREL congeneric factor analyses? *Personality and Individual Differences, 11,* 1175–1181.

Bracken, B. A. (1987). Limitations of preschool instruments and standards for minimal levels of technical adequacy. *Journal of Psychoeducational Assessment, 5,* 313–326.

Bracken, B. A. (1988). Ten psychometric reasons why similar tests produce dissimilar results. *Journal of School Psychology, 26,* 155–166.

Bracken, B. A. (1994). Advocating for effective preschool assessment practices: A comment on Bagnato and Neisworth. *School Psychology Quarterly, 9,* 103–108.

Bracken, B. A. (1998). *Bracken Basic Concept Scale–Revised.* San Antonio: The Psychological Corporation.

Bracken, B. A., & McCallum, R. S. (1998). *Universal Nonverbal Intelligence Test.* Itasca, IL: Riverside Publishing.

Bretherton, I. (1993). Theoretical contributions from developmental psychology. In P. G. Boss, W. J. Doherty, R. LaRossa, W. R. Schumm, & S. K. Steinmetz (Eds.), *Sourcebook of family theories and methods: A contextual approach* (pp. 275–297). New York: Plenum.

Brodsky, S. (1991). *Testifying in court: Guidelines and maxims for the expert witness.* Washington, DC: American Psychological Association.

Brody, N. (1992). *Intelligence* (2nd ed.). San Diego: Academic Press.

Brody, N. (1997). Malleability and change in intelligence. In H. Nyborg (Ed.), *The scientific study of human nature: Tribute to Hans J. Eysenck at eighty* (pp. 311–330). Oxford, England: Pergamon.

Broman, S. H., & Nichols, P. L. (1975, September). *Early mental development, social class, and school-age IQ.* Paper presented at the meeting of the American Psychological Association, Chicago, IL.

Brooks, R. (1979). Psychoeducational assessment: A broader perspective. *Professional Psychology, 10,* 708–722.

Brooks-Gunn, J., & Lewis, M. (1983). Screening and diagnosing handicapped infants. *Topics in Early Childhood Special Education, 3,* 14–28.

Brophy, J. E. (1983). Research on the self-fulfilling prophecy and teacher expectations. *Journal of Educational Psychology, 75,* 631–661.

Brophy, J. E., & Good, T. L. (1970). Teachers' communication of differential expectations for children's classroom performance: Some behavioral data. *Journal of Educational Psychology, 61,* 365–374.

Brown, A. L., & French, L. A. (1979). The zone of potential development: Implications for intelligence testing in the year 2000. *Intelligence, 3,* 255–273.

Brown, L., Sherbenou, R. J., & Johnsen, S. K. (1997). *Test of Nonverbal Intelligence–Third Edition.* Austin, TX: Pro-Ed.

Brown, T. L., & Morgan, S. B. (1991). Concurrent validity of the Stanford-Binet, 4th Edition: Agreement with the WISC-R in classifying learning disabled children. *Psychological Assessment, 3,* 247–253.

Brown, V. L., Cronin, M., & McEntire, E. (1994). *Test of Mathematical Abilities–Second Edition.* Austin, TX: Pro-Ed.

Brown, V. L., Hammill, D. D., & Wiederholt, J. L. (1995). *Test of Reading Comprehension–Third Edition.* Austin, TX: Pro-Ed.

Bryant, B. R., & Wiederholt, J. L. (1991). *Gray Oral Reading Test–Diagnostic.* Austin, TX: Pro-Ed.

Burke, H. R. (1958). Raven's Progressive Matrices: A review and critical evaluation. *Journal of Genetic Psychology, 93,* 199–228.

Burke County Public Schools. (undated). *Transitional planning checklist.* Raleigh, NC: Author.

Burlington v. Massachusetts Department of Education, 471 U.S. 359 (1996), LEXIS 6.

Camilli, G. (1993). The case against item bias detection techniques based on internal criteria: Do item bias procedures obscure test fairness issues? In P. W. Holland & H. Wainer (Eds.), *Differential item functioning* (pp. 397–437). Hillsdale, NJ: Erlbaum.

Campbell, J. M. (1998). Internal and external validity of seven Wechsler Intelligence Scale for Children–Third Edition short forms in a sample of psychiatric inpatients. *Psychological Assessment, 10,* 431–434.

Campbell, S. B. (1989). Developmental perspectives. In T. H. Ollendick & M. Hersen (Eds.), *Handbook of child psychopathology* (pp. 5–28). New York: Plenum.

Campione, J. C., & Brown, A. L. (1978). Toward a theory of intelligence: Contributions from research with retarded children. *Intelligence, 2,* 279–304.

Canivez, G. L. (1995). Validity of the Kaufman Brief Intelligence Test: Comparisons with the Wechsler Intelligence Scale for Children–Third Edition. *Assessment, 2,* 101–111.

Canivez, G. L. (1996). Validity and diagnostic efficiency of the Kaufman Brief Intelligence Test in reevaluating students with learning disability. *Journal of Psychoeducational Assessment, 14,* 4–19.

Canivez, G. L., & Watkins, M. W. (1998). Long-term stability of the Wechsler Intelligence Scale for Children–Third Edition. *Psychological Assessment, 10,* 285–291.

Canivez, G. L., & Watkins, M. W. (1999). Long-term stability of the Wechsler Intelligence Scale for Children–Third Edition among demographic subgroups: Gender, race/ethnicity, and age. *Journal of Psychoeducational Assessment, 17,* 300–313.

Carlisle Area School v. Scott P., 62 F.3d 520 (3rd Cir. 1995), LEXIS 21415.

Carlson, J. S., & Jensen, C. M. (1980). The factorial structure of the Raven Coloured Progressive Matrices Test: A reanalysis. *Educational and Psychological Measurement, 40,* 1111–1116.

Carroll, J. B. (1993a). *Human cognitive abilities: A survey of factor-analytic studies.* New York: Cambridge University Press.

Carroll, J. B. (1993b). What abilities are measured by the WISC-III? *Monograph Series of the Journal of Psychoeducational Assessment, Wechsler Intelligence Scale for Children: Third Edition,* 134–143.

Carroll, J. B. (1995). [Review of the book *Assessment of cognitive processes: The PASS theory of intelligence*]. *Journal of Psychoeducational Assessment, 13,* 397–409.

Carroll, J. B. (1997a). Commentary on Keith and Witta's hierarchical and cross-age confirmatory factor analysis of the WISC-III. *School Psychology Quarterly, 12,* 108–109.

Carroll, J. B. (1997b). Psychometrics, intelligence, and public perception. *Intelligence, 24,* 25–52.

Carroll, J. B. (1997c). The three-stratum theory of cognitive abilities. In D. P. Flanagan, J. L. Genshaft, & P. L. Harrison (Eds.), *Contemporary intellectual assessment: Theories, tests, and issues* (pp. 122–130). New York: Guilford.

Carroll, J. B., & Horn, J. L. (1981). On the scientific basis of ability testing. *American Psychologist, 36,* 1012–1020.

Carrow-Woolfolk, E. (1995). *Oral and Written Language Scales.* Circle Pines, MN: American Guidance Service.

Carrow-Woolfolk, E. (1999a). *Comprehensive Assessment of Spoken Language.* Circle Pines, MN: American Guidance Service.

Carrow-Woolfolk, E. (1999b). *Test of Auditory Comprehension of Language–Third Edition.* Austin, TX: Pro-Ed.

Carter, R. B. (1977). A study of attitudes: Mexican American and Anglo American elementary teachers' judgments of Mexican American bilingual children's speech. *Dissertation Abstracts International, 37,* 4941A–4942A. (University Microfilms No. 77–1502)

Caruso, J. C., & Cliff, N. (1999). The properties of equally and differentially weighted WAIS–III factor scores. *Psychological Assessment, 11,* 198–206.

Carvajal, H. H., & Gerber, J. (1987). 1986 Stanford-Binet abbreviated forms. *Psychological Reports, 61,* 285–286.

Carvajal, H. H., Gerber, J., Hewes, P., & Weaver, K. A. (1987). Correlations between scores on Stanford-Binet IV and Wechsler Adult Intelligence Scale–Revised. *Psychological Reports, 61,* 83–86.

Carvajal, H. H., Gerber, J., & Smith, P. D. (1987). Relationship between scores of young adults on Stanford-Binet IV and Peabody Picture Vocabulary Test–Revised. *Perceptual and Motor Skills, 65,* 721–722.

Carvajal, H. H., Hardy, K. M., Harmon, K., Seller, T. A., & Holmes, C. B. (1987). Relationship among scores on the Stanford-Binet IV, Peabody Picture Vocabulary Test–Revised, and Columbia Mental Maturity Scale. *Bulletin of the Psychonomic Society, 25,* 275–276.

Carvajal, H. H., Hardy, K. M., Smith, K. L., & Weaver, K. A. (1988). Relationships between scores on Stanford-Binet IV and Wechsler Preschool and Primary Scale of Intelligence. *Psychology in the Schools, 25,* 129–131.

Carvajal, H. H., Hayes, J. E., Lackey, K. L., Rathke, M. L., Wiebe, D. A., & Weaver, K. A. (1993). Correlations between scores on the Wechsler Intelligence Scale for Children–III and the General Purpose Abbreviated Battery of the Stanford-Binet IV. *Psychological Reports, 72,* 1167–1170.

Carvajal, H. H., Hayes, J. E., Miller, H. R., Holly, R., Wiebe, D. A., & Weaver, K. A. (1993). Comparisons of the vocabulary scores and IQs on the Wechsler Intelligence Scale for Children–III and the Peabody Picture Vocabulary Test–Revised. *Perceptual and Motor Skills, 76,* 28–30.

Carvajal, H. H., Karr, S. K., Hardy, K. M., & Palmer, B. L. (1988). Relationships between scores on Stanford-Binet IV and scores on McCarthy Scales of Children's Abilities. *Bulletin of the Psychonomic Society, 26,* 349.

Carvajal, H., & McKnab, P. (1990). Relationships between scores of gifted students on Stanford-Binet IV and the SRA Educational Ability Series. *Gifted Child Quarterly, 34,* 80–82.

Carvajal, H. H., McKnab, P., Gerber, J., Hewes P., & Smith, K. L. (1989). Counseling college-bound students: Can ACT scores be predicted? *School Counselor, 36,* 186–191.

Carvajal, H. H., McVey, S., Sellers, T., Weyand, K., & McKnab, P. (1987). Relationships between scores on the General Purpose Abbreviated Battery of Stanford-Binet IV, Peabody Picture Vocabulary Test–Revised, Columbia Mental Maturity Scale, and Goodenough-Harris Drawing Test. *Psychological Record, 37,* 127–130.

Carvajal, H. H., Parks, C. S., Parks, J. P., Logan, R. A., & Page, G. L. (1993). A concurrent validity study of the Wechsler Preschool and Primary Scale of Intelligence–Revised and Columbia Mental Maturity Scale. *Bulletin of the Psychonomic Society, 31,* 33–34.

Carvajal, H. H., Parks, J. P., Bays, K. J., Logan, R. A., Lujano, C. I., Page, G. L., & Weaver, K. A. (1991). Relationships between scores on Wechsler Preschool and Primary Scale of Intelligence–Revised and Stanford-Binet IV. *Psychological Reports, 69,* 23–26.

Carvajal, H. H., Parks, J. P., Logan, R. A., & Page, G. L. (1992). Comparisons of the IQ and vocabulary scores on Wechsler Preschool and Primary Scale of Intelligence–Revised and Peabody Picture Vocabulary Test–Revised. *Psychology in the Schools, 29,* 22–24.

Carvajal, H. H., & Weyand, K. (1986). Relationships between scores on Stanford-Binet IV and Weschler Intelligence Scale for Children–Revised. *Psychological Reports, 59,* 963–966.

Cattell, R. B. (1963). Theory of fluid and crystalized intelligence: A critical experiment. *Journal of Educational Psychology, 54,* 1–22.

Ceci, S. J. (1991). How much does schooling influence general intelligence and its cognitive components? A reassessment of the evidence. *Developmental Psychology, 27,* 703–722.

Ceci, S. J., Rosenblum, T., de Bruyn, E., & Lee, D. Y. (1997). A bio-ecological model of intellectual development: Moving beyond h2. In R. J. Sternberg & E. Grigorenko (Eds.), *Intelligence, heredity, and environment* (pp. 303–322). New York: Cambridge University Press.

Cedar Rapids Community School District v. Garret F., 119 S. Ct. 992 (1999), LEXIS 1709.

Chae, P. K. (1999). Correlation study between WISC–III scores and TOVA performance. *Psychology in the Schools, 36,* 179–185.

Chandler, J. T., & Plakos, J. (1969). Spanish-speaking pupils classified as educable mentally retarded. *Integrated Education, 7,* 28–33.

Chatman, S. P., Reynolds, C. R., & Willson, V. L. (1984). Multiple indexes of test scatter on the Kaufman Assessment Battery for Children. *Journal of Learning Disabilities, 17,* 523–531.

Chavez, E. L. (1982). Analysis of a Spanish translation of the Peabody Picture Vocabulary Test. *Perceptual and Motor Skills, 54,* 1335–1338.

Chung, R. C.-Y., & Lin, K.-M. (1994). Help-seeking behavior among Southeast Asian refugees. *Journal of Community Psychology, 22,* 109–120.

Clarizio, H. F. (1994). *Assessment and treatment of depressions in children and adolescents* (2nd ed.). Brandon, VT: Clinical Psychology Publishing Company.

Cleary, T. A., Humphreys, L. G., Kendrick, S. A., & Wesman, A. G. (1975). Educational uses of tests with disadvantaged students. *American Psychologist, 30,* 15–41.

Cleveland Heights–University Heights City School District v. Boss, 144 F.3d 391 (6th Cir. 1998), LEXIS 8829.

Cole, N. S. (1981). Bias in testing. *American Psychologist, 36,* 1067–1077.

Coll, C. T. G., & Meyer, E. C. (1993). The sociocultural context of infant development. In C. H. Zeanah, Jr. (Ed.), *Handbook of infant mental health* (pp. 56–69). New York: Guilford.

Collinsgru v. Palmyra Board of Education, 161 F.3d 225 (3rd Cir. 1998), LEXIS 29806.

Compas, B. E., Hinden, B. R., & Gerhardt, C. A. (1995). Adolescent development: Pathways and processes of risk and resilience. *Annual Review of Psychology, 46,* 265–293.

Connaway, S. (1996). ABCs for teachers who suspect child abuse. *NRCCSA News, 5,* 4–5.

Connolly, A. J. (1988). *KeyMath–Revised: A Diagnostic Inventory of Essential Mathematics.* Circle Pines, MN: American Guidance Service.

Connolly, A. J. (1997). *Manual for Keymath–Revised.* Circle Pines, MN: American Guidance Service.

Coon, H., Carey, G., & Fulker, D. W. (1992). Community influences on cognitive ability. *Intelligence, 16,* 169–188.

Cooper, H. M. (1989). *Integrating research. A guide for literature reviews.* Newbury Park, CA: Sage.

Corman, L., & Budoff, M. (1974). Factor structures of Spanish-speaking and non-Spanish-speaking children on Raven's Progressive Matrices. *Educational and Psychological Measurement, 34,* 977–981.

Cormier, W. H., & Cormier, L. S. (1979). *Interviewing strategies for helpers: A guide to assessment, treatment, and evaluation.* Monterey, CA: Brooks/Cole.

County of San Diego v. California Special Education Hearing Office, Grossmont Union High School District, 93 F.3d 1458 (9th Cir. 1996), LEXIS 22406.

Crary, M. A., Voeller, K. S., & Haak, J. J. (1988). Questions of developmental neurolinguistic assessment. In M. G. Tramontana & S. R. Hooper (Eds.), *Assessment issues in child neuropsychology* (pp. 249–279). New York: Plenum.

Crawford et al. v. Honig et al., 37 F.3d 485 (9th Cir. 1994), LEXIS 27359.

Cronkite v. Long Beach Unified School District, 176 F.3d 482 (9th Cir. 1999), LEXIS 16485.

Crowe, S. F. (2000). Does the Letter–Number Sequencing task measure anything more than Digit Span? *Psychological Assessment, 7,* 113–117.

Cypress–Fairbanks Independent School District v. Michael F., 118 F.3d 245 (5th Cir. 1997), LEXIS 17603.

Daniel Hoffman v. The Board of Education of the City of New York, 410 N. Y. S.2d 99 and 400 N.E.2d 317–49 N.Y.2d 121.

Danielson, G. I. (1991). An initial reaction to the WISC–III. *Communiqué, 20,* 23.

Das, J. P. (1973). Cultural deprivation and cognitive competence. In N. R. Ellis (Ed.), *International review of research in mental retardation* (Vol. 6, pp. 1–53). New York: Academic Press.

Das, J. P., Carlson, J., Davidson, M. B., & Longe, K. (1997). *PREP: PASS remedial program.* Seattle: Hogrefe.

Das, J. P., Naglieri, J. A., & Kirby, J. R. (1994). *Assessment of cognitive processes: The PASS theory of intelligence.* Needham Heights, MA: Allyn & Bacon.

Davis, F. B. (1959). Interpretation of differences among averages and individual test scores. *Journal of Educational Psychology, 50,* 162–170.

Dean, R. S. (1977a). Analysis of the PIAT with Anglo and Mexican-American children. *Journal of School Psychology, 15,* 329–333.

Dean, R. S. (1977b). Reliability of the WISC–R with Mexican-American children. *Journal of School Psychology, 15,* 267–268.

Dean, R. S. (1979a). Distinguishing patterns for Mexican-American children on the WISC–R. *Journal of Clinical Psychology, 35,* 790–794.

Dean, R. S. (1979b). Predictive validity of the WISC–R with Mexican-American children. *Journal of School Psychology, 17,* 55–58.

Dean, R. S. (1980). Factor structure of the WISC–R with Anglos and Mexican Americans. *Journal of School Psychology, 18,* 234–239.

Deary, I. J., & Caryl, P. G. (1993). Intelligence, EEG, and evoked potentials. In P. A. Vernon (Ed.), *Biological approaches to the study of human intelligence* (pp. 259–315). Norwood, NJ: Ablex.

Deary, I. J., & Stough, C. (1996). Intelligence and inspection time: Achievements, prospects, and problems. *American Psychologist, 51,* 599–608.

DeAvila, E. A., & Havassy, B. (1974). The testing of minority children: A neo-Piagetian approach. *Today's Education, 63,* 72–75.

DeBord v. Board of Education of the Ferguson-Florissant School District, 126 F.3d 1102 (8th Cir. 1997), LEXIS 27851.

DeLamatre, J. E., & Hollinger, C. L. (1990). Utility of the Stanford-Binet IV abbreviated form for placing exceptional children. *Psychological Reports, 67,* 973–974.

Delany, E., & Hopkins, T. (1987). *Examiner's handbook: An expanded guide for Fourth Edition users.* Chicago: Riverside Publishing.

DeMauro, G. E. (1998). Review of the Diagnostic Achievement Test for Adolescents, Second Edition. In J. C. Impara & B. S. Plake (Eds.), *The thirteenth mental measurements yearbook.* Lincoln: University of Nebraska Press.

Deno, S. L., & Fuchs, L. S. (1987). Developing curriculum-based measurement systems for data-based special education problem solving. *Focus on Exceptional Children, 19,* 1–16.

Detterman, D. K. (1986). Human intelligence is a complex system of separate processes. In R. J. Sternberg & D. K. Detterman (Eds.), *What is intelligence?* (pp. 57–61). Norwood, NJ: Ablex.

Detterman, D. K. (1987). What does reaction time tell us about intelligence? In P. A. Vernon (Ed.), *Speed of information-processing and intelligence* (pp. 177–200). Norwood, NJ: Ablex.

Detterman, D. K. (1994). Intelligence and the brain. In P. A. Vernon (Ed.), *The neuropsychology of individual differences* (pp. 35–57). San Diego: Academic Press.

Deutsch, M., Fishman, J. A., Kogan, L., North, R., & Whiteman, M. (1964). Guidelines for testing minority group children. *Journal of Social Issues, 20,* 129–145.

Diana v. State Board of Education, Civ. Act. No. C-70–37 (N. D. Cal., 1970, *further order,* 1973).

Diaz, R. M., & Klinger, C. (1991). Towards an explanatory model of the interaction between bilingualism and cognitive development. In E. Bialystok (Ed.), *Language processing in bilingual children* (pp. 167–192). Cambridge, England: Cambridge University Press.

Dillon, R. F., Pohlmann, J. T., & Lohman, D. F. (1981). A factor analysis of Raven's Advanced Progressive Matrices freed of difficulty factors. *Educational and Psychological Measurement, 41,* 1295–1302.

Dodwell, P. C. (1961). Children's understanding of number concepts: Characteristics of an individual and of a group test. *Canadian Journal of Psychology, 15,* 29–36.

Doe v. Board of Education of Baltimore County, 162 F.3d 289 (4th Cir. 1998), LEXIS 37365.

Doe v. Board of Education of Oak Park, 115 F.3d 1273 (7th Cir. 1997), LEXIS 12351.

Doe v. Board of Education of the Elyria City Schools, 149 F.3d 1182 (6th Cir. 1998), LEXIS 22759.

Doe v. Metropolitan Nashville Public Schools, 133 F.3d 384 (6th Cir. 1998), LEXIS 5553.

Doll, B., & Boren, R. (1993). Performance of severely language-impaired students on the WISC–III, Language Scales, and Academic Achievement Measures. *Monograph Series of the Journal of Psychoeducational Assessment, Wechsler Intelligence Scale for Children: Third Edition,* 77–86.

Donald B. v. Board of School Commissioners of Mobile County, 117 F.3d 1371 (11th Cir. 1997), LEXIS 19968.

Donders, J. (1995). Validity of the Kaufman Brief Intelligence Test (K-BIT) in children with traumatic brain injury. *Assessment, 2,* 219–224.

Donders, J. (1997). A short form of the WISC–III for clinical use. *Psychological Assessment, 9,* 15–20.

Donders, J., & Warchausky, S. (1997). WISC–III factor index score pattern after traumatic head injury in children. *Child Neuropsychology, 3,* 71–78.

Drasgow, F. (1987). Study of the measurement bias of two standardized psychological tests. *Journal of Applied Psychology, 72,* 19–29.

Dresser, N. (1996). *Multicultural manners.* New York: Wiley.

DuBois, P. H. (1972). *Increase in educational opportunity through measurement.* Proceedings of the 1971 Invitational Conference on Testing Problems. Princeton, NJ: Educational Testing Service.

Dudek, S. Z., Lester, E. P., Goldberg, J. S., & Dyer, G. B. (1969). Relationship of Piaget measures to standard intelligence and motor scales. *Perceptual and Motor Skills, 28,* 351–362.

Dugbartey, A. T., Sanchez, P. N., Rosenbaum, J. G., Mahurin, R. K., Davis, J. M., & Townes, B. D. (1999). WAIS–III Matrix Reasoning test performance in a mixed clinical sample. *The Clinical Neuropsychologist, 13,* 396–404.

Dumont, R., Cruse, C. L., Price, L., & Whelley, P. (1996). The relationships between the Differential Ability Scales (DAS) and the Wechsler Intelligence Scale for Children–Third Edition (WISC–III) for students with learning disability. *Psychology in the Schools, 33,* 203–209.

Dumont, R., & Faro, C. (1993). A WISC–III short form for learning-disabled students. *Psychology in the Schools, 30,* 212–219.

Dumont, R., Farr, L. P., Willis, J. O., & Whelley, P. (1998). 30-second interval performance on the Coding subtest of the WISC–III: Further evidence of WISC folklore? *Psychology in the Schools, 35,* 111–117.

Dumont, R., & Willis, J. O. (1995). Intrasubtest scatter on the WISC–III for various clinical samples vs. the standardization sample: An examination of WISC folklore. *Journal of Psychoeducational Assessment, 13,* 271–285.

Dumont, R., Willis, J. O., Farr, L. P., McCarthy, T., & Price, L. (2000). The relationship between the Differential Ability Scales (DAS) and the Woodcock-Johnson Tests of Cognitive Ability–Revised (WJ–R COG) for students referred for special education evaluations. *Journal of Psychoeducational Assessment, 18,* 27–38.

Duncan, G., Brooks-Gunn, J., & Klebanov, P. (1994). Economic deprivation and early childhood development. *Child Development, 65,* 296–318.

Duncan, S. E., & DeAvila, E. A. (1990). *Language Assessment Scales–Oral.* Monterey, CA: CTB/McGraw-Hill.

Duncan, S. E., & DeAvila, E. A. (1994). *Language Assessment Scales Reading–Writing.* Monterey, CA: CTB/McGraw-Hill.

Dunn, L. M., & Dunn, L. M. (1997). *Peabody Picture Vocabulary Test–III.* Circle Pines, MN: American Guidance Services.

Dunst, C. J. (1980). *A clinical and educational manual for use with the Uzgiris and Hunt Scales of Infant Psychological Development.* Baltimore: University Park Press.

Dusek, J. B., & O'Connell, E. J. (1973). Teacher expectancy effects on the achievement test performance of elementary school children. *Journal of Educational Psychology, 65,* 371–377.

Ebel, R. L. (1971). Criterion-referenced measurements: Limitations. *School Review, 79,* 282–288.

Ebel, R. L. (1975). Educational tests: Valid? Biased? Useful? *Phi Delta Kappan, 57,* 83–89.

Edelbrock, C. S. (1984). Developmental considerations. In T. H. Ollendick & M. Hersen (Eds.), *Child behavioral assessment: Principles and procedures* (pp. 20–37). New York: Pergamon.

Eklund, S., & Scott, M. (1965). Effects of bilingual instructions on test responses of Latin American children. *Psychology in the Schools, 2,* 280–282.

Elkind, D. (1961). Children's discovery of the conservation of mass, weight, and volume: Piaget replication study II. *Journal of Genetic Psychology, 98,* 219–227.

Elkind, D. (1974). *Children and adolescents: Interpretive essays on Jean Piaget* (2nd ed.). New York: Oxford University Press.

Elkind, D. (1981). *Children and adolescents: Interpretive essays on Jean Piaget* (3rd ed.). New York: Oxford University Press.

Elliott, C. D. (1990a). *DAS administration and scoring manual.* San Antonio: The Psychological Corporation.

Elliott, C. D. (1990b). *DAS introductory and technical handbook.* San Antonio: The Psychological Corporation.

Emanuelsson, I., & Svensson, A. (1990). Changes in intelligence over a quarter of a century. *Scandinavian Journal of Educational Research, 34,* 171–187.

Emmons, R. (1996, December 27). Black English has its place. *Los Angeles Times,* p. B9.

Erford, B. T., Vitali, G. J., & Slosson, S. W. (1999). *Slosson Intelligence Test–Primary.* East Aurora, NY: Slosson Educational Publications.

Erin, J. N., & Koenig, A. J. (1997). The student with a visual disability and a learning disability. *Journal of Learning Disabilities, 30,* 309–320.

Estes, W. K. (1974). Learning theory and intelligence. *American Psychologist, 29,* 740–749.

Estes, W. K. (1986). Where is intelligence? In R. J. Sternberg & D. K. Detterman (Eds.), *What is intelligence?* (pp. 63–67). Norwood, NJ: Ablex.

E. S. v. Independent School District, No. 196, 135 F.3d 566 (8th Cir. 1998), LEXIS 1278.

Evans, R. G. (1985). Accuracy of the Satz-Mogel procedure in estimating WAIS–R IQs that are in the normal range. *Journal of Clinical Psychology, 41,* 100–103.

Everett, F., Proctor, N., & Cartmell, B. (1983). Providing psychological services to American Indian children and families. *Professional Psychology: Research and Practice, 14,* 588–603.

Exceptional Children Division, Department of Public Instruction. (July, 2000). *North Carolina state forms.* Raleigh, NC: Author.

Eysenck, H. J. (1967). Intelligence assessment: A theoretical and experimental approach. *British Journal of Educational Psychology, 37,* 81–98.

Eysenck, H. J., & Schoenthaler, S. J. (1997). Raising IQ level by vitamin and mineral supplementation. In R. J. Sternberg & E. L. Grigorenko (Eds.), *Intelligence, heredity, and environment* (pp. 363–392). New York: Cambridge University Press.

Eysenck, M. W. (1994). *Individual differences: Normal and abnormal. Principles of psychology.* Hove, England: Erlbaum.

Fagan, J. F. (1984a). The intelligent infant: Theoretical implications. *Intelligence, 8,* 1–9.

Fagan, J. F. (1984b). The relationship of novelty preferences during infancy to later intelligence and later recognition memory. *Intelligence, 8,* 339–346.

Fagan, J. F., & Singer, L. T. (1983). Infant recognition memory as a measure of intelligence. *Advances in Infancy Research, 2,* 31–78.

Farrell, A. D. (1991). Computers and behavioral assessment: Current applications, future possibilities, and obstacles to routine use. *Behavioral Assessment, 13,* 159–179.

Faust, D. S., & Hollingsworth, J. O. (1991). Concurrent validation of the Wechsler Preschool and Primary Scale of Intelligence–Revised (WPPSI–R) with two criteria of cognitive abilities. *Journal of Psychoeducational Assessment, 9,* 224–229.

Ferrara, S. (1998). Review of the Wechsler Individual Achievement Test. In J. C. Impara & B. S. Plake (Eds.), *The thirteenth mental measurements yearbook.* Lincoln: University of Nebraska Press.

Finkelson, L., & Stavrou, E. (1999, April). *The stability of IQ in learning disabled students.* Paper presented at the National Association of School Psychologists annual convention, Las Vegas, NV.

Finkle, L. J., Hanson, D. P., & Hostetler, S. K. (1983). The assessment of profoundly handicapped children. *School Psychology Review, 12,* 75–81.

Fischbein, S. (1980). IQ and social class. *Intelligence, 4,* 51–64.

Fish, B. (1985). Children's Psychiatric Rating Scale–A. *Psychopharmacology Bulletin, 21,* 753, 764.

Fisher, G. L., Jenkins, S. J., Bancroft, J. J., & Kraft, L. M. (1988). The effects of K-ABC-based remedial teaching strategies on word recognition skills. *Journal of Learning Disability, 21,* 307–312.

Fishler, K., Graliker, B. V., & Koch, R. (1965). The predictability of intelligence with Gesell Developmental Scales in mentally retarded infants and young children. *American Journal of Mental Deficiency, 69,* 515–525.

Fishman, M. A., & Palkes, H. S. (1974). The validity of psychometric testing in children with congenital malformations of the central nervous system. *Developmental Medicine and Child Neurology, 16,* 180–185.

Fitzsimmons, R. J., & Loomer, B. B. (1978). *Spelling: Learning and instruction.* Iowa City: University of Iowa.

Flanagan, D. P., & Alfonso, V. C. (1995). A critical review of the technical characteristics of new and recently revised intelligence tests for preschool children. *Journal of Psychoeducational Assessment, 13,* 66–90.

Flanagan, D. P., McGrew, K. S., & Ortiz, S. O. (2000). *The Wechsler intelligence scales and Gf-Gc theory: A contemporary approach to interpretation.* Boston: Allyn & Bacon.

Flaugher, R. L. (1974). Some points of confusion in discussing the testing of black students. In L. P. Miller (Ed.), *The testing of black students: A symposium* (pp. 11–16). Englewood Cliffs, NJ: Prentice-Hall.

Flaugher, R. L. (1978). The many definitions of test bias. *American Psychologist, 33,* 671–679.

Florence County School District Four v. Carter, 510 U.S. 7 (1993), LEXIS 7154.

Flynn, J. R. (1984). The mean IQ of Americans: Massive gains 1932–1978. *Psychological Bulletin, 95,* 29–51.

Flynn, J. R. (1987). Massive IQ gains in 14 nations: What IQ tests really measure. *Psychological Bulletin, 101,* 171–191.

Flynn, J. R. (1998). WAIS–III and WISC–III IQ gains in the United States from 1972 to 1995: How to compensate for obsolete norms. *Perceptual and Motor Skills, 86,* 1231–1239.

Foley v. Special School District of St. Louis County, 153 F.3d 863 (8th Cir. 1998), LEXIS 18814.

Fort Zumwalt School District v. Clynes, 119 F.3d 1997 (8th Cir. 1997), LEXIS 17214.

Frederiksen, N. (1986). Toward a broader conception of human intelligence. *American Psychologist, 41,* 445–452.

Freeman, F. S. (1955). *Theory and practice of psychological testing.* New York: Holt, Rinehart, and Winston.

Freeman, F. S. (1962). *Theory and practice of psychological testing* (3rd ed.). New York: Holt, Rinehart and Winston.

Freides, D. (1993). Proposed standard of professional practice: Neuropsychological reports display all quantitative data. *The Clinical Neuropsychologist, 7,* 234–235.

Frisby, C. L. (1993). One giant step backward: Myths of black cultural learning styles. *School Psychology Review, 22,* 535–557.

Fry, A. F., & Hale, S. (1996). Processing speed, working memory, and fluid intelligence: Evidence for a developmental cascade. *Psychological Science, 7,* 237–241.

Fuchs, D., & Fuchs, L. S. (1989). Effects of examiner familiarity on Black, Caucasian, and Hispanic children: A meta-analysis. *Exceptional Children, 55,* 303–308.

Fuchs, L. S., & Fuchs, D. (1986). Curriculum-based assessment of progress through long-term and short-term goals. *Journal of Special Education, 20,* 69–82.

Galvan, R. R. (1967). Bilingualism as it relates to intelligence test scores and school achievement among culturally deprived Spanish-American children. *Dissertation Abstracts International, 28,* 3021A. (University Microfilms No. 68–1131)

Gardner, H. (1983). *Frames of mind: The theory of multiple intelligences.* New York: Basic Books.

Gardner, H. (1998). Are there additional intelligences? The case for naturalist, spiritual, and existential intelligences. In J. Kane (Ed.), *Education, information, and transformation* (pp. 111–131). Englewood Cliffs, NJ: Prentice-Hall.

Gardner, H., Kornhaber, M. L., & Wake, W. K. (1996). *Intelligence: Multiple perspectives.* Ft. Worth, TX: Harcourt Brace College.

Garrett, H. E. (1946). A developmental theory of intelligence. *American Psychologist, 1,* 372–378.

Gaskill, F. W., III, & Brantley, J. C. (1996). Changes in ability and achievement scores over time: Implications for children classified as learning disabled. *Journal of Psychoeducational Assessment, 14,* 220–228.

Gearheart, B. R., & Willenberg, E. P. (1980). *Application of pupil assessment information* (3rd ed.). Denver: Love.

Genshaft, J. L., & Hirt, M. (1974). Language differences between black children and white children. *Developmental Psychology, 10,* 451–456.

Georgia State Conference of Branches of NAACP v. State of Georgia, 775 F.2d 1403 (11th Cir. 1985), LEXIS 24517.

Gerken, K. C. (1978). Performance of Mexican American children on intelligence tests. *Exceptional Children, 44,* 438–443.

Gerken, K. C., & Hodapp, A. F. (1992). Assessment of preschoolers at-risk with the WPPSI–R and the Stanford-Binet L-M. *Psychological Reports, 71,* 659–664.

Giger, J. N., & Davidhizar, R. F. (Eds.). (1991). *Transcultural nursing: Assessment and intervention.* St. Louis: Mosby.

Ginsburg, H. P., & Baroody, A. J. (1990). *Test of Early Mathematics Ability–Second Edition.* Austin, TX: Pro-Ed.

Glasser, A. J., & Zimmerman, I. L. (1967). *Clinical interpretations of the Wechsler Intelligence Scale for Children.* New York: Grune & Stratton.

Glaub, V. E., & Kamphaus, R. W. (1991). Construction of a nonverbal adaptation of the Stanford-Binet Fourth Edition. *Educational & Psychological Measurement, 51,* 231–241.

Gleason, J. B. (1997). *The development of language.* Needham Heights, MA: Allyn & Bacon.

Glutting, J. J., Adams, W., & Sheslow, D. (2000). *Wide Range Intelligence Test.* Wilmington, DE: Wide Range, Inc.

Glutting, J. J., McDermott, P. A., & Konold, T. R. (1997). Ontology, structure, and diagnostic benefits of a normative subtest taxonomy from the WISC–III standardization sample. In D. P. Flanagan, J. L. Genshaft, & P. L. Harrison (Eds.), *Contemporary intellectual assessment: Theories, tests, and issues* (pp. 349–372). New York: Guilford.

Glutting, J. J., McDermott, P. A., & Stanley, J. C. (1987). Resolving differences among methods of establishing confidence limits for test scores. *Educational & Psychological Measurement, 37,* 607–614.

Glutting, J. J., & Oakland, T. D. (1993). *Guide to the assessment of test session behavior for the WISC–III and the WIAT: Manual.* San Antonio: The Psychological Corporation.

Glutting, J. J., Watkins, M. W., & Youngstrom, E. A. (in press). Multifactored and cross-battery ability assessments: Are they worth the effort? In C. R. Reynolds & R. W. Kamphaus (Eds.), *Handbook of psychological and educational assessment of children: Intelligence and achievement* (2nd ed). New York: Guilford.

Glutting, J. J., Youngstrom, E. A., Oakland, T. D., & Watkins, M. W. (1996). Situational specificity and generality of test behaviors for samples of normal and referred children. *School Psychology Review, 25,* 94–107.

Glutting, J. J., Youngstrom, E. A., Ward, T., Ward, S., & Hale, R. L. (1997). Incremental efficacy of WISC–III factor scores in predicting achievement: What do they tell us? *Psychological Assessment, 9,* 295–301.

G. M. v. New Britain Board of Education, 173 F.3d 77 (2nd Cir. 1999), LEXIS 6915.

Goddard, H. H. (1908). The Binet and Simon tests of intellectual capacity. *Training School, 5,* 3–9.

Goddard, H. H. (1910). A measuring scale of intelligence. *Training School, 6,* 146–155.

Goetz, E. T., & Hall, R. J. (1984). Evaluation of the Kaufman Assessment Battery for Children from an information-processing perspective. *Journal of Special Education, 18,* 281–296.

Goh, D. S. (1978). *New method in the design of intelligence test short forms–the WISC–R example.* Paper presented at the meeting of the American Psychological Association, Toronto, Canada.

Goldfarb, L. P., Plante, T. G., Brentar, J. T., & DiGregorio, M. (1995). Administering the Digit Span subtest of the WISC–III: Should the examiner make eye contact or not? *Assessment, 2,* 313–318.

Goldschmid, M. L. (1967). Different types of conservation and nonconservation and their relation to age, sex, I.Q., M.A., and vocabulary. *Child Development, 38,* 1229–1246.

Goldstein, D. J., Fogle, E. E., Wieber, J. L., & O'Shea, T. M. (1995). Comparison of the Bayley Scales of Infant Development–Second Edition and the Bayley Scales of Infant Development with premature infants. *Journal of Psychoeducational Assessment, 13,* 391–396.

Goldstein, G. (1987). Neuropsychological assessment for rehabilitation: Fixed batteries, automated systems, and non-psychometric methods. In M. J. Meier, A. L. Benton, & L. Diller (Eds.), *Neuropsychological rehabilitation* (pp. 18–40). Edinburgh: Churchill Livingstone.

Good, T. L., & Brophy, J. E. (1972). Behavioral expression of teacher attitudes. *Journal of Educational Psychology, 63,* 617–624.

Goslin, D. A. (1963). *The search for ability: Standardized testing in social perspective.* New York: Russell Sage.

Gottfried, A. W., & Brody, N. (1975). Interrelationships between and correlates of psychometric and Piagetian scales of sensorimotor intelligence. *Developmental Psychology, 11,* 379–387.

Gottlieb, J., Alter, M., & Gottlieb, B. W. (1991). Mainstreaming mentally retarded children. In J. L. Matson & J. A. Mulick (Eds.), *Handbook of mental retardation* (2nd ed., pp. 60–73). New York: Pergamon.

Graf, M., & Hinton, R. N. (1997). Correlations for the developmental visual-motor integration test and the Wechsler Intelligence Scale for Children–III. *Perceptual and Motor Skills, 84,* 699–702.

Granier, M. J., & O'Donnell, L. (1991). *Children's WISC–III scores: Impact of parent education and home environment.* San Antonio: The Psychological Corporation.

Green, B. F., Jr. (1978). In defense of measurement. *American Psychologist, 33,* 664–670.

Green, B. F., Jr. (1981). A primer of testing. *American Psychologist, 36,* 1001–1011.

Greenberg, R. D., Stewart, K. J., & Hansche, W. J. (1986). Factor analysis of the WISC–R for white and black children evaluated for gifted placement. *Journal of Psychoeducational Assessment, 4,* 123–130.

Greene, A. C., Sapp, G. L., & Chissom, B. (1990). Validation of the Stanford-Binet Intelligence Scale: Fourth Edition with exceptional black male students. *Psychology in the Schools, 27,* 35–41.

Grice, J. W., Krohn, E. J., & Logerquist, S. (1999). Cross-validation of the WISC–III factor structure in two samples of children with learning disabilities. *Journal of Psychoeducational Assessment, 17,* 236–248.

Gridley, B. E., & McIntosh, D. E. (1991). Confirmatory factor analysis of the Stanford-Binet: Fourth Edition for a normal sample. *Journal of School Psychology, 29,* 237–248.

Guilford, J. P. (1967). *The nature of human intelligence.* New York: McGraw-Hill.

Gunter, C. M., Sapp, G. L., & Green, A. C. (1995). Comparison of scores on WISC–III and WISC–R of urban learning disabled students. *Psychological Reports, 77,* 473–474.

Gutentag, S. S., Naglieri, J. A., & Yeates, K. O. (1998). Performance of children with traumatic brain injury on the Cognitive Assessment System. *Assessment, 5,* 263–272.

Gutkin, T. B., & Reynolds, C. R. (1981). Factorial similarity of the WISC–R for white and black children from the standardization sample. *Journal of Educational Psychology, 73,* 227–231.

Guy, D. P. (1977). Issues in the unbiased assessment of intelligence. *School Psychology Digest, 6,* 14–23.

Gyurke, J. S., Prifitera, A., & Sharp, S. A. (1991). Frequency of verbal and performance IQ discrepancies on the WPPSI–R at various levels of ability. *Journal of Psychoeducational Assessment, 9,* 230–239.

Gyurke, J. S., Stone, B. J., & Beyer, M. (1990). A confirmatory factor analysis of the WPPSI–R. *Journal of Psychoeducational Assessment, 8,* 15–21.

Hack, M., Breslau, N., Aram, D., Weissman, B., Klein, M., & Borawski-Clark, E. (1992). The effect of very low birth weight and social risk on neurocognitive abilities at school age. *Journal of Developmental & Behavioral Pediatrics, 13,* 412–420.

Haier, R. J. (1990). The end of intelligence research. *Intelligence, 14,* 371–374.

Hall, V. C., Huppertz, J. W., & Levi, A. (1977). Attention and achievement exhibited by middle- and lower-class black and white elementary school boys. *Journal of Educational Psychology, 69,* 115–120.

Hall, V. C., Turner, R. R., & Russell, W. (1973). Ability of children from four subcultures and two grade levels to imitate and comprehend crucial aspects of standard English: A test of the different language explanation. *Journal of Educational Psychology, 64,* 147–158.

Hammill, D. D. (1998). *Detroit Tests of Learning Aptitude–Fourth Edition.* Austin, TX: Pro-Ed.

Hammill, D. D., Brown, V. L., Larsen, S. C., & Wiederholt, J. L. (1994). *Test of Adolescent Language–Third Edition.* Austin, TX: Pro-Ed.

Hammill, D. D., Hresko, W. P., Ammer, J., Cronin, M., & Quinby, S. (1998). *Hammill Multiability Achievement Test.* Austin, TX: Pro-Ed.

Hammill, D. D., & Larsen, S. C. (1996). *Test of Written Language–Third Edition.* Austin, TX: Pro-Ed.

Hammill, D. D., Mather, N., & Roberts, R. (2001). *Illinois Test of Psycholinguistic Abilities.* Austin, TX: Pro-Ed.

Hammill, D. D., Pearson, N. A., & Wiederholt, J. L. (1997). *Comprehensive Test of Nonverbal Intelligence.* Austin, TX: Pro-Ed.

Hanson, R. A. (1975). Consistency and stability of home environmental measures related to IQ. *Child Development, 46,* 470–480.

Harrington, R. G., Kimberly, J., & Dai, X. (1992). The relationship between the Woodcock-Johnson Psycho-Educational Battery–Revised (Early Development) and the Wechsler Preschool and Primary Scale of Intelligence–Revised. *Psychology in the Schools, 29,* 116–125.

Hartley, L. L. (1990). Assessment of functional communication. In D. E. Tupper & K. D. Cicerone (Eds.), *The neuropsychology of everyday life: Assessment of basic competencies* (pp. 125–168). Boston: Kluwer.

Hartmann v. Loudoun County Board of Education, 118 F.3d 996 (4th Cir. 1997), LEXIS 16795.

Hartwig, S. S., Sapp, G. L., & Clayton, G. A. (1987). Comparison of the Stanford-Binet Intelligence Scale: Form L-M and the Stanford-Binet Intelligence Scale Fourth Edition. *Psychological Reports, 60,* 1215–1218.

Harver, J. R. (1977). Influence of presentation dialect and orthographic form on reading performance of black inner-city children. *Educational Research Quarterly, 2,* 9–16.

Hay, D. (1999). The developmental genetics of intelligence. In M. Anderson (Ed.), *The development of intelligence* (pp. 75–104). Hove, England: Psychology Press.

Hayden, D. C., Furlong, M., & Linnemeyer, S. (1988). A comparison of the Kaufman Assessment Battery for Children and the Stanford-Binet for the assessment of gifted children. *Psychology in the Schools, 25,* 239–243.

Heath, S. B. (1989). Oral and literate traditions among Black Americans living in poverty. *American Psychology, 44,* 367–373.

Heather S. v. State of Wisconsin, 125 F.3d 1045 (7th Cir. 1997), LEXIS 24927.

Heffernan, L., & Black, F. W. (1984). Use of the Uzgiris and Hunt Scales with handicapped infants: Concurrent validity of the Dunst age norms. *Journal of Psychoeducational Assessment, 2,* 159–168.

Hegde, M. N. (1995). *Introduction to communication disorders* (2nd ed.). Austin, TX: Pro-Ed.

Hendershott, J. L., Searight, H. R., Hatfield, J. L., & Rogers, B. J. (1990). Correlations between the Stanford-Binet, Fourth Edition and the Kaufman Assessment Battery for Children for a preschool sample. *Perceptual and Motor Skills, 71,* 819–825.

Henderson, N. B., Butler, B. V., & Goffeney, B. (1969). Effectiveness of the WISC and Bender-Gestalt Test in predicting arithmetic and reading achievement for white and nonwhite children. *Journal of Clinical Psychology, 25,* 268–271.

Henderson, N. B., Fay, W. H., Lindemann, S. J., & Clarkson, Q. D. (1973). Will the IQ test ban decrease the effectiveness of reading prediction? *Journal of Educational Psychology, 65,* 345–355.

Herrell, J. M., & Golland, J. H. (1969). Should WISC subjects explain Picture Arrangement stories? *Journal of Consulting and Clinical Psychology, 33,* 761–762.

Herrera-Graf, M., Dipert, Z. J., & Hinton, R. N. (1996). Exploring the effective use of the Vocabulary/Block Design short form with a special school population. *Educational & Psychological Measurement, 56,* 522–528.

Herring, R. D. (1992). Biracial children: An increasing concern for elementary and middle school counselors. *Elementary School Guidance & Counseling, 27,* 123–130.

Herrnstein, R. J., & Murray, C. (1994). *The bell curve: The reshaping of American life by differences in intelligence.* New York: Free Press.

Herschell, A. D., Greco, L. A., Filcheck, H. A., & McNeil, C. B. (in press). Who is testing whom: Ten suggestions for managing disruptive behavior during testing. *Intervention in School and Clinic.*

Hewett, J. B., & Bolen, L. M. (1996). Performance changes on the K–TEA: Brief Form for learning-disabled students. *Psychology in the Schools, 33,* 97–102.

Hines v. Tullahoma City School System, Nos. 97–5103, 97–5104, 1998 U.S. Court of Appeals for the Fourth Circuit, LEXIS 26035.

Hishinuma, E. S., & Yamakawa, R. (1993). Construct and criterion-related validity of the WISC–III for exceptional students and those who are "at risk." *Monograph Series of the Journal of Psychoeducational Assessment, Wechsler Intelligence Scale for Children: Third Edition,* 94–104.

Hobby, K. L. (1980). *WISC–R split-half short form manual.* Los Angeles: Western Psychological Services.

Hodapp, A. F., & Hass, J. K. (1997). Correlations between Wechsler Intelligence Scale for Children–III and Peabody Picture Vocabulary Test–Revised. *Psychological Reports, 80,* 491–495.

Hoekstra v. Independent School District, 103 F.3d 624 (8th Cir. 1996), LEXIS 33334.

Holland, W. R. (1960). Language barrier as an educational problem of Spanish-speaking children. *Exceptional Children, 27,* 42–50.

Hollinger, C. L., & Baldwin, C. (1987). *Comparing the Stanford-Binet, Fourth Edition with the WISC-R among exceptional children.* Unpublished manuscript, Cleveland State University at Cleveland.

Hollinger, C. L., & Baldwin, C. (1990a). Comparing scores on the Stanford-Binet, Fourth Edition with the WISC–R for exceptional children. *Psychological Reports, 66,* 979–984.

Hollinger, C. L., & Baldwin, C. (1990b). The Stanford-Binet, Fourth Edition: A small study of concurrent validity. *Psychological Reports, 66,* 1331–1336.

Holmes, J. M. (1988). Testing. In R. G. Rudel (Ed.), *Assessment of developmental learning disorders* (pp. 166–201). New York: Basic Books.

Honaker, L. M., & Fowler, R. D. (1990). Computer-assisted psychological assessment. In G. Goldstein & M. Hersen (Eds.), *Handbook of psychological assessment* (2nd ed., pp. 521–546). New York: Pergamon.

Hoover, H. D. (1984). The most appropriate scores for measuring educational development in the elementary schools: GE's. *Educational Measurement: Issues & Practice, 3,* 8–14.

Horn, J. L. (1967). Intelligence–why it grows, why it declines. *Trans-action, 5,* 23–31.

Horn, J. L. (1968). Organization of abilities and the development of intelligence. *Psychological Review, 75,* 242–259.

Horn, J. L. (1978a). Human ability systems. In P. B. Baltes (Ed.), *Life-span development and behavior* (Vol. 1, pp. 211–256). New York: Academic Press.

Horn, J. L. (1978b). The nature and development of intellectual abilities. In R. T. Osborne, C. E. Noble, & N. Weyl (Eds.), *Human variation: The biopsychology of age, race, and sex* (pp. 107–136). New York: Academic Press.

Horn, J. L. (1979). Trends in the measurement of intelligence. *Intelligence, 3,* 229–239.

Horn, J. L. (1985). Remodeling old models of intelligence. In B. Wolman (Ed.), *Handbook of intelligence* (pp. 267–300). New York: Wiley.

Horn, J. L. (1987). A context for understanding information processing studies of human abilities. In P. A. Vernon (Ed.), *Speed of information-processing and intelligence* (pp. 201–238). Norwood, NJ: Ablex.

Horn, J. L. (1998). A basis for research on age differences in cognitive capabilities. In J. J. McArdle & R. W. Woodcock (Eds.), *Human cognitive abilities in theory and practice* (pp. 57–87). Mahwah, NJ: Erlbaum.

Horn, J. L., & Cattell, R. B. (1967). Age differences in fluid and crystallized intelligence. *Acta Psychologica, 26,* 107–129.

Horn, J. L., & Knapp, J. R. (1973). On the subjective character of the empirical base of Guilford's structure-of-intellect model. *Psychological Bulletin, 80,* 33–43.

Hornby, G. (1992). Integration of children with special educational needs: Is it time for a policy review? *Support for Learning, 7,* 130–134.

Horowitz, F. D., & O'Brien, M. (1989). In the interest of the nation: A reflective essay on the state of our knowledge and the challenges before us. *American Psychologist, 44,* 441–445.

Houston Independent School District (HISD) v. Bobby, Joyce, and Caius R., 200 F.3d 341 (5th Cir. 2000), LEXIS 715.

Howell, K. K., & Bracken, B. A. (1992). Clinical utility of the Bracken Basic Concept Scale as a preschool intellectual screener: Comparison with the Stanford-Binet for African-American children. *Journal of Clinical Child Psychology, 21,* 255–261.

Hresko, W. P., Herron, S. R., & Peak, P. K. (1996). *The Test of Early Written Language–Second Edition.* Austin, TX: Pro-Ed.

Hresko, W. P., Reid, D. K., & Hammill, D. D. (1999). *Test of Early Language Development–Third Edition.* Austin, TX: Pro-Ed.

Hresko, W. P., & Schlieve, P. L. (1993). *DATA–2 pro-score system.* Austin, TX: Pro-Ed.

Huberty, T. J., & Koller, J. R. (1984). WISC–R test ages as predictors of achievement. *Educational & Psychological Research, 4,* 73–79.

Hudson, L. (1972). The context of the debate. In K. Richardson, D. Spears, & M. Richards (Eds.), *Race and intelligence: The fallacies behind the race-IQ controversy* (pp. 10–16). Baltimore: Penguin Books.

Humphreys, L. G. (1971). Theory of intelligence. In R. Cancro (Ed.), *Intelligence: Genetic and environmental influences* (pp. 31–42). New York: Grune & Stratton.

Humphreys, L. G. (1973). Statistical definitions of test validity for minority groups. *Journal of Applied Psychology, 58,* 1–4.

Humphreys, L. G. (1979). The construct of general intelligence. *Intelligence, 3,* 105–120.

Humphreys, L. G. (1985). General intelligence: An integration of factor, test, and simplex theory. In B. B. Wolman (Ed.), *Handbook of intelligence: Theories, measurements, and applications* (pp. 201–224). New York: Wiley.

Humphreys, L. G. (1986). Commentary. *Journal of Vocational Behavior, 29,* 421–437.

Humphreys, L. G., & Davey, T. C. (1988). Continuity in intellectual growth from 12 months to 9 years. *Intelligence, 12,* 183–197.

Humphreys, L. G., & Parsons, C. K. (1979). Piagetian tasks measure intelligence and intelligence tests assess cognitive development: A reanalysis. *Intelligence, 3,* 369–382.

Humphreys, L. G., Parsons, C. K., & Park, R. K. (1979). Dimensions involved in differences among school means of cognitive measures. *Journal of Educational Measurement, 16,* 63–76.

Hunt, E. (1985). The correlates of intelligence. *Current Topics in Human Intelligence, 1,* 157–178.

Hunt, E. (1987). The next work on verbal ability. In P. A. Vernon (Ed.), *Speed of information-processing and intelligence* (pp. 347–392). Norwood, NJ: Ablex.

Hunt, E. (1997). Nature vs nurture: The feeling of vujà dé. In R. J. Sternberg & E. Grigorenko (Eds.), *Intelligence, heredity, and environment* (pp. 531–551). New York: Cambridge University Press.

Hunt, E., & Pellegrino, J. (1985). Using interactive computing to expand intelligence testing: A critique and prospectus. *Intelligence, 9,* 207–236.

Hunt, P. L. (1987). Black clients: Implications for supervision of trainees. *Psychotherapy, 24,* 114–119.

Hunter, J. E. (1986). Cognitive ability, cognitive aptitudes, job knowledge, and job performance. *Journal of Vocational Behavior, 29,* 340–362.

Hunter, J. E., & Hunter, R. F. (1984). Validity and utility of alternative predictors of job performance. *Psychological Bulletin, 96,* 72–98.

Hunter, J. E., & Schmidt, F. L. (1990). *Methods of meta-analysis: Correcting error and bias in research findings.* Newbury Park, CA: Sage.

Hutton, U., Wilding, J., & Hudson, R. (1997). The role of attention in the relationship between inspection time and IQ in children. *Intelligence, 24,* 445–460.

Hyde, J. S., & McKinley, N. M. (1997). Gender differences in cognition: Results from meta-analyses. In P. J. Caplan, M. Crawford, J. S. Hyde, & J. T. E. Richardson (Eds.), *Gender differences in human cognition* (pp. 30–51). New York: Oxford University Press.

Illingworth, R. S., & Birch, L. B. (1959). The diagnosis of mental retardation in infancy. A follow-up study. *Archives of Disease in Childhood, 34,* 269–273.

Iverson, G. L., & Franzen, M. D. (1994). The Recognition Memory Test, Digit Span, and Knox Cube Test as markers of malingered memory impairment. *Assessment, 1,* 323–334.

Jackson v. New Hyde Park Memorial High School, No. 98–7978, 1999, U.S. Court of Appeals for the Second Circuit, LEXIS 5741.

Jacob-Timm, S., & Hartshorne, T. S. (1998). *Ethics and law for school psychologists* (3rd ed.). New York: Wiley.

Jacoby, R., & Glauberman, N. (Eds.). (1995). *The bell curve debate: History, documents, opinions.* New York: Times Books.

Jason D. W. v. Houston Independent School District, 158 F.3d 205 (5th Cir. 1998), LEXIS 26589.

Jenkins, J. J., & Paterson, D. G. (Eds.). (1961). *Studies in individual differences.* New York: Appleton-Century-Crofts.

Jensen, A. R. (1974a). How biased are culture-loaded tests? *Genetic Psychology Monographs, 90,* 185–244.

Jensen, A. R. (1974b). Review of the book *Genetic diversity and human equality. Perspectives in Biology and Medicine, 17,* 430–434.

Jensen, A. R. (1975). The price of inequality. *Oxford Review of Education, 1,* 59–71.

Jensen, A. R. (1979). g: Outmoded theory or unconquered frontier? *Creative Science and Technology, 11,* 16–29.

Jensen, A. R. (1993). Spearman's g: Links between psychometrics and biology. *Annals of the New York Academy of Sciences, 702,* 103–129.

Jensen, A. R. (1998). *The g factor: The science of mental ability.* Westport, CT: Praeger.

Jensen, A. R., & Osborne, R. T. (1979). *Forward and Backward Digit Span interaction with race and IQ: A longitudinal developmental comparison.* Berkeley: University of California. (ERIC Document Reproduction Service No. ED 173 384)

Jensen, A. R., & Reynolds, C. R. (1982). Race, social class and ability patterns on the WISC–R. *Personality and Individual Differences, 3,* 423–438.

Jensen, A. R., & Vernon, P. A. (1986). Jensen's reaction time studies: A reply to Longstreth. *Intelligence, 10,* 153–179.

Johnson, D. L., Howie, V. M., Owen, M., Baldwin, C. D., & Luttman, D. (1993). Assessment of three-year-olds with the Stanford-Binet Fourth Edition. *Psychological Reports, 73,* 51–57.

Johnson, R. C., McClearn, G. E., Yuen, S., Nagoshi, C. T., Ahern, F. M., & Cole, R. E. (1985). Galton's data a century later. *American Psychologist, 40,* 875–892.

Johnson v. Duneland School Corporation, 92 F.3d 554 (7th Cir. 1996), LEXIS 20185.

Johnston, W. T., & Bolen, L. M. (1984). A comparison of the factor structure of the WISC–R for blacks and whites. *Psychology in the Schools, 21,* 42–44.

Kahn, J. V. (1983). Sensorimotor period and adaptive behavior development of severely and profoundly mentally retarded children. *American Journal of Mental Deficiency, 88,* 69–75.

Kamphaus, R. W., Benson, J., Hutchinson, S., & Platt, L. O. (1994). Identification of factor models for the WISC–III. *Educational & Psychological Measurement, 54,* 174–186.

Kanfer, R., Eyberg, S. M., & Krahn, G. L. (1992). Interviewing strategies in child assessment. In C. E. Walker & M. C. Roberts (Eds.), *Handbook of clinical child psychology* (2nd ed., pp. 49–62). New York: Wiley.

Kaplan, C. H. (1992). Ceiling effects in assessing high-IQ children with the WPPSI–R. *Journal of Clinical Child Psychology, 21,* 403–406.

Kaplan, C. H., Fox, L. M., & Paxton, L. (1991). Bright children and the revised WPPSI: Concurrent validity. *Journal of Psychoeducational Assessment, 9,* 240–246.

Kaplan, E., Fein, D., Kramer, J., Delis, D., & Morris, R. (1999). *WISC–III PI.* San Antonio: The Psychological Corporation.

Kaplan, E., Fein, D., Morris, R., & Delis, D. C. (1991). *WAIS–R as a neuropsychological instrument.* San Antonio: The Psychological Corporation.

Kaplan, S. L., & Alfonso, V. C. (1997). Confirmatory factor analysis of the Stanford-Binet Intelligence Scale: Fourth Edition with preschoolers with developmental delays. *Journal of Psychoeducational Assessment, 15,* 226–236.

Kari H. v. Franklin Special School District, Nos. 96–5066, 96–5178, 1997 U.S. Court of Appeals for the Sixth Circuit, LEXIS 21724.

Karr, S. K., Carvajal, H., Elser, D., Bays, K., Logan, R. A., & Page, G. L. (1993). Concurrent validity of the WPPSI–R and the McCarthy Scales of Children's Abilities. *Psychological Reports, 72,* 940–942.

Karr, S. K., Carvajal, H., & Palmer, B. L. (1992). Comparison of Kaufman's short form of the McCarthy Scales of Children's Abilities and the Stanford-Binet Intelligence Scales–Fourth Edition. *Perceptual and Motor Skills, 74,* 1120–1122.

Kathleen H., Larry H., and Daniel H. v. Massachusetts Department of Education et al., 154 F.3d 8 (1st Cir. 1998), LEXIS 22054.

Kaufman, A. S. (1972). Piaget and Gesell: A psychometric analysis of tests built from their tasks. *Child Development, 42,* 1341–1360.

Kaufman, A. S. (1975). Factor analysis of the WISC–R at 11 age levels between 6½ and 16½ years. *Journal of Consulting and Clinical Psychology, 43,* 135–147.

Kaufman, A. S. (1979). *Intelligent testing with the WISC–R.* New York: Wiley.

Kaufman, A. S. (1990). *Assessing adolescent and adult intelligence.* Needham Heights, MA: Allyn & Bacon.

Kaufman, A. S. (1994). *Intelligent testing with the WISC–III.* New York: Wiley.

Kaufman, A. S., & DiCuio, R. F. (1975). Separate factor analyses of the McCarthy Scales for groups of black and white children. *Journal of School Psychology, 13,* 10–18.

Kaufman, A. S., & Doppelt, J. E. (1976). Analysis of WISC–R standardization data in terms of the stratification variables. *Child Development, 47,* 165–171.

Kaufman, A. S., & Hollenbeck, G. P. (1974). Comparative structure of the WPPSI for blacks and whites. *Journal of Clinical Psychology, 30,* 316–319.

Kaufman, A. S., Kaufman, J. C., Balgopal, R., & McLean, J. E. (1996). Comparison of three WISC–III short forms: Weighing psychometric, clinical, and practical factors. *Journal of Clinical Child Psychology, 25,* 97–105.

Kaufman, A. S., & Kaufman, N. L. (1983). *Kaufman Assessment Battery for Children.* Circle Pines, MN: American Guidance Service.

Kaufman, A. S., & Kaufman, N. L. (1985). *Kaufman Test of Educational Achievement Brief Form.* Circle Pines, MN: American Guidance Service.

Kaufman, A. S., & Kaufman, N. L. (1990). *Kaufman Brief Intelligence Test.* Circle Pines, MN: American Guidance Service.

Kaufman, A. S., & Kaufman, N. L. (1993). *Kaufman Adolescent & Adult Intelligence Test.* Circle Pines, MN: American Guidance Service.

Kaufman, A. S., & Kaufman, N. L. (1998). *Manual for the Kaufman Test of Educational Achievement–Comprehensive Form.* Circle Pines, MN: American Guidance Service.

Keasey, C. T., & Charles, D. C. (1967). Conservation of substance in normal and mentally retarded children. *Journal of Genetic Psychology, 111,* 271–279.

Keating, D. P. (1975). Precocious cognitive development at the level of formal operations. *Child Development, 46,* 276–280.

Keir, G. (1949). The Progressive Matrices as applied to school children. *British Journal of Psychology, Statistical Section, 2,* 140–150.

Keith, T. Z. (1985). Questioning the K-ABC: What does it measure? *School Psychology Review, 14,* 9–20.

Keith, T. Z. (1990). Confirmatory and hierarchical confirmatory analysis of the Differential Ability Scales. *Journal of Psychoeducational Assessment, 8,* 391–405.

Keith, T. Z. (1997). What does the WISC–III measure? A reply to Carroll and Kranzler. *School Psychology Quarterly, 12,* 117–118.

Keith, T. Z., Cool, V. A., Novak, C. G., White, L. J., & Pottebaum, S. M. (1988). Confirmatory factor analysis of the Stanford-Binet Fourth Edition: Testing the theory-test match. *Journal of School Psychology, 26,* 253–274.

Keith, T. Z., Quirk, K. J., Schartzer, C., & Elliott, C. D. (1999). Construct bias in the differential ability scales? Confirmatory and hierarchical factor structure across three ethnic groups. *Journal of Psychoeducational Assessment, 17,* 249–268.

Keith, T. Z., & Witta, E. L. (1997). Hierarchical and cross-age confirmatory factor analysis of the WISC–III: What does it measure? *School Psychology Quarterly, 12,* 89–107.

Kelly, T. P., & Brittion, P. G. (1996). Sex differences on an adaptation of the Digit Symbol subtest of the Wechsler Intelligence Scale for Children–III. *Perceptual and Motor Skills, 83,* 843–847.

Kennedy, W. A., Van de Riet, V., & White, J. C., Jr. (1963). A normative sample of intelligence and achievement of Negro elementary school children in the southeastern United States. *Monographs of the Society for Research in Child Development, 28,* 1–112.

Keogh, B. K., & Kopp, C. B. (1978). From assessment to intervention: An elusive bridge. In F. D. Minifie & L. L. Lloyd (Eds.), *Communicative and cognitive abilities–early behavioral assessment* (pp. 523–547). Baltimore: University Park Press.

Keogh, B. K., Major-Kingsley, S., Omori-Gordon, H., & Reid, H. P. (1982). *A system of marker variables for the field of learning disabilities.* Syracuse, NY: Syracuse University Press.

Kessler, J. W. (1988). *Psychopathology of childhood* (2nd ed.). Englewood Cliffs, NJ: Prentice Hall.

Keston, M. J., & Jimenez, C. (1954). A study of the performance on English and Spanish editions of the Stanford-Binet Intelligence Test by Spanish American children. *Journal of Genetic Psychology, 85,* 263–269.

Kirk, S. A., McCarthy, J. J., & Kirk, W. D. (1968). *The Illinois Test of Psycholinguistic Abilities.* Urbana: University of Illinois Press.

Klassen, R. M., & Kishor, N. (1996). A comparative analysis of practitioners' errors on WISC–R and WISC–III. *Canadian Journal of School Psychology, 12,* 35–43.

Klein, N. K., Hack, M., & Breslau, N. (1989). Children who were very low birth weight: Development and academic achievement at nine years of age. *Journal of Developmental & Behavioral Pediatrics, 10,* 32–37.

Kleinmuntz, B. (1967). *Personality measurement: An introduction.* Homewood, IL: Dorsey Press.

Kline, R. B. (1989). Is the Fourth Edition Stanford-Binet a four-factor test? Confirmatory factor analysis of alternative models for ages 2 through 23. *Journal of Psychoeducational Assessment, 7,* 4–13.

Kluckhohn, F. R. (1958). Family diagnosis: 1. Variations in the basic values of family systems. *Social Casework, 39,* 63–72.

Knight, B. C., Baker, E. H., & Minder, C. C. (1990). Concurrent validity of the Stanford-Binet: Fourth Edition and Kaufman Assessment Battery for Children with learning-disabled students. *Psychology in the Schools, 27,* 116–120.

Knobloch, H., & Pasamanick, B. (1960). Environmental factors affecting human development before and after birth. *Pediatrics, 26,* 210–218.

Koh, T., Abbatiello, A., & McLoughlin, C. S. (1984). Cultural bias in WISC subtest items: A response to Judge Grady's suggestion in relation to the PASE case. *School Psychology Review, 13,* 89–94.

Kolin, P. C., & Kolin, J. L. (1980). *Professional writing for nurses in education, practice, and research.* St. Louis: Mosby.

Komm, R. A. (1978). A comparison of the Black Intelligence Test of Cultural Homogeneity with the Wechsler Intelligence Scale for Children (Revised), as measured by a conventional achievement test within a black population at different social class levels. *Dissertation Abstracts International, 39,* 6031A–6032A. (University Microfilms No. 79–05059)

Konold, T. R. (1999). Evaluating discrepancy analysis with the WISC–III and WIAT. *Journal of Psychoeducational Assessment, 17,* 24–35.

Konold, T. R., Glutting, J. J., McDermott, P. A., Kush, J. C., & Watkins, M. W. (1999). Structure and diagnostic benefits of a normative subtest taxonomy developed from the WISC–III standardization sample. *Journal of School Psychology, 37,* 29–48.

Konold, T. R., Kush, J. C., & Canivez, G. L. (1997). Factor replication of the WISC–III in three independent samples of children receiving special education. *Journal of Psychoeducational Assessment, 15,* 123–137.

Konold, T. R., Maller, S. J., & Glutting, J. J. (1998). Measurement and non-measurement influences of test-session behavior on individually administered measures of intelligence. *Journal of School Psychology, 36,* 417–432.

Koocher, G. P., & Keith-Spiegel, P. C. (1990). *Children, ethics, and the law: Professional issues and cases.* Lincoln: University of Nebraska Press.

Kranzler, J. H. (1997). What does the WISC–III measure? Comments on the relationship between intellgence, working memory capacity, and information processing speed and efficiency. *School Psychology Quarterly, 12,* 110–116.

Kranzler, J. H., & Keith, T. Z. (1999). Independent confirmatory factor analysis of the Cognitive Assessment System (CAS): What does CAS measure? *School Psychology Review, 28,* 117–144.

Kreutzer, J. S., Harris-Marwitz, J., & Myers, S. L. (1990). Neuropsychological issues in litigation following traumatic brain injury. *Neuropsychology, 4,* 249–259.

Krohn, E. J., & Lamp, R. E. (1989). Concurrent validity of the Stanford-Binet Fourth Edition and K-ABC for Head Start children. *Journal of School Psychology, 27,* 59–67.

K. R. v. Anderson Community School Corporation, 125 F.3d 1017 (7th Cir. 1997), LEXIS 2295.

Kumabe, K. T., Nishida, C., & Hepworth, D. H. (1985). *Bridging ethnocultural diversities in social work and health.* Honolulu: University of Hawaii.

Kush, J. C. (1996). Factor structure of the WISC–III for students with learning disabilities. *Journal of Psychoeducational Assessment, 14,* 32–40.

Kush, J. C., & Watkins, M. W. (1997). Construct validity of the WISC–III verbal and performance factors for Black special education students. *Assessment, 4,* 297–304.

LaFromboise, T. D., Trimble, J. E., & Mohatt, G. V. (1990). Counseling intervention and American Indian tradition: An integrative approach. *Counseling Psychologist, 18,* 628–654.

Lahey, M. (1988). *Language development and language disorders.* New York: Macmillan.

Lambeau v. Arlington County School Board, 114 F.3d 1176 (4th Cir. 1997), LEXIS 20660.

Lamp, R. E., & Krohn, E. J. (1990). Stability of the Stanford-Binet Fourth Edition and K-ABC for young Black and White children from low income families. *Journal of Psychoeducational Assessment, 8,* 139–149.

Larry P. v. Riles, 343 F. Supp. 1306 (D.C. N. D. Cal., 1972), aff'd., 502 F.2d 963 (9th Cir. 1974), *further proceedings,* 495 F. Supp. 926 (D.C. N. D. Cal., 1979), *aff'd.,* 502 F.2d 693 (9th Cir. 1984).

Larsen, S. C., Hammill, D. D., & Moats, L. C. (1999). *Test of Written Spelling–Fourth Edition.* Austin, TX: Pro-Ed.

Lassiter, K. S., & Bardos, A. N. (1995). The relationship between young children's academic achievement and measures of intelligence. *Psychology in the Schools, 32,* 170–177.

Laughlin, T. (1995). The school readiness composite of the Bracken Basic Concept Scale as an intellectual screening instrument. *Journal of Psychoeducational Assessment, 13,* 294–302.

Lavin, C. (1996a). Scores on the Wechsler Intelligence Scale for Children–Third Edition and Woodcock-Johnson Tests of Achievement–Revised for a sample of children with emotional handicaps. *Psychological Reports, 79,* 1291–1295.

Lavin, C. (1996b). The relationships between the Wechsler Intelligence Scale for Children–Third Edition and the Kaufman Test of Educational Achievement. *Psychology in the Schools, 33,* 119–123.

Lavin, C. (1996c). The Wechsler Intelligence Scale for Children–Third Edition and the Stanford- Binet–Fourth Edition: A preliminary study of validity. *Psychological Reports, 78,* 491–496.

Law, J. G., Jr., & Faison, L. (1996). WISC–III and KAIT results on adolescent delinquent males. *Journal of Clinical Psychology, 52,* 699–703.

Lawlis, G. F., Stedman, J. M., & Cortner, R. H. (1980). Factor analysis of the WISC–R for a sample of bilingual Mexican-Americans. *Journal of Clinical Child Psychology, 9,* 57–58.

Lawson, T. T., & Evans, L. D. (1996). Stanford-Binet: Fourth Edition short forms with underachieving and learning disabled students. *Psychological Reports, 49,* 47–50.

Lester, E. P., Muir, R., & Dudek, S. Z. (1970). Cognitive structure and achievement in the young child. *Canadian Psychiatric Association Journal, 15,* 279–287.

Levandowski, B. (1975). The difference in intelligence test scores of bilingual students on an English version of the intelligence test as compared to a Spanish version of the test. *Illinois School Research, 11,* 47–51.

Levenson, R. L., Jr., Golden-Scaduto, C. J., Aiosa-Karpas, C. J., & Ward, A. W. (1988). Effects of examiners' education and sex on presence and type of clerical errors made on WISC–R protocols. *Psychological Reports, 62,* 659–664.

Levinson, E. M., & Folino, L. (1994). Correlations of scores on the Gifted Evaluation Scale with those on WISC–III and Kaufman Brief Intelligence Test for students referred for gifted evaluation. *Psychological Reports, 74,* 419–424.

Levy, B. B., & Cook, H. (1973). Dialect proficiency and auditory comprehension in standard and black nonstandard English. *Journal of Speech and Hearing Research, 16,* 642–649.

Lewis-O'Donnell, M. (1986). *A comparison study of the performance of inpatient emotionally disturbed non-psychotic children and the standardization sample using the Stanford-Binet (Fourth Edition).* Unpublished doctoral dissertation, Biola University, La Mirada, CA.

Light, R. J., & Pillemer, D. B. (1984). *Summing up. The science of reviewing research.* Cambridge, MA: Harvard University Press.

Linden, K. W., & Linden, J. D. (1968). *Modern mental measurement: A historical perspective.* Boston: Houghton Mifflin.

Linville, J. N., Rust, J. O., & Kim, J. K. (1999). The Information and Picture Completion dyad of the WISC–III as a screening test for gifted referrals. *Journal of Instructional Psychology, 26,* 98–104.

Lipsetz, J. D., Dworkin, R. H., & Erlenmeyer-Kimling, L. (1993). Wechsler Comprehension and Picture Arrangement subtests and social adjustment. *Psychological Assessment, 5,* 430–437.

Little, S. G. (1992). The WISC–III: Everything old is new again. *School Psychology Quarterly, 7,* 136–142.

Livesay, K. K. (1986, October). *Comparisons of the Stanford-Binet: Fourth Edition to the S-B L-M and WISC–R with gifted referrals.* Paper presented at the annual conference of the Florida Association of School Psychologists, Jacksonville, FL.

LoBello, S. G., & Gulgoz, S. (1991). Factor analysis of the Wechsler Preschool and Primary Scale of Intelligence–Revised. *Psychological Assessment: A Journal of Consulting and Clinical Psychology, 3,* 130–132.

LoBello, S. G., Thompson, A. P., & Evani, V. (1998). Supplementary WAIS–III tables for determining subtest strengths and weaknesses. *Journal of Psychoeducational Assessment, 16,* 196–200.

Locurto, C. (1990). The malleability of IQ as judged from adoption studies. *Intelligence, 14,* 275–292.

Loehlin, J. C., Horn, J. M., & Willerman, L. (1989). Modeling IQ change: Evidence from the Texas Adoption Project. *Child Development, 60,* 993–1004.

Loehlin, J. C., Horn, J. M., & Willerman, L. (1994). Differential inheritance of mental abilities in the Texas Adoption Project. *Intelligence, 19,* 325–336.

Loehlin, J. C., Lindzey, G., & Spuhler, J. N. (1975). *Race differences in intelligence.* San Francisco: W. H. Freeman.

Logue v. Unified School District No. 512, Shawnee Mission, 153 F.3d 727 (10th Cir. 1998), LEXIS 25930.

Long, P. A., & Anthony, J. J. (1974). The measurement of mental retardation by a culture-specific test. *Psychology in the Schools, 11,* 310–312.

Lozoff, B. (1989). Nutrition and behavior. *American Psychologist, 44,* 231–236.

Luiselli, J. K. (1989). Health-threatening behaviors. In J. K. Luiselli (Ed.), *Behavioral medicine and developmental disabilities* (pp. 114–151). New York: Springer-Verlag.

Lukens, J. (1988). Comparison of the Fourth Edition and the L-M edition of the Stanford-Binet used with mentally retarded persons. *Journal of School Psychology, 26,* 87–89.

Lukens, J. (1990). Stanford-Binet, Fourth Edition and the WISC–R for children in the lower range of intelligence. *Perceptual and Motor Skills, 70,* 819–822.

Lukens, J., & Hurrell, R. M. (1996). A comparison of the Stanford-Binet IV and the WISC–III with mildly retarded children. *Psychology in the Schools, 33,* 24–27.

Luria, A. R. (1966a). *Higher cortical functions in man.* New York: Basic Books.

Luria, A. R. (1966b). *Human brain and psychological processes.* New York: Harper & Row.

Lynch, E. W., & Hanson, M. J. (Eds.). (1992). *Developing cross-cultural competence: A guide for working with young children and their families.* Baltimore: Paul H. Brookes.

Lynn, R. (1977). The intelligence of the Japanese. *Bulletin of the British Psychological Society, 30,* 69–72.

Lynn, R. (1987). Japan: Land of the rising IQ: A reply to Flynn. *Bulletin of the British Psychological Society, 40,* 464–468.

Lynn, R. (1990). The role of nutrition in secular increases in intelligence. *Personality & Individual Differences, 11,* 273–285.

Lyon, M. A. (1995). A comparison between WISC–III and WISC–R scores for learning disabilities reevaluations. *Journal of Learning Disabilities, 28,* 253–255.

MacArthur, R. S. (1960). The Coloured Progressive Matrices as a measure of general intelligence ability for Edmonton grade III boys. *Alberta Journal of Educational Research, 6,* 67–75.

MacArthur, R. S., & Elley, W. B. (1963). The reduction of socio-economic bias in intelligence testing. *British Journal of Educational Psychology, 33,* 107–119.

Mackinson, J. A., Leigh, I. W., & Anthony, S. (1997). Validity of the TONI–2 with deaf and hard of hearing children. *American Annals of the Deaf, 142,* 294–299.

Mainstream English is the key. (1996, December 22). *Los Angeles Times,* p. M4.

Maller, S. J., & Ferron, J. (1997). WISC–III factor invariance across deaf and standardization samples. *Educational & Psychological Measurement, 57,* 987–994.

Marie O., Gabriel C., and Kyle G. v. Edgar, Governor of Illinois, and Spagnolo, State Superintendent of Education, 131 F.3d 610 (7th Cir. 1997), LEXIS 33978.

Marin, G., & Marin, B. V. (1991). *Research with Hispanic populations.* Newbury Park, CA: Sage.

Marjoribanks, K. (1972). Environment, social class, and mental abilities. *Journal of Educational Psychology, 63,* 103–109.

Mark, R., Beal, A. L., & Dumont, R. (1998). Validation of a WISC–III short-form for the identification of Canadian gifted students. *Canadian Journal of School Psychology, 14,* 1–10.

Markwardt, F. C. (1989). *Peabody Individual Achievement Test–Revised.* Circle Pines, MN: American Guidance Service.

Markwardt, F. C. (1997). *Peabody Individual Achievement Test–Revised.* Circle Pines, MN: American Guidance Service.

Marquardt, T. P., Stoll, J., & Sussman, H. (1988). Disorders of communication in acquired cerebral trauma. *Journal of Learning Disabilities, 21,* 340–351.

Marshall v. Georgia, U.S. District Court for the Southern District of Georgia, CV 482–233, June 28, 1994; amended August 24, 1984.

Marston, D. B. (1989). A curriculum-based measurement approach to assessing academic performance: What it is and why do it. In M. R. Shinn (Ed.), *Curriculum-based measurement: Assessing special children* (pp.18–78). New York: Guilford.

Martelle, Y., & Smith, D. K. (1994). *Relationship of the WIAT and WJ–R Tests of Achievement in a sample of students referred for learning disabilities.* Paper presented at the annual meeting of the National Association of School Psychologists, Seattle. (ERIC Document Reproduction Services ED 381976)

Mason, E. M. (1992). Percent of agreement among raters and rater reliability of the Copying subtest of the Stanford-Binet Intelligence Scale: Fourth Edition. *Perceptual and Motor Skills, 74,* 347–353.

Massey, J. O. (1964). *WISC scoring criteria.* Palo Alto, CA: Consulting Psychologists Press.

Masten, A. S., & Braswell, L. (1991). Developmental psychopathology: An integrative framework. In P. R. Martin (Ed.), *Handbook of behavior therapy and psychological science: An integrative approach* (pp. 35–56). New York: Pergamon.

Matarazzo, J. D., Daniel, M. H., Prifitera, A., & Herman, D. O. (1988). Inter-subtest scatter in the WAIS–R standardization sample. *Journal of Clinical Psychology, 44,* 940–950.

Matarazzo, R. (1995). Psychological report standards in neuropsychology. *The Clinical Neuropsychologist, 9,* 249–250.

Matt, G. E., & Cook, T. D. (1994). Threats to the validity of research syntheses. In H. M. Cooper & L. V. Hedges (Eds.), *Handbook of research synthesis* (pp. 503–520). New York: Russell Sage.

Matthews, J. R., Bowen, J. M., & Matthews, R. W. (1996). *Successful scientific writing: A step-by-step guide for the biological and medical sciences.* New York: Cambridge University Press.

Mattie T. v. Holladay, No. DC-75–31-S (N. D. Miss. 1979).

Mattis, P. J., Hannay, J., & Meyers, C. A. (1992). Efficacy of the Satz-Mogel Short Form WAIS–R for tumor patients with lateralized lesions. *Psychological Assessment, 4,* 357–362.

M. C. and G. C. v. Central Regional School District, 81 F.3d 389 (3rd Cir. 1996), LEXIS 8717.

McArdle, J. M., Prescott, C. A., Hamagami, F., & Horn, J. L. (1998). A contemporary method for developmental-genetic analyses of age changes in intellectual abilities. *Developmental Neuropsychology, 14,* 69–114.

McCall, R. B. (1977). Childhood IQ's as predictors of adult educational and occupational status. *Science, 197,* 482–483.

McCall, R. B. (1979). The development of intellectual functioning in infancy and the prediction of later I.Q. In J. D. Osofsky (Ed.), *Handbook of infant development* (pp. 707–741). New York: Wiley.

McCall, R. B. (1994). Commentary on Plomin, R. (1994): Advice to the new social genetics: Lessons partly learned from the genetics of mental development. *Social Development, 3,* 54–59.

McCall, R. B., Appelbaum, M. I., & Hogarty, P. S. (1973). Developmental changes in mental performance. *Monographs of the Society for Research in Child Development, 38*(3), 1–83.

McCall, R. B., & Carriger, M. S. (1993). A meta-analysis of infant habituation and recognition memory performance as predictors of later IQ. *Child Development, 64,* 57–79.

McCall, R. B., & Mash, C. W. (1995). Infant cognition and its relation to mature intelligence. *Annals of Child Development, 4,* 27–56.

McCall, V. W., Yates, B., Hendricks, S., Turner, K., & McNabb, B. (1989). Comparison between the Stanford-Binet: L–M and the Stanford-Binet: Fourth Edition with a group of gifted children. *Contemporary Educational Psychology, 14,* 93–96.

McCallum, R. S., & Karnes, F. A. (1987). Comparison of intelligence tests: Responses of gifted pupils to the Stanford-Binet Intelligence Scale (4th ed.), the British Ability Scales, and the Wechsler Intelligence Scale for Children–Revised. *School Psychology International, 8,* 133–139.

McCallum, R. S., & Karnes, F. A. (1990). Use of a brief form of the Stanford-Binet Intelligence Scale (Fourth) for gifted children. *Journal of School Psychology, 28,* 279–283.

McCrowell, K. L., & Nagle, R. J. (1994). Comparability of the WPPSI–R and the S-B:IV among preschool children. *Journal of Psychoeducational Assessment, 12,* 126–134.

McGrew, K. S., & Flanagan, D. P. (1998). *The intelligence test desk reference (ITDR): Gf-Gc cross-battery assessment.* Boston: Allyn & Bacon.

McGrew, K. S., Werder, J. K., & Woodcock, R. W. (1991). *WJ–R technical manual: A reference on theory and current research.* Itasca, IL: Riverside.

McLoyd, V. C. (1998). Socioeconomic disadvantage and child development. *American Psychologist, 53,* 185–204.

McShane, D. A., & Plas, J. M. (1984). The cognitive functioning of American Indian children: Moving from the WISC to the WISC–R. *School Psychology Review, 13,* 61–73.

Mealer, C., Morgan, S., & Luscomb, R. (1996). Cognitive functioning of ADHD and non-ADHD boys on the WISC–III and WRAML: An analysis within a memory model. *Journal of Attention Disorders, 1,* 133–145.

Melton, G. B. (1994). Doing justice and doing good: Conflicts for mental health professionals. *The Future of Children, 4,* 102–118.

Mercer, J. R. (1976). Pluralistic diagnosis in the evaluation of Black and Chicano children: A procedure for taking sociocultural variables into account in clinical assessment. In C. A. Hernandez, M. J. Haug, & N. N. Wagner (Eds.), *Chicanos: Social and psychological perspectives* (2nd ed., pp. 183–195). St. Louis: Mosby.

Mercy, J. A., & Steelman, L. C. (1982). Familial influence on the intellectual attainment of children. *American Sociological Review, 47,* 532–542.

Meyer, W. J., & Goldstein, D. (1971). *Performance characteristics of middle-class and lower-class preschool children on the Stanford-Binet, 1960 Revision.* (ERIC Document Reproduction Service No. ED 044 429)

Michael, W. B. (1998). Review of the Woodcock-McGrew-Weder Mini-Battery of Achievement. In J. C. Impara & B. S. Plake (Eds.), *The thirteenth mental measurements yearbook.* Lincoln: University of Nebraska Press.

Miele, F. (1979). Cultural bias in the WISC. *Intelligence, 3,* 149–164.

Miller, C. K., & Chansky, N. M. (1972). Psychologists' scoring of WISC protocols. *Psychology in the Schools, 9,* 144–152.

Miller, C. K., Chansky, N. M., & Gredler, G. R. (1970). Rater agreement on WISC protocols. *Psychology in the Schools, 7,* 190–193.

Miller, L. T., & Vernon, P. A. (1992). The general factor in short-term memory, intelligence, and reaction time. *Intelligence, 16,* 5–29.

Miller, L. T., & Vernon, P. A. (1996). Intelligence, reaction time, and working memory in 4- to 6-year-old children. *Intelligence, 22,* 155–190.

Millon, T. (1987). On the nature of taxonomy in psychopathology. In C. G. Last & M. Hersen (Eds.), *Issues in diagnostic research* (pp. 3–85). New York: Plenum.

Milrod, R. J., & Rescorla, L. (1991). A comparison of the WPPSI–R and WPPSI with high-IQ children. *Journal of Psychoeducational Assessment, 9,* 255–262.

Molfese, V., Yaple, K., Helwig, S., Harris, L., & Connell, S. (1992). Stanford-Binet Intelligence Scale (Fourth Edition): Factor structure and verbal subscale scores for 3-year-olds. *Journal of Psychoeducational Assessment, 10,* 47–58.

Moore, C., O'Keefe, S. L., & Lawhon, D. (1998). Concurrent validity of the Snijders-Oomen Nonverbal Intelligence Test 2nd Primary Scale of Intelligence–Revised. *Psychological Reports, 82,* 619–625.

Moore, M. V. (1969). Pathological writing. *Asha, 11,* 535–538.

Morales, E. S., & George, C. (1976, September). *Examiner effects in the testing of Mexican-American children.* Paper presented at the meeting of the American Psychological Association, Washington, DC.

Morsbach, G., McGoldrick, G., & Younger, J. (1978). Inter-scorer reliability of the Geometric Design subtest of the WPPSI. *Journal of Behavioural Science, 2,* 279–284.

Morsbach, H. (1988). The importance of silence and stillness in Japanese nonverbal communication: A cross-cultural approach. In P. Fernando (Ed.), *Cross-cultural perspectives in nonverbal communication* (pp. 201–216). Göttingen, Federal Republic of Germany: Hogrefe.

Morton Community Unit School District No. 709 v. J. M., 152 F.3d 583 (7th Cir. 1998), LEXIS 17079.

Mrs. B. v. Milford Board of Education, 103 F.3d 1114 (2nd Cir. 1997), LEXIS 1114.

Muller v. Committee on Special Education of the East Islip Union Free School District, 145 F.3d 95 (2nd Cir. 1998), LEXIS 10313.

Muñoz-Sandoval, A. F., Cummins, J., Alvarado, C. G., & Ruef, M. L. (1998). *Bilingual Verbal Ability Tests.* Itasca, IL: Riverside.

Murphy, K. P. (1957). Tests of abilities and attainments. In A. W. G. Ewing (Ed.), *Educational guidance and the deaf child* (pp. 213–251). Manchester, England: Manchester University Press.

Murphy v. UPS, 119 S. Ct. 1331 (1999), LEXIS 2238.

Myers, B., & Goldstein, D. (1979). Cognitive development in bilingual and monolingual lower-class children. *Psychology in the Schools, 16,* 137–142.

Myers, J. E. (1993). Expert testimony regarding child sexual abuse. *Child Abuse & Neglect, 17,* 175–185.

Nagle, R. J., & Bell, N. L. (1993). Validation of Stanford-Binet Intelligence Scale: Fourth Edition abbreviated batteries with college students. *Psychology in the Schools, 30,* 227–231.

Naglieri, J. A. (1999a). *Essentials of CAS assessment.* New York: Wiley.

Naglieri, J. A. (1999b). How valid is the PASS theory and CAS? *School Psychology Review, 28,* 145–162.

Naglieri, J. A., & Das, J. P. (1990). Planning, attention, simultaneous, and successive (PASS) cognitive processes as a model for intelligence. *Journal of Psychoeducational Assessment, 8,* 303–337.

Naglieri, J. A., & Das, J. P. (1997). *Cognitive Assessment System.* Itasca, IL: Riverside.

Naglieri, J. A., & Yazzie, C. (1983). Comparison of the WISC–R and PPVT–R with Navajo children. *Journal of Clinical Psychology, 39,* 598–600.

Neisser, U. (Ed.). (1998). *The rising curve: Long-term gains in IQ and related measures.* Washington, DC: American Psychological Association.

Nelson, N. W. (1993). *Childhood language disorders in context: Infancy through adolescence.* New York: Macmillan.

Nettelbeck, T. (1987). Inspection time and intelligence. In P. A. Vernon (Ed.), *Speed in information-processing and intelligence* (pp. 295–346). Norwood, NJ: Ablex.

Neuhaus, M. (1967). Modifications in the administration of the WISC Performance subtests for children with profound hearing losses. *Exceptional Children, 33,* 573–574.

Newcomer, P. L. (1990). *Diagnostic Achievement Battery–Second Edition.* Austin, TX: Pro-Ed.

Newcomer, P. L., & Bryant, B. R. (1993). *Diagnostic Achievement Test for Adolescents–Second Edition.* Austin, TX: Pro-Ed.

Newcomer, P. L., & Hammill, D. D. (1997). *The Test of Language Development–Intermediate: Third Edition.* Austin, TX: Pro-Ed.

Newman, R. (1991). The role of the psychologist expert witness: Provider of perspective and input. *Neuropsychology Review, 2,* 241–249.

Nichols, P. L. (1971). The effects of heredity and environment on intelligence test performance in 4 and 7 year white and Negro sibling pairs. *Dissertation Abstracts International, 32,* 101B-102B. (University Microfilms No. 71–81, 874)

Norton v. Orinda Union School District, No. 97–17029, 1999, U.S. Court of Appeals for the Ninth Circuit, LEXIS 3121.

Oakland, T. D. (1980). An evaluation of the ABIC, pluralistic norms, and estimated learning potential. *Journal of School Psychology, 18,* 3–11.

Oakland, T. D. (1983). Concurrent and predictive validity estimates for the WISC–R IQs and ELPs by racial-ethnic and SES groups. *School Psychology Review, 12,* 57–61.

Oakland, T. D., & Feigenbaum, D. (1979). Multiple sources of test bias on the WISC–R and Bender-Gestalt Test. *Journal of Consulting and Clinical Psychology, 47,* 968–974.

Oberti v. Board of Education of the Borough of Clementon School District, 995 F.2d 1204 (3rd Cir. 1993), LEXIS 12641.

O'Conner, P. T. (1996). *Woe is I: The grammarphobe's guide to better English in plain English.* New York: Putnam.

Ojai Unified School District v. Jackson, 4 F.3d 1467 (9th Cir. 1993), LEXIS 24095.

Okazaki, S., & Sue, S. (1995). Methodological issues in assessment research with ethnic minorities. *Psychological Assessment, 7,* 367–375.

Olea, M. M., & Ree, M. J. (1994). Predicting pilot and navigator criteria: Not much more than *g. Journal of Applied Psychology, 79,* 845–851.

Olivier, K., & Barclay, A. G. (1967). Stanford-Binet and Goodenough-Harris Test performances of Head Start children. *Psychological Reports, 20,* 1175–1179.

O'Neil, M. (1984). *The general method of social work practice.* Englewood Cliffs, NJ: Prentice-Hall.

O'Neill, A. M. (1981). "…On the other foot." *Journal of School Psychology, 19,* 71–72.

Orpet, R. E., Yoshida, R. K., & Meyers, C. E. (1976). The psychometric nature of Piaget's conservation of liquid for ages six and seven. *Journal of Genetic Psychology, 129,* 151–160.

Osgood, C. E. (1957). Motivational dynamics of language behavior. In *Nebraska symposium on motivation* (Vol. 5, pp. 348–424). Lincoln: University of Nebraska Press.

O'Toole v. Olathe District Schools Unified School District No. 233, 144 F.3d 692 (10th Cir. 1997), LEXIS 10126.

Owens, R. E. (1995). *Language disorders: A functional approach to assessment and intervention* (2nd ed.). Needham Heights, MA: Allyn & Bacon.

Ownby, R. L., & Carmin, C. N. (1988). Confirmatory factor analyses of the Stanford-Binet Intelligence Scale, Fourth Edition. *Journal of Psychoeducational Assessment, 6,* 331–340.

Ownby, R. L., & Wallbrown, F. H. (1983). Evaluating school psychological reports, Part I: A procedure for systematic feedback. *Psychology in the Schools, 20,* 41–45.

Palmer, M., & Gaffney, P. D. (1972). Effects of administration of the WISC in Spanish and English and relationship of social class to performance. *Psychology in the Schools, 9,* 61–64.

Panter, J. (1997). *Assessing the school readiness of kindergarten children.* Unpublished doctoral dissertation, University of Memphis, Memphis.

Paolo, A. M., & Ryan, J. J. (1993). WAIS–R abbreviated forms in the elderly: A comparison of the Satz-Mogel with a seven-subtest short form. *Psychological Assessment, 5,* 425–429.

Parents in Action on Special Education v. Joseph P. Hannon, 506 F. Supp. 831 (N. D. Ill. 1980).

Parker, K. C. H., & Atkinson, L. (1994). Factor space of the Wechsler Intelligence Scale for Children–Third Edition: Critical thoughts and recommendations. *Psychological Assessment, 6,* 201–208.

Peck v. Lansing School District, 148 F.3d 619 (6th Cir. 1998), LEXIS 13710.

Pellegrino, J. W. (1986). Intelligence: The interaction of culture and cognitive processes. In R. J. Sternberg & D. K. Detterman (Eds.), *What is intelligence?* (pp. 113–115). Norwood, NJ: Ablex.

Perkins, D. A., & Grotzer, T. A. (1997). Teaching intelligence. *American Psychologist, 52,* 1125–1133.

Peterson, J. (1925). *Early conceptions and tests of intelligence.* Yonkers-on-Hudson, NY: World Book.

Phelps, L. (1989). Comparison of scores for intellectually gifted students on the WISC–R and the Fourth Edition of the Stanford-Binet. *Psychology in the Schools, 26,* 125–129.

Phelps, L. (1996). Discriminative validity of the WRAML with ADHD and LD children. *Psychology in the Schools, 33,* 5–12.

Phelps, L., Bell, M. C., & Scott, M. J. (1988). Correlations between the Stanford-Binet: Fourth Edition and WISC–R with a learning disabled population. *Psychology in the Schools, 25,* 380–382.

Phelps, L., Leguori, S., Nisewaner, K., & Parker, M. (1993). Practical interpretations of the WISC–III with language-disordered children. *Monograph Series of the Journal of Psychoeducational Assessment, Wechsler Intelligence Scale for Children: Third Edition,* 71–76.

Pilgrim, B. M., Meyers, J. E., Bayless, J., & Whetstone, M. M. (1999). Validity of the Ward seven-subtest WAIS–III short form in a neuropsychological population. *Applied Neuropsychology, 6,* 243–246.

Plante, L. G., Plante, T. G., Rahm, P., Brentar, J. T., & Couchman, C. (1997). Administering the Digit Span subtest of the WISC–III to children with attentional, emotional, and learning difficulties: Should the examiner make eye contact or not? *Assessment, 4,* 351–357.

Plomin, R., & DeFries, J. C. (1980). Genetics and intelligence: Recent data. *Intelligence, 4,* 15–24.

Plomin, R., DeFries, J. C., & Fulker, D. W. (1988). *Nature and nurture during infancy and early childhood.* New York: Cambridge University Press.

Plomin, R., & Petrill, S. A. (1997). Genetics and intelligence: What's new? *Intelligence, 24,* 53–77.

Poolaw v. Bishop, 67 F.3d 830 (9th Cir. 1995), LEXIS 27778.

Poole, D. A., & Lamb, M. E. (1997). *Investigative interviews of children: A guide for helping professionals.* Washington, DC: American Psychological Association.

Pope, K. S., Butcher, J. N., & Seelen, J. (1993). *The MMPI, MMPI–2, and MMPI–A in court: Assessment, testimony, and cross-examination for expert witnesses and attorneys.* Washington, DC: American Psychological Association.

Post, J. M. (1970). The effects of vocalization on the ability of third grade students to complete selected performance subtests from the Wechsler Intelligence Scale for Children. *Dissertation Abstracts International, 31,* 1579A. (University Microfilms No. 70–19, 602)

Poteat, G. M., Wuensch, K. L., & Gregg, N. B. (1988). An investigation of differential prediction with the WISC–R. *Journal of School Psychology, 26,* 59–68.

Poythress, N. G. (1992). Expert testimony on violence and dangerousness: Roles for mental health professionals. *Forensic Reports, 5,* 135–150.

Prewett, P. N. (1992). Short forms of the Stanford-Binet Intelligence Scale: Fourth Edition. *Journal of Psychoeducational Assessment, 10,* 257–264.

Prewett, P. N. (1995). A comparison of two screening tests (the Matrix Analogies Test–Short Form and the Kaufman Brief Intelligence Test) with the WISC–III. *Psychological Assessment, 7,* 69–72.

Prewett, P. N., & Farhney, M. R. (1994). The concurrent validity of the Matrix Analogies Test–Short Form with the Stanford-Binet: Fourth Edition and KTEA-BF (academic achievement). *Psychology in the Schools, 31,* 20–25.

Prewett, P. N., & McCaffery, L. K. (1993). A comparison of the Kaufman Brief Intelligence Test (K-BIT) with the Stanford-Binet, a two-subtest short form, and the Kaufman Test of Educational Achievement (K-TEA) Brief Form. *Psychology in the Schools, 30,* 299–304.

Prifitera, A., Weiss, L. G., & Saklofske, D. H. (1998). The WISC–III in context. In A. Prifitera & D. Saklofske (Eds.), *WISC–III clinical use and interpretation* (pp. 1–38). San Diego: Academic.

Quay, L. C. (1972). Negro dialect and Binet performance in severely disadvantaged black four-year-olds. *Child Development, 43,* 245–250.

Quay, L. C. (1974). Language dialect, age, and intelligence-test performance in disadvantaged black children. *Child Development, 45,* 463–468.

Quereshi, M. Y., & Seitz, R. (1994). Non-equivalence of WPPSI, WPPSI–R, and WISC–R scores. *Current Psychology: Developmental, Learning, Personality, Social, 13,* 210–225.

Ramey, C. T., & Ramey, S. L. (1990). Intensive educational intervention for children of poverty. *Intelligence, 14,* 1–9.

Ramirez, M., III. (1991). *Psychotherapy and counseling with minorities: A cognitive approach to individual and cultural differences.* Elmsford, NY: Pergamon.

Rapaport, D., Gill, M. M., & Schafer, R. (1968). *Diagnostic psychological testing* (rev. ed.). New York: International Universities Press.

Raven, J., Raven, J. C., & Court, J. H. (1998a). *Advanced Progressive Matrices.* Oxford, England: Oxford Psychologists Press.

Raven, J., Raven, J. C., & Court, J. H. (1998b). *Coloured Progressive Matrices.* Oxford, England: Oxford Psychologists Press.

Raven, J., Raven, J. C., & Court, J. H. (1998c). *Standard Progressive Matrices.* Oxford, England: Oxford Psychologists Press.

Raven, J. C. (1938). *Progressive Matrices.* London: Lewis.

Raven, J. C. (1960). *Guide to using the Standard Progressive Matrices.* London: Lewis.

Raven, J. C. (1965). *The Coloured Progressive Matrices Test.* London: Lewis.

Raven, J. C., Court, J. H., & Raven, J. (1983). *Manual for Raven's Progressive Matrices and Vocabulary Scales (Section 3)–Standard Progressive Matrices (1983 edition).* London: Lewis.

Raven, J. C., Court, J. H., & Raven, J. (1986). *Manual for Raven's Progressive Matrices and Vocabulary Scales (Section 2)–Coloured Progressive Matrices (1986 edition, with U.S. norms).* London: Lewis.

Raven, J. C., & Summers, B. (1986). *Manual for Raven's Progressive Matrices and Vocabulary Scales–Research supplement no. 3.* London: Lewis.

Reed, M. (1970). Deaf and partially hearing children. In P. Mittler (Ed.), *The psychological assessment of mental and physical handicaps* (pp. 403–441). London: Methuen.

Reed, V. A. (1994). *An introduction to children with language disorders* (2nd ed.). Englewood Cliffs, NJ: Merrill.

Reid, D. K., Hresko, W. P., & Hammill, D. D. (1989). *The Test of Early Reading Ability–Second Edition.* Austin, TX: Pro-Ed.

Reschly, D. J. (1978). WISC–R factor structures among Anglos, blacks, Chicanos, and native-American Papagos. *Journal of Consulting and Clinical Psychology, 46,* 417–422.

Reschly, D. J., & Reschly, J. E. (1979). Validity of WISC–R factor scores in predicting achievement and attention for four sociocultural groups. *Journal of School Psychology, 17,* 355–361.

Reschly, D. J., & Sabers, D. L. (1979). Analysis of test bias in four groups with the regression definition. *Journal of Educational Measurement, 16,* 1–9.

Resnick, L. B. (1979). The future of IQ testing in education. *Intelligence, 3,* 241–253.

Reynolds, C. R., & Gutkin, T. B. (1980). A regression analysis of test bias on the WISC–R for Anglos and Chicanos referred for psychological services. *Journal of Abnormal Child Psychology, 8,* 237–243.

Reynolds, C. R., & Hartlage, L. (1979). Comparison of WISC and WISC–R regression lines for academic prediction with black and with white referred children. *Journal of Consulting and Clinical Psychology, 47,* 589–591.

Reynolds, C. R., Kamphaus, R. W., & Rosenthal, B. L. (1988). Factor analysis of the Stanford-Binet Fourth Edition for ages 2 years through 23 years. *Measurement & Evaluation in Counseling & Development, 21,* 52–63.

Reynolds, C. R., & Nigl, A. J. (1981). A regression analysis of differential validity in intellectual assessment for black and for white inner city children. *Journal of Clinical Child Psychology, 10,* 176–179.

Reynolds, C. R., Sanchez, S., & Willson, V. L. (1996). Normative tables for calculating the WISC–III Performance and Full Scale IQs when Symbol Search is substituted for Coding. *Psychological Assessment, 8,* 378–382.

Ridgewood Board of Education v. N. E., 172 F.3d 238 (3rd Cir. 1999), LEXIS 5751.

Rimoldi, H. J. (1948). A note on Raven's Progressive Matrices Test. *Educational and Psychological Measurement, 8,* 347–352.

Robinson, N. M., Dale, P. S., & Landesman, S. (1990). Validity of Stanford-Binet IV with linguistically precocious toddlers. *Intelligence, 14,* 173–186.

Robinson, N. M., & Harris, S. R. (1980). *Tricks of the trade: Testing infants and preschoolers.* Unpublished manuscript, University of Washington at Seattle, Child Development and Mental Retardation Center.

Rodgers, J. L., Rowe, D. C., & May, K. (1994). DF analysis of NLSY IQ/achievement data: Nonshared environmental influences. *Intelligence, 19,* 157–177.

Rodiriecus v. Waukegan School District No. 60, 90 F.3d 249 (7th Cir. 1996), LEXIS 18366.

Rogers, S. J. (1977). Characteristics of the cognitive development of profoundly retarded children. *Child Development, 48,* 837–843.

Roid, G. H., & Miller, L. J. (1997). *Leiter International Performance Scale–Revised.* Wood Dale, IL: Stoelting.

Roid, G. H., Prifitera, A., & Weiss, L. G. (1993). Replication of the WISC–III factor structure in an independent sample. *Monograph Series of the Journal of Psychoeducational Assessment, Wechsler Intelligence Scale for Children: Third Edition,* 6–21.

Roid, G. H., & Worrall, W. (1997). Replication of the Wechsler Intelligence Scale for Children–Third Edition: Four-factor model in the Canadian normative sample. *Psychological Assessment, 9,* 512–515.

Rose, S. A., & Feldman, J. F. (1995). Prediction of IQ and specific cognitive abilities at 11 years from infancy measures. *Developmental Psychology, 31,* 685–696.

Rose, S. A., Feldman, J. F., Wallace, I. F., & Cohen, P. (1991). Language: A partial link between infant attention and later intelligence. *Developmental Psychology, 27,* 798–805.

Rosenthal, R. (1966). *Experimenter effects in behavioral research.* New York: Appleton-Century-Crofts.

Rosenthal, R. (1984). *Meta-analytic procedures for social research.* Beverly Hills, CA: Sage.

Rotheram, M. J., & Phinney, J. S. (1986). Introduction: Definitions and perspectives in the study of children's ethnic socialization. In J. S. Phinney & M. J. Rotheram (Eds.), *Children's ethnic socialization: Pluralism and development* (pp. 10–28). Newbury Park, CA: Sage.

Rothlisberg, B. A. (1987). Comparing the Stanford-Binet, Fourth Edition to the WISC–R: A concurrent validity study. *Journal of School Psychology, 25,* 193–196.

Rothlisberg, B. A. (1990). The relation of the Stanford-Binet: Fourth Edition to measures of achievement: A concurrent validity study. *Psychology in the Schools, 27,* 120–125.

Rothlisberg, B. A., & McIntosh, D. E. (1991). Performance of a referred sample on the Stanford-Binet IV and the K-ABC. *Journal of School Psychology, 29,* 367–370.

Rousey, A. (1990). Factor structure of the WISC–R Mexicano. *Educational & Psychological Measurement, 50,* 351–357.

Rozencwajg, P. (1991). Analysis of problem solving strategies on the Kohs Block Design Test. *European Journal of Psychology of Education, 6,* 73–88.

Russman v. Board of Education of the Enlarged City School District of the City of Watervliet, 150 F.3d 219 (2nd Cir. 1998), LEXIS 17026.

Rust, J. O., & Lindstrom, A. (1996). Concurrent validity of the WISC–III and Stanford-Binet IV. *Psychological Reports, 79,* 618–620.

Rust, J. O., & Yates, A. G. (1997). Concurrent validity of the Wechsler Intelligence Scale for Children–Third Edition and the Kaufman Assessment Battery for Children. *Psychological Reports, 80,* 89–90.

Ryan, J. J. (1999). Two types of tables for use with the seven-subtest short forms of the WAIS–III. *Journal of Psychoeducational Assessment, 17,* 145–151.

Ryan, J. J., Ament, P. A., & Axelrod, B. N. (2000, August). *Validity of WAIS–III 7–subtest short forms for African Americans.* Paper submitted for presentation at the 108th annual meeting of the American Psychological Association, Washington, DC.

Ryan, J. J., Arb, J. D., Paul, C. A., & Kreiner, D. S. (2000). Reliability of the WAIS–III subtests, indexes, and IQs in a sample of persons with substance abuse disorders. *Assessment, 7,* 151–156.

Ryan, J. J., & Lopez, S. J. (1999, August). *Exploratory factor analysis of the WAIS–III in a mixed patient sample.* Poster session presented at the 107th annual meeting of the American Psychological Association, Boston.

Ryan, J. J., Lopez, S. J., & Werth, T. R. (1998). Administration time estimates for the WAIS–III subtests, scales, and short forms in a clinical sample. *Journal of Psychoeducational Assessment, 16,* 315–323.

Ryan, J. J., Lopez, S. J., & Werth, T. R. (1999). Development and preliminary validation of a Satz-Mogel short form of the WAIS–III in a sample of persons with substance abuse disorders. *International Journal of Neuroscience, 98,* 131–140.

Ryan, J. J., Paolo, A. M., & Brungardt, T. M. (1992). WAIS–R testretest stability in normal persons 75 years and older. *Clinical Neuropsychologist, 6,* 3–8.

Ryan, J. J., Sattler, J. M., & Lopez, S. J. (2000). Age effects on Wechsler Adult Intelligence Scale–III subtests. *Archives of Clinical Neuropsychology, 15,* 311–317.

Ryan, J. J., & Ward, L. C. (1999). Validity, reliability, and standard errors of measurement for two seven-subtest short forms of the Wechsler Adult Intelligence Scale–III. *Psychological Assessment, 11,* 207–211.

Sabatino, D. A., Spangler, R. S., & Vance, H. B. (1995). The relationship between the Wechsler Intelligence Scale for Children–Revised and the Wechsler Intelligence Scale for Children–III scales and subtests with gifted children. *Psychology in the Schools, 32,* 18–23.

Sacramento City School District v. Rachel H., 14 F.3d 1398 (9th Cir. 1994), LEXIS 1124.

Saklofske, D. H., Schwean, V. L., & O'Donnell, L. (1996). WIAT performance of children with ADHD. *Canadian Journal of School Psychology, 12,* 55–59.

Saklofske, D. H., Schwean, V. L., Yackulic, R. A., & Quinn, D. (1994). WISC–III and SB:FE performance of children with attention deficit hyperactivity disorder. *Canadian Journal of School Psychology, 10,* 167–171.

Salend, S. J. (1990). *Effective mainstreaming.* New York: Macmillan.

Sameroff, A. J., Seifer, R., Baldwin, A., & Baldwin, C. (1993). Stability of intelligence from preschool to adolescence: The influence of social and family risk factors. *Child Development, 64,* 80–97.

Sandoval, J. (1979). The WISC–R and internal evidence of test bias with minority groups. *Journal of Consulting and Clinical Psychology, 47,* 919–927.

Sandoval, J., & Miille, M. P. W. (1980). Accuracy of judgments of WISC–R item difficulty for minority groups. *Journal of Consulting and Clinical Psychology, 48,* 249–253.

Sandoval, J., Zimmerman, I. L., & Woo-Sam, J. M. (1983). Cultural differences on WISC–R verbal items. *Journal of School Psychology, 21,* 49–55.

Sanford, E. (1998). Review of the Woodcock-McGrew-Weder Mini-Battery of Achievement. In J. C. Impara & B. S. Plake (Eds.), *The thirteenth mental measurements yearbook* (pp. 363–364). Lincoln: University of Nebraska Press.

Sapp, G. L., Abbott, G., Hinckley, R., & Rowell, A. (1997). Examination of the validity of the WISC–III with urban exceptional students. *Psychological Reports, 81,* 1163–1168.

Sattler, J. M. (1969). Effects of cues and examiner influence on two Wechsler subtests. *Journal of Consulting and Clinical Psychology, 33,* 716–721.

Sattler, J. M. (1970). Racial "experimenter effects" in experimentation, testing, interviewing, and psychotherapy. *Psychological Bulletin, 73,* 137–160.

Sattler, J. M. (1973). Racial experimenter effects. In K. S. Miller & R. M. Dreger (Eds.), *Comparative studies of blacks and whites in the United States* (pp. 8–32). New York: Seminar Press.

Sattler, J. M. (1976). Scoring difficulty of the WPPSI Geometric Design subtest. *Journal of School Psychology, 14,* 230–234.

Sattler, J. M. (1982). *Assessment of children's intelligence and special abilities* (2nd ed.). Needham Heights, MA: Allyn & Bacon.

Sattler, J. M. (1988). *Clinical and forensic interviewing of children and families: Guidelines for the mental health, education, pediatric, and child maltreatment fields.* San Diego: Jerome M. Sattler, Publisher.

Sattler, J. M. (1991). How good are federal judges in detecting differences in item difficulty on intelligence tests for ethnic groups? *Psychological Assessment, 3,* 125–129.

Sattler, J. M. (1992). *Assessment of children* (revised and updated 3rd ed.). San Diego: Jerome M. Sattler, Publisher.

Sattler, J. M., & Altes, L. M. (1984). Performance of bilingual and monolingual Hispanic children on the Peabody Picture Vocabulary Test–Revised and the McCarthy Perceptual Performance Scale. *Psychology in the Schools, 21,* 313–316.

Sattler, J. M., Andres, J. R., Squire, L. S., Wisely, R., & Maloy, C. F. (1978). Examiner scoring of ambiguous WISC–R responses. *Psychology in the Schools, 15,* 486–489.

Sattler, J. M., & Atkinson, L. (1993). Item equivalence across scales: The WPPSI–R and WISC–III. *Psychological Assessment, 5,* 203–206.

Sattler, J. M., Avila, V., Houston, W. B., & Toney, D. H. (1980). Performance of bilingual Mexican American children on Spanish and English versions of the Peabody Picture Vocabulary Test. *Journal of Consulting and Clinical Psychology, 46,* 782–784.

Sattler, J. M., & Gwynne, J. (1982). White examiners generally do not impede the intelligence test performance of black children: To debunk a myth. *Journal of Consulting and Clinical Psychology, 50,* 196–208.

Sattler, J. M., & Ryan, J. J. (1998). *Comparison of two methods of computing short-form Deviation Quotients on the WAIS–III.* Unpublished manuscript, Central Missouri State University at Warrensburg.

Satz, P., & Mogel, S. (1962). An abbreviation of the WAIS for clinical use. *Journal of Clinical Psychology, 18,* 77–79.

Sbordone, R. J. (1988). Assessment and treatment of cognitive-communicative impairments in the closed-head-injury patient: A neurobehavioral-systems approach. *Journal of Head Trauma Rehabilitation, 3*(2), 55–62.

Scarr, S. (1978). From evolution to Larry P., or what shall we do about IQ tests? *Intelligence, 2,* 325–342.

Scarr, S. (1991). Theoretical issues in investigating intellectual plasticity. In S. E. Brauth, W. S. Hall, & R. J. Dooling (Eds.), *Plasticity of development* (pp. 57–71). Cambridge: MIT Press.

Scarr, S. (1997a). Behavior-genetic and socialization theories of intelligence: Truce and reconciliation. In R. J. Sternberg & E. L. Grigorenko (Eds.), *Intelligence, heredity, and environment* (pp. 3–41). New York: Cambridge University Press.

Scarr, S. (1997b). The development of individual differences in intelligence and personality. In H. W. Reese & M. D. Franzen (Eds.), *Biological and neuropsychological mechanisms: Lifespan developmental psychology* (pp. 1–22). Mahwah, NJ: Lawrence Erlbaum.

Schinka, J. A., Vanderploeg, R. D., & Curtiss, G. (1997). WISC–III subtest scatter as a function of highest subtest scaled score. *Psychological Assessment, 9,* 83–88.

Schinka, J. A., Vanderploeg, R. D., & Greblo, P. (1998). Frequency of WISC–III and WAIS–R pairwise subtest differences. *Psychological Assessment, 10,* 171–175.

Schmidtke, A., & Schaller, S. (1980). Comparative study of factor structure of Raven's Coloured Progressive Matrices. *Perceptual and Motor Skills, 51,* 1244–1246.

Schneider, B. H., & Gervais, M. D. (1991). Identifying gifted kindergarten students with brief screening measures and the WPPSI–R. *Journal of Psychoeducational Assessment, 9,* 201–208.

Schoenfeld v. Parkway School District, 138 F.3d 379 (8th Cir. 1998), LEXIS 4035.

Schuerger, J. M., & Witt, A. C. (1989). The temporal stability of individually tested intelligence. *Journal of Clinical Psychology, 45,* 294–302.

Schultz, L. G. (1990). Social workers as expert witnesses in child abuse cases: A format. *Journal of Independent Social Work, 5,* 69–87.

Schultz, M. K. (1997). WISC–III and WJ–R tests of achievement: Concurrent validity and learning disability identification. *Journal of Special Education, 31,* 377–386.

Schwean, V. L., & Saklofske, D. H. (1998). WISC–III assessment of children with attention deficit/hyperactivity disorder. In A. Prifitera & D. H. Saklofske (Eds.), *WISC–III clinical use and interpretation* (pp. 91–118). San Diego: Academic.

Schwebel, A. I., & Bernstein, A. J. (1970). The effects of impulsivity on the performance of lower-class children on four WISC subtests. *American Journal of Orthopsychiatry, 40,* 629–636.

Searls, E. F. (1975). *How to use WISC scores in reading diagnosis.* Newark, DE: International Reading Association.

Seattle School District No. 1 v. B. S., 82 F.3d 1493 (9th Cir. 1996), LEXIS 10904.

Sellers v. School Board of the City of Manassas, Virginia, 141 F.3d 524 (4th Cir. 1998), LEXIS 5628.

Semler, I. J., & Iscoe, I. (1966). Structure of intelligence in Negro and white children. *Journal of Educational Psychology, 57,* 326–336.

Sewell, T. E. (1979). Intelligence and learning tasks as predictors of scholastic achievement in black and white first-grade children. *Journal of School Psychology, 17,* 325–332.

Sewell, T. E., & Severson, R. A. (1974). Learning ability and intelligence as cognitive predictors of achievement in first-grade black children. *Journal of Educational Psychology, 66,* 948–955.

Sherman, M., Chinsky, J. M., & Maffeo, P. (1974). Wechsler Preschool and Primary Scale of Intelligence Animal House as a measure of learning and motor abilities. *Journal of Consulting and Clinical Psychology, 42,* 470.

Shevtsov v. Los Angeles Unified School District, 134 F.3d 379 (9th Cir. 1998), LEXIS 4248.

Shindell, S. (1989). Assessing the visually impaired older adult. In T. Hunt & C. J. Lindley (Eds.), *Testing older adults.* Austin, TX: Pro-Ed.

Shinn, M. R. (Ed.). (1989). *Curriculum-based measurement: Assessing special children.* New York: Guilford.

Shinn, M. R. (Ed.). (1998). *Advanced applications of curriculum-based measurement.* New York: Guilford.

Shull-Senn, S., Weatherly, M., Morgan, S. K., & Bradley-Johnson, S. (1995). Stability reliability for elementary-age students on the Woodcock-Johnson Psychoeducational Battery–Revised (Achievement Section) and the Kaufman Test of Educational Achievement. *Psychology in the Schools, 32,* 86–92.

Siegler, R. S. (1992). The other Alfred Binet. *Developmental Psychology, 28,* 179–190.

Siegler, R. S., & Richards, D. D. (1982). The development of intelligence. In R. J. Sternberg (Ed.), *Handbook of human intelligence* (pp. 897–971). Cambridge: Cambridge University Press.

Silvaroli, N. J. (1997). *Classroom reading inventory* (8th ed.). Boston: McGraw-Hill.

Silver, A. A., & Hagin, R. S. (1990). *Disorders of learning in childhood.* New York: Wiley.

Silverstein, A. B. (1973). Note on prevalence. *American Journal of Mental Deficiency, 77,* 380–382.

Silverstein, A. B. (1982). Note on the constancy of the IQ. *American Journal of Mental Deficiency, 87,* 227–228.

Silverstein, A. B. (1984). Pattern analysis: The question of abnormality. *Journal of Consulting and Clinical Psychology, 52,* 936–939.

Silverstein, A. B. (1989). Reliability and abnormality of scaled-score ranges. *Journal of Clinical Psychology, 45,* 926–929.

Silverstein, A. B. (1990a). Critique of a Doppelt-type short form of the WAIS–R. *Journal of Clinical Psychology, 46,* 333–339.

Silverstein, A. B. (1990b). Notes on the reliability of Wechsler short forms. *Journal of Clinical Psychology, 46,* 194–196.

Silverstein, A. B. (1990c). Short forms of individual intelligence tests. *Psychological Assessment: A Journal of Consulting and Clinical Psychology, 2,* 3–11.

Sink, C., & Tracy, L. (1988). Educating the head injured: A continuum of programs and services. *Cognitive Rehabilitation, 6,* 34–37.

Slate, J. R. (1994). WISC–III correlations with the WIAT. *Psychology in the Schools, 31,* 278–285.

Slate, J. R. (1995). Two investigations of the validity of WISC–III. *Psychological Reports, 76,* 299–306.

Slate, J. R., & Hunnicutt, L. C., Jr. (1988). Examiner errors on the Wechsler scales. *Journal of Psychoeducational Assessment, 6,* 280–288.

Slate, J. R., & Jones, C. H. (1995). Preliminary evidence of the validity of the WISC–III for African American students undergoing special education evaluation. *Educational & Psychological Measurement, 55,* 1039–1046.

Slate, J. R., Jones, C. H., Coulter, C., & Covert, T. L. (1992). Practitioners' administration and scoring of the WISC–R: Evidence that we do err. *Journal of School Psychology, 30,* 77–82.

Slate, J. R., Jones, C. H., Graham, L. S., & Bower, J. (1992). *Correlations of WRAT–R and PPVT–R scores with WISC–III scores in a sample of students with mental retardation.* Unpublished manuscript, Arkansas State University at Jonesboro.

Slate, J. R., Jones, C. H., Graham, L. S., & Bower, J. (1994). Correlations of WISC–III, WRAT–R, KM–R, and PPVT–R scores in students with specific learning disabilities. *Learning Disabilities Research & Practice, 9,* 104–107.

Slate, J. R., & Saarino, D. A. (1995). Differences between WISC–III and WISC–R IQs: A preliminary investigation. *Journal of Psychoeducational Assessment, 13,* 340–346.

Slosson, R. L. (1996). *Slosson Intelligence Test–Revised.* East Aurora, NY: Slosson Educational Publications.

Slosson, R. L. (1998). *Slosson Intelligence Test–Revised: Technical manual–Calibrated norms tables.* East Aurora, NY: Slosson Educational Publications.

Smith, D. K., St. Martin, M. E., & Lyon, M. A. (1989). A validity study of the Stanford-Binet: Fourth Edition with students with learning disabilities. *Journal of Learning Disabilities, 22,* 260–261.

Smith, M. L. (1980). Meta-analysis of research on teacher expectations. *Evaluation in Education, 4,* 53–55.

Smith, T. D., Smith, B. L., Bramlett, R. K., & Hicks, N. (1999, April). *WISC–III stability over a three-year period in students with learning disabilities.* Paper presented at the meeting of the National Association of School Psychologists, Las Vegas, NV.

Smith, T. D., Smith, B. L., & Smithson, M. M. (1995). The relationship between the WISC–III and the WRAT–3 in a sample of rural referred children. *Psychology in the Schools, 32,* 291–295.

Snow, R. E. (1986). On intelligence. In R. J. Sternberg & D. K. Detterman (Eds.), *What is intelligence? Contemporary viewpoints on its nature and definition* (pp. 133–139). Norwood, NJ: Ablex.

Snyderman, M., & Rothman, S. (1987). Survey of expert opinion on intelligence and aptitude testing. *American Psychologist, 42,* 137–144.

Sokal, M. M. (Ed.). (1987). *Psychological testing and American society, 1890–1930*. New Brunswick, NJ: Rutgers University Press.

Soroko v. Arlington County Public Schools, 125 F.3d 848 (4th Cir. 1997), LEXIS 34718.

Spearman, C. E. (1923). *The nature of intelligence and the principles of cognition*. London: MacMillan.

Spearman, C. E. (1927). *The abilities of man*. New York: MacMillan.

Spencer, M. B., & Markstrom-Adams, C. (1990). Identity processes among racial and ethnic minority children in America. *Child Development, 61*, 290–310.

Spiegel, J. (1982). An ecological model of ethnic families. In M. McGoldrick, J. Pearce, & L. Giordano (Eds.), *Ethnicity and family therapy* (pp. 31–51). New York: Guilford.

Spitz, H. H. (1996). Commentary on the contributions to this volume. In D. K. Detterman (Ed.), *Current topics in human intelligence: Vol. 5. The environment* (pp. 173–177). Norwood, NJ: Ablex.

Springer v. Fairfax County School Board, 134 F.3d 659 (4th Cir. 1998), LEXIS 937.

Spruill, J. (1988). Two types of tables for use with the Stanford-Binet Intelligence Scale: Fourth Edition. *Journal of Psychoeducational Assessment, 6*, 78–86.

Spruill, J. (1996). Composite SAS of the Stanford-Binet Intelligence Scale, Fourth Edition: Is it determined by only one area SAS? *Psychological Assessment, 8*, 328–330.

Stankov, L., & Roberts, R. D. (1997). Mental speed is not the "basic" process of intelligence. *Personality & Individual Differences, 22*, 69–84.

Stavrou, E., & Flanagan, R. (1996, March). *The stability of WISC–III scores in learning disabled children*. Paper presented at the annual convention of the National Association of School Psychologists, Atlanta, GA.

Stern, W. (1914). *The psychological methods of testing intelligence*. Baltimore: Warwick & York.

Sternberg, R. J. (1985). Human intelligence: The model is the message. *Science, 230*, 1111–1118.

Sternberg, R. J. (1986). *Intelligence applied: Understanding and increasing your intellectual skills*. New York: Harcourt Brace Jovanovich.

Sternberg, R. J. (1990). *Metaphors of mind: Conceptions of the nature of intelligence*. New York: Cambridge University Press.

Sternberg, R. J. (1991). Death, taxes, and bad intelligence tests. *Intelligence, 15*, 257–269.

Sternberg, R. J. (1996). *Successful intelligence*. New York: Simon & Schuster.

Sternberg, R. J., & Berg, C. A. (1986). Quantitative integration: Definitions of intelligence: A comparison of the 1921 and 1986 symposia. In R. J. Sternberg & D. K. Detterman (Eds.), *What is intelligence?* (pp. 155–162). Norwood, NJ: Ablex.

Sternberg, R. J., & Detterman, D. K. (Eds.). (1986). *What is intelligence? Contemporary viewpoints on its nature and definition*. Norwood, NJ: Ablex.

Sternberg, R. J., & Kaufman, J. C. (1998). Human abilities. *Annual Review of Psychology, 49*, 479–502.

Stetson, E. G. (1989a). *The Stetson Spelling Program: Instructor's manual*. Austin, TX: Pro-Ed.

Stetson, E. G. (1989b). *The Stetson Spelling Program: Teacher's manual*. Austin, TX: Pro-Ed.

Stewart, K. J., & Moely, B. E. (1983). The WISC–R third factor: What does it mean? *Journal of Consulting and Clinical Psychology, 51*, 940–941.

Stockton v. Barbour County Board of Education, 112 F.3d 510 (4th Cir. 1997), LEXIS 14435.

Stoddard, G. D. (1943). *The meaning of intelligence*. New York: Macmillan.

Stone, B. J. (1992). Joint confirmatory factor analysis of the DAS and WISC–R. *Journal of School Psychology, 30*, 185–195.

Strommen, E. (1988). Confirmatory factor analysis of the Kaufman Assessment Battery for Children: A reevaluation. *Journal of School Psychology, 26*, 13–23.

St. Tammany Parish School Board v. State of Louisiana, 142 F.3d 776 (5th Cir. 1998), LEXIS 10466.

Sue, D. W. (1990). Culture-specific strategies in counseling: A conceptual framework. *Professional Psychology: Research and Practice, 21*, 424–433.

Sullivan, P. M. (1978). *A comparison of administration modifications on the WISC–R Performance Scale with different categories of deaf children*. Unpublished doctoral dissertation, University of Iowa, Iowa City.

Sutton, G. W., Koller, J. R., & Christian, B. T. (1982). The Stanford-Binet mental age and the WISC–R test age: A comparison study. *Psychology in the Schools, 19*, 287–289.

Sutton v. United Airlines, 119 S. Ct. 2139 (1999), LEXIS 4371.

Svanum, S., & Bringle, R. G. (1982). Race, social class, and predictive bias: An evaluation using the WISC, WRAT, and teacher ratings. *Intelligence, 6*, 275–286.

Swanson, E. N., & DeBlassie, R. (1971). Interpreter effects on the WISC performance of first grade Mexican-American children. *Measurement and Evaluation in Guidance, 4*, 172–175.

Swanson, H. L. (1985). Assessing learning disabled children's intellectual performance: An information processing perspective. In K. D. Gadow (Ed.), *Advances in learning and behavioral disabilities* (Vol. 4, pp. 225–272). Greenwich, CT: JAI.

Tarnowski, K. J., & Rohrbeck, C. A. (1992). Disadvantaged children and families. In T. H. Ollendick & R. J. Prinz (Eds.), *Advances in clinical child psychology* (Vol. 15, pp. 41–79). New York: Plenum.

Taylor, E. M. (1961). *Psychological appraisal of children with cerebral defects*. Cambridge: Harvard University Press.

Taylor, R. L., & Ziegler, E. W. (1987). Comparison of the first principal factor on the WISC–R across ethnic groups. *Educational & Psychological Measurement, 47*, 691–694.

Teeter, A., Moore, C. L., & Petersen, J. D. (1982). WISC–R Verbal and Performance abilities of native American students referred for school learning problems. *Psychology in the Schools, 19*, 39–44.

Teglasi, H., & Freeman, R. W. (1983). Rapport pitfalls of beginning testers. *Journal of School Psychology, 21*, 229–240.

Tellegen, A., & Briggs, P. F. (1967). Old wine in new skins: Grouping Wechsler subtests into new scales. *Journal of Consulting Psychology, 31*, 499–506.

Tellegen, P. (1997). An addition and correction to the Jenkinson et al. (1996) Australian SON–R 2½–7 validation study. *Journal of Psychoeducational Assessment, 15*, 67–69.

Terman, L. M. (1911). The Binet-Simon Scale for measuring intelligence: Impressions gained by its application. *Psychological Clinic, 5*, 199–206.

Terman, L. M. (1916). *The measurement of intelligence*. Boston: Houghton Mifflin.

Terman, L. M. (1921). A symposium: Intelligence and its measurement. *Journal of Educational Psychology, 12,* 127–133.

Terman, L. M., & Childs, H. G. (1912). A tentative revision and extension of the Binet-Simon Measuring Scale of Intelligence. *Journal of Educational Psychology, 3,* 61–74, 133–143, 198–208, 277–289.

Tharp, R. G. (1989). Psychocultural variables and constants: Effects on teaching and learning in schools. *American Psychologist, 44,* 349–359.

The Psychological Corporation. (1992). *Wechsler Individual Achievement Test.* San Antonio: Author.

The Psychological Corporation. (1997). *WAIS–III—WMS–III Technical Manual.* San Antonio: Author.

The Psychological Corporation (1999). *Wechsler Abbreviated Scale of Intelligence.* San Antonio: Author.

Thomas, P. J. (1977). Administration of a dialectical Spanish version and standard English version of the Peabody Picture Vocabulary Test. *Psychological Reports, 40,* 747–750.

Thomas R. W. v. Massachusetts Department of Education, et al., 130 F.3d 477 (1st Cir. 1997), LEXIS 33348.

Thompson, A. P., Browne, J., Schmidt, F., & Boer, M. (1997). Validity of the Kaufman Brief Intelligence Test and a four-subtest WISC–III short form with adolescent offenders. *Assessment, 4,* 385–394.

Thompson, A. P., & Sota, D. D. (1998). Comparison of the WAIS–R and the WISC–III scores with a sample of 16-year-old youth. *Psychological Reports, 82,* 1339–1346.

Thompson, B., Wasserman, J. D., & Matula, K. (1996). The factor structure of the Behavior Rating Scale of the Bayley Scales of Infant Development–II. *Educational and Psychological Measurement, 56,* 460–474.

Thompson v. Board of the Special School District No. 1, 144 F.3d 574 (8th Cir. 1998), LEXIS 9880.

Thorndike, E. L. (1927). *The measurement of intelligence.* New York: Bureau of Publications, Teachers College, Columbia University.

Thorndike, R. L., & Hagen, E. P. (1977). *Measurement and evaluation in psychology and education* (4th ed.). New York: Wiley.

Thorndike, R. L., Hagen, E. P., & Sattler, J. M. (1986a). *Guide for administering and scoring the Stanford-Binet Intelligence Scale: Fourth Edition.* Chicago: Riverside.

Thorndike, R. L., Hagen, E. P., & Sattler, J. M. (1986b). *Technical manual, Stanford-Binet Intelligence Scale: Fourth Edition.* Chicago: Riverside.

Thorndike, R. M. (1990). Would the real factors of the Stanford-Binet Fourth Edition please come forward? *Journal of Psychoeducational Assessment, 8,* 412–435.

Thurstone, L. L. (1938). Primary mental abilities. *Psychometric Monographs,* No. 1.

Todd v. Elkins School District No. 10, 149 F.3d 1188 (8th Cir. 1998), LEXIS 22489.

Torgesen, J. K. (1979). What shall we do with psychological processes? *Journal of Learning Disabilities, 12,* 514–521.

Tucker v. Calloway County Board of Education, 136 F.3d 495 (6th Cir. 1998), LEXIS 31393.

Tuddenham, R. D. (1962). The nature and measurement of intelligence. In L. J. Postman (Ed.), *Psychology in the making* (pp. 469–525). New York: Knopf.

Tulsky, D. S., & Ledbetter, M. F. (2000). Updating to the WAIS–III and WMS–III: Considerations for research and clinical practice. *Psychological Assessment, 12,* 253–262.

Tulsky, D. S., Rolfhus, E. L., & Zhu, J. (2000). Two-tailed versus one-tailed base rates of discrepancy scores in the WAIS–III. *The Clinical Neuropsychologist, 14*(3), (page numbers not available).

Tulsky, D. S., Zhu, J., & Prifitera, A. (1999). Assessing adult intelligence with the WAIS–III. In G. Goldstein (Ed.), *The handbook of psychological assessment* (3rd ed.). Amsterdam, Netherlands: Elsevier Science.

Tupa, D. J., Wright, M. O., & Fristad, M. A. (1997). Confirmatory factor analysis of the WISC–III with child psychiatric inpatients. *Psychological Assessment, 9,* 302–306.

Turk, D. C., & Kerns, R. D. (1985). Assessment in health psychology: A cognitive-behavioral perspective. In P. Karoly (Ed.), *Measurement strategies in health psychology* (pp. 335–372). New York: Wiley.

Turnbull, H. R., III. (1993). *Free appropriate public education: The law and children with disabilities* (4th ed.). Denver: Love.

Turnbull, W. W. (1979). Intelligence testing in the year 2000. *Intelligence, 3,* 275–282.

Uba, L. (1994). *Asian Americans: Personality patterns, identity, and mental health.* New York: Guilford.

University of Chicago Press. (1993). *The Chicago manual of style* (14th ed.). Chicago: Author.

U.S. Department of Education. (1994). *Elementary and secondary school compliance reports.* Washington, DC: U.S. Department of Education, Office of Civil Rights.

U.S. Department of Education. (1998). *To assure the free appropriate public education of all children with disabilities: Twentieth annual report to Congress on the implementation of the Individuals with Disabilities Education Act.* Washington, DC: Author.

U.S. Department of Education. (1999). *To assure the free appropriate public education of all children with disabilities: Twenty-first annual report to Congress on the implementation of the Individuals with Disabilities Education Act.* Washington, DC: Author.

U.S. Department of Health and Human Services. (1985). *The impact of Head Start on children, families and communities: Head Start synthesis project* (Contract No. 105–81–C-026). Washington, DC: CSR. (ERIC Document Reproduction Service No. ED 263984)

Uzgiris, I. C., & Hunt, J. McV. (1975). *Assessment in infancy: Ordinal scales of psychological development.* Urbana: University of Illinois Press.

Valdé, G., & Figueroa, R. A. (1994). *Bilingualism and testing: A special case of bias.* Norwood, NJ: Ablex.

Vance, H. B., & Fuller, G. B. (1995). Relation of scores on WISC–III and WRAT–3 for a sample of referred children and youth. *Psychological Reports, 76,* 371–374.

Vance, H. B., Huelsman, C. B., Jr., & Wherry, R. J. (1976). The hierarchical factor structure of the Wechsler Intelligence Scale for Children as it relates to disadvantaged white and black children. *Journal of General Psychology, 95,* 287–293.

Vance, H. B., Maddux, C. D., Fuller, G. B., & Awadh, A. M. (1996). A longitudinal comparison of WISC–III and WISC–R scores of special education students. *Psychology in the Schools, 33,* 113–118.

Vance, H. B., & Wallbrown, F. H. (1978). The structure of intelligence for black children: A hierarchical approach. *Psychological Record, 28,* 31–39.

Vanderploeg, R. D., Schinka, J. A., Baum, K. M., Tremont, G., & Mittenberg, W. (1998). WISC–III premorbid prediction strategies: Demographic and best performance approaches. *Psychological Assessment, 10,* 277–284.

VanderVeer, B., & Schweid, E. (1974). Infant assessment: Stability of mental functioning in young retarded children. *American Journal of Mental Deficiency, 79,* 1–4.

Vernon, P. A. (1983). Speed of information processing and general intelligence. *Intelligence, 7,* 53–70.

Vernon, P. A. (1997). Behavioral genetic and biological approaches to intelligence. In H. Nyborg (Ed.), *The scientific study of human nature: Tribute to Hans J. Eysenck at eighty* (pp. 240–258). Oxford, England: Pergamon.

Vernon, P. E. (1950). *The structure of human abilities.* New York: Wiley.

Vernon, P. E. (1965). Ability factors and environmental influences. *American Psychologist, 20,* 723–733.

Wachs, T. D. (1975). Relation of infants' performance on Piaget scales between twelve and twenty-four months and their Stanford-Binet performance at thirty-one months. *Child Development, 46,* 929–935.

Wagoner, R. (1988). *Scoring errors made by practicing psychologists on the WISC–R.* Unpublished masters thesis, Western Carolina University at Cullowhee, North Carolina.

Walczak v. Florida Union Free School District, 142 F.3d 119 (2nd Cir. 1998), LEXIS 7797.

Wallace, G., & Hammill, D. D. (1994). *Comprehensive Receptive and Expressive Vocabulary Test.* Austin, TX: Pro-Ed.

Ward, L. C. (1990). Prediction of verbal, performance, and full scale IQs from seven subtests of the WAIS–R. *Journal of Clinical Psychology, 46,* 436–440.

Ward, S., Garcia, M., Trebon, B., Ward, R., & Erwin, H. (1995, March). *The relationship of the WISC–III and achievement across age levels.* Paper presented at the 27th annual meeting of the National School Psychology Association Convention, Chicago.

Warner v. Independent School District No. 625, 134 F.3d 1333 (8th Cir. 1998), LEXIS 4931.

Wasik, B. H., & Wasik, J. L. (1976). Patterns of conservation acquisition and the relationship of conservation to intelligence for children of low income. *Perceptual and Motor Skills, 43,* 1147–1154.

W. B. v. Matula, 67 F.3d 484 (3rd Cir. 1995), LEXIS 28925.

Weaver, A. S. (1968). The prediction of first grade reading achievement in culturally disadvantaged children. *Dissertation Abstracts International, 28,* 3789A. (University Microfilms No. 68–2, 887)

Wechsler, D. (1939). *The measurement of adult intelligence.* Baltimore: Williams & Wilkins.

Wechsler, D. (1949). *Wechsler Intelligence Scale for Children.* San Antonio: The Psychological Corporation.

Wechsler, D. (1958). *The measurement and appraisal of adult intelligence* (4th ed.). Baltimore: Williams & Wilkins.

Wechsler, D. (1974). *Wechsler Intelligence Scale for Children–Revised.* San Antonio: The Psychological Corporation.

Wechsler, D. (1981). *Wechsler Adult Intelligence Scale–Revised.* San Antonio: The Psychological Corporation.

Wechsler, D. (1989). *Wechsler Preschool and Primary Scale of Intelligence–Revised.* San Antonio: The Psychological Corporation.

Wechsler, D. (1991). *Wechsler Intelligence Scale for Children–Third Edition.* San Antonio: The Psychological Corporation.

Wechsler, D. (1997). *Wechsler Adult Intelligence Scale–Third Edition.* San Antonio: The Psychological Corporation.

Weiss, L. G. (1995). WISC–III IQ's: New norms raise queries. A review of 22 studies comparing WISC–R to WISC–III IQ scores. *Assessment Focus, 1(2).* San Antonio: The Psychological Corporation.

Weiss, L. G., & Prifitera, A. (1995). An evaluation of differential prediction of WIAT achievement scores from WISC–III FSIQ across ethnic and gender groups. *Journal of School Psychology, 33,* 297–304.

Weiss, L. G., Prifitera, A., & Roid, G. H. (1993). The WISC–III and the fairness of predicting achievement across ethnic and gender groups. *Monograph Series of the Journal of Psychoeducational Assessment, Wechsler Intelligence Scale for Children: Third Edition,* 35–42.

Welsh, M. C., & Pennington, B. F. (1988). Assessing frontal lobe functioning in children: Views from developmental psychology. *Developmental Neuropsychology, 4,* 199–230.

Wenger v. Canastota Central School District, 146 F.3d 123 (2nd Cir. 1998), LEXIS 12510.

Werner, E. E., Honzik, M. P., & Smith, R. S. (1968). Prediction of intelligence and achievement at ten years from twenty months pediatric and psychologic examinations. *Child Development, 39,* 1063–1075.

Wesman, A. G. (1968). Intelligent testing. *American Psychologist, 23,* 267–274.

Whitten, J., Slate, J. R., Jones, C. H., & Shine, A. (1994). Examiners' errors in administering and scoring the WPPSI–R. *Journal of Psychoeducational Assessment, 12,* 49–54.

Wiederholt, J. L., & Bryant, B. R. (1992). *Gray Oral Reading Test* (3rd ed.). Austin, TX: Pro-Ed.

Wiedl, K. H., & Carlson, J. S. (1976). The factorial structure of the Raven Coloured Progressive Matrices Test. *Educational and Psychological Measurement, 36,* 409–413.

Wilkinson, G. S. (1993). *Wide Range Achievement Test–Revision 3.* Wilmington, DE: Jastak Associates.

Willerman, L., & Fiedler, M. F. (1977). Intellectually precocious preschool children: Early development and later intellectual accomplishments. *Journal of Genetic Psychology, 131,* 13–20.

Williams, K. T. (1997). *Expressive Vocabulary Test.* Circle Pines, MN: American Guidance Service.

Williams, R. L. (1970). From dehumanization to black intellectual genocide: A rejoinder. *Clinical Child Psychology Newsletter, 9,* 6–7.

Williams, R. L. (1972, September). *The BITCH-100: A culture-specific test.* Paper presented at the meeting of the American Psychological Association, Honolulu.

Willis, J. O., Dumont, R., & Cruse, C. L. (1997). Review of Woodcock-McGrew-Wender Mini-Battery of Achievement. *Journal of Psychoeducational Assessment, 15,* 270–280.

Wilson, M. (undated). *Triennial review work sheet.* Unpublished manuscript, Bedford County Public Schools at Bedford, VA.

Wilson, R. S. (1978a). Sensorimotor and cognitive development. In F. D. Minifie & L. L. Lloyd (Eds.), *Communicative and cognitive abilities–early behavioral assessment* (pp. 135–149). Baltimore: University Park Press.

Wilson, R. S. (1978b). Synchronies in mental development: An epigenetic perspective. *Science, 202,* 939–948.

Wilson, R. S. (1983). The Louisville Twin Study: Developmental synchronies in behavior. *Child Development, 54,* 298–316.

Wissler, C. (1901). The correlation of mental and physical tests. *Psychological Review, 3* (Monograph Suppl. 16).

Wodrich, D. L., & Kush, J. C. (1998). Kaufman Adolescent and Adult Intelligence Test (KAIT): Concurrent validity of fluid ability for preadolescents and adolescents with central nervous system disorders and scholastic concerns. *Journal of Psychoeducational Assessment, 16,* 215–225.

Wolf, F. M. (1986). *Meta-analysis. Quantitative methods for research synthesis.* Sage University Paper Series on Quantitative Applications in the Social Sciences, 07–001. Beverly Hills, CA: Sage.

Wolf, R. (1966). The measurement of environments. In A. Anastasi (Ed.), *Testing problems in perspective* (pp. 491–503). Washington, DC: American Council on Education.

Wolf, T. H. (1969). The emergence of Binet's conceptions and measurement of intelligence: A case history of the creative process. Part II. *Journal of the History of the Behavioral Sciences, 5,* 207–237.

Woodcock, R. W. (1987). *Woodcock Reading Mastery Tests–Revised.* Circle Pines, MN: American Guidance Services.

Woodcock, R. W. (1991). *Woodcock Language Proficiency Battery–Revised.* Itasca, IL: Riverside.

Woodcock, R. W. (1997). *Woodcock Diagnostic Reading Battery.* Itasca, IL: Riverside.

Woodcock, R. W. (1998). The *Woodcock Reading Mastery Tests–Revised.* Circle Pines, MN: American Guidance Service.

Woodcock, R. W., & Johnson, M. B. (1989). *Woodcock-Johnson Psychoeducational Battery–Revised.* Itasca, IL: Riverside.

Woodcock, R. W., McGrew, K. S., & Mather, N. (2001). *The Woodcock-Johnson® III.* Itasca, IL: Riverside.

Woodcock, R. W., McGrew, K. S., & Werder, J. K. (1994). *Woodcock-McGrew-Werder Mini-Battery of Achievement.* Itasca, IL: Riverside.

Woodcock, R. W., & Muñoz-Sandoval, A. F. (1993). *Woodcock-Muñoz Language Survey.* Itasca, IL: Riverside.

Yankton School District v. Schramm, 93 F.3d 1369 (8th Cir. 1996), LEXIS 21479.

Yell, M. L. (1998). *The law and special education.* Upper Saddle River, NJ: Merrill.

Yerkes, R. M. (1917). The Binet versus the point scale method of measuring intelligence. *Journal of Applied Psychology, 1,* 111–122.

Ylvisaker, M. (1986). Language and communication disorders following pediatric head injury. *Journal of Head Trauma Rehabilitation, 1,* 48–56.

Yoshida, R. K., & Meyers, C. E. (1975). Effects of labeling as educable mentally retarded on teachers' expectancies for change in a student's performance. *Journal of Educational Psychology, 67,* 521–527.

Youngstrom, E. A., Kogos, J. L., & Glutting, J. J. (1999) Incremental efficacy of the Differential Ability Scales factor scores in predicting individual achievement criteria. *School Psychology Quarterly, 14,* 26–39.

Yudin, L. W. (1966). An abbreviated form of the WISC for use with emotionally disturbed children. *Journal of Consulting Psychology, 30,* 272–275.

Z. A. & Bobby A. v. San Bruno Park School District, 165 F.3d 1273 (9th Cir. 1999), LEXIS 1047.

Zajonc, R. B. (1976). Family configuration and intelligence. *Science, 192,* 227–236.

Zambrana, R. E., & Silva-Palacios, V. (1989). Gender differences in stress among Mexican immigrant adolescents in Los Angeles, California. *Journal of Adolescent Research, 4,* 426–442.

Zehnder, M. M. (1994). *Using expert witnesses in child abuse and neglect cases.* St. Paul: Minnesota County Attorneys Association.

Zhu, J. J., Tulsky, D. S., & Rolfhus, E. (1999, November). *WAIS-III reliability data for special clinical groups.* Paper presented at the 19th annual meeting of the National Academy of Neuropsychology, San Antonio, TX.

Zhu, J. J., Woodell, N. M., & Kreiman, C. L. (1997, August). *Three year re-evaluation stability of the WISC–III: A learning disabled sample.* Paper presented at the annual convention of the American Psychological Association, Chicago, IL.

Zigler, E. (1982, August). *On the definition and classification of mental retardation.* Paper presented at the meeting of the American Psychological Association, Washington, DC.

Zigler, E., Balla, D., & Hodapp, R. M. (1984). On the definition and classification of mental retardation. *American Journal of Mental Deficiency, 89,* 215–230.

Zigler, E., & Butterfield, E. C. (1968). Motivational aspects of changes in IQ test performances of culturally deprived nursery school children. *Child Development, 39,* 1–14.

Zigler, E., & Farber, E. A. (1985). Commonalities between the intellectual extremes: Giftedness and mental retardation. In F. D. Horowitz & M. O'Brien (Eds.), *The gifted and talented: Developmental perspectives* (pp. 387–408). Washington, DC: American Psychological Association.

Zima, J. P. (1983). *Interviewing: Key to effective management.* Chicago: Science Research Associates.

Zimmerman, I. L., & Woo-Sam, J. M. (1985). Clinical applications. In B. B. Wolman (Ed.), *Handbook of intelligence: Theories, measurements, and applications* (pp. 873–898). New York: Wiley.

Zimmerman, I. L., & Woo-Sam, J. M. (1997). Review of the criterion-related validity of the WISC–III: The first five years. *Perceptual and Motor Skills, 85,* 531–546.

Zipperer v. The School Board of Seminole County, Florida, 111 F.3d 847 (11th Cir. 1997), LEXIS 9984.

Zobrest v. Catalina Foothills School District, No. 92–94, 509 U.S. 1 (1993), LEXIS 4211.

Zumbo, B. D. (1999). *A handbook on the theory and methods of differential item functioning (DIF): Logistic regression modeling as a unitary framework for binary and Likert-type (ordinal) item scores.* Ottawa, ON: Directorate of Human Resources Research and Evaluation, Department of National Defense. Available: http://quarles.unbc.ca/psyc/zumbo/DIF/index.html

NAME INDEX

SUBJECT INDEX

Table BC-1
Percentile Ranks for Deviation IQs and Composite Scores

IQ	NCE	Percentile rank Any test with SD = 15	Percentile rank Any test with SD = 16	IQ	NCE	Percentile rank Any test with SD = 15	Percentile rank Any test with SD = 16	IQ	NCE	Percentile rank Any test with SD = 15	Percentile rank Any test with SD = 16
155	99	99.99	99.97	118	75	88	87	81	23	10	12
154	99	99.98	99.96	117	74	87	86	80	22	9	11
153	99	99.98	99.95	116	73	86	84	79	20	8	9
152	99	99.97	99.94	115	71	84	83	78	19	7	8
151	99	99.97	99.93	114	69	82	81	77	17	6	8
150	99	99.96	99.91	113	68	81	79	76	15	5	7
149	99	99.95	99.89	112	67	79	77	75	15	5	6
148	99	99.93	99.87	111	66	77	75	74	13	4	5
147	99	99.91	99.83	110	64	75	73	73	13	4	5
146	99	99.89	99.80	109	63	73	71	72	10	3	4
145	99	99.87	99.75	108	61	70	69	71	10	3	4
144	99	99.83	99.70	107	60	68	67	70	7	2	3
143	99	99.79	99.64	106	59	66	65	69	7	2	3
142	99	99.74	99.57	105	57	63	62	68	7	2	2
141	99	99.69	99	104	56	61	60	67	1	1	2
140	99	99.62	99	103	54	58	57	66	1	1	2
139	99	99.53	99	102	53	55	55	65	1	1	1
138	99	99	99	101	52	53	52	64	1	1	1
137	99	99	99	100	50	50	50	63	1	1	1
136	99	99	99	99	48	47	48	62	1	1	1
135	99	99	99	98	47	45	45	61	1	.47	1
134	99	99	98	97	46	42	43	60	1	.38	1
133	99	99	98	96	44	39	40	59	1	.31	1
132	93	98	98	95	43	37	38	58	1	.26	.43
131	93	98	97	94	41	34	35	57	1	.21	.36
130	93	98	97	93	40	32	33	56	1	.17	.30
129	90	97	96	92	39	30	31	55	1	.13	.25
128	90	97	96	91	37	27	29	54	1	.11	.20
127	87	96	95	90	36	25	27	53	1	.09	.17
126	87	96	95	89	34	23	25	52	1	.07	.13
125	85	95	94	88	33	21	23	51	1	.05	.11
124	85	95	93	87	32	19	21	50	1	.04	.09
123	83	94	92	86	31	18	19	49	1	.03	.07
122	81	93	92	85	29	16	17	48	1	.03	.06
121	80	92	91	84	27	14	16	47	1	.02	.05
120	78	91	89	83	26	13	14	46	1	.02	.04
119	77	90	88	82	25	12	13	45	1	.01	.03

Note. NCE = normal curve equivalent.